Freedom in the World
2021

D0861078

The findings of *Freedom in the World 2021* include events from January 1, 2020, through December 31, 2020.

Freedom in the World 2020
The Annual Survey of
Political Rights & Civil Liberties

Sarah Repucci
General Editor

Shannon O'Toole
Managing Editor

Elisha Aaron, Noah Buyon, Isabel Linzer,
David Meijer, Tyler Roylance, Amy Slipowitz, Tessa Weal
Associate Editors

Freedom House • New York, NY, and Washington, DC

ROWMAN & LITTLEFIELD
Lanham • Boulder • New York • London

Published by Rowman & Littlefield
An imprint of The Rowman & Littlefield Publishing Group, Inc.
4501 Forbes Boulevard, Suite 200, Lanham, Maryland 20706
www.rowman.com

86-90 Paul Street, London EC2A 4NE, United Kingdom

Copyright © 2022 by Freedom House, Inc.

All rights reserved. No part of this book may be reproduced in any form or by any electronic or mechanical means, including information storage and retrieval systems, without written permission from the publisher, except by a reviewer who may quote passages in a review.

British Library Cataloguing in Publication Information Available

Library of Congress Cataloging-in-Publication Data

ISBN: 978-1-5381-5180-8 (paper)
ISBN: 978-1-5381-5181-5 (electronic)

♾™ The paper used in this publication meets the minimum requirements of American National Standard for Information Sciences—Permanence of Paper for Printed Library Materials, ANSI/NISO Z39.48-1992.

*To Arch Puddington, a lifelong champion of democracy and mainstay
of Freedom House's research and analysis division for 26 years*

Contents

Acknowledgments

Freedom in the World 2021 could not have been completed without the contributions of numerous Freedom House staff members and consultants. The section titled "Survey Team" contains a detailed list of the writers and advisers without whose efforts this project would not have been possible.

Sarah Repucci served as the project director for this year's survey and Mai Truong served as the research director for management and strategy. Elisha Aaron, Ever Bussey, Noah Buyon, Cathryn Grothe, Isabel Linzer, David Meijer, Shannon O'Toole, Tyler Roylance, Nate Schenkkan, Amy Slipowitz, and Tessa Weal provided extensive research, analytical, editorial, and administrative assistance. Jacqueline Laks Gorman, M. L. Liu, and Peter Schmidtke served as fact-checkers on country reports. Overall guidance for the project was provided by Michael J. Abramowitz, president of Freedom House. A number of other Freedom House staff offered valuable additional input on the country reports and ratings process.

This edition of *Freedom in the World* is dedicated to Arch Puddington, a lifelong champion of democracy who retired in 2020 after serving for 26 years as a mainstay of Freedom House's research and analysis division.

Freedom House would like to acknowledge the generous financial support for *Freedom in the World* by National Endowment for Democracy, the Merrill Family Foundation, and the Lilly Endowment. Freedom House is solely responsible for the report's content.

Freedom in the World 2021
Democracy under Siege

By Sarah Repucci and Amy Slipowitz

As a lethal pandemic, economic and physical insecurity, and violent conflict ravaged the world in 2020, democracy's defenders sustained heavy new losses in their struggle against authoritarian foes, shifting the international balance in favor of tyranny. Incumbent leaders increasingly used force to crush opponents and settle scores, sometimes in the name of public health, while beleaguered activists—lacking effective international support—faced heavy jail sentences, torture, or murder in many settings.

These withering blows marked the 15th consecutive year of decline in global freedom. The countries experiencing deterioration outnumbered those with improvements by the largest margin recorded since the negative trend began in 2006. The long democratic recession is deepening.

The impact of the long-term democratic decline has become increasingly global in nature, broad enough to be felt by those living under the cruelest dictatorships, as well as by citizens of long-standing democracies. Nearly 75 percent of the world's population lived in a country that faced deterioration last year. The ongoing decline has given rise to claims of democracy's inherent inferiority. Proponents of this idea include official Chinese and Russian commentators seeking to strengthen their international influence while escaping accountability for abuses, as well as antidemocratic actors within democratic states who see an opportunity to consolidate power. They are both cheering the breakdown of democracy and exacerbating it, pitting themselves against the brave groups and individuals who have set out to reverse the damage.

The malign influence of the regime in China, the world's most populous dictatorship, was especially profound in 2020. Beijing ramped up its global disinformation and censorship campaign to counter the fallout from its cover-up of the initial coronavirus outbreak, which severely hampered a rapid global response in the pandemic's early days. Its efforts also featured increased meddling in the domestic political discourse of foreign democracies, transnational extensions of rights abuses common in mainland China, and the demolition of Hong Kong's liberties and legal autonomy. Meanwhile, the Chinese regime has gained clout in multilateral institutions such as the UN Human Rights Council, which the United States abandoned in 2018, as Beijing pushed a vision of so-called noninterference that allows abuses of democratic principles and human rights standards to go unpunished while the formation of autocratic alliances is promoted.

As COVID-19 spread during the year, governments across the democratic spectrum repeatedly resorted to excessive surveillance, discriminatory restrictions on freedoms like movement and assembly, and arbitrary or violent enforcement of such restrictions by police and nonstate actors. Waves of false and misleading information, generated deliberately by political leaders in some cases, flooded many countries' communication systems, obscuring reliable data and jeopardizing lives. While most countries with stronger democratic institutions ensured that any restrictions on liberty were necessary and proportionate to the threat posed

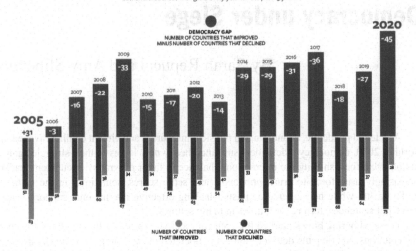

A Growing Democracy Gap: 15 Years of Decline

Countries with aggregate score declines in *Freedom in the World* have outnumbered those with gains every year for the past 15 years.

by the virus, a number of their peers pursued clumsy or ill-informed strategies, and dictators from Venezuela to Cambodia exploited the crisis to quash opposition and fortify their power.

The expansion of authoritarian rule, combined with the fading and inconsistent presence of major democracies on the international stage, has had tangible effects on human life and security, including the frequent resort to military force to resolve political disputes. As long-standing conflicts churned on in places like Libya and Yemen, the leaders of Ethiopia and Azerbaijan launched wars last year in the regions of Tigray and Nagorno-Karabakh, respectively, drawing on support from authoritarian neighbors Eritrea and Turkey and destabilizing surrounding areas. Repercussions from the fighting shattered hopes for tentative reform movements in both Armenia, which clashed with the Azerbaijani regime over Nagorno-Karabakh, and Ethiopia.

India, the world's most populous democracy, dropped from Free to Partly Free status in *Freedom in the World 2021*. The government of Prime Minister Narendra Modi and its state-level allies continued to crack down on critics during the year, and their response to COVID-19 included a ham-fisted lockdown that resulted in the dangerous and unplanned displacement of millions of internal migrant workers. The ruling Hindu nationalist movement also encouraged the scapegoating of Muslims, who were disproportionately blamed for the spread of the virus and faced attacks by vigilante mobs. Rather than serving as a champion of democratic practice and a counterweight to authoritarian influence from countries such as China, Modi and his party are tragically driving India itself toward authoritarianism.

The parlous state of US democracy was conspicuous in the early days of 2021 as an insurrectionist mob, egged on by the words of outgoing president Donald Trump and his refusal to admit defeat in the November election, stormed the Capitol building and temporarily disrupted Congress's final certification of the vote. This capped a year in which the administration attempted to undermine accountability for malfeasance, including by dismissing inspectors general responsible for rooting out financial and other misconduct in government; amplified false allegations of electoral fraud that fed mistrust among much of the US population; and condoned disproportionate violence by police in response to massive protests calling for an end to systemic racial injustice. But the outburst of political violence at the symbolic heart of US democracy, incited by the president himself, threw the country into even greater crisis. Notwithstanding the inauguration of a new president in keeping with the law and the constitution, the United States will need to work vigorously to strengthen its institutional safeguards, restore its civic norms, and uphold the promise of its core principles for all segments of society if it is to protect its venerable democracy and regain global credibility.

The widespread protest movements of 2019, which had signaled the popular desire for good governance the world over, often collided with increased repression in 2020. While successful protests in countries such as Chile and Sudan led to democratic improvements, there were many more examples in which demonstrators succumbed to crackdowns, with oppressive regimes benefiting from a distracted and divided international community. Nearly two dozen countries and territories that experienced major protests in 2019 suffered a net decline in freedom the following year.

Although *Freedom in the World*'s better-performing countries had been in retreat for several years, in 2020 it was struggling democracies and authoritarian states that accounted for more of the global decline. The proportion of Not Free countries is now the highest it has been in the past 15 years. On average, the scores of these countries have declined by about 15 percent during the same period. At the same time, the number of countries worldwide earning a net score improvement for 2020 was the lowest since 2005, suggesting that the prospects for a change in the global downward trend are more challenging than ever. With India's decline to Partly Free, less than 20 percent of the world's population now lives in a Free country, the smallest proportion since 1995. As repression intensifies in already unfree environments, greater damage is done to their institutions and societies, making it increasingly difficult to fulfill public demands for freedom and prosperity under any future government.

A Shifting International Balance

In 2020, the number of Free countries in the world reached its lowest level since the beginning of a 15-year period of global democratic decline, while the number of Not Free countries reached its highest level.

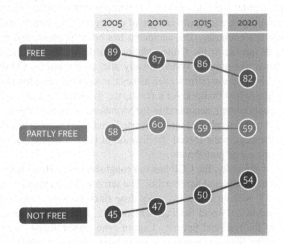

The enemies of freedom have pushed the false narrative that democracy is in decline because it is incapable of addressing people's needs. In fact, democracy is in decline because its most prominent exemplars are not doing enough to protect it. Global leadership and solidarity from democratic states are urgently needed. Governments that understand the value of democracy, including the new administration in Washington, have a responsibility to band together to deliver on its benefits, counter its adversaries, and support its defenders. They must also put their own houses in order to shore up their credibility and fortify their institutions against politicians and other actors who are willing to trample democratic principles in the pursuit of power. If free societies fail to take these basic steps, the world will become ever more hostile to the values they hold dear, and no country will be safe from the destructive effects of dictatorship.

THE SHIFTING INTERNATIONAL BALANCE

Over the past year, oppressive and often violent authoritarian forces tipped the international order in their favor time and again, exploiting both the advantages of nondemocratic systems and the weaknesses in ailing democracies. In a variety of environments, flickers of hope were extinguished, contributing to a new global status quo in which acts of repression went unpunished and democracy's advocates were increasingly isolated.

The Chinese Communist Party (CCP), faced with the danger that its authoritarian system would be blamed for covering up and thus exacerbating the COVID-19 pandemic, worked hard to convert the risk into an opportunity to exert influence. It provided medical supplies to countries that were hit hard by the virus, but it often portrayed sales as donations and orchestrated propaganda events with economically dependent recipient governments. Beijing sometimes sought to shift blame to the very countries it claimed to be helping, as when Chinese state media suggested that the coronavirus had actually originated in Italy. Throughout the year, the CCP touted its own authoritarian methods for controlling the contagion, comparing them favorably with democracies like the United States while studiously ignoring the countries that succeeded without resorting to major abuses, most notably Taiwan. This type of spin has the potential to convince many people that China's censorship and repression are a recipe for effective governance rather than blunt tools for entrenching political power.

Beyond the pandemic, Beijing's export of antidemocratic tactics, financial coercion, and physical intimidation have led to an erosion of democratic institutions and human rights protections in numerous countries. The campaign has been supplemented by the regime's moves to promote its agenda at the United Nations, in diplomatic channels, and through worldwide propaganda that aims to systematically alter global norms. Other authoritarian states have joined China in these efforts, even as key democracies abandoned allies and their own values in foreign policy matters. As a result, the mechanisms that democracies have long used to hold governments accountable for violations of human rights standards and international law are being weakened and subverted, and even the world's most egregious violations, such as the large-scale forced sterilization of Uighur women, are not met with a well-coordinated response or punishment.

In this climate of impunity, the CCP has run roughshod over Hong Kong's democratic institutions and international legal agreements. The territory has suffered a massive decline in freedom since 2013, with an especially steep drop since mass prodemocracy demonstrations were suppressed in 2019 and Beijing tightened its grip in 2020. The central government's imposition of the National Security Law in June erased almost overnight many of Hong Kong's remaining liberties, bringing it into closer alignment with the system on the mainland. The Hong Kong government itself escalated its use of the law early in 2021 when more than 50 prodemocracy activists and politicians were arrested, essentially for holding a primary and attempting to win legislative elections that were ultimately postponed by a year; they face penalties of up to life in prison. In November the Beijing and Hong Kong governments had colluded to expel four prodemocracy members from the existing Legislative Council, prompting the remaining 15 to resign in protest. These developments reflect a dramatic increase in the cost of opposing the CCP in Hong Kong, and the narrowing of possibilities for turning back the authoritarian tide.

The use of military force by authoritarian states, another symptom of the global decay of democratic norms, was on display in Nagorno-Karabakh last year. New fighting erupted in September when the Azerbaijani regime, with decisive support from Turkey, launched an offensive to settle a territorial dispute that years of diplomacy with Armenia had failed to resolve. At least 6,500 combatants and hundreds of civilians were killed, and tens of thousands of people were newly displaced. Meaningful international engagement was absent, and the war only stopped when Moscow imposed a peacekeeping plan on the two sides, fixing in place the Azerbaijani military's territorial gains but leaving many other questions unanswered.

The fighting in Nagorno-Karabakh has had spillover effects for democracy. In addition to strengthening the rule of Azerbaijan's authoritarian president, Ilham Aliyev, the conflict threatens to destabilize the government in Armenia. A rare bright spot in a region replete with deeply entrenched authoritarian leaders, Armenia has experienced tentative gains in freedom since mass antigovernment protests erupted in 2018 and citizens voted in a more reform-minded government. But Prime Minister Nikol Pashinyan's capitulation in the war sparked a violent reaction among some opponents, who stormed the parliament in November and physically attacked the speaker. Such disorder threatens the country's hard-won progress, and could set off a chain of events that draws Armenia closer to the autocratic tendencies of its neighbors.

Ethiopia had also made democratic progress in recent years, as new prime minister Abiy Ahmed lifted restrictions on opposition media and political groups and released imprisoned journalists and political figures. However, persistent ethnic and political tensions remained. In July 2020, a popular ethnic Oromo singer was killed, leading to large protests in the Oromia Region that were marred by attacks on non-Oromo populations, a violent response by security forces, and the arrest of thousands of people, including many opposition figures. The country's fragile gains were further imperiled after the ruling party in the Tigray Region held elections in September against the will of the federal authorities and labeled Abiy's government illegitimate. Tigrayan forces later attacked a military base, leading to an overwhelming response from federal forces and allied ethnic militias that displaced tens of thousands of people and led to untold civilian casualties. In a dark sign for the country's democratic prospects, the government enlisted military support from the autocratic regime of neighboring Eritrea, and national elections that were postponed due to the pandemic will now either take place in the shadow of civil conflict or be pushed back even further.

In Venezuela, which has experienced a dizzying 40-point score decline over the last 15 years, some hope arose in 2019 when opposition National Assembly leader Juan Guaidó appeared to present a serious challenge to the rule of dictator Nicolás Maduro. The opposition named Guaidó as interim president under the constitution, citing the illegitimacy of the presidential election that kept Maduro in power, and many democratic governments recognized his status. In 2020, however, as opponents of the regime continued to face extrajudicial execution, enforced disappearances, and arbitrary detention, Maduro regained the upper hand. Tightly controlled National Assembly elections went forward despite an opposition boycott, creating a new body with a ruling party majority. The old opposition-led legislature hung on in a weakened state, extending its own term as its electoral legitimacy ebbed away.

Largest 10-Year Declines
Dramatic declines in freedom have been observed in every region of the world.

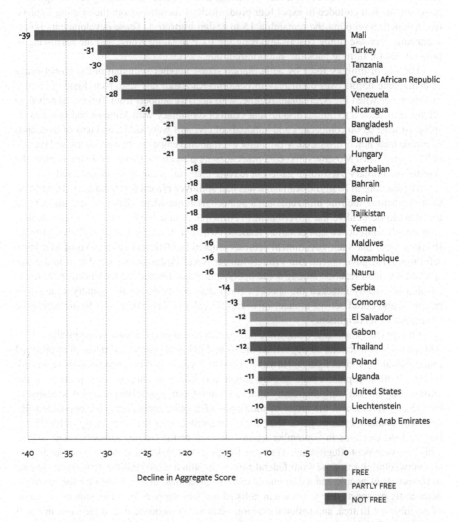

Country	Decline
Mali	-39
Turkey	-31
Tanzania	-30
Central African Republic	-28
Venezuela	-28
Nicaragua	-24
Bangladesh	-21
Burundi	-21
Hungary	-21
Azerbaijan	-18
Bahrain	-18
Benin	-18
Tajikistan	-18
Yemen	-18
Maldives	-16
Mozambique	-16
Nauru	-16
Serbia	-14
Comoros	-13
El Salvador	-12
Gabon	-12
Thailand	-12
Poland	-11
Uganda	-11
United States	-11
Liechtenstein	-10
United Arab Emirates	-10

Decline in Aggregate Score

FREE
PARTLY FREE
NOT FREE

Belarus emerged as another fleeting bright spot in August, when citizens unexpectedly rose up to dispute the fraudulent results of a deeply flawed election. Alyaksandr Lukashenka's repressive rule had previously been taken for granted, but for a few weeks the protests appeared to put him on the defensive as citizens awakened to their democratic potential despite brutal crackdowns, mass arrests, and torture. By the start of 2021, however, despite ongoing resistance, Lukashenka remained in power, and protests, more limited in scale, continued to be met with detentions. Political rights and civil liberties have become even more restricted than before, and democracy remains a distant aspiration.

In fact, Belarus was far from the only place where the promise of increased freedom raised by mass protests eventually curdled into heightened repression. Of the 39 countries and territories where Freedom House noted major protests in 2019, 23 experienced a score decline for 2020—a significantly higher share than countries with declines represented in the world at large. In settings as varied as Algeria, Guinea, and India, regimes that protests had taken by surprise in 2019 regained their footing, arresting and prosecuting demonstrators, passing newly restrictive laws, and in some cases resorting to brutal crackdowns, for which they faced few international repercussions.

The fall of India from the upper ranks of free nations could have a particularly damaging impact on global democratic standards. Political rights and civil liberties in the country have deteriorated since Narendra Modi became prime minister in 2014, with increased pressure on human rights organizations, rising intimidation of academics and journalists, and a spate of bigoted attacks, including lynchings, aimed at Muslims. The decline only accelerated after Modi's reelection in 2019. Last year, the government intensified its crackdown on protesters opposed to a discriminatory citizenship law and arrested dozens of journalists who aired criticism of the official pandemic response. Judicial independence has also come under strain; in one case, a judge was transferred immediately after reprimanding the police for taking no action during riots in New Delhi that left over 50 people, mostly Muslims, dead. In December, Uttar Pradesh, India's most populous state, approved a law that prohibits forced religious conversion through interfaith marriage, which critics fear will effectively restrict interfaith marriage in general; authorities have already arrested a number of Muslim men for allegedly forcing Hindu women to convert to Islam. Amid the pandemic the government imposed an abrupt COVID-19 lockdown in the spring, which left millions of migrant workers in cities without work or basic resources. Many were forced to walk across the country to their home villages, facing various forms of mistreatment along the way. Under Modi, India appears to have abandoned its potential to serve as a global democratic leader, elevating narrow Hindu nationalist interests at the expense of its founding values of inclusion and equal rights for all.

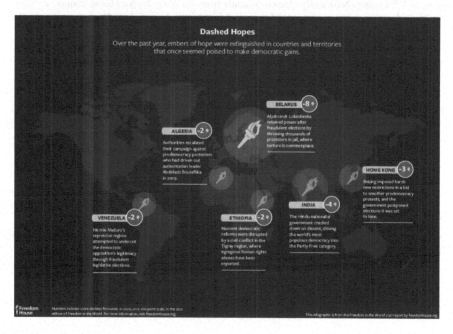

Dashed Hopes

Over the past year, embers of hope were extinguished in countries and territories that once seemed poised to make democratic gains.

BELARUS -8 ◆
Alyaksandr Lukashenka retained power after fraudulent elections by throwing thousands of protesters in jail, where torture is commonplace.

ALGERIA -2 ◆
Authorities escalated their campaign against prodemocracy protesters who had driven out authoritarian leader Abdelaziz Bouteflika in 2019.

HONG KONG -3 ◆
Beijing imposed harsh new restrictions in a bid to smother prodemocracy protests, and the government postponed elections it was set to lose.

INDIA -4 ◆
The Hindu nationalist government cracked down on dissent, driving the world's most populous democracy into the Partly Free category.

VENEZUELA -2 ◆
Nicolás Maduro's repressive regime attempted to undercut the democratic opposition's legitimacy through fraudulent legislative elections.

ETHIOPIA -2 ◆
Nascent democratic reforms were disrupted by a civil conflict in the Tigray region, where egregious human rights abuses have been reported.

Freedom House. Numbers indicate score declines for events in 2020, on a 100-point scale, in the 2021 edition of *Freedom in the World*. For more information, visit freedomhouse.org.

This infographic is from the *Freedom in the World* 2021 report by freedomhouse.org

To reverse the global shift toward authoritarian norms, democracy advocates working for freedom in their home countries will need robust solidarity from like-minded allies abroad.

THE ECLIPSE OF US LEADERSHIP

The final weeks of the Trump presidency featured unprecedented attacks on one of the world's most visible and influential democracies. After four years of condoning and indeed pardoning official malfeasance, ducking accountability for his own transgressions, and encouraging racist and right-wing extremists, the outgoing president openly strove to illegally overturn his loss at the polls, culminating in his incitement of an armed mob to disrupt Congress's certification of the results. Trump's actions went unchecked by most lawmakers from his own party, with a stunning silence that undermined basic democratic tenets. Only a serious and sustained reform effort can repair the damage done during the Trump era to the perception and reality of basic rights and freedoms in the United States.

The year leading up to the assault on the Capitol was fraught with other episodes that threw the country into the global spotlight in a new way. The politically distorted health recommendations, partisan infighting, shockingly high and racially disparate coronavirus death rates, and police violence against protesters advocating for racial justice over the summer all underscored the United States' systemic dysfunctions and made American democracy appear fundamentally unstable. Even before 2020, Trump had presided over an accelerating decline in US freedom scores, driven in part by corruption and conflicts of interest in the administration, resistance to transparency efforts, and harsh and haphazard policies on immigration and asylum that made the country an outlier among its Group of Seven peers.

But President Trump's attempt to overturn the will of the American voters was arguably the most destructive act of his time in office. His drumbeat of claims—without evidence—that the electoral system was ridden by fraud sowed doubt among a significant portion of the population, despite what election security officials eventually praised as the most secure vote in US history. Nationally elected officials from his party backed these claims, striking at the foundations of democracy and threatening the orderly transfer of power.

Though battered, many US institutions held strong during and after the election process. Lawsuits challenging the result in pivotal states were each thrown out in turn by independent courts. Judges appointed by presidents from both parties ruled impartially, including the three Supreme Court justices Trump himself had nominated, upholding the rule of law and confirming that there were no serious irregularities in the voting or counting processes. A diverse set of media outlets broadly confirmed the outcome of the election, and civil society groups investigated the fraud claims and provided evidence of a credible vote. Some Republicans spoke eloquently and forcefully in support of democratic principles, before and after the storming of the Capitol. Yet it may take years to appreciate and address the effects of the experience on Americans' ability to come together and collectively uphold a common set of civic values.

The exposure of US democracy's vulnerabilities has grave implications for the cause of global freedom. Rulers and propagandists in authoritarian states have always pointed to America's domestic flaws to deflect attention from their own abuses, but the events of the past year will give them ample new fodder for this tactic, and the evidence they cite will remain in the world's collective memory for a long time to come. After the Capitol riot, a spokesperson from the Russian foreign ministry stated, "The events in Washington show that the US electoral process is archaic, does not meet modern standards, and is prone to violations." Zimbabwe's president said the incident "showed that the US has no moral right to punish another nation under the guise of upholding democracy."

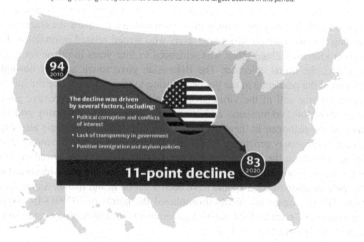

United States in Decline

Over the past 10 years, the United States' aggregate *Freedom in the World* score has declined by 11 points, placing it among the 25 countries that have suffered the largest declines in this period.

94
2010

The decline was driven
by several factors, including:
• Political corruption and conflicts of interest
• Lack of transparency in government
• Punitive immigration and asylum policies

11-point decline

83
2020

‡ Freedom House. Note: The US received a score of 94 in the 2011 edition of *Freedom in the World*, covering the events of 2010. It received a score of 83 in the 2021 edition, covering 2020. All scores are on a scale of 0 to 100. For more information on the methodology, visit freedomhouse.org. This infographic is from the *Freedom in the World* 2021 report by freedomhouse.org.

For most of the past 75 years, despite many mistakes, the United States has aspired to a foreign policy based on democratic principles and support for human rights. When adhered to, these guiding lights have enabled the United States to act as a leader on the global stage, pressuring offenders to reform, encouraging activists to continue their fight, and rallying partners to act in concert. After four years of neglect, contradiction, or outright abandonment under Trump, President Biden has indicated that his administration will return to that tradition. But to rebuild credibility in such an endeavor and garner the domestic support necessary to sustain it, the United States needs to improve its own democracy. It must strengthen institutions enough to survive another assault, protect the electoral system from foreign and domestic interference, address the structural roots of extremism and polarization, and uphold the rights and freedoms of all people, not just a privileged few.

Everyone benefits when the United States serves as a positive model, and the country itself reaps ample returns from a more democratic world. Such a world generates more trade and fairer markets for US goods and services, as well as more reliable allies for collective defense. A global environment where freedom flourishes is more friendly, stable, and secure, with fewer military conflicts and less displacement of refugees and asylum seekers. It also serves as an effective check against authoritarian actors who are only too happy to fill the void.

THE LONG ARM OF COVID-19

Since it spread around the world in early 2020, COVID-19 has exacerbated the global decline in freedom. The outbreak exposed weaknesses across all the pillars of democracy, from elections and the rule of law to egregiously disproportionate restrictions on freedoms of assembly and movement. Both democracies and dictatorships experienced successes and failures in their battle with the virus itself, though citizens in authoritarian states had fewer tools to resist and correct harmful policies. Ultimately, the changes precipitated by the pandemic left many societies—with varied regime types, income levels, and demographics—in worse political condition; with more pronounced racial, ethnic, and gender inequalities; and vulnerable to long-term effects.

Transparency was one of the hardest-hit aspects of democratic governance. National and local officials in China assiduously obstructed information about the outbreak, including by carrying out mass arrests of internet users who shared related information. In December, citizen journalist Zhang Zhan was sentenced to four years in prison for her reporting from Wuhan, the initial epicenter. The Belarusian government actively downplayed the seriousness of the pandemic to the public, refusing to take action, while the Iranian regime concealed the true toll of the virus on its people. Some highly repressive governments, including those of Turkmenistan and Nicaragua, simply ignored reality and denied the presence of the pathogen in their territory. More open political systems also experienced significant transparency problems. At the presidential level and in a number of states and localities, officials in the United States obscured data and actively sowed misinformation about the transmission and treatment of the coronavirus, leading to widespread confusion and the politicization of what should have been a public health matter. Similarly, Brazilian president Jair Bolsonaro repeatedly downplayed the harms of COVID-19, promoted unproven treatments, criticized subnational governments' health measures, and sowed doubt about the utility of masks and vaccines.

Freedom of personal expression, which has experienced the largest declines of any democracy indicator since 2012, was further restrained during the health crisis. In the midst of a heavy-handed lockdown in the Philippines under President Rodrigo Duterte, the authorities stepped up harassment and arrests of social media users, including those who criticized the government's pandemic response. Cambodia's authoritarian prime minister, Hun Sen, presided over the arrests of numerous people for allegedly spreading false information linked to the virus and criticizing the state's performance. Governments around the world also deployed intrusive surveillance tools that were often of dubious value to public health and featured few safeguards against abuse.

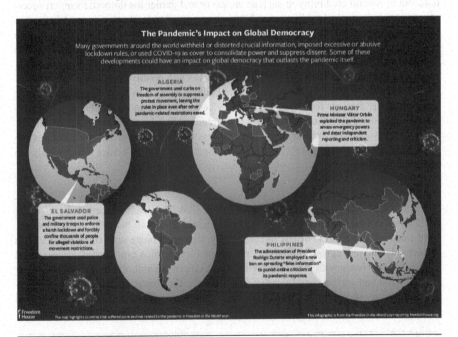

The Pandemic's Impact on Global Democracy

Many governments around the world withheld or distorted crucial information, imposed excessive or abusive lockdown rules, or used COVID-19 as cover to consolidate power and suppress dissent. Some of these developments could have an impact on global democracy that outlasts the pandemic itself.

ALGERIA
The government used curbs on freedom of assembly to suppress a protest movement, leaving the rules in place even after other pandemic-related restrictions eased.

HUNGARY
Prime Minister Viktor Orbán exploited the pandemic to amass emergency powers and deter independent reporting and criticism.

EL SALVADOR
The government used police and military troops to enforce a harsh lockdown and forcibly confine thousands of people for alleged violations of movement restrictions.

PHILIPPINES
The administration of President Rodrigo Duterte employed a new ban on spreading "false information" to punish online criticism of its pandemic response.

Freedom House

The map highlights countries that suffered score declines related to the pandemic in Freedom in the World 2021.

This infographic is from the Freedom in the World 2021 report by freedomhouse.org

But beyond their impact in 2020, official responses to COVID-19 have laid the ground-work for government excesses that could affect democracy for years to come. As with the response to the terrorist attacks of September 11, 2001, when the United States and many other countries dramatically expanded their surveillance activities and restricted due process rights in the name of national security, the COVID-19 pandemic has triggered a shift in norms and the adoption of problematic legislation that will be challenging to reverse after the virus has been contained.

In Hungary, for example, a series of emergency measures allowed the government to rule by decree despite the fact that coronavirus cases were negligible in the country until the fall. Among other misuses of these new powers, the government withdrew financial assis-tance from municipalities led by opposition parties. The push for greater executive authority was in keeping with the gradual concentration of power that Prime Minister Viktor Orbán has been orchestrating over the past decade. An indicative move came in December, when the pliant parliament approved constitutional amendments that transferred public assets into the hands of institutions headed by ruling-party loyalists, reduced independent oversight of government spending, and pandered to the ruling party's base by effectively barring same-sex couples from adopting children.

In Algeria, President Abdelmadjid Tebboune, who had recently taken office through a tightly controlled election after longtime authoritarian leader Abdelaziz Bouteflika resigned under public pressure, banned all forms of mass gatherings in March. Even as other restrictions were eased in June, the prohibition on assembly remained in place, and authorities stepped up arrests of activists associated with the prodemocracy protest movement. Many of the arrests were based on April amendments to the penal code, which had been adopted under the cover of the COVID-19 response. The amended code increased prison sentences for defamation and criminalized the spread of false information, with higher penalties during a health or other type of emergency—provisions that could continue to suppress critical speech in the future.

Indonesia turned to the military and other security forces as key players in its pandemic response. Multiple military figures were appointed to leading positions on the country's COVID-19 task force, and the armed services provided essential support in developing emergency hospitals and securing medical supplies. In recent years, observers have raised concerns about the military's growing influence over civilian governance, and its heavy involvement in the health crisis threatened to accelerate this trend. Meanwhile, restrictions on freedoms of expression and association have worsened over time, pushing the country's scores deeper into the Partly Free range.

In Sri Lanka, President Gotabaya Rajapaksa dissolved the parliament in early March, intending to hold elections the following month. The pandemic delayed the vote, however, giving Rajapaksa the opportunity to rule virtually unchecked and consolidate power through various ministerial appointments. After his party swept the August elections, the new par-liament approved constitutional amendments that expanded presidential authority, including by allowing Rajapaksa to appoint electoral, police, human rights, and anticorruption com-missions. The changes also permitted the chief executive to hold ministerial positions and dissolve the legislature after it has served just half of its term.

The public health crisis is causing a major economic crisis, as countries around the world fall into recession and millions of people are left unemployed. Marginalized populations are bearing the brunt of both the virus and its economic impact, which has exacerbated income inequality, among other disparities. In general, countries with wider income gaps have weaker protections for basic rights, suggesting that the economic fallout from the pandemic could have harmful implications for democracy. The global financial crisis of 2008–09 was notably followed by political instability and a deepening of the democratic decline.

Largest One-Year Gains and Declines in 2020

Gains in aggregate score reflect improvements in conditions for political rights and civil liberties.

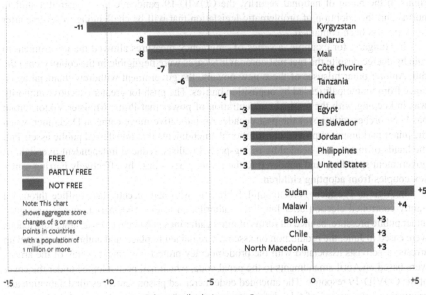

Gain or Decline in Aggregate Score

The COVID-19 pandemic is not the only current global emergency that has the potential to hasten the erosion of democracy. The effects of climate change could have a similar long-term impact, with mass displacement fueling conflict and more nationalist, xenophobic, and racist policies. Numerous other, less predictable crises could also surface, including new health emergencies. Democracy's advocates need to learn from the experience of 2020 and prepare for emergency responses that respect the political rights and civil liberties of all people, including the most marginalized.

THE RESILIENCE OF DEMOCRACY

A litany of setbacks and catastrophes for freedom dominated the news in 2020. But democracy is remarkably resilient and has proven its ability to rebound from repeated blows.

A prime example can be found in Malawi, which made important gains during the year. The Malawian people have endured a low-performing democratic system that struggled to contain a succession of corrupt and heavy-handed leaders. Although mid-2019 national elections that handed victory to the incumbent president were initially deemed credible by local and international observers, the count was marred by evidence that Tipp-Ex correction fluid was used to alter vote tabulation sheets. The election commission declined to call for a new vote, but opposition candidates took the case to the constitutional court. The court resisted bribery attempts and issued a landmark ruling in February 2020, ordering fresh elections. Opposition presidential candidate Lazarus Chakwera won the June rerun vote by a comfortable margin, proving that independent institutions can hold abuse of power in check. While Malawi is a country of 19 million people, the story of its election rerun has wider implications, as courts

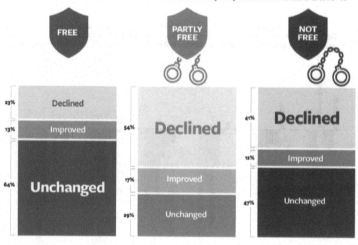

The Resilience of Democracy

Democracies and dictatorships alike have been affected by a global decline in freedom over the past 15 years. But in 2020 most Free countries resisted further declines, while many Partly Free and Not Free countries could not.

in other African states have asserted their independence in recent years, and the nullification of a flawed election—for only the second time in the continent's history—will not go unnoticed.

Taiwan overcame another set of challenges in 2020, suppressing the coronavirus with remarkable effectiveness and without resorting to abusive methods, even as it continued to shrug off threats from an increasingly aggressive regime in China. Taiwan, like its neighbors, benefited from prior experience with SARS, but its handling of COVID-19 largely respected civil liberties. Early implementation of expert recommendations, the deployment of masks and other protective equipment, and efficient contact-tracing and testing efforts that prioritized transparency—combined with the country's island geography—all helped to control the disease. Meanwhile, Beijing escalated its campaign to sway global opinion against Taiwan's government and deny the success of its democracy, in part by successfully pressuring the World Health Organization to ignore early warnings of human-to-human transmission from Taiwan and to exclude Taiwan from its World Health Assembly. Even before the virus struck, Taiwanese voters defied a multipronged, politicized disinformation campaign from China and overwhelmingly reelected incumbent president Tsai Ing-wen, who opposes moves toward unification with the mainland.

More broadly, democracy has demonstrated its adaptability under the unique constraints of a world afflicted by COVID-19. A number of successful elections were held across all regions and in countries at all income levels, including in Montenegro, and in Bolivia, yielding improvements. Judicial bodies in many settings, such as The Gambia, have held leaders to account for abuses of power, providing meaningful checks on the executive branch and contributing to slight global gains for judicial independence over the past four years. At the same time, journalists in even the most repressive environments like China sought to shed light on government transgressions, and ordinary people from Bulgaria to India to Brazil continued to express discontent on topics ranging from corruption and systemic inequality to the mishandling of the health crisis, letting their leaders know that the desire for democratic governance will not be easily quelled.

Declines Across the Board

The 15 years of decline have affected all regions and *Freedom in the World* subcategories.

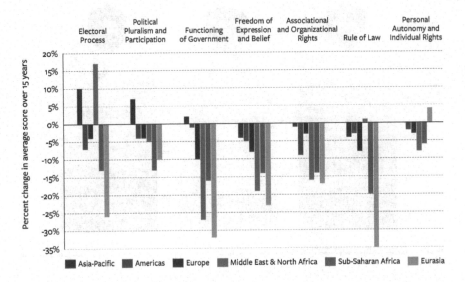

The Biden administration has pledged to make support for democracy a key part of US foreign policy, raising hopes for a more proactive American role in reversing the global democratic decline. To fulfill this promise, the president will need to provide clear leadership, articulating his goals to the American public and to allies overseas. He must also make the United States credible in its efforts by implementing the reforms necessary to address considerable democratic deficits at home. Given many competing priorities, including the pandemic and its socioeconomic aftermath, President Biden will have to remain steadfast, keeping in mind that democracy is a continuous project of renewal that ultimately ensures security and prosperity while upholding the fundamental rights of all people.

Democracy today is beleaguered but not defeated. Its enduring popularity in a more hostile world and its perseverance after a devastating year are signals of resilience that bode well for the future of freedom.

COUNTRIES IN THE SPOTLIGHT

The following countries—and one territory—featured important developments in 2020 that affected their democratic trajectory and deserve special scrutiny in 2021.

- **Armenia:** Prime Minister Nikol Pashinyan's reformist government is in political jeopardy as the country grapples with the fallout from the war with Azerbaijan.
- **Côte d'Ivoire:** President Alassane Ouattara defied constitutional term limits and secured election to a third term in a process marred by candidate disqualifications, an opposition boycott, and widespread political violence.
- **El Salvador:** President Nayib Bukele has used security forces to strongarm the parliament and enforce brutal pandemic-related restrictions on movement.
- **Ethiopia:** The initially reformist government responded to political and ethnic unrest with mass arrests and a military offensive in the Tigray Region, leading to widespread and egregious human rights violations.

- **Hong Kong:** Beijing's imposition of a draconian National Security Law in 2020 has resulted in arrests of prodemocracy activists, increased self-censorship, and a weakening of due process safeguards.
- **Jordan:** Authorities disbanded a major teachers' union and enforced excessive restrictions on assembly during the pandemic, suppressing dissent and harming the quality of parliamentary elections.
- **Malawi:** A flawed 2019 election was annulled by the Constitutional Court, the rerun election was better managed, and the resulting government made progress in fighting corruption.
- **North Macedonia:** The recently reelected government of Prime Minister Zoran Zaev has reversed years of democratic backsliding, but the country continues to be denied a chance to join the European Union.
- **Peru:** The dubious impeachment of one president was quickly followed by the resignation of his replacement, highlighting deep political dysfunction that has disrupted anticorruption efforts.
- **Sri Lanka:** A pandemic-related delay in elections allowed President Gotabaya Rajapaksa to rule without a legislature for five months, and once elected, the new parliament approved constitutional amendments to expand the president's authority.

Countries in the Spotlight

The following countries—and one territory—featured important developments in 2020 that affected their democratic trajectory, and deserve special scrutiny in 2021.

Armenia: Prime Minister Nikol Pashinyan's reformist government is in political jeopardy as the country grapples with the fallout from the war with Azerbaijan.

Côte d'Ivoire: President Alassane Ouattara defied constitutional term limits and secured election to a third term in a process marred by candidate disqualifications, an opposition boycott, and widespread political violence.

El Salvador: President Nayib Bukele has used security forces to strongarm the parliament and enforce brutal pandemic-related restrictions on movement.

Ethiopia: The initially reformist government responded to political and ethnic unrest with mass arrests and a military offensive in the Tigray Region, leading to widespread and egregious human rights violations.

Hong Kong: Beijing's imposition of a draconian National Security Law in 2020 has resulted in arrests of prodemocracy activists, increased self-censorship, and a weakening of due process safeguards.

Jordan: Authorities disbanded a major teachers' union and enforced excessive restrictions on assembly during the pandemic, suppressing dissent and harming the quality of parliamentary elections.

Malawi: A flawed 2019 election was annulled by the Constitutional Court, the rerun election was better managed, and the resulting government made progress in fighting corruption.

North Macedonia: The recently reelected government of Prime Minister Zoran Zaev has reversed years of democratic backsliding, but the country continues to be denied a chance to join the European Union.

Peru: The dubious impeachment of one president was quickly followed by the resignation of his replacement, highlighting deep political dysfunction that has disrupted anticorruption efforts.

Sri Lanka: A pandemic-related delay in elections allowed President Gotabaya Rajapaksa to rule without a legislature for five months, and once elected, the new parliament approved constitutional amendments to expand the president's authority.

AMERICAS: LOCKDOWN VIOLENCE, FREE SPEECH RESTRICTIONS, AND LEGISLATIVE TUMULT

People in a number of countries in the Americas faced violence and other abuses in the enforcement of harsh COVID-19 lockdowns. Police and military units in El Salvador and Venezuela reportedly engaged in arbitrary detentions and torture, while paramilitary groups policed civilian movement in Venezuela and Colombia. Even in Argentina, where democratic institutions are stronger, reports emerged of police firing rubber bullets at alleged quarantine breakers. Separately, the president of Mexico downplayed the harms of the coronavirus, leaving citizens with less access to life-saving information and resources.

Freedom of expression suffered elsewhere in the region. Cuban authorities unleashed a wave of intimidation, arbitrary detentions, and illegal house arrests against independent journalists and a group of dissident artists with whom the government had at one point promised an open dialogue. A harsh new cybercrimes law in Nicaragua mandated prison sentences for spreading "false information" online.

Flawed voting and political dysfunction prompted concern in some settings. In El Salvador, President Nayib Bukele shocked the country by ordering troops into the parliament in an attempt to secure extra funding for security forces. Guyana's legislative elections were marred by media bias and interference with the tabulation that favored the incumbent government, though a recount ordered by the Supreme Court eventually confirmed an opposition victory. Peru was rocked by the Congress's impeachment of one president on dubious grounds, followed a week later by the resignation of his replacement under intense public pressure. The chaotic events, which were seen as a blow to anticorruption efforts, resulted in a status decline from Free to Partly Free for Peru.

In a more positive development, Suriname emerged from the domineering rule of President Dési Bouterse after he was ousted in May elections, and the new government operated with greater transparency. Similarly, the presidential election in Bolivia was administered impartially, and the results were recognized by all competing parties, capping a period of serious political turmoil. And in Chile, following 2019 protests against inequality that featured property destruction and police violence, an overwhelming majority of voters approved the creation of a constitutional convention tasked with replacing the existing charter, which had originally been drafted under the dictatorship of Augusto Pinochet.

AMERICAS: STATUS BY POPULATION   **AMERICAS: STATUS BY COUNTRY**

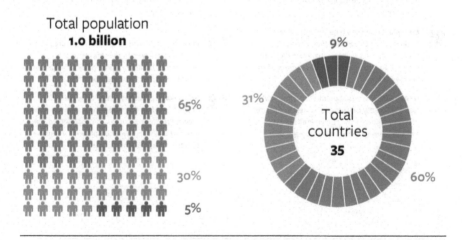

Total population
1.0 billion

65%
30%
5%

31%
9%
60%

Total countries
35

ASIA-PACIFIC: GROWING THREATS TO EXPRESSION AND ASSEMBLY

Cambodia's one-party legislature adopted a new emergency law that effectively empowered the government to surveil and arrest anyone who expresses dissent. Students and academics in Indonesia were arrested and beaten by authorities seeking to discourage public criticism of the government on a variety of issues. In the Philippines, President Rodrigo Duterte's government shuttered a major broadcaster, arrested social media users for critical posts during the pandemic, and adopted a vaguely worded new antiterrorism law that allowed people to be arbitrarily labeled as terrorists and detained without a warrant or charges, including for speech-related offenses.

Authorities in several countries restricted public assembly. Even before the February 2021 coup in Myanmar, students and activists there experienced a uptick in detentions for their involvement in public protests during 2020, while an extended internet shutdown in Rakhine State made it difficult for people to organize online and gather in public. Increasing arrests and prosecutions in Singapore have left residents less able to protest without a permit, and demonstrations by migrant workers in the Maldives led to arrests and deportations. Protests in Thailand calling for democratic reforms were met with arrests and use of water cannons against demonstrators. The Thai military's violent crackdown on dissent and the abolition of a popular opposition party reversed previous democratic progress, and as a result Thailand's status changed from Partly Free to Not Free.

ASIA-PACIFIC: STATUS BY POPULATION

ASIA-PACIFIC: STATUS BY COUNTRY

Total population
4.2 billion

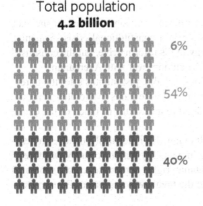

6%
54%
40%

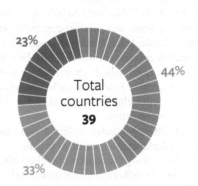

23%
44%
Total countries
39
33%

EURASIA: POWER GRABS, STALLED REFORMS, AND ARMED CONFLICT

Blatantly fraudulent parliamentary elections in Kyrgyzstan touched off protests that were quickly co-opted by criminal elements, and Sadyr Japarov—a nationalist politician serving time on a kidnapping conviction—seized power as both prime minister and president. At year's end, Japarov had advanced a new draft constitution that could reshape Kyrgyzstan's political system in the mold of its authoritarian neighbors. The country earned an 11-point score decline—the largest in *Freedom in the World 2021*—and its status declined to Not Free.

The second-largest decline in this year's report occurred in Belarus, which lost eight points as security forces attempted to crush antigovernment demonstrations triggered by the fraudulent reelection of Alyaksandr Lukashenka. The crackdown left a handful of protesters dead and hundreds at risk of torture in the country's jails.

EURASIA: STATUS BY POPULATION   **EURASIA: STATUS BY COUNTRY**

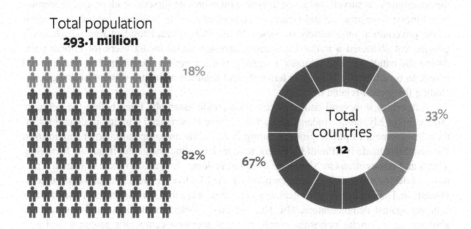

Total population
293.1 million

18%

82%

67%

Total countries
12

33%

Other problematic elections took place across the region. In Russia, President Vladimir Putin was handed the right to stay in power through 2036 in a rigged referendum, with official results showing 78 percent approval. Comparatively free but flawed parliamentary elections in Georgia deepened that country's political crisis, as the second round of voting was boycotted by the opposition.

In Ukraine, President Volodymyr Zelenskyy's reform campaign faltered in the face of the pandemic and political corruption, culminating in a constitutional crisis. Armenian prime minister Nikol Pashinyan made some headway in his reform drive, but the consensus behind his government was shattered by defeat in the autumn war with Azerbaijan.

That war brought death and despair to Nagorno-Karabakh, just months after the unrecognized territory held historically competitive elections. These gains evaporated amid the fighting, which claimed scores of civilian lives and led to an exodus of much of the ethnic Armenian population.

COVID-19 inflicted suffering everywhere, although the notoriously opaque government of Turkmenistan remained in denial, claiming implausibly that the country was free of the virus. Among the pandemic's other effects on human rights across the region, separatist authorities closed down humanitarian corridors into the breakaway regions of Eastern Donbas in Ukraine and South Ossetia in Georgia.

EUROPE: DEMOCRACIES WILT UNDER THE PANDEMIC

COVID-19 placed the democracies of Europe, the top-performing region in *Freedom in the World 2021*, under severe strain. Leaders confronted hard choices, postponing elections and locking down cities, and their decisions were implemented imperfectly: enforcement of restrictions on movement, for example, often discriminated against marginalized groups, including immigrants in France and Roma in Bulgaria. As they failed to contain the virus, many governments, including those of the United Kingdom and Spain, sought to limit public scrutiny of their decision-making processes, while inadequate labor protections in the Netherlands and elsewhere compounded the risk of illness for low-wage workers.

In countries where democratic institutions were already under attack, right-wing populists actively exploited the pandemic. Hungary's parliament handed expansive emergency powers to Prime Minister Viktor Orbán, ostensibly so the government could better respond

EUROPE: STATUS BY POPULATION   **EUROPE: STATUS BY COUNTRY**

Total population
629.7 million

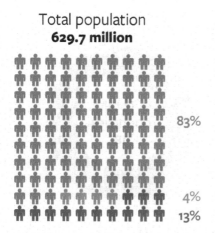

83%

4%

13%

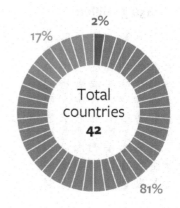

2%

17%

Total
countries
42

81%

to COVID-19. In Poland, the ruling party cited the health crisis as justification for an illegal, last-minute attempt to bypass the electoral commission and unilaterally arrange postal voting for the presidential election. Though this failed and the election was held at a later date, it was marred by the misuse of state resources and criminal charges against LGBT+ activists.

The Western Balkans saw both setbacks and progress. Flawed parliamentary elections dealt a grievous blow to Serbia's multiparty system. In Kosovo, the political old guard ousted Prime Minister Albin Kurti's short-lived government and formed a new one, unconstitutionally. Conversely, Montenegro bucked a six-year string of score declines, as elections resulted in the first transfer of power to the opposition in the country's independent history. North Macedonia's reformist government was reelected, and its institutions have largely recovered from damage inflicted by the fugitive former prime minister, Nikola Gruevski.

To the southeast, Turkey's government continued to clamp down on domestic dissent and intervened in the presidential vote of the unrecognized Turkish Republic of Northern Cyprus. Along the Turkish-Greek border, migrants and refugees endured violent "pushbacks," a phenomenon also seen on the Croatian-Bosnian border.

MIDDLE EAST AND NORTH AFRICA: COVID-19 CRACKDOWNS AND UNACCOUNTABLE REGIMES

A number of governments in the Middle East and North Africa took advantage of the pandemic to tamp down protests. In Jordan, emergency laws enacted in response to the pandemic were among those used to detain thousands of teachers who participated in massive strikes and protests led by the Teachers' Syndicate, which was ultimately dissolved. In light of its blanket ban on protests and the closure of the union, as well as an electoral framework that gave significant advantages to progovernment forces during the year's elections, Jordan's status declined from Partly Free to Not Free.

The Iranian regime was especially opaque in its response to COVID-19, using censorship and prosecutions to suppress independent reporting on the true extent of one of the region's largest early outbreaks. Similar tactics were employed to contain information about the previous year's bloody crackdown on antigovernment protests and the security forces' accidental destruction of a civilian airliner in January.

Lack of state accountability was also linked to the loss of human life in Lebanon, where a series of government failures led to a tremendous chemical explosion in Beirut's port

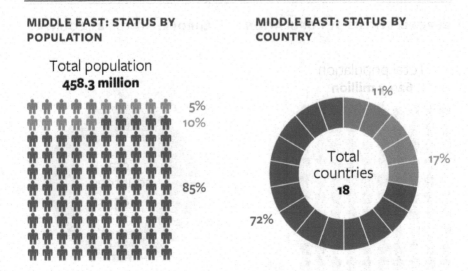

MIDDLE EAST: STATUS BY POPULATION

Total population
458.3 million

5%
10%
85%

MIDDLE EAST: STATUS BY COUNTRY

Total countries
18

11%
17%
72%

complex that killed scores of people, injured thousands, and inflicted massive structural damage across the city. An investigation into the blast encountered considerable resistance from incumbent political forces.

The steady collapse of freedom in Egypt continued for the eighth straight year, as the regime of President Abdel Fattah al-Sisi stage-managed parliamentary elections and worked to silence the country's remaining independent journalists and civil society activists, including by harassing the Egypt-based families of dissidents living abroad.

SUB-SAHARAN AFRICA: ISOLATED GAINS AMID BROADER DEMOCRATIC BACKSLIDING

Important democratic progress was reported in Malawi, which held its successful re-run of the flawed 2019 elections, and Sudan, whose ongoing reforms improved academic freedom, banned female genital mutilation, and repealed a law restricting women's travel abroad. Nevertheless, a larger number of countries registered declines due to new limits on freedom of movement as well as violent, fraudulent elections that extended incumbent presidents' already lengthy tenures.

Elections in Tanzania and the Central African Republic, for example, were characterized by government repression and violence. The presidential election in Togo was marred by accusations of fraud, with only a small pool of observers allowed to monitor the flawed process that handed President Faure Gnassingbé his fourth term in office. Accusations of fraud and the use of COVID-19 restrictions to hinder voter registration cast doubt on the presidential election in Guinea, where the incumbent secured a third term after engineering a referendum to lift term limits. In Côte d'Ivoire, where President Alassane Ouattara also claimed a constitutionally dubious third term after a favorable court ruling on the matter, some citizens were excluded from the election through the closure of polling stations, while others faced intimidation from the police, military, and ruling-party allies. Mali's democratically elected leaders were overthrown in a military coup, and its status declined from Partly Free to Not Free as a result.

Forced displacement and restrictions on freedom of movement contributed to score declines in five countries, including Ethiopia, where the conflict in the Tigray Region

**SUB-SAHARAN AFRICA:
STATUS BY POPULATION**

**SUB-SAHARAN AFRICA:
STATUS BY COUNTRY**

Total population
1.1 billion

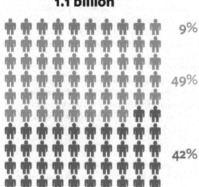

9%
49%
42%

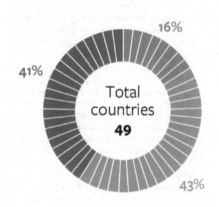

16%
41%
43%

Total
countries
49

forced tens of thousands of people from their homes. In Cameroon, conflict between the government and separatist groups also pushed people out of their communities, with the separatists enforcing their own movement restrictions and targeting students and teachers in Anglophone regions. Violence and forced displacement expanded in Mozambique, whose Cabo Delgado Province has been the site of a growing insurgency. Burkina Faso was also under attack by Islamist insurgents, and its population had to contend with abusive progovernment paramilitaries and disproportionate COVID-19 restrictions as well. Rwanda's public health rules were aggressively implemented, with scores of people arrested and abused in custody.

WORLD: STATUS BY POPULATION

WORLD: STATUS BY COUNTRY

Total population
7.8 billion

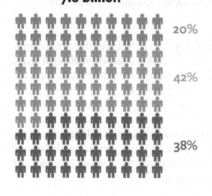

20%
42%
38%

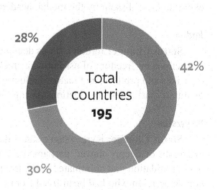

28%
42%
30%

Total
countries
195

Freedom in the World 2021 Status Changes

India

▼ India's status declined from Free to Partly Free due to a multiyear pattern in which the Hindu nationalist government and its allies presided over rising violence and discriminatory policies affecting the Muslim population and pursued a crackdown on expressions of dissent by the media, academics, civil society groups, and protesters.

Jordan

▼ Jordan's status declined from Partly Free to Not Free due to harsh new restrictions on freedom of assembly, a crackdown on the teachers' union following a series of strikes and protests, and factors including a lack of adequate preparations that harmed the quality of parliamentary elections during the COVID-19 pandemic.

Kyrgyzstan

▼ Kyrgyzstan's status declined from Partly Free to Not Free because the aftermath of deeply flawed parliamentary elections featured significant political violence and intimidation that culminated in the irregular seizure of power by a nationalist leader and convicted felon who had been freed from prison by supporters.

Mali

▼ Mali's status declined from Partly Free to Not Free due to legislative elections that were marred by political violence and a subsequent military coup that removed the country's elected civilian leadership.

Peru

▼ Peru's status declined from Free to Partly Free due to extended political clashes between the presidency and Congress since 2017 that have heavily disrupted governance and anticorruption efforts, strained the country's constitutional order, and resulted in an irregular succession of four presidents within three years.

Seychelles

▲ The Seychelles' status improved from Partly Free to Free because a strengthened electoral framework contributed to a more open and competitive presidential election, resulting in the country's first transfer of power to an opposition party.

Thailand

▼ Thailand's status declined from Partly Free to Not Free due to the dissolution of a popular opposition party that had performed well in the 2019 elections, and the military-dominated government's crackdown on youth-led protests calling for democratic reforms.

Zimbabwe

▼ Zimbabwe's status declined from Partly Free to Not Free due to the authorities' intensifying persecution of opposition figures and civic activists.

FREEDOM IN THE WORLD STATUS CHANGES

India

Status Change: India's status declined from Free to Partly Free due to a multiyear pattern in which the Hindu nationalist government and its allies presided over rising violence and discriminatory policies affecting the Muslim population and pursued a crackdown on expressions of dissent by the media, academics, civil society groups, and protesters.

Jordan

Status Change: Jordan's status declined from Partly Free to Not Free due to harsh new restrictions on freedom of assembly, a crackdown on the teachers' union following a series of strikes and protests, and factors including a lack of adequate preparations that harmed the quality of parliamentary elections during the COVID-19 pandemic.

Kyrgyzstan

Status Change: Kyrgyzstan's status declined from Partly Free to Not Free because the aftermath of deeply flawed parliamentary elections featured significant political violence and intimidation that culminated in the irregular seizure of power by a nationalist leader and convicted felon who had been freed from prison by supporters.

Mali

Status Change: Mali's status declined from Partly Free to Not Free due to legislative elections that were marred by political violence and a subsequent military coup that removed the country's elected civilian leadership.

Peru

Status Change: Peru's status declined from Free to Partly Free due to extended political clashes between the presidency and Congress since 2017 that have heavily disrupted governance and anticorruption efforts, strained the country's constitutional order, and resulted in an irregular succession of four presidents within three years.

Seychelles

Status Change: The Seychelles' status improved from Partly Free to Free because a strengthened electoral framework contributed to a more open and competitive presidential election, resulting in the country's first transfer of power to an opposition party.

Thailand

Status Change: Thailand's status declined from Partly Free to Not Free due to the dissolution of a popular opposition party that had performed well in the 2019 elections, and the military-dominated government's crackdown on youth-led protests calling for democratic reforms.

Zimbabwe

Status Change: Zimbabwe's status declined from Partly Free to Not Free due to the authorities' intensifying persecution of opposition figures and civic activists.

Introduction

The *Freedom in the World 2021* survey contains reports on 195 countries and 15 territories. Each country report begins with a section containing the following information: **population, capital**, and **freedom status** (Free, Partly Free, or Not Free). Each territory report begins with a section containing the same information, except for the capital. The population figures are drawn primarily from the *2020 World Population Data Sheet* of the Population Reference Bureau.

The **political rights** and **civil liberties** ratings range from 1 to 7, with 1 representing the most free and 7 the least free. The **status** designation of Free, Partly Free, or Not Free, which is determined by the average of the political rights and civil liberties ratings, indicates the general state of freedom in a country or territory. A brief explanation of status changes is provided for each country or territory as required. Any improvements or declines in the ratings since the previous survey are noted next to the relevant number in each report. For a full description of the methods used to determine the survey's ratings, please see the chapter on the survey's methodology.

Following the section described above, each country and territory report is composed of three parts: an **overview**, bullets on **key developments**, and an analysis of **political rights and civil liberties**. The overview provides a succinct, general description that explains the country or territory's place on the 0–7 rating scale; bullets on key developments summarize key events that took place in 2020; and the section on political rights and civil liberties analyzes the degree of respect for the rights and liberties that Freedom House uses to evaluate freedom in the world. This section is composed of seven parts that correspond to the seven main subcategories in the methodology and justify a country or territory's score for each indicator. The scores for each indicator, subcategory, and category, along with any changes from the previous year, are noted next to the relevant subheading.

Country Reports

Afghanistan

Population: 38,966,000
Capital: Kabul
Freedom Status: Not Free
Electoral Democracy: No

Overview: Afghanistan's constitution provides for a unitary state, headed by a directly elected president, with significant checks from the parliament and a wide range of rights guaranteed to citizens. However, an insurgency waged by Islamist militants has undermined the writ of the state in much of the rural hinterland, severely restricting the franchise. Political rights and civil liberties are curtailed in practice by violence, corruption, patronage, and flawed electoral processes.

KEY DEVELOPMENTS IN 2020

- In February, the Independent Election Commission (IEC) announced that President Ghani had claimed victory in the September 2019 presidential poll, and he was inaugurated for his second term in March. Challenger Abdullah Abdullah refused to accept the result and held a parallel inauguration. In May, the two teams signed a political agreement to work together in a government headed by Ghani.
- The United States signed an agreement with the Taliban in February according to which the Americans announced a conditional troop withdrawal timetable, and intra-Afghan negotiations were to commence. These negotiations, between the Taliban and a government delegation, convened in Doha in September but had made no substantive progress by year end.
- Conflict between Afghan government forces and the Taliban continued. After the US-Taliban agreement, US forces exercised restraint on the battlefield, intervening only to support Afghan positions during Taliban attacks. The Taliban refrained from high-casualty attacks on population centers or on international forces, but stepped up attacks against Afghan security forces, as well as targeted killings in Kabul and other cities.
- The World Health Organization (WHO) recorded over 50,000 COVID-19 infections, and 2,000 related deaths, and the country imposed limited lockdown measures early in the year. Afghanistan suffered fewer direct effects from the pandemic than many other countries, however, and the ongoing conflict had a greater impact on everyday life.

POLITICAL RIGHTS: 13 / 40
A. ELECTORAL PROCESS: 3 / 12
A1. Was the current head of government or other chief national authority elected through free and fair elections? 1 / 4

Afghanistan's president is directly elected for up to two five-year terms and has the power to appoint ministers, subject to parliamentary approval. In February 2020, the Independent Election Commission (IEC) announced that Ashraf Ghani had won the September 2019 presidential election with 50.64 percent of votes cast. However, his leading opponent, former foreign minister Abdullah Abdullah, contested the result, and held a parallel inauguration alongside Ghani's on March 9. The electoral dispute was resolved in a May 17 political agreement between the Ghani and Abdullah camps that confirmed Ashraf Ghani as president, heading a cabinet whose members were nominated by both teams. Abdullah in turn headed a new High Reconciliation Council charged with running Afghanistan's peace process.

The 2019 election process featured several flaws and challenges. Final turnout was approximately 1.8 million—a historic low for a presidential election. The campaign was hampered by uncertainty over whether the election would take place or not. The election authorities successfully rolled out an electoral roll and biometric voter verification (BVV) technology, but there were major problems in the BVV implementation. Over a million initially reported votes had to be thrown out because of the lack of any corresponding BVV; other controversies centered on the handling of separate discrepancies in the BVV record. Finally, the commissioners and their secretariats struggled to maintain the confidence of candidate teams and to allay suspicions of political interference.

A2. Were the current national legislative representatives elected through free and fair elections? 1 / 4

In the directly elected lower house of the National Assembly, the 249-seat Wolesi Jirga (House of the People), members stand for five-year terms. In the 102-seat Meshrano Jirga (House of Elders), the upper house, the provincial councils elect two-thirds of members for three- or four-year terms, and the president appoints the remaining third for five-year terms. The constitution envisages the election of district councils, which would also send members to the Meshrano Jirga, though these have not been established. Ten Wolesi Jirga seats are reserved for the nomadic Kuchi community, including at least three women, and 65 of the chamber's general seats are reserved for women.

Parliamentary elections originally scheduled for 2014 were postponed amid security concerns, and the president extended the legislature's mandate with an apparently unconstitutional decree until elections were finally held in October 2018. Despite security threats from the Taliban, which threatened to punish people for voting, and poor organization by the Independent Election Commission (IEC), more than four million people voted (approximately half of registered voters). The vote count and adjudication process were protracted and contested, amidst allegations of corruption by members of the electoral commissions. Other problems included a poll worker shortage, attributed to fears of violence, and difficulties with the then-untested biometric identification system that contributed to delays in opening polling stations, and long lines. Many people reportedly waited hours to vote, and some left before casting their ballots.

A3. Are the electoral laws and framework fair, and are they implemented impartially by the relevant election management bodies? 1 / 4

Elections are administered by the IEC, and disputes are adjudicated by the Electoral Complaints Commission (ECC). Following the highly contested vote count and audit process that accompanied the 2018 parliamentary elections, both election management bodies were disbanded in February 2019, and several members of the bodies were prosecuted, found guilty of corruption, and jailed. Members of the new IEC and ECC were nominated by political parties and civil society organizations, voted on by the presidential candidates, and sworn in in March 2019. The bodies also included international experts inducted as nonvoting members. Nevertheless, candidates continued to question the independence and competence of IEC and ECC members and their secretariats during the 2019 presidential election.

Parliamentary and provincial council elections are conducted using a Single Non-Transferable Vote (SNTV) system, in multimember constituencies, which tends to award most seats to candidates with a low vote share. Political parties have been unsuccessful in their attempts to replace SNTV with a proportional system. A new voter roll and biometric voter verification were introduced in 2018 and 2019 and have helped limit the mass fraudulent voting that marred earlier elections. But recent electoral complaints reflected concerns that the election management bodies may have colluded in circumventing the new safeguards.

B. POLITICAL PLURALISM AND PARTICIPATION: 7 / 16

B1. Do the people have the right to organize in different political parties or other competitive political groupings of their choice, and is the system free of undue obstacles to the rise and fall of these competing parties or groupings? 2 / 4

Afghans have the right to form or join a political party and there is a highly competitive field of parties, espousing a range of traditional, Islamist, and liberal ideologies. In practice, most candidates for elected office run as independents and participate in fluid alliances linked to local and regional patronage networks. While political parties have been free to seek registration since 2005, they have yet to consolidate mass support. The main parties are typically defined in relation to prominent figures or factions who had a role in earlier stages of the country's ongoing conflict.

B2. Is there a realistic opportunity for the opposition to increase its support or gain power through elections? 2 / 4

Multiple opposition leaders and parties seek power through elections. However, the question of whether these elections provide a realistic route to power for a democratic opposition remains unsettled.

The Afghan president's control over administrative and security-sector appointments throughout the country and influence in financial-resource allocation offers the incumbent significant electoral advantages, and the 2019 presidential election and its aftermath left open the question of whether the opposition has a route to power through elections. The balance of power in the government formed after the May 2020 political agreement depended on negotiations, protests, coalition-building, control of the electoral institutions, and exercise of patronage, in addition to the direct appeal to voters.

B3. Are the people's political choices free from domination by forces that are external to the political sphere, or by political forces that employ extrapolitical means? 1 / 4

The dominant threat to the free exercise of Afghans' political choices is the insurgency waged by the Taliban movement, which exerts complete or partial control over most rural areas and conducts intimidation in some urban areas. The Taliban are opposed to the current political system on the basis that they consider electoral democracy un-Islamic. They have thus sought to disrupt elections and have targeted civilians whom they accuse of being apologists for the government or political system more generally.

In addition to the Taliban insurgency, in many parts of the country former military commanders have emerged as important local power brokers, often with patronage links to the government and influence in the security forces or informal militias. These local power brokers typically exercise disproportionate influence over the population in their areas and attempt to speak on behalf of the community when dealing with government.

The civil administration and moneyed elites also exert undue influence over the electoral apparatus, and these concerns were reflected in the justice system, when members of the electoral commissions were tried and convicted of fraud in 2019. The expectation of fraud and sense that actual votes would not count likely contributed to low turnout in areas where there was little Taliban threat to polling.

B4. Do various segments of the population (including ethnic, racial, religious, gender, LGBT+, and other relevant groups) have full political rights and electoral opportunities? 2 / 4

The constitution recognizes multiple ethnic and linguistic minorities and provides more guarantees of equal status to minorities than historically have been available in Afghanistan. Since 2001, the traditionally marginalized Shiite Muslim minority, which includes most ethnic Hazaras, has enjoyed increased levels of political representation and participation in national institutions. Over the past three presidential elections, the main tickets have included vice presidents from the minority ethnic groups as a way of broadening the appeal of the ticket. Through this tradition of coalition building, Tajiks, Hazaras and Uzbeks have all had a stake in the electoral contest.

Women's political participation has been constrained by threats, harassment, and social restrictions on traveling alone and appearing in public. The proportion of women registered as voters declined from 41 percent in 2010 to 34 percent in 2018. In 2018, over 400 women competed for the 68 parliamentary seats allocated to female representatives. All candidates running in the 2019 presidential poll were men.

C. FUNCTIONING OF GOVERNMENT: 3 / 12

C1. Do the freely elected head of government and national legislative representatives determine the policies of the government? 1 / 4

The ability of the president and their cabinet, acting in concert with the legislature, to set and implement state policies is limited by a number of factors. The government remains heavily dependent on military and economic support from the United States and its allies, and it is unable to enforce its laws and decisions in parts of the country controlled by the Taliban and other insurgents. Parliament exercises weak oversight over the executive, is often disregarded by the government, and very rarely adopts legislation on its own initiative.

During 2020, the peace initiative led by the US special representative Zalmay Khalilzad highlighted the challenge faced by the president in retaining effective control over national policy while facing an armed insurgency and remaining dependent on the United States and other allies for military and economic assistance. While the agreement that was ultimately signed between the United States and the Taliban had strong implications for the Afghan government, the government had no role in agreement's negotiation. In particular, the agreement committed the United States to ensuring that the Afghan authorities released 5,000 Taliban prisoners, despite President Ghani being unconvinced of the wisdom of releasing so many prisoners. However, after organizing a consultative assembly (Loya Jirga), he obtained a mandate to proceed with the releases. Similarly, in the final stages of the first round of talks, the president found himself under intense pressure to accept a compromise favored by the US-led diplomatic team facilitating the talks.

C2. Are safeguards against official corruption strong and effective? 1 / 4

There have been periodic arrests, prosecutions, and dismissals of civilian and military officials accused of corruption, and an Anti-Corruption Justice Centre (ACJC) was established in 2016, bringing together specialized police, prosecutors, and courts to focus on high-level malfeasance. Nevertheless, corruption remains an endemic problem, law enforcement agencies and the judiciary are themselves compromised by graft and political pressure, and the most powerful officials and politicians effectively enjoy impunity.

During the process of government formation after the May 2020 political agreement, numerous reports claimed that key senior appointments could only be secured through cash payment to the appointing authority.

C3. Does the government operate with openness and transparency? 1 / 4

Government operations are largely opaque, and corruption is endemic in the management of public-sector contracting. The ownership of mining companies that receive government contracts often goes undisclosed, effectively allowing individuals and entities legally prohibited from winning contracts, such as members of parliament, to participate. The National Procurement Commission, established in 2014 and chaired by the president to guide the National Procurement Authority (NPA), has made some positive progress in reforming procurement processes.

CIVIL LIBERTIES: 14 / 60

D. FREEDOM OF EXPRESSION AND BELIEF: 6 / 16

D1. Are there free and independent media? 2 / 4

Afghanistan has a vibrant media sector, with multiple outlets in print, radio, and television that collectively carry a wide range of views and are generally uncensored. Media providers include independent and commercial firms, as well as a state broadcaster and outlets tied to specific political interests.

However, journalists face the threat of harassment and attack by the Taliban, Islamic State (IS) militant group, and government-related figures attempting to influence how they are covered in the news. Restrictions on freedom of expression have been justified in the name of avoiding incitement to or support of terrorism. The Afghan authorities ban the live television coverage of terrorist incidents, which can restrict on-the-ground television reporting. The Committee to Protect Journalists (CPJ) recorded five journalists killed in 2020, and named Afghanistan in the top three countries for retaliatory killings against journalists.

A rapid expansion in the availability of mobile phones, the internet, and social media has granted many Afghans greater access to diverse views and information. The Afghan government has publicly supported media freedom and cooperated with initiatives to counter security threats to media workers. Nevertheless, high-level officials, including Ghani, periodically question the validity of stories critical of the government and attempt to discredit journalists.

D2. Are individuals free to practice and express their religious faith or nonbelief in public and private? 1 / 4

While religious freedom has improved since 2001, it is still hampered by violence and discrimination aimed at religious minorities and reformist Muslims. The constitution establishes Islam as the official religion and guarantees freedom of worship to other religions. Blasphemy and apostasy by Muslims are considered capital crimes, and non-Muslim proselytizing is strongly discouraged in practice. Conservative social attitudes, intolerance, and the inability or unwillingness of law enforcement officials to defend individual freedoms mean that those perceived as violating religious and social norms are highly vulnerable to abuse.

Terrorist attacks against places of worship, funerals, and sites associated with religious and sectarian minority groups continued during 2020. In March, a suicide attack on a gurdwara in Kabul killed 25 people. Thirty-six people were killed in an attack the same month on a gathering in west Kabul to commemorate Shia leader Abdul Ali Mazari, who was slain in 1995. In May, 24 people were killed in a maternity hospital located in a Shia-dominated area of Kabul. Some observers have interpreted these attacks as attempts to stoke sectarian tensions where they have not historically existed.

D3. Is there academic freedom, and is the educational system free from extensive political indoctrination? 1 / 4

Academic freedom is largely tolerated in government-controlled areas, where public schools and universities enjoy full autonomy from the government (though there are serious shortages of qualified instructors and up-to-date teaching materials).

The conflict continues to directly impact the education system. In November, 35 people were killed when Islamist militants stormed the campus of Kabul University. Government security forces and the Taliban have both taken over schools to use as military posts. The expansion of Taliban control in rural areas has left an increasing number of public schools outside of government control. The Taliban operate an education commission in parallel to the official Ministry of Education. Although their practices vary between areas, some schools under Taliban control reportedly allow teachers to continue teaching, but ban certain subjects and replace them with Islamic studies.

D4. Are individuals free to express their personal views on political or other sensitive topics without fear of surveillance or retribution? 2 / 4

Although private discussion in government-held areas is largely free and unrestrained, discussion of a political nature is more dangerous for Afghans living in contested or Taliban-controlled areas. Government security agencies have increased their ability to monitor the internet, including social media platforms. However, this monitoring has not yet had a perceptible impact on social media use.

E. ASSOCIATIONAL AND ORGANIZATIONAL RIGHTS: 4 / 12

E1. Is there freedom of assembly? 2 / 4

The constitution guarantees the right to peaceful assembly, subject to some restrictions, but this right is upheld erratically from region to region. The police sometimes fire live ammunition when attempting to break up demonstrations, and in past years demonstrations have been subject to devastating and deadly terrorist or militant attacks. The Taliban suppresses demonstrations in areas it controls.

E2. Is there freedom for nongovernmental organizations, particularly those that are engaged in human rights- and governance-related work? 1 / 4

The constitution guarantees the right to form nongovernmental organizations (NGOs), and both the legal framework and the national authorities are relatively supportive of civil society groups. NGOs play an important role in the country, particularly in urban areas, where thousands of cultural, welfare, and sports associations operate.

However, NGOs are sometimes hampered by official corruption and bureaucratic reporting requirements, and the threat of violence by armed groups is a major obstacle to their activities. The Taliban operates its own commission to regulate the affairs of companies and organizations. While the Taliban have to some extent allowed access for NGOs to areas which they control, the commission and field commanders often impose arbitrary restrictions, in particular against organizations deemed to be close to the Afghan government.

E3. Is there freedom for trade unions and similar professional or labor organizations? 1 / 4

Despite broad constitutional protections for workers, labor rights are not well defined in law, and no effective enforcement or dispute-resolution mechanisms are currently in place. Unions are largely absent from the informal and agricultural sectors, which account for most Afghan workers.

F. RULE OF LAW: 2 / 16

F1. Is there an independent judiciary? 1 / 4

The judicial system operates haphazardly, and justice in many places is administered on the basis of a mixture of legal codes by inadequately trained judges. Corruption in the judiciary is extensive, with judges and lawyers often subject to threats and bribes from local leaders or armed groups. Informal justice systems, employing variants of both customary law and Sharia (Islamic law), are widely used to arbitrate disputes, especially in rural areas. The Taliban have installed their own judiciary in areas they control, but many Taliban commanders impose arbitrary punishments without reference to this system.

F2. Does due process prevail in civil and criminal matters? 0 / 4

Prosecutions and trials suffer from a number of weaknesses, including lack of proper representation, excessive reliance on uncorroborated witness testimony, lack of reliable forensic evidence, arbitrary decision-making, and failure to publish court decisions. The police force is heavily militarized and primarily focused on its role as a first line of defense against insurgents in administrative centers. There are high levels of corruption and complicity in organized crime among police, particularly near key smuggling routes. There is an entrenched culture of impunity for the country's political and military power brokers.

F3. Is there protection from the illegitimate use of physical force and freedom from war and insurgencies? 0 / 4

The Afghan population remains acutely vulnerable to the full range of threats from armed conflict, including violence to the person, loss of property and livelihood, chronic insecurity, and encroachment on liberty by the arbitrary rule of armed groups. The experience of the war varies dramatically between different sections of the population and areas.

The US government continued to drive a peace process during 2020, with the Taliban scaling back attacks in the week preceding the agreement reached in February. The Taliban also paused violence for three days over each of the two Eids. Under the February deal, the United States announced a conditional troop withdrawal timetable, and intra-Afghan negotiations (IAN) were to commence. The IAN convened in Doha in September but had made no substantive progress by year's end, and the Taliban declared their intention to sustain their military campaign against Afghan forces. When the negotiation teams assembled in Doha, the Taliban made it clear that they were uninterested in discussing an early ceasefire.

After the US-Taliban agreement, US forces exercised new restraint on the battlefield, only intervening to support Afghan security forces while they were being attacked by the Taliban. For their part, the Taliban generally refrained from high-casualty attacks on population centers or on international forces. But Taliban stepped up attacks on Afghan security forces and mounted an intensified campaign of targeted killings of Afghans, in Kabul and other cities, whom they deemed to be apologists for the government or political system. The Taliban avoided claiming responsibility for the urban target-killing, but both the Afghan government and diplomatic missions in Kabul concluded that the killings were conducted by the group.

As a result of these shifts in the conflict, civilians in many rural areas controlled by the Taliban experienced less violence due to reduced bombardment and ground offensives. But in areas contested by Taliban and government, such as around district centers, there was an intensification of violence. And in urban areas, the risk of being caught in suicide bombings was replaced by the chronic insecurity of the targeted-killing campaign.

The US-led peace process only involved the Taliban, and not the Islamic State (IS). In the spring, the Taliban launched a successful ground offensive against the last enclave controlled by Islamic State, in Kunar Province. Thereafter, the Islamic State survived as an underground terrorist network, conducting occasional attacks. But the loss of territory and dispersal of many of its fighters left the Islamic State militarily severely weakened.

There were contradictory trends in and claims about the overall levels of violence during the year. On the one hand, the UN Assistance Mission in Afghanistan (UNAMA) noted a significant reduction in civilian casualties relative to recent years: 5,939 civilian casualties in the first three quarters of 2020 (2,117 killed and 3,822 injured). This was equivalent to a 30 percent drop in civilian casualties relative to the same period in 2019. Those who were optimistic about the negotiation process in Doha attributed this fall to the voluntary restraint, or a "reduction in violence," which US negotiators said the Taliban had promised, while signing the February agreement. By other indicators, violence intensified after the US-Taliban agreement. The hopeful trends in the UNAMA figures were attributable to a decline in mass-casualty suicide attacks, which in turn reflected both the decline of the IS and the pause of the Taliban bombing campaign in Kabul. The decline also reflected the reduction in aerial bombardment of the Taliban by US forces. The decline in civilians killed by the Taliban was modest.

Meanwhile, Afghan authorities produced figures that reflected increased intensity of Taliban attacks. For example, the Afghan National Security Council reported that the third week of June was the deadliest of the conflict so far, with Taliban carrying out 422 attacks in 32 provinces, killing 291 members of the Afghan National Security Forces and wounding 550 others. In August, President Ghani reported that Taliban had inflicted 12,279 military and civilian casualties since their February agreement with the United States.

F4. Do laws, policies, and practices guarantee equal treatment of various segments of the population? 1 / 4

Despite some legal protections, members of religious, ethnic and other minority groups remain subject to harassment and discrimination, including in employment and education. Ethnic-based patronage practices affect different groups' access to jobs depending on the local context. The population of non-Muslim minorities such as Hindus and Sikhs has shrunk to a tiny fraction of its former size due to emigration in recent decades. Women face severe disadvantages in the justice system, access to employment, and other matters, with harmful societal norms often overriding legal guarantees.

There is no legal protection for LGBT+ people, who face societal disapproval and abuse by police. Same-sex sexual activity is considered illegal under the penal code and Sharia.

G. PERSONAL AUTONOMY AND INDIVIDUAL RIGHTS: 2 / 16

G1. Do individuals enjoy freedom of movement, including the ability to change their place of residence, employment, or education? 0 / 4

The constitution grants Afghans freedom of movement, residence, and travel abroad. However, these freedoms are severely circumscribed in practice by the ongoing civil conflict, which continued to cause mass displacement and render travel unsafe in much of the country. Amnesty International reported that were are as many as 4 million internally displaced people, driven from their homes by conflict, natural disaster, and climate change. Many of them have remained in displaced persons camps for much of the current twenty-year conflict. Some 114,000 people were reported newly displaced in the first six months of 2020.

Opportunities for Afghans to seek refuge abroad have been curtailed in recent years, as the European Union (EU) has attempted to reinforce its external border and member states have increased deportations of failed asylum seekers, Iran and Pakistan have compelled hundreds of thousands of refugees to return home, and the United States has decreased the number of refugees permitted annually.

G2. Are individuals able to exercise the right to own property and establish private businesses without undue interference from state or non-state actors? 1 / 4

Citizens are formally free to own property, buy and sell land, and establish businesses. However, economic freedoms are constrained by corruption, and the dominant economic role of a narrow, politically connected elite. Over the past two decades the most profitable activities available to Afghans have been government and defense contracting, narcotics trafficking, and property and minerals development. Investors in all of these sectors have depended on connections to those in power. Land theft backed by the threat of force is a serious problem.

A combination of harassment, extortion, and arbitrary taxation make for a highly unfavorable business climate for any investor hoping to operate within the law. Companies are only able to operate in areas the Taliban controls by paying illegal taxes. The movement now also routinely extorts money from traders in government-controlled towns.

G3. Do individuals enjoy personal social freedoms, including choice of marriage partner and size of family, protection from domestic violence, and control over appearance? 0 / 4

Domestic violence against women remains pervasive. In 2017, the Ministry of Public Health estimated that 51 percent of women experience domestic violence in their lifetimes. However, women's rights activists maintain that only a small proportion of actual incidents are reported. According to a May 2018 report published by the United Nations, many cases of violence against women are dealt with by traditional mediation, rather than through the criminal justice system; this largely enables impunity for perpetrators.

Women's choices regarding marriage and divorce remain restricted by custom and discriminatory laws. The forced marriage of young girls to older men or widows to their husbands' male relations is a problem, and many girls continue to be married before the legal age of 16. The courts and the detention system have been used to enforce social control of women, for example by jailing those who defy their families' wishes regarding marriage.

G4. Do individuals enjoy equality of opportunity and freedom from economic exploitation? 1 / 4

The constitution bans forced labor and gives all citizens the right to work. However, debt bondage remains a problem, as does child labor, which is particularly prevalent in the carpet industry. Most human trafficking victims in Afghanistan are children trafficked internally to work in various industries, become domestic servants, settle debts, or be subjected to sexual exploitation. Children are also vulnerable to recruitment by armed militant groups, and to a lesser extent by government security forces.

Albania

Population: 2,800,000
Capital: Tirana
Freedom Status: Partly Free
Electoral Democracy: Yes

Overview: Albania has a record of competitive elections, though political parties are highly polarized and often organized around leading personalities. Religious freedom and freedom of assembly are generally respected. Corruption and organized crime remain serious problems despite recent government efforts to address them, and the intermingling of powerful business, political, and media interests inhibits the development of truly independent news outlets.

KEY DEVELOPMENTS IN 2020

- In January, the parliament established the Political Council, tasked with creating a plan to address electoral reforms recommended by the Organization for Security and Co-operation in Europe (OSCE). By October, the parliament had adopted most of the Council's plan, including policies to gradually depoliticize election administration, introduce electronic identification of voters where technically possible, and restructure the Central Election Commission (CEC), among other changes.
- Due to the COVID-19 pandemic, the government passed a state of emergency that, among other restrictions, banned public gatherings. However, in December, several hundred protesters clashed with police for several days after a police officer killed an unarmed civilian who had violated a coronavirus-related curfew. Demonstrators threw stones, flares, and firecrackers at officers who used tear gas and water cannon to disperse them.

POLITICAL RIGHTS: 27 / 40
A. ELECTORAL PROCESS: 8 / 12
A1. Was the current head of government or other chief national authority elected through free and fair elections? 3 / 4

The president is the head of state and is chosen by the parliament for a maximum of two five-year terms; the office does not hold executive power, though the president heads the military and plays a key role in selecting senior judges. The prime minister is the head of government and is designated by the majority party or coalition. Because both the president and prime minister are selected by lawmakers, their legitimacy is generally dependent on the conduct of parliamentary elections.

In April 2017, Ilir Meta, the head of the Socialist Movement of Integration (LSI), was selected as president. Socialist Party (PS) leader Edi Rama retained his position as prime minister following the June 2017 parliamentary election.

In July 2020, the parliament initiated an impeachment procedure against President Meta. The committee that conducted the impeachment inquiry concluded in October that, though Meta had overstepped his constitutional authority by postponing a series of local elections in June 2019, his impeachment was not justified.

A2. Were the current national legislative representatives elected through free and fair elections? 3 / 4

Albania is a parliamentary republic. The unicameral, 140-member Kuvendi (Assembly) is elected through proportional representation in 12 regional districts of varying size. All members serve four-year terms.

Events preceding the 2017 legislative election reflected ongoing distrust between the opposition Democratic Party (PD) and the ruling PS. In late 2016, the president called the parliamentary election for the following June. The PD boycotted the election in February 2017, claiming the PS would commit massive electoral fraud. A standoff ensued, with tensions escalating that May, when the PD held a large protest in Tirana. Mediators from the

United States and European Union (EU) facilitated an agreement between the parties later that month; the PD was guaranteed several ministerial positions, the chair of the Central Election Commission (CEC), and directorships of several public agencies.

The election was held in June 2017, a week later than initially scheduled. The PS won 74 seats, enough to govern alone, on voter turnout of 46.8 percent. Organization for Security and Co-operation in Europe (OSCE) election monitors praised the contest's conduct, but noted that the mediated agreement resulted in the "selective and inconsistent application" of electoral law. The mission also noted vote-buying and voter intimidation allegations.

Municipal elections held in June 2019 were also marred by vote-buying allegations. PD and LSI lawmakers resigned their seats in February and threatened to boycott the coming local elections. After months of opposition-led protests, President Meta attempted to delay the contests in June, just before the elections, but the parliament reversed his decree and censured him for his actions. The contests proceeded as scheduled, but opposition parties boycotted local races; PS candidates won most mayoral contests and local council seats on a turnout of 23 percent.

While OSCE monitors said the contests were generally orderly, they also reported significant irregularities; parties tracked voter participation, impinging on voters' rights to participate without fear of retribution. Some voters also reported that they were threatened with loss of employment or the withdrawal of social service support depending on their vote. The PD denounced the contest, claiming that turnout figures had been inflated.

A3. Are the electoral laws and framework fair, and are they implemented impartially by the relevant election management bodies? 2 / 4

After the 2017 election, the OSCE voiced concerns that the CEC was not operating transparently and sometimes failed to sanction parties that committed electoral violations, such as failing to adhere to gender quota requirements. In January 2020, the parliament established the Political Council, comprised of representatives of the three largest parties, to create a plan to address needed electoral reforms recommended by the OSCE. In July, the parliament partially adopted provisions of the Council's plan to gradually depoliticize election administration, introduce electronic identification of voters where technically possible, and restructure the CEC, among other changes. In October, some reforms that required more thorough legislative changes were enacted by the parliament.

B. POLITICAL PLURALISM AND PARTICIPATION: 12 / 16

B1. Do the people have the right to organize in different political parties or other competitive political groupings of their choice, and is the system free of undue obstacles to the rise and fall of these competing parties or groupings? 3 / 4

Albanian citizens generally have the right to organize in political parties. The two main parties, the PS and the PD, are sharply polarized and given to personality-driven rivalry. Candidates for legislative elections who do not belong to a party currently seated in the parliament must collect a set number of signatures in order to run.

B2. Is there a realistic opportunity for the opposition to increase its support or gain power through elections? 3 / 4

Albania's multiparty system provides ample opportunity for opposition parties to participate in the political process, and elections have resulted in the rotation of power among parties. The PD and LSI boycotted the June 2019 local contests, leaving fewer options for Albanians who voted.

B3. Are the people's political choices free from domination by forces that are external to the political sphere, or by political forces that employ extrapolitical means? 3 / 4

While individuals are generally free to make their own political choices, powerful economic actors can also shape the political sphere through their media holdings and influence on electoral campaigns. Criminal organizations are also known to influence Albanian politics.

B4. Do various segments of the population (including ethnic, racial, religious, gender, LGBT+, and other relevant groups) have full political rights and electoral opportunities? 3 / 4

Albanian law guarantees political rights for citizens regardless of their ethnic, racial, lingual, or religious identity. Electoral officials provided voter education materials in minority languages for the 2017 parliamentary poll, though not for the June 2019 local elections.

Roma and other marginalized people remain vulnerable to political exploitation. OSCE monitors noted that Romany individuals faced difficulty registering to vote in 2019 due to a lack of a permanent address.

Women are underrepresented both in politics and election administration roles; 36 women held parliamentary seats in 2019.

C. FUNCTIONING OF GOVERNMENT: 7 / 12

C1. Do the freely elected head of government and national legislative representatives determine the policies of the government? 3 / 4

In 2017, elections, and thus the timely formation of a new government, were threatened by an impasse between the PD and PS that persisted until international mediators facilitated a political agreement. Once installed, the government was largely able to formulate and implement policy, though its ability to do so was somewhat impacted by the February 2019 opposition boycott.

C2. Are safeguards against official corruption strong and effective? 2 / 4

Corruption is pervasive, and the EU has repeatedly called for rigorous implementation of antigraft measures, particularly for corruption within the judiciary. The Special Prosecutor Service was established as part of 2016 reforms, and is tasked with prosecuting high-level corruption. In a process monitored by EU and US experts, the government has been vetting judges and prosecutors since 2018, so as to identify and prevent corruption in the justice system. A March 2020 European Commission report praised Albania's anticorruption efforts.

C3. Does the government operate with openness and transparency? 2 / 4

A robust law on access to information is not well implemented. Public procurement processes and public finances are frequently opaque, though parliamentary procedures are more open.

CIVIL LIBERTIES: 39 / 60 (−1)

D. FREEDOM OF EXPRESSION AND BELIEF: 13 / 16

D1. Are there free and independent media? 2 / 4

While the constitution guarantees freedom of expression, the intermingling of powerful business, political, and media interests inhibits the development of independent news outlets; most are seen as biased toward either the PS or the PD. Reporters have little job security and remain subject to lawsuits, intimidation, and occasional physical attacks by those facing media scrutiny. Print media has continued to experience declining revenue, which has driven down journalists' salaries.

In December 2019, the parliament passed two laws allowing government agencies to hear complaints from individuals alleging defamation from television stations and news sites. Under the legislation, these agencies will have the power to fine journalists or restrict the activities of outlets found to have engaged in defamation. The Council of Europe criticized the law for its vague parameters and its potential to deter online reporting.

D2. Are individuals free to practice and express their religious faith or nonbelief in public and private? 4 / 4

The constitution provides for freedom of religion, which is generally upheld in practice.

D3. Is there academic freedom, and is the educational system free from extensive political indoctrination? 3 / 4

The government typically does not limit academic freedom, though teachers in several districts have faced pressure ahead of elections to participate in political rallies. Access to higher education is affected by corruption.

D4. Are individuals free to express their personal views on political or other sensitive topics without fear of surveillance or retribution? 4 / 4

There are no significant restrictions on free and open private discussion, including for online blogs and social media.

E. ASSOCIATIONAL AND ORGANIZATIONAL RIGHTS: 8 / 12 (−1)
E1. Is there freedom of assembly? 3 / 4 (−1)

Freedom of assembly is generally respected. Demonstrations by opposition parties and civic groups are common. Opposition protests were frequently held between April and June 2019, ahead of June's local elections, and sometimes turned violent.

In 2020, the government banned public gatherings as a part of the state of emergency declared due to the coronavirus pandemic. However, in May, protestors confronted police after the unpopular demolition of the National Theater in Tirana. In December, also in Tirana, several hundred protesters clashed with police for several days after a police officer killed an unarmed civilian who had violated a coronavirus-related curfew. Demonstrators threw stones, flares, and firecrackers at officers who used tear gas and water cannon to disperse them. Witnesses saw police chasing protesters through city squares. During the first two days, over 62 people were arrested, and 116 people were charged for holding an illegal protest, arson, or breaching public order.

Score Change: The score declined from 4 to 3 due to increased violence between demonstrators and police at separate protests during the year.

E2. Is there freedom for nongovernmental organizations, particularly those that are engaged in human rights- and governance-related work? 3 / 4

Nongovernmental organizations (NGOs) generally function without restriction, but have limited funding due to dependence on foreign donors and policy influence.

E3. Is there freedom for trade unions and similar professional or labor organizations? 2 / 4

The constitution guarantees workers the rights to organize and bargain collectively, and most have the right to strike. However, effective collective bargaining remains limited, and union members have little protection against discrimination by employers.

F. RULE OF LAW: 9 / 16

F1. Is there an independent judiciary? 2 / 4

The constitution provides for an independent judiciary, but the underfunded courts are subject to political pressure and influence, and public trust in judicial institutions is low. Corruption in the judiciary remains a serious problem, and convictions of high-ranking judges for corruption and abuse of power are historically rare.

In 2016, the parliament approved a variety of reforms designed to boost the judiciary's independence and capacity, including the evaluation of current and prospective judges and prosecutors based on their professionalism, moral integrity, and independence by an international team of career judges and prosecutors, called the Independent Qualification Commission (IQC). Vetting processes are ongoing and were praised by the European Commission in a March 2020 report; in 2020, judges were dismissed or resigned due to their unexplained assets.

F2. Does due process prevail in civil and criminal matters? 2 / 4

Constitutional guarantees of due process are upheld inconsistently. Trial procedures can be affected by corruption within the judicial system, and are sometimes closed to the public. Legal counsel is not always provided to those that cannot afford their own.

F3. Is there protection from the illegitimate use of physical force and freedom from war and insurgencies? 2 / 4

Reports of police abuse of detainees continues. Prison inmates suffer from poor living conditions and a lack of adequate medical treatment. Drug-related crime remains a problem, as Albania is a transit country for heroin smugglers.

Tribal law is practiced in parts of northern Albania, and sometimes involves revenge killings.

F4. Do laws, policies, and practices guarantee equal treatment of various segments of the population? 3 / 4

Roma face significant discrimination in education, health care, employment, and housing. A 2010 law bars discrimination based on race and several other categories, including sexual orientation and gender identity, and a 2013 reform of the criminal code introduced protections against hate crimes and hate speech based on sexual orientation and gender identity. However, bias against LGBT+ people remains strong in practice. Women are underrepresented in the workforce. Women living in rural areas, in particular, have fewer opportunities for employment and education than do men.

G. PERSONAL AUTONOMY AND INDIVIDUAL RIGHTS: 9 / 16

G1. Do individuals enjoy freedom of movement, including the ability to change their place of residence, employment, or education? 3 / 4

Albanians generally enjoy freedom of movement, though criminal activity and practices related to historically predominant honor codes limit these rights in some areas. People are generally free to change their place of residence or employment.

G2. Are individuals able to exercise the right to own property and establish private businesses without undue interference from state or nonstate actors? 2 / 4

Numerous property-restitution cases related to confiscations during the communist era remain unresolved. Illegal construction is a major problem, as is bribery linked to government approval of development projects.

G3. Do individuals enjoy personal social freedoms, including choice of marriage partner and size of family, protection from domestic violence, and control over appearance? 2 / 4

The government generally does not place explicit restrictions on social freedoms. Authorities in the past have indicating a willingness to recognize same-sex marriages, but no policy developments have followed.

Domestic violence is widespread, and while the parliament has adopted some measures to combat the problem in recent years, few cases are prosecuted. Police are poorly equipped to handle cases of domestic violence or spousal rape, which is often not understood to be a crime. According to a UN Women survey released in May 2019, 47 percent of female Albanian respondents experienced domestic violence from intimate partners in their lifetime.

G4. Do individuals enjoy equality of opportunity and freedom from economic exploitation? 2 / 4

Albania has relatively robust labor laws, but lacks the capacity to enforce workplace safety and other protections. Conditions in the manufacturing, construction, and mining sectors are often substandard and put workers at risk.

While Albania continues to struggle with human trafficking, authorities are becoming more proactive in addressing the issue, according to the US State Department's 2020 *Trafficking in Persons Report*. Though the government continued to delay funding for shelters managed by NGOs, the government cooperated with civil society leaders to create the Advisory Board of Victims of Trafficking and increased victim assistance in criminal proceedings with a new Development Center for Criminal Justice for Minors.

Algeria

Population: 44,400,000
Capital: Algiers
Freedom Status: Not Free
Electoral Democracy: No

Overview: Political affairs in Algeria have long been dominated by a closed elite based in the military and the ruling party, the National Liberation Front (FLN). While there are multiple opposition parties in the parliament, elections are distorted by fraud, and electoral processes are not transparent. Other concerns include the suppression of street protests, legal restrictions on media freedom, and rampant corruption. The rise of the Hirak protest movement in 2019 has put pressure on the regime, leading it to crack down on dissent and engineer a presidential transition that protesters rejected as a continuation of the status quo.

KEY DEVELOPMENTS IN 2020

- Beginning in March, cases of COVID-19 gradually increased, spiked over the summer, and surged again in November. By year's end more than 2,700 deaths had been recorded by the World Health Organization.
- In response to the health crisis, in March the government introduced restrictions on freedom of movement and assembly, but authorities continued to suppress protests after other lockdown measures were eased beginning in June. The restrictions effectively put an end to the Hirak protest movement's weekly demonstrations calling for democratic reforms, and the government intensified its efforts to prosecute activists, journalists, and ordinary citizens who voiced dissent online.

- In September, Parliament approved a wide-ranging constitutional revision that was intended to address some of the demands of the protest movement. However, critics argued that it fell short in a number of ways, including by leaving the president with power over the judiciary and retaining vaguely defined limits on freedom of information. The new constitution was reportedly approved in a November referendum by 67 percent of participating voters, though turnout was less than 24 percent amid pandemic concerns and calls for a boycott.

POLITICAL RIGHTS: 10 / 40

A. ELECTORAL PROCESS: 3 / 12

A1. Was the current head of government or other chief national authority elected through free and fair elections? 1 / 4

The president, who is directly elected for up to two five-year terms, remains the dominant figure in the executive branch, though some authority was shifted to the prime minister under constitutional reforms adopted in 2020. In 2008, term limits were removed, allowing President Abdelaziz Bouteflika to serve four terms, but they were reinstated in 2016 when Parliament passed a constitutional reform package. President Bouteflika's decision to seek another term, which would have been his fifth, sparked the Hirak protests in 2019. Bouteflika resigned in April of that year, after losing the support of the armed forces.

Bouteflika ally Abdelkader Bensalah, the head of Parliament's upper house, served as interim president during a transitional period of several months, and a presidential election was held in December 2019. Former prime minister Abdelmajid Tebboune won in the first round with 58 percent of the vote, defeating four other candidates. Abdelaziz Belaïd, a 2014 presidential candidate and the only contestant who had not served in cabinet posts under Bouteflika, won 7 percent of the vote. The Constitutional Council reported a record low voter turnout of just under 40 percent, and one outside expert suggested an actual figure as low as 20 percent. Protesters called the election a sham and orchestrated a boycott. Outside observers were not allowed to enter the country to monitor the poll.

A2. Were the current national legislative representatives elected through free and fair elections? 1 / 4

The 462 members of the People's National Assembly, the lower house of Parliament, are directly elected to five-year terms, which can only be renewed once under the 2020 constitutional reforms. In the 2017 elections, the ruling FLN and the allied Democratic National Rally (RND) won a combined 261 seats. Several other parties each won a far smaller share of seats. An unpublished European Union (EU) assessment of the polls, acquired by Algerian newspaper *Liberté*, noted serious deficiencies in the electoral process, highlighting the inaccessibility of voter rolls and opaque vote-counting procedures. Opposition parties and other observers alleged widespread fraud, and media outlets carried videos recorded by voters that appeared to show ballot-box stuffing and other irregularities.

The president appoints one-third of the members of the upper legislative house, the Council of the Nation, which has 144 members serving six-year terms. The other two-thirds are indirectly elected by local and provincial assemblies. Half of the chamber's mandates come up for renewal every three years. The FLN secured 29 of the 48 indirectly elected seats at stake in December 2018, with the RND and smaller factions or independents taking the remainder.

A3. Are the electoral laws and framework fair, and are they implemented impartially by the relevant election management bodies? 1 / 4

Algeria's elections, which were previously administered by the Interior Ministry, were often subject to government interference, but pressure from protesters in 2019 forced the government to establish the Independent National Authority for Elections (ANIE). Other changes adopted that year lowered the number of signatures required to add candidates to the presidential ballot from 60,000 to 50,000 and abolished the requirement for presidential candidates to receive 600 signatures from other elected officials.

However, the slate of presidential candidates that was ultimately announced ahead of the December 2019 presidential election was dominated by former Bouteflika administration officials, raising doubts about the efficacy of the electoral reforms. The absence of international election monitors also drew criticism from Algerian civil society.

The 2020 constitutional reforms were adopted by Parliament in September and then approved in a November referendum, with support from 67 percent of participating voters. However, turnout was reported at less than 24 percent; opponents of the package—including activists from the Hirak protest movement—had called for a boycott after they were prevented from campaigning for a "no" vote or airing their views on state media.

B. POLITICAL PLURALISM AND PARTICIPATION: 4 / 16

B1. Do the people have the right to organize in different political parties or other competitive political groupings of their choice, and is the system free of undue obstacles to the rise and fall of these competing parties or groupings? 1 / 4

The Interior Ministry must approve political parties before they can operate legally. Parties cannot form along explicitly ethnic lines. The Islamic Salvation Front (FIS), which swept the 1990 local and 1991 national elections that preceded Algeria's decade-long civil war, remains banned. In 2019, the Interior Ministry legalized 10 new parties, but other parties still lack official recognition, and in practice the authorities routinely interfere with opposition party activities.

B2. Is there a realistic opportunity for the opposition to increase its support or gain power through elections? 1 / 4

Opposition parties play a marginal role in the national legislature, and their campaigns are regularly curtailed by the government. Election boycotts by opposition groups are not uncommon.

Since the beginning of the Hirak in 2019, the government has curbed the ability of opposition parties to assemble and seek public support, and restrictions related to the COVID-19 pandemic further limited such activities beginning in March 2020. In September, the Rally for Culture and Democracy (RCD) denounced the Algiers authorities' decision to block its planned national conference at a hotel; the conference had to be moved to the party's main office.

Opposition leaders have also been subject to detention and prosecution. In March 2020, an appeals court sentenced Karim Tabbou, spokesperson for the Democratic and Social Union (UDS), an unrecognized political party, to one year in prison and a 50,000 dinar ($400) fine for inciting violence and "harming national security." Tabbou, a former official in the Socialist Forces Front (FFS), had been arrested in 2019 after publicly criticizing General Ahmed Gaïd Salah, then the army chief of staff. In July 2020, he was provisionally released, but in December he was sentenced in a separate case to a one-year suspended prison term and a fine of 100,000 dinars ($800) for "undermining national security." In February 2020, after nine months in jail, Labour Party leader Louisa Hanoune was released when a military court in Blida overturned a previous sentence of 15 years in prison for "harming the authority of the army" and "conspiracy against the authority of the state."

B3. Are the people's political choices free from domination by forces that are external to the political sphere, or by political forces that employ extrapolitical means? 1 / 4

Since President Bouteflika's resignation, the military has maintained its long-standing influence on decision making, with General Gaïd Salah playing a key role until his death in December 2019. Under the leadership of General Saïd Chengriha as of 2020, the military remains the most influential political actor in Algeria, thanks to its lack of accountability and vast resources.

In recent years, there have been allegations and scandals involving corruption and financial influence in the selection of political candidates, as well as vote-buying during elections. After Bouteflika's resignation, Gaïd Salah initiated an anticorruption campaign targeting entrepreneurs and officials linked with the former administration, which he claimed was aimed at reducing the improper influence of these groups on domestic political decisions.

B4. Do various segments of the population (including ethnic, racial, religious, gender, LGBT+, and other relevant groups) have full political rights and electoral opportunities? 1 / 4

No specific ethnic or religious group dominates the main state institutions, which tend to include both Arabs and Amazigh (Berber) officials. Kabylie-based parties associated with the Amazigh community, like the RCD and the FFS, control a handful of municipalities, but their activities are often curtailed by the military, and some ethnic Berbers have been targeted by the authorities for mobilizing in support of their political interests. In 2019, 19 Amazigh activists were handed six-month prison sentences for carrying Amazigh flags during demonstrations, having been accused of endangering Algeria's territorial integrity.

Women have gradually played a larger role in politics, but they remain reluctant to run for office, are often unable to secure meaningful influence within Parliament, and are more likely to lose intraparty debates. Women hold only 26 percent of seats in the lower house and 6 percent in the upper house of Parliament.

LGBT+ people are politically marginalized and have little practical ability to advocate for their political interests.

C. FUNCTIONING OF GOVERNMENT: 3 / 12
C1. Do the freely elected head of government and national legislative representatives determine the policies of the government? 1 / 4

The military has historically served as the ultimate arbiter of policy disputes in Algeria, and elected leaders have relied on its support to maintain office. The loss of military backing played a significant role in President Bouteflika's resignation in 2019. The army chief of staff continues to wield considerable influence in government under Bouteflika's successor.

C2. Are safeguards against official corruption strong and effective? 1 / 4

Inadequate anticorruption laws, a lack of official transparency, low levels of judicial independence, and bloated bureaucracies contribute to widespread corruption at all levels of government. The anticorruption investigations that do occur are often used to settle scores between factions within the regime.

The courts issued a series of harsh sentences against Bouteflika's former political and economic allies after his resignation in 2019 as part of an anticorruption campaign initiated by General Gaïd Salah. In September 2019, the former president's brother Saïd Bouteflika and two former intelligence chiefs were sentenced to 15 years in prison for "plotting against the state" and "undermining the army," but a retrial was ordered by the Supreme Court in November 2020. Among other figures sentenced during 2020 were former prime ministers, several former cabinet ministers, key members of well-connected business families, and a former prefect of Algiers.

The constitutional reforms passed by Parliament in September 2020 included provisions for an Authority for Transparency and for the Prevention of and Fight against Corruption, as well as a ban on combining roles in public office and private business.

C3. Does the government operate with openness and transparency? 1 / 4

The country lacks legislation that guarantees citizens' access to official information. There is considerable opacity surrounding official decision-making procedures, the publication of official acts is rarely timely, and rules on asset disclosure by government officials are weak and poorly enforced. The 2020 constitutional revision introduced a requirement for all appointed and elected officials to declare their assets at the beginning and end of their terms, and obliges the public administration to justify its decisions within a time period to be determined by law. While the revised constitution nominally guarantees the right to access information, it includes vague exceptions for "the rights of others, the legitimate interests of businesses, and the requirements of national security."

CIVIL LIBERTIES: 22 / 60 (−2)

D. FREEDOM OF EXPRESSION AND BELIEF: 6 / 16 (−1)

D1. Are there free and independent media? 1 / 4

Although some newspapers are privately owned and some journalists remain aggressive in their coverage of government affairs, most papers rely on government agencies for printing and advertising, encouraging self-censorship. Authorities sometimes block distribution of independent news outlets that are based abroad or online. In April 2020, the websites of media outlets Maghreb Emergent, Radio M, and Interlignes became unavailable to Algerian users. In August the website of L'Avant-Garde Algérie also became inaccessible from within the country. Additional news websites were blocked in December, including Tariq News, Shihab Presse, UltraSawt, TSA Algérie, and Twala. Viewers can access unlicensed private television channels located in Algeria but legally based outside the country, though these are subject to government crackdowns.

In April 2020, Parliament approved a new law criminalizing "fake news" that undermines public order and security, with sentences ranging from one to five years in prison. In December the government issued a decree requiring news websites to be directed by Algerian nationals and based physically in Algeria, to report income sources, and to keep an archive of at least six months of their publications. Websites in French or other foreign languages must be approved by a special authority for online media.

Authorities use these and other legal mechanisms to harass the media and censor or punish controversial reporting. Journalists and bloggers are frequently subjected to brief detentions, short jail terms, suspended sentences, or fines for offenses including defamation and "undermining national unity," and this pattern continued in 2020. In addition, journalists covering demonstrations or who are close to the protest movement have been arbitrarily arrested and interrogated. A number of foreign correspondents were expelled from Algeria in 2019, but no such incidents were reported in 2020.

D2. Are individuals free to practice and express their religious faith or nonbelief in public and private? 1 / 4

Algeria's population is overwhelmingly Sunni Muslim. Members of religious minorities, including Christians and non-Sunni Muslims, suffer from state persecution and interference. Proselytizing by non-Muslims is illegal. Authorities have cracked down on the small Ahmadi minority, claiming that its members denigrate Islam, threaten national security, and violate laws on associations. Religious communities may only gather to worship at state-approved locations.

In January 2020, the authorities shuttered two Protestant churches in Oran, continuing a multiyear crackdown on the Algerian Protestant Church (EPA) that began in late 2017. Before this period, the EPA had maintained its status as a legally recognized organization since 1974.

Accusations of nonbelief or blasphemy can draw criminal punishments, and such charges are sometimes used for political purposes. In October 2020, Amazigh and Hirak activist Yacine Mebarki received a sentence of 10 years in prison and a fine of 10 million dinars ($77,000) for offenses including "supporting atheism" and "offending Islam," after police found a slightly damaged Quran in his house during a search the previous month.

D3. Is there academic freedom, and is the educational system free from extensive political indoctrination? 2 / 4

Authorities generally do not interfere directly with the operations of universities, but debate is circumscribed in practice due to restrictive laws that limit speech more broadly. Academic work is also affected by state censorship of domestically published and imported books. Student organizations have been active in the Hirak protests that began in 2019, with members calling for political reforms. The authorities have occasionally resorted to violence to suppress these demonstrations.

D4. Are individuals free to express their personal views on political or other sensitive topics without fear of surveillance or retribution? 2 / 4 (−1)

Private discussion and the public expression of personal views are relatively unhindered when they do not focus on certain sensitive topics, but social media users are subject to prosecution for critical comments that touch on the government or religion. The government monitors internet activity in the name of national security and does not disclose information about the program's targets or range, which is thought to be extensive.

The authorities stepped up prosecutions of social media users, particularly Hirak supporters, during 2020. In April, for example, Walid Kechida was arrested on charges of insulting the president and Islamic morals by sharing memes and images that were considered offensive. In May, activist Soheib Debaghi was sentenced to one year in prison over his antigovernment Facebook posts; he was released in November. Also in May, Larbi Tahar and Boussif Mohamed Boudiaf received sentences of 18 months in prison following the publication of Facebook posts that targeted President Tebboune; they were pardoned in July. In September, a former police officer was sentenced to two years in prison after he used Facebook to denounce the repression of Hirak protesters by police.

Score Change: The score declined from 3 to 2 due to the arrest and imprisonment of activists and supporters of the antigovernment protest movement for expressing their views on social media.

E. ASSOCIATIONAL AND ORGANIZATIONAL RIGHTS: 3 / 12 (−1)

E1. Is there freedom of assembly? 1 / 4 (−1)

Legal restrictions on freedom of assembly remain in place, but are inconsistently enforced. The Hirak protests, which began in 2019, have sometimes been tolerated by the authorities. However, security personnel have resorted to the use of tear gas, water cannons, arbitrary arrests, and excessive force to preempt or disrupt some of the rallies.

Beginning in March 2020, all gatherings and demonstrations were banned due to the COVID-19 emergency. While Hirak activists initially accepted this decision, many later called for an end to the ban, especially after the government in June announced the gradual lifting of other COVID-19 restrictions. During this initial period and through the end of the year, the authorities prosecuted activists for participation in past protests and carried out new arrests as protesters attempted to hold unauthorized demonstrations despite the official prohibition. The Algerian League for the Defense of Human Rights estimated that about 200 activists were arrested from March to mid-June. Among other cases during the year, an Algiers court in March sentenced activists Karim Boutata and Ahcene Kadi to six months in jail and a 20,000 dinar ($150) fine for their participation in a 2019 demonstration. In June, Merzoug Touati, Yanis Adjila, and Amar Beri were arrested after they attempted to organize a demonstration to show solidarity with political prisoners. In September, another Hirak activist, Brahim Laalami, received a sentence of three years in prison, while former lawmaker Khaled Tazaghart was sentenced to one year in prison for his participation in the protest movement.

Score Change: The score declined from 2 to 1 because a March ban on demonstrations remained in place even after other pandemic-related restrictions were lifted, and the government arrested hundreds of activists for their role in the antigovernment protest movement that began in 2019.

E2. Is there freedom for nongovernmental organizations, particularly those that are engaged in human rights- and governance-related work? 1 / 4

The 2012 law on associations effectively restricts the formation, funding, and activities of nongovernmental organizations (NGOs). Permits and receipts of application submission are required to establish and operate NGOs, but organizations often face considerable delays and bureaucratic obstacles when attempting to obtain such documents, leaving them in a legally precarious position.

NGOs must notify the government of staffing changes and submit detailed reports on their funding; those that accept foreign funding without government approval risk fines or imprisonment.

Authorities have taken a particular interest in Rassemblement Actions Jeunesse (RAJ), a human rights organization that has supported the Hirak. In 2019, several members, including the NGO's president, Abdelouhab Fersaoui, were arrested and detained in the Harrach prison in Algiers. Fersaoui was initially sentenced to a year in prison in April 2020 over his Facebook posts, but the sentence was then reduced in May, and he was released with credit for time served in pretrial detention. In December, a court in Sidi M'hamed acquitted five other RAJ activists.

E3. Is there freedom for trade unions and similar professional or labor organizations? 1 / 4

The country's main labor federation, the General Union of Algerian Workers (UGTA), has been criticized for its close relationship to the government and for its failure to advocate for workers' interests.

Workers require government approval to establish new unions, and this is difficult to obtain in practice, leaving many unions without legal status. Authorities routinely clamp down on independent unions. SNATEG, an independent union that represents workers at the public gas and electricity utility SONELGAZ, has been repeatedly harassed by the authorities in recent years. In February 2020, police closed and banned all entry to a SNATEG office in Algiers.

In 2019, Kaddour Chouicha, president of the independent higher education workers' union SESS, was arrested and given a one-year prison sentence for his criticism of the military and support for the protest movement. Chouicha is also the vice president of the Algerian League for the Defense of Human Rights. In March 2020, an Oran court acquitted him on appeal.

F. RULE OF LAW: 6 / 16

F1. Is there an independent judiciary? 1 / 4

The judiciary is susceptible to pressure from the civilian government and the military. Judges are appointed by the High Council of the Judiciary, which is headed by the president, although the 2020 constitutional reforms removed the justice minister and attorney general from the body. Two representatives of the judges' union and the chair of the National Human Rights Council were added to the council.

Concerns regarding the judiciary's independence persist. In September 2020, members of the Algiers bar association went on strike for a week and took part in a sit-in, demanding an independent judiciary and "respect for the rights of the defense." The protest, which was supported by the national bar association with a two-day solidarity strike, was triggered by an incident in which a judge rejected a request by the president of the Algiers bar association to postpone a hearing in a politically fraught corruption case—a decision that defense lawyers said was part of a pattern of unfair or abusive treatment by judges serving the interests of the government.

F2. Does due process prevail in civil and criminal matters? 1 / 4

The lack of independence on the part of judges and prosecutors often erodes the due process rights of defendants, particularly in politically sensitive trials against former officials or civic activists. Lengthy delays in bringing cases to trial are common. Prosecutors' requests to extend pretrial detention periods are typically granted. Security forces frequently conduct warrantless searches and engage in arbitrary arrests and short-term detentions.

F3. Is there protection from the illegitimate use of physical force and freedom from war and insurgencies? 2 / 4

A 2006 reconciliation law gave immunity to Islamist and state perpetrators of serious crimes during the civil war, while compensating families of those who were subject to such crimes, which included forced disappearances. The reconciliation law was also notable for criminalizing public discussion on the fate of the disappeared.

Allegations of torture have decreased since the end of the war, but human rights activists still accuse the police of using excessive force and abusing detainees. Prison conditions have deteriorated since the beginning of the Hirak in 2019. In June 2020, the online media site Algérie Part reported on the poor conditions at Algiers' Harrach prison, where the occupancy rate was estimated at around 130 percent, detainees routinely slept on the floor, hygiene was poor, and medical services were unable to cope with the COVID-19 emergency. In July, two prisoners at the facility, including a former minister, died after contracting COVID-19, while eight detainees were hospitalized and five more had to be put in isolation.

Terrorist groups, including Al-Qaeda in the Islamic Maghreb (AQIM) and the Islamic State militant group, continue to operate in Algeria. However, attacks have grown less frequent in recent years. In the only attacks reported in 2020, a car bomb exploded in February near the border with Mali, killing one soldier, and another soldier was killed in an ambush in June.

F4. Do laws, policies, and practices guarantee equal treatment of various segments of the population? 2 / 4

Officials have made gradual efforts to address the Amazigh community's cultural demands. Tamazight, the Berber language, became a national language in 1995, allowing it to be taught officially in schools serving Amazigh areas, and it received the status of an official language nationwide through a 2016 constitutional amendment, meaning it could be used in administrative documents. The constitutional revisions adopted in 2020 made it impossible to change the status of Tamazight as a national language. However, Arabic remains the prevailing language of government.

The constitution guarantees gender equality, but women continue to face both legal and societal discrimination. Many women receive lower wages than men in similar positions, and there are few women in company leadership positions. Sexual harassment, while punishable with fines and jail time, is nevertheless common in workplaces. NGOs dedicated to women's rights have become more vocal as part of the Hirak, calling for a renewed commitment to the constitutional promise of gender equality.

LGBT+ people face discrimination and violence, and many LGBT+ activists have fled the country. Same-sex sexual activity is punishable with prison sentences as long as two years. While prosecutions for such acts have declined in recent years, LGBT+ Algerians face mistreatment at the hands of police and discrimination by health providers and employers. In September 2020, a court in El Khroub sentenced two people to three years in prison and 42 others to one-year suspended sentences after they were arrested at a clandestine gay wedding in Constantine in July.

About 175,000 Sahrawis from Western Sahara live in refugee camps in the Tindouf area, near the border with Morocco. The camps have been present since 1975, in a remote desert region with very limited job opportunities. About 90,000 of the residents are considered "vulnerable" by the Office of the UN High Commissioner for Refugees (UNHCR), as they rely on humanitarian assistance for food, water, and education. In 2020, an epidemic ravaging local livestock and the COVID-19 restrictions negatively affected the livelihoods and living conditions of Sahrawi refugees and increased their food insecurity.

Sub-Saharan African migrants, including refugees and asylum seekers, are subject to racial discrimination in Algeria, and they are often arbitrarily arrested and deported from the country—or simply abandoned at the southern desert borders—without being given the opportunity to challenge the actions in court. Human Rights Watch in October 2020 reported that since early September, authorities had expelled to Niger some 3,400 sub-Saharan migrants, including women, children, and asylum seekers registered with the UNHCR; this raised the total number of expulsions for the year to date to more than 16,000.

G. PERSONAL AUTONOMY AND INDIVIDUAL RIGHTS: 7 / 16

G1. Do individuals enjoy freedom of movement, including the ability to change their place of residence, employment, or education? 2 / 4

While most citizens are relatively free to travel domestically and abroad, the authorities closely monitor and limit access to visas for non-Algerians. Men of military draft age are not allowed to leave the country without official consent. The land border between Algeria and Morocco remains closed. Police reportedly limit the movement of sub-Saharan African migrants attempting to reach the Mediterranean coast. Married women younger than 18 must obtain the permission of their husbands to travel abroad.

In response to the COVID-19 pandemic, the authorities in March 2020 imposed significant restrictions on domestic and international freedom of movement; curfews and other controls fluctuated in the second half of the year along with the rates of infection.

G2. Are individuals able to exercise the right to own property and establish private businesses without undue interference from state or nonstate actors? 2 / 4

The government plays a dominant role in the economy, leaving little room for private competitors. Cronyism is also a major obstacle to private enterprise, with businesspeople who are not aligned with the regime often facing harassment by the authorities. Numerous regulations and their flawed implementation make Algeria one of the most difficult environments in the world in which to establish and operate a business. Inheritance rules favor men over women.

G3. Do individuals enjoy personal social freedoms, including choice of marriage partner and size of family, protection from domestic violence, and control over appearance? 2 / 4

Women do not enjoy equal rights in marriage and divorce under the family code, which is based on Islamic law. Among other provisions, women must obtain a male guardian's permission to marry, and the father is the legal guardian of his children. Domestic violence is common, and the laws against it are weak; for example, cases can be dropped if the victim forgives the alleged abuser. Women's rights groups report that between 100 and 200 women are killed in domestic abuse incidents each year. No law addresses spousal rape. In October 2020, the rape and killing of a young woman near Boumerdes sparked outrage and a mobilization by women's rights groups calling for better protection and harsher sentences. According to Féminicides Algérie, there were 54 cases of femicide in the country during 2020.

G4. Do individuals enjoy equality of opportunity and freedom from economic exploitation? 1 / 4

The weak rule of law, government involvement in the economy, and bureaucratic obstacles pose major barriers to economic opportunity and social mobility. Laws against unsafe or abusive working conditions are poorly enforced.

A 2009 law criminalized all forms of trafficking in persons, and Algeria reported its first conviction under the law in 2015. In recent years, the government has made an effort to enforce the ban through prosecutions and has provided protection for victims, though not systematically. Undocumented sub-Saharan African migrants are particularly susceptible to labor exploitation, including through the practice of debt bondage, as well as sexual exploitation.

Andorra

Population: 80,000
Capital: Andorra la Vella
Freedom Status: Free
Electoral Democracy: Yes

Overview: Andorra has a parliamentary system of government and regularly holds free and fair elections. Political rights and civil liberties are generally respected. However, the country has strict naturalization criteria, and more than 50 percent of the population consists of noncitizens who do not have the right to vote. Among other outstanding concerns, abortion remains completely prohibited, and there is a notable wage gap between men and women. The small Muslim and Jewish communities lack dedicated cemeteries, and the country has no recognized mosque.

KEY DEVELOPMENTS IN 2020

- Women's rights activists continued to call on the government to decriminalize abortion, objecting to the fact that reform has been blocked in part by resistance from one of the country's two unelected heads of state, the Roman Catholic bishop of La Seu d'Urgell. In July, a leading activist was charged with slander against state institutions after she testified about the issue before a UN committee in 2019.
- The authorities were successful at containing the spread of COVID-19 for most of the year, implementing an extensive testing program and social-distancing measures, including temporary restrictions on movement. Several hundred cases were reported in the spring, followed by a larger surge that began in October; 84 deaths had been recorded by late December.

POLITICAL RIGHTS: 38 / 40 (−1)

A. ELECTORAL PROCESS: 12 / 12

A1. Was the current head of government or other chief national authority elected through free and fair elections? 4 / 4

Andorra has a parliamentary system, with a prime minister elected by and accountable to the legislature. The legitimacy of the prime minister, usually the head of the party with the most seats, rests largely on the conduct of parliamentary elections, which have historically been competitive and credible. Xavier Espot Zamora, the new leader of the ruling Democrats for Andorra (DA) party, was chosen as prime minister in May 2019 following the previous month's elections. The DA had lost its parliamentary majority, but it formed a coalition government with two smaller liberal parties. Espot replaced outgoing prime minister Antoni Martí Petit, who had held the post since 2011.

Two "co-princes," the French president and the Roman Catholic bishop of La Seu d'Urgell, Spain, serve jointly as Andorra's ceremonial heads of state.

A2. Were the current national legislative representatives elected through free and fair elections? 4 / 4

Members of the unicameral, 28-member Consell General are directly elected every four years through a mixed voting system. In the April 2019 elections, the DA led with 11 seats, followed by the Social Democratic Party (PS) with 7, the Liberals of Andorra (LA) and the new conservative party Third Way (TV) with 4 each, and the new social-liberal party Committed Citizens (CC) with 2. The LA and CC joined the DA in the new governing coalition. The polls were generally considered competitive, credible, and well administered.

A3. Are the electoral laws and framework fair, and are they implemented impartially by the relevant election management bodies? 4 / 4

The Electoral Law, which was last changed in 2014 to introduce regulations on campaign finance, provides a sound framework for free and fair elections. The Electoral Board supervises elections impartially. However, the law does not provide a formal role for international or citizen observers.

B. POLITICAL PLURALISM AND PARTICIPATION: 15 / 16

B1. Do the people have the right to organize in different political parties or other competitive political groupings of their choice, and is the system free of undue obstacles to the rise and fall of these competing parties or groupings? 4 / 4

Political parties may form and operate freely, and there are a number of active parties in Andorra. Two new parties, TV and CC, made their debut in the 2019 elections.

B2. Is there a realistic opportunity for the opposition to increase its support or gain power through elections? 4 / 4

The country has experienced multiple democratic transfers of power between rival parties, most recently in 2011, when the DA replaced a government led by the PS. Opposition parties are well represented in the Consell General and deprived the DA of its outright majority in the 2019 elections.

B3. Are the people's political choices free from domination by forces that are external to the political sphere, or by political forces that employ extrapolitical means? 4 / 4

Citizens and political figures are generally able to make political choices without undue interference from external forces.

B4. Do various segments of the population (including ethnic, racial, religious, gender, LGBT+, and other relevant groups) have full political rights and electoral opportunities? 3 / 4

More than 50 percent of the population consists of noncitizens—mostly from nearby states—who do not have the right to vote in national elections or run for elected office. Under Andorra's restrictive naturalization criteria, one must marry a resident Andorran or live in the country for more than 20 years to qualify for citizenship. Prospective citizens are also required to learn Catalan, the national language.

There are no specific policies to encourage the political participation of women, but women are active in politics, and after the 2019 elections they held 50 percent of the seats in the legislature. LGBT+ people are also free to participate in politics, and a number of parties advocate for their interests.

C. FUNCTIONING OF GOVERNMENT: 11 / 12 (−1)

C1. Do the freely elected head of government and national legislative representatives determine the policies of the government? 3 / 4 (−1)

The elected government and parliament generally exercise their powers without improper influence from unelected or nonstate actors. However, in recent years the bishop of La Seu d'Urgell, Joan-Enric Vives i Sicília, has repeatedly threatened to resign as co-prince if the Andorran government were to decriminalize abortion, a move that would result in a constitutional crisis. Similar threats were made in 2009 by the other co-prince, then French president Nicolas Sarkozy, who stated that he would resign if Andorra failed to reform its banking system. Neither co-prince is elected, directly or indirectly, by Andorran voters, and the bishop's intervention on such a high-profile policy matter continued to draw objections from reform advocates during 2020.

Score Change: The score declined from 4 to 3 because the bishop of La Seu d'Urgell, an unelected co-prince of Andorra, has obstructed a movement to legalize abortion in recent years by warning that he would abdicate and trigger a constitutional crisis if such a measure were passed.

C2. Are safeguards against official corruption strong and effective? 4 / 4

Government corruption is not viewed as a pressing issue in Andorra. Over the past several years, the government has made progress on financial-sector reforms designed to prevent abuses of the country's banking system that could facilitate either domestic or transnational corruption. A law that renounced banking secrecy and required certain disclosures about accounts held by nonresidents entered into force at the start of 2018. In 2019, the parliament adopted legislation to strengthen existing safeguards against money laundering and terrorist financing, which drew praise from the Council of Europe's Committee of Experts on the Evaluation of Anti-Money Laundering Measures and the Financing of Terrorism.

Nevertheless, in a new compliance report published in October 2020, the Council of Europe's Group of States against Corruption (GRECO) expressed disappointment with the progress of other anticorruption legislation, finding that only three of its 13 recommendations had been satisfactorily addressed. The report noted in particular that members of parliament are still not obliged to report conflicts of interest or declare assets.

C3. Does the government operate with openness and transparency? 4 / 4

While proposals for a general law on transparency and access to information were still under consideration during 2020, the government makes efforts to operate openly in practice. Among other resources, it publishes a regular bulletin, accessible online, that documents government activity, budgetary processes, public procurement, and asset disclosures. Since 2017 the Ministry of Territorial Planning has sponsored a participatory budget process, allowing members of the public to help set spending priorities. The parliamentary rules of procedure were amended in 2019, obliging the parliament to inform the public about all of its activities.

CIVIL LIBERTIES: 55 / 60
D. FREEDOM OF EXPRESSION AND BELIEF: 14 / 16
D1. Are there free and independent media? 3 / 4

There are a number of daily and weekly newspapers, and the country's only domestic television station is operated by the public broadcaster Ràdio i Televisió d'Andorra. Residents have access to a variety of foreign media services. While press freedom is generally respected, criminal defamation laws remain on the books, and business, political, and religious interests have historically influenced media coverage; reporting on the activities of Andorra's banks has been particularly difficult.

D2. Are individuals free to practice and express their religious faith or nonbelief in public and private? 3 / 4

Freedom of religion is generally upheld, but the Roman Catholic Church enjoys a privileged position that allows it to draw on some state support and to bypass some bureaucratic processes that other faith groups must adhere to.

Despite years of negotiations between the Muslim community and the government, there is no recognized mosque for the country's roughly 2,000 Muslims. The government has organized meetings with Jewish and Muslim communities to discuss the possible establishment of a special cemetery where those groups could conduct burials according to their customs and beliefs, but there has been little progress on the proposal.

D3. Is there academic freedom, and is the educational system free from extensive political indoctrination? 4 / 4

There are no restrictions on academic freedom, and the educational system is free from indoctrination.

D4. Are individuals free to express their personal views on political or other sensitive topics without fear of surveillance or retribution? 4 / 4

There are no significant constraints on personal expression or freedom of private discussion. Authorities are not known to illegally monitor private online communications.

E. ASSOCIATIONAL AND ORGANIZATIONAL RIGHTS: 11 / 12

E1. Is there freedom of assembly? 4 / 4

Andorran law provides for freedom of assembly, and the government respects this right in practice. Demonstrations against government policies and in response to other social and political controversies take place on occasion. In 2019, protests against Andorra's strict prohibition on abortion drew hundreds of participants. Authorities imposed temporary restrictions on large gatherings during 2020 to limit the spread of COVID-19.

E2. Is there freedom for nongovernmental organizations, particularly those that are engaged in human rights- and governance-related work? 4 / 4

Various nongovernmental organizations (NGOs) are active in the country and function without restriction. Human rights groups are generally able to publish their findings and advocate for improvements without repercussions.

However, Vanessa Mendoza Cortés, leader of the women's rights organization Stop Violence, was charged in July 2020 with slandering the co-princes and state institutions through her 2019 testimony before a UN body about conditions for women in Andorra, including the abortion ban. The maximum penalty for the slander charge was four years in prison; an initial hearing in the case was pending at year's end.

E3. Is there freedom for trade unions and similar professional or labor organizations? 3 / 4

The right to unionize is protected by law and the constitution, and a new labor law that took effect in 2019 established regulations for collective bargaining and the right to strike. However, unions and the political opposition characterized the law as a setback, arguing in part that it placed unnecessary constraints on the right to strike and increased job insecurity. There are no laws in place to penalize antiunion discrimination.

In 2018, Andorra experienced its first major strike in 85 years, when civil servants walked out to protest reforms to their contracts proposed by the Martí government.

F. RULE OF LAW: 15 / 16

F1. Is there an independent judiciary? 4 / 4

The judiciary is impartial and independent, and is generally free from pressure from the government. Judges are appointed and supervised by the Higher Council of Justice; the two co-princes, the speaker of parliament, and the prime minister each select one of the council's five members, and the fifth is elected by judges and magistrates. In its October 2020 compliance report, GRECO called for a larger proportion of the council's membership to be elected by judges and magistrates.

F2. Does due process prevail in civil and criminal matters? 4 / 4

Defendants enjoy the presumption of innocence and the right to a fair trial, and due process is generally upheld in the criminal justice system. The constitution prohibits arbitrary arrest and imprisonment, but police can detain suspects for up to 48 hours without charge.

F3. Is there protection from the illegitimate use of physical force and freedom from war and insurgencies? 4 / 4

Andorra is free from war and insurgencies, violent crimes rates are low, and law enforcement agents are not known to use excessive force against civilians. Prison conditions are adequate.

F4. Do laws, policies, and practices guarantee equal treatment of various segments of the population? 3 / 4

In 2019, the parliament adopted a law on equal treatment and nondiscrimination. While it was focused primarily on combating gender discrimination, it included comprehensive protections against discrimination based on race, ethnicity, age, disability, sexual orientation, gender identity or expression, and other such categories; the legislation also featured enforcement mechanisms, including fines. To address a persistent gender pay gap estimated at 22 percent and as high as 40 percent in some sectors, the new law specifically required equal pay for equal work. A report published by a women's rights organization in March 2020 described ongoing problems including discrimination in the labor market and gender-based violence.

Andorra provides temporary protection and services to refugees and asylum seekers, but there is no law allowing the government to grant asylum or refugee status.

G. PERSONAL AUTONOMY AND INDIVIDUAL RIGHTS: 15 / 16

G1. Do individuals enjoy freedom of movement, including the ability to change their place of residence, employment, or education? 4 / 4

There are few restrictions on freedom of movement, and people are generally free to change their place of residence, employment, and education. The government imposed temporary restrictions on travel and internal movement during 2020 in response to the COVID-19 pandemic, including an initial lockdown from March to May, though the measures were largely seen as proportionate to the public health threat.

G2. Are individuals able to exercise the right to own property and establish private businesses without undue interference from state or nonstate actors? 4 / 4

The legal and regulatory framework is generally supportive of property rights and entrepreneurship, and there are few undue obstacles to private business activity in practice.

G3. Do individuals enjoy personal social freedoms, including choice of marriage partner and size of family, protection from domestic violence, and control over appearance? 3 / 4

Personal social freedoms are generally respected, though there are some restrictions for same-sex couples, who can form civil unions but not marry or adopt children. Domestic violence is prohibited by law and punishable with prison sentences; the government pursues domestic violence cases and provides resources for victims. Nevertheless, such violence remains a serious problem, and sometimes involves violence against children. The Council of Europe's November 2020 report on Andorra's implementation of the Istanbul Convention—a treaty on preventing and combating violence against women and domestic violence—listed a number of shortcomings in the collection of data and the support system for victims of sexual violence.

Andorra remains one of the few countries in Europe where abortion is completely prohibited, with penalties for both doctors and patients who undergo the procedure. Abortion is relatively accessible in neighboring France and Spain, though this option can be expensive for Andorrans.

G4. Do individuals enjoy equality of opportunity and freedom from economic exploitation? 4 / 4

Andorran laws provide protections for most workers, including migrant workers. However, temporary workers are in a precarious position, as they must leave the country when their employment contract expires, exposing those with expired contracts to potential abuse by employers. The Labor Inspections Office is proactive in addressing violations of workers' rights.

A 2019 report from the Council of Europe's Group of Experts on Action against Trafficking in Human Beings (GRETA) found that Andorra had made legislative and policy progress on combating trafficking, but called on authorities to scrutinize high-risk sectors for possible victims and raise awareness of the threat among law enforcement bodies. Confirmed cases of trafficking have been rare in practice.

Angola

Population: 32,500,000
Capital: Luanda
Freedom Status: Not Free
Electoral Democracy: No

Overview: Angola has been ruled by the same party since independence, and authorities have systematically repressed political dissent. Corruption, due process violations, and abuses by security forces remain common. Since President João Lourenço's election in 2017, the government eased some restrictions on the press and civil society, but challenges persist.

KEY DEVELOPMENTS IN 2020

- Lourenço announced in September that what would have been Angola's first-ever municipal elections, planned for later in the year, would be postponed due to complications related to the COVID-19 pandemic. A new date was not set, and some analysts attributed the move to government reluctance to relinquish its power to appoint subnational officials.
- In 2020, the government privatized a number of media outlets officials said were owned by members of the political and military elite but funded by the state. Journalists' groups expressed concern about a lack of transparency regarding the privatizations, and afterward, about censorship at some of the outlets.
- The COVID-19 pandemic led to the declaration of a state of emergency for two months, from late March to late May, and other restrictions thereafter, which were enforced with violence by police and the military. Numerous killings by security forces were linked to enforcement of confinement measures.

POLITICAL RIGHTS: 10 / 40 (−1)

A. ELECTORAL PROCESS: 3 / 12

A1. Was the current head of government or other chief national authority elected through free and fair elections? 0 / 4

The 2010 constitution abolished direct presidential elections. Instead, the head of the national list of the political party receiving the most votes in general elections becomes president, without any confirmation process by the elected legislature. The constitution permits the president to serve a maximum of two five-year terms, and to directly appoint the vice president, cabinet, and provincial governors.

In 2016, the ruling Popular Movement for the Liberation of Angola (MPLA) announced that Defense Minister João Lourenço, who was also the MPLA vice president, would be its presidential candidate in 2017. The decision was made by the MPLA's political bureau, without public consultation. The MPLA retained power in the 2017 legislative elections, and Lourenço succeeded José Eduardo dos Santos, who had been in power for 38 years.

A2. Were the current national legislative representatives elected through free and fair elections? 2 / 4

Angola's 220-seat, unicameral National Assembly, whose members are elected to five-year terms by proportional representation, has little power, and most legislation originates in the executive branch.

In the 2017 legislative polls, the MPLA won 61 percent of the vote and 150 seats, while the opposition National Union for the Total Independence of Angola (UNITA) took 27 percent and 51 seats, and the Broad Convergence for the Salvation of Angola–Electoral Coalition (CASA–CE) won 9 percent and 16 seats. Two smaller parties won the remainder. An African Union (AU) monitoring mission praised the elections' conduct, noting that they were peaceful and that there was a broad consensus that polling preparations and processes were better organized than in past elections. However, the prevalence of biased progovernment media, deficiencies in voter registration processes, and the MPLA's use of public resources in its campaign disadvantaged the opposition. There were also reports of postelection violence in some locations.

Alleging grave irregularities at the National Election Commission (CNE), including manipulation of the vote count, opposition leaders called the 2017 polls fraudulent and jointly disputed the results. The Constitutional Court dismissed their claim, citing a lack of evidence. Opposition figures elected to the National Assembly ultimately took their seats— a move that prompted intense criticism from their political base.

Lourenço announced in September 2020 that the country's first-ever municipal elections, planned for later in the year, would be postponed because the COVID-19 pandemic had interfered with the process of drafting relevant electoral legislation. A new date was not set, and some analysts attributed the decision to government reluctance to relinquish the power to appoint subnational officials.

A3. Are the electoral laws and framework fair, and are they implemented impartially by the relevant election management bodies? 1 / 4

The law states that the makeup of the CNE should reflect the disposition of power in the National Assembly, which gives an advantage to the MPLA. The political opposition, in its challenge of the 2017 election results, cited serious misconduct and a lack of transparency on the part of the CNE.

The opposition rejected the nomination, in February 2020, of the new CNE president, citing a lack of independence from the MPLA, past cases of corruption, and alleged fraud committed during the process of his appointment. He was later confirmed by the MPLA-led National Assembly; opposition protesters defied a ban on demonstrations in Luanda to oppose the confirmation and were met with violence by police.

B. POLITICAL PLURALISM AND PARTICIPATION: 5 / 16 (−1)

B1. Do the people have the right to organize in different political parties or other competitive political groupings of their choice, and is the system free of undue obstacles to the rise and fall of these competing parties or groupings? 1 / 4 (−1)

While there is a multiparty system in place, competition is limited. The process for creating new political parties is fraught with bureaucratic obstacles and attempts at cooptation, factors that severely hinder public confidence in new parties.

Citing irregularities in the process, the Constitutional Court in August 2020 rejected the legalization of a new opposition party, PRA-JA Servir Angola, led by Abel Chivukuvuku. The decision also placed bureaucratic limits on the ability of Chivukuvuku and the party's other promoters to attempt to establish a new, different party in the coming years. The court's decision was appealed.

Score Change: The score declined from 2 to 1 because the government-aligned Constitutional Court refused to permit Abel Chivukuvuku's opposition grouping, PRA-JA Servir Angola, to register as a political party.

B2. Is there a realistic opportunity for the opposition to increase its support or gain power through elections? 1 / 4

There is little space for the opposition to increase its parliamentary representation, much less gain power through elections. Angola has never experienced a transfer of power between rival parties. Nevertheless, opposition parties have been building public support in recent years, particularly in and around the capital, Luanda.

No municipal elections are held in the country for opposition parties to contest, though the national government has been working to change this since 2015. However, citing delays in voter registration, in September 2020 authorities announced the postponement of local elections set for later in the year, without indicating whether they would take place in 2021.

B3. Are the people's political choices free from domination by forces that are external to the political sphere, or by political forces that employ extrapolitical means? 1 / 4

MPLA-aligned economic oligarchies nurture a system of dependency and patronage that can subvert candidates' and voters' ability to freely express their political choices.

B4. Do various segments of the population (including ethnic, racial, religious, gender, LGBT+, and other relevant groups) have full political rights and electoral opportunities? 2 / 4

While societal pressures can discourage women from active political participation, women's rights advocates have an increasingly vocal presence in political life.

Government and state institutions are controlled by the MPLA, which draws much of its support from Kimbundu ethnic group, while the Ovimbundo and Kikongo ethnicities are predominant, respectively, in UNITA and FNLA.

Discussion of issues affecting LGBT+ people have historically been considered taboo, and such topics have been absent from political debate. This has changed somewhat with the parliament's adoption of a new penal code that decriminalized same-sex relations in January 2019.

C. FUNCTIONING OF GOVERNMENT: 2 / 12

C1. Do the freely elected head of government and national legislative representatives determine the policies of the government? 1 / 4

The country has been ruled by the MPLA since independence, and the president is expected to consult routinely with the party's political bureau. Former president dos Santos retained his position as head of the MPLA for a year after President Lourenço's election. In 2018, dos Santos was finally replaced by Lourenço as party leader, enabling the new president to consolidate his authority.

Executive powers are broad and varied, leaving the parliament to act largely as a rubber stamp in approving the president's policies. Like his predecessor, President Lourenço frequently adopts legislation by presidential decree.

C2. Are safeguards against official corruption strong and effective? 1 / 4

After decades of MPLA rule, corruption and patronage have become entrenched in nearly all segments of public and private life. President Lourenço stressed his willingness to fight endemic corruption since his 2017 election campaign, and a few high-profile dos Santos-era officials have been convicted of corruption, including, in 2020, José Filomeno dos Santos, the son of the former president. His sister, Isabel dos Santos, had her assets seized in Angola and Portugal after she was accused of siphoning public funds from the state oil firm, Sonangol.

Other figures under judicial inquiry and facing seizure of assets include two close aides of the former president, Manuel Hélder Vieira Dias "Kopelipa" and Leopoldino do Nascimento, as well as Carlos São Vicente, son-in-law of dos Santos. However, prosecution of high-profile individuals not directly connected to the family of the former president has seldom led to trial. Charges of mismanagement and coercion levied against former minister and Luanda governor Higino Carneiro were dismissed by the Constitutional Court in July 2020, for example; and no charges have been brought against Manuel Vicente, who for more than a decade led the state oil company Sonangol, the epicenter of corruption during the Santos era.

C3. Does the government operate with openness and transparency? 0 / 4

Government operations are generally opaque. In 2018, the government announced the formation of the National Oil, Gas, and Biofuels Agency (ANPG) to oversee the industry beginning in February 2019. However, its leadership has been sourced from Sonangol; ANPG head Paulino Jerónimo previously served as the state oil firm's chief executive in the 2010s.

CIVIL LIBERTIES: 21 / 60

D. FREEDOM OF EXPRESSION AND BELIEF: 7 / 16

D1. Are there free and independent media? 1 / 4

The Angolan state owns most media in the country, and state-owned media report favorably on the government and rarely carry critical coverage. In 2020, government-controlled outlets declined to cover large youth marches at which participants demanded employment opportunities, for example. Most ostensibly private outlets also act as mouthpieces of the regime. However, foreign news outlets, including Portuguese news agency Lusa, French news agency RFI, and Voice of America (VOA), are widely read.

In 2020, the government privatized a number of outlets they said were owned by members of the political and military elite but funded by the state. Journalists' groups expressed concern about a lack of transparency regarding the privatizations, and afterward, about claims that reports critical of the government had been censored at several of those outlets.

Insult and defamation are both considered criminal offenses. The criminal code also includes "abuse of press freedom," a charge that can be levied against those accused of engaging in incitement, hate speech, defense of fascist or racist ideologies, or "fake news."

D2. Are individuals free to practice and express their religious faith or nonbelief in public and private? 2 / 4

The constitution guarantees religious freedom, but the government imposes onerous criteria on religious groups for official recognition, which is required for the legal construction of houses of worship. Notably, many Pentecostal churches—which have had a profound social impact in Angola—remain unregistered.

There are no registered Muslim groups, and Muslim communities have been vocal in their demands for recognition and the right to worship freely. In September 2020, the government reauthorized religious celebrations on Saturday and Sunday, leaving out the Muslim holy weekday, Friday. (Large religious celebrations had been prohibited under COVID-19-related restrictions.)

D3. Is there academic freedom, and is the educational system free from extensive political indoctrination? 2 / 4

Academics must maintain a façade of agreement with the MPLA's preferred narratives and refrain from open criticism of the party, or risk losing their positions. Those who voice dissent are often monitored by security services.

D4. Are individuals free to express their personal views on political or other sensitive topics without fear of surveillance or retribution? 2 / 4

In recent years, there has been somewhat less fear of retribution for expressing criticism of the government or controversial opinions in private conversations. However, self-censorship persists, fueled by concerns that a perceived intent to organize against the government could result in reprisals. While internet access is increasing in Angola, the government actively monitors online activity. Known surveillance of civil society groups, journalists, and academics can leave people reluctant to speak out.

The results of an Afrobarometer poll, released in August 2020, indicated that 32 percent of individuals surveyed considered themselves "not at all free" to express their political views, and another 16 percent said they felt "not completely free." Together, this was greater than the percentage of individuals who said they considered themselves totally or partially free to express such views.

E. ASSOCIATIONAL AND ORGANIZATIONAL RIGHTS: 6 / 12

E1. Is there freedom of assembly? 2 / 4

Constitutional guarantees of freedom of assembly are poorly upheld. While the Lourenço administration has shown more tolerance for public demonstrations than its predecessor, peaceful marches are still at times met with violence and arrests by the security forces. In February 2020, police violently dispersed and made arrests at a protest against the nomination of the new president of the electoral commission, and journalists were also injured amid the upheaval. Police responded similarly in August, when a group marched for access to water, and in September, at a march where participants demanded greater employment opportunities. Grassroots protest marches in October and November were likewise met with disproportionate force, resulting in several unlawful killings.

Separatists in the oil-rich Cabinda region were also targeted by the government in 2020. In November, several activists in were arrested at a march in support of local political leaders who had been detained.

E2. Is there freedom for nongovernmental organizations, particularly those that are engaged in human rights- and governance-related work? 2 / 4

Nongovernmental organizations (NGOs) working on human rights and governance are closely monitored. The MPLA traditionally made vocal attempts to discredit their work and sometimes threatened such groups with lawsuits and outright closure, prompting many to curtail their activities. However, the environment for NGOs has improved since 2018, with a reduction in interference and a greater willingness on the part of the government to engage in dialogue with civil society groups.

E3. Is there freedom for trade unions and similar professional or labor organizations? 2 / 4

Certain employees who provide services considered essential—including prison guards and firefighters, but also workers in the oil sector—may not legally strike. Unions not associated with the MPLA have faced interference and harassment. However, the government in recent years has allowed more strikes to proceed without interference or repression.

F. RULE OF LAW: 5 / 16

F1. Is there an independent judiciary? 1 / 4

The president appoints Supreme Court judges to life terms without legislative input. Corruption and political pressure from the MPLA contribute to the judiciary's general inefficacy and undermine its independence.

Under President Lourenço, the judiciary has seized assets of some high-profile MPLA officials and members of the former presidential family, a few of whom have been put on trial. Whether the developments reflect lasting improvement in judicial independence remains to be seen.

F2. Does due process prevail in civil and criminal matters? 1 / 4

Constitutional guarantees of due process are poorly upheld. Many defendants are unable to afford legal counsel, and the state largely fails to provide qualified legal aid to those who need it. Arbitrary arrest and lengthy pretrial detention remain problems.

Legal representatives for several leading political activists in Cabinda who were detained in 2020 claimed violations of judicial procedures by local authorities and courts.

F3. Is there protection from the illegitimate use of physical force and freedom from war and insurgencies? 1 / 4

Security forces enjoy impunity for violent acts, including torture and extrajudicial killings committed against detainees, activists, and others. In 2020, a medical doctor was killed while in police custody, reportedly after he was arrested for not properly wearing his face mask. Angolan prisons are reported to be overcrowded, unhygienic, lacking in necessities, and plagued by sexual abuse.

According to government statistics, violent crime, including robberies, assaults, and homicides, has increased in Luanda in recent years.

The low-level separatist insurgency in the isolated Cabinda region continues to pose a security threat. The Front for the Liberation of the Enclave of Cabinda (FLEC) claims to have engaged in guerrilla activity against Angolan soldiers, but the government has not verified these claims.

F4. Do laws, policies, and practices guarantee equal treatment of various segments of the population? 2 / 4

Women face discrimination in the workplace that makes it difficult for them to rise to senior positions. There have been reports of abuse of women and children accused of practicing witchcraft.

Same-sex relations were banned in Angola until January 2019, when the parliament adopted a new criminal code that did not include a historical "vices against nature" statute. Lawmakers also banned discrimination based on sexual orientation the same month.

Semi-nomadic Khoi and San tribes in southern provinces have been particularly hard-hit by a prolonged drought, which has been largely neglected by the government. These hardships were aggravated by the COVID-19 pandemic.

Security forces allegedly harass and abuse immigrant communities, and the government has failed to adequately protect refugees and asylum seekers. United Nations representatives expressed concern about the forced expulsion of Congolese migrants in 2020, suggesting it violated international directives on the treatment of refugees.

G. PERSONAL AUTONOMY AND INDIVIDUAL RIGHTS: 3 / 16

G1. Do individuals enjoy freedom of movement, including the ability to change their place of residence, employment, or education? 1 / 4

Several organizations have been working to remove land mines that were placed during Angola's 1975–2002 civil war. Land mines inhibit agriculture, construction, and freedom of movement, particularly in rural areas.

There have been reports by local NGOs, namely the Justice, Peace, and Democracy Association (AJPD), that the authorities and private security groups that guard Lunda Norte Province's diamond mines restrict the movements of local residents, and some local farmers abandoned their land.

The process for securing entry and exit visas remains difficult and mired in corruption. Bribes are frequently required in order to obtain employment and residence.

Restrictions on movement and other activity enacted in response to the COVID-19 pandemic were frequently enforced with violence, with Amnesty International and local NGOs reporting at least seven resulting deaths.

G2. Are individuals able to exercise the right to own property and establish private businesses without undue interference from state or nonstate actors? 1 / 4

Predatory Angolan elites tend to either disrupt or coopt emerging new businesses. Authorities at times have expropriated land and demolished homes without providing compensation. Customary law practices can leave women with unequal inheritance rights.

G3. Do individuals enjoy personal social freedoms, including choice of marriage partner and size of family, protection from domestic violence, and control over appearance? 1 / 4

Domestic violence is widespread in Angola, and perpetrators are rarely prosecuted. Child marriage remains common, particularly in rural areas.

G4. Do individuals enjoy equality of opportunity and freedom from economic exploitation? 0 / 4

Public oil revenues are not equitably distributed or used to benefit the entire population. Rural regions in particular have inadequate infrastructure and access to services, leading to inequities in economic opportunity.

Child labor is a major problem, and foreign workers are vulnerable to sex trafficking and forced labor in the construction and mining industries. The authorities have failed to effectively investigate human trafficking or prosecute offenders.

Antigua and Barbuda

Population: 100,000
Capital: St. John's
Freedom Status: Free
Electoral Democracy: Yes

Overview: Antigua and Barbuda is a democracy that holds regular elections. Corruption in government is a concern, and women and LGBT+ people are underrepresented in politics and experience some discrimination. In 2017, Hurricane Irma devastated Barbuda: the entire island was evacuated, and many residents lost their livelihoods; some have yet to return home. The government has since sought to weaken the island's longstanding system of communal land rights.

KEY DEVELOPMENTS IN 2020

- In July, groups protested outside Parliament against what they claimed were unfair restrictions implemented by the government to prevent the spread of COVID-19; restrictions for tourists were lighter than those imposed upon residents. Prime Minister Gaston Browne blamed the opposition for the protest and suggested that the young people who made up a majority of the protesters were ignorant of what the government was doing to protect lives. According to government statistics provided to the World Health Organization (WHO), 159 people had tested positive for coronavirus and 5 people had died during the year.
- In August, the Barbuda Council called for secession from Antigua, due to rising tensions over the control of land on Barbuda stemming from a dispute over the right to develop a multimillion-dollar private resort, supported by the central government. In September, the government threatened to remove the Barbuda Council from the country's constitution by means of a referendum.

POLITICAL RIGHTS: 33 / 40
A. ELECTORAL PROCESS: 12 / 12
A1. Was the current head of government or other chief national authority elected through free and fair elections? 4 / 4

The country's 1981 constitution establishes a parliamentary system, with a governor general representing the British monarch as ceremonial head of state. The prime minister is the head of government and is typically the leader of the majority party elected to Parliament. Antigua and Barbuda Labour Party (ABLP) leader Gaston Browne once again became prime minister after his party won a majority in the 2018 parliamentary elections.

A2. Were the current national legislative representatives elected through free and fair elections? 4 / 4

The bicameral parliament is composed of a 17-seat Senate, whose members are appointed by the governor general, and the House of Representatives, whose 17 members are directly elected in single-seat constituencies, by means of a simple majority; representatives serve five-year terms.

In February 2018, citing a need to demonstrate state stability to investors, Prime Minister Browne called snap elections for March, a year ahead of schedule. The campaign period was at times rancorous, with the Commonwealth Observer Group noting a "surge of vitriolic and personal attacks exchanged between political parties and candidates." The governing ABLP took 59 percent of the total vote and won 15 constituencies, up from 14 previously. The main opposition United Progressive Party (UPP) took 37 percent of the vote, but only one constituency. The Barbuda People's Movement (BPM) won the Barbuda constituency, which had previously been held by the ABLP. Observers deemed the polls generally competitive and credible. Turnout was high, at about 76 percent.

A3. Are the electoral laws and framework fair, and are they implemented impartially by the relevant election management bodies? 4 / 4

Electoral laws are generally fair and are implemented impartially by the relevant election management bodies. However, in 2018, polling for all Barbudans took place on Antigua as a result of Hurricane Irma, requiring that many people travel between the islands to vote. The government provided services to those needing to travel, and 87 percent of eligible Barbudans participated.

Separately, since 1984, the electoral boundaries of Antigua and Barbuda have shifted only slightly. Consequently, there is now a significant disparity in constituency size, from 1,138 (St. Phillip South) to 4,878 (St. George).

B. POLITICAL PLURALISM AND PARTICIPATION: 13 / 16

B1. Do the people have the right to organize in different political parties or other competitive political groupings of their choice, and is the system free of undue obstacles to the rise and fall of these competing parties or groupings? 3 / 4

Political parties can organize and operate freely. While there are several small political parties in the country, elections have been won by either the ABLP or the UPP since 1994.

Inadequate campaign finance regulations allow candidates and parties to accept donations without disclosing donors' identities.

B2. Is there a realistic opportunity for the opposition to increase its support or gain power through elections? 4 / 4

There are realistic opportunities for opposition parties to increase their support or gain power through elections. Power has alternated frequently between the ABLP and UPP.

B3. Are the people's political choices free from domination by forces that are external to the political sphere, or by political forces that employ extrapolitical means? 3 / 4

People's political choices are generally free from the influence of nondemocratic actors. However, a lack of transparency for party and campaign financing has given rise to concerns about the potential influence of unknown domestic and foreign interests over political candidates. The most significant case was that of R. Allen Stanford, a United States citizen, who was an influential figure in Antigua (the second largest employer in the country at one point) and used the country to run a multibillion-dollar Ponzi scheme. Separately, the Brazilian multinational Odebrecht SA purchased Meinl Bank (Antigua) Ltd in 2010 as part of its scheme to bribe government officials in various countries. The ABLP, then in opposition, has called on key members of the UPP to disclose their involvement in the purchase. Prime Minister Browne has denied any involvement in the Odebrecht scandal.

B4. Do various segments of the population (including ethnic, racial, religious, gender, LGBT+, and other relevant groups) have full political rights and electoral opportunities? 3 / 4

Women are underrepresented in politics, and only two women were elected to the House of Representatives in 2018. LGBT+ people are marginalized and face discrimination, impacting their ability to engage fully in political processes.

A. FUNCTIONING OF GOVERNMENT: 8 / 12

C1. Do the freely elected head of government and national legislative representatives determine the policies of the government? 3 / 4

The elected prime minister, cabinet, and parliament determine government. There are some concerns about the influence of businesses on policymaking.

Tensions between the central government and residents and representatives from Barbuda have grown since the 2016 dissolution of the Barbuda Land Act of 2007, which guaranteed that land was communally owned by Barbudans and that their consent was required for its purchase and development. The 2016 law allows privatization without communal consent. The Barbuda Council and the Browne government have been at odds over a plan to build a multimillion-dollar resort, endorsed by the government, but resisted by the Council due to concerns over potential environmental damage. The rising tensions led to the Council calling for the secession of Barbuda in August 2020. In September, the government accused the Council of treason and threatened to remove it from the country's constitution by means of a referendum.

C2. Are safeguards against official corruption strong and effective? 2 / 4

Government corruption remains a concern, and anticorruption laws are enforced unevenly. Authorities have been criticized for doing little to investigate local official wrongdoing in the case of R. Allen Stanford. Several other company officials have faced justice, but only in the United States. Similarly, few prosecutions have emerged from the Odebrecht corruption scandal.

In May 2018, Asot Michael, the minister of investment and trade, resigned over allegations (which he denied) that he had engaged in illegal campaign financing and bribe-taking while previously serving as the energy minister. The Antiguan Integrity Commission indicated it would investigate the allegations, but no charges appeared to have been filed. The ABLP tried to discipline Michael, but he has challenged the party's punishments.

Antigua's Citizenship by Investment program (CBI) and Permanent Residence Certificate (PRC), in which individuals can be granted citizenship or residency in exchange for a sizable business investment or contribution, have been heavily scrutinized in recent years. In 2018, the US Department of State noted that the CBI left the country vulnerable to financial crimes and raised questions about the program's autonomy from politicians who might seek to misuse it. The Organisation for Economic Co-operation and Development (OECD) has also raised concerns about the programs.

C3. Does the government operate with openness and transparency? 3 / 4

Antigua and Barbuda has gradually improved its accountability structures since 2004, when the government enacted a Freedom of Information Act. The Public Accounts Committee can also expose governmental improprieties and wrongdoings, but historically has not functioned effectively. There have been lengthy delays in submission of the auditor general's report. Public officials must disclose all income, assets, and personal gifts received in their official capacity in a confidential report to the Integrity Commission per the 2004 Integrity in Public Life Act. Resource deficiencies have impeded the commission's ability to investigate corrupt individuals. Despite the Procurement and Contract Management Act of 2011, concerns remain about public procurement in relation to the expertise of officials in positions mandated by the law, the completeness of documentation, and that some applications are made retrospectively, with often a waiver being requested.

Accountability for elected officials has increased somewhat in recent years. In January 2020, Minister of Agriculture, Fisheries and Barbuda Affairs Dean Jonas was suspended for six months after allegations that he mistreated staff. In November, Minister of Education Michael Browne was removed from his position after he was charged with an undisclosed crime.

CIVIL LIBERTIES: 52 / 60

A. FREEDOM OF EXPRESSION AND BELIEF: 15 / 16

D1. Are there free and independent media? 3 / 4

Press freedom is generally respected in Antigua and Barbuda. Criminal defamation was abolished in 2015. However, under the Sedition and Undesirable Publications Act, seditious libel is a criminal offence punishable by a maximum of two years in prison and a maximum fine of $5,000. Critical journalists remain at risk of libel suits from unhappy politicians. The prime minister has characterized the frequently critical *Observer* as "fake news" and a threat to the country.

Most media outlets are concentrated among a small number of firms affiliated with either the current ABLP government or the UPP.

D2. Are individuals free to practice and express their religious faith or nonbelief in public and private? 4 / 4

The constitution provides for freedom of worship as well as the right to practice and change religion, and these freedoms are generally respected. A law outlawing blasphemous language is not enforced.

D3. Is there academic freedom, and is the educational system free from extensive political indoctrination? 4 / 4

Academic freedom is generally respected.

D4. Are individuals free to express their personal views on political or other sensitive topics without fear of surveillance or retribution? 4 / 4

Individuals are generally free to express their personal views on political or other sensitive topics.

E. ASSOCIATIONAL AND ORGANIZATIONAL RIGHTS: 10 / 12

E1. Is there freedom of assembly? 4 / 4

Freedom of assembly is guaranteed under the constitution, and the government generally respects these rights in practice. In July 2020, groups protested outside Parliament against what they claimed were unfair restrictions implemented by the government to prevent the spread of COVID-19; restrictions for tourists were lighter than those imposed upon residents. Prime Minister Browne blamed the UPP for the protest and suggested that the young people who made up a majority of the protesters were ignorant of what the government was doing to protect lives. However, the government did not restrict political demonstrations.

E2. Is there freedom for nongovernmental organizations, particularly those that are engaged in human rights–and governance-related work? 3 / 4

The country's few nongovernmental organizations (NGOs) are active, though inadequately funded and often influenced by the government.

E3. Is there freedom for trade unions and similar professional or labor organizations? 3 / 4

Labor unions can organize freely and bargain collectively. Workers providing essential services must give notice two weeks before intent to strike. However, the International Labour Organization (ILO) has described the list of essential services as excessively broad. Strikes are fairly rare.

F. RULE OF LAW: 14 / 16

F1. Is there an independent judiciary? 4 / 4

The constitution provides for an independent judiciary, which is generally respected by the government. In November 2018, voters rejected in a referendum the adoption of the Caribbean Court of Justice as their highest appellate court. Thus, the Judicial Committee of the Privy Council, based in London, retains that role.

In recent years, the courts have increasingly asserted independence from the ABLP government—which had a history of manipulating the judicial system—with the support of the Eastern Caribbean Supreme Court. The High Court of Justice has issued several rulings since 2018 that have slowed government-backed development plans for Barbuda. In October 2020, the Court of Appeal ruled that the Privy Council should decide whether the Antiguan government or the Barbuda Council controls land sales on Barbuda.

F2. Does due process prevail in civil and criminal matters? 3 / 4

Constitutional guarantees of due process are mostly upheld. However, prisoners on remand often remain in jail for an average of three to four years before their cases are heard.

F3. Is there protection from the illegitimate use of physical force and freedom from war and insurgencies? 4 / 4

Residents of Antigua and Barbuda do not face any significant security threats. However, prisons are severely overcrowded, and conditions within them are poor.

F4. Do laws, policies, and practices guarantee equal treatment of various segments of the population? 3 / 4

The 2005 Equal Opportunity Act bars discrimination on the basis of race, gender, class, political affinity, or place of origin. There are no specific laws prohibiting discrimination against people with disabilities, or LGBT+ individuals. Societal norms discourage participation of women in some sectors of the economy, and few women hold leadership positions.

Same-sex sexual activity remains criminalized under a 1995 law; however, the law is not strictly enforced. In November 2019, the Eastern Caribbean Alliance for Diversity and Equality (ECADE) announced it would file official legal challenges against colonial era laws against same-sex sexual activity in Antigua and Barbuda and four other Caribbean countries. The government announced it would not support, nor enact, any such legal changes.

Gender stereotypes and discrimination can make finding employment a challenge for women. Mental health services require improvement and people with physical disabilities are stigmatized and underemployed.

G. PERSONAL AUTONOMY AND INDIVIDUAL RIGHTS: 13 / 16

G1. Do individuals enjoy freedom of movement, including the ability to change their place of residence, employment, or education? 4 / 4

Individuals enjoy freedom of movement, including the ability to change their place of residence, employment, or education.

G2. Are individuals able to exercise the right to own property and establish private businesses without undue interference from state or non-state actors? 3 / 4

Many Barbudans forced to evacuate the island due to Hurricane Irma opposed moves by lawmakers in Antigua to eliminate the communal land ownership system that governed the island for almost two centuries, and instead establish private land ownership. The government argues that the change is necessary to assist Barbuda's recovery.

The development of a multimillion-dollar private resort on Barbuda, led by the Peace Love and Happiness partnership, has driven tensions between the Browne government and Barbudan population and their representatives, who are concerned about the environmental impacts of the development. The Browne government has threatened those who attempt to obstruct the plans with jail time; in July 2020, the Barbudan Council Secretary, Paul Need, was arrested for blocking passage to a public road with his vehicle.

G3. Do individuals enjoy personal social freedoms, including choice of marriage partner and size of family, protection from domestic violence, and control over appearance? 3 / 4

The Domestic Violence Act of 2015 strengthened the measures that can be taken against the perpetrators of domestic violence and laid out a process for victims to obtain an order of protection. However, domestic violence remains a serious problem. Same-sex marriage and civil partnerships are not recognized. In November 2020, local advocacy groups called for the Minister of Gender Affairs Dean Jonas to resign after he suggested that girls who are still legal minors could consent to having sex with older men.

G4. Do individuals enjoy equality of opportunity and freedom from economic exploitation? 3 / 4

Antigua and Barbuda is a destination and transit country for the trafficking of men, women, and children for the purposes of forced labor and sexual exploitation. Government efforts to address the problem are inadequate, but progress is being made, according to the US State Department's *2020 Trafficking in Persons* report. Compulsory labor is prohibited by law. In September 2019, the Industrial Court ruled against Antigua and Barbuda's Department of Immigration, confirming that it has been breaching the rights of its workers for at least the last two decades, during which time the department did not paid employees for sick days, holidays worked, and overtime.

Argentina

Population: 45,400,000
Capital: Buenos Aires
Freedom Status: Free
Electoral Democracy: Yes

Overview: Argentina is a vibrant representative democracy with competitive elections, lively media and civil society sectors, and unfettered public debate. Economic instability, corruption in the government and judiciary, and drug-related violence are among the country's most serious challenges.

KEY DEVELOPMENTS IN 2020

- In response to the COVID-19 pandemic, Argentina imposed one of the strictest and most prolonged lockdowns in the world, which lasted for more than six months. In addition to steps taken by the central government, some provinces and towns erected irregular roadblocks and arbitrarily impeded legal transit. Despite these measures, by the end of 2020 more than 43,000 people had died from COVID-19, according to data gathered by Johns Hopkins University.
- Enforcement of the national quarantine produced a rise in police brutality, including several deaths, with young people from marginalized sectors particularly vulnerable.

- The pandemic and the measures to contain it deepened Argentina's economic crisis. The country has been in a recession since 2018 and the economy contracted by more than 10 percent in 2020, driving the poverty rate from 25 percent in 2017 to more than 40 percent in mid-2020.
- Since taking office in late 2019, President Alberto Fernández and Vice President Cristina Fernández de Kirchner (no relation) have attacked the judiciary for its alleged politicization and launched initiatives that, if enacted, could diminish judicial independence. In 2020 this included verbal attacks on the Supreme Court and a proposed judicial reform that would allow the administration to appoint new judges in key federal courts.

POLITICAL RIGHTS: 35 / 40

A. ELECTORAL PROCESS: 11 / 12

A1. Was the current head of government or other chief national authority elected through free and fair elections? 4 / 4

The constitution provides for a president to be elected for a four-year term, with the option of reelection for one additional term. Presidential candidates must win 45 percent of the vote to avoid a runoff. Alberto Fernández, a center-left figure who aside from a brief time in the Buenos Aires city legislature had never held elected office before, was elected president in the first round of elections in October 2019 with 48.24 percent of the vote, against incumbent Mauricio Macri's 40.28 percent. The poll was deemed competitive and credible by international observers.

Fernández's victory was widely viewed as benefiting from having political veteran and former president Cristina Fernández de Kirchner on his ticket. A member of the populist Peronist movement, she was the subject of multiple allegations of corruption at the time of the election.

A2. Were the current national legislative representatives elected through free and fair elections? 4 / 4

The National Congress consists of a 257-member Chamber of Deputies, whose representatives are directly elected for four-year terms with half of the seats up for election every two years; and the 72-member Senate, whose representatives are directly elected for six-year terms, with one-third of the seats up for election every two years. Legislators are elected through a proportional representation system with closed party lists.

Legislative elections, including the most recent ones held in October 2019 together with the presidential vote, are generally free and fair. In the lower chamber, there were 130 seats contested in 2019, of which President Fernández's Frente de Todos won 64, former president Macri's Juntos por el Cambio won 56, and a number of smaller coalitions won between one and three seats each. The Senate saw 25 seats contested in 2019, of which Frente de Todos won 13, Juntos por el Cambio won 8, and Frente Cívico por Santiago won 2. Frente de Todos holds the greatest number of seats in both houses.

A3. Are the electoral laws and framework fair, and are they implemented impartially by the relevant election management bodies? 3 / 4

Argentina has a clear, detailed, and fair legislative framework for conducting elections. There is universal suffrage. Voting is compulsory for people between 18 and 70 years old, and voluntary between 16 and 18, and for people older than 70. However, the system suffers from some shortcomings, including inconsistent enforcement of electoral laws and campaign finance regulations. Further, aspects of election management fall under the purview of the executive branch, as Argentina's National Electoral Chamber (CNE) works in conjunction with the National Electoral Directorate, a department of the Ministry of the Interior.

B. POLITICAL PLURALISM AND PARTICIPATION: 16 / 16

B1. Do the people have the right to organize in different political parties or other competitive political groupings of their choice, and is the system free of undue obstacles to the rise and fall of these competing parties or groupings? 4 / 4

Argentina has competitive political parties that operate without encountering undue obstacles. Primary elections are mandatory for presidential and legislative elections, and only party candidates that obtain 1.5 percent of the national vote can move on to the general election.

B2. Is there a realistic opportunity for the opposition to increase its support or gain power through elections? 4 / 4

Argentina's multiparty political system affords opposition candidates the realistic opportunity to compete for political power, and opposition parties command significant popular support and hold positions in national and subnational government.

The 2019 elections marked the return of Peronism to national power after a 4-year-hiatus under Macri, who in December 2019 became the first elected non-Peronist to complete a presidential term since 1928.

B3. Are the people's political choices free from domination by forces that are external to the political sphere, or by political forces that employ extrapolitical means? 4 / 4

Argentines' political choices are generally free from domination by groups that are not democratically accountable.

B4. Do various segments of the population (including ethnic, racial, religious, gender, LGBT+, and other relevant groups) have full political rights and electoral opportunities? 4 / 4

Members of ethnic and religious minority groups have full political rights in Argentina. However, in practice, the government frequently ignores legal obligations to consult with Indigenous communities about legislation and government actions that affect them.

Women and women's interests are reasonably well represented in the legislature. The 2019 legislative elections, in which a portion of seats were contested, were the first conducted under a new law that mandates all party lists to have full gender parity, with men and women alternating. Women now hold 42 percent of seats in the Chamber of Deputies, and 38 percent in the Senate. Previously, the law required that at least 30 percent of a party's legislative candidates be women. In December 2019, President Fernández created the Ministry of Women, Genders, and Diversity, with a focus on promoting equality and combating gender-based violence. In practice, however, top government, judicial, and political positions at the national level continue to be dominated by men, especially from the city and province of Buenos Aires.

LGBT+ people are also reasonably well represented in Argentina. Robust legal protections for LGBT+ people are codified in the law, and Argentina in 2010 became the first country in the Americas to legalize same-sex marriage.

C. FUNCTIONING OF GOVERNMENT: 8 / 12

C1. Do the freely elected head of government and national legislative representatives determine the policies of the government? 3 / 4

Argentina's elected officials are duly installed in office without interference. However, the political system is characterized by a powerful executive, with the president having authority to implement some policies by decree, thereby bypassing the legislative branch. Provincial governors are also powerful and tend to influence lawmakers representing their provinces.

In December 2019, Congress granted President Fernández broad emergency powers for one year. This package weakened oversight mechanisms and allowed Fernández to impose new taxes, determine wage and pension increases by decree, and renegotiate foreign debt, among other measures. In March 2020, the president used this authority to respond to the incipient COVID-19 pandemic by decreeing a one-year health emergency that authorized the government to circumvent existing regulations and make direct purchases of health equipment without public bidding.

Cristina Fernández de Kirchner is arguably the most influential vice president in the country's history: she is the driving force behind the electoral coalition that brought Alberto Fernández to power and handpicked him as the presidential candidate.

C2. Are safeguards against official corruption strong and effective? 2 / 4

Corruption scandals are common, and several prominent members of the political class, including former presidents, have been charged with or found guilty of malfeasance in recent years. However, weak anticorruption bodies and the politicization of the judicial system hamper institutional safeguards against corruption. For instance, the country's main anticorruption office is part of the Justice Ministry and is headed by a presidential appointee, leaving it vulnerable to improper influence by the executive. Further, many politicians hold immunity in connection with their elected posts and are thus shielded from legal consequences for corrupt behavior.

Vice President Cristina Fernández de Kirchner faces numerous investigations for alleged corruption during her time as president, from 2007 to 2015, and has been indicted on several occasions. Judges have requested her pretrial arrest, but she was protected through legislative immunity as a senator between 2017 and 2019, and as vice president thereafter. The government has attacked the Supreme Court and the judiciary for processing corruption cases involving the vice president and other *kirchnerista* officials. Several prominent kirchneristas, including Amado Boudou, who served as Fernández de Kirchner's vice president before being convicted in 2018 on corruption charges, were controversially granted conditional, coronavirus-related humanitarian releases from prison in 2020.

C3. Does the government operate with openness and transparency? 3 / 4

In recent years the government has taken steps to improve transparency at the national level, including by presenting periodic action plans as part of its membership in the Open Government Partnership. Authorities have digitized state records and procedural documents and have published more information online, including on public procurement and contracting bids, as part of an effort to join the Organization for Economic Cooperation and Development (OECD).

In 2017, Argentina enacted an access to information law that established a Public Information Agency, through which citizens may request information from state agencies and other state-funded institutions. The implementation of the law has been uneven, and the agency is located within the office of the Chief of Cabinet of Ministers, who is appointed by the president. Adherence to and enforcement of public-asset disclosure regulations is inconsistent. Further, there has been limited progress to promote transparency at the provincial and municipal levels, and in the judiciary.

The health emergency declared in March 2020 relaxed procurement regulations, reducing transparency in government purchases.

CIVIL LIBERTIES: 49 / 60 (−1)

D. FREEDOM OF EXPRESSION AND BELIEF: 15 / 16

D1. Are there free and independent media? 3 / 4

Argentine law guarantees freedom of expression, and Congress decriminalized libel and slander in 2009. While media ownership is concentrated among large conglomerates that frequently favor a political grouping, Argentineans nevertheless enjoy a robust and lively media environment, and there is no official censorship. In October 2020, the governmental Ombudsman's Office announced the creation of a media observatory intended to monitor instances of fake news and symbolic violence such as hate speech; press freedom advocates expressed concern about the project's ambiguous mission and alleged ideological bias.

Journalists face occasional harassment and violence. In addition, those covering discrimination against LGBT+ people report frequent threats on social media. Some journalists have faced corruption or other charges in connection with their investigative work. An audit of Argentina's intelligence service led to a June 2020 announcement that the government had amassed dossiers on hundreds of journalists during the Macri administration, including classifications of reporters' perceived political leanings.

D2. Are individuals free to practice and express their religious faith or nonbelief in public and private? 4 / 4

Argentina's constitution guarantees freedom of religion. While the population is largely Roman Catholic, public education is secular, and religious minorities express their faiths freely. The government has formally acknowledged more than 5,300 non-Catholic organizations, granting them tax-exempt status and other benefits.

D3. Is there academic freedom, and is the educational system free from extensive political indoctrination? 4 / 4

Academic freedom is guaranteed by law and largely observed in practice.

D4. Are individuals free to express their personal views on political or other sensitive topics without fear of surveillance or retribution? 4 / 4

Private discussion is vibrant and unrestricted. However, in April 2020 the minister of security announced the creation of "cyberpatrols" to monitor social media and punish those who spread false information regarding the COVID-19 pandemic, a campaign that resulted in the initiation of several criminal cases.

E. ASSOCIATIONAL AND ORGANIZATIONAL RIGHTS: 11 / 12

E1. Is there freedom of assembly? 4 / 4

Freedom of assembly is generally respected, and citizens frequently organize protests to make their voices heard. Peaceful antigovernment demonstrations were common in Buenos Aires and other cities throughout 2020, despite lockdown restrictions.

E2. Is there freedom for nongovernmental organizations, particularly those that are engaged in human rights- and governance-related work? 4 / 4

Nongovernmental organizations (NGOs) generally operate without restrictions. Civic organizations, especially those focused on human rights and abuses committed under the 1976–83 dictatorship, are robust and play a major role in society, although some fall victim to Argentina's pervasive corruption.

E3. Is there freedom for trade unions and similar professional or labor organizations? 3 / 4

Organized labor remains dominated by Peronist unions, and union influence remains significant, although it has decreased in recent years. Most labor unions have been controlled by the same individuals or groups since the 1980s, and internal opposition to union leadership has been limited by fraud and intimidation.

F. RULE OF LAW: 10 / 16

F1. Is there an independent judiciary? 2 / 4

Inefficiencies and delays plague the judicial system, which is susceptible to political manipulation, particularly at lower levels. Some federal judges are known to maintain close ties with political actors, and to engage in corrupt practices. Judicial cases tend to follow political trends: several former officials and businessmen involved in corruption allegations during the previous government of Fernández de Kirchner were imprisoned during Macri's presidency, but many were released soon before or after Alberto Fernández's electoral win.

Since taking office in December 2019, the president and vice president have attacked the judiciary for its alleged politicization and launched initiatives that, if enacted, could diminish judicial independence. In June 2020, the government presented a broad judicial reform to expand the number of federal courts in Buenos Aires from 12 to 46, which would allow President Fernández and the Peronist-controlled Senate to appoint many new judges. The president also appointed a commission of experts that proposed other changes to the judiciary, including the creation of new tribunals that would reduce the influence of the Supreme Court. Critics questioned the commission's composition: among the members was the vice president's personal lawyer. In addition, the Senate voted to change the rules on the appointment of the attorney general, reducing the confirmation requirement from two-thirds to a simple majority. As of the years end, neither the judicial nor the prosecutorial reforms had been approved by the Chamber of Deputies, where the government's majority is fragile.

In September 2020, the Senate acted to remove three judges from a federal court tasked with key decisions in corruption cases involving the vice president, her family, and close associates. In a display of its relative independence, the Supreme Court ruled that the judges must remain in their posts until Senate-confirmed replacements are appointed following an open competition, which could take years. Overall, the Supreme Court has pushed back against executive overreach during the Kirchner, Macri, and Fernández administrations. In December, the vice president issued a polemical public letter in which she directly accused Supreme Court members of protecting Macri and engaging in "lawfare" against her.

F2. Does due process prevail in civil and criminal matters? 3 / 4

Due process rights are protected by the constitution and are generally upheld. However, the justice system and security forces, especially at the provincial level, have long stood accused of using excessive violence and having ties with drug-trafficking operations.

The UN Special Rapporteur on torture issued a report in 2019 stating that six out of ten people held in Argentine prisons had yet to reach the final stage in their trial, and were thus being held despite having not been convicted of any crime. The report also highlighted prison overcrowding and excessive violence against inmates and people under interrogation by police forces, among other forms of ill-treatment.

Court cases dating from the mid-2000s have allowed the prosecution of crimes against humanity committed during the brutal 1976–83 dictatorship. Hundreds of military and police officers have been convicted of torture, murder, and forced disappearance and sentenced to long prison terms, helping to combat a culture of impunity. Many victims of state-sponsored terrorism, including kidnapped children, have never been found.

F3. Is there protection from the illegitimate use of physical force and freedom from war and insurgencies? 2 / 4

Drug-related violence remained a serious issue in 2020 as international criminal organizations used the country as both an operational base and a transit route; the northern and central regions are particularly affected. Rosario—the country's third largest city and an important port in Santa Fe province—has been at the center of a spike in drug-related violence and unrest that has featured armed attacks against courts and intimidation of public officials.

Police misconduct, including torture and brutality against suspects in custody, is endemic. Prisons are overcrowded, and conditions remain substandard throughout the country. Arbitrary arrests and abuses by police are rarely punished in the courts, and police collusion with drug traffickers is common.

In 2020, enforcement of the coronavirus-induced lockdown led to a rise in cases of excessive force, especially against the poor. In August, Amnesty International reported more than 30 cases of police brutality during the enforcement of the national lockdown. A case that drew significant attention was the April disappearance of 22-year old Facundo Astudillo Castro, who went missing after being detained by Buenos Aires province police for violating the lockdown. His body was found in August, with drowning ruled as the cause of death; an enforced disappearance investigation remained open as of December, and no suspects had been detained.

F4. Do laws, policies, and practices guarantee equal treatment of various segments of the population? 3 / 4

Argentina has robust antidiscrimination laws, but enforcement is uneven outside well-off urban areas. Argentina's Indigenous peoples, who comprise approximately 2.4 percent of the population, are largely neglected by the government and suffer disproportionately from extreme poverty and poor access to public services. Only 11 of Argentina's 23 provinces have constitutions recognizing the rights of Indigenous peoples. Displays of xenophobia against migrants and race-based discrimination are common. Women enjoy legal equality, but continue to face economic discrimination and gender-based wage gaps.

Argentina's LGBT+ population enjoys full legal rights, including marriage, adoption, and the right to serve in the military. However, LGBT+ people face some degree of societal discrimination, and occasionally, serious violence. LGBT+ people were at times subjected to excessive force by the police in the context of lockdown enforcement.

G. PERSONAL AUTONOMY AND INDIVIDUAL RIGHTS: 13 / 16 (−1)

G1. Do individuals enjoy freedom of movement, including the ability to change their place of residence, employment, or education? 3 / 4 (−1)

The government generally respects citizens' constitutional right to free travel both inside and outside of Argentina. People are free to change their place of education or employment.

In response to the COVID-19 pandemic, Argentina implemented one of the strictest and most prolonged lockdowns in the world. All domestic flights were cancelled and almost all international travel was banned from March to October 2020. Many provinces erected *de facto* internal borders with vague regulations that were sometimes implemented in an arbitrary way, ignoring legally sanctioned exceptions to national restrictions and at times imposing unnecessary hardship on families suffering medical emergencies. The province of San Luis banned even the entry of ambulances from neighboring areas in Córdoba and prevented people from seeking medical treatment. There were further reports of security agents enforcing lockdown measures with disproportionate force, including with tear gas and rubber bullets. Human rights groups criticized the measures as excessive and unclear, and in September the Supreme Court ordered provincial governments to enact the restrictions in accordance with human rights norms, international treaty obligations, and exceptions provided by official regulations. In November, the Court ordered the province of Formosa to allow the entry of 7,500 provincial residents who had not been able to return to their homes for months.

Score Change: The score declined from 4 to 3 due to harsh COVID-19 movement restrictions that were often arbitrarily implemented, with reports of disproportionate force used by law enforcement agents assigned to enforce the lockdown.

G2. Are individuals able to exercise the right to own property and establish private businesses without undue interference from state or nonstate actors? 3 / 4

Citizens generally enjoy the right to own property and establish private businesses. However, cumbersome regulations, bureaucratic abuses, and corruption continue to affect the private sector at all levels.

Approximately 70 percent of the country's rural Indigenous communities lack titles to their lands, and forced evictions, while technically illegal, still occur. Indigenous communities continue to struggle to defend their land rights against oil and gas prospectors, and to reclaim traditional lands.

G3. Do individuals enjoy personal social freedoms, including choice of marriage partner and size of family, protection from domestic violence, and control over appearance? 4 / 4

Argentineans enjoy broad freedom regarding marriage and divorce. Same-sex marriage and adoption by same-sex couples has been legal nationwide since 2010. A 2012 gender identity law allows people to legally change their gender.

Violence against women remains a serious problem. Activists continue to hold highly visible protests and events aimed at drawing attention to the issue. According to official data, lockdown measures enacted in response to the coronavirus pandemic led to a sharp rise in violence against women, with a two-thirds year-on-year increase in calls to a domestic violence hotline in April 2020.

Following years of civil society mobilization and an unsuccessful legislative effort in 2018, in December 2020 Congress legalized abortions up to the 14th week of pregnancy, a development with few precedents in Latin America. President Fernández and top government officials had strongly backed the bill and were key to its approval in the Senate.

G4. Do individuals enjoy equality of opportunity and freedom from economic exploitation? 3 / 4

Some industries like garment and brick production profit from the forced labor of men, women, and children from Argentina as well as from neighboring countries; forced labor is also present in the agriculture sector and among domestic workers and street vendors. Exploitation is made easier by the prevalence of informal work: nearly half of all Argentine workers operate in the informal sector, without proper benefits or formal legal protections. Workers in the informal economy were severely affected by pandemic lockdown measures, deepening social inequalities.

Men, women, and children are subject to sex trafficking. The government maintained the use of a hotline to facilitate investigations and has worked to identify more victims, deliver antitrafficking trainings, and prosecute officials involved in trafficking, according to the US State Department's 2020 *Trafficking in Persons Report*.

Armenia

Population: 3,000,000
Capital: Yerevan
Freedom Status: Partly Free
Electoral Democracy: No

Note: The numerical scores and status listed above do not reflect conditions in Nagorno-Karabakh, which is examined in a separate report. *Freedom in the World* reports assess the level of political rights and civil liberties in a given geographical area, regardless of whether they are affected by the state, nonstate actors, or foreign powers. Disputed territories are sometimes assessed separately if they meet certain criteria, including boundaries that are sufficiently stable to allow year-on-year comparisons. For more information, see the report methodology and FAQ.

Overview: Armenia is in the midst of a significant transition following mass antigovernment protests and elections in 2018 that forced out an entrenched political elite. The new government has pledged to deal with long-standing problems including systemic corruption, opaque policymaking, a flawed electoral system, and weak rule of law. The country's politics were seriously destabilized, and more than 2,400 soldiers were killed in 2020, when fighting with Azerbaijan broke out over control of the territory of Nagorno-Karabakh.

KEY DEVELOPMENTS IN 2020

- Armenia and Azerbaijan began fighting over control of Nagorno-Karabakh in September, before a cease-fire agreement favoring Azerbaijan was finalized in November; over 2,400 Armenian soldiers were killed in the fighting, while 90,000 of the territory's residents fled to Armenia proper. The government of Nikol Pashinyan faced widespread criticism over the agreement, with protesters temporarily seizing the parliament's chambers soon after the cease-fire was announced, but it remained in power at year's end.
- The government declared martial law in September, as the conflict with Azerbaijan began. Despite these restrictions, major protests were held after a cease-fire was secured in November, including the one that led to the parliament takeover. The government rescinded most martial law restrictions in early December, and antigovernment protests continued through year's end.
- Authorities made continued progress in anticorruption efforts throughout the year. In February, a corruption trial against former president Serzh Sargsyan held its first session, while Prosperous Armenia party leader Gagik Tsarukyan was arrested on tax evasion charges in September. In December, the cabinet submitted a bill finalizing the creation of a new anticorruption office, which is expected to begin its work in 2021.
- The government declared a COVID-19-related state of emergency in March. Mass gatherings were heavily restricted, and Armenians were largely prevented from leaving their homes during the lockdown. Most lockdown measures ended in May, though the state of emergency did not expire until September.

POLITICAL RIGHTS: 22 / 40 (+1)

A. ELECTORAL PROCESS: 6 / 12

A1. Was the current head of government or other chief national authority elected through free and fair elections? 2 / 4

In late 2015, a voters approved constitutional changes that, among other things, transformed the country from a semipresidential to a parliamentary republic. The president, who had been directly elected for up to two five-year terms, would henceforth be chosen by the parliament for a single seven-year term, and most executive power would shift to the prime minister, who would also be chosen by a parliamentary majority. The new system took effect in 2018, when Serzh Sargsyan completed his second consecutive presidential term. The parliament elected diplomat Armen Sarkissian as president; though Sargsyan pledged to refrain from extending his rule by seeking the premiership, the then ruling Republican Party (HHK) nevertheless nominated him and ushered him into the post. This prompted mass antigovernment protests and led to Sargsyan's resignation after less than a week in office. Nikol Pashinyan, a deputy with the opposition Yelq Alliance who emerged as the leader of the demonstrations, sought and gained appointment as interim prime minister later in 2018.

Executive elections held before 2018 were dominated by the HHK, with incumbent elites benefiting from the abuse of administrative resources and severe limitations imposed on opposition candidates. However, Pashinyan and his new My Step Alliance swept the December 2018 parliamentary elections, which were markedly freer and fairer than elections in previous years, and took office in January 2019.

A2. Were the current national legislative representatives elected through free and fair elections? 2 / 4

The National Assembly consists of a minimum of 101 members elected for five-year terms through a combination of national and district-based proportional representation. Up to four additional seats are reserved for ethnic minority representatives, and further seats can be added to ensure that opposition parties hold at least 30 percent of the seats.

Pashinyan announced his resignation as prime minister in October 2018 in order to trigger snap parliamentary elections that December. Reports by local and international observers noted that the elections were credible. The Organization for Security and Co-operation in Europe (OSCE) found that "the general absence of electoral malfeasance, including of vote-buying and pressure on voters, allowed for genuine competition." The My Step Alliance won 70 percent of the vote and was allotted 88 seats, including the four ethnic minority mandates. Prosperous Armenia, headed by wealthy businessman Gagik Tsarukyan, took 8 percent and 26 seats, while Bright Armenia, a small liberal party that had been part of the Yelq Alliance, took 6 percent and 18 seats. The HHK failed to cross the 5 percent threshold for representation.

A3. Are the electoral laws and framework fair, and are they implemented impartially by the relevant election management bodies? 2 / 4

Members of Central Election Commission (CEC) are recommended and then confirmed by the National Assembly for six-year terms. In the past, the CEC was generally subservient to the HHK, and showed reluctance to investigate alleged electoral violations by the party. This resulted in a low level of public trust in the electoral process and the CEC. However, the commission reportedly exhibited more professional conduct during the 2018 snap election, making preparations on a shortened timeline, conducting voter education campaigns, and handling voter rolls, candidate registration, and publication of results in a transparent manner.

Critics of Armenia's preexisting electoral code argued that its complex system for voting and seat allocation gave an undue advantage to the HHK and affiliated business magnates. In 2019, a parliamentary working group was formed to consider major reforms to the country's electoral system. In February 2020, Pashinyan assembles a constitutional reform commission to consider electoral reforms, and its work was continuing at year's end.

B. POLITICAL PLURALISM AND PARTICIPATION: 10 / 16

B1. Do the people have the right to organize in different political parties or other competitive political groupings of their choice, and is the system free of undue obstacles to the rise and fall of these competing parties or groupings? 3 / 4

The HHK's political dominance and control of administrative resources has historically prevented a level playing field among the country's many competing parties. However, the protest movement that forced Sargsyan from office also increased pressure on the HHK to refrain from interfering in party activities, giving opposition groups significantly more freedom to operate ahead of the 2018 election. Political parties have since operated in a much freer environment, though they were largely unable to hold rallies due to COVID-19-related restrictions and the declaration of martial law during the conflict with Azerbaijan. However, small political parties were especially active in their public opposition to the November 2020 cease-fire agreement ending the conflict in Nagorno-Karabakh.

In late December 2020, amendments to the Law on Parties gained parliamentary approval. The amendments will tie public funding of political parties to female and nationwide representation, and will cap individual donations.

B2. Is there a realistic opportunity for the opposition to increase its support or gain power through elections? 3 / 4

The HHK had been the main ruling party since 1999, and opposition groups had little chance of winning power in the flawed elections before 2018. However, that year's election transformed the political landscape, leaving the HHK with no parliamentary representation and paving the way for My Step to form the government. In 2018, opposition parties also defeated the HHK in municipal elections that it had long dominated, including in the capital city of Yerevan.

The ruling party and two largest opposition groups declined to field candidates for the September 2019 municipal elections, allowing current and former HHK members to retain the mayoralties of five villages. In May 2020, the three parties supported a bill abolishing direct mayoral elections in towns and some villages in favor of a party-list system. Local elections due in 2020 were postponed to 2021 due to the ongoing COVID-19 pandemic, with voters expected to participate under the new system.

B3. Are the people's political choices free from domination by forces that are external to the political sphere, or by political forces that employ extrapolitical means? 2 / 4

The HHK and its allies historically used vote buying, voter intimidation, and the abuse of administrative resources to distort the popular will, but the parliament adopted legislation that criminalized various acts related to vote buying in 2018. That year's snap election and local elections in 2018 and 2019 saw a decline in these practices.

B4. Do various segments of the population (including ethnic, racial, religious, gender, LGBT+, and other relevant groups) have full political rights and electoral opportunities? 2 / 4

A system introduced as part of the 2015 constitutional reforms mandates the inclusion of up to four members of parliament representing ethnic minorities; all four must be elected on a party list. In 2018, My Step won all four minority seats, representing ethnic Russians, Yazidis, Assyrians, and Kurds.

No openly LGBT+ people have run in elections or been appointed to a public office in Armenia. Women remain underrepresented in politics and government, and most parties do little to address women's interests aside from meeting the gender quota on candidate lists. Armenia's first female mayor was elected in 2018.

Despite his praise of women's involvement in the 2018 protests, Pashinyan included only one woman, labor and social affairs minister Zaruhi Batoyan, in the cabinet in 2019. Batoyan was dismissed after the cease-fire agreement with Azerbaijan was announced in November 2020, leaving Armenia with an all-male cabinet.

C. FUNCTIONING OF GOVERNMENT: 6 / 12 (+1)

C1. Do the freely elected head of government and national legislative representatives determine the policies of the government? 2 / 4

Through its significant majority, gained in a free and fair election, My Step controlled parliamentary decision-making throughout the year, despite significant pressure placed on it in the aftermath of the conflict over Nagorno-Karabakh.

The HHK previously dominated policymaking, but it gained this power through a series of deeply flawed elections. Wealthy businesspeople, some of whom maintained close ties to the HHK, can still exert some influence over policymaking, though the Pashinyan government has worked to loosen their grip since taking office.

Russia also wields influence in Armenia, and its strategic priorities have prompted some significant policy changes in the past. Moscow refrained from interfering with the 2018 antigovernment demonstrations and the transfer of power, but did facilitate the cease-fire agreement ending the September-to-November 2020 conflict over Nagorno-Karabakh.

C2. Are safeguards against official corruption strong and effective? 2 / 4 (+1)

Relationships between politicians, public servants, and businesspeople have historically influenced policy and contributed to selective application of the law. The HHK government included some of Armenia's wealthiest business leaders, who continued private entrepreneurial activities despite conflicts of interest.

However, the Pashinyan government has made steady progress in investigating past wrongdoing and fortifying anticorruption mechanisms. In April 2020, the parliament passed legislation expanding the ability of prosecutors to investigate corrupt acts of former officials. Under the new law, prosecutors can more easily request the seizure of ill-gotten assets if their status is proven in court, and are allowed to investigate acts going back ten years. In early December, the cabinet submitted a bill finalizing the creation of the Anti-Corruption Committee (ACC), which was originally envisioned in 2019 as part of a three-year anticorruption plan. The ACC, as well as a specialized anticorruption court, are scheduled to begin operating in 2021.

Law enforcement agencies initiated high-profile investigations when Pashinyan took office, and those activities continued in 2020. A corruption trial against former president Serzh Sargsyan began in February; Sargsyan, along with former agriculture minister Sergo Karapetyan, two other officials, and the head of a fuel supplier, were accused of manipulating a government tender in the supplier's favor in December 2019. The trial was ongoing at year's end.

Sargsyan's son in law, Mikayel Minasyan, who formerly served as the Armenian ambassador to the Vatican, was indicted on money laundering and income falsification allegations in April, and businesses connected to him were seized by prosecutors in June

2020. However, an appeals court voided an arrest warrant against Minasyan, who denied the allegations, in December.

Former finance minister Gagik Khachatryan faces several charges, including embezzlement of public funds, abuse of power, suppression of competition, and tax evasion. His son, Gurgen Khachatryan, was accused of aiding his activities in January 2020; Gurgen avoided arrest and vowed to remain at large in May, calling the investigation itself illegal. The cases against both individuals were ongoing at year's end.

Prosperous Armenia leader Gagik Tsarukyan was questioned by authorities investigating vote-buying and tax-evasion allegations in June 2020, and was stripped of parliamentary immunity later that month. He was arrested by the National Security Service in late September and was later bailed, though he faced continued questioning over the accusations in early December. The case against Tsarukyan was ongoing at year's end.

Score Change: The score improved from 1 to 2 due to a new law that strengthened Armenia's anticorruption framework and the prosecution of former government officials and their associates for economic crimes.

C3. Does the government operate with openness and transparency? 2 / 4

Transparency has historically been limited, and enforcement of asset-declaration rules for public officials has been weak. However, in 2020, the National Assembly made strides in enhancing transparency, including by strengthening asset-declaration requirements.

The Pashinyan government has also worked to expand the public's access to information, speaking more frequently to the press and the general population, including through live video streaming on social media. However, the government faced protracted criticism for withholding information on fatalities during the conflict with Azerbaijan, and for signing a cease-fire agreement with little public discussion.

CIVIL LIBERTIES: 33 / 60 (+1)
D. FREEDOM OF EXPRESSION AND BELIEF: 9 / 16
D1. Are there free and independent media? 2 / 4

Independent and investigative outlets operate relatively freely in Armenia, and generally publish online. Small independent outlets provided robust coverage of the 2018 protests, challenging the narratives of state broadcasters and other establishment media. By comparison, most print and broadcast outlets are affiliated with political or larger commercial interests.

Violence against journalists has declined since 2018, but still occurs; the Committee to Protect Freedom of Expression (CPFE), a local nongovernmental organization (NGO), counted six injuries among journalists in the second quarter of 2020. In August, former police chief Vladimir Gasparyan physically threatened two Radio Free Europe/Radio Liberty (RFE/RL) journalists reporting on a government plan to dismantle illegally constructed homes near Lake Sevan, and attempted to run them down with his vehicle. A criminal investigation into Gasparyan's behavior was opened a day later.

Journalists also face legal action in the course of their work. The CPFE counted 22 cases lodged against journalists in its second- and third-quarter reports.

In March 2020, the government used COVID-19 state-of-emergency powers to restrict media outlets from reporting on information from unofficial sources, and several outlets and journalists were compelled to edit stories and social media posts that month. Bowing to pressure from journalists and media advocacy groups, the restriction was lifted in April, but the government vowed to monitor media outlets.

D2. Are individuals free to practice and express their religious faith or nonbelief in public and private? 2 / 4

Article 18 of the constitution recognizes the Armenian Apostolic Church as a "national church" responsible for the preservation of Armenian national identity; 94 percent of the population identifies as Armenian Apostolic. Religious minorities have reported some discrimination in the past. A temple for Yazidis—one of the country's main religious minorities—opened in the village of Aknalich in 2019.

D3. Is there academic freedom, and is the educational system free from extensive political indoctrination? 2 / 4

Although the constitution protects academic freedom, administrative and accreditation processes remain open to political influence. There is some self-censorship among academics on politically sensitive subjects.

D4. Are individuals free to express their personal views on political or other sensitive topics without fear of surveillance or retribution? 3 / 4

Private discussion is relatively free and vibrant. The law prohibits wiretapping or other electronic surveillance without judicial approval, though the judiciary lacks independence and has been accused of excessive deference to law enforcement agencies requesting consent.

E. ASSOCIATIONAL AND ORGANIZATIONAL RIGHTS: 8 / 12

E1. Is there freedom of assembly? 3 / 4

The right to assemble is legally guaranteed but inconsistently upheld in practice. In 2018, mass antigovernment demonstrations were organized across the country under the slogan Reject Serzh, aiming to stop the outgoing president from governing as prime minister. Despite some violent interference by police and the temporary detention of protesters, the demonstrations encountered fewer obstacles than in the past.

While conditions improved under the Pashinyan government, public assemblies were restricted when it introduced COVID-19-related emergency measures in March 2020, which prohibited gatherings of over 20 people. While the national lockdown ended in May, limits on the assemblies persisted through the end of the year; 252 people were arrested for violating social-distancing rules while rallying to support Prosperous Armenia leader Tsarukyan in June.

Assemblies were also restricted when the Armenian government declared martial law in September, as the conflict with Azerbaijan began. Despite these restrictions, major protests were held after a cease-fire was secured in November. Several hundred protesters occupied the parliament's chambers soon after the cease-fire announcement, with police reportedly doing little to disperse the crowds. Two days after the cease-fire was made public, an opposition rally was called off after police cited martial law to order its cancellation.

The government rescinded most martial law restrictions in early December, including restrictions on assemblies, and antigovernment protests continued through year's end. In late December, 77 demonstrators were arrested after clashes occurred in front of a Yerevan government building.

E2. Is there freedom for nongovernmental organizations, particularly those that are engaged in human rights- and governance-related work? 3 / 4

Outspoken NGOs operate in Armenia, with most of them based in Yerevan. These NGOs lack significant local funding and often rely on foreign donors. Despite this impediment, civil society was active in the 2018 protests, and consulted with the government on policy matters in 2020, most notably on electoral, constitutional, and anticorruption reform.

E3. Is there freedom for trade unions and similar professional or labor organizations? 2 / 4

The law protects the rights of workers to form and join independent unions, strike, and engage in collective bargaining. However, these protections are not well enforced, and employers are generally able to block union activity in practice.

F. RULE OF LAW: 6 / 16

F1. Is there an independent judiciary? 1 / 4

The courts face systemic political influence, and judicial institutions are undermined by corruption. Judges reportedly feel pressure to work with prosecutors to convict defendants, and acquittal rates are extremely low. The government, which published a five-year judicial-reform strategy in 2019, embarked on continued reforms in 2020.

In late June, the parliament approved constitutional amendments requiring all Constitutional Court judges to abide by 12-year term limits, in a session boycotted by Prosperous Armenia and Bright Armenia parliamentarians. As a result, three Constitutional Court members who had served for longer than 12 years were immediately removed, and their successors were selected in a September parliamentary session.

Hrayr Tovmasyan, who previously served as chair, remained on the bench, but was forced to give the chair up as a result of the amendments. The Pashinyan government was previously embroiled in a conflict over his tenure; in June 2019, justice Vahe Grigoryan—a government ally—unsuccessfully attempted to claim the chair via a legislative technicality. That October, the government attempted to strip Tovmasyan's powers, saying his HHK affiliation made him incapable of hearing the case of former president Robert Kocharyan, who was accused of playing a role in fatal clashes between protesters and police during the 2008 presidential campaign.

The trial against Kocharyan, which began in May 2019 and remained in session at year's end, was a challenging matter for the judiciary. A judge assigned to preside over the case was harassed by two of Kocharyan's supporters in Yerevan that September. Kocharyan's lawyers later, and unsuccessfully, called on the judge to recuse herself three times, most recently in March 2020.

F2. Does due process prevail in civil and criminal matters? 1 / 4

Authorities apply the law selectively, and due process is not guaranteed in civil or criminal cases. Lengthy pretrial detention remains a problem, and the Armenian judiciary is largely distrusted by the public.

The raft of corruption investigations aimed at HHK elites and allies have prompted concerns about the ability of the country's judicial and investigative mechanisms to ensure fair application of the law.

F3. Is there protection from the illegitimate use of physical force and freedom from war and insurgencies? 2 / 4

Reports of police abuse of detainees and poor conditions in prisons persist. After the change in government in 2018, law enforcement agencies renewed dormant investigations into past cases of physical violence by police. Former president Kocharyan was controversially charged that year with attempting to overthrow the constitutional order over his involvement in the fatal clashes of 2008.

Conditions in areas adjacent to Azerbaijan and Nagorno-Karabakh, an ethnic Armenian-majority territory that previously gained de facto independence from Azerbaijan in 1994, worsened throughout 2020. In July, Armenian and Azerbaijani forces fought along the border, causing the deaths of four Azerbaijani soldiers.

In late September, the countries engaged in a full-scale military conflict over Nagorno-Karabakh; population centers in the territory were targeted during the fighting, causing civilian casualties and forcing residents to flee. A Russian-brokered cease-fire was agreed in early November; under its terms, parts of Nagorno-Karabakh taken by Azerbaijani forces remained under Azerbaijani control, along with neighboring territories formerly held by Armenia. The Armenian government reported the deaths of at least 2,425 soldiers in the conflict, while Azerbaijan reported the loss of 2,783. At least 143 civilians were killed, while over 90,000 of the territory's residents were displaced into Armenia proper. Dozens of Armenian prisoners of war reportedly remained in Azerbaijani custody at year's end. Some were reportedly tortured while in detention.

F4. Do laws, policies, and practices guarantee equal treatment of various segments of the population? 2 / 4

Women reportedly face discrimination in employment and education, despite legal protections.

Although same-sex sexual activity was decriminalized in 2003, LGBT+ people continue to face violence and mistreatment at the hands of police and civilians, and no antidiscrimination legislation exists to benefit this group.

In April 2020, an appeals court ruled that authorities did not appropriately investigate a 2018 assault against LGBT+ activists in the southern village of Shurrnukh, in which six people were injured, and ordered a new investigation. Authorities had initially declined to prosecute the assailants after some of the accused were granted amnesty.

G. PERSONAL AUTONOMY AND INDIVIDUAL RIGHTS: 10 / 16 (+1)

G1. Do individuals enjoy freedom of movement, including the ability to change their place of residence, employment, or education? 3 / 4

The law protects freedom of movement and the rights of individuals to change their place of residence, employment, and education. In practice, access to higher education is somewhat hampered by a culture of bribery.

Authorities restricted the ability of Armenians to leave their homes or attend mass gatherings when a COVID-19-related lockdown was instituted in March 2020. The national lockdown ended in May, though the government maintained a COVID-19-related state of emergency through September. The September-to-November conflict over Nagorno-Karabakh also constrained freedom of movement along some border areas.

G2. Are individuals able to exercise the right to own property and establish private businesses without undue interference from state or nonstate actors? 3 / 4 (+1)

Economic diversification and simpler regulations have increased the ease of doing business in recent years, but a lack of transparency and persistent cronyism created unfair advantages for those with ties to public officials during the HHK government's tenure. However, much of this has subsided since the 2018 change in government. Businesspeople, especially those connected to small- and medium-sized firms, previously faced arbitrary expropriation of assets and bribery demands at the hands of prominent HHK supporters, but this activity has become less common since the party's departure from office.

Armenian law adequately protects property rights, though officials have not always upheld them in the past.

Score Change: The score improved from 2 to 3 because undue interference in business activities by HHK affiliates has subsided since the 2018 change in government.

G3. Do individuals enjoy personal social freedoms, including choice of marriage partner and size of family, protection from domestic violence, and control over appearance? 2 / 4

The constitution defines marriage as a union between a man and a woman. Domestic violence is common and not adequately prosecuted, and services for victims are inadequate. A new law on domestic violence that took effect in 2018 placed an emphasis on "restoring family harmony," raising concerns that it would deter victims from leaving dangerous situations. In October 2019, the government introduced amendments to remove that reference and expand the definition of what constituted domestic violence. In early January 2020, a women's rights activist reported that police became more responsive to domestic violence cases after the law's introduction.

The HHK government signed the Istanbul Convention, a Council of Europe (CoE) document that binds participating countries to bolster their efforts to combat violence against women, in 2018. The Pashinyan government attempted to ratify it in 2019, but the Apostolic Church publicly opposed the effort that year. While the government has not yet ratified the Istanbul Convention, the parliament did approve the ratification of the Lanzarote Convention, a CoE document that requires signatories to address sexual violence against children, in May 2020.

G4. Do individuals enjoy equality of opportunity and freedom from economic exploitation? 2 / 4

Legal protections against exploitative or dangerous working conditions are poorly enforced, and about half of workers are employed in the informal sector, where they may be more exposed to such conditions. Armenians are subjected to sex and labor trafficking abroad, and some children in the country work in agriculture and other sectors. Children residing in care institutions face a particularly heightened risk of trafficking. According to the US State Department, the government has made efforts to address trafficking in persons in recent years, in part by raising awareness of the problem and training law enforcement authorities, but it has done little to identify victims proactively, and the number of successful prosecutions remains small.

Australia

Population: 25,800,000
Capital: Canberra
Freedom Status: Free
Electoral Democracy: Yes

Overview: Australia has a strong record of advancing and protecting political rights and civil liberties. Challenges to these freedoms include the threat of foreign political influence, harsh policies toward asylum seekers, discrimination against LGBT+ people, increasingly stringent checks against the press, and ongoing difficulties ensuring the equal rights of First Nations Australians.

KEY DEVELOPMENTS IN 2020

- To combat the spread of the COVID-19 pandemic, Australian authorities enforced long, strict lockdowns at different times throughout the year. In some instances, restrictions like the closure of internal state and territory borders were implemented with little warning; in December, the border between Victoria and New South Wales was closed with just over a day's notice, stranding many people who were visiting family for the holidays. Individuals who needed to cross state borders to access health care and other essential services had difficulty obtaining exemptions.
- In June, people inspired by the Black Lives Matter (BLM) movement in the United States gathered in several cities to protest the mistreatment of and systemic inequity faced by Aboriginal and Torres Strait Islander people. In New South Wales, police forcefully dispersed peaceful protesters, including by using tear gas.
- In April, the High Court of Australia ruled that the 2019 warrant the Australian Federal Police (AFP) had used to raid *Sunday Telegraph* editor Annika Smethurst's home was invalid. Smethurst had overseen the publication of a controversial piece covering leaked plans to expand the government's spying powers; charges against her were dropped in May.

POLITICAL RIGHTS: 40 / 40

A. ELECTORAL PROCESS: 12 / 12

A1. Was the current head of government or other chief national authority elected through free and fair elections? 4 / 4

The Australian government is a parliamentary democracy under a constitutional monarchy. The leader of the popularly elected majority party or coalition is designated as prime minister and serves as head of government. Scott Morrison, the head of the Liberal Party, became prime minister in 2018 after successfully challenging Malcolm Turnbull for the leadership. Morrison's ascension continued a pattern in which prime ministers failed to serve full terms due to "leadership coups," which have drawn criticism for failing to reflect the will of the electorate. After becoming Liberal leader, Morrison took steps in late 2018 to limit "coups" in the party with new rules; a two-thirds majority of Liberal members of parliament is now required to remove a party leader who has ascended to the country's premiership. Morrison won a new term as prime minister when the Liberal Party and its coalition partner, the National Party, won a free and fair election in May 2019.

A governor-general, appointed on the recommendation of the prime minister, represents the monarch of the United Kingdom (UK) as head of state. The powers of the monarchy are extremely limited. Retired general David Hurley was appointed governor-general in July 2019.

A2. Were the current national legislative representatives elected through free and fair elections? 4 / 4

The bicameral legislative branch consists of a 151-member House of Representatives and 76-member Senate. Lower house members are elected through a ranked-choice ballot, and serve three-year terms. Senators are elected through a ranked-choice ballot and serve staggered six-year terms.

The Liberal–National coalition won 77 seats in the House of Representatives in the May 2019 election, earning a one-seat majority over all other parties. The Labor Party won 68, while the Greens won 1. Independents took the remaining 5 seats.

Forty seats in the Senate were filled in the same contest. The Liberal–National coalition won 19 of the seats up for reelection, while Labor won 13, the Greens won 6, and 2 were won by independents. Turnout for the election stood at 91.9 percent.

A3. Are the electoral laws and framework fair, and are they implemented impartially by the relevant election management bodies? 4 / 4

Australian electoral laws and procedures are generally fair and impartial. The Australian Electoral Commission (AEC)—an independent federal agency—coordinates all federal elections and referendums, draws seat boundaries, and keeps the electoral rolls. Voting is compulsory, and a registered voter's failure to vote may result in a small fine, which if unpaid can increase, and ultimately lead to a criminal conviction.

B. POLITICAL PLURALISM AND PARTICIPATION: 16 / 16

B1. Do the people have the right to organize in different political parties or other competitive political groupings of their choice, and is the system free of undue obstacles to the rise and fall of these competing parties or groupings? 4 / 4

Australians may organize political parties without restrictions. Registration and recognition as a political party requires a party constitution and either one member in Parliament, or at least 500 members on the electoral roll.

B2. Is there a realistic opportunity for the opposition to increase its support or gain power through elections? 4 / 4

Power rotates between parties frequently, traditionally alternating between the Labor Party and the Liberal–National coalition. The Greens and smaller left-leaning parties tend to ally with Labor, while rural-oriented and conservative parties often ally with the Liberals.

B3. Are the people's political choices free from domination by forces that are external to the political sphere, or by political forces that employ extrapolitical means? 4 / 4

Political participation in Australia is largely free from undue domestic influence. The UK's monarch remains the Australian head of state, but the monarchy's power is strictly limited by the Australian constitution and legal precedent.

Concerns about foreign interference in politics, particularly from China, have persisted for several years. Chinese actors have allegedly funded candidates and parties, and a 2020 AFP foreign interference investigation named some Chinese consular officials in their warrants. The government banned foreign donations to political parties, independent candidates, and other political campaign groups in 2018. Additionally, the Foreign Influence Transparency Scheme, which came into force that year, requires persons who engage in political activities, such as lobbying on behalf of a foreign government or other entity, to register publicly.

B4. Do various segments of the population (including ethnic, racial, religious, gender, LGBT+, and other relevant groups) have full political rights and electoral opportunities? 4 / 4

Political rights and electoral opportunities are granted to all Australians. However, the interests of women are inadequately represented, and women in Parliament have reported being intimidated and harassed by their male colleagues. Only 46 seats in the lower house are held by women, representing 30.7 percent of the body. The opposition Labor Party employs an internal quota specifying that 40 percent of its candidates must be women; this quota will rise to 50 percent in 2025. The governing Liberal Party also aims for equal gender representation by 2025 but does not use a quota system.

Some voting restrictions—including the requirement that voters hold a fixed address and a ban on voting by prisoners serving long sentences—disproportionately affect First Nations Australians, who are also underrepresented in Parliament. The lower house's first Aboriginal man won a seat in 2010, and the first Aboriginal woman won a seat in 2016. The

Australian government has considered reforms to strengthen Aboriginal and Torres Strait Islander people's political voice, including a proposed representative body that would advise Parliament on policy matters that affect them. Prime Minister Morrison had dismissed the proposition in 2018, calling it a de facto third chamber of Parliament, even though it would not be constitutionally enshrined. The government formed a 19-member panel to consider the idea in November 2019.

LGBT+ representatives have served in Parliament since the 1990s, when Green senator Bob Brown became the first openly gay member of the upper house. The first openly gay member of the House of Representatives was elected in a 2016 by-election.

C. FUNCTIONING OF GOVERNMENT: 12 / 12

C1. Do the freely elected head of government and national legislative representatives determine the policies of the government? 4 / 4

The freely elected government is generally able to develop and implement policy.

C2. Are safeguards against official corruption strong and effective? 4 / 4

Laws against official corruption are generally well enforced, but the absence of a federal anticorruption body makes enforcement more difficult. All states and territories operate local anticorruption bodies; the first state-level agency was formed in 1989, when Queensland created its Criminal Justice Commission.

Prime Minister Morrison has faced increasing pressure from independent legislators and the nongovernmental organization (NGO) Transparency International to create a federal equivalent. In late 2018, he proposed the creation of the Commonwealth Integrity Commission (CIC), which would monitor law enforcement agencies as well as other federal bodies, but would have no authority to hold public hearings and would be unable to investigate allegations of corruption without receiving a referral. Draft legislation to create the body was released in November 2020.

In early 2020, a report by the Australian National Audit Office revealed that, leading up to the 2019 election, the ruling Liberal–National coalition misappropriated A$100 million (US$75.5 million) by favoring safe and marginal coalition seats for funding for community sporting groups and omitting organizations in safe Labor or independent electorates that had as much, and in some cases more, merit. The Audit office found that the prime minister was implicated in the scandal, and in February, sports minister Bridget McKenzie resigned.

C3. Does the government operate with openness and transparency? 4 / 4

Government operations are characterized by a high degree of transparency, and political affairs are openly discussed in Parliament and in the media. Parliamentary records and commissioned reports are readily available. The Freedom of Information Act allows people to access a wide range of government documents, though some government agencies have been criticized for long delays and unnecessary refusals of freedom of information requests.

CIVIL LIBERTIES: 57 / 60

D. FREEDOM OF EXPRESSION AND BELIEF: 15 / 16

D1. Are there free and independent media? 3 / 4

Though the constitution does not explicitly protect press freedom, journalists scrutinize lawmakers and the government, covering controversial topics generally without serious obstacles or risk of harassment or violence.

However, the use of leaked government documents by the press prompted two controversial raids by the Australian Federal Police (AFP) in June 2019. Police raided the publicly owned Australian Broadcasting Corporation's (ABC) Sydney office after the broadcaster published in 2017 the "Afghan Files," a series of stories based on leaked documents that focused on misconduct and unlawful killings by Australian soldiers in Afghanistan. The ABC sued to block the review of the seized documents, though their case was dismissed in February 2020.

The day before the ABC raid, the AFP searched the home of *Sunday Telegraph* political editor Annika Smethurst, in response to a 2018 story covering leaked plans to expand the government's spying powers. In April 2020, the High Court of Australia ruled that the warrant relied upon by the AFP in the Smethurst raid was invalid, as it lacked basic details about the nature of the alleged offense. Although the High Court declined to prohibit the evidence produced by the search from use by prosecutors, the AFP subsequently confirmed that it would not pursue charges against Smethurst.

Members of the press have also been constricted by the use of judicial suppression orders while covering criminal cases. A judge in the state of Victoria issued a suppression order to limit reporting on the trial of Cardinal George Pell, an Australian Vatican official convicted of sexual assault in December 2018. Victoria state prosecutors warned nearly 100 journalists with a February 2019 letter that reporting on the Pell case could result in contempt of court charges if their explanations for doing so were deemed insufficient. Some staff members of publications that covered the case received these letters even though they did not report on the case themselves. Prosecutors filed charges against 36 individual journalists and organizations in April 2019, and a trial commenced in the Victorian Supreme Court in November 2020. The prosecution dropped 13 charges against journalists and publications. Proceedings remained ongoing at the end of the year.

In July 2020, the Australian Competition and Consumer Commission proposed a News Media Bargaining Code that would compel online platforms to pay news media companies for use of their content. Google and Facebook have strenuously opposed the proposed regulations, launching aggressive countercampaigns, and Facebook has threatened to remove all news from its Australian platforms if the code is adopted.

D2. Are individuals free to practice and express their religious faith or nonbelief in public and private? 4 / 4

The constitution explicitly prohibits laws that would either impose or restrict religious expression, and individuals are generally able to express religious beliefs or nonbelief.

D3. Is there academic freedom, and is the educational system free from extensive political indoctrination? 4 / 4

Academic freedom is generally respected. However, in 2017, federal officials warned of Chinese attempts to monitor Chinese students in Australia, and to question academics in Australia whose views differed with those of the Chinese government. Some students have expressed fears of foreign surveillance, prompting them to wear masks while protesting Chinese government actions, so as to protect their identities. Some universities receive significant amounts of foreign funding, particularly from China, which has further raised concerns over Beijing's influence on curriculums and university governance.

D4. Are individuals free to express their personal views on political or other sensitive topics without fear of surveillance or retribution? 4 / 4

Generally, people in Australia may freely discuss personal views on sensitive topics, though the government passed a number of laws in recent years increasing its surveillance powers. A data retention law requires telecommunications companies to store users' metadata for two years. The law sparked concerns about the government's ability to track mobile and online communications, the potential for data breaches, and potential violations of civil liberties. In July 2019, the AFP disclosed that it accessed Australians' metadata nearly 20,000 times, and reviewed the metadata of journalists 58 times during its 2017–18 reporting period.

The 2018 Assistance and Access Act requires technology companies to provide law enforcement agencies access to encrypted communications, on grounds that include preventing terrorism and crime. Civil rights groups criticized the new law's broad reach, relative lack of oversight, and steep fines for companies that do not comply. Vault Systems, an Australian provider of cloud services, warned in July 2019 that multinational companies were increasingly housing their data in other countries because of the legislation.

Additionally, in August 2019, the High Court ruled against Michaela Banerji, who had been dismissed from the Department of Immigration and Border Protection in 2013 in connection with a pseudonymous Twitter account in which she criticized government policies on immigration and the treatment of detainees. She had sued for wrongful dismissal.

E. ASSOCIATIONAL AND ORGANIZATIONAL RIGHTS: 12 / 12

E1. Is there freedom of assembly? 4 / 4

Freedom of assembly is not explicitly codified in law, but the government generally respects the right to peaceful assembly. There are some limited restrictions meant to ensure public safety, and some incidents of police using excessive force against protesters have been reported.

Following the police killing of George Floyd in the United States in May, Black Lives Matter protests occurred in a number of Australian cities focusing on the treatment of First Nations Australians. In June, the New South Wales (NSW) Supreme Court ruled against protest organizers who sought a license to assemble despite coronavirus lockdown measures, though this was overturned by the NSW Court of Appeals shortly before the protest's planned start. As people were leaving a BLM protest in Sydney that month, police used tear gas to disperse the crowd. In October, a Sydney University law professor observing peaceful student protests was knocked to the ground, arrested, and fined by police.

E2. Is there freedom for nongovernmental organizations, particularly those that are engaged in human rights- and governance-related work? 4 / 4

NGOs are generally free to form, function, and receive funding. A 2018 bill intended to limit foreign interference in the political sphere also sought to limit donations to certain charities from foreign entities, which raised concerns that it would severely impact the ability of NGOs to function. However, after pressure from the Labor and Green parties, the bill was amended to specify that it does not apply to charities and advocacy groups.

E3. Is there freedom for trade unions and similar professional or labor organizations? 4 / 4

Workers can freely organize and bargain collectively, and trade unions actively engage in political debates and campaigns. However, strikes are only allowed when negotiating new union agreements, and may only pertain to issues under negotiation. In 2017, a High Court ruling prohibited organizations that had previously violated orders from the Fair Work Commission from holding strikes during negotiations. The court described the right to strike as a "privilege."

F. RULE OF LAW: 15 / 16

F1. Is there an independent judiciary? 4 / 4

The Australian judiciary is generally independent. However, a lengthy investigation in September and October 2019 by independent media outlet Crikey revealed that the Liberal–National government consciously worked to install individuals affiliated with the Liberal Party—including former candidates, donors, and party members—to the Administrative Appeals Tribunal (AAT), a body that reviews the merits of administrative decisions by government agencies.

F2. Does due process prevail in civil and criminal matters? 4 / 4

The right to due process is generally respected. Defendants and detainees are presumed innocent until proven guilty and can only be held for 24 hours without being charged for a crime, with exceptions for terrorism cases.

People living in rural areas, and in particular Aboriginal people, face significant barriers to accessing the justice system. Judges, lawyers, and prosecutors must be flown into remote communities, providing little time to prepare cases or be briefed by clients. Courtrooms are often in ad hoc, repurposed buildings, and lengthy case dockets are a prominent issue. Judges travelling these circuits work large caseloads as a result of understaffing and under-funding, which could impact their health and their court decisions. Significant case backlogs cause individuals to wait years for their cases to be heard, which can place some, like those who have experienced domestic violence, in further danger.

F3. Is there protection from the illegitimate use of physical force and freedom from war and insurgencies? 4 / 4

Australia provides protection from the illegitimate use of force, and Australians have means to seek redress for harm. Prison conditions mostly meet international standards. However, conditions at numerous juvenile detention centers are substandard. Some children have instead been detained in adult prisons. In May 2019, an ABC investigative program reported on the practice of placing minor detainees in "watch houses," maximum security facilities usually reserved for violent adult offenders.

The use of solitary confinement has become controversial, with the Victoria state ombudsman calling for the end of its use in September 2019. The ombudsman noted that children and adolescents were sometimes placed in solitary confinement.

F4. Do laws, policies, and practices guarantee equal treatment of various segments of the population? 3 / 4

First Nations Australians continue to lag behind other groups in key social and economic indicators; suffer higher rates of incarceration; and report routine mistreatment by police and prison officials. Aboriginal and Torres Strait Islander children are placed in detention at a rate 22 times higher than that of non-Aboriginal children. Additionally, people with disabilities make up almost one-third of the prison population, and face harassment and violence in prisons.

Men and women have the same legal rights, and discrimination based on sexual orientation or gender identity is prohibited. In practice, women and LGBT+ people experience employment discrimination and harassment.

Religious exemptions within the Sex Discrimination Act of 1984 allow for the expulsion of students and dismissal of teachers on the basis of their sexual orientation. While this power is rarely exercised, this act has sometimes been used to discriminate. Prime Minister Morrison faced pressure from rights groups to remove the exemptions, and from religious groups to retain and bolster them. In response, Morrison unveiled a bill at the end of 2018, aimed at protecting LGBT+ students from discrimination.

The Liberal–National government spent much of 2019 drafting a bill meant to limit religious discrimination in Australian society, which remained under consideration at the end 2020. LGBT+ advocates objected to the draft legislation, warning that the bill would allow health providers to deny treatment to LGBT+ patients for religious reasons. In July 2020, Equality Australia, an LGBT+ advocacy group, called on the government to introduce stronger hate speech legislation alongside the proposed bill. The NGO also warned that state-level antidiscrimination laws could be superseded by the federal legislation.

Australia's harsh asylum and immigration policies continued to be enforced in 2020. Rights groups objected to the detention of refugees and asylum seekers in offshore facilities, characterized by poor living conditions, inadequate safety for women and children, and a lack of sufficient healthcare and education services. Asylum seekers can wait years for their applications to be processed; in one severe case, a man seeking asylum from Sri Lanka who fled to Australia in 2009 was still being held in immigration detention at the end of 2020. The processing center on Manus Island in Papua New Guinea closed in 2017, and asylum seekers in offshore detention centers in Nauru have been increasingly transferred to Australia. The United Nations special rapporteurs on migrant rights called on the government to continue that practice, warning in a June 2019 statement that the lack of medical care on Manus Island and Nauru amounted to cruel and inhuman treatment. Despite this, Parliament repealed a law allowing offshore detainees to seek emergency medical care in Australia in December 2019, only ten months after it was enacted. At the end of 2020, hundreds of asylum seekers remained indefinitely detained in on- and offshore immigration detention.

In 2020, the coronavirus pandemic exacerbated the difficulties faced by asylum seekers and other temporary visa holders, who were denied access to the government's welfare packages for those affected by the coronavirus. As a result, many temporary visa holders, including refugees, were forced to rely on food banks and charities to survive. Advocacy groups criticized their exclusion from the government's coronavirus relief that placed temporary visa holders at greater risk of homelessness and destitution. In August, Multicultural Affairs Minister Alan Tudge said the government would "make no apology" for prioritizing Australian citizens and residents over temporary visa holders in allocating welfare.

G. PERSONAL AUTONOMY AND INDIVIDUAL RIGHTS: 15 / 16

G1. Do individuals enjoy freedom of movement, including the ability to change their place of residence, employment, or education? 4 / 4

The government respects freedom of movement, and neither state nor nonstate actors interfere with the choice of residence, employment, or institution of higher education.

In response to the coronavirus pandemic, some state and territory governments closed their internal borders at different times during the year. The process to obtain an exemption from travelling between states was difficult and often significantly delayed. Some who were reliant on cross-border services including access to employment or health care, suffered as a result of the closures. In December, the border between Victoria and New South Wales was closed with the public given just over a day's warning, stranding many cross-border travelers who had visited family for the holidays.

G2. Are individuals able to exercise the right to own property and establish private businesses without undue interference from state or nonstate actors? 4 / 4

With an open and free market economy, businesses and individuals enjoy a high level of economic freedom and strong protections for property rights.

G3. Do individuals enjoy personal social freedoms, including choice of marriage partner and size of family, protection from domestic violence, and control over appearance? 4 / 4

The government generally does not restrict social freedoms. In 2017, Parliament legalized same-sex marriage following a nationwide, nonbinding postal survey in which more than 60 percent of participants favored legalization. Same-sex couples have also won the right to adopt children at the state level, with the Northern Territory becoming the last state or territory to legalize LGBT+ adoption in 2018. Discrimination based on gender identity was prohibited under a 2013 amendment to the Sex Discrimination Act of 1984.

Gender-based violence remains a national concern, particularly for Aboriginal and Torres Strait Islander women. In addition, women who kill domestic abusers in self-defense are often jailed, with Aboriginal and Torres Strait Islander women representing the majority of this incarcerated group. In September 2019, the attorney general pledged that the government would pass legislation facilitating defendants' ability to claim and submit evidence of self-defense in court. Following the brutal murder of a Queensland woman, Hannah Clarke, and her three children by Clarke's estranged husband in February 2020, there were multiple calls to criminalize coercive control as part of the arsenal for combating domestic and intimate partner violence.

Abortion law is decided by state and territory governments. New South Wales was the last state to decriminalize abortion when it overturned a 119-year-old law in September 2019. Access to abortions is also proscribed in some states despite its legality, forcing women in those areas to seek assistance from private providers instead of public health systems.

G4. Do individuals enjoy equality of opportunity and freedom from economic exploitation? 3 / 4

Australians generally enjoy robust economic opportunities and freedom from exploitation. However, Aboriginal and Torres Strait Islander people continue to face economic hardship; Census data from 2016 revealed that employment rates in remote areas declined since 2006, impeding their upward social mobility.

In 2018, Parliament passed the Modern Slavery Act, requiring large businesses to be more transparent about potential slavery in their supply chains and to make efforts to address the problem. While the law, which took effect in early 2019, has been largely viewed favorably, some critics have noted that it fails to impose penalties for noncompliance.

Austria

Population: 8,900,000
Capital: Vienna
Freedom Status: Free
Electoral Democracy: Yes

Overview: Austria has a democratic system of government that guarantees political rights and civil liberties. The country has historically been governed by a grand coalition of the center-left Social Democratic Party of Austria (SPÖ) and the center-right Austrian People's Party (ÖVP). In recent years, the political system has faced pressure from the Freedom Party of Austria (FPÖ), a right-wing, populist party that openly entertains nationalist and xenophobic sentiments.

KEY DEVELOPMENTS IN 2020

- The ÖVP formed a coalition with the Green Party in January, marking the first time the Green Party entered national government. The previous ÖVP–FPÖ coalition collapsed in 2019 after a video of the then FPÖ leader offering state contracts in return for donations and favorable media coverage was made public in the so-called Ibizagate affair.

- In November, 4 people were killed and 23 were injured by an assailant in Vienna, who was later killed by police. The attacker was previously imprisoned for attempting to join the Islamic State (IS) militant group and participated in a deradicalization program before receiving parole.

- In December, the Constitutional Court (VfGH) overturned a 2019 law banning students under the age of 10 from wearing headscarves in elementary schools, ruling that it discriminated against Muslims.

- The authorities instituted a COVID-19-related lockdown between March and May and issued new restrictions on mass gatherings in September. New lockdowns were imposed in November and December as cases rose. Austrian authorities reported over 356,000 cases and 6,086 deaths to the World Health Organization by year's end.

POLITICAL RIGHTS: 37 / 40

A. ELECTORAL PROCESS: 12 / 12

A1. Was the current head of government or other chief national authority elected through free and fair elections? 4 / 4

Executive elections in Austria are generally free and fair. The president is elected for a six-year term and has predominantly ceremonial duties. The president does, however, appoint the chancellor, who also needs the support of the legislature to govern. President Alexander Van der Bellen, a former Green Party leader, was elected in 2016 after a close and controversial poll that featured a repeat of the runoff between Van der Bellen and FPÖ candidate Norbert Hofer. The runoff was repeated after the VfGH established that there had been problems with the handling of postal ballots.

Following snap elections in 2019, an ÖVP–Green Party government took office in January 2020, marking the first time the Green Party has participated in a national government. Sebastian Kurz of the ÖVP, who led the previous ÖVP–FPÖ coalition, returned as chancellor.

A2. Were the current national legislative representatives elected through free and fair elections? 4 / 4

Legislative elections in Austria are generally considered credible. The National Council, the lower house, has 183 members chosen through proportional representation at the district, state, and federal levels. Members serve five-year terms. The 61 members of the upper house, the Federal Council (Bundesrat), are chosen by state legislatures for five- or six-year terms.

Snap National Council elections took place in September 2019, after the Ibizagate affair triggered the previous ÖVP–FPÖ coalition's collapse. The ÖVP was the clear winner with 71 seats, though it did not win a parliamentary majority. The Green Party returned after a two-year absence from parliament, winning 26 seats. Support for the FPÖ collapsed, with the party losing 20 seats and holding 31. The SPÖ won 40, while the liberal NEOS claimed 15. Voter turnout was around 75.5 percent.

A3. Are the electoral laws and framework fair, and are they implemented impartially by the relevant election management bodies? 4 / 4

Austria's electoral laws and framework are fair and generally implemented impartially by the relevant bodies.

B. POLITICAL PLURALISM AND PARTICIPATION: 15 / 16

B1. Do the people have the right to organize in different political parties or other competitive political groupings of their choice, and is the system free of undue obstacles to the rise and fall of these competing parties or groupings? 4 / 4

Austria has competitive political parties that form and operate without encountering undue obstacles. Recent years have seen the rise and fall of various competing parties and coalitions through democratic processes.

B2. Is there a realistic opportunity for the opposition to increase its support or gain power through elections? 4 / 4

Opposition parties have a realistic opportunity to gain representation. Until recently, Austria has often been governed by grand coalitions, a trend that has fostered some public disillusionment with the political process. An ÖVP–FPÖ government, which collapsed in 2019, was succeeded by an ÖVP–Green Party coalition in January 2020.

B3. Are the people's political choices free from domination by forces that are external to the political sphere, or by political forces that employ extrapolitical means? 4 / 4

Austrians are generally free to make their own political choices without pressure from the military, business leaders, or other groups that are not democratically accountable.

B4. Do various segments of the population (including ethnic, racial, religious, gender, LGBT+, and other relevant groups) have full political rights and electoral opportunities? 3 / 4

The participation of Slovene, Hungarian, and Romany minorities in local government remains limited. There is little minority representation in the legislature. The number of people who have been naturalized (thus gaining certain political rights) has fallen since the establishment of a more restrictive national integration policy in 2009. Individuals must have lived in Austria for 10 years, 5 of them as a permanent resident, to qualify for naturalization.

Several political parties include support for gender equality in their platforms. In the 2019 elections, 39 percent of the members elected to the parliament were women, a slight increase compared to 2017. The country's first majority-female cabinet was appointed in January 2020.

C. FUNCTIONING OF GOVERNMENT: 10 / 12

C1. Do the freely elected head of government and national legislative representatives determine the policies of the government? 4 / 4

The freely elected president and legislative representatives work with the chancellor, vice chancellor, and cabinet ministers to determine the policies of the government.

C2. Are safeguards against official corruption strong and effective? 3 / 4

Public-sector corruption is problematic, and the political class is widely perceived as corrupt. The Council of Europe's (CoE) Group of States against Corruption has criticized Austria for weak party-finance legislation and for failing to adequately regulate lobbying and prevent corruption amongst parliamentarians. Austria has seen an increase in indictments for, and the rising costs of, corruption in recent years.

Investigations into Ibizagate—which began with the 2019 release of a video of then FPÖ leader Heinz-Christian Strache offering state contracts in exchange for donations and favorable media coverage—continued in 2020. A parliamentary inquiry into the affair launched in June and was continuing at year's end. In December, an Austrian who allegedly filmed the video in 2017 was arrested in Germany. A decision on his extradition was pending at year's end.

Former finance minister Karl-Heinz Grasser, who faced bribery and embezzlement charges for providing inside information on a 2004 sale of public housing, received an eight-year prison sentence in December 2020, though he vowed to appeal.

In 2017, the Ministry of Defense accused European aircraft manufacturer Airbus of fraud by overcharging the government in a 2003 transaction to account for the cost of kickbacks. In April 2020, a Vienna court ruled that a subsequently launched criminal probe should end. In November, prosecutors elected to close their investigation into Airbus.

C3. Does the government operate with openness and transparency? 3 / 4

Austria's government has frequently been criticized for inadequate transparency. Official secrecy remains enshrined in the constitution. For over six years, a draft freedom-of-information law has been mired in parliamentary procedures. It remained so at the end of 2020, despite the ÖVP–Green government's pledge to improve transparency. Austria's overall legal framework on access to information, containing vague criteria for compliance and lacking a strong appeals mechanism, is weak.

Transparency on COVID-19-related expenditures was also lacking. Spending related to the government's stimulus plan, valued at €50 billion ($60.5 billion) by June 2020, was routed through a government-controlled company, limiting the parliament's ability to scrutinize outlays.

CIVIL LIBERTIES: 56 / 60
D. FREEDOM OF EXPRESSION AND BELIEF: 14 / 16
D1. Are there free and independent media? 3 / 4

The federal constitution and the Media Law of 1981 provide the basis for free media in Austria, and the government generally respects these provisions. However, libel and slander laws protect politicians and government officials, many of whom—particularly members of the FPÖ—have filed defamation suits in recent years. Media ownership remains highly concentrated, particularly in the provinces.

The government exerts some influence on the state broadcaster, the Austrian Broadcasting Corporation (ORF). In November 2020, ORF board member Hans Peter Haselsteiner resigned, voicing disapproval over perceived political interference and the stalling of reforms meant to bolster the broadcaster's independence.

The Austrian government was opaque in some of its dealings with the press in the context of the COVID-19 pandemic. In April 2020, the Association of the Foreign Press criticized the government's use of COVID-19 measures to allow only ORF and Austrian Press Agency correspondents at its press conferences, effectively barring foreign journalists from attending in person.

While there is no official censorship, Austrian law prohibits any form of neo-Nazism or antisemitism, as well as the public denial, approval, or justification of Nazi crimes, including the Holocaust.

D2. Are individuals free to practice and express their religious faith or nonbelief in public and private? 3 / 4

Religious freedom is constitutionally guaranteed. Austrian law divides religious organizations into three legal categories: officially recognized religious societies, religious confessional communities, and associations. Many religious minority groups allege that the law impedes their legitimate claims for recognition and demotes them to second– or third-class status.

Foreign funding for Muslim houses of worship and imams is prohibited by a 2015 law; Orthodox Christian and Jewish groups with similarly strong links to communities abroad face no such restrictions. In 2019, constitutional courts confirmed the legality of a 2015 law that enabled the expulsion of 40 imams from Turkey in 2018. The FPÖ has been criticized for stoking anti-Muslim sentiment through controversial advertising campaigns. In recent years, antisemitic and anti-Islamic tendencies have become more prevalent.

Full-face coverings were banned in 2017, which was generally interpreted as targeting women who wear burqas and niqabs (facial veils), even though very few women in Austria wear those garments. In 2019, the government banned the wearing of headscarves at elementary schools for students under the age of 10. It did not apply to children wearing a kippa. While the January 2020 ÖVP–Green coalition agreement included a commitment to renew and expand the law to apply to students as old as 14, the VfGH overturned it in December, saying it discriminated against Muslims.

D3. Is there academic freedom, and is the educational system free from extensive political indoctrination? 4 / 4

Academic freedom is generally upheld, and the educational system is free from extensive political indoctrination.

D4. Are individuals free to express their personal views on political or other sensitive topics without fear of surveillance or retribution? 4 / 4

Private discussion in Austria is generally free and unrestricted. However, there have been some difficulties related to the balance between ensuring freedom of speech and enforcing legal prohibitions on hate speech. A debate surrounding more extensive online surveillance through state authorities is ongoing.

In September 2020, the ÖVP–Green government published a draft bill that would mandate the deletion of online content deemed illegal within 24 hours. Reporters Without Borders (RSF) criticized the bill, warning that individual users would have little recourse if their content were removed. The bill remained under consideration at year's end.

E. ASSOCIATIONAL AND ORGANIZATIONAL RIGHTS: 12 / 12

E1. Is there freedom of assembly? 4 / 4

Freedom of assembly is constitutionally protected and respected in practice. However, the authorities did limit assemblies under COVID-19-related measures. Gatherings of more than five people were banned in March 2020, though restrictions were loosened in May. New limits on assembly were introduced in September, and new lockdowns were instituted in November and December as cases rose.

E2. Is there freedom for nongovernmental organizations, particularly those that are engaged in human rights– and governance-related work? 4 / 4

Nongovernmental organizations operate without restrictions.

E3. Is there freedom for trade unions and similar professional or labor organizations? 4 / 4

Trade unions are free to organize and to strike, and they are considered an essential partner in national policymaking. According to government statistics, some 1.4 million workers are members of trade unions.

F. RULE OF LAW: 15 / 16

F1. Is there an independent judiciary? 4 / 4

The judiciary is independent, and the Constitutional Court examines the compatibility of legislation with the constitution without political influence or interference. The CoE's Consultative Council of European Judges criticized a slight lack of independence in an analysis of the Administrative Court of Vienna conducted in 2019. Austrian judges are appointed by the executive instead of a politically independent body, which the CoE criticized as an insufficient separation of the state government from the judicial system.

F2. Does due process prevail in civil and criminal matters? 4 / 4

Due process generally prevails in civil and criminal matters. However, scandals involving Austria's intelligence apparatus in recent years raised concerns about the potential politicization of the justice system, as well as respect for due process.

F3. Is there protection from the illegitimate use of physical force and freedom from war and insurgencies? 4 / 4

People in Austria are generally free from the illegitimate use of physical force, war, and insurgencies. However, terrorist threats are a concern. In November 2020, 4 people were killed and 23 were injured in Vienna by an assailant who was then killed by police. The government disclosed that the assailant, Kujtim Fejzulai, was previously imprisoned for attempting to travel to Syria to join the IS. Fejzulai participated in a deradicalization program while imprisoned and was subsequently paroled.

In December, Austrian authorities arrested five individuals accused of participating in a far-right group and confiscated over 70 weapons. Interior Minister Karl Nehammer reported that the weapons cache may have been meant for a "far-right militia," and noted that the unnamed suspects were known neo-Nazis.

Conditions in prisons generally meet high European standards.

F4. Do laws, policies, and practices guarantee equal treatment of various segments of the population? 3 / 4

Some marginalized groups face difficulty exercising their human rights before the law. Strong rhetoric has been directed against refugees and migrants in recent years. Some asylum seekers can be deported while appeals are pending. In 2019, the Office of the UN High Commissioner for Human Rights (OHCHR) said the Austrian asylum system did not meet international human rights standards. The ÖVP–Green coalition espoused a strict stance on asylum in its January 2020 coalition agreement, vowing to preemptively detain asylum seekers who are deemed dangerous. Asylum seekers were also affected by COVID-19 measures; in May 2020, a group of 300 asylum seekers were quarantined in a Vienna facility despite a face-mask shortage. Some residents attempted to escape, fearing they were to be deported.

LGBT+ people face some societal discrimination. Hate-crime legislation prohibits incitement based on sexual orientation. However, no law prohibits service providers from denying services on that basis.

Despite some improvement since 2005, gender equality remains an issue in Austria. According to Eurostat, Austrian men earned 19.9 percent more than women in 2019.

G. PERSONAL AUTONOMY AND INDIVIDUAL RIGHTS: 15 / 16

G1. Do individuals enjoy freedom of movement, including the ability to change their place of residence, employment, or education? 4 / 4

Austrian citizens enjoy freedom of movement and choice of residence. However, Austrians faced strict limits on movement in March 2020 under COVID-19-related measures. Those restrictions expired in May, though new lockdowns were imposed in November and December as cases increased.

Roma and other ethnic minorities face discrimination in the labor and housing markets. The Labor Ministry has sought to promote integration of younger immigrants by providing German-language instruction and job training.

G2. Are individuals able to exercise the right to own property and establish private businesses without undue interference from state or nonstate actors? 4 / 4

Austrians may freely exercise the right to own property and establish businesses.

G3. Do individuals enjoy personal social freedoms, including choice of marriage partner and size of family, protection from domestic violence, and control over appearance? 4 / 4

Same-sex marriage became legal in Austria in 2019. Restrictions on same-sex couples adopting children ended in 2016.

The 2009 Second Protection against Violence Act increased penalties for perpetrators of domestic violence and authorized further punitive measures against chronic offenders.

G4. Do individuals enjoy equality of opportunity and freedom from economic exploitation? 3 / 4

A 1979 law guarantees women's freedom from discrimination in various areas, including the workplace. However, the income gap between men and women remains significant.

According to the US State Department's 2020 *Trafficking in Persons Report*, the Austrian government is making significant efforts to fight human trafficking, with convicted traffickers receiving significant sentences. In June, the CoE lauded Austria's progress in fighting trafficking, though it also noted that survivors were not consistently compensated.

Media reports from June and September 2020 noted that seasonal farm workers often lived in poor conditions and did not receive the minimum wage.

Azerbaijan

Population: 10,100,000
Capital: Baku
Freedom Status: Not Free
Electoral Democracy: No

Note: The numerical scores and status listed above do not reflect conditions in Nagorno-Karabakh, which is examined in a separate report. *Freedom in the World* reports assess the level of political rights and civil liberties in a given geographical area, regardless of whether they are affected by the state, nonstate actors, or foreign powers. Disputed territories are sometimes assessed separately if they meet certain criteria, including boundaries that are sufficiently stable to allow year-on-year comparisons. For more information, see the report methodology and FAQ.

Overview: Power in Azerbaijan's authoritarian regime remains heavily concentrated in the hands of Ilham Aliyev, who has served as president since 2003, and his extended family. Corruption is rampant, and the formal political opposition has been weakened by years of persecution. The authorities have carried out an extensive crackdown on civil liberties in recent years, leaving little room for independent expression or activism. In 2020, Azerbaijan won a conflict over control of Nagorno-Karabakh, at the cost of over 2,700 soldiers.

KEY DEVELOPMENTS IN 2020

- Azerbaijan and Armenia engaged in armed conflict over control of the territory of Nagorno-Karabakh between September and November, when a Russian-backed cease-fire was finalized; over 2,700 Azerbaijani soldiers died in the fighting. Under the agreement's terms, Azerbaijan maintained control over parts of the territory gained during the conflict, along with adjacent land previously occupied by Armenia.
- The ruling Yeni (New) Azerbaijan Party (YAP) maintained control of the parliament in snap elections held in February. The contest was marred by procedural and tabulation concerns, electoral misconduct, and an opposition boycott; authorities arrested opposition leaders along with activists planning to hold a protest over the elections' conduct later that month.
- Azerbaijani authorities sought to restrict media freedom and limit online discussion regarding the COVID-19 pandemic. Several journalists received prison sentences or detention for reporting on the crisis, while some internet users were forced to remove material critical of the government's pandemic response from social media platforms and websites.

POLITICAL RIGHTS: 2 / 40

A. ELECTORAL PROCESS: 0 / 12

A1. Was the current head of government or other chief national authority elected through free and fair elections? 0 / 4

The president is directly elected for seven-year terms. There are no term limits. Since the early 1990s, elections have not been considered credible or competitive by international observers. A February 2018 presidential decree moved that year's presidential election, originally planned for October, up to April. President Ilham Aliyev—who succeeded his father, Heydar, in 2003—won a fourth term with some 86 percent of the vote amid evidence of electoral fraud and a boycott by the main opposition parties. Organization for Security and Co-operation in Europe (OSCE) observers found that the election lacked genuine competition due to a restrictive political environment in which the seven nominal opposition candidates did not openly confront or criticize the president.

In 2017, President Aliyev appointed his wife, Mehriban Aliyeva, as vice president. The post had been created via constitutional changes that were pushed through in 2016 without meaningful parliamentary debate or public consultation.

The prime minister and cabinet are appointed and dismissed by the president. In October 2019, Prime Minister Novruz Mammadov—in office since April 2018—was replaced by Ali Asadov.

A2. Were the current national legislative representatives elected through free and fair elections? 0 / 4

The 125 seats in Azerbaijan's unicameral Milli Mejlis, or National Assembly, are filled through elections in single-member districts, with members serving five-year terms.

Aliyev dissolved the parliament in December 2019, and snap elections were held in February 2020. The ruling YAP won 70 parliamentary seats, while independents won 41 and the remainder were won by smaller parties; contests for 4 seats were not immediately decided. Turnout stood at 46.8 percent. A major opposition alliance, the National Council of Democratic Forces (NCDF), boycotted the elections. OSCE monitors criticized the conduct of the poll, noting procedural and tabulation concerns and ultimately questioning "whether the results were established honestly."

A3. Are the electoral laws and framework fair, and are they implemented impartially by the relevant election management bodies? 0 / 4

The electoral laws and framework fall short of international standards and do not ensure free and fair elections. The nomination process for members of electoral commissions places the bodies under the influence of the ruling party. Commission members have been known to unlawfully interfere with the election process and obstruct the activities of observers. Complaints of electoral violations do not receive adequate or impartial treatment.

Election observers have repeatedly condemned restrictions on freedom of assembly, the inability of candidates to obtain permission to hold rallies or appear on television, political interference with courts investigating electoral violations, and noncompliance with past European Court of Human Rights (ECtHR) decisions on election issues. OSCE monitors present during the February 2020 parliamentary elections noted pervasive electoral misconduct, including verbal and physical abuse directed against candidates' representatives and monitors.

B. POLITICAL PLURALISM AND PARTICIPATION: 2 / 16

B1. Do the people have the right to organize in different political parties or other competitive political groupings of their choice, and is the system free of undue obstacles to the rise and fall of these competing parties or groupings? 1 / 4

The political environment in Azerbaijan is neither pluralistic nor competitive. The ability of opposition parties to operate and engage with the public is limited by the dominance of the YAP. A number of laws restrict candidates' efforts to organize and hold rallies, and the opposition has virtually no access to coverage on television, which remains the most popular news source. The regime has cracked down violently on any Islamic political movement that reaches national prominence.

B2. Is there a realistic opportunity for the opposition to increase its support or gain power through elections? 0 / 4

The Aliyev family has held the presidency since 1993. The biased electoral framework and repressive media and political environment effectively make it impossible for opposition parties to gain power through elections. The traditional opposition parties boycotted the most recent parliamentary, presidential, and municipal elections rather than take part in an unfair process.

Opposition figures complained that moving the 2018 presidential election forward by six months further disadvantaged them by leaving inadequate time to prepare their campaigns. Similar concerns were raised about the February 2020 snap parliamentary elections.

Opposition politicians and party officials are subject to arbitrary arrest on dubious charges, physical violence, and intimidation. Musavat (Equality) Party leader Arif Hajili and

Republican Alternative (ReAL) leader Ilgar Mammadov were arrested ahead of a planned rally in front of CEC headquarters in mid-February 2020. (Mammadov had previously been imprisoned in 2014 over accusations of stoking unrest but was allowed early release in 2018 and was acquitted in April 2020.)

In March 2020, Musavat vice chairman Tofiq Yaqublu was arrested over a traffic incident that observers believe was fabricated. Yaqublu received a four-year prison sentence over charges of hooliganism in September but was transferred to house arrest later that month after engaging in a hunger strike. Yaqublu was previously imprisoned between 2013 and 2014 over politically motivated charges and was reportedly tortured during a short detention in October 2019.

B3. Are the people's political choices free from domination by forces that are external to the political sphere, or by political forces that employ extrapolitical means? 1 / 4

The authoritarian system in Azerbaijan excludes the public from any genuine and autonomous political participation. The regime relies on abuse of state resources, corrupt patronage networks, and control over the security forces and criminal justice system to maintain its political dominance.

B4. Do various segments of the population (including ethnic, racial, religious, gender, LGBT+, and other relevant groups) have full political rights and electoral opportunities? 0 / 4

The political system does not allow women or minority groups to organize independently or advocate for their respective interests. There are no meaningful mechanisms to promote increased representation of women and ethnic or religious minorities. The government has worked to stifle public expressions of ethnic Talysh and Lezgin identity, among other targeted groups.

Internally displaced persons (IDPs) who left Nagorno-Karabakh and settled in other parts of Azerbaijan after the 1994 cease-fire have been unable to participate in municipal elections where they subsequently settled and are instead directed to vote for their former districts. IDPs have not historically pursued office in Azerbaijan since the 1994 cease-fire.

C. FUNCTIONING OF GOVERNMENT: 0 / 12
C1. Do the freely elected head of government and national legislative representatives determine the policies of the government? 0 / 4

Neither the president nor members of parliament are elected in a free or fair manner, and the parliament is unable to serve as a meaningful check on the powerful presidency. Lawmakers and lower-level elected officials essentially carry out the instructions of the ruling party.

C2. Are safeguards against official corruption strong and effective? 0 / 4

Corruption is pervasive. In the absence of a free press and independent judiciary, officials are held accountable for corrupt behavior only when it suits the needs of a more powerful or well-connected figure.

Investigative reports published by foreign media in recent years have revealed evidence that Aliyev family used their positions to amass large private fortunes. In 2017, a network of international media outlets exposed a $2.9 billion slush fund that was held within United Kingdom-registered shell companies and linked to the Azerbaijani ruling elite, including the Aliyev family. The resources were reportedly used in part to improperly influence the Parliamentary Assembly of the Council of Europe in order to minimize criticism of electoral conduct and alleged rights abuses. In September 2020, the *Times of Israel* reported that a publicly owned Israeli aerospace firm transferred at least $155 million to that slush fund, though the firm's specific purpose was unclear.

C3. Does the government operate with openness and transparency? 0 / 4

Government operations are opaque. Although public officials are nominally required to submit financial disclosure reports, procedures and compliance remain unclear, and the reports are not publicly accessible. There are legal guarantees for citizens' access to information, but also broad exceptions to this right, and authorities at all levels systematically refuse to respond to information requests.

In 2017, Azerbaijan withdrew from the Extractive Industries Transparency Initiative (EITI), an international platform that promotes good governance and transparency in resource-rich countries. Azerbaijan, an important producer of oil and gas, had been suspended due to ongoing noncompliance with EITI human rights standards.

CIVIL LIBERTIES: 8 / 60
D. FREEDOM OF EXPRESSION AND BELIEF: 2 / 16
D1. Are there free and independent media? 0 / 4

Constitutional guarantees for press freedom are routinely and systematically violated, as the government works to maintain a tight grip on the information landscape. Defamation remains a criminal offense. Journalists—and their relatives—face harassment, violence, and intimidation by authorities. Legal amendments passed in 2017 extended government control over online media, allowing blocking of websites without a court order if they are deemed to contain content that poses a danger to the state or society. Independent news sites are regularly blocked or struck with cyberattacks.

Journalists face detention or imprisonment on false charges, along with travel bans. The Committee to Protect Journalists (CPJ) counted four imprisoned journalists in the country in 2020. In November, Azel.tv editor in chief Afgan Sadygov received a seven-year prison sentence for bribery, a charge the CPJ reported was fabricated. Later that month, Polad Aslanov, editor in chief of news site Press-az, received a 16-year prison sentence for selling state secrets to Iran. Aslanov, who planned to appeal, claimed that he was targeted for reporting on corruption.

The authorities are known to restrict artistic expression. Azerbaijani musician Parviz Guluzade was given a 30-day administrative sentence in December 2019 for public intoxication after making a critical reference to a bank connected to the Aliyev family in one of his songs. Guluzade, who was tortured in detention, was released in late January 2020.

Azerbaijani authorities also sought to restrict media freedom after COVID-19-related measures were instituted in late March 2020. In late April, the International Press Institute reported that three journalists covering the government's COVID-19 response had been jailed by courts, while another was detained.

D2. Are individuals free to practice and express their religious faith or nonbelief in public and private? 0 / 4

The regime exercises control over religion through state-affiliated entities such as the Caucasus Muslim Board. Religious communities that attempt to operate independently face burdensome registration requirements, interference with the importation and distribution of printed religious materials, and arrest and harassment of religious leaders with international ties or a significant following. For example, Haji Taleh Bagirzade and members of his Muslim Unity Movement, a nonviolent conservative Shiite group, have been subjected to mass arrests, torture, and imprisonment as part of a crackdown that began in 2015.

A number of mosques have been closed in recent years, ostensibly for registration or safety violations. Jehovah's Witnesses face harassment as well as prosecution for evading military service.

D3. Is there academic freedom, and is the educational system free from extensive political indoctrination? 1 / 4

The authorities have long curtailed academic freedom. Some educators have reported being dismissed for links to opposition groups, and students have faced expulsion and other punishments for similar reasons. The Azerbaijani history curriculum is known to include negative and discriminatory references to Armenians.

D4. Are individuals free to express their personal views on political or other sensitive topics without fear of surveillance or retribution? 1 / 4

Law enforcement bodies monitor private telephone and online communications—particularly of activists, political figures, and foreign nationals—without judicial oversight. The escalation of government persecution of critics and their families has undermined the assumption of privacy among ordinary residents and eroded the openness of private discussion. Even state officials have been punished for their and their family members' social media activity, and activists have been imprisoned—on unrelated fabricated charges—for critical Facebook posts. In recent years, activists have been targeted by spear-phishing campaigns designed to install malicious software on their computers or steal personal information. Activists report that harassment on social media, often highly sexualized for female activists, is commonplace.

In March 2020, the parliament amended the Law of Information to allow the prosecution of those accused of disseminating purportedly false news in response to the COVID-19 pandemic. Human Rights Watch (HRW) counted at least 10 cases where the internet users were subsequently compelled to remove material criticizing the government's pandemic response by year's end.

Social media users and antiwar activists who signed a statement calling for a peaceful resolution to the September-to-November 2020 conflict over control of Nagorno-Karabakh were harassed and threatened online, prompting at least one activist to remove their signature.

E. ASSOCIATIONAL AND ORGANIZATIONAL RIGHTS: 1 / 12

E1. Is there freedom of assembly? 0 / 4

The law imposes tight restrictions on freedom of assembly, which is contingent on the protection of "public order and morals." Activists have complained that in practice, the obstacles to public gatherings include additional, extralegal measures. Unsanctioned assemblies can draw a harsh police response and fines for participants, and the government largely stopped issuing permits for rallies in Baku in 2019. Even when permits are issued, the government typically confines demonstrations to relatively isolated locations, where it can track attendees through facial-recognition technology and mobile-phone data.

In February 2020, police in Baku arrested several dozen protesters who intended to demonstrate against the conduct of that month's parliamentary elections in front of CEC headquarters, along with opposition leaders. In July, as many as 30,000 demonstrators in Baku called for war against Armenia after Azerbaijani and Armenian forces fought earlier that month. While that protest was tolerated, security forces clashed with a group of participants who then broke into the parliament building, with President Aliyev subsequently blaming the opposition Azerbaijan Popular Front Party (AXFP) for the incident.

Some 17 party members were among at least 80 people detained on charges that observers considered spurious.

E2. Is there freedom for nongovernmental organizations, particularly those that are engaged in human rights- and governance-related work? 0 / 4

Repressive laws on NGOs have been used to pressure both local and foreign organizations, many of which have suspended operations when their bank accounts were frozen or their offices raided. Nearly all organizations or networks that work on human rights are forced by the state to operate in a legal gray zone. The government has refused to permit the European Union to provide grant support for local civil society groups. Civic activists are routinely subjected to harassment, intimidation, detention, and abuse by police.

Activists also faced government scrutiny during the September-to-November 2020 conflict over Nagorno-Karabakh. Civil society activist Giyas Ibrahimov was briefly detained over his activity in September. In October, he was questioned by prosecutors for signing a petition calling for a peaceful resolution along with activist Narmin Shahmarzade.

E3. Is there freedom for trade unions and similar professional or labor organizations? 1 / 4

Although the law permits the formation of trade unions and the right to strike, the majority of unions remain closely affiliated with the government, and many categories of workers are prohibited from striking. Most major industries are dominated by state-owned enterprises, in which the government controls wages and working conditions.

F. RULE OF LAW: 0 / 16
F1. Is there an independent judiciary? 0 / 4

The judiciary is corrupt and subservient to the executive. Judges are appointed by the parliament on the proposal of the president. The courts' lack of political independence is especially evident in the many trumped-up or otherwise flawed cases brought against opposition figures, activists, and critical journalists.

F2. Does due process prevail in civil and criminal matters? 0 / 4

Constitutional guarantees of due process are not upheld. Arbitrary arrest and detention are common, and detainees are often held for long periods before trial. Political detainees have reported restricted access to legal counsel, fabrication and withholding of evidence, and physical abuse to extract confessions.

In 2019, the so-called Ganja case provided prominent examples of due process violations. The case stemmed from a 2018 incident where two police officers died during a demonstration, following the attempted assassination of the mayor of Ganja. In response, police charged 77 suspects, 10 of whom died in custody or while being detained. The government claimed that the protests were an attempted Islamist uprising, despite significant evidence to the contrary. Authorities were unable to provide a coherent version of events in trials held in 2019.

Although nominally independent, the Azerbaijani Bar Association acts on the orders of the Ministry of Justice and is complicit in the harassment of human rights lawyers. Legal amendments that took effect in 2018 stipulated that only Bar Association members could represent clients in court. Since then, the association has disbarred, suspended, or threatened most of the country's active human rights lawyers for speaking to the media about violations of their clients' rights. In nearly all disciplinary cases, the courts have upheld the Bar Association's decisions without a thorough assessment or public justification.

F3. Is there protection from the illegitimate use of physical force and freedom from war and insurgencies? 0 / 4

International observers have consistently concluded that both torture and impunity for the perpetrators of such abuse are endemic in the Azerbaijani criminal justice system. Police regularly administer beatings during arrest or while breaking up protests. In April 2020, five Ganga-case defendants accused the authorities of torturing them and forcing them to sign documents implicating themselves in criminal activity in an ECtHR filing.

Prison conditions are substandard. Medical care is generally inadequate, and overcrowding is common. Prisoners are also at risk of contracting COVID-19; in June 2020, relatives of inmates held in a Baku prison warned that most of the population had COVID-19 symptoms, despite government claims to the contrary. Adherence to some mitigation measures, like the use of face masks, is reportedly inconsistent in prisons.

Azerbaijanis were affected by armed conflict with Armenia during 2020. In July, Azerbaijani and Armenian forces fought along the border, resulting in the deaths of four Azerbaijani soldiers. The two countries engaged in a full-scale conflict over control of Nagorno-Karabakh in late September, with civilian and military casualties reported on both sides. In October, the city of Ganga was bombed, with one death reported. The conflict ended in early November after a Russian-brokered cease-fire was agreed; under its terms, Azerbaijan would retain control of parts of Nagorno-Karabakh gained during the fighting, along with adjacent land held by Armenia. In early December, the Azerbaijani government reported 2,783 soldiers died in the fighting, while at least 143 civilians on both sides were killed.

The conflict was marked by reported acts of mistreatment, desecration, and vandalism. In early December 2020, HRW accused Azerbaijani forces of physically abusing Armenian prisoners of war, several dozen of whom were reportedly in Azerbaijani custody at year's end. Later in December, Azerbaijani prosecutors accused two soldiers of desecrating the corpses of Armenian soldiers and accused two others of vandalizing gravestones in Nagorno-Karabakh.

F4. Do laws, policies, and practices guarantee equal treatment of various segments of the population? 0 / 4

Members of ethnic minority groups have complained of discrimination in areas including education, employment, and housing. Women are subject to discrimination in employment, including both de facto bias and formal exclusion from certain types of work under the labor code.

While IDPs from the Nagorno-Karabakh conflict that ended in 1994 are entitled to special assistance, they face severe infringements on their economic and social rights and freedom of movement. Many are housed in dormitories or substandard housing and are unable to change their place of residence, which is often located out of range of sources of employment or adequate medical care.

Although same-sex sexual activity is legal, LGBT+ people experience societal discrimination and risk harassment by the police. In 2017, police fined or detained dozens of people for weeks in a coordinated crackdown that led many LGBT+ residents to flee the country.

G. PERSONAL AUTONOMY AND INDIVIDUAL RIGHTS: 5 / 16

G1. Do individuals enjoy freedom of movement, including the ability to change their place of residence, employment, or education? 1 / 4

The government restricts freedom of movement, particularly foreign travel, for opposition politicians, journalists, and civil society activists. While travel bans were lifted for some dissidents during 2019, many others remained in place, including for some of the political prisoners released that March; others fled the country to avoid further persecution. Some travel bans remained in effect in 2020.

IDPs from the previous Nagorno-Karabakh conflict enjoy freedom of movement in law, but not in practice. IDPs are legally registered at their place of initial resettlement, which are sometimes in rural areas and far from any source of employment. The process of changing registration is difficult, and IDPs who change their place of registration risk losing their status and accompanying state assistance. As a result, many families are separated, with usually male wage-earners relocating to urban centers for work while their families remain at their place of registration.

Freedom of movement was curtailed under COVID-19 measures for much of 2020. In late March, the government introduced a national quarantine, extending those measures in April and May. While some restrictions were relaxed in May, others were retained; measures were tightened in October, and wide-ranging restrictions were reintroduced in December as COVID-19 cases increased.

People with disabilities and psychiatric patients are routinely institutionalized; there is no clear procedure to review their confinement.

G2. Are individuals able to exercise the right to own property and establish private businesses without undue interference from state or nonstate actors? 1 / 4

Property rights are affected by government-backed development projects that often entail forced evictions, unlawful expropriations, and demolitions with little or no notice. Corruption and the economic dominance of state-owned companies and politically connected elites pose obstacles to ordinary private business activity.

G3. Do individuals enjoy personal social freedoms, including choice of marriage partner and size of family, protection from domestic violence, and control over appearance? 2 / 4

The law generally grants women and men the same rights on personal status matters such as marriage, divorce, and child custody. Domestic violence is a notable problem, and related legal protections are inadequate. Conservative social norms contribute to the widespread view that domestic violence is a private matter, which discourages victims from reporting perpetrators to the police. However, the growth of social media and the movement of rural populations to Baku in recent years have spurred public discussion of the issue.

The hijab has been formally banned in Azerbaijani schools since 2011, and women who choose to wear it have increasingly complained of discrimination by both private and public employers.

G4. Do individuals enjoy equality of opportunity and freedom from economic exploitation? 1 / 4

Legal safeguards against exploitative working conditions are poorly enforced, and many employers reportedly ignore them without penalty. Children are vulnerable to forced labor, especially in the agriculture sector. A 2019 US Department of Labor report also noted that some children were forced to engage in the sex trade.

The government has taken some steps to combat forced labor and sex trafficking, including by prosecuting traffickers and providing services to victims, but the problem persists, notably among Romany children and foreign household workers. In 2017, the authorities extended a preexisting moratorium on workplace inspections through 2020.

As a result of corruption and a lack of public accountability for the allocation of resources, the state's oil and gas revenues tend to benefit privilege elites rather than the general population, narrowing access to economic opportunity.

Bahamas

Population: 400,000
Capital: Nassau
Freedom Status: Free
Electoral Democracy: Yes

Overview: The Bahamas is a stable democracy where political rights and civil liberties are generally respected. However, the islands have a relatively high homicide rate. Harsh immigration policies, which mainly affect Haitian-Bahamians and Haitian migrants, are often executed in the absence of due process. Government corruption is a serious problem that is thought to have had significant economic consequences.

KEY DEVELOPMENTS IN 2020

- The Bahamas received emergency funds from the International Monetary Fund (IMF) to cope with the economic fallout of the COVID-19 pandemic. As part of receiving these funds, the government committed to publishing public procurement contracts intended to address the public health emergency, the ownership information of the companies receiving those contracts, and the results of a specific audit of COVID-19 expenditures. According to government statistics provided to the World Health Organization (WHO), over 7,800 people tested positive for coronavirus and 170 people died during the year.
- In November, Peter Turnquest, the deputy prime minister and finance minister, resigned after allegations emerged that he was involved in a fraud scheme worth over $20 million, though he was not charged. Prime Minister Hubert Minnis assumed the finance minister role and appointed Desmond Bannister as the new deputy.

POLITICAL RIGHTS: 38 / 40

A. ELECTORAL PROCESS 12 / 12

A1. Was the current head of government or other chief national authority elected through free and fair elections? 4 / 4

The Bahamas is governed under a parliamentary system, and a mostly ceremonial governor-general is appointed by the British monarch as head of state. The prime minister is head of government and is appointed by the governor-general; the office is usually held by the leader of the largest party in Parliament or the head of a parliamentary coalition. Hubert Minnis became prime minister following the victory of his party, the Free National Movement (FNM), in the May 2017 legislative elections.

A2. Were the current national legislative representatives elected through free and fair elections? 4 / 4

Members of the lower chamber of the bicameral parliament, the 39-member House of Assembly, are directly elected to five-year terms. The 16 members of the Senate are appointed for five-year terms by the governor-general based on recommendations made by the prime minister and the opposition leader.

In the May 2017 general elections, the ruling Progressive Liberal Party (PLP) was defeated by the FNM, which won 35 out of 39 seats in the House of Assembly; Minnis, the FNM leader, was then appointed prime minister. International monitors praised the electoral process but expressed concern about an outdated voter-registration system, the replacement of the parliamentary commissioner—a key administrative official—and the redrawing of electoral districts before the polls.

A3. Are the electoral laws and framework fair, and are they implemented impartially by the relevant election management bodies? 4 / 4

The electoral process is regulated by the Parliamentary Elections Act and generally well managed by the Parliamentary Registration Department. The parliamentary commissioner heads the department and is appointed by the governor-general acting on the recommendation of the prime minister after consultation with the opposition leader. The COVID-19 pandemic prompted passage of legislation that established a permanent voter register to reduce in-person registration.

B. POLITICAL PLURALISM AND PARTICIPATION 16 / 16

B1. Do the people have the right to organize in different political parties or other competitive political groupings of their choice, and is the system free of undue obstacles to the rise and fall of these competing parties or groupings? 4 / 4

Political parties may organize freely and operate unhindered. However, as electoral financing is not regulated, there is no legal obligation to disclose funding sources and no limit on campaign spending.

B2. Is there a realistic opportunity for the opposition to increase its support or gain power through elections? 4 / 4

Opposition parties operate without undue interference. Political power has alternated between the PLP and the FNM since the country achieved independence in 1973.

B3. Are the people's political choices free from domination by forces that are external to the political sphere, or by political forces that employ extrapolitical means? 4 / 4

Voters and candidates are generally able to exercise their political choices freely. However, a lack of campaign-finance regulations leaves open avenues for the outsized role of money in politics.

B4. Do various segments of the population (including ethnic, racial, religious, gender, LGBT+, and other relevant groups) have full political rights and electoral opportunities? 4 / 4

Only citizens may vote, and protracted citizenship and naturalization proceedings make achieving citizenship difficult for children born in the Bahamas to foreign parents. This predominately affects children of Haitian immigrants. Though women and women's interests remain underrepresented in politics, 7 out of 16 Senators are women, including both the Senate president and vice president. LGBT+ people are underrepresented in politics but continued to be more visible. Advocates for LGBT+ rights reported productive engagement during 2019 with the Office of the Attorney General.

C. FUNCTIONING OF GOVERNMENT 10 / 12

C1. Do the freely elected head of government and national legislative representatives determine the policies of the government? 4 / 4

Freely elected officials are generally able to determine national policies in a free and unhindered manner. At the onset of the COVID-19 pandemic, Parliament approved the prime minister's state-of-emergency declaration, which implemented a lockdown in the country. Emergency measures remained in place at year's end.

C2. Are safeguards against official corruption strong and effective? 3 / 4

The country's anticorruption mechanisms are relatively weak, and there is no agency specifically empowered to handle allegations of government corruption. Rates of reporting corruption are low, as whistleblowers fear retaliation.

In November 2020, the deputy prime minister and finance minister, Peter Turnquest, resigned after allegations emerged that he was involved in a fraud scheme worth over $20 million, though he was not charged. Prime Minister Minnis assumed the finance minister role and appointed Desmond Bannister as the new deputy. In February, members of the former PLP government were named in a federal lawsuit in the United States alleging they were paid to ignore a decades-long sex trafficking operation. Separately, bribery cases against former labor minister Shane Gibson and former housing and environment minister Kenred Dorsett were dismissed, decisions widely viewed as politicized.

Legislation to establish an independent anticorruption body and an ombudsman remained stalled in 2020. The government committed to anticorruption safeguards that would prevent misuse of public funds intended to handle the COVID-19 public health crisis.

C3. Does the government operate with openness and transparency? 3 / 4

Government procurement processes lack transparency, and political parties and campaigns are not required to disclose their finances. The 2017 Freedom of Information Act and its whistleblower protections were still not fully implemented in 2020. Legislators and other high-ranking public officials must disclose their income and assets under the Public Disclosure Act but often fail to submit the required information on time, without penalty.

A 2019 Fiscal Responsibility Law aims to improve transparency of public sector spending, but its independent oversight and enforcement body was not operational at the end of 2020. Additional bills to manage public debt, improve transparency in public finance and comply with international best practices were opened for consultation.

The Bahamas received emergency funds from the International Monetary Fund (IMF) to cope with the economic fallout of the COVID-19 pandemic. As part of receiving these funds, the government committed to publishing public procurement contracts intended to address the public health emergency, publish the ownership information of the companies receiving those contracts, and publish the results of a specific audit of COVID-19 expenditures.

CIVIL LIBERTIES: 53 / 60
D. FREEDOM OF EXPRESSION AND BELIEF 15 / 16
D1. Are there free and independent media? 3 / 4

Press freedom in the Bahamas is constitutionally guaranteed and generally respected in practice. The country's privately owned newspapers and radio broadcasters freely express a variety of views, although partisanship is common.

Libel is a criminal offense punishable by up to two years in prison. Though rarely enforced, Gorman Bannister, who ran news and commentary pages on social media, was charged with libel in 2019 for allegedly posting insults and defamatory statements against a former cabinet minister. He was again arraigned in 2020 for a threatening Facebook voice note against another minister. He was released on bail on both occasions. The Supreme Court also upheld a criminal libel charge related to an acrimonious Facebook exchange.

D2. Are individuals free to practice and express their religious faith or nonbelief in public and private? 4 / 4

Religious freedom is generally respected.

D3. Is there academic freedom, and is the educational system free from extensive political indoctrination? 4 / 4

Academic institutions are generally free from political pressure and other interference.

D4. Are individuals free to express their personal views on political or other sensitive topics without fear of surveillance or retribution? 4 / 4

People can freely express personal views in private and in public without fear of retribution or surveillance. Correctional officers were warned they might lose their jobs for complaining about COVID-19-related prison safety issues.

E. ASSOCIATIONAL AND ORGANIZATIONAL RIGHTS 12 / 12

E1. Is there freedom of assembly? 4 / 4

Freedom of assembly is protected by the constitution, and the government respects this right in practice. Protests sometimes faced police opposition and restrictions implemented to curb the spread of the coronavirus pandemic led to some arrests in 2020.

E2. Is there freedom for nongovernmental organizations, particularly those that are engaged in human rights– and governance-related work? 4 / 4

Freedom of association is generally protected, and a variety of nongovernmental organizations (NGOs) operate in the country. A new 2019 NGO registration law required NGOs to declare sources of contributions and donations and account for annual income and expenditures. Many NGOs failed to register by the 2020 deadline and faced fines; their members faced possible imprisonment.

E3. Is there freedom for trade unions and similar professional or labor organizations? 4 / 4

Labor, business, and professional organizations are generally free from government interference. Unions have the right to strike, and collective bargaining is prevalent, but union organizers met government resistance during the COVID-19 pandemic. In February 2020, a Supreme Court injunction prevented members of the Bahamas Utilities Services and Allied Workers Union from striking. Related litigation and proceedings before the industrial tribunal were ongoing at the end of the year.

F. RULE OF LAW 13 / 16

F1. Is there an independent judiciary? 4 / 4

The judicial system is headed by the Supreme Court and a court of appeals, with the additional right of appeal to the Privy Council in London under certain circumstances. The Bahamian judiciary is predominantly independent. There have been no major reports in recent years of attempts by powerful figures to use their influence to secure favorable rulings. The Bahamas Bar Association called for a transparent and merit-based selection process for judicial officers; the Inter-American Development Bank suggested separating the Offices of the Public Prosecutor and the Attorney General to ensure independence.

F2. Does due process prevail in civil and criminal matters? 3 / 4

Due process in civil and criminal matters generally prevails. However, the government only appoints counsel to defendants in capital cases, leaving some people without legal representation. Generally, noncitizens, asylum seekers, and migrants do not enjoy due process before detention or deportation. In February 2020, the prime minister created a "strike force" to pursue Haitian migrants. Reports of long-term detention of immigrants and arbitrary detention of asylum seekers persisted.

F3. Is there protection from the illegitimate use of physical force and freedom from war and insurgencies? 4 / 4

Homicide and violent crime rates in the Bahamas remain among the highest in the Caribbean. In 2019, murders increased, though initial reports from 2020 suggest that the crime rate is down. However, state security agents generally do not engage in the illegal use of force against civilians, and the population is not threatened by large-scale violence or insurgencies.

Prison conditions are poor. Violence against prisoners by guards continued to be reported in 2020.

F4. Do laws, policies, and practices guarantee equal treatment of various segments of the population? 2 / 4

The constitution does not prohibit gender-based discrimination and discrimination based on sexual orientation. LGBT+ people continue to report discrimination in employment and housing. Advocates for LGBT+ rights celebrated the country's first Pride week in October 2020, despite backlash from religious groups.

Harsh immigration policies enacted in 2014 target Bahamian-Haitians and Haitian migrants, requiring them to carry a passport and residency permits. The government prioritizes Bahamian citizens for hiring, land grants, and shelter in hurricane relief centers, and pursued removal of shantytowns that primarily house migrants.

G. PERSONAL AUTONOMY AND INDIVIDUAL RIGHTS 13 / 16

G1. Do individuals enjoy freedom of movement, including the ability to change their place of residence, employment, or education? 3 / 4

The freedom of movement is protected. However, curfews during the COVID-19 pandemic resulted in the arrests of homeless people and migrants. Migrants' and Haitian-Bahamians' lack of Bahamian identity documents affected their ability to move freely; choose their places of residence, employment, and education; and seek medical attention during the coronavirus health crisis.

Roadblocks have been erected as part of immigration enforcement actions.

G2. Are individuals able to exercise the right to own property and establish private businesses without undue interference from state or non-state actors? 4 / 4

The country has a strong private sector, and the economy relies mostly on tourism and financial services. Individuals are free to establish businesses, subject to generally non-onerous legal requirements.

Efforts to get rid of shantytowns continued in 2020. Emergency powers were invoked to defend demolitions on land impacted by the hurricane but an injunction halting service disconnections or evictions in shantytowns remained in effect.

G3. Do individuals enjoy personal social freedoms, including choice of marriage partner and size of family, protection from domestic violence, and control over appearance? 3 / 4

The government does not place explicit restrictions on social freedoms. However, the Bahamian constitution distinguishes between Bahamian men and women in the transmission of citizenship to a spouse or child, resulting in distinctions in treatment of married Bahamian women's children and their foreign-born husbands. A May Supreme Court decision granting Bahamian citizenship to a Bahamian-born child regardless of the gender of their Bahamian parent was appealed by the government.

Violence against women, including domestic violence and marital rape, is a serious issue. Same-sex marriage is not legalized.

G4. Do individuals enjoy equality of opportunity and freedom from economic exploitation? 3 / 4

The Bahamas is a source, destination, and transit country for men, women, and children for forced labor and sexual exploitation. According to the US State Department's *2020 Trafficking in Persons* report, the government fully complies with minimum international standards to address the problem. Migrant workers, many of whom arrive in the Bahamas to work in the agricultural sector and in domestic services, are particularly vulnerable to exploitation.

Bahrain

Population: 1,500,000
Capital: Manama
Freedom Status: Not Free
Electoral Democracy: No

Overview: Bahrain's Sunni-led monarchy dominates state institutions, and elections for the lower house of parliament are no longer competitive or inclusive. Since violently crushing a popular prodemocracy protest movement in 2011, the authorities have systematically eliminated a broad range of political rights and civil liberties, dismantled the political opposition, and cracked down harshly on persistent dissent concentrated among the Shiite population.

KEY DEVELOPMENTS IN 2020

- Sheikh Khalifa bin Salman al-Khalifa—the king's uncle and the country's only prime minister since independence—died in November at age 84. The king appointed the crown prince, Sheikh Salman bin Hamad al-Khalifa, to replace him.
- Confirmed cases of COVID-19 during the year were concentrated disproportionately among migrant workers, who tended to live in crowded accommodations and were also the most vulnerable to losing their jobs, housing, and residency. By year's end, roughly 94,000 cases and more than 350 deaths had been reported overall.
- In September, the government agreed to normalize relations with Israel in a pact brokered by the United States. The deal prompted protests by some Bahrainis.

POLITICAL RIGHTS: 2 / 40 (+1)

A. ELECTORAL PROCESS: 2 / 12

A1. Was the current head of government or other chief national authority elected through free and fair elections? 0 / 4

The 2002 constitution gives the king power over the executive, legislative, and judicial authorities. The monarch appoints and dismisses the prime minister and cabinet members, who are responsible to him rather than the legislature. Khalifa bin Salman al-Khalifa, the uncle of the current king, Hamad bin Isa al-Khalifa, was the country's only prime minister between independence from Britain in 1971 and his death in November 2020. The crown prince and eldest son of the king, Salman bin Hamad al-Khalifa, was appointed as the new prime minister.

A2. Were the current national legislative representatives elected through free and fair elections? 1 / 4

The king appoints the 40-member Consultative Council, the upper house of the National Assembly. The lower house, or Council of Representatives, consists of 40 elected members serving four-year terms. Formal political parties are not permitted, but members of "political societies" have participated in elections in practice.

Lower house elections were held in November 2018, with a runoff round in December, but with bans on the country's main opposition groups in place, the exercise featured little meaningful competition. A law adopted earlier that year prohibited the candidacy of anyone who belonged to dissolved political societies, had boycotted or been expelled from the parliament, or had received a prison sentence of at least six months. Most seats went to independents, though small Sunni Islamist groups won several seats, and a leftist group won two. As in previous years, turnout figures were disputed amid a lack of independent election monitoring.

A3. Are the electoral laws and framework fair, and are they implemented impartially by the relevant election management bodies? 1 / 4

Bahrain's electoral framework is unfair, with electoral districts deliberately designed to underrepresent Shiites, who form a majority of the citizen population but have never been able to obtain majority representation in the parliament. The government has also allegedly drawn district borders to put certain political societies, including leftist and Sunni Islamist groups, at a disadvantage. The government directorate responsible for administering elections is headed by the justice minister, a member of the royal family, and is not an independent body.

Voters' passports are stamped to indicate that they have voted, and there is a widespread belief that people who do not have these stamps are at a higher risk of being prevented from travelling. The government has previously punished people who call for election boycotts.

B. POLITICAL PLURALISM AND PARTICIPATION: 0 / 16

B1. Do the people have the right to organize in different political parties or other competitive political groupings of their choice, and is the system free of undue obstacles to the rise and fall of these competing parties or groupings? 0 / 4

Formal political parties are illegal. A 2005 law makes it illegal to form political associations based on class, profession, or religion, while a 2016 amendment prohibits serving religious clerics from engaging in political activity. The law permits "political societies," with some of the functions of a political party, to operate after registering with the government, but the authorities have closed down almost all opposition political societies since 2016 and jailed many of their leaders. The most popular, the Shiite Islamist society Al-Wefaq, was forcibly disbanded that year for allegedly encouraging violence. The second-largest opposition group, the secularist National Democratic Action Society (Wa'ad), was banned in 2017.

Individual opposition leaders and activists routinely face harassment, and the regime has forced many into prison or exile. In 2019, the country's top court upheld a sentence of life in prison that had been imposed on Al-Wefaq's general secretary, Ali Salman, in 2018 for alleged espionage on behalf of Qatar. He had been in detention on various charges since 2014.

B2. Is there a realistic opportunity for the opposition to increase its support or gain power through elections? 0 / 4

The ruling family maintains a monopoly on political power, with members holding many cabinet seats directly. The system's structure excludes the possibility of a change in government through elections, and the parliament has been dominated by progovernment lawmakers since the dissolution of the main opposition parties.

B3. Are the people's political choices free from domination by forces that are external to the political sphere, or by political forces that employ extrapolitical means? 0 / 4

The monarchy generally excludes the public from any meaningful or genuinely independent political participation. Since 2011 it has used the security forces to isolate the country's Shiite population and suppress political dissent. There have also been repeated allegations that the royal court uses its patronage networks to influence candidates and elections.

B4. Do various segments of the population (including ethnic, racial, religious, gender, LGBT+, and other relevant groups) have full political rights and electoral opportunities? 0 / 4

Although Shiites make up a majority of the country's citizens, they have tended to be underrepresented in both chambers of the National Assembly and the cabinet. The regime, which is controlled by a Sunni ruling family, is committed to preventing Shiites from organizing independently to advance their political interests. However, the dominant role of the monarchy means that even Sunnis face restrictions on their ability to engage in independent political activity. Senior positions in politics and government are often allocated to members of the royal family and a number of affiliated Sunni tribes. Certain wealthy Shiite families also enjoy a privileged position.

Women formally enjoy full political rights, but they are typically marginalized in practice. Six women were elected to the lower house in 2018, up from three, and a woman was chosen as speaker for the first time; nine women were named to the upper house. One woman serves in the cabinet as minister of health; the first woman minister was appointed in 2004.

Noncitizens make up just over half of the total population, and most have no political rights, but the minority of expatriates who own property in the kingdom are allowed to vote in municipal elections. Citizenship generally must be inherited from a Bahraini father, and foreign men married to Bahraini women do not have access to naturalization.

LGBT+ identity is generally not recognized openly, including in political contexts.

C. FUNCTIONING OF GOVERNMENT: 2 / 12

C1. Do the freely elected head of government and national legislative representatives determine the policies of the government? 0 / 4

There are no elected officials with executive authority. The National Assembly may propose legislation to the government, but it is the government that drafts and submits the bills for consideration by the legislature. With the main opposition groups no longer present in the National Assembly, the body has become silent on politically sensitive topics, even if it does feature some debate on economic reforms, austerity measures, and public services. When the government agreed to normalize relations with Israel in September 2020, the parliament welcomed the move, though it was not consulted beforehand.

Bahrain is fiscally and economically dependent on Saudi Arabia and the United Arab Emirates, which gives their governments significant influence over its foreign policy.

C2. Are safeguards against official corruption strong and effective? 2 / 4

There are some laws in place to combat corruption, but enforcement is weak, and high-ranking officials or members of the royal family who are suspected of corruption are rarely punished. The 2013–18 national anticorruption strategy called for the creation of a national anticorruption authority, but this has not been implemented. The generally pliant parliament is unable to serve as an effective check on malfeasance, and the media are not sufficiently free to independently air allegations of corruption against powerful figures. Civil society anticorruption efforts are also restricted; activists who highlight such problems have been prohibited from traveling or otherwise harassed.

C3. Does the government operate with openness and transparency? 0 / 4

Parliamentary proceedings are public, and the parliament is entitled to scrutinize the government budget, but in practice the executive issues orders and laws without providing insight or allowing meaningful public consultation on their development. The limited availability of data on actual expenditures, as opposed to annual spending targets, hinders scrutiny. No law guaranteeing public access to government information has been adopted, and officials are not obliged to disclose their assets or income.

ADDITIONAL DISCRETIONARY POLITICAL RIGHTS QUESTION
Is the government or occupying power deliberately changing the ethnic composition of a country or territory so as to destroy a culture or tip the political balance in favor of another group? –2 / 0 (+1)

Over the past two decades, the government has made concerted efforts to erode the Shiite citizen majority and tip the country's demographic balance in favor of the Sunni minority, mostly by recruiting foreign-born Sunnis to serve in the security forces and become citizens. No data on the sectarian makeup of the population are made public, but the annual rate of growth in the number of citizens has slowed significantly since 2016. This may indicate that the unofficial policy of rapidly naturalizing selected Sunni Muslims from other countries has eased, though it could also reflect other factors, such as reduced birth rates or migration abroad for economic reasons.

Meanwhile, hundreds of Bahrainis have had their citizenship revoked in recent years, including a large number of Shiite leaders and activists. After a mass revocation in 2019 prompted an international outcry, the king decreed that citizenship would be restored to 551 people, and courts reinstated another 147 people as citizens. By late that year, according to the United Kingdom–based Bahrain Institute for Rights and Democracy, nearly two-thirds of the people whose citizenship had been revoked over the previous seven years had had it restored, leaving nearly 300 denationalized. Citizenship was not restored to the most prominent opposition activists affected by the practice, and the government retains the authority to revoke citizenship without meaningful due process.

Score Change: The score improved from –3 to –2 due to recent restorations of citizenship to many Shiite residents whose rights had been revoked, as well as a lack of clear evidence that foreign-born Sunnis were being recruited and granted citizenship at the same rate as in previous years, though both practices were believed to continue.

CIVIL LIBERTIES: 10 / 60
D. FREEDOM OF EXPRESSION AND BELIEF: 2 / 16
D1. Are there free and independent media? 0 / 4

The government owns all national broadcast media outlets, and the private owners of Bahrain's main newspapers have close ties to the state. The only independent newspaper, *Al-Wasat*, was banned in 2017. Self-censorship is encouraged by the vaguely worded Press Law, which allows the state to imprison journalists for criticizing the king or Islam or for threatening national security. Insulting the king is punishable by up to seven years in prison. A 2016 edict requires newspapers to apply for a one-year renewable license to publish online. The government selectively blocks online content, including opposition websites and content that criticizes religion or highlights human rights abuses. Authorities have blocked online access to Qatari news outlets since diplomatic relations with Qatar broke down in 2017.

Journalists face legal and bureaucratic obstacles to their work in practice. The authorities have refused to renew the credentials of several Bahraini journalists working with foreign media outlets. Six journalists remained behind bars as of late 2020, according to the Committee to Protect Journalists, and one imprisoned journalist was temporarily moved to solitary confinement in April after he shared a video in which he disputed official claims about measures being taken to protect prisoners from COVID-19. International journalists often face difficulty obtaining a visa to enter Bahrain.

D2. Are individuals free to practice and express their religious faith or nonbelief in public and private? 1 / 4

Islam is the state religion, and the penal code criminalizes blasphemy-related offenses. However, non-Muslim minority groups are generally free to practice their faiths. Both Muslim and non-Muslim religious groups are required to register with government ministries. Muslim religious groups register with the Ministry of Justice and Islamic Affairs through the Sunni or Shiite awqaf (endowments) that oversee mosques and prayer houses; their directors are appointed by royal decree and paid by the government.

Although Shiite communities are free to carry out religious observances, Shiite clerics and community leaders often face harassment, interrogation, prosecution, and imprisonment. An estimated 45 Shiite religious sites were demolished or vandalized in 2011 in apparent reprisal for the role of Shiite opposition groups in that year's protests. The Islamic Ulema Council, a group of Shiite clerics, was banned in 2014. The government revoked the citizenship of senior Shiite cleric Isa Qassim in 2016, and he was given a suspended one-year prison sentence for money laundering in 2017; he left Bahrain in 2018. Other Shiite clergy have been detained or questioned for taking part in protests or being suspected of doing so. Protests and police restrictions periodically obstruct access to mosques.

Most religious gatherings and processions were suspended in the spring of 2020 due to the COVID-19 pandemic. Mosques gradually reopened for group prayer during the second half of the year, though some safety measures remained in place.

D3. Is there academic freedom, and is the educational system free from extensive political indoctrination? 0 / 4

Academic freedom is not formally restricted, but scholars who criticize the government have in the past been subject to dismissal, and universities are affected by a broader climate in which criticism is frequently equated with disloyalty. In 2011, a number of faculty members and administrators were fired for supporting the call for democracy, and hundreds of students were expelled. Those who remained were forced to sign loyalty pledges.

D4. Are individuals free to express their personal views on political or other sensitive topics without fear of surveillance or retribution? 1 / 4

The penal code includes a variety of punishments for offenses such as insulting the king or state institutions and spreading false news. Many Bahrainis have been convicted and jailed for political speech, including on social media. Authorities have also warned against online expression that contradicts the foreign policy priorities of Bahrain and its regional allies. In 2019, the Interior Ministry warned that Bahrainis could be found guilty of cybercrimes simply for following or sharing content from social media accounts deemed to promote "sedition."

The security forces are believed to use networks of informers, and the government monitors the personal communications of activists, critics, and opposition members.

E. ASSOCIATIONAL AND ORGANIZATIONAL RIGHTS: 1 / 12

E1. Is there freedom of assembly? 0 / 4

A permit is required to hold demonstrations, and a variety of onerous restrictions make it difficult to organize a legal gathering in practice. Police regularly use force to break up political protests, most of which occur in Shiite villages. Participants can face long jail terms, particularly if the demonstrations involve clashes with security personnel. Some protests were held without permission in 2020, mostly in opposition to the government's September agreement to normalize relations with Israel. Organizers and participants were reportedly summoned by authorities and compelled to sign pledges that they would cease their activities.

E2. Is there freedom for nongovernmental organizations, particularly those that are engaged in human rights- and governance-related work? 0 / 4

NGOs are prohibited from operating without a permit, and authorities have broad discretion to deny or revoke permits. The government also reserves the right to replace the boards of NGOs. Bahraini human rights defenders and their family members are subject to harassment, intimidation, and prosecution. Many of them were either in prison or in exile as of 2020. Nabeel Rajab, leader of the banned Bahrain Center for Human Rights, was released on probation in June, having been in detention since 2016.

E3. Is there freedom for trade unions and similar professional or labor organizations? 1 / 4

Bahrainis have the right to establish independent labor unions, but workers must give two weeks' notice before a strike, and strikes are banned in a variety of economic sectors. Trade unions cannot operate in the public sector, and collective-bargaining rights are limited even in the private sector. Harassment and firing of unionist workers occurs in practice. Domestic, agricultural, and temporary workers do not have the right to join or form unions.

F. RULE OF LAW: 1 / 16

F1. Is there an independent judiciary? 0 / 4

The king appoints all judges and heads the Supreme Judicial Council, which administers the courts and proposes judicial nominees. The courts are subject to government pressure in practice. The country's judicial system is seen as corrupt and biased in favor of the royal family and its allies, particularly in politically sensitive cases.

F2. Does due process prevail in civil and criminal matters? 1 / 4

Law enforcement officers reportedly violate due process during arrests and detention, in part by obstructing detainees' access to attorneys. Detainees are sometimes held incommunicado. Judicial proceedings often put defendants at a disadvantage, with judges denying bail requests or restricting defense attorneys' attendance or arguments without explanation. Prominent defense lawyers who represent dissidents have themselves been prosecuted on various charges. One such attorney, Abdullah al-Shamlawi, was convicted in June 2020 and sentenced to eight months in prison over 2019 social media posts in which he criticized certain Shiite religious traditions; after an appeal, the penalty was reduced to a six-month suspended sentence in September.

In 2017, the government restored the National Security Agency's power to make arrests, despite widespread allegations that it had engaged in torture and other abuses, and the constitution was amended to permit military trials for civilians in security-related cases, further weakening due process rights.

F3. Is there protection from the illegitimate use of physical force and freedom from war and insurgencies? 0 / 4

Torture is criminalized, but detainees frequently report mistreatment by security forces and prison officials, who are rarely held accountable. The Interior Ministry ombudsman's office has failed to provide a meaningful check on such impunity. Political prisoners have alleged denial of medical care and religious discrimination against Shiite inmates. In March 2020, nearly 1,500 prisoners were released amid concerns about the spread of COVID-19, but the releases did not include activists, opposition leaders, human rights defenders, or journalists.

Three executions in 2017 marked the first uses of the death penalty since 2010, and another three men were put to death in 2019. UN special rapporteurs and experts have raised concerns that individuals sentenced to death were forced to confess under torture, among other flaws in their cases.

Police have been targeted in small bombings and armed attacks in recent years, though no major incidents were reported in 2019 or 2020.

F4. Do laws, policies, and practices guarantee equal treatment of various segments of the population? 0 / 4

Women enjoy legal equality on some issues, and gender-based discrimination in employment is prohibited, but discrimination is common in practice.

Shiites of both Arab and Persian ethnicity face de facto discrimination in matters including employment. They are largely excluded from the security forces, except when serving as unarmed community police officers. There is a general perception that Shiite public employees are relegated to nonsecurity ministries, like those focused on health and education, which may put Sunni applicants at a disadvantage in such sectors. The government does not publish socioeconomic data that are broken down by religious sect.

Discrimination based on sexual orientation is common. The law does not provide protections against such bias, though same-sex sexual activity is not criminalized for those aged 21 and older. Public displays of same-sex affection could fall afoul of public decency laws.

Bahrain is not a signatory to the 1951 refugee convention and does not recognize refugee status.

G. PERSONAL AUTONOMY AND INDIVIDUAL RIGHTS: 6 / 16

G1. Do individuals enjoy freedom of movement, including the ability to change their place of residence, employment, or education? 1 / 4

Authorities sometimes restrict movement inside the country for residents of largely Shiite villages outside Manama, where the government maintains a heavy security presence. The government also obstructs foreign travel by numerous opposition figures and activists.

Bahrain established a "flexible" permit for foreign workers in 2017, aiming to ease the workers' ability to change jobs; the traditional sponsorship system ties migrant workers to a specific employer. However, participation in the new scheme has been limited by numerical caps and other restrictions.

A contact-tracing mobile application promoted by the government during the COVID-19 pandemic in 2020 was criticized by human rights groups for its intrusive features, including centralized, real-time location tracking; the app was mandatory for those ordered to self-isolate.

G2. Are individuals able to exercise the right to own property and establish private businesses without undue interference from state or nonstate actors? 2 / 4

Although registered businesses are largely free to operate, obtaining approval can be difficult in practice. For the wealthy elites who dominate the business sector, property rights are generally respected, and expropriation is rare. However, Shiite citizens encounter difficulties obtaining affordable housing and in some cases face bans on purchasing land. Much of the country's scarce land is occupied by royal properties and military facilities. Noncitizens can only own property in designated areas. Women may inherit property, but their rights are not equal to those of men.

G3. Do individuals enjoy personal social freedoms, including choice of marriage partner and size of family, protection from domestic violence, and control over appearance? 2 / 4

Personal status issues such as marriage, divorce, and child custody are governed by a 2017 unified family law applying to both Sunni and Shiite Muslim families. The law's provisions are based on Sharia (Islamic law) principles that put women at a disadvantage on many topics.

Accused rapists can avoid punishment by marrying their victims, and spousal rape is not specifically outlawed. Adultery is illegal, and those who kill a spouse caught in the act of adultery are eligible for lenience in sentencing.

G4. Do individuals enjoy equality of opportunity and freedom from economic exploitation? 1 / 4

Migrant workers are vulnerable to exploitation. Some employers subject them to forced labor and withhold their salaries and passports, although this is illegal. The government has taken significant steps to combat human trafficking in recent years, but its enforcement efforts focus mainly on sex trafficking rather than forced labor, according to the US State Department.

Migrant workers reportedly accounted for a disproportionate share of COVID-19 cases in 2020. While the government made efforts to ensure less crowded temporary accommodations for some and encouraged voluntary repatriation for others, migrants who lost their jobs often faced eviction, denial of services, or deportation. Migrant workers also received fewer emergency benefits than citizens.

Revenues from oil and gas exports are used to fund public employment and services that benefit all citizens, but access to public-sector jobs and promotion opportunities often depends on one's social and sectarian background and personal connections.

Bangladesh

Population: 169,800,000
Capital: Dhaka
Freedom Status: Partly Free
Electoral Democracy: No

Overview: The ruling Awami League (AL) has consolidated political power through sustained harassment of the opposition and those perceived to be allied with it, as well as of critical media and voices in civil society. Corruption is a serious problem, and anticorruption efforts have been weakened by politicized enforcement. Due process guarantees are poorly upheld and security forces carry out a range of human right abuses with near impunity.

KEY DEVELOPMENTS IN 2020

- In March, the government temporarily released leader of the opposition Bangladesh Nationalist Party (BNP) Khaleda Zia from jail to receive medical treatment at home; her release was extended another six months in September. Zia remained sidelined from politics, which severely hampered the competitiveness of the BNP.
- Citing the outbreak of the COVID-19 pandemic, in April, the government quarantined over 300 Rohingya refugees on Bhasan Char, a silt island off the Bangladesh coastline that critics say lacks adequate facilities and is prone to flooding. Though the quarantine was supposed to be temporary, the original 300 refugees remained on the island through the end of the year. In December, the government sent over 1,000 refugees there, and announced plans to send over 2,500 refugees to the island in total, despite condemnation of the decision from rights groups and the United Nations.

POLITICAL RIGHTS: 15 / 40

A. ELECTORAL PROCESS: 4 / 12

A1. Was the current head of government or other chief national authority elected through free and fair elections? 1 / 4

A largely ceremonial president, who serves for five years, is elected by the legislature. President Abdul Hamid was elected to his second term in 2018.

The leader of the party that wins the most seats in the unicameral National Parliament assumes the position of prime minister and wields effective power. Sheikh Hasina was sworn in for her third term as prime minister in early 2019 following the AL's overwhelming victory in the 2018 elections, which were marked by violence, intimidation of opposition candidates and supporters, allegations of fraud benefiting the ruling party, and the exclusion of nonpartisan election monitors. Hamid also swore in 24 cabinet ministers, 19 ministers of state, and 3 deputy ministers.

A2. Were the current national legislative representatives elected through free and fair elections? 1 / 4

The National Parliament is composed of 350 members, 300 of whom are directly elected. Political parties select a total of 50 women members based on the parties' share of elected seats.

The AL overwhelmingly won the December 2018 polls, with the party and its alliance partners taking 288 of the 300 directly elected seats. Election day and the campaign that preceded it were marked by political violence in which at least 17 people were killed, as well as legal and extralegal harassment of government opponents. The opposition Bangladesh Nationalist Party (BNP) claimed that thousands of its supporters and nearly a dozen of its candidates had been arrested ahead of the elections, and that its candidates were subject to intimidation and violence.

In the election's wake, the BNP alleged that the AL had benefitted from widespread electoral fraud carried out by AL supporters with the complicity of law enforcement agents and the army. The government also faced criticism for long delays in approving the accreditation of the Asian Network for Free Elections (ANFREL), which ultimately canceled its election monitoring mission. A number of domestic and international missions were also unable to observe the elections due to similar delays or authorities' outright denial of accreditation.

The previous general election in 2014 was boycotted by the BNP, the main opposition party, and was disrupted by significant violence.

A3. Are the electoral laws and framework fair, and are they implemented impartially by the relevant election management bodies? 2 / 4

The independence of the Election Commission (EC) and its ability to investigate complaints has long been questioned by opposition parties and outside observers, including by foreign governments and international organizations that have withdrawn financial assistance to the commission over such concerns. The EC's stewardship of the 2018 national election lent further credence to complaints that it favors the ruling party. In the run-up to the 2018 polls, the commission disproportionately disqualified opposition candidates for various violations. Moreover, the EC failed to order additional security measures following outbreaks of political violence that preceded the vote, or to meaningfully address many complaints filed by opposition figures about election-related violence and other electoral irregularities. After the election, the EC affirmed the results without investigating widespread allegations of fraud. In 2020, controversial municipal elections in Dhaka city and by-elections for several vacated parliamentary seats raised further concerns about electoral integrity and the EC's independence.

B. POLITICAL PLURALISM AND PARTICIPATION: 7 / 16

B1. Do the people have the right to organize in different political parties or other competitive political groupings of their choice, and is the system free of undue obstacles to the rise and fall of these competing parties or groupings? 2 / 4

Bangladesh has a multiparty system in which power has historically alternated between political coalitions led by the AL and the BNP; third parties have traditionally had difficulty achieving traction. Both parties are nondemocratic in terms of internal structure, and are led by families that have competed to lead Bangladesh since independence, along with a small coterie of advisers. A crackdown on the BNP ahead of the 2018 elections significantly disrupted its operations. However, the government eased restrictions on opposition protests and rallies after the polls.

The constitution bans religiously based political parties, and the Jamaat-i-Islami (JI) party was prohibited from taking part in the 2014 and 2018 elections because of its overtly Islamist charter, though some JI members ran as independents. Bangladesh's International Crimes Tribunal—named as such despite lacking international oversight—was created in 2010 by Hasina to try people suspected of committing war crimes during Bangladesh's 1971 war of independence from Pakistan. Critics of the tribunal claim it was established to persecute Hasina's political opponents, notably those in JI.

B2. Is there a realistic opportunity for the opposition to increase its support or gain power through elections? 1 / 4

The main opposition party, the BNP, has been weakened by regular harassment and arrests of key members that have significantly harmed its ability to challenge the AL in elections. The 2018 election campaign was characterized by a crackdown on dissent that saw thousands of people and several political candidates arrested. There were also several acts of violence committed against opposition figures.

In the run-up to the 2018 parliamentary polls, former prime minister and BNP leader Khaleda Zia was convicted on corruption charges in two separate court cases, sentenced to over a decade in prison, and later banned from electoral competition. In March 2020, the government temporarily released Zia from jail to receive medical treatment at home, though she was not permitted to leave the country; her release was extended another six months in September. Zia remained sidelined from politics, which severely hampered the competitiveness of the BNP.

A JI spokesman said more than 1,850 party members were arrested ahead of the 2018 elections, and some party members claimed they had been subject to torture while in custody.

In the first half of 2019, the BNP and other opposition parties boycotted local elections, which saw historically low turnout, but the BNP has since returned to political competition. In 2020, the BNP participated in municipal and other local elections.

B3. Are the people's political choices free from domination by forces that are external to the political sphere, or by political forces that employ extrapolitical means? 2 / 4

The rival AL and BNP parties dominate politics and limit political choices for those who question internal party structures or hierarchy, or who would create alternative parties or political groupings.

Animosity between Hasina and Zia, as well as between lower-level cadres, has contributed to continued political violence. In 2020, human rights group Odhikar registered 73 deaths and 2,883 people injured because of political violence, and 2,339 injured in intraparty clashes. Violent political protests and election-related violence also persisted in 2020.

B4. Do various segments of the population (including ethnic, racial, religious, gender, LGBT+, and other relevant groups) have full political rights and electoral opportunities? 2 / 4

In the National Parliament, 50 seats are allotted to women, who are elected by political parties based on their overall share of elected seats. Women lead both main political parties. Nevertheless, societal discrimination against women, as well as against as well against LGBT+ people, limits their participation in politics in practice. Religious, ethnic, and other marginalized groups remain underrepresented in politics and state agencies. In 2019, several transgender women competed for women's reserved seats in parliament. None were selected.

C. FUNCTIONING OF GOVERNMENT: 4 / 12

C1. Do the freely elected head of government and national legislative representatives determine the policies of the government? 1 / 4

Policy is set by the ruling AL, and weaknesses in the country's institutions have reduced checks on its processes and decision-making. Low representation of opposition lawmakers in the National Parliament significantly reduces its ability to provide thorough scrutiny of or debate on government policies, budgets, and proposed legislation.

Problems with the 2018 election including violence, intimidation of opposition candidates and supporters, and allegations of fraud benefiting the ruling party undermined the legitimacy of the AL government that was seated in January 2019.

C2. Are safeguards against official corruption strong and effective? 1 / 4

Under the AL government, anticorruption efforts have been weakened by politicized enforcement and subversion of the judicial process. In particular, the Anti-Corruption Commission (ACC) has become ineffective and subject to overt political interference. The government continues to bring or pursue politicized corruption cases against BNP party leaders. In 2020, AL politicians continued to be accused of corruption, despite the party's increased actions and rhetoric against it. In April, over two dozen AL local leaders and government officials were charged with corruption for allegedly stealing COVID-19 relief supplies that were designated for low-income people who had been particularly affected by the pandemic.

Media outlets and civil society face restrictions and are therefore less able to expose government corruption.

C3. Does the government operate with openness and transparency? 2 / 4

Endemic corruption and criminality, weak rule of law, limited bureaucratic transparency, and political polarization have long undermined government accountability. The 2009 Right to Information Act mandates public access to all information held by public bodies and overrides secrecy legislation. Although it has been unevenly implemented, journalists and civil society activists have had some success in using it to obtain information from local governing authorities.

CIVIL LIBERTIES: 24 / 60

D. FREEDOM OF EXPRESSION AND BELIEF: 6 / 16

D1. Are there free and independent media? 1 / 4

Journalists and media outlets face many forms of pressure, including frequent lawsuits, harassment, and serious or deadly physical attacks. Throughout 2020, journalists were beaten by uniformed security forces, forced to disappear, or sued for defamation. Journalists have been arrested or attacked in connection with reporting on topics including crimes committed during the 1971 war and election irregularities during both the 2018 parliamentary polls and 2019 local polls. A climate of impunity for attacks on media workers remains the norm, and there has been little progress made to ensure justice for a series of blogger murders since 2015. Dozens of bloggers remain in hiding or exile.

The 2018 Digital Security Act allows the government to conduct searches or arrest individuals without a warrant, criminalizes various forms of speech, and was vehemently opposed by journalists.

Forms of artistic expression contained in books, films, and other materials are occasionally banned or censored.

D2. Are individuals free to practice and express their religious faith or nonbelief in public and private? 2 / 4

Islam is designated as the official religion, though the constitution designates secularism as among the "high ideals" the charter is grounded in. Although religious minorities have the right to worship freely, they occasionally face legal repercussions for proselytizing. Members of minority groups—including Hindus, Christians, Buddhists, and Shiite and Ahmadiyya Muslims—face harassment and violence, including mob violence against their houses of worship. In October 2019, a Muslim mob attacked Hindu residences in Barisal after false rumors circulated that a Hindu man posted blasphemous content on Facebook. In May 2020, in the same town, a mob attacked a Hindu man's shop and subsequently clashed with police, injuring 10 people. These incidents are part of a pattern in recent years in which violence against religious or other minorities appears to have been deliberately provoked through social media.

Those with secular or nonconformist views can face societal opprobrium and attacks from hardline Islamist groups.

D3. Is there academic freedom, and is the educational system free from extensive political indoctrination? 1 / 4

In recent years, Bangladesh's academic institutions have faced frequent threats from a variety of actors, resulting in reduced autonomy and rising self-censorship. Faculty hiring and promotion are often linked to support for the AL, and campus debate is often stifled by the AL's student wing. Throughout 2020, several academics were fired or censured for criticizing the government's response to the COVID-19 pandemic and other issues. In September 2019, members of the AL student wing attacked a nonviolent protest and beat a student to death after he posted criticism of the AL on Facebook.

Islamist groups have growing influence on government policy and standards. In 2017, Islamist groups compelled changes to educational content they deemed "atheistic" in widely used Bengali-language textbooks. Separately, Islamic extremists have attacked secular professors.

D4. Are individuals free to express their personal views on political or other sensitive topics without fear of surveillance or retribution? 2 / 4

Open discussion of sensitive religious and political issues is restrained by fears of harassment and violence. In the lead-up to national and local elections between 2018 and 2020, repression of dissent created a climate of fear and self-censorship. Censorship of digital content and surveillance of telecommunications and social media have become increasingly common. In June 2020, a 15-year-old boy was arrested for criticizing Prime Minister Hasina on Facebook.

E. ASSOCIATIONAL AND ORGANIZATIONAL RIGHTS: 5 / 12
E1. Is there freedom of assembly? 2 / 4

The constitution provides for the rights of assembly and association, but this is upheld inconsistently. Protesters are frequently injured and occasionally killed during clashes in which police use excessive force. Many demonstrations took place in 2020, though authorities sometimes tried to prevent rallies by arresting party activists. During the COVID-19 pandemic in April, garment-industry workers disregarded COVID-19 lockdown restrictions to protest for backpay and safer working conditions.

E2. Is there freedom for nongovernmental organizations, particularly those that are engaged in human rights- and governance-related work? 2 / 4

Many nongovernmental organizations (NGOs) operate in Bangladesh and are able to function without onerous restrictions, but the use of foreign funds must be cleared by the NGO Affairs Bureau, which can also approve or reject individual projects. The 2016 Foreign Donations (Voluntary Activities) Regulation Act made it more difficult for NGOs to obtain foreign funds and gave officials broad authority to deregister NGOs. Democracy, governance, and human rights NGOs are regularly denied permission for proposed projects and are subject to harassment and surveillance. In September 2019, the government banned two NGOs from working in the Rohingya refugee camps after the allegedly supported an antirepatriation campaign to Myanmar.

In 2020, authorities continued to invoke digital security laws to arrest several rights activists for online speech, citing offenses including hurting religious sentiment and undermining law and order. Pressure and intimidation from Islamist groups also limit NGO activities on some issues such as LGBT+ rights and protection for minority religious groups.

E3. Is there freedom for trade unions and similar professional or labor organizations? 1 / 4

Legal reforms in 2015 eased restrictions on the formation of unions. However, union leaders who attempt to organize or unionize workers continue to face dismissal or physical intimidation. Organizations that advocate for labor rights have faced increased harassment. Worker grievances fuel unrest at factories, particularly in the garment industry, where protests against low wages and unsafe working conditions are common. Protesting workers often face violence, arrest, and dismissal.

F. RULE OF LAW: 4 / 16

F1. Is there an independent judiciary? 1 / 4

Politicization of and pressure against the judiciary persists. In 2017, the Chief Justice of the Supreme Court retired; he left the country and said, in an autobiography published in September 2018, that he had been forced to retire after the Bangladeshi military intelligence threatened him because of rulings he had made against the government. In July 2019, Bangladesh's Anti-Corruption Commission charged the former chief justice with corruption in absentia. Other allegations of political pressure on judges are common, as are allegations that unqualified AL loyalists were being appointed to court positions.

F2. Does due process prevail in civil and criminal matters? 1 / 4

Individuals' ability to access the justice system is compromised by endemic corruption within the courts and severe case backlogs. Pretrial detention is often lengthy, and many defendants lack counsel. Suspects are routinely subject to arbitrary arrest and detention, demands for bribes, and physical abuse by police. Criminal cases against ruling party activists are regularly withdrawn on the grounds of "political consideration," undermining the judicial process and entrenching a culture of impunity.

The 1974 Special Powers Act permits arbitrary detention without charge, and the criminal procedure code allows detention without a warrant. A 2009 counterterrorism law includes a broad definition of terrorism and generally does not meet international standards. Concerns have repeatedly been raised that the International Crimes Tribunal's procedures and verdicts do not meet international standards on issues such as victim and witness protection, the presumption of innocence, defendant access to counsel, and the right to bail. Since 2013, the tribunal has sentenced at least 45 people to death or long prison sentences.

F3. Is there protection from the illegitimate use of physical force and freedom from war and insurgencies? 1 / 4

Terrorist attacks by Islamist militant groups have remained low following the government's increased counterterrorism efforts since the 2016 Holey Artisan Bakery terrorist attack. However, the Islamic State (IS) militant group claimed credit for several nonlethal bomb attacks on police officers in Dhaka in 2019 and 2020.

A range of human rights abuses by law enforcement agencies—including enforced disappearances, custodial deaths, arbitrary arrests, and torture—have continued unabated. A 2017 Human Rights Watch (HRW) report documented the use of detention and enforced disappearance against members of the political opposition, despite the government's promise to address the issue. In 2018, the government initiated a "war on drugs," during which thousands were arrested and over 100 people were killed.

The human rights NGO Odhikar reported 159 extrajudicial killings perpetrated by law enforcement agencies in the first half of 2020. A statement from the International Federation for Human Rights released in August 2020 said at least 572 people had been subject to enforced disappearance between 2009 and July 2020. Prison conditions are extremely poor; severe overcrowding is common, and juveniles are often incarcerated with adults.

F4. Do laws, policies, and practices guarantee equal treatment of various segments of the population? 1 / 4

Members of ethnic and religious minority groups face some discrimination under law as well as harassment and violations of their rights in practice. Indigenous people in the Chittagong Hill Tracts (CHT), religious minorities, and other ethnic groups remain subject to physical attacks, property destruction, land grabs by Bengali settlers, and occasional abuses by security forces.

Over a million ethnic Rohingyas have fled Myanmar and entered Bangladesh since the 1990s. The vast majority do not have official refugee status; suffer from a complete lack of access to health care, employment, and education; and are subject to substantial harassment. Since a sharp escalation in violence directed against Rohingyas in Myanmar's Rakhine State began in 2017, over 700,000 refugees have poured across the border into Bangladesh, creating a humanitarian crisis. Most refugees live in precarious camps that lack basic services. Authorities reached a repatriation agreement with Myanmar in October 2018, but the United Nations refugee agency said conditions in Myanmar were not fit for the refugees' return and that safeguards for them were "absent." Subsequent efforts to repatriate Rohingya have failed, and the government has become increasingly hostile toward the refugees. In 2019, authorities cut off cell phone service in refugee camps (restored in August 2020 after international pressure) and erected barbed wire fencing around them.

Citing the coronavirus pandemic, in April 2020, the government quarantined over 300 Rohingya refugees on Bhasan Char, a silt island off the Bangladesh coastline that critics say lacks adequate facilities and is prone to flooding. Though the quarantine was supposed to be temporary, the original 300 refugees remained on the island through the end of the year. In refugee camps on the mainland, gang violence and other lawlessness escalated. In December, the government transferred over a thousand refugees to Bhasan Char and announced plans to move over 2,500 refugees there in total, despite condemnation of the decision from rights groups and the United Nations. Reports alleged that authorities had forced refugees to consent to the relocation.

A criminal ban on same-sex relations is rarely enforced, but societal discrimination remains the norm, and dozens of attacks on LGBT+ individuals are reported every year. A number of LGBT+ individuals remain in exile following the 2016 murder of Xulhaz Mannan, a prominent LGBT+ activist, by Islamist militants. Some legal recognition is available for transgender people, though in practice they face severe discrimination.

G. PERSONAL AUTONOMY AND INDIVIDUAL RIGHTS: 9 / 16

G1. Do individuals enjoy freedom of movement, including the ability to change their place of residence, employment, or education? 3 / 4

The ability to move within the country is relatively unrestricted, as is foreign travel, though there are some rules on travel into and around the CHT districts by foreigners as well as into Rohingya refugee camps. During the COVID-19 pandemic, the government implemented some movement restrictions that were limited in scope and duration.

There are few legal restrictions regarding choice of education or employment.

G2. Are individuals able to exercise the right to own property and establish private businesses without undue interference from state or nonstate actors? 2 / 4

Property rights are unevenly enforced, and the ability to engage freely in private economic activity is somewhat constrained. Corruption and bribery, inadequate infrastructure, and official bureaucratic and regulatory hurdles hinder business activities throughout the country. State involvement and interference in the economy is considerable. The 2011 Vested Properties Return Act allows Hindus to reclaim land that the government or other individuals seized, but it has been unevenly implemented. Tribal minorities have little control over land decisions affecting them, and Bengali-speaking settlers continue to illegally encroach on tribal lands in the CHT.

G3. Do individuals enjoy personal social freedoms, including choice of marriage partner and size of family, protection from domestic violence, and control over appearance? 2 / 4

Under personal status laws affecting all religions, women have fewer marriage, divorce, and inheritance rights than men, and face discrimination in social services and employment. Rape, acid throwing, and other forms of violence against women occur regularly despite laws offering some level of protection. A law requiring rape victims to file police reports and obtain medical certificates within 24 hours of the crime in order to press charges prevents most cases from reaching the courts. In October 2020, the government introduced the death penalty for rape in response to large protests after a series of high-profile incidents of rape and sexual assault.

Giving or receiving dowry is a criminal offense, but coercive requests still occur. Bangladesh ranks among the top 10 countries with the highest rates of child marriage. Despite a stated government commitment in 2014 to abolish the practice by 2041, in 2017 parliament approved a law that would permit girls under the age of 18 to marry under certain circumstances, reversing a previous legal ban on the practice.

G4. Do individuals enjoy equality of opportunity and freedom from economic exploitation? 2 / 4

Socioeconomic inequality is widespread. Working conditions in the garment industry remain extremely unsafe in most factories despite the renewal of a legally binding accord between unions and clothing brands to improve safety practices. During the COVID-19 pandemic, over a quarter of workers in the garment industry, approximately 1 million people, were laid off. Comprehensive reforms of the industry are hampered by the fact that a growing number of factory owners are also legislators or influential businesspeople.

Bangladesh remains both a major supplier of and transit point for trafficking victims, with tens of thousands of people trafficked each year. Women and children are trafficked both overseas and within the country for the purposes of domestic servitude and sexual exploitation, while men are trafficked primarily for labor abroad. A comprehensive 2013 antitrafficking law provides protection to victims and increased penalties for traffickers, but enforcement remains inadequate.

Barbados

Population: 300,000
Capital: Bridgetown
Freedom Status: Free
Electoral Democracy: Yes

Overview: Barbados is a democracy that regularly holds competitive elections and upholds civil liberties. Challenges include official corruption and a lack of government transparency, discrimination against LGBT+ people, violent crime, and poverty.

KEY DEVELOPMENTS IN 2020

- In September, the Barbadian government announced that it would remove the British monarch as head of state and become a republic by November 2021. Further, Prime Minister Mia Mottley publicized that the government would hold a referendum to legalize same-sex civil unions.
- In March, the first people in Barbados tested positive for COVID-19, prompting the government to impose a lockdown, which included a curfew. These measures were time-bound and relied on public health data; experts praised the Mottley government's openness and transparency in providing information to the public about the pandemic. By yearend, 372 people had tested positive for the virus and 7 people had died, according to government statistics provided to the World Health Organization (WHO).

POLITICAL RIGHTS: 38 / 40

A. ELECTORAL PROCESS: 12 / 12

A1. Was the current head of government or other chief national authority elected through free and fair elections? 4 / 4

The prime minister, usually the leader of the largest party in Parliament, is head of government. The British monarch is head of state, represented by a governor general. In September 2020, however, the Barbadian government announced that it would remove the British monarch as head of state and become a republic by November 2021. Dame Sandra Mason was appointed governor general in 2018.

Mia Mottley of the Barbados Labour Party (BLP) was appointed prime minister after her party decisively won the May 2018 general elections, unseating Freundel Stuart of the Democratic Labour Party (DLP). The polls were regarded as competitive and credible.

A2. Were the current national legislative representatives elected through free and fair elections? 4 / 4

Members of the 30-seat House of Assembly, the lower house, are directly elected for five-year terms. The governor general appoints the 21 members of the upper house, the Senate: 12 on the advice of the prime minister, 2 on the advice of the leader of the opposition, and the remaining 7 at their own discretion. Senators serve five-year terms.

The results of parliamentary elections held in May 2018 were accepted by all stakeholders. The opposition BLP took all 30 seats in the House of Assembly. Bishop Joseph Atherley, originally a BLP member who was elected in the May 2018 polls, subsequently sat as an independent to become the leader of the opposition.

A3. Are the electoral laws and framework fair, and are they implemented impartially by the relevant election management bodies? 4 / 4

The independent Electoral and Boundaries Commission (EBC) oversees elections in Barbados in a professional manner. Its five commissioners are chosen based on their expertise by the prime minister and the opposition for a maximum term of five years.

B. POLITICAL PLURALISM AND PARTICIPATION: 16 / 16

B1. Do the people have the right to organize in different political parties or other competitive political groupings of their choice, and is the system free of undue obstacles to the rise and fall of these competing parties or groupings? 4 / 4

Political parties form and operate freely. New parties emerged in 2018 to challenge the traditionally dominant BLP and DLP, but all failed to win any seats. In June 2019, Atherley launched the People's Party for Democracy and Development—a self-described socialist and Christian movement that was joined by two opposition senators.

B2. Is there a realistic opportunity for the opposition to increase its support or gain power through elections? 4 / 4

Opposition parties have a realistic chance of gaining power, which has historically rotated peacefully between the BLP and DLP. The BLP's landslide victory over the DLP in 2018 highlighted the political system's competitiveness.

B3. Are the people's political choices free from domination by forces that are external to the political sphere, or by political forces that employ extrapolitical means? 4 / 4

Voters and candidates are generally able to express their political choices without interference from actors that are not democratically accountable.

B4. Do various segments of the population (including ethnic, racial, religious, gender, LGBT+, and other relevant groups) have full political rights and electoral opportunities? 4 / 4

Barbados's population is fully enfranchised, with adult citizens, Commonwealth citizens, and foreigners with seven years' residency able to vote. Laws protect the political rights of women, but conservative, discriminatory attitudes and societal marginalization can discourage women from running for office. Although Mia Mottley became the country's first woman to be prime minister in 2018, politics remain dominated by men. Women make up only 20 percent of the House of Assembly.

C. FUNCTIONING OF GOVERNMENT: 10 / 12

C1. Do the freely elected head of government and national legislative representatives determine the policies of the government? 4 / 4

The prime minister and members of Parliament are largely unimpeded in their ability to craft and implement policy, notwithstanding the powerful role played by labor unions, the demands of international creditors, and the growing influence of China.

C2. Are safeguards against official corruption strong and effective? 3 / 4

Barbados's government has failed to implement key anticorruption measures. Civil society groups, business figures, and the attorney general have complained of serious incidences of corruption, but no major officials have faced arrest under the Mottley administration. Potential whistleblowers fear costly defamation suits.

Barbados is one of just seven countries in the Americas to have neither signed nor ratified the Inter-American Convention on Mutual Assistance in Criminal Matters. The government is also yet to ratify the UN Convention against Corruption (UNCAC), having signed the treaty in 2003. However, in January 2018 the government ratified the Inter-American Convention against Corruption, which it signed in 2001.

Concerns over major alleged irregularities prior to the Mottley administration at eight state-owned enterprises, including the Barbados Water Authority (BWA), surfaced in June 2020.

In Transparency International's Global Corruption Barometer published in September 2019, perceived corruption in Barbados was the lowest in the Americas, with 55 percent of respondents believing that the Mottley administration is doing a good job in fighting corruption.

C3. Does the government operate with openness and transparency? 3 / 4

Academic experts praised the BLP government's transparency during the COVID-19 pandemic, including the use of regular press briefings. However, Barbados lacks key laws to ensure this openness persists, notably, a long-promised Freedom of Information Act. A long-promised Integrity in Public Life Bill—which would require politicians and senior officials to declare their personal wealth and would create a new Integrity Commission—was passed by the House of Assembly in July 2020 but failed to pass the Senate in August. Information on the country's national budget is difficult to obtain.

The Mottley administration passed a Public Finance Management Act, involving greater oversight of state-owned enterprises, in 2019, and an ongoing Public Sector Modernisation Project aims to improve citizens' access to public spending information.

In October 2020, the European Council added Barbados to a list of noncooperative jurisdictions for tax purposes, reflecting a "partially compliant" rating given to the country by the Organisation for Economic Co-operation and Development in April 2020.

CIVIL LIBERTIES: 57 / 60
D. FREEDOM OF EXPRESSION AND BELIEF: 16 / 16
D1. Are there free and independent media? 4 / 4

The media are free from censorship and government control. Newspapers, including the two major dailies, are privately owned. Four private and two government-run radio stations operate in the country. The government-owned Caribbean Broadcasting Corporation (CBC) is the only local television station and is broadly balanced.

D2. Are individuals free to practice and express their religious faith or nonbelief in public and private? 4 / 4

The constitution guarantees freedom of religion, which is widely respected for mainstream religious groups. However, members of Barbados's small Rastafarian and Muslim communities have reported some discrimination.

D3. Is there academic freedom, and is the educational system free from extensive political indoctrination? 4 / 4

Academic freedom is respected, though members of the government occasionally disparage academics who criticize government policy.

D4. Are individuals free to express their personal views on political or other sensitive topics without fear of surveillance or retribution? 4 / 4

Freedom of speech is largely respected in Barbados, with commentators and members of the public free to express their views on most topics without encountering negative consequences.

E. ASSOCIATIONAL AND ORGANIZATIONAL RIGHTS: 12 / 12
E1. Is there freedom of assembly? 4 / 4

Barbados's legal framework guarantees freedom of assembly, which is upheld in practice. Several protests took place peacefully in 2020, including Black Lives Matter demonstrations in June.

E2. Is there freedom for nongovernmental organizations, particularly those that are engaged in human rights- and governance-related work? 4 / 4

Nongovernmental organizations (NGOs) operate without restriction or surveillance. There are many NGOs active in the country, which primarily focus on cultural issues, homelessness, environmentalism, and women's rights.

E3. Is there freedom for trade unions and similar professional or labor organizations? 4 / 4

The right to form labor unions is respected, and unions are active and politically influential. In February 2020, construction workers staged a successful strike for wage increases. In May, healthcare workers, organized by the National Union of Public Workers (NUPW), staged a brief walkout over the government's failure to distribute sanitary and personal protective equipment, among other issues, during the COVID-19 crisis. After meeting with Prime Minister Mottley, they returned to work.

F. RULE OF LAW: 14 / 16

F1. Is there an independent judiciary? 4 / 4

The judiciary generally operates with independence. The Supreme Court includes a high court and a court of appeals. The Caribbean Court of Justice is the highest appellate court for Barbados.

F2. Does due process prevail in civil and criminal matters? 4 / 4

Constitutional guarantees of due process are generally upheld. In January 2020, the government appointed two more judges (making a total of five), and plans to appoint more prosecutors, to address the large backlog of nearly 1,000 cases it inherited from the previous administration in 2018. However, progress remains slow.

In 2017, the judiciary adopted a protocol to prevent gender discrimination in the administration of justice. The protocol, drafted with UN support, was the first of its kind in the Caribbean Community (CARICOM).

F3. Is there protection from the illegitimate use of physical force and freedom from war and insurgencies? 3 / 4

Barbados is free from war and insurgencies. However, complaints that the Royal Barbados Police Force physically abuses suspects to coerce individuals to provide information have been reported in recent years. In March 2020, charges against murder suspect Roger Sealy were dismissed after evidence showed that police had abused Sealy to gain information from him.

The number of homicides has risen steadily in recent years, although the figure for 2020 (39) was somewhat below 2019 levels (49).

The government has taken some positive steps to address prison overcrowding and abuse. Legal changes in April 2019 complied with a June 2018 ruling by the Caribbean Court of Justice that the mandatory death penalty in Barbados for those convicted of murder was unconstitutional. However, by April 2020, several prisoners on death row were still awaiting resentencing and more than 70 prisoners were waiting to be tried for murder. The death penalty remains on the statute book, though the last execution was carried out in 1984 and the last sentence was given in 2016.

F4. Do laws, policies, and practices guarantee equal treatment of various segments of the population? 3 / 4

Women make up half of the country's workforce, although they earn less than men for comparable work. As of 2017, workplaces have been required to articulate a policy against sexual harassment. LGBT+ people face discrimination in housing, employment, and health care, and reported verbal harassment from the authorities when seeking assistance during the pandemic.

In February 2020, a transgender activist filed a lawsuit with the Employment Rights Tribunal (ERT), the first of its kind, alleging that her employer had fired her for changing her name to reflect her gender identity.

G. PERSONAL AUTONOMY AND INDIVIDUAL RIGHTS: 15 / 16

G1. Do individuals enjoy freedom of movement, including the ability to change their place of residence, employment, or education? 4 / 4

Individuals in Barbados are generally free to move, live, and work across the territory as they see fit.

G2. Are individuals able to exercise the right to own property and establish private businesses without undue interference from state or nonstate actors? 4 / 4

The legal framework generally supports property rights and private-business activity. The government has worked to ensure a healthy environment for business and to attract domestic and foreign investment, particularly in the tourism industry.

G3. Do individuals enjoy personal social freedoms, including choice of marriage partner and size of family, protection from domestic violence, and control over appearance? 3 / 4

Violence against women remains widespread, and laws addressing domestic violence are not well enforced. Reports of child abuse have increased in recent years, according to the US State Department. In September 2020, the Mottley administration said it would put same-sex civil unions to a referendum. Same-sex relations remain punishable with jail sentences, though the law is not enforced.

G4. Do individuals enjoy equality of opportunity and freedom from economic exploitation? 4 / 4

Residents generally have access to economic opportunity, and the law provides some protections against exploitative labor practices. However, prior to the COVID-19 pandemic nearly 18 percent of the population lived in poverty. Some estimates suggest the unemployment rate rose to over 50 percent by the end of 2020, largely reflecting the impact of the pandemic.

The government has taken steps to crack down on human trafficking, including police raids, screening of vulnerable people, training officials to detect possible trafficking victims, and awareness campaigns. However, partly reflecting a lack of resources and government inattention, there have been no prosecutions for trafficking since 2013 and no trafficking convictions to date.

Belarus

Population: 9,400,000
Capital: Minsk
Freedom Status: Not Free
Electoral Democracy: No

Overview: Belarus is an authoritarian state in which elections are openly rigged and civil liberties are severely restricted. After permitting limited displays of dissent as part of a drive to pursue better relations with the European Union (EU) and the United States, the government in 2020 cracked down on a massive antigovernment protest movement, sparked by a fraudulent presidential election, and severely limited fundamental civil liberties.

KEY DEVELOPMENTS IN 2020

- The government claimed that the incumbent president Alyaksandr Lukashenka won the August presidential election with 80 percent of the vote, though the results were widely denounced as fraudulent. The campaign and election period featured an unfair candidate registration process, the detention of candidates, widespread internet disruptions on election day, and the violent crackdown on peaceful protesters demanding their right to a fair vote.
- A prodemocracy movement led largely by presidential candidates and opposition movement leaders Sviatlana Tsikhanouskaya and Veronika Tsepkalo emerged in the run-up to the election and grew massively in numbers after the fraudulent poll. Armed riot police and plainclothes officers used disproportionate, sometimes deadly force to break up the mass demonstrations, and detained over 32,000 people. Reports of beatings, torture, and other human rights abuses of people in detention have since emerged, and security forces beat, arrested, fined, and in some cases shot Belarusian and foreign journalists covering events.
- After the election, authorities imprisoned the founders of a would-be new party and prosecuted the members of the opposition Coordination Council, which united a broad spectrum of civic and political leaders calling for dialogue and peaceful negotiations with the government to resolve the post-election crisis. By the fall, scores of activists and opposition leaders, including Tsikhanouskaya and Tsepkalo, were expelled or had fled the country.
- As the COVID-19 pandemic spread across the country, President Alyaksandr Lukashenka dismissed concerns about the virus as "psychosis" and refused to implement mitigation measures.

POLITICAL RIGHTS: 2 / 40 (−3)

A. ELECTORAL PROCESS: 0 / 12

A1. Was the current head of government or other chief national authority elected through free and fair elections? 0 / 4

The president is elected for five-year terms, and there are no term limits. President Alyaksandr Lukashenka was first elected in 1994, in the country's only democratic election. The 2020 campaign period was heavily controlled by authorities, who permitted only 15 of 55 applicants to register as candidates. The government arrested two major candidates, Siarhei Tsikhanouski and Viktar Babaryka, and forced another candidate, Valery Tsepkalo, to flee the country before voting day. Scores of activists were similarly arrested or fled the country. Sviatlana Tsikhanouskaya and Veronika Tsepkalo, who led the largest opposition rallies in the country since the fall of the Soviet Union, both became popular candidates after their husbands were arrested and forced to flee. They experienced severe pressure from authorities and eventually went into exile after the election. Authorities failed to send an invitation to the Organization for Security and Co-operation in Europe (OSCE) on time, and the elections took place without an independent monitoring mission.

The government claimed that Lukashenka won the poll with 80 percent of the vote, though this was widely denounced as fraudulent. A parallel vote count using the mobile application "Golos," with data from just under 23 percent of polling stations, revealed that Tsikhanouskaya likely received 13 times more votes than were reported. Protests after the announcement of the results were met with disproportionate police force, including the use of live ammunition, and mass, arbitrary detentions, among other abuses. Documentation by human rights organizations showed that by the end of the year, 169 people were being held as political prisoners and the government had opened more than 900 criminal cases, all related to the election period.

In September, amid ongoing massive protests and growing calls for a repeat election, Lukashenka inaugurated himself in a secret, unannounced ceremony. Democratic states worldwide have refused to recognize Lukashenka's legitimacy.

A2. Were the current national legislative representatives elected through free and fair elections? 0 / 4

Legislative elections in Belarus are tightly restricted. The 110 members of the Chamber of Representatives, the lower house of the National Assembly, are elected by popular vote to four-year terms from single-mandate constituencies. The upper chamber, the Council of the Republic, consists of 64 members serving four-year terms: regional councils elect 56 and the president appoints 8.

A parliamentary election was held in November 2019, nearly a year ahead of schedule. Candidates loyal to President Lukashenka won every seat in the lower house, while independent candidates won none. OSCE election monitors reported some ballot boxes were stuffed, and that observers were often prohibited from observing ballot boxes or papers.

A3. Are the electoral laws and framework fair, and are they implemented impartially by the relevant election management bodies? 0 / 4

The legal framework for elections fails to meet democratic standards, and authorities have dismissed OSCE recommendations to improve it. Electoral commission members of all levels are politically aligned with and dependent on the government, and independent observers have no access to ballot-counting processes. Out of the 1,989 members of local electoral commissions formed for the presidential election, authorities allowed only two representatives of independent political parties to register, dismissing thousands of other independent applications.

B. POLITICAL PLURALISM AND PARTICIPATION: 1 / 16 (−2)
B1. Do the people have the right to organize in different political parties or other competitive political groupings of their choice, and is the system free of undue obstacles to the rise and fall of these competing parties or groupings? 0 / 4 (−1)

Involvement in political activism can result in a loss of employment, expulsion from educational institutions, smear campaigns in the media, fines, and the confiscation of property. Political parties face formidable challenges when seeking official registration.

After the 2020 election, an unprecedented grassroots political movement emerged, seeking to resolve the postelection conflict and hold a repeat poll. The regime has deliberately tried to undermine these initiatives. In August, Maryia Kalesnikava, who campaigned with Tsikhanouskaya, and Babaryka, announced the creation of a new political party called "Together." One week later, Kalesnikava was kidnapped and later incarcerated, effectively ending the initiative. That same month, Tsikhanouskaya and other activists, including the winner of the 2015 Nobel Prize in Literature, Sviatlana Aleksiyevich, formed the Coordination Council, a civil society group that sought a peaceful resolution to the postelection violence and a rerun of the presidential poll. The government responded to the group's creation by arresting and prosecuting several of its leaders, claiming that they were attempting to seize power illegally and that they were a national security threat.

Score Change: The score declined from 1 to 0 because the government intensified its efforts to shut independent organizations out of the political process, including by imprisoning the founders of a would-be new party and by prosecuting the members of the opposition Coordination Council.

B2. Is there a realistic opportunity for the opposition to increase its support or gain power through elections? 0 / 4

There is effectively no opportunity for independent candidates to gain power through elections, and Belarus has never experienced a democratic transfer of power. During the 2020 presidential election, vast numbers of Belarusians responded enthusiastically to the participation of opposition candidates. This interest manifested itself at the early stages of campaign and, in spite of regime's attempts to eliminate challengers, developed into a broad civil resistance movement. However, Lukashenka's regime has proven unyielding to the popular demand for political change.

B3. Are the people's political choices free from domination by the military, foreign powers, religious hierarchies, economic oligarchies, or any other powerful group that is not democratically accountable? 0 / 4 (−1)

Private citizens and political candidates are limited in their opportunities to express their views and make political choices. Meaningful participation in politics is generally not possible. The police and military used severe, sometimes fatal violence, and arrested and detained over 32,000 people to crack down on the peaceful prodemocracy protests in August 2020, ensuring that Lukashenka would maintain his power.

Score Change: The score declined from 1 to 0 because the military and police used violence and intimidation to suppress mass protests against the incumbent president's fraudulent reelection and have played a central role in perpetuating his rule.

B4. Do various segments of the population (including ethnic, racial, religious, gender, LGBT+, and other relevant groups) have full political rights and electoral opportunities? 1 / 4

No registered party represents the specific interests of ethnic or religious minority groups. Women formally enjoy equal political rights and make up 40 percent of legislators elected in November 2019. However, women are underrepresented in leadership positions. Women's advocacy groups have diverging positions on promoting the political rights of women, with some such groups taking the position that there is no need for gender equality initiatives in Belarus. There has been some visible activism by women's groups seeking to raise awareness of gender-based violence, but the government has largely refrained from addressing their concerns.

C. FUNCTIONING OF GOVERNMENT: 1 / 12 (−1)

C1. Do the freely elected head of government and national legislative representatives determine the policies of the government? 0 / 4

Though Lukashenka claimed victory in the 2020 presidential elections, the legitimacy of his office is disputed both domestically and internationally. The constitution vests power in the president, stating that presidential decrees have higher legal force than legislation. Lukashenka considers himself the head of all branches of government, including the parliament, which always supports his policies and rarely initiates legislation on its own.

C2. Are safeguards against official corruption strong and effective? 1 / 4

The state controls at least 70 percent of the economy, and graft is encouraged by a lack of transparency and accountability in government. There are no independent bodies to investigate corruption cases, and graft trials are typically closed. Presidential clemency has been issued occasionally to free convicted corrupt officials, some of whom Lukashenka has returned to positions of authority.

C3. Does the government operate with openness and transparency? 0 / 4 (−1)

The government largely fails to adhere to legal requirements providing for access to information. In recent years, authorities have moved to make some basic information about government operations available online. However, the COVID-19 pandemic further revealed the government's inability to provide transparent information to the public. President Lukashenka frequently provided conflicting and misleading information and guidance about the dangers of the coronavirus and ways to reduce its spread. Evidence from the United Nations (UN) suggested that the government's reported COVID-19 case numbers and mortality rate were vastly inaccurate.

Similarly, the regime has deliberately kept silent about important matters, such as talks with Russia about economic and other issues.

Score Change: The score declined from 1 to 0 because the government systematically concealed or provided misleading information about essential matters of public interest, including the COVID-19 pandemic and relations with Russia.

CIVIL LIBERTIES: 9 / 60 (−5)
D. FREEDOM OF EXPRESSION AND BELIEF: 2 / 16
D1. Are there free and independent media? 0 / 4

The government exercises unrestricted control over mainstream media. The 2008 media law secures a state monopoly over information about political, social, and economic affairs. Libel is both a civil and criminal offense, and the criminal code contains provisions protecting the "honor and dignity" of high-ranking officials. The government owns the only internet service provider and controls the internet through legal and technical means. The official definition of mass media includes websites and blogs, placing them under the Information Ministry's supervision. Most independent journalists operate under the assumption that they are under surveillance by the Committee for State Security (KGB). Journalists are subject to fines, detention, and criminal prosecution for their work. The government has used antiextremism legislation to curtail media activity.

In 2020, security forces beat, arrested, fined, and in some cases shot Belarusian and foreign journalists in hundreds of documented cases. Before and especially after the presidential election, authorities systemically disrupted the work of independent domestic and international media, detaining 477 journalists and prosecuting 9 with criminal charges. On voting day and for three days after the presidential election during the height of the mass prodemocracy protests, the government shut down the internet in almost the entire country, limiting the ability of reporters to provide accurate information to the public.

D2. Are individuals free to practice and express their religious faith or nonbelief in public and private? 1 / 4

Despite constitutional guarantees of religious equality, government decrees and registration requirements maintain restrictions on religious activity. Legal amendments in 2002 provided for government censorship of religious publications and barred foreigners from leading religious groups. The amendments also placed strict limitations on religious groups active in Belarus for less than 20 years. In 2003, the government signed a concordat with the Belarusian Orthodox Church, which is controlled by the Russian Orthodox Church, giving it a privileged position.

After the 2020 elections, Lukashenka attempted to weaken the Catholic Church's influence, which had denounced state violence against peaceful prodemocracy protesters. In December, the government denied Tadeusz Kondrusiewicz, a Belarusian citizen and Archbishop of Minsk–Mohilev, reentry to the country. He was allowed to return only after negotiations with the Vatican and intense international pressure.

D3. Is there academic freedom, and is the educational system free from extensive political indoctrination? 0 / 4

Academic freedom remains subject to intense state ideological pressures, and academic personnel face harassment and dismissal if they use a liberal curriculum or are suspected of disloyalty. Students and professors who join opposition protests face threat of dismissal and revocation of degrees.

The government pressures schoolchildren to join the pro-Lukashenka group Belarusian Republican Union of Youth (BRSM). The government has announced plans to tighten control over private schools, which noticed significant rise in demand after the 2020 election; many public school teachers were linked to the falsification of voting results.

Student activity at universities rose sharply in 2020, as many were involved in the August 2020 prodemocracy protests. Authorities responded with unprovoked brutality and repression, as plainclothes security forces attacked peaceful student protests within and outside of University campuses. Lukashenka replaced at least eight deans at different universities.

D4. Are individuals free to express their personal views on political or other sensitive topics without fear of surveillance or retribution? 0 / 4

The use of wiretapping and other surveillance by state security agencies limits the right to free private discussion. Private citizens often avoid discussing sensitive issues over the phone or via internet communication platforms, for fear that state security agents are monitoring conversations.

During and after the 2020 election period and prodemocracy protests, authorities threatened, harassed, and arrested protesters, presidential candidates, professionals in the cultural sphere, academics, theater troupes, athletes, medical professionals, public figures, private individuals, and others who spoke out against Lukashenka and the postelection violence. Police routinely coerced, threatened, and tortured detained individuals, forcing them to open their mobile devices in search of photos, videos, and correspondence that confirmed their participation in the prodemocracy protests. Authorities also monitored social media activity of people who were arrested to find evidence of their participation in the protests and potentially increase the criminal charges they would face. The private company Synesis, which was sanctioned by the European Union (EU), reportedly helped authorities identify and arrest demonstrators by providing video surveillance technology with facial recognition.

E. ASSOCIATIONAL AND ORGANIZATIONAL RIGHTS: 1 / 12 (−2)

E1. Is there freedom of assembly? 0 / 4 (−1)

The government restricts freedom of assembly. Protests require permission from local authorities, who often arbitrarily deny it.

In the summer of 2020, unprecedented prodemocracy protests, demonstrations, and campaign rallies for Tsikhanouskaya occurred across the country—in the form of street chains, marches, and block parties with concerts and performances—assembling hundreds of thousands of people. Police and military forces only partially succeeded in blocking people from congregating before voting day on August 9. But in the weeks that followed, the government deployed military equipment and armed riot police, who attacked and arrested people brutally and indiscriminately, at times opening fire with live ammunition, killing several. More than 32,000 people were arrested and later tried, jailed, or fined. Numerous instances of cruel treatment, beatings, and torture of protesters were recorded, with total impunity for the security forces involved.

Score Change: The score declined from 1 to 0 because security forces employed serious violence, torture, mass arrests, and thousands of arbitrary detentions as part of their crackdown on a large and sustained antigovernment protest movement.

E2. Is there freedom for nongovernmental organizations, particularly those that are engaged in human rights and governance-related work? 1 / 4

Freedom of association is severely restricted. Registration of groups remains selective, and regulations ban foreign assistance to entities and individuals deemed to promote foreign meddling in internal affairs. Few human rights groups continue to operate because of resource shortages and pressure from the authorities, and staff and supporters risk prosecution and fines for their activism. Activists involved in the 2020 prodemocracy movement have been arrested by the thousands, and many more have fled the country.

Participation in unregistered or liquidated organizations, which had been criminalized in 2005, was decriminalized in 2018. Instead, the Criminal Code introduced the prospect of large fines, which obscures civil liberties infringements from the eyes of human rights watchdogs and democratic governments.

E3. Is there freedom for trade unions and similar professional or labor organizations? 0 / 4 (−1)

Independent labor unions face harassment, and their leaders are frequently fired and prosecuted for engaging in peaceful protests. No independent unions have been registered since 1999, when Lukashenka issued a decree setting extremely restrictive registration requirements.

Independent unions were prominent in the prodemocracy movement in the summer of 2020, striking to protest the fraudulent presidential election and police violence toward peaceful demonstrators. The state increasingly targeted and pressured workers to prevent them from going on strike. Union leaders and rank-and-file members were arrested, fined, dismissed from their posts, sent to psychiatric institutions, and forced into exile.

Score Change: The score declined from 1 to 0 because union leaders and rank-and-file members faced fines, dismissal, and detention for striking or threatening to strike as part of the postelection protest movement.

F. RULE OF LAW: 1 / 16 (−1)

F1. Is there an independent judiciary? 0 / 4

Courts are entirely subservient to President Lukashenka, who appoints Supreme Court justices with the approval of the rubber-stamp parliament.

F2. Does due process prevail in civil and criminal matters? 0 / 4 (−1)

The right to a fair trial is not respected and often flatly dismissed in cases with political overtones. In a departure from international norms, the power to extend pretrial detention lies with a prosecutor rather than a judge. The absence of independent oversight allows police to routinely and massively violate legal procedures. The government regularly attacks attorneys, who often are the only connection between imprisoned activists and their families and society.

During and after the presidential campaign of 2020, arbitrary arrests, police brutality and torture, and the denial of due process rights continued with impunity. Lawyers were often denied the right to meet with their defendants. Several lawyers defending political prisoners from the prodemocracy protests were disbarred or arrested.

Score Change: The score declined from 1 to 0 because the authorities systematically denied basic due process rights to detainees during election-related crackdowns, with even the lawyers for some detained protesters facing arrest and disbarment.

F3. Is there protection from the illegitimate use of physical force and freedom from war and insurgencies? 0 / 4

Law enforcement agencies have broad powers to employ physical force against suspects, who have little opportunity for recourse if they are abused. Human rights groups continue to document instances of beatings, torture, and intimidation during detention. During and after the presidential election period, detained peaceful prodemocracy protesters experienced cruel and dehumanizing treatment during their arrests, while being transported to detention centers, and when incarcerated.

F4. Do laws, policies, and practices guarantee equal treatment of various segments of the population? 1 / 4

Authorities have sought to increase the dominance of the Russian language. Official Usage of Belarusian remains rare. The UN Educational, Scientific, and Cultural Organization (UNESCO) recognizes Belarusian as "vulnerable." Since Lukashenka became president, the share of first graders who study in Belarusian fell from 40 to under 10 percent in 2019.

Women are prohibited from entering 181 different occupations, and societal norms in much of the country hold that women should be mothers or housewives. However, Tsikhanouskaya's mass support in the prodemocracy movement has become a slight counter to long-standing gender roles.

LGBT+ people face widespread societal discrimination, and law enforcement authorities are reluctant to investigate and prosecute attacks against them.

G. PERSONAL AUTONOMY AND INDIVIDUAL RIGHTS: 5 / 16 (−2)

G1. Do individuals enjoy freedom of movement, including the ability to change their place of residence, employment, or education? 1 / 4 (−1)

Opposition activists are occasionally detained at the border for lengthy searches. Passports are used as a primary identity document in Belarus, and authorities are known to harass people living in a different location than indicated by domestic stamps in their passport.

On numerous occasions, authorities forced the expulsion of politically active Belarusians in 2020. Prominent prodemocracy figure Tsikhanouskaya, Archbishop of the Belarusian Catholic Church Kondrusiewicz, and other public figures were forced to leave the country in August. Maryia Kalesnikava, who campaigned with Tsikhanouskaya, refused to leave Belarus and was later kidnapped and had her passport torn apart. In September, she was arrested and tried in a criminal case for threatening national security. In December 2020, authorities prohibited Belarusians from leaving the country at land border crossings, except with Russia, ostensibly to prevent the spread of COVID-19; the policy was likely enforced to prevent political dissidents from fleeing.

Score Change: The score declined from 2 to 1 because numerous civic and opposition activists and their supporters fled or were forced out of the country, and border officials imposed restrictions on their reentry.

G2. Are individuals able to exercise the right to own property and establish private businesses without undue interference from state or nonstate actors? 1 / 4 (−1)

Limits on economic freedom have eased in recent years, allowing for greater property ownership and small business operations. However, state interference still affects the economy and profitable business owners are never secure from arbitrary government pressure and harassment. Many businesspeople that became involved in the postelection prodemocracy efforts, often to support victims of human rights abuses or to incentivize policemen to resign from law enforcement, were criminally prosecuted on groundless claims. Other businesses and their owners who supported candidates other than Lukashenka have been arrested under false pretense. Multiple businesses relocated their employees to neighboring countries fearing that they would be harassed or prosecuted by the state.

Score Change: The score declined from 2 to 1 because authorities interfered with businesses and arrested owners in their efforts to put down the year's prodemocracy protest movement.

G3. Do individuals enjoy personal social freedoms, including choice of marriage partner and size of family, protection from domestic violence, and control over appearance? 2 / 4

Domestic violence is a pervasive problem in Belarus, and police register about 150,000 incidents per year. In 2018, Lukashenka blocked a draft law on the prevention of domestic violence jointly developed by the law enforcement agencies and civil society representatives. He called attitudes against the corporal punishment of children "nonsense from the West" and insisted that "good" punishment of children could be useful to them.

The constitution explicitly bans same-sex marriage. The Belarusian government led an effort in 2016 to block LGBT+ rights from being part of a UN international initiative focused on urban areas.

G4. Do individuals enjoy equality of opportunity and freedom from economic exploitation? 1 / 4

Mandatory unpaid national workdays, postgraduate employment allocation, compulsory labor for inmates in state rehabilitation facilities, and restrictions on leaving employment in certain industries have led labor activists to conclude that all Belarusian citizens experience forced labor at some stage of their life. Many women become victims of the international sex trade.

In 2018, based on a presidential decree, the government effectively revived a plan to tax the unemployed by mandating full payment for housing and utility services starting in 2019. An attempt to impose the tax in 2017 was met with mass protests that were brutally suppressed.

Belgium

Population: 11,500,000
Capital: Brussels
Freedom Status: Free
Electoral Democracy: Yes

Overview: Belgium is a stable electoral democracy with a long record of peaceful transfers of power. Political rights and civil liberties are legally guaranteed and largely respected. Major concerns in recent years have included the threat of terrorism, corruption scandals, and rising right-wing nationalism and xenophobia.

KEY DEVELOPMENTS IN 2020

- A political deadlock in place since the May 2019 elections lasted until September 2020, when an unstable seven-party governing coalition under the leadership of Prime Minister Alexander De Croo was formed by the Flemish-speaking and francophone wings of the Liberal, Social Democrat, and Green parties, along with the Flemish Christian Democrats.
- Belgium suffered one of the highest death rates in Europe during the COVID-19 pandemic, with insufficient protection in nursing homes leading to numerous deaths and garnering national and international criticism. The new government responded to a severe second wave in autumn by imposing stringent restrictions that rapidly reduced cases. According to researchers at the University of Oxford, the country registered nearly 650,000 cases and 20,000 deaths by year's end.

POLITICAL RIGHTS: 39 / 40

A. ELECTORAL PROCESS: 12 / 12

A1. Was the current head of government or other chief national authority elected through free and fair elections? 4 / 4

The Belgian monarchy is largely ceremonial, although the king retains constitutional authority to mediate the process of government formation. He was particularly active in this role in 2020 as negotiations over a new government stalled. The prime minister, who is the leader of the majority party or coalition, is appointed by the monarch and approved by the legislature. In October 2019, Sophie Wilmès was appointed prime minister of the caretaker, interim government while governing coalition talks continued. In late September 2020, seven parties forged a parliamentary majority under the leadership of Flemish Liberal Alexander De Croo, who was sworn in as prime minister in October.

Belgium's multilayered subnational administrative units have their own governments with varying degrees of autonomy. In addition to the three main geographic divisions of French-speaking Wallonia in the south, Flemish-speaking Flanders in the north, and the bilingual Brussels capital region, there are overlapping governments for the French community, the Flemish community, and the much smaller German-speaking community. Beneath these are provincial and various local governments. In late 2019, the German-speaking community launched a system of participatory democracy in which citizens are selected by lot to join a Citizens' Council, which provides input on policy matters and features a mechanism to monitor the regional parliament's response.

A2. Were the current national legislative representatives elected through free and fair elections? 4 / 4

Belgium's federal parliament consists of two houses: the Chamber of Representatives and the Senate. The 150 members of the lower house (the Chamber) are elected directly by proportional representation. The Senate is composed of 50 members selected by community and regional parliaments, and an additional 10 members chosen by the first 50 based on the results of the Chamber of Representatives elections. Members serve five-year terms in both houses, and elections are generally free and fair.

In the May 2019 elections, establishment parties lost significant shares of support to parties on the far left and far right of the political spectrum. The right-wing, nationalist New Flemish Alliance (N-VA), lost some power, taking 25 seats in the Chamber of Representatives (down 8 seats), but the far-right, separatist Flemish Interest (VB) party won 18 seats, a gain of 15. The francophone Socialist Party (PS) won 20 seats, down 3 from the previous election. The Greens, composed of the francophone Ecolo (in Wallonia and Brussels) and their Flemish-speaking counterpart Groen (in Flanders and Brussels) won 21 seats, a significant increase. The francophone Liberals (MR) of incumbent prime minister Charles Michel won 14 seats, while the Christian Democratic party (CD&V), the Workers' Party of Belgium (PvdA in Flemish, PTB in French) and the Flemish Liberals (VLD) took 12 seats each. It took until September 2020 to form a new government, a delay that is not historically unusual for Belgium.

Regional elections held concurrently in May 2019 showed a similar trend, with losses by establishment parties in all parts of the country. However, the N-VA remained the biggest party in Flanders and was able to form a government in coalition with the CD&V and the VLD that October. The PS remained the biggest party in Wallonia and formed a new coalition government with Ecolo and MR in September. In Brussels, a coalition was formed between PS and Socialist Party Differently (SP.A), Ecolo and Groen, the liberal VLD, and the francophone party DéFI.

A3. Are the electoral laws and framework fair, and are they implemented impartially by the relevant election management bodies? 4 / 4

Despite the complexity of the political system, the electoral laws and framework are generally fair and impartially implemented.

B. POLITICAL PLURALISM AND PARTICIPATION: 16 / 16

B1. Do the people have the right to organize in different political parties or other competitive political groupings of their choice, and is the system free of undue obstacles to the rise and fall of these competing parties or groupings? 4 / 4

The party system is robust but highly fragmented, with separate Flemish and Francophone political parties representing various positions on the left-right spectrum.

B2. Is there a realistic opportunity for the opposition to increase its support or gain power through elections? 4 / 4

Belgium's coalition-based politics allow individual parties to move easily in and out of government, and there is a long record of peaceful transfers of power between rival parties at the federal level. However, the 2019 regional and federal elections showed decreasing support for establishment parties and increasing support for far-right, far-left, and green parties across the country. The increasing power of the Flemish right-wing N-VA and the far-right VB makes coalitional majorities that exclude these nationalist parties increasingly difficult to assemble. The N-VA and VB, in turn, criticized the formation of a government lacking the participation of the biggest parties in one of the two main regions, with several thousand participants mounting a protest near Brussels in September.

B3. Are the people's political choices free from domination by forces that are external to the political sphere, or by political forces that employ extrapolitical means? 4 / 4

The political choices of voters and candidates are generally free from undue interference.

B4. Do various segments of the population (including ethnic, racial, religious, gender, LGBT+, and other relevant groups) have full political rights and electoral opportunities? 4 / 4

Members of racial, ethnic, religious, and other minority groups are free to participate in national and subnational politics, and women also enjoy full political rights. In the 2019 elections, women were elected to 65 seats out of 150 in the Chamber of Representatives; this 43 percent share represented a rise of 4 percentage points from the 2014 elections. The Senate must have a minimum of 20 women senators.

In general, the larger parties incorporate members of minority groups, including in senior positions. In 2019, Belgians elected Petra de Sutter, an openly transgender member of the Green party, as a member of the European Parliament; in 2020 de Sutter also became deputy prime minister in the new government.

C. FUNCTIONING OF GOVERNMENT: 11 / 12

C1. Do the freely elected head of government and national legislative representatives determine the policies of the government? 4 / 4

Elected officials generally adopt and implement laws and policies without improper interference from unelected entities, though the difficulty of forming majority coalitions has sometimes disrupted governance over the past decade.

C2. Are safeguards against official corruption strong and effective? 3 / 4

Public officials can face heavy fines and up to 10 years' imprisonment for corruption-related offenses, and enforcement of anticorruption legislation is generally adequate. However, recent corruption scandals have drawn attention to abuses involving politicians who hold multiple positions on the boards of public and private entities, with some officials holding more than a dozen paid positions. The Group of States against Corruption (Greco), a Council of Europe anticorruption body, has repeatedly warned about Belgium's lethargic implementation of recommended anticorruption reforms.

C3. Does the government operate with openness and transparency? 4 / 4

The law provides mechanisms for the public to access government information, and these procedures generally function in practice. Legislators and other high-ranking elected officials are required by law to regularly disclose their assets as well as paid or unpaid mandates, executive functions, and occupations to the Court of Audit. Information about asset declarations is not publicly accessible, but declarations of interests are published in the official government gazette.

CIVIL LIBERTIES: 57 / 60

D. FREEDOM OF EXPRESSION AND BELIEF: 15 / 16

D1. Are there free and independent media? 4 / 4

Freedom of the press is guaranteed by the constitution and generally respected by the government, though some law enforcement actions affecting journalists have raised concerns in recent years. Belgians have access to numerous public and private media outlets that present a range of views. Internet access is unrestricted. Although online harassment cases remain rare, journalist Florence Hainaut was the victim of sustained digital harassment in July 2020 after writing an opinion piece criticizing bans on Islamic headscarves. A draft law introduced in 2019 received criticism for threatening whistleblowers and journalists with criminal penalties for revealing classified information; the government pledged revisions to the bill, which remained pending throughout 2020.

D2. Are individuals free to practice and express their religious faith or nonbelief in public and private? 3 / 4

More than half of the country's population identifies as Roman Catholic. Freedom of religion is generally protected, but members of minority religious groups have complained of discrimination and harassment. A ban on the partial or total covering of the face in public locations, which is understood to target Muslims, has been in effect since 2011. The 2020 US Department of State *Report on International Religious Freedom* noted that anti-Muslim and antisemitic incidents continue to affect the Jewish and Muslim communities. The rise of nationalist and far-right parties in Flanders has contributed to the normalization of anti-Muslim rhetoric in some political discourse. In June 2020, the Constitutional Court received criticism following a ruling that higher education institutions are allowed to ban headscarves and other religious symbols.

In December 2019, the town of Aalst renounced the United Nations Educational, Scientific, and Cultural Organization (UNESCO) designation associated with its Carnival, after a long dispute over a racially insensitive float in the Carnival parade. Town officials claim the float—featuring stereotypical depictions of a Jew with a hooked nose, sitting on piles of money—is meant to be humorous, while UNESCO, Jewish groups, and the European Union (EU) have condemned its antisemitic message, reminiscent of 1930s Nazi propaganda. In 2020, the Carnival again featured grotesque caricatures of Jews.

D3. Is there academic freedom, and is the educational system free from extensive political indoctrination? 4 / 4

The government does not restrict academic freedom. Schools are free from political indoctrination, and there are no significant impediments to scholarly research or discussion.

D4. Are individuals free to express their personal views on political or other sensitive topics without fear of surveillance or retribution? 4 / 4

Private discussion is open and vibrant, and freedom of expression is guaranteed by the constitution, though there are laws banning incitement to hatred and other such offenses, which occasionally lead to prosecutions, fines, and jail terms.

E. ASSOCIATIONAL AND ORGANIZATIONAL RIGHTS: 12 / 12
E1. Is there freedom of assembly? 4 / 4

Freedom of assembly is protected by law and generally respected in practice.

E2. Is there freedom for nongovernmental organizations, particularly those that are engaged in human rights– and governance-related work? 4 / 4

Freedom of association is guaranteed by the constitution, and nongovernmental organizations operate without undue restrictions.

E3. Is there freedom for trade unions and similar professional or labor organizations? 4 / 4

Workers at companies that employ more than 50 people have the right to organize and join unions and to bargain collectively. Employers found guilty of firing workers because of union activities are required to reinstate the workers or pay an indemnity.

F. RULE OF LAW: 15 / 16
F1. Is there an independent judiciary? 4 / 4

The judiciary is independent by law and in practice, and court rulings are duly enforced by other state entities.

F2. Does due process prevail in civil and criminal matters? 4 / 4

The judicial process generally guarantees a fair trial, and the authorities typically observe safeguards against arbitrary arrest and detention. Extraordinary security measures adopted in the period surrounding terrorist attacks in 2015 and 2016 have eased significantly in the years since, though a 2017 legal change increased the maximum length of detention in police custody without a judicial order from 24 to 48 hours.

F3. Is there protection from the illegitimate use of physical force and freedom from war and insurgencies? 4 / 4

Although conditions in prisons and detention centers meet most international standards, the facilities continue to suffer from overcrowding and other problematic living conditions.

F4. Do laws, policies, and practices guarantee equal treatment of various segments of the population? 3 / 4

Antidiscrimination legislation prohibits bias and acts of hatred and incitement based on categories including gender, race, ethnicity, nationality, and sexual orientation. Nevertheless, some groups, including immigrants, Belgians of African descent, and Romany residents, continue to face a degree of discrimination in practice.

In February 2019, UN experts stated that racial discrimination is institutionally endemic in Belgium and called for recognition of the country's history of human rights abuses during its colonial rule over what is now the Democratic Republic of the Congo. Following debates prompted by the Black Lives Matter protests in the spring of 2020, King Philippe expressed regrets over Belgian colonial rule. Although politicians have gradually become aware of the need for critical discussion about the country's past, the rising influence of hard-right, nationalist parties in Flanders has been accompanied by racism and xenophobia.

In April 2020, the death of a young adult of Moroccan descent after a police chase in Brussels resulted in brief riots and prompted discussion of police discrimination against Belgians with racial or ethnic minority backgrounds who reside in areas of high poverty. The Interfederal Centre for Equal Opportunities (UNIA), which acts as the state antidiscrimination agency, has received hundreds of complaints of police mistreatment and abuse of migrants and members of ethnic and racial minority groups in recent years. The agency logged a nearly 50 percent increase in discrimination complaints in 2020.

G. PERSONAL AUTONOMY AND INDIVIDUAL RIGHTS: 15 / 16

G1. Do individuals enjoy freedom of movement, including the ability to change their place of residence, employment, or education? 4 / 4

The law provides for freedom of domestic movement and foreign travel, and the government upholds these rights in practice. There are no restrictions on the right to change one's place of residence, employment, or education.

G2. Are individuals able to exercise the right to own property and establish private businesses without undue interference from state or nonstate actors? 4 / 4

The legal framework supports property rights, and commercial activity is regulated without arbitrary interference.

G3. Do individuals enjoy personal social freedoms, including choice of marriage partner and size of family, protection from domestic violence, and control over appearance? 4 / 4

There are few significant restrictions on personal social freedoms. Belgium legalized same-sex marriage in 2003, and in 2006 same-sex couples gained the right to adopt children.

G4. Do individuals enjoy equality of opportunity and freedom from economic exploitation? 3 / 4

Immigration has increased in recent years, but non-EU immigrants and their native-born children remain poorly integrated into the labor market.

Despite government efforts to combat the problem, Belgium remains a destination country for human trafficking, particularly for sexual exploitation and domestic labor; victims generally originate in Eastern Europe, Asia, and Africa.

Belize

Population: 400,000
Capital: Belmopan
Freedom Status: Free
Electoral Democracy: Yes

Overview: Belize is a democracy that has experienced regular rotations of power through competitive elections. Civil liberties are mostly respected. Government corruption is a concern, as is the high rate of violent crime. Authorities have been slow to address persistent problems of police brutality and human trafficking within the country's borders.

KEY DEVELOPMENTS IN 2020

- Belize was seriously affected in 2020 by both the COVID-19 pandemic and a sharp economic contraction that accompanied it. By year's end, the country had registered over 10,000 COVID-19 cases and over 240 deaths, according to researchers at the University of Oxford.
- A series of high-profile cases of misuse of public funds and corruption made headlines during the year, with several prominent scandals and court rulings involving the ruling United Democratic Party (UDP).
- In general elections held in November, the opposition People's United Party (PUP), under the leadership of Johnny Briceño, won an overwhelming 26 of parliament's 31 seats, garnering nearly 60 percent of the vote.

POLITICAL RIGHTS: 34 / 40 (−1)

A. ELECTORAL PROCESS: 12 / 12

A1. Was the current head of government or other chief national authority elected through free and fair elections? 4 / 4

The prime minister, usually the leader of the largest party in the parliament, is head of government. Formally, the prime minister is appointed by the governor general, who represents the British monarch as head of state. The legitimacy of the prime minister is largely dependent on the conduct of legislative elections, which are typically credible and well administered. After 17 years in opposition, the PUP, under the leadership of Johnny Briceño, won a convincing victory in the November 2020 elections.

A2. Were the current national legislative representatives elected through free and fair elections? 4 / 4

The 31 members of the House of Representatives are directly elected to five-year terms. The Senate has 12 seats. The ruling party, the opposition, and several civil associations select the senators, who are then appointed by the governor general.

In the 2020 legislative polls, the opposition PUP won a landslide victory, taking 26 of the 31 seats. Turnout was over 81 percent, the highest since 1998. Observers from the Caribbean Community (CARICOM) commended "the smooth and timely opening of the polls; the seamless voting process, and the efficient closing of the polls and tallying of votes." The observers also noted that "there were no incidents of intimidation of voters inside or outside of the polling stations," and that the COVID-19 safe-voting protocols were effective, even as the country dealt with widespread damage inflicted by Tropical Storm Eta.

A3. Are the electoral laws and framework fair, and are they implemented impartially by the relevant election management bodies? 4 / 4

Electoral laws are generally fair. The Organization of American States (OAS) has suggested that the role of the Elections and Boundaries Commission and the Elections and Boundaries Department be strengthened, and that authorities work to reduce partisanship associated with the confirmation of their appointees. In 2019 opposition parties and civil society groups brought a case to force a revision of Belize's highly malapportioned constituencies, but an opposition-party request for an injunction stopping the 2020 elections pending resolution of the redistricting issue was denied in October 2020.

B. POLITICAL PLURALISM AND PARTICIPATION: 14 / 16

B1. Do the people have the right to organize in different political parties or other competitive political groupings of their choice, and is the system free of undue obstacles to the rise and fall of these competing parties or groupings? 4 / 4

Political parties can organize freely. The effects of the country's "first-past-the-post" electoral system have entrenched the two largest parties. While a number of smaller parties have competed, only the PUP and UDP have won seats in the parliament.

B2. Is there a realistic opportunity for the opposition to increase its support or gain power through elections? 4 / 4

The political system allows for opposition parties to increase their support or gain power through elections. Since 1984 there have been fairly regular transfers of power between the two main parties.

B3. Are the people's political choices free from domination by forces that are external to the political sphere, or by political forces that employ extrapolitical means? 4 / 4

Recent elections, including those in 2020, have been viewed as generally free of undue interference from entities outside the democratic political sphere. However, the OAS has raised concerns about the potential impact of unregulated campaign financing on the transparency of the political process.

B4. Do various segments of the population (including ethnic, racial, religious, gender, LGBT+, and other relevant groups) have full political rights and electoral opportunities? 2 / 4

Women are reasonably well represented in the political system, holding four seats in the current House of Representatives and five seats in the Senate. There were 13 women candidates out of a total of 88 in the 2020 elections. In municipal elections held in March 2018, women won 18 of the 67 seats, though no mayorships.

Indigenous people, particularly those of Mayan descent, are not well represented in politics. Mestizo Belizeans and Afro-Indigenous peoples are better integrated into the political system. LGBT+ people face discrimination, and this affects their ability to engage fully in political and electoral processes. A collection of religious denominations nominate one member of the Senate, but non-Christian groups are not included in the process.

C. FUNCTIONING OF GOVERNMENT: 8 / 12 (−1)
C1. Do the freely elected head of government and national legislative representatives determine the policies of the government? 4 / 4

The elected prime minister, cabinet, and national legislative representatives are duly seated following elections and are able to freely determine the policies of the government.

C2. Are safeguards against official corruption strong and effective? 2 / 4

Belize continues to struggle with corruption, and there is little political will to address the problem. Anticorruption laws are poorly enforced; for example, no one has ever been prosecuted under the Prevention of Corruption in Public Life Act, which has been on the books for over 20 years.

Several high-profile cases of corruption and fraud in 2020 were connected to the UDP. John Saldivar resigned as leader-elect of the party in February after allegations that he had received payments from a US businessman accused of fraud. Another case involved businessman Nestor Vasquez, the owner of television station Channel 7 and a prominent UDP member, who resigned in September from the boards of several national agencies after being accused of charging personal expenditures to the state-owned Belize Telemedia Limited. In July, a Belizean businessman was found liable in a United States court and ordered to pay $120 million in connection with a massive real estate scam; in 2019 a US Federal Trade Commission (FTC) filing had highlighted government officials' ties to the scheme.

C3. Does the government operate with openness and transparency? 2 / 4 (−1)

The government generally engages in policymaking with openness and transparency. However, a Supreme Court ruling in January 2020 that the UDP government improperly spent $645 million highlighted the sidelining of the legislature on budgetary and finance matters. The court stated that the spending violated both the constitution and the Finance and Audit Reform Act. There are also persistent problems with procurement processes and officials' financial disclosure statements. While the law requires public officials to submit annual financial disclosure statements for review by the Integrity Commission, the body was defunct for years until members were finally appointed in 2017, and its resources remain limited. There is little chance for the public to challenge disclosures.

Members of Belize's business community allege that favoritism influences the government's awarding of licenses and public contracts. The International Monetary Fund (IMF) in its 2019 mission report recommended that authorities implement and enforce asset declaration rules and strengthen the rules on conflicts of interest.

Score Change: The score declined from 3 to 2 due to a Supreme Court ruling that the government had engaged in $645 million dollars' worth of spending without having secured parliamentary approval, in violation of the constitution and statutory law.

CIVIL LIBERTIES: 53 / 60 (+2)
D. FREEDOM OF EXPRESSION AND BELIEF: 16 / 16 (+1)
D1. Are there free and independent media? 4 / 4 (+1)

The constitution guarantees freedom of the press, though it includes exceptions for interests such as national security, public order, and morality. While reporting generally covers a wide range of viewpoints in practice, journalists sometimes face threats, physical harassment, or assault in the course of their work.

Score Change: The score improved from 3 to 4 because have been no significant constraints on independent media in recent years.

D2. Are individuals free to practice and express their religious faith or nonbelief in public and private? 4 / 4

Religious freedom is constitutionally protected and largely respected in practice. Religious groups must register with the authorities, and foreign missionaries are required to obtain a visa and permit, but the procedures are not onerous.

D3. Is there academic freedom, and is the educational system free from extensive political indoctrination? 4 / 4

Academic freedom is generally respected.

D4. Are individuals free to express their personal views on political or other sensitive topics without fear of surveillance or retribution? 4 / 4

There are no significant constraints on individual expression regarding politics or other such matters, whether in private discussion or on social media.

E. ASSOCIATIONAL AND ORGANIZATIONAL RIGHTS: 11 / 12

E1. Is there freedom of assembly? 4 / 4

Freedom of assembly is constitutionally protected, and the government generally respects this right.

E2. Is there freedom for nongovernmental organizations, particularly those that are engaged in human rights-and governance-related work? 4 / 4

Nongovernmental organizations are generally free from government interference.

E3. Is there freedom for trade unions and similar professional or labor organizations? 3 / 4

Unions are free to form and operate, and employers have been penalized for violating union rights under the labor code. However, while labor unions are active and politically influential, their ability to protect workers' rights is limited in practice. There are some restrictions on the right to strike, including an official definition of "essential" workers that is broader than the International Labour Organization's standard. In July 2020, the police's Gang Suppression Unit fired rubber bullets and tear gas to suppress a labor protest by union workers at the Port of Belize.

F. RULE OF LAW: 13 / 16 (+1)

F1. Is there an independent judiciary? 4 / 4 (+1)

The judiciary is generally independent, despite inadequate resources and periodic attempts by political and business interests to interfere with its composition. In a dispute that stretched from 2012 to 2018, a group of companies controlled by businessman Michael Ashcroft tried unsuccessfully to have Samuel Awich removed as a judge on the Court of Appeal, Belize's highest judicial body, on the basis of excessive delays in Awich's judgments. In December 2020, the new PUP government stated that Supreme Court judges would be required to deliver judgments within a set time limit, and pledged to provide greater resources to the judiciary.

Score Change: The score improved from 3 to 4 because there have been no major incidents in which judicial independence was compromised.

F2. Does due process prevail in civil and criminal matters? 3 / 4

Detainees and defendants are guaranteed a range of legal rights, which are mostly respected in practice. However, police have reportedly detained suspects without charge for longer than is permitted by the law, and have used the threat of extended detention to intimidate suspects. Judicial delays and a large backlog of cases contribute to lengthy trials and other procedures, with many defendants spending years in pretrial detention.

F3. Is there protection from the illegitimate use of physical force and freedom from war and insurgencies? 3 / 4

Belize is free from major threats to physical security, such as war and insurgencies, but the long-running border dispute with Guatemala remains unresolved. Tensions have lessened in recent years, but there are occasional incidents.

Belize remains among the countries with the highest per capita murder rates in the world, although authorities recorded 102 homicides in 2020, a significant decrease from the 134 in 2019—likely due to lockdown restrictions aimed at curbing the spread of COVID-19. The violence is localized around the south side of Belize City, though some violent crime has spread to other parts of the country. From July to October 2020 a state of emergency was imposed on the south side of Belize City in response to gang violence.

Cases of police brutality continue to be reported. The Police Amendment Act, promulgated in April 2018, was designed to improve disciplinary procedures and increase penalties for police misconduct. In August 2020, three high-ranking police officers were suspended for two months in connection with police violence against protesting port workers in July.

In October, the largest prison break in Belizean history took place when 28 prisoners staged a violent escape from the Belize Central Prison. News reports suggested that two prison guards helped to abet the escape.

F4. Do laws, policies, and practices guarantee equal treatment of various segments of the population? 3 / 4

The constitution and laws protect against many forms of discrimination, but there are no specific provisions addressing sexual orientation or gender identity.

Discrimination against LGBT+ people persists. In 2016, the Supreme Court struck down a provision of the criminal code that outlawed same-sex sexual activity. The government accepted the decriminalization, but in September 2017 it appealed the portion of the judgment finding that unconstitutional discrimination based on sex includes sexual orientation. In December 2019, the Court of Appeal upheld the unconstitutionality of the criminal code article and confirmed that constitutional freedom of expression and antidiscrimination protections include sexual orientation. Following the ruling, the government proposed the Equal Opportunities Bill, which would have ensured explicit protections against discrimination for all Belizeans, but the bill was withdrawn in September 2020 after encountering strong opposition from religious groups.

Women face employment discrimination and are less likely than men to hold managerial positions. However, the government has actively pursued programs aimed at encouraging gender equality and protecting women's rights.

No separate legal system or laws specifically protect Indigenous people.

G. PERSONAL AUTONOMY AND INDIVIDUAL RIGHTS: 13 / 16

G1. Do individuals enjoy freedom of movement, including the ability to change their place of residence, employment, or education? 4 / 4

The government generally respects freedom of internal movement and foreign travel.

G2. Are individuals able to exercise the right to own property and establish private businesses without undue interference from state or non-state actors? 3 / 4

Individuals have the right to own property and establish private businesses. However, legal regulations are at times poorly enforced. Leaders of the Indigenous Maya community say their ancestral land rights are not protected, particularly with regard to oil exploration and logging activities. In 2016 the Belizean government responded to a Caribbean Court of Justice ruling requiring recognition of Mayan land rights by setting up a commission to facilitate implementation of the court's decision, but progress has been slow. The government responded dismissively to reports by Mayan communities that illegal surveying activities were being conducted on their traditional lands in October 2020.

G3. Do individuals enjoy personal social freedoms, including choice of marriage partner and size of family, protection from domestic violence, and control over appearance? 3 / 4

Personal social freedoms are generally respected, though domestic violence remains a serious problem despite government measures to combat it. Rape is illegal, but reporting and conviction rates are low, and sentences are sometimes light.

G4. Do individuals enjoy equality of opportunity and freedom from economic exploitation? 3 / 4

Some legal protections against exploitative working conditions are respected and enforced. However, Belizean and foreign women and girls are vulnerable to sex trafficking, and migrant workers are sometimes subjected to forced labor in agriculture, fisheries, and retail businesses. The US State Department's *Trafficking in Persons Report* for 2020 acknowledged the government's "significant efforts" to combat trafficking, but noted that "the government did not demonstrate overall increasing efforts" and stated that "alleged trafficking-related complicity by government officials remains a problem."

Benin

Population: 12,200,000
Capital: Porto-Novo
Freedom Status: Partly Free
Electoral Democracy: No

Overview: Benin had been among the most stable democracies in sub-Saharan Africa, but President Patrice Talon began using the justice system to attack his political opponents after taking office in 2016, and new electoral rules effectively excluded all opposition parties from the 2019 parliamentary elections. Protests surrounding those elections were met with harsh restrictions on civil liberties, including an internet shutdown and deadly police violence against demonstrators.

KEY DEVELOPMENTS IN 2020
- In March, authorities restricted travel and public gathering sizes in response to the COVID-19 pandemic, though some restrictions were loosened in May. The informal employment sector was severely affected by the pandemic, with some Beninese workers facing food insecurity.
- Local elections were held in May, despite an African Court on Human and Peoples' Rights (AfCHPR) order to suspend them and ensure opposition participation. Pro-government parties won the majority of local council seats.

- The media regulator banned "unauthorized" online news outlets in July, prompting at least one to temporarily close. Media owners criticized the decision, warning it would restrict press freedom and destabilize the sector.

POLITICAL RIGHTS: 21 / 40
A. ELECTORAL PROCESS: 5 / 12
A1. Was the current head of government or other chief national authority elected through free and fair elections? 3 / 4

The president is elected by popular vote for up to two five-year terms and serves as both the chief of state and head of government. In the 2016 presidential election, Patrice Talon defeated former prime minister Lionel Zinsou of the then incumbent Cowry Forces for an Emerging Benin (FCBE) with 65 percent of the vote. Talon, Benin's richest businessman, ran as an independent, supported by the business sector and a number of small political parties. The election was generally held in accordance with international standards, although voter card shortages and the late delivery of materials to polling stations led to some delays.

A2. Were the current national legislative representatives elected through free and fair elections? 1 / 4

Delegates to the 83-member, unicameral National Assembly serve four-year terms and are elected by proportional representation. The April 2019 legislative elections were neither free nor fair, as new electoral rules effectively prevented all opposition parties from participating. Observers canceled poll-monitoring plans for fear of violence, turnout fell to about a quarter of eligible voters amid an opposition boycott, there was an internet shutdown on election day, and security forces violently suppressed protests before and after balloting, resulting in several deaths.

Only the progovernment Progressive Union and Republican Bloc won seats, taking 47 and 36 respectively. That November, the new National Assembly adopted constitutional amendments, including provisions imposing three-term limits on legislators, expanding the body to 109 seats, and extending terms to five years beginning in 2026 to align them with those of the president. The next legislative elections would still occur in 2023. In December 2020, the AfCHPR called for their repeal before the next presidential election.

Municipal elections were held in May 2020, ignoring an April AfCHPR order to suspend them and ensure opposition participation. Sébastien Ajavon, a businessman living in exile after receiving a drug trafficking conviction in 2018, had sued after opposition parties were barred from participating. The Progressive Union and the Republican Bloc won most local council seats, while the FCBE, the only opposition group to field candidates, won 14 percent of them.

A3. Are the electoral laws and framework fair, and are they implemented impartially by the relevant election management bodies? 1 / 4

Elections are conducted by the Autonomous National Electoral Commission (CENA). Following the passage of a restrictive electoral law in 2018, the Constitutional Court—headed by Talon's former personal lawyer—ruled that parties must obtain a "certificate of conformity" from the interior ministry. In March 2019, CENA approved only two party lists, both loyal to the president. Despite electoral-code and constitutional reforms approved that November, key rules barring opposition parties remained in force.

CENA barred opposition groups from the May 2020 local elections, again favoring progovernment parties.

B. POLITICAL PLURALISM AND PARTICIPATION: 9 / 16

B1. Do the people have the right to organize in different political parties or other competitive political groupings of their choice, and is the system free of undue obstacles to the rise and fall of these competing parties or groupings? 2 / 4

After multiparty elections were restored in 1991, Benin generally had a large number of active political parties. However, the 2018 electoral code established restrictive rules including an unusually high 10 percent national threshold and an onerous increase in obligatory financial deposits, though sums for presidential candidates were reduced in November 2019.

All opposition parties were excluded from the 2019 parliamentary contest, though the FCBE gained legal recognition that September. A second opposition party, the Democrats, which was formed after a split within the FCBE, won recognition in December 2020.

B2. Is there a realistic opportunity for the opposition to increase its support or gain power through elections? 1 / 4

Talon's defeat of Zinsou, former president Thomas Boni Yayi's chosen successor in the 2016 election, marked Benin's fourth presidential transfer of power between rival groups since 1991.

However, the government has since introduced significant obstacles to opposition parties and presidential candidates, and leading opposition figures faced harassment and prosecution. Ajavon, who received an in absentia conviction in 2018, remained in France in 2020. In June 2019, Boni Yayi fled Benin after being placed under de facto house arrest for 52 days. That August, Zinsou received a suspended six-month prison sentence in absentia and a five-year ban on running for office over alleged 2016 campaign violations. In April 2020, former finance minister Komi Koutché received a 20-year sentence in absentia for embezzlement.

Under the 2019 constitutional amendments, no president can serve more than two terms in their life, even if they are nonconsecutive; some alleged this was aimed at Boni Yayi. Future presidential and vice-presidential candidates must also obtain endorsement from 10 percent of mayors and National Assembly deputies.

B3. Are the people's political choices free from domination by forces that are external to the political sphere, or by political forces that employ extrapolitical means? 3 / 4

Politics have generally been free from military interference, though soldiers and police used lethal force to disperse opposition protests in 2019. However, 20 people, including 10 soldiers, were arrested over a so-called destabilization effort in February 2020. Some 15 soldiers were arrested in late June on suspicion of plotting a coup d'état.

The role of personal wealth in politics has increased in recent years, with higher campaign costs and clientelist structures boosting the careers of wealthier politicians. Talon developed his private businesses in part by financing the campaigns of Boni Yayi and other elites and then securing lucrative contracts. After becoming president, Talon allegedly attempted to bribe lawmakers during while attempting to secure passage of constitutional amendments.

B4. Do various segments of the population (including ethnic, racial, religious, gender, LGBT+, and other relevant groups) have full political rights and electoral opportunities? 3 / 4

Women and minority groups are not legally excluded from political participation, but cultural factors limit women's engagement. Women won just 7 percent of the seats in the 2019 parliamentary elections. Constitutional amendments passed that November reserved 24 seats for women in the next legislative term.

Benin has historically been divided between northern and southern ethnic groups, and political parties often rely on ethnic bases of support. Southern-born Talon selected most of his political appointees from the southern Gbe-speaking region. The 2019 election of a southerner as National Assembly president broke with a tradition where legislative leaders and chief executives come from different regions.

C. FUNCTIONING OF GOVERNMENT: 7 / 12

C1. Do the freely elected head of government and national legislative representatives determine the policies of the government? 2 / 4

The president and the legislature generally determine government policy. However, the current National Assembly was not elected freely or fairly, and its lack of opposition members seriously undermines its role as an independent branch of government.

The government does not consistently implement policy throughout Benin. In many rural areas, the state struggles to deliver basic services, and citizens instead rely on local customary and religious leaders.

C2. Are safeguards against official corruption strong and effective? 2 / 4

Corruption remains widespread. Corrupt officials rarely face prosecution, contributing to a culture of impunity.

The National Anti-Corruption Authority (ANLC) hears complaints and sends cases to courts, but has no independent law enforcement capacity. In April 2020, the cabinet announced its intention to replace the ANLC with a High Commission for the Prevention of Corruption and forwarded legislative amendments to lawmakers.

The Court of Punishment of Economic Crimes and Terrorism (CRIET) was established in 2018 to prosecute corruption, drug trafficking, and terrorism cases, but critics claim it targets political opponents and journalists. CRIET issued convictions against Ajavon in 2018 and Koutché in April 2020.

C3. Does the government operate with openness and transparency? 3 / 4

The 2015 Information and Communication Code provides for public access to government records. However, information deemed sensitive, including national security, trade, and judicial documents, remains restricted.

As a West African Economic and Monetary Union member, Benin was obliged to convert the Chamber of Accounts into a more independent Court of Auditors that would examine government finances. Its creation was mandated in a 2019 constitutional amendment package, but it remained inactive as recently as September 2020. The General Inspectorate of Finance, which the president directly controls, has harassed the opposition rather than promoted transparency.

CIVIL LIBERTIES: 44 / 60 (–1)

D. FREEDOM OF EXPRESSION AND BELIEF: 14 / 16 (–1)

D1. Are there free and independent media? 2 / 4 (–1)

Constitutional guarantees of freedom of expression are somewhat respected, and print outlets have expressed a wide variety of viewpoints. However, media outlets have encountered new scrutiny and restrictions under the Talon administration.

Defamation remains a crime punishable by fines, and media outlets critical of the government have increasingly risked suspension. The High Authority for Audiovisual Media and Communication (HAAC) shuttered four broadcasters in 2016 and suspended a major newspaper in 2018. One broadcaster, Ajavon-owned Sikka TV, was ordered reopened in a

2017 court ruling but remained shuttered within Benin, instead broadcasting online and via satellite. Ajavon-owned Soleil FM was shuttered in December 2019 after HAAC declined to renew its license, and its staff was dismissed in January 2020.

In July 2020, HAAC banned all "unauthorized" online news outlets, despite their efforts to attain authorization. Media owners criticized the decision, warning it would restrict press freedom and destabilize the sector. At least one outlet closed, albeit temporarily, after the announcement.

A 2017 digital media law allows for the prosecution and imprisonment of journalists for online content that is purportedly false or harasses individuals. In April 2019, newspaper editor Casimir Kpédjo was arrested for publishing "false" information about the national debt; Kpédjo was bailed a month later, and his case remained pending at the end of 2020. In December 2019, Ignace Sossou of Bénin Web TV received an 18-month sentence for "harassment" after quoting a public prosecutor. Sossou was released in June 2020 after his sentence was reduced. In January 2020, an online news editor was detained for a week for reporting on a speculated ambassadorial appointment.

Score Change: The score declined from 3 to 2 because the media regulator ordered the closure of online media outlets it considered "unauthorized," despite their attempts to gain official authorization.

D2. Are individuals free to practice and express their religious faith or nonbelief in public and private? 4 / 4

Religious freedom is constitutionally guaranteed and generally respected in practice.

D3. Is there academic freedom, and is the educational system free from extensive political indoctrination? 4 / 4

Academic freedom is largely respected.

D4. Are individuals free to express their personal views on political or other sensitive topics without fear of surveillance or retribution? 4 / 4

There are no major restrictions on personal expression. Individuals generally are not subject to surveillance or reprisals when discussing political or other sensitive matters.

E. ASSOCIATIONAL AND ORGANIZATIONAL RIGHTS: 9 / 12
E1. Is there freedom of assembly? 2 / 4

Freedom of assembly has traditionally been respected; permit and registration requirements for demonstrations are not always enforced. However, in the months before the 2019 elections, some local authorities issued blanket protest bans. Authorities forcibly dispersed opposition protests, sometimes resulting in fatalities.

In January 2020, protesters in the town of Savé clashed with police after a resident was arrested. Two people died later that month during a police operation to arrest participants in the earlier clash.

Authorities banned noncommercial gatherings of more than 10 people in March 2020 in response to the COVID-19 pandemic. Restrictions on other gatherings of over 50 people were still in place in December.

E2. Is there freedom for nongovernmental organizations, particularly those that are engaged in human rights- and governance-related work? 4 / 4

Nongovernmental organizations (NGOs), including human rights groups, generally operate freely. However, Beninese NGOs can no longer bring cases to the AfCHPR, after Benin withdrew from a relevant protocol in April 2020.

E3. Is there freedom for trade unions and similar professional or labor organizations? 3 / 4

The right to form unions is respected. However, public-sector employees face collective bargaining restrictions. In 2018, the Constitutional Court reinstated a law prohibiting public employees in the defense, health, justice, and security sectors from striking, and a new law limited strikes to a maximum of 10 days per year for private-sector workers and public employees not covered by the existing ban.

F. RULE OF LAW: 11 / 16

F1. Is there an independent judiciary? 2 / 4

Although the judiciary has demonstrated some independence, the courts are susceptible to corruption, Judges are not nominated or promoted transparently.

Judicial independence was undermined when President Talon's personal lawyer, Joseph Djogbénou, was named Constitutional Court president in 2018. The court's quick decision to reverse an earlier ruling on public-sector strikes intensified concerns about its autonomy, as did a 2019 decision requiring parties to obtain conformity certificates to compete in that year's parliamentary elections.

Critics argue CRIET also lacks independence. CRIET has allegedly been used to prosecute Talon's political opponents. Judges were appointed by decree in 2018, in lieu of a transparent confirmation process.

F2. Does due process prevail in civil and criminal matters? 3 / 4

Due process usually prevails in criminal and civil matters. However, judicial inefficiency, corruption, and a shortage of attorneys in the north inhibit the right to a fair trial. Lack of resources contributes to often lengthy pretrial detentions. Arbitrary arrests and detentions occasionally occur.

F3. Is there protection from the illegitimate use of physical force and freedom from war and insurgencies? 3 / 4

The population is free from war and other major physical threats, though the threat of terrorism may be growing in the north. In February 2020, a police station in a northern village was attacked by armed individuals, and one officer was killed.

Prison conditions are harsh. Prisoners face overcrowding, lack of access to food and water, and occasional physical abuse. Police brutality remains a problem, including beatings and torture of suspects. Superiors often shield perpetrators from prosecution.

F4. Do laws, policies, and practices guarantee equal treatment of various segments of the population? 3 / 4

Relations among Benin's ethnic groups are generally amicable, despite recent political tensions. Minority ethnic groups have typically been represented in government agencies, the civil service, and the armed forces. The constitution prohibits discrimination based on race, gender, and disability, but not sexual orientation. The 1996 penal code imposes a higher age of consent for same-sex sexual activity (21) than for heterosexual activity (13). LGBT+ people face social stigma and discrimination in practice.

Women experience discrimination in employment and access to credit, health care, and education.

G. PERSONAL AUTONOMY AND INDIVIDUAL RIGHTS: 10 / 16

G1. Do individuals enjoy freedom of movement, including the ability to change their place of residence, employment, or education? 3 / 4

Individuals can generally move freely throughout Benin. However, in some rural areas, cultural traditions force women to remain indoors for extended periods. Police roadblocks can make travel difficult, and officers occasionally demand bribes from travelers seeking to pass through. Public transport was suspended in March 2020 due to COVID-19-related restrictions, but resumed later in the year, while some movement restrictions persisted.

G2. Are individuals able to exercise the right to own property and establish private businesses without undue interference from state or nonstate actors? 3 / 4

Reforms to the business registration process, anticorruption efforts, and other regulatory changes since 2010 improved the business environment. However, property registration is difficult, and contract enforcement is inconsistent. Despite laws guaranteeing equal rights to inheritance for women, many women are denied the right to inherit property in practice.

G3. Do individuals enjoy personal social freedoms, including choice of marriage partner and size of family, protection from domestic violence, and control over appearance? 2 / 4

Domestic violence remains a serious problem, and women are often reluctant to report domestic abuse. A 2003 law that prohibits female genital mutilation reduced the incidence of the practice, but it still persists. Marriage for those under 18 years old is prohibited, though exceptions are allowed for 14- to 17-year-olds with parental consent. Child marriage and forced marriage remain common in rural areas.

G4. Do individuals enjoy equality of opportunity and freedom from economic exploitation? 2 / 4

Legal protections against forced labor and other exploitative working conditions are unevenly enforced. Poor conditions are prevalent in the large informal sector, which was impacted by the COVID-19 pandemic. Human trafficking is widespread, despite a recent uptick in prosecutions for the crime. The practice of sending young girls to wealthy families to work as domestic servants has led to cases of exploitation and sexual slavery. Children are also exploited for agricultural labor and work in various trades.

Bhutan

Population: 700,000
Capital: Thimphu
Freedom Status: Partly Free
Electoral Democracy: Yes

Overview: Bhutan is a constitutional monarchy that has made significant strides toward democratic consolidation and adherence to the rule of law over the past decade. It has held multiple credible elections and undergone transfers of power to opposition parties. Ongoing problems include discrimination against Nepali-speaking and non-Buddhist minorities, media self-censorship, and, increasingly, the use of libel and defamation cases to silence journalists.

KEY DEVELOPMENTS IN 2020

- Bhutan's response to the COVID-19 pandemic was considered highly effective in preventing rapid spread without resorting to onerous limitations on freedom. According to researchers at the University of Oxford, by the end of 2020 the country had registered approximately 670 cases, and no deaths.
- In December, Bhutan's Parliament voted to decriminalize same-sex relations, and at year's end the bill awaited royal approval.
- Bhutan's increasingly contentious relations with China saw another setback in June, when China claimed an area of eastern Bhutan.

POLITICAL RIGHTS: 30 / 40 (+1)

A. ELECTORAL PROCESS: 10 / 12

A1. Was the current head of government or other chief national authority elected through free and fair elections? 3 / 4

King Jigme Khesar Namgyel Wangchuck formally succeeded his father in 2008. The monarch is head of state, appoints a number of high officials in consultation with other bodies, and retains a waning degree of influence over ministerial positions; the monarch also nominates the leader of the majority party in the elected National Assembly to serve as prime minister. The 2018 National Assembly election, held that September and October, was free and fair, and resulted in a sizable victory for the United Party of Bhutan (DNT), which was formerly in the opposition. After the DNT's victory, the king appointed Lotay Tshering as prime minister.

A2. Were the current national legislative representatives elected through free and fair elections? 4 / 4

The constitution provides for a bicameral Parliament, with a 25-seat upper house, the National Council, and a 47-seat lower house, the National Assembly. Members of both houses serve five-year terms. The king appoints five members of the nonpartisan National Council, and the remaining 20 are popularly elected as independents; the National Assembly is entirely elected. The April 2018 upper-house election saw record turnout; some observers ascribed the higher turnout to reforms designed to encourage voting and make casting ballots easier for residents, such as a new system of voting by post. The National Assembly election was held in two rounds in September and October 2018, with the two parties that won the most support in the first round advancing to the second. The DNT, which launched in 2013, won 30 out of 47 seats, followed by the Bhutan Peace and Prosperity Party (DPT), which won 17 seats. The then ruling People's Democratic Party (PDP) did not advance to the runoff.

A3. Are the electoral laws and framework fair, and are they implemented impartially by the relevant election management bodies? 3 / 4

Elections are administered by the Election Commission of Bhutan (ECB). The commission is thought to act impartially, although some of its regulations regarding which parties can compete in elections are controversial.

B. POLITICAL PLURALISM AND PARTICIPATION: 12 / 16 (+1)

B1. Do the people have the right to organize in different political parties or other competitive political groupings of their choice, and is the system free of undue obstacles to the rise and fall of these competing parties or groupings? 3 / 4

Citizens must receive government approval to form political parties. Obtaining approval is sometimes difficult, and the government has denied registration to several newly formed parties.

B2. Is there a realistic opportunity for the opposition to increase its support or gain power through elections? 4 / 4

The opposition has a realistic chance to win elections, and there is now regular turnover in control of government. In 2018, the DNT won control of Parliament for the first time, and another opposition party, the DPT, finished second, despite having won no seats in 2013.

B3. Are the people's political choices free from domination by forces that are external to the political sphere, or by political forces that employ extrapolitical means? 3 / 4 (+1)

India still has some influence over the choices of Bhutanese voters and politicians. China does not have an official diplomatic relationship with Bhutan but has assiduously courted Bhutanese leaders in recent years. The relationship between India, Bhutan, and China has become more complicated and dangerous in recent years, as India and China have clashed near Bhutanese territory. In June 2020, Chinese officials made a new claim to territory in Bhutan's east; the claim appeared to be a coercive tactic connected to efforts to resolve a long-standing border dispute. In November 2020, satellite imagery appeared to show that China was building a Chinese village inside Bhutanese territory.

The royal family retains significant influence, although it has significantly retreated in recent years, refraining from interference with policymaking and allowing for democratic consolidation. Most members of the political elite, including members of Parliament, steadfastly support the king and are hesitant to take any positions in direct opposition to the royal family. The king played an active role in marshaling public support for measures to contain the COVID-19 pandemic, but neither he nor elected politicians attempted to use the pandemic to consolidate political power.

Score Change: The score improved from 2 to 3 because the monarchy's role and influence in partisan politics and elections have continued to recede in recent years.

B4. Do various segments of the population (including ethnic, racial, religious, gender, LGBT+, and other relevant groups) have full political rights and electoral opportunities? 2 / 4

Electoral rules stipulate that political parties must not be limited to members of any regional, ethnic, or religious group. There is no party that represents Nepali speakers. Citizenship rules are strict, and many Nepali-speaking people have not attained citizenship, effectively disenfranchising them. International election monitors have noted that Nepali speakers have been turned away from voting.

Women are underrepresented in public office, but the proportion of women in the National Assembly increased from 8 percent to 15 percent following the 2018 election. Women won 2 of the 20 elected National Council seats in 2018. Traditional customs inhibit women's political participation, though electoral reforms introduced for the 2018 polling also boosted turnout, including among women. The government has supported several programs to empower women and increase their engagement in politics.

C. FUNCTIONING OF GOVERNMENT: 9 / 12

C1. Do the freely elected head of government and national legislative representatives determine the policies of the government? 3 / 4

Bhutan has made a successful transition from a system in which the monarch and his advisers dominated governance to one in which policies and legislation are mostly determined by elected officials.

While Chinese influence has been an important factor in recent years, India too maintains significant influence on Bhutanese policymaking, providing considerable foreign aid and shaping Bhutanese foreign policy based on a bilateral treaty between the two countries, first signed in 1947. As a result, the Bhutanese government is hesitant to make policies that will upset the relationship with India.

C2. Are safeguards against official corruption strong and effective? 3 / 4

The government generally enforces anticorruption laws effectively. The 2006 Anti-Corruption Act established whistleblower protections. The Anti-Corruption Commission (ACC) is tasked with investigating and preventing graft, and has successfully prosecuted several high-profile cases.

Nepotism and favoritism in public procurement and government employment remain problematic.

C3. Does the government operate with openness and transparency? 3 / 4

Although Bhutan lacks comprehensive freedom of information legislation, the government has strengthened transparency by making the salaries of officials public and making the central and local budgets more open to review. A right to information law passed by the National Assembly in 2014 was designed to put the onus on government officials and agencies to release information. However, the National Council still has not approved the bill.

ADDITIONAL DISCRETIONARY POLITICAL RIGHTS QUESTION
Is the government or occupying power deliberately changing the ethnic composition of a country or territory so as to destroy a culture or tip the political balance in favor of another group? −1 / 0

The government has for decades attempted to diminish and repress the rights of ethnic Nepalis, forcing many of them to leave Bhutan. The government expelled a large percentage of Nepali speakers in the early 1990s; in 1992, well over 100,000 refugees living in Nepal were denied reentry to Bhutan. A resettlement effort aimed at transferring the refugees to other countries began in 2007, resulting in the resettlement of the majority of refugees. However, 7,000 refugees remain in Nepal, and while the UN High Commissioner for Refugees has pressured Nepal to absorb the remaining refugees, some continue to seek repatriation to Bhutan.

CIVIL LIBERTIES: 31 / 60 (+1)
D. FREEDOM OF EXPRESSION AND BELIEF: 9 / 16
D1. Are there free and independent media? 2 / 4

While there are multiple private media outlets, many depend on advertising from state bodies, and Bhutan's media environment remains subject to a high degree of self-censorship, especially regarding criticism of the royal family. Powerful individuals can use defamation laws to retaliate against critics. In 2018, a journalist was sentenced to three months in prison for libel after she posted on Facebook about a woman who had allegedly mistreated her stepdaughter.

The Bhutan Information Communications and Media Act 2018 came into force that January; the government said it would strengthen the independence of the media and promote a free and vibrant media industry. The legislation mandated the establishment of an independent Media Council, which became operational in 2019, to monitor the media for harmful or offensive content. Press freedom advocates fear that the body will erode press freedom and contribute to greater self-censorship.

D2. Are individuals free to practice and express their religious faith or nonbelief in public and private? 2 / 4

The constitution protects freedom of religion, but local authorities are known to harass non-Buddhists. While Bhutanese of all faiths can worship freely in private, some experience pressure to participate in Buddhist ceremonies and practices.

Christian churches have often been unable to obtain registration from the government, which means that they cannot raise funds or buy property, placing constraints on their activities. Christian children are sometimes not allowed into schools based on their religion.

D3. Is there academic freedom, and is the educational system free from extensive political indoctrination? 2 / 4

Few restrictions on academic freedom have been reported. However, Bhutanese university students are often hesitant to speak out on controversial political issues and practice self-censorship.

D4. Are individuals free to express their personal views on political or other sensitive topics without fear of surveillance or retribution? 3 / 4

Freedom of expression is constitutionally guaranteed and generally respected. However, under the National Security Act, speech that creates or attempts to create "hatred and disaffection among the people" or "misunderstanding or hostility between the government and people," among other offenses, can be punished with imprisonment. The broad language of the law makes it vulnerable to misuse.

E. ASSOCIATIONAL AND ORGANIZATIONAL RIGHTS: 5 / 12
E1. Is there freedom of assembly? 2 / 4

The constitution guarantees freedom of assembly, but this right is limited by government-imposed restrictions. Public gatherings require government permission, which is sometimes denied. Curfews and restrictions on the location of demonstrations also serve to curtail assembly rights.

E2. Is there freedom for nongovernmental organizations, particularly those that are engaged in human rights- and governance-related work? 2 / 4

Nongovernmental organizations (NGOs) that work on issues related to ethnic Nepalis are not allowed to operate, but other local and international NGOs work with increasing freedom on a wide range of issues. Under the 2007 Civil Society Organization Act, all new NGOs must register with the government. Registration is granted to NGOs that are determined by the government to be "not harmful to the peace and unity of the country."

E3. Is there freedom for trade unions and similar professional or labor organizations? 1 / 4

The constitution nominally guarantees the right of workers to form unions, but the right to strike is not legally protected. Workers may bargain collectively, and antiunion discrimination is prohibited. Most of the country's workforce is engaged in small-scale agriculture and is therefore not unionized.

F. RULE OF LAW: 8 / 16

F1. Is there an independent judiciary? 3 / 4

The independence of the judiciary is largely respected. Senior judges are appointed by the king on the recommendation of the National Judicial Commission. However, the rulings of judges often lack consistency, and many people view the judiciary as corrupt.

F2. Does due process prevail in civil and criminal matters? 2 / 4

Although the right to a fair trial is largely guaranteed and arbitrary arrest is not a widespread problem, plaintiffs and defendants in civil disputes often represent themselves. Many people who are unable to repay debts are held in detention, which is considered arbitrary under international law.

A number of political prisoners who were detained before Bhutan transitioned to its current democratic system remain imprisoned. In 2019, the Working Group on Arbitrary Detention of the UN High Commissioner for Human Rights reported that individuals detained under national security laws, including political prisoners, suffered due process violations including the lack of legal representation. In December 2019, a campaign group that included members of the Bhutanese diaspora and resettled refugees petitioned for the prisoners' release, but they remained in jail throughout 2020.

Overall, however, the rule of law and due process has improved substantially in civil and criminal matters, and Bhutan's courts are relatively effective.

F3. Is there protection from the illegitimate use of physical force and freedom from war and insurgencies? 2 / 4

The civilian police force generally operates within the law, and incidents of excessive force are rare. In recent years, crime rates have generally been low. However, insurgents from the Indian state of Assam sometimes enter Bhutan and undermine security. Occasional instances of kidnapping and robbery occur along the border with India.

F4. Do laws, policies, and practices guarantee equal treatment of various segments of the population? 1 / 4

The constitution protects against discrimination based on sex, race, disability, language, religion, or societal status. However, Nepali-speaking people reportedly face employment discrimination and other forms of bias.

LGBT+ people experience societal discrimination and social stigma, and there are no specific legal protections for transgender people. In December 2020, both houses of Parliament completed a final vote to repeal criminal code provisions that criminalize same-sex relations; the law awaited the king's assent at the end of the year.

Despite recent gains, discrimination in employment and education persists for women in Bhutan.

G. PERSONAL AUTONOMY AND INDIVIDUAL RIGHTS: 9 / 16 (+1)

G1. Do individuals enjoy freedom of movement, including the ability to change their place of residence, employment, or education? 2 / 4

Bhutanese citizens generally have the freedom to travel domestically and internationally. However, the government has established different categories of citizenship, which restricts foreign travel for some. These restrictions reportedly have the greatest effect on Nepali speakers. Bhutanese security forces sometimes arrest Nepali people seeking to enter the country.

G2. Are individuals able to exercise the right to own property and establish private businesses without undue interference from state or nonstate actors? 3 / 4 (+1)

Individuals generally have rights to own property and establish businesses, but the process of registering property or a new business can be cumbersome and hinder business development. In recent years, the legal system has become more consistent, and establishing businesses has become easier. However, some ethnic Nepalis who lack a security clearance certificate face difficulties in starting a business.

Score Change: The score improved from 2 to 3 because the government has gradually strengthened the legal and regulatory framework to support property rights and business activity, and state authorities have reduced their reliance on coercive tactics.

G3. Do individuals enjoy personal social freedoms, including choice of marriage partner and size of family, protection from domestic violence, and control over appearance? 2 / 4

Reports of domestic violence have increased in recent years, with an additional rise in 2020 attributed to the COVID-19 lockdown. Societal taboos lead many incidents of rape and domestic violence to go unreported. Child marriage still occurs with some frequency.

G4. Do individuals enjoy equality of opportunity and freedom from economic exploitation? 2 / 4

Female household workers, who often come from rural areas or India, are vulnerable to forced labor and other abuse, as are foreign workers in the construction and hydropower sectors. Child labor continued to be a problem in 2020, mostly in the agriculture and construction sectors.

Sex trafficking remained a problem in 2020, and the government's enforcement efforts were inadequate. However, the US State Department's *Trafficking in Persons Report 2020* upgraded Bhutan's status because the government has made more intensive efforts to meet international standards, including prosecutions and an investigation into reports of labor exploitation.

Bolivia

Population: 11,600,000
Capital: La Paz (administrative), Sucre (judicial)
Freedom Status: Partly Free
Electoral Democracy: Yes

Overview: Bolivia is a democracy where credible elections have been held regularly. While mass protests and violence erupted after the disputed 2019 elections, new general elections held in 2020 were credible and fair, and stakeholders accepted the results. Child labor and violence against women are persistent problems, independent and investigative journalists face harassment, and the judiciary is politicized and hampered by corruption.

KEY DEVELOPMENTS IN 2020

- Repeat general elections held in October were competitive and credible, and polling took place peacefully. The Movement for Socialism (MAS) won a majority in the legislature and its candidate, Luis Arce, won the presidency with 55 percent of the vote. The elections had been delayed twice due to the COVID-19 pandemic; over 158,000 people tested positive for the coronavirus during the year, according to data the government provided to the World Health Organization (WHO).

- In September, the interim government charged former president Evo Morales with terrorism, after having already prosecuted hundreds of individuals associated with his administration. The next month, the MAS-dominated legislature approved the indictment of 11 ministers from the interim government, and recommended interim president Áñez be prosecuted for her alleged role in encouraging violence at protests in 2019. Rights groups and others expressed concern that the prosecutions were a continuation of Bolivian authorities' long-problematic use of the justice system to persecute political opponents.

- In July, the Second Constitutional Chamber of the La Paz Department Tribunal overturned a decision of the civil registry office that had denied a same-sex couple registration of their civil union. The couple's union was officially approved in December.

- In May, Health Minister Marcelo Navajas was arrested for corruption related to the purchase of ventilators to aid people suffering from severe COVID-19 symptoms. He allegedly authorized payments that totaled approximately $4.7 million, over $27,000 for each unit, which was more than double what was stipulated in the contract.

POLITICAL RIGHTS: 27 / 40 (+2)
A. ELECTORAL PROCESS: 10 / 12 (+2)
A1. Was the current head of government or other chief national authority elected through free and fair elections? 4 / 4 (+1)

Bolivia's president is both chief of state and head of government, and is directly elected to a five-year term. The presidential election in October 2020 took place after the results of the 2019 election was annulled. Early results of the October 2019 presidential election suggested that a runoff between incumbent Evo Morales of the Movement for Socialism (MAS) and the main opposition candidate, former president Carlos Mesa of the Comunidad Ciudadana (Citizen Community) party, was likely. Soon after, election officials released an updated vote count showing Morales with an outright victory, prompting mass demonstrations. An Organization of American States (OAS) electoral observation mission criticized the tally that showed Morales with an outright victory, saying it contradicted independent counts and that a runoff round should go forward—though the credibility of this criticism has since been disputed by some independent analysts. Morales maintained that his victory was legitimate, but also invited the OAS to audit the election, and it sent a delegation of experts to do so.

As protests, counterprotests, and accompanying violence intensified in the weeks following the 2019 poll, Morales, vice president Álvaro García Linera, and the heads of the Senate and the lower chamber resigned in November, after Morales lost the support of the military and police forces. Days later, Jeanine Áñez Chavez, a senior senator and the highest-ranking official in the line of succession who had not yet resigned, was approved by the Constitutional Court to assume the presidency on an interim basis. Áñez indicated that she would only serve until a new election could be held, though in January 2020, she announced her candidacy for president in the next election. She eventually withdrew from the race in September in order to unify the MAS-opposition.

An agreement between the interim government and the parliament, mediated by the United Nations, the European Union (EU), and the Catholic Church, established a new election date and a new Supreme Electoral Tribunal (TSE), whose actions were widely considered independent and free from undue political influence. The election was supposed to be held in May 2020; however it was postponed twice due to the COVID-19 pandemic, first to September, and then to October. In August, MAS supporters organized roadblocks for two weeks to protest the second delay of the election.

The results of the October 2020 poll showed a clear victory for MAS candidate Luis Arce, who won over 55 percent of the vote, precluding the need for a runoff. Former president Mesa won 28 percent of the vote. Voter turnout was recorded at 84 percent. Multiple independent observer missions, including one from the OAS, deemed the poll credible and fair, and competing parties and civil society stakeholders accepted the results.

Score Change: The score improved from 3 to 4 because the presidential election was organized and administered impartially, and its results were recognized by all competing parties and the international community.

A2. Were the current national legislative representatives elected through free and fair elections? 4 / 4

The Plurinational Legislative Assembly (ALP) consists of a 130-member Chamber of Deputies and a 36-member Senate. Legislative terms are five years.

Due to allegations of irregularities in the 2019 general elections, the results of the vote for legislative representatives were considered invalid, and the ALP passed a law in November 2019 calling for new legislative elections alongside the October 2020 presidential election. In October, the MAS won 75 of the 130 seats in the Chamber of Deputies and 21 seats in the Senate. The Citizen Community party secured 39 seats in the lower house and 11 seats in the upper house. The Creemos party won 16 and 4 seats in the Chamber of Deputies and the Senate, respectively.

A3. Are the electoral laws and framework fair, and are they implemented impartially by the relevant election management bodies? 2 / 4 (+1)

The final report of the OAS on the 2019 elections claimed that the elections' overall results were not verifiable, due to "willful manipulation" abetted by a biased TSE. In particular, the report excoriated TSE members for allowing electronic voting results to be diverted to shadowy external servers, "destroying all trust in the electoral process" and "making data manipulation and tally sheet forgery possible." However, in 2020 the methodology and credibility of the OAS report was disputed by the *Washington Post, New York Times,* and other independent analysts. After Morales's resignation in November 2019, the parliament agreed on a transparent formula to reconstitute an independent TSE in December.

In the 2020 elections, the TSE's actions were widely considered independent and free from undue political influence. Though the day of the vote was postponed twice due to the coronavirus pandemic, the body nevertheless administered a safe vote with high turnout, successfully implementing necessary public health measures such as social distancing and separate timeslots for voting.

For years, Bolivian politics were characterized by MAS efforts to abolish presidential term limits. In 2017, MAS lawmakers overturned the articles in the constitution setting presidential term limits by consulting a constitutional tribunal the lawmakers themselves had appointed, despite voters rejecting this measure by referendum in 2016.

Score Change: The score improved from 1 to 2 because the newly appointed Supreme Electoral Tribunal provided more independent and transparent oversight of the presidential election, despite a number of weaknesses in the legal framework.

B. POLITICAL PLURALISM AND PARTICIPATION: 10 / 16

B1. Do the people have the right to organize in different political parties or other competitive political groupings of their choice, and is the system free of undue obstacles to the rise and fall of these competing parties or groupings? 3 / 4

Citizens have the right to organize political parties. MAS has dominated politics since Morales's election to the presidency in 2005, drawing support from social movements, trade unions, and civil society actors. Morales's maneuvers to achieve a reelection bid were a core issue in the rancorous 2019 campaign period. The most prominent opposition party, Citizen Community, attracted individuals who opposed his persistent efforts to extend his term. Opposition leaders have criticized the 2018 Political Organizations Law, which contains a provision requiring intraparty primaries.

In the 2020 election, a new political party called Creemos emerged, headed by the regional leader from Santa Cruz, Luis Fernando Camacho, who organized a wave of protests that led to Morales's resignation. Creemos is the leading party in Santa Cruz, Bolivia's richest region, and received 16 percent of the vote in the presidential election.

B2. Is there a realistic opportunity for the opposition to increase its support or gain power through elections? 2 / 4

There are no formal institutional barriers that prevent opposition parties from participating in elections. However, the overwhelming dominance of the MAS, aided by its use of public resources to back its campaigns, made it difficult for opposition parties to gain power through elections. Further, some electoral rules and regulations endanger the maintenance of a level political playing field and hinder the opposition's ability to realistically challenge the MAS. The 2018 Political Organizations Law also mandates that coalitions be finalized months before their required intraparty primaries are held, which obstructs the formation of a realistic opposition force.

Interim president Áñez initially announced in January 2020 her candidacy for president, but, after a series of scandals including alleged abuse of administrative resources, withdrew from the race in September in order to unite the MAS-opposition.

In the 2019 presidential election, the OAS observer mission claimed that the results of the vote were manipulated so as to prevent a runoff between Morales and Mesa, the second-place candidate. However, the *Washington Post*, *New York Times*, and other independent analysts later disputed these allegations.

B3. Are the people's political choices free from domination by forces that are external to the political sphere, or by political forces that employ extrapolitical means? 2 / 4

People are generally free to make political decisions without undue influence from the military, foreign powers, or other influential groups. Over the course of Morales's tenure, however, public employees were coerced by their employers to attend progovernment rallies.

Several violent confrontations occurred between supporters of competing parties in the run-up to the 2020 election. However, leaders of all parties called for their supporters to allow everyone to campaign freely and peacefully in each region. The interventions, protests, roadblocks, and violence that preceded and followed the 2019 elections were not as severe in 2020.

B4. Do various segments of the population (including ethnic, racial, religious, gender, LGBT+, and other relevant groups) have full political rights and electoral opportunities? 3 / 4

The constitution recognizes 36 Indigenous nationalities within a plurinational state, and formalizes political autonomy in Indigenous territories. Adult citizens enjoy universal and equal suffrage. Although they are well represented in government, the interests of Indigenous groups are often overlooked by politicians.

Formally, Bolivia has progressive legislation that guarantees equal political representation for women and seeks to protect them from political violence. While women are well-represented in politics, elected to 46 percent of seats in the Chamber of Deputies and nearly 56 percent of those in the Senate in 2020, sexism and patriarchal attitudes undermine their work, particularly at local levels.

C. FUNCTIONING OF GOVERNMENT: 7 / 12

C1. Do the freely elected head of government and national legislative representatives determine the policies of the government? 3 / 4

Elected officials are free to set and implement government policy without undue interference from nonstate actors. However, opposition members charge that the MAS majority in the legislature, combined with Morales's powerful presidency, has opened the space for strong executive influence on legislative processes.

During 2020, the parliament, dominated by the MAS, clashed consistently with interim president Áñez. Áñez, who initially recognized that her only mandate as the unelected interim president was to administer new elections, attempted to implement policies that reversed Morales administration decisions and enact new legislation. Tensions between the executive and the legislative branches of government impeded the passage and implementation of legislation throughout the year.

C2. Are safeguards against official corruption strong and effective? 2 / 4

Anticorruption laws are poorly enforced, and corruption affects a range of government entities and economic sectors, including law enforcement bodies and extractive industries. Public procurement processes are frequently compromised by bribery.

During the COVID-19 pandemic, former minister of health Marcelo Navajas was fired and later arrested on suspicion of corruption after intentionally overpaying for artificial ventilators. The government paid $4.7 million to a Spanish company to purchase 179 ventilators, each costing $27,683. The manufacturer offered the ventilators for between $10,312 and $11,941 per unit, and stipulated less than half of $4.7 million in total in the contract.

C3. Does the government operate with openness and transparency? 2 / 4

Bolivia has no law guaranteeing access to public information. Elected officials by law must make asset declarations, but these are unavailable to the public.

CIVIL LIBERTIES: 39 / 60 (+1)

D. FREEDOM OF EXPRESSION AND BELIEF: 14 / 16

D1. Are there free and independent media? 2 / 4

While the constitution guarantees freedom of expression, in practice, journalists encounter harassment in connection with critical or investigative reporting. Harassment of critical media outlets has at times come from MAS government officials, who have characterized journalists as liars and participants in an international conspiracy against Morales. This harassment continued under interim president Áñez's administration. Media outlets with editorial positions that were perceived as hostile under the Morales administration were denied access to public advertising contracts. Bolivia's National Press Association documented 87 instances of physical attacks against journalists in 2019, mostly from both Morales and opposition supporters, 14 incidents of violence at the premises of media outlets, and 16 cases of authorities threatening and harassing members of the press. These attacks continued in 2020, though mostly by demonstrators.

In March 2020, the interim government issued a decree that provided for the criminal prosecution of journalists and members of the general public who published what authorities deemed to be misinformation about the COVID-19 pandemic and the government's policies to address it. Facing pressure from civil society organizations and the international community, the government withdrew that provision of the decree in May.

D2. Are individuals free to practice and express their religious faith or nonbelief in public and private? 4 / 4

Freedom of religion is guaranteed by the constitution and generally upheld in practice. The 2009 constitution ended the Roman Catholic Church's official status, and created a secular state.

D3. Is there academic freedom, and is the educational system free from extensive political indoctrination? 4 / 4

Academic freedom is legally guaranteed and upheld in practice.

D4. Are individuals free to express their personal views on political or other sensitive topics without fear of surveillance or retribution? 4 / 4

Private discussion is robust and generally free from interference or surveillance.

E. ASSOCIATIONAL AND ORGANIZATIONAL RIGHTS: 9 / 12 (+1)

E1. Is there freedom of assembly? 3 / 4 (+1)

Bolivian law protects the right to peaceful assembly. However, many past protests have been marred by clashes between demonstrators and police, as well as physical confrontations between protesters and counterprotesters around divisive issues.

In 2019, after Morales's resignation, the interim government deployed security forces to disperse protesting Morales sympathizers, who at times also fought with opposition supporters. The use of force by authorities during the 2019 postelectoral unrest resulted in the deaths of at least 30 people, and hundreds of injuries. The Inter-American Commission on Human Rights (IACHR) and the UN High Commissioner for Human Rights reported that police had committed serious human rights violations.

In August 2020, after the presidential election was delayed a second time, nearly 150,000 protesters blockaded streets and marched in numerous cities, seeking the resignation of interim president Áñez. Health officials said these roadblocks prevented crucial medical supplies from reaching parts of the country, significantly delaying the Red Cross's and other medical convoys, likely resulting in the deaths of approximately 30 people who had COVID-19. Unlike in 2019, there were no reports of major incidents of overt violence at the 2020 protests.

Score Change: The score improved from 2 to 3 because demonstrations during the year generally featured less violence and police interference than in 2019, when clashes between protesters and security forces resulted in dozens of deaths.

E2. Is there freedom for nongovernmental organizations, particularly those that are engaged in human rights- and governance-related work? 3 / 4

Many nongovernmental organizations (NGOs) operate but are subject to some legal restrictions. In 2016, the country's Plurinational Constitutional Tribunal (TCP) dismissed a petition arguing that two statutes in the country's NGO laws gave the government license to dissolve NGOs. Government officials from all political affiliations have at times smeared rights groups as antigovernment conspirators.

E3. Is there freedom for trade unions and similar professional or labor organizations? 3 / 4

Labor and peasant unions are an active force wielding significant political influence.

The country's official labor code is inconsistent with Bolivian law; for example, it prohibits public sector unions, yet many public sector workers are able to legally unionize. A National Labor Court hears cases of antiunion discrimination, but tends to hand down verdicts slowly, and penalties for antiunion discrimination are not consistently applied.

F. RULE OF LAW: 6 / 16

F1. Is there an independent judiciary? 1 / 4

Bolivia stands as the sole country that appoints justices via popular elections. However, judges on the Supreme Court, the TCP, and other entities are first nominated through a two-thirds vote in the legislature. For years, this allowed the MAS to dominate the candidate selection process, producing a lenient judiciary. The popular election of judges has politicized and factionalized appointments, creating further opportunities for corruption. In addition to its politicization, the judiciary remains overburdened and beset by corruption.

The use of the judiciary to prosecute opposition leaders was a common practice during the Morales administration and continued under interim president Áñez's government, which pressured prosecutors to pursue criminal cases against hundreds of individuals associated with the Morales administration. In September 2020, the government accused Morales himself of terrorism and issued a warrant for his arrest, though it was eventually annulled in court. In October 2020, the outgoing legislature approved the indictment of 11 ministers from the interim government, and recommended that interim president Áñez be prosecuted for her role in worsening the violence at protests in 2019, alleging that she and other ministers had committed "genocide and other offenses."

F2. Does due process prevail in civil and criminal matters? 1 / 4

Many people have difficulty accessing the justice system because they lack resources to travel to courts and other relevant offices, and also because services, where provided, are often insufficient and inefficient. In criminal matters, people accused of committing crimes can go years before they have a formal trial. Police are poorly paid and receive inadequate training, and corruption within the police force remains a problem.

F3. Is there protection from the illegitimate use of physical force and freedom from war and insurgencies? 2 / 4

Morales supporters and opponents fought violently in several cities following the 2019 elections and Morales's resignation. Both sympathizers and detractors of Morales had access to explosives, including dynamite, homemade rocket launchers, and Molotov cocktails, and used them against each other and the security forces. Morales opponents were reportedly shot at in the localities of Montero and Vila. The houses of journalists and activists who had been critical of Morales were burnt, as were a number of public buses in La Paz. By year's end, a political dialogue backed by the EU, the UN, and the Episcopal Conference, among others, opened, and violence receded before reaching the point of civil war or insurgency.

F4. Do laws, policies, and practices guarantee equal treatment of various segments of the population? 2 / 4

The 2010 antiracism law contains measures to combat discrimination and impose criminal penalties for discriminatory acts. However, racism and associated discrimination is common in the country, especially against Indigenous groups.

Bolivia has laws in place that prohibit discrimination against LGBT+ people. However, these laws are rarely enforced, and LGBT+ people experience widespread societal discrimination. Chi Hyun Chung, a Presbyterian minister who considers homosexuality to be an illness requiring psychiatric treatment, ran for president in 2019 and 2020, with an anti-LGBT+ rights agenda as part of his platform; he came in third in 2019 but lost most of his support in 2020.

G. PERSONAL AUTONOMY AND INDIVIDUAL RIGHTS: 10 / 16

G1. Do individuals enjoy freedom of movement, including the ability to change their place of residence, employment, or education? 3 / 4

There are no formal limits on people's ability to change their place of residence, employment, or education, but choices can be limited by socioeconomic difficulties. Roads are occasionally blockaded as part of protest actions, impeding free movement.

G2. Are individuals able to exercise the right to own property and establish private businesses without undue interference from state or nonstate actors? 2 / 4

Women enjoy the same formal rights to property ownership as men, but discrimination is common, leading to disparities in property ownership and access to resources.

The rights of Indigenous people to prior consultation in cases of natural resource extraction and land development are not fully upheld by law or in practice.

G3. Do individuals enjoy personal social freedoms, including choice of marriage partner and size of family, protection from domestic violence, and control over appearance? 3 / 4

The constitution reserves marriage as a bond between a man and a woman, and makes no provision for same-sex civil unions. However, in July 2020, the Second Constitutional Chamber of the La Paz Department Tribunal overturned a decision of the civil registry office denying a same-sex couple registration of their civil union, which was officially approved in December.

Gender-based violence is a serious problem, and laws criminalizing violence against women are not well enforced. Cases of femicide and violence against women increased dramatically during the COVID-19 pandemic, with over 14,464 cases recorded by the government Special Force to Combat Violence (FELCV) between January and August 2020. Many women lack access to birth control and reproductive health care

G4. Do individuals enjoy equality of opportunity and freedom from economic exploitation? 2 / 4

Bolivia is a source country for the trafficking of men, women, and children for forced labor and prostitution, and the country faced increased international criticism over permissive legislation regarding child labor in 2018, when the country changed the minimum working age to 14 years old.

Bosnia and Herzegovina

Population: 3,300,000
Capital: Sarajevo
Freedom Status: Partly Free
Electoral Democracy: No

Overview: Bosnia and Herzegovina (BiH) is a highly decentralized parliamentary republic whose complex constitutional regime is embedded in the Dayton Peace Agreement, which ended the 1992–95 Bosnian War. Political affairs are characterized by severe partisan gridlock among nationalist leaders from the country's Bosniak, Serb, and Croat communities. Corruption remains a serious problem in the government and elsewhere in society.

KEY DEVELOPMENTS IN 2020

- Opposition parties made breakthroughs in November's municipal elections, as well as in a Mostar's special election, securing seats in various assemblies. (An internationally brokered agreement had paved the way for municipal elections in Mostar, which were held for the first time since 2008.)
- In May, Federation prime minister Fadil Novalić was implicated in a respirator-procurement scandal and was briefly taken into custody by state anticorruption police. He and two codefendants were indicted in December on charges of corruption and embezzlement.
- Some 8,300 migrants, refugees, and asylum seekers were stranded in the country at year's end, with most living in camps that lacked basic services and offered little protection against winter weather. Reports emerged of violence against migrants by local authorities, as well as by Croatian border guards who have repeatedly been accused of illegal pushbacks.

POLITICAL RIGHTS: 19 / 40

A. ELECTORAL PROCESS: 6 / 12

A1. Was the current head of government or other chief national authority elected through free and fair elections? 2 / 4

The 1995 Dayton Accords that ended the civil war in BiH created a loosely knit state composed of two entities—the Federation, whose residents are mainly Bosniak and Croat, and the Serb-dominated Republika Srpska (RS)—that operate under a weak central government. The position of head of state is held by a three-member presidency comprising one Bosniak, one Serb, and one Croat; they are each elected to a four-year term, which they serve concurrently.

The chair of the Council of Ministers, or prime minister, is nominated by the presidency and approved by the House of Representatives. The chair in turn nominates other ministers for approval by the House.

The October 2018 elections were once again dominated by the country's three entrenched nationalist blocs: the Bosniak nationalist Party of Democratic Action (SDA), the Croat nationalist Croatian Democratic Union (HDZ-BiH), and the Serb nationalist Alliance of Independent Social Democrats (SNSD). Milorad Dodik of the SNSD, the longtime president of the RS entity, won the Serb seat in BiH's state presidency, and Šefik Džaferović of the SDA won the Bosniak seat. However, Željko Komšić of the center-left Democratic Front party decisively defeated the HDZ-BiH incumbent for the Croat seat of the presidency.

International observers raised concerns about the integrity of the elections, including about a high number of ballots disqualified by the Central Electoral Commission (CIK).

Two years after the last general elections, no new government has yet been formed in the Federation entity, the larger of the country's two administrative entities.

A2. Were the current national legislative representatives elected through free and fair elections? 2 / 4

The Parliamentary Assembly, a state-level body, has two chambers. The 15-seat upper house, the House of Peoples, consists of five members from each of the three main ethnic groups, elected by the Federation and RS legislatures for four-year terms. The lower house, the House of Representatives, has 42 popularly elected members serving four-year terms, with 28 seats assigned to representatives from the Federation and 14 to representatives from the RS.

The SDA, HDZ-BiH, and SNSD dominated the 2018 general elections, capturing nine, five, and six seats in the highly fragmented House of Representatives and many other legislative posts at the entity, canton, and municipal levels. However, they faced stiff competition from other parties, particularly the Social Democratic Party, which took five House of Representatives seats, and the left-wing Democratic Front–Civic Alliance, which won three. Nine smaller parties also won representation at the state level. Election monitors noted significant irregularities and a decline in overall quality as compared with prior polls. Turnout was down slightly, at about 53 percent.

Municipal elections originally planned for October 2020 were delayed until November because of a funding dispute between the three leading nationalist blocs. Opposition parties made breakthroughs in Sarajevo, Banja Luka, Tomislavgrad, and several other locales, as well as in Mostar's special election. The HDZ- and SDA-backed list came in first and second, respectively, in Mostar. However, the opposition BH Bloc, composed of the Social Democratic Party (SDP) and Naša Stranka (Our Party), secured 6 councilors in the 35-seat city assembly—enough to determine the shape of the eventual governing majority, even if they are not formally part of it.

A3. Are the electoral laws and framework fair, and are they implemented impartially by the relevant election management bodies? 2 / 4

Under BiH's constitutional regime, the CIK administers elections with the help of municipal election commissions. Both are subject to significant political party interference. The CIK is a largely ineffectual body, unable to act decisively without political support.

Conflicts over fair ethnic representation continue to surround aspects of the constitution and electoral laws. For example, BiH citizens who do not identify as members of the country's Bosniak, Serb, or Croat "constitutive peoples" remain barred from the presidency and membership in the House of Peoples, despite 2009 and 2016 rulings by the European Court of Human Rights that the exclusion of members of other ethnic groups violated the European Convention on Human Rights. The Federation's upper house, also known as the House of Peoples, was not fully seated until several months after the 2018 elections due to a legal dispute over its system of ethnic seat allocations. The dispute also held up the formation of the state-level House of Peoples, whose members are appointed by the entity legislatures.

B. POLITICAL PLURALISM AND PARTICIPATION: 9 / 16

B1. Do the people have the right to organize in different political parties or other competitive political groupings of their choice, and is the system free of undue obstacles to the rise and fall of these competing parties or groupings? 3 / 4

Political parties typically organize and operate freely, though the political arena in the Federation is generally limited to Bosniaks and Croats, while Serbs control politics in the RS. Coalitions at all levels of government shift frequently, but incumbent parties have maintained their positions with the help of vast patronage networks, making it difficult for smaller reform-oriented forces to achieve meaningful breakthroughs.

B2. Is there a realistic opportunity for the opposition to increase its support or gain power through elections? 2 / 4

There are no explicit legal barriers preventing opposition parties from entering government, but expansive veto powers granted to the constitutive peoples and their representatives have helped the dominant nationalist parties to manipulate the system and shut out reformist or multiethnic challengers. However, in the 2020 municipal elections, opposition parties made breakthroughs in Sarajevo, Banja Luka, Tomislavgrad, and several other locales, as well as in Mostar's special election.

B3. Are the people's political choices free from domination by forces that are external to the political sphere, or by political forces that employ extrapolitical means? 2 / 4

In addition to domestic problems like the politicization of public resources and the influence of corrupt patronage networks, certain foreign powers wield outsized influence in the Bosnian political sphere. Serbia and Croatia exert leverage through their respective local allies, the SNSD and the HDZ-BiH. Russia and Turkey have also offered support to preferred parties and candidates.

The Office of the High Representative (OHR), which was created by the Dayton Accords, operates under the auspices of the United Nations and has the authority to remove elected officials if they are deemed to be obstructing the peace process. The OHR has not intervened in Bosnian politics in recent years.

B4. Do various segments of the population (including ethnic, racial, religious, gender, LGBT+, and other relevant groups) have full political rights and electoral opportunities? 2 / 4

Political rights in BiH are in large part contingent on one's ethnic background and place of residence. Jews and Roma are constitutionally barred from the presidency and from membership in the House of Peoples, despite the European Court of Human Rights rulings against those provisions. Serbs who live in the Federation and Croats and Bosniaks who live in the RS are also excluded from the presidency. Some Croats argue that their rights to representation are violated by electoral laws allowing non-Croats a significant voice in the selection of the Croat member of the presidency and Croat members of the House of Peoples. Critics of the Croat nationalist HDZ bloc counter, however, that the party has manipulated the discourse surrounding this issue to obstruct civic and liberal reforms of the country's constitutional order. Women are underrepresented in politics and government.

C. FUNCTIONING OF GOVERNMENT: 4 / 12

C1. Do the freely elected head of government and national legislative representatives determine the policies of the government? 2 / 4

Government formation and policy implementation are seriously impeded by the country's complex system of ethnic representation. Under the Dayton Accords, representatives from each of the three major ethnic groups, at both the state and entity levels, may exercise a veto on legislation deemed harmful to their interests. The state government is also undercut by movements within each of BiH's entities for greater autonomy.

Dodik, who serves as the Serb member of the state-level presidency and holds significant influence in the RS, continues to speak openly of his desire for the RS to secede from BiH.

C2. Are safeguards against official corruption strong and effective? 1 / 4

Corruption remains widespread and systemic, and legislation designed to combat the problem is poorly enforced. When corruption probes are actually opened, they rarely result in convictions.

In May 2020, Federation prime minister Fadil Novalić was implicated in a respirator-procurement scandal, and briefly taken into custody by the state anticorruption police. He and two codefendants were indicted in December on charges of corruption and embezzlement. Also in May, Košarac, the foreign trade and economic relations minister, was caught on film at a party in a Sarajevo restaurant while a COVID-19 lockdown was in force. He survived a consequent confidence vote in the BiH parliament.

C3. Does the government operate with openness and transparency? 1 / 4

Government operations remain largely inaccessible to the public. Procurement awards are often made in secret and public institutions often do not comply with freedom of information laws. Candidates for major offices are obliged to make financial disclosures, but the relevant laws do not meet international standards, and the resulting disclosures are considered unreliable. Debate and decisions on matters of public interest, including legislation and subjects pertaining to European Union (EU) accession, routinely occur during interparty negotiations that take place behind closed doors, outside of government institutions.

CIVIL LIBERTIES: 34 / 60

D. FREEDOM OF EXPRESSION AND BELIEF: 10 / 16

D1. Are there free and independent media? 2 / 4

Freedom of expression is legally guaranteed but limited in practice. Journalists face political pressure as well as harassment, threats, and assaults in the course of their work. There is a large private media sector, including outlets that are affiliated with local political parties and those that belong to major international news networks. Public broadcasters in both entities, and at the canton level, often operate as partisan platforms; this is especially pronounced with the entity broadcaster in the RS, Radio-Television Republika Srpska (RTRS), whose coverage serves the interests of the SNSD.

D2. Are individuals free to practice and express their religious faith or nonbelief in public and private? 3 / 4

Religious freedom is not subject to formal restrictions, but in practice religious communities face some discrimination in areas where they constitute a minority. Acts of vandalism against religious sites continue to be reported.

D3. Is there academic freedom, and is the educational system free from extensive political indoctrination? 2 / 4

The education system is racked by corruption and clientelism, and the curriculum is politicized at all levels of education. There is evidence of political interference in the operations of university student groups, in particular by the SDA at the University of Sarajevo. At some schools in the Federation, Bosniak and Croat students are still divided into separate classes on the basis of their ethnicity. Some Bosniak returnees in the RS have sent their children to temporary alternative schools to avoid curriculums they find discriminatory, and some Serb families have described discriminatory educational environments in the Federation.

D4. Are individuals free to express their personal views on political or other sensitive topics without fear of surveillance or retribution? 3 / 4

Freedom of expression for individuals is generally protected from overt government interference. However, peer pressure and the risk of an adverse public reaction remain significant curbs on the discussion of sensitive topics. The news media often report on "controversial" social media posts by members of the public.

E. ASSOCIATIONAL AND ORGANIZATIONAL RIGHTS: 7 / 12

E1. Is there freedom of assembly? 3 / 4

Freedom of assembly is generally respected in BiH, and peaceful protests are common. However, demonstrators sometimes encounter administrative obstacles or police violence.

In 2018, persistent and often large-scale protests followed the unexplained death—and presumed murder—that March of David Dragičević, a 21-year-old Banja Luka resident whose case touched on broader concerns about policing and the rule of law in the RS. Dragičević's father and opposition leaders accused the RS police, prosecutor's office, and political leadership of either playing a role in or covering up his son's death. In 2019 and 2020, RS police continued to ban and disperse "Justice for David" protests.

E2. Is there freedom for nongovernmental organizations, particularly those that are engaged in human rights- and governance-related work? 2 / 4

The nongovernmental organization (NGO) sector in BiH remains robust but is sometimes exposed to government pressure and interference, with more difficult conditions in the RS, where there have been reports of prolonged tax investigations of NGOs by the RS government. Many organizations rely on government funding, posing a potential conflict if they seek to criticize the authorities.

E3. Is there freedom for trade unions and similar professional or labor organizations? 2 / 4

Labor unions operate freely in the whole of BiH, although workers often have limited bargaining power in practice. The right to strike is legally protected, but labor laws in the Federation pose significant barriers to the exercise of this right. Legal protections against antiunion action by employers are weakly enforced. The leading political blocs in the country exercise significant control over unions in their respective strongholds.

F. RULE OF LAW: 7 / 16

F1. Is there an independent judiciary? 1 / 4

The judiciary is formally independent, but weak in practice, and the Constitutional Court continues to face challenges from the SNSD and HDZ-BiH in particular. Dozens of Constitutional Court decisions have been disregarded by political leaders, as has some jurisprudence from the European Court of Human Rights. Individual judges are also subject to political pressure, interference, and intimidation regarding the cases before them. The High Judicial and Prosecutorial Council of Bosnia and Herzegovina (HJPC), which appoints judges, has been racked by scandal and is widely perceived as corrupt. Facing international pressure to resign, the body's leader, Milan Tegeltija, stepped down in December 2020, in light of allegations of corruption and cronyism.

The existence of four separate court systems—for the central state, the RS, the Federation, and the self-governing Brčko district—contributes to overall inefficiency.

F2. Does due process prevail in civil and criminal matters? 2 / 4

Guarantees of due process are inconsistently upheld, with judges often failing to manage trials effectively and contributing to extensive delays. Access to adequate legal counsel can be contingent on one's financial standing. Police corruption is a problem and sometimes stems from links to organized crime. Public prosecutors are widely reputed to be corrupt and under political control.

The process of prosecuting war crimes in domestic courts has been slow, with political interference and courts' lack of resources and capacity exacerbating a large backlog of cases. Despite efforts to reinvigorate the process, impunity for war crimes including killings and sexual violence has persisted.

The 2019 assassination of business owner Slaviša Krunić, a prominent critic of the RS government, remains unsolved. Three suspects were formally charged with carrying out the murder in December 2019, but little was publicly known about the motives or potential organizers behind the crime.

In September 2020, evidence surfaced implicating RS prime minister Radovan Višković, in covering up mass graves containing the remains of men killed in the 1995 Srebrenica genocide. The Office of the Prosecutor of Bosnia and Herzegovina confirmed it was reviewing evidence; Višković has denied the allegations, and local authorities have not opened a formal investigation.

F3. Is there protection from the illegitimate use of physical force and freedom from war and insurgencies? 2 / 4

Although overall violent crime rates are not unusually high for the region, organized crime is a significant problem, and high-profile incidents in recent years have fueled public frustration with the police and judicial system. Harassment by police remains routine for vulnerable groups, including significant numbers of migrants transiting through the country. Many prisons are overcrowded or feature other substandard conditions, and detainees are subject to physical abuse by prison authorities. Active land mines dating to the 1990s continue to pose a threat to civilians.

F4. Do laws, policies, and practices guarantee equal treatment of various segments of the population? 2 / 4

Laws guaranteeing equal treatment are unevenly upheld. Discrimination against members of the Romany minority is widespread. Bosniaks and Croats in the RS experience difficulties accessing social services. People who returned to their homes after being displaced during the war face discrimination in employment and housing in regions where their ethnic group constitutes a minority; Bosniak returnees in the RS entity face notable discrimination and harassment. Women are legally entitled to full equality with men but encounter discrimination in the workplace in practice. Members of the LGBT+ community face discrimination, harassment, and occasional physical attacks, and authorities often fail to adequately investigate and prosecute crimes against LGBT+ people.

More than 50,000 migrants, refugees, and asylum seekers arrived in the country during 2018 and 2019, marking a sharp increase from previous years; arrivals began to slow in 2020, reaching around 16,000. While the vast majority travel on to other locations, some 8,300 remained stranded in BiH as of late 2020, most of whom live in squalid migrants camps that lack basic services or protection against the elements. Authorities in the RS entity have refused to allow any migrant centers, and the burden of care has been thrust almost entirely on a handful of municipalities in the country's northwest. Many migrants are exposed to routine violence by local authorities, as well as by Croatian border guards who have repeatedly been accused of illegal pushbacks. Instances of violence between migrants and local community members continue, including at least one reported murder of a migrant in the Herzegovina region in October 2019.

G. PERSONAL AUTONOMY AND INDIVIDUAL RIGHTS: 10 / 16

G1. Do individuals enjoy freedom of movement, including the ability to change their place of residence, employment, or education? 3 / 4

The law protects freedom of movement, and this right is generally upheld in practice. Land mines limit movement in some areas.

G2. Are individuals able to exercise the right to own property and establish private businesses without undue interference from state or nonstate actors? 2 / 4

Although the legal framework broadly supports property rights and private business activity, widespread corruption and patronage remain major barriers to free enterprise. Individuals who returned to their homes after being displaced by the 1992–95 war have faced attacks on their property. The European Commission has called for further progress on compensating people for property that cannot be returned.

G3. Do individuals enjoy personal social freedoms, including choice of marriage partner and size of family, protection from domestic violence, and control over appearance? 3 / 4

Individual freedom on personal status matters such as marriage and divorce is generally protected. Same-sex marriage is not recognized, though in 2020 the Federation government appointed a working group to consider ways to regulate such partnerships.

Domestic violence remains a serious concern despite some government efforts to combat it. Incidents of abuse are believed to be considerably underreported, and civic groups have found that law enforcement authorities are often reluctant to intervene or impose strong penalties.

G4. Do individuals enjoy equality of opportunity and freedom from economic exploitation? 2 / 4

Legal protections against exploitative working conditions are poorly enforced, and workers in some industries face hazardous conditions. Patronage and clientelism continue to adversely affect hiring practices and contribute to de facto restrictions on economic opportunity.

According to the US State Department's 2020 *Trafficking in Persons Report*, both Bosnian and foreign adults and children are subject to trafficking for the purposes of sexual exploitation and forced labor in BiH, with Romany children particularly vulnerable to forced begging and forced marriages that amount to domestic servitude. The report found that the government-maintained efforts toward prosecuting perpetrators and protecting victims and increased efforts in preventing trafficking during the coverage period.

Botswana

Population: 2,300,000
Capital: Gaborone
Freedom Status: Free
Electoral Democracy: Yes

Overview: While it is considered one of the most stable democracies in Africa, Botswana has been dominated by a single party since independence. Media freedom remains under threat. The indigenous San people, as well as migrants, refugees, and LGBT+ people, face discrimination.

KEY DEVELOPMENTS IN 2020

- In July, the government gazetted a bill that would effectively prohibit national and local legislators from defecting to other parties. The bill progressed through Parliament and awaited President Mokgweetsi Masisi's signature by December, though it had not been signed by year's end.
- President Masisi declared a COVID-19-related state of emergency in March, and wide-ranging emergency legislation was gazetted in April. The Emergency Powers Act (EPA) prohibited the right to strike and prohibited the dissemination of purportedly false pandemic-related news among other provisions. Authorities reported 14,205 COVID-19 cases and 40 deaths to the World Health Organization (WHO) by year's end.

POLITICAL RIGHTS: 28 / 40

A. ELECTORAL PROCESS: 10 / 12

A1. Was the current head of government or other chief national authority elected through free and fair elections? 3 / 4

The president is indirectly elected by the National Assembly for a five-year term and is eligible for reelection. The vice president is appointed by the president and confirmed by the National Assembly. The president holds significant power, including the authority to prolong or dismiss the National Assembly. In 2018, Vice President Mokgweetsi Masisi was named interim president when the term of predecessor Ian Khama expired. The Botswana Democratic Party (BDP) won a majority of parliamentary seats in the October 2019 elections. Masisi was sworn into office that November.

A2. Were the current national legislative representatives elected through free and fair elections? 4 / 4

Parliament includes a unicameral, 65-seat National Assembly and an advisory House of Chiefs. Voters directly elect 57 National Assembly members to five-year terms, while 6 members are nominated by the president and approved by the National Assembly. The president and attorney general are ex officio members. The 34-member House of Chiefs is composed mostly of traditional leaders, representatives they elect, and representatives appointed by the president. It advises legislators on tribal issues, land matters, and the constitution.

The BDP won 38 National Assembly seats with 52.7 percent of the vote in the October 2019 elections, while the Umbrella for Democratic Change (UDC) won 15 seats and 35.9 percent, the Botswana Patriotic Front (BPF) won 3 seats and 4.4 percent, and the Alliance of Progressives (AP) won 1 seat and 5.1 percent.

Southern African Development Community (SADC) and African Union (AU) observers called the poll free and fair but criticized the lack of indelible ink and the use of translucent ballot boxes. The UDC claimed that voters were allowed to cast multiple ballots, and that voters and election officials were bribed. The UDC petitioned the High Court to throw the results out, but their case was dismissed in December 2019. The Court of Appeal agreed to hear the matter in January 2020, but dismissed it later that month, citing a lack of jurisdiction.

A3. Are the electoral laws and framework fair, and are they implemented impartially by the relevant election management bodies? 3 / 4

The Independent Electoral Commission (IEC) administers elections and is generally considered independent and capable. However, the IEC was affected by budgetary constraints and a staff shortage during the 2019 electoral period, impacting its voter-education and registration drives.

The Electoral Amendment Act of 2016 (EAA), which mandated electronic voting for the 2019 elections, caused controversy after its passage. The opposition Botswana Congress Party (BCP) claimed that electronic voting was susceptible to pro-BDP manipulation and threatened to boycott the 2019 polls. The government withdrew the electronic-voting mandate and other provisions of the EAA in 2018, and the BCP settled a lawsuit against the government in 2019.

B. POLITICAL PLURALISM AND PARTICIPATION: 10 / 16

B1. Do the people have the right to organize in different political parties or other competitive political groupings of their choice, and is the system free of undue obstacles to the rise and fall of these competing parties or groupings? 3 / 4

The right of political parties to form and operate is legally guaranteed and is respected in practice. However, the opposition has alleged that the BDP abuses state resources, including the influential state media, to its own benefit. The lack of a public-financing system also leaves opposition parties at a disadvantage. However, the 2018 withdrawal of an EAA provision that had increased candidates' fees brought some relief to opposition parties.

The UDC and its leader, Duma Boko, reported harassment and interference from government agencies during the 2019 election campaign, including the harassment of Boko's family members and the impounding of an UDC-owned light aircraft.

In July 2020, amid concerns that BDP parliamentarians intended to join other parties, the government gazetted a bill that would effectively prohibit local and national legislators from doing so. While the bill awaited Masisi's signature by December, he did not sign it into law by year's end.

B2. Is there a realistic opportunity for the opposition to increase its support or gain power through elections? 2 / 4

The BDP, drawing on the advantages of its long incumbency, has dominated the political landscape since 1966; no opposition party has ever won power.

In 2012, several opposition parties formed the UDC to contest elections. However, subsequent infighting within the UDC threatened its competitiveness during the 2019 contests. The opposition vote was further split when former president Khama quit the BDP in 2019 and helped form the BPF. In October 2020, the AP, BPF, and UDC signed an agreement to cooperate in future by-elections.

B3. Are the people's political choices free from domination by forces that are external to the political sphere, or by political forces that employ extrapolitical means? 3 / 4

People's political choices are largely free from domination by unelected outside groups. While observers noted the potential for tribal chiefs to influence voters, an Afrobarometer survey published in January 2020 showed that most respondents did not see chiefs as influential.

Election monitors noted that Batswana political parties rely on foreign donations, which could allow for external interference in domestic politics.

There have been some past reports of vote buying during elections.

B4. Do various segments of the population (including ethnic, racial, religious, gender, LGBT+, and other relevant groups) have full political rights and electoral opportunities? 2 / 4

Women have full political rights, but cultural factors limit their participation, and their interests are not necessarily addressed by elected leaders. Only 11 female candidates ran for seats in 2019, a decline from the 17 who participated in 2014. Seven women currently sit in the National Assembly.

Smaller ethnic and tribal groups tend to be left out of the political process, with observers noting that members are disadvantaged by the country's first-past-the-post electoral system. People with disabilities have participated at low levels in recent parliamentary elections. Parties generally do not represent the interests of LGBT+ people.

C. FUNCTIONING OF GOVERNMENT: 8 / 12

C1. Do the freely elected head of government and national legislative representatives determine the policies of the government? 3 / 4

Elected officials determine government policies. However, opposition parties have criticized the executive for dominating the National Assembly and rushing legislation without adequate deliberation or consultation.

In 2016, lawmakers approved an amendment increasing number of National Assembly members appointed by the president from four to six. Opposition leaders argued that the change would strengthen executive power at the legislature's expense.

In 2018, Masisi transferred the Directorate of Intelligence and Security Services (DISS) and the Financial Intelligence Agency from their respective ministries to the president's office, prompting concerns over the improper centralization of power.

President Masisi declared a COVID-19 state of emergency in March 2020 while Emergency Powers Act (EPA), which gave the president wide-ranging powers, was gazetted in April. The state of emergency remained in force through year's end after Parliament approved an extension in September.

C2. Are safeguards against official corruption strong and effective? 3 / 4

Botswana has a comprehensive legislative anticorruption framework. Whistleblower-protection legislation was passed in 2016. In 2019, legislators passed the Declaration of Assets and Liabilities Act (DALA), though opposition parties questioned its effectiveness in fighting corruption. DALA called for the creation of the Ethics and Integrity Directorate, which became operational in January 2020.

The main anticorruption agency, the Directorate on Corruption and Economic Crime (DCEC) has been accused of ineffectiveness in pursuing high-level cases, and its independence was questioned when it was transferred to the president's office in 2012. In July 2020, then DCEC director general Joseph Mathambo voiced concerns over the agency's budgetary resources in front of a parliamentary committee. Mathambo was dismissed in August.

High-profile cases, including that of former DISS head Isaac Seabelo Kgosi, who was originally accused of tax evasion, continued during the year. In February 2020, Kgosi was formally accused of misusing money from National Petroleum Fund, but was acquitted in December along with several codefendants.

C3. Does the government operate with openness and transparency? 2 / 4

Botswana lacks a freedom-of-information law, which limits government transparency. Budget processes are opaque and public contracts are often awarded through patronage networks. Section 44 of the Corruption and Economic Crime Act prohibits publishing information on DCEC investigations. Public officers and the heads of private organizations are subject to DALA. In August 2020, legislators passed the Income Tax Amendment Bill, which is meant to improve transparency on tax matters.

CIVIL LIBERTIES: 44 / 60
D. FREEDOM OF EXPRESSION AND BELIEF: 12 / 16
D1. Are there free and independent media? 2 / 4

Freedom of expression is constitutionally guaranteed. However, incidents of intimidation and harassment against journalists have been reported under the Masisi administration.

State-run media outlets dominate the broadcasting sector and have exhibited progovernment bias. A government ban on private-media advertising remains in place, harming the competitiveness and viability of many outlets.

The 2008 Media Practitioners Act established a statutory media regulator and mandated the registration of all media workers and outlets—including websites and blogs—with violations punishable by a fine or imprisonment. Journalistic activity is also affected by provisions of the National Security Law, DALA, and the DISS Act.

Journalistic activity was also affected by COVID-19 measures. Under the EPA, Batswana were prohibited from using sources other than the government or the WHO.

D2. Are individuals free to practice and express their religious faith or nonbelief in public and private? 4 / 4

Religious freedom is generally respected, though all religious organizations must register with the government.

D3. Is there academic freedom, and is the educational system free from extensive political indoctrination? 3 / 4

Although academic freedom is generally respected, professors often practice self-censorship when addressing sensitive topics. Foreign academics have previously been deported for publishing work that criticized the government, contributing to cautiousness among many scholars.

D4. Are individuals free to express their personal views on political or other sensitive topics without fear of surveillance or retribution? 3 / 4

Freedom of expression is constitutionally protected but is restricted in practice, prompting self-censorship amongst Batswana. Insulting the president, a lawmaker, or a public official is punishable by a fine. The 2008 Public Service Act restricts the ability of public-sector workers to air political views. The DISS is able to monitor private online communications.

Batswana were also affected by restrictions when discussing the COVID-19 pandemic. In late March 2020, the communications regulator issued a public notice warning that the penal code and Communications Regulatory Act prohibited so-called false-news dissemination. The EPA included COVID-19-related false-news provisions. Offenders face a $10,000 fine, imprisonment of up to five years, or both.

E. ASSOCIATIONAL AND ORGANIZATIONAL RIGHTS: 10 / 12
E1. Is there freedom of assembly? 4 / 4

Freedom of assembly is constitutionally guaranteed and largely upheld in practice. However, the Public Order Act requires citizens to seek police permission to exercise this right. The constitutionality of this clause has been questioned in the past, and police have sometimes denied requests for unclear reasons.

The government declared a COVID-19-related state of emergency in March 2020, restricting the size of public assemblies; assembly restrictions remained in effect through year's end.

E2. Is there freedom for nongovernmental organizations, particularly those that are engaged in human rights- and governance-related work? 4 / 4

Nongovernmental organizations, including human rights groups, generally operate without restrictions.

E3. Is there freedom for trade unions and similar professional or labor organizations? 2 / 4

The right to form a union is respected, but the Trade Dispute Act places restrictions on who can strike. As a result, the government declares many strikes illegal, putting employees' jobs at risk. The law does not always protect workers from antiunion discrimination by employers.

In 2018, the government attempted to derecognize public-service unions for alleged noncompliance with provisions of the Public Service Act of 2008, but a trade court blocked the attempt. President Masisi promised to restore the dormant Public Service Bargaining Council that year but has not yet done so.

The right to strike was restricted by the EPA.

F. RULE OF LAW: 11 / 16

F1. Is there an independent judiciary? 3 / 4

The judiciary is generally independent and free from interference. However, there have been calls to improve the transparency, impartiality, and public oversight of the selection and appointment processes for judges. While the Judicial Service Commission advertises vacancies and interviews potential members of the High Court, the appointment process for Court of Appeal judges is relatively nontransparent.

F2. Does due process prevail in civil and criminal matters? 3 / 4

The right to a fair trial is constitutionally protected and generally upheld in practice. However, the judiciary lacks human and financial resources, leading to case backlogs, lengthy pretrial detentions, and the postponement of cases.

Attorneys are provided to defendants in capital cases, but defendants in noncapital cases must pay for their own counsel. The DISS can arrest suspects without a warrant if agents believe they have committed or will commit a crime.

While courts were affected by COVID-19 mitigation measures, they remained largely operational during the year.

F3. Is there protection from the illegitimate use of physical force and freedom from war and insurgencies? 3 / 4

Although citizens are largely protected from the illegitimate use of force, corporal punishment is sometimes imposed. The DISS has historically been accused of corrupt activity, unlawful arrests, and extrajudicial killings. Instances of police brutality have been reported, and perpetrators are rarely held accountable.

Antipoaching operations have resulted in fatal incidents over the past two decades. In 2018, President Masisi ended an unwritten shoot-to-kill policy originally adopted in at least 2013 to deter wildlife poachers. The poaching ban was revoked altogether in 2019. However, in April 2020, soldiers killed 5 suspected poachers, while another was killed in June.

Motswana law allows for capital punishment, with three people being executed in February and March 2020. In October, Amnesty International called for a moratorium on executions.

F4. Do laws, policies, and practices guarantee equal treatment of various segments of the population? 2 / 4

Customary law, commonly applied in rural areas, often discriminates against women. The indigenous San people tend to be economically marginalized and lack access to education and other public services. There have been reports of beatings, abuse, and arbitrary arrests of San by police and park rangers. Botswana has no human rights body to investigate violations.

Same-sex relations were criminalized until 2019, when the High Court ruled that ban unconstitutional. The government took its case to the Court of Appeal, which was considering the matter in 2020.

Refugees in Botswana have been detained in encampments and have been denied the ability to work and integrate into local communities. In June 2020, the Office of the UN High Commissioner for Refugees's (UNHCR) Botswana mission chief called on the government to facilitate the integration of refugees. Defense, Justice, and Security Minister Kagiso Mmusi offered to open a dialogue on the issue later that month.

G. PERSONAL AUTONOMY AND INDIVIDUAL RIGHTS: 11 / 16

G1. Do individuals enjoy freedom of movement, including the ability to change their place of residence, employment, or education? 3 / 4

Most citizens can move freely throughout the country and travel internationally, though refugees and asylum seekers face movement restrictions. San people have limited access to their traditional lands in the Central Kalahari Game Reserve. The government's long-standing policy has been to relocate San out of the reserve, and those who still have relatives living there must apply for a permit to visit them. In October 2020, San signatories sent a petition to President Masisi calling on the government to recommit to a dialogue to resolve the land-access dispute.

Movement restrictions were imposed when a COVID-19-related state of emergency was declared in March 2020, with Batswana requiring permits to travel within the country in some cases. International travel restrictions were in effect for much of 2020, but were loosened beginning in November.

G2. Are individuals able to exercise the right to own property and establish private businesses without undue interference from state or nonstate actors? 3 / 4

Botswana has generally sound legal protections for property rights which are enforced in practice. The country's regulatory framework is considered conducive to establishing and operating private businesses. Land rights for wives, widows, and orphans were improved in September 2020, when President Masisi signed amendments to the Land Policy of 2015 into law.

G3. Do individuals enjoy personal social freedoms, including choice of marriage partner and size of family, protection from domestic violence, and control over appearance? 2 / 4

Gender-based violence (GBV), including domestic violence and rape, is pervasive. Spousal rape is not considered a crime. Customary law restricts women's rights within a marriage. When husbands and wives separate, custody is traditionally granted to the father.

Child and forced marriages still occur under customary law. Women can experience harassment for not dressing conservatively.

In 2018, Parliament passed the Penal Code Amendment Bill, which introduced stronger penalties for rape and raised the age of consent from 16 to 18. In September 2020, the government published a draft of the Sexual Offenders Registry Bill, which would impose a registration and monitoring system for sex offenders among other provisions. The bill passed a parliamentary reading in December, proceeding to the committee stage.

In August 2020, the Botswana Nurses Union warned that GBV incidents increased after the COVID-19 pandemic took hold. In November, 25 dedicated courts were established to adjudicate GBV cases.

G4. Do individuals enjoy equality of opportunity and freedom from economic exploitation?
3 / 4

Workers enjoy protections against exploitative labor practices. However, employer abuses in the retail, tourism, and private-security sectors are an ongoing problem. Botswana lacks a strong regulatory framework for labor brokers that dispatch workers to clients on short-term contracts, in which exploitation is common.

Human trafficking remains an ongoing challenge. The Anti-Human Trafficking Act of 2014 was amended in 2018 to include stiffer financial penalties. However, the US State Department reported that the judiciary was unfamiliar with the legislation in the 2020 edition of its *Trafficking in Persons Report*, hindering antitrafficking efforts.

Brazil

Population: 211,800,000
Capital: Brasília
Freedom Status: Free
Electoral Democracy: Yes

Overview: Brazil is a democracy that holds competitive elections, and the political arena, though polarized, is characterized by vibrant public debate. However, independent journalists and civil society activists risk harassment and violent attack, and the government has struggled to address high rates of violent crime and disproportionate violence against and economic exclusion of minorities. Corruption is endemic at top levels, contributing to widespread disillusionment with traditional political parties. Societal discrimination and violence against LGBT+ people remains a serious problem.

KEY DEVELOPMENTS IN 2020

- Brazil was one of the world's worst-affected countries during the COVID-19 pandemic. According to University of Oxford researchers, the country registered over 190,000 deaths and 2 million cases by the end of 2020, and public health specialists decried the dismissive attitude and misinformation-laden response by national authorities, especially President Jair Bolsonaro.
- Tension between President Bolsonaro and other members of the political establishment remained high throughout the year, as the president clashed with state governors over the COVID-19 response and with Congress and the Supreme Court over various policy and oversight issues.

- In April, Minister of Justice Sérgio Moro, an influential anticorruption crusader, resigned after alleging that President Bolsonaro had attempted to interfere with management of the Federal Police in order to favor Bolsonaro's own interests.

POLITICAL RIGHTS: 31 / 40

A. ELECTORAL PROCESS: 10 / 12

A1. Was the current head of government or other chief national authority elected through free and fair elections? 3 / 4

Brazil is a federal republic governed under a presidential system. The president is elected by popular vote for a four-year term and is eligible for reelection to a second term.

In the 2018 race, candidates made their cases to voters disillusioned by persistent, high-level corruption scandals, and increasingly concerned by a difficult economic environment and a rise in violent crime. Jair Bolsonaro, then of the far-right Social Liberal Party (PSL), won the election, taking 55.1 percent of the vote in a runoff against Fernando Haddad of the leftist Workers' Party (PT). Bolsonaro's campaign was characterized by a disdain for democratic principles and aggressive pledges to wipe out corruption and violent crime. An Organization of American States (OAS) election observation mission generally praised the poll's administration, and stakeholders quickly accepted its result. However, the highly polarized campaign was marred by the spread of fake news, conspiracy theories, and aggressive rhetoric on social networks and online messaging services (notably WhatsApp). There were also frequent preelection threats and violence targeting candidates, political supporters, journalists, and members of the judiciary. While most of the reported incidents appeared to involve attacks by Bolsonaro supporters, his backers were also targeted, and Bolsonaro was stabbed at a rally in early September, forcing him to cut back on public appearances a month before the election.

Municipal elections were held throughout the country in November 2020. Centrist and conservative parties not aligned with the president made gains and PT mayoral candidates suffered losses, while Bolsonaro-backed candidates performed poorly.

A2. Were the current national legislative representatives elected through free and fair elections? 3 / 4

Legislative elections are generally free and fair. The bicameral National Congress is composed of an 81-member Senate and a 513-member Chamber of Deputies. Senators serve staggered eight-year terms, with one- to two-thirds coming up for election every four years. Members of the Chamber of Deputies serve four-year terms.

In the October 2018 elections, the PT lost seats but remained the largest party in the lower house, with 56 deputies. Bolsonaro's PSL captured 52 seats, up from just a single seat previously. In the Senate, the center-right Brazilian Democratic Movement (MDB, previously PMDB) maintained its lead with a total of 12 seats, while the Brazilian Social Democratic Party (PSDB) holds 9, followed by the Social Democratic Party (PSD), Democrats (DEM), and PT, which each hold 4 seats. The PSL entered the chamber after capturing 4 seats.

The 2018 legislative elections were held concurrently with the first round of the presidential election; campaigning thus took place in the same highly polarized environment, marked by aggressive rhetoric and instances of political violence.

A3. Are the electoral laws and framework fair, and are they implemented impartially by the relevant election management bodies? 4 / 4

Brazilian election laws are generally well enforced. A Supreme Electoral Court (TSE) presides over cases related to violations of electoral law.

In late 2019 and early 2020 the TSE published new rules and standards and established a task force to rapidly respond to digital disinformation networks and campaigns. The coordination involved collaboration with both civil society groups and tech companies such as Facebook and Google. Politicians and their allies continued to spread digital disinformation in the run-up to the November 2020 municipal elections, though not as intensively as in the 2018 general elections. Investigations by the TSE into the role of Bolsonaro and close supporters in coordinating disinformation networks continued throughout the year.

B. POLITICAL PLURALISM AND PARTICIPATION: 14 / 16

B1. Do the people have the right to organize in different political parties or other competitive political groupings of their choice, and is the system free of undue obstacles to the rise and fall of these competing parties or groupings? 4 / 4

Brazil has an unfettered multiparty system marked by vigorous competition among rival parties. The electoral framework encourages the proliferation of parties, a number of which are based in a single state. Some parties display little ideological consistency. Party switching is common by members of Congress, rendering electoral coalitions fragile. The sheer number of parties means that the executive branch must piece together diverse and often ideologically incoherent coalitions to pass legislation. In late 2019, Bolsonaro left the PSL to create the Alliance for Brazil (APB), but the party had not achieved formal registration and the president remained unaffiliated as of the end of 2020.

Ahead of the 2018 elections, 35 parties were registered, 30 of which won seats in the lower chamber—the largest number of parties seated there since Brazil's return to electoral politics in 1985. However, political parties operate with little transparency and under no governance rules, and often are targets of investigations into the misuse of public funds.

B2. Is there a realistic opportunity for the opposition to increase its support or gain power through elections? 4 / 4

Opposition parties are able to compete freely and gain power through elections at both the federal and subnational levels. Ahead of the 2018 polls, Bolsonaro's former small, far-right PSL succeeded in attracting widespread support in a short amount of time. Elected officials in subnational positions are often influential political actors, and prominent opposition to Bolsonaro has come from these leaders.

B3. Are the people's political choices free from domination by forces that are external to the political sphere, or by political forces that employ extrapolitical means? 3 / 4

Recent investigations into corruption have exposed how powerful business interests undermine democratic accountability by facilitating or encouraging corruption among elected officials. Criminal groups have carried out attacks against political candidates. In 2018, Rio de Janeiro councilwoman Marielle Franco, a Black lesbian politician who was an outspoken advocate for minorities, was murdered. Investigations into the crime revealed corruption schemes and the growing power of militia groups in Rio de Janeiro State, whose membership includes active and retired members of the local police force. Although two alleged perpetrators were detained in 2019, the mastermind of the crime remained unknown. Militias and other criminal organizations—which may exercise significant control over campaigning and other political activity within their territories—were partly blamed for a rise in violence as the 2020 municipal elections approached; at least 25 candidates were killed prior to the November balloting.

B4. Do various segments of the population (including ethnic, racial, religious, gender, LGBT+, and other relevant groups) have full political rights and electoral opportunities? 3 / 4

The constitution guarantees equal rights without prejudice, but some groups have greater political representation than others. Afro-Brazilians and women and their interests remain underrepresented in electoral politics and in government.

The 2020 municipal elections produced improvements for several underrepresented groups: self-identified Afro-Brazilians garnered approximately 44 percent of city council seats; the number of Indigenous mayors and council members rose nearly 30 percent; LGBT+ candidates won a record number of seats; and the number of women elected rose modestly compared to 2016. Gains in diversity were abetted by a September TSE ruling that parties must distribute public campaign funds equitably between White and non-White candidates.

C. FUNCTIONING OF GOVERNMENT: 7 / 12

C1. Do the freely elected head of government and national legislative representatives determine the policies of the government? 3 / 4

Widespread corruption undermines the government's ability to make and implement policy without undue influence from private or criminal interests.

During the 2010s, the functioning of government was severely hampered by a rolling political crisis that saw the removal of President Dilma Rousseff following charges she had improperly manipulated the state budget. Her term was completed by Michel Temer, who had been vice president; Temer soon became the subject of separate charges by the attorney general of bribery and obstruction of justice, which the lower house subsequently blocked. Corruption was a chief concern for voters during the 2018 elections that brought Bolsonaro to power—as well as a more autonomous legislature.

Given Bolsonaro's lack of a stable governing coalition, congressional leaders have gained political prominence since he came to power. This influence was preserved in 2020, as Congress helped fill a vacuum in responding to the COVID-19 pandemic. State governors also played an active role during the pandemic, with many insisting on more stringent restrictions and vocally objecting to Bolsonaro's management.

The presence of thousands of active-duty and retired military officials in the Bolsonaro administration, along with the expansion of military missions to areas like environmental protection, has prompted unease about growing armed forces influence in politics. These concerns were particularly acute in mid-2020, when the press reported on a meeting in which the president, with the support of several generals, came close to ordering a shutdown of Congress and the Supreme Court.

C2. Are safeguards against official corruption strong and effective? 2 / 4

Corruption and graft are endemic in Brazil, especially among elected officials. Beginning in 2014, an investigation known as Operation Car Wash focused on bribery, money laundering, and bid-rigging involving state oil company Petrobras and private construction companies. In addition to former Petrobras executives and heads of major construction firms, its findings have also implicated elected officials from across the political spectrum. Sérgio Moro, then serving as a crusading judge, became the face of the crackdown, and subsequently joined the incoming Bolsonaro administration as justice minister.

However, a series of investigative reports known as Car Wash Leaks, published by the online outlet The Intercept Brasil in 2019, exposed an improper relationship between Moro (in his role as judge) and federal prosecutors, in which Moro had shared advice on how to prosecute high-level corruption cases. One such case was that of former president Luiz Inácio "Lula" da Silva, who was convicted on corruption charges and imprisoned in 2018 before being freed in November 2019, after the Supreme Court ruled that defendants must be released while appeals are pending. Investigations related to Operation Car Wash continued throughout 2020, but the primary task force was substantially dismantled.

In April 2020, Moro resigned in protest from the Justice Ministry after President Bolsonaro attempted to interfere with the federal police—one of the agencies tasked with investigating Bolsonaro's family members and associates. Criminal inquiries have targeted multiple members of Bolsonaro's family, and in October, one of the president's sons, Senator Flavio Bolsonaro, was charged for diverting public resources when he was a state deputy in Rio de Janeiro.

Numerous corruption allegations also occurred amid Brazil's widely criticized response to the COVID-19 pandemic. In September, Rio de Janeiro state governor Wilson Witzel was suspended from office as a federal probe investigated graft stemming from pandemic-related procurement processes.

C3. Does the government operate with openness and transparency? 2 / 4

Brazil enacted a Freedom of Information Act in 2012, but in practice, the government does not always release requested information, and when doing so, not always in machine-readable formats. Compliance with the legislation also varies among Brazil's 26 states and the Brasília Federal District.

The Bolsonaro administration undermined transparency and the president routinely spread misinformation about the virus, labeling it a "little flu" and advocating use of discredited medications, particularly hydroxychloroquine. In April 2020, Bolsonaro attempted to limit requirements to respond to information requests, but the Supreme Court blocked the initiative. Coronavirus-related transparency portals maintained by subnational governments partially compensated for federal shortcomings by providing information on emergency contracts, donations, and social protection measures.

CIVIL LIBERTIES: 43 / 60 (−1)
D. FREEDOM OF EXPRESSION AND BELIEF 14 / 16
D1. Are there free and independent media? 3 / 4

The constitution guarantees freedom of expression, and the media scene is vibrant. However, investigative journalists, particularly those who cover corruption and crime, face threats, harassment, obstruction, and violence, which in some cases has been deadly.

Journalists who criticized Bolsonaro face online and offline harassment, and outlets that carried such criticism face economic pressure from the government. Reporters Without Borders (RSF) tallied 580 attacks in 2020 linked to the "Bolsonaro system" of harassment and abuse, mostly disseminated through social media. In August, the president threatened to punch a journalist who asked about his family's links to corruption allegations. This environment emboldened presidential allies such as Marcelo Crivella, the mayor of Rio de Janeiro, who assigned municipal employees to intimidate interviewees and hinder journalistic coverage of the COVID-19 pandemic. As of August 2020, Article 19 had tallied 82 pandemic-related attacks on reporters.

The legal framework provides inadequate protection for freedom of expression. Defamation is subject to criminal penalties, and in 2020 high-ranking officials requested criminal investigations of several journalists and a Supreme Court justice for criticisms of the government's response to the pandemic. A bill purportedly intended to combat disinformation passed the Senate in June 2020, but multiple provisions were criticized by domestic and international press freedom and human rights groups, and the bill remained pending in the lower house at year's end.

D2. Are individuals free to practice and express their religious faith or nonbelief in public and private? 4 / 4

The constitution guarantees freedom of religion, and the government generally respects this right in practice. However, violence against Afro-Brazilian religious groups is frequent, especially in Rio de Janeiro's favelas. The Commission to Combat Religious Intolerance, composed of judges and public prosecutors, registered over 200 Afro-Brazilian temples ("terreiros") closed in 2019 after assaults or threats from evangelical drug dealers; these groups operate and claim territory like other Brazilian drug-trafficking operations, but also seek to repress faiths that do not align with their own.

D3. Is there academic freedom, and is the educational system free from extensive political indoctrination? 4 / 4

Academic debate is vibrant and freedom is generally unrestricted in schools and universities. Education policy has become increasingly politicized under the Bolsonaro administration, and some professors and researchers have sought temporary refuge abroad following threats in Brazil. In June 2020, Bolsonaro used the COVID-19 pandemic to justify a regulation strengthening executive branch control over the appointment of rectors of federal universities, but the measure was dropped following civil society and congressional opposition.

D4. Are individuals free to express their personal views on political or other sensitive topics without fear of surveillance or retribution? 3 / 4

People are generally able to express personal views in public without fear of surveillance or retaliation. However, in the tense 2018 campaign atmosphere, some political speech was met with acts of violence. A prevalence of violent homophobic rhetoric in recent years has contributed to a sense of fear among many that open discussion of LGBT+ rights and issues could be met with harassment or attack.

Intimidation and harassment by progovernment troll groups on social media remains a serious problem in Brazil. Investigations into the role of Bolsonaro allies, including family members, in the disinformation campaigns continued throughout 2020.

In June 2020, the Ministry of Justice compiled a set of dossiers of 579 federal and state security officials, along with three academics, identified as "antifascists;" in August, the Supreme Court barred the production and use of such profiles. This followed Bolsonaro supporters' dissemination on social media of several similar lists of "antifascist" private citizens.

E. ASSOCIATIONAL AND ORGANIZATIONAL RIGHTS: 9 / 12

E1. Is there freedom of assembly? 3 / 4

While freedom of assembly is generally respected, police or other security agents sometimes use excessive force against demonstrations.

E2. Is there freedom for nongovernmental organizations, particularly those that are engaged in human rights- and governance-related work? 3 / 4

Nongovernmental organizations (NGOs) are able to operate freely in a variety of fields. However, activists working on land rights and environmental protection issues have faced harassment, threats, and violence in recent years, along with verbal hostility from Bolsonaro and other administration officials.

In November 2020 media reports circulated regarding Bolsonaro administration plans to control NGO activity in the Amazon, generating concerned reaction by Brazilian groups and European parliamentarians, but no concrete actions had been taken by year's end.

E3. Is there freedom for trade unions and similar professional or labor organizations? 3 / 4

Industrial labor unions are well organized, and although they are politically connected, Brazilian unions tend to be freer from political party control than their counterparts in other Latin American countries. However, controversial labor reforms enacted in 2017 diminished the strength and role of unions in collective bargaining with businesses.

F. RULE OF LAW: 8 / 16

F1. Is there an independent judiciary? 3 / 4

The judiciary, though largely independent, is overburdened, inefficient, and often subject to intimidation and other external influences, especially in rural areas. Despite these shortcomings, the country's progressive constitution has resulted in an active judiciary that often rules in favor of citizens over the state.

The Supreme Court has maintained its role as an autonomous counterweight to the executive. Tensions remained high in 2020, with allies of the president frequently issuing verbal attacks and threats against the court. Starting in April, right-wing Bolsonaro supporters held a series of demonstrations demanding the chamber's closure, leading to investigations by the court and the attorney general's office that continued during the rest of the year. Despite the interbranch hostility, in September Bolsonaro appointed a relative moderate to fill an open court seat.

F2. Does due process prevail in civil and criminal matters? 2 / 4

The judiciary generally upholds the right to a fair trial. However, federal, state, and appellate courts are severely backlogged. The state struggles to provide legal counsel for defendants and prisoners who are unable to afford an attorney. Access to justice also varies greatly due to Brazil's high level of income inequality. Under a 2017 law, members of the armed forces and military police accused of certain serious crimes against civilians can be tried in military, rather than civilian, courts.

F3. Is there protection from the illegitimate use of physical force and freedom from war and insurgencies? 1 / 4

Brazil has a high homicide rate, though it decreased in 2018 and 2019 before rising slightly in the first nine months of 2020, according to *O Globo* newspaper's Violence Monitor. Victims are often caught in crossfire between highly organized and well-armed drug-trafficking outfits, as well as between those outfits and security forces.

Brazil's police force remains mired in corruption, and serious police abuses, including extrajudicial killings, continued in 2020. Police officers are rarely prosecuted for abuses, and those charged are almost never convicted. A 2020 Brazilian Public Security Forum report indicated increasing significant rises in police violence in recent years, peaking at 6,357 deaths—of whom 80 percent were Black or brown—in 2019.

Police violence is particularly acute in Rio de Janeiro: law enforcement agents killed over 1,800 people in 2019, and the pace was similar through May 2020. In June 2020, however, the Supreme Court forbade most police operations in Rio de Janeiro's slums during the COVID-19 pandemic, leading to a sharp decline in police violence in the following months.

Conditions in Brazil's severely overcrowded prisons are life-threatening, characterized by disease, a lack of adequate food, and deadly gang-related violence. Violence is more likely to affect poor, Black prisoners. Although courts ordered the release of over 50,000 prisoners to ease overcrowding amid the COVID-19 pandemic, the coronavirus had caused the deaths of over 200 prisoners and facility staff as of October.

F4. Do laws, policies, and practices guarantee equal treatment of various segments of the population? 2 / 4

Some populations are not able to fully exercise their human rights in practice. Many Indigenous communities—who comprise about 1 percent of the population—suffer from poverty and lack adequate sanitation and education services.

Just over half of Brazil's population identifies as Black or of mixed race. Afro-Brazilians suffer from high rates of poverty and illiteracy, and almost 80 percent of Brazilians living in extreme poverty are Black or mixed race. Victims of violence in Brazil are predominantly young, Black, and poor: according to a 2020 report by the Brazilian Public Security Forum, nearly 75 percent of violence victims in 2019 were Black. The same group noted that the number of femicides grew approximately 7 percent in 2019, and an additional 2 percent in the first half of 2019.

Although Brazil has a largely tolerant society, it reportedly has one of the world's highest levels of violence against LGBT+ people. According to Grupo Gay da Bahia, an LGBT+ advocacy organization, 297 LGBT+ people were killed in 2019 as a result of homophobic violence, marking a nearly 30 percent drop from the group's figures for the previous year. Grupo Gay reported 152 murders of transgender Brazilians between October 2019 and September 2020, a small rise from the previous period.

In 2019, despite intense pressure from some religious and political leaders, the Supreme Court ruled LGBT+ people are protected under a criminal law that prohibits discrimination on the basis "race, color, ethnicity, religion, and national origin."

Indigenous lands have been subject to increased pressure since Bolsonaro took office, encouraged by his rhetoric and support for easing environmental laws. Indigenous groups were severely affected by the COVID-19 pandemic, and Congress was forced to override Bolsonaro's veto of several provisions of an aid package designed to help protect Indigenous peoples from the virus.

G. PERSONAL AUTONOMY AND INDIVIDUAL RIGHTS: 12 / 16 (−1)

G1. Do individuals enjoy freedom of movement, including the ability to change their place of residence, employment, or education? 4 / 4

Brazilians enjoy freedom to travel within and outside of the country, and to make decisions about their places of residence and employment, though access to high-quality education across all levels remains a challenge. Gang violence in favelas at times has impeded free movement, and has prompted schools to shut down temporarily.

G2. Are individuals able to exercise the right to own property and establish private businesses without undue interference from state or nonstate actors? 3 / 4

While property rights are generally enforced, laws granting indigenous populations exclusive use of certain lands are not always upheld, sometimes leading to violent conflicts. According to figures released by the Pastoral Land Commission, at least 18 people were murdered over land and resource disputes in 2020, and invasions of indigenous lands rose markedly. According to Human Rights Watch, the federal government almost completely ceased collecting environmental fines starting in late 2019 and continuing into 2020, even as illegal deforestation increased.

Requirements for starting new businesses are often onerous, but authorities have taken some steps to ease the process. Legislation approved in August 2019 loosened licensing and inspection requirements for small businesses, for example. Corruption and organized crime can pose obstacles to private business activity.

G3. Do individuals enjoy personal social freedoms, including choice of marriage partner and size of family, protection from domestic violence, and control over appearance? 3 / 4

The government generally does not restrict social freedoms. Same-sex marriage became legal in 2013. However, while a 2006 law sought to address Brazil's high rates of impunity for domestic violence, violence against women and girls remains widespread. Abortion is legal only in the case of rape, a threat to the mother's life, or a rare and usually fatal brain deformity in the fetus, and in August 2020 the Ministry of Health imposed new reporting requirements on clinicians in cases of rape victims seeking abortions. These restrictions limit women's reproductive choices and impinge on family planning.

G4. Do individuals enjoy equality of opportunity and freedom from economic exploitation? 2 / 4 (−1)

Slavery-like working conditions pose a significant problem in rural and urban zones. A 2012 constitutional amendment allows the government to confiscate all property of landholders found to be using slave labor, a measure often criticized by Bolsonaro. Deeply entrenched patterns of discrimination, including precarious employment in the informal economy, contributed to Afro-Brazilians suffering higher infection and mortality as a result of the COVID-19 pandemic.

Since 2013 the Brazilian economy has suffered from mismanagement, including negligence and corruption in large state-owned mining and oil enterprises, and successive administrations have failed to address distortions caused by economic concentration. A 20-year budgetary spending cap enacted in 2016 resulted in cuts to public services and poses a serious obstacle to using state spending to ameliorate inequality of opportunity.

At the outset of the COVID-19 pandemic, poverty and inequality in Brazil had risen more since 2014 than in any other country in Latin America, and the pandemic led to record unemployment and workforce reductions. An emergency aid program provided to offset coronavirus-induced disruptions reduced poverty rates in 2020, but was scheduled to phase out in 2021 and did not include any structural changes to counter the trend toward higher inequality.

Score Change: The score declined from 3 to 2 due to a multiyear trend of rising poverty, income inequality, and barriers to social mobility, combined with the economic effects of the COVID-19 pandemic, which created record unemployment and left many Brazilians dependent on temporary public assistance.

Brunei

Population: 500,000
Capital: Bandar Seri Begawan
Freedom Status: Not Free
Electoral Democracy: No

Overview: Brunei is an absolute monarchy in which the sultan exercises executive power. There are no elected representatives at the national level. Freedoms of the press and assembly are significantly restricted. Online speech is monitored by authorities, but is lively nevertheless.

KEY DEVELOPMENTS IN 2020

- Brunei made new commitments to combat trafficking, ratifying the Association of Southeast Asian Nations (ASEAN) Convention against Trafficking in Persons, and additionally acceded to the United Nations Trafficking in Persons protocol.
- Authorities adopted one of the most effective responses to COVID-19 in Asia, issuing clear restrictions on mass gatherings and travel, providing information about the risks of exposure, and offering guidance on how people could protect themselves. However, this transparency did not carry over into other areas of governance in Brunei.

POLITICAL RIGHTS: 7 / 40

A. ELECTORAL PROCESS: 0 / 12

A1. Was the current head of government or other chief national authority elected through free and fair elections? 0 / 4

The hereditary sultan, Hassanal Bolkiah Mu'izzaddin Waddaulah, is the head of state and prime minister, and continues to wield broad powers under a long-standing state of emergency imposed in 1984.

In recent years, Brunei has appeared to be paving the way for Hassanal's son, Prince Al-Muhtadee Billah, to take power. There are no indications that any transition would involve moving away from a traditional monarchy.

A2. Were the current national legislative representatives elected through free and fair elections? 0 / 4

The unicameral Legislative Council has no political standing independent of the sultan, who appoints its members. Brunei has not held direct legislative elections since 1962.

Elections are held for village-level councils that play a consultative role, though candidates are vetted by the government.

A3. Are the electoral laws and framework fair, and are they implemented impartially by the relevant election management bodies? 0 / 4

There are no national-level electoral laws, and there have not been any national, direct legislative elections in over five decades.

B. POLITICAL PLURALISM AND PARTICIPATION: 3 / 16

B1. Do the people have the right to organize in different political parties or other competitive political groupings of their choice, and is the system free of undue obstacles to the rise and fall of these competing parties or groupings? 1 / 4

Genuine political activity by opposition groups remains extremely limited. The National Development Party (NDP) was permitted to register in 2005 after pledging to work as a partner with the government and swearing loyalty to the sultan; it is the only registered party.

B2. Is there a realistic opportunity for the opposition to increase its support or gain power through elections? 0 / 4

There are no national-level elections in which opposition forces could gain power. Since the National Solidarity Party was deregistered without explanation in 2007, the NDP has been Brunei's sole legal political party. It has no formal political role, few activities in practice, and a small membership, and is unable to challenge the sultan's power in any meaningful way.

B3. Are the people's political choices free from domination by forces that are external to the political sphere, or by political forces that employ extrapolitical means? 1 / 4

With the dominance of the sultan and lack of elections, residents have few avenues for genuine and autonomous political participation. However, people have some very limited ability to challenge unpopular policies through the organization of social movements.

B4. Do various segments of the population (including ethnic, racial, religious, gender, LGBT+, and other relevant groups) have full political rights and electoral opportunities? 1 / 4

Members of ethnic, religious, and other minority groups have few opportunities for political participation, even on a local level. Village council candidates must be Muslim, and ministers and deputy ministers must be Muslim and Malay unless the sultan grants an exception. Since many ethnic Chinese in Brunei remain permanent residents and not citizens, they are further excluded from the limited participation in politics available.

C. FUNCTIONING OF GOVERNMENT: 4 / 12

C1. Do the freely elected head of government and national legislative representatives determine the policies of the government? 0 / 4

None of Brunei's national-level policymakers are chosen through elections. The sultan wields broad powers and is counseled by appointed advisory bodies and the appointed legislature.

C2. Are safeguards against official corruption strong and effective? 3 / 4

In 2015, the government enacted amendments to the Prevention of Corruption Act, which strengthened the anticorruption framework by establishing new conflict of interest rules for public officials, among other provisions. The government claims to have a zero-tolerance policy on corruption, and its Anti-Corruption Bureau has successfully prosecuted a number of lower-level officials.

C3. Does the government operate with openness and transparency? 1 / 4

Although the appointed Legislative Council has no independent power, it formally passes the state budget and engages in question-and-answer sessions with government officials. The council meets once each year for a session lasting approximately two weeks. However, in general there is little transparency in the operations of the Brunei government.

CIVIL LIBERTIES: 21 / 60

D. FREEDOM OF EXPRESSION AND BELIEF: 6 / 16

D1. Are there free and independent media? 1 / 4

Officials may close newspapers without cause and fine and imprison journalists for up to three years for reporting deemed "false and malicious." Brunei's only television station is state-run. The country's main English-language daily newspaper, the *Borneo Bulletin*, is controlled by the sultan's family and its journalists often practice self-censorship. Another former English-language newspaper, the *Brunei Times*, closed abruptly in 2016, allegedly after complaints from the Saudi embassy in Brunei over critical coverage of Saudi hajj policies. A new online outlet, the *Scoop*, which launched in 2017, contains somewhat independent coverage of Brunei society and politics.

D2. Are individuals free to practice and express their religious faith or nonbelief in public and private? 1 / 4

The state religion is the Shafi'i school of Sunni Islam, but the constitution allows for the practice of other religions. Non-Shafi'i forms of Islam are actively discouraged, and marriage between Muslims and non-Muslims is not allowed. Muslims require permission from the Ministry of Religious Affairs to convert to other faiths. Christians are allowed to hold low-key Christmas celebrations inside churches or at homes, but not outdoors or at shopping malls. Brunei again limited some aspects of Chinese New Year celebrations in 2020.

In 2014, Brunei implemented new criminal regulations based on Sharia (Islamic law), which include limits on the use of certain words and expressions deemed to be sacred to Islam in reference to other religions. The code also includes a ban on proselytizing of a religion other than Islam to Muslims or atheists and requires Muslims to participate in religious observances. In April 2019, the government implemented a second phase that mandated death by stoning for insulting the prophet Muhammad, though a moratorium on capital punishment was issued in May 2019.

D3. Is there academic freedom, and is the educational system free from extensive political indoctrination? 2 / 4

Academic freedom is respected to some extent, although institutions must seek approval from authorities to host visiting scholars, public lectures, and conferences. Scholars reportedly practice self-censorship or release their work under pseudonyms in overseas publications.

D4. Are individuals free to express their personal views on political or other sensitive topics without fear of surveillance or retribution? 2 / 4

The government utilizes an informant system to monitor suspected dissidents, and online communications are monitored for subversive content. Nevertheless, Brunei has an active online discussion community, although there are reports of self-censorship online regarding issues related to the monarchy.

In December 2019, a former civil servant who criticized the government's halal certification policy in a 2017 Facebook post was given an 18-month sentence in absentia. The civil servant, who was the first to be convicted under the Sedition Act, fled to Canada to seek asylum, stating that he fears returning to Brunei because he is gay and risks harsh punishment under laws prohibiting same-sex intimacy.

E. ASSOCIATIONAL AND ORGANIZATIONAL RIGHTS: 3 / 12
E1. Is there freedom of assembly? 1 / 4

Long-standing state-of-emergency laws continue to restrict freedom of assembly. No more than 10 people can assemble for any purpose without a permit, and these laws are frequently enforced. The government further limited public gatherings amidst the pandemic, but relaxed these curbs in August.

E2. Is there freedom for nongovernmental organizations, particularly those that are engaged in human rights- and governance-related work? 1 / 4

Most nongovernmental organizations (NGOs) are professional or business groups, although a few work on issues related to social welfare. All groups must register, registration can be refused for any reason, and registered groups can be suspended.

E3. Is there freedom for trade unions and similar professional or labor organizations? 1 / 4

The law guarantees the right to form and join a union, but the agreement that had permitted Brunei's only active union, the Brunei Oilfield Workers Union, is now expired. Strikes are illegal, and collective bargaining is not recognized.

F. RULE OF LAW: 5 / 16

F1. Is there an independent judiciary? 1 / 4

Brunei has a dual judicial system of secular and Sharia courts; all senior judges are appointed by the sultan. The courts appear to act independently when handling civil matters, and have yet to be tested in political cases or under the new regulations recently phased in.

F2. Does due process prevail in civil and criminal matters? 2 / 4

Civil and criminal law is based on English common law and is enforced in secular courts, while Sharia is enforced in Sharia courts. People detained under the Internal Security Act (ISA) lack due process rights including the presumption of innocence.

The country's controversial penal code, based on Sharia, was delayed for several years; Brunei introduced the first phase in 2014 but held off on implementing the second of three envisioned phases, which contains penalties including amputations and death by stoning, until April 2019. Many of the Sharia rules overlap with existing provisions of the civil and criminal laws, but there are different sentences and burdens of proof under the new code.

The government only provides an attorney to indigent defendants in death penalty cases. To address this gap in access to justice, the Law Society of Brunei launched a pilot program for the country's first legal aid fund in 2018. The program has continued, and the Law Society has encouraged its members to take on pro bono cases.

F3. Is there protection from the illegitimate use of physical force and freedom from war and insurgencies? 1 / 4

Brunei retained the death penalty for crimes including drug trafficking before the new Sharia code was launched. However, no individual has been executed since 1957. Prison conditions generally meet international standards.

Sharia-based criminal statutes implemented in April 2019 contain more severe penalties for violations including consensual same-sex relations, theft, and adultery; they vary from whippings to amputations and death by stoning. In May 2019, the sultan issued a "de facto moratorium on capital punishment," but did not issue clarification on the other provisions.

F4. Do laws, policies, and practices guarantee equal treatment of various segments of the population? 1 / 4

Brunei citizenship is inherited from citizen fathers. Citizen mothers must complete an application to pass citizenship on to children born to a noncitizen father. Thousands of stateless residents of Brunei, including longtime ethnic Chinese residents, are denied the full rights and benefits granted to citizens.

LGBT+ people living in Brunei are subject to severe penalties for same-sex relations under Sharia-based laws. Under regulations introduced in April 2019, consensual same-sex acts can be punished by death, or by whipping if the offenders are female.

G. PERSONAL AUTONOMY AND INDIVIDUAL RIGHTS 7 / 16

G1. Do individuals enjoy freedom of movement, including the ability to change their place of residence, employment, or education? 2 / 4

Freedom of movement is respected, and Brunei's success in combating COVID-19 meant that it lifted restrictions on movement and gathering relatively early in the year. All government employees, domestic and foreign, must apply for permission to travel abroad, but permission is easily obtained. Stateless children do not have free access to education and instead must apply to enroll in schools; if accepted they sometimes have to pay tuition not required of citizens.

G2. Are individuals able to exercise the right to own property and establish private businesses without undue interference from state or nonstate actors? 2 / 4

Brunei citizens are able to own property and can establish businesses with relative ease, but protections for private property are not strong. State-linked firms dominate many sectors of the economy and the government heavily subsidizes a number of industries.

G3. Do individuals enjoy personal social freedoms, including choice of marriage partner and size of family, protection from domestic violence, and control over appearance? 1 / 4

Women are disadvantaged in Brunei under Islamic law in matters involving divorce and child custody. The new Sharia penal code criminalizes "indecent behavior," enjoins women to dress "modestly," and makes abortion and extramarital sex capital offenses. There is no specific law against domestic violence, and although rape is a capital crime, spousal rape is not criminalized.

Transgender people are prohibited from dressing in line with their gender identity under the Sharia-based penal code.

G4. Do individuals enjoy equality of opportunity and freedom from economic exploitation? 2 / 4

There is no private-sector minimum wage in Brunei. Labor inspections are frequent, but are often aimed at identifying undocumented migrant workers. Migrants who come to Brunei to serve as household workers are often coerced into involuntary servitude or debt bondage, and can be subject to varying forms of abuse. Workers who overstay visas are regularly imprisoned and, in some cases, caned.

According to the US State Department's 2020 *Trafficking in Persons Report*, Brunei is on the Tier 2 Watchlist, at risk of being dropped into the lowest tier, because it has made little progress in fighting human trafficking over the previous year and did not prosecute or convict any traffickers for the third straight year. However, Brunei did ratify the ASEAN Convention against Trafficking in Persons in January and acceded to the United Nations Trafficking in Persons protocol in March. The government operates a shelter for women and boys who are trafficked, but adult males do not receive shelter or services.

Bulgaria

Population: 6,900,000
Capital: Sofia
Freedom Status: Free
Electoral Democracy: Yes

Overview: Multiple parties compete in Bulgaria's democratic system, and there have been several transfers of power between rival parties in recent decades. The country continues to struggle with political corruption and organized crime. While the media sector remains pluralistic, ownership concentration is a growing problem. Journalists at times encounter threats or violence in the course of their work. Ethnic minorities, particularly Roma, face discrimination. Despite funding shortages and other obstacles, civil society groups have been active and influential.

KEY DEVELOPMENTS IN 2020

- The COVID-19 outbreak dominated public life and discourse from early March to mid-May, with the government commanding high levels of support due to its relatively well-managed and effective response. However, authorities' response to the pandemic's second wave was hesitant, and at the end of December, the country had one of the highest rates in the world of COVID-19-related deaths, as measured by number of deaths per million people.
- Romany neighborhoods were placed under harsher COVID-19 restrictions than neighborhoods where Roma did not constitute a majority. The severe restrictions placed on Roma drew statements of alarm from local and international rights groups, who said that in addition to unduly restricting movement, the rules harmed the ability of Romany people to access work, services, and education.
- Mass antigovernment protests erupted in July in response to a series of corruption scandals and continued through most of the year. The protests, at which participants called for the resignation of Prime Minister Boyko Borisov and his government, and the prosecutor general, featured occasional violence against participants and journalists by police, but were largely peaceful.
- The European Commission's new rule-of-law report, issued in September, reiterated long-standing concerns about the sweeping powers of and lack of accountability for the prosecutor general. The prosecutor's decision to conduct a raid of the offices of President Rumen Radev's staff was among the numerous catalysts of the year's antigovernment protest movement; Radev had tried to block the appointment of the prosecutor general, Ivan Geshev, in 2019.

POLITICAL RIGHTS: 33 / 40 (−1)

A. ELECTORAL PROCESS: 11 / 12

A1. Was the current head of government or other chief national authority elected through free and fair elections? 4 / 4

The president, who is directly elected for up to two five-year terms, is the head of state but has limited powers. In 2016, former air force commander Rumen Radev, an independent candidate supported by the opposition Bulgarian Socialist Party (BSP), defeated parliament speaker Tsetska Tsacheva of the ruling Citizens for European Development of Bulgaria (GERB) party. The election was generally well administered, and stakeholders accepted the results.

The legislature chooses the prime minister, who serves as head of government. Prime Minister Borisov, of the center-right GERB, returned to office after his party's victory in the 2017 early parliamentary elections.

A2. Were the current national legislative representatives elected through free and fair elections? 4 / 4

The unicameral National Assembly, with 240 members, is elected every four years in 31 multimember constituencies. The 2017 early elections were deemed free and fair by international observers.

A3. Are the electoral laws and framework fair, and are they implemented impartially by the relevant election management bodies? 3 / 4

The Central Election Commission (CEC) administers Bulgaria's elections and generally works professionally and impartially, though some flaws have been reported in past elections. High numbers of invalid ballots (including 4.6 percent of ballots cast in 2017 parliamentary elections) has prompted concern and calls for reform by the Organization for Security and Co-operation in Europe (OSCE). Other OSCE recommendations have questioned restrictions on voting rights of prisoners and persons with disabilities, as well as restrictions on the ability of ethnic minority members campaigning in their preferred language.

The parliament passed controversial reforms to the electoral laws in 2016, introducing compulsory voting and new rules on voting abroad that reduced the number of polling places and led to protests throughout the diaspora. In 2017, the Constitutional Court struck down the law on compulsory voting.

Controversial changes to electoral code were introduced in September 2020, just six months ahead of elections set for March 2021. These mandated a "mixed" mode of voting, using both paper ballots and voting machines. Claiming that the expected chaos would allow governing parties to steal the next election, the opposition vehemently criticized the changes and President Radev imposed a veto, which was overruled by the majority in Parliament.

B. POLITICAL PLURALISM AND PARTICIPATION: 14 / 16

B1. Do the people have the right to organize in different political parties or other competitive political groupings of their choice, and is the system free of undue obstacles to the rise and fall of these competing parties or groupings? 4 / 4

Bulgaria's party system is competitive and quite volatile, featuring both established parties like the BSP and Movement for Rights and Freedoms (DPS), as well as cycles in which new parties emerge while others decline or disappear. GERB first won seats in parliament in 2009, and the 2017 elections featured the emergence of the United Patriots (UP) alliance, which won 27 seats. New political parties emerged in 2020 as well, one of which was polling third at year's end.

B2. Is there a realistic opportunity for the opposition to increase its support or gain power through elections? 4 / 4

There have been multiple peaceful transfers of power between rival parties through elections since the end of communist rule in 1990. In the 2017 early parliamentary elections, the BSP, currently the main opposition party, gained 41 additional seats compared with the previous balloting. Two new parties that emerged in 2020 are likely to enter next parliament in 2021, and could become governing coalition members.

B3. Are the people's political choices free from domination by forces that are external to the political sphere, or by political forces that employ extra-political means? 3 / 4

Bulgarians are generally free to make independent political choices. However, limited public funding and unlimited private funding for political parties leaves parties vulnerable to the undue influence of private donors.

Economic oligarchs dominate major political parties, and prominent businessmen exert influence over party platforms and policy decisions. The problem of business influence is exacerbated by a lack of transparency in campaign finance law.

B4. Do various segments of the population (including ethnic, racial, religious, gender, LGBT+, and other relevant groups) have full political rights and electoral opportunities? 3 / 4

While marginalized groups generally have full political rights, the law dictates that electoral campaigns must be conducted in the Bulgarian language, which hinders outreach to non- Bulgarian-speaking minority groups. The ethnic Turkish minority is represented by the DPS, but the Roma are more marginalized. Small Romany parties are active, and many Roma reportedly vote for the DPS, though none hold seats in the parliament. Courts have continued to deny registration to the political party OMO Ilinden, which seeks legal recognition of a Macedonian ethnic minority in Bulgaria; this issue was featured in a critical European Parliament resolution on the rule of law and fundamental rights in Bulgaria, adopted in October 2020.

Members of far-right nationalist parties, including the current government junior coalition partner UP, have engaged in hate speech against Roma, ethnic Turks, Jews, Muslims, migrants, and refugees, among other groups, particularly during election periods.

There are currently 62 women in the 240-seat parliament, and the representation of women and women's issues in politics is generally lacking.

So-called oligarchs exert influence on the vote in smaller municipalities and within marginalized groups in particular, an issue referred to as the "controlled vote."

C. FUNCTIONING OF GOVERNMENT: 8 / 12 (−1)
C1. Do the freely elected head of government and national legislative representatives determine the policies of the government? 3 / 4 (−1)

Elected executive and legislative officials in general are able to set and implement policies without undue interference from external or unelected entities. However, "oligarch" politicians in the last several years have had increasing influence on policy making.

The informal influence on government of the nominally opposition party DPS and its honorary chair Ahmed Dogan, and the widespread perception that aspects of the state have been "captured" by dubious business figures, were among the triggers of the mass antigovernment protests that shook the country in July 2020 and continued throughout most of the year. In one of the year's most discussed political incidents, it was revealed that sections of a public beach had been reserved for Dogan's exclusive use, and that state security agents were tasked with keeping citizens away from the area. The businessman and DPS lawmaker Delyan Peevski is also suspected of having had influence over policymaking, and of having played a role in securing the appointment of Geshev as the country's controversial prosecutor general. In July, as protests continued, Borisov replaced several of his cabinet ministers and GERB released a statement saying the dismissals were necessary to "eliminate insinuations that GERB and the three are directly controlled by the DPS and Peevski."

Score Change: The score declined from 4 to 3 due to evidence of the ability of politicians and businesspeople to exert informal, opaque, and outsized influence on elected leaders and state institutions.

C2. Are safeguards against official corruption strong and effective? 2 / 4

Bulgaria, which joined the European Union (EU) in 2007, has struggled to meet the bloc's anticorruption requirements amid resistance from much of the political class.

Anticorruption laws are not adequately enforced, including in high-profile cases, contributing to a culture of impunity. The country remains subject to long-term monitoring by the EU's cooperation and verification mechanism, whose annual reports have called for new legislative efforts to combat corruption.

In January 2018, the parliament overrode a presidential veto and adopted legislation that created a centralized anticorruption commission to replace multiple existing bodies. The record of the commission's achievements is mixed to date; despite having extensive prerogatives that were further boosted at the end of 2018, some of its flagship cases were overturned in court, while analysts have raised serious concerns that some of the organization's actions are politically motivated. Corruption scandals involving oligarchs who until recently had enjoyed government favors helped bring about mass antigovernment protests at which participants demanded the resignation of the public prosecutor for allegedly serving illegitimate interests.

C3. Does the government operate with openness and transparency? 3 / 4

Although Bulgaria has laws meant to ensure that the government operates with transparency, they are only partially enforced. While the transparency in the work of Parliament, the cabinet, and municipal bodies has increased considerably in recent years, public access to information about budgets and spending of various government agencies is sometimes inadequate or presented in an inaccessible way.

CIVIL LIBERTIES: 45 / 60 (−1)
D. FREEDOM OF EXPRESSION AND BELIEF: 13 / 16
D1. Are there free and independent media? 2 / 4

The constitution protects freedom of expression, including for the press, but journalists face threats and pressure from private owners or public media management. Even though the media sector remains pluralistic, many outlets are dependent on financial contributions from the state (through advertising), effectively resulting in pressure to run government-friendly material. Media ownership remains opaque, with this issue being among those prominently covered in the 2020 European Commission's Rule of Law Report on Bulgaria, as well as by the European Parliament's 2020 Resolution on the rule of law and fundamental rights in Bulgaria.

Assaults on journalists continued in 2020. Journalist Polina Paunova was attacked while attempting to interview participants at a GERB party conference, while another journalist, Dimiter Kenarov, was subject to police violence during his coverage of the antigovernment protests in September.

D2. Are individuals free to practice and express their religious faith or nonbelief in public and private? 3 / 4

Religious freedom is generally respected, but members of minority faiths in what is a mostly Orthodox Christian country have reported instances of harassment and discrimination, and some local authorities have prohibited proselytizing and other religious activities by such groups. A 2016 law that imposed fines for the wearing of face-covering garments in public locations was widely understood to be directed against Muslims. UP, along with other parties, have tried to limit foreign donations to religious denominations as well as proselytizing by foreign nationals. The Religious Denominations Act, which entered into force in early 2019, thwarted those efforts.

D3. Is there academic freedom, and is the educational system free from extensive political indoctrination? 4 / 4

Academic freedom is generally upheld in practice.

D4. Are individuals free to express their personal views on political or other sensitive topics without fear of surveillance or retribution? 4 / 4

Freedom of expression is guaranteed by the constitution. However, in 2020, Penal Code amendments included in coronavirus-related state-of-emergency measures sought to curb the spread of "false information" with heavy fines and prison terms; these were successfully vetoed by President Radev. Nevertheless, the prosecutorial office on several occasions brought charges for sparking panic, most notably against the President of Bulgarian Pharmaceutical Union, prompting public outcry. A court dismissed the charges.

E. ASSOCIATIONAL AND ORGANIZATIONAL RIGHTS: 11 / 12
E1. Is there freedom of assembly? 4 / 4

The authorities generally respect constitutional guarantees of freedom of assembly. However, a COVID-19-related state of emergency that lasted for two months in the spring of 2020 featured a ban on mass gatherings.

Mass antigovernment demonstrations erupted in July, after a series of public scandals involving the prime minister, the prosecutorial office, and various politicians. Though state authorities generally respected the right to peaceful protest during the protests, tolerating even unauthorized street blockades, on at least two occasions police used excessive force against participants, prompting criticism in the country and from international organizations.

E2. Is there freedom for nongovernmental organizations, particularly those that are engaged in human rights- and governance-related work? 4 / 4

Nongovernmental organizations (NGOs) operate freely and have a degree of influence, though they experience funding shortages, often rely on foreign donors, and sometimes face hostility from politicians and interest groups. The long-standing hostility of the UP toward NGOs that accept funds form out-of-country donors took legal form in July 2020, when its lawmakers submitted amendments to the Non-profit Legal Entities Act. Under the guise of "improved transparency for the activity of public-benefit NGOs," they aimed to limit both the powers of the newly established Public Council of Civil Society Organizations—where representatives of NGOs critical of government were elected as members—and, to curb the activities of foreign-funded NGOs. The amendments were pending at year's end.

E3. Is there freedom for trade unions and similar professional or labor organizations? 3 / 4

Workers have the right to join trade unions, which are generally able to operate, but some public employees cannot legally strike. Collective bargaining is legal—collective contracts are listed in a specialized public registry. Trade unions are partners to the government and business in discussing public budgets and other issues (retirement age, pensions reforms, and healthcare reforms, for example), yet their voice and influence is weak.

F. RULE OF LAW: 10 / 16
F1. Is there an independent judiciary? 3 / 4

Bulgaria's judiciary has benefited from legal and institutional reforms associated with EU membership, but it is still prone to politicization. A Supreme Judicial Council (SJC), responsible for judicial and prosecutorial appointments and management, was installed under revised rules in 2017, with half the members (six judges, four prosecutors, and an investigator) elected by their peers and half by a two-thirds parliamentary majority.

Tensions have increased in recent years between the prosecutor general's office and some of the courts, with high-ranking prosecutors verbally attacking the Supreme Court of Cassation (SCC), its court decisions, and its chair. The SJC, taking the side of the prosecutors, has launched disciplinary procedures against judges critical of it, which are widely seen as politically motivated.

The Justice Minister was among the five ministers that resigned amid mass antigovernment, anticorruption protests in 2020.

F2. Does due process prevail in civil and criminal matters? 2 / 4

Constitutional rights to due process are not always upheld. Police have been accused of misconduct, including arbitrary arrests and failure to inform suspects of their rights. Public trust in the justice system is low due to its reputed vulnerability to political and outside pressure.

The selection of the new prosecutor general in 2019 sparked controversy, amid suspicions of undue political influence on the choice. The long, seven-year mandate and the lack of effective accountability measures for the position have long been noted as major problems with the prosecutorial office, weakening due process and the rule of law in the country. Though the Constitutional Court ruled in July 2020 that any prosecutor may launch an investigation on the activities of the prosecutor general, his strong position both with regard to career promotion within the prosecutorial office, and within SJC, does not de facto permit such investigations to take place. This leaves the most powerful figure within the judicial system without effective mechanisms of control over their actions. A series of international organizations, including the EU in its 2020 rule-of-law report, have issued recommendations to address these problems, to little effect.

A series of scandals involving the prosecutorial office, including alleged raids of private businesses, actions suppressing voices critical of the government, as well as a raid of the offices of the Bulgarian president, were among the triggers of the 2020 antigovernment protests.

F3. Is there protection from the illegitimate use of physical force and freedom from war and insurgencies? 3 / 4

Although the population faces few acute threats to physical security, police brutality, including abuse of suspects in custody, remains a problem. Overcrowding and violence plague many of Bulgaria's prisons. Organized crime is still a major issue, and scores of suspected contract killings since the 1990s are unsolved. Arrests of ordinary citizens by the police during a protest in September 2020 prompted investigation for disproportionate use of force, which at year's end had not yet been concluded.

F4. Do laws, policies, and practices guarantee equal treatment of various segments of the population? 2 / 4

Ethnic minorities, particularly Roma, face discrimination in employment, health care, education, and housing, though the government and NGOs operate a number of programs meant to improve their social integration. Authorities periodically demolish illegally constructed or irregular housing—mostly in areas occupied by Roma—without providing alternative shelter.

Migrants and asylum seekers have reportedly faced various forms of mistreatment by Bulgarian authorities, including beatings and extortion.

Discrimination based on sexual orientation or gender identity is illegal, but societal bias against LGBT+ people persists. In July 2018, the Constitutional Court ruled that the Council of Europe's Istanbul Convention on preventing gender-based violence was unconstitutional, finding fault with its conceptualization of gender. Conservative critics argued that the convention would create a basis for expanded rights for LGBT+ people. The annual pride celebration in Sofia is routinely attacked by nationalist groups. In October 2020, a widely circulated video depicted youths attacking people they suspected of being gay, while police stood by; an investigation was subsequently launched.

A gender equality law passed in 2016 was designed to foster equal opportunity for women, but discrimination in employment persists: women are employed less often and paid less than men.

COVID-19-related restrictions were unevenly enforced, with the Romany minority subject to more severe restrictions. Human rights watchdogs in the country and abroad raised serious concerns that COVID-19 had exacerbated racism against the Roma in Bulgaria.

G. PERSONAL AUTONOMY AND INDIVIDUAL RIGHTS: 11 / 16 (−1)

G1. Do individuals enjoy freedom of movement, including the ability to change their place of residence, employment, or education? 3 / 4 (−1)

For the most part, Bulgarians have faced few major restrictions on their freedom of movement. However, the COVID-19-related state of emergency featured selective blockades of mostly Romany-populated neighborhoods in several towns. This was achieved by placing severe limits on the movement of people and only allowing exceptions for work on permanent employment contracts, which very few of the inhabitants of such neighborhoods possessed. As the pandemic progressed, local municipalities used other excuses to introduce stricter limits on Romany communities, the most often quoted being insufficient compliance within the respective neighborhoods with the anti-COVID-19 measures—but only in a few cases were strict blockades introduced as a result of actual spike in cases. This prompted local NGOs including the Bulgarian Helsinki Committee and Amalipe Center; international NGOs such as Amnesty International, the European Roma Right Centre, and the Open Society Foundations; and international human rights protection bodies to express alarm over the discriminatory treatment of Roma during the pandemic, as well as for the disproportionate negative effect of COVID-19 outbreak on access to education and employment for this minority group.

Corruption and bias can sometimes hamper efforts to change one's place of employment. In 2017, the government issued a rule that restricted the ability of asylum seekers to move outside of the district where they are housed.

Score Change: The score declined from 4 to 3 due to disproportionate and discriminatory restrictions on the movement of members of the Romany minority connected to COVID-19.

G2. Are individuals able to exercise the right to own property and establish private businesses without undue interference from state or nonstate actors? 3 / 4

The legal and regulatory framework is generally supportive of property rights and private business, though property rights are not always respected in practice, and corruption continues to hamper business and investment. The gray economy of undeclared business activity has been estimated at nearly 30 percent of the country's economy. Attempts at business raiding, including with the suspected assistance of state institutions and the prosecutorial office, are perceived to be on the rise and were among the triggers of the antigraft protests in 2020.

G3. Do individuals enjoy personal social freedoms, including choice of marriage partner and size of family, protection from domestic violence, and control over appearance? 3 / 4

The law generally grants equal rights to men and women regarding personal status matters such as marriage and divorce. Domestic violence remains a problem. People who have experienced domestic violence and NGOs addressing gender-based violence claim that state authorities are often ineffective in providing protection and pursuing criminal charges when abuse is reported.

Same-sex marriage is illegal in Bulgaria, and same-sex couples are barred from adopting children.

G4. Do individuals enjoy equality of opportunity and freedom from economic exploitation? 2 / 4

Labor laws provide basic protections against exploitative working conditions, but they do not extend in practice to gray-market employment. Roma and other ethnic minorities are particularly vulnerable to trafficking for sexual and labor exploitation. Although the government has continued to step up efforts to combat trafficking, shelter victims, and punish perpetrators, these measures have not matched the scale of the problem, and punishments remain light in practice.

Burkina Faso

Population: 20,900,000
Capital: Ouagadougou
Freedom Status: Partly Free
Electoral Democracy: Yes

Overview: Presidential and legislative elections held in 2015 and 2020 have laid a foundation for the continued development of democratic institutions in Burkina Faso. While civil society and organized labor remain strong forces for democracy, Burkinabè also face continued insecurity and violence at the hands of armed militant groups, militia groups, and government forces.

KEY DEVELOPMENTS IN 2020

- In November, President Roch Marc Christian Kaboré of the People's Movement for Progress (MPP) won a second term in office, while the MPP won a plurality of National Assembly seats in concurrent legislative elections. The polls were considered fair but were marred by ongoing insecurity.
- Armed groups attacked security forces and civilians during the year, causing numerous casualties and internal displacement. In January, 39 people were killed by armed assailants in Soum Province, while 15 were killed when a traders' convoy was attacked in Loroum in May. Over 1 million people were internally displaced as of August.
- Security forces and an affiliated militia group engaged in extrajudicial killings during the year. In April, 31 people were executed after being detained during a counterterrorism operation, while gendarmes and militia members were accused of killing 12 detainees in May.

- Authorities banned demonstrations and public gatherings to lessen the spread of COVID-19 in March and restricted freedom of movement, issuing strict quarantines in areas with confirmed COVID-19 cases. Burkinabè accused of violating curfews faced ill-treatment while in custody. The government reported 6,537 cases and 82 deaths to the World Health Organization (WHO) by year's end.

POLITICAL RIGHTS: 23 / 40

A. ELECTORAL PROCESS: 7 / 12

A1. Was the current head of government or other chief national authority elected through free and fair elections? 2 / 4

The president is head of state and is directly elected to no more than two five-year terms. Roch Marc Christian Kaboré of the MPP was reelected in November 2020, winning 57.7 percent of the vote in the first round. Insecurity impeded electoral organization in some areas, particularly in the north and east. Voting did not occur in 15 communes as a result. Islamist militants also threatened violence against voters. Opposition figures initially alleged fraud, but observers considered the election fair; no formal objections were received by the time the results were certified in December.

The prime minister is head of government and is appointed by the president with the approval of the National Assembly. The prime minister recommends a cabinet that is formally appointed by the president. Christophe Dabiré was appointed in January 2019.

A2. Were the current national legislative representatives elected through free and fair elections? 2 / 4

The 127 members of the National Assembly are directly elected to five-year terms via proportional representation. The November 2020 legislative elections, held concurrently with the presidential election, were generally viewed as open and fair, despite ongoing insecurity. Voter turnout was reportedly low in some areas due to insecurity and a lack of polling stations. The MPP won 56 seats, while the Congress for Democracy and Progress (CDP) won 20.

Municipal elections were last held in 2016 and showed an erosion of support for the then ruling CDP in favor of the MPP. Observers from local civil society groups and international missions noted minor irregularities in those polls. However, election-related violence prevented polling in some districts which reportedly contributed to low turnout. Makeup elections for several constituencies were held peacefully in 2017, though some candidates were reportedly excluded.

A3. Are the electoral laws and framework fair, and are they implemented impartially by the relevant election management bodies? 3 / 4

The Independent National Electoral Commission is responsible for organizing elections, and the November 2020 polls were generally well administered. Local observers noted irregularities, such as a lack of ballot papers at some precincts, but reported that these issues did not affect the contests' integrity.

In August 2020, the National Assembly adopted a revised electoral code that drew criticism from opposition politicians. Under the code, the president can refer cases of "force majeure or exceptional circumstances" that impede electoral organization to the Constitutional Council. The code allows the validation of results on the basis of polling stations that operate on election day, with the court's agreement. In December, the Constitutional Council annulled votes from 200 polling places due to irregularities including discrepancies in reported vote totals.

B. POLITICAL PLURALISM AND PARTICIPATION: 10 / 16

B1. Do the people have the right to organize in different political parties or other competitive political groupings of their choice, and is the system free of undue obstacles to the rise and fall of these competing parties or groupings? 2 / 4

The constitution guarantees the right to form political parties, but their ability to participate in political life is sometimes restricted by the government. The government authorized 146 political groups to participate in the November 2020 elections.

Major parties, such as the MPP, CDP, and Union for Progress and Change, have extensive patronage networks and disproportionate access to media coverage, making it difficult for other parties to build their support bases. Presidential candidates must also provide a 25 million CFA franc ($42,800) deposit.

B2. Is there a realistic opportunity for the opposition to increase its support or gain power through elections? 3 / 4

The end of former president Blaise Compaoré's 27-year regime in 2014 gave way to a freer environment in which opposition parties can consolidate popular support and gain power through elections. However, a history of rotation of power between parties has yet to be firmly established.

B3. Are the people's political choices free from domination by forces that are external to the political sphere, or by political forces that employ extrapolitical means? 2 / 4

The Burkinabè military maintains a significant presence in the political sphere, and the history of military intervention poses a threat to democratic stability. In 2015, the presidential guard, which was loyal to Compaoré, attempted to stage a coup d'état. The maneuver sparked widespread protests and failed after the army's chief of staff moved to support the transitional government.

B4. Do various segments of the population (including ethnic, racial, religious, gender, LGBT+, and other relevant groups) have full political rights and electoral opportunities? 3 / 4

The constitution enshrines full political rights and electoral opportunities for all segments of the population. However, a small educated elite, the military, and labor unions have historically dominated political life.

Women are underrepresented in political leadership positions; while they held 13.4 percent of seats in the previous parliament, they only won 6.3 percent in November 2020. Within parties, women are frequently relegated to women's secretariats that have little influence. In January 2020, the National Assembly adopted a 30 percent gender quota for party lists and introduced an alternating system meant to improve the position of female candidates on those lists.

C. FUNCTIONING OF GOVERNMENT: 6 / 12

C1. Do the freely elected head of government and national legislative representatives determine the policies of the government? 2 / 4

Laws are promulgated and debated by the National Assembly. While democratic institutions continue to develop, they are not yet strong enough to withstand the influence of the military and other elite groups. Attacks by Islamic militants, which have increased in frequency in recent years, severely impede the government's ability to implement its policies in the insecure north and east.

C2. Are safeguards against official corruption strong and effective? 2 / 4

Corruption is widespread, particularly among customs officials and municipal police. Anticorruption laws and bodies are generally ineffective, though local nongovernmental organizations (NGOs) provide some accountability by publicizing official corruption and its effects.

In May 2020, following allegations made by the National Anti-Corruption Network, former defense minister Jean-Claude Bouda was taken into custody over corruption charges. Proceedings against Bouda were ongoing at year's end. In July, a former National Social Security Fund human-resources director and chief of staff were convicted of charges including nepotism over their management of an employee-recruitment process in 2018. Both defendants received three-year prison terms.

C3. Does the government operate with openness and transparency? 2 / 4

The successful 2015 elections and installation of a civilian government signified a marked improvement in government accountability and transparency. However, government procurement processes are opaque, and procedures meant to increase transparency are often not followed. Government officials are required to make financial disclosures, but the information is rarely made public, and penalties for noncompliance do not appear to be enforced.

CIVIL LIBERTIES: 31 / 60 (−2)

D. FREEDOM OF EXPRESSION AND BELIEF: 11 / 16

D1. Are there free and independent media? 2 / 4

The media environment has improved since the end of Compaoré's rule. Since then, defamation has been decriminalized, reporters at the public broadcaster have experienced less political interference, and private outlets operate with relative freedom. However, a 2019 penal-code revision made disseminating information about terrorist attacks and security-force activity, along with the "demoralization" of defense and security forces, criminal offenses punishable by prison terms of up to 10 years.

In January 2020, an unknown assailant attempted to use an incendiary device to damage a vehicle belonging to investigative journalist Yacouba Ladji Bama. The government later ruled the incident an accident. In June, five people—including the editor of social-media news outlet Proximité.info—were arrested for defaming a public official. All five were convicted on charges including public insult and incitement to violence in July and received 12- to 36-month sentences.

D2. Are individuals free to practice and express their religious faith or nonbelief in public and private? 3 / 4

Burkina Faso is a secular state, and freedom of religion is generally respected. The population is predominately Muslim with a large Christian minority. Followers of both religions often engage in syncretic practices.

However, Muslims and Christians faced violent attacks from armed groups and assailants during 2020. In February, Islamist militants kidnapped seven people who visited a pastor's home in the town of Sebba; five of them, including the pastor, were subsequently found dead. That same month, assailants attacked a church in the northern village of Pansi, killing at least 24 people. In August, Djibo imam Souaibou Cissé was found dead several days after he was abducted from a bus. President Kaboré condemned the killing of Cissé, calling it an attack on the country's "model of religious tolerance." In November, unidentified assailants threw an incendiary device into a Kossodo mosque during a religious service.

D3. Is there academic freedom, and is the educational system free from extensive political indoctrination? 3 / 4

Academic freedom is unrestricted, though due to the former regime's repressive tactics against student-led protests, a legacy of tension between the government and academic organizations persists.

Islamic militant groups in the north have threatened teachers in an effort to force them to adopt Islamic teachings, resulting in the closure of schools. Human Rights Watch (HRW) reported that militant groups launched at least 45 attacks on educational targets in 2020.

D4. Are individuals free to express their personal views on political or other sensitive topics without fear of surveillance or retribution? 3 / 4

Private discussion is unrestricted in much of the country. However, attacks and intimidation by militant Islamic groups in the north and east, an increased security presence in response to their activities, and 2019 penal-code revisions have dissuaded people from speaking about local news, politics, and other sensitive topics.

E. ASSOCIATIONAL AND ORGANIZATIONAL RIGHTS: 8 / 12
E1. Is there freedom of assembly? 3 / 4

The constitution guarantees freedom of assembly, which is sometimes upheld in practice. Under the new government, space for demonstrations and protests has opened. In March 2020, the government suspended all demonstrations and public gatherings to lessen the spread of COVID-19. The suspension was used to ban a planned trade-union demonstration that month. Some demonstrations were nevertheless held; in late April, Ouagadougou traders calling for a reopening of a local market blocked a road.

In December 2019, government extended a state of emergency that was originally declared in 14 provinces in 2018. The state of emergency, which will remain in force through mid-January 2021, allows the government to restrict the freedom of assembly.

E2. Is there freedom for nongovernmental organizations, particularly those that are engaged in human rights- and governance-related work? 2 / 4

While many NGOs operate openly and freely, human rights groups have reported abuses by security forces in the past. NGOs still face harassment in carrying out their work, and NGO leaders argue that some legal provisions, including vaguely worded terrorism laws, are vulnerable to being misused to silence human rights defenders. NGO members and activists also risk punishment under the 2019 penal-code revisions.

NGO workers also face the risk of violence; in 2019, two Democratic Youth Organization (ODJ) activists were killed while traveling to meet a government official in Yagha Province. In May 2020, the ODJ denounced the government over its handling of the case, noting that autopsies had not been performed.

E3. Is there freedom for trade unions and similar professional or labor organizations? 3 / 4

The constitution guarantees the right to strike. Unions frequently and freely engage in strikes and collective bargaining, and coordinate with civil society to organize demonstrations on social issues. However, the government has used legal means to suppress union activity, including the denial of permits for planned demonstrations.

F. RULE OF LAW: 5 / 16 (−1)
F1. Is there an independent judiciary? 2 / 4

The judiciary is formally independent but has historically been subject to executive influence and corruption.

A military trial against 84 people accused of involvement in the 2015 coup commenced in 2018. While analysts expressed concerns that the defendants would not receive a fair trial, at least 10 were convicted in 2019; one defendant received a 30-year sentence in absentia, while others received 15- to 20-year sentences.

F2. Does due process prevail in civil and criminal matters? 1 / 4 (−1)

Constitutional due-process guarantees are undermined by corruption and inefficacy of the judiciary and police force. The judicial system is also affected by ongoing insecurity. As of July 2020, no terrorism-related trial proceeded since the outbreak of militant violence in 2016. Some detainees accused of terrorist activities have remained in pretrial detention for several years. The High Court of Djibo was closed due to insecurity in 2019.

In April 2020, HRW reported that 31 people who had been detained during a counterterrorism operation in Djibo were executed by security forces. Witnesses reported that the unarmed victims were members of the Fulani ethnic group. In May, gendarmes were accused of extrajudicially killing 12 detainees in Est Region. Witnesses reported that the gendarmes were assisted by members of the Volunteers for the Defense of the Fatherland (VDP) militia, and that the victims were also Fulani. In July, HRW reported that Djibo residents discovered the bodies of at least 180 people between November 2019 and June 2020, and that government forces were likely responsible for their deaths. According to the residents, most of the victims, who were restrained before they were killed, were Fulani.

Score Change: The score declined from 2 to 1 because Burkinabè security forces and an affiliated militia engaged in extrajudicial killings of civilians, many of them members of the Fulani ethnic group, in several incidents during the year.

F3. Is there protection from the illegitimate use of physical force and freedom from war and insurgencies? 0 / 4

The security environment has declined in recent years due to activity by Islamic militant groups, bandits, and militias. Traditional leaders, government officials, lawmakers, and civilians are regularly targeted for kidnapping or assassination by assailants, including Islamic militants. In January 2020, an official in the eastern town of Pama was kidnapped by unknown assailants before being released. Five soldiers and the mayor of Pensa were among eight people killed in a July attack.

Security forces and civilians also faced attacks from armed groups, causing numerous casualties. The government blamed armed assailants for killing 39 people in Soum Province in January. In late May, 15 people were killed when a guarded convoy of traders was attacked in Loroum Province. Over 1 million Burkinabè were internally displaced as of August.

Militia groups also engaged in violence in 2020. In January, the National Assembly adopted legislation creating the VDP, which was implicated in the extrajudicial killings of 12 Fulani men in May. Members of the Koglwéogo militia, meanwhile, were accused of raiding three villages in Yatenga Province in March, killing at least 43 people. In September, video of a Koglwéogo member mistreating a child accused of theft was disseminated online.

Security forces engaged in violent operations in 2020, with targets including refugees and members of the Fulani ethnic group. Security forces executed 23 people in the village of Sissé in March, while HRW reported on the discovery of at least 180 deceased Fulani in Djibo in July. In May, security forces physically abused Malian refugees living in the Mentao camp.

Allegations of torture and abuse of suspects in custody by police are common, and prison conditions are poor. In March 2020, the Burkinabè Movement for Human and Peoples' Rights condemned reports of torture and ill-treatment against individuals arrested for violating COVID-19-related curfews.

F4. Do laws, policies, and practices guarantee equal treatment of various segments of the population? 2 / 4

Discrimination against ethnic minorities occurs, but is not widespread. LGBT+ people, as well as those living with HIV, routinely experience discrimination. While illegal, gender discrimination remains common in employment and education.

Members of the Fulani ethnic group have historically expressed dissatisfaction over government neglect.

G. PERSONAL AUTONOMY AND INDIVIDUAL RIGHTS: 7 / 16 (−1)

G1. Do individuals enjoy freedom of movement, including the ability to change their place of residence, employment, or education? 1 / 4 (−1)

Due to insecurity, the government has established heavily guarded checkpoints on roads and has instituted curfews and states of emergency in some provinces. Travelers are sometimes subjected to bribery or harassment by security forces at checkpoints. Armed groups are also known to erect roadblocks, notably blockading Djibo for much of 2020.

Schools are a common target of armed groups, with Islamist militants targeting schools that operate in French instead of Arabic.

In late March 2020, the government restricted freedom of movement in towns with more than one confirmed case of COVID-19 under a wide-ranging quarantine policy. These measures were lifted in early May.

Score Change: The score declined from 2 to 1 because freedom of movement for Burkinabè was impeded by reported bribery at checkpoints, ongoing insecurity, and COVID-19-related restrictions.

G2. Are individuals able to exercise the right to own property and establish private businesses without undue interference from state or nonstate actors? 2 / 4

In recent years, the government has implemented reforms to reduce the amount of capital necessary to start a business, facilitating the ability to obtain credit information, and improving the insolvency resolution process. However, the business environment is hampered by corruption.

G3. Do individuals enjoy personal social freedoms, including choice of marriage partner and size of family, protection from domestic violence, and control over appearance? 2 / 4

Women face discrimination in cases involving family rights and inheritance. Early marriage remains an issue, especially in the north. The practice of female genital mutilation (FGM) is less common than in the past, but still occurs. Domestic violence remains a problem despite government efforts to combat it.

G4. Do individuals enjoy equality of opportunity and freedom from economic exploitation? 2 / 4

Burkina Faso is a source, transit, and destination country for human trafficking. Child labor is present in agriculture and mining, with 20,000 children working in gold mines. Women from neighboring countries are recruited by traffickers and transported to Burkina Faso, where they are forced into prostitution.

According to the 2020 edition of the US Department of State's *Trafficking in Persons Report*, the Burkinabè government has worked to assist forced-begging victims and has adopted a strategy to combat the trafficking of children. However, no investigations, prosecutions, or convictions of suspected traffickers were reported, as the justice system has been overwhelmed by terrorism-related cases.

Burundi

Population: 11,900,000
Capital: Gitega
Freedom Status: Not Free
Electoral Democracy: No

Overview: Burundi has been in political and economic crisis since 2015. Democratic gains made after the 12-year civil war ended in 2005 have been undone by a shift toward authoritarian politics and violent repression against anyone perceived to oppose the ruling party, the National Council for the Defense of Democracy–Forces for the Defense of Democracy (CNDD–FDD).

KEY DEVELOPMENTS IN 2020

- Former army general and cabinet minister Évariste Ndayishimiye of the ruling CNDD–FDD won the May presidential election, while the party secured a lower-house majority in concurrent legislative contests. The elections were affected by a pervasive campaign of intimidation and violence targeting the opposition and a shutdown of social media and messaging services.
- Outgoing president Pierre Nkurunziza, who served three terms as chief executive, died in June; the government reported his death was unexpected and was caused by a heart attack. However, speculation that Nkurunziza died of COVID-19 persisted.
- The Burundian government did little to provide information or issue restrictions in response to the COVID-19 pandemic; health-care workers were warned from publicly discussing the crisis, testing was irregularly conducted, and mitigation measures were not consistently enforced. However, President Ndayishimiye vowed to strengthen the government's response to the pandemic during his swearing-in ceremony.

POLITICAL RIGHTS: 4 / 40 (+1)
A. ELECTORAL PROCESS: 1 / 12 (+1)
A1. Was the current head of government or other chief national authority elected through free and fair elections? 1 / 4 (+1)

Burundi adopted a new constitution in 2005 after a series of agreements ended the country's 12-year civil war. The constitution was amended in 2018 via a referendum. Among other provisions, the amended constitution lengthened presidential terms from five years to seven, consolidating the rule of then president Pierre Nkurunziza–who had served three terms–and the CNDD–FDD.

In January 2020, CNDD–FDD insiders selected Évariste Ndayishimiye, a former army general and interior minister, as the party's candidate to succeed Nkurunziza for the May election. Ndayishimiye won 71.5 percent of the vote that month, while Agathon Rwasa of the National Congress for Liberty (CNL) received 25.2 percent. Gaston Sindimwo of the Union for National Progress (UPRONA) received 1.7 percent, while others received 1.6 percent.

The contest was marred by a wide-ranging campaign of repression, which the UN Commission of Inquiry on Burundi said included the intelligence services, police, and the ruling party's youth wing in an August report. However, violence and repression were less common during 2020 election period when compared to 2015. Relatively few COVID-19 mitigation measures were enforced during the 2020 campaign, with the CNDD–FDD encouraging large election rallies. Several days before election day, the government expelled World Health Organization (WHO) officials who voiced concern over the campaigning. International observers were also barred. The CNL claimed that the results were fraudulent, though the Constitutional Court upheld the results in June. Outgoing president Nkurunziza died days after the election, with Ndayishimiye consequently succeeding him that month, ahead of schedule.

The president appoints a vice president, who must be approved separately by a two-thirds majority in both houses of Parliament. The 2018 constitutional amendments reintroduced the position of prime minister. In late June 2020, Prosper Bazombanza was named vice president, while former public security minister Alain-Guillaume Bunyoni was named prime minister.

Score Change: The score improved from 0 to 1 because the outgoing president was replaced through an electoral process that, while deeply flawed, featured less violence and repression than the 2015 election period.

A2. Were the current national legislative representatives elected through free and fair elections? 0 / 4

Parliament's lower house, the National Assembly, includes 100 members who are directly elected via proportional representation along with 23 "co-opted" members to ensure that 60 percent of the house is represented by members of the Hutu ethnic group and 40 percent is Tutsi. Members serve five-year terms. The upper house, the Senate, consists of 39 members, 36 of whom are chosen by locally elected officials for five-year terms. Some 3 seats are reserved for the Twa ethnic group.

National Assembly elections took place concurrently with the presidential elections in May 2020, amid the COVID-19 pandemic and a campaign to repress opposition groups. The ruling CNDD–FDD secured 86 seats, while the CNL secured 32 and UPRONA secured 2. Members of the Twa ethnic group received 3 seats via co-option. One CNL candidate was originally removed from an electoral list due to a previous incarceration but was reinstated and allowed to take her parliamentary seat due to a June Constitutional Court ruling.

Senators were indirectly elected in July 2020; the CNDD–FDD received 34 seats, while the CNL and UPRONA each received 1 seat. Twa members held 3 seats.

A3. Are the electoral laws and framework fair, and are they implemented impartially by the relevant election management bodies? 0 / 4

The five-member Independent National Electoral Commission (CENI) is under the effective control of the ruling CNDD–FDD. In 2015, two members who fled the country amid that year's unrest were replaced with pro-Nkurunziza appointments approved by a CNDD–FDD–controlled Parliament. Constitutional amendments extending presidential term limits, consolidating power in the executive, and allowing for a future revision of the Burundian ethnic power-sharing system were approved in a 2018 referendum that was marred by a violent intimidation campaign conducted by the CNDD–FDD.

CNL presidential candidate Rwasa challenged the conduct of the May 2020 presidential election, alleging incidents of ballot-box stuffing, falsified election reports, and votes counted from deceased or exiled citizens, though the Constitutional Court rejected that challenge in June.

B. POLITICAL PLURALISM AND PARTICIPATION: 3 / 16

B1. Do the people have the right to organize in different political parties or other competitive political groupings of their choice, and is the system free of undue obstacles to the rise and fall of these competing parties or groupings? 1 / 4

While political party formation is legally allowed, the activities of parties and political leaders perceived as opposing the CNDD–FDD are severely discouraged by the threat of retaliatory violence, repression, or arrest. Local rights groups and Amnesty International reported that the CNDD–FDD continued to deploy those tactics ahead of the May 2020 parliamentary and presidential elections, with opposition members facing arrest, torture, and murder.

Many political parties include youth branches that intimidate and attack opponents, the most prominent of which is the ruling party's Imbonerakure.

An electoral code passed in 2019 prohibits coalitions of independent candidates.

B2. Is there a realistic opportunity for the opposition to increase its support or gain power through elections? 0 / 4

The opposition has little realistic opportunity to increase its popular support through elections. Opposition parties, politicians, and their supporters face harassment, intimidation, and assassination in Burundi, and many opposition politicians and groups operate in exile. The National Council for the Respect of the Arusha Agreement (CNARED), an opposition-in-exile group, attempted to negotiate with the CNDD–FDD to participate in the 2020 elections, but was unsuccessful in securing an accord.

B3. Are the people's political choices free from domination by forces that are external to the political sphere, or by political forces that employ extrapolitical means? 0 / 4

The Imbonerakure, National Intelligence Service (SNR), and Burundian police are allies of the CNDD–FDD and use violence and intimidation to influence people's political choices.

B4. Do various segments of the population (including ethnic, racial, religious, gender, LGBT+, and other relevant groups) have full political rights and electoral opportunities? 2 / 4

The 2005 constitution requires power-sharing between Hutus and Tutsis in Parliament, and additionally stipulates that women and representatives of the Twa minority be seated in both houses. However, the constitutional revisions approved in 2018 require that these ethnic quotas be reviewed over the next five years, opening the door for their elimination and the potential exclusion of ethnic minorities from politics.

Women face social pressure that can deter active political participation, and few women hold political office at senior levels. The August 2020 Commission of Inquiry report noted that women also face state-sanctioned violence "for their supposed or actual political opinions, their refusal to join the ruling party or their links with an armed movement."

The current political environment is characterized by the dominance of the CNDD–FDD and repression of its opponents, reducing meaningful openings for effective political representation of ethnic and religious minorities and other distinct groups. In June 2020, however, President Ndayishimiye appointed Imelde Sabushimike as human rights minister; Sabushimike is the country's first Twa cabinet minister.

The CNDD–FDD apparatus has violently targeted returning refugees on suspicion of opposition sympathies.

C. FUNCTIONING OF GOVERNMENT: 0 / 12

C1. Do the freely elected head of government and national legislative representatives determine the policies of the government? 0 / 4

The ruling CNDD–FDD, whose election to power fell far short of standards for free and fair elections, controls policy development and implementation.

C2. Are safeguards against official corruption strong and effective? 0 / 4

Corruption is endemic, though President Ndayishimiye vowed to address corruption during his swearing-in ceremony. Corrupt officials generally enjoy impunity, even when wrongdoing is exposed by nongovernmental organizations (NGOs) and other actors. Anticorruption organizations are underresourced and ineffective.

C3. Does the government operate with openness and transparency? 0 / 4

Government operations are opaque, and government officials are generally unaccountable to voters. There are few opportunities for civil society actors and others to participate in policymaking. Due to recurrent assassinations and assassination attempts, politicians are wary of organizing town hall–style meetings or making other public appearances before voters.

The government was nontransparent during the COVID-19 pandemic, with authorities providing little factual information on the illness. According to a June 2020 Human Rights Watch (HRW) report, COVID-19 testing is inconsistent, and health-care workers are warned from publicly discussing the course of the pandemic.

The authorities were perceived as opaque about possible COVID-19 infections amongst high-ranking officials; while the government reported President Nkurunziza's June 2020 death was the result of cardiac arrest, widespread speculation persisted that he had been infected with COVID-19.

CIVIL LIBERTIES: 10 / 60

D. FREEDOM OF EXPRESSION AND BELIEF: 4 / 16

D1. Are there free and independent media? 0 / 4

Freedom of expression is constitutionally guaranteed, but severely restricted in practice by draconian press laws and a dangerous operating environment for media workers, who risk threats, harassment, and arrest in response to their coverage. A 2013 media law limits the protection of journalistic sources, requires journalists to meet certain educational and professional standards, and bans content related to national defense, security, public safety, and the state currency. The government dominates the media through its ownership of the public television broadcaster, radio stations, and *Le Renouveau*, the only daily newspaper. Key independent news outlets destroyed in the political violence of 2015 have yet to be re-established. Many journalists have fled the country since 2015, and some have been forcibly disappeared. The Burundian government has banned the British Broadcasting Corporation (BBC) and Voice of America (VOA) since 2018.

Government harassment and intimidation of journalists continued in 2020. In January, four journalists from the *Iwacu* newspaper, who were arrested in October 2019 while covering protests in the west of the country, were convicted of attempting to undermine state security, and sentenced to two and a half years in prison. The government also shut down social media sites and messaging applications on election day in May 2020, impeding the ability of journalists to report on the contests.

D2. Are individuals free to practice and express their religious faith or nonbelief in public and private? 3 / 4

While freedom of religion has generally been observed in Burundi, relations between the government and the Roman Catholic Church, of which a majority of Burundians are members, have worsened in recent years. In 2017, the government set up a commission to monitor religious groups and guard against political subversion within them. In September 2019, the Commission of Inquiry reported that the government was exerting more control over churches to curb political dissent. The same month, senior government officials called for the defrocking of a group of Catholic bishops who accused the ruling party of instigating political violence.

D3. Is there academic freedom, and is the educational system free from extensive political indoctrination? 1 / 4

Both university students and staff who support the CNDD–FDD receive preferential treatment at academic institutions. Continued intimidation of opposition supporters has created an atmosphere of fear and limited free speech on university campuses. Reports indicate that teachers allied to the CNDD–FDD have intimidated students seen as not supporting the party, in some cases preventing them from attending school. Teachers are increasingly screened for political loyalty to the ruling party.

Some schools had barred students of voting age who had not made contributions to the 2020 elections from attending class, though the practice was prohibited in February 2019. That March, authorities arrested several students for allegedly doodling on a photo of Nkurunziza in their schoolbooks, though the charges were eventually dropped.

D4. Are individuals free to express their personal views on political or other sensitive topics without fear of surveillance or retribution? 0 / 4

The SNR and the Imbonerakure actively surveil private citizens. There is a reluctance to engage in speech which could be perceived as critical of the ruling party due to fears of harassment, threats of violence, and other reprisals. In 2019, the Imbonerakure used surveillance and harassment tactics previously employed in the run-up to the 2018 referendum, such as ensuring citizens paid election taxes and attacking those who had not, while they assaulted individuals expressing opposition to the ruling party. Social media and messaging applications were notably blocked on election day in May 2020.

E. ASSOCIATIONAL AND ORGANIZATIONAL RIGHTS: 1 / 12

E1. Is there freedom of assembly? 0 / 4

Opposition or antigovernment meetings and rallies are usually prevented or dispersed, and participants in gatherings seen as antigovernment face harassment or arrest. Many people who participated in 2015 protests against late president Nkurunziza fled Burundi amid a subsequent crackdown.

Major election rallies were held during the run-up to the May 2020 poll, despite concerns that they would facilitate the spread of COVID-19. That same month, four WHO staff members were forced to leave Burundi after voicing concerns over the rallies.

E2. Is there freedom for nongovernmental organizations, particularly those that are engaged in human rights- and governance-related work? 0 / 4

NGOs in Burundi face restrictive registration laws and persecution for activity seen as hostile to the government. A number of human rights and other groups perceived as antigovernment have been banned, and many of their members have fled the country rather than face surveillance, intimidation, arrest, or assassination in Burundi.

E3. Is there freedom for trade unions and similar professional or labor organizations? 1 / 4

The constitution provides protections for organized labor, and the labor code guarantees the right to strike. However, it is unlikely that union members would feel free to exercise the collective bargaining rights guaranteed by the law in the current political climate.

F. RULE OF LAW: 1 / 16

F1. Is there an independent judiciary? 0 / 4

The judiciary is hindered by corruption and a lack of resources and training, and is generally subservient to the executive. In 2015, Constitutional Court justices were reportedly intimidated into ruling in favor of Nkurunziza's decision to stand for a third term. The executive regularly interferes in the criminal justice system to protect CNDD–FDD and Imbonerakure members, as well as persecute the political opposition.

In June 2020, the Constitutional Court partially checked the power of the ruling party by upholding an opposition challenge to the disqualification of an opposition parliamentary candidate. However, the court did not entertain a challenge to over the conduct of the presidential election, despite evidence of widespread fraud and intimidation. The August Commission of Inquiry report also noted the involvement of the judiciary in a repression campaign that targeted the opposition ahead of the elections.

F2. Does due process prevail in civil and criminal matters? 0 / 4

The courts, police, and security forces do not operate independently or professionally, and constitutional guarantees of due process are generally not upheld. Arbitrary arrest and lengthy pretrial detention are common. There have been reports that detainees' families were able to secure their release only upon making large payments to the SNR or Imbonerakure.

Defendants must provide their own legal representation, making trial rights dependent on the ability to afford a lawyer. Some detainees accused of participating in the 2015 protests or subsequent antigovernment violence did not have access to lawyers and were forced to make false confessions under threat of death.

In 2017, the International Criminal Court (ICC) opened an investigation into alleged crimes against humanity committed by government actors. Two days after the investigation's launch, Burundi left the ICC, becoming the first country ever to do so.

The Burundian prison system is overcrowded, with the World Prison Brief reporting the prison population at 304 percent of capacity as of December 2020. Prisoners were at risk of contracting COVID-19, with health-care workers reporting that quarantine measures were insufficiently enforced within the prison system.

F3. Is there protection from the illegitimate use of physical force and freedom from war and insurgencies? 0 / 4

The security situation in Burundi remains extremely poor. A 2019 UN report found that widespread human rights violations persist; violations include forced disappearance, summary execution, sexual violence, torture, and arbitrary arrest and detention. The report identified the Imbonerakure as the principal perpetrators but noted the role of the SNR and other state agents. A 2018 investigative report by the BBC found that the government operated at least 22 secret facilities where political dissidents have reportedly been tortured and killed. The government responded to the report by calling it "fake" and threatening to sue the BBC. The government similarly rejected the UN report.

The UN High Commissioner for Refugees reported that over 312,000 Burundian refugees resided in nearby countries as of December 2020, with nearly half of them residing in Tanzania.

F4. Do laws, policies, and practices guarantee equal treatment of various segments of the population? 1 / 4

Despite quotas for representation in the National Assembly, the Twa population remains marginalized relative to the Hutu and Tutsi ethnic groups. People living with albinism face systematic discrimination and violence in Burundi. LGBT+ people also experience official and societal discrimination. The 2009 penal code criminalizes same-sex sexual activity, and punishments include up to two years in prison.

Discrimination against women is common in access to education, healthcare, and employment.

G. PERSONAL AUTONOMY AND INDIVIDUAL RIGHTS: 4 / 16

G1. Do individuals enjoy freedom of movement, including the ability to change their place of residence, employment, or education? 1 / 4

Since 2015, concerns for personal safety have restricted free movement, particularly in neighborhoods regarded as opposition strongholds, where security forces frequently conduct search operations. According to the August 2020 Commission of Inquiry report, the Imbonerakure maintains a checkpoint system to control population movement, despite official instructions for the organization to refrain from such activity. Some local authorities have imposed curfews on women and girls.

G2. Are individuals able to exercise the right to own property and establish private businesses without undue interference from state or nonstate actors? 1 / 4

Land conflict has been an explosive issue in Burundi for decades, which was exacerbated by the return of displaced populations after the civil war ended in 2005. Many of the returnees found new owners occupying their land, and the courts have often failed to fairly adjudicate land disputes. There are additional reports that some refugees who fled in 2015 are returning to find their land occupied.

Due to customary law, women typically are unable to inherit property. The deteriorating security situation hampers private business activity in the country, as does rampant corruption.

G3. Do individuals enjoy personal social freedoms, including choice of marriage partner and size of family, protection from domestic violence, and control over appearance? 1 / 4

Sexual and domestic violence are serious problems but are rarely reported to law enforcement agencies. Rights monitors continue to report sexual violence carried out by security forces and Imbonerakure, who act with impunity. Women are often targeted for rape if they or their spouses refuse to join the CNDD–FDD, and men sometimes experience sexual abuse while in government custody.

According to the citizenship code, a Burundian woman married to a foreign national cannot pass on her citizenship to her husband or children.

G4. Do individuals enjoy equality of opportunity and freedom from economic exploitation? 1 / 4

Individuals not allied with the ruling party may lose their employment. Community service requirements have taken on political overtones, such as building offices for the CNDD–FDD, amounting to what a 2019 UN report called forced labor.

Women have limited opportunities for advancement in the workplace. Much of the population is impoverished. In 2017, "vagrancy" and begging by able-bodied persons became formal offenses under the penal code. The ongoing political and humanitarian crisis has contributed to an economic decline, less access to basic services, and deteriorating living conditions.

The government has conducted some trainings for government officials on handling cases of human trafficking. However, the government has largely failed to prevent domestic human trafficking, to protect victims, and to prosecute perpetrators.

Cabo Verde

Population: 600,000
Capital: Praia
Freedom Status: Free
Electoral Democracy: Yes

Overview: Cabo Verde is a stable democracy with competitive elections and periodic transfers of power between rival parties. Civil liberties are generally protected, but access to justice is impaired by an overburdened court system, and crime remains a concern. Other outstanding problems include persistent inequities for women and migrant workers.

KEY DEVELOPMENTS IN 2020

- As a result of the COVID-19 pandemic, the government pushed back the August municipal elections to October, when 65 candidates competed from the MpD, PAICV, the Democratic and Independent Cabo Verdean Union (UCID), and the Popular Party (PP), and 12 groups of independent citizens on different candidate lists, such as the Movement in Defense of Justice of Labor. Public health measures for the electoral campaign and voting successfully limited the spread of the virus at the polls, and included restrictions on public gatherings and discouragement of door-to-door contact with voters. According to government statistics provided to the World Health Organization (WHO), over 11,800 people tested positive for the coronavirus, and 113 people died by the end of the year.
- In November, the government announced they would be expanding the controversial surveillance camera system into São Vicente, Sal, and Boa Vista, as part

of its Smart City project. In February, the government released statistics that the surveillance system had helped prevent over 2,000 crimes in Praia.

POLITICAL RIGHTS: 38 / 40

A. ELECTORAL PROCESS: 12 / 12

A1. Was the current head of government or other chief national authority elected through free and fair elections? 4 / 4

The president is directly elected for up to two consecutive five-year terms. The prime minister, who holds most executive authority, is nominated by, is accountable to the National Assembly, and is formally appointed by the president.

Incumbent Jorge Carlos Fonseca of the Movement for Democracy (MpD) was reelected as president in late 2016 with 74 percent of the vote. Ulisses Correia e Silva, also of the MpD, was appointed as prime minister in early 2016, a month after the legislative elections.

A2. Were the current national legislative representatives elected through free and fair elections? 4 / 4

Members of the 72-seat National Assembly are directly elected in multimember constituencies to serve five-year terms. In the 2016 legislative election, the MpD, then in opposition, won 40 seats. The African Party for the Independence of Cabo Verde (PAICV) was reduced to 29 seats, and the UCID took 3. International observers assessed the elections as largely free and fair.

With the support of all political parties, the government announced in August 2020 that municipal elections for the country's 22 municipalities would be held in October 2020. A total of 65 candidates competed from the MpD, PAICV, the Democratic and Independent Cabo Verdean Union (UCID), and the Popular Party (PP), and 12 groups of independent citizens on different candidate lists, such as the Movement in Defense of Justice of Labor. As a result of the COVID-19 pandemic, the government adopted public health measures for the electoral campaign and voting periods. Public gatherings and door-to-door contact with voters were not recommended; candidates used both traditional media and social media for their campaigns. Simple safety provisions (using hand sanitizer, wearing masks, and maintaining socially distanced voter lines) were in place during the polls.

The ruling MpD received fewer votes than it did the last municipal elections in 2016. The party won 14 municipalities, losing 5 it had controlled and its absolute majority in 2 others. The PAICV won eight municipalities; in 2016, the party had only won two municipalities.

A3. Are the electoral laws and framework fair, and are they implemented impartially by the relevant election management bodies? 4 / 4

The legal framework provides for fair and competitive elections. The National Elections Commission (CNE), whose members are elected by a two-thirds majority in the National Assembly, is generally considered impartial. Prior to the 2020 municipal elections, the CNE successfully managed hundreds of complaints regarding the election.

B. POLITICAL PLURALISM AND PARTICIPATION: 16 / 16

B1. Do the people have the right to organize in different political parties or other competitive political groupings of their choice, and is the system free of undue obstacles to the rise and fall of these competing parties or groupings? 4 / 4

There are no significant impediments to the formation and competition of political parties. A number of different parties are active, though only the PAICV and the MpD have held power at the national level. Groups of independent citizens have an active role in the political life, participating in elections.

B2. Is there a realistic opportunity for the opposition to increase its support or gain power through elections? 4 / 4

The opposition has a realistic opportunity to gain power through elections. There have been three democratic transfers of power between the PAICV and the MpD since independence in 1975, the most recent in 2016.

B3. Are the people's political choices free from domination by forces that are external to the political sphere, or by political forces that employ extrapolitical means? 4 / 4

The political choices of voters and candidates are free from undue external influence. However, there were some reports of vote buying and of voters being pressured near polling stations during the 2016 elections.

B4. Do various segments of the population (including ethnic, racial, religious, gender, LGBT+, and other relevant groups) have full political rights and electoral opportunities? 4 / 4

Women have full and equal political rights and have become more involved in politics in the last decade. Nevertheless, social constraints have somewhat impaired their participation, with women currently holding 36 percent of seats in the parliament. The enforcement of the 2019 Gender Parity Law, which introduced a 40 percent gender quota for candidate lists at the national and local levels, has proven to be difficult. The gender quota was not respected for the October 2020 municipal elections and in the nomination of trustees for a newly formed public company.

C. FUNCTIONING OF GOVERNMENT: 10 / 12

C1. Do the freely elected head of government and national legislative representatives determine the policies of the government? 4 / 4

The prime minister and cabinet determine the policies of the government, under the supervision of the National Assembly and the president. The government is able to implement laws and policies without undue interference from unelected entities.

C2. Are safeguards against official corruption strong and effective? 3 / 4

Cabo Verde has relatively low levels of corruption overall, but bribery and nepotism are problems at the municipal level. Allegations of graft continue to surround costly infrastructure projects and other spending measures, public procurements, public companies, and management of public lands.

C3. Does the government operate with openness and transparency? 3 / 4

The current government has taken numerous steps to improve transparency, including by publishing more information about state operations and finances online; it generally adheres to legal guarantees of public access to information. However, many officeholders fail to comply with rules requiring them to declare their personal assets and income. The government in 2020 ensured factual information about the COVID-19 pandemic was accessible to the public, holding daily press conferences and setting up a website with regularly updated data.

CIVIL LIBERTIES: 54 / 60
D. FREEDOM OF EXPRESSION AND BELIEF: 16 / 16

D1. Are there free and independent media? 4 / 4

Press freedom is guaranteed by law and generally respected in practice, though Article 105 of the electoral code prohibits media organizations from disseminating opinions on or criticism of parties and candidates after a certain date during a campaign period. Though the publicly owned Radio and Television of Cabo Verde (RTC) respected the right of all candidates to free airtime during the October 2020 municipal elections' campaign period, the candidate from the Movement in Defense of Justice of Labor accused the media of manipulating the political landscape. The PAICV in September 2020 announced that it was filing a complaint against RTC, alleging discrimination in news coverage.

Publicly and privately owned media outlets are largely free of government control. The government in 2019 gave up its power to nominate trustees for RTC, reinforcing the independence of the public broadcasting company, which installed a new independent board of governors in July 2020. However, precarious finances at many outlets can undermine journalists' job security and their ability to undertake investigative reporting projects. A lack of funding has contributed to the closure of several privately owned newspapers, decreasing the diversity of information in the print sector.

During the COVID-19 pandemic, the government did not restrict freedom of information but issued legal threats to media outlets that promoted misinformation about the coronavirus, which drew concern from the Cape Verdean Association of Journalists (AJOC).

D2. Are individuals free to practice and express their religious faith or nonbelief in public and private? 4 / 4

The constitution establishes the separation of church and state, though the Roman Catholic Church receives some privileges, such as the recognition of Catholic marriages under civil law. While all religious groups are required to register with the Justice Ministry to obtain tax and other benefits, the process is not restrictive, and there are no limitations on freedom of worship.

D3. Is there academic freedom, and is the educational system free from extensive political indoctrination? 4 / 4

Academic freedom is respected, and the educational system is not affected by political indoctrination. Due to COVID-19, in-person classes were suspended in March 2020 and replaced with online learning and educational television classes through the RTC.

D4. Are individuals free to express their personal views on political or other sensitive topics without fear of surveillance or retribution? 4 / 4

There are no significant constraints on individuals' freedom of expression. The government is not known to engage in online surveillance or improper monitoring of personal communications. Social media is widely used to express private and political opinions.

E. ASSOCIATIONAL AND ORGANIZATIONAL RIGHTS: 11 / 12
E1. Is there freedom of assembly? 4 / 4

Freedom of assembly is legally guaranteed and observed in practice. In 2020 as a result of the COVID-19 pandemic, freedom of assembly was temporarily suspended. Several demonstrations, however, did take place in 2020.

E2. Is there freedom for nongovernmental organizations, particularly those that are engaged in human rights and governance-related work? 4 / 4

Numerous nongovernmental organizations (NGOs) operate freely in the country, focusing on a variety of social, economic, environmental, and cultural issues. International human rights institutions, local organizations, and journalists are able to monitor prison conditions and other human rights indicators without government interference.

E3. Is there freedom for trade unions and similar professional or labor organizations? 3 / 4

The constitution protects the right to unionize, and workers may form and join unions in practice. However, the government restricts the right to strike in broadly defined essential industries, and formal collective bargaining is reportedly uncommon in the private sector. Workers in the public and private sectors held strikes in 2020, including staff at the National Institute of Meteorology and Geophysics.

F. RULE OF LAW: 14 / 16
F1. Is there an independent judiciary? 4 / 4

The judiciary is independent, though the courts are overburdened and understaffed. Despite the COVID-19 pandemic in 2020, the courts improved their performance, reducing the number of pending cases. The government established a small claims court, inaugurated in October 2020, and new judges were appointed during the year. Work went on during 2020 to revise the penal code to clarify rules for parole and to add penalties for gang-related crimes.

F2. Does due process prevail in civil and criminal matters? 3 / 4

Police and prosecutors generally observe legal safeguards against arbitrary arrest and detention. Defense attorneys are provided to indigent defendants. However, due to the limited capacity of the court system, there are often delays in detainees' first hearings before a judge, and many cases are dropped because defendants in detention are denied a timely trial.

F3. Is there protection from the illegitimate use of physical force and freedom from war and insurgencies? 4 / 4

Law enforcement officials are sometimes accused of excessive force, but perpetrators are often investigated and punished by oversight bodies. Cabo Verde is generally free of major crime or unrest. Nevertheless, violent crime does occur, and street crime, smuggling, and drug trafficking are perceived as consistent problems. As of November 2020, 97.1 percent of the prison population were men.

In 2017, the government permitted Chinese technology firm Huawei to install surveillance cameras in Praia and three other cities as part of its Safe City project. While observers voiced privacy concerns, the government has maintained its support for the program. In February 2020, the government reported that the camera system helped prevent 2,000 crime cases in Praia. In November, authorities announced they would be expanding the system into São Vicente, Sal, and Boa Vista.

Prison conditions are poor and often overcrowded, but the government has been working to improve conditions, which includes changes in legislation, the implementation of a social reintegration program for prisoners, and the construction of more cells and bathrooms.

F4. Do laws, policies, and practices guarantee equal treatment of various segments of the population? 3 / 4

Gender discrimination is prohibited by law, but wage discrimination and unequal access to education persist for women. No comprehensive antidiscrimination legislation exists for the entire population. Immigrants often face discriminatory treatment by employers. As per a measure adopted in July 2020, the government established a High Authority for Immigration to help in the integration of immigrants in Cabo Verde. Same-sex relations are not criminalized, and the law protects against employment discrimination based on sexual orientation. However, LGBT+ people are reportedly subject to physical violence and verbal abuse.

G. PERSONAL AUTONOMY AND INDIVIDUAL RIGHTS: 13 / 16

G1. Do individuals enjoy freedom of movement, including the ability to change their place of residence, employment, or education? 4 / 4

Individual freedom of movement is recognized by law, and there are no significant restrictions in practice. People may freely change their place of employment or education. During the state of emergency declared in March 2020 due to COVID-19, freedom of movement was temporarily suspended. Further, the media reported alleged illegal detentions and violence perpetrated by law enforcement officials implementing government restrictions. However, these abuses seem to have been isolated incidents and only took place in the capital, Praia.

G2. Are individuals able to exercise the right to own property and establish private businesses without undue interference from state or nonstate actors? 3 / 4

Property rights are generally respected. The legal framework and government policies are supportive of private business activity, though obstacles such as corruption and legal and bureaucratic inefficiency remain a concern. Small and medium-size businesses are one of the main sources of income for families whose members are not directly employed in the public services.

G3. Do individuals enjoy personal social freedoms, including choice of marriage partner and size of family, protection from domestic violence, and control over appearance? 3 / 4

Personal social freedoms are generally protected, including in matters of marriage and family law. Authorities enforce laws against rape and domestic abuse, but such violence remains a serious problem, and insufficient public resources are dedicated to supporting and protecting victims. During 2020, a number of public demonstrations called for stronger enforcement of the law against gender-based violence. According to statistics, 11 percent of Cabo Verdean women are victims of physical violence and 5.8 percent over the age of 15 experience sexual violence. Due to an increase in sexual abuse of minors, the National Assembly late in 2020 held debates to strengthen the penalties against those convicted of such crimes and the criminalizing of sexting to minors and sex tourism involving minors.

Same-sex marriages are not recognized.

G4. Do individuals enjoy equality of opportunity and freedom from economic exploitation? 3 / 4

The law prohibits forced labor and other exploitative practices, and the government actively enforces such safeguards in the formal sector. However, a high percent of the Cabo Verdean workforce continues to work informally.

Immigrant workers who lack employment contracts remain vulnerable to abuses, and children are reportedly exposed to sex trafficking and illegal work in agriculture or domestic service.

Cambodia

Population: 16,500,000
Capital: Phnom Penh
Freedom Status: Not Free
Electoral Democracy: No

Overview: Cambodia's political system has been dominated by Prime Minister Hun Sen and the Cambodian People's Party (CPP) for more than three decades. While the country conducted semicompetitive elections in the past, the 2018 polls were held in a severely repressive environment. Since then, Hun Sen's government has maintained pressure on opposition party members, independent press outlets, and demonstrators with intimidation, politically motivated prosecutions, and violence.

KEY DEVELOPMENTS IN 2020

- The government arrested and tried scores of opposition activists, union leaders, journalists, and other opponents throughout the year—often on charges of "incitement," or over crimes ostensibly related to the COVID-19 pandemic, which had a relatively minimal impact in Cambodia. In August, the European Union imposed trade sanctions on Cambodia in response to Hun Sen's extensive, ongoing repression.
- Citing the need to respond to the COVID-19 pandemic, the government enacted legislation that gave Hun Sen power to declare a state of emergency that would grant him vast, virtually unchecked power. If invoked, the designation would increase government surveillance capabilities and allow Hun Sen to further restrict media, assembly, travel, and business activities.
- A prominent Thai dissident vanished from Cambodia in June, reportedly shoved into a black sedan by armed men and then disappearing. He is one of many Thai activists who have disappeared or were found dead in Cambodia, Laos, and Vietnam in recent years.
- Judges sitting in the Extraordinary Chambers in the Courts of Cambodia (ECCC), which oversees the trials of surviving members of the genocidal Khmer Rouge regime, terminated a case against a defendant charged with committing genocide against a Muslim group, likely marking an end to the body's work.

POLITICAL RIGHTS: 5 / 40

A. ELECTORAL PROCESS: 1 / 12

A1. Was the current head of government or other chief national authority elected through free and fair elections? 0 / 4

King Norodom Sihamoni is chief of state but has little political power. The prime minister is head of government and is appointed by the monarch from among the majority coalition or party in parliament following legislative elections. Hun Sen first became prime minister in 1985. He was nominated most recently after 2018 National Assembly polls, which offered voters no meaningful choice. Most international observation groups were not present due to the highly restrictive nature of the contest.

A2. Were the current national legislative representatives elected through free and fair elections? 0 / 4

The bicameral parliament consists of the 62-seat Senate and the 125-seat National Assembly. Members of parliament and local councilors indirectly elect 58 senators, and the king and National Assembly each appoint 2. Senators serve six-year terms, while National Assembly members are directly elected to five-year terms.

In 2018, the CPP won every seat in both chambers in elections that were considered neither free nor fair by established international observers and prompted condemnation from many democracies. In the lead-up to the vote the Supreme Court had banned the main opposition Cambodia National Rescue Party (CNRP); many of its members were jailed, and numerous media outlets were closed. Several small, obscure new "opposition parties" ran candidates in the lower-house elections, though many of these were believed to have been manufactured by government allies to suggest multiparty competition.

A3. Are the electoral laws and framework fair, and are they implemented impartially by the relevant election management bodies? 1 / 4

In 2015, Cambodia passed two new election laws that permit security forces to take part in campaigns, punish parties that boycott parliament, and mandate a shorter campaign period of 21 days. The laws have been broadly enforced.

Voting is tied to a citizen's permanent-resident status in a village, township, or urban district, and this status cannot be changed easily.

The CPP has complete control over the nine seats of the National Election Committee (NEC). In 2018, the NEC sought to aid the CPP's campaign by threatening to prosecute any figures that urged an election boycott and informing voters that criticism of the CPP was prohibited.

B. POLITICAL PLURALISM AND PARTICIPATION: 2 / 16

B1. Do the people have the right to organize in different political parties or other competitive political groupings of their choice, and is the system free of undue obstacles to the rise and fall of these competing parties or groupings? 0 / 4

Following the 2018 elections, Cambodia is a de facto one-party state. The main opposition CNRP was banned and its leaders have been charged with crimes, while other prominent party figures have fled the country. Although several small opposition parties contested the 2018 lower-house elections, none won seats. All of the smaller parties were permitted to run by the CPP-controlled NEC, and both domestic and international observers questioned their authenticity.

CNRP members and supporters and a broad range of other opposition activists were subject to harassment and arrests throughout 2020. At least 100 party members and civil society representatives were put on trial together late in the year, including leading opposition figures Sam Rainsy and Mo Sochua, who stood trial in absentia. In August, security forces arrested four opposition activists, and separately arrested Suong Sophorn, the president of a minor opposition party. In July, the police broke up a protest by CNRP supporters, and at least 16 CNRP activists were detained between January and June.

The government has continued a prosecution against CNRP official Kem Sokha, who was originally accused of treason in 2017 over a speech he gave four years earlier in which he disclosed having received US training on building grassroots support. Kem Sokha, who maintains his innocence, spent a year in solitary confinement before he was released on bail in late 2018. In November 2019, he was freed from house arrest, but at the end of 2020 remained under court supervision ahead of his impending trial.

B2. Is there a realistic opportunity for the opposition to increase its support or gain power through elections? 0 / 4

The political opposition has been quashed through an ongoing government campaign of harassment, arrests, and convictions of opposition figures, supporters, and perceived supporters, carried out alongside severe restrictions on press freedom, free assembly, and civil society. The high rate of spoiled ballots in the 2018 lower house election—8.6 percent of all votes, according to the NEC—suggested strong popular discontent with the lack of choice, especially given that Hun Sen had repeatedly warned Cambodians not to spoil ballots.

B3. Are the people's political choices free from domination by forces that are external to the political sphere, or by political forces that employ extrapolitical means? 1 / 4

The ruling party is not democratically accountable, and top leaders, especially Hun Sen, use the police and armed forces as instruments of repression. The military has stood firmly behind Hun Sen and his crackdown on opposition. Hun Sen has built a personal bodyguard unit in the armed forces that he reportedly uses to harass and abuse CPP opponents.

B4. Do various segments of the population (including ethnic, racial, religious, gender, LGBT+, and other relevant groups) have full political rights and electoral opportunities? 1 / 4

Ethnic Vietnamese are regularly excluded from the political process and scapegoated by both parties. Women make up 15 percent of the National Assembly, but their interests, like those of most citizens, are poorly represented.

C. FUNCTIONING OF GOVERNMENT: 2 / 12

C1. Do the freely elected head of government and national legislative representatives determine the policies of the government? 0 / 4

Hun Sen has increasingly centralized power, and figures outside of his close circle have little impact on policymaking. Analysts also believe the prime minister is grooming his son, General Hun Manet, to succeed him. Hun Manet has gained several key posts during his father's rule, including the commander of the Royal Cambodian Armed Forces (RCAF). Hun Sen's June 2020 remarks that he wanted to "support my son and train him so that he is capable" were interpreted as confirmation of these suspicions, though Hun Sen also has said that he wants to remain in charge for another decade.

C2. Are safeguards against official corruption strong and effective? 1 / 4

Anticorruption laws are poorly enforced, and corruption is pervasive in public procurement and tax administration, to the benefit of Prime Minister Hun Sen and his family. In 2018, anticorruption nongovernmental organization (NGO) Global Witness claimed that the prime minister's family benefited from ownership stakes in firms worth over $200 million; these companies were involved in projects varying from gold mining to the construction of Phnom Penh's international airport.

Members of the prime minister's family have also used their positions to keep millions of dollars in assets abroad and have acquired Cypriot passports through its Citizenship by Investment program; participants must invest at least €2 million ($2.4 million) in order to qualify.

Senior CPP senators have been implicated in acts of corruption, benefiting from smuggling operations and illegal land concessions.

C3. Does the government operate with openness and transparency? 1 / 4

Nepotism and patronage undermine the functioning of a transparent bureaucratic system. A draft access to information law was made public in 2018 and was finalized in 2019, but the government added the bill to its long-term strategic plan, delaying its implementation to 2023. Human Rights Watch (HRW) and ARTICLE 19, a British NGO that advocates for greater freedom of information worldwide, criticized the bill in December 2019, warning it did not meet international standards.

CIVIL LIBERTIES: 19 / 60 (−1)
D. FREEDOM OF EXPRESSION AND BELIEF: 7 / 16 (−1)
D1. Are there free and independent media? 1 / 4

The government uses lawsuits, criminal prosecutions, massive tax bills, and occasionally violent attacks to intimidate the media. There are private print and broadcast outlets, but many are owned and operated by the CPP.

Since 2017, the government has engaged in an intense crackdown on independent media. The independent English-language newspaper *Cambodia Daily* closed that year after it was issued an onerous tax bill. It has since been relaunched as an online news aggregator. In 2018, the *Phnom Penh Post*, an independent newspaper, was sold to a Malaysian investor with links to Hun Sen, and many of its editors and reporters quit or were fired.

Chinese investments also influence Cambodian press output. Fresh News, a progovernment news site, has distributed content from Chinese state media since accepting outside investment in 2018.

While progovernment media organizations operate freely, foreign media groups operate with more severe restrictions and in some instances forced out of the country altogether. Radio Free Asia (RFA), which reported on forced evictions and corruption in the country, was forced to close its Phnom Penh bureau in late 2017. Two of its journalists, Uon Chhin and Yeang Sothearin, were arrested and charged with espionage soon after. Their trial began in July 2019, and in 2020 courts twice rejected their petitions to dismiss the charges.

Two former staff members of the *Cambodia Daily*, Cambodian Aun Pheap and Canadian Zsombor Peter, were charged with incitement to commit a felony in 2017 after writing about local elections being held that May. Both journalists subsequently fled the country, and the charges against them were dropped in November 2020. A number of journalists faced incitement charges in 2020, including Ros Sokhet, publisher of the private *Cheat Khmer* newspaper, who was arrested in June; Sok Oudom, owner of the Rithysen Radio News Station, detained in May; and Sovann Rithy of the TVFB news outlet, charged in April.

D2. Are individuals free to practice and express their religious faith or nonbelief in public and private? 3 / 4

The majority of Cambodians are Theravada Buddhists and can practice their faith freely, but societal discrimination against religious and ethnic minorities persists. The government has increasingly used Facebook to spread disinformation about or smear activist monks; one such monk, Luon Sovath, fled the country in 2020 after being targeted.

D3. Is there academic freedom, and is the educational system free from extensive political indoctrination? 2 / 4

Teachers and students practice self-censorship regarding discussions about Cambodian politics and history. Criticism of the prime minister and his family is often punished.

D4. Are individuals free to express their personal views on political or other sensitive topics without fear of surveillance or retribution? 1 / 4 (−1)

Open criticism of the prime minister and government by private citizens can result in reprisals, notably during the run-up to elections.

Free expression has come under further restriction in 2020. In April, several weeks after authorities announced such plans, the government enacted legislation that gave Hun Sen the power to declare a state of emergency that granted authorities vast powers to conduct digital surveillance, ban assemblies, ban or limit broadcasting, fix prices, and confiscate equipment, among other provisions that amounted to virtually unchecked powers. While a state of emergency was never declared, Hun Sen issued numerous threats as the global pandemic became apparent: for example, warning in early March that anyone who spread "fake news" would be considered a terrorist. A number of people, including private citizens and those considered political opponents, were indeed arrested throughout year on the pretext of spreading false information about COVID-19 or purportedly contravening government narratives about public health.

Score Change: The score declined from 2 to 1 due to numerous arrests predicated on spreading false information about the COVID-19 pandemic, as well as the adoption of a new emergency law that further empowers the government to conduct surveillance and punish expressions of dissent.

E. ASSOCIATIONAL AND ORGANIZATIONAL RIGHTS: 3 / 12
E1. Is there freedom of assembly? 1 / 4

Authorities are openly hostile to free assembly. Gatherings by the now-banned major opposition party are prohibited. The authorities repeatedly broke up protests, often using violence, throughout 2020.

E2. Is there freedom for nongovernmental organizations, particularly those that are engaged in human rights- and governance-related work? 1 / 4

Activists and civil society groups dedicated to justice and human rights risk violence and typically face state harassment, as do activists involved in land disputes.

E3. Is there freedom for trade unions and similar professional or labor organizations? 1 / 4

Cambodia has a small number of independent trade unions, and workers have the right to strike, but many face retribution for doing so. A 2016 law on unions imposed restrictions such as excessive requirements for union formation. In July 2020, authorities arrested union leader Rong Chhun on incitement charges.

F. RULE OF LAW: 3 / 16
F1. Is there an independent judiciary? 0 / 4

The judiciary is marred by corruption and a lack of independence. Judges have facilitated the government's ability to pursue charges against a broad range of opposition politicians.

F2. Does due process prevail in civil and criminal matters? 1 / 4

Due process rights are poorly upheld in Cambodia. Abuse by law enforcement officers and judges remains extremely common. Sham trials are frequent, while elites generally enjoy impunity.

F3. Is there protection from the illegitimate use of physical force and freedom from war and insurgencies? 1 / 4

Cambodians live in an environment of repression and fear. The torture of suspects and prisoners is frequent. The security forces are regularly accused of using excessive force against detained suspects.

The work of the Extraordinary Chambers in the Courts of Cambodia (ECCC), established to try the leaders of the former Khmer Rouge regime, has brought convictions for crimes against humanity, homicide, torture, and religious persecution. In 2018, the tribunal found Nuon Chea and Khieu Samphan, two surviving leaders of the Khmer Rouge, guilty of genocide and crimes against humanity. They both received life sentences; both had already been sentenced to life in prison for past convictions of crimes against humanity. The convictions marked the first time the Khmer Rouge crimes were legally defined as genocide. Nuon Chea died in August 2019 and Kaing Guak Eav, or Duch, died in August 2020.

Three defendants remain under the jurisdiction of the ECCC; the body was split over whether to continue the trial against one, Ao An, leading to an impasse. Ultimately, in August 2020 the court terminated the case against Ao An, who was accused of overseeing the genocide of the Cham Muslim minority during the Khmer Rouge period. It seems unlikely the tribunal will hear any further cases.

A prominent Thai dissident vanished from Cambodia in June 2020, reportedly shoved into a black sedan by armed men and then disappearing.

F4. Do laws, policies, and practices guarantee equal treatment of various segments of the population? 1 / 4

Ethnic minorities, especially those of Vietnamese descent, often face legal and societal discrimination. The Cambodian government frequently refuses to grant refugee protections to Montagnards fleeing Vietnam, where they face persecution by the Vietnamese government. LGBT+ individuals have no legal protection against discrimination.

G. PERSONAL AUTONOMY AND INDIVIDUAL RIGHTS: 6 / 16

G1. Do individuals enjoy freedom of movement, including the ability to change their place of residence, employment, or education? 2 / 4

The constitution guarantees the rights to freedom of travel and movement, and the government generally respects these rights in practice. However, restrictions do occur, notably when the government tries to prevent activists from traveling around the country. The new emergency law allows the government to restrict movement severely if invoked.

G2. Are individuals able to exercise the right to own property and establish private businesses without undue interference from state or nonstate actors? 1 / 4

Land and property rights are regularly abused for the sake of private development projects. Over the past several years, hundreds of thousands of people have been forcibly removed from their homes, with little or no compensation, to make room for commercial plantations, mine operations, factories, and high-end residential developments. Land disputes are common, and security forces typically respond to protests with force.

G3. Do individuals enjoy personal social freedoms, including choice of marriage partner and size of family, protection from domestic violence, and control over appearance? 2 / 4

The government does not frequently repress personal social freedoms, but women suffer widespread social discrimination. Rape and violence against women are common.

G4. Do individuals enjoy equality of opportunity and freedom from economic exploitation? 1 / 4

Equality of opportunity is severely limited in Cambodia, where a small elite controls most of the economy. Labor conditions can be harsh, sometimes sparking protests, and the government cracked down on labor protests in 2020.

Cambodia is a country of origin, destination point, and transit point for sex and labor trafficking. In its 2020 *Trafficking in Persons* report, the US State Department noted that Cambodia is on the Tier 2 watch list, potentially to be dropped into Tier 3, as while it is working to prosecute traffickers and establishing long-term plans to combat trafficking, it failed to show improved efforts in these areas compared to 2019.

Cameroon

Population: 26,600,000
Capital: Yaoundé
Freedom Status: Not Free
Electoral Democracy: No

Overview: President Paul Biya has ruled Cameroon since 1982. His Cameroon People's Democratic Movement (CPDM) has maintained power by rigging elections, using state resources for political patronage, and limiting the activities of opposition parties. Press freedom and nongovernmental organizations (NGOs) are restricted, and due process protections are poorly upheld. A conflict between security forces and separatists in the Anglophone Northwest and Southwest regions is ongoing and has resulted in widespread civilian deaths and displacements.

KEY DEVELOPMENTS IN 2020

- The ruling Cameroon People's Democratic Movement (CPDM) dominated legislative elections in February, as well as the country's first-ever regional elections in December.
- Authorities cracked down on the opposition Cameroon Renaissance Movement (CRM) throughout the year, banning their rallies and arresting demonstrators who defied the bans. On September 22, over 500 protesters including two party leaders were arrested in multiple cities and accused of crimes including insurrection. A day before, CRM leader Maurice Kamto was placed on house arrest, where he remained until December 8.
- The conflict in the Anglophone regions wore on, with frequent reports of violence by separatists and government forces. Separatists maintained an atmosphere of terror in the regions, including through deadly attacks on students, teachers, and schools.
- Rights groups and journalists reported a massacre of 21 civilians by government forces and armed ethnic Fulani militiamen in February, in Ngarbuh, Northwest Region. In April, authorities acknowledged some of the events there and pledged to investigate.

POLITICAL RIGHTS: 7 / 40

A. ELECTORAL PROCESS: 1 / 12

A1. Was the current head of government or other chief national authority elected through free and fair elections? 0 / 4

The president is head of state, is directly elected to a seven-year term in a single voting round and may serve an unlimited number of terms. President Paul Biya won a seventh term in the October 2018 presidential election, taking 71 percent of the vote in a process marked by low turnout and a lack of genuine democratic competition. Maurice Kamto of the CRM came in second, with 14 percent of the vote. The election was tainted by irregularities including unsigned results sheets, and intimidation and fear in the Anglophone regions kept many from casting their votes. A television report after the election depicted supposed Transparency International observers praising the electoral process, but Transparency International quickly issued a statement asserting that they had no election observers in Cameroon.

In the Anglophone Northwest and Southwest Regions, separatists called for an election boycott, and armed militants used threats and intimidation to keep voters away from the polls. Out of 2,300 polling stations in the Northwest Region, only 74 opened on election day. Approximately 15 percent of registered voters cast ballots in the Southwest Region, while turnout was only 5 percent in the Northwest Region.

A2. Were the current national legislative representatives elected through free and fair elections? 1 / 4

The upper chamber of Cameroon's bicameral Parliament is the 100-member Senate. Senators serve five-year terms; 70 are elected through indirect suffrage by regional councils, while the remaining 30 are appointed by the president. The 180 members of the National Assembly, the lower chamber, are directly elected in multimember constituencies to five-year terms.

The ruling CPDM won 63 of 70 contested seats in March 2018 Senate elections. The opposition Social Democratic Front (SDF), won the remaining 7 seats, all based in the Northwest Region. The 30 remaining senators, appointed by the president at his prerogative, all belong to the CPDM. The SDF alleged fraud and intimidation in the Northwest and Southwest Regions, and petitioned the Constitutional Council to cancel election results in the Southwest Region, but the council rejected the petition.

Long-delayed National Assembly elections were finally held in Cameroon in February 2020, together with municipal elections. The CRM refused to put up candidates, though the SDF participated, as did the National Union for Democracy and Progress (UNDP), which is allied with the CPDM. The CPDM retained its majority, winning 139 of the 167 seats contested. The Constitutional Council invalidated the results in 11 constituencies of the Anglophone Northwest and Southwest Regions, where boycotts and ongoing tensions resulted in low turnout; separatists claimed that 98 percent of eligible voters had boycotted the election. Reruns took place in March, and the incumbent CPDM won all 13 of the seats at stake.

On December 6, 2020, the first-ever regional elections took place despite calls for boycott by opposition parties, who rejected the government's characterization that they would lead to greater regional autonomy in the country, and threats by separatist groups in the Anglophone regions to arrest would-be voters. In the indirect election, a 24,000-member electoral college composed of regional delegates and traditional chiefs chose 900 regional councilors in all 10 regions (90 for each region). Biya's CPDM party won the majority.

A3. Are the electoral laws and framework fair, and are they implemented impartially by the relevant election management bodies? 0 / 4

The independence and integrity of Cameroon's electoral framework has long been compromised by accusations of partisanship by election management bodies. The Constitutional Council—created in in February 2018, just eight months before the presidential election—has the power to validate election results and adjudicate election disputes, and the majority of its 11 members have ties to the ruling party. The council rejected all 18 petitions to cancel the presidential election results filed by opposition parties in 2018, despite credible allegations of fraud and intimidation.

The Elections Cameroon (ELECAM) electoral body was created in 2006 to address concerns about the fair management of previous elections. However, President Biya chooses its members, and CPDM partisans have historically dominated the body.

B. POLITICAL PLURALISM AND PARTICIPATION: 3 / 16

B1. Do the people have the right to organize in different political parties or other competitive political groupings of their choice, and is the system free of undue obstacles to the rise and fall of these competing parties or groupings? 1 / 4

The ability to organize in political groups, and their freedom to operate, is severely limited, and opposition leaders risk arrest and imprisonment. Opposition rallies are frequently prohibited by the government, and such events were frequently banned in 2020, with police at times using force to disperse them. In September, the CRM defied a government ban and staged peaceful protests in multiple cities including Douala and Yaoundé, at which police arrested over 500 party members and supporters. Two CRM officers were detained at the central prison of Yaoundé in connection with the event, and Kamto was placed on house arrest for weeks in apparent connection with the event before being freed in December.

In addition, the government of Cameroon halted a fundraising campaign initiated by Kamto to fight the spread of the coronavirus. The government deemed the effort illegal, ordered two telephone operators to close the mobile accounts opened for the purpose, and rejected donations of protective masks and screening tests.

B2. Is there a realistic opportunity for the opposition to increase its support or gain power through elections? 0 / 4

Despite the existence of hundreds of registered political parties, Cameroon remains essentially a one-party state. The organizational advantages of the ruling party's long incumbency, its dominance over electoral bodies, and its superior access to media and public resources to achieve partisan gains, disadvantage opposition candidates. Opposition parties are highly fragmented, preventing any one of them from becoming a viable alternative to the ruling CPDM. Frequent harassment, intimidation, and arrests of opposition figures further reduce the ability of opposition parties to gain power through elections.

B3. Are the people's political choices free from domination by forces that are external to the political sphere, or by political forces that employ extrapolitical means? 1 / 4

State patronage and President Biya's control of high-level appointments help the CPDM retain power.

Insecurity in the Anglophone regions caused by violence between armed militants and the military made voting nearly impossible in the 2018 presidential election, effectively denying voters a political choice. The ongoing crisis also affected the 2020 parliamentary, municipal, and regional elections; supporters of Ambazonia called for boycotts, resulting in low turnout.

B4. Do various segments of the population (including ethnic, racial, religious, gender, LGBT+, and other relevant groups) have full political rights and electoral opportunities? 1 / 4

Groups advocating for greater self-determination in the Anglophone regions remain marginalized and excluded from political debate, as reflected by the 2017 banning of the Southern Cameroons National Council (SCNC), an Anglophone political group. LGBT+ people, and some ethnic minorities, such as the Bamiléké, are generally excluded from positions of political influence, and their interests are poorly represented by elected officials.

The government has expressed a commitment to increasing women's representation in Parliament. There were 61 women deputies elected in 2020, an increase of four from the previous election, and women have some ability to advocate for their interests within the CPDM.

C. FUNCTIONING OF GOVERNMENT: 3 / 12

C1. Do the freely elected head of government and national legislative representatives determine the policies of the government? 1 / 4

President Biya has extensive executive authority, including wide-ranging appointment powers and strong control over state institutions. Many policies are generated by the government and adopted by presidential decree, with minimal involvement by the parliament. When it is involved, the parliament shows little independence and largely acts as a rubber stamp for the president's policy initiatives.

C2. Are safeguards against official corruption strong and effective? 1 / 4

Corruption is systemic and bribery is commonplace in all sectors, despite anticorruption initiatives including the creation of the National Anticorruption Commission (CONAC). A number of former high-level government officials are serving prison terms for corruption, though these efforts are often perceived as moves by Biya to persecute political adversaries, who are oftentimes his former allies.

C3. Does the government operate with openness and transparency? 1 / 4

Decisions, especially those made by presidential decree, are often adopted with no public consultation. Cameroon lacks an access to information law, and it is difficult to gain access to government documents or statistics in practice. The websites of most ministries do not provide substantial information.

CIVIL LIBERTIES: 9 / 60 (-2)
D. FREEDOM OF EXPRESSION AND BELIEF: 4 / 16

D1. Are there free and independent media? 0 / 4

Independent and critical journalists face pressure and the risk of detention or arrest in connection with their work, with the Committee to Protect Journalists (CPJ) reporting that eight journalists were imprisoned at the end of 2020. Defamation remains a criminal offense, and the National Communications Council (CNC), a media regulatory body, has a history of harassing journalists and outlets. State-run CRTV has been criticized for favoring the CPDM in its coverage. The government continued to suppress media coverage of the Anglophone crisis in 2020.

In June 2020, the military acknowledged the death in state custody of journalist Samuel Wazizi, who covered the violent conflict in the Anglophone regions, among other topics. The head of the Cameroon Journalists' Trade Union and a number of independent analysts said Wazizi had been tortured by state forces; his death had not been investigated at year's end.

D2. Are individuals free to practice and express their religious faith or nonbelief in public and private? 2 / 4

Religious freedom is somewhat restricted in northern areas affected by the presence of the Boko Haram extremist group, which has carried out violent attacks against places of worship. In addition, random attacks against believers and facilities in connection with the conflict in the Northwest and Southwest regions are common. In November 2020, Roman Catholic cardinal Christian Tumi was kidnapped by gunmen in Cameroon's Northwest Region, but was freed shortly after.

D3. Is there academic freedom, and is the educational system free from extensive political indoctrination? 1 / 4

There are no legal restrictions on academic freedom, but state security informants operate on university campuses and academics can face negative repercussions for criticizing the government or discussing its political opponents. Law lecturer Felix Agbor Bala was dismissed from the University of Buea in May 2020 over an exam question probing the causes of the Anglophone crisis that authorities considered "seditious."

Academic freedom has been severely impacted by the crisis in the Anglophone regions, with separatists enforcing a boycott of schools and carrying out acts of violence against teachers and students. Elsewhere, numerous teachers in 2020 reported acts of violence against them by their students.

D4. Are individuals free to express their personal views on political or other sensitive topics without fear of surveillance or retribution? 1 / 4

Public criticism of the government and membership in opposition political parties can have a negative consequences for professional opportunities and advancement. Cameroonians tend to avoid discussing sensitive political issues for fear of reprisals, notably the potential for a return to a federal system that would grant the Anglophone regions more autonomy, or the regions' outright secession. Social media users and individuals who possess or distribute antigovernment material have also faced arrest.

E. ASSOCIATION AND ORGANIZATIONAL RIGHTS: 2 / 12

E1. Is there freedom of assembly? 0 / 4

Freedom of assembly is subject to significant restrictions. Authorities continued to ban and violently disperse events perceived as antigovernment in 2020, notably those staged by the opposition CRM.

E2. Is there freedom for nongovernmental organizations, particularly those that are engaged in human rights- and governance-related work? 1 / 4

The influence of civil society has weakened over the years, with many nongovernmental organizations (NGOs) relying entirely on foreign assistance, and others coopted by the regime. Anglophone activists have faced harassment, violence, and arrest for their activities. LGBT+ organizations have also been targeted by law enforcement. The government has restricted the work of international NGOs, denying their staff access to the country.

E3. Is there freedom for trade unions and similar professional or labor organizations? 1 / 4

Trade unions and collective bargaining are legally permitted, although unions are still subject to numerous restrictions in the exercise of their rights. Strikes are theoretically permitted, but the government has used force to disrupt them in practice.

F. RULE OF LAW: 0 / 16 (−1)

F1. Is there an independent judiciary? 0 / 4

The judiciary is subordinate to the Ministry of Justice, with corruption and political influence, including by the executive, weakening courts. The president appoints judges, and can dismiss them at will. Prosecutors have been pressured to stop pursuing corruption cases against some high-profile officials.

F2. Does due process prevail in civil and criminal matters? 0 / 4 (−1)

Due process rights are poorly upheld. Lengthy pretrial detentions are commonplace. Civilians accused of terrorism are frequently not afforded the right to a fair trial. French legal norms are regularly imposed upon Cameroonians in Anglophone regions.

Acts of violence against lawyers are increasing. In July 2020, then president of the Cameroon Bar Association, Patie Charles Tchakoute, filed a formal complaint with the defense secretary about police assaults against lawyers. Later, in November, hundreds of lawyers who turned out to a Douala bail hearing in support of colleagues being prosecuted for "contempt of court, attempted corruption, and fraud" were assaulted by security forces. In response to this and other incidents, the Cameroon Bar Association went on strike, once from November 30 to December 4, and again indefinitely, beginning December 7.

The government has invoked charges of terrorism, rebellion, and insurrection against opposition leaders and separatist supporters in 2019 and 2020, and they are often detained in the absence of due process and without realistic avenues for challenging their detention. A number of people arrested in the aftermath of the September 2020 CRM antigovernment rallies face charges in military courts.

State security forces have carried out extrajudicial killings and arbitrary detentions in connection with the Anglophone crisis, and in the Far North regions in response to Boko Haram activities. In September, Ambazonian leader Sisiku AyukTabe received a confirmation of his life sentence from a military court for charges of insurrection and terrorism, along with nine supporters. One of AyukTabe's lawyers claimed that the ruling was prearranged, and local activists called the trial a sham.

Score Change: The score declined from 1 to 0 because due process protections have collapsed across much of the country.

F3. Is there protection from the illegitimate use of physical force and freedom from war and insurgencies? 0 / 4

Active conflicts involving both Boko Haram and Anglophone separatists threaten the security of millions of people in Cameroon. Human Rights Watch (HRW) reported that government forces destroyed several hundred homes in the Anglophone regions, and carried out violent attacks against civilians throughout the year. Rights groups and journalists reported the massacre of 21 civilians by government forces and armed ethnic Fulani militiamen in February 2020, in Ngarbuh, Northwest Region. In April, authorities acknowledged some of the events there and pledged to investigate.

In August, the Islamist armed group Boko Haram reportedly sent child suicide bombers to a site for displaced people in the Far North region of Cameroon, killing at least 17 civilians. Security forces operating in the Far North Region have been accused of torturing alleged Boko Haram collaborators, many of whom have been held without charge.

In 2018, Biya established a National Disarmament, Demobilization, and Reintegration Committee (NDDRC) for ex-fighters of Boko Haram and armed Anglophone separatist groups. Its inaugural session took place in September 2020, in Yaoundé.

F4. Do laws, policies, and practices guarantee equal treatment of various segments of the population? 0 / 4

Discrimination against Anglophone Cameroonians and individuals from certain ethnic groups, including the Bamiléké, is common. The government imposes the French language in Anglophone regions, and Anglophone Cameroonians are frequently denied senior jobs in the civil service.

Discrimination against the LGBT+ community is rife, and violence against LGBT+ people is common. The penal code forbids same-sex relations; those convicted face prison sentences as long as five years. A cybercrime law punishes those who solicit same-sex relations online with two-year prison sentences. People are frequently prosecuted with no evidence of sexual activity, but rather on suspicions that they are gay.

The ongoing Boko Haram and Anglophone conflicts have forced large numbers of people to flee their homes. As of November 30, 2020, the UN Office for the Coordination of Humanitarian Affairs (UNOCHA) estimated that there were 711,056 internally displaced persons (IDPs) in the Northwest and Southwest regions, and 321,886 in the Far North Region. IDPs often struggle to access food, education, and other basic needs, and displaced women are vulnerable to gender-based violence.

G. PERSONAL AUTONOMY AND INDIVIDUAL RIGHTS: 3 / 16 (-1)

G1. Do individuals enjoy freedom of movement, including the ability to change their place of residence, employment, or education? 0 / 4 (-1)

Free movement is severely limited in parts of the Far North Region due to the Boko Haram activity, and in the two Anglophone regions due to the ongoing crisis there.

The Anglophone crisis has exacted a heavy toll on children, many of whom have been deprived of their right to education. Thousands of schools have closed, and attacks and kidnappings of students and teachers at those operating are frequent. Among instances over just a matter of weeks in 2020, at least eight students were killed in an October attack on a private school in Kumba, Southwest Region, perpetrated by likely Anglophone separatists. In a separate incident, children from Bamenda, Northwest Region, were kidnapped on their way home from school; six were released the next day, with several having to be hospitalized after being subjected to torture. On November 4, gunmen attacked a high school, Kulu Memorial College, in Limbe, Southwest Region, ordering students and teachers to remove their clothing before setting the school on fire.

Score Change: The score declined from 1 to 0 because armed groups have continued to launch deadly attacks against students, teachers, and schools.

G2. Are individuals able to exercise the right to own property and establish private businesses without undue interference from state or nonstate actors? 1 / 4

Harassment of small business owners by state agents is common. Agribusinesses and logging operations are often carried out without consulting local inhabitants. In many regions, women are still dispossessed of their inheritance rights.

In August 2020, the minister of domains and land affairs, Henri Eyébé Ayissi announced the suspension of a provisional lease between the state and cocoa producer Neo Industry SA in Ntem Valley, in South Province. The decision followed local opposition to Neo's plans to begin development of parts of an ancestral reserve.

G3. Do individuals enjoy personal social freedoms, including choice of marriage partner and size of family, protection from domestic violence, and control over appearance? 1 / 4

The constitution guarantees equal rights to men and women, but traditional legal values and practices often take precedence and do not always provide women with full rights. The Boko Haram conflict has exacerbated the already prevalent practice of child marriage and sexual abuse of minors in the Far North Region. Customary law can allow rapists to escape punishment if the victim consents to marriage. Despite laws guaranteeing equal rights to men and women to file for divorce, in practice courts often disadvantage women by making proceedings prohibitively expensive or lengthy. Cases of domestic violence and rape continue to be widespread in 2020, and perpetrators are rarely prosecuted.

G4. Do individuals enjoy equality of opportunity and freedom from economic exploitation? 1 / 4

Despite a 2011 law against human trafficking, Cameroon remains a source, transit, and destination country for forced labor and sex trafficking of children, as well as a source country for women who are subject to forced labor and prostitution in Europe. Some internally displaced women have also resorted to prostitution in the cities of Yaoundé and Douala. Child labor remains common, and child workers are frequently exposed to hazardous working conditions, particularly when collecting scrap metal for sale.

Canada

Population: 38,200,000
Capital: Ottawa
Freedom Status: Free
Electoral Democracy: Yes

Overview: Canada has a strong history of respect for political rights and civil liberties, though in recent years citizens have been concerned about fair elections and transparent governance; humane treatment of prisoners; citizens' right to privacy; and religious and journalistic freedom. While Indigenous peoples and other vulnerable populations still face discrimination and other economic, social, and political challenges, the federal government has acknowledged and made some moves to address these issues.

KEY DEVELOPMENTS IN 2020

- Provincial elections were held in New Brunswick, British Columbia, and Saskatchewan in September and October, despite the COVID-19 pandemic. Options for mail-in ballots and early voting were expanded and procedures were put in place at polling stations, such as physical distancing and sanitization protocols, to ensure that the coronavirus did not spread. There were over 572,000 confirmed cases of COVID-19 and over 15,000 deaths throughout the year, according to government statistics provided to the World Health Organization (WHO).
- In January, demonstrators blockaded construction roads, freight and passenger railways, and government buildings across the country in support of Indigenous peoples's opposition to the development of the Coastal GasLink natural gas pipeline in northern British Columbia. In response, the Alberta government in May passed the Critical Infrastructure Defence Act that instituted fines of up to $25,000, six months in jail, or both, for blocking the construction of "essential infrastructure," which included highways, pipelines, railways, and oil and gas rigs.

POLITICAL RIGHTS: 40 / 40

A. ELECTORAL PROCESS: 12 / 12

A1. Was the current head of government or other chief national authority elected through free and fair elections? 4 / 4

The British monarch is head of state, represented by a ceremonial governor general, currently Julie Payette, who is appointed on the advice of the prime minister. The prime minister is the head of government and is invited to the post by the governor general after elections; the office is usually held by the leader of the majority party or governing coalition in parliament. Justin Trudeau resumed his position as prime minister after the Liberal Party maintained control of government in the October 2019 federal elections.

A2. Were the current national legislative representatives elected through free and fair elections? 4 / 4

The parliament consists of an elected 338-member House of Commons, and an appointed 105-member Senate. Lower-house elections are held every four years on fixed dates; early elections may be called by the governor general if the government loses a parliamentary vote of no confidence, or on the advice of the prime minister.

The most recent federal election was held in October 2019, in which the center-left Liberal Party lost their majority government by losing 20 seats but maintained a plurality. The Conservative Party and Bloc Québécois gained 23 and 22 seats (131 and 34 in total), respectively, and the left-leaning New Democratic Party (NDP) lost 15 (24 in total). The Organization for Security and Co-operation in Europe (OSCE) did a preliminary investigation in advance of the 2019 election and found "full stakeholder confidence in the overall integrity of the electoral process."

New Brunswick, British Columbia, and Saskatchewan all held provincial elections in the fall of 2020, despite the COVID-19 pandemic. Options for mail-in ballots and early voting were expanded and procedures were put in place at polling stations, such as physical distancing and sanitization protocols, to ensure that the coronavirus did not spread. In New Brunswick and British Columbia, opposition parties complained that the premiers called for elections to take advantage of their parties' increased popularity during the pandemic.

A3. Are the electoral laws and framework fair, and are they implemented impartially by the relevant election management bodies? 4 / 4

Electoral laws are generally fair and well enforced by the relevant bodies. However, some critics expressed concern about the 2014 Fair Elections Act, arguing that its stringent voter identification requirements placed Indigenous peoples (or First Nations peoples) at a disadvantage. In December 2018, the Liberal government passed a bill relaxing some of the criticized provisions. This 2018 law restricts spending by political parties and other actors during elections, gives voting rights to all Canadians living abroad, improves the privacy of voters' information within the databases of political parties, and increases the power of the commissioner of Canada Elections to investigate violations of election rules. It further bans foreign donations for partisan campaigns and requires major online platforms, such as Facebook and Google, to create a registry of digital political advertisements.

B. POLITICAL PLURALISM AND PARTICIPATION: 16 / 16

B1. Do the people have the right to organize in different political parties or other competitive political groupings of their choice, and is the system free of undue obstacles to the rise and fall of these competing parties or groupings? 4 / 4

Canadians are free to organize in different political parties, and the system is open to the rise and fall of competing groups. However, a small number of parties have traditionally dominated electorally. A total of 21 political parties were registered in the 2019 election.

B2. Is there a realistic opportunity for the opposition to increase its support or gain power through elections? 4 / 4

Opposition parties have a realistic chance of gaining power through elections. In 2015, the Conservatives lost power to a Liberal majority, and in 2019 the Liberals' control of parliament diminished to a minority government.

B3. Are the people's political choices free from domination by forces that are external to the political sphere, or by political forces that employ extrapolitical means? 4 / 4

People's political choices are generally free from domination by actors that are not democratically accountable.

B4. Do various segments of the population (including ethnic, racial, religious, gender, LGBT+, and other relevant groups) have full political rights and electoral opportunities? 4 / 4

Members of religious minorities and Indigenous people are seated in the parliament, as are many women; Prime Minister Trudeau's cabinet has full gender parity. However, the political interests of many groups are not always well represented. For example, critical issues facing Indigenous peoples, including clean drinking water, mental health and addiction services, and compensation for Indigenous children who were taken from their homes, received minimal attention during the 2019 electoral campaign.

The rights and interests of LGBT+ people are protected. A 2017 law explicitly prohibits discrimination based on gender identity or gender expression, affording transgender individuals, among others, more protection against hate crimes.

C. FUNCTIONING OF GOVERNMENT: 12 / 12

C1. Do the freely elected head of government and national legislative representatives determine the policies of the government? 4 / 4

After some initial delays, federal and provincial governments in Canada were able to continue their legislative business during the COVID-19 pandemic by limiting the number of lawmakers allowed to meet in-person in Parliament and provincial assemblies and moving most legislative committees to online platforms. Emergency powers for the federal finance minister to spend money on pandemic-related measures without parliamentary approval were granted in March 2020 and were subsequently extended through the end of the year.

C2. Are safeguards against official corruption strong and effective? 4 / 4

Canada has a reputation for clean government and a record of vigorous prosecution of corruption cases. The governing Liberal Party faced accusations of corruption in August 2020, related to a government contract given to a charity to which Prime Minister Trudeau's family has financial connections. Conservative Party ministers accused the Liberals of intentionally ending the August parliamentary session to avoid an inquiry into the scandal.

C3. Does the government operate with openness and transparency? 4 / 4

Canadians may request public information under the provisions of the Access to Information Act, but they may face delays or excessive costs. In 2017, the Liberal government proposed a number of reforms to the act, but the measures have been criticized as inadequate. The information commissioner of Canada argued that the proposal would instead "result in a regression of existing rights," creating new hurdles for requests and giving agencies additional grounds for refusal. The bill passed in Parliament in late 2017 and was passed unamended by the Senate in June 2019.

CIVIL LIBERTIES: 58 / 60

D. FREEDOM OF EXPRESSION AND BELIEF: 16 / 16

D1. Are there free and independent media? 4 / 4

Canada's media are generally free; journalists are mostly protected from violence and harassment in their work and are able to express diverse viewpoints. A law permitting journalists' greater ability to protect their sources took effect in 2017. It stipulates that they cannot be required to disclose confidential sources unless a Superior Court judge is persuaded that the information cannot be obtained through other means, and that it is in the public interest for the source to be revealed. In September 2019, the Supreme Court applied this law and found that a Canadian Broadcasting Corporation (CBC) journalist did not have to reveal her sources for information on political corruption in Quebec.

D2. Are individuals free to practice and express their religious faith or nonbelief in public and private? 3 / 4

The Canadian constitution and other legislation protect religious freedom. However, in June 2019, the Quebec provincial government passed Bill 21, leading to a reduction of religious freedom in the province, where over a quarter of Canadians live. The bill bans certain government employees in positions of authority from wearing religious symbols such as a hijab, crucifix, turban, or kippah while at work. The list of such persons includes judges, police officers, government lawyers, and teachers. The bill has a grandfather clause for government employees already wearing symbols—they can keep wearing them until they change institutions or take a promotion.

D3. Is there academic freedom, and is the educational system free from extensive political indoctrination? 4 / 4

Academic freedom is generally respected.

D4. Are individuals free to express their personal views on political or other sensitive topics without fear of surveillance or retribution? 4 / 4

Private discussion in Canada is generally free and unrestrained. However, in 2015, the former Conservative government passed a controversial antiterrorism law granting the Canadian Security Intelligence Service (CSIS) wider authority to conduct surveillance and share information about individuals with other agencies. Its passage elicited considerable condemnation from Canadian intellectuals and both domestic and foreign civil liberties watchdogs, who warned that it undermined the concept of privacy and could harm freedom of expression.

In 2017, the Liberal government introduced a bill that would reverse some of the law's provisions and establish an independent review and complaints body as well as a parliamentary committee to monitor Canada's intelligence-gathering agencies. However, the 2017 law has also been criticized for allowing Canada's spy agencies excessive powers to perform surveillance on Canadians without their knowledge, and for failing to explicitly prohibit the use of intelligence gathered by foreign entities through torture. The bill was passed unamended by the Senate in June 2019.

E. ASSOCIATIONAL AND ORGANIZATIONAL RIGHTS: 12 / 12
E1. Is there freedom of assembly? 4 / 4

Freedom of assembly is constitutionally protected and generally upheld in practice. In January 2020, demonstrators blockaded construction roads, freight and passenger railways, and government buildings across the country in support of Indigenous peoples' opposition to the development of the Coastal GasLink natural gas pipeline in northern British Columbia. In response, the Alberta government in May passed the Critical Infrastructure Defence Act that instituted fines of up to $25,000, six months in jail, or both for blocking the construction of "essential infrastructure" such as highways, pipelines, railways, and oil and gas rigs. Environmental and labor activists criticized the act, in effect since June, for its overly broad definition of "essential infrastructure," which could limit people's ability to protest, and excessively harsh penalties.

Protests occurred throughout the country during the COVID-19 pandemic, with widespread Black Lives Matter demonstrations emerging in the summer of 2020.

E2. Is there freedom for nongovernmental organizations, particularly those that are engaged in human rights- and governance-related work? 4 / 4

Nongovernmental organizations (NGOs) operate freely and frequently inform policy discussions.

E3. Is there freedom for trade unions and similar professional or labor organizations? 4 / 4

Trade unions and business associations enjoy high levels of membership and are well organized.

F. RULE OF LAW: 15 / 16
F1. Is there an independent judiciary? 4 / 4

Canada's judiciary is generally independent.

F2. Does due process prevail in civil and criminal matters? 4 / 4

Constitutionally protected due process rights are generally upheld in practice. Canada's criminal law is based on legislation enacted by parliament; its tort and contract laws are based on English common law, with the exception of those in Quebec, where they are based on the French civil code.

F3. Is there protection from the illegitimate use of physical force and freedom from war and insurgencies? 4 / 4

The use of solitary confinement for extended periods of time in Canada's prisons has been controversial. Many critics charge that the time that inmates are excluded from the general population of prisoners has become excessive, and that prisoners with mental health issues are harmed due to frequent placement in solitary confinement. The government's 2018 legislation that responded to this criticism was further denounced by legal advocates for prisoners, who claimed the bill would have little practical effect. This bill passed the Senate and became law in June 2019 with the addition of some minor amendments, including increased judicial oversight on decisions to isolate prisoners, more support for inmates with mental illnesses, and community-based options for rehabilitating indigenous people and members of other vulnerable populations. An advisory panel report released in October 2020 found that the length of solidarity confinement and the frequency of its use has not substantially changed since the introduction of the new law.

F4. Do laws, policies, and practices guarantee equal treatment of various segments of the population? 3 / 4

The government has made increasing efforts to enforce equal rights and opportunities for minority groups, although some problems persist. First Nations people remain subject to widespread discrimination, struggle with food insecurity, and unequal access to education, health care, public services, and employment.

The government's 2015 Truth and Reconciliation Commission of Canada (TRC) called for the creation of the National Inquiry into Missing and Murdered Indigenous Women and Girls (MMIWG) in 2019. The Inquiry investigated the government's complicity and involvement in the disappearance or murder of more than 4,000 Indigenous women and girls over the past 30 years. The authors concluded that the sum of historical and contemporary injustices, longstanding and extant state policy and indifference, and an epidemic of violence against Indigenous peoples amounted to genocide. The MMIWG also made recommendations to improve the lives of Canada's First Nations populations. However, the release of the federal government's action plan to implement the MMIWG's 2019 recommendations was delayed due to the COVID-19 pandemic, and an analysis published in December 2019 by the Yellowhead Institute found that only 9 out of 94 TRC calls to action had been completed since 2015.

G. PERSONAL AUTONOMY AND INDIVIDUAL RIGHTS: 16 / 16

G1. Do individuals enjoy freedom of movement, including the ability to change their place of residence, employment, or education? 4 / 4

Freedom of movement is constitutionally protected and upheld in practice. Due to the COVID-19 pandemic, provincial and municipal governments at various times throughout the year limited people's movements in order to prevent the spread of the virus, and roughly half of provinces mandated that all travelers self-isolate upon arrival. From July to November, the provincial governments of New Brunswick, Nova Scotia, Prince Edward Island, and Newfoundland and Labrador created an interprovincial "bubble," for residents within that zone; the federal government required individuals to self-isolate after international travel, but all residents of the four "bubble" provinces could move freely within the four provinces' borders. The rules were enforced with monetary fines, though compliance was common and fines were given quite rarely.

G2. Are individuals able to exercise the right to own property and establish private businesses without undue interference from state or nonstate actors? 4 / 4

Property rights are not constitutionally guaranteed but are generally well protected by law and through the enforcement of contracts.

G3. Do individuals enjoy personal social freedoms, including choice of marriage partner and size of family, protection from domestic violence, and control over appearance? 4 / 4

Canada legalized same-sex marriage in 2005. Domestic violence is a problem that disproportionately affects women, particularly indigenous women, and is underreported. There have been initiatives in recent years to better train police in handling domestic violence cases. Since the Liberal Party entered government in 2015, there has been a marked improvement in gender equality, according to the most recent United Nations (UN) Gender Inequality Index (2017).

G4. Do individuals enjoy equality of opportunity and freedom from economic exploitation? 4 / 4

There have been some reports of forced labor in the agricultural, food processing, construction, and other sectors, as well as among domestic workers. However, the government, aided by NGOs that work to reveal forced labor and sex trafficking, do attempt to hold perpetrators accountable and to provide aid to victims.

There is no national minimum wage, though provinces have set their own. Occupational safety standards are robust and generally well enforced. However, young workers, migrants, and new immigrants remain vulnerable to abuses in the workplace.

Central African Republic

Population: 4,800,000
Capital: Bangui
Freedom Status: Not Free
Electoral Democracy: No

Overview: The Central African Republic (CAR) suffers from pervasive insecurity and an absence of state authority in much of the country. A series of peace deals between the government and various armed groups have not produced improvements in the security situation and have been repeatedly breached by both parties. Violent attacks against civilians, including sexual violence, are an acute risk in many areas. There is little support for independent journalists, and workers with nongovernmental organizations (NGOs), particularly aid workers, operate at great personal risk.

KEY DEVELOPMENTS IN 2020

- In December, the Constitutional Court excluded former president François Bozizé from running in the presidential election. Bozizé took power in a coup in 2003 and had ruled until 2013; he currently faces an international arrest warrant for crimes against humanity and incitement of genocide. The court also excluded several dozen members of armed groups from participating in the legislative elections. Earlier, in June, it struck down a draft law to delay elections due to the COVID-19 pandemic, saying it would have effectively extended President Faustin-Archange Touadéra's term.
- In December, the main signatories of the February 2019 peace agreement joined forces in a new rebel alliance, the Coalition of Patriots for Change (CPC). They said the government was incapable of holding free and fair elections, called for a national consultation, and engaged in armed battles with the Central African Armed Forces (FACA), supported by MINUSCA (United Nations Multidimensional Integrated Stabilization Mission in the Central African Republic), during election week.
- The presidential and legislative elections eventually took place as scheduled on December 27, amid widespread insecurity. Polls were marred by violence, threats of reprisals against voters by rebel forces, the inability of residents living in rebel-held areas to participate in the election, and allegations of ballot-box seizures and other fraud. Provisional results were expected in January 2021.
- According to statistics from the UN Children's Fund (UNICEF), 4,971 positive cases of COVID-19 were reported during the year, and 63 virus-related deaths. The agency cautioned that this was likely an undercount, because relatively few coronavirus tests were performed. In March, the government implemented lockdown

measures in Bangui, which lasted for several months, and Touadéra encouraged people to take precautions to protect public health.

POLITICAL RIGHTS: 3 / 40 (–1)

A. ELECTORAL PROCESS: 3 / 12 (–1)

A1. Was the current head of government or other chief national authority elected through free and fair elections? 0 / 4 (–1)

The president is chief of state and is directly elected to up to two five-year terms. President Faustin-Archange Touadéra was elected in February 2016. Fears of widespread electoral violence were not realized, but there were many reports of serious fraud at the polls.

Despite delays and irregularities in the voter registration, and after more than a week of sporadic fighting outside the capital, the first round of the latest presidential election took place on December 27, 2020. While the government and its international partners described the election as credible and legitimate, opposition parties denounced the polls, which took place alongside legislative elections, as marred by widespread ballot-box stuffing and vote buying. Many citizens, moreover, were prevented from voting due to threats and attacks perpetrated by the new rebel coalition. There were no national or international independent observers outside of the capital, Bangui. The Constitutional Court was set to announce provisional results in January 2021.

Score Change: The score declined from 1 to 0 because the December election was marred by violence related to the country's ongoing civil war, threats of reprisals against voters lodged by rebel forces, the inability of residents living in rebel-held areas to participate in the election, and reports of ballot-box seizures.

A2. Were the current national legislative representatives elected through free and fair elections? 1 / 4

Members of Parliament are directly elected to five-year terms. The constitution adopted in 2015 stipulated the creation of a Senate, but it has not been established.

The current parliament was elected in February 2016, followed by a second round of by-elections that March. A first round had to be nullified following a slew of allegations of fraud and other misconduct.

Like the presidential polls, the first round of the legislative elections took place on December 27, 2020, and was plagued by insecurity, voter intimidation, and allegations of fraud.

A3. Are the electoral laws and framework fair, and are they implemented impartially by the relevant election management bodies? 1 / 4

The electoral laws of the Central African Republic permit multiparty competition, and adult citizens enjoy universal and equal suffrage. However, electoral authorities operate in an opaque manner.

In April 2020, the ruling party proposed amending the Constitution and extending President Faustin-Archange Touadéra's mandate should elections need to be postponed due to the COVID-19 pandemic. In June, the Constitutional Court rejected the draft law on grounds that it would entail changes to the presidential term limits.

A law regulating the National Elections Authority (ANE) was approved in July 2020, and among other provisions, sought to rapidly bring in new ANE commissioners to replace past ones whose performance had been criticized by the opposition. The new board named in October 2020 was still largely controlled by the ruling party. Separately, Parliament amended the electoral law to extend the period for voter registration in September, three months before the year's elections. The opposition coalition contested the bill, instead calling for a national consultation. The election ultimately was marred by irregularities surrounding voter registration.

B. POLITICAL PLURALISM AND PARTICIPATION: 2 / 16

B1. Do the people have the right to organize in different political parties or other competitive political groupings of their choice, and is the system free of undue obstacles to the rise and fall of these competing parties or groupings? 1 / 4

While political parties are legally able to form and operate, party members conducting political activities are at risk of intimidation and violence by the national police in Bangui and other security bodies, and by armed groups in the areas they control.

B2. Is there a realistic opportunity for the opposition to increase its support or gain power through elections? 1 / 4

Several opposition parties exist in the parliament. The most prominent opposition leaders—including former President Bozizé—joined forces within the Coalition for Democratic Opposition (COD-2020), initiated in November 2019 and formally created in February 2020, to overcome increasing government repression.

However, most of the candidates to the 2020 presidential and legislative elections were not able to run their electoral campaign outside of the capital due to widespread violence and direct threats and aggression by armed rebel groups outside the capital. Also, the Constitutional Court rejected the pleas submitted on December 24, 2020, by six presidential candidates from the opposition, who invoked article 115 of the electoral code and asked the court to postpone elections due to the withdrawal of another candidate (Jean-Serge Bokassa) from the presidential race because of insecurity.

B3. Are the people's political choices free from domination by forces that are external to the political sphere, or by political forces that employ extrapolitical means? 0 / 4

Citizens are vulnerable to pressure and intimidation from national police and nonstate armed groups. Due to enduring insecurity, voters outside the capital are largely unable to participate in political processes.

A Russian military presence in Central African Republic persists. President Touadéra has named a former Russian intelligence agent as his special advisor and assigned his personal security to the Wagner Group, a Russian security company with links to Russian President Vladimir Putin.

B4. Do various segments of the population (including ethnic, racial, religious, gender, LGBT+, and other relevant groups) have full political rights and electoral opportunities? 0 / 4

Enduring discrimination and an accompanying lack of access to political processes prevents members of many ethnic, religious, and other minority groups from achieving political representation. Sectarian violence against Muslims continues to affect their ability to participate in politics. Women are underrepresented in politics, and just 11 sit in the 140-seat parliament, though the electoral law passed in 2019 requires that 35 percent of candidates be women. Societal and legal discrimination against LGBT+ people prevent them from working to see their interests represented in the political sphere.

Due to the long-lasting tribalization of politics, the country's public institutions and army are dominated by its ethnic majority, the Gbaya, to which belongs former President Bozizé. President Touadéra has followed the same path, promoting members of his groups, the Mbaka-Mandja, to key senior positions and to the presidential guard.

C. FUNCTIONING OF GOVERNMENT: 0 / 12

C1. Do the freely elected head of government and national legislative representatives determine the policies of the government? 0 / 4

Presidential and parliamentary elections held in early 2016 led to a peaceful transfer of power from the National Transitional Council to an elected government. However, while the elected representatives can determine the policies of the government, the weak authority of the state outside the capital severely limits the government's ability to implement policy decisions.

C2. Are safeguards against official corruption strong and effective? 0 / 4

Corruption and nepotism have long been pervasive in all branches of government, and addressing public-sector corruption is difficult given the lack of political will. Members of the president's party appear to benefit from impunity. In March 2020, the vice president of the parliament, Jean-Symphorien Mapenzi, was reelected to his post despite the leak in February of an audio recording in which he was heard admitting to having fixed a parliamentary vote on a finance bill. The year before, the second vice president of the parliament, Mathurin Dimbélé-Nakoé, escaped sanctions in a case of corruption involving mining licenses granted to Chinese companies.

C3. Does the government operate with openness and transparency? 0 / 4

Government operations are largely nontransparent, and civil society groups and others have limited opportunity to comment upon or influence impending policy decisions. Citizens outside of the capital have limited access to their elected representatives in the national legislature. In July 2020, the UN Panel of Experts reported on an expansion of the presidential guard that was not provided for in the national defense plan nor in the security sector reform process.

ADDITIONAL DISCRETIONARY POLITICAL RIGHTS QUESTION

Is the government or occupying power deliberately changing the ethnic composition of a country or territory so as to destroy a culture or tip the political balance in favor of another group? −1 / 0

Targeted religious- and ethnic-based violence continued in 2020 in northwestern and eastern regions of the country. Hundreds of thousands of civilians remain internally displaced or confined to ethnic and sectarian enclaves.

CIVIL LIBERTIES: 6 / 60

D. FREEDOM OF EXPRESSION AND BELIEF: 4 / 16

D1. Are there free and independent media? 1 / 4

There is little support for independent media, and in Bangui, outlets are increasingly aligned with national politicians and foreign governments, especially Russia. Media (and social media) often carry material meant to incite hate, discrimination, or violence, mainly against minority groups, with a spike in such material during the 2020 preelection period. Although the High Commission of Communication has played an active role in media regulation since 2017, the situation has not improved.

In July 2018, three Russian journalists were ambushed and killed near the city of Sibut (two hours' drive from Bangui). The killing remains unpunished. In June 2019, two AFP journalists were arrested and beaten in Bangui by the police, during a demonstration by an opposition group.

D2. Are individuals free to practice and express their religious faith or nonbelief in public and private? 0 / 4

Officially, Central African Republic is a secular state, but ethnic and religious cleavages often overlap with the country's political divisions. Muslims and Christian residents in Bangui remain partially segregated in separate enclaves, and fears of identity-based or sectarian violence by armed actors impedes free religious expression.

D3. Is there academic freedom, and is the educational system free from extensive political indoctrination? 2 / 4

Although extremely dysfunctional, the educational system is generally free of extensive political indoctrination. However, clientelism and corruption are widespread in many schools and universities.

D4. Are individuals free to express their personal views on political or other sensitive topics without fear of surveillance or retribution? 1 / 4

Public discussion and political debates are generally free from surveillance by state authorities. However, political instability and the risk of violent retaliation for challenging the presence of armed groups or expressing opinions on other sensitive topics inhibits free expression.

E. ASSOCIATIONAL AND ORGANIZATIONAL RIGHTS: 1 / 12

E1. Is there freedom of assembly? 0 / 4

Although freedom of assembly and the right to political protest is guaranteed under the constitution, these liberties are curtailed due to government repression of the opposition in Bangui, and threats posed by armed groups that control areas outside of the capital. Limitations imposed to prevent the spread of COVID-19 also hampered free association in 2020, though there were no major reports of abuses in enforcement of lockdown measures.

E2. Is there freedom for nongovernmental organizations, particularly those that are engaged in human rights- and governance-related work? 0 / 4

The operations of NGOs are limited by poor security conditions, and aid workers are particularly vulnerable. According to the International NGO Safety Organization (INSO), there were 361 recorded security incidents in 2020 involving relief workers, resulting in 2 aid workers killed, 13 injured, and 13 abducted.

E3. Is there freedom for trade unions and similar professional or labor organizations? 1 / 4

Trade unions and collective bargaining are permitted, although union organizers are sometimes subject to arbitrary detention or arrest. Small-scale agricultural organizations and cooperatives exist throughout the country, including organizations for women farmers.

F. RULE OF LAW: 1 / 16

F1. Is there an independent judiciary? 1 / 4

Courts are generally inefficient and frequently hampered by corruption. The government has limited authority to enforce judicial decisions. Judicial salaries have often gone unpaid. Judicial personnel are often untrained and are reluctant to be deployed outside of the capital. The Special Criminal Court (SCC), created in 2015, although considered relatively independent, had yet to complete any prosecutions at year's end 2020.

The Constitutional Court continued to display a high degree of independence in 2020, including by striking down the draft law intended to extend presidential term limits, and by playing a watchdog role during the electoral process.

In February 2020, the parliament passed a bill establishing a Truth, Justice, Reconciliation and Reparations Commission (TJRRC). The commission will be given a four-year mandate to investigate the violent events in the country over a period of 60 years (1959–2019). The commission was mostly conceived as a convenient vehicle to achieve political accommodation during peace negotiations, and it may never become fully empowered.

F2. Does due process prevail in civil and criminal matters? 0 / 4

Arbitrary detention and lengthy pretrial detention are commonplace, and the state justice system has limited presence beyond Bangui. Impunity for violence, economic crimes, and human rights violations remained widespread in 2020.

In December 2019, former President François Bozizé returned to Bangui from exile despite UN sanctions and an international arrest warrant for crimes against humanity and incitement to genocide. After entering the country in January 2020, former President Michel Djotodia, who overthrew Bozizé in the 2013 coup, announced in September his return to Bangui from exile, and engaged in political maneuvers to support President Touadéra.

In December 2019, the International Criminal Court (ICC) confirmed the charges of war crimes and crimes against humanity against two former anti-Balaka militia leaders, Alfred Yekatom and Patrice-Edouard Ngaïssona, arrested in 2018.

F3. Is there protection from the illegitimate use of physical force and freedom from war and insurgencies? 0 / 4

In Bangui, the officials of the Central African Office for the Repression of Banditry (OCRB) are often accused of abuse of power and excessive use of force. Outside of the capital, armed nonstate actors continue to operate with impunity, despite the 2019 peace deal. These groups were responsible for violent attacks against civilians, often on the basis of ethnic and religious identity, as well as attacks against international peacekeeping forces and humanitarian workers.

Violent competition among insurgent groups for control of territory and natural resources kept about 681,930 Central Africans internally displaced in 2020, and there were 634,687 refugees living outside the country at year's end. The UN Office for the Coordination of Humanitarian Affairs (OCHA) reported that insecurity and fear of attacks ahead of the general elections had led 55,000 people to flee their homes. Conflict between farmers and nomadic pastoralists further destabilized the country in 2020.

In September 2019, the UN Security Council voted unanimously to relax an arms embargo established in 2013.

F4. Do laws, policies, and practices guarantee equal treatment of various segments of the population? 0 / 4

Same-sex sexual acts are illegal, and punishable by fines and imprisonment. While enforcement of these laws is uncommon, societal discrimination against LGBT+ people remains acute. Discrimination continues against the Muslim minority, nomadic pastoralist groups, and the forest-dwelling Ba'aka.

The independent High Authority for Good Governance is tasked with protecting the rights of members of minority groups and people with disabilities, though its reach is limited.

Due to the tribalization of politics, the Gbaya and the Mbaka-Mandja groups may continue to enjoy unfair advantages.

G. PERSONAL AUTONOMY AND INDIVIDUAL RIGHTS: 0 / 16

G1. Do individuals enjoy freedom of movement, including the ability to change their place of residence, employment, or education? 0 / 4

Free movement by citizens is inhibited by the lack of security and targeted violence. Transportation routes are threatened by banditry and theft in many areas. Limitations of movement imposed to prevent the spread of COVID-19 have economically affected Central Africans during the peak of the pandemic. Schools were closed during parts of the year to prevent the virus's spread.

G2. Are individuals able to exercise the right to own property and establish private businesses without undue interference from state or nonstate actors? 0 / 4

Businesses and homes are regularly looted or extorted by armed militants, with little prospect for compensation or legal recourse for victims. The agricultural economy—the livelihood of the majority of the population—remains restricted by ongoing violence and insecurity.

The family code does not discriminate against women when it comes to inheritance rights. However, in practice, the possibility for women to inherit faces many challenges, including eviction from the family home after the death or disappearance of men during conflict.

G3. Do individuals enjoy personal social freedoms, including choice of marriage partner and size of family, protection from domestic violence, and control over appearance? 0 / 4

Women and girls are by far the primary victims of sexual violence, but men and boys are also affected. Sexual violence is used as a deliberate tool of warfare, and attackers enjoy broad impunity. Such acts that are not related to ethnic conflict are most often perpetrated within communities by family or neighbors. Constitutional guarantees for women's rights are rarely enforced, especially in rural areas. Sexual abuses by UN peacekeeping forces have been documented, but many instances have not been investigated or prosecuted.

G4. Do individuals enjoy equality of opportunity and freedom from economic exploitation? 0 / 4

Economic opportunity is heavily restricted by the widespread corruption and the presence of armed groups in many areas of the country. Many armed groups exploit gold and diamond mines, and forced labor and child recruitment for soldiering are common practices. The government has made significant efforts to eliminate trafficking, though it has not yet fully met minimum standards, according to the US State Department's 2020 *Trafficking in Persons* report.

Chad

Population: 16,900,000
Capital: N'Djamena
Freedom Status: Not Free
Electoral Democracy: No

Overview: Chad has held regular presidential elections since 1996, but no election has ever produced a change in power. Legislative elections are routinely delayed, and have not been held since 2011. Opposition activists risk arrest and severe mistreatment while in detention. The state faces multiple insurgencies led by rebel militants in the north, and Boko Haram in the Lake Chad Basin.

KEY DEVELOPMENTS IN 2020

- In late March, militant fighters affiliated with Boko Haram killed 98 soldiers while attacking the village of Boma. In response, the government launched a counteroffensive in the Lake Chad Basin, and claimed to have killed 1,000 militant fighters during the operation.
- In July, the Independent National Electoral Commission (CENI) announced a delay to legislative elections, which are now scheduled for October 2021. The next presidential election, meanwhile, is due that April.
- In December, the National Assembly voted to approve constitutional amendments creating an indirectly elected Senate, allowing the president to name a vice president, and lowering the age of eligibility for presidential candidates from 45 years to 40, among other provisions. President Idriss Déby Itno promulgated the amendments later that month.
- President Déby issued a COVID-19-related state of emergency in April, which included restrictions on movement; some were loosened in June, though others remained in force in parts of Chad through year's end. Authorities also used pandemic-related measures to limit assemblies and target political opponents.

POLITICAL RIGHTS: 3 / 40

A. ELECTORAL PROCESS: 1 / 12

A1. Was the current head of government or other chief national authority elected through free and fair elections? 1 / 4

The president is directly elected to a five-year term. President Idriss Déby Itno took power in 1990 during a rebellion, and then overwhelmingly won elections in 1996, 2001, 2006, and 2011. In the 2016 poll, he received just under 60 percent of the vote, defeating opposition leader Saleh Kebzabo, who took 13 percent. The opposition rejected the result, citing electoral irregularities.

In July 2020, the Independent National Electoral Commission (CENI) announced that the next presidential election would be held in April 2021.

The position of prime minister was abolished by the 2018 constitution. In December 2020, legislators approved constitutional amendments allowing the president to appoint a vice president, among other provisions. The amendments were promulgated by Déby later that month.

A2. Were the current national legislative representatives elected through free and fair elections? 0 / 4

The unicameral National Assembly currently consists of 188 members elected to four-year terms. The ruling political party, Déby's Patriotic Salvation Movement (MPS), and allied parties control 117 seats. Elections have not been organized since 2011, with legislative elections due in 2015 having been repeatedly postponed. In July 2020, CENI announced another delay, this time to October 2021.

Constitutional reforms promulgated in December 2020 provide for the creation of an indirectly elected Senate, with members serving staggered six-year terms. No senators were seated at year's end, with its envisioned powers remaining with the lower house.

A3. Are the electoral laws and framework fair, and are they implemented impartially by the relevant election management bodies? 0 / 4

The CENI's leadership is appointed by the country's entrenched political class through the National Framework for Political Dialogue (CNDP), and civil society is excluded from the process. In 2019, the CNDP adopted a revised electoral code that will reduce the number of lower-house members from 188 to 161 in the next legislature, over the objection of opposition members.

In December 2020, the National Assembly—whose mandate had long expired—approved constitutional reforms that, among other changes, reduced the age of eligibility for presidential candidates to from 45 years to 40. Opposition politicians denounced the adoption of the reform package by a legislative body with expired mandates and the lack of a popular referendum on the proposals.

B. POLITICAL PLURALISM AND PARTICIPATION: 1 / 16

B1. Do the people have the right to organize in different political parties or other competitive political groupings of their choice, and is the system free of undue obstacles to the rise and fall of these competing parties or groupings? 1 / 4

There are more than 130 registered political parties in Chad, though most of them are aligned with the ruling party. The MPS enjoys significant influence, and has held a majority in the National Assembly since 1997.

Opposition parties are subject to government harassment. For several days in late October and early November 2020, after opposition politicians and civil society members criticized a government-led forum on political reform, the headquarters of several parties and nongovernmental organizations (NGOs) were surrounded by police.

B2. Is there a realistic opportunity for the opposition to increase its support or gain power through elections? 0 / 4

The mandate of the current legislature expired in 2015 and elections have been repeatedly postponed, leaving the opposition no avenue to increase support or gain power through elections. The political opposition is legally recognized, but opposition leaders who publicly criticize the government risk harassment and arrest. Opposition leaders have disappeared after entering state custody.

B3. Are the people's political choices free from domination by forces that are external to the political sphere, or by political forces that employ extrapolitical means? 0 / 4

Extensive kinship networks tied to the president and his family have resulted in a concentration of political and economic power. The government is not accountable to voters in practice, and voters have few effective means of influencing or participating in politics.

The military also wields considerable influence, and President Déby has closely affiliated himself with the armed forces to hold political power. In August 2020, as Chad celebrated 60 years of independence from France, the MPS-controlled legislature awarded Déby the title of marshal.

B4. Do various segments of the population (including ethnic, racial, religious, gender, LGBT+, and other relevant groups) have full political rights and electoral opportunities? 0 / 4

Members of the Beri ethnic group control Chad's political, economic, and military spheres, causing resentment among the country's other ethnic groups. Christians in the south are largely excluded from political power; some Christians hold government positions, but their voice is limited. Cabinet members and some officials were previously required to be sworn in on a Bible or Quran, but that requirement was eliminated by constitutional amendments promulgated in December 2020.

Women hold few senior positions in government and political parties and are largely excluded from local governance bodies in rural areas. LGBT+ people are severely marginalized, impacting their ability to engage in political processes and advocate for their interests.

C. FUNCTIONING OF GOVERNMENT: 1 / 12

C1. Do the freely elected head of government and national legislative representatives determine the policies of the government? 1 / 4

Déby enjoys unlimited discretionary power over the composition of the government and routinely reshuffles the cabinet. Déby did so in July 2020, expanding its size from 31 members to 35. The elimination of the prime minister's office in 2018 further concentrated power in the presidency. The influence of the presidential office impedes the National Assembly from steering national policies.

C2. Are safeguards against official corruption strong and effective? 0 / 4

Corruption, bribery, and nepotism are endemic in Chad. Journalists, labor leaders, and religious figures have faced harsh reprisals for speaking out about corruption, including arrest, prosecution, and expulsion from the country. Corruption charges against high-level officials that do go forward are widely viewed as selective prosecutions meant to discredit those who pose a threat to Déby or his allies.

Chadian officials are also known to facilitate regional drug trafficking, using the profits to influence members of the security services and the judiciary. In July 2020, 10 officials, including three military officers and a National Security Agency (ANS) official, received prison terms and fines for their involvement in that trade, after a shipment of medication bound for Libya was seized in January.

C3. Does the government operate with openness and transparency? 0 / 4

Chad has no law establishing the right to access official information. Déby, his family, and his associates dominate government and have little incentive to share basic information about government operations with the public.

CIVIL LIBERTIES: 14 / 60

D. FREEDOM OF EXPRESSION AND BELIEF: 6 / 12

D1. Are there free and independent media? 1 / 4

The constitution provides for freedom of the press, but press freedom is restricted in practice. Although criticism of the government is generally permitted within certain boundaries, reporters and editors self-censor to avoid reprisals. Journalists can face arrest, detention, and imprisonment on charges including defamation.

In January 2020, a court in Mongo handed radio journalist Ali Hamata Achène a six-month prison term for charges including defamation over a 2019 social media post criticizing the length of pretrial detentions in that city. In May, Mbainaissem Gedeon Mbeibaroum, a correspondent for news site Alwihda Info, was arrested and briefly detained while attempting to cover intercommunal violence in Hadjer-Lamis Region. After his arrest, a local official claimed that journalists working for private outlets were not allowed to cover events in their district.

D2. Are individuals free to practice and express their religious faith or nonbelief in public and private? 1 / 4

The state imposes a number of religious restrictions, primarily against certain Muslim sects. Several sects deemed to promote violence are banned, despite limited evidence of such activity. Imams are subject to governance by the semipublic High Council for Islamic Affairs, which is led by a group of imams belonging to the Tijanyya Sufi order. Wearing burqas is banned by ministerial decree, and the government detains individuals who wear them in public.

D3. Is there academic freedom, and is the educational system free from extensive political indoctrination? 2 / 4

The government does not restrict academic freedom, but funds meant for the education system, as well as government-funded stipends, are regularly in arrears.

D4. Are individuals free to express their personal views on political or other sensitive topics without fear of surveillance or retribution? 2 / 4

Space for open and free private discussion exists but tends to be self-censored due to fears of reprisal from the state. Between July and October 2020, the government throttled internet speeds and limited access to some social media platforms after a video of a soldier purportedly shooting two mechanics was disseminated online.

E. ASSOCIATIONAL AND ORGANIZATIONAL RIGHTS: 4 / 12
E1. Is there freedom of assembly? 1 / 4

Constitutional guarantees of free assembly are not upheld by authorities, who routinely ban gatherings and persecute organizers. In February 2020, authorities used tear gas to disperse a N'Djamena rally held by university students, injuring at least 11 demonstrators. In August, authorities banned an opposition march calling on the government to address insecurity in southern Chad.

The authorities also sought to limit assemblies using COVID-19-related restrictions. In late November 2020, authorities used those measures to arrest organizers and participants of a civil society–led forum on political reform.

E2. Is there freedom for nongovernmental organizations, particularly those that are engaged in human rights– and governance-related work? 1 / 4

NGOs must receive government approval to operate legally, but few such applications are approved. Government regulations stipulate that 1 percent of foreign NGOs' project budgets must be paid to a body consisting of government authorities and other NGO representatives, which assesses the organizations' in-country activities. In March 2020, Economy Minister Issa Doubragne warned that NGOs that did not comply with government regulations would be prohibited from operating in Chad.

In August 2020, the N'Djamena High Court suspended the secretary general of the Chadian Convention for the Defense of Human Rights (CTDDH), Mahamat Nour Ahmat

Ibédou, from his post. Civil society observers considered the suspension to be politically motivated, noting Ibédou's previous criticism of the Déby government.

E3. Is there freedom for trade unions and similar professional or labor organizations? 2 / 4

The constitution guarantees the rights to strike and unionize, but a 2007 law imposed limits on public sector workers' right to strike. In January 2020, the government and public-sector unions signed a pact to address labor disagreements, though the unions claimed the government was not fulfilling its obligations within the pact in September.

F. RULE OF LAW: 1 / 16

F1. Is there an independent judiciary? 0 / 4

The rule of law and judicial system remain weak because the political leadership, especially the executive, heavily influences the courts. The executive is known to suspend magistrates by decree.

F2. Does due process prevail in civil and criminal matters? 1 / 4

Security forces routinely ignore constitutional protections regarding search, seizure, and detention. Detained persons may be denied access to lawyers, notably those detained in connection with their involvement in antigovernment protests or activities. Many people suspected of committing crimes are held for lengthy periods without charge.

F3. Is there protection from the illegitimate use of physical force and freedom from war and insurgencies? 0 / 4

Civilian leaders do not maintain control of the security forces, who stand accused of killing and torturing with impunity. In addition, tensions amongst ethnic groups have been known to escalate into violent conflict.

The Boko Haram militant group, which operates near Lake Chad, was active in 2020. In late March, militants launched an attack in the village of Boma, killing 98 soldiers. Later that month, the army launched a counteroffensive, which was personally supervised by President Déby. The government claimed that over 1,000 militant fighters were killed during the operation, which ended in April.

The military previously blockaded the northern town of Miski, which was controlled by self-defense militias, following a local uprising. A preliminary agreement to end the blockade was reached in November 2019. In September 2020, the Miski self-defense committee withdrew from the agreement, claiming the Déby government was aiming to exploit the region's gold reserves.

Prison conditions often do not conform to international standards. In April 2020, the government announced that 44 Boko Haram fighters died by suicide in a N'Djamena prison. However, in August, the National Human Rights Commission concluded that the dead were arbitrarily arrested civilians who died in overcrowded cells without adequate provisions. In November, the CTTDH reported the existence of prisons operated by the ANS, in which prisoners are reportedly mistreated.

F4. Do laws, policies, and practices guarantee equal treatment of various segments of the population? 0 / 4

Due to cultural stigmatization, LGBT+ citizens are forced to conceal their sexual orientation and gender identity. The current penal code criminalizes same-sex sexual activity. Women face pervasive discrimination. Girls have limited access to education.

Ethnic disparities in the justice system have been reported, with officials refraining from enforcing court orders against people who share the same ethnic identity.

While discrimination against people living with disabilities is legally prohibited, NGOs claim that these provisions go unenforced.

The government struggles to provide services to internally displaced persons (IDPs). In December 2020, the Office of the UN High Commissioner for Refugees counted 336,000 IDPs, along with over 478,000 refugees from other countries residing in Chad. That same month, the government adopted legislation extending protections to refugees and asylum-seekers.

G. PERSONAL AUTONOMY AND INDIVIDUAL RIGHTS: 3 / 16

G1. Do individuals enjoy freedom of movement, including the ability to change their place of residence, employment, or education? 1 / 4

Although constitutional guarantees for the freedom of movement exist, in practice militant activity and government restrictions have limited movement. In January 2020, authorities lifted a state of emergency that was instituted in the provinces of Ouaddaï, Sila, and Tibesti in August 2019 following intercommunal violence there.

In April 2020, President Déby instituted a state of emergency in response to the COVID-19 pandemic, which included strict restrictions on movement. While some restrictions were loosened in June, others remained in force in some areas through year's end.

Public resource constraints restrict citizens' ability to pursue employment or educational opportunities outside of their local areas. The delivery of administrative documents is often slowed by bureaucratic constraints, limiting access to official documentation.

G2. Are individuals able to exercise the right to own property and establish private businesses without undue interference from state or nonstate actors? 1 / 4

Laws establishing land and property rights are nominally in force, but are functionally irrelevant to the majority of the country's population owing to the state's minimal presence in rural areas; customary law governs land ownership and use rights in practice. Laws protecting the right of women to inherit land are not enforced.

Establishing and operating a business in Chad is extremely difficult, due in part to corruption.

G3. Do individuals enjoy personal social freedoms, including choice of marriage partner and size of family, protection from domestic violence, and control over appearance? 0 / 4

Violence against women is common. Female genital mutilation is illegal but widely practiced.

The penal code bans child marriage, setting the legal age of marriage at 18, but the courts rarely hold those who practice it accountable.

G4. Do individuals enjoy equality of opportunity and freedom from economic exploitation? 1 / 4

Chad has adopted minimum wage and occupational safety laws, but they are not well enforced. Many workers are unaware of or lack access to formal channels through which they may seek redress for mistreatment; corruption also impedes workers from obtaining redress. Unpaid wages are a problem in many sectors.

Chad is a source, transit, and destination country for child trafficking. Chad has made efforts to counter human trafficking, such as initiating judicial proceedings against suspected traffickers, but criminal proceedings that return verdicts are rare.

Chile

Population: 19,500,000
Capital: Santiago
Freedom Status: Free
Electoral Democracy: Yes

Overview: Chile is a stable democracy that has experienced a significant expansion of political rights and civil liberties since the return of civilian rule in 1990. Ongoing concerns include corruption and unrest linked to land disputes with Indigenous Mapuche people. In 2019, Chile experienced massive and at times violent protests against the government and societal inequality. The demands for change culminated in a national plebiscite in October 2020, in which voters chose to replace the dictatorship-era constitution with a new charter to be drafted starting in 2021.

KEY DEVELOPMENTS IN 2020

- In an October plebiscite, an overwhelming majority of voters decided to replace the dictatorship-era 1980 constitution with a new charter, which will be drafted by a 155-member constitutional convention set to be elected in April 2021.
- In March, President Sebastián Piñera declared a state of emergency in response to the COVID-19 pandemic that included a stringent national lockdown, which continued throughout most of the year. Nonetheless, Chile suffered over 600,000 cases and 16,000 related deaths by the end of 2020, according to researchers at the University of Oxford.
- The massive protests and subsequent police repression that erupted in October 2019 declined significantly amid measures to contain the COVID-19 crisis, but sporadic protests and police abuses continued throughout the year.

POLITICAL RIGHTS: 38 / 40
A. ELECTORAL PROCESS: 12 / 12
A1. Was the current head of government or other chief national authority elected through free and fair elections? 4 / 4

Presidential elections in Chile are free and fair. The president is elected to a four-year term, and consecutive terms are not permitted. Piñera was elected in December 2017 to serve his second term; he had served as president previously, from 2010 to 2014.

A2. Were the current national legislative representatives elected through free and fair elections? 4 / 4

The 2017 legislative elections were the first to take place under new rules that established more proportional districts, and increased the number of seats in both houses. The Chamber of Deputies now has 155 seats, up from 120 previously. The number of Senate seats was increased from 38 to 50, but the new seats will be introduced gradually, with the Senate reaching its new 50-seat capacity in 2022.

Senators serve eight-year terms, with half up for election every four years, and members of the Chamber of Deputies are elected to four-year terms. Since 1990, congressional elections have been widely regarded as free and fair.

A3. Are the electoral laws and framework fair, and are they implemented impartially by the relevant election management bodies? 4 / 4

Chile's electoral framework is robust and generally well implemented. In October 2020, a national plebiscite was held on replacing the 1980 constitution, considered by its critics an ideological embodiment of the dictatorship led by General Augusto Pinochet. An overwhelming 78 percent of voters supported replacement, and 79 percent endorsed the election of a 155-member constitutional convention to draft the new charter. Elections to the convention were set for April 2021. The balloting will be held concurrently with subnational elections, including for governors, who will be elected for the first time following a 2018 legal reform.

B. POLITICAL PLURALISM AND PARTICIPATION: 15 / 16

B1. Do the people have the right to organize in different political parties or other competitive political groupings of their choice, and is the system free of undue obstacles to the rise and fall of these competing parties or groupings? 4 / 4

Chile has a multiparty political system in which parties operate freely. The current Congress, which held its first session in March 2018, includes representatives from more than a dozen political parties, as well as several independent candidates. Multiple new parties were registered or began organizing in 2020, motivated by interest in participating in the constitutional convention set to be elected in April 2021.

B2. Is there a realistic opportunity for the opposition to increase its support or gain power through elections? 4 / 4

Power alternation between parties occurs regularly, both in Congress and for the presidency.

B3. Are the people's political choices free from domination by forces that are external to the political sphere, or by political forces that employ extrapolitical means? 4 / 4

People are generally free to exercise their political choices without undue influence from actors that are not democratically accountable.

B4. Do various segments of the population (including ethnic, racial religious, gender, LGBT+, and other relevant groups) have full political rights and electoral opportunities? 3 / 4

The constitutional convention set to be elected in April 2021 will feature gender parity among its 155 members, and 17 seats will be reserved for members of Indigenous communities.

Women are represented in government, and the electoral system includes a quota for women in the legislature. However, women report difficulty gaining influence in intraparty debates.

The interests of the Mapuche minority, which represents about 9 percent of the population, are present in political life, with Mapuche activists regularly making their voices heard in street demonstrations. However, this activism has yet to translate into significant legislative power. In 2017, one Mapuche candidate was elected to the Senate, and one to the Chamber of Deputies.

Public officials from affluent backgrounds, including family-based political networks, remain overrepresented in positions of political power.

C. FUNCTIONING OF GOVERNMENT: 11 / 12

C1. Do the freely elected head of government and national legislative representatives determine the policies of the government? 4 / 4

While lobbying and interest groups exist and work to shape policy, there is little significant intervention by actors who are not democratically accountable in policymaking processes.

C2. Are safeguards against official corruption strong and effective? 3 / 4

Anticorruption laws are generally enforced, though high-level corruption scandals crop up with some regularity. In June 2019, General Juan Miguel Fuente-Alba became the first former army commander in chief to face corruption charges in a criminal court; he remained under house arrest throughout 2020, as investigations into military corruption continued to expand. In November 2018, Piñera dismissed 21 army generals amid multiple corruption scandals in the military, bringing about the most significant change in the army's high command since 1990.

C3. Does the government operate with openness and transparency? 4 / 4

The government operates with relative transparency. In 2009 the Transparency and Access to Public Information Law came into force; it increases public access to information and created a Council on Transparency. Agencies have generally been responsive to information requests, and failures to comply with the law or other measures designed to encourage transparent operations have been punished with fines.

In September 2019 the government replaced the decades-old Copper Law, in what was viewed as a major step toward improving transparency in the wake of series of corruption scandals involving the armed forces. The previous legislation had stipulated that 10 percent of the state-run copper giant Codelco's export sales be channeled to the armed forces without oversight.

CIVIL LIBERTIES: 55 / 60 (+3)
D. FREEDOM OF EXPRESSION AND BELIEF: 16 / 16 (+1)
D1. Are there free and independent media? 4 / 4

Guarantees of free speech are generally respected, though some laws barring defamation of state institutions remain on the books. Media ownership is highly concentrated.

During the 2019 protest movement, the offices of at least two newspapers were set on fire, looted, and otherwise vandalized: *El Líder* in San Antonio, and *El Mercurio de Valparaíso* in Valparaíso. Another outlet in the El Mercurio group, *El Mercurio de Antofagasta*, was attacked by protesters in January 2020.

D2. Are individuals free to practice and express their religious faith or nonbelief in public and private? 4 / 4

The constitution provides for religious freedom, and the government generally upholds this right in practice.

D3. Is there academic freedom, and is the educational system free from extensive political indoctrination? 4 / 4 (+1)

Generally, academic freedom is unrestricted in Chile. In 2019, protesters occupied, vandalized, and looted some universities, forcing several educational establishments to finish the semester early or move classes online. Some academics were publicly harassed, especially on social media. However, in 2020 academic freedom was restored to its previous level after the government implemented restrictions in response to the COVID-19 pandemic, which severely dampened both the protest movement and on-campus activity in general.

Score Change: The score improved from 3 to 4 because the protest-related disturbances, closures, and intimidation that affected university campuses in 2019 largely subsided in 2020.

D4. Are individuals free to express their personal views on political or other sensitive topics without fear of surveillance or retribution? 4 / 4

Chileans enjoy open and free private discussion.

E. ASSOCIATIONAL AND ORGANIZATIONAL RIGHTS: 11 / 12 (+1)

E1. Is there freedom of assembly? 3 / 4 (+1)

The right to assemble peacefully has traditionally been widely respected. However, peaceful protest activity that arose in 2019, when people took to the streets to demonstrate against the government and against societal inequality, was severely disrupted by a variety of factors including people who took advantage of the protest movement's cover to engage in looting, arson, and vandalism; and by widespread police violence and a restrictive state of emergency that was imposed in response to the unrest.

In March 2020, the COVID-19 pandemic prompted President Piñera to declare a new state of emergency, and the government took measures that restricted civil liberties, including a stringent lockdown and a ban on public gatherings of more than 50 people.

Due in large part to pandemic-related restrictions, both civilian violence and police repression decreased significantly in comparison to 2019. However, sporadic protests did occur, and a minority of the thousands of Chileans who gathered in a central square in Santiago on the first anniversary of the start of the 2019 upheaval looted, rioted, firebombed a police headquarters, and burned two churches. The police continued to engage in acts of repression, including an October incident in which a member of the *carabineros* (the national police) allegedly threw a teenager off a bridge in Santiago; the officer was charged with attempted murder. In late November, protesters demanding Piñera's resignation clashed with carabineros in Santiago, resulting in the detention of 74 people.

Score Change: The score improved from 2 to 3 because, while violent incidents were reported, there was a significant decrease in protest-related violence compared with 2019.

E2. Is there freedom for nongovernmental organizations, particularly those that are engaged in human rights- and governance-related work? 4 / 4

Nongovernmental organizations (NGOs) form and operate without interference.

E3. Is there freedom for trade unions and similar professional or labor organizations? 4 / 4

There are strong laws protecting worker and union rights, but some limited antiunion practices by private sector employers continue to be reported.

F. RULE OF LAW: 13 / 16

F1. Is there an independent judiciary? 4 / 4

The constitution provides for an independent judiciary, and the courts are generally free from political interference.

F2. Does due process prevail in civil and criminal matters? 4 / 4

The right to legal counsel is constitutionally guaranteed and due process generally prevails in civil and criminal matters. However, indigent defendants do not always receive effective legal representation.

In December 2020, opposition senators introduced a bill proposing a general amnesty for the hundreds of protesters arrested during the main wave of upheaval in late 2019. President Piñera repeatedly declared that he would veto any such law, and the bill remained pending at year's end. The Public Prosecutor's Office stated in October that more than 5,000 indictments related to protest violence had led to 725 convictions for various crimes, with 648 people still detained pending resolution of their cases.

Hundreds of carabineros also remain under investigation by prosecutors for alleged human rights violations, but as of October only one police officer had been convicted, and local human rights advocates criticized prosecutors' alleged lack of political will to investigate and prosecute state agents.

Human rights groups and the United Nations have criticized the government's use of antiterrorism laws, which do not guarantee due process, to prosecute acts of violence by Mapuche activists.

F3. Is there protection from the illegitimate use of physical force and freedom from war and insurgencies? 2 / 4

While the government has developed mechanisms to investigate and punish police abuses, excessive force and human rights abuses committed by the carabineros still occur, and such abuses intensified during the social upheaval that started in 2019. The protest movement was also marked by a general state of unrest in many places, as some took advantage of the uprising to commit acts of arson, looting, and other vandalism.

By the end of 2019, at least 29 civilians had been killed and more than 3,000 injured, including over 350 eye injuries inflicted due to security forces' use of rubber bullets and pellets. More than 2,700 members of security forces were also injured during the unrest. The government's National Institute for Human Rights, Human Rights Watch (HRW), and Amnesty International all accused the carabineros and the military of perpetrating human rights violations during the protests, including excessive use of force against protesters, as well as torture and sexual abuse of people held in detention. Significant property damage that took place during the protests also contributed to a threatening and unstable environment.

In 2020, the scale of abuses committed by the security forces fell because of the decline in protests amid the COVID-19 pandemic and associated restrictions, but criticism of security force tactics continued. In November, the head of the carabineros, Mario Rozas, resigned after police officers shot and wounded two minors in a raid at a state-run foster home; Rozas had faced heavy criticism for the police's handling of the social crisis in 2019.

F4. Do laws, policies, and practices guarantee equal treatment of various segments of the population? 3 / 4

While indigenous people still experience societal discrimination and police brutality, their poverty levels have declined somewhat, aided by government scholarships, land transfers, and social spending.

LGBT+ people continue to face societal bias, despite a 2012 antidiscrimination law that covers sexual orientation and gender identity. In November 2018, the president signed a gender-identity law allowing for gender identity to be changed on the civil registry.

In practice, elites benefit from systematic favorable legal treatment, and widespread grievances about social inequality were a major driver of the 2019 protests.

G. PERSONAL AUTONOMY AND INDIVIDUAL RIGHTS: 15 / 16 (+1)

G1. Do individuals enjoy freedom of movement, including the ability to change their place of residence, employment, or education? 4 / 4 (+1)

The constitution protects the freedom of movement, and the government respects this right in practice. Freedom of movement was constrained in 2019 due to the roadblocks, damage to train stations, and vandalism associated with the social unrest that began in October. In 2020, the transit impact of civil unrest ceased, and by the end of the year the only constraints on freedom of movement stemmed from governmental measures to control the spread of the coronavirus.

Score Change: The score improved from 3 to 4 because the roadblocks, disruption to public transportation, and other restrictions on movement associated with the protests of 2019 were alleviated in 2020.

G2. Are individuals able to exercise the right to own property and establish private businesses without undue interference from state or nonstate actors? 4 / 4

Individuals generally have the right to own property and establish and operate private businesses, and are able to do so without interference from the government or other actors. However, Mapuche activists continue to demand greater territorial rights to land, ancestral waters, and natural resources, and ongoing tensions in the Araucanía Region produced violent clashes in August 2020 between Mapuche activists and non-Indigenous groups supported by the carabineros.

G3. Do individuals enjoy personal social freedoms, including choice of marriage partner and size of family, protection from domestic violence, and control over appearance? 4 / 4

The government generally does not restrict personal social freedoms. However, violence against children and women remains a problem. A law against femicide went into force in 2010. A total of 40 femicides were reported as of December 2020. According to HRW, emergency calls reporting gender-based violence and harassment rose significantly in the first half of 2020.

In 2017, a law introduced by then-president Michelle Bachelet that decriminalized abortion in the events of rape, an inviable fetus, or danger to the life of the woman, took effect.

A 2015 law recognizes civil unions for same-sex and different-sex couples, but same-sex marriages are not recognized.

G4. Do individuals enjoy equality of opportunity and freedom from economic exploitation? 3 / 4

While compulsory labor is illegal, forced labor, particularly among foreign citizens, continues to occur in the agriculture, mining, and domestic service sectors.

Although there have been improvements in fighting child labor, minors still suffer commercial sexual exploitation and work unprotected in the agricultural sector. Moreover, there is limited public information about forced child labor.

China

Population: 1,402,400,000
Capital: Beijing
Freedom Status: Not Free
Electoral Democracy: No

Note: The numerical scores and status listed above do not reflect conditions in Hong Kong or Tibet, which are examined in separate reports. *Freedom in the World* reports assess the level of political rights and civil liberties in a given geographical area, regardless of whether they are affected by the state, nonstate actors, or foreign powers. Territories are sometimes assessed separately if they meet certain criteria, including boundaries that are sufficiently stable to allow year-on-year comparisons. For more information, see the report methodology and FAQ.

Overview: China's authoritarian regime has become increasingly repressive in recent years. The ruling Chinese Communist Party (CCP) is tightening its control over the state bureaucracy, the media, online speech, religious groups, universities, businesses, and civil society associations, and it has undermined its own already modest rule-of-law reforms. The CCP leader and state president, Xi Jinping, has consolidated personal power to a degree not seen in China for decades, but his actions have also triggered rising discontent among elites within and outside the party. The country's human rights movements continue to seek avenues for protecting basic liberties despite a multiyear crackdown.

KEY DEVELOPMENTS IN 2020

- The outbreak of COVID-19 at the beginning of the year provided justification for the acceleration of existing programs to track, surveil, and control the behavior of citizens through new mobile-phone applications and other technologies. Using draconian methods, the government was largely successful in containing the virus after the initial outbreak in Hubei Province, with fewer than 4,800 deaths reported by the World Health Organization at year's end. However, the CCP leadership worked to suppress independent sources of information and criticism about its early cover-up and mishandling of the contagion, punishing whistleblowers and citizen journalists and promoting disinformation that deflected blame for the pandemic to other countries.
- Throughout the year, the government pushed ahead with repressive programs aimed at changing demographics and ensuring "social stability" in ethnic minority areas, particularly Xinjiang, Tibet, and Inner Mongolia. New evidence indicated the massive scale of projects involving the forced relocation of rural residents, the forced sterilization of Uighur women, the mass detention of Uighurs in "political reeducation" centers, and the imprisonment of tens of thousands of others by the courts. Credible reports of abuse and deaths in custody also emerged during the year.
- In August, ethnic Mongolian students, parents, teachers, and administrators mounted strikes and demonstrations to protest a required reduction in the use of Mongolian as the language of instruction in the Inner Mongolia region. The government responded with mass arrests, enforced disappearances, termination of employment, expulsion of students, property confiscations, and the threat of long prison terms. The authorities used various forms of harassment and coercion to pressure parents to send their children back to school.
- The authorities continued a years-long crackdown on independent civil society, with new arrests and criminal prosecutions of journalists and activists, as well as onerous scrutiny of foreign nongovernmental organizations (NGOs). Authorities also increased restrictions on religious practice by Chinese Buddhists, Christians, and Muslims throughout China under 2018 regulations on religious affairs, and persecution of the banned spiritual movement Falun Gong continued unabated.

- The space for independent academic discussion and research reached new lows, with professors and students facing reprisals—in the form of censored writings, travel restrictions, demotions, arrests, or imprisonment—for expressing views that were deemed critical of CCP governance.

POLITICAL RIGHTS: −2 / 40 (−1)

A. ELECTORAL PROCESS: 0 / 12

A1. Was the current head of government or other chief national authority elected through free and fair elections? 0 / 4

There are no direct or competitive elections for national executive leaders. The National People's Congress (NPC) formally elects the state president for five-year terms and confirms the premier after he is nominated by the president, but both positions are decided in advance by the top CCP leadership and announced at the relevant party congress. The CCP's seven-member Politburo Standing Committee (PSC), headed by Xi Jinping in his role as the party's general secretary, sets government and party policy in practice. Xi also holds the position of state president and serves as chairman of the state and party military commissions.

Xi was awarded a second five-year term as CCP general secretary at the 19th Party Congress in October 2017, and at the NPC session in March 2018 he was confirmed for a second five-year term as state president. Also at that session, the NPC approved amendments to China's constitution that abolished the two-term limit for the state presidency and vice presidency. Combined with the absence of a designated successor for Xi on the new PSC, the move reinforced predictions that he planned to break with precedent and remain China's paramount leader for three or more terms.

A2. Were the current national legislative representatives elected through free and fair elections? 0 / 4

The 3,000 NPC members are formally elected for five-year terms by subnational congresses, but in practice all candidates are vetted by the CCP. Only the NPC's standing committee meets regularly, with the full congress convening for just two weeks a year to approve proposed legislation; party organs and the State Council, or cabinet, effectively control lawmaking decisions. The current NPC was seated in March 2018.

A3. Are the electoral laws and framework fair, and are they implemented impartially by the relevant election management bodies? 0 / 4

Political positions are directly elected only at the lowest levels. Independent candidates who obtain the signatures of 10 supporters are by law allowed to run for seats in the county-level people's congresses, and elections for village committees are also supposed to give residents the chance to choose their representatives. In practice, however, independent candidates for these posts are often kept off the ballot or out of office through intimidation, harassment, fraud, and in some cases detention. Only a very small number of independent candidates have gained office in elections, though some attempt to do so in each election cycle.

Elections are not administered by an independent body. The indirect elections that populate people's congresses at various levels are conducted by those congresses' standing committees, while village-level elections are conducted by a village electoral committee that answers to the local party committee.

B. POLITICAL PLURALISM AND PARTICIPATION: 0 / 16

B1. Do the people have the right to organize in different political parties or other competitive political groupings of their choice, and is the system free of undue obstacles to the rise and fall of these competing parties or groupings? 0 / 4

The CCP seeks to monopolize all forms of political organization and does not permit any meaningful political competition. Eight small noncommunist parties are allowed to play a minor role in China's political system and are represented on the Chinese People's Political Consultative Conference (CPPCC), an official advisory body. However, their activities are tightly circumscribed, and they must accept the CCP's leadership as a condition for their existence.

Citizens who seek to establish genuinely independent political parties or otherwise advocate for democracy are harshly punished. In 2020, the authorities continued to round up and punish prodemocracy activists and lawyers who had attended an informal gathering in Xiamen, Fujian Province, in late December 2019. One attendee, New Citizens' Movement founder and legal activist Xu Zhiyong, was detained in February after weeks in hiding; he was formally arrested in June on charges of "inciting subversion of state power," which can carry a prison term of 15 years. He remained in incommunicado detention at year's end.

B2. Is there a realistic opportunity for the opposition to increase its support or gain power through elections? 0 / 4

China's one-party system rigorously suppresses the development of any organized political opposition, and the CCP has ruled without interruption since winning a civil war against the Nationalist Party (Kuomintang) in 1949. While factions within the CCP have always existed, they do not compete openly or democratically, and they remain unaccountable to the public. Xi Jinping has steadily increased his personal power and authority within the party since 2012. He exercises direct supervision over a variety of policy areas; his official contributions to party ideology were formally added to the CCP and national constitutions in 2017 and 2018, respectively; and the CCP Central Committee's plenary meeting in 2019 reaffirmed the primacy of "Xi Jinping Thought."

The government's initial cover-up and mishandling of the COVID-19 outbreak led to criticism of Xi's leadership, including from some within the CCP, but these voices were quickly silenced. Ren Zhiqiang, an influential party figure and businessman, went missing in March 2020 after publishing an essay that sharply critiqued Xi's management of the crisis; it was later announced that he had been expelled from the CCP, and he was sentenced in September to 18 years in prison on charges of corruption and embezzlement.

B3. Are the people's political choices free from domination by forces that are external to the political sphere, or by political forces that employ extrapolitical means? 0 / 4

The authoritarian CCP is not accountable to voters and denies the public any meaningful influence or participation in political affairs. Among other coercive methods of suppressing independent political engagement, in 2020 the authorities continued their heavy reliance on plainclothes personnel, rather than uniformed police officers, to intimidate and harass activists and subject them to extrajudicial detention.

B4. Do various segments of the population (including ethnic, racial, religious, gender, LGBT+, and other relevant groups) have full political rights and electoral opportunities? 0 / 4

The political system is dominated in practice by ethnic Han Chinese men. Societal groups such as women, ethnic and religious minorities, and LGBT+ people have no opportunity to gain meaningful political representation and—as with the rest of the population—are barred from advancing their interests outside the formal structures controlled by the CCP. Nominal representatives of ethnic minority groups such as Tibetans, Uighurs, and Mongolians participate in party and state bodies like the NPC, but their role is largely symbolic. Women are severely underrepresented in top CCP and government positions, and the situation has grown slightly worse in recent years. Just one woman was named to the 25-member Politburo at the 19th Party Congress in 2017, down from the previous two. No woman has ever sat on the PSC.

C. FUNCTIONING OF GOVERNMENT: 1 / 12 (−1)

C1. Do the freely elected head of government and national legislative representatives determine the policies of the government? 0 / 4

None of China's national leaders are freely elected, and the legislature plays a minimal role in policymaking and the development of new laws. The continuing concentration of power in Xi Jinping's hands, an emerging cult of personality, and Xi's calls for greater ideological conformity and party supremacy have further reduced the limited space for policy debate even within the CCP.

C2. Are safeguards against official corruption strong and effective? 1 / 4

Since becoming CCP leader in 2012, Xi has pursued an extensive anticorruption campaign. Well over a million officials have been investigated and punished, according to official figures, including senior state and party officials from the security apparatus, the military, the Foreign Ministry, state-owned enterprises, and state media. The campaign continued during 2020.

The anticorruption effort has generated a chilling effect among officials and reduced ostentatious displays of wealth, but corruption is believed to remain extensive at all levels of government. Moreover, the initiative has been heavily politicized, as many of the elites targeted were seen as Xi's former or potential rivals, and a 2017 change to party regulations shifted the focus of disciplinary inspections to enforcing party ideology and loyalty.

The authorities have failed to adopt basic reforms that would address corruption more comprehensively, such as requiring officials to publicly disclose their assets, creating genuinely independent oversight bodies, and allowing independent media, courts, and civic activists to function as watchdogs. Instead, in 2018 the NPC established the highly centralized and powerful National Supervisory Commission (NSC), which merged the anticorruption functions of various state and party entities and is tasked with enforcing political and ideological discipline in addition to compliance with the law.

C3. Does the government operate with openness and transparency? 0 / 4 (−1)

The Chinese government and the CCP are notoriously opaque. Since open-government regulations took effect in 2008, more official documents and information have been made available to the public and posted on official websites. However, resistance on the part of government organs to providing specific information requested by citizens has undercut the impact of the measures, and minimal budgetary information is made available to the public.

The scope for public input and consultation on laws and policies has narrowed further in recent years as many policy advocacy NGOs have been shut down and academics and intellectuals operate under intense pressure, including those working in areas that were previously not considered sensitive, such as the environment, public health, women's rights, and the economy.

At the outset of the COVID-19 pandemic in early 2020, authorities suppressed information about the disease and punished health professionals who tried to raise the alarm. Even after the full public health response was underway, officials continued to censor independent information, withhold or distort key data, and generally resist transparency, including on crucial issues like vaccine development. Meanwhile, state media promoted propaganda and disinformation about the pandemic, including conspiracy theories and suggestions that the virus had originated outside of China.

Score Change: The score declined from 1 to 0 due to a multiyear deterioration in the government's provision of information in the public interest, culminating in an extensive censorship and disinformation campaign surrounding the COVID-19 pandemic.

ADDITIONAL DISCRETIONARY POLITICAL RIGHTS QUESTION
Is the government or occupying power deliberately changing the ethnic composition of a country or territory so as to destroy a culture or tip the political balance in favor of another group? −3 / 0

The government continued in 2020 to aggressively pursue policies—including large-scale resettlement, work-transfer programs, forced sterilizations, and mass internment—that are altering the demography of ethnic minority regions, especially Xinjiang, Tibet, and Inner Mongolia. Further evidence emerged during the year of the government's systematic program of forced sterilizations of Uighur and other Muslim women in Xinjiang, particularly those with two or more children. Official documents also state explicitly that violations of birth-control measures or having too many children are punishable by extrajudicial internment and fines, often the equivalent of several years' income for an average family. Birth-control violations were one of the top reasons Uighurs were sent to internment camps, in which an estimated 1.8 million Uighurs and other Muslims have been detained.

The government's program of relocating "surplus rural laborers" accelerated during the year. An official white paper released in September stated that 2.6 million individuals in Xinjiang had been relocated in the year prior to June 2020, and 1.8 million during the year prior to June 2019, primarily from poor rural areas in the region's south. While the government claims that the program is voluntary and beneficial to participants, the evidence suggests conditions tantamount to forced labor, with ethnic minorities housed separately in near prison-like environments, subjected to political indoctrination, and economically exploited.

The government also continued to implement policies meant to attract Han Chinese migrants to ethnic minority regions. Programs aimed at encouraging marriages between Han Chinese and ethnic minorities through financial and other incentives, such as an advantage on the university entrance exam for children from such marriages, were expanded in 2020.

Other official policies effectively deprive ethnic minority communities of their right to access, enjoy, and pass down their distinct cultures, religions, and identities. New evidence uncovered in 2020 showed a rapid increase in the number of children in Xinjiang being held in state-run boarding schools and orphanages, many of whom have either one or both parents in detention; the number of boarding students at the primary and middle-school levels was reported to have reached 880,500 by the end of 2019. These institutions, many of which are surrounded by barbed-wire fencing and aim to be fully Chinese-language environments, expose Uighur and other Muslim children to intense political indoctrination without independent guidance from their families.

In Inner Mongolia, education officials announced in August that all primary and middle schools would have to use Chinese as the language of instruction for certain subjects, a decision that led to widespread protests—including class walkouts and boycotts—and a subsequent government crackdown. The authorities arrested or detained thousands of people, subjecting many others to enforced disappearances, house arrests, dismissal from employment, property confiscation, expulsions from school, and the threat of long prison terms.

CIVIL LIBERTIES: 11 / 60

D. FREEDOM OF EXPRESSION AND BELIEF: 1 / 16

D1. Are there free and independent media? 0 / 4

China is home to one of the world's most restrictive media environments and its most sophisticated system of censorship, particularly online. The CCP maintains control over news reporting via direct ownership, accreditation of journalists, harsh penalties for comments critical of party leaders or the CCP, and daily directives to media outlets and websites that guide coverage of breaking news stories. State management of the telecommunications infrastructure enables the blocking of websites, removal of smartphone applications from the domestic market, and mass deletion of social media posts and user accounts that touch on banned political, social, economic, and religious topics. Thousands of websites have been blocked, many for years, including major news and social media hubs like the *New York Times*, YouTube, Twitter, and Facebook.

The government continues to exert control over apolitical spaces such as online music stores and platforms for live streaming, dating, celebrity gossip, and blockchain technology, in part by suspending or tightening scrutiny of features that enable real-time communication. The multipurpose social media tool WeChat increasingly employs artificial intelligence to scan and delete images that are deemed to include banned content.

According to the Committee to Protect Journalists (CPJ), 47 journalists were behind bars in connection with their work as of December 2020, although the actual number of people held for uncovering or sharing newsworthy information is much greater. In an unusually harsh penalty, journalist Chen Jieren was sentenced to 15 years in prison in April for publishing critical online material about the CCP, including allegations of official corruption in Hunan Province. Authorities expelled at least 17 foreign journalists during the year, many of whom had been reporting on sensitive topics. Chris Buckley of the *New York Times* was forced to leave in May after officials refused to renew his visa; he had been personally attacked by state media for his reporting on COVID-19.

Numerous citizen journalists were also detained, disappeared, and in some cases criminally charged for their reporting on the pandemic. In early 2020, security forces in Wuhan detained three citizen journalists—Fang Bin, Chen Qiushi and Li Zehua—who had filmed and uploaded videos of themselves from within the city during its coronavirus lockdown; their videos ran counter to official narratives and were disseminated widely. Li and Chen were both later released, with Chen reportedly under tight surveillance at his parents' home in Shandong Province. Zhang Zhan, another citizen journalist and former human rights lawyer, was sentenced to four years in prison in December for "picking quarrels and stirring up trouble," after her videos from Wuhan highlighted government incompetence and lack of transparency. Separately, at least three people were detained in April for their involvement with the Terminus 2049 Project, a website that archives censored articles and information; documents and other information related to the pandemic had been stored on the site.

Despite the heavy restrictions on media freedom, Chinese journalists, grassroots activists, and internet users have continued to seek out and exploit new ways to expose official misconduct, access uncensored information, and share incisive political commentary, although they risk reprisals when doing so. Tens of millions of people use circumvention tools like virtual private networks (VPNs) to reach the uncensored global internet or accessed blocked overseas broadcasts via satellite. Those who illegally sell VPN services can be sentenced to prison, and individuals have faced fines simply for using a VPN to reach uncensored material.

D2. Are individuals free to practice and express their religious faith or nonbelief in public and private? 0 / 4

The CCP regime has established a multifaceted apparatus to control all aspects of religious activity, including by vetting religious leaders for political reliability, placing limits on the number of new monastics or priests, and manipulating religious doctrine according to party priorities. The ability of believers to practice their faith varies dramatically based on religious affiliation, location, and registration status. Many do not necessarily feel constrained, particularly if they are Chinese Buddhists or Taoists. However, a 2017 Freedom House report found that at least 100 million believers belong to groups facing high or very high levels of religious persecution, namely Protestant Christians, Tibetan Buddhists, Uighur Muslims, and Falun Gong practitioners.

The government continued to tighten control over religious communities and carry out demolitions of allegedly unauthorized places of worship in 2020, both during and after COVID-19 lockdowns. The online magazine *Bitter Winter* reported the destruction of hundreds of Buddhist and folk temples across rural China, including in Sichuan, Hebei, Henan, Zhejiang and Fujian Provinces. Persecution of unofficial Protestant groups also continued during the year. The police broke up the Easter Sunday service of the unregistered Early Rain Covenant Church in Chengdu, Sichuan Province, which was being held online due to the coronavirus. The service was shut down, and eight members were detained in raids on their homes. The church's pastor, Wang Yi, had been sentenced in 2019 to nine years in prison on charges of "inciting subversion of state power."

The Vatican and the Chinese government in October 2020 confirmed a two-year extension of their 2018 agreement on the selection of Roman Catholic bishops. The unpublished agreement reportedly allows the government to nominate bishops and the Vatican to exercise a veto. The status of some existing bishops recognized by the Vatican but not by the government remained unclear. Clergy who lack state recognition have complained of intimidation and pressure to sign registration forms.

In Xinjiang, intrusive restrictions on the practice of Islam affect the wearing of religious attire, attendance at mosques, fasting during Ramadan, choice of baby names, and other basic forms of religious expression. Many categories of individuals are barred from certain activities; for example, children under 18 cannot enter mosques or receive religious instruction. In 2020, authorities in the region reportedly prohibited recipients of state benefits from performing daily prayers. Peaceful religious practices are routinely punished under charges of "religious extremism," resulting in detention, prison sentences, and indoctrination for many Uighur, Kazakh, and Hui Muslims.

The regime's campaign to eradicate the Falun Gong spiritual group continued in 2020. Hundreds of Falun Gong practitioners have received long prison terms in recent years, and many others are arbitrarily detained in various "legal education" facilities. Detainees typically face torture aimed at forcing them to abandon their beliefs, sometimes resulting in deaths in custody.

D3. Is there academic freedom, and is the educational system free from extensive political indoctrination? 0 / 4

Academic freedom is heavily restricted, and the space for academic discussion and research that departs from CCP guidelines has been reduced further in recent years, even regarding what were previously less sensitive topics, such as labor rights, constitutional law, or economics. Efforts to police classroom discussions have increased at all levels of education, including via installation of surveillance cameras in some classrooms, large-scale recruitment of student informants, and the creation of special departments to supervise the political thinking of teaching staff. The CCP controls the appointment of top university officials, and many scholars practice self-censorship to protect their careers and personal safety.

Political indoctrination, including the study of "Xi Jinping Thought," is a required component of the curriculum at all levels of education. Increased government funding to support research promoting party ideology has spurred the establishment of dozens of centers dedicated to "Xi Jinping Thought." Professors and students face reprisals—ranging from censored writings, travel restrictions, and demotions to arrest and imprisonment—for expressing views that are deemed critical of the CCP's governance and of Xi Jinping's slogans. In January 2020, the national teaching materials committee banned all foreign teaching materials for primary through secondary schools and required all materials to be submitted for political review in advance. A new directive published in April empowered the central government to review and approve for publication all academic research on the origins of the coronavirus. In August, Peking University issued new regulations requiring teachers and students to register and seek approval before participating in international online conferences.

A series of outspoken liberal academics have been harassed and persecuted by the authorities, especially since 2018. Tsinghua University law professor Xu Zhangrun was detained for a week in July 2020, with police reportedly accusing him of soliciting prostitutes. In 2019 Xu had been stripped of his teaching duties, placed under investigation, and subjected to a wage cut in connection with publications that criticized Xi Jinping's authoritarian policies and called for political reforms. Geng Xiaonan, a publisher, and her husband were detained in September and charged in October with "illegal business operations" after publicly expressing support for Xu.

D4. Are individuals free to express their personal views on political or other sensitive topics without fear of surveillance or retribution? 1 / 4

The government's ability to monitor citizens' lives and communications has increased dramatically in recent years, inhibiting online and offline conversations. Social media applications like WeChat are known to closely monitor user discussions so as to conform with government content restrictions and surveillance requests. Surveillance cameras, increasingly augmented with facial-recognition software, cover many urban areas and public transportation, and are expanding into rural regions. The country's evolving Social Credit System rates citizens' trustworthiness based on a wide range of data, including financial records, purchasing behavior, video gaming habits, social acquaintances, and adherence to rules in public spaces. Devices used by police to quickly extract and scan data from smartphones, initially deployed in Xinjiang, have spread nationwide.

Databases with the personal details of certain categories of individuals—including users of drugs, petitioners, members of ethnic minorities, religious believers, foreigners, and migrant workers—have been purchased by police throughout the country. The 2017 Cybersecurity Law requires companies to store Chinese users' data in China and submit to potentially intrusive security reviews, and telecommunications companies are now required to obtain facial scans of new internet or mobile phone users as part of the real-name registration process.

In 2020, the authorities leveraged the COVID-19 pandemic to justify even more intrusive surveillance methods. Mandatory "health code" mobile apps were introduced as part of the government's effort to track and contain the spread of the virus; the apps monitored users' locations and interactions to determine their risk of infection, then limited their access to certain public spaces and services accordingly. Independent analysts found that the apps lacked privacy protections and in at least some cases shared data with police.

Electronic surveillance is supplemented with offline monitoring by neighborhood party committees, "public security volunteers" who are visible during large events, and an especially heavy police presence in places like Xinjiang. The ability of Uighurs and other Muslim minorities in Xinjiang to express themselves freely in private has been further undermined in recent years by a policy of having Chinese officials stay in their homes to monitor and indoctrinate them. In some cases male officials reside in close quarters with women and children whose adult male family members are in detention.

Court verdicts have cited private social media communications, public surveillance video, and personal meetings as evidence in cases where citizens were punished for expressing their views on political or religious topics. In addition to legal penalties, a growing number of internet users have faced account closures, job dismissals, and police interrogation because of politically sensitive or even humorous comments made on social media platforms.

The February 2020 death of Li Wenliang—one of several whistleblowing health professionals who shared warnings about the new coronavirus and were then detained by police—from COVID-19 led to an outpouring of public anger toward the authorities on social media, including widespread demands for freedom of speech. The government responded with censorship and arrests. One NGO documented 897 cases involving internet users who were punished for speech about the coronavirus between January 1 and March 26. The Ministry of Public Security reported on February 21 that police had handled 5,111 cases of "fabricating and deliberately disseminating false and harmful information."

E. ASSOCIATIONAL AND ORGANIZATIONAL RIGHTS: 2 / 12
E1. Is there freedom of assembly? 1 / 4

The constitution protects the right of citizens to demonstrate, but in practice protesters rarely obtain approval and risk punishment for assembling without permission. Spontaneous demonstrations have thus become a common form of protest. Some are met with police violence, and organizers often face reprisals, even in cases where local officials ultimately concede to protesters' demands. Armed police have been accused of opening fire during past protests in Xinjiang.

E2. Is there freedom for nongovernmental organizations, particularly those that are engaged in human rights- and governance-related work? 0 / 4

The ability of civil society organizations to engage in work related to human rights and governance is extremely constrained and has decreased under a 2017 law on foreign NGOs and 2016 legislation governing philanthropy, which significantly reduced civic groups' access to funding from foreign sources and increased supervision and funding from the government. The space for organizations to operate without formal registration, a previously common practice, has also diminished, although some continue to do so. Several prominent NGOs that focused on policy advocacy, including in less politically sensitive areas like public health or women's rights, have been shuttered in recent years under government pressure. Hundreds of thousands of NGOs are formally registered, but many operate more as government-sponsored entities and focus on service delivery. Government-sanctioned organizations dominated the charitable response to COVID-19 in 2020, but many civic groups found ways to provide assistance despite the bureaucratic barriers, and the authorities eased restrictions slightly to facilitate such work.

The foreign NGO law that took effect in 2017 restricts the operations of foreign NGOs in China, requires them to find a Chinese sponsor entity and register with the Ministry of Public Security, and gives police the authority to search NGOs' premises without a warrant, seize property, detain personnel, and initiate criminal procedures. Hundreds of foreign NGOs have registered offices or temporary activities, though the vast majority are trade and agricultural associations, or groups involved in issues such as cultural exchange, public health, education, or the rights of people with disabilities. A list of sponsoring Chinese entities documented by the ChinaFile NGO Project indicated a heavy presence of state and CCP-affiliated organizations. The number of foreign NGOs that choose to deregister rather than attempt to comply with the law has increased each year since its adoption.

E3. Is there freedom for trade unions and similar professional or labor organizations? 1 / 4

The only legal labor union organization is the government-controlled All-China Federation of Trade Unions (ACFTU), which has long been criticized for failing to properly defend workers' rights, but has reportedly become even less of an ally to workers in recent years.

The authorities continued to suppress labor activism in 2020. Several young activists were released during the year after pledging to abandon their efforts to help organize factory workers in Guangdong Province. They were among dozens involved in the unionization campaign who were detained in 2018 and 2019, and the workers' attempts to establish independent collective bargaining were eventually defeated.

Despite the constraints on union activity, strikes and labor protests continued to be reported across the country in 2020, particularly over wage arrears. Factory closures during the COVID-19 lockdown led to a smaller number of such incidents early in the year, but the *China Labour Bulletin* documented some 500 incidents during the second half of the year, for a total of about 800.

F. RULE OF LAW: 2 / 16

F1. Is there an independent judiciary? 1 / 4

The CCP dominates the judicial system, with courts at all levels supervised by party political-legal committees that have influence over the appointment of judges, court operations, and verdicts and sentences. CCP oversight is especially evident in politically sensitive cases, and most judges are CCP members. In 2019, the annual work report of Supreme People's Court president Zhou Qiang emphasized that judges should conform to CCP ideology and uphold the party's "absolute leadership" of the courts.

Incremental reforms aimed at improving judicial performance, while maintaining party supremacy, were introduced beginning in 2014. The changes focused on increasing transparency, professionalism, and autonomy from local authorities. Many judges complain about local officials interfering in cases to protect powerful litigants, support important industries, or avoid their own potential liability.

F2. Does due process prevail in civil and criminal matters? 1 / 4

Reforms to the criminal justice system in recent decades have sought to guarantee better access to lawyers, allow witnesses to be cross-examined, and establish other safeguards to prevent wrongful convictions. However, violations of due process—including excessive use of pretrial and incommunicado detention—are widespread, and a multiyear crackdown on human rights lawyers has weakened defendants' access to independent legal counsel.

Prosecutions rely heavily on confessions, many of which are obtained through torture. The law encourages judges to exclude such evidence, but it is commonly used in practice. The NGO Safeguard Defenders documented 87 televised confessions between mid-2013 and early 2020, finding that they often involved physical and other forms of coercion. Human rights lawyer Wang Quanzhang, who was released in April 2020 after nearly five years in prison on charges of "subversion" in connection with his defense of activists and persecuted religious believers, filed a rare complaint in July against public security officials in Tianjin, alleging that he was tortured in an attempt to extract a guilty plea and requesting that his conviction be overturned.

Criminal trials are frequently closed to the public, and the conviction rate is estimated at 98 percent or more. While adjudication of routine civil and administrative disputes is considered more fair, cases that touch on politically sensitive issues or the interests of powerful groups are subject to decisive "guidance" from political-legal committees.

Extrajudicial forms of detention remain widespread, despite the abolition of "reeducation through labor" camps at the end of 2013. Large numbers of people—particularly petitioners, grassroots rights activists, Falun Gong adherents, and Uighur Muslims—are still held in various types of arbitrary detention. A new form of extrajudicial detention for targets of anticorruption and official misconduct investigations, known as *liuzhi*, was introduced in 2018, in tandem with the establishment of the NSC. Individuals can be held in *liuzhi* for up to six months without access to legal counsel. Separately, the criminal procedure law allows "residential surveillance in a designated location," in which individuals can be held for up to six months in an undisclosed location.

F3. Is there protection from the illegitimate use of physical force and freedom from war and insurgencies? 0 / 4

Conditions in places of detention are harsh, with reports of inadequate food, regular beatings, and deprivation of medical care. In addition to their use to extract confessions, torture and other forms of coercion are widely employed by the authorities to force political and religious dissidents to recant their beliefs. Security agents routinely flout legal protections, and impunity is the norm for police brutality and suspicious deaths in custody. While some such deaths are reported to family members, there are likely many more that are never officially recognized, particularly when the victims belong to persecuted ethnic minority populations. Citizens who seek redress for abuse in custody or suspicious deaths often meet with reprisals or imprisonment.

The government has gradually reduced the number of crimes that carry the death penalty, which totaled 46 as of 2020, but it is estimated that thousands of inmates are executed each year; the figure is considered a state secret. The government claims it has ended the transplantation of organs from executed prisoners. However, the scale of the transplantation industry and the speed with which some organs are procured far exceed what is feasible via the country's nascent voluntary donation system, and there is growing international attention to possible crimes against humanity in connection with the practice.

F4. Do laws, policies, and practices guarantee equal treatment of various segments of the population? 0 / 4

Chinese laws formally prohibit discrimination based on nationality, ethnicity, race, gender, religion, or health condition, but these protections are often violated in practice. Several laws bar gender discrimination in the workplace, and gender equality has reportedly improved over the past decade. Nevertheless, bias remains widespread, including in job recruitment and college admissions. The #MeToo movement against sexual harassment and assault, which began in the United States and has spread to China in recent years, has helped to raise awareness of the problem, but activists have often had their online accounts deleted, or been harassed or detained. Ethnic and religious minorities, LGBT+ people, people with disabilities, and people with illnesses such as HIV/AIDS and hepatitis B also face widespread discrimination in employment and access to education. Religious and ethnic minorities are disproportionately targeted and abused by security forces and the criminal justice system. In addition to being held in extrajudicial detention, members of these communities tend to be sentenced to longer prison terms than Han Chinese convicts.

Despite China's international obligation to protect the rights of asylum seekers and refugees, law enforcement agencies continue to repatriate North Korean defectors, who face imprisonment or execution upon return.

Foreign residents of China, particularly Africans and people of African descent, faced discrimination in the enforcement of COVID-19 restrictions during 2020. Many were arbitrarily forced to quarantine, evicted from their homes, refused services, and denied entry to certain locations or public transportation.

G. PERSONAL AUTONOMY AND INDIVIDUAL RIGHTS: 6 / 16

G1. Do individuals enjoy freedom of movement, including the ability to change their place of residence, employment, or education? 1 / 4

China's *hukou* (household registration) system prevents roughly 290 million internal migrants from enjoying full legal status as residents in cities where they work. In 2020, the government restated its goal of reforming the system in order to expand the benefits of urban residency to 100 million migrants based on their education, employment record, and housing status, with the most stringent requirements in major cities like Shanghai and Beijing and looser standards applied in smaller municipalities. The plan would still leave a large majority of migrants without equal rights or full access to social services such as education for their children in local schools. One significant constraint on the government's goals has been the requirement that migrants give up land rights in their rural home regions; many are reluctant to permanently surrender these rights in exchange for uncertain employment prospects in towns and cities.

Many other Chinese citizens also face obstacles to freedom of movement within the country. Police checkpoints throughout Xinjiang limit residents' ability to travel or even leave their hometowns. Elsewhere in China, the developing Social Credit System has reportedly led to restrictions on air and train travel for millions of citizens with low scores. While China's constitution gives individuals the right to petition the government concerning a grievance or injustice, in practice petitioners are routinely intercepted in their efforts to reach Beijing, forcefully returned to their hometowns, or extralegally detained in "black jails," psychiatric institutions, and other sites.

Millions of people are affected by government restrictions on their access to foreign travel and passports, with Uighurs and Tibetans experiencing the greatest difficulty in obtaining a passport. Overseas Chinese nationals who engage in politically sensitive activities are at risk of being prevented from returning to China or may choose not to return for fear of being arrested.

The pandemic-related lockdowns of early 2020 featured abusive enforcement methods, with inadequate access to essential supplies and reports that some residents were physically sealed into their homes. Meanwhile, the "health code" mobile apps that were introduced to help limit the spread of the virus often restricted users' freedom of movement based on opaque or arbitrary criteria.

G2. Are individuals able to exercise the right to own property and establish private businesses without undue interference from state or nonstate actors? 1 / 4

The authorities dominate the economy through state-owned enterprises in key sectors such as banking and energy, and through state ownership of land. Chinese citizens are legally permitted to establish and operate private businesses. However, those without strong informal ties to powerful officials often find themselves at a disadvantage in legal disputes with competitors, in dealings with regulators, or in the context of politicized anticorruption campaigns. Foreign companies and executives can face arbitrary regulatory obstacles, debilitating censorship, demands for bribes, travel restrictions, or negative media campaigns. Many private companies in China have internal party organizations or committees. In September 2020, the CCP issued an "opinion" document calling for the private sector to be brought more closely under the guidance of the party.

Property rights protection remains weak. Urban land is owned by the state, with only the buildings themselves in private hands. Rural land is collectively owned by villages. Farmers enjoy long-term lease rights to the land they work, but they have been restricted in their ability to transfer, sell, or develop it. Low compensation and weak legal protections have facilitated land seizures by local officials, who often evict residents and transfer the land rights to developers. Corruption is endemic in such projects, and local governments rely on land development as a crucial source of revenue. The COVID-19 pandemic provided opportunities for further violations of property rights. In February 2020, Guangdong Province passed emergency legislation that allowed local governments to requisition property, equipment, and other goods, without adequate safeguards against abuse.

G3. Do individuals enjoy personal social freedoms, including choice of marriage partner and size of family, protection from domestic violence, and control over appearance? 2 / 4

A legal amendment allowing all families to have two children—effectively abolishing the one-child policy that had long applied to most citizens—took effect in 2016. While the authorities continue to regulate reproduction, the change means that fewer Han Chinese families are likely to encounter the punitive aspects of the system, such as high fines, job dismissal, reduced government benefits, and occasionally detention. Abuses such as forced abortions and sterilizations are less common for Han Chinese citizens than in the past, but they continue to occur. By law, ethnic minority couples are still permitted to have up to three children, but in practice ethnic Tibetans and Uighur and other Muslims in Xinjiang have been subject to abusive policies aimed at limiting their reproduction through forced sterilizations and birth control.

Muslims in Xinjiang face restrictions and penalties related to aspects of their appearance with religious connotations, such as headscarves on women or beards on men.

The country's first law designed to combat domestic violence came into effect in 2016, but domestic violence continues to be a serious problem, affecting one-quarter of Chinese women, according to official figures. Activists have complained that the law fails to provide support for victims and does not criminalize spousal rape, and that it remains extremely difficult for victims to win court cases or even obtain protection orders against their abusers.

G4. Do individuals enjoy equality of opportunity and freedom from economic exploitation? 2 / 4

While workers in China are afforded important protections under existing laws, violations of labor and employment regulations are widespread. Local CCP officials have long been incentivized to focus on economic growth rather than the enforcement of labor laws. Exploitative employment practices such as wage theft, excessive overtime, student labor, and unsafe working conditions are pervasive in many industries. In one deadly incident in September 2020, 16 coal miners were killed in an underground fire at a site operated by a state-owned power company. The company had failed a government inspection months earlier. Forced labor and trafficking are common, frequently affecting rural migrants, and Chinese nationals are similarly trafficked abroad. Forced labor is the norm in prisons and other facilities for criminal, political, and religious detainees.

Colombia

Population: 49,400,000
Capital: Bogotá
Freedom Status: Partly Free
Electoral Democracy: Yes

Overview: Colombia is among the longest-standing democracies in Latin America, but one with a history of widespread violence and serious human rights abuses. Public institutions have demonstrated the capacity to check executive power and enforce the rule of law, and violence declined as the government and the country's main left-wing guerrilla group moved toward a peace accord signed in 2016. Nonetheless, Colombia still faces enormous challenges in consolidating peace and guaranteeing political rights and civil liberties outside of major urban areas.

KEY DEVELOPMENTS IN 2020

- With over 1.6 million cases and over 40,000 deaths reported by the government, Colombia was severely afflicted by the COVID-19 pandemic. The outbreak initially centered on the Atlantic coast region, but also affected Bogotá and other major cities; in rural areas, illegal armed groups violently enforced unofficial quarantines.
- In December, President Iván Duque announced that nearly one million Venezuelans without legal status would be excluded from Colombia's coronavirus vaccination program. Some 1.7 million Venezuelans, many sick or impoverished, had settled in Colombia in recent years after fleeing a devastating economic crisis at home; some returned during the year, even as closure of the two nations' border thwarted legal passage.
- The peace accord signed in 2016 between the government and the left-wing Revolutionary Armed Forces of Colombia (FARC) rebel group remained intact during the year, but implementation delays—which were exacerbated by restrictions imposed to control the coronavirus pandemic—and the continued rearming of some former rebels prompted concern about the pact's durability.
- Powerful former president Álvaro Uribe was subjected to a detention order in August amid an investigation into witness tampering and intimidation allegations.
- Abuses by state security forces led to repeated public outcry. In February, news outlets exposed an illegal surveillance operation run by the Colombian military, and in June revelations emerged of soldiers committing a series of alleged sexual assaults. In September, a police killing in Bogota sparked violent protests that resulted in the deaths of 13 people.

- A multiyear wave of lethal attacks against human rights defenders and other social activists continued throughout 2020. Scores of activists—which were concentrated among marginalized indigenous and Afro-Colombian communities—were murdered, and the perpetrators of such crimes generally enjoyed impunity.

POLITICAL RIGHTS: 29 / 40

A. ELECTORAL PROCESS: 10 / 12

A1. Was the current head of government or other chief national authority elected through free and fair elections? 4 / 4

The president is directly elected to a four-year term. As part of a series of 2015 constitutional amendments, presidential reelection was eliminated.

The peace accord between the government and the FARC was a significant issue in the 2018 election. President Duque, a protégé of former president and chief peace-accord critic Álvaro Uribe, pledged throughout the campaign to alter the pact's terms, which he characterized as overly magnanimous toward the guerrillas. No candidate garnered an outright majority in the first round; following a polarized runoff campaign, Duque defeated left-wing former Bogotá mayor Gustavo Petro with 54 percent of the vote. The balloting was considered competitive and credible, though election observers logged sporadic reports of vote buying and other violations in both the first and second rounds.

Local and regional elections are generally characterized by greater opacity and more frequent violence than national elections, including over 100 attacks and 7 murders in the run-up to the October 2019 balloting. In the most prominent race, for mayor of Bogotá, Green Alliance candidate Claudia López won; she became the city's first woman and first openly gay mayor. Opposition-aligned candidates also won the governorship in Antioquia—the heartland of Uribe and the Democratic Center (CD)—along with the mayoralties of Medellín and Cali.

A2. Were the current national legislative representatives elected through free and fair elections? 3 / 4

Congress is composed of the Senate and the Chamber of Representatives, with all seats up for election every four years. The nation at large selects 100 Senate members using a proportional representation system; two additional members are chosen by indigenous communities, one seat is awarded to the runner-up in the presidential election, and another five seats were reserved in 2018 and 2022 for the FARC under the peace accord. The Chamber of Representatives consists of 172 members, with 161 elected by proportional representation in multimember districts, two chosen by Afro-Colombian communities, one each by indigenous and expatriate voters, one seat reserved for the runner-up vice presidential candidate, and five seats reserved for the FARC, as in the Senate.

The March 2018 legislative elections were relatively peaceful, though observers noted accusations of fraud, vote buying, and connections between candidates and organized crime figures. Senate seats were dispersed, with six parties winning 10 or more seats, led by Duque's CD with 19. In the Chamber of Representatives, five parties won 21 or more seats, led by the Liberal Party with 35; the CD garnered 32 seats. In its first balloting as a legal party, the FARC took no seats aside from the five guaranteed to it in each chamber.

A3. Are the electoral laws and framework fair, and are they implemented impartially by the relevant election management bodies? 3 / 4

The legal framework generally allows for competitive balloting in practice, though the nine-member National Electoral Council (CNE)—which oversees the conduct of the country's elections, including the financing of political campaigns and the counting of votes—has faced criticism for ineffective enforcement of electoral laws, blamed in part on the partisan selection system for its members.

B. POLITICAL PLURALISM AND PARTICIPATION: 11 / 16

B1. Do the people have the right to organize in different political parties or other competitive political groupings of their choice, and is the system free of undue obstacles to the rise and fall of these competing parties or groupings? 3 / 4

Colombia's historically rigid two-party system has undergone a protracted process of realignment and diversification in recent years. The 2018 elections brought into the legislature a mix of parties from the left, right, and center. This balance, coupled with intraparty splits, left Duque with an unstable governing coalition in each legislative chamber, though the government maintained a working majority during most of 2020. The FARC, whose acronym now stands for Common Alternative Revolutionary Force, reorganized as a political party in 2017; the congressional seats it received under the peace accord gave it far more representation than it would have earned through normal voting.

B2. Is there a realistic opportunity for the opposition to increase its support or gain power through elections? 3 / 4

Democratic transfers of power between rival parties are routine at both the national level and in the regions, though significant areas remain under the long-term control of machine-style political clans with ties to organized crime. Petro's performance in the 2018 presidential election marked the strongest showing for the political left in a modern presidential campaign, and a number of candidates from outside traditional parties were able to win regional-level races in 2019. Numerous prominent politicians occupy the political space between the extremes of Petro and the CD, and in 2020 jockeying began among prospective candidates in anticipation of the 2022 elections.

B3. Are the people's political choices free from domination by forces that are external to the political sphere, or by political forces that employ extrapolitical means? 2 / 4

Despite the peace accord with the FARC, activity by the smaller National Liberation Army (ELN) leftist guerrilla group, the successors of previously disbanded right-wing paramilitary groups, and criminal gangs has continued to impair the ability of citizens in some areas to participate freely in the political process, as evidenced by the attacks during the 2019 regional campaigns. In March 2020, audio emerged of a murdered rancher affiliated with drug traffickers discussing arrangements to distribute cash to voters in support of Duque's second-round campaign in 2018, in areas along the Caribbean coast; investigations were ongoing at year's end.

B4. Do various segments of the population (including ethnic, racial, religious, gender, LGBT+, and other relevant groups) have full political rights and electoral opportunities 3 / 4

Lighter-skinned Colombians occupy a disproportionate share of government posts. While progress remains slow, the government has undertaken a series of steps to incorporate Indigenous and Afro-Colombian voices into national political debates in recent years. The 2016 peace accord included provisions for improving consultation mechanisms for marginalized groups, but issues affecting Afro-Colombians and Indigenous groups are rarely priorities in national policymaking. An Indigenous senator, Feliciano Valencia, was the victim of an assassination attempt in October 2020.

Women enjoy equal political rights, and at least 30 percent of the candidates on party lists must be women. About 20 percent of the seats in each congressional chamber are currently held by women. Colombia's vice president, Marta Lucía Ramírez, is a woman.

In October 2019, Green Alliance candidate Claudia López won the mayorship of Bogotá, becoming the city's first woman and first openly gay mayor.

C. FUNCTIONING OF GOVERNMENT: 8 / 12

C1. Do the freely elected head of government and national legislative representatives determine the policies of the government? 3 / 4

Elected officials generally determine government policy without interference. However, the Colombian state has long struggled to establish a secure presence in all parts of its territory, meaning threats from guerrilla groups and criminal gangs can disrupt policymaking and implementation in certain regions and localities. The emergency decree powers granted to the president amid the 2020 coronavirus pandemic raised concern among some observers that Congress's role was being unduly bypassed.

C2. Are safeguards against official corruption strong and effective? 2 / 4

Corruption occurs at multiple levels of public administration. Graft scandals have emerged in recent years within an array of federal agencies, but investigations do result in convictions, including against senior officials. Numerous members of the two Uribe administrations (2002–10) were convicted of corruption, trading favors, and spying on political opponents.

A multicountry bribery scandal centered on the Brazilian construction firm Odebrecht led to charges in 2017 and 2018 against two senators and multiple former legislators and bureaucrats. In 2020, numerous fraud investigations were opened in relation to emergency COVID-19 spending, especially at the local level. Scrutiny of politicians by the national attorney general and inspector general has increased. In December 2020, the head of the National Police was forced to resign while facing a conflict of interest investigation by the inspector general. However, whistleblowers lack sufficient legal protection; for example, in October 2020 an employee of a state-owned media agency faced criminal charges after providing a watchdog group with evidence of internal censorship at the agency.

C3. Does the government operate with openness and transparency? 3 / 4

Government information is generally available to the public, though information related to military and security affairs can be difficult to access. A proposal that was put to a referendum in 2018 would have committed lawmakers to passing a set of reforms meant to establish far-reaching increases in government transparency; although support for the measures was nearly unanimous, turnout narrowly failed to clear the threshold for the outcome to be binding.

CIVIL LIBERTIES: 36 / 60 (–1)

D. FREEDOM OF EXPRESSION AND BELIEF: 12 / 16

D1. Are there free and independent media? 2 / 4

The constitution guarantees freedom of expression, and opposition views are commonly aired in the media. However, journalists face intimidation, kidnapping, and violence both in the course of reporting and as retaliation for their work. The government has prosecuted several notorious cases of murdered journalists in recent years, but convictions are rare. In 2020, local press watchdog Foundation for Press Freedom registered 445 attacks on press freedom, including one killing, for which military involvement was under investigation. In

May the newsweekly *Semana* published an explosive report detailing military surveillance operations that targeted scores of domestic and foreign journalists as well as politicians, judges, and activists, leading to the firing of 11 soldiers, with additional investigations ongoing at year's end.

Self-censorship is common, and slander and defamation remain criminal offenses. In July 2020, Vice President Marta Lucía Ramirez filed criminal charges against an Insight Crime journalist after an article mentioned ties between her husband and an accused drug trafficker; she dropped the case several days later. The government does not restrict access to the internet, nor does it censor websites. Twitter and other social media platforms have become important arenas for political discourse, but large areas of Colombia remain without local news coverage.

D2. Are individuals free to practice and express their religious faith or nonbelief in public and private? 4 / 4

The constitution provides for freedom of religion, and the government generally respects this right in practice.

D3. Is there academic freedom, and is the educational system free from extensive political indoctrination? 3 / 4

Academic freedom is generally respected. University debates are often vigorous, though armed groups maintain a presence on some campuses to generate political support and intimidate opponents. Students were among the most active protesters during large-scale mobilizations in November and December 2019, in which demonstrators had expressed a litany of grievances with government policies.

D4. Are individuals free to express their personal views on political or other sensitive topics without fear of surveillance or retribution? 3 / 4

Individual expression is generally protected in major urban centers, but it remains inhibited in more remote areas where the state, insurgents, and criminals vie for control.

E. ASSOCIATIONAL AND ORGANIZATIONAL RIGHTS: 6 / 12
E1. Is there freedom of assembly? 2 / 4

Although provided for in the constitution, freedom of assembly is restricted in practice by violence. Due in part to the need for social distancing, no planned protests achieved the scale of the dramatic wave that shook Bogotá and other cities in late 2019. However, dissemination of footage of a police killing in Bogotá in September generated a massive reaction. Protesters destroyed dozens of police posts, while the police responded with gunfire, leaving 13 dead and hundreds wounded. The government blamed the unrest on subversives and proposed new restrictions on protest activity, while opposition officials, including Bogotá mayor López, strongly criticized the police response. In September, the Supreme Court ordered state institutions to respect the right to protest and establish protocols to prevent abuses by the security forces.

E2. Is there freedom for nongovernmental organizations, particularly those that are engaged in human rights and governance-related work? 2 / 4

The legal framework generally supports nongovernmental organizations, and civil society is diverse and active, but the threat of violent reprisal poses a major obstacle to freedom of association. While the government provides protection to thousands of threatened human rights workers, trust in the service varies widely, and the COVID-19 pandemic posed additional challenges to effective protection. Hundreds of activists have been murdered in recent years, mostly by insurgents or the criminal organizations that succeeded right-wing paramilitary groups that demobilized in the mid-2000s; impunity is widespread, though indictments and convictions have occurred in some cases.

Although the Duque administration has reiterated its respect for civil society groups and repeatedly committed to developing more effective protection policies, violations against activists have continued at a high level. As of mid-December 2020, the UN had registered 120 killings of social leaders and human rights defenders during the year. Among the most frequent victims are land rights, victims' rights, and ethnic and Indigenous rights advocates targeted by illegal armed groups and other powerful interests seeking to control local illicit economies or halt the implementation of rural development plans, especially coca substitution programs.

E3. Is there freedom for trade unions and similar professional or labor organizations? 2 / 4

Workers may form and join trade unions, bargain collectively, and strike, and antiunion discrimination is prohibited. Over the past two decades, Colombia's illegal armed groups have killed more than 2,600 labor union activists and leaders. Killings have declined substantially from their peak in the early 2000s, though 14 trade unionists were murdered between January 2019 and March 2020, according to the International Trade Union Confederation. A special prosecutorial unit has substantially increased prosecutions for such assassinations since 2007, but few investigations have targeted those who ordered the killings.

F. RULE OF LAW: 9 / 16

F1. Is there an independent judiciary? 3 / 4

The justice system remains compromised by corruption and extortion. The Constitutional Court and the Supreme Court have consistently exhibited independence from the executive, though corruption allegations involving members of both courts have damaged their credibility in recent years.

The Constitutional Court has repeatedly been asked to mediate polarizing political disputes, especially with respect to the Special Jurisdiction for Peace (JEP), a parallel court structure or tribunal that lies at the heart of the 2016 peace accord's transitional justice system. Critics of the peace accord, led by former president Uribe, continued to call for shutting down the JEP throughout 2020. In August, the Supreme Court ordered Uribe confined to house arrest amid a witness tampering and bribery investigation. He subsequently resigned from the Senate, leading to the transfer of the case to the attorney general's office, and was granted conditional release in October.

F2. Does due process prevail in civil and criminal matters? 2 / 4

Colombia's prosecutorial service is relatively professional and due process protections have improved, but they remain weak overall, and trial processes move very slowly. The two key transitional justice bodies, the JEP and the Truth Commission, began operations in 2018; by late 2020 they had amassed enormous volumes of evidence and received testimony from thousands of people. In 2020 operations were slowed by the coronavirus pandemic, but investigations and testimony continued, including public acknowledgement by former FARC combatants that guerrillas had engaged in recruitment of minors, sexual assault, and kidnapping, and carried out several prominent assassinations. However, uncertainty remains about the extent to which the bodies will be able to render a comprehensive historical and judicial accounting of Colombia's conflict.

F3. Is there protection from the illegitimate use of physical force and freedom from war and insurgencies? 2 / 4

Many soldiers operate with limited civilian oversight, though the government has in recent years increased human rights training and investigated violations by security forces personnel. Collaboration between security forces and illegal armed groups has declined, but rights groups report official toleration of paramilitary successor groups in some regions. The police are more professional than many in neighboring countries but lack necessary resources, are occasionally abusive, and are largely absent from many rural areas where the most dangerous groups are active.

Civil-military relations have been a source of significant tension in recent years. A portion of the armed forces opposed the peace process, and the ability of accused human rights violators within the military to receive benefits under the transitional justice system is one of the most controversial elements of the process. The systematic killing of civilians to fraudulently inflate guerrilla death tolls resulted in as many as 3,000 murders by the military between 2002 and 2008. Such killings plummeted after the scandal was exposed, but in 2019 the *New York Times* reported that the military was again emphasizing body counts, with a corresponding rise in extrajudicial executions. Additional scandals involving both corruption and rights violations buffeted the military in 2019, resulting in the forced resignation of defense minister Guillermo Botero in November and army chief Nicacio Martínez in December. The military's image was further dented by new revelations in 2020, particularly a large-scale surveillance operation exposed in May and several cases of soldiers raping Indigenous minors reported in June. The state responded to the wave of scandals by removing some soldiers and commanders and forming several investigative commissions, but as of November they had yet to yield institutional reforms. Similarly, police violence in September in Bogotá—and longstanding impunity for alleged brutality—prompted calls to remove the police from the Ministry of Defense, but the Duque administration rejected such proposals.

Some parts of the country, particularly resource-rich zones and drug-trafficking corridors, remain highly insecure. Remnant guerrilla forces—including both the ELN and dissident factions of the FARC—and paramilitary successor groups regularly abuse the civilian population, especially in coca-growing areas. In 2020, the strict lockdown that accompanied the COVID-19 pandemic led to numerous crimes committed by armed groups against the population under the guise of quarantine enforcement. This pattern reflected a general conflict fragmentation and intensification in some areas, illustrated by a dramatic rise in the number of massacres—defined as incidents in which three or more people are murdered—with local NGO Indepaz registering 91 massacres. Though the acreage under cultivation has stabilized, coca growing has reached historic highs in recent years. Impunity for crime in general is rampant, and most massacres that took place during the conflict have gone unpunished. Prison conditions remain harsh; in March 2020, 24 inmates died in a Bogotá prison riot that began as a protest regarding insufficient protection from the coronavirus.

A steady trickle of former FARC combatants have returned to clandestine life, with the total number of "dissidents" estimated at around 2,500. In 2019, several high-ranking FARC members officially announced their return to insurgency, alleging government failure to abide by the accord's terms. Although observers characterize reintegration of ex-combatants as partially successful, as of November 2020 the JEP reported that 249 demobilized FARC members had been killed since the peace agreement. Despite a coronavirus-related ELN partial ceasefire in April 2020, prospects for an accord between the government and the rebels remained poor throughout the year.

Despite these problems, violence overall has significantly subsided since the early 2000s. The national homicide rate in 2020 was approximately 24 per 100,000 people, and other crimes also appeared to decline as a result of the coronavirus lockdown in 2020.

F4. Do laws, policies, and practices guarantee equal treatment of various segments of the population? 2 / 4

The legal framework provides protections against various forms of discrimination based on gender, race and ethnicity, sexual orientation and gender identity, and other categories, and the government takes some measures to enforce these protections. Nevertheless, several vulnerable groups suffer serious disadvantages in practice.

Afro-Colombians, who account for as much as 25 percent of the population, make up the largest segment of the more than 7 million people who have been displaced by violence, and some 80 percent of Afro-Colombians live below the poverty line. Areas with concentrated Afro-Colombian populations continue to suffer vastly disproportionate levels of abuse by guerrillas, security forces, and criminal groups.

Most of Colombia's Indigenous inhabitants, who make up more than 3 percent of the population, live on approximately 34 million hectares granted to them by the government, often in resource-rich, strategic regions that are highly contested by armed groups. Indigenous people have been targeted by all sides in the country's various conflicts. In 2020, Indigenous communities in the departments of Chocó, Cauca, and Nariño suffered increasing violence and displacement perpetrated by the ELN, former FARC members, and paramilitary successors, prompting a protest gathering in Bogotá in October to demand greater protection. The coronavirus pandemic caused additional deprivation, particularly for the Wayúu group living near the Venezuelan border.

Women face employment discrimination and sexual harassment in the workplace, as well as gender-based violence. Killings of women spiked in 2020, and women were also disproportionately harmed by the economic dislocation wrought by the pandemic-induced lockdown.

LGBT+ people suffer societal discrimination and abuse, and there are also high levels of impunity for crimes committed against them. According to the governmental ombudsman's office, 63 LGBT+ people were murdered in the first 8 months of 2020.

As many as 1.7 million Venezuelan migrants have entered Colombia in recent years, and the government has offered work permits, access to services, and other accommodations to those who register. The influx created increasing strain in 2020; public opinion toward migrants hardened, and the economic disruption inflicted by the COVID-19 pandemic caused a reverse migration toward Venezuela, even as closure of the two nations' border thwarted legal passage. In December, President Duque stirred controversy by announcing that the nearly one million Venezuelans without legal status would be excluded from Colombia's coronavirus vaccination program.

G. PERSONAL AUTONOMY AND INDIVIDUAL RIGHTS: 9 / 16 (−1)

G1. Do individuals enjoy freedom of movement, including the ability to change their place of residence, employment, or education? 2 / 4 (−1)

Freedom of movement improved substantially in tandem with the peace process, but it remains restricted by ongoing violence in certain regions, particularly for vulnerable minority groups. Travel in some remote areas is further limited by illegal checkpoints operated by criminal and guerrilla groups. These problems were exacerbated by both the strict official lockdown from March through August 2020 and the even harsher unofficial lockdown imposed by illegal armed groups, which was violently enforced in at least 11 departments.

Score Change: The score declined from 3 to 2 because armed groups have illegally enforced strict pandemic-related lockdowns, murdered people at informal checkpoints, forced some to flee their homes, and trapped human rights defenders and social leaders in locations where they face threats of violence.

G2. Are individuals able to exercise the right to own property and establish private businesses without undue interference from state or nonstate actors? 2 / 4

Violence and instability in some areas threaten property rights and the ability to establish businesses. Guerrillas, paramilitary successor groups, and common criminals regularly extort payments from business owners. Corruption as well as undue pressure exerted on prosecutors and members of the judiciary can disrupt legitimate business activity.

Progress remains slow on the implementation of the landmark 2011 Victims and Land Law, which recognized the legitimacy of claims by victims of conflict-related abuses, including those committed by government forces. While affected citizens continue receiving compensation, the legal process for land restitution is heavily backlogged, and the resettlement of those who were displaced during the conflict continues to move slowly, with the Duque administration demonstrating little will to accelerate the process.

G3. Do individuals enjoy personal social freedoms, including choice of marriage partner and size of family, protection from domestic violence, and control over appearance? 3 / 4

Personal social freedoms, such as those related to marriage and divorce, are largely respected. In 2016, after several years of contradictory judicial and administrative decisions regarding same-sex unions, the Constitutional Court voted to legalize them. In October 2018 the Constitutional Court reaffirmed a 2006 ruling that allowed abortion in cases of rape or incest, severe fetal malformation, or a threat to the life of the mother, but Congress's refusal to pass implementing regulations created confusion in the health care sector. A case involving the constitutionality of criminal penalties for abortion remained under review at the court as of the end of 2020.

G4. Do individuals enjoy equality of opportunity and freedom from economic exploitation? 2 / 4

Child labor, the recruitment of children by illegal armed groups, and related sexual abuse are serious problems in Colombia; recruitment declined following the peace accord, but rose again amid pandemic-related disruption and violence in 2020. A 2011 free trade agreement with the United States and a subsequent Labor Action Plan called for enhanced investigation of abusive labor practices and rights violations, but progress remains deficient in several areas. In coca-growing zones, armed groups exert coercive pressure on farmers to engage in coca cultivation and shun crop-substitution programs.

Comoros

Population: 900,000
Capital: Moroni
Freedom Status: Partly Free
Electoral Democracy: No

Overview: Comoros's volatile political history includes coups and attempted coups, though some recent presidential and legislative elections were reasonably well administered. A controversial 2018 referendum introduced major systemic changes, and opponents of the referendum and its main proponent, President Azali Assoumani, were severely persecuted. Since winning the referendum and securing reelection in 2019, Azali has consolidated power by cracking down on the opposition and limiting press freedom. Systemic corruption and poverty remain problems.

KEY DEVELOPMENTS IN 2020

- The ruling Convention for the Renewal of the Comoros (CRC) and allied candidates won every seat in the January and February legislative elections, which were marred by an opposition boycott and disagreements over voter turnout.
- President Azali was the reported target of an unsuccessful April bombing attempt, which the authorities blamed on a terrorist organization. Some 19 people were detained over the incident by May.
- Comorian authorities suspended travel to the French territories of Mayotte and Réunion in March and implemented a COVID-19-related overnight curfew in April, which remained in effect at year's end. Public gatherings were prohibited for much of the year. The government reported 765 cases and 9 deaths to the World Health Organization at year's end.

POLITICAL RIGHTS: 16 / 40 (−2)

A. ELECTORAL PROCESS: 5 / 12 (−1)

A1. Was the current head of government or other chief national authority elected through free and fair elections? 1 / 4

Under the 2001 constitution, the president was directly elected for a single five-year term, with eligibility rotating among the main islands of Grande Comore (Ngazidja), Anjouan, and Mohéli. However, a new constitution, approved in a controversial 2018 referendum that was boycotted by the opposition, allows the president to run for two consecutive five-year terms, and abolished the system of rotating power among the islands. The referendum allowed President Azali Assoumani of the CRC to contest the March 2019 presidential election.

The Supreme Court barred seven contestants from participating ahead of election day, including former president Ahmed Abdallah Mohamed Sambi. On election day, the 12 opposition candidates reported that some polling stations opened several hours early, with full ballot boxes. Acts of violence and intimidation were also reported in some regions.

The Independent National Electoral Commission (CENI) initially reported that Azali won the election in the first round with 60.8 percent of the vote, while Ahamada Mahamoudou of the Juwa Party won 14.6 percent; in early April, the Supreme Court validated results stating that Azali earned 59 percent of the vote. The 12 opposition candidates immediately rejected the results. Observers from the African Union (AU), the Common Market for Eastern and Southern Africa, and the East Africa Standby Force, an AU-backed regional defense organization, said the contest was marred by irregularities.

A2. Were the current national legislative representatives elected through free and fair elections? 2 / 4 (−1)

The unicameral Assembly of the Union consists of 24 directly elected members who serve five-year terms. Another 9 members were previously selected by the three islands' assemblies, but those seats were eliminated via a 2019 ordinance.

The 2020 legislative elections, held in two rounds in January and February, were boycotted by the major opposition parties. Progovernment candidates won every seat; the CRC won 20, the allied Orange Party won 2, and progovernment independent candidates won the remaining 2. AU monitors who observed the January round called the contest generally peaceful, but noted a lack of public interest due to the opposition boycott. Opposition groups claimed that first-round turnout stood at 10 percent, rejecting the CENI figure of 61.5 percent. Members of the Comorian diaspora were unable to participate, with the government denying the opposition's calls to ensure their inclusion.

Score Change: The score declined from 3 to 2 because the January and February legislative elections were marred by disagreements over voter turnout and an opposition boycott, leaving Comorians effectively unable to vote for the candidates of their choice.

A3. Are the electoral laws and framework fair, and are they implemented impartially by the relevant election management bodies? 2 / 4

The CENI, while historically able to run credible elections, has faced more recent accusations of bias and corruption.

The 2018 constitutional referendum, which the CENI said passed with 93 percent of the vote, was marred by an opposition boycott. Opposition groups denounced it as an unconstitutional power grab by Azali and said Azali's dismissal of the Constitutional Court ahead of the vote rendered it illegal. There were also allegations of voter intimidation and fraud. Later, upon facing growing dissent in the parliament, Azali dismissed the CENI's top opposition representative.

The new constitution allows the president to run for two consecutive terms, abolished the system of rotating power among the islands, abolished the three vice-presidential posts (one representing each island), and declared Sunni Islam the national religion. It also transferred the competencies of the Constitutional Court, which was considered impartial in deciding electoral matters, to a new Supreme Court chamber.

B. POLITICAL PLURALISM AND PARTICIPATION: 7 / 16 (−1)

B1. Do the people have the right to organize in different political parties or other competitive political groupings of their choice, and is the system free of undue obstacles to the rise and fall of these competing parties or groupings? 2 / 4

Political parties are mainly formed around specific leaders and draw on island or ethnic bases of support. In the past, parties have generally operated freely, though the government occasionally disrupted opposition parties' activities by denying them meeting and assembly space.

The authorities systematically cracked down on opposition figures who publicly criticized the 2018 constitutional referendum. That December, two dozen opposition figures received prison sentences for opposing the referendum or the president, including former vice president Djaffar Said Ahmed Hassane and Juwa secretary general Ahmed el-Barwane. El-Barwane was among 17 opposition figures pardoned by Azali in 2019.

Despite those pardons, his government has maintained pressure on the opposition in the aftermath of the 2019 presidential election. Presidential candidates Achmet Said Mohamed and Soilihi Mohamed were briefly detained that March, though both were later released. Soilihi, who led a National Transitional Council (CNT) that unsuccessfully attempted to force Azali from office through civil disobedience and industrial action, agreed to refrain from further involvement after his release that April.

B2. Is there a realistic opportunity for the opposition to increase its support or gain power through elections? 1 / 4 (−1)

In the past, numerous opposition parties had a realistic chance of gaining power through elections, though they were impeded by occasional government interference. Allegations of misuse of state resources by incumbents were not uncommon. However, the arrests, convictions, and harsh sentences against opposition leaders who spoke out against the 2018 constitutional referendum hampered the ability of opposition parties to compete in elections. The 2020 legislative elections, which were marred by an opposition boycott, ended with progovernment candidates winning every seat.

Score Change: The score declined from 2 to 1 because progovernment candidates won every legislative seat in the January and February elections after an opposition boycott, leaving no opposition presence in the body.

B3. Are the people's political choices free from domination by forces that are external to the political sphere, or by political forces that employ extrapolitical means? 2 / 4

While individuals are generally free to exercise their political choices, the influence of Comoros's powerful army—which cracked down on dissent during the 2018 constitutional referendum—as well as of religious authorities can place pressure on voters and candidates.

The army was used to intimidate and detain opposition figures during and after the 2019 presidential campaign. Gendarmes arrested Soilihi after he announced his CNT involvement that March. Gendarmes also interrogated the spouse of presidential candidate Achmet, who served as a CNT spokesperson, that April.

B4. Do various segments of the population (including ethnic, racial, religious, gender, LGBT+, and other relevant groups) have full political rights and electoral opportunities? 2 / 4

There are no laws preventing various segments of the population from enjoying full political rights and electoral opportunities. However, traditional attitudes discourage women from participating in politics. Only four women won legislative seats in the 2020 polls. Legal and societal discrimination against LGBT+ people makes political advocacy for LGBT+ rights difficult.

C. FUNCTIONING OF GOVERNMENT: 4 / 12

C1. Do the freely elected head of government and national legislative representatives determine the policies of the government? 2 / 4

According to the constitution, the president decides on the policies of the state, which are executed by the government. However, irregular legislative activity hampered representative policymaking in previous years.

C2. Are safeguards against official corruption strong and effective? 1 / 4

There are reports of corruption at all levels, including within the judiciary, civil service, and security forces. The Azali administration dissolved the National Commission for Preventing and Fighting Corruption in 2016.

In 2018, former president Sambi was arrested for corruption, embezzlement, and forgery in connection with a passport-sales scheme. A parliamentary report revealed that the scheme cost Comoros as much as $971 million. Sambi remained under house arrest at the end of 2020.

C3. Does the government operate with openness and transparency? 1 / 4

Government operations are characterized by opacity. Various reform initiatives have been unsuccessful. Financial asset disclosures by public officials are not released to the public. Comoros provides no opportunities for public engagement in the budget process.

CIVIL LIBERTIES: 26 / 60

D. FREEDOM OF EXPRESSION AND BELIEF: 8 / 16

D1. Are there free and independent media? 1 / 4

The constitution and laws provide for freedom of speech and of the press. However, the use of censorship laws to prosecute legitimate journalistic work, and other pressure, has prompted widespread self-censorship. Press freedom was restricted in 2018 with the closings of private radio stations, as criticism of Azali and the constitutional referendum gained traction.

Journalistic activity remained restricted in 2020. In January, *Masiwa Komor* reporter Ali Mbaé and FCBK FM reporter Oubeidillah Mchangama were arrested while planning to cover an opposition rally on Grande Comore. That same month, news director Binti Mhadjou and editor in chief Moinadjoumoi Papa Ali, both of the public Comoros Radio and Television Office, were suspended by the information minister for purportedly giving favorable coverage to strike participants. They returned to their roles in March. In December, Oubeidillah was arrested for disturbing "public order" after reporting on the possibility of a fuel shortage, but was provisionally released later that month.

D2. Are individuals free to practice and express their religious faith or nonbelief in public and private? 2 / 4

Some 98 percent of the population is Sunni Muslim. Sunni Islam was made the state religion in 2018, resulting in wariness of the government among adherents of minority religions. Previously, the state religion had been "Islam"; some observers suggested the change reflected Azali's efforts to bring Comoros closer to Saudi Arabia and to counter the influence of former president Sambi, who is seen as close to Iran.

Anti-Shia sentiments have been publicly expressed by some government figures, while many Christians keep their faith private to avoid harassment. Proselytizing and public religious ceremonies are prohibited for all religions except Sunni Islam.

D3. Is there academic freedom, and is the educational system free from extensive political indoctrination? 3 / 4

Comoros has two types of schools: madrassas, where the Quran is integral, and state-run schools with French instruction. Academic freedom is generally respected, though the education system is sometimes affected by unrest from student protests and teacher strikes.

D4. Are individuals free to express their personal views on political or other sensitive topics without fear of surveillance or retribution? 2 / 4

Private discussion is generally free. However, the legacies of the country's volatile political history, which involves coups and attempted coups, the opposition crackdown during the 2018 constitutional referendum, authorities' monitoring of social media during the 2019 presidential campaign, and a one-day shutdown of telecommunications services that March, can discourage people from openly discussing politics in some situations.

E. ASSOCIATIONAL AND ORGANIZATIONAL RIGHTS: 6 / 12

E1. Is there freedom of assembly? 1 / 4

Freedoms of assembly and association are constitutionally protected, but these freedoms have been inconsistently upheld, and deteriorated significantly since 2018. Opposition rallies held before and soon after the March 2019 presidential election were violently dispersed. Public gatherings were banned under COVID-19-related measures during much of 2020, and those measures remained in effect at year's end.

E2. Is there freedom for nongovernmental organizations, particularly those that are engaged in human rights- and governance-related work? 2 / 4

Nongovernmental organizations (NGOs) sometimes face bureaucratic interference, including requirements to secure permits from high-level officials to visit prisons. Some NGO representatives have spoken out against the atmosphere of repression in recent years, but did so at some risk in light of the broad crackdown on dissent.

E3. Is there freedom for trade unions and similar professional or labor organizations? 3 / 4

Workers have the right to form unions, bargain collectively, and strike. In cases of national interest, the government may require essential personnel to return to work. No law prohibits antiunion discrimination or protects workers from retribution for striking. There are some laws that impose mandatory arbitration processes for labor disputes.

F. RULE OF LAW: 6 / 16

F1. Is there an independent judiciary? 1 / 4

The judicial system is based on both Sharia (Islamic law) and the French legal code. Though the law establishes mechanisms for the selection of judges and attorneys, the executive often disregards these and simply appoints people to their positions. Court decisions are not always upheld.

The 2018 referendum abolished the Constitutional Court and established a new constitutional chamber of the Supreme Court. This chamber ruled in favor of the government during the March 2019 election period by barring several candidates from running and by validating the results, despite widespread concerns over voting irregularities.

F2. Does due process prevail in civil and criminal matters? 1 / 4

All defendants have the right to a fair public trial, but they often face lengthy delays. Due-process rights are affected by corruption.

Political figures, including candidates, have been denied due process; 2019 presidential candidates Achmet and Soilihi were arrested for CNT-related activities that March, for example. Former president Sambi's pretrial detention period ended in April 2019 with no progress on pending corruption charges, and he remained under house arrest at the end of 2020.

F3. Is there protection from the illegitimate use of physical force and freedom from war and insurgencies? 2 / 4

The law prohibits the illegitimate use of physical force, but security agents have engaged in excessive force, and are generally not held accountable for such behavior. There are questions about the will or capacity of the army to identify and punish abuses within its ranks.

President Azali has been the reported target of violent attacks. In March 2019, Azali was reportedly targeted in a bombing while traveling to a campaign rally, though no one was injured. Azali was also the reported target of an unsuccessful April 2020 bombing attempt; 22 people were initially charged for their alleged involvement, and 19 were in detention by May. The authorities reported that a terrorist organization was suspected of orchestrating the incident.

F4. Do laws, policies, and practices guarantee equal treatment of various segments of the population? 2 / 4

The law provides for equality of persons. However, same-sex sexual activity is illegal, with punishments of a fine and up to five years' imprisonment. Few women hold positions of responsibility in business outside of elite families. Laws requiring that services be provided for people with disabilities are not well enforced.

G. PERSONAL AUTONOMY AND INDIVIDUAL RIGHTS: 6 / 16

G1. Do individuals enjoy freedom of movement, including the ability to change their place of residence, employment, or education? 2 / 4

Internal and external freedom of movement is constitutionally and legally protected. While these rights are generally respected in practice, poverty frequently prevents travel between the islands as well as access to higher education.

The authorities introduced pandemic-related movement restrictions in March 2020, suspending travel to Mayotte and Réunion. An overnight curfew was imposed in April and remained in effect at year's end.

G2. Are individuals able to exercise the right to own property and establish private businesses without undue interference from state or nonstate actors? 2 / 4

In accordance with civil and some customary laws, women have equal rights in inheritance matters. Local cultures on Grande Comore and Mohéli are matrilineal, with women legally possessing all inheritable property. However, this is complicated by the concurrent application of Sharia, interpretations of which can limit gender equality. In addition, a poor land-registration system and women's difficulties in securing loans hampers their right to own land.

Endemic corruption and a lack of transparency hampers normal business activity.

G3. Do individuals enjoy personal social freedoms, including choice of marriage partner and size of family, protection from domestic violence, and control over appearance? 1 / 4

Early and forced marriages have been reported in Comoros. The law prohibits domestic violence, but courts rarely fine or order the imprisonment of convicted perpetrators, and women and children rarely file official complaints. Sexual violence and workplace harassment are believed to be widespread but are rarely reported to authorities.

G4. Do individuals enjoy equality of opportunity and freedom from economic exploitation? 1 / 4

The Comorian economy, which is primarily agricultural, relies heavily on remittances from Comorian citizens in France. Many young people struggle to find sustainable opportunities for employment. Poverty has driven many people to attempt the dangerous trip to Mayotte.

Government efforts to identify and prosecute human trafficking are minimal, and trafficking cases, if addressed, are often done so through informal mediation processes. These mechanisms have sometimes facilitated the return of trafficking victims to traffickers.

Congo, Republic of (Brazzaville)

Population: 5,500,000
Capital: Brazzaville
Freedom Status: Not Free
Electoral Democracy: No

Overview: President Denis Sassou Nguesso has maintained nearly uninterrupted power for over 40 years by severely repressing the opposition. Corruption and decades of political instability have contributed to poor economic performance and high levels of poverty. Abuses by security forces are frequently reported and rarely investigated. While a variety of media operate, independent coverage is limited by widespread self-censorship and the influence of owners. Human rights and governance-related nongovernmental organizations (NGOs) scrutinize state abuses, but also self-censor to avoid reprisals. Religious figures are also known to self-censor.

KEY DEVELOPMENTS IN 2020:

- The Sassou Nguesso government continued detaining members of opposition groups during the year. Four members of the Embody Hope group who were arrested in 2019 remained in detention through at least April.
- In January, NGO Global Witness reported that the state-run National Petroleum Company of Congo (SNPC) held as much as $3.3 billion in previously undisclosed liabilities, while it was owed nearly $1.2 billion by unidentified debtors.
- Authorities closed borders in response to the COVID-19 pandemic in March, instituting a nationwide curfew that was lifted outside of Brazzaville and Pointe-Noire in September. The government resisted open discussion of the pandemic, with one journalist being suspended from their post after questioning a minister over Congo's response in April. The authorities reported 6,200 cases and 100 deaths to the World Health Organization by year's end.

POLITICAL RIGHTS: 2 / 40
A. ELECTORAL PROCESS: 0 / 12

A1. Was the current head of government or other chief national authority elected through free and fair elections? 0 / 4

The president is directly elected to five-year terms. The 2002 constitution restricted the president to two terms and set an age limit of 70. However, a 2015 constitutional referendum proposed by President Denis Sassou Nguesso removed those restrictions, allowing him to run again. The referendum passed, amidst widespread protests and claims of fraud.

Sassou Nguesso has held power since 1979, with the exception of a five-year period in the 1990s. In March 2016, he secured a third presidential term since returning to power in 1997, winning 60 percent of the vote in an election marked by fraud, intimidation, and an internet shutdown.

A2. Were the current national legislative representatives elected through free and fair elections? 0 / 4

Congo's parliament consists of a 72-seat Senate and a 151-seat National Assembly. Councilors from every department elect senators to six-year terms. National Assembly members are directly elected to five-year terms.

The July 2017 legislative elections were boycotted by several opposition parties amid credible allegations that the vote would be rigged. Sassou Nguesso's Congolese Labor Party (PCT) claimed 96 lower-house seats and its allies won 12, in a process tainted by widespread fraud and low voter turnout. Elections were indefinitely postponed in nine districts in the Pool Region, where the military had been engaged in a campaign against a rebel group accused of launching attacks on Brazzaville.

A3. Are the electoral laws and framework fair, and are they implemented impartially by the relevant election management bodies? 0 / 4

The 2015 constitutional referendum to increase presidential term limits consolidated the PCT's dominance of the political system by allowing Sassou Nguesso to run for a third term. Elections are administered by the Independent National Electoral Commission, which was established in 2016 and is widely regarded as an instrument of presidential authority.

B. POLITICAL PLURALISM AND PARTICIPATION: 2 / 16

B1. Do the people have the right to organize in different political parties or other competitive political groupings of their choice, and is the system free of undue obstacles to the rise and fall of these competing parties or groupings? 1 / 4

Political groupings exist, but the government represses those not aligned with the PCT, including by persecuting their leaders. In 2016, opposition leader Paulin Makaya of the United for Congo party was sentenced to two years' imprisonment for inciting disorder over his participation in protests against the constitutional referendum. Makaya was released in 2018 but was blocked from boarding international flights on at least two subsequent occasions. Members of groups that oppose the PCT remained in detention for at least part of 2020. Four members of Embody Hope, who were arrested in late 2019 for endangering state security, remained in detention through at least April 2020.

Sassou Nguesso's two most prominent opponents in the 2016 presidential election received prison terms after that contest. In 2018, retired general Jean-Marie Michel Mokoko was sentenced to 20 years' imprisonment for threatening state security. Mokoko was allowed to travel to Turkey to seek medical care in July 2020, after his health deteriorated. In 2019, André Okombi Salissa, who had led the opposition Initiative for Democracy in Congo coalition, was sentenced to 20 years of forced labor for the same charge.

Political parties are sometimes denied registration without cause. During the 2017 legislative campaign, the Yuki party was denied official party status, forcing its candidates to run independently.

The government banned private campaign contributions in 2016, leaving opposition parties and candidates dependent on limited public financing.

B2. Is there a realistic opportunity for the opposition to increase its support or gain power through elections? 0 / 4

There is little opportunity for the opposition to gain power through elections, and opposition leaders frequently experience harassment, intimidation, and arrest. Two of Sassou Nguesso's rivals in the 2016 presidential race—Mokoko and Okombi Salissa—were repeatedly harassed during the election campaign and were subsequently imprisoned.

B3. Are the people's political choices free from domination by forces that are external to the political sphere, or by political forces that employ extrapolitical means? 0 / 4

The Sassou Nguesso government routinely uses military and police forces to intimidate citizens. Employers engage in widespread discrimination in hiring and regarding other decisions, based on political beliefs.

B4. Do various segments of the population (including ethnic, racial, religious, gender, LGBT+, and other relevant groups) have full political rights and electoral opportunities? 1 / 4

Although there are no legal restrictions on political participation by religion, gender, sexual identity, or ethnic group, members of Sassou Nguesso's northern Mbochi ethnic group occupy key government posts. Insofar as the government includes representatives from other regional and ethnic groups, their ability to shape policy is very limited. The government also routinely suppresses political parties that draw support from Congo's southern regions, which have long opposed Sassou Nguesso.

Women are underrepresented in government, holding just 17 National Assembly seats and 13 Senate seats. Societal constraints limit women's political participation in practice.

C. FUNCTIONING OF GOVERNMENT: 0 / 12

C1. Do the freely elected head of government and national legislative representatives determine the policies of the government? 0 / 4

Government policy is set by President Sassou Nguesso, who was reelected in a deeply flawed process in 2016. There is little oversight from the parliament, which is dominated by the ruling PCT and protects the executive from accountability.

C2. Are safeguards against official corruption strong and effective? 0 / 4

Corruption is endemic, and domestic prosecutions for corruption are often politically motivated. The president's family and advisers effectively control the SNPC without meaningful oversight, and offshore companies are allegedly used to embezzle SNPC funds.

Sassou Nguesso's family has long been dogged by credible allegations of corruption by foreign governments, prominent NGOs, and journalists, prompting demands for accountability from civil society. In February 2020, French news outlet *Challenges* reported that Denis Christel Sassou Nguesso, the president's son and a Congolese parliamentarian, was indicted by French authorities over money-laundering allegations in late 2019.

C3. Does the government operate with openness and transparency? 0 / 4

Government operations are opaque. Although the constitution guarantees access to information, there is no implementing legislation, nor is there a specific law mandating public access to official information. Public procurement procedures are nontransparent. Authorities generally do not publish draft legislation or regulations.

In January 2020, Global Witness reported that the SNPC held as much as $3.3 billion in undisclosed liabilities, some of which resulted from activities unrelated to oil production, while dividends owed to the government had gone missing. The NGO also reported that the SNPC was owed nearly $1.2 billion by unidentified debtors at the end of 2018.

CIVIL LIBERTIES: 18 / 60

D. FREEDOM OF EXPRESSION AND BELIEF: 7 / 16

D1. Are there free and independent media? 1 / 4

While the constitution provides for freedom of speech and press, the government routinely pressures, threatens, and incarcerates journalists. While there are numerous media outlets, many are owned by government allies who influence their coverage. Widespread self-censorship among journalists discourages independent reporting in practice.

Rocil Otouna, a journalist for state broadcaster Télé Congo, was suspended from his post after questioning the justice minister on Congo's COVID-19 response in late April 2020. In May, the Higher Council for Freedom of Communication, Congo's media regulator, called for Otouna to be returned to his post.

D2. Are individuals free to practice and express their religious faith or nonbelief in public and private? 3 / 4

Although religious freedom is generally respected, pastors are reticent to make statements that could be construed as hostile to the Sassou Nguesso government. In 2015, the government banned the wearing of the niqab, the full-face veil, in public, citing security and terrorism concerns.

D3. Is there academic freedom, and is the educational system free from extensive political indoctrination? 1 / 4

Academic freedom is tenuous. Most university professors avoid discussions of or research on politically sensitive topics. In 2018, the government announced that it would ban a book, published in Paris, about widespread human rights abuses perpetrated by the military in the Pool Region between 2016 and 2017.

D4. Are individuals free to express their personal views on political or other sensitive topics without fear of surveillance or retribution? 2 / 4

The government reportedly surveils electronic communications of private individuals, and those who speak out against the government are occasionally arrested.

E. ASSOCIATIONAL AND ORGANIZATIONAL RIGHTS: 4 / 12
E1. Is there freedom of assembly? 1 / 4

The government restricts freedom of assembly. Groups must receive official authorization from local and federal authorities to hold public assemblies, and permission is routinely denied. Government forces sometimes employ violence against protesters or disperse assemblies. The government used COVID-19-related measures to ban gatherings of more than 50 people. That ban remained in place through year's end.

E2. Is there freedom for nongovernmental organizations, particularly those that are engaged in human rights- and governance-related work? 1 / 4

Although the constitution guarantees freedom of association, NGOs must register with the Ministry of Interior. Those critical of the government often encounter a more burdensome registration process. Arbitrary arrests of civil society figures have continued in recent years, contributing to a reduction in activity. Groups still operating commonly curtail reporting on human rights abuses, or word criticism of authorities carefully, in order to avoid reprisals or harassment.

E3. Is there freedom for trade unions and similar professional or labor organizations? 2 / 4

Although union rights are nominally protected, laws protecting union members are not always enforced. The government has intervened in labor disputes by harassing and arresting laborers and pressuring union leaders, particularly against the country's largest labor union, the Congolese Trade Union Confederation.

F. RULE OF LAW: 1 / 16

F1. Is there an independent judiciary? 0 / 4

Congo's judiciary is dominated by Sassou Nguesso's allies, crippled by lack of resources, and vulnerable to corruption and political influence. In 2015, the Constitutional Court's confirmation of the constitutional referendum results was viewed as a rubber-stamp approval of Sassou Nguesso's efforts to remain in power.

F2. Does due process prevail in civil and criminal matters? 1 / 4

Defendants, including the government's political opponents, are routinely denied due process. Arbitrary arrests and detentions are common, despite being prohibited by the constitution. Other fair-trial rights guaranteed by law, including the right to legal assistance for those who cannot afford it, are not always honored in practice.

F3. Is there protection from the illegitimate use of physical force and freedom from war and insurgencies? 0 / 4

Citizens in some neighborhoods are at risk of intimidation and violent crime by groups of young men known as *bébés noirs*. There have also been reports of arbitrary arrests and physical abuses by police attempting to curb the activities of such groups. Reports of human rights violations by security forces are generally not investigated by the government.

In May 2020, video emerged of security forces physically attacking individuals who did not wear face masks as they enforced COVID-19-related measures.

F4. Do laws, policies, and practices guarantee equal treatment of various segments of the population? 0 / 4

Employment discrimination against women persists. The government prevents refugees and other foreign workers from holding certain jobs, and refugees sometimes face harassment and arrest by authorities.

While no law specifically prohibits same-sex sexual relations between adults, LGBT+ people experience occasional police harassment.

Minority ethnic groups experience severe discrimination in employment, housing, and education. Some communities often live in substandard housing on the outskirts of villages, and occasionally are targeted in acts of violence committed by members of the majority Bantu population.

The government exhibits widespread discrimination against residents of Congo's southern regions. They are routinely denied high-paying public-sector jobs, as well as admission to the public university. By contrast, residents of Congo's northern regions are disproportionately appointed to key government positions and the civil service.

G. PERSONAL AUTONOMY AND INDIVIDUAL RIGHTS: 6 / 16

G1. Do individuals enjoy freedom of movement, including the ability to change their place of residence, employment, or education? 2 / 4

Although private citizens generally enjoy freedom of movement, activists and opposition leaders can face restrictions and confiscation of their passports.

The 2016–17 conflict in Pool led to the displacement of many of its residents. An estimated 81,000 people left their homes.

The government imposed a COVID-19-related curfew in late March 2020 and closed the country's borders except for cargo traffic. Authorities also restricted nonessential travel in and out of Brazzaville and Pointe-Noire in May. Movement restrictions were loosened outside of those areas that month, as interregional travel resumed. Curfews were lifted outside of Brazzaville and Pointe-Noire in late September. Only Brazzaville and Pointe-Noire were subject to overnight curfews by December.

G2. Are individuals able to exercise the right to own property and establish private businesses without undue interference from state or nonstate actors? 2 / 4

Legal protections for business and property rights can be undermined by bureaucracy, poor judicial safeguards, and corruption. The government directly or indirectly controls property in key industries such as oil, minerals, and aviation.

G3. Do individuals enjoy personal social freedoms, including choice of marriage partner and size of family, protection from domestic violence, and control over appearance? 1 / 4

Violence against women, including domestic violence and rape, is widespread, but rarely reported. There are no specific laws forbidding domestic violence other than general assault statutes.

Men are legally considered the head of the household, and divorce settlements are thus skewed against women. Adultery is illegal for both men and women, but women convicted of the crime face a potential prison sentence, while the penalty for men is a fine.

G4. Do individuals enjoy equality of opportunity and freedom from economic exploitation? 1 / 4

Congo is a source and destination country for human trafficking, and allegations of complicity have been lodged against government officials. However, the US State Department reported in its 2020 *Trafficking in Persons Report* that authorities strengthened their efforts to address the problem by providing more assistance to victims, adopting broad antitrafficking laws, and prosecuting more alleged traffickers.

According to local NGOs, members of minority groups have been conscripted into forced farm labor by members of the Bantu ethnic majority. Child labor laws are reportedly not effectively enforced.

Congo, Democratic Republic of (Kinshasa)

Population: 89,600,000
Capital: Kinshasa
Freedom Status: Not Free
Electoral Democracy: No

Overview: The political system in the Democratic Republic of Congo (DRC) has been paralyzed in recent years by the manipulation of the electoral process by political elites. Citizens are unable to freely exercise basic civil liberties, and corruption is endemic. Physical security is tenuous due to violence and human rights abuses committed by government forces, as well as armed rebel groups and militias that are active in many areas of the country.

KEY DEVELOPMENTS IN 2020

- In April, President Félix Tshisekedi's chief of staff, Vital Kamerhe, became the highest-ranking public official to face corruption charges and was sentenced to

20 years' forced labor in June. Fulgence Lobota Bamaros, another official and an ally of former president Joseph Kabila, was convicted of embezzlement in June, receiving a three-year sentence.

- The Tshisekedi administration successfully appointed several high-ranking judges during the year, replacing several judges accused of corruption in February and appointing three Constitutional Court members in July. The judiciary also showed new signs of independence during the year, resisting intimidation and political opposition to its efforts to hear major corruption cases.
- In December, Tshisekedi announced the dissolution of a power-sharing government that had included the Course for Change (CACH) coalition and the Common Front for Congo (FCC) of former president Kabila. The coalition government, which was formed in 2019, was marred by disagreements between the two factions over matters including government appointments and oversight.
- The authorities restricted assemblies and instituted lockdowns in March, as the COVID-19 pandemic became a critical concern, but those restrictions were inconsistently enforced to disrupt antigovernment assemblies. The World Health Organization reported 17,000 cases and 584 deaths at the end of the year.

POLITICAL RIGHTS: 5 / 40 (+1)
A. ELECTORAL PROCESS: 1 / 12
A1. Was the current head of government or other chief national authority elected through free and fair elections? 0 / 4

According to the constitution, the president is chief of state and is elected for a maximum of two five-year terms. The prime minister is head of government, and is formally appointed by the president.

Former president Joseph Kabila overstayed his constitutional mandate by two years, leaving the DRC without an elected head of government for a period starting in late 2016. A Constitutional Court ruling that year allowed him to remain in office until a successor was in place, but elections were repeatedly postponed by the Independent National Electoral Commission (CENI), despite mediation effects by the Roman Catholic Church's National Episcopal Conference of Congo (CENCO), until late December 2018.

In January 2019, Félix Tshisekedi was declared the victor of the preceding month's presidential election with 38.6 percent of the vote, defeating Martin Fayulu of the Lamuka (Wake Up) coalition, who secured 34.8 percent according to CENI. Tshisekedi, a leader of the Course for Change (CACH) coalition, was believed to have secured the presidency via a backroom deal—meant to preserve political influence for Kabila—under which he allied himself with the Kabila-led Common Front for Congo (FCC). The FCC had previously backed Emmanuel Ramazani Shadary, who received 23.9 percent of the vote as the People's Party for Reconstruction and Democracy (PPRD) candidate. Several opposition candidates were barred from competing in the poll.

The polls were heavily criticized due to voter suppression and electoral fraud. Observers from the Catholic Church and the civil society coalition Synergy of Citizen Election Observation Missions reported massive fraud and irregularities. CENCO reported widespread ballot-validation procedure violations, large vote-counting discrepancies, and confusion over the locations of vote-counting centers. CENCO's tally—reportedly reviewed by multiple independent auditors—supported their contention that Fayulu won 60 percent of the vote. Election observers were denied access to polling stations in some cases, and foreign observers were not allowed to participate.

CENI only released a national tally, impeding observers in their efforts to determine where tampering occurred. However, 1.2 million voters were disenfranchised when citizens in three opposition areas—Beni territory and Butembo in North Kivu Province and Yumbi in Mai-Ndombe Province—were prevented from voting, officially for security and public health concerns; residents viewed the decision as politically motivated. Official results reported a margin of victory that was a little over half the number of voters disenfranchised in opposition areas.

In May 2019, Sylvestre Ilunga Ilukamba, a Kabila ally, was appointed prime minister, and remained in his post at the end of 2020.

A2. Were the current national legislative representatives elected through free and fair elections? 1 / 4

The DRC has a bicameral national legislature with a 500-seat National Assembly directly elected for five-year terms, and a 108-seat Senate elected by provincial assemblies. Senators hold a five-year mandate. The DRC's 715 provincial legislators elect national senators and provincial governors. Eight Senate seats are reserved for customary chiefs.

National Assembly elections were held concurrently with the presidential vote in December 2018 and were also criticized as deeply flawed. The FCC won 341 seats, Lamuka took 112, and the CACH took 47. Because elections were postponed until March 2019 in opposition areas of Beni, Butembo, and Yumbi, voters in these areas were prevented from influencing the National Assembly race.

Senate elections were held in March 2019, with the FCC taking 91 seats. As former president, Kabila holds a lifetime Senate appointment. Provincial elections, last held in December 2018, were compromised by vote buying, so national senators are not freely elected.

A3. Are the electoral laws and framework fair, and are they implemented impartially by the relevant election management bodies? 0 / 4

The country's electoral framework does not ensure transparent elections in practice. Opposition parties and civil society frequently criticize CENI and the Constitutional Court for lacking independence and for pro-Kaliba bias. Throughout 2018 and 2019, the political opposition repeatedly protested that the electoral process was unfair, and Fayulu unsuccessfully appealed the presidential election's result to the Constitutional Court in January 2019. One month later, the United States announced diplomatic sanctions on the then president and vice president of CENI, the National Assembly president, and the chief judge of the Constitutional Court, for electoral fraud.

In July 2020, the National Assembly nominated CENI secretary general Ronsard Malonda, a Kabila ally, as the electoral authority's president. Lamuka, civil society groups, and the Catholic Church objected, noting Malonda's tenure as secretary general while compromised provincial elections were held in 2018. The nomination prompted protests that month, and President Tshisekedi rejected the nomination soon after.

B. POLITICAL PLURALISM AND PARTICIPATION: 2 / 16

B1. Do the people have the right to organize in different political parties or other competitive political groupings of their choice, and is the system free of undue obstacles to the rise and fall of these competing parties or groupings? 1 / 4

People have the right to organize political parties. Hundreds of parties exist, with many configured along ethnic or regional lines. However, most lack national reach, and their ability to function is limited in practice. Opposition leaders and supporters are often intimidated and face restrictions on movements and rights to campaign or organize public events.

Opposition and government coalitions shifted before and after the December 2018 elections. In 2018, Kabila formed the FCC, which included parliamentary leaders, governors, and some civil society members and journalists. Lamuka, meanwhile, selected Fayulu as its presidential candidate and counts former rebel leader Jean-Pierre Bemba Gombo as a senior official. Tshisekedi leads the Union for Democracy and Social Progress (UDPS), a member of CACH.

CACH finalized a power-sharing government with the FCC in August 2019. However, that power-sharing government was felled by major disagreements between the two factions, leading President Tshisekedi to announce its collapse and vow to assemble a new coalition in December 2020.

Under the Tshisekedi administration, some opposition members have been released from prison, and some politicians living in exile were permitted to return. However, political party officials still faced reprisals for criticizing the power-sharing government. In May 2020, Henri Magie, the leader of the PPRD's youth wing, was accused of contempt for suggesting that Tshisekedi did not win the 2018 elections, and received an 18-month prison sentence in July.

B2. Is there a realistic opportunity for the opposition to increase its support or gain power through elections? 0 / 4

Although opposition groups enjoy significant public support, the repeated postponement of and government interference in elections have prevented the opposition from gaining power through electoral competition.

The government prevented an opposition coalition from rising to power despite evidence that it won the vote in 2018. In the run-up to those elections, the CENI rejected the candidacy of six opposition politicians, including Bemba and former Katanga governor Moïse Katumbi, who had entered self-imposed exile in 2016 and returned to the DRC in 2019. Government authorities regularly blocked or delayed the campaign activities of opposition candidates. Authorities helped facilitate the movement and campaign activities of Kabila's favored candidate. Nonstate armed groups also obstructed candidate movements.

B3. Are the people's political choices free from domination by forces that are external to the political sphere, or by political forces that employ extrapolitical means? 0 / 4

The military, security services, and armed rebel or militia groups interfere with citizens' political choices. Systematic repression in major cities across the country intensified in the lead-up to the December 2018 elections, including excessive force against opposition demonstrators by government personnel who employed tear gas and live ammunition, as well as reports of people being paid to provoke violence during opposition rallies. In some areas, soldiers and armed groups at polling stations reportedly coerced voters to cast ballots for the FCC. Armed groups also hindered citizens' ability to participate in the political process.

B4. Do various segments of the population (including ethnic, racial, religious, gender, LGBT+, and other relevant groups) have full political rights and electoral opportunities? 1 / 4

Lack of access to public services and state institutions in rural areas hinders political participation. While women are politically underrepresented, female politicians hold more seats in the parliament selected in 2018 and 2019 than in the previous body, holding 64 lower-house seats and 23 Senate seats. Internally displaced people throughout the country, meanwhile, face practical obstacles to participating in elections.

C. FUNCTIONING OF GOVERNMENT: 2 / 12 (+1)

C1. Do the freely elected head of government and national legislative representatives determine the policies of the government? 0 / 4

Massive electoral fraud and irregularities prevent democratically elected officials from determining government policies. Prior to the December 2018 and March 2019 elections, the incumbent president, national legislature, and provincial assemblies had exceeded their electoral mandates by two years or more.

While former president Kabila maintained political power through the FCC's governing agreement with CACH, the two coalitions came into conflict throughout the year, impeding the business of government. In January, for example, Tshisekedi claimed that pro-Kaliba legislators were obstructing his government, and threatened to dissolve the body.

C2. Are safeguards against official corruption strong and effective? 1 / 4 (+1)

Corruption in the government, security forces, and mineral extraction industries is extensive and has corroded public services and development efforts. Appointments to high-level positions in government are often determined by nepotism. Accountability mechanisms are weak, and impunity is commonplace.

President Tshisekedi publicly committed the government to fighting corruption, and created a Corruption Prevention and Combating Agency (APLC) by decree in March 2020. However, the creation of the APLC, which possesses broad powers, was controversial, with an opposition legislator publicly criticizing the fact that the APLC was not created via legislation. In December, agency head Ghislain Kikangalao was arrested on suspicion of embezzling funds from a Nigerian bank.

Major corruption cases surfaced during 2020. In April, Tshisekedi's chief of staff, Vital Kamerhe, was charged with embezzling over $50 million in public funds earmarked for an infrastructure program. Kamerhe, the highest-ranking DRC politician to face such a prosecution, was convicted in late June, receiving a 20-year forced-labor sentence that he vowed to appeal. Also in April, the Court of Cassation issued an arrest warrant for public official Patient Sayiba Tambwe, who was accused of misappropriating public funds; Sayiba was detained and interrogated for several days in September before he was released. In April, prosecutors issued a warrant against Kaliba ally Fulgence Lobota Bamaros for misappropriating $50 million in infrastructure funds. In June, Lobota received a three-year labor sentence.

In June 2020, Deputy Health Minister Albert M'peti Biyombo warned Prime Minister Ilukamba that other cabinet members may have participated in a kickback scheme that involved the DRC's COVID-19 response efforts.

Score Change: The score improved from 0 to 1 due to signs of greater political will to combat corruption, including the conviction of President Tshisekedi's chief of staff in an embezzlement case.

C3. Does the government operate with openness and transparency? 1 / 4

Despite previous, incremental improvements in revenue reporting, there is little transparency in the state's financial affairs. The law does not provide for public access to government information, and citizens often lack the practical ability to obtain records on public expenditures and state operations. Required financial disclosures from top officials have not typically been made public.

CIVIL LIBERTIES: 15 / 60 (+1)

D. FREEDOM OF EXPRESSION AND BELIEF: 7 / 16

D1. Are there free and independent media? 1 / 4

Although press freedom is constitutionally guaranteed, journalists often face criminal defamation suits, threats, detentions, arbitrary arrests, and physical attacks in the course of their work. Radio is the dominant medium, and newspapers and state-sponsored news channels are found in large cities. While journalists frequently criticize authorities, political harassment of reporters is common, and authorities have sometimes attempted to shutter media outlets. Some foreign reporters were barred from the country during the last national elections. Artists also face government reprisal.

When President Tshisekedi came to power in 2019, he pledged to improve the DRC's media environment. Despite this pledge, journalists continued to face detention, government scrutiny, and physical attack in 2020, with authorities sometimes using COVID-19 measures to justify those actions. In late March, police officers in the city of Likasi chased and physically attacked reporter Tholi Totali Glody after he informed them that he was covering the COVID-19 lockdown. In May, journalist Fabrice Ngani was arrested along with three local activists for delivering a critical letter to the governor of Mongala Province. Ngani was released in June, but was banned from reporting by the provincial government. In November, nongovernmental organization (NGO) Journalists in Danger reported that a total of 40 journalists were detained, 1 was killed, and another was missing in the DRC in the year to date.

D2. Are individuals free to practice and express their religious faith or nonbelief in public and private? 3 / 4

The constitution guarantees freedom of religion, and authorities generally respect this right in practice. Although religious groups must register with the government to be recognized, unregistered groups typically operate unhindered. Some church facilities, personnel, and services have been affected by violence in conflict areas. Despite this overall tolerance, the authorities responded aggressively to protest activities by the Catholic Church and some Protestant groups following the announcement of election results in 2019, sometimes entailing in violence in and around places of worship.

The government has also used violence in its efforts to suppress the Bundu dia Kongo (BDK), a religious movement that calls for autonomy in Kongo Central Province. In late April 2020, police in the town of Songololo killed at least 15 people when firing into, and then setting fire to, a home where BDK members were meeting. Several days later, BDK leader Zacharie Badiengila was detained in Kinshasa after negotiations to secure his surrender failed; Human Rights Watch (HRW) reported that at least 33 BDK members were killed in the subsequent raid.

D3. Is there academic freedom, and is the educational system free from extensive political indoctrination? 2 / 4

There are no formal restrictions on academic freedom. Primary and secondary school curriculums are regulated but not strongly politicized. However, political events and protests at universities and schools are subject to violent repression. Armed group attacks have also targeted schools, preventing children from accessing education.

D4. Are individuals free to express their personal views on political or other sensitive topics without fear of surveillance or retribution? 1 / 4

Open political dissent is routinely suppressed, though Congolese can express their views on some subjects. When presidential chief of staff Kamerhe was tried for corruption in 2020, many Congolese openly discussed systemic corruption on social media platforms.

E. ASSOCIATIONAL AND ORGANIZATIONAL RIGHTS: 3 / 12

E1. Is there freedom of assembly? 1 / 4

The constitution guarantees freedom of assembly, and demonstrations are held regularly, but those who participate risk arrests, beatings, and lethal violence. Assemblies of larger than 20 people were banned in March 2020, under COVID-19 restrictions that were used to disrupt opposition protests.

Despite these historical and pandemic-related restrictions, major assemblies and rallies were nevertheless held in 2020. In April, 300 supporters of Vital Kamerhe blocked a road in the town of Bukavu in opposition to his arrest on corruption charges. Demonstrators opposed FCC-backed reforms to the prosecutorial system in protests held in June; some of the participants in the Kinshasa demonstration used incendiary devices and blocked traffic, and security forces used tear gas to disperse them. In July, nationwide protests were held in opposition to the attempted appointment of Ronsard Malonda to the CENI presidency. At least six people died in those protests, and authorities in Kinshasa used tear gas to disperse another anti-Malonda protest held later in the month.

E2. Is there freedom for nongovernmental organizations, particularly those engaged in human rights– and governance-related work? 1 / 4

Thousands of NGOs are active in the DRC, but many face obstacles to their work. Domestic human rights advocates in particular are subject to harassment, arbitrary arrest, and detention. In May 2020, the UN Joint Human Rights Office in Congo publicly criticized their ongoing treatment.

Female NGO workers in the health-care field have been subjected to sexual exploitation in the DRC. In September 2020, the New Humanitarian and Reuters reported that individuals supporting an Ebola response effort in the DRC were regularly forced to engage in sex acts to gain employment from NGOs and the Health Ministry.

E3. Is there freedom for trade unions and similar professional or labor organizations? 1 / 4

A number of national labor unions and professional associations, covering parts of the public and private sectors, operate legally in the DRC, but the overwhelming majority of workers are informally employed. Some civil servants and members of state security forces are not permitted to unionize and bargain collectively. Violations of the procedures for a legal strike can result in prison terms. Although it is against the law for employers to retaliate against workers for union activities, such legal protections are poorly enforced.

F. RULE OF LAW: 1 / 16 (+1)

F1. Is there an independent judiciary? 1 / 4 (+1)

The judiciary is often seen as corrupt and subject to political manipulation. It often shows bias against the opposition and civil society, while government allies typically enjoy impunity for abuses.

The Tshisekedi administration replaced several judges suspected of corruption in February 2020, when it appointed six high-ranking judges. In July, Tshisekedi appointed three judges to the Constitutional Court, who were sworn in at an October ceremony despite FCC claims that their appointments were unconstitutional.

The judicial branch also showed greater independence in trying officials suspected of wrongdoing in 2020. In April, then justice minister Célestin Tunda called on the Court of Cassation to rescind its warrant against government official Patient Sayiba Tambwe, but the court declined. The judiciary also oversaw the notable corruption trial of Vital Kamerhe despite the suspicious death of the trial's first judge in May.

Score Change: The score improved from 0 to 1 due to the replacement of flawed judicial officials and the courts' ability to resist attempted political interference in high-profile corruption cases.

F2. Does due process prevail in civil and criminal matters? 0 / 4

Courts are concentrated in urban areas; rural areas rely on customary courts. Informal justice mechanisms are common throughout the country. Civilians are often tried in military courts, which have weak safeguards for defendants' rights, poor witness protection mechanisms, and are subject to interference from high-ranking military personnel. Arbitrary arrests and detentions are common, as is prolonged pretrial detention. Much of the prison population consists of pretrial detainees.

Courts have inconsistently provided justice for killings or other severe crimes in recent years. In November 2020, a military court convicted militia leader Ntabo Ntaberi Sheka and two codefendants of war crimes perpetrated in the Walikale and Masisi territories, with Sheka and one codefendant receiving life sentences. However, courts have failed to provide justice for police killings or massacres in South Kivu Province and the Beni territory in North Kivu Province that have together resulted in over 3,000 civilian deaths over the past six years. DRC courts have officially granted reparations to the targets of sexual violence and other serious crimes, but these are rarely paid in practice.

Pro-Kabila legislators sought to lessen the independence of prosecutors through a legislative proposal that would have given the justice minister more prosecutorial control in June 2020. The proposal was denounced by CACH and Lamuka legislators and President Tshisekedi. The parliament suspended its consideration in early July. Pro-Kaliba Justice Minister Tunda resigned later that month after facing accusations of bypassing the government to support the proposal.

F3. Is there protection from the illegitimate use of physical force and freedom from war and insurgencies? 0 / 4

Prison conditions are life-threatening, and torture of detainees is common. Civilian authorities do not effectively control security forces. The military is notoriously undisciplined. Incidents of soldiers exchanging intelligence and weapons with rebel or militia groups continued during 2020. Soldiers and police regularly commit serious human rights abuses, including rape and other physical attacks, and high-ranking military officials enjoy impunity for crimes.

Government forces have participated in summary killings and forced disappearances, and the judicial system has not held officials accountable. Senior intelligence officials accused of serious human rights abuses have not been tried for their acts. In July 2020, General Gabriel Amisi Kumba, who was sanctioned by the United States and European Union for human rights abuses, was appointed army chief, succeeding another general who faced sanctions.

Armed groups have contributed to years of conflicts and communal violence that have had a catastrophic impact on civilians, with over five million conflict-related deaths since

1998. Despite continued attempts to demobilize combatants, the Kivu Security Tracker counted approximately 130 armed groups in the DRC in 2020.

F4. Do laws, policies, and practices guarantee equal treatment of various segments of the population? 0 / 4

Ethnic discrimination is common, and is both a contributing factor and an outcome of armed conflicts across the country. While the constitution prohibits discrimination against people with disabilities, they often encounter obstacles to finding employment, attending school, or accessing government services. Discrimination based on HIV status is also prohibited, but people with HIV similarly face difficulties accessing health care and education. LGBT+ people can be prosecuted for same-sex sexual activity under public decency laws.

Although the constitution prohibits discrimination against women, in practice they face discrimination in nearly every aspect of their lives, especially in rural areas. The family code assigns women a subordinate role in the household. Young women are increasingly seeking professional work outside the home, particularly in urban centers, though they continue to face disparities in wages and promotions. When families are short on money to pay school fees, boys are often favored over girls to receive education.

Across the country, people seen as "outsiders" to a specific town or province face discrimination. In Haut-Katanga Province, for example, tensions exist between residents and migrants from the Kasaï regions, many of whom are members of the Luba tribe. The BDK, meanwhile, has called for the expulsion of "nonnative" residents from areas where they are active. Members of the Banyarwanda lingual group have faced a lack of clarity over their political status within the DRC and, in some cases, internal displacement at the hands of militia groups.

G. PERSONAL AUTONOMY AND INDIVIDUAL RIGHTS: 4 / 16

G1. Do individuals enjoy freedom of movement, including the ability to change their place of residence, employment, or education? 1 / 4

Freedom of movement is protected by law but seriously curtailed in practice, in large part due to armed conflicts and other security problems. An estimated 5.5 million people were internally displaced at the end of 2019 according to the Internal Displacement Monitoring Centre. Various armed groups and government forces impose illegal tolls on travelers passing through territory under their control.

G2. Are individuals able to exercise the right to own property and establish private businesses without undue interference from state or nonstate actors? 1 / 4

Individuals have the right to own property and establish private businesses. In conflict zones, armed groups and government soldiers have seized private property and destroyed homes. Property ownership and business activity are also hampered by pervasive corruption and a complicated system of taxation and regulation that encourages bribery.

Although the constitution prohibits discrimination against women, some laws and customary practices put women at a disadvantage with respect to inheritance and land ownership.

G3. Do individuals enjoy personal social freedoms, including choice of marriage partner and size of family, protection from domestic violence, and control over appearance? 1 / 4

Sexual and gender-based violence is common; sex crimes affect women, girls, men, and boys. Rebel fighters and government soldiers have regularly been implicated in rape and sexual abuse. Rebel commanders have abducted girls into forced marriages. Convictions for these offenses remain rare. Abortion is prohibited except to save the life of a pregnant woman, and illegal abortions can draw lengthy prison sentences.

The family code obliges wives to obey their husbands, who are designated as the heads of their households. Married women are under the legal guardianship of their husbands. Although the legal minimum age for marriage is 18, many women are married earlier.

G4. Do individuals enjoy equality of opportunity and freedom from economic exploitation? 1 / 4

Formal protections against economic exploitation are poorly enforced, and most Congolese are informally employed. Although the law prohibits all forced or compulsory labor, such practices are common and include forced child labor in mining, street vending, domestic service, and agriculture. Some government forces and other armed groups force civilians to work for them, and the recruitment and use of child soldiers remains widespread. Working conditions can be life threatening. Accidents are common in the mining sector, and safety precautions are rarely enforced.

Costa Rica

Population: 5,100,000
Capital: San José
Freedom Status: Free
Electoral Democracy: Yes

Overview: Costa Rica has a long history of democratic stability, with a multiparty political system and regular rotations of power through credible elections. Freedoms of expression and association are robust. The rule of law is generally strong, though presidents have often been implicated in corruption scandals. Among other ongoing concerns, Indigenous people face discrimination, and land disputes involving Indigenous communities persist.

KEY DEVEOPMENTS IN 2020

- Costa Rica successfully managed the first wave of the COVID-19 pandemic, but cases rose continuously during the second half of the year; according to researchers at the University of Oxford, the country registered over 169,000 cases and nearly 2,200 deaths by year's end.
- In May, Costa Rica became the first Central American country to permit same-sex marriage.
- Attacks against Indigenous activists related to land disputes were a cause for serious concern, with one leader killed and another wounded in February.
- Large-scale protests broke out in October in response to a proposed tax hike linked to an International Monetary Fund (IMF) loan agreement. Protesters responded violently to police sent to dismantle road blockades, resulting in arrests and injuries.

POLITICAL RIGHTS: 38 / 40

A. ELECTORAL PROCESS: 12 / 12

A1. Was the current head of government or other chief national authority elected through free and fair elections? 4 / 4

The president is directly elected for a four-year term and can seek a nonconsecutive second term. Presidential candidates must win 40 percent of the vote to avoid a runoff. In April 2018, Carlos Alvarado Quesada of the governing Citizen Action Party (PAC) was elected president in the second round of voting. Alvarado faced Fabricio Alvarado Muñoz of the evangelical National Restoration Party (PRN) in the runoff and won decisively, with over 60 percent of the vote.

A2. Were the current national legislative representatives elected through free and fair elections? 4 / 4

Elections for the 57-seat unicameral Legislative Assembly occur every four years, and deputies are elected by proportional representation. Deputies may not run for two consecutive terms, but may run again after skipping a term. In the February 2018 legislative elections, which were held concurrently with the first round of the presidential poll, no party came close to winning a majority. The PAC took 10 seats, the PRN won 14, and the National Liberation Party (PLN), historically one of the most powerful parties in Costa Rican politics, won 17 seats.

A3. Are the electoral laws and framework fair, and are they implemented impartially by the relevant election management bodies? 4 / 4

A special chamber of the Supreme Court appoints the independent national election commission, the Supreme Electoral Tribunal (TSE), which is responsible for administering elections. The TSE carries out its functions impartially and the electoral framework is fair.

B. POLITICAL PLURALISM AND PARTICIPATION: 15 / 16

B1. Do the people have the right to organize in different political parties or other competitive political groupings of their choice, and is the system free of undue obstacles to the rise and fall of these competing parties or groupings? 4 / 4

People have the right to organize in different political parties without undue obstacles. The historical dominance of the PLN and the Social Christian Unity Party (PUSC) has waned in recent years, as newly formed parties have gained traction, leading to the collapse of the traditional two-party system. (Seven parties won seats in the 2018 legislative elections). The PRN, which was founded in 2005, emerged as a major force in politics in 2018, as evidenced by Alvarado Muñoz's second-place finish in the presidential election and the party's relatively strong showing in the legislative elections.

B2. Is there a realistic opportunity for the opposition to increase its support or gain power through elections? 4 / 4

Power regularly alternates in Costa Rica and opposition parties compete fiercely in presidential and legislative elections. Parties along a wide spectrum of the political order freely competed in the 2018 elections, and the PRN made major gains, winning 14 seats in the legislature after capturing just 1 seat in the 2014 contest.

B3. Are the people's political choices free from domination by forces that are external to the political sphere, or by political forces that employ extrapolitical means? 4 / 4

Citizens' political choices are free from domination by unelected elites and other undemocratic powers.

B4. Do various segments of the population (including ethnic, racial, religious, gender, LGBT+, and other relevant groups) have full political rights and electoral opportunities? 3 / 4

Members of religious, racial, ethnic, and other minority groups enjoy full political rights in Costa Rica, though some groups remain underrepresented in government. Indigenous rights have not historically been prioritized by politicians, and there are no Indigenous representatives in the legislature. Afro-Costa Ricans are also underrepresented in national-level government, though in 2018 Epsy Campbell Barr became the first Afro-Costa Rican woman to serve as vice president. In May 2020, Eduardo Cruickshank became the first Afro-Costa Rican to be elected president of the legislature. In 2018, the first openly gay legislative deputy was elected.

The government has introduced initiatives to increase women's political participation, such as the institution of gender quotas in order to ensure gender parity in political parties. Women and women's interests are represented in government—46 percent of seats in the Legislative Assembly are held by women following the 2018 elections.

C. FUNCTIONING OF GOVERNMENT: 11 / 12

C1. Do the freely elected head of government and national legislative representatives determine the policies of the government? 4 / 4

Costa Rica's freely elected government and lawmakers set and implement state policy without interference. However, legislative gridlock remains a systemic issue.

C2. Are safeguards against official corruption strong and effective? 3 / 4

Costa Rica's anticorruption laws are generally well enforced. However, despite its functioning anticorruption mechanisms, nearly every president since 1990 has been accused of corruption after leaving office. In 2017, former president Luis Guillermo Solís was implicated in the Cementazo scandal, involving influence peddling related to Chinese cement exports to Costa Rica. A legislative commission found that close to 30 people, including prominent officials from all three branches of government, were involved in the scandal. Although he was cleared of wrongdoing by the Public Ethics Office of the Attorney General in April 2018, in July 2019 the attorney general announced that Solís was being investigated.

C3. Does the government operate with openness and transparency? 4 / 4

Citizens generally have access to government information. However, there are some deficiencies in the reporting of budgets to the public, including a lack of transparency in communicating the objectives of the annual budget. Senior government officials are required to make financial disclosures, but that information is not available to the public.

CIVIL LIBERTIES: 53 / 60
D. FREEDOM OF EXPRESSION AND BELIEF: 16 / 16
D1. Are there free and independent media? 4 / 4

Freedom of the press is largely respected in Costa Rica. Defamation laws are on the books, but imprisonment was removed as a punishment for defamation in 2010.

D2. Are individuals free to practice and express their religious faith or nonbelief in public and private? 4 / 4

Roman Catholicism is the official religion, but the constitution guarantees the freedom of religion, which is generally respected in practice.

D3. Is there academic freedom, and is the educational system free from extensive political indoctrination? 4 / 4

Academic freedom is constitutionally protected and generally upheld.

D4. Are individuals free to express their personal views on political or other sensitive topics without fear of surveillance or retribution? 4 / 4

Private discussion is free and the government is not known to surveil the electronic communications of Costa Ricans.

E. ASSOCIATIONAL AND ORGANIZATIONAL RIGHTS: 11 / 12

E1. Is there freedom of assembly? 4 / 4

Freedom of assembly is constitutionally protected, and this right is largely upheld in practice. A diverse range of groups, including LGBT+ and environmental organizations, hold regular rallies and protests without government interference. In October 2020, widespread protests forced the government to withdraw a proposed tax increase and IMF loan agreement. Some of the protests turned violent; authorities reported that more than 100 police officers were injured, including when protesters responded with firebombs and other violence as officers tried to dismantle roadblocks.

E2. Is there freedom for nongovernmental organizations, particularly those that are engaged in human rights- and governance-related work? 4 / 4

Nongovernmental organizations (NGOs), including those engaged in human rights work, are active and do not encounter undue obstacles.

In March 2019, Indigenous land rights activist Sergio Rojas was murdered at his home. Prosecutors sought to close the case without resolution in September 2020, but a court ruled in December that the investigation must continue.

E3. Is there freedom for trade unions and similar professional or labor organizations? 3 / 4

Although labor unions are free to organize and mount frequent protests and strikes with minimal governmental interference, the law requires a minimum of 12 employees to form a union, which may negatively impact union rights at small enterprises. Rates of union membership in the private sector are low, due in part to discrimination by employers against union members. Employers have been known to occasionally fire workers who attempt to form unions.

There were recurring strikes in 2019, including a strike by Social Security Service workers. In January 2020, President Alvarado signed into law a bill restricting strikes by public sector employees. Among its features are limits on permitted justifications for strikes, and salary suspensions for workers who participate in strikes deemed illegal.

F. RULE OF LAW: 13 / 16

F1. Is there an independent judiciary? 4 / 4

The judicial branch is generally independent and impartial. Supreme Court judges are elected by a supermajority of the legislature. Prosecutors and the judges are able to investigate public officials. In February 2020, the Attorney General's Office opened a criminal investigation into President Alvarado and other high-ranking officials in connection with alleged misuse of Costa Ricans' personal information by a data analysis office within the presidency. The investigation, along with a parallel inquiry by legislators, continued at year's end.

F2. Does due process prevail in civil and criminal matters? 3 / 4

Due process rights are enshrined in the constitution, and they are protected for the most part. However, there are often substantial delays in judicial processes, at times resulting in lengthy pretrial detention.

F3. Is there protection from the illegitimate use of physical force and freedom from war and insurgencies? 3 / 4

Violent crime in Costa Rica has increased in recent years. In 2020, the country documented 568 murders, a rate of approximately 11.1 murders per 100,000 people. Criminal groups transport drugs along the Pacific coast, and the government has reported that many homicides there are related to organized crime and drug trafficking. There are reports of occasional police abuses of detainees and civilians, including violence and degrading treatment; confirmed cases are generally investigated and prosecuted.

Overcrowding, poor sanitation, insufficient access to health care, and violence remain serious problems in Costa Rica's prisons. Although Costa Rica did not have a reported case of COVID-19 in prisons until July 2020, by mid-December over 2,700 prisoners and staff had tested positive for the virus, and 13 prisoners had died. Recurrent abuse by prison police has not been thoroughly investigated due to victims' reluctance to file formal complaints.

F4. Do laws, policies, and practices guarantee equal treatment of various segments of the population? 3 / 4

The constitution outlines equal rights for all people, but these rights are upheld unevenly. Indigenous people, who compose 3 percent of the population, continue to face discrimination, particularly in regard to land rights and access to basic services. Land disputes between Indigenous and non-Indigenous peoples have been a source of tension for years. A 1977 Indigenous Law formalized Indigenous groups' exclusive rights to some territories, but the government has failed to implement the law or provide compensation to non-Indigenous settlers who continue to occupy the land. Conflict with settlers has resulted in Indigenous groups being targeted in recent years by harassing lawsuits and violence committed with impunity. Bribri leader Sergio Rojas was murdered in 2019, and in February 2020 Brörán leader Yehry Rivera was killed and Bribri leader Mainor Ortíz Delgado was shot and wounded in connection with land disputes. All three had previously been granted protectionary measures by the Inter-American Commission on Human Rights (IACHR).

Costa Ricans of African descent have also faced discrimination in health care, education, and employment. In July 2020, the legislature passed a law punishing acts of racism and xenophobia that occur in sports venues.

Women experience discrimination due to entrenched gender stereotypes, which can limit their equal access to employment, health services, and the justice system. Executive orders prohibit discrimination on the basis of sexual orientation and gender identity, and the government has expressed commitment to the protection of LGBT+ people. However, law enforcement officials have discriminated against LGBT+ people, and there have been reports of attacks by police on transgender sex workers.

In 2016, a new law provided disabled people greater personal autonomy. Prior to the law's passage, family members often had legal guardianship over disabled people.

In 2019, the government modified the General Law on HIV/AIDS to facilitate condom distribution and expand screenings, counseling, and privacy protections for HIV/AIDS patients.

The number of asylum seekers from Nicaragua has increased sharply since a political crisis erupted there in 2018. More than 80,000 Nicaraguans have fled to Costa Rica, and approximately 50,000 have applied for asylum. Although the law entitles asylum seekers to access public services, discrimination sometimes prevents them from taking advantage of those benefits, and legal restrictions limit employment opportunities for asylum seekers. Anti-Nicaraguan discrimination rose in 2020 as a result of the COVID-19 pandemic, even as Nicaraguan migrants' economic precarity increased.

G. PERSONAL AUTONOMY AND INDIVIDUAL RIGHTS: 13 / 16

G1. Do individuals enjoy freedom of movement, including the ability to change their place of residence, employment, or education? 4 / 4

Freedom of movement is constitutionally guaranteed and Costa Ricans enjoy relative freedom in their choice of residence and employment. During the October 2020 protests, nearly 60 roadblocks were erected throughout the country, preventing free movement for several weeks.

G2. Are individuals able to exercise the right to own property and establish private businesses without undue interference from state or nonstate actors? 3 / 4

Property rights are generally protected. Individuals are free to establish businesses, and the business and investment climate is relatively open, although the complicated bureaucracy can deter entrepreneurs seeking to establish a business. In 2020, the Superintendency of Financial Institutions (SUGEF) was given oversight over real estate agencies to improve the transparency of real estate transactions. Costa Rica was also removed in 2020 from the Office of the United States Trade Representative's watch list regarding the protection of intellectual property rights.

G3. Do individuals enjoy personal social freedoms, including choice of marriage partner and size of family, protection from domestic violence, and control over appearance? 3 / 4

Despite the existence of domestic violence protections, violence against women and children remains a problem. In 2019 the president signed a bill increasing the statute of limitations in child sexual abuse cases from 10 to 25 years.

In 2018, the Supreme Court, following an IACHR advisory opinion, ruled that the prohibition of same-sex marriage was unconstitutional and gave the legislature 18 months to pass legislation overturning the ban. In May 2020, the 18-month period concluded with no legislative consensus and Costa Rica became the first Central American country to permit same-sex marriage.

Abortion is illegal in Costa Rica except when a woman's health is in danger due to a pregnancy. In December 2019, President Alvarado signed a technical decree intended to facilitate limited access to abortion by outlining the circumstances under which an abortion may be performed legally, though the conditions remain restrictive. For example, in addition to a woman's health being deemed at risk, she must agree to mandatory evaluation by three medical professionals.

G4. Do individuals enjoy equality of opportunity and freedom from economic exploitation? 3 / 4

Despite legal protections, domestic workers, particularly migrant workers, are subject to exploitation and forced labor. Employers often ignore minimum wage and social security laws, and the resulting fines for violations are insignificant. Child labor is a problem in the informal economy.

Sex trafficking and child sex tourism are also serious problems. The US State Department's 2020 *Trafficking in Persons Report* noted an increased number of investigations and convictions and an increase in anti-trafficking funds. However, the report noted ongoing failures to adequately disburse anti-trafficking funds and effectively coordinate referral mechanisms with civil society groups.

Côte d'Ivoire

Population: 26,200,000
Capital: Yamoussoukro (official), Abidjan (de facto)
Freedom Status: Partly Free
Electoral Democracy: No

Overview: Côte d'Ivoire continues to recover from an armed conflict that ended in 2011. Several root causes of the country's violent conflict remain, including ethnic and regional tensions, land disputes, corruption, and impunity. While civil liberties were better protected in recent years, an outbreak of election-related violence in 2020 brought significant setbacks. Women are significantly underrepresented in politics.

KEY DEVELOPMENTS IN 2020

- At least 22,000 people contracted and 130 people died from COVID-19 in Côte d'Ivoire during the year. The government declared a state of emergency in response to the pandemic and took advantage of the crisis to change the electoral code by emergency decree.
- In July, former prime minister and presidential candidate Amadou Gon Coulibaly died suddenly, prompting President Ouattara, a member of the same party, to step in as the presidential candidate despite having assured the opposition that he would not run for a third term. Ouattara won the election in October though it was neither free nor fair, was marred by violence, and was boycotted by the opposition.
- In November, security forces raided the homes of multiple opposition party leaders, arrested and detained over 20 people on charges of conspiracy and sedition, and held some incommunicado for several days.
- From August through November, opposition supporters, progovernment supporters, and militias armed with machetes and guns clashed on the streets in several towns and cities, claiming over 80 lives and prompting more than 3,000 people to flee the country.

POLITICAL RIGHTS: 16 / 40 (−3)
A. ELECTORAL PROCESS: 5 / 12 (−2)
A1. Was the current head of government or other chief national authority elected through free and fair elections? 2 / 4 (−1)

The October 2020 presidential election was neither free nor fair. Former prime minister and presidential candidate of the Rally of the Houphouëtists for Democracy and Peace (RHDP) Amadou Gon Coulibaly died unexpectedly in July 2020. President Alassane Ouattara, who had spent two five-year presidential terms in office, reversed his previous decision not to run and was nominated in August by the RDHP, which claimed Ouattara was eligible for two more terms because the 2016 Constitution's two-term limit was adopted after Ouattara's second election; some critics charged that Ouattara had moved forward with the new constitution to enable his third term. His nomination was met by major protests from opposition parties.

The Constitutional Council rejected 40 of the 44 candidates for the presidential election and validated the candidacy of only four individuals: Alassane Ouattara, Henri Konan Bédié, Pascal Affi N'Guessan, and Bertin Konan Kouadio. Rejected candidates were unable to appeal the Council's decisions, and the government ignored a ruling from African Court of Human and People's Rights (ACHPR) to allow prominent opposition leader Guillaume Soro and former president Laurent Gbagbo to run. Several leading opposition parties, including those of Soro and Gbagbo, refused to participate in the polls and called for a boycott of and protests against the election. The government banned all public demonstrations throughout the election period, and those that occurred were met with violence. The campaign period itself was marred by instances of violence between progovernment and antigovernment supporters, resulting in dozens of deaths.

The opposition boycotted the October election outright, while many would-be voters were prevented from casting ballots due to security concerns. Ouattara won the poll with 94 percent of the vote, according to the government, which put turnout at 54 percent. These numbers were contested by independent observers from the Electoral Institute for Sustainable Democracy in Africa (EISA), which reported that only 54 percent of polling stations opened and only 41 percent of voter cards were distributed before the vote. The group also said the electoral roll had issues with the comprehensiveness of its data, and included a large number of deceased individuals, and that the election commission lacked transparency and heavily favored the ruling party in administering the election.

The prime minister is the head of government, is appointed by the president, and is responsible for designating a cabinet, which is also approved by the president. In July 2020 after the death of Coulibaly, Hamed Bakayoko was appointed prime minister.

Score Change: The score declined from 3 to 2 because the incumbent president was elected in a contest that featured restrictions on the opposition that resulted in a boycott, and was marred by state and nonstate violence throughout the campaign period and after.

A2. Were the current national legislative representatives elected through free and fair elections? 2 / 4

The bicameral parliament consists of a 255-seat lower house, the National Assembly, and a 99-seat Senate, which was envisaged by the 2016 constitution and seated in March 2018. National Assembly members are directly elected to five-year terms. Of the Senate's 99 seats, 66 are indirectly elected by the National Assembly and members of various local councils, and 33 members are appointed by the president; all members serve five-year terms.

The members of the current National Assembly were directly elected in credible, largely peaceful polls held in 2016. The RHDP won 167 seats. Independent candidates took the majority of the remaining seats. In the 2018 Senate election, RHDP candidates won 50 of the 66 elected seats, and independent candidates took the remaining 16; the opposition boycotted the vote over allegations of bias by the Independent Electoral Commission (CEI), as well as over claims that the CEI's establishment would help Ouattara consolidate power. (The opposition previously boycotted the referendum on the draft constitution that established the CEI.)

A3. Are the electoral laws and framework fair, and are they implemented impartially by the relevant election management bodies? 1 / 4 (−1)

In 2016, the ACHPR ruled that the CEI was biased in favor of the government and ordered amendments to the electoral law. President Ouattara conceded to the CEI's reorganization, increasing the number of civil society members in the CEI from four to six by parliamentary amendment in 2019. Civil society criticized the reforms, warning that the government would still exert influence due to its continued ability to nominate members, and changes that could make the body more independent were only partially implemented.

Recent allegations of irregularities in CEI appointment and other procedures and related changes in staff, as well as opposition boycotts of staffing processes for district-level posts, have left the CEI mostly run by members of the ruling party.

In April 2020, the government amended the electoral code by emergency executive ordinance—enabled because of the COVID-19 pandemic's state of emergency measures—without consultation with the election's participants. The updated electoral roll was opaque and regionally unbalanced, and the CEI refused to report detailed data and submit to an independent audit.

Score Change: The score declined from 2 to 1 because changes to the country's electoral code were made by executive decree, and because the election commission operates opaquely, in the general absence of oversight by opposition-appointed members.

B. POLITICAL PLURALISM AND PARTICIPATION: 7 / 16 (−1)

B1. Do the people have the right to organize in different political parties or other competitive political groupings of their choice, and is the system free of undue obstacles to the rise and fall of these competing parties or groupings? 2 / 4

The Ivorian constitution permits multiparty competition, and recent presidential and legislative elections have been contested by a large number of parties and independent candidates. The ruling RHDP, dominated by Ouattara's Rally of the Republicans (RDR), holds a virtual lock on political power, but has faced increased competition in recent years. In 2018, the Democratic Party of Côte d'Ivoire (PDCI) of former president Henri Konan Bédié split with the coalition after disagreement over the RHDP's 2020 presidential nominee; a faction of PDCI candidates ran against the RHDP in the 2018 municipal elections. In February 2019, former rebel commander and former premier Guillaume Soro resigned as National Assembly speaker. He later formed the Generations and People in Solidarity (GPS) party, and declared his presidential candidacy in October.

B2. Is there a realistic opportunity for the opposition to increase its support or gain power through elections? 2 / 4

The Ivorian Popular Front of former president Gbagbo holds seats in parliament, but it is relatively weak, has strong internal divisions, and is disorganized. The Ivorian Popular Front (FPI) has been split into two factions; one that is directly attached to Gbagbo and another that is more moderate. Each faction put forward a candidate in the 2020 presidential elections, though only the moderate faction's N'Guessan was allowed to run.

In August 2020, the Constitutional Council rejected the candidacy of 40 of the 44 parties and individuals who submitted a nomination for the presidential election, including Soro and former president Laurent Gbagbo. International observer missions noted there was no appeals process for the rejected candidates to have their candidacy recognized, and that the election was not genuinely competitive. The government ignored the ACHPR's ruling to accept Soro's and Gbagbo's candidacies.

The opposition largely boycotted the October 2020 presidential elections. After election day, security forces arrested and detained opposition figures, and some were prevented from contacting a lawyer or their families. Opposition leaders including N'Guessan and dozens of opposition party members were detained at the house of Henri Konan Bédié, allegedly for "conspiracy" and "sedition." N'Guessan was detained and held incommunicado for over 60 hours. Between August and October, police arrested over 40 political dissidents, mainly for their participation in protests.

B3. Are the people's political choices free from domination by forces that are external to the political sphere, or by political forces that employ extrapolitical means? 1 / 4 (−1)

Individuals faced intimidation, threats, and physical violence when participating in the 2020 presidential election. Opposition parties boycotted the polls and staged multiple marches, sit-ins, and demonstrations leading up to election day in October, despite the government's ban on all protests from August through October. Security forces used violence to disperse protesters, killing several demonstrators during the campaigning period. Members of leading civil society institutions, like academics, suggested that participating in public debate about the elections would be seen as protest by their superiors.

Supporters of the opposition faced threats from the police and the military, who further failed to keep citizens safe during and after election day. More than 50 people were killed by militia members who attacked citizens with impunity. Opposition and government supporters clashed on the streets with machetes, clubs, and hunting rifles in Abidjan and at least eight other towns.

Score Change: The score declined from 2 to 1 because voters faced intimidation from police forces, the military, and heads of academic institutions who supported the president, reducing people's ability to make independent political choices.

B4. Do various segments of the population (including ethnic, racial, religious, gender, LGBT+, and other relevant groups) have full political rights and electoral opportunities? 2 / 4

Citizenship has been a source of tension since the 1990s, when Ivorian nationalists adopted former president Bédié's concept of "Ivoirité" to exclude perceived foreigners, including Ouattara, from the political process. A law relaxing some conditions for citizenship went into effect in 2014 but its application remains uneven. Hundreds of thousands of individuals, mostly northerners, lack documentation.

Women are poorly represented in in the parliament, holding 12 percent of seats in the National Assembly and 19 percent in the Senate at year's end.

A north-south, Muslim-Christian schism has been a salient feature of Ivorian life for decades and was exacerbated by the 2002–11 crisis. However, the schism has since receded, and the current government coalition includes Muslims and Christians. Political parties are not ethnically homogenous—Côte d'Ivoire comprises people from more than 60 ethnicities—though each tends to be dominated by specific ethnic groups.

C. FUNCTIONING OF GOVERNMENT: 4 / 12

C1. Do the freely elected head of government and national legislative representatives determine the policies of the government? 2 / 4

Though defense and security forces are nominally under civilian control, problems of parallel command and control systems within the armed forces, known as the Republican Forces of Côte d'Ivoire (FRCI), remain significant. In 2016, the government instituted a law meant to reduce the size of the officer corps and refine the military's command structure, but these changes have largely gone unimplemented. Nonstate armed actors and former rebels enjoy significant influence, especially in the north and west.

Additionally, after several years of relative calm, military mutinies in 2017 exposed the fragility of the civilian government's control over the state armed forces. Civilian control was tested again in September 2019, when special forces members scuffled with Abidjan police in an effort to free an arrested colleague; this incident ended without violence, however.

C2. Are safeguards against official corruption strong and effective? 1 / 4

Corruption and bribery remain endemic, and particularly affect the judiciary, police, and government contracting operations. Petty bribery also hampers citizens' access to services ranging from obtaining a birth certificate to clearing goods through customs. A public anticorruption body, the High Authority for Good Governance (HABG), was established in 2013, but is considered ineffective. Perpetrators at all levels seldom face prosecution.

C3. Does the government operate with openness and transparency? 1 / 4

The government generally awards contracts in a nontransparent manner. Access to up-to-date information from government ministries is difficult for ordinary citizens to acquire, although some ministries do publish information online. In 2013, the National Assembly passed an access to information law, but enforcement has been inconsistent. The HABG requires public officials to submit asset declarations, but this is not well enforced.

CIVIL LIBERTIES: 28 / 60 (−4)

D. FREEDOM OF EXPRESSION AND BELIEF: 9 / 16 (−2)

D1. Are there free and independent media? 2 / 4

Conditions for the press have improved since the end of the 2010–11 conflict, and incidents of serious violence against journalists are rare. However, journalists face intimidation and occasional violence by security forces in connection with their work. Most national media sources, especially newspapers, exhibit partisanship in their news coverage, consistently favoring either the government or the opposition. Many journalists were arrested, detained, and beaten by police while covering protests and violence during and after the 2020 election period.

D2. Are individuals free to practice and express their religious faith or nonbelief in public and private? 3 / 4

Legal guarantees of religious freedom are typically upheld, and individuals are free to practice their faith in public and private. Relations between Muslims and Christians were exacerbated by the 2002–11 crisis, but tensions have largely receded. In May 2019, police closed Danané's great mosque, after the supporters of two imams vying for its leadership clashed.

D3. Is there academic freedom, and is the educational system free from extensive political indoctrination? 2 / 4 (−1)

Public universities were closed and used as military bases during the 2010–11 conflict, and now suffer from a lack of adequate resources and facilities. Classes were disrupted when teachers and university lecturers launched a nationwide strike over salaries, bonuses, and housing aid in late January 2019; the strike was suspended that March when unions held talks with the government.

Academics faced threats and intimidation if they addressed or critiqued the ruling party and other politically sensitive topics during the 2020 election cycle. Legal scholars were unable to organize a public debate on the constitutionality of President Ouattara's third term, as many feared their participation would be considered a form of illegal protest. Individuals at institutions with leadership that support the ruling party engaged in self-censorship.

Score Change: The score declined from 3 to 2 due to a widespread perception among professors and students that debating sensitive political topics involving the 2020 election would be met with retaliation from the government.

D4. Are individuals free to express their personal views on political or other sensitive topics without fear of surveillance or retribution? 2 / 4 (−1)

Though people are free to engage in political discussion and debate, politics and the ruling party became dangerous topics during the 2020 election cycle. During and after the elections, militias and unknown actors attacked opposition supporters demonstrating and meeting during the opposition's boycott of the election. Security forces largely overlooked the violence against opposition supporters, which discouraged individuals from openly expressing their political views.

Score Change: The score declined from 3 to 2 because Ivorians engaged in self-censorship due to concerns about harassment or retaliation by the government and militia forces during the election period.

E. ASSOCIATIONAL AND ORGANIZATIONAL RIGHTS: 6 / 12 (−2)
E1. Is there freedom of assembly? 1 / 4 (−1)

Freedom of assembly was restricted by June 2019 criminal code revisions, which include one- to three-year prison sentences for organizing "undeclared or prohibited" assemblies and a vague definition of "public order" that can be broadly interpreted by authorities.

President Ouattara banned public demonstrations and protests throughout the 2020 election period. Police violently dispersed protests and other acts of civil disobedience that stemmed from the opposition's election boycott. Armed militias brutally attacked unarmed protesters throughout the election period with impunity. Progovernment groups and opposition supporters frequently clashed. Over 50 people were killed because of violence at public demonstrations.

Score Change: The score declined from 2 to 1 because police forces allowed armed militias to attack peaceful protesters who opposed President Ouattara's reelection.

E2. Is there freedom for nongovernmental organizations, particularly those that are engaged in human rights- and governance-related work? 2 / 4 (−1)

Domestic and international nongovernmental organizations (NGOs) are generally free to operate. However, poor security conditions—especially in north and west—are a constraint for some organizations.

In 2020, authorities arrested many activists, including several well-known leaders of the Alternative Citoyenne Ivoirienne (ACI), on a range of illegitimate charges, from "undermining public order" to "undermining national defense." Those arrested had been critical of Ouattara's candidacy for president.

Score Change: The score declined from 3 to 2 because the government targeted leaders and members of governance-oriented NGOs with arrest and detention during the election cycle.

E3. Is there freedom for trade unions and similar professional or labor organizations? 3 / 4

The right to organize and join labor unions is constitutionally guaranteed. Workers have the right to bargain collectively. Côte d'Ivoire typically has various professional strikes every year, though sometimes strikes have become violent. Teachers and university lecturers held a nationwide strike over salaries, bonuses, and housing aid from January through March 2019.

F. RULE OF LAW: 6 / 16

F1. Is there an independent judiciary? 1 / 4

The judiciary is not independent, and judges are highly susceptible to external interference and bribes. Processes governing the assignment of cases to judges are opaque. The judiciary was fully mobilized to support President Ouattara's third term.

F2. Does due process prevail in civil and criminal matters? 1 / 4

The constitution guarantees equal access to justice and due process for all citizens, but these guarantees are poorly upheld in practice. The state struggles to provide attorneys to defendants who cannot afford legal counsel. Security officials are susceptible to bribery and are rarely held accountable for misconduct. Prolonged pretrial detention is a serious problem for both adults and minors, with some detainees spending years in prison without trial. In late 2018, the lower house adopted a new Code of Criminal Procedure that included a circuit of criminal courts to address the backlog.

F3. Is there protection from the illegitimate use of physical force and freedom from war and insurgencies? 2 / 4

Physical violence against civilians in the form of extortion, banditry, and sexual violence, sometimes perpetrated by members of the state armed forces, remain common. Disputes over land use and ownership between migrants, and those who claim customary land rights, sometimes turn violent. The country's prisons are severely overcrowded, and incarcerated adults and minors are not always separated.

Concerns about impunity, victor's justice, and reconciliation have persisted after the close of the 2010–11 conflict. To date, only a handful of individuals have been put on trial for crimes committed during that period, and most prosecutions have focused on figures associated with Gbagbo. In 2018, Ouattara pardoned 800 people accused or convicted of committing violent acts during the 2010–11 conflict, including former first lady Simone Gbagbo, ostensibly to foster reconciliation. In January 2019, the International Criminal Court acquitted former president Gbagbo of crimes against humanity during the 2010–11 conflict, and Gbagbo was conditionally released.

In November 2020, the United Nations reported that over 3,000 people fled Côte d'Ivoire because of postelection violence.

F4. Do laws, policies, and practices guarantee equal treatment of various segments of the population? 2 / 4

Same-sex relations are not criminalized in Côte d'Ivoire, but LGBT+ people can face prosecution under criminal code language amended in 2019 that references "unnatural acts" and "moral sensitivity." No law prohibits discrimination based on sexual orientation. LGBT+ people face societal prejudice as well as harassment by state security forces.

Intercommunal tensions over land rights frequently involve migrants from neighboring countries, who sometimes experience violent intimidation.

G. PERSONAL AUTONOMY AND INDIVIDUAL RIGHTS: 7 / 16

G1. Do individuals enjoy freedom of movement, including the ability to change their place of residence, employment, or education? 2 / 4

Freedom of movement has improved since 2011. However, irregular checkpoints and acts of extortion continue in some areas, particularly in the west and north, and near gold and diamond-producing regions. The government's efforts to combat these practices have been undermined by inconsistent financial support and a failure to investigate and prosecute perpetrators. Women are generally afforded equal freedom of movement, though risks of insecurity and sexual violence hinder this in practice.

G2. Are individuals able to exercise the right to own property and establish private businesses without undue interference from state or nonstate actors? 2 / 4

Citizens have the right to own and establish private businesses, and the country has attracted significant investment since 2011. However, property and land rights remain weak, especially in the west, where conflict over land tenure remains a significant source of tension. Under a new marriage law passed in July 2019, women are legally entitled to use inherited property as collateral for loans. Migrants may be discriminated over land issues even though they have legal documents of their property title.

G3. Do individuals enjoy personal social freedoms, including choice of marriage partner and size of family, protection from domestic violence, and control over appearance? 1 / 4

Women suffer significant legal and economic discrimination, and sexual and gender-based violence are widespread. Legal protections from gender-based violence are weak and are often ignored. Impunity for perpetrators also remains a problem, and when it is prosecuted, rape is routinely reclassified as indecent assault. Costly medical certificates are often essential for convictions yet are beyond the means of victims who are impoverished.

Child marriage is historically widespread, though the July 2019 marriage law set the minimum age for marriage at 18 for both sexes. Customary and religious marriages, more common outside urban areas, were not affected by the law. The July 2019 law also banned same-sex marriage.

G4. Do individuals enjoy equality of opportunity and freedom from economic exploitation? 2 / 4

Despite efforts by the government and international industries in recent years to counter the phenomenon, child labor is a frequent problem, particularly in the cocoa industry. Human trafficking is prohibited by the new constitution, but government programs for victims of trafficking—often children—are inadequate.

Croatia

Population: 4,000,000
Capital: Zagreb
Freedom Status: Free
Electoral Democracy: Yes

Overview: Croatia is a parliamentary republic that regularly holds free elections. Civil and political rights are generally respected, though corruption in the public sector is a serious issue. The Roma and ethnic Serbs face discrimination, as do LGBT+ people. In recent years, concerns about the presence of far-right groups and figures espousing discriminatory values in public life have increased.

KEY DEVELOPMENTS IN 2020

- In January, former prime minister Zoran Milanović defeated incumbent Kolinda Grabar-Kitarović in the second round of the country's presidential election, winning 52.7 percent of the vote. Voter turnout was 55 percent.

- Prime Minister Andrej Plenković of the Croatian Democratic Union (HDZ) called for the 2020 parliamentary election to occur in July, a few months early. Critics claimed that he moved the date forward to capitalize on the public's positive perception of his party's handling of the COVID-19 pandemic. The HDZ resecured its plurality in parliament and formed a coalition government with two smaller parties.

POLITICAL RIGHTS: 36 / 40

A. ELECTORAL PROCESS: 12 / 12

A1. Was the current head of government or other chief national authority elected through free and fair elections? 4 / 4

The president, who is head of state, is elected by popular vote for a maximum of two five-year terms. The prime minister is head of government and is appointed by the president with parliamentary approval.

Former Social Democratic Party (SDP) prime minister Zoran Milanović defeated incumbent Kolinda Grabar-Kitarović in the second round of the country's presidential elections in January 2020, capturing 52.7 percent of the vote. Voter turnout was 55 percent.

Chairman of the HDZ Andrej Plenković remained prime minister following the 2020 legislative elections.

A2. Were the current national legislative representatives elected through free and fair elections? 4 / 4

Members of the 151-member unicameral parliament, called the Hrvatski Sabor, are elected to four-year terms.

Prime Minister Plenković called for the 2020 parliamentary election to occur in July, a few months ahead of schedule. Critics claimed he moved the date forward in order to capitalize on the public's perception of the governing HDZ's success in addressing the COVID-19 pandemic. In the July election, the HDZ captured 66 seats, which enabled the party to form a coalition government with two smaller parties. The main opposition party, the SDP, won 41 seats, the far-right Homeland Movement party secured 16, and the new left-wing We Can party took 8. Though the elections were deemed free and fair, ethnic Serb candidates experienced harassment during the campaigning period.

A3. Are the electoral laws and framework fair, and are they implemented impartially by the relevant election management bodies? 4 / 4

While some concerns about the use of public funds for political campaigns persist, in general, the State Election Commission implements robust electoral laws effectively.

B. POLITICAL PLURALISM AND PARTICIPATION: 14 / 16

B1. Do the people have the right to organize in different political parties or other competitive political groupings of their choice, and is the system free of undue obstacles to the rise and fall of these competing parties or groupings? 4 / 4

Citizens may freely organize and participate in the activities of a wide variety of political parties. A slate of new right- and left-wing populist parties and candidates emerged in the 2019 European Parliament elections. Two new coalitions made breakthroughs in the July 2020 parliamentary election: the far-right Homeland Movement and the new left-wing coalition We Can, a pact of civic and progressive groups largely centered in Zagreb.

B2. Is there a realistic opportunity for the opposition to increase its support or gain power through elections? 4 / 4

The SDP-led opposition coalition holds a significant bloc of seats in the legislature and is generally able to operate free from restrictions or intimidation. In general, however, the HDZ has dominated politics and draws support from the Roman Catholic Church, veterans, and a growing number of conservative nongovernmental organizations (NGOs). The main SDP-led opposition bloc has won the most seats in only two parliamentary elections since 1991, although the country was headed by an SDP president from 2010 to 2015 and an SDP president was elected in 2020, as well as a non-HDZ and non-SDP executive from 2000 to 2010.

B3. Are the people's political choices free from domination by forces that are external to the political sphere, or by political forces that employ extrapolitical means? 3 / 4

While voters and candidates are generally able to freely express their political choices, many public servants obtained their positions through patronage networks, and thus risk becoming beholden to a party or special interest group as a result. Patronage networks are particularly influential in Zagreb, which has been under the stewardship of HDZ-affiliated Mayor Milan Bandić—considered one of the country's most powerful politicians—almost continuously for the past 20 years. Bandić's tenure has been marked by corruption allegations and credible allegations of improper hiring practices and public procurement deals.

The Catholic Church remains influential in Croatia and has begun associating with conservative and far-right civil society groups, which have become a bigger factor in local politics in recent years. Veterans groups are also influential in Croatian politics, especially in regard to the still contentious memory politics of the Independence War (1991–1995) and the position of ethnic Serbs in Croatian society.

B4. Do various segments of the population (including ethnic, racial, religious, gender, LGBT+, and other relevant groups) have full political rights and electoral opportunities? 3 / 4

Eight parliamentary seats are set aside for ethnic minorities, including three for ethnic Serbs. However, the political interests of marginalized groups, notably Roma and Serbs, are underrepresented.

Women are represented across political parties, and women have held Croatia's presidency between 2015 and 2019 and the prime minister's office between 2009 and 2011. However, the number of women in parliament decreased in 2016 after the Constitutional Court struck down a law requiring 40 percent of a party's candidates be women. In the 2020 parliamentary election, 35 women won seats in parliament from various political parties.

The treatment of ethnic Serbs in public office in Croatia has deteriorated in recent years. In September 2018, sitting lawmaker and Independent Democratic Serb Party (SDS) leader Milorad Pupovac was pelted with food items by a protester in Zagreb. Pupovac claimed the incident reflected growing hostility toward the Serb population from ascendant right-wing and nationalist movements in the country, many of which appear to enjoy the tacit support of the HDZ. Pupovac remained the target verbal attacks throughout 2019, and his party's election posters were repeatedly defaced during the European Parliament elections. Similar incidents marred the 2020 parliamentary campaign.

Societal discrimination discourages LGBT+ people from participating in politics, and elements of the political establishment have espoused discriminatory attitudes in their activism.

C. FUNCTIONING OF GOVERNMENT: 10 / 12

C1. Do the freely elected head of government and national legislative representatives determine the policies of the government? 4 / 4

Democratically elected representatives are duly installed into office and are generally able to make public policy without undue external influence or pressure.

C2. Are safeguards against official corruption strong and effective? 3 / 4

A criminal code in effect since 2013 enforces stiffer penalties for various forms of corruption. While some progress has been made, official corruption—including nepotism, bribery, fraud, and patronage—remains a serious problem. Numerous high-level corruption cases, like the one involving the government's mismanagement and collapse of Croatia's largest employer, Agrokor, have been filed in recent years, but many are yet to see a verdict. The European Commission singled out corruption as a major issue facing the country and local NGOs have observed that the problem has actually worsened since the country joined the bloc in 2013.

In November 2020, former prime minister Ivo Sanader was sentenced to eight years in prison for taking money from public companies to create slush funds for the HDZ. The HDZ was fined and compelled to return millions of illegally obtained funds.

C3. Does the government operate with openness and transparency? 3 / 4

In 2013, Croatia adopted the Law on the Right of Access to Information. The legislation created a proportionality and public-interest test designed to balance reasons for disclosing information and reasons for restricting it. It also established an independent information commissioner to monitor compliance. However, government bodies do not always release requested information in a timely manner.

Media reports in 2018 suggested that former economy minister Martina Dalić and a group of well-connected businesspeople and lawyers crafted a 2017 law allowing the government to take over management of the troubled agricultural company Agrokor. The entire drafting process took place outside of official proceedings and in private meetings. Facing conflict-of-interest allegations, Dalić resigned in May 2018.

CIVIL LIBERTIES: 49 / 60

D. FREEDOM OF EXPRESSION AND BELIEF: 13 / 16

D1. Are there free and independent media? 3 / 4

Media in Croatia is highly polarized but generally free from overt political interference or manipulation. However, journalists continue to face threats, harassment, and occasional attacks—sometimes at the hands of police—which has created an atmosphere of self-censorship. The European Federation of Journalists and local journalist associations have warned of growing political pressure and attacks on the Croatian press under the HDZ government. A 2020 European Commission report warned about deteriorating media freedoms in Croatia.

In April 2020, unidentified men attacked two reporters documenting an Easter Mass held during the coronavirus state of emergency, when the government had banned public gatherings.

D2. Are individuals free to practice and express their religious faith or nonbelief in public and private? 3 / 4

The Croatian constitution guarantees freedom of religion, and this is generally upheld in practice. However, the small Serb Orthodox community remains vulnerable to harassment, and members have reported vandalism of their churches. Jewish communities and other groups have expressed increasing concern about Holocaust denial and displays by right-wing nationalists of symbols and slogans associated with the fascist Ustaša regime that governed Croatia during the Second World War. Revisionist accounts of the Ustaša period continued to be promoted by far-right groups and newspapers in 2020.

D3. Is there academic freedom, and is the educational system free from extensive political indoctrination? 3 / 4

While there are generally no overt restrictions on speech in schools and universities, critics continue to allege inappropriate political interference at all levels of education. While aspects of a long-planned modernization of school curriculums were approved by Parliament in 2018, the HDZ has long sought to delay the updates and has moved to install its own members into the group tasked with developing its policies—including extremely conservative members opposed to sex education.

Far-right groups have had an increasing presence and influence on academic freedom, as evidenced by their unsuccessful 2018 campaign to fire three academics at the University of Zagreb for a paper the academics had published on the increase in far-right political activity in the country.

D4. Are individuals free to express their personal views on political or other sensitive topics without fear of surveillance or retribution? 4 / 4

People are generally free to engage in discussions of a sensitive nature without fearing surveillance or retribution, although there have been some reports of police arresting individuals voicing criticism of the government.

E. ASSOCIATIONAL AND ORGANIZATIONAL RIGHTS: 12 / 12
E1. Is there freedom of assembly? 4 / 4

Freedom of assembly is protected and respected in Croatia.

E2. Is there freedom for nongovernmental organizations, particularly those that are engaged in human rights- and governance-related work? 4 / 4

NGOs in Croatia are robust, active, and free from restrictions. However, many groups have complained of growing political pressure from parts of the government and the HDZ against journalists and civil society activists.

In September 2019, Prime Minister Plenković verbally attacked a local NGO which had shed light on the allegedly illicit financial dealings of Croatia's candidate for the "Democracy and Demography" portfolio of the European Commission.

E3. Is there freedom for trade unions and similar professional or labor organizations? 4 / 4

The constitution allows workers to form and join trade unions, and this right is generally respected in practice.

F. RULE OF LAW: 11 / 16
F1. Is there an independent judiciary? 3 / 4

While judicial independence is generally respected, there have been recent concerns about the influence of extreme right-wing groups on the judiciary. For example, in 2017, a court reversed a 1945 conviction of an academic who was complicit in atrocities committed by the fascist Ustaša regime. Critics allege the courts have been ruling in line with the views of right-wing NGOs and the HDZ, while the courts maintain that they are redressing partisan rulings of the Yugoslav communist era.

F2. Does due process prevail in civil and criminal matters? 3 / 4

Due process rights are generally upheld, but the system tends to work more efficiently for individuals with abundant resources or high social standing.

In November 2018, Ivica Todorić, the former owner of Agrokor under investigation for fraud in relation to the company's collapse, was extradited from the United Kingdom. He was arrested upon arrival in Croatia but released days later after posting the €1 million bail. Todorić was acquitted in one trial in October 2020 but still faced other charges.

The International Commission on Missing Persons has criticized Croatia for its slow progress in identifying human remains of victims of the 1991–95 conflicts and in making reparations to survivors and their families.

F3. Is there protection from the illegitimate use of physical force and freedom from war and insurgencies? 3 / 4

Violence by state and nonstate actors is uncommon. Prison conditions do not meet international standards due to overcrowding and inadequate medical care.

F4. Do laws, policies, and practices guarantee equal treatment of various segments of the population? 2 / 4

Ethnic and religious minorities and LGBT+ people in Croatia face discrimination. Analysts have expressed concerns that the increasing visibility of far-right, nationalist groups has spread discriminatory rhetoric. Occasionally, the government's actions suggest their endorsement of far-right groups, and observers have expressed concern that the government has tacitly approved of discriminatory behavior. A group of NGOs in December 2018 criticized the government for lacking a comprehensive human rights policy, and warned of the continuing deterioration of protection of human rights in the country, especially for marginalized groups and women.

The constitution prohibits gender discrimination, but women earn less than men for comparable work and hold fewer leadership positions.

Police violence against migrants, refugees, and asylum-seekers increased in 2020, according to the Danish Refugee Council (DRC). Most such incidents took place along the border with Bosnia and Herzegovina, rather than Serbia, as in the past. The DRC has produced photographs and testimony of serious abuses allegedly committed by border police toward migrants and refugees, including sexual violence and torture.

G. PERSONAL AUTONOMY AND INDIVIDUAL RIGHTS: 13 / 16

G1. Do individuals enjoy freedom of movement, including the ability to change their place of residence, employment, or education? 4 / 4

Freedom of movement is protected by the constitution and upheld in practice. People may freely change their place of residence, employment, or education.

G2. Are individuals able to exercise the right to own property and establish private businesses without undue interference from state or nonstate actors? 3 / 4

Property rights are generally well protected. However, corruption can inhibit normal business operations.

G3. Do individuals enjoy personal social freedoms, including choice of marriage partner and size of family, protection from domestic violence, and control over appearance? 3 / 4

In 2014, following a 2013 referendum that banned same-sex marriage, the parliament passed a law allowing same-sex civil unions. The law affords same-sex couples equal rights in inheritance, social benefits, and taxation, but not the right to adopt children.

Domestic violence remains a concern. Convictions for rape and domestic violence can bring lengthy prisons terms, although Amnesty International noted that the vast majority of cases receive light sentences of one year or less. Police sometimes fail to adhere to recommended procedures for handling reports of domestic violence.

In April 2018, lawmakers ratified the Istanbul Convention, a treaty on preventing and combating gender-based and domestic violence. The treaty was unpopular among conservative and far-right groups who believed its tenets could lead to the legal introduction of same-sex marriage, a third gender category, or school curriculum changes. In response, the government adopted a statement saying the treaty's adoption would not change the legal definition of marriage. Amnesty International criticized the Croatian government for failing to harmonize its legislative and policy framework with the treaty's terms.

G4. Do individuals enjoy equality of opportunity and freedom from economic exploitation? 3 / 4

Worker protection laws are robust, and the Office of the Labor Inspectorate actively investigates work sites. However, labor violation remain a problem within the hospitality sector. Workers in the informal sector have less access to legal protections.

Human trafficking remains a problem, sentences for those convicted of it can be light, and witness statements are not always given the appropriate consideration in court cases.

Cuba

Population: 11,300,000
Capital: Havana
Freedom Status: Not Free
Electoral Democracy: No

Overview: Cuba's one-party communist state outlaws political pluralism, bans independent media, suppresses dissent, and severely restricts basic civil liberties. The government continues to dominate the economy despite recent reforms that permit some private-sector activity. The regime's undemocratic character has not changed despite a generational transition in political leadership between 2018 and 2019 that included the introduction of a new constitution.

KEY DEVELOPMENTS IN 2020

- The government achieved some success in controlling the COVID-19 pandemic, reporting just 145 deaths to the World Health Organization by year's end, but the global crisis took a heavy toll on the economy. In July, partly in response, the government announced that it would liberalize rules regulating the tiny private sector, including by allowing private businesses to trade more freely and obtain legal status as enterprises, eliminating the restrictive list of permitted occupations for self-employment, and expanding experiments with nonagricultural cooperatives.
- The government at times cited the pandemic to justify crackdowns on dissident gatherings. In November, when members of the Movimiento San Isidro (MSI)—a

collective of dissident artists—gathered and went on hunger strike to protest the arrest of rapper Denis Solís, police violently detained them on the pretext of controlling the spread of the coronavirus. This led to a sit-in by numerous artists and intellectuals at the Ministry of Culture. While the government initially agreed to negotiate with the group, protest participants later reported police harassment, intimidation, and charges of violating health restrictions.

- During the year, the government continued to expand its list of so-called *regulados*, the more than 200 Cuban citizens who are not allowed to travel abroad due to their dissident political activities, human rights advocacy, or practice of independent journalism. The government also stepped up interrogations, threats, detentions, raids, and exorbitant fines targeting independent journalists and activists who publishing critical stories on foreign websites or social media.

POLITICAL RIGHTS: 1 / 40

A. ELECTORAL PROCESS: 0 / 12

A1. Was the current head of government or other chief national authority elected through free and fair elections? 0 / 4

Under the 2019 constitution, the president and vice president of the republic are chosen to serve up to two five-year terms by the National Assembly, and the prime minister and other members of the Council of Ministers are designated by the National Assembly upon the proposal of the president. In practice, these processes ratify candidates who have been preselected by the ruling Communist Party of Cuba (PCC).

Miguel Díaz-Canel was elected as president of the republic under the new constitutional system in a nearly unanimous National Assembly vote in October 2019. In December of that year, he named Manuel Marrero as prime minister. Díaz-Canel had been the president of the Council of State, Cuba's top executive office under the old constitution, since 2018, when he succeeded Raúl Castro in a tightly controlled transfer of power. However, Castro, who had succeeded his brother Fidel in 2008, continued to wield considerable power as first secretary of the PCC as of 2020.

A2. Were the current national legislative representatives elected through free and fair elections? 0 / 4

The unicameral National Assembly is directly elected to serve five-year terms, but a PCC-controlled commission designates all candidates, presenting voters with a single candidate for each seat. Those who receive more than 50 percent of the valid votes cast are deemed elected. The National Assembly in turn selects the 21 members of the Council of State, a body that exercises legislative power between the assembly's two brief annual sessions.

In the 2018 National Assembly elections, all 605 of the approved candidates were deemed elected.

A3. Are the electoral laws and framework fair, and are they implemented impartially by the relevant election management bodies? 0 / 4

The only Cuban elections that offer a choice of more than one candidate per office are those for municipal assemblies, but no campaigning is allowed. This did not change under the new electoral law unanimously approved in 2019 following ratification of the new constitution, which retained the system of PCC-controlled electoral and candidacy commissions. However, the new law eliminated provincial assemblies, calling instead for municipal assemblies to approve provincial governors proposed by the president, and cut the number of National Assembly delegates to 474 as of the 2023 elections.

B. POLITICAL PLURALISM AND PARTICIPATION: 0 / 16

B1. Do the people have the right to organize in different political parties or other competitive political groupings of their choice, and is the system free of undue obstacles to the rise and fall of these competing parties or groupings? 0 / 4

The constitution identifies the PCC as the "superior driving force of the society and the state." All other political parties are illegal. Political dissent is a punishable offense, and dissidents are systematically harassed, detained, physically assaulted, and imprisoned for minor infractions. Supposedly spontaneous mob attacks, known as "acts of repudiation," are often used to silence political dissidents.

The Cuban Observatory of Human Rights (OCDH), a nongovernmental organization based in Madrid, reported about 1,800 arbitrary detentions of peaceful dissidents during 2020. As has been typical in recent years, these detentions normally took place without legal oversight and were combined with home raids, fines, confiscation of belongings, beatings, and threats. Such brief politically motivated detentions of political dissidents and independent journalists were a key repressive tactic under the government of Raúl Castro, and they have continued in a similar fashion under Díaz-Canel.

B2. Is there a realistic opportunity for the opposition to increase its support or gain power through elections? 0 / 4

The PCC has monopolized government and politics in Cuba since the mid-1960s, allowing no electoral competition and preventing any alternative force from succeeding it through a democratic transfer of power. Dissident groups mounted an unprecedented attempt to field independent candidates in the 2017 municipal elections, but the authorities successfully blocked their candidacies, ensuring that none of them appeared on the ballot. Similarly, security forces mobilized to suppress any opposition activity during both the February 2019 constitutional referendum and the October 2019 election of the president by the National Assembly.

B3. Are the people's political choices free from domination by forces that are external to the political sphere, or by political forces that employ extrapolitical means? 0 / 4

The authoritarian one-party system in Cuba largely excludes the public from any genuine and autonomous political participation. The military and intelligence agencies play an important role in suppressing dissent and wield deep influence over virtually every aspect of the state. Members of dissident groups and even independent actors in the arts, journalism, and other fields are systematically surveilled and periodically interrogated in order to intimidate them or turn them into informants.

State employees who express political dissent or disagreement with the authorities often face harassment or summary dismissal. Professionals dismissed from their jobs in the state sector have difficulty continuing their careers, as licenses for professions are not available in the private sector.

B4. Do various segments of the population (including ethnic, racial, religious, gender, LGBT+, and other relevant groups) have full political rights and electoral opportunities? 0 / 4

The PCC leadership has exhibited greater gender and racial diversity in recent years. However, since political rights are denied to all Cuban citizens, women, Afro-Cubans, and members of other demographic groups are unable to choose their representatives or organize independently to assert their political interests.

At the 2016 party congress, the proportion of women on the PCC Central Committee rose to 44.4 percent, from 41.7 percent in 2011. Afro-Cubans accounted for 35.9 percent, up from 31.3 percent in 2011. Women also now hold more than half of the 605 National Assembly seats; Cubans of African and mixed-race descent make up about half of the assembly. The Afro-Cuban PCC stalwart Esteban Lazo simultaneously holds the powerful positions of National Assembly president and head of the Council of State.

The political interests of LGBT+ people are not well represented. Some public advocacy is permitted, but only with the permission of the PCC. The only openly gay member of the National Assembly, Luis Ángel Adán Roble, stepped down in November 2019 after a rift with the National Center for Sex Education (CENESEX), an institution headed by the daughter of Fidel Castro that seeks to control and direct LGBT+ advocacy.

C. FUNCTIONING OF GOVERNMENT: 1 / 12

C1. Do the freely elected head of government and national legislative representatives determine the policies of the government? 0 / 4

None of Cuba's nominally elected officials are chosen through free and fair contests, and major policy decisions are reserved for the PCC leadership in practice. The National Assembly, which the constitution describes as the "supreme organ of state power," has little independent influence, meets for brief sessions twice a year, and votes unanimously on nearly all matters before it.

C2. Are safeguards against official corruption strong and effective? 1 / 4

Corruption remains a serious problem in Cuba, with widespread illegality permeating everyday life. The state enjoys a monopoly on most large business transactions, and there are no independent mechanisms to hold officials accountable for wrongdoing.

The government has at times pursued anticorruption campaigns, and long prison sentences have been imposed on high-level Cuban officials and foreign businessmen found guilty of corruption-related charges. However, internal reforms that would make the system more transparent and less prone to abuse have been rejected, and the authorities do not tolerate civil society groups, independent journalists, or independent courts that might serve as external checks on government malfeasance.

In 2020, as the COVID-19 pandemic exacerbated economic hardship, state media publicized an official crackdown on illegal commercial activity that featured a distinct lack of due process.

C3. Does the government operate with openness and transparency? 0 / 4

Cuba lacks effective laws that provide for freedom of information and access to official records. Major state events frequently take place behind closed doors, and the government withholds many types of statistics from the public. Most decisions surrounding the government's response to the pandemic in 2020 were made and implemented without transparency or consultation.

CIVIL LIBERTIES: 12 / 60 (−1)

D. FREEDOM OF EXPRESSION AND BELIEF: 4 / 16 (−1)

D1. Are there free and independent media? 0 / 4 (−1)

Cuba has one of the most restrictive media environments in the world. The formal media sector is owned and controlled by the state, and the constitution prohibits privately owned media. The country's independent press operates outside the law, its publications are considered "enemy propaganda," and its journalists are routinely harassed, detained, interrogated, threatened, defamed in the official press, and prohibited from traveling abroad. Government agents regularly accuse them of being mercenaries and even terrorists, and many face charges of "usurpation of legal capacity," "diffusion of false news," or other vaguely defined offenses. For example, in September 2020, journalist Roberto Quiñones completed a one-year prison sentence after refusing to pay a fine for "resistance" and "disobedience" in custody; he had initially been arrested and beaten while covering a trial for the news website CubaNet.

Decree Law 370, enacted in 2019, bans Cuban citizens from hosting their writings on foreign servers—including social media platforms like Facebook—and prohibits the circulation of "information contrary to the social interest, morals, good customs, and integrity of people." Authorities increased their use of the law against independent journalists during 2020, subjecting dozens of individuals to arbitrary arrests, fines, or confiscation of their devices. The crackdown frequently included threats against the journalists' families as well as pressure to delete and discontinue their critical coverage of the government.

In addition to independent journalism, the government closely monitors and persecutes perceived dissidents within the artistic community and has increasingly turned its attention to more mainstream artists and media figures who air independent or critical views. Members of the artists' collective MSI—formed in response to Decree Law 349 of 2018, which requires Ministry of Culture approval for public and private cultural activities and bans artistic content based on ill-defined criteria such as harm to "ethical and cultural values"—were repeatedly harassed and intimidated during 2020. After rapper Denis Solís was arrested, tried, and sentenced to eight months in jail for "contempt of authority" in November, fellow MSI members organized protests and a hunger strike. The movement's headquarters, at the Havana home of artist Luis Manuel Otero Alcántara, was besieged by the authorities, who ultimately raided the house and detained 14 people, citing violations of pandemic-related health restrictions. The next day, on November 27, a larger group of artists, writers, and supporters held a sit-in protest at the Culture Ministry, prompting the government to offer negotiations. Officials soon reneged on their promises, however, and in December the regime carried out a wave of extralegal house arrests, arbitrary detentions, and mob violence against leading independent journalists and artists associated with the movement. Some also had their phone and internet service cut off, and state media conducted smear campaigns against key journalists and outlets.

The intensified repression during 2020 was driven in part by the expansion of mobile internet service in recent years, as many Cubans have used their access to share independent news and information, criticize government performance, and post popular hashtags associated with protests and dissidents. Solís was notably detained after posting a video on social media in which he confronted a police officer who had entered his home.

Score Change: The score declined from 1 to 0 due to an increase in the government's use of detentions, house arrest, fines, harassment, and other reprisals to suppress independent journalism and expressions of dissent among artists and writers.

D2. Are individuals free to practice and express their religious faith or nonbelief in public and private? 3 / 4

Religious freedom has improved over the past decade, but official obstacles still make it difficult for churches to operate without interference. Certain church groups have struggled to obtain registration, and association with an unregistered group is a criminal offense. The Roman Catholic Church has enjoyed an expansion of its pastoral rights, including periodic access to state media and public spaces and the ability to build new churches and distribute its own publications. Protestant and evangelical groups tend to face greater restrictions, though they too have experienced improved conditions in recent years.

D3. Is there academic freedom, and is the educational system free from extensive political indoctrination? 0 / 4

Academic freedom is restricted in Cuba. Private schools and universities have been banned since the early 1960s, teaching materials often contain ideological content, and educators commonly require PCC affiliation for career advancement. University students have been expelled for dissident behavior. Despite the elimination of exit visas in 2013, university faculty must still obtain permission to travel to academic conferences abroad, and officials often prevent dissident intellectuals from attending such events. Officials also deny entry to prominent intellectuals who have been critical of the regime. Recent years have featured numerous cases of academics being dismissed from positions in reprisal for their political opinions or activities.

D4. Are individuals free to express their personal views on political or other sensitive topics without fear of surveillance or retribution? 1 / 4

Cubans often engage in robust private discussions regarding everyday issues like the economy, food prices, foreign travel, and difficulties gaining internet access, but they tend to avoid discussing more sensitive political issues such as human rights and civil liberties. Neighborhood-level "Committees for the Defense of the Revolution" assist security agencies by monitoring, reporting, and suppressing dissent.

The authorities also monitor expressions of dissent on social media and through surveillance of electronic communications, punishing users with criminal charges or other forms of reprisal. Decree Law 389, approved in 2019, authorizes investigators to engage in electronic surveillance without prior judicial approval and use the resulting information as evidence in criminal cases. Anonymity and encryption technologies are legally prohibited, but many Cubans with mobile internet access use encrypted services such as WhatsApp and Telegram to communicate privately among trusted friends.

E. ASSOCIATIONAL AND ORGANIZATIONAL RIGHTS: 0 / 12

E1. Is there freedom of assembly? 0 / 4

Restrictions on freedom of assembly remain a key form of political control. Security forces and government-backed assailants routinely break up peaceful gatherings or protests by political dissidents and civic activists.

During 2020, the government took advantage of the pandemic to expand its control over public assembly, exercising emergency powers without legal restraint and in some cases using the threat of contagion to justify raids on protests and dissident gatherings, as with the raid on MSI hunger strikers in late November. Although the action provoked an unprecedented day-long solidarity sit-in by more than 150 mainstream artists and intellectuals in front of the Ministry of Culture, many of the leading participants—and independent journalists who covered the movement—were later subjected to various forms of harassment and intimidation by the authorities.

E2. Is there freedom for nongovernmental organizations, particularly those that are engaged in human rights- and governance-related work? 0 / 4

Citing the 1985 Law on Associations, the government refuses to register any new organization that is not state supervised. Nearly all politically motivated short-term detentions in recent years have targeted members of independent associations, think tanks, human rights groups, political parties, or trade unions.

A number of independent civil society organizations suffered repression during 2020, with some activists detained on arbitrary charges, imprisoned, prevented from traveling abroad, or forced into exile. In addition to the MSI, the dissident groups most commonly persecuted by the government include the Ladies in White, the Patriotic Union of Cuba (UNPACU), the Christian Liberation Movement (MCL), the United Anti-Totalitarian Forum (FAU), and the Cuban Association of Electoral Observers (ACOE).

E3. Is there freedom for trade unions and similar professional or labor organizations? 0 / 4

Cuban workers do not have the right to strike or bargain collectively, and independent labor unions are illegal.

F. RULE OF LAW: 2 / 16

F1. Is there an Independent Judiciary? 0 / 4

According to the constitution, the National Assembly controls judicial appointments and suspensions, and the Council of State exercises these powers when the assembly is not in session. The Council of State is also empowered to issue "instructions of a general character" to the courts, whose rulings typically conform to the interests of the PCC in practice. Judges are tasked with enforcing laws on vaguely defined offenses such as "public disorder," "contempt," "disrespect for authority," "precriminal dangerousness," and "aggression," which are used to prosecute the regime's political opponents.

F2. Does due process prevail In civil and criminal matters? 0 / 4

The regime's systematic violation of due process is regularly illustrated by trumped-up criminal cases against dissidents and independent journalists, many of which were reported during or continued into 2020. They included cases against UNPACU leader José Daniel Ferrer, artist Luis Manuel Otero Alcántara, rapper Denis Solís, journalist Roberto Quiñones, and Silverio Portal, an activist who completed a four-year prison sentence for "contempt" and "public disorder" in December. While many political detainees are held for short periods or eventually released from prison, they remain subject to new charges and extralegal confinement or harassment by the authorities.

F3. Is there protection from the illegitimate use of physical force and freedom from war and insurgencies? 1 / 4

Although violent crime rates are believed to be relatively low, physical security for the population is undermined by government-backed violence. Opposition activists, human rights defenders, and other perceived enemies of the regime are routinely subjected to public assaults, excessive use of force by police during raids and arrests, and abuse in custody.

The government has repeatedly refused to allow international monitoring of its prisons. Prison conditions are poor, featuring overcrowding, forced labor, inadequate sanitation and medical care, and physical abuse.

F4. Do laws, policies, and practices guarantee equal treatment of various segments of the population? 1 / 4

Article 42 of the 2019 constitution extended protection from discrimination to a wider array of vulnerable groups, explicitly adding categories such as ethnic origin, gender identity, sexual orientation, age, and disability to the existing safeguards regarding race, sex, national origin, and religion. PCC control of the government and justice system limits their ability to enforce such guarantees impartially or effectively, and independent calls for equal treatment can draw state reprisals.

Women enjoy legal equality and are well represented in most professions, though their labor force participation rate lags well behind that of men, suggesting persistent economic disparities and cultural double standards.

While racial discrimination has long been outlawed, Cubans of African descent have reported widespread discrimination and profiling by police. Many lack access to the dollar economy. A 2017–18 survey found that more than three-quarters of those receiving crucial remittances from abroad were White, leaving Afro-Cubans at an even greater disadvantage.

Discrimination based on sexual orientation is illegal in areas such as employment and housing, and Mariela Castro Espín, Raúl Castro's daughter and the director of CENESEX, has advocated on behalf of LGBT+ people. However, the advocacy efforts of independent LGBT+ groups and activists are either ignored or suppressed.

G. PERSONAL AUTONOMY AND INDIVIDUAL RIGHTS: 6 / 16

G1. Do individuals enjoy freedom of movement, including the ability to change their place of residence, employment, or education? 1 / 4

Freedom of movement and the right to change one's residence and place of employment are restricted. Cubans who move to Havana without authorization are subject to removal. Cubans still face extremely high passport fees, and Cuban doctors, diplomats, and athletes who "defect" abroad are prohibited from visiting for eight years. Some dissidents and journalists are barred from foreign travel, despite a 2013 migration law that rescinded the exit-visa requirement. The number of these individuals, known as *regulados*, rose sharply during 2020, with estimates exceeding 200 by late in the year.

G2. Are individuals able to exercise the right to own property and establish private businesses without undue interference from state or nonstate actors? 1 / 4

The 2019 constitution recognized private property as one form of ownership, though opportunities to obtain property and operate private enterprises remain restricted. In 2020, the government's largely successful measures to contain COVID-19, combined with the pandemic's impact on the global economy, had a severe effect on the country's fragile private sector. As of May, nearly 40 percent of the more than 600,000 licensed self-employed workers had temporarily closed their businesses due to public health–related constraints.

Partly in response to the crisis, the government in July announced plans for a series of economic reforms, including the legalization of small and medium-sized enterprises, the elimination of the restrictive list of permitted self-employment occupations, the opening of wholesale markets to self-employed workers, and a move to allow private businesses to import materials and export their products through state companies. In addition, the government said it would enable the growth of cooperatives outside the agricultural sector.

G3. Do individuals enjoy personal social freedoms, including choice of marriage partner and size of family, protection from domestic violence, and control over appearance? 3 / 4

Individuals enjoy broad freedom in their interpersonal, romantic, and sexual relationships. While divorce is common, men and women have equal rights to marital goods and child custody. The 2019 constitution does not contain language that defines marriage as a union between a man and a woman, raising the possibility that same-sex marriage could be legalized in the future. A proposed constitutional change that would have more explicitly supported legalization was ultimately rejected. Abortion is legal in Cuba.

The country lacks specific legislation to address gender-based or domestic forms of violence, and police are reportedly unresponsive to complaints of such abuse.

G4. Do individuals enjoy equality of opportunity and freedom from economic exploitation? 1 / 4

Average official salaries remain extremely low. The national currency is very weak, encouraging an exodus of trained personnel into the private and tourism sectors, where the convertible peso—pegged to the US dollar—is used. Cubans employed by foreign firms are often much better remunerated than their fellow citizens, even though most are contracted through a state employment agency that siphons off the bulk of their wages and uses political criteria in screening applicants.

Cyprus

Population: 1,200,000
Capital: Nicosia
Freedom Status: Free
Electoral Democracy: Yes

Note: The numerical scores and status listed here do not reflect conditions in Northern Cyprus, which is examined in a separate report. *Freedom in the World* reports assess the level of political rights and civil liberties in a given geographical area, regardless of whether they are affected by the state, nonstate actors, or foreign powers. Disputed territories are sometimes assessed separately if they meet certain criteria, including boundaries that are sufficiently stable to allow year-on-year comparisons. For more information, see the report methodology and FAQ.

Overview: The Republic of Cyprus is a democracy that has de jure sovereignty over the entire island. In practice, however, the government controls only the southern, largely Greek-speaking part of the island, as the northern area is ruled by the self-declared Turkish Republic of Northern Cyprus (TRNC), recognized only by Turkey. Political rights and civil liberties are generally respected in the Republic of Cyprus. Ongoing concerns include corruption, societal discrimination against minority groups, and weaknesses in the asylum system.

KEY DEVELOPMENTS IN 2020

- The first cases of COVID-19 in Cyprus were confirmed in March. The government adopted temporary lockdown measures, including restrictions on incoming travelers and the closure of most businesses for two months. The virus remained well controlled for most of the year, though cases began to rise in the autumn. A total of 22,000 confirmed cases and 119 deaths had been reported by year's end.
- Due in part to the pandemic, the country received only about 7,000 new asylum applications in 2020, down from 13,600 in 2019. However, there were still nearly 20,000 cases yet to be processed at the end of the year, and the Cypriot coast guard reportedly pushed back some vessels carrying refugees from ports in Turkey and Lebanon.
- A media investigation published in August implicated politicians and state officials in an alleged scheme to facilitate citizenship applications by foreign investors with criminal records.

POLITICAL RIGHTS: 38 / 40

A. ELECTORAL PROCESS: 12 / 12

A1. Was the current head of government or other chief national authority elected through free and fair elections? 4 / 4

The president is elected by popular vote for five-year terms. The current president, Nicos Anastasiades of the center-right Democratic Rally (DISY), won a second term with 56 percent of the vote in a 2018 runoff against Stavros Malas, who was backed by the left-wing Progressive Party of Working People (AKEL). The two had outpolled seven other candidates in the first round. International observers found that the overall election process adhered to democratic principles.

A2. Were the current national legislative representatives elected through free and fair elections? 4 / 4

The unicameral House of Representatives has 80 seats filled through proportional representation for five-year terms. The Turkish Cypriot community has 24 reserved seats, which have been unfilled since Turkish Cypriot representatives withdrew from the chamber in 1964.

In the 2016 legislative elections, which were held in accordance with international standards, DISY led the voting with 18 seats, down slightly from 2011, followed by AKEL with 16, also a decline. The Democratic Party (DIKO) received 9 seats, the Movement for Social Democracy (EDEK) took 3, and the Green Party secured 2. Three new parties won seats for the first time: the far-right National Popular Front (ELAM) took 2, while 3 each went to the center-left Citizens' Alliance (SYPOL) and the right-wing Solidarity, an offshoot of DISY.

A3. Are the electoral laws and framework fair, and are they implemented impartially by the relevant election management bodies? 4 / 4

Electoral laws are generally fair. In their report on the 2018 presidential vote, election monitors from the Organization for Security and Co-operation in Europe (OSCE) noted some improvements since the 2013 contest, including 2017 legal changes that abolished most mandatory-voting provisions and established a ceiling of €1 million ($1.1 million) for candidates' campaign spending. The report found that the election was administered in a "highly professional, efficient, and transparent manner."

B. POLITICAL PLURALISM AND PARTICIPATION: 15 / 16

B1. Do the people have the right to organize in different political parties or other competitive political groupings of their choice, and is the system free of undue obstacles to the rise and fall of these competing parties or groupings? 4 / 4

A wide array of parties compete in the political system. Cyprus's two main parties, DISY on the right and AKEL on the left, usually split the largest share of the vote, but neither has dominated politics, and other parties are often able to play significant roles. Both DISY and AKEL lost seats in the 2016 parliamentary elections, and despite an increase in the vote threshold for representation, from 1.8 percent to 3.6 percent, three new parties were able to enter the parliament. In the May 2019 European Parliament (EP) elections, four parties won representation: DISY and AKEL with two seats each, and DIKO and EDEK with one each.

B2. Is there a realistic opportunity for the opposition to increase its support or gain power through elections? 4 / 4

Cyprus has experienced regular democratic transfers of power between rival parties in recent decades, and multiple opposition parties are able to gain representation in the legislature.

B3. Are the people's political choices free from domination by forces that are external to the political sphere, or by political forces that employ extrapolitical means? 4 / 4

People are generally able to express their political choices without undue interference from outside actors.

B4. Do various segments of the population (including ethnic, racial, religious, gender, LGBT+, and other relevant groups) have full political rights and electoral opportunities? 3 / 4

Three recognized Christian minority groups—the Armenians, the Latins, and the Maronites—each have one nonvoting representative in the parliament. Members of these communities vote in special elections for their representatives, as well as in the general elections. The 24 seats reserved for the Turkish Cypriot population remain unfilled. However, in the 2019 EP elections, Niyazi Kızılyürek of AKEL became the first Turkish Cypriot to be elected to the EP or to win office in the Republic of Cyprus since 1964.

Women in Cyprus have equal political rights, but they are underrepresented in political parties. No parliamentary party is led by a woman, and parties have failed to meet internal quotas mandating that 30 to 35 percent of their candidates be women. Women hold about a fifth of the seats in the House of Representatives. No women ran for president in 2018. Sexism and patriarchal attitudes discourage women from playing a more active role in politics.

The interests of the LGBT+ community, which still faces significant discrimination from some sectors of society, are not always well represented in the political system.

C. FUNCTIONING OF GOVERNMENT: 11 / 12

C1. Do the freely elected head of government and national legislative representatives determine the policies of the government? 4 / 4

The freely elected government is able to make and implement policy without improper interference from unelected entities.

C2. Are safeguards against official corruption strong and effective? 3 / 4

Cyprus has strong anticorruption laws that are, for the most part, adequately enforced. However, there have been a number of high-profile corruption scandals in recent years, and critics of the government's record have raised concerns about early releases and pardons of individuals convicted on corruption charges.

In August 2020, Al Jazeera released an investigative report on Cyprus's citizenship-by-investment program. It revealed that at least 30 of the roughly 1,400 wealthy applicants who received European Union (EU) citizenship by investing €2 million ($2.2 million) in Cyprus had criminal convictions or pending charges; another 40 were identified as "politically exposed persons," meaning they held senior positions in governments or state-owned enterprises. This led some analysts to conclude that members of the Cypriot government may have knowingly facilitated the problematic applications in violation of the law. Demetris Syllouris, the speaker of the Cypriot parliament, and another lawmaker, Christakis Giovanis, resigned in October after being implicated in the media investigation; several state officials were also accused of wrongdoing. The government terminated the citizenship-by-investment program in November.

C3. Does the government operate with openness and transparency? 4 / 4

In general, the government operates with openness and transparency. The country enacted a long-awaited freedom of information law in late 2017, though civil society activists had argued that the bill's exemptions were too broad.

CIVIL LIBERTIES: 56 / 60
D. FREEDOM OF EXPRESSION AND BELIEF: 15 / 16
D1. Are there free and independent media? 4 / 4

Freedom of speech is constitutionally guaranteed, and media freedom is generally respected. A vibrant independent press frequently holds the authorities to account. Numerous private outlets compete with public media, and there are no restrictions on access to online news sources.

In 2019, the auditor general threatened to withhold state subsidies from the English-language daily *Cyprus Mail* after the newspaper used a Turkish geographical name in its reports. Separately, in February 2020, the auditor general and the *Kathimerini* newspaper—along with its parent company—filed lawsuits against one another for alleged defamation.

In March 2020, in a rare act of violence against the media, a pipe bomb exploded at the offices of MC Digital Media Group, which owns the *Cyprus Times* and other outlets. No one was injured in the attack, and it did not cause extensive damage.

D2. Are individuals free to practice and express their religious faith or nonbelief in public and private? 4 / 4

Freedom of religion is guaranteed by the constitution and generally protected in practice. Nearly 90 percent of those living in government-controlled Cyprus are Orthodox Christians, and the Orthodox Church enjoys certain privileges, including religious instruction and some religious services in public schools. Non-Orthodox students may opt out of such activities. The government recognizes Muslim religious institutions and facilitates crossings at the UN buffer zone between north and south for the purpose of worship at religious sites.

Muslim groups have occasionally faced obstacles in the operation of their religious sites or discrimination by the general public. For example, the nongovernmental organizations (NGOs) Caritas and Action for Equality, Support, Antiracism (KISA) have reported cases of private employers refusing to hire women who wore hijabs. However, according to Caritas, Muslim students have faced less discrimination recently than in previous years. Members of other religious minorities sometimes encounter isolated incidents of discrimination.

D3. Is there academic freedom, and is the educational system free from extensive political indoctrination? 3 / 4

Academic freedom is respected in Cyprus. However, state schools use textbooks containing negative language about Turkish Cypriots and Turkey, and there is some political pressure regarding schools' treatment of sensitive historical and unification-related issues.

D4. Are individuals free to express their personal views on political or other sensitive topics without fear of surveillance or retribution? 4 / 4

People are generally free to engage in political and other sensitive discussions without fear of retribution or surveillance.

E. ASSOCIATIONAL AND ORGANIZATIONAL RIGHTS: 12 / 12
E1. Is there freedom of assembly? 4 / 4

Freedom of assembly is constitutionally guaranteed and generally respected.

E2. Is there freedom for nongovernmental organizations, particularly those that are engaged in human rights- and governance-related work? 4 / 4

NGOs are generally free to operate without government interference. However, in June 2020, the Supreme Court ordered KISA to pay a €10,000 ($11,000) fine for defamation over a document that criticized two government appointees. In August, the parliament amended the law on associations, empowering the Ministry of Interior to swiftly deregister NGOs it deems inactive or noncompliant with the law's filing requirements. The ministry deregistered KISA in December, despite the group's claims that the action was illegal and unconstitutional. An appeal was pending at year's end.

E3. Is there freedom for trade unions and similar professional or labor organizations? 4 / 4

Workers have the right to strike, form independent trade unions, and engage in collective bargaining. The law provides remedies for antiunion discrimination, though enforcement is uneven.

F. RULE OF LAW: 15 / 16
F1. Is there an independent judiciary? 4 / 4

The judiciary is independent in practice. Supreme Court judges are appointed by the president on the recommendation of the court's existing members, and lower court judges are appointed by Supreme Court judges in their capacity as the Supreme Council of Judicature.

F2. Does due process prevail in civil and criminal matters? 4 / 4

The justice system generally upholds due process standards. Law enforcement agencies largely observe safeguards against arbitrary arrest and detention, and criminal defendants have access to counsel and fair trial procedures.

F3. Is there protection from the illegitimate use of physical force and freedom from war and insurgencies? 4 / 4

Residents of Cyprus are free from major threats to physical security, though human rights monitors have noted cases of police brutality. Overcrowding and other problematic conditions have been reported at prisons and migrant detention centers.

In an attempt to block Cyprus's efforts to explore for offshore oil and gas, the Turkish government has threatened to use force against drilling vessels. Ankara argues that the maritime areas in question are under the jurisdiction of either Turkey or the TRNC. Tensions rose in August 2020 when a Turkish survey ship with military escorts entered disputed waters west of Cyprus. In December, the EU approved sanctions against Turkish officials and entities in response to the action.

F4. Do laws, policies, and practices guarantee equal treatment of various segments of the population? 3 / 4

Despite government efforts to combat prejudice and inequality, members of non–Greek Cypriot minority groups, including migrants and asylum seekers, face discrimination and occasional violence.

More than 7,000 new asylum applications were filed in 2020. While this represented a decrease from the roughly 13,600 applications in 2019, due in part to the COVID-19 pandemic, the influx in recent years has created a large backlog of asylum cases, which can take several years to process. The Cypriot Asylum Service estimated that there were 19,660 applications pending at the end of 2020. A specialized administrative court began operating in June 2019 to handle appeals. While many newcomers are quickly released from overburdened reception centers, they often lack access to other housing. Overcrowding and other poor conditions at the Pournara center were exacerbated in 2020 by COVID-19 lockdowns, prompting protests by the residents. Separately, in March and September, the Cypriot coast guard reportedly pushed back vessels that were carrying refugees and migrants from ports in Turkey and Lebanon.

Gender discrimination in the workplace remains a problem, including with respect to hiring practices, salaries, and sexual harassment; laws against it have not been adequately enforced.

Antidiscrimination laws generally prohibit bias based on sexual orientation, and there are legal protections for transgender people on some issues as well. For example, laws barring incitement to hatred apply to both sexual orientation and gender identity. However, the LGBT+ community continues to face societal discrimination in practice.

G. PERSONAL AUTONOMY AND INDIVIDUAL RIGHTS: 14 / 16

G1. Do individuals enjoy freedom of movement, including the ability to change their place of residence, employment, or education? 3 / 4

There are few impediments to freedom of movement within the government-controlled area of the Republic of Cyprus. The UN buffer zone dividing the island remains in place, though travel between north and south has improved since 2004 due to an increase in the number of border crossings. Two new crossing points opened in 2018. However, in response to the COVID-19 pandemic, the border was closed for parts of 2020.

G2. Are individuals able to exercise the right to own property and establish private businesses without undue interference from state or nonstate actors? 4 / 4

Property rights are generally respected in Cyprus. A 1991 law stipulates that property left by Turkish Cypriots after 1974, when a Turkish invasion divided the island, belongs to the state. Under the law in the north, Greek Cypriots can appeal to the Immovable Property Commission (IMP), which in 2010 was recognized by the European Court of Human Rights as a responsible authority for the resolution of property disputes. However, its work has been seriously impaired in recent years by a lack of funding from the TRNC and Ankara.

G3. Do individuals enjoy personal social freedoms, including choice of marriage partner and size of family, protection from domestic violence, and control over appearance? 4 / 4

Personal social freedoms are largely unrestricted. Same-sex civil unions are allowed under a 2015 law, but it did not include adoption rights for same-sex couples. Since 2017, the government has been considering legislation that would establish a procedure to correct one's legal gender. Domestic violence remains a problem despite official efforts to prevent and punish it. Two government-funded shelters are open to survivors of domestic abuse.

G4. Do individuals enjoy equality of opportunity and freedom from economic exploitation? 3 / 4

The legal framework generally protects workers against exploitative conditions of employment, and the government has made genuine progress in combating human trafficking. However, persistent problems include insufficient resources for labor inspectors and illegally low pay for undocumented migrant workers. Migrant workers and asylum seekers remain vulnerable to sexual exploitation and forced labor.

Czech Republic

Population: 10,700,000
Capital: Prague
Freedom Status: Free
Electoral Democracy: Yes

Overview: The Czech Republic is a parliamentary democracy in which political rights and civil liberties are generally respected. However, in recent years, the country has experienced several corruption scandals and political disputes that have hampered normal legislative activity. Illiberal rhetoric and the influence of powerful business entities in the political arena are increasingly visible.

KEY DEVELOPMENTS IN 2020

- In March, at the beginning of the coronavirus pandemic's outbreak in the Czech Republic, Prime Minister Babiš announced inaccurate information about the number of COVID-19 testing sites opened by the government and declared that medical staff at testing sites were performing tests on everyone who had shown symptoms of the virus, which was false. Though the government later corrected Babiš's announcements, the conflicting reports were an example the government's lack of transparency around the public health crisis. By the end of the year, over 718,000 people tested positive for the virus, and over 11,500 people died, according to government statistics provided to the World Health Organization (WHO).
- In October, the Interior Ministry proposed a legislative amendment that would allow officials to withhold information pertaining to crisis situations that they believe, if made public, would endanger the management of that crisis. Critics argued that this restriction of oversight would give authorities an excuse to hide sensitive information from the public.

POLITICAL RIGHTS: 36 / 40

A. ELECTORAL PROCESS: 12 / 12

A1. Was the current head of government or other chief national authority elected through free and fair elections? 4 / 4

The president is the head of state but holds limited powers and is directly elected to up to two five-year terms. The January 2018 presidential election was considered credible. President Miloš Zeman of the Party of Civic Rights was reelected, defeating his opponent, Jiří Drahoš, in the second round of voting.

The prime minister is the head of government and holds most executive power. In December 2017, controversial billionaire Andrej Babiš of the Action of Dissatisfied Citizens (ANO) party was sworn in as prime minister, following elections that were held in accordance with international standards.

A2. Were the current national legislative representatives elected through free and fair elections? 4 / 4

The 200 members of the Chamber of Deputies, the lower house of Parliament, are elected to four-year terms by proportional representation. The Senate, the upper chamber, which holds limited legislative power, has 81 members elected for six-year terms, with one-third up for election every two years.

The Babiš-led ANO won 78 seats in the Chamber of Deputies in the October 2017 legislative elections, followed by the Civic Democratic Party (ODS) with 25, and the populist, anti-immigration Freedom and Direct Democracy (SPD) party with 22. The polls were generally well administered, and the results were broadly accepted by stakeholders.

Mainstream parties refused to cooperate with Babiš after his late 2017 appointment as prime minister, and he struggled to assemble a coalition. In July 2018, after almost nine months of negations, corruption allegations, and a vote of no confidence in January, ANO and the Czech Social Democratic Party (ČSSD) with the support of the Communist Party of Bohemia and Moravia (KSČM) formed a coalition government. Since then, the coalition has experienced several crises, with ČSSD threatening to leave the coalition multiple times.

Elections for 27 Senate seats were held in October 2020. The center-right opposition party Mayors and Independents (STAN) won the most seats (10). The elections were administered fairly, with public health measures implemented to prevent the spread of the COVID-19 pandemic. Opposition parties accused Prime Minister Babiš of delaying action on the coronavirus crisis out of fear that unpopular public health measures may decrease the coalition government's support.

A3. Are the electoral laws and framework fair, and are they implemented impartially by the relevant election management bodies? 4 / 4

The electoral framework is robust and generally well implemented by the State Election Commission. However, the body does not always operate with transparency, and a 2017 Organization for Security and Co-operation in Europe (OSCE) needs-assessment mission expressed concern that its meetings were typically closed to the public and opposition representatives. The OSCE mission also criticized the decentralized procedures surrounding the maintenance of voter lists, which made the lists difficult to verify.

B. POLITICAL PLURALISM AND PARTICIPATION: 15 / 16

B1. Do the people have the right to organize in different political parties or other competitive political groupings of their choice, and is the system free of undue obstacles to the rise and fall of these competing parties or groupings? 4 / 4

Political parties are free to form and operate. Since the 2013 elections, the establishment parties ODS and the ČSSD have lost support, and space has opened up for the populist ANO, anti-immigration and nationalist SPD, and liberal Czech Pirate Party.

B2. Is there a realistic opportunity for the opposition to increase its support or gain power through elections? 4 / 4

Power rotates between parties regularly. The opposition holds a large majority in the Senate.

B3. Are the people's political choices free from domination by forces that are external to the political sphere, or by political forces that employ extrapolitical means? 4 / 4

The influence of politically connected media outlets has been a growing concern since a significant controversy arose in 2017 involving the daily newspaper *MF Dnes*, which is among the assets Babiš placed in a trust to comply with 2016 conflict-of-interest legislation. Critics have accused him of using *MF Dnes* and another newspaper his trust owns, *Lidove noviny*, as tools to advance his political and business interests. In October 2019, Petr Kellner, the country's wealthiest man, acquired the company that operates one of the most influential Czech television channels, TV Nova. Reports suggest Kellner has helped mobilize a network of experts and journalists to improve China's image in the country, which he refutes.

B4. Do various segments of the population (including ethnic, racial, religious, gender, LGBT+, and other relevant groups) have full political rights and electoral opportunities? 3 / 4

By law, all citizens have full political rights and electoral opportunities. However, the Roma lack meaningful political representation. Women hold 45 of the 200 seats in the Chamber of Deputies, and 12 of the 81 seats in the Senate. However, women remain under-represented in politics and public bodies generally.

C. FUNCTIONING OF GOVERNMENT: 9 / 12

C1. Do the freely elected head of government and national legislative representatives determine the policies of the government? 4 / 4

Elected officials are duly installed and generally able to craft and implement policy. Political polarization and the controversy surrounding Babiš contributed to drawn-out negotiations that left the country without a governing coalition through the first half of 2018. In addition to the ČSSD threatening to leave the government multiple times in 2019, the prime minister's escalating dispute with President Zeman deepened the nation's political instability.

In late August and early September 2020, president of the Senate Miloš Vystrčil visited Taiwan despite the disapproval of both the coalition government and the president. The visit was met with pressure and threats from the Chinese government. In response, President Zeman announced that he would not include Vystrčil in foreign policy briefings.

C2. Are safeguards against official corruption strong and effective? 2 / 4

Corruption remains a problem in Czech politics, but institutions have generally been responsive to corruption allegations and scandals. In 2017, Czech police and the European Anti-Fraud Office began an investigation into Prime Minister Babiš, following allegations of improprieties, known as the Stork's Nest fraud scandal, regarding the disbursement of European Union (EU) subsidy funds to one of his firms Agrofert, which Babiš still had de facto ownership over, according to a leaked 2018 European Commission legal opinion. The scandal was not resolved in 2020.

C3. Does the government operate with openness and transparency? 3 / 4

The government often fails to proactively publish information about procurement processes, public officials' salaries, and public spending. Members of the public must request a time-sensitive password to view asset declarations online. In 2018, new legislation came into force requiring that the "ultimate beneficial owners" of companies and trust funds be disclosed in a register. Although the register is not available to the public, law enforcement agencies, the courts, and several other entities can access it.

In March 2020, at the beginning of the coronavirus pandemic's outbreak in the country, Prime Minister Babiš announced inaccurate information about the number of COVID-19 testing sites opened by the government and declared incorrectly that medical staff at testing sites were performing tests on everyone who had shown symptoms of the virus. Government reports later corrected Babiš's announcements.

In October 2020, the Interior Ministry proposed a legislative amendment that would allow officials to withhold information pertaining to crisis situations that they believe, if made public, would endanger the management of that crisis. Critics argued that this restriction of oversight and would give authorities an excuse to not share sensitive information with the public.

CIVIL LIBERTIES: 55 / 60

D. FREEDOM OF EXPRESSION AND BELIEF: 14 / 16

D1. Are there free and independent media? 3 / 4

The media operate relatively freely, and the government does not place undue restrictions on content. Legislation protects private ownership of media outlets, but concerns remain about the extent to which the media is controlled by wealthy business figures and its potential impact on journalists' ability to investigate commercial interests.

Although Prime Minister Babiš placed his significant media holdings in a trust, the trust is controlled in part by his close associates. Critics have accused both of his newspapers of biased coverage, claiming that they are being used as tools to advance the prime minister's political interests. Another Czech billionaire, Petr Kellner, announced in October 2019 his upcoming acquisition of Central European Media Enterprises (CME), which owns 30 television channels broadcasting to five countries. Among the most influential television stations in the Czech Republic is TV Nova, now operated by CME. Analysts note that media outlets serve as a means of influence in the region, and although Kellner denies any political motives, his acquisition of CME has raised questions about his influence on public discourse.

In November 2020, the Czech Television Council, a portion of which was newly elected, controversially dismissed its Supervisory Commission, raising questions about the public broadcaster's independence.

D2. Are individuals free to practice and express their religious faith or nonbelief in public and private? 3 / 4

The government generally upholds freedom of religion. Tax benefits and financial support are provided to registered religious groups. The state has initiated a process to return land confiscated from churches by the former communist regime, which will take place over the next 30 years.

D3. Is there academic freedom, and is the educational system free from extensive political indoctrination? 4 / 4

Academic freedom is respected. Ceremonial presidential approval is required for academic positions.

In November 2019, reports emerged that four faculty members at Prague's Charles University had received secret Chinese payments, prompting an investigation and the firing of the faculty members involved. Analysts have voiced concerns that China might use its ties with prominent politicians to build a foothold in Czech academia.

D4. Are individuals free to express their personal views on political or other sensitive topics without fear of surveillance or retribution? 4 / 4

People are generally able to express controversial or political opinions without fear of surveillance or retribution.

E. ASSOCIATIONAL AND ORGANIZATIONAL RIGHTS: 12 / 12

E1. Is there freedom of assembly? 4 / 4

Freedom of assembly is upheld in practice, and demonstrations take place frequently and without incident. In 2019, demonstrations in Prague with approximately 300,000 participants demanded Prime Minister Babiš's resignation over corruption allegations. Protests in 2020 focused on COVID-19 restrictions; police used tear gas and water cannon to disperse protesters in October in Prague.

E2. Is there freedom for nongovernmental organizations, particularly those that are engaged in human rights- and governance-related work? 4 / 4

Tens of thousands of registered nongovernmental organizations (NGOs) operate in the country, generally without interference from the government or security forces. However, the environment for civil society has grown increasingly antagonistic as the government and its allies have harshly criticized some outspoken NGOs.

E3. Is there freedom for trade unions and similar professional or labor organizations? 4 / 4

Trade unions and professional associations function freely, though they are weak in practice. Workers have the right to strike, though this right is limited for essential public employees, such as hospital workers and air traffic controllers.

F. RULE OF LAW: 14 / 16
F1. Is there an independent judiciary? 3 / 4

The judiciary is largely independent, though its complexity and multilayered composition have led to slow delivery of judgments. In 2019, the appointment of Marie Benešová as Justice Minister raised concerns over the independence of the judiciary. She took office in April of that year, following Minister Jan Kněžínek's resignation one day after police investigators proposed charging Babiš with subsidy fraud.

F2. Does due process prevail in civil and criminal matters? 4 / 4

The rule of law generally prevails in civil and criminal matters. Despite corruption and political pressure within law enforcement agencies, the office of the public prosecutor has become more independent in recent years.

However, the recent investigation of Prime Minister Babiš and his nomination for Justice Minister, Marie Benešová, showed that political interests may interfere with due process. In September 2019, President Zeman openly stated he would use his constitutional authority to dismiss potential criminal charges of fraud against the prime minister.

F3. Is there protection from the illegitimate use of physical force and freedom from war and insurgencies? 4 / 4

The Czech Republic is free from war in insurgencies. However, prisons are over-crowded and at times unsanitary.

F4. Do laws, policies, and practices guarantee equal treatment of various segments of the population? 3 / 4

The 2009 Antidiscrimination Act provides for equal treatment regardless of sex, race, age, disability, belief, or sexual orientation. However, high-level public officials—including the Public Defender of Rights appointed in February 2020—have made insensitive comments that some critics have called discriminatory. The Roma face discrimination in the job market and significantly poorer housing conditions than non-Roma, as well as occasional threats and violence from right-wing groups. Many Roma children attend ethnically segregated schools. The COVID-19 pandemic deepened inequality particularly for low-income families with more than one child and Roma students, as classes were moved online and required stable internet connection and often multiple computers per household.

Women are underrepresented at the highest levels of business. According to data from the European Commission, the gender pay gap in the Czech Republic is one of the largest in the EU.

Anti-Muslim attitudes have increased in the wake of the refugee crisis confronting European states, and the country's legal battle with the EU about accepting refugee quotas. The populist and anti-immigration SPD continued to spread Islamophobic rhetoric characterizing Islam as "incompatible with freedom and democracy." These positions are episodically approved by some of the highest representatives of state.

Asylum seekers are routinely detained, and conditions in detention centers are generally poor. Only 1 in 10 applicants were granted asylum in 2020.

G. PERSONAL AUTONOMY AND INDIVIDUAL RIGHTS: 15 / 16

G1. Do individuals enjoy freedom of movement, including the ability to change their place of residence, employment, or education? 4 / 4

Individuals enjoy freedom of movement, including the ability to change their place of residence, employment, or education. In 2020, the government twice restricted movement due to a surge in coronavirus cases, though the measures were in line with public health guidance.

G2. Are individuals able to exercise the right to own property and establish private businesses without undue interference from state or nonstate actors? 4 / 4

The rights to own property and operate private businesses are established in the law and upheld in practice.

G3. Do individuals enjoy personal social freedoms, including choice of marriage partner and size of family, protection from domestic violence, and control over appearance? 4 / 4

Authorities generally do not restrict social freedoms, though same-sex marriages are not legally recognized. While gender discrimination is legally prohibited, sexual harassment in the workplace appears to be fairly common.

Parliament has yet to ratify the Council of Europe's Istanbul Convention on preventing and combating violence against women. Reports show that only a small number of perpetrators of gender-based violence face criminal charges.

During the 2020 coronavirus pandemic, organizations supporting victims of gender-based violence reported a 42 percent increase in calls received, and an almost 50 percent increase in contact with victims, who were often forced to stay in the same household as their abusers.

In September 2019, the government cut funding for NGOs providing support for survivors of gender-based and domestic violence by 70 percent. This severely limited counseling services and legal support to those who have experienced gender-based violence.

G4. Do individuals enjoy equality of opportunity and freedom from economic exploitation? 3 / 4

Human trafficking remains a problem as organized criminal groups use the country as a source, transit, and destination point; women and children are particularly vulnerable to being trafficked for the purpose of sexual exploitation. The government has made serious efforts to fund protective services and other resources for survivors and to prosecute perpetrators.

Denmark

Population: 5,800,000
Capital: Copenhagen
Freedom Status: Free
Electoral Democracy: Yes

Overview: Denmark is a robust democracy with regular free and fair elections. Citizens enjoy full political rights, the government protects free expression and association, and the judiciary functions independently. However, Denmark has struggled to uphold fundamental freedoms for immigrants and other newcomers.

KEY DEVELOPMENTS IN 2020

- By December, 10 individuals who had been deemed "foreign fighters" were administratively deprived of their Danish citizenship. The minister for immigration and integration was granted permanent authorization to carry out this procedure, aimed at people who fight abroad for extremist groups, the same month. It is applicable only to those with dual citizenship.
- At year's end, more than 52,000 citizens had signed a motion to bring the measure known as the "ghetto law" before Parliament, with a view to halting further implementation. The law, applicable to neighborhoods identified as having high unemployment and crime rates and a high percentage of foreign-born residents, permits housing demolition, strict early-education requirements, and more severe penalties for crimes committed in the designated areas.
- Amendments to the Epidemic Act that allowed authorities to sharply curtail individual freedoms were passed in March, but the initial restrictions implemented were relaxed later in the year. In December, a revised proposal that better ensured transparency and democratic control of pandemic measures was proposed, with strong backing from lawmakers and the health care sector.
- In December, lawmakers passed a measure that criminalized sex without explicit consent. Previously, proof of violence or serious threat had been required to bring rape charges.

POLITICAL RIGHTS: 40 / 40

A. ELECTORAL PROCESS: 12 / 12

A1. Was the current head of government or other chief national authority elected through free and fair elections? 4 / 4

The constitution retains a monarch, currently Queen Margrethe II, with mostly ceremonial duties. The monarch chooses the prime minister, usually the leader of the largest party or government coalition. Mette Frederiksen of the Social Democratic Party (SDP) was appointed by Queen Margrethe in June 2019, after that party emerged as Parliament's largest in the election held that month.

A2. Were the current national legislative representatives elected through free and fair elections? 4 / 4

The 179 members of Denmark's unicameral Parliament (Folketinget) are elected to four-year terms through a system of modified proportional representation.

Since the June 2019 elections, Frederiksen has headed an SDP-led government with the support of the Red-Green Alliance, the Socialist People's Party (SF), and the Social Liberal Party (SLP). The election was considered free and fair, and the results were accepted by stakeholders and the public.

A3. Are the electoral laws and framework fair, and are they implemented impartially by the relevant election management bodies? 4 / 4

Robust electoral laws are upheld impartially by the various bodies tasked with implementation.

B. POLITICAL PLURALISM AND PARTICIPATION: 16 / 16

B1. Do the people have the right to organize in different political parties or other competitive political groupings of their choice, and is the system free of undue obstacles to the rise and fall of these competing parties or groupings? 4 / 4

Numerous political parties compete freely.

B2. Is there a realistic opportunity for the opposition to increase its support or gain power through elections? 4 / 4

The Danish political system is open to the rise of opposition parties through elections. In recent years, the most significant political ascent has been that of the Danish People's Party (DF), which supported the 2015–19 Liberal-led government; however, the DF has since seen a dramatic decrease in voter confidence due to internal disagreements and power struggles.

The Nye Borgerlige (New Right) party was established in 2015 by former DF members, and espouses an anti-immigrant, anti-European Union (EU), and libertarian-leaning agenda. In June 2019, it won four parliamentary seats. The new Vegan Party is expected to contest next general elections, having gathered the required number of signatures.

B3. Are the people's political choices free from domination by forces that are external to the political sphere, or by political forces that employ extrapolitical means? 4 / 4

Voters and political figures are generally free from undue influences by actors who are not democratically accountable.

B4. Do various segments of the population (including ethnic, racial, religious, gender, LGBT+, and other relevant groups) have full political rights and electoral opportunities? 4 / 4

The electoral laws guarantee universal suffrage for citizens, as well as representation in regional and municipal elections for permanent residents. Refugees and other immigrants may vote in municipal and regional but not general elections, after having obtained permanent residence at least three years before an election date. Women, LGBT+ people, persons living with disabilities, and members of ethnic and religious minority groups are represented in prominent positions.

In contrast, figures who have voiced discriminatory views have been able to draw attention in the political arena, and their rhetoric may discourage open political participation by the targeted groups. The Hard Line (Stram Kurs) party was formed in 2017 and espouses an anti-Muslim agenda; founder Rasmus Paludan burned copies of the Koran during campaign events in 2019. Hard Line fell short of the two-percent popular-vote threshold to gain parliamentary representation in the 2019 election.

The territories of Greenland and the Faroe Islands each have two representatives in Parliament. They also have their own elected institutions, which have power over almost all areas of governance, except foreign and financial policy.

C. FUNCTIONING OF GOVERNMENT: 12 / 12
C1. Do the freely elected head of government and national legislative representatives determine the policies of the government? 4 / 4

Denmark's freely elected government is able to craft and implement policy. Danish governments most often control a minority of seats in Parliament, ruling with the aid of one or more supporting parties. Since 1909, no single party has held a majority of seats, helping to create a tradition of compromise.

C2. Are safeguards against official corruption strong and effective? 4 / 4

Anticorruption laws and bodies are generally effective, and corruption is not considered an urgent problem in Denmark.

C3. Does the government operate with openness and transparency? 4 / 4

Government operations are generally transparent.

CIVIL LIBERTIES: 57 / 60
D. FREEDOM OF EXPRESSION AND BELIEF: 16 / 16
D1. Are there free and independent media? 4 / 4

Domestic media reflect a wide variety of political opinions and are frequently critical of the government.

D2. Are individuals free to practice and express their religious faith or nonbelief in public and private? 4 / 4

Freedom of worship is legally protected. However, the Evangelical Lutheran Church is subsidized by the government as the official state religion. The faith is taught in public schools, though students may withdraw from religious classes with parental consent.

In 2015, a Danish citizen of Palestinian origin launched an attack on a freedom of expression event and then on a Copenhagen synagogue, killing several people. Since the attack, the government has provided security for Jewish religious and cultural facilities considered to be at risk of attack.

In 2018, a general ban on the public wearing of face coverings, widely referred to as a "burqa ban" applicable to Muslim women, took effect. By July 2020, 60 people had been charged with violating the ban, out of which only some cases addressed specifically the wearing of burqas. Fines for defying the ban range from $150 to $300.

In 2018, Parliament adopted a law requiring mandatory participation in a ceremony for confirmation of newly granted Danish citizenship, with guidelines including a require-ment for shaking hands. The provision was viewed as a means of requiring Muslims who refuse to touch someone of a different gender on religious grounds to adopt practices seen as "Danish." In February 2020, one man rejected the handshake—not for religious reasons, but out of principle—and as a consequence was not granted citizenship. A large number of mayors in municipalities across the country have protested against the regu-lation, which also lacks support from the current government. When COVID-19 struck Denmark in March 2020, all citizenship ceremonies were put on hold, but they were later resumed; as a temporary measure, the handshake was suspended and replaced with the signing of a statement.

D3. Is there academic freedom, and is the educational system free from extensive political indoctrination? 4 / 4

Academic freedom is generally respected.

D4. Are individuals free to express their personal views on political or other sensitive topics without fear of surveillance or retribution? 4 / 4

Private discussion is vibrant and unrestricted.

E. ASSOCIATIONAL AND ORGANIZATIONAL RIGHTS: 12 / 12

E1. Is there freedom of assembly? 4 / 4

The constitution provides for freedom of assembly, which is upheld in practice.

E2. Is there freedom for nongovernmental organizations, particularly those that are engaged in human rights- and governance-related work? 4 / 4

Nongovernmental organizations (NGOs) operate freely in Denmark, and frequently inform policy debates.

E3. Is there freedom for trade unions and similar professional or labor organizations? 4 / 4

Workers are free to organize and bargain collectively.

F. RULE OF LAW: 14 / 16

F1. Is there an independent judiciary? 4 / 4

The judiciary is independent. Judges are formally appointed by the monarch but are recommended by the Justice Minister in consultation with the independent Judicial Appointments Council.

F2. Does due process prevail in civil and criminal matters? 3 / 4

Citizens enjoy full due-process rights. However, restrictions imposed especially on rejected asylum seekers remain in force. Individuals who were denied asylum in Denmark, but whom the government is for various reasons unable to deport, may be subject to administrative measures parallel to those imposed on people with criminal convictions. Many such individuals live in isolated centers with poor facilities where they are subject to travel restrictions and have no legal option to challenge their placement.

In 2019, the Youth Crime Board was established to deal with individuals between the ages of 10 and 17 who violate the law or are at risk of criminal behavior. Youths may be placed in secure institutions where conditions closely resemble those in the detention system. Professionals have criticized the mechanism for reinforcing criminal identity among youth, in addition to effectively lowering the age of criminal responsibility below the age of 15, as outlined by law.

In October 2019, Parliament adopted legislation that would allow the minister of immigration and integration to strip citizenship from individuals who fight abroad for extremist groups, namely the Islamic State (IS); the minister only has the power to do so for those holding dual citizenship. By December 2020, 10 individuals considered to be "foreign fighters" had been stripped of their Danish citizenship, with one additional case pending. Five of the cases were brought to court. By virtue of its "sunset clause," the law was due to expire in 2021, but the government made it permanent in December 2020. Furthermore, children born to Danish parents in conflict zones are henceforth not granted Danish citizenship at birth, and the Danish foreign service may deny fighters in foreign conflicts consular assistance.

F3. Is there protection from the illegitimate use of physical force and freedom from war and insurgencies? 4 / 4

People in Denmark are generally free from violent crime and physical abuse by state authorities.

However, in September 2020, Denmark was found guilty by the European Court of Human Rights (ECHR) of inhuman or degrading treatment when a complainant, Niels Lund Aggerholm, who had been placed in a psychiatric institution for violent behavior and diagnosed with paranoid schizophrenia, was chained to his bed for an uninterrupted period of 23 hours.

F4. Do laws, policies, and practices guarantee equal treatment of various segments of the population? 3 / 4

Danish immigration laws have long been some of the harshest in Europe, and immigration laws and asylum policies were tightened in response to large numbers of refugees and asylum seekers entering Europe beginning in 2015. While Denmark recorded 21,000 asylum applications that year, the figure stood at 2,716 in 2019. In 2020, with the closing of borders due to the COVID-19 pandemic, this number decreased further to an all-time low of 1,547 applicants for asylum in Denmark. Out of these, less than half progressed to substantial consideration by the administration. This represents a sharp drop from previous years, indicating that the Danish refugee policy under the current government remains as restrictive as under previous governments.

Denmark loosened some restrictions for refugees and asylum seekers in 2019. That June, the SDP committed to accepting refugees under a UN-backed quota system in return for parliamentary support for its government. In November, the government declared that families living at a facility in Sjælsmark would be moved to a new, less restrictive, facility in 2020; they are now in a different facility with only slightly improved conditions for the families. In December 2019, lawmakers amended existing legislation to allow children and adolescents who were previously removed under the Integration Law to return to Denmark and secure their own residency. However, the UN Committee on Economic, Social and Cultural Rights criticized Denmark in an October 2019 report, noting that refugees lacked universal access to interpretation services while using Denmark's health system and that municipalities were not obligated to provide housing to refugees.

Discrimination, including based on gender identity or sexual orientation, is prohibited by law.

The Greenlandic Inuit community faces social marginalization in Denmark, though the government has implemented programs to address this issue.

G. PERSONAL AUTONOMY AND INDIVIDUAL RIGHTS: 15 / 16

G1. Do individuals enjoy freedom of movement, including the ability to change their place of residence, employment, or education? 4 / 4

Freedom of movement is protected by law and generally respected by the government. However, in 2018, the previous government of Lars Løkke Rasmussen proposed an "antighetto" initiative, applicable to neighborhoods identified as having high unemployment and crime rates, and a high percentage of foreign-born residents. It aims to shift the areas' demographics, institute day care requirements for foreign children that would integrate them into Danish society through language and culture lessons and enact stricter punishments for crimes committed there. Legislation to demolish certain housing structures to meet demographic quotas passed that November, and the daycare provision was approved that December. The Frederiksen government continued these initiatives during 2019, and by 2020, several public housing areas had found themselves on the "hard ghetto" list, a consequence of which will be that public housing in the area will have to be demolished or transformed into cooperative or privately owned housing. This would have a strongly detrimental effect on the freedom of residence of affected individuals, with a further discriminatory effect. However, given that the COVID-19 crisis has meant a sharp rise in unemployment affecting these areas, there is some political will to consider stalling some of the more comprehensive effects of the regulations. By December 2020, more than 52,000 citizens had signed a motion to bring the "ghetto law" before Parliament, with a view to halting further implementation including demolitions and other significant measures.

Since 2015, Denmark has enacted measures that restrict the movement of people who seek to join, or have joined, extremist groups abroad—notably the IS. Some of the measures have been criticized for having a low evidentiary threshold or for lacking appropriate oversight mechanisms.

G2. Are individuals able to exercise the right to own property and establish private businesses without undue interference from state or nonstate actors? 4 / 4

Private business activity is free from undue influence by government officials or nonstate actors.

G3. Do individuals enjoy personal social freedoms, including choice of marriage partner and size of family, protection from domestic violence, and control over appearance? 3 / 4

Refugees and other newcomers face lengthy waiting times for family reunification, including in cases involving small children, and restrictions on family reunification were tightened in the wake of the 2015 refugee crisis. The SDP, under pressure from partners in the Red Bloc, committed to loosening some restrictions in return for their support in forming the government in June 2019, and specifically committed to reviewing strict requirements for children seeking permanent residence in Denmark.

Restrictive amendments to the Epidemic Act were passed by Parliament in March 2020, during the early months of the COVID-19 pandemic. A measure authorizing forced vaccinations and other limitations of individual freedoms was reversed by the government later in the year, and in December 2020, a much-revised form of the bill ensuring transparency and democratic control was presented, with the support of most lawmakers and the health-care sector.

In 1989, Denmark became the first country in the world to adopt same-sex civil unions, and in 2012, Parliament overwhelmingly passed same-sex marriage legislation enabling couples to wed in the Lutheran state church of their choosing. Priests are not obligated to officiate but, when requested to do so, must find a colleague who will.

In December 2020, lawmakers passed a measure that criminalized sex without explicit consent. Previously, proof of violence or serious threat had been required to bring rape charges.

G4. Do individuals enjoy equality of opportunity and freedom from economic exploitation? 4 / 4

Public- and private-sector workers are generally free from exploitation by employers. However, migrants engaged in forced labor can be found in some sectors, including the agricultural and service industries. Women and children, also primarily migrants, can be found engaged in forced sex work. The government and NGOs work, frequently in conjunction, to identify and prevent human trafficking and to provide aid to survivors.

Djibouti

Population: 1,000,000
Capital: Djibouti
Freedom Status: Not Free
Electoral Democracy: No

Overview: Djibouti is a republic ruled by a powerful president, Ismail Omar Guelleh, who has been in office since 1999 and is not subject to term limits. While Djibouti technically has a multiparty political system, the ruling Union for a Presidential Majority (UMP) uses authoritarian means to maintain its dominant position. The opposition's ability to operate is severely constrained, and journalists and activists who air criticism of Guelleh or the UMP are regularly harassed or arrested.

KEY DEVELOPMENTS IN 2020

- The COVID-19 outbreak in Djibouti was most acute in May. Authorities successfully curbed the spread of the virus through border controls, mass testing, and contact tracing, as well as movement restrictions and social-distancing rules that began in March and were eased in June. At year's end the country had reported 61 deaths from the virus.
- In June and July, police used excessive force, including live ammunition, to suppress demonstrations against the government's detention and alleged mistreatment of an air force lieutenant who had been arrested in April after criticizing authorities on social media and attempting to flee the country. *Journalists who sought to cover the case and corresponding protests were arrested or forced into hiding.*

POLITICAL RIGHTS: 5 / 40
A. ELECTORAL PROCESS: 2 / 12
A1. Was the current head of government or other chief national authority elected through free and fair elections? 0 / 4

The president, who holds most executive power, serves five-year terms under current rules. President Guelleh was elected to a fourth term in 2016, having been credited with 87 percent of the vote. The opposition fractured, with some groups boycotting the poll and others participating. The lead-up to the election featured restrictions on the media and the harassment or detention of opposition figures. On election day, opposition parties complained that their monitors were turned away from polling sites.

A2. Were the current national legislative representatives elected through free and fair elections? 1 / 4

The 65 members of the unicameral National Assembly are directly elected for five-year terms. Constitutional changes in 2010 called for the creation of an upper house, but the new Senate had yet to be established as of 2020.

Most of the opposition boycotted legislative elections held in 2018, citing the government's failure to honor a 2014 political agreement by implementing electoral reforms. The polls were marked by irregularities, and the ruling UMP increased its majority to 57 of 65 seats. The opposition Union for Democracy and Justice–Djiboutian Democratic Party (UDJ-PDD) won seven seats, and the Center of Unified Democrats (CDU) took one.

A3. Are the electoral laws and framework fair, and are they implemented impartially by the relevant election management bodies? 1 / 4

A core element of the 2014 political agreement—meant to end the opposition's boycott of the legislature following deeply flawed elections in 2013—was a pledge to reform the Independent National Electoral Commission (CENI), which the opposition has accused of bias. These reforms had not been carried out as of 2020. Other electoral provisions favor the dominant party, for example by awarding at least 80 percent of the seats in each multimember parliamentary district to the party that wins a majority in that district.

B. POLITICAL PLURALISM AND PARTICIPATION: 3 / 16

B1. Do the people have the right to organize in different political parties or other competitive political groupings of their choice, and is the system free of undue obstacles to the rise and fall of these competing parties or groupings? 1 / 4

While Djibouti technically has a multiparty political system, parties must register with the government to operate legally. The authorities have denied recognition to a number of opposition parties; members of such parties have been periodically harassed, arrested, and prosecuted, and their offices have been raided by police. The law requires the leaders of political parties to have clean criminal records, and the government has pursued spurious charges against opposition figures to disqualify them or their parties.

B2. Is there a realistic opportunity for the opposition to increase its support or gain power through elections? 0 / 4

President Guelleh has been in power since 1999, when he succeeded his uncle, the only other president since independence in 1977. The 2013 elections marked the first time that the opposition had won any seats in the National Assembly. Opposition parties have traditionally been disadvantaged by Djibouti's electoral system, media controls, abuse of state resources to favor incumbents, and arrests and harassment of opposition leaders and supporters.

B3. Are the people's political choices free from domination by forces that are external to the political sphere, or by political forces that employ extrapolitical means? 1 / 4

The ruling party dominates the state apparatus and uses security forces and other administrative resources to marginalize, disrupt, and suppress independent political activity.

B4. Do various segments of the population (including ethnic, racial, religious, gender, LGBT+, and other relevant groups) have full political rights and electoral opportunities? 1 / 4

The constitution prohibits political parties based on gender or on ethnic, religious, or regional identity. Minority groups, including the Afar, Yemeni Arabs, and non-Issa Somalis, are represented at all levels of the government, but the president's majority Issa group holds paramount positions in the ruling party, the civil service, and the security forces.

Women are underrepresented in leadership positions. A legal quota ensures that women hold at least 25 percent of the seats in the National Assembly, and the actual number is only slightly above that level.

In practice, the authoritarian political system restricts the ability of women and members of ethnic and religious minorities to organize independently and advance their respective interests.

C. FUNCTIONING OF GOVERNMENT: 0 / 12

C1. Do the freely elected head of government and national legislative representatives determine the policies of the government? 0 / 4

The president, who is not freely elected, effectively controls policymaking and governance, and the UMP-dominated parliament does not serve as a meaningful check on executive power.

C2. Are safeguards against official corruption strong and effective? 0 / 4

Corruption is a serious problem that is enabled and sustained by the dominant position of President Guelleh and his ruling party in every aspect of public administration. All significant business deals reportedly go through the president himself.

State bodies tasked with combating corruption lack the resources and independence to function effectively. Prosecutions of senior officials are rare.

C3. Does the government operate with openness and transparency? 0 / 4

The government operates in an opaque manner and resists attempts to shed light on its policymaking, budgetary, and contracting decisions. There is no law establishing the right to access public information. The government has made no effort to explain to citizens how it spends revenue collected from foreign powers that lease land for military bases in Djibouti.

There is also little transparency on Guelleh's investment deals with Chinese and other foreign entities, which have provided Djibouti with loans, built critical infrastructure, and operated special economic zones. The agreements have resulted in a massive amount of public debt and spread discontent among local communities that were not consulted on the location or terms of foreign development projects.

CIVIL LIBERTIES: 19 / 60
D. FREEDOM OF EXPRESSION AND BELIEF: 6 / 16
D1. Are there free and independent media? 0 / 4

Despite constitutional protections, freedom of expression is not upheld in practice, and j*ournalists engage in self-censorship*. Defamation and distribution of false information are criminal offenses. The National Communication Commission distributes licenses to media outlets; the National Security Service reportedly has a role in approving such licenses. The government owns the dominant newspaper, television station, and radio broadcaster, as well as printing presses. According to Reporters Without Borders, domestic media content generally reflects government views. Journalists affiliated with outlets based abroad or small opposition publications are subject to harassment and arbitrary arrest. The websites of the overseas opposition radio station La Voix de Djibouti, run by exiles in Europe, and the Association for Respect for Human Rights in Djibouti (ARDHD) are sometimes blocked by the state-owned internet service provider.

In 2020, a number of journalists, some of whom worked for La Voix de Djibouti, were arrested, harassed by authorities, or forced into hiding due to their coverage of the detention of dissident air force lieutenant Fouad Youssouf Ali and corresponding protests. In some cases police also harassed journalists' family members.

D2. Are individuals free to practice and express their religious faith or nonbelief in public and private? 2 / 4

Islam is the state religion, and 94 percent of the population is Sunni Muslim. The Ministry of Islamic Affairs oversees religious matters; under a 2013 law and 2014 implementing decree, the ministry has direct authority over mosques and imams, who are civil service employees, and vets their Friday sermons. Registered non-Muslim religious groups operate freely, and unregistered groups are able to worship in private, though public proselytizing is illegal.

D3. Is there academic freedom, and is the educational system free from extensive political indoctrination? 2 / 4

Academic freedom is not always respected. Teachers have at times been detained for alleged affiliation with opposition groups. The state oversees the curriculums of the secular public school system and private Islamic schools.

D4. Are individuals free to express their personal views on political or other sensitive topics without fear of surveillance or retribution? 2 / 4

Open discussion of sensitive political issues is impeded by restrictive laws on defamation and other such offenses. The government reportedly monitors social media and conducts surveillance on perceived opponents. Individuals are subject to arrest for posting critical content about the government online.

In March 2020, air force lieutenant Fouad Youssouf Ali fled to Ethiopia and released a video on social media that accused a military official of corruption and clan-based discrimination and called for an armed uprising. After Ethiopian authorities deported him back to Djibouti in April, the government arrested him on charges of treason, defamation of the armed forces, and incitement to hatred and rebellion. In June, he released a video from prison and alleged inhumane treatment. After his initial attempt to flee in March, his wife, two children, and more than a dozen other family members had been temporarily detained, and they subsequently reported harassment.

E. ASSOCIATIONAL AND ORGANIZATIONAL RIGHTS: 3 / 12

E1. Is there freedom of assembly? 0 / 4

Freedom of assembly is protected under the constitution but not respected in practice. Permits are required for public gatherings. Police regularly use violence to disperse unauthorized protests and arrest participants. In June and July 2020, authorities used live ammunition and other excessive force to suppress demonstrations against the government's arrest and alleged mistreatment of air force lieutenant Fouad Youssouf Ali. An estimated 100 to 200 people were arrested.

E2. Is there freedom for nongovernmental organizations, particularly those that are engaged in human rights– and governance-related work? 1 / 4

Local human rights groups that work on politically sensitive matters cannot operate freely, face difficulties in registering with the authorities, and are subject to government harassment. Organizations that focus on social and economic development, including women's rights groups, are generally tolerated by the government. Individual activists are regularly arrested for their work.

E3. Is there freedom for trade unions and similar professional or labor organizations? 2 / 4

While workers may legally join unions and strike, the union registration process is onerous and subject to government discretion, which the Labor Ministry has used to favor progovernment unions and deny registration to independent labor groups. The government has been known to intimidate labor leaders and obstruct union activities. Teachers' union activists have reported being dismissed, transferred, demoted, or denied access to wages.

F. RULE OF LAW: 4 / 16

F1. Is there an independent judiciary? 0 / 4

The courts are not independent of the government and suffer from corruption. Supreme Court judges are appointed by the president, with the advice of a judicial council dominated by presidential and UMP nominees. The president and parliamentary majority also control appointments to the Constitutional Council.

F2. Does due process prevail in civil and criminal matters? 2 / 4

Security forces frequently make arrests without the required court approval, and lengthy pretrial detention is a problem, with detainees often waiting years to go to trial. Allegations of politically motivated prosecutions are common, and opposition groups consistently accuse the government of sanctioning arbitrary arrests and detentions. The government has used counterterrorism laws to target political opponents.

F3. Is there protection from the illegitimate use of physical force and freedom from war and insurgencies? 1 / 4

Security forces regularly engage in physical abuse and torture during arrest and detention. Prison conditions are reportedly poor, with pretrial and convicted prisoners often held together due to overcrowding. The authorities released hundreds of prisoners in 2020 to address concerns about the spread of COVID-19 behind bars.

F4. Do laws, policies, and practices guarantee equal treatment of various segments of the population? 1 / 4

Though the law provides for equal treatment of all Djiboutian citizens, Somali Issas control the ruling party and dominate government positions, while members of minority ethnic groups and clans suffer from discrimination that contributes to their social and economic marginalization.

Women have fewer employment opportunities and are paid less than men for the same work. While the law requires at least 20 percent of upper-level public service positions to be held by women, this rule has not been enforced.

Same-sex sexual activity is not specifically banned, but such conduct has been penalized under broader morality laws, and there are no laws in place to prevent discrimination against LGBT+ people. Matters of sexual orientation and gender identity are generally not discussed publicly.

Djibouti hosts roughly 30,000 refugees and asylum seekers. Slow processing of asylum claims leaves many asylum seekers at risk of deportation. A 2017 law allows registered refugees to work without a permit and provides access to health care and education.

G. PERSONAL AUTONOMY AND INDIVIDUAL RIGHTS: 6 / 16

G1. Do individuals enjoy freedom of movement, including the ability to change their place of residence, employment, or education? 2 / 4

The government has been accused of suspending the travel privileges of political opponents. Civilian movement is restricted in militarized border areas due to past activity by the Front for the Restoration of Unity and Democracy (FRUD-Armé), a rebel group, and tensions with Eritrea.

Movement restrictions and social-distancing measures associated with the COVID-19 pandemic were most intense between March and May 2020, and included stay-at-home orders for all but essential workers. Some constraints remained in place for the rest of the year, with adjustments in response to changing case numbers. The government's management of the crisis broadly conformed to international guidelines and was relatively successful at curbing the outbreak.

G2. Are individuals able to exercise the right to own property and establish private businesses without undue interference from state or nonstate actors? 2 / 4

Private property protections are weak, and court proceedings on business and property matters are affected by corruption and political influence.

Customary practices and personal status rules based on Sharia (Islamic law) place women at a disadvantage regarding inheritance and property ownership.

G3. Do individuals enjoy personal social freedoms, including choice of marriage partner and size of family, protection from domestic violence, and control over appearance? 1 / 4

Female genital mutilation is illegal, but most women and girls have undergone the procedure. Domestic violence is rarely reported and prosecuted, and spousal rape is not specifically criminalized. The Sharia-based family code requires women to obtain a guardian's consent to marry, among other discriminatory provisions surrounding marriage and divorce.

G4. Do individuals enjoy equality of opportunity and freedom from economic exploitation? 1 / 4

Many residents have difficulty finding employment in the formal sector, as the president and his allies tightly control all large-scale economic activity, especially around the military bases leased by foreign powers. Legal safeguards against exploitative working conditions are poorly enforced; migrant workers and refugees are especially vulnerable to abuse.

A 2016 law on human trafficking includes strong penalties for perpetrators, but authorities have struggled to secure convictions and to effectively identify and assist victims.

Dominica

Population: 70,000
Capital: Roseau
Freedom Status: Free
Electoral Democracy: Yes

Overview: Dominica is a parliamentary democracy and has been governed by the Dominica Labor Party (DLP) since 2000. While the country is committed to democratic governance and civil liberties are generally upheld, a number of concerns persist; these include effective management of elections, judicial efficiency, and government corruption—notably relating to the country's Citizenship by Investment (CBI) program.

KEY DEVELOPMENTS IN 2020

- In June, the Eastern Caribbean Supreme Court (ECSC) overturned a High Court decision, saying allegations that the DLP in its 2014 campaign had engaged in "treating" of voters—referring to the practice of improperly seeking to secure votes through the provision of gifts and services—must be heard in court. At issue were two free concerts hosted by the DLP ahead of the polls that featuring internationally known performers.
- There were just under 100 COVID-19 cases during the year, according to World Health Organization (WHO) data, and no reported deaths. As the pandemic's

extent became apparent, Prime Minister Roosevelt Skerrit urged citizens to protect themselves and to avoid sensationalism and fake news about the virus. Authorities provided information about virus-mitigation measures, and there were no notable abuses reported under the state of emergency that lasted from March through June.

POLITICAL RIGHTS: 37 / 40

A. ELECTORAL PROCESS: 11 / 12

A1. Was the current head of government or other chief national authority elected through free and fair elections? 4 / 4

The president, who is the ceremonial head of state, is nominated by the prime minister and opposition leader and elected by the House of Assembly for a five-year term. The prime minister is head of government and is appointed by the president.

The leader of the governing DLP, Roosevelt Skerrit, retained his position as prime minister after his party won a majority of the parliamentary seats in the 2019 general elections. Despite the overall credibility of the elections, the campaign was marred by unrest linked to opposition concerns over the lack of electoral reform, and a corruption scandal involving Skerrit. To ensure the elections passed without incident, the government requested that personnel from the Regional Security System of the Caribbean—an organization composed of several Eastern Caribbean states—be deployed to Dominica four days before the election.

In October 2018, the government reelected former minister of security Charles Savarin as president. Savarin received the full support of the DLP, but the opposition United Workers' Party (UWP) walked out of the parliamentary confirmation session in protest of what they said was an irregular nominating process that failed to adhere to constitutional procedures.

A2. Were the current national legislative representatives elected through free and fair elections? 4 / 4

Dominica's unicameral House of Assembly consists of 30 members who serve five-year terms; 21 members are directly elected, 5 senators are appointed by the prime minister, and 4 are appointed by the opposition leader. There are two ex officio members: the House speaker and the clerk of the House.

The DLP won 18 seats in the 2019 general elections, and the UWP captured 3. Turnout was historically low, with only 54 percent of eligible voters participating. The polls were monitored by the Caribbean Community (CARICOM), the Organization of American States (OAS), and the Commonwealth of the United Kingdom. They generally concluded that voters were able to cast their ballots without intimidation or fear, and that the results reflected the will of the people. However, the campaign was marred by unrest linked to opposition concerns over the lack of electoral reform. To help ensure the elections passed without incident, members of the Regional Security System of the Caribbean were deployed.

A3. Are the electoral laws and framework fair, and are they implemented impartially by the relevant election management bodies? 3 / 4

The Electoral Commission manages and organizes the election process, and the electoral laws are generally fair. However, concerns persist. In the aftermath of the 2014 elections, the results of which were were challenged by the UWP, there was an expectation that the government would support some reforms. These included updating voter rolls and issuing voter identification cards—which among other things would address concerns about voting by members of the Dominican diaspora. However, the government did not adopt any new measures.

Opposition protests turned violent in the lead-up to the December 2019 elections. After the polls, the OAS recommended a series of changes, such as issuing photo ID cards to voters; introducing an electronic voting system; undertaking a review of the voter list; and introducing legislation to regulate political party and campaign financing. In response to the pressures for reform, the government appointed a commission in mid-December to advise on possible improvements to the electoral system. At the end of December, the opposition challenged the results in ten constituencies; the case continued in 2020.

A case relating to the 2014 election also remains open. In June 2020, the Eastern Caribbean Court of Justice overturned a High Court decision, arguing that the DLP must answer in court to the alleged "treating" of voters. The allegations focus on two concerts organised by the DLP in the run-up to the election, which the complainants say were acts of treating meant to improperly influence the polls' outcome.

B. POLITICAL PLURALISM AND PARTICIPATION: 16 / 16
B1. Do the people have the right to organize in different political parties or other competitive political groupings of their choice, and is the system free of undue obstacles to the rise and fall of these competing parties or groupings? 4 / 4

Political parties are free to organize and operate. The effects of the country's first-past-the-post electoral system has entrenched two-party politics, and while there are a number of small political parties in the country, since 2005 only the DLP and UWP have won seats in Parliament.

B2. Is there a realistic opportunity for the opposition to increase its support or gain power through elections? 4 / 4

Opposition parties are unencumbered by formal restrictions and are generally free to operate. There has not been a change of party in government since 2000, but this has more to do with the weakness of the opposition than any unfairness in the electoral system.

After a series of antigovernment protests in 2017, the government denied several demonstration permits to the opposition, citing public security grounds.

B3. Are the people's political choices free from domination by forces that are external to the political sphere, or by political forces that employ extrapolitical means? 4 / 4

Voters and candidates are generally able to express their political choices without undue influence from actors that are not democratically accountable.

B4. Do various segments of the population (including ethnic, racial, religious, gender, LGBT+, and other relevant groups) have full political rights and electoral opportunities? 4 / 4

All adult citizens may vote. Women are underrepresented in politics generally. Out of 42 candidates in the 2019 elections, only 13 were women, and 8 won seats—although this was an improvement from the 2014 elections. There are three women serving as senators out of nine positions. The position of House speaker is held by a woman.

The Indigenous Carib-Kalinago population participates in the political process, with members generally supporting one of the two major political parties. LGBT+ people face discrimination and are marginalized, impacting their ability to engage fully in political processes.

C. FUNCTIONING OF GOVERNMENT: 10 / 12
C1. Do the freely elected head of government and national legislative representatives determine the policies of the government? 4 / 4

The freely elected prime minister, cabinet, and national legislative representatives determine the policies of the government.

C2. Are safeguards against official corruption strong and effective? 3 / 4

While the government generally implements anticorruption laws effectively, domestic and international observers have raised concerns over corruption within Dominica's Citizenship by Investment (CBI) program, which allows foreigners to gain citizenship through an economic investment in the country. In March 2020, the US State Department, which has long been critical of the program, said in its International Narcotics Control Strategy Report that Dominica "accepts a large number of applicants and sometimes issues passports despite adverse information on applicants uncovered during the vetting process."

In 2017, the prime minister announced an interim policy to tighten the issuance of diplomatic passports, following a controversy in which an Iranian businessman ensnared in a corruption scandal in Iran was found to be holding a Dominican diplomatic passport. More information was exposed in 2019, when Al Jazeera published a story claiming that Dominican officials from both major parties, including the prime minister, were willing to receive money in return for political appointments. Prime Minister Skerrit allegedly received hundreds of thousands of dollars in return for appointing an Iranian businessman as the Dominican ambassador to Malaysia.

C3. Does the government operate with openness and transparency? 3 / 4

The government of Dominica generally operates with openness and transparency, though there are concerns that the long-incumbent DLP has been less forthcoming in recent years with information on some programs, including CBI. Government officials are required to submit financial accounts, but these accounts are frequently incomplete. Access to information is not protected by law, but the government makes efforts to provide information on many topics, and posts information related to the budget online.

CIVIL LIBERTIES: 56 / 60

D. FREEDOM OF EXPRESSION AND BELIEF: 15 / 16

D1. Are there free and independent media? 3 / 4

Freedom of expression is constitutionally guaranteed, and the press is generally free in practice. However, defamation remains a criminal offense punishable by imprisonment or fines. Defamation lawsuits and threats of lawsuits are commonly used by the Skerrit government against members of the media, resulting in some self-censorship.

D2. Are individuals free to practice and express their religious faith or nonbelief in public and private? 4 / 4

Freedom of religion is protected under the constitution and other laws, and is generally respected in practice.

D3. Is there academic freedom, and is the educational system free from extensive political indoctrination? 4 / 4

Academic freedom is generally respected.

D4. Are individuals free to express their personal views on political or other sensitive topics without fear of surveillance or retribution? 4 / 4

Individuals are generally free to express their personal views on political or other sensitive topics.

E. ASSOCIATIONAL AND ORGANIZATIONAL RIGHTS: 11 / 12

E1. Is there freedom of assembly? 3 / 4

Freedom of assembly is guaranteed under the constitution, and the government has generally respected these rights, including under a COVID-related state of emergency. However, protests sometimes become violent, or give way to looting or acts of vandalism.

Some unrest took place at opposition protests in 2017, and the prime minister characterized them as threats to state security. Later, several UWP members, including leader Lennox Linton, were charged with incitement and obstruction. The trials had not concluded by the end of 2020. In December 2018, riot police used tear gas against demonstrators with the Concerned Citizens Movement—a civil society group that often criticizes the government—who blocked a road and refused calls to disperse. UWP protests during the lead-up to the 2019 elections at times featured burning debris, and while confrontations between protesters and riot police took place on several instances, there were no major injuries.

E2. Is there freedom for nongovernmental organizations, particularly those that are engaged in human rights–and governance-related work? 4 / 4

Nongovernmental organizations (NGOs) and advocacy groups generally operate without interference.

E3. Is there freedom for trade unions and similar professional or labor organizations? 4 / 4

Workers have the right to organize, strike, and bargain collectively, and laws prohibit antiunion discrimination by employers. However, the country's definition of "essential" workers is broad, extending to those in the agricultural sector, and there are burdensome restrictions on the ability of these workers to strike.

F. RULE OF LAW: 15 / 16

F1. Is there an independent judiciary? 4 / 4

An independent judiciary is provided for in the constitution, and judicial independence is generally respected. Courts are subordinate to the interisland Eastern Caribbean Supreme Court (ECSC).

F2. Does due process prevail in civil and criminal matters? 4 / 4

The constitution provides for due process rights, and these are generally observed in practice. While the judicial system generally operates efficiently, staffing shortages remain a problem and can result in prolonged pretrial detention, in some cases lasting as long as 24 months.

F3. Is there protection from the illegitimate use of physical force and freedom from war and insurgencies? 4 / 4

People in Dominica generally enjoy freedom from illegitimate force.

F4. Do laws, policies, and practices guarantee equal treatment of various segments of the population? 3 / 4

Women's rights are not fully protected. Laws on sexual harassment are weak. Cases of rape are underreported, with significant stigma attached to the crime and little support available for victims.

Same-sex sexual relations are illegal, though the relevant provisions of the Sexual Offences Act are not enforced, a position that has been made clear by Prime Minister Skerrit. In July 2019, a gay man filed a claim against the colonial-era law.

Members of the small Indigenous population, the Carib-Kalinago, face discrimination and a variety of accompanying challenges, including high poverty levels and difficulties in obtaining loans from banks. Rastafarians have reported discrimination and profiling by police.

G. PERSONAL AUTONOMY AND INDIVIDUAL RIGHTS: 15 / 16

G1. Do individuals enjoy freedom of movement, including the ability to change their place of residence, employment, or education? 4 / 4

Individuals in Dominica generally enjoy freedom of movement, though those outside the established Carib-Kalinago community must apply for special access to the Carib Reserve area, which is granted by the Carib Council. There are no restrictions on people's ability to change their place of employment or education.

G2. Are individuals able to exercise the right to own property and establish private businesses without undue interference from state or non-state actors? 4 / 4

The government of Dominica supports both domestic and foreign investment. Property rights are generally safeguarded. However, women have more limited rights because traditionally property is deeded to the head of household, who is usually a man.

G3. Do individuals enjoy personal social freedoms, including choice of marriage partner and size of family, protection from domestic violence, and control over appearance? 3 / 4

Women and children have some limitations on their personal freedoms, including freedom from violence. There is little protection against domestic abuse, and both violence against women and child abuse remain widespread problems.

G4. Do individuals enjoy equality of opportunity and freedom from economic exploitation? 4 / 4

Revisions to labor laws have strengthened worker protections in recent years, though there are reports of violations of overtime laws in the tourism sector. The labor commissioner operates within the Justice Department and is under resourced. The government has made efforts to address poverty and unemployment, including in the wake of Hurricane Maria, which devastated the island in 2017.

According to the most recent (2019) *Findings on the Worst Forms of Child Labor* report from the United States' Department of Labor, Dominica made minimal improvements in efforts to eliminate the most severe forms of child labor. The report also noted that children from the Kalinago community have poor access to secondary education, which "could make them more vulnerable to the worst forms of child labor."

Dominican Republic

Population: 10,500,000
Capital: Santo Domingo
Freedom Status: Partly Free
Electoral Democracy: Yes

Overview: The Dominican Republic holds regular elections that are relatively free, though recent years have been characterized by controversies around implementing a new electoral framework. Pervasive corruption undermines state institutions. Discrimination against

Dominicans of Haitian descent and Haitian migrants, as well as against LGBT+ people, remain serious problems.

KEY DEVELOPMENTS IN 2020

- Though the COVID-19 pandemic delayed the May presidential and legislative elections until July, election observers from the Organization of American States (OAS) commended the credible polling administration and efforts to reduce the spread of the coronavirus. Luis Abinader and the Modern Revolutionary Party (PRM) won the presidential and legislative votes respectively, ending the Dominican Liberation Party's (PLD) 16 years of governance. Observers noted low voter turnout, electoral technology issues, and a lack of implementation campaign finance laws.
- In November, the Anti-Corruption Office (PEPCA) commenced "Operation Anti Pulpo," which charged 11 former government officials with administrative corruption, including the brother and sister of former president Danilo Medina. Seven defendants were detained pending trial and others were under house arrest at the end of the year.

POLITICAL RIGHTS: 26 / 40
A. ELECTORAL PROCESS: 9 / 12
A1. Was the current head of government or other chief national authority elected through free and fair elections? 3 / 4

The president is both head of state and chief of government and is elected to a four-year term. A 2015 constitutional amendment allowed presidents to run for a second term. Luis Abinader of the PRM was elected president over the PLD's Gonzalo Castillo, ending the PLD's 16-year tenure. The COVID-19 pandemic delayed elections from May to July 2020. Voter turnout was low at 49.6 percent, compared to 68 percent in 2016.

Observers from the Organization of American States (OAS) monitored the elections and deemed the polls credible. They lauded the Central Electoral Board's (JCE's) measures to reduce the possibility of spreading the coronavirus at polling stations and the consensus among political forces in postponing the election.

Inconsistent enforcement of social distancing and curfew measures implemented due to the pandemic benefited the PLD and both parties used pandemic-related food, services, and medical supplies to incentivize voters. OAS observers reiterated issues with electronic voting that delayed municipal elections earlier in the year and repeated calls for compliance with parity requirements for women candidates and better supervision of parties' and candidates' finances under existing regulations.

A2. Were the current national legislative representatives elected through free and fair elections? 3 / 4

The Dominican Republic's bicameral National Congress consists of the 32-member Senate and the 190-member Chamber of Deputies, with members of both chambers directly elected to four-year terms. The PRM gained majorities in both chambers in the July 2020 legislative elections, which were held alongside the presidential election.

A3. Are the electoral laws and framework fair, and are they implemented impartially by the relevant election management bodies? 3 / 4

The February 2019 Electoral Regime Law and the August 2018 Law of Political Parties, Groups, and Movements establish the country's new electoral framework. A Special

Prosecutor for Investigation and Persecution of Electoral Crimes and Offences was instituted by the Electoral Regime Law, but election observers expressed concerns about its political independence. The July 2020 elections exposed gaps in the implementation of campaign finance laws—demonstrated by unregulated distribution of gifts and humanitarian aid, candidates' failure to submit required budgets and income and expenditure reports, and a lack of transparency in public fund allocations to candidates. Challenges to both electoral laws were still pending at the end of 2020.

Despite the JCE's shortcomings, the body operates with some transparency and cooperates with election monitors, opposition parties, and other relevant groups; it held a series of postelection meetings to improve the existing electoral framework.

B. POLITICAL PLURALISM AND PARTICIPATION: 10 / 16

B1. Do the people have the right to organize in different political parties or other competitive political groupings of their choice, and is the system free of undue obstacles to the rise and fall of these competing parties or groupings? 3 / 4

Political parties are generally free to form and operate. However, newer and smaller parties struggle to access public financing and secure equal media coverage. They can be dissolved if they do not achieve at least one percent of votes. Provisions of the 2018 electoral law that required a minimum amount of time that competing candidates must be associated with their party were declared unconstitutional in 2019.

B2. Is there a realistic opportunity for the opposition to increase its support or gain power through elections? 3 / 4

Opposition parties and candidates generally do not face selective restrictions during election periods but are disadvantaged by elements of the electoral framework. In July 2020, the main opposition party, the PRM, ended the PLD's 16-year tenure and won a majority in the National Congress.

B3. Are the people's political choices free from domination by forces that are external to the political sphere, or by political forces that employ extrapolitical means? 3 / 4

People are generally free to exercise their political choices. A history of violent police responses to social and political demonstrations may deter political participation by some, and economic oligarchies and organized crime groups have some influence over the political sphere. Electoral laws require some accountability for campaign finances, but political parties and presidential candidates do not always comply.

B4. Do various segments of the population (including ethnic, racial, religious, gender, LGBT+, and other relevant groups) have full political rights and electoral opportunities? 1 / 4

Gender parity laws requiring between 40 and 60 percent of candidates for the National Congress be women were not respected during the July 2020 elections. Women hold 47 seats in the House and 4 in the Senate.

A 2013 Constitutional Tribunal decision stripped Dominican-born descendants of Haitian migrants of their citizenship, and thus their right to vote. Discriminatory attitudes and occasional acts of targeted violence against Black Dominicans (perceived to be Haitians) and LGBT+ people discourage their political participation.

C. FUNCTIONING OF GOVERNMENT: 7 / 12

C1. Do the freely elected head of government and national legislative representatives determine the policies of the government? 3 / 4

Government and legislative representatives are generally able to determine national policies in a free and unhindered manner. President Abinader's government was duly installed six weeks after the elections, and the legislature approved 94 initiatives in the first hundred days. In March 2020, Congress authorized former president Medina to declare a state of emergency for 25 days due to the COVID-19 pandemic, which was extended throughout the year including after President Abinader took power. A state of emergency was still in place at year's end.

Though remote work and restricted in-person sessions were implemented during the pandemic, the Chamber of Deputies and the Senate still operated freely, advancing hundreds of legislative initiatives.

C2. Are safeguards against official corruption strong and effective? 2 / 4

Corruption remains a serious, systemic problem at all levels of the government, judiciary, and security forces, and in the private sector. Reports indicate that politicians routinely accept bribes. A US Justice Department investigation into the Brazilian construction company Odebrecht, the results of which became public in late 2016, revealed that $92 million had been paid to public officials in the Dominican Republic to obtain contracts for major infrastructure projects in the country during three consecutive governments. Numerous officials from prior administrations were linked to the scandal, but only seven were formally charged. Trials for six defendants resumed in September 2020 but stalled in December due to the absence of a key witness, a former Odebrecht employee. This led the Anti-Corruption Office (PEPCA) to explore canceling the agreement that grants Odebrecht immunity from criminal prosecution.

The new government committed to significant anticorruption policies and announced that it would cease its contractual relationships with Odebrecht. In November 2020, PEPCA commenced "Operation Anti Pulpo," which charged 11 former government officials with administrative corruption, including the brother and sister of former president Medina. Seven defendants are detained pending trial and others were under house arrest at the end of the year.

C3. Does the government operate with openness and transparency? 2 / 4

The government does not always operate with transparency. Although state agencies generally respond to information requests, they often provide inaccurate or incomplete responses. Public officials are required to publicly disclose assets, but nongovernmental organizations (NGOs) have cast doubt upon the accuracy of these disclosures. Public contracting and purchasing processes are opaque and allow for high levels of corruption. The government used digital channels and apps to share information in 2020 about the coronavirus pandemic.

CIVIL LIBERTIES: 41 / 60

D. FREEDOM OF EXPRESSION AND BELIEF: 14 / 16

D1. Are there free and independent media? 2 / 4

The law guarantees freedom of speech and of the press. Several national daily newspapers and many local publications operate in the country. There are more than 300 privately owned radio stations and several private television networks alongside the state-owned Radio Televisión Dominicana (RTVD), though ownership of private outlets is highly concentrated and public funding of media lacks transparency. The economic effects of the coronavirus pandemic resulted in suspensions of radio and television opinion programs and staff reductions at major newspapers.

Journalists risk intimidation and violence when investigating drug trafficking and corruption and may also face legal or regulatory pressure as a result of their investigations. During the pandemic, state authorities threatened, attacked, arrested and detained journalists, although the press members were exempt from curfew restrictions. Charges for defamation and insult brought against journalist Marino Zapete in 2019, following corruptions allegations he levied against the sister of the country's public prosecutor, were dropped in September 2020, and his accuser was fined.

D2. Are individuals free to practice and express their religious faith or nonbelief in public and private? 4 / 4

Religious freedom is generally upheld. However, the Catholic Church receives special privileges from the state including funding for construction, and exemptions from custom duties.

D3. Is there academic freedom, and is the educational system free from extensive political indoctrination? 4 / 4

Constitutional guarantees regarding academic freedom are generally observed.

D4. Are individuals free to express their personal views on political or other sensitive topics without fear of surveillance or retribution? 4 / 4

People are generally free to express personal views in public and privately without fear of retribution or surveillance.

E. ASSOCIATIONAL AND ORGANIZATIONAL RIGHTS: 10 / 12
E1. Is there freedom of assembly? 3 / 4

Freedom of assembly is guaranteed by the constitution, and demonstrations are common, but sometimes subject to violent dispersal by police. Dominican-Haitian activists were arrested after a peaceful antiracism demonstration in June 2020.

E2. Is there freedom for nongovernmental organizations, particularly those that are engaged in human rights- and governance-related work? 4 / 4

Freedom of association is constitutionally guaranteed, and the government respects the right to form civic groups.

E3. Is there freedom for trade unions and similar professional or labor organizations? 3 / 4

Workers other than military and police personnel may form and join unions, though over 50 percent of workers at a workplace must be union members in order to engage in collective bargaining. Workers must exhaust mediation measures and meet other criteria for a strike to be considered legal. In practice, union membership is discouraged, and workers risk dismissal for joining.

In September 2020, the National Confederation of Trade Unions pushed the government to pay a holiday bonus and extend social assistance for workers suspended during the coronavirus pandemic. In October, the government announced plans to pay pensions to cane-cutters after decades-long protests.

F. RULE OF LAW: 8 / 16
F1. Is there an independent judiciary? 3 / 4

Judicial independence is hampered by corruption and the judiciary is susceptible to political pressure. Justices of the Supreme Court and Constitutional Court are appointed to seven- and nine-year terms, respectively, by the National Council of the Judiciary. The body is comprised of the president, the leaders of both chambers of Congress, the Supreme Court president, and a congressional representative from an opposition party; its composition has led to claims that the body is susceptible to politicization. Transparency International's office in the Dominican Republic identified judicial delay, judicial autonomy, and curbing inefficient spending among necessary reforms.

In October 2020, the Dominican Republic Lawyers College won a challenge to reopen all courts to prevent the possibility of politicized decisions in virtual proceedings during the pandemic.

Reports of selective prosecution and the improper dismissal of cases continue.

F2. Does due process prevail in civil and criminal matters? 2 / 4

Corruption and politicization of the justice system have significant impact on due process, and strongly limit access to justice for people without resources or political connections. Corruption within law enforcement agencies remains a serious challenge.

In May 2020, 63 percent of people being held in prisons were in pretrial detention.

F3. Is there protection from the illegitimate use of physical force and freedom from war and insurgencies? 2 / 4

Rates of murder and other violent crime are high. Local organization The Citizens' Security Observatory reported a modest 3.9 percent reduction in the 2019 homicide rate, and the National Human Rights Commission and NGOs reported that security forces had committed at least 80 extrajudicial killings. Police occasionally used violence to implement pandemic-related measures.

Prisons are severely overcrowded.

F4. Do laws, policies, and practices guarantee equal treatment of various segments of the population? 1 / 4

Dominicans with European features or lighter skin color enjoy systemic advantages. Dominican-Haitians and Haitian migrants face persistent discrimination, including obstacles in securing legal documents such as identification, birth certificates, and marriage licenses, and have difficulty registering their children as Dominican citizens. Without identification, they are ineligible for any social assistance. Women experience a significant amount of workplace discrimination, and the gender pay gap is 20 percent, as of 2020.

Before he left office, President Medina issued a resolution granting naturalized citizenship to 750 individuals denationalized by a 2013 court judgment, which was being challenged before the Constitutional Tribunal.

LGBT+ people experience occasional violence, as well as discrimination in employment, education, and health services. They are barred from working in certain public sectors, such as the police and armed forces. An antidiscrimination bill remained stalled in Parliament at the end of 2020.

G. PERSONAL AUTONOMY AND INDIVIDUAL RIGHTS: 9 / 16

G1. Do individuals enjoy freedom of movement, including the ability to change their place of residence, employment, or education? 2 / 4

While citizens are generally free to move around the country, during the COVID-19 pandemic, thousands were arrested for violating restrictions on public gatherings. At times, police unlawfully detained and acted violently toward those who violated coronavirus-related restrictions. Asylum seekers and refugees must pay a fee to gain travel documents.

People of Haitian descent without identification cards cannot attend university or obtain formal jobs.

G2. Are individuals able to exercise the right to own property and establish private businesses without undue interference from state or non-state actors? 3 / 4

Private business activity remains susceptible to undue influence by organized crime and corrupt officials.

G3. Do individuals enjoy personal social freedoms, including choice of marriage partner and size of family, protection from domestic violence, and control over appearance? 2 / 4

Violence and discrimination against women remain pervasive. Poor medical care has left the country with one of the highest maternal mortality rates in the region. A 2015 Constitutional Tribunal decision effectively reinstated a complete ban on abortion. The new president expressed support for decriminalization in cases of rape or incest, risk to the life of the mother, and fetal abnormality, which mirrored a 2018 national public opinion survey.

G4. Do individuals enjoy equality of opportunity and freedom from economic exploitation? 2 / 4

Many workers in the country are employed informally, leaving them without legal protections.

The Dominican Republic remains a source, transit, and destination country for the trafficking of men, women, and children for sexual exploitation and forced labor. Haitians who lack documentation and clear legal status are particularly susceptible to forced labor but are often overlooked by antitrafficking initiatives.

The 2020 *Trafficking in Persons* report issued by the US State Department highlighted fewer convictions of traffickers, inadequate sentencing, insufficient victims' services, and a lack of transparency regarding official complicity in trafficking.

Ecuador

Population: 17,500,000
Capital: Quito
Freedom Status: Partly Free
Electoral Democracy: Yes

Overview: Elections take place regularly, and some key state institutions have recently displayed greater independence. A leftist government led by President Rafael Correa was elected in 2007, and the subsequent decade was characterized by both economic growth and severe strain on democratic institutions. President Lenín Moreno was elected in 2017 as Correa's chosen successor, and he subsequently adopted more conservative economic policies, while allowing greater space for civil society and the press. The government's popularity plummeted following a harsh crackdown on a 2019 protest movement against austerity measures and the severe economic and public health impacts of the COVID-19 pandemic.

KEY DEVELOPMENTS IN 2020

- By the end of the year, over 212,000 people had been infected with the coronavirus, and at least 14,000 had died, according to researchers at the University of

Oxford. The country was particularly hard-hit by the pandemic's first wave, featuring one of the highest infection rates in Latin America.
- Several corruption scandals involving public health expenditures emerged during the pandemic, resulting in the investigations and arrests of multiple state officials.
- In April, exiled former president Rafael Correa was convicted of overseeing bribery schemes during his presidency (2007–17). In August, the National Court of Justice confirmed his 8-year prison sentence, leaving him unable to run for vice president in the 2021 elections.

POLITICAL RIGHTS: 27 / 40

A. ELECTORAL PROCESS: 8 / 12

A1. Was the current head of government or other chief national authority elected through free and fair elections? 3 / 4

The 2008 constitution provides for a directly elected president. The president has the authority to dissolve the legislature, which triggers new elections for both the assembly and the presidency. In 2018, voters approved a referendum that restored term limits, which had been eliminated in a 2015 constitutional amendment under former president Correa; the president can now serve up to two terms, which effectively bars Correa from reclaiming the presidency.

In April 2017, Lenín Moreno of the Proud and Sovereign Fatherland (PAIS) alliance won the presidential runoff with 51 percent of the vote, defeating Guillermo Lasso of the Creating Opportunities–Society United for More Action (CREO–SUMA) alliance, who took 49 percent. Some observers expressed concerns about the use of state resources to produce materials favoring Moreno.

Lasso denounced the results as fraudulent and refused to concede, but failed to provide strong evidence to support his claims. Meanwhile, international observers generally praised the election's conduct. Following a partial recount that did not reveal any significant discrepancy from the previous count, the National Electoral Council (CNE) ratified the election's result.

Local and provincial elections in 2019 took place without incident; the PAIS alliance lost some mayoralties to other establishment and some newer parties.

A2. Were the current national legislative representatives elected through free and fair elections? 3 / 4

Ecuador has a 137-seat unicameral National Assembly, with 116 members directly elected, 15 elected by proportional representation, and 6 elected through multiseat constituencies for Ecuadorians living abroad; following the 2018 referendum, members serve a maximum of two four-year terms. International and domestic observers generally praised the 2017 legislative elections, though an Organization of American States (OAS) mission urged reforms including removing the names of deceased persons from the voter rolls and additional training for various actors in the electoral process. The ruling PAIS alliance won 74 out of 137 seats, followed by the opposition CREO–SUMA, which took 28. The rest of the seats were captured by nine other parties.

A3. Are the electoral laws and framework fair, and are they implemented impartially by the relevant election management bodies? 2 / 4

During the Correa era, the CNE had generally been considered government-controlled. The body faced some criticism for its administration of the 2017 elections, including for slow vote counting and irregularities in the voter rolls. In response to the criticism, the transitional National Council of Citizen Participation and Social Control (CPCCS), which is responsible for appointing CNE members, dismissed all sitting CNE members in July 2018, and that November, five newly appointed members began a six-year term.

The new members displayed greater independence and transparency than the previous group, and oversaw the successful 2019 local elections, but have also incurred controversy. In January 2020, CNE president Diana Atamaint narrowly avoided an impeachment trial amid accusations of influence peddling, although she continued to face criticism during the year. The CNE also faced scrutiny as preparations began for the February 2021 presidential elections. In July, the CNE suspended the registration of Correa's Social Commitment Force (FCS) party and several others due to registration irregularities. However, in October, the CNE allowed the inscription of Andrés Arauz, the candidate endorsed by Correa, as the candidate of the Union of Hope (UNES) coalition, despite additional allegations of irregularities.

B. POLITICAL PLURALISM AND PARTICIPATION: 12 / 16

B1. Do the people have the right to organize in different political parties or other competitive political groupings of their choice, and is the system free of undue obstacles to the rise and fall of these competing parties or groupings? 3 / 4

According to the 2008 constitution, political organizations must collect voters' signatures equivalent to 1.5 percent of the electoral rolls to register and participate in general elections. If a party or grouping fails to win 5 percent of the vote for two consecutive elections, its registration can be revoked, disadvantaging smaller parties. The 2019 local and provincial elections featured the participation of 278 parties and movements. Inscription for the 2021 elections closed in October 2020 with a record 17 presidential precandidates and 18 legislative party lists.

B2. Is there a realistic opportunity for the opposition to increase its support or gain power through elections? 3 / 4

For decades, Ecuador's political parties have been largely personality based, clientelist, and fragile. The ruling PAIS alliance, the largest bloc in the legislature, split into two factions after Moreno came to power, with one faction loyal to Moreno and the other loyal to former president Correa; ahead of the 2019 polls the latter group resigned from the ruling party and joined the new Citizens' Revolution party. Establishment parties such as the Social Christian Party and newer parties like Lasso's CREO performed well in the 2019 local elections, winning 43 and 34 mayoral races, respectively, compared with 27 won by the ruling PAIS alliance.

There was little suppression of opposition and new parties in either the 2019 local elections or the registration process for the 2021 elections, although the latter was characterized by internal party tensions, administrative confusion, and occasional cross-party contention.

B3. Are the people's political choices free from domination by forces that are external to the political sphere, or by political forces that employ extrapolitical means? 3 / 4

The people's political choices are generally free from domination by powerful groups that are not democratically accountable. However, wealthy business interests can undermine democratic accountability by facilitating or encouraging corruption among elected officials.

B4. Do various segments of the population (including ethnic, racial, religious, gender, LGBT+, and other relevant groups) have full political rights and electoral opportunities? 3 / 4

Ecuador's constitution promotes nondiscrimination and provides for the adoption of affirmative action measures to promote equality and representation of marginalized groups.

In practice, however, Indigenous groups often lack a voice in key decisions pertaining to their land and resources. Nonetheless, Indigenous groups are an important force in national politics. At the end of 2020, an Indigenous presidential candidate, Yaku Pérez of the Pachakutik party, was one of the front-runners in the February 2021 election.

An LGBT+ rights activist, Pamela Troya, registered as the only openly gay candidate for the 2021 legislative elections. In October 2020, she filed a complaint after being mocked by a prosecutorial staffer while reporting that she had received death threats.

C. FUNCTIONING OF GOVERNMENT: 7 / 12

C1. Do the freely elected head of government and national legislative representatives determine the policies of the government? 3 / 4

Elected officials are generally free to set and implement government policy without undue interference from nonstate actors. However, the executive has exhibited a strong influence on other branches of the government, and political actors are susceptible to manipulation by powerful business interests.

President Moreno has taken steps to reduce the dominance of the executive. Additionally, the fracturing of the PAIS alliance, with more than one-third of its members in the parliament defecting in January 2018 to a new coalition that backs Correa, compelled Moreno to work with opposition lawmakers to advance legislation.

C2. Are safeguards against official corruption strong and effective? 2 / 4

Ecuador has long been racked by corruption, and the weak judiciary and lack of investigative capacity in government oversight agencies contribute to an environment of impunity. Although the Moreno administration initially emphasized anticorruption efforts and several prominent politicians faced investigation and prosecution in recent years, corruption scandals rocked the country during the COVID-19 pandemic, illustrating the depth of the challenge of effectively combating graft.

In May 2020, media outlets reported on cases of corruption in public hospitals, including irregularities in the purchase of protective equipment and body bags. Another large corruption network that allegedly sold medical supplies to state hospitals at vastly inflated prices was linked to former president Abdalá Bucaram and two of his sons, all of whom remained under investigation at year's end. In June, Guayas Province governor Carlos Luis Morales was arrested for allegedly collaborating with family members to defraud the government on contracts for medical supplies; Morales died of a heart attack later that month.

The most politically significant corruption-related development in 2020 was the April conviction of former president Correa on charges that he and political allies orchestrated a system in which illegal payments from state contractors were diverted to finance political campaigns. Along with 17 other former officials and contractors, he was sentenced to eight years in prison and barred from participating in politics. Following confirmation of the sentence on appeal at the National Court of Justice in September, Correa's attempt to stand for the vice presidency in the 2021 elections was disallowed. Correa, who claimed the evidence used to convict him was doctored, has resided in Belgium since leaving office; as of year's end, he had not returned to Ecuador to serve his sentence or confront the multiple additional judicial processes that remain pending against him.

C3. Does the government operate with openness and transparency? 2 / 4

The law guarantees citizens' right to access public information, and although compliance has improved over the years, some government bodies remain reluctant to disclose it. In 2018, the government took steps to enhance access to information, including the establishment of a transparency-monitoring mechanism to ensure that public agencies provide relevant information online. Public procurement processes are frequently opaque, as illustrated by repeated corruption scandals involving the purchase of overpriced medical supplies and the distribution of public works contracts to friends and family members of public officials. At the height of the COVID-19 pandemic's first wave in April—and following heavy criticism from the media and civil society—President Moreno admitted that the government's stated numbers of cases and deaths represented a significant undercount.

CIVIL LIBERTIES: 40 / 60 (+2)

D. FREEDOM OF EXPRESSION AND BELIEF: 13 / 16 (+1)

D1. Are there free and independent media? 3 / 4 (+1)

Media freedom improved after President Moreno took office in 2017. Upon his election, Moreno met with the owners of private media outlets and pledged to usher in a new, more open environment for journalists. His administration has permitted more diverse coverage in the country's state-run media, which had previously shown clear bias toward Correa and the PAIS alliance.

In 2018, the National Assembly approved a reform of the restrictive Organic Communications Law, including the elimination of the notorious Superintendency of Information and Communication (SUPERCOM), which monitored media content, investigated journalists, and issued fines and other sanctions.

In 2020, investigative journalism, which was effectively muzzled during the Correa government, played a key role in Ecuador, including by discrediting official COVID-19 statistics, exposing corruption in the public health sector, and revealing new details about the mechanics of corruption in the Correa administration.

Major challenges to press freedom still remain. Reporters and media operations were severely affected by the COVID-19 pandemic: local press freedom group Fundamedios reported that 24 journalists died from the virus during the year, even as the pandemic-induced economic contraction led to hundreds of layoffs. As in previous years, reporters and media outlets suffered threats and occasional physical attacks. Some forms of defamation remain criminalized, and in October, journalist Juan Sarmiento received a 10-day prison sentence and fine following a conviction on charges that his criticisms of the Napo provincial government's coronavirus response dishonored the province's governor.

Score Change: The score improved from 2 to 3 due to continued improvements in the freedom and capacity of private media, which played an important role in exposing multiple high-profile instances of corruption and official misdeeds during the year.

D2. Are individuals free to practice and express their religious faith or nonbelief in public and private? 4 / 4

Freedom of religion is constitutionally guaranteed and generally respected in practice.

D3. Is there academic freedom, and is the educational system free from extensive political indoctrination? 3 / 4

In 2018, the National Assembly approved reforms to the Organic Law on Higher Education, which restores public funding for research at universities that operate in Ecuador under international agreements. The legislation that removed the funding, passed in 2016, had threatened the viability of two graduate institutions, Universidad Andina Simón Bolívar and FLACSO Ecuador.

D4. Are individuals free to express their personal views on political or other sensitive topics without fear of surveillance or retribution? 3 / 4

Discussion of controversial topics among private citizens is generally free. However, crackdowns on social media have led some online outlets to disable sections for public commentary for fear of reprisals, limiting the freedom of private discussion online.

E. ASSOCIATIONAL AND ORGANIZATIONAL RIGHTS: 9 / 12 (+1)

E1. Is there freedom of assembly? 3 / 4 (+1)

Numerous protests occur throughout the country without incident, and restrictions on assembly rights initially eased under President Moreno. However, national security legislation provides a broad definition of sabotage and terrorism, extending to acts against persons and property by unarmed individuals, which can be used to limit assembly rights. In May 2020 the Ministry of Defense issued a regulation authorizing soldiers' use of lethal force in situations that potentially included protests. Following a challenge by rights groups, the Constitutional Court suspended the regulation in June pending a full decision, which had not occurred at year's end.

In October 2019, a government move to eliminate fuel subsidies triggered massive, countrywide demonstrations and strike actions by unions, Indigenous movements, and other sectors of society. Some demonstrations turned violent, featuring looting, clashes between protesters and police, and attacks on private property. In response, the government declared a nationwide state of emergency that imposed a curfew and other limits on freedom of assembly rights. A number of demonstrations also saw mass arrests of participants and excessive police violence against protesters. After days of negotiations, Moreno canceled the order eliminating subsidies for gasoline and diesel, and activists in turn called off the demonstrations.

No similar violence or mass arrests occurred in 2020, although several smaller-scale protests were repressed by police, including demonstrations in May against the government's inadequate COVID-19 response in Guayaquil and a September protest in Quito by medical students demanding wages owed by the government.

In March 2020, assembly rights were restricted throughout the country under the state of emergency declared by President Moreno as the pandemic struck. While the Constitutional Court validated the legality of the emergency restrictions, the court imposed a monitoring mechanism to ensure fundamental rights were not curtailed. In August, the court ruled against additional extensions of the state of emergency, which subsequently expired in September.

Score Change: The score improved from 2 to 3 because there were fewer instances of protest-related violence and mass arrests compared with the previous year.

E2. Is there freedom for nongovernmental organizations, particularly those that are engaged in human rights- and governance-related work? 3 / 4

In 2017, the Moreno administration rescinded controversial Correa-era decrees that had introduced onerous requirements for forming a nongovernmental organization (NGO), granted officials broad authority to dissolve organizations, and obliged NGOs to register all members. However, while observers say the new regime for NGO regulation is an improvement, it has also drawn criticism for retaining excessive government regulatory power. For example, current NGO regulations allow authorities to close an NGO deemed to be performing activities different from those for which it was created, or to be participating in politics.

E3. Is there freedom for trade unions and similar professional or labor organizations? 3 / 4

Private-sector labor unions have the right to strike, though the labor code limits public-sector strikes. Only a small portion of the general workforce is unionized, partly because many people work in the informal sector. In 2018, the National Union of Educators (UNE), which had been dissolved by the government in 2016 under restrictive NGO regulations, was able to resume operations when it was registered as a union.

F. RULE OF LAW: 8 / 16

F1. Is there an independent judiciary? 2 / 4

Ecuador's highest-ranking judicial bodies are the 21-member National Court of Justice and the 9-member Constitutional Court. Both courts faced attacks on their autonomy during the Correa era, but judicial independence has increased during the Moreno administration. One of the measures passed in the 2018 referendum involved restructuring the National Council of Citizen Participation and Social Control (CPCCS), a powerful body responsible for appointing the attorney general, and the Judiciary Council, which appoints judges. The referendum's passage led to the sacking of all CPCCS members, who were considered allies of the Correa government. In 2018, the transitional CPCCS appointed by Moreno replaced all members of the Judiciary Council.

More controversially, the transitional CPCCS had significant influence over the composition of the Constitutional Court, despite the CPCCS's lack of jurisdiction over the court under the terms of the referendum. The transitional CPCCS voted to remove all nine judges on the court, citing corruption and a lack of independence within the body, and then created a committee to select the court's new members. The new Constitutional Court members were selected in early 2019 and approved by the transitional CPCCS; later in the year, the new court ratified the legality of the transitional CPCCS's actions. The CPCCS has remained unstable: four members were removed by congress in 2019, and the council's president was removed in November 2020 for improperly obtaining a disability certificate that confers tax benefits.

F2. Does due process prevail in civil and criminal matters? 2 / 4

Judicial processes remain slow, and procedures designed to expedite cases have been implemented at the detriment of defendants' due process rights. Many people are held in pretrial detention for longer than is permitted by law. While the number of public defenders has increased in recent years, the state is still unable to provide adequate legal counsel for all defendants who are unable to supply their own.

During his tenure, former president Correa and his allies frequently intervened in court cases, telling judges how they should rule, and sometimes removing judges who refused to comply. Under President Moreno, such blatant interference in court proceedings has diminished, allowing defendants more fair public hearings of their cases.

Following the March 2020 declaration of a state of emergency, reports that judicial institutions were failing to address human rights and due process violations prompted an April ruling by the Constitutional Court directing the Judiciary Council to ensure continued access to justice.

F3. Is there protection from the illegitimate use of physical force and freedom from war and insurgencies? 2 / 4

Allegations of police abuse of suspects and detainees continue. In October 2020, municipal police officers in Durán were filmed attacking a mentally disabled woman who was caught selling toothpaste outside a public building. The officers involved were detained.

Accountability efforts related to the 2019 protest violence remained limited in 2020. As of October, hundreds of investigations were open, but only a handful of trials had begun; nearly all focused on protesters accused of inciting or committing violence, some of whom were indigenous leaders or members of the political opposition. Multiple groups that conducted investigations, including the Inter-American Commission on Human Rights (IACHR), Human Rights Watch (HRW), and the governmental Ombudsman's Office, found that state agents committed human rights violations during the protests, but investigations had not yielded charges as of October.

F4. Do laws, policies, and practices guarantee equal treatment of various segments of the population? 2 / 4

Indigenous people continue to suffer widespread societal discrimination, and oil-drilling and mining projects on Indigenous lands are frequently carried out without consulting local Indigenous communities, as required by the constitution. In July 2020, the Constitutional Court issued a ruling that reinforced consultation requirements for proposed changes to the status of Indigenous ancestral territories.

Ecuador is one of the largest recipients of refugees in Latin America. According to the UN High Commissioner for Refugees (UNHCR), Ecuador hosted over 415,000 Venezuelans as of the end of 2020. In October 2020, the government announced that it had granted over 44,000 humanitarian visas to migrants from Venezuela. Many Venezuelan immigrants have reported facing discrimination and xenophobia, amid unfounded accusations that their arrival has caused a spike in crime and violence in the country. In addition, approximately 250,000 refugees from Colombia have entered Ecuador since the late 1990s, and thousands are still there.

G. PERSONAL AUTONOMY AND INDIVIDUAL RIGHTS: 10 / 16

G1. Do individuals enjoy freedom of movement, including the ability to change their place of residence, employment, or education? 3 / 4

Freedom of movement outside and inside the country is largely unrestricted. Workers in the palm oil industry, however, have faced restrictions on their movement imposed by employers, including curfews. Individuals may generally determine their place of employment and education.

G2. Are individuals able to exercise the right to own property and establish private businesses without undue interference from state or nonstate actors? 2 / 4

The government does not impose significant restrictions on the right to own property and establish private businesses. However, widespread corruption by both public officials and private-sector actors can obstruct normal business activity and weakens the protection of property rights.

G3. Do individuals enjoy personal social freedoms, including choice of marriage partner and size of family, protection from domestic violence, and control over appearance? 3 / 4

In June 2019, the Constitutional Court, by a vote of 5–4, ruled that the marriage ban on same-sex couples was unconstitutional, based on a previous opinion by the Inter-American Court of Human Rights that recommended the recognition of same-sex marriage. The Constitutional Court ruling divided public opinion, but same-sex couples successfully applied for marriage licenses in the following months. Civil unions had previously been recognized in Ecuador.

In a May 2020 report, the UN Special Rapporteur on violence against women highlighted significant ongoing challenges in protecting women from violence and abuse, and cited a study from the National Institute of Statistics and Censuses (INEC) that found that 65 percent of Ecuadorian women had suffered abuse in some form during their lives. Abortion remains a crime in Ecuador, and in September 2020, President Moreno vetoed an ambitious health code reform that would have decriminalized abortions resulting from obstetric emergencies.

G4. Do individuals enjoy equality of opportunity and freedom from economic exploitation? 2 / 4

Men, women, and children are sometimes subjected to forced labor and sex work in Ecuador; Indigenous and Afro-Ecuadorian individuals, as well as migrants and refugees, remain most vulnerable. According to data published in a 2020 World Bank report, 6.6 percent of Venezuelans in Ecuador reported being subjected to forced labor within the previous month, and the economic disruption caused by the COVID-19 pandemic further increased migrants' economic precarity and vulnerability.

The government has taken some action to address the problem of economic exploitation, including by increasing trafficking-related law enforcement operations. However, services for victims are inadequate, and some public officials believed to be complicit in trafficking operations have escaped punishment.

Egypt

Population: 100,800,000
Capital: Cairo
Freedom Status: Not Free
Electoral Democracy: No

Overview: President Abdel Fattah al-Sisi, who first took power in a 2013 coup, has governed Egypt in an increasingly authoritarian manner. Meaningful political opposition is virtually nonexistent, as expressions of dissent can draw criminal prosecution and imprisonment. Civil liberties, including press freedom and freedom of assembly, are tightly restricted. Security forces engage in human rights abuses with impunity. Discrimination against women, LGBT+ people, and other groups remain serious problems, as does a high rate of domestic violence.

KEY DEVELOPMENTS IN 2020
- Restrictive new emergency measures were justified as a response to the COVID-19 pandemic. In May, amendments to the Emergency Law banned all forms of public gatherings, gave police greater powers to make arrests, and expanded the jurisdiction of military courts. Authorities also used the pandemic to justify skipping renewal hearings for pretrial detention orders. A number of doctors were arrested for speaking out about a lack of personal protective equipment (PPE) and coronavirus tests.
- Tightly controlled parliamentary elections took place over several months in the second half of the year. The polls were marred by low turnout, claims of fraud, vote buying, severe interference by security apparatuses, and detention and intimidation of individuals who criticized the process. No credible domestic or international

groups were allowed to monitor the elections, which delivered control both chambers of the parliament to the ruling regime.

- In September, small antigovernment protests erupted in a number of villages. The regime responded with harsh repression, arresting hundreds of people, including children, and killing two men. Most of those detained faced charges of protesting illegally, calling for unauthorized protests, joining a terrorist group, spreading false news, and misusing social media.
- Authorities escalated repression of perceived dissidents throughout the year, arresting and jailing scores, including several high-profile journalists, and activists with the country's remaining major human rights organizations. Egypt-based family members of dissidents abroad faced persecution, including home raids, arrest, and confiscation of passports.

POLITICAL RIGHTS: 6 / 40 (−1)

A. ELECTORAL PROCESS: 2 / 12

A1. Was the current head of government or other chief national authority elected through free and fair elections? 0 / 4

The president is elected by popular vote for up to two terms. President Abdel Fattah al-Sisi, who first took power in a 2013 coup while serving as Egypt's defense minister and armed forces commander, has never been elected in a fair contest. He won elections in 2014 and 2018, the latter with 97 percent of the vote after pressuring the opposition candidates to withdraw and approving a loyal challenger, Mousa Mostafa Mousa, head of the Al-Ghad Party, who had campaigned for Sisi before entering the race. Voting in 2018 was marred by low turnout, the use of state resources and media to support Sisi's candidacy, voter intimidation, and vote buying. The electoral commission threatened nonvoters with fines in an attempt to increase participation.

Constitutional amendments adopted in 2019 added two years to Sisi's current term, extending it through 2024, at which point he will be allowed to seek an additional six-year term. Beyond this, future presidents will be limited to two six-year terms.

A2. Were the current national legislative representatives elected through free and fair elections? 1 / 4

The 2019 amendments to the 2014 constitution reestablished the Egyptian parliament as a bicameral body in which members serve five-year terms. The upper house, the Senate, is made up of 300 seats, and has almost no significant legislative competences. Two-thirds of the Senate members are elected (of those, half through closed party lists and half through individual seats) and one-third are appointed by the president. The House of Representatives is made up of 568 members, half elected through closed party lists, and half to individual seats. The president has the right to appoint 28 additional members to the House.

The 2020 elections to both bodies of the parliament were neither free nor fair, and were marred by the widespread detention and intimidation of individuals who criticized the process, low turnout, claims of fraud, vote buying, and severe interference by security apparatuses. No credible domestic or international groups were allowed to monitor the elections.

Elections for the Senate took place in two stages in August and October. Without any competitor lists, the Unified National List, headed by the regime-allied Mostaqbal Watan (Nation's Future) Party, won all of the 100 party-list seats, and 88 of the individual seats. Another proregime party, the Republican People's Party, won 6 individual seats. Independents took the remaining 6 seats. In October, President Sisi appointed 100 mostly proregime members to the Senate.

Elections for the House of Representative took place in October and November. The regime-allied lists headed by Mostaqbal Watan won all 284 seats allocated for party-list seats, and the overall majority in the House was easily secured by the proregime parties and candidates. Mostaqbal Watan wound up with 315 seats, while the Republican People's Party took 50. The Wafd Party, the Guardians of the Nation party, and the Modern Egypt Party took smaller proportions.

Egypt has not hold elections for local councils since 2008. The last elected local councils were dissolved in 2011 after the Egyptian uprising. Since then, government-appointed officials have controlled local governance.

A3. Are the electoral laws and framework fair, and are they implemented impartially by the relevant election management bodies? 1 / 4

In 2019, following a tightly controlled constitutional referendum, the 2014 constitution was amended to hand more power to President Sisi. The referendum was marred by reports of vote buying and other irregularities, and no organized opposition was permitted to challenge the well-resourced "yes" campaign. Nearly 89 percent of participants backed the amendments, according to official results.

While the electoral laws themselves provide some basis for credible elections, electoral authorities largely fail in practice to ensure an open and competitive campaign environment. The board of the National Electoral Commission (NEC) consists of senior judges drawn from some of Egypt's highest courts, who serve six-year terms. The NEC's establishing legislation phases out direct judicial supervision of elections by 2024, which critics argue will damage the integrity of elections and reduce public trust in the results.

B. POLITICAL PLURALISM AND PARTICIPATION: 2 / 16 (−1)

B1. Do the people have the right to organize in different political parties or other competitive political groupings of their choice, and is the system free of undue obstacles to the rise and fall of these competing parties or groupings? 0 / 4

Political parties are legally allowed to form and operate, but in practice there are no political parties that offer meaningful opposition to the incumbent leadership.

Activists, parties, and political movements that criticize the regime continued to face arrests, harsh prison terms, death sentences, extrajudicial violence, and other forms of pressure. In 2019, 15 individuals were detained in response to their peaceful political activities; the arrests, including of former parliamentarian and human rights lawyer Zyad el-Elaimy, as well as journalists and politicians Hossam Moanis and Hisham Fouad, were viewed as a signal ahead of the 2020 elections that political organizing would not be tolerated. Members of this group were reportedly subjected to torture while in detention. Thousands of dissidents, activists, and opposition figures remain in prison, where they live in squalid conditions.

Parties formed on the basis of religion are forbidden. While some Islamist parties still operate in a precarious legal position, the Muslim Brotherhood was outlawed in 2013 as a terrorist organization, and its political party was banned. Since then, authorities have systematically persecuted its members.

B2. Is there a realistic opportunity for the opposition to increase its support or gain power through elections? 0 / 4

By extending the presidential term lengths and limits in 2019, controlling the electoral process, intimidating presidential and parliamentary candidates, and denying credible opposition parties the space to function, the regime makes it nearly impossible for the opposition to gain power through elections. Families of dissidents abroad have increasingly faced persecution by state authorities.

B3. Are the people's political choices free from domination by forces that are external to the political sphere, or by political forces that employ extra political means? 1 / 4

Since the 2013 coup, the military has dominated the political system, with most power and patronage flowing from Sisi and his domestic allies in the armed forces and security agencies. Most of Egypt's provincial governors are former military or police commanders. Vaguely worded 2019 constitutional amendments further strengthened the legal under-pinnings of the military's political influence, calling on it to "protect the constitution and democracy, and safeguard the basic components of the state and its civilian nature, and the people's gains, and individual rights and freedoms." Regional allies, such as Saudi Arabia and the United Arab Emirates, have assisted the regime through financial and other support.

B4. Do various segments of the population (including ethnic, racial, religious, gender, LGBT+, and other relevant groups) have full political rights and electoral opportunities? 1 / 4 (−1)

The constitution and Egyptian laws grant political rights to all citizens regardless of religion, gender, race, ethnicity, or any other such distinction. However, women, Christians, Shiite Muslims, people of color, and LGBT+ people face discrimination and are denied access to a number of rights, which in turn affects their ability to participate in political life. In light of increasing control by Sisi and the military over elections and other aspects of society, these groups are generally only able to represent their interests within the narrow scope of officially sanctioned politics, and risk harsh penalties for transgressing stated and unstated red lines. The diminishing power of the legislature further undercuts avenues for meaningful representation.

Human Rights Watch (HRW) in October 2020 published a review of the cases of 13 LGBT+ individuals prosecuted between 2017 and 2020. After being detained by police officers, some were tortured, subjected to purported virginity tests or otherwise sexually assaulted, and denied medical care and access to legal counsel.

Coptic Christians, who account for some 10 percent of the population, obtained 31 seats in the House of Representatives in 2020, 28 through the party-list seats and 3 through individual seats. Thanks in large part to quotas, the number of women in the House of Representatives increased to 148 of the 596 seats, or almost 25 percent, women also make up about 13 percent of the Senate, and in December 2020, President Sisi appointed a woman as one of the deputy chief justices of the Supreme Constitutional Court. Three months earlier, Sisi approved a bill to protect the privacy of sexual assault survivors, to encourage them to report assaults and harassments. However, women generally struggle to see their interests represented in Egyptian politics.

Score Change: The score declined from 2 to 1 because the regime's tighter control over elections and the dwindling autonomy of the parliament over the past five years has reduced the ability of women and religious and other minority groups to organize independently and meaningfully advocate for their interests through the political system.

C. FUNCTIONING OF GOVERNMENT: 2 / 12

C1. Do the freely elected head of government and national legislative representatives determine the policies of the government? 0 / 4

President Sisi, who was not freely elected, dominates the policymaking process. The parliament, led by security apparatuses, has neither a significant role in forming and debating laws, nor the ability to provide a meaningful check on executive power. Rather, many laws originate in the cabinet.

The 2019 constitutional amendments further consolidated Sisi's authority, and increased the military's already considerable independence from civilian oversight and its constitutional role in civilian governance. In addition to the language tasking the military with protecting "the constitution and democracy," the amendments allow the Supreme Council of the Armed Forces to permanently control the appointment of the defense minister, who is also the commander in chief; that power had previously been limited to the first two presidential terms after the 2014 constitution took effect.

C2. Are safeguards against official corruption strong and effective? 1 / 4

Corruption is pervasive at all levels of government. Official mechanisms for investigating and punishing corrupt activity remain weak and ineffective. The Administrative Control Authority (ACA), the body responsible for most anticorruption initiatives, is under the control of Sisi. It lacks credibility, transparency, and impartiality and is not allowed to monitor the economic activities of the military. Thus, the ACA is believed to be an instrument in the president's hand to control the bureaucracy, to manage key patronage networks, to serve the regime's propaganda.

C3. Does the government operate with openness and transparency? 1 / 4

The Sisi administration has provided very little transparency regarding government spending and operations. Civil society groups and independent journalists have few opportunities to comment on or influence state policies, legislation, and public spending priorities. The military is notoriously opaque with respect to both its core expenditures and its extensive business interests, including in major infrastructure and land-development projects. This leads to an almost complete lack of accountability for any malpractice.

The government's dealing with the COVID-19 pandemic was characterized by opacity, misinformation about the numbers of cases and deaths, and the further spread of misinformation by the regime-allied outlets that dominate the media sector. A number of doctors were arrested for speaking out about a lack of personal protective equipment (PPE) and coronavirus tests.

CIVIL LIBERTIES: 12 / 60 (−2)

D. FREEDOM OF EXPRESSION AND BELIEF: 3 / 16 (−1)

D1. Are there free and independent media? 0 / 4 (−1)

The Egyptian media sector is dominated by progovernment outlets; most critical or opposition-oriented outlets were shut down in the wake of the 2013 coup. More recently, a number of private television channels and newspapers have been launched or acquired by businesspeople and individuals tied to the military and intelligence services. Independent reporting is suppressed through restrictive laws, intimidation, and other means, but a few independent outlets still operate, including Mada Masr and al-Manassa.

Egyptian journalists risk arrest in connection with their work, and among those detained in 2020 were Nora Younis, editor of the independent news website Al-Manassa, who was arrested in June; and Lina Attalah, editor-in-chief of Mada Masr, who was arrested in May. Another prominent journalist, Mohamed Monir, died in July after contracting COVID-19 while in pretrial detention. In December 2020, the Committee to Protect Journalists (CPJ) found that Egypt was the third-worst jailer of journalists in the world, with 27 in detention.

Foreign journalists face obstruction by the state. In March, Egypt expelled *Guardian* reporter Ruth Michaelson over her critical coverage of the government's response to

COVID-19. Police raided the Cairo offices of Turkish Anadolu News Agency in January, arresting at least four people on charges of operating without a license and spreading false news. Separately, in 2019, the public prosecutor's office established a media monitoring wing tasked with advising the media on the proper coverage of cases.

Two laws ratified in 2018 pose additional threats to press freedom. The Media Regulation Law prescribes prison sentences for journalists who "incite violence" and permits censorship without judicial approval, among other provisions. The Anti-Cyber and Information Technology Crimes Law allows authorities to block any website considered to be a threat to national security, a broad stipulation that is vulnerable to abuse. Websites of independent news and information entities are regularly blocked. According to the domestic digital rights group Masaar, 628 links and 596 websites had been blocked in Egypt as of September 2020.

Score Change: The score declined from 1 to 0 due to restrictive new legislation, a pattern of arbitrary arrests and detentions of journalists, expulsions of and travel restrictions on foreign reporters, and the widespread blocking of websites.

D2. Are individuals free to practice and express their religious faith or nonbelief in public and private? 1 / 4

While Article 2 of the 2014 constitution declares Islam to be the official religion, Article 64 states that "freedom of belief is absolute." Most Egyptians are Sunni Muslims. Coptic Christians form a substantial minority, and there are smaller numbers of Shiite Muslims, non-Coptic Christian denominations, and other groups. Religious minorities and atheists have faced persecution and violence, with Copts in particular suffering numerous cases of forced displacement, physical assaults, bomb and arson attacks, and blocking of church construction in recent years. Informal reconciliation sessions following instances of sectarian conflict have denied Copts justice for acts of violence against them.

D3. Is there academic freedom, and is the educational system free from extensive political indoctrination? 1 / 4

The state controls education and curriculums in public schools and to a lesser degree in some of the country's private institutions. Faculty members and departments have some autonomy in shaping specific courses, though many scholars self-censor to avoid any punitive measures.

Under a 2014 law, university heads are appointed by presidential decree. A 2015 decree allows for the dismissal of university professors who engage in on-campus political activity, and in 2016 the government reportedly began imposing more systematic requirements for academics to obtain approval from security officials for travel abroad. A number of prominent academics are in prison, including political science professor Hazem Hosny, who has criticized Sisi and was arrested in September 2019.

Since 2013, university students have faced reprisals for political activism that include arrests, disciplinary sanctions such as expulsion, military trials, and extrajudicial killings. In December 2020, prosecutors in Egypt said that charges would not be filed against five state security officers thought to be responsible for the 2016 torturing and killing of Giulio Regeni, an Italian Cambridge University graduate student who had been researching independent trade unions in Egypt.

D4. Are individuals free to express their personal views on political or other sensitive topics without fear of surveillance or retribution? 1 / 4

Increasingly since 2013, individuals expressing personal views contrary to preferred state narratives have been subject to reprisals. Arrests of activists over social media posts and other activities are common and send a clear message that voicing dissent is intolerable, which contributes to self-censorship among ordinary Egyptians. Progovernment media figures and state officials regularly call for national unity and suggest that only enemies of the state would criticize the authorities.

The security services use sophisticated surveillance equipment and techniques to monitor social media platforms and mobile phone applications. The 2018 Anti-Cyber and Information Technology Crimes Law requires telecommunications companies to store users' data for 180 days, further enabling widespread government surveillance, and language in the law vaguely criminalizes online expression that "threatens national security." The 2018 Media Regulation Law subjects any social media user with more than 5,000 followers to government monitoring and regulation, threatening online expression.

E. ASSOCIATIONAL AND ORGANIZATIONAL RIGHTS: 1 / 12
E1. Is there freedom of assembly? 0 / 4

According to the constitution, freedom of assembly should not be restricted. However, a 2013 law, as amended in 2017, allows the Interior Ministry to ban, postpone, or relocate protests with a court's approval. Among other restrictions, unauthorized gatherings of 10 or more people are subject to forced dispersal, protests at places of worship are prohibited, and protest organizers must inform police of their plans at least three days in advance. Thousands of people have been arrested under the 2013 law, and some jailed protesters have received death sentences. The severity of the crackdown on assembly rights has made protests extremely rare.

However, in September 2020, scattered demonstrations erupted over several days in a number of villages. The protests came in response to the government's decision to demolish unregistered houses, but people also turned out to voice other grievances and to mark the anniversary of protests the previous year. The regime responded to the 2020 demonstrations with repression, using tear gas, batons, birdshot, and even live ammunition. Two men were killed, while hundreds, including dozens of children, were detained; defendants reported being subjected to torture. Most of those detained faced charges of protesting illegally, calling for unauthorized protests, joining a terrorist group, spreading false news, and misusing social media.

E2. Is there freedom for nongovernmental organizations, particularly those that are engaged in human rights- and governance-related work? 0 / 4

Nongovernmental organizations (NGOs) have faced mass closures as well as harassment in the form of office raids, arrests of members, lengthy legal cases, and restrictions on travel in recent years. A restrictive 2019 law provides for large fines against NGOs deemed to threaten national security, public morals, and public order; essentially stipulates that NGOs are limited to development work; and imposes onerous reporting requirements and intrusive monitoring systems. NGOs in violation of the rules may be shuttered for one year.

In 2020, authorities escalated repression of human rights advocates. In August, Bahey el-Din Hassan, a prominent human rights defender and cofounder of the Cairo Institute for Human Rights Studies (CIHRS), was sentenced in absentia to 15 years in prison over critical tweets he had published. (Hassan left Egypt in 2014, and lives in exile.) In February, Patrick George Zaki, a researcher with the Egyptian Initiative for Personal Rights (EIPR), was detained and reportedly tortured. In November, security forces arrested three other EIPR staff members, including Executive Director Gasser Abdel-Razek, after EIPR met with 13 ambassadors and other diplomats to discuss human rights in Egypt. Abdel Razek and the two others were released in December after international pressure, but Zaki remained in prison at the end of the year.

E3. Is there freedom for trade unions and similar professional or labor organizations? 1 / 4

The government only recognizes unions affiliated with the state-controlled Egyptian Trade Union Federation. While Article 15 of the constitution provides for the right to organize peaceful strikes, they are not tolerated in practice, and the law on protests prohibits gatherings that impede labor and production. Striking workers are regularly arrested and prosecuted, particularly since a spate of labor protests in 2016; workers at military-owned businesses are subject to trials by military courts.

A new law enacted in August 2019 eased many of the restrictions imposed by a 2017 law on trade unions, which had effectively compelled them to join the state-controlled federation and imposed controls on their structures, by-laws, and elections. Among other changes, the new law lowered the threshold for union formation from 150 to 50 workers, and imposed fines rather than prison terms for violations. It remained unclear whether the legislation would lead to actual improvements in the recognition, registration, and operational autonomy of independent unions.

F. RULE OF LAW: 2 / 16 (−1)

F1. Is there an independent judiciary? 1 / 4

The executive branch exerts influence over the courts, which typically protect the interests of the government, military, and security apparatus and have often disregarded due process and other basic safeguards in cases against the government's political opponents or where there is perceived dissent. The 2019 constitutional amendments further strengthened the president's supervisory powers over the judiciary and undermined its independence. The changes allow the president to appoint the heads of judicial bodies and authorities, choosing from among several candidates nominated by their governing councils. The president will also serve as the veto-wielding head of the Supreme Council for Judicial Bodies and Authorities, which controls appointments and disciplinary matters for the judiciary. The chief justice of the Supreme Constitutional Court will be chosen by the president from among its most senior members.

Many detained government critics and opposition figures have been prosecuted in the Emergency State Security Courts created when President Sisi declared a state of emergency in 2017; the state of emergency has been repeatedly renewed and remained in effect at the end of 2020. Decisions in these courts are subject to executive-branch approval, as the president can suspend any of their rulings and order retrials.

F2. Does due process prevail in civil and criminal matters? 0 / 4 (−1)

Although the constitution limited military trials of civilians to crimes directly involving the military, its personnel, or its property, a 2014 presidential decree placed all "public and vital facilities" under military jurisdiction, resulting in the referral of thousands of civilian defendants to military courts. That expansion of jurisdiction was effectively incorporated into the constitution in 2019.

Restrictive new emergency measures enacted in 2020 were justified as a response to the COVID-19 pandemic. In May, President Sisi approved and signed into law amendments to Emergency Law no. 162 of 1958 that banned all forms of public gatherings and demonstrations, and gave police greater powers to make arrests. It further expanded the jurisdiction of the military judicial system over civilians by giving the president the power to authorize the military to investigate and prosecute crimes that violate the Emergency Law. Authorities also used the COVID-19 pandemic to justify skipping renewal hearings for pretrial detention orders.

Sisi continues to rule in a style that entrenches military privilege and shields the armed forces from legal accountability for their actions. Charges brought in military courts are often vague or fabricated, defendants are denied due process, and basic evidentiary standards are routinely disregarded. The Emergency State Security Courts also disregard due process protections, including the right to appeal convictions.

Score Change: The score declined from 1 to 0 due to the enactment of amendments to emergency and antiterrorism laws that expanded the power of the military justice system to prosecute civilians and increased the risk of arbitrary punishment for individuals and organizations.

F3. Is there protection from the illegitimate use of physical force and freedom from war and insurgencies? 0 / 4

Police brutality and impunity for abuses by security forces were catalysts for the 2011 uprising against President Hosni Mubarak, but no reforms have since been enacted and security forces continue to wield illegitimate force with impunity. Antiterrorism laws provide a vague definition of terrorism and grant law enforcement personnel sweeping powers and immunity in enforcement.

Reports of torture, alleged extrajudicial killings, and forced disappearances continued through 2020. Prison conditions are very poor, and prisons were grossly unequipped to prevent the spread of COVID-19 or to treat it. Inmates are subject to physical abuse, overcrowding, a lack of sanitation, and denial of medical care. Use of the death penalty has increased dramatically since Sisi took power, despite serious concerns about due process violations and politicized prosecutions. In 2020, there was a steady rise in the number of death sentences issued and in the number of people sentenced to death. In October alone, according to the EIPR, 53 people were executed.

Conflict continues between security forces and adherents of the Islamic State (IS) militant group based in the North Sinai region. Both terrorist attacks and military operations have resulted in civilian casualties.

F4. Do laws, policies, and practices guarantee equal treatment of various segments of the population? 1 / 4

Women enjoy legal equality on many issues, and their court testimony is equal to that of men except in cases involving personal status matters such as divorce, which are more influenced by religious law. In practice, women face extensive discrimination in employment, among other disadvantages. Other segments of the population that are subject to various forms of harassment and discrimination include religious minorities, people of color from southern Egypt, migrants and refugees from sub-Saharan Africa, people with disabilities, and LGBT+ people.

While same-sex sexual conduct is not explicitly banned, people suspected of such activity can be charged with prostitution or "debauchery." The police have carried out dozens of such arrests in recent years.

G. PERSONAL AUTONOMY AND INDIVIDUAL RIGHTS: 6 / 16
G1. Do individuals enjoy freedom of movement, including the ability to change their place of residence, employment, or education? 1 / 4

The constitution guarantees freedom of movement, but internal travel and access are restricted tightly in North Sinai and to a lesser extent in other governorates along Egypt's borders. Sinai residents are subject to curfews, checkpoints, and other obstacles to travel.

Individuals seeking to change their place of employment or education can encounter bureaucratic barriers and scrutiny from security officials. In addition, a growing list of rights activists, journalists, political party members, bloggers, and academics have been subjected to arbitrary bans on international travel in recent years. A number of foreign researchers or activists have been expelled or denied entry to the country.

G2. Are individuals able to exercise the right to own property and establish private businesses without undue interference from state or nonstate actors? 2 / 4

While a 2017 investment law was designed to encourage private investment in underdeveloped areas, bureaucratic barriers and related corruption remain serious problems, and the outsized role of military-affiliated companies has sidelined private businesses and hindered economic development. Property rights in Sinai and other border areas are affected by the activities of security forces.

Women are at a legal disadvantage in property and inheritance matters, typically receiving half the inheritance due to a man. Societal biases also discourage women's ownership of land.

G3. Do individuals enjoy personal social freedoms, including choice of marriage partner and size of family, protection from domestic violence, and control over appearance? 2 / 4

Domestic violence, sexual harassment, and female genital mutilation (FGM) are still among the most acute problems in Egyptian society. The country has adopted laws to combat these practices in recent years, and FGM is reportedly becoming less common over time. However, the effectiveness of such laws is hindered by societal resistance, poor enforcement, abuses by the police themselves, and lack of adequate protection for witnesses, all of which deter victims from contacting authorities. Spousal rape is not a crime.

Personal status rules based on religious affiliation put women at a disadvantage in marriage, divorce, and custody matters. Muslim women cannot marry non-Muslim men, for example, and the Coptic Church rarely permits divorce.

G4. Do individuals enjoy equality of opportunity and freedom from economic exploitation? 1 / 4

Egyptian women and children, migrants from sub-Saharan Africa and Asia, and Syrian refugees are vulnerable to forced labor and sex trafficking in Egypt. The Egyptian authorities routinely punish individuals for offenses that stemmed directly from their circumstances as trafficking victims. Military conscripts are exploited as cheap labor to work on military- or state-affiliated development projects.

El Salvador

Population: 6,500,000
Capital: San Salvador
Freedom Status: Partly Free
Electoral Democracy: Yes

Overview: Elections in El Salvador are largely credible and free. However, widespread corruption undermines democracy and the rule of law, and lack of physical security remains a grave problem. Authorities have pursued a harsh, militarized response to the country's powerful criminal gangs, resulting in extrajudicial killings and other abuses. There is an active civil society sector and a lively press, though journalists risk harassment and violence in connection with coverage of organized crime or corruption.

KEY DEVELOPMENTS IN 2020

- President Nayib Bukele ordered security forces to occupy the national legislature for one day in early February, in an attempt to compel its approval of a security funding request. Most legislators declined to appear at the emergency session called by Bukele, and the Constitutional Chamber of the Supreme Court ruled the president's actions unconstitutional in October.
- Salvadorans endured a strict COVID-19 lockdown between March and June; residents were largely confined to their homes and faced arrest and arbitrary detention in centers run by the security forces for perceived violations. The Bukele administration resisted judicial orders to curtail the detentions before the lockdown measures expired; much of the economy was reopened by late August.
- The Bukele administration sought to withhold information related to its pandemic response and other activities throughout the year. In March, the public information agency's hearings were suspended, and the same agency withheld documents related to an investigation into Bukele's estate in October, after the president appointed three new members to its governing body.

POLITICAL RIGHTS: 30 / 40 (–2)

A. ELECTORAL PROCESS: 11 / 12

A1. Was the current head of government or other chief national authority elected through free and fair elections? 4 / 4

El Salvador's president is directly elected for a single five-year term. In February 2019, Grand Alliance for National Unity (GANA) candidate Nayib Bukele won the presidential election in the first round with 53.1 percent of the vote, followed by Nationalist Republican Alliance (ARENA) candidate Carlos Calleja with 31.72 percent and Farabundo Martí National Liberation Front (FMLN) candidate Hugo Martínez with 14.41 percent. Voter turnout was 51.88 percent. Organization of American States (OAS) observers called the election free and generally fair, and lauded the losing candidates' willingness to concede on election night.

A2. Were the current national legislative representatives elected through free and fair elections? 3 / 4

The 84-member, unicameral Legislative Assembly is elected for three years. In the March 2018 elections, ARENA won 37 seats, the FMLN won 23, GANA won 11, and the National Conciliation Party (PCN) won 8; the rest went to smaller parties and coalitions. Votes for ARENA and the FMLN declined compared with previous legislative elections. Turnout was roughly 46 percent.

A European Union (EU) observation mission declared the elections well organized, transparent, and the calmest since the 1992 peace accords that ended the country's 1980–92 civil war. However, observers also noted a lack of voter education, particularly regarding the issue of cross-voting, a procedure that allows voters to select candidates from more than one party list.

A3. Are the electoral laws and framework fair, and are they implemented impartially by the relevant election management bodies? 4 / 4

The country's electoral framework has undergone a number of changes in recent years, at times contributing to inefficiencies and confusion surrounding electoral processes. Implementation of a 2015 reform that called on citizens, as opposed to partisan representatives, to oversee vote counting was delayed ahead of the 2018 polls, resulting in inadequate training for the citizens who were drafted. In addition, the Supreme Electoral Tribunal (TSE) reportedly dismissed nonpartisans in favor of partisans.

In 2018, a list of political donors who gave between 2006 and 2017 was published for the first time, marking an improvement in campaign-finance transparency.

B. POLITICAL PLURALISM AND PARTICIPATION: 13 / 16

B1. Do the people have the right to organize in different political parties or other competitive political groupings of their choice, and is the system free of undue obstacles to the rise and fall of these competing parties or groupings? 4 / 4

Salvadorans are free to organize in different political parties or organizations. While two parties, the leftist FMLN and the right-wing ARENA, have dominated politics since the end of the civil war, new parties have emerged and are able to participate and compete in political processes. In 2018, the first independent candidate was elected to the legislature, and the two major parties saw their share of the vote decline.

Campaign donation records released in 2018 showed that between 2006 and 2017, ARENA received more donations than any other party, and that most of its donations had come from companies. The FMLN collected the second-most donations, with most of those funds coming from individuals.

B2. Is there a realistic opportunity for the opposition to increase its support or gain power through elections? 4 / 4

Opposition parties are able to increase support and gain power through elections. Historically, executive elections were closely contested between the two main parties, while smaller parties performed better in the legislature. President Bukele's 2019 election marked a break in the two main parties' executive dominance; while they commanded a combined 88 percent of the vote in the first round of the 2014 presidential election, they received 46 percent in 2019.

B3. Are the people's political choices free from domination by forces that are external to the political sphere, or by political forces that employ extrapolitical means? 2 / 4

Criminal groups hold significant influence over political life. Political candidates face threats from these groups, but parties are also known to engage in transactions with them. For example, party leaders negotiate with criminal groups in order to operate in gang-controlled areas; police have asserted that all major parties engage in such bargains, and some politicians have openly admitted to the practice. Parties have paid gangs to coerce or intimidate voters to cast ballots in their favor and have hired gangs to provide security for their events. Parties are known to provide gang leaders with special access to politicians and have sometimes pledged to provide social services to gang members' families.

Several of these negotiations came to light during 2020. In January, Attorney General Raúl Melara accused legislator Norman Quijano of negotiating with members of the MS-13 gang to secure votes for his 2014 presidential campaign, but a legislative attempt to strip Quijano of immunity failed in May. In July, former president Mauricio Funes (2009–14), who fled to Nicaragua in 2016 while facing a corruption investigation, was accused of offering concessions to gang members in return for a truce. Former defense minister David Munguía Payés was accused of spearheading negotiations with Funes's approval and was placed under house arrest in late July. The case against Munguía was ongoing at year's end.

The Bukele administration has also been implicated in such behavior. In September 2020, the news site El Faro reported that the government was working to negotiate a truce with, and secure electoral support from, MS-13 members. Bukele denied the allegations.

Since the transition to democracy, the military has largely been an apolitical institution—though it has not always cooperated with civilian authorities. The military retains a significant role in public security operations, even though the 1992 peace accord originally prohibited its involvement.

B4. Do various segments of the population (including ethnic, racial, religious, gender, LGBT+, and other relevant groups) have full political rights and electoral opportunities? 3 / 4

All citizens have full political rights and electoral opportunities under the law, regardless of gender, ethnicity, religion, or sexual orientation, but women and minority groups are underrepresented in the legislature and in high-level government positions. In 2018, the country's first openly transgender political candidate ran for a seat on the San Salvador Municipal Council. A 2013 statute requires that 30 percent of legislative and municipal candidates be women, and just over 30 percent of the seats in the Legislative Assembly were held by women following the 2018 elections. However, only 10 percent of mayoral seats were held by women after that year's municipal elections, and women's interests are poorly represented in practice. President Bukele's inaugural cabinet marked an improvement, attaining gender parity in 2019.

C. FUNCTIONING OF GOVERNMENT: 6 / 12 (−2)

C1. Do the freely elected head of government and national legislative representatives determine the policies of the government? 2 / 4 (−1)

The government lacks authority over areas controlled by criminal groups, and public officials are known to collaborate with criminal organizations. Several mayors have been accused of facilitating extortion rackets and assassinations and buying campaign support from gangs and criminal networks.

The Bukele administration repeatedly sought to interfere with the legislature's ability to determine policy in 2020. For one day in February, Bukele ordered security forces to occupy the legislative chamber and attempted to compel lawmakers to approve a loan meant to bolster security funding. Most Legislative Assembly members declined to appear, and the Supreme Court instructed the administration to refrain from deploying security forces again; in October, the court's Constitutional Chamber ruled Bukele's actions unconstitutional. Separately in October, El Faro reported that the July resignation of Finance Minister Nelson Fuentes came after Bukele pressured him to freeze legislators' salaries over their resistance to his funding request.

President Bukele also sought to override the legislature regarding the response to COVID-19. In May, he issued an emergency decree to extend pandemic-related measures without legislative approval, though the Supreme Court suspended his declaration. In mid-June, Bukele issued a decree aiming to manage the withdrawal of lockdown measures, but he ultimately acquiesced to the country's staged reopening after lockdown measures legally expired.

The United States wields significant influence over the government's ability to execute policy; El Salvador currently relies on an August 2019 bilateral agreement to bolster its capacity to deal with asylum seekers and maintain internal security. Some Salvadorans have also expressed concern that multinational corporations have excessive influence over local and national government officials.

Score Change: The score declined from 3 to 2 due to a pattern of attempts by President Bukele to exceed his legal powers, including his deployment of troops in the legislative chamber as part of a bid to secure increased funding for security agencies.

C2. Are safeguards against official corruption strong and effective? 2 / 4

Corruption is widespread in El Salvador, despite efforts to combat it. In March 2019, the Supreme Court used a narrow reading of the constitution to limit investigations by its Probity Section, which examines illicit enrichment, to public officials who have left office within the past 10 years. The decision effectively closed pending cases against officials whose terms of service ended before 2009.

In September 2019, President Bukele announced the creation of the International Commission against Impunity in El Salvador (CICIES), an OAS-supported anticorruption agency. CICIES cannot independently launch prosecutions, but it provides technical assistance to Salvadoran prosecutors upon request.

In November 2020, the attorney general's office launched a criminal investigation into the suspected misuse of COVID-19-related funds, based on information provided by CICIES. Finance Minister Alejandro Zelaya and Health Minister Francisco Alabí were among those under investigation for misdirecting funds at year's end.

The justice system continues to grapple with multiple corruption cases involving previous administrations. In August 2020, former Funes-era defense ministers Munguía and José Atilio Benítez Parada were charged with receiving ill-gotten funds related to a weapons-modernization program during their tenure; that case was ongoing at year's end.

C3. Does the government operate with openness and transparency? 2 / 4 (−1)

While there have been advances in the implementation of access-to-information legislation in the past, the government sought to limit transparency as the COVID-19 pandemic took hold in 2020. The Access to Public Information Agency (IAIP) suspended hearings as a national lockdown was declared in late March; individuals were notably impeded in efforts to gain information about quarantine conditions and COVID-19 test results as a consequence.

Government officials sought to withhold information on COVID-19-related expenditures. In May, President Bukele declined to submit legally mandated spending reports to the legislature. That same month, five members of a special oversight committee resigned, saying the government bypassed it when making spending decisions. In late October, citing alleged violations of public health rules, the Labor Ministry closed two Court of Auditors offices that were reportedly monitoring the Finance Ministry and Bukele's office. In early December, Deputy Security Minister Mauricio Arriaza resigned after he was accused of failing to ensure the finance minister's compliance with instructions to report on pandemic-related spending. Despite these obstructions, some pandemic-related information did become public, with El Faro relying on IAIP records to report on the government's acquisition of faulty face masks from a company connected to a legislator in July.

The Bukele administration also sought to reduce transparency on other subjects, including the president's own affairs. In September, Bukele enacted changes to existing access-to-information legislation, giving the government more time to respond to requests and giving the executive more discretion over the release of records. In October, after the president installed three new IAIP commissioners, the agency reversed an earlier decision that had allowed a journalist to receive documents related to a Probity Section investigation into Bukele's estate.

The government had previously elected to withhold information on its crime-fighting efforts; in July 2019, it announced that it would stop including deaths resulting from encounters with security forces in official homicide data, potentially obscuring both extrajudicial killings and the true homicide rate.

Score Change: The score declined from 3 to 2 because government resistance to required disclosures, political pressure on the public information agency, and a suspension of the agency's activities during a COVID-19 lockdown all reduced transparency regarding state spending and other matters of public interest.

CIVIL LIBERTIES: 33 / 60 (−1)
D. FREEDOM OF EXPRESSION AND BELIEF: 11 / 16
D1. Are there free and independent media? 2 / 4

The constitution provides for freedom of the press. While the media scene is robust, reporters face significant challenges. Harassment and acts of violence in response to coverage of corruption and organized crime have often led journalists to engage in self-censorship. Access to the internet is not restricted, and online outlets like El Faro and Revista Factum are critical sources of independent reporting. However, most Salvadorans rely on privately owned television and radio networks for news, and ownership in the broadcast sector is highly concentrated. The government launched a daily newspaper, *Diario El Salvador*, in October 2020, under the aegis of a publicly owned energy company.

Police officers and government officials have sought to prevent press coverage of controversial or sensitive matters in recent years. Human Rights Watch has noted cases in which police officers barred journalists from visiting homicide scenes.

President Bukele used verbal attacks and the threat of criminal charges to put pressure on critical journalists and outlets in 2020. In September, he announced via social media that Héctor Silva Avalos, a writer for the nongovernmental organization (NGO) InSight Crime, was under criminal investigation, though Silva reported that he had received no official notification. Later that month, Bukele announced a money-laundering investigation targeting El Faro, and accused several other outlets of "attacking" the administration.

D2. Are individuals free to practice and express their religious faith or nonbelief in public and private? 3 / 4

Religious freedom is generally respected by the government. However, congregants and religious leaders have increasingly faced gang violence and extortion in recent years. People in some communities have been unable to access their churches due to territorial disputes between gangs. In addition, religious leaders working with former gang members have faced harassment and the threat of murder.

D3. Is there academic freedom, and is the educational system free from extensive political indoctrination? 3 / 4

Academic freedom is respected, and the educational system is generally free from extensive political indoctrination. However, teachers and students continue to face intimidation and violence by gang members.

D4. Are individuals free to express their personal views on political or other sensitive topics without fear of surveillance or retribution? 3 / 4

While private discussion and personal expression are generally free, the prevalence of gang activity leads many Salvadorans to curtail speech about organized crime and other sensitive topics outside of their homes.

E. ASSOCIATIONAL AND ORGANIZATIONAL RIGHTS: 8 / 12

E1. Is there freedom of assembly? 3 / 4

Freedom of assembly is generally upheld, and public protests and gatherings are permitted. However, the persistent threat of violence by security forces or gang members serves as a deterrent to participation.

E2. Is there freedom for nongovernmental organizations, particularly those that are engaged in human rights- and governance-related work? 3 / 4

NGOs operate freely and play an important role in society and policymaking. However, groups that work on human rights and governance-related topics sometimes face threats and extortion attempts from criminal groups. Impunity for such attacks, as well as occasional pressure on NGOs by police, has prompted some observers to question the government's commitment to the protection of freedom of association and human rights in general.

Several NGOs and associations have reported discovering microphones or other listening devices on their premises in recent years, including the National Association of Private Companies (ANEP), the Salvadoran Foundation for Economic and Social Development (FUSADES), and the National Development Foundation (FUNDE).

E3. Is there freedom for trade unions and similar professional or labor organizations? 2 / 4

Labor unions have long faced obstacles in a legal environment that favors business interests, including by mandating only light penalties for employers who interfere with strikes. The law prohibits strikes in sectors deemed essential, and the designation is vaguely defined.

F. RULE OF LAW: 7 / 16

F1. Is there an independent judiciary? 2 / 4

Judicial independence is not consistently respected by the government, and the judicial system is hampered by corruption. Elected officials do not always observe Supreme Court rulings. Powerful individuals can evade justice by exerting pressure on the judiciary.

The Bukele administration repeatedly defied or criticized court orders related to its COVID-19 response during 2020. After the Supreme Court issued rulings in March and April that limited the government's ability to detain people during the pandemic, Bukele called on law enforcement personnel to ignore the rulings. In May, after the Supreme Court's Constitutional Chamber suspended a state-of-emergency declaration, Bukele threatened to sue the body at the Inter-American Court of Human Rights.

F2. Does due process prevail in civil and criminal matters? 2 / 4

Due process rights are constitutionally guaranteed but inconsistently upheld. Interpreters are not always provided for defendants who do not speak Spanish. Rights advocates report that police have carried out arbitrary arrests and detentions as part of the country's crackdown on gangs.

The authorities routinely denied due process to individuals accused of violating the strict COVID-19 lockdown measures. In April 2020, the human rights ombudsman's office (PDDH) reported that it had received 778 complaints in the lockdown's first month; the PDDH's report to the Legislative Assembly also highlighted incidents involving excessive use of force and arbitrary detention. Security forces reportedly continued to carry out such detentions after the Constitutional Chamber of the Supreme Court issued three rulings to curtail the practice in March and April.

Progress on addressing crimes committed during the civil war has been inconsistent. In 2016, the Supreme Court struck down a 1993 law preventing the investigation and prosecution of war crimes. In February 2020, the legislature passed a new reconciliation bill that rights groups warned would offer amnesty for war criminals. Bukele vetoed the measure, which was then placed under the review of the Supreme Court's Constitutional Chamber, where it remained at year's end.

The Bukele administration resisted calls to cooperate in the ongoing El Mozote trial, in which 17 high-ranking military officers stand accused of massacring nearly 1,000 people in the northeastern town of El Mozote in 1981. The administration continued to ignore an October 2019 judicial order requiring it to open defense archives on El Mozote and other military operations. In September 2020, a magistrate investigating the massacre was prevented from examining a military archive and was told that Bukele and Defense Minister René Merino Monroy prohibited the inspection. In October, El Faro reported that "declassified" documents released by the Bukele administration were in fact previously released by former president Salvador Sánchez Cerén (2014–19).

Also in October, the Supreme Court ordered the closure of criminal proceedings in a separate civil war–era case involving the 1989 killings of six Jesuit priests at the hands of the military.

F3. Is there protection from the illegitimate use of physical force and freedom from war and insurgencies? 1 / 4

Crime and other violence, much of which is linked to gang activity, remain grave problems. The government reported 697 murders in the first half of 2020, a decline from the 1,630 recorded in the first half of 2019. Deaths resulting from security operations were not included in official homicide figures beginning in 2019.

Civilians in El Salvador are vulnerable to forced disappearances, with the attorney general's office counting 1,225 missing persons in 2020 through mid-November. Relatives of the disappeared often fear reprisals for discussing their cases publicly.

Police and other security forces have been implicated in hundreds of extrajudicial killings as part of the government's militarized response to organized crime. In August 2019, the PDDH released a report documenting evidence of extrajudicial executions by police during its 2014–18 reporting period, noting that most victims were unarmed. Witnesses who spoke to the PDDH said officers commonly hid evidence, moved bodies, and engaged in acts of torture and sexual assault against their victims. Extrajudicial killings allegedly continued under the cover of the COVID-19 pandemic. In May 2020, authorities claimed that the apparent victim of an extrajudicial killing had instead died of COVID-19, despite evidence that the individual was beaten. Meanwhile, gangs continue to engage in targeted violence against security officers and their families, among other victims.

Prisons remain extremely overcrowded, and conditions for inmates can be lethal due to disease, lack of adequate medical care, and the risk of attack by other inmates. In 2018, the legislature voted to make permanent the "extraordinary measures" implemented in 2016 to increase security in prisons. Human rights groups and UN officials criticized the decision, with the latter saying the move would "dehumanize" detainees. In April 2020, President Bukele ordered a lockdown in prisons in response to a spike in murders. Prison authorities restricted gang members to their cells for a 24-hour period, and members of rival gangs were forced to share cells.

F4. Do laws, policies, and practices guarantee equal treatment of various segments of the population? 2 / 4

Women are granted equal rights under the law, but are often subject to discrimination. Indigenous people disproportionately face poverty, unemployment, and labor discrimination. Certain other populations, particularly internally displaced persons and LGBT+ people, also have inadequate access to the justice system. Discrimination on the basis of sexual orientation is prevalent, and LGBT+ people are often the targets of hate crimes and violence, including by state security agents. In February 2019, a transgender woman who had been deported from the United States died from a violent assault committed in January. In August 2020, three police officers were convicted of aggravated homicide for killing her, and they received 20-year prison terms.

Local NGOs supporting transgender Salvadorans reported that their clients had difficulty accessing medication and financial resources during the COVID-19 lockdown in 2020, and faced heightened risks of violence and housing insecurity.

In 2018, in a sign of increased attention to discrimination against LGBT+ people, the government approved an Institutional Policy for the Care of the LGBT Population. Officials indicated the government's commitment to its tenets in public statements and events, though its practical effects remain unclear.

The government restricted the rights of asylum seekers by signing an agreement with the United States in September 2019, whereby El Salvador would accept asylum seekers trying to reach the United States and stop them from traveling north. Human rights groups objected, warning that the country was unsafe, but the two governments reportedly finalized the agreement in December 2020.

G. PERSONAL AUTONOMY AND INDIVIDUAL RIGHTS: 7 / 16 (−1)

G1. Do individuals enjoy freedom of movement, including the ability to change their place of residence, employment, or education? 1 / 4 (−1)

Freedom of travel within El Salvador is complicated by gang activity. MS-13 and another major gang, Barrio 18, control certain neighborhoods of Salvadoran cities, making it dangerous for residents to travel, work, and attend school. The Internal Displacement Monitoring Center has estimated that hundreds of thousands of people have been displaced by violence in recent years. In mid-2018, the Supreme Court ruled that the government failed in its obligations to those displaced by violence, instituting a six-month deadline for the development of a new policy to address their needs. While the government missed this deadline, it did enact legislation meant to address the issue in January 2020.

Salvadorans faced additional movement restrictions when the government instituted a strict COVID-19 lockdown in March 2020. Residents were only allowed to leave home for basic goods, medical appointments, or work that was considered essential, and some people reportedly ran low on vital supplies as the lockdown continued. For two days in April, the town of La Libertad was cordoned off by the military, with residents unable to purchase basic goods. Mass transit was suspended nationwide for 15 days in May.

In May, President Bukele attempted to declare another state of emergency to extend pandemic-related restrictions but conceded to the lockdown's expiration in mid-June. The economy largely reopened by August, though authorities reserved the right to restrict travel in municipalities reporting high COVID-19 positivity rates. As many as 23,000 police officers were deployed to enforce the government's lockdown, and by August over 16,000 people had spent periods of forced confinement in quarantine centers overseen by the police and military.

Score Change: The score declined from 2 to 1 due to excessively harsh and lengthy COVID-19 lockdown measures that restricted free movement and featured abusive enforcement by security agencies.

G2. Are individuals able to exercise the right to own property and establish private businesses without undue interference from state or nonstate actors? 2 / 4

Businesses and private citizens are regularly subject to extortion. According to a 2018 report from the National Council of Small Businesses in El Salvador, some 90 percent of small businesses are affected by extortion. A 2019 report from InSight Crime and the Global Initiative against Transnational Organized Crime found that businesses and individuals pay extortion fees worth 1.7 percent of the country's gross domestic product.

Indigenous people, the majority of whom belong to the Nahua-Pipil ethnic group, face difficulties in securing land rights and accessing credit. Most Indigenous Salvadorans live on communal land or in rented accommodations.

G3. Do individuals enjoy personal social freedoms, including choice of marriage partner and size of family, protection from domestic violence, and control over appearance? 2 / 4

Men and women have equal legal rights on matters such as marriage and divorce, and there are few formal restrictions on such decisions. However, same-sex marriage remains illegal in El Salvador. The rights of transgender people were slightly expanded in January 2019, when a judge in the southern city of Zacatecoluca ruled in favor of a transgender woman who sought to update her name and gender on government-issued identification documents.

Abortion is punishable by imprisonment, including in cases where the pregnant person's life is at risk. Some women have been jailed despite credible claims that their pregnancies ended due to miscarriage; in March 2020, the UN Working Group on Arbitrary Detention warned that three Salvadoran women were unfairly imprisoned for abortion-related crimes, and called on the government to reconsider their cases. At least one woman received a sentence commutation or acquittal in 2020, though this remains rare.

The prevalence of adolescent pregnancy is a serious problem, accounting for approximately a third of all pregnancies, and many are the result of sexual assault. Female students with children often leave school, sometimes under pressure from their principals. Gender-based violence, including domestic violence, sexual violence, and femicide, is also common. An April 2019 report by the Organization of Salvadoran Women for Peace (ORMUSA) indicated that the majority of sexual-assault survivors were girls between the ages of 12 and 17. El Salvador has Latin America's highest femicide rate.

These issues were exacerbated by the COVID-19 pandemic. In August 2020, women's rights campaigners warned that over 100 girls had become pregnant as the result of sexual assault during the lockdown. ORMUSA reported 878 cases of familial domestic violence against women during the first half of the year, along with 84 cases of femicide in the first eight months of the year. The majority of the femicides took place during the lockdown.

There have been several reported incidents in recent years of femicide-suicide, in which women and girls die by suicide as a result of abuse. El Salvador remains one of the only countries in the world where this is considered a crime, and the first conviction was handed down in March 2019.

G4. Do individuals enjoy equality of opportunity and freedom from economic exploitation? 2 / 4

El Salvador remains a source, transit, and destination country for the trafficking of women, children, and LGBT+ people. There are instances of forced labor in the construction and informal sectors. According to the 2020 edition of the US State Department's *Trafficking in Persons Report,* the government has bolstered its ability to prosecute traffickers and enacted legislation granting temporary residency rights to trafficking survivors. However, shelter and public services for survivors remain insufficient.

Children are vulnerable to economic exploitation, and child labor is a serious problem. Children perform dangerous jobs in agriculture and are recruited by gangs and other criminal elements to carry out illegal activities. While the government has made improvements in collecting and publishing data on these issues and continues to implement a National Policy for the Protection of Children and Adolescents, progress in combating child exploitation remains slow.

Equatorial Guinea

Population: 1,400,000
Capital: Malabo
Freedom Status: Not Free
Electoral Democracy: No

Overview: Equatorial Guinea holds regular elections, but the voting is neither free nor fair. The current president, who took power in a military coup that deposed his uncle, has led a highly repressive authoritarian regime since 1979. Oil wealth and political power are concentrated in the hands of the president's family. The government frequently detains the few opposition politicians in the country, cracks down on civil society groups and censors journalists. The judiciary is under presidential control, and security forces engage in torture and other violence with impunity.

KEY DEVELOPMENTS IN 2020

- In January, two judges were arrested without warrants and dismissed by presidential decree. A former head of the Supreme Court who had spoken out against government corruption and violations of judicial independence narrowly avoided arrest in February and later fled the country.
- In August, the prime minister and cabinet submitted their resignations after the president criticized them for economic mismanagement. However, nearly all of the same officials were included in the new cabinet later that month.
- The government effectively expelled a World Health Organization (WHO) representative from the country in May, accusing her of inflating data on COVID-19 infections. By year's end, more than 5,200 cases and 86 deaths had been confirmed. Also during the year, authorities disbanded two religious organizations for allegedly violating social-distancing rules and arrested a nurse for privately raising her concerns about lack of oxygen in a hospital, and several journalists were suspended for reporting that security forces had beaten people while enforcing lockdown regulations.

POLITICAL RIGHTS: 0 / 40

A. ELECTORAL PROCESS: 0 / 12

A1. Was the current head of government or other chief national authority elected through free and fair elections? 0 / 4

President Teodoro Obiang Nguema Mbasogo, Africa's longest-serving head of state, has held power since 1979. He was awarded a new seven-year term in the 2016 presidential election, reportedly winning 93.5 percent of the vote. The main opposition party at the time, Convergence for Social Democracy (CPDS), boycotted the election, and other factions faced police violence, detentions, and torture. One opposition figure who had been barred from running for president, Gabriel Nsé Obiang Obono, was put under house arrest during the election, and police used live ammunition against supporters gathered at his home.

A2. Were the current national legislative representatives elected through free and fair elections? 0 / 4

The bicameral parliament consists of a 70-seat Senate and a 100-seat Chamber of Deputies, with members of both chambers serving five-year terms. Fifteen senators are appointed by the president, 55 are directly elected, and there can be several additional ex officio members. The Chamber of Deputies is directly elected.

In the 2017 legislative elections, the ruling Democratic Party of Equatorial Guinea (PDGE) and its subordinate allied parties won 99 seats in the lower house, all 55 of the elected seats in the Senate, and control of all municipal councils. The opposition Citizens for Innovation (CI), led by Nsé Obiang, took a single seat in the Chamber of Deputies and a seat on the capital's city council. The preelection media environment was tightly controlled, and a wave of arrests of CI supporters began when police dispersed an opposition rally ahead of the vote. Among other irregularities on election day, a ban on private vehicles prevented many voters from reaching distant polling stations, and polls closed one hour earlier than scheduled.

A3. Are the electoral laws and framework fair, and are they implemented impartially by the relevant election management bodies? 0 / 4

Equatorial Guinea does not have an independent electoral body; the head of the National Election Commission during the 2017 elections was also the country's interior minister and a member of the PDGE. Elections are not fairly managed in practice.

B. POLITICAL PLURALISM AND PARTICIPATION: 0 / 16

B1. Do the people have the right to organize in different political parties or other competitive political groupings of their choice, and is the system free of undue obstacles to the rise and fall of these competing parties or groupings? 0 / 4

The PDGE is the dominant party, operating in conjunction with a number of subordinate parties in its coalition. The opposition CI was officially banned as a political party in 2018, and its members face imprisonment and regular threats of imprisonment by the state.

Other opposition leaders and members are also subject to arrest, detention, and trial. Two members of the Coalition for the Restoration of Democracy (CORED), who were seized in Togo, and dissident members of the ruling PDGE were among a group of 130 defendants tried in March 2019 for their alleged involvement in a 2017 coup attempt. Opposition leaders living in exile were tried in absentia. The court ultimately convicted 112 people and imposed harsh prison terms in May 2019. After appeals, the convictions were confirmed by the Supreme Court in November 2020.

Among other recent cases, CPDS member Luis Mba Esono was detained without charge in July 2019 and released in February 2020. Separately, the opposition Movement for the Liberation of Equatorial Guinea 3rd Republic (MLGE3R) reported in November 2019 that four of its members had been abducted in South Sudan. They were transferred to Equatorial Guinea, and in March 2020 a military court convicted them along with six others on treason and spying charges.

B2. Is there a realistic opportunity for the opposition to increase its support or gain power through elections? 0 / 4

Equatorial Guinea has never experienced a peaceful transfer of power through elections. President Obiang appointed his son, Teodoro "Teodorín" Nguema Obiang Mangue, as vice president in 2016, paving the way for a dynastic succession.

There was no opposition representative in the legislature as of 2020. Jesús Mitogo Oyono, then CI's only lower house member, was not allowed to return to his seat after he was imprisoned on charges of sedition in 2018, even though he was pardoned and released later that year. He sought asylum in the United States in May 2020 and was expelled from the party.

In July 2020, the opposition Center Right Union (UCD) agreed to enter the ruling party's coalition, and UCD leader Avelino Mocache Menga was appointed as secretary of state for fisheries and water resources in August.

B3. Are the people's political choices free from domination by forces that are external to the political sphere, or by political forces that employ extrapolitical means? 0 / 4

The regime routinely uses the security forces to attack and intimidate opposition supporters, and political loyalty to the ruling party is treated as a condition for obtaining and keeping public-sector employment.

B4. Do various segments of the population (including ethnic, racial, religious, gender, LGBT+, and other relevant groups) have full political rights and electoral opportunities? 0 / 4

The ethnic Fang majority dominates political life in Equatorial Guinea, leaving minority ethnic groups with little influence; power is concentrated in the hands of the president's family and allies from their region of origin in particular. Women formally enjoy equal political rights, holding a few positions in government, 23 percent of the seats in the Chamber of Deputies, and 17 percent of the seats in the Senate. However, they have little opportunity to independently advocate for their interests or organize politically. While no law explicitly prevents LGBT+ people from exercising their political rights, societal discrimination discourages them from participating openly and advocating for their communities.

C. FUNCTIONING OF GOVERNMENT: 0 / 12

C1. Do the freely elected head of government and national legislative representatives determine the policies of the government? 0 / 4

The executive branch—headed by the president, who is not freely elected—sets and implements government policy, leaving the legislature with no meaningful role in the policymaking process.

In August 2020, the president accepted the resignation of the prime minister and cabinet after criticizing them for mismanagement of the economy and failing to address other pressing problems. However, most of the ministers were reappointed days later, including Prime Minister Francisco Pascual Obama Asue, who had held his post since 2016. Some observers attributed the incident to factional struggles within the ruling elite.

C2. Are safeguards against official corruption strong and effective? 0 / 4

There are no independent anticorruption mechanisms, and the government is marred by nepotism and graft. Hiring and promotions within the government, army, and civil service favor those with ties to the president and his family. One of the president's sons, Gabriel Mbega Obiang Lima, is the minister of mines and hydrocarbons, granting him sweeping control over the country's natural resources and chief source of revenue. Teodorín, the vice president, has been the focus of money-laundering investigations in multiple countries for several years. In 2017, a French court convicted him of money-laundering charges in absentia, handing him a suspended sentence and a suspended $34 million fine. The court also seized his assets in France, including a luxurious building in Paris, which the government of Equatorial Guinea claimed belonged to its diplomatic presence; this was denied by the host country, and the International Court of Justice upheld France's position in December 2020.

The government has taken some steps to address corruption in response to international pressure. It ratified the UN Convention against Corruption in 2018 and the African Union's Convention on Preventing and Combating Corruption in 2019. In November 2019, a government commission was formed to draft legislation that would bring the country into compliance with both conventions. The government also committed to strengthening its anticorruption efforts in order to receive a loan from the International Monetary Fund in December 2019; however, the measures laid out in the anticorruption plan were not fully implemented during 2020.

C3. Does the government operate with openness and transparency? 0 / 4

The government's budget process and procurement system are opaque, as are the finances of state-owned companies. A significant percentage of revenue from the country's oil reserves are funneled to Obiang's allies through noncompetitive, nontransparent construction contracts, often for projects of questionable value. International financial organizations and human rights groups have criticized the government for pouring resources into wasteful infrastructure initiatives while neglecting health and social spending.

The Extractive Industries Transparency Initiative (EITI) agreed to consider Equatorial Guinea's latest application for membership in 2019, but in February 2020 the EITI board concluded that the government had provided inadequate evidence of its commitment to transparency requirements.

The authorities repeatedly attempted to suppress information about both the COVID-19 pandemic and the official response during 2020. In May, the government forced the WHO to withdraw its representative from the country, accusing her of inflating the case count. The move disrupted the reporting of data for several weeks.

CIVIL LIBERTIES: 5 / 60 (−1)
D. FREEDOM OF EXPRESSION AND BELIEF: 2 / 16 (−1)
D1. Are there free and independent media? 0 / 4

Press freedom is severely limited, despite constitutional protections. Most journalists consistently exercise self-censorship, and those who do criticize the regime are subject to dismissal and other reprisals. The country's only private television and radio broadcaster, RTV-Asonga, is controlled by Teodorín. The handful of private newspapers and magazines in operation face intense financial and political pressure and are unable to publish regularly. The government has sought to block access to the websites of opposition parties and exile groups since 2013, and online versions of Spanish newspapers are regularly blocked. The government has obstructed access to the internet in times of political tension.

In April 2020, seven journalists from an Asonga TV talk show were suspended after they aired images of soldiers beating a man who had allegedly violated COVID-19-related movement restrictions.

D2. Are individuals free to practice and express their religious faith or nonbelief in public and private? 1 / 4 (−1)

The constitution protects religious freedom, though in practice it is sometimes affected by the country's broader political repression and endemic corruption. The Roman Catholic Church is the dominant faith and is exempt from registration and permit requirements that apply to other groups. Government officials have reportedly been required to attend Catholic masses on ceremonial occasions, such as the president's birthday.

In April 2020, the government issued a decree to disband two religious groups on the grounds that they did not comply with COVID-19-related bans on church services and other gatherings. The decree took effect without due process and included deportation orders for foreign pastors associated with the groups.

Score Change: The score declined from 2 to 1 because the government abruptly disbanded two religious groups without due process, accusing them of violating COVID-19-related restrictions.

D3. Is there academic freedom, and is the educational system free from extensive political indoctrination? 1 / 4

Academic freedom is politically constrained, and self-censorship among faculty is common. University professors and teachers have reportedly been hired or dismissed due to their political affiliations.

D4. Are individuals free to express their personal views on political or other sensitive topics without fear of surveillance or retribution? 0 / 4

Freedoms of personal expression and private discussion are restricted. The government uses informants and electronic surveillance to monitor members of the opposition, nongovernmental organizations (NGOs), and journalists, including the few members of the foreign press in the country. Critics of the government are subject to arbitrary arrest, physical abuse, and trumped-up charges.

In April 2020, a nurse was arrested after using WhatsApp to express concerns to a friend about the lack of oxygen in a Malabo hospital; the message was shared widely beyond its original recipient. The nurse was released later in the month.

E. ASSOCIATIONAL AND ORGANIZATIONAL RIGHTS: 0 / 12

E1. Is there freedom of assembly? 0 / 4

Freedom of assembly is severely restricted. Opposition gatherings are typically blocked or dispersed by security forces, and citizens are sometimes pressured to attend progovernment events.

E2. Is there freedom for nongovernmental organizations, particularly those that are engaged in human rights- and governance-related work? 0 / 4

All associations must register with the government through an onerous process, and independent NGOs face state persecution. In 2019, the Center for Studies and Initiatives for the Development of Equatorial Guinea (CEID-GE) was dissolved by government decree just a few months after its leader was placed under house arrest to prevent him from receiving a human rights award at a ceremony hosted by the French and German embassies.

Two civic activists who had been arrested in separate cases in 2019, Joaquín Eló Ayeto and Luis Nzó, were released in February and March 2020, reportedly without explanation. In May, however, a group of soldiers stormed Eló Ayeto's house in an apparent act of intimidation.

E3. Is there freedom for trade unions and similar professional or labor organizations? 0 / 4

The constitution provides for the right to organize unions, but there are many legal and practical barriers to union formation, collective bargaining, and strikes. The government has refused to register a number of trade unions; a farmers' organization is the only legal union.

F. RULE OF LAW: 0 / 16

F1. Is there an independent judiciary? 0 / 4

The judiciary is not independent, and judges in sensitive cases often consult with the office of the president before issuing important rulings. Under the constitution, the president is the nation's first magistrate. He also oversees the body that appoints judges. The court system's impartiality is further undermined by corruption.

In January 2020, Antonio Ondo Abaga Maye, a judge in Malabo, was arrested without a warrant on orders from the government, apparently because he had released two individuals in an investigation under his purview. He was allegedly tortured while in detention. Separately that month, another judge, Ruben Fernando Mba Obama Mangue, was also arrested without a warrant, and both were subsequently removed from their positions by presidential decree.

In February, security forces surrounded the home of former Supreme Court president Juan Carlos Ondó Angué, but the arrival of Spanish, French, and US diplomats reportedly prevented his arrest; he was accused of involvement in the alleged 2017 coup attempt. Ondó Angué had been dismissed from his judicial post in 2018 after expressing support for a colleague who had allegedly resisted a government-backed corruption scheme and then died in detention. After the incident at his home, Ondó Angué went into hiding and fled the country.

F2. Does due process prevail in civil and criminal matters? 0 / 4

Security forces routinely detain people without charge. Those who are tried can be subjected to proceedings that lack due process. In 2019, as the trial against alleged participants in the 2017 coup attempt was underway, President Obiang unilaterally appointed new magistrates and prosecutors by decree. The American Bar Association (ABA), which observed the trial, noted a dearth of evidence against the accused and reported that a military officer in the audience was seen relaying messages to prosecutors and judges. The court convicted 112 of the defendants despite these failings, with some receiving 97-year prison sentences, and the verdicts were upheld on appeal in November 2020.

Military courts, which are empowered to try civilians for certain crimes, have even fewer due process protections than civilian courts and lack an avenue for appeal. In March 2020, a military court convicted 10 people suspected of links to MLGE3R after a closed-door trial held in a prison facility. They were found guilty of treason, espionage, and verbal abuse and insult of the head of state, receiving sentences of up to 90 years in prison.

F3. Is there protection from the illegitimate use of physical force and freedom from war and insurgencies? 0 / 4

Beatings and torture by security forces are reportedly common. Defendants who were tried in 2019 for alleged involvement in the 2017 coup attempt claimed that they were tortured in an effort to extract confessions. The ABA reported that two of the defendants died in custody. Prisons are overcrowded and feature harsh conditions, including physical abuse, poor sanitation, and denial of medical care.

F4. Do laws, policies, and practices guarantee equal treatment of various segments of the population? 0 / 4

Women face discrimination in employment and other matters, particularly in rural areas. Ethnic minority groups such as the Bubi, Ndowe, and Annobonese suffer persistent societal discrimination in the form of harassment from law enforcement officials or difficulties accessing public services.

Immigrants, including irregular migrants, are subject to raids, physical abuse, and extortion by police. Same-sex sexual activity is not illegal, but LGBT+ people face social stigma and mistreatment including street harassment, discrimination in the workplace, and forced pregnancies.

G. PERSONAL AUTONOMY AND INDIVIDUAL RIGHTS: 3 / 16

G1. Do individuals enjoy freedom of movement, including the ability to change their place of residence, employment, or education? 1 / 4

Freedom of movement is protected by law but restricted in practice through measures such as police checkpoints, which often require the payment of bribes. Authorities have denied opposition members and other dissidents reentry from abroad or restricted their movements within the country.

Amid the travel restrictions imposed in response to the COVID-19 pandemic in 2020, individuals with dual nationality who were trying to return to their countries of residency abroad were pressured to give up their Equatoguinean nationality at the airport.

G2. Are individuals able to exercise the right to own property and establish private businesses without undue interference from state or nonstate actors? 1 / 4

Pervasive corruption and onerous bureaucratic procedures serve as major impediments to private business activity. Property rights are inconsistently respected by the government, which is known to seize land and offer little recourse for those affected. Members of the Bubi minority have reported cases of land grabs by elites and the government in recent years.

Most women face disadvantages regarding inheritance and property rights under both the civil code and customary practices, though women enjoy greater customary rights among the Bubi.

G3. Do individuals enjoy personal social freedoms, including choice of marriage partner and size of family, protection from domestic violence, and control over appearance? 1 / 4

The civil code and customary law put women at a disadvantage with respect to personal status matters like marriage and child custody, with some exceptions among the Bubi. Laws against rape and domestic violence are not enforced effectively. The government does little to collect data, raise awareness, or support civil society efforts to combat such problems, which include sexual violence against minors and LGBT+ people. Child marriage is common, with the UN Children's Fund estimating that 30 percent of Equatoguinean women between the ages of 20 and 24 were married before age 18. The Education Ministry requires female students to take pregnancy tests and bars pregnant girls from attending school.

G4. Do individuals enjoy equality of opportunity and freedom from economic exploitation? 0 / 4

The country's oil wealth is concentrated among the ruling elite, leaving much of the population without access to basic services. Equatorial Guinea continues to score poorly on social and economic development indicators, and economic conditions have worsened amid low oil prices in recent years.

Foreign workers in the oil and construction industries and a variety of other sectors are subject to passport confiscation and forced labor. Equatoguineans from rural areas are also vulnerable to forced labor, including in the sex trade. Corrupt officials are often complicit in human trafficking, according to the US State Department.

Eritrea

Population: 3,500,000
Capital: Asmara
Freedom Status: Not Free
Electoral Democracy: No

Overview: Eritrea is a militarized authoritarian state that has not held a national election since independence from Ethiopia in 1993. The People's Front for Democracy and Justice (PFDJ), headed by President Isaias Afwerki, is the sole political aparty. Arbitrary detention is commonplace, and citizens are required to perform national service, often for their entire working lives. The government shut down all independent media in 2001.

KEY DEVELOPMENTS IN 2020

- The Tigrayan People's Liberation Front (TPLF)—which accused Eritrea of supporting the Ethiopian military campaign against it—launched three rocket attacks against Asmara in November. Details on damage or casualties were unclear.
- Eritrean authorities released several groups of religious prisoners during the year. A group of Muslims detained in 2018 was reportedly released by August, while as many as 69 Christians were released between September and October. Some 28 Jehovah's Witnesses were released in December.
- The government instituted a strict COVID-19-related lockdown in April and maintained travel restrictions within the country through at least early December. Authorities also used COVID-19 measures to disrupt trade routes and limit access to fishing areas used by members of the Afar ethnic group, straining their food supply. The government reported 1,252 cases and 1 death to the World Health Organization at year's end.

POLITICAL RIGHTS: 1 / 40

A. ELECTORAL PROCESS: 0 / 12

A1. Was the current head of government or other chief national authority elected through free and fair elections? 0 / 4

Following Eritrea's formal independence from Ethiopia in 1993, an unelected Transitional National Assembly chose Isaias to serve as president until elections could be held under a new constitution. He has remained in office since then, without ever obtaining a mandate from voters.

A2. Were the current national legislative representatives elected through free and fair elections? 0 / 4

A constitution ratified in 1997 but never instituted calls for an elected 150-seat National Assembly, which would choose the president from among its members by a majority vote. National elections have been postponed indefinitely, and the transitional assembly has not met since 2002. National elections have never been conducted. Periodic local and regional assembly elections are carefully orchestrated by the PFDJ and offer no meaningful choice to voters.

A3. Are the electoral laws and framework fair, and are they implemented impartially by the relevant election management bodies? 0 / 4

The 1997 constitution calls for an electoral commission whose head is appointed by the president and confirmed by the National Assembly, but it has never been established. Electoral laws have not been finalized.

B. POLITICAL PLURALISM AND PARTICIPATION: 0 / 16

B1. Do the people have the right to organize in different political parties or other competitive political groupings of their choice, and is the system free of undue obstacles to the rise and fall of these competing parties or groupings? 0 / 4

The PFDJ is the only legally recognized political party in Eritrea. Alternative groups must operate from abroad among the diaspora. Groups were hosted in Ethiopia in the past, but its government ordered many of them to cease operations after the two countries sought rapprochement in 2018.

The Eritrean government holds prominent dissidents and family members in detention; a group of 11 has reportedly been held incommunicado since 2001. Reports in 2018 suggested that one of these individuals, former foreign minister Haile "Durue" Woldensae, died in detention. In 2012, the government captured Ciham Ali Abdu, daughter of former information minister Ali Abdu Ahmed, while she tried to flee to Sudan; she was still detained incommunicado at the end of 2020. Authorities have detained former finance minister Berhane Abrehe since 2018, though his wife was released in 2019.

B2. Is there a realistic opportunity for the opposition to increase its support or gain power through elections? 0 / 4

President Isaias and the PFDJ have been in power without interruption since independence. Since multiparty elections have never been allowed, opposition groups have had no opportunity to compete or enter government.

B3. Are the people's political choices free from domination by forces that are external to the political sphere, or by political forces that employ extrapolitical means? 0 / 4

Eritrean society is dominated by the military, with most citizens required to perform open-ended military or other national service. The authorities' intolerance of dissent and the absence of elections or opposition parties leaves individuals with no political options other than loyalty to the PFDJ, imprisonment, or illegal emigration.

B4. Do various segments of the population (including ethnic, racial, religious, gender, LGBT+, and other relevant groups) have full political rights and electoral opportunities? 0 / 4

Women and various ethnic groups are nominally represented within the PFDJ but have no practical ability to organize independently or advocate for their interests through the political system.

C. FUNCTIONING OF GOVERNMENT: 1 / 12

C1. Do the freely elected head of government and national legislative representatives determine the policies of the government? 0 / 4

Power is concentrated in the hands of the unelected president, who reportedly determines policy with the help of an informal circle of advisers, leaving the cabinet and security officials to merely carry out his decisions. In 2016, the United Nations Human Rights Council (UNHRC) noted that military personnel are overrepresented among the president's closest associates.

C2. Are safeguards against official corruption strong and effective? 1 / 4

Petty bribery and influence peddling are thought to be endemic, and larger-scale corruption is a problem among some party officials and military leaders. The government's control over foreign exchange effectively gives it sole authority over imports. Those in the regime's favor profit from the smuggling and sale of scarce goods such as food, building materials, and alcohol. Senior military officials have allegedly profited from smuggling Eritreans out of the country. There are no independent agencies or mechanisms in place to prevent or punish corruption. Special anticorruption courts overseen by the military nominally exist but are mostly inactive.

C3. Does the government operate with openness and transparency? 0 / 4

The government operates without public scrutiny. Basic data about the state budget and its appropriations are not publicly disclosed, and officials are not required to disclose their assets.

CIVIL LIBERTIES: 1 / 60

D. FREEDOM OF EXPRESSION AND BELIEF: 0 / 16

D1. Are there free and independent media? 0 / 4

The government shut down all independent media outlets in 2001. Several outlets provide coverage to Eritreans from outside the country, including the British Broadcasting Corporation (BBC), Paris-based Radio Erena and satellite station Asena TV. According to the Committee to Protect Journalists, 16 journalists were imprisoned for their work in Eritrea, almost all of them since 2001.

D2. Are individuals free to practice and express their religious faith or nonbelief in public and private? 0 / 4

The government places strict limits on the exercise of religion. Eritrea officially recognizes only four faiths: Sunni Islam, Orthodox Christianity, Roman Catholicism, and Evangelical Lutheranism. Jehovah's Witnesses face severe persecution, including denial of citizenship and travel papers. Religious practice is prohibited among members of the military.

Followers of other denominations are subject to arrest. In April 2020, 15 Christians worshipping in a private home in Asmara were arrested. In June, authorities arrested 30 individuals who attended a Christian wedding in the capital.

The government also interferes in the practice of faiths it recognizes. The Eritrean Orthodox Church's patriarch, Abune Antonios, was deposed and placed under house arrest in 2006. In 2019, church bishops expelled Antonios for "heresy." In February 2020, an Ethiopian Roman Catholic cardinal was denied entry into Eritrea, despite possessing an entry visa.

The Eritrean government released several groups of religious prisoners in 2020. A group of Muslims, who were originally detained after 2018 protests sparked by the death of Islamic school chairman Musa Mohammed Nur, were reportedly released by August. As many as 69 Christians were released between September and October. In December, 28 Jehovah's Witnesses were released.

D3. Is there academic freedom, and is the educational system free from extensive political indoctrination? 0 / 4

Academic freedom is greatly constrained. Students in their last year of secondary school must perform military service at the Sawa military training center. In 2019, Human Rights Watch (HRW) reported that widespread physical and sexual abuse took place at Sawa. Former students say they were given insufficient food and were forced to perform manual labor. While international observers called on the government to release students held at Sawa to lessen their risk of contracting COVID-19, HRW reported in September 2020 that a new group of students was sent there.

From 2017 to 2019, the government took steps to nationalize an Islamic school in Asmara along with seven other schools operated by religious organizations, as part of a broader policy to assert state control of the education system.

D4. Are individuals free to express their personal views on political or other sensitive topics without fear of surveillance or retribution? 0 / 4

Freedoms of expression and private discussion are severely inhibited by fear of government informants and the likelihood of arrest and arbitrary detention for any airing of dissent. The authorities regularly block access to social media platforms and shutter internet cafés.

Members of the Eritrean diaspora are, by comparison, better able to express dissent online. Activists have used internet platforms and protests to oppose the government as part of the *Yiakl* (Enough) campaign in 2020. However, members of the diaspora are also subject to government surveillance and harassment.

E. ASSOCIATIONAL AND ORGANIZATIONAL RIGHTS: 0 / 12
E1. Is there freedom of assembly? 0 / 4

Freedom of assembly is not recognized by the authorities. Those who protest face the threat of deadly force at the hands of state security officers, or arbitrary detention. Gatherings of more than 10 people were restricted in March 2020 as part of the government's COVID-19 response.

E2. Is there freedom for nongovernmental organizations, particularly those that are engaged in human rights- and governance-related work? 0 / 4

The law requires all nongovernmental organizations (NGOs) to undergo an onerous and arbitrary annual registration process and limits their activities to providing humanitarian relief. In reality, there are no independent civil society organizations based in Eritrea. The government continues to deny permission for external human rights organizations to enter the country.

In January 2020, Finland-based Finn Church Aid ended activities in Eritrea after the government halted the NGO's teacher-training program, which reportedly sought participants outside of the national-service apparatus.

E3. Is there freedom for trade unions and similar professional or labor organizations? 0 / 4

There are no independent trade unions in Eritrea. The only union umbrella group, the National Confederation of Eritrean Workers, is affiliated with the PFDJ. According to reports to the UNHRC, the government has prevented new unions from being formed. However, in May 2020, the UN's special rapporteur on human rights in Eritrea reported that the government ratified the International Labour Organization's eight fundamental conventions.

F. RULE OF LAW: 0 / 16

F1. Is there an independent judiciary? 0 / 4

The judiciary has no independence from the executive branch. The Supreme Court called for in the constitution has never been established, nor has a Judicial Commission tasked with appointing judges. The president controls the appointment and dismissal of all judges; even nominally elected judges in local community courts are controlled by the Justice Ministry, according to UN investigators. Many judges are military officers.

F2. Does due process prevail in civil and criminal matters? 0 / 4

Basic principles of due process are systematically violated. Arbitrary arrests and detentions are common; targets include those who evade military service, try to flee the country, or are suspected of practicing an unauthorized religion. Eritreans who offend high-ranking government or party officials are also reportedly subject to arbitrary arrest.

Prisoners, including children, former members of the government, and their family members, are routinely held incommunicado for indefinite periods without charge or trial, with the authorities refusing even to inform family members whether they are still alive. There is no operational system of public defense lawyers. Thousands of political prisoners and prisoners of conscience remain imprisoned.

F3. Is there protection from the illegitimate use of physical force and freedom from war and insurgencies? 0 / 4

UN investigators have described the routine and systematic use of physical and psychological torture in both civilian and military detention centers. Deaths in custody or in military service due to torture and other harsh conditions have been reported, though authorities do not investigate such incidents. Security forces employ lethal violence arbitrarily and with impunity. Individuals attempting to escape military service or flee the country have been fired on by soldiers.

In April 2020, the UN special rapporteur called on the government to release low-risk detainees to limit the spread of COVID-19, though she reported that the authorities did not take such measures in her May report.

Eritrea supported the Ethiopian government when it launched its military campaign against the TPLF in November 2020, though Eritrean officials initially denied involvement. The TPLF, which accused Eritrea of committing troops, launched three rocket attacks on Asmara that month, though details on damage or casualties were unclear.

F4. Do laws, policies, and practices guarantee equal treatment of various segments of the population? 0 / 4

There are allegations that two of Eritrea's nine recognized ethnic groups, the Kunama and Afar, face severe discrimination, including exclusion from the government's poverty alleviation programs.

Laws mandate equal educational opportunity for women and equal pay for equal work. However, traditional societal discrimination against women persists in the countryside, and the deeply flawed legal system does not effectively uphold their formal rights.

Same-sex relations are criminalized, and LGBT+ people enjoy no legal protections from societal discrimination.

G. PERSONAL AUTONOMY AND INDIVIDUAL RIGHTS: 1 / 16

G1. Do individuals enjoy freedom of movement, including the ability to change their place of residence, employment, or education? 0 / 4

Freedom of movement is heavily restricted. Eritreans young enough for national service are rarely given permission to go abroad, and those who try to travel outside the country without obtaining an exit visa face imprisonment. Individuals also require permits to travel within the country. Eritrean refugees and asylum seekers who are repatriated from other countries are subject to detention under harsh conditions.

The opening of the border with Ethiopia in 2018 prompted tens of thousands of Eritreans to flee, and individuals have continued in their efforts to leave since that border's 2019 closure. Eritrean troops supporting the Ethiopian campaign against the TPLF have reportedly repatriated refugees residing in Ethiopia.

Authorities instituted strict COVID-19-related restrictions on movement. A lockdown was imposed in early April 2020, and pandemic-related travel restrictions remained in force through at least early December. In July, Human Rights Concern–Eritrea reported that the authorities used pandemic-related measures to disrupt the Afar ethnic group's access to fishing sites and trade routes, risking their food supply.

G2. Are individuals able to exercise the right to own property and establish private businesses without undue interference from state or nonstate actors? 0 / 4

The national conscription system denies much of the working-age population the opportunity to establish and run their own businesses. Both the authorities and private actors with the regime's support can confiscate property and evict occupants without due process.

G3. Do individuals enjoy personal social freedoms, including choice of marriage partner and size of family, protection from domestic violence, and control over appearance? 1 / 4

Men and women have equal rights under laws governing marriage, nationality, and other personal status matters. However, girls in rural areas remain vulnerable to early or forced marriage. Rape of women and sexualized forms of violence against men are common in detention and in military service. Sexual assault of female conscripts is endemic and has not been thoroughly investigated by the authorities.

The government has banned the practice of female genital mutilation (FGM). In May 2020, the UN special rapporteur noted the government's formation of a steering committee and adoption of a national action plan to halt FGM and other forms of gender-based violence (GBV). However, FGM remains widespread in rural areas.

G4. Do individuals enjoy equality of opportunity and freedom from economic exploitation? 0 / 4

Eritrea's conscription system ties most able-bodied men and women—including those under 18 who are completing secondary school—to obligatory military service, which can also entail compulsory, unpaid labor for enterprises controlled by the political elite. National service is supposed to last 18 months but is open-ended in practice. UN human rights experts have described this system as enslavement.

Estonia

Population: 1,300,000
Capital: Tallinn
Freedom Status: Free
Electoral Democracy: Yes

Overview: Estonia's democratic institutions are generally strong, and both political rights and civil liberties are widely respected. However, more than 5 percent of the population remains stateless and cannot participate in national elections. Corruption is a persistent challenge, as is discrimination against ethnic Russians, Roma, LGBT+ people, and others. Far-right and Euroskeptic forces have becoming increasingly vocal in Estonian politics in recent years.

KEY DEVELOPMENTS IN 2020

- In March, the government declared a state of emergency in response to the COVID-19 pandemic. The emergency lasted until May and was then replaced with a less rigorous set of movement restrictions and social-distancing measures. The country successfully suppressed the virus for most of the year, but the number of infections began to rise in the fall, and some nationwide restrictions were reintroduced in November. By the end of the year, Estonia had reported nearly 28,000 confirmed cases of COVID-19 and 229 deaths.
- In October, the ruling coalition announced plans to organize a nonbinding referendum proposed by the far-right Conservative People's Party of Estonia (EKRE) that would ask voters to support a constitutional amendment defining marriage as a union between a man and a woman, effectively restricting the rights of same-sex couples. The parliament passed the referendum bill in its first reading in December, with opposition parties pledging to block the measure from advancing further. A second reading was scheduled for January 2021.
- The durability of the ruling coalition was tested during the year by multiple ministerial resignations as well as continued controversial statements by EKRE representatives. One of the party's leaders, Mart Helme, resigned as interior minister in November after a radio broadcast in which he verbally attacked US president-elect Joseph Biden and the validity of his victory.

POLITICAL RIGHTS: 38 / 40

A. ELECTORAL PROCESS: 12 / 12

A1. Was the current head of government or other chief national authority elected through free and fair elections? 4 / 4

The prime minister, who serves as head of government, is nominated by the president and approved by the parliament. Prime Minister Jüri Ratas of the Center Party was reappointed in 2019 following that year's parliamentary elections and the formation of a coalition comprising the centrist-populist Center Party, the far-right EKRE, and the conservative Isamaa party.

The president is elected by the parliament to a five-year term, filling a largely ceremonial role as head of state. Current president Kersti Kaljulaid was elected as a nonpartisan consensus candidate in a sixth round of voting in 2016. Although the overall election process was free and fair, it was criticized as lengthy and not entirely transparent.

A2. Were the current national legislative representatives elected through free and fair elections? 4 / 4

The constitution establishes a 101-seat, unicameral parliament, called the Riigikogu, whose members are elected for four-year terms using proportional representation in multi-member constituencies.

The March 2019 parliamentary elections met democratic standards. Like in previous elections in 2015, the voter turnout was about 64 percent. Five parties cleared the 5 percent vote threshold for representation, with the main opposition center-right Reform Party capturing a plurality with 34 seats. Electoral support for EKRE more than doubled, which translated into 19 seats. The incumbent Center Party won 26 seats, down one. The number of seats won by Isamaa and the left-wing Social Democratic Party (SDE) dropped to 12 and 10, respectively.

A3. Are the electoral laws and framework fair, and are they implemented impartially by the relevant election management bodies? 4 / 4

The legal framework for conducting elections is clear and fairly administered. Online voting is common and has gained in popularity. The 2019 parliamentary elections featured record turnout online, with some 44 percent of participating voters using this method and demonstrating strong public confidence in the system.

B. POLITICAL PLURALISM AND PARTICIPATION: 15 / 16

B1. Do the people have the right to organize in different political parties or other competitive political groupings of their choice, and is the system free of undue obstacles to the rise and fall of these competing parties or groupings? 4 / 4

Estonia's political parties organize and operate freely, and the political landscape remains open and competitive.

B2. Is there a realistic opportunity for the opposition to increase its support or gain power through elections? 4 / 4

The country has undergone multiple democratic transfers of power between rival parties following elections over the past three decades, and opposition parties have a strong presence in the parliament.

B3. Are the people's political choices free from domination by forces that are external to the political sphere, or by political forces that employ extrapolitical means? 4 / 4

People's political choices are generally not subject to undue interference. However, there were increasing concerns about the influence of online disinformation ahead of and after the 2019 elections.

B4. Do various segments of the population (including ethnic, racial, religious, gender, LGBT+, and other relevant groups) have full political rights and electoral opportunities? 3 / 4

More than 5 percent of the country's population—mostly ethnic Russians—remain stateless and cannot participate in national elections. Resident noncitizens are permitted to vote in local and European Parliament elections but may not run as candidates or join political parties. The authorities have adopted policies to assist those seeking naturalization.

President Kaljulaid is the first woman in the country's history to hold her office. While a record total of 29 women were elected to the 101-seat Riigikogu in 2019, representation for women in government remains a challenge.

EKRE's entry into a coalition government in 2019 raised political equality concerns among domestic and international observers due to the party's history of racist, sexist, anti-LGBT+, and White nationalist sentiments. EKRE cabinet ministers have advocated anti-LGBT+ policy goals and expressed a variety of extremist views, including conspiracy theories, discriminatory falsehoods about immigration and refugees, and antisemitic sentiments.

C. FUNCTIONING OF GOVERNMENT 11 / 12

C1. Do the freely elected head of government and national legislative representatives determine the policies of the government? 4 / 4

Both the government and the parliament are freely elected and function without interference from external or nonstate actors.

However, the coalition government formed in 2019 suffered from instability amid multiple personnel changes, including separate resignations by three ministers in November 2020 alone. Mart Helme, who resigned as interior minister that month after verbally attacking US president-elect Joseph Biden and the legitimacy of his election victory in a radio broadcast, was the sixth EKRE minister to step down since the ruling coalition was established the previous year.

C2. Are safeguards against official corruption strong and effective? 3 / 4

The legal framework and independent law enforcement institutions provide important checks on corruption, and cases against high-profile defendants have been brought to court in recent years, though the results have been mixed. A trial that began in 2017 focused on Edgar Savisaar—former leader of the Center Party and Tallinn city mayor—and a number of codefendants who were accused of bribery, money laundering, and embezzlement. Savisaar was excused from the trial due to poor health in 2018, and defendants including the Center Party itself were punished with fines. Several government officials and businessmen in the case were acquitted in January 2020, but an appeal by the prosecution was pending at year's end. Separate trials concerning recent corruption scandals in Tallinn and Tartu municipalities and the Tallinn seaport ended in 2019 and 2020, again with some key defendants acquitted or released due to poor health. Early in 2020, new charges involving alleged corruption in the health sector were announced.

In May 2020, the ruling coalition introduced a bill that would abolish the Supervisory Committee on Party Financing (ERJK) and delegate its tasks to the National Audit Office. Opposition parties protested the move, noting several recent verdicts of the ERJK regarding the finances of the Center Party; the bill had not been passed at year's end. It was reported in January 2020 that Estonian political parties on the whole had spent more than they took in during 2019, which could leave them vulnerable to improper influence by private interests. There are no comprehensive rules for the protection of whistleblowers, and lobbying is not sufficiently regulated. Separately in January, the appointment of coalition party members to a committee responsible for selecting the directors of state-owned enterprises raised concerns about conflicts of interest.

C3. Does the government operate with openness and transparency? 4 / 4

Estonia is known for its high degree of government transparency and well-developed e-governance services.

Public access to government information and the asset declarations of officials is provided for both in law and in practice. According to the latest European Union (EU) reports, Estonia stands out as one of best performers in the EU in ensuring a transparent and effective public procurement system.

CIVIL LIBERTIES: 56 / 60
D. FREEDOM OF EXPRESSION AND BELIEF: 16 / 16
D1. Are there free and independent media? 4 / 4

The government generally respects freedom of the press. Public and private television and radio stations broadcast freely, and there are a number of independent newspapers. However, EKRE leaders have verbally attacked journalists, raising concerns about self-censorship, and observers have noted a trend toward ownership concentration in recent years, especially at the regional level. Citing interference by the owner of *Postimees*, the country's oldest newspaper, most of the journalists on the paper's investigative and opinion desks resigned in late 2019. Economic dislocation associated with the COVID-19 pandemic led to sharp declines in advertising revenue during 2020, which could exacerbate the media's vulnerability to editorial pressure. Separately, judges have increasingly used the criminal procedure code to restrict media coverage in various cases of public interest, particularly those concerning corruption.

D2. Are individuals free to practice and express their religious faith or nonbelief in public and private? 4 / 4

Religious freedom is respected in law and in practice. During the state of emergency declared between March and May 2020 in response to the COVID-19 pandemic, public gatherings including religious services were restricted. In May, before the restrictions were eased, religious authorities called for the sounding of church bells as a form of pressure on the government to allow the resumption of group worship.

D3. Is there academic freedom, and is the educational system free from extensive political indoctrination? 4 / 4

Academic freedom is generally respected. However, by law, public Russian-language high schools must teach 60 percent of their curriculum in the Estonian language.

D4. Are individuals free to express their personal views on political or other sensitive topics without fear of surveillance or retribution? 4 / 4

There are no significant constraints on the freedoms of personal expression and private discussion.

E. ASSOCIATIONAL AND ORGANIZATIONAL RIGHTS: 12 / 12

E1. Is there freedom of assembly? 4 / 4

The constitution guarantees freedom of assembly, and the government upholds this right in practice. Gatherings were temporarily restricted during 2020 in response to the COVID-19 pandemic, but demonstrations on various topics proceeded peacefully when the health rules were not in place.

E2. Is there freedom for nongovernmental organizations, particularly those that are engaged in human rights- and governance-related work? 4 / 4

The government upholds freedom of association and does not restrict or control the activities of nongovernmental organizations.

E3. Is there freedom for trade unions and similar professional or labor organizations? 4 / 4

The law recognizes workers' rights to organize, strike, and bargain collectively, although public servants at the municipal and state levels may not strike. While these rights are largely upheld in practice, union membership has gradually declined, and employers in some sectors have resisted bargaining efforts.

F. RULE OF LAW: 14 / 16

F1. Is there an independent judiciary? 4 / 4

The judiciary is independent and generally free from government or other interference.

F2. Does due process prevail in civil and criminal matters? 4 / 4

Legal processes in civil and criminal matters are generally free and fair. Laws prohibiting arbitrary arrest and detention and ensuring the right to a fair trial are largely observed.

F3. Is there protection from the illegitimate use of physical force and freedom from war and insurgencies? 3 / 4

While Estonians generally enjoy physical security, the country's steadily declining intentional homicide rate remains one of the highest in the EU. There have been reports of law enforcement officials using excessive force when arresting suspects. Some inmates reportedly have inadequate access to health care. Estonia has a relatively high incarceration rate, with about 184 people per 100,000 residents in prisons as of 2020.

F4. Do laws, policies, and practices guarantee equal treatment of various segments of the population? 3 / 4

The constitution and laws provide broad safeguards against discrimination based on race, gender, language, sexual orientation, and other such categories. However, Russian-speaking residents continue to face societal discrimination, and some statutes lack robust protections against such bias. The Equal Treatment Act, for example, does not consider Estonian linguistic requirements for public officials to be discriminatory. Gender discrimination is also a problem, particularly in employment. Women in Estonia earn on average 21.7 percent less than men, according to 2019 Eurostat data; while the gap has declined, it remains the highest among EU countries. Roma face employment discrimination and disparities in educational outcomes.

The rhetoric and ideological beliefs of many active EKRE members have raised the prominence of hostile and extremist views toward the Jewish community, LGBT+ people, and Muslims, as well as other marginalized groups.

G. PERSONAL AUTONOMY AND INDIVIDUAL RIGHTS: 14 / 16

G1. Do individuals enjoy freedom of movement, including the ability to change their place of residence, employment, or education? 4 / 4

Citizens and residents enjoy free movement inside Estonia, and there are no significant restrictions on international travel. Movement restrictions imposed during 2020 in response to the COVID-19 pandemic were generally regarded as proportionate to the health threat.

G2. Are individuals able to exercise the right to own property and establish private businesses without undue interference from state or nonstate actors? 4 / 4

The legal and regulatory framework is generally supportive of property rights and entrepreneurship, and residents can freely engage in private business activity in practice.

G3. Do individuals enjoy personal social freedoms, including choice of marriage partner and size of family, protection from domestic violence, and control over appearance? 3 / 4

While individual freedom on personal status issues such as marriage and divorce is generally upheld, same-sex marriage is not recognized. At the end of 2020, the parliament had yet to adopt necessary amendments for the implementation of a 2014 law permitting same-sex civil unions. Moreover, the ruling coalition announced in October 2020 that it would proceed with an EKRE-backed plan to hold a nonbinding referendum in 2021 on whether to define marriage in the constitution as a union between a man and a woman. The necessary legislation passed its first reading in the parliament in December, and a second reading was scheduled for January 2021.

Gender-based violence, including domestic violence, remains a serious problem. Reports of domestic violence to police increased dramatically during the pandemic in 2020, and at the same time victims were less able to report the crimes promptly. Cases resulting in serious injuries and deaths also increased.

G4. Do individuals enjoy equality of opportunity and freedom from economic exploitation? 3 / 4

There are legal safeguards against exploitative working conditions, and they are generally enforced in practice. The government makes serious and sustained efforts to prosecute those responsible for human trafficking and provide services to victims, though it has encountered difficulties in adequately punishing convicted traffickers and identifying victims, according to the US State Department.

Estonia's unemployment rate jumped to almost 8 percent by late 2020 due to the effects of the COVID-19 pandemic. Nearly a quarter of the population remains at risk of poverty or social exclusion. The government adopted an extraordinary pension hike in April 2020 to help address the problem.

Eswatini

Population: 1,100,000
Capital: Mbabane (administrative), Lobamba (legislative, royal)
Freedom Status: Not Free
Electoral Democracy: No

Overview: Eswatini (known internationally as Swaziland until 2018) is a monarchy currently ruled by King Mswati III. The king exercises ultimate authority over all branches of the national government and effectively controls local governance through his influence over traditional chiefs. Political dissent and civic and labor activism are subject to harsh punishment under sedition and other laws. Additional human rights problems include impunity for security forces and discrimination against women and LGBT+ people.

KEY DEVELOPMENTS IN 2020

- King Mswati issued an emergency declaration in response to the COVID-19 in March, which included restrictions on assemblies and in-person education and largely lasted through the year. A journalist fled Eswatini after his news outlet reported on Mswati's apparent COVID-19 diagnosis, and Prime Minister Ambrose Mandvulo Dlamini died of the illness in December.
- In August, the government published a draft cybercrime bill that would institute large fines or prison sentences against those accused of disseminating purportedly false news. While the government withdrew it from consideration in November after facing heavy criticism, it introduced a social media bill in December, which remained under consideration at year's end.

POLITICAL RIGHTS: 1 / 40

A. ELECTORAL PROCESS: 0 / 12

A1. Was the current head of government or other chief national authority elected through free and fair elections? 0 / 4

The king is the chief executive authority and is empowered to appoint and dismiss the prime minister and members of the cabinet. Mswati III took the throne in 1986, four years after the death of his father, King Sobhuza II.

The prime minister is ostensibly the head of government but has little practical power. Ambrose Mandvulo Dlamini, a former banker, was appointed prime minister in October

2018. Dlamini died of COVID-19 in December 2020. Deputy Prime Minister Themba Ma-suku succeeded him on an acting basis.

Traditional chiefs govern their respective localities and typically report directly to the king. While some chiefs inherit their positions according to custom, others are appointed through royal interventions, as allowed by the constitution.

A2. Were the current national legislative representatives elected through free and fair elections? 0 / 4

The 73-member House of Assembly, the lower chamber of the bicameral Parliament, includes 59 members elected by popular vote within the *tinkhundla* system, which allows local chiefs to vet candidates and influence outcomes in practice; the king appoints 10 members. If female representation does not exceed 30 percent of the lower house, an additional four women may be elected by the body; parliamentarians did so in November 2018.

The king appoints 20 members of the 30-seat Senate, the upper chamber, with the remainder selected by the House of Assembly. All members of Parliament serve five-year terms. After the parliamentary elections in September 2018, the king appointed six members of the royal family to the House of Assembly and eight to the Senate. The elections, which were tightly controlled and featured a slate of candidates almost entirely loyal to the king, did not offer voters a genuine choice.

In 2018, a senior official at the Elections and Boundaries Commission (EBC) reported that members of the House of Assembly were accepting bribes in exchange for their votes in Senate elections, but no apparent consequences followed.

A3. Are the electoral laws and framework fair, and are they implemented impartially by the relevant election management bodies? 0 / 4

The EBC is not considered impartial. It is financially and administratively dependent on the executive, and its members are appointed by the king on the advice of the Judicial Service Commission, whose members are also royal appointees. Details of the results of September 2018 parliamentary elections were only made public in March 2019.

Traditional chiefs also play an important role in elections, as candidates effectively need their approval to run for office.

B. POLITICAL PLURALISM AND PARTICIPATION: 1 / 16

B1. Do the people have the right to organize in different political parties or other competitive political groupings of their choice, and is the system free of undue obstacles to the rise and fall of these competing parties or groupings? 0 / 4

Election to public office is based on "individual merit," according to the constitution. There is no legal avenue for parties to register and participate in elections, though some political associations exist without legal recognition. Over the years, political parties seeking legal recognition have suffered court defeats, including a Supreme Court ruling in 2018 rejecting a challenge by the Swazi Democratic Party (SWADEPA) to the ban on political parties competing in elections.

A number of prodemocracy organizations and trade unions have continued to lobby for political reforms and have publicly challenged Mswati's grip on power, even given the serious risks involved. In May 2019, political activist Goodwill Sibiya filed a legal complaint over the king's management of the Tibiyo Taka Ngwane (Wealth of the Nation) investment fund. Sibiya was then arrested on suspicion of sedition and membership in the People's United Democratic Movement (PUDEMO), though he was released by May 2020. Civil servants held protests in August and September 2019. In December 2019, the police raided the homes of prominent opposition leaders, arresting and briefly detaining individuals including PUDEMO secretary general Wandile Dludlu. Although the police denied targeting prodemocracy activists, the arrests indicated the authorities' intolerance of political reform efforts.

B2. Is there a realistic opportunity for the opposition to increase its support or gain power through elections? 0 / 4

The king has tight control over the political system in law and in practice, leaving no room for the emergence of an organized opposition with the potential to enter government. The vast majority of candidates who contested the 2018 general elections were supporters of the king.

B3. Are the people's political choices free from domination by forces that are external to the political sphere, or by political forces that employ extrapolitical means? 0 / 4

Traditional chiefs, as the king's representatives, wield enormous influence over their subjects. In addition to vetting prospective candidates for office, they have been accused of ordering residents to vote or not vote for certain candidates.

B4. Do various segments of the population (including ethnic, racial, religious, gender, LGBT+, and other relevant groups) have full political rights and electoral opportunities? 1 / 4

There are virtually no members of minority groups in the government, as most officials have some connection to the royal family or its broader clan. Women are politically marginalized, with the lower house of Parliament falling well short of a 30 percent gender quota after the 2018 elections. Even after the invocation of the Election of Women Members to the House of Assembly Act, which allowed for the selection of another four female legislators, women only represent 9.6 percent of the House of Assembly. Women hold 40 percent of seats in the Senate, which is not directly elected.

Customary restrictions on widows in mourning—a period that can last from one to three years—effectively bar women from participating in public affairs during that time. LGBT+ people and people with disabilities are also politically marginalized.

C. FUNCTIONING OF GOVERNMENT: 0 / 12

C1. Do the freely elected head of government and national legislative representatives determine the policies of the government? 0 / 4

The king and his government determine policy and legislation; members of Parliament hold no real power and effectively act as a rubber stamp in approving the king's legislative priorities. Parliament cannot initiate legislation and has little oversight or influence on budgetary matters. The king is also constitutionally empowered to veto any legislation. The absolute authority of the king was demonstrated by his decision to rename the country in 2018 without any constitutional process or parliamentary approval.

C2. Are safeguards against official corruption strong and effective? 0 / 4

Corruption is a major problem, and implicated officials generally enjoy impunity. The Anti-Corruption Commission (ACC) is perceived to be ineffective, with civil society groups accusing it of pursuing politically motivated cases and serving the interests of the prime minister. The ACC, which reports to the Justice Ministry, lacks adequate financial and human resources and must consult with the minister on hiring. In 2018, a cabinet committee was established to develop a zero-tolerance policy on corruption in government, but its ability to create an effective anticorruption framework remains unclear. The Tibiyo Taka Ngwane fund has reportedly been used for the king's personal gain, with PUDEMO accusing Mswati of using it to bolster his personal income as far back as 2011.

C3. Does the government operate with openness and transparency? 0 / 4

Eswatini lacks access-to-information laws, and there is no culture of proactive disclosure of government information. Public requests for information are largely ignored in practice, and the budgeting process lacks transparency. The authorities tightly restrict access to data on spending by the royal family and the security forces. Transparency was further reduced by Parliament's passage of the Public Service Act in 2018, which broadly prevents officials from providing public information to the media unless given express permission by the secretary of the cabinet.

CIVIL LIBERTIES: 18 / 60

D. FREEDOM OF EXPRESSION AND BELIEF: 5 / 16

D1. Are there free and independent media? 1 / 4

A variety of laws, including the Sedition and Subversive Activities Act (SSAA) and defamation laws, can be used to restrict media coverage by criminalizing publications that are alleged to be seditious, as well as the use of words that are alleged to be seditious, for example, those that "may excite disaffection" against the king. Journalists often face harassment, assault, and intimidation, and self-censorship is reportedly common. The state broadcaster is tightly controlled by the government, and the *Swazi Observer*, a major newspaper, is effectively owned by the king.

Several journalists faced questioning, detention, or other forms of scrutiny for their reporting or their own political activity during the year. Swaziland News editor Zweli Martin Dlamini fled Eswatini twice in 2020; in February, he left the country after being detained and physically assaulted by police for reporting on the king. In late April, he fled to South Africa after the outlet reported on King Mswati's apparent COVID-19 diagnosis. In April, police interrogated and seized documents from *Swati Newsweek* managing editor Eugene Dube, who fled Eswatini in May. In November, *Swazi Observer* managing editor Mbongeni Mbingo was suspended from his post for his reported membership in Vuka Sive, which is considered an antimonarchical political group.

D2. Are individuals free to practice and express their religious faith or nonbelief in public and private? 2 / 4

The constitution guarantees religious freedom and bars discrimination based on religion. Rules requiring registration of religious organizations are not strictly enforced. However, members of the Muslim minority allege discrimination by officials and Christian residents, and police reportedly monitor mosques. Non-Christian groups are also denied airtime on state broadcasters. Construction of religious buildings must be approved by the government or local chiefs. Christian education is compulsory in public schools, and in 2017, the government banned the teaching of other religions in the public-school curriculum.

D3. Is there academic freedom, and is the educational system free from extensive political indoctrination? 1 / 4

Academic freedom is limited by restrictive laws such as the Suppression of Terrorism Act (STA) and the SSAA. Student activists face potential violence, arrest, and suspension. In early 2018, police arrested 11 students protesting the administration at Swaziland Christian University and used excessive force to break up the demonstration. In August 2019, police detained seven students who had been part of a demonstration organized by the Swaziland National Union of Students (SNUS) to call for scholarships for higher education students; the government-aligned *Swazi Observer* said the students had engaged in property damage, while the protesters said they were mistreated in custody. In addition, students at a number of colleges and universities boycotted classes in November 2019 after the government failed to make payment of allowances, but the action did not appear to be met with interference.

D4. Are individuals free to express their personal views on political or other sensitive topics without fear of surveillance or retribution? 1 / 4

Constitutional rights to free expression are severely restricted in practice. Security agencies reportedly monitor personal communications, social media, and public gatherings, and criticism of the king or other elements of the regime can be punished under laws such as the SSAA, the STA, and the Public Order Act. Under revisions to the Public Order Act passed in 2017, any criticism of Swazi culture and traditions or defacement of national symbols—including the king's image—can draw fines and up to two years in prison.

In August 2020, the government published a draft cybercrime bill that would penalize the dissemination of purportedly false news with heavy fines or imprisonment of up to 10 years. The bill was heavily criticized by legislators, who warned it would impinge on media and individual freedoms, and the government withdrew it in November after a parliamentary committee rejected the bill's false-news provisions. In December, the government introduced a social media bill which remained under consideration at year's end.

E. ASSOCIATIONAL AND ORGANIZATIONAL RIGHTS: 3 / 12
E1. Is there freedom of assembly? 1 / 4

Freedom of assembly is restricted. Surveillance of protests is common, and the information collected is reportedly used to deny protesters access to government jobs and services. Demonstrations, notably by public workers demanding higher wages, are often violently dispersed by police, and protesters risk arrest and detention. Nevertheless, labor and prodemocracy protests have taken place in spite of these risks. Demonstrations that are not perceived as a direct challenge to the king, meanwhile, have been allowed to go forward. Assemblies of greater than 50 people were restricted by King Mswati in March 2020 as part of the country's COVID-19 response.

E2. Is there freedom for nongovernmental organizations, particularly those that are engaged in human rights- and governance-related work? 1 / 4

The operation of nongovernmental organizations (NGOs) has been inhibited by broadly written sedition and terrorism laws as well as police monitoring and interference. Organizations that advocate for democracy remain banned.

Despite the restrictions, it appears there is limited tolerance of some forms of human rights-based legal activism. For example, Women and Law Southern Africa–Swaziland was allowed to bring a case on gender equality in divorce settlements, with the court deciding in its favor in 2019. In October 2020, the Southern Africa Litigation Centre was allowed to submit an opinion on the pending cybercrime bill to Parliament.

E3. Is there freedom for trade unions and similar professional or labor organizations? 1 / 4

Eswatini has active, vocal labor unions, but workers' rights are poorly upheld in practice. Although workers in most sectors, with the exception of essential services defined by the labor minister, can join unions, strikes and other labor activism routinely trigger crackdowns and arrests by the police. A number of prodemocracy activists and former trade unions are exiled in South Africa, where they have been accommodated by South Africa's Congress of South African Trade Unions (COSATU)—whose members periodically picket against the Eswatini government on South Africa's border with the country.

F. RULE OF LAW: 5 / 16

F1. Is there an independent judiciary? 2 / 4

Although the judiciary displays a degree of independence in some cases, the king holds ultimate authority over the appointment and removal of judges, acting on advice from the Judicial Service Commission made up of royal appointees.

In a rare instance of judicial review that sought to change gender power relations, the High Court of Eswatini in August 2019 ruled in favor of gender equality in civil marriages regarding property rights in the event of divorce. The High Court's full bench unanimously ruled that sections of the Marriage Act, in existence since 1964, were discriminatory toward women and violated the constitutional right to equality because women could not inherit property. While the original applicant of the case withdrew, the NGO she collaborated with, Women and Law Southern Africa–Swaziland, was allowed to proceed with the application on its own.

F2. Does due process prevail in civil and criminal matters? 1 / 4

Safeguards against arbitrary arrest and detention, such as time limits on detention without charge, are not always respected in practice. Detainees are generally granted access to lawyers, though only those facing life imprisonment or capital punishment can obtain counsel at public expense. Lengthy pretrial detention is common.

F3. Is there protection from the illegitimate use of physical force and freedom from war and insurgencies? 1 / 4

Despite the 2018 passage of the Police Service Act, which prescribes disciplinary measures for police officers who use illegitimate force, physical abuse of suspects and inmates by law enforcement officials is an ongoing problem, and investigations into such abuse lack independence and transparency. Some prisons also suffer from overcrowding and other harsh conditions.

F4. Do laws, policies, and practices guarantee equal treatment of various segments of the population? 1 / 4

Women's rights remain restricted in law and in practice. Both civil and customary law treat women as dependents of their fathers or husbands, and societal discrimination further impairs their access to education and employment. Residents who are not ethnic Swazis also face de facto discrimination. People with disabilities experience social stigma as well as discrimination in education and employment. In 2018, King Mswati signed the Persons with Disabilities Act, intended to address many of the inequities experienced by disabled residents.

Discrimination against LGBT+ people is not prohibited by law and is widespread in practice. A criminal ban on same-sex sexual activity is not regularly enforced. In October 2020, the High Court considered a challenge from an NGO advocating for LGBT+ rights, Eswatini Sexual and Gender Minorities, to be added to the government's registrar of companies. The court's decision was pending at year's end.

G. PERSONAL AUTONOMY AND INDIVIDUAL RIGHTS: 5 / 16

G1. Do individuals enjoy freedom of movement, including the ability to change their place of residence, employment, or education? 2 / 4

The constitution guarantees freedom of movement. However, minority ethnic groups and political activists have faced delays in obtaining passports and other citizenship documents. Traditional chiefs regulate movement and residence within their communities and generally deny access to groups advocating for human rights or democracy. Individuals who violate customary rules can face eviction from their localities. Widows in mourning are barred from approaching chiefs or the king and excluded from certain public places and activities. While free movement is restricted in these cases, no broad-based policies or practices prevent or punish internal movement generally.

G2. Are individuals able to exercise the right to own property and establish private businesses without undue interference from state or nonstate actors? 1 / 4

The constitution provides legal protections for property rights, but women generally face limitations under customary rules that subordinate them to male relatives. Widows in particular face expropriation by the deceased husband's family. Chiefs have broad authority to allocate and withdraw rights to communal land. However, some progress was made in 2019, when the High Court ruled in favor of gender equality in civil marriages, granting women property rights in the event of divorce.

Individuals can face expropriation due to land claims by state-owned companies and powerful private interests, and constitutional guarantees of fair compensation are not upheld.

In 2019, the finance minister promised to institute wide-ranging economic reforms that would see state-owned monopolies—considered key to the monarchy's control of the country's finances—loosen their grip on the economy. Progress in this reform effort was slow in 2020.

G3. Do individuals enjoy personal social freedoms, including choice of marriage partner and size of family, protection from domestic violence, and control over appearance? 1 / 4

Women's social freedoms are restricted by both civil and customary law, which puts them at a disadvantage regarding marriage, divorce, and child custody. Customary law allowed girls as young as 13 to marry. Sexual and domestic violence remains extremely common; in March 2020, the UN resident coordinator for Eswatini reported that 48 percent of Swazi women and girls experience sexual violence in their lifetimes. Punishment for perpetrators is often lenient.

The Eswatini government did made make progress on women's rights by amending the 1964 Marriage Act to prohibit marriages of persons under the age of 18 and passing the Sexual Offences and Domestic Violence Act, which criminalizes nonconsensual sex between spouses, in 2019.

G4. Do individuals enjoy equality of opportunity and freedom from economic exploitation? 1 / 4

Residents have some access to formal employment and economic opportunity, but the majority of the population lives in poverty. Forced labor remains a problem, with some chiefs compelling Swazis, including children, to work in their communities or the king's fields. Among other forms of child labor, girls are particularly vulnerable to domestic servitude and commercial sexual exploitation. The royal family has extensive privileges compared to ordinary citizens.

Ethiopia

Population: 114,900,000
Capital: Addis Ababa
Freedom Status: Not Free
Electoral Democracy: No

Overview: Ethiopia is undergoing a turbulent period of political change set off by the 2018 appointment of Prime Minister Abiy Ahmed, who came to power after Prime Minister Haile-mariam Desalegn resigned in the face of mass protests at which demonstrators demanded greater political rights. Abiy pledged to reform Ethiopia's authoritarian state and has overseen a revision of some laws used by his predecessors to suppress dissent. However, long-awaited August 2020 general elections were postponed due to the COVID-19 pandemic, posing an obstacle to the country's democratic transition. Moreover, Abiy's ruling Prosperity Party—a reconfiguration of the ethnoregional coalition that ruled Ethiopia since 1991—has partly reverted to authoritarian tactics, jailing opposition leaders and limiting media freedom in the face of growing regional and intercommunal violence. Most notably, the Ethiopian military has been engaged in a prolonged conflict with the security forces of the Tigray Region in a bid to arrest senior members of the Tigrayan People's Liberation Front (TPLF).

KEY DEVELOPMENTS IN 2020

- In March, amid the worsening COVID-19 pandemic, authorities postponed general elections set for August; the planned multiparty poll would have been a milestone in the country's democratic transition. At year's end, the National Electoral Board of Ethiopia (NEBE) scheduled polls for June 2021. While there was broad agreement on the need to postpone the elections, there was very little agreement on what would happen after the mandate of the government expired at the beginning of October, and it remains unclear how the de facto extension of the government's mandate was legally justified.
- The killing of Oromo musician Hachalu Hundessa in June triggered violent protests across Oromia regional state. According to federal police, 239 people were killed during the unrest, including many civilians in targeted attacks against minorities in Oromia, as well as in clashes with security forces. The Ethiopian government responded with a wave of arrests, including the detention of several high-profile opposition leaders, and imposed an internet shutdown. At least two suspects have been arrested on suspicion of involvement the singer's death.
- In September, the Tigrayan Regional Council held regional elections, defying the decision to postpone all elections due to the pandemic. Results showed a landslide victory for the TPLF. The federal government deemed the regional Tigray government unlawful, and withdrew budget subsidies from the Tigray Regional Council. The Tigray Regional Council responded by withdrawing recognition of the legislative and executive branches of the federal government.
- In November, the dispute between the federal government and the TPLF escalated into violence when Abiy ordered the deployment of federal troops into the Tigray Region after TPLF forces had attacked the Ethiopian military's Northern Command. The ensuing violent conflict involved a number of militia groups, as well as special police forces, and displaced thousands of refugees to Sudan. While allegation of the massacre of civilians and of rape by federal and regional security forces have trickled out, the number of casualties is unknown, as the flow of information in and out of Tigray was severely disrupted by internet and telecommunications blackouts and interference with journalists trying to cover the unrest.

POLITICAL RIGHTS: 9 / 40 (−1)

A. ELECTORAL PROCESS: 2 / 12

A1. Was the current head of government or other chief national authority elected through free and fair elections? 0 / 4

The president is the head of state and is indirectly elected to a six-year term by both chambers of Parliament. The prime minister is head of government, and is selected by the largest party in Parliament after elections, or in the case of a resignation.

Prime Minister Abiy Ahmed—a former military officer from Ethiopia's largest ethnic group, the Oromo, and a longstanding member of the ruling Ethiopian People's Revolutionary Democratic Front (EPRDF)—was sworn in as prime minister in April 2018, succeeding Hailemariam Desalegn, who had resigned in February 2018 amid growing protests at which demonstrators demanded greater political rights. Abiy was reconfirmed at the EPRDF party congress in October 2018 and was expected to lead the EPRDF's successor, the Prosperity Party, into the next election. The election had been slated for August 2020, but was postponed as a result of the COVID-19 pandemic. In December, the NEBE set the elections for June 2021.

A2. Were the current national legislative representatives elected through free and fair elections? 0 / 4

The bicameral Parliament includes the 153-seat House of Federation, whose members are elected by state assemblies to five-year terms, and the House of People's Representatives, with 547 members directly elected to five-year terms.

The 2015 parliamentary and regional elections were tightly controlled by the EPRDF, with reports of voter coercion, intimidation, and registration barriers. The opposition lost its sole parliamentary seat, as the EPRDF and its allies took all 547 seats in the House of People's Representatives. The Prosperity Party, the successor party of the EPRDF, largely controls both houses, except for representatives of the Tigrayan People's Liberation Front (TPLF), who left the EPRDF coalition when it was merged into the Prosperity Party.

The Tigrayan Regional Council held regional elections in September 2020, defying the National Electoral Board of Ethiopia's decision to postpone all elections due to the COVID-19 pandemic. Several parties participated and the results showed a landslide victory for the TPLF, though the Prosperity Party and the Tigray Democratic Party boycotted the poll. Following the election, the federal government deemed the regional Tigray government unlawful, and withdrew budget subsidies from the Tigray Regional Council. TPLF parliamentarians were recalled to the regional capital, and the Tigrayan Regional Council said it no longer recognized the executive and legislative branches of the federal government.

In December, the NEBE set the next parliamentary elections for June 2021, but its schedule did not include polls in Tigray Region.

A3. Are the electoral laws and framework fair, and are they implemented impartially by the relevant election management bodies? 2 / 4

The 2015 elections were held on time and official results were released within a month. However, opposition parties repeatedly questioned the independence of the NEBE, and the Unity for Democracy and Justice (UDJ) party alleged that it blocked its leaders from registering as candidates.

A number of reforms to the electoral system and its oversight have taken shape under Prime Minister Abiy. In November 2018, parliament confirmed Birtukan Mideksa, a prominent, previously exiled former opposition leader, to serve as head of the NEBE. In August 2019, Parliament unanimously passed the Ethiopian Election, Political Parties Registration, and Election Ethics law. Some opposition parties claimed that consultations ahead of the bill's approval were inadequate. The law provides an updated and more complete framework for the 2020 elections than had been mandated previously and represented a step toward multiparty democracy. With the postponement of the election, however, electoral laws could again be amended ahead of the planned 2021 polls. One member of the NEBE, Gethahun Kassa, resigned in September, signaling tensions within the electoral board.

While there was broad agreement on the need to postpone the elections slated for August 2020, there was very little agreement on what would happen after the mandate of the government expired at the beginning of October. In order to resolve this constitutional crisis, the government called upon the Council of Constitutional Inquiry to lead a number of consultations with experts and produce recommendations. These consultations were televised nationally and largely viewed as productive. However, they were largely ignored by the CCI and it remains unclear how the decision-making process regarding the postponement of the election and the de facto extension of the government's mandate was legally justified.

Separately, in June 2019, the parliament postponed a planned census due to unrest associated with various ethnic conflicts. The completion of the census is a key step toward demarcating constituencies.

B. POLITICAL PLURALISM AND PARTICIPATION: 4 / 16 (-1)

B1. Do the people have the right to organize in different political parties or other competitive political groupings of their choice, and is the system free of undue obstacles to the rise and fall of these competing parties or groupings? 1 / 4 (-1)

During the premierships of Abiy's predecessors, opponents of the EPRDF found it nearly impossible to operate inside Ethiopia and were subject to prosecution under restrictive antiterrorism and other legislation. However, political reforms starting in 2018, as well as that year's approval of a widespread amnesty, have permitted increasing political plurality and mobilization.

However, Ethiopia's political party landscape underwent major changes in 2020, particularly after the postponement of elections in March and the assassination of Oromo musician Hachalu Hundessa and its aftermath in June. The deadly attacks on members of ethnic minority groups in parts of Oromia resulted in a crackdown on political parties and leaders. Among these are prominent opposition politicians Jawar Mohammed, Bekele Gerba, Eskinder Nega, and Lidetu Ayele, who were all arrested for alleged involvement in the violent aftermath of Hachalu's assassination. Public protests in support of these individuals have been suppressed violently. Most of the most vocal opponents of the government were in jail at year's end.

Score Change: The score declined from 2 to 1 due to mass arrests of high-profile politicians and their supporters from across the political spectrum following unrest sparked by the assassination of Oromo musician Hachalu Hundessa.

B2. Is there a realistic opportunity for the opposition to increase its support or gain power through elections? 1 / 4

The changes Prime Minister Abiy's government began to implement in 2018 had started to improve conditions for opposition groupings, though the Prosperity Party still maintains numerous formal and informal advantages over opposition parties due to its effective incumbency.

New freedoms for opposition politicians and parties resulting from 2018 reforms deteriorated in 2020. However, despite the arrests of high-profile opposition politicians and the growing impasse between the Tigray regional government and the federal government, the government's rhetorical commitment to inclusive multiparty elections has remained, and the opposition camp stands a better chance than in previous elections to curb the ruling party's complete hold on power.

B3. Are the people's political choices free from domination by forces that are external to the political sphere, or by political forces that employ extrapolitical means? 1 / 4

The authoritarian one-party system in Ethiopia has largely excluded the public from genuine political participation, though nascent attempts by Abiy to include more diverse voices in the political system are starting to yield mixed results. Moreover, Abiy has taken steps to curtail the role of Ethiopia's powerful military in the country's politics in some parts of the country, while maintaining a stronghold in others.

Patronage networks, often based on ethnicity, continue to drive political decision making, especially in rural regions.

B4. Do various segments of the population (including ethnic, racial, religious, gender, LGBT+, and other relevant groups) have full political rights and electoral opportunities? 1 / 4

Women hold nearly 39 percent of seats in the lower house and 32 percent in the upper house, but in practice, the interests of women are not well represented in politics. Prime Minister Abiy has made some effort to include women in high-level decision-making processes. In 2018, women were appointed to a number of prominent positions including the presidency, head of the NEBE, president of the Supreme Court, and to half of all cabinet posts.

Since 1991, political parties in Ethiopia have primarily been based on ethnicity. The country's major ethnic parties have been allied with the EPRDF but have historically had little room to effectively advocate for their constituents. The Prosperity Party has developed a national platform under the leadership of Prime Minister Abiy. This development has raised the profile of ruling-party structures in Ethiopia's peripheral regions, where local ruling parties had previously been denied full membership in the EPRDF. (Populations in Afar, Somali, Gambella, and Benishangul Gumuz—officially termed "emerging regions"— were notably underrepresented in national politics since their local ruling parties were affiliates rather than full members of the EPRDF coalition.) At the same time, the merger has increased demands for more regional autonomy, particularly in Tigray; Oromia; and the Southern Nations, Nationalities, and People's Region. It has also rekindled long-standing fears of smaller regions of being dominated by the more populous ethnic groups.

C. FUNCTIONING OF GOVERNMENT: 3 / 12

C1. Do the freely elected head of government and national legislative representatives determine the policies of the government? 0 / 4

None of Ethiopia's nominally elected officials were chosen through credible elections. The country's governance institutions have long been dominated by the EPRDF and subsequently the Prosperity Party. The elections slated for August 2020 were postponed due to the COVID-19 pandemic. The Tigrayan Regional Council was elected in September of 2020, although these elections were labelled illegal by the House of Federations and the results are not recognized at the federal level.

C2. Are safeguards against official corruption strong and effective? 2 / 4

Corruption and unequal resource distribution are significant problems that have contributed to the unrest that has plagued Ethiopia in recent years. The government has taken some steps to address the issue, which remains a priority for Prime Minister Abiy's administration.

Numerous high-profile military and government officials were arrested and charged with corruption in 2018 and 2019. In May 2020, Bereket Simon, a former communications minister and prime minister, was convicted on corruption charges and sentenced to six years in prison in Bahir Dar. Proceedings in many other cases continued throughout 2020.

The most notable safeguard introduced against corruption in 2020 was the introduction of new bank notes in September. The government announced that all old bank notes were being withdrawn from circulation within three months to fight corruption, embezzlement, and contraband. The new notes have additional design and security features that makes the production of counterfeits very difficult.

C3. Does the government operate with openness and transparency? 1 / 4

The Prosperity Party has attempted to be less opaque than its predecessors, but the events leading up to the postponement of the elections and subsequent to Hachalu Hundessa's death reflect some inability or unwillingness of authorities to operate with openness and transparency. Moreover, a series of political assassinations and high-profile deaths in the last two years remain unresolved, with little government communication about the matter.

In the aftermath of Hachalu Hundessa's assassination and the violence that ensued in Oromia, the internet was shut down for 3 weeks, making the entire population dependent on state-run news channels for information. The mass arrests that followed were also not handled transparently. Similarly, very little information was released about numerous killings by militias in the Metekel Zone of the Benishangul-Gumuz Region.

Very little information is available about the conflict in Tigray Region, and what does emerge is difficult or impossible to verify. Internet and telephone lines were cut for almost two months, while independent journalists were denied access to the region. The nature of the involvement of Eritrean soldiers, the status of camps, the humanitarian situation in the region all remain opaque.

Government procurement processes remain largely opaque. The renovation of Meskel Square, and the development of Friendship Park and Entoto Park were awarded to companies without full transparency of the tender and decision-making processes.

CIVIL LIBERTIES: 13 / 60 (−1)
D. FREEDOM OF EXPRESSION AND BELIEF: 4 / 16
D1. Are there free and independent media? 1 / 4

After years of severe restrictions on press freedom, the government took initial steps to increase freedoms for independent media in 2018, when a number of prominent journalists were released from prison.

Ethiopia's media landscape is dominated by state-owned broadcasters and government-oriented newspapers. Since Abiy took office in 2018, the government has eased restrictions on independent media, permitting both greater freedom for journalists and a more diverse range of news for consumers. That year, the government lifted bans on 264 websites (including news sites and blogs) and television networks.

However, after the assassination of Hachalu Hundessa, Oromo Media Network (OMN), which has been banned before 2018, was again shut down and charged with inciting violence through its platforms. Similarly, Tigray TV is no longer available outside of Tigray, and has similarly been accused by the government of inciting violence and spearheading misinformation campaigns. A large number of journalists were jailed in July and August, including Kenyan journalist Yassin Juma. This prompted the Ethiopian Foreign Correspondents' Association (FCA) to write an open letter condemning the government's activities. Juma was released in September with several other journalists.

During the conflict in Tigray, a number of journalists have been arrested, had their licenses revoked, or were deported, and internet and telecommunications blackouts affected the flow of information in and out of the region. Ethiopia's state-owned telecommunications monopoly, Ethio Telecom, also suspended internet service for in Western Oromia for more than three months from January through March, and then again for three weeks in early July 2020 following the assassination of Hachalu Hundessa. Social media and communications platforms such as Facebook, Twitter, and WhatsApp have been blocked intermittently.

Hate speech and the deliberate spreading of misinformation on social media have been blamed for fanning the flames of violent conflict in regions of Ethiopia. In February 2020, the government approved a new a hate speech law that makes the intentional publication, distribution, and possession of false information illegal. However, Amnesty International and Human Rights Watch criticized the proposed law as vague and as potentially opening the door for misuse by public authorities to curb freedom of expression. In December, the Council of Ministers approved a draft media proclamation to serve as a legal framework for media, with an emphasis on freedom of information and expression. It remains to be seen how this will be implemented.

D2. Are individuals free to practice and express their religious faith or nonbelief in public and private? 1 / 4

The Ethiopian constitution guarantees religious freedom, and different faith groups have coexisted in the country for centuries. Prime Minister Abiy has promoted reconciliation between Ethiopia's main faith groups, including through the 2018 release of Muslim activists who had been arrested in 2015 for protesting the government's treatment of Muslims.

However, religion has increasingly become a divisive factor in Ethiopian politics, and local conflicts have featured violence along religious lines. The mass violence in July 2020 has taken on a religious dimension in parts of Bale and Arsi, in the Oromia region, with the targeting of followers of the Ethiopian Orthodox Tewahedo Church (EOTC).

D3. Is there academic freedom, and is the educational system free from extensive political indoctrination? 1 / 4

Academic freedom remains restricted in Ethiopia, though academics have become markedly more vocal on political and economic matters since the lifting of the state of emergency in 2018. Conferences and lectures at state universities have addressed controversial topics and featured a number of speakers who criticized the ruling party. Academics have been able to voice their critiques of the government through social media and various media outlets including the *Addis Standard* and Ethiopia Insight, discussing issues including federalism, election postponement, the administration's COVID-19 response, and the importance of national dialogue.

Direct political indoctrination of university students—through mandatory trainings on government policy or pressure to join the ruling party—also seems to have abated under Abiy, mainly as a consequence of the weakening of the party structures in general.

With few exceptions, institutions of higher education are funded and administered by the federal government, which also sets admission standards and student quotas. The Ministry of Education still monitors and regulates official curricula.

D4. Are individuals free to express their personal views on political or other sensitive topics without fear of surveillance or retribution? 1 / 4

The gains made in 2018, including the release of political prisoners and lifting of bans against prominent government critics in the media and other sectors, had fostered a more open atmosphere for free expression among ordinary people. However, following the assassination of Hachalu Hundessa, arbitrary arrests, extrajudicial activities, widespread surveillance in parts of Oromia, and nontransparent court proceedings have once again led individuals to be more reluctant to express political views openly. This has been further escalated by the violent conflict in the Tigray Region, where a state of emergency proclamation has led to a greater wariness of surveillance.

E. ASSOCIATIONAL AND ORGANIZATIONAL RIGHTS: 4 / 12
E1. Is there freedom of assembly? 1 / 4

Severe restrictions on assembly under the EPRDF government eased after the political transition in 2018, when formerly banned opposition movements returned from exile and held political rallies with thousands of supporters. However, the Abiy administration has continued to break up political meetings and arrest activists, particularly in Addis Ababa and Oromia regional state. In January 2020, dozens of supporters of the opposition Oromo Liberation Front were arrested across Oromia, and security forces used violence to disperse crowds of protesters after the killing of Hachalu Hundessa. Clashes between protestors and local security forces were also reported from the Afar Region.

Freedom of assembly was formally suspended between April and September, when strict social distancing rules prohibited meetings of four or more people unless approved by local authorities. While the state of emergency ended in September, social distancing norms continued to limit mass assemblies of people compared to previous years. The state of emergency announcement in November in Tigray has once again prohibited assembly.

E2. Is there freedom for nongovernmental organizations, particularly those that are engaged in human rights- and governance-related work? 2 / 4

The passage of a new civil society law in February 2019 dispensed with many restrictions that had been placed on nongovernmental organizations (NGOs) by the draconian 2009 Charities and Societies Proclamation, which prohibited work on political and human rights issues and had forced international NGOs working on human rights and democratic governance to leave the country. Institutions like Amnesty International and Human Rights Watch returned after the law's approval. International funding for local advocacy organizations has resumed, too, resulting in a much more active and visible human rights community. The Ethiopian Human Rights Commission, which has previously functioned as a government mouthpiece, has been more independent following the appointment of Daniel Bekele, previously Africa director at Human Rights Watch, as its commissioner in 2019. On the eve of the conflict in Tigray, the Ethiopian Human Rights Commission held a dialogue on the "Structural Human Rights Challenges of Ethiopia" that included dozens of domestic civil society organizations.

However, the federal Civil Society Organizations Agency retains broad powers. Moreover, while NGOs are more able to legally operate in the human rights and governance spheres, practically many of these organizations are unable to access large parts of Ethiopia either due to security challenges or a lack of official approval, as was the case in Tigray. While the discourse around NGOs is more open, many of the practical realities have not improved.

Relations between federal government and human rights NGOs soured in 2020. Amnesty International and others published reports throughout the year criticizing the administration's response to political protests in Oromia and pointing to human rights violations by security forces, which were downplayed by government officials.

E3. Is there freedom for trade unions and similar professional or labor organizations? 1 / 4

The Ethiopian Constitution recognizes the right of workers to join trade unions, and a 2019 labor law has further bolstered their legal status. More than 500,000 workers are organized under the umbrella of the Confederation of Ethiopian Trade Unions (CETU). However, CETU has refrained from openly challenging the government, and independent unions have faced harassment in the past. There has not been a legal strike in Ethiopia since 1993.

On the employer side, a large number of chambers of commerce and business associations exist for different industries and locations. The largest and oldest among them, the Addis Ababa Chamber of Commerce, is a regular critic of government policy. The federally organized Ethiopian Chamber of Commerce, of which the Addis chamber is a member, has been more aligned with official policy.

F. RULE OF LAW: 2 / 16

F1. Is there an independent judiciary? 1 / 4

The judiciary is officially independent, but in practice it is subject to political interference, and judgments rarely deviate from government policy. The appointment of lawyer and civil society leader Meaza Ashenafi as president of the Supreme Court in November 2018 as well as the selection of constitutional scholar Gideon Timotewos as attorney general in August 2020 have raised hopes for reform and greater independence of the courts. However, Ethiopia's security forces have maintained significant influence over the judicial process, especially in cases against opposition leaders and other political adversaries. A number of approved bail orders by courts were also overruled by the police during the year.

F2. Does due process prevail in civil and criminal matters? 0 / 4

Due process rights are generally not respected. While more than 10,000 people who had been arbitrarily detained were released after the change of political leadership in 2018, several waves of summary arrests have taken place since. More than 9,000 individuals—many of them supporters of local opposition groups, but also law enforcement and local government officials— were arrested in the aftermath of the violence that followed the killing of Hachalu Hundessa in June 2020. In September, the government brought charges against about 2,000 of them, denying that the investigations were politically motivated.

The right to a fair trial is often not respected, particularly for opponents of the government charged under the antiterrorism law. In civil matters, due process is hampered by the limited capacity of the Ethiopian courts system, especially in the peripheral regions where access to government services is weak. As a result, routine matters regularly take years to be resolved. The temporary closure of the court system in 2020 due to the COVID-19 pandemic further contributed to the backlog in cases.

F3. Is there protection from the illegitimate use of physical force and freedom from war and insurgencies? 0 / 4

Ethnic violence and unrest continued in numerous regions of Ethiopia in 2020. A government campaign to suppress armed opposition forces in western Oromia has led to repeated clashes and widespread displacement from there. Ethnic rivalries along the border of Amhara and Benishangul Gumuz as well as Afar and Somali regional states also resulted in bloodshed. The situation in the border region between Amhara and Tigray remains tense due to a boundary dispute. Most notable, however, is the conflict in Tigray, which at year's end led to the fleeing of 50,000 people and an unknown number of deaths, estimated likely to be in the thousands. Security forces, both regional and federal, have been accused of war crimes, including the massacring of civilians and rape.

Conflicts in other parts of the country, notably along the border between Oromia and Somali state, grew less intense in 2020.

F4. Do laws, policies, and practices guarantee equal treatment of various segments of the population? 1 / 4

There are major regional discrepancies between Ethiopia's "highland" regional states—Oromia, Amhara, Tigray, Southern Nations, Nationalities and Peoples' Region, and the new Sidama State—and the "lowland" states of Afar, Somali, Gambella, and Benishangul Gumuz. Populations in the latter four states continue to have less access to government services. A split between the Abiy administration and the TPLF removed the previously dominant Tigrayan political elite from power. The mutual nonrecognition and the violent conflict that ensued in 2020 has had financial and other implications for the Tigray Region and Tigrayans more broadly, the rights of civilians are limited under the state of emergency, and people are vulnerable to abusive practices by security forces.

Same-sex sexual activity is prohibited by law and punishable by up to 15 years' imprisonment. Women face discrimination in education. A gender gap persists in many aspects of economic life including women's wages relative to their male counterparts in similar positions; according to the World Bank's Gender Innovation Lab, women have far lower wage incomes (44 percent lower) and business sales (79 percent lower) than do men.

A government campaign to support internally displaced people (IDPs) to return to their home communities has led to a significant decline in their numbers. According to the International Organization for Migration, there were 1.8 million IDPs in Ethiopia in mid-2020, down from a peak of more than 3 million the previous year.

G. PERSONAL AUTONOMY AND INDIVIDUAL RIGHTS: 3 / 16 (−1)

G1. Do individuals enjoy freedom of movement, including the ability to change their place of residence, employment, or education? 0 / 4 (−1)

While the constitution establishes freedom of movement, local conflicts impede people's ability to travel freely. In early 2020, blockades and temporary road closures were reported from the border of Amhara and Tigray, Somali and Afar, as well as from several parts of Oromia. Measures to contain the COVID-19 pandemic introduced additional restrictions: state governments temporarily suspended travel between regions, the federal government instituted limitations on the capacity of public transport, and the Addis Ababa city administration briefly restricted the circulation of private cars.

From March to September 2020, Ethiopia closed all its land borders in response to the COVID-19 pandemic. The border with Eritrea has remained shut since April 2019; it had been opened in 2018 for the first time in two decades, but Eritrean officials ordered the border crossing closed when the peace process between the two countries stalled.

Violent conflict, fueled by ethnic tensions, armed groups, as well as security clampdowns in parts of Oromia and Benishangul Gumuz, have significantly reduced interregional travel, with most Ethiopians feeling safer in their home region than in other states. The escalation of violence in Oromia following the death of Hachalu Hundessa led to a security crackdown during which grave crimes were committed. Movement inside and into Oromia was consequently reduced, with roadblocks set up both by protesters and security forces.

The violent conflict in Tigray has made movement within and to the region as well as northern Amhara difficult, with curfews set by the military to control movement.

Score Change: The score declined from 1 to 0 because increased violence between ethnic groups has caused mass displacement and severely impaired civilians' ability to travel safely within the country.

G2. Are individuals able to exercise the right to own property and establish private businesses without undue interference from state or nonstate actors? 1 / 4

Private business opportunities are limited by heavy government regulation of key industries and the dominance of state-owned enterprises in many sectors. State monopolies persist in the telecommunication, shipping, and aviation industries, while the financial sector is closed to foreign competition and effectively controlled by state-owned banks. In 2020, the Abiy government advanced its plans for a liberalization of the economy, and the deadline for a partial sale of the state-owned EthioTelecom was set for early 2021.

All land must be leased from the state. The government has evicted Indigenous groups from various areas to make way for infrastructure projects, such as the Gibe III dam in the Lower Omo Valley. Urban development projects in Addis Ababa and other cities have also repeatedly led to the forced resettlement of local tenants.

A gender gap persists in many aspects of economic life including land ownership and access to finance.

G3. Do individuals enjoy personal social freedoms, including choice of marriage partner and size of family, protection from domestic violence, and control over appearance? 1 / 4

Legislation protects women's rights, but these rights are routinely violated in practice. Enforcement of laws against rape and domestic abuse is inconsistent, and cases routinely stall in the courts. According to government estimates, incidences of rape and domestic violence rose by about 25 percent during the COVID lockdown period.

Forced child marriage is illegal but common in Ethiopia, and prosecutions for the crime are rare. Female genital mutilation (FGM) is also illegal, but the law is inconsistently enforced, and the 2016 Ethiopian Demographic and Health Survey found that 65 percent of women between the ages of 15 and 49 had undergone the practice. However, reports suggest that FGM rates have reduced in recent years due to efforts by both NGOs and the government to combat the practice.

G4. Do individuals enjoy equality of opportunity and freedom from economic exploitation? 1 / 4

Despite near-universal primary school enrollment, access to quality education and other social services varies widely across regions and is particularly poor in the "emerging" lowland states. A new labor law adopted in 2019 expanded workers' rights, such by extending paid maternity leave, and raised the working age to 15 years. However, reports from Ethiopia's industrial parks suggest that working conditions can be precarious, and child labor is prevalent in many agricultural households.

In April 2020, the Ethiopian government adopted a new antitrafficking law which stipulates strict punishments for crimes such as sexual exploitation and the smuggling of persons.

Fiji

Population: 900,000
Capital: Suva
Freedom Status: Partly Free
Electoral Democracy: Yes

Overview: The repressive climate that followed a 2006 coup has eased since democratic elections were held in 2014 and 2018. However, the ruling party frequently interferes with opposition activities, the judiciary is subject to political influence, and military and police brutality is a significant problem.

KEY DEVELOPMENTS IN 2020

- Throughout the year, the government rejected permits for marches and public demonstrations, citing restrictions on public gatherings implemented to prevent the spread of COVID-19. In June, police shut down protests at the University of the South Pacific. By year's end, 49 people had tested positive for COVID-19, and 2 people had died, according to government statistics provided to the World Health Organization (WHO).
- In May, the opposition Socialist Democratic Liberal Party (SODELPA) was suspended for a month for allegedly breaching party registration rules, after an internal feud over the leadership of the party split it into two factions. In June, police raided the offices of both major opposition parties, SODELPA and the National Federation Party, allegedly looking for payments related to social media posts.

POLITICAL RIGHTS: 24 / 40
A. ELECTORAL PROCESS: 8 / 12
A1. Was the current head of government or other chief national authority elected through free and fair elections? 3 / 4

The prime minister is the head of government. The party that wins the most seats in parliamentary elections selects the prime minister, who is then appointed by the president. In the 2018 parliamentary elections, Prime Minister Bainimarama's FijiFirst Party won 50 percent of the total vote and 27 seats in the 51-member parliament. The Multinational Observer Group reported that the polling "was transparent and credible overall and the outcome broadly represented the will of Fijian voters."

The president is elected by Parliament, which chooses between two candidates: one named by the prime minister and one by the leader of the opposition. As head of state, the president—who is elected to a three-year term and is eligible for reelection—holds a largely ceremonial role. President George Konrote, from the Polynesian island of Rotuma, was sworn in to a second term in November 2018.

A2. Were the current national legislative representatives elected through free and fair elections? 2 / 4

Parliament is Fiji's unicameral legislative body, with 51 members elected to serve four-year terms. International observers of the 2018 parliamentary elections found polling largely credible, although civil society participation was limited.

Municipal councils continue to be run by government-appointed administrators, having been dissolved in 2009 in the wake of the abrogation of the 1997 constitution. As a result, municipal elections have not been held since 2005.

A3. Are the electoral laws and framework fair, and are they implemented impartially by the relevant election management bodies? 3 / 4

The legal framework for Fijian elections is considered fair. However, the structure of the electoral system has raised concerns about potential political interference. FijiFirst's secretary general, Aiyaz Sayed-Khaiyum, serves as minister of elections, as well as attorney general. Opposition parties claim that this creates a bias in the Electoral Commission, which administers elections, and affects the independence of the body.

B. POLITICAL PLURALISM AND PARTICIPATION: 9 / 16

B1. Do the people have the right to organize in different political parties or other competitive political groupings of their choice, and is the system free of undue obstacles to the rise and fall of these competing parties or groupings? 3 / 4

The right to form political parties is constitutionally guaranteed, but the government has eligibility requirements that discourage the formation of smaller parties: prospective parties must submit 5,000 signatures to become registered. The 5 percent nationwide threshold for representation in Parliament further disincentivizes the formation of smaller parties.

B2. Is there a realistic opportunity for the opposition to increase its support or gain power through elections? 1 / 4

The dominance of FijiFirst in parliament and its popularity with the public has left little space for opposition forces to assert themselves politically. However, the major opposition party, the Social Democratic Liberal Party (SODELPA), won 21 seats in 2018, up from 15 in 2014. FijiFirst has used state resources to advance its political campaigns. The Multinational Observer Group noted that during the 2018 parliamentary campaign, government ministers and high-level officials engaged in high-profile activities, such as opening buildings, signing commercial contracts, and disbursing government grants and funds, which could have provided an electoral advantage to FijiFirst.

Opposition figures have been targeted by corruption charges they claim are politically motivated. Before the 2018 election, the Fiji Independent Commission Against Corruption (FICAC) charged Sitiveni Rabuka with making a false declaration of assets. He was acquitted, but FICAC appealed the decision, and the case was ultimately dismissed two days before the elections in November. Had he been convicted, Rabuka would have been barred from the contest.

In May 2020, SODELPA was suspended for a month for allegedly breaching the party registration rules, after an internal feud over the leadership of the party split it into two factions. In June, Police raided the offices of both major opposition parties, SODELPA and the National Federation Party, allegedly looking for payments related to social media posts.

B3. Are the people's political choices free from domination by forces that are external to the political sphere, or by political forces that employ extrapolitical means? 2 / 4

The military has a history of interference in Fijian politics. The leaders of the two major political parties are both former military commanders, which contributes to the perception that the military has undue political influence.

B4. Do various segments of the population (including ethnic, racial, religious, gender, LGBT+, and other relevant groups) have full political rights and electoral opportunities? 3 / 4

The law does not restrict the participation of minorities and women in politics. However, both Indigenous and Indo-Fijian women are underrepresented by political parties. Only 10 out of the 51 members of Parliament are women.

Small minority groups, including Banabans, Chinese, and the descendants of people from the Solomon Islands, lack significant political representation.

Historically, political affiliations have been associated with ethnicity. The Bainimarama government has pushed for a national identity transcending ethnicity, race, and religion.

C. FUNCTIONING OF GOVERNMENT: 7 / 12

C1. Do the freely elected head of government and national legislative representatives determine the policies of the government? 3 / 4

The executive branch under Prime Minister Bainimarama determines the policies of government. With FijiFirst holding a strong parliamentary majority, the government has frequently pushed through bills and budgets with minimal scrutiny from the opposition.

C2. Are safeguards against official corruption strong and effective? 2 / 4

Safeguards against corruption are limited in their effectiveness. The FICAC has had limited success combatting institutional corruption. Corruption remains a serious problem. FICAC has also allegedly pursued politically motivated corruption cases. In June and September 2020, FICAC launched corruption investigations into the activities of 10 opposition parliamentarians and one government minister.

C3. Does the government operate with openness and transparency? 2 / 4

Since the restoration of elective democracy in 2014, government transparency and openness has improved. The government now organizes an annual briefing for civil society organizations on the budget. Parliamentary sessions are broadcast live, and the Hansard (an official report of parliamentary proceedings) is updated regularly. Although candidates for elections are required to declare their assets, there is no law requiring public asset disclosures by members of parliament. Fiji lacks an access to information law, and requests for information from the media and the public are sometimes denied. In recent years, FijiFirst has used its parliamentary majority to rewrite parliamentary standing orders in a manner that limits debate on legislation and scrutiny of official statements.

CIVIL LIBERTIES: 36 / 60

D. FREEDOM OF EXPRESSION AND BELIEF: 12 / 16

D1. Are there free and independent media? 2 / 4

Fiji has an active media sector, with several private television stations, radio stations, and newspapers. The political opposition and other critics of the FijiFirst government have accused the state of using its power to silence critics. For example, the vaguely worded Media Industry Development Decree bans reporting that is critical of the government or harmful to "national interest public order." Restrictive press laws are sometimes enforced by the government, which leads to self-censorship. In April 2020, Jone Kalouniwai, a senior military officer, defended the government's right to censor the press during the COVID-19 pandemic.

D2. Are individuals free to practice and express their religious faith or nonbelief in public and private? 4 / 4

Freedom of religion is generally respected, though in the past there have been many cases of vandalism of Hindu temples.

D3. Is there academic freedom, and is the educational system free from extensive political indoctrination? 3 / 4

Academic freedom is not overtly constrained, but government control over funding has been used to exert influence over tertiary institutions. The University of the South Pacific prohibits the majority of its employees from taking an official position with a political party or running for office. The government withdrew its funding for the Fiji-based University of the South Pacific in September, after the Fijian Attorney General claimed the university's leadership had engaged in misconduct. Vice Chancellor Pal Ahluwalia had launched an investigation into irregularities under his predecessor, who was known to be close to the Fiji government.

D4. Are individuals free to express their personal views on political or other sensitive topics without fear of surveillance or retribution? 3 / 4

There were few confirmed reports of the government restricting private discussion on political matters or other sensitive topics during 2020. However, the government places constraints on free speech, such as a law banning the burning of the national flag.

E. ASSOCIATIONAL AND ORGANIZATIONAL RIGHTS: 7 / 12

E1. Is there freedom of assembly? 2 / 4

The constitution gives the government wide latitude to prohibit protests, including on the basis of public safety and morality. In 2020, the government rejected permits for marches and public demonstrations, citing restrictions on public gatherings implemented to prevent the spread of COVID-19. In June, police shut down protests at the University of the South Pacific. Fiji has refused entry into the country for the United Nations Special Rapporteur on the rights to freedom of assembly since 2014.

E2. Is there freedom for nongovernmental organizations, particularly those that are engaged in human rights- and governance-related work? 3 / 4

Fiji has an extensive nongovernmental organization (NGO) network, which largely operates without government interference. Strict sedition laws, which criminalize criticism of the government, place constraints on the range of initiatives that NGOs can undertake. NGOs have been critical of the proposed Parliamentary Powers and Privileges Bill, which they claim further penalizes criticism of parliament and could further erode civic space.

E3. Is there freedom for trade unions and similar professional or labor organizations? 2 / 4

Restrictions on trade union protests remain. Union members' political activities are also restricted: they are prohibited from becoming members of Parliament and face obstacles to joining political parties.

In February 2020, government suspended five unions for failing to submit audit reports. General Secretary of the National Workers Union Felix Anthony appeared in court in February and again in August over his activities during a 2019 protest by water authority workers. Amnesty International reported a rise in harassment of trade unionists in the leadup to these protests and other important union meetings.

F. RULE OF LAW: 7 / 16

F1. Is there an independent judiciary? 2 / 4

While the constitution guarantees an independent judiciary, there have been credible allegations of political interference among judges. The prime minister has substantial appointment powers, with the authority to both appoint and dismiss judges on the Supreme Court and other high courts. These powers leave the judiciary vulnerable to interference and abuse by the executive. Fiji has refused entry into the country for the United Nations Special Rapporteur on the independence of judges since 2014.

F2. Does due process prevail in civil and criminal matters? 1 / 4

Due process rights are often not respected in practice. Corruption is a major problem in the police force. Due to resource shortages, lengthy pretrial detentions are common. The law allows suspects to be arrested without a warrant for violating the Crimes Decree. Politically motivated criminal charges are not uncommon.

F3. Is there protection from the illegitimate use of physical force and freedom from war and insurgencies? 2 / 4

Torture and beatings by police remain a serious issue. Police officers and military officials who commit abuses are rarely brought to justice, and those who are convicted of crimes are frequently pardoned or have their convictions overturned on appeal. Prisons are often overcrowded, lack sanitation, and provide inadequate health services. Fiji refuses entry into the country for the United Nations Special Rapporteur on torture. In May 2020, four former prison officers seeking asylum in Australia claimed that the commissioner of the Corrections Service, Francis Kean, was responsible for a culture of violence and intimidation inside Fiji's prisons. That same month, opposition parliamentarian Pio Tikoduadua was arrested for posting a video showing police throwing a man off a bridge. The director of public prosecutions declined to press charges against Tikoduadua. Nine police officers were subsequently suspended.

F4. Do laws, policies, and practices guarantee equal treatment of various segments of the population? 2 / 4

LGBT+ people face discrimination in employment and access to healthcare. Prime Minister Bainimarama has been criticized for making prejudiced remarks against LGBT+ people, and declared in August 2019 that, so long as FijiFirst remained in power, same-sex marriage would remain outlawed. Fiji Rugby Union chair Francis Kean withdrew his nomination to the World Rugby Council in April 2020 after recordings emerged of his homophobic comments while he oversaw Fiji's prisons.

Women experience discrimination in employment as well, and a gender pay gap persists.

Relations between Indigenous Fijians and Indo-Fijians remain strained. Indigenous Fijians previously enjoyed legal advantages in education and political representation. However, the interim government installed after the 2006 coup removed many of these privileges in a bid to foster a sense of national unity.

G. PERSONAL AUTONOMY AND INDIVIDUAL RIGHTS: 10 / 16

G1. Do individuals enjoy freedom of movement, including the ability to change their place of residence, employment, or education? 3 / 4

Citizens enjoy the freedom to travel, live, work, and seek education inside and outside the country. However, the law gives the government broad powers to restrict both internal and foreign travel. The government did not utilize the law to impose any new restrictions on travel in 2020.

G2. Are individuals able to exercise the right to own property and establish private businesses without undue interference from state or nonstate actors? 3 / 4

Property rights are generally respected. However, it is difficult to obtain land titles. The government amended the Land Sales Act in 2014 to require foreign nationals who fail to build a dwelling on their land within two years of acquisition to pay a fine equivalent to 10 percent of the land value every six months. Under the law, urban residential freehold land cannot be sold to foreigners.

G3. Do individuals enjoy personal social freedoms, including choice of marriage partner and size of family, protection from domestic violence, and control over appearance? 2 / 4

Domestic violence remains a problem in Fiji, and perpetrators who are convicted of the crime often receive light sentences. The Fiji Women's Crisis Center warns that there was a spike in domestic violence cases during the government's lockdown, implemented to prevent the spread of COVID-19.

Although there is a growing movement in support of marriage equality in Fiji, Prime Minister Bainimarama has openly stated he does not support it.

G4. Do individuals enjoy equality of opportunity and freedom from economic exploitation? 2 / 4

Sex trafficking of children remained a problem in 2020, and the government was ineffective in addressing it. The US State Department's *2020 Trafficking in Persons Report* found no improvement in Fiji's record on human trafficking during the year. In July, reports of an 11-year-old victim of sex trafficking emerged. Safety standards at workplaces are not always adequately enforced. Long work hours are common in some jobs, including transportation and shipping.

Finland

Population: 5,500,000
Capital: Helsinki
Freedom Status: Free
Electoral Democracy: Yes

Overview: Finland's parliamentary system features free and fair elections and robust multiparty competition. Corruption is not a significant problem, and freedoms of speech, religion, and association are respected. The judiciary is independent under the constitution and in practice. Women and ethnic minority groups enjoy equal rights, though harassment and hate speech aimed at minority groups does occur.

KEY DEVELOPMENTS IN 2020

- In response to the COVID-19 pandemic, the Finnish government declared a state of emergency in March, which was in place for three months. Authorities closed down the capital and restricted movement into and out of the country; no curfew was imposed, and all business remained open. According to government statistics provided to the World Health Organization (WHO), over 36,100 people tested positive for COVID-19 and over 500 people died by year's end.
- In September, the Nordic Resistance Movement, a far-right, neo-Nazi organization, lost their Supreme Court appeal against their 2019 ban. The court issued a cease-and-desist order for the organization and declared the group had abused the rights to free assembly and free expression, with the aim of overturning democracy and limiting human rights.

POLITICAL RIGHTS: 40 / 40
A. ELECTORAL PROCESS: 12 / 12
A1. Was the current head of government or other chief national authority elected through free and fair elections? 4 / 4

The president, whose role is mainly ceremonial, is directly elected for up to two six-year terms. In 2018, former finance minister and incumbent president Sauli Niinistö, originally of the center-right National Coalition Party (KOK), won a second presidential term with 62.6 percent of the vote, defeating several challengers. The election was considered broadly free and fair.

The prime minister, the head of government, is selected by Finland's freely elected parliament. Following parliamentary elections in April 2019, Antti Rinne of the Social Democratic Party became prime minister in June. However, he resigned due to criticism within the governing coalition over his handling of a postal workers' strike in November 2019, and Sanna Marin was chosen by the party to replace him in December 2019.

A2. Were the current national legislative representatives elected through free and fair elections? 4 / 4

Representatives in the 200-seat, unicameral parliament, the Eduskunta, are elected to serve four-year terms. In March 2019, the coalition government headed by Prime Minister Sipilä of the Center Party, which had been in power since 2015, resigned after failing to secure parliamentary support for a reform of the health care system, one of its key priorities. The move triggered the elections held in April 2019. After a preliminary needs-assessment mission to Finland before the 2019 parliamentary elections, the Organization for Security and Co-operation in Europe (OSCE) expressed "a high level of confidence in all the aspects of the electoral process" and concluded that it was not necessary to send an election observation mission.

The Social Democratic Party won the largest share of the vote, taking 40 seats. The right-wing Finns Party placed second with 39 seats. The new government formed in June 2019 comprised the Social Democratic Party, the Center Party (31 seats), the Green League (20 seats), the Left Alliance (16 seats), and the Swedish People's Party of Finland (9 seats). The remainder of seats went to KOK (38), the Christian Democrats (5), the new Movement Now (1), and the Åland Coalition (1).

A3. Are the electoral laws and framework fair, and are they implemented impartially by the relevant election management bodies? 4 / 4

Finland's electoral laws are robust and generally well implemented by the relevant authorities. The OSCE in 2019 found no new electoral problems to address since its previous review.

B. POLITICAL PLURALISM AND PARTICIPATION: 16 / 16

B1. Do the people have the right to organize in different political parties or other competitive political groupings of their choice, and is the system free of undue obstacles to the rise and fall of these competing parties or groupings? 4 / 4

There are no significant constraints on political parties' ability to organize and operate, and they compete freely in practice.

B2. Is there a realistic opportunity for the opposition to increase its support or gain power through elections? 4 / 4

Finland regularly experiences peaceful transfers of power between rival political parties through elections, with governments typically consisting of multiparty coalitions. The 2019 elections produced the country's first Social Democratic prime minister since 2003.

B3. Are the people's political choices free from domination by forces that are external to the political sphere, or by political forces that employ extrapolitical means? 4 / 4

People's political choices are generally free from undue interference by forces that are not democratically accountable.

B4. Do various segments of the population (including ethnic, racial, religious, gender, LGBT+, and other relevant groups) have full political rights and electoral opportunities? 4 / 4

Citizens from the Finnish majority and all ethnic minorities enjoy full political rights. The Åland Islands—an autonomous region located off the southwestern coast whose inhabitants speak Swedish—have their own 30-seat parliament, as well as one seat in the national legislature. The Sámi of northern Finland, an Indigenous people who number about 10,000, have a legislature with limited powers, but they do not have guaranteed representation in the parliament. Members of the Sámi community continue to call for greater inclusion in political decision-making processes.

Women and women's interests are reasonably well represented in politics, as are LGBT+ people and their respective interests. Prime Minister Marin is the third woman to serve as Finland's head of government. Her installation also marked the first time that all parties in a Finnish governing coalition were headed by women.

C. FUNCTIONING OF GOVERNMENT: 12 / 12

C1. Do the freely elected head of government and national legislative representatives determine the policies of the government? 4 / 4

Finland's freely elected government and lawmakers are generally able to develop and implement policy without undue interference from unelected entities.

In March 2020, the government declared a state of emergency due to the COVID-19 pandemic. The government attempted to introduce the Infectious Diseases Act, which would give them more powers than the current Emergency Powers Act, enabling them, for example, to order the closure of gyms and group exercise facilities. Concerns over restrictions of economic freedom brought the bill to a stall, and it had not been approved by Parliament by year's end.

C2. Are safeguards against official corruption strong and effective? 4 / 4

Corruption is not a significant problem in Finland and is generally punished under relevant laws when discovered. However, in 2018 the Council of Europe's anticorruption body urged Finland to bolster corruption prevention and detection policies within government and law enforcement agencies, including by increasing whistleblower protections. It further warned of possible conflicts of interest between the public and private sectors in the Sipilä government's planned health care and social service reforms.

C3. Does the government operate with openness and transparency? 4 / 4

Laws permitting access to public information are generally well enforced, though there are some limits on the disclosure of information related to national security, foreign affairs, trade secrets, and criminal investigations. All citizens, including government officials, are required by law to make public asset declarations, though there are no penalties for noncompliance. While companies perceive corruption risks and favoritism within public procurement as low, informal networks and personal associations, notably at the local level, are still believed to hold influence over procurement decisions.

CIVIL LIBERTIES: 60 / 60

D. FREEDOM OF EXPRESSION AND BELIEF: 16 / 16

D1. Are there free and independent media? 4 / 4

Freedom of expression is protected by Article 12 of the constitution and the 2003 Act on the Exercise of Freedom of Expression in Mass Media. Media outlets in Finland are typically independent and free from political pressure or censorship, and the media environment is strong.

However, journalists sometimes face harassment for their work, notably those who cover topics related to immigrants and immigration. Journalists also face the risk of defamation charges. In April 2019, investigative reporter Johanna Vehkoo was convicted of defaming a far-right politician and ordered to pay more than $7,000 in fines and compensation.

D2. Are individuals free to practice and express their religious faith or nonbelief in public and private? 4 / 4

Religious freedom is guaranteed in the constitution and generally respected in practice. However, far-right hate speech and incidents of vandalism directed at the Jewish and Muslim communities are ongoing concerns.

D3. Is there academic freedom, and is the educational system free from extensive political indoctrination? 4 / 4

Academic freedom is generally respected.

D4. Are individuals free to express their personal views on political or other sensitive topics without fear of surveillance or retribution? 4 / 4

There are few impediments to personal expression, and the authorities are not known to engage in improper surveillance of personal communications. However, in March 2019 the parliament gave final approval to two bills that strengthen the authority of the intelligence service and defense forces to access private communications involving national security threats. Work on the measures had begun after what was considered the country's first-ever terrorist attack in 2017.

E. ASSOCIATIONAL AND ORGANIZATIONAL RIGHTS: 12 / 12

E1. Is there freedom of assembly? 4 / 4

Freedom of assembly is protected by law and upheld in practice. As a response to the COVID-19 pandemic, the government restricted public events—including protests—to no more than 50 people in March 2020. This restriction was removed in October.

In October 2020, police used pepper spray against protesters obstructing traffic, who were associated with the environmental activist group Extinction Rebellion and calling on the government to take more significant measures to combat the climate crisis. In December, the National Police Board and the prosecutor general opened an inquiry into accusations of assault levied against the police for their actions.

E2. Is there freedom for nongovernmental organizations, particularly those that are engaged in human rights- and governance-related work? 4 / 4

Nongovernmental organizations operate without restriction.

E3. Is there freedom for trade unions and similar professional or labor organizations? 4 / 4

Workers have the right to organize and bargain collectively, though public-sector workers who provide services deemed essential may not strike. Approximately 70 percent of workers belong to trade unions, which actively advocate for members' interests.

F. RULE OF LAW: 16 / 16

F1. Is there an independent judiciary? 4 / 4

The constitution provides for an independent judiciary, and the courts operate without political interference in practice.

F2. Does due process prevail in civil and criminal matters? 4 / 4

Due process is generally respected in Finland. Authorities largely uphold safeguards against arbitrary arrest and detention and provide the conditions for fair trials.

F3. Is there protection from the illegitimate use of physical force and freedom from war and insurgencies? 4 / 4

There are few significant threats to physical security, and violent crime is uncommon, although it has increased in recent years.

F4. Do laws, policies, and practices guarantee equal treatment of various segments of the population? 4 / 4

The constitution guarantees the Sámi people cultural autonomy and the right to pursue their culturally significant livelihoods, which include fishing and reindeer herding. However, representatives of the community have said that they cannot fully exercise their rights in practice and face restrictions on land use. While Roma comprise a very small percentage of Finland's population, they are significantly disadvantaged and marginalized.

Women enjoy equal legal rights. Despite an equal pay law, women earn only about 83 percent as much as men on average. In February 2020, the government initiated a new policy that grants new parents seven months of parental leave, regardless of gender.

A June 2019 report by the European Commission against Racism and Intolerance (ECRI) noted an increase in racist and intolerant hate speech in Finland, especially toward Muslims and refugees. Hate speech on the internet was also a concern, with targets including immigrants, people of African descent, LGBT+ people, the Jewish community, and Roma. A 2020 report by Finland's Non-Discrimination Ombudsman further highlighted racism against people of African descent. The report noted that 20 percent of those surveyed said they had experienced ethnic profiling by police or security guards, 70 percent said they had experienced discrimination in education, and 60 percent said they had not been treated equally when applying for jobs. Further, 60 percent said they had not filed any official complaints on discriminatory behavior.

The Nordic Resistance Movement, a neo-Nazi organization that the National Police Board has called "violent and openly racist," was banned in March 2019. In September 2020, Finland's Supreme Court denied their appeal and issued a cease-and-desist order against them. NRM had appealed the ban on the basis of their rights to freedom of assembly and freedom of speech. However, the Supreme Court ruled that the organization's activities constituted abuse of those same freedoms. This is the first time an organization has been given a cease-and-desist order in Finland since the 1970s.

In 2016, the Finnish government amended its asylum law to limit the aid available to asylum seekers. The amendments prompted concern from the UN refugee agency, which suggested that authorities had abandoned good practices and sought to align their policies with the minimum required by international treaties governing the treatment of refugees.

G. PERSONAL AUTONOMY AND INDIVIDUAL RIGHTS: 16 / 16

G1. Do individuals enjoy freedom of movement, including the ability to change their place of residence, employment, or education? 4 / 4

Individuals in Finland are free to travel abroad and domestically. The country has one of the most expansive "freedom to roam" policies in the world, allowing people to use any public or private land for recreational purposes so long as the privacy of a private residence is not violated, and no environmental damage is incurred. There are no undue restrictions on people's ability to change their place of residence, education, or employment.

During the COVID-19 pandemic in 2020, Finland ensured that citizens had the right to return to Finland and all persons had the right to leave the country. Restrictions on entry into the country for noncitizens were implemented temporarily. In November 2020, new rules required passengers entering Finland to have a certificate of a negative COVID-19 test taken less than 72 hours before arrival.

G2. Are individuals able to exercise the right to own property and establish private businesses without undue interference from state or nonstate actors? 4 / 4

Intellectual and physical property rights are upheld. There are no major obstacles to establishing a business, and the country boasts a well-regulated, transparent, and open economy.

G3. Do individuals enjoy personal social freedoms, including choice of marriage partner and size of family, protection from domestic violence, and control over appearance? 4 / 4

People's choices on personal status matters are for the most part unrestricted. Same-sex marriage has been allowed since 2017. However, legislation requires that transgender people be sterilized and have a mental health diagnosis in order to obtain legal recognition of their gender. In 2017, the UN Human Rights Council (UNHRC) called for Finland to eliminate these impediments to legal gender recognition. The ECRI echoed this call in 2019. The UNHRC has also recommended that Finland amend its criminal code to no longer define rape according to the degree of violence used by the perpetrator. The new coalition government in 2019 placed this matter on its agenda, and in July 2020 the Ministry of Justice issued a recommendation to include consent in the definition of rape. The proposal is unlikely to go to Parliament for consideration until spring 2021. Domestic violence is an ongoing concern.

G4. Do individuals enjoy equality of opportunity and freedom from economic exploitation? 4 / 4

The authorities generally uphold protections against exploitative working conditions. Asylum seekers and migrants are most vulnerable to sex and labor trafficking. According to the US State Department, the government actively prosecutes trafficking offenses, and survivors have access to protection and assistance, though alleged perpetrators often receive lighter charges and penalties due to lack of specialized training for investigators.

France

Population: 66,900,000
Capital: Paris
Freedom Status: Free
Electoral Democracy: Yes

Overview: The French political system features vibrant democratic processes and generally strong protections for civil liberties and political rights. However, successive governments have responded to deadly terrorist attacks in recent years by curtailing constitutional protections and empowering law enforcement to infringe upon personal freedoms. Anti-Muslim and anti-immigrant sentiment continue to be rife throughout the country.

KEY DEVELOPMENTS IN 2020

- Restrictions implemented to prevent the spread of COVID-19 were disproportionately enforced upon members of marginalized groups. During the first lockdown from March through May, Amnesty International reported fines for breaching lockdown rules were given at a rate three times higher in Seine-Saint-Denis, the poorest department in mainland France, than elsewhere in the country, even though residents in Seine-Saint-Denis followed the rules at the same rate as others in the country. According to government statistics provided to the World Health Organization (WHO), over 2,578,000 people tested positive for the virus and more than 64,000 people died by year's end.
- In October, the schoolteacher Samuel Paty was murdered after displaying cartoon images of the prophet Muhammad in his classroom. The government subsequently drafted the Reinforcing Republican Principles Law, which it claimed sought to combat "religious separatism." However, the legislation increases surveillance of mosques and Muslim associations, and would require Muslim organizations to sign a contract of "respect for Republican values" when applying for state subsidies.
- In November, four police officers brutally assaulted Michel Zecler, a Black music producer, inside the entrance of his recording studio; Zecler was initially detained for allegedly breaking COVID-19 rules by not wearing a mask in the street. The officers involved were charged with assault.

POLITICAL RIGHTS 38 / 40

A. ELECTORAL PROCESS 12 / 12

A1. Was the current head of government or other chief national authority elected through free and fair elections? 4 / 4

The French president is chief of state, and is elected to five-year terms by direct, universal suffrage in a two-round system. The prime minister is head of government and is appointed by the president. Emmanuel Macron, a centrist newcomer to politics, won the second round of the 2017 presidential election against Marine Le Pen from the far-right National Front (FN).

The Organization for Security and Co-operation in Europe expressed confidence in the integrity of French elections.

A2. Were the current national legislative representatives elected through free and fair elections? 4 / 4

Members of the lower house of Parliament, the 577-seat National Assembly, are elected to five-year terms in a two-round system. The upper house, the 348-seat Senate, is an indirectly elected body whose members serve six-year terms. In the June 2017 legislative elections, Macron's La République en Marche! (LREM) and its centrist ally won a majority 350 seats in the National Assembly.

The government adjusted polling practices for the 2020 local elections due to the COVID-19 pandemic. Controversially, the first round of voting took place on March 15 (at the beginning of the coronavirus outbreak), and the second round was held on June 28. Voter turnout reached 44.7 percent for the first round, and 41.6 percent for the second round, record lows.

A3. Are the electoral laws and framework fair, and are they implemented impartially by the relevant election management bodies? 4 / 4

France's electoral laws and framework are fair and implemented impartially. Legislation passed in June 2020 to facilitate proxy voting and mail voting were not applied to the year's local elections.

B. POLITICAL PLURALISM AND PARTICIPATION: 15 / 16

B1. Do the people have the right to organize in different political parties or other competitive political groupings of their choice, and is the system free of undue obstacles to the rise and fall of these competing parties or groupings? 4 / 4

Parties are generally able to organize and operate freely. Elections in recent years have been competitive and less dominant parties have gained more visibility.

B2. Is there a realistic opportunity for the opposition to increase its support or gain power through elections? 4 / 4

The recent elections have demonstrated that parties outside the political mainstream can gain power through elections.

B3. Are the people's political choices free from domination by forces that are external to the political sphere, or by political forces that employ extrapolitical means? 4 / 4

People's political choices are generally free from domination.

B4. Do various segments of the population (including ethnic, racial, religious, gender, LGBT+, and other relevant groups) have full political rights and electoral opportunities? 3 / 4

No laws restrict the political participation of women, LGBT+ people, and other marginalized groups. However, far-right parties and their nationalist ideologies have become more mainstream and have emboldened racist commentary in public discourse, further excluding marginalized groups from the political sphere.

C. FUNCTIONING OF GOVERNMENT: 10 / 12

C1. Do the freely elected head of government and national legislative representatives determine the policies of the government? 4 / 4

The elected head of government and national legislative representatives determine the policies of the government. However, the government has increasingly used Article 49.3 of the constitution—the *ordonnance* process— to forego parliamentary debate and change government policy.

In 2020, Parliament twice declared a "health state of emergency," enabling the prime minister to implement restrictions to respond to the public health crisis.

C2. Are safeguards against official corruption strong and effective? 3 / 4

Despite a 2017 law seeking to reduce conflicts of interest, corruption allegations have been lodged against several high-level government officials in recent years—including against Alexis Kohler, general secretary of the Elysée Palace, for unlawful conflicts of interest.

C3. Does the government operate with openness and transparency? 4 / 4

The government generally operates with openness and transparency, although it has increasingly used the ordonnance process and an accelerated procedure—which limits Parliament's discussion of draft legislation—to enact policies without parliamentary debate or public scrutiny. These powers were used to push through a contentious pension reform proposal in February 2020 (though it was suspended due to the COVID-19 pandemic), the controversial Reinforcing Republican Principles Bill, and the much-criticized Global Security Bill. and Global Security Bill.

The government's response to the COVID-19 pandemic was inconsistent and lacked transparency. An April 2020 investigation by the news outlet Mediapart found that the government withheld information about its shortage of personal protective equipment. A December 2020 report from parliament's investigative committee on the management of the pandemic criticized the health sector's lack of preparedness and its chaotic and erratic decision-making processes.

In January 2020, the Group of States against Corruption (GRECO) raised concerns over a lack of transparency around relationships between the French executive and lobbyists.

CIVIL LIBERTIES: 52 / 60

D. FREEDOM OF EXPRESSION AND BELIEF: 14 / 16

D1. Are there free and independent media? 4 / 4

The media generally operate freely and represent a wide range of political opinions. There were some incidents of violence against journalists in 2020.

The 2020 National Law Enforcement Doctrine stipulates that there are no exceptions for journalists covering protests when police disperse public demonstrations. This doctrine was formalized in Global Security Bill, adopted by the National Assembly in November, which controversially outlawed the spread of identifiable images of police "when aimed at the physical or mental integrity of police officers." However, the government promised to rewrite this provision (Article 24) after video recordings of two incidents showed police misconduct; video of the brutal dismantling of a refugee camp in Paris in November; and footage of the violent arrest of Michel Zecler, a Black music producer.

In December 2020, two journalists initiated legal actions for having been prevented access to refugee camp evacuations in the North and Pas-de-Calais departments.

D2. Are individuals free to practice and express their religious faith or nonbelief in public and private? 3 / 4

The constitution protects freedom of religion. Antidefamation laws penalize religiously motivated abuse, and Holocaust denial is illegal. The government maintains the policy of *laïcité* (secularism), whereby religion and state affairs are strictly separated, though it also has official relationships with organizations representing the country's three major religions—Christianity, Islam, and Judaism.

The government drafted the Reinforcing Republican Principles Law, which was still in discussion at the end of 2020, after the October murder of Samuel Paty, a schoolteacher who had shown caricatures of the Islamic prophet Muhammad in his class when teaching about freedom of expression. The law ostensibly would combat "religious separatism." However, the legislation would increase surveillance of mosques and Muslim associations and would require Muslim organizations to sign a contract of "respect for Republican values" when applying for state subsidies. Critics have warned that the law stigmatizes Muslims and could increase Islamophobic sentiments.

D3. Is there academic freedom, and is the educational system free from extensive political indoctrination? 4 / 4

There are no formal restrictions on academic freedom in France.

A December 2020 draft bill passed by the Senate includes provisions that criminalize on-campus gatherings that "trouble the tranquility" of the university and that enable increased government scrutiny over the ideological basis of scholarly research in France. University staff strongly pushed back against the draft law.

D4. Are individuals free to express their personal views on political or other sensitive topics without fear of surveillance or retribution? 3 / 4

A law aiming at tackling hate speech on the internet has been largely rejected by the Constitutional Council in June 2020, after critics raised that it would pose a serious threat to freedom of expression.

In December 2020, three government decrees extended the compiling of information for three public security files that will enable authorities to keep records on political militants and activists, including on their families and underage children, on their health, or on their activities on social media.

E. ASSOCIATIONAL AND ORGANIZATIONAL RIGHTS: 11 / 12
E1. Is there freedom of assembly? 3 / 4

Freedom of assembly is normally respected. However, the government's restrictions on public gatherings in response to the COVID-19 pandemic was declared unconstitutional by the Council of State in June 2020, after the Council deemed the restrictions disproportionate to the public health risk at the time.

Throughout 2020, police frequently and unnecessarily used excessive force against protesters. Police violently dispersed a feminist march in March; a demonstration by health care workers in June; and Black Lives Matter protests in June against police violence and racism, following the murder of George Floyd in the United States.

E2. Is there freedom for nongovernmental organizations, particularly those that are engaged in human rights- and governance-related work? 4 / 4

Nongovernmental organizations generally operate freely. The National Law Enforcement Doctrine has complicated and obstructed NGO reports around protests and police actions.

The Reinforcing Republican Principles Bill eases the government's ability to dismantle associations that do not respect the "values of the Republic." After the October 2020 murder of Samuel Paty, authorities ordered the dissolution of the Collective against Islamophobia in France (CCIF) in November, claiming the organization had taken actions to provoke terrorist acts, and defended and promoted an overly broad notion of Islamophobia.

E3. Is there freedom for trade unions and similar professional or labor organizations? 4 / 4

Trade unions are free to operate without any undue restrictions.

F. RULE OF LAW: 13 / 16
F1. Is there an independent judiciary? 4 / 4

France has an independent judiciary, and the rule of law generally prevails in court proceedings.

F2. Does due process prevail in civil and criminal matters? 3 / 4

Due process generally prevails in civil and criminal matters. However, antiterrorism legislation passed in 2017, which replaced a state of emergency instituted after the 2015 terror attacks in Paris, enshrined controversial administrative control measures into law.

A March 2020, decree extended the maximum amount of time allowed for pretrial detentions, with little oversight.

F3. Is there protection from the illegitimate use of physical force and freedom from war and insurgencies? 3 / 4

The threat of terrorism exists in France. In October 2020, the schoolteacher Samuel Paty was murdered after displaying cartoon images of the prophet Muhammad in his classroom. Police shot Paty's killer shortly thereafter, though two of his students and five others were charged for being complicit in what was declared a terrorist murder. The same month in Nice, a man killed three people outside of the city's Notre Dame Basilica. The killer had entered France a month earlier, and had no clear connections to known terrorist groups, though authorities claimed the attacker was likely motivated by extremist ideology.

The number of complaints of police violence sent to the police's internal disciplinary body (IPGN) has sharply increased since 2018, as have suspicions that the IGPN is too lenient on police forces.

Instances of unnecessary and excessive police violence continued to be documented throughout 2020. In November and December, police violently dismantled and evacuated refugee camps in Paris, Calais, and Grande Synthe (North), pulling up tents and leaving people thrown to the ground. Also in November, four police officers brutally assaulted Michel Zecler, a Black music producer, inside the entrance of his recording studio; Zecler was initially detained for allegedly breaking COVID-19 rules by not wearing a mask in the street. The officers involved were charged with assault.

The Interior Ministry announced in June 2020 that it would ban police from using the chokehold technique—which led to the death of Cédric Chouviat in January 2020—and later stated that it would reform the IPGN. However, it reversed the decision on chokeholds after police unions expressed discontent.

F4. Do laws, policies, and practices guarantee equal treatment of various segments of the population? 3 / 4

Migrants and refugees in France continue to suffer both from societal discrimination and abuse from authorities. During the COVID-19 pandemic, they received reduced aid, were heavily policed, and experienced dangerous sanitary conditions.

Anti-Muslim sentiment, attacks against mosquegoers, reports of vandalism of mosques, and verbal assaults have increased in recent years. A variety of antisemitic conspiracy theories surged after the emergence of the coronavirus pandemic. The far-right has become increasingly successful in shaping French public discourse, using racist language against minority ethnic groups.

Restrictions implemented to prevent the spread of COVID-19 were disproportionately enforced upon members of marginalized groups. During the first lockdown, Amnesty International reported that the number of fines for breaching lockdown rules was three times higher in Seine-Saint-Denis, the poorest department in mainland France, than elsewhere in the country, even though residents in Seine-Saint-Denis followed the rules at the same rate as others in the country.

Research published in October 2020 by the European Trade Union Confederation revealed that the French gender pay gap has only narrowed by 0.1 percent since 2010. The efficacy of government efforts to address gender inequality is unclear. Sexual harassment of women is a prominent issue.

French law forbids the categorization of people according to ethnic origin, and no official statistics are collected on ethnicity. Discrimination based on sexual orientation is prohibited by law.

G. PERSONAL AUTONOMY AND INDIVIDUAL RIGHTS: 14 / 16

G1. Do individuals enjoy freedom of movement, including the ability to change their place of residence, employment, or education? 4 / 4

While there are normally no restrictions on freedom of travel or choice of residence or employment in France, the COVID-19 pandemic led to exceptional restrictions on freedom of movement. The French government instituted two lockdowns to prevent the virus's spread during 2020, one from March to June, and a second one from late October to December. Authorities were criticized for discriminatory enforcement of the rules, as police restricted the movement of marginalized groups far more than the rest of the population.

G2. Are individuals able to exercise the right to own property and establish private businesses without undue interference from state or nonstate actors? 4 / 4

Private businesses are free to operate.

G3. Do individuals enjoy personal social freedoms, including choice of marriage partner and size of family, protection from domestic violence, and control over appearance? 3 / 4

Individuals generally enjoy personal social freedoms—including choice of marriage partner and size of family. In September 2020, the National Assembly voted to double the duration of paternity leave to 28 days. Though the National Assembly had voted to legalize medically assisted procreation for all women, the Senate rejected it for single women and lesbian couples in July 2020.

During the two COVID-19 lockdowns in 2020, reports of domestic violence rose sharply, despite government measures to prevent this. Authorities implemented mechanisms to report violence and set up safe zones, for which legislation was adopted in June 2020. However, the appointment of Gérald Darmanin, who is being criminally investigated for rape, as Interior Minister in July 2020 caused shock and anger among feminist activists and government critics.

Muslim women remain the target of several laws enacted in recent years preventing them from wearing clothing that involves religious practice, forcing some women to dress against their will.

G4. Do individuals enjoy equality of opportunity and freedom from economic exploitation? 3 / 4

Employment discrimination against women, French Muslims, immigrants of North African descent, and others outside the historical elite hinders equality of opportunity. While France's government acts against human trafficking, the problem persists in the commercial sex trade; some victims are also forced into domestic labor.

Gabon

Population: 2,200,000
Capital: Libreville
Freedom Status: Not Free
Electoral Democracy: No

Overview: Although Gabon holds multiparty elections, President Ali Bongo Ondimba maintains political dominance through a combination of patronage and repression, having succeeded his father when he died in 2009 after more than 40 years in power. The executive branch effectively controls the judiciary. Other significant problems include discrimination against immigrants, marginalization of minority groups, and legal and de facto inequality for women.

KEY DEVELOPMENTS IN 2020

- In March, the first person in Gabon tested positive for COVID-19, which prompted the government to declare a state of emergency and implement a lockdown, including a 12-hour curfew, that lasted over a month. In some areas, the lockdown was so strict that some people claimed they were unable to access essential commodities. According to government statistics provided to the World Health Organization (WHO), 9,571 people tested positive for coronavirus and 64 people died by year's end.
- In June, the government passed a law decriminalizing homosexuality, though same-sex marriage remains illegal. Some LGBT+ people feared there would be a backlash from groups that opposed the law, though no significant incidents were reported on by year's end.

POLITICAL RIGHTS: 3 / 40

A. ELECTORAL PROCESS: 0 / 12

A1. Was the current head of government or other chief national authority elected through free and fair elections? 0 / 4

The president, who wields executive authority, is elected by popular vote for seven-year terms. Presidential term limits were abolished in 2003. The president nominates and can dismiss the prime minister at will.

The August 2016 presidential election pitted incumbent Ali Bongo Ondimba against Jean Ping of the opposition Union of Forces for Change (UFC). The electoral commission declared Bongo the winner with 49.8 percent of the vote, compared with 48.2 percent for Ping. In Haut-Ogooué Province, a Bongo family stronghold, the commission claimed a turnout rate of 99.9 percent, with 95 percent for Bongo, even though turnout in the rest of the country was just 54 percent. Both Ping and observers from the European Union (EU) called for a recount.

Meanwhile, violent protests erupted, and security forces stormed Ping's headquarters. Although the government claimed the death toll from the unrest was under 10, journalists and opposition leaders estimated that more than 50 people had died, and hundreds were arrested.

The Constitutional Court, headed by a longtime Bongo family ally, rebuffed an observation mission from the African Union (AU) during the recount. Following the recount, the president was credited with 50.66 percent of the vote, leaving Ping with 47.24 percent. Ping rejected the results.

A2. Were the current national legislative representatives elected through free and fair elections? 0 / 4

Gabon's Parliament consists of the National Assembly, whose members are elected by popular vote for five-year terms, and the Senate, which is indirectly elected by regional and municipal officials for six-year terms. Under the 2018 constitution, the size of the National Assembly increased from 120 to 143 seats, and the Senate was set to decrease in size from 102 to 52 members at its next elections, originally scheduled for December 2020 but postponed to early 2021. The most recent Senate elections were held in 2014, with Bongo's Gabonese Democratic Party (PDG) claiming 81 seats.

National Assembly elections were originally due in 2016 but were repeatedly postponed. The incumbent assembly was finally dissolved in April 2018, leaving the Senate as the only legislative body for most of the year. The PDG claimed 98 seats in the National Assembly elections that October, which were boycotted by several opposition parties due to the government's failure to create a genuinely independent electoral commission. PDG allies won roughly 10 more seats, and no single party other than the PDG took more than 11. The elections were marked by credible allegations of fraud and repression. The president's eldest daughter was credited with more than 99 percent of the vote for the seat she won.

A3. Are the electoral laws and framework fair, and are they implemented impartially by the relevant election management bodies? 0 / 4

Gabon's electoral laws and framework do not ensure credible elections. The electoral commission, the Interior Ministry, and the Constitutional Court all play important roles in managing elections, and all are widely seen as loyal to the president.

In January 2018, Parliament gave its final approval to constitutional amendments that were developed in an opaque process without meaningful input from opposition parties or civil society. Among other changes, the amendments introduced a runoff system for presidential elections if no candidate wins a majority in the first round, and required ministers to pledge allegiance to the president. Lawmakers rejected opposition proposals including the imposition of presidential term limits.

B. POLITICAL PLURALISM AND PARTICIPATION: 2 / 16

B1. Do the people have the right to organize in different political parties or other competitive political groupings of their choice, and is the system free of undue obstacles to the rise and fall of these competing parties or groupings? 1 / 4

The PDG dominates the nominally multiparty system. Opposition parties remain fragmented, and the government has disrupted their activities by denying them permits for public gatherings, arresting participants in their largely peaceful protests, and incarcerating their leaders.

B2. Is there a realistic opportunity for the opposition to increase its support or gain power through elections? 0 / 4

The PDG has monopolized the executive branch since the 1960s, and there is no realistic opportunity for the opposition to gain power through elections. In 2017, Ping called for a civil disobedience campaign, arguing that he had exhausted all institutional remedies for the fraudulent 2016 election. He and some other opposition leaders boycotted the 2018 National Assembly elections.

B3. Are the people's political choices free from domination by forces that are external to the political sphere, or by political forces that employ extrapolitical means? 0 / 4

The Bongo family and its associates have acquired enormous wealth and economic control after decades in power. These resources are allegedly used to sustain political patronage networks and fund vote-buying during elections. The leadership also relies on security forces to intimidate the opposition. Ahead of the 2018 National Assembly elections, there were some reports of opposition candidates and supporters being detained and threatened with violence.

B4. Do various segments of the population (including ethnic, racial, religious, gender, LGBT+, and other relevant groups) have full political rights and electoral opportunities? 1 / 4

Ethnic minorities have little ability to organize independently and gain political representation, given the dominance of the PDG. Key government and military posts are held by loyalists from the major ethnic groups. Though Parliament decriminalized homosexuality in 2020, LGBT+ people are not openly represented politically, in practice.

In July 2020, Rose Christiane Ossouka Raponda of the PDG became the first woman appointed prime minister in Gabon.

C. FUNCTIONING OF GOVERNMENT: 1 / 12

C1. Do the freely elected head of government and national legislative representatives determine the policies of the government? 0 / 4

Government policy is set by the president and his senior aides. President Bongo suffered a massive stroke in October 2018, and his cognitive fitness for office remains uncertain. In November 2018, the Constitutional Court unilaterally altered the constitution to allow the vice president to assume some of the president's functions if he is "temporarily unavailable." The constitution had only provided for the president's permanent incapacitation, in which case the Senate president would serve as interim president and an election would be called within 60 days.

Parliament is dominated by the PDG and provides little oversight of the executive branch.

C2. Are safeguards against official corruption strong and effective? 1 / 4

Both corruption and impunity remain major problems. Authorities have reportedly used anticorruption efforts to target regime opponents. In 2017, the government criticized an ongoing French corruption probe focused on Marie-Madeleine Mborantsuo, a Bongo family ally who serves as president of the Constitutional Court. A special criminal court for cases involving the theft of public funds was established in 2018, but critics say prosecutions remain selective. In January 2020, civil society organizations filed a lawsuit in Libreville accusing Noureddin Bongo of corruption and money laundering. The public prosecutor dismissed the complaint in February.

Brice Laccruche Alihanga, who was dismissed as the president's chief of staff in November 2019, was charged with corruption and incarcerated in late 2019. Lawyers representing Laccruche filed a lawsuit in French courts in January 2020 against an unidentified party—likely, against Noureddin Bongo—for his arbitrary detention and death threats.

C3. Does the government operate with openness and transparency? 0 / 4

The government operates with minimal transparency. The presidency's budget is not subject to the same oversight as those for other institutions. High-level civil servants are required to disclose their assets, but the declarations are not made public. The government has refused to disclose any information about Bongo's health condition, despite sustained public demands and efforts to position his son, Noureddin Bongo Valentin—who was appointed General Coordinator of Presidential Affairs in 2019—to compete in the 2023 presidential elections.

CIVIL LIBERTIES: 19 / 60

D. FREEDOM OF EXPRESSION AND BELIEF: 8 / 16

D1. Are there free and independent media? 1 / 4

Press freedom is guaranteed by law but is restricted in practice, and self-censorship to avoid legal repercussions for critical reporting is common. The 2017 communications code contains provisions that restricted media freedom, including an obligation for media to promote "the country's image and national cohesion."

A new state media regulator created in February 2018, the High Authority of Communication (HAC), imposed suspensions on three news outlets in August 2018 in response to reporting on government corruption, and another newspaper was suspended for three months that November for an article on President Bongo's health. In April 2020, the HAC suspended the news site Gabon Media Time for three months after its representatives ignored a summons to attend an HAC meeting on a libel complaint; the HAC had suspended the site for a month in July 2019 after it criticized Gabon's hospitals' financial management. Landry Amiang Washington, an activist blogger arrested in 2016, was released from prison in January 2020.

D2. Are individuals free to practice and express their religious faith or nonbelief in public and private? 3 / 4

Although religious freedom is enshrined in the constitution and generally respected, some heterodox religious groups reportedly have difficulty obtaining registration from the government.

D3. Is there academic freedom, and is the educational system free from extensive political indoctrination? 2 / 4

Omar Bongo University, Gabon's main center for tertiary education, is state run, and academic freedom there is tenuous. Professors are believed to self-censor to protect their positions and avoid conflicts with the authorities.

D4. Are individuals free to express their personal views on political or other sensitive topics without fear of surveillance or retribution? 2 / 4

Ordinary individuals' freedom to express criticism of the government is limited by restrictive laws and deterred by the authorities' surveillance and detention of opposition figures and activists.

E. ASSOCIATIONAL AND ORGANIZATIONAL RIGHTS: 3 / 12
E1. Is there freedom of assembly? 1 / 4

Freedom of assembly is limited. In recent years the government has repeatedly denied permits for meetings, used tear gas, and arrested demonstrators to disperse unauthorized gatherings. A 2017 law further limited the freedom to assemble, in part by making organizers responsible for offenses committed during a public gathering.

E2. Is there freedom for nongovernmental organizations, particularly those that are engaged in human rights- and governance-related work? 1 / 4

Relatively few nongovernmental organizations (NGOs) are able to operate in Gabon. Freedom of association is guaranteed by the constitution, but the process for formally registering NGOs is onerous and implemented inconsistently, leaving groups vulnerable to accusations that they are not in compliance with the law.

E3. Is there freedom for trade unions and similar professional or labor organizations? 1 / 4

Workers are legally permitted to join unions, engage in collective bargaining, and strike, but the government has disrupted sit-ins and other labor activism in recent years, and has arrested participants.

F. RULE OF LAW: 3 / 16
F1. Is there an independent judiciary? 0 / 4

The courts are subordinate to the president. The judiciary is accountable to the Ministry of Justice, through which the president has the power to appoint and dismiss judges. Under the amended constitution, the country's highest judicial body, the Constitutional Court, is composed of three members appointed by the president, two by the National Assembly, one by the Senate, and three by the Superior Council of the Judiciary, which itself is headed by the president and justice minister. The 2018 constitution also created a new special court, the Court of Justice of the Republic, which alone has the authority to judge top executive and judicial officials. It consists of seven members appointed by the Superior Council of the Judiciary and six members of Parliament. The Constitutional Court is headed by a longtime Bongo family ally.

In August 2019, a Libreville appellate court agreed to hear a lawsuit filed by civil society groups that would have required President Bongo to undergo a medical exam to determine his fitness for office. The government suspended the judge who made the ruling and blocked the proceedings. In February 2020, the government similarly refused to hear a lawsuit brought forward the previous month by civil society activists charging Noureddin Bongo with corruption.

F2. Does due process prevail in civil and criminal matters? 1 / 4

Legal safeguards against arbitrary arrest and detention are not upheld by police, and detainees are often denied access to lawyers. Lengthy pretrial detention is common. Cases of arbitrary arrests linked to opposition activism have reportedly increased since the 2016 election crisis. Several detained opposition figures have been denied due process, and prisoners have occasionally died in state custody.

F3. Is there protection from the illegitimate use of physical force and freedom from war and insurgencies? 1 / 4

Prison conditions are harsh, and facilities are severely overcrowded, with limited access to proper medical care. Torture is outlawed by the constitution, but detainees and inmates continue to face physical abuse. In January, former head of the state-run Gabon Oil Company Patrichi Christian Tanasa, in prison as the result of a corruption investigation, alleged that he had been tortured and sexually assaulted while in custody. Violent crime and ritual killings remain serious concerns in Gabon.

F4. Do laws, policies, and practices guarantee equal treatment of various segments of the population? 1 / 4

The country's large population of noncitizen African immigrants is subject to harassment and extortion, including by police. Members of some minority groups reportedly experience discrimination in the workplace and often live in extreme poverty.

Women have equal legal rights on some issues but face significant de facto discrimination in employment and other economic matters. Sexual harassment in the workplace, which is not prohibited by law, is reportedly common.

In June 2020, the government passed a law decriminalizing homosexuality. Some LGBT+ people feared that there would be a backlash from groups that opposed the law. Same-sex marriage remains illegal and LGBT+ individuals are still subject to widespread social stigma. Those who are open about their gender identity or sexual orientation risk housing and employment discrimination.

G. PERSONAL AUTONOMY AND INDIVIDUAL RIGHTS: 5 / 16

G1. Do individuals enjoy freedom of movement, including the ability to change their place of residence, employment, or education? 2 / 4

There are no laws restricting internal travel, but police often monitor travelers at checkpoints and demand bribes. Married women seeking to obtain a passport or travel abroad must have permission from their husbands. The government has imposed travel bans on opposition leaders in recent years.

G2. Are individuals able to exercise the right to own property and establish private businesses without undue interference from state or nonstate actors? 1 / 4

Bureaucratic and judicial delays can pose difficulties for businesses. Enforcement of contracts and property rights is weak, and the process for property registration is lengthy. Bongo and his associates play a dominant role in the economy, impairing fair competition and favoring those with connections to the leadership.

G3. Do individuals enjoy personal social freedoms, including choice of marriage partner and size of family, protection from domestic violence, and control over appearance? 1 / 4

Personalized forms of violence are believed to be widespread, and perpetrators generally enjoy impunity. Rape and domestic abuse are rarely reported to authorities or prosecuted. Spousal rape is not specifically prohibited. Abortion is a punishable crime under most circumstances. The minimum age for marriage is 15 for women and 18 for men. The civil code states that a wife must obey her husband as the head of household.

G4. Do individuals enjoy equality of opportunity and freedom from economic exploitation? 1 / 4

Wage standards and laws against forced labor are poorly enforced, particularly in the informal sector and with respect to foreign workers. Both adults and children are exploited in a number of different occupations, and foreign women are trafficked to Gabon for prostitution or domestic servitude.

The Gambia

Population: 2,400,000
Capital: Banjul
Freedom Status: Partly Free
Electoral Democracy: No

Overview: The Gambia was ruled for over two decades by former president Yahya Jammeh, who consistently violated political rights and civil liberties. The 2016 election resulted in a surprise victory for opposition candidate Adama Barrow. Fundamental freedoms including the rights to free assembly, association, and expression initially improved thereafter, but the progress toward the consolidation of the rule of law is slow. The Barrow government has faced increasing criticism over corruption. LGBT+ individuals face severe discrimination and violence against women remains a serious problem.

KEY DEVELOPMENTS IN 2020

- In January, authorities forcefully dispersed a Banjul demonstration against President Barrow's decision to remain in office beyond a three-year timetable. Authorities arrested 137 people including high-ranking members of the Three Years Jotna (Three Years Is Enough) pressure group; the group was banned that

month and eight members received charges including rioting, which remained pending at year's end.
* In September, legislators rejected a draft constitution that would have introduced term limits for presidents.
* President Barrow imposed a COVID-19-related state of emergency in March, which expired in September. Public assemblies were restricted in March and a curfew was instituted in August, though most restrictions were rescinded or loosened by year's end. The authorities reported nearly 3,800 cases and 124 deaths to the World Health Organization at year's end.

POLITICAL RIGHTS: 20 / 40
A. ELECTORAL PROCESS: 7 / 12
A1. Was the current head of government or other chief national authority elected through free and fair elections? 2 / 4

The president is directly elected to a five-year term and faces no term limits. International observers were not allowed into The Gambia ahead of the 2016 presidential election. The Independent Electoral Commission (IEC) nevertheless conducted an impartial vote count, and declared that Adama Barrow, the candidate of an opposition coalition, won.

President Jammeh initially conceded defeat, but reversed his position, and had not stepped down by the time Barrow was inaugurated in Senegal in early 2017. The Economic Community of West African States (ECOWAS) mobilized troops under a previous authorization to intervene militarily if a peaceful transfer of power did not begin by the last day of Jammeh's mandate. Within days of its deployment, Jammeh conceded defeat and left the country, allowing Barrow to take office.

A2. Were the current national legislative representatives elected through free and fair elections? 3 / 4

Of the 58 members of the unicameral National Assembly, 53 are elected by popular vote and the remainder are appointed by the president; members serve five-year terms. The 2017 parliamentary elections were transparent, peaceful, and neutrally managed. Weaknesses included low turnout, incomplete updating of the voter registry, and poor organization of vote-collation processes. Nevertheless, most polling stations operated on time and vote counting was transparent. The United Democratic Party (UDP), which had backed Barrow and had previously been in opposition, won 31 seats and an absolute majority.

The IEC delayed a legislative by-election scheduled for April 2020 to November because of the COVID-19 pandemic. The Barrow-led National People's Party (NPP) gained that seat. Local residents accused the NPP of buying votes and misusing government resources.

A3. Are the electoral laws and framework fair, and are they implemented impartially by the relevant election management bodies? 2 / 4

The IEC adequately managed the 2017 National Assembly elections and 2018 local elections but faces serious challenges. Election observers have called for improvements to voter registration processes, improved polling station conditions, standardized counting and collation processes, and the redrawing of election district boundaries.

In late 2019, the Constitutional Review Commission released a draft of a new constitution, which would have introduced term limits for presidents. However, the National Assembly did not adopt the draft in a September 2020 vote. Later that month, the government introduced a draft electoral bill that would eliminate a directly elected legislative seat, among other provisions. The varying sizes of legislative districts were not addressed in the bill, which remained under consideration at year's end.

B. POLITICAL PLURALISM AND PARTICIPATION: 9 / 16
B1. Do the people have the right to organize in different political parties or other competitive political groupings of their choice, and is the system free of undue obstacles to the rise and fall of these competing parties or groupings? 2 / 4

There were 16 political parties registered in The Gambia as of February 2020. To register a new party, organizers must pay a 1 million dalasi ($19,000) registration fee and garner the signatures of 10,000 registered voters, with at least 1,000 from each of the country's regions. Parties centered on a particular religion, ethnicity, or region are banned. Parties are required to submit annual audits to the IEC.

Prior to the 2016 presidential election, Jammeh's Alliance for Patriotic Reorientation and Construction (APRC) had long dominated politics. The UDP subsequently became the dominant party before Barrow split from party leader Ousainou Darboe. In late 2019, the IEC approved the NPP's formation.

B2. Is there a realistic opportunity for the opposition to increase its support or gain power through elections? 3 / 4

The UDP won a legislative majority in 2017, displacing the APRC. However, the UDP split from Barrow, who went on to launch the NPP, in late 2019. The UDP also expelled eight legislators for reportedly supporting Barrow's decision to serve a full term that November; Barrow was originally expected to step down by January 2020, in line with the timetable agreed by the coalition that backed him, but ultimately did not do so.

In November 2020, Barrow stated that he would consider bringing the NPP into an alliance with the APRC or the UDP ahead of the scheduled 2021 presidential election.

B3. Are the people's political choices free from domination by forces that are external to the political sphere, or by political forces that employ extrapolitical means? 2 / 4

While Gambians' political choices are freer from the undue dominance of unelected groups since Jammeh's 22-year rule ended, military forces and foreign powers remain influential in Gambian politics.

The ECOWAS Mission in The Gambia (ECOMIG) was originally scheduled to end in 2018, but its mandate has been repeatedly extended at the request of the Barrow government to facilitate security-sector reform, and due to ongoing concerns that pro-Jammeh loyalists in the military could cause political instability. Barrow most recently requested an extension of the ECOMIG mission in September 2020, which ECOWAS agreed to.

B4. Do various segments of the population (including ethnic, racial, religious, gender, LGBT+, and other relevant groups) have full political rights and electoral opportunities? 2 / 4

While political rights and electoral opportunities have improved, women remain underrepresented in politics. The National Assembly elected in 2017 included the first-ever woman speaker and parliamentarian living with disabilities; both were presidential appointees. Only five women held National Assembly seats in 2020.

There is concern that Gambian politics are being defined by ethnic divisions. Ethnic tensions escalated toward the end of the Jammeh regime, with the former president criticizing members of the plurality Mandinka ethnic group before leaving office. Members of the Jola ethnic group were subsequently perceived as supporting the APRC, while Mandinkas were perceived as supporting the UDP.

C. FUNCTIONING OF GOVERNMENT: 4 / 12

C1. Do the freely elected head of government and national legislative representatives determine the policies of the government? 2 / 4

Nonstate actors, armed forces, and foreign governments do not appear to enjoy preponderant influence over the Barrow government.

President Barrow imposed a COVID-19-related state of emergency in March 2020 and issued an executive order to extend it in May, after losing a legislative vote on the matter that month. The state of emergency ended in September.

C2. Are safeguards against official corruption strong and effective? 1 / 4

The Barrow government has undertaken limited initiatives to reduce corruption, which remains a serious problem. Allegations of corruption by officials at all levels of government are frequently lodged, and both state and semistate agencies face allegations of improperly funneling money to private citizens. While legislators adopted anticorruption legislation in 2019, an envisioned anticorruption commission has not yet been finalized.

In October 2020, news outlet Malagen reported that the Fisheries Ministry's permanent secretary, Bamba Banja, accepted bribes from Chinese fishing companies over a three-year period. Banja was suspended from his post, and a police investigation remained open as of December.

C3. Does the government operate with openness and transparency? 1 / 4

Government operations are generally opaque. Government officials must make asset declarations to the ombudsman, but declarations are not open to public and media scrutiny. There are widespread allegations of corruption in public procurement. Key licensing processes, especially for industries reliant on natural resources, are not transparent.

CIVIL LIBERTIES: 26 / 60

D. FREEDOM OF EXPRESSION AND BELIEF: 8 / 16

D1. Are there free and independent media? 2 / 4

The media environment has improved under the Barrow administration. More people are entering the profession, exiled journalists have returned to the country, and there has been a proliferation of private print, online, radio, and television outlets. In 2019, the government exempted print media from a levy that media groups argued was designed to restrict press freedom. Nevertheless, some restrictive media laws remain in effect, and some have been upheld by courts. Reports of harassment of journalists by police continue.

In January 2020, journalists Pa Modou Bojang and Gibbi Jallow were arrested along with two radio technicians, and radio stations Home Digital FM and King FM were shuttered for reporting on demonstrations against President Barrow's continued tenure in office. All four individuals were released from custody, though Bojang and Jallow received incitement charges.

D2. Are individuals free to practice and express their religious faith or nonbelief in public and private? 2 / 4

The Barrow government has maintained that The Gambia is a secular society in which all faiths can practice freely. In practice, non-Sunni Islamic groups experience discrimination. Ahmadiyya Muslims have been publicly denounced as non-Muslims by the quasigovernmental Supreme Islamic Council, and a 2015 fatwa by the council denied Ahmadiyya burial rights in Muslim ceremonies. The 2019 draft constitution, which did not attain legislative approval in 2020, omitted a reference to The Gambia as a secular country, prompting concern among civil society.

D3. Is there academic freedom, and is the educational system free from extensive political indoctrination? 2 / 4

Academic freedom was severely limited at the University of The Gambia under Jammeh. However, since Barrow took office, the environment for the free exchange of ideas among students and professors has improved, despite lingering challenges. Lecturers still face political pressure.

D4. Are individuals free to express their personal views on political or other sensitive topics without fear of surveillance or retribution? 2 / 4

Gambians have more freedom to express political views under the Barrow administration. However, sedition laws remain on the books, which some analysts argued could be used to criminalize criticism of the government on social media. The government considered criminalizing statements deemed offensive or insulting to public officials in 2019, but refrained from officially proposing it after a leak of the draft language provoked public outcry.

E. ASSOCIATIONAL AND ORGANIZATIONAL RIGHTS: 6 / 12
E1. Is there freedom of assembly? 2 / 4

The constitution guarantees freedom of assembly, but the Public Order Act (POA), which was used by Jammeh to restrict protests, remains in force. Under the POA, permits from the police inspector general are required for public assemblies.

Three Years Jotna, a pressure group that called for President Barrow to step down in line with his original three-year timetable, organized an approved January 2020 demonstration in Banjul. However, participants faced a violent response from the authorities after deviating from their original route, with security forces using tear gas and physically attacking demonstrators. The authorities arrested 137 people, including high-ranking Three Years Jotna members. The group itself was banned later in January and eight of its members received charges including rioting and unlawful assembly, which remained pending at year's end.

President Barrow imposed a COVID-19-related state of emergency in March 2020, banning public assemblies. Other social gatherings were banned in August. Most pandemic-related restrictions were rescinded or relaxed by year's end, however.

E2. Is there freedom for nongovernmental organizations, particularly those that are engaged in human rights- and governance-related work? 2 / 4

There are a number of nongovernmental organizations (NGOs) in The Gambia focused on human rights and governance issues. NGO workers faced detention and other reprisals under Jammeh.

While there have been relatively few reports of such suppression under Barrow, human rights advocate Madi Jobarteh did face false-news charges in June 2020, after he criticized the government's handling of cases where individuals were allegedly killed by ECOMIG and government personnel. While the charges were dropped in July, Jobarteh was told that he was under government surveillance that month.

Environmental groups have reported harassment by security forces.

E3. Is there freedom for trade unions and similar professional or labor organizations? 2 / 4

Workers—except for civil servants, household workers, and security forces—may form unions, strike, and bargain for wages, but the labor minister has the discretion to exclude other categories of workers. The Gambia has multiple trade unions that operate without government restrictions, although several lack organization and funds.

F. RULE OF LAW: 6 / 16

F1. Is there an independent judiciary? 2 / 4

The Barrow government has taken steps to improve the judiciary, which was hampered by Jammeh-era corruption and inefficiency. These steps include ending the use of contract judges, the establishment of additional courts to address the backlog of cases, and giving courts greater budgetary autonomy. The government also reconstituted the Judicial Service Commission, which appoints lower-court magistrates and advises the president on higher-level appointments, court efficiency, and operations. Nonetheless, the executive still dominates judicial appointments. The Supreme Court showed independence of the Barrow government when it ruled against its efforts to appoint a National Assembly member in January 2020.

F2. Does due process prevail in civil and criminal matters? 1 / 4

Constitutional due process guarantees remain poorly upheld. While political dissidents faced less risk of arrest and prosecution during the Barrow administration, high-ranking members of Three Years Jotna did face criminal charges after organizing an anti-Barrow protest in January 2020.

The government has taken steps to arrest and prosecute security officers responsible for Jammeh-era human rights abuses. In August 2020, Nyima Sonko, the widow of UDP official Ebrima Solo Sandeng, criticized the government over a lack of progress in investigating his 2016 death in detention.

F3. Is there protection from the illegitimate use of physical force and freedom from war and insurgencies? 2 / 4

The use of illegitimate physical force by security agents has been less frequent under the Barrow administration. There have been some attempts to improve prison conditions, though they remain dire. A Human Rights Commission began operating in 2019 after commissioners were appointed.

The Truth, Reconciliation, and Reparations Commission, established in 2018 to investigate Jammeh-era human rights abuses, continued to hold hearings in 2020. However, testimony has not yet led to any prosecutions, and the release of some perpetrators has been controversial.

F4. Do laws, policies, and practices guarantee equal treatment of various segments of the population? 1 / 4

Several groups encounter serious difficulties in exercising their human rights. Legal protections for disabled persons require strengthening and enforcement. LGBT+ people face severe societal discrimination, and same-sex relations remain criminalized. The 1997 constitution prohibits discrimination, but this "does not apply in respect to adoption, marriage, divorce, burial, and devolution of property upon death."

G. PERSONAL AUTONOMY AND INDIVIDUAL RIGHTS: 6 / 16

G1. Do individuals enjoy freedom of movement, including the ability to change their place of residence, employment, or education? 2 / 4

There are no legal restrictions on freedom to change one's place of residence or employment. In practice, the endurance of strong kinship networks, unclear land-ownership rules, and economic speculation impact Gambians' ability to change residence.

Travel was restricted by the pandemic-related state of emergency in March 2020, with the land border with Senegal closed and nonmedical flights banned. A nationwide curfew was introduced in August but expired by December.

G2. Are individuals able to exercise the right to own property and establish private businesses without undue interference from state or nonstate actors? 2 / 4

Gambian law provides formal protection of property rights, although Sharia (Islamic law) provisions on family law and inheritance can facilitate discrimination against women. Corruption hampers legitimate business activity. Land ownership is a contentious issue in The Gambia, with conflicts sometimes escalating into violence. These disputes are exacerbated by unclear division of responsibilities between traditional and state authorities.

G3. Do individuals enjoy personal social freedoms, including choice of marriage partner and size of family, protection from domestic violence, and control over appearance? 1 / 4

Rape and domestic violence are illegal, but common. There are no laws prohibiting polygamy or levirate marriage, in which a widow is married off to the younger brother of her spouse. Female genital mutilation (FGM) was outlawed in 2015, but is still practiced by some; there is evidence that rates of FGM and child marriage have increased since the end of the Jammeh regime. The Barrow government has undertaken steps to address child marriage and gender-based violence (GBV) and announced a national campaign to address domestic and sexual violence in December 2020.

G4. Do individuals enjoy equality of opportunity and freedom from economic exploitation? 1 / 4

Enforcement of labor laws is inconsistent. Women enjoy less access to higher education, justice, and employment than men. Although child labor and forced labor are illegal, some women and children are subject to sex trafficking, domestic servitude, and forced begging.

In the 2020 edition of its *Trafficking in Persons Report*, the US State Department noted the government's efforts to identify trafficking victims and improve security at shelters, but also reported that the government did not secure a trafficking conviction during the reporting year. The government launched a "zero tolerance" policy to combat trafficking in January, vowing to assign more investigators and better document trafficking cases.

Georgia

Population: 3,700,000
Capital: Tbilisi
Freedom Status: Partly Free
Electoral Democracy: Yes

Note: The numerical scores and status listed above do not reflect conditions in Abkhazia and South Ossetia, which are examined in separate reports. *Freedom in the World* reports assess the level of political rights and civil liberties in a given geographical area, regardless of whether they are affected by the state, nonstate actors, or foreign powers. Disputed territories are sometimes assessed separately if they meet certain criteria, including boundaries that are sufficiently stable to allow year-on-year comparisons. For more information, see the report methodology and FAQ.

Overview: Georgia holds regular and competitive elections. Its democratic trajectory showed signs of improvement during the period surrounding a change in government in 2012–13, but recent years have featured backsliding. Oligarchic influence affects the country's political affairs, policy decisions, and media environment, and the rule of law is undermined by politicization. Civil liberties are inconsistently protected.

KEY DEVELOPMENTS IN 2020

- Parliament introduced a new mixed electoral system in June, which was implemented in the elections held that autumn. Under the new system, most seats are filled through proportional representation, and the vote threshold for entering Parliament via proportional representation was lowered from 5 percent to 1 percent.
- The ruling Georgian Dream party won a third term in government in the October and November parliamentary elections, though the contest was marred by vote buying, instances of violence, and apparent tabulation errors that prompted an opposition boycott of the November runoff. Voter turnout in that round stood at 26 percent, the lowest since independence.
- Movement and travel restrictions were in force between March and May as part of the government's response to the COVID-19 pandemic, and were reintroduced in November as case counts rose. While the restrictions were largely proportionate to the threat, progovernment businesspeople notably won public-health procurement tenders as the pandemic progressed.

POLITICAL RIGHTS: 23 / 40 (−1)

A. ELECTORAL PROCESS: 7 / 12 (−1)

A1. Was the current head of government or other chief national authority elected through free and fair elections? 2 / 4

Georgia has a dual executive, with the prime minister serving as head of government and the president as head of state. Under constitutional changes approved in 2017, the president elected in 2018 is to serve a six-year term, after which a 300-member electoral college comprising national lawmakers and regional and local officials will choose presidents.

In 2018, Salome Zourabichvili, an independent former foreign minister supported by Georgian Dream, won about 60 percent of the vote in the second round of the presidential election, defeating Grigol Vashadze, a former foreign minister running for the opposition United National Movement (UNM). While the electoral environment was largely peaceful, significant problems in the preelection period and voter intimidation on election day marred the quality of the runoff. Abuse of administrative resources and limited instances of vote buying and ballot-box stuffing were reported. Outside many voting stations, the presence of Georgian Dream activists created an intimidating atmosphere. Just days before the runoff, a charitable foundation controlled by former prime minister Bidzina Ivanishvili, the Georgian Dream chairman, promised to write off the debts of over 600,000 Georgians—about one in six eligible voters.

The president formally appoints the prime minister, whom Parliament nominates. Giorgi Gakharia, the prime minister since September 2019, was reappointed in December 2020 after Georgian Dream won that year's parliamentary elections.

A2. Were the current national legislative representatives elected through free and fair elections? 2 / 4 (−1)

The unicameral Parliament is composed of 150 members, with 120 selected through nationwide proportional representation and 30 directly elected in single-member districts. This system was introduced in June 2020; previously, nearly half of lawmakers were elected in single-member districts. All members serve four-year terms.

In the October parliamentary elections and November runoffs, Georgian Dream won 90 seats, including all 30 single-member district seats. The UNM-led coalition won 36, all via proportional representation, and seven smaller groups won the remaining seats. Election observers, including the Organization for Security and Co-operation in Europe (OSCE) Office for Democratic Institutions and Human Rights (ODIHR), considered the vote competitive but noted numerous shortcomings, including the use of administrative resources, vote buying, interference with observers, disorganized precinct-level electoral commissions, preelection violence, limited instances of election-day violence, violations of voting secrecy, and intimidation of government employees, party activists, and voters.

After the first round, preliminary Central Election Commission (CEC) figures showed some Georgian Dream candidates winning over 100 percent of the votes in their races, which the commission blamed on a technical error. A parallel tabulation from the International Society for Fair Elections and Democracy (ISFED), a nongovernmental organization (NGO), suggested major discrepancies, though ISFED disclosed an error in its own data in December.

In early November, opposition parties announced a boycott of that month's runoff and refused to enter the new Parliament. Voter turnout for the runoff stood at 26 percent, the lowest recorded since independence. Georgian Dream responded in December by introducing legislation that would deny public funding and free media airtime to parties that boycott Parliament sessions. The public defender's office and the US ambassador to Georgia criticized the bill, which remained under consideration at year's end.

Score Change: The score declined from 3 to 2 due to significant shortcomings in the year's elections, including voter intimidation, misuse of administrative resources, vote buying, election-related violence, and apparent tabulation discrepancies, which prompted opposition parties to boycott the runoff.

A3. Are the electoral laws and framework fair, and are they implemented impartially by the relevant election management bodies? 3 / 4

The country's electoral laws are generally fair, and the bodies that implement them have typically done so impartially. However, Georgian Dream's dominance in precinct-level commissions, complicated complaints procedures, and short timelines for filing complaints impair election quality.

The current electoral system for Parliament was introduced in June 2020 and implemented for the first time in the October and November elections. The new system expanded the use of proportional representation and reduced the vote threshold for entering Parliament via proportional representation from 5 percent to 1 percent.

Under 2017 constitutional amendments, Parliament was set to be elected through a fully proportional system beginning in 2024. Georgian Dream offered to accelerate the new system's introduction after major protests in June 2019, but the necessary constitutional amendments were rejected in Parliament that November.

B. POLITICAL PLURALISM AND PARTICIPATION: 9 / 16

B1. Do the people have the right to organize in different political parties or other competitive political groupings of their choice, and is the system free of undue obstacles to the rise and fall of these competing parties or groupings? 2 / 4

Georgia hosts a dynamic multiparty system, and new political parties have often been able to form and operate without major obstacles. However, a pattern of single-party dominance since the 2000s has inhibited the development and stability of competing groups. In July 2019, Mamuka Khazaradze, the founder of one of Georgia's largest banks, and his business partner were charged with money laundering two weeks after Khazaradze stated his intention to form a political party. That party, Lelo for Georgia, won four seats in the October and November 2020 parliamentary elections, though Khazaradze himself remained under investigation as recently as October.

B2. Is there a realistic opportunity for the opposition to increase its support or gain power through elections? 3 / 4

Georgia last underwent a peaceful transfer of power between rival groups in 2012–13, when Georgian Dream defeated the UNM in parliamentary and presidential elections. A faction of the UNM split off in 2017, leaving behind two smaller parties that were less capable of mounting a credible opposition challenge. Georgian Dream won most mayoral and gubernatorial posts, including the Tbilisi mayoralty, that year.

While smaller parties could more easily enter Parliament in 2020 due to the new 1 percent vote threshold, their fragmentation limits their ability to form coalitions and attain power.

B3. Are the people's political choices free from domination by forces that are external to the political sphere, or by political forces that employ extrapolitical means? 2 / 4

Ivanishvili, the wealthy businessman who founded Georgian Dream in 2011, resigned as party chairman and premier in 2013, but remained the party's primary financial backer and continued to control it informally. His successors as prime minister and party chairman were close confidants and former employees. Ivanishvili was reelected as chairman of Georgian Dream at a party congress in 2018, and he remained in that post at the end of 2020.

Recent elections have featured allegations of various forms of vote buying and intimidation, including pressure on public employees and recipients of social benefits to support the ruling party.

B4. Do various segments of the population (including ethnic, racial, religious, gender, LGBT+, and other relevant groups) have full political rights and electoral opportunities? 2 / 4

No laws prevent women or ethnic and religious minorities from participating in politics. Electoral reforms introduced in June 2020 included a gender quota for the proportional representation component of parliamentary elections; at least one in every four candidates on a party's list must be a woman. Nevertheless, women and minority groups and their interests remain underrepresented at all levels of government. Although a woman did become president in 2018, women won only 31 seats in the 2020 parliamentary elections. Ethnic minority groups make up an estimated 13 percent of the population, with ethnic Armenians and Azerbaijanis forming the largest communities. Some 17 candidates from these groups ran in the 2020 elections, though only a fraction of them won seats.

C. FUNCTIONING OF GOVERNMENT: 7 / 12

C1. Do the freely elected head of government and national legislative representatives determine the policies of the government? 2 / 4

The ability of elected officials to determine and implement government policy is impaired by the informal role of Ivanishvili, who holds no government office but exerts significant influence over executive and legislative decision-making. His de facto authority was demonstrated in 2018, when Prime Minister Giorgi Kvirikashvili resigned due to disagreements with Ivanishvili.

Ivanishvili's policy influence has also been visible in the authorities' generally favorable treatment of his financial and business interests, and in particular the multibillion-dollar Georgian Co-Investment Fund (GCF), which was unveiled in 2013 and is active in large real-estate development projects in Tbilisi.

C2. Are safeguards against official corruption strong and effective? 2 / 4

While petty corruption has become less common, corruption within government persists. In some cases, it has allegedly taken the form of nepotism or cronyism in government hiring and procurement. Effective application of anticorruption laws and regulations is impaired by a lack of independence among law enforcement bodies and the judiciary, and successful cases against high-ranking officials who are on good terms with the Georgian Dream leadership remain rare.

Businesspeople with links to Georgian Dream received COVID-19-related public contracts during 2020; between April and June, a contributor to President Zourabichvili's campaign received several tenders, including a $1.3 million deal with the Health Ministry. In April, a firm owned by another party supporter secured a contract to produce four million face masks for a foundation controlled by Ivanishvili.

C3. Does the government operate with openness and transparency? 3 / 4

Government operations are generally subject to scrutiny by auditing bodies, the media, civil society organizations, and the public. However, the Institute for the Development of Freedom of Information, a Georgian advocacy group, reports that access to public information has been uneven since 2010. While public officials do declare assets, the Georgia chapter of Transparency International (TI) warned in September 2020 that the monitoring of such declarations is inconsistent and does not focus on conflicts of interest or potential corruption.

CIVIL LIBERTIES: 37 / 60

D. FREEDOM OF EXPRESSION AND BELIEF: 10 / 16

D1. Are there free and independent media? 2 / 4

The media environment is pluralistic but partisan. The public broadcaster has been accused of favoring the government. Several staff members at Adjara TV and Radio, a publicly funded regional outlet, were dismissed or reassigned between March and July 2020 after Georgian Dream criticized the outlet's editorial stance and employees protested over political interference; at least some of the affected staff members were later reinstated after further protests.

In July 2019, a long-running legal dispute over the ownership of the opposition-aligned television station Rustavi 2 was decided at the European Court of Human Rights, leading to the station being transferred to a former owner who was more sympathetic to Georgian Dream. A newly appointed director then dismissed key employees. A large share of the staff quit to join a new station, Mtavari Arkhi (Main Channel), which began broadcasting in September 2019. Its founder, Giorgi Rurua, was subsequently arrested on gun possession charges, which were considered to be politically motivated, that November. Rurua received a four-year prison term in July 2020.

In December 2019, Facebook announced that it had taken down hundreds of Georgian accounts and pages for fraudulently posing as media outlets and news organizations. Their content supported the Georgian Dream government, and Facebook traced them to the government and a Georgian advertising agency. In May 2020, ISFED identified continued inauthentic pro–Georgian Dream social media activity.

D2. Are individuals free to practice and express their religious faith or nonbelief in public and private? 2 / 4

The constitution guarantees freedom of religion but grants unique privileges to the Georgian Orthodox Church. COVID-19-related gathering restrictions were not enforced against the church, though many congregants reportedly did not attend church ceremonies.

Georgia's religious minorities—among them Jehovah's Witnesses, Baptists, Pentecostals, and Muslims—have reported discrimination and hostility, including from Georgian Orthodox priests and adherents, and are insufficiently protected by the state.

D3. Is there academic freedom, and is the educational system free from extensive political indoctrination? 3 / 4

Academic freedom is generally respected. However, in August 2018, Georgian authorities froze the assets of the International Black Sea University and prevented it from accepting students for the new academic year, citing tax arrears that were allegedly owed by the institution. The asset freeze was eventually lifted that October after the debt was paid, though the university maintained that the tax claim was unlawful. The university is associated with the movement led by Turkish Islamic preacher Fethullah Gülen, which the Turkish government has declared a terrorist organization. In 2017, Georgian authorities closed two schools associated with the movement, citing regulatory violations. The seemingly disproportionate and arbitrary nature of the enforcement actions raised suspicions that they were carried out under Turkish pressure.

D4. Are individuals free to express their personal views on political or other sensitive topics without fear of surveillance or retribution? 3 / 4

Georgians generally enjoy freedom of expression, including in their online communications. However, watchdog groups have expressed concerns in recent years that various security-related laws empower state agencies to conduct surveillance and data collection without adequate oversight. A 2017 law created a new electronic surveillance agency under the umbrella of the State Security Service that would have the authority to fine service providers for failure to cooperate with its work. Privacy advocates questioned whether the law complied with earlier Constitutional Court rulings on state surveillance.

In recent years, multiple public figures—including opposition and ruling party politicians—have been subjected to intimidation through the threatened or actual release of surreptitiously recorded sex videos, contributing to an atmosphere that deters free expression on politics.

E. ASSOCIATIONAL AND ORGANIZATIONAL RIGHTS: 7 / 12
E1. Is there freedom of assembly? 2 / 4

Freedom of assembly is often respected, but police sometimes respond to demonstrations with excessive force. In November 2020, the police used water cannons to disperse largely peaceful demonstrators protesting apparent electoral violations outside the CEC building in Tbilisi. The public defender's office and other watchdogs called the use of water cannons excessive and illegal.

Water cannons, tear gas, and rubber bullets were previously used in June 2019, when protesters attempted to enter the Parliament building after a Russian lawmaker appeared in the speaker's chair to address an Interparliamentary Assembly on Orthodoxy meeting. Hundreds of people were injured. Police also used water cannons and tear gas to disperse protesters gathered outside Parliament that November, after the body failed to pass electoral reforms.

Separately in 2019, the government declined to guarantee protection for a planned LGBT+ pride rally in Tbilisi. In 2020, right-wing protesters gathered outside the offices of an LGBT+ pride organization and reportedly vandalized the building's exterior.

E2. Is there freedom for nongovernmental organizations, particularly those that are engaged in human rights- and governance-related work? 3 / 4

The civil society sector is fairly robust. Some groups are included in policy discussions, though others report facing political pressure, largely in the form of public criticism by government officials and opposition figures.

In January 2020, the judge presiding over the case against Giorgi Rurua refused an amicus curiae brief offered by the TI chapter in Georgia. The organization criticized the judge's conduct in a September statement, accusing him of demonstrating progovernment bias.

E3. Is there freedom for trade unions and similar professional or labor organizations? 2 / 4

Workers are legally allowed to organize, bargain collectively, and strike, though there are some restrictions on the right to strike, including a ban on strikes by certain categories of workers. Legal protections against antiunion discrimination by employers are weak and poorly enforced in practice.

F. RULE OF LAW: 8 / 16
F1. Is there an independent judiciary? 2 / 4

Despite ongoing judicial reforms, executive and legislative interference in the courts remains a substantial problem, as does a lack of transparency and professionalism surrounding judicial proceedings.

Under the constitutional framework that took effect after the 2018 presidential election, the High Council of Justice rather than the president nominates Supreme Court judges; Parliament then approves the judges. A judicial self-governing body elects most council members. In December 2018, the council presented a list of Supreme Court nominees, but a coalition of NGOs argued that it had used an opaque process and selected judges with tainted reputations. Later that month, the head of the legal affairs committee in Parliament resigned to protest what she called the "hasty and unacceptable" nomination process. In December 2019, Parliament ultimately confirmed 14 Supreme Court justices, though opposition members refused to participate. Observers from the Council of Europe and other institutions criticized the appointments, saying the candidates did not demonstrate the requisite knowledge or impartiality to serve.

Parliament passed further judicial reforms in September 2020, preempting an opinion from the Venice Commission of the Council of Europe. In an October statement, the council's representatives noted that some of its recommendations had been implemented, but criticized Parliament's decision to preempt the review, which the government had requested.

F2. Does due process prevail in civil and criminal matters? 2 / 4

The law guarantees due process, but the related safeguards are not always respected. The office of the country's public defender, or ombudsperson, has reported problems including a failure to fully implement Constitutional Court rulings on due process matters, administrative delays in court proceedings, the violation of the accused's right to a presumption of innocence, failure to observe rules surrounding detention and interrogation, and the denial of access to a lawyer upon arrest. A number of perceived opponents of the government have faced prosecutions in recent years that were widely seen as selective or politically motivated.

F3. Is there protection from the illegitimate use of physical force and freedom from war and insurgencies? 2 / 4

Human rights watchdogs and the ombudsperson continue to express concern about the physical abuse of detainees during arrest and in police custody, and have noted the lack of an independent system for supervising police conduct and addressing claims of mistreatment. A 2018 law established a new state inspector's office tasked with investigating police abuses, but it is not independent from the prosecutor's office, a shortcoming that drew criticism from human rights groups. The new office went into operation in November 2019. Violence and harsh conditions in prisons remain a problem.

F4. Do laws, policies, and practices guarantee equal treatment of various segments of the population? 2 / 4

A 2014 antidiscrimination law provides protection against discrimination on the basis of various factors, including race, gender, age, sexual orientation, and gender identity, but it is enforced unevenly. Women and people with disabilities suffer from discrimination in employment, among other problems. LGBT+ people face societal discrimination and are occasionally the targets of serious violence. Transgender people in particular receive little protection, and prosecutors rarely designate crimes against transgender people (or other minorities) as hate crimes, despite evidence supporting such designations.

G. PERSONAL AUTONOMY AND INDIVIDUAL RIGHTS: 12 / 16

G1. Do individuals enjoy freedom of movement, including the ability to change their place of residence, employment, or education? 4 / 4

There are ongoing restrictions on travel to and from the separatist territories of Abkhazia and South Ossetia, and individuals who approach their de facto borders can face detention, generally for short periods. A COVID-19-related state of emergency from March to May 2020 included a curfew and transportation restrictions; similar rules were reintroduced in November and remained in force through year's end, as cases of the virus increased. Nevertheless, the constraints were largely proportionate to the public health threat, and Georgians are otherwise free to travel and change their place of residence, employment, and education without undue interference.

G2. Are individuals able to exercise the right to own property and establish private businesses without undue interference from state or nonstate actors? 3 / 4

The legal framework and government policies are generally supportive of private business activity. However, protection for property rights remains weak, and deficiencies in judicial independence and government transparency hamper economic freedom.

G3. Do individuals enjoy personal social freedoms, including choice of marriage partner and size of family, protection from domestic violence, and control over appearance? 3 / 4

Personal social freedoms are generally respected. However, constitutional changes approved in 2017 define marriage as "a union between a man and a woman for the purpose of creating a family." There is no law allowing civil unions for same-sex couples.

Domestic violence remains a problem in Georgia, and the response from police is often inadequate, though changing societal attitudes have contributed to more frequent reporting and some improvements in enforcement in recent years. Spousal rape is not specifically criminalized.

G4. Do individuals enjoy equality of opportunity and freedom from economic exploitation? 2 / 4

Unsafe conditions and inadequate legal protections for workers continue to contribute to a high rate of workplace deaths and injuries, notably in the country's mines, though the number of such incidents has fallen in recent years. The number of workplace deaths reached 59 in 2018 before slipping to 38 in 2019 and 22 in the first nine months of 2020. In September, Parliament passed a labor reform law that introduced new rules for overtime, shift breaks, and other working conditions, while strengthening the labor inspector's office.

Georgia is a source, destination, and transit country for human trafficking linked to sexual exploitation and forced labor and displaced people from Abkhazia and South Ossetia are among the populations most vulnerable to trafficking. However, according to the US State Department's latest *Trafficking in Persons Report*, the government continued its enforcement efforts and improved its performance on victim identification.

Germany

Population: 83,300,000
Capital: Berlin
Freedom Status: Free
Electoral Democracy: Yes

Overview: Germany is a representative democracy with a vibrant political culture and civil society. Political rights and civil liberties are largely assured both in law and practice. The political system is influenced by the country's totalitarian past, with constitutional safeguards designed to prevent authoritarian rule. Although Germany has generally been stable since the mid-20th century, political tensions have grown following an influx of asylum seekers into the country, and the growing popularity of a right-wing populist party.

KEY DEVELOPMENTS IN 2020

- In February, Thuringia state legislators from the right-wing populist Alternative for Germany (AfD) secured the installation of Thomas Kemmerich of the Free Democratic Party (FDP) as minister-president, sparking widespread criticism. Kemmerich resigned within days, and his predecessor, Bodo Ramelow of the Left, was reselected in March.
- In May, the Federal Constitutional Court (BVerfG) ruled that provisions of the Federal Intelligence Service (BND) Act were unconstitutional, in part because they impinged on the privacy of journalistic sources. The federal cabinet agreed on proposed revisions to the BND Act in December, though Reporters Without Borders (RSF) criticized the proposal for offering insufficient protections for journalists.
- In June, payment processing firm Wirecard filed for bankruptcy after its auditor refused to back financial statements over evidence of fraud. Wirecard's collapse prompted a parliamentary inquiry, which was still ongoing at year's end, as well as a rebuke of German regulators by the European Securities and Markets Authority (ESMA) via a November report.
- While the German government instituted public-assembly restrictions in response to the COVID-19 pandemic, the BVerfG upheld those rights for protesters who followed social-distancing requirements in April. Major protests against COVID-19 measures were held as the year progressed, with some turning violent. The World Health Organization counted 1.71 million cases and 33,071 deaths at year's end.

POLITICAL RIGHTS: 39 / 40

A. ELECTORAL PROCESS: 12 / 12

A1. Was the current head of government or other chief national authority elected through free and fair elections? 4 / 4

Germany's head of state is a largely ceremonial president, chosen by the Federal Convention, a body formed jointly by the Bundestag (Federal Parliament) and state representatives. The president can serve up to two five-year terms. Former foreign minister Frank-Walter Steinmeier of the Social Democratic Party (SPD) was elected president in early 2017.

The federal chancellor—the head of government—is elected by the Bundestag and usually serves for the duration of a legislative session. The chancellor's term can be cut short only if the Bundestag chooses a replacement in a so-called constructive vote of no confidence. Angela Merkel won a fourth term as chancellor following free and fair Bundestag elections in 2017. After negotiations of an unprecedented length, she formed a coalition government in 2018 between her center-right Christian Democratic Union (CDU), its Bavarian sister party, the Christian Social Union (CSU), and the center-left SPD. The current term is expected to be her last term in office.

A2. Were the current national legislative representatives elected through free and fair elections? 4 / 4

The parliament includes a lower house, the Bundestag, as well as an upper house, the 69-seat Bundesrat (Federal Council), which represents the country's 16 federal states. The Bundestag is elected at least every four years through a mixture of proportional representation and single-member districts, which can lead the number of seats to vary from the minimum of 598. The 2017 elections saw 709 lower-house representatives elected. Organization for Security and Co-operation in Europe (OSCE) monitors deemed the elections transparent and free from manipulation.

The CDU–CSU won 246 seats, while its coalition partner in the last government, the SPD, took 153 seats. Both parties posted their worst results since 1949. The right-wing populist AfD entered the Bundestag for the first time in its history, taking 94 seats, posting particularly strong results in the former German Democratic Republic (DDR). The FDP won 80 seats. The far-left party the Left, widely viewed as a successor to the East German communists, took 69. The Greens won 67.

In Germany's federal system, state governments have considerable authority over matters such as education, policing, taxation, and spending. State governments appoint Bundesrat members, and in this manner can influence national policies. In February 2020, members of Thuringia's state legislature selected Thomas Kemmerich of the FDP to replace Bodo Ramelow of the Left as minister-president; Kemmerich received support from the CDU and the AfD, which secured nearly 24 percent of the vote in the October 2019 state election. Kemmerich's installation was met with widespread criticism. Chancellor Merkel called for a reversal of the decision. Kemmerich resigned days after his installation, and an Ramelow-led Left–SPD–Green coalition was formed in March 2020. New elections are due in Thuringia in 2021.

A3. Are the electoral laws and framework fair, and are they implemented impartially by the relevant election management bodies? 4 / 4

Germany's electoral laws and framework are fair and impartial. A failure to reform the problem of so-called overhang seats led to an inflated number of Bundestag members following the 2017 elections: German voters cast two ballots—one for a candidate in their constituency and another for a party, with the latter vote determining the total number of seats a party will hold in the Bundestag. If a party wins more seats in the first vote than are permitted by results of the second, it gets to keep these "overhang" seats. The extra seats are costly and have previously been deemed unconstitutional for allowing a party more seats than it is formally allotted. With 709 lower-house members, Germany now has the world's second-largest national parliament, after China.

B. POLITICAL PLURALISM AND PARTICIPATION: 15 / 16

B1. Do the people have the right to organize in different political parties or other competitive political groupings of their choice, and is the system free of undue obstacles to the rise and fall of these competing parties or groupings? 4 / 4

While the CDU–CSU and the SPD have historically dominated German politics, other parties have increased their support in recent years. Parties do not face undue restrictions on registration or operation. Under electoral laws that, for historical reasons, are intended to restrict the far left and far right, a party must receive either 5 percent of the national vote or win at least three directly elected seats to gain representation in the parliament. The constitution makes it possible to ban political parties, although a party must be judged to pose a threat to democracy for a ban to be legal, and no party has been successfully banned since 1956. In 2017, the Federal Constitutional Court (BVerfG) found the extreme-right National Democratic Party to be unconstitutional but ruled that it did not pose a great enough threat to merit a ban.

Support for the AfD has risen in recent years, as the party has moved further to the right of the political spectrum. The AfD held seats in the Bundestag and all state parliaments in 2020. While its popularity has shaken the German political system, most parties oppose the AfD and eschew coalitions that include it.

B2. Is there a realistic opportunity for the opposition to increase its support or gain power through elections? 4 / 4

While German government is very much consensus oriented, opposition parties have a realistic opportunity to increase their support and gain power through elections. Chancellor Merkel has presided over coalitions of several configurations during her time in office.

B3. Are the people's political choices free from domination by forces that are external to the political sphere, or by political forces that employ extrapolitical means? 4 / 4

The German government is democratically accountable to the voters, who are free to throw their support behind their preferred candidates and parties without undue influence.

B4. Do various segments of the population (including ethnic, racial, religious, gender, LGBT+, and other relevant groups) have full political rights and electoral opportunities? 3 / 4

The constitution gives all citizens age 18 or older the right to vote, and this guarantee applies regardless of gender, ethnicity, religion, sexual orientation, or gender identity. However, some groups are politically underrepresented. Women hold only 31.5 percent of Bundestag seats as of December 2020, the lowest number since 1998. Some 8 percent of Bundestag members are from immigrant backgrounds, having at least one parent who was born without German citizenship.

Naturalization rates are low, leading to large numbers of long-term residents who cannot vote in federal elections. Nearly eight million foreign-born residents were unable to vote in the 2017 federal elections, due in part to restrictive citizenship and voting laws.

C. FUNCTIONING OF GOVERNMENT: 12 / 12

C1. Do the freely elected head of government and national legislative representatives determine the policies of the government? 4 / 4

Democratically elected representatives decide and implement policy without undue interference.

C2. Are safeguards against official corruption strong and effective? 4 / 4

While Germany generally maintains strong and effective corruption safeguards, the regulatory framework on lobbying members of parliament has been considered insufficient. For example, there is no central lobbying register in Germany. The Council of Europe's Group of States against Corruption regularly criticizes Germany for its opaque party-financing regime and for a lack of lobbying regulations.

In June 2020, German media reported that CDU parliamentarian Philipp Amthor used his legislative post to lobby the federal Ministry for Economic Affairs and Energy on behalf of US technology firm Augustus Intelligence, and received a board seat and stock options for his efforts. Transparency International's German office criticized the revelation, warning that Amthor's behavior may have violated the criminal code. Amthor remained in the Bundestag but resigned from the firm's board and surrendered his stock options.

The June 2020 collapse of payment processing firm Wirecard, meanwhile, brought scrutiny on the German financial regulatory system. Wirecard filed for bankruptcy after its accounting firm refused to sign off on financial statements over evidence of fraud. Its chief executive, Markus Braun, was arrested in June and again in July over fraud and embezzlement charges and remained in pretrial custody at year's end. In November, the ESMA rebuked the Federal Financial Supervisory Authority—which had filed criminal complaints against journalists for reporting on irregularities at Wirecard—over a lack of independence from the government, a failure of internal controls, and other deficiencies. A parliamentary inquiry into the collapse was ongoing at year's end.

Germany is obligated to enhance legal protections for whistleblowers under a European Union (EU) directive issued in 2019. In November 2020, Justice Minister Christine Lambrecht announced a bill meant to ensure compliance, though the draft was not published by year's end.

C3. Does the government operate with openness and transparency? 4 / 4

The government is held accountable for its performance through open parliamentary debates, which are covered widely in the media. In 2018, the government introduced question time, in which the chancellor answers questions from the parliament three times per year. However, transparency is limited by an overburdened bureaucracy and inconsistent state-level standards.

CIVIL LIBERTIES: 55 / 60

D. FREEDOM OF EXPRESSION AND BELIEF 14 / 16

D1. Are there free and independent media? 4 / 4

Freedom of expression is enshrined in the constitution, and the media are largely free and independent. Hate speech, such as racist agitation or antisemitism, is punishable by law. It is also illegal to advocate for Nazism, deny the Holocaust, or glorify the ideology of Hitler.

Journalists face harassment and abuse, especially via social media, as well as physical attacks when reporting on right-wing demonstrations. Such attacks were common in 2020, especially against journalists reporting on Querdenken (Lateral Thinking) demonstrations against COVID-19 restrictions.

The privacy of communications between journalists and their sources have been affected by provisions of the BND Act. In May 2020, the BVerfG ruled BND Act's surveillance provisions unconstitutional and mandated its revision. A revised bill was approved by the cabinet in December, but was criticized by RSF, which warned that it offered insufficient protections for journalists. The revision remained under consideration at year's end.

D2. Are individuals free to practice and express their religious faith or nonbelief in public and private? 3 / 4

Freedom of belief is legally protected. However, eight states have passed laws prohibiting schoolteachers from wearing headscarves, while Berlin and the state of Hesse have adopted legislation banning headscarves for civil servants.

Antisemitism in Germany is seen to be on the rise. In October 2020, the head of the Federal Office for the Protection of the Constitution warned of increasing verbal and physical attacks against Jewish individuals and organizations. In December, an assailant who killed two people in an assault a synagogue in the city of Halle in 2019 received a life sentence.

Islamophobia also remains a concern. German police recorded 632 politically motivated attacks against Muslim individuals and institutions in the first three quarters of 2020.

D3. Is there academic freedom, and is the educational system free from extensive political indoctrination? 4 / 4

Academic freedom is generally respected, though legal prohibitions on extremist speech are enforceable in school and university settings. Debates about freedom of expression on campuses have continued in recent years. In February 2020, a survey commissioned by the Konrad Adenauer Foundation and the German Association of University Professors and Lecturers found that nearly a third of university educators felt constrained by institutional guidelines.

D4. Are individuals free to express their personal views on political or other sensitive topics without fear of surveillance or retribution? 3 / 4

Private discussion and internet access are generally unrestricted, but recent developments have prompted concern about government surveillance of private communications. In 2017, the Bundestag passed a law allowing police to use spyware to conduct surveillance of encrypted online messaging services like WhatsApp when conducting criminal investigations. In October 2020, the federal cabinet opened discussions on a proposal to give intelligence agencies the ability to access such messages.

In 2018, the controversial Network Enforcement Act came into full effect. The law compels social media companies to delete content deemed to clearly constitute illegal hate speech within 24 hours of being reported, and content that appears to be illegal hate speech within seven days. According to RSF, social media companies have subsequently removed thousands of posts that should not be considered hate speech.

Watchdogs continue to express concern about a controversial 2015 data-retention law that requires telecommunications companies to store users' telephone and internet data for 10 weeks. Critics view the law as a threat to general privacy and to whistleblowers, who could be punished under a section detailing illegal data handling. After the law was suspended and found to be incompatible with EU law by several German courts, the European Court of Justice (ECJ) is expected to consider the issue. A November 2020 Bundestag report warned that the ECJ is unlikely to sustain the law, based on its rulings on data-retention legislation in other EU member states. The ECJ case was still pending at year's end.

In recent surveys, a majority of Germans said they are careful when publicly stating their opinion, especially on migration, for fear of repercussions.

E. ASSOCIATIONAL AND ORGANIZATIONAL RIGHTS: 12 / 12

E1. Is there freedom of assembly? 4 / 4

The right to peaceful assembly is enshrined in the constitution and is generally respected in practice, except in the case of outlawed groups, such as those advocating Nazism or opposing democratic order.

Assembly rights were restricted under COVID-19-related measures, but an April 2020 BVerfG ruling upheld rights for protesters who abided by social-distancing requirements. Several large demonstrations against COVID-19 measures—some of which turned violent—were held in 2020. In late August, for example, 38,000 protesters rallied in Berlin, most of them peacefully. However, several hundred demonstrators belonging to the far-right Realm Citizens group then tried to breach the Reichstag building before they were repelled by police. In early November, 20,000 protesters assembled in Leipzig under the Querdenken banner. Far-right participants reportedly clashed with police during those demonstrations, while the Union of German Journalists counted at least 32 attacks on the press during the incident.

E2. Is there freedom for nongovernmental organizations, particularly those that are engaged in human rights- and governance-related work? 4 / 4

Germany has a vibrant sphere of nongovernmental organizations (NGOs) and associations, which operate freely. However, in 2019, several NGOs lost their tax-exempt status after the Federal Financial Court ruled that they took part in political partisanship. In December 2020, the parliament passed a revised tax law that explicitly allowed more NGOs operating in areas including climate change and LGBT+ issues to claim tax-exempt status.

E3. Is there freedom for trade unions and similar professional or labor organizations? 4 / 4

Trade unions, farmers' groups, and business confederations are generally free to organize, and play an important role in shaping Germany's economic model.

F. RULE OF LAW: 14 / 16

F1. Is there an independent judiciary? 4 / 4

The judiciary is independent, and generally enforces the rights provided by Germany's laws and constitution.

F2. Does due process prevail in civil and criminal matters? 4 / 4

The rule of law prevails in Germany. Civil and criminal matters are treated according to legal provisions and with due process. However, under "preventive detention" practices, those convicted of certain violent crimes can be detained after serving their full sentence if they are deemed to pose a danger to the public. In 2019, the ECJ ruled that German prosecutors were not allowed to issue European arrest warrants because of their dependence on state-level justice ministers. In November 2020, the Thuringia justice minister offered a draft proposal on enhancing prosecutorial independence to the Bundesrat.

In recent years, several state governments adopted laws that increased the surveillance powers of law enforcement. These laws have been criticized for enabling police to take preemptive action if they believe there is an "impending danger," a vaguely defined term could allow for abuses according to critics. The Berlin state government introduced a draft reform package in June 2020, which was still under consideration at year's end. Modest reforms were introduced in Bremen in November.

The professionalism of law-enforcement officers has come under question after the 2018 discovery of a neo-Nazi network within the Frankfurt police. Since then, police in several cities and states have been accused of espousing extremist and discriminatory sentiments. In June 2020, for example, 25 Berlin officials were discovered to have participated in a far-right chat network. Some 30 North Rhine–Westphalia officers, meanwhile, were suspended for participating in a similar group in September. Despite earlier reluctance, the federal Ministry of the Interior agreed to launch a study in October, though the Left and the FDP criticized the move as insufficient.

F3. Is there protection from the illegitimate use of physical force and freedom from war and insurgencies? 3 / 4

Politically motivated crimes against public officials and politicians have increased in recent years. The political establishment was notably shaken by the 2019 murder of Hesse politician Walter Lübcke at the hands of a far-right extremist. In February 2020, the Federal Criminal Police Office reported that 1,451 politically motivated attacks took place in 2019, compared to 1,256 in 2018. Politically motivated attacks were also reported in 2020. In January, bullet holes were found in the office of SPD parliamentarian Karamba Diaby, who also received a death threat. In October, an arsonist targeted the Robert Koch Institute, the public disease-control agency, in what police consider a politically motivated attack.

Several mass-casualty incidents were reported in 2020. In late February, a German who espoused far-right views killed nine people when attacking two shisha bars in the western city of Hanau. Chancellor Merkel later reported that the assailant, who died by suicide, was likely motivated by racist tendencies. In August, an individual suspected of Islamist tendencies attacked several motorists on a Berlin highway, injuring six. In December, five people in the city of Trier were killed by an individual driving into a pedestrian zone, though no political motive was immediately identified.

Attacks on refugees and refugee housing continued to decline from a peak of 3,500 in 2016. In 2019, nearly 1,750 such attacks were reported.

F4. Do laws, policies, and practices guarantee equal treatment of various segments of the population? 3 / 4

The constitution and other laws guarantee equality and prohibit discrimination on the basis of origin, gender, religion or belief, disability, age, or sexual orientation. However, a number of obstacles stand in the way of equal treatment of all segments of the population. Race-based discrimination is commonplace. Women, meanwhile, face a gender-based pay gap, while men are likelier to hold full-time employment. In July 2020, the federal cabinet adopted Germany's first gender-equality strategy, focusing on pay, political representation, and other issues.

In 2018, restrictive new asylum and migration policies were passed, which include building camps along Germany's international borders to hold asylum seekers and deporting any asylum seeker who had previously applied for asylum in another EU country. The implementation of these policies thus far has been slow.

G. PERSONAL AUTONOMY AND INDIVIDUAL RIGHTS: 15 / 16

G1. Do individuals enjoy freedom of movement, including the ability to change their place of residence, employment, or education? 4 / 4

Freedom of movement is legally protected and generally respected, although the refugee crisis and security concerns related to activity by the Islamic State (IS) militant group have led to some restrictions on travel. In 2015, the government introduced legislation allowing the confiscation of identity documents from German citizens suspected of terrorism to prevent them from traveling abroad, particularly to Iraq and Syria.

Nationwide movement restrictions were not instituted during the first wave of the COVID-19 pandemic, though the states of Bavaria and Saarland did institute a lockdown in March 2020. Several states required visitors to present negative COVID-19 tests during the school vacation period in October. Bavaria also instituted a nighttime curfew in December 2020, as coronavirus cases increased.

G2. Are individuals able to exercise the right to own property and establish private businesses without undue interference from state or nonstate actors? 4 / 4

The rights to own property and engage in commercial activity are respected.

G3. Do individuals enjoy personal social freedoms, including choice of marriage partner and size of family, protection from domestic violence, and control over appearance? 4 / 4

The government generally does not restrict social freedoms. Women's rights are protected under antidiscrimination laws. However, a considerable gender wage gap persists, with women earning approximately 20 percent less in gross wages than men according to 2019 statistics. A law requiring large German companies to reserve at least 30 percent of nonexecutive-board seats for women took effect in 2016, but this law affects a limited number of companies. The federal government considered instituting a similar quota for executive boards in November 2020, though a decision was not reached at year's end.

Adoption and tax legislation passed in 2014 gave equal rights to same-sex couples in these areas. The government legalized same-sex marriage in 2017.

In 2019, a Nazi-era law banning doctors from providing information on or advertising abortion services was reformed. Clinics and doctors may disclose abortion services, but a ban on providing further information was maintained. Human-rights campaigners criticized the reform as insufficient.

G4. Do individuals enjoy equality of opportunity and freedom from economic exploitation? 3 / 4

According to the US State Department's 2020 *Trafficking in Persons Report*, migrants from Eastern Europe, Africa, and Asia are targeted for sex trafficking and forced labor. Ethnic Roma are notably vulnerable to sex trafficking and to other forms of sex work.

Employees of meat producer Tönnies, many of whom are Bulgarian, North Macedonian, Polish, and Romanian, face poor working and living conditions. Tönnies workers also risked COVID-19 infection; by June 2020, over 1,000 workers at a meat-processing plant in the city of Rheda-Wiedenbrück had tested positive.

Ghana

Population: 31,100,000
Capital: Accra
Freedom Status: Free
Electoral Democracy: Yes

Overview: Since 1992, Ghana has held competitive multiparty elections and undergone peaceful transfers of power between the two main political parties. Although the country has a relatively strong record of upholding civil liberties, discrimination against women and LGBT+ people persists. There are some weaknesses in judicial independence and the rule of law, corruption presents challenges to government performance, and political violence is a growing concern.

KEY DEVELOPMENTS IN 2020

- President Nana Akufo-Addo of the New Patriotic Party (NPP) won a second term in December, defeating predecessor John Mahama of the National Democratic Congress (NDC) in an effective rematch. While election observers considered the polls well-managed, Mahama called the results fraudulent and NDC supporters held protests; the immediate postelection period was marred by violence, with police reporting five deaths several days after the polls.
- The NPP and NDC ended the concurrent parliamentary elections with a tie, with each party winning 137 seats. An independent legislator agreed to support the NPP later that month, giving it a bare majority.
- In March, the government instituted COVID-19-related movement and gathering restrictions and promulgated an Imposition of Restrictions Act (IRA) that was criticized by the NDC and legal observers for its disproportionality. A lockdown was also instituted in the Accra and Kumasi areas, though they were relaxed in late April. At year's end, the World Health Organization reported a total of 54,771 COVID-19 cases and 335 deaths.

POLITICAL RIGHTS: 35 / 40

A. ELECTORAL PROCESS: 12 / 12

A1. Was the current head of government or other chief national authority elected through free and fair elections? 4 / 4

The president, who serves as head of state and head of government, is directly elected for up to two four-year terms. President Nana Akufo-Addo of the NPP won a second term in the December 2020 presidential election with 51.3 percent of the vote, while his predecessor, John Mahama (2012–17) of the NDC, took 47.3 percent. African Union (AU) and European Union (EU) electoral observers called the contest well-organized and generally peaceful, though EU monitors criticized a lack of campaign finance regulation and a misuse of state resources. However, Mahama rejected the results, alleging fraud, and issued a legal challenge that was pending at year's end.

The immediate postelection period was marred by violence, with the national police reporting at least five deaths in the days following the vote. NDC supporters held protests in parts of Ghana in December, notably marching on the Electoral Commission (EC) headquarters in Accra in the middle of the month.

A2. Were the current national legislative representatives elected through free and fair elections? 4 / 4

Members of the unicameral, 275-seat Parliament are elected directly in single-member constituencies to serve four-year terms.

The NPP, which held a majority in the previous parliament, and the NDC each won 137 seats in December 2020 elections held concurrently with the presidential contest. One seat was won by an independent who agreed to support the NPP, giving that party a bare de facto majority. Monitors lauded the elections' overall conduct.

A3. Are the electoral laws and framework fair, and are they implemented impartially by the relevant election management bodies? 4 / 4

Domestic and international observers consider the EC a capable manager of the electoral process. However, its composition has been the subject of political disagreement in the past; the 2018 appointment of Jean Mensah as its chairwoman was criticized by the NDC, which called her appointment partisan. Civil society largely lauded Mensah's selection, however.

In 2019, the EC announced plans to compile a new voter register ahead of the December 2020 elections. During a six-week period between June and August, and for one day in October, the EC registered voters through an updated biometric system. While this drive was largely successful, a number of minors and foreign-born residents were reportedly able to register, and NPP and NDC supporters clashed at some registration sites. AU electoral observers ultimately lauded the registration process and the EC's overall performance in a December statement.

B. POLITICAL PLURALISM AND PARTICIPATION: 13 / 16

B1. Do the people have the right to organize in different political parties or other competitive political groupings of their choice, and is the system free of undue obstacles to the rise and fall of these competing parties or groupings? 3 / 4

The constitution guarantees the right to form political parties, and this right is generally respected. However, civil society groups have expressed concern about the rising involvement of partisan vigilante groups in inter- and intraparty disputes.

Candidates, especially from smaller parties, were impeded in their ability to compete by an increase in registration fees. In September 2020, Mensah announced that presidential candidates were responsible for filing fees totaling 100,000 cedi ($17,200), double the 2016 amount, while fees for parliamentary candidates stood at 10,000 cedi ($1,730).

B2. Is there a realistic opportunity for the opposition to increase its support or gain power through elections? 4 / 4

There have been multiple peaceful transfers of power between the NPP and NDC and parties in opposition have meaningful opportunities to increase their public support and win office. Mahama's defeat in the 2016 presidential race marked the first time since the 1992 reintroduction of multiparty politics that an incumbent stood for reelection and lost.

While Ghanaian political contests are generally peaceful, candidates are sometimes victims of violence. In October 2020, NPP member of Parliament (MP) Ekow Quansah Hayford was shot and killed by several assailants in an apparent robbery, as he left the campaign trail. In mid-December, days after parliamentary elections were held, NDC MP Kwame Gakpe was attacked in his home and was subsequently hospitalized; the party alleged that NPP supporters attacked him.

B3. Are the people's political choices free from domination by forces that are external to the political sphere, or by political forces that employ extrapolitical means? 3 / 4

Ghanaians are generally free from undue interference with their political choices by powerful groups that are not democratically accountable. However, voters and candidates are threatened by vigilantism and politically motivated violence despite the 2019 promulgation of the Vigilantism and Related Offences Act, which bans all political and other vigilante groups.

NPP and NDC supporters clashed at several voter registration sites in July 2020—despite an agreement between the two parties to refrain from such activity—resulting in one death. Then special development minister Mavis Hawa Koomson was publicly criticized for firing warning shots at a registration center in her constituency that month, and said she did so to protect herself.

B4. Do various segments of the population (including ethnic, racial, religious, gender, LGBT+, and other relevant groups) have full political rights and electoral opportunities? 3 / 4

Ghanaian laws provide for equal participation in political life by the country's various cultural, religious, and ethnic groups. Women formally enjoy political equality, but hold comparatively few leadership positions in practice. However, in July 2020, the NDC selected Jane Naana Opoku-Agyemang as its vice-presidential candidate, the first time a woman was placed on a major party's presidential ticket. Women won 40 parliamentary seats in the December elections, a slight increase over the 2016 results and the largest share since the reintroduction of multiparty politics.

The National House of Chiefs, Ghana's highest body of customary authority, has been under pressure to include women as members.

C. FUNCTIONING OF GOVERNMENT: 10 / 12

C1. Do the freely elected head of government and national legislative representatives determine the policies of the government? 4 / 4

Elected officials are generally free to set and implement government policy without improper influence from unelected entities. However, the president gained the ability to more easily enact states of emergency under the Imposition of Restrictions Act (IRA). The IRA, which was passed by Parliament and signed by Akufo-Addo in March 2020 as the COVID-19 pandemic became a global crisis, limited the ability of Parliament to easily revoke presidentially declared states of emergency. The IRA was criticized by the NDC and legal scholars, who warned that the legislation was disproportionate and gave the executive wide-ranging powers. The IRA expired in December, though the government vowed to renew it later that month.

C2. Are safeguards against official corruption strong and effective? 3 / 4

Political corruption remains a problem despite active media coverage, fairly robust laws and institutions, and government antigraft initiatives. Legislation adopted in 2017 established the Office of the Special Prosecutor (OSP) to investigate political corruption. President Akufo-Addo appointed former attorney general Martin Amidu, a NDC member, as special prosecutor in 2018.

Amidu resigned in November 2020, citing a lack of resources as one of his reasons. Amidu also claimed that Akufo-Addo sought to interfere in a report on the transfer of mineral royalties to publicly owned Agyapa Royalties. The OSP warned that the plan, which envisioned Accra selling shares in the firm, could lead to "bid rigging" or "illicit financial flows." Akufo-Addo sent the proposed transaction back to Parliament for consideration that month, where it remained at year's end. Amidu's deputy, Jane Cynthia Naa Torshie Lamptey, became the acting special prosecutor in late November.

The administrations of former presidents John Atta Mills (2009–12) and Mahama were implicated in a bribery scheme in January 2020, when European aircraft maker Airbus admitted to bribing individuals in Ghana and several other countries between 2011 and 2015. President Akufo-Addo referred the matter to the OSP in February; it named Mahama's brother a person of interest in March and reported that Mahama himself was directly implicated in July. However, Amidu elected not to open an investigation against Mahama before resigning as special prosecutor. The probe remained active at year's end.

C3. Does the government operate with openness and transparency? 3 / 4

The government operates with relative transparency, though there are weaknesses in the legal framework. In 2019, Akufo-Addo signed the Right to Information Act, which grants citizens the right to seek, access, and receive information from public as well as some private institutions. The law came into effect in January 2020.

CIVIL LIBERTIES: 47 / 60

D. FREEDOM OF EXPRESSION AND BELIEF: 14 / 16

D1. Are there free and independent media? 3 / 4

Freedom of the press is constitutionally guaranteed and generally respected in practice. Ghana has a diverse and vibrant media landscape that includes state- and privately-owned television and radio stations as well as a number of independent newspapers and magazines. Online news media operate without government restrictions. Government agencies occasionally limit press freedom by harassing and arresting journalists, especially those reporting on politically sensitive issues.

Journalists were also impeded in their work under the cover of COVID-19-related restrictions. In April 2020, Zuria FM manager Yussif Abdul-Ganiyu was physically attacked by a soldier while reporting on the lockdown in the city of Kumasi and was later detained before he was ultimately released without charge. Several days later, soldiers enforcing a lockdown assaulted TV Africa journalist Samuel Adobah in Greater Accra as while he reported on a fire there. Journalists also faced detention, threats, and harassment while covering the December 2020 elections.

D2. Are individuals free to practice and express their religious faith or nonbelief in public and private? 3 / 4

Religious freedom is constitutionally and legally protected, and the government largely upholds these protections in practice. However, public schools feature mandatory religious education courses drawing on Christianity and Islam, and Muslim students have allegedly been required to participate in Christian prayer sessions and church services in some publicly funded Christian schools.

D3. Is there academic freedom, and is the educational system free from extensive political indoctrination? 4 / 4

Academic freedom is legally guaranteed and generally upheld in practice.

D4. Are individuals free to express their personal views on political or other sensitive topics without fear of surveillance or retribution? 4 / 4

Private discussion is both free and vibrant. The government does not restrict individual expression on social media.

E. ASSOCIATIONAL AND ORGANIZATIONAL RIGHTS: 11 / 12

E1. Is there freedom of assembly? 4 / 4

The right to peaceful assembly is constitutionally guaranteed and generally respected. Permits are not required for meetings or demonstrations. However, President Akufo-Addo instituted COVID-19-related movement and gathering restrictions in March 2020. Assembly restrictions were relaxed, though not totally rescinded, at the end of May and again in late July.

Despite the pandemic and related restrictions, notable protests occurred during the year. In June 2020, some 60 people attended an Accra vigil held under the Black Lives Matter banner in response to the May killing of George Floyd in the United States. Attendees clashed with Accra police after they arrested the event's organizer, and officers later fired into the air to disperse the gathering. NDC supporters who rejected the results of the December elections held protests in several parts of the country in the days after the polls. Later that month, Accra police secured a restraining order to prohibit further opposition protests in the capital.

E2. Is there freedom for nongovernmental organizations, particularly those that are engaged in human rights– and governance-related work? 4 / 4

Nongovernmental organizations are generally able to operate freely and play an important role in ensuring government accountability and transparency.

E3. Is there freedom for trade unions and similar professional or labor organizations? 3 / 4

Under the constitution and 2003 labor laws, workers have the right to form and join trade unions. However, the government forbids or restricts organized labor action in a number of sectors, including fuel distribution and utilities, public transportation, and ports and harbor services.

F. RULE OF LAW: 11 / 16

F1. Is there an independent judiciary? 2 / 4

Judicial independence is constitutionally and legally enshrined. While the judiciary has demonstrated greater levels of impartiality in recent years, corruption and bribery continue to pose challenges.

F2. Does due process prevail in civil and criminal matters? 3 / 4

Constitutional protections for due process and defendants' rights are mostly upheld. However, police have been known to accept bribes, make arbitrary arrests, and hold people without charge for longer than the legally permitted limit of 48 hours. The government is not obliged to provide the accused with legal counsel, and many people unable to afford lawyers are forced to represent themselves in court.

F3. Is there protection from the illegitimate use of physical force and freedom from war and insurgencies? 3 / 4

Prisons are overcrowded, and conditions can be life threatening, though the prison service has attempted to reduce congestion and improve the treatment of inmates in recent years.

Communal and ethnic violence is known to take place in parts of Ghana. Communal violence that began in 2018 between members of the Konkomba and Chokosi ethnic groups in North East Region escalated in 2019. In April 2020, the Internal Displacement Monitoring Centre reported that 2,300 people had been internally displaced by that conflict, which began over a land dispute.

Islamic militants and other armed groups active in the Sahel have reportedly taken refuge in the northern reaches of Ghana in recent years.

F4. Do laws, policies, and practices guarantee equal treatment of various segments of the population? 3 / 4

Despite equal rights under the law, women face societal discrimination, especially in rural areas, where their opportunities for education and employment are limited. However, women's enrollment in universities is increasing. People with disabilities and LGBT+ people also face societal discrimination. Same-sex sexual activity remains criminalized, encouraging police harassment and impunity for violence against LGBT+ people.

G. PERSONAL AUTONOMY AND INDIVIDUAL RIGHTS: 11 / 16

G1. Do individuals enjoy freedom of movement, including the ability to change their place of residence, employment, or education? 3 / 4

Freedom of movement is guaranteed by the constitution and is generally respected by the government. However, poorly developed road networks and banditry can make travel outside the capital and tourist areas difficult. Police have been known to set up illegal checkpoints to demand bribes from travelers. Bribery is also rife in the education sector.

Movement restrictions were introduced in March 2020, as the government formulated a response to the COVID-19 pandemic. Lockdowns were introduced in the Accra and Kumasi metropolitan areas, though they were relaxed beginning in late April. Restrictions on domestic flights were lifted in early May.

G2. Are individuals able to exercise the right to own property and establish private businesses without undue interference from state or nonstate actors? 3 / 4

Although the legal framework generally supports property ownership and private business activity, weaknesses in the rule of law, corruption, and an underregulated property rights system remain impediments. Bribery is a common practice when starting a business and registering property.

G3. Do individuals enjoy personal social freedoms, including choice of marriage partner and size of family, protection from domestic violence, and control over appearance? 3 / 4

While personal social freedoms are upheld in many respects and among large segments of the population, domestic violence and rape are serious problems, and harmful traditional practices including female genital mutilation and early or forced marriage persist in certain regions.

The government has worked to combat gender-based violence, including by expanding the police's domestic violence and victim support units and creating special courts for gender-based violence, though such services are reportedly underresourced.

G4. Do individuals enjoy equality of opportunity and freedom from economic exploitation? 2 / 4

Most workers are employed in the informal sector, limiting the effectiveness of legal and regulatory safeguards for working conditions. The exploitation of children in the agricultural and mining sectors remains a problem. Similar abuses in the fishing industry have also been reported, especially in the region surrounding Lake Volta.

In the 2020 edition of its *Trafficking in Persons Report*, the US State Department reported that the Ghanaian government had bolstered its efforts to identify trafficking survivors and prosecute suspects. However, the State Department also noted that the government's efforts were underresourced, and that corruption affected its ultimate success.

Greece

Population: 10,700,000
Capital: Athens
Freedom Status: Free
Electoral Democracy: Yes

Overview: Greece's parliamentary democracy features vigorous competition between political parties and a strong if imperfect record of upholding civil liberties. Ongoing concerns include corruption, discrimination against immigrants and minority groups, and poor conditions for irregular migrants and asylum seekers.

KEY DEVELOPMENTS IN 2020

- Although Greece initially reported relatively few cases of COVID-19, the country experienced a much deadlier second wave of infections later in the year and reintroduced a full lockdown in November. By year's end, nearly 138,000 cases and 4,800 deaths had been documented.
- In March, amid a surge in irregular border crossings from Turkey, the government suspended processing of asylum applications and allegedly began engaging in arbitrary pushbacks of people entering by land and sea.
- The overcrowded Moria reception center on the island of Lesbos was ravaged by fire in September, temporarily depriving more than 12,000 migrants and asylum seekers of shelter.
- In October, after a protracted trial, leaders of the far-right party Golden Dawn, including former members of parliament, were found guilty of operating a criminal organization. The convicted defendants appealed their prison sentences, which ranged up to 13 years.

POLITICAL RIGHTS: 37 / 40
A. ELECTORAL PROCESS: 12 / 12
A1. Was the current head of government or other chief national authority elected through free and fair elections? 4 / 4

The largely ceremonial president is elected by a parliamentary supermajority for a five-year term. The prime minister is chosen by the president and is usually the leader of the largest party in the parliament. Kyriakos Mitsotakis, head of the center-right party New Democracy (ND), took office as prime minister after the July 2019 elections, replacing incumbent Alexis Tsipras of the Coalition of the Radical Left (SYRIZA). Katerina Sakellaropoulou, a longtime judicial official who had been nominated by ND but was also supported by SYRIZA and the center-left Movement for Change (KINAL), was elected president in January 2020.

A2. Were the current national legislative representatives elected through free and fair elections? 4 / 4

The 300 members of the unicameral Hellenic Parliament are elected to serve four-year terms through a mixture of 8 single-member constituencies, 48 multimember constituencies, and a national constituency with 12 seats. Under the electoral law in effect for the 2019 elections, the party with the most votes received a 50-seat bonus, making it easier to form a governing majority.

In the 2019 elections, ND won a single-party majority of 158 seats. SYRIZA lost its leading position, falling to 86 seats, while KINAL won 22. Among smaller parties, the Communist Party of Greece (KKE) took 15, the right-wing Greek Solution took 10, and the left-wing European Realistic Disobedience Front (MeRA25) secured 9. The far-right Golden Dawn failed to win representation.

A3. Are the electoral laws and framework fair, and are they implemented impartially by the relevant election management bodies? 4 / 4

The country has generally fair electoral laws, equal campaigning opportunities, and a weakly enforced system of compulsory voting. If passed with a two-thirds supermajority, changes to the electoral laws are implemented for the next elections. If passed with a simple majority, they go into effect in the following elections. An electoral law passed by the SYRIZA-led government with a simple majority in 2016 abolished the 50-seat bonus awarded to the winning party and was set to take effect during the elections after those in 2019. In January 2020, the ND government secured passage of legislation that would restore a bonus system, awarding between 20 and 50 bonus seats to the leading party depending on its share of the national vote. The new law also passed with a simple majority, meaning it would take effect only after the next elections.

B. POLITICAL PLURALISM AND PARTICIPATION: 15 / 16

B1. Do the people have the right to organize in different political parties or other competitive political groupings of their choice, and is the system free of undue obstacles to the rise and fall of these competing parties or groupings? 4 / 4

The political system features vigorous competition among a variety of parties. Six parties were represented in the parliament as of 2020. Many other parties participated in the last elections but did not reach the 3 percent vote threshold to secure representation.

B2. Is there a realistic opportunity for the opposition to increase its support or gain power through elections? 4 / 4

Greece has established a strong pattern of democratic transfers of power between rival parties, with the Panhellenic Socialist Movement (PASOK) and ND alternating in government for most of the past four decades. SYRIZA entered government for the first time in 2015, and ND succeeded it after the 2019 elections.

B3. Are the people's political choices free from domination by forces that are external to the political sphere, or by political forces that employ extrapolitical means? 4 / 4

No group or institution from outside the political system exerts undue influence over the choices of voters and candidates.

B4. Do various segments of the population (including ethnic, racial, religious, gender, LGBT+, and other relevant groups) have full political rights and electoral opportunities? 3 / 4

Greece's largest recognized minority population, the Muslim community of Thrace, has full political rights, and three members of the community won seats in the 2019 parliamentary elections. The authorities have rejected some ethnic groups' attempts to secure official recognition or to register associations with names referring to their ethnic identity, affecting their ability to organize and advocate for their political interests, though such associations are generally able to operate without legal recognition. Since 2010, documented immigrants have been allowed to vote in municipal elections.

There are no significant legal or practical barriers to women's political participation, and women hold more than a fifth of the seats in the parliament. In January 2020, Katerina Sakellaropoulou became the first woman to be elected as president of Greece. Despite this symbolic development, sexism and patriarchal attitudes continue to dissuade many women from playing a more active role in politics.

C. FUNCTIONING OF GOVERNMENT: 10 / 12

C1. Do the freely elected head of government and national legislative representatives determine the policies of the government? 4 / 4

Greek elected officials generally set and implement government policies without undue interference, and the influence of international creditor institutions has receded over the past decade.

C2. Are safeguards against official corruption strong and effective? 3 / 4

Corruption remains a problem in Greece, and institutions tasked with combating it have inadequate resources. Tax officials in past years have been implicated in tax evasion schemes, which seriously complicate the government's fiscal reform efforts. A new criminal code and a new code of criminal procedure that were adopted in 2019 allow prison time for the bribery of politicians and are more broadly aligned with relevant international conventions. However, the Organization for Economic Co-operation and Development (OECD) Working Group on Bribery expressed serious concerns that the main active bribery offense was converted from a felony to a misdemeanor.

Overall, there has been gradual improvement in enforcement of anticorruption laws. In mid-2020, authorities began investigating police officers who allegedly offered to overlook illegal activity in exchange for bribes. Cases implicating the police made up almost 45 percent of all corruption cases investigated in 2019.

C3. Does the government operate with openness and transparency? 3 / 4

A number of laws and government programs are designed to ensure the transparency of official decisions and provide public access to information. Officials are required to make public declarations of their assets and income. The transparency of state procurement contracts remains a concern. Past years have featured prosecutions of former officials for contract-related bribery schemes, and in 2020, the government was accused of favoring politically connected companies in spending programs related to COVID-19. Many contracts were reportedly awarded directly using opaque, expedited procedures.

CIVIL LIBERTIES: 50 / 60 (−1)

D. FREEDOM OF EXPRESSION AND BELIEF: 14 / 16

D1. Are there free and independent media? 3 / 4

The constitution includes provisions guaranteeing freedom of the press, and these are generally upheld in practice, though the law imposes some limits related to defamation, hate speech, and other such content. While citizens continue to enjoy access to a broad array of print, broadcast, and online news outlets, ownership concentration and editorial interference from owners remain concerns, and the government has been accused of directing public funds toward friendly private media.

Journalists are sometimes subject to assaults or other mistreatment, particularly while attempting to cover protests or report on migration issues. Among other incidents during 2020, separate German media teams reporting on the migration crisis were temporarily detained by police on the islands of Lesbos and Samos, and an Italian crew was detained on Lesbos in December.

D2. Are individuals free to practice and express their religious faith or nonbelief in public and private? 3 / 4

The constitution guarantees freedom of religion, and this is generally respected in practice. However, the Orthodox Church of Greece—which has a special constitutional status as the "prevailing religion" of the country—receives government subsidies, and its clergy's salaries and pensions are paid for by the state. The constitution prohibits proselytizing, but this restriction is rarely enforced. Members of some minority religions face discrimination and legal barriers, such as permit requirements to open houses of worship.

D3. Is there academic freedom, and is the educational system free from extensive political indoctrination? 4 / 4

There are no significant constraints on academic freedom in Greece, and the educational system is free of political indoctrination. Legislation adopted in 2019 eliminated an academic "asylum" rule that had prevented police from entering university campuses without permission, except under specified circumstances. While the political opposition denounced the change as antidemocratic, the government argued that the rule had led to impunity for criminal activity that disrupted academic life.

D4. Are individuals free to express their personal views on political or other sensitive topics without fear of surveillance or retribution? 4 / 4

The government does not engage in improper monitoring of personal expression. Individuals are generally free to discuss their views in practice.

E. ASSOCIATIONAL AND ORGANIZATIONAL RIGHTS: 11 / 12 (−1)
E1. Is there freedom of assembly? 3 / 4 (−1)

Freedom of assembly is guaranteed by the constitution, and the government generally protects this right. However, some protests have become violent, and police at times have used excessive force to disperse demonstrators. In February 2020, for example, police on Lesbos reportedly used tear gas and flash grenades against protesting asylum seekers, including children. Similar confrontations occurred later in the year, particularly in the context of a devastating fire at the Moria camp in September.

Beginning in March 2020, large gatherings were prohibited as part of the response to the COVID-19 pandemic. A number of protests went forward despite the restrictions, which were periodically adjusted depending on the health situation. The government banned an annual demonstration in November marking a 1973 student uprising, citing health reasons; hundreds of people who assembled were dispersed using tear gas and a water cannon, and some were arrested. Similarly, dozens of people who gathered to commemorate a teenager's 2008 killing by police in December were arrested for violating health restrictions.

In July, the government secured passage of a law requiring protest organizers to notify authorities of planned events and exposing them to liability for protest-related damage or injury if they fail to follow legal procedures. Authorities could ban planned demonstrations on public safety grounds with the approval of a judge, according to the law. Nongovernmental organizations (NGOs), labor unions, and opposition parties opposed the law, and thousands of demonstrators protested its introduction in central Athens, leading to violent clashes between civilians throwing firebombs and police officers using tear gas and flash grenades.

Score Change: The score declined from 4 to 3 because the parliament enacted new legal restrictions on protests, and because multiple demonstrations during the year resulted in violence, arrests, and excessive use of force by police.

E2. Is there freedom for nongovernmental organizations, particularly those that are engaged in human rights- and governance-related work? 4 / 4

NGOs generally operate without interference from the authorities. However, during 2020 the government made a series of changes to the registration requirements for organizations working on asylum and migration issues, generally increasing the regulatory burden on the NGOs and giving government officials significant discretion to deny registrations. In September, police announced criminal charges against 33 foreign NGO workers and two other individuals for allegedly facilitating irregular crossings from Turkey.

E3. Is there freedom for trade unions and similar professional or labor organizations? 4 / 4

Most workers have the right to form and join unions, bargain collectively, and strike. The law provides protections against discrimination toward union members, and the government generally upholds union rights.

F. RULE OF LAW: 11 / 16

F1. Is there an independent judiciary? 3 / 4

The judiciary is largely independent, though its autonomy is undermined somewhat by corruption. Judges are appointed by the president on the advice of the Supreme Judicial Council, which is mostly composed of other judges. They serve until retirement age and cannot be removed arbitrarily.

F2. Does due process prevail in civil and criminal matters? 3 / 4

The law provides safeguards against arbitrary arrest and detention, ensures access to defense counsel, and provides for fair trial conditions. Persistent problems include court backlogs that lead to prolonged pretrial detention as well as improper detention of asylum seekers.

F3. Is there protection from the illegitimate use of physical force and freedom from war and insurgencies? 3 / 4

While overall rates of violent crime are low, there are occasional acts of politically motivated violence and vandalism by left- or right-wing extremist groups. For example, in recent years the anarchist group Rouvikonas has damaged the property or ransacked the premises of NGOs, corporations, universities, churches, government buildings, embassies, and consulates, among other targets.

Some prisons and detention centers suffer from substandard conditions, and law enforcement personnel have been accused of physical abuse, particularly against vulnerable groups such as migrants and asylum seekers.

F4. Do laws, policies, and practices guarantee equal treatment of various segments of the population? 2 / 4

Women generally enjoy equality before the law, though they continue to face workplace discrimination in practice.

Violence targeting immigrants, refugees, and LGBT+ people remains a problem. Members of the Romany minority are also subject to discrimination despite legal protections. According to the Racist Violence Recording Network (RVRN) annual report for 2019, incidents of organized violence had decreased since 2013, but there were still "a significant number of attacks showing signs of structured organizations or committed by organized groups targeting refugees and migrants." In October 2020, after a trial lasting five years, leaders and members of the far-right party Golden Dawn, including 18 former lawmakers, were convicted of operating a criminal organization. Some defendants were also found guilty of specific xenophobic attacks, including violent assaults on Egyptian fishermen. Those convicted received prison sentences of up to 13 years, though they reportedly filed appeals.

Since 2016, when the EU reached an agreement with Turkey to curb the westward flow of migrants and refugees, the number entering Greece has been significantly reduced. It fell sharply in 2020, partly due to the pandemic; there were a total of 15,696 new arrivals in the country during 2020, compared with 74,613 during 2019, according to the Office of the UN High Commissioner for Refugees (UNHCR). Many of the refugees and asylum seekers are housed in Reception and Identification Centers on the Aegean islands or in camps on the mainland. Some of these sites feature harsh living conditions, violence, harassment of women, and endangerment of children. A fire broke out in the overcrowded Moria center on Lesbos in September 2020, leaving some 13,000 people temporarily without shelter. Under pressure from NGOs, officials have attempted to close the worst facilities and increase the use of urban accommodation. Many of these relocation attempts are protested by local communities.

Greek authorities have been accused of forcibly returning migrants and asylum seekers who attempt to enter irregularly from Turkey by land and sea. Beginning in late February 2020, the Turkish government actively encouraged irregular crossings, and Greek forces were accused of using excessive violence to repel the thousands of people who responded. The Greek government also suspended processing of asylum applications, resuming the service only in May. The immediate crisis eased later in March as international borders were closed due to COVID-19, but Greek forces allegedly continued to push back people attempting to cross by sea from Turkey.

G. PERSONAL AUTONOMY AND INDIVIDUAL RIGHTS: 14 / 16

G1. Do individuals enjoy freedom of movement, including the ability to change their place of residence, employment, or education? 4 / 4

Freedom of movement is generally unrestricted for most residents.

Due to the COVID-19 pandemic, the government imposed tight movement restrictions in March 2020. The measures were initially successful in containing the virus, and the country was able to ease restrictions during the spring and summer months. Cases began rising again in August, and the government introduced new limits on movement and large gatherings. Curfews were reintroduced in October, and the country went into lockdown in November. Police were accused of using violent or abusive tactics while enforcing the social-distancing rules in some cases.

G2. Are individuals able to exercise the right to own property and establish private businesses without undue interference from state or nonstate actors? 3 / 4

The government and legal framework are generally supportive of property rights and entrepreneurship, but bureaucratic obstacles can inhibit business activity. Those who have political connections or are willing to pay bribes can sometimes expedite official procedures. In an effort to put pressure on tax-evading property owners who misrepresent the value of their assets, the Independent Authority for Public Revenue announced significant fines for this offense in 2019.

G3. Do individuals enjoy personal social freedoms, including choice of marriage partner and size of family, protection from domestic violence, and control over appearance? 4 / 4

There are no major constraints on personal social freedoms, though domestic violence remains a problem.

A 2018 law stipulated that civil courts have priority over Sharia (Islamic law) courts in adjudicating family law disputes among the Muslim population in Thrace, and that the Sharia bodies could only handle cases in which all parties have agreed to the arrangement. The system in place before the change had been criticized as discriminatory.

A 2017 law allowed unmarried transgender people over age 15 to change their legal gender on identity documents without undergoing gender confirmation surgery or other such procedures, subject to validation by a judge. In 2018, the parliament approved legislation that permitted same-sex couples to serve as foster parents.

G4. Do individuals enjoy equality of opportunity and freedom from economic exploitation? 3 / 4

Most residents enjoy legal protections against exploitative working conditions, but labor laws are not always adequately enforced. Migrants and asylum seekers are especially vulnerable to trafficking for forced labor or sexual exploitation, and government efforts to combat the problem, while increasing, remain insufficient, according to the US State Department.

Grenada

Population: 100,000
Capital: St. George's
Freedom Status: Free
Electoral Democracy: Yes

Overview: Grenada is a parliamentary democracy that regularly holds credible elections. Ongoing concerns include corruption, discrimination against LGBT+ people, and violence against women and children.

KEY DEVELOPMENTS IN 2020

- According to researchers at the University of Oxford, Grenada recorded 127 COVID-19 cases and no deaths as of the end of 2020. The virus inflicted considerable economic damage, with gross domestic product declining an estimated 13.5 percent during the year.
- In July, the governing New National Party (NNP) retracted the Coronavirus Disease (COVID-19) Control Bill following criticism that that it would create an indefinite state of emergency and increase the potential for arbitrary state action.

POLITICAL RIGHTS: 37 / 40
A. ELECTORAL PROCESS: 11 / 12
A1. Was the current head of government or other chief national authority elected through free and fair elections? 4 / 4

The prime minister, usually the leader of the largest party in Parliament, is head of government. The prime minister is appointed by the governor general, who represents the British monarch as head of state.

Following the March 2018 elections, New National Party (NNP) leader Keith Mitchell was sworn in for a second consecutive term as prime minister. Cécile La Grenade was sworn in as Grenada's first woman to be governor general in 2013.

A2. Were the current national legislative representatives elected through free and fair elections? 4 / 4

The bicameral parliament consists of the directly elected, 15-seat House of Representatives, whose members serve five-year terms, and the 13-seat Senate, which is appointed by the governor general. Ten Senate seats are appointed on the advice of the prime minister, and the remaining three on the advice of the opposition leader; senators also serve five-year terms.

The NNP won the elections held in March 2018, capturing all 15 seats in the House of Representatives with 59 percent of the vote. The NDC received 41 percent of the vote. The electoral observation mission of the Organization of American States (OAS) expressed concern over a lack of campaign finance regulations and other issues, but deemed the polls credible.

A3. Are the electoral laws and framework fair, and are they implemented impartially by the relevant election management bodies? 3 / 4

Electoral laws are generally fair, and they are usually implemented impartially by the supervisor of elections, who heads the Parliamentary Elections Office.

In Grenada's 2016 constitutional referendum, all proposals failed to pass—including setting a three-term limit for the prime minister, establishing fixed dates for elections, and reforming the electoral authority and the body that sets constituency boundaries. Voter turnout was low, at just 32 percent.

The unbalanced size of constituencies has resulted in unequal voting power among citizens. For example, in a country of 100,000 people, the largest of Grenada's 15 constituencies has around 6,000 more registered voters than the smallest. This long-standing discrepancy has not been addressed.

B. POLITICAL PLURALISM AND PARTICIPATION: 16 / 16

B1. Do the people have the right to organize in different political parties or other competitive political groupings of their choice, and is the system free of undue obstacles to the rise and fall of these competing parties or groupings? 4 / 4

Political parties can organize freely. While a number of small parties have competed in elections, the first-past-the-post system encourages two-party politics, and since 1999 only the NNP and NDC have won seats in Parliament. Additionally, weak campaign finance laws potentially create an unfair advantage for certain parties.

B2. Is there a realistic opportunity for the opposition to increase its support or gain power through elections? 4 / 4

There are realistic opportunities for opposition parties to increase their support or gain power through elections, and power has rotated on several occasions since the first election in 1984, after democracy was restored to Grenada. However, the NNP has won a majority of the elections since then, and the NDC failed to win any seats in the House of Representatives in both the 2013 and 2018 elections.

B3. Are the people's political choices free from domination by forces that are external to the political sphere, or by political forces that employ extrapolitical means? 4 / 4

People are generally able to express their political choices without encountering pressure from outside actors. However, the OAS has expressed concern about a lack of transparency and regulation of campaign finance procedures, which could create avenues for undue influence over candidates and voters by business or other special interest groups.

B4. Do various segments of the population (including ethnic, racial, religious, gender, LGBT+, and other relevant groups) have full political rights and electoral opportunities? 4 / 4

Grenada's constitution guarantees universal suffrage for adult citizens. Political representation largely reflects a population that is over 90 percent of African or mixed descent.

However, other ethnic groups have a voice in politics and are represented in Parliament. Women remain underrepresented in politics, though 7 out of 15 seats in the House of Representatives were won by women in 2018. Women's advocacy groups have influence in the general political sphere. The marginalization of LGBT+ people impacts their ability to engage fully in political and electoral processes.

C. FUNCTIONING OF GOVERNMENT: 10 / 12

C1. Do the freely elected head of government and national legislative representatives determine the policies of the government? 4 / 4

The appointed prime minister and cabinet and freely elected representatives are able to determine the policies of the government. However, because of concerns over the lack of an opposition in the House of Representatives, three NDC members were appointed to the Senate after the 2013 and 2018 elections.

C2. Are safeguards against official corruption strong and effective? 3 / 4

Corruption remains a prominent issue in Grenada, despite safeguards enshrined in the Prevention of Corruption Act and the Integrity in Public Life Act. Several suggested amendments in the 2016 constitutional reform package would have strengthened anticorruption safeguards, but all were voted down by significant margins.

Grenada's Citizenship by Investment (CBI) Program, which allows foreigners to gain citizenship through an economic investment in the country, continued to trouble some analysts due to the potential for fraud and abuse, despite the tightening of rules governing it in 2017. In April 2019, the government passed reforms to ensure the completion of projects and protect investors. However, that November, Al Jazeera reported that politicians in Grenada had allegedly accepted campaign contributions or future kickbacks off of government contracts from wealthy foreign businesspeople in exchange for diplomatic passports or ambassadorships, all connected to the CBI program. Although the prime minister and the NNP denied the report, the story heightened concern about the CBI program's susceptibility to corruption.

C3. Does the government operate with openness and transparency? 3 / 4

The government of Grenada generally operates with transparency. A decree passed in 2013 under the authority of the Integrity in Public Life Act requires all public officials to declare their personal assets. An appointed commission monitors and verifies declarations but does not disclose them publicly except in court. In 2017, Parliament passed an amendment to the Mutual Exchange of Information on Tax Matters Bill, which allows Grenadian authorities to request financial information about its citizens residing abroad in an effort to prevent tax avoidance. In August 2020, the Fiscal Responsibility Oversight Committee, an external body charged with monitoring the state's fiscal position, noted that the opacity of data involving state-run entities and other financial liabilities impeded it from fulfilling its role.

There is no law to ensure public access to information, even though the government has pledged to introduce such an act.

CIVIL LIBERTIES: 52 / 60

D. FREEDOM OF EXPRESSION AND BELIEF: 15 / 16

D1. Are there free and independent media? 3 / 4

In 2012, Grenada became the first Caribbean country to decriminalize defamation, but seditious libel remains a criminal offense. Politicians have initiated defamation lawsuits against the media, contributing to self-censorship among journalists who may not be able to afford legal costs or resulting fines.

Press freedom advocates have criticized censorship at the country's largest broadcaster, the Grenada Broadcasting Network (GBN), which is partly owned by the government. In July 2019 the GBN was accused by the NDC of deliberately sabotaging coverage of the party after the screen went blank at the beginning of an NDC news conference, with coverage resuming at the conclusion of the party's remarks. GBN denied the accusations, and stated that the disruption was due to an electrical outage.

D2. Are individuals free to practice and express their religious faith or nonbelief in public and private? 4 / 4

Freedom of religion is protected under the constitution and is generally respected in practice.

D3. Is there academic freedom, and is the educational system free from extensive political indoctrination? 4 / 4

The government generally respects academic freedom.

D4. Are individuals free to express their personal views on political or other sensitive topics without fear of surveillance or retribution? 4 / 4

Individuals are free to express their personal views on political or other sensitive topics.

E. ASSOCIATIONAL AND ORGANIZATIONAL RIGHTS: 11 / 12

E1. Is there freedom of assembly? 4 / 4

Freedom of assembly is constitutionally guaranteed, and that right is generally respected in practice. The widespread criticism of the proposed Coronavirus Disease (COVID-19) Control Bill, 2020 came in part over concerns that it would indefinitely curtail freedom of assembly, accompanied by objections to the potential for arbitrary arrest and excessive powers granted to the minister of health. The government withdrew the legislation, though social distancing protocols remained in place.

E2. Is there freedom for nongovernmental organizations, particularly those that are engaged in human rights–and governance-related work? 4 / 4

Nongovernmental organizations (NGOs) are generally free to operate.

E3. Is there freedom for trade unions and similar professional or labor organizations? 3 / 4

The right of workers to form and join labor unions is constitutionally protected, though unions and labor activists face some obstacles. Workers have the right to strike, organize, and bargain collectively, though employers are not legally bound to recognize a union if a majority of workers do not join. Essential services workers may strike, but compulsory arbitration can be used to resolve disputes. The list of essential services is extensive and includes services that should not be considered as such according to International Labour Organization (ILO) standards.

In 2020, the NNP faced increasing opposition from farmers to its plans to merge the cooperative associations that manage the important nutmeg and cocoa industries under a plan that would include additional state control and potential market liberalization. The government backed off on plans to assert control of the board of directors of a merged association, and discussions continued throughout the year.

F. RULE OF LAW: 13 / 16

F1. Is there an independent judiciary? 4 / 4

An independent judiciary is constitutionally guaranteed. Courts have demonstrated independence in recent years, as evidenced by a 2017 Supreme Court decision that prevented the government from expropriating property owned by the company Rex Resorts. There has not been tangible evidence of political interference in the judiciary in recent years.

Grenada is a member of the Organization of Eastern Caribbean States court system, and is a charter member of the Caribbean Court of Justice, but the judiciary relies on the Judicial Committee of the Privy Council in London as its final court of appeal. In 2016, Parliament approved legislation to eliminate the Privy Council as the final court, but the measure was defeated in the year's constitutional referendum. A second referendum on the matter failed again in 2018.

F2. Does due process prevail in civil and criminal matters? 3 / 4

Detainees and defendants are guaranteed a range of legal rights, including the presumption of innocence and the right to trial without delay, which are mostly respected in practice. However, case backlogs have rendered trial delays common in practice. Additionally, staffing shortages prevent the state from providing legal counsel to some indigent defendants.

F3. Is there protection from the illegitimate use of physical force and freedom from war and insurgencies? 3 / 4

Grenada is free from war and insurgencies. Flogging remains a punishment for petty crimes, and the prison system is overcrowded. The 2019 occupancy rate was over 230 percent, high by regional standards. Although considered one of the safer Caribbean islands, there has been a rise in reports of sexual assault in recent years.

F4. Do laws, policies, and practices guarantee equal treatment of various segments of the population? 3 / 4

Same-sex sexual activity between men is a criminal offense, although the law is rarely enforced. In October 2020, the Director of Public Prosecutions declined to pursue charges against two men who were engaged in sex in a video that was circulated online, labeling the provision of the criminal code "obsolete." Nonetheless, LGBT+ people face significant societal discrimination; one of the men in the video said that he had received death threats and experienced hostile treatment from the public.

The law does not prohibit discrimination in employment or occupation regarding sexual orientation, HIV-positive status, or gender identity. The 2016 constitutional referendum included an amendment to protect the equal treatment of people in Grenada, but that amendment was overwhelmingly rejected due to concerns that language in the amendment might lead to the legalization of same-sex marriage.

G. PERSONAL AUTONOMY AND INDIVIDUAL RIGHTS: 13 / 16

G1. Do individuals enjoy freedom of movement, including the ability to change their place of residence, employment, or education? 4 / 4

Freedom of movement is constitutionally guaranteed, and this right is generally respected in practice.

G2. Are individuals able to exercise the right to own property and establish private businesses without undue interference from state or non-state actors? 3 / 4

The government of Grenada has actively encouraged both national and foreign investors to operate businesses in the country, but procedures involved in establishing a new business are onerous. In 2017 and 2018 the government attempted to expropriate the Grenadian Hotel from its owners, Rex Resorts, abandoning its claim only after the hotel had been sold to another company. In the World Bank's Doing Business 2020 rankings, Grenada placed 146 out of 190, the lowest ranked English-speaking Caribbean nation.

G3. Do individuals enjoy personal social freedoms, including choice of marriage partner and size of family, protection from domestic violence, and control over appearance? 3 / 4

Violence against women and children is a widespread issue in Grenada. According to a 2018 survey released in August 2020, 29 percent of Grenadian women reported experiencing physical or sexual violence in their lifetime. Domestic violence legislation came into effect in 2011, but enforcement has been limited. In 2018, the Royal Grenada Police Force launched the Special Victims Unit to handle cases of sexual assault, domestic violence, and child abuse, as well as a new hotline for reporting sexual abuse.

G4. Do individuals enjoy equality of opportunity and freedom from economic exploitation? 3 / 4

Poverty and unemployment are pervasive and hamper the social mobility of many Grenadians. In 2018, Grenada ratified the ILO's Domestic Workers Convention, to improve work conditions of domestic workers, who are mainly women. It came into effect in November 2019. Children are not explicitly prohibited from doing hazardous work.

A 2015 law punishes human trafficking with up to 25 years in jail and large fines. However, reports of human trafficking are rare.

Guatemala

Population: 18,100,000
Capital: Guatemala City
Freedom Status: Partly Free
Electoral Democracy: Yes

Overview: While Guatemala holds regular elections that are generally free, organized crime and corruption severely impact the functioning of government. Violence and criminal extortion schemes are serious problems, and victims have little recourse to justice. Journalists, activists, and public officials who confront crime, corruption, and other sensitive issues risk attack.

KEY DEVELOPMENTS IN 2020
- COVID-19 cases began to spike in Guatemala in May and reached a peak in July. By year's end, over 138,000 people had been infected and over 4,800 died, according to researchers at the University of Oxford. The government closed borders, instituted a stringent lockdown, and approved a large relief package under emergency powers.
- Following the 2019 departure of the UN-backed International Commission against Impunity in Guatemala (CICIG), efforts to tackle systemic corruption and impunity

deteriorated, prosecutions stalled, and attacks against judges, prosecutors, and civil society actors intensified.
* The election of justices to high courts has been delayed for over a year due to procedural irregularities, alleged corruption, and the legislature's noncompliance with selection criteria required by the Constitutional Court.
* The approval of a controversial 2021 budget set off massive protests in November, which were met with repression and arrests.

POLITICAL RIGHTS: 21 / 40

A. ELECTORAL PROCESS: 7 / 12

A1. Was the current head of government or other chief national authority elected through free and fair elections? 2 / 4

The constitution stipulates a four-year presidential term, and prohibits reelection. In the August 2019 runoff, Alejandro Giammattei of the Vamos party won 58 percent of the vote, defeating former first lady Sandra Torres of the center-left National Unity for Hope party (UNE). While the results were judged as credible, Organization of American States (OAS) electoral observers noted irregularities including disturbances, ballot burning, voter intimidation, and acts of violence. Giammattei took office in January 2020.

The campaign was also marked by successful efforts to disqualify presidential candidates. Union of National Change (UCN) candidate Mario Estrada was disqualified after he was arrested on charges of drug trafficking in the United States in April 2019, and Fuerza party candidate Mauricio Radford was barred over an ongoing corruption case. Zury Ríos, the Valor party candidate and daughter of former dictator Efraín Ríos Montt, was disqualified because of a legal provision that bars members of his family from holding office. Former attorney general Thelma Aldana, who pursued a high-profile corruption case against former president Otto Peréz Molina (2012–15), was barred and fled to the United States after receiving threats, allegedly issued by the targets of her investigations. Electoral crimes prosecutor Óscar Schaad fled Guatemala days before the first round in June 2019 after he and his family were threatened; Schaad resigned in November.

A2. Were the current national legislative representatives elected through free and fair elections? 3 / 4

Members of the unicameral, 160-seat Congress are elected to four-year terms. Legislators were elected in June 2019, concurrently with the first round of the presidential election and 340 mayoral races. The UNE won 53 seats while President Giammattei's Vamos party won 16 seats. The UCN won 12, and the remaining 79 seats were split between 16 parties, none of which won more than 10 seats.

The 2019 election results were deemed credible, but observers noted irregularities, disturbances, and threats of violence. A number of local races were nullified or rescheduled by the Supreme Electoral Tribunal (TSE) due to death threats against electoral officials and violent incidents. Election monitors received complaints from female officeholders and candidates who reported discrimination.

A3. Are the electoral laws and framework fair, and are they implemented impartially by the relevant election management bodies? 2 / 4

Authorities and lawmakers in recent years have taken some steps to reform election administration. In 2016, the legislature approved reforms that included stronger oversight of party finances and enhanced sanctioning powers for the TSE. The 2019 elections were the first to be held under the new system, but the implementation of these reforms was incomplete.

The 2016 reforms included a provision to restrict the practice of switching party affiliation, or *transfuguismo*, for legislators. However, OAS election monitors reported that this provision was inconsistently applied during the 2019 elections.

In March 2020, after months of delay and amid the onset of the COVID-19 pandemic, Congress elected new TSE magistrates (2020–26) in a session featuring little transparency. Several of those elected are reportedly associated with officials accused of corruption.

B. POLITICAL PLURALISM AND PARTICIPATION: 10 / 16

B1. Do the people have the right to organize in different political parties or other competitive political groupings of their choice, and is the system free of undue obstacles to the rise and fall of these competing parties or groupings? 3 / 4

Political groups and organizations generally operate without encountering legal restrictions. However, new groups sometimes face bureaucratic delays from the TSE when attempting to register.

Elections take place within an inchoate multiparty system in which new parties are frequently created, often without sufficient resources and infrastructure to gain broad support. A historic lack of party finance regulations has allowed some candidates and parties access to vast resources.

B2. Is there a realistic opportunity for the opposition to increase its support or gain power through elections? 3 / 4

Elections at the national and local levels are competitive, and new parties routinely gain significant quotas of power. Guatemalan politics are unstable and power rotates between parties frequently, which can discourage a traditional opposition from coalescing. Political candidates risk attack during campaign periods; civil society organization Electoral Watch reported that at least 10 candidates were killed during the 2019 election period.

B3. Are the people's political choices free from domination by forces that are external to the political sphere, or by political forces that employ extrapolitical means? 2 / 4

Verbal harassment and physical violence against voters are common during elections, and can deter political participation. Weak campaign finance regulations have historically permitted lopsided resource advantages, as well as financing of candidates by special interests and organized criminal groups, distorting the political choices of citizens. Presidential candidate Estrada, who was arrested in the United States, was accused of promising cabinet positions to Sinaloa drug cartel associates in return for their support. Observers reported that armed groups and criminal organizations have attempted to sway the results of local races. Direct vote buying is also common.

B4. Do various segments of the population (including ethnic, racial, religious, gender, LGBT+, and other relevant groups) have full political rights and electoral opportunities? 2 / 4

Members of ethnic and other minority groups struggle to fully exercise their political rights, and there are no affirmative measures in place to promote the election of representatives of Indigenous peoples. While as much as 60 percent of the population is Indigenous, only one Indigenous presidential candidate ran in 2019. No Indigenous persons or Afro-Guatemalans hold cabinet-level positions.

Women are underrepresented in politics, though small women's rights groups, mainly those working on addressing violence against women, have some visibility in the political sphere. President Giammattei has appointed three woman ministers to his cabinet. Only 19 percent of the Congress is female.

The first openly gay man to enter Congress was elected in 2019; in 2020, he was the target of attacks and homophobic messages from fellow legislators. Political opportunities remain rare for the LGBT+ community.

C. FUNCTIONING OF GOVERNMENT: 4 / 12

C1. Do the freely elected head of government and national legislative representatives determine the policies of the government? 2 / 4

The elected government and legislature determine government policies, but they are frequently subject to influence by outside interests. President Giammattei came to the presidency backed by a group of former military officials; such networks possess significant economic power and frequently oppose the peace process that Guatemala has been fitfully implementing since 1996.

Recent investigations of electoral and party finance corruption have shed light on the influence of unelected and illicit groups over the government. There are serious allegations of links between drug trafficking and the political elite. In August 2020, US prosecutors charged a former minister of the economy with laundering millions of dollars in drug money. Business groups continue to hold significant sway over the executive and legislative branches.

C2. Are safeguards against official corruption strong and effective? 1 / 4

Corruption, which is often related to organized crime, remains a serious problem. The CICIG operated for 12 years before the government succeeded in shutting it down in 2019. Since its closure, authorities and lawmakers have continued to obstruct the fight against corruption, prosecutions have stalled, and many high-profile cases have lost momentum due to a lack of support. The Special Prosecutor's Office against Impunity (FECI) has pressed forward with investigations of high-level officials in current and past administrations. However, lack of support for FECI from the Attorney General's Office (FGR) has furthered weakened efforts to curb corruption.

Since the CICIG's departure, judges, prosecutors and civil society actors have increasingly been the targets of attacks, threats, lawsuits, and defamation campaigns for their prior support of CICIG and continuing commitment to tackling corruption.

The COVID-19 pandemic provided opportunities for corruption due to the easing of regulations for contract procurement and decreased access to government information. In April, two deputy health ministers were fired and placed under investigation for allegedly engaging in pandemic-related graft.

C3. Does the government operate with openness and transparency? 1 / 4

Public information offices frequently fail to publish data about public expenditures as required. The Law on Access to Information is poorly enforced, and dedicated nongovernmental organizations (NGOs) continue to file grievances over its nonapplication and, together with the Office of the Human Rights Ombudsman (PDH), work to encourage the government to adhere to its provisions.

The government's contracting and budgeting processes are opaque and racked with corruption. This worsened in 2020 due to the easing of procurement requirements in response to the COVID-19 pandemic, which strained the already precarious health system and made it harder for relief to reach affected communities in a timely manner. Civil society observers also criticized the government's general mismanagement of the pandemic, including severe deficiencies in transparency and accuracy regarding case numbers and regional patterns.

CIVIL LIBERTIES: 31 / 60

D. FREEDOM OF EXPRESSION AND BELIEF: 11 / 16

D1. Are there free and independent media? 2 / 4

While the constitution protects freedom of speech, journalists face threats and self-censor when covering sensitive topics including drug trafficking, corruption, organized crime, and human rights violations. Threats come from public officials, illicit actors, the police, and individuals aligned with companies operating on Indigenous lands. Physical attacks against journalists occur regularly. The Association of Guatemalan Journalists registered dozens of acts of intimidation, threats, and assaults in 2020, and at least two journalists were killed during the year: Bryan Guerra was murdered in Chiquimula in February, and Mario Ortega was shot in November in San José. Journalists have demanded that the government implement a protection program that was agreed to in 2012, but little progress has been made. Media ownership is also highly concentrated. The country's cybercrime laws have failed to protect outlets and reporters from harassment by trolls for hire, while officials abuse unrelated laws to censor media outlets.

Rural, Indigenous, and women journalists are afforded little protection from discrimination, threats, and frivolous legal action, and reporters covering regional news suffered attacks and detentions on several occasions in 2020. In September, Indigenous journalist Anastasia Mejía Tiriquiz was arrested and charged with multiple serious offenses, including sedition and arson, after covering protests regarding alleged corruption by local authorities.

Journalists raised serious concerns regarding obstacles to covering the COVID-19 pandemic, including difficulty in accessing official information, censorship by government officials, arbitrary detentions, and defamation campaigns. President Giammattei was highly combative with reporters throughout the year, and journalists Marvin del Cid and Sonny Figueroa, who have published articles examining alleged misdeeds by the president and members of his inner circle, faced repeated threats and police harassment.

D2. Are individuals free to practice and express their religious faith or nonbelief in public and private? 4 / 4

The constitution guarantees religious freedom, and individuals are free to practice and express their religious faith or nonbelief in practice. Public religious gatherings were prohibited as part of the pandemic-related restrictions. In September religious services were allowed to restart, with face masks, attendance restrictions, and social distancing required.

D3. Is there academic freedom, and is the educational system free from extensive political indoctrination? 3 / 4

Although the government does not interfere with academic freedom, scholars have received death threats for questioning past human rights abuses or continuing injustices.

D4. Are individuals free to express their personal views on political or other sensitive topics without fear of surveillance or retribution? 2 / 4

Many Guatemalans take precautions when speaking about social and political issues outside of their homes due to a high level of insecurity in the country. Journalists and human rights defenders reported incidents of harassment and surveillance throughout 2020. This stepped-up surveillance, along with increased intimidation and harassment of perceived opponents of the government, has encouraged greater self-censorship among ordinary citizens.

E. ASSOCIATIONAL AND ORGANIZATIONAL RIGHTS: 6 / 12
E1. Is there freedom of assembly? 2 / 4

The constitution guarantees freedom of assembly, but this right is not always protected. Police frequently threaten force, and at times use violence against protesters. Protests related to environmental or Indigenous rights issues have been met with harsh resistance from the police and armed groups.

In March 2020, the government declared a state of emergency due to the outbreak of COVID-19 and instituted mandatory curfews and restrictions on gatherings and activities. By September, the police had detained more than 40,000 people for violating the curfew restrictions.

In November, massive protests erupted following the congressional approval of the 2021 budget, which included sharp cuts to key services while allocating money to agencies plagued by corruption allegations. While most protesters—many of whom demanded President Giammattei's resignation—were peaceful, sporadic violence occurred, including the setting of a fire that damaged Congress. Journalists and the PDH reported excessive use of force by the security forces against demonstrators; at least 22 people were injured, two of them with severe eye injuries. At least 35 protesters were detained, though most charges were later dismissed.

E2. Is there freedom for nongovernmental organizations, particularly those that are engaged in human rights- and governance-related work? 2 / 4

The constitution guarantees freedom of association, and a variety of NGOs operate. However, groups associated with human rights, Indigenous rights, and environmental rights face increasing violence and criminalization of their work. The Unit for the Protection of Human Rights Defenders in Guatemala (UDEFEGUA), an NGO, documented 15 killings and 22 assassination attempts in 2020, as well as hundreds of less severe incidents. Despite a 2014 ruling by the Inter-American Court of Human Rights requiring a comprehensive public policy to protect human rights defenders, the government failed to advance such a policy; indeed, rights advocates criticized the closure of several agencies that were central to implementation of human rights provisions of the 1996 peace accords.

In February, legislators approved an amendment to the law governing NGOs that introduces a more onerous registration process, expands the state's authority to deregister groups, and restricts NGOs' control of funds received from abroad. In March, however, the Constitutional Court provisionally suspended enactment of the law; at year's end, a final ruling had not been issued.

E3. Is there freedom for trade unions and similar professional or labor organizations? 2 / 4

Guatemala is home to a vigorous labor movement, but workers are frequently denied the right to organize and face mass firings and blacklisting. Trade union members are also subject to intimidation, violence, and murder, particularly in rural areas. Labor laws obstruct union membership and impede strikes.

F. RULE OF LAW: 6 / 16
F1. Is there an independent judiciary? 2 / 4

The judiciary is hobbled by corruption, inefficiency, incapacity, and intimidation of judges, prosecutors, and witnesses, both by outside actors and influential figures within the judiciary. The Constitutional Court (CC) demonstrated independence in several rulings in 2020. However, continued attempts to remove CC magistrates and public attacks against them, along with consistent refusal by Congress and the Supreme Court to comply with CC rulings, raised serious concerns about the weakening of the judiciary's independence.

Corruption also affected the process to select new Supreme Court and appellate court judges, who were supposed to assume office in 2019. In February 2020, FECI uncovered a corruption network seeking to influence nominations, prompting the CC to suspend the selection process. In May, the CC issued a ruling laying out clear guidelines for the selection of justices to the high courts. However, as of year's end, Congress had refused to abide by the ruling and carry out the selection process.

In June and again in November, the Supreme Court granted requests to lift the immunity of four CC magistrates, alleging that their ruling on the judicial selection process amounted to criminal conduct. Civil society groups described the efforts as retaliation for CC rulings upholding the rule of law.

In November, the Supreme Court pushed through the election of Roberto Molina Barreto to the CC, despite questions about the process and Molina's independence, given his vote to overturn Ríos Montt's genocide conviction in 2013 and subsequent run for vice president on a ticket with Zury Ríos in the 2019 election.

F2. Does due process prevail in civil and criminal matters? 1 / 4

Due process rights are guaranteed in the constitution, but those rights are inconsistently upheld, due in part to corruption in the judiciary and an ineffective police force in which many officers routinely violate the law and the rights of citizens. Access to justice remains difficult, especially for the Indigenous community. Conviction rates are low.

In recent years, judges and prosecutors have reported threats and harassment, been targeted by smear campaigns, and been subjected to malicious criminal and disciplinary complaints in apparent retaliation for their work on sensitive cases related to corruption and human rights abuses. More than 40 lawsuits have been filed against FECI prosecutors in an attempt to close down its investigations. In October 2020, the FGR approved nine administrative complaints against FECI prosecutors, filed mostly by individuals facing FECI investigations. PDH head Jordán Rodas, regarded as an independent advocate for human rights, also faced criminal complaints and legislative motions for his removal on the basis of allegedly promoting abortion rights and displaying pro-LGBT+ bias.

F3. Is there protection from the illegitimate use of physical force and freedom from war and insurgencies? 2 / 4

High levels of violence, kidnappings, and extortion at the hands of the police, drug traffickers, and street gangs continue, with related fears and risks routinely affecting the lives of ordinary people. Links between the state, politicians, the military, and illicit actors complicate a cohesive response to the country's security challenges. Despite these challenges, the homicide rate dropped for the 11th straight year; the authorities reported a 28 percent drop in homicides in 2020 compared to 2019. Prison facilities are grossly overcrowded and rife with gang and drug-related violence and corruption. Prison riots are common, and are frequently deadly.

Since taking office in January 2020, the Giammattei administration has also declared states of siege, which restrict constitutional guarantees and allow for the deployment of security forces, in eight municipalities. Authorities justified the measures on the presence of armed groups and need to restore order, but no specific events were cited, and NGOs and Indigenous groups raised concerns that the orders were intended to facilitate evictions and promote megaprojects in the affected areas. In some areas, the measures resulted in the illegal detention of community leaders.

Efforts to bring perpetrators of past human rights abuses to justice continued in 2020, but progress was mixed. In November, a former special forces officer was ordered to stand trial for his participation in the infamous 1982 Dos Erres massacre; six former military officers have previously been sentenced in connection with the case. The COVID-19 pandemic paralyzed judicial activity, resulting in the temporary suspension of judicial proceedings in several ongoing civil war–era criminal trials. In January 2019, Congress began considering legal measures to offer amnesty for civil war–era crimes. Despite a Constitutional Court provisional ruling to suspend debate later that year, the bill remained pending in Congress throughout 2020.

F4. Do laws, policies, and practices guarantee equal treatment of various segments of the population? 1 / 4

Equal rights are guaranteed in the constitution, but minorities continue to face unequal treatment. Indigenous communities suffer from high rates of poverty, illiteracy, and infant mortality. Indigenous women are particularly marginalized. Discrimination against the Mayan community is a major concern.

LGBT+ people face discrimination, violence, and police abuse and are unprotected by legislation. The PDH has stated that people living with HIV/AIDS also face discrimination.

The constitution prohibits discrimination based on gender, but women continue to face gender-based inequality; women are usually paid less for their labor than men, and sexual harassment in the workplace is not penalized.

In March 2020, an agreement signed with the United States in 2019 that forces migrants passing through Guatemala to claim asylum there first was temporarily suspended due to the coronavirus pandemic. However, the United States continued to deport migrants, many of whom tested positive for COVID-19, and deportees were at times subjected to social ostracism upon their return due to fears of contagion.

G. PERSONAL AUTONOMY AND INDIVIDUAL RIGHTS: 8 / 16

G1. Do individuals enjoy freedom of movement, including the ability to change their place of residence, employment, or education? 3 / 4

While there are no permanent restrictions on free movement, violence and the threat of violence by gangs and organized criminal groups inhibits this right in practice, and has prompted the displacement of thousands of people. Guatemalans saw their freedom of movement restricted due to the COVID-19-linked state of emergency, as did communities living in regions where states of siege were implemented.

G2. Are individuals able to exercise the right to own property and establish private businesses without undue interference from state or nonstate actors? 2 / 4

Protections for property rights and economic freedom rarely extend beyond Guatemalans with wealth and political connections. Land protections are especially limited for the Indigenous community, and for women in particular. A series of Constitutional Court rulings in June and July 2020 reinforced communal landholding rights in Indigenous communities. In September, however, the Inter-American Commission on Human Rights condemned a wave of murders of Indigenous land rights' defenders.

Business activity is hampered by criminal activity including extortion and fraud. An inefficient state bureaucracy, rife with unclear and complicated regulations, also contributes to difficulties in establishing and operating a business.

G3. Do individuals enjoy personal social freedoms, including choice of marriage partner and size of family, protection from domestic violence, and control over appearance? 2 / 4

Physical and sexual violence against women and children remains high, with perpetrators rarely facing prosecution. According to the police, 358 women were killed in

Guatemala in 2020, and more than 3,000 have been killed since 2015. The law permits abortion only when a pregnancy threatens the life of the woman. Teen pregnancy remains high; in 2017, a decree banned marriages for children under the age of 18, though the law is not effectively enforced. The coronavirus lockdown resulted in increased reports of violence against women throughout the country, while transport reductions limited women's access to support services.

G4. Do individuals enjoy equality of opportunity and freedom from economic exploitation?
1 / 4

The Indigenous community's access to economic opportunities and socioeconomic mobility remains limited, with more than 70 percent of the Indigenous population living in poverty. Income distribution is among the most unequal worldwide, with the wealthiest 10 percent of the population holding nearly 50 percent of the national wealth. Significant barriers to accessing education persist, particularly for girls, Indigenous children, and rural residents. These obstacles were exacerbated by the COVID-19 pandemic, which shuttered classrooms throughout the country, as well as by hurricanes Eta and Iota, which struck in November and left at least 60 people dead and tens of thousands displaced, along with large-scale damage to crops and property centered in majority-indigenous areas.

Child labor persists, especially among Indigenous children, as does sexual exploitation of vulnerable groups including children, LGBT+ people, and Indigenous people. Gangs often force children and young men to join their organizations or perform work for them.

Guinea

Population: 12,600,000
Capital: Conakry
Freedom Status: Partly Free
Electoral Democracy: No

Overview: Guinea returned to civilian rule in 2010, following a 2008 military coup and decades of authoritarian governance. Since then, the country has held multiparty elections, which have been plagued by violence, delays, and other flaws. The government uses restrictive criminal laws to discourage dissent, and ethnic divisions and pervasive corruption often exacerbate political disputes. Regular abuse of civilians by military and police forces reflects a deep-seated culture of impunity. In March 2020, President Alpha Condé won approval of a new constitution that allowed him to seek a third term in office over the objections of opposition groups.

KEY DEVELOPMENTS IN 2020
- In March, Guinean voters approved a proposed constitution that, among other provisions, institutes six-year presidential terms, allows presidents to serve beyond the end of their terms in some circumstances, and effectively resets term limits for incumbent Alpha Condé. According to the official results, nearly 92 percent of voters approved the constitution on a turnout of 61 percent.
- Parliamentary elections were concurrently held with the constitutional referendum in March. The ruling Rally of the Guinean People (RPG) of President Condé won a parliamentary majority in a contest that was impacted by concerns over voter-roll

integrity, communications disruptions, attacks on polling stations, and an opposition boycott. While the RPG won 79 seats, no other party won more than 10.

- President Condé won a third term in October, winning 59.5 percent of the vote in the first round. Other candidates, including main challenger Cellou Dalein Diallo, accused Condé of engaging in fraud, but the Constitutional Court rejected their claims in November. The presidential election was marred by a government crackdown on protests, with security forces using tear gas and live ammunition to disperse them.
- The Guinean government introduced restrictions on public gatherings and movement in response to the COVID-19 pandemic, restricting travel into Greater Conakry and establishing roadblocks. Restrictions on public gatherings remained in force through most of the year, though they were loosened in December. The World Health Organization (WHO) reported 13,700 cases and 81 deaths at year's end.

POLITICAL RIGHTS: 14 / 40 (−1)

A. ELECTORAL PROCESS: 4 / 12 (−1)

A1. Was the current head of government or other chief national authority elected through free and fair elections? 2 / 4 (−1)

The president is elected by popular vote for up to two six-year terms according to the 2020 constitution. In the October presidential election, incumbent Alpha Condé won a third term, with the Constitutional Court declaring him the winner in early November. According to the official results, Condé won 59.5 percent of the vote in the first round. Condé's main challenger, Union of Democratic Forces of Guinea (UFDG) candidate Cellou Dalein Diallo—who officially won 33.5 percent of the vote—challenged the results along with three other candidates, but the court rejected their accusations of fraud in November.

African Union (AU) and Economic Community of West African States (ECOWAS) monitors called the election's conduct sound days after the vote, though the European Commission's high commissioner for foreign policy questioned the results later in October. Some Guineans who sought to register for the vote were effectively unable to do so, due to COVID-19-related restrictions.

The immediate postelection period was marred by violence, the sequestering of high-profile opposition figures, and disruptions to communications services. The home of UFDG candidate Diallo was surrounded for several days in late October, after he declared himself the victor, while several high-profile supporters were arrested. Security forces cracked down on opposition protests in Conakry; the UFDG claimed that as many as 46 people were killed by early November, while the government separately reported 21 deaths by late October. Internet communications were disrupted in the days following the election, though services were restored by late October.

Score Change: The score declined from 3 to 2 because some Guineans were unable to register to vote for the presidential election to vote due to COVID-19-related restrictions; the election itself was marred by opposition allegations of fraud, communications disruptions, and a violent crackdown.

A2. Were the current national legislative representatives elected through free and fair elections? 1 / 4 (+1)

The unicameral National Assembly includes 114 seats. Some 76 members are elected via proportional representation, while another 38 are directly elected. Members serve five-year terms.

Parliamentary elections were held in late March 2020, allowing voters to replace a body that had served beyond its electoral mandate. The ruling Rally of the Guinean People (RPG) won 79 seats, while the UFDG and the Union of Republican Forces (UFR) boycotted the contest and won none. No other party won more than 10 seats. The Independent National Electoral Commission (CENI) reported that turnout stood at 61 percent. The AU, ECOWAS, and the International Organization of La Francophonie (OIF) declined to send observers over concerns about the integrity of the voter rolls.

The immediate preelection period was marked by arrests and enforced disappearances of opposition members. On election day, security forces in Conakry used tear gas and live ammunition to disperse demonstrators, some of whom established roadblocks. Security Minister Albert Damatang Camara reported that six people died in Conakry on election day. Polling stations were also attacked throughout the country, as opponents of a concurrently held constitutional referendum clashed with supporters and security forces. Several dozen people were reportedly killed nationwide, with Human Rights Watch (HRW) counting at least 32 deaths over a three-day period in the city of Nzérékoré.

Score Change: The score improved from 0 to 1 because a new legislature was elected despite concerns over voter-roll integrity and widespread violence, replacing a body whose democratic mandate expired.

A3. Are the electoral laws and framework fair, and are they implemented impartially by the relevant election management bodies? 1 / 4 (−1)

While the Guinean electoral framework has allowed credible elections to proceed in the past, the composition of electoral bodies has been the subject of disagreement. In 2018, the parliament reduced the number of CENI commissioners from 25 to 17 and mandated that the governing and opposition parties each hold 7 commission seats. The 2018 law also mandated that parties must hold at least two parliamentary seats and must have contested the last presidential election to gain CENI representation. CENI chair Kabinet Cissé was selected in April 2020, after predecessor Amadou Salif Kébé died of COVID-19.

CENI was responsible for a voter registration drive ahead of the February 2020 parliamentary elections, which were delayed to March. In February, the OIF warned that 2.4 million names were unverifiable due to technical issues. ECOWAS recommended the removal of those names, and CENI acceded to that request in mid-March.

The 2020 constitution, which was concurrently approved during the March parliamentary elections, proved controversial. The new constitution instituted six-year terms for the chief executive compared to the previous document's five. New language on term limits was interpreted as a reset for President Condé, who was term-limited under the old constitution. The referendum itself was marred by attacks on polling stations in opposition areas. After the final text was published in April, the African Network for Constitutional Lawyers criticized the removal of a clause allowing independent candidates to run for president. The final text also allows incumbent presidents to maintain their posts beyond their mandates in certain circumstances.

Score Change: The score declined from 2 to 1 because a March constitutional referendum allowing the incumbent to remain in power was marred by attacks on polling places in opposition areas.

B. POLITICAL PLURALISM AND PARTICIPATION: 7 / 16

B1. Do the people have the right to organize in different political parties or other competitive political groupings of their choice, and is the system free of undue obstacles to the rise and fall of these competing parties or groupings? 2 / 4

More than 130 parties are registered, with most having clear ethnic or regional bases. Relations between the ruling RPG and opposition parties are strained. Government and opposition supporters are known to engage in violent clashes during elections.

Members of the National Front for the Defense of the Constitution (FNDC), a coalition of civil society groups, political parties, and labor unions, face intimidation and arrests. Two leaders were arrested in March 2020 and were denied access to legal counsel for part of their detention. They were bailed in mid-March, and charges against them were dismissed in July. Another FNDC leader, Oumar Sylla, was arrested for disseminating false information in April, but was released in August. However, he was rearrested in late September after calling for demonstrations. Sylla, who launched a hunger strike in December, remained in custody at year's end.

B2. Is there a realistic opportunity for the opposition to increase its support or gain power through elections? 2 / 4

Although multiparty elections take place, Guinea has not established a pattern of peaceful democratic power transfers between rival parties. Before becoming president in 2010, Condé was an opposition leader under longtime president Lansana Conté. However, rather than defeating an incumbent leader, Condé won the first election after a period of military rule that followed Conté's death in 2008. The 2020 constitution's language on term limits also allowed for Condé to continue as president, despite being term-limited under the old constitution.

Security forces frequently attack rallies and protests organized by the opposition, making it more difficult for opposition parties to mobilize their supporters. The government banned and forcefully dispersed demonstrations organized by opposition parties and the FNDC in 2020.

B3. Are the people's political choices free from domination by forces that are external to the political sphere, or by political forces that employ extrapolitical means? 1 / 4

While the military's role in politics has waned since the return to civilian rule, ethnic loyalty continues to play an outsized role in the political choices of voters and party leaders. Rather than organizing around policy platforms or political ideologies and trying to attract new supporters, each party tacitly pledges allegiance to its respective ethnic group, contributing to the threat of mutual hostility and violence.

While President Condé and his allies mounted their campaign to win the approval of the new constitution, the administration received rhetorical and other support from powerful external actors. For example, the Russian ambassador to Guinea called Condé "legendary" and endorsed his constitution project in a 2019 state television appearance, adding that it would be beneficial to the country if Condé remained in power. There is widespread speculation that lucrative, foreign-owned mining interests in Guinea, including Russian and Chinese operations, back Condé because they view him as best positioned to protect their interests.

B4. Do various segments of the population (including ethnic, racial, religious, gender, LGBT+, and other relevant groups) have full political rights and electoral opportunities? 2 / 4

Women and minority groups have full political rights, but ethnic divisions and gender bias limit their participation in practice. Under a law passed in May 2019, women must constitute 50 percent of electoral lists. Parties did not previously adhere to older legal obligations mandating that women were to represent 30 percent of proportional representation lists for parliamentary elections. Despite these historical and current requirements, women remain underrepresented in the parliament, holding under 17 percent of its seats in May 2020.

C. FUNCTIONING OF GOVERNMENT: 3 / 12

C1. Do the freely elected head of government and national legislative representatives determine the policies of the government? 1 / 4

The flawed electoral process undermines the legitimacy of executive and legislative officials. In addition, their ability to determine and implement laws and policies without undue interference is impeded by impunity and rampant corruption.

C2. Are safeguards against official corruption strong and effective? 1 / 4

The National Anti-Corruption Agency (ANLC), which reports directly to the presidency, is underfunded and understaffed. A government audit whose findings were released in 2016 uncovered thousands of civil-service positions held by absent or deceased workers. Some lower-level officials have been prosecuted on corruption charges in recent years, but major cases involving senior politicians and the lucrative mining industry have mainly been pursued in foreign courts.

In 2017, the National Assembly adopted an anticorruption law that restructured the ANLC and established new procedures for receiving corruption complaints and protecting whistleblowers. The law has still not been applied.

C3. Does the government operate with openness and transparency? 1 / 4

Government operations are generally opaque. An access-to-information law was previously adopted but not enacted. Parliamentarians adopted a new access-to-information law in November 2020.

In 2019, the Natural Resource Governance Institute reported some improvements related to government transparency. These were mostly related to reforms of rules and practices related to of the Ministry of Mines and Geology, as well as to revenue management.

CIVIL LIBERTIES: 24 / 60 (−1)

D. FREEDOM OF EXPRESSION AND BELIEF: 10 / 16 (−1)

D1. Are there free and independent media? 2 / 4

The 2020 constitution guarantees media freedom, but Guinea has struggled to uphold freedom of expression in practice. A criminal code adopted in 2016 retained penalties of up to five years in prison for defamation or insult of public figures, contributing to self-censorship among journalists. A cybersecurity law passed that year criminalized similar offenses online, as well as the dissemination of information that is false, protected on national security grounds, or "likely to disturb law and order or public security or jeopardize human dignity." Several dozen newspapers publish regularly in Guinea, though most have small circulations. More than 30 private radio stations and some private television stations compete with the public broadcaster, Radio Télévision Guinéenne. Due to the high illiteracy rate, most of the population accesses information through radio.

The climate for journalists has improved somewhat in recent years, with fewer violent attacks and prosecutions for defamation. However, journalists at private outlets were reportedly harassed by the government in 2020. Journalists reporting on the March and October elections also faced communications disruptions and regulatory scrutiny; in late March, infrastructure firm GUILAB conducted maintenance work on undersea cables, which interrupted telephone and internet access as the polls were held. In October, the media regulator, the High Authority for Communication, suspended news site guinéematin.com, though that suspension was lifted in early November. Internet disruptions were also reported for several days in late October, after the presidential election was held.

D2. Are individuals free to practice and express their religious faith or nonbelief in public and private? 3 / 4

Religious rights are generally respected in practice. Some non-Muslim government workers have reported occasional discrimination. People who convert from Islam to Christianity sometimes encounter pressure from their community.

D3. Is there academic freedom, and is the educational system free from extensive political indoctrination? 3 / 4

Academic freedom has historically faced political restrictions under authoritarian regimes. The problem has eased in recent years, particularly since the return to civilian rule in 2010, though self-censorship still tends to reduce the vibrancy of academic discourse.

D4. Are individuals free to express their personal views on political or other sensitive topics without fear of surveillance or retribution? 2 / 4 (−1)

There are few practical limits on private discussion, though ethnic tensions and laws restricting freedom of expression may deter open debate in some circumstances. Discussion on the new constitution, which was approved by voters in March 2020, was discouraged as the government moved to harass and detain activists who addressed the subject. Social media users also faced connection disruptions ahead of the March vote and in the days following the October presidential election.

Score Change: The score declined from 3 to 2 because the government maintained a campaign of harassment and detention against those who opposed the constitutional referendum, and disrupted communications services during preelection and postelection periods.

E. ASSOCIATIONAL AND ORGANIZATIONAL RIGHTS: 4 / 12

E1. Is there freedom of assembly? 1 / 4

Freedom of assembly is enshrined in the constitution, but this right is often restricted. Assemblies held without notification as required by Guinean law are considered unauthorized, and are often violently dispersed, leading to deaths, injuries, and arrests. Restrictions on public gatherings were introduced in April 2020 as part of the government's efforts to limit the spread of COVID-19. Modified restrictions remained in force through much of the year but were loosened in December.

Despite these restrictions, major demonstrations occurred during the year. Protests against President Conté's constitution project, which began in 2019, continued in 2020, though they were partially suspended due to pandemic-related measures. In October, Amnesty International counted at least 50 deaths and 200 injuries resulting from the crackdown against that campaign, along with other protests, between October 2019 and July 2020. Protests related to the March and October elections were also dispersed violently. Amnesty International reported that security forces used live ammunition and tear gas against demonstrators in October.

Guineans also protested against the imposition of COVID-19 restrictions and faced violent government responses. For example, in May 2020, protesters in the town of Coyah clashed with security forces over travel restrictions and accusations of corrupt enforcement. Five people were killed in that incident.

E2. Is there freedom for nongovernmental organizations, particularly those that are engaged in human rights– and governance-related work? 1 / 4

Civil society remains weak, ethnically divided, and subject to periodic harassment and intimidation. Intimidation, harassment, and imprisonment of nongovernmental organization (NGO) workers and activists increased in 2020, especially against those opposing the new constitution. Guinean NGOs also struggle due to poor access to funding, leadership struggles, the restriction of civic space, and safety issues.

E3. Is there freedom for trade unions and similar professional or labor organizations? 2 / 4

Although workers are allowed to form trade unions, strike, and bargain collectively, they must provide 10 days' notice before striking, and strikes are banned in broadly defined essential services. In practice, unions are relatively active.

F. RULE OF LAW: 4 / 16

F1. Is there an independent judiciary? 1 / 4

While the judicial system has demonstrated a limited degree of independence since 2010, it remains subject to political influence and corruption. The judiciary also suffers from a lack of resources and dearth of personnel.

F2. Does due process prevail in civil and criminal matters? 1 / 4

Security forces engage in arbitrary arrests, often disregarding legal safeguards. Most detainees are people in prolonged pretrial detention, though justice reforms in recent years have reduced their numbers. Due-process rights pertaining to trials are frequently denied, and many disputes are settled informally through traditional justice systems.

Security personnel implicated in abuses ahead of the March and October 2020 elections did not face significant judicial scrutiny, due to limited judicial capacity and the unwillingness of witnesses to participate in subsequent proceedings.

F3. Is there protection from the illegitimate use of physical force and freedom from war and insurgencies? 1 / 4

The new criminal code adopted in 2016 eliminated the death penalty and explicitly outlawed torture for the first time. However, human rights advocates noted that the criminal code categorized a number of acts that fall within the international definition of torture as merely "inhuman and cruel," a category that does not carry any explicit penalties in the code. In practice, security forces continue to engage in torture and other forms of physical violence with apparent impunity.

The justice system has largely failed to hold perpetrators accountable for past atrocities under military rule. In November 2019, then justice minister Mohammed Lamine Fofana said the trial of 13 suspects indicted for the 2009 Conakry stadium massacre, in which over 150 opposition protesters were killed by security forces, would be held by June 2020. However, the trial has not yet commenced. Several defendants have been in custody longer than the legal pretrial limit.

F4. Do laws, policies, and practices guarantee equal treatment of various segments of the population? 1 / 4

Women face pervasive societal discrimination and disadvantages in both the formal and traditional justice systems. Various ethnic groups engage in mutual discrimination with respect to hiring and other matters. Antidiscrimination laws do not protect LGBT+ people. Same-sex sexual activity is a criminal offense that can be punished with up to three years in prison; although this law is rarely enforced, LGBT+ people have been arrested on lesser charges.

G. PERSONAL AUTONOMY AND INDIVIDUAL RIGHTS: 6 / 16

G1. Do individuals enjoy freedom of movement, including the ability to change their place of residence, employment, or education? 2 / 4

Guineans enjoyed some freedom of movement for both domestic and international travel in 2020. However, rampant crime in some neighborhoods can impede movement. Travel into Greater Conakry was also restricted in March 2020 as part of the government's response to the COVID-19 crisis, with the authorities establishing roadblocks as part of their enforcement efforts. A nationwide curfew was also instituted, though it expired outside of Greater Conakry by July. An overnight curfew in that region remained in force through year's end.

G2. Are individuals able to exercise the right to own property and establish private businesses without undue interference from state or nonstate actors? 2 / 4

Private business activity is hampered by corruption and political instability, among other factors. A centralized Agency for the Promotion of Private Investments aims to ease the business registration process. Following recent reforms, property registration processes have become faster and less expensive.

Women face gender-based disadvantages in laws and practices governing inheritance and property rights.

G3. Do individuals enjoy personal social freedoms, including choice of marriage partner and size of family, protection from domestic violence, and control over appearance? 1 / 4

Rape and domestic violence are common but underreported due to fears of stigmatization, and there is no specific legislation meant to address domestic abuse. Female genital mutilation (FGM) is nearly ubiquitous despite a legal ban, affecting up to 97 percent of girls and women in the country. The new criminal code adopted in 2016 set the legal age for marriage at 18, but early and forced marriages remained common.

In 2019, the parliament amended the civil code to make monogamy the general regime of marriage, except in case of "explicit agreement" of the first wife. This reflected a major change to a bill passed in late 2018 legalizing polygamy, which was rejected by President Condé.

G4. Do individuals enjoy equality of opportunity and freedom from economic exploitation? 1 / 4

The 2016 criminal code specifically criminalized trafficking in persons and debt bondage, but reduced the minimum penalties for such crimes, and enforcement has been weak. In some mining areas, child labor is a major issue. There are also cases of women and children being trafficked for sexual exploitation to other parts of West Africa as well as Europe, the Middle East, and the United States.

Guinea-Bissau

Population: 1,900,000
Capital: Bissau
Freedom Status: Partly Free
Electoral Democracy: No

Overview: Guinea-Bissau's political system has been hampered in recent years by divisions between the president and the parliament, and within the main political party. Conditions for civil liberties have gradually improved as the country has recovered from the aftermath of a military coup in 2012, though police continue to disrupt some demonstrations. Corruption is a major problem that has been exacerbated by organized criminal activity, including drug trafficking.

KEY DEVELOPMENTS IN 2020

- In January, Domingos Simões Pereira appealed Umaro Sissoco Embaló's victory in the 2019 presidential election, claiming that widespread fraud had taken place. Though the Supreme Court ordered the National Election Commission (CNE) to conduct a full audit of the results, the CNE refused and reconfirmed Embaló's victory.
- In February, Embaló held an inauguration for his presidency despite the ongoing court appeal, with key military chiefs and the outgoing president José Mário Vaz in attendance. The African Party for the Independence of Guinea-Bissau and Cabo Verde (PAIGC), which lost the presidential election but has a majority in the parliament, ignored Embaló's ceremony and appointed an interim president, Cipriano Cassamá, resulting in a two-day period during which there were two presidents. Cassamá stepped down after one day, saying he feared for his safety.
- In March, upon President Embaló's request, military troops occupied the Supreme Court, other public institutions, and public broadcasting outlets, "in order to enable the formation of the new cabinet." For multiple days, the state radio was silent, and the state television channel showed a blank screen. The troops left after Embaló's new cabinet had been installed.
- The government enforced a state of emergency due to the COVID-19 pandemic, which included restrictions that banned assemblies of more than 25 people, preventing protesters from gathering during a period of high political tension. However, in September, while assembly restrictions were still in force, President Embaló organized an event to celebrate the anniversary of the country's independence with more than 15,000 people in attendance.

POLITICAL RIGHTS: 17 / 40
A. ELECTORAL PROCESS: 7 / 12
A1. Was the current head of government or other chief national authority elected through free and fair elections? 2 / 4

The president is elected through a two-round voting system for up to two consecutive terms of five years. The prime minister is appointed by the president "in accordance with the election results" after consulting with the parliamentary parties, and the government must be dissolved if the parliament rejects its proposed budget.

Umaro Sissoco Embaló of the Movement for Democratic Alternation (Madem G15) party, supported by former president José Mário Vaz —who placed fourth in the first round—and a coalition of opposition parties, won the December 2019 presidential election's run-off with 53.6 percent of the vote, defeating Domingos Simões Pereira of the African Party for the Independence of Guinea-Bissau and Cabo Verde (PAIGC) who won 46.4 percent of the vote. According to the National Election Commission (CNE), voter turnout was 72.7 percent. The African Union's (AU) election observation mission found that the administration of the run-off vote was free and transparent, despite challenges with the first round of voting. Internationally bodies such as the Economic Community of West African States (ECOWAS) acknowledged Embaló's victory in April 2020.

However, in January 2020, Pereira contested the results in the Supreme Court, alleging widespread fraud. The CNE refused to conduct a full audit of the results as ordered by the court. In February, Embaló held an inauguration in a symbolic ceremony that was not constitutionally binding, as it was not conducted by the president of the parliament. Key military chiefs, including the Armed Forces chief of staff, as well as the outgoing president José Mário Vaz were in attendance at the ceremony. Meanwhile, the parliament appointed an interim president, Cipriano Cassamá, who then resigned after one day, saying he feared for his safety. A few days after Embaló's ceremony, upon his request, military troops occupied the Supreme Court and several public broadcasting outlets "in order to enable the formation of the new cabinet." Later, the court was unable to meet due to the COVID-19 pandemic and because the presiding judge had fled the country, saying he feared for his safety. The court ultimately rejected Pereira's appeal in September.

In February 2020, Embaló appointed Nuno Gomes Nabiam as prime minister.

A2. Were the current national legislative representatives elected through free and fair elections? 3 / 4

Members of the 102-seat National People's Assembly are elected by popular vote for four-year terms. In the March 2019 elections, the PAIGC remained the largest single party with 47 seats, though it lost its outright majority. Madem G15 won 27, the Party of Social Renewal (PRS) took 21, the United People's Assembly–Democratic Party of Guinea-Bissau (APU-PDGB) took 5, and the Union for Change (UM) and the Party for a New Democracy (PND) each secured a single seat. The PAIGC formed a majority coalition with the latter three parties, but APU-PDGB leader Nuno Gomes Nabiam renounced the deal, after PAIGC leader Pereira decided he would be the party's presidential candidate.

The United Nations and European Union praised the 2019 parliamentary elections as peaceful and orderly, and an observation mission from the AU deemed them free and fair, though it noted some flaws in the process.

A3. Are the electoral laws and framework fair, and are they implemented impartially by the relevant election management bodies? 2 / 4

There are some problems with the country's electoral laws and framework, including weak controls on campaign spending, vote buying, and a lack of legal provisions for domestic poll observers. Elections have been subject to delays in recent years, due in part to lack of funding and stalled voter registration processes.

In the run-up to the first round of the 2019 presidential election, the PAIGC-led government decided to review the voter registry in order to include some 25,000 people who were not able to vote in the parliamentary elections due to technical errors. The PRS and Madem G15 claimed that the changes were fraudulent, but ECOWAS rejected the opposition's demand for a new registration process.

B. POLITICAL PLURALISM AND PARTICIPATION: 8 / 16

B1. Do the people have the right to organize in different political parties or other competitive political groupings of their choice, and is the system free of undue obstacles to the rise and fall of these competing parties or groupings? 3 / 4

There are no major constraints on party formation. Dozens of political parties are active in Guinea-Bissau, and 21 competed in the 2019 parliamentary elections, up from 15 in 2014. However, the political crisis since 2015—when former president Vaz dismissed then prime minister Pereira—has led to some instances of violence and intimidation among partisan groups.

After President Embaló dismissed former prime minister Aristides Gomes in February 2020, several members of the Gomes administration were prevented from leaving the country. Former minister of justice and human rights Ruth Monteiro took refuge in the Portuguese embassy in Bissau, claiming that the new regime was using security forces to harass and threaten members of the Gomes government. Gomes himself took refuge in the United Nations headquarters in Bissau in March, fearing for his own safety. PAIGC leader and former presidential candidate Pereira also fled the country. In December, the prosecutor general issued a warrant for his arrest.

B2. Is there a realistic opportunity for the opposition to increase its support or gain power through elections? 2 / 4

Guinea-Bissau has a limited record of democratic power transfers between rival political parties, as the PAIGC or military rulers have governed for most of the period since independence. In 2014, Vaz succeeded an independent who had served as acting president in the wake of the 2012 coup. Nevertheless, opposition forces increased their representation in the 2019 legislative elections. President Embaló of the new party Madem G15 succeeded former president Vaz of the PAIGC, who lost in the first round of the 2019 presidential election. However, Embaló's use of the military to complete his installation in office raised concerns.

B3. Are the people's political choices free from domination by forces that are external to the political sphere, or by political forces that employ extrapolitical means? 1 / 4

The military has apparently refrained from interfering in politics since 2014, though they were used by President Embaló to complete his installment in office. The choices of voters and politicians continue to be influenced by corruption and patronage networks. Organized crime linked to drug trafficking and money laundering has contributed to the country's political instability in recent decades.

B4. Do various segments of the population (including ethnic, racial, religious, gender, LGBT+, and other relevant groups) have full political rights and electoral opportunities? 2 / 4

Women enjoy equal political rights, but their participation is limited in practice by cultural obstacles, and they are underrepresented in leadership positions. Just 14 women won seats in the March 2019 parliamentary elections, the same number as in 2014. A 2018 law requires 36 percent of candidates on party lists to be women.

Ethnicity plays a role in politics, reducing the extent to which all groups' interests are represented. For example, one of the larger groups, the Balanta, has traditionally dominated the military and cast votes for the PRS.

C. FUNCTIONING OF GOVERNMENT: 2 / 12

C1. Do the freely elected head of government and national legislative representatives determine the policies of the government? 1 / 4

Governance has been impaired by the political crisis that began in 2015, and election delays have undermined the democratic legitimacy of incumbent officials. The original term of the parliament that was replaced by the March 2019 elections had expired nearly a year earlier. The full legislature has convened only sporadically in recent years.

In late February and into March 2020, a constitutional crisis emerged when Embaló organized his inauguration unconstitutionally. The PAIGC, which has a slim parliamentary majority but lost the presidential election, ignored Embaló's inauguration and appointed an interim president, Cipriano Cassamá. However, Cassamá resigned after one day in office, saying he feared for his safety. Embaló was eventually recognized by the parliament.

C2. Are safeguards against official corruption strong and effective? 1 / 4

Corruption is pervasive, including among senior government figures. Both military and civilian officials have been accused of involvement in the illegal drug trade. Critics of past corruption investigations targeting former high-ranking officials have argued that they were politically motivated.

In February 2020, minister of justice and human rights Monteiro and director of the Judiciary Police Filomena Lopes—who had been instrumental in the country's anticorruption efforts and praised by the United Nations for their work—were fired by President Embaló.

C3. Does the government operate with openness and transparency? 0 / 4

There are no effective legal provisions to facilitate public access to government information, and government officials do not disclose their personal financial information as required by law. The political impasse and related parliamentary dysfunction have further obstructed oversight of government spending in recent years. The lack of transparency contributes to chronic budget shortfalls, frequent delays in public-sector wages, and doubts about the management of foreign assistance.

CIVIL LIBERTIES: 27 / 60 (–2)
D. FREEDOM OF EXPRESSION AND BELIEF: 10 / 16 (–1)
D1. Are there free and independent media? 1 / 4 (–1)

The constitution provides for freedom of the press, and there is some media diversity. However, journalists regularly face harassment and intimidation, including pressure regarding their coverage from political figures and government officials.

In late February and early March 2020, soldiers occupied the facilities of the state radio and television broadcasters for several days. The stations were closed and under armed guard at the request of President Embaló. For multiple days, the state radio was silent, and the state television channel showed a blank screen.

In July, armed men in national guard uniforms smashed equipment and vandalized the property of the privately owned Radio Capital FM station, which is allied to Embaló's opposition, the PAIGC, temporarily silencing the broadcaster. Before the July attack, the station, which had received threats for years, was warned to stop a talk program in which listeners called in to express their opinions on matters including the government.

Score Change: The score declined from 2 to 1 due to the use of armed forces to intimidate media outlets, including soldiers' occupation of the national television and radio stations and an extralegal attack on a popular private radio broadcaster.

D2. Are individuals free to practice and express their religious faith or nonbelief in public and private? 3 / 4

Religious freedom is legally protected and usually respected in practice. Government licensing requirements are not onerous and are often disregarded. Some Muslims have reportedly raised concerns about the influence of foreign imams who preach a more rigorous or austere form of Islam, threatening religious tolerance.

D3. Is there academic freedom, and is the educational system free from extensive political indoctrination? 3 / 4

Academic freedom is guaranteed and generally upheld, though the education system is poor in terms of access, quality, and basic resources. Public schools were closed for much of 2018 and 2019 due to ongoing teachers' strikes, and in 2020 as a consequence of COVID-19 restrictions.

D4. Are individuals free to express their personal views on political or other sensitive topics without fear of surveillance or retribution? 3 / 4

Individuals are relatively free to express their views on political topics in the private and social sphere, though some more public figures have faced the threat of arrest or charges in retaliation for their remarks in recent years.

E. ASSOCIATIONAL AND ORGANIZATIONAL RIGHTS: 7 / 12 (-1)

E1. Is there freedom of assembly? 1 / 4 (-1)

Freedom of assembly is frequently restricted. The authorities repeatedly interfere with demonstrations linked to the political tensions between the presidency and the legislature. The state of emergency enforced due to the COVID-19 pandemic banned assemblies of more than 25 people. The restrictions were prolonged by President Embaló for nearly six months and prevented protesters from gathering during a period of high political tension. However, the restrictions were not equally enforced: in September, Embaló organized an event to celebrate the anniversary of the country's independence that was attended by more than 15,000 people. Embaló also held several rallies during the lockdown. Restrictions were only partially lifted in December 2020.

Score Change: The score declined from 2 to 1 because authorities used the COVID-19 pandemic as a pretext to curtail assembly rights for political opposition groups.

E2. Is there freedom for nongovernmental organizations, particularly those that are engaged in human rights- and governance-related work? 3 / 4

Nongovernmental organizations (NGOs) are generally able to operate. Some groups have faced intimidation and other obstacles, particularly those that are associated with street demonstrations, but no major cases of repressive measures against NGOs were reported during 2020.

E3. Is there freedom for trade unions and similar professional or labor organizations? 3 / 4

Workers are allowed to form and join independent trade unions, but few work in the wage-earning formal sector. Private employers sometimes engage in improper interference with union organizing and other activities. The right to strike is protected, and government workers frequently exercise it, although the prolonged state of emergency due to the COVID-19 pandemic restricted this right.

F. RULE OF LAW: 5 / 16

F1. Is there an independent judiciary? 1 / 4

Judges are highly susceptible to corruption and political pressure, and the court system as a whole lacks the resources and capacity to function effectively.

F2. Does due process prevail in civil and criminal matters? 0 / 4

Corruption is common among police, and officers often fail to observe legal safeguards against arbitrary arrest and detention. Very few criminal cases are brought to trial or successfully prosecuted, partly due to the limited material and human resources available to investigators. Most of the population lacks access to the justice system in practice.

F3. Is there protection from the illegitimate use of physical force and freedom from war and insurgencies? 2 / 4

Conditions in prisons and detention centers are often extremely poor, and law enforcement personnel generally enjoy impunity for abuses. Because of its weak institutions and porous borders, Guinea-Bissau has become a transit point for criminal organizations trafficking various types of contraband. The armed forces and some other state entities have been linked to drug trafficking. In recent years, authorities have made some progress in combating the drug trade and organized crime. Violence associated with political unrest has continued to recede since the restoration of elected civilian rule.

A low-intensity conflict in Senegal's Casamance region occasionally affects security across the border in Guinea-Bissau, where the Senegalese rebels sometimes operate.

F4. Do laws, policies, and practices guarantee equal treatment of various segments of the population? 2 / 4

Women face significant societal discrimination and traditional biases, despite some legal protections. They generally do not receive equal pay for similar work and have fewer opportunities for education and employment.

There are virtually no effective legal protections against discrimination on other grounds, including ethnicity, sexual orientation, and gender identity, though same-sex relations are not specifically criminalized.

G. PERSONAL AUTONOMY AND INDIVIDUAL RIGHTS: 5 / 16

G1. Do individuals enjoy freedom of movement, including the ability to change their place of residence, employment, or education? 2 / 4

There are few formal restrictions on freedom of movement, but widespread corruption among police and other public officials can limit this right in practice, as can criminal activity. At times, Senegalese rebel activity may restrict movement in the border area.

G2. Are individuals able to exercise the right to own property and establish private businesses without undue interference from state or nonstate actors? 1 / 4

Illegal economic activity, including logging, by organized groups remains a problem. The quality of enforcement of property rights is generally poor, and the formal procedures for establishing a business are relatively onerous.

Women, particularly those from certain ethnic groups in rural areas, face restrictions on their ability to own and inherit property.

G3. Do individuals enjoy personal social freedoms, including choice of marriage partner and size of family, protection from domestic violence, and control over appearance? 1 / 4

There are multiple constraints on personal social freedoms. Early and forced marriages remain common, especially in rural areas. The government, international organizations, and community leaders have worked to eliminate female genital mutilation (FGM), though nearly half of the country's women have suffered from such violence. Despite the existence of legislation to address gender-based violence, the problem is reportedly widespread; victims of rape and domestic abuse rarely report the crimes to authorities.

G4. Do individuals enjoy equality of opportunity and freedom from economic exploitation? 1 / 4

Guinea-Bissau is one of the world's poorest countries, with most families relying on unstable employment in the informal economy or remittances from migrant workers abroad. Public services have deteriorated in recent years amid irregular payment of public-sector workers.

Boys are vulnerable to organized exploitation through forced begging and to forced labor in sectors including mining and agriculture. A rising number of Muslim children from Guinea-Bissau are trafficked by money-making schemes disguised as religious Koranic schools, particularly into Senegal.

Girls are frequently victims of sexual exploitation or domestic servitude. Government officials have been accused of complicity in trafficking activity, including sex tourism schemes in the Bijagós islands.

Guyana

Population: 800,000
Capital: Georgetown
Freedom Status: Free
Electoral Democracy: Yes

Overview: Guyana is a parliamentary democracy with a lively press and a robust civil society. However, elections in March 2020 were marred by attempted fraud perpetrated by the incumbent government, and violent crime and discrimination against Indigenous and LGBT+ people remain significant problems. The recent discovery of rich offshore oil and natural gas reserves has raised the stakes of anticorruption reforms and revived traditional ethnopolitical divisions.

KEY DEVELOPMENTS IN 2020

- Irfaan Ali of the opposition People's Progressive Party/Civic (PPP/C) was sworn in as president in August after being declared the winner of the March general election. Former president David Granger, leading a coalition of the A Partnership for National Unity (APNU) and the Alliance for Change (AFC), had declared himself the winner, but evidence of irregularities prompted a recount that favored Ali, and court decisions and international pressure eventually led the Granger government to hand over power.
- Following a rise in racial tensions during the election crisis, violence between Indo-Guyanese and Afro-Guyanese villagers in September left four people dead in Berbice Region.
- Guyana largely avoided the global first wave of the COVID-19 pandemic, but cases began a steady rise in August; according to researchers at the University of Oxford, the country registered over 6,300 cases and over 160 deaths by year's end.

POLITICAL RIGHTS: 30 / 40 (−1)

A. ELECTORAL PROCESS: 9 / 12 (−1)

A1. Was the current head of government or other chief national authority elected through free and fair elections? 3 / 4

The president, who serves as both chief of state and head of government, appoints the cabinet, though ministers are collectively responsible to the National Assembly. Parties designate a presidential candidate ahead of National Assembly elections, with the winning party's candidate assuming the presidency for a maximum of two five-year terms.

Irfaan Ali of the opposition PPP/C became president in August 2020 following a hotly contested recount of the March election and multiple rounds of litigation. Balloting had been due since March 2019, after Granger and the APNU-AFC coalition lost a vote of confidence in December 2018. However, government stalling and a series of procedural disputes followed, and elections were not called until October 2019. Results announced by the government following the March 2020 election were based on a tally that included alterations to the count from the country's largest voting district, leading to accusations of government fraud. Following protests and lawsuits, Guyana's High Court ordered a recount, but political maneuvering and courtroom battles continued for months until the government finally accepted the recount results establishing Ali's narrow victory.

A2. Were the current national legislative representatives elected through free and fair elections? 3 / 4 (−1)

Members of the unicameral, 65-seat National Assembly are elected to five-year terms; 25 representatives are elected in 10 geographical constituencies, while 40 are elected by proportional representation in one nationwide constituency. Up to seven unelected cabinet ministers and parliamentary officials may also hold ex-officio seats.

In the 2020 elections, the PPP/C won 33 seats and the APNU-AFC coalition secured 31 seats, while the union of A New United Guyana (ANUG), the Liberty and Justice Party (LJP) and The New Movement (TNM) was allocated 1 seat. European Union (EU) observers reported that the March election was competitive and vote casting was generally free, although polarization, unregulated party and campaign finance, and a lack of transparency characterized the preelectoral period. Moreover, according to the EU observation mission, the integrity of the entire vote was "seriously compromised" by the manipulation of results in the largest electoral district, Region 4, by senior officials from the Guyana Elections Commission (GECOM). The electoral crisis stretched for months and included a disputed, month-long recount, the attempted invalidation of tens of thousands of votes by GECOM's chief elections officer, significant international pressure, and sometimes contradictory interventions from both Guyanese courts and the Caribbean Court of Justice. The eventual allocation of seats was based on the recount, completed in June and judged to be accurate by Caribbean Community (CARICOM) observers.

Score Change: The score declined from 4 to 3 due to irregularities that marred the preelectoral period and vote-tallying process and amounted to an unsuccessful attempt by the former government to change the election's outcome.

A3. Are the electoral laws and framework fair, and are they implemented impartially by the relevant election management bodies? 3 / 4

Although observers characterized the balloting as generally free, both Guyana's election laws and GECOM's management received harsh criticism. In its final report, the EU observation mission described GECOM as dysfunctional, riven by polarization, opaque in its decision making, and derelict in its duty to control its officials from interfering with the election results. The mission recommended an overhaul of GECOM's composition and practices. Following the change of government, multiple GECOM members faced criminal charges for abetting the fraudulent vote tabulation, including Chief Elections Officer Keith Lowenfield, who was arrested in September.

B. POLITICAL PLURALISM AND PARTICIPATION: 13 / 16

B1. Do the people have the right to organize in different political parties or other competitive political groupings of their choice, and is the system free of undue obstacles to the rise and fall of these competing parties or groupings? 4 / 4

Political parties may form freely, and they generally operate without interference. A long-standing deadlock between two major parties with different ethnic bases had softened somewhat in recent years, with the multiethnic AFC emerging alongside the predominantly Afro-Guyanese APNU and the mainly Indo-Guyanese PPP/C. However, ethnopolitical divisions have sharpened as an anticipated influx of oil and gas revenues raises the stakes of controlling the distribution of state resources.

New parties emerged to contest the 2020 elections, with ANUG, LJP and TNM joining forces to gain one shared seat. There are no legal provisions allowing independent candidates to stand for the presidency.

B2. Is there a realistic opportunity for the opposition to increase its support or gain power through elections? 4 / 4

The PPP/C ruled from 1992 to 2015, and the APNU-AFC from 2015 to 2020. The PPP/C took power through elections in 2020, but significant pressure from the international community—especially the United States and CARICOM—and civil society was required to carry out a comprehensive recount and ensure a declaration of the PPP/C as the winner based on the recount results.

B3. Are the people's political choices free from domination by forces that are external to the political sphere, or by political forces that employ extrapolitical means? 3 / 4

Voters are largely free to make their own political choices. However, there is concern that politics may be improperly influenced by the largely Indo-Guyanese economic elite.

B4. Do various segments of the population (including ethnic, racial, religious, gender, LGBT+, and other relevant groups) have full political rights and electoral opportunities? 2 / 4

Women and ethnic minorities have equal political rights, though ethnic divisions have long played a powerful role in politics. Indigenous people, who make up about 10 percent of the population, remain politically marginalized. At least one third of each party's candidate list must consist of women, and 25 out of 70 seats in the National Assembly were won by women in 2020.

A consultation process on constitutional reform with Indigenous groups promised in late 2019 has largely failed to materialize. The small LJP party nominated Indigenous rights activist Lenox Shuman for president in 2020; although he was disqualified by GECOM for holding dual Canadian citizenship, Shuman became the deputy speaker of the National Assembly in September.

C. FUNCTIONING OF GOVERNMENT: 8 / 12

C1. Do the freely elected head of government and national legislative representatives determine the policies of the government? 4 / 4

The president and the legislative majority are generally able to create and implement policy without improper interference. The political stalemate in the aftermath of the 2020 election resulted in a period of policy paralysis, including delayed public spending due to the lack of a budget approved by parliament.

C2. Are safeguards against official corruption strong and effective? 2 / 4

In recent years, the government has made progress in introducing durable safeguards against corruption, notably by strengthening controls on money laundering and empowering a new agency to audit state-owned companies. However, graft remains widespread, and the discovery of rich oil and natural gas reserves beneath the country's coastal waters has added urgency to the need for effective anticorruption reforms.

C3. Does the government operate with openness and transparency? 2 / 4

Laws designed to ensure government transparency are inconsistently upheld. A 2013 Access to Information Act allows the government to refuse requests with little or no justification.

A government integrity commission tasked with reviewing officials' asset disclosures was reestablished in 2018 after a long dormancy.

In 2017, Guyana joined the Extractive Industries Transparency Initiative (EITI), which requires countries to submit reports detailing the use of revenue obtained from the extraction of their natural resources, though as of the end of 2020 the government had published an EITI report for only the 2017 fiscal year. Critics have suggested that Guyana's negotiation of its initial set of oil contracts, conducted in private negotiations with individual companies rather than through open auctions, resulted in unfavorable terms for the government.

CIVIL LIBERTIES: 43 / 60

D. FREEDOM OF EXPRESSION AND BELIEF: 15 / 16

D1. Are there free and independent media? 3 / 4

Although freedom of the press is generally respected, government officials have filed defamation cases and occasionally threatened journalists. Criminal defamation charges can draw up to two years in prison.

The Guyana National Broadcasting Authority, whose board is appointed by the president, has been accused of partisan bias in its regulatory and licensing decisions. According to EU observers, state-run print and television outlets displayed "overt bias" in favor of the ruling APNU+AFC during the 2020 election campaign, while several private outlets provided highly favorable coverage to the PPP/C.

D2. Are individuals free to practice and express their religious faith or nonbelief in public and private? 4 / 4

Religious freedom is constitutionally guaranteed and generally respected in practice. Rules limiting visas for foreign missionaries and barring blasphemous libel are not actively enforced. Religious groups can register places of worship and receive associated benefits without difficulty.

D3. Is there academic freedom, and is the educational system free from extensive political indoctrination? 4 / 4

Academic freedom is largely upheld.

D4. Are individuals free to express their personal views on political or other sensitive topics without fear of surveillance or retribution? 4 / 4

People are generally free to express their views without fear of retaliation or other repercussions. However, a 2018 cybercrime law contains provisions that could be used to stifle dissent online, according to critics.

E. ASSOCIATIONAL AND ORGANIZATIONAL RIGHTS: 11 / 12

E1. Is there freedom of assembly? 4 / 4

The authorities generally uphold the right to peaceful assembly. In September 2020, police used tear gas and pellets to disperse protesters after demonstrations over the killings of two Afro-Guyanese teenagers turned violent; peaceful demonstrations linked to the same incident proceeded without incident.

E2. Is there freedom for nongovernmental organizations, particularly those that are engaged in human rights- and governance-related work? 4 / 4

Nongovernmental organizations (NGOs) operate freely. The government has consulted with NGOs on various policy initiatives, including measures designed to combat human trafficking. In July 2020, the nongovernmental Guyana Human Rights Association suffered an arson attack on its offices.

E3. Is there freedom for trade unions and similar professional or labor organizations? 3 / 4

The rights to form labor unions, bargain collectively, and strike are generally upheld, and unions are well organized. However, laws against antiunion discrimination are poorly enforced. In September and October 2020, health care workers engaged in protests and threatened strikes over pay and working conditions, prompting the government to threaten criminal and civil penalties before acceding to negotiations.

F. RULE OF LAW: 8 / 16

F1. Is there an independent judiciary? 2 / 4

The courts are impaired by political disputes, staff shortages, and lack of resources. The president must obtain the agreement of the leader of the opposition to appoint the chancellor of the judiciary and the chief justice; both positions remained in the hands of acting placeholders as of 2020 due to the ongoing failure to agree on appointments. Other judges are appointed by the president on the advice of a Judicial Service Commission, which is also selected with input from the opposition. Guyana's courts played a mixed role during the 2020 election crisis. A June decision by the Court of Appeal bolstered the Granger government's position that large numbers of votes should be invalidated. However, when the Caribbean Court of Justice—which serves as Guyana's apex judicial body—overruled this decision, the Court of Appeal confirmed that GECOM must declare a winner based on the recount-based vote tally, which favored the PPP/C.

F2. Does due process prevail in civil and criminal matters? 2 / 4

Observance of due process safeguards is uneven. Defendants are often held in pretrial detention for periods longer than their maximum possible sentence. As of November 2020, the prison population stood at over 140 percent of capacity, with 40 percent of inmates in pretrial detention. A new attorney general and legal affairs minister, Anil Nandlall, took office in August 2020 promising to reduce the use of custodial sentences in favor of community service. Police officers do not always operate with professionalism; some have reportedly accepted bribes and committed a variety of other crimes.

F3. Is there protection from the illegitimate use of physical force and freedom from war and insurgencies? 2 / 4

Reports of police violence, abuse of detainees, and harsh prison conditions persist. The rate of violent crime has fallen somewhat in recent years, but remains stubbornly high.

The threat of territorial conflict with Venezuela remained present in 2020. In December, the International Court of Justice ruled that it had jurisdiction and would adjudicate the border dispute.

F4. Do laws, policies, and practices guarantee equal treatment of various segments of the population? 2 / 4

Indo-Guyanese people, who make up 40 percent of the total population, predominate within the business sector, while Afro-Guyanese hold most public sector positions. A history of interethnic violence and the organization of politics along ethnic lines makes communal violence a perennial concern. In September 2020, two Afro-Guyanese teenagers were murdered in a largely Indo-Guyanese region, leading to protests and the killings of two Indo-Guyanese people.

Laws barring discrimination based on race, gender, and other categories are not effectively enforced. Women continue to suffer from workplace bias and significantly lower pay. Guyana's nine principal Indigenous groups still face disparities in the provision of health care, education, and justice. Same-sex sexual activity is punishable with harsh jail terms, and the LGBT+ community is subject to police harassment and discrimination.

G. PERSONAL AUTONOMY AND INDIVIDUAL RIGHTS: 9 / 16

G1. Do individuals enjoy freedom of movement, including the ability to change their place of residence, employment, or education? 3 / 4

There are no undue legal restrictions on freedom of movement, including with respect to residency, employment, and education. However, factors including bribery, racial polarization, and neglected infrastructure in some regions limit this right in practice.

G2. Are individuals able to exercise the right to own property and establish private businesses without undue interference from state or nonstate actors? 2 / 4

The legal framework generally supports the rights to own property and operate private businesses, but complex regulations are unevenly enforced, and corruption and organized crime sometimes inhibit business activity. The land rights of Indigenous communities are impaired by flawed legal procedures, as well as by unauthorized encroachment and resource exploitation by outsiders.

G3. Do individuals enjoy personal social freedoms, including choice of marriage partner and size of family, protection from domestic violence, and control over appearance? 2 / 4

Individual freedom on personal status matters such as marriage and divorce is generally respected, though same-sex marriage and civil unions are prohibited. Marriage before age 18 is allowed with judicial or parental permission, and such marriages are reportedly common. Domestic abuse is widespread, and conviction rates for such abuse and for sexual offenses are low.

G4. Do individuals enjoy equality of opportunity and freedom from economic exploitation? 2 / 4

Legal protections against exploitative working conditions are not enforced consistently. Those working in the informal sector and extractive industries in the country's interior are particularly vulnerable to abuses.

The US State Department detailed Guyana's continued efforts to address human trafficking in 2020, citing legal reforms, a successful trafficking conviction and sentencing, and new plans aimed at eliminating child labor. However, investigations and prosecutions remained inadequate, male victims went largely unsupported, and labor inspectors remained unprepared to effectively combat trafficking.

Haiti

Population: 11,400,000
Capital: Port-au-Prince
Freedom Status: Partly Free
Electoral Democracy: No

Overview: As a result of political instability, street protests, and rampant gang violence, the Haitian government struggles to meet the most basic needs of its citizens. The criminal justice system lacks the resources, independence, and integrity to uphold due process and ensure physical security for the population. Antigovernment protests often result in excessive use of force by police.

KEY DEVELOPMENTS IN 2020

- In May, President Jovenel Moïse prohibited the sharing of photos or videos of the bodies of people who died from COVID-19. The government claimed the law was intended to prevent social stigmatization for people who contracted the virus. Anticorruption activists and human rights groups criticized the rules as laying the groundwork for the government to further restrict free speech in the future. According to government data provided to the World Health Organization (WHO), there were only 10,000 confirmed cases of COVID-19 and 236 deaths during the year, though many believe case numbers were far higher, as testing sites were limited and distrust in the health care system is widespread.
- In January, the parliament dissolved after legislative and mayoral elections that were due in October 2019 were postponed indefinitely, and the mandates of the incumbents expired. President Moïse attempted to consolidate power in the executive branch and passed decrees without legislative approval. Major antigovernment protests that took place throughout the year called for his resignation over allegations of corruption, his various decrees, and the mismanagement of the coronavirus pandemic.
- In August, constitutional scholar and head of the Port-au-Prince Bar Association Monferrier Dorval was assassinated hours after he denounced Moïse administration policies on a public radio show. Gang violence and criminality continued to rise during the year, deepening the country's rule-of-law and humanitarian crisis.

POLITICAL RIGHTS: 15 / 40 (−1)

A. ELECTORAL PROCESS: 4 / 12 (−1)

A1. the current head of government or other chief national authority elected through free and fair elections? 2 / 4

In Haiti's semipresidential system, the president is directly elected for a five-year term. The prime minister is appointed by the president and confirmed by Parliament.

Jovenel Moïse of the Haitian Tet Kale Party (PHTK), the handpicked successor of Michel Martelly, won the 2015 presidential election, but the contest was nullified due to extensive fraud. Moïse went on to win a repeat election in 2016, taking 55.6 percent of the vote. He was inaugurated in early 2017 after an electoral tribunal verified the election result, citing irregularities but no evidence of widespread fraud. Civil society groups claimed that fraud in the vote tally, inconsistent voter registration lists, voter disenfranchisement, and a low voter turnout of 21 percent undermined the new president's mandate.

After a series of four prime ministers between 2017 and 2019, Joseph Jouthe, a trained civil engineer, was appointed prime minister by presidential decree in March 2020. Jouthe was unable to receive parliamentary approval after Parliament dissolved in January, when the terms of most parliamentarians expired. Jouthe replaced Fritz-William Michel, a former finance ministry official, who had also been appointed by Moïse without parliamentary confirmation.

A2. Were the current national legislative representatives elected through free and fair elections? 0 / 4 (−1)

The directly elected, bicameral Parliament is composed of a Senate, with 30 members who serve six-year terms, and a Chamber of Deputies, with 119 members who serve four-year terms. The 2015 legislative elections were plagued by disorder, fraud, and violence. Despite concerns about the elections' credibility, 92 lawmakers took office in early 2016. Elections for a portion of the Senate and the runoff elections for the remaining seats in the Chamber of Deputies were held in 2016 along with the repeat presidential election, and the contests were marred by low voter turnout and fraud. The PHTK emerged as the largest single party in both chambers, followed by Vérité (Truth), though most of the seats were divided among a large number of smaller parties.

Elections for the Chamber of Deputies, two-thirds of the Senate, and local mayoralties were canceled in October 2019 and were not held in 2020. As a result, the parliament was dissolved in January 2020 and did not function throughout the year.

Score Change: The score declined from 1 to 0 because no new parliament was elected or installed during the year, even though the mandates of lower house members and most senators expired in January.

A3. Are the electoral laws and framework fair, and are they implemented impartially by the relevant election management bodies? 2 / 4

The Provisional Electoral Council (CEP) was established in the late 1980s as a temporary body, but it continues to be responsible for managing the electoral process. Although the constitution has provisions to prevent executive dominance of the CEP, the executive branch asserts significant control over it in practice. Legislative elections were not held from 2011 until 2015 because a number of electoral councils appointed by former president Martelly did not meet constitutional requirements or receive parliamentary approval; critics claimed that CEP members would have been beholden to Martelly. A new CEP was appointed in September 2020 by presidential decree. Human rights observers claim the CEP's appointment and its mandate given by the president's decree, which tasks the body with drafting a constitutional referendum, were unconstitutional. The CEP announced that an electoral calendar and draft electoral decree were underway, though neither were released by the end of the year.

B. POLITICAL PLURALISM AND PARTICIPATION: 7 / 16

B1. Do the people have the right to organize in different political parties or other competitive political groupings of their choice, and is the system free of undue obstacles to the rise and fall of these competing parties or groupings? 2 / 4

Legal and administrative barriers that prevented some parties from registering or running in past elections have largely been eliminated. The number of members required to form a political party was reduced from 500 to 20 in 2014, leading to the creation of dozens of new parties. However, the risk of violence continues to impair normal political activity. Opposition party leaders are sometimes threatened, and protests organized by opposition parties are regularly met with repressive force by the government.

B2. Is there a realistic opportunity for the opposition to increase its support or gain power through elections? 1 / 4

Haiti has a poor record of peaceful democratic transfers of power. It remains difficult for the opposition to increase its support or gain power through elections, which are regularly disrupted by violence, marred by accusations of fraud, and postponed. The PHTK has consolidated power in the legislature and at the local level, in part through alliances with smaller parties.

B3. Are the people's political choices free from domination by forces that are external to the political sphere, or by political forces that employ extrapolitical means? 2 / 4

Haitians' political choices are free from explicit domination by the military and other forces outside the political system. However, many politicians rely on money linked to drug trafficking, gangs, and other illegal sources of funding to finance their campaigns, which has a considerable influence over political outcomes in the country. Politicians from the ruling PHTK and opposition groups have hired gangs to either incite or halt residents' involvement in protests and other political activities, according to local human rights activists.

B4. Do various segments of the population (including ethnic, racial, religious, gender, LGBT+, and other relevant groups) have full political rights and electoral opportunities? 2 / 4

Haitian women are underrepresented in political life, with only four out of 149 parliamentary seats held by women from 2017–2019. The constitution mandates that 30 percent of public officials be women, but there are no penalties for noncompliance. Election-related violence and social and cultural norms discourage women from participating in politics. Due to societal discrimination, the interests of LGBT+ people are not represented in the political system, and there are no openly LGBT+ politicians.

C. FUNCTIONING OF GOVERNMENT: 4 / 12

C1. Do the freely elected head of government and national legislative representatives determine the policies of the government? 1 / 4

Parliament was dissolved in January 2020 as the mandates of two-thirds of Senate members and all Chamber of Deputy members expired and no new elections were held. President Moïse attempted to rule by decree, though the legitimacy of his power was questioned as only members of parliament have the constitutional authority to pass laws. Legitimacy questions also undermined the mandates of the prime minister and various government ministries. Corruption, instability, and security threats hinder the government from carrying out its own policies and providing basic services across the country.

C2. Are safeguards against official corruption strong and effective? 1 / 4

Corruption is widespread in Haiti, as are allegations of impunity for government officials. A 2017 law reduced the independence and powers of the Central Financial Intelligence Unit (UCREF), which was responsible for investigating money-laundering cases. That same year, Moïse replaced the heads of the Anticorruption Unit (ULCC) and the UCREF with political allies and former members of the Martelly administration; both units had been investigating Moïse for potential money laundering.

In August 2020, the Superior Court of Auditors and Administrative Disputes (CSCCA) issued its third and final report on corruption among government officials involving a low-interest development-loan program operated by Venezuela. A prior report alleged that Moïse embezzled millions of dollars from a road rehabilitation project funded by the program in 2016 before he took office, which the president refuted. None of the ministers or state officials implicated in the corruption scandal were prosecuted by the end of 2020. In September 2020, against objections from the CSCCA's president, Moïse issued a decree that rendered the court's opinions on public procurement contracts advisory and nonbinding, which would allow for the awarding of state contracts without prior court approval.

C3. Does the government operate with openness and transparency? 2 / 4

Haitians' general distrust of the government stems in large part from the absence of transparency and accountability measures that are needed to reduce corruption. There are no laws providing the public with access to state information, and it is reportedly very difficult to obtain government documents and data in practice. All government officials must file financial disclosure forms within 90 days of taking office and within 90 days of leaving office, though these requirements are not well enforced, and the reports are not made public.

In November 2020, President Moïse created the National Intelligence Agency (ANI) to gather information on and prevent terrorist acts, under an expanded definition of the term. The presidential decree that created the body granted the ANI total secrecy and the ability to conduct surveillance of individuals and businesses at any time, even if there is no relevant ongoing investigation.

CIVIL LIBERTIES: 22 / 60
D. FREEDOM OF EXPRESSION AND BELIEF: 10 / 16
D1. Are there free and independent media? 2 / 4

The constitution includes protections for press freedom, and the media sector is pluralistic, but the work of journalists is constrained by threats and violence, government interference, and a lack of financial resources.

In May 2020, President Moïse issued decrees to combat the COVID-19 pandemic that included prohibition of the sharing of photos or videos of the bodies of people who died from the virus. The government claimed the laws were intended to prevent the stigmatization of people who had contracted coronavirus. Anticorruption activists and human rights groups criticized the rules as laying the groundwork for the government to further restrict free speech in the future.

Attacks on journalists occur frequently. In July 2020, journalist Setoute Yvens survived a shooting attempt, and Pradel Alexandre received death threats in retaliation for their work in Haiti. In April, a group of journalists were attacked as they investigated whether the National Identification Office was violating COVID-19 protocols. In October 2019, Radio Panic FM and Radio Méga reporter Néhémie Joseph was found dead in the city of Mirebalais; Joseph, who criticized the government in social media posts, had accused former mayor Élionel Casséus and Senator Rony Célestin, both members of the ruling PHTK, of threatening his life the month before. Though a suspect was arrested in January 2020, the case was transferred to a second judge after the first judge refused to work without security guarantees; no conviction had been reported by the end of the year.

D2. Are individuals free to practice and express their religious faith or nonbelief in public and private? 3 / 4

Freedom of religion is constitutionally guaranteed, and religious groups generally practice freely. However, the traditionally dominant Roman Catholic and Protestant churches and schools receive certain privileges from the state, while Vodou religious leaders experience social stigmatization and violence for their beliefs and practices. The government has denied registration to the small Muslim community.

D3. Is there academic freedom, and is the educational system free from extensive political indoctrination? 2 / 4

Educational institutions and academics choose their curriculum freely, but university associations and student groups that protest government actions are often met with police violence.

D4. Are individuals free to express their personal views on political or other sensitive topics without fear of surveillance or retribution? 3 / 4

There are few significant constraints on freedom of private discussion. The government does not engage in widespread surveillance, nor is it known to illegally monitor private online communications. However, the penal code includes defamation-related offenses, and the risk of violent reprisals may also serve as a deterrent to unfettered discussion of sensitive issues such as corruption, gangs, and organized crime.

E. ASSOCIATIONAL AND ORGANIZATIONAL RIGHTS: 3 / 12

E1. Is there freedom of assembly? 1 / 4

The constitution enshrines freedom of assembly, but this right is often violated in practice by police that use excessive force such as tear gas and live rounds of ammunition in targeted areas to disperse protesters. Antigovernment protests and marches took place through much of 2020, with participants calling for Moïse's resignation over corruption allegations, the country's dire economic prospects, and the mismanagement of the COVID-19 crisis.

In October 2020, student Grégory Saint-Hilaire was shot and killed during a protest against the government's education policy. Student protests escalated after human rights observers attributed the death to the Haitian police.

E2. Is there freedom for nongovernmental organizations, particularly those that are engaged in human rights- and governance-related work? 1 / 4

Human rights defenders and activists with NGOs that address sensitive topics are subject to threats and violence, which creates a climate of fear. Violence against activists is rarely investigated or prosecuted. The head of the Port-au-Prince Bar Association, Monferrier Dorval, was assassinated in August 2020 hours after he spoke out against the government on the radio, sparking protests by lawyers and judges around the country. The investigation into the suspicious death in November 2019 of Jeudy Charlot, founder of LGBT+ advocacy group Kouraj (Courage), was still stalled without an arrest at the end of 2020.

E3. Is there freedom for trade unions and similar professional or labor organizations? 1 / 4

Workers' right to unionize is protected under the law, and strikes are not uncommon, though the union movement in Haiti is weak and lacks collective bargaining power in practice. Most citizens are informally employed. Workers who engage in union activity frequently face harassment, suspension, termination, and other repercussions from employers.

F. RULE OF LAW: 4 / 16

F1. Is there an independent judiciary? 1 / 4

Despite constitutional guarantees of independence, the judiciary is susceptible to pressure from the executive and legislative branches. A lack of resources has contributed to bribery throughout the judicial system, and weak oversight means that most corrupt officials are not held accountable. When Moïse's government took power, all 18 chief prosecutors from each jurisdiction were replaced; this opened new avenues for executive interference in the judiciary, since prosecutors can determine which cases end up before a judge. The mandates of 33 out of 185 lower court judges were not renewed between 2019 and 2020.

F2. Does due process prevail in civil and criminal matters? 1 / 4

Constitutionally protected due process rights are regularly violated in practice. Arbitrary arrest is common, as are extortion attempts by police and in all levels of the legal system. Most suspects do not have legal representation, and even those who do suffer from long delays and case mismanagement. The pretrial detention rate increased from 72 percent in 2019 to 78 percent in 2020, due to frequent court closures caused by antigovernment protests and the coronavirus pandemic, in addition to an existing backlog of cases and resource constraints. Many have never appeared before a judge despite the legal requirement of a court hearing within 48 hours of arrest.

In November 2020, President Moïse published two decrees that expanded the definition of "terrorism" and created the National Intelligence Agency (ANI) to gather information on and prevent terrorist acts that ostensibly threaten national security. Human rights groups have denounced the decrees, criticizing that the new definition of "terrorist act," which includes robbery, extortion, arson, and the destruction of public and private goods, threatens residents' civil rights and the rule of law. Further, the decrees authorize the ANI to have total secrecy and conduct surveillance at any time, even if there is no relevant ongoing investigation. ANI staff will be recruited from the Haitian National Police and from the military and will not be subject to legal recourse without prior authorization from the president.

F3. Is there protection from the illegitimate use of physical force and freedom from war and insurgencies? 1 / 4

A culture of impunity in law enforcement leaves civilians in Haiti with little protection from the illegitimate use of force. Crime statistics are difficult to authenticate, and crimes are underreported, but the UN Secretary General recorded that 701 killings in Haiti were reported to police between March and August 2020. Police are regularly accused of abusing suspects and detainees. Conditions in Haiti's prisons, which are among the world's most overcrowded, are extremely poor.

Criminal groups also exert considerable influence, operating with relative impunity as they fight for territory and extort residents living in areas under their control. At least 111 people were reportedly murdered, and 48 people went missing in June and July 2020 due to gang violence in Cité Soleil, a slum of Port-au-Prince. In late October, high school student Evelyne Sincère was kidnapped and brutally killed. Her killing sparked mass protests, particularly among the Haitian diaspora, demanding government accountability for the rise in gang violence and kidnappings that disproportionately affects women and girls.

F4. Do laws, policies, and practices guarantee equal treatment of various segments of the population? 1 / 4

Discrimination against women, the LGBT+ community, and people with disabilities is pervasive. Among other problems, women face bias in employment and disparities in access to financial services.

A new penal code reform was published in June 2020 by executive decree, prohibiting harassment and discrimination on the basis of sexual orientation, which occurs regularly. The reform was met with sharp resistance and public protest by conservative cultural and religious groups.

G. PERSONAL AUTONOMY AND INDIVIDUAL RIGHTS: 5 / 16

G1. Do individuals enjoy freedom of movement, including the ability to change their place of residence, employment, or education? 1 / 4

The government generally does not restrict travel or place limits on the ability to change one's place of employment or education. However, insecurity prevented free movement, particularly in Port-au-Prince, as roads were blockaded in frequent protests and people stayed in their homes due to widespread gang violence. In addition, the government's flawed response to natural disasters has prevented many displaced residents from returning to their homes, forcing them to live in poor conditions for extended periods. At the end of 2019 (the most recent statistics as of this writing), around 33,000 people were living in camps for the internally displaced. More than 6,125 people (1,500 households) were displaced when their houses were burned down by armed gangs in October 2020.

G2. Are individuals able to exercise the right to own property and establish private businesses without undue interference from state or nonstate actors? 2 / 4

Although the legal framework protects property rights and private business activity, it is difficult in practice to register property, enforce contracts, and obtain credit. Poor record keeping and corruption contribute to inconsistent enforcement of property rights.

G3. Do individuals enjoy personal social freedoms, including choice of marriage partner and size of family, protection from domestic violence, and control over appearance? 2 / 4

Basic freedoms related to marriage, divorce, and custody are generally respected. However, there are no laws addressing domestic violence, which is a widespread problem. Both domestic violence and rape are underreported and rarely result in successful prosecutions, with justice officials often favoring reconciliation or other forms of settlement.

G4. Do individuals enjoy equality of opportunity and freedom from economic exploitation? 0 / 4

Socioeconomic mobility is obstructed by entrenched poverty, with a national literacy rate of 61.7 percent for the population aged 15 and older. Over 50 percent of Haitians live on less than $2.41 a day. Legal protections against exploitative working conditions in formal employment are weakly enforced, and most workers are informally employed. As many as 300,000 children work as domestic servants, often without pay or access to education; they are especially vulnerable to physical or sexual abuse. Other forms of child labor are common. In August 2020, in the rural southern town of Beamont, reports emerged that 84 high school students were pregnant when school reopened and many of them had dropped out. Nearly half of the 84 students were minors who had been impregnated by men between the ages of 22 and 60, in what human rights group suspect are cases of exploitation of impoverished adolescent girls and young women.

Honduras

Population: 9,900,000
Capital: Tegucigalpa
Freedom Status: Partly Free
Electoral Democracy: No

Overview: Institutional weakness, corruption, violence, and impunity undermine the overall stability of Honduras. Journalists, political activists, and women are often the victims of violence, and perpetrators are rarely brought to justice. While Honduras holds regular elections, irregularities surrounding the 2017 presidential poll prompted election monitors to call the result into question.

KEY DEVELOPMENTS IN 2020

- Honduras registered over 120,000 cases of COVID-19 and 3,100 deaths by the end of 2020, according to University of Oxford researchers.
- In January 2020, the Organization of American States (OAS) and the Honduran government failed to reach an agreement to renew the mandate of the Mission to Support the Fight against Corruption and Impunity in Honduras (MACCIH), despite public support for renewal, and several prominent corruption cases ended in dismissal or acquittal during the year.
- In June, a new criminal code took effect that that lowers sentences in corruption and drug trafficking cases, and includes provisions criticized by human rights groups as risks to free expression, association, and assembly.
- Aggression against the Garifuna community escalated, with one community leader killed in June and five leaders subjected to enforced disappearance in July.

POLITICAL RIGHTS: 19 / 40

A. ELECTORAL PROCESS: 7 / 12

A1. Was the current head of government or other chief national authority elected through free and fair elections? 2 / 4

The president is both chief of state and head of government, and is elected by popular vote to four-year terms. The leading candidate is only required to win a plurality; there is no runoff system.

In a controversial 2015 decision, the Honduran Supreme Court voided Article 239 of the constitution, which had limited presidents to one term. President Juan Orlando Hernández of the National Party (PN) was subsequently reelected in 2017 by a narrow margin. The OAS noted numerous issues with the electoral process, which it said "was characterized by irregularities and deficiencies, with very low technical quality and lacking integrity," and appealed for new elections to be held. The government dismissed the OAS petition, and by year's end the United States, the European Union (EU), and Canada had recognized Hernández as the winner of the election.

A2. Were the current national legislative representatives elected through free and fair elections? 3 / 4

Members of the 128-seat, unicameral National Congress are elected for four-year terms using proportional representation by department. In the 2017 polls, the governing PN acquired an additional 13 seats, but fell short of a legislative majority. The opposition Liberty and

Refoundation (LIBRE) party and Liberal Party (PL) lost seven seats and one seat, respectively. While the 2017 presidential and parliamentary votes were held concurrently, stakeholders accepted the results of the legislative elections; only the presidential poll was disputed.

A3. Are the electoral laws and framework fair, and are they implemented impartially by the relevant election management bodies? 2 / 4

The Supreme Electoral Council (TSE) came under heavy criticism for its administration of the 2017 presidential poll. A preliminary vote count had showed challenger Salvador Nasralla with a significant lead, but subsequent updates and the final result—which was released three weeks after the elections—showed a victory by Hernández. The delay prompted protests and widespread allegations of TSE incompetence and bias toward the ruling party. Authorities dismissed the OAS's recommendation for a rerun of the poll.

An UN-sponsored national dialogue did not produce an agreement on electoral reform in 2018, but a subsequent effort between the OAS and Honduras resulted in Congress's 2019 creation of two new electoral bodies to replace the TSE, the Electoral Court of Justice (TJE) and National Electoral Council (CNE). As of the end of 2020, no new electoral law had been implemented, despite the imminent start of the 2021 campaign.

B. POLITICAL PLURALISM AND PARTICIPATION: 8 / 16

B1. Do the people have the right to organize in different political parties or other competitive political groupings of their choice, and is the system free of undue obstacles to the rise and fall of these competing parties or groupings? 3 / 4

Political parties are largely free to operate, though power has mostly been concentrated in the hands of the PL and the PN since the early 1980s. In 2013, LIBRE and the Anti-Corruption Party (PAC) participated in elections for the first time, winning a significant share of the vote and disrupting the dominance of the PL and the PN. PAC lost all but one of its seats in 2017, but LIBRE maintained its position as the second-largest party in the parliament.

B2. Is there a realistic opportunity for the opposition to increase its support or gain power through elections? 2 / 4

Opposition parties are competitive, and in 2017, opposition candidates took a significant portion of the vote in both the legislative and presidential elections. However, the many serious irregularities surrounding the TSE's administration of the 2017 presidential election prompted EU and OAS election monitors to question the validity of the vote count, and the opposition insisted that a PN-aligned TSE had denied the opposition candidate victory in the presidential race.

B3. Are the people's political choices free from domination by forces that are external to the political sphere, or by political forces that employ extrapolitical means? 1 / 4

Political and economic elites have traditionally exerted significant influence over political parties, limiting people's political choices. The military, after decades of ruling Honduras, remains politically powerful. President Hernández's appointments of military officials to civilian posts, many related to security, have underscored that influence. There were numerous reports of vote buying during the 2017 polling period.

B4. Do various segments of the population (including ethnic, racial, religious, gender, LGBT+, and other relevant groups) have full political rights and electoral opportunities? 2 / 4

Adult citizens may vote, and voting is compulsory. Members of ethnic minority groups remain underrepresented in Honduras's political system and in the political sphere generally, though there have been modest efforts by the government to encourage their participation and representation. After being criticized for failing to do so in past elections, electoral authorities in 2017 printed voter information materials in Indigenous and Afro-Honduran languages. However, no representatives of the Afro-Honduran (Garifuna) population were elected to Congress in 2017.

Women are also underrepresented in politics. In the 2017 elections, women won 27 of 128 congressional races and 23 of 298 mayoral posts. In October 2020 Congress passed a law requiring additional ballot slots for women in the 2021 elections, although it was unclear how effective the law would be in practice.

C. FUNCTIONING OF GOVERNMENT: 4 / 12

C1. Do the freely elected head of government and national legislative representatives determine the policies of the government? 2 / 4

In 2014, the Hernández administration eliminated five cabinet-level ministries and created seven umbrella ministries in an effort to cut costs. Critics have argued that the restructuring concentrated power in too few hands. Two new executive decrees passed in 2018 further consolidated power in the executive branch. The military, which has traditionally maintained substantial autonomy from civilian oversight, has played an increasing role in both internal security and programs unrelated to security in recent years, prompting the UN Office of the High Commissioner on Human Rights (OHCHR) to call for demilitarization and a return of nondefense matters to civilian control.

C2. Are safeguards against official corruption strong and effective? 1 / 4

Corruption remains rampant in Honduras, despite efforts to bolster its anticorruption mechanisms in recent years. The MACCIH, which was established in 2016, facilitated anticorruption legislation aimed at preventing illicit campaign donations, and cooperated with the Attorney General's Special Prosecutor's Unit Against Impunity and Corruption (UFE-CIC) in its work. In April 2019, MACCIH reported that 120 individuals were being prosecuted for corruption, including 70 government officials. That December, Congress—some members of which were implicated in corruption by MACCIH's work—advised President Hernández not to renew the MACCIH's mandate. After the OAS and the Honduran government failed to reach an extension agreement, the mission ended in January 2020.

The shuttering of the MACCIH was just one marker of a pattern of regression in Honduran anticorruption efforts in 2020. In March, the Supreme Court vacated the conviction of former first lady Rosa Elena Bonilla, who had been convicted of fraud and embezzlement in 2019, and in July she was released from prison pending a new trial. The new criminal code that took effect in June 2020 eased penalties for multiple crimes public officials are regularly accused of, including corruption and drug trafficking. The new code also contributed to the dismissal of charges or acquittal of officials implicated in several emblematic corruption cases, including one that exposed large-scale embezzlement in the public health sector. The COVID-19 pandemic resulted in additional public health-related graft allegations, with revelations centered on fraudulent contracts and inflated prices for medical supplies and mobile hospital facilities.

President Hernández was directly implicated in corruption in 2019, when United States prosecutors identified him and former president Porfirio Lobo as coconspirators in a drug smuggling operation run by Juan Antonio Hernández, the president's brother. In October 2019, a United States jury convicted the president's brother; his sentencing was still pending as of the end of 2020. In May 2020, US prosecutors indicted Juan Carlos Bonilla, a notorious former Honduran police chief; the indictment's language included suggestions that Bonilla had acted in collusion with the Hernández brothers.

C3. Does the government operate with openness and transparency? 1 / 4

Government operations are generally opaque. Journalists and interest groups have difficulty obtaining information from the government. Secrecy laws passed in 2014 allow authorities to withhold information on security and national defense for up to 25 years. The laws cover information regarding the military police budget, which is funded by a security tax, as well as information related to the Supreme Court and the Foreign Affairs and International Cooperation Directorate.

During the COVID-19 pandemic in 2020, civil society groups criticized a lack of transparency for medical supply and food aid distribution. The November creation of a Ministry of Transparency was also criticized by civil society representatives as an effort to undermine the efficacy of existing transparency mechanisms.

CIVIL LIBERTIES: 25 / 60 (−1)
D. FREEDOM OF EXPRESSION AND BELIEF: 9 / 16
D1. Are there free and independent media? 1 / 4

Authorities systematically violate the constitution's press freedom guarantees. Reporters and outlets covering sensitive topics or who are perceived as critical of authorities risk assaults, threats, blocked transmissions, and harassment. In 2020, television host German Vallecillo, Jr. was killed along with cameraman Jorge Posas in La Ceiba in July, while Facebook-based reporter Luis Alonzo Almendares was shot dead in Comayagua in September. Although a government program exists to provide protection to threatened journalists, both domestic press advocacy groups and the OHCHR describe it as inadequate.

The Committee for Free Expression, a local press freedom group, noted that the state of emergency declared in March inhibited reporting and led to dozens of press freedom violations, including at least nine attacks perpetrated by members of the security forces between March and mid-June.

Journalists are also targeted by various types of defamation laws. In March 2019, the Supreme Court upheld the 2016 defamation conviction of Globo TV host David Romero Ellner, and he was taken into custody to serve a 10-year prison sentence; in July 2020, Romero died in prison after contracting COVID-19. According to the Committee to Protect Journalists (CPJ), while defamation was decriminalized under the new criminal code, insult and slander continue to be subject to criminal penalties.

D2. Are individuals free to practice and express their religious faith or nonbelief in public and private? 4 / 4

Religious freedom is generally respected in Honduras.

D3. Is there academic freedom, and is the educational system free from extensive political indoctrination? 2 / 4

Academic freedom is undermined by criminal groups, who control all or parts of schools in some areas and subject staff to extortion schemes. Authorities sometimes move to suppress student demonstrations by arresting participants and dispersing the events, and violent clashes between police and student protesters sometimes occur.

D4. Are individuals free to express their personal views on political or other sensitive topics without fear of surveillance or retribution? 2 / 4

Under the Special Law on Interception of Private Communications, passed in 2011, the government can intercept online and telephone messages. Violence, threats, and intimidation by state and nonstate actors curtails open and free private discussion among the general population.

E. ASSOCIATIONAL AND ORGANIZATIONAL RIGHTS: 4 / 12

E1. Is there freedom of assembly? 1 / 4

Freedom of assembly is constitutionally protected, but the government consistently uses force to disperse participants. Ongoing protests roiled the country for much of 2019, after President Hernández announced austerity measures for the country's health and education sectors in April. Congress suspended the measures, but hundreds of protests were held throughout Honduras in the following months, with demonstrators calling for the president's resignation. Hernández's implication in his brother's drug-smuggling operation drove additional protests in Tegucigalpa. Amnesty International reported that authorities regularly used tear gas and live ammunition against demonstrators and bystanders, and that six people were killed during protests or government reprisals by year's end.

The COVID-19-linked state of emergency included restrictions on freedom of assembly, though the OHCHR logged hundreds of protests in 2020, many of them related to pandemic-related deprivation. State security forces were accused of excessive force in enforcing the assembly restrictions. In December, three UN special rapporteurs sent a joint letter calling for revisions of sections of the new criminal code that threaten assembly rights, including vague invocations of the word "terrorism" that potentially jeopardized protest organizers.

E2. Is there freedom for nongovernmental organizations, particularly those that are engaged in human rights- and governance-related work? 1 / 4

NGOs and their staff, especially in the human rights and environmental fields, face significant threats, including harassment, surveillance, smear campaigns aimed at undermining their work, and violence. The Inter-American Commission on Human Rights (IACHR) reported that between January 2014 and August 2018, at least 65 human rights defenders were murdered. At least eight additional rights activists were killed in 2020, according to the OHCHR. Activists from the Garifuna community have been especially targeted in recent years, a pattern that continued in 2020. In June, Garifuna leader Antonio Bernárdez was found murdered, and in July, five community leaders were abducted by a large group of armed men, some of whom wore clothing bearing police agency insignia. All of the men remained missing at year's end.

In 2018, a court convicted seven suspects in the prominent 2016 killing of environmental and indigenous rights activist Berta Cáceres; they received multidecade sentences in 2019. In August 2020, trial began for the president of the company constructing the hydroelectric dam Cáceres had opposed, though human rights advocates expressed concern about persistent delays in the process.

E3. Is there freedom for trade unions and similar professional or labor organizations? 2 / 4

Labor unions are well organized and can strike, though labor actions have resulted in clashes with security forces. The government does not always honor formal agreements entered with public-sector unions. Union leaders and labor activists in both the public and private sector face harassment, dismissal, and violence for their activities. According to a report published in June 2020 by the Network Against Anti-Union Violence, 36 trade unionists were murdered between 2009 and 2019, including two in 2019.

F. RULE OF LAW: 4 / 16 (−1)

F1. Is there an independent judiciary? 1 / 4

Political and business elites exert excessive influence over the judiciary, including the Supreme Court. Judicial appointments are made with little transparency, and the UN Special Rapporteur on the independence of judges and lawyers reported in June 2020 that the

Supreme Court maintains excessive control over lower-level judicial appointments. Judges have been removed from their posts for political reasons, and a number of legal professionals have been killed in recent years.

The Special Rapporteur also noted Congress's excessive power over the judiciary. In 2012, Congress voted to remove four of the five justices in the Supreme Court's constitutional chamber, and in 2013, the legislature granted itself greater removal power over officials from other branches, curtailed the power of the Supreme Court's constitutional chamber, and revoked the right of citizens to challenge the constitutionality of laws. Corruption cases involving legislators are heard by the Supreme Court, and the Court has shelved or delayed cases of graft allegations involving scores of legislators.

F2. Does due process prevail in civil and criminal matters? 1 / 4 (−1)

Due process is limited due to a compromised judiciary and a corrupt and often inept police force, in which many officers have engaged in criminal activities including drug trafficking and extortion. The government has increasingly utilized the armed forces to combat crime and violence. Arbitrary arrests and detentions are common, as is lengthy pretrial detention. In 2017, authorities established several new courts in an attempt to address lengthy trial delays. Authorities in the armed forces have dishonorably discharged members accused of rights violations before their trials have taken place. The OHCHR noted that cases in the already backlogged justice system faced additional delays and complications in 2020 as a result of the COVID-19 pandemic.

The new criminal code entered into force in June despite criticism by human rights groups, including over the continued criminalization of insult and slander, definitions of torture and enforced disappearance that were inconsistent with international standards, and a litany of ambiguously worded provisions that could affect free association and assembly rights. According to the OHCHR, the code did contain alternative sentencing provisions that could alleviate severe overcrowding in the country's prisons.

Score Change: The score declined from 2 to 1 because a new criminal code contained vaguely worded provisions that expose citizens to arbitrary and abusive enforcement.

F3. Is there protection from the illegitimate use of physical force and freedom from war and insurgencies? 1 / 4

The homicide rate has declined notably over the last decade, but violent crime and gang violence remain serious problems, and have prompted large-scale internal displacement and migration. In response to widespread violence, the government has empowered the Military Police of Public Order (PMOP) and other security forces to combat security threats, and these units often employ excessive force when conducting operations. The OHCHR reported several deaths that constituted potential human rights abuses in 2020, including the April killing of a man in Cortés department by PMOP officers enforcing the pandemic lockdown and a suspected extrajudicial execution during a joint police-military operation in San Pedro Sula.

Prisons are overcrowded and underequipped, and prison violence remains rampant due in large part to pervasive gang presence. Despite the military taking control of prison security in late 2019, InSight Crime registered at least 55 inmates murdered between December 2019 and August 2020.

F4. Do laws, policies, and practices guarantee equal treatment of various segments of the population? 1 / 4

Violence and discrimination against LGBT+ people and Indigenous and Garifuna populations persist at high levels in Honduras. Lesbian Network Cattrachas, a local NGO, reported that at least 20 LGBT+ people were killed in 2020. Cattrachas registered an impunity rate of 91 percent in the 373 murders of LBGT+ people between 2009 and 2020. According to the OHCHR and the UN Working Group on Business and Human Rights, lands inhabited by Indigenous and Afro-Honduran people are particularly vulnerable to expropriation for development projects without adequate prior consultation, and communities that contest such projects are unable to effectively assert their rights.

Honduras has among the highest femicide rates in the world, and these murders are rarely investigated. According to the National Autonomous University of Honduras, 406 women were murdered in 2019, and 217 women were killed in the first eight months of 2020.

Asylum seekers from Honduras and other countries can find themselves held in Honduran territory due to a bilateral agreement signed with the United States in 2019. As part of the agreement, Honduras agreed to house asylum seekers whose claims were either rejected or not processed by the United States, even if they did not originate in Honduras.

G. PERSONAL AUTONOMY AND INDIVIDUAL RIGHTS: 8 / 16

G1. Do individuals enjoy freedom of movement, including the ability to change their place of residence, employment, or education? 2 / 4

While authorities generally do not restrict free movement, ongoing violence and impunity have reduced personal autonomy for the country's residents. Those living in gang-controlled territories face extortion, and dangerous conditions limit free movement and options for education and employment. The Office of the UN High Commissioner for Refugees (UNHCR) estimated that over 247,000 people were internally displaced in Honduras at the end of 2019. According to the OHCHR, movement restrictions associated with the COVID-19 pandemic increased the difficulties faced by vulnerable communities, including Indigenous Hondurans and migrants.

G2. Are individuals able to exercise the right to own property and establish private businesses without undue interference from state or nonstate actors? 2 / 4

Corruption, crime, and gang activity inhibits the ability to conduct business activities freely and dissuades entrepreneurs from establishing new businesses. Those who work in the transportation sector (taxi and bus drivers) are notable targets of gangs, but many are unable to flee for fear of retaliatory violence against themselves and their families. According to Human Rights Watch (HRW), the government uses force to prevent people from attempting to flee the country.

G3. Do individuals enjoy personal social freedoms, including choice of marriage partner and size of family, protection from domestic violence, and control over appearance? 2 / 4

Same-sex marriage remains illegal in Honduras. In 2019, a law came into force banning same-sex couples from adopting children despite the objection of activists, who called the bill superfluous and discriminatory. Abortion is illegal in Honduras, including in cases of rape or incest, with criminal sanctions including imprisonment for those accused of terminating their pregnancies. Emergency contraception is also prohibited. Domestic violence remains widespread, and most such attacks go unpunished.

G4. Do individuals enjoy equality of opportunity and freedom from economic exploitation? 2 / 4

Lack of socioeconomic opportunities combined with high levels of crime and violence limit social mobility for most Hondurans, and exacerbate income inequality. High youth unemployment and low levels of education help to perpetuate the cycle of crime and violence; these issues, especially access to education, were exacerbated by the COVID-19 pandemic as well as Hurricanes Eta and Iota, which struck in November 2020 and affected over 4 million people, killed nearly 100, and caused significant damage.

Human trafficking is a significant issue in Honduras, which serves as a source country for women and children forced into prostitution; adults and children are also vulnerable to forced labor in the agriculture, mining, and other sectors, and as domestic servants.

Hungary

Population: 9,800,000
Capital: Budapest
Freedom Status: Partly Free
Electoral Democracy: Yes

Overview: After taking power in 2010 elections, Prime Minister Viktor Orbán's Alliance of Young Democrats–Hungarian Civic Union (Fidesz) party pushed through constitutional and legal changes that have allowed it to consolidate control over the country's independent institutions. More recently, the Fidesz-led government has moved to institute policies that hamper the operations of opposition groups, journalists, universities, and nongovernmental organizations (NGOs) who criticize it or whose perspectives it otherwise finds unfavorable.

KEY DEVELOPMENTS IN 2020

- In March, the first COVID-19 cases were reported in Hungary, and by the end of the year over 322,000 people had tested positive for the virus and over 9,500 people had died. The government used the pandemic to justify giving the prime minister power to rule by decree, without parliamentary oversight, for an indefinite amount of time.
- In April, the parliament amended the criminal code to broaden the offense of "scaremongering" to include the intentional spreading of false or distorted information during a state of emergency, punishable with a five-year prison sentence.
- In May, the Court of Justice of the European Union (CJEU) ruled that the use of "transit zones" to hold asylum seekers while processing their claims amounted to unlawful detention and was a violation of European Union (EU) law. The government closed down the transit zones in response, though the new legal framework further restricts access to asylum in Hungary.
- In November, the parliament passed a law that severely restricts same-sex couples' ability to adopt children, declaring legally that the parents of a child must be a woman and a man.

POLITICAL RIGHTS: 26 / 40 (−1)
A. ELECTORAL PROCESS: 9 / 12
A1. Was the current head of government or other chief national authority elected through free and fair elections? 3 / 4

The National Assembly elects both the president and the prime minister, meaning the democratic legitimacy of these votes rests largely on the fairness of parliamentary elections.

The president's duties are mainly ceremonial, but they may influence appointments and return legislation for further consideration before signing it into law. The president is limited to a maximum of two terms. János Áder, a founding member of Fidesz, has been president since 2012, having won a second five-year term in 2017.

The prime minister holds most executive power. Orbán has been prime minister since 2010, winning reelection in 2014 and 2018.

A2. Were the current national legislative representatives elected through free and fair elections? 3 / 4

Voters elect representatives every four years to a 199-seat, unicameral National Assembly under a mixed system of proportional and direct representation (106 from single-member districts and 93 from compensatory party lists). The coalition of Fidesz and its junior partner, the Christian Democratic People's Party (KDNP), won the April 2018 parliamentary elections with 49.3 percent of the vote, capturing exactly two-thirds (133) of the seats. The far-right Movement for a Better Hungary (Jobbik) took 26 seats, a coalition led by the center-left Hungarian Socialist Party (MSZP) won 20 seats, and smaller parties and individuals divided the remainder.

An election-monitoring mission performed by the Organization for Security and Co-operation in Europe (OSCE) said the elections were generally well administered, but it noted an "overlap between state and ruling party resources," and added that opaque campaign finance, media bias, and "intimidating and xenophobic rhetoric" hampered voters' ability to make informed choices. While there was no evidence of electoral fraud that could have affected the elections' outcome, some irregularities were reported, and the OSCE found that rigid adherence to formal regulations by the National Election Commission (NVB) had in effect limited access to legal remedy.

Fidesz took advantage of access to state resources to promote its candidate in an October 2020 by-election, who ultimately won.

A3. Are the electoral laws and framework fair, and are they implemented impartially by the relevant election management bodies? 3 / 4

Members of the NVB are nominated by the president and confirmed to nine-year terms by the parliament. There is no formal parliamentary debate or public consultation process to inform the selection of current NVB members, and observers have raised concerns about the body's impartiality. The OSCE report on the 2018 election noted the NVB's tendency to favor the ruling party when considering complaints over advertising materials. However, the NVB has on a few occasions ruled against Fidesz; they fined Prime Minister Orbán in 2018 for posting an election campaign video in a kindergarten classroom online without permission from the parents.

Nevertheless, Orbán's government has been largely successful in superseding impartiality requirements. In 2019, the Supreme Court effectively neutralized a long-standing neutrality requirement for state institutions during election campaigns.

The OSCE's 2018 assessment also indicated that citizens were not permitted to participate in election observation at polling places, and that "intimidating rhetoric by the government" discouraged public involvement in election-related activities. Numerous local election commissions operated without an opposition or nonpartisan presence during the 2018 polls.

After Fidesz took power in 2010, it used its parliamentary supermajority to redraw constituency boundaries in its favor. Electoral bodies frequently reject referendums proposed by the opposition while approving government proposals of dubious constitutionality, including a controversial 2016 referendum on an EU asylum quota plan.

B. POLITICAL PLURALISM AND PARTICIPATION: 11 / 16

B1. Do the people have the right to organize in different political parties or other competitive political groupings of their choice, and is the system free of undue obstacles to the rise and fall of these competing parties or groupings? 3 / 4

Political parties can organize legally, but they face some practical impediments in their efforts to garner popular support. Changes to party registration and financing systems that took effect ahead of the 2014 parliamentary polls encouraged the registration of new parties, but these reforms were criticized as a means for Fidesz to divide the opposition. Opposition parties are disadvantaged by the politicized distortion of the advertising market, notably including the market for the country's many billboards.

Individual politicians face smear campaigns in progovernment media outlets. Opposition parties faced bogus competitors in the 2014 and 2018 elections that may have been created by the government for the purpose of splitting the opposition vote. Authorities have also interfered with opposition figures' peaceful political activities.

In 2020, the government cut party funding and halved state subsidies for political parties in order to increase funds dedicated to fight the COVID-19 pandemic. These measures disproportionately affected opposition parties. The parliament further amended the electoral framework to require that political parties field candidates in 71 (instead of 27) single-member constituencies on a single list, forcing small opposition parties to combine and field one consolidated list of candidates.

B2. Is there a realistic opportunity for the opposition to increase its support or gain power through elections? 2 / 4

Fidesz has dominated the political landscape since the 2010 election. The opposition remains fragmented, and opposition parties increasingly contend with obstacles and restrictions that detract from their ability to gain power through elections. These include unequal access to media, smear campaigns, politicized audits, and a campaign environment skewed by the ruling coalition's mobilization of state resources.

While the 2018 parliamentary polls were generally well administered, the proliferation of obstacles faced by opposition parties and candidates diminished their ability to freely compete with Fidesz. The OSCE cited the "pervasive overlap between state and ruling party resources," which often made extensive government advertising campaigns indistinguishable from Fidesz promotional materials. The ruling party also harnessed Hungary's public broadcaster to disseminate its message, with the OSCE's media monitoring mission describing "clear patterns of political bias" in its election-related programming. Finally, the national government maintains effective control of the State Audit Office (ÁSZ), which monitors campaign activities and party spending. In recent years, ÁSZ has imposed sanctions only on opposition parties for financial irregularities, while condoning or overlooking problematic spending of state subsidies by the ruling party.

Nevertheless, Fidesz lost control of several cities, including the capital of Budapest, in 2019 local elections. Gergely Karácsony, the winner of Budapest's mayoral election, commanded over 50 percent of the vote; opposition politicians also wrested control of Budapest's local council.

B3. Are the people's political choices free from domination by forces that are external to the political sphere, or by political forces that employ extrapolitical means? 3 / 4

Individuals are largely able to participate in public affairs without encountering undue influence over their political choices. However, Fidesz has increasingly harnessed its members' political and economic power to sideline opposition groups and prevent them from presenting a meaningful challenge to its dominant position. The 2018 OSCE report found that Roma and other economically marginalized groups were vulnerable to pressure to vote for the ruling parties because of "the fear of losing access to the limited public works funds."

B4. Do various segments of the population (including ethnic, racial, religious, gender, LGBT+, and other relevant groups) have full political rights and electoral opportunities? 3 / 4

Women are underrepresented in political life, and the share of women in the parliament remains low. Only 25 of 199 National Assembly members, or 13 percent, and only 3 out of 14 cabinet ministers are women. Ruling party ministers and progovernment media occasionally make derogatory and sexist remarks toward women in the parliament.

Hungary's constitution guarantees the right of ethnic minority populations to form self-governing bodies, and all 13 recognized minorities have done so. Minorities can also register to vote for special minority lists—with a preferential vote threshold—in parliamentary elections. Most ethnic minority groups, given their small size degree to which they have assimilated into Hungarian society, are unable win a preferential mandate. Minorities without a parliamentary mandate can send a "national minority advocate" to the parliament without voting rights. Only one of the 13 recognized minorities managed to elect a representative with voting rights to the National Assembly in 2018. A former Fidesz politician, who suspended their party membership, won a seat to represent the German minority that year.

Roma have long been underrepresented in politics and government and have been the target of derogatory rhetoric from Fidesz members in recent years. Voter turnout is low among Roma, even though the number of registered Romany voters increased from 2014 to 2018. The 2018 OSCE election report found that Roma are increasingly exposed to pressures like intimidation and vote-buying.

C. FUNCTIONING OF GOVERNMENT: 6 / 12 (−1)

C1. Do the freely elected head of government and national legislative representatives determine the policies of the government? 2 / 4 (−1)

The governing coalition is effectively able to draft and implement laws and policies without undue interference. Fidesz continues to dominate governance through a parliamentary supermajority that it acquired in problematic elections. Prime Minister Orbán, the party's leader, exerts considerable influence over the legislature. The ability of the opposition to check government activities remains limited.

December 2019 amendments to rules governing the National Assembly further weakened legislators' ability to exercise their influence. Parliamentarians lost the ability to cross the political aisle and were prohibited from entering state institutions without prior notification or permission. Lawmakers have also had their behavior in the National Assembly restricted in other ways after Fidesz won its third term, with the speaker disciplining and fining lawmakers for occupying the lectern and bringing signs onto the floor. A September 2020 temporary resolution further restricted independent ministers' ability to introduce legislation, requiring draft laws to be supported by the leader of a party.

In March 2020, in response to the COVID-19 pandemic, the government declared a "state of danger" and passed the widely denounced Authorization Act, conferring sweeping emergency powers to the executive. The legislation enables the prime minister to rule by decree for an indefinite time without parliamentary approval, and to suspend or depart from any law or take any extraordinary measure. In June, the state of danger was replaced by a state of medical emergency, regulated by the Health Care Act, which was also amended to extend the power of the executive to rule by decree with neither meaningful parliamentary oversight nor a set end date.

The National Assembly adopted the Ninth Amendment of the Fundamental Law in December 2020, which rewrote the rules for special legal orders. The new legal regime, which will enter into force in 2023, significantly extends the powers of the executive.

Score Change: The score declined from 3 to 2 because a series of legal and rule changes in recent years, including 2020 emergency legislation, expanded the prime minister's ability to rule by decree, further reducing the parliament's capacity to meaningfully check executive power.

C2. Are safeguards against official corruption strong and effective? 2 / 4

Corruption remains a problem in Hungary, and instances of high-level government corruption have not been properly investigated. Prosecutors have also been reluctant to investigate long-standing allegations of the public misuse of development funds disbursed by the EU, despite the severity of the problem. Fidesz has also established broad control over auditing and investigative bodies, including the ÁSZ.

The 2020 annual report of the European Anti-Fraud Office (OLAF) warned that Hungary was the worst-performing EU member state regarding the misappropriation of EU funds, and nearly 4 percent of EU-provided funds were misused during its 2015–19 reporting period.

The latest report of the Group of States against Corruption (GRECO) held that Hungary performed poorly in complying with its recommendations on implementing anticorruption measures in relation to ministers, judges, and prosecutors. Transparency International's Hungarian chapter has warned that a number of companies with close ties to the government are supported primarily by public funds.

C3. Does the government operate with openness and transparency? 2 / 4

Hungary's Freedom of Information Act contains numerous exemptions, permits agencies to charge fees for the release of information, and is inconsistently enforced. In many cases, information is only made available as a result of litigation. In November 2020, the parliament amended the Fundamental Law's definition of what constitutes public funds. The new, narrow definition can render public oversight of a large amount of public money impossible.

In March 2020, the parliament classified the plans for the Budapest-Belgrade railway project, 85 percent of which is financed by Chinese loans.

Major legislation is frequently rushed through the parliament, leaving citizens and interest groups little time to provide feedback or criticism. Important proposals are hidden in long omnibus bills, and the government tends to submit substantial bills overnight. Journalists, meanwhile, have been curtailed from performing their duties while covering events in the parliament, with the speaker prohibiting audio and video recording in corridors surrounding the plenary chamber, entrances, and on-site cafeterias in October 2019.

When emergency laws were introduced in April 2020 because of the COVID-19 pandemic, the government significantly extended the deadline for fulfilling freedom of information requests. Critics denounced the extension as unconstitutional and a hindrance to effectively coping with the crisis. Important epidemiological data was not accessible to the public, and pandemic-related government measures that seriously constrained individual rights were often published just a few hours or minutes before they entered into force.

CIVIL LIBERTIES: 43 / 60
D. FREEDOM OF EXPRESSION AND BELIEF: 10 / 16
D1. Are there free and independent media? 2 / 4

The constitution protects freedom of the press, but Fidesz has undermined this guarantee through legislation that has politicized media regulation. While private, opposition-aligned media outlets exist, national, regional, and local media are increasingly dominated by progovernment outlets, which are frequently used to smear political opponents and highlight false accusations. Government advertising and sponsorships favor progovernment outlets, leaving independent and critical outlets in a financially precarious position.

Members of Prime Minister Orbán's governing coalition and their allies have worked to close or acquire critical media outlets since 2015, when news outlet Origo was taken over by progovernment investors. The 2016 closure of Hungary's largest independent daily, *Népszabadság*, represented a particularly serious blow to media diversity. In late 2018, around 470 progovernment media outlets were merged under the Central European Press and Media Foundation (KESMA). The government declared the merger to be of "national strategic importance" to exempt it from competition laws, and won the court case that challenged the move.

In March 2020, a businessman close to Fidesz bought 50 percent of the Indamedia Group, a partner of *Index*, the country's largest independent news outlet. In June, the editor in chief of *Index* was dismissed for voicing his concerns about the outlet's independence. Almost the entire staff subsequently resigned, and *Index* resumed operating with a completely new editorial team.

The April changes to the "scaremongering" law, ostensibly to fight false or distorted information about COVID-19, ultimately challenged journalists' ability to secure reliable sources to report on the crisis, as many individuals, especially health care workers, feared retaliation if they provided information publicly.

D2. Are individuals free to practice and express their religious faith or nonbelief in public and private? 3 / 4

The constitution guarantees religious freedom and provides for the separation of church and state, though these guarantees were weakened in the 2011 version of the constitution, whose preamble makes direct references to Christianity. Constitutional amendments enacted in 2018 and 2020 reinforced those references, obliging all state organs to protect "Christian culture" and guaranteeing children's right to education based on Christian values.

The government has led xenophobic campaigns in recent years, fueling anti-Muslim sentiment, and sought to establish links between the spread of the pandemic and illegal migration in 2020.

After the adoption of a 2011 law on churches, some 300 religious communities lost their status as incorporated churches and were relegated to the new category of "religious organizations." When that law was later found in violation of the European Convention on Human Rights, the government adopted a new law in 2018 to fulfill the same goals. That legislation created a four-tier recognition scheme, leaving the parliament to determine where organizations would fall in the new system. The law does not rectify the earlier deregistration of churches.

D3. Is there academic freedom, and is the educational system free from extensive political indoctrination? 2 / 4

The Fidesz-led government has maintained its efforts to bring schools and universities under close supervision. A gradual overhaul of the public education system raised concerns about excessive government influence on school curriculums, and legislation adopted in 2014 allows for government-appointed chancellors empowered to make financial decisions at public universities. The government has increasingly threatened the academic autonomy of well-established institutions, pulling support, interfering in their affairs, and landing progovernment supporters in leading positions. In 2018, the government revoked accreditation from all gender studies programs, with senior officials questioning the rationale for this field of academic study.

Progovernment media outlets commonly target activists, academics, programs, and institutions, often by calling them "Soros agents," referring to Hungarian-born financier and philanthropist George Soros, or "mercenaries." Legal changes enacted by the parliament in 2017 targeted the Central European University (CEU), a graduate school founded by Soros, by changing the requirements for foreign universities to operate in Hungary. The CJEU later ruled the 2017 changes were incompatible with EU law.

The Fidesz government also targeted the Hungarian Academy of Sciences (MTA) and stripped the 200-year-old MTA of its network of research institutions in 2019, handing them over to a new governing body. The controversy later abated when the government agreed that the MTA would maintain much of its funding and operational autonomy. However, in 2020, the MTA elected a new president, well-known for his support of the Fidesz government.

D4. Are individuals free to express their personal views on political or other sensitive topics without fear of surveillance or retribution? 3 / 4

While freedom of expression is constitutionally protected, ongoing efforts to sideline voices and perspectives that authorities find unfavorable, including many found at the Hungarian Academy of Sciences, CEU, NGOs, and media outlets, have discouraged open criticism of the government and other politically sensitive speech.

In April 2020, at the onset of the COVID-19 pandemic, the parliament broadened the criminal code's definition of "scaremongering" to include the intentional spreading of false or distorted information during a state of emergency and extended the maximum prison sentence to five years. More than 130 criminal proceedings were initiated on account of the new crime by June. Some individuals were arrested and interrogated for being critical of government measures on social media.

E. ASSOCIATIONAL AND ORGANIZATIONAL RIGHTS: 10 / 12

E1. Is there freedom of assembly? 4 / 4

The constitution provides for freedom of assembly, and the government generally respects this right in practice. Fidesz's electoral victory in 2018 prompted large crowds to turn out for peaceful antigovernment demonstrations.

In April 2020, a total ban on public gatherings was introduced, though some demonstrations were organized. The police imposed heavy fines on the participants of car demonstrations ("honking protests"), organized by two opposition ministers.

E2. Is there freedom for nongovernmental organizations, particularly those that are engaged in human rights- and governance-related work? 2 / 4

NGOs whose activities conflict with government priorities have come under continued pressure. Since taking power, Fidesz has instituted burdensome registration and reporting requirements for NGOs, and police illegally raided the offices of one group, the Ökotárs Foundation, in 2015. NGOs assisting asylum seekers have also been subject to Hungary's "Stop Soros" laws in 2018, which heavily restricted the right to asylum and criminalized activities supporting asylum seekers. An infringement procedure based on the "Stop Soros" legislation is currently pending before the CJEU.

The government continues to stigmatize NGOs as "foreign agents" or "Soros agents", and frequently scapegoat them for developments unfavorable to the government or deemed unpopular in the eyes of the public.

In June 2020, the CJEU found that the 2017 Act on the Transparency of Organizations, requiring organizations that receive donations from abroad to register as such, was not compatible with EU jurisprudence. So far, the government has failed to execute the judgment, the relevant law is still in force.

E3. Is there freedom for trade unions and similar professional or labor organizations? 4 / 4

Workers' rights to form associations and bargain collectively are generally recognized, but the 2012 Labor Code weakened the position of trade unions by curtailing their rights. There are significant limitations on what can be considered a lawful strike, and union membership is low. Trade unions are present in less than 25 percent of workplaces, and only 7 percent of workers belong to one.

F. RULE OF LAW: 10 / 16

F1. Is there an independent judiciary? 2 / 4

Judicial independence remains a matter of concern. All of the 11 judges appointed to the Constitutional Court between 2010 and 2014 were named by the Fidesz government. Only when Fidesz temporarily lost its supermajority was it willing to include a small opposition party into the nomination process for four judges, which took place in 2016. Rulings in recent years on politically sensitive cases have favored government interests. High-ranking government officials and progovernment media berate judgments that are detrimental to the interests of the government.

The government has also interfered with the administration of the judicial branch in recent years. Significant powers are vested in the president of National Judicial Office (NJO), a position occupied by Tünde Handó from 2012 to 2020. The powers of the judicial self-governing body, the National Judicial Council (NJC), which supervises the president of the NJO, are relatively weak. Handó has been regarded as an ally of the Fidesz government in curtailing judicial independence and has come into conflict with the NJC many times. Handó was appointed to the Constitutional Court in 2020, and was replaced by György Barna Senyei, another Fidesz ally.

The parliament sought to create a new administrative court system in 2018, which would have given the Minister of Justice broad powers to appoint and promote judges. Instead, in late December 2019, the government passed an omnibus bill effectively resurrecting the administrative court circuit. The legislation also restricted judicial interpretation of existing case law and allowed members of the Constitutional Court to assume a seat on the Supreme Court without nomination. In October 2020, Constitutional Court justice András Varga, who had written several decisions favorable to the government, was elected president of the Supreme Court, despite the NJC's overwhelming opposition. In addition, administrative authorities were also given the chance to challenge unfavorable rulings directly before the Constitutional Court.

F2. Does due process prevail in civil and criminal matters? 3 / 4

Due process rights are enshrined in the constitution and are generally respected. However, the former head of the NJO, Tünde Handó, was criticized for using her authority to transfer certain cases to courts of her choice. Litigation costs are relatively high, while access to legal aid is limited. There have been concerns about the quality of lawyers appointed for defendants who are unable or unwilling to retain legal counsel on their own.

Hungarian courts have also shown continued resistance to European judicial oversight on due process matters in 2019. That September, Hungary's Supreme Court sided with Prosecutor General Péter Polt in his efforts to limit the European Court of Justice's (ECJ) oversight over an ongoing case, which began when a lower-level judge suspended a criminal trial and sought the ECJ's opinion on its compliance with EU regulations. Polt argued that the judge's request itself was unlawful.

F3. Is there protection from the illegitimate use of physical force and freedom from war and insurgencies? 3 / 4

Inadequate medical care and poor sanitation in the country's prisons and detention centers remain problems. The coronavirus presented further challenges to the safety of prisoners and prison staff. In 2020, the government created new facilities that added significantly more space in prisons and detention centers, bringing prison capacities under 100 percent.

Physical abuse by police is a problem, and there are systematic deficiencies in reporting, indicting, investigating and sanctioning such conduct.

F4. Do laws, policies, and practices guarantee equal treatment of various segments of the population? 2 / 4

The rights of refugees and asylum seekers are routinely violated in Hungary, where frequent changes to asylum policy—including the uncontestable declaration, by law, of Serbia as a safe third country—and the construction of barriers along the country's southern border made it nearly impossible for individuals to apply for asylum and receive protection. Since 2018, only two asylum seekers are formally permitted to enter the country per day. Once allowed in, asylum seekers were frequently detained in poorly equipped transit zones, and few were recognized by Hungarian authorities as refugees. In May 2020, the CJEU ruled that Hungarian asylum procedures were incompatible with EU law and placing asylum seekers in the transit zones constituted unlawful detention. The government subsequently closed the transit zones, but passed legislation requiring asylum seekers to present their documentation at diplomatic missions in other countries.

European courts have heavily criticized Hungarian asylum and immigration policy, ruling that the policies and actions were incompatible with EU law and at times amounted to human rights violations. Despite this, the government has maintained its stance; it continues to train special police units with wide powers to remove migrants from the country.

Roma are Hungary's largest ethnic minority and face widespread discrimination, societal exclusion, violence, and poverty. Roma students continue to be segregated or improperly placed in schools for children with mental disabilities, a practice that led the European Commission (EC) to begin an infringement procedure in 2016. In early 2020, Prime Minister Orbán launched an anti-Roma campaign in response to a court awarding pecuniary damages to Roma pupils for school segregation in the town of Gyöngyöspata. The parliament amended public education laws to prevent courts from awarding pecuniary damages for similar future claims. Roma were disproportionately impacted by the COVID-19 pandemic in 2020, and the government failed to address the health, economic, and social needs of Romany communities.

Women in Hungary are subject to employment discrimination and tend to be underrepresented in high-level business positions.

The Fidesz government has proven to be increasingly discriminatory towards LGBT+ people. In May 2020, the parliament voted to end the legal recognition of gender identity, requiring "sex at birth" to be used on identification documents. In November, it passed a law that severely restricts same-sex couples' ability to adopt children, declaring in law the parents of a child to be a woman and a man. Senior Fidesz politicians have made homophobic statements in public; Prime Minister Orbán compared same-sex relationships to pedophilia in a radio interview in October 2020.

Antisemitism persists in Hungary, and anti-Soros campaigns pander to individuals with those sentiments.

G. PERSONAL AUTONOMY AND INDIVIDUAL RIGHTS: 13 / 16

G1. Do individuals enjoy freedom of movement, including the ability to change their place of residence, employment, or education? 4 / 4

There are no significant restrictions on Hungarians' freedom of travel or the ability to change their place of residence or employment. However, a July 2019 law restricts the ability of students and parents to avoid the centralized school system and limits their access to alternative schools.

Movement restrictions and curfews related to the COVID-19 pandemic were instituted based on epidemiological data.

G2. Are individuals able to exercise the right to own property and establish private businesses without undue interference from state or nonstate actors? 3 / 4

Individuals have the right to own property and establish private businesses. However, the success of a business is somewhat dependent upon its owner's government connections. Businesspeople whose activities are not in line with the financial or political interest of the government are likely to face harassment and intimidation, and subject to increasing administrative pressure for a possible takeover.

G3. Do individuals enjoy personal social freedoms, including choice of marriage partner and size of family, protection from domestic violence, and control over appearance? 3 / 4

The constitution enshrines the concept of marriage as a union between a man and a woman. LGBT+ Hungarians are allowed to pursue civil unions, but they remain prohibited from adopting children.

In 2020, the National Assembly ended the legal recognition of gender identity for transgender people. As a result of the Ninth Amendment of the Fundamental Law, the constitution now stipulates that "the mother is a woman, the father is a man", and "Hungary protects the right of children to self-identify in line with their birth sex." Furthermore, the new law effectively limits the right to adoption only to married couples, excluding single people and non-married partners—among them same-sex couples—from this right. Human rights NGOs condemned the amendments for stigmatizing and discriminating against LGBT+ people.

Domestic violence and spousal rape are illegal, but the definition of rape hinges on the use of force or coercion, not on lack of consent. NGOs describe government responses to violence against women as inadequate. In May 2020, the parliament rejected the ratification of the Istanbul Convention over what parliamentarians considered to be the destructive nature of the convention's gender ideology and the document's preferential treatment for asylum seekers on the basis of gender.

The right to life from conception is constitutionally protected, but access to abortion is today largely unrestricted.

G4. Do individuals enjoy equality of opportunity and freedom from economic exploitation?
3 / 4

Hungary is a transit point, source, and to a lesser extent, destination for trafficked persons, including women trafficked for prostitution. Prevention, coordination efforts, and processes to identify and support victims remain inadequate, while trafficking investigations and enforcement of relevant laws are unreliable. In 2020, the government adopted a National Strategy against Human Trafficking for 2020–23, which included harsher sanctions for traffickers. The parliament also amended the relevant laws primarily to protect children against sexual exploitation.

A 2018 labor code amendment significantly raised the maximum hours of overtime employers are allowed to ask for per year. Changes in 2020, made during the state of emergency caused by the coronavirus, extended the length of time over which cumulative overtime hours would be counted.

Iceland

Population: 400,000
Capital: Reykjavík
Freedom Status: Free
Electoral Democracy: Yes

Overview: Iceland is a parliamentary democracy with a long history of upholding political rights and civil liberties. However, links between elected representatives and business interests remain a concern, as does the concentration of private media ownership. Reports of systematic exploitation of immigrant labor and maltreatment of asylum seekers continue.

KEY DEVELOPMENTS IN 2020
- President Guðni Thorlacius Jóhannesson, who serves as a largely ceremonial head of state, won a second term in June with 92.2 percent of the vote.
- Parliament adopted legislation to protect whistleblowers in May, while conflict-of-interest legislation that will apply to ministers and other officials was adopted in June. Both pieces of legislation will take effect in 2021.
- Icelandic authorities did not impose a wide-ranging COVID-19 lockdown during the year, relying instead on border restrictions, public-assembly restrictions, quarantining, isolation, and contact tracing. The authorities reported 5,754 cases and 29 deaths to the World Health Organization (WHO) at year's end.

POLITICAL RIGHTS: 37 / 40

A. ELECTORAL PROCESS: 12 / 12

A1. Was the current head of government or other chief national authority elected through free and fair elections? 4 / 4

The president serves as a largely ceremonial chief of state, is directly elected to a four-year term, and is not subject to term limits. President Guðni Thorlacius Jóhannesson was reelected in June 2020 with 92.2 percent of the vote. Guðmundur Franklín Jónsson received 7.8 percent.

The prime minister is head of government. The leader of the ruling party or coalition usually becomes prime minister; the legitimacy of the prime minister rests primarily on the conduct of the parliamentary polls. The current prime minister, Katrín Jakobsdóttir of the Left-Green Movement (LGM), took office in 2017, following parliamentary elections that were viewed as credible by international observers.

A2. Were the current national legislative representatives elected through free and fair elections? 4 / 4

The unicameral Parliament is elected for four-year terms. The 2017 election was the third parliamentary election in four years, following the dissolution of the governing coalition in the wake of a scandal involving then prime minister Bjarni Benediktsson.

Organization for Security and Co-operation in Europe (OSCE) monitors found the elections well administered and in line with international standards. The Independence Party (IP) won 16 seats, the LGM won 11, and the Progressive Party won 8. The three parties formed a coalition government after several weeks of talks.

A3. Are the electoral laws and framework fair, and are they implemented impartially by the relevant election management bodies? 4 / 4

The constitution, the election law of 2000, and related legislation establish a clear and detailed framework for conducting elections. Electoral laws are implemented impartially by a variety of national- and regional-level authorities. However, the division of responsibilities between the relevant bodies is not always well defined.

An extensive constitutional reform process, launched by popular initiative in 2009, led to the drafting of a new constitution that, among other things, would have harmonized the number of votes per seat in all constituencies. The draft was approved by referendum in 2012, but the initiative subsequently stalled in the legislature.

Discussions over constitutional matters continued in 2020, with Prime Minister Jakobsdóttir vowing to propose amendments via legislation in October. A cross-party parliamentary committee began a review of the current constitution late in the year.

B. POLITICAL PLURALISM AND PARTICIPATION: 15 / 16

B1. Do the people have the right to organize in different political parties or other competitive political groupings of their choice, and is the system free of undue obstacles to the rise and fall of these competing parties or groupings? 4 / 4

Political parties form and operate freely, rising and falling according to political developments and the will of the public. In 2017, two new parties, the Center Party and the People's Party, gained parliamentary representation.

B2. Is there a realistic opportunity for the opposition to increase its support or gain power through elections? 4 / 4

Opposition parties can gain power through free elections, as evidenced by the LGM's gains in 2017 and subsequent inclusion in the coalition government. However, the IP has only rarely lost its status as the largest party in Parliament and is usually part of the ruling coalition.

B3. Are the people's political choices free from domination by forces that are external to the political sphere, or by political forces that employ extrapolitical means? 3 / 4

No military, foreign, or religious entities exert undemocratic influence over voters' choices. However, some politicians and parties are closely linked with businesses, which in turn exert significant political influence. Fisheries Minister Kristján Þór Júlíusson is closely affiliated with Samherji, an Icelandic fishing company that was implicated in a scheme to bribe Namibian officials in 2019.

B4. Do various segments of the population (including ethnic, racial, religious, gender, LGBT+, and other relevant groups) have full political rights and electoral opportunities? 4 / 4

All Icelandic citizens of adult age may vote in local and national elections. Foreigners can vote in municipal elections if they have been residents for at least five years, or three years if they are citizens of Nordic countries. In Reykjavík´s 2018 municipal election, an unprecedented number of immigrants ran for office.

The interests of women and LGBT+ people are well represented in politics.

C. FUNCTIONING OF GOVERNMENT: 10 / 12

C1. Do the freely elected head of government and national legislative representatives determine the policies of the government? 4 / 4

The freely elected head of government and national legislative representatives determine the policies of the government.

C2. Are safeguards against official corruption strong and effective? 3 / 4

While Iceland maintains robust anticorruption laws, public officials and major companies have engaged in corrupt behavior. Some officials implicated in corrupt or unsavory behavior have often continued to serve in government.

A report published by the Council of Europe's Group of States against Corruption (GRECO) in 2018 criticized the inadequate enforcement of conflict-of-interest rules and urged the government to strengthen rules on accepting third-party gifts. Legislation protecting whistleblowers was adopted by Parliament in May 2020. In June, Parliament adopted conflict-of-interest legislation that will apply to ministers, their advisers, and permanent secretaries. Both laws will take effect in 2021. In November 2020, GRECO reported that Iceland was in partial compliance with its recommendations.

C3. Does the government operate with openness and transparency? 3 / 4

Iceland's Information Act, passed in 2013 to strengthen existing legislation on transparency and freedom of information, has been criticized by press freedom advocates as having weak provisions. Public officials have sought to conceal information that may be embarrassing or implicate them in wrongdoing.

CIVIL LIBERTIES: 57 / 60

D. FREEDOM OF EXPRESSION AND BELIEF 15 / 16

D1. Are there free and independent media? 3 / 4

The constitution guarantees freedom of speech and of the press. The autonomous Icelandic National Broadcasting Service (RÚV) competes with private radio and television stations. Private media ownership is concentrated, with the media company 365 controlling most major private television and radio outlets, as well as free newspaper *Fréttablaðið*, which enjoys the highest circulation in the print market.

D2. Are individuals free to practice and express their religious faith or nonbelief in public and private? 4 / 4

The constitution provides for freedom of religion, which is generally upheld in practice. About 70 percent of Icelanders belong to the Evangelical Lutheran Church. The state supports the church through a special tax, which citizens can choose to direct to the University of Iceland instead.

D3. Is there academic freedom, and is the educational system free from extensive political indoctrination? 4 / 4

Academic freedom is respected, and the education system is free of excessive political involvement.

D4. Are individuals free to express their personal views on political or other sensitive topics without fear of surveillance or retribution? 4 / 4

People in Iceland may freely discuss personal views on sensitive topics without fear or surveillance or retribution.

E. ASSOCIATIONAL AND ORGANIZATIONAL RIGHTS: 12 / 12
E1. Is there freedom of assembly? 4 / 4

Freedom of assembly is generally upheld. In recent years, however, police have faced criticism for arresting or forcefully dispersing peaceful protesters under a broadly worded provision of the Police Law of 1996.

Icelandic authorities issued varying public-assembly restrictions during the year based on the spread of COVID-19.

E2. Is there freedom for nongovernmental organizations, particularly those that are engaged in human rights- and governance-related work? 4 / 4

Nongovernmental organizations (NGOs) may form, operate, and fundraise freely, and frequently inform policy discussions.

E3. Is there freedom for trade unions and similar professional or labor organizations? 4 / 4

The labor movement is robust, with more than 80 percent of all eligible workers belonging to unions. Most unions have the right to strike, except for the National Police Federation.

The Icelandic Nurses Association planned a June 2020 strike over wages and working conditions, though it suspended that action to enter arbitration; a tribunal issued a ruling to resolve the dispute in September. Coast Guard mechanics launched a strike in November, though Parliament passed legislation to end their action that month. Negotiations to resolve that dispute were ongoing after the legislation was passed.

F. RULE OF LAW: 15 / 16
F1. Is there an independent judiciary? 4 / 4

The judiciary is generally independent. Judges are proposed by an Interior Ministry selection committee, are formally appointed by the president, and are not subject to term limits. However, the selection process for the Court of Appeals was interfered with by former justice minister Sigríður Andersen in 2017, when she selected nominees who were considered unqualified to that court. In December 2020, the Grand Chamber of the European Court of Human Rights (ECtHR) ruled that the government violated the European Convention on Human Rights (ECHR) when an Icelandic defendant was judged by one of Andersen's nominees.

F2. Does due process prevail in civil and criminal matters? 4 / 4

The law does not provide for trial by jury, but many trials and appeals use panels of several judges. Prison conditions generally meet international standards.

F3. Is there protection from the illegitimate use of physical force and freedom from war and insurgencies? 4 / 4

Police are generally responsive to incidents of violence. War and insurgencies are not a concern.

F4. Do laws, policies, and practices guarantee equal treatment of various segments of the population? 3 / 4

The constitution states that all people shall be treated equally before the law, regardless of sex, religion, ethnic origin, race, or other status. However, in 2017, the European Commission against Racism and Intolerance noted an apparent rise in racist discourse in Iceland in recent years.

The rate of refugee recognition in Iceland is low compared to other northern European countries. In 2019, authorities deported an Albanian family, including a heavily pregnant woman, despite receiving medical certification that she was unfit to fly. The family was deported even though an appeal against their deportation was still under consideration, and they were ultimately removed from Iceland.

Immigrants who do not fluently speak Icelandic can face barriers to employment. Noncitizens were previously prohibited from holding public-sector employment, though this restriction ended in 2019.

G. PERSONAL AUTONOMY AND INDIVIDUAL RIGHTS: 15 / 16

G1. Do individuals enjoy freedom of movement, including the ability to change their place of residence, employment, or education? 4 / 4

Freedom of movement is constitutionally protected and respected in practice. Travel into Iceland was limited due to the COVID-19 pandemic in March 2020, though authorities announced a loosening of restrictions in June and maintained a quarantine policy for incoming travelers.

G2. Are individuals able to exercise the right to own property and establish private businesses without undue interference from state or nonstate actors? 4 / 4

There is generally no undue government interference in business or private property ownership.

G3. Do individuals enjoy personal social freedoms, including choice of marriage partner and size of family, protection from domestic violence, and control over appearance? 4 / 4

Parliament unanimously passed a law legalizing same-sex marriage in 2010, and a 2006 law established full and equal rights for same-sex couples in matters of adoption and assisted pregnancy. A comprehensive law on transgender issues adopted in 2012 aimed to simplify legal issues pertaining to gender reassignment surgery, to ensure full and equal rights for transgender people, and to guarantee relevant health care.

Individuals seeking an abortion after the 16th week of a pregnancy previously required special approval to undergo the procedure, but Parliament amended the law to allow abortions through the 22nd week in 2019.

G4. Do individuals enjoy equality of opportunity and freedom from economic exploitation? 3 / 4

Citizens generally enjoy fair access to economic opportunity. However, the systematic exploitation of migrant workers, including underpaying employees and denying overtime, has become a significant problem in recent years, especially in the tourism industry.

Employers who exploit workers have largely acted with impunity due to an inadequate government response. Wage theft is not punishable by law. There are reports of forced labor, primarily involving migrants, in the construction and service industries, and of forced sex work in nightclubs.

Iceland criminalized human trafficking in 2009. In the 2020 edition of its *Trafficking in Persons Report*, the US State Department reported that no one had been prosecuted or convicted of trafficking since 2010. However, the State Department did note an increase in victim-assistance funding to NGOs.

India

Population: 1,400,100,000
Capital: New Delhi
Freedom Status: Partly Free
Electoral Democracy: Yes

Status Change: India's status declined from Free to Partly Free due to a multiyear pattern in which the Hindu nationalist government and its allies have presided over rising violence and discriminatory policies affecting the Muslim population and pursued a crackdown on expressions of dissent by the media, academics, civil society groups, and protesters.

Note: The numerical scores and status listed above do not reflect conditions in Indian Kashmir, which is examined in a separate report. *Freedom in the World* reports assess the level of political rights and civil liberties in a given geographical area, regardless of whether they are affected by the state, nonstate actors, or foreign powers. Disputed territories are sometimes assessed separately if they meet certain criteria, including boundaries that are sufficiently stable to allow year-on-year comparisons. For more information, see the report methodology and FAQ.

Overview: While India is a multiparty democracy, the government led by Prime Minister Narendra Modi and his Hindu nationalist Bharatiya Janata Party (BJP) has presided over discriminatory policies and increased violence affecting the Muslim population. The constitution guarantees civil liberties including freedom of expression and freedom of religion, but harassment of journalists, nongovernmental organizations (NGOs), and other government critics has increased significantly under Modi. Muslims, scheduled castes (Dalits), and scheduled tribes (Adivasis) remain economically and socially marginalized.

KEY DEVELOPMENTS IN 2020

- In February, more than 50 people, mostly Muslims, were killed amid communal and protest-related violence in Delhi that followed weeks of demonstrations against discriminatory changes to the country's citizenship law.
- Authorities filed criminal charges against journalists, students, and private citizens under colonial-era sedition laws as well as the 2000 Information Technology (IT) Act in response to speech perceived as critical of the government, notably including expressions of opposition to the new citizenship legislation and discussion of the official response to the COVID-19 pandemic.

- India's internal migrant population endured significant hardships as a result of the government's pandemic-related lockdown, which was imposed in March and gradually eased beginning in May. Many migrant laborers were unable to access basic supplies and services in cities, forcing millions to travel hundreds of miles—often on foot—to their home villages. Harsh restrictions on movement were violently enforced by police and citizen vigilantes, with Muslims often scapegoated as potential spreaders of the virus.
- In September, several BJP leaders who were credibly accused of orchestrating the demolition of a historic mosque in 1992 were acquitted by a special court. Modi the previous month had signaled his support for the construction of a Hindu temple on the contested site.

POLITICAL RIGHTS: 34 / 40

A. ELECTORAL PROCESS: 12 / 12

A1. Was the current head of government or other chief national authority elected through free and fair elections? 4 / 4

Executive elections and selection procedures are generally regarded as free and fair. Executive power is vested in a prime minister, typically the leader of the majority party in the Lok Sabha (House of the People), and a cabinet of ministers nominated by the prime minister. They are appointed by the president and responsible to the Lok Sabha. Narendra Modi was sworn in for a second term as prime minister after the BJP's victory in the 2019 Lok Sabha elections.

The president, who plays a largely symbolic role, is chosen for a five-year term by state and national lawmakers. Current president Ram Nath Kovind, a Dalit and a veteran BJP politician, was elected in 2017.

A2. Were the current national legislative representatives elected through free and fair elections? 4 / 4

Members of the 545-seat Lok Sabha, the lower house of Parliament, are directly elected in single-member constituencies for five-year terms. Most members of the less powerful 245-seat upper house, the Rajya Sabha (Council of States), are elected by state legislatures using a proportional-representation system to serve staggered six-year terms; up to 12 members are appointed by the president.

The most recent Lok Sabha elections were held in seven phases in April and May 2019. The ruling BJP won 303 seats, giving its National Democratic Alliance coalition a stable majority of 353 seats. The opposition Indian National Congress party placed a distant second with 52 seats, for a total of 92 seats with its partners in the United Progressive Alliance. Smaller parties and independents took the remainder. Voter turnout was 67 percent. The elections were considered generally free and fair, though some violations of campaign rules were reported.

A3. Are the electoral laws and framework fair, and are they implemented impartially by the relevant election management bodies? 4 / 4

Elections for the central and state governments are overseen by the independent Election Commission of India. The head of the commission is appointed by the president and serves a fixed six-year term. The commission is generally respected and had been thought to function without undue political interference. In 2019, however, its impartiality and competence were called into question. The panel's decisions concerning the timing and phasing of national elections, and allegations of selective enforcement of the Model Code of Conduct, which regulates politicians' campaign behavior and techniques, suggested bias toward the ruling BJP.

B. POLITICAL PLURALISM AND PARTICIPATION: 13 / 16

B1. Do the people have the right to organize in different political parties or other competitive political groupings of their choice, and is the system free of undue obstacles to the rise and fall of these competing parties or groupings? 4 / 4

Political parties are generally able to form and operate without interference, and a wide variety of parties representing a range of views and interests compete in practice. However, the opaque financing of political parties—notably through electoral bonds that allow donors to obscure their identities—remains a source of concern.

B2. Is there a realistic opportunity for the opposition to increase its support or gain power through elections? 4 / 4

Different parties regularly succeed one another in government at the state and national levels. Modi and the BJP took power after the 2014 elections, ending 10 years of government by the Congress party, and was reelected by a wide margin in the 2019 parliamentary elections. In 2020, the BJP lost regional elections in Delhi, but its coalition scored a narrow victory in state elections in Bihar.

B3. Are the people's political choices free from domination by forces that are external to the political sphere, or by political forces that employ extrapolitical means? 3 / 4

Political participation, while generally free, is hampered by insurgent violence in certain areas. Separately, some political actors have sought to inflame communal tensions with the goal of energizing their own supporters while potentially intimidating opponents.

B4. Do various segments of the population (including ethnic, racial, religious, gender, LGBT+, and other relevant groups) have full political rights and electoral opportunities? 2 / 4

Women and members of religious and ethnic minorities vote in large numbers and have opportunities to gain political representation. In 2019, for the first time, the rate of women's voting in national elections equaled that of men. Quotas for the Lok Sabha ensure that 84 and 47 seats are reserved for the so-called scheduled castes and scheduled tribes, respectively. State assemblies and local bodies feature similar quotas for these historically disadvantaged groups, as well as for women representatives. However, marginalized segments of the population continue to face practical obstacles to full political representation. Muslim candidates notably won 27 of 545 seats in the 2019 Lok Sabha elections, up from 22 previously. However, this amounted to just 5 percent of the seats in the chamber, whereas Muslims make up some 14 percent of the population.

The political rights of India's Muslims continue to be threatened. In December 2019, Parliament adopted the Citizenship Amendment Act (CAA), which grants special access to Indian citizenship to non-Muslim immigrants and refugees from neighboring Muslim-majority states. At the same time, the government moved forward with plans for the creation of a national register of citizens. Many observers believe the register's purpose is to disenfranchise Muslim voters by effectively classifying them as illegal immigrants. Importantly, Muslims disproportionately lack documentation attesting to their place of birth. Undocumented non-Muslims, meanwhile, would be eligible for citizenship through a fast-track process under the CAA.

The citizenship status of nearly two million residents of Assam remains in doubt after a citizens' register was finalized in the northeastern state in 2019. The state is home to a significant Muslim minority population, as well as many people classified as members of scheduled tribes.

Under constitutional amendments introduced by the BJP-led government in December 2019, Lok Sabha seats reserved for two appointed members representing Indians of European descent were eliminated as of January 2020, as were similarly reserved seats in some state legislatures.

C. FUNCTIONING OF GOVERNMENT: 9 / 12

C1. Do the freely elected head of government and national legislative representatives determine the policies of the government? 4 / 4

India's elected leaders have the authority to set government policies, draft and enact legislation, and govern the country's territory in practice.

C2. Are safeguards against official corruption strong and effective? 2 / 4

Large-scale political corruption scandals have repeatedly exposed bribery and other malfeasance, but a great deal of corruption is thought to go unreported and unpunished, and the authorities have been accused of selective, partisan enforcement.

The Lokpal and Lokayuktas Act of 2014 created independent national and state bodies tasked with receiving complaints of corruption against public servants or politicians, investigating such claims, and pursuing convictions through the courts. However, the new agencies have been slow to begin operations; the first leaders of the national and a number of the state bodies were appointed in 2019.

C3. Does the government operate with openness and transparency? 3 / 4

The public generally has some access to information about government activity, but the legal framework meant to ensure transparency has been eroded in recent years. The 2014 Whistleblowers Protection Act was regarded as limited in scope, and subsequent amendments have drawn criticism for further undermining it. Millions of requests are made annually under the 2005 Right to Information (RTI) Act, and responses have been used to improve transparency and expose corrupt activities. However, most requesters do not receive the information sought, including those seeking information about core government policies, and noncompliant bureaucrats generally go unpunished. Dozens of right-to-information users and activists have been murdered since the act's introduction, and hundreds have been assaulted or harassed. In 2019, Parliament adopted amendments to the RTI Act that placed the salaries and tenures of the central and state-level information commissioners under the control of the central government, potentially exposing the commissioners to political pressure. Vacancies impede the workings of the Central Information Commission that was established by the RTI Act: 6 of its 11 positions were unfilled for most of 2020. There are concerns that the positions that have been filled are held by ruling-party loyalists.

CIVIL LIBERTIES: 33 / 60 (−4)

D. FREEDOM OF EXPRESSION AND BELIEF: 9 / 16 (−1)

D1. Are there free and independent media? 2 / 4

The private media are vigorous and diverse, and investigations and scrutiny of politicians do occur. However, attacks on press freedom have escalated dramatically under the Modi government, and reporting has become significantly less ambitious in recent years. Authorities have used security, defamation, sedition, and hate speech laws, as well as contempt-of-court charges, to quiet critical voices in the media. Hindu nationalist campaigns aimed at discouraging forms of expression deemed "antinational" have exacerbated self-censorship. Online disinformation from inauthentic sources is ubiquitous in the run-up to elections. Separately, revelations of close relationships between politicians, business executives, and lobbyists, on one hand, and leading media personalities and owners of media outlets, on the other, have dented public confidence in the press.

In 2020, dozens of journalists whose reporting was critical of the government's handling of the coronavirus pandemic were arrested, and media outlets faced pressure to praise the government's response. In a March video conference with the heads of India's largest newspapers, Prime Minister Modi called on media to help prevent the spread of "pessimism, negativity, and rumor mongering," which many perceived to be a warning not to criticize officials' management of the pandemic.

Journalists risk harassment, death threats, and physical violence in the course of their work. Such attacks are rarely punished, and some have taken place with the complicity or active participation of police. Two deadly attacks on journalists were reported in 2020, according to the Committee to Protect Journalists (CPJ). No journalists were killed in connection with their work in 2019, but five were murdered in 2018, and four in 2017.

D2. Are individuals free to practice and express their religious faith or nonbelief in public and private? 2 / 4

While Hindus make up about 80 percent of the population, the Indian state is formally secular, and freedom of religion is constitutionally guaranteed. However, a number of Hindu nationalist organizations and some media outlets promote anti-Muslim views, a practice that the government of Prime Minister Modi has been accused of encouraging. Attacks against Muslims and others in connection with the alleged slaughter or mistreatment of cows, which are held to be sacred by Hindus, continued in 2020. The nonprofit group IndiaSpend documented 45 killings by cow vigilantes between 2012 and 2018. More than 120 cases of cow-related violence, including lynchings, have been reported since Modi came to power, and the BJP has faced criticism for failing to mount an adequate response.

In 2020, during the early weeks of the COVID-19 pandemic, the country's Muslims were widely and speciously blamed for spreading the coronavirus, including by ruling-party officials. Separately, in September, 32 individuals charged with orchestrating the illegal 1992 demolition of a prominent mosque in the state of Uttar Pradesh were acquitted by a special court, despite substantial evidence of their culpability. Among those exonerated were several high-profile members of the BJP. Modi had laid the foundation stone for a new Hindu temple on the site a month earlier, after a long-awaited 2019 Supreme Court judgment had permitted the construction of a temple there. The mosque had stood on the site for centuries prior to its unlawful destruction.

Legislation in several states criminalizes religious conversions that take place as a result of "force" or "allurement," which can be broadly interpreted to prosecute proselytizers. Some states require government permission for conversion.

D3. Is there academic freedom, and is the educational system free from extensive political indoctrination? 2 / 4

Academic freedom has significantly weakened in recent years, as intimidation of professors, students, and institutions over political and religious issues has increased. Members of the student wing of the Hindu nationalist organization Rashtriya Swayamsevak Sangh (RSS)—from which the ruling BJP is widely regarded to have grown—have engaged in violence on campuses across the country, including attacks on students and professors. Academics face pressure not to discuss topics deemed sensitive by the BJP government, particularly India's relations with Pakistan and conditions in Indian Kashmir.

D4. Are individuals free to express their personal views on political or other sensitive topics without fear of surveillance or retribution? 3 / 4 (−1)

Personal expression and private discussion in India had long been open and free. However, colonial-era and other laws are increasingly invoked to penalize perceived criticism of the government by ordinary citizens. Activists, Muslims, and members of other marginalized communities are routinely charged with sedition for criticizing the government and its policies.

Numerous sedition cases were brought during 2020 against people who protested in opposition to the CAA, including an apparent mass criminal complaint filed by police in Jharkhand State in January against some 3,000 people who participated in such a demonstration. The same month, police brought a sedition case against a student in Karnataka for holding up a "Free Kashmir" poster. Also during the year, authorities invoked a section of the IT Act to penalize online speech, including critical discussion of the COVID-19 pandemic. In March, Kolkata police arrested a woman under the IT Act for allegedly spreading false information about a doctor contracting the virus. Similar arrests under the act in response to discussion of the pandemic were reported in Uttar Pradesh, Karnataka, Mizoram, and Rajasthan.

Several government-designed mobile applications that were introduced to help stem the spread of COVID-19 by aiding the enforcement of a strict lockdown were viewed as invasive by human rights lawyers. In some cases, private information about individuals' health status was released without their consent.

A nationwide Central Monitoring System launched in 2013 is meant to enable authorities to intercept any digital communication in real time without judicial oversight, raising concerns about abusive surveillance practices.

Score Change: The score declined from 4 to 3 due to the frequent use of sedition and other charges in recent years to deter free speech, including discussion of a discriminatory citizenship law and the COVID-19 pandemic.

E. ASSOCIATIONAL AND ORGANIZATIONAL RIGHTS: 7 / 12 (−1)

E1. Is there freedom of assembly? 2 / 4

There are legal restrictions on freedom of assembly, including a provision of the criminal procedure code that empowers authorities to restrict public gatherings and impose curfews whenever "immediate prevention or speedy remedy" is required. State and central governments have repeatedly suspended mobile and internet service to curb protests in recent years, including in 2020. Peaceful demonstrations take place regularly in practice, although the pandemic led to fewer such events being held in 2020.

The national government and some state governments used assembly bans, internet blackouts, and live ammunition between December 2019 and March 2020 to quell widespread protests against the CAA and proposals to roll out a citizens' registration process across the country. Protesters, including students and academics, were detained, denied access to legal representation, and subjected to harsh treatment. In February, more than 50 people were killed in protest-related violence in Delhi; there were reports of indiscriminate attacks against Muslims and police officers failing to respond, as well as some attacks against the police and Hindu residents. Critics alleged that the country's COVID-19 lockdown, which was imposed in March and gradually eased beginning in May, was conceived by the government in part to forestall further CAA protests and to silence dissent.

E2. Is there freedom for nongovernmental organizations, particularly those that are engaged in human rights- and governance-related work? 2 / 4 (−1)

A wide variety of NGOs operate, but some, particularly those involved in the investigation of human rights abuses, continue to face threats, legal harassment, excessive police force, and occasionally lethal violence. Under certain circumstances, the Foreign Contributions Regulation Act (FCRA) permits the federal government to deny NGOs access to foreign funding, and authorities have been accused of exploiting this power to target perceived political opponents. Since 2015, the government has deregistered nearly 15,000 associations under the FCRA. Amendments to the FRCA that were passed in 2020, without consulting civil society groups, tightened restrictions on foreign funding.

In September 2020, Amnesty International shuttered its operations in India after authorities froze its bank accounts for alleged foreign funding violations. The organization is thought to have been punished in reprisal for a series of reports that criticized the government's actions in Kashmir and the Delhi police's complicity in the February 2020 communal violence, in which Muslims were the main victims. An Amnesty International report released in June also detailed an apparent coordinated spyware campaign targeting a number of human rights activists.

Score Change: The score declined from 3 to 2 because the government enacted legislation to tighten restrictions on foreign funding for NGOs and separately froze the assets of Amnesty International, forcing it to shutter its operations in the country.

E3. Is there freedom for trade unions and similar professional or labor organizations? 3 / 4

Although workers in the formal economy regularly exercise their rights to bargain collectively and strike, laws including the Essential Services Maintenance Act have enabled the government to ban certain strikes. Public employees have more limited organizing rights, and private employers are not legally obliged to recognize unions or engage in bargaining.

Mass strikes by farmers and others who objected to new government-backed agriculture laws were gaining momentum at the end of 2020; the laws, passed rapidly by Parliament in September, introduced market-based reforms that many farmers saw as a threat to their livelihoods.

F. RULE OF LAW: 8 / 16 (−1)
F1. Is there an independent judiciary? 2 / 4 (−1)

The judiciary is formally independent of the political branches of government. Judges, particularly at the Supreme Court level, have displayed autonomy and activism in response to public-interest litigation. However, lower levels of the judiciary suffer from corruption, and the courts have shown signs of increasing politicization. Several key Supreme Court rulings in recent years have been favorable to the BJP, including the 2019 decision allowing the construction of a Hindu temple on the site of a historic mosque, and the court's March 2020 decision to deny bail to a scholar and prominent critic of Modi who was charged with supporting a banned Maoist group.

Also in 2020, the president appointed a recently retired chief justice to the upper house of Parliament, a rare move that critics viewed as a threat to the constitutional separation of powers. Earlier in the year, a judge was transferred in February to a less desirable position after he issued rulings that criticized Delhi police for their failure to address communal violence and related hate speech by BJP politicians.

Score Change: The score declined from 3 to 2 because the unusual appointment of a recently retired chief justice to the upper house of Parliament, a pattern of more progovernment decisions by the Supreme Court, and the high-profile transfer of a judge after he ruled against the government's political interests all suggested a closer alignment between the judicial leadership and the ruling party.

F2. Does due process prevail in civil and criminal matters? 2 / 4

Due process rights are not consistently upheld. Citizens face substantial obstacles in the pursuit of justice, including demands for bribes and difficulty getting the police to file a First Information Report, which is necessary to trigger an investigation of an alleged crime. Corruption within the police force remains a problem. The justice system is severely backlogged and understaffed, leading to lengthy pretrial detention for suspects, many of whom remain in jail longer than the duration of any sentence they might receive if convicted. A number of security laws allow detention without charge or based on vaguely defined offenses.

F3. Is there protection from the illegitimate use of physical force and freedom from war and insurgencies? 2 / 4

Torture, abuse, and rape by law enforcement and security officials have been reported. A bill intended to prevent torture remains pending. Abuses by prison staff against prisoners, particularly those belonging to marginalized groups, are common. Figures reported by the National Human Rights Commission (NHRC) suggest that 1,723 deaths occurred in judicial or police custody from January to December 2019.

Security forces battling regional insurgencies continue to be implicated in extrajudicial killings, rape, torture, kidnappings, and destruction of homes. While the criminal procedure code requires that the government approve the prosecution of security force members, approval is rarely granted, leading to impunity.

The Maoist insurgency in the east-central hills region of India continues, though the annual number of casualties linked with it has decreased significantly since a peak in 2010. Among other abuses, the rebels have allegedly imposed illegal taxes, seized food and places of shelter, and engaged in abduction and forced recruitment of children and adults. Local civilians and journalists who are perceived to be progovernment have been attacked. Tens of thousands of civilians have been displaced by the violence and live in government-run camps.

Separately, in India's seven northeastern states, more than 40 insurgent factions—seeking either greater autonomy or complete independence for their ethnic or tribal groups—continue to attack security forces and engage in intertribal violence. Such fighters have been implicated in bombings, killings, abductions, and rapes of civilians, and they operate extensive extortion networks.

F4. Do laws, policies, and practices guarantee equal treatment of various segments of the population? 2 / 4

The constitution bars discrimination based on caste, and laws set aside quotas in education and government jobs for historically underprivileged scheduled tribes, Dalits, and groups categorized by the government as "other backward classes." However, members of these populations face routine discrimination and violence, and the criminal justice system fails to provide equal protection to marginalized groups.

In parts of the country, particularly in rural areas, informal community councils issue edicts concerning social customs. Their decisions sometimes result in violence or persecution aimed at those perceived to have transgressed social norms, especially women and members of scheduled castes. Other forms of discrimination faced by women include workplace bias and sexual harassment. Indian participation in the international #MeToo movement against sexual harassment and assault has raised awareness of the problem, but women have also endured reprisals after reporting cases.

In 2018, the Supreme Court ruled that the use of Section 377 of the Indian penal code to ban same-sex intercourse was unconstitutional. However, discrimination continues against LGBT+ people, including violence and harassment in some instances.

G. PERSONAL AUTONOMY AND INDIVIDUAL RIGHTS: 9 / 16 (−1)

G1. Do individuals enjoy freedom of movement, including the ability to change their place of residence, employment, or education? 2 / 4 (−1)

The constitution grants citizens the right to reside and settle in any part of the territory of India. However, freedom of movement is hampered in some parts of the country by insurgent violence or communal tensions. Several states have recently enacted legislation requiring companies to reserve jobs for locals, limiting opportunities for interstate migration, although reports point to limited enforcement of the quotas thus far.

India's large internal migrant population suffered significant hardships during the early stages of the 2020 pandemic. The government imposed an excessively harsh lockdown in March that offered little assistance or security to low-paid workers, millions of whom were consequently compelled to travel from cities to their native villages for lack of employment and essential supplies; many were unable to access basic services, including transportation, and were forced to walk hundreds of miles. Also during the lockdown, which was gradually eased beginning in May, reports emerged of violent enforcement by police and civilian vigilantes, with Muslims often singled out for abuse.

Score Change: The score declined from 3 to 2 due to an excessively harsh pandemic-related lockdown that triggered the displacement of millions of low-paid migrant workers under dangerous conditions and featured violent and discriminatory enforcement by police and civilian vigilantes.

G2. Are individuals able to exercise the right to own property and establish private businesses without undue interference from state or nonstate actors? 3 / 4

Although the legal framework generally supports the right to own property and engage in private business activity, property rights are somewhat tenuous for tribal groups and other marginalized communities, and members of these groups are often denied adequate resettlement opportunities and compensation when their lands are seized for development projects. While many states have laws to prevent transfers of tribal land to nontribal groups, the practice is reportedly widespread, particularly with respect to the mining and timber industries. Muslim personal status laws and traditional Hindu practices discriminate against women in terms of property rights and inheritance.

G3. Do individuals enjoy personal social freedoms, including choice of marriage partner and size of family, protection from domestic violence, and control over appearance? 2 / 4

Rape and other sexual abuse are serious problems and scheduled-caste and tribal women are especially vulnerable. Mass demonstrations after the fatal gang rape of a woman on a Delhi bus in 2012 prompted the government to enact significant legal reforms, but egregious new rape cases continued to surface in 2020, and the criminal justice system has been repeatedly faulted for its poor handling of such matters.

Despite criminalization and hundreds of convictions each year, dowry demands surrounding marriage persist, sometimes resulting in violence. A 2006 law banned dowry-related harassment, widened the definition of domestic violence to include emotional or verbal abuse, and criminalized spousal sexual violence. However, reports indicate that enforcement is poor.

Muslim personal status laws and traditional Hindu practices feature gender discrimination on matters such as marriage, divorce, and child custody. A Muslim divorce custom allowing a man to unilaterally and summarily divorce his wife was criminalized in 2019. The malign neglect of female children after birth remains a concern, as does the banned use of prenatal sex-determination tests to selectively abort female fetuses.

G4. Do individuals enjoy equality of opportunity and freedom from economic exploitation? 2 / 4
The constitution bans human trafficking, and bonded labor is illegal, but estimates of the number of workers still affected by the practice range from 20 to 50 million. A 2016 law allows children below the age of 14 to engage in "home-based work," as well as other occupations between the ages of 14 and 18. Children are not permitted to work in potentially hazardous industries, though the rule is routinely flouted. There have been reports of complicity by law enforcement officials in human trafficking.

Indonesia

Population: 271,700,000
Capital: Jakarta
Freedom Status: Partly Free
Electoral Democracy: Yes

Overview: Indonesia has made impressive democratic gains since the fall of an authoritarian regime in 1998, establishing significant pluralism in politics and the media and undergoing multiple, peaceful transfers of power between parties. However, the country continues to struggle with challenges including systemic corruption, discrimination and violence against minority groups, separatist tensions in the Papua region, and the politicized use of defamation and blasphemy laws.

KEY DEVELOPMENTS IN 2020
- In April, the government issued a directive to police to combat alleged disinformation about the COVID-19 pandemic and criticism of the government and president's response to it. Police had arrested 51 individuals under this policy by June. Other legislation and policies enacted after the outbreak of the pandemic were used to limit freedoms and silence dissent.
- A controversial omnibus law passed in October severely limited workers' rights and environmental protections. Passed with minimal public consultation, the law, among other things, stripped worker protections such as the length of severance pay and allowable overtime.
- In October, protests against the new omnibus law erupted countrywide, and were violently suppressed by police. Hundreds of protesters were arrested in 18 different provinces, and police reportedly used tear gas and water cannons to disperse them.
- In June, a group of activists and students known as the Balikpapan Seven were convicted and sentenced to up to 11 months' imprisonment for treason related to their involvement in 2019 antiracist protests in Jayapura, Papua. Treason charges were brought against other students and activists involved in protests against racism and attacks on Papuans, as well as against those involved in flag raisings of the Papuan Morning Star and the Republic of South Moluccas (RMS) flags.

POLITICAL RIGHTS: 30 / 40

A. ELECTORAL PROCESS: 11 / 12

A1. Was the current head of government or other chief national authority elected through free and fair elections? 4 / 4

The president is directly elected and serves as both head of state and head of government. Presidents and vice presidents can serve up to two five-year terms. Joko Widodo ("Jokowi"), the candidate of the Indonesian Democratic Party of Struggle (PDI-P), won a second term in the April 2019 election with 55.5 percent of the vote, defeating former general Prabowo Subianto, the Great Indonesia Movement Party (Gerindra) candidate.

Limited voting irregularities were reported, but the contest was largely considered free and fair by international election monitors. Prabowo's campaign claimed the election was marred by widespread fraud and vote rigging, but this claim was rejected by the Constitutional Court in June 2019. Jokowi appointed Prabowo as his defense minister.

A2. Were the current national legislative representatives elected through free and fair elections? 4 / 4

The House of Representatives (DPR), the main parliamentary chamber, consists of 575 members elected in 34 multimember districts. The 136-member House of Regional Representatives (DPD) is responsible for monitoring laws related to regional autonomy and may also propose bills on the topic. All legislators serve five-year terms with no term limits.

Legislative elections were held concurrently with the presidential race and local contests in April 2019. The PDI-P, led by former president Megawati Sukarnoputri, won 19.3 percent of the vote and 128 seats. Golkar, the party of former authoritarian president Suharto, won 85 seats with 12.3 percent of the vote, followed by Gerindra with 78 seats and 12.6 percent of the vote. Partai NasDem won 59 seats, while the Democratic Party (PD) of former president Susilo Bambang Yudhoyono won 54. Two Islamic parties—the National Mandate Party (PAN) and the United Development Party (PPP)—lost seats from the last parliament, returning with 44 and 19 seats, respectively. Two other Islamic parties, the National Awakening Party (PKB) and the Prosperous Justice Party (PKS), increased their representation, winning 58 and 50 seats, respectively.

A3. Are the electoral laws and framework fair, and are they implemented impartially by the relevant election management bodies? 3 / 4

The legal framework for elections is largely democratic, and electoral authorities are mostly seen as impartial. However, some legal provisions are problematic. Under a 2012 law, the hereditary sultan of Yogyakarta is that region's unelected governor.

A 2016 revision to the law governing local elections requires that the Election Oversight Agency (Bawaslu) and the General Elections Commission (KPU) conduct a binding consultation with the parliament and the government before issuing any new regulations or decisions. Activists expressed concerns that the rules would reduce electoral authorities' independence.

B. POLITICAL PLURALISM AND PARTICIPATION: 13 / 16

B1. Do the people have the right to organize in different political parties or other competitive political groupings of their choice, and is the system free of undue obstacles to the rise and fall of these competing parties or groupings? 4 / 4

The right to organize political parties is respected, and the system features competition among several major parties. Four new parties contested the 2019 elections, two of them led by children of former president Suharto.

However, election laws favor large parties by increasing eligibility requirements. The 2017 General Elections Law requires new parties to undergo a "factual verification" process which involves confirming the accuracy of submitted documents on parties' management, membership, and operations.

Communist parties are banned, and those who disseminate communist symbols or promote communism can face prison sentences of up to 12 years.

B2. Is there a realistic opportunity for the opposition to increase its support or gain power through elections? 4 / 4

Indonesia has established a pattern of democratic power transfers between rival parties since 1999. The most recent handover occurred in 2014, when the PDI-P returned to power after losing the previous two presidential elections. However, the 2017 General Elections Law requires parties or coalitions fielding presidential candidates to hold 20 percent of the seats in the parliament or 25 percent of the national vote in the most recent parliamentary election. The provision effectively bars new or smaller parties from fielding candidates in the presidential race.

B3. Are the people's political choices free from domination by forces that are external to the political sphere, or by political forces that employ extrapolitical means? 3 / 4

While voters and candidates are generally free from undue interference, the military remains influential, with former commanders playing prominent, and growing roles in politics. Intimidation by nonstate actors—including Islamist radical groups—remains a problem.

B4. Do various segments of the population (including ethnic, racial, religious, gender, LGBT+, and other relevant groups) have full political rights and electoral opportunities? 2 / 4

Women enjoy full political rights, and political parties are also subject to 30 percent gender quotas for steering committees and candidates. However, they remain underrepresented in electoral politics, holding 21 percent of the DPR's seats, though they do sometimes win leadership positions. Puan Maharani, daughter of former president Megawati and granddaughter of former president Sukarno, was elected in 2019 as the first woman to be speaker of the parliament.

Ethnic Chinese are poorly represented in politics, and often abstain from voting. However, two parties with ethnic Chinese leaders, the Indonesian Solidarity Party (PSI) and United Indonesian Party (Perindo), contested the April 2019 elections. Both parties fell below the 4-percent threshold to earn seats.

Some local governments have discriminated against religious minorities by restricting access to identification cards, birth certificates, marriage licenses, and other bureaucratic necessities, limiting their political rights and electoral opportunities.

LGBT+ people are also poorly represented in electoral politics.

C. FUNCTIONING OF GOVERNMENT: 6 / 12
C1. Do the freely elected head of government and national legislative representatives determine the policies of the government? 3 / 4

Elected officials generally determine the policies of the government, though national authorities have faced difficulties in implementing their decisions due to resistance at the local level. Separately, observers have warned that the military is regaining its influence over civilian governance and economic affairs. These concerns increased during the COVID-19 pandemic in 2020, as military generals served as the heads of both the National Task Force for COVID-19 Management and the Ministry of Health.

C2. Are safeguards against official corruption strong and effective? 1 / 4

Corruption remains endemic in the national and local legislatures, civil service, judiciary, and police. From January to June 2020, according to information released by Indonesia Corruption Watch in October, 1,008 cases with 1,043 defendants were heard at the Corruption Crime Court, High Court, and Supreme Court combined, with average sentences handed down of three years. The most common offenses were embezzlement of state funds, bribery, and extortion. Acrimony between rival agencies—particularly the Corruption Eradication Commission (KPK) and the National Police—has hindered anticorruption efforts, and civilian investigators have no jurisdiction over the military. In September 2019, the parliament passed legislation weakening the KPK; under the new act, the KPK can only employ investigators from the National Police, is restricted in its ability to wiretap suspects, and is supervised in its work by an independent panel appointed by the president.

C3. Does the government operate with openness and transparency? 2 / 4

Although civil society groups are able to comment on and influence pending policies or legislation, government transparency is limited by broad exemptions in the freedom of information law and obstacles such as a 2011 law that criminalizes leaking vaguely defined "state secrets" to the public.

The 2020 omnibus law, which was passed by the DPR in October and signed by Jokowi in November, included many individual pieces of new legislation, the proposals of which had sparked nationwide protests in 2019, as well as revisions to 79 existing laws. Indonesian critics have argued the government did not adequately consult the public on the content of the law, consultations they claim were deliberately avoided to sow confusion over the law's provisions; its passage was also rushed through the parliament.

CIVIL LIBERTIES: 29 / 60 (−2)

D. FREEDOM OF EXPRESSION AND BELIEF: 9 / 16 (−1)

D1. Are there free and independent media? 3 / 4

Indonesia hosts a vibrant and diverse media environment, though legal and regulatory restrictions hamper press freedom. The 2008 Law on Electronic Information and Transactions extended libel to online media, and criminalized the distribution or accessibility of information or documents that are "contrary to the moral norms of Indonesia," or involve gambling, blackmail, or defamation. In January and February 2020, police detained journalist Muhammad Asrul for more than a month for alleged criminal defamation arising from a series of articles published in 2019 about a corruption scandal. At the beginning of his detention, he was held for two days without notice to his family or employer and without access to legal counsel. In this case and others, the police violated the terms set out in the 2018 memorandum of understanding between the Press Council and the police chief.

According to the Indonesian group the Alliance of Independent Journalists (AJI), violence against journalists in Indonesia hit an all-time high in 2020, with 84 reports of violent incidents received by AJI over the course of the year. In October, the AJI reported 28 cases of police action against journalists, including intimidation, physical violence, and detention, targeting those covering the mass demonstrations against the 2020 omnibus law. Many journalists showed their press identification, yet were still targeted. Foreign journalists visiting Papua and West Papua continue to report bureaucratic obstacles and deportations. Internet blackouts during protests in Jakarta and Papua in recent years as well as self-censorship have also inhibited press activity. Journalists covering sensitive subjects, including LGBT+ issues, face harassment and threats.

There are growing concerns that the government has used the COVID-19 pandemic to tighten restrictions on journalists, including criminalizing criticism of the government. A new directive issued by the Criminal Investigation Agency in April 2020 allows for up to 18 months of imprisonment for "hostile information about the president and government" or disinformation about the coronavirus. By June, police had arrested 51 individuals for allegedly spreading misinformation about COVID-19. Several Indonesian media outlets during the year experienced digital attacks including hacking, doxing, and distributed denial-of-service (DDOS) attacks after publishing pieces critical of the government's COVID-19 response.

D2. Are individuals free to practice and express their religious faith or nonbelief in public and private? 1 / 4

Indonesia officially recognizes Islam, Protestantism, Roman Catholicism, Hinduism, Buddhism, and Confucianism. Individuals may leave the "religion" section on their identity cards blank, but those who do—including adherents of unrecognized faiths—often face discrimination. Atheism is not accepted, and the criminal code contains provisions against blasphemy, penalizing those who "distort" or "misrepresent" recognized faiths.

National and local governments fail to protect religious minorities and exhibit bias in investigations and prosecutions. Building a new house of worship requires the signatures of 90 congregation members and 60 local residents of different faiths.

Violence and intimidation against Ahmadi and Shiite communities persists, and the central government continues to tolerate persecution of these groups. However, in December 2020, the newly appointed religious affairs minister, Yaqut Cholil Qoumas—who is chair of the Islamic group Nahdlatul Ulama's youth wing, Ansor—pledged to protect Shia and Ahmadiyah minorities and, promote dialogue among different religious groups.

D3. Is there academic freedom, and is the educational system free from extensive political indoctrination? 2 / 4 (−1)

Threats to academic freedom have increased in recent years. Hard-line groups and others are known to threaten discussions on LGBT+ matters, interfaith issues, Papua, police violence, and the 1965–66 anticommunist massacres.

Academics have been charged with defamation and removed from their posts for criticism of public officials. Throughout 2020, academics, students, and researchers received threats—including death threats—and experienced hacking of their online accounts, physical intimidation, and violence for organizing discussions on topics apparently perceived as critical of the government.

Academic discussions on Papua and West Papua have been canceled and organizers surveilled and threatened. Four students from Khairun University in North Maluku were expelled in December 2019 for their involvement that month in peaceful protests over human rights abuses in Papua and West Papua; one of the students was charged with treason in July 2020. Students, student union leaders, and others involved in campus protests against anti-Papuan racism continued to face intimidation, arrest, and treason charges, with authorities linking the antiracism protests to secessionist movements.

Score Change: The score declined from 3 to 2 due to an escalating pattern of arrests, prosecutions, physical attacks, and intimidation aimed at students and academics who engage in public discussion of politically sensitive topics.

D4. Are individuals free to express their personal views on political or other sensitive topics without fear of surveillance or retribution? 3 / 4

Laws against blasphemy, defamation, and certain other forms of speech sometimes inhibit the expression of personal views on sensitive topics, including on social media. The chief of the National Police in October 2020 issued instructions for online surveillance of activists and engagement in progovernment counternarratives. Research from the Indonesia Survey Institute has found that these laws and state practices have had a chilling effect: Indonesians surveyed in 2019 increasingly reported feeling that they cannot freely voice their opinions online.

The government is known to surveil and detain individuals who discuss separatism in Maluku or Papua or fly the Papuan or the RMS flags. An elderly couple were convicted of treason in 2019 and sentenced to five years in prison for displaying the RMS flag inside their home.

Civil servants are also subject to stringent restrictions on online activity; in late 2019, the government formed a task force to review "radical" social media comments from civil servants, including speech believed to insult or criticize the official *Pancasila* ideology, the state motto, the constitution, or the government. The decree governing this new task force also prohibits civil servants from joining organizations deemed to insult the country's governing principles.

E. ASSOCIATIONAL AND ORGANIZATIONAL RIGHTS: 6 / 12 (−1)

E1. Is there freedom of assembly? 2 / 4

Freedom of assembly is usually upheld, and peaceful protests are common. However, assemblies addressing sensitive political topics—such as the 1965–66 massacres or regional separatism—are regularly dispersed, with participants facing intimidation or violence from vigilantes or police.

In April 2020, police arrested 23 activists in Maluku for alleged participation in flag-raising ceremonies. In October, three of them were found guilty of treason for taking part in protests and received prison sentences of two to three years. A group of activists and students known as the Balikpapan Seven were convicted of treason in June 2020 for their involvement in 2019 antiracist protests in Jayapura, Papua, and sentenced to ten to eleven months' imprisonment each. The Seven included two student union leaders from prominent universities, two other students, two members of the National Committee of West Papua, and well-known Papuan independence activist and former political prisoner Buchtar Tabuni.

Thousands of protesters demonstrated against the passage of the Omnibus Law in 18 provinces in October 2020, led by student activists and workers. Police arrested hundreds of people and used tear gas and water cannons, injuring dozens.

E2. Is there freedom for nongovernmental organizations, particularly those that are engaged in human rights- and governance-related work? 2 / 4

While nongovernmental organizations (NGOs) are active in Indonesia, they are subject to government monitoring and interference. A 2013 law requires all NGOs to register with the government and submit to regular reviews of their activities. It limits the types of activities NGOs can undertake and bars them from committing blasphemy or espousing ideas that conflict with the official *Pancasila* ideology, such as atheism and communism. The government is empowered to dissolve noncompliant organizations without judicial oversight.

Authorities and influential Muslim organizations have continued to intimidate and harass LGBT+ people and activists. Nahdlatul Ulama, Indonesia's largest Muslim organization, has called for LGBT+ activism to be criminalized. The cumulative effect of this campaign has been to drive the LGBT+ activist community underground, and to hamper groups seeking to provide services to LGBT+ people.

Activists working to address Papuan issues are also targeted by the government.

E3. Is there freedom for trade unions and similar professional or labor organizations? 2 / 4 (−1)

Workers can join independent unions, bargain collectively, and with the exception of civil servants, stage strikes. Legal strikes can be unduly delayed by obligatory arbitration processes, and laws against antiunion discrimination and retaliation are not well enforced. As a result of a memorandum of understanding signed in 2018, the military can assist police in dealing with strikes and demonstrations.

The 2020 omnibus law challenged workers' rights by abolishing sectoral minimum wages, opting instead for a provincial minimum wage set by governors. This limits labor unions' negotiating power as wages are set by geography rather than sector. The law also reversed hard-won labor protections—including the length of severance pay and allowable overtime—reduced labor protections and job security by decreasing the number of statutory days off from two to one per week, and considerably extended outsourcing permissions for companies, which was previously limited to five sectors. The government's lack of consultation with existing unions over the law and its opacity about the law's contents demonstrated the narrowing of space for trade unions and labor organizations in Indonesia, and the growing, significant challenges to workers' rights. At the end of the year, the omnibus law was awaiting review by the Constitutional Court after challenges were filed by a number of unions and NGOs.

Score Change: The score declined from 3 to 2 due to the passage of omnibus legislation that removed key labor protections and weakened the position of trade unions.

F. RULE OF LAW: 5 / 16

F1. Is there an independent judiciary? 2 / 4

The judiciary has demonstrated its independence in some cases, particularly in the Constitutional Court. However, the court system remains plagued by corruption and other weaknesses. Judicial decisions can also be influenced by religious considerations.

F2. Does due process prevail in civil and criminal matters? 1 / 4

Police reportedly engage in arbitrary arrests and detentions, particularly of protesters or activists suspected of separatism. Existing safeguards against coerced confessions are ineffective, and defendants are sometimes denied proper access to legal counsel, including in death penalty cases.

A number of districts and provinces have ordinances based on Sharia (Islamic law) that are unconstitutional and contradict Indonesia's international human rights commitments.

F3. Is there protection from the illegitimate use of physical force and freedom from war and insurgencies? 1 / 4

Military service members accused of crimes against civilians are tried in military courts, which lack impartiality and often impose light punishments, even for serious human rights violations. In September 2020, he National Human Rights Commission (Komnas HAM) reported that security forces tortured and murdered a pastor in Intan Jaya, Papua, while searching for stolen military weapons. The military had yet to take action against any officer by the end of the year.

Deadly confrontations between security forces remain common in Papua and West Papua. There were at least eight deaths from violence between security forces and communities in September and October 2020 alone, including two members of security forces, church workers, and activists. In November, one teenager was killed and another injured in a shootout with police in Gome District, West Papua.

Torture by law enforcement agencies is not specifically criminalized. Prisons are overcrowded and corrupt, leading to riots, protests, and jailbreaks. Violence related to natural resource extraction remains a problem. In Aceh, regulations under Sharia permit provincial authorities to use caning as punishment for offenses related to gambling, alcohol consumption, and illicit sexual activity.

F4. Do laws, policies, and practices guarantee equal treatment of various segments of the population? 1 / 4

Papuans face racial discrimination, including from authorities. Inspired by the Black Lives Matter movement, the hashtag #PapuanLivesMatter spread across Indonesia after a Papuan student was shot by security forces while out fishing in April 2020.

Some national laws and numerous local ordinances discriminate against women either explicitly or in effect.

LGBT+ people suffer from widespread discrimination, and authorities continue to target them with inflammatory and discriminatory rhetoric. LGBT+ people also risk attacks by hard-line Islamist groups, sometimes with support from local authorities. The military has dismissed 16 soldiers for same-sex relations, including one soldier in 2020, who in addition to being dismissed was sentenced to one year in prison for having relations with another service member. The military has defended its stance against homosexuality, and the police force has also taken action against LGBT+ members of the force.

Ethnic Chinese, who make up approximately one percent of the population but reputedly hold much of the country's wealth, are also vulnerable to harassment.

Indonesia grants temporary protection to refugees and migrants, but is not party to the 1951 Refugee Convention and does not accept refugees for asylum and resettlement.

G. PERSONAL AUTONOMY AND INDIVIDUAL RIGHTS: 9 / 16

G1. Do individuals enjoy freedom of movement, including the ability to change their place of residence, employment, or education? 3 / 4

The freedoms to travel and change one's place of residence, employment, or higher education are generally respected. However, Indonesians engaging in these administrative processes are sometimes vulnerable to bribery.

G2. Are individuals able to exercise the right to own property and establish private businesses without undue interference from state or nonstate actors? 2 / 4

A robust private sector exists, but business activity is hampered by corruption. Property rights are sometimes threatened by state appropriation and licensing of communally owned land to companies, particularly for those with unregistered or customary land rights. Women have relatively poor rights to marital property, as well. Ethnic Chinese in Yogyakarta face restrictions on private property ownership under a 1975 decree that contravenes national laws.

G3. Do individuals enjoy personal social freedoms, including choice of marriage partner and size of family, protection from domestic violence, and control over appearance? 2 / 4

Abortion is illegal except to save a woman's life or in instances of rape. Adults over the age of 15 must have corroboration and witnesses to bring rape charges.

Sharia-based ordinances in a number of districts impose restrictions on dress, gambling, alcohol use, and sexual activity; these ordinances are disproportionately enforced against women and LGBT+ people. In June 2020, the district head of Central Lombok required female Muslim civil servants to wear Islamic face coverings instead of masks to combat COVID-19.

Public displays of affection are banned in Aceh Province under Sharia-based regulations.

Marriages must be conducted under the supervision of a recognized religion, which obstructs interfaith marriages. The minimum age for marriage, defined in the 1974 Marriage Law, was 16 for women and 19 for men; child marriage was historically common for girls. In 2018, the Constitutional Court ruled the minimum age of 16 for women to marry unconstitutional. The parliament complied with the ruling in September 2019, amending the law to make the minimum age for marriage 19 for women.

G4. Do individuals enjoy equality of opportunity and freedom from economic exploitation? 2 / 4

National, provincial, and local authorities set standards for working conditions and compensation, but enforcement is inconsistent. Indonesian workers are trafficked abroad, including women in domestic service and men in the fishing industry.

Iran

Population: 84,200,000
Capital: Tehran
Freedom Status: Not Free
Electoral Democracy: No

Overview: The Islamic Republic of Iran holds elections regularly, but they fall short of democratic standards due in part to the influence of the hard-line Guardian Council, an unelected body that disqualifies all candidates it deems insufficiently loyal to the clerical establishment. Ultimate power rests in the hands of the country's supreme leader, Ayatollah Ali Khamenei, and the unelected institutions under his control. These institutions, including the security forces and the judiciary, play a major role in the suppression of dissent and other restrictions on civil liberties.

KEY DEVELOPMENTS IN 2020

- Iran struggled during the year to contain one of the worst outbreaks of COVID-19 in the Middle East, and the authorities used censorship and criminal prosecutions to suppress independent reporting on the true extent of the contagion.
- Hard-line politicians cemented their control over the parliament after several thousand candidates, including many reformists and independents, were prohibited from running in the February elections. The balloting, which drew record-low turnout, was held just days after the country's first coronavirus cases were officially confirmed, fueling suspicions that the authorities had delayed informing the public of the already surging outbreak in order to ensure smooth elections.
- The authorities continued to detain many political prisoners despite the threat from COVID-19 in places of incarceration, though prominent rights activist Narges Mohammadi was released in October amid concerns about her health. Executions of high-profile dissidents and antigovernment protesters also continued during the year.

POLITICAL RIGHTS: 6 / 40 (−1)

A. ELECTORAL PROCESS: 3 / 12

A1. Was the current head of government or other chief national authority elected through free and fair elections? 1 / 4

The supreme leader, who has no fixed term, is the highest authority in the country. He is the commander in chief of the armed forces and appoints the head of the judiciary, the heads of state broadcast media, and the Expediency Council—a body tasked with mediating disputes between the Guardian Council and the parliament. He also appoints six members of the Guardian Council; the other six are jurists nominated by the head of the judiciary and confirmed by the parliament, all for six-year terms. The supreme leader is appointed by the Assembly of Experts, which monitors his work. However, in practice his decisions appear to go unchallenged by the assembly, whose proceedings are kept confidential. The current supreme leader, Ali Khamenei, succeeded Islamic Republic founder Ruhollah Khomeini in 1989.

The president, the second-highest ranking official in the Islamic Republic, appoints a cabinet that must be confirmed by the parliament. He is elected by popular vote for up to two consecutive four-year terms. In the 2017 presidential election, only six men were allowed to run, out of some 1,600 candidates who had applied. All 137 women candidates were disqualified by the Guardian Council. The main challenger to incumbent president Hassan Rouhani, a self-proclaimed moderate, was hard-line cleric Ebrahim Raisi. In the run-up to the election, the authorities intensified their crackdown on the media, arresting several journalists and administrators of reformist channels on Telegram, the popular messaging application. However, Rouhani's victory, with 57 percent of the vote amid roughly 70 percent turnout, appeared to reflect the choice of the electorate among the available candidates.

A2. Were the current national legislative representatives elected through free and fair elections? 1 / 4

Members of the 290-seat parliament are elected to four-year terms. Elections for the body were held in February 2020, with most seats going to hard-liners and conservatives loyal to the supreme leader. Ahead of the vote, the Guardian Council disqualified more than 9,000 of the 16,000 people who had registered to run, including large numbers of reformist and moderate candidates. Voter turnout, the lowest for parliamentary elections in the history of the Islamic Republic at 42.6 percent, was likely depressed by factors including the mass disqualifications and the announcement of the first coronavirus cases just two days before the balloting. The outbreak was believed to have begun weeks earlier, raising suspicions that the authorities delayed disclosing it for political reasons; Khamenei denounced foreign "propaganda" for supposedly exaggerating the health threat to frighten voters.

Elections for the Assembly of Experts, a group of 86 clerics chosen by popular vote to serve eight-year terms, were last held in 2016. Only 20 percent of the would-be candidates were approved to run, a record low. A majority of the new assembly ultimately chose hard-line cleric Ahmad Jannati, head of the Guardian Council, as the body's chairman.

A3. Are the electoral laws and framework fair, and are they implemented impartially by the relevant election management bodies? 1 / 4

The electoral system in Iran does not meet international democratic standards. The Guardian Council, controlled by hard-line conservatives and ultimately by the supreme leader, vets all candidates for the parliament, the presidency, and the Assembly of Experts. The council typically rejects candidates who are not considered insiders or deemed fully loyal to the clerical establishment, as well as women seeking to run in the presidential election. As a result, Iranian voters are given a limited choice of candidates.

B. POLITICAL PLURALISM AND PARTICIPATION: 2 / 16

B1. Do the people have the right to organize in different political parties or other competitive political groupings of their choice, and is the system free of undue obstacles to the rise and fall of these competing parties or groupings? 0 / 4

Only political parties and factions loyal to the establishment and to the state ideology are permitted to operate. Reformist groups have come under increased state repression, especially since 2009, and affiliated politicians are subject to arbitrary detention and imprisonment on vague criminal charges. In August 2020, six reformist political activists were sentenced to one year in prison for their criticism of the crackdown on antigovernment protesters in November 2019.

B2. Is there a realistic opportunity for the opposition to increase its support or gain power through elections? 1 / 4

While there is some space for shifts in power between approved factions within the establishment, the unelected components of the constitutional system represent a permanent barrier to opposition electoral victories and genuine rotations of power.

Top opposition leaders face restrictions on their movement and access to the media. Mir Hossein Mousavi, Zahra Rahnavard, and Mehdi Karroubi—leaders of the reformist Green Movement, whose protests were violently suppressed following the disputed 2009 presidential election—have been under house arrest without formal charges since 2011. Reformist former president Mohammad Khatami is the subject of a media ban that prohibits the press from mentioning him and publishing his photos. Former hard-line president Mahmoud Ahmadinejad, who fell out of favor for challenging Khamenei, was barred from running in the 2017 presidential election.

B3. Are the people's political choices free from domination by forces that are external to the political sphere, or by political forces that employ extrapolitical means? 0 / 4

The choices of both voters and politicians are heavily influenced and ultimately circumscribed by Iran's unelected state institutions and ruling clerical establishment.

B4. Do various segments of the population (including ethnic, racial, religious, gender, LGBT+, and other relevant groups) have full political rights and electoral opportunities? 1 / 4

Men from the Shiite Muslim majority population dominate the political system. Women remain significantly underrepresented in politics and government. In 2017, Rouhani appointed two women among his several vice presidents but failed to name any women as cabinet ministers. No women candidates have ever been allowed to run for president.

Five seats in the parliament are reserved for recognized non-Muslim minority groups: Jews, Armenian Christians, Assyrian and Chaldean Christians, and Zoroastrians. However, members of non-Persian ethnic minorities and especially non-Shiite religious minorities are rarely awarded senior government posts, and their political representation remains weak.

C. FUNCTIONING OF GOVERNMENT: 1 / 12 (−1)

C1. Do the freely elected head of government and national legislative representatives determine the policies of the government? 1 / 4

The elected president's powers are limited by the supreme leader and other unelected authorities. The powers of the elected parliament are similarly restricted by the supreme leader and the unelected Guardian Council, which must approve all bills before they can become law. The council often rejects bills it deems un-Islamic. Nevertheless, the parliament has been a platform for heated political debate and criticism of the government, and legislators have frequently challenged presidents and their policies.

C2. Are safeguards against official corruption strong and effective? 0 / 4

Corruption remains endemic at all levels of the bureaucracy, despite regular calls by authorities to tackle the problem. Powerful actors involved in the economy, including the Islamic Revolutionary Guard Corps (IRGC) and bonyads (endowed foundations), are above scrutiny in practice, and restrictions on the media and civil society activists prevent them from serving as independent watchdogs to ensure transparency and accountability.

In 2019, the judiciary launched a crackdown on corruption amid accusations that the effort was politically motivated. The initiative continued in 2020 and included high-profile prosecutions of former politicians and court officials.

C3. Does the government operate with openness and transparency? 0 / 4 (−1)

The transparency of Iran's governing system is extremely limited in practice, and powerful elements of the state and society are not accountable to the public. A 2009 access to information law, for which implementing regulations were finally adopted in 2015, grants broadly worded exemptions allowing the protection of information whose disclosure would conflict with state interests, cause financial loss, or harm public security, among other stipulations.

The ruling establishment actively suppressed or manipulated information on a number of important topics during 2020. In January, for example, a Ukrainian passenger jet was shot down near Tehran, killing all 176 people on board, many of whom were Canadian citizens. After initially denying reports that one of its missiles had destroyed the airliner, the IRGC admitted days later that its personnel had targeted the plane after mistaking it for an incoming missile amid heightened tensions with the United States following the US assassination of Qasem Soleimani, commander of the IRGC's elite Quds force, in neighboring Iraq. A Canadian government report subsequently criticized Iran for what it called a secretive investigation of the incident, and no senior official was known to have resigned or been punished. Meanwhile, as of May authorities had sentenced at least 13 people to prison terms for protesting the disaster and criticizing the initial denial of responsibility.

During the COVID-19 outbreak, the authorities engaged in increased censorship to conceal its actual extent. Journalists were reportedly told to use only official statistics, while hospital workers were allegedly warned not to discuss the number of infections and fatalities with the media. Official data leaked to foreign media in August suggested that the true death toll was nearly three times higher than what the government publicly claimed. In addition to censorship, some officials promoted disinformation and conspiracy theories, warning that the virus could be a US biological weapon.

A year after the violent crackdown on antigovernment protests in November 2019, authorities continued to intimidate the families of victims and obstruct efforts to clarify the number of protesters killed.

Score Change: The score declined from 1 to 0 due to the government's restriction of information on a series of major events, including mass protests and a related crackdown in late 2019, the military's accidental destruction of a civilian airliner in January 2020, and the spread of COVID-19.

CIVIL LIBERTIES: 10 / 60
D. FREEDOM OF EXPRESSION AND BELIEF: 2 / 16
D1. Are there free and independent media? 0 / 4

Media freedom is severely limited both online and offline. The state broadcasting company is tightly controlled by hard-liners and influenced by the security apparatus. News and analysis are heavily censored, while critics and opposition members are rarely, if ever, given a platform on state-controlled television, which remains a major source of information for many Iranians. State television has a record of airing confessions extracted from political prisoners under duress, and it routinely carries reports aimed at discrediting dissidents and opposition activists.

Newspapers and magazines face censorship and warnings from authorities about which topics to cover and how. Tens of thousands of foreign-based websites are filtered, including news sites and major social media services. Satellite dishes are banned, and Persian-language broadcasts from outside the country are regularly jammed. Police periodically raid private homes and confiscate satellite dishes. Iranian authorities have pressured journalists working for Persian-language media outside the country by summoning and threatening their families in Iran.

In 2020, the government stepped up censorship and harassment of journalists in response to the COVID-19 pandemic. A number of journalists were summoned by authorities after reporting information that contradicted official statements about the health crisis. In late March, a public health task force temporarily suspended all newspaper printing, delivery, and distribution, citing the need to reduce the spread of the virus. Two journalists with a semiofficial news agency were detained in April after a cartoon posted on one of the outlet's social media accounts suggested that Khamenei supported fake treatments to ward off the coronavirus. The cartoon was deleted minutes after it was posted. The business daily *Jahan Sanaat* was temporarily suspended in August after it reported the comments of an epidemiologist on the task force who suggested that the real numbers of infections and deaths could be up to 20 times higher than what was officially reported.

The Committee to Protect Journalists reported that at least 15 journalists were imprisoned in Iran as of December 2020. Among those sentenced during the year was award-winning journalist Mohammad Mosaed, who in August received a term of four years and nine months in prison followed by a two-year ban on journalistic activity; he had been arrested for his coverage of the November 2019 crackdown on protests and of the coronavirus pandemic. In December, authorities executed exile journalist Rouhollah Zam, the editor of the Amad News channel on the Telegram messaging application; a resident of France, he was abducted while in Iraq in 2019 and taken to Iran, where he was accused of stirring violence during 2017 antigovernment protests.

D2. Are individuals free to practice and express their religious faith or nonbelief in public and private? 0 / 4

Iran is home to a majority Shiite Muslim population and Sunni Muslim, Baha'i, Christian, and Zoroastrian minorities. The constitution recognizes only Zoroastrians, Jews, and certain Christian communities as non-Muslim religious minorities, and these small groups are relatively free to worship. The regime cracks down on Muslims who are deemed to be at variance with the state ideology and interpretation of Islam.

Sunni Muslims complain that they have been prevented from building mosques in major cities and face difficulty obtaining government jobs. In recent years, there has been increased pressure on the Sufi Muslim order Nematollahi Gonabadi, including destruction of its places of worship and the jailing of some of its members.

The government also subjects some non-Muslim minorities to repressive policies and discrimination, including Baha'is and unrecognized Christian groups. Baha'is are systematically persecuted, sentenced to prison, and banned from access to higher education. Among other acts of repression during 2020, security forces raided the homes of dozens of Baha'is in cities across the country in November, seizing religious books and other material.

D3. Is there academic freedom, and is the educational system free from extensive political indoctrination? 1 / 4

Academic freedom remains limited in Iran, and universities have experienced harsh repression since 2009. Khamenei has warned that universities should not be turned into centers for political activities. Students have been prevented from continuing their studies for political reasons or because they belong to the Baha'i community.

Foreign scholars visiting Iran are vulnerable to detention on trumped-up charges. In October 2020, authorities temporarily released Iranian-French anthropologist Fariba Adelkhah, who had been arrested in June 2019 and sentenced in May to five years in prison for alleged offenses against national security. In November, Kylie Moore-Gilbert, a British-Australian researcher detained in 2018 and accused of spying for Israel, was released in exchange for the release of three Iranians jailed abroad. Iranian-Swedish physician and academic Ahmadreza Djalali was reportedly at risk of execution during the year, having been arrested in 2016 and sentenced to death for alleged espionage.

D4. Are individuals free to express their personal views on political or other sensitive topics without fear of surveillance or retribution? 1 / 4

Iran's vaguely defined restrictions on speech, harsh criminal penalties, and state monitoring of online communications are among several factors that deter citizens from engaging in open and free private discussion. Despite the risks and limitations, many do express dissent on social media, in some cases circumventing official blocks on certain platforms.

E. ASSOCIATIONAL AND ORGANIZATIONAL RIGHTS: 1 / 12

E1. Is there freedom of assembly? 0 / 4

The constitution states that public demonstrations may be held if they are not "detrimental to the fundamental principles of Islam." In practice, only state-sanctioned demonstrations are typically permitted, while other gatherings have in recent years been forcibly dispersed by security personnel, who detain participants.

In addition to thousands of arrests, hundreds of people were killed and thousands were injured in the protests that erupted in mid-November 2019. Estimates of the death toll ranged from more than 300 to 1,500. A temporary internet shutdown imposed by authorities suppressed communication about the demonstrations, but videos that showed security forces firing directly at protesters still emerged. Rallies were organized in support of the regime later in November, and they received live coverage from state media. Ahead of the one-year anniversary of the protests, authorities pressured the families of some victims to remain silent and warned them not to hold public memorials for their loved ones.

E2. Is there freedom for nongovernmental organizations, particularly those that are engaged in human rights- and governance-related work? 0 / 4

Nongovernmental organizations that seek to address human rights violations are generally suppressed by the state. For example, the Center for Human Rights Defenders remains closed, with several of its members in jail. Even groups that focus on more apolitical issues are subject to crackdowns. In June 2020, the founder of the Imam Ali Popular Students Relief Society, an influential charity dedicated to helping the poor and victims of natural disasters, was arrested along with two of his aides on unknown charges. In 2019, six environmental activists who had been detained in a larger wave of arrests in 2018 were sentenced to between six and 10 years in prison based on dubious charges of collaboration with the United States.

E3. Is there freedom for trade unions and similar professional or labor organizations? 1 / 4

Iran does not permit the creation of labor unions; only state-sponsored labor councils are allowed. Labor rights groups have come under pressure in recent years, with key leaders and activists sentenced to prison on national security charges. Workers who engage in strikes are vulnerable to dismissal and arrest. Several detained labor activists received heavy prison terms of 14 years or more during 2019. One prominent figure, Sepideh Gholian, was released on bail that year but returned to prison in June 2020 after she refused to ask the supreme leader for clemency.

F. RULE OF LAW: 3 / 16

F1. Is there an independent judiciary? 1 / 4

While the courts have a degree of autonomy within the ruling establishment, the judicial system is regularly used as a tool to silence regime critics and opposition members. The head of the judiciary is appointed by the supreme leader for renewable five-year terms; Ebrahim Raisi was named to the post in 2019. Political dissidents and advocates of human and labor rights have continued to face arbitrary judgments, and the security apparatus's influence over the courts has reportedly grown in recent years.

F2. Does due process prevail in civil and criminal matters? 1 / 4

The authorities routinely violate basic due process standards, particularly in politically sensitive cases. Activists are arrested without warrants, held indefinitely without formal charges, and denied access to legal counsel or any contact with the outside world. Many are later convicted on vague security charges in trials that sometimes last only a few minutes. Lawyers who take up the cases of dissidents have been jailed and banned from practicing, and a number have been forced to leave the country to escape prosecution. In 2019, prominent human rights lawyer Nasrin Sotoudeh was reportedly sentenced to an additional 33 years in prison and 148 lashes for her activities; she had been in prison serving a five-year sentence since mid-2018. In October 2020, she was temporarily released amid concerns about her health following a hunger strike.

Dual nationals and those with connections abroad have also faced arbitrary detention, trumped-up charges, and denial of due process rights in recent years. Several such individuals remained behind bars in 2020.

F3. Is there protection from the illegitimate use of physical force and freedom from war and insurgencies? 0 / 4

Former detainees have reported being beaten during arrest and subjected to torture until they confess to crimes dictated by their interrogators. Some crimes can be formally punished with lashes in addition to imprisonment or fines. Prisons are overcrowded, and prisoners often complain of poor detention conditions, including denial of medical care. Political prisoners have repeatedly engaged in hunger strikes in recent years to protest mistreatment in custody. In 2020, authorities temporarily released tens of thousands of prisoners to prevent the spread of COVID-19 behind bars. Very few political prisoners were reportedly among those granted leave, though prominent rights activist Narges Mohammadi was released in October after her sentence was reduced amid concerns about her health; she had first been arrested in 2015. The number of coronavirus infections in prisons was allegedly larger than acknowledged by authorities.

Iran has generally been second only to China in the number of executions it carries out, putting hundreds of people to death each year. Convicts can be executed for offenses other than murder, such as drug trafficking, and for crimes they committed when they were younger than 18 years old. Legislation enacted in 2017 significantly increased the quantity of illegal drugs required for a drug-related crime to incur the death penalty, prompting sentence reviews for thousands of death-row inmates. In September 2020, wrestler Navid Afkari was executed for allegedly murdering a state employee during 2018 antiestablishment protests; a global campaign had called for a fair retrial, as Afkari had reportedly confessed under torture and was subjected to a closed trial. Separately, the death sentences of three young men arrested in connection with the November 2019 protests were suspended in July 2020 following a social media campaign on their behalf; a retrial was pending at year's end.

The country faces a long-term security threat from terrorist and insurgent groups that recruit from disadvantaged Kurdish, Arab, and Sunni Muslim minority populations.

F4. Do laws, policies, and practices guarantee equal treatment of various segments of the population? 1 / 4

Women do not receive equal treatment under the law and face widespread discrimination in practice. For example, a woman's testimony in court is given half the weight of a man's, and the monetary compensation awarded to a female victim's family upon her death is half that owed to the family of a male victim.

A majority of the population is of Persian ethnicity, and ethnic minorities experience various forms of discrimination, including restrictions on the use of their languages. Some provinces with large non-Persian populations remain underdeveloped. Activists campaigning for the rights of ethnic minority groups and greater autonomy for their respective regions have come under pressure from the authorities, and some have been jailed.

Members of the LGBT+ community face harassment and discrimination, though the problem is underreported due to the criminalized and hidden nature of these groups in Iran. The penal code criminalizes all sexual relations outside of traditional marriage, and Iran is among the few countries where individuals can be put to death for consensual same-sex conduct.

G. PERSONAL AUTONOMY AND INDIVIDUAL RIGHTS: 4 / 16

G1. Do individuals enjoy freedom of movement, including the ability to change their place of residence, employment, or education? 1 / 4

Freedom of movement is restricted, particularly for women and perceived opponents of the regime. Many journalists and activists have been prevented from leaving the country. Women are banned from certain public places and can generally obtain a passport to travel abroad only with the permission of their fathers or husbands.

G2. Are individuals able to exercise the right to own property and establish private businesses without undue interference from state or nonstate actors? 1 / 4

Iranians have the legal right to own property and establish private businesses. However, powerful institutions like the IRGC play a dominant role in the economy, limiting fair competition and opportunities for entrepreneurs, and bribery is said to be widespread in the business environment, including for registration and obtaining licenses. Women are denied equal rights in inheritance matters.

G3. Do individuals enjoy personal social freedoms, including choice of marriage partner and size of family, protection from domestic violence, and control over appearance? 1 / 4

Social freedoms are restricted in Iran. All residents, but particularly women, are subject to obligatory rules on dress and personal appearance, and those who are deemed to have violated the rules face state harassment, fines, and arrest.

Police conduct raids on private gatherings that breach rules against alcohol consumption and the mixing of unrelated men and women. Those attending can be detained and fined or sentenced to corporal punishment in the form of lashes.

Women do not enjoy equal rights in divorce and child custody disputes. In 2019, the Guardian Council approved a legal amendment that would enable Iranian women married to foreign men to request Iranian citizenship for their children.

G4. Do individuals enjoy equality of opportunity and freedom from economic exploitation? 1 / 4

The government provides no protection to women and children forced into sex trafficking, and both Iranians and migrant workers from countries like Afghanistan are subject to forced labor and debt bondage. The IRGC has allegedly used coercive tactics to recruit thousands of Afghan migrants living in Iran to fight in Syria. Human Rights Watch has reported that children as young as 14 are among those recruited.

The population faces widespread economic hardship driven by a combination of US-led trade sanctions and mismanagement by the regime. The crisis has resulted in the rapid devaluation of the national currency and soaring prices for many basic goods. The United States continued to impose new sanctions during 2020 despite international concern that they could hinder Iran's ability to secure supplies of food and drugs as it struggled with the coronavirus. Some Iranian officials blamed the country's poor handling of the pandemic on the effects of the sanctions.

Iraq

Population: 39,700,000
Capital: Baghdad
Freedom Status: Not Free
Electoral Democracy: No

Overview: Iraq holds regular, competitive elections, and the country's various partisan, religious, and ethnic groups generally enjoy representation in the political system. However, democratic governance is impeded in practice by corruption and security threats. In the Kurdistan region, democratic institutions lack the strength to contain the influence of long-standing power brokers. Increasingly, Iran has been able to influence politics in Baghdad. Civil liberties are generally respected in Iraqi law, but the state has limited capacity to prevent and punish violations.

KEY DEVELOPMENTS IN 2020

- The COVID-19 pandemic deeply impacted Iraq's already dilapidated health sector, which struggled to cope with the large number of people who contracted the virus. The lockdowns imposed by Iraqi and Kurdistan Regional Government (KRG) authorities exacerbated the financial hardships of low-wage workers and small business owners.

- In May, following aborted attempts by two other candidates for prime minister, Mustafa al-Kadhimi succeeded in forming a government that was approved by Parliament.
- In April and May, authorities in Iraq, particularly in the Kurdistan region, exploited the COVID-19 lockdowns to put down protests and severely curtail press freedom, assembly rights, and opposition activity.
- Reconstruction of areas liberated from the Islamic State (IS) militant group's control continued at a slow pace throughout the year. Almost 1.3 million Iraqis remained internally displaced as of December, and the threat of terrorism persisted.

POLITICAL RIGHTS: 16 / 40 (−1)

A. ELECTORAL PROCESS: 8 / 12

A1. Was the current head of government or other chief national authority elected through free and fair elections? 2 / 4

After national elections, the Council of Representatives (CoR) chooses the largely ceremonial president, who in turn appoints a prime minister nominated by the largest bloc in the parliament. The prime minister, who holds most executive power and forms the government, serves up to two four-year terms. The May 2018 national elections were generally viewed as credible by international observers, despite low turnout and allegations of fraud, which were particularly prevalent in the Kurdish provinces and neighboring Kirkuk. That October, after a five-month delay, the new CoR chose Kurdish politician Barham Salih as president, and Adel Abdul Mahdi, a Shiite independent, was appointed prime minister. Mahdi resigned in December 2019. In May 2020, the major blocs in parliament and their foreign backers agreed to name the independent Mustafa al-Kadhimi. The formation of the government was completed a month later.

The Kurdistan Regional Government (KRG), composed of Iraq's northernmost provinces, is ostensibly led by a president with extensive executive powers. The draft Kurdish constitution requires presidential elections every four years and limits presidents to two terms. However, after eight years as president, Masoud Barzani of the Kurdistan Democratic Party (KDP) had his term extended in a 2013 political agreement with another party, the Patriotic Union of Kurdistan (PUK).

After Barzani stepped down in 2017, the presidency remained vacant, and executive power was held by Prime Minister Nechirvan Barzani, his nephew. After the September 2018 Kurdish parliamentary elections, the KDP nominated Nechirvan Barzani to become president and Masrour Barzani—Masoud Barzani's son—to serve as prime minister. In May 2019, Nechirvan Barzani was elected president by the Iraqi Kurdish parliament and sworn in a month later, after the position had been vacant for nearly two years. Masrour Barzani was appointed and sworn in as prime minister the same month. Both Barzanis, the president and prime minister, are from the KDP.

A2. Were the current national legislative representatives elected through free and fair elections? 3 / 4

The 329 members of the CoR are elected every four years from multimember open lists in each province, though a December 2019 reform significantly changed the framework for future polls. The May 2018 elections, held under the party-list system, were generally viewed as credible by international observers, despite some allegations of fraud. The Sairoon alliance, led by Shiite cleric Moqtada al-Sadr, won the most seats with 54, followed by the Conquest coalition led by Hadi al-Amiri with 48, outgoing prime minister Haider al-Abadi's Victory alliance with 42, and the State of Law coalition headed by former prime minister Nouri al-Maliki with 25. The top four alliances were all led by Shiite parties, though they made varying efforts to reach across sectarian lines. Among the several Kurdish parties, the KDP won 25 seats and the PUK won 19. The remaining seats were divided among Sunni-led coalitions, smaller parties, and independents. After the resignation of former prime minister Mahdi in December 2019, a new government formed in June 2020 under Prime Minister al-Kadhimi.

Following repeated delays, provincial council elections originally scheduled for 2017 were postponed indefinitely by the CoR in November 2019. Kirkuk, the subject of a dispute between the KRG and the central government, has not held provincial council elections since 2005.

In the Kurdistan region, the 111-seat Kurdistan Parliament is elected through closed party-list proportional representation in a single district, with members serving four-year terms. The September 2018 elections, originally due in 2017, resulted in the governing KDP increasing its plurality to 45 seats. The PUK received 21 seats, Gorran took 12, and several smaller parties and minority representatives accounted for the remainder. The elections were plagued by fraud allegations and other irregularities, and Gorran and other smaller parties rejected the results.

A3. Are the electoral laws and framework fair, and are they implemented impartially by the relevant election management bodies? 3 / 4

The Independent High Electoral Commission (IHEC) is responsible for managing elections in Iraq. The IHEC generally enjoys the confidence of the international community and, according to some polls, the Iraqi public. It faced criticism in 2018 from opposition leaders and outgoing prime minister Haider al-Abadi over its handling of electronic voting challenges and the subsequent recount, but international organizations praised the body for its professionalism and impartiality.

Under electoral reforms approved in December 2019, each of the country's 18 provinces would be divided into a number of new electoral districts, with one legislator elected for every 100,000 people. The reforms moreover abolished the existing party-list voting system and replaced it with one in which voters select individual candidates from the new districts, which at year's end had yet to be delineated. It was unclear how that procedure would commence in the absence of recent census data, as a national census has not been conducted since 1987; this lack of current data had already resulted in skewed parliamentary seat allocations.

The Kurdistan Independent High Electoral and Referendum Commission (IHERC) administers elections in the Kurdistan region. In addition to the 2018 legislative balloting, the IHERC conducted the 2017 independence referendum, in which 93 percent of voters favored independence, though the exercise—which was not monitored by international observers—was allegedly marred by intimidation and fraud.

B. POLITICAL PLURALISM AND PARTICIPATION: 7 / 16 (−1)

B1. Do the people have the right to organize in different political parties or other competitive political groupings of their choice, and is the system free of undue obstacles to the rise and fall of these competing parties or groupings? 3 / 4

The constitution guarantees the freedom to form and join political parties, with the exception of the pre-2003 dictatorship's Baath Party, which is banned. A 2016 law strengthened the ban, criminalizing Baathist protests and the promotion of Baathist ideas. The measure applies to any group that supports racism, terrorism, sectarianism, sectarian cleansing, and other ideas contrary to democracy or the peaceful transfer of power.

Individual Iraqis' freedom to run for office is also limited by a vague "good conduct" requirement in the electoral law.

In practice, Iraqis can generally form parties and operate without government interference. Party membership and multiparty alliances shift frequently. The IHEC registered 205 parties for the 2018 elections, reflecting both a relatively open political environment and deep fragmentation.

The electoral reforms approved in late 2019 in response to protesters' demands are expected to make independent candidacies more viable.

B2. Is there a realistic opportunity for the opposition to increase its support or gain power through elections? 2 / 4 (−1)

Elections are competitive, but most parties are dominated by one sectarian or ethnic group, meaning large and established parties representing the Shiite majority have tended to govern. Minority groups have only gained power as part of a cross-sectarian party or bloc. A number of new parties that are more secular and national in orientation participated in the 2018 elections, but Shiite parties continued to play the leading role. The strong performance of the newly formed Conquest coalition, which finished second, raised some concerns due to its inclusion of members associated with the Popular Mobilization Forces (PMF)—state-sponsored militia groups that fought against IS and have been accused of war crimes and ties with Iran. The former ruling party, Dawa, split into the State of Law coalition and the Victory coalition, led by former prime ministers al-Maliki and al-Abadi, respectively. The split created an opening for other lists, like Sairoon and Conquest, to gain seats and influence government formation. The 2018 transfer of power proceeded far more smoothly than in 2014, when former prime minister al-Maliki stepped down only after intense domestic and international pressure.

In the Kurdistan region, the traditional dominance of the KDP and the PUK was for a time challenged by the rise of the reformist group Gorran, but the repeated postponement of presidential and legislative elections before 2018 allowed entrenched interests to remain in power. Although the damaging crisis that followed the 2017 independence referendum appeared to threaten the KDP's electoral prospects, it ultimately retained its leading position in the 2018 legislative elections. The PUK replaced Gorran as the second-largest party in the Kurdish parliament after Gorran lost much of its reformist appeal for joining the KRG cabinet and being plagued by corruption scandals.

In 2019 and 2020, Kurdish Regional Government authorities continued to intensify their repression of the activities of the New Generation opposition party and its affiliated media outlet, Nalia Radio and Television (NRT), which is owned by the party leader Shaswar Abdul Wahid. In April 2019, security forces detained over 80 members of the New Generation party, allegedly for defamation and insulting a state employee. In August 2020, authorities unlawfully shut and raided two NRT offices for over a month. In December, they raided two other offices and suspended the outlet's broadcasting license. The Ministry of Culture and Youth, which issued the suspension, claimed that NRT had broken rules regulating broadcast media, though they did not specify which rules had been broken. NRT had covered violence during antigovernment protests throughout the year.

Score Change: The score declined from 3 to 2 due to a multiyear crackdown by Kurdish regional authorities on a Kurdish opposition party's members and affiliated media outlet.

B3. Are the people's political choices free from domination by forces that are external to the political sphere, or by political forces that employ extrapolitical means? 1 / 4

Iraq's political system remains distorted by interference from foreign powers, most notably Iran, which physically and politically threatens Iraqi policymakers who challenge its interests, while at other times, buys off their support. The PMF have strong links to Iran, and dozens of figures associated with these militias ran in the 2018 elections and won seats in the CoR.

The ability of IS to suppress normal political activity has waned significantly since 2017, when government forces successfully drove the group out of the territory it formerly controlled.

B4. Do various segments of the population (including ethnic, racial, religious, gender, LGBT+, and other relevant groups) have full political rights and electoral opportunities? 1 / 4

Despite legal and constitutional measures designed to protect the political rights of various religious and ethnic groups, the dominant role of ethno-sectarian parties and the allocation of key offices according to informal religious or ethnic criteria reduce the likelihood that politicians will act in the interests of the whole population.

Sunni Arabs, the largest ethno-sectarian minority, are represented in the parliament but often argue that the Shiite majority excludes them from positions of real influence. The presidency and premiership are reserved in practice for a Kurd and a Shiite; the position of parliament speaker goes to a Sunni. Muhammad al-Halbusi was named speaker in September 2018.

A system of reserved seats ensures a minimum representation in the CoR for some of Iraq's smaller religious and ethnic minorities. There are five seats reserved for Christians and one each for Fayli Kurds (added in 2018), Yazidis, Sabean Mandaeans, and Shabaks. The Kurdish parliament reserves five seats for Turkmen, five for Christians, and one for Armenians. The political rights of minorities have been severely impeded by widespread displacement from formerly IS-occupied areas. Although polling stations were set up at encampments for the country's nearly two million internally displaced people (IDPs), in May 2018 the parliament voted to annul the votes of IDPs due to fraud claims.

The CoR and the Kurdish parliament reserve 25 percent and 30 percent of their seats for women, respectively, though such formal representation has had little obvious effect on state policies toward women, who are typically excluded from political debates and leadership positions. LGBT+ people are unable to enjoy equal political rights in practice due to harsh societal discrimination, and the main political parties do not advocate for the interests of LGBT+ people in their platforms.

C. FUNCTIONING OF GOVERNMENT: 2 / 12

C1. Do the freely elected head of government and national legislative representatives determine the policies of the government? 1 / 4

Several factors, including low institutional capacity, widespread corruption and extensive Iranian influence, have hindered the ability of elected officials to independently set and implement laws and policies. The existence of the PMF, which is officially part of Iraqi state institutions but in reality, sets its own policies, undermines the ability of the government to set and implement its own domestic and foreign agendas, as can be seen in the repression of protests, kidnapping and assassinations of activists, and attacks on US targets in Iraq. The United States and its allies also exert some policy influence through their support for Iraqi security forces and other state institutions. Iraq's fragmented politics can lead to gridlock and dysfunction, as demonstrated by the protracted negotiations on government formation following the May 2018 elections.

In the Kurdistan region, Masoud Barzani effectively suspended the parliament in 2015 after the speaker and many members opposed his extended presidential mandate. The

Kurdish legislature that was elected in September 2018 met and approved a new government in July 2019, but tension was still high between the KDP and PUK, due to the KDP's and Barzanis' dominance of KRG politics.

C2. Are safeguards against official corruption strong and effective? 0 / 4

Corruption remains a major problem in Iraq, and was a key contributor to the protest movement in Baghdad and other cities that erupted in 2019. Political parties, which siphon funds from the ministries they control and take kickbacks for government contracts, resist anticorruption efforts, while whistleblowers and investigators are subject to intimidation and violence. The judicial system, itself hampered by politicization and corruption, takes action on only a fraction of the cases investigated by the Integrity Commission, one of three governmental anticorruption bodies. The KRG suffers from similar corruption problems.

C3. Does the government operate with openness and transparency? 1 / 4

A few policies that promote openness have been adopted, including rules requiring public officials to disclose their assets, but the government does not generally operate with transparency. The CoR debates the budget, and interest groups are often able to access draft legislation. However, security conditions make elected representatives, who usually live and work in a restricted part of the capital, relatively inaccessible to the public. The public procurement system is nontransparent and corrupt, with no legal recourse available for unsuccessful bidders. The oil and gas industry also lacks transparency, and the government has failed to make adequate progress in meeting its commitments to the Extractive Industries Transparency Initiative. The government has not yet passed a comprehensive law on access to information.

ADDITIONAL DISCRETIONARY POLITICAL RIGHTS QUESTION
Is the government or occupying power deliberately changing the ethnic composition of a country or territory so as to destroy a culture or tip the political balance in favor of another group? −1 / 0

IS's loss of territorial control in 2017 largely halted its campaign to alter religious demography. However, hundreds of thousands of Iraqis who were displaced by IS remain unable to return to their homes, for both security and economic reasons. Kurdish authorities encouraged local and substate forces to prevent thousands of Arab families displaced by the IS conflict from returning to villages near the Syria-Iraq border and in disputed areas under de facto KRG control, in an apparent attempt to change the region's demography. Displaced families with perceived links to IS who continue to reside in and outside of camps are particularly vulnerable to assault and sexual abuse. Many cannot return to their homes because their original communities reject their return or Iraqi authorities prohibit it. As of December 2020, approximately 4.7 million Iraqis displaced by the 2014 IS offensive had returned to their home regions, while more than 1.2 million people remained internally displaced.

CIVIL LIBERTIES: 13 / 60 (−1)
D. FREEDOM OF EXPRESSION AND BELIEF: 4 / 16 (−1)
D1. Are there free and independent media? 1 / 4

The constitution allows limits on free expression to preserve "public order" and "morality." Iraq's media scene appears lively and diverse, but there are few politically independent news sources. Journalists who do not self-censor can face legal repercussions or violent retaliation. Media outlets face restrictions and obstruction in response to their coverage.

Journalists covering the antigovernment protests in Iraq and the Kurdistan region were obstructed, threatened, and endangered by authorities. On January 20, 2020, Iraqi security forces opened fire on protesters in Tahrir Square in Baghdad, killing photojournalist Youssef Sattar, and wounding others. On August 12, Huner Rasool, a journalist with Gali Kurdistan TV, died while attempting to escape clashes between Kurdish security forces and protesters in Ranya.

Militias have shot, arrested and kidnapped journalists for their work. Four journalists and one media executive were killed in 2020, according to Reporters without Borders (RSF). In early 2020, Ahmed Abdul Samad and Safaa Ghali, both working for local Iraqi station Dijlah TV, and executive director of al-Rasheed TV Nizar Thanoun in Baghdad, were gunned down. The three individuals were seemingly targeted by militias for their critical reporting on the militias' repression of protesters.

In 2020, KRG authorities intensified the persecution and harassment of media outlets and journalists, particularly those covering anti-KRG protests relating to economic hardship and corruption.

D2. Are individuals free to practice and express their religious faith or nonbelief in public and private? 1 / 4

The constitution guarantees freedom of belief, but in practice many Iraqis have been subjected to violence and displacement due to their religious identity. Places of worship have often been targets for terrorist attacks. Blasphemy laws remain in the legal code, although enforcement is rare. A 2015 religious conversion law automatically designates the children of a parent who has converted to Islam as Muslim, even if the other parent is a non-Muslim. Restaurants serving alcohol and liquor stores have faced harassment and attacks, further eroding religious freedom.

Most political leaders expressed support for religious pluralism after IS's defeat, and minorities living in liberated areas have largely able to practice their religion freely since.

D3. Is there academic freedom, and is the educational system free from extensive political indoctrination? 1 / 4

Educators have long faced the threat of violence or other repercussions for teaching subjects or discussing topics that powerful state or nonstate actors find objectionable. The country's official curriculum is often augmented in the classroom by religious or sectarian viewpoints.

Political activism by university students can result in harassment or intimidation.

D4. Are individuals free to express their personal views on political or other sensitive topics without fear of surveillance or retribution? 1 / 4 (−1)

Social media posts on controversial topics sometimes result in retribution. Certain topics, including corruption and, to a somewhat lesser extent, criticism of Iran, are considered to be off limits and at times prompted arrest, docking of salaries, torture, and criminal lawsuits. Social media users and bloggers have faced defamation lawsuits for criticizing local authorities' poor response to the COVID-19 pandemic.

Iranian-backed militias have threatened, kidnapped, tortured, and assassinated many perceived critics, including prominent Iraqi analyst, Hisham al-Hashimi, who was shot in July 2020. Over 30 private citizens involved in the 2019-2020 protests, including at least one minor, were abducted in 2019 and 2020; their whereabouts were unknown at year's end. Many vocal activists have left the country or relocated to the Kurdistan region, fearing for their lives.

Political speech in the Kurdistan region can also prompt arbitrary detentions or other reprisals from government or partisan forces. Kurdish authorities arrested protesters and organizers, as well as bloggers, for criticizing COVID-19 lockdown measures, corruption, and the non-payment of state salaries. In December 2020, Kurdish authorities also arrested dozens of young men for calling for protests in their social media posts.

Score Change: The score declined from 2 to 1 due to a pattern of arrests, abductions, and disappearances of individuals who expressed opposition to Iranian-backed militias through protests or social media posts.

E. ASSOCIATIONAL AND ORGANIZATIONAL RIGHTS: 4 / 12

E1. Is there freedom of assembly? 0 / 4

The constitution guarantees freedom of assembly, but protesters are frequently at risk of violence or arrest, and these dangers became acute during the 2019–20 protest movement. Security forces used curfews, tear gas, and live ammunition to suppress demonstrations in Baghdad and other southern cities that began in October 2019 against corruption, poor infrastructure and government services, and high unemployment. By mid-December, some 25,000 people had been injured during the protests, and at least 700 were killed. Iraqi security forces and pro-Iranian militias routinely opened live fire at protesters. Iraqi officials and journalists reported that snipers under the command of Iranian-backed militia units used live ammunition to shoot at protesters from rooftops and carried out a wave of kidnappings of protest organizers and activists. Iranian media and media outlets linked to Iranian-backed militias spread false reports about activists to justify their targeting.

Authorities in Iraq, particularly in Kurdistan, exploited COVID-19 lockdowns to ban protests and restrict the ability of individuals to reach protest sites. In May 2020, KRG security forces in Dohuk opened fire and arrested protesters who were demanding improvement in living conditions, an end to corruption, and payment of unpaid state salaries.

E2. Is there freedom for nongovernmental organizations, particularly those that are engaged in human rights- and governance-related work? 2 / 4

Nongovernmental organizations (NGOs) enjoy societal support and a relatively hospitable regulatory environment, though they must register with the government and obtain approval from the commission responsible for suppressing Baathism. For international NGOs registration is cumbersome and often requires payment of bribes. In the Kurdistan region, NGOs must renew their registration annually.

In 2020, a number of antigovernment activists were kidnapped as the protest movement continued. In August, gunmen killed Reham Yacoub and Tahseen Osama and attempted to assassinate Lodya Remon Albarty, three prominent civil society activists in Basra. In October and December, activists were arrested in the Kurdistan region for calling and engaging in protests against the region's ruling parties.

E3. Is there freedom for trade unions and similar professional or labor organizations? 2 / 4

Labor laws allow for collective bargaining (even by nonunionized workers), protect the rights of subcontractors and migrant workers, and permit workers to strike, among other rights. However, public-sector workers are not allowed to unionize, there is no legal prohibition against antiunion discrimination, and workers do not have access to legal remedies if fired for union activity. Some state officials and private employers discourage union activity with threats, demotions, and other deterrents.

F. RULE OF LAW: 1 / 16

F1. Is there an independent judiciary? 0 / 4

The judiciary is influenced by corruption, political pressure, tribal forces, and religious interests. The lines between the executive, legislative, and judicial branches are frequently blurred, and executive interference in the judiciary is widespread. Due to distrust of or lack of access to the courts, many Iraqis have turned to tribal bodies to settle disputes, even those involving major crimes.

F2. Does due process prevail in civil and criminal matters? 0 / 4

Criminal proceedings in Iraq are deeply flawed. Arbitrary arrests, including arrests without a warrant, are common. Terrorism cases in particular have been prone to fundamental violations of due process, with human rights groups describing systematic denial of access to counsel and short, summary trials with little evidence that the defendants committed specific crimes other than association with IS. In 2018, some trials of suspected IS members that resulted in death sentences lasted as little as 20 minutes, and hundreds of family members of suspected IS fighters have been arbitrarily detained.

Several senior military commanders were removed from their posts in October 2019 following a violent crackdown on protesters. The actions were rejected by many Iraqis as inadequate and had little deterrent effect on members of the security forces who fatally injured many demonstrators throughout the year. Despite a public vow by Prime Minister al-Kadhimi in August 2020 to investigate and punish those responsible for the disappearances and assassinations, the perpetrators continued to roam free. A new mechanism to locate victims has not successfully obtained the release of those who disappeared.

F3. Is there protection from the illegitimate use of physical force and freedom from war and insurgencies? 1 / 4

The end of large-scale combat with IS significantly improved the security environment. Though the organization remained active as a clandestine terrorist group in 2020, it no longer controlled Iraqi territory or civilian populations, and its ability to operate was diminished.

Tensions between Iran and the United States continued to play out on Iraqi soil, as Iranian-backed militias used small-scale rockets and improvised explosive device (IED) towards American forces and personnel, endangering Iraqi residents. In January 2020, the United States assassinated Iranian General Qassim Suleimani at the Baghdad airport, as well as several prominent Iraqi militia members.

In 2020, Turkish military forces launched operations into Kurdish territory and in June began to set up multiple military bases in Iraq, ostensibly to increase their own border security.

The use of torture to obtain confessions is widespread, including in death penalty cases. Detainees are often held in harsh, overcrowded conditions, and forced disappearances, particularly of suspected IS fighters, have been reported.

F4. Do laws, policies, and practices guarantee equal treatment of various segments of the population? 0 / 4

Women face widespread societal bias and discriminatory treatment under laws on a number of topics. Sexual harassment in the workplace is prohibited, but it is reportedly rare for victims to pursue formal complaints.

Members of a given ethnic or religious group tend to suffer discrimination or persecution in areas where they represent a minority, leading many to seek safety in other neighborhoods or provinces. Same-sex relations are not explicitly prohibited, but LGBT+ people risk violence if they are open about their identity. People of African descent suffer from high rates of extreme poverty and discrimination.

G. PERSONAL AUTONOMY AND INDIVIDUAL RIGHTS: 4 / 16

G1. Do individuals enjoy freedom of movement, including the ability to change their place of residence, employment, or education? 1 / 4

Freedom of movement improved somewhat as areas formerly controlled by IS were brought back under government control. However, large-scale destruction of housing and infrastructure, the presence of sectarian or partisan militias, and the ongoing threat of violence made it difficult for many displaced people to return home. Almost 1.3 million Iraqis remained internally displaced as of December 2020.

The movement of women is limited by legal restrictions. Women require the consent of a male guardian to obtain a passport and the Civil Status Identification Document, which is needed to access employment, education, and a number of social services.

In March and April 2020, both the Baghdad government and the KRG imposed lockdowns due to COVID-19, severely restricting movement between provinces and closing international borders. The KRG imposed particularly harsh and prolonged lockdowns throughout the year: the first from March through mid-May, another in early June, and another in early July.

G2. Are individuals able to exercise the right to own property and establish private businesses without undue interference from state or non-state actors? 1 / 4

Iraqis are legally free to own property and establish businesses, but observance of property rights has been limited by corruption and conflict. Business owners face demands for bribes, threats, and violent attempts to seize their enterprises. Contracts are difficult to enforce. Women are legally disadvantaged with respect to inheritance rights and may face pressure to yield their rights to male relatives.

G3. Do individuals enjoy personal social freedoms, including choice of marriage partner and size of family, protection from domestic violence, and control over appearance? 1 / 4

Forced and early marriages are common, especially in the context of displacement and poverty. Nearly one in four Iraqi women aged 20 to 24 were married by age 18, and marriage between 15 and 18 is legal with parental approval. Laws on marriage and divorce favor men over women. In 2020, Iraq witnessed a spike in domestic violence cases. Renewed efforts by Iraqi women's rights organizations to compel the parliament to pass a law banning gender-based violence have been unsuccessful. Rapists can avoid prosecution if they marry their victims; spousal rape is not prohibited. The law also allows reduced sentences for those convicted of so-called honor killings, which are seldom punished in practice.

Both men and women face pressure to conform to conservative standards on personal appearance. A number of high-profile women associated with the beauty and fashion industries were murdered in 2018. The assailants remain unknown, but the government blamed extremist groups for the murders.

G4. Do individuals enjoy equality of opportunity and freedom from economic exploitation? 1 / 4

After the military defeat of IS, many Yazidi women who had been forced into sex slavery remained missing. Exploitation of children, including through forced begging and the recruitment of child soldiers by some militias, is a chronic problem. Foreign migrant workers frequently work long hours for low pay, and they are vulnerable to forced labor.

Human trafficking is also a problem, and internally displace people are particularly vulnerable. Government efforts to enforce trafficking laws have been inadequate.

Ireland

Population: 5,000,000
Capital: Dublin
Freedom Status: Free
Electoral Democracy: Yes

Overview: Ireland is a stable democracy in which political rights and civil liberties are respected and defended. There is some limited societal discrimination, especially against the traditionally nomadic Irish Travellers. Corruption scandals have plagued the police force, and domestic violence remains a problem.

KEY DEVELOPMENTS IN 2020
- In the historic February general elections, Sinn Féin won 37 seats (24.5 percent), its best result ever and only one less than Fianna Fáil's 38 seats (22.2 percent). Fine Gael won 35 seats (20.9 percent), and the Green Party 12 (7.1 percent). Fine Gael and Fianna Fáil formed a government—the two rival parties had never before governed together—with the Green Party in June.
- The government passed the Health (Preservation and Protection and other Emergency Measures in the Public Interest) Act 2020 in March in order to combat the coronavirus pandemic. The law gave new emergency powers to government ministries and the police to enforce lockdowns and curfews. By the end of the year, over 91,000 people had tested positive for the virus, and 2,237 people had died, according to government statistics provided to the World Health Organization (WHO).

POLITICAL RIGHTS: 39 / 40
A. ELECTORAL PROCESS: 12 / 12
A1. Was the current head of government or other chief national authority elected through free and fair elections? 4 / 4
The Taoiseach, or prime minister, is nominated by the House of Representatives (Dàil Eireann) and formally appointed by the president. Thus, the legitimacy of the prime minister is largely dependent on the conduct of Dàil elections, which historically have been free and fair. The Dàil elected Micheál Martin as Taoiseach in June 2020 following a general election in February, to lead the coalition government between Fianna Fáil, Fine Gael, and the Green Party.

The president is elected to up to two seven-year terms, and as chief of state has mostly ceremonial duties. Michael D. Higgins was reelected in 2018. Voting in presidential elections has historically been free and fair.

A2. Were the current national legislative representatives elected through free and fair elections? 4 / 4
The Dàil's 160 members are elected in multimember districts through a proportional representation system, and their terms last five years. The Senate (Seanad Éireann) contains 60 seats; 43 members are indirectly chosen through an electoral college, while 11 are

selected by the Taoiseach and 6 are selected from constituencies that represent some higher education institutions.

The February 2020 Dàil election saw no major irregularities or unequal campaigning. In a historic result, Sinn Féin won 37 seats (24.5 percent), its best result ever and only one less than Fianna Fáil's 38 seats (22.2 percent). Fine Gael won 35 seats (20.9 percent), and the Green Party 12 (7.1 percent). In June, Fianna Fáil formed a historic coalition government with Fine Gael—the two rivals had never before governed together—and the Green Party.

A3. Are the electoral laws and framework fair, and are they implemented impartially by the relevant election management bodies? 4 / 4

Ireland's electoral framework is strong and government bodies hold credible polls. The government renewed its commitments to establish an Electoral Commission in the 2020 Programme for Government, released in June.

Ireland frequently holds referendums, especially on European Union (EU) treaties.

B. POLITICAL PLURALISM AND PARTICIPATION: 16 / 16

B1. Do the people have the right to organize in different political parties or other competitive political groupings of their choice, and is the system free of undue obstacles to the rise and fall of these competing parties or groupings? 4 / 4

Political parties in Ireland are free to form and compete. Among the main parties, Fianna Fáil and Fine Gael do not differ widely in ideology, despite their long history as rivals; they represent the successors of opposing sides in the nation's 1922–23 civil war. Other key parties include Sinn Féin—a left-wing republican party that leads the opposition—the Labour Party, and the Green Party.

B2. Is there a realistic opportunity for the opposition to increase its support or gain power through elections? 4 / 4

Opposition parties generally do not encounter restrictions or harassment that affects their ability to gain power through elections, and most of the main parties have been part of government at some point in the history of the state.

B3. Are the people's political choices free from domination by forces that are external to the political sphere, or by political forces that employ extrapolitical means? 4 / 4

People's political choices are generally free from domination by the military, foreign powers, religious hierarchies, and other powerful groups.

B4. Do various segments of the population (including ethnic, racial, religious, gender, LGBT+, and other relevant groups) have full political rights and electoral opportunities? 4 / 4

Women are active in politics but are underrepresented, holding 22.5 percent of the Dàil's seats.

While ethnic minority and marginalized groups are generally free to participate in politics, Irish Travellers and Roma have little representation. However, in June 2020, Eileen Flynn became the first Irish Traveller woman to be appointed as a Senator. Travellers were formally recognized as an Indigenous ethnic group in 2017, the same year the National Traveller and Roma Inclusion Strategy 2017–21 was launched.

C. FUNCTIONING OF GOVERNMENT: 11 / 12

C1. Do the freely elected head of government and national legislative representatives determine the policies of the government? 4 / 4

Elected officials freely determine government policy. In March 2020, the government passed the Health (Preservation and Protection and other Emergency Measures in the Public Interest) Act 2020 to combat the coronavirus pandemic. The law gave new emergency powers to government ministries and the police to enforce lockdowns and curfews.

C2. Are safeguards against official corruption strong and effective? 3 / 4

Ireland has a recent history of problems with political corruption but has introduced anticorruption legislation in recent years. The Corruption Offences Act, which took effect in 2018, modernized and consolidated existing anticorruption laws, though critics claimed that the legislation did not adequately address bribery.

Scandals involving Ireland's police (An Garda Síochána) have raised concerns about a lack of safeguards against corruption in that sector. In November 2020, eight members of the Garda were suspended following an inquiry into corruption.

A multi-agency review group examining anticorruption and antifraud structures in Ireland, established after the government completed a 2017 study of white-collar crime, made numerous recommendations in December 2020, including establishing an Advisory Council against Economic Crime and Corruption.

C3. Does the government operate with openness and transparency? 4 / 4

The public has broad access to official information under the 2014 Freedom of Information Act, though partial exemptions remain for the police and some other agencies. A Transparency Code requires open records on the groups and individuals that advise public officials on policy.

The government has been criticized for failing to consult meaningfully with civil society groups and relevant stakeholders in policy formulation, particularly regarding the Roma, Travellers, and people living with disabilities.

CIVIL LIBERTIES: 58 / 60
D. FREEDOM OF EXPRESSION AND BELIEF: 16 / 16
D1. Are there free and independent media? 4 / 4

Irish media are free and independent, and present a variety of viewpoints. However, the media sector is highly concentrated, with Independent News and Media (INM) controlling much of the newspaper market. The government has promised reforms of Ireland's restrictive defamation laws, which continue to receive criticism, including from the European Commission.

D2. Are individuals free to practice and express their religious faith or nonbelief in public and private? 4 / 4

Freedom of religion is constitutionally guaranteed. Although religious oaths are still required from senior public officials, there is no state religion, and adherents of other faiths face few impediments to religious expression. In recent years, the Roman Catholic Church has notably declined in the public eye, following a series of sexual abuse and other scandals involving the Church and its clergy.

D3. Is there academic freedom, and is the educational system free from extensive political indoctrination? 4 / 4

Academic freedom is respected. The Catholic Church operates approximately 90 percent of Ireland's schools, most of which include religious education from which parents may exempt their children. The constitution requires equal funding for schools run by different denominations.

D4. Are individuals free to express their personal views on political or other sensitive topics without fear of surveillance or retribution? 4 / 4

There are no significant impediments to open and free private discussion, including in personal online communications. However, Ireland's national identity card—the Public Services Card (PSC)—continued to cause controversy in 2020 due to data storage and privacy concerns.

E. ASSOCIATIONAL AND ORGANIZATIONAL RIGHTS: 12 / 12

E1. Is there freedom of assembly? 4 / 4

The right to assemble freely is respected, and peaceful demonstrations are held each year. However, emergency lockdown legislation adopted due to the COVID-19 pandemic in 2020 placed major restrictions on freedom of assembly. Arrests for violating lockdown regulations took place at protests in Dublin. The Irish Council for Civil Liberties (ICCL) criticized a criminal investigation into a Black Lives Matter protest held in Dublin in June.

E2. Is there freedom for nongovernmental organizations, particularly those that are engaged in human rights- and governance-related work? 4 / 4

Freedom of association is upheld, and nongovernmental organizations (NGOs) can operate freely.

E3. Is there freedom for trade unions and similar professional or labor organizations? 4 / 4

Labor unions operate without hindrance, and collective bargaining is legal and unrestricted.

F. RULE OF LAW: 14 / 16

F1. Is there an independent judiciary? 4 / 4

Ireland has a generally independent judiciary and a legal system based on common law. The long-awaited Judicial Council, a body which promotes judicial excellence, good conduct, and the independence of the judiciary, was established in December 2019 and met for the first time in February 2020.

F2. Does due process prevail in civil and criminal matters? 4 / 4

Due process generally prevails in civil and criminal matters. However, the police force has been affected by repeated corruption scandals in recent years. A new police commissioner was appointed in 2018; his predecessor resigned in 2017 after the irregular use of breathalyzer tests and questions about her approach toward whistleblowers stoked controversy.

The police received new powers to prosecute people who violated lockdown restrictions in 2020, as a part of legislation passed to combat the COVID-19 pandemic. In October, the police were criticized for searching student accommodations in Cork after they broke up a house party the previous month that had violated lockdown rules.

F3. Is there protection from the illegitimate use of physical force and freedom from war and insurgencies? 3 / 4

Irish prisons and detention facilities are frequently dangerous, unsanitary, overcrowded, and ill-equipped for prisoners with mental illness. However, the Irish Prison Service appears to have coped relatively well with the impact of COVID-19, submitting a "best practice" report to the World Health Organization (WHO) in June 2020.

Some politicians and communities have expressed concern about the impact of the United Kingdom's departure from the EU (known as Brexit) on aspects of the 1998 Good Friday Agreement, which ended a period of sectarian conflict in Northern Ireland known as the Troubles; some concerns relate to a perceived risk of unrest at the Northern Ireland border. However, the threat of violence in Ireland remained low in 2020.

A series of official inquiries in recent years have detailed decades of past physical, sexual, and emotional abuse—including forced labor as recently—against women and children in state institutions and by Catholic priests and nuns from the early 20th century until 1996, as well as collusion to hide the abuse. In 2015, the government launched a compensation scheme for sexual abuse survivors, though there were some instances of applicants being inappropriately denied compensation. In 2019, former prime minister Leo Varadkar issued a state apology over sexual abuse in schools. In December 2020, the government commission investigating the Catholic Church's and the State's complicity in the system that enabled the abuse announced that a final report regarding the Church-run "Mother and Baby Homes" would be published in January 2021.

F4. Do laws, policies, and practices guarantee equal treatment of various segments of the population? 3 / 4

According to a report from the Irish Network Against Racism, the number of reported racist incidents in Ireland in 2020 was almost double that in 2019. While existing legislation bans hate speech, Ireland lacks comprehensive hate-crime laws, and civil society organizations have criticized the laws that do exist as being out of date and ineffective. Following public consultations throughout the year, in December 2020 the justice minister announced plans to introduce new hate crime legislation in 2021 that would make it a criminal offense.

The EU Agency for Fundamental Rights reported in September 2020 that two-thirds of the Irish Travellers and Roma in Ireland face discrimination based on their ethnicity. The Council of Europe called the National Traveller and Roma Inclusion Strategy 2017–21 ineffective in a June 2019 report, and the government has committed to reviewing the strategy as part of its 2020 Programme for Government.

In 2020, concerns continued to be raised that people with disabilities face housing issues, are persistently institutionalized, and have suffered a severe reduction of social benefits in recent years. Advocacy groups criticized the government for underfunding disability services during the COVID-19 pandemic. There also have been concerns raised about Department of Health's guidance on ethical considerations of those in critical care as they relate to people with long-term conditions.

Irish law prohibits discrimination based on sexual orientation, but some social stigma against LGBT+ people persists.

The asylum application process is complex, and asylum seekers can be housed for lengthy periods in poor living conditions in a system known as Direct Provision. An advisory group recommended in October 2020 that the government end Direct Provision by 2023.

The 2015 International Protection Law expedites asylum procedures but focuses on enabling deportations rather than identifying and processing cases. In August 2020, the Irish Refugee Council (IRC), an NGO that supports asylum seekers, published a report which showed that 55 percent of asylum seekers interviewed felt unsafe and 50 percent felt they were unable to socially distance during the pandemic; a temporary Direct Provision center set up in March 2020 experienced a large COVID-19 outbreak.

Discrimination in the workplace on the basis of gender is illegal, though there is still a substantial gender pay gap.

G. PERSONAL AUTONOMY AND INDIVIDUAL RIGHTS: 16 / 16

G1. Do individuals enjoy freedom of movement, including the ability to change their place of residence, employment, or education? 4 / 4

There are ordinarily no restrictions on travel or the ability to change one's place of residence, employment, or education. However, emergency legislation due to the COVID-19 pandemic in 2020 has placed major restrictions on freedom of movement to and from Ireland but also within it, though the measures were usually implemented in conjunction with a rise of coronavirus cases. The pandemic is likely to exacerbate Ireland's housing crisis, particularly for low-income workers, according to a December 2020 KBC Bank.

G2. Are individuals able to exercise the right to own property and establish private businesses without undue interference from state or nonstate actors? 4 / 4

Private businesses are free to operate, and property rights are generally respected.

G3. Do individuals enjoy personal social freedoms, including choice of marriage partner and size of family, protection from domestic violence, and control over appearance? 4 / 4

Individuals in Ireland have gained expanded social freedoms in recent years. In a 2015 referendum, voters extended marriage rights to same-sex couples. That same year, the Children and Family Relationships Act extended adoption rights to same-sex and cohabiting couples, and the Gender Recognition Act allowed transgender individuals to obtain legal recognition without medical or state intervention, and—for married transgender people—without divorcing. In a 2018 referendum, voters abolished a constitutional amendment that made nearly all abortions illegal, and health providers began performing abortions in January 2019.

That same month, Ireland enacted the Domestic Violence Act 2018, which criminalized forms of emotional and psychological abuse. However, domestic and sexual violence against women remain serious problems, and marginalized and immigrant women have particular difficulty accessing support. In June 2020, figures released by An Garda Síochána showed a 25 percent rise in cases of domestic violence, linked to the COVID-19 pandemic.

G4. Do individuals enjoy equality of opportunity and freedom from economic exploitation? 4 / 4

People generally enjoy equality of opportunity. Workers have rights and protections under employment legislation. Although the government works to combat human trafficking and protect victims, undocumented migrant workers remain at risk of trafficking and labor exploitation. During the COVID-19 pandemic, journalists reported that working conditions in Ireland's meat processing plants were unsafe and posed a high risk of spreading the virus.

Israel

Population: 9,200,000
Capital: Jerusalem
Freedom Status: Free
Electoral Democracy: Yes

Note: The numerical scores and status listed above do not reflect conditions in the Gaza Strip or the West Bank, which are examined in separate reports. Although the international community generally considers East Jerusalem to be part of the occupied West Bank, it may be mentioned in this report when specific conditions there directly affect or overlap with conditions in Israel proper. Prior to its 2011 edition, *Freedom in the World* featured one report for Israeli-occupied portions of the West Bank and Gaza Strip and another for Palestinian-administered portions. *Freedom in the World* reports assess the level of political rights and civil liberties in a given geographical area, regardless of whether they are affected by the state, nonstate actors, or foreign powers. Disputed territories are sometimes assessed separately if they meet certain criteria, including boundaries that are sufficiently stable to allow year-on-year comparisons. For more information, see the report methodology and FAQ.

Overview: Israel is a multiparty democracy with strong and independent institutions that guarantee political rights and civil liberties for most of the population. Although the judiciary is comparatively active in protecting minority rights, the political leadership and many in society have discriminated against Arab and other ethnic or religious minority populations, resulting in systemic disparities in areas including political representation, criminal justice, education, and economic opportunity.

KEY DEVELOPMENTS IN 2020

- After two successive elections in 2019 failed produce a governing majority, new parliamentary elections were held in March, and right-leaning incumbent prime minister Benjamin Netanyahu formed a coalition government that included his centrist rival, Benny Gantz, in May. However, the coalition collapsed in December 2020, and elections were scheduled for March 2021.
- Netanyahu remained in office throughout the year despite being on trial for three separate corruption charges. For several months, his critics maintained weekly protests outside his residence in Jerusalem and at other locations across the country.
- Israeli officials were fairly successful at containing the COVID-19 pandemic in the first half of the year, and related restrictions on assembly and movement were not unusually long lasting or widely disproportionate to the health threat. A surge in cases that began in the summer led to a second lockdown, and a third round of restrictions were imposed in December as case numbers spiked again.

POLITICAL RIGHTS: 33 / 40

A. ELECTORAL PROCESS: 12 / 12

A1. Was the current head of government or other chief national authority elected through free and fair elections? 4 / 4

A largely ceremonial president is elected by the Knesset for one seven-year term. In 2014, Reuven Rivlin of the conservative Likud party was elected to replace outgoing president Shimon Peres, receiving 63 votes in a runoff against Meir Sheetrit of the centrist Hatnuah party.

The prime minister is usually the leader of the largest faction in the Knesset. In 2014, in a bid to create more stable governing coalitions, the electoral threshold for parties to win representation was raised from 2 percent to 3.25 percent, and the no-confidence procedure was revised so that opponents hoping to oust a sitting government must simultaneously vote in a new one.

The incumbent prime minister in 2020, Benjamin Netanyahu of Likud, had been in office since 2009. However, he served in a caretaker capacity from December 2018 through May 2020, as two elections in 2019 failed to result in a governing coalition. The March 2020 elections led to the formation of a unity government in which Netanyahu would serve as prime minister for the first 18 months and Benny Gantz of the centrist Blue and White bloc would then replace him. However, the agreement collapsed in December, and Netanyahu returned to his caretaker status pending new elections in March 2021.

A2. Were the current national legislative representatives elected through free and fair elections? 4 / 4

Members of the 120-seat Knesset are elected by party-list proportional representation for four-year terms, and elections are typically free and fair.

In the March 2020 elections, Likud won 36 seats, Blue and White won 33, and the Joint List—a coalition of parties representing Arab citizens of Israel, who often identify as Palestinian—took 15. Two ultra-Orthodox parties, Shas and United Torah Judaism, took 9 and 7 seats; the left-leaning alliance Labour-Gesher-Meretz won 7; and the right-wing parties Yisrael Beiteinu and Yemina captured 7 and 6 seats, respectively.

Objecting to the formation of the unity government, more than a dozen members of Blue and White formed an opposition faction in the Knesset called Yesh Atid–Telem. Also in opposition during 2020 were the Joint List, Yisrael Beiteinu, Yamina, and Meretz.

A3. Are the electoral laws and framework fair, and are they implemented impartially by the relevant election management bodies? 4 / 4

The fairness and integrity of elections are guaranteed by the Central Elections Committee (CEC), which is composed of delegations representing the various political groups in the Knesset and chaired by a Supreme Court judge. Elections are generally conducted in a peaceful and orderly manner, and all parties usually accept the results.

B. POLITICAL PLURALISM AND PARTICIPATION: 13 / 16

B1. Do the people have the right to organize in different political parties or other competitive political groupings of their choice, and is the system free of undue obstacles to the rise and fall of these competing parties or groupings? 3 / 4

Israel hosts a diverse and competitive multiparty system. However, parties or candidates that deny Israel's Jewish character, oppose democracy, or incite racism are prohibited. Under a 2016 law, the Knesset can remove any members who incite racism or support armed struggle against the state of Israel with a three-quarters majority vote; critics allege that the law is aimed at silencing Arab representatives. Two far-right Jewish candidates were barred from running in the September 2019 elections. In February 2020, the Supreme Court rejected a bid to exclude Joint List candidate Heba Yazbak, and she went on to win a Knesset seat in March.

B2. Is there a realistic opportunity for the opposition to increase its support or gain power through elections? 4 / 4

Israel has undergone multiple, peaceful rotations of power among rival political groups during its history. Opposition parties control several major cities, including Tel Aviv, and many Arab-majority towns are run by mayors from the Joint List parties.

B3. Are the people's political choices free from domination by forces that are external to the political sphere, or by political forces that employ extrapolitical means? 4 / 4

Israeli voters are generally free from coercion or undue influence by interest groups outside the political sphere. A 2017 law imposes funding restrictions on organizations that are not political parties but seek to influence elections. While it was aimed at limiting political interference by outside groups and wealthy donors, critics of the law said its provisions could affect civil society activism surrounding elections and infringe on freedoms of association and expression.

B4. Do various segments of the population (including ethnic, racial, religious, gender, LGBT+, and other relevant groups) have full political rights and electoral opportunities? 2 / 4

Political power in Israel is held disproportionately by Jewish men; while Ashkenazim (Jews of European descent) have historically enjoyed particular advantages, Mizrahim (Jews of Middle Eastern descent) have gained representation in recent decades.

Women generally enjoy full political rights in law and in practice, though they remain somewhat underrepresented in leadership positions and can encounter additional obstacles in parties and communities—both Jewish and Arab—that are associated with religious or cultural conservatism. Shas and United Torah Judaism continued to exclude women from their candidate lists in 2020, while Ra'am, an Islamist party on the Joint List, elected its first woman Knesset member.

In 2018, the Knesset adopted a new "basic law" known as the nation-state law, which introduced the principle that the right to exercise self-determination in the State of Israel belongs uniquely to the Jewish people, among other discriminatory provisions. The basic laws of Israel are considered equivalent to a constitution, and critics of the nation-state law said it created a framework for the erosion of non-Jewish citizens' political and civil rights.

Arab or Palestinian citizens of Israel already faced some discrimination in practice, both legal and informal. No Arab party has ever been formally included in a governing coalition, and Arabs generally do not serve in senior positions in government. However, in the immediate aftermath of the 2020 elections, the Joint List supported Benny Gantz for prime minister, marking the first time the Arab parties have endorsed a candidate since Yitzhak Rabin in 1992. Arab voter turnout also surged to nearly 65 percent in 2020, up from 49 percent in April 2019 and the highest level since 1999.

The roughly 600,000 Jewish settlers in the West Bank and East Jerusalem are Israeli citizens and can participate in Israeli elections. Arab residents of East Jerusalem have the option of obtaining Israeli citizenship, though most decline for political reasons. While these noncitizens are entitled to vote in municipal as well as Palestinian Authority (PA) elections, most have traditionally boycotted Israeli municipal balloting, and Israel has restricted PA election activity in the city. A Palestinian Jerusalem resident who is not a citizen cannot become mayor under current Israeli law. Israeli law strips noncitizens of their Jerusalem residency if they are away for extended periods, and a law adopted in 2018 empowers the interior minister to revoke such residency for those deemed to be involved in terrorism or treason-related offenses. Citizenship and residency status are denied to Palestinian residents of the West Bank or Gaza Strip who are married to Israeli citizens.

Courts can revoke the citizenship of any Israeli convicted of spying, treason, or aiding the enemy. Separately, it was reported during 2017 that the Interior Ministry had revoked the citizenship of dozens and possibly thousands of Bedouins over several years, citing decades-old registration errors.

Jewish immigrants and their immediate families are granted Israeli citizenship and residence rights. Other immigrants must apply for these rights, and it is difficult in practice for non-Jewish migrant workers and asylum seekers to obtain citizenship.

C. FUNCTIONING OF GOVERNMENT: 8 / 12

C1. Do the freely elected head of government and national legislative representatives determine the policies of the government? 3 / 4

The government and parliament are free to set and implement policies and laws without undue interference from unelected entities. Military service plays an important role in both political and civilian life, with many top officers entering politics at the end of their careers, but elected civilian institutions remain in firm control of the military.

In 2019, the failure of two successive elections to yield a governing majority meant that the country lacked a fully empowered government for the entire year, with the incumbents remaining in place in a caretaker capacity. The instability continued in 2020, as the government formed in the wake of the March elections collapsed after about seven months in office, necessitating the fourth round of balloting in just two years.

C2. Are safeguards against official corruption strong and effective? 2 / 4

High-level corruption investigations are relatively frequent, with senior officials implicated in several scandals and criminal cases in recent years. In November 2019, Netanyahu was indicted on separate charges of fraud, bribery, and breach of trust; police had recommended the charges in 2018 after conducting three investigations into his alleged acceptance of expensive gifts, his apparent attempt to collude with the owner of the newspaper *Yedioth Ahronoth* to secure positive coverage, and the granting of regulatory favors to telecommunications operator and media conglomerate Bezeq in return for positive coverage. Netanyahu denied the charges against him, accused law enforcement bodies of perpetrating "an attempted coup," and called for a commission to "investigate the investigators." He refused to step down as prime minister after the indictment and continued to hold office through 2020. He also pursued legislative approval of an immunity bill that would shield him and other lawmakers from prosecution while in office, though the measure had not passed at year's end. Pretrial hearings proceeded during the year, with the prosecution scheduled to formally open its case in early 2021.

Also during 2020, prosecutors continued to investigate Netanyahu's former personal attorney, a former navy commander, and a number of other former officials for alleged bribery related to a contract to purchase naval vessels. Police had recommended charges in 2018.

A law passed in 2017 limits the circumstances under which the police can file indictment recommendations when investigating elected officials and senior civil servants and increases the penalties for leaking a police recommendation or other investigative materials. While the law did not apply to existing investigations, the parliamentary opposition at the time accused the majority of trying to weaken law enforcement agencies to protect its political leadership.

C3. Does the government operate with openness and transparency? 3 / 4

Israel's laws, political practices, civil society groups, and independent media generally ensure a substantial level of governmental transparency, though recent corruption cases have illustrated persistent shortcomings. The Freedom of Information Law grants every citizen and resident of Israel the right to receive information from a public authority. However, the law includes blanket exemptions that allow officials to withhold information on the armed forces, intelligence services, the Atomic Energy Agency, and the prison system, potentially enabling the concealment of abuses.

CIVIL LIBERTIES: 43 / 60

D. FREEDOM OF EXPRESSION AND BELIEF: 12 / 16

D1. Are there free and independent media? 3 / 4

The Israeli media sector as a whole is vibrant and free to criticize government policy. While the scope of permissible reporting is generally broad, print articles on security matters are subject to a military censor. According to the results of a freedom of information request, in 2019 the military partially redacted a total of 1,973 news items and fully barred publication of 202 others, out of 8,127 stories submitted for review; both figures represented a decline from the previous year. The Government Press Office has occasionally withheld press cards from journalists to restrict them from entering Israel, citing security considerations.

A 2017 law allows police and prosecutors to obtain court orders that require the blocking of websites found to publish criminal or offensive content. Freedom of expression advocates warned that the measure could permit the suppression of legitimate speech.

Netanyahu's dual role as prime minister and communications minister between 2014 and 2017 raised questions about conflicts of interest involving the ministry's regulatory functions. He was forced to resign as communications minister in light of the police investigations into his alleged attempts to arrange favorable coverage from certain private media outlets. While the next two communications ministers were considered close allies of the prime minister, a Blue and White member, Yoaz Hendel, took the post as part of the unity government formed in May 2020.

D2. Are individuals free to practice and express their religious faith or nonbelief in public and private? 3 / 4

While Israel defines itself as a Jewish state, freedom of religion is largely respected. Christian, Muslim, and Baha'i communities have jurisdiction over their own members in matters of marriage, divorce, and burial. The Orthodox establishment governs personal status matters among Jews, drawing objections from many non-Orthodox and secular Israelis. Most ultra-Orthodox Jews, or Haredim, have been excused from compulsory military service under a decades-old exemption for those engaged in full-time Torah study. The Supreme Court, having struck down the existing exemption law as unconstitutional in 2017, has called for the Knesset to adopt new guidelines or begin enforcing normal conscription rules, repeatedly extending deadlines for it to do so. No new legislation had been adopted as of 2020.

Although the law protects the religious sites of non-Jewish groups, they face discrimination in the allocation of state resources as well as persistent cases of vandalism or harassment, which usually go unsolved.

Citing security concerns, Israeli authorities have set varying limits on access to the Temple Mount/Haram al-Sharif in East Jerusalem in recent years, affecting worshippers across the broader area. However, in 2018 the government lifted restrictions on Jewish lawmakers visiting the site that had been in place for nearly three years.

D3. Is there academic freedom, and is the educational system free from extensive political indoctrination? 3 / 4

Primary and secondary education is universal, though divided into multiple public school systems (state, state-religious, Haredi, and Arabic). School quality and resources are generally lower in mostly non-Jewish communities. A 2018 law bans groups that are in favor of legal action abroad against Israeli soldiers, or that otherwise undermine state educational goals by criticizing the military, from entering Israeli schools or interacting with students.

Israel's universities have long been centers for dissent and are open to all students, though security-related restrictions on movement limit access for West Bank and Gaza residents in practice.

D4. Are individuals free to express their personal views on political or other sensitive topics without fear of surveillance or retribution? 3 / 4

While private discussion in Israel is generally open and free, there are some restrictions on political expression. For example, the 2011 Boycott Law exposes Israeli individuals and groups to civil lawsuits if they advocate an economic, cultural, or academic boycott of the state of Israel or West Bank settlements.

E. ASSOCIATIONAL AND ORGANIZATIONAL RIGHTS: 9 / 12

E1. Is there freedom of assembly? 3 / 4

Protests and demonstrations are widely permitted and typically peaceful. However, some protest activities—such as desecration of the flag of Israel or a friendly country—can draw serious criminal penalties, and police have sometimes attempted to restrict peaceful demonstrations. Antigovernment protest activity continued throughout 2020 despite varying pandemic-related rules on social distancing. For several weeks, the authorities prohibited individuals from participating in protests more than a kilometer from their homes.

E2. Is there freedom for nongovernmental organizations, particularly those that are engaged in human rights- and governance-related work? 2 / 4

The environment for nongovernmental organizations (NGOs) has deteriorated in recent years. A law that took effect in 2012 requires NGOs to submit financial reports four times a year on support received from foreign government sources. Under a 2016 law, NGOs that receive more than half of their funding from foreign governments must disclose this fact publicly and in any written or oral communications with elected officials. The measure mainly affects groups associated with the political left that oppose Israel's policies toward the Palestinians; foreign funding for right-leaning groups that support Jewish settlements in the West Bank, for example, more often comes from private sources.

A 2017 law bars access to the country for any foreign individuals or groups that publicly support a boycott of Israel or its West Bank settlements. The measure was criticized by civil society organizations as an obstacle to the activities of many pro-Palestinian and human rights groups. In 2019, the Supreme Court upheld a deportation order that authorities had issued the previous year against Human Rights Watch's regional director, Omar Shakir, in part because the organization had called on businesses to stop operating in West Bank settlements to avoid complicity in human rights abuses. In a separate 2018 case, authorities sought to bar entry to a US student pursuing a graduate degree in Israel on the grounds that she had been involved with a proboycott organization in the past. The Supreme Court ruled later the same year that the 2017 law did not apply to the student, in part because it was meant to be preventive rather than punitive.

E3. Is there freedom for trade unions and similar professional or labor organizations? 4 / 4

Workers may join unions and have the right to strike and bargain collectively. Most of the workforce either belongs to Histadrut, the national labor federation, or is covered by its social programs and bargaining agreements.

F. RULE OF LAW: 11 / 16

F1. Is there an independent judiciary? 4 / 4

The judiciary is independent and regularly rules against the government. The Supreme Court has historically played a crucial role in protecting minority groups and overturning decisions by the government and the parliament when they threaten human rights. The court hears direct petitions from both Israeli citizens and Palestinian residents of the West Bank and Gaza Strip, and the state generally adheres to court rulings.

Some right-wing politicians have advocated reforms that would allow the Knesset to override the Supreme Court when it strikes down legislation. However, lawmakers overwhelmingly rejected such a bill in August 2020, with Likud members abstaining to avoid a rupture in the governing coalition.

F2. Does due process prevail in civil and criminal matters? 3 / 4

Although due process is largely guaranteed in ordinary cases, those suspected of security-related offenses are subject to special legal provisions. Individuals can be held in administrative detention without trial for renewable six-month terms. According to the human rights group B'Tselem, there were a total of 4,279 Palestinians from the occupied territories in Israeli Prison Service facilities at the end of June 2020, including 357 in administrative detention. Under criminal law, individuals suspected of security offenses can be held for up to 96 hours without judicial review under certain circumstances and be denied access to an attorney for up to 21 days.

According to Defense for Children International (DCI) Palestine, 151 Palestinian children (aged 12–17) from the occupied territories were being held in Israeli military detention as of June 2020. Although Israeli law prohibits the detention of children younger than 12, some are occasionally held. Most Palestinian child detainees are serving sentences—handed down by a special military court for minors created in 2009—for throwing stones or other projectiles at Israeli troops in the West Bank; acquittals on such charges are very rare, and the military courts have been criticized for a lack of due process protections. East Jerusalem Palestinian minors are tried in Israeli civilian juvenile courts.

F3. Is there protection from the illegitimate use of physical force and freedom from war and insurgencies? 2 / 4

Israeli border communities receive occasional rocket and artillery fire from Syria and the Gaza Strip. Israeli security forces and civilians also face the ongoing threat of small-scale terrorist attacks, most often involving stabbings or vehicular assaults. Human rights groups have sometimes accused police of using deadly force against stone throwers or perpetrators of stabbing and vehicular attacks when they did not pose a lethal threat.

The Supreme Court banned torture in a 1999 ruling, but said physical coercion might be permissible during interrogations in cases involving an imminent threat. Human rights organizations accuse the authorities of continuing to use some forms of physical abuse and other measures such as isolation, sleep deprivation, psychological threats and pressure, painful binding, and humiliation.

F4. Do laws, policies, and practices guarantee equal treatment of various segments of the population? 2 / 4

Jewish citizens, particularly those of Ashkenazi descent, typically enjoy practical advantages relative to the rest of the population on matters including legal treatment and socioeconomic conditions.

Arab or Palestinian citizens of Israel face de facto discrimination in education, social services, and access to housing and related permits. Aside from the Druze minority, they are exempted from military conscription, though they may volunteer. Those who do not serve are ineligible for the associated benefits, including scholarships and housing loans. The 2018 nation-state law downgraded Arabic from an official language of the country to a language with "special status," while another clause said the change would not "affect the status given to the Arabic language before this law came into force," suggesting that it would be a largely symbolic demotion. In 2019, the Organisation for Economic Co-operation and Development (OECD) released a report that found a significant and growing gap between the abilities of Hebrew-speaking students and those of their Arabic-speaking peers in Israeli schools.

The 2018 nation-state law also declared that the state "views the development of Jewish settlement as a national value and shall act to encourage and promote its establishment and strengthening." The Jewish National Fund (JNF-KKL), which owns about 13 percent of the land in Israel, has effectively maintained a Jewish-only land-leasing policy thanks to a land-swap arrangement with the Israel Land Authority, which grants the JNF-KKL replacement property whenever an Arab bidder obtains a parcel of its land.

Many of Israel's Bedouin citizens live in towns and villages that are not recognized by the state. Those in unrecognized villages cannot claim social services, are in some cases off the electricity grid, and have no official land rights, and the government routinely demolishes their unlicensed structures.

Israelis of Ethiopian origin suffer from discrimination—including in the criminal justice system—and lag behind the general population economically despite government integration efforts. In 2019, Ethiopian Israelis staged several days of demonstrations against police brutality after the fatal shooting of a teenager of Ethiopian descent by an off-duty police officer.

Women are treated equally in criminal and civil courts and have achieved substantial parity within Israeli society, though economic and other forms of discrimination persist, particularly among Arab and religious Jewish communities. Arab women are far less likely to be employed than either Arab men or Jewish women.

Discrimination based on sexual orientation is illegal, though LGBT+ people continue to face bias in some communities. Gay and transgender Israelis are permitted to serve openly in the military.

Individuals who enter the country irregularly, including asylum seekers, can be detained for up to a year without charges. Asylum applications, when fully processed, are nearly always rejected. In recent years the authorities have pressured thousands of African migrants and asylum seekers who entered the country irregularly—mostly from Eritrea and Sudan—to agree to be repatriated or deported to a third country, such as Rwanda or Uganda. There have been few new irregular entries since a barrier along the border with Egypt was completed in 2013, though there were more than 30,000 asylum seekers in the country as of 2020.

G. PERSONAL AUTONOMY AND INDIVIDUAL RIGHTS: 11 / 16
G1. Do individuals enjoy freedom of movement, including the ability to change their place of residence, employment, or education? 3 / 4

Security measures can sometimes present obstacles to freedom of movement, though military checkpoints are restricted to the West Bank. Informal local rules that prevent driving on the Sabbath and Jewish holidays can also hamper free movement. Some movement restrictions were imposed for public health purposes during 2020, but they were generally limited in duration and grounded in genuine epidemiological concerns.

G2. Are individuals able to exercise the right to own property and establish private businesses without undue interference from state or nonstate actors? 3 / 4

Property rights within Israel are effectively protected, and business activity is generally free of undue interference. Businesses face a low risk of expropriation or criminal activity, and corruption is not a major obstacle for private investors. However, the authorities' general commitment to property rights has been called into question given their handling of unrecognized Bedouin villages and settlement policies in the West Bank.

G3. Do individuals enjoy personal social freedoms, including choice of marriage partner and size of family, protection from domestic violence, and control over appearance? 3 / 4

Personal social freedoms are generally guaranteed. However, since religious courts oversee personal status issues, women face some disadvantages in divorce and other matters. Many ultra-Orthodox Jewish communities attempt to enforce unofficial rules on gender separation and personal attire. Marriages between Jews and non-Jews are not recognized by the state unless conducted abroad, nor are marriages involving a Muslim woman and a non-Muslim man. Israel recognizes same-sex marriages conducted abroad. Nonbiological parents in same-sex partnerships are eligible for guardianship rights. A 2018 law extended surrogacy rights to women without a male partner but not to men without a female partner, effectively excluding gay men.

G4. Do individuals enjoy equality of opportunity and freedom from economic exploitation? 2 / 4

Israel remains a destination for human-trafficking victims, and African migrants and asylum seekers residing in the country are especially vulnerable to forced labor and sex trafficking. The government works actively to combat trafficking and protect victims. Israel's legal foreign workers are formally protected from exploitation by employers, but these guarantees are poorly enforced. A smaller number of foreigners work in the country illegally. Histadrut has opened membership to foreign workers and called on employers to grant them equal rights. Discrimination against and exploitation of Palestinians from the occupied territories working in Israel remains commonplace.

Italy

Population: 60,300,000
Capital: Rome
Freedom Status: Free
Electoral Democracy: Yes

Overview: Italy's parliamentary system features competitive multiparty elections. Civil liberties are generally respected, but concerns about the rights of migrants persist, and regional inequalities are substantial and persistent. Endemic problems of corruption and organized crime pose an enduring challenge to the rule of law and economic growth.

KEY DEVELOPMENTS IN 2020

- Italy was the first country in Europe to experience a major COVID-19 outbreak, and remained one of the countries most severely afflicted by the pandemic. The government introduced rigid restrictions in March, including a nationwide lockdown and restrictions on commercial and industrial activities. Restrictions were eased during the summer, but reintroduced as a new pandemic wave began in autumn. According to researchers at the University of Oxford, the country registered over 2.1 million cases and 74,000 deaths by the end of 2020.
- In a September referendum, Italians voted overwhelmingly in favor of cutting the size of parliament by more than one third. The vote was held concurrently with several key regional elections that resulted in a boost to the fragile ruling coalition.

POLITICAL RIGHTS: 36 / 40

A. ELECTORAL PROCESS: 12 / 12

A1. Was the current head of government or other chief national authority elected through free and fair elections? 4 / 4

Parliament and regional representatives elect the president, whose role is largely ceremonial but sometimes politically influential, for a seven-year term. The legitimacy of the presidential vote rests largely on the fairness of legislative elections. Sergio Mattarella, a former constitutional judge backed by the center-left Democratic Party, was elected president in 2015.

The president appoints the prime minister, who serves as head of government and is often, but not always, the leader of the largest party in the Chamber of Deputies, Italy's lower house. The prime minister proposes a Council of Ministers that requires confirmation by parliament.

In August 2019 Giuseppe Conte, an independent law professor who was not a member of parliament, was reinstated as prime minister of a new center-left government formed by the Five Star Movement, the Democratic Party (PD), the Free and Equals (LeU), and Italia Viva.

A2. Were the current national legislative representatives elected through free and fair elections? 4 / 4

The bicameral parliament consists of the 630-member Chamber of Deputies and the 315-member Senate. Members of both houses are popularly elected for five-year terms, though the president can appoint five additional senators, and former presidents are also entitled to Senate seats.

The March 2018 elections were considered free and fair by international observers. A center-right coalition government led by the League party and the Five Star Movement was formed in June 2018, but it collapsed in August 2019 amid a coalitional crisis provoked by League leader Matteo Salvini. That September, a new government was forged by a coalition including the Five Star Movement, the PD, and LeU, later joined by Italia Viva. In 2020, a rise in public trust helped stabilize the government during the first phase of the COVID-19 crisis, but the coalition entered another period of fragility in December amid a second pandemic wave and sharp debate within the coalition regarding the prime minister's plan for economic recovery.

In a referendum held in September, 70 percent of Italians voted in favor of cutting the Chamber of Deputies to 400 seats, and the Senate to 200. Proponents of the change, particularly members of the Five Star Movement, argued that the move would reduce costs, while critics contended the shift would weaken parliamentary authority of and deliver minimal cost savings. Concurrent elections in nine regions led to gains for the League, but the governing PD maintained control of several key regions, and the balloting was perceived as a setback for right-wing opposition leader Matteo Salvini. The changes will take effect in 2023.

A3. Are the electoral laws and framework fair, and are they implemented impartially by the relevant election management bodies? 4 / 4

While Italy's electoral framework and campaign-finance regulations are complex, the elections they enable have consistently been deemed fair and credible.

The current electoral law, adopted by parliament in 2017, introduced a mixed system in both houses, with 36 percent of seats allocated using the first-past-the-post method, and 64 percent using a proportional, party-list method. The law encouraged coalition governments, as demonstrated by the 2018 election results.

In June 2020, the coalition-leading PD and Five Star parties presented a new electoral reform centered on a fully proportional, closed-list system, including a 5 percent threshold for electoral representation. However, disagreements among coalition members stymied progress on the bill during the rest of the year.

B. POLITICAL PLURALISM AND PARTICIPATION: 14 / 16

B1. Do the people have the right to organize in different political parties or other competitive political groupings of their choice, and is the system free of undue obstacles to the rise and fall of these competing parties or groupings? 4 / 4

Political parties are generally able to form and operate freely, and the political landscape features a high level of pluralism and competition. Since the beginning of the 1990s, politics have been characterized by unstable coalitions and the frequent emergence of new parties.

B2. Is there a realistic opportunity for the opposition to increase its support or gain power through elections? 4 / 4

Italy has a long record of frequent changes in the governing coalition, with multiple transfers of power since the early 1990s.

The September 2020 regional elections shifted the regional balance of power further to the right, with 14 of 20 Italian regions now ruled by right-wing or center-right coalitions. Opposition leader Salvini faced a challenge from a far-right ally, the Brothers of Italy, which won the regional presidency of Marche in 2020.

B3. Are the people's political choices free from domination by forces that are external to the political sphere, or by political forces that employ extrapolitical means? 3 / 4

The public is generally free to make political choices without undue interference. However, organized crime groups retain some ability to intimidate and influence politicians, especially at the local level, and to establish corruption networks abetted by public administrators. In 2020, the government used its authority to dissolve 11 town councils over ties to local mafia-like groups, leaving a total of 39 local governments under special administration as of year's end.

B4. Do various segments of the population (including ethnic, racial, religious, gender, LGBT+, and other relevant groups) have full political rights and electoral opportunities? 3 / 4

Electoral laws contain provisions designed to encourage political participation by linguistic minorities and promote gender parity, though progress toward full political representation for women and LGBT+ people remains slow.

The extremely limited political participation rights accorded to migrants limits their voice in national politics, a dynamic exacerbated by the emergence of a xenophobic and nationalist discourse in recent years. In October 2020, the government amended the tightened restrictions on citizenship and naturalization enacted in 2018, but maintained several provisions that imposed barriers to citizenship, including a lengthy processing period and an Italian-language proficiency requirement.

C. FUNCTIONING OF GOVERNMENT: 10 / 12

C1. Do the freely elected head of government and national legislative representatives determine the policies of the government? 4 / 4

Elected officials are able to craft and implement policy without improper interference from unelected entities. Prime Minister Conte has led two coalition governments since the 2018 elections without having won a seat in parliament. The coalition formed in

September 2019 commanded a legislative majority and generally was able to determine policies throughout 2020.

C2. Are safeguards against official corruption strong and effective? 3 / 4

Corruption remains a serious problem despite long-term efforts to combat it, and its impact is exacerbated when officials and members of organized crime networks jointly carry out graft schemes. Since 2018 Italy has strengthened its anticorruption framework. An anticorruption law adopted in 2019 tightened sanctions for corruption, reformed statutes of limitation to limit stalling tactics, and extended existing antimafia investigative tools to include corruption offenses. Despite this increased capacity, many sectors require additional reforms to limit graft, including public procurement.

C3. Does the government operate with openness and transparency? 3 / 4

The legal framework mandates administrative transparency and access to public information through a Freedom of Information Act (FOIA) adopted in 2016. Although the legislation designates access to information as a fundamental right, efforts to ensure compliance with FOIA requests by public administrators remain incomplete.

CIVIL LIBERTIES: 54 / 60 (+1)
D. FREEDOM OF EXPRESSION AND BELIEF: 15 / 16
D1. Are there free and independent media? 3 / 4

Freedom of the press is constitutionally guaranteed. Despite the rapid growth of the online news industry, traditional media still play a large role in news consumption. There are more than 100 daily newspapers, most of them locally or regionally based, as well as political party papers, free papers, and weekly publications. Concentration of ownership remains a major concern, but many media viewpoints are available. Internet access is generally unrestricted.

The Ministry of Interior registered 163 acts of intimidation against journalists in 2020, a sharp spike from the 87 such events recorded in 2019. Organized crime threats—which have resulted in permanent police protection for over a dozen journalists—accounted for 17 percent of the acts, while 42 percent were attributed to social or political motivations, including a series of attacks by protesters opposed to the COVID-19 lockdowns.

Defamation remains criminalized in Italy, and lawmakers have repeatedly failed to address the persistent use of frivolous lawsuits intended to deter factual reporting; a legislative reform effort initiated in 2019 stalled in November 2020.

D2. Are individuals free to practice and express their religious faith or nonbelief in public and private? 4 / 4

Religious freedom is constitutionally guaranteed and respected in practice. There is no official religion; while the Roman Catholic Church receives certain benefits under a treaty with the state, other groups have access to similar benefits through their own accords.

Some local governments have raised obstacles to the construction and recognition of mosques, and right-wing political parties have stoked anti-Muslim attitudes. Antisemitic acts have also trended upward in recent years.

D3. Is there academic freedom, and is the educational system free from extensive political indoctrination? 4 / 4

Academic freedom is generally respected.

D4. Are individuals free to express their personal views on political or other sensitive topics without fear of surveillance or retribution? 4 / 4

There are no major restrictions on people's ability to discuss controversial or sensitive topics in public without fear of surveillance or retribution.

E. ASSOCIATIONAL AND ORGANIZATIONAL RIGHTS: 12 / 12

E1. Is there freedom of assembly? 4 / 4

The freedom to assemble peacefully is guaranteed in the constitution and typically upheld in practice. COVID-19 containment measures included restrictions on freedom of assembly, though a series of demonstrations against lockdown measures took place throughout the year.

E2. Is there freedom for nongovernmental organizations, particularly those that are engaged in human rights- and governance-related work? 4 / 4

Nongovernmental organizations (NGOs) are generally free to organize and operate. During the first Conte government, Italian authorities engaged in repeated standoffs with NGO-operated ships involved in rescue operations of trafficked and smuggled migrants and refugees in the Mediterranean Sea. In 2019 new decrees limited access to Italian ports, leading to extended wait times for disembarkation that created serious health risks for migrants, and imposed large potential fines for noncompliance. In October 2020, the second Conte government amended the decrees, lowering—though not eliminating—the fines.

E3. Is there freedom for trade unions and similar professional or labor organizations? 4 / 4

Trade unions are generally free to organize and operate. The constitution recognizes the right to strike but places restrictions on strikes by employees in essential sectors like transportation, sanitation, and health, as well as by some self-employed individuals, including lawyers, doctors, and truck drivers.

COVID-19 containment measures did not include restrictions on the right to strike, and unions organized several work stoppages throughout the year to demand effective workplace sanitation and safety measures.

F. RULE OF LAW: 13 / 16 (+1)

F1. Is there an independent judiciary? 4 / 4 (+1)

The judiciary is generally independent and autonomous. Allegations of abuse of power and corruption involving members of the High Council of the Judiciary, which controls internal governance of the judiciary, have led to reform efforts, including an August 2020 proposal to improve the Council's accountability and transparency; the bill remained pending in parliament as of the end of 2020.

Organized crime networks continue to threaten judges and prosecutors involved in anti-mafia processes, particularly in Calabria, but state protection measures function adequately, and both attacks and the incidence of mafia-related judicial corruption have declined overall in recent years.

Score Change: The score improved from 3 to 4 due to declines in both judicial corruption and efforts to intimidate judges in recent years.

F2. Does due process prevail in civil and criminal matters? 3 / 4

Due process rights are largely upheld. However, judicial procedures are often characterized by lengthy delays; Italy has one of the lowest numbers of judges per capita in the European Union. The government has been criticized for denying detained migrants access to lawyers.

F3. Is there protection from the illegitimate use of physical force and freedom from war and insurgencies? 3 / 4

While the population is generally free from major threats to physical security, there have been reports of excessive use of force by police and prison guards, particularly against undocumented migrants. Asylum seekers and undocumented migrants have been often held in overcrowded and unhygienic conditions. At the outset of the coronavirus pandemic, prisoners angry about increased isolation and fearful of disease transmission in overcrowded facilities rioted in dozens of prisons, leaving at least 13 prisoners dead and several hundred injured inmates and guards.

F4. Do laws, policies, and practices guarantee equal treatment of various segments of the population? 3 / 4

The law prohibits discrimination based on gender, race, sexual orientation, and other categories, and these protections are generally enforced. However, members of the Romany minority have unequal access to housing, and many live in segregated settlements that lack adequate infrastructure. LGBT+ people face societal discrimination and occasional acts of violence. Police registered 1,119 hate crimes in 2019; over 70 percent involved racism and xenophobia, with approximately 10 percent linked to sexual orientation or gender identity.

Italy's treatment of migrants, refugees, and asylum seekers has been subject to significant criticism in recent years. In late 2018, parliament approved legal changes that tightened conditions for granting asylum and humanitarian protection, reduced access to services, and eased deportation conditions. Following the 2019 coalitional realignment, Prime Minister Conte promised to roll back the anti-immigrant policies. The decree enacted in October 2020 allows migrants and refugees to apply for residency on humanitarian protection grounds if they "risk being subjected to torture or inhumane treatment" at home and expands access to public services, but does not offer regularized status to those who lost legal residency under the 2018 decrees.

G. PERSONAL AUTONOMY AND INDIVIDUAL RIGHTS: 14 / 16

G1. Do individuals enjoy freedom of movement, including the ability to change their place of residence, employment, or education? 4 / 4

Individuals are generally free to travel and to change their place of residence, employment, and education.

G2. Are individuals able to exercise the right to own property and establish private businesses without undue interference from state or nonstate actors? 3 / 4

The legal and regulatory framework supports property rights and the operation of private businesses, but corruption and organized crime can hinder normal business activity, as can onerous bureaucratic obstacles. Delays in court proceedings often undermine enforcement of protections for property rights.

According to experts on organized crime, mafia groups exploited the social and economic crises provoked by the COVID-19 pandemic, distributing goods and expanding control of cash-starved local businesses via loan-sharking and money-laundering operations.

G3. Do individuals enjoy personal social freedoms, including choice of marriage partner and size of family, protection from domestic violence, and control over appearance? 4 / 4

The law protects individual freedom on personal status issues such as marriage and divorce. Same-sex civil unions with nearly all the benefits of marriage are permitted, and courts have begun to recognize second-parent adoption rights for same-sex couples. Though public awareness of the problem of domestic violence is increasing due to advocacy campaigns, it remains a persistent issue, and calls to the national domestic violence rose significantly during the COVID-19 lockdown.

G4. Do individuals enjoy equality of opportunity and freedom from economic exploitation?
3 / 4

In the last few years, Italy has adopted measures to combat human trafficking and labor exploitation, but both phenomena remain concerns, especially with respect to asylum seekers, refugees, and migrants from Eastern Europe. The COVID-19 pandemic increased migrants' vulnerability to exploitation and worsened labor and living conditions, even as many were excluded from large-scale government aid programs instituted in response to the crisis. In May the government passed a law allowing undocumented workers to apply for short-term residency permits, but critics suggested the program left out workers in many sectors and would do little to combat exploitation, especially of mistreated workers in the agricultural sector. During the year, the government assented to demands by Italy's major trade union confederations and repeatedly extended a ban on firing workers amid the coronavirus emergency.

The trafficking of women and girls for sexual exploitation remains a concern. In a positive step, the October amendments to the 2018 immigration decrees ended asylum seekers' exclusion from access to reception centers, which had left victims of trafficking without assistance.

Jamaica

Population: 2,800,000
Capital: Kingston
Freedom Status: Free
Electoral Democracy: Yes

Overview: Jamaica's political system is democratic and features competitive elections and orderly rotations of power. However, corruption remains a serious problem, and long-standing relationships between officials and organized crime figures are thought to persist. Violent crime remains a concern, as does harassment and violence against LGBT+ people.

KEY DEVELOPMENTS IN 2020

- During most of the year, Jamaica was less severely afflicted by the COVID-19 pandemic than many countries in the Americas, but cases began to rise steadily from late August; according to researchers at the University of Oxford, the country registered approximately 13,000 cases and over 300 deaths by year's end.
- General elections held in September produced a convincing win for the governing Jamaica Labour Party (JLP) and Prime Minister Andrew Holness. The JLP gained 57 percent of the vote and 49 of 63 seats in the House of Representatives, while the opposition People's National Party (PNP) received 43 percent and 14 seats.

POLITICAL RIGHTS: 34 / 40

A. ELECTORAL PROCESS: 12 / 12

A1. Was the current head of government or other chief national authority elected through free and fair elections? 4 / 4

The British monarch is the ceremonial head of state and is represented by a governor general. The prime minister is the head of government; the position is appointed after elections by the governor general, and usually goes to the leader of the majority party or coalition. The prime minister's legitimacy rests largely on the conduct of legislative elections, which in Jamaica are generally free and fair. Jamaica Labour Party (JLP) leader Holness became prime minister after the party's narrow win in the 2016 election; he retained and strengthened his position in the 2020 election.

A2. Were the current national legislative representatives elected through free and fair elections? 4 / 4

Jamaica's bicameral Parliament consists of a 63-member House of Representatives, elected for five years, and a 21-member Senate, with 13 senators appointed on the advice of the prime minister and 8 on the advice of the opposition leader. Senators also serve five-year terms.

In 2020, the governing JLP won a convincing victory, taking 57 percent of the vote; given the dynamics of Jamaica's first-past-the-post electoral system, this translated to wins in 49 districts. The opposition People's National Party (PNP) performed poorly, winning 43 percent and only 14 seats. The elections were considered free and fair. However, due to COVID-19 and voter apathy, turnout was by far the lowest in the country's history (other than the PNP-boycotted election in 1983), at just 37 percent. A Jamaican nongovernmental organization (NGO), Citizens Action for Free and Fair Elections, said that it was satisfied that the elections were "conducted fairly and in the main free from fear."

A3. Are the electoral laws and framework fair, and are they implemented impartially by the relevant election management bodies? 4 / 4

Electoral laws are generally fair, and they are implemented impartially by the Electoral Commission of Jamaica.

B. POLITICAL PLURALISM AND PARTICIPATION: 13 / 16

B1. Do the people have the right to organize in different political parties or other competitive political groupings of their choice, and is the system free of undue obstacles to the rise and fall of these competing parties or groupings? 4 / 4

Political parties form and operate without restriction. Although various smaller parties are active, politics at the national level are dominated by the social democratic PNP and the more conservative JLP.

B2. Is there a realistic opportunity for the opposition to increase its support or gain power through elections? 4 / 4

Opposition parties operate freely, and political power has alternated between the PNP and JLP.

B3. Are the people's political choices free from domination by forces that are external to the political sphere, or by political forces that employ extrapolitical means? 2 / 4

Powerful criminal organizations can influence voters who live in areas under their control. These organizations have used intimidation or other tactics to ensure high voter turnout for particular candidates or parties in exchange for political favors; there were scattered reports of such activity in the 2020 election.

B4. Do various segments of the population (including ethnic, racial, religious, gender, LGBT+, and other relevant groups) have full political rights and electoral opportunities? 3 / 4

Women are underrepresented in politics. Eleven women were elected to the lower house in 2016, amounting to 17.5 percent of the body. The situation improved somewhat in 2020, with a record eighteen women elected, or 29 percent. During the campaign, PNP leader Peter Phillips stated that domestic labor obligations are among the factors inhibiting women's political involvement, sparking debate about how to increase women's participation.

The LGBT+ community experiences harassment and violence, and this limits the ability of openly LGBT+ people to engage in political and electoral processes. Political attacks are often couched in anti-LGBT+ rhetoric.

C. FUNCTIONING OF GOVERNMENT: 9 / 12

C1. Do the freely elected head of government and national legislative representatives determine the policies of the government? 4 / 4

The elected prime minister and national legislative representatives determine the policies of the government. However, powerful criminal groups, as well as corruption in politics, can affect democratic policymaking.

C2. Are safeguards against official corruption strong and effective? 3 / 4

Long-standing links between officials and organized crime figures persist. Government bodies continue to pursue corruption investigations, and cases often end in convictions. However, there are criticisms in the media and from NGOs that authorities are reluctant to pursue some cases, while others are subject to extensive delays. Government whistleblowers are not well protected. In December 2020, for example, newspapers reported that several employees of the Jamaica Cultural Development Commission had faced intimidation after an audit report suggesting irregularities in the use of taxpayers' money was leaked to the press.

New legal efforts to fight corruption have been mounted in recent years. These include the approval of the Integrity Commission Act of 2017, which requires lawmakers and public officials to disclose their income, liabilities, and assets; the act also streamlined anticorruption laws and empowered a single commission to monitor compliance. The Integrity Commission began its work in 2018. However, its effectiveness has been limited by several high-profile resignations, delays in issuing reports, and a lack of prosecutions resulting from its work. In August 2020, the Integrity Commission was criticized for its decision not to reveal the names of five current and former parliamentarians who had been referred to prosecutors in connection with deficient asset declarations.

In a 2019 report to the Senate, the Integrity Commission warned that managers at oil refining firm Petrojam had spent J$2.6 million ($19,700) on birthday parties, and that the firm was unable to justify major outlays. Investigations into graft at Petrojam continued throughout 2020; in June, the Commission submitted additional reports to Parliament and prosecutors, even as observers raised concerns that a member of the Integrity Commission also served on the Petrojam board.

In October 2019, former education minister Ruel Reid, two relatives, and Caribbean Maritime University president Fritz Pinnock were arrested on suspicion of corruption, fraud, and the misappropriation of as much as J$50 million ($380,000) in public funds for their personal use. The case remained pending as of the end of 2020, but further arrests were made during the year.

C3. Does the government operate with openness and transparency? 2 / 4

An access to information law has been in effect since 2004, though it contains a number of exemptions. Legislative processes are often opaque.

In September 2020, the JLP government rescinded an informal convention that placed six pivotal parliamentary oversight committees under opposition leadership; officials cited alleged PNP ineffectiveness to justify appointing government legislators to head four of the committees.

CIVIL LIBERTIES: 46 / 60 (+2)

D. FREEDOM OF EXPRESSION AND BELIEF: 15 / 16

D1. Are there free and independent media? 4 / 4

The constitutional right to free expression is generally respected. Most newspapers are privately owned and express a variety of views. Broadcast media are largely publicly owned, but espouse similarly pluralistic points of view. Journalists occasionally face intimidation, especially in the run up to elections.

In June 2020, Parliament completed passage of a data-protection bill that critics suggested was overly broad in scope and could allow authorities to compel journalists investigated under its provisions to reveal their sources.

D2. Are individuals free to practice and express their religious faith or nonbelief in public and private? 4 / 4

Freedom of religion is constitutionally protected and generally respected in practice. While laws banning Obeah—an Afro-Caribbean shamanistic religion—remain on the books, they are not actively enforced.

D3. Is there academic freedom, and is the educational system free from extensive political indoctrination? 4 / 4

The government does not restrict academic freedom.

D4. Are individuals free to express their personal views on political or other sensitive topics without fear of surveillance or retribution? 3 / 4

Individuals are generally free to express their personal views on political or other sensitive topics. However, the presence of powerful criminal groups in some urban neighborhoods can discourage people from talking openly about such groups' activities.

In 2017, the House of Representatives passed a bill establishing the groundwork for a National Identification System (NIDS). Privacy advocates expressed concern about possible overcollection of people's personal information, and in 2019, the Supreme Court ruled the NIDS unconstitutional, stating that a requirement that citizens submit biometric data infringed on Jamaicans' privacy. In 2020, the government revised the bill, making enrollment voluntary; passage remained pending at year's end.

E. ASSOCIATIONAL AND ORGANIZATIONAL RIGHTS: 11 / 12 (+1)

E1. Is there freedom of assembly? 4 / 4 (+1)

Freedom of assembly is provided for by the constitution and is largely respected in practice. Protests are occasionally marred by violence or otherwise unsafe conditions, though such events in recent years have been held without major incident.

Score Change: The score improved from 3 to 4 because there have been no recent crackdowns or serious threats to free assembly.

E2. Is there freedom for nongovernmental organizations, particularly those that are engaged in human rights-and governance-related work? 4 / 4

Jamaica has a robust and vibrant civil society with many active community groups. However, some struggle financially or have difficulty attracting volunteers, negatively impacting their levels of engagement. Others are funded by the central government, but for the most part act autonomously. NGOs are well represented in the education, health, and environment sectors, and many provide support for the most marginalized groups in society.

E3. Is there freedom for trade unions and similar professional or labor organizations? 3 / 4

Around 20 percent of the workforce is unionized, and antiunion discrimination is illegal. Labor unions are politically influential and have the right to strike. However, workers in essential services must undergo an arbitration process with the Ministry of Labor and Social Security before they may legally strike, and the definition of the work constituting "essential services" is broad. There are reports of private employers laying off unionized workers and then later hiring them as contract workers.

The Industrial Disputes Tribunal (IDT) is allowed to reinstate workers whose dismissals are found to be unjustified, although cases before the IDT often take much longer to settle than the 21 days stipulated by the law.

F. RULE OF LAW: 9 / 16 (+1)

F1. Is there an independent judiciary? 4 / 4 (+1)

Judicial independence is guaranteed by the constitution, and while the judiciary is widely considered independent, corruption remains a problem in some lower courts.

Score Change: The score improved from 3 to 4 because there have been no major incidents in recent years suggesting that judicial independence is compromised.

F2. Does due process prevail in civil and criminal matters? 2 / 4

A large backlog of cases and a shortage of court staff at all levels continue to undermine the justice system. The vast majority of arrests are made without a warrant, detainees frequently lack access to legal counsel, and trials are often delayed for many years or dismissed due to systemic failures. In order to reduce the backlog, the government passed the 2017 Criminal Justice (Plea Negotiations and Agreements) Act, which increased avenues for the resolution of cases outside of trial. Since its passage, prosecutors, judges, and government officials have noted an unwillingness from some defendants to consider plea deals.

F3. Is there protection from the illegitimate use of physical force and freedom from war and insurgencies? 2 / 4

Killings by police remain a serious problem in Jamaica. According to the Independent Commission of Investigations, 115 people were shot and killed by security personnel in 2020. This represented an increase from the 86 killings in 2019, though police killings have declined overall in recent years. Prosecutions for illegal killings by members of the security forces remain rare.

Gang and vigilante violence remain common. Police reported 1,323 murders in 2020—a similar figure to the previous two years—giving Jamaica the highest homicide rate (approximately 47 per 100,000) in the Americas in 2020. The country is a transit point for cocaine, and much of the island's violence is the result of warfare between drug-trafficking organizations. Kingston's insular "garrison" communities, home to scores of gangs, remain the epicenter of violence and serve as safe havens for criminal groups. Many initiatives to address the problem have been undertaken by successive governments, but crime and violence remain deeply entrenched.

States of emergency (SOEs), which provide expanded authority to the security forces, are frequently imposed in response to localized spikes in violence, but in June 2020 the government announced that the various SOEs in place across the country would be allowed to expire in July in anticipation of the general election.

F4. Do laws, policies, and practices guarantee equal treatment of various segments of the population? 1 / 4

Harassment and violence targeting LGBT+ people remains a major concern, and such instances are frequently ignored by the police. Anti-LGBT+ discrimination is pervasive.

In 2014, the government expanded the Offences Against the Person Act to criminalize the promotion of violence against any category of persons, including LGBT+ individuals, via audio or visual materials. Jamaica's first public pride event took place in 2015, and subsequent events have grown larger, though they are still met with government reticence. Some high-profile politicians have also spoken out publicly in support of the Jamaica Forum of Lesbians, All-Sexuals and Gays (J-FLAG), a rights group, in recent years. In November 2020, the government accepted several recommendations made by the UN Human Rights Council, including strengthening antidiscrimination policies and improving investigations in cases of violence against LGBT+ people.

Legislation against sodomy, which is punishable by 10 years in prison with hard labor, has been challenged in court and at the Inter-American Commission on Human Rights (IACHR). In 2018, a parliamentary subcommittee proposed a national referendum on repealing Jamaica's antisodomy law, but the move was criticized by LGBT+ activists, who felt legislators should scrap the law themselves; resolution remained pending throughout 2020.

Women enjoy the same legal rights as men but suffer employment discrimination and tend to earn less than men for performing the same job. Acceptance of Rastafarians is increasing, but discrimination persists, particularly in schools; in 2020, Rastafarian advocates criticized a July Supreme Court decision that a school did not violate a child's constitutional rights when it barred her attendance unless she cut her dreadlocks.

G. PERSONAL AUTONOMY AND INDIVIDUAL RIGHTS: 11 / 16

G1. Do individuals enjoy freedom of movement, including the ability to change their place of residence, employment, or education? 3 / 4

Although there are constitutional guarantees of freedom of movement, political and communal violence frequently precludes the full enjoyment of this right. States of emergency that were enacted during much of 2019 and 2020 restricted movement, with residents of affected areas facing roadblocks, random searches, and identity checks. There are no formal restrictions on people's ability to change their place of employment or education.

G2. Are individuals able to exercise the right to own property and establish private businesses without undue interference from state or non-state actors? 3 / 4

Jamaica has an active private sector and a powerful probusiness lobby. Individuals are free to establish businesses subject to legal requirements, which are not onerous. Recent reforms have included expediting the incorporation process, making electricity in Kingston more consistent, and easing the import process. However, corruption and crime can still hamper normal business activity. The World Bank's 2020 *Doing Business* report noted difficulties in paying taxes, registering property, and enforcing contracts.

G3. Do individuals enjoy personal social freedoms, including choice of marriage partner and size of family, protection from domestic violence, and control over appearance? 2 / 4

Legal protections for women and girls are poorly enforced, and violence and discrimination remain widespread. There is no blanket ban on spousal rape, nor are there laws against sexual harassment. Child abuse, including sexual abuse, is widespread.

G4. Do individuals enjoy equality of opportunity and freedom from economic exploitation? 3 / 4

Residents of neighborhoods where criminal groups are influential are at a heightened risk of becoming victims of human traffickers. Because of the poverty in certain communities and high-profile tourism industry, child sex tourism is present in some of Jamaica's resort areas, according to local NGOs.

Japan

Population: 126,000,000
Capital: Tokyo
Freedom Status: Free
Electoral Democracy: Yes

Overview: Japan is a multiparty parliamentary democracy. The ruling Liberal Democratic Party (LDP) has governed almost continuously since 1955, with stints in opposition from 1993 to 1994 and 2009 to 2012. Political rights and civil liberties are generally well respected. Outstanding challenges include ethnic and gender-based discrimination and claims of improperly close relations between government and the business sector.

KEY DEVELOPMENTS IN 2020

- In August, Prime Minister Shinzō Abe announced that he would step down for health reasons. The ruling LDP held a party caucus in September and chose Yoshihide Suga as its new leader; Suga took office as prime minister two days later.
- It was reported in October that the prime minister's office had refused to confirm the nominations of six professors to the Science Council of Japan, an independent science advisory panel, raising concerns about academic freedom.
- The first case of COVID-19 in Japan was confirmed in January. Case counts declined after a first peak in April, rose again for a period in late July and early August, and surged for a third time in November and December. By year's end the cumulative number of cases was more than 240,000, and more than 3,500 deaths had been reported. The government declared a state of emergency from April to late May, but the move did not give it the authority to enforce lockdowns or restrict movement within the country. The Olympic Games, originally scheduled to take place in July and August, were postponed until 2021 as a result of the pandemic.

POLITICAL RIGHTS: 40 / 40

A. ELECTORAL PROCESS: 12 / 12

A1. Was the current head of government or other chief national authority elected through free and fair elections? 4 / 4

The prime minister is the head of government and is chosen by the freely elected parliament. The prime minister selects the cabinet, which can include a limited number of ministers who are not members of the parliament. Japan's emperor serves as head of state in a ceremonial capacity.

Shinzō Abe, who had become the country's longest-serving prime minister since taking office for a second time in 2012, announced in August 2020 that he would step down for health reasons. The LDP chose Chief Cabinet Secretary Yoshihide Suga as its new leader at a party caucus in September, and the parliament voted to confirm him as prime minister two days later.

A2. Were the current national legislative representatives elected through free and fair elections? 4 / 4

The parliament, or Diet, has two chambers. The more powerful lower house, the House of Representatives, has 465 members elected to maximum four-year terms through a mixture of single-member districts and proportional representation. The upper house, the House of Councillors, has 245 members serving fixed six-year terms, with half elected every three years using a mixture of nationwide proportional representation and prefecture-based voting. The prime minister and his cabinet can dissolve the lower house, but not the upper house. The lower house can also pass a no-confidence resolution that forces the cabinet to either resign or dissolve the lower house.

Legislative elections in Japan are free and fair. In the most recent lower house elections, held in 2017, the LDP won 284 seats, and an allied party, Komeito, took 29. The opposition Constitutional Democratic Party (CDP) won 55, the Party of Hope secured 50, and smaller parties and independents captured the remainder. In July 2019 elections for the upper house, the LDP-led coalition retained 71 seats out of the 124 contested, giving it a comfortable majority of 141 seats in the chamber, although it fell short of the two-thirds supermajority required to revise the constitution. The CDP won 17 seats, and other seats went to smaller parties and independents.

A3. Are the electoral laws and framework fair, and are they implemented impartially by the relevant election management bodies? 4 / 4

Japan's electoral laws are generally fair and well enforced. Campaigning is heavily regulated, which typically benefits incumbents, although the rules are applied equally to all candidates. In June 2020, a former justice minister and his wife, an LDP lawmaker, were arrested on suspicion of violating the election law by handing out cash to politicians and supporters; they were indicted the following month.

Malapportionment in favor of the rural districts from which the LDP draws significant support has been a persistent problem, despite a series of reforms to reduce the disparity with urban districts. A November 2020 Supreme Court ruling upheld the constitutionality of the most recent upper house elections, but called on lawmakers to address the remaining gap in voting power between the most and least populated constituencies.

B. POLITICAL PLURALISM AND PARTICIPATION: 16 / 16
B1. Do the people have the right to organize in different political parties or other competitive political groupings of their choice, and is the system free of undue obstacles to the rise and fall of these competing parties or groupings? 4 / 4

Parties generally do not face undue restrictions on registration or operation. In August 2020, two opposition parties—the CDP and the Democratic Party for the People—agreed to merge in an attempt to form a united front against the ruling LDP. Some new parties gained seats in the 2019 upper house elections.

B2. Is there a realistic opportunity for the opposition to increase its support or gain power through elections? 4 / 4

While the LDP has governed for most of Japan's postwar history, there have been democratic transfers of power to and from alternative parties. Opposition parties are represented in the parliament and govern at the subnational level.

B3. Are the people's political choices free from domination by forces that are external to the political sphere, or by political forces that employ extrapolitical means? 4 / 4

People's political choices are generally free from improper interference by powerful interests that are not democratically accountable.

B4. Do various segments of the population (including ethnic, racial, religious, gender, LGBT+, and other relevant groups) have full political rights and electoral opportunities? 4 / 4

Citizens enjoy equal rights to vote and run in elections regardless of gender, ethnicity, religion, sexual orientation, or gender identity.

Women remain underrepresented in government. There were no women contenders in the September 2020 contest to select a new LDP president, with male-led factions appearing to hinder their rise. A nonbinding 2018 gender parity law urges parties to nominate equal numbers of male and female candidates. In the 2019 upper house elections, 28.1 percent of all candidates and 22.6 of winning candidates were women, both record highs in Japan.

Around 600,000 ethnic Koreans born in Japan hold special residency privileges but not Japanese citizenship, meaning they are ineligible to participate in any elections at the national and local levels. Most but not all are South Korean nationals, and they have the option of applying for Japanese citizenship.

The Ainu, an Indigenous people numbering at least 20,000, live mostly on the northern island of Hokkaido. The Ainu Party was launched in 2012 to increase their political representation, though it has yet to win seats in the Diet.

C. FUNCTIONING OF GOVERNMENT: 12 / 12

C1. Do the freely elected head of government and national legislative representatives determine the policies of the government? 4 / 4

Elected officials are free to govern without interference, though senior civil servants have some influence over policy.

C2. Are safeguards against official corruption strong and effective? 4 / 4

The prevalence of corruption in government is relatively low, media coverage of political corruption scandals is widespread and vigorous, and officials who are implicated face criminal prosecution. For instance, in December 2019, an LDP incumbent in the lower house was indicted on charges of taking bribes from a Chinese company. He was arrested again in August 2020 on charges of offering witnesses money in exchange for falsely testifying in court. Separately, it was reported in December 2020 that two former agriculture ministers had taken bribes from a food company.

Some government officials have close relations with business leaders and retiring bureaucrats often quickly secure high-paying positions with companies that receive significant government contracts.

C3. Does the government operate with openness and transparency? 4 / 4

The government generally operates with openness and transparency. Access to information legislation allows individuals to request information from government agencies, though in practice the law has not always been implemented effectively. Government officials have at times withheld information from lawmakers and the public in connection with political scandals. In December 2020, prosecutors charged one of Abe's aides with failing to report financial details related to annual banquets for the former prime minister's political supporters that allegedly violated campaign spending laws. Both Abe and Suga publicly apologized for making false statements in connection with the case.

CIVIL LIBERTIES: 56 / 60

D. FREEDOM OF EXPRESSION AND BELIEF: 15 / 16

D1. Are there free and independent media? 3 / 4

Freedom of the press is guaranteed in the constitution, and Japan has a highly competitive media sector. However, press freedom advocates have expressed concern about a 2014 law that allows journalists to be prosecuted for revealing state secrets, even if the information was unknowingly obtained. A 2017 report by the UN special rapporteur on freedom of expression noted concern about pressure on the media from the government, and recommended the repeal of Article 4 of the Broadcast Act, which gives the government the power to determine what information is "fair" and thus acceptable for public broadcast.

Under the traditional *kisha kurabu* (press club) system, institutions such as government ministries and corporate organizations have restricted the release of news to journalists and media outlets with membership in their clubs. In 2020, in order to maintain social distancing during the COVID-19 pandemic, the Cabinet Office limited access to its briefings for freelancers and foreign correspondents, while guaranteeing access for members of the cabinet press club. While the club system has been criticized for privileging the major dailies and other established outlets that belong to it and potentially encouraging self-censorship, in recent years online media and weekly newsmagazines have challenged the daily papers' dominance of political news with more aggressive reporting.

D2. Are individuals free to practice and express their religious faith or nonbelief in public and private? 4 / 4

Freedom of religion is guaranteed by the constitution, and there are no substantial barriers to religious expression or the expression of nonbelief.

D3. Is there academic freedom, and is the educational system free from extensive political indoctrination? 4 / 4

Academic freedom is constitutionally guaranteed and mostly respected in practice, but education and textbooks have long been a focus of public and political debate. While there is not a national curriculum or single official history text, the Ministry of Education's screening process has approved textbooks that downplay Japan's history of imperialism and war atrocities.

In October 2020, it was reported that the prime minister's office had refused to confirm the nomination of six professors to the Science Council of Japan, an independent advisory panel. The nominees had opposed government-backed security legislation, and human rights activists argued that the unusual move to reject them raised concerns about academic freedom.

D4. Are individuals free to express their personal views on political or other sensitive topics without fear of surveillance or retribution? 4 / 4

The government generally does not restrict personal expression or private discussion. Some observers have raised concerns that antiterrorism and anticonspiracy legislation that went into effect in 2017 could permit undue surveillance.

E. ASSOCIATIONAL AND ORGANIZATIONAL RIGHTS: 12 / 12
E1. Is there freedom of assembly? 4 / 4

Freedom of assembly is protected under the constitution, and peaceful demonstrations take place frequently. In 2020, protests were held on topics including opposition to proceeding with the Olympic Games in 2021, racial discrimination and support for the Black Lives Matter movement, human rights violations by the Chinese government, and the controversy surrounding nominations to the Science Council of Japan.

E2. Is there freedom for nongovernmental organizations, particularly those that are engaged in human rights- and governance-related work? 4 / 4

Nongovernmental organizations (NGOs) are generally free from undue restrictions and remained diverse and active in 2020.

E3. Is there freedom for trade unions and similar professional or labor organizations? 4 / 4

Most workers have the legal right to organize, bargain collectively, and strike. However, public-sector workers are barred from striking, and some, such as firefighters and prison staff, cannot form unions. Labor unions are active and exert political influence through the Japanese Trade Union Confederation and other groupings.

F. RULE OF LAW: 15 / 16
F1. Is there an independent judiciary? 4 / 4

Japan's judiciary is independent. For serious criminal cases, a judicial panel composed of professional judges and *saiban-in* (lay judges), selected from the general public, render verdicts.

F2. Does due process prevail in civil and criminal matters? 4 / 4

Constitutional guarantees of due process are generally upheld. However, observers have argued that trials often favor the prosecution. There are reports that suspects have been detained on flimsy evidence, arrested multiple times for the same alleged crime, or subjected to lengthy interrogations that yield what amount to forced confessions. Police can detain suspects for up to 23 days without charge. Access to those in pretrial detention is sometimes limited.

New legislation adopted in 2017 added nearly 300 categories of conspiracy offenses to the criminal code in order to help unravel terrorist plots and organized crime networks. Critics of the changes raised concerns that they gave the government too much authority to restrict civil liberties.

F3. Is there protection from the illegitimate use of physical force and freedom from war and insurgencies? 4 / 4

People in Japan are generally protected from the illegitimate use of physical force and the threat of war and insurgencies. Violent crime rates are low. However, organized crime is fairly prominent, particularly in the construction and nightlife sectors; crime groups also run drug-trafficking and loansharking operations.

No executions were carried out in 2020, marking the first such year since 2011. Prisoners facing death sentences or accused of crimes that could carry the death penalty are held in solitary confinement, sometimes for years at a time. There are frequent reports of substandard medical care in prisons. Human Rights Watch in April 2020 called for a reduction in the population of detention facilities in Japan, arguing that COVID-19 prevention and treatment measures in the prison system were inadequate.

F4. Do laws, policies, and practices guarantee equal treatment of various segments of the population? 3 / 4

Societal discrimination against various minority groups has generally declined over time, but it can affect access to housing and employment.

A law adopted in 2016 was intended to eliminate discrimination against Japan's estimated three million *burakumin*—descendants of feudal-era outcasts. The law obliges national and local governments to provide advice, support, and education on the issue, but it does not assign penalties for acts of discrimination.

A 2019 law officially recognized the Ainu as an Indigenous people of Japan, though critics noted that it failed to offer an apology for past mistreatment.

Japan-born descendants of colonial subjects (particularly ethnic Koreans and Chinese) also experience discrimination. A 2016 hate speech law calls on the government to take steps to eliminate discriminatory speech against ethnic minorities, but it does not carry any penalties for perpetrators.

LGBT+ people face social stigma and in some cases harassment. There is no national law barring discrimination based on sexual orientation or gender identity. In 2016, sexual harassment regulations for national public officials were modified to prohibit harassment on the basis of sexual orientation or gender identity. Employment discrimination and sexual harassment against women are common.

Asylum is granted to less than 1 percent of those who apply each year under Japan's strict screening process, and very few refugees are accepted for third-country resettlement in Japan.

G. PERSONAL AUTONOMY AND INDIVIDUAL RIGHTS: 14 / 16

G1. Do individuals enjoy freedom of movement, including the ability to change their place of residence, employment, or education? 4 / 4

There are few significant restrictions on internal or international travel, or on individuals' ability to change their place of residence, employment, and education.

The government was criticized for its restrictions on entry for foreign travelers during the COVID-19 pandemic, as the limits applied even to permanent residents seeking reentry; the rules were eased for residents in September 2020. Internal travel was discouraged, but the government had no legal authority to impose lockdowns.

G2. Are individuals able to exercise the right to own property and establish private businesses without undue interference from state or nonstate actors? 4 / 4

Property rights are generally respected. People are free to establish private businesses, although Japan's economy is heavily regulated.

G3. Do individuals enjoy personal social freedoms, including choice of marriage partner and size of family, protection from domestic violence, and control over appearance? 3 / 4

While personal social freedoms are mostly protected, there are some limitations. The country's system of family registration, *koseki*, recognizes people as members of a family unit and requires married couples to share a surname, which usually defaults to the husband's last name. This can create legal complications for women as well as children born out of wedlock or to divorced parents, among others.

There is no legal recognition of same-sex marriage in Japan, though some municipal and prefectural governments have passed local legislation allowing the registration of same-sex partnerships.

Domestic violence is punishable by law, and protective orders and other services are available for victims, but such abuse often goes unreported.

G4. Do individuals enjoy equality of opportunity and freedom from economic exploitation?
3 / 4

Individuals generally enjoy equality of opportunity, and the legal framework provides safeguards against exploitative working conditions. However, long workdays are common in practice and have been criticized as harmful to workers' health.

Many workers are temporary or contract employees with substantially lower wages, fewer benefits, and less job security than regular employees.

Commercial sexual exploitation remains a problem. Traffickers frequently bring foreign women into the country for forced sex work by arranging fraudulent marriages with Japanese men.

Jordan

Population: 10,700,000
Capital: Amman
Freedom Status: Not Free
Electoral Democracy: No

Status Change: Jordan's status declined from Partly Free to Not Free due to harsh new restrictions on freedom of assembly, a crackdown on the teachers' union following a series of strikes and protests, and factors including a lack of adequate preparations that harmed the quality of parliamentary elections during the COVID-19 pandemic.

Overview: Jordan is a monarchy in which the king plays a dominant role in politics and governance. The parliament's lower house is elected, but the electoral system puts the opposition at a disadvantage, and the chamber wields little power in practice. The media and civil society groups are hampered by restrictive laws and government pressure. The judicial system lacks independence and often fails to ensure due process.

KEY DEVELOPMENTS IN 2020

- Jordanian authorities initiated one of the world's harshest COVID-19 lockdowns in March, after King Abdullah II invoked a preexisting defense law. Jordanians were confined to their homes, and grocery stores and pharmacies were among the establishments shuttered during a three-day lockdown that month. While many measures were lifted in June, nightly curfews and mass-gathering limits remained in force at year's end.
- The government shuttered the country's teacher's union in July, after it accused the government of reneging on a salary deal reached in 2019. Authorities forcibly dispersed demonstrations against the closure—arresting over 250 people by August—and forced detainees to sign pledges promising to refrain from future demonstrations to secure their release.

- Voters elected a new parliament in November, with tribal elites and progovernment businesspeople representing the bulk of the new body. The Islamic Action Front (IAF)—the political arm of the Muslim Brotherhood in Jordan—won five seats in contest marred by a dearth of campaigning, lower turnout due to the ongoing COVID-19 pandemic, and continued malapportionment.

POLITICAL RIGHTS: 11 / 40 (−1)

A. ELECTORAL PROCESS: 2 / 12 (−1)

A1. Was the current head of government or other chief national authority elected through free and fair elections? 0 / 4

Jordan's hereditary monarch, King Abdullah II, holds broad executive powers. He appoints and dismisses the prime minister and cabinet and may dissolve the bicameral National Assembly at his discretion. Constitutional amendments adopted in 2016 empowered the king to make a number of other appointments, including the crown prince and a regent, without a royal decree countersigned by the prime minister or other cabinet ministers.

Abdullah II dissolved the parliament in September 2020, and Omar al-Razzaz, a former World Bank economist and education minister, resigned in early October. Al-Razzaz was succeeded by Bisher al-Khasawneh, a veteran diplomat and royal adviser, who was named to the post several days later.

A2. Were the current national legislative representatives elected through free and fair elections? 1 / 4

The king appoints the 65 members of the upper house of the parliament, the Senate. The lower house, the 115-seat House of Representatives, is elected for four-year terms or until the parliament is dissolved. Its members win office through races in 23 multimember districts, with 15 seats reserved for the leading women candidates who failed to capture district seats. Twelve district seats are reserved for religious and ethnic minorities.

The royal court announced its intention to trigger an election in a July 2020 statement, and Abdullah II dissolved the parliament in late September. However, uncertainty over the early-November polling date amid the ongoing COVID-19 pandemic prompted some candidates to delay campaign efforts. International observers, who regularly monitor parliamentary elections, were largely absent.

Independents, many of whom were tribal figures and businesspeople considered loyal to the monarchy, won 133 seats. The IAF won five, along with the Islah Alliance and the Muslim Center Party. Voter turnout stood at 29.9 percent, down from 36 percent in 2016. Vote buying, which was observed in 2016, became more common during the November 2020 contest, partially due to the dire economic situation caused by the pandemic.

Elections were held in 2017 for mayors, local and municipal councils, and 12 new governorate councils created under a 2015 decentralization law. However, 15 percent of the governorate council seats are appointed, and the councils have no legislative authority. A quarter of the seats in the Amman municipal council are also appointed by the government. As with the parliamentary elections, independent tribal candidates won the vast majority of seats, while the IAF and its allies won a plurality of the few seats captured by party-based candidates.

A3. Are the electoral laws and framework fair, and are they implemented impartially by the relevant election management bodies? 1 / 4 (−1)

Elections are administered by the Independent Election Commission (IEC), which generally receives positive reviews from international monitors in terms of technical management, though irregularities continue to be reported. IEC members are appointed by royal decree.

The 2016 electoral-law reform introduced multiple-vote proportional representation for parliamentary elections, replacing a single nontransferable vote system that favored progovernment businesspeople and tribal elites over opposition-oriented political parties. The new law also redrew district lines in an attempt to mitigate acute malapportionment that has long placed urban voters at a severe disadvantage.

Even after these changes, rural and tribal voters, who make up the regime's support base, remain heavily overrepresented. For example, 59,000 eligible voters in the district of Ma'an elected four legislators after the new system was introduced, whereas the first district of Zarqa, which is dominated by Jordanian citizens of Palestinian origin, had over 450,000 voters electing six legislators. After the November 2020 poll, tribal elites and progovernment businesspeople remained overrepresented within the parliament itself.

The legal framework for elections is unstable. Major changes are often introduced weeks before polling day, hindering campaign efforts. Candidate registration is reportedly easier in some progovernment areas. The IEC has also shown inconsistency managing voter rolls in recent elections, though voter registration was made automatic ahead of the 2016 poll.

Score Change: The score declined from 2 to 1 because weaknesses in the existing legal framework and continued malapportionment allowed an environment favoring progovernment candidates to persist during the 2020 elections.

B. POLITICAL PLURALISM AND PARTICIPATION: 6 / 16

B1. Do the people have the right to organize in different political parties or other competitive political groupings of their choice, and is the system free of undue obstacles to the rise and fall of these competing parties or groupings? 2 / 4

Political parties based on ethnicity, race, gender, or religion are banned in Jordan. Parties must receive approval from the Ministry of Political and Parliamentary Affairs. Authorities have reportedly intimidated individuals attempting to form political parties and there is a long-standing fear of creating or joining political parties due to the regime's historically harsh repression of them.

While the IAF has been tolerated, it suffers from electoral malapportionment, which affects its urban support base. Its parent organization, the Muslim Brotherhood, has been targeted by the authorities for several years. In 2015, the government licensed the offshoot Muslim Brotherhood Society (MBS) and moved to invalidate the original organization's legal registration. The Muslim Brotherhood's offices were forcibly shuttered in 2016, after the regime prevented it from holding internal elections, exacerbating preexisting divisions and weakening it politically. In July 2020, the organization lost an appeal against the transfer of its offices to the MBS, with the Court of Cassation ordering its dissolution in its ruling. The Muslim Brotherhood vowed to appeal, and the IAF participated in the November 2020 poll despite the ruling.

The electoral system favors tribally affiliated independents over political parties with specific ideologies and platforms, as does the patronage-based political culture. In October 2020, the al-Hayat Center for Civil Society Development, a local nongovernmental organization (NGO), reported that only 12 percent of candidates relied on party lists to earn votes.

B2. Is there a realistic opportunity for the opposition to increase its support or gain power through elections? 1 / 4

The political system—including the overrepresentation of rural voters—limits the ability of any party-based opposition to make significant gains. The IAF and the Islah Alliance, which it supported in the November 2020 poll, won a combined nine percent of lower-house seats. Moreover, the constitutional authority of the monarchy means that no opposition force can win control of the executive branch by democratic means alone.

B3. Are the people's political choices free from domination by forces that are external to the political sphere, or by political forces that employ extrapolitical means? 1 / 4

While voters and candidates are generally free from overt threats or violence, they remain heavily influenced by tribal affiliations and the state-sponsored patronage networks that accompany them. The Jordanian intelligence service is widely believed to influence the electoral process. Citizens' political participation is also constrained by the fact that many important positions are appointed rather than elected.

B4. Do various segments of the population (including ethnic, racial, religious, gender, LGBT+, and other relevant groups) have full political rights and electoral opportunities? 2 / 4

Women have equal political rights, and female candidates previously won seats beyond the legal quotas set for the parliament and subnational councils, but cultural prejudices remain an obstacle to women's full participation in practice. Four women won off-quota seats on governorate councils in 2017. Women performed well at the municipal and local levels that year, but none won mayoral posts. No women won parliamentary seats beyond the 15-seat quota in the November 2020 poll.

Nine lower-house seats are reserved for Christians and three for ethnic Circassians and Chechens together. Christians are not permitted to contest nonreserved seats. Citizens of Palestinian origin, who tend to live in urban areas, make up a majority of the overall population but remain politically underrepresented.

C. FUNCTIONING OF GOVERNMENT: 3 / 12

C1. Do the freely elected head of government and national legislative representatives determine the policies of the government? 0 / 4

The king dominates policymaking and the legislative process. The appointed government submits all draft legislation to the House of Representatives, which may approve, reject, or amend bills, though they require approval from the appointed Senate and the king to become law. Groups of 10 or more lawmakers can propose legislation, but the House must then refer it to the government before it can return to the chamber as a draft law. Among other royal prerogatives, the king unilaterally appoints the heads of the armed forces, the intelligence service, and the gendarmerie.

C2. Are safeguards against official corruption strong and effective? 2 / 4

The government has undertaken some efforts to combat widespread corruption, and the Integrity and Anti-Corruption Commission (IACC) is tasked with investigating allegations. However, successful prosecutions—particularly of high-ranking officials—are historically rare. Anticorruption efforts are undermined by a lack of genuinely independent enforcement institutions and restrictions on investigative journalism and civil society activism.

In June 2020, the government launched a crackdown targeting businesspeople and politicians suspected of tax evasion, money laundering, and customs evasion, after expanding the IACC's powers. By July, authorities raided 650 firms and were reportedly examining the tax records of 70 individuals. While Jordanians cautiously welcomed the crackdown, observers warned that political opponents were also targeted by the government.

C3. Does the government operate with openness and transparency? 1 / 4

Access-to-information laws are vague, lack procedural detail, and contain sweeping exceptions. Officials are not required to make public declarations of their income and assets. The National Assembly does not exercise effective or independent oversight of the government's budget proposals. Activists and journalists who attempt to investigate state or royal finances are subject to arrest on defamation and other charges.

CIVIL LIBERTIES: 23 / 60 (–2)

D. FREEDOM OF EXPRESSION AND BELIEF: 7 / 16

D1. Are there free and independent media? 1 / 4

Jordanian media laws are restrictive, vague, and arbitrarily enforced. Various statutes penalize defamation, criticism of the king or state institutions, harming Jordan's relations with foreign states, blasphemy, and any content considered to lack objectivity. Government gag orders and informal instructions to media outlets regarding news coverage are common. News sites face onerous registration requirements that, if not met, can serve as a justification for blocking. Journalists rarely face serious violence or significant jail time for their work, but they often practice self-censorship.

Journalists faced severe restrictions under COVID-19-related measures. In March 2020, the cabinet halted the publication of all newspapers for two weeks. In April, the government issued a vaguely worded decree prohibiting the dissemination of pandemic-related information that would "cause panic." According to the Committee to Protect Journalists, four journalists operating in Jordan were arrested for reporting or commenting on the ongoing pandemic as the year progressed, and two were still in custody at year's end.

The government also sought to restrict media coverage of other subjects as the year progressed. Immediately after the July 2020 closure of the country's Teachers' Syndicate, the attorney general issued a wide-ranging gag order prohibiting discussion of the subject. Human Rights Watch counted the detention—and subsequent release—of two journalists for reporting on the matter by late August, while two others were assaulted by authorities during that period.

D2. Are individuals free to practice and express their religious faith or nonbelief in public and private? 2 / 4

Islam is the state religion. The government monitors sermons at mosques for political, sectarian, or extremist content and issues prescribed texts and themes. Muslim clerics require government authorization to preach or dispense religious guidance. Many Christian groups are recognized as religious denominations or associations and can worship freely, though they cannot proselytize among Muslims. While converts from Islam are not prosecuted for apostasy, they face bureaucratic obstacles and harassment in practice. Unrecognized religious groups are allowed to practice their faiths but suffer from a number of disadvantages stemming from their lack of legal status. Atheists and agnostics are required to list a religious affiliation on government documents.

D3. Is there academic freedom, and is the educational system free from extensive political indoctrination? 2 / 4

Intelligence services reportedly monitor academic events and campus life, and administrators work with state officials to scrutinize scholarly material for politically sensitive content.

D4. Are individuals free to express their personal views on political or other sensitive topics without fear of surveillance or retribution? 2 / 4

Open discussion of topics such as politics, the monarchy, religious affairs, and security issues is inhibited by the threat of punishment under the various laws governing expression. The telecommunications law requires companies to enable the tracking of private communications upon the issuance of a court order, and authorities are allowed to order surveillance of people suspected of terrorism. Many Jordanians hold a long-standing belief that government agents routinely listen to their phone calls and monitor their online activities.

Under cybercrime legislation, internet users can face fines or prison terms as long as three months if they are convicted of defamation for online comments. A number of activists and protesters arrested in 2020 were charged with offenses related to social media posts in which they criticized the government.

E. ASSOCIATIONAL AND ORGANIZATIONAL RIGHTS: 1 / 12 (−2)
E1. Is there freedom of assembly? 0 / 4 (−1)

Jordanian law limits free assembly. Authorities require prior notification for any demonstration or event and have broad discretion to disperse public gatherings. At times, the Interior Ministry cancels planned public events without advance notice or explanation. Violations of the law on assembly can draw fines and jail time. Security forces are known to engage in violent confrontations with protesters.

The government further restricted the right to assemble in response to the ongoing COVID-19 pandemic. In March 2020, it used the Defense Law to restrict public gatherings of more than 10 people, and later 20; restrictions on assembly persisted even after other measures were rolled back in June. Authorities used these powers to disperse demonstrations after the Teachers' Syndicate was closed in late July. Several dozen protesters were arrested in an Amman demonstration held several days after the union's closure, and some were physically attacked by police. Security forces similarly attacked participants of protests held in several cities in July and August. Some protesters were later pressured to sign pledges promising to refrain from further activity, under penalty of hefty fines. In addition, the authorities restricted Facebook Live, limiting the ability of social media users to view footage of the demonstrations.

Score Change: The score declined from 1 to 0 because the government used emergency powers to place strict limits on assembly, forcibly dispersed protests against the closure of the Teachers' Syndicate in July and August, and restricted communications services used to broadcast those protests.

E2. Is there freedom for nongovernmental organizations, particularly those that are engaged in human rights- and governance-related work? 1 / 4

While many local and international NGOs are able to operate in the country, there are significant restrictions on civil society. The Ministry of Social Development has the authority to deny registration and requests for foreign funding, and can disband organizations it finds objectionable. The ministry has broad supervisory powers over NGO operations and activities, and board members must be vetted by state security officials. In practice, these regulations are applied in an opaque and arbitrary manner.

E3. Is there freedom for trade unions and similar professional or labor organizations? 0 / 4 (−1)

Workers have the right to form unions, but only in 17 designated industries. Groups must obtain government approval and join the country's semiofficial union federation, the General Federation of Jordanian Trade Unions (GFJTU). The right to strike is limited by requirements for advance notice and mediation, and participants in an illegal strike are subject to dismissal. No new trade unions have been allowed to form in Jordan since 1976. Although the kingdom has agreed to many of the International Labour Organization's fundamental conventions, it has failed to ratify the Freedom of Association and Protection of the Right to Organise Convention of 1948.

In 2013, a dozen unofficial trade unions formed the Jordanian Federation of Independent Trade Unions (FITU). Lacking official status, they are not allowed to establish headquarters, collect fees from their members, or engage in collective bargaining. They also face heavy pressure from the GFJTU and governmental bodies to cease their activities and shut down.

The Teachers' Syndicate began the longest public-sector strike in Jordanian history in September 2019, which ended after a deal was struck that October. The union later accused the government of reneging on the deal, with its leader criticizing then premier al-Razzaz in a July 2020 speech. Later that month, the government ordered a two-year closure of the syndicate, shuttering offices and arresting its 13-member board. Over 250 people were subsequently detained as protests opposing the shuttering continued through August. In late December, a court handed one-year sentences to five syndicate leaders and ordered the organization's permanent dissolution, though the defendants vowed to appeal and were bailed.

Score Change: The score declined from 1 to 0 because authorities raided and closed the headquarters and branch offices of the teachers' union, jailed hundreds of its members in July and August, and ordered the organization's permanent dissolution in a December court ruling.

F. RULE OF LAW: 7 / 16

F1. Is there an independent judiciary? 2 / 4

The judiciary's independence is limited. Under 2016 constitutional amendments, the king unilaterally appoints the entire Constitutional Court and the chair of the Judicial Council, which nominates civil court judges and is mostly comprised of senior judiciary members. Judges of both the civil and the Sharia (Islamic law) courts—which handle personal status matters for Muslims—are formally appointed by royal decree. The Justice Ministry has the power to monitor judges, promote them, and determine their salaries, further weakening the branch's autonomy.

F2. Does due process prevail in civil and criminal matters? 1 / 4

Police can hold suspects for up to six months without filing formal charges, and governors are empowered to impose administrative detention for up to one year. In practice, the authorities often ignore procedural safeguards against arbitrary arrest and detention, holding individuals incommunicado or beyond legal time limits. Criminal defendants generally lack access to counsel before trial, impairing their ability to mount a defense. Despite a constitutional prohibition, courts allegedly accept confessions extracted under torture.

F3. Is there protection from the illegitimate use of physical force and freedom from war and insurgencies? 2 / 4

Torture and other mistreatment in custody are common and rarely draw serious penalties. Prison conditions are generally poor, and inmates reportedly suffer from beatings and other abuse by guards. Terrorist attacks remain a threat to physical security. In November 2019, Jordanian authorities said they had disrupted a plot to attack US and Israeli targets in the country earlier in the year; two suspects who were allegedly inspired by the Islamic State militant group went on trial that month.

F4. Do laws, policies, and practices guarantee equal treatment of various segments of the population? 2 / 4

Women face discrimination in law and in practice. For example, women's testimony is not equal to men's in Sharia courts, and certain social benefits favor men over women. Jordanians of Palestinian origin are often excluded from jobs in the public sector and security forces, which are dominated by East Bank tribes. Discrimination against LGBT+ people is prevalent and includes the threat of violence, though consensual same-sex sexual activity is not specifically prohibited by law. The authorities have denied registration to NGOs that support LGBT+ rights.

Refugees and asylum seekers have not historically received permanent settlement in Jordan, though individuals residing in the country are usually allowed to remain while UN agencies seek their placement in third countries. Refugees often lack access to work permits, and work informally. Jordan is not a signatory to the Convention and Protocol Relating to the Status of Refugees.

The Office of the UN High Commissioner for Refugees (UNHCR) counted 752,000 refugees in Jordan in November 2020, and separately reported 662,000 hailing from Syria at the beginning of November. The government, which claims to host nearly double that number, has taken inconsistent steps in supporting this population; it agreed to issue 200,000 work permits in return for a loan-and-investment package in a 2016 compact, and reached the 190,000-permit mark in July 2020. In 2018, it legalized the status of several thousand Syrian refugees living outside of camps, but also prohibited refugees from accessing subsidized health care. Syrian refugees are at risk of refoulement, with at least 16 refugees forcibly transferred to the Rukban camp near the Syrian border in August 2020. Amnesty International reported that some refugees who arrived there in July returned to Syria, while another was forcefully sent to territory controlled by Syrian authorities.

Citizens living in Jordan proper risk the arbitrary revocation of citizenship or documentation if they are of Palestinian descent.

G. PERSONAL AUTONOMY AND INDIVIDUAL RIGHTS: 8 / 16

G1. Do individuals enjoy freedom of movement, including the ability to change their place of residence, employment, or education? 2 / 4

Jordanians generally enjoy freedom of domestic movement and international travel, though international flights were restricted between March and September 2020 due to COVID-19-related measures. Refugees and migrant workers face impediments to travel, and are often unable to change employers. Employers reportedly confiscate migrant workers' passports. Children of Jordanian mothers and non-Jordanian fathers, who lack citizenship themselves, have difficulty accessing jobs, education, and health care without a special identity card that is difficult to obtain.

G2. Are individuals able to exercise the right to own property and establish private businesses without undue interference from state or nonstate actors? 2 / 4

The legal framework generally supports property rights for citizens, but women do not have equal access to property under Sharia-based inheritance rules. Private business activity is hampered by obstacles such as corruption and the abuse of political or other connections.

G3. Do individuals enjoy personal social freedoms, including choice of marriage partner and size of family, protection from domestic violence, and control over appearance? 2 / 4

Personal social freedoms are limited by the country's conservative culture and specific laws. The government does not recognize marriages between Muslim women and non-Muslim men. Matters such as marriage and divorce are handled by religious courts, which place women and converts from Islam at a disadvantage and restrict some interfaith marriages. Women are not allowed to pass citizenship onto their children.

However, modest legal improvements have been enacted in recent years. In 2017, the parliament adopted legislation to better regulate the processing of domestic violence complaints. Other laws enacted that year abolished a penal code provision that allowed rapists to avoid punishment by marrying their victims. Reduced sentences are still possible for those who murder a spouse caught committing adultery, and spousal rape is not a crime.

G4. Do individuals enjoy equality of opportunity and freedom from economic exploitation?
2 / 4

Migrant workers, who are the majority of the Jordanian garment industry's workforce, are especially vulnerable to exploitative labor practices. Labor rights organizations have raised concerns about poor working conditions, forced labor, and sexual abuse in Qualifying Industrial Zones, where mostly female and foreign factory workers process goods for export. Rules governing matters such as the minimum wage, working hours, and safety standards are not well enforced, particularly in certain sectors like agriculture and construction, and among migrant workers. The influx of Syrian refugees has exacerbated the situation by expanding the pool of laborers willing to work in the informal sector for low wages. According to official data from 2016, the number of child laborers in the country had doubled since 2007.

Kazakhstan

Population: 18,700,000
Capital: Nur-Sultan
Freedom Status: Not Free
Electoral Democracy: No

Overview: President Nursultan Nazarbayev ruled Kazakhstan from 1990 to 2019, when he stepped down, and still maintains significant influence over governance of the country. Parliamentary and presidential elections are neither free nor fair, and major parties exhibit continued political loyalty to the government. The authorities have consistently marginalized or imprisoned genuine opposition figures. The dominant media outlets are either in state hands or owned by government-friendly businessmen. Freedoms of speech and assembly remain restricted, and corruption is endemic.

KEY DEVELOPMENTS IN 2020

- The government exploited the COVID-19 pandemic to further monitor the social media of critics of the regime. In January, Duman Aitzhanov, a doctor, had a criminal case initiated against him after sharing a video on WhatsApp that stated the number of confirmed COVID-19 cases in Kazakhstan and the necessary measures needed to halt the spread of the disease. There were over 202,000 people who tested positive for the virus and over 2,700 people who died during the year, according to government statistics provided to the World Health Organization (WHO).
- In February, violent clashes in villages near the Kazakh-Kyrgyz border occurred between ethnic Kazakhs and ethnic Dungans. Eleven people were killed, close to

200 injured, and 20,000 people were reportedly displaced, having fled over the border to Kyrgyzstan.

POLITICAL RIGHTS: 5 / 40

A. ELECTORAL PROCESS: 1 / 12

A1. Was the current head of government or other chief national authority elected through free and fair elections? 0 / 4

According to the constitution, the president, who holds most executive power, is directly elected for up to two five-year terms. However, former president Nazarbayev's special status as Kazakhstan's "first president" exempted him from term limits. In July 2018, Nazarbayev signed a decree making him chairman of the Security Council for life. The decree gave the Security Council significant constitutional powers, which could allow Nazarbayev to maintain power despite his resignation from the presidency in March 2019, after nearly 30 years in office. Senate chairman Kasym-Zhomart Tokayev was appointed acting president, and then won a five-year term in the June 2019 election with 71 percent of the vote. Amirzhan Kosanov of the Ult Tagdyry party won 16.2 percent and Daniya Yespayeva of Ak Zhol won 5.1 percent. Other candidates earned 7.7 percent of the vote.

The 2019 presidential election was not credible. President Tokayev benefited from the support of the ruling Nur Otan party, state media, and his predecessor, while none of his opponents were considered genuine competitors. Observers from the Organization for Security and Co-operation in Europe (OSCE) noted incidents of ballot box stuffing, the falsification of ballots, and the use of identical voter signatures on election day.

Despite his resignation, former president Nazarbayev still wields significant power in Kazakhstan. He remains leader of Nur Otan, and as the Security Council's lifelong chair he is responsible for the appointment of ministers and key officials, with the exception of the foreign, interior, and defense portfolios.

A2. Were the current national legislative representatives elected through free and fair elections? 0 / 4

The upper house of the bicameral Parliament is the 49-member Senate, with 34 members chosen by directly elected regional councils and 15 appointed by the president. The senators, who are officially nonpartisan, serve six-year terms, with half of the elected members up for reelection every three years. The lower house, the Mazhilis, has 107 deputies, with 98 elected by proportional representation on party slates and 9 appointed by the Assembly of the People of Kazakhstan, which ostensibly represents the country's various ethnic groups. Members serve five-year terms.

Legislative elections do not meet democratic standards. Irregularities including ballot box stuffing, group and proxy voting, and manipulation of voter lists have been reported, and the ruling party benefits from a blurred distinction between it and the state. In the 2016 Mazhilis elections, Nur Otan took 84 of the 98 elected seats, winning 82.2 percent of the popular vote. Ak Zhol and the Communist People's Party, which are both considered loyal to the government, each secured 7 seats, with 7.2 percent and 7.1 percent of the vote respectively. No genuine opposition party was able to win representation. New parliamentary elections were scheduled for January 2021.

A3. Are the electoral laws and framework fair, and are they implemented impartially by the relevant election management bodies? 1 / 4

Kazakhstan's legal framework is not sufficient to ensure free and fair elections, and safeguards that do exist are not properly enforced. Electoral laws make it difficult for opposition parties to obtain parliamentary representation. Parties must clear a 7 percent vote threshold to enter the Mazhilis, and are barred from forming electoral blocs, preventing them from pooling votes and campaign resources. Presidential candidates must also pass a Kazakh language test with unclear evaluation criteria. Moreover, the Assembly of the People of Kazakhstan is appointed by the president at his discretion, giving the executive branch influence over the nine Mazhilis members chosen by the assembly.

Election laws introduced in 2017 imposed further restrictions on who can become a presidential candidate, requiring at least five years of experience in public service or elected positions and the submission of medical records. The latter rule raised the possibility that candidates could be arbitrarily disqualified for health reasons. These legal changes also banned self-nomination of presidential candidates, effectively excluding independents and requiring a nomination from a registered party or public association. Changes to the electoral code in May 2020 established a quota system of 30 percent for women and young people under the age of 29 to be included in all parliamentary party lists and local representative bodies (*maslikhats*). Critics claim the quota system only pays lip-service to gender equality, as there is no requirement that parties should allocate their seats according to the quota.

B. POLITICAL PLURALISM AND PARTICIPATION: 3 / 16

B1. Do the people have the right to organize in different political parties or other competitive political groupings of their choice, and is the system free of undue obstacles to the rise and fall of these competing parties or groupings? 1 / 4

The 2002 Law on Political Parties was revised in 2020, reducing the number of members required to register a party with the Ministry of Justice from 40,000 to 20,000. Critics argue that the measure does not ease the onerous registration process, and officials have broad discretion to delay or deny party registration in practice. The law still prohibits parties based on ethnic origin, religion, or gender.

Opposition parties have been banned or marginalized through laws against extremism; their leaders have faced criminal charges, and their followers in Kazakhstan have had their activities restricted.

B2. Is there a realistic opportunity for the opposition to increase its support or gain power through elections? 0 / 4

Kazakhstan experienced its first peaceful transfer of power through an election in 2019, though it was neither free nor fair. Nazarbayev stood down as president that March, and acting president Tokayev won the election to replace him in June. Only one opposition candidate, Amirzhan Kosanov, earned over 10 percent of the vote.

Opposition parties are similarly locked out of gaining power or influence through legislative elections. The ruling Nur Otan party holds a preponderance of seats in the Mazhilis, and the second- and third-largest parties in the body are considered loyal to Nur Otan.

In May 2020, Parliament approved a bill formalizing parliamentary opposition in the Mazhilis. The new law provides non–Nur Otan deputies the right to initiate hearings, set the agenda for government questioning, propose legislation, and chair one of the seven standing parliamentary committees. The lack of real opposition parties in Parliament throws the import of the law into question.

The opposition party Democratic Choice of Kazakhstan remains banned and considered a terrorist organization by the authorities. Activists associated with the party often receive prison sentences on politically motivated charges. No opposition parties are set to participate in the January 2021 parliamentary elections.

B3. Are the people's political choices free from domination by forces that are external to the political sphere, or by political forces that employ extrapolitical means? 1 / 4

While voters and candidates are not subject to undue influence by the military or foreign powers, the political system is dominated by a small group of elites surrounding Nazarbayev and his family. The country's politics are shaped largely by competition among these elites for resources and positions. In May 2020, this competition took place at the highest levels when President Tokayev removed the former president's daughter, Dariga Nazarbayeva, as speaker of the Senate, the constitutionally designated position for presidential succession should the sitting president step down or die in office.

B4. Do various segments of the population (including ethnic, racial, religious, gender, LGBT+, and other relevant groups) have full political rights and electoral opportunities? 1 / 4

The legal ban on parties with an ethnic, religious, or gender focus—combined with the dominance of Nur Otan—limits the ability of women and minority groups to organize independently and advocate for their interests through the political system. Women currently hold 27 percent of the seats in the Mazhilis and less than 11 percent of the seats in the Senate. The language test for presidential candidates also presents an obstacle for non-Kazakh ethnic minorities, as well as many Kazakhs.

C. FUNCTIONING OF GOVERNMENT: 1 / 12

C1. Do the freely elected head of government and national legislative representatives determine the policies of the government? 0 / 4

Government policies are determined by the executive branch, which is not freely elected, irrespective of the constitutionally defined roles of the executive, judiciary, and legislature. Parliament does not serve as an effective check on the executive, and instead largely provides formal approval for the government's legislative initiatives.

However, changes to the constitution adopted by Parliament and the president in 2017 shifted some powers from the president to the Mazhilis. The amendments gave Parliament greater influence over the choice of prime minster and cabinet members and the authority to dismiss them. They also limited the president's ability to rule by decree.

President Tokayev has also been forced to share power with former president Nazarbayev, who retains significant influence by leading the ruling Nur Otan party and by holding powerful official positions.

C2. Are safeguards against official corruption strong and effective? 1 / 4

Corruption is widespread at all levels of government. Corruption cases are often prosecuted at the local and regional levels, but charges against high-ranking political and business elites are rare, typically emerging only after an individual has fallen out of favor with the leadership. Journalists, activists, and opposition figures are often prosecuted for supposed financial crimes. In November 2020, former Health Minister Elzhan Birtanov was arrested and detained in custody on charges of embezzling 526 million tenges ($1.2 million).

In December 2020, a British court froze assets connected to alleged fraud against BTA Bank, owned by the Kazakhstan government. The bank accused its former chair of embezzlement with the assistance of Bolat Otemuratov, a Kazakh business tycoon and longtime associate of former president Nursultan Nazarbayev.

President Tokayev, like his predecessor, has highlighted the importance of tackling corruption. In September 2020, the government prohibited officials and their families from having bank accounts abroad. A new October law seeks to fight corruption by banning civil servants and their families from receiving gifts, material rewards, or services for their work.

C3. Does the government operate with openness and transparency? 0 / 4

The government and legislature offer little transparency on their decision-making processes, budgetary matters, and other operations. The media and civil society do not have a meaningful opportunity to provide independent commentary and input on pending laws and policies. A law on public access to government information was adopted in 2015, but it is poorly implemented in practice. Officials' asset and income declarations are not publicly available.

CIVIL LIBERTIES: 18 / 60

D. FREEDOM OF EXPRESSION AND BELIEF: 4 / 16

D1. Are there free and independent media? 0 / 4

Media independence is severely limited in Kazakhstan. While the constitution provides for freedom of the press, most of the media sector is controlled by the state or government-friendly owners, and the government has repeatedly harassed or shut down independent outlets. Self-censorship is common. The authorities also use internet blackouts to restrict access to media outlets.

Legislation introduced in 2018 requires journalists to verify the accuracy of information prior to publication by consulting with relevant government bodies or officials, obtaining consent for the publication of personal or otherwise confidential information, and acquiring accreditation as foreign journalists if they work for foreign outlets.

Defamation was decriminalized in June 2020, but libel remains a criminal offense, and the criminal code prohibits insulting the president and other officials. Journalists critical of the regime often face harassment. Throughout 2020, several journalists found themselves subject to prospective criminal cases, including three who were charged for disseminating false information about the COVID-19 pandemic; the charges against them were eventually dropped.

D2. Are individuals free to practice and express their religious faith or nonbelief in public and private? 1 / 4

The constitution guarantees freedom of worship, and some religious communities practice without state interference. However, activities by unregistered religious groups are banned, and registered groups are subject to close government supervision. The government has broad authority to outlaw organizations it designates as "extremist."

The 2011 Law on Religious Activities and Religious Associations prohibited the distribution of religious literature outside places of worship, required the state approval of all religious literature, and prohibited unregistered missionary activity, among other provisions. In 2018, Parliament considered amendments that would have further restricted religious education, proselytizing, and the publication of materials, but these amendments were recalled in January 2019.

Local officials continue to harass groups defined as "nontraditional," including Protestant Christians, Jehovah's Witnesses, and Muslims who do not adhere to the government-approved version of Islam. According to Forum 18, a nongovernmental organization (NGO) that tracks religious freedom in Eurasia, authorities launched 168 prosecutions against individuals and groups for unsanctioned religious activity in 2019. Restrictions on gathering for worship were placed on religious groups under the COVID-19 state of emergency legislation and were used as a pretext to charge a Baptist congregation in Pavlodar not just for breaking coronavirus health measures, but also for being an unregistered religious community.

D3. Is there academic freedom, and is the educational system free from extensive political indoctrination? 2 / 4

Academic freedom remains constrained by political sensitivities surrounding certain topics, including the former president, his inner circle, and relations with Russia. Self-censorship on such topics is reportedly common among scholars and educators. In 2018, a new law was passed giving universities greater freedom to choose the content of their academic programs.

D4. Are individuals free to express their personal views on political or other sensitive topics without fear of surveillance or retribution? 1 / 4

Authorities are known to monitor social media, and users are regularly prosecuted on charges such as inciting social and ethnic hatred, insulting government officials, and promoting separatism or terrorism. The media law that came into force in 2018 also made it impossible for internet users to leave anonymous comments online, further limiting free expression.

Since 2019, the authorities have stepped up their efforts to surveil and block access to material it deemed inappropriate. Mobile service providers have instructed their customers to install encryption software on mobile phones that would allow security services to intercept data traffic and circumvent email and messaging applications' encryption. The government claimed the encryption software was required in order protect citizens from online fraud and hacker attacks. Those who did not install the software faced difficulties in accessing the Internet, particularly social networking sites.

Government monitoring of social media was especially acute during the COVID-19 pandemic, which authorities exploited to clamp down on critics of the regime. An Almaty court in June 2020 convicted political and human rights activist Alnur Ilyashev for spreading false information and sentenced him to a three-year noncustodial sentence of "restricted freedom." Ilyashev had called the government's and Nur Otan's response to the pandemic incompetent. In January, Duman Aitzhanov, a doctor, had a criminal case initiated against him after sharing a video on WhatsApp that stated the number of confirmed COVID-19 cases in Kazakhstan and the necessary measures needed to halt the spread of the disease.

E. ASSOCIATIONAL AND ORGANIZATIONAL RIGHTS: 2 / 12

E1. Is there freedom of assembly? 1 / 4

Despite constitutional guarantees, the government imposes tight restrictions on freedom of assembly. President Tokayev revised the public assembly law in May 2020 to no longer require groups to obtain permission from state authorities to gather in public. Instead, groups are required to give notification three to seven days in advance and then wait for approval by the local administration. Critics argue that the state continues to restrict who can protest and where, as only officially registered groups are allowed to give notification, and gatherings are only allowed in state-approved sites, which are often located far from the center of cities.

Organizers and participants who fall outside of the new law continue to be subject to fines and jail terms. More than 100 people were detained by police in February outside of a rally organized by the unregistered Democratic Party of Kazakhstan. Authorities have continued to block protests by the Democratic Choice of Kazakhstan (DVK), a party headed by its exiled leader, Mukhtar Ablyazov.

The government used social distancing measures, introduced as part of the state of emergency response to the COVID-19 pandemic, as a pretext to break up the Democratic Party of Kazakhstan's and DVK's unsanctioned rallies in June 2020. However, in November the Democratic Party was allowed to hold a rally protesting the parliamentary elections scheduled for January 2021.

E2. Is there freedom for nongovernmental organizations, particularly those that are engaged in human rights- and governance-related work? 1 / 4

NGOs continue to operate but face government harassment when they attempt to address politically sensitive issues. There are extensive legal restrictions on the formation and operation of NGOs, including onerous financial rules and harsh penalties for noncompliance. Organizations can incur fines and other punishments for vaguely defined offenses like interfering with government activities or engaging in work outside the scope of their charters.

Civil and human rights activists accused the government of using the COVID-19 state-of-emergency measures as an excuse to crack down on activists and critics, charging them with violating coronavirus restrictions and spreading false information about the pandemic.

In October and November 2020, a series of tax violations were levied against at least 13 NGOs for allegedly breaking the law on the reporting of foreign financial donations. The NGOs claimed the investigations sought to halt their activities in the run-up to the January 2021 parliamentary elections.

E3. Is there freedom for trade unions and similar professional or labor organizations? 0 / 4

Workers have limited rights to form and join trade unions or participate in collective bargaining. The government is closely affiliated with the largest union federation and major employers, while genuinely independent unions face repressive actions by the authorities. The country's major independent trade union body, the Confederation of Independent Trade Unions (KNPRK), was dissolved in 2017, and key leaders were later sentenced to prison for protesting the group's termination. Subsequent efforts to register the group have been denied. Kazakhstan's restrictions on union activity gained the attention of the International Labor Organization (ILO), which criticized the country's stance in a June 2019 statement.

May 2020 revisions to the Law on Trade allowed smaller local trade unions the opportunity to join with larger oblast level organizations, as well as international trade union federations. Though authorities claimed this enhanced the freedom of trade unions, critics claimed the changes were minimal, as independent unions critical of government policy had already been banned.

F. RULE OF LAW: 4 / 16

F1. Is there an independent judiciary? 1 / 4

The judiciary is effectively subservient to the executive branch, with the president nominating or directly appointing judges based on the recommendation of the Supreme Judicial Council, which is itself appointed by the president. Judges are subject to political influence, and corruption is a problem throughout the judicial system.

F2. Does due process prevail in civil and criminal matters? 1 / 4

Police reportedly engage in arbitrary arrests and detentions and violate detained suspects' right to assistance from a defense lawyer. Prosecutors, as opposed to judges, are empowered to authorize searches and seizures. Defendants are often held in pretrial detention for long periods. Politically motivated prosecutions and prison sentences against activists, journalists, and opposition figures are common.

F3. Is there protection from the illegitimate use of physical force and freedom from war and insurgencies? 1 / 4

Conditions in pretrial detention facilities and prisons are harsh. According to family and advocates of multiple inmates interviewed by Radio Free Europe/Radio Liberty, prison conditions deteriorated during the COVID-19 pandemic. Prisoners were only allowed out of their cells for a very limited time, conditions were cramped and unsanitary, no face masks or protective equipment were proved, and no medical treatment was given to inmates who contracted the virus.

Police at times use excessive force during arrests, and torture is widely employed to obtain confessions, with numerous allegations of physical abuse and other mistreatment documented each year. In February 2020, civil rights activist Dulat Agadil died suspiciously while in custody for just a few hours at a pretrial holding center in Nur-Sultan. An official investigation claimed the cause of death was a heart attack, although friends and civil rights activists have contested that the police were responsible.

Violent clashes occurred in villages near the Kazakh-Kyrgyz border in February 2020 between ethnic Kazakhs and ethnic Dungans. Eleven people were killed, close to 200 were injured, and 20,000 people were reportedly displaced, having fled over the border to Kyrgyzstan.

Terrorist violence within the country is rare, though some Kazakhstanis have traveled abroad to support the Islamic State (IS) militant group.

F4. Do laws, policies, and practices guarantee equal treatment of various segments of the population? 1 / 4

While the constitution guarantees equality before the law and prohibits discrimination based on gender, race, and other categories, it does not explicitly prohibit discrimination based on sexual orientation or gender identity. Major segments of society face discrimination in practice. Traditional cultural biases limit economic and professional opportunities for women, and the law offers no protection against sexual harassment in the workplace. Members of the sizable Russian-speaking minority have complained of discrimination in employment and education.

LGBT+ people continue to face societal discrimination, harassment, and violence, despite the decriminalization of same-sex relations in 1998. In June 2020, the government appeared to take advantage of diminished public oversight during the COVID-19 lockdown to introduce a draft "anti-gender" bill, which would eliminate the idea of gender and gender equality. The social stigma experienced by LGBT+ people has also disproportionally affected their access to health care during the pandemic. Transgender individuals in particular have been subjected to unethical treatment and abuse.

Under pressure from Beijing, the Kazakhstan government at times detains ethnic Kazakhs fleeing neighboring China and threatens them with the prospect of deportation, even though they are subject to discrimination and torture upon return.

G. PERSONAL AUTONOMY AND INDIVIDUAL RIGHTS: 8 / 16

G1. Do individuals enjoy freedom of movement, including the ability to change their place of residence, employment, or education? 2 / 4

Kazakhstani citizens can travel freely but must register their permanent residence with local authorities. New rules that went into effect in 2017 under the pretext of fighting terrorism require citizens to register even temporary residences lasting more than a month with local authorities or face fines. The change increases the ability of the authorities to monitor internal movement and migration, but critics also suggested that it would lead to corruption and create a black market for false registration documents. The government locked down and restricted people's movement in many Kazakh cities, towns, and villages in response to the coronavirus pandemic.

G2. Are individuals able to exercise the right to own property and establish private businesses without undue interference from state or nonstate actors? 2 / 4

While the rights of entrepreneurship and private property are formally protected, they are limited in practice by bureaucratic hurdles and the undue influence of politically connected elites, who control large segments of the economy.

G3. Do individuals enjoy personal social freedoms, including choice of marriage partner and size of family, protection from domestic violence, and control over appearance? 2 / 4

NGOs continue to report instances of early and forced marriage, particularly in rural areas. Women are also encouraged to support large families; those who raise at least six children receive a medal from the government, along with tax breaks and modest monthly benefits.

Domestic violence is a serious problem that often goes unpunished, as police are reluctant to intervene in what are regarded as internal family matters. The Union of Crisis Centers of Kazakhstan, a network of 16 local NGOs, reported that these crimes occurred in one out of every eight families in the country as recently as 2018. The Committee on the Elimination of Discrimination against Women (CEDAW), a UN body, warned in a 2019 report that domestic violence had been effectively decriminalized. Incidents of domestic violence reportedly increased and intensified during the COVID-19 pandemic.

In December 2020, Symbat Kulzhagharova died after falling from her 11th floor apartment. Despite claims her passing was suicide, many speculated her death was related to domestic violence. In the aftermath of her passing a petition to increase punishment for domestic violence in Kazakhstan was signed by over 70,000 people.

G4. Do individuals enjoy equality of opportunity and freedom from economic exploitation? 2 / 4

Migrant workers from neighboring countries often face poor working conditions and a lack of effective legal safeguards against exploitation. Both migrants and Kazakhstani workers from rural areas are vulnerable to trafficking for the purposes of forced labor and prostitution in large cities. The authorities reportedly make little effort to assist foreign victims of trafficking.

Kenya

Population: 53,500,000
Capital: Nairobi
Freedom Status: Partly Free
Electoral Democracy: No

Overview: Kenya holds regular multiparty elections. However, pervasive corruption and brutality by security forces remain serious problems. The country's media and civil society sectors are vibrant, even as journalists and human rights defenders remain vulnerable to restrictive laws and intimidation.

KEY DEVELOPMENTS IN 2020

- Over 96,000 people tested positive for COVID-19, and 1,670 people died from the virus during the year, according to government figures reported by the World Health Organization (WHO). Authorities imposed strict lockdown measures, including a curfew and movement restrictions, which police implemented with excessive, sometimes fatal force.

- In March, 13-year-old Yassin Moyo was struck by a police bullet fired as officers were violently enforcing a coronavirus lockdown in his Nairobi neighborhood. Moro was among at least 20 people killed by police enforcing the lockdown.
- In July, police teargassed and arrested activists at a Nairobi protest against police brutality during the enforcement of coronavirus curfew measures.
- In September, a probe by the Ethics and Anti-Corruption Commission (EACC) found that at least 15 top government officials and businesspeople had misused millions of dollars designated for the Kenya Medical Supplies Authority's purchase and distribution of funds and supplies to prevent the spread of COVID-19.

POLITICAL RIGHTS: 19 / 40

A. ELECTORAL PROCESS: 6 / 12

A1. Was the current head of government or other chief national authority elected through free and fair elections? 1 / 4

The president and deputy president, who can serve up to two five-year terms, are directly elected by majority vote; they are also required to win 25 percent of the votes in at least half of Kenya's 47 counties.

President Kenyatta was reelected in 2017 in a disputed election, the rerun of which was boycotted by the main opposition candidate. The first election, held that August, returned a solid victory by Kenyatta, which many analysts had predicted; this was annulled the following month by the Supreme Court, which ruled that vote-counting procedures by the Independent Electoral and Boundaries Commission (IEBC) had been severely flawed, and that a rerun should be held. The main opposition coalition, the National Super Alliance (NASA), threatened to boycott the rerun unless a number of reforms were implemented at the IEBC. When some of these reforms were not met, opposition candidate Raila Odinga boycotted the rerun, urging his supporters not to participate.

The final results showed that Kenyatta won the rerun with 98.3 percent of the vote. Turnout for the rerun was only 38.8 percent—much lower than turnout for the August polls, which reached nearly 80 percent. Odinga continued to harshly criticize the election process after the second vote, and Kenyatta began his final term facing a significant legitimacy crisis.

Violence and intimidation marred the 2017 election period. Chris Msando, the IEBC member in charge of the vote-counting system, was murdered days ahead of the August vote, with his body showing signs of torture. In the weeks between the annulled election and the rerun, one IEBC commissioner fled Kenya for the United States, prompting the IEBC chairman to assert that the body could not guarantee a free election given the atmosphere of intimidation. Police in Nairobi and Kisumu used excessive force in an attempt to quell sometimes-violent opposition protests. Several dozen people were reportedly killed by police in the capital alone, according to Human Rights Watch (HRW).

A2. Were the current national legislative representatives elected through free and fair elections? 3 / 4

The bicameral Parliament consists of the 349-seat National Assembly and the 67-seat Senate. In the National Assembly, 290 members are directly elected from single-member constituencies. A further 47 special women representatives are elected from the counties, and political parties nominate 12 additional members according to their share of seats won. The Senate has 47 elected members representing the counties, 16 special women representatives nominated by political parties based on the share of seats won, and four nominated members representing youth and people with disabilities. Both houses have speakers who are ex-officio members.

In 2017, Kenyatta's Jubilee Coalition secured majorities in both the National Assembly and the Senate, and stakeholders broadly accepted the results. Irregularities and violations were reported, but they were not systematic and did not harm or benefit any specific party.

A3. Are the electoral laws and framework fair, and are they implemented impartially by the relevant election management bodies? 2 / 4

The IEBC is mandated with conducting free and fair elections, and operates under a robust electoral framework. However, the IEBC faces frequent allegations of favoritism toward the incumbent Jubilee Coalition, and in 2017 its members experienced violence and intimidation severe enough to prompt its chairman to declare that he could not guarantee the integrity of the presidential rerun. After the annulment of the first presidential election in 2017, the National Assembly approved controversial measures mandating that if a candidate withdraws from a rerun election, then the other candidate automatically wins the poll. The amendments additionally limited the Supreme Court's power to annul election results. The measures took effect a few days after the rerun was held.

In May 2018, after a public reconciliation, Kenyatta and Odinga formed the Building Bridges Initiative (BBI). Under the initiative, a task force was convened, and entrusted with studying public opinion on the problems that plague Kenyan politics such as ethnic strife, corruption, and political dysfunction, and ultimately producing recommendations for reform. The BBI report was launched in November 2019 and was officially sent to the president in October 2020. Its recommendations were geared toward changing some structures of the government in advance of the 2022 elections, including introducing a prime minister and reducing the size of the cabinet, among other measures that aimed to encourage whistleblowers and boost local development.

B. POLITICAL PLURALISM AND PARTICIPATION: 8 / 16

B1. Do the people have the right to organize in different political parties or other competitive political groupings of their choice, and is the system free of undue obstacles to the rise and fall of these competing parties or groupings? 2 / 4

Citizens are free to organize into political parties. Kenyan parties represent a range of ideological, regional, and ethnic interests, but are notoriously weak, and are often amalgamated into coalitions designed only to contest elections. Under the Political Parties Act, parties that receive at least 5 percent of the votes cast in a national election are eligible for public funds. As of October 2020, there were 71 fully registered and 9 provisionally registered parties.

A March 2018 rapprochement between Kenyatta and Odinga helped deescalate political tensions somewhat, though little has been done to bring to justice the perpetrators of political violence that took place in the previous years.

B2. Is there a realistic opportunity for the opposition to increase its support or gain power through elections? 2 / 4

Opposition parties and candidates are competitive in Kenyan elections, and the 2017 polls saw a high number of incumbents voted out of office. However, Odinga's decision to boycott the rerun election in protest of a lack of reforms at the IEBC left Kenyatta opponents without a viable candidate to vote for, effectively guaranteeing Kenyatta's reelection.

Politics have been unstable since March 2018, when Kenyatta and Odinga publicly reached a truce in an event that became popularly known as "the handshake." Some analysts say the handshake dealt a blow to the foundations of both the ruling Jubilee Coalition and the opposing NASA, because each party's opposition to the other had served as a key factor in keeping them each united. Odinga was later named African Union High Representative for Infrastructure Development in October 2018, a role that distanced him from national politics. In October 2020, Jubilee officials recommended stripping the sitting deputy president, William Ruto, of his post as deputy party leader, deepening rifts in the ruling coalition that have surfaced since their victory in 2017.

B3. Are the people's political choices free from domination by forces that are external to the political sphere, or by political forces that employ extrapolitical means? 2 / 4

While people's political choices are somewhat free from undue influence by powerful, democratically unaccountable actors, groups such as Mungiki, a Kikuyu-affiliated gang, exert control over daily services such as matatu (minibus) routes in some regions, and may use violence, intimidation, and other extrapolitical means to influence local and national electoral outcomes.

B4. Do various segments of the population (including ethnic, racial, religious, gender, LGBT+, and other relevant groups) have full political rights and electoral opportunities? 2 / 4

Ethnicity remains the most salient organizing principle in Kenyan politics, and two ethnic groups—the Kikuyu and Kalenjin—have dominated the presidency since independence. The 2010 constitution intended to reduce the role of ethnicity in elections, and fiscal and political devolution, implemented in 2013, has served to generate more intraethnic competition at the county level. Nevertheless, the ongoing politicization of ethnicity at the national level hinders effective representation of different segments of Kenya's diverse population, limits voter choice, and impedes meaningful policy debates.

The stipulation that all voters possess a National Identity Card hinders historically marginalized groups from obtaining greater access to the political process, particularly the nearly seven million pastoralists from the upper Rift Valley and the North Eastern Province. There are significant implicit barriers to the participation of non-Christian and LGBT+ people in national politics. Somali Kenyans, especially in the Eastleigh community of Nairobi and in the coastal and northeastern parts of the country, have been the target of government crackdowns in the name of combatting the militant group Shabaab, and are underrepresented politically. Coastal communities have historically been politically marginalized and received less government support, fueling a sense of grievance and fostering political instability.

C. FUNCTIONING OF GOVERNMENT: 5 / 12

C1. Do the freely elected head of government and national legislative representatives determine the policies of the government? 2 / 4

The ability of elected officials to set and implement policy is undermined by corruption and other dysfunctions. Although the 2010 constitution reduced the powers of the executive branch and improved the oversight role of Parliament, corruption limits the independence of the legislative branch, and in practice, the parliament is generally subordinate to the president.

C2. Are safeguards against official corruption strong and effective? 1 / 4

Corruption continues to plague national and county governments in Kenya, and state institutions tasked with combating corruption have been ineffective. The Ethics and Anti-Corruption Commission (EACC) lacks prosecutorial power and has been largely unsuccessful in pursuing corruption cases. The EACC's weakness is compounded by shortcomings at the Office of the Director of Public Prosecutions (ODPP) and within the judiciary.

However, following the April 2018 appointment of Noordin Haji as the Director of Public Prosecutions (DPP), the ODPP stepped up anticorruption investigations, arresting and charging a number of high-profile officials, and in 2019, Finance Minister Henry Rotich and the prominent governor of Nairobi County, Mike "Sonko" Mbuvi, were both served with corruption charges. In September 2020, the EACC recommended charges be brought against several officials and businesspeople in connection with the Kenya Medical Supplies Authority's misuse of funds intended to combat COVID-19. In December, the head of the Energy and Petroleum Regulatory Authority was arrested for allegedly accepting bribes.

C3. Does the government operate with openness and transparency? 2 / 4

Elaborate rules govern public finance in Kenya, but enforcement is often lacking. Parliament's Budget and Appropriations Committee effectively delegates the budget process to the Treasury, and the legislature has demonstrated limited willingness to ensure that the Treasury respects budget-making procedures. When budget information is made available, it is generally released long after the planning stages during which stakeholders could offer input.

Many of the central government's expenditures are not disclosed. At the county level, while the number of budgeting documents published increased somewhat in 2020, the availability of financial information still falls below levels that would allow for adequate public participation in local-government budgetary processes.

CIVIL LIBERTIES: 29 / 60
D. FREEDOM OF EXPRESSION AND BELIEF: 10 / 16
D1. Are there free and independent media? 2 / 4

Kenya has one of the more vibrant media landscapes on the African continent, with journalists actively working to expose government corruption and other wrongdoing. However, several laws restrict press freedom, and the government and security forces harass journalists, incidents that are rarely investigated by police. For example, in October 2020, the personal assistant of a member of Parliament attacked a reporter in Meru County because the assistant believed the reporter had encouraged interviewees to criticize the parliamentarian. The combination of restrictive laws on press freedom and the potential for harassment and violence leads to self-censorship in some cases.

In March 2020, Kenyan officials threatened those who publish misinformation about COVID-19 with two years in jail and a $50,000 fine. The nongovernmental organization (NGO) Article 19 reported that arbitrary arrests and cases of harassment and assault have increased since the coronavirus outbreak began, with journalists, bloggers, and online activists accused of spreading false information about the pandemic. In October, the National Security Advisory Committee released guidelines that allow for the Multi-Agency Team on Public Order "to monitor, document, and enforce compliance" with media broadcasting laws and social media usage guidance ahead of the 2022 general election, guidelines that have been severely criticized by a large coalition of media stakeholders.

D2. Are individuals free to practice and express their religious faith or nonbelief in public and private? 2 / 4

The government generally respects the constitutional guarantee of freedom of religion. However, counterterrorism operations against the Somalia-based Shabaab militant group have left Muslims exposed to state violence and intimidation. Shabaab militants have at times specifically targeted Christians in Kenya.

D3. Is there academic freedom, and is the educational system free from extensive political indoctrination? 3 / 4

Academic freedom in Kenya is traditionally robust. However, student union elections have led to allegations of fraud, and violent protests. In addition, there is evidence that ethnic considerations have influenced university hiring, leaving the staff of some institutions with significant ethnic imbalances. In January 2020, the Cabinet Secretary for Education disbanded the council of the University of Nairobi and revoked the appointment of a new vice chancellor (who had been officially installed five months earlier), a struggle that underscored long-standing tensions around the appropriate level of autonomy from state interference of academic institutions.

D4. Are individuals free to express their personal views on political or other sensitive topics without fear of surveillance or retribution? 3 / 4

The relatively unfettered freedom of private discussion in Kenya has suffered somewhat from state counterterrorism operations, intimidation by security forces, and ethnically affiliated gangs. The government in recent years has used its broadly defined surveillance powers to monitor mobile phone and internet communications. Still, over 80 percent of Kenyans access social media sites, and "Kenyans on Twitter" have their own hashtag, #KOT, demonstrating their influence. Likewise, political candidates have increased their use of social media to reach younger voters.

E. ASSOCIATIONAL AND ORGANIZATIONAL RIGHTS: 7 / 12
E1. Is there freedom of assembly? 2 / 4

The constitution guarantees the freedom of assembly. However, the law requires organizers of public meetings to notify local police in advance, and in practice police have regularly prohibited gatherings on security or other grounds, and violently dispersed assemblies that they had not explicitly banned.

In July 2020, police teargassed and arrested activists at a Nairobi protest against police's use of disproportionate force while enforcing coronavirus curfew measures. Police also violently dispersed a protest in August, which activists had organized in response to the EACC investigation into theft and corruption within the Kenya Medical Supplies Authority.

E2. Is there freedom for nongovernmental organizations, particularly those that are engaged in human rights- and governance-related work? 2 / 4

Kenya has an active nongovernmental organization (NGO) sector, but civil society groups have faced growing obstacles in recent years, including repeated government attempts to deregister hundreds of NGOs for alleged financial violations. The government has still not implemented the Public Benefits Organizations (PBO) Act, which was passed in 2013 to improve the regulatory framework for NGOs and offer greater freedom for them to operate.

E3. Is there freedom for trade unions and similar professional or labor organizations? 3 / 4

The 2010 constitution affirmed the rights of trade unions to establish their own agendas, bargain collectively, and strike. Unions are active in Kenya, with approximately 57 unions representing 2.6 million workers in 2018. However, labor leaders sometimes experience intimidation, notably in the wake of strike actions. A number of strikes have taken place in the past several years, including those organized by medical workers and university staff, who faced additional pressures and resource constraints in 2020 as they dealt with the coronavirus pandemic.

F. RULE OF LAW: 5 / 16

F1. Is there an independent judiciary? 2 / 4

The judiciary is generally considered to be independent, but judicial procedures are inefficient. The government has occasionally refused to comply with court orders. In 2018, it refused to release opposition politician and Odinga supporter Miguna Miguna and halt his deportation, as ordered, and to end the shutdown of several television stations. In September 2020, the Chief Justice recommended that President Kenyatta dissolve Parliament because it had failed to meet the constitutionally required two-thirds gender quota, a move the High Court suspended pending further deliberation.

After the High Court annulled the first 2017 presidential election, members of the ruling Jubilee Coalition threatened and intimidated judges. In June 2018, President Kenyatta signed an appropriations bill that reduced the budget for the judiciary to $143 million, compared to $173 million the previous year, which some critics claimed was retaliation for the 2017 election annulment. The National Assembly's Budget and Appropriations Committee further reduced allocations to the judiciary for the 2020–21 financial year.

F2. Does due process prevail in civil and criminal matters? 1 / 4

Constitutional guarantees of due process are poorly upheld. There remains a significant backlog of court cases. The police service is thoroughly undermined by corruption and criminality.

F3. Is there protection from the illegitimate use of physical force and freedom from war and insurgencies? 1 / 4

Following their January 2019 two-day terrorist attack on the DusitD2 hotel and office complex in Nairobi, which left more than 20 people dead, the Islamist militant group the Shabaab continued to pose a security threat in 2020. In June, the group attacked a passenger bus in northeastern Kenya, injuring eight people.

Violence against suspects and detainees by security forces, including extrajudicial killings, remains a serious concern, and abuses are rarely punished. Extrajudicial killings are especially prevalent in low-income areas in Nairobi. Some officers have posted photos of executed victims on social media.

These trends accelerated in 2020 as Kenyan police utilized excessive and sometimes lethal force to impose coronavirus curfew measures. According to the Deadly Force database kept by the *Nation Newsplex*, 137 people were killed by police in 2020, exceeding the death toll for 2019 by 12 percent. In a widely publicized case, an officer shot and killed 13-year-old Yassin Moyo, who was standing on his family's balcony in a low-income neighborhood of Nairobi as police enforced curfew in late March. Other incidents are believed to have gone unreported.

F4. Do laws, policies, and practices guarantee equal treatment of various segments of the population? 1 / 4

Consensual same-sex sexual activity is criminalized under the penal code, with a maximum penalty of 14 years in prison. In May 2019, the High Court dismissed a challenge to the law. LGBT+ people face discrimination, abuse, and violent attacks. Reports of police abuses against refugees and asylum seekers continue. Somali Kenyans are often stereotyped as refugees and terrorists, a misconception that has been exacerbated by the Shabaab's successive attacks in Kenya since the 2010s, and have been the target of government crackdowns as a result. Coastal communities have long experienced government underinvestment, resulting in worse educational, health, and economic outcomes in the region.

G. PERSONAL AUTONOMY AND INDIVIDUAL RIGHTS: 7 / 16

G1. Do individuals enjoy freedom of movement, including the ability to change their place of residence, employment, or education? 2 / 4

While the constitution provides protections for freedom of movement and related rights, they are impeded in practice by security concerns and ethnic tensions that lead many residents to avoid certain parts of the country. The enforcement of COVID-19 lockdown measures were disproportionate and often excessively implemented. Police beat, tortured, and sometimes killed individuals allegedly for breaking curfew—including some essential workers—who were returning home from their place of employment. Some incidents occurred before curfew was in effect.

G2. Are individuals able to exercise the right to own property and establish private businesses without undue interference from state or nonstate actors? 1 / 4

Organized crime continues to threaten legitimate business activity in Kenya. Political corruption and ethnic favoritism also affect the business sector and exacerbate existing imbalances in wealth and access to economic opportunities, including public sector jobs. Forced evictions without compensation are prevalent in low-income areas, particularly in Nairobi.

G3. Do individuals enjoy personal social freedoms, including choice of marriage partner and size of family, protection from domestic violence, and control over appearance? 2 / 4

The constitution recognizes marriage as a union between two people of the opposite sex, but otherwise does not place explicit restrictions on social freedoms. Polygamy is legal, and approximately 10 percent of the married population are in polygamous marriages, according to the most recent data. Rape and domestic violence remain common and are rarely prosecuted.

G4. Do individuals enjoy equality of opportunity and freedom from economic exploitation? 2 / 4

Kenya remains an unequal society, with wealth generally concentrated in towns and cities. The arid and semiarid north and northeastern parts of the country have particularly high poverty rates.

Refugees and asylum seekers from neighboring countries, particularly children, have been vulnerable to sex trafficking and forced labor in Kenya, though Kenyan children are also subject to such abuses. Kenyan workers are recruited for employment abroad in sometimes exploitative conditions, particularly in the Middle East.

Kiribati

Population: 100,000
Capital: Tarawa
Freedom Status: Free
Electoral Democracy: Yes

Overview: Kiribati is a multiparty democracy that holds regular elections and has experienced peaceful transfers of power between competing groups. Civil liberties are generally upheld, though outstanding problems include a ban on same-sex sexual activity and some forms of gender discrimination.

KEY DEVELOPMENTS IN 2020

- Recognition of the Beijing-based Chinese government versus the government of Taiwan dominated June's presidential race, with the pro-Beijing leader, President Taneti Maamau, winning a solid victory over pro-Taiwan challenger, Banuera Berina. Berina had opposed the government's move in 2019 to cut off diplomatic relations with Taiwan and switch recognition to Beijing.
- The Chinese government opened an embassy in Kiribati in May, joining Australia, New Zealand, and Cuba as the only countries with a diplomatic presence on the islands.
- Tangariki Reete became the first woman parliament speaker following legislative elections in April.
- Kiribati recorded no cases of COVID-19 during the year. The government banned foreign arrivals in March, as the extent of the virus became apparent, with extremely limited exceptions. The ban remained in effect through the rest of the year.

POLITICAL RIGHTS: 37 / 40

A. ELECTORAL PROCESS: 12 / 12

A1. Was the current head of government or other chief national authority elected through free and fair elections? 4 / 4

The president is elected through a nationwide popular vote and may serve up to three four-year terms. Three to four presidential candidates are nominated by the legislature from among its members, and cabinet members must also be members of the legislature. The president can be removed through a no-confidence vote, but this also triggers general elections.

Maamau of the Tobwaan Kiribati Party (TKP) was reelected president in June 2020, winning decisively over Berina, of the Kiribati Moa Party (KPM), in a free and fair vote. The issue of recognition of the Beijing-based Chinese government versus the government of Taiwan dominated the race, with the pro-Beijing leader, President Maamau, prevailing over his pro-Taiwan challenger, Berina, who had opposed the government's move in 2019 to cut off diplomatic relations with Taiwan and switch recognition to China.

A2. Were the current national legislative representatives elected through free and fair elections? 4 / 4

The unicameral House of Assembly (Maneaba ni Maungatabu) has 46 members, 44 of whom are elected through a two-round runoff system from 26 constituencies. An appointed member is selected by representatives of people originally from the island of Banaba (Ocean Island) who now live on Fiji's Rabi Island, having been displaced by phosphate mining during the 20th century. The attorney general holds a seat ex officio.

A free and fair legislative election was held in April 2020. The Tobwaan Kiribati Party (TKP) took the most seats, 13 of 44. Following the elections, Boutokaan te Koaua (BTK) and the KMP joined to create the new Boutokaan Kiribati Moa (BKM). When the new parliament opened, TKP and BTK—counting their members and respective allies—each held 22 seats. A record four women won seats in the parliament, and Tangarik Reete became the first woman parliament speaker.

A3. Are the electoral laws and framework fair, and are they implemented impartially by the relevant election management bodies? 4 / 4

The constitution and legal framework provide for democratic elections, and balloting is well administered in practice. Losing candidates and parties typically accept the final outcome of elections, and rarely raise accusations of malfeasance.

B. POLITICAL PLURALISM AND PARTICIPATION: 15 / 16

B1. Do the people have the right to organize in different political parties or other competitive political groupings of their choice, and is the system free of undue obstacles to the rise and fall of these competing parties or groupings? 4 / 4

There are no constraints on the formation of or competition between political parties. The country's parties are relatively loose alliances that lack formal platforms and are subject to periodic mergers and reconfigurations. Geographic and ancestral ties continue to play an important role in political affiliation.

B2. Is there a realistic opportunity for the opposition to increase its support or gain power through elections? 4 / 4

Kiribati has a history of smooth and democratic transfers of power between government and opposition parties.

B3. Are the people's political choices free from domination by forces that are external to the political sphere, or by political forces that employ extrapolitical means? 4 / 4

There are no significant constraints on the choices of voters and candidates imposed by forces not democratically accountable.

B4. Do various segments of the population (including ethnic, racial, religious, gender, LGBT+, and other relevant groups) have full political rights and electoral opportunities? 3 / 4

All citizens enjoy full political rights. However, women's political participation is somewhat inhibited in practice by traditional social norms. The number of women elected to the legislature increased from three to four in the 2020 election. A woman, Tangariki Reete, was also elected speaker for the first time.

C. FUNCTIONING OF GOVERNMENT: 10 / 12

C1. Do the freely elected head of government and national legislative representatives determine the policies of the government? 4 / 4

The president and cabinet are able to both form and implement their policy agenda without undue interference, while the legislature provides oversight and a check on executive authority. The government's ability to enact policy depends on its ability to win legislative approval.

C2. Are safeguards against official corruption strong and effective? 3 / 4

While there is virtually no large-scale corruption in Kiribati, petty graft and nepotism in public appointments remain problems.

C3. Does the government operate with openness and transparency? 3 / 4

Kiribati lacks comprehensive regulations on public asset disclosure for officials, access to government information, and other transparency matters. In 2017, a former president told lawmakers that he was denied access to basic data on the production of copra, a coconut product, despite multiple requests. Later that year, the president signed a new law, the Kiribati Audit Act, which strengthened the autonomy of the Audit Office and established an independent board to oversee its work. (The office previously reported to the Finance Ministry.) The law also laid out enforcement mechanisms and broadened the Audit Office's mandate, allowing more thorough assessments of budgets, expenditures, and government performance.

The government responded to the 2018 *Butiraoi* ferry disaster, which killed 95 people, with opacity. After receiving public criticism over its failure to release a report on the incident, the government vowed to make the report public after the completion of a police investigation. The report was issued in October 2019, but authorities only allowed individuals to read it under strict supervision; the report attributed the ferry disaster to the vessel's poor condition and noted that the crew was regularly inebriated.

CIVIL LIBERTIES: 56 / 60

D. FREEDOM OF EXPRESSION AND BELIEF: 16 / 16

D1. Are there free and independent media? 4 / 4

While the market does not support a large and diverse media sector, there are no significant restrictions on the flow of news and information, which is often disseminated informally. A small number of private news and media outlets operate freely. Wave TV, which launched in March 2019, was reportedly the first to produce content locally. Foreign radio services are available.

Foreign journalists can perform their roles in Kiribati only after receiving a permit. In October 2019, a group of Australian journalists was restricted to a Tarawa hotel after the government claimed they arrived without the requisite permit. The journalists had visited Kiribati to report on the government's decision to end its recognition of Taiwan.

D2. Are individuals free to practice and express their religious faith or nonbelief in public and private? 4 / 4

The constitution guarantees freedom of religion. Religious organizations of a certain size are required to register with the government, but there are no penalties for failing to do so. Two islands in the southern part of the archipelago have overwhelmingly Protestant populations and maintain a "one religion" tradition. However, foreign missionaries may operate freely there upon requesting permission from local authorities.

D3. Is there academic freedom, and is the educational system free from extensive political indoctrination? 4 / 4

The school system is free of political indoctrination, and religious education by various denominations is available in public schools but not mandatory. There are no restrictions on academic freedom in the country, which hosts a campus of the Fiji-based University of the South Pacific as well as a teachers' college and technical training centers.

D4. Are individuals free to express their personal views on political or other sensitive topics without fear of surveillance or retribution? 4 / 4

The government does not impose constraints on freedom of speech or the expression of personal views.

E. ASSOCIATIONAL AND ORGANIZATIONAL RIGHTS: 12 / 12

E1. Is there freedom of assembly? 4 / 4

Freedom of assembly is constitutionally protected and generally upheld in practice.

E2. Is there freedom for nongovernmental organizations, particularly those that are engaged in human rights- and governance-related work? 4 / 4

There are no undue constraints on nongovernmental organizations (NGOs). The Kiribati Association of Non-Governmental Organisations (KANGO) serves as an umbrella group for a number of local NGOs, including church-based groups and health associations.

E3. Is there freedom for trade unions and similar professional or labor organizations? 4 / 4

Workers have the right to organize unions, strike, and bargain collectively. The Kiribati Trade Union Congress (KTUC), an affiliate of the International Trade Union Confederation (ITUC), includes unions and associations representing nurses, teachers, fishermen, and seafarers.

F. RULE OF LAW: 15 / 16

F1. Is there an independent judiciary? 4 / 4

The judicial system is modeled on English common law, and the courts are independent in practice. The chief justice is appointed by the president on the advice of the cabinet and the Public Service Commission (PSC); other High Court judges are appointed by the president on the advice of the chief justice and the PSC. Judges cannot be removed unless a special tribunal and the legislature find evidence of misbehavior, or an inability to perform their functions.

F2. Does due process prevail in civil and criminal matters? 4 / 4

Due process guarantees are typically respected during arrests, initial detentions, and trials. Detainees have access to lawyers, and defendants are usually granted bail while awaiting trial.

F3. Is there protection from the illegitimate use of physical force and freedom from war and insurgencies? 4 / 4

Police brutality is uncommon, and procedures for punishing such abuse are effective. Prison conditions are not considered harsh or inhumane. Kiribati has no army, relying on Australia and New Zealand to provide defense assistance under bilateral agreements. The use of traditional communal justice systems, which can include corporal punishment, is increasingly rare.

F4. Do laws, policies, and practices guarantee equal treatment of various segments of the population? 3 / 4

Women face legal discrimination on some issues as well as societal bias that limits their access to employment in practice. Citizenship laws favor men over women, for example by allowing fathers but not mothers to confer citizenship on children.

Same-sex sexual activity is a criminal offense, though the ban is rarely enforced; discrimination in employment based on sexual orientation is prohibited.

In 2018, Kiribati launched its first national disability action plan. The plan, which runs through 2021, aims to help Kiribati implement the UN Convention on the Rights of Persons with Disabilities, to which it became a signatory in 2013.

G. PERSONAL AUTONOMY AND INDIVIDUAL RIGHTS: 13 / 16

G1. Do individuals enjoy freedom of movement, including the ability to change their place of residence, employment, or education? 4 / 4

There are no significant constraints on freedom of movement.

G2. Are individuals able to exercise the right to own property and establish private businesses without undue interference from state or nonstate actors? 3 / 4

The government operates a system of land registration and generally upholds property rights. Land is owned on either an individual or a kinship basis, and inheritance laws pertaining to land favor sons over daughters. The World Bank has reported some bureaucratic obstacles to private business activity.

G3. Do individuals enjoy personal social freedoms, including choice of marriage partner and size of family, protection from domestic violence, and control over appearance? 3 / 4

Same-sex marriage is not permitted. Domestic violence is criminalized but remains a serious and widespread problem. A 2019 survey of domestic violence in South Tarawa found that 38 percent of women had experienced physical or sexual violence by a male partner. Cultural norms deter formal complaints and police interventions.

G4. Do individuals enjoy equality of opportunity and freedom from economic exploitation? 3 / 4

There are few economic opportunities in Kiribati, with most citizens engaged in subsistence agriculture. Although forced labor and other exploitative working conditions are uncommon, local women and girls are vulnerable to commercial sexual exploitation, often involving the crews of visiting ships.

In 2015, Kiribati adopted the Occupational Safety and Health Act, which restricted children and adolescents from a list of professions considered dangerous. That same year, it adopted the Employment and Industrial Relations Act, which set the minimum employment age for most work at 14 years and the minimum age for "hazardous" work at 18.

Kiribati is considered among the world's most environmentally vulnerable countries as a result of climate change and associated rising sea levels, which will affect coastal regions. The effects will likely have a detrimental impact on farming, fishing, and people's access to fresh water.

Kosovo

Population: 1,800,000
Capital: Priština
Freedom Status: Partly Free
Electoral Democracy: Yes

Overview: Kosovo holds credible and relatively well-administered elections, but its institutions remain weak, and rampant corruption has given rise to deep public distrust in the government. Journalists face serious pressure, and risk being attacked in connection with their reporting. The rule of law is inhibited by executive interference in the judiciary.

KEY DEVELOPMENTS IN 2020

- In February, the nationalist party Vetëvendosje (Self-Determination) formed a coalition government and installed Albin Kurti as prime minister. However, the Kurti government was ousted after 51 days by a vote of no-confidence orchestrated by the political old guard, including former president Thaçi, and the junior coalition partner Democratic League of Kosovo (LDK). The LDK then formed a government with Avdullah Hoti as prime minister, winning parliamentary confirmation with the bare minimum 61 votes. In December, the Constitutional Court determined that the Hoti government had been illegitimately elected, as one lawmaker had been convicted of fraud before voting. The courts called for new elections in 2021.

- In November, Hashim Thaçi resigned from the presidency after being indicted by an international tribunal based out of The Hague for war crimes committed during the wars in former Yugoslavia in the 1990s. Vjosa Osmani became acting president, to be replaced after the 2021 parliamentary elections.
- In March and April, when the first people tested positive for COVID-19, residents in northern Kosovo were initially provided medical treatment by the Serbian government, not the Kosovar government. Throughout the year, residents were often unsure if they should follow lockdown restrictions imposed by the Serbian or Kosovar government. According to government statistics provided to the World Health Organization (WHO), over 51,000 people tested positive for COVID-19 and 1,300 died.

POLITICAL RIGHTS: 23 / 40 (−2)

A. ELECTORAL PROCESS: 8 / 12 (−1)

A1. Was the current head of government or other chief national authority elected through free and fair? 2 / 4 (−1)

Kosovo is a parliamentary republic, with the prime minister indirectly elected for a four-year term by at least a two-thirds majority (61 votes) of the unicameral Assembly. In February 2020, Albin Kurti, leader of the nationalist party Vetëvendosje, became prime minister after the Assembly approved the party's coalition government with 66 votes; talks had been ongoing since the October 2019 elections between Vetëvendosje and the LDK, which had emerged as the two largest parties in the election.

In March 2020, Kurti's government collapsed, and though Kurti favored holding snap elections, the Constitutional Court ruled in May that new elections were not necessary; Avdullah Hoti of the LDK came to power in June with the bare minimum 61 parliamentary votes. In December, the Constitutional Court ruled that the Hoti government had been illegitimately elected, as one lawmaker had already been convicted of fraud before voting. The courts called for new elections in 2021.

The president is elected by the Assembly for a five-year term by a two-thirds majority. If after two rounds no candidate has received a two-thirds majority, the president is elected by a simple majority. Former president Hashim Thaçi resigned in November 2020 after being indicted by an international tribunal based out of The Hague for war crimes committed during wars in former Yugoslavia in the 1990s. Vjosa Osmani became acting president, to be replaced after the 2021 parliamentary elections.

Score Change: The score declined from 3 to 2 after the parliament installed the government of Prime Minister Avdullah Hoti by a single-vote margin with the support of one lawmaker with an active prison sentence, which was later nullified by the Constitutional Court.

A2. Were the current national legislative representatives elected through free and fair elections? 3 / 4

The unicameral Assembly contains 120 seats and members are elected to four-year terms; 100 are directly elected by proportional representation, while 10 seats are reserved for ethnic Serbs and another 10 are reserved for other ethnic communities.

The October 2019 election was marked by a relatively high turnout of 44.6 percent. Vetëvendosje won 31 seats, the LDK won 30, and the Democratic Party of Kosovo (PDK) won 25. The Alliance for the Future of Kosovo (AAK) and the Social Democratic Party (PSD) won 14 seats in an electoral alliance. The Serb List won 10. Other parties won the remaining 10 seats. While the election was considered credible by local and European

Union (EU) observers, vote-counting issues were noted, along with incidents of voter intimidation in Serb areas.

The Vetëvendosje-LDK coalition government, approved in February 2020, was ousted after 51 days by a no-confidence vote. The LDK then formed a coalition government in June with the minimum number of votes needed (61). In December, the Constitutional Court ruled that the Hoti government's ascension was invalid, as one lawmaker had already been convicted of fraud before voting. The courts called for new elections in 2021.

A3. Are the electoral laws and framework fair, and are they implemented impartially by the relevant election management bodies? 3 / 4

The Central Election Commission (CEC), which administers elections, is generally transparent and fair. The CEC was largely successful in organizing the October 2019 snap election, and was able to provide real-time electoral updates on its website. However, the body was unable to fully update voter rolls, which contained some deceased voters. Overall, the government has failed to implement effective electoral reforms, as recommended by the European Commission.

B. POLITICAL PLURALISM AND PARTICIPATION: 10 / 16 (−1)

B1. Do the people have the right to organize in different political parties or other competitive political groupings of their choice, and is the system free of undue obstacles to the rise and fall of these competing parties or groupings? 3 / 4

A proliferation of parties competes in Kosovo. However, political parties sometimes face intimidation and harassment that can negatively impact their ability to operate. The Serb List has been accused of harassing rival parties and creating an environment where voters fear supporting alternatives.

Formerly a political movement, Vetëvendosje transformed into a political party and won the 2019 parliamentary elections, a significant power shift away from mainstream political parties.

B2. Is there a realistic opportunity for the opposition to increase its support or gain power through elections? 3 / 4 (−1)

Opposition parties have a somewhat reasonable chance of gaining power through elections. Vetëvendosje and the LDK defeated the governing PANA coalition, which included the AAK, PDK, and Social Democratic Initiative (NISMA), in the October 2019 snap election. However, the political old guard, including former president Thaçi, and the junior coalition partner LDK, helped oust the Vetëvendosje government by pushing forward a no-confidence vote. The collapse of the Vetëvendosje government raised questions in relation to the reasonable ability of the opposition to gain and maintain power.

Candidates competing in Serb areas from parties other than the Serb List encountered intimidation during the 2019 election campaign. Three ethnic Serb parties and alliances competed with the Serb List but were unable to pass the 5 percent vote threshold to enter the parliament.

Score Change: The score declined from 4 to 3 after the political old guard engineered the downfall of the first government ever led by the Vetëvendosje party, which had only been in power for 51 days.

B3. Are the people's political choices free from domination by forces that are external to the political sphere, or by political forces that employ extrapolitical means? 2 / 4

Corruption and clientelism often pressure voters' choices during elections. Powerful businesspeople in Kosovo may influence their employees' political choices.

Serbia continues to exert influence on the platform of the Serb List, as well as the political choices of ethnic Serbs generally. EU election monitors noted that the Serbian government and Serb List officials explicitly directed ethnic Serbs in Kosovo to vote for the party during the 2019 election campaign.

Major political figures in Kosovo, including former president Thaçi and former prime minister Haradinaj, have links to organized crime and high-level corruption, which play powerful roles in politics and influence the installation of key leaders.

B4. Do various segments of the population (including ethnic, racial, religious, gender, LGBT+, and other relevant groups) have full political rights and electoral opportunities? 2 / 4

While several political parties compete for the votes of ethnic Serbs, the population is not fully integrated into the electoral process or Kosovo's institutions. Seven minority groups are officially recognized and politically represented through parliamentary quotas.

Women hold 38 out of 120 seats in the parliament and gender quotas are enshrined in the constitution. However, women have historically been underrepresented in politics. Though parties are legally required to achieve gender parity in their candidate lists, no party met the requirement in 2019. Media coverage during the 2019 election campaign provided more reporting on male candidates.

LGBT+ people are politically marginalized, and their interests are not represented in Kosovar politics.

C. FUNCTIONING OF GOVERNMENT: 5 / 12

C1. Do the freely elected head of government and national legislative representatives determine the policies of the government? 2 / 4

Kosovo had three governments during 2020. Former prime minister Haradinaj's caretaker government was replaced in February by the short-lived, reformist Kurti government. The Hoti government took office in June, but was unable to function effectively due to its narrow majority in the Assembly; decision-making was nearly impossible, and the opposition boycotted parliamentary sessions. In December, the Constitutional Court declared the Hoti government was illegitimate, and called for new elections in 2021.

Serbia still maintains influence in northern Kosovo, where Kosovar institutions do not have a strong presence. In recent years, the government has decentralized, granting self-rule to Serb enclaves in the southern part of Kosovo; this weakened parallel structures run by the Serbian government in those areas. A 2015 agreement between Kosovo and Serbia laid the groundwork for the Community of Serb Municipalities, a body intended to promote the interests of Serbs, which includes a proposed legislature for the Serb community. The establishment of the community remained at an impasse at the end of 2020.

Government communication with the Serbian community regarding the coronavirus was poor. People who contracted COVID-19 in northern Kosovo were initially provided medical treatment by the Serbian government. The local population was often confused as to whether to follow coronavirus restrictions imposed by the Serbian or Kosovar government.

The Chinese and Turkish governments have exerted influence over government processes in Kosovo in recent years.

State capture is a prominent issue and is often a result of clientelism—the illegal giving of favors to officials from wealthy individuals or groups, should officials pursue the interest of those who reward them.

C2. Are safeguards against official corruption strong and effective? 1 / 4

According to the European Commission's October 2020 report on Kosovo, corruption and state capture are widespread and of serious concern, and the institutional framework to combat them is weak. The mandates of Kosovo's four main anticorruption bodies overlap, and they have difficulty coordinating their efforts. Authorities have shown little commitment to prosecuting high-level corruption, and when top officials are prosecuted, convictions are rare. The short-lived Kurti government of early 2020 made some efforts to fight corruption and introduced a working group to study vetting in the judicial system. Multiple corruption scandals involving government officials were exposed during the Hoti government.

In October 2020, the Hoti government abolished the Special Anti-Corruption Taskforce that had operated under the Kosovo Police for more than 10 years and had investigated cases of high-level corruption among senior politicians. It had interviewed Hoti in 2019 as part of an ongoing corruption investigation.

C3. Does the government operate with openness and transparency? 2 / 4

The COVID-19 pandemic exacerbated existing challenges with government transparency. Despite the adoption of the Law on Access to Public Documents in 2010, which was intended to make government documents available upon request, government institutions frequently deny those requests with little or no justification; the COVID-19 pandemic provided officials another excuse to avoid fulfilling requests. Courts have been very slow to respond to complaints from those denied government information due to persistent backlogs in the judicial system.

CIVIL LIBERTIES: 31 / 60
D. FREEDOM OF EXPRESSION AND BELIEF: 9 / 16
D1. Are there free and independent media? 2 / 4

The constitution guarantees press freedom, and a variety of media outlets operate in Kosovo, including the publicly operated Radio Television.

Political influence over the media sector remains at concerning levels, and a number of journalists were attacked in 2020. The increasing tensions around political events in Kosovo during the year also resulted in an increase in the number of journalists threatened or harassed on social media.

D2. Are individuals free to practice and express their religious faith or nonbelief in public and private? 2 / 4

The constitution guarantees religious freedom. However, the Law on Freedom of Religion prevents some religious communities from registering as legal entities, a designation that would allow them to more easily buy and rent property, access burial sites, establish bank accounts, and carry out other administrative activities. In 2020, the government again failed to pass draft legislation that would incorporate the recommendations of the Venice Commission of the Council of Europe by allowing the legal registration of currently unrecognized religious communities.

Measures put in place by the government during 2020 to deal with the COVID-19 pandemic, such as a ban on public gatherings, prevented people from practicing their faith at houses of worship, though these measures followed public-health guidance.

Tensions between Muslims and Orthodox Christians occasionally flare up, though interreligious relations are generally peaceful.

D3. Is there academic freedom, and is the educational system free from extensive political indoctrination? 2 / 4

In recent years, the European Association for Quality Assurance in Higher Education has expressed concern that the independence of the Kosovo Accreditation Agency (KAA) has been compromised and is subject to political influence. In July 2019, three universities that were established between 2009 and 2015 lost their accreditation due to the poor quality of their curriculums and administrative failures. PDK officials were involved in establishing these schools, and members of the outgoing 2019 PDK coalition were installed in some leadership positions.

D4. Are individuals free to express their personal views on political or other sensitive topics without fear of surveillance or retribution? 3 / 4

Individuals are largely free to express their political views without fear of retribution. In recent years, limited space has opened up for discussion on sensitive topics such as ethnic relations and LGBT+ matters.

E. ASSOCIATIONAL AND ORGANIZATIONAL RIGHTS: 8 / 12
E1. Is there freedom of assembly? 3 / 4

Freedom of assembly is generally respected, though demonstrations are occasionally restricted for security reasons. A number of protests were held without incident in 2020, with participants respecting COVID-19 safety measures: they stood masked, distanced themselves from each other, and gathered at their windows and on their balconies, banging pots and pans.

E2. Is there freedom for nongovernmental organizations, particularly those that are engaged in human rights- and governance-related work? 3 / 4

Nongovernmental organizations (NGOs) function freely, though the courts can ban groups that infringe on the constitutional order or encourage ethnic hatred. NGOs occasionally experience pressure to curtail criticism of the government, though many continue to criticize the authorities and have largely been able to engage in advocacy work without interference. Funding for NGOs remained an issue in 2020, as international sources of support have declined in recent years. Despite the uncertainty of how the pandemic would affect their funding, civil society organizations continued to provide aid throughout the year.

E3. Is there freedom for trade unions and similar professional or labor organizations? 2 / 4

The constitution protects the right to establish and join trade unions, but employers frequently do not respect collective bargaining rights. It is difficult to form a private sector union because employers often intimidate workers to prevent them from organizing. As a result, few private sector unions exist in Kosovo. Several public sector unions denounced a June 2020 Constitutional Court ruling that the law on salaries adopted in 2019, which would have increased their wages, was unconstitutional.

F. RULE OF LAW: 6 / 16
F1. Is there an independent judiciary? 1 / 4

Political interference in the judiciary, particularly from the executive branch, remains a problem, despite the December 2020 ruling that the Hoti government was elected illegitimately. Widespread judicial corruption also negatively impacts the branch's independence. Resource constraints and a lack of qualified judges hinder the performance of the judiciary. In early 2020, the Kurti government introduced a working group to study vetting in the judicial system; the Hoti government later appointed a new working group on the matter. Judges' ability to work has been seriously impacted by the COVID-19 pandemic, which limited in-person court hearings.

F2. Does due process prevail in civil and criminal matters? 1 / 4

Prosecutors and courts remain susceptible to political interference and corruption by powerful political and business elites, undermining due process.

Although the law states that defendants should not be detained before trial unless they are likely to flee or tamper with evidence, judges often order suspects detained without cause. Lengthy pretrial detentions are common due to judicial inefficiency and resource constraints.

In April 2019, Kosovo repatriated 110 people who previously lived in territory controlled by the Islamic State (IS) militant group. While they are provided public services and legal counsel, individuals within this group have also been subject to detention or house arrest upon their return.

F3. Is there protection from the illegitimate use of physical force and freedom from war and insurgencies? 2 / 4

Although the EU brokered an agreement in 2015 between Kosovo and Serbia to disband the Serb Civilna Zastita (Civil Protection) security force in northern Kosovo, there have been reports that the force is still operating illegally. Prison conditions have improved in recent years, but violence and poor medical care remain problems. The police sometimes abuse detainees in custody.

In October 2019, prosecutors reopened an investigation into the death of Vetëvendosje activist Astrit Dehari, who was accused of attacking the Assembly building in 2016. Dehari died in detention that year, and his death was ruled a suicide; prosecutors launched their probe after his family commissioned a report from a Swiss forensic institute that concluded Dehari did not die by suicide. No further information was reported by the end of 2020.

In November 2020, a number of former Kosovo Liberation Army (KLA) members—including former president Thaçi, leader of the PDK Kadri Veseli, former head of Parliament Jakup Krasniqi, and member of Parliament Rexhep Selimi—were charged with war crimes by the Kosovo Specialist Chambers (KSC), a tribunal in The Hague investigating war crimes committed during Kosovo's 1998–99 war for independence. Thaçi resigned from his position and the four were being held in detention in The Hague at year's end. The government previously attempted to stop the work of the KSC through efforts to repeal or renegotiate the 2015 law establishing its existence. Some former KLA members have been convicted by other courts.

F4. Do laws, policies, and practices guarantee equal treatment of various segments of the population? 2 / 4

Kosovo's Roma, Ashkali, and Gorani populations continue to face discrimination in education, employment, and access to social services; they were particularly impacted by the COVID-19 pandemic.

LGBT+ people face social pressure to hide their sexual orientation or gender identity and face obstacles in making legal changes on the latter. The Civil Code of Kosovo continues to exclude same-sex partnerships from legal recognition.

Women experience discrimination in employment, particularly in regard to hiring for high-level positions in government and the private sector. The Law on Gender Equality seeks to ensure that the governing boards of private companies have gender parity, but this has not been widely implemented.

G. PERSONAL AUTONOMY AND INDIVIDUAL RIGHTS: 8 / 16

G1. Do individuals enjoy freedom of movement, including the ability to change their place of residence, employment, or education? 3 / 4

Freedom of movement and residence is somewhat impaired in Kosovo, especially for those living in Serb areas. The government refuses to accept travel documents issued by the Serbian government that show towns in Kosovo as the place of residence, hindering travel for many Serbs. Meanwhile, Serbs living in Kosovo do not benefit from Serbia's visa waiver agreement with the EU, making travel with a Serbian passport relatively difficult for those living in the enclaves. Kosovars have also been hindered from traveling to Bosnia and Herzegovina by the need for visas in recent years.

In 2020, the government restricted movement and enforced curfews at different times throughout the year to prevent the spread the COVID-19 pandemic. These public health measures were time-bound and depended on the severity of the outbreak.

G2. Are individuals able to exercise the right to own property and establish private businesses without undue interference from state or nonstate actors? 1 / 4

The legal framework on property rights is poorly outlined, and those rights are inadequately enforced in practice. While the law states that inheritance must be split equally between male and female heirs, strong patriarchal attitudes lead to pressure on women to relinquish their rights to male family members. A number of policies incentivize co-ownership, where couples who wish to register their properties jointly have their municipal taxes and fees waived. However, this has not significantly increased the percentage of properties owned by women. Property reclamation by displaced persons is hindered by threats of violence and resistance to accepting returnees from local communities.

G3. Do individuals enjoy personal social freedoms, including choice of marriage partner and size of family, protection from domestic violence, and control over appearance? 2 / 4

Domestic violence remains a problem, despite the government's five-year strategy that was launched in 2017 to address the issue, and is considered a civil matter unless the victim is physically harmed. The number of cases of domestic violence rose dramatically in 2020 during the COVID-19 pandemic. When criminal cases are referred, prosecutions and convictions are rare. Rape is illegal, but spousal rape is not addressed by the law. Courts often give convicted rapists sentences that are lighter than the prescribed minimum.

G4. Do individuals enjoy equality of opportunity and freedom from economic exploitation? 2 / 4

Equal opportunity is inhibited by persistently high levels of unemployment. Kosovo is a source, transit point, and destination for human trafficking, and corruption within the government enables perpetrators. Children are at particular risk of exploitation by traffickers, who can force them to beg or engage in sex work.

Kuwait

Population: 4,700,000
Capital: Kuwait City
Freedom Status: Partly Free
Electoral Democracy: No

Overview: Kuwait is a constitutional emirate ruled by the Sabah family. While the monarchy holds executive power and dominates most state institutions, the elected parliament plays an influential role, often challenging the government. State authorities impose some constraints on civil liberties, including speech and assembly, and the country's large population of non-citizen workers faces particular disadvantages.

KEY DEVELOPMENTS IN 2020

- Sheikh Nawaf al-Ahmad al-Jaber al-Sabah, aged 83, was installed as the new emir in September after his predecessor and half-brother, Sheikh Sabah al-Ahmad al-Jaber al-Sabah, died at age 91. In October, Sheikh Nawaf appointed his half-brother Sheikh Meshaal al-Ahmad al-Jaber al-Sabah, aged 80, as the new heir apparent.
- As a result of the COVID-19 pandemic, authorities imposed a nationwide lockdown in March, subsequently lifting the restrictions in phases through August. However, a ban on public gatherings remained in place. Migrant workers, who suffered from loss of employment and overcrowded living conditions during the year, mounted protests despite the ban. By year's end the country had reported more than 150,000 confirmed cases of the coronavirus and about 940 deaths.
- In August, the parliament passed Kuwait's first law to combat domestic violence, following years of campaigning by women's rights activists.
- Parliamentary elections were held in December, and 24 of the 50 winning candidates were broadly aligned with the political opposition. Many incumbents lost their seats, including the sole female member.

POLITICAL RIGHTS: 14 / 40 (+1)
A. ELECTORAL PROCESS: 3 / 12 (+1)
A1. Was the current head of government or other chief national authority elected through free and fair elections? 0 / 4

The hereditary emir holds extensive executive powers. Sheikh Nawaf al-Ahmad al-Jaber al-Sabah became the new ruler in September 2020, after the death of his half-brother and predecessor, Sheikh Sabah al-Ahmad al-Jaber al-Sabah, who was 91 and had reigned since 2006. Sheikh Nawaf appointed another half-brother, Sheikh Meshaal al-Ahmad al-Jaber al-Sabah, as his heir apparent in October. The parliament, which must approve the choice of heir by majority vote, did so unanimously, though the ruling family has been under growing pressure to plan a transition to a younger generation.

The emir chooses the prime minister and appoints cabinet ministers on the prime minister's recommendation. At least one cabinet minister must be an elected member of parliament. The parliament can remove cabinet ministers through a vote of no confidence, and the emir can respond to a similar vote against the prime minister either by forming a new cabinet or by dissolving the parliament and holding elections. All prime ministers and most senior cabinet ministers have been members of the ruling family. Current prime minister Sabah al-Khalid al-Sabah was appointed in 2019.

A2. Were the current national legislative representatives elected through free and fair elections? 2 / 4 (+1)

The 50-member National Assembly (parliament) is elected by popular vote on a formally nonpartisan basis. The emir may appoint up to 15 cabinet ministers who were not elected members of the assembly, and these are considered additional ex-officio members, though no ministers can take part in confidence votes.

The parliament serves terms of up to four years. The emir and the Constitutional Court, which lacks independence, have the power to dissolve the assembly, and the executive can thereby determine the timing of elections to suit its political priorities. This has occurred four times since 2011, usually when serious disputes arose between lawmakers and senior ministers from the ruling family. However, the parliament elected in 2016 served its full four-year term.

Elections were held on schedule in December 2020, with a reported voter turnout of about 70 percent. As in the 2016 elections, 24 of the successful candidates were broadly aligned with the opposition, including Islamist and liberal blocs, but there was also significant turnover, with just 19 of the 43 incumbents who ran winning seats. Nine candidates who did not win seats launched an appeal claiming that there were irregularities including vote buying, falsified voter addresses, and failure to check the identities of voters. Alleged vote buying has been a long-standing problem.

A local nongovernmental organization (NGO), the Kuwait Transparency Society, observed the 2020 polls, but only five observers were allowed, rather than the usual 15, ostensibly because of COVID-19 restrictions. Pandemic-related constraints also prevented normal election rallies, but there was extensive online campaigning ahead of the vote.

Score Change: The score improved from 1 to 2 because parliamentary elections were held at the end of the legislature's full term, breaking a pattern of early dissolutions and snap voting that disadvantaged the opposition, and because the balloting proved relatively competitive despite some chronic flaws and new public health constraints.

A3. Are the electoral laws and framework fair, and are they implemented impartially by the relevant election management bodies? 1 / 4

Elections are administered by the Interior Ministry rather than an independent institution, and the electoral system lacks transparency, as evidenced by an opaque voter registration process. Kuwaiti elections are relatively competitive by the standards of the region, but they are not typically observed by independent, well-established monitoring organizations, and corruption in campaigns remain a concern.

The emir has implemented changes to electoral laws in close proximity to elections. In 2012, two months ahead of elections, Sheikh Sabah issued a decree that reduced the number of candidates elected in each district from four to one; opposition forces claimed that the move was designed to reduce their strength, as they had been able to build successful alliances under the previous system.

B. POLITICAL PLURALISM AND PARTICIPATION: 7 / 16

B1. Do the people have the right to organize in different political parties or other competitive political groupings of their choice, and is the system free of undue obstacles to the rise and fall of these competing parties or groupings? 2 / 4

Formal political parties are banned, and while parliamentary blocs are permitted and exist in practice, the prohibition on parties tends to inhibit political organization among like-minded candidates.

Politicians have some space to criticize the government, but those who have seriously challenged the emir's authority have faced criminal charges. In 2018 the Cassation Court ordered the imprisonment of a group of opposition figures, including two sitting and several former lawmakers, on long-contested charges related to the storming of the parliament building during 2011 protests calling for the resignation of the prime minister. One of the former lawmakers who was imprisoned, prominent opposition leader

Musallam al-Barrak, had completed a two-year prison term in 2017 on separate charges of insulting the emir; those charges stemmed from his strong public opposition to the new 2012 electoral law.

B2. Is there a realistic opportunity for the opposition to increase its support or gain power through elections? 2 / 4

The constitutional system does not allow democratic transfers of power at the executive level. Opposition blocs are able to gain representation in the parliament, but after their victory in early 2012 was controversially annulled, they boycotted elections in late 2012 and 2013; since the changes to the electoral laws in 2012 they have not held a majority.

Candidates aligned with the opposition won 24 out of 50 seats in the parliament elected in December 2020, including three members of the local affiliate of the Muslim Brotherhood, an Islamist group that is banned in most other Persian Gulf monarchies.

B3. Are the people's political choices free from domination by forces that are external to the political sphere, or by political forces that employ extrapolitical means? 2 / 4

The hereditary emir and the ruling family frequently interfere in political processes, including through the harassment of political and media figures, and the government impedes the activities of opposition parliamentary blocs. It has been alleged that senior members of the ruling family provide economic resources to favored politicians and journalists in order to exert political influence.

In the absence of political parties, major tribes hold their own informal and technically illegal primary elections to unite their members behind certain parliamentary candidates, who then typically use their public office to generate economic benefits for members of their tribe.

B4. Do various segments of the population (including ethnic, racial, religious, gender, LGBT+, and other relevant groups) have full political rights and electoral opportunities? 1 / 4

The electorate consists of men and women over 21 years of age who have been citizens for at least 20 years and who have a Kuwaiti father. Most members of state security agencies are barred from voting.

Access to citizenship is tightly restricted. About 70 percent of the country's residents are noncitizens, primarily from South Asian and other Arab countries, who have no right to vote even if they are lifelong residents. Naturalization is extremely rare for people born abroad or without a Kuwaiti father, and it is not permitted for non-Muslims. More than 100,000 residents, known as bidoon, are stateless; many of them claim Kuwaiti nationality and descent, but official processes to verify their eligibility for citizenship are slow, opaque, and largely ineffective. Individuals have at times had their Kuwaiti citizenship revoked for political reasons.

The Shiite Muslim community makes up about a third of the citizen population but is not well represented in the political system. Shiite candidates won six out of 50 seats in both the 2016 and 2020 parliamentary elections.

Women have had the right to vote and run for office since 2005, and a few have been elected to the parliament, but the legislature was left without any women after the sole female incumbent lost her seat in the December 2020 elections. Entrenched societal attitudes hamper more active participation by women in the political process, and the interests of women are poorly represented in practice. Neither the political groupings nor the tribes generally promote women's participation as candidates. Societal and legal discrimination against LGBT+ people prevents them from playing any open role in political affairs.

C. FUNCTIONING OF GOVERNMENT: 4 / 12

C1. Do the freely elected head of government and national legislative representatives determine the policies of the government? 1 / 4

While some laws initiated by elected members of parliament are adopted and implemented, policymaking authority is concentrated in the hands of the hereditary emir and his appointed government. The emir has repeatedly used his power to dissolve the National Assembly when it imposes checks on the executive. He can also veto legislation and issue executive decrees when the assembly is not in session.

Interactions between the executive and legislature are affected by succession-related rivalries within the ruling family. Powerful members of the family are able to put pressure on rivals who are government ministers by cultivating allies in the parliament who can question them and scrutinize their performance.

C2. Are safeguards against official corruption strong and effective? 1 / 4

Corruption is pervasive. An Anti-Corruption Authority began operating in 2015, and it has referred some cases for prosecution, but in general its activities appear insufficient given the perceived scale of the problem. In 2019 the Constitutional Court struck down a 2018 law meant to regulate conflicts of interest among officials, finding that it failed to precisely define what amounted to a conflict of interest.

Allegations of malfeasance lodged by lawmakers against government ministers have been at the heart of the country's recurring political crises. Members of the ruling elite regularly disregard parliamentary calls for accountability and often obstruct elected officials' efforts to investigate graft and abuse of power. In November 2019, the cabinet resigned after members of the parliament criticized some ministers for misusing public funds and threatened a no-confidence vote against the interior minister. Shortly afterward, the outgoing defense minister, Sheikh Nasser Sabah al-Ahmad al-Sabah, who was also the son of the then emir and seen as a possible successor, accused the interior minister of embezzling public funds. The Justice Ministry banned media discussion of the matter.

C3. Does the government operate with openness and transparency? 2 / 4

Transparency on government spending is inadequate, and there are few mechanisms that encourage officials to disclose information about government operations. Kuwait does not have any legislation guaranteeing the right to access public information. The State Audit Bureau provides some oversight on revenue and expenditures, reporting to both the government and the National Assembly, though not necessarily to the public. Defense spending is particularly opaque, with no detailed breakdown available to the parliament.

CIVIL LIBERTIES: 23 / 60

D. FREEDOM OF EXPRESSION AND BELIEF: 6 / 16

D1. Are there free and independent media? 1 / 4

Kuwaiti law assigns penalties for the publication of material that insults Islam, criticizes the emir, discloses information considered secret or private, or calls for the regime's overthrow. Journalists also risk imprisonment under a restrictive 2016 cybercrimes law that criminalizes the dissemination of similar content online.

Thousands of books have been banned in the country for political or moral reasons, and the government has instructed internet service providers to block certain websites on similar grounds. The media regulator, the Commission for Mass Communications and Information Technology, has sweeping powers to monitor, block, and censor online material. Foreign media outlets operate relatively freely in Kuwait.

D2. Are individuals free to practice and express their religious faith or nonbelief in public and private? 2 / 4

Islam is the state religion, and blasphemy is a punishable offense. The government appoints Sunni imams and oversees their sermons. Shiite Muslims have their own religious institutions, including Sharia (Islamic law) courts, though the government does not permit training of Shiite clerics in the country. Several Christian churches are officially registered, and members of other non-Muslim minority groups are generally permitted to practice their faiths in private; they are forbidden from proselytizing.

D3. Is there academic freedom, and is the educational system free from extensive political indoctrination? 2 / 4

Academic freedom is impeded by self-censorship on politically sensitive topics, as well as by broader legal restrictions on freedom of expression, including the prohibitions on insulting the emir and defaming Islam.

D4. Are individuals free to express their personal views on political or other sensitive topics without fear of surveillance or retribution? 1 / 4

Freedom of expression is curtailed by state surveillance and the criminalization of some forms of critical speech, especially if it touches on the emir or the rulers of other Arab countries. The cybercrimes law that took effect in 2016 imposes prison sentences of up to 10 years as well as fines for online speech that criticizes the emir, judicial officials, religious figures, or foreign leaders.

Activists and other individuals are often summoned for questioning over their online comments, and some have been prosecuted. Beginning in March 2020, the Ministry of Information issued repeated warnings about spreading false news or rumors in the context of the COVID-19 pandemic, and Amnesty International reported that those referred for prosecution included a user accused of spreading false information about the spread of the virus in Egypt.

Individuals who criticize the government on social media also tend to be harassed by online trolls and automated "bot" accounts, and local activists and academics have expressed concerns that some of this activity may be state sponsored.

E. ASSOCIATIONAL AND ORGANIZATIONAL RIGHTS: 4 / 12

E1. Is there freedom of assembly? 1 / 4

Freedom of assembly is constrained in practice. Organizers must notify officials of a public meeting or protest, and those who participate in unauthorized protests are subject to prison terms or, for noncitizens, deportation. Nevertheless, some peaceful protests have been allowed without a permit.

In July 2019 the authorities arrested 15 advocates for the rights of bidoon after they took part in a protest triggered by the suicide of a young stateless man who was denied civil documents that are required to study or work. They were tried on charges that included calling for and attending unauthorized protests. In January 2020, two of them were sentenced to 10 years in prison, though an appeals court later overturned the penalties; the remainder of those in detention were reportedly acquitted or otherwise released after signing good-conduct pledges.

In March 2020, the government banned public gatherings as part of the COVID-19 lockdown, but the ban was kept in place later in the year after other lockdown restrictions were lifted.

E2. Is there freedom for nongovernmental organizations, particularly those that are engaged in human rights- and governance-related work? 2 / 4

The government restricts the registration and licensing of NGOs, forcing many groups to operate without legal standing. Representatives of licensed NGOs must obtain government permission to attend foreign conferences, and critical groups may be subject to harassment. Kuwaiti NGOs were largely absent from the country's Universal Periodic Review process at the UN Human Rights Council in January 2020.

E3. Is there freedom for trade unions and similar professional or labor organizations? 1 / 4

Private-sector workers who are Kuwaiti citizens have the right to join labor unions and bargain collectively, and a limited right to strike, but labor laws allow for only one national union federation. Noncitizen migrant workers do not enjoy these rights and can face dismissal and deportation for engaging in union or strike activity. In 2019 the Kuwait Trade Union Federation opened an office to provide migrant workers with advice on legal disputes. Civil servants and household workers are also denied union rights; most citizen workers are public employees and do not have the right to strike.

Migrant workers have sometimes participated in risky illegal labor actions to protest nonpayment of wages and other abuses. For instance, in May 2020, during the COVID-19 pandemic, Egyptian migrant workers protested after being confined to shelters while awaiting repatriation. The demonstrations, which authorities described as riots, were broken up by police using tear gas.

F. RULE OF LAW: 7 / 16

F1. Is there an independent judiciary? 1 / 4

Kuwait lacks an independent judiciary. The emir has the final say on judicial appointments, which are proposed by a Supreme Judicial Council made up of senior judges as well as the attorney general and deputy justice minister, and the executive branch approves judicial promotions. Judges who are Kuwaiti citizens are appointed for life, while noncitizens receive contracts for up to three years, reflecting a wider tendency to keep noncitizens employed on precarious short-term contracts. The courts frequently rule in favor of the government in cases related to politics.

F2. Does due process prevail in civil and criminal matters? 2 / 4

Arbitrary arrests and detentions sometimes occur despite legal safeguards. Authorities may detain suspects for four days without charge. Noncitizens arrested for minor offenses are subject to detention and deportation without due process or access to the courts. In 2019, nine Egyptians were deported to Egypt because they were deemed to be members of the Muslim Brotherhood, which is banned in Egypt.

F3. Is there protection from the illegitimate use of physical force and freedom from war and insurgencies? 2 / 4

Kuwait is generally free from armed conflict, no major terrorist attacks have been reported since 2015, and there are relatively low levels of criminal violence. However, while the constitution prohibits torture and other forms of cruel and unusual punishment, these protections are not always upheld. Detainees, especially bidoon, continue to experience torture and beatings in custody. Overcrowding and unsanitary conditions are significant problems at prisons and deportation centers.

In 2017, the government carried out its first execution in four years, and a total of seven people were executed by hanging that year. Human Rights Watch has reported violations of due process in capital cases. No executions were reported in 2020.

F4. Do laws, policies, and practices guarantee equal treatment of various segments of the population? 2 / 4

Despite some legal protections from bias and abuse, women remain underrepresented in the workforce and face unequal treatment in several areas of law and society. Women account for a majority of university students, but the government enforces gender segregation in educational institutions. LGBT+ people face societal discrimination, and the penal code prescribes prison sentences for sex between men and "imitating the opposite sex."

Officials consider the country's more than 100,000 bidoon to be illegal residents, and they lack the protections and benefits associated with citizenship. They often live in poor conditions and have difficulty accessing public services and obtaining formal employment.

Noncitizen migrant workers are also excluded from the legal protections granted to citizens on a variety of topics. During the COVID-19 lockdown in 2020, many migrant workers were left without wages, while most Kuwaiti citizens, who tend to work in the public sector, continued to receive income.

G. PERSONAL AUTONOMY AND INDIVIDUAL RIGHTS: 6 / 16

G1. Do individuals enjoy freedom of movement, including the ability to change their place of residence, employment, or education? 2 / 4

Kuwait generally does not place constraints on citizens' movement, but migrant workers often face de facto restrictions on travel and choice of residence. The labor sponsorship system limits migrant workers' freedom to change jobs without permission from their existing employer.

In 2020 the country was under lockdown for several months as a result of the COVID-19 pandemic. Three areas that are home to large numbers of migrant workers—Mahboula, Jleeb al-Shuyoukh, and Al-Farwaniya—were under lockdown for months longer than the rest of the country. Many migrant workers were confined to overcrowded living quarters that increased their risk of infection, and infection rates overall were significantly higher among noncitizens than among citizens.

G2. Are individuals able to exercise the right to own property and establish private businesses without undue interference from state or nonstate actors? 1 / 4

Kuwaiti law allows citizens and foreign nationals, but not bidoon, to own private property. Although the law permits the establishment of businesses, bureaucratic obstacles sometimes slow the process. Companies are legally prohibited from conducting business with citizens of Israel.

Sharia-based inheritance rules, particularly those pertaining to Sunni families, put women at a disadvantage.

G3. Do individuals enjoy personal social freedoms, including choice of marriage partner and size of family, protection from domestic violence, and control over appearance? 2 / 4

Personal status laws favor men over women in matters of marriage, divorce, and child custody. For example, Sunni women must have the approval of a male guardian in order to marry, and they are only permitted to seek a divorce when deserted or subjected to domestic violence. Domestic abuse and spousal rape are not specifically prohibited by law, and rapists can avoid punishment if they marry their victims.

Article 153 of the penal code classifies crimes in which a man kills a close female relative whom he has caught in "an unsavory sexual act" as misdemeanors, punishable by at most three years in prison. Such incidents are rare but not entirely unknown; a local civil society campaign seeks to eliminate the penal code provision.

In August 2020, the parliament passed Kuwait's first law to combat domestic violence, following years of campaigning by women's rights activists. It provides for shelters, restraining orders, and legal assistance for victims, among other components. However, it does not criminalize domestic violence or cover gender-based violence outside the immediate household. The importance of such deficiencies was underlined by a case in September in which a pregnant woman was shot in a hospital by a family member who reportedly opposed her choice of husband.

G4. Do individuals enjoy equality of opportunity and freedom from economic exploitation? 1 / 4

Foreign household workers and other migrant workers are highly vulnerable to abuse and exploitation, often forced to live and work in poor or dangerous conditions for low pay. Despite some legal protections designed to prevent mistreatment, many employers reportedly confiscate their household workers' passports, subject them to excessive working hours, and restrict their movements outside the home. International media reports during 2019 highlighted cases in which recruiting agents held female migrant workers for ransom, demanding money from their families before they could return home. Other migrant workers have been repatriated by the state labor bureau after being refused payment or otherwise harassed or abused by their employers.

Kyrgyzstan

Population: 6,600,000
Capital: Bishkek
Freedom Status: Not Free
Electoral Democracy: No

Status Change: Kyrgyzstan's status declined from Partly Free to Not Free because the aftermath of deeply flawed parliamentary elections featured significant political violence and intimidation that culminated in the irregular seizure of power by a nationalist leader and convicted felon who had been freed from prison by supporters.

Overview: After two revolutions that ousted authoritarian presidents in 2005 and 2010, Kyrgyzstan adopted a parliamentary form of government. Governing coalitions have proven unstable, however, and corruption remains pervasive. Before it split, the Social Democratic Party of Kyrgyzstan (SDPK) consolidated power over several years, using the justice system to suppress political opponents and civil society critics. Unrest surrounding the annulled 2020 parliamentary elections led to significant political upheaval.

KEY DEVELOPMENTS IN 2020

- Protesters damaged government offices and forcibly released high-profile prisoners in October amid demonstrations against the conduct of that month's parliamentary elections. While the results were annulled two days after the polls, violence continued as the month progressed; supporters of nationalist politician Sadyr Japarov, who was among those freed from custody, intimidated and attacked opposition groups seeking to form a transitional government.

- Japarov became acting president and prime minister in mid-October, after the protests prompted the resignation of President Sooronbay Jeenbekov and Prime Minister Kubatbek Boronov. Japarov resigned from both posts in November to qualify for a presidential election due in January 2021.
- Kyrgyzstani officials were opaque in their response to the COVID-19 pandemic, denying reports that the country's health-care system was overwhelmed despite evidence of overcrowding. Bloggers, journalists, and medical professionals who criticized the COVID-19 response were forced to apologize for their statements by the authorities in March and April.
- Uzbek human rights activist Azimjan Askarov, who was accused of organizing riots after acts of violence were perpetrated against ethnic Uzbeks in southern Kyrgyzstan in 2010, died of pneumonia while in custody in July. Askarov, who was tortured in detention, had remained imprisoned despite his deteriorating health and repeated calls for his release.

POLITICAL RIGHTS: 4 / 40 (−8)
A. ELECTORAL PROCESS: 2 / 12 (−2)
A1. Was the current head of government or other chief national authority elected through free and fair elections? 0 / 4 (−1)

The directly elected president, who shares executive power with a prime minister, serves a single six-year term with no possibility of reelection. Prime ministers are appointed by the president after receiving the parliament's nomination.

The 2017 presidential election was marked by inappropriate use of government resources in support of Sooronbay Jeenbekov of the SDPK, who had served as prime minister under his predecessor, Almazbek Atambayev.

Birimdik (Unity), a political party affiliated with Jeenbekov, was among those implicated in vote buying and the misuse of administrative resources during the October 2020 parliamentary elections. Major protests over the poll's conduct took place in Bishkek the day after it was held and turned violent; demonstrators had clashed with police, forcibly freed prisoners held by the State Committee for National Security (GKNB), and set fire to the building housing the parliament and the president's office by the morning of October 6.

On October 14, Jeenbekov accepted the parliament's nomination of Sadyr Japarov of the Mekenchil (Patriotic) party—who days before had been freed from GKNB custody while serving a prison sentence for kidnapping—as prime minister. Jeenbekov resigned on October 15th, as Japarov supporters threatened to march on his residence.

Parliament speaker Kanat Isayev was next in the line of succession but declined to assume the presidency, after Japarov supporters called for Isayev's resignation and arrest. The parliament made Japarov acting president on October 16, though he had publicly declared himself acting president the day before. He served until November, when he resigned to qualify for an early presidential election scheduled for January 2021. Talant Mamytov, who had replaced Isayev as speaker, then became interim president.

Earlier, Prime Minister Mukhammedkaliy Abylgaziyev resigned in June 2020 after a corruption probe focusing on the government's management of radio frequencies implicated him in improper behavior. Successor Kubatbek Boronov resigned in October amid that month's unrest. Japarov resigned in November to contest the January 2021 presidential election, and was succeeded by First Deputy Prime Minister Artem Novikov.

Score Change: The score declined from 1 to 0 because Sadyr Japarov assumed the role of acting president before being appointed by the parliament amid threats of violence against his predecessor, and also became acting prime minister through opaque means.

A2. Were the current national legislative representatives elected through free and fair elections? 1 / 4 (−1)

The unicameral parliament currently consists of 120 deputies elected by party list in a single national constituency to serve five-year terms. No single party is allowed to hold more than 65 seats.

The Central Commission for Elections and Referenda (CEC) originally reported that four parties exceeded the threshold to secure seats in the October 2020 parliamentary elections, three of them affiliated with Jeenbekov. Birimdik topped the poll, reportedly winning 24.5 percent of the vote. Mekenim Kyrgyzstan (My Homeland Kyrgyzstan) won 23.9 percent; it is affiliated with the family of former customs official Raimbek Matraimov, who was implicated in money laundering and tax evasion that siphoned as much as $700 million out of Kyrgyzstan between 2011 and 2016. The progovernment Kyrgyzstan Party and nationalist Butun Kyrgyzstan (Whole Kyrgyzstan) also earned representation. The SDPK, which held most of the previous parliament's seats, split in 2019, and did not field candidates in the October 2020 poll.

Opposition parties refused to accept the results, accusing the victors of vote buying and intimidation; vote-buying evidence was disseminated on social media. Journalists and civil society also accused the victors of misusing administrative resources. The CEC annulled the results two days after the vote was held, selecting a December date for a rerun. However, parliamentarians in late October decided to delay the poll, which could be held as late as June 2021. When the parliament's term expired around the same time, parliamentarians voted to extend their own mandates.

Score Change: The score declined from 2 to 1 because electoral authorities annulled the results of the October 2020 parliamentary elections due to vote buying and other irregularities, and because the parliament subsequently postponed a new poll and extended its own mandate.

A3. Are the electoral laws and framework fair, and are they implemented impartially by the relevant election management bodies? 1 / 4

The CEC exhibited political bias during the 2017 presidential election, according to international observers. Electoral-law amendments enacted ahead of that poll made it more difficult for nongovernmental organizations (NGOs) to field observers and appeal decisions by election officials.

A 2016 referendum on constitutional amendments was conducted hastily, with little transparency or opportunities for public debate on the proposed changes. It ultimately won adoption. Administrative resources were reportedly used to support a "yes" vote, and state employees faced pressure to participate in the effort.

In November 2020, parliamentarians published a draft constitution that would strengthen the presidency and allow the next officeholder to appoint new CEC and Constitutional Chamber members before a new parliament is installed. A constitutional convention formed that month was tasked with formalizing the document, and continued its work at year's end.

B. POLITICAL PLURALISM AND PARTICIPATION: 3 / 16 (-2)

B1. Do the people have the right to organize in different political parties or other competitive political groupings of their choice, and is the system free of undue obstacles to the rise and fall of these competing parties or groupings? 1 / 4 (-1)

Citizens have the freedom to organize political parties and groupings, especially at the local level. Political parties are primarily vehicles for a handful of strong personalities, rather than mass organizations with clear ideologies and policy platforms. The SDPK split in 2019 as former presidents Jeenbekov and Atambayev competed for influence, with high-ranking members subsequently joining parties including Birimdik and Mekenim Kyrgyzstan.

Parties must pass a threshold to earn parliamentary seats, along with at least 0.7 percent of the vote in each of Kyrgyzstan's nine regional divisions. Electoral amendments passed in late October 2020 lowered the national threshold from 7 percent to 3 percent, and significantly reduced registration fees for parties.

Political parties were impeded by violence in the aftermath of the October 2020 parliamentary elections. Opposition parties excluded from the parliament attempted to collaborate in the formation of a transitional government but supporters of Japarov, acting with groups believed to maintain criminal connections, engaged in a campaign of street violence to intimidate supporters, with security forces failing to intervene.

Score Change: The score declined from 2 to 1 because Japarov supporters and groups believed to maintain criminal connections engaged in violence and intimidation to prevent opposition groups from collaborating to form a transitional government after the October 2020 elections.

B2. Is there a realistic opportunity for the opposition to increase its support or gain power through elections? 1 / 4

The 2010 constitutional reforms aimed to ensure political pluralism and prevent the reemergence of an authoritarian, superpresidential system. Since 2012, however, observers noted the SDPK's consolidation of power and its use of executive agencies to target political enemies. Opposition members and outside observers also accused the SDPK of attempting to improperly influence electoral and judicial outcomes. In recent years, opposition leaders have faced politically motivated criminal investigations and prosecutions, significantly reducing the public legitimacy of the justice system.

The proposed constitution published in November 2020 would reintroduce a superpresidential system while shrinking the size and role of the parliament.

B3. Are the people's political choices free from domination by forces that are external to the political sphere, or by political forces that employ extrapolitical means? 0 / 4 (-1)

While largely free from military domination, Kyrgyzstani politics are subject to the influence of organized crime and economic oligarchies. Political affairs are generally controlled by a small group of elites who head competing patronage networks.

Criminal violence and intimidation marred the aftermath of the October 2020 elections. Japarov supporters attacked an October 9 rally meant to bolster a potential transitional government, injuring its proposed prime minister and forcing several other politicians to flee. Speaker Isayev was also threatened by Japarov supporters before declining to serve as interim president later that month.

Score Change: The score declined from 1 to 0 because Japarov supporters engaged in a campaign of violence and threats of violence against sitting officials and political opponents to secure their preferred government in October 2020.

B4. Do various segments of the population (including ethnic, racial, religious, gender, LGBT+, and other relevant groups) have full political rights and electoral opportunities? 1 / 4

Ethnic minority groups face political marginalization. Politicians from the Kyrgyz majority have used ethnic Uzbeks as scapegoats on various issues in recent years, and minority populations remain underrepresented in elected offices, even in areas where they form a demographic majority.

Women enjoy equal political rights and have attained some notable leadership positions, but they are also underrepresented, having won 19 percent of the seats in the 2015 parliamentary election despite a 30 percent gender quota for party candidate lists. Legislation enacted in August 2019 extended the 30 percent gender quota to local municipal councils.

C. FUNCTIONING OF GOVERNMENT: 0 / 12 (−4)

C1. Do the freely elected head of government and national legislative representatives determine the policies of the government? 0 / 4 (−1)

Unresolved constitutional ambiguities regarding the division of power among the president, the prime minister, and the parliament—combined with the need to form multiparty coalitions—have contributed to the instability of governments in recent years. The prime minister has been replaced over a dozen times since 2010.

President Jeenbekov worked to steadily consolidate control of the government following his election in 2017, though predecessor Atambayev maintained significant influence until losing a power struggle against Jeenbekov in 2019. After Jeenbekov resigned amid protests in October 2020, neither his presidential successors nor their concurrently serving prime ministers were freely selected. The parliament also continued beyond the expiration of its democratic mandate.

Score Change: The score declined from 1 to 0 because neither the chief executive nor the legislators serving at the end of the year were freely elected.

C2. Are safeguards against official corruption strong and effective? 0 / 4 (−1)

Corruption is pervasive in politics and government. Political elites use government resources to reward clients—including organized crime figures—and punish opponents. An anticorruption office within the GKNB was formed in 2012, but has primarily been used to target the administration's political enemies in the parliament and municipal governments. Former prime ministers Sapar Isakov and Jantoro Satybaldiyev, who were aligned with former president Atambayev, were arrested on corruption charges in 2018; both were convicted and received prison sentences in December 2019.

A 2019 international investigation led by the Organized Crime and Corruption Reporting Project (OCCRP) implicated former customs official Raimbek Matraimov and his family in an operation that siphoned hundreds of millions of dollars out of Kyrgyzstan. Later that year, Chinese Uighur businessperson Aierken Saimaiti, who collaborated in the operation and served as a source for news articles on the subject, was murdered in Istanbul shortly before the OCCRP report was released.

The government was resistant to the investigation's findings for much of the year. In February 2020, the State Customs Service announced an investigation into a low-ranking official named in the report. In June, the GKNB accused the journalists who reported on the Matraimov case of corruption. Matraimov was eventually detained over his activity in October, after Japarov installed new leaders in the customs office and the GKNB. However, Matraimov was placed under de facto house arrest the next day after agreeing to return only

$24.6 million to the state, taking advantage of "economic amnesty" offered to officials who agreed to return ill-gotten gains by Japarov.

Score Change: The score declined from 1 to 0 because officials ignored and resisted the results of an investigation revealing pervasive corruption, and because Japarov offered "economic amnesty" to officials who benefited from ill-gotten gains after taking power in October 2020.

C3. Does the government operate with openness and transparency? 0 / 4 (−2)

Kyrgyzstani access-to-information laws are considered relatively strong, but implementation is poor in practice. Similarly, although public officials are obliged to disclose information on their personal finances, powerful figures are rarely held accountable for noncompliance or investigated for unexplained wealth. Oversight of public contracts is inadequate; corruption scandals in recent years have often centered on procurement deals or sales of state assets. Abylgaziyev, for example, resigned as prime minister in June 2020 when his government was accused of selling radio frequency access at below-market prices.

Kyrgyzstani officials were not transparent in disclosing COVID-19 infections or deaths, and are widely believed to have undercounted the toll of the pandemic. Death certificates of individuals who exhibited COVID-19 symptoms often listed pneumonia as the cause of death. Officials also denied reports that the Kyrgyzstani health-care system was overwhelmed by the pandemic, though evidence of overcrowding in hospitals was disseminated on social media in July.

Government decisions were made, and key posts were claimed, in an opaque fashion in the aftermath of the annulled October 2020 elections. Japarov notably claimed the powers of the presidency immediately after Jeenbekov's resignation but before the parliament appointed him to the role. Meanwhile, the parliament eschewed a mandatory public comment period when deciding to amend the electoral code that month. The decision to delay the next parliamentary election to 2021 was made after relevant legislation was considered and passed in one day. Parliamentarians were similarly nontransparent when considering the draft constitution in November, with one purported author learning about the draft's contents via social media.

Score Change: The score declined from 2 to 0 because government officials and legislators made key decisions in a nontransparent fashion after the October 2020 parliamentary elections were annulled, with Japarov claiming presidential powers before parliamentarians formerly installed him to the post and lawmakers passing key legislation without public comment.

ADDITIONAL DISCRETIONARY POLITICAL RIGHTS QUESTION
Is the government or occupying power deliberately changing the ethnic composition of a country or territory so as to destroy a culture or tip the political balance in favor of another group? −1 / 0

Southern Kyrgyzstan has yet to fully recover from the ethnic upheaval of 2010, which included numerous documented instances of government involvement or connivance in violence against ethnic Uzbeks in the region, with the aim of tipping the political and economic balance in favor of the Kyrgyz elite. Many Uzbek homes and businesses were destroyed or seized. While intimidation has continued and little has been done to reverse the outcomes of the violence, some steps have been taken to restore Uzbek-language media in the region, and fears of further unrest have eased over time.

CIVIL LIBERTIES: 24 / 60 (-3)
D. FREEDOM OF EXPRESSION AND BELIEF: 10 / 16
D1. Are there free and independent media? 2 / 4

The media landscape is relatively diverse but divided along ethnic lines, and prosecutions for inciting ethnic hatred have tended to focus on minority writers despite the prevalence of openly racist and antisemitic articles in Kyrgyz-language media. A 2014 law criminalized the publication of "false information relating to a crime or offense" in the media, which international monitors saw as a contradiction of the country's 2011 decriminalization of defamation. The law assigns penalties of up to three years in prison, or five years if the claim serves the interests of organized crime or is linked to the fabrication of evidence.

Journalists and bloggers covering major events, including ongoing corruption cases, the COVID-19 response, and the October 2020 elections, faced intimidation, detention, physical attack, and interference as they conducted their work. In January, Bolot Temirov, editor in chief of news site Factcheck, was assaulted in Bishkek several weeks after the site reported on the Matraimov affair. Several bloggers who discussed the pandemic response were forced to apologize for their remarks in March and April, including a doctor who commented on working conditions at his hospital. Several Radio Free Europe/Radio Liberty (RFE/RL) journalists were physically attacked during the October election period, while one RFE/RL journalist was prevented from entering a police station in the city of Osh before the poll was conducted. Other outlets received intimidating and threatening messages during the October protests, with some of them relying on volunteers to protect their offices.

The draft constitution published in November 2020 would allow the government to censor material that violates "generally recognized moral values," without defining those values or offering an avenue for appealing such decisions.

D2. Are individuals free to practice and express their religious faith or nonbelief in public and private? 2 / 4

All religious organizations must register with the authorities, a process that is often cumbersome and arbitrary. Groups outside the traditional Muslim and Orthodox Christian mainstream reportedly have difficulty obtaining registration, and the 2009 Law on Religion deems all unregistered groups illegal. Organizations such as the Jehovah's Witnesses often face police harassment. The government also monitors and restricts some Islamic groups, including the nonviolent Islamist movement Hizb ut-Tahrir and Yakyn Inkar, which practices strict asceticism. Some unregistered religious communities have nevertheless been able to practice their faiths without state intervention, and authorities have investigated and punished relatively rare acts of violence against religious figures or minorities.

D3. Is there academic freedom, and is the educational system free from extensive political indoctrination? 3 / 4

The government does not formally restrict academic freedom, though teachers and students have reportedly faced pressure to participate in political campaigns and voting, including in the 2017 presidential election.

D4. Are individuals free to express their personal views on political or other sensitive topics without fear of surveillance or retribution? 3 / 4

Private discussion is generally free in the country, and prosecutions of individuals for the expression of personal views on social media are rare. However, state and local authorities regularly raid homes where they believe members of banned groups like Hizb ut-Tahrir or certain religious minorities, such as Jehovah's Witnesses, meet to discuss their beliefs.

E. ASSOCIATIONAL AND ORGANIZATIONAL RIGHTS: 5 / 12 (−1)

E1. Is there freedom of assembly? 1 / 4 (−1)

A 2012 law allows peaceful assembly, and small protests and civil disobedience actions, such as blocking roads, take place regularly. Nevertheless, domestic and international watchdogs have voiced concerns over violations of assembly rights, including arrests and other forms of interference. Far-right groups and criminal organizations are also known to intimidate and attack demonstrators.

Demonstrators faced campaigns of violence and detention in 2020. Masked men attacked women activists attending a Bishkek march commemorating International Women's Day in March, resulting in several injuries. Police then detained over 70 activists as well as 3 journalists, denying them access to legal counsel or explaining why they were detained; few of the assailants were arrested. In June, a Bishkek court ruled that the demonstration was not authorized and fined 11 participants. In November, however, the Supreme Court found the police action unconstitutional.

Protests held after the October 2020 elections were also marred by violence. Over 600 people were injured in clashes within two days of the poll, and one person was reportedly killed. The building housing the parliament and president's office was damaged after protests on October 6. Then president Jeenbekov declared martial law in Bishkek on October 9, though a state of emergency was rolled back several days later.

Japarov supporters attacked and intimidated protesters and opposition groups after the annulled elections, notably disrupting a rally held to support a potential anti-Japarov transitional government on October 9. Ata-Meken parliamentary candidate Tilek Toktogaziyev was seriously injured during the rally, while a car carrying former president Atambayev, who was freed from GKNB custody earlier that month and attended the rally, was shot at. Protests opposing the draft constitution were held in November.

Score Change: The score declined from 2 to 1 because peaceful protesters objecting to the conduct of the October 2020 elections faced violence from Japarov supporters, and because then president Jeenbekov declared martial law in an effort to curtail mass gatherings.

E2. Is there freedom for nongovernmental organizations, particularly those that are engaged in human rights- and governance-related work? 2 / 4

NGOs are active in civic and political life. Public advisory councils were established in the parliament and most ministries in 2011, permitting improved monitoring and advocacy by NGOs. However, human rights workers, including those who support ethnic Uzbek victims, LGBT+ people, and women's groups, face threats, harassment, and physical attacks. Ultranationalists have harassed US and European NGOs as well as domestic counterparts that are perceived to be favored by foreign governments and donors.

E3. Is there freedom for trade unions and similar professional or labor organizations? 2 / 4

Kyrgyzstani law provides for the formation of trade unions, which are generally able to operate without obstruction. However, parliamentarians have considered legislative amendments that would limit their ability to organize and would force them to affiliate with the Federation of Trade Unions of Kyrgyzstan (FTUK), which would serve as the country's only national union. The amendments, which were introduced in 2019, received a second reading in November 2020 and remained under consideration at year's end.

Strikes are prohibited in many sectors. Legal enforcement of union rights is weak, and employers do not always respect collective-bargaining agreements.

F. RULE OF LAW: 2 / 16 (−2)

F1. Is there an independent judiciary? 0 / 4 (−1)

The judiciary is dominated by the executive branch. Corruption among judges is widespread. In 2019, the GKNB announced corruption charges against seven judges, including three sitting Supreme Court justices; the judges were accused of issuing rulings that favored organized criminal groups.

The judiciary provided little resistance to the opaque and procedurally questionable installation of Sadyr Japarov as prime minister and president. In October 2020, the Supreme Court overturned his 2012 conviction for attempting to overthrow the government. Japarov's 2013 conviction for kidnapping a regional governor was also overturned.

Also in October, the Supreme Court refused to consider a CEC appeal over the parliament's decision to delay a rerun election. In December, the Constitutional Chamber ruled the parliament's decision to extend its own term constitutional.

Score Change: The score declined from 1 to 0 because the judiciary overturned Japarov's criminal convictions as he assumed executive power, and because the judiciary allowed the parliament to delay an election and remain in office beyond its electoral mandate.

F2. Does due process prevail in civil and criminal matters? 0 / 4 (−1)

Defendants' rights, including the presumption of innocence, are not always respected, and evidence allegedly obtained through torture is regularly accepted in courts.

Due process was not consistently upheld for high-profile prisoners released from GKNB custody in October 2020. While Japarov's convictions were overturned after his release, former president Atambayev, who received a corruption-related prison sentence in June and was released along with Japarov, was rearrested on charges of inciting unrest in October. Other politicians who escaped the GKNB during the protests were also sent back into custody.

Score Change: The score declined from 1 to 0 because individuals—including Japarov— were released from prison without due process during the October 2020 protests, and because Japarov was allowed to remain free and assume executive power while others were taken back into custody.

F3. Is there protection from the illegitimate use of physical force and freedom from war and insurgencies? 1 / 4

There are credible reports of torture during arrest and interrogation, in addition to physical abuse in prisons. Most such reports do not lead to investigations and convictions.

Uzbek human rights activist Azimjan Askarov, who was accused of organizing riots after acts of violence were perpetrated against ethnic Uzbeks in southern Kyrgyzstan in 2010, died of pneumonia while in custody in July 2020. Askarov, who was tortured in detention, remained imprisoned despite his deteriorating health and repeated calls for his release. Meanwhile, few perpetrators of the 2010 violence have been brought to justice.

F4. Do laws, policies, and practices guarantee equal treatment of various segments of the population? 1 / 4

Legal bans on gender discrimination in the workplace are not effectively enforced. Traditional biases also put women at a disadvantage regarding education and access to services. Ethnic minorities—particularly Uzbeks, who make up nearly half of the population of the city of Osh—continue to face discrimination on economic, security, and other matters. Uzbeks are often targeted for harassment, arrest, and mistreatment by law enforcement agencies based on dubious terrorism or extremism charges. Same-sex sexual activity is not illegal, but discrimination against and abuse of LGBT+ people at the hands of police are pervasive. Ultranationalist groups have also engaged in intimidation of LGBT+ and feminist activists.

In June 2019, the government announced its intention to repatriate Kyrgyzstanis in Iraqi and Syrian territory previously controlled by the Islamic State militant group. Plans to repatriate those still living in Iraq stalled during 2020.

G. PERSONAL AUTONOMY AND INDIVIDUAL RIGHTS: 7 / 16

G1. Do individuals enjoy freedom of movement, including the ability to change their place of residence, employment, or education? 2 / 4

The government generally respects the right of unrestricted travel to and from Kyrgyzstan, though journalists and human rights activists sometimes face bans and other obstacles. Barriers to internal migration include a requirement that citizens obtain permits to work and settle in particular areas of the country.

G2. Are individuals able to exercise the right to own property and establish private businesses without undue interference from state or nonstate actors? 2 / 4

The misuse of personal connections, corruption, and organized crime impair private business activity. The ethnic violence of 2010 has affected property rights in the south, as many businesses, mainly owned by ethnic Uzbeks, were destroyed or seized.

G3. Do individuals enjoy personal social freedoms, including choice of marriage partner and size of family, protection from domestic violence, and control over appearance? 2 / 4

Cultural constraints and inaction by law enforcement officials discourage victims of domestic violence and rape from contacting the authorities. Legislation enacted in 2017 aimed to broaden the definition of domestic abuse and improve both victim assistance and responses from law enforcement bodies, but the law is weakly enforced.

The practice of bride abduction persists despite the strengthening of legal penalties in 2013, and few perpetrators are prosecuted.

G4. Do individuals enjoy equality of opportunity and freedom from economic exploitation? 1 / 4

The government does not actively enforce workplace health and safety standards. Child labor is restricted by law but reportedly occurs, particularly in the agricultural sector. The trafficking of women and girls into forced prostitution abroad is a serious problem. Police have been accused of complicity in the trafficking and exploitation of sex trafficking victims, and reportedly accept bribes from traffickers. Kyrgyzstani men are especially vulnerable to trafficking for forced labor abroad.

Laos

Population: 7,200,000
Capital: Vientiane
Freedom Status: Not Free
Electoral Democracy: No

Overview: Laos is a one-party state in which the ruling Lao People's Revolutionary Party (LPRP) dominates all aspects of politics and harshly restricts civil liberties. There is no organized opposition and no truly independent civil society. News coverage of the country is limited by the remoteness of some areas, repression of domestic media, and the opaque nature of the regime. Economic development has led to a rising tide of disputes over land and environmental issues, and growing debt to China. In recent years, a wide-ranging anti-corruption campaign has had some positive impact.

KEY DEVELOPMENTS IN 2020

- Laos handled the COVID-19 pandemic with a high, and unusual, degree of government transparency, proactively producing accurate and useful public information campaigns. The International Federation of Red Cross and Red Crescent Societies praised the government's work in informing the public. By the end of the year, 41 people had tested positive for coronavirus, according to government statistics provided to the World Health Organization (WHO).
- In October, reports revealed that four Lao Christians had been jailed for several months for planning Christian funeral rites. That same month, a group of Lao Christians were evicted from their homes; they fled into a forest because they would not renounce their faith.

POLITICAL RIGHTS: 2 / 40

A. ELECTORAL PROCESS: 0 / 12

A1. Was the current head of government or other chief national authority elected through free and fair elections? 0 / 4

Laos is a one-party communist state and the ruling Lao People's Revolutionary Party (LPRP)'s 61-member Central Committee, under the leadership of the 11-member Politburo, makes all major decisions. The LPRP vets all candidates for election to the National Assembly, whose members elect the president and prime minister.

The LPRP selected new leaders through an opaque process at a party congress in 2016. After that year's tightly controlled National Assembly elections, lawmakers chose Bounnhang Vorachith to serve as president, and Thongloun Sisoulith to serve as prime minister. The next party congress will be held in early 2021.

A2. Were the current national legislative representatives elected through free and fair elections? 0 / 4

National Assembly elections are held every five years, but are not free or fair, and international observers are not permitted to monitor them. The LPRP won 144 of 149 seats in the 2016 legislative elections, with the remainder going to carefully vetted independents.

A3. Are the electoral laws and framework fair, and are they implemented impartially by the relevant election management bodies? 0 / 4

The electoral laws and framework are designed to ensure that the LPRP, the only legal party, dominates every election and controls the political system.

B. POLITICAL PLURALISM AND PARTICIPATION: 0 / 16

B1. Do the people have the right to organize in different political parties or other competitive political groupings of their choice, and is the system free of undue obstacles to the rise and fall of these competing parties or groupings? 0 / 4

The constitution makes the ruling LPRP the sole legal political party and grants it a leading role at all levels of government.

B2. Is there a realistic opportunity for the opposition to increase its support or gain power through elections? 0 / 4

Although the LPRP is the only legal party, National Assembly candidates are not required to be members. However, all candidates must be approved by National Assembly–appointed committees.

B3. Are the people's political choices free from domination by forces that are external to the political sphere, or by political forces that employ extrapolitical means? 0 / 4

The authoritarian one-party system in Laos excludes the public from any genuine and autonomous political participation.

B4. Do various segments of the population (including ethnic, racial, religious, gender, LGBT+, and other relevant groups) have full political rights and electoral opportunities? 0 / 4

The right to vote and run for office are guaranteed in the constitution, but due to the one-party system, no portion of the population may exercise full political rights and electoral opportunities. Nominal representatives of ethnic minorities hold positions in the Politburo, Central Committee, and National Assembly, but they are limited in their ability to advocate for policies that benefit minorities. Women hold 27.5 percent of the National Assembly's seats, but their presence in the legislature similarly does not guarantee that the interests of women are represented in politics.

C. FUNCTIONING OF GOVERNMENT: 2 / 12

C1. Do the freely elected head of government and national legislative representatives determine the policies of the government? 0 / 4

None of the country's nominally elected officials are chosen through free and fair contests, and major policy decisions are reserved for the LPRP. In recent years, the government has more frequently passed laws, rather than decrees, to govern, though due to the choreographed nature of elections, the representatives approving these bills do not clearly represent the electorate.

C2. Are safeguards against official corruption strong and effective? 1 / 4

Corruption by government officials is widespread. Laws aimed at curbing graft are not well enforced, and government regulation of virtually every facet of life provides many opportunities for bribery and fraud.

However, Prime Minister Thongloun has initiated an anticorruption drive since taking office in 2016, empowered the State Audit Organization (SAO) to conduct financial and budget investigations. The SAO has since uncovered several instances of misappropriated state funds and unreported expenditures, and some LPRP officials have apparently returned money that they stole to the national treasury.

Thongloun has also taken steps to address illegal or environmentally harmful extraction industries, like mining and timber, that have been conduits for corrupt activity since he took office in 2016, though his actions have largely been unsuccessful.

Though the National Assembly has become more rhetorically assertive on the matter—with members criticizing corruption, bribery, and the lack of judicial independence in various sessions—little real progress was made in 2020 through the government's anticorruption efforts. Punishments varied, and included acts of party discipline, demotion, and in some cases, "reeducation." Relatively few of the officials suspected of corruption have been pursued through judicial means.

C3. Does the government operate with openness and transparency? 1 / 4

There is no access to information law in Laos. However, the 2012 Law on Making Legislation increased legislative transparency by requiring bills proposed at the central and provincial levels to be published for comment for 60 days and, once passed, to be posted for 15 days before coming into force. The prime minister has repeatedly promised to make government more transparent to the citizenry, although how he will do so is unclear.

Authorities have also withheld information about a 2018 dam collapse, which resulted in 43 deaths. The government received a report on the incident in March 2019, which blamed the collapse on substandard construction; however, the report was never fully made public. In May 2020, Laos submitted a plan to build a new dam on the Mekong River, despite the 2018 dam collapse and the dangers of the dam to the Mekong ecosystem.

However, in 2020, the government was very transparent in regard to the severity of the COVID-19 outbreak. Authorities gave useful information to citizens and provided accurate statistics to international bodies, according to the International Federation of Red Cross and Red Crescent Societies (IFRC).

CIVIL LIBERTIES: 11 / 60 (–1)
D. FREEDOM OF EXPRESSION AND BELIEF: 3 / 16 (–1)
D1. Are there free and independent media? 0 / 4

Authorities use legal restrictions and intimidation tactics against state critics, and as a result, self-censorship is widespread. The state owns nearly all media, though some independent outlets, primarily entertainment magazines that steer clear of political commentary, have emerged in recent years. Coverage of the catastrophic 2018 dam collapse was suppressed within the country.

In July 2019, the government required news outlets that disseminate material through social media networks to register themselves, threatening fines and prison sentences for those who did not comply; the Information Ministry claimed the move was meant to arrest the spread of "fake news." In October, the government again warned online news outlets to register with the national government or be banned from publishing on social media platforms.

D2. Are individuals free to practice and express their religious faith or nonbelief in public and private? 1 / 4 (–1)

Religious freedom is guaranteed in the constitution, but in practice is constrained, in part through the LPRP's control of clergy training and supervision of Buddhist temples. There have been multiple cases in recent years of Christians being briefly detained or sentenced to jail for unauthorized religious activities or being pressured by authorities to renounce their faith. A ban on public proselytizing is generally enforced, and authorities make efforts to monitor the importation of religious materials. In October 2020, reports revealed that four Lao Christians had been jailed for several months for planning Christian funeral rites. That same month, a group of Lao Christians were evicted from their homes and moved into a forest because they would not renounce Christianity.

Score Change: The score declined from 2 to 1 due to increasing persecution of members of the Christian minority that included the jailing of Lao Christians for planning religious funeral rites.

D3. Is there academic freedom, and is the educational system free from extensive political indoctrination? 1 / 4

University professors cannot teach or write about politically sensitive topics, though Laos has invited select foreign academics to teach courses in the country.

D4. Are individuals free to express their personal views on political or other sensitive topics without fear of surveillance or retribution? 1 / 4

Government surveillance of the population has been scaled back in recent years, but security agencies and LPRP-backed mass organizations continue to monitor for public dissent, which is punishable under a variety of laws. As a result, there is little space for open and free private discussion of sensitive issues. The government attempts to monitor social media usage for content and images that portray Laos negatively. Courts hand down heavy sentences in response to the posting of such material. In November 2019, a court sentenced a Laotian citizen to five years in prison for criticizing the government in a Facebook post. In August 2020, authorities detained a citizen for criticizing government corruption on Facebook, though he was released on bail a month later.

E. ASSOCIATIONAL AND ORGANIZATIONAL RIGHTS: 0 / 12

E1. Is there freedom of assembly? 0 / 4

Although protected in the constitution, the government severely restricts freedom of assembly. Protests are rare, and those deemed to be participating in unsanctioned gatherings can receive lengthy prison sentences. The government occasionally allows demonstrations that pose little threat to the LPRP.

In November 2019, police detained eight activists who planned a prodemocracy protest in Vientiane; six were released, while the whereabouts of the other two remain unclear.

E2. Is there freedom for nongovernmental organizations, particularly those that are engaged in human rights- and governance-related work? 0 / 4

Alongside LPRP-affiliated mass organizations, there are some domestic nongovernmental welfare and professional groups, but they are prohibited from pursuing political agendas. Registration and regulatory mechanisms for nongovernmental organizations (NGOs) are onerous and allow for arbitrary state interference. A new decree on associations, which came into force in 2017, mandates that NGOs secure government approval for their initiatives and funding, among other new restrictions.

Human rights and prodemocracy activists are also at risk of unexplained disappearances. In August 2019, prodemocracy activist Od Sayavong disappeared in Bangkok, where he resided. His whereabouts were unknown at the end of 2020. In November 2019, Phetphouthon Philachane, a Laotian citizen who demonstrated in front of the Laotian embassy in Bangkok earlier in the year, disappeared after returning to Laos. Scores of participants in a cancelled November 2019 prodemocracy rally also went missing.

The 2012 disappearance of prominent antipoverty activist Sombath Somphone remained unsolved in 2020. Multiple Thai dissidents have disappeared, or turned up dead, in Laos and neighboring states in recent years.

E3. Is there freedom for trade unions and similar professional or labor organizations? 0 / 4

Most unions belong to the official Lao Federation of Trade Unions. Strikes are not expressly prohibited, but workers rarely stage walkouts. Collective bargaining is legally permitted, but rarely exercised by workers, as workers who try to engage in collective bargaining are usually punished.

F. RULE OF LAW: 2 / 16

F1. Is there an independent judiciary? 0 / 4

The courts are wracked by corruption and subject to LPRP influence. Major decisions are often made secretly.

F2. Does due process prevail in civil and criminal matters? 0 / 4

Due process rights are outlined in the law, but these rights are routinely denied. Defendants are often presumed guilty, and long procedural delays in the judicial system are common. Appeals processes are often nonexistent or delayed, sometimes indefinitely. Searches without warrants occur and arbitrary arrests continue. Villages are encouraged to settle noncriminal disputes in local mediation units, which are outside the formal judicial system.

F3. Is there protection from the illegitimate use of physical force and freedom from war and insurgencies? 1 / 4

Security forces often illegally detain suspects. Prison conditions are substandard, with reports of inadequate food and medical facilities.

Prisoners are also subject to torture: a group of villagers from Xékong Province, who were detained after their 2017 protest, were reportedly tortured while in detention. A villager from Salavan Province, who was detained in 2011, died in custody in May 2019; neighbors feared he was tortured.

F4. Do laws, policies, and practices guarantee equal treatment of various segments of the population? 1 / 4

Equal rights are constitutionally guaranteed but are not upheld in practice. Discrimination against members of ethnic minority tribes is common. The Hmong, who fielded a guerrilla army allied with US forces during the Vietnam War, are particularly distrusted by the government and face harsh treatment, and some other ethnic minorities like Khmu are also often discriminated against. Asylum for refugees is protected by law, but not always granted.

There have been multiple violent attacks, including murders, of Chinese nationals in Laos in recent years.

While same-sex relations are legal and violence against LGBT+ people is rare, no legislation provides explicit protection against discrimination based on sexual preference or gender identity; gender-based discrimination and violence are widespread. Discriminatory norms and religious practices have contributed to women's limited access to education, employment opportunities, and worker benefits.

G. PERSONAL AUTONOMY AND INDIVIDUAL RIGHTS: 6 / 16

G1. Do individuals enjoy freedom of movement, including the ability to change their place of residence, employment, or education? 2 / 4

The dominance of the LPRP over most aspects of society can effectively restrict individuals' ability to choose their place of residence, employment, or education. Freedom of movement is sometimes restricted for ethnic Hmong. Security checkpoints in central Laos can hamper travel, though the military has in recent years reduced controls in the region.

G2. Are individuals able to exercise the right to own property and establish private businesses without undue interference from state or nonstate actors? 1 / 4

All land is owned by the state, though citizens have rights to use it. However, in recent years land rights have become an increasing source of public discontent. Construction began on a high-speed rail line from China through Laos at the end of 2016, resulting in the displacement of over 4,000 families; many villagers remain uncertain of what kind of compensation they will receive. In March 2020, authorities detained a villager involved in a land dispute in Saysettha district.

Villagers who live on or near the sites of planned dams on the Mekong River are increasingly caught up in land disputes and are often forced to leave their homes. As many as 465 families in Louangphabang Province were reportedly displaced in July 2019, as construction proceeded on one of the dams. Apparent deficiencies revealed by the catastrophic dam collapse in southern Laos in 2018, which killed dozens of people and left thousands homeless, have not prompted the government to reevaluate dam-building projects.

Foreign investors are subject to expropriation of joint ventures without due process in Laotian courts.

G3. Do individuals enjoy personal social freedoms, including choice of marriage partner and size of family, protection from domestic violence, and control over appearance? 2 / 4

Social freedoms can be restricted, especially for women and children. A 2016 survey supported by the UN and the World Health Organization (WHO) revealed that nearly a third of women in Laos had experienced domestic violence. Abortion is illegal and only permitted when the mother's life is at risk. Underage marriage is permitted with parental permission.

G4. Do individuals enjoy equality of opportunity and freedom from economic exploitation? 1 / 4

Trafficking in persons, especially to Thailand, is common, and enforcement of antitrafficking measures is hindered by a lack of transparency and weak rule of law. The building of new roads through Laos in recent years has aided trafficking operations.

Children as young as 12 years old may be legally employed in Laos. Inspections of workplaces, including those for industries considered hazardous, are required by law but do not take place regularly.

Latvia

Population: 1,900,000
Capital: Riga
Freedom Status: Free
Electoral Democracy: Yes

Overview: Latvia is a multiparty democracy whose elections are regarded as free and fair. Civil liberties are generally respected in law and in practice. However, corruption remains a major problem affecting politics, the judiciary, and the wider criminal justice system. The country's ethnic Russian population faces disadvantages in matters such as education and employment.

KEY DEVELOPMENTS IN 2020

- In March, a state of emergency was declared as a result of the COVID-19 pandemic. It lasted until June, when it was replaced by less extreme social-distancing measures. A second state of emergency was declared in November in response to a new wave of COVID-19 cases. In late December, a New Year curfew was imposed, and the emergency restrictions were extended until February 2021. As of the end of the year, Latvia had reported roughly 40,000 confirmed COVID-19 cases and more than 600 deaths.

- In June, the parliament approved an overhaul of local government, including a reduction in the number of municipalities. The reform was set to be fully implemented after the 2021 local elections.
- In August, the Development/For!/Progressives alliance won the Riga city council elections, defeating the Harmony party, which had long governed the city but suffered from a series of corruption scandals. The victorious alliance formed a governing coalition with other groups and installed a new mayor in October.

POLITICAL RIGHTS: 37 / 40
A. ELECTORAL PROCESS: 12 / 12
A1. Was the current head of government or other chief national authority elected through free and fair elections? 4 / 4

The Saeima (parliament) elects the president, who may serve up to two four-year terms. The prime minister, who holds most executive authority, is nominated by the president and approved by the parliament. After legislative elections in October 2018 and lengthy negotiations, a ruling coalition of five parties was formed in January 2019. A former economy minister and member of the European Parliament, Krišjānis Kariņš of the center-right group New Unity, was confirmed that month as the new prime minister.

In May 2019, the Saeima selected European Court of Justice judge Egils Levits to succeed Raimonds Vējonis as president.

A2. Were the current national legislative representatives elected through free and fair elections? 4 / 4

The constitution provides for a unicameral, 100-seat Saeima, whose members are elected to four-year terms. The 2018 parliamentary elections were viewed as competitive and credible, and stakeholders accepted the results.

The 2018 elections featured significant losses for all three previously governing parties—the Union of Greens and Farmers (ZZS), New Unity, and the conservative National Alliance—which jointly took 32 seats. The center-left opposition party Harmony, which relies on support from Latvia's ethnic Russians, took 23 seats, one fewer than in the previous elections. Newly founded movements took the remaining 45: the populist Who Owns the State? (KPV LV) and the right-wing New Conservative Party (JKP) each took 16 seats, and the liberal coalition Development/For! (A/P!) took the remaining 13. Kariņš of New Unity successfully formed a coalition with the National Alliance, JKP, a majority of KPV LV lawmakers, and A/P! in January 2019.

In August 2020, an alliance between A/P! and the Progressives won the Riga city council elections, receiving 26 percent of the vote. Harmony, which had governed in the city since 2009, finished a distant second with 17 percent, having been weakened in part by corruption scandals. The winning bloc formed a coalition with the National Alliance, New Unity, and the JKP, and Mārtiņš Staķis of A/P! was installed as mayor in October.

A3. Are the electoral laws and framework fair, and are they implemented impartially by the relevant election management bodies? 4 / 4

In general, the electoral framework is implemented fairly by the Central Election Commission and regional and local election administrations.

The president has traditionally been elected through a closed vote, but in late 2018 the outgoing Saeima amended the constitution to make future balloting open.

In June 2020, the parliament passed legislation to reorganize local government in the country. The reform, which would take full effect after the 2021 local elections, included a reduction in the number of municipalities from 119 to 42.

B. POLITICAL PLURALISM AND PARTICIPATION: 15 / 16

B1. Do the people have the right to organize in different political parties or other competitive political groupings of their choice, and is the system free of undue obstacles to the rise and fall of these competing parties or groupings? 4 / 4

Latvia's political parties organize and compete freely, and elections often result in representation for newly founded parties or coalitions. However, candidates cannot run as independents, and those who belonged to communist or pro-Soviet organizations after 1991 may not hold public office.

B2. Is there a realistic opportunity for the opposition to increase its support or gain power through elections? 4 / 4

The country has experienced numerous peaceful transfers of power between rival parties, and opposition parties typically have a strong presence in the Saeima and in local governments. However, Harmony and predecessor parties that were mostly supported by Latvia's Russian-speaking population have never been invited to participate in forming a government.

B3. Are the people's political choices free from domination by forces that are external to the political sphere, or by political forces that employ extrapolitical means? 4 / 4

Politically connected businesspeople have historically exercised undue influence in the country, using patronage networks, corruption, and other opaque means to infringe on the autonomy of voters and candidates. However, the 2018 election defeat of the ZZS—whose most prominent politician has long faced corruption allegations—and subsequent efforts by the new government to combat graft and money laundering have reinforced an apparent decline in improper influence by such figures.

Authorities and other observers continue to express concern about the presence of Russian government disinformation and propaganda in Latvian media, among other attempts by Moscow to influence domestic politics.

B4. Do various segments of the population (including ethnic, racial, religious, gender, LGBT+, and other relevant groups) have full political rights and electoral opportunities? 3 / 4

More than 200,000 of Latvia's registered residents are stateless, and most of them are ethnic Russians. They may not vote, hold public office, work in government offices, or establish political parties. Under a 2019 law that took effect in January 2020, the Latvian-born children of noncitizen residents are granted Latvian citizenship by default, unless both parents agree on conferring the citizenship of another country. The measure was intended to further reduce the stateless population over time.

Women have made gains in political participation in recent years. Women candidates won 31 percent of the Saeima seats in 2018, up from 19 percent previously.

LGBT+ people are poorly represented in Latvian politics, and parties have been reluctant to address their interests. However, the Saeima elected in 2018 included two openly LGBT+ members, Foreign Minister Edgars Rinkēvičs and A/P! lawmaker Marija Golubeva.

C. FUNCTIONING OF GOVERNMENT: 10 / 12

C1. Do the freely elected head of government and national legislative representatives determine the policies of the government? 4 / 4

The country's elected leadership is able to set and implement government policies without improper interference from foreign or unelected entities, and the politically diverse legislature provides a meaningful check on executive authority.

C2. Are safeguards against official corruption strong and effective? 3 / 4

Latvian anticorruption and auditing bodies have historically been subject to politicization attempts, funding shortfalls, and a dearth of qualified personnel. However, the Corruption Prevention and Combating Bureau (KNAB) has recently expanded its activities. The bureau initiated 47 criminal proceedings during 2019, representing an increase of 24 percent over the previous year and the largest number in the last decade.

The courts were adjudicating several high-profile corruption cases in 2020. The long-running trial of ZZS power broker Aivars Lembergs—the former mayor of Ventspils and one of the richest people in the country—continued during the year, as did the case of longtime central bank governor Ilmārs Rimšēvičs, who was charged with bribery in 2018 and money laundering in 2019. Separately, in the wake of a procurement scandal in Riga's municipal government in late 2018, Nils Ušakovs of Harmony was forced to resign as mayor in 2019, and in February 2020 the Saeima dissolved Riga's city council and appointed an interim government. That move triggered Riga's snap municipal elections in August.

In June 2020, the parliament established a specialized Economic Affairs Court to deal with cases of economic and financial crimes. The legislation was criticized by the Council for the Judiciary, which expressed doubts that the new court would improve quality and efficiency.

C3. Does the government operate with openness and transparency? 3 / 4

The legislative framework features extensive provisions intended to ensure government transparency. However, there is a notable lack of transparency in the functioning of state-owned companies and in public procurement processes.

CIVIL LIBERTIES: 52 / 60

D. FREEDOM OF EXPRESSION AND BELIEF: 14 / 16

D1. Are there free and independent media? 3 / 4

While Latvian media outlets publicize a wide range of political views in both Latvian and Russian, government offices, courts, and politically connected businesspeople sometimes interfere with their work. The National Electronic Mass Media Council (NEPLP), the country's media regulator, is perceived to be vulnerable to political influence. Libel remains a criminal offense.

Authorities have occasionally restricted access to Russian radio and news websites, citing concerns about propaganda in some cases. In June 2020, the NEPLP banned seven television channels operated by the Russian state-owned network RT, arguing that they were under the effective control of Dmitry Kiselyov, who heads another Russian state media group and had been sanctioned by the European Union (EU). The move was criticized by Reporters Without Borders. Separately, it was reported in July that the NEPLP had started infringement procedures against the Russian-language television channel PBK on the grounds that it improperly rebroadcast content from other outlets and failed to provide a minimum of local coverage. In December, the authorities charged several journalists with violating EU sanctions, apparently because they worked for units of Kiselyov's media group in Latvia.

D2. Are individuals free to practice and express their religious faith or nonbelief in public and private? 4 / 4

Freedom of religion is generally respected. However, Latvia's small Muslim population has faced some social pressure since a 2015 refugee crisis. Instances of antisemitic and Islamophobic hate speech have appeared on social media and the internet but are rarely reported to the police.

D3. Is there academic freedom, and is the educational system free from extensive political indoctrination? 3 / 4

While academic freedom is largely upheld, lawmakers have begun to place some limitations on instruction in recent years. A 2015 law mandated that schools provide a "moral education" that coincides with the values of the constitution, including traditional views on marriage and family life. A law that took effect in 2017 enabled the firing of teachers found to be "disloyal to the state."

Authorities in 2018 endeavored to discourage or eliminate the use of minority languages in schools and universities, and the measures were generally viewed as targeting Russian-language instruction. The Saeima amended the Education Law to phase out the use of minority languages in public and private high schools, and to significantly reduce their use in primary schools. The Kariņš government has pledged to maintain these policies.

D4. Are individuals free to express their personal views on political or other sensitive topics without fear of surveillance or retribution? 4 / 4

There are few restrictions on personal expression or private discussion. However, legal constraints include a ban on the public display of Soviet or Nazi symbols as well as prohibitions on incitement to ethnic hatred and denial of historical crimes.

E. ASSOCIATIONAL AND ORGANIZATIONAL RIGHTS: 12 / 12
E1. Is there freedom of assembly? 4 / 4

Freedom of assembly is protected by law and generally respected in practice.

E2. Is there freedom for nongovernmental organizations, particularly those that are engaged in human rights– and governance-related work? 4 / 4

The government does not restrict the activities of nongovernmental organizations (NGOs). However, advocacy by NGOs is increasingly viewed as partisan activity.

E3. Is there freedom for trade unions and similar professional or labor organizations? 4 / 4

Workers may establish trade unions, strike, and engage in collective bargaining, and antiunion discrimination is prohibited. In practice, the share of workers covered by collective-bargaining agreements has declined over time. A 2019 law imposed fines on employers that refuse to negotiate a collective agreement, among other potential violations.

F. RULE OF LAW: 12 / 16
F1. Is there an independent judiciary? 3 / 4

While judicial independence is generally respected, inefficiency, politicization, and corruption within the judicial system persist.

Legislation that took effect in 2020 increased transparency and the judiciary's role in the selection of both new judges and the country's prosecutor general, with candidates applying through an open competition.

F2. Does due process prevail in civil and criminal matters? 3 / 4

The legal framework provides safeguards against arbitrary arrest and guarantees for fair trial procedures. However, the court system is hampered by corruption and inefficiency, and defendants with adequate resources have exploited these weaknesses to delay or obstruct prosecutions. Criminal suspects are sometimes interrogated without the presence of a lawyer, and lengthy or unnecessary pretrial detention remains a concern.

F3. Is there protection from the illegitimate use of physical force and freedom from war and insurgencies? 3 / 4

Latvians are generally free from major threats to physical security, though the country has comparatively high levels of violent crime by EU standards. According to the statistics agency Eurostat, Latvia had the bloc's highest intentional homicide rate in 2018, the latest year for which data were available. Latvia also has one of the EU's higher prison population rates, with some 179 incarcerated people per 100,000 residents in 2020. Some prison facilities reportedly suffer from poor physical conditions and episodes of violence.

F4. Do laws, policies, and practices guarantee equal treatment of various segments of the population? 3 / 4

The constitution guarantees equality before the law and the protection of human rights without discrimination, and a number of safeguards are specified in law. However, a 2018 report by the UN Committee on the Elimination of Racial Discrimination urged Latvia to adopt a comprehensive antidiscrimination law and expressed concern that state language policies could discriminate against ethnic minority groups in education, employment, and access to services. Women continue to suffer from a gender-based pay gap in practice, and members of Latvia's Romany minority face discrimination in schools and workplaces. Discrimination in employment based on sexual orientation is prohibited, but the law does not provide broader protection against discrimination for LGBT+ people.

G. PERSONAL AUTONOMY AND INDIVIDUAL RIGHTS: 14 / 16

G1. Do individuals enjoy freedom of movement, including the ability to change their place of residence, employment, or education? 4 / 4

Citizens and noncitizens may travel freely within the country and internationally. Movement restrictions imposed during the COVID-19 pandemic in 2020 were generally seen as legitimate responses to the evolving public health threat.

G2. Are individuals able to exercise the right to own property and establish private businesses without undue interference from state or nonstate actors? 4 / 4

The legal and regulatory framework supports an environment in which property rights are respected and people may freely operate businesses, though corruption can impede business activities.

G3. Do individuals enjoy personal social freedoms, including choice of marriage partner and size of family, protection from domestic violence, and control over appearance? 3 / 4

Individual freedom regarding personal status matters such as marriage and divorce is generally upheld, but a constitutional ban on same-sex marriage was adopted in 2005. While lawmakers have repeatedly declined to recognize same-sex partnerships, most recently in October 2020, the Constitutional Court ruled in favor of parental leave for same-sex couples in November, finding that the constitution required the state to protect the rights of such families.

Laws on domestic violence encompass various forms of abuse and provide for protection orders and criminal charges. However, police do not always take meaningful action when cases are reported. Latvia had not ratified the Council of Europe's Istanbul Convention on violence against women as of 2020.

G4. Do individuals enjoy equality of opportunity and freedom from economic exploitation?
3 / 4

Legal protections against exploitative working conditions are generally upheld, though enforcement is uneven in the large informal sector of the economy. Informal workers are more vulnerable to labor abuses and recruitment into criminal enterprises. About 27 percent of Latvia's population was at risk of social exclusion or poverty as of 2019, according to Eurostat.

The US State Department reports that Latvians are subject to trafficking for sexual exploitation, domestic servitude, and forced labor abroad, while a growing number of foreign migrant workers in Latvia are exposed to labor exploitation. Latvia maintains an assistance mechanism for trafficking survivors, but prosecutors have had relatively little success in convicting alleged perpetrators.

Lebanon

Population: 6,800,000
Capital: Beirut
Freedom Status: Partly Free
Electoral Democracy: No

Overview: Lebanon's political system ensures representation for its officially recognized religious communities, but limits competition and impedes the rise of cross-communal or civic parties. While residents enjoy some civil liberties and media pluralism, they also suffer from pervasive corruption and major weaknesses in the rule of law. The country's large population of noncitizens, including refugees and migrant workers, remain subject to legal constraints and societal attitudes that severely restrict their access to employment, freedom of movement, and other fundamental rights.

KEY DEVELOPMENTS IN 2020

- In August, more than 200 people died and thousands were injured in a massive chemical explosion in the port of Beirut that devastated much of the capital. The official response was characterized by a lack of transparency, and key politicians refused to cooperate with a judicial investigation into possible criminal negligence.
- Prime Minister Hassan Diab resigned after the explosion, but the official designated to replace him withdrew in September after failing to form a government, and former prime minister Saad Hariri was nominated instead. Hariri had yet to organize a new cabinet at year's end, and Diab remained in place as a caretaker prime minister.
- A lockdown imposed early in the year was fairly successful in containing the COVID-19 pandemic, but cases began to rise in the late summer and fall after restrictions were eased, and attempts to regain control were hampered by the effects of the Beirut blast and the country's worsening economic and governance problems. By year's end, 1,443 deaths had been reported by the World Health Organization.

POLITICAL RIGHTS: 13 / 40 (-1)
A. ELECTORAL PROCESS: 5 / 12
A1. Was the current head of government or other chief national authority elected through free and fair elections? 1 / 4

The president, who is elected to a six-year term by the parliament, appoints the prime minister after consulting with the parliament. The president and prime minister choose the cabinet, which holds most formal executive power. According to long-standing agreements on sectarian power-sharing, the president must be a Maronite Christian, the prime minister must be a Sunni Muslim, and the speaker of parliament must be a Shiite Muslim.

In 2016, after a two-year vacancy, lawmakers elected former military commander Michel Aoun as president. While the move eased the country's broader political deadlock, the parliament at the time had been operating with an expired electoral mandate for three years, undermining the democratic legitimacy of the presidential election.

In January 2020, Hassan Diab—a former education minister and a vice president at the American University of Beirut—was sworn in as prime minister along with a new cabinet. He succeeded Saad Hariri, who had resigned in October 2019 following widespread anticorruption protests. Diab's government collapsed in August 2020 after the devastating chemical explosion in Beirut, and he announced his resignation. Mustapha Adib, Lebanon's ambassador to Germany, was nominated to replace Diab, but he withdrew in September after failing to form a technocratic government. Hariri returned as the new prime minister–designate, though he had yet to organize a government at year's end, and Diab remained in office in a caretaker capacity.

A2. Were the current national legislative representatives elected through free and fair elections? 2 / 4

Members of the 128-seat National Assembly are elected for five-year terms. The most recent elections were held in 2018, after a five-year delay; the parliament elected in 2009 had repeatedly extended its own term, citing the need for electoral reforms as well as security concerns related to the civil war in Syria.

In the 2018 elections, the Shiite militant group Hezbollah and its allies, including Christian factions linked to President Aoun, made gains overall, leaving them with a clear majority of seats. The Hezbollah-led bloc's chief rival, Hariri's Sunni-led Future Movement, lost more than a third of its seats, though its main Christian partners performed well, nearly doubling their representation. While the elections were conducted peacefully and were free and fair in many respects, vote buying was rampant, and the electoral framework retained a number of fundamental structural flaws associated with the sectarian political system. Turnout was less than 50 percent nationally and even lower in several contested districts.

A3. Are the electoral laws and framework fair, and are they implemented impartially by the relevant election management bodies? 2 / 4

Lebanon does not have an independent electoral commission; instead, the Interior Ministry oversees elections. Parliamentary seats are divided among major sects under a constitutional formula that does not reflect their current demographic weight. There has been no official census in Lebanon since the 1930s, prior to independence. The electoral framework is inclusive and supports pluralism, but it is the product of bargaining among established leaders and tends to entrench the existing sectarian and communalist political system.

The 2017 electoral law introduced proportional representation and preferential voting, and improved opportunities for diaspora voting. However, the rules for redistricting and seat allocation still favor incumbent parties. The law sharply raised registration fees for candidates as well as spending caps for campaigns, while allowing private organizations and foundations to promote coalitions and candidates, effectively increasing advantages accorded to wealthier groups and individuals. As under past electoral laws, members of the military and citizens who have been naturalized for less than 10 years cannot participate in elections.

B. POLITICAL PLURALISM AND PARTICIPATION: 7 / 16

B1. Do the people have the right to organize in different political parties or other competitive political groupings of their choice, and is the system free of undue obstacles to the rise and fall of these competing parties or groupings? 3 / 4

Citizens are formally free to organize in different political groupings, and scores of parties compete in practice. While parties do rise and fall based on their performance and voters' preferences, most of Lebanon's political parties are vehicles for an established set of communal leaders who benefit from patronage networks, greater access to financing, and other advantages of incumbency.

B2. Is there a realistic opportunity for the opposition to increase its support or gain power through elections? 1 / 4

The elites who dominate Lebanese politics include traditional leaders, military veterans, former militia leaders, and wealthy businessmen. Under the country's power-sharing system, none of the parties they control consistently behave as opposition groups. Consolidation of power among political elites also hampers intraparty competition.

Despite the new electoral system introduced in 2017, the political parties and alliances that prevailed before the reform have maintained their positions. They not only benefited from advantages under laws they shaped, but also used intimidation, social pressure, and propaganda to marginalize new political forces.

B3. Are the people's political choices free from domination by forces that are external to the political sphere, or by political forces that employ extrapolitical means? 1 / 4

A variety of forces that are not democratically accountable—including entrenched patronage networks, religious institutions, armed nonstate actors such as Hezbollah, and competing foreign powers—use a combination of financial incentives and intimidation to exert influence on Lebanese voters and political figures. The 2018 elections featured credible allegations of corruption, as well as analyses pointing to the role of establishment parties' patronage networks in mobilizing or incentivizing voters.

B4. Do various segments of the population (including ethnic, racial, religious, gender, LGBT+, and other relevant groups) have full political rights and electoral opportunities? 2 / 4

Lebanon officially recognizes 18 religious communities, and the political system ensures that nearly all of these groups are represented, though not according to their actual shares of the population. Individuals who are not, or do not wish to be, affiliated with the recognized groups are effectively excluded. Moreover, the country's large refugee population, including Palestinian refugee camp residents and Syrians who fled their country's civil war, are not eligible to acquire citizenship and have no political rights.

Women formally have the same political rights as men. In practice, women remain marginalized due to religious restrictions, institutionalized inequality, hidden legal obstacles, political culture, and societal discrimination. Neither the 2017 electoral law nor informal understandings regarding power-sharing include rules to guarantee women's participation in politics. Few women serve in the parliament as a result, though more female candidates participated in the 2018 elections than in previous contests: 111 women registered, with 86 ultimately running as candidates. Only six women were elected.

LGBT+ people have little political representation. However, more politicians have expressed support for their rights in recent years; nearly 100 parliamentary candidates in 2018 publicly called for the decriminalization of same-sex relations.

C. FUNCTIONING OF GOVERNMENT: 1 / 12 (−1)

C1. Do the freely elected head of government and national legislative representatives determine the policies of the government? 1 / 4

When the government is able to develop policies, they tend to be the result of negotiation among the country's dominant political figures, regardless of formal titles and positions; meanwhile, the legislature generally facilitates these policies rather than serving as an independent institutional check on the government. The authority of the government is also limited in practice by the power of autonomous militant groups like Hezbollah and foreign states with interests in Lebanon.

The elections of a president, parliament, parliament speaker, and prime minister between 2016 and 2019 eased the country's years-long political deadlock. However, since then prime minister Saad Hariri resigned in late 2019, the system has been unstable; the Diab government was seen as unable and unwilling to set its own agenda or pursue its own policies without approval or acquiescence from the elites who backed it. After Diab resigned in August 2020, he and his cabinet served only as caretakers through the end of the year, lacking the power in law and in practice to govern effectively.

C2. Are safeguards against official corruption strong and effective? 0 / 4

Corruption is endemic. Political and bureaucratic corruption is widespread, businesses routinely pay bribes and cultivate ties with politicians to win contracts or avoid unfavorable state actions, anticorruption laws are loosely enforced, and patronage networks generally operate unchecked. State expenditures remain irregular, with few mechanisms for effective oversight. Institutions such as the Central Inspection Bureau and Supreme Disciplinary Board are woefully underfunded and understaffed. When anticorruption institutions do take action, it tends to be selective or politicized. Chronic corruption has affected state-owned companies and utilities, contributing to poor service delivery and routine electricity blackouts.

C3. Does the government operate with openness and transparency? 0 / 4 (−1)

Political leaders and government officials often operate behind closed doors, outside of state institutions, and with little regard for formal procedures. Although civil society groups have some ability to influence pending policies or legislation, and may along with the media discuss proposals that have been made public, their influence is often contingent on participation in opaque processes. The National Assembly approved an access to information law in 2017, but it is not fully implemented, and government documents remain difficult to obtain in practice.

In the aftermath of the Beirut port explosion in August 2020, the state responded in opaque and arbitrary ways, withholding information and obstructing both policy input and accountability efforts. Different security services seemed to work at cross-purposes and without communicating clearly to the public, and special powers associated with emergency declarations were employed intermittently or selectively. The justice minister, through a nontransparent process, appointed a judge to lead an investigation of the explosion, which was caused by dangerous chemicals that had been left for years in a port warehouse. In December the judge charged Diab and three former cabinet ministers with criminal negligence, but leading political figures denounced the decision, and some officials refused to cooperate with the probe.

Separately in 2020, an ongoing collapse of the country's currency reverberated through the financial system and the broader economy, underscoring concerns about transparency at the central bank and accountability for years of mismanagement that led to the crisis.

Score Change: The score declined from 1 to 0 due to the government's opaque and disjointed responses to a series of national crises in recent years, including a currency collapse and a massive explosion in Beirut's port complex that devastated much of the capital.

CIVIL LIBERTIES: 30 / 60
D. FREEDOM OF EXPRESSION AND BELIEF: 11 / 16
D1. Are there free and independent media? 2 / 4

Press freedom is constitutionally guaranteed but inconsistently upheld. While the country's media are among the most open and diverse in the region, nearly all outlets depend on the patronage of political parties, wealthy individuals, or foreign powers, and consequently practice some degree of self-censorship. Books, movies, plays, and other artistic works are subject to censorship, especially when the content involves politics, religion, sex, or Israel, and the artists responsible for work deemed controversial by the government or major religious groups face official interference. It is a criminal offense to criticize or defame the president or security services. Authorities sometimes use such laws to harass and detain journalists, and those detained are often forced to sign pledges to refrain from writing content viewed as defamatory by the government.

Authorities have failed to protect the media from violence or intimidation by members of political, religious, and other influential groups. Supporters of political parties attacked reporters covering protests in January and February 2020, and several journalists experienced harassment online throughout the year—with partisans often threatening to kill or otherwise harm them. Journalists were also assaulted by security personnel and demonstrators during protests that followed the Beirut port explosion in August. A photographer who was reportedly among the first to arrive at the scene of the blast was assassinated in December, stirring speculation about possible motives for the killing.

Despite the legal and practical obstacles they faced, many journalists in 2020 were able to report and comment on sensitive topics such as state corruption, elite malfeasance, and the behavior of armed factions like Hezbollah.

D2. Are individuals free to practice and express their religious faith or nonbelief in public and private? 3 / 4

The constitution protects freedom of conscience, and the state does not typically interfere with the practice or expression of religious faith or nonbelief. While blasphemy is a criminal offense, enforcement varies and is generally lax. Individuals may face societal pressure to express faith or allegiance to a confessional community. Leaders and members of different communities discourage proselytizing by other groups.

D3. Is there academic freedom, and is the educational system free from extensive political indoctrination? 3 / 4

Academic freedom is generally unimpaired. Individuals are mostly free to select subjects for research and disseminate their findings. However, various laws and customary standards—including restrictions on defamation, blasphemy, and work or opinions related to Israel—limit debate on certain issues. The state does not engage in extensive political indoctrination through education, though religious and other nonstate entities do seek to reinforce communal identities and perspectives.

D4. Are individuals free to express their personal views on political or other sensitive topics without fear of surveillance or retribution? 3 / 4

Private discussion and public expression of personal views are somewhat uninhibited. Lebanese citizens routinely engage in debates about political and other controversial topics, both online and offline. However, repressive laws that criminalize defamation or otherwise restrict speech remain on the books, and individuals sometimes face police questioning, arrests, short detentions, or fines if they criticize the government, the military, foreign heads of state, or other powerful entities. Noncitizens, including refugees and migrant workers, have fewer legal protections and may be especially reluctant to engage in speech that could draw the attention of the security services. Lebanese authorities often use cameras to record people in public places, and regularly monitor social media and electronic communications—including of prominent individuals such as politicians, dissidents, and journalists. Authorities also fail to protect people from nonstate actors, such as political parties or militant groups and their supporters, that may monitor and punish them for expressing critical opinions.

E. ASSOCIATIONAL AND ORGANIZATIONAL RIGHTS: 8 / 12
E1. Is there freedom of assembly? 3 / 4

The authorities generally respect the right to assemble, which is protected under the constitution, and people routinely gather without permits or coordination with security services in practice. Demonstrators have been able to mount protests against government dysfunction and lack of services in recent years, including in 2020. While most participants have remained peaceful, smaller groups have occasionally engaged in violence.

Authorities, political parties, militia groups, and individuals have sometimes responded to peaceful demonstrations with violence. For example, riot police used force to disperse protesters in downtown Beirut in January 2020, as cabinet formation was underway, and after the Beirut port explosion in August. Supporters of various political parties also beat protesters or attacked their encampments during the year.

Organizers of other types of gatherings—such as LGBT+ pride events, concerts featuring LGBT+ performers, or public discussions with authors and activists who hold certain positions on the Syrian civil war—may also face threats from hostile nonstate groups and lack effective protection from the government.

E2. Is there freedom for nongovernmental organizations, particularly those that are engaged in human rights-and governance-related work? 3 / 4

NGOs tend to operate freely in Lebanon, though they must comply with the Law on Associations, which has not been thoroughly updated since 1909, and other applicable laws relating to labor, finance, and immigration. NGOs must also register with the Interior Ministry, which may oblige them to undergo an approval process and can investigate a group's founders, officers, and staff. NGOs sometimes face bureaucratic obstruction or intimidation by security services, depending on their line of work or particular initiatives. Groups that focus on Syria-related matters or are led and staffed by Syrian refugees are especially prone to scrutiny and interference.

E3. Is there freedom for trade unions and similar professional or labor organizations? 2 / 4

Individuals may establish, join, and leave trade unions and other professional organizations. However, the Labor Ministry has broad authority over the formation of unions, union elections, and the administrative dissolution of unions. The state regulates collective bargaining and strikes, and many unions are linked to political parties and serve as tools of influence for political leaders. Public employees, agricultural workers, and household workers are not protected by the labor code and have no legal right to organize, though they have formed unrecognized representative organizations. While noncitizen legal residents may join unions under the law, migrant workers have fewer union rights, and large numbers of refugees lack legal status or the right to work.

F. RULE OF LAW: 5 / 16

F1. Is there an independent judiciary? 1 / 4

Lebanon's judiciary is not independent. Political leaders exercise significant influence over judicial appointments, jurisdiction, processes, and decisions, which are also affected by corruption and the undue influence of other prominent people.

F2. Does due process prevail in civil and criminal matters? 1 / 4

Due process is subject to a number of impediments, including violations of defendants' right to counsel and extensive use of lengthy pretrial detention. Due process guarantees are particularly inadequate in the country's exceptional courts, including the military courts, whose judges do not require a background in law and are authorized to try civilians and juveniles in security-related cases. In practice, military courts have asserted jurisdiction over cases involving human rights activists and protesters in addition to those focused on alleged spies and militants.

F3. Is there protection from the illegitimate use of physical force and freedom from war and insurgencies? 2 / 4

Armed militias, terrorist groups, and criminal organizations continue to undermine security in Lebanon. Residents in southern Lebanon have lived with the risk of land-mine detonation since the 1975–90 civil war. Hundreds of thousands of mines were deployed during the war by multiple groups, including the Israeli military and Lebanese militias. The UN Interim Force in Lebanon (UNIFIL) has worked to remove these mines since 2006, along with the Mines Advisory Group (MAG), a UK-based NGO.

Prisons and detention centers are badly overcrowded and poorly equipped, and the use of torture by law enforcement, military, and state security personnel continues despite the passage of antitorture legislation and the creation of institutional mechanisms to halt the practice.

In 2020, the incumbent interior minister admitted in a television interview that he had killed two people during the civil war and that Aoun, the current president, had protected him from repercussions; he did not clarify the circumstances of the killings. The admission coincided with abuses by security services under the interior minister's control during the year. In August, for instance, security personnel assaulted and harassed citizens for insulting the president or engaging in protests after the Beirut port explosion.

F4. Do laws, policies, and practices guarantee equal treatment of various segments of the population? 1 / 4

The country's legal system is meant to protect members of recognized confessional communities against mistreatment by the state, but groups have engaged in discriminatory behavior toward one another in practice, and people who do not belong to a recognized community have difficulty obtaining official documents, government jobs, and other services.

Women face discrimination in wages, benefits, and societal standards and practices, and are barred from certain types of employment.

LGBT+ people face both official and societal discrimination and harassment. In 2018, an appeals court ruled that private same-sex intercourse between consenting adults was not illegal, though the decision was not binding beyond the case in question, and the criminal code provision barring same-sex sexual relations remains in force. LGBT+ people who violate this law risk a one-year prison sentence.

More than a million Syrians reside in Lebanon. Of that number, some 865,000 were officially registered as refugees as of the end of 2020 by the Office of the UN High Commissioner for Refugees; the government has barred the agency from registering new Syrian refugees since 2015. Syrian refugees have faced arbitrary arrests and other forms of harassment, and most live in poverty due in part to limitations on their employment options. The government has also enforced housing regulations to compel Syrian refugees to destroy their informal camps, threatening to use the military against those who did not comply. Syrians have sometimes been deported despite the risk of mistreatment by Syrian authorities.

About 477,000 Palestinian refugees resided in Lebanon as of mid-2020. Some 45 percent of those already residing in Lebanon prior to the Syrian civil war live in 12 designated refugee camps and are restricted from 39 professions, contributing to widespread poverty, unemployment, and underemployment. In 2019, Lebanese authorities issued new regulations requiring foreigners to possess work permits, further restricting Palestinians' access to the labor market.

G. PERSONAL AUTONOMY AND INDIVIDUAL RIGHTS: 6 / 16

G1. Do individuals enjoy freedom of movement, including the ability to change their place of residence, employment, or education? 1 / 4

Citizens enjoy constitutional and legal rights to freedom of movement. With few formal restrictions, they are able to travel within Lebanon. Nevertheless, citizens find it extremely difficult to transfer official places of residence for voting purposes. They also face de facto sectarian boundaries and militia checkpoints in some areas.

Noncitizens are subject to much harsher restrictions on movement. Many Palestinians classified as refugees live in designated camps, and access to those areas is controlled and often constrained by Lebanese security services. Many Syrian refugees live in informal camps or smaller settlements, and are subject to curfews and other obstacles to movement. In 2020, many municipalities introduced special COVID-19-related curfews and restrictions that applied only to Syrian refugees.

Migrant workers face severe restrictions on movement under a sponsorship system that revokes their residency rights if they are dismissed by their designated employers. Employers often confiscate migrant workers' passports, further reducing their autonomy.

G2. Are individuals able to exercise the right to own property and establish private businesses without undue interference from state or nonstate actors? 2 / 4

Lebanese law protects citizens' rights to own property and operate private businesses, but powerful groups and individuals sometimes engage in land-grabbing and other infringements without consequence, and business activity is impaired by bureaucratic obstacles and corruption.

Refugees, including longtime Palestinian residents, have few property rights. Women have weaker property rights than men under the religious codes that govern inheritance and other personal status issues in Lebanon, and they often face family pressure to transfer property to male relatives.

G3. Do individuals enjoy personal social freedoms, including choice of marriage partner and size of family, protection from domestic violence, and control over appearance? 2 / 4

Because the religious codes and courts of each confessional community determine personal status law in Lebanon, people's rights regarding marriage, divorce, and child custody depend on their affiliation, though women are typically at a disadvantage compared with men. Partners seeking to enter an interfaith marriage often travel abroad, as Lebanon recognizes civil marriages performed elsewhere. Women cannot pass Lebanese citizenship to non-Lebanese spouses or children of non-Lebanese fathers.

In 2017, the parliament repealed Article 522 of the penal code, which allowed rapists to evade criminal prosecution if they subsequently married their victims for a period of at least three years. However, the change did not affect a similar article related to sex with a minor, and spousal rape is still not a criminal offense.

LGBT+ marriage remains illegal within Lebanon. However, transgender people have some legal precedent allowing them to live publicly based on their gender identity; in 2016, the Court of Appeals allowed a transgender man to legally change his gender in the civil registry, and supported the plaintiff's desire to seek gender confirmation surgery in its ruling.

G4. Do individuals enjoy equality of opportunity and freedom from economic exploitation? 1 / 4

Citizens' communal affiliation can either enhance or restrict their economic opportunities in a given area, company, or public-sector entity, depending on which group is in a dominant position. Individuals must also contend with political patronage and clientelism, layered on top of communally enabled corruption, in the public and private sectors.

Noncitizens, such as refugees and migrant workers, enjoy even less opportunity and are especially vulnerable to exploitative working conditions and sex trafficking. The authorities do not effectively enforce laws against child labor, which is common among Syrian refugees, rural Lebanese, and segments of the urban poor.

Household workers and migrant workers who operate under the sponsorship system routinely suffer from economic exploitation. Employers are favored in legal cases involving migrant workers, discouraging the latter from reporting denial of wages as well as physical, psychological, and sexual abuse. In 2020, as the Lebanese economy collapsed, some employers abandoned their non-Lebanese employees near their home countries' embassies, often without fulfilling their contractual obligation to provide for the workers' return flights.

Lesotho

Population: 2,100,000
Capital: Maseru
Freedom Status: Partly Free
Electoral Democracy: Yes

Overview: Lesotho is a constitutional monarchy. In recent years, the army's involvement in the country's already fragile politics has resulted in political instability and a security crisis. Corruption remains a challenge. Customary practice and law restrict women's rights in areas such as property, inheritance, and marriage and divorce.

KEY DEVELOPMENTS IN 2020

- In March, Prime Minister Thomas Thabane suspended Parliament for three months in what he said was part of government efforts to combat the COVID-19 pandemic. Shortly before the suspension, the National Assembly, Parliament's lower house, had passed a bill preventing Thabane from calling for new elections if he lost a no-confidence vote. In April, the Constitutional Court overturned the suspension of Parliament, and a day later Thabane deployed the army to restore order and peace against what he called "rogue" elements destabilizing his government.
- In May, Prime Minister Thabane, who was being investigated for the 2017 murder of his estranged former wife, resigned after months of political uncertainty and calls from within his government for his resignation. Moeketsi Majoro became the new prime minister later that month under a new coalition between the All Basotho Convention (ABC) and the opposition Democratic Congress (DC).
- In December, DC leader and deputy prime minister Mathibeli Mokhothu, was linked in a court case to Rana Qamar, a Pakistani national well-known for human trafficking who has allegedly donated extensively to the DC. Qamar has been accused of using two cabinet ministers, including Mokhothu, to pressure an immigration official into letting two Pakistanis into Lesotho without visas.

POLITICAL RIGHTS: 27 / 40

A. ELECTORAL PROCESS: 10 / 12

A1. Was the current head of government or other chief national authority elected through free and fair elections? 3 / 4

Lesotho is a constitutional monarchy. King Letsie III serves as the ceremonial head of state. The prime minister is head of government; the head of the majority party or coalition automatically becomes prime minister following elections, making the prime minister's legitimacy largely dependent on the conduct of the polls. Thomas Thabane became prime minister after the All Basotho Convention (ABC) won a plurality in a snap election in 2017. In May 2020, the coalition government collapsed and Thabane, who was being investigated for the 2017 murder of his estranged former wife, resigned after months of political uncertainty and increasing pressure from within the ABC and among coalition partners calling for his resignation. The ABC and opposition Democratic Congress (DC) formed a new coalition government with Moeketsi Majoro as prime minister later that month.

The prime minister can advise the king to dissolve Parliament and call a new election, but members of the lower house voted to restrict this ability by constitutional amendment in October 2019. The amendment was still under consideration in the upper house at year's end.

A2. Were the current national legislative representatives elected through free and fair elections? 4 / 4

The lower house of Parliament, the National Assembly, has 120 seats; 80 are filled through first-past-the-post constituency votes, and the remaining 40 through proportional representation. The Senate—the upper house of Parliament—consists of 22 principal chiefs who wield considerable authority in rural areas and whose membership is hereditary, along with 11 other members appointed by the king and acting on the advice of the Council of State. Members of both chambers serve five-year terms.

In 2017, the coalition government of former prime minister Pakalitha Mosisili—head of the DC—lost a no-confidence vote, triggering the third legislative election since 2012. Election observers declared the contest peaceful, generally well administered, and competitive.

However, isolated instances of political violence were noted, as was a heavy security presence at many polling places, which electoral officials said intimidated some voters. The ABC won a plurality of seats and formed a coalition government.

In May 2020, the coalition government collapsed after Thabane's resignation, and the ABC formed a new coalition with the DC later in the month.

A3. Are the electoral laws and framework fair, and are they implemented impartially by the relevant election management bodies? 3 / 4

Although the Independent Electoral Commission (IEC) faces capacity constraints, and the credibility of the voters' roll has been questioned in the past, the IEC has been commended for its independence and its efforts to uphold electoral laws and oversee credible elections. International observers broadly commended the IEC's administration of the 2017 snap poll but noted deficiencies they linked to a lack of capacity, including late disbursement of campaign funds to political parties.

IEC chairperson Mahapela Lehohla and two other commissioners attempted to remain in their posts after their terms expired in January 2019 and sued the government to lengthen their mandates that May. Lesotho's political parties opposed their efforts, and the Transformation Resource Centre, a local nongovernmental organization (NGO), filed a legal challenge at the Constitutional Court in July. The court rejected the commissioners' case that October and Lehohla's appeal that December, leaving the IEC with no active members. After IEC workers appealed to Parliament, in November 2020, King Letsie III appointed three IEC commissioners based on the advice of the Council of State.

B. POLITICAL PLURALISM AND PARTICIPATION: 11 / 16

B1. Do the people have the right to organize in different political parties or other competitive political groupings of their choice, and is the system free of undue obstacles to the rise and fall of these competing parties or groupings? 3 / 4

Political parties may form freely and are allocated funding by the IEC, and 27 parties contested the 2017 election. However, politics have been unstable since a failed 2014 coup. In recent years, the country has seen politically motivated assassinations and assassination attempts, and political leaders operate within the country at some risk to their personal safety. For example, Nqosa Mahao, the leader of a faction that was fighting Thabane for control of the ABC, reported that he was targeted by an assassination plot in June 2019.

B2. Is there a realistic opportunity for the opposition to increase its support or gain power through elections? 3 / 4

Opposition parties have a realistic chance of gaining power through elections, and power has rotated frequently between DC- and ABC-led coalitions. However, political instability and associated violence and intimidation has at times prompted opposition leaders to flee the country. The South African Development Community (SADC) facilitated a governance reform process to address these concerns, culminating in the creation of the *National Reforms Authority* (NRA) in August 2019. The 59 members of the NRA were sworn into office in February 2020 and are expected to complete their work at least 6 months before the 2022 elections.

B3. Are the people's political choices free from domination by forces that are external to the political sphere, or by political forces that employ extrapolitical means? 2 / 4

Recent political instability is largely related to disputes among factions of the Lesotho Defence Force (LDF). Although the heavy military presence at voting stations during the 2017 election was questioned, no reports of voter interference surfaced. However, in June 2019, then defense minister Tefo Mapesela claimed that senior police officers threatened him after he criticized an army commander and a senior intelligence official in a phone conversation.

Principal chiefs wield some political influence over their rural subjects.

In 2018, Lesotho-based Chinese businessman Yan Xie claimed that he heavily donated to most of Lesotho's political parties. Critics argued that Yan's financial clout gave him considerable influence over the country's political elites, exemplified by his 2017 appointment as a "head of special projects" and special trade envoy. In June 2020, Yan reportedly fled to Australia after learning that he was being investigated for corruption.

B4. Do various segments of the population (including ethnic, racial, religious, gender, LGBT+, and other relevant groups) have full political rights and electoral opportunities? 3 / 4

The constitution guarantees political rights for all. However, societal norms discourage women from running for office, and no parliamentary or party-list gender quota exists to ensure their representation. After the 2017 election, only 23 percent of seats in Parliament were held by women, down from 25 percent before the contest. Women's involvement in local government has also declined; women held 49 percent of local positions in 2011, but only 40 percent in 2017. The inaccessibility of some polling stations to persons living with disabilities was raised as a concern during the 2017 election. LGBT+ individuals generally face societal discrimination, and this discourages them from advocating for their rights in the political sphere.

C. FUNCTIONING OF GOVERNMENT: 6 / 12

C1. Do the freely elected head of government and national legislative representatives determine the policies of the government? 2 / 4

While elections are held without delays and representatives are duly seated, persistent political instability disrupts normal government operations. Reports of Prime Minister Thabane and his current wife's involvement in the 2017 murder of his estranged wife and his initial resistance to resigning from office in early 2020 destabilized much of the government and focused Parliament's energies on managing the political crisis. In March 2020, Thabane suspended Parliament for three months in what he said was part of government efforts to combat the COVID-19 pandemic. Shortly before the suspension, the National Assembly had passed a bill preventing him from calling for new elections if he lost a no-confidence vote. This was overturned in April by the Constitutional Court, and a day later Thabane deployed the army to restore order and peace against what he called "rogue" elements destabilizing his government. In May, Parliament rejected a move to extend the state of emergency by six months; the prime minister was instead advised to use powers provided for under the Disaster Management Act.

The *National Reforms Authority* (NRA) was inaugurated in February 2020 to oversee the implementation of reforms backed by the Southern African Development Community (SADC) that are meant to bring about lasting political stability, peace, and security in Lesotho.

C2. Are safeguards against official corruption strong and effective? 2 / 4

Official corruption and impunity remain significant problems. The main anticorruption agency, the Directorate on Corruption and Economic Offence (DCEO), lacks full prosecutorial powers and faces capacity and funding challenges. The Asset Forfeiture Unit, which was established in 2016 to recover property connected to corruption cases, is largely ineffective. In July 2020, DCEO Director General Mahlomola Manyokole reported that Acting Chief Justice 'Maseforo Mahase had approved plans for the establishment of a specialized anticorruption court. That same month, Parliament made amendments to the DCEO Act to grant the agency powers to investigate money-laundering crimes beyond Lesotho's borders. Anticorruption officials have claimed that individuals and companies have used state capture tactics to obtain immunity for corrupt dealings.

While DCEO officers work to fulfill the directorate's mandate, the agency took few corruption cases to court in 2020. In February, Mahali Phamotse, the Gender, Youth, Sports and Recreation Minister, was charged with corruption over a 2015 tender for school textbooks. She was released on bail and continued in her role. In September 2020, the DCEO issued a directive to the Ministry of Health to stop payments to all suppliers due to corruption allegations in the awarding of tenders for medical supplies intended to combat the COVID-19 crisis.

In December 2020, DC leader and deputy prime minister Mathibeli Mokhothu, was linked in a court case to Rana Qamar, a Pakistani national well-known for human trafficking whohas allegedly donated extensively to the DC. Qamar has been accused of using two cabinet ministers, including Mokhothu, to pressure an immigration official into letting two Pakistanis into Lesotho without visas.

C3. Does the government operate with openness and transparency? 2 / 4

Lesotho has no access to information law, and responses to information requests are not guaranteed or responded to by information officers in a timely manner. The management of public finances is shrouded in secrecy. Government procurement decisions and tenders generally cannot be accessed online. Although high-level government and elected officials are required to disclose their assets and business interests—which Prime Minister Majoro and his cabinet did in June 2020—these declarations are not made public. Enforcement of the rules is limited by resource constraints. The appointment process for judges lacks transparency, though in December 2020, the Minister of Law and Justice won a Constitutional Court decision in December that effectively stops the Judicial Services Commission (JSC) from recommending names for appointment without the participation of a majority of its members.

CIVIL LIBERTIES: 36 / 60
D. FREEDOM OF EXPRESSION AND BELIEF: 12 / 16
D1. Are there free and independent media? 2 / 4

Freedom of the press is only indirectly protected under constitutional guarantees of freedom of expression. Journalists are subject to threats and intimidation from the authorities and private citizens. State and private media outlets have also been accused of open bias.

Journalists additionally face statutory barriers that interfere in their work, including criminal code provisions that bar sedition and offenses against the "dignity of the royal family." The Penal Code, adopted in 2010, allows police officers to force journalists to reveal their sources. In July 2020, the bodyguards of Deputy Police Commissioner Paseka Mokete physically assaulted a *Lesotho Times* photographer and asked him to delete photos he had taken of Mokete, who was appearing in court on charges of sexually assaulting a junior police officer. In November 2020, one journalist was shot by members the Lesotho Mounted Police Service (LMPS) while reporting on the youth protests known as #BachaShutDown.

In October 2020, the government proposed restrictions on social media use, including provisions that allow regulators to investigate online posts and order their removal.

D2. Are individuals free to practice and express their religious faith or nonbelief in public and private? 4 / 4

The constitution provides legal protections for freedom of religion and prohibits religious discrimination, and religious freedom is generally upheld in practice.

D3. Is there academic freedom, and is the educational system free from extensive political indoctrination? 3 / 4

Academic freedom is generally respected in practice, though the government does interfere in the administration of institutions of higher education. In September 2019, National University of Lesotho (NUL) officials warned that the institution risked closure due to government funding cuts.

D4. Are individuals free to express their personal views on political or other sensitive topics without fear of surveillance or retribution? 3 / 4

The constitution provides legal protections for freedom of expression. However, political violence in recent years has discouraged open political debate. In October 2020, the Lesotho Communications Authority (LCA) proposed regulations for online content that would require users with at least 100 followers or a reach of at least 100 to register as internet broadcasters and obtain a certificate from the LCA, which has the authority to investigate and order the removal of posts that do not comply with Lesotho Telecommunications Authority (Broadcasting) Rules of 2004.

E. ASSOCIATIONAL AND ORGANIZATIONAL RIGHTS: 7 / 12

E1. Is there freedom of assembly? 2 / 4

Protests and demonstrations are permitted, but organizers must seek a permit seven days in advance. Demonstrations take place each year and are sometimes broken up violently by police. In 2020, various groups, including health care professionals, garment workers, and transport operators staged protests during the COVID-19 lockdown, with demands ranging from the payment of unpaid wages to the provision of personal protective equipment in hospitals. Police shot one journalist and violently detained others at the #BachaShutDown youth protests in November 2020.

E2. Is there freedom for nongovernmental organizations, particularly those that are engaged in human rights- and governance-related work? 3 / 4

NGOs generally operate without restrictions. However, some civil society groups act cautiously when working on politically sensitive issues. In addition, government rules on registering NGOs are strict; those who are accused of neglecting to register their organization risk a five-year prison sentence. No NGOs have been held to account for failure to register in recent years.

E3. Is there freedom for trade unions and similar professional or labor organizations? 2 / 4

While labor and union rights are constitutionally guaranteed, the union movement is weak and highly fragmented, and these challenges have undermined unions' ability to advance the rights of workers. The government has previously been accused of undermining bodies like the National Advisory Committee on Labour (NACOLA), Wages Advisory Board, and Industrial Relations Council.

Many employees in the textile sector—Lesotho's largest formal employer—face obstacles when attempting to join unions. In August 2020, Bull Clothing fired more than 200 workers for participating in a June strike action, during which police reportedly used excessive force. The company later rehired the workers on probationary contracts with significantly reduced benefits and wages. The workers' union took the matter to the Directorate of Dispute Prevention and Resolution (DDPR) conciliation tribunal; the case had not been heard by year's end.

F. RULE OF LAW: 8 / 16

F1. Is there an independent judiciary? 2 / 4

The constitution protects judicial independence, but the judiciary lacks resources and faces a shortage of judicial officers. The *Lesotho Times* reported in October 2020 that the judicial system was on the verge of collapse due to a lack of funds and infrastructural disrepair. Judges do rule against the government, including on politically sensitive issues. In May 2020, Prime Minister Majoro admitted that factional battles within the ruling ABC had eroded the independence of the judiciary. The SADC and the government decided in 2018 to engage foreign judges on high-profile and politically sensitive cases. In April, the Constitutional Court ruled Prime minister Thabane's suspension of Parliament was unconstitutional.

The judicial appointment process lacks transparency, and members of the JSC at times act without proper oversight.

F2. Does due process prevail in civil and criminal matters? 2 / 4

While the courts generally uphold due process, a large backlog of cases has left individuals subject to trial delays and lengthy pretrial detention. In the first eight months of 2019, the government appointed three foreign judges to preside over high-profile criminal cases that were affected by the ongoing backlog. In June 2020, reports emerged that one of the foreign judges had resigned over poor working conditions. The other two had intended to resign citing similar concerns but did not when they received significant pay increases.

The COVID-19 pandemic exacerbated issues within the courts system, though the Court of Appeal operated during the lockdown period in 2020, holding remote hearings.

F3. Is there protection from the illegitimate use of physical force and freedom from war and insurgencies? 2 / 4

Lesotho faced years of violence related to factional disputes within the army; the SADC appointed a facilitation team to create a reform process that would partially focus on the security sector. The SADC's work culminated in the creation of the NRA, though the country did not meet the original May 2019 deadline for full implementation of the SADC-backed program. Members of the NRA were sworn into office in February 2020 and were expected to complete their work by mid-2021.

The constitution provides legal protections against torture, but allegations of torture have been levied against police forces, the LDF, and prison authorities. The enforcement of COVID-19 regulations in 2020 was marked by numerous reports of police brutality and excessive use of force. In March 2020, Lesotho Lawyers for Human Rights filed an application seeking a court declaration that the state of emergency had not authorized law enforcement agencies to torture civilians who violated the regulations. In September, a civilian from Mafeteng was tortured to death by the police.

Lesotho does not have an independent administrative body to investigate human rights abuses.

F4. Do laws, policies, and practices guarantee equal treatment of various segments of the population? 2 / 4

Rights are restricted for some groups. Same-sex relations between men are illegal, though this law is not enforced. LGBT+ individuals face societal discrimination challenges accessing services, like health care. Discrimination based on sexual orientation or gender identity is not prohibited by law. Customary laws and other social norms discriminate against women. For example, women are considered minors under the guardianship of their fathers before marriage and their husbands after marriage. Schools often lack facilities for students with disabilities. Parliament failed to pass the Disability Equity Bill in 2020, which would advance the rights of people with disabilities.

G. PERSONAL AUTONOMY AND INDIVIDUAL RIGHTS: 9 / 16

G1. Do individuals enjoy freedom of movement, including the ability to change their place of residence, employment, or education? 3 / 4

The constitution protects freedom of movement, which is generally upheld. In recent years, a high incidence of rape on a path near the Ha Lebona and Ha Koeshe villages has prompted some women to reduce travel in the area.

COVID-19 regulations in 2020 restricted free movement in order to curtail the spread of the virus. Some restrictions were lifted late in the year, including on international travel.

G2. Are individuals able to exercise the right to own property and establish private businesses without undue interference from state or nonstate actors? 2 / 4

The constitution protects property rights, though related laws are inconsistently upheld. Women's rights are restricted in areas such as property and inheritance, including chieftainships which can only be inherited by men. Expropriation is provided for in the constitution but is uncommon and subject to fair compensation. Government instability and the country's volatile politics hampers normal business activity. In November 2020, Parliament adopted new regulations that will reserve a list of 47 business activities for the Basotho ethnic group. Foreigners can only participate in these activities as minority shareholders.

G3. Do individuals enjoy personal social freedoms, including choice of marriage partner and size of family, protection from domestic violence, and control over appearance? 2 / 4

Prominent social norms and harmful patriarchal attitudes negatively affect women. Women's rights are restricted in marriage and divorce. Violence against women is high, and there is no domestic violence law despite government promises to enact one. Forced and child marriages remain an ongoing problem. Advocacy organizations in 2020 reported increases in cases of gender-based violence (GBV) during the COVID-19 lockdown. In September 2020, a study by the Commonwealth Secretariat reported that one in three women in Lesotho had experienced physical or sexual violence, often at the hands of their partners. Accountability for the perpetrators of gender-based violence is not consistent.

In August 2019, former constitutional affairs minister Mootsi Lehata, who served under former prime minister Mosisili, reached a settlement to avoid a trial over a 2018 rape accusation. Lehata was accused of raping a 17-year-old girl, who subsequently became pregnant, that January; the survivor withdrew her claim as part of the settlement.

G4. Do individuals enjoy equality of opportunity and freedom from economic exploitation? 2 / 4

Human trafficking remains an ongoing challenge for Lesotho. The US State Department's 2020 *Trafficking in Persons Report* found that the Lesotho authorities did not meet minimum standards to eliminate trafficking or make any significant progress in addressing it. Few victims are identified, and few support services are made available to them or the appropriate NGOs. The legal framework for prosecuting trafficking remains weak, without strong penalties to deter offenders. In November 2020, the National Assembly passed amendments to the Anti-Trafficking in Persons Law which introduce tougher sentences for convicted persons, including life imprisonment if the victim is a child, and abolished fines for offenses.

In December 2020, the DC party leader and deputy prime minister Mathibeli Mokhothu was reportedly linked in a court case to Rana Qamar, a Pakistani national well-known for human trafficking. Qamar has been accused of using two cabinet ministers, including Mokhothu, to pressure an immigration official into letting two Pakistanis into Lesotho without visas.

Child labor and forced labor for both men and women remains a problem.

Liberia

Population: 5,100,000
Capital: Monrovia
Freedom Status: Partly Free
Electoral Democracy: Yes

Overview: Liberia has enjoyed nearly two decades of peace and stability since the second civil war ended in 2003. During this time, the country has made considerable progress rebuilding government capacity, reestablishing the rule of law, and ensuring the political rights and civil liberties of citizens, and 2017 saw the first peaceful transfer of power between leaders since 1944. However, Liberia still faces serious issues with corruption, impunity, and violence against women.

KEY DEVELOPMENTS IN 2020

- Voters cast ballots for 15 Senate seats in December, with the opposition Collaborating Political Parties (CPP) alliance taking an early lead in several contests. While voting was largely peaceful, isolated incidents of fraud were reported, and an independent candidate in Gbarpolu County was kidnapped ahead of a partial rerun before an alliance of women's groups rescued her. Final results remained pending at year's end.
- Voters signaled their early approval of proposed constitutional amendments—which would shorten the terms of the president, vice president, and legislators while ending a dual-citizenship ban—in a referendum held concurrently with Senate elections. Opposition groups called for a ban, fearing President George Weah would use the amendments to seek a future third term, and the results were thrown into doubt by the prevalence of invalid ballots; the results remained uncertified at year's end.
- President Weah declared a COVID-19-related state of emergency in April, heavily restricting the movement of Liberians and relying on the army to enforce those restrictions until the declaration expired in July. Journalists who reported on the pandemic faced questioning, interference, and, in some cases, physical attack from the authorities. The government reported 1,800 cases and 83 deaths to the World Health Organization by year's end.

POLITICAL RIGHTS: 27 / 40
A. ELECTORAL PROCESS: 8 / 12
A1. Was the current head of government or other chief national authority elected through free and fair elections? 3 / 4

Liberia's president is directly elected and can serve up to two six-year terms. Since the end of the civil wars in 2003, Liberia has had three peaceful presidential elections. The most recent election, held in 2017, was assessed by domestic and international observers as generally peaceful and credible, though difficulties including long queues at polling places and challenges related to voter identification were noted.

A runoff between George Weah of the Coalition for Democratic Change (CDC) and incumbent vice president Joseph Boakai of the Unity Party (UP), the top two finishers in the first round of the 2017 poll, was delayed when third-place finisher Charles Brumskine of the Liberty Party (LP) challenged the first-round results on grounds of fraud. The Supreme Court found his claim unsupported by the evidence, and the runoff was held several weeks later than scheduled, in late December. Weah won with 61.5 percent of the vote, and Boakai conceded defeat. Observers noted procedural and administrative improvements in the runoff compared to the first round. Weah's 2018 inauguration marked the first peaceful transfer of power since 1944.

A2. Were the current national legislative representatives elected through free and fair elections? 3 / 4

Liberia has a bicameral legislature composed of a 30-member Senate and a 73-member House of Representatives; senators are elected to nine-year terms, and representatives to six-year terms.

Lower-house elections were held concurrently with the first round of the presidential election in October 2017. The CDC won 21 seats, while the UP won 20. The People's Unification Party, which was allied to the ruling CDC, won 5 seats. The LP won 3 seats. The remaining 24 seats were won by independents and other parties. Despite administrative problems, observers considered the elections generally peaceful and well administered, with only minor incidents of violence during the campaign.

Fifteen Senate seats were contested in December 2020 elections. According to preliminary results from the NEC, the CPP—which includes the LP, UP, the All Liberian Party, and the Alternative National Congress—took an early lead in several seats.

The vote was largely peaceful, but the campaign period was marred by incidents of fraud and violence. Several voters were caught carrying multiple registration cards on election day. The Gbarpolu County election was disrupted when a local chief seized ballot boxes, forcing a partial rerun in mid-December. A candidate contesting that seat, independent Botoe Kanneh, was assaulted and kidnapped before that rerun, but was rescued by several women's groups. A final declaration for that contest was still pending at year's end. Final results for races in Nimba and Grand Kru counties were also unresolved by year's end.

A3. Are the electoral laws and framework fair, and are they implemented impartially by the relevant election management bodies? 2 / 4

While the NEC's independence is mandated by law, its capacity is limited and it has struggled to enforce electoral laws. The National Code of Conduct Act is not consistently followed by officials.

President Weah nominated a slate of commissioners in March 2020, but the CPP voiced concerns over the nominees' independence and criticized the fact that the nominated chairman, A. Ndubisi Nwabudike, is not Liberian by birth. The Liberia Immigration Service reported it had no records on his naturalization in early April. Nwabudike did not provide sufficient proof of his status during his nomination hearing, sparking controversy. Weah rescinded Nwabudike's nomination in April and nominated commissioner Davidetta Browne Lansanah to the chair in June. Browne Lansanah remained as acting chairwoman at year's end.

In September 2020, the CPP accused the commission of collaborating with the CDC to delay that month's scheduled Senate elections to December. Also in September, the CPP sued to force the NEC to fully revise a preexisting voter roll, but the Supreme Court ruled against the CPP in October. The Liberian Election Observation Network criticized the NEC's voter-registration efforts in October, calling its information campaign insufficient.

The NEC also managed a constitutional referendum, which was concurrently held with the December Senate elections. The proposed amendments would shorten the terms of the president, the vice president, and lower-house legislators from six years to five, would shorten senators' terms from nine years to seven, and would end a ban on dual citizenship. The opposition, which feared that President Weah would use the amendments to seek a third term, called for a boycott. In November, the Supreme Court ordered the referendum's cancellation over a ballot-design issue but reversed itself several days later, after the NEC offered a remedy. While voters appeared to approve the amendments, a large number of invalid votes put the results into doubt. The NEC's certification of the results was still pending at year's end.

B. POLITICAL PLURALISM AND PARTICIPATION: 12 / 16

B1. Do the people have the right to organize in different political parties or other competitive political groupings of their choice, and is the system free of undue obstacles to the rise and fall of these competing parties or groupings? 3 / 4

Political parties generally do not face undue legal or practical obstacles that prevent them from forming or operating. The People's Liberation Party was certified by the NEC in late December 2020. However, the Council of Patriots (COP), an opposition group, claimed in August that the Liberia Business Registry's nonresponse to its application was due to partisanship. The ruling party has been known to use public resources to fund campaigns during election periods—notably by taking advantage of state-owned vehicles and facilities.

Opposition parties can form coalitions; the CPP, which was formed in 2019, received its own NEC certification in August 2020. The seven-party Rainbow Alliance was certified later that month.

B2. Is there a realistic opportunity for the opposition to increase its support or gain power through elections? 3 / 4

Opposition parties and independent candidates have a realistic chance of gaining office and power through the ballot box. In 2017, President Weah, of the then opposition CDC, won his post over the former ruling party's candidate. Opposition candidates found success in the December 2020 Senate elections, with the NEC reporting early leads for CPP contestants.

However, candidates and their staff also faced physical attacks during the election period. In early December, CDC supporters attacked a convoy belonging to the CPP candidate in Grand Cape Mount County, destroying the vehicles. Gbarpolu County candidate Kanneh was kidnapped while campaigning in mid-December. The alliance of women's groups that rescued her reported that security officers who were apparently involved in the kidnapping also raped two members of her campaign team and assaulted Kanneh's brother.

B3. Are the people's political choices free from domination by forces that are external to the political sphere, or by political forces that employ extrapolitical means? 3 / 4

Allegations of undue influence or pressure on voters by powerful groups not democratically accountable to the people are somewhat rare. A general wariness of election-related violence persists in Liberia, however.

B4. Do various segments of the population (including ethnic, racial, religious, gender, LGBT+, and other relevant groups) have full political rights and electoral opportunities? 3 / 4

Members of Lebanese and Asian minority groups whose families have lived in Liberia for generations are denied citizenship and cannot participate in political processes. While former president Ellen Johnson Sirleaf (2006–18) was the first elected female head of state in Africa, and Liberia's current vice president is a woman, women are poorly represented in national politics and hold few leadership positions in political parties. Only one woman held a seat in the outgoing Senate, while eight sat in the lower house in December 2020. Social stigma against LGBT+ people discourages them from advocating for their rights in the context of Liberian politics.

C. FUNCTIONING OF GOVERNMENT: 7 / 12

C1. Do the freely elected head of government and national legislative representatives determine the policies of the government? 3 / 4

Once elected, government officials are duly installed in office, and elected legislators generally operate without interference. However, bribery and corruption can influence policy prioritization.

C2. Are safeguards against official corruption strong and effective? 2 / 4

Many institutions are devoted to fighting corruption, but they lack the resources and capacity to function effectively, and corruption remains pervasive.

The naturalization status of Liberia Anti-Corruption Commission (LACC) head A. Ndubusi Nwabudike, who was nominated to lead the NEC in March 2020, came into question. While that nomination was rescinded—and the Liberia National Bar Association expelled him from its ranks in June, over his inability to prove his naturalization status—Nwabudike remained at his LACC post at year's end.

Charles Sirleaf, a former deputy central bank director and son of former president Sirleaf, stood trial for his alleged involvement in the disappearance of several billion Liberian dollars from the central bank along with four other defendants in 2019. The charges against four defendants, including Sirleaf, were dropped in May 2020. Former bank governor Milton Weeks was acquitted in August.

C3. Does the government operate with openness and transparency? 2 / 4

The Freedom of Information Act is rarely used, and the government responds slowly to information requests. Transparency guidelines for public procurement processes are not fully enforced. In 2020, many new public officials, including most in the executive branch, failed to declare their assets as required by law. The LACC, which collects asset declarations, is not obligated to disclose those submitted by executive branch members, and efforts by civil society and media to gain access to President Weah's declaration have been unsuccessful.

CIVIL LIBERTIES: 33 / 60

D. FREEDOM OF EXPRESSION AND BELIEF: 11 / 16

D1. Are there free and independent media? 2 / 4

Liberia's constitution provides for freedom of speech and the press, but these rights are sometimes restricted in practice. Investigative reporters receive threats, including by members of the government who have vowed to sue in response to journalistic inquiries. President Weah has previously taken an adversarial stance toward media, denouncing "fake news" that purportedly threatened national stability. Liberia also maintained onerous criminal and civil libel laws, though libel, "sedition," and "criminal malevolence" were effectively decriminalized via the Press Freedom Act in 2019. Defamation remains a civil offense, and journalists risk jail time for nonpayment.

The Committee to Protect Journalists reported the death of one journalist in 2020; Zenu Koboi Miller, who was attacked by President Weah's bodyguards near a Monrovia stadium in January, died in February. Miller's wife claimed that he died of internal bleeding, though his death certificate listed hypertension as the cause.

In January 2020, the Liberia Telecommunications Authority (LTA) announced it would begin issuing five-year licenses to FM radio stations, replacing one-year licenses issued under the old regulatory regime. Radio operators called the related fees onerous, but the LTA's chairwoman defended the new regulatory regime in August, saying it was meant to ensure stability and regulatory compliance. The original announcement came a day after a civil court restored the license of Punch FM, which was suspended in 2018; Punch FM's operators alleged that it was targeted for its presumed antigovernment stance.

Journalists reporting on the COVID-19 pandemic faced intimidation, scrutiny, and attack from the authorities. In mid-March 2020, for example, *Integrity Watch* publisher Charles Bioma Yates was questioned by the National Security Agency over social media posts criticizing government policy. In late April, Solicitor General Seyma Syrenius Cephus threatened to shutter media outlets disseminating purportedly false news, after President Weah was speculated to have contracted COVID-19. That same day, Deputy Information Minister Eugene Fahngon announced that existing press passes were void and would be replaced with new documents. Journalists carrying the old passes were stopped by the authorities, and the general manager of Spoon FM temporarily shuttered its newsroom due to the subsequent disruption.

D2. Are individuals free to practice and express their religious faith or nonbelief in public and private? 3 / 4

Religious freedom is protected in the constitution, and there is no official religion. However, about 86 percent of the population is Christian, and the Muslim minority reports discrimination in government appointments. In 2015, a proposal to amend the constitution to establish Christianity as the official religion contributed to interreligious tensions. Former president Sirleaf shelved the proposal, but discussion reemerged during the 2017 campaign. Since his election, President Weah has made efforts to reach out to the Muslim population.

D3. Is there academic freedom, and is the educational system free from extensive political indoctrination? 3 / 4

The government does not restrict academic freedom, though educational quality and infrastructure remain inadequate.

D4. Are individuals free to express their personal views on political or other sensitive topics without fear of surveillance or retribution? 3 / 4

People are generally free to engage in private discussion while in public spaces, but some topics are taboo, such as discussion of issues affecting LGBT+ people. The government is not known to illegally monitor online communications. However, in May 2020, COP member Menipakei Dumoe was arrested after criticizing the government's COVID-19 response, saying "we the poor in Monrovia need AK-47s so our leaders can take us seriously" in a social media post. Authorities searched Dumoe's home for weapons before arresting him. Dumoe was released a day later.

E. ASSOCIATIONAL AND ORGANIZATIONAL RIGHTS: 7 / 12
E1. Is there freedom of assembly? 2 / 4

Freedom of assembly is constitutionally guaranteed, and some rallies were held in 2020. The COP held a demonstration in Monrovia in early January, with participants calling the dismissal of the government's economic team. The authorities forcefully dispersed the rally. In August, protesters in Monrovia called for the government to declare rape a national emergency after a child survived rape and genital mutilation. The authorities used tear gas to disperse the protests on the third day.

E2. Is there freedom for nongovernmental organizations, particularly those that are engaged in human rights- and governance-related work? 3 / 4

Numerous civil society groups, including human rights organizations, operate in Liberia. However, groups focused on LGBT+ issues tend to keep a low profile due to fears of retribution for their activism.

Staff members of two human rights groups received threats after Agnes Reeves Taylor—the ex-wife of former president Charles Taylor (1997–2003)—returned to Liberia in July 2020. Reeves Taylor was previously accused of torture while her husband led an insurgency during the 1989–96 civil war, but was released from a United Kingdom prison in 2019.

E3. Is there freedom for trade unions and similar professional or labor organizations? 2 / 4

Unions are free to form and mobilize and are well organized. The rights of workers to strike, organize, and bargain collectively are recognized. However, the law does not protect workers from employer retaliation for legal strike activity. Labor disputes can turn violent, particularly at the country's various mines and rubber plantations.

F. RULE OF LAW: 6 / 16
F1. Is there an independent judiciary? 1 / 4

The constitution provides for an independent judiciary, but it is impeded by corruption, backlogs, and funding shortfalls.

The judiciary has also been affected by political interference. In 2019, the Senate voted to remove Supreme Court associate justice Kabineh Ja'neh from the bench, finding him guilty of official misconduct after he issued a writ in favor of petroleum dealers who opposed a gasoline sale levy. Ja'neh appealed to the Economic Community of West African States Court of Justice that September. The court ruled in Ja'neh's favor in November 2020, awarding him $200,000 in damages along with back pay. The court also instructed the government to either reinstate him or allow him to retire. The Senate declined to issue a response, citing the lack of a quorum ahead of the December elections.

F2. Does due process prevail in civil and criminal matters? 1 / 4

The right to due process under the law is guaranteed by the constitution but poorly upheld. Many people accused of crimes spend more time in pretrial detention than the length they would serve for a guilty sentence. Citizens of means may be able to bribe judges to rule in their favor. Reports of arbitrary arrest by law enforcement agents continue.

F3. Is there protection from the illegitimate use of physical force and freedom from war and insurgencies? 2 / 4

The security environment in Liberia has improved dramatically in the years since warfare ended in 2003. However, the police force is still viewed as corrupt, and lacks the financial support to provide robust protection for Liberia's people. Prison conditions are very poor, and reports of abuse and threats against detainees and prisoners by law enforcement agents and prison guards continue. In May 2020, a criminal court judge stated that he would not sentence individuals suspected of COVID-19 exposure to prison, but instead would seek the advice of health officials. However, prison authorities were reluctant to release inmates because of the pandemic, instead electing to ban visits and employ screening measures.

F4. Do laws, policies, and practices guarantee equal treatment of various segments of the population? 2 / 4

Some minority ethnic groups continue to be stigmatized as outsiders, and the Muslim population experiences some discrimination. LGBT+ people face social stigma and the threat of violence. The penal code makes "voluntary sodomy" a misdemeanor offense that can carry up to a year in prison, and this provision can be invoked against LGBT+ people. In a 2017 presidential debate with nine candidates, none supported same-sex marriage.

G. PERSONAL AUTONOMY AND INDIVIDUAL RIGHTS: 9 / 16

G1. Do individuals enjoy freedom of movement, including the ability to change their place of residence, employment, or education? 3 / 4

While some unofficial border checkpoints remain, at which border patrol agents sometimes attempt to extract bribes, people have enjoyed a gradual increase in the right to move about freely in the years since large-scale violence ended.

President Weah declared a COVID-19-related state of emergency in early April 2020, heavily restricting the movement of Liberians. COVID-19 restrictions were aggressively enforced by the military. Residents of several counties were subsequently prohibited from leaving their homes without passes, and authorities used force to ensure compliance. A curfew was also instituted, though it was loosened in May. The state of emergency expired in late July, and soldiers were recalled to their barracks.

G2. Are individuals able to exercise the right to own property and establish private businesses without undue interference from state or nonstate actors? 2 / 4

Conflicts over land remain pervasive. Many of these conflicts originated in the civil wars and subsequent displacement and resettlement. Others are the result of opaque concession agreements granting foreign corporations access to lands for mining and for the production of timber and palm oil.

In 2018, legislators passed the Land Rights Act, which formalized community ownership of ancestral land. In 2019, the Liberia Land Authority (LLA) signed memorandums of understanding with 24 communities to control a total of two million acres of land under the law. That August, the LLA launched a public awareness program to educate residents on their rights under the legislation.

Customary law practices that prevail in large parts of the country disadvantage women in matters of land rights and inheritance.

G3. Do individuals enjoy personal social freedoms, including choice of marriage partner and size of family, protection from domestic violence, and control over appearance? 2 / 4

While men and women enjoy equal legal rights under civil law, gender disparities are common in customary law, which remains dominant in much of Liberia and disadvantages women in matters including inheritance and child custody. Violence against women and children, particularly rape, is pervasive. In 2017, the Senate voted to make rape a bailable offense, prompting protests by women's rights activists. Despite the vote, rape remained a nonbailable offense in 2020. In 2019, President Weah signed the Domestic Violence Act, which was originally proposed in 2014, into law. The legislation mandates stricter punishment for those convicted of domestic violence, though restrictions on female genital mutilation (FGM) were not included.

Incidents of sexual violence, including rape, surged during the COVID-19-related state of emergency, with the Ministry of Justice counting 600 rape cases in the first half of 2020. In September, a month after protests were held in Monrovia, President Weah declared a national emergency over gender-based violence (GBV), vowing to name a special prosecutor to pursue rape cases, create a sex offender registry, and establish a national task force. However, progress on this initiative stalled by year's end.

G4. Do individuals enjoy equality of opportunity and freedom from economic exploitation?
2 / 4

Human trafficking for the purpose of forced labor and prostitution remains a problem, with most victims trafficked from rural areas to cities. Many trafficking victims are children, who can be found working in diamond mines, agricultural operations, or as domestic laborers, or engaged in forced begging or prostitution. Individuals working in mining operations face unsafe conditions; in May 2020, at least two people died when a mine shaft collapsed.

Libya

Population: 6,900,000
Capital: Tripoli
Freedom Status: Not Free
Electoral Democracy: No

Overview: Libya has been racked by internal divisions and intermittent civil conflict since a popular armed uprising in 2011 deposed longtime dictator Mu'ammar al-Qadhafi. International efforts to bring rival administrations together in a unity government have repeatedly failed, and interference from regional powers has exacerbated the fighting. A proliferation of weapons and autonomous militias, flourishing criminal networks, and the presence of extremist groups have all contributed to the country's lack of physical security. The ongoing violence has displaced hundreds of thousands of people, and human rights conditions have steadily deteriorated.

KEY DEVELOPMENTS IN 2020
- Fighting between the rival blocs based in the east and west of the country intensified in the first months of the year, after Turkey intervened in January to support the government in Tripoli. The eastern military alliance led by Khalifa Haftar, which had launched an offensive targeting the capital in April 2019, pulled back in June, leading to negotiations and a UN-brokered cease-fire in October. A political dialogue process intended to establish an interim government and set a timeline for national elections was underway at year's end.
- The government in Tripoli and local authorities imposed various travel restrictions over the course of the year in an attempt to curb COVID-19 transmission, but confirmed cases surged in the late summer and fall, and roughly 100,000 cases and 1,500 deaths had been reported by late December.

- Citizen protests erupted episodically across the country in response to electricity blackouts, water shortages, high fuel prices, and frustration with government mismanagement and corruption. Protesters in both the eastern and western regions were met with excessive force, including live gunfire, as well as detentions and abuse in custody.

POLITICAL RIGHTS: 1 / 40

A. ELECTORAL PROCESS: 0 / 12

A1. Was the current head of government or other chief national authority elected through free and fair elections? 0 / 4

Libya remained divided between rival administrations in 2020. The Government of National Accord (GNA), led by Prime Minister Fayez al-Serraj, was based in Tripoli and had military allies that controlled much of western Libya. It was formed as part of the 2015 Libyan Political Agreement (LPA), an internationally brokered pact meant to end the political gridlock and armed conflict that had started in 2014 between factions loyal to the Tubruk-based House of Representatives (HoR), elected that year, and the Tripoli-based General National Congress (GNC), which was elected in 2012 and rejected the outcome of the 2014 elections. The LPA text granted a one-year mandate to the GNA upon its approval by the HoR, with a one-time extension if necessary. However, the HoR never granted its approval. Instead, an interim government affiliated with the HoR persisted in the east, under the protection of Haftar and his Libyan National Army (LNA), renamed the Libyan Arab Armed Forces (LAAF) during 2019.

The United Nations sought to resolve the rift by convening inclusive talks in April 2019, but the effort was derailed when Haftar's forces launched a campaign to seize the capital and the rest of western Libya. The LAAF and its foreign allies were forced to retreat from western Libya in June 2020, and an informal truce led to a formal cease-fire in October. A UN-led Libyan Political Dialogue Forum (LPDF) was then tasked with drafting plans for an interim government and a timeline for national elections. As the forum's discussions continued at year's end, al-Serraj remained in place as prime minister in Tripoli, and Abdullah al-Thani held the premiership in Tubruk, though both had offered to resign and were expected to hand power to the planned interim government.

A2. Were the current national legislative representatives elected through free and fair elections? 0 / 4

Under the 2015 LPA, the unicameral, 200-seat HoR was to remain in place as the interim legislature. The agreement also created the High Council of State (HCS), a secondary consultative body composed of some members of the rival GNC. However, the HoR never formally approved the LPA's provisions or recognized the GNA.

Members of the HoR were elected in 2014 in polls that were marked by violence and drew the participation of only about 15 percent of the electorate. Its mandate formally expired in 2015; while it unilaterally extended its tenure, it has rarely achieved a quorum in practice. Following the launch of Haftar's offensive against Tripoli in 2019, the HoR became further divided, with members opposed to the campaign meeting in Tripoli and other members continuing to meet in Tubruk. There were attempts to reunify the body in the context of the LPDF process in late 2020, but the dispute remained unresolved.

A3. Are the electoral laws and framework fair, and are they implemented impartially by the relevant election management bodies? 0 / 4

An August 2011 constitutional declaration, issued by an unelected National Transitional Council, serves as the governing document for the ongoing transitional period between the revolution against al-Qadhafi and the adoption of a permanent constitution. Despite some legal developments, Libya lacks a functioning electoral framework in practice.

An electoral law was published in the aftermath of the 2011 revolution, and members of the High National Election Commission (HNEC) were appointed. A Constitutional Drafting Assembly (CDA) that was elected in 2014 voted to approve a draft constitution in 2017. In the fall of 2018, the HoR approved a law containing a framework for a constitutional referendum, along with several accompanying amendments to the 2011 constitutional declaration. It then submitted the former, the Referendum Law, to the HNEC, but there was speculation that the new law and amendments would face legal challenges. There was no substantive progress on the constitution in 2019 or 2020. Participants in the UN-led LPDF agreed in November that presidential and parliamentary elections should be held in December 2021.

B. POLITICAL PLURALISM AND PARTICIPATION: 1 / 16
B1. Do the people have the right to organize in different political parties or other competitive political groupings of their choice, and is the system free of undue obstacles to the rise and fall of these competing parties or groupings? 1 / 4

A range of political parties organized to participate in the 2012 GNC elections, but all candidates were required to run as independents in the 2014 HoR elections. Civilian politics have since been overshadowed by the activities of armed groups, which wield significant power and influence on the ground. While various political factions and coalitions exist, the chaotic legal and security environment does not allow for normal political competition.

B2. Is there a realistic opportunity for the opposition to increase its support or gain power through elections? 0 / 4

Libya remained divided between rival political and military factions throughout 2020. The LAAF's withdrawal from western Libya in June cleared the way for the October cease-fire and the resumption of talks on future elections, but political influence was still heavily dependent on military strength.

B3. Are the people's political choices free from domination by forces that are external to the political sphere, or by political forces that employ extrapolitical means? 0 / 4

Ordinary citizens have no role in Libya's political affairs, which are currently dominated by armed factions, foreign governments, oil interests, smuggling syndicates, and other extrapolitical forces. Citizens and civilian political figures are subject to violence and intimidation by the various armed groups.

Foreign powers backed opposing sides in the 2019–20 conflict, and in some cases their involvement grew as the fighting intensified. Russia, Egypt, the United Arab Emirates, Saudi Arabia, France, and others have lent support to the LAAF, while Turkey and Qatar have been the most prominent supporters of the GNA. Turkey's direct intervention in the fighting beginning in January 2020 helped to push the LAAF and its allies back to the central coastal city of Sirte and set the stage for the cease-fire and political dialogue. The cease-fire agreement called for all foreign fighters to depart Libya by the end of January 2021, though it was unclear whether this provision would be honored.

B4. Do various segments of the population (including ethnic, racial, religious, gender, LGBT+, and other relevant groups) have full political rights and electoral opportunities? 0 / 4

The political impasse and armed conflict prevented all segments of the population from exercising their basic political rights in 2020. Communities that lacked an affiliation with a powerful militia were especially marginalized.

The CDA featured two reserved seats each for three non-Arab ethnic minority groups: Amazigh, Tebu, and Tuareg. The Amazigh, however, largely boycotted the 2014 CDA elections and had no representatives in the body, and the two Tebu members rejected the draft constitution it adopted in 2017. The draft was approved by the CDA despite rules requiring support from at least one member from each of the three minority groups.

Representation for ethnic minority groups remained lacking in the 2020 LPDF process. Amazigh and Tuareg organizations denounced the UN-led dialogue for excluding their communities.

C. FUNCTIONING OF GOVERNMENT: 0 / 12

C1. Do the freely elected head of government and national legislative representatives determine the policies of the government? 0 / 4

Neither the GNA nor Haftar's camp had electoral legitimacy or full control over the national territory in 2020, and both remained dependent on fractious militia groups and foreign powers for their security. To the extent that civilian government institutions continued to function, they were bifurcated. For example, de facto authorities in the eastern part of the country have established a parallel central bank and state oil company.

In January 2020, Haftar imposed a blockade on the country's oil production facilities, denying revenue to the GNA and disrupting electricity and other basic services. After Russian-mediated talks on the matter, Haftar lifted the blockade, and oil production and sales resumed in October.

C2. Are safeguards against official corruption strong and effective? 0 / 4

Corruption is pervasive among government officials, and opportunities for graft and criminal activity abound in the absence of functioning fiscal, judicial, and other institutions. Public frustration with corruption contributed to public protests during 2020.

C3. Does the government operate with openness and transparency? 0 / 4

There are no effective laws guaranteeing public access to government information, and none of the competing authorities engage in transparent budget-making and contracting practices.

CIVIL LIBERTIES: 8 / 60
D. FREEDOM OF EXPRESSION AND BELIEF: 4 / 16
D1. Are there free and independent media? 1 / 4

There is a diverse array of Libyan media outlets based inside and outside the country. However, most are highly partisan, producing content that favors one of the country's political and military factions, and in many cases promoting propaganda, hate speech, or disinformation in coordination with foreign backers. The civil conflict and related violence by criminal and extremist groups have made objective reporting dangerous, and journalists are subject to intimidation, arbitrary detention, and physical abuse by both sides in the conflict. Among other incidents during 2020, in May an LAAF-controlled military court in Benghazi sentenced freelance journalist Abuzreiba al-Zway to 15 years in prison for working with a Turkey-based television station. Despite the risks, some independent journalists and outlets have made efforts to engage in fact-based reporting, particularly in light of the COVID-19 pandemic.

D2. Are individuals free to practice and express their religious faith or nonbelief in public and private? 1 / 4

Religious freedom is often violated in practice. Nearly all Libyans are Sunni Muslims, but Christian and other minority communities have been attacked by armed groups, including local affiliates of the Islamic State (IS) militant group. In eastern Libya, hard-line Salafi Muslims aligned with Haftar's forces control Benghazi's mosques and religious programming. Salafi militants, who reject the veneration of saints, have destroyed or vandalized Sufi Muslim shrines with impunity.

D3. Is there academic freedom, and is the educational system free from extensive political indoctrination? 1 / 4

There are no effective laws guaranteeing academic freedom. The armed conflict has damaged many university facilities and altered classroom dynamics; for example, professors can be subject to intimidation by students who are aligned with militias.

D4. Are individuals free to express their personal views on political or other sensitive topics without fear of surveillance or retribution? 1 / 4

Although the freedom of private discussion and personal expression improved dramatically after 2011, the ongoing hostilities have taken their toll, with many Libyans increasingly withdrawing from public life or avoiding criticism of powerful figures. Numerous examples of kidnappings and killings of activists, politicians, and journalists have added to the general deterrent effect. Conditions for personal expression are considerably worse in the LAAF-controlled east than in the west, where residents have somewhat more freedom to criticize the GNA, though violent reprisals for critical speech have been reported in both areas.

Among other cases during 2020, a rapper was allegedly kidnapped in Tripoli in July after he released a song that criticized armed groups. In November, masked assailants in Benghazi murdered Hanan al-Barassi, a lawyer and activist who had criticized corruption within the LAAF on social media.

E. ASSOCIATIONAL AND ORGANIZATIONAL RIGHTS: 2 / 12

E1. Is there freedom of assembly? 1 / 4

A 2012 law on freedom of assembly is generally compatible with international human rights principles, but in practice the armed conflict and related disorder seriously deter peaceful assemblies in many areas.

In 2020, waves of protests erupted in response to electricity cuts, water shortages, high fuel prices, a surge in COVID-19 cases, and frustration with widespread corruption. Demonstrations were reported in multiple cities in western Libya beginning in August and in eastern regions beginning in September. These mostly peaceful protests were met with excessive force by armed groups, which used live ammunition to disperse assemblies and detained and tortured some participants. At least two civilians were reportedly killed.

E2. Is there freedom for nongovernmental organizations, particularly those that are engaged in human rights- and governance-related work? 1 / 4

The number of active nongovernmental organizations (NGOs) has declined in recent years due to armed conflict and the departure of international donors. Militias with varying political, tribal, and geographic affiliations have attacked civil society activists with impunity. Many NGO workers have fled abroad or ceased their activism in the wake of grave threats to themselves or their families.

Despite these obstacles, Libyan humanitarian groups worked with municipal leaders to raise awareness of the COVID-19 pandemic and provide masks and testing kits.

E3. Is there freedom for trade unions and similar professional or labor organizations? 0 / 4

Some trade unions, previously outlawed, formed after 2011. However, normal collective-bargaining activity has been impossible in the absence of basic security and a functioning legal system.

F. RULE OF LAW: 0 / 16

F1. Is there an independent judiciary? 0 / 4

The role of the judiciary remains unclear without a permanent constitution, and judges, lawyers, and prosecutors face frequent threats and attacks. The national judicial system has essentially collapsed, with courts unable to function in much of the country. In some cases, informal dispute-resolution mechanisms have filled the void, and a military court system operates in affiliation with the LAAF in eastern Libya.

F2. Does due process prevail in civil and criminal matters? 0 / 4

Since the 2011 revolution, the right of citizens to a fair trial and due process has been challenged by the continued interference of armed groups and an inability to access lawyers and court documents. Militias and semiofficial security forces regularly engage in arbitrary arrests, detentions, and intimidation with impunity. Thousands of individuals remain in custody without any formal trial or sentencing. The LAAF's military courts routinely flout basic standards of due process and are used to suppress dissent.

F3. Is there protection from the illegitimate use of physical force and freedom from war and insurgencies? 0 / 4

Libya's warring militias and their foreign partners operate with little regard for the physical security of civilians. Various armed groups have carried out indiscriminate shelling of civilian areas, torture of detainees, summary executions, rape, and the destruction of property. Militias also engage in criminal activity, including extortion and other forms of predation on the civilian population.

The fighting associated with the LAAF's campaign against Tripoli between April 2019 and June 2020 killed more than 1,000 people and displaced more than 200,000. The offensive featured urban warfare and indiscriminate attacks on civilian targets, such as hospitals and airports, most of which were allegedly committed by the LAAF. Following the withdrawal of Haftar's forces in June, the GNA reported finding evidence of atrocities in areas it recaptured, including hundreds of bodies in mass graves and other locations. Separately, reports of growing insecurity in eastern cities like Benghazi have included unexplained bombings, murders, and kidnappings.

F4. Do laws, policies, and practices guarantee equal treatment of various segments of the population? 0 / 4

Libyans from certain tribes and communities—often those perceived as pro-Qadhafi, including natives of the town of Tawergha—have faced discrimination, violence, and displacement. The Tebu and Tuareg minorities in the south also face discrimination. Foreign migrant workers, asylum seekers, and refugees have been subject to severe mistreatment, including detention in squalid facilities by both state authorities and other armed groups. In at least two incidents during 2020, groups of migrants were reportedly killed by those detaining them.

Women are not treated equally under the law and face practical restrictions on their ability to participate in the workforce. Widows and displaced women in particular are vulnerable to economic deprivation and other abuses.

Under Libya's penal code, sexual activity between members of the same sex is punishable by up to five years in prison. LGBT+ people face severe discrimination and harassment and have been targeted by militant groups.

G. PERSONAL AUTONOMY AND INDIVIDUAL RIGHTS: 2 / 16

G1. Do individuals enjoy freedom of movement, including the ability to change their place of residence, employment, or education? 0 / 4

The 2011 constitutional declaration guarantees freedom of movement, but militia checkpoints restrict travel within Libya, while combat and poor security conditions more generally affect movement as well as access to education and employment.

Airports in Benghazi, Tripoli, Sabha, and Misrata have been attacked and damaged, severely limiting access to air travel. During the LAAF's 2019–20 offensive on the capital, the city's Mitiga airport was attacked. Beginning in March 2020, the GNA and local authorities imposed travel restrictions and a series of curfews to contain the spread of COVID-19. All ports and airports were closed for some periods, and special chartered planes were reserved for humanitarian assistance, citizen repatriation, and travel by political elites. In August, curfews that the GNA imposed on public health grounds coincided with anticorruption protests, leading to accusations that the restrictions were politically motivated.

G2. Are individuals able to exercise the right to own property and establish private businesses without undue interference from state or nonstate actors? 1 / 4

While Libyans formally have the right to own property and can start businesses, legal protections are not upheld in practice. Businesses and homes have been damaged amid fighting or other unrest, or confiscated by militias, particularly in Libya's eastern regions. Ongoing insecurity has severely disrupted ordinary commerce, allowing armed groups to dominate smuggling networks and informal markets.

G3. Do individuals enjoy personal social freedoms, including choice of marriage partner and size of family, protection from domestic violence, and control over appearance? 1 / 4

Laws and social customs based on Sharia (Islamic law) disadvantage women in personal status matters including marriage and divorce. Libyan women with foreign husbands do not enjoy full citizenship rights and cannot transfer Libyan citizenship to their children. There are no laws that specifically address or criminalize domestic violence, and most such violence goes unreported due to social stigma and the risk of reprisals. The law imposes penalties for extramarital sex and allows rapists to avoid punishment by marrying their victims. Rape and other sexual violence have become increasingly serious problems in the lawless environment created by the civil conflict.

G4. Do individuals enjoy equality of opportunity and freedom from economic exploitation? 0 / 4

There are few protections against exploitative labor practices. Forced labor, sexual exploitation, abuse in detention facilities, and starvation are widespread among migrants and refugees from sub-Saharan Africa, the Middle East, and South Asia, many of whom are beholden to human traffickers. The International Organization for Migration reported that there were more than 574,000 migrants in Libya as of December 2020.

Libya lacks comprehensive laws criminalizing human trafficking, and the authorities have been either incapable of enforcing existing bans or complicit in trafficking activity.

Traffickers have taken advantage of civil unrest to establish enterprises in which refugees and migrants are loaded into overcrowded boats that are then abandoned in the Mediterranean Sea, where passengers hope to be rescued and taken to Europe. The voyages often result in fatalities. Libyan coast guard forces, which receive support from European governments, work to block such departures and have reportedly abused and exploited the passengers they intercept. In October 2020, GNA authorities arrested a coast guard commander accused of human trafficking and other crimes.

Liechtenstein

Population: 40,000
Capital: Vaduz
Freedom Status: Free
Electoral Democracy: Yes

Overview: The Principality of Liechtenstein combines a powerful monarchy with a parliamentary system of government. The prince has an influential political role, which was enhanced by a constitutional referendum in 2003. Human rights and civil liberties are generally respected in the country.

KEY DEVELOPMENTS IN 2020

- In an August referendum, voters rejected a proposed change to the constitution that would have promoted equal representation for women in politics. Proposals to allow dual citizenship for naturalized citizens and to fund a railway expansion were also voted down.
- The government imposed social-distancing rules in March in response to the COVID-19 pandemic, but it began easing the restrictions in late April when it appeared that the virus had been contained, with only a few dozen cases and one death. Officials tightened the rules again from October through December as cases rose sharply. By year's end, the country had reported more than 2,200 confirmed cases and 44 deaths.

POLITICAL RIGHTS: 33 / 40

A. ELECTORAL PROCESS: 10 / 12

A1. Was the current head of government or other chief national authority elected through free and fair elections? 2 / 4

Liechtenstein has one of the most politically powerful hereditary monarchies in Europe. In a 2003 constitutional referendum, voters granted significantly more power to the prince. As head of state, the prince appoints the prime minister and cabinet on the recommendation of the parliament and has the authority to dismiss the government and dissolve the parliament.

Prince Hans-Adam II is the current head of state, but he delegated his governmental authority to his son, Hereditary Prince Alois, in 2004. Adrian Hasler, the prime minister as of 2020, first took office in 2013, when his Progressive Citizens' Party (FBP) won legislative elections.

A2. Were the current national legislative representatives elected through free and fair elections? 4 / 4

The Landtag, the unicameral parliament, consists of 25 deputies chosen by proportional representation every four years. International observers considered the 2017 parliamentary elections to be credible. The ruling conservative FBP led the voting with nine seats, followed by its coalition partner, the center-right Patriotic Union (VU), with eight. The right-wing populist Independents (DU) and the center-left Free List (FL) won five and three seats, respectively. The next elections were due in 2021.

A3. Are the electoral laws and framework fair, and are they implemented impartially by the relevant election management bodies? 4 / 4

The electoral framework provides a sound basis for democratic balloting. There are no formal provisions for election observation, but domestic and international observers are free to monitor the process. While voting is compulsory under the law, the rule is not enforced.

B. POLITICAL PLURALISM AND PARTICIPATION: 13 / 16

B1. Do the people have the right to organize in different political parties or other competitive political groupings of their choice, and is the system free of undue obstacles to the rise and fall of these competing parties or groupings? 4 / 4

There are no onerous limits on the establishment or activities of political parties. The 8 percent vote threshold for representation in the parliament is comparatively high, though the 2013 elections marked the first time that four parties had won seats. In 2019, an administrative court ruled that a new political group, Democrats for Liechtenstein, should be recognized by the government as a political party, which entitled it to public financing. The party was founded in 2018 by three members of parliament who left DU.

B2. Is there a realistic opportunity for the opposition to increase its support or gain power through elections? 3 / 4

The unelected prince wields significant governmental authority, meaning the extent to which power can change hands through elections is limited. The FBP and VU have traditionally dominated the parliament, competing with each other and usually forming coalition governments. The FL has long served as a smaller opposition party, and DU gained ground after entering the legislature with four seats in 2013, winning an additional seat in 2017. However, the 2018 splintering of DU cast doubt on its future prospects.

B3. Are the people's political choices free from domination by forces that are external to the political sphere, or by political forces that employ extrapolitical means? 3 / 4

Although citizens' political choices are largely free from undue interference, the prince has the power to veto the outcome of national referendums and popular initiatives. He has occasionally threatened to use this power, thereby influencing the results. In a 2012 constitutional referendum, however, 76 percent of voters rejected a proposal to limit the prince's veto power.

Transparency of political financing remains a concern. In response to calls for reform by the Council of Europe's Group of States against Corruption (GRECO), the parliament in 2019 passed a modification of the law on party financing, stipulating that parties may no longer accept anonymous donations exceeding 300 Swiss francs ($315). However, the law did not require parties to publicly disclose their known donors.

B4. Do various segments of the population (including ethnic, racial, religious, gender, LGBT+, and other relevant groups) have full political rights and electoral opportunities? 3 / 4

Approximately one-third of the population consists of foreign nationals—mostly from neighboring countries—who do not have political rights. Under Liechtenstein's restrictive naturalization criteria, one must live in the country for 30 years, or marry a resident Liechtenstein citizen and live in the country for more than 10 years, to qualify for citizenship. In an August 2020 referendum, voters rejected a proposal that would have allowed naturalized Liechtenstein citizens from European Economic Area countries and Switzerland to retain their original nationality as well.

Women and members of ethnic minority groups generally enjoy formal political equality, though some disparities persist in practice. The number of women in the parliament declined in 2017 from six to three, which led to calls for the introduction of a gender quota. However, as part of the August 2020 referendum, voters rejected a proposed change to the constitution that would have required the promotion of equal representation for women in politics.

C. FUNCTIONING OF GOVERNMENT: 10 / 12

C1. Do the freely elected head of government and national legislative representatives determine the policies of the government? 2 / 4

Although elected executive and legislative officials set the policy agenda, the prince has significant governmental authority with no electoral mandate. He can dismiss the government and the parliament and veto both legislation and the outcome of public plebiscites; he also plays a powerful role in the appointment of judges.

C2. Are safeguards against official corruption strong and effective? 4 / 4

Anticorruption laws are effectively implemented, and levels of corruption are reportedly low. A 2018 GRECO compliance report applauded Liechtenstein for the recent implementation of reforms to the criminal code, including the addition of charges for bribery in the private sector and the expansion of the definition of "public officials" to include a wider range of personnel, including all Landtag members and parliamentary employees. However, a 2020 update of this report observed that Liechtenstein still lacked a code of conduct for members of parliament, who are not currently required to declare assets or conflicts of interest.

C3. Does the government operate with openness and transparency? 4 / 4

Although there is no constitutional guarantee of access to information, laws are in place to provide for government transparency, and these are largely respected in practice.

The government has made efforts in recent years to increase transparency in the banking sector. The country's large financial industry has historically been criticized for enabling foreign clients to hide wealth from their respective governments and potentially aiding corruption or other criminal activity. A 2019 report by the Organization for Economic Co-operation and Development's Global Forum on Transparency and Exchange of Information for Tax Purposes concluded that Liechtenstein is largely compliant with international standards regarding beneficiary ownership, accounting, and banking.

CIVIL LIBERTIES: 57 / 60

D. FREEDOM OF EXPRESSION AND BELIEF: 16 / 16

D1. Are there free and independent media? 4 / 4

The constitution guarantees freedom of the press, which is respected in practice. Liechtenstein has one private television station, one public radio station, and two main newspapers that are owned by the two major political parties. The local media sector lacks pluralism, but residents have access to foreign news outlets, including broadcasts from Germany, Austria, and Switzerland.

D2. Are individuals free to practice and express their religious faith or nonbelief in public and private? 4 / 4

Although the constitution establishes Roman Catholicism as the state religion, religious freedom is constitutionally guaranteed and protected in practice. Catholic or Protestant education is mandatory in all primary schools, but exemptions are routinely granted. Islamic religious classes have been offered in some primary schools since 2008. All religious groups have tax-exempt status. Muslim groups have yet to obtain permission to establish a mosque or a dedicated Muslim cemetery; there is one Islamic prayer room, and churches open their facilities for use by other faiths upon request.

D3. Is there academic freedom, and is the educational system free from extensive political indoctrination? 4 / 4

Academic freedom is largely respected, with no significant restrictions by state or nonstate actors.

D4. Are individuals free to express their personal views on political or other sensitive topics without fear of surveillance or retribution? 4 / 4

The law guarantees freedom of expression, but prohibits public insults directed against a race or ethnic group. The government is not known to improperly monitor private communications.

E. ASSOCIATIONAL AND ORGANIZATIONAL RIGHTS: 12 / 12
E1. Is there freedom of assembly? 4 / 4

The constitution guarantees freedom of assembly, and this right is respected in practice.

E2. Is there freedom for nongovernmental organizations, particularly those that are engaged in human rights- and governance-related work? 4 / 4

Domestic and international nongovernmental organizations are able to function freely.

E3. Is there freedom for trade unions and similar professional or labor organizations? 4 / 4

The law facilitates the formation of trade unions and collective bargaining, and workers enjoy freedom of association in practice. The principality has at least one trade union. While a 2008 legal change removed a ban on strikes for civil servants, the right to strike in general is not explicitly protected by law. Major labor disputes are rare in the country.

F. RULE OF LAW: 14 / 16
F1. Is there an independent judiciary? 3 / 4

The judiciary is generally independent and impartial, but the constitution gives the prince a powerful influence over the appointment of judges, meaning the process lacks a key element of democratic accountability. The selection board for judicial candidates is chaired by the prince or his deputy, whose assent is required for candidate recommendations; the rest of the board consists of the prince's appointees and representatives of the government and parliamentary parties. The recommended candidates are submitted for approval by the parliament and appointment by the prince. The 2020 GRECO report called for the selection board to include judges chosen by their peers, and for the appointment procedure to feature specific integrity criteria that candidates must meet.

F2. Does due process prevail in civil and criminal matters? 4 / 4

The constitution provides for the right to a fair trial, and the rights of defendants are usually respected. Most trials are public, and defendants are considered innocent until proven guilty. In a 2017 report, the Council of Europe's Committee for the Prevention of Torture expressed concerns about some aspects of police custody procedures, including the fact that police can deny the presence of a lawyer during initial questioning.

F3. Is there protection from the illegitimate use of physical force and freedom from war and insurgencies? 4 / 4

People in Liechtenstein are largely free from the illegitimate use of physical force. Violent crime is extremely rare. While the country's small prison facility can hold up to 16 men and four women in short-term detention, those serving longer sentences are incarcerated in neighboring Austria.

F4. Do laws, policies, and practices guarantee equal treatment of various segments of the population? 3 / 4

The legal framework prohibits discrimination on various grounds, though some shortcomings remain. In 2018, the European Commission against Racism and Intolerance (ECRI) reiterated the need for Liechtenstein to ratify Protocol 12 to the European Convention on Human Rights, which provides a general prohibition against discrimination.

Despite the presence of antidiscrimination laws, women, particularly Muslim women, and LGBT+ people experience employment discrimination. Women continue to earn significantly less on average than their male counterparts. LGBT+ individuals face social stigma, and according to a leading human rights group, often do not disclose their sexual orientation or gender identity out of fear of bias.

G. PERSONAL AUTONOMY AND INDIVIDUAL RIGHTS: 15 / 16

G1. Do individuals enjoy freedom of movement, including the ability to change their place of residence, employment, or education? 4 / 4

There are no significant restrictions on freedom of movement in Liechtenstein. The social-distancing rules imposed for parts of 2020 were generally seen as a legitimate response to the public health threat posed by COVID-19.

G2. Are individuals able to exercise the right to own property and establish private businesses without undue interference from state or nonstate actors? 4 / 4

The legal framework generally protects property rights and supports private business activity without undue restrictions. Nonresidents are not allowed to establish a business in Liechtenstein, but prospective business owners exploit loopholes to work around the law.

G3. Do individuals enjoy personal social freedoms, including choice of marriage partner and size of family, protection from domestic violence, and control over appearance? 3 / 4

Personal social freedoms are largely protected. Same-sex registered partnerships are legal, but the prince has expressed opposition to adoption rights for same-sex couples. While single LGBT+ people can adopt children, same-sex couples cannot.

Domestic violence and spousal rape are illegal in Liechtenstein, and authorities effectively prosecute offenders and protect victims. Abortion is criminalized unless the pregnant person is at risk of death or serious harm, or was under age 14 at the time of conception. A 2011 referendum proposal to expand the conditions for legal abortion was defeated by voters.

G4. Do individuals enjoy equality of opportunity and freedom from economic exploitation? 4 / 4

Liechtenstein is largely free from economic exploitation and human trafficking. Despite the country's overall wealth and low unemployment rates, however, relative poverty persists among some communities. Immigrants in particular often struggle to achieve economic security and social mobility.

Lithuania

Population: 2,800,000
Capital: Vilnius
Freedom Status: Free
Electoral Democracy: Yes

Overview: Lithuania is a democracy in which political rights and civil liberties are generally respected. Chronic problems including corruption and socioeconomic inequality often arouse public dissatisfaction with the government, political parties, and other institutions. Women, LGBT+ people, members of the Romany minority, and some other groups experience varying degrees of discrimination and underrepresentation in politics.

KEY DEVELOPMENTS IN 2020

- The main opposition party, the center-right Homeland Union–Lithuanian Christian Democrats (TS-LKD), won a plurality of seats in October parliamentary elections and formed a coalition government with two other parties in November. Ingrida Šimonytė was sworn in as prime minister in December.
- The government imposed national social-distancing rules and movement restrictions for three months beginning in March in response to the COVID-19 pandemic. After a period of reduced restrictions, the measures were reinstated in November due to a rise in cases and further tightened the following month. By the end of the year, Lithuania had reported more than 145,000 confirmed cases and some 1,800 deaths.

POLITICAL RIGHTS: 38 / 40

A. ELECTORAL PROCESS: 12 / 12

A1. Was the current head of government or other chief national authority elected through free and fair elections? 4 / 4

The president, whose main competencies as head of state pertain to foreign affairs, is directly elected for up to two five-year terms. The prime minister, who as head of government holds most executive authority, is appointed by the president with the approval of the parliament.

Centrist nonpartisan candidate Gitanas Nausėda was elected as the new president in 2019 after his predecessor, Dalia Grybauskaitė, completed her second term of office. Nausėda took 66 percent of the vote in the runoff round, defeating Ingrida Šimonytė, an independent lawmaker backed by the TS-LKD, who took 33 percent. Šimonytė was appointed as prime minister following the October 2020 parliamentary elections and took office in December. Both the presidential election and the appointment of the prime minister were in accordance with democratic standards.

A2. Were the current national legislative representatives elected through free and fair elections? 4 / 4

The unicameral, 141-seat Seimas (parliament) consists of 71 members elected in single-mandate constituencies and 70 chosen by proportional representation, all for four-year terms.

In the October 2020 elections, the center-right opposition TS-LKD captured 50 seats, leaving the incumbent centrist-populist Farmers and Greens Union (LVŽS) in second place with 32 seats. Another centrist-populist party, the Labor Party, won 10 seats, while the Lithuanian Social Democratic Party (LSDP) received 13. The junior coalition partners in the LVŽS government—Electoral Action of Poles in Lithuania–Christian Families Alliance (LLRA-KŠS) and the Lithuanian Social Democratic Labor Party (LSDLP)—won three seats each. Two liberal and business-oriented parties—the Liberal Movement and the Freedom Party—won 13 and 11 seats, respectively, and formed a new governing coalition with the TS-LKD in November.

The elections were considered free and fair, with few irregularities reported. However, the outgoing LVŽS government's decision to distribute cash benefits for pensioners and other social groups just before the balloting was widely criticized as politically motivated.

A3. Are the electoral laws and framework fair, and are they implemented impartially by the relevant election management bodies? 4 / 4

The legislative framework for conducting elections is consistent with democratic standards and generally well implemented. The Central Electoral Commission has typically operated and adjudicated election-related complaints in a fair manner.

B. POLITICAL PLURALISM AND PARTICIPATION: 16 / 16

B1. Do the people have the right to organize in different political parties or other competitive political groupings of their choice, and is the system free of undue obstacles to the rise and fall of these competing parties or groupings? 4 / 4

Political parties generally operate freely. Citizens of other European Union (EU) member states are eligible to join Lithuanian political parties but cannot found them.

Small parties and some civic organizations argue that the minimum number of members for political parties (2,000) is a burdensome requirement that hampers the creation of new parties and the maintenance of small ones. Public funding rules generally favor the main parliamentary forces, as private financing of political organizations is tightly restricted. The state subsidies are calculated according to the results of the previous elections and represent the main source of revenue for parties. Public election committees—a way for groups of citizens to run for municipal councils without joining or establishing a political party—have been an option since 2010, though they are not permitted for parliamentary elections.

B2. Is there a realistic opportunity for the opposition to increase its support or gain power through elections? 4 / 4

Regular transfers of power between rival parties after elections have been the norm since the early 1990s, with left- and right-leaning coalitions alternating in government. Parties in opposition retain a significant presence in the Seimas.

B3. Are the people's political choices free from domination by forces that are external to the political sphere, or by political forces that employ extrapolitical means? 4 / 4

Sporadic cases of vote buying during national elections have been observed, and clientelism can influence politics at the local level. However, voters and candidates are generally free to exercise their political autonomy without undue influence or interference.

B4. Do various segments of the population (including ethnic, racial, religious, gender, LGBT+, and other relevant groups) have full political rights and electoral opportunities? 4 / 4

There are no formal restrictions on the political participation of women, LGBT+ people, or members of ethnic, religious, and other minority groups. Women and women's interests remain underrepresented in politics, though women candidates won 27 percent of the seats in the October 2020 parliamentary elections—an increase from 21 percent in the previous Seimas. Moreover, the three main leaders of the new governing coalition were women, including Prime Minister Šimonytė and Seimas speaker Viktorija Čmilytė-Nielsen, who heads the Liberal Movement. Šimonytė's cabinet approached gender balance, with women holding six of the 14 ministerial posts.

Political parties that are supportive of equal rights for LGBT+ people increased their parliamentary representation in 2020. The Freedom Party, founded in 2019, campaigned for marriage equality and had an openly gay candidate among its leaders, garnering 9 percent of the national vote.

The LLRA-KŠS, which represents members of the ethnic Polish minority, failed to clear the 5 percent vote threshold for proportional-representation seats in 2020, having succeeded in the 2012 and 2016 Seimas elections. Nevertheless, it captured three seats in single-mandate districts.

C. FUNCTIONING OF GOVERNMENT: 10 / 12

C1. Do the freely elected head of government and national legislative representatives determine the policies of the government? 4 / 4

The country's elected officials are able to determine and implement government policies without improper interference from unelected or foreign entities. However, corruption scandals have periodically raised concerns about the influence of major businesses on governance.

C2. Are safeguards against official corruption strong and effective? 3 / 4

Corruption remains an issue in Lithuania, and certain sectors, including health care and construction, are perceived as prone to malfeasance. While anticorruption bodies are active, there are usually considerable delays in the investigation and prosecution of political corruption cases.

The protection of whistleblowers and journalists who report on corruption cases is legally guaranteed, though such safeguards are upheld inconsistently at the local level.

C3. Does the government operate with openness and transparency? 3 / 4

Lithuanian law grants the public the right to access official information, and the government generally complies with such requests. However, the operations of state companies remain somewhat opaque and prone to financial misconduct. Reforms intended to improve the transparency and fairness of public procurement have been limited. In recent years, politicians' attempts to reduce the scope of accessible public information concerning themselves have increased.

CIVIL LIBERTIES: 52 / 60 (−1)

D. FREEDOM OF EXPRESSION AND BELIEF: 15 / 16 (−1)

D1. Are there free and independent media? 3 / 4 (−1)

The government generally respects freedom of the press, and the media market is vibrant. However, the increasing concentration of media ownership in the hands of a small number of companies raises the risk of editorial interference by powerful political and business interests. Journalists often engage in self-censorship when reporting on certain large companies. The economic impact of the COVID-19 pandemic in 2020 left the media more vulnerable to undue influence.

In July, the Radio and Television Commission of Lithuania banned five television channels operated by the Russian state-owned network RT, following a recommendation from the Foreign Ministry. It cited links between RT and Dmitry Kiselyov, who heads another Russian state media group and had been sanctioned by the EU. Reporters Without Borders criticized the ban.

In October, the Court of Appeal found former Lithuanian president Rolandas Paksas and Lietuvos Rytas media group owner Gedvydas Vainauskas guilty in an influence-peddling case. Vainauskas, who received a fine, was accused of bribing Paksas, who received a suspended three-year prison sentence, to help secure regulators' support for a business project in 2015. An appeal to the Supreme Court was pending at year's end.

Because of a vaguely worded law restricting the dissemination of information that "abases family values," public and private media outlets have faced pressure to limit coverage of the LGBT+ community and its interests.

Score Change: The score declined from 4 to 3 because journalists' autonomy has been curtailed in recent years by ongoing consolidation of media ownership and related editorial pressure to support owners' business and political interests.

D2. Are individuals free to practice and express their religious faith or nonbelief in public and private? 4 / 4

Freedom of religion is guaranteed by law and largely upheld in practice. However, nine so-called traditional religious communities, and particularly the Roman Catholic Church, enjoy certain government benefits, including annual subsidies that are not granted to other groups. Despite the presence of a small Muslim community, Vilnius remained without a mosque in 2020.

D3. Is there academic freedom, and is the educational system free from extensive political indoctrination? 4 / 4

Academic freedom is respected, and the educational system is generally free from political influence.

D4. Are individuals free to express their personal views on political or other sensitive topics without fear of surveillance or retribution? 4 / 4

The freedoms of personal expression and private discussion are generally robust and unrestricted. However, due to concerns about the Russian government's aggressive foreign policy, individuals who criticize government stances on security-related issues—including energy policy, military spending, conscription, and sanctions against authoritarian regimes—can face institutional scrutiny and societal marginalization.

E. ASSOCIATIONAL AND ORGANIZATIONAL RIGHTS: 11 / 12
E1. Is there freedom of assembly? 4 / 4

Freedom of assembly is generally respected. Demonstrations on topics including LGBT+ people's rights and solidarity with antigovernment protesters in Belarus proceeded without incident in 2020, when public health conditions permitted.

E2. Is there freedom for nongovernmental organizations, particularly those that are engaged in human rights- and governance-related work? 4 / 4

Nongovernmental organizations (NGOs) are able to register without facing serious obstacles, and they generally operate without undue restrictions in practice.

E3. Is there freedom for trade unions and similar professional or labor organizations? 3 / 4

Workers have the right to form and join trade unions and engage in collective bargaining, though there have been reports of employees being punished for attempting to organize. Less than 10 percent of workers are trade union members, and the share of workers covered by collective agreements is similarly low. Changes to the labor code in 2017 required employers with at least 20 workers to initiate the election of a work council to represent employees' interests, if a union was not already established, though only unions can engage in collective bargaining. Strikes are relatively uncommon due to strict regulations, lack of strike funds, and the absence of a culture of industrial action.

F. RULE OF LAW: 12 / 16

F1. Is there an independent judiciary? 3 / 4

Although public confidence in the courts has been steadily improving in recent years, judicial corruption remains a significant concern. An extensive bribery scandal in 2019 led to criminal charges against eight senior judges, including a member of the Supreme Court.

In April 2020, the parliament rejected all three of the proposed candidates to replace three outgoing judges of the Constitutional Court, including its chairperson; the three were nominated by the president, the Seimas speaker, and the acting head of the Supreme Court, respectively. Lawmakers also rejected a permanent appointment for the acting Supreme Court chief, which had been proposed by President Nausėda. The votes left both of the country's highest judicial institutions without permanent leadership at the end of the year.

F2. Does due process prevail in civil and criminal matters? 3 / 4

Defendants generally enjoy the presumption of innocence and freedom from arbitrary arrest and detention, but detained suspects are not always granted timely access to an attorney. The law states that pretrial detention should only be employed in exceptional circumstances, and its use has declined from previously high levels in recent years.

F3. Is there protection from the illegitimate use of physical force and freedom from war and insurgencies? 3 / 4

The population is largely free from major threats to physical security, and the homicide rate has declined in recent years, though it remains one of the highest in the EU, according to the statistics agency Eurostat.

Although the government has taken measures to improve the situation, conditions at some prisons are substandard, violence among prisoners remains a problem, and physical abuse of prisoners by correctional officers persists.

F4. Do laws, policies, and practices guarantee equal treatment of various segments of the population? 3 / 4

The constitution guarantees equality before the law and forbids discrimination based on gender, race, language, and other categories. The laws provide similar protections, including against discrimination based on sexual orientation, though gender identity is not addressed. In practice, women generally earn less than men per hour worked, and both LGBT+ people and members of the Romany minority experience societal discrimination. Ethnic Poles and members of other national minority groups have objected to limits on the use of their languages; public signs must be written only in Lithuanian, even in areas predominantly inhabited by people who speak different languages.

G. PERSONAL AUTONOMY AND INDIVIDUAL RIGHTS: 14 / 16

G1. Do individuals enjoy freedom of movement, including the ability to change their place of residence, employment, or education? 4 / 4

Residents of Lithuania may leave the country and travel internally without significant obstacles. Movement restrictions related to the COVID-19 pandemic in 2020 were generally considered to be proportionate measures aimed at protecting public health.

G2. Are individuals able to exercise the right to own property and establish private businesses without undue interference from state or nonstate actors? 4 / 4

Successive Lithuanian governments have worked to maintain a well-regulated market economy, and the legal framework generally protects property rights and the freedom to operate private businesses.

G3. Do individuals enjoy personal social freedoms, including choice of marriage partner and size of family, protection from domestic violence, and control over appearance? 3 / 4

Individual freedom regarding personal status matters such as marriage and divorce is generally upheld, but the constitution defines marriage as a union between a man and a woman, and same-sex partnerships are not legally recognized. In 2019, the Constitutional Court ruled that Lithuania must grant residence permits for foreigners in same-sex marriages or registered partnerships with Lithuanian citizens that were established abroad. Separately, legal provisions that would allow gender-confirmation surgery and related procedures are not in place.

Domestic violence remains a problem; it is one of the country's most reported crimes, second only to burglary, but the rates of investigation and prosecution remain inadequate. Eight out of 10 victims of domestic violence in Lithuania are women.

G4. Do individuals enjoy equality of opportunity and freedom from economic exploitation? 3 / 4

The law provides protections against exploitative working conditions, and these are enforced in practice. However, according to Eurostat data as of 2018, the incidence rate for fatal workplace accidents in Lithuania was nearly twice the EU average. Foreign workers in sectors such as construction and transportation are vulnerable to labor trafficking, and Lithuanian women and children have been exploited for sex trafficking. The government actively works to prosecute traffickers and provides aid to victims in conjunction with NGOs.

Luxembourg

Population: 600,000
Capital: Luxembourg
Freedom Status: Free
Electoral Democracy: Yes

Overview: Luxembourg is a constitutional monarchy with a democratically elected government. Political rights and civil liberties are generally respected. Ongoing concerns include insufficient government transparency and inadequate safeguards against conflicts of interest.

KEY DEVELOPMENTS IN 2020

- In April, the Belgian conglomerate Mediahuis's purchased the Saint-Paul group, the owner of the country's largest daily newspaper, the *Luxemburger Wort*. Mediahuis announced plans to shift more coverage online, evidence of the growing prominence of online media in Luxembourg. Though the company claimed that the acquisition would result in no job losses, 70 *Luxemburger Wort* employees were let go in December, a move criticized by analysts as potentially weakening the country's media environment.
- Authorities implemented travel restrictions throughout 2020 to combat the spread of the COVID-19 pandemic. The government implemented a curfew and ordered businesses closed in March, and again in December. According to government statistics provided to the World Health Organization, over 46,700 people tested positive for coronavirus and 498 people died by year's end.

POLITICAL RIGHTS: 38 / 40
A. ELECTORAL PROCESS: 12 / 12
A1. Was the current head of government or other chief national authority elected through free and fair elections? 4 / 4

The prime minister is the head of government and serves five-year terms. The leader of the majority coalition formed after parliamentary elections is appointed prime minister by the hereditary monarch, the grand duke, whose powers are largely ceremonial.

Incumbent prime minister Xavier Bettel of the Democratic Party (DP) was appointed to form a new government in October 2018 following that month's parliamentary election. The new government, which took office that December, was based on the existing coalition of the DP, the Luxembourg Socialist Workers' Party (LSAP), and the Greens (DG). The election was viewed as credible.

A2. Were the current national legislative representatives elected through free and fair elections? 4 / 4

The unicameral legislature, the Chamber of Deputies, consists of 60 members elected to five-year terms by proportional representation. In the October 2018 election, the DP led the ruling coalition parties with 12 seats, followed by the LSAP with 10 and the Green Party with 9. The main opposition party, the Christian Social People's Party (CSV), won 21 seats. The populist right-wing Alternative Democratic Reform Party (ADR) won 4 seats, while the Pirate Party and the Left each took 2. The contest was generally seen as free and fair, though the campaign was marked by some antisemitic vandalism of DP candidate posters.

Luxembourgers participated in the May 2019 European Parliament (EP) election; the DP won 21.4 percent of the vote, while the CSV won 21.1 percent, the DG won 18.9 percent, and the LSAP won 12.2 percent.

A3. Are the electoral laws and framework fair, and are they implemented impartially by the relevant election management bodies? 4 / 4

The electoral laws and framework are considered fair, and they are generally implemented impartially. Voting is compulsory. In 2017, the government passed a law allowing postal ballots for all citizens.

A multiparty Constitutional Revision Committee completed its draft of a new constitution in 2018. The charter, which did not include major changes to the political system, would take effect only after it had been approved by the parliament and by the public in a referendum. The draft remained pending at the end of 2020.

B. POLITICAL PLURALISM AND PARTICIPATION: 16 / 16

B1. Do the people have the right to organize in different political parties or other competitive political groupings of their choice, and is the system free of undue obstacles to the rise and fall of these competing parties or groupings? 4 / 4

The political system is open to the establishment of new parties, which do not face undue obstacles in their formation or activities. Three parties have traditionally dominated politics: the CSV, historically aligned with the Catholic Church; the LSAP, a formerly radical but now center-left party representing the working class; and the DP, which favors free-market economic policies. Four smaller parties, the DG, the ADR, the Left, and the Pirate Party have also won representation. While constituting a party is relatively easy, the structure and size of electoral constituencies, as well as the 10 percent electoral threshold, favor larger parties.

B2. Is there a realistic opportunity for the opposition to increase its support or gain power through elections? 4 / 4

The country has a record of peaceful transfers of power between rival parties. Both the DP and the DG were in the opposition before forming the governing coalition with the LSAP in 2013. The CSV, which had played a leading role in most governments since 1945, was forced into opposition in 2013 for the first time since 1979, and it remained out of government following the 2018 election.

B3. Are the people's political choices free from domination by forces that are external to the political sphere, or by political forces that employ extrapolitical means? 4 / 4

Citizens are generally able to make political choices without undue interference from any democratically unaccountable groups. However, close links between the country's financial center and its law-making elites is regularly a topic of concern for the opposition and outside observers.

B4. Do various segments of the population (including ethnic, racial, religious, gender, LGBT+, and other relevant groups) have full political rights and electoral opportunities? 4 / 4

Women engage actively in politics, and the government has taken measures to encourage greater participation. A 2016 law mandates that at least 40 percent of each party's electoral candidates be women; parties risk losing a portion of their public financing if they do not meet the quota. However, only 18 women held elected seats at the end of 2019, which accounts for 30 percent of Parliament. Citizens who belong to ethnic minorities and LGBT+ people enjoy full political rights and are free to participate in practice. In 2013, Prime Minister Bettel became the nation's first openly gay person to hold his position.

About 49 percent of the population consists of foreign nationals, most of whom are citizens of other European Union (EU) member states, with Portugal accounting for the largest single contingent. The law allows naturalization and dual nationality, and children automatically gain citizenship when a parent is naturalized. Foreign residents are entitled to vote in municipal elections and EU foreigners can participate in EU elections. However, they are excluded from national elections. Notably, politicians of foreign origin remain rare in Luxembourg, despite the background of nearly half the population.

C. FUNCTIONING OF GOVERNMENT: 10 / 12

C1. Do the freely elected head of government and national legislative representatives determine the policies of the government? 4 / 4

The prime minister, cabinet, and parliament determine and implement the government's policies without improper interference from unelected entities.

C2. Are safeguards against official corruption strong and effective? 3 / 4

Corruption is not widespread in Luxembourg, and allegations of corruption are generally investigated and prosecuted. However, the Council of Europe's Group of States Against Corruption (GRECO) has previously criticized the government for failing to develop a comprehensive strategy to prevent graft. In addition, rules on accepting gifts, lobbying, and mitigating conflicts of interest after government officials leave office are lacking.

In January 2020, after a scandal broke out about mismanagement at the royal court, the government triggered a reform process that aimed at making the missions of the royal family more transparent. The main issue was the role the Grand duchess attributed to herself: without a constitutional right, she saw herself as a political actor more than a ceremonial representative.

C3. Does the government operate with openness and transparency? 3 / 4

While the legislative process and government operations are largely transparent, there is no comprehensive freedom of information law in place, and in practice the media and civil society groups often have difficulty obtaining official information. Cabinet members are obligated to disclose any shares in companies that they own, but there are no penalties for those who do not cooperate.

In late November 2019, Luxembourg was one of 12 EU member states that blocked a proposed directive requiring firms to more fully disclose revenues and tax payments throughout the bloc. The directive was billed as an effort to reduce corporate tax avoidance within the EU.

CIVIL LIBERTIES: 59 / 60 (–1)

D. FREEDOM OF EXPRESSION AND BELIEF: 16 / 16

D1. Are there free and independent media? 4 / 4

Freedom of the press is guaranteed by the constitution and generally respected in practice. Luxembourg's media market is regulated by the Independent Luxembourg Broadcasting Authority (ALIA). A single conglomerate, RTL Télé Lëtzebuerg (RTL), dominates broadcast radio and television, though numerous print, online, and foreign news sources are also available and present a broad range of views. Internet access is not restricted.

The written press has historically tended to align with traditional parties. In April 2020, the Belgian conglomerate Mediahuis's purchased the Saint-Paul group, the owner of the country's largest daily newspaper, the *Luxemburger Wort*. Mediahuis announced plans to shift more coverage online, evidence of the growing prominence of online media. Though Mediahuis claimed that the acquisition would result in no job losses, 70 *Luxemburger Wort* employees were let go in December, a move criticized by analysts as potentially weakening the country's media environment.

D2. Are individuals free to practice and express their religious faith or nonbelief in public and private? 4 / 4

Freedom of religion is largely respected in practice. The state has historically paid the salaries of clergy from a variety of Christian groups, but a 2016 law ended the practice for all clergy hired after that point. Under the law, the government continued to provide some funding to six major recognized religious communities, including the Muslim community, based on their size. Religious instruction in secondary and primary schools was phased out in 2016–17. In 2018, the parliament adopted legislation that banned face coverings in schools, medical facilities, public buildings, public transport, and retirement homes. The law was widely understood to be aimed at Muslims, though the wearing of such garments is extremely rare in the country.

D3. Is there academic freedom, and is the educational system free from extensive political indoctrination? 4 / 4

Academic freedom is generally respected in practice.

D4. Are individuals free to express their personal views on political or other sensitive topics without fear of surveillance or retribution? 4 / 4

Freedom of expression is largely respected, and individuals can voice their political views without fear of retribution.

E. ASSOCIATIONAL AND ORGANIZATIONAL RIGHTS: 12 / 12
E1. Is there freedom of assembly? 4 / 4

Freedom of assembly is guaranteed by the constitution and generally respected in practice.

E2. Is there freedom for nongovernmental organizations, particularly those that are engaged in human rights- and governance-related work? 4 / 4

Nongovernmental organizations (NGOs) are largely free to operate without any undue restrictions.

E3. Is there freedom for trade unions and similar professional or labor organizations? 4 / 4

Workers are free to organize in trade unions and bargain collectively. The right to strike is guaranteed once conciliation procedures are formally exhausted. Employers are subject to penalties for antiunion discrimination.

F. RULE OF LAW: 15 / 16 (−1)
F1. Is there an independent judiciary? 4 / 4

Judicial independence is generally upheld. Judges are appointed by the grand duke and cannot be removed arbitrarily.

Parliament conducted ongoing discussions in 2020 regarding a constitutional amendment that strengthens the independence of judiciary by establishing a Council of Justice, competent to nominate candidates for all judicial posts prior to their formal appointment by the executive (and formally by the grand duke). Composed of nine members, the council would also develop ethical standards and act as a watchdog for judges.

F2. Does due process prevail in civil and criminal matters? 4 / 4

Due process is largely upheld in civil and criminal matters. Defendants have the right to a fair and public trial, and this right is generally respected. Police typically observe safeguards against arbitrary arrest and detention.

F3. Is there protection from the illegitimate use of physical force and freedom from war and insurgencies? 4 / 4

There are no major threats to civilians' physical security. Prison conditions and protections against the illegitimate use of force are adequate, and violent crime is rare.

F4. Do laws, policies, and practices guarantee equal treatment of various segments of the population? 3 / 4 (−1)

Discrimination on the basis of race, religion, disability, age, sex, gender identity, or sexual orientation is prohibited by law. The rights of LGBT+ people are generally respected.

In April 2020, Luxembourg accepted 11 unaccompanied underage asylum seekers from Greek refugee camps.

Women have benefited from reductions in the gender pay gap and an increase in their labor participation rate in recent years, though women still hold significantly fewer senior positions than men.

The Luxembourg government has placed an onerous language requirement public sector jobs and employment. Individuals in the public sector must speak German, French, and Luxembourgish fluently. However, very few official documents are in Luxembourgish, and exceptions to this requirement are made for high-level positions due to a lack of qualified candidates. The requirement funnels citizens into public sector positions, which are lucrative and secure, pushing immigrant workers into the unstable private sector in which there are other barriers to entry. Moreover, discrimination in the education system limits somewhat the economic potential of nonnationals.

Score Change: The score declined from 4 to 3 because language requirements for public sector positions limit the ability of immigrant workers to participate in segments of the labor market.

G. PERSONAL AUTONOMY AND INDIVIDUAL RIGHTS: 16 / 16

G1. Do individuals enjoy freedom of movement, including the ability to change their place of residence, employment, or education? 4 / 4

Individuals generally enjoy freedom of movement, and there are no significant restrictions on their ability to change their place of residence, employment, or institution of higher education. Authorities implemented travel restrictions throughout 2020 to combat the spread of the COVID-19 pandemic. However, the government implemented a curfew and ordered businesses closed in March, and again in December. Restrictions varied throughout the year, depending on the rate of infection.

G2. Are individuals able to exercise the right to own property and establish private businesses without undue interference from state or nonstate actors? 4 / 4

The rights to own property and operate private businesses are legally protected and respected in practice.

G3. Do individuals enjoy personal social freedoms, including choice of marriage partner and size of family, protection from domestic violence, and control over appearance? 4 / 4

Individual freedoms on issues such as marriage and divorce are generally guaranteed. Same-sex marriage has been legal since 2014, and same-sex couples have full adoption rights. Abortions are legal on request within the first trimester of pregnancy; later abortions require two doctors to determine that the pregnancy threatens the woman's life or health. The authorities generally uphold laws and practices meant to address rape and domestic violence.

G4. Do individuals enjoy equality of opportunity and freedom from economic exploitation? 4 / 4

The country's residents largely enjoy equality of opportunity, and the government enforces legal protections against exploitative working conditions. Occasional cases of forced labor in the construction and food-service industries have been reported, especially among migrant workers.

Madagascar

Population: 27,700,000
Capital: Antananarivo
Freedom Status: Partly Free
Electoral Democracy: Yes

Overview: An unelected administration governed Madagascar following a 2009 coup, but the country returned to electoral politics in 2013. Politics have been unstable, and government corruption and a lack of accountability persist. Defamation and other laws restrict press freedom. Authorities deny permits for demonstrations and disperse some that take place. The government has struggled to manage lawlessness and poverty, particularly in the south. However, the courts have shown increasing independence, and in 2018 issued rulings that calmed an escalating political crisis.

KEY DEVELOPMENTS IN 2020

- In August, prisoners staged a massive riot and breakout at Farafangana Prison, in the south-eastern part of the island, after enduring inhumane conditions that had only been exacerbated by the COVID-19 pandemic. Due to the coronavirus, familial visits had been prohibited, and the squalid, unsanitary conditions enabled the virus to spread rapidly and pervasively throughout the prison population. The number of prisoners who contracted COVID-19 was unknown at year's end. Prison guards and security forces shot and killed 23 prisoners.
- In the December Senate elections, President Andry Rajoelina's political alliance won 10 out of the 12 elected seats, in a contest boycotted by the opposition. Earlier in the year, the National Assembly had reduced the number of senators in the body from 63 to 18, including 6 appointed by the President.

POLITICAL RIGHTS: 26 / 40 (+1)
A. ELECTORAL PROCESS: 9 / 12

A1. Was the current head of government or other chief national authority elected through free and fair elections? 3 / 4

Madagascar is a semipresidential republic, with a president elected for a five-year term and a prime minister nominated by the National Assembly and appointed by the president.

Andry Rajoelina defeated Marc Ravalomanana, both former presidents, in the 2018 presidential election's second round of voting in December with 55.7 percent of the vote, which the High Constitutional Court (HCC) confirmed in January 2019 despite allegations of fraud. The bitter rivalry between Rajoelina and Ravalomanana did not obstruct campaigning in 2018, which was relatively peaceful. Most election observers, particularly those from the European Union (EU), the African Union (AU), and the Southern Africa Development Community (SADC), recognized the election as generally free and fair.

Prime Minister Christian Ntsay, who was appointed by former president Hery Rajaonarimampianina in 2018 after the HCC ordered him to dissolve the government and name a consensus prime minister, was reappointed by President Rajoelina in July 2019.

A2. Were the current national legislative representatives elected through free and fair elections? 3 / 4

The bicameral legislature consists of the 151-seat National Assembly and the Senate. Members of the National Assembly are directly elected to five-year terms.

In March 2020, the National Assembly passed a measure, approved by President Rajoelina, that reduced the size of the Senate from 63 to 18 seats. Six of these seats are appointed by the president; the remaining 12 are indirectly elected from an electoral college. Senators serve five-year terms. While Rajoelina was within his constitutional mandate and claimed the reduction of Senate seats raised funds for public universities, opposition groups claimed the change was politically motivated, as former president Rajaonarimampianina's New Forces for Madagascar (HVM) party had dominated the Senate and used it as a stronghold of the opposition. The senatorial elections in December 2020 were boycotted by almost all opposition parties in protest. Rajoelina's political alliance won 10 out of the 12 seats; the vote was deemed free and fair by most election observers, despite the boycott.

A political alliance led by President Rajoelina won 84 National Assembly seats in the May 2019 parliamentary elections, while presidential candidate Ravalomanana's I Love Madagascar (TIM) party won 16; the remaining 51 were won by other parties and independent candidates. The contest was deemed free and fair by election observers, though some political parties claimed that the results were marred by fraud.

A3. Are the electoral laws and framework fair, and are they implemented impartially by the relevant election management bodies? 3 / 4

The CENI is subject to some influence by the executive, which controls member nomination and budget allocation processes. A new electoral code was adopted in 2018, though provisions that would have prevented Rajoelina and Ravalomanana from running prompted mass demonstrations and were ruled unconstitutional by the HCC later that year.

The independence and credibility of the CENI has been seriously undermined by its lack of resources and expertise in different domains (particularly in database management and information technology). CENI vice president Thiery Rakotonarivo revealed in March 2020 that over one million people likely had the same national identity card numbers as others on the voter roll, a problem that has existed for many years because voter registration is done manually. The president of the CENI, Hery Rakotomanana, forced Rakotonarivo to resign later in the month and claimed the issue should not have affected any recent election results.

B. POLITICAL PLURALISM AND PARTICIPATION: 11 / 16

B1. Do the people have the right to organize in different political parties or other competitive political groupings of their choice, and is the system free of undue obstacles to the rise and fall of these competing parties or groupings? 3 / 4

Almost 200 registered political parties are registered in Madagascar. However, the political parties law is widely viewed as a flawed document that places undue burdens on individual candidates, effectively mandating a high cost for political candidacy. Political leaders frequently use religion, ethnicity, and caste as instruments to mobilize voters.

B2. Is there a realistic opportunity for the opposition to increase its support or gain power through elections? 3 / 4

Opposition parties can increase their support through elections, but most political parties lack the financial resources to engage in vibrant competition. The government has historically denied opposition parties permits to hold demonstrations. Opposition and independent political figures were harassed and arrested by authorities in 2020.

The TIM claimed an August 2019 revision to a law on opposition parties prohibiting individuals who do not hold a legislative seat from serving as the official opposition targeted their party leader Ravalomanana. The Senate proposed an amendment to the bill later that month, effectively delaying its passage; it remained unresolved in the upper house at the end of 2020.

In March 2020, the National Assembly passed a measure that reduced the size of the Senate from 63 seats to 18, ostensibly to increase available funds for investment in public universities. Opposition parties claim the change was politically motivated and boycotted the December 2020 Senate elections in protest.

B3. Are the people's political choices free from domination by forces that are external to the political sphere, or by political forces that employ extrapolitical means? 3 / 4

Economic networks compete for power through strategic support of political candidates. In turn, a narrow group of political elites maintain their status by supporting the interests of their private-sector patrons. As a result, lines between public and private expenditures are blurry.

The military has some influence over politics, and it threatened to intervene during a 2018 political crisis. However, the military did not interfere in the 2019 election, and election observers called the contest credible.

B4. Do various segments of the population (including ethnic, racial, religious, gender, LGBT+, and other relevant groups) have full political rights and electoral opportunities? 2 / 4

The constitution guarantees political and electoral rights for all citizens, but in practice, discrimination impedes the political representation of some groups. The members of the Merina ethnic group are overrepresented in governmental institutions compared to the members of the other seventeen prominent ethnic groups. While some LGBT+ people are active politically in the capital, they face social stigma that discourages political participation and open advocacy for LGBT+ rights.

Cultural norms restrict the political participation of women, who hold 18 percent of National Assembly seats and 11 percent of Senate seats. Muslims are disproportionately affected by the nationality code, which can make it difficult for them to secure citizenship documents and thus voting rights. Ethnicity and caste are important political determinants, but generally do not affect political rights.

C. FUNCTIONING OF GOVERNMENT: 7 / 12 (+1)

C1. Do the freely elected head of government and national legislative representatives determine the policies of the government? 3 / 4 (+1)

Following a 2009 coup, the country returned to electoral politics in 2013. Government instability has since been reflected in the frequent replacement of the prime minister and frequent changes to the composition of the cabinet.

However, since the election of Rajoelina in 2018, the government has become more stable. Though the opposition boycotted the senatorial elections in December 2020, election observers deemed the polls free and fair. The successful senate elections and the as-of-yet secure tenure of Rajoelina's cabinet are evidence of increased stability in the political landscape.

According to the constitution, the president determines policies, and Parliament writes laws and votes on them. However, the Parliament lacks the strength to act as an effective check on executive power. Additionally, economic elites exert significant influence on elected officials.

Score Change: The score improved from 2 to 3 because of increased government stability in recent years, as seen in the successful Senate elections.

C2. Are safeguards against official corruption strong and effective? 2 / 4

Corruption remains a serious problem in Madagascar, though a series of recent reforms and anticorruption strategies aim to address it. Investigations and prosecutions of corruption by the Independent Anticorruption Bureau (BIANCO) were infrequent and rarely targeted high-profile individuals, but the agency has become more independent in recent years. A May 2019 BIANCO report implicated 79 lawmakers for accepting bribes to adopt 2018 electoral reforms favoring then-president Rajaonarimampianina. Prosecutors were expected to review the report and consider indictments against the legislators, but no major updates were reported by the end of 2020. In November 2019, BIANCO submitted a report to the High Court of Justice (HCJ) implicating three former ministers in acts of corruption. However, the file remained unreviewed, as the some of the HCJ's seats remained unfilled.

C3. Does the government operate with openness and transparency? 2 / 4

The constitution provides for the right to information, but no law defines a formal procedure for requesting government information. However, ministers and officials often hold press briefings, and laws, decrees, and high court decisions are posted on the internet. In March 2019, the government launched a new online contact form for Malagasy to send messages to President Rajoelina and key aides.

There is little oversight of procurement processes. Asset declarations are required for most government officials, and while many complied with these laws, there are few practical consequences for those who refuse.

CIVIL LIBERTIES: 33 / 60 (−2)

D. FREEDOM OF EXPRESSION AND BELIEF: 10 / 16 (−1)

D1. Are there free and independent media? 2 / 4

The constitution provides for freedom of the press. However, this guarantee has been undermined by criminal libel laws and other restrictions, as well as safety risks involved in the investigation of sensitive subjects such as cattle rustling and the illicit extraction and sale of natural resources.

During the COVID-19 pandemic in 2020, the government targeted and harassed journalists and media outlets who allegedly spread "false information" about the coronavirus and the government's response to the pandemic.

D2. Are individuals free to practice and express their religious faith or nonbelief in public and private? 3 / 4

Religious freedom is provided for in the constitution, though this right is upheld inconsistently. Religious leaders have noted that some workers were unable to practice their religion due to poor enforcement of labor laws. The government has historically restricted the Muslim community's access to education by threatening to close down Islamic schools. Several church facilities have been attacked by armed individuals, some apparently attempting robberies, in recent years.

D3. Is there academic freedom, and is the educational system free from extensive political indoctrination? 3 / 4

Academic freedom is generally respected. However, a lack of resources and frequent strikes hamper normal operations of public universities.

D4. Are individuals free to express their personal views on political or other sensitive topics without fear of surveillance or retribution? 2 / 4 (−1)

There were no official reports of the government monitoring online activity. However, a cybercrimes law prohibits online defamation and spreading "false information," and has been used to prosecute social media users.

In October 2020, former communications minister Harry Laurent Rahajason was sentenced to 44 months in prison after supporting a protest through social media online against President Rajoelina's claims that an herbal drink could cure patients with coronavirus. His arrest and the detention of a journalist who wrote on social media about the COVID-19 pandemic, has deterred others from speaking freely online.

Score Change: The score declined from 3 to 2 because arrests and prosecutions of individuals who criticized the government's response to the COVID-19 pandemic deterred others from expressing their views.

E. ASSOCIATIONAL AND ORGANIZATIONAL RIGHTS: 8 / 12 (−1)
E1. Is there freedom of assembly? 2 / 4 (−1)

The constitution guarantees freedom of assembly, but authorities have sometimes declined requests for protests and rallies in the name of public security.

In 2020, the government denied authorization of opposition protests and cracked down on those that happened, using the pretext of the COVID-19 pandemic. In June 2020, security forces used tear gas and warning shots to disperse several groups of individuals protesting COVID-19 lockdown measures in the city of Toamasina. In the capital city Antananarivo, opposition parties complained that they were not given authorization to hold public meetings and protests.

Score Change: The score declined from 3 to 2 because unlike in the previous year, the government consistently cracked down on antigovernment demonstrations, often citing COVID-19 as justification.

E2. Is there freedom for nongovernmental organizations, particularly those that are engaged in human rights- and governance-related work? 3 / 4

Freedom of association is provided for in the constitution and is generally respected. A wide variety of nongovernmental organizations (NGOs) are active, but many domestic human rights groups lack resources. Although no restrictions are placed on NGOs, the government is not always receptive to their opinions. Groups focused on the environment or human rights face pressure from powerful interests. Raleva Rajoany (known as Raleva) was arrested and given a two-year suspended sentence in 2017, and again in September 2020, for his activism against a gold mine owned by a Chinese company that pollutes a river in Mananjary. In October 2020, he appeared before a judge and was released.

E3. Is there freedom for trade unions and similar professional or labor organizations? 3 / 4

Workers have the right to join unions, engage in collective bargaining, and strike. However, more than 80 percent of workers are engaged in agriculture, fishing, and forestry at a subsistence level, and therefore have no access to unions.

F. RULE OF LAW: 7 / 16

F1. Is there an independent judiciary? 2 / 4

The executive influences judicial decisions through the reassignment of judges. Trial outcomes are frequently predetermined, and the Malagasy people generally regard the judiciary as corrupt. Local tribunals are seen as overburdened and corrupt.

In 2018 and 2019, key HCC rulings have reflected its growing independence from the executive. In 2018, it struck down election laws that would have prevented key figures from competing against former president Rajaonarimampianina in that year's election. In April 2019, the HCC forced President Rajoelina to delay a constitutional referendum that aimed to dissolve the Senate and give more power to regional authorities. However, the HCC has at times approved Rajoelina's actions despite legitimate protests from the opposition.

F2. Does due process prevail in civil and criminal matters? 1 / 4

Due process rights are poorly upheld. A lack of training, resources, and personnel hampers the effectiveness of the criminal justice system. Many people held in pretrial detention do not have access to lawyers, and the successful assertion of due process rights is often tied to the ability of family and friends to intercede on behalf of the accused.

The government has increased funding for the judiciary, launched capacity-building efforts, and pardoned individuals detained over minor offenses as part of a new policy supported by the UN Office of the High Commissioner for Human Rights (OHCHR). In October 2019, the government also instituted the use of "fair ground hearings" to alleviate the pretrial backlog.

F3. Is there protection from the illegitimate use of physical force and freedom from war and insurgencies? 2 / 4

The police and military are unable to assert authority over the entire country, and areas in southern Madagascar are subjected to raids and violence by bandits and criminal groups. Security forces operate with little oversight or accountability for extrajudicial killings, particularly against cattle thieves, known as *dahalo*.

Detainees and prisoners suffer from harsh and sometimes life-threatening conditions due to overcrowding in detention facilities, and substandard hygiene and health care. In August 2020, prisoners staged a massive riot and breakout at the Farafangana Prison to escape the inhumane conditions they endured, which had been exacerbated by the COVID-19 pandemic. Prison guards and security forces shot and killed 23 prisoners, which Amnesty International described as "an appalling attack on the right to life." Due to the coronavirus, familial visits had been prohibited, and the squalid, unsanitary conditions enabled the virus to spread rapidly and pervasively throughout the prison population. The number of prisoners who contracted COVID-19 is unknown.

People convicted of crimes can be sentenced to hard labor.

F4. Do laws, policies, and practices guarantee equal treatment of various segments of the population? 2 / 4

Legal provisions prohibit discrimination based on race, gender, disability, and social status, but these are upheld inconsistently. Conservative cultural and social norms can prevent women from having the same opportunities as men. Some ethnic groups face discrimination outside of their home regions. There are no legal protections against discrimination based on sexual orientation or gender identity; LGBT+ people face social stigma, particularly in rural areas, and experience employment discrimination and occasional acts of violence. The age of consent for same-sex relations is 21, but 14 for heterosexual relations. In March 2020, a woman was arrested because of her relationship with a 19-year-old woman.

G. PERSONAL AUTONOMY AND INDIVIDUAL RIGHTS: 8 / 16

G1. Do individuals enjoy freedom of movement, including the ability to change their place of residence, employment, or education? 3 / 4

The government generally does not interfere in freedom of movement; individuals are allowed to move freely in the country and can travel internationally. However, bandit attacks in the south and west have made traveling across the island difficult. Authorities seized 112 weapons and arrested 48 people in a May 2019 operation against bandits. In 2020, the government restricted movement to curtail the spread of the COVID-19 pandemic.

G2. Are individuals able to exercise the right to own property and establish private businesses without undue interference from state or nonstate actors? 2 / 4

Madagascar's legal structure provides protections for private property rights, though enforcement of these protections is inconsistent, in part because most farmers do not hold official rights to their land. There is a history of competition between the state-recognized property rights system and customary land use practices, as well as attempts by the state to permit mining, commercial agriculture, and other economic pursuits on land where ownership is disputed.

In recent years, Madagascar has made it easier to start a business by reducing the number of registration procedures and simplifying the payment of registration fees. In May 2019, the government launched a financing program to support Malagasy establishing new businesses.

G3. Do individuals enjoy personal social freedoms, including choice of marriage partner and size of family, protection from domestic violence, and control over appearance? 2 / 4

Women and children have limited social freedoms in Madagascar, especially in rural areas. Forced child marriage and domestic abuse are common. Although sexual harassment is illegal, the law is not enforced, and harassment is common. Abortion is illegal in Madagascar.

G4. Do individuals enjoy equality of opportunity and freedom from economic exploitation? 1 / 4

Most people work in subsistence agriculture, making advancement in the local economy extremely challenging.

According to the US State Department's 2020 *Trafficking in Persons Report*, the Malagasy government does not scrutinize officials implicated in trafficking, though it does provide some services to victims and convicted traffickers for the first time since 2016.

Malawi

Population: 19,100,000
Capital: Lilongwe
Freedom Status: Partly Free
Electoral Democracy: Yes

Overview: Malawi holds regular elections and has undergone multiple transfers of power between political parties, most recently in June 2020. Political rights and civil liberties are for the most part respected by the state. However, corruption is endemic, police brutality and arbitrary arrests are common, and discrimination and violence toward women, members of minority groups, and people with albinism remain problems.

KEY DEVELOPMENTS IN 2020

- By the end of the year, over 6,500 people had tested positive for COVID-19 and 189 people had died. Despite the pandemic, the electoral commission was able to successfully administer the year's repeat presidential election.
- In February, the Constitutional Court annulled the May 2019 presidential election due to widespread, systematic irregularities. The court ordered a new presidential election and determined the threshold for victory to be 50 percent and one vote, instead of the simple plurality that had been used in previous elections.
- In June, Lazarus Chakwera of the Malawi Congress Party (MCP), who led the "Tonse" coalition of nine opposition parties, won the presidential election with 59 percent of the vote. The elections were well-administered, competitive, and credible, and the results were accepted by all stakeholders.
- In September, President Chakwera operationalized the long-stalled 2017 Access to Information Act. Further, the executive office instituted weekly news conferences, opening the space for journalists to report on government activity.

POLITICAL RIGHTS: 29 / 40 (+3)

A. ELECTORAL PROCESS: 9 / 12 (+1)

A1. Was the current head of government or other chief national authority elected through free and fair elections? 3 / 4

The president is directly elected for five-year terms and exercises considerable executive authority. Following the Constitutional Court's annulment of the 2019 presidential election, a new poll was held in June 2020, which Lazarus Chakwera of the Malawi Congress Party (MCP) won with 58.6 percent of the vote. The incumbent, Peter Mutharika, of the ruling Democratic Progressive Party (DPP), came second with 39.4 percent. Although election observers were not present due to travel restrictions as a result of the COVID-19 pandemic, the elections were well-administered, competitive, and credible, and reflected the will of Malawian voters.

A2. Were the current national legislative representatives elected through free and fair elections? 3 / 4

The unicameral National Assembly is composed of 193 members elected by popular vote to serve five-year terms. Legislative elections were held concurrently with the annulled presidential election in May 2019 and experienced some of the same irregularities and logistical problems that marred the presidential poll. As many as 29 legislative candidates challenged the results in court, three of whom were successful. Six of the cases remained undecided by the end of 2020. In the 2019 legislative poll, the DPP won 62 seats, followed by the MCP with 55, the United Democratic Front (UDF) with 10, the People's Party (PP) with 5, the United Transformation Movement (UTM) with 4, and the Alliance for Democracy with 1. Independent candidates won 55 seats. Six legislative by-elections were held during 2020, and the MCP and the UDF each won two seats, and independent candidates won the remaining two seats.

A3. Are the electoral laws and framework fair, and are they implemented impartially by the relevant election management bodies? 3 / 4 (+1)

Several 2020 legislative changes improved the quality of the year's repeat presidential elections. The Constitutional Court determined presidential elections must be won with a majority of the vote, not just a plurality, which Parliament operationalized by legislative amendment. Other ancillary changes extended the mandate of the current parliament from five to six years, so that the next legislative elections would be held concomitantly with the 2025 presidential poll. Malawi Electoral Commission (MEC) officers who presided over the 2019 elections appeared before Parliament in February 2020, who recommended their dismissal. However, President Mutharika declined to fire them, letting their terms expired in early June 2020.

To minimize COVID-19 transmission during polling, the MEC provided masks to polling staff and handwashing facilities to voters while promoting social distancing guidelines at polling stations. Despite the COVID-19 pandemic, funding shortfalls, and a short time frame, the June 2020 presidential election was competently managed.

Score Change: The score improved from 2 to 3 because electoral laws were updated in keeping with Constitutional Court rulings following the annulment of the 2019 presidential election, and observers regarded the new electoral commission's management of the 2020 presidential election as competent.

B. POLITICAL PLURALISM AND PARTICIPATION: 12 / 16

B1. Do the people have the right to organize in different political parties or other competitive political groupings of their choice, and is the system free of undue obstacles to the rise and fall of these competing parties or groupings? 3 / 4

There are few significant obstacles to the formation of political parties, though the government has at times held up the registration of new groups. While several parties compete in practice, they are loosely organized, with politicians frequently moving between parties or forming their own breakaway groups. Many candidates choose to run as independents. Following the Constitutional Court's interpretation of majority to mean over half of the vote, political parties created coalitions for the 2020 presidential election. These included an electoral alliance between the then-ruling DPP and opposition UDF supporting incumbent Mutharika, with UDF leader Atupele Muluzi as the vice president candidate. The second major coalition, dubbed the Tonse Alliance, brought together nine opposition political parties, led by MCP's Chakwera, with Saulos Chilima of the UTM party as the candidate for vice president.

B2. Is there a realistic opportunity for the opposition to increase its support or gain power through elections? 3 / 4

Malawi has experienced peaceful transfers of power between rival groups. Opposition parties hold seats in Parliament and, ahead of the June 2020 elections, were able to mobilize and pass several laws to facilitate the fairness of the polls, despite resistance from the ruling party. Opposition parties are generally able to campaign freely throughout the country. The 2020 elections were the first time an opposition party defeated an incumbent since the transition to democracy in 1994.

However, the governing party generally has a campaigning advantage. Before the June 2020 election, opposition parties faced violence and intimidation from the police and ruling party agents. The state-owned broadcaster, the Malawi Broadcasting Corporation (MBC), was again accused of favoring the ruling party in its coverage, compelling the opposition to rely on private media to convey its message to the public.

B3. Are the people's political choices free from domination by forces that are external to the political sphere, or by political forces that employ extrapolitical means? 3 / 4

Traditional chiefs, who wield some authority and receive government honoraria, are supposed to be nonpartisan figures under the law, but they frequently seek to influence voter choices in practice. Some chiefs publicly endorsed the incumbent president ahead of the June 2020 election and even threatened opposition candidates seeking to campaign in their regions.

The Political Parties Act, which came into force in 2018, bans politicians from using cash handouts and other incentives to garner votes. Despite this, a 2020 study by Afrobarometer found that around 16 percent of Malawians had reported being offered food, a gift, or money in return for their vote by a candidate or someone from a political party in the 2019 elections.

B4. Do various segments of the population (including ethnic, racial, religious, gender, LGBT+, and other relevant groups) have full political rights and electoral opportunities? 3 / 4

All ethnic, religious, and gender groups have full political rights under the law. However, women remain underrepresented in politics despite gradual gains, and according to Afrobarometer, they are less likely than men to become politically involved. The 2020 presidential candidates did not include any women. The number of women in the legislature remained unchanged at 44, and Catherine Gotani Hara continued to serve as the speaker of parliament. In the 31-member cabinet appointed by Chakwera, there were 11 women, although only 4 were full ministers, the rest being deputies.

Political parties generally do not advocate for the rights of LGBT+ people, who are subject to legal and societal discrimination.

C. FUNCTIONING OF GOVERNMENT: 8 / 12 (+2)

C1. Do the freely elected head of government and national legislative representatives determine the policies of the government? 3 / 4

Executive and legislative representatives are typically able to determine the policies of government without hindrance. However, patronage and clientelism are common, and wealthy business leaders often influence policymaking.

C2. Are safeguards against official corruption strong and effective? 2 / 4 (+1)

Corruption is endemic in Malawi, though the Chakwera government has taken steps to address the issue. Civil society leaders have accused the Anti-Corruption Bureau (ACB), which is responsible for investigating corruption, of being ineffective and politically compromised. In 2020, the new Chakwera government fulfilled its pledge to fully fund the ACB's budget requests. In June, the Human Rights Defenders Coalition (HRDC) began implementing a whistleblower campaign that has resulted in the reporting of multiple cases of corruption to the ACB. During the second half of the year, several high-profile public officials were arrested on corruption charges and a former cabinet minister in the DPP government was convicted and sentenced for abuse of office.

Score Change: The score improved from 1 to 2 because the government fully funded the country's anticorruption bureau, and authorities carried out a series of arrests and successful prosecutions in high-profile corruption cases during the year.

C3. Does the government operate with openness and transparency? 3 / 4 (+1)

Malawi lacks budgetary transparency and the government does not make year-end budget audit reports public, though President Chakwera's policy changes have improved government openness. The long-stalled Access to Information Act, which was enacted in 2017, was made operational in September 2020. President Chakwera provided regular updates on his government in weekly radio addresses throughout the year. Chakwera has also appeared twice before Parliament to answer questions from legislators, a tradition required by law but previously not honored. The new administration further instituted weekly press conferences, where reporters ask questions about government affairs.

High-level officials are legally required to declare their assets and other financial interests while in public service, which Chakwera did in August 2020.

Score Change: The score improved from 2 to 3 because a long-stalled law on access to information was finally implemented in September, and the Chakwera government stepped up its public engagement with the media, increased compliance with parliamentary oversight, and abided by asset declaration rules.

CIVIL LIBERTIES: 37 / 60 (+1)

D. FREEDOM OF EXPRESSION AND BELIEF: 13 / 16

D1. Are there free and independent media? 2 / 4

Freedom of the press is legally guaranteed and historically respected in practice. However, news outlets have experienced intimidation and undue regulatory interference in recent years. The public Malawi Broadcasting Corporation (MBC) has historically been biased in favor of the former ruling party, the DPP. Most private media houses are owned by political families and often take partisan positions. Journalists sometimes face physical violence while reporting on demonstrations or police activity. In May 2020, journalists were attacked by suspected ruling-party loyalists while traveling to cover an opposition campaign rally.

A vaguely worded 2016 cybersecurity law criminalizes the posting of "offensive" content online, which could place journalists at risk of prosecution.

D2. Are individuals free to practice and express their religious faith or nonbelief in public and private? 4 / 4

The constitution upholds freedom of religion, and this right is generally respected in practice. Squabbles between Christians and Muslims occasionally flare up but are often peacefully resolved.

D3. Is there academic freedom, and is the educational system free from extensive political indoctrination? 4 / 4

Malawi's education system is largely free from political indoctrination. University students and professors are able to engage in research and political activities without interference.

D4. Are individuals free to express their personal views on political or other sensitive topics without fear of surveillance or retribution? 3 / 4

Citizens are typically free to express their personal views without fear of surveillance or retribution. According to a 2020 Afrobarometer survey, 62 percent of Malawians said that they are free to say what they think. However, according to the survey, many Malawians do not feel comfortable criticizing the government and engage in self-censorship. In addition to the 2016 cybercrime law's ban on posting "offensive" content, a law against insulting the leader of Malawi remains in the legal code, though it is rarely enforced. Civil society leaders have expressed suspicions that the government monitors their electronic communications with technology introduced in 2017.

E. ASSOCIATIONAL AND ORGANIZATIONAL RIGHTS: 8 / 12 (+1)
E1. Is there freedom of assembly? 3 / 4 (+1)

Freedom of assembly is guaranteed in the constitution. Prior to the February 2020 Constitutional Court ruling on the disputed 2019 presidential election, the HRDC continued to organize a series of street protests against the 2019 election's irregularities. In March, the outgoing government arrested and charged HRDC leaders after they called for nationwide antigovernment protests, though these charges were dropped by the new government. Many other postelection demonstrations have occurred peacefully, without violence from security agents. Prominent among the year's protests were demonstrations in October and November, criticizing the government's failure to implement the Gender Equality Act (GEA) and speaking out against the increasing rate of gender-based violence.

Score Change: The score improved from 2 to 3 because there was no repetition of the protest-related violence and intimidation reported during 2019, with major protests largely proceeding peacefully in 2020.

E2. Is there freedom for nongovernmental organizations, particularly those that are engaged in human rights- and governance-related work? 2 / 4

Nongovernmental organizations (NGOs) are active in Malawi, but leading civil society figures have been subject to intimidation, and NGO operations are somewhat constrained by onerous regulations. Under the NGO Act, an organization's registration can be suspended if it is deemed to have departed from its original purpose, engaged in partisan politics, or violated any provisions of the law, among other grounds. The NGO Board has threatened to deregister NGOs, though this had not yet occurred as of 2020.

E3. Is there freedom for trade unions and similar professional or labor organizations? 3 / 4

The rights to organize labor unions and to strike are legally protected, though workers in poorly defined essential services have only a limited right to strike. Unions are active and collective bargaining is practiced, but retaliation against unregistered unions and strikers is not illegal.

F. RULE OF LAW: 9 / 16
F1. Is there an independent judiciary? 3 / 4

Judicial independence is generally respected, particularly in the higher courts. The decision of the Constitutional Court to annul the 2019 elections and its upholding by the Malawi Supreme Court underscored the high levels of judicial independence in Malawi. However, judges sometimes face political pressure and are offered bribes to sway their decisions. The appointment process for judges lacks transparency, and the judiciary is underfunded, which can also undercut judicial autonomy. In October 2020, President Chakwera allocated funds for and appointed four new Supreme Court justices and 12 Constitutional Court judges, appointments that may help ease the financial pressures on the judiciary.

F2. Does due process prevail in civil and criminal matters? 2 / 4

Arbitrary arrests and detentions are common. Defendants are entitled to legal representation, but in practice they are frequently forced to represent themselves in court. Although the law requires that suspects be released or charged with a crime within 48 hours of arrest, these rights are often denied. Case backlogs contribute to lengthy pretrial detention; those awaiting trial make up about 18 percent of the prison population.

F3. Is there protection from the illegitimate use of physical force and freedom from war and insurgencies? 2 / 4

Police are poorly trained and often ineffective. Police brutality and extrajudicial killings are not uncommon. Prison conditions are dire, characterized by overcrowding and extremely poor health care; many inmates die from disease.

F4. Do laws, policies, and practices guarantee equal treatment of various segments of the population? 2 / 4

The constitution explicitly guarantees the rights of all humans. A 2020 Afrobarometer survey found that 76 percent of Malawians said they have never experienced unfair treatment based on their ethnic identity. However, same-sex relations remains a crime punishable by up to 14 years in prison. LGBT+ people are subject to arbitrary arrest and detention and are sometimes physically assaulted while in custody.

Despite constitutional guarantees of equal protection, women experience discrimination in education, politics, employment, business, and other aspects of life.

People with albinism experience discrimination and have been attacked, abducted, killed, and mutilated. In the 2020–21 national budget, the government provided resources to create an action plan to protect people living with albinism.

G. PERSONAL AUTONOMY AND INDIVIDUAL RIGHTS: 7 / 16

G1. Do individuals enjoy freedom of movement, including the ability to change their place of residence, employment, or education? 2 / 4

The constitution establishes freedom of internal movement and foreign travel, which are generally respected in practice for Malawians. However, during the election campaigns, militant opposition party and ruling party supporters sometimes set up no-go zones for political opponents. Police roadblocks are ubiquitous in Malawi and bribes are common at these checkpoints. According to the United Nations, the government's policy of confining refugees to designated camps restricts their freedom of movement and impairs their ability to earn a living. Police frequently round up those found outside of the camps and return them.

G2. Are individuals able to exercise the right to own property and establish private businesses without undue interference from state or nonstate actors? 2 / 4

Property rights are inadequately protected. Most land is held under customary tenure, and the process of creating titles that would allow legal ownership of land has moved slowly. Women are at a disadvantage regarding property ownership and inheritance. Starting a business can be a cumbersome process that is worsened by corruption in key government agencies.

G3. Do individuals enjoy personal social freedoms, including choice of marriage partner and size of family, protection from domestic violence, and control over appearance? 1 / 4

Domestic violence is common, but victims rarely come forward, and police generally do not intervene in domestic violence cases. Child sexual abuse is prevalent. Approximately 42 percent of women marry before they turn 18, in violation of the law. Traditional chiefs have spoken out against, and in some cases forced the annulment of underage marriages. Police have taken more action against perpetrators of sexual abuse in recent years.

In August 2020, the High Court ruled that security forces must compensate women who were raped, defiled, and sexually assaulted by police officers, and ordered the arrest of law enforcers who were implicated. However, at the end of the year, the police had yet to execute the order.

G4. Do individuals enjoy equality of opportunity and freedom from economic exploitation? 2 / 4

Revenues from large, state-run industries tend to benefit the political elite. Income inequality remains a problem and inhibits economic mobility.

The enforcement of labor laws is weak, and employees are often paid extremely low wages, despite minimum-wage laws. Child labor is a persistent problem, particularly on tobacco estates.

Malaysia

Population: 32,800,000
Capital: Kuala Lumpur
Freedom Status: Partly Free
Electoral Democracy: No

Overview: The Barisan Nasional (BN) political coalition ruled Malaysia from independence in 1957 until 2018, maintaining power by manipulating electoral districts, appealing to ethnic nationalism, and suppressing criticism through restrictive speech laws and politicized prosecutions of opposition leaders. The BN lost to an opposition alliance in the May 2018 general elections. However, a period of political turbulence and realignment in early 2020 culminated in a new governing coalition that included parties central to the pre-2018 regime. The current government has been resistant to governance reforms, and there are escalating concerns about narrowing freedoms.

KEY DEVELOPMENTS IN 2020

- The Pakatan Harapan (PH) coalition government collapsed in February 2020 following turbulence that prompted Prime Minister Mahathir Mohamad to resign. A week of political machinations and uncertainty concluded with the formation of a new coalition, the Perikatan Nasional (PN), led by Prime Minister Muhyiddin Yassin.
- In July, a Malaysian court sentenced former prime minister Najib Razak to 12 years in prison after finding him guilty of multiple counts of corruption and abuse of power related to the embezzlement of billions of dollars from state investment fund 1MDB.
- State officials invoked the COVID-19 pandemic to justify crackdowns on free speech and movement. Independent news outlets were often excluded from official COVID-19 briefings, parliamentary sessions, and other events of public interest as a purported safety precaution. Thousands of people were arrested for violating various pandemic-related movement restrictions, with migrant workers at times disproportionately targeted.
- Additionally, a number of journalists, activists, and others were charged during the year with sedition, defamation, or violation of the 1998 Communications and Multimedia Act (CMA) for speech critical or perceived as critical of authorities.

POLITICAL RIGHTS: 21 / 40

A. ELECTORAL PROCESS: 6 / 12

A1. Was the current head of government or other chief national authority elected through free and fair elections? 2 / 4

The prime minister is the head of government and chief executive. Though formally appointed by the monarch, the authority of the prime minister and cabinet is based on the support of a majority in the lower house of Parliament. Muhyiddin Yassin of the Malaysian United Indigenous Party (PPBM) was not elected through free and fair elections. Instead, he was appointed prime minister following Mahathir Mohamad's resignation and the PPBM's decision to leave the PH coalition in order to form the new PN coalition alongside the United Malays National Organisation (UMNO), the Islamic Party (PAS), and smaller parties.

The monarch, known as the Yang di-Pertuan Agong, is elected for five-year terms by and from the hereditary rulers of 9 of Malaysia's 13 states. Sultan Abdullah of Pahang was chosen as head of state in 2019, following the abdication of his predecessor.

A2. Were the current national legislative representatives elected through free and fair elections? 2 / 4

The upper house of the bicameral Parliament, the Senate or Dewan Negara, consists of 44 members appointed by the monarch on the advice of the prime minister and 26 members elected by the 13 state legislatures, serving three-year terms. The Senate has limited power to amend or block legislation passed by the lower house. The House of Representatives, or Dewan Rakyat, has 222 seats filled through direct elections in single-member constituencies.

The PH victory in 2018 occurred despite lopsided electoral conditions that gave the BN significant advantages, such as gerrymandered and seriously malapportioned voting districts, weak regulation of campaign spending, and legal constraints on media independence and expressions of dissent.

The PN government that took power in 2020 is composed of the same parliamentary representatives elected in May 2018, but some parliamentarians changed parties following the coalition realignment. At the time Prime Minister Muhyiddin was sworn in in March, the PN ruling coalition and its supporting members of parliament collectively held 113 seats in the House of Representatives, compared to 109 seats held by the PH opposition coalition and its independent supporters. A federal by-election in January 2020 gave an additional parliamentary seat to UMNO, part of the PN coalition.

A3. Are the electoral laws and framework fair, and are they implemented impartially by the relevant election management bodies? 2 / 4

The Election Commission (EC), which administers elections and is responsible for voter rolls and the delineation of electoral boundaries, was seen as subservient to the government under the BN, with members appointed by the king on the advice of the prime minister. The EC chairman appointed in 2018 under the PH government was considered a reformist, but following the takeover of the PN coalition in 2020, he resigned to become the parliamentary speaker. A new chairman was appointed in August 2020, while the other commissioners appointed by the PH in 2019 were not removed. In August 2020, an Electoral Reform Committee submitted a report containing 49 recommendations for revamping electoral laws, including the regulation of political party funding and replacing the first-past-the-post electoral system with proportional representation. Although action on the recommendations remained pending at year's end, the government announced that in 2021 it would implement constitutional amendments lowering the voting age to 18 and establishing automatic voter registration.

Sabah state elections were held in September 2020. Election watchdog group Bersih noted widespread vote-buying efforts, but commended the EC's administration of the balloting. However, the Human Rights Commission of Malaysia (SUHAKAM) noted insufficient adherence to sanitary protections, and campaigners returning from Sabah to the Kuala Lumpur area were cited by health officials as a trigger for the wave of COVID-19 cases that continued to rise at year's end.

B. POLITICAL PLURALISM AND PARTICIPATION: 9 / 16

B1. Do the people have the right to organize in different political parties or other competitive political groupings of their choice, and is the system free of undue obstacles to the rise and fall of these competing parties or groupings? 2 / 4

The party system in Malaysia is diverse and competitive, but groups that challenged BN rule prior to 2018 often faced obstacles such as unequal access to the media, restrictions on campaigning and freedom of assembly, and politicized prosecutions. The Registrar of Societies (ROS) oversees the registration of political parties and was known to issue politicized decisions under the BN government. Several opposition parties formed by PPBM defectors in 2020, including Mahathir's new party, alleged in December that the ROS was stalling on registration approval.

B2. Is there a realistic opportunity for the opposition to increase its support or gain power through elections? 3 / 4

Although opposition parties had long governed in a number of Malaysia's states, the 2018 elections that brought the PH coalition to power represented the country's first democratic transfer of power between rival political groups at the federal level since independence in 1957.

In 2019, the UMNO and PAS formed an opposition bloc; the PPBM joined them to form the core of the PN government following Mahathir's resignation as prime minister in February 2020. This coalitional realignment produced a new government without an election, while the PH alliance returned to opposition status. In the September 2020 Sabah state elections, a coalition aligned with the PN federal government defeated the incumbent, PH-aligned state government.

Although the PN's narrow majority spurred recurrent opposition claims that it had sufficient members of parliament to form a new government, the PN government successfully passed a 2021 budget in December, demonstrating the coalition's continuing majority.

B3. Are the people's political choices free from domination by forces that are external to the political sphere, or by political forces that employ extrapolitical means? 2 / 4

The military is not active in politics, and foreign powers do not directly meddle in domestic political affairs, though the BN's increasingly close ties with China were a prominent issue in the 2018 election campaign. In 2020, the PN reverted to the version of a China-funded infrastructure megaproject that was negotiated by the BN but had been suspended and then altered by the PH.

During its decades in power, the BN built strong connections with Malaysia's business elites and used these relationships to influence electoral outcomes, including through favorable coverage by mainstream private media and greater access to financial resources. Since returning to power in March 2020, parties within the PN coalition have used government-linked companies (GLCs), official monopolies for certain goods and services, and state investment vehicles for political purposes. In May, UMNO's president stated explicitly that politicians were made heads of GLCs to ensure that PN government policies would be implemented.

B4. Do various segments of the population (including ethnic, racial, religious, gender, LGBT+, and other relevant groups) have full political rights and electoral opportunities? 2 / 4

Suffrage in Malaysia is universal for adult citizens. However, social and legal restrictions limit political participation among some minority groups. UMNO and the PAS are defenders of long-standing policies that favor the ethnic Malay and Muslim majority. The PN coalition featured minimal representation and participation of Chinese and Indian minorities, but did include representatives of ethnic groups from Sabah and Sarawak states, which are located on the island of Borneo.

Women's interests remain significantly underrepresented in politics. The PN's ministry in charge of women's affairs offered misogynistic advice for women during the COVID-19 lockdown period, suggesting they maintain household harmony by wearing makeup and not nagging their husbands.

Sabah and Sarawak, which are home to distinct ethnic groups, have sought greater autonomy in recent years. States' natural resource rights have been increasingly recognized, and national oil company Petronas paid hundreds of millions of dollars to the Sarawak government in September 2020.

C. FUNCTIONING OF GOVERNMENT: 6 / 12

C1. Do the freely elected head of government and national legislative representatives determine the policies of the government? 2 / 4

While elected officials determine and implement government policy, the unfair electoral framework has historically weakened their legitimacy. Decision-making power has typically been concentrated in the hands of the prime minister and his close advisers.

C2. Are safeguards against official corruption strong and effective? 2 / 4

High-level corruption was a critical weakness of the BN government, and former prime minister Najib Razak's efforts to avoid accountability for the 1MDB scandal damaged the country's anticorruption mechanisms more generally. Najib and his successor as UMNO leader, former deputy prime minister Ahmad Zahid Hamidi, were arrested in 2018 and indicted for numerous corruption-related offenses.

The Malaysian Anti-Corruption Commission (MACC) launched a National Anti-Corruption Plan under the PH. Although the PN government committed to carrying out the plan, observers questioned the government's political will to implement it. Several high-profile corruption cases were dropped in 2020, including dozens of timber concessions-related graft charges against former Sabah chief minister Musa Aman, and the 1MDB-related charges against Najib's stepson, Riza Aziz. However, Najib was convicted in July 2020 on seven counts of criminal breach of trust, money laundering, and abuse of power. He received a total sentence of 42 years in prison, but the most severe charge carried a 12-year term, with the rest served concurrently. A prolonged appeals process was expected to follow; Najib also faced a series of additional trials on related charges.

Transparency International's Global Corruption Barometer, published in November 2020, showed that two-thirds of those surveyed thought the government was doing a good job at fighting corruption, though 40 percent of Malaysians felt that corruption had increased in the previous 12 months, and 13 percent had paid a bribe in the preceding year.

C3. Does the government operate with openness and transparency? 2 / 4

A lack of independent oversight regarding state-affiliated companies and investment funds has long created conditions conducive to corruption. Efforts towards enacting a freedom of information act and other reforms stalled after the PN government took power.

Although the government was initially open and transparent regarding Malaysia's COVID-19 status and the state's response, observers faulted the government's data transparency as the late-year coronavirus wave accelerated. In addition, no legislative action on economic stimulus occurred until Parliament convened in May, and no debate was permitted during the parliamentary session. The government made its pandemic-related financial expenditures public, but there was no external review of spending.

CIVIL LIBERTIES: 30 / 60 (−1)

D. FREEDOM OF EXPRESSION AND BELIEF: 8 / 16 (−1)

D1. Are there free and independent media? 2 / 4 (−1)

Prior to the 2018 elections, most private news publications and television stations were controlled by political parties or businesses allied with the BN, and state news outlets similarly reflected government views. The market began to change after the PH took power, as independent outlets benefited from a reduction in political pressure and harassment. The PH pledged to reform restrictive media laws, and in 2019 it achieved repeal of the 2018 Anti-Fake News Act, but several problematic laws remained in force at the end of its tenure.

A draft bill on the establishment of a Malaysian Media Council that would encourage both media freedom and press accountability remained pending at year's end. Press freedom watchdog group Article 19 noted that the draft failed to clarify the relationship between the prospective Media Council and the Malaysian Communication and Multimedia Commission (MCMC), which monitors websites and can order the removal of material considered provocative or subversive. A 2012 amendment to the 1950 Evidence Act holds owners and editors of websites, providers of web-hosting services, and owners of computers or mobile devices accountable for information published through their services or property.

The change of government in March 2020 brought increased government pressure on private media. State officials invoked the COVID-19 pandemic to justify the exclusion of independent outlets from official COVID-19 briefings, parliamentary sessions, and other events of public interest. The government also initiated investigations and prosecutions of multiple reporters and outlets for alleged crimes including sedition, defamation, and violations of the 1998 Communications and Multimedia Act (CMA). In August, the police raided the office of international news outlet Al-Jazeera and two local broadcasters in Kuala Lumpur as part of its investigation into an Al-Jazeera documentary that included footage of law enforcement raids targeting migrants in Malaysia during the pandemic. Additional state actions criticized by press freedom advocates were the investigation of an editor of an online health news portal who allegedly violated the Official Secrets Act by reporting the findings of an independent inquiry into a hospital fire, and the filing of contempt of court charges against online news outlet Malaysiakini and one of its editors for hosting reader comments that allegedly insulted the judiciary.

Score Change: The score declined from 3 to 2 due to increased government pressure on private media, including law enforcement actions in response to critical coverage and the government's use of the COVID-19 pandemic as a pretext to prevent independent outlets from covering key events.

D2. Are individuals free to practice and express their religious faith or nonbelief in public and private? 1 / 4

While Malaysia is religiously diverse, legal provisions restrict religious freedom. Ethnic Malays are constitutionally defined as Muslim and are not entitled to renounce their faith. The powerful Malaysian Islamic Development Department (JAKIM) has played a central role in shaping and enforcing the practice of Islam in Malaysia, and state-level authorities perform their own enforcement functions. Muslim children and civil servants are required to receive religious education using government-approved curriculums and instructors. Practicing a version of Islam other than Sunni Islam is prohibited, and Shiites and other sects face discrimination. More than 30 people were arrested for practicing Shia Islam in the states of Selangor and Johor during 2019.

Non-Muslims are not able to build houses of worship as easily as Muslims, and the state retains the right to demolish unregistered religious statues and houses of worship. In 2018, a dispute over the relocation of a Hindu temple triggered rioting, with assailants allegedly linked to a property developer storming the temple and beating worshippers.

Strict regulations were established for places of worship during the pandemic, and foreigners were not allowed to attend services.

D3. Is there academic freedom, and is the educational system free from extensive political indoctrination? 2 / 4

There is some degree of academic freedom in Malaysia. Under the BN government, instructors and students who espoused antigovernment views or engaged in political activity were subject to disciplinary action under the Universities and University Colleges Act (UUCA) of 1971. Under the PH government in 2018, Parliament amended the UUCA to allow students to engage in political activity on campus.

The government continues to control appointments of top officials at public universities; in 2018 the PH education minister, Maszlee Malik, organized the replacement of several university chairmen who had been installed by the BN. Maszlee himself was appointed as president of the International Islamic University of Malaysia, but he resigned that post in January 2019 following protests. The PH government was seeking to abolish the UUCA when the government changed hands in 2020, and the PN government announced that the law would remain in force.

D4. Are individuals free to express their personal views on political or other sensitive topics without fear of surveillance or retribution? 3 / 4

The PH government's initial statements and initiatives created a more open environment for public discussion of issues that had previously been considered off limits. However, the government did not fulfill a promise to repeal the Sedition Act, and other restrictive laws, including criminal prohibitions on blasphemy, remained in place, impeding individual expression on sensitive political and religious topics.

In May 2020, the government announced it would pursue legal action against people who disseminate supposed fake news related to COVID-19 under laws including the Sedition Act, the Penal Code, and the CMA; at least 270 such cases had been opened by October.

E. ASSOCIATIONAL AND ORGANIZATIONAL RIGHTS: 6 / 12
E1. Is there freedom of assembly? 2 / 4

Freedom of assembly can be limited on the grounds of maintaining security and public order. In 2019 Parliament amended the 2012 Peaceful Assembly Act, reducing the mandatory police notification period from 10 days to 7 days before the planned event, among other changes. However, the law still imposed criminal penalties for violations, lacked provisions to allow spontaneous assemblies, banned those under age 21 from organizing an assembly, and prohibited participation by minors and noncitizens. While demonstrations are often held in practice, police continue to enforce such restrictions and investigate participants in allegedly illegal protests. In 2020, the government used COVID-19 restrictions to press charges against hospital union activists who picketed alleged mistreatment of hospital workers.

E2. Is there freedom for nongovernmental organizations, particularly those that are engaged in human rights- and governance-related work? 2 / 4

A wide array of nongovernmental organizations (NGOs) operate in Malaysia, and they have a strong record of campaigning for electoral, anticorruption, and other reforms. However, NGOs must be approved and registered by the government, which has refused or revoked registrations for political reasons in the past. Some international human rights organizations have been forbidden from forming local branches. Numerous individual activists remained subject to police harassment and criminal charges—particularly for speech-related offenses—under both the PH and PN governments.

Following the accession of the PN government in March 2020, a number of activists were subjected to criminal investigation under the CMA. In June the government opened an investigation of prominent activist Cynthia Gabriel for a public letter criticizing the manner of the PN coalition's accession to power. Another activist was investigated under the Peaceful Assembly Act for urging citizens to protest against the PN government.

E3. Is there freedom for trade unions and similar professional or labor organizations? 2 / 4

Most Malaysian workers can join trade unions, but the law contravenes international guidelines by restricting unions to representing workers in a single or similar trade. The director general of trade unions can refuse or withdraw registration arbitrarily. Collective bargaining rights are limited, particularly in designated high-priority industries, as is the right to strike.

A new labor law passed in 2019 shifted some discretionary powers from the minister for human resources to the director general of industrial relations and replaced the penalty of imprisonment for illegal strikes with higher fines, among other changes. The Malaysia Trade Union Congress (MTUC) objected to the measure, arguing that its provisions allowing rival unions to compete for sole bargaining rights at a workplace would effectively empower employers and their preferred unions. The ROS suspended the MTUC and threatened it with deregistration over allegations of mismanagement in December 2019; the suspension was lifted in January 2020, and the organization advocated for workers' economic and health rights throughout the year.

F. RULE OF LAW: 7 / 16

F1. Is there an independent judiciary? 2 / 4

Judicial independence has historically been compromised by extensive executive influence, with courts frequently issuing arbitrary or politically motivated verdicts in high-profile cases. However, a series of judicial appointments in 2018 and 2019 improved confidence in the independence of the higher courts and prospects for reform. In May 2019, Datuk Tengku Maimun Tuan Mat became the first woman to hold the chief justice post at the Federal Court, and she continued to emphasize anticorruption and efficiency-enhancing reforms in 2020.

The July 2020 guilty verdict in former prime minister Najib Razak's corruption trial signaled a degree of judicial independence. Conversely, allegations of misconduct by senior judges prompted SUHAKAM to reiterate previous calls for the formation of a royal commission of inquiry during the year.

F2. Does due process prevail in civil and criminal matters? 2 / 4

Several existing laws undermine due process guarantees. The 2012 Security Offences (Special Measures) Act allows police to detain anyone for up to 28 days without judicial review for broadly defined "security offenses," and suspects may be held for 48 hours before being granted access to a lawyer. It was renewed for another five years in 2017. Also that year, lawmakers amended the Prevention of Crime Act—a law ostensibly aimed at combating organized crime—to revoke detainees' right to address the government-appointed Prevention of Crime Board, which is empowered to order the detention of individuals listed by the Home Ministry for renewable two-year terms without trial or legal representation. The 2015 Prevention of Terrorism Act, together with the National Security Council (NSC) Act from the same year, gives the NSC—led by the prime minister—wide powers of arrest, search, and seizure without a warrant in areas deemed as security risks and in the context of countering terrorism. The PH government proposed the formation of an Independent Police Complaints and Misconduct Commission, but in 2020 the PN government introduced a bill that would establish a weaker version with little independent authority.

Malaysia's secular legal system is based on English common law. However, Muslims are subject to Sharia (Islamic law), the interpretation of which varies by state, and the constitution's Article 121 stipulates that all matters related to Islam should be heard in Sharia courts. This results in different treatment of Muslims and non-Muslims in "moral" and family law cases.

F3. Is there protection from the illegitimate use of physical force and freedom from war and insurgencies? 2 / 4

Torture and abuse in police custody remain problems, and prisons are often overcrowded and unsafe. A number of criminal offenses can be punished with caning, including immigration violations.

The death penalty can be applied in Malaysia for numerous offenses; most of the roughly 1,300 people facing execution in Malaysian prisons were convicted under the country's harsh laws on drug trafficking. Despite imposing a moratorium on executions in 2018, the PH government announced in 2019 that it would retain the death penalty but seek to end its mandatory application for certain offenses. Movement toward reform stalled in 2020, as the PN government declined to push legislative changes and refused to publicly release the findings of a death penalty review committee established in 2019.

The Malaysian government initially received credit during the COVID-19 pandemic for pledging not to jail people for violating movement restrictions. However, a policy shift resulted in thousands of individuals being arrested, detained, and prosecuted for alleged breaches of the movement control order, and rights groups characterized the social distancing protocols at jails as insufficient. As of the end of July, over 21,000 people had been arrested and charged in court for violations of movement restrictions.

F4. Do laws, policies, and practices guarantee equal treatment of various segments of the population? 1 / 4

Although the constitution provides for equal treatment of all citizens, it grants a "special position" to ethnic Malays and other indigenous people, known collectively as *bumiputera*. The government maintains programs intended to boost the economic status of bumiputera, who receive preferential treatment in areas including property ownership, higher education, civil service jobs, business affairs, and government contracts.

Women are placed at a disadvantage by a number of laws, particularly Sharia-related provisions. They are legally barred from certain occupations and work schedules, and they suffer from de facto discrimination in employment.

LGBT+ Malaysians face widespread discrimination and harassment. Same-sex sexual relations are punishable by up to 20 years in prison under the penal code, though this is generally not enforced. Some states apply their own penalties to Muslims under Sharia statutes. Transgender people can also be punished under state-level Sharia laws. In November 2019, five men in the state of Selangor were sentenced to fines, up to seven months in prison, and six cane strokes for "attempted" same-sex sexual activity following a police raid on a private event. LGBT+ advocates reported that during the COVID-19 lockdown, law enforcement agents engaged in harassment based on individuals' perceived sexual orientation. In April, a viral social media post claimed that COVID-19 was divine punishment for the rise in LGBT+ people and associated "immoral" acts.

Migrant workers and refugees do not enjoy effective legal protections, and individuals in these communities experienced discrimination during the COVID-19 pandemic. Routine mistreatment of Rohingya asylum seekers and a government crackdown on undocumented migrants in May were harshly criticized by human rights organizations and a group of United Nations experts.

G. PERSONAL AUTONOMY AND INDIVIDUAL RIGHTS: 9 / 16

G1. Do individuals enjoy freedom of movement, including the ability to change their place of residence, employment, or education? 3 / 4

Citizens are generally free to travel within and outside of Malaysia, as well as to change residence and employment. However, professional opportunities and access to higher education are affected by regulations and practices that favor bumiputera and those with connections to political elites. Although the practice is illegal, employers of migrant workers commonly hold their passports, preventing them from leaving abusive situations. The COVID-19 pandemic resulted in a series of movement restrictions of varying intensity throughout 2020, with thousands of arrests for violating the law.

G2. Are individuals able to exercise the right to own property and establish private businesses without undue interference from state or nonstate actors? 3 / 4

Malaysia has a vibrant private sector. Bribery, however, is common in the business world, and the close nexus between political and economic elites distorts normal business activity and fair competition. Some laws pertaining to property and business differentiate between bumiputera and non-bumiputera, and Sharia-based inheritance rules for Muslims often favor men over women.

G3. Do individuals enjoy personal social freedoms, including choice of marriage partner and size of family, protection from domestic violence, and control over appearance? 2 / 4

While some personal social freedoms are protected, Muslims face legal restrictions on marriage partners and other social choices. Societal pressures may also regulate dress and appearance, especially among Malay women. Sharia courts often favor men in matters of divorce and child custody. The minimum age for marriage is generally 16 for girls and 18 for boys, but Sharia courts in some states allow younger people to marry, and child marriage is a common occurrence. Although the PH government attempted to raise the minimum age to 18 for Muslims and non-Muslims of both genders, only one state did so by the end of 2019. Reports of domestic violence increased substantially during the COVID-19 lockdown period.

G4. Do individuals enjoy equality of opportunity and freedom from economic exploitation? 1 / 4

Rural residents and foreign workers, especially those working illegally, are vulnerable to exploitative or abusive working conditions, including forced labor or debt bondage.

Foreign workers make up over a fifth of the country's workforce; about two million are documented, and estimates of the undocumented range from two million to more than four million. The authorities' periodic crackdowns on illegal foreign workers can result in punishment rather than protection for victims of human trafficking. Investigations into forced labor in Malaysia's palm oil industry resulted in several large companies being barred from shipping to the United States in 2020.

In 2020, the government initially offered medical assistance to undocumented migrant workers, but then reversed course and engaged in a series of immigration raids, while blocking migrants and asylum seekers from aid programs.

There have been no convictions of Malaysians for involvement in a network of human trafficking camps along the Thai-Malaysian border since the sites were discovered in 2015. The camps included mass graves holding the bodies of dozens of victims, and corrupt Malaysian officials were thought to have been complicit in the operation.

Maldives

Population: 500,000
Capital: Malé
Freedom Status: Partly Free
Electoral Democracy: No

Overview: An opposition victory in the 2018 presidential election resulted in initial efforts to revise antidemocratic laws and establish transitional justice mechanisms. Despite improvements since the election, many basic freedoms remain restricted, and government-led efforts to reform the justice system remain nascent.

KEY DEVELOPMENTS IN 2020

- Maldives suffered major economic damage from the COVID-19 pandemic, as well as a significant public health toll; according to researchers at the University of Oxford, the country registered over 13,000 cases and 48 deaths during the year.
- Migrant workers were especially affected by restrictions and other policies enacted in light of the pandemic. Dozens of were arrested after violating a ban on protests when they turned out to decry inhumane conditions and nonpayment of wages. According to Human Rights Watch (HRW), thousands were deported during the year, sometimes without being paid wages.
- Corruption remained a major issue. Former vice president Ahmed Adeeb was convicted of corruption in October 2020 and sentenced to 20 years' imprisonment, while procurement processes related to COVID-19 were the subject of graft investigations throughout much of the year.

POLITICAL RIGHTS: 19 / 40 (+1)
A. ELECTORAL PROCESS: 7 / 12
A1. Was the current head of government or other chief national authority elected through free and fair elections? 2 / 4

The president is directly elected for up to two five-year terms. The run-up to the September 2018 election was marred by the misuse of state resources on behalf of incumbent president Abdulla Yameen of the Progressive Party of Maldives (PPM), police interference with opposition campaign efforts, and various forms of manipulation by electoral officials. The Maldivian Democratic Party (MDP) and other opposition groups endorsed Ibrahim Mohamed Solih, an MDP lawmaker, after former president Mohamed Nasheed was disqualified over a dubious 2015 terrorism conviction. Despite the impediments to his campaign, Solih won the election with over 58 percent of the vote amid high turnout, leaving Yameen with less than 42 percent. The current government coalition includes the MDP, the Jumhooree Party (JP) led by Qasim Ibrahim, the Maldives Reform Movement (MRM) led by former president Maumoon Abdul Gayoom, and the religiously conservative Adhaalath Party.

A2. Were the current national legislative representatives elected through free and fair elections? 3 / 4

The unicameral People's Majlis is composed of 85 seats, with members elected from individual districts to serve five-year terms. Elections held in April 2019 were largely transparent and competitive, with Commonwealth observers reporting that vote buying—while still a problem—appeared less prevalent than in previous elections. The MDP captured 65 seats, with Nasheed winning a seat representing a district in Malé. The PPM suffered a sharp decline, winning only five seats. The JP also won five seats, the Maldives Development Alliance won two, and independents took an additional seven. Nasheed was elected speaker. In 2020, the chamber continued its sessions online during the national lockdown prompted by the COVID-19 pandemic.

A3. Are the electoral laws and framework fair, and are they implemented impartially by the relevant election management bodies? 2 / 4

The independence of the Elections Commission, whose members are appointed by the president with approval from the parliament, has been seriously compromised in recent years, with key decisions favoring the PPM. In the run-up to the 2018 presidential election, its officials were accused of tampering with the voter reregistration process and arbitrarily changing vote-counting procedures, among other controversial actions.

The Elections Commission was credited with an improved and more impartial performance in its administration of the 2019 parliamentary elections—earning praise from Commonwealth observers—and in its preparations for 2020 local council elections.

The local council elections initially set for April 2020 were delayed due to the COVID-19 pandemic, with the terms of current local government officials extended via a constitutional amendment, and legal complications addressed in a bill passed in May.

B. POLITICAL PLURALISM AND PARTICIPATION: 8 / 16 (+1)

B1. Do the people have the right to organize in different political parties or other competitive political groupings of their choice, and is the system free of undue obstacles to the rise and fall of these competing parties or groupings? 3 / 4

Political pluralism and participation deteriorated during Yameen's presidency, as authorities subjected opposition leaders and their supporters to judicial harassment. Restrictions on and dispersals of political rallies, raids on opposition offices, and arbitrary detentions and convictions of opposition politicians were common for most of 2018, but virtually no such abuses have been reported since that year's presidential election.

Yameen was arrested on money-laundering charges in February 2019, but was released from detention the following month, and the PPM and its allies were able to compete in the April parliamentary elections. Former authoritarian president Maumoon Abdul Gayoom aligned himself with the opposition under Yameen, and in November 2019, the MRM was able to officially register as a party.

B2. Is there a realistic opportunity for the opposition to increase its support or gain power through elections? 2 / 4

The country has rarely experienced transfers of power between rival parties through elections. Under Yameen, the government and the PPM used the politicized justice system and the security forces to undermine the competitiveness of the opposition and maintain control of the legislature. The opposition secured victory in the 2018 presidential election only due to deep public dissatisfaction with Yameen's rule and a reported turnout of nearly 90 percent, overcoming wide-ranging efforts by Yameen and his allies to subvert the election and rig the outcome. The MDP's victory in the 2019 parliamentary elections completed its latest progression from opposition to ruling party, though its coalition had secured a de facto legislative majority by late 2018.

B3. Are the people's political choices free from domination by forces that are external to the political sphere, or by political forces that employ extrapolitical means? 2 / 4 (+1)

The Yameen government exerted improper influence over a number of state institutions to restrict the political choices of voters and politicians. In addition to using security forces, the Elections Commission, and the justice system to suppress dissent, Yameen's allies reportedly threatened public and private sector employees with dismissal for participating in opposition protests or other political activities. Such workers were also forced to attend progovernment events. While such abuses have waned under Solih, intimidation by hard-line Islamist groups continues to affect the political system. Vote buying remains a problem during elections, and allegations of bribery and corruption have surrounded instances of party switching in recent years.

Score Change: The score improved from 1 to 2 due to a reduction in the use of security forces to exert political and electoral control since the end of the Yameen administration.

B4. Do various segments of the population (including ethnic, racial, religious, gender, LGBT+, and other relevant groups) have full political rights and electoral opportunities? 1 / 4

The constitution and laws require all citizens to be Muslims and all candidates for elected office to be followers of Sunni Islam, explicitly excluding adherents of minority religions. High-level positions in state institutions or independent bodies, including the Human Rights Commission of the Maldives, also require individuals to be a Sunni Muslim Maldivian. Societal discrimination against women has limited their political participation; four women won seats in the parliament in 2019, down from five in 2014. LGBT+ people are unable to openly take part in political affairs, given the criminalization of same-sex intimacy and the prevalence of societal bias. Foreign workers, who make up between a quarter and a third of the population, have no political rights.

C. FUNCTIONING OF GOVERNMENT: 4 / 12

C1. Do the freely elected head of government and national legislative representatives determine the policies of the government? 2 / 4

Elected officials generally determine and implement government policies, but the functioning of the parliament was seriously impaired from mid-2017 to late 2018 by then president Yameen's heavy-handed attempts to retain control in the face of defections to the opposition, including detentions of lawmakers and deployments of security forces in and around the chamber. The situation improved dramatically after the change in administration, and the parliament was able to operate without similar obstructions during 2019 and 2020.

C2. Are safeguards against official corruption strong and effective? 1 / 4

Corruption remains endemic at all levels of government. The Anti-Corruption Commission has been only moderately effective, often launching investigations and taking other actions in response to public complaints, but rarely holding powerful figures to account for abuses. Whistleblowers and journalists reporting on corruption have been jailed or forced into exile in the face of political persecution.

The new government took a number of initial steps intended to combat corruption. An anonymous whistleblower web portal was launched in February 2019, and President Solih signed a bill providing legal protections for whistleblowers into law that October. In November 2019, former president Yameen was convicted of money laundering, sentenced to five years in prison, and ordered to pay a $5 million fine; the case centered on $1 million in government fees that had been diverted to a personal bank account. Yameen appealed, and in October 2020, the Supreme Court ruled that his accounts were frozen unlawfully; the appeal of his criminal conviction remained ongoing at year's end. Former vice president Ahmed Adeeb pleaded guilty to corruption charges in September 2020 and was sentenced to 20 years' imprisonment in October, though he was transferred to house arrest due to health concerns.

According to the Anti-Corruption Commission (ACC), the state response to the COVID-19 pandemic had prompted 34 corruption complaints as of December 2020. The most prominent case involved allegations of corruption in the purchase of ventilators by the Health Ministry, which resulted in the resignation of the minister of health in October. The case was exposed by the Auditor General in August 2020; prosecutors declined to press charges in October, but ACC inquiries continued and parliament voted to pursue charges in December.

C3. Does the government operate with openness and transparency? 1 / 4

Large state contracts for infrastructure and other projects have regularly been awarded through opaque processes, in which bribery and kickbacks are widely believed to play a role. The Solih administration did not immediately revise antidemocratic changes made to public finance rules by the previous government.

The president, cabinet ministers, and members of parliament are required by the constitution to submit annual asset declarations, but it is not required that these be made public, and the relevant agencies have resisted disclosing how many officials comply with the rule. In 2019 Solih and members of his cabinet publicly disclosed their personal finances, but the Maldives branch of Transparency International called the disclosures "incomplete"; seven of the ministers declared that they had no assets, and some of the other disclosures appeared dubious or contradictory.

CIVIL LIBERTIES: 21 / 60 (−1)
D. FREEDOM OF EXPRESSION AND BELIEF: 3 / 16
D1. Are there free and independent media? 1 / 4

The constitution guarantees freedom of expression so long as it is exercised in a manner that is "not contrary to any tenet of Islam," a vague condition that encourages self-censorship in the media. State-run media and regulatory bodies, especially the Maldives Broadcasting Commission (MBC), have typically displayed bias in favor of the government and restricted coverage of the opposition.

Journalists continue to face the threat of violence in reprisal for their work, particularly by Islamist militants. The Presidential Commission on Investigation of Murders and Enforced Disappearances, established in November 2018 by President Solih, confirmed in

September 2019 that journalist Ahmed Rilwan, who disappeared in 2014, had been abducted and murdered by a local affiliate of the terrorist group Al-Qaeda. A trial of suspects in the 2017 murder of liberal blogger Yameen Rasheed has experienced repeated delays, and made little progress in 2020. The presidential commission reportedly found evidence that officials under the previous administration had interfered with the police investigations in both cases. In August 2020, the commission stated it was seeking international expertise in the Rilwan case, and a foreign expert reportedly arrived in November.

D2. Are individuals free to practice and express their religious faith or nonbelief in public and private? 0 / 4

Freedom of religion is severely restricted. Islam is the state religion, and all citizens are required to be Muslims. Imams must use government-approved sermons. Non-Muslim foreigners are allowed to observe their religions only in private. In recent years, growing religious extremism, stoked in part by the Yameen administration, has led to an increase in threatening rhetoric and physical attacks against those perceived to be insulting or rejecting Islam. Secularist writers and defenders of freedom of conscience have faced pressure from the authorities as well as death threats. Mohamed Rusthum Mujuthaba, who was arrested on blasphemy allegations in September 2019 over social media comments, remained imprisoned throughout 2020.

D3. Is there academic freedom, and is the educational system free from extensive political indoctrination? 1 / 4

Islam is a compulsory subject in schools and is incorporated into all other subject areas. School and university curriculums have come under increased influence from hard-line religious leaders, resulting in some content that denigrates democracy and promotes jihadist narratives. Academics and teachers who express views deemed objectionable by state and nonstate actors risk punishment or reprisals. In 2019, a college was vandalized and its chairman was threatened after he criticized supporters of a death sentence against a woman accused of extramarital sex.

D4. Are individuals free to express their personal views on political or other sensitive topics without fear of surveillance or retribution? 1 / 4

Although the Solih administration was expected to be more tolerant of public criticism than its predecessor, individuals who speak out on behalf of minority groups or basic freedoms are still at significant risk of attack from violent nonstate actors. Local human rights groups have had to relocate several social media users who received death threats for exercising their freedom of expression. In June 2020 a public sector employee was reportedly fired for social media posts that allegedly defamed President Solih and Majlis Speaker Nasheed.

E. ASSOCIATIONAL AND ORGANIZATIONAL RIGHTS: 5 / 12 (−1)
E1. Is there freedom of assembly? 2 / 4 (−1)

Respect for freedom of assembly is uneven. A 2016 law requires protest organizers to obtain police permission for their events and restricts demonstrations to certain designated areas. Assemblies were banned during a 2018 state of emergency but allowed in the run-up to the September 2018 presidential election after authorities faced growing international pressure. In 2019, opposition supporters and hard-line Islamists were able to hold protests related to Yameen's money-laundering case and demands that the government shut down the MDN for supposedly insulting Islam.

In July 2020, the Solih government, citing the need to address the COVID-19 pandemic, violated a campaign pledge by applying the 2016 law to limit protests. Migrant workers decrying inhumane conditions and nonpayment of wages were especially affected by the tightened restrictions; dozens of protesting migrants were detained.

Score Change: The score declined from 3 to 2 because the government resumed enforcement of a restrictive law on demonstrations and responded to protests by migrant workers with arrests and detentions.

E2. Is there freedom for nongovernmental organizations, particularly those that are engaged in human rights– and governance-related work? 1 / 4

Nongovernmental organizations (NGOs) operate in a restrictive environment. They are required to obtain government approval before seeking domestic or foreign funding, and regulators have broad discretion to investigate and dissolve NGOs. The Human Rights Commission of Maldives is not independent in practice. In recent years, Maldivian human rights groups have increasingly become targets of surveillance, harassment, threats of violence, and blasphemy allegations, including from extremist nonstate actors.

In October 2019, Islamist groups denounced the MDN as "anti-Islamic" after content from its 2015 report on radicalization and violent extremism circulated on social media, and the government suspended the NGO's activities that month. That November, the NGO Registrar under the Ministry of Youth, Sports, and Community Empowerment decided to dissolve the MDN, and the dissolution took effect in December. A criminal blasphemy investigation against the authors of the 2015 report remained ongoing in 2020, and donor funds in MDN bank accounts were arbitrarily frozen in December 2019 and January 2020.

Starting in June 2020, Islamist extremist groups targeted women's rights NGO Uthema with a campaign of social media harassment for producing an allegedly anti-Islamic report on Maldives' compliance with the United Nations Convention on the Elimination of All Forms of Discrimination against Women.

E3. Is there freedom for trade unions and similar professional or labor organizations? 2 / 4

The constitution and labor laws allow workers to form trade unions, and a number of unions are active. However, collective bargaining is not protected, and strikes are prohibited in many sectors, including the crucial tourism industry.

F. RULE OF LAW: 6 / 16

F1. Is there an independent judiciary? 1 / 4

Judicial independence is seriously compromised. Many judges are unqualified, and the courts are widely considered vulnerable to corruption or political influence. The Supreme Court has repeatedly intervened in political affairs and apparently exceeded its constitutional authority, typically acting according to political interests.

In February 2018, acting under Yameen's state of emergency, the military raided the Supreme Court and arrested two of its justices, including the chief justice, in response to court decisions favoring jailed opposition leaders and lawmakers who had been arbitrarily expelled. The three justices remaining on the Supreme Court after the raid subsequently reversed those decisions. That March, parliament passed legislation—in conflict with the constitution—specifying the removal of judges upon Supreme Court confirmation of criminal convictions. In May and June 2018, the detained Supreme Court justices received prison terms for "obstruction of justice" and other offenses; after their appeals were denied, they were formally removed. Following the change in government, the jailed former justices and other wrongfully arrested officials were released to house arrest. By October 2019, both former justices were free after completing their sentences or having them overturned, though they were not reinstated.

The new government used its parliamentary majority to reshape the Supreme Court, but without the extreme and extraconstitutional tactics used by the previous administration. The parliament, acting on the recommendations of the Judicial Service Commission, voted to remove one justice for corruption in August 2019 and two more—including the chief justice—for a litany of violations that November. Separately, the government followed through on the appointment of the first two female justices to the Supreme Court in September despite Islamist objections to the nominations. In September 2020, a female judge was appointed to the Criminal Court bench for the first time in the country's history.

F2. Does due process prevail in civil and criminal matters? 1 / 4

Police have regularly engaged in arbitrary arrests in recent years, often to disrupt opposition activities, protests, or the work of journalists. Due process rights are not well enforced in practice, and under Yameen, opposition figures were subjected to deeply flawed trials on politically motivated charges, according to human rights groups and international monitors. The new government has yet to undertake comprehensive reforms of the criminal justice system.

F3. Is there protection from the illegitimate use of physical force and freedom from war and insurgencies? 2 / 4

The constitution and the Anti-Torture Act ban torture, but police brutality and the abuse of detainees and prison inmates remain problems, and impunity remains the norm. Flogging and other forms of corporal punishment are authorized for some crimes, and flogging sentences are issued in practice for offenses such as extramarital sex. Prisons are overcrowded, inmates reportedly lack proper access to medical care, and human rights groups have reported numerous unexplained deaths in custody.

In December 2020, President Solih signed into law a bill establishing a transitional justice mechanism to investigate and redress human rights abuses from 1953–2018. The bill had been revised in response to concerns by the United Nations and local human rights groups that the draft version proposed in 2019 was overly narrow in scope.

F4. Do laws, policies, and practices guarantee equal treatment of various segments of the population? 2 / 4

Gender-based discrimination in employment is prohibited by law, but women continue to face discrimination in practice. Girls and women from underprivileged backgrounds are disproportionately affected by Sharia (Islamic law) penalties for crimes like fornication and adultery.

Migrant workers—who account for approximately one-third of the population—encounter disparate treatment by state authorities and have difficulty accessing justice. In 2020, thousands of migrant workers with unclear immigration status were arbitrarily deported during the COVID-19 pandemic.

Same-sex sexual acts and marriage are prohibited by law and can draw prison sentences, corporal punishment, and even threats of citizenship revocation. As a result, LGBT+ people rarely report societal discrimination or abuse. In June 2020, a man from Makunudhoo island was arrested following allegations of same-sex relations.

G. PERSONAL AUTONOMY AND INDIVIDUAL RIGHTS: 7 / 16

G1. Do individuals enjoy freedom of movement, including the ability to change their place of residence, employment, or education? 2 / 4

Freedom of movement is provided for by law, but there are some restrictions in practice. Authorities have at times imposed travel bans on members of opposition parties and other perceived government opponents. Migrant workers are also subject to constraints on their movement, including through retention of their passports by employers.

G2. Are individuals able to exercise the right to own property and establish private businesses without undue interference from state or nonstate actors? 2 / 4

Property rights are limited, with most land owned by the government and leased to private entities or commercial developers through what is often an opaque process. Residents sometimes face displacement by development projects without adequate consultation or compensation.

G3. Do individuals enjoy personal social freedoms, including choice of marriage partner and size of family, protection from domestic violence, and control over appearance? 1 / 4

Personal social freedoms are restricted by Sharia-based laws and growing religious extremism in society. Among other rules on marriage and divorce, citizen women are barred from marrying non-Muslim foreigners, while citizen men can marry non-Muslim foreigners only if they are Christian or Jewish. Extramarital sex is criminalized, and there is a high legal threshold to prove rape allegations. Women face increasing pressure to dress more conservatively, in keeping with hard-line interpretations of Islam. Violence against women is rarely investigated and punished, although sexual assault charges were filed in November against Ali Waheed, who had served as minister of tourism until numerous assault allegations led to his firing in July.

G4. Do individuals enjoy equality of opportunity and freedom from economic exploitation? 2 / 4

The legal framework provides some protections against worker exploitation, including rules on working hours and bans on forced labor. However, migrant workers are especially vulnerable to abuses such as debt bondage and withholding of wages, a problem that was exacerbated during the economic contraction caused by the COVID-19 pandemic and resulting collapse of tourism. Women and children working in domestic service may also be subject to exploitative conditions.

Mali

Population: 20,300,000
Capital: Bamako
Freedom Status: Not Free
Electoral Democracy: No

Status Change: Mali's status declined from Partly Free to Not Free due to legislative elections that were marred by political violence and a subsequent military coup that removed the country's elected civilian leadership.

Overview: Mali experienced a political transition away from authoritarian rule beginning in the early 1990s, and gradually built up its democratic institutions for about 20 years. However, the country displayed characteristics of state fragility along the way that eventually contributed to a 2012 military coup, and a rebellion in northern Mali that erupted the same year. Though constitutional rule was restored and a peace agreement signed in the north in 2015, the events have left an enduring situation of insecurity and political tensions that culminated in another coup in 2020.

KEY DEVELOPMENTS IN 2020

- The government of President Ibrahim Boubacar Keïta, which was weakened by a March and April parliamentary contest marred by violence and low turnout, was overthrown in a coup d'état in August. The military government, which named a new president and prime minister in September and named members of an unelected transitional legislature in December, remained in power at year's end.
- Before the civilian administration was overthrown, Malians held major antigovernment protests between June and August. Security forces killed at least 14 protesters over a three-day period in Bamako in July, which sparked continued protests against the Keïta government.
- Malian authorities initiated a COVID-19-related lockdown in March, but notably allowed that month's parliamentary contests to go ahead. The military government declared a COVID-19-related state of emergency in December, citing a rise in cases; the World Health Organization reported 7,029 COVID-19 cases and 269 deaths at the end of the year.

POLITICAL RIGHTS: 9 / 40 (−8)

A. ELECTORAL PROCESS: 2 / 12 (−3)

A1. Was the current head of government or other chief national authority elected through free and fair elections? 0 / 4 (−2)

The president, who is chief of state, is normally elected by popular vote and may serve up to two five-year terms. In a two-round presidential election in 2018, incumbent president Ibrahim Boubacar Keïta took 67 percent of the vote; he defeated the late Soumaïla Cissé, a former finance minister, who took 33 percent. International election observers said the polling was relatively well conducted.

Keïta's hold on the presidency weakened after the flawed March and April 2020 parliamentary elections, the March kidnapping of Soumaïla Cissé, and a violent response to protests ended with at least 14 fatalities over three days in July. In August, a group of military personnel known as the National Committee for the Salvation of the People (CNSP) launched a coup d'état, abducted Keïta, and compelled him to resign. In September, the CNSP selected Bah N'Daou, a former military officer and Keïta-era defense minister, as acting president. Colonel Assimi Goïta, the CNSP's leader, was made vice president.

The prime minister is head of government, and is appointed by the president. Boubou Cissé was appointed in April 2019, but was removed by the CNSP in August 2020. Former foreign minister Moctar Ouane was named prime minister by N'Daou in September.

Score Change: The score declined from 2 to 0 because the elected president and prime minister were overthrown in a coup d'état.

A2. Were the current national legislative representatives elected through free and fair elections? 0 / 4 (−1)

Members of the 147-seat unicameral National Assembly normally serve five-year terms. Thirteen seats were reserved to represent Malians living abroad. Keïta's Rally for Mali (RPM) party won 66 seats in legislative elections held in 2013, and its allies took an additional 49 seats. Soumaïla Cissé's Union for the Republic and Democracy (URD) won 17, and the third-largest party, the Alliance for Democracy (ADEMA), won 16.

A two-round parliamentary contest was held in March and April 2020, but the contest was marred by violence, low turnout, and disagreement over the results. Opposition leader Soumaïla Cissé was kidnapped days before the first round and was not released until October. Voters, especially in the north and center of Mali, were subjected to intimidation, while observers reported vote-buying incidents. COVID-19 restrictions, which were introduced in March, also impacted the poll. A group of civil society observers reported a first-round turnout figure of 7.5 percent.

The National Assembly was dissolved by Keïta in August after he was detained by the CNSP along with then prime minister Cissé and other officials. The coup d'état was condemned by regional and international actors including the Economic Community of West African States (ECOWAS), which called on the CNSP to appoint civilian transitional leaders and commit to the reintroduction of civilian rule.

A 121-member National Transitional Council (CNT) was formed in December, with CNSP member Colonel Malick Diaw named as its president. Security forces control 22 seats, while political parties and organizations hold 11. The June 5th Movement—Rally of Patriotic Forces (M5-RFP), an alliance of opposition parties and civil society groups, separately holds 8 seats.

Score Change: The score declined from 1 to 0 because an elected parliament was replaced by an unelected transitional body as the result of a coup d'état.

A3. Are the electoral laws and framework fair, and are they implemented impartially by the relevant election management bodies? 2 / 4

Electoral operations are normally divided among three administrative bodies in Mali—the Ministry of Territorial Administration and Decentralization, the Independent National Electoral Commission, and the General Office of Elections. The Constitutional Court also participates in the electoral process by validating election results and resolving disputes.

The Constitutional Court overturned the results for 31 parliamentary seats in late April 2020, increasing the RPM's representation by 10 seats in the interim. Protests over the court's decision were held that same month. Keïta dismissed several Constitutional Court judges in July, following a ECOWAS proposal to resolve the political impasse, and offered to organize a rerun of the invalidated contests. New judges were appointed in early August, though the news that a Keïta ally was involved in their selection was met with criticism.

B. POLITICAL PLURALISM AND PARTICIPATION: 5 / 16 (−3)

B1. Do the people have the right to organize in different political parties or other competitive political groupings of their choice, and is the system free of undue obstacles to the rise and fall of these competing parties or groupings? 2 / 4

The creation and the functioning of political parties are determined by a legal framework known as the Political Parties Charter, which is generally fair. The Charter prohibits the creation of political parties on an "ethnic, religious, linguistic, regionalist, sexist, or professional basis."

There are more than 100 registered political parties in Mali, though fewer than 20 are active. Parties are relatively weak, and are usually based around support for a particular personality, and policy differences between parties are not always clear. Parties are often poorly funded, which hampers their ability to effectively organize and win voter support.

B2. Is there a realistic opportunity for the opposition to increase its support or gain power through elections? 1 / 4 (−1)

Electoral competition is normally open to opposition forces. A 2014 law institutionalized specific privileges for opposition parties in the parliament, such as the ability to choose an official leader of the opposition. However, in 2016 the ruling majority passed, over the objections of opposition parties, amendments to the electoral code that favored establishment and majority parties by requiring candidates to make a significant financial campaign deposit, and to receive support from national councilors.

Opposition figures faced violent attack during the March and April 2020 parliamentary elections. Late URD leader Soumaïla Cissé and members of his entourage were kidnapped while traveling through the town of Niafunké, and one bodyguard was killed. Several people were freed a day later, and Cissé himself was freed in October after the military government agreed to release 200 individuals suspected of militant activity. (Cissé died of COVID-19 in December.)

Score Change: The score declined from 2 to 1 because opposition leaders and candidates faced physical violence and intimidation during the March and April parliamentary elections, limiting their ability to fully participate in the contest.

B3. Are the people's political choices free from domination by forces that are external to the political sphere, or by political forces that employ extrapolitical means? 0 / 4 (−2)

Before the August 2020 coup d'état, political choices were the privilege of the Malian people, though these choices were occasionally influenced by the promise of patronage appointments or other benefits in exchange for political support. The military government that took power has since appointed key officials, including the acting president, vice president, and prime minister. The same military government initially sought to govern Mali for three years, though it subsequently agreed to hold new elections within 18 months.

Score Change: The score declined from 2 to 0 because a military-led transitional government superseded the ability of voters to make meaningful political choices.

B4. Do various segments of the population (including ethnic, racial, religious, gender, LGBT+, and other relevant groups) have full political rights and electoral opportunities? 2 / 4

No law limits the political rights of minorities, and no single ethnic group dominates the government or security forces. Tuareg pastoralist groups in the north have historically occupied a marginal position in national political life.

Societal attitudes can discourage women from participating in political processes. In the country's 2018 presidential election, Djeneba N'Diaye was the sole female candidate. While a 2015 gender quota bill mandates that 30 percent of elected and appointed positions are to be filled by women, the military government named only four women to a 25-member cabinet in October 2020, and 27 percent of the CNT's seats are held by women.

C. FUNCTIONING OF GOVERNMENT: 2 / 12 (−2)
C1. Do the freely elected head of government and national legislative representatives determine the policies of the government? 0 / 4 (−2)

President Keïta was elected in a generally credible poll in 2018, while the National Assembly elected in 2013 was also freely elected. That parliament remained in place beyond the end of its mandate, however, with elections held in March and April 2020. The August coup d'état replaced an elected national government with a military one, which remained in power at year's end.

The volatile security situation in northern and central Mali has limited government activity there.

Score Change: The score declined from 2 to 0 because an elected government was overthrown during the year and was therefore unable to determine policy.

C2. Are safeguards against official corruption strong and effective? 1 / 4

Corruption remains a problem in government, notably in public procurement. Bribery and embezzlement of public funds is common and impunity for corrupt officials is the norm. The Office of the Auditor General is an independent office responsible for analyzing public spending, but despite identifying sizable embezzlement cases, very few prosecutions have been made. Its 2018 annual report, submitted to Keïta in July 2019, highlighted significant financial irregularities. The arrest of the mayor of Bamako that October as part of a corruption investigation, as well as the detention of other state officials, may have reflected a new resolve on the part of the civilian government to tackle corruption. After the August 2020 coup d'état, the CNSP launched a crackdown on apparent abuses by government officials, but took little action to fight corruption within the military.

C3. Does the government operate with openness and transparency? 1 / 4

Government operations remain generally opaque. Mali does not have a comprehensive freedom of information regime, although numerous laws do provide for public access to some official documents and information. However, such laws are replete with extensive and vague exceptions, and journalists have faced obstacles when attempting to obtain information, particularly about military expenditure.

In February 2020, the civilian government joined the Global Forum on Transparency and Exchange of Information for Tax Purposes, a working group backed by the Organization for Economic Co-operation and Development to fight tax evasion and improve transparency.

CIVIL LIBERTIES: 24 / 60
D. FREEDOM OF EXPRESSION AND BELIEF: 10 / 16
D1. Are there free and independent media? 2 / 4

The media environment in Bamako and in the rest of the south is relatively open, though there are sporadic reports of censorship, self-censorship, and threats against journalists. Reporting on the situation in the north remains dangerous due to the presence of active militant groups. Defamation is a crime that can draw fines or prison time.

Journalists and media outlets covering antigovernment protests faced detention, transmission disruptions, and acts of vandalism in July 2020. Protesters occupied the headquarters of public broadcaster Office de Radio-Télévision du Mali (ORTM), which briefly went off the air, and stole equipment during the demonstrations. A Liberté TV journalist was arrested by police while filing a report on the protests that month, though she was released a day later. Social media services were disrupted for several days in July.

Press freedom was restricted after the August 2020 coup d'état. Sud FM correspondent Sory Ibra Maiga was forced to leave a September press conference after asking about the deployment of law enforcement agents to secure a transitional government meeting. Later that month, journalist Ibrahim Adiawiakoye was arrested after publishing an article commenting on former youth minister Harouna Touré's ties to the CNSP. Adiawiakoye was released a day later after Touré withdrew a defamation complaint. Journalists Adama Diarra and Seydou Oumar Traoré were detained in October and November, respectively, after they were accused of criminally defaming members of the judiciary.

D2. Are individuals free to practice and express their religious faith or nonbelief in public and private? 2 / 4

Freedom of religion is constitutionally guaranteed in Mali, which is a secular state, and discrimination of the basis of religion is prohibited. The population is predominantly Sunni Muslim, and Sufism plays a role in the beliefs of most residents.

The 2012 Islamist uprising shattered the image of Mali as a religiously tolerant country. Armed extremist groups have terrorized northern and central Mali, and have attacked those whom they perceive as failing to follow their strict interpretation of Islam. They have occasionally carried out targeted kidnappings of Christians and subjected them to sometimes violent harassment. In 2017, several Christian churches in central Mali were attacked by alleged Islamist gunmen.

D3. Is there academic freedom, and is the educational system free from extensive political indoctrination? 3 / 4

Academic freedom is upheld in areas with a consolidated government presence but restricted in areas with a heavy militant presence.

D4. Are individuals free to express their personal views on political or other sensitive topics without fear of surveillance or retribution? 3 / 4

Private discussion is generally open and free in areas under government control but is more restricted in areas with a militant presence or where intercommunal violence has flared.

E. ASSOCIATIONAL AND ORGANIZATIONAL RIGHTS: 6 / 12

E1. Is there freedom of assembly? 2 / 4

The constitution guarantees freedom of assembly, but participants in public gatherings risk violence by state security forces, and the government has occasionally restricted social media use to prevent activists from organizing protests.

Protesters rallied against the late April 2020 Constitutional Court decision to overturn the election results in 31 parliamentary seats that month, and regular antigovernment protests were held beginning in early June, days after the M5-RFP's formation was announced. Protests grew violent during a three-day period in July, with some participants engaging in looting. The authorities responded with force, resulting in at least 14 deaths in Bamako over three days. Several high-ranking M5-RFP members were also detained in July, but were released several days later.

Despite the violence, protests largely continued through August; security forces forcibly dispersed another rally in Bamako that month, using tear gas and water cannons to clear a city square. On August 17th, opposition groups vowed to launch daily protests, but President Keïta and Prime Minister Cissé were detained by the CNSP the next day.

E2. Is there freedom for nongovernmental organizations, particularly those that are engaged in human rights- and governance-related work? 2 / 4

Many nongovernmental organizations (NGOs) operate in Mali without state interference. However, large, established NGOs with ties to the political elite are influential, and can overshadow smaller and more innovative groups, particularly in the competition for funding. Ongoing insecurity in some parts of the country hampers NGO efforts to provide aid and services to returning refugees and others affected by instability. A European Commission report issued in October 2020 counted 150 incidents affecting humanitarian NGOs in the first eight months of the year.

E3. Is there freedom for trade unions and similar professional or labor organizations? 2 / 4

The constitution guarantees workers the right to form unions and to strike, with some limitations for essential services workers, and requirements involving compulsory arbitration. The government has broad discretionary power over the registration of unions and recognition of collective bargaining, and the authorities do not effectively enforce laws against antiunion discrimination.

The National Union of Workers of Mali (UNTM) held two strikes in November and December 2020 over pay disagreements. The UNTM and military government held negotiations on the matter in December, though the UNTM briefly suspended its participation after President N'Daou harshly criticized the strike in a speech.

F. RULE OF LAW: 4 / 16

F1. Is there an independent judiciary? 2 / 4

Judges are appointed by the president, while the minister of justice supervises both law enforcement and judicial functions. The judiciary is beholden to the executive, despite constitutional guarantees of judicial independence. Additionally, the overall efficiency of the judicial system remains low.

In July 2020, Keïta announced the removal of Constitutional Court judges as part of an effort to resolve the country's political impasse. In August, nine judges were appointed to the court; three were named by Keïta, three by National Assembly president Moussa Timbine, and three by a judicial council. The appointments were met with criticism due to the involvement of a Keïta ally in the judges' installation.

Militant attacks against judicial personnel have prompted some judges to vacate their posts. In 2017, judge Soungalo Koné was kidnapped in central Mali by armed men who asked for the release of detained militants in exchange for his freedom. In February 2019, the magistrates' union announced that he had died the previous month, still in captivity, from an illness.

F2. Does due process prevail in civil and criminal matters? 1 / 4

Due process rights are inconsistently upheld. Detainees are not always charged within the 48-hour period set by law, and arbitrary arrests are common. Since a deadly 2015 hotel attack in Bamako, a national state of emergency remained in force for several years, and was last extended in October 2019. The emergency designation gave security services greater authority to search homes without a warrant, detain suspects, and restrict protests. The military government suspended that state of emergency after taking power in August 2020, though a COVID-19-related state of emergency was declared in late December.

Detainees face extended pretrial detention periods. The trial of Amadou Sanogo, who staged a coup d'état in 2012 and was accused of killing 21 soldiers who sought to oppose him that year, began in 2016 but was quickly adjourned. Sanogo was not bailed until late January 2020, though his release was criticized by human rights groups; the case against him remained pending at year's end.

Due process rights were not consistently upheld for high-ranking officials detained by the military in the August 2020 coup d'état. Former prime minister Sissé, former National Assembly president Timbine, and eight generals who were detained were released in October, but were warned that they "remain at the disposition of the courts."

The Truth, Justice and Reconciliation Commission created in 2014 is responsible for investigating human rights violations committed since 1960, but its activities are restricted by the rise of terrorist activities and intercommunal tensions within Mali's borders.

F3. Is there protection from the illegitimate use of physical force and freedom from war and insurgencies? 0 / 4

Islamist militant groups not party to a 2015 peace agreement continued to carry out acts of violence against civilians in the northern and central regions. Ongoing instability has contributed to the spread of organized crime and accompanying violence and kidnappings. Late opposition leader Soumaïla Cissé, who was abducted in March 2020, was released by the Support Group for Islam and Muslims (GSIM), a militant group with reported links to al-Qaeda, in October. In return for the release of Cissé, French aid worker Sophie Pétronin, and two Italian hostages, the GSIM secured the release of 200 individuals.

Several violent attacks occurred during 2020. In October, 13 soldiers and 12 civilians were killed in a terrorist attack in the central region of Mopti. Several days later, one UN peacekeeper was killed and another was injured in separate attacks. That same month, at least 20 people from the central village of Farabougou were abducted by suspected Islamist militants, and the town was effectively blockaded. A search party looking for the abducted residents came under fire days later; six people were killed and 22 were injured in that incident. The military liberated Farabougou in late October, though access to the village remained limited at year's end. In November, unidentified assailants killed an imam in the town of Débougou.

Malian military personnel have been known to engage in human rights violations, and have been accused of committing summary executions. In June 2020, the UN Multidimensional Integrated Stabilization Mission in Mali reported that Malian forces were responsible for 119 extrajudicial killings, 32 forced disappearances, and 116 arbitrary arrests, many of them in the regions of Mopti and Ségou, in the first three months of the year.

Prisons are characterized by overcrowding, insufficient medical care, and a lack of proper food and sanitation. The COVID-19 pandemic also affected prisons, with the authorities releasing or pardoning over 1,600 prisoners to reduce the spread of the virus in 2020.

F4. Do laws, policies, and practices guarantee equal treatment of various segments of the population? 1 / 4

Members of a northern caste known as black Tamasheqs face societal discrimination, including slavery-like treatment and hereditary servitude. Authorities sometimes deny them official documents or discriminate against them in housing, schooling, and police protection.

Arabs and Tuaregs also face discrimination. In October 2020, Arab and Tuareg merchants in the city of Timbuktu rallied against attacks on their businesses, with participants saying they commonly faced blame for criminal and jihadist activity in the region.

Same-sex sexual acts are legal, but LGBT+ people face discrimination, including cases of violence from family members meant as a corrective punishment.

Although equal rights are provided for in the constitution, the law does not provide for the same legal status for women and men, and women are required by law to obey their husbands. Sexual harassment is not prohibited by law and is a common practice in schools and the workplace.

Conditions in northern Mali have left many refugees unable or unwilling to return, as continuing insecurity in the region complicates resettlement. The UN High Commissioner for Refugees (UNHCR) counted 140,000 Malian refugees living in asylum countries and nearly 251,000 internally displaced persons in May 2020.

G. PERSONAL AUTONOMY AND INDIVIDUAL RIGHTS: 4 / 16

G1. Do individuals enjoy freedom of movement, including the ability to change their place of residence, employment, or education? 1 / 4

Freedom of movement and choice of residence remain affected by insecurity, especially in northern and central Mali. According to UN Children's Fund, 1,113 schools were closed as of December 2019. Schools have been targeted in militant attacks.

G2. Are individuals able to exercise the right to own property and establish private businesses without undue interference from state or nonstate actors? 1 / 4

Citizens have the right to own property and conduct business activity, but these rights are not consistently respected, and widespread corruption hampers normal business activities. It is generally necessary to pay bribes in order to operate a business.

Traditional customs sometimes undermine the right of women to own property. The law discriminates against women in matters of marriage, divorce, and inheritance.

G3. Do individuals enjoy personal social freedoms, including choice of marriage partner and size of family, protection from domestic violence, and control over appearance? 1 / 4

Rape and domestic violence against women are widespread, and most such crimes go unreported. There are no specific laws prohibiting spousal rape or domestic violence. Female genital mutilation is legal and commonly practiced in the country. LGBT+ couples cannot adopt children in Mali.

G4. Do individuals enjoy equality of opportunity and freedom from economic exploitation? 1 / 4

Although trafficking in persons is a criminal offense, prosecutions are infrequent. Many judicial officials remain unaware of the antitrafficking law, and the police lack adequate resources to combat trafficking. Traditional forms of slavery and debt bondage persist, particularly in the north, with thousands of people estimated to be living in such conditions.

Although the government has taken steps to eliminate child labor, it is a significant concern, especially in the agricultural and artisanal gold-mining sectors. Armed groups also regularly recruited and use child soldiers.

Malta

Population: 500,000
Capital: Valletta
Freedom Status: Free
Electoral Democracy: Yes

Overview: Malta is a parliamentary democracy with regular, competitive elections and periodic rotations of power. Civil liberties are generally respected. New and smaller political parties encounter difficulties in challenging the dominance of the two main parties, and official corruption is a serious problem.

KEY DEVELOPMENTS IN 2020

- Robert Abela succeeded Joseph Muscat as leader of the Labour Party and prime minister in January. Muscat announced his intention to resign in December 2019 after his chief of staff was implicated in the 2017 assassination of journalist Daphne Caruana Galizia.
- In July, legislators approved a package of constitutional reforms that, among other provisions, will strengthen the Maltese anticorruption agency and require future presidents to win a two-thirds majority in the parliament to win their post. The Council of Europe (CoE) voiced its support for reforms in October, though it also criticized the lack of debate over the package.
- While Malta avoided a major COVID-19 outbreak in the early months of the pandemic, cases began to increase in August. The World Health Organization reported nearly 12,600 cases and 215 deaths at year's end.

POLITICAL RIGHTS: 35 / 40

A. ELECTORAL PROCESS: 12 / 12

A1. Was the current head of government or other chief national authority elected through free and fair elections? 4 / 4

The president is head of state and is elected by the parliament for a five-year term. Under constitutional reforms passed in July 2020, future presidents will require the support of two-thirds of the parliament. George Vella of the Labour Party was selected by the parliament in April 2019, running unopposed.

The president nominates the prime minister, who must be a member of parliament (MP) and is usually the leader of the majority party or coalition. George Muscat won a second five-year term as prime minister when the Labour Party won a snap election in June 2017. Muscat announced that he would leave the Labour leadership and the post of prime minister in December 2019, when it emerged that police were preparing to question his chief of staff, Keith Schembri, over the 2017 murder of journalist Daphne Caruana Galizia, and as demonstrators called for him to step down. Robert Abela succeeded Muscat as Labour leader and prime minister in January 2020.

A2. Were the current national legislative representatives elected through free and fair elections? 4 / 4

Members of the unicameral parliament are elected for a five-year term through a single-transferable-vote (STV), proportional representation voting system in multimember districts. National elections are considered free and fair. The ruling Labour Party won snap elections in June 2017, earning 55 percent of the vote and 37 seats. The opposition Nationalist Party and allies won 30 seats.

A3. Are the electoral laws and framework fair, and are they implemented impartially by the relevant election management bodies? 4 / 4

The constitution and the electoral law provide for democratic elections. Members of the Electoral Commission are appointed by the president, and both major parties are represented on it.

Since 1987, when constitutional amendments were passed, improvements have been made to ensure more proportionality between votes and parliamentary seats won by the parties. However, a party needs to win 16 to 17 percent of the valid votes in one of Malta's 13 electoral districts to enter the parliament.

B. POLITICAL PLURALISM AND PARTICIPATION: 14 / 16

B1. Do the people have the right to organize in different political parties or other competitive political groupings of their choice, and is the system free of undue obstacles to the rise and fall of these competing parties or groupings? 3 / 4

There are no significant restrictions to political party formation, although the ruling party benefits from progovernment bias in the state media. Smaller parties have difficulty competing against the two established parties, which have superior access to private donations. The Democratic Party won two seats in 2017 by fielding candidates via the Nationalists' party list.

The 2015 Financing of Political Parties Act aims to improve transparency of party fundraising. Compliance is overseen by the Electoral Commission, which is dominated by Labour and Nationalist members. The law caps individual donations, but imposes no ceiling on electoral spending. Parties are not obliged to identify donors contributing less than €7,000 ($7,900). In 2017, the Nationalists were accused of using false invoicing to conceal unreported donations. In 2018, the Constitutional Court upheld a Nationalist appeal to halt the Electoral Commission's investigation, ruling that it could not simultaneously investigate and judge such issues. A government pledge to amend the law to comply with that ruling was still pending in 2020.

B2. Is there a realistic opportunity for the opposition to increase its support or gain power through elections? 4 / 4

The Labour and Nationalist parties have regularly alternated in power since independence from the United Kingdom in 1964, establishing a strong pattern of peaceful democratic transfers of power.

B3. Are the people's political choices free from domination by forces that are external to the political sphere, or by political forces that employ extrapolitical means? 3 / 4

Voters are free from undue interference in their political choices. However, powerful economic interests influence the main political parties.

B4. Do various segments of the population (including ethnic, racial, religious, gender, LGBT+, and other relevant groups) have full political rights and electoral opportunities? 4 / 4

Women and minority groups enjoy full political rights and electoral opportunities, though women's participation in politics remains low. Women held only nine of the parliament's seats at year's end.

C. FUNCTIONING OF GOVERNMENT: 9 / 12

C1. Do the freely elected head of government and national legislative representatives determine the policies of the government? 4 / 4

While elected representatives are freely able to make policy, the Council of Europe's (CoE) Venice Commission criticized Malta for the disproportionate power of the executive in a 2018 report. In early July 2020, the government submitted a constitutional reform package meant to address those concerns, and won parliamentary approval for the proposals later that month. The Venice Commission welcomed the reforms in an October report, but criticized the lack of debate on the proposals, which were passed before the commission could publish a formal opinion.

C2. Are safeguards against official corruption strong and effective? 2 / 4

Maltese anticorruption efforts are considered weak, and government officials and businesspeople have been linked to corruption and influence peddling in recent years. The Permanent Commission against Corruption (PCAC), created in 1988, lacked independent prosecutorial powers. Under the reform package passed in July 2020, the PCAC will be empowered to send its findings to the attorney general. In addition, the PCAC chairperson will be chosen by legislators, not the prime minister.

The Panama Papers—a trove of documents leaked from a Panama-based law firm and made public in 2016—have led to multiple corruption allegations against Maltese officials, and related investigations were ongoing in 2020. Investigation targets included former prime minister Muscat's chief of staff, Keith Schembri, and former energy minister Konrad Mizzi, for establishing trusts in New Zealand and secret accounts in Panama shortly after taking office in 2013. Schembri and Mizzi resigned in November 2019 amid turmoil surrounding the 2017 murder of Daphne Caruana Galizia, who had accused both individuals of corruption. Mizzi was expelled from the Labour Party in June 2020, though he remained an MP. Schembri, meanwhile, was arrested in September over a kickback scheme connected to the distribution of passports.

Caruana Galizia had alleged that Michelle Muscat, the wife of the former prime minister, owned Egrant, an offshore firm. In 2018, an inquiry concluded there was no evidence linking the firm to the Muscat family. In June 2020, the Civil Society Network called for a new inquiry to determine the firm's ultimate owner. Later that month, the head of the Maltese police force's Economic Crimes Unit, Ian Abdilla—who participated in the Egrant inquiry—was dismissed after facing long-running allegations of ineffectiveness.

Caruana Galizia had also accused energy firm Electrogas Malta of corruption, and the National Audit Office (NAO) found "multiple instances of noncompliance" in the firm's bid to construct a power station in Delimara in a 2018 report. According to August 2020 testimony from a police inspector, the police believed Caruana Galizia's death was linked to her ongoing investigations into Electrogas Malta. Businessman Yorgen Fenech, a stakeholder in the firm, was accused of orchestrating her murder in November 2019. After his arrest, Fenech claimed that Schembri was intent on murdering the journalist, and that Joseph Muscat was aware of the plot. Fenech was awaiting trial at the end of 2020.

Two 2019 CoE reports—by the Group of States against Corruption, published that April, and the Committee of Experts on the Evaluation of Anti-Money Laundering Measures and the Financing of Terrorism (MONEYVAL), published that September—highlighted significant problems with Malta's ongoing fight against corruption and money laundering. The government committed to implementing the MONEYVAL report's recommendations and submitted a report in October 2020, in an effort to avoid Malta being declared a high-risk country for financial crime. MONEYVAL is due to decide on that designation in 2021.

C3. Does the government operate with openness and transparency? 3 / 4

Malta has a freedom-of-information law and asset disclosure rules for public officials. However, information requests are not always answered. Details of government contracts are sometimes withheld from the public.

Land-use and construction decisions are nontransparent. In December 2020, a group of farmers and residents living near the locality of Qormi claimed that Infrastructure Malta, the public road-management agency, maintained an undisclosed plan to seize land in order to expand a highway.

CIVIL LIBERTIES: 55 / 60

D. FREEDOM OF EXPRESSION AND BELIEF: 14 / 16

D1. Are there free and independent media? 3 / 4

The media are generally free and diverse. Residents have full access to international services and domestic outlets, though state-owned media has often favored the government. Maltese journalists also face harassment and libel accusations.

The 2017 murder of Caruana Galizia demonstrated the physical dangers faced by journalists, especially those investigating corruption. In October 2020, MediaToday managing editor Saviour Balzan stated that Maltese journalists were reluctant to publish some stories in the aftermath of her death.

Libel was decriminalized in 2018 but remains a civil offense, and journalists face civil libel suits. In February 2020, Matthew Caruana Galizia, one of the late journalist's sons, disclosed that his mother faced a total of over 40 libel cases, and noted that the family was still contesting them. A July report provided to the European Parliament's civil liberties committee noted the heavy use of lawsuits to impede the work of Maltese journalists.

In June 2020, the Broadcasting Authority, the Maltese media regulator, instructed publicly run Television Malta (TVM) not to air journalists' questions of government officials during live press conferences, claiming the order was meant to avoid partisan coverage. The order sparked controversy after TVM interrupted the broadcast of an August press conference on Malta's COVID-19 response. The Institute of Maltese Journalists denounced the instruction that month, calling it an act of censorship.

D2. Are individuals free to practice and express their religious faith or nonbelief in public and private? 4 / 4

The constitution establishes Roman Catholicism as the state religion, but religious minorities worship freely. A 2016 legal reform decriminalized the vilification of religion, and blasphemy, and banned the incitement of religious hatred.

The Maltese parliament considered an equality bill that, among other provisions, would prohibit workplace discrimination based on several characteristics, including religious identity. Catholic schools, parents' associations, and bishops objected to the bill, warning it would limit their ability to hire educators. While Justice Minister Edward Zammit Lewis narrowed the bill's scope in December 2020, removing a clause that would have allowed the bill to supersede other laws, it remained under consideration at year's end.

D3. Is there academic freedom, and is the educational system free from extensive political indoctrination? 4 / 4

The education system is free from extensive political indoctrination.

D4. Are individuals free to express their personal views on political or other sensitive topics without fear of surveillance or retribution? 3 / 4

Individuals are generally free to express their personal views on political or other sensitive topics without fear of surveillance or retribution. However, many Maltese, particularly public-service employees, fear retribution for expressing criticism of powerful actors. Harassment via social media platforms, especially against journalists, is widespread.

E. ASSOCIATIONAL AND ORGANIZATIONAL RIGHTS: 12 / 12

E1. Is there freedom of assembly? 4 / 4

The constitution provides for freedom of assembly, and this right is respected. In early June 2020, several hundred demonstrators rallied in front of the parliament building under the

Black Lives Matter banner to object to the 2019 murder of Ivorian Lassana Cisse. A small group of counterprotesters also held a rally during that event. Later that month, nongovernmental organizations (NGOs) organized an anticorruption protest in front of the parliament.

E2. Is there freedom for nongovernmental organizations, particularly those that are engaged in human rights- and governance-related work? 4 / 4

NGOs, including human rights defenders, usually operate without state interference. However, in 2019, Claus Peter Reisch, captain of the *MV Lifeline*, a vessel that rescued migrants stranded at sea, was fined €10,000 ($11,400) by a Maltese court for entering national waters without proper registration. In January 2020, an criminal appeals court overturned the verdict.

E3. Is there freedom for trade unions and similar professional or labor organizations? 4 / 4

The law recognizes the right to form and join trade unions, engage in collective bargaining, and strike. Antiunion discrimination by employers is relatively uncommon.

F. RULE OF LAW: 15 / 16
F1. Is there an independent judiciary? 4 / 4

The judiciary is generally independent. A 2016 constitutional reform created a Judicial Appointments Committee (JAC) to make recommendations to the prime minister on appointments to the judiciary except for the chief justice, who serves as JAC chair.

A 2018 Venice Commission report noted weaknesses in the justice system that undermined judicial independence and favored the executive. A June 2020 report from the commission lauded the government's efforts to address this imbalance, though its subsequent October report called for continued judicial reforms.

In 2019, arguing that the prime minister maintained "arbitrary discretion" over judicial matters, NGO Repubblika initiated court proceedings to send the law on the appointment of judges to the Court of Justice of the European Union (CJEU) for review. In December 2020, the CJEU advocate general ruled that the Maltese judicial selection process did not violate the 1992 Maastricht Treaty.

F2. Does due process prevail in civil and criminal matters? 4 / 4

Police and prosecutors typically observe due process guarantees, including access to defense counsel and protection against arbitrary arrest. However, court cases are known to progress slowly within the justice system.

In January 2020, Police Commissioner Lawrence Cutajar, who was accused by civil society observers of deferring to the Muscat government and faced criticism over his handling of the Caruana Galizia murder investigation, resigned. In June, a magistrate opened an investigation into allegations that then commissioner Cutajar had leaked information to Melvin Theuma, who is considered a "middleman" in the Caruana Galizia murder.

F3. Is there protection from the illegitimate use of physical force and freedom from war and insurgencies? 4 / 4

Maltese authorities do not engage in torture or ill-treatment of detainees. Rates of violent crime are low, though various forms of organized crime remain a problem. A series of car bombings preceded the 2017 assassination of Caruana Galizia.

F4. Do laws, policies, and practices guarantee equal treatment of various segments of the population? 3 / 4

Discrimination based on gender, race, sexual orientation, and religion is prohibited by law, which is generally enforced, but a gender pay gap persists. Transgender people may legally express their gender identity on government documents.

Malta largely complies with international and European Union rules on refugees and asylum seekers. Since 2017, asylum seekers can appeal decisions on asylum claims. However, Malta has been criticized for resisting acceptance of migrants rescued at sea, and NGOs working with migrants and refugees sometimes report police harassment and hostility by far-right groups. Many asylum seekers are confined in overcrowded and squalid detention centers.

G. PERSONAL AUTONOMY AND INDIVIDUAL RIGHTS: 14 / 16

G1. Do individuals enjoy freedom of movement, including the ability to change their place of residence, employment, or education? 4 / 4

Residents enjoy full freedom of movement.

G2. Are individuals able to exercise the right to own property and establish private businesses without undue interference from state or nonstate actors? 4 / 4

There are no significant restrictions on property rights, and the legal framework is supportive of private business activity.

G3. Do individuals enjoy personal social freedoms, including choice of marriage partner and size of family, protection from domestic violence, and control over appearance? 3 / 4

Divorce was legalized in 2011, and subsequent laws have legalized same-sex marriage and permitted adoption by same-sex couples.

Abortion is prohibited, although involuntary abortions resulting from secondary effects when a woman is undergoing medical treatment are not prosecuted.

Reported cases of domestic violence are increasing. In May 2020, Home Affairs Minister Byron Camilleri reported that domestic violence cases increased by 7 percent in the first calendar quarter of the year over the same period in 2019.

G4. Do individuals enjoy equality of opportunity and freedom from economic exploitation? 3 / 4

Residents generally enjoy fair access to economic opportunity and protection from labor exploitation, though migrant workers are vulnerable to labor and sex trafficking or conditions that amount to forced labor. The leader of a leading Maltese trade union has claimed that some migrants are being paid less than one euro an hour for their labor.

Marshall Islands

Population: 60,000
Capital: Majuro
Freedom Status: Free
Electoral Democracy: Yes

Overview: The Republic of the Marshall Islands (RMI) is a stable democracy with regular, competitive elections, an independent judiciary, and a free press. Civil liberties are generally respected. Persistent problems include corruption, gender discrimination, domestic violence, and human trafficking.

KEY DEVELOPMENTS IN 2020

- In January, David Kabua, son of the first president of the Marshall Islands, Amata Kabua, was elected as president by Parliament. Former president Hilda Heine regained her seat as a representative in the November elections, but her coalition lost significant support and she was unable to retain her position as prime minister.
- In March, travel restrictions were implemented to prevent the spread of the COVID-19 pandemic: all travel into the Marshall Islands, including for Marshallese citizens, was banned for much of the year, as was, at times, all outbound travel. These restrictions were an extension of the state-of-emergency declaration already in place because of an outbreak of Dengue Fever that had begun in 2019. In October, two US Army Garrison workers tested positive for the coronavirus—the only two individuals who contracted COVID-19 throughout the year—and were required to quarantine at the army base.

POLITICAL RIGHTS: 38 / 40

A. ELECTORAL PROCESS: 12 / 12

A1. Was the current head of government or other chief national authority elected through free and fair elections? 4 / 4

The president, who is elected by the unicameral legislature from among its members for four-year terms, nominates fellow lawmakers to serve as cabinet ministers, and they are formally appointed by the parliament speaker.

The RMI parliament elected David Kabua, son of the first president of the Marshall Islands, Amata Kabua, as the new president in January 2020. He replaced Hilda Heine, the first woman to be head of state of a Pacific Island country, who lost her coalition after the general elections in November.

A2. Were the current national legislative representatives elected through free and fair elections? 4 / 4

The parliament, known as the Nitijela, consists of 33 members, with 19 seats directly elected in single-member districts and five multimember districts with between 2 and 5 seats. Elections are officially nonpartisan, and lawmakers are free to form alliances and change party affiliations after taking office.

There were no reports of violence or complaints of fraud or irregularities at the November 2019 election, which experienced a notably low voter turnout. Fewer than 40 percent of registered voters cast their ballots. The opposition coalition made significant gains in the parliament. Two incumbents on the main atoll (the reefs of coral that form the Marshall Islands) Majuro and multiple others across the islands were voted out of office and replaced with several newcomers.

A3. Are the electoral laws and framework fair, and are they implemented impartially by the relevant election management bodies? 4 / 4

The constitutional and legal framework provides for democratic elections, and it is implemented impartially.

B. POLITICAL PLURALISM AND PARTICIPATION: 16 / 16

B1. Do the people have the right to organize in different political parties or other competitive political groupings of their choice, and is the system free of undue obstacles to the rise and fall of these competing parties or groupings? 4 / 4

Parliamentary elections are technically nonpartisan, but politicians can organize in groupings that compete freely and do not encounter obstacles from state or nonstate actors. These groups tend to function as loose coalitions among lawmakers, and representatives switching between them is common.

B2. Is there a realistic opportunity for the opposition to increase its support or gain power through elections? 4 / 4

The country has an established record of democratic transfers of power between rival groups. Some governments have been replaced as a result of elections, while others have been toppled by no-confidence votes.

B3. Are the people's political choices free from domination by forces that are external to the political sphere, or by political forces that employ extrapolitical means? 4 / 4

There are no significant undue constraints on the political choices of voters or candidates. Traditional chiefs play an influential but gradually waning role in politics.

B4. Do various segments of the population (including ethnic, racial, religious, gender, LGBT+, and other relevant groups) have full political rights and electoral opportunities? 4 / 4

Naturalized citizens were allowed to run as candidates in the 2015 and subsequent elections, after a court ruling found that a 1980 law requiring parliamentary candidates to have at least one Marshallese parent and traditional land rights was unconstitutional.

Women have full political rights, though entrenched gender roles limit their participation to some extent. Heine is the country's first woman to be elected president. Only two women entered parliament in 2019—Hilda Heine and newly elected Kitlang Kabua.

In October 2019, the Supreme Court removed a 2016 law that banned absentee voting. However, the undoing of the law did not take effect in the November elections, as the court recognized that there was too little time for the government to implement the changes. An estimated 30,000 Marshallese citizens, around a third of the country's citizenry, live in the United States and had a growing influence in the 2011 and 2015 parliamentary and mayoral elections, before the law was set in place.

C. FUNCTIONING OF GOVERNMENT: 10 / 12

C1. Do the freely elected head of government and national legislative representatives determine the policies of the government? 4 / 4

There are no undue restrictions on the elected government's ability to form and implement laws and policies. A body of chieftains from the Ralik and Ratak Island chains, the Council of Iroij, has an advisory role under the constitution. Its 12 members can offer joint opinions and request reconsideration of any bill affecting customary law, traditional practices, land tenure, and related matters. Concerns of Chinese influence on the country's independence persist, despite the RMI's trade deal with Taiwan and deep ties to the United States. In October 2020, a senior RMI official denounced China's attempts at coercion in the region.

The Republic of the Marshall Islands has close relations with the United States under a 1986 Compact of Free Association, which allows the US military to operate in the country in exchange for defense guarantees and development assistance. A component of the compact in force through 2023 calls for the United States to provide annual aid, including contributions to a trust fund for the country.

C2. Are safeguards against official corruption strong and effective? 3 / 4

Corruption has been a chronic problem, though auditing bodies and the independent courts are somewhat effective in detecting abuses and holding officials accountable. High-ranking public officials, however, are rarely prosecuted for corruption. Corruption is most prevalent in the allocation of foreign aid, government procurement, and transfers. In the 2018 audit of Marshallese embassies, over $2.5 million of funds were allegedly misappropriated by various offices. All instances of potential theft of government assets received neither investigation nor proper accounting, according to an independent auditor. In August 2020, the United Nations and the government of New Zealand launched a regional anti-corruption project, with over $16 million in funds that would operate in 13 Pacific Island countries, including the Marshall Islands.

The number of fraud cases prosecuted by the Marshallese Auditor General increased in both 2019 and 2020, potentially a sign of the system working more effectively as a result of a new funds from the World Bank. In September 2020, Auditor General Junior Patrick reported a total of 13 corruption allegations since January, including embezzlement, misappropriation of public assets, abuse of office, and tax evasion, among other malpractice. A total of 46 cases of suspected illegal conduct in government have been reported since a significant audit was conducted in 2018. During the 2020 reporting period that ended in August, there were eight active investigations.

In March 2020, a three-year review of the government's passport program found numerous internal control and compliance problems. Over 500 passports had been issued to non-Indigenous Marshallese who did not have evidence of legal citizenship. In several instances, passport applications were approved without the required documentation at the instruction of high-ranking officials.

In March 2019, the European Union (EU) added the Republic of the Marshall Islands to their list of tax havens in the world. The list, set up to crack down on tax avoidance by corporations and wealthy individuals, added the RMI because of alleged facilitation of offshore structures to attract capital without real economic substance. RMI could potentially face sanctions or restrictions from EU countries as a result of its presence on the list.

C3. Does the government operate with openness and transparency? 3 / 4

There is no strong legal mechanism for obtaining access to government information, but documents can often be obtained through the courts. Auditors have repeatedly found invalid or poorly documented spending practices at government ministries, agencies, and state-owned enterprises.

CIVIL LIBERTIES: 55 / 60

D. FREEDOM OF EXPRESSION AND BELIEF: 16 / 16

D1. Are there free and independent media? 4 / 4

The government generally respects the freedoms of speech and the press. A privately owned newspaper, the *Marshall Islands Journal*, publishes articles in English and Marshallese. Broadcast outlets include both government- and church-owned radio stations, and cable television offers a variety of international news and entertainment programs. Internet access is expanding, reaching nearly 40 percent of the population in 2018, but it remains limited due to poor infrastructure and high costs.

D2. Are individuals free to practice and express their religious faith or nonbelief in public and private? 4 / 4

Religious freedoms are respected in practice. Religious groups are not required to register with the government, but those that register as nonprofits are eligible for tax exemptions.

D3. Is there academic freedom, and is the educational system free from extensive political indoctrination? 4 / 4

There are no significant restrictions on academic freedom.

D4. Are individuals free to express their personal views on political or other sensitive topics without fear of surveillance or retribution? 4 / 4

Citizens are generally free to discuss their political opinions, and there are no reports of improper government surveillance.

E. ASSOCIATIONAL AND ORGANIZATIONAL RIGHTS: 11 / 12
E1. Is there freedom of assembly? 4 / 4

The government upholds constitutional guarantees of freedom of assembly. Protests in recent years have addressed issues including climate change, women's rights, and the legacy of US nuclear weapons tests in the country.

E2. Is there freedom for nongovernmental organizations, particularly those that are engaged in human rights- and governance-related work? 4 / 4

Civil society groups, many of which are sponsored by or affiliated with church organizations and provide social services, operate freely.

E3. Is there freedom for trade unions and similar professional or labor organizations? 3 / 4

Constitutional and legal provisions that protect freedom of association also apply to trade unions. However, there are no laws regulating the right to strike, and few employers are large enough to support union activity among their workers.

F. RULE OF LAW: 15 / 16
F1. Is there an independent judiciary? 4 / 4

The constitution provides for an independent judiciary, and the judiciary generally operates without political interference. Judges are appointed by the cabinet on the recommendation of the Judicial Service Commission, and the legislature confirms the appointments. High Court and Supreme Court judges can only be removed by a two-thirds vote in the Nitijela, for clear failure or inability to perform their duties or for serious crimes or abuses.

F2. Does due process prevail in civil and criminal matters? 4 / 4

The authorities generally observe legal safeguards against arbitrary arrest and detention. The state provides lawyers for indigent defendants, and due process standards for trials are upheld.

F3. Is there protection from the illegitimate use of physical force and freedom from war and insurgencies? 4 / 4

Violent street crime and other such threats to physical security are relatively rare, though conditions in the country's few prison and jail facilities are sometimes overcrowded or otherwise below international standards.

The *LA Times* uncovered in November the extent of dangerous radiation levels on various atolls in the Marshall Islands—similar to the levels at Fukushima and Chernobyl—caused and hidden by the United States military and government. From the 1940s through the 1950s, the US military displaced Marshallese living on various atolls, detonated 67 nuclear bombs, destroyed entire islands, and dumped 130 tons of irradiated soil from Nevada into the Runit Dome on the atoll Enewetak. Further, the American government withheld key information about the contents of the Dome and claimed it would be safe for the Marshallese to return (which was false), before signing the 1986 Compact of Free Association. An international tribunal created by the RMI and United States in 1988 acknowledged \$2.3 billion in claims to be paid by the US government; only \$4 million had been paid out by 2010. In November 2019, RMI President Heine called for the US government to pay to repair the Runit Dome, which was found to be leaking in July 2019, further endangering the population living near and on the island.

In July 2020, the United States government declared that the Runit Dome was safe, despite evidence provided by RMI government reports to the contrary. The RMI's Nuclear Commission claims that the US report contains no new analysis and ignores evidence and information from local communities.

F4. Do laws, policies, and practices guarantee equal treatment of various segments of the population? 3 / 4

Women generally enjoy equal treatment under the law, but there is no explicit ban on discrimination in employment, and women face disadvantages in the workplace in practice. While same-sex sexual activity was decriminalized in 2005, discrimination based on sexual orientation and gender identity is not prohibited by law.

G. PERSONAL AUTONOMY AND INDIVIDUAL RIGHTS: 13 / 16

G1. Do individuals enjoy freedom of movement, including the ability to change their place of residence, employment, or education? 4 / 4

Freedom of movement is generally respected. Marshallese citizens have the right to live and work in the United States and to travel there without a visa. In recent years, sea level rise due to climate change has become a more prominent impetus for Marshallese citizens to move to the United States, in a trend that has been called voluntary out-migration.

In August 2019, due to an outbreak of dengue fever, the government imposed a domestic travel ban throughout the Marshall Islands, declaring a state of emergency. The outbreak was severe, and the state of emergency was extended into 2020. In March 2020, restrictions were further tightened to prevent the spread of the COVID-19 pandemic: all travel into the Marshall Islands, including for Marshallese citizens, was banned for much of the year, as was, at times, all outbound travel. In October 2020, two US Army Garrison workers tested positive for the coronavirus—the only two individuals who contracted COVID-19 throughout the year—and were required to quarantine at the army base.

G2. Are individuals able to exercise the right to own property and establish private businesses without undue interference from state or nonstate actors? 3 / 4

Individuals have the rights to own property and establish private businesses, and these rights are largely observed in practice.

G3. Do individuals enjoy personal social freedoms, including choice of marriage partner and size of family, protection from domestic violence, and control over appearance? 3 / 4

Personal social freedoms are mostly upheld. However, the minimum age for marriage is 16 for women and 18 for men; about a quarter of women aged 20–24 were married by age 18. While domestic violence remains widespread, reporting of the problem has increased in recent years possibly due to improved processes for obtaining orders of protection.

G4. Do individuals enjoy equality of opportunity and freedom from economic exploitation? 3 / 4

The government enforces a minimum wage law, though it does not apply to the informal sector. Some local and East Asian women are subjected to forced prostitution in a trade that depends on visiting freight or fishing vessels. According to the US State Department's 2020 *Trafficking in Persons Report*, the RMI government did not increase its efforts to combat trafficking and did not report providing assistance to any potential or confirmed victims during the reporting period. In February 2020, the government charged a Chinese national for sex trafficking, though the case was ongoing at the end of the year.

In March 2019, three Marshallese people were charged in the Marshall Islands for their role in a human trafficking ring. The three charged had been working with US elected official Paul Petersen to connect families looking to adopt children from pregnant Marshallese, falsifying their travel and visa documents, and housing them in the United States in what was described by multiple investigators and news outlets as a "baby mill."

Mauritania

Population: 4,600,000
Capital: Nouakchott
Freedom Status: Partly Free
Electoral Democracy: No

Overview: Mohamed Ould Abdel Aziz, who first came to power through a military coup in 2008 and won a second term in a deeply flawed 2014 election, stepped down peacefully after Mohamed Ould Ghazouani won the presidency in a relatively credible 2019 election. The poll came on the heels of successful legislative elections held in 2018, which were more pluralistic than past elections. A variety of media outlets operate, but journalists risk arrest for reporting on sensitive topics and many self-censor. Black Mauritanians, the Haratin population, women, and LGBT+ people face discrimination. The government has taken increased steps to implement laws that address the problem of institutionalized slavery and discrimination but continues to arrest antislavery and antidiscrimination activists.

KEY DEVELOPMENTS IN 2020

- The authorities quashed legal proceedings targeting three prominent critics of the former Ould Abdel Aziz administration in February. Arrest warrants against two of them, businessman Mohamed Bouamatou and Moustapha Ould Limam Chafi—who had advised former Burkinabè president Blaise Compaoré (1987–2014)—were suspended, and Ould Limam Chafi returned to Mauritania in October.
- In July, a legislative inquiry publicized evidence of corruption and embezzlement during the Ould Abdel Aziz administration. The former president, who refused to appear before legislators that month, was questioned for a week in August and had his passport seized; his son in law was also questioned by authorities that month. Neither man was charged by year's end.
- Mauritanian authorities imposed a COVID-19-related overnight curfew and closed mosques in March, though the mosque-closure measure was reversed in May. Interregional travel was restricted in May, and a new curfew was introduced in December as cases rose. The government reported 13,642 COVID-19 cases and 324 deaths to the World Health Organization at year's end.

POLITICAL RIGHTS: 14 / 40 (+1)

A. ELECTORAL PROCESS: 6 / 12

A1. Was the current head of government or other chief national authority elected through free and fair elections? 2 / 4

The president is chief of state and is directly elected to up to two five-year terms by popular vote. In June 2019, Mauritanians elected Mohamed Ould Ghazouani to replace Mohamed Ould Abdel Aziz, whose second term came to an end. Six candidates, including those from major opposition parties, competed in the election. Ould Ghazouani, who represented the ruling Union for the Republic (UPR) and is reputedly close to Ould Abdel Aziz, won 52 percent of the vote in the first round. Antislavery activist Biram Dah Abeid came second with 19 percent. Mohamed Ould Boubacar, the Islamist party Tawassoul's candidate, won 18 percent.

The authorities dismissed opposition claims of electoral misconduct and fraud. Local and international observers noted irregularities but praised the poll's peaceful conduct and found it generally satisfactory. For the first time in its history, Mauritania experienced a peaceful transfer of power after the incumbent completed his term, signaling a departure from a history of military coups.

The prime minister is head of government and is appointed by the president. President Ould Ghazouani named Mohamed Ould Bilal, a longtime public official, to succeed Ismaïl Ould Bedda Ould Cheikh Sidiya in August 2020. Ould Bilal's predecessor resigned after he and several other ministers were implicated in Ould Abdel Aziz–era corruption.

A2. Were the current national legislative representatives elected through free and fair elections? 2 / 4

Constitutional reforms adopted through a 2017 referendum dissolved the Senate, leaving the 157-seat National Assembly as the country's legislative body. Members are directly elected to five-year terms in a mixed system of direct and plurality voting; four members are directly elected by the diaspora.

Ninety-eight political parties participated in the September 2018 National Assembly elections, including members of the opposition National Front for the Defense of Democracy (FNDU), a coalition that boycotted previous elections. The ruling UPR won 89 seats, while Tawassoul, the largest opposition party, won 14.

A coalition of opposition groups called the elections fraudulent, but most Mauritanian politicians as well as African Union (AU) observers deemed them credible. AU observers said "imperfections" in the process did not appear to have affected the polls' credibility.

Abeid, a 2014 and 2019 presidential candidate and head of the Initiative for the Resurgence of the Abolitionist Movement in Mauritania (IRA Mauritania), an antislavery group, won a seat in the parliament in 2018. However, Abeid was held in pretrial detention during the elections as authorities investigated claims that he had threatened a journalist. His arrest was reportedly carried out in the absence of a warrant. IRA Mauritania denied the allegations against him. In December 2018, Abeid was released after receiving a sentence shorter than time served.

The UPR posted a strong performance in concurrent municipal elections.

A3. Are the electoral laws and framework fair, and are they implemented impartially by the relevant election management bodies? 2 / 4

In 2018, the government appointed a new Independent National Electoral Commission (CENI) following a series of dialogues with some opposition parties. However, the FNDU, which had boycotted the dialogue process, rejected the commission and demanded its dissolution. That July, the government appointed a former FNDU member as CENI president. Despite the controversies over its composition, the new commission organized 2018 elections that were generally viewed as successful. In May 2019, prior to the presidential elections, government and opposition groups agreed to a compromise that allowed members of the opposition greater participation in the CENI.

B. POLITICAL PLURALISM AND PARTICIPATION: 4 / 16 (+1)

B1. Do the people have the right to organize in different political parties or other competitive political groupings of their choice, and is the system free of undue obstacles to the rise and fall of these competing parties or groupings? 2 / 4 (+1)

Several obstacles prevent parties from successfully mobilizing their bases. A 2018 decree commanded the government to dissolve all political parties unable to gain at least 1 percent of votes in two consecutive district elections. In March 2019, 76 parties were disbanded under the decree.

Demonstrations organized by political parties are often prevented or dispersed. Authorities have denied registration to activist parties, including the Forces of Progress for Change, which opposes racial discrimination. The party's legal petition to gain recognition has been pending before the Supreme Court since 2015. The ruling party is frequently successful in efforts to co-opt leaders of smaller parties with comparatively fewer resources.

The environment for opposition figures did improve during 2020. In February, the government quashed legal proceedings against three prominent critics of former president Ould Abdel Aziz. Arrest warrants were withdrawn against two, businessman Mohamed Bouamatou and Moustapha Ould Limam Chafi, who previously advised former Burkinabè president Compaoré. Ould Limam Chafi, who had not resided in Mauritania since 2011, returned in October 2020.

Score Change: The score improved from 1 to 2 because the government dropped charges against political critics, and one exiled opposition figure returned to the country during the year.

B2. Is there a realistic opportunity for the opposition to increase its support or gain power through elections? 1 / 4

Most opposition parties lack an institutional base. Many are formed by splinter factions of the UPR that later rejoin it, sometimes because of active co-optation. After boycotting elections for years, opposition parties participated in recent presidential and legislative elections. Although the UPR benefitted from incumbency advantages in the 2019 presidential election, opposition parties managed to gain sizable number of votes, totaling over 47 percent.

Most opposition parties boycotted both the 2013 parliamentary elections and the 2014 presidential election, citing a system dominated by the ruling UPR, which since its creation in 2009 has won every election handily. Though opposition parties took part in the September 2018 elections, the UPR remained dominant, winning a large legislative majority. Opposition parties fared somewhat better in the municipal and regional elections.

B3. Are the people's political choices free from domination by forces that are external to the political sphere, or by political forces that employ extrapolitical means? 1 / 4

The political choices of Mauritanians are greatly influenced by the military, which plays a key role in the political system. Since 1978, Mauritania has either been under military rule or led by a military leader, with the exception of 18 months of civilian government between 2007 and 2008. President Ould Ghazouani is a former defense minister and general, though he was elected in a competitive and democratic poll. In recent years, the overt influence of the military in politics has receded somewhat.

B4. Do various segments of the population (including ethnic, racial, religious, gender, LGBT+, and other relevant groups) have full political rights and electoral opportunities? 0 / 4

The Bidhan ethnic group dominates the Mauritanian government, while Black Mauritanians and the Haratin ethnic group are underrepresented in elected positions and in high-level government roles. Discrimination hinders the ability of these groups to gain power. Thousands of Black Mauritanians who were forced out of their villages by the military in 1989 have been allowed to return, but face difficulties when trying to enroll in the census and register to vote.

Women participate in politics at lower levels than men, largely due to traditional cultural norms, and women's interests are poorly represented in national politics in practice. Women hold 31 National Assembly seats.

C. FUNCTIONING OF GOVERNMENT: 4 / 12

C1. Do the freely elected head of government and national legislative representatives determine the policies of the government? 1 / 4

The executive dominates the legislative branch. The president has the power to dissolve the National Assembly, but the legislature has no impeachment power over the president. The military maintains a great deal of influence on policymaking.

C2. Are safeguards against official corruption strong and effective? 2 / 4

The government has adopted numerous anticorruption laws, and signed the African Union Convention on Preventing and Combating Corruption in 2005. Money-laundering and terror-financing measures were adopted by the government and banks in 2019. Nevertheless, corruption remains widespread and laws are not effectively enforced. Public contracts are typically awarded in exchange for bribes or on the basis of patronage. Bribes are often necessary for ordinary government processes like obtaining licenses and permits.

The former Ould Abdel Aziz administration was suspected of corrupt behavior for several years. A 2017 report from Sherpa, a nongovernmental organization (NGO), documented multiple cases of corruption that had gone unpunished. In July 2020, a legislative inquiry publicized evidence of Ould Abdel Aziz–era corruption and embezzlement. Legislators founded a High Court of Justice to try presidents and ministers of "high treason" that month, after the former president refused to testify, and forwarded the inquiry's findings to prosecutors in August. Ould Abdel Aziz was detained later that month and faced questioning for a week before he was released, and his passport was seized. The former president's son in law, who was implicated in the inquiry, was also questioned by police in August. No charges were brought against either individual by year's end.

C3. Does the government operate with openness and transparency? 1 / 4

The government does not operate with transparency, particularly in granting mining and fishing licenses, land distribution, government contracts, and tax payments. The construction of a new airport in Nouakchott that opened in 2016 drew criticism—a company with no experience in airport construction won a contract to build the facility through an opaque procurement process.

CIVIL LIBERTIES: 21 / 60
D. FREEDOM OF EXPRESSION AND BELIEF: 9 / 16
D1. Are there free and independent media? 2 / 4

Mauritania has a vibrant media landscape, with several privately owned newspapers, television stations, and radio stations in operation. However, journalists who cover sensitive topics or scrutinize the political elite may face harassment and wiretapping. Criminal defamation laws remain on the books and are sometimes enforced against journalists. Most journalists practice a degree of self-censorship when covering issues such as the military, corruption, and slavery.

In January 2020, blogger Mohamed Ali Abdel Aziz was arrested for publishing a social media video criticizing President Ould Ghazouani; authorities claimed the video included insulting and racist language. Later that month, journalist Cheikh Ould Mami and video producer Abdou Ould Tajeddine were arrested in connection with the video's publication. All three were released later that month.

D2. Are individuals free to practice and express their religious faith or nonbelief in public and private? 2 / 4

Mauritania is an Islamic republic. Non-Muslims cannot proselytize or become citizens, and those who convert from Islam to another religion lose their citizenship. In practice, however, non-Muslim communities are generally not targeted for persecution.

Apostasy is a crime punishable by death. To date, no one has been executed for the crime. However, in 2018, the parliament passed a law strengthening capital punishment for certain blasphemy offenses. The new law removes the possibility of repentance to avoid a death sentence for committing some forms of blasphemy. In June 2020, journalist Eby Ould Zeidane was accused of blasphemy after he called for Ramadan to be held on fixed dates. Ould Zeidane was released that month and repented in July.

In March 2020, authorities ordered the closure of mosques in response to COVID-19, though they were allowed to reopen in May. An imam accused of violating the closure order was arrested in Nouakchott in April, though he was released from detention while awaiting trial in May.

D3. Is there academic freedom, and is the educational system free from extensive political indoctrination? 3 / 4

Academic freedom is largely respected. However, in 2018, the government instituted a new rule prohibiting high school graduates aged 25 and above to register in public universities. The rule was suspended in late 2019, after police violently dispersed a protest against the policy.

The increasing use of Arabic as the language of instruction in universities has hindered access to education for Black Mauritanians, who mainly speak other languages. Student activists sometimes face pressure from university administrators, including threats of expulsion and intimidation.

D4. Are individuals free to express their personal views on political or other sensitive topics without fear of surveillance or retribution? 2 / 4

Individuals have faced reprisals for expressing views critical of the government on social media, including termination of employment from government agencies. In 2019, two bloggers were arrested and then imprisoned for over two months for sharing on Facebook information about a corruption scandal that implicated individuals close to then president Ould Abdel Aziz.

In 2018, the government adopted a new law that mandated severe penalties for discrimination and racism. In mid-April 2020, IRA Mauritania activist Mariem Cheikh was arrested and charged with making "racist comments through social media" for commenting on racial discrimination and slavery but was released later that month.

In June 2020, the parliament approved legislation punishing the dissemination of purportedly false news, the creation of false identities online, and other offenses. Offenders could receive prison sentences as long as five years and fines ranging from 50,000 to 200,000 Ouguiya ($1,380 to $5,500).

E. ASSOCIATIONAL AND ORGANIZATIONAL RIGHTS: 4 / 12
E1. Is there freedom of assembly? 1 / 4

While the constitution guarantees freedom of assembly, organizers are required to obtain consent from the government for large gatherings, which is often denied. While the government imposed COVID-19-related restrictions on assemblies in March 2020, protests did occur as the year progressed. In November, relatives of Mauritanians who died during the 1989–91 period of unrest called for the repeal of an amnesty law in Nouakchott and Bababe protests. Authorities arrested over 40 people, who were later released.

E2. Is there freedom for nongovernmental organizations, particularly those that are engaged in human rights- and governance-related work? 1 / 4

NGOs, particularly antislavery organizations, frequently encounter intimidation, violence, and repression in carrying out their activities. Under the Law of Associations of 1964, associations required government approval to register, which could be denied for a variety of reasons. The cabinet sent a draft bill meant to replace this legislation to the parliament in September 2020; the bill would allow associations to automatically gain legal status after filing bylaws with the government, though the Interior Ministry would be allowed to temporarily suspend associations without notice. The bill remained under consideration as recently as November.

IRA Mauritania has repeatedly been denied permission to register as an NGO. In 2018, Abeid, its leader, spent five months in prison awaiting trial on charges of incitement to hatred and violence following a complaint by a journalist he allegedly threatened. He was released that December.

The Alliance for the Refoundation of the Mauritanian State, which opposes the country's caste system, has also faced government scrutiny. Authorities arrested 14 people who attended its inaugural meeting on two occasions in February 2020. Five were kept in pretrial detention and were convicted of "violating the sanctity of God" in October; two received prison sentences shorter than their detention and were released, while the other three were released later that month. Another three received sentences and fines in absentia.

E3. Is there freedom for trade unions and similar professional or labor organizations? 2 / 4

Workers have the legal right to unionize, but unions require approval from the public prosecutor to operate and often confront hostility from employers. The right to collective bargaining is not always respected, and the government sometimes pressures union members to withdraw their membership. The right to strike is limited by notice requirements and other onerous regulations.

F. RULE OF LAW: 4 / 16
F1. Is there an independent judiciary? 1 / 4

Mauritania's judiciary lacks independence. The president has the power to unilaterally appoint many key judges, including three of the six judges on the Constitutional Court and the chair of the Supreme Court. The courts are subject to political pressure from the executive branch. Instances of judges facing retaliatory measures for issuing rulings against the government have been reported.

F2. Does due process prevail in civil and criminal matters? 1 / 4

Due process rights are often not respected in practice. Suspects are frequently arrested without being informed of the charges against them. Lengthy pretrial detentions are common. Arbitrary arrests of opposition politicians, journalists, and human rights activists occur with some frequency.

F3. Is there protection from the illegitimate use of physical force and freedom from war and insurgencies? 1 / 4

Torture and abuse at Mauritania's prisons and detention centers remain problematic, and perpetrators are rarely held accountable. Prisons are plagued by violence, are overcrowded, and lack basic sanitation. Food shortages are also common in prisons. Children are sometimes held with the adult prison population.

Police frequently beat suspects following arrest. In May 2020, three police officers were dismissed for assaulting a group they had arrested in Nouakchott, after one of them published a video of the incident online.

F4. Do laws, policies, and practices guarantee equal treatment of various segments of the population? 1 / 4

Same-sex sexual activity is illegal in Mauritania and punishable by death for men. LGBT+ individuals generally hide their sexual orientation or gender identity due to severe discrimination. Racial and ethnic discrimination remains a serious problem. In January 2020, eight men attending a birthday celebration in a Nouakchott restaurant were arrested for "imitating women," along with a woman, who received a suspended sentence, and the restaurant's owner. The owner was acquitted, but the eight other defendants received two-year sentences for charges including indecency in February, after police had described them as "sodomizers" to the court. In early March, an appeals court upheld their convictions but suspended the sentences of seven men and reduced the sentence of the eighth.

Sharia law as it is applied in Mauritania discriminates against women. The testimony of two women is equal to that of one man. Female victims of crime are entitled to only half the financial compensation that male victims receive. In the past few years, the parliament has twice rejected a bill that aimed to sanction gender-based violence (GBV).

G. PERSONAL AUTONOMY AND INDIVIDUAL RIGHTS: 4 / 16
G1. Do individuals enjoy freedom of movement, including the ability to change their place of residence, employment, or education? 1 / 4

While the Bidhan population is relatively free to make personal decisions about residence, employment, and education, the choices of Black Mauritanians and the Haratin are often constrained by racial and caste-based discrimination. People lacking government identity cards are not allowed to travel in some regions, which disproportionately affects Black Mauritanians.

COVID-19-related restrictions on movement were imposed in March 2020, when the government introduced an overnight curfew. Interregional travel was restricted in May. Another curfew was introduced in December, after an increase in cases.

G2. Are individuals able to exercise the right to own property and establish private businesses without undue interference from state or nonstate actors? 2 / 4

Though the law guarantees property rights, these rights are not always enforced in practice, as it can be difficult to get property disputes fairly adjudicated in court. Complex laws and an opaque bureaucracy present challenges to starting a business.

Many Black Mauritanians who left their homes in the Senegal River Valley in the wake of the 1989 conflict have returned but have been unable to regain ownership of their land. Local authorities reportedly allow the Bidhan to appropriate land used by the Haratin and Black Mauritanians.

G3. Do individuals enjoy personal social freedoms, including choice of marriage partner and size of family, protection from domestic violence, and control over appearance? 1 / 4

Many girls are married before the age of 18. In 2017, the government sent the parliament a bill that would ban marriage for girls under 18. The bill failed in the National Assembly, largely due to pressure from religious leaders.

Female genital mutilation (FGM) is illegal, but the law is rarely enforced and the practice remains common. Domestic violence and rape remain problems, victims rarely seek legal redress, and convictions for these crimes are rare. Laws banning adultery and morality offenses discourage sexual-assault survivors from reporting incidents to police.

G4. Do individuals enjoy equality of opportunity and freedom from economic exploitation? 0 / 4

Despite amendments to the antislavery law passed in 2015 meant to address the problem more robustly, slavery and slavery-like practices continued in 2020, with many former slaves still reliant on their former owners due to racial discrimination, poverty, and other socioeconomic factors. The government cracks down on NGOs that push for greater enforcement of the law and rarely prosecutes perpetrators but has shown an increased commitment to enforcing antislavery laws. In July 2020, two slave owners received 10- and 15-year sentences, while a third received a suspended sentence. The court also ordered the government to ensure the legal status of the former slaves and their relatives.

Mauritius

Population: 1,300,000
Capital: Port Louis
Freedom Status: Free
Electoral Democracy: Yes

Overview: Mauritius is home to an open, multiparty system that has allowed for the regular handover of power between parties through free and fair elections. Civil liberties are generally upheld. However, the political leadership remains dominated by a few families, ethnic divisions are increasingly prominent in politics. Corruption is a problem, journalists occasionally face harassment and legal pressure, integration of women into the political system has been slow, and LGBT+ people face threats and discrimination.

KEY DEVELOPMENTS IN 2020

- In February, Kaushik Jadunundun—a member of the Information and Communication Technologies (ICT) Act's governance body, the Information and

Communication Technologies Authority (ICTA)—was arrested for defamation and spent the night in jail. He resigned in April because of his arrest. The arrest of Jadunundun and another individual who posted comments on Facebook about a sitting parliamentarian, were both under provisions of the ICT Act.

- The COVID-19 Act, passed in May, has been criticized for limiting workers' rights, including through reductions of additional pay for night-workers and overtime, annual days of leave, and other protections in the Workers' Rights Act (WRA) of 2019. The COVID-19 Act also specifically targets low-income, essential workers by enabling employers to bypass union negotiations and make direct requests to a Redundancy Board created by the WRA.

POLITICAL RIGHTS: 37 / 40
A. ELECTORAL PROCESS: 12 / 12

A1. Was the current head of government or other chief national authority elected through free and fair elections? 4 / 4

The president, whose role is mostly ceremonial is elected by the unicameral National Assembly to a five-year term. Pritivirajsing Roopun, a lawmaker from the Militant Socialist Movement (MSM), was elected president in December 2019, following the previous month's parliamentary elections.

Executive power resides with the prime minister who is appointed by the president from the party or coalition with the most seats in the legislature. Pravind Jugnauth of the MSM, who had succeeded his father as prime minister when the latter stepped down in 2017, was reinstalled after the 2019 elections, which were generally considered credible.

A2. Were the current national legislative representatives elected through free and fair elections? 4 / 4

Of the National Assembly's 70 members, 62 are directly elected in 21 constituencies, including 2 members from a constituency representing the autonomous island of Rodrigues. Up to 8 "best losers" are appointed from among unsuccessful candidates who gained the largest number of votes, in order to ensure fair representation of the country's different ethnic communities. The members of the National Assembly serve five-year terms. Rodrigues has its own elected Regional Assembly.

The MSM's Morisian Alliance won 42 seats in the November 2019 National Assembly elections. The opposition National Alliance, led by former prime minister Navinchandra Ramgoolam's Mauritian Labor Party (PTR), took 17 seats, followed by former prime minister Paul Bérenger's Mauritian Militant Movement (MMM) with 9, and the Organization of the People of Rodrigues (OPR) with 2. Opposition leaders filed court challenges over alleged irregularities, but African Union (AU) election observers concluded that polling was conducted peacefully and professionally. Voter turnout was approximately 77 percent.

A3. Are the electoral laws and framework fair, and are they implemented impartially by the relevant election management bodies? 4 / 4

The Electoral Supervisory Commission has impartially supervised the electoral process. There is no law on the financing of electoral campaigns. Long-running discussions on electoral reform and party financing laws have led to no concrete action as of the end of 2020.

B. POLITICAL PLURALISM AND PARTICIPATION: 15 / 16

B1. Do the people have the right to organize in different political parties or other competitive political groupings of their choice, and is the system free of undue obstacles to the rise and fall of these competing parties or groupings? 4 / 4

Political parties are generally free to form and operate. More than 70 parties competed in the 2019 elections, only four formed the government.

B2. Is there a realistic opportunity for the opposition to increase its support or gain power through elections? 4 / 4

Since independence, political power has peacefully rotated among the three largest parties—the PTR, the MSM, and the MMM. The MSM has been in power since 2014, when it defeated the PTR.

B3. Are the people's political choices free from domination by the military, foreign powers, religious hierarchies, economic oligarchies, or any other powerful group that is not democratically accountable? 4 / 4

Voters and candidates are generally able to express their political choices without pressure from actors who are not democratically accountable. However, money plays an important role in politics, and there is no law on the financing of electoral campaigns. The Jugnauth and Ramgoolam families have long-running holds on political leadership positions, which may influence intraparty politics.

B4. Do various segments of the population (including ethnic, racial, religious, gender, LGBT+, and other relevant groups) have full political rights and electoral opportunities? 3 / 4

The government officially recognizes four distinct communities: Hindus, Muslims, Sino-Mauritians, and the general population, which includes Mauritian Creoles, Franco-Mauritians, and people of African descent. Ethnic minority groups such as Rodriguais and Chagossians are considered Creole. The Truth and Justice Commission (TJC) and the Equal Opportunities Commission (EOC) sought to ensure that all ethnic minority groups hold equal legal rights and access, though in practice linguistic nationalism has maintained a social hierarchy that marginalizes Mauritian Creoles politically and favors the Hindu majority, who hold most positions of political influence.

Women hold a handful of cabinet seats and other high-level political positions but are generally underrepresented in politics. Fourteen women secured seats in the 2019 parliamentary elections. Local elections require that at least one-third of political parties' candidates in each district be women.

Discrimination against LGBT+ people can discourage their active political participation.

C. FUNCTIONING OF GOVERNMENT: 10 / 12

C1. Do the freely elected head of government and national legislative representatives determine the policies of the government? 4 / 4

Elected representatives are duly seated, and the government has been able to make policy without interference or major political disruptions.

C2. Are safeguards against official corruption strong and effective? 3 / 4

The country's anticorruption framework is robust but inconsistently applied.

In 2018, former president Ameenah Gurib-Fakim, who was the first woman to be elected president in Mauritius, resigned after allegations emerged in the media that she had made thousands of dollars in personal purchases using a credit card issued to her by a nongovernmental organization.

C3. Does the government operate with openness and transparency? 3 / 4

The government openly debates the country's budget in the National Assembly, publishes it and other legislation online and in the press, and maintains a National Open Data Portal. However, Transparency International has noted concerns about opaque hiring processes that may be affected by nepotism and cronyism. In 2020, the corruption watch-dog warned of government opacity in the management of medical supplies during the COVID-19 pandemic, as well as ways in which nepotism led to the Wakashio oil spill. There are no laws that guarantee the right to access government information.

In May 2020, the National Assembly passed the Quarantine Act and the COVID-19 Act, which was criticized for increasing the discretionary powers of the prime minister without transparency requirements. Further, the prime minister does not need to consult with public health officials when setting public health guidelines. Policies instituted under the two laws do not need to incorporate an expiration date (sunset clause) for their implementation.

CIVIL LIBERTIES: 50 / 60 (–2)
D. FREEDOM OF EXPRESSION AND BELIEF: 14 / 16 (–1)
D1. Are there free and independent media? 3 / 4

The constitution guarantees freedom of expression. Several private daily and weekly publications report on the ruling and opposition parties, but the state-owned Mauritius Broadcasting Corporation's radio and television services generally reflect government view-points. A small number of private radio stations compete with the state-run media.

Journalists occasionally face legal pressure. One of the main newspapers, *L'Express*, has faced verbal attacks by authorities, who have also reduced advertising with the outlet. Its journalists have faced legal and other harassment, though no reporter has been imprisoned and most are broadly perceived as operating freely.

D2. Are individuals free to practice and express their religious faith or nonbelief in public and private? 4 / 4

Religious freedom is generally upheld. The government grants subsidies to Hindu, Roman Catholic, Muslim, Anglican, Presbyterian, and Seventh-day Adventist communities, but not to smaller groups, though all religious groups may apply for tax-exempt status. Tensions between Muslim and Hindu communities continue to be reported.

D3. Is there academic freedom, and is the educational system free from extensive political indoctrination? 4 / 4

Academic freedom is generally upheld.

D4. Are individuals free to express their personal views on political or other sensitive topics without fear of surveillance or retribution? 3 / 4 (–1)

Private discussion is generally unrestricted. However, 2019 saw the first impacts of the October 2018 amendments to the Information and Communication Technologies (ICT) Act making the online publication of material deemed false, harmful, or illegal punishable by up to 10 years in prison.

In 2020, multiple individuals were arrested under the ICT Act for expressing criticism of the government and its policies. In February, Kaushik Jadunundun—a member of the ICT governance body, the Information and Communication Technologies Authority

(ICTA)—was arrested for defamation and spent the night in jail. He resigned in April because of his arrest. In July, a Facebook user was arrested for allegedly insulting a member of Parliament in one of their posts.

Score Change: The score declined from 4 to 3 due to the arrests under the ICT Act of an individual who allegedly insulted a politician online and a member of the ICT governing authority, who subsequently left his position.

E. ASSOCIATIONAL AND ORGANIZATIONAL RIGHTS: 11 / 12 (−1)
E1. Is there freedom of assembly? 4 / 4

Freedom of assembly is usually upheld, though authorities' responses to some protests have raised concerns in recent years. The May 2020 passages of the COVID-19 Act and Quarantine Act have been cited by some as government overreach. All assembly was banned during the government-imposed lockdown, and provisions of the laws increased policing powers to enforce this provision and others.

In August and September 2020, tens of thousands of people took to the streets to protest the poor handling of the Wakashio oil spill.

E2. Is there freedom for nongovernmental organizations, particularly those that are engaged in human rights- and governance-related work? 4 / 4

Civil society groups operate freely. However, many are reliant upon government funding that could compromise their independence.

E3. Is there freedom for trade unions and similar professional or labor organizations? 3 / 4 (−1)

Unions regularly meet with government leaders, protest, and advocate for improved compensation and workers' rights. There are more than 300 unions in Mauritius. However, the COVID-19 Act, passed in May 2020, has been criticized for limiting workers' rights, including through reductions of additional pay for night-workers and overtime, annual days of leave, and other protections in the Workers' Rights Act (WRA) of 2019. The COVID-19 Act also specifically targets workers earning less than 50,000 Mauritian rupees ($1,303) per month who work in sectors deemed essential. The new law enables employers to bypass union negotiations and make direct requests for the mass termination of workers' contracts to a Redundancy Board created by the WRA; before the Act, employers had to negotiate with unions to find alternatives. Whereas before workers could file a grievance with the Commission for Conciliation and Mediation, under the COVID-19 Act, all decisions are made by the Redundancy Board. If the Board rules in favor of the worker, the worker receives one-time financial compensation.

Score Change: The score declined from 4 to 3 because the COVID-19 Act exempts employers of essential workers from processes designed to protect the rights of workers and union members.

F. RULE OF LAW: 13 / 16
F1. Is there an independent judiciary? 3 / 4

The generally independent judiciary administers a legal system that combines French and British traditions. However, judicial independence has been questioned in some cases involving politicians.

Mauritius has maintained the right of appeal to the Privy Council in London.

F2. Does due process prevail in civil and criminal matters? 4 / 4

Constitutional guarantees of due process are generally upheld. However, Mauritian criminal law allows for police to charge suspects provisionally and then hold them for months until a formal charge is issued. Due to court backlogs, many of those being held in prison are in pretrial detention, and some detainees reportedly wait years before facing trial.

F3. Is there protection from the illegitimate use of physical force and freedom from war and insurgencies? 3 / 4

Mauritius is free from war and insurgencies, and the 2016 Independent Police Complaints Commission (IPCC) was formed to manage complaints. However, allegations of abuses by police continue. Under the Quarantine Act passed in May 2020, police powers were extended to include boarding a ship or aircraft, entering private premises without a warrant, and arresting someone without a warrant believed to be in violation of the Act.

F4. Do laws, policies, and practices guarantee equal treatment of various segments of the population? 3 / 4

Though the law and the EOC do not allow for discrimination in the workforce, some citizens view economic leadership to be closed to ethnic minority groups. Chagossians and other minorities form an underclass, while Hindu Mauritians are more privileged, albeit within a differentiated ethnic structure with remnants of a caste system. Women generally earn less money than men for equal work.

LGBT+ people face discrimination and the risk of targeted violence. Laws that criminalize same sex relations remain on the books, even if rarely invoked.

G. PERSONAL AUTONOMY AND INDIVIDUAL RIGHTS: 12 / 16

G1. Do individuals enjoy freedom of movement, including the ability to change their place of residence, employment, or education? 4 / 4

Citizens are generally allowed to move freely within Mauritius, but there are restrictions on travel to the Chagos Islands. Mauritians are free to change their place of residence, employment, and education.

G2. Are individuals able to exercise the right to own property and establish private businesses without undue interference from state or nonstate actors? 3 / 4

Mauritius is considered among the most business-friendly countries in Africa. However, the Non-Citizen Property Restriction Act limits most noncitizens from owning or acquiring property. Corruption can hamper business activity.

G3. Do individuals enjoy personal social freedoms, including choice of marriage partner and size of family, protection from domestic violence, and control over appearance? 3 / 4

The government generally does not limit social freedoms, though same-sex unions are not recognized. Rape is against the law, but spousal rape is not specifically criminalized. Domestic violence is illegal but remains a significant concern.

G4. Do individuals enjoy equality of opportunity and freedom from economic exploitation? 2 / 4

Women and children are vulnerable to sex trafficking. While the government has made some efforts to prosecute traffickers and provide services to victims, these efforts are generally inadequate.

The position of migrant workers in the manufacturing and construction sectors can be precarious. During the COVID-19 pandemic, Mauritian labor rights advocacy organizations have claimed that the government's rolling back of labor protection laws have led to more exploitation of migrant workers.

Mexico

Population: 127,800,000
Capital: Mexico City
Freedom Status: Partly Free
Electoral Democracy: Yes

Overview: Mexico has been an electoral democracy since 2000, and alternation in power between parties is routine at both the federal and state levels. However, the country suffers from severe rule of law deficits that limit full citizen enjoyment of political rights and civil liberties. Violence perpetrated by organized criminals, corruption among government officials, human rights abuses by both state and nonstate actors, and rampant impunity are among the most visible of Mexico's many governance challenges.

KEY DEVELOPMENTS IN 2020

- With over 125,000 deaths and 1.4 million cases, people in Mexico was severely affected by the COVID-19 pandemic. The government initially hid the virus's true toll from the public, and the actual numbers of cases and deaths caused by the coronavirus are unknown.
- In July, authorities identified the bone fragments of one of the 43 missing Guerrero students, further undermining stories about the controversial case told by the Peña Nieto administration.
- Also in July, former head of the state oil company PEMEX Emilio Lozoya was implicated in several multimillion-dollar graft schemes involving other high-ranking former officials. Extradited from Spain, he testified against his former bosses and peers, including former presidents Calderón and Peña Nieto.
- In December, the Committee to Protect Journalists (CPJ) named Mexico the most dangerous country in the world for members of the media. At least nine reporters were killed in Mexico this year—including three in a 10-day span in November—which accounts for one third globally of all journalists killed during the year.

POLITICAL RIGHTS: 27 / 40

A. ELECTORAL PROCESS: 9 / 12

A1. Was the current head of government or other chief national authority elected through free and fair elections? 3 / 4

The president is elected to a six-year term and cannot be reelected. However, a 2019 constitutional amendment enables citizens to initiate a recall referendum halfway through the president's term.

Andrés Manuel López Obrador of the left-leaning National Regeneration Movement (MORENA) won the 2018 poll with a commanding 53 percent of the vote. His closest rival, Ricardo Anaya—the candidate of the National Action Party (PAN) as well as of the Democratic Revolution Party (PRD) and Citizens' Movement (MC)—took 22 percent. The results of the 2018 poll represented a stark repudiation of outgoing president Enrique Peña Nieto and the Institutional Revolutionary Party (PRI), which, took just 16 percent of the vote.

The election campaign was marked by violence and threats against candidates for state and local offices; at least 145 people died because of election-related violence. Accusations of illicit campaign activities remained frequent at the state and municipal level.

A2. Were the current national legislative representatives elected through free and fair elections? 3 / 4

Senators are elected for six-year terms through a mix of direct voting and proportional representation, with at least two parties represented in each state's delegation. In the Chamber of Deputies, the lower house of the bicameral Congress, 300 members are elected through direct representation and 200 through proportional representation, each for three-year terms. Under 2013 electoral reforms, current members of Congress are no longer barred from reelection and candidates are permitted to run as independents. For legislators elected in 2018, senators will be eligible to serve up to two six-year terms, and deputies will be permitted to serve up to four three-year terms.

In the 2018 elections, MORENA achieved a 255-seat majority in the Chamber of Deputies, and with the support of its coalition allies, the Workers' Party (PT) and the Social Encounter Party (PES), held just over 300 seats, enough to amend the constitution. The PAN won 79 seats, while the PRI plummeted from winning 202 seats in the 2015 midterms to just 47 seats in 2018. Similarly, the MORENA-led coalition now commands a clear majority in the 128-member Senate with 70 seats, compared to 24 for the PAN and 15 for the PRI.

Accusations of illicit campaign activities are frequent at the state and federal level, and violations including vote buying, ballot stealing, and misuse of public funds were reported in 2018.

A3. Are the electoral laws and framework fair, and are they implemented impartially by the relevant election management bodies? 3 / 4

Mexico's National Electoral Institute (INE) supervises elections and enforces political party laws, including strict regulations on campaign financing and the content of political advertising, although control is uneven in practice. While the 2018 elections were generally considered free and fair, the INE and the Federal Electoral Tribunal (TEPJF) struggled to comprehensively address problems including misuse of public funds, vote buying, ballot stealing, and ensuring of transparent campaign financing. Frequent verbal attacks by MORENA, along with steps to cut the INE's budget, prompted accusations that the administration sought to lessen electoral oversight and give itself an advantage in future elections, though new INE officers selected in 2020 were regarded as professional. Campaign finance issues were prominent in scandals in 2020, including evidence that the president's brother accepted $90,000 in cash for use in campaigns in Chiapas. In November, the Financial Intelligence Unit found no wrongdoing on his part.

President López Obrador has extolled the use of informal, extralegal referendums—known as citizen consultations—which are not supervised by the INE. A series of consultations since 2018 on infrastructure and social spending have been criticized as skewed toward the president's preferred outcomes, and they have featured the participation of only a small proportion of Mexican voters. In March 2020, a consultation in Mexicali regarding construction of a large brewery featured participation of less than 5 percent of the electorate.

B. POLITICAL PLURALISM AND PARTICIPATION: 13 / 16

B1. Do the people have the right to organize in different political parties or other competitive political groupings of their choice, and is the system free of undue obstacles to the rise and fall of these competing parties or groupings? 4 / 4

Mexico's multiparty system features few official restrictions on political organization and activity. Though moribund at the national level, opposition parties are competitive in many states, and independent candidacies are becoming more common. President López Obrador's victory reflected the political system's openness to pluralistic competition, and ended fears on the left that powerful actors would block their electoral path to power. MORENA includes a wide range of ideological and political currents, and tensions were visible throughout 2020 as various factions competed in a bitterly fought campaign for party head, with legislator Mario Delgado declared the winner in October. In September, the INE denied registration to the party Mexico Libre led by former president Calderón and his wife, Margarita Zavala, on the basis of opaque funding sources.

No gubernatorial elections occurred in 2020. Victories in the 2019 gubernatorial races in in Baja California and Puebla reinforced MORENA's gradually growing strength at the subnational level. MORENA officials now govern six states and Mexico City, and control 20 of the 32 state legislatures.

B2. Is there a realistic opportunity for the opposition to increase its support or gain power through elections? 4 / 4

Power has routinely changed hands at the national level since 2000. The dominant victory of López Obrador and MORENA in 2018 followed six years of government control by the PRI, which had ruled Mexico without interruption from 1929 to 2000, before losing consecutive presidential races to the right-leaning PAN in 2000 and 2006.

In May 2020, the Supreme Court struck down a widely criticized law passed by the Baja California legislature that retroactively extended the term of its governor, Jaime Bonilla, to five years from the two-year term he won in June 2019.

Because of MORENA dominance at the federal level, leadership of the political opposition increasingly devolved to state governors in 2020. The López Obrador administration's budgetary austerity measures prompted non-MORENA governors, particularly in northern Mexico, to label themselves the Federalist Alliance and advocate for a renegotiation of basic fiscal structures.

B3. Are the people's political choices free from domination by forces that are external to the political sphere, or by political forces that employ extrapolitical means? 2 / 4

Criminal groups, while increasingly fragmented, exert powerful influence on the country's politics through threats and violence against candidates, election officials, and campaign workers, particularly at the local level. At least 145 politicians were murdered between fall 2017 and election day in July 2018. Scores of politicians are believed to have withdrawn 2018 candidacies due to fears of violence.

Separately, in states and municipalities with lower levels of multiparty participation, locally dominant political actors often govern in a highly opaque manner that limits political activity and citizen participation.

B4. Do various segments of the population (including ethnic, racial, religious, gender, LGBT+, and other relevant groups) have full political rights and electoral opportunities? 3 / 4

Mexico has a large indigenous population, and Indigenous people and groups are free to participate in politics. There are some provisions for the integration of Indigenous community customs in electing leaders in some states, though only for local authorities. Parties serving Indigenous communities' interests often compete in states with large Indigenous populations. However, in practice, Indigenous people remain severely underrepresented in political institutions. Mexico's small Afro-Mexican population is similarly underrepresented in national politics, though they are recognized in the constitution.

The 2018 election confirmed the success of gender requirements for candidacies and party lists: 48 percent of representatives in the Chamber of Deputies and 49 percent in the Senate are women. In December 2020, the Federal Electoral Tribunal ruled that each party must have at least seven women among their candidates in the 15 gubernatorial elections in 2021.

C. FUNCTIONING OF GOVERNMENT: 5 / 12

C1. Do the freely elected head of government and national legislative representatives determine the policies of the government? 2 / 4

Organized crime and related violence have limited the effective governing authority of elected officials in some areas of the country, as well as of the federal government. Members of organized crime groups have persisted in their attempts to infiltrate local governments in order to plunder municipal coffers and ensure their own impunity. The notorious and still unsolved mass disappearance of 43 students in Guerrero in 2014 was linked to a deeply corrupt local government collaborating with a drug gang, as well as corrupt or complicit members of various state security forces. In the most violent regions, the provision of public services has become more difficult, as public-sector employees face extortion and pressure to divert public funds.

C2. Are safeguards against official corruption strong and effective? 1 / 4

Official corruption remains a serious problem. The billions of dollars in illegal drug money that enter the country each year from the United States profoundly affect politics, as does rampant public-contract fraud and other forms of siphoning off state funds. Attempts to prosecute officials for alleged involvement in corrupt or criminal activity have often failed due to the weakness of the cases brought by the state.

The López Obrador administration has made the pursuit of corruption a priority, and several prominent figures from the Peña Nieto administration have been indicted or arrested on graft charges. However, critics have seen López Obrador's anticorruption efforts as heavily politicized. Emilio Lozoya, the former head of state oil company PEMEX, was accused of involvement in several multimillion-dollar graft schemes involving high-ranking officials and was extradited from Spain in July 2020. Upon his return to Mexico, he provided testimony regarding corruption among his former bosses and peers, including former presidents Calderón and Peña Nieto and multiple prominent officials from the PRI and the PAN. In August, Lozoya's testimony from the Attorney General's Office was leaked, potentially tainting the legal process.

C3. Does the government operate with openness and transparency? 2 / 4

Despite some limitations, several freedom of information laws passed since 2002 have successfully strengthened transparency at the federal level, though enforcement is uneven across states. In recent years, the government has failed to release relevant information on some of the country's most controversial issues, including abuses by the security forces and the investigation into the missing 43 students in Guerrero. The military, assigned ever-expanding roles under López Obrador, is one of the least transparent state institutions. President López Obrador has been openly critical of the system that enables the public to access information about his administration.

Throughout the COVID-19 pandemic, government officials were accused of inadequate and incompetent management, including opacity about the virus's true toll, which was estimated to be far higher than the official figures.

CIVIL LIBERTIES: 34 / 60 (−1)

D. FREEDOM OF EXPRESSION AND BELIEF: 13 / 16

D1. Are there free and independent media? 2 / 4

The security environment for journalists remains highly challenging. Reporters probing police issues, drug trafficking, and official corruption face serious, sustained risk of physical harm. The Committee to Protect Journalists (CPJ) named Mexico the deadliest country for journalists in 2020, and recorded the deaths of at least nine journalists in Mexico in connection with their work in 2020, with another five killings of reporters under investigation. Self-censorship has increased, with many newspapers in violent areas avoiding publication of stories concerning organized crime. Press watchdog groups have decried the slow pace of the federal government's special prosecutor for crimes against freedom of expression since the office gained authority in 2013. Several convictions in cases of murdered journalists occurred in 2020, though 90 percent of cases of journalists who are murdered are unresolved. In October, the CPJ noted that no new cases had been federalized since López Obrador took office.

The Federal Protection Mechanism for Human Rights Defenders and Journalists within the Interior Secretariat, created in 2012, has successfully protected hundreds of activists and reporters, providing them safe houses, panic buttons, and bodyguards. However, the mechanism is underfunded—in October 2020 the trust fund financing it was dissolved—and has been unable to include many journalists.

Diversity of viewpoints in print and online media remains high, but broadcast television has been dominated by the duopoly of Televisa and TV Azteca since the 1990s. Media outlets depend on government advertising and subsidies. Congress enacted legislation to regulate the distribution of government resources in 2018 and President López Obrador cut spending on state advertising in July 2020. However, media watchdogs note continued opacity and politicization of government media support. Throughout 2020, López Obrador continued his daily morning news conferences, dominating news cycles and often chastising and demeaning specific reporters and news outlets.

Mexico has been at the forefront of citizen-led efforts to ensure internet access. The 2013 amendments to Article 6 of the constitution made access to the internet a civil right. However, gangs have engaged in threats and violence against bloggers and online journalists who report on organized crime. In July 2020, state-owned news outlet Notimex was accused of exacerbating the polarized online environment by sponsoring and coordinating online troll attacks on reporters and outlets perceived as hostile to the administration.

The COVID-19 pandemic deeply affected journalists' safety throughout 2020. Article 19 registered 52 media workers who died of the disease, and numerous others who were exposed to the infection due to a lack of protective gear.

D2. Are individuals free to practice and express their religious faith or nonbelief in public and private? 4 / 4

Religious freedom is protected by the constitution and is generally respected in practice, though religious minorities, particularly Indigenous Evangelical communities in Chiapas, face occasional persecution by local authorities.

D3. Is there academic freedom, and is the educational system free from extensive political indoctrination? 4 / 4

The government does not restrict academic freedom, though university students and some academics are occasionally threatened for their political activism. University research was expected to be subject to cuts following the controversial October 2020 rescission of dozens of public trust funds that included funding for research centers, many of which are housed within universities.

D4. Are individuals free to express their personal views on political or other sensitive topics without fear of surveillance or retribution? 3 / 4

While there are no formal impediments to free and open discussion, fear of criminal monitoring restricts citizens' willingness to converse publicly about crime in some areas of the country.

E. ASSOCIATIONAL AND ORGANIZATIONAL RIGHTS: 7 / 12
E1. Is there freedom of assembly? 3 / 4

The constitution guarantees the right to peacefully assemble. Protests are frequent, though political and civic expression is restricted in some regions, and police frequently use excessive force and detain protesters arbitrarily. Human rights watchdogs expressed concern that the 2019 National Use of Force Law, which enabled the creation of the National Guard, would increase the abuse of protesters. As of the end of 2020, the Supreme Court had not ruled on challenges to the law.

Several instances of protest-related violence caused controversy in 2020. In March, tens of thousands of women protested against violence against women and other forms of gender discrimination in Mexico City and initiated a one-day strike. In November, police fired live ammunition at a feminist protest in Cancún, resulting in at least 10 injuries; the police chief and state security minister were subsequently forced out of their jobs.

E2. Is there freedom for nongovernmental organizations, particularly those that are engaged in human rights– and governance-related work? 2 / 4

Although highly active, nongovernmental organizations (NGOs) sometimes face violent resistance; the Office of the United Nations (UN) High Commissioner for Human Rights counted seven activist deaths by September 2020. Environmental activists and representatives of Indigenous groups contesting large-scale infrastructure projects have been particularly vulnerable. Revelations emerged in 2017 that government agencies had allegedly attempted to spy on the electronic communications of a number of civil society activists.

The Federal Protection Mechanism for Human Rights Defenders and Journalists has provided physical security for hundreds of activists since its 2012 inception, though rights groups consider it sluggish and subject to government neglect. The trust fund that finances the mechanism was eliminated in October 2020, prompting concern that its efficacy will further diminish.

Civil society members freely criticize state policies, but López Obrador's penchant for dismissing criticism and insulting perceived opponents generated tension between the president and NGOs throughout 2020.

E3. Is there freedom for trade unions and similar professional or labor organizations? 2 / 4

Trade union membership has diminished significantly in recent decades. In 2019 major labor reform brought hope of an end to the rampant use of informal, nontransparent negotiations between employers and politically connected union leaders creating in "protection contracts" never seen by workers. Several important provisions of the law took effect in 2020, but the June arrest in Tamaulipas of labor leader Susana Prieto, one of the country's most visible trade unionists, prompted both domestic and international criticism.

F. RULE OF LAW: 5 / 16

F1. Is there an independent judiciary? 2 / 4

The Supreme Court (SCJN) has been regarded in recent years as generally independent, but several 2019 appointments of justices viewed as close to the government raised concerns about diminished autonomy. Such concerns were amplified by the SCJN's approval of a national citizen consultation in 2021 on whether to open investigations into potential misdeeds during the administrations of López Obrador's five immediate presidential predecessors. The ruling condoned a constitutionally illegitimate exercise intended to gain political advantage. A December 2020 judicial reform bill intends to improve judicial careers and competence, though observers warn that it concentrates the judiciary's power in the SCJN.

F2. Does due process prevail in civil and criminal matters? 1 / 4

Mexico's justice system is plagued by delays, unpredictability, and corruption, which often lead to impunity for perpetrators of crimes. A 2008 constitutional reform replaced the civil-inquisitorial trial system with an oral-adversarial one. Implementation of the adversarial system was technically completed in 2016 and did show some improvements, but it needs more capacity to fulfill the project's goals. A lack of political commitment to prosecutorial autonomy and the attorney general's resistance to reform, has limited the efficacy of the 2018 overhaul of the prosecutorial agency.

Widespread bribery, limited capacity, and weak coordination undermine the lower courts' and law enforcement's integrity. According to a December 2020 government report, the vast majority of crimes committed in 2019 went unreported, largely because underpaid police were viewed as either inept or in league with criminals. When investigations were conducted, only a tiny handful of crimes ended in convictions.

Widely publicized raids often result in the release of accused criminals due to grave procedural deficiencies. Rather than improve investigative and prosecutorial competence and efficacy, however, the López Obrador administration's legislative initiatives have mostly sought to harden penalties and limit defendants' rights.

F3. Is there protection from the illegitimate use of physical force and freedom from war and insurgencies? 1 / 4

Mexicans are subject to the threat of violence at the hands of multiple actors, including individual criminals, criminal gangs that operate with impunity, and police officers who are often susceptible to bribery. A missing-persons registry—which continues to grow despite increased government efforts in recent years—reflects an epidemic of enforced disappearances. Mexicans in police or military custody are at risk of torture by the authorities, and must also navigate a prison system that respects neither due process nor physical safety.

Abuses during arrests and criminal investigations are rife, and detainees report routine physical abuse while being held. The 2017 comprehensive General Law on Torture established a prohibition on the use of torture and disqualified evidence obtained through its use. Though it has contributed to mild progress in excluding torture-based confessions from prosecutions, impunity remains almost universal. A series of deaths in police custody in 2020 sparked protests, and the fatal beating of a Jalisco man led to violent clashes between police and protesters in Guadalajara in June.

Human rights advocates consistently express concern about a lack of accountability for abuses committed by members of the military, including torture, forced disappearances, and extrajudicial executions. Only a handful of soldiers have been convicted in civilian courts for abuses against civilians, despite myriad NGO and National Human Rights Commission (CNDH) reports implicating state security forces in grave human rights abuses. Rights advocates and elected officials have criticized the leader of the CNDH, a close ally of the president, for passivity and mismanagement.

Forced disappearances and killings remain a crisis in Mexico, despite recent efforts to be more responsive to victims. The 2017 General Law on Disappearances removed the statute of limitations on missing-persons crimes. In August 2020, a new protocol took effect to abet the search and identification of disappearance victims; cases in the national registry numbered over 73,000 as of July.

The kidnapping and presumed deaths of 43 students in Guerrero in 2014 remains controversial. President López Obrador created a presidential commission to investigate the case after taking office, and in 2019 a new special prosecutor was assigned to manage it. Multiple arrest warrants were issued in 2020, though the missing students' fates remained unknown at year's end. The identification of one student's bone fragments in July 2020 further undermined the story presented by the Peña Nieto administration.

The government's primary response to insecurity hotspots was the deployment of militarized forces. In 2019, President López Obrador established a nominally civilian-led gendarmerie that would draw from the Army, Navy, and federal police, and would rely on military officers for its top ranks. This new National Guard has been sharply criticized by rights advocates for reinforcing the militarization of public security. Reform advocates and rights groups, as well as the local office of the Office of the UN High Commissioner for Human Rights, denounced the May 2020 announcement that regular military troops would remain actively deployed in a policing role, and questioned the increasing reliance on the military to carry out a broadening array of tasks.

Deaths attributed to organized crime remained at historic highs in 2020. Violence was particularly acute Guanajuato, where a multi-year battle to control gasoline theft and drug trafficking routes continued. While large organizations like the Jalisco New Generation Cartel (CJNG) and the Sinaloa Cartel continue to drive insecurity in some areas, the splintering of other criminal groups, along with the diversification of their revenue sources, has made efforts to combat the violence even more daunting. Over 500 police were killed during the year; in June, an attack attributed to the CJNG targeted the police chief of Mexico City, who was wounded.

Mexican prisons remain highly unsafe, with inmates commonly engaging in criminal activity while incarcerated. As of mid-October, the CNDH had registered 232 confirmed and 236 suspected deaths of COVID-19 in prisons. Fears about the spread of disease in overcrowded prisons provided impetus to pass an Amnesty Law in April 2020, but the measure was limited in scope and no prisoners were released under its provisions during the year. The prison population increased by nearly 14,000 inmates in 2020, and the percentage of prisoners in pretrial detention rose from 37 to 42 percent.

F4. Do laws, policies, and practices guarantee equal treatment of various segments of the population? 1 / 4

Mexican law bans discrimination based on ethnic origin, gender, age, religion, and sexual orientation. Nevertheless, lighter-skinned Mexicans enjoy substantial social advantage compared to Indigenous people and other distinct groups. The large Indigenous population experience social and economic discrimination, and approximately 70 percent of Indigenous people live in poverty. Southern states with high concentrations of Indigenous residents suffer from deficient services, a problem that had particularly negative health and educational consequences during the COVID-19 pandemic. Because Indigenous groups are in particular danger from criminal violence, communities in Guerrero and Michoacán have formed self-defense groups, some of which were subsequently legalized. Afro-Mexicans face discrimination, though the 2020 census included an option for Afro-Mexican self-identification for the first time.

LGBT+ people have strong legal protections, but they are not uniformly enforced. Transgender women in particular face discrimination and violence.

Migrants from Central America, many of whom move through Mexico to reach the United States, have long faced persecution and criminal predation. The López Obrador administration initially sought to protect migrants, but reversed course in 2019 when the United States threatened to seal its border with Mexico and institute punitive tariffs. In response, the National Guard was ordered to arrest migrants moving northward—a policy that led to complaints of rights abuses throughout 2020—established immigration checkpoints along major roads, and raided migrant shelters in the country.

The government cooperated with the implementation of Migrant Protection Protocols (MPP), a United States policy forcing asylum seekers to remain in Mexico until their cases are processed. Tens of thousands have been forced to wait in border cities like Ciudad Juárez and Nuevo Laredo for their hearings, finding themselves at risk of kidnapping and extortion in the interim, with near-total impunity for their attackers. These policies remained in place in 2020; the COVID-19 pandemic exacerbated the harsh migrant shelter conditions. The government has made some remediation efforts, including a November 2020 reform to protect child and adolescent migrants and the firing of hundreds of allegedly corrupt migration agents.

G. PERSONAL AUTONOMY AND INDIVIDUAL RIGHTS: 9 / 16 (−1)

G1. Do individuals enjoy freedom of movement, including the ability to change their place of residence, employment, or education? 3 / 4

Citizens are generally free to change their place of residence, employment, or education. However, criminals have impeded freedom of movement by blocking major roads in several states in recent years, and ordinary citizens avoid roads in many rural areas after dark. Although some states restricted freedom of movement in response to the COVID-19 pandemic, restrictions were less harsh than most countries suffering outbreaks of similar severity.

G2. Are individuals able to exercise the right to own property and establish private businesses without undue interference from state or nonstate actors? 2 / 4

Property rights in Mexico are protected by a modern legal framework, but the weakness of the judicial system, frequent solicitation of bribes by bureaucrats and officials, and the high incidence of criminal extortion harm security of property for many individuals and businesses. Large-scale development projects, including high-priority López Obrador initiatives, have been accompanied by corruption and rights-related controversy in recent years, exemplified in 2020 by the dispute over a train line, primarily serving tourists, in the Yucatan Peninsula.

G3. Do individuals enjoy personal social freedoms, including choice of marriage partner and size of family, protection from domestic violence, and control over appearance? 2 / 4 (−1)

Sexual abuse and domestic violence against women are common, and perpetrators are rarely punished. Implementation of a 2007 law designed to protect women from such crimes remains halting, particularly at the state level, and impunity is the norm for the killers of hundreds of women each year. State authorities can issue "gender alerts" that trigger greater scrutiny and an influx of resources to combat an epidemic of violence against women, but the mechanism has proven ineffective. Femicides rose in the first half of 2020, and the COVID-19 pandemic led to a spike in domestic abuse complaints.

The government has made some efforts to combat violence and promote gender equality, but López Obrador has also cut funding for women's services and dismissed feminist protesters as aligned with the political opposition.

Abortion has been a contentious issue in recent years. Many states reacted to Mexico City's 2007 liberalization of abortion laws by strengthening their own criminal bans on the procedure. In September 2019 Oaxaca became only the second state to decriminalize first-trimester abortions.

Mexico has taken steps toward equality for LGBT+ people, though significant cultural and legal barriers persist. A 2015 Supreme Court decision overruled state laws defining the purpose of marriage as procreation. The passage of legislation in Puebla in November 2020 and Tlaxcala in December, Mexico City and 21 other states had legalized same-sex marriage. In October 2020, Sonora became the tenth state to allow gender changes on identification documents.

Score Change: The score declined from 3 to 2 because the government has resisted calls to address gender-based violence, particularly domestic violence, and cut funding for related services despite significant increases in the scale of the problem.

G4. Do individuals enjoy equality of opportunity and freedom from economic exploitation? 2 / 4

Economic opportunity is limited in Mexico, which maintains a high rate of economic inequality. Migrant agricultural workers face brutally exploitative conditions in several northern states, and the COVID-19 pandemic prompted a spike in workers' rights abuse complaints. In 2018, the Supreme Court ruled that Mexico's millions of domestic workers—the vast majority of whom are women—must be incorporated into the formal sector and receive social security and health benefits. The López Obrador administration has increased some forms of redistributive spending, and in recent years has sharply increased Mexico's minimum wage.

Mexico is a major source, transit, and destination country for trafficking in persons, including women and children, many of whom are subject to forced labor and sexual exploitation. Organized criminal gangs are heavily involved in human trafficking in Mexico and into the United States. This danger has been exacerbated since 2019 by the United States' denial of entry to asylum seekers presenting themselves at the border under the MPP program, which has forced thousands of migrants to wait in nearby cities like Ciudad Juárez.

Micronesia

Population: 100,000
Capital: Palikir
Freedom Status: Free
Electoral Democracy: Yes

Overview: The Federated States of Micronesia (FSM) is a relatively stable democracy that holds regular, competitive elections. However, secessionist movements have sometimes unsettled the country's politics and threatened its unity. The judiciary is independent, and civil liberties are generally respected. Ongoing problems include underreporting of domestic violence and the exploitation of migrant workers.

KEY DEVELOPMENTS IN 2020

- In February, a referendum on independence for the state of Chuuk was delayed to 2022.
- A constitutional convention was convened in January but went into recess in March due to COVID-19 mitigation measures.
- President David Panuelo declared a COVID-19-related state of emergency in January and individuals who had traveled to China were prohibited from entering the FSM that month. All four states halted inbound travel by March. While outbound restrictions ended in November, a ban on inbound travel persisted through year's end. No cases or deaths were reported in 2020.

POLITICAL RIGHTS: 37 / 40
A. ELECTORAL PROCESS: 12 / 12

A1. Was the current head of government or other chief national authority elected through free and fair elections? 4 / 4

The president is both chief of state and head of government and receives assistance from the vice president. Both offices are indirectly elected for four-year terms by members of Congress, with candidates from among the legislature's four at-large, directly elected state representatives, known as senators. In March 2019, David Panuelo, the senator representing the state of Pohnpei, was chosen as president, defeating incumbent Peter Christian. Vice President Yosiwo George was reelected.

Each of the four states (Yap, Chuuk, Pohnpei, and Kosrae) has its own elected governor.

A2. Were the current national legislative representatives elected through free and fair elections? 4 / 4

The 14-member unicameral Congress includes 4 senators, 1 from each state, who serve four-year terms and are elected by proportional representation. Another 10 members serve two-year terms in single-member districts allocated by population. Each state also has its own elected legislature.

In March 2019, the FSM held full congressional elections. Incumbent president Christian lost his post to Panuelo. The senators from the three other states are Vice President George from Kosrae, Wesley Simina from Chuuk, and Joseph Urusemal from Yap. There were no reports of fraud or irregularities in the election's administration. Voters also approved the FSM's fourth Constitutional Convention, which was convened in January 2020 but went into recess in March due to COVID-19.

A3. Are the electoral laws and framework fair, and are they implemented impartially by the relevant election management bodies? 4 / 4

Elections in the FSM, which are generally considered free and fair, are administered by a government agency headed by a national election director and one commissioner from each state. Constitutional amendments must be approved by three-quarters of voters in at least three of the four states.

B. POLITICAL PLURALISM AND PARTICIPATION: 15 / 16
B1. Do the people have the right to organize in different political parties or other competitive political groupings of their choice, and is the system free of undue obstacles to the rise and fall of these competing parties or groupings? 4 / 4

There are no formal political parties, but there are no restrictions on their formation. All candidates run as independents.

B2. Is there a realistic opportunity for the opposition to increase its support or gain power through elections? 4 / 4

The FSM has an established record of democratic power transfers. Under an informal agreement, the presidency has typically rotated among the four states, but Congress has sometimes deviated from this pattern.

B3. Are the people's political choices free from domination by forces that are external to the political sphere, or by political forces that employ extrapolitical means? 4 / 4

Traditional leaders and institutions exercise significant influence in society, especially at the village level. However, neither these nor donor countries like the United States and China exert undue control over the political choices of voters or candidates. Investments from United States and China have been met with pushback in recent years, as citizens are concerned about how those funds might impinge upon the FSM's political, economic, and cultural independence.

B4. Do various segments of the population (including ethnic, racial, religious, gender, LGBT+, and other relevant groups) have full political rights and electoral opportunities? 3 / 4

Women and minority groups formally have full political rights, and they are free to participate in practice, though women's political engagement is limited to some extent by discriminatory attitudes. The FSM remains one of the few countries in the world with no women in its national legislature. A small number of women were elected to state-level legislatures.

C. FUNCTIONING OF GOVERNMENT: 10 / 12
C1. Do the freely elected head of government and national legislative representatives determine the policies of the government? 4 / 4

Elected officials determine and implement policy and legislation at the federal level, though considerable authority is vested in the states and their elected governments. Some leading politicians from Chuuk, by far the most populous state, have advocated independence from the FSM in recent years, and the issue remained a topic of public discussion under the guidance of the Chuuk Political Status Commission. Opponents of Chuuk's secession have argued that its separation from the FSM would be unconstitutional. A referendum was planned for 2019, but was delayed that year and again in February 2020; it is now scheduled for 2022.

The FSM relies on defense guarantees and economic assistance from the United States under a 1986 Compact of Free Association (CoFA), which extends through 2023. In 2019, the funding and security commitments of the CoFA were reaffirmed by the United States.

China has become an increasingly important partner for trade and development aid in recent years, though its role does not amount to an undue interference in FSM governance, and citizens and officials have been wary of it becoming so. In late 2019, China pledged $72 million worth of development support to the FSM.

C2. Are safeguards against official corruption strong and effective? 3 / 4

Official corruption is a problem and a source of public discontent. Complaints about misuse of public resources are frequent, particularly from US authorities overseeing aid funds. Government entities responsible for combating corruption, including the attorney general's office and public auditor, are independent and fairly effective, though some corrupt officials reportedly enjoy impunity.

C3. Does the government operate with openness and transparency? 3 / 4

Government operations and legislative processes are generally transparent, though there is no comprehensive law guaranteeing public access to government information. Limited technical capacity and the country's sprawling geography pose practical barriers to openness and accountability in the FSM. Officials are not legally obliged to submit asset disclosures.

In March 2020, the Chuuk Office of the Public Auditor warned that records related to the state debt-relief fund were improperly maintained, and that financial statements did not fully report liabilities to the public.

CIVIL LIBERTIES: 55 / 60
D. FREEDOM OF EXPRESSION AND BELIEF: 16 / 16
D1. Are there free and independent media? 4 / 4

The news media operate freely. Print outlets include government-published newsletters and several small, privately owned weekly and monthly newspapers. There are several radio stations, cable television is available, and satellite television is increasingly common. More than a third of the population has internet access.

Lack of resources is a problem for the broadcasting of important meteorological forecasts for the population of Chuuk, which will face rising sea levels and extreme weather events.

In 2019, several members of the Yap Council of Chiefs, which oversees traditional and cultural matters on the island, unsuccessfully demanded the expulsion of journalist Joyce McClure, asserting that McClure wrote misleading news articles. McClure claimed the demand was prompted by critical reports on Chinese presence and influence on the island.

D2. Are individuals free to practice and express their religious faith or nonbelief in public and private? 4 / 4

Religious freedom is generally respected, and religious groups are not required to register with the government. About 96 percent of the population is Roman Catholic or Protestant. A small Ahmadi Muslim community has reported some instances of discrimination and vandalism. Intolerance for non-Christian religions in several of states is a growing concern.

D3. Is there academic freedom, and is the educational system free from extensive political indoctrination? 4 / 4

The educational system is free from extensive indoctrination.

D4. Are individuals free to express their personal views on political or other sensitive topics without fear of surveillance or retribution? 4 / 4

The constitution guarantees freedom of expression, and there are no significant constraints on this right in practice. The government does not improperly monitor personal communications or social media activity.

E. ASSOCIATIONAL AND ORGANIZATIONAL RIGHTS: 11 / 12
E1. Is there freedom of assembly? 4 / 4

Freedom of assembly is constitutionally protected and demonstrations typically proceed peacefully.

E2. Is there freedom for nongovernmental organizations, particularly those that are engaged in human rights- and governance-related work? 4 / 4

Citizens are free to organize in civic groups, and a number of students' and women's organizations are active.

E3. Is there freedom for trade unions and similar professional or labor organizations? 3 / 4

Union rights are generally respected, and there are no laws to prevent workers from forming unions, engaging in collective bargaining, or striking. However, such activities are not specifically protected or regulated by law, and few employers are large enough to support unionization in practice.

F. RULE OF LAW: 15 / 16
F1. Is there an independent judiciary? 4 / 4

The judiciary is independent. The chief justice, who administers the judicial system, and the associate justices of the Supreme Court are appointed by the president with the approval of a two-thirds majority in Congress. They are appointed for life-long terms and cannot be removed arbitrarily.

F2. Does due process prevail in civil and criminal matters? 4 / 4

The police respect legal safeguards against arbitrary arrest and detention, and defendants are generally provided with basic due process guarantees surrounding trials and appeals. However, a shortage of lawyers may sometimes impair detainees' access to counsel in practice.

F3. Is there protection from the illegitimate use of physical force and freedom from war and insurgencies? 4 / 4

Criminal activity does not pose a major threat to physical security, though police have struggled to deal with illegal fishing. Law enforcement officials have intercepted several shipments of weapons and ammunition bound for the FSM during 2020.

Mistreatment of individuals in custody is known to occur; in March 2020, the Justice Department filed charges against three correctional officers who allegedly assaulted a prisoner.

In October 2019, the acting attorney general on Yap, American Rachelle Bergeron, was murdered; her murder was allegedly connected to her work cracking down on human trafficking in the FSM. Two men were accused of conspiring to murder Bergeron that month, though the trial against them was delayed to October 2020 due to the COVID-19 pandemic.

F4. Do laws, policies, and practices guarantee equal treatment of various segments of the population? 3 / 4

The constitution gives citizens equal protection under the law and prohibits discrimination based on race, ancestry, national origin, gender, sexual orientation, language, or social status. In 2018, Congress passed a landmark law prohibiting discrimination based on sexual orientation, which then president Christian signed. However, the law did not mention gender identity, leaving transgender people vulnerable to continued discrimination.

Half as many women enjoy formal employment as do men, and women generally participate far less in the formal and informal labor markets.

G. PERSONAL AUTONOMY AND INDIVIDUAL RIGHTS: 13 / 16

G1. Do individuals enjoy freedom of movement, including the ability to change their place of residence, employment, or education? 4 / 4

Freedom of movement is generally respected. Under the CoFA, Micronesians are free to travel to the United States without visas for residence, education, and employment. Many Micronesians have migrated to US Pacific states or territories such as Hawaii and Guam.

Travel out of the FSM was severely impacted by COVID-19-related measures, however, with inbound travel effectively halted by March 2020. Outbound travel restrictions ended in November, though inbound restrictions remained through year's end.

G2. Are individuals able to exercise the right to own property and establish private businesses without undue interference from state or nonstate actors? 3 / 4

Property rights are protected by law, and individuals are able to operate private businesses; most such enterprises are small and family-owned in practice. Property and business rights are somewhat restricted for foreigners. Noncitizens are legally prohibited from owning land, and a number of regulations limit the kinds of businesses that they can own and operate.

G3. Do individuals enjoy personal social freedoms, including choice of marriage partner and size of family, protection from domestic violence, and control over appearance? 3 / 4

Personal social freedoms are largely protected. However, there are no specific laws against spousal rape, and both rape and domestic violence are rarely prosecuted due to societal inhibitions against reporting such crimes. The FSM's first support center for survivors of gender-based violence (GBV) opened in Chuuk in March 2020.

G4. Do individuals enjoy equality of opportunity and freedom from economic exploitation? 3 / 4

Forced labor is prohibited, and the government enforces basic standards for working conditions in the formal sector. Foreign migrant workers nevertheless remain vulnerable to exploitative labor practices, including on foreign fishing vessels in FSM waters. Micronesian women are at risk of sex trafficking.

The 2020 edition of the US State Department's *Trafficking in Persons Report* noted the government's efforts to address trafficking, including the opening of an antitrafficking division in the Justice Department. However, services for survivors and professional knowledge of trafficking issues within law enforcement and the judiciary remained lacking.

Moldova

Population: 3,500,000
Capital: Chişinău
Freedom Status: Partly Free
Electoral Democracy: Yes

Note: The numerical scores and status listed above do not reflect conditions in Transnistria, which is examined in a separate report. *Freedom in the World* reports assess the level of political rights and civil liberties in a given geographical area, regardless of whether they are affected by the state, nonstate actors, or foreign powers. Disputed territories are sometimes assessed separately if they meet certain criteria, including boundaries that are sufficiently stable to allow year-on-year comparisons. For more information, see the report methodology and FAQ.

Overview: Moldova has a competitive electoral environment, and freedoms of assembly, speech, and religion are mostly protected. Nonetheless, pervasive corruption in the government sector, links between major political figures and powerful economic interests, as well as critical deficiencies in the justice sector and the rule of law continue to hamper democratic governance.

KEY DEVELOPMENTS IN 2020

- Former premier Maia Sandu of the Action and Solidarity Party (PAS) became Moldova's first female president, defeating incumbent Igor Dodon in a free and fair two-round November election.
- While authorities instituted largely proportional COVID-19-related restrictions, some businesses and individuals received arbitrary fines and the media regulator unsuccessfully attempted to limit journalists' ability to quote unofficial sources. Nearly 144,000 COVID-19 cases and 3,000 deaths were recorded by year's end.
- Oligarch Vladimir Plahotniuc, who fled Moldova in 2019, was charged by prosecutors for his alleged involvement in a banking scandal in May. Despite attempts to extradite him from the United States and Turkey, Plahotniuc remained at large at year's end.

POLITICAL RIGHTS: 26 / 40
A. ELECTORAL PROCESS: 9 / 12
A1. Was the current head of government or other chief national authority elected through free and fair elections? 4 / 4

The president is elected by direct popular vote for up to two consecutive four-year terms. If no candidate receives more than 50 percent of the votes in the first round, the two leading candidates compete in a second round. Former premier Maia Sandu of the PAS defeated incumbent president Igor Dodon in the two-round November 2020 contest. Sandu won 57.7 percent of the second-round vote, while Dodon won 42.3 percent. Organization for Security and Co-operation in Europe (OSCE) observers called the election competitive, but reported that electoral authorities did not investigate allegations of first-round irregularities.

A prime minister nominated by the president and confirmed by Parliament holds most executive authority. Ion Chicu, who became prime minister in November 2019, resigned in December 2020. Sandu nominated Foreign Minister Aureliu Ciocoi as acting prime minister on New Year's Eve.

A2. Were the current national legislative representatives elected through free and fair elections? 3 / 4

Voters elect the 101-seat unicameral Parliament to four-year terms. In February 2019, Moldova held its first parliamentary elections using a mixed electoral system, under which 51 lawmakers were elected in single-member constituencies through the first-past-the-post system and 50 were elected through proportional representation from closed party lists in one national constituency.

OSCE observers considered the elections competitive, but noted shortcomings including credible allegations of pressure on public employees, indications of vote buying, and abuse of public resources for partisan electoral aims. Outcomes were also affected by limited space for independent media to present alternative viewpoints to voters. Five parties entered Parliament—the PSRM with 35 seats, the Democratic Party of Moldova (PDM) with 30, the ACUM ("Now") bloc of the PAS and the Dignity and Truth (DA) party with 26, and the Șor Party with 7—3 independent candidates also won seats.

ACUM and the PSRM subsequently formed a short-lived coalition led by Sandu. After that government fell in November 2019, the PSRM and PDM supported Chicu, who was succeeded by Ciocoi in December 2020.

A3. Are the electoral laws and framework fair, and are they implemented impartially by the relevant election management bodies? 2 / 4

The February 2019 parliamentary elections were governed by a 2017 revision to electoral rules that introduced a mixed system featuring both single-member constituencies and seats allocated proportionally by party lists. The Venice Commission of the Council of Europe had opposed the new system. Parliament restored the old proportional system that July.

The OSCE 2019 election observation mission noted "a lack of inclusive public debate and meaningful consultation with relevant stakeholders and no broad consensus" on the 2017 electoral rule amendments. The monitors otherwise assessed that year's elections positively, and considered their administration professional and transparent.

Local elections held in October and November 2019 were competitive and mostly compliant with electoral standards, though observers noted a number of shortcomings, including cumbersome registration processes and a lack of adherence to gender parity laws.

OSCE monitors largely lauded the November 2020 presidential contest, noting that polling stations were calm and orderly. However, they reported that complaints regarding alleged irregularities were largely dismissed by the Central Electoral Commission.

B. POLITICAL PLURALISM AND PARTICIPATION: 12 / 16

B1. Do the people have the right to organize in different political parties or other competitive political groupings of their choice, and is the system free of undue obstacles to the rise and fall of these competing parties or groupings? 3 / 4

Political party legislation in Moldova is generally liberal, but does include restrictions. Parties seeking legal registration must enlist 4,000 members coming from at least half of Moldovan districts. These requirements effectively disallow regional, municipal, and local parties, as well as parties representing geographically concentrated ethnolinguistic minorities (for example, Gagauzians and Bulgarians). Despite these limitations, 14 political parties and one bloc participated in the February 2019 parliamentary elections, of which four gained seats. Three independent candidates, meanwhile, won single-member constituency seats. In February 2020, the Constitutional Court ruled those provisions unconstitutional, instructing Parliament to revise the Law on Political Parties by July 2021.

B2. Is there a realistic opportunity for the opposition to increase its support or gain power through elections? 4 / 4

Opposition parties have a strong presence in Parliament and other elected offices, and can gain support through elections. Following the February 2019 parliamentary elections, the three then opposition parties—the PAS, DA, and PSRM—came to power, ousting the PDM. Following the November 2019 fall of the Sandu government, the ACUM bloc returned to opposition.

B3. Are the people's political choices free from domination by forces that are external to the political sphere, or by political forces that employ extrapolitical means? 2 / 4

Oligarchs and business interests strongly influence and corrupt national and local political institutions, undermining political accountability.

B4. Do various segments of the population (including ethnic, racial, religious, gender, LGBT+, and other relevant groups) have full political rights and electoral opportunities? 3 / 4

Women and minorities do not face direct legal barriers to political participation, but social obstacles prevent women from having a proportional role in Moldovan politics. Representation of women, people with disabilities, and Roma remains low, though women and members of ethnic minorities attain office.

Some 25 women hold parliamentary seats, representing just under a quarter of the body. Lawmakers from Moldova's ethnic minorities, including Gagauzian, Bulgarian, Armenian, and Romany, also hold seats. The October and November 2019 local elections brought slightly more women and Roma into elected local positions. Maia Sandu became Moldova's first female president in November 2020.

LGBT+ people organize and advocate for equal rights, are discouraged from political engagement due to harassment.

C. FUNCTIONING OF GOVERNMENT: 5 / 12

C1. Do the freely elected head of government and national legislative representatives determine the policies of the government? 3 / 4

Before resigning as PDM head and fleeing Moldova in June 2019, oligarch Vladimir Plahotniuc played a key role in policymaking, despite holding no elected office and enjoying little public support. Since the 2019 establishment of two governments—in June and then in November—business elites have exerted less control over the state.

Before his electoral defeat in November 2020, former president Dodon, despite holding a nonexecutive, nonpartisan office, interfered with the executive agenda and supported the PSRM, which he led before becoming president.

In early December, PSRM and allied lawmakers attempted to shift control over the Security and Intelligence Service (SIS) from the presidency to Parliament, which would have undercut incoming president Sandu's authority. However, the Constitutional Court suspended the legislation after a legal challenge.

C2. Are safeguards against official corruption strong and effective? 1 / 4

Corruption remains entrenched in all levels of government, and existing anticorruption laws are inadequately enforced. Moldova is still recovering from a 2014 banking scandal involving the central bank, in which $1 billion was stolen. In 2016, former prime minister Vlad Filat received a nine-year prison sentence in connection with the scandal, but was conditionally paroled in December 2019. Two key actors in the fraud, Plahotniuc and Ilan Şor, left Moldova in 2019.

The scandal continued to reverberate in 2020. In March, authorities detained four central bank board members for their alleged involvement, and their cases remained pending at year's end. In May, a video of former president Dodon purportedly receiving a bribe from Plahotniuc was published online, sparking a criminal complaint against Dodon. That same month, the prosecutor general charged Plahotniuc for his involvement in the scandal. Prosecutors sought Plahotniuc's extradition from the United States in June and from Turkey in September, but he remained at large at year's end.

C3. Does the government operate with openness and transparency? 1 / 4

Although the governments in power since June 2019 were more transparent than their predecessors, serious issues, including the late publication of plans, draft policies, and bills for consultation, persist. Efforts to transparently appoint public officials have been marred by procedural failures.

Moldovan authorities were also opaque in COVID-19-related decision-making. In March 2020, access-to-information fulfillment deadlines were extended by 30 working days. In April, the Moldovan chapter of Transparency International criticized the use of email to transmit health-care tender offers, warning that such a method was vulnerable to abuse.

CIVIL LIBERTIES: 35 / 60 (+1)

D. FREEDOM OF EXPRESSION AND BELIEF: 12 / 16 (+1)

D1. Are there free and independent media? 2 / 4

The media environment is dominated by outlets connected to political parties. With few exceptions, nationally broadcasting television stations are owned by people affiliated with political parties. Reporters have previously faced difficulty accessing publicly important information and threats of legal action from public figures and politicians.

Journalists were also affected by the government's COVID-19 response. In March 2020, the Moldovan media regulator attempted to restrict outlets from quoting unofficial sources, before rescinding that decision a day later. Journalists also faced longer waits for the fulfillment of access-to-information requests due to COVID-19-related policy changes.

D2. Are individuals free to practice and express their religious faith or nonbelief in public and private? 3 / 4

While constitution proclaims religious freedom and separation of state from religion, the law also provides special status to the Moldovan Orthodox Church. Orthodox symbols have been placed in public institutions, and Orthodox churches are sometimes present within public hospitals and some schools. Muslims have sometimes been summarily targeted by negative messages and comments in media and by figures including former president Dodon.

D3. Is there academic freedom, and is the educational system free from extensive political indoctrination? 3 / 4

There is a good degree of academic freedom in Moldova. However, the Orthodox Church strongly indoctrinates the Moldovan educational system, with educational officials at all levels frequently promoting the church and Orthodox beliefs.

D4. Are individuals free to express their personal views on political or other sensitive topics without fear of surveillance or retribution? 4 / 4 (+1)

Individuals have generally been able to engage in discussions of political nature without fear of retribution. However, under the PDM's rule, there were credible concerns that criticizing the government or affiliated actors could lead to damaged career prospects. Private discussion was curtailed by surveillance against the opposition, journalists, and civil society actors. However, these fears subsided after the 2019 fall of the PDM government.

Score Change: The score improved from 3 to 4 because private discussion is generally free and unfettered following the 2019 collapse of the PDM government.

E. ASSOCIATIONAL AND ORGANIZATIONAL RIGHTS: 8 / 12
E1. Is there freedom of assembly? 3 / 4

Freedom of assembly is constitutionally guaranteed and mostly upheld in practice. While the government limited public gatherings and restricted access to public areas in response to the COVID-19 pandemic, major protests were held during 2020. Veterans held antigovernment demonstrations in Chişinău in early March, and called for an increase to benefits in a late May protest. During a veterans' protest in July, several participants were arrested and beaten by security forces in front of the Parliament building in Chişinău. In early December, some 20,000 Moldovans demonstrated and called for snap elections after Parliament attempted to strip incoming president Sandu of control over the SIS.

E2. Is there freedom for nongovernmental organizations, particularly those that are engaged in human rights- and governance-related work? 3 / 4

The nongovernmental organization (NGO) sector is active but has been affected by recent legislative changes. In June 2020, Parliament approved legislation simplifying registration and revoking related fees for NGOs. However, the new law also prohibited NGOs from supporting electoral candidates.

E3. Is there freedom for trade unions and similar professional or labor organizations? 2 / 4

Trade unions do not encounter major obstacles in Moldova. However, trade unions are not active or visible, and do not play an active role in protecting workers' rights.

F. RULE OF LAW: 6 / 16
F1. Is there an independent judiciary? 1 / 4

Moldova's judicial branch continues to be highly susceptible to political pressures that hamper its independence, and judicial appointment processes lack transparency.

F2. Does due process prevail in civil and criminal matters? 1 / 4

Due process rights are poorly upheld in the Moldovan justice system. Lengthy pretrial detentions are common.

Politically motivated prosecutions occurred under previous governments, targeting opposition figures and lawyers defending perceived enemies of the elite. In February 2020, the general prosecutor's office vowed to examine dozens of politically motivated prosecutions, and several cases were closed in October.

In 2018, seven Turkish teachers of the Orizont Lyceum were deported to Turkey, in violation of national and international norms, and eventually received prison terms for their alleged links to the Gulenist movement. In February 2020, former SIS chief Vasile Botnari was detained for facilitating the deportation, but was issued a modest fine and a five-year ban on holding public office in August. Other individuals who allegedly facilitated the deportation avoided justice, and judicial review of the case has largely been opaque.

A criminal trial against Ilan Şor, who was accused of involvement in the 2014 banking scandal and fled Moldova in 2019, is still ongoing, but court hearings have been repeatedly postponed.

F3. Is there protection from the illegitimate use of physical force and freedom from war and insurgencies? 2 / 4

Prisoners and detainees face maltreatment and torture, and those who engage in such behavior face little consequence. Individuals responsible for 2009 acts of torture and maltreatment against postelection protesters remain largely uninvestigated and unsentenced.

Those involved in the case of Andrei Braguța, who died in police custody in 2017 after a traffic violation, have not yet been adequately sentenced.

Overcrowding and inhumane conditions are common in Moldovan prisons. Health care in pretrial and penitentiary institutions remains poor. COVID-19 clusters were identified in some of these facilities as the pandemic progressed.

F4. Do laws, policies, and practices guarantee equal treatment of various segments of the population? 2 / 4

The 2012 Moldovan Law on Ensuring Equality provides an adequate normative framework for preventing and addressing discrimination. The law's main operational body, the Equality Council, has been praised for effective work and principled stance on difficult and complex discrimination issues, but has been underfunded by successive governments.

Women, persons with disabilities, Roma people, linguistic minorities, Muslims and other non-Orthodox believers, people of African and Asian descent, older persons, and LGBT+ people often face employment discrimination. Some of these groups also face discrimination in education, housing, and public service. Hate speech against minority groups is often promoted by some media outlets and public figures. Some of these groups were additionally affected by the COVID-19 pandemic; for example, migrants, COVID-19 survivors, and minority groups faced hate speech during the pandemic.

Schools and universities generally do not provide education in the Ukrainian, Gagauz, Bulgarian, or Romani languages. Low-quality public schools in the south, populated by many Gagauzians and Bulgarians, often fail to prepare graduates for admission to Romanian-language universities.

G. PERSONAL AUTONOMY AND INDIVIDUAL RIGHTS: 9 / 16

G1. Do individuals enjoy freedom of movement, including the ability to change their place of residence, employment, or education? 3 / 4

The law protects freedom of internal movement and foreign travel, and the government generally respects these rights. There are no formal restrictions on the right to change one's place of employment or education, but bribery is not uncommon in educational institutions. Travel to Transnistria is subject to checks by the de facto territorial authorities.

While Moldovan authorities issued largely proportional COVID-19-related movement restrictions, large fines were sometimes issued for those who violated them.

G2. Are individuals able to exercise the right to own property and establish private businesses without undue interference from state or nonstate actors? 2 / 4

Although Moldovan law guarantees property rights, they are undermined by a weak and corrupt judiciary. Widespread corruption affects fair competition and normal business activity. Allies of powerful individuals have been accused of benefiting economically from selective enforcement of business regulations. Some businesses also complained of receiving arbitrary COVID-19-related fines.

G3. Do individuals enjoy personal social freedoms, including choice of marriage partner and size of family, protection from domestic violence, and control over appearance? 2 / 4

Most personal social freedoms are protected, but domestic violence and sexual abuse are common. A 2016 report by several Moldovan NGOs found that more than 63 percent of women and girls over the age of 15 had experienced some form of gender-based violence in their lifetime, while over 20 percent of men admitted to having had nonconsensual sex with a woman. Domestic and gender-based violence laws are inadequately enforced, and abuses that do not result in significant injury are subject only to administrative penalties. Local groups reported an increase in violence against women during the country's COVID-19 lockdown.

Sexual harassment in the workplace remains common, and such incidents are inadequately addressed.

Child marriages are reported in the Romany community. Neither marriage nor civil unions for same-sex couples are legally recognized.

G4. Do individuals enjoy equality of opportunity and freedom from economic exploitation? 2 / 4

Due to weak labor rights protection and enforcement by authorities and trade unions, reports of exploitative labor practices, including long work hours, low wages, and fully or partially undocumented work or wages, are common. The rural population, women, and Roma are especially vulnerable to these practices. Regulations meant to prevent exploitative or unsafe working conditions remain poorly enforced. Human trafficking remains a problem, although the authorities do attempt to prosecute traffickers.

Monaco

Population: 40,000
Capital: Monaco
Freedom Status: Free
Electoral Democracy: Yes

Overview: The Principality of Monaco is a constitutional monarchy headed by Prince Albert II. The prince appoints the government, which is responsible only to him. Legislative power is exercised jointly by the prince and the freely elected parliament. Civil liberties are generally respected.

KEY DEVELOPMENTS IN 2020

- In a report published in February, the Council of Europe's Group of States against Corruption (GRECO) concluded that Monaco had made insufficient progress in the prevention of corruption by members of parliament, judges, and prosecutors.
- In September, the prince appointed Pierre Dartout as Monaco's new minister of state. Dartout replaced Serge Telle, who had held the office since 2016.
- The principality was relatively successful in containing the spread of COVID-19 during the year, with authorities using a combination of testing, social-distancing measures, and temporary stay-at-home orders when case levels were rising. By year's end, a total of about 850 cases and just three deaths had been reported.

POLITICAL RIGHTS: 26 / 40
A. ELECTORAL PROCESS: 8 / 12
A1. Was the current head of government or other chief national authority elected through free and fair elections? 0 / 4

The hereditary monarch holds extensive executive authority, including the exclusive right to change the government, and there are no constitutional provisions allowing citizens to alter this system. The current prince, Albert II, took the throne after his father's death in

2005. The head of government, known as the minister of state, is traditionally appointed by the monarch from a candidate list of three French nationals submitted by the French government. Pierre Dartout took office as minister of state in September 2020, replacing Serge Telle, who had served for four years.

A2. Were the current national legislative representatives elected through free and fair elections? 4 / 4

The 24 members of the unicameral National Council are elected for five-year terms; the 16 candidates who receive the most votes are elected, and the remaining 8 seats are filled through list-based proportional representation. The 2018 elections were evaluated as credible by international observers. The new political movement Priorité Monaco, led by veteran politician Stéphane Valeri and defectors from the more established Horizon Monaco, won 58 percent of the vote and 21 seats. Horizon Monaco itself took 26 percent and 2 seats, while the Union Monégasque took 16 percent and the remaining seat. After the elections, Valeri became president of the National Council, which is regarded as the most powerful elected office in Monaco.

A3. Are the electoral laws and framework fair, and are they implemented impartially by the relevant election management bodies? 4 / 4

The legal framework provides an adequate basis for credible elections, and a number of recent changes have improved the conduct of elections, including the modification of campaign finance rules in 2017 and the broadening of suffrage rights for detainees in 2014. However, in a 2018 report, the Organization for Security and Co-operation in Europe (OSCE) argued that the campaign finance system could be further strengthened.

Municipal authorities, led by the mayor of Monaco, form an Electoral Committee that administers elections with support from the Interior Ministry, and observers consider their conduct to be credible. However, technical meetings in preparation for elections are not open to the public, limiting the committee's transparency.

B. POLITICAL PLURALISM AND PARTICIPATION: 10 / 16

B1. Do the people have the right to organize in different political parties or other competitive political groupings of their choice, and is the system free of undue obstacles to the rise and fall of these competing parties or groupings? 3 / 4

Political associations, groupings of people who hold similar political viewpoints, compete in Monaco, rather than traditional parties. There are no undue restrictions on the formation of new political associations. However, office seekers are prohibited from running as individual independent candidates; independents must instead form a list of at least 13 candidates to participate in elections.

B2. Is there a realistic opportunity for the opposition to increase its support or gain power through elections? 2 / 4

Opposition political associations are able to gain seats in the parliament. In 2018, the new political movement Priorité Monaco, also known as Primo!, won 21 seats, while Horizon Monaco fell from 20 seats to just 2. However, there are structural limits on the opposition's ability to secure executive power through elections, as the cabinet—appointed by the prince—is not responsible to the elected parliament.

B3. Are the people's political choices free from domination by forces that are external to the political sphere, or by political forces that employ extrapolitical means? 2 / 4

The fact that the head of government is a French national appointed from a list submitted by the French government, and that the powerful head of state is an unelected monarch, means that people's political participation is heavily circumscribed by democratically unaccountable forces. Nevertheless, voters' and candidates' choices with respect to parliamentary representation are largely free from domination by such entities.

B4. Do various segments of the population (including ethnic, racial, religious, gender, LGBT+, and other relevant groups) have full political rights and electoral opportunities? 3 / 4

Only about 9,000 of Monaco's residents—roughly a quarter of the total—are citizens, and noncitizens do not have the right to vote or run for office, though a number of legal routes to naturalization are available. Most noncitizen residents are nationals of neighboring France or Italy.

Among the citizen population, women and members of racial or ethnic minority groups are free to participate in elections, both as voters and candidates, but women's interests are not always well represented in the political system, and only eight women were elected to the parliament in 2018. The six-member council of ministers included one woman as of 2020.

C. FUNCTIONING OF GOVERNMENT: 8 / 12

C1. Do the freely elected head of government and national legislative representatives determine the policies of the government? 2 / 4

The hereditary prince has significant governing authority, including the exclusive power to initiate legislation, conduct foreign policy, and approve changes to the constitution. However, all legislation and the budget require parliamentary approval, and the parliament is generally free from interference by unelected groups.

C2. Are safeguards against official corruption strong and effective? 3 / 4

Despite recent improvements in the legal framework for combating corruption, several loopholes remain. The parliament lacks a code of conduct on accepting gifts or potential conflicts of interest. High-level corruption is a problem, and officials sometimes act with impunity. A February 2020 report by GRECO concluded that Monaco had made insufficient progress in the prevention of corruption by members of parliament, judges, and prosecutors. Only two of the Council of Europe organization's 16 recommendations had been satisfactorily addressed.

In 2017, Philippe Narmino resigned as director of judicial services, or justice minister, after it was revealed that wealthy Russian businessman Dmitriy Rybolovlev gave him gifts in exchange for pursuing fraud charges against an art dealer. The Rybolovlev case revealed extensive corruption in Monaco's judicial system. In 2019, Laurent Anselmi was replaced as justice minister months after he unexpectedly turned down a request for a term renewal from the judge overseeing the investigation into the Rybolovlev scandal. However, Anselmi then became Monaco's foreign minister. The original criminal probe against the art dealer was finally dismissed in July 2020, while the corruption investigation continued.

C3. Does the government operate with openness and transparency? 3 / 4

The law generally provides for public access to government information, including draft laws and proposed legislation. The 2020 GRECO report highlighted shortcomings in the transparency of parliamentary work, including a lack of consultation with the public on proposed legislation and the confidentiality of committee meetings. There are no financial disclosure laws in place for lawmakers or officials appointed by the prince.

CIVIL LIBERTIES: 57 / 60

D. FREEDOM OF EXPRESSION AND BELIEF: 16 / 16

D1. Are there free and independent media? 4 / 4

The constitution provides for freedom of expression, and press freedom is generally respected in practice. Monaco has a weekly government newspaper, an English-language monthly, and several online publications. There is one major private broadcaster based in the country. French and Italian broadcast and print media are widely available, and internet access is not restricted.

D2. Are individuals free to practice and express their religious faith or nonbelief in public and private? 4 / 4

Roman Catholicism is the official state religion, but the constitution guarantees freedom of religion and public worship, and this is largely respected in practice. Jehovah's Witnesses have struggled to secure official recognition as a religious association despite favorable rulings by the Supreme Court.

D3. Is there academic freedom, and is the educational system free from extensive political indoctrination? 4 / 4

There are no undue restrictions on academic freedom.

D4. Are individuals free to express their personal views on political or other sensitive topics without fear of surveillance or retribution? 4 / 4

People are generally free to express their personal views without fear of retribution. Insulting the ruling family is illegal and can result in prison sentences of up to five years, but the law is infrequently enforced.

E. ASSOCIATIONAL AND ORGANIZATIONAL RIGHTS: 12 / 12

E1. Is there freedom of assembly? 4 / 4

The constitution provides for freedom of assembly, which is generally respected in practice.

E2. Is there freedom for nongovernmental organizations, particularly those that are engaged in human rights- and governance-related work? 4 / 4

No significant restrictions are imposed on the formation or operation of nongovernmental organizations (NGOs).

E3. Is there freedom for trade unions and similar professional or labor organizations? 4 / 4

The law grants workers the right to establish unions and bargain collectively, and anti-union discrimination is prohibited. All workers except government employees have the right to strike. Unions and employers engage in collective bargaining in practice.

F. RULE OF LAW: 14 / 16

F1. Is there an independent judiciary? 3 / 4

The constitution provides for an independent judiciary. The prince names five full members and two judicial assistants to the Supreme Court based on nominations by the National Council, government bodies, and the lower courts. The recruitment process for judges lacks transparency, which contributes to a perception that they may lack independence. The Judicial Service Commission is ostensibly responsible for ensuring the independence of the judiciary, but in practice it does not have enforcement power. The director of judicial services, who oversees the judicial and law enforcement systems, is responsible only to the prince. Approximately half of the judges in Monaco are Monegasque nationals, and the other half are French nationals.

Concerns about the independence of the judiciary resurfaced in 2019, when the director of judicial services turned down a request for a three-year term renewal from the judge overseeing the investigation into the Rybolovlev corruption scandal. The director was replaced later that year, and the corruption probe continued as of 2020.

F2. Does due process prevail in civil and criminal matters? 4 / 4

Due process rights are generally respected. Defendants are presumed innocent until proven guilty and are informed of the charges against them promptly. Defendants have access to attorneys and sufficient time to prepare a defense.

F3. Is there protection from the illegitimate use of physical force and freedom from war and insurgencies? 4 / 4

The population faces no major threats to physical security. Violent crime and excessive use of force by police are both rare in Monaco.

F4. Do laws, policies, and practices guarantee equal treatment of various segments of the population? 3 / 4

Monaco lacks a law that broadly prohibits discrimination based on race or ethnicity, though insults and defamation on such grounds are illegal. In the absence of a comprehensive law, Article 14 of the European Convention on Human Rights is used to prevent and punish discrimination. The government established the Office of the High Commissioner for the Protection of Rights, Liberties, and for Mediation in 2013 to address discrimination.

The law prohibits discrimination based on gender, and women's rights are generally respected. However, the European Commission against Racism and Intolerance has noted that women do not enjoy the same rights to social benefits as their male counterparts, as men receive head-of-household status by default, and has called for the establishment of a program guaranteeing the equal treatment of LGBT+ people.

G. PERSONAL AUTONOMY AND INDIVIDUAL RIGHTS: 15 / 16

G1. Do individuals enjoy freedom of movement, including the ability to change their place of residence, employment, or education? 4 / 4

There are no significant restrictions on freedom of internal movement or foreign travel. Temporary movement restrictions that were imposed during the COVID-19 pandemic in 2020 were generally considered legitimate measures to protect public health.

G2. Are individuals able to exercise the right to own property and establish private businesses without undue interference from state or nonstate actors? 3 / 4

Property rights are respected, and noncitizens holding a residence permit may purchase property and establish businesses. However, obtaining government approval to start a business is often a lengthy and complex process, and related costs can be prohibitively expensive.

G3. Do individuals enjoy personal social freedoms, including choice of marriage partner and size of family, protection from domestic violence, and control over appearance? 4 / 4

Personal social freedoms are generally respected. Abortion remains illegal except under special circumstances, including rape and a risk to the pregnant person's life or physical health. In 2019, however, the parliament passed legislation that removed criminal punishments for people who undergo abortions; health professionals could still face penalties for performing an abortion in Monaco. Also in 2019, the parliament adopted a law that allows civil partnerships for all couples, including those of the same sex. Domestic violence is outlawed in Monaco, and there are few reported incidents. The government and NGOs provide a network of support services for victims of domestic violence.

G4. Do individuals enjoy equality of opportunity and freedom from economic exploitation? 4 / 4

Legal protections against labor exploitation are adequately enforced.

Mongolia

Population: 3,400,000
Capital: Ulaanbaatar
Freedom Status: Free
Electoral Democracy: Yes

Overview: Following a peaceful revolution in 1990, Mongolia began holding multiparty elections and established itself as an electoral democracy. Political rights and civil liberties have been firmly institutionalized, though the two dominant parties continue to rely on patronage networks, and widespread corruption hampers further development.

KEY DEVELOPMENTS IN 2020

- The Mongolian People's Party (MPP) secured a parliamentary majority in June elections, winning 62 seats. Several parliamentary candidates were detained or faced scrutiny over corruption during the election period, despite a law mandating the electoral commission's consent for the detention of candidates.
- Former prime ministers Jargaltulgyn Erdenebat and Sanjaagiin Bayar received prison sentences over separate accusations of corruption in July. Erdenebat, who won a parliamentary seat for the MPP in June, was not seated during the year.
- Authorities shut the Mongolian-Chinese border in January and restricted other external travel in March in response to the spread of COVID-19. Local transmission was detected in November, prompting a national lockdown that was loosened in December. Authorities reported 1,195 cases and no deaths to the World Health Organization (WHO) by year's end.

POLITICAL RIGHTS: 36 / 40

A. ELECTORAL PROCESS: 11 / 12

A1. Was the current head of government or other chief national authority elected through free and fair elections? 4 / 4

Under the 1992 constitution, the president is directly elected for up to two four-year terms. Under constitutional amendments adopted in November 2019, presidents will only serve one six-year term beginning in 2025. Khaltmaa Battulga of the Democratic Party (DP) was elected in 2017 following a campaign marked by accusations of corruption and relatively little policy discussion. The contest required a runoff, a first in the country's democratic history. Organization for Security and Co-operation in Europe (OSCE) monitors called the poll credible but noted a lack of analytical media coverage.

The prime minister, who holds most executive power in Mongolia's hybrid parliamentary-presidential system, is nominated by the party or coalition with the most parliamentary seats and is approved by lawmakers with the president's agreement. Ukhnaagiin Khürelsükh took the post in 2017 and remained there at year's end.

A2. Were the current national legislative representatives elected through free and fair elections? 4 / 4

Members of the 76-seat parliament, the State Great Hural, are elected for four-year terms. All members were elected to multimember constituencies in the June 2020 elections, with 48 elected via simple-majority voting and 28 via proportional representation. The MPP won 62 seats while the DP won 11. The Mongolian People's Revolutionary Party, the National Labor Party (HUN), and an independent each won 1 seat. Turnout stood at 73.7 percent. No international monitors observed the polls due to COVID-19-related travel restrictions. One MPP parliamentarian, former prime minister Erdenebat, was not seated due to a corruption trial.

A3. Are the electoral laws and framework fair, and are they implemented impartially by the relevant election management bodies? 3 / 4

Electoral laws are generally fair, though they are often changed shortly before elections and tend to favor the two largest parties.

In late 2019, the parliament approved changes that eased eligibility regulations and tightened campaign-finance laws. The parliament also mandated the use of a plurality-at-large voting system for the June 2020 elections. The electoral map used in the elections favored rural voters, with disproportionately few seats drawn in the capital of Ulaanbaatar.

While the General Election Commission (GEC) is often regarded with suspicion over political influence, no major complaints arose from its management of the June 2020 elections. Several parliamentary candidates were detained or faced scrutiny related to corruption accusations during the electoral period, however, despite a 2019 election law requiring the GEC's consent for the detention of candidates.

B. POLITICAL PLURALISM AND PARTICIPATION: 16 / 16

B1. Do the people have the right to organize in different political parties or other competitive political groupings of their choice, and is the system free of undue obstacles to the rise and fall of these competing parties or groupings? 4 / 4

While the Mongolian political system features multiple parties, it is also marked by the dominance of the MPP and DP. Parties are built around patronage networks rather than political ideologies. Representatives of large business groups play an important role in funding and directing the MPP and DP.

New political movements may form and operate freely, with the HUN entering the parliament for the first time in June 2020.

B2. Is there a realistic opportunity for the opposition to increase its support or gain power through elections? 4 / 4

There are no undue barriers preventing opposition parties from gaining power through elections, though there are practical hurdles. The MPP and DP have remained the two largest political forces in the country, regularly alternating in government and establishing a record of peaceful transfers of authority.

B3. Are the people's political choices free from domination by forces that are external to the political sphere, or by political forces that employ extrapolitical means? 4 / 4

Powerful business interests have some influence over candidates and have supported them through a nontransparent party-finance system. However, candidates and voters are generally free to make political choices without excessive outside influence, in part because corporate interests are balanced across various factions of the two main parties.

B4. Do various segments of the population (including ethnic, racial, religious, gender, LGBT+, and other relevant groups) have full political rights and electoral opportunities? 4 / 4

All adult citizens other than those who are incarcerated are entitled to full political rights, and these are generally observed in practice. However, despite quotas supporting gender diversity, women remain underrepresented in politics, holding about 17 percent of parliamentary seats and few senior government posts. Ethnic Kazakh parliamentarians are regularly elected in Bayan-Ölgii, which is predominantly Kazakh.

LGBT+ people face some societal discrimination that hampers their ability to advocate for their interests in the political sphere, though such advocacy has been increasing.

C. FUNCTIONING OF GOVERNMENT: 9 / 12

C1. Do the freely elected head of government and national legislative representatives determine the policies of the government? 4 / 4

Freely elected representatives are duly seated and generally able to craft government policy without improper interference. However, corporations, aided by opaque party-finance procedures, have also been able to influence policymaking.

Parliamentarians were previously allowed to hold concurrent cabinet positions, effectively making a relatively large number of members bound to the premier. Constitutional amendments passed in 2019 limited the number of parliamentarians who could serve in a cabinet.

C2. Are safeguards against official corruption strong and effective? 2 / 4

Corruption, which is endemic in Mongolia, is widely perceived to have worsened in recent years, particularly with respect to state involvement in the mining sector. Anticorruption laws are vaguely written and infrequently enforced. Corruption investigations are often dropped by prosecutors before reaching definitive conclusions.

The Independent Authority Against Corruption (IAAC) has been criticized as ineffective in pursuing cases. The IAAC's independence was weakened in 2019 when emergency legislation allowed the National Security Council (NSC) to recommend the chief's dismissal before the end of their term. The chief and the prosecutor general, who had called for prosecutions against parliamentarians implicated in corruption, were dismissed that year.

High-profile corruption cases were nevertheless resolved in 2020. In May, former prime minister Mendsaikhany Enkhsaikhan received a four-and-a-half-year prison sentence for corruption, though his sentenced was reduced in November. In July, Erdenebat received a six-year sentence and a ban from public office. Also in July, former prime minister Bayar received a five-year sentence over allegations that he manipulated a mining contract. In August, former parliamentarian Batbayar Undarmaa received a two-and-a-half-year prison sentence for inappropriately receiving a loan from a government fund.

C3. Does the government operate with openness and transparency? 3 / 4

While there are many laws and regulations designed to maintain government transparency and accountability, implementation and enforcement is inconsistent. The 2011 Law on Information Transparency and Right to Information contains exemptions allowing certain types of information to be withheld from the public. Authorities often invoke these exemptions, as well as the State Secrets Law, to limit disclosures.

Constitutional amendments approved in 2019 established an auditing body that would maintain independent powers over government finances.

The E-Mongolia platform, which is meant to make government services more accessible, launched in October 2020.

CIVIL LIBERTIES: 48 / 60

D. FREEDOM OF EXPRESSION AND BELIEF: 14 / 16

D1. Are there free and independent media? 3 / 4

Press freedom is generally respected, and media outlets collectively present a wide range of views. However, coverage can be partisan; the OSCE noted xenophobic rhetoric and unsupported allegations of corruption in the media during the 2017 election campaign. Ownership of media companies remains opaque and subject to speculation. Many journalists self-censor to avoid offending political or business interests and facing costly libel suits. Journalists can also be forced to pay administrative fines for publishing false and defamatory information under a broadly worded 2017 law.

Authorities imposed criminal penalties for the dissemination of purported disinformation in March 2020, as the COVID-19 pandemic took hold worldwide. Journalists reportedly engaged in self-censorship while reporting on the pandemic.

D2. Are individuals free to practice and express their religious faith or nonbelief in public and private? 4 / 4

Individuals are free to practice their religion under the law and in practice, though religious groups are required to register with the government and the ease of registration procedures varies by region and locality.

D3. Is there academic freedom, and is the educational system free from extensive political indoctrination? 4 / 4

Academic freedom is generally respected.

D4. Are individuals free to express their personal views on political or other sensitive topics without fear of surveillance or retribution? 3 / 4

There are few significant impediments to free and open private discussion. Fear of repercussions from powerful actors continue to deter open expression for some.

E. ASSOCIATIONAL AND ORGANIZATIONAL RIGHTS: 11 / 12

E1. Is there freedom of assembly? 4 / 4

Freedom of assembly is upheld in practice, though public assembly was restricted for much of 2020 under COVID-19-related measures.

E2. Is there freedom for nongovernmental organizations, particularly those that are engaged in human rights– and governance-related work? 4 / 4

Numerous environmental, human rights, and social welfare groups operate without restrictions, though most are small. Individual activists sometimes report incidents of intimidation and harassment.

E3. Is there freedom for trade unions and similar professional or labor organizations? 3 / 4

Trade unions are independent and active, and the government generally respects their rights to bargain collectively and engage in legal strike actions. However, labor rights are restricted for certain groups, such as foreign and temporary workers, and there are some reports of employers unlawfully disrupting union activity.

F. RULE OF LAW: 11 / 16

F1. Is there an independent judiciary? 2 / 4

Judges are appointed by the president on the recommendation of the Judicial General Council, whose five members in turn are nominated by the three tiers of courts, the bar association, and the Justice Ministry. However, legislation passed in 2019 allows the NSC to recommend the dismissal of judges; Battulga dismissed the Supreme Court's chief justice that year. That June, another 17 judges, including five Supreme Court justices, were dismissed by the NSC. While additional legislation was supposed to regulate appointments to the judiciary under constitutional amendments, this did not occur by year's end.

Corruption and political influence in the daily work of judges remain concerns.

F2. Does due process prevail in civil and criminal matters? 3 / 4

Due process rights are generally respected, but cases of arbitrary arrest and detention have been reported. The right to a fair trial can be undermined by intimidation or bribery.

F3. Is there protection from the illegitimate use of physical force and freedom from war and insurgencies? 3 / 4

While Mongolians face few major threats to physical security, there have been reports of police illegally using physical abuse to obtain confessions. Some prison and detention facilities feature insufficient nutrition, heat, and medical care.

F4. Do laws, policies, and practices guarantee equal treatment of various segments of the population? 3 / 4

There are no formal barriers to equal treatment under the law. Discrimination based on gender, race, sexual orientation, gender identity, and other categories is prohibited. However, women and LGBT+ people continue to face societal discrimination and harassment, including in the workplace. Public events in support of LGBT+ equality have grown in attendance and visibility over the past several years.

Rape and other acts of sexual violence against LGBT+ people have historically gone unprosecuted. A 2017 criminal code revision includes stronger protections for this community; law enforcement officials have gradually received training to comply with the new code.

G. PERSONAL AUTONOMY AND INDIVIDUAL RIGHTS: 12 / 16

G1. Do individuals enjoy freedom of movement, including the ability to change their place of residence, employment, or education? 4 / 4

The government respects freedom of movement. Exit bans imposed on individuals involved in legal cases are overseen by the courts.

The border with China was closed in January 2020 and other external travel was restricted in March as COVID-19 spread worldwide, while an internal quarantine was declared in Ulaanbaatar and other cities in March. A national lockdown was imposed in November when local transmission was detected and was maintained through December.

G2. Are individuals able to exercise the right to own property and establish private businesses without undue interference from state or nonstate actors? 3 / 4

People are generally free to own property and establish private businesses, though state-owned enterprises play a prominent role in some sectors. Corruption also hampers many private business activities. Officials have reportedly withheld operating licenses and other documentation from businesses until bribes are paid. There is a history of corruption and government interference in the mining industry.

G3. Do individuals enjoy personal social freedoms, including choice of marriage partner and size of family, protection from domestic violence, and control over appearance? 3 / 4

Individual rights on personal-status issues such as marriage and divorce are protected by law. However, domestic violence remains a problem. The government has initiated programs to encourage better police responses to domestic-violence complaints in recent years. A government survey conducted with the UN and published in 2018 found that nearly a third of women faced physical or sexual abuse from a partner. Just 10 percent of those who had suffered severe sexual violence by a nonpartner reported the crimes to the authorities. Sexual harassment is not explicitly restricted and is widespread.

G4. Do individuals enjoy equality of opportunity and freedom from economic exploitation? 2 / 4

The government has struggled to cope with economic inequality, particularly as large numbers of rural Mongolians migrate to cities that lack sufficient housing and infrastructure. New housing continues to be constructed, but many existing residents have reportedly been left homeless by urban redevelopment projects.

Women, children, people living in poverty, and other vulnerable segments of the population are at some risk of becoming trafficking victims, and can be compelled to engage in sex work, forced labor, or begging. Mining workers are subject to exploitative conditions, as are contract workers from China. The government has taken efforts to better prosecute trafficking cases, but corruption and a lack of will to address the issue impede progress.

Montenegro

Population: 600,000
Capital: Podgorica
Freedom Status: Partly Free
Electoral Democracy: Yes

Overview: An opposition coalition came to power in late 2020 following elections held that August, ending three decades of rule by the Democratic Party of Socialists (DPS). At the end of 2020 the new administration was still working to streamline operations and meet international standards for transparency but had been responsive to criticism from civil society and its political opponents, signaling a shift from the previous administration. Corruption remains a problem, and there are serious deficiencies in the judiciary and a lack of guarantees for due process.

KEY DEVELOPMENTS IN 2020

- In the run-up to parliamentary elections in August, the opposition organized into three factions—representing, broadly, right-wing, center-right, and center-left views—which refused to attack one another. Analysts attributed the opposition's narrow victory to this strategy, pointing to the emergence of a reformist majority that cut across ethnopolitical lines and overcame the DPS, despite the incumbent party's significant institutional advantages.
- In December, lawmakers voted to approve a new technocratic, reformist government, led by Prime Minister Zdravko Krivokapić, who confirmed the country's membership in the North Atlantic Treaty Organization and its European Union (EU) trajectory. However, as a government of nonpartisan experts, it is a de facto minority government supported by an ideologically heterogenous parliamentary majority, leaving it vulnerable to instability as its work begins in earnest.
- Protests against a controversial law that appeared to permit the transfer of Serbian Orthodox Church (SOC) property to the Monetengrin state continued during the year. The demonstrations drew massive crowds—as well as the ire of President Milo Đukanović, who characterized them as threatening the state—and at times were marred by police violence against protesters. In late December, in somewhat rushed procedure, the new parliamentary majority approved amendments removing the disputed sections of the law.
- The National Coordination Body (NCB), established in March to launch a response to the COVID-19 pandemic, faced criticism over its ability to bypass parliament in enacting emergency procedures, and for a lack of independent experts on its staff. Led by prominent DPS members or their relatives, the NCB additionally faced allegations of partisanship, including over its statement in July that leaders of the opposition Democratic Front (DF) were bringing COVID-19 into the country via their visits to neighboring Serbia. In December, the NCB was disbanded and new bodies were established to coordinate the COVID-19 response.

POLITICAL RIGHTS: 24 / 40 (+2)

A. ELECTORAL PROCESS: 9 / 12 (+1)

A1. Was the current head of government or other chief national authority elected through free and fair elections? 3 / 4

The president is chief of state and is directly elected for up to two five-year terms. In April 2018, Milo Đukanović of the DPS, who has served as either prime minister or president for most of the last three decades, was elected president with 53.9 percent of the vote. Independent candidate Mladen Bojanić finished second with 33.4 percent. Đukanović refused to participate in public debates with the other candidates during the campaign. While some irregularities such as misuse of public resources were reported, the Organization for Security and Co-operation in Europe (OSCE), which monitored the election, stated that the polling was generally credible and respected fundamental rights. However, the mission noted that Đukanović and the DPS enjoyed significant institutional advantages that reduced the poll's competitiveness.

The president nominates the prime minister, who requires legislative approval. Following the parliamentary elections in August 2020, Đukanović nominated Zdravko Krivokapić, leader of the strongest electoral list in the new post-election coalition, for the post. Krivoka-pić's government was then approved in December.

A2. Were the current national legislative representatives elected through free and fair elections? 3 / 4 (+1)

Members of the unicameral, 81-seat Parliament—the Skupština—are directly elected for four-year terms.

While the DPS once again posting the strongest performance by a single party in the 2020 parliamentary election, taking 30 seats, it failed to secure a majority with its traditional coalition partners. With a narrow majority with 41 seats, the new ruling alliance is composed of three coalitions: For the Future of Montenegro (27 seats), Peace is Our Nation (10), and In Black and White (4). Turnout was high, at 76.64 percent.

The OSCE and the European Network of Election Monitoring Organizations (EN-EMO) noted that the polls took place in an atmosphere of high polarization over issues including church affiliation and national identity. They also said the elections in some ways violated provisions of the constitution, including because the early election date was never harmonized with other legal obligations; because pandemic-restrictions on movement and assembly impeded campaign activities; and because several lawmakers were arrested or charged with various offenses without their parliamentary immunity first being waived. The line between the ruling parties and the state was again blurred during the campaign, additionally, as the DPS and its coalition partners gained undue advantage through the widespread misuse of state resources, thus affecting the principle of equal opportunity in the campaign.

Nevertheless, the polls were widely considered an improvement from previous years' contests, with monitors and other analysts concluding that they were conducted in a more se-cure, orderly, and transparent manner and featured robust participation from across society.

Score Change: The score improved from 2 to 3 because parliamentary elections held in August, while not free from irregularities, were less affected by issues that compromised previous polls.

A3. Are the electoral laws and framework fair, and are they implemented impartially by the relevant election management bodies? 3 / 4

The conduct of elections in Montenegro is facilitated by a comprehensive legal and administrative framework, but opposition parties have long claimed that this framework was seriously flawed. In October 2018, Parliament voted to form a committee, composed of seven members from the ruling coalition and seven from the opposition, tasked with crafting legislation to reform electoral laws, taking into consideration recent recommendations of the OSCE and the European Commission (EC). However, numerous opposition parties refused to participate in the committee's efforts and insisted on the establishment of a technocratic government as the key precondition for any new electoral framework to be implemented and to yield results.

Nevertheless, in 2020 opposition parties participated in polls run under a framework many had previously characterized as unfair.

B. POLITICAL PLURALISM AND PARTICIPATION: 10 / 16 (+1)

B1. Do the people have the right to organize in different political parties or other competitive political groupings of their choice, and is the system free of undue obstacles to the rise and fall of these competing parties or groupings? 2 / 4

Political parties are for the most part able to form and operate without direct interference. While the 2020 DPS campaign featured familiar attempts to delegitimize opposition activity by equating it with threats to the state or to public order, the party lost its parliamentary majority, and a new technocratic, reformist government was established that December. However, it is a *de facto* minority government supported by a highly heterogeneous parliamentary majority, leaving it susceptible to future instability.

During 2020, several party and civil society activists were arrested for taking part in political protests across the country.

B2. Is there a realistic opportunity for the opposition to increase its support or gain power through elections? 3 / 4 (+1)

Prior to the 2020 elections, the DPS had been in power since 1991, which has provided it with significant structural advantages over opposition parties.

In 2020, the opposition gathered in three coalitions, some led by figures relatively new to national politics; the coalitions refused to attack each other and focused criticism instead on the DPS and what they perceived as "satellite parties" that were clear in their intention of joining a postelection coalition with the DPS. In the context of weakened DPS and the church issue, which cut across existing ethnopolitical divides, this proved to be a winning strategy despite the DPS's institutional advantages. The approval of the new government in December marked the end of three decades of DPS rule.

Score Change: The score improved from 2 to 3 because an opposition coalition defeated the long-ruling Democratic Party of Socialists (DPS), which had been in power for three decades.

B3. Are the people's political choices free from domination by forces that are external to the political sphere, or by political forces that employ extrapolitical means? 2 / 4

While voters are generally free to express their political choices, extensive patronage systems and widespread corruption encourage loyalty to the DPS, which had been in power for nearly three decades. Many members of the DPS are believed to have ties to organized crime, resulting in opportunities for illicit pressure on voters and candidates. Both public-sector workers, and private-sector employees working for companies with links to the state, have long faced pressure to vote for the former ruling party.

B4. Do various segments of the population (including ethnic, racial, religious, gender, LGBT+, and other relevant groups) have full political rights and electoral opportunities? 3 / 4

All citizens have full political rights and electoral opportunities. Small political parties representing interests of ethnic, religious, and other minority groups participate in the political sphere, and members of these minorities are also represented within larger parties—though the Romany population remains underrepresented. In the 2020 elections, voter materials were provided in the Albanian language, but not Romany.

Women are underrepresented in political leadership positions and politics generally. The government has taken steps to increase women's participation, including through gender quotas on electoral lists, though implementation is uneven. Draginja Vuksanović, the first female presidential candidate in Montenegrin history, won 8 percent of the vote in the 2018 elections.

C. FUNCTIONING OF GOVERNMENT: 5 / 12

C1. Do the freely elected head of government and national legislative representatives determine the policies of the government? 2 / 4

Đukanović has wielded vast personalized power for decades through his tenure as both prime minister and president, as well as during his time outside of government as chair of the DPS. Although the constitution provides for a parliamentary system of government, Parliament passed a new law after Đukanović's April 2018 election that expanded presidential powers, including by allowing the president to form councils, committees, and working groups within the presidency.

The Montenegrin parliament has had limited capacity to exercise its oversight functions, and for years functioned as a rubber stamp for legislation proposed by the DPS-led government. An opposition boycott from 2016 to 2020 further diminished the power of the legislative branch to act as a check. However, since the 2020 election, lawmakers have been working to restore parliamentary powers and oversight capabilities.

The National Coordination Body (NCB), established in March 2020 to coordinate a response to the COVID-19 pandemic, faced criticism over its ability to bypass parliament in enacting emergency procedures, among other issues.

C2. Are safeguards against official corruption strong and effective? 1 / 4

Corruption and cronyism remain widespread, and modest efforts by authorities to address the problem, prompted in part by EU accession requirements, have not produced significant results. A new anticorruption agency began its work in 2016, but EC Progress Reports have been continuously questioned the integrity, credibility, impartiality, independence, accountability, and priority-setting of the agency. The 2020 report characterizes its institutional capacity as weak, producing limited results in its key areas of monitoring, and expressed concern about the prevalence of high-level corruption in government and an overall lack of independence of various public institutions. Senior officials implicated in corruption schemes rarely face prosecution. Civil society organizations and independent media provide some accountability by reporting on official corruption and its effects.

C3. Does the government operate with openness and transparency? 2 / 4

The government publishes some information online, but citizens have few opportunities for meaningful participation in public consultations on legislation and policy reforms. Budget plans are not widely available, nor is information on government contracts.

CIVIL LIBERTIES: 39 / 60 (–1)
D. FREEDOM OF EXPRESSION AND BELIEF: 10 / 16
D1. Are there free and independent media? 2 / 4

A variety of independent media operate in Montenegro, and media coverage tends to be partisan and combative. The DPS government frequently denied opposition media outlets advertising contracts from publicly owned or controlled entities, and the public broadcaster, RTCG, remains under tight control of the DPS. Journalists self-censor to avoid threats, political pressure, costly defamation suits, or job loss. Reporters who cover corruption and organized crime risk violence. Some of the most prominent physical attacks on investigative reporters, such as Olivera Lakić (2018) and Vladimir Otašević (2019), remain unresolved. In contrast, investigative journalist Jovo Martinović was found guilty of participating in drug trafficking, despite the protests of Montenegrin journalists and international organizations and clear that evidence he was working undercover as part of an investigation at the time of his alleged crimes.

Several instances in early 2020 brought attention to the issue of intimidation of reporters. In March, two RTCG journalists were subject to disciplinary proceedings in connection with critical comments about an RTCG documentary, which they had posted on their private social media accounts. Earlier, several journalists were detained on allegations of causing panic and disorder in connection with separate reporting on an explosion, and on protests. There were several instances of journalists being pressured by law enforcement agents to reveal their sources during the year, according to the most recent EC report; additionally, during the campaign period in August, the EC report noted anonymous harassment of journalists critical of the DPS, apparently coordinated on a website created for that purpose.

D2. Are individuals free to practice and express their religious faith or nonbelief in public and private? 3 / 4

The constitution guarantees freedom of religious belief, but in recent years Serbian Orthodox Church (SOC) and its adherents have been the subject of discrimination and hate speech, and its clergy has been characterized by the DPS as enemies of the state.

In late December 2019, a wave of protests erupted against the newly adopted and controversial Law on Freedom of Religion or Belief and the Legal Status of Religious Communities, which contained language SOC leaders said would allow the transfer of SOC church buildings and other property to the Montenegrin state. It was adopted after rancorous sessions of Parliament that saw, among other things, the arrest of opposition lawmakers. Discontent among the SOC religious community—the largest confessional group in Montenegro—eventually lead to a wave of the SOC-organized, large-scale peaceful protest rallies against the law. President Đukanović characterized the demonstrations as "a lunatic movement," and claimed that participants were not against the disputed law, but rather opposed to Montenegrin statehood and independence. Nevertheless, the protests were reportedly the largest in the history of Montenegro, amounting at certain points to a fifth of the population in the streets across the country. In June 2020, members of the United States Commission on International Religious Freedom stated the Serbian Orthodox Church in Montenegro "rightly fears that the law serves as an excuse to confiscate property."

Attempts at dialogue between the government and the church failed to produce an agreement. In late December 2020, in somewhat rushed procedure, the new parliamentary majority adopted changes to the law, removing the controversial parts regulating property rights and ownership of church buildings and estates.

D3. Is there academic freedom, and is the educational system free from extensive political indoctrination? 3 / 4

Academic freedom is guaranteed by law and generally upheld. However, in 2017, the rector of the University of Montenegro, who was appointed in 2014 and enacted a series of reforms, was removed by the new government, violating university autonomy. In March 2020, the Supreme Court upheld the Podgorica High Court's previous ruling that her removal was unlawful. In general, university professors and researchers remain disengaged from critical discussions of the sociopolitical situation in the country, as they may face repercussions.

D4. Are individuals free to express their personal views on political or other sensitive topics without fear of surveillance or retribution? 2 / 4 (−1)

People are generally free to engage in public discussions. In 2020, however, a number of people were arrested in connection with posts to public and private Facebook pages that contained satirical content about state symbols or remarks insulting or perceived as insulting to authorities, as well as for sharing unverified news sources or misinformation.

The existence of extensive, DPS-linked patronage networks has fostered an environment where vocal opposition to the government or its policies is still widely believed to jeopardize employment opportunities, both in the public and private sector.

Score Change: The score decreased from 3 to 2 because a number of citizens were arrested for public and private social media posts perceived as critical of the DPS.

E. ASSOCIATIONAL AND ORGANIZATIONAL RIGHTS: 9 / 12

E1. Is there freedom of assembly? 3 / 4

While citizens generally enjoy freedom of assembly, authorities in the past have attempted to limit protests organized by the opposition Democratic Front (DF) party, violence at demonstrations had erupted occasionally, and DPS-controlled media has referred to opposition protests as "antistate." Some protests in 2020 were marred by arrests and excessive use of force against peaceful demonstrators.

E2. Is there freedom for nongovernmental organizations, particularly those that are engaged in human rights– and governance-related work? 3 / 4

Although most NGOs operate without interference, those that investigate corruption or that criticized the former DPS government have faced pressure. During his 2018 presidential campaign, Đukanović made a number of inflammatory statements directed at civil society, saying in a television appearance that some NGOs and members of the media are "unscrupulous fighters for power," willing to destroy the government in the pursuit of foreign donations. In 2020, Đukanović accused the NGO sector (and independent media) of being responsible for the "bad image of Montenegro in the international community."

Krivokapić's government, which took power at the end of 2020, has declared civil society actors its strategic partners in comprehensive reforms.

E3. Is there freedom for trade unions and similar professional or labor organizations? 3 / 4

There is freedom for trade unions, which remain relatively strong in the public sector. However, reports of intimidation of labor activists by employers continue.

F. RULE OF LAW: 9 / 16

F1. Is there an independent judiciary? 2 / 4

Efforts to bolster judicial independence continue, though the judiciary remains susceptible to pressure from the government, and judicial corruption remains a problem. There are serious deficiencies in transparency, openness, professionalism, and accountability of the judicial system. In July 2020, the DPS minister of justice called on the president of the Supreme Court and presidents of basic courts who had held their positions for more than two mandates to resign, which they refused to do.

Secret audio recordings and official documents leaked in 2019 implicated Supreme State Prosecutor Ivica Stanković and president of the Supreme Court Vesna Medenica in bribery and corruption affairs, and these issues were not resolved in 2020. Responsibility for prosecutions remains under the tight grip of the DPS, and selective justice remains a fundamental problem.

F2. Does due process prevail in civil and criminal matters? 1 / 4

Constitutional guarantees of due process are inconsistently upheld. Legal proceedings are lengthy and often highly bureaucratic, particularly when involving business dealings. Police frequently hold suspects in extended pretrial detention while completing investigations. Courts are poorly funded and often overburdened.

Two DF leaders, Andrija Mandić and Milan Knežević, who were charged with plotting an attempted coup in 2016, were found guilty in May 2019 and were each given sentences of up to five years in prison. Legal procedures surrounding the trial were chaotic and opaque, several witnesses recanted testimony, and many details of the alleged plot remained murky after the trial closed. Aspects of the long-running case were denounced by the opposition as attempts by the DPS to bolster its dominant political position, and overall the affair reflected a lack of due process and adherence to proper procedures in criminal matters.

F3. Is there protection from the illegitimate use of physical force and freedom from war and insurgencies? 3 / 4

Violent crime is not a significant problem, although several apparent executions by criminal gangs of rivals have taken place in recent years. Prison conditions do not meet international standards for education or health care, and prison guards reportedly abuse inmates regularly and with impunity.

F4. Do laws, policies, and practices guarantee equal treatment of various segments of the population? 3 / 4

Members of the Romany, Ashkali, Egyptian, and other ethnic minority groups, and LGBT+ people, face discrimination. Women in Montenegro are legally entitled to equal pay for equal work, but patriarchal attitudes often limit their salary levels, as well as their educational opportunities.

G. PERSONAL AUTONOMY AND INDIVIDUAL RIGHTS: 11 / 16

G1. Do individuals enjoy freedom of movement, including the ability to change their place of residence, employment, or education? 3 / 4

The freedom of movement and the right of citizens to change their residence, employment, and institution of higher education, are generally respected in practice. However, many jobs are awarded through patronage, limiting access for those without connections.

G2. Are individuals able to exercise the right to own property and establish private businesses without undue interference from state or nonstate actors? 2 / 4

The state sector dominates much of Montenegro's economy, and related clientelism, as well as corruption, pose obstacles to normal business activity. The minister of Sustainable Development and Tourism resigned in November 2019 after a video recording leaked showing two inspectors from the ministry demanding a kickback from a local businessman.

G3. Do individuals enjoy personal social freedoms, including choice of marriage partner and size of family, protection from domestic violence, and control over appearance? 3 / 4

The government for the most part does not place restrictions on personal social freedoms. In July 2020, Montenegro legalized same-sex civil partnerships.

Domestic violence remains a problem.

G4. Do individuals enjoy equality of opportunity and freedom from economic exploitation? 3 / 4

Most workers employed in the private sector remain unprotected from exploitation and arbitrary decisions of their employers. Trafficking in persons for the purposes of prostitution and forced labor remains a problem. The government does not fully meet the minimum standards for the elimination of trafficking but is making increasing efforts in this regard, according to the US State Department's 2020 *Trafficking in Persons Report*.

Morocco

Population: 36,000,000
Capital: Rabat
Freedom Status: Partly Free
Electoral Democracy: No

Note: The numerical scores and status listed above do not reflect conditions in Western Sahara, which is examined in a separate report. *Freedom in the World* reports assess the level of political rights and civil liberties in a given geographical area, regardless of whether they are affected by the state, nonstate actors, or foreign powers. Disputed territories are sometimes assessed separately if they meet certain criteria, including boundaries that are sufficiently stable to allow year-on-year comparisons. For more information, see the report methodology and FAQ.

Overview: Morocco holds regular multiparty elections for Parliament, and reforms in 2011 shifted some authority over government from the monarchy to the elected legislature. Nevertheless, King Mohammed VI maintains dominance through a combination of substantial formal powers and informal lines of influence in the state and society. Many civil liberties are constrained in practice.

KEY DEVELOPMENTS IN 2020

- Moroccan authorities instituted mass-gathering restrictions, arrested individuals accused of spreading purportedly false information, and maintained internal movement restrictions in response to the COVID-19 pandemic, though some restrictions were relaxed in May. Infections and deaths rose beginning in October, and the World Health Organization recorded 437,000 cases and 7,355 deaths at year's end.
- Several journalists who were previously surveilled or targeted by authorities were detained during the year. *Akhbar al-Youm* editor in chief Soulaimane Raissouni was accused of sexual assault in May, Le Desk reporter Omar Radi was accused of rape and collaborating with foreign intelligence services in July, and *Al-Quds al-Arabi* contributor Maati Monjib was accused of money laundering in late December; all three remained in custody at year's end.
- In December, Morocco normalized relations with Israel under an agreement supported by the United States, which recognized Morocco's claim over the territory of Western Sahara that month. Police in Rabat, meanwhile, prevented protesters from demonstrating over the agreement.

POLITICAL RIGHTS: 13 / 40

A. ELECTORAL PROCESS: 5 / 12

A1. Was the current head of government or other chief national authority elected through free and fair elections? 1 / 4

Constitutional reforms in 2011 required the king to appoint the prime minister from the party that wins the most seats in parliamentary elections, but the reforms nevertheless preserved nearly all of the king's existing powers. The monarch can disband the legislature, rule by decree, and dismiss or appoint cabinet members.

After the 2016 parliamentary elections, political disagreement over the composition of a new government consumed more than five months. In 2017, King Mohammed VI used his royal prerogative to appoint Saad Eddine al-Othmani, a former Party of Justice and Development (PJD) foreign minister, as prime minister, replacing Abdelilah Benkirane, also of the PJD. However, technocrats loyal to the palace obtained key economic portfolios, and the PJD was similarly excluded from the "strategic ministries" of interior, foreign affairs, justice, and Islamic affairs.

The Party of Progress and Socialism (PPS) left the governing coalition in October 2019, and a new cabinet was announced later that month. The palace engineered a cabinet that was reduced in size, from 39 to 23 ministers, and numerous technocrats were appointed, though some of the most important ministries remained essentially unchanged.

A2. Were the current national legislative representatives elected through free and fair elections? 2 / 4

The lower house of Parliament, the Chamber of Representatives, has 395 directly elected members who serve five-year terms. Of these, 305 are elected from 92 multimember constituencies. The remaining 90 are elected from a single nationwide constituency, with 60 seats reserved for women and 30 for people under the age of 40. Members of the 120-seat upper house, the Chamber of Counselors, are chosen by an electoral college—made up of professional, labor, and business organizations as well as local and regional officials—to serve six-year terms.

In the 2016 parliamentary elections, the PJD placed first with 125 seats in the Chamber of Representatives, followed by the royalist Party of Authenticity and Modernity (PAM) with 102. Both increased their share of seats compared with 2011. Istiqlal (Independence) fell by 14 seats to 46; the National Rally of Independents declined by 15 seats to 37; the Popular Movement dropped 5 seats to 27; and the Socialist Union of Popular Forces fell by 19 seats to 20. The PPS won 12 seats, a decline of 6. Official turnout was 43 percent of registered voters, lower than the 45 percent in 2011 and representing only 23 percent of eligible voters.

Authorities placed limits on some foreign electoral observers, and instances of vote buying and other irregularities were reported, but the elections provided a degree of choice to voters.

A3. Are the electoral laws and framework fair, and are they implemented impartially by the relevant election management bodies? 2 / 4

The constitutional and legal framework allows for competitive legislative elections, but the transparency of the process is not guaranteed. Elections are overseen by the Interior Ministry, with some participation by the Justice Ministry, rather than an independent electoral commission. Approximately three million Moroccans live abroad, and the electoral laws made it exceedingly difficult for voters outside of Morocco to cast their ballots in 2016.

B. POLITICAL PLURALISM AND PARTICIPATION: 5 / 16

B1. Do the people have the right to organize in different political parties or other competitive political groupings of their choice, and is the system free of undue obstacles to the rise and fall of these competing parties or groupings? 2 / 4

Morocco has a vibrant multiparty system, but parties are generally unable to assert themselves relative to the power of the palace. Of the two largest parties, the PJD polls strongly in urban areas, while the PAM dominates rural areas. Smaller parties tend to be unstable and are sometimes built around the personalities of their leaders. Venerable parties like Istiqlal, the USFP, and the RNI, meanwhile, have lost influence.

Justice and Charity (Al-Adl wa al-Ihsan) is an illegal Islamist movement that does not participate in elections. Nevertheless, it enjoys widespread support, and authorities largely tolerate its activities. More recent social movements such as the reformist February 20th Movement, which emerged from the 2011 Arab Spring protests, and *Hirak Rif*, a campaign against inequality that began in Morocco's largely Amazigh Rif region in 2016, enjoy considerable popular support, but have also faced government repression.

B2. Is there a realistic opportunity for the opposition to increase its support or gain power through elections? 1 / 4

Prior to 2011, the PJD was a vocal opposition party, and its entry into government showed that the system allowed some rotation of power. However, this opportunity is permanently limited by the presence and influence of the monarchy, both formally and in practice. Although the PJD won a plurality of seats in the 2016 elections, it struggled to form a governing coalition, and its ability to exercise power has been undermined by the king's support for parties loyal to the palace.

The October 2019 reshuffle was led by the monarch and resulted in a smaller cabinet with a large share of palace-approved technocrats, leaving elected political parties with less representation and authority.

B3. Are the people's political choices free from domination by forces that are external to the political sphere, or by political forces that employ extrapolitical means? 1 / 4

The constitution and informal practice give the king overwhelming influence over political affairs, including government formation. The monarch and his circle of advisers and associates—known in Morocco as the *Makhzen* ("central storehouse")—wield enormous private economic power that can be used to shape political outcomes through patronage networks.

B4. Do various segments of the population (including ethnic, racial, religious, gender, LGBT+, and other relevant groups) have full political rights and electoral opportunities? 1 / 4

The political system features universal suffrage, but parties based on religious, ethnic, or regional identity are prohibited, and the concerns and interests of women and the Amazigh population are not adequately addressed.

At least 40 percent of the population is Amazigh, and the majority of Moroccans have Amazigh roots. Amazigh elites enjoy access to the monarchy and also have their interests represented in Parliament, but the bulk of the population is socially and economically marginalized. Recent unrest in Al Hoceïma, the surrounding Rif region, and other cities across Morocco stemmed in large part from inequities experienced by many Amazigh residents and their inability to find redress for their grievances through the political system.

A system of reserved seats for women is meant to encourage their participation in the electoral process at the national and local levels, partly offsetting traditional social pressures that deter such engagement. Women won a greater share of parliamentary seats in 2016, taking 21 percent of the lower house, compared with 17 percent in 2011. Nevertheless, women remain underrepresented in party and cabinet leadership positions.

The 2019 conviction of journalist Hajar Raissouni for supposedly having an illegal abortion and engaging in extramarital sex underscored the need for greater political mobilization on behalf of women's rights, prompting a nationwide petition calling for an end to outmoded and discriminatory laws. The ongoing Outlaws campaign continued to gather signatures in its efforts to trigger criminal-code changes through 2020.

C. FUNCTIONING OF GOVERNMENT: 3 / 12

C1. Do the freely elected head of government and national legislative representatives determine the policies of the government? 1 / 4

While elected officials are duly installed in government, their power to shape policy is sharply constrained by the king, who sets domestic and foreign policy and commands the armed forces and intelligence services, and the Makhzen. Royal commissions tend to wield more power than ministries.

C2. Are safeguards against official corruption strong and effective? 1 / 4

Corruption is rife in state institutions and the economy. Despite official rhetoric about combating corruption, the palace and government have a mixed record on enforcement. The Central Authority for the Prevention of Corruption was strengthened in 2015 and was renamed the National Commission for Integrity and Anti-Corruption. In late 2018, the king appointed the commission's leader after the post remained vacant for three years.

While profound reforms are needed to combat corruption, progress has been slowed by a lack of political will, low institutional capacity, and the influence of elites who benefit from the status quo.

C3. Does the government operate with openness and transparency? 1 / 4

Overall transparency is limited. Civil society leaders have faulted a controversial 2018 access to information law for provisions that criminalize "misuse" of government information or "distortion of content." The government publishes budget and financial information online, and public officials—including parliamentarians, judges, and civil servants—are required to declare their assets. However, the monarchy itself, with its vast array of economic interests, is not subject to these rules.

Transparency is sometimes lacking with respect to the king's health, a subject which is considered taboo. In September 2019, the palace made a rare statement on Mohammed VI's health, reporting that a pending overseas trip was cancelled due to a respiratory ailment. In June 2020, the state news agency reported that Mohammed VI had undergone heart surgery,

CIVIL LIBERTIES: 24 / 60

D. FREEDOM OF EXPRESSION AND BELIEF: 7 / 16

D1. Are there free and independent media? 1 / 4

The state dominates the broadcast media, but affluent Moroccans have access to foreign satellite television channels. Although the independent press enjoys a significant degree of freedom when reporting on economic and social policies, the authorities use a number of financial and legal mechanisms to punish critical journalists, particularly those who focus on the king, his family, the status of Western Sahara, or Islam. The authorities also occasionally disrupt websites and internet platforms. Bloggers are harassed for posting content that offends the monarchy, although many online activists operate anonymously.

Several journalists, all of whom have previously faced government surveillance or prosecution, were detained by authorities during 2020. In May, *Akhbar al-Youm* editor in chief Soulaimane Raissouni, the uncle of Hajar Raissouni, was detained on suspicion of sexual assault, and remained in detention at year's end. In July, Omar Radi, a reporter at news site Le Desk, was arrested on charges including rape and working with foreign intelligence agencies. Observers doubted the veracity of the claims against Radi, who remained in detention at year's end, noting the authorities' use of sexual assault charges to stifle criticism and the government's previous surveillance and targeting of Radi. In December, *Al-Quds al-Arabi* contributor Maati Monjib, who was also harassed and surveilled by the authorities in the past, was detained on suspicion of money laundering.

Media freedoms were also restricted by COVID-19-related measures. In March 2020, the Culture Ministry halted the printing and distribution of newspapers. Authorities also began arresting individuals accused of spreading purportedly false news that same month.

Human rights groups continued to criticize the government's efforts to suppress reporting on the restive Rif region in 2020.

D2. Are individuals free to practice and express their religious faith or nonbelief in public and private? 2 / 4

Nearly all Moroccans are Muslims, and the king, identified as "commander of the faithful" in the constitution, has ultimate authority over religious affairs. Imams are required to obtain state certification, and mosques are monitored by the authorities. The government operates a well-financed training program for imams and female religious counselors tasked with promoting a state-sanctioned version of "moderate Islam," which some critics charge is also intended to promote political quiescence.

Despite deep societal prejudices, the small Jewish community is permitted to practice its faith, though many synagogues are unmarked. The Christian community, which numbers approximately 50,000, also experiences prejudice. Christian marriages are not legally recognized by the government.

D3. Is there academic freedom, and is the educational system free from extensive political indoctrination? 2 / 4

Universities generally provide a more open space for discussion, but professors practice self-censorship when dealing with sensitive topics like Western Sahara, the monarchy, and Islam. Salafists, adherents of a fundamentalist form of Islam, are closely monitored in universities. Periodic violence between university student groups, often stoked by Morocco's political, ethnic, and sectarian differences, inhibits the right to peaceful student activism.

In 2019, Parliament passed a law reestablishing French as the language of instruction for math, science, and other technical subjects, in part to help prepare students for French-language instruction at universities. Some opponents expressed preference for Chinese or English to improve Morocco's global economic competitiveness, while traditionalists preferred the reinforcement of Moroccan Arabic.

D4. Are individuals free to express their personal views on political or other sensitive topics without fear of surveillance or retribution? 2 / 4

There is some freedom of private discussion, but state surveillance of online activity and personal communications is a serious concern, and the arrests of journalists, bloggers, and activists for critical speech serve as a deterrent to uninhibited debate among the broader population. In 2019, Amnesty International reported that spyware was used to surveil journalist Maati Monjib and reported that similar tactics were used against Omar Radi in June 2020.

The government also sought to restrict social media activity with a draft law that the cabinet adopted in March 2020. The law would have allowed for the censorship of material that is considered a security threat, penalties against service providers, and prison sentences and fines for social media users who call for consumer boycotts. The draft was temporarily withdrawn in May after its publication sparked an outcry.

In June 2020, the Health Ministry launched the Wiqaytna (Our Protection) COVID-19 tracing application. Wiqaytna's launch sparked concerns over user privacy, with civil society groups noting the relative weakness of existing data-protection legislation.

E. ASSOCIATIONAL AND ORGANIZATIONAL RIGHTS: 5 / 12
E1. Is there freedom of assembly? 1 / 4

Freedom of assembly is restricted. The authorities sometimes use excessive force and violence to disperse protests, and harass activists involved in organizing demonstrations that express criticism of the government.

The government suppressed protests in the Rif region that erupted after the 2016 death of Al Hoceïma fish vendor Mohcine Fikri. The ensuing Hirak Rif protest movement against corruption and economic deprivation gained support from activists across Morocco, but those protests were dispersed in 2017. Nasser Zefzafi and other protest leaders were arrested that year and received 20-year prison sentences in 2018, while 50 other activists received shorter sentences. The charges were upheld by an appeals court in 2019, and Zefzafi remained imprisoned at year's end.

Despite existing and COVID-19-related assembly restrictions, major protests occurred in 2020. In late February, several thousand protesters marched in Casablanca, calling for an expansion of human rights and the release of imprisoned Hirak Rif participants. In September, demonstrators in Rabat rallied against the normalization of Israeli ties with Bahrain and the United Arab Emirates. In December, police in Rabat moved to prevent protests after the Moroccan government announced the normalization of ties with Israel.

E2. Is there freedom for nongovernmental organizations, particularly those that are engaged in human rights- and governance-related work? 2 / 4

While civil society organizations are active, they are subject to legal harassment, travel restrictions, intrusive surveillance, and other impediments to their work. The authorities routinely deny registration to nongovernmental organizations (NGOs) with links to Justice and Charity or that assert the rights of marginalized communities.

The Moroccan Association for Human Rights (AMDH), one of Morocco's most prominent NGOs, is frequently targeted by the government. The authorities have cancelled numerous AMDH events in recent years and are known to impede its efforts to rent space and open bank accounts. In April 2020, AMDH vice president Omar Naji was charged with defamation for criticizing the COVID-19-related confiscation of street merchants' goods in the city of Nador, while AMDH member Siham el-Makrini was arrested for incitement in May after commenting on teachers' rights in a social media post. Both individuals were acquitted in November.

Amnesty International has been prohibited from carrying out research in Morocco since 2015.

E3. Is there freedom for trade unions and similar professional or labor organizations? 2 / 4

Workers are permitted to form and join independent trade unions, and the 2004 labor law prevents employers from punishing workers who do so, but there are undue legal and employer restrictions on collective bargaining and strikes. The authorities sometimes forcibly break up labor-related protests. Unions are often closely affiliated with political parties.

Teachers held several strikes over promotions and pay in 2020. Contract teachers held a five-day strike in November over promotions and pay deductions, while full-time teachers called for a strike later that month over promotions. Contract teachers held another strike in late December, claiming that the government reneged on a previous agreement to offer them full-time posts. Postal workers, meanwhile, announced a strike over working conditions at the end of December.

F. RULE OF LAW: 5 / 16

F1. Is there an independent judiciary? 1 / 4

The court system is not independent of the monarch, who chairs the Supreme Council of the Judiciary. In practice, the courts are regularly used to punish perceived opponents of the government, including dissenting Islamists, human rights and anticorruption activists, and critics of Moroccan rule in Western Sahara.

F2. Does due process prevail in civil and criminal matters? 1 / 4

Due process is often neglected. Law enforcement officers frequently violate legal and procedural safeguards against arbitrary arrest and detention, and many convictions rely on confessions that may have been coerced. Pretrial detainees are reportedly held beyond a one-year limit in practice, and there are no provisions in the law allowing for pretrial detainees to challenge their detentions in court. Some suspects, particularly those accused of terrorism, are held in secret detention for days or weeks before formal charges are filed.

The convictions of Hirak Rif protesters were reportedly based on confessions obtained through torture, which the defendants all retracted during trial. Among other flaws in the process, the defendants were denied prompt access to lawyers after their arrests, and defense lawyers faced obstacles in accessing and presenting trial evidence.

The case against Hajar Raissouni also illustrated serious due process deficiencies. She and her fiancé were arrested in August 2019 and sentenced to a year's imprisonment that September on charges of extramarital sex and obtaining an illegal abortion, in what was considered a politically motivated prosecution. Raissouni, her fiancé, and her doctors, who were also prosecuted, received royal pardons that October.

The 2020 cases against Omar Radi and Soulaimane Raissouni were also regarded as politically motivated. Radi, for example, faced prolonged interrogation sessions in June, and was placed into pretrial detention in July, even though his lawyers argued that such treatment should not have applied in his case.

F3. Is there protection from the illegitimate use of physical force and freedom from war and insurgencies? 2 / 4

Cases of excessive force by police and torture in custody continue to occur. A number of the protesters detained in recent years have reported being beaten and injured during arrest, and some have been subjected to prolonged solitary confinement while awaiting trial.

Prisons often suffer from overcrowding, and prisoners faced heightened risks of contracting COVID-19. In April 2020, Mohammed VI pardoned over 5,600 prisoners and ordered their release in an effort to limit the spread of the coronavirus. Nevertheless, a prison in Drâa-Tafilalet Province became the site of at least 68 infections later that month.

Terrorism remains a threat to physical security in Morocco, though the authorities have had some success in preventing attacks. In July 2019, three assailants, who were avowed supporters of the Islamic State militant group, were sentenced to death for murdering two Scandinavian women while they hiked in the Atlas Mountains in 2018. However, Morocco has not carried out an execution since 1993.

F4. Do laws, policies, and practices guarantee equal treatment of various segments of the population? 1 / 4

Constitutional reforms in 2011 granted official status to Tamazight languages, which have been promoted in schools along with Amazigh culture. Nevertheless, Amazigh and other communities that do not identify with the dominant Arab culture tend to face educational and economic disadvantages. Civil society groups that promote Amazigh rights have faced government interference.

Gender equality was also recognized in the 2011 constitution, but women continue to face significant discrimination at the societal level and are underrepresented in the labor force. LGBT+ people face harsh discrimination and occasional violence. Same-sex sexual relations can be punished with up to three years in prison.

The government has granted temporary residency permits to refugees and migrants as part of an effort to regularize their status and provide them with basic services, which earned Morocco international praise in recent years. However, many registered refugees living in Morocco still do not possess residency or work permits. Authorities notably launched a crackdown on refugees, asylum seekers, and migrants from sub-Saharan Africa in 2018, arresting thousands of people in a series of raids that year and subsequently abandoning them near the Algerian border. The arrests were condemned by international rights groups for violating international law, as well as the basic human rights of those affected.

G. PERSONAL AUTONOMY AND INDIVIDUAL RIGHTS: 7 / 16

G1. Do individuals enjoy freedom of movement, including the ability to change their place of residence, employment, or education? 2 / 4

Moroccan law guarantees freedom of movement and the ability to change one's place of employment or education, but in practice poor economic conditions and corruption limit these rights. Widespread bribery, nepotism, and misconduct within the educational sector constrain merit-based advancement.

Movement was also restricted under COVID-19-related measures, with the government instituting a lockdown in March 2020. While some measures were relaxed in May, some internal movement restrictions were maintained throughout the rest of the year.

G2. Are individuals able to exercise the right to own property and establish private businesses without undue interference from state or nonstate actors? 2 / 4

Well over a third of the land is collectively owned by tribes and managed by the Interior Ministry, and in recent years it has been subject to private development without fair compensation to previous occupants. Moreover, under tribal rules of inheritance, women cannot hold the rights to occupy and use such lands, leaving them more vulnerable to displacement. Ordinary inheritance rules also put women at a disadvantage, generally granting them half the property of an equivalent male heir.

Private business activity is hampered in part by the dominant role of the king and his family. Among other assets, Mohammed VI has a majority stake in the National Investment Company, a massive conglomerate with businesses in virtually every economic sector, including mining, tourism, food, banking, construction, and energy.

G3. Do individuals enjoy personal social freedoms, including choice of marriage partner and size of family, protection from domestic violence, and control over appearance? 2 / 4

The 2004 family code granted women increased rights in the areas of marriage, divorce, and child custody, though a number of inequities and restrictions remain, and implementation of the code has been uneven.

All extramarital sexual activity is illegal, which deters rape survivors from bringing charges, among other repercussions.

Domestic violence is rarely reported or punished due to social stigma, though Moroccan NGOs offer support to domestic-violence survivors. A 2018 law criminalized domestic violence and forced marriage and imposed more stringent penalties on those convicted of rape. Although the law was considered a step forward, critics faulted the legislation for failing to outlaw spousal rape, not providing a clear definition of domestic violence, and not mandating the government to provide greater support for survivors. In July 2020, a network of NGOs reported that domestic violence increased during the country's COVID-19 lockdown.

G4. Do individuals enjoy equality of opportunity and freedom from economic exploitation? 1 / 4

Poverty is widespread, and economic opportunities are scarce for a large portion of the population. The deaths of two coal miners working in dangerous conditions in the town of Jerada in 2018 sparked protests and underscored chronic problems related to inequality and government neglect of certain industries and communities.

Child laborers, especially girls working as domestic helpers, are denied basic rights and are frequently abused by their employers. A 2018 labor law meant to protect young women employed as household workers requires employers to use written contracts, sets a minimum working age of 18 (after a five-year phase-in period during which 16- and 17-year-olds are allowed to work), mandates a day off each week, and sets a minimum wage. Rights groups criticized the legislation for failing to provide support to reintegrate domestic workers into society, and for permitting girls under 18 to work until 2023.

A 2016 law criminalized human trafficking; existing measures had defined and banned only some forms of trafficking and left many victims unprotected. Immigrant laborers, especially from sub-Saharan Africa, are often employed informally and subject to significant exploitation.

Mozambique

Population: 31,200,000
Capital: Maputo
Freedom Status: Partly Free
Electoral Democracy: No

Overview: The ruling party's unbroken incumbency before and since the introduction of multiparty elections in 1994 has allowed it to establish significant control over state institutions. The opposition has disputed the results of recent elections, and its armed wing fought a low-level conflict against government forces that persisted until a truce was signed in 2016. Hundreds of thousands of people have since been internally displaced due to an ongoing Islamist insurgency. Mozambique also struggles with corruption, and journalists who report on it and other sensitive issues risk violent attacks.

KEY DEVELOPMENTS IN 2020

- The Mozambican government declared a COVID-19-related state of emergency in late March, instituting restrictions on assembly and movement. A new state of emergency was introduced in August and was lifted in September, though some restrictions remained in force afterwards. The World Health Organization reported nearly 18,400 COVID-19 cases at the end of the year, along with 163 deaths.
- The ongoing Islamist insurgency in Cabo Delgado Province intensified during the year, with insurgents notably capturing the port town of Moçimboa da Praia in August. In December, the Office of the UN High Commissioner for Refugees

(UNHCR) reported that over 530,000 people were internally displaced, most of them due to the conflict.

POLITICAL RIGHTS: 14 / 40

A. ELECTORAL PROCESS: 3 / 12

A1. Was the current head of government or other chief national authority elected through free and fair elections? 1 / 4

The president, who appoints the prime minister, is elected by popular vote for up to two five-year terms. President Filipe Nyusi of the Front for the Liberation of Mozambique (FRELIMO) won the presidential contest in 2019 with 73 percent of the vote, an increase of 20 percentage points over his 2014 victory. Additionally, because FRELIMO won the most votes in all provinces, it received the right to select all 10 of the country's provincial governors. Turnout was reported at just over 50 percent.

The campaign was marred by violence, much of which targeted opposition members or their supporters, and several politicians and activists were killed. Anastácio Matavel, a respected independent election observer, was killed that October, with members of an elite police unit accused of carrying out the murder. Further violence was reported at dozens of polling stations on election day, as were instances of harassment of poll workers, notably those appointed by the opposition, with police taking part in the intimidation. Additionally, there were credible reports of ballot-box stuffing; interference with the registration of election observers; serious voting-register inaccuracies, particularly in Gaza Province; and tabulation irregularities. As in past elections, FRELIMO enjoyed a strong advantage due to its use of state resources to fund campaign activities and secure media coverage. A number of opposition rallies were prevented by authorities.

Opposition parties denounced the election as fraudulent, while civil society organizations denounced the polls, saying they were neither free, fair, nor transparent; that the ruling party had captured the electoral machinery through the National Elections Commission's (CNE) appointment process; and that the polls were the worst since the introduction of multiparty democracy in 1994. International observers from the Community of Portuguese Language Countries, the European Union, and the US embassy expressed concern about the reports of irregularities and election-related violence, but ultimately recognized the presidential election's outcome.

In January 2020, President Nyusi reappointed incumbent Carlos Agostinho do Rosário to the prime ministership.

A2. Were the current national legislative representatives elected through free and fair elections? 1 / 4

Members of the 250-seat unicameral Assembly of the Republic are elected to five-year terms. The 2019 legislative elections were held concurrently with the presidential election. FRELIMO took 184 seats, up from 144 previously. The Mozambique National Resistance (RENAMO) won 60 seats, down from 89 previously, and the Democratic Movement of Mozambique (MDM) took 6 seats, down from 17 previously.

The legislative polls were marred by the same violence, irregularities, and fraud allegations as the presidential election. Similarly, international observers objected to their conduct but accepted the results, while opposition parties rejected the elections, and a coalition of civil society groups called them patently flawed.

A3. Are the electoral laws and framework fair, and are they implemented impartially by the relevant election management bodies? 1 / 4

Elections are administered by the CNE and a support body, the Technical Secretariat for Electoral Administration. While the CNE's members hail from FRELIMO, RENAMO, the MDM, and civil society, FRELIMO effectively controls the selection process. Domestic and international observers have long argued that this structure has led to the politicization of the body, and deeply undermines stakeholder confidence in its operations. Seven new CNE members were selected by the FRELIMO-controlled parliament in December 2020.

The CNE's administration of the 2019 elections drew sharp domestic and international criticism. Among other issues—including irregularities in distribution of campaign finance funding and ballot printing, and general opacity of operations—large discrepancies emerged between the CNE's voter rolls and records kept by the National Institute of Statistics, notably in Gaza Province, a FRELIMO stronghold. CNE records showed more than 300,000 more registered voters in Gaza than voting-age adults counted in the 2017 census.

B. POLITICAL PLURALISM AND PARTICIPATION: 7 / 16

B1. Do the people have the right to organize in different political parties or other competitive political groupings of their choice, and is the system free of undue obstacles to the rise and fall of these competing parties or groupings? 2 / 4

The right to form political parties is largely respected. While many parties compete, most lack resources to campaign effectively and build a public following. Opposition leaders face harassment and threats for speaking out against the government. Figures within FRELIMO perceived as acting in conflict with the aims of the party can encounter obstacles, including intraparty disciplinary measures.

B2. Is there a realistic opportunity for the opposition to increase its support or gain power through elections? 1 / 4

FRELIMO first took power when Mozambique gained independence in 1975, and has remained in power since the 1992 agreement that ended the country's 1977–92 civil war and the introduction of multiparty elections in 1994. Since then, FRELIMO's use of public resources to fund campaign activities has provided it with an unfair electoral advantage.

In 2018, the parliament overwhelmingly approved constitutional reforms that in coming years would allow the indirect election of provincial governors, district administrators, and mayors. The changes were viewed as beneficial to RENAMO and a step toward greater decentralization and political stability. However, FRELIMO harnessed pressure tactics, the advantages of incumbency, and apparent fraud to secure an overwhelming victory in the 2019 elections. Because the party won the most votes in all provinces, it may select all of the country's provincial governors, effectively making the previous year's constitutional reforms moot. Many analysts have expressed concern that the failure to balance the share of power through the 2018 reforms threatens the precarious peace in Mozambique.

B3. Are the people's political choices free from domination by forces that are external to the political sphere, or by political forces that employ extrapolitical means? 2 / 4

Unelected elites in FRELIMO, including military members and powerful business figures, retain great influence and play a large role in shaping the party's platform. Civil servants face acute pressure to campaign and vote for the ruling party, and to make financial contributions to it. Those who openly support opposition candidates face intimidation by elements of the party embedded in state administration, and by police.

B4. Do various segments of the population (including ethnic, racial, religious, gender, LGBT+, and other relevant groups) have full political rights and electoral opportunities? 2 / 4

Ethnic minorities are generally able to participate fully in political life, and people from various ethnic groups hold high-level government positions. However, FRELIMO's support base lies in the extreme north and extreme south, and ethnic groups concentrated in other regions, such as the Ndau and Macua, are underrepresented. In 2019, three districts affected by the regional conflict in Cabo Delgado Province could not vote for security reasons. The decision effectively disenfranchised the many ethnic-minority voters who live there, notably members of the Makonde and Mwani ethnic groups that are concentrated in the region.

Women hold 42.4 percent of the parliament's seats as of July 2020. Women were appointed to notable cabinet roles in a January reshuffle, including the foreign affairs and education posts, though key positions were maintained by male politicians.

C. FUNCTIONING OF GOVERNMENT: 4 / 12

C1. Do the freely elected head of government and national legislative representatives determine the policies of the government? 1 / 4

Power remains generally centralized in the executive branch, which dominates the parliament and all other branches of government. The 2018 constitutional reforms introduced some measures to reduce centralization, but these reforms were in effect overridden by FRELIMO's victory in the year's severely flawed elections.

Foreign donors have significant influence on policymaking, specifically as it relates to economic policy and public-sector reform. Business elites connected to FRELIMO have a strong impact on government decisions, particularly on those related to foreign investment in the oil, gas, and agriculture sectors.

C2. Are safeguards against official corruption strong and effective? 1 / 4

Corruption remains widespread at the highest levels of government. Patronage networks are deeply entrenched, with various groupings competing for state resources. The anticorruption legal framework is undermined by a variety of loopholes: for example, embezzlement is not included in the Anti-Corruption Law. A judiciary susceptible to pressure from the executive branch further complicates attempts to enforce anticorruption laws.

In August 2020, Center for Public Integrity (CIP), a Mozambican nongovernmental organization (NGO), warned that the government's COVID-19-related procurement processes allowed for the possibility of overcharging and conflicts of interest.

C3. Does the government operate with openness and transparency? 2 / 4

Despite the passage of a freedom of information law in 2014, it is difficult to obtain government information in practice. The government is especially opaque regarding the Islamist insurgency in Cabo Delgado Province. In September 2020, Amnesty International called on the government to investigate acts of murder and torture committed by security forces in the province, but the authorities called the related evidence false.

CIVIL LIBERTIES: 29 / 60 (−2)

D. FREEDOM OF EXPRESSION AND BELIEF: 9 / 16

D1. Are there free and independent media? 2 / 4

State-run outlets dominate the Mozambican media sector, and authorities often direct such outlets to provide coverage favorable to the government. However, a number of smaller independent outlets provide important coverage. Journalists frequently experience government pressure, harassment, and intimidation, which encourages self-censorship. The government is known to retaliate against journalists who criticize it by cancelling public advertising contracts. Journalists and political commentators appearing on television programs have been the targets of attacks and kidnappings in recent years.

In April 2020, radio journalist Ibraimo Abú Mbaruco was forcibly disappeared in Cabo Delgado Province, and has not been heard from since. In June, Omardine Omar, a reporter for news site Carta de Moçambique, was convicted of civil disobedience and received a 15-day sentence that was converted to a fine. Omar, who was engaged in an extortion investigation for the news site when he was arrested, had been accused of violating COVID-19-related measures. In late August, the Maputo offices of newspaper *Canal de Moçambique* were destroyed in a fire; the newspaper had been investigating accusations of corruption within the Ministry of Mineral Resources and Energy.

D2. Are individuals free to practice and express their religious faith or nonbelief in public and private? 3 / 4

Religious freedom is generally respected, but government responses to attacks by armed Islamists have involved closing mosques and detaining Muslim leaders, alarming human rights activists.

D3. Is there academic freedom, and is the educational system free from extensive political indoctrination? 2 / 4

There are no legal restrictions on academic freedom. However, academics have been hesitant to criticize the government since law professor Gilles Cistac was murdered after supporting RENAMO in a televised appearance in 2015. Indoctrination at primary schools has been reported, particularly in Gaza Province, where some teachers have added FRELIMO propaganda to their curricula.

D4. Are individuals free to express their personal views on political or other sensitive topics without fear of surveillance or retribution? 2 / 4

Civil society groups claim that authorities monitor criticism of the government posted online. There have been reports of government intelligence agents monitoring the e-mails of opposition party members.

E. ASSOCIATIONAL AND ORGANIZATIONAL RIGHTS: 6 / 12

E1. Is there freedom of assembly? 2 / 4

Freedom of assembly is constitutionally guaranteed, but the right to assemble is subject to notification and timing restrictions. The government frequently disallows protests on the basis of errors in the organizers' official applications.

Despite these restrictions, protests did occur during 2020. In March, Maputo street vendors protested in response to official instructions to halt the sale of goods, and clashed with security forces. In April, taxi drivers in Nacala-a-Velha held a protest over COVID-19 measures, and also clashed with the authorities.

E2. Is there freedom for nongovernmental organizations, particularly those that are engaged in human rights- and governance-related work? 2 / 4

Most NGOs operate without significant legal restriction. However, rights defenders and members of groups perceived as critical of the government continue to report acts of intimidation, and these increased ahead of the 2019 election. NGOs involved in election-monitoring activity reported significant obstruction and harassment, including death threats.

The Mozambican Association for the Defense of Sexual Minorities (LAMBDA) applied for registration in 2008, but had no success attaining registration in subsequent years, even after multiple resubmissions. While LAMBDA has operated with the occasional cooperation of local authorities, its legal status remained unresolved as recently as 2019.

E3. Is there freedom for trade unions and similar professional or labor organizations? 2 / 4

Workers have the right to form unions, but a number of restrictions impede the right to strike and make the practice rare. Public-sector workers are not allowed to strike.

F. RULE OF LAW: 6 / 16 (−1)

F1. Is there an independent judiciary? 2 / 4

Judicial independence is hampered by the dominance of the executive branch. The attorney general is directly appointed by the president, with no legislative confirmation process. Pressure from FRELIMO's leadership often impedes investigations into corruption and fraud. While former president Armando Guebuza and members of his administration have been implicated in fraud and embezzlement, prosecutions were not promptly launched against them, though Guebuza-era finance minister Manuel Chang was eventually charged for corruption in November 2020. Observers claim that this historical inaction results from the influence of FRELIMO's leadership.

F2. Does due process prevail in civil and criminal matters? 2 / 4

Although due process rights are constitutionally guaranteed, these rights are not always respected in practice. RENAMO leaders assert that the police arrest members of their party arbitrarily. Due to resource constraints and an understaffed judiciary, lengthy pretrial detentions are common.

F3. Is there protection from the illegitimate use of physical force and freedom from war and insurgencies? 0 / 4 (−1)

Fighting between RENAMO and FRELIMO lasted for over a year before the parties agreed to a truce in late 2016. While a formal agreement was reached in August 2019, a dissident group of RENAMO fighters resisted demobilization. In August and September 2020, this group reportedly launched several attacks against civilians in central Mozambique, leading to several dozen deaths.

Residents of Cabo Delgado Province continue to suffer from violence and displacement as a result of an ongoing Islamist insurgency. Insurgents made progress capturing towns in the north during the year, notably capturing the port town of Moçimboa da Praia in August. In October, insurgents captured the village of Muatide and reportedly executed at least 50 residents. Security forces deployed to fight the insurgents have also been accused of extrajudicial killings, kidnappings, and other abuses.

Score Change: The score declined from 1 to 0 due the effects of an escalating Islamist insurgency in Cabo Delgado Province.

F4. Do laws, policies, and practices guarantee equal treatment of various segments of the population? 2 / 4

Mozambican police reportedly discriminate against Zimbabwean, Somali, and Chinese immigrants. People with albinism continued to face discrimination, persecution, and violence. Government efforts to protect people with albinism have been inadequate.

Women experience discrimination in education and employment; on average, women are less educated and earn less than men. Sexual harassment in the workplace and at schools remains widespread.

Homosexuality was decriminalized in 2015, but LGBT+ people face significant discrimination. The LGBT+ advocacy group LAMBDA has held training sessions for police officers aimed at helping them to address discrimination, including instances in which community members demand the arrest of LGBT+ people under defunct antigay laws.

Members of the Mwani ethnic group, many of whom practice Islam, face employment discrimination, and have sometimes been subjected to the expropriation of the land they occupy.

G. PERSONAL AUTONOMY AND INDIVIDUAL RIGHTS: 8 / 16 (−1)

G1. Do individuals enjoy freedom of movement, including the ability to change their place of residence, employment, or education? 2 / 4 (−1)

Although Mozambicans face no formal restrictions on domestic or international travel, movement is hampered by the presence of checkpoints manned by corrupt police officials, who often harass and demand bribes from travelers.

Hundreds of thousands of Mozambicans have been displaced from their residences due to the ongoing insurgency in Cabo Delgado Province, which grew more intense in 2020. In December, the Office of the UN High Commissioner for Refugees (UNHCR) counted over 530,000 internally displaced persons (IDPs) in Mozambique, most of them from Cabo Delgado. As many as 130,000 IDPs resided in the provincial capital of Pemba that same month.

Score Change: The score declined from 3 to 2 because the insurgency in Cabo Delgado Province has impaired freedom of movement in the area and caused the forced displacement of many residents.

G2. Are individuals able to exercise the right to own property and establish private businesses without undue interference from state or nonstate actors? 2 / 4

The law does not recognize private property outside urbanized areas; citizens instead obtain land use rights from the government. Many citizens are uninformed about the land law and fail to properly register their holdings. The government must approve all formal transfers of land use rights in an often opaque and protracted process. As a result, most land transactions occur on an extralegal market.

There is no legal restriction to private business. However, businesspeople do face kidnappings and extortion.

Under customary law, women usually cannot inherit property. The government does not frequently intervene to protect women's property rights when inheritance is denied.

G3. Do individuals enjoy personal social freedoms, including choice of marriage partner and size of family, protection from domestic violence, and control over appearance? 2 / 4

Domestic violence is pervasive in Mozambique and laws against it are infrequently enforced. Early and forced marriages remain common in rural areas.

Mozambique has historically possessed one of the world's highest rates of child marriage, though the government passed legislation closing a loophole that previously allowed the practice in 2019.

G4. Do individuals enjoy equality of opportunity and freedom from economic exploitation? 2 / 4

Many women and girls from rural areas are at risk of becoming drawn into sex trafficking and domestic servitude. Government efforts to confront trafficking are improving but remain inadequate, according to the US State Department's most recent *Trafficking in Persons Report*, which also stated that the authorities did not proactively identify survivors outside of criminal cases and have not enacted an action plan or legislation that would better support them.

Child labor is permitted for children between 15 and 17 years old with a government permit. However, children under 15 frequently labor in the agriculture, mining, and fishing sectors, where they often work long hours and do not attend school. According to a 2017 Ministry of Labor report, more than one million children between the ages of 7 and 17 are actively employed.

Myanmar

Population: 54,700,000
Capital: Nay Pyi Taw
Freedom Status: Not Free
Electoral Democracy: No

Overview: Myanmar's transition from military dictatorship to democracy stalled under the leadership of the National League for Democracy (NLD), which came to power in relatively free elections in 2015. The military, known as the Tatmadaw, retained significant influence over politics, and the government largely failed to uphold human rights and to prioritize peace and security in areas affected by armed conflict. A 2017 military operation and ongoing conflict have forced hundreds of thousands of people from the Rohingya minority, a mostly Muslim ethnic group, to seek refuge in Bangladesh, and those remaining in Rakhine State continue to face the threat of genocide. Journalists, activists, and ordinary people risked criminal charges and detention for voicing dissent during 2020, while a lengthy internet shutdown impaired access to vital news and information in Rakhine and Chin States.

KEY DEVELOPMENTS IN 2020

- Though few people tested positive for COVID-19 in the spring, over 123,000 people had tested positive and more than 2,600 people had died from the virus by year's end. Citing the pandemic, the government prohibited in-person campaigning ahead of the November parliamentary elections, which benefited the incumbent NLD.
- The NLD's sweeping election victory was marred by an ongoing internet shutdown in some areas, limited media coverage and election monitoring, and the cancellation of balloting for almost one million voters in a number of conflict-prone districts.
- Fighting between the Tatmadaw and ethnic minority rebels in Chin, Kachin, Karen, Rakhine, and Shan States continued, displacing thousands of civilians and limiting free movement. More than 900,000 Rohingya refugees from Rakhine State remained in Bangladesh.
- In September, video testimony by two Tatmadaw soldiers that was provided to the International Criminal Court (ICC) corroborated claims that the army had committed grave human rights abuses against the Rohingya.
- Also in September, student protesters were arrested and charged for distributing materials that criticized the government or military and for demonstrating against the internet shutdown and ongoing conflict in Rakhine State. Some of those arrested were convicted and given lengthy prison sentences.

POLITICAL RIGHTS: 13 / 40 (−1)

A. ELECTORAL PROCESS: 5 / 12

A1. Was the current head of government or other chief national authority elected through free and fair elections? 2 / 4

The legislature elects the president, who serves as chief of state and head of government and makes a number of key ministerial appointments. Military members of the legislature have the right to nominate one of the three presidential candidates, and the elected members of each chamber nominate the other two. The candidate with the largest number of votes in a combined parliamentary vote wins the presidency; the other two candidates become vice presidents, ensuring that a military nominee is always either president or vice president.

Htin Kyaw, the NLD candidate, won the presidency in 2016, following the 2015 parliamentary elections. He resigned in 2018 and was replaced by Win Myint, one of NLD leader Aung San Suu Kyi's aides. A new president was set to be selected in early 2021, in the wake of the November 2020 parliamentary elections.

Aung San Suu Kyi continued to hold the powerful position of state counselor as of 2020. The post, akin to that of a prime minister, was created for her in 2016 through legislation designed to circumvent provisions in the 2008 military-drafted constitution that had barred her from running for president on the grounds that members of her immediate family hold foreign citizenship.

The commander in chief of the armed forces retained broad powers under the constitution, including control over security-related cabinet ministries (home, defense, and border affairs), and is selected through an opaque process by the military-dominated National Defense and Security Council (NDSC).

A2. Were the current national legislative representatives elected through free and fair elections? 2 / 4

The bicameral Assembly of the Union consists of the 440-seat lower House of Representatives and the 224-seat upper House of Nationalities. Representatives serve five-year terms. A quarter of the seats in both houses are reserved for the military and are filled through appointment by the commander in chief of the armed forces. The remainder are filled through direct elections in a first-past-the-post system.

The 2020 parliamentary elections featured significant flaws. Existing rules allowed for the exclusion of many Muslim candidates and the disenfranchisement of hundreds of thousands of Rohingya. In addition, the Union Election Commission (UEC) canceled voting in a number of conflict-affected districts in Rakhine and other states, preventing about one million people from electing new representatives. Analysts raised concerns that the cancellations benefited the NLD at the expense of ethnic-based opposition parties, such as the Arakan National Party (ANP). Opposition parties faced unequal access to state-run media during the campaign period, and pandemic-related restrictions on in-person campaigning disproportionately affected smaller parties and lesser-known candidates. The main opposition party—the military-supported Union Solidarity and Development Party (USDP)—and more than 20 others called for the voting to be postponed in light of the pandemic. The UEC argued that its provisions, including an increase in the number of polling stations, would be sufficient to ensure a safe and fair process.

Due to the various restrictions on travel and free movement, external election observers and journalists were not able to monitor the 2020 polls. In August, the independent, Myanmar-based People's Alliance for Credible Elections (PACE) was denied accreditation to monitor polls because it received foreign funding.

The NLD won a convincing majority in the overall popular vote, taking 138 of the 168 elected seats in the upper house, 258 of the 330 elected seats in the lower house, and 501 of 660 elected seats across 14 state and regional legislatures. The USDP placed a distant second with 7 seats in the upper house, 26 in the lower house, and 38 in the states and regions. The remaining seats were captured by ethnic minority parties, other small parties, and independents. At year's end the USDP was alleging fraud, and adjudication of its claims was expected in early 2021.

A3. Are the electoral laws and framework fair, and are they implemented impartially by the relevant election management bodies? 1 / 4

Various features of the electoral framework undermine the democratic nature of the country's elections. These include the military's role in presidential nominations and appointments to both chambers of parliament, as well as rigid citizenship laws and excessive residency requirements that prevent large numbers of people from voting or standing for office.

The UEC, which is responsible for electoral administration, is empowered to adjudicate complaints against itself. Its members are appointed by the president and confirmed by the legislature, which has only limited authority to reject nominees. The decision of the UEC to limit or cancel voting in several dozen townships populated by ethnic minority groups was criticized as lacking sufficient transparency and disenfranchising voters, as were UEC-imposed rules surrounding access to and censorship of broadcast time allotted to political parties.

B. POLITICAL PLURALISM AND PARTICIPATION: 8 / 16 (−1)

B1. Do the people have the right to organize in different political parties or other competitive political groupings of their choice, and is the system free of undue obstacles to the rise and fall of these competing parties or groupings? 3 / 4

Party competition in the lead-up to the 2020 elections was robust, with 7,000 candidates from more than 90 parties participating. Alongside the NLD, the USDP, and regionally based ethnic parties, a number of new parties emerged, including Shwe Mann's Union Betterment Party and Thet Thet Khine's People's Pioneer Party. However, the response to COVID-19 restricted parties' ability to convene meetings and large rallies throughout the country, making it more difficult for newer and smaller parties to build support among voters.

Competition remains skewed in part by the USDP's systematic support from the military. The constitution contains a requirement that political parties be loyal to the state, which carries the potential for abuse. Laws allow penalties, including deregistration, for political parties that accept support from foreign governments or religious bodies, or that are deemed to have abused religion for political purposes or disrespected the constitution.

B2. Is there a realistic opportunity for the opposition to increase its support or gain power through elections? 2 / 4 (−1)

The military's constitutional prerogatives, as well as its close ties to the USDP, limit the degree to which any other force can secure control over the executive or the legislature through elections.

At the same time, pandemic-related measures—particularly a number of restrictions imposed in September 2020, as COVID-19 cases rose dramatically—disproportionately affected opposition parties and privileged the ruling NLD and sitting lawmakers ahead of the November elections. Stay-at-home orders circumscribed electoral activities in some areas, including Yangon and Rakhine State, and much of the campaigning had to shift online. In areas affected by internet shutdowns and fighting between the military and ethnic insurgent groups, campaigning was all but impossible. The ability of smaller parties and lesser-known candidates to campaign was further hindered by unequal access to state-owned media and the cancellation or delay of polling in dozens of townships.

Score Change: The score declined from 3 to 2 due to a variety of electoral obstacles—including unequal access to state-run media outlets, pandemic-related restrictions on in-person campaigning, and internet shutdowns and canceled balloting in some districts—that effectively privileged the ruling NLD and put opposition ethnic minority parties at a particular disadvantage.

B3. Are the people's political choices free from domination by forces that are external to the political sphere, or by political forces that employ extrapolitical means? 2 / 4

Despite its waning ability to influence electoral outcomes, the military retains considerable power over political affairs, particularly in conflict areas. This continued in 2020, as the country's institutions responded to the COVID-19 pandemic. The UEC granted the military leadership the authority to determine whether populations in conflict areas would be able to vote, allowing it to help shape political representation.

B4. Do various segments of the population (including ethnic, racial, religious, gender, LGBT+, and other relevant groups) have full political rights and electoral opportunities? 1 / 4

Members of the country's Buddhist and ethnic Bamar majority hold most senior leadership positions in the major national political parties and in government. Members of ethnic and religious minority groups face restrictions on their political rights and electoral opportunities, including through discriminatory citizenship, residency, and party registration laws.

The 1982 Citizenship Law does not allow for anyone who entered the country or is descended from someone who entered the country after 1948 to become a full citizen with political rights. Naturalization of spouses is only allowed if the spouse holds a Foreigner's Registration Certificate from before the law's enactment.

The majority of the mainly Muslim Rohingya were rendered stateless by the 1982 Citizenship Law, which also dictates that only those who are descended from ethnic groups deemed to be native to the country prior to 1823 are considered full citizens who can run for public office. Six of the dozen Rohingya who filed to run as candidates in 2020 were disqualified on citizenship grounds. In 2015, the president issued a decree—later upheld by a Constitutional Tribunal—revoking the temporary identification cards, or "white cards," that had allowed Rohingya to vote in previous elections. Most of the 600,000 Rohingya remaining in Myanmar were unable to vote in the 2020 elections. However, a small number of Rohingya and other Muslims with citizenship documents were able to vote, and several dozen Muslims ran as candidates, including two NLD members who were both elected.

Because the military prevented polling in some regions, certain ethnic-based parties such as the ANP lost seats, and ethnic minority groups like the Karen, Kachin, and Shan were effectively disenfranchised. The ability of residents of Rakhine State to participate in the elections was compromised by the ongoing internet shutdown, as well as continued armed conflict that limited access to voter registration and polling stations.

Women remain underrepresented in the government and civil service, due largely to societal biases that discourage their political participation. Notwithstanding the prominence of Aung San Suu Kyi, whose father led Myanmar's independence struggle and who gained respect as an opposition leader and political prisoner during military rule, few women have achieved ministerial-level appointments.

C. FUNCTIONING OF GOVERNMENT: 4 / 12

C1. Do the freely elected head of government and national legislative representatives determine the policies of the government? 2 / 4

Although elected officials are able to set policy in some subject areas, the military is guaranteed control over the Defense, Home Affairs, and Border Affairs Ministries. The military also effectively controls at least six seats on the powerful 11-member NDSC.

The 2008 constitution allows the military to dissolve the civilian government and the parliament and rule directly if the president declares a state of emergency. The military also retains a veto on amendments to the constitution. In 2019 the NLD announced the formation of a parliamentary committee on constitutional change, but in March 2020 military delegates blocked NLD proposals to reduce the military's representation in the parliament.

Effective governance and control over territory in some regions is contested between the armed forces and ethnic minority rebel groups.

C2. Are safeguards against official corruption strong and effective? 1 / 4

Despite government initiatives aimed at curbing official corruption, it remains rampant at both the national and local levels. An Anti-Corruption Commission (ACC), established in 2014 and reformed in 2017 with 12 members appointed by the president, has brought a number of cases against high-ranking officials. The former chief minister of Tanintharyi Region was sentenced in May 2020 to 30 years in prison for bribery.

Privatization of state-owned companies and other economic reforms in recent years have allegedly benefited family members and associates of senior officials. The government ignores tax evasion by the country's wealthiest companies and individuals.

C3. Does the government operate with openness and transparency? 1 / 4

The government does not operate with openness and transparency. A 2017 draft Right to Information Law remained stalled in Parliament as of 2020. A proposed law on access to government archives that was publicized in July included heavy financial penalties and potential prison time for unauthorized access to certain information.

Some information about the budget has been released in recent years, but official spending receives limited parliamentary scrutiny. The military owns an extensive network of "crony companies" whose revenues enable it to avoid accountability and public oversight and engage in human rights violations with impunity, according to a UN report released in 2019.

ADDITIONAL DISCRETIONARY POLITICAL RIGHTS QUESTION

Is the government or occupying power deliberately changing the ethnic composition of a country or territory so as to destroy a culture or tip the political balance in favor of another group? -4 / 0

The central authorities have long used violence, displacement, and other tactics to alter the demographics of states with ethnic unrest or insurgencies. The Rohingya in Rakhine State have faced particularly harsh restrictions for decades, including limits on family size and the ability and right to marry, the denial of legal status and social services, and disenfranchisement and loss of citizenship. Human rights experts and the United Nations have labeled the abuses against the Rohingya as crimes against humanity and ethnic cleansing, and many have argued that they constitute either genocide or a precursor to genocide.

Repression of the Rohingya escalated in 2017, after rebels from the Arakan Rohingya Salvation Army (ARSA) attacked multiple police posts with rudimentary weapons. The military launched a severe, ongoing counteroffensive against Rohingya communities across the northern part of the state, leading to reports of torture, rape, indiscriminate killings, and the burning of villages, worsening already dire humanitarian conditions and causing 740,000 Rohingya refugees to join the 200,000 others already in Bangladesh. Aung San Suu Kyi did not explicitly acknowledge or condemn such organized official violence against Rohingya civilians. There has been little meaningful accountability for the atrocities; for example, two low-ranking officers and a soldier were court-martialed in June 2020.

The UN Independent International Fact-Finding Mission on Myanmar released its final report in September 2019, finding that the 600,000 Rohingya still in Rakhine State remained "under threat of genocide." In November 2019, the ICC began an investigation into allegations of genocide and other crimes against the Rohingya. In September 2020, video testimony from two Tatmadaw soldiers at an ICC hearing supported allegations of mass human rights violations against the Rohingya, including rape, executions, and mass burials.

The International Court of Justice (ICJ) ruled against Myanmar on this issue in January 2020, urging the government to implement emergency measures to protect the Rohingya and preserve evidence of the crimes against them. A September 2020 report to the UN Human Rights Council by UN High Commissioner for Human Rights Michelle Bachelet noted that ongoing civilian casualties in Rakhine may amount to further war crimes. In October, Human Rights Watch likened the conditions for the approximately 130,000 Rohingya kept in several dozen camps in Rakhine State to apartheid, with severe restrictions on travel and education, as well as access to health care, food, and shelter.

CIVIL LIBERTIES: 15 / 60 (−1)

D. FREEDOM OF EXPRESSION AND BELIEF: 5 / 16

D1. Are there free and independent media? 1 / 4

Media freedom is restricted. The authorities are empowered by law to deny licenses to outlets whose reporting is considered insulting to religion or a threat to national security, and the risk of prosecution under criminal defamation and a range of other restrictive laws encourages self-censorship. While internet access has expanded in recent years, online activity is also subject to criminal punishment under several broadly worded legal provisions, and dozens of journalists and social media users have faced defamation and incitement cases filed by the military and politicians. An internet shutdown affecting parts of Rakhine and Chin States has remained in place since June 2019, blocking access to a variety of digital services and news sources, which was particularly problematic during the COVID-19 pandemic and the 2020 election period.

The military-controlled Home Affairs Ministry routinely surveils journalists, and reporters covering sensitive topics risk harassment, physical violence, and imprisonment. In March 2020, the government issued orders to block 220 websites, including a number of ethnic media outlets; authorities also arrested a prominent editor, U Nay Myo Lin of the Voice of Myanmar, for interviewing the rebel Arakan Army's spokesman. Also in March, police raided the office of the Rakhine media group Narinjara News, detained three reporters, and seized equipment and files.

COVID-19-related restrictions on movement that were enacted in September 2020 in Rakhine State, Yangon, and other cities did not exempt private media, further limiting independent coverage of the election campaign.

D2. Are individuals free to practice and express their religious faith or nonbelief in public and private? 1 / 4

The constitution provides for freedom of religion. It distinguishes Buddhism as the majority religion, but also recognizes Christianity, Islam, Hinduism, and animism. The government occasionally interferes with religious assemblies and attempts to control the Buddhist clergy. Authorities discriminate against minority religious groups—particularly Muslims—in practice, refusing them permission to hold gatherings and restricting educational activities, proselytization, and construction and repair of houses of worship.

Anti-Muslim hate speech and discrimination have been amplified by social media, and by some state institutions and mainstream news websites. The officially illegal Buddha Dhamma Parahita Foundation, formerly known as Ma Ba Tha, agitates for the protection of Buddhist privileges, urges boycotts against Muslim-run businesses, and disseminates anti-Muslim propaganda; respected mainstream monks such as Sitagu Sayadaw have also allegedly stoked religious hatred. Muslims face systematic discrimination in obtaining identity cards, and "Muslim-free" villages have been established with the complicity of officials.

D3. Is there academic freedom, and is the educational system free from extensive political indoctrination? 1 / 4

Political activity on university campuses is generally restricted, and universities are not autonomous. Student unions—which have historically been important advocates for human rights—are discouraged, have no formal registration mechanisms, and are viewed with suspicion by authorities. A 2018 directive from the Ministry of Education required students to get permission from their universities and the ministry itself to hold events on campus, obliging them to submit names and biographies of speakers, titles of public talks, and the number of people expected to attend. In September 2020, more than a dozen students were detained and others faced charges for distributing materials that were critical of government policies.

D4. Are individuals free to express their personal views on political or other sensitive topics without fear of surveillance or retribution? 2 / 4

Private discussion and personal expression are constrained by state surveillance and laws that inhibit online speech. Dozens of defamation cases involving online commentary have been filed under Section 66(d) of the 2013 Telecommunications Law, which includes bans on online activity deemed to be threatening or defamatory.

Social media users and those quoted in the media have faced prosecution for expressing their views on particular topics, particularly when they entail criticism of the authorities. Five members of the Peacock Generation satirical poetry troupe, detained in April 2019 for performances posted on Facebook that were critical of the military, were sentenced that October to a year in prison; during 2020 they faced additional charges.

E. ASSOCIATIONAL AND ORGANIZATIONAL RIGHTS: 5 / 12 (−1)

E1. Is there freedom of assembly? 1 / 4 (−1)

Unauthorized demonstrations are punishable with up to six months in prison under the Peaceful Assembly and Peaceful Procession Law; a variety of other vaguely defined violations can draw lesser penalties. Protesters focused on issues such as land rights and the rights of ethnic minority groups are regularly charged and sentenced to jail terms under the law. The internet shutdown in Rakhine State has severely impeded the ability of activists and ordinary citizens to organize protests.

A blanket ban on protests in 11 townships of central Yangon has been in place since 2017, though it is selectively enforced. Authorities occasionally employ excessive force against peaceful protesters. Protesters no longer have to ask permission for assemblies, but they do need to notify authorities 48 hours in advance, and local officials often treat this process as a request for permission in practice.

The government detained and prosecuted significantly more students and activists for protest activities in 2020 than in previous years. For example, in September, dozens of students and others were arrested and faced criminal charges after taking part in demonstrations or distributing materials to protest the internet shutdown and ongoing conflict in Rakhine State. As of November, at least two students were reported to have received sentences amounting to seven years in prison.

Score Change: The score declined from 2 to 1 due to an extended shutdown of internet service in Rakhine State, which disrupted the organization of public gatherings, and an increase in the number of protest-related detentions of students and activists during the year.

E2. Is there freedom for nongovernmental organizations, particularly those that are engaged in human rights- and governance-related work? 2 / 4

Although nongovernmental organizations (NGOs) comment on human rights issues and engage in governance work, barriers to their interaction with government ministries have increased in recent years. The Home Affairs Ministry issued regulations in 2015 that require NGOs to obtain government approval prior to registration. Police routinely arrest civil society activists for voicing dissent on a variety of politically sensitive topics.

E3. Is there freedom for trade unions and similar professional or labor organizations? 2 / 4

A ban on independent trade unions was lifted in 2011, and union activity has taken root in Myanmar. Strikes by workers protesting poor labor conditions or the denial of rights take place regularly. However, trade unionists continue to face retaliation for their efforts, and legal protections against abuse by employers are weak. Several hundred workers were fired from two clothing factories in May 2020, after the workers formed a union; the management blamed COVID-19 for the layoffs.

F. RULE OF LAW: 1 / 16

F1. Is there an independent judiciary? 0 / 4

The judiciary is not independent. Judges are nominated by the president, and lawmakers can reject the choice only if it is clearly proven that the nominee does not meet the legal qualifications for the post. The courts generally adjudicate cases in accordance with the government's interests, particularly in major cases with political implications.

F2. Does due process prevail in civil and criminal matters? 1 / 4

Administrative detention laws allow individuals to be held without charge, trial, or access to legal counsel for up to five years if they are deemed a threat to state security or sovereignty.

Although the parliament in 2016 repealed several legal provisions that were used to imprison dissidents, numerous individuals who are considered political prisoners continued to be held in 2020. According to the Assistance Association for Political Prisoners (AAPP), as of December there were a total of 601 political prisoners in Myanmar, with 42 serving sentences, 196 in pretrial detention, and 363 others awaiting trial outside prison.

F3. Is there protection from the illegitimate use of physical force and freedom from war and insurgencies? 0 / 4

The NLD government's efforts to negotiate peace agreements with ethnic rebel groups remained stymied in 2020 by military offensives against the insurgents, particularly in Shan, Kachin, and Kayin States; attacks by such groups against security forces; and continued divisions among signatories and nonsignatories to a 2015 national cease-fire agreement.

The NLD's approach to dealing with ethnic minorities has also been faulted for inhibiting peace efforts. Following the outbreak of COVID-19 in 2020, several armed ethnic groups called for a cease-fire.

Indiscriminate shelling, extrajudicial killings, forced disappearances, and other abuses by the military continue to be reported, while rebel groups engage in forced disappearances and forced recruitment. Areas in the north remain riddled with landmines planted by both rebels and the army. Authorities at times prevent aid groups from reaching populations affected by violence. Civilians continued to flee fighting in Shan, Kachin, Kayin, and Chin States in 2020, leaving tens of thousands displaced at year's end. An intensification of military action in northern Rakhine State, following attacks on police posts by the ethnic Rakhine Arakan Army in January 2019, continued unabated in 2020, killing dozens of people and displacing more than 70,000. The Arakan Army has also conducted indiscriminate attacks on civilians, and in March 2020 the government classified it as a terrorist group. Attacks by the military in May targeted Rakhine Buddhist villages.

Prisons in Myanmar are severely overcrowded, and conditions for inmates are sometimes life-threatening. In April 2020, almost 25,000 prisoners were released from the overcrowded prison system in the largest annual amnesty in years, according to the AAPP.

F4. Do laws, policies, and practices guarantee equal treatment of various segments of the population? 0 / 4

Some of the country's worst human rights abuses, commonly committed by government troops, are against ethnic and religious minority populations. The government's failure to protect victims, conduct investigations, and punish perpetrators is well documented.

Ethnic minority groups such as the Shan, Mon, Chin, Karen, and Kachin, as well as non-Rohingya Muslims, also face some societal discrimination, while the ethnic Bamar, Buddhist majority retains a privileged position.

In addition to conflict-related violence, women are subject to discrimination in employment, against which there are no explicit legal protections. A number of laws create a hostile environment for LGBT+ residents. Same-sex sexual activity is criminalized, and police reportedly harass, extort, and physically and sexually abuse LGBT+ people.

G. PERSONAL AUTONOMY AND INDIVIDUAL RIGHTS: 4 / 16

G1. Do individuals enjoy freedom of movement, including the ability to change their place of residence, employment, or education? 1 / 4

Freedom of internal travel for Myanmar citizens is generally respected outside of conflict zones, but due to an intensification of the country's armed conflicts in recent years, travel in a number of states has been further restricted. In addition, Myanmar's large population of stateless residents are subject to significant restrictions on their movement, particularly the 600,000 Rohingya who remain in Rakhine State and are confined to designated camps and villages; those who attempt to travel outside these areas are regularly arrested and detained.

Numerous exiled activists who returned to the country after the transition to partial civilian rule have experienced substantial delays and evasion from government authorities when attempting to renew visas and residency permits. Separately, illegal toll collection by state and nonstate actors remains a problem in some areas.

In 2020, the government imposed COVID-19-related restrictions on movement in the spring and again in the fall. While many of the constraints themselves were generally recognized as legitimate, hundreds of people were either heavily fined or imprisoned for violating curfew or quarantine regulations, and rights groups criticized these penalties as disproportionate.

G2. Are individuals able to exercise the right to own property and establish private businesses without undue interference from state or nonstate actors? 1 / 4

Disputes over land grabbing and business projects that violate human rights are common. Myanmar's property-transfer laws prohibit transfers to or from a foreigner except in certain state-approved cases of inheritance, and require registration of foreign-owned property. Stateless residents, including the Rohingya, cannot legally buy or sell property or set up a business.

Instances of forced eviction and displacement, confiscation, lack of sufficient compensation, and direct violence against landholders by state security officials abound. Court cases are frequently brought against farmers for trespassing on land that was taken from them. A 2018 amendment to the Vacant, Fallow, and Virgin Lands Management Law required anyone living on land thus categorized (about 30 percent of Myanmar's land, predominantly in ethnic minority states and regions) to apply by March 2019 for a permit to continue using it; violators could face two-year prison terms. Surveys and analysis indicate that the majority of those affected—particularly from ethnic minority and refugee communities—were not aware of the law, putting their use of the land at risk.

Multiple sources continued to report in 2020 that Rohingya land and property have been razed, confiscated, appropriated, or built on, often with the direct involvement of the military, and sometimes under the guise of development assistance.

G3. Do individuals enjoy personal social freedoms, including choice of marriage partner and size of family, protection from domestic violence, and control over appearance? 1 / 4

Men and women formally enjoy equal rights on personal status issues, though there are restrictions on marriages of Buddhist women to non-Buddhist men. Laws that might protect women from domestic abuse and rape are weak and poorly enforced, and such violence is an acute and persistent problem. The army has a record of using rape as a weapon of war against ethnic minority women, and security personnel typically enjoy impunity for sexual violence.

G4. Do individuals enjoy equality of opportunity and freedom from economic exploitation? 1 / 4

Human trafficking, forced labor, child labor, and the recruitment of child soldiers all remain serious problems in Myanmar, and the government's efforts to address them are inadequate. Child soldiers are enlisted by the military and ethnic rebel groups, which also recruit civilians for forced labor. Various commercial and other interests continue to use forced labor despite a formal ban on the practice. Trafficking victims include women and girls subjected to forced sex work and domestic servitude, as well as women who are sold as brides to men in China—an expanding practice in some ethnic minority states. People displaced by ongoing conflicts are especially vulnerable to sexual and labor exploitation.

Namibia

Population: 2,500,000
Capital: Windhoek
Freedom Status: Free
Electoral Democracy: Yes

Overview: While Namibia is a multiparty democracy, the ruling South West Africa People's Organisation (SWAPO) has ruled since independence. Protections for civil liberties are generally robust. Minority ethnic groups accuse the government of favoring the majority

Ovambo in allocating services. The nomadic San people suffer from poverty and marginalization. Other human rights concerns include police brutality, the criminalization of same-sex sexual relations, and discrimination against women.

KEY DEVELOPMENTS IN 2020

- Nationwide protests against gender-based violence (GBV) were held in October after the remains of a missing woman were found in Walvis Bay. Police forcefully responded; at least 27 people were arrested, including 3 journalists.
- Local and regional elections were held in November. While SWAPO won a majority of regional votes, it fell short of its 2015 performance and lost control of the Windhoek municipal council to opposition groups.
- Namibian authorities relied on public-assembly restrictions, travel restrictions, and other measures to limit the spread of COVID-19. Despite these efforts, the country faced infection waves in August and December. Some 23,333 cases and 196 deaths were reported to the World Health Organization (WHO) by year's end.

POLITICAL RIGHTS: 31 / 40

A. ELECTORAL PROCESS: 11 / 12

A1. Was the current head of government or other chief national authority elected through free and fair elections? 4 / 4

The president is both chief of state and head of government and is directly elected for up to two five-year terms. In November 2019, Hage Geingob of SWAPO was reelected with 56.3 percent of the vote. While international observers deemed polls peaceful and credible, concerns were raised about the lack of verifiable paper trail, long waiting times, and delays in the counting and release of results.

In February 2020, the Supreme Court ruled the use of electronic voting machines without a paper trail invalid but did not accept an opposition call to overrule the 2019 results.

A2. Were the current national legislative representatives elected through free and fair elections? 4 / 4

The National Council, the upper chamber of the bicameral parliament, has 42 seats, with members appointed by regional councils for six-year terms. The lower house, the National Assembly, has 96 seats filled by popular election for five-year terms using party-list proportional representation. International observers considered the November 2019 polls competitive and credible, though some logistical glitches with electronic voting machines were reported, and concerns were raised about other aspects of the electoral process.

SWAPO won a lower-house majority in those elections, though its dominant position was challenged. It won 63 seats and 65.5 percent of the vote. Opposition parties performed well. The Popular Democratic Movement (PDM) won 16 seats, while the Landless People's Movement (LPM) won 4.

Local and regional elections were held in November 2020. SWAPO won a majority of votes cast in regional polls but fell short of its 2015 performance. SWAPO notably lost control of the Windhoek municipal council to opposition groups. In December, the Electoral Court accepted a motion from the Electoral Commission of Namibia (ECN) to reject some regional-council and local-authority results due to the delivery of ballots meant for other races and the premature closure of a polling station.

A3. Are the electoral laws and framework fair, and are they implemented impartially by the relevant election management bodies? 3 / 4

The electoral framework is robust and generally well implemented. The controversy around use of electronic machines dominated the 2019 elections, with some party leaders expressing doubt about the results for want of a verifiable paper trail. The 2019 results were declared free and fair by the Commonwealth Observer Group and the South African Development Community, although they raised concerns over other aspects of the electoral process.

The use of electronic voting machines without paper trails was ruled invalid in February 2020. In July, the High Court ruled that the ECN acted unconstitutionally when it removed names from a PDM candidate list.

B. POLITICAL PLURALISM AND PARTICIPATION: 12 / 16

B1. Do the people have the right to organize in different political parties or other competitive political groupings of their choice, and is the system free of undue obstacles to the rise and fall of these competing parties or groupings? 3 / 4

Political parties may form and operate freely. Registration requirements are not onerous and there were no time limits for parties wishing to register and participate in the 2019 elections. However, candidate-registration fees and campaign financing can place an undue burden on smaller parties. Parties that hold parliamentary seats receive annual public support based on parliamentary representation, which disproportionately benefits SWAPO. Small parties lack financial resources or broad nationwide membership bases, making it difficult to mobilize electoral support. Some 18 parties nevertheless registered for the November 2020 local and regional elections.

B2. Is there a realistic opportunity for the opposition to increase its support or gain power through elections? 3 / 4

Opposition parties may freely compete in elections and generally do not encounter intimidation or harassment during election campaigns. Although opposition parties have historically been regarded as weak and fragmented, they gained several seats in the 2019 elections, dislodging SWAPO from the two-thirds majority it held since 2014. Eleven of the 15 parties that registered for the 2019 parliamentary elections secured seats. Opposition parties also did well in the November 2020 local and regional elections, though only six parties won regional seats.

B3. Are the people's political choices free from domination by forces that are external to the political sphere, or by political forces that employ extrapolitical means? 3 / 4

People are generally able to express their political choices without undue influence from external actors, including the church and traditional leaders. However, the historic domination of SWAPO—an ideologically diverse party that often faces intraparty disputes—limits voters' ability to directly express a preference for particular policies.

B4. Do various segments of the population (including ethnic, racial, religious, gender, LGBT+, and other relevant groups) have full political rights and electoral opportunities? 3 / 4

The constitution guarantees political rights for all, and the government works to uphold these rights in practice. Namibia has made great strides in increasing female parliamentary representation; women held 46 National Assembly seats as of December 2020. Nevertheless, women are often discouraged from running for office and few women contested the November 2020 regional and local elections.

Almost all ethnic groups are represented in the parliament and in senior political positions. However, members of the San ethnic group have faced restrictions on their political rights due to widespread discrimination and marginalization. LGBT+ people face discrimination that hampers their ability to openly advocate for their interests.

In December 2020, the Namibian Federation for the Visually Impaired lauded the ECN's production of Braille ballot papers and voter-education efforts intended for the visually impaired.

C. FUNCTIONING OF GOVERNMENT: 8 / 12

C1. Do the freely elected head of government and national legislative representatives determine the policies of the government? 3 / 4

The democratically elected government freely determines policies. However, 2014 reforms increased executive power, including by adding parliamentarians who are appointed by the president and by limiting the National Council's power to review certain bills.

A growing Chinese presence, and Chinese ties to Namibian political elites, have prompted questions over the country's influence. In September 2020, an LPM parliamentarian alleged that over 3,500 Chinese troops were stationed in Namibia, which Defence Minister Peter Hafeni Vilho neither confirmed nor denied later that month.

C2. Are safeguards against official corruption strong and effective? 3 / 4

While Namibia has a sound legal anticorruption framework, concerns remain that anticorruption laws are inconsistently enforced, and difficulties in accessing government-held information present barriers to gathering evidence. Light sentences on high-profile cases and low prosecution and conviction rates undermine the work of the Anti-Corruption Commission (ACC). The ACC is also underfunded; in June 2020, director general Paulus Noa warned that the agency would stop work on 17 high-profile cases due to shortfalls. In October, the government used a contingency fund to direct resources to the ACC.

Despite these challenges, high-profile anticorruption activity continued during the year. Six people, including former ministers and other officials, were accused of corruption in 2019 for allegedly colluding with Icelandic fishing company Samherji, which sought preferential access to Namibian waters. The case was ongoing as of September 2020.

The Witness Protection Act and the Whistleblower Protection Act, which were signed in 2017, remained unimplemented as of September 2020. That month, Justice Minister Yvonne Dausab reported that the government would need to spend N$160 million ($9.2 million) annually to implement the Witness Protection Act.

C3. Does the government operate with openness and transparency? 2 / 4

Namibia lacks access-to-information laws despite government promises to finalize this legislation. While a draft was tabled in June 2020, it was not passed by year's end.

Namibia also lacks an institutional culture of openness and transparency. A veil of secrecy exists over the extractive industry, military spending, statehouse upgrades, state security infrastructure, and private funding of political parties. In September 2020, Minister Vilho announced that some defense-spending information would not be shared with the National Assembly.

According to a September 2020 report from the Media Institute of Southern Africa, Namibian government agencies denied some requests for information using the COVID-19 pandemic as a reason.

While a commission of inquiry sent a report on ancestral land issues to President Geingob in July, his office did not make the report public by December, despite promises to do so.

CIVIL LIBERTIES: 46 / 60

D. FREEDOM OF EXPRESSION AND BELIEF: 14 / 16

D1. Are there free and independent media? 3 / 4

The constitution guarantees media freedom and freedom of expression. In practice, journalists face few legal restrictions and generally work without risking their personal safety. While self-censorship is common in state media, private media remain critical of the government. The absence of information laws obstructs investigative journalism, however.

Journalists did face impediments during the COVID-19 crisis, or under the pretext of the pandemic. In June 2020, the president's office apologized after journalists were blocked from attending the opening ceremony of a COVID-19 isolation facility in Windhoek; two female journalists who attended reportedly filed assault complaints against police over their treatment. In August, the Namibia Press Agency was criticized for distancing itself from correspondent Edward Mumbuu, who asked Geingob a question about the Samherji affair during a July COVID-19 press conference.

D2. Are individuals free to practice and express their religious faith or nonbelief in public and private? 4 / 4

Religious freedom is generally respected in practice.

D3. Is there academic freedom, and is the educational system free from extensive political indoctrination? 4 / 4

Academic freedom is guaranteed by law and generally respected in practice.

D4. Are individuals free to express their personal views on political or other sensitive topics without fear of surveillance or retribution? 3 / 4

Freedom of expression is legally guaranteed and generally observed in practice. However, Namibia lacks cyber-harassment or data-protection legislation.

Social media is increasingly used to express political dissent, though most citizens avoid criticizing the government. In October 2020, activists organized nationwide protests against GBV under the #ShutItAllDown hashtag.

The government reportedly maintains significant capabilities to surveil citizens. However, the legal framework for doing so remains questionable.

E. ASSOCIATIONAL AND ORGANIZATIONAL RIGHTS: 11 / 12

E1. Is there freedom of assembly? 3 / 4

Freedom of assembly is guaranteed in law and is usually observed in practice. Public-assembly restrictions were imposed under a COVID-19-related state of emergency. A ban on outdoor assemblies of over 100 people remained in force at year's end.

Protests nevertheless took place during 2020. In July, antiabortion activists held an event in Windhoek. #ShutItAllDown protests were held nationwide in October, after the remains of a missing woman were found in Walvis Bay. Police used force against some protesters; at least 27 people were arrested, including 3 journalists.

E2. Is there freedom for nongovernmental organizations, particularly those that are engaged in human rights- and governance-related work? 4 / 4

Human rights groups generally operate without interference, though government leaders sometimes use public platforms against civil society.

E3. Is there freedom for trade unions and similar professional or labor organizations? 4 / 4

Constitutionally guaranteed union rights are respected and observed in practice, though essential public-sector workers do not have the right to strike. Collective bargaining is not widely practiced outside the public-service sector and the mining, construction, and agriculture industries. Union membership has declined in recent years, with 25 percent of the labor force unionized.

Despite COVID-19-related restrictions, labor activity took place during 2020. In May, the Namibia Food and Allied Workers Union backed protests against a Windhoek hotel, prompted by layoffs and pay cuts.

F. RULE OF LAW: 11 / 16

F1. Is there an independent judiciary? 3 / 4

By law and in practice, the separation of powers is observed, and judges are not frequently subject to undue influence. The 2015 establishment of the Office of the Judiciary affords the system administrative and financial independence. However, the judiciary lacks adequate resources and is vulnerable to budget cuts.

Judges are appointed by the president upon the recommendation of the Judicial Service Commission, which the president has some influence over. Public access to court documents and proceedings has been restricted in recent years; in 2019, documents implicating the president and justice minister in a fraud case were kept out of public view by a court ruling. In February 2020, the Legal Assistance Centre criticized a proposed rule that would allow case files to be kept from public view.

F2. Does due process prevail in civil and criminal matters? 3 / 4

The rule of law and fair-trial rights are constitutionally protected, though equal access to justice is obstructed by factors including economic and geographic barriers, a shortage of public defenders, a lack of resources, and backlogs. A pilot program meant to address the backlog launched in September 2019; Chief Justice Peter Shivute is expected to comment on the program's success in 2021.

Due process was impacted by COVID-19 measures; while courts functioned during the lockdown, some cases were postponed and services were relatively limited.

F3. Is there protection from the illegitimate use of physical force and freedom from war and insurgencies? 3 / 4

Namibia is free from war and insurgencies. However, police brutality and the abuse of suspects in custody are problems. In March 2020, an individual in Ohangwena Region died after he was allegedly assaulted by police. While two officers faced accusations related to his death, they remained on duty after receiving bail. In July, three officers received 10-year sentences for murdering a suspect in 2013.

F4. Do laws, policies, and practices guarantee equal treatment of various segments of the population? 2 / 4

While the constitution guarantees the right to equality and prohibits discrimination, challenges remain. The San people face widespread societal discrimination and marginalization and lack land access.

Same-sex sexual relations remain criminalized, though the prohibition is not enforced. LGBT+ people and women face widespread discrimination. In April 2020, video of a local community leader verbally insulting and physically assaulting a transgender woman in the eastern city of Gobabis was made public. Police reportedly turned the woman away when she attempted to press charges, though charges were filed after a nongovernmental organization (NGO) intervened.

Increased government support and NGO educational programs about the condition of people living with albinism, who are targeted by ritual killings, has helped improve their living experiences.

In October 2020, an organization representing members of the Baster and Zambesi groups noted widespread discrimination in a report to the Office of the UN High Commissioner for Human Rights (OHCHR).

G. PERSONAL AUTONOMY AND INDIVIDUAL RIGHTS: 10 / 16

G1. Do individuals enjoy freedom of movement, including the ability to change their place of residence, employment, or education? 3 / 4

Freedom of movement is constitutionally guaranteed and generally observed in practice. However, authorities imposed COVID-19-related restrictions when a state of emergency was declared in March 2020. Some movement restrictions were relaxed in May, though a tighter lockdown was imposed in August as cases rose.

The illegal fencing of communal land and its impact on freedom of movement and access to resources found in communal areas remains a challenge.

G2. Are individuals able to exercise the right to own property and establish private businesses without undue interference from state or nonstate actors? 3 / 4

Private property rights are guaranteed in law and largely respected in practice. The constitution prohibits expropriation without compensation. There are no legal barriers to women's access to land. However, customs regarding inheritance procedures and property rights limit women.

Parliamentarians considered a National Equitable Economic Empowerment Bill (NEEEB) in 2020. Independent Patriots for Change leader Panduleni Itula criticized it in September, saying it would restrict ownership rights. NEEEB remained under consideration at year's end.

Land rights remain a contentious and unresolved issue. The Commission of Inquiry into Ancestral Land Rights and Restitution presented its report to President Geingob in July 2020, though the report was not made public as of December. In April, the indigenous Hai// om group sued the government in an effort to gain recognition for its ancestral rights to land in the Etosha National Park.

G3. Do individuals enjoy personal social freedoms, including choice of marriage partner and size of family, protection from domestic violence, and control over appearance? 2 / 4

LGBT+ people face harassment, discrimination, attacks, and impeded access to public services. Same-sex marriages are not recognized, and many churches have indicated their unwillingness to recognize or perform them. Legal challenges from people in same-sex partnerships exist in the courts, seeking either residency permits or recognition of their marriages. Sodomy laws exist, though there have been no recent convictions. Rates of GBV are high.

Abortion is only available for those in medical danger and for survivors of rape and incest. Forced and child marriages occur; 7 percent of girls are married before turning 18.

G4. Do individuals enjoy equality of opportunity and freedom from economic exploitation? 2 / 4

Slavery and servitude are constitutionally outlawed. However, forced child labor is prevalent in the agricultural sector and in domestic settings. San and Zemba children are especially at risk. In the 2020 edition of its *Trafficking in Persons Report*, the US State Department reported that Namibia nevertheless met antitrafficking standards.

Nauru

Population: 10,000
Capital: Yaren District
Freedom Status: Free
Electoral Democracy: Yes

Overview: People in Nauru generally enjoy political rights and civil liberties, though the government has taken steps to sideline its political opponents—particularly the Nauru 19, an activist group who had been charged with a variety of crimes in connection with a 2015 antigovernment protest. Corruption is a serious problem. Asylum seekers and refugees housed in Nauru under an agreement with Australia live in dire conditions, and the country has attracted sustained international criticism over the persistent reports of abuses against them.

KEY DEVELOPMENTS IN 2020

- To prevent the spread of coronavirus in the country, Nauruan authorities severely restricted international travel to and from the country and introduced severe penalties for breaching public health measures, such as the government-imposed curfew. By the end of the year, no one in Nauru tested positive for COVID-19, according to government statistics provided to the World Health Organization (WHO).
- In October, the United States government agreed to resettle over 1,100 asylum seekers, many of whom were in detention in the Nauru processing center, by early 2021. The agreement would leave less than 80 asylum seekers on the island.

POLITICAL RIGHTS: 34 / 40
A. ELECTORAL PROCESS: 12 / 12
A1. Was the current head of government or other chief national authority elected through free and fair elections? 4 / 4

Nauru is a parliamentary republic, and the parliament chooses the president and vice president from among its members.

In the August 2019 parliamentary elections, which were independently monitored by the Pacific Islands Forum, incumbent president Baron Waqa lost reelection in his constituency, and thus the opportunity to be reelected president. Lionel Aingimea was subsequently chosen to be president, winning with 12 votes to 6 over rival David Adeang.

A2. Were the current national legislative representatives elected through free and fair elections? 4 / 4

The 19-member unicameral Parliament is popularly elected from eight constituencies for three-year terms. In the August 2019 parliamentary elections, observed by the Pacific

Islands Forum monitoring mission, then-president Waqa was accused of manipulating the electoral rolls by granting citizenship to around 118 foreigners. However, the 2019 elections were generally regarded as free and fair, and Waqa did not win reelection.

In February 2019, former president Waqa proposed changing the constitution to extend representatives terms to four years. However, no such changes were made by the end of 2020.

A3. Are the electoral laws and framework fair, and are they implemented impartially by the relevant election management bodies? 4 / 4

The electoral laws are generally fair and implemented impartially. The Nauru Electoral Commission is responsible for managing the entire election process. Voting is compulsory.

In the August 2019 elections, a recount was conducted for the Ubenide electorate after six paper ballots were discovered in the parliamentary chamber. The recount did not change the outcome of the election, and there was no evident manipulation of the initial tally.

B. POLITICAL PLURALISM AND PARTICIPATION: 14 / 16

B1. Do the people have the right to organize in different political parties or other competitive political groupings of their choice, and is the system free of undue obstacles to the rise and fall of these competing parties or groupings? 4 / 4

Although political parties are permitted, most candidates run as independents.

A contempt-of-court law enacted in May 2018 was criticized as being designed to intimidate opposition figures and others who supported the Nauru 19 activist group.

In 2019, the government continued its prosecution and persecution of the Nauru 19, in what legal experts had declared an example of a "bullying government, using the arms of the state to persecute its opponents." Despite this, government interference into the lives of members of the Nauru 19 reportedly eased in September 2019, although newly elected president Lionel Aingimea denied that the government had ever taken steps to prevent them from traveling or gaining employment.

B2. Is there a realistic opportunity for the opposition to increase its support or gain power through elections? 3 / 4

Intense political rivalries created political instability prior to 2013. However, former president Waqa served two full terms before losing his seat as a representative and being replaced by Lionel Aingimea in 2019.

The 2019 elections also featured significant turnover of representatives, with about half of incumbents losing their seats in parliament.

B3. Are the people's political choices free from domination by forces that are external to the political sphere, or by political forces that employ extrapolitical means? 4 / 4

People's political choices are generally free from domination by powerful interests that are not democratically accountable. In July 2019, a former representative alleged that bribery was rife in the electoral process, claiming that candidates routinely buy motorcycles and kitchenware for constituents.

B4. Do various segments of the population (including ethnic, racial, religious, gender, LGBT+, and other relevant groups) have full political rights and electoral opportunities? 3 / 4

The constitution provides for universal suffrage. However, widely held biases regarding the role of women in society have discouraged women's participation in politics and elections; just two women won seats in Parliament in August 2019, one of whom was an incumbent. Including those two representatives, only three women have been elected in Nauru's modern history.

C. FUNCTIONING OF GOVERNMENT: 8 / 12

C1. Do the freely elected head of government and national legislative representatives determine the policies of the government? 3 / 4

The freely elected Parliament, led by the speaker, sets and makes policy. However, the Australian government has had considerable influence over politics due to the processing center for asylum seekers they base on Nauru. Australian authorities have detained many refugees on the island indefinitely, which is a significant source of income for Nauru's government.

In February 2019, the Nauruan government rushed through regulations that enabled them to block medical referrals, made by overseas doctors, for asylum seekers and refugees held in the processing center. This regulation came after new laws were passed in Australia that allowed doctors to compel the transfer of sick refugees from Nauru to Australia (called the "Medevac" law).

C2. Are safeguards against official corruption strong and effective? 3 / 4

Corruption remains a problem. Allegations of improper payments to senior government officials, including former President Waqa, by an Australian phosphate company emerged in 2016, and an investigation by Australian federal police remained ongoing in 2020. Legal proceedings related to the scandal also took place in Singapore in 2018, where a local company was fined for bribing a Nauruan member of Parliament.

The Australian Broadcasting Corporation reported in 2018 that many family members of Nauruan politicians owned shares of the land where the Australian-run processing center is situated; they disproportionately benefit from their ability to collect high rents or secure high-paying jobs or other contracts at the center.

In April 2019, former president Sprent Dabwido—who had signed the offshore asylum seeker detention deal with Australia during his time as president—claimed that the money Nauru received from Australia for hosting of the asylum processing center had led to vast amounts of corruption. The government and then-president Waqa denied these allegations.

C3. Does the government operate with openness and transparency? 2 / 4

Nauru lacks a law on access to public information, but the Government Information Office releases some budget figures. Government officials are not required to disclose financial information. A 2017 audit of the 2013–14 government accounts ended a 15-year gap between government audits, a gap which officials blamed on an absence of qualified staff.

CIVIL LIBERTIES: 43 / 60

D. FREEDOM OF EXPRESSION AND BELIEF: 13 / 16

D1. Are there free and independent media? 2 / 4

Freedom of expression is constitutionally guaranteed but not always respected in practice. Foreign journalists have a particularly difficult time operating in Nauru, as the government has implemented restrictions that appear to be aimed at deterring outside coverage of conditions for asylum seekers and refugees. Since 2014, foreign journalists have been subject to a visa application fee of roughly AUD $8,000 ($5,500), up from approximately AUD $150 ($103) previously. The media visa fee remained unchanged at the end of 2020.

Ahead of the 2018 Pacific Islands Forum, held in Nauru, the government banned the Australian Broadcasting Corporation from entering the country, describing it as an "activist media organization."

The 2016 Crimes Act introduced criminal charges for defamation, now punishable with up to three years in prison. Similarly, the Administration of Justice Act, a contempt-of-court law passed in 2018, serves as a deterrent for journalists to publish pieces critical of the government and the judiciary.

D2. Are individuals free to practice and express their religious faith or nonbelief in public and private? 4 / 4

The constitution provides for freedom of religion, which the government generally respects in practice.

D3. Is there academic freedom, and is the educational system free from extensive political indoctrination? 4 / 4

Academic freedom is generally respected.

Reports emerged in 2020 that the University of the South Pacific, a regional university with campuses located in various countries in the South Pacific including Nauru, was plagued by allegations of corruption and large-scale improper spending. President Aingimea, who assumed the role of chancellor of the university in July 2020, acknowledged that the governance of the university needed improvement.

D4. Are individuals free to express their personal views on political or other sensitive topics without fear of surveillance or retribution? 3 / 4

Authorities are not known to illegally monitor private online communications. For three years, the government blocked Facebook, citing a need to protect users from obscene and pornographic content; the policy more likely represented another example of the government attempting to restrict coverage of the Australian processing center for asylum seekers. The ban was ultimately lifted in 2018.

In June 2020, the president presented the National Disaster Risk Management (Amendment) Bill 2020, which outlawed publishing or posting messages on social or mass media that are intended to cause fear, mislead the public, or distort official information, with severe punishments. The new law also expands police powers to act in a national disaster without a warrant. How the new law will be applied and what level of oversight will be exercised, was unclear at the end of 2020.

E. ASSOCIATIONAL AND ORGANIZATIONAL RIGHTS: 9 / 12

E1. Is there freedom of assembly? 3 / 4

The constitution upholds the right to assemble peacefully, but this right has not always been respected in practice. Demonstrations related to the treatment of asylum seekers housed at the Australian processing center are often repressed. Members of the Nauru 19 group, who were arrested for their 2015 antigovernment protests, were sentenced to jail time in December 2019.

Failure to adhere to public gather restrictions that were introduced to curtail the spread of COVID-19, including social distancing regulations, can result in hefty fines of up to AUD $5,000 ($3,438) or imprisonment.

E2. Is there freedom for nongovernmental organizations, particularly those that are engaged in human rights- and governance-related work? 3 / 4

There are no legal restrictions on the formation of nongovernmental organizations (NGOs) in Nauru. There are several advocacy groups for women, as well as development-focused and religious organizations. However, authorities have interfered with the operations of activists seeking to improve the treatment of asylum seekers.

E3. Is there freedom for trade unions and similar professional or labor organizations? 3 / 4

There are no formal trade unions and only limited labor protection laws, partly because there is little large-scale private employment. The rights to strike and to collectively bargain are not protected by law.

F. RULE OF LAW: 9 / 16

F1. Is there an independent judiciary? 2 / 4

There have been concerns about undue influence on the judiciary from government officials, who have been accused of dismissing judges for unfavorable rulings. Many are concerned that government officials have pressured the judiciary in connection with the Nauru 19 case.

The Supreme Court is the highest authority on constitutional issues in Nauru. Appeals had previously been heard in the high court of Australia, but in March 2018, Nauruan Justice Minister David Adeang announced that the country would sever links with Australia's justice system, citing both onerous costs associated with case proceedings in another country and the need for Nauru to establish greater independence. However, some skeptics viewed the development as a means of denying members of the Nauru 19 activist group an avenue to appeal their cases. Nauru later signed memoranda with neighboring Pacific countries, including Papua New Guinea, Kiribati, Solomon Islands, and Vanuatu, to provide justices for Nauru's new Court of Appeals.

The Nauruan government has been accused of interfering with the judicial process and undermining the rule of law. The May 2018 contempt-of-court law makes criticism of witnesses, judicial officers, or legal representatives in a pending court matter illegal, as well as undermining judicial officials or the authority of courts. Violations of the law, which contains exemptions for government officials deemed to be acting in good faith or the interests of national security, are punishable by fines of up to AUD $20,000 ($15,469) for individuals and AUD $50,000 ($38,673) for corporations.

Australian Supreme Court Justice Geoffrey Muecke claimed the government terminated his contract as a result of his granting a permanent stay in 2018 for the Nauru 19 court proceedings. He claimed the government also pressured the sentencing magistrate to issue maximum penalties to members of the group. In December 2019, the Nauru government accused supporters of the Nauru 19 of being in contempt of court, while Nauru's chief justice insisted that the government had not interfered in the proceedings of the Nauru 19 case. President Aingimea claimed that neither he nor the preceding government had interfered with the judiciary's independence. The members of the Nauru 19 were ultimately convicted and sentenced to jail time in December 2019. As a result of the events surrounding the Nauru 19 case, the New Zealand government withdrew its financial support of the Nauruan judiciary.

F2. Does due process prevail in civil and criminal matters? 2 / 4

Though the constitution provides for due process rights, the resumption of legal proceedings against members of the Nauru 19 as well as changes to the appellate jurisdiction indicate that due process is not always respected in practice.

In 2017, the government passed a law that distinguishes between public servants who testify in favor of the government or against it. Analysts said it appeared that those who miss work to testify against the government would be placed on leave without pay, and that the law appeared to represent an attempt to discourage civil servants from testifying in favor of the Nauru 19.

Legal proceedings against the Nauru 19, which had been permanently stayed in September 2018 by Justice Muecke, were renewed after the stay was overturned by the Nauru Appeals Court in June 2019. Muecke had been fired after granting the stays. In October 2019, the protesters launched a new appeal, seeking again to have a permanent stay placed on the charges. However, this appeal was denied by the courts, and the Nauru 19 were sentenced to jail time in December 2019.

Legal experts in Australia and New Zealand criticized the entire legal and judicial process for the Nauru 19 case as unjust. During its four-year period, reports emerged of plagiarism, corruption, exploitation, and mistreatment of judges (specifically, Geoffrey Muecke, who claimed that parts of his contract had not been paid), bias in the judiciary, denial of legal representation, and more. While court proceedings were ongoing, the members of the group were jailed. Critics claimed that the entire process represented a breakdown of the rule of law and set a "chilling precedent" for the future of the Nauruan justice system.

F3. Is there protection from the illegitimate use of physical force and freedom from war and insurgencies? 3 / 4

Civilian authorities control the small police force. Nauru has no armed forces; Australia provides defense assistance under an informal agreement.

The Australian processing center for asylum seekers has received considerable international criticism for poor treatment of asylum seekers housed there. Few arrests have been made in connection with alleged abuses of its residents.

F4. Do laws, policies, and practices guarantee equal treatment of various segments of the population? 2 / 4

The constitution provides for equal treatment regardless of race, country of origin, ethnicity, politics, or gender, but those rights are not always protected in practice. There are few legal protections against discrimination, which is notably a problem for women in the workplace. In 2016, the government decriminalized homosexuality, which had previously been punishable by up to 14 years of hard labor.

Several reports have detailed widespread abuse of refugees and asylum seekers forcibly transferred to Nauru under its agreement with Australia. Crimes committed against asylum seekers outside the processing center, where most refugees are housed, frequently go uninvestigated. The asylum seekers suffer from grossly inadequate housing; denial of health care for life-threatening conditions; and a high rate of self-harm attempts among residents—who wait, at times, for years for their asylum applications to be processed. Rates of self-harm among refugees was found to be 200 times more likely than that of Australian citizens. Thoughts of self-harm among children were particularly alarming, and reports of this mental health issue were ignored by authorities. The last children were evacuated from Nauru and resettled in the United States in February 2019. In March 2019, reports from the Australian Broadcasting Corporation (ABC) found that refugees had been exposed to asbestos for prolonged periods. In November 2019, the Nauruan government denied the medical evacuation of over 20 individuals, all of whom had been vouched for by Australian doctors.

In October 2020, the United States agreed to resettle over 1,100 asylum seekers who were in the Nauru and Papua New Guinea processing centers by early 2021. The agreement would leave 80 asylum seekers on the two islands.

G. PERSONAL AUTONOMY AND INDIVIDUAL RIGHTS: 12 / 16

G1. Do individuals enjoy freedom of movement, including the ability to change their place of residence, employment, or education? 3 / 4

Most people in Nauru are free to move around the island. However, while asylum seekers were granted freedom of movement across the island in 2015, there are limits on their ability to leave, including in order to accompany family members who receive emergency medical care in Australia, and they face significant difficulties in obtaining employment and education. Many asylum seekers had lived in tents and converted storage containers at the Australian processing center, where they were under heavy surveillance. In October 2018, the aid group Doctors Without Borders (MSF) was asked by Nauru officials to stop providing care for asylum seekers, and the group subsequently left the country. In the days afterward, MSF condemned conditions for the asylum seekers and refugees in Nauru and claimed they had been forced out. As of March 31, 2020, 209 asylum seekers transferred to Nauru from Australia remained in the country.

The government has withheld the passports of some political opponents in recent years, including at least three people associated with the Nauru 19, among them two former opposition lawmakers. These two opposition lawmakers blame the government for the death of former president and Nauru 19 member Sprent Dabwido. Legal action, filed in July 2019 by the two former lawmakers, claims that the Nauruan government delayed in returning Dabwido his passport, preventing him from receiving treatment for cancer in Australia in time to be cured.

To prevent the introduction of COVID-19 into the country, Nauruan stopped most international flights landing in March 2020 and imposed quarantine requirements for most international arrivals, except for those arriving from a regularly updated list of "safe countries" deemed to have sufficiently low levels of COVID-19 in their respective populations. Other movement restrictions, including curfews, were enforced with strict punishments.

G2. Are individuals able to exercise the right to own property and establish private businesses without undue interference from state or nonstate actors? 3 / 4

The constitution protects the right to own property and people in Nauru are able to freely establish businesses. However, as of 2014, foreigners must pay approximately $4,500 USD a year for a business visa, up from $300.

In his ruling on the Nauru 19 case, Judge Muecke said that the government of Nauru maintained an unwritten blacklist under which the Nauru 19 were denied employment and the right to conduct business on the island.

G3. Do individuals enjoy personal social freedoms, including choice of marriage partner and size of family, protection from domestic violence, and control over appearance? 3 / 4

Domestic violence, which mostly affects women, remains a serious problem, and children are also vulnerable to violence. However, authorities have taken some efforts to address these problems, notably by approving the new protections within the 2017 Domestic Violence and Family Protection Bill, and the 2016 Child Protection and Welfare Act. In 2020, the government simplified the process for victims of domestic violence to obtain safety and protection orders against their abusers. Marital rape was also made a criminal offense in 2016. In June 2020, the government of Nauru announced that it would introduce harsher laws for sex offenders, including by reducing the ability of sex offenders to receive bail and introducing laws that prevent the age of the perpetrator a mitigating factor in sex offences.

Same-sex marriage is not recognized by law. Abortion is only allowed when the mother's life is in danger, but not in cases of rape; the ban on abortion in cases of rape sparked controversy in 2016, regarding the treatment of a pregnant asylum seeker who said she was raped at the Australian-run processing center.

G4. Do individuals enjoy equality of opportunity and freedom from economic exploitation?
3 / 4

With the exception of asylum seekers, individuals generally enjoy equal economic opportunities. However, economic opportunities are limited to sectors such as phosphate mining and the public sector.

There are no health and safety laws to protect workers outside the public sector, and issues relating to dust exposure for phosphate miners are of serious concern. According to the U.S. State Department, there have been no reports of human trafficking in Nauru in recent years.

Nepal

Population: 30,000,000
Capital: Kathmandu
Freedom Status: Partly Free
Electoral Democracy: Yes

Overview: Since the end of a decade-long civil war in 2006, Nepal has held a series of competitive elections and adopted a permanent constitution. As politics have stabilized, pressure on journalists has decreased, and authorities have been more tolerant of peaceful assembly. However, political protests are still occasionally marred by violence, and corruption remains endemic in politics, government, and the judicial system. Other problems include gender-based violence (GBV), underage marriage, and bonded labor. Transitional justice bodies have struggled to fulfill their mandates.

KEY DEVELOPMENTS IN 2020
- The ruling Nepal Communist Party (NCP) won 16 of the 18 upper-house seats contested in January elections.
- Prime Minister Khadga Prasad Sharma Oli triggered the dissolution of the parliament in December after his authority over the NCP weakened due to an ongoing dispute with former rebel leader Pushpa Kamal Dahal. Over 10,000 people protested the dissolution in Kathmandu later that month.
- Nepali authorities imposed a lockdown to mitigate the spread of COVID-19 in late March before loosening it in July. The government faced ongoing public dissent over its perceived inability to competently respond to the pandemic, while migrant workers reportedly faced poor conditions in quarantine facilities. Local transmission accelerated in the second half of the year, with authorities reporting over 260,000 cases and 2,758 deaths to the World Health Organization (WHO) by year's end.

POLITICAL RIGHTS: 25 / 40
A. ELECTORAL PROCESS: 10 / 12
A1. Was the current head of government or other chief national authority elected through free and fair elections? 3 / 4

The president is the head of state and is elected to up to two five-year terms by a parliamentary electoral college and state assemblies. The prime minister is elected by the parliament. The legitimacy of executive office holders is largely determined by the conduct of legislative and provincial elections.

Khadga Prasad Sharma Oli was sworn in as prime minister in February 2018 after his party, the Communist Party of Nepal–Unified Marxist-Leninist (CPN-UML), won majorities in the upper and lower houses of the Federal Parliament in late 2017. European Union observers declared the 2017 polls largely credible, despite incidents of preelectoral violence at some campaign events.

The current president, Bidhya Devi Bhandari, was reelected in March 2018.

A2. Were the current national legislative representatives elected through free and fair elections? 4 / 4

Members of the 275-seat House of Representatives are elected to five-year terms; 165 are directly elected in single-seat constituencies, while 110 are elected by proportional representation. The National Assembly has 59 members; 56 are indirectly elected to six-year terms by an electoral college comprised of provincial and local leaders, while 3 are appointed by the president on the government's recommendation.

Local elections—the first since 1997—were held in several stages in 2017. National and provincial elections were held late in the year. The polls were generally well conducted and saw healthy turnout, and the results were accepted by participants. However, the Rastriya Janata Party–Nepal (RJP-N), an umbrella group representing ethnic Madhesis, boycotted several rounds of local polls due to grievances related to the 2015 constitution.

While the 2017 polls were more peaceful than in 2013, violence did occur, with four deaths reported during the year's electoral periods. There was a significant uptick in violence in the south, which were related to interparty tensions and separatist opposition.

Elections were held for 18 National Assembly seats in January 2020. The NCP, the product of a 2018 merger between the CPN-UML and the Communist Party of Nepal–Maoist (UCPN-M), won 16 seats, while the RJP-N won the other 2.

A3. Are the electoral laws and framework fair, and are they implemented impartially by the relevant election management bodies? 3 / 4

The legal framework for elections is sound and facilitates the conduct of credible polls. However, the parliament has yet to address the grievances that many have with the 2015 constitution, including province demarcation and proportional representation based on population.

B. POLITICAL PLURALISM AND PARTICIPATION: 10 / 16

B1. Do the people have the right to organize in different political parties or other competitive political groupings of their choice, and is the system free of undue obstacles to the rise and fall of these competing parties or groupings? 3 / 4

Political parties are generally free to form and operate. Opposition figures do sometimes face arrest. Alliance for Independent Madhesh (AIM) leader CK Raut was arrested in 2018 on charges of disturbing law and order and voicing views against the state and nationality but was released in 2019 after agreeing to refrain from supporting an independent Madhesi state. That May, AIM—renamed the Janamat (Mandate) Party—endorsed Raut's agreement.

In 2018, the UCPN-M and the CPN-UML, which formed an alliance to contest the 2017 parliamentary election, merged to form the NCP. The NCP underwent an internal split in 2020, based on disagreements between Prime Minister Oli and former rebel leader Pushpa

Kamal Dahal, better known as Prachanda, of the UCPN-M. While Oli and Prachanda committed to a power-sharing deal in September, Oli triggered the dissolution of the parliament in December after his authority within the NCP weakened.

B2. Is there a realistic opportunity for the opposition to increase its support or gain power through elections? 3 / 4

Opposition parties have a realistic chance of gaining power through elections. The CPN-UML, then in opposition, won the 2017 elections. Smaller opposition parties have difficulty gaining power at the national level, partly due to a 3 percent threshold for proportional-representation seats in the lower house. Smaller parties perform better at the local level.

B3. Are the people's political choices free from domination by forces that are external to the political sphere, or by political forces that employ extrapolitical means? 2 / 4

People's ability to freely exercise their political choices is occasionally limited by sporadic outbursts of political violence, as well as by security agents who at times have cracked down on political demonstrations. Vote buying has been reported in recent elections.

B4. Do various segments of the population (including ethnic, racial, religious, gender, LGBT+, and other relevant groups) have full political rights and electoral opportunities? 2 / 4

Though the constitution has requirements for the participation of women and minorities in the legislature, social discrimination continues to hinder their political involvement. A limited definition of citizenship has resulted in the disenfranchisement of stateless people. Bhandari is Nepal's first female president, and 32.7 percent of lower-house lawmakers are female; however, few women hold senior political positions.

Indigenous Nepalis and members of the Dalit group are underrepresented in politics and in the civil service, despite policies meant to bolster their participation. Members of the Chhettri and Hill Brahmin groups, meanwhile, are relatively overrepresented.

C. FUNCTIONING OF GOVERNMENT: 5 / 12

C1. Do the freely elected head of government and national legislative representatives determine the policies of the government? 3 / 4

Nepal ratified a new constitution in 2015, an important step in its democratic transition. Successful elections were held in 2017 and in 2020, though representative rule is not fully consolidated.

C2. Are safeguards against official corruption strong and effective? 1 / 4

Corruption is endemic in Nepali politics and government and often goes unpunished. Corruption by officials obstructed the delivery of foreign aid provided to Nepal after a 2015 earthquake, though aid has slowly been distributed since.

The top Nepali anticorruption agency, the Commission for Investigation of Abuse of Authority (CIAA) has been more active in recent years. In 2017, it accused Chudamani Sharma, a former tax official, of embezzlement and granting improper tax exemptions. However, the CIAA has been accused of excessively focusing on low-level cases; in July 2020, a special court posthumously acquitted a tax official accused of accepting a 1,000 rupee ($9) bribe. The official died by suicide in 2019, after he was released from CIAA custody.

C3. Does the government operate with openness and transparency? 1 / 4

The government generally operates with opacity. The Election Commission, the Truth and Reconciliation Commission (TRC), and the Commission of Investigation on Enforced

Disappeared Persons (CIEDP), among others, have been criticized for lack of transparency. Mechanisms for utilizing the 2007 Right to Information Act are poorly defined, and the law is inconsistently enforced.

CIVIL LIBERTIES: 31 / 60

D. FREEDOM OF EXPRESSION AND BELIEF: 10 / 16

D1. Are there free and independent media? 2 / 4

The 2015 constitution guarantees freedom of expression and prohibits prior restraints on press freedom, though these rules can be suspended in a national emergency. The constitution does not prohibit future press restraints for national security reasons. In addition, high-level government officials attempt to muzzle media criticism through pressure, intimidation, and legal maneuvers.

A 2018 criminal code revision criminalizes publicizing private information about a person without consent, photographing an individual without consent, and "disrespectful" satire. Press freedom advocates argued that the code could be used to prosecute journalists engaged in newsgathering. Authorities have used the National Transaction Act (NTA), which is meant to fight cybercrime, to target journalists and artists.

The parliament began considering an Information Technology Bill, which would replace the NTA; a Media Council Bill; and a Mass Communications Bill, which would create a new media regulator, in 2019. Amnesty International criticized the Information Technology Bill in January 2020, calling it vague and overly broad. The Media Council Bill originally included a 1 million rupee ($8,000) maximum fine against journalists who violated a code of conduct, though the National Assembly removed the provision when endorsing it in February 2020. All three bills remained under consideration at year's end.

Journalists reporting on the COVID-19 pandemic faced harassment and detention over their work. In April 2020, *Nagarik* reporter Dilip Paudel received threatening messages after reporting on the eviction of an individual suspected of contracting COVID-19. That same month, Radio Dhangadhi reporter Lok Karki was detained after filming an argument over the distribution of pandemic-related aid. In May, Radio Janakpur manager Shital Sah was harassed by several individuals after reporting on COVID-19 tracking efforts.

D2. Are individuals free to practice and express their religious faith or nonbelief in public and private? 2 / 4

Like the interim constitution before it, the 2015 constitution identifies Nepal as secular, signaling a break with the Hindu monarchy that was toppled after the 1996–2006 civil war and formally abolished in 2008. Religious freedom is constitutionally protected and tolerance is broadly practiced, though some religious minorities occasionally report harassment. Muslims in Nepal are particularly impoverished, occupying a marginalized space. Proselytizing is prohibited under a 2017 law, and some Christians have been prosecuted under this law.

D3. Is there academic freedom, and is the educational system free from extensive political indoctrination? 3 / 4

The government does not restrict academic freedom. Much scholarly activity takes place freely, including on political topics. Authorities exercise some control over the primary education curriculum but have relatively little over universities. Neither professors nor students face repercussions for political speech, and peaceful campus protests are tolerated. However, student unions affiliated with major political parties sometimes clash violently, and police occasionally use force to disperse them. Student clashes have become less common in recent years.

Minorities, including Hindi- and Urdu-speaking Madhesi groups, have complained that Nepali is enforced as the language of education in government schools.

D4. Are individuals free to express their personal views on political or other sensitive topics without fear of surveillance or retribution? 3 / 4

While the freedom to engage in private discussions on sensitive topics has expanded somewhat with Nepal's political stabilization, authorities have occasionally cracked down on individuals who criticize the government on social media.

The parliament also continued considering legislation that would impact online expression, namely the Information Technology Bill and Mass Communications Bill, in 2020. The parliament also considered the Special Service Bill, which would give the Nepali intelligence agency wide-ranging surveillance and interception powers, during 2020. The bills remained under consideration at year's end.

E. ASSOCIATIONAL AND ORGANIZATIONAL RIGHTS: 7 / 12
E1. Is there freedom of assembly? 3 / 4

Although the constitution guarantees freedom of assembly, security forces have been known to violently disperse protests and demonstrations, particularly in the south, where a large Madhesi population and related secessionist movement exist.

Major protests were held during the year, despite COVID-19-related restrictions. Nationwide protests were held in June 2020 over the government's pandemic response. Police responded to protests forcefully; 10 people who were near the prime minister's residence were arrested in mid-June, while police used water cannon, batons, and tear gas in response to protests elsewhere. In late December, protesters rallied against Prime Minister Oli's decision to dissolve the parliament earlier that month. Police reported that at least 10,000 people participated in protests in Kathmandu, in defiance of COVID-19 restrictions.

E2. Is there freedom for nongovernmental organizations, particularly those that are engaged in human rights– and governance-related work? 2 / 4

Although the constitution allows NGOs to form and operate in Nepal, legal restrictions make this difficult in practice. The District Administration Office (DAO), which is responsible for registering NGOs, is often understaffed and lacks essential resources. Foreign NGOs must enter project-specific agreements with the Nepali government. There is a widespread view that NGOs should not be overly political, which hinders some groups from engaging in certain forms of public advocacy.

E3. Is there freedom for trade unions and similar professional or labor organizations? 2 / 4

The 2015 constitution provides for the right to form trade unions. Labor laws protect the freedom to bargain collectively, and unions generally operate without state interference. Workers in a broad range of "essential" industries cannot stage strikes.

F. RULE OF LAW: 6 / 16
F1. Is there an independent judiciary? 2 / 4

The 2015 constitution provides for an independent judiciary. However, judicial independence is compromised by endemic corruption in many courts.

The state has generally ignored local court verdicts, Supreme Court decisions, and National Human Rights Commission (NHRC) recommendations addressing crimes committed during the 1996–2006 civil war. In 2019, the government sought to weaken the NHRC with a proposed amendment to human rights law that would give the attorney general the power to bring human rights cases and would prohibit the NHRC from opening regional and local offices. The amendment appeared to remain pending in 2020.

F2. Does due process prevail in civil and criminal matters? 1 / 4

Constitutional due process guarantees are poorly upheld in practice. Arbitrary arrests do occur. Heavy case backlogs and a slow appeals process result in long pretrial detentions. The government provides legal counsel to those who cannot afford their own, but only at a defendant's request. Those unaware of this right often end up representing themselves.

F3. Is there protection from the illegitimate use of physical force and freedom from war and insurgencies? 2 / 4

Rights advocates continue to criticize Nepal for failing to punish abuses and war crimes committed during the 1996–2006 civil war.

Due to a lack of will on the part of the security forces and political parties, neither the TRC nor the CIEDP, key transitional justice bodies, have implemented reforms demanded by the UN or the Supreme Court. Although the TRC and CIEDP have received thousands of reports of human rights violations and enforced disappearances, no alleged perpetrators have been prosecuted. In January 2020, the government appointed new commissioners to both bodies with little consultation while ignoring calls for the amendment of the underlying legal framework.

F4. Do laws, policies, and practices guarantee equal treatment of various segments of the population? 1 / 4

The 2015 constitution includes rights for sexual minorities. The first passport on which the holder was permitted to select a third gender was issued in 2015. However, LGBT+ people face continued harassment by the authorities and other citizens, particularly in rural areas.

The constitution frames the protection of fundamental human rights for Nepali citizens only. This potentially leaves equal rights of noncitizens, including migrants and people who cannot prove citizenship, unprotected.

Tibetans in Nepal face difficulty achieving formal refugee status due to Chinese pressure on the Nepali government. Women often do not receive the same educational and employment opportunities as men.

Muslims enjoy greater freedom to practice their religion under the 2015 constitution but continue to face widespread discrimination.

Children living with disabilities are sometimes excluded from the education system, or face segregation in the classroom.

G. PERSONAL AUTONOMY AND INDIVIDUAL RIGHTS: 8 / 16

G1. Do individuals enjoy freedom of movement, including the ability to change their place of residence, employment, or education? 3 / 4

Freedom of movement is generally respected in Nepal. There are legal limits on the rights of refugees to move freely, but restrictions are rarely enforced. Citizens generally enjoy choice of residence, though bribery is common in the housing market as well as the university admittance process.

In rural areas, women remain subject to *chaupadi*, a traditional practice in which menstruating women are physically separated from their families and communities; the practice was criminalized under a 2018 law. The first arrest under this law took place in 2019. when a Nepali man was arrested after his sister-in-law died of smoke inhalation in a *chaupadi* hut.

G2. Are individuals able to exercise the right to own property and establish private businesses without undue interference from state or nonstate actors? 2 / 4

Although citizens have the right to own private businesses, starting a business in Nepal often requires bribes to a wide range of officials. Licensing and other red tape can be extremely onerous. Women face widespread discrimination when starting businesses, and customs and border police are notoriously corrupt in dealing with cross-border trade. Foreigners generally cannot own land.

G3. Do individuals enjoy personal social freedoms, including choice of marriage partner and size of family, protection from domestic violence, and control over appearance? 2 / 4

GBV remains a major problem. Nepali police reported 2,144 cases of rape during the 2019–20 reporting period, a slightly lower figure than in the 2018–19 period but higher than the 1,480 cases counted in 2017–18.

The 2009 Domestic Violence Act provides for monetary compensation and psychological treatment for victims, but authorities rarely prosecute domestic violence cases, and these are sometimes handled informally.

Underage marriage, especially of girls, is widespread. In 2019, the UN Children's Fund (UNICEF) reported that Nepal had one of the world's highest child marriage rates.

Foreign men married to Nepali women must wait 15 years to obtain naturalized citizenship, while foreign women married to Nepali men can immediately become citizens. Children of foreign-born fathers and Nepali mothers must apply for naturalized citizenship, while children of foreign-born mothers and Nepali fathers are automatically granted citizenship. In June 2020, a parliamentary committee endorsed an amendment to the Citizenship Act that would require foreign-born wives to wait 7 years before attaining their own citizenship. The amendment remained under consideration at year's end.

G4. Do individuals enjoy equality of opportunity and freedom from economic exploitation? 1 / 4

Trafficking of children and women from Nepal for prostitution in India is common, and police rarely intervene. Bonded labor is illegal but remains a serious problem. Child labor also remains a problem; children can be found working in the brickmaking, service, and other industries, as well as in forced begging and sex work.

The 2015 earthquake left millions of people homeless. Many of those affected lack opportunities for social mobility as they struggle to recover from the disaster.

Netherlands

Population: 17,500,000
Capital: Amsterdam
Freedom Status: Free
Electoral Democracy: Yes

Overview: The Netherlands is a parliamentary democracy with a strong record of safeguarding political rights and civil liberties. Nevertheless, Muslims and immigrants experience harassment and discrimination, and polarization around cultural identity issues has increased. Harsh asylum policies have been a source of controversy. The Kingdom of the Netherlands also has overall responsibility for human rights compliance on six Caribbean islands. Corruption, prison conditions and asylum policies are of concern on the islands.

KEY DEVELOPMENTS IN 2020

- The government restricted assembly rights periodically throughout the year to prevent the spread of COVID-19. During the first government-imposed lockdown in March, police dispersed antilockdown protesters for not respecting social-distancing rules. In September, authorities in The Hague, the location of many of these protests, implemented stricter rules on spontaneous assemblies that normally would be tolerated by police. According to government statistics provided to the World Health Organization (WHO), more than 795,000 people tested positive for coronavirus and nearly 11,400 people died by year's end.

- In October, research released by the International Institute of Social Studies in The Hague showed that migrant workers, mainly from Eastern Europe, were living in degrading conditions, were not ensured proper compensation, and were housed illegally. Between a third and half of all workers in the agricultural sector are migrant workers at risk of exploitation.

POLITICAL RIGHTS: 40 / 40

A. ELECTORAL PROCESS: 12 / 12

A1. Was the current head of government or other chief national authority elected through free and fair elections? 4 / 4

The Netherlands is a parliamentary constitutional monarchy. The prime minister is the head of government, appointed by the parliament after elections. Prime Minister Mark Rutte won a third term following elections in March 2017, leading a cabinet of his People's Party for Freedom and Democracy (VVD) alongside the Christian Democratic Appeal (CDA), the Democrats 66 (D66), and the Christian Union. Elections are generally well administered, and the results are accepted by all parties.

A2. Were the current national legislative representatives elected through free and fair elections? 4 / 4

The Netherlands has a parliament that consists of the First Chamber, elected indirectly by the members of the twelve provincial councils, and the Second Chamber, members of which are directly elected to terms of four years. After losing its majority in the First Chamber in 2019, the governing coalition led by Prime Minister Rutte has since lost its majority in the Second Chamber, as well. Subsequently, the coalition has become even more dependent on ad hoc majorities to have bills signed off and its policies approved.

The nationalist Forum for Democracy (FvD) party gained a plurality of the vote in the March 2019 Provincial Council elections (14.5 percent). Party leader Thierry Baudet was criticized for attempting to justify sexist and white supremacist statements as legitimate cultural commentary, leading to some defections of elected representatives in provincial councils and the First Chamber.

A3. Are the electoral laws and framework fair, and are they implemented impartially by the relevant election management bodies? 4 / 4

Elections are administered by the Electoral Council, which works impartially and professionally. Throughout 2020, the Minister of Interior began preparing for the March 2021 parliamentary elections, incorporating public health measures to prevent the spread of COVID-19.

B. POLITICAL PLURALISM AND PARTICIPATION: 16 / 16

B1. Do the people have the right to organize in different political parties or other competitive political groupings of their choice, and is the system free of undue obstacles to the rise and fall of these competing parties or groupings? 4 / 4

Political parties operate freely. The Elections Law does not impose any undue restrictions on the creation of political parties and the registration of candidates for elections.

Government funding extends to all parties with at least 1,000 members and at least one seat in Parliament.

B2. Is there a realistic opportunity for the opposition to increase its support or gain power through elections? 4 / 4

In the 2017 Second Chamber elections, several opposition parties gained seats and three of them joined the new government. In the March 2019 provincial elections, newcomer FvD made significant gains, winning the most votes of any individual party, and removing the governing coalition's majority from the upper chamber.

B3. Are the people's political choices free from domination by forces that are external to the political sphere, or by political forces that employ extrapolitical means? 4 / 4

The people are free to make their own political choices without pressure from groups that are not democratically accountable.

B4. Do various segments of the population (including ethnic, racial, religious, gender, LGBT+, and other relevant groups) have full political rights and electoral opportunities? 4 / 4

Marginalized groups participate freely in the political process. Several political parties specifically cater to the (perceived) interests of religious groups or ethnic minorities. Underrepresentation in politics of persons without higher education is sometimes identified as a problem.

C. FUNCTIONING OF GOVERNMENT: 12 / 12

C1. Do the freely elected head of government and national legislative representatives determine the policies of the government? 4 / 4

Government policies reflect the choices of freely elected members of Parliament. Inordinate influence of corporate interests over government policies continued to be criticized by investigative journalists and nongovernmental organizations (NGOs).

C2. Are safeguards against official corruption strong and effective? 4 / 4

The Netherlands has low levels of corruption and anticorruption mechanisms are generally effective.

In response to the Council of Europe's Group of States against Corruption (GRECO) recommendation to strengthen integrity safeguards for parliamentarians, the Second Chamber created a Code of Conduct in September 2020 with an independent complaints body (to begin working in 2021), a stronger mechanism than the one created in 2019 by the First Chamber.

C3. Does the government operate with openness and transparency? 4 / 4

Laws are in place recognizing the right to request government information, and they are generally enforced, although critics contend that long delays in responding to requests for information are common. The COVID-19 crisis was cited several times as an additional reason for delay in 2020. A bill initiated in 2012 that would require the government to make documents available online rather than by request continued to await parliamentary discussion.

Reports emerged about significant malpractice within the Tax Administration's collection processes, including illegal practices involving childcare allowances beginning in 2012. The Dutch Personal Data Protection Authority concluded that discriminatory use had been made of data on the (double) nationality of certain applicants. In May 2020, the government filed a formal complaint to the public prosecutor, asking them to investigate Tax Administration officers for extortion and discrimination. In December 2020, a special parliamentary committee reported that families were punished illegitimately, and, when legitimate, to disproportionate extremes. Between 9,000 and 26,000 families are entitled to compensation.

CIVIL LIBERTIES: 58 / 60 (−1)

D. FREEDOM OF EXPRESSION AND BELIEF: 16 / 16

D1. Are there free and independent media? 4 / 4

A free and independent press thrives in the Netherlands.

D2. Are individuals free to practice and express their religious faith or nonbelief in public and private? 4 / 4

The constitution guarantees freedom of religion, which is generally respected in practice. A prohibition of burqas and niqabs in public establishments and on public transport came into force in August 2019. However, a report by *de Volkskrant* showed that no fines had been issued at all as of October 2020.

Religious schools became a contentious political issue with respect to Islamic establishments, after the government antiterrorism agency claimed that teachers at one secondary school seemed to foment hatred toward nonbelievers. This caused significant controversy, especially after the school was refused government funding, though this refusal was reversed by an administrative court decision in November 2019.

D3. Is there academic freedom, and is the educational system free from extensive political indoctrination? 4 / 4

Academic freedom is largely respected in the Netherlands.

D4. Are individuals free to express their personal views on political or other sensitive topics without fear of surveillance or retribution? 4 / 4

There are no restrictions on freedom of speech or expression, apart from the criminalization of hate speech. The exact interpretation of hate speech provisions continued to be debated in 2020. The court rejected Geert Wilders's appeal of his conviction for hate speech, after he called for the reduction of the number of Moroccans in the Netherlands, but annulled charges against him for incitement to discriminate.

E. ASSOCIATIONAL AND ORGANIZATIONAL RIGHTS: 12 / 12

E1. Is there freedom of assembly? 4 / 4

Freedom of assembly is constitutionally guaranteed and generally respected by authorities. The government restricted assembly rights periodically throughout the year to prevent the spread of COVID-19. During the first lockdown in March 2020, police dispersed anti-lockdown protesters for not respecting social distancing rules. In September, authorities in The Hague, the location of many of these protests, implemented stricter rules on spontaneous assemblies that normally would be tolerated by police.

Demonstrations following the May 2020 death of George Floyd in the United States drew thousands of participants, a number not seen in antiracism demonstrations in a generation. In particular, protesters demonstrated in support of removing the figure Black Pete from Saint Nicholas celebrations.

E2. Is there freedom for nongovernmental organizations, particularly those that are engaged in human rights- and governance-related work? 4 / 4

NGOs operate freely and without interference from the government or nonstate actors.

A draft bill proposed in December 2020 would enable local authorities and prosecutors to gather information from civil society organizations on any foreign funding that the organizations receive. The memo accompanying the draft bill links the proposal to concerns over foreign funding of religious groups in migrant communities. Civil society organizations voiced concerns over the possibility that the law would be applied arbitrarily and in a discriminatory manner.

E3. Is there freedom for trade unions and similar professional or labor organizations? 4 / 4

Workers' rights to organize, bargain collectively, and strike are protected.

F. RULE OF LAW: 15 / 16

F1. Is there an independent judiciary? 4 / 4

The judiciary is independent, and the rule of law generally prevails in civil and criminal matters.

F2. Does due process prevail in civil and criminal matters? 4 / 4

The right to a fair trial is legally guaranteed and respected in practice. By June 2020, extra judicial capacity was allocated to deal with the case backlog that was a result of the COVID-19 pandemic. The courts employed retired judges and more frequently used single-judge panels.

F3. Is there protection from the illegitimate use of physical force and freedom from war and insurgencies? 4 / 4

The police are under civilian control, and prison conditions mostly meet international standards. To prevent the spread of COVID-19 among prison populations, the government allowed the early release of detainees who had almost completed their sentence. Prison capacity went down from 85.8 percent at the end of 2019 to 78.2 percent as of mid-April 2020.

Sub-standard prison conditions continued to be reported on islands in the Caribbean under the jurisdiction of the Netherlands, notably on the island of Sint Maarten.

F4. Do laws, policies, and practices guarantee equal treatment of various segments of the population? 3 / 4

The Netherlands has antidiscrimination laws and hate speech laws on the books. Rising anti-immigrant sentiment in recent years has been accompanied by more open expression of anti-Islamic views.

Muslims and people with a migrant background experience harassment and intimidation. Persistent labor market discrimination on ethnic grounds, of older people, of pregnant women, and of disabled people continued to be documented in 2020. The Netherlands Institute for Human Rights (College voor de Rechten van de Mens) criticized the government's inadequate policies to counter discrimination in the public sphere.

Protests in the Netherlands in June following the death of George Floyd in the United States strengthened the movement to remove the figure Black Pete from Saint Nicholas celebrations; mainstream political leaders, including the prime minister, supported the change.

Discussion of the country's the colonial past of the country and its role in the slave trade also gained prominence; Amsterdam and other cities issued formal apologies.

Actions by NGOs on ethnic profiling by the police focused particularly on the Royal Netherlands Marechaussee, a gendarmerie force, whose tasks include border controls and checks on illegal residents. Reports emerged in 2020 that the use of racist language was prominent among the Rotterdam police force.

Dutch asylum policies have long drawn criticism for being unduly harsh. Dutch officials routinely register children born to those who have been trafficked or to asylum seekers under the category "nationality unknown" as opposed to "stateless." This practice has reportedly affected more than 13,000 children under age 10, according to the most recent Dutch Central Bureau of Statistics data from September 2016. In December 2020, the UN Human Rights Committee urged the government to review its legislation and establish a procedure for determining statelessness.

Increasing delays in decision-making on asylum applications, for which the government was obliged to pay asylum seekers fees, led to the government reportedly paying €1 million in administrative penalties per week in 2020. Emergency legislation was introduced in July 2020 to suspend for one year the government's obligation to compensate asylum seekers if their application had been unduly delayed.

Unlike other European Union (EU) member states, Dutch authorities refused to accept a contingent of young unaccompanied asylum seekers from refugee camps in Greece. After the fire at the Moria camp in September 2020, the government decided to accept 100 persons from the camp for resettlement, though this number would be subtracted from the 2021 quota of 500 refugees that are accepted annually from around the world.

The Caribbean islands that are part of the Netherlands lack well-developed asylum procedures. NGOs continued to call for more government action to support Venezuelan refugees on the islands of Aruba and Curaçao; reports suggest that many are regularly expelled from Curaçao. In 2020, about 16,000 Venezuelans resided on Curaçao without a residence permit, living off wages from informal jobs. After the COVID-19 pandemic destroyed the informal economy on those islands, NGOS stepped in to provide food to migrants and destitute citizens of the islands.

G. PERSONAL AUTONOMY AND INDIVIDUAL RIGHTS: 15 / 16 (−1)

G1. Do individuals enjoy freedom of movement, including the ability to change their place of residence, employment, or education? 4 / 4

Residents generally enjoy freedom of movement and choice of residence, employment, and institution of higher education. Though the government did implement a lockdown to curb the spread of the COVID-19 pandemic, these measures were largely in line with public health guidance.

G2. Are individuals able to exercise the right to own property and establish private businesses without undue interference from state or non-state actors? 4 / 4

Property rights are legally protected and generally upheld in practice.

G3. Do individuals enjoy personal social freedoms, including choice of marriage partner and size of family, protection from domestic violence, and control over appearance? 4 / 4

Personal social freedoms are largely respected.

Domestic violence is a persistent problem. According to data published in December 2020 by the Domestic Violence and Sexual Violence Prevalence Monitor created by

Statistics Netherlands, nearly half of all young adult women have experienced some form of sexual violence.

G4. Do individuals enjoy equality of opportunity and freedom from economic exploitation?
3 / 4 (−1)

Increased efforts were set in motion in 2019 by government to prevent and fight human trafficking. The independent government-appointed National Rapporteur on Trafficking in Human Beings and Sexual Violence against Children highlighted in 2020 the lack of attention for trafficking of young people and children who experience sexual abuse, both in the Netherlands and at refugee reception centers after they have applied for asylum.

Long-standing concerns over exploitative working and housing conditions for migrants, particularly in the agricultural and meat-processing sector, deepened in 2020. In October, research released by the International Institute of Social Studies in The Hague showed that migrant workers, mainly from Eastern Europe, were living in degrading conditions, were not ensured proper compensation, and were housed illegally. Between a third and half of all workers in the agricultural sector are migrant workers at risk of exploitation. Government policies created in December 2019 were widely considered insufficient and have not properly regulated temporary employment agencies, which are often the cause of the problem.

Score Change: The score declined from 4 to 3 because migrant workers face exploitative or unsafe working and housing conditions in some industries, despite government efforts to address their treatment.

New Zealand

Population: 5,000,000
Capital: Wellington
Freedom Status: Free
Electoral Democracy: Yes

Overview: New Zealand is a parliamentary democracy with a long record of free and fair elections and of guaranteeing political rights and civil liberties. Concerns include discrimination against the Māori and other minority populations, as well as reports of foreign influence in politics and the education sector.

KEY DEVELOPMENTS IN 2020

- In October elections, Prime Minister Jacinda Arden's Labour Party won an absolute majority in the New Zealand parliament, and candidates of Indigenous or other minority backgrounds made record gains.
- New Zealand was lauded for its relatively successful management of the COVID-19 pandemic; as of year's end, the country had registered 2,162 cases and 25 deaths, according to researchers at the University of Oxford. The government's response included nationwide lockdowns and ongoing restrictions, as well as a one-month delay in parliamentary elections amid a second wave of the virus in August.
- Following the March 2019 extremist attack on mosques in Christchurch, New Zealand authorities successfully prosecuted the offender and took measures to

combat extremist ideologies and foster community reconciliation. In December 2020, Prime Minister Ardern apologized to the country's Muslim community for the state's failure to prevent the attack.

POLITICAL RIGHTS: 40 / 40

A. ELECTORAL PROCESS: 12 / 12

A1. Was the current head of government or other chief national authority elected through free and fair elections? 4 / 4

A governor general, appointed by the United Kingdom's Queen Elizabeth II on advice from the prime minister, represents the British monarch as New Zealand's ceremonial head of state. The prime minister, who is head of government, is appointed by the governor general and is usually the leader of the majority party or coalition in the directly elected parliament. Jacinda Ardern, leader of the Labour Party, was reelected as prime minister in 2020 following legislative elections, which were considered well administered and credible.

A2. Were the current national legislative representatives elected through free and fair elections? 4 / 4

The 120 members of parliament's single chamber, the House of Representatives, serve three-year terms. The mixed electoral system combines voting in geographic districts with proportional representation. Elections in New Zealand are generally well administered, and their results considered credible.

In the October 2020 elections, the Labour Party secured a 65-seat majority in the 120-seat parliament. The opposition National Party claimed 33 seats, a decrease of 23 compared to the 2017 election, while the leftist Green Party won 10 seats. The anti-immigration New Zealand First party, which had been in coalition with Labour, lost all nine of the seats it won in 2017. The Māori Party, representing New Zealand's Indigenous Māori people, reentered Parliament with two seats. The 2020 election was originally scheduled for September , but was delayed by a month amid a nascent second wave of the COVID-19 pandemic in Auckland. The delay of the election was considered lawful, and no concerns were voiced about electoral irregularities resulting from it.

A3. Are the electoral laws and framework fair, and are they implemented impartially by the relevant election management bodies? 4 / 4

The legal framework supports democratic elections, and elections are implemented fairly in practice. The independent New Zealand Electoral Commission administers polls and referendums, promotes compliance with electoral laws, and provides public education on electoral issues.

B. POLITICAL PLURALISM AND PARTICIPATION: 16 / 16

B1. Do the people have the right to organize in different political parties or other competitive political groupings of their choice, and is the system free of undue obstacles to the rise and fall of these competing parties or groupings? 4 / 4

New Zealanders are able to organize political parties without undue legal restrictions or other obstacles, and parties are free to operate and campaign for support.

B2. Is there a realistic opportunity for the opposition to increase its support or gain power through elections? 4 / 4

The political system has experienced regular democratic transfers of power between rival parties. Power has traditionally alternated between the center-left Labour Party and the center-right National Party. Currently, the National Party serves as a strong opposition force in parliament.

B3. Are the people's political choices free from domination by forces that are external to the political sphere, or by political forces that employ extrapolitical means? 4 / 4

People are generally able to act on their political preferences without undue influence from powerful groups. However, several studies in recent years have raised concerns over the likelihood that sizable political donations from Chinese businesspeople and other Chinese figures have influenced the policy positions of political parties and lawmakers.

B4. Do various segments of the population (including ethnic, racial, religious, gender, LGBT+, and other relevant groups) have full political rights and electoral opportunities? 4 / 4

Political rights and electoral opportunities are granted to all New Zealand citizens, and permanent residents have the right to vote. The New Zealand Bill of Rights Act 1990 codifies civil and political rights and all draft legislation is assessed against that Act. Seven of Parliament's constituency seats are reserved for representatives of the Māori population, though Māori may also vote or run in general electoral districts.

In the 2020 elections saw victories by New Zealand's first lawmakers of African, Latin American, and Sri Lankan background. Iranian refugee Golriz Ghahraman was reelected to a second term, while the Māori Party returned to parliament for the first time since 2017.

Women are relatively well represented in politics, and the government has taken steps to encourage their participation. Ardern is the third woman to serve as the country's prime minister. The 2020 elections were the second in New Zealand's history to be contested with both major parties led by women. National Party leader Judith Collins remained leader of the opposition despite her party's loss in the balloting.

C. FUNCTIONING OF GOVERNMENT: 12 / 12

C1. Do the freely elected head of government and national legislative representatives determine the policies of the government? 4 / 4

The prime minister and cabinet ministers, with the support of a majority in the House of Representatives, determine and implement the government's policy agenda without improper interference from any unelected entity. In 2020, the pandemic affected the functioning of parliament, with parliamentary sittings suspended for five weeks between late March and early May.

C2. Are safeguards against official corruption strong and effective? 4 / 4

Government corruption is not considered a significant problem in New Zealand, and cases of official malfeasance are routinely investigated and prosecuted.

Despite the country's strong anticorruption record, there is some concern about a "revolving door" between political or government posts and private-sector lobbying groups, which could entail conflicts of interest. The government's Serious Fraud Office, which is in charge of investigating suspected corruption, has increased its attention to political party funding, and several investigations yielded charges for alleged campaign finance violations in 2020; the most prominent case involved unnamed defendants tied to a foundation associated with the New Zealand First party.

C3. Does the government operate with openness and transparency? 4 / 4

The government operates with a high level of transparency, and new legislation is openly discussed in parliament and the media. Parliamentary records, government policies, and commissioned reports are published online and readily available as required by law. The government upholds transparency in budgetary procedures, and members of parliament must submit annual financial disclosure statements.

CIVIL LIBERTIES: 59 / 60 (+2)

D. FREEDOM OF EXPRESSION AND BELIEF: 16 / 16

D1. Are there free and independent media? 4 / 4

New Zealand has a free and robust independent media sector, including a Māori-language public network and radio station.

In November 2020, New Zealand media giant Stuff issued a public apology after an internal investigation revealed systemic racism in its reporting, particularly in portrayals of Māori people.

D2. Are individuals free to practice and express their religious faith or nonbelief in public and private? 4 / 4

Religious freedom is protected by law and generally respected in practice. Only religious organizations that wish to collect donations and receive tax benefits need to register with the government, and the process is not onerous.

D3. Is there academic freedom, and is the educational system free from extensive political indoctrination? 4 / 4

Academic freedom typically prevails at all levels of instruction. However, concerns persist regarding Chinese interference in New Zealand's higher education sector. Beginning in late 2017 and throughout 2018, a prominent China studies professor at the University of Canterbury in Christchurch was subjected to an intimidation campaign. Reports of Chinese government attempts to influence student groups and monitor Chinese students in New Zealand also emerged in 2017.

D4. Are individuals free to express their personal views on political or other sensitive topics without fear of surveillance or retribution? 4 / 4

New Zealanders are free to discuss personal views on sensitive topics. However, new intelligence and security legislation adopted in 2017 allows law enforcement agencies to access private communications under certain conditions in order to protect national security.

In December 2019, Parliament passed the Terrorism Suppression (Control Orders) Act, which had been criticized by the privacy commissioner for authorizing an overly intrusive regime of monitoring and restrictions on individuals designated as having been involved in terrorism activities abroad.

E. ASSOCIATIONAL AND ORGANIZATIONAL RIGHTS: 12 / 12

E1. Is there freedom of assembly? 4 / 4

The government generally respects freedom of assembly. Public gatherings were severely restricted in March in response to the COVID-19 pandemic's arrival in New Zealand, but controls were eased starting in April following successful containment measures; looser restrictions were imposed in response to the smaller second wave in August.

In June, demonstrations in support of the Black Lives Matter (BLM) movement took place in several New Zealand cities. The protests, which sought to call attention to structural and racial discrimination in New Zealand, including against the Indigenous Māori, were mostly peaceful and were not impeded by police.

E2. Is there freedom for nongovernmental organizations, particularly those that are engaged in human rights- and governance-related work? 4 / 4

There are no significant restrictions on nongovernmental organizations' ability to form, operate, and solicit funds.

E3. Is there freedom for trade unions and similar professional or labor organizations? 4 / 4

Workers may freely organize and bargain collectively, and trade unions actively engage in political debates and campaigns. Workers also have the right to strike, with the exception of uniformed police personnel.

F. RULE OF LAW: 15 / 16 (+1)

F1. Is there an independent judiciary? 4 / 4

The New Zealand judiciary is generally independent. Most judges are appointed by the governor general on the recommendation of the attorney general, who first consults with senior jurists.

F2. Does due process prevail in civil and criminal matters? 4 / 4

Law enforcement practices and court procedures provide for due process protections in civil and criminal matters. Defendants and detainees are presumed innocent until proven guilty and by law must immediately be notified of the charges against them.

Pretrial detention durations have increased in recent years, as authorities have tightened bail requirements and relaxed the time limit in which cases must be concluded.

F3. Is there protection from the illegitimate use of physical force and freedom from war and insurgencies? 4 / 4 (+1)

Rates of violent crime are relatively low, and residents have legal recourse to seek redress for violations of their physical security. The March 2019 Christchurch terrorist attack was the worst mass shooting in New Zealand's modern history. The shooting, which took place at two mosques and killed 51 people, was preplanned and accompanied by an 87-page document filled with anti-immigrant and anti-Muslim hate speech. Following the attack, government representatives collaborated with tech companies, including Google and Facebook, to ensure the removal of material on online platforms depicting the attack and prevent livestreaming of potential future attacks. In March 2020, the perpetrator of the shootings, Australian man Brenton Tarrant, pleaded guilty to 51 counts of murder, 40 counts of attempted murder, and one charge of terrorism; he received a life sentence in August. A Royal Commission inquiry into the causes of the attack identified serious failures by the country's intelligence services, and Prime Minister Ardern apologized to New Zealand's Muslim community in December.

Prison conditions generally meet international standards, though some facilities are poorly equipped to house detainees with disabilities or mental health problems.

Score Change: The score improved from 3 to 4 because there were no further instances of terrorist violence following the attacks of 2019.

F4. Do laws, policies, and practices guarantee equal treatment of various segments of the population? 3 / 4

The 1993 Human Rights Act protects all people in New Zealand from discrimination on the basis of gender, religion, ethnicity, and sexual orientation, among other categories, and its provisions are generally respected in practice. However, Māori—who account for approximately 16 percent of the population—and Pacific Islanders experience some discrimination in schools, the workplace, and the health system. Indigenous people are also disproportionately represented in the penal system, accounting for just over half of the prison population as of May 2019. Recent campaigns to recruit more officers of Māori, Pacific Islander, and Asian descent aim to improve cultural and ethnic sensitivity within the police force, and to combat profiling and discrimination.

The arrival of the coronavirus in New Zealand resulted in some incidents of racism targeting members of East Asian communities, including public harassment and discriminatory media treatment.

The yearly Child Poverty Monitor Technical Report outlines the national issue of child poverty in New Zealand. Children of Māori and Pacific Islander descent are especially vulnerable to this problem. The Ardern government has been criticized for its ineffective efforts to combat the issue of child poverty, despite it being a priority on its policy agenda.

Women continue to face some disparities in employment, including a gender pay gap and underrepresentation in leadership positions in both the public and private sectors. The government enforces strong legislation protecting the rights of LGBT+ people. However, LGBT+ people report workplace discrimination and poorer physical and mental health compared to the general population.

The New Zealand Human Rights Commission has raised concerns that refugees are not always given sufficient information to enable them to access important services such as interpreters, housing, and English-language instruction. Separately, asylum seekers are sometimes detained alongside criminal inmates while their identity is being confirmed. Despite these issues, the government has been accepting of refugees, and has increased the number allowed entry in recent years. In 2019, the government ended restrictions on the number of refugees from Africa and the Middle East.

G. PERSONAL AUTONOMY AND INDIVIDUAL RIGHTS: 16 / 16 (+1)

G1. Do individuals enjoy freedom of movement, including the ability to change their place of residence, employment, or education? 4 / 4

The government respects freedom of movement, and neither state nor nonstate actors place undue restrictions on people's ability to change their place of residence, employment, or education.

G2. Are individuals able to exercise the right to own property and establish private businesses without undue interference from state or nonstate actors? 4 / 4

New Zealand's legal and regulatory frameworks are broadly supportive of private business activity and provide strong protections for property rights.

G3. Do individuals enjoy personal social freedoms, including choice of marriage partner and size of family, protection from domestic violence, and control over appearance? 4 / 4

Personal social freedoms are broadly protected, including on issues like marriage and divorce. Same-sex marriage was legalized in 2013, and same-sex couples may jointly adopt children. However, violence against women and children remains a critical problem in many communities. A government survey released in 2020 reported that over one in three women has been a victim of sexual violence in her lifetime. Abortion is legal in New Zealand; in March 2020 Parliament removed all restrictions up to 20 weeks of pregnancy and fully decriminalized the procedure.

G4. Do individuals enjoy equality of opportunity and freedom from economic exploitation? 4 / 4 (+1)

Residents generally have access to economic opportunities, but the Māori and Pacific Islander populations have disproportionately high rates of unemployment, affecting their economic and social mobility. Women and Pacific people are among the most likely groups to receive lower pay for equal work. In December 2020 the Human Rights Commission announced an inquiry into the unequal pay and equal employment discrimination faced by Pacific workers.

Migrant workers are vulnerable to exploitative conditions including forced labor in industries such as fishing, agriculture, construction, hospitality, and domestic service. The government has taken action to combat these abuses, and in August 2020 authorities announced a crackdown on exploitation and protections to help migrant workers escape exploitative environments.

Score Change: The score improved from 3 to 4 due to improved protections for migrant workers, and because worker protections are generally upheld in practice.

Nicaragua

Population: 6,600,000
Capital: Managua
Freedom Status: Not Free
Electoral Democracy: No

Overview: The election of Sandinista leader Daniel Ortega in 2006 began a period of democratic deterioration marked by the consolidation of all branches of government under his party's control, the limitation of fundamental freedoms, and unchecked corruption in government. In 2018, state forces, with the aid of informally allied armed groups, responded to a mass antigovernment movement with violence and repression. The rule of law collapsed as the government moved to put down the movement, with rights monitors reporting the deaths of at least 325 people, extrajudicial detentions, disappearances, and torture. Arbitrary arrests and detentions have since continued, perceived government opponents report surveillance and monitoring, and talks with the opposition have floundered.

KEY DEVELOPMENTS IN 2020

- The government refused to implement social distancing measures to manage the COVID-19 pandemic, intentionally underreported cases, and fired health workers who criticized authorities' handling of the issue.
- Attacks against Indigenous populations continued with impunity, as settlers continued to invade Indigenous lands.
- In October, the government passed two laws viewed as attempts to suffocate opposition: the Foreign Agents Law, which requires any Nicaraguan receiving funds from abroad to register as a foreign agent with the Interior Ministry, and prohibits such agents from engaging in political activities or holding public office; and the Special Cybercrimes Law, which criminalizes the dissemination of "false or distorted" information using communications technology.
- In December, the government passed a law enabling officials to bar individuals labeled as "terrorists" or "traitors" from running for or holding public office. The country's next presidential election will take place in November 2021.

POLITICAL RIGHTS: 10 / 40

A. ELECTORAL PROCESS: 3 / 12

A1. Was the current head of government or other chief national authority elected through free and fair elections? 1 / 4

The constitution provides for a directly elected president, and elections are held every five years. Constitutional reforms in 2014 eliminated term limits and required the winner of the presidential ballot to secure a simple plurality of votes.

President Ortega was reelected in 2016 with over 72 percent of the vote in a severely flawed election that was preceded by the Supreme Court's move to strip the main opposition candidate, Eduardo Montealegre, of control of his Independent Liberal Party (PLI), leaving him no political vehicle upon which to run for president. The decision severely disrupted the operations of the PLI, and Ortega's closest competitor, Maximino Rodríguez of the Constitutionalist Liberal Party (PLC), received just 15 percent of the vote, with no other candidate reaching 5 percent. Ortega's wife, Rosario Murillo, ran as his vice presidential candidate.

Ortega's Sandinista National Liberation Front (FSLN) won 135 of 153 mayorships contested in 2017 municipal elections. There were reports ahead of the polls that the FSLN had ignored local primary surveys in order to put its preferred candidates up for election. Seven people were killed in postelection clashes between government and opposition supporters, according to the Nicaraguan Center of Human Rights (CENIDH).

A2. Were the current national legislative representatives elected through free and fair elections? 1 / 4

The constitution provides for a 92-member unicameral National Assembly. Two seats in the legislature are reserved for the previous president and the runner-up in the most recent presidential election. Legislative elections are held every five years.

In the 2016 legislative elections, Ortega's FSLN increased its majority to 70 seats in the National Assembly, followed by the PLC with 13 seats. The PLI won just 2 seats, in contrast to the 26 seats it won in the 2011 election. Ortega refused to allow international election monitoring. Montealegre was expelled from the PLI a few months ahead of the polls, severely damaging the party's competitiveness.

Nicaragua's North Caribbean Coast Autonomous Region (RACCN) and South Caribbean Coast Autonomous Region (RACCS) have regional councils, for which elections were held in March 2019; the FSLN won the largest share of the vote in each. The only independent observer group reported a number of irregularities, including the participation of voters from ineligible areas; low turnout; and a heavy military presence in several municipalities while polling took place.

A3. Are the electoral laws and framework fair, and are they implemented impartially by the relevant election management bodies? 1 / 4

The Supreme Electoral Council (CSE) and judiciary generally serve the interests of the FSLN. In 2016, the CSE pushed 16 opposition members of the National Assembly from their seats in response to their failure to recognize the Supreme Court's move to expel Montealegre from the PLI; later that year it certified Ortega's reelection following a severely flawed electoral process.

Both the acting head of the CSE, Lumberto Campbell, and the previous CSE president, Roberto Rivas, are on the United States' list of sanctioned individuals for the CSE's role in facilitating Nicaragua's highly flawed elections.

B. POLITICAL PLURALISM AND PARTICIPATION: 4 / 16

B1. Do the people have the right to organize in different political parties or other competitive political groupings of their choice, and is the system free of undue obstacles to the rise and fall of these competing parties or groupings? 1 / 4

Political parties face legal and practical obstacles to formation and operations. Party leaders are easily co-opted or disqualified by Ortega-aligned institutions. Membership in the FSLN is often required in order to hold civil service positions, discouraging people from registering as members of other parties. Under 2014 constitutional reforms, legislators must follow the party vote or risk losing their seats.

The Foreign Agents Law passed in October 2020 requires anyone receiving funds from foreign governments, organizations, or individuals to register as a foreign agent, and prohibits such agents from engaging in political activities or holding public office. In December 2020, congress passed a law that would prohibit individuals designated as "traitors" from running for or holding public office. International watchdogs including Human Rights Watch and domestic government opponents viewed the new laws as indications the government intended to clamp down on opposition and prevent competition in the 2021 elections.

B2. Is there a realistic opportunity for the opposition to increase its support or gain power through elections? 0 / 4

Years of political repression under Ortega, including through politicized court rulings and other measures that prevented opposition figures from participating in politics, severely limit the ability of the opposition to gain power through elections, and very few opposition figures hold legislative seats or other government positions. In 2018, police and progovernment armed groups employed lethal force against peaceful opposition and antigovernment protesters; thousands of protest participants were arbitrarily detained and arrested, and thousands more fled into exile. While such large-scale violence was not repeated in 2019 and 2020, heavy-handed repression of the opposition has continued, with frequent reports of harassment, arbitrary detention, and violence. The government has refused to discuss electoral reforms or early elections as called for by the Nicaraguan population.

B3. Are the people's political choices free from domination by forces that are external to the political sphere, or by political forces that employ extrapolitical means? 1 / 4

President Ortega has consolidated all branches of government and most public institutions, as well as the country's media, under his party's control, allowing him and the FSLN great influence over people's political choices.

Public-sector workers experienced pressure to keep away from the antigovernment protest movement in 2018. Hundreds of health professionals were dismissed from public hospitals for providing assistance to protesters or for their alleged role in antigovernment demonstrations.

Police and state-allied armed groups were the primary perpetrators of violence during the 2018 crisis, and in 2020 they continued to attack perceived regime opponents. In a report released in December, the Inter-American Commission on Human Rights (IACHR) identified a "revolving door" system of short-term arbitrary detentions intended to intimidate and disrupt regime opponents.

In November 2020, hurricanes Eta and Iota devastated sections of the country. As damage assessment and aid efforts got underway, accusations emerged that the government was prioritizing Sandinista-led areas, as well as hindering independent journalistic coverage of the crisis.

B4. Do various segments of the population (including ethnic, racial religious, gender, LGBT+, and other relevant groups) have full political rights and electoral opportunities? 2 / 4

Minority groups, especially the Indigenous inhabitants of Nicaragua's eastern and Caribbean regions, are politically underrepresented across parties, and the government and FSLN largely ignore their grievances. Indigenous and Afro-descendent populations are underrepresented in the National Assembly; in 2020 there was only one Indigenous representative, Brooklyn Rivera of the Yatama party, and two Kriol representatives.

The 2018 crackdown signaled Ortega's intolerance of activism that could be perceived as challenging his government, including by Indigenous activists and other segments of the population seeking greater political rights. During the brief congressional debate on the 2020 Foreign Agents Law, Rivera expressed concern that the law could disproportionately impact underrepresented political groups.

As per a new municipal electoral law approved in 2012, half of each party's candidates for mayoralties and council seats must be women. Women also hold 45 percent of National Assembly seats. In practice, successful political advocacy by women is generally restricted to initiatives that enjoy the support of the FSLN, which has not prioritized women's policy concerns.

C. FUNCTIONING OF GOVERNMENT: 3 / 12

C1. Do the freely elected head of government and national legislative representatives determine the policies of the government? 1 / 4

The FSLN dominates most public institutions. The tripartite alliance between government, private business, and organized labor, which is recognized in Article 98 of the constitution, has become less functional since the private sector began to distance itself from the government upon the violent events of 2018. The manipulation of the 2016 election and the expulsion of 16 opposition politicians from the legislature prevented elected representatives from determining government policies.

Under constitutional reforms in 2014, Ortega has a wide degree of discretionary powers to set policy. Executive dominance of the highly polarized legislature results in a consistent lack of oversight.

C2. Are safeguards against official corruption strong and effective? 1 / 4

Because the justice system and other public bodies are generally subservient to Ortega and the FSLN, there is little chance that allegations of corruption against government officials will see a thorough investigation or prosecution. Corruption charges against high-ranking government officials are rare, while corruption cases against opposition figures are often criticized for being politically motivated.

The intermixing of Ortega family, Sandinista party, and government interests have long been criticized as presenting significant conflicts of interest and opportunities for corruption. Ortega's sons and daughters have been appointed to prominent positions such as ambassador and presidential adviser. Several of the president's sons are among the multiple Nicaraguan officials sanctioned by the US Treasury Department for alleged involvement in corrupt activities, including one who was added to the sanctions list in July 2020.

C3. Does the government operate with openness and transparency? 1 / 4

Government operations and policymaking are generally opaque. The 2007 Law on Access to Public Information requires public entities and private companies doing business with the state to disclose certain information. Government agencies at all levels generally ignore this law.

Ortega rarely holds press conferences. The Communications and Citizenry Council, which oversees the government's press relations, is directed by Vice President Murillo and has been accused of limiting access to information.

Independent observers allege that the government intentionally underreported the number of COVID-19 cases in the country, and the Pan-American Health Organization was denied access to Nicaraguan hospitals. Many people whose deaths were attributed to "atypical pneumonia" were nonetheless given express burials that family members were barred from attending. Health workers were reportedly prevented from using personal protective equipment and implementing safety protocols in public hospitals, and dozens of nurses and doctors were fired for signing a letter criticizing the government's response to the pandemic.

CIVIL LIBERTIES: 20 / 60 (−1)

D. FREEDOM OF EXPRESSION AND BELIEF: 7 / 16

D1. Are there free and independent media? 1 / 4

The press has faced increased political and judicial harassment since 2007, when Ortega returned to power, with the administration engaging in systematic efforts to obstruct and discredit media critics. Journalists have been subject to threats, arrest, and physical attacks. The IACHR has granted protectionary measures to several journalists in light of harassment and death threats.

Repression of journalists has become acute since the current political crisis broke out in 2018. The state has ordered television companies and mobile phone service providers to stop transmitting several independent news channels through their systems. Numerous outlets have been raided and closed. Journalists have been arrested and charged with terrorism; as of April 2020, over 90 media workers had gone into exile. Restrictions on ink and paper forced the newspaper *El Nuevo Diario* to close in 2019. In February 2020, the government lifted restrictions on newsprint to *La Prensa*, but the state continued to hold property confiscated in 2018 from critical outlets, apply criminal defamation laws, and seize assets throughout 2020, while government supporters continued to harass and attack journalists with impunity. In late 2020, violently broke up a press conference held by journalist Carlos Fernando Chamorro, at which he called on the government to return the building that had housed the *Confidencial* and *Esta Semana*.

In October, congress passed the Special Cybercrimes Law, which criminalizes the dissemination through communications technology of "false news," coverage or remarks that harm the reputation of a public officials, and publishing material that "incites hatred and violence, [or] endangers economic stability, public order, public health or national security." In addition to criticizing the law's vague language, press freedom advocates noted that it would obstruct investigative journalism and exposure of corruption by prohibiting the publication of information leaked by sources within the government.

D2. Are individuals free to practice and express their religious faith or nonbelief in public and private? 2 / 4

Religious freedom was generally respected prior to the 2018 crisis, though some Catholic and evangelical church leaders had reported retaliation by the government for criticism of the Ortega administration, including the confiscation or delay of imported goods and donations. Since the political crisis ignited, however, church officials have been denounced and smeared by authorities for accompanying or defending antigovernment protestors, pro-government mobs have attacked churches where antigovernment protesters were sheltering, and members of the clergy have received threats and experienced surveillance. There have been reports that Ortega supporters have infiltrated parishes and harassed or intimidated parishioners at church services. In 2020, Ortega accused local bishops of participating in a plot to overthrow him, and the United States' Commission for International Religious Freedom (USCIRF) released a report expressing concern about the repression of Catholics.

Faith leaders have criticized attempts by the Ortega administration to co-opt religious belief for political ends. The government has required public employees to attend government-sponsored religious festivals, making them miss official Catholic Church events.

D3. Is there academic freedom, and is the educational system free from extensive political indoctrination? 2 / 4

Prior to the 2018 crisis, academic freedoms were generally respected, although some academics refrained from open criticism of the government. Since then, teachers have reported being required to attend training that promotes government views and reaffirms the government's version of the 2018 political crisis. In the public primary and secondary school system, there have been reports of students being required to attend progovernment rallies, and of pro-FSLN materials displayed in school buildings.

D4. Are individuals free to express their personal views on political or other sensitive topics without fear of surveillance or retribution? 2 / 4

In 2020, repression and intimidation by state and progovernment forces contributed to a generalized climate of fear and terror that continues to restrict free expression. The families of victims of regime violence are subjected to routine monitoring and surveillance, and returnees from abroad reported being subjected to surveillance upon return. In 2019, the Special Rapporteurship on Economic, Social, Cultural, and Environmental Rights (REDESCA) of the IACHR reported concerns about discrimination and retaliatory threats against state employees who disagreed with or acted against state policy.

The 2020 Cybercrimes Law criminalized the spread of "false news" and targeted whistleblowing by government employees. The law also gives the government broad access to user data. Additionally, in November congress passed the first of two required readings of a constitutional amendment to allow for life sentences for hate crimes. Ortega has often referred to opposition actions as hate crimes, and analysts feared the law would be used to target political opponents.

E. ASSOCIATIONAL AND ORGANIZATIONAL RIGHTS: 2 / 12

E1. Is there freedom of assembly? 0 / 4

Freedom of assembly deteriorated severely in 2018, when at least 325 people were killed and at least 2,000 were injured in a ferocious crackdown on an antigovernment protest movement that began that April, after authorities announced social security reforms; it soon turned into a broader antigovernment movement aimed at forcing the regime from power. A majority of the abuses have been attributed to the national police and armed allied groups, which the UN Office of the High Commissioner for Human Rights (OHCHR) said in an August 2018 report operate with "total impunity." In September of that year, the national police issued a statement declaring unauthorized marches and demonstrations "illegal." Police have since denied permits for public demonstrations, and have occupied public spaces to prevent protests.

Police continued to block or disperse attempted demonstrations in 2019 and 2020. More than 100 people were arrested March 2019 for attempting to protest in Managua, but ultimately released. Attempts to gather in 2020 faced violent obstruction, including protesters marching in support of political prisoners in February who were beaten by police, a series of rallies on International Women's Day in March that encountered police blockades and assaults, and a student-led, satire-based protest in October that was attacked by police and civilian armed groups.

An amnesty law passed in 2019 states that protesters who are released must not take part in actions that lead to further "crimes," effectively prohibiting them from again participating in antigovernment demonstrations.

E2. Is there freedom for nongovernmental organizations, particularly those that are engaged in human rights- and governance-related work? 0 / 4

Groups critical of the government or that focus on issues like corruption have operated within an increasingly restrictive environment under the Ortega administration, which among other measures has used registration laws to choke off their sources of funding. Since April 2018, human rights defenders and leaders of civil society organizations have experienced severe harassment, arbitrary detention, and arbitrary expulsion. Twelve NGOs, most of which focused on democracy, human rights, or press freedom, saw their registration cancelled at the close of 2018.

Human rights organizations reported continued monitoring and surveillance in 2020. In September, a group of domestic and regional human rights NGOs, including Amnesty International and the Washington Office on Latin America, decried a wave of repression of activists, including sexual assaults of women activists. The government also suppressed actions by NGOs and church groups to provide public health assistance in response to the COVID-19 pandemic.

The Foreign Agents Law enacted in 2020 threatened to further impede the operations of independent groups. Recipients of foreign funding who register as foreign agents must also provide monthly reports detailing all income, along with actual and planned expenditures.

E3. Is there freedom for trade unions and similar professional or labor organizations? 2 / 4

The FSLN controls many of the country's labor unions, and the legal rights of non-FSLN unions are not fully guaranteed in practice. Although the law recognizes the right to strike, approval from the Ministry of Labor is almost never granted. Employers sometimes form their own unions to avoid recognizing legitimate organizations. Employees have reportedly been dismissed for union activities, and citizens have no effective recourse when those in power violate labor laws.

F. RULE OF LAW: 3 / 16 (−1)

F1. Is there an independent judiciary? 1 / 4

The judiciary remains dominated by FSLN and PLC appointees, and the Supreme Court is a largely politicized body controlled by Sandinista judges.

F2. Does due process prevail in civil and criminal matters? 0 / 4

Since protests erupted in April 2018, UN investigators and other human rights organizations have documented rampant violations of due process. These include widespread arbitrary arrests and detentions by police and allied progovernment forces, failure to produce search or arrest warrants, no discussion of detainees' rights, no public registry of detainees or their location, and individuals being held incommunicado during initial detention. Due process has continued to deteriorate in 2020 as a result of repressive new laws and lack of oversight by independent entities.

The government announced in February 2019 that it would release political prisoners detained during the 2018 protests. Between mid-March and mid-June, the government released nearly 400 people imprisoned for activities related to the 2018 protests, and another

91 were released in late December; most were released under house arrest while charges against them remained active. Released prisoners were subjected to harassment and surveillance. Defense attorneys of political prisoners also reported being harassed. The IACHR reported 94 political prisoners still in custody as of September 2020.

An amnesty law passed in June 2019 covers crimes committed during the 2018 protests. Although the law acknowledges that crimes covered by international treaties, such as crimes against humanity, would be excluded from the amnesty, critics feared that the law would be used to shield the state and its agents from responsibility for past abuses. The pervasive lack of effective due process intensified activist concerns regarding implementation of the Foreign Agents Law, the Cybersecurity Law, and the anti-traitors law, all of which were passed in late 2020, as well as the pending constitutional amendment on hate crimes.

F3. Is there protection from the illegitimate use of physical force and freedom from war and insurgencies? 1 / 4

The 2018 antigovernment protest movement was met with violent repression by police and informally allied armed forces, resulting in the deaths of at least 325 people. In an August 2018 report on repression of the protest movement, the OHCHR detailed severe abuses including psychological and physical torture of detainees, including sexual violence, forced confessions, disappearances, and extrajudicial killings. In 2019 there were reports of dozens of antigovernment activists being killed in more remote parts of the country, allegedly by police and paramilitaries.

Changes to the military code and national police passed in 2014 give the president power to deploy the army for internal security purposes and appoint the national police chief, and permitted the police to engage in political activity. The 2015 sovereign security law has been criticized for militarizing civilian agencies.

In March 2020, the Office of the UN High Commissioner for Refugees (UNHCR) estimated that more than 100,000 Nicaraguans had fled the country, with more than 77,000 in Costa Rica.

Prisons are often characterized by overcrowding and poor sanitation. To prevent the spread of COVID-19 within prison walls, the government released over 2,800 prisoners to house arrest in May 2020, but political prisoners were not among those freed.

F4. Do laws, policies, and practices guarantee equal treatment of various segments of the population? 1 / 4 (−1)

The constitution and laws nominally recognize the rights of indigenous communities, but those rights have not been respected in practice. Approximately 5 percent of the population is Indigenous and lives mostly in the RACCN and the RACCS. While Indigenous populations have been granted legal rights and protections to land, the government does not enforce these laws.

Attacks against Indigenous populations and land incursions in recent years have been perpetrated with impunity. In March 2020, the IACHR rebuked Nicaragua's failure to protect Indigenous people from violence and expulsion from their traditional lands. As of December, 12 members of the Mayangna and Miskito communities had been murdered in 2020, adding to a toll of nearly 50 since 2015. Indigenous communities sustained large-scale damage from the November 2020 hurricanes, with rights advocates warning of a potential rise in settler incursions into protected lands.

The country's LGBT+ population is subject to intermittent threats and discriminatory treatment.

Score Change: The score declined from 2 to 1 because the government has failed to protect Indigenous peoples from violent land grabs by settlers.

G. PERSONAL AUTONOMY AND INDIVIDUAL RIGHTS: 8 / 16

G1. Do individuals enjoy freedom of movement, including the ability to change their place of residence, employment, or education? 2 / 4

The 2018 collapse of institutions, that year's bloody crackdown on dissenters, and continuing government repression since have created a climate of fear and mistrust that discourages free movement. Poor infrastructure limits movement in some majority-indigenous areas.

G2. Are individuals able to exercise the right to own property and establish private businesses without undue interference from state or nonstate actors? 2 / 4

Property rights are protected on paper but can be tenuous in practice. Titles are often contested, and individuals with connections to the FSLN sometimes enjoy an advantage during property disputes. Conflict over land in the RACCS and RACCN between Indigenous residents and settlers continued in 2020, resulting in numerous deaths. The Center for Justice and International Law (CEJIL) warned in a 2019 report that Miskito communities in the north could be at risk of extinction due to land invasions.

Individuals and communities in the construction zone for a planned interoceanic canal have reported intimidation by surveyors and anonymous actors, though the project appeared to have stalled.

G3. Do individuals enjoy personal social freedoms, including choice of marriage partner and size of family, protection from domestic violence, and control over appearance? 2 / 4

Individuals enjoy broad freedom in their interpersonal relationships and in their personal appearance.

Domestic violence remains widespread and underreported, and few cases are ever prosecuted. The 2012 Comprehensive Law against Violence toward Women addresses both physical and structural forms of violence, and recognizes violence against women as a matter of public health and safety. A 2013 reform to the law allows mediation between the victim and accuser, despite concerns from rights groups. The family code includes protections for pregnant minors and the elderly, establishes equal duties of mothers and fathers, and prohibits physical punishment of children. It defines marriage as a union between a man and a woman and, as such, deprives same-sex couples the right to adopt children or the ability to receive fertility treatment.

Abortion is illegal and punishable by imprisonment, even when performed to save the pregnant person's life or in cases of rape or incest. The criminalization of abortion can cause women to seek out risky illegal abortions that can jeopardize their health.

G4. Do individuals enjoy equality of opportunity and freedom from economic exploitation? 2 / 4

Nicaragua is a source country for women and children forced into prostitution; adults and children are also vulnerable to forced labor, notably in the agriculture and mining sectors, and as domestic servants. The 2020 US State Department's *Trafficking in Persons Report* downgraded the country to Tier 3, alleging that the while the government initiated a handful of investigations and one prosecution, it decreased its overall prosecution, protection, and prevention efforts in 2019, and did not cooperate with NGOs in the anti-trafficking coalition.

Much of the economy is informal, and workers in these sectors lack legal protections associated with formal employment. The legal minimum wage is inadequate to cover the cost of basic goods.

Niger

Population: 24,200,000
Capital: Niamey
Freedom Status: Partly Free
Electoral Democracy: No

Overview: The current government in Niger was democratically elected in 2011 and reelected in 2016 in a polling process plagued by serious irregularities. The struggle to meet security challenges posed by active militant groups has served as an alibi for the government to restrict civil liberties. Security, transparency, and gender equality are limited.

KEY DEVELOPMENTS IN 2020

- Nigeriens voted for outgoing president Mahamadou Issoufou's successor and for the parliament in late December elections, which observers called largely calm. The vote marked what was expected to be the first peaceful transfer of power in Niger, though results were not finalized by year's end.
- A government audit completed in February reported that as much as 76 billion CFA francs ($130 million) in public money was diverted through the manipulation of defense contracts between 2014 and 2019. However, no prosecutions were launched based on the audit by year's end.
- Militant groups launched several attacks against civilian and military targets during the year. Militants were reportedly responsible for killing 89 soldiers in a January attack, while Boko Haram was blamed for attacking a village in Diffa Region and killing 28 people the day before local elections were held in December.
- In March, the government closed borders and imposed an overnight curfew in Niamey in response to the COVID-19 pandemic, though the curfew was lifted in May. Protests were restricted by pandemic-related measures and at least one journalist was arrested over pandemic-related reporting. The authorities reported 3,110 cases and 96 deaths to the World Health Organization at year's end.

POLITICAL RIGHTS: 20 / 40

A. ELECTORAL PROCESS: 6 / 12

A1. Was the current head of government or other chief national authority elected through free and fair elections? 2 / 4

The president is directly elected to up to two five-year terms. Nigeriens voted to replace term-limited incumbent Mahamadou Issoufou in late December 2020. Former interior minister Mohamed Bazoum, the candidate of the ruling Nigerien Party for Democracy and Socialism (PNDS Tarayya), competed against 29 others, including former president Mahamane Ousmane (1993–96).

The Constitutional Court disqualified several candidates in November, including Nigerien Democratic Movement for an African Federation candidate Hama Amadou; Amadou was disqualified over a 2017 human-trafficking conviction which he called bogus. The polls were marked by isolated reports of attempted vote buying, but were largely peaceful. The Independent National Electoral Commission (CENI) did not release provisional results by year's end.

A2. Were the current national legislative representatives elected through free and fair elections? 2 / 4

There are 171 seats in the unicameral National Assembly, 158 of which are directly elected from 8 multimember constituencies; 8 which are reserved for minority representatives, who are elected directly from special single-seat constituencies; and 5 that are reserved for Nigeriens living abroad.

Nigeriens abroad were unable to participate in the late December 2020 parliamentary elections due to the COVID-19 pandemic, but voters within Niger voted to fill the 166 domestic seats concurrently with the presidential contest. Economic Community of West African States (ECOWAS) observers called the elections relatively free and fair, and lauded the participation of young and female voters. Results for the parliamentary elections were not finalized by year's end.

Regional and local elections were held in mid-December 2020. The night before these polls opened, the Boko Haram militant group reportedly launched an attack on a village in Diffa Region, killing at least 28 people.

A3. Are the electoral laws and framework fair, and are they implemented impartially by the relevant election management bodies? 2 / 4

The electoral code offers a framework for fair elections. However, the opposition, pointing to reports of widespread irregularities in recent elections, among other issues, has cast doubt over the impartiality of the CENI and the Constitutional Court, which together approve lists of candidates and validate election results. In 2017, the government and the opposition disagreed over the appointment of a new commission to organize the 2020 presidential and legislative elections; the government unilaterally appointed the new commission after the opposition boycotted the process.

In 2019, parliamentarians adopted a new electoral code. That same year, the CENI launched the process of enrollment in a biometric voter list. ECOWAS and the Organization of La Francophonie called the new voter file reliable after reviewing it in September 2020.

While 41 candidates registered to participate in the December 2020 presidential elections, 11 were disqualified by the Constitutional Court in November. Most were disqualified because they did not pay the required registration fee.

B. POLITICAL PLURALISM AND PARTICIPATION: 8 / 16

B1. Do the people have the right to organize in different political parties or other competitive political groupings of their choice, and is the system free of undue obstacles to the rise and fall of these competing parties or groupings? 2 / 4

By law, political parties may freely organize and conduct their activities. However, the PNDS Tarayya–led government has employed a variety of tactics to interfere in the operation of opposition parties, including persecution of opposition leaders and the co-optation of key opposition figures. Over 150 political parties were registered as of November 2020.

B2. Is there a realistic opportunity for the opposition to increase its support or gain power through elections? 2 / 4

In theory, the opposition can mobilize support and increase its membership. However, the opposition has suffered from a lack of leadership, partly due to the absence of Amadou, who previously served a prison sentence and lived in exile. Opposition parties have been divided into several coalitions and face serious difficulties in challenging the PNDS Tarayya's dominance. In addition, a history of government-led repression and co-option has hindered their ability to gain power through elections.

Members of the opposition have expressed concern over the rising insecurity in several regions, particularly in the opposition stronghold of Tillabéri. Such insecurity has hindered the parties' ability to campaign and disturbed polling operations in the region. Tillabéri voter-enlistment agents have been targeted by militants, who threatened to attack anyone participating in elections. In September 2020, the CENI reported Tillabéri voter-registration figures that fell below the national average.

B3. Are the people's political choices free from domination by forces that are external to the political sphere, or by political forces that employ extrapolitical means? 2 / 4

Niger has experienced several military coups, most recently in 2010, and the influence of the military still looms over the political sphere. The government claimed to have foiled a coup attempt in 2015, though it did not produce evidence. In late 2018, multiple military officers were arrested; the timing and circumstances of the arrests appear similar to those of the alleged 2015 incident.

B4. Do various segments of the population (including ethnic, racial, religious, gender, LGBT+, and other relevant groups) have full political rights and electoral opportunities? 2 / 4

The law provides for equal opportunity for all Nigeriens to seek political office and participate in political processes. However, women have been underrepresented both in elected and cabinet positions. A parity law calls for women to hold 10 percent of parliamentary seats and 25 percent of cabinet positions. While 16 percent of the parliament was female as of 2016, the quota has historically not been respected, nor does it guarantee that women participate equally once elected or appointed to cabinet positions.

While the Hausa and Zarma (or Djerma) ethnic groups have dominated many government positions, ethnic minorities are increasingly visible in politics, particularly Tuareg and Arabs. Nomadic groups, including the Fulani, are underrepresented in elected positions and have difficulty registering to vote.

C. FUNCTIONING OF GOVERNMENT: 6 / 12

C1. Do the freely elected head of government and national legislative representatives determine the policies of the government? 2 / 4

Elected representatives were duly installed into office following the 2016 polls. However, the harassment of the opposition during the 2016 electoral period, as well as irregularities in the elections themselves, damaged the government's legitimacy.

C2. Are safeguards against official corruption strong and effective? 2 / 4

There are several anticorruption authorities and programs. The High Authority for Combating Corruption and Related Crimes (HALCIA) is the official anticorruption body. The government operates an anticorruption hotline and has established an anticorruption initiative focused on the judiciary. The HALCIA actively tracks corruption cases and informs the public of its activities. However, the government often has refused to carry through HALCIA recommendations or pursue identified corruption cases in court. Corruption is thought to be particularly high in Nigerien taxation agencies. Bribes are sometimes required to gain access to public services.

A government audit completed in February 2020 reported that as much as 76 billion CFA francs ($130 million) in public money was diverted due to the manipulation of defense procurements between 2014 and 2019. In August, the Organized Crime and Corruption Reporting Project (OCCRP) reported that two businessmen with government ties had orchestrated the diversion of funds. No prosecutions were launched based on the audit by year's end.

In recent years, the International Crisis Group (ICG) has found increasing evidence of relationships between traffickers and politicians. In 2019, an adviser to the National Assembly president was arrested in Guinea-Bissau while transporting cocaine, though there was no proof of involvement on the part of the legislature's president.

C3. Does the government operate with openness and transparency? 2 / 4

Implementation and enforcement of the 2011 Charter on Access to Public Information and Administrative Documents has been uneven. Government information related to the mining, uranium, and oil sectors, and state-operated companies, is often not disclosed.

In February 2020, Niger resumed its participation in the Extractive Industries Transparency Initiative (EITI). In 2017, Niger, a global leader in uranium production, withdrew from EITI after the organization suspended the country; EITI cited its failure to meet standards for transparent licensing allocation and contract disclosure, lack of a comprehensive public license register, and other concerns.

CIVIL LIBERTIES: 28 / 60

D. FREEDOM OF EXPRESSION AND BELIEF: 10 / 16

D1. Are there free and independent media? 2 / 4

In 2010, Niger adopted a press law eliminating prison terms for media offenses and reducing the threat of libel cases. However, journalists still face difficulties, including occasional police violence while covering protests, and detention or prosecution in response to critical or controversial reporting. Niger Search editor Samira Ibrahim Sabou was arrested in June 2020 after outgoing president Issoufou's son accused her of defamation. Sabou was released in July.

Journalists also faced scrutiny for reporting on the COVID-19 pandemic. In early March 2020, journalist Kaka Touda Mamane Goni was arrested after reporting on a suspected COVID-19 case in a Niamey hospital, which filed a complaint. Mamane was handed a suspended sentence and freed later that month.

D2. Are individuals free to practice and express their religious faith or nonbelief in public and private? 2 / 4

Freedom of religion is legally guaranteed, but there are some constraints on religious expression and worship in practice. The rise of militant groups has increased the threat of violence against Christians.

In March 2020, the government shuttered places of worship as part of its COVID-19 response; the decision was heavily criticized by Muslims, who represent the overwhelming majority of the population, and sparked protests.

In 2019, citing security concerns, the government adopted a new law that imposed greater control over religious activities, including building worship places, preaching, and religious education.

D3. Is there academic freedom, and is the educational system free from extensive political indoctrination? 3 / 4

Academic freedom is generally upheld, but insecurity and heavy-handed responses to campus protests can impede academic freedom.

D4. Are individuals free to express their personal views on political or other sensitive topics without fear of surveillance or retribution? 3 / 4

Freedom of expression is generally upheld in Niger. However, the government has shown some intolerance of criticism, and has prosecuted people over social media comments. In May 2020, Amnesty International reported that at least 10 people were arbitrarily detained over alleged cybercrime violations since March. In one of these cases, authorities gained access to an individual's WhatsApp conversations.

E. ASSOCIATIONAL AND ORGANIZATIONAL RIGHTS: 6 / 12

E1. Is there freedom of assembly? 2 / 4

Freedom of assembly is constitutionally guaranteed, but authorities do not always respect this right in practice, and police have at times used force to break up demonstrations. In 2017, the government announced the prohibition of public protests on "business days."

In March 2020, at least 15 civil society activists who organized a protest over procurement-related corruption were arrested by the authorities, and 6 were kept in detention. Authorities also used force to disperse the Niamey rally, which had been prohibited under COVID-19 measures; 3 people in a market were killed after a tear gas canister reportedly ignited the structure. Three of the detained individuals were bailed in late April, while the other three were provisionally released in late September.

E2. Is there freedom for nongovernmental organizations, particularly those that are engaged in human rights- and governance-related work? 2 / 4

The government occasionally restricts the operations of nongovernmental organizations (NGOs), and a lack of security in certain regions also impedes their functioning. The government has restricted the movement of UN personnel and aid workers without military escort in some areas, impacting the delivery of humanitarian assistance. In August 2020, staff members of NGO ACTED were among six French and two Nigeriens killed by armed assailants at a wildlife reserve.

E3. Is there freedom for trade unions and similar professional or labor organizations? 2 / 4

While the constitution and other laws guarantee workers the right to join unions and bargain for wages, a large portion of the workforce is employed informally and lacks access to formal union representation. The legal definition of "essential" workers not permitted to strike is broad, and the can invoke mandatory arbitration processes to settle strikes.

F. RULE OF LAW: 6 / 16

F1. Is there an independent judiciary? 1 / 4

The constitution provides for an independent judiciary, and courts have shown some level of independence, though the judicial system is subject to executive interference. Recent rulings against opposition leaders and civil society activists have decreased trust in the judiciary.

F2. Does due process prevail in civil and criminal matters? 2 / 4

Arbitrary arrests and imprisonments are frequent. Many people accused of crimes are held in pretrial detention for extended periods of time, sometimes in the same population as people convicted of crimes. In 2018, several military officers accused of plotting a 2015 coup against the Issoufou government received 5- to 15-year prison sentences, after spending over 2 years in pretrial detention.

States of emergency declared in several regions allow the army to engage in mass arrests and detain those suspected of links with terrorist organizations.

F3. Is there protection from the illegitimate use of physical force and freedom from war and insurgencies? 1 / 4

Nigeriens face insecurity due to ongoing militant activity. Several militant groups, including Boko Haram, are active within Nigerien territory. Militants launched several attacks against civilians and military personnel in 2020. Some 89 soldiers were killed by suspected militants who attacked an army base in the western town of Chinagodrar in January. At least 50 Boko Haram fighters were reportedly killed when government forces repelled a March attack on a military installation in Toumour. In May, Boko Haram reportedly attacked an army base in Diffa Region; at least 12 soldiers were killed. The day before local elections were held in December, Boko Haram reportedly attacked a village in Diffa, killing at least 28 people.

Criminal groups from Nigeria were observed in the southern region of Maradi in 2019, and engaged in village raids, kidnappings, sexual violence, and killings.

A reliance on nonstate armed groups to conduct counterterrorism operations has inflamed intercommunal tensions near the Niger-Mali border, leading to instances of violence. Furthermore, increased attacks on the Burkina Faso border have prompted concerns about militant activity there. The government has imposed states of emergency within the regions of Diffa, Tillabéri, and Tahoua over ongoing insecurity.

F4. Do laws, policies, and practices guarantee equal treatment of various segments of the population? 2 / 4

The rights of ethnic minority groups are protected by law. While two ethnic groups, Hausa and Zarma (or Djerma), have dominated economic leadership positions, Tuareg and Arabs are increasingly represented. Same-sex sexual activity is not illegal in Niger, but same-sex relationships are highly stigmatized, and there is no protection against discrimination based on sexual orientation. Although the 2010 constitution prohibits gender discrimination, women suffer widespread discrimination in practice. The application of the law by customary courts often discriminates against women.

Niger has made efforts to welcome Malian and Nigerian refugees and other forcibly displaced populations.

G. PERSONAL AUTONOMY AND INDIVIDUAL RIGHTS: 6 / 16

G1. Do individuals enjoy freedom of movement, including the ability to change their place of residence, employment, or education? 2 / 4

The constitution guarantees freedom of movement, but this is hampered by militant activity and bribery by security officials who guard checkpoints. COVID-19-related movement restrictions were also introduced in March 2020, when authorities closed external borders. A curfew was imposed in Niamey that month, though it was loosened in late April and lifted in May. While air travel resumed in August, authorities again tightened borders in October.

G2. Are individuals able to exercise the right to own property and establish private businesses without undue interference from state or nonstate actors? 2 / 4

Several complications undermine legal guarantees of the right to own property. Few people hold formal ownership documents for their land, though customary law provides some protection. However, the enforcement of both state and customary law often gives way to tension and confusion. Women have less access to land ownership than men due to inheritance practices and inferior status in property disputes.

G3. Do individuals enjoy personal social freedoms, including choice of marriage partner and size of family, protection from domestic violence, and control over appearance? 1 / 4

Family law gives women inferior status in divorce proceedings. Female genital mutilation (FGM) was criminalized in 2003 and has declined, but it continues among a small percentage of the population. Penalties for rape are heavy, but societal attitudes and victims' fears of retribution discourage reporting, and when rape is reported it is often poorly investigated. Domestic violence is not explicitly criminalized, though women may lodge criminal allegations of battery against partners. Some cases have resulted in convictions, but reporting is similarly discouraged in practice.

G4. Do individuals enjoy equality of opportunity and freedom from economic exploitation? 1 / 4

Although slavery was criminalized in 2003 and banned in the 2010 constitution, it remains a problem in Niger. Estimates of the number of enslaved people vary widely but is generally counted in the tens of thousands. Niger remains a source, transit point, and destination for human trafficking.

Nigeria

Population: 206,100,000
Capital: Abuja
Freedom Status: Partly Free
Electoral Democracy: No

Overview: While Nigeria has made significant improvements to the quality of its elections since the 1999 transition to democratic rule, the 2019 presidential and National Assembly elections, which saw President Muhammadu Buhari reelected and the All Progressives Caucus (APC) regain its legislative majority, were marred by irregularities. Corruption remains endemic in the key petroleum industry. Security challenges, including the ongoing insurgency by the Boko Haram militant group, kidnappings, and communal and sectarian violence in the Middle Belt region, threaten the human rights of millions of Nigerians. The military and law-enforcement agencies often engage in extrajudicial killings, torture, and other abuses. Civil liberties are undermined by religious and ethnic bias, while women and LGBT+ people face pervasive discrimination. The vibrant media landscape is impeded by criminal defamation laws, as well as the frequent harassment and arrests of journalists who cover politically sensitive topics.

KEY DEVELOPMENTS IN 2020

- In July, acting Economic and Financial Crimes Commission (EFCC) chief Ibrahim Magu was questioned by a presidential tribunal over allegations of ethics breaches. Magu was suspended that month, but no permanent chairperson was selected by year's end.
- Widespread protests were held in October, after a recording of Special Anti-Robbery Squad (SARS) officers killing an individual in Delta State was made public.

Some protests were reportedly hijacked, leading to clashes and deaths. Soldiers and police indiscriminately fired into a crowd of protesters camped near a Lagos toll gate in late October, killing at least 12.

- Insurgent violence continued throughout the year—in June, a Boko Haram splinter group abducted five aid workers in Borno State and claimed responsibility for killing them in July; the same group made four unsuccessful assassination attempts against the state's governor during the year. Boko Haram also continued its campaign, killing at least 50 soldiers in Yobe State in March and over 70 people in Borno in November.
- Nigerian states imposed COVID-19 lockdowns in March and April and a nationwide curfew was introduced in May. Security forces were excessive in their enforcement, with the National Human Rights Commission (NHRC) reporting 18 extrajudicial killings by mid-April. Some 86,576 cases and 1,278 deaths were reported to the World Health Organization by year's end.

POLITICAL RIGHTS: 21 / 40 (−1)

A. ELECTORAL PROCESS: 6 / 12

A1. Was the current head of government or other chief national authority elected through free and fair elections? 2 / 4

The president can serve a maximum of two four-year terms and is elected by a qualified majority vote. The president must also win at least 25 percent of the votes cast in 24 states. President Buhari of the APC was reelected in February 2019, winning 53 percent of the vote. People's Democratic Party (PDP) candidate Atiku Abubakar won 39 percent. Other candidates shared 8 percent of the vote.

A one-week voting delay, announced on the morning of the election, undermined confidence in the Independent National Electoral Commission (INEC). International observers noted serious irregularities when the election was held, including election-related violence, vote buying, and the intimidation of election officials and voters. Turnout, recorded at 35.7 percent, was the lowest ever recorded in Nigeria. Abubakar legally challenged the results that March, but the Supreme Court dismissed his appeal that October.

Gubernatorial and assembly elections, held in 29 states in 2019, were marred by reports of intimidation. Gubernatorial contests in Edo and Ondo states, held in September and October 2020, respectively, were relatively well conducted. However, domestic observers reported incidents of violence and intimidation in both contests. PDP candidate Godwin Nogheghase Obaseki won in Edo, while Ondo governor Oluwarotimi Akeredolu of the APC was reelected.

A2. Were the current national legislative representatives elected through free and fair elections? 2 / 4

Members of the bicameral National Assembly, consisting of the 109-seat Senate and the 360-seat House of Representatives, are elected for four-year terms.

Legislative elections were held concurrently with the February 2019 presidential election. According to INEC, the APC won 212 seats, while the PDP won 127, the All Progressives Grand Alliance (APGA) won 10, and another 7 parties won the remainder. In the Senate, the APC won 63 seats, while the PDP won 44 and the Young Progressives Party (YPP) won 1. One Senate seat was reported vacant.

Observers reported irregularities including violence, intimidation of voters and officials, and vote buying; observers noted incidents where party officials directed some voters on how to cast ballots at polling stations. INEC declined to certify winning candidates in two races because local returning officers operated under duress.

By-elections for 6 Senate seats and 9 local races that were originally scheduled for October 2020 were held in December. Turnout for these races was reportedly low.

A3. Are the electoral laws and framework fair, and are they implemented impartially by the relevant election management bodies? 2 / 4

The 1999 constitution and the Electoral Act of 2010 provide Nigeria's legal electoral framework. In 2018 and 2019, the National Assembly passed Electoral Act amendments designed to strengthen equal airtime obligations for broadcasters, make the voter register and election results more accessible to voters, and extend federal electoral regulations to local races. President Buhari vetoed the bill four times during this period, citing inconsistencies with existing law. The bill remained under consideration in the lower house as recently as November 2020.

European Union observers reported that the 2019 national elections were administered in general accordance with existing procedures but warned that the delay to presidential and congressional races that February affected voter turnout, confused voters, and undermined confidence in the electoral process. Other observers noted INEC's apparent lack of preparedness to fulfill some of its obligations; its electoral security committee, cochaired by the national security adviser, was not in operation by election day. Domestic observers considered the 2020 gubernatorial elections relatively well conducted, but those contests were affected by INEC's decision to postpone them.

B. POLITICAL PLURALISM AND PARTICIPATION: 10 / 16

B1. Do the people have the right to organize in different political parties or other competitive political groupings of their choice, and is the system free of undue obstacles to the rise and fall of these competing parties or groupings? 3 / 4

Nigerians generally have the right to organize in different political parties. There were 91 registered parties and 73 presidential candidates in 2019, the largest number of parties and candidates since the 1999 transition to democracy. INEC removed 74 parties from the register in February 2020, citing their inability to win the support of a sufficient number of voters and lack of representation nationwide. After 22 parties won an appeals-court judgment in August, INEC vowed to bring its case to the Supreme Court. That case remained pending at year's end.

A constitutional amendment signed by President Buhari in 2018 allowed independent candidates to compete in federal and state elections. The president also signed a "Not Too Young to Run" bill that same month, lowering the age of eligibility to run for political office from 40 to 35 years. However, a lack of internal party democracy and high fees make it difficult for prospective candidates to vie for major-party nominations.

B2. Is there a realistic opportunity for the opposition to increase its support or gain power through elections? 3 / 4

Nigeria's multiparty system provides an opportunity for opposition parties to gain power through elections, as demonstrated by President Buhari's 2015 victory over predecessor Goodluck Jonathan. Buhari's election marked the first time in Nigerian history that a sitting president was peacefully replaced. Opposition parties can also gain influence when legislators cross the aisle; a wave of APC legislators defected to the PDP during the 2015–19 legislative session, depriving that party of its majority.

New political parties have successfully entered the National Assembly in recent years; the YPP won its first Senate seat in 2019. The APGA, which was formed in 2003, won 10 lower-house seats in 2019. However, the APC and PDP still overshadow their competitors, occupying most elected offices in Nigeria.

B3. Are the people's political choices free from domination by forces that are external to the political sphere, or by political forces that employ extrapolitical means? 2 / 4

Citizens' political choices remain impaired or undermined by vote buying and intimidation, the influence of powerful domestic and international economic interests, and the local domination of either the military or illegal armed groups in certain regions of the country. Wealthy political sponsors, or "godfathers," dispense patronage and use their considerable influence to cultivate support for candidates who, in return, use their political offices to further enrich their backers.

Military personnel and armed gangs have been known to interfere in the voting process. INEC reported that voting stations in Rivers State were invaded by soldiers and gangs during the 2019 gubernatorial election, and local officials were unlawfully arrested.

B4. Do various segments of the population (including ethnic, racial, religious, gender, LGBT+, and other relevant groups) have full political rights and electoral opportunities? 2 / 4

Nigeria's legal framework generally provides for equal participation in political life by the country's various cultural, religious, and ethnic groups. However, politicians and parties often rely on voters' ethnic loyalties, and the interests of a given group may be poorly addressed in areas where it forms a minority or when affiliated parties are not in power.

Women enjoy formal political equality, but restrictive societal norms limit their participation in practice. Only eight women held Senate seats after the 2019 legislative elections, while 21 women were present in the House of Representatives in December 2020. Women are poorly represented in the cabinet, holding 7 of 43 posts after President Buhari named his cabinet in July 2019.

Same-sex relationships were criminalized and LGBT+ advocacy groups were banned in 2014, when former president Jonathan signed the Same-Sex Marriage (Prohibition) Act. Openly LGBT+ people are deterred from running for office or working to advance their political interests.

C. FUNCTIONING OF GOVERNMENT: 5 / 12 (−1)

C1. Do the freely elected head of government and national legislative representatives determine the policies of the government? 2 / 4

Elected officials generally make and implement policy in Nigeria, but are impaired by factors including corruption, partisan conflict, poor control over areas where militant groups are active, and the president's undisclosed health problems, which have caused him to seek treatment abroad in recent years.

President Buhari has demonstrated a willingness to obstruct government bodies while in office. In September 2019, Buhari appointed an economic advisory council that superseded a constitutionally mandated economic-management body chaired by Vice President Yemi Osinbajo. That November, Nigerian media reported that Buhari had dismissed 35 of Osinbajo's aides, and that Osinbajo was bypassed on several presidential decisions. Access to the president was also tightly controlled by a powerful chief of staff, Abba Kyari, who died of COVID-19 in April 2020.

C2. Are safeguards against official corruption strong and effective? 1 / 4 (−1)

The government has attempted to reduce corruption in public and private institutions, but the practice remains pervasive, particularly in the oil and security sectors. A whistleblower policy introduced in 2016, which rewards Nigerians who provide information on government corruption, led to the recovery of 594 billion naira ($1.6 billion) by late 2019, according to the finance ministry.

Nigeria has sought to recover funds reportedly stolen by late president Sani Abacha (1993–98), though members of his family have contested those efforts. In February 2020, over $300 million in funds laundered through the US financial system and held by a family member were returned.

Nigerian politicians have been locked in an effort to curb corruption in the petroleum sector since at least 2001, when legislators first considered an expansive Petroleum Industry Bill (PIB). Legislators later split the PIB into several components to secure its passage. The National Assembly passed the first component, a Petroleum Industry Governance Bill, in 2018, which Buhari refused to sign. Buhari introduced a new PIB to the National Assembly in September 2020, which remained under legislative consideration at year's end.

Nigerian customs officials have also been susceptible to corruption, allowing smuggled goods to enter the country through porous customs checks in return for bribes. In response, Nigeria closed its borders with Benin and Niger in 2019. The Nigeria Employers' Consultative Association, an umbrella organization for private businesses, criticized the decision and called for a campaign to improve customs practices instead. The Economic Community of West African States (ECOWAS), which counts all three countries as members, also objected, warning that the border closure would hamper the region's free-trade agreement. The Nigerian government reopened the borders in mid-December 2020.

In July 2020, acting EFCC chief Ibrahim Magu, who held the post since 2016, was reportedly arrested by security agents and compelled to attend a presidential tribunal over allegations that he sold seized assets and engaged in other ethics breaches. While the government denied that he was detained, Magu was suspended that month. EFCC operations chief Mohammed Umar was named acting chairman, though a permanent chairperson was not selected by year's end.

Score Change: The score declined from 2 to 1 because the chairman of the country's financial crimes commission was suspended on suspicion of corruption in July.

C3. Does the government operate with openness and transparency? 2 / 4

The 2011 Freedom of Information Act (FOIA) guarantees the right to access public records, but nongovernmental organizations (NGOs) have criticized government agencies for routinely refusing to release information sought through the law. The law has also encountered resistance in some states. In 2018, Lagos State declined to make its education budget public in response to a freedom-of-information request. In 2019, an Edo state court ruled that the federal act did not apply in states that did not adopt it. In April 2020, the *Premium Times* reported that 16 states had not adopted the FOIA or developed a parallel transparency mechanism.

CIVIL LIBERTIES: 24 / 60 (−1)

D. FREEDOM OF EXPRESSION AND BELIEF: 9 / 16

D1. Are there free and independent media? 2 / 4

Freedoms of speech, expression, and the press are constitutionally guaranteed. However, these rights are limited by sedition, criminal defamation, and so-called false-news laws. Sharia (Islamic law) statutes in 12 northern states impose severe penalties for alleged press offenses. Internet service providers (ISPs) sometimes block websites at the request of the Nigerian Communications Commission, particularly those advocating independence for the secessionist state of Biafra, which collapsed in 1970. The government has accused journalists of undermining national security when reporting on operations against Boko Haram. Officials restrict press freedom by publicly criticizing, harassing, and arresting journalists, especially when they cover corruption, human-rights violations, separatist and communal violence, or other politically sensitive topics.

At least two Nigerian journalists were killed in 2020. In January, *Regent Africa Times* editor Alex Ogbu died while covering an Abuja protest organized by the Islamic Movement of Nigeria (IMN). While the authorities claimed Ogbu accidentally died, news site Sahara Reporters reported that Ogbu was shot by police. In October, Gboah TV reporter Onifade Emmanuel Pelumi died in Lagos State; Pelumi, who was covering an attempted robbery, was reportedly shot by police and was taken into custody before he was later found dead.

Nigerian authorities also used COVID-19 measures to detain journalists or impede their work. In April 2020, police in Ebonyi State arrested *Sun* correspondent Chijioke Agwu, who the governor accused of publishing "false and damaging" information. Agwu was later released without charge.

D2. Are individuals free to practice and express their religious faith or nonbelief in public and private? 1 / 4

Religious freedom is constitutionally protected, but the government has also embarked on crackdowns against religious groups that have questioned its authority. Nigeria has been locked in a long struggle against Boko Haram, a militant group that has itself targeted moderate Muslims and Christians along with their respective houses of worship. State and local governments have been known to endorse de facto official religions in their territory, placing limits on religious activity.

The government's conflict with the IMN, a Shiite Muslim group that advocates for Islamic rule in Nigeria, escalated in August 2019, when an Abuja court banned it and labeled it a terrorist organization. The move came after the IMN and security forces in Abuja clashed that July. The IMN considers its leader, Sheikh Ibrahim el-Zakzaky, to be the ultimate source of authority in Nigeria, and does not recognize the government in Abuja.

The government has responded violently to IMN activity in recent years. In 2015, security forces raided el-Zakzaky's compound, arrested him and his wife, and killed at least 300 IMN members. Dozens more were killed in a 2018 army operation. Despite a 2016 court order to release him, el-Zakzaky and his wife were only freed in 2019 to seek medical attention in India. El-Zakzaky elected to return to custody in Nigeria, claiming his medical team was altered without his permission and objecting to security restrictions in India. In November 2020, the Nigerian *Guardian* newspaper reported that a homicide trial against el-Zakzaky and his wife had begun in the Kaduna High Court.

Individuals who express nonbelief can face legal consequences. In April 2020, Mubarak Bala, a humanist, was arrested in Kaduna State for social media comments criticizing Islam. Bala, who was charged with blasphemy, was transferred to Kano State, and remained detained at year's end.

D3. Is there academic freedom, and is the educational system free from extensive political indoctrination? 3 / 4

The federal government generally respects academic freedom. However, some state governments mandate religious instruction in elementary and secondary curriculums and student admission and faculty hiring policies are subject to political interference. Boko Haram's assault on secular education has included the closure or destruction of primary, secondary, and tertiary institutions. In 2018, the UN Children's Fund (UNICEF) reported that as many as three million children in the north were left without access to a school as a result. Boko Haram has continued targeting schoolchildren; in December 2020, it claimed responsibility for the disappearance of over 300 students in Katsina State, though they were released a week later.

Students have faced ill-treatment in unregulated Islamic schools, which have operated for decades. Some parents have patronized these schools for corrective services, as a robust juvenile-rehabilitation system is lacking in much of Nigeria.

D4. Are individuals free to express their personal views on political or other sensitive topics without fear of surveillance or retribution? 3 / 4

Nigerians are generally free to engage in discussions on politics and other topics, though expression of critical views on political leaders or sensitive subjects like the military, religion, and ethnicity occasionally leads to arrests or violent reprisals.

By 2018, the National Assembly passed a Digital Rights and Freedom Bill, which would expand freedom of expression online by regulating government surveillance and prohibiting the suspension of internet services. The bill was sent to the president in 2019, but Buhari declined to sign it, stating that it covered too many technical subjects and did not address them extensively. A revised bill was under legislative consideration at the end of 2020.

Legislators considered bills on hate speech and on the dissemination of purportedly false statements in 2020. The false-statements bill would impose fines, a one-year prison sentence, or both against offenders, while the hate-speech bill would allow the death penalty for speech that is linked to the death of another person. NGOs including Amnesty International and the Nigerian Union of Journalists harshly criticized the false-statements bill in front of the Senate judiciary committee in March. Both bills remained under consideration at year's end.

E. ASSOCIATIONAL AND ORGANIZATIONAL RIGHTS: 6 / 12 (−1)
E1. Is there freedom of assembly? 1 / 4 (−1)

The right to peaceful assembly is constitutionally guaranteed. However, federal and state governments frequently ban public events perceived as threats to national security, including those that could incite political, ethnic, or religious tension. Rights groups have criticized federal and state governments for prohibiting or dispersing protests that are critical of authorities or associated with controversial groups, including the separatist Indigenous People of Biafra. IMN activities were banned in 2019 after an Abuja court classified it as a terrorist organization.

Nigerians held regular protests against police brutality in October 2020, days after a recording of SARS officers killing an individual in Delta State was made public. An early protest in Abuja was met with force, with officers using tear gas on participants. Government agencies also employed other methods to target protesters and organizers, with the Central Bank of Nigeria ordering a freeze on the accounts of NGOs and individuals suspected of involvement. While Inspector General Mohammed Adamu announced the dissolution of SARS on October 11th, widespread protests over police conduct continued.

While most protests held under the #EndSARS banner were peaceful, Amnesty International Nigeria reported that some were hijacked, leading to violent clashes and deaths. On October 20th, Lagos state governor Babajide Sanwo-Olu ordered a one-day curfew in response. That evening, soldiers and police opened fire on protesters camped near a toll gate in the city, killing at least 12 and injuring scores more; Human Rights Watch (HRW) reported that protest-ers were indiscriminately shot, while Amnesty International reported that closed-circuit televi-sion (CCTV) cameras were removed in "a clear attempt to hide evidence." In late November, Inspector General Adamu reported that 102 people died during the protests.

Score Change: The score declined from 2 to 1 because the authorities responded to October demonstrations against the conduct of Nigerian police with force, using tear gas to disperse a protest, indiscriminately firing on a group of protesters later in the month, and working to hide evidence of their activities.

E2. Is there freedom for nongovernmental organizations, particularly those that are engaged in human rights- and governance-related work? 2 / 4

Nigeria has a broad and vibrant civil society. However, members of some organizations face intimidation and physical harm for speaking out against Boko Haram, or encounter obstacles when investigating alleged human rights abuses committed by the military against Boko Haram suspects. Aid workers operating in the northeast are additionally impeded by restrictions imposed by civilian and military officials. Groups operating in the restive Niger Delta region, meanwhile, also face intimidation.

The Islamic State West Africa Province (ISWAP), a Boko Haram splinter group, an-nounced that it would target humanitarian workers in June 2020, and abducted five aid workers in Borno State that month. The group claimed responsibility for killing them in July. ISWAP abducted two local officials and an aid worker in Borno in December.

E3. Is there freedom for trade unions and similar professional or labor organizations? 3 / 4

Under the constitution, workers have the right to form and join trade unions, engage in collective bargaining, and conduct strikes. Nevertheless, the government forbids strike action in some essential services, including public transportation and security. In February 2020, the Academic Staff Union of Universities launched a strike over the nonpayment of allowances and the implementation of a new payment system; the two sides reached an agreement in December. The National Association of Resident Doctors launched strikes in June and Sep-tember over matters including pay and a lack of personal protective equipment (PPE).

F. RULE OF LAW: 4 / 16

F1. Is there an independent judiciary? 2 / 4

Judicial independence is constitutionally and legally enshrined. The judiciary has achieved some degree of independence and professionalism in practice, but political inter-ference, corruption, equipment, and training remain important problems.

Former Supreme Court chief justice Walter Onnoghen was suspended over his alleged maintenance of undisclosed assets in January 2019. His suspension was announced weeks before the presidential election, sparking fears of a politically motivated effort to remove Onnoghen. Onnoghen was convicted of falsely declaring assets that April, receiving a 10-year ban from holding public office. While an appeals court ruled that Onnoghen's suspen-sion violated his fair-hearing rights, his passport was seized that December. A lawyer acting as a concerned citizen sued over the seizure and the reported lack of severance, but that suit was dismissed in October 2020.

Funding is also a problem for the judiciary. In May 2020, President Buhari signed an executive order ostensibly giving state-level judiciaries and legislatures financial autonomy. The country's 36 state governors sued the federal government in September, alleging that it sought to avoid its financial responsibilities through the order.

F2. Does due process prevail in civil and criminal matters? 1 / 4

There have been numerous allegations of extortion and bribe taking within the police force. Federal and state authorities have been criticized for disregarding due process, with prolonged pretrial detention of suspects even after courts ordered their release on bail.

According to a 2019 HRW report, thousands of children suspected of supporting Boko Haram were detained by the military; detained children reportedly received no educational services and were sometimes abused by soldiers. In July 2020, the United Nations reported that children with suspected Boko Haram ties still faced military detention, but UN staff could not report on how many children were held between January 2017 and December 2019 because they lacked access to detention facilities. The Nigerian military released nearly 1,600 children during that reporting period. Authorities released another 223 children in March 2020. A UN working group on children and conflict called on Nigeria to release all children in detention in December.

F3. Is there protection from the illegitimate use of physical force and freedom from war and insurgencies? 0 / 4

The military has been repeatedly criticized by local and international human rights groups for extrajudicial killings, torture, and other abuses, including during counterinsurgency efforts in the northeast and operations against separatist movements in the southeast. Police forces have been accused of similar behavior; in June 2020, Amnesty International reported that SARS was responsible for at least 82 cases of torture, ill-treatment, or extrajudicial killings between 2017 and May 2020.

Sharia courts that operate in Nigeria are known to impose the death penalty. In August 2020, a Sharia court in Kano State handed Yahaya Sharif-Aminu a death sentence over recorded comments that were considered blasphemous. Sharif-Aminu appealed the verdict in September, and a state appeals court was expected to hear the case in November.

Boko Haram continued to attack government forces and civilians in 2020. In March, Boko Haram killed at least 50 soldiers in an ambush in Yobe State. In November, over 70 people in Borno State, most of them farmers, were killed by Boko Haram fighters in an incident the United Nations called "the most violent direct attack against innocent civilians in Nigeria this year." The Council on Foreign Relations (CFR) reported that Boko Haram was responsible for 2,720 deaths in Borno State alone in 2020, compared to 1,136 in 2019. Top of Form

ISWAP also attacked officials and civilians in 2020. Borno state governor Babagana Zulum was targeted by the group four times during the year, surviving a July attack on his convoy, two attacks in September, and a late-November attack. ISWAP was also blamed for an attack in Borno State that killed as many as 81 people in June, along with twin attacks that killed dozens more several days later.

A rolling conflict between farmers and the Fulani, a seminomadic Muslim ethnic group, continued to destabilize northern Nigeria in 2020. The Fulani have abandoned degraded grasslands in the north, coming into increased conflict with farmers as they travel south to find new grazing lands. Banditry in the northwestern states of Kaduna, Katsina, and Zamfara have also resulted in fatalities; at least 57 people died in a bandit attack on six villages in Katsina in June 2020. In May, the International Crisis Group reported that over 200,000 people have been displaced in the northwest since 2011, with some fleeing to Niger.

Various vigilante groups are active in Nigeria, with the National Assembly attempting to give official recognition to the Vigilante Group of Nigeria (VGN) in 2017. Buhari refused to sign legislation recognizing the group in 2018, though legislators attempted to secure recognition again in 2019. In September 2020, the VGN called on the federal government to incorporate it in a new community-policing initiative, but it still lacked official recognition at year's end.

Kidnapping has become an acute concern in Nigeria. While Boko Haram is known to employ this tactic, the US Consulate General in Lagos also noted its increasing use by criminals demanding ransom, as well as by factions in intercommunal conflicts. In May 2020, a Nigerian consulting firm reported that as much as $18 million was paid in ransom since 2011.

F4. Do laws, policies, and practices guarantee equal treatment of various segments of the population? 1 / 4

Despite constitutional safeguards against ethnic discrimination, many ethnic minorities experience bias by state governments and other societal groups in areas including employment, education, and housing.

Women are subject to widespread societal discrimination regarding matters such as education and employment. Many poor families choose to send sons to school while daughters become street vendors or domestic workers. Women also face significant legal disadvantages in states governed by Sharia statutes.

LGBT+ Nigerians face widespread discrimination by the government and society at large. Nigerians convicted of engaging in same-sex relationships can be imprisoned for as long as 14 years due to federal legislation enacted in 2014, while 12 northern states maintain the death penalty for same-sex relations. LGBT+ people are also subject to assault by police officers during arrests, extortion attempts, and discrimination when accessing public and private services. A 2019 survey showed widespread opposition to LGBT+ rights, with 74 percent of respondents supporting prison sentences for those engaging in same-sex activity.

G. PERSONAL AUTONOMY AND INDIVIDUAL RIGHTS: 5 / 16

G1. Do individuals enjoy freedom of movement, including the ability to change their place of residence, employment, or education? 1 / 4

While the freedom of movement is legally guaranteed, security officials frequently impose dusk-to-dawn curfews and other movement restrictions in areas affected by communal violence or by Boko Haram activities. According to the UN High Commissioner for Refugees, over 2.1 million people were internally displaced nationwide at the end of 2020.

Freedom of movement was also curtailed by COVID-19 measures, with states imposing lockdowns in March and April and a nationwide curfew being imposed in May. In mid-April 2020, the NHRC recorded 27 incidents of freedom-of-movement violations or unlawful arrests, along with 18 extrajudicial killings by authorities enforcing pandemic-related measures. A nationwide curfew remained in effect at year's end.

G2. Are individuals able to exercise the right to own property and establish private businesses without undue interference from state or nonstate actors? 2 / 4

Nigeria's poorly regulated property rights system hinders citizens and private businesses from engaging in the efficient and legal purchase or sale of property, including land. Bribery is a common practice when starting a business and registering property. However, the climate for private enterprise in recent years has benefited from advancements in credit accessibility, ease of starting a business, ease of paying taxes, and property registration.

Women belonging to certain ethnic groups are often denied equal rights to inherit property due to customary laws and practices.

G3. Do individuals enjoy personal social freedoms, including choice of marriage partner and size of family, protection from domestic violence, and control over appearance? 1 / 4

Despite the existence of strict laws against rape, domestic violence, female genital mutilation (FGM), and child marriage, these offenses remain widespread, with low rates of reporting and prosecution. Women and girls in camps for displaced persons have reported sexual abuse by members of the military and other authorities. Boko Haram's attacks on women's rights have been particularly egregious, with victims often subjected to forced marriage and rape, among other acts.

Governors in all 36 states declared a state of emergency over sexual violence in June 2020, after the May rape and murder of a woman in an Edo State church, the rape and murder of a woman in Oyo State in June, and the rape of a girl in Jigawa State triggered protests. In their declaration, the governors vowed to impose federal laws and establish sex-offender registries.

Abortion is illegal unless the life of the mother is in danger. As a result, many women seek out dangerous illegal abortions, finding themselves at risk of medical complications. Women who face such complications often do not receive further medical treatment.

G4. Do individuals enjoy equality of opportunity and freedom from economic exploitation? 1 / 4

Nigerian organized crime groups are heavily involved in human trafficking. Boko Haram has subjected children to forced labor and sex slavery. Both Boko Haram and a civilian vigilante group that opposes the militants have forcibly recruited child soldiers, according to the US State Department.

Meanwhile, implementation of the 2003 Child Rights Act, which protects children from sexual exploitation and other abuses, remains uneven; in 2019, a UNICEF child protection specialist noted that 11 northern states have not implemented the legislation.

The National Agency for the Prohibition of Trafficking in Persons (NAPTIP) continues to rescue trafficking survivors and prosecute some suspected traffickers, but its funding is reportedly inadequate, and few prosecutions against labor traffickers are uncommon. Trafficking survivors often find their freedom of movement withheld by NAPTIP in poorly managed shelters, and experience discrimination when seeking access to public services after their release.

North Korea

Population: 25,800,000
Capital: Pyongyang
Freedom Status: Not Free
Electoral Democracy: No

Overview: North Korea is a one-party state led by a dynastic totalitarian dictatorship. Surveillance is pervasive, arbitrary arrests and detention are common, and punishments for political offenses are severe. The state maintains a system of camps for political prisoners where torture, forced labor, starvation, and other atrocities take place. While some social and economic changes have been observed in recent years, including a growth in small-scale private business activity, human rights violations are still widespread, grave, and systematic.

KEY DEVELOPMENTS IN 2020

- Authorities closed North Korea's borders beginning in January in an effort to prevent the spread of COVID-19 into the country. The government also sharply restricted internal movement and enforced lockdowns and quarantines for high-risk areas and people. Those who violated the rules near the border risked summary execution. North Korea did not officially report any domestic cases of COVID-19 during the year, despite numerous reports of suspected cases.

- There were no formal diplomatic negotiations with either the United States or South Korea in 2020, and relations remain strained. In June, North Korean authorities destroyed the inter-Korean liaison office in Kaesong and threatened broader military measures, but these did not ultimately materialize.

- In September, a South Korean fisheries official crossed into North Korean waters in a possible attempt to defect to the North. Soldiers who found the official shot him and then burned his body, apparently following disease-control protocols. While North Korean leader Kim Jong-un sent an apology to the South Korean president for the incident, South Korean and international authorities called for further investigation.

POLITICAL RIGHTS: 0 / 40

A. ELECTORAL PROCESS: 0 / 12

A1. Was the current head of government or other chief national authority elected through free and fair elections? 0 / 4

Kim Jong-un became the country's supreme leader after the death of his father, Kim Jong-il, in 2011. The elder Kim had led North Korea since the 1994 death of his own father, Kim Il-sung, to whom the office of president was permanently dedicated in a 1998 constitutional revision. In 2016, the State Affairs Commission (SAC) was established as the country's top ruling organ, and Kim Jong-un was named its chairman. Kim has held a variety of other titles, including first chairman of the National Defense Commission—previously the highest state body—and supreme commander of the Korean People's Army.

In March 2019, Kim was reelected as SAC chairman by the Supreme People's Assembly (SPA), the country's legislature, and given the new title of "supreme representative of all the Korean people and the supreme leader of the Republic." Choe Ryong-hae, a highly placed aide to Kim who also holds multiple titles, became vice-chairman of the SAC and head of the SPA's 15-member Presidium, a standing committee that manages the legislature's day-to-day affairs when the full body is not in session.

In August 2020, reports suggested that Kim Jong-un had delegated more power to senior officials, including his sister, Kim Yo-jong, who is now understood to be in charge of relations with the United States and South Korea.

A2. Were the current national legislative representatives elected through free and fair elections? 0 / 4

Members of the 687-seat SPA, North Korea's unicameral legislature, are elected to five-year terms. All candidates are preselected by the Democratic Front for the Reunification of the Fatherland (DFRF), a coalition dominated by the ruling Korean Workers' Party (KWP) alongside a handful of subordinate parties and organizations. Each candidate then runs unopposed. Voting is compulsory for citizens who are at least 17 years old, and turnout commonly approaches 100 percent.

Elections for the SPA were held in March 2019, with voters endorsing preselected candidates for all 687 seats. Turnout was reported at 99.99 percent. Local elections were held in late July 2019, filling 27,876 posts; voter turnout was reported at 99.98 percent.

A3. Are the electoral laws and framework fair, and are they implemented impartially by the relevant election management bodies? 0 / 4

Although there is a clear framework for conducting elections, including official election monitors, the system's structure denies voters any choice and rules out any opposition to the incumbent leadership. The government uses the mandatory elections as an unofficial census, keeping track of whether and how people voted, and interprets any rejection of the preselected candidates as treason.

B. POLITICAL PLURALISM AND PARTICIPATION: 0 / 16

B1. Do the people have the right to organize in different political parties or other competitive political groupings of their choice, and is the system free of undue obstacles to the rise and fall of these competing parties or groupings? 0 / 4

North Korea is effectively a one-party state. Although a small number of minor parties and organizations legally exist, all are members of the DFRF.

B2. Is there a realistic opportunity for the opposition to increase its support or gain power through elections? 0 / 4

Any political dissent or opposition is prohibited and harshly punished. The country has been ruled by the KWP since its founding, and the party itself has always been controlled by the Kim family; Kim Jong-un became chairman of the KWP in 2016. His late father, Kim Jong-il, was dubbed the "eternal general secretary" of the party after his death.

B3. Are the people's political choices free from domination by forces that are external to the political sphere, or by political forces that employ extrapolitical means? 0 / 4

The general public has no opportunity for political participation, and even KWP elites operate under the threat of extreme penalties for perceived dissent or disloyalty. The party is subject to regular purges aimed at reinforcing the leader's personal authority, and the regime has executed senior officials who have fallen out of favor with Kim Jong-un.

B4. Do various segments of the population (including ethnic, racial, religious, gender, LGBT+, and other relevant groups) have full political rights and electoral opportunities? 0 / 4

North Korea is ethnically homogeneous, with only a small Chinese population and a few non-Chinese foreign residents. Foreigners are not allowed to join the KWP or serve in the military or government. Religious groups are harshly suppressed and unable to organize politically. Women hold few leadership positions in the ruling party and hold only 121 of the SPA's 687 seats; the system does not allow these representatives to independently address the interests of women. The government typically denies the existence of LGBT+ people in North Korea.

C. FUNCTIONING OF GOVERNMENT: 0 / 12

C1. Do the freely elected head of government and national legislative representatives determine the policies of the government? 0 / 4

North Korea has no freely elected officials. Kim Jong-un and his inner circle determine the policies of the government, and the SPA gathers periodically to unanimously approve all decisions. In 2020, the SPA held sessions in April and November.

C2. Are safeguards against official corruption strong and effective? 0 / 4

Corruption is believed to be endemic at every level of the state and economy, and government officials commonly engage in bribery. There are no independent or impartial anticorruption mechanisms.

Small-scale local markets have become a prime target of corrupt police officers, who solicit bribes from the operators and detain those who cannot pay. Market participants also pay bribes to supervisors at their official workplaces, to avoid discipline or imprisonment for abandoning their state-assigned roles. A 2020 Human Rights Watch report on the country's prison system noted that North Koreans often paid bribes to avoid arrest, mitigate their treatment while in detention, and secure family visits.

C3. Does the government operate with openness and transparency? 0 / 4

The government is neither transparent in its operations nor accountable to the public. Information about the functioning of state institutions is tightly controlled for both domestic and external audiences.

The authorities heavily restricted information about the status of the COVID-19 pandemic during 2020. Officials disclosed only fragmentary data regarding key aspects of its response, such as quarantines and testing. The government eventually reported thousands of "suspected" cases, but claimed that no infections were confirmed and attributed no deaths to the virus.

CIVIL LIBERTIES: 3 / 60
D. FREEDOM OF EXPRESSION AND BELIEF: 0 / 16
D1. Are there free and independent media? 0 / 4

All domestic media outlets are run by the state. Televisions and radios are permanently fixed to state channels, and all publications and broadcasts are subject to strict supervision and censorship. The government occasionally allows a small number of foreign books, films, and television programs to be distributed and aired in the country, but this remains rare.

In recent years, several foreign news agencies have established bureau offices in Pyongyang. North Korea allowed the Associated Press (AP) to open the country's first foreign bureau in 2012, though it is no longer active. The AP was followed by Japanese agency Kyodo News, China's Xinhua, and Agence France-Presse (AFP), which still maintain a physical presence in the country. Access for these organizations is tightly controlled, and the government has been known to expel media crews in retaliation for their work. Select foreign media services are often invited to the country to cover key political events and holidays, although authorities strictly manage their visits.

Voice of America (VOA), Radio Free Asia (RFA), the British Broadcasting Corporation (BBC), and several South Korean outlets broadcast shortwave and medium-wave Korean-language radio programming into North Korea, though the government works to jam these stations.

Campaigns to send information into the country via USB thumb drives, SD cards, and leaflets have been common, and North Koreans have constructed homemade radios to receive foreign broadcasts. However, in December 2020, the South Korean authorities banned the act of sending leaflets and other information across the border without government permission. The consumption of foreign radio broadcasts and possession of contraband devices are subject to severe punishment, potentially including the death penalty, if detected by North Korean authorities.

D2. Are individuals free to practice and express their religious faith or nonbelief in public and private? 0 / 4

Although freedom of religion is guaranteed by the constitution, it does not exist in practice. State-sanctioned churches maintain a token presence in Pyongyang, and some

North Koreans are known to practice their faith furtively. However, intense state indoctrination and repression preclude free and open exercise of religion. Crackdowns are common, and North Koreans caught practicing a religious faith are arrested and subjected to harsh punishments, including imprisonment in labor camps. Foreigners caught proselytizing also risk arrest and detention.

D3. Is there academic freedom, and is the educational system free from extensive political indoctrination? 0 / 4

There is no academic freedom. The state must approve all curriculums, including those of educational programs led by foreigners. Although some North Koreans are permitted to study abroad at both universities and short-term educational training programs, those granted such opportunities are subject to monitoring and reprisals for perceived disloyalty.

D4. Are individuals free to express their personal views on political or other sensitive topics without fear of surveillance or retribution? 0 / 4

Nearly all forms of private communication are monitored by a huge network of informants. Domestic third-generation (3G) mobile service has been available since 2008, with an estimated five or six million users nationally. Mobile phones operating on this network are used as surveillance tools by the state, which can review individuals' application usage and intranet browsing history and take screenshots of their activity. Newer mobile phones have been designed to block users' efforts to consume contraband media.

Ordinary mobile users do not have access to the global internet, but can connect to a state-run intranet. Only a small number of elites have internet access, reaching it through their own service. Domestic and international mobile services are kept strictly separate, and crackdowns on users with Chinese-origin phones have been reported.

E. ASSOCIATIONAL AND ORGANIZATIONAL RIGHTS: 0 / 12

E1. Is there freedom of assembly? 0 / 4

Freedom of assembly is not recognized, and participants in any unauthorized gatherings are subject to severe punishment, including prison sentences.

E2. Is there freedom for nongovernmental organizations, particularly those that are engaged in human rights- and governance-related work? 0 / 4

There are no legal associations or organizations other than those created by the state and ruling party.

E3. Is there freedom for trade unions and similar professional or labor organizations? 0 / 4

Strikes, collective bargaining, and other organized labor activities are illegal and can draw severe punishment for participants, including prison sentences.

F. RULE OF LAW: 0 / 16

F1. Is there an independent judiciary? 0 / 4

North Korea's judiciary is subordinate to the political leadership in law and in practice. According to the constitution, the Central Court, the country's highest court, is accountable to the SPA, and its duties include protecting "state power and the socialist system."

F2. Does due process prevail in civil and criminal matters? 0 / 4

Fundamental due process rights, including freedom from arbitrary detention and the right to a fair trial, are systematically denied. As many as 120,000 political prisoners are thought to be held in internment camps in the country. Foreign visitors are also at risk of arbitrary detention. At least four South Korean citizens, the first of whom was seized in 2013, remained in custody as of 2020; they were accused of a range of crimes, including espionage and kidnapping.

In April 2020, unofficial reports claimed that the government had granted a mass amnesty to inmates who had displayed model behavior during their sentences. In August, the SPA Presidium was reported to have decreed an amnesty for those who had been convicted of "crimes against the country and the people," set to take effect in September. It remained unclear how many prisoners were affected by the two reported amnesties.

F3. Is there protection from the illegitimate use of physical force and freedom from war and insurgencies? 0 / 4

Documented North Korean human rights violations include widespread torture, public executions, forced labor by detainees, and death sentences for political offenses. Defectors who seek safety in third countries are sometimes returned to North Korea, where they are subject to torture and disproportionate punishment. China's government considers North Korean escapees to be irregular economic migrants and regularly turns them back, in violation of international law.

In September 2020, North Korean soldiers reportedly shot and burned the body of a missing South Korean fisheries official who may have been attempting to defect across the maritime border. According to media reports, the North Korean regime had recently ordered security personnel to open fire in the event of unauthorized entries into restricted border zones, ostensibly as part of its effort to prevent the spread of COVID-19. Kim Jong-un offered an apology for the incident; South Korean and international authorities called for an investigation.

The unresolved conflict with South Korea remains a threat to physical security, as does North Korea's nuclear weapons program in particular. Negotiations with Seoul and the United States remained stalled in 2020. North Korean forces test-launched a series of short-range missiles and projectiles in March and April. In June, the regime cut off all communication with the South after human rights groups sent leaflets over the border. It then destroyed the inter-Korean liaison office located near the border town of Kaesong.

F4. Do laws, policies, and practices guarantee equal treatment of various segments of the population? 0 / 4

The most prevalent form of discrimination is based on perceived political and ideological nonconformity rather than ethnicity. All citizens are classified according to their family's level of loyalty and proximity to the leadership under a semihereditary caste-like system known as *songbun*. Those who are classified as "wavering" or "hostile" under the system, as opposed to "loyal," face official discrimination in employment, live in poorer housing, and receive limited access to education, though the rules can be manipulated through bribery. Family members of suspected political and ideological dissidents are also subject to punishment in what amounts to guilt by association.

Members of the ethnic Chinese population in North Korea have limited options for education and employment, though they have somewhat more freedom to travel across the border and engage in trade. In January 2020, there were reports that Chinese residents were required to participate in North Korean political events and related monetary contributions, from which they were historically exempted.

Women have legal equality, but they face rigid discrimination in practice and are poorly represented in public employment and the military. Although they have fewer opportunities in the formal sector, women are economically active outside the socialist system, which can expose them to arbitrary state interference.

The law does not explicitly prohibit same-sex relations, but the government maintains that the practice does not exist in the country.

North Korea has historically denied the rights of people living with disabilities. Defectors report that disabled people have been quarantined, exiled, forcibly sterilized, experimented on, and sometimes executed. The UN special rapporteur for disability rights visited North Korea in 2017 but was escorted by government minders, prohibited from reviewing internal data, and denied access to a mental health institution during her trip.

G. PERSONAL AUTONOMY AND INDIVIDUAL RIGHTS: 3 / 16

G1. Do individuals enjoy freedom of movement, including the ability to change their place of residence, employment, or education? 0 / 4

Residents have no freedom of movement, and forced internal resettlement is routine. Emigration is illegal. In recent years, North Korean authorities have employed stricter domestic controls in an effort to arrest the flow of defectors. While more than 2,700 defectors arrived in South Korea in 2011, the annual number had plunged to just over 1,000 by 2019, and only 229 were reported in 2020 amid tighter pandemic-related travel restrictions across the region.

The regime imposed severe new limits on movement in response to COVID-19 during the year, including the reported "shoot on sight" orders for security forces patrolling restricted border zones. In November, South Korean officials said the North had executed a citizen for violating quarantine measures by bringing goods through customs in the border city of Sinuiju. In addition to promptly closing borders in January, the government initially closed schools, postponed major events, and required the use of protective clothing while on public transportation. Tens of thousands of people were held in quarantine during the year; state authorities said they had released more than 32,000 people from quarantine as of October, but the total number of people quarantined was not disclosed.

A person's *songbun* classification affects his or her place of residence as well as employment and educational opportunities, access to medical facilities, and even access to stores. All foreign travel—whether for work, trade, or educational opportunities—is strictly controlled by the government. Freedom of movement for foreigners in North Korea is also limited and subject to arbitrary constraints.

Most North Korean workers are unable to freely choose their employment, with the government assigning men and unmarried women to their positions and often denying monetary compensation. Workers, especially women, seek informal employment to earn an income, and pay bribes to their official employers to cover their absences.

G2. Are individuals able to exercise the right to own property and establish private businesses without undue interference from state or nonstate actors? 1 / 4

The formal economy remains both centrally planned and grossly mismanaged. Business activity is also hobbled by a lack of infrastructure, a scarcity of energy and raw materials, an inability to borrow on world markets or from multilateral banks because of sanctions, lingering foreign debt, and ideological isolationism.

However, expanding informal and government-approved private markets and service industries have provided many North Koreans, especially women, with a growing field of activity that is somewhat free from government control. The Korea Institute for National Unification (KINU), a South Korean government agency, reported that women earned over 70 percent of household income in North Korea as recently as 2018, attributing this to their participation in local markets.

Local officials have had some discretion in the management of special economic zones and over small-scale experiments with market-oriented economic policies.

G3. Do individuals enjoy personal social freedoms, including choice of marriage partner and size of family, protection from domestic violence, and control over appearance? 1 / 4

Men and women have formal equality in personal status matters such as marriage and divorce. However, sexual and physical violence against women—in the home, in prisons and labor camps, and in other situations—is common, and victims have little legal recourse. There are no specific legal penalties for domestic violence. UN bodies have noted the use of forced abortions and infanticide against women who are pregnant when forcibly repatriated from China.

G4. Do individuals enjoy equality of opportunity and freedom from economic exploitation? 1 / 4

Forced labor is common in prison camps, mass mobilization programs, and state-run contracting arrangements in which North Korean workers are sent abroad. Criminal human-trafficking networks, sometimes operating with the assistance of government officials, target North Korean women; those ensnared by this activity are subject to sex slavery and forced marriages, often in neighboring China.

Some women in North Korea have also turned to prostitution to survive in recent years, and are exploited by their employers and by police officers. In August 2020, six people were allegedly executed by firing squad for their involvement in a prostitution ring consisting of officials and female performing-arts university students. More than 50 students were reportedly sent to a labor camp, and others were punished with reeducation sessions.

Economic opportunity has been affected by escalating international sanctions in response to North Korea's weapons tests and threats of military aggression. Since 2016, sanctions have targeted civilian industries including textiles and seafood. North Korea has also been cut off from the international banking system. While this has not deterred North Korea's pursuit of nuclear weapons, it has created growing difficulties for those dependent on markets and quasi-private businesses. Agricultural reforms in previous years have allowed larger percentages of crop yields to be kept by households, but productivity suffers from lack of access to supplies and modern equipment.

North Macedonia

Population: 2,100,000
Capital: Skopje
Freedom Status: Partly Free
Electoral Democracy: Yes

Overview: North Macedonia is a parliamentary republic. A left-leaning government has calmed tensions in the wake of a 2017 parliamentary crisis that paralyzed normal political activity. North Macedonia continues to struggle with corruption, and while the media and civil society participate in vigorous public discourse, journalists and activists face pressure and intimidation.

KEY DEVELOPMENTS IN 2020

- July's parliamentary elections produced a virtual tie, with the governing Social Democratic Union of Macedonia (SDSM) taking 35.89 percent of the vote, and the Internal Macedonian Revolutionary Organization–Democratic Party for Macedonian Unity (VMRO–DPMNE) winning 34.57 percent. The polls were competitive, credible, and took place without major incident, and the SDSM formed a governing coalition with smaller parties shortly thereafter.
- A new public prosecutor law was approved in February, following some controversy about last-minute changes to the measure's provisions. The law was part of an ongoing reform drive aimed at open accession talks with the European Union (EU).
- In October, the EU signaled that it was prepared to start accession negotiations before the end of the year. In November, though, the Bulgarian government blocked the start of talks.
- Authorities enacted various measures restricting movement and other activities in response to the COVID-19 pandemic, and a state of emergency was in place at year's end. Violators could be fined, but were not subject to violence or other forms of disproportionate enforcement. According to the country's public health office, 75,500 COVID-19 cases had been confirmed by mid-December.

POLITICAL RIGHTS: 27 / 40 (+3)

A. ELECTORAL PROCESS: 9 / 12 (+2)

A1. Was the current head of government or other chief national authority elected through free and fair elections? 3 / 4 (+1)

The president is elected to as many as two five-year terms through a direct popular vote. President Stevo Pendarovski of the SDSM won his first term in May 2019, taking 51.7 percent of the vote against opponent Gordana Siljanovska-Davkova's 44.8 percent. Voter turnout was 46.7 percent—a low figure, but one consistent with recent North Macedonian elections. The Organization for Security and Co-operation in Europe (OSCE) sent a monitoring mission that determined that the election was free and credible, despite some technical challenges involving voter rolls and technological infrastructure, among other issues.

The unicameral Assembly elects the prime minister, who is head of government and holds most executive power. Parliamentary elections held in July 2020 resulted in a virtual tie, with the SDSM barely ahead of the VMRO–DPMNE. The SDSM was able to easily form a coalition government with smaller left-wing and ethnic minority parties. The VMRO–DPMNE did not significantly obstruct the process as in years prior, and Prime Minister Zoran Zaev's new cabinet was approved by the end of August.

Score Change: The score improved from 2 to 3 due to the orderly formation and approval of a government after July's parliamentary elections.

A2. Were the current national legislative representatives elected through free and fair elections? 3 / 4 (+1)

Members of the 120-seat Assembly are elected by proportional representation to four-year terms.

The July 2020 polls showed improvement from previous years, with instances of vote-buying, intimidation, and other misconduct reported less frequently. The elections were originally scheduled for November 2020; moved up to April 2020 after the EU in October

2019 refused to green light accession talks with Skopje; and finally pushed back to July due to public health–related concerns amid the COVID-19 pandemic. The OSCE monitoring mission observing the elections concluded that they were well-managed and free, but criticized last-minute changes to the electoral framework by the government. The SDSM won 35.89 percent of the vote and 46 seats, while the VMRO–DPMNE won 34.57 percent and 44 seats, with the remainder divided among smaller parties.

Score Change: The score improved from 2 to 3 because the parliamentary elections saw fewer instances of vote-buying, voter intimidation, and other acts of misconduct compared to previous polls.

A3. Are the electoral laws and framework fair, and are they implemented impartially by the relevant election management bodies? 3 / 4

Election laws have deficiencies, though the overall accessibility of election results and reporting by the State Election Commission has improved since 2019. Ambiguities in election laws that have yet to be addressed include regulations governing the registration of candidates, and resolution mechanisms for election-related disputes. Additionally, OSCE observers, in both 2019 and 2020, expressed concerns about inaccuracies in the electoral roll.

In September 2018, the government held a controversial referendum to approve the Prespa Agreement, signed with Greece in June 2018, to change the country's name to North Macedonia. Voter turnout was only 37 percent, below the 50 percent required for the results to count—though 90 percent of participants voted in favor of the change. OSCE observers assessed the referendum results as credible, but said content had been inadequately explained to the public, and the election commission lacked transparency in carrying out the poll. Analysts expressed concern about a social media disinformation campaign, which reportedly originated in Russia, urging Macedonians to boycott the vote.

In January 2019, the government ratified the Prespa Agreement, despite inadequate voter turnout for the referendum, and the country's name change, from Macedonia to North Macedonia, was confirmed by parliament.

B. POLITICAL PLURALISM AND PARTICIPATION: 11 / 16

B1. Do the people have the right to organize in different political parties or other competitive political groupings of their choice, and is the system free of undue obstacles to the rise and fall of these competing parties or groupings? 3 / 4

While the constitution protects the right to establish and join political parties, vast patronage networks hamper democratic competition. Violence occurred in parliament in 2017 in response to the election of an SDSM-backed parliament speaker. Around 100 people were injured in the altercation. Tensions between the parties have decreased since 2018. Both the main center-left and center-right blocs lost votes in the 2020 parliamentary elections to ethnic Albanian minority parties, and a far-left party, Levica, which won two seats and entered the parliament for the first time.

B2. Is there a realistic opportunity for the opposition to increase its support or gain power through elections? 3 / 4

In 2017, power rotated from the right-wing nationalist party, the VMRO–DPMNE—which had governed since 2006—to the left-leaning SDSM, which had governed through much of the 1990s and early 2000s. Before taking power in 2017, SDSM had boycotted parliament on several occasions over claims of electoral fraud, as well as following a scandal in which the administration of former prime minister Nikola Gruevski allegedly directed the secret service to operate a massive wiretapping and surveillance program. However, competitive elections in 2019 and 2020 and the credible 2018 referendum reflected improvements in the North Macedonian electoral system and greater ability of opposition parties to campaign freely and win support through elections.

B3. Are the people's political choices free from domination by forces that are external to the political sphere, or by political forces that employ extrapolitical means? 2 / 4

While voters are largely free to make political decisions, reports of intimidation and vote buying remain common. Patronage networks remain influential in political life and can influence political outcomes.

B4. Do various segments of the population (including ethnic, racial, religious, gender, LGBT+, and other relevant groups) have full political rights and electoral opportunities? 3 / 4

Ethnic Albanians make up about 25 percent of the population, and a political party representing Albanians has sat in each ruling coalition. Certain types of legislation must pass with a majority of legislators from both major ethnic groups (Albanians and Macedonians). In March 2018, the SDSM-led government passed a new language law extending the official use of Albanian to all state-level institutions, including the parliament.

North Macedonia's Romany community remains politically marginalized. The country's Turkish, Serbian, and Bosnian minorities are comparatively well integrated.

Despite the introduction of parity laws and joint initiatives on behalf of nongovernmental organizations (NGOs) and electoral authorities, societal attitudes discourage women from participating in politics. Some women are disenfranchised through the practice of family voting. Despite these challenges, the first woman defense minister was appointed in 2017. Women currently make up 47 percent of parliament.

Small LGBT+ advocacy groups are politically active, but LGBT+ people have little representation in politics.

C. FUNCTIONING OF GOVERNMENT: 7 / 12 (+1)

C1. Do the freely elected head of government and national legislative representatives determine the policies of the government? 3 / 4 (+1)

For much of 2017, parliament did not function effectively due to VMRO–DPMNE attempts to prevent the formation of an SDSM-led government, as well as the parliamentary altercation in which Zaev and other SDSM lawmakers were injured. However, the formation of the new government in the middle of 2017 ushered in a return to more normal parliamentary activity, which has since continued. Nevertheless, post-Prespa legislative activity is still marked by a tense atmosphere.

The election of Stevo Pendarovski as president in May 2019 resolved an impasse between the legislature and executive that had existed for much of the previous three years, as both bodies are now governed by the SDSM. The SDSM-led parliament has continued to govern responsibly and in dialogue with its partners in the ethnic Albanian blocs.

Score Change: The score improved from 2 to 3 to reflect a steady, multiyear decline in obstructionism in the parliament.

C2. Are safeguards against official corruption strong and effective? 2 / 4

Corruption remains a serious problem, and there has been widespread impunity for corrupt government officials, including members of parliament and the judiciary. While the

2020 EU progress report praised North Macedonia's steady reforms, serious corruption and procurement scandals continue to emerge.

The August 2019 arrest on extortion charges of Katica Janeva, the outgoing special prosecutor appointed in 2015 to investigate the revelations of the wiretapping program, shook public trust in anticorruption efforts. Local papers reported that Janeva allegedly joined two others, including reality television star Bojan Jovanovski, in blackmailing the well-known businessman Orce Kamcev. In June 2020, Janeva was found guilty of abuse of office and sentenced to a seven-year prison term.

C3. Does the government operate with openness and transparency? 2 / 4

The law on open access to public information is inconsistently implemented. While the government has pledged to undertake reforms aimed at increasing its transparency, it has yet to register concrete progress.

In 2020, legal experts expressed concern about significant, last-minute changes to a draft public prosecutor law, made quickly just before the law's approval. Lawmakers passed the measure in February 2020 as part of a drive to open EU accession talks.

CIVIL LIBERTIES: 39 / 60
D. FREEDOM OF EXPRESSION AND BELIEF: 12 / 16
D1. Are there free and independent media? 3 / 4

North Macedonia's media landscape is deeply polarized along political lines, and private media outlets are often tied to political or business interests that influence their content. However, a wide collection of critical and independent outlets operate and are found mainly online.

North Macedonian journalists remain subject to political pressure and harassment, and physical attacks continue to be reported.

D2. Are individuals free to practice and express their religious faith or nonbelief in public and private? 3 / 4

The constitution guarantees freedom of religion. However, Islamophobia is present in the rhetoric of politicians and in public discourse, and is directed primarily at the ethnic Albanian community and the Roma.

D3. Is there academic freedom, and is the educational system free from extensive political indoctrination? 3 / 4

Academic freedom is largely respected, but corruption in universities is significant. Many textbooks minimally cover the postindependence period, primarily because ethnic Macedonians and ethnic Albanians interpret the 2001 civil conflict differently.

D4. Are individuals free to express their personal views on political or other sensitive topics without fear of surveillance or retribution? 3 / 4

Allegations of widespread wiretapping and monitoring of private citizens, journalists, politicians, and religious leaders by the previous VMRO–DPMNE government helped bring about its ouster. The SDSM-led government has taken some steps to reform the national security service, which was widely believed to have carried out the surveillance program under former prime minister Gruevski's direction. Notably, in December 2018, the parliament passed a law that rolled back the power of the secret police to conduct surveillance activities.

E. ASSOCIATIONAL AND ORGANIZATIONAL RIGHTS: 8 / 12

E1. Is there freedom of assembly? 3 / 4

Constitutional guarantees of freedom of assembly are generally well respected. However, demonstrations are typically monitored by riot police, who in the past have employed disproportionate force against demonstrators, and protests sometimes give way to property damage.

In September 2020, members of the Romany community protested police violence against their community, after footage emerged of an officer beating a Romany man in Bitola. The protests took place peacefully, without interference by authorities.

E2. Is there freedom for nongovernmental organizations, particularly those that are engaged in human rights- and governance-related work? 3 / 4

The government has expressed support for civil society. However, groups that focus on human rights– and governance-related work, and particularly those that receive foreign funding, face pressure from the VMRO–DPMNE and its supporters. Since the change in government in 2017, the work of nongovernmental organizations (NGOs) has become freer and safer, and public institutions have become more responsive to the work and engagement of the civil society sector.

E3. Is there freedom for trade unions and similar professional or labor organizations? 2 / 4

Workers may organize and bargain collectively, though trade unions lack stable financing and skilled managers, and journalists have reportedly been fired for their union activities.

F. RULE OF LAW: 9 / 16

F1. Is there an independent judiciary? 2 / 4

Concerns remain about the efficacy and independence of the judiciary. The EU stressed judicial reforms as a key priority for the government's accession bid. In 2018, the government adopted a number of reforms aimed at enhancing judicial independence, including the strengthening of mechanisms to address misconduct by judges. However, not all of the judicial reforms promised by the government have been implemented.

F2. Does due process prevail in civil and criminal matters? 2 / 4

Due process rights remain compromised by corruption and patronage within the justice system, in which the public has little confidence. Political interference in the work of prosecutors remains a problem. The selective application of justice also persists, although the government has carried out some reforms intended to ameliorate the issue. The 2019 arrest of the special prosecutor has also weakened the SDSM government's overall anticorruption agenda.

In February 2020, as part of efforts to open accession talks with the EU, lawmakers approved a measure allowing the transfer of cases from the former special prosecutor's office to ordinary state prosecutors, with some limitations on when illegally wiretapped conversations may be introduced as evidence. Another section of the law stipulated a new process for the appointment of the prosecutor for organized crime and corruption cases, which envisioned that that official would be voted on by other prosecutors across the country ahead of formal appointment by the Council of Public Prosecutors. The law prompted complaints from the VMRO–DPMNE, which alleged that the SDSM was attempting to establish influence within the justice system. Both the VMRO–DPMNE and legal experts voiced disapproval of significant, last-minute changes to the text, apparently the result of political bargaining that ensured the law's approval.

F3. Is there protection from the illegitimate use of physical force and freedom from war and insurgencies? 3 / 4

The threat of physical violence has subsided significantly under the tenure of the SDSM government. In February 2019, police successfully prevented an attack planned by supporters of the Islamic State (IS).

There have been occasional outbreaks of interethnic violence in North Macedonia. In 2015, 18 people were killed in violent clashes between police and a group of Albanian extremists in Kumanovo as well as near the border with Kosovo. However, such incidents have been less frequent in recent years.

F4. Do laws, policies, and practices guarantee equal treatment of various segments of the population? 2 / 4

A 2010 antidiscrimination law does not prohibit discrimination on the basis of sexual orientation or gender identity, and anti-LGBT+ sentiment is widespread. In August 2019, Prime Minister Zaev faced an outcry after using a homophobic slur in responding to a question on the corruption charges against former special prosecutor Janeva. His statement and subsequent apology were severely criticized as inadequate by local journalists, as well as by the North Macedonian office of the Helsinki Committee for Human Rights.

Laws prohibit workplace sexual harassment, but the issue persists, and most instances are rarely reported.

Albanians suffer from discrimination in employment and anti-Albanian sentiment has flared in recent years. The Romany people face employment and other discrimination. Footage in September 2020 of a police officer brutalizing a Romany man in Bitola once again highlighted the marginalized position and routine violence that members of the Romany community face in North Macedonia.

G. PERSONAL AUTONOMY AND INDIVIDUAL RIGHTS: 10 / 16

G1. Do individuals enjoy freedom of movement, including the ability to change their place of residence, employment, or education? 3 / 4

Travel and movement are generally unrestricted. Corruption can hamper people's ability to freely choose their place of employment or education.

G2. Are individuals able to exercise the right to own property and establish private businesses without undue interference from state or nonstate actors? 3 / 4

The right to own property and establish private businesses is generally respected, though corruption remains a barrier to free enterprise.

G3. Do individuals enjoy personal social freedoms, including choice of marriage partner and size of family, protection from domestic violence, and control over appearance? 2 / 4

Rape, including spousal rape, is illegal, as is domestic violence, which remains common; both are infrequently reported. The government and some NGOs provide services to victims of domestic violence.

A 2017 ruling by the Administrative Court allowed people to change their gender in the country's official registry to match their gender identity.

G4. Do individuals enjoy equality of opportunity and freedom from economic exploitation? 2 / 4

Laws do not impose rigid barriers to social mobility, though rampant corruption can effectively hamper individuals from rising to higher income levels. The informal economy is large, leaving many workers vulnerable to employer abuse.

Human trafficking remains a problem. The government has taken some steps to better identify trafficking victims, notably at government-run transit centers that house migrants and refugees. However, government support to NGOs that aid trafficking victims has decreased.

Norway

Population: 5,400,000
Capital: Oslo
Freedom Status: Free
Electoral Democracy: Yes

Overview: Norway is one of the most robust democracies in the world. Elections are free and fair, and power regularly rotates between parties. Civil liberties are respected, with independent media and civil society actors holding the government to account. Discrimination against Roma and other marginalized groups remains a problem.

KEY DEVELOPMENTS IN 2020

- In August, the Norwegian Journalists' Association, Verdens Gang, and the Norwegian Editors' Association sued the Attorney General for denying access to documents in a court case concerning police handling of guns. The case was with the Supreme Court at year's end.
- As part of the government's response to the COVID-19 pandemic, freedom of movement was limited during the year. In March, strict rules prohibited travel outside of residents' home county. Essential health workers were prohibited from traveling abroad, and only Norwegian nationals or residents were permitted to reenter Norway. By the end of the year, 48,278 people had tested positive for coronavirus, and 436 people had died, according to government statistics provided to the World Health Organization (WHO).

POLITICAL RIGHTS: 40 / 40

A. ELECTORAL PROCESS: 12 / 12

A1. Was the current head of government or other chief national authority elected through free and fair elections? 4 / 4

The constitutional monarch, currently King Harald V, appoints the prime minister, who is the leader of the majority party or coalition in the parliament. While the monarch is officially the head of state and commander in chief of the armed forces, his duties are largely ceremonial. The prime minister, Conservative Party leader Erna Solberg, took office in 2013 and received a new mandate following her center-right coalition's victory in the 2017 general election.

A2. Were the current national legislative representatives elected through free and fair elections? 4 / 4

Norway's unicameral parliament, the Storting, has 169 members who are directly elected for four-year terms through a system of proportional representation in multimember districts.

An election monitoring mission from the Organization for Security and Co-operation in Europe (OSCE) concluded that the 2017 elections were well conducted, offering notable praise for the country's early voting mechanisms. However, the mission found that visually impaired voters experienced some difficulties. The opposition Labour Party led the voting with 49 seats, followed by the ruling Conservatives with 45 seats, the right-wing populist Progress Party with 27, the Centre Party with 19, the Socialist Left Party with 11, the Christian Democratic Party and the Liberal Party with 8 each, and the Green Party and Red Party with 1 each. The Conservatives renewed their governing coalition with the Progress Party, with the Liberal Party joining the bloc in early 2018 and the Christian Democrats joining in January 2019. In January 2020, however, the Progress Party left the governing coalition due to political differences over the government's decision to bring home a woman and her two children from Syria. The governing coalition is now a minority government.

A3. Are the electoral laws and framework fair, and are they implemented impartially by the relevant election management bodies? 4 / 4

Elections are regulated by the constitution and the Representation of the People Act of 2002. The National Electoral Committee, whose members are appointed by the king from all parliamentary parties, oversees the conduct of elections with the support of local-level committees. The 2017 OSCE election monitoring mission noted a high degree of public confidence in the country's electoral infrastructure.

B. POLITICAL PLURALISM AND PARTICIPATION: 16 / 16

B1. Do the people have the right to organize in different political parties or other competitive political groupings of their choice, and is the system free of undue obstacles to the rise and fall of these competing parties or groupings? 4 / 4

A range of political parties operate freely in Norway.

B2. Is there a realistic opportunity for the opposition to increase its support or gain power through elections? 4 / 4

Norway has a long history of democratic and peaceful transfers of power after elections. The center-left Labour Party on the one hand, and center-right coalitions led by the Conservatives or the Christian Democrats on the other, have typically rotated in and out of government. Smaller parties wield influence by participating in national and local coalitions.

B3. Are the people's political choices free from domination by forces that are external to the political sphere, or by political forces that employ extrapolitical means? 4 / 4

Citizens are generally free from undue interference in their political choices, and no military, foreign, or religious entities exert undemocratic pressure on voters. Public funding is the main source of party revenue, though the 2017 OSCE election monitoring mission noted a sharp increase in private contributions and conveyed concerns that this could allow wealthy donors to acquire undue influence over Norwegian politics.

B4. Do various segments of the population (including ethnic, racial, religious, gender, LGBT+, and other relevant groups) have full political rights and electoral opportunities? 4 / 4

Women and minority groups enjoy full political rights and electoral opportunities. Women are well represented in Norwegian politics: The posts of prime minister, foreign minister, and justice minister, among others, were held by women in 2020, and 41 percent of parliamentarians are women. Minority ethnic groups and the interests of LGBT+ people are addressed through robust antidiscrimination laws and various protections for same-sex couples.

The Indigenous Sami population, in addition to participating in the national political process, has its own legislature, the Sameting, which has worked to protect the group's language and cultural rights and to influence the national government's decisions about Sami land and resources. The national government has a deputy minister tasked specifically with handling Sami issues.

C. FUNCTIONING OF GOVERNMENT: 12 / 12

C1. Do the freely elected head of government and national legislative representatives determine the policies of the government? 4 / 4

The freely elected government and parliament develop and implement policy without undue influence from actors who are not democratically accountable. In March 2020, in response to the COVID-19 pandemic, the parliament approved a law that gave the government discretionary powers to address the public health crisis. The draft law enabled the government to make exceptions from current laws without going through the parliament for up to six months. Parliamentary consultations adjusted the law to only apply in urgent cases when ordinary parliamentary procedures would not be possible and to only last one month.

C2. Are safeguards against official corruption strong and effective? 4 / 4

Provisions of the penal code criminalizing corrupt activity are generally upheld. Official corruption is not viewed as a significant problem in Norway, though cases of corruption have surfaced at major firms in recent years. Norwegian bank DNB faced a money laundering probe in November 2019 after an Icelandic news outlet reported that it was used to route funds from Icelandic fishing company Samherji to shell firms; those funds were allegedly used to bribe Namibian officials.

C3. Does the government operate with openness and transparency? 4 / 4

The government generally operates with transparency. Several audits of public grants and other government spending were conducted in 2017, with auditors finding evidence of inadequate management.

The 2006 Freedom of Information Act provides for access to government documents, though it contains exemptions for some information pertaining to national security and foreign policy. Investigative journalists have previously complained that senior government officials use various tactics to avoid or delay inquiries that would expose negligence or wrongdoing.

CIVIL LIBERTIES: 60 / 60

D. FREEDOM OF EXPRESSION AND BELIEF: 16 / 16

D1. Are there free and independent media? 4 / 4

Freedom of the press is constitutionally guaranteed and generally respected in practice. Norwegians have access to news and commentary from a wide variety of independent outlets. In recent years, the courts have grappled with legal questions related to the protection of journalists' sources in criminal cases. In 2017, the European Court of Human Rights (ECHR) ruled that the Norwegian government could not compel journalists to reveal their sources, even if the source had come forward independently. In August 2020, the Norwegian Journalists' Association, Verdens Gang, and the Norwegian Editors' Association sued the Attorney General for denying access to documents in a case concerning police handling of guns. The case was with the Supreme Court at year's end.

D2. Are individuals free to practice and express their religious faith or nonbelief in public and private? 4 / 4

Freedom of religion is protected by the constitution and generally upheld in practice. However, religiously motivated hate crimes do occur. The government also launched an action plan against discrimination and hatred against Muslims, which includes requirements for police to separately register anti-Muslim crimes.

D3. Is there academic freedom, and is the educational system free from extensive political indoctrination? 4 / 4

Academic freedom is generally respected.

D4. Are individuals free to express their personal views on political or other sensitive topics without fear of surveillance or retribution? 4 / 4

Private discussion in Norway is free and vibrant.

E. ASSOCIATIONAL AND ORGANIZATIONAL RIGHTS: 12 / 12
E1. Is there freedom of assembly? 4 / 4

The right to freedom of assembly is generally respected. There have been tensions in recent years over demonstrations by extremist groups and their potential threat to public security, with some critics calling for far-right marches to be prohibited. Public health measures instituted in 2020 to prevent the spread of COVID-19 limited the size of public gatherings. In June 2020, Black Lives Matter protests in response to the killing of George Floyd in the United States and against racism in Norway took place despite these regulations. The protests in Oslo and Bergen drew thousands of protestors, and other demonstrations took place across Norway. Police requested that those who took part stay home after participating and get tested if they showed symptoms of the virus.

E2. Is there freedom for nongovernmental organizations, particularly those that are engaged in human rights- and governance-related work? 4 / 4

Nongovernmental organizations (NGOs) form and operate without undue restrictions.

E3. Is there freedom for trade unions and similar professional or labor organizations? 4 / 4

The right to strike is legally guaranteed—except for members of the military and senior civil servants—and is generally respected in practice. All workers have the right to engage in collective bargaining.

F. RULE OF LAW: 16 / 16
F1. Is there an independent judiciary? 4 / 4

The judiciary is generally considered independent, and the court system, headed by the Supreme Court, operates fairly at the local and national levels. The king appoints judges on the advice of the Judicial Appointments Board, which is composed of legal and judicial professionals as well as representatives of the public.

F2. Does due process prevail in civil and criminal matters? 4 / 4

Law enforcement agencies and the courts generally observe legal safeguards against arbitrary arrest and detention. Criminal defendants have access to counsel at the government's expense, and the principles of due process are typically respected during trial.

In October 2019, the Norwegian Labor and Welfare Administration (NAV) was found to have wrongfully imprisoned at least 48 people on charges of welfare fraud, having misinterpreted European Union (EU) rules on social security when it denied benefits to over 2,400 people who travelled to EU and European Economic Area (EEA) states since 2012. In

September 2020, the NAV requested that individuals affected by the scandal contact them, to attempt to resolve the issue. They had already processed about 42,000 cases.

F3. Is there protection from the illegitimate use of physical force and freedom from war and insurgencies? 4 / 4

The police are under civilian control, and physical abuse by law enforcement authorities is rare. Prison conditions generally meet international standards.

Far-right and extremist violence is a recognized threat in Norway; the national Police Security Service has warned of an increased risk of far-right terrorism. In August 2019, a Neo-Nazi sympathizer murdered his adopted sister, an ethnic Chinese woman, before unsuccessfully attacking a mosque in the southwestern municipality of Bærum. In June 2020, he was sentenced to 21 years in prison with a minimum term of 14 years for the murder of his sister in June 2020.

F4. Do laws, policies, and practices guarantee equal treatment of various segments of the population? 4 / 4

The equality and antidiscrimination ombudsman enforces the Gender Equality Act, the Antidiscrimination Act, and other laws designed to protect the basic rights of women, minorities, and other groups at risk of mistreatment. These laws are generally upheld in practice.

Norwegian authorities reported 761 hate crimes in 2019, the majority of which were based on race, ethnicity, religion or sexual orientation. A Neo-Nazi group conspicuously handed out leaflets outside the Synagogue in Oslo during the Jewish New Year service.

The national government also supports Sami-language instruction and media outlets in the relevant regions. The Norwegian national human rights institution, however, has highlighted that Norway does not currently disaggregate statistical data by ethnicity or Indigenous status, which limits the evidence base for human rights monitoring and improving policy and service delivery for Indigenous groups such as the Sami.

In the 2020 UN Committee on Economic, Social and Cultural Rights report on Norway, it noted concern over evidence of people with visual impairments facing technological barriers at work; persons with an immigrant background continue to face discrimination in employment and access to healthcare; one third of older persons in hospitals and in health and care services are malnourished or at risk of malnutrition; and women still face a persistent pay gap of 12.4 percent as of 2019.

In recent years, the Council of Europe has encouraged Norwegian authorities to address widespread discriminatory attitudes toward Roma, and to ensure that they have equal access to education and employment.

Norway is increasingly coming under scrutiny for its restrictive refugee and asylum policies. In November 2020, 18-year-old Mustafa Hasan—who came to Norway as a 6-year-old—was deported by an Immigration Appeals Board because his mother had provided inaccurate information. The case stoked widespread criticism of the country's asylum policies. In December, the government increased the requirements for permanent residency from 3 to 5 years of living in Norway.

G. PERSONAL AUTONOMY AND INDIVIDUAL RIGHTS: 16 / 16

G1. Do individuals enjoy freedom of movement, including the ability to change their place of residence, employment, or education? 4 / 4

Freedom of movement in Norway is generally respected. People can change their place of residence, employment, and education. However, some EU- and EEA-born welfare recipients living in Norway reportedly refrained from traveling abroad for fear of losing benefits;

in November 2019, local NGO Caritas reported that several thousand were discouraged or stopped from traveling abroad in recent years.

As part of the government's response to the COVID-19 pandemic, freedom of movement was limited in 2020. In March, strict rules prohibited travel outside of residents' home county. Essential health workers were prohibited from travelling abroad, and only Norwegian nationals or residents were permitted to reenter Norway. Regulations in place at the end of 2020 require that anyone coming into Norway from countries or areas with a high infection rate must present a negative COVID-19 test to officials and quarantine upon arrival for 10 days.

G2. Are individuals able to exercise the right to own property and establish private businesses without undue interference from state or nonstate actors? 4 / 4

The rights to own property and operate private businesses are established in Norwegian law and upheld in practice.

G3. Do individuals enjoy personal social freedoms, including choice of marriage partner and size of family, protection from domestic violence, and control over appearance? 4 / 4

The government generally does not restrict personal social freedoms. The Gender Equality Act provides equal rights for men and women with respect to marriage, divorce, and other personal status matters.

Domestic violence is a problem. In June 2019, Norway's Institute for Human Rights (NIM) estimated that 150,000 people experience domestic violence annually. Later that summer, the government launched a plan of action to combat domestic violence, which included a specific focus on Sami communities. Amnesty International has also expressed concern that the penal code does not use a consent-based definition of rape and imposes a limited set of qualifying circumstances.

In 2018, the parliament passed a government-proposed law that bans face coverings, including the niqab and burqa, from teaching environments at all levels of education, effectively placing limits on individuals' choice of dress and personal appearance. The ban did not apply outside classroom settings, for instance during recess or staff meetings.

G4. Do individuals enjoy equality of opportunity and freedom from economic exploitation? 4 / 4

The principle of equality of opportunity and legal protections against economic exploitation are generally upheld. The government has been active in combating labor and sex trafficking and works to provide services to victims. There have been reports of forced labor in the agriculture and construction sectors, including a case of Bangladeshi migrants being exploited on Norwegian farms through a Portuguese trafficker.

Oman

Population: 4,700,000
Capital: Muscat
Freedom Status: Not Free
Electoral Democracy: No

Overview: Oman is a hereditary monarchy, and power is concentrated in the hands of the sultan. The regime restricts virtually all political rights and civil liberties, imposing criminal penalties for criticism and dissent.

KEY DEVELOPMENTS IN 2020

- Sultan Qaboos bin Said died in January; he had ruled Oman since 1970. He was succeeded by his cousin, Sultan Haitham bin Tariq, who in August delegated to his cabinet ministers some of the responsibilities Qaboos had formally maintained, including the appointment of the Minister of Foreign Affairs.
- In May, the Ministry of Interior announced that the municipal elections set for 2020 would be postponed indefinitely due to the COVID-19 pandemic; the existing councils would continue until new elections could be held. According to government statistics provided to the World Health Organization (WHO), over 128,000 people had tested positive for the virus, and 1,499 people had died by year's end.

POLITICAL RIGHTS: 6 / 40

A. ELECTORAL PROCESS: 2 / 12

A1. Was the current head of government or other chief national authority elected through free and fair elections? 0 / 4

In January 2020, Sultan Haitham succeeded his cousin, Sultan Qaboos, who died that month and had governed Oman since seizing power from his father, Sultan Said bin Taimur, in 1970. Sultan Haitham delegated to his cabinet ministers some of the responsibilities Sultan Qaboos had formally maintained, including the appointment of a Minister of Foreign Affairs, in August 2020.

A2. Were the current national legislative representatives elected through free and fair elections? 1 / 4

The 1996 basic law, promulgated by decree, created a bicameral body consisting of an appointed Council of State (Majlis al-Dawla) and a wholly elected Consultative Council (Majlis al-Shura). Citizens elect the Consultative Council for four-year terms, but the chamber has no legislative powers and can only recommend changes to new laws.

Consultative Council elections were held in October 2019, with 637 nonpartisan candidates, including 40 women, competing for the council's 86 seats. Two women were elected. In November 2019, the sultan appointed the 86 members of the Council of State for a four-year term, including 15 women.

Oman held its first-ever municipal council elections in 2012. In the most recent elections in 2016, voters chose among 731 nonpartisan candidates to fill 202 seats on the 11 councils, which correspond to Oman's 11 governorates. Turnout was about 49 percent. In May 2020, the Ministry of Interior announced that the municipal elections set for 2020 would be postponed indefinitely due to the COVID-19 pandemic; the existing councils would continue until new elections could be held.

A3. Are the electoral laws and framework fair, and are they implemented impartially by the relevant election management bodies? 1 / 4

The electoral framework allows all citizens over the age of 21 to vote unless they are in the military or security forces. However, the framework applies only to the Consultative Council and municipal councils, which serve largely as advisory bodies. Elections are administered by the Ministry of Interior rather than by an independent commission.

B. POLITICAL PLURALISM AND PARTICIPATION: 2 / 16

B1. Do the people have the right to organize in different political parties or other competitive political groupings of their choice, and is the system free of undue obstacles to the rise and fall of these competing parties or groupings? 0 / 4

Political parties are not permitted, and the authorities do not tolerate other forms of organized political opposition. A 2014 law allows the revocation of citizenship for Omanis who join organizations deemed harmful to national interests.

B2. Is there a realistic opportunity for the opposition to increase its support or gain power through elections? 0 / 4

The sultan maintains a monopoly on political power. The structure of the constitutional system excludes the possibility of a change in government through elections.

B3. Are the people's political choices free from domination by forces that are external to the political sphere, or by political forces that employ extrapolitical means? 1 / 4

The nonpartisan nature of Oman's limited elections, the overwhelming dominance of the sultan in Omani society, and the authorities' suppression of dissent leave voters and candidates with little autonomy in their political choices.

B4. Do various segments of the population (including ethnic, racial, religious, gender, LGBT+, and other relevant groups) have full political rights and electoral opportunities? 1 / 4

Noncitizens, who make up about 44 percent of the population, have no political rights or electoral opportunities. Citizenship is generally transmitted from Omani fathers. Foreign residents must live legally in the country for 20 years to qualify for citizenship, or 15 and 10 years for foreign husbands and wives of Omani citizens, respectively, if they have a son. These and other conditions make naturalizations relatively rare.

Omani women can legally vote and run for office, but they have few practical opportunities to organize independently and advance their interests in the political system. Two women were elected to the Consultative Council in 2019, up from one in 2015, and seven women won seats on municipal councils in 2016, up from four in 2012. Fifteen women serve on the appointed Council of State.

C. FUNCTIONING OF GOVERNMENT: 2 / 12

C1. Do the freely elected head of government and national legislative representatives determine the policies of the government? 0 / 4

Government policy is set by the sultan and an inner circle of advisers and senior ministers. The Council of State and the Consultative Council are advisory bodies with no lawmaking powers.

C2. Are safeguards against official corruption strong and effective? 2 / 4

Oman's legal code does not provide an effective framework for the prevention, exposure, and impartial prosecution of corruption. However, government officials are required to declare their assets and sources of wealth, and several high-profile corruption cases involving government officials and executives from Oman's oil industry have resulted in convictions and prison terms in recent years.

C3. Does the government operate with openness and transparency? 0 / 4

The law does not provide freedom of information guarantees. Openness and transparency are limited in practice by the concentration of power and authority in a small inner circle around the sultan. The State Audit Institution monitors ministerial spending, conflicts of interest, and state-owned companies, but its findings are not released to the public, and it does not cover the sultan's court or the military.

CIVIL LIBERTIES: 17 / 60

D. FREEDOM OF EXPRESSION AND BELIEF: 5 / 16

D1. Are there free and independent media? 1 / 4

Freedom of expression is limited, and criticism of the sultan is prohibited. There are private media outlets in addition to those run by the state, but they typically accept government subsidies, practice self-censorship, and face punishment if they cross political redlines. The government has broad authority to close outlets, block websites, revoke licenses, and prosecute journalists for content violations, and it has used this authority on multiple occasions in recent years.

The government's efforts to suppress critical news and commentary extend to online activity and social media. In June 2020, the Court of First Instance in Muscat sentenced Adel al-Kasbi, a broadcaster, and Salem al-Awfi, a former member of the Consultative Council, to a year in prison for "using information technology to spread harm to public order" through critical Twitter posts.

D2. Are individuals free to practice and express their religious faith or nonbelief in public and private? 2 / 4

Islam is the state religion. Non-Muslims have the right to worship, but they are banned from proselytizing. Religious organizations must register with the government. The Ministry of Awqaf (religious charitable bequests) and Religious Affairs distributes standardized texts for mosque sermons, and imams are expected to stay within the content outlines of these texts.

D3. Is there academic freedom, and is the educational system free from extensive political indoctrination? 1 / 4

The government restricts academic freedom by preventing the publication of material on politically sensitive topics and placing controls on contacts between Omani universities and foreign institutions.

D4. Are individuals free to express their personal views on political or other sensitive topics without fear of surveillance or retribution? 1 / 4

The authorities reportedly monitor personal communications, and the growing number of arrests, interrogations, and jail terms related to criticism of the government on social media has encouraged self-censorship among ordinary citizens in recent years. A new penal code issued by the government in 2018 increased the maximum penalties for slander of the sultan and blasphemy to 7 and 10 years in prison, respectively, from three years for both under the old code.

In June 2020, Awad al-Sawafi was sentenced to a suspended one-year term of imprisonment and banned from social media for a year by the Ibri Court of First Instance after being arrested and charged with "incitement" and "misuse of social media." Al-Sawafi had posted on Twitter a comment critical of government agencies that had threatened citizens. In July 2020, Ghazi al-Awlaki was detained by the Internal Security Service in the Dhofar Governorate after posting on Facebook about Arab governments' "virtual armies" on social media platforms. Al-Awlaki was held without charge or access to a lawyer for seven weeks before being released in September.

E. ASSOCIATIONAL AND ORGANIZATIONAL RIGHTS: 3 / 12

E1. Is there freedom of assembly? 0 / 4

A limited right to peaceful assembly is provided for in Oman's basic law. However, all public gatherings require official permission, and the government has the authority to prevent organized public meetings without any appeals process. The 2018 penal code prescribes prison terms and fines for individuals who initiate or participate in a gathering of more than 10 people that threatens security or public order, or who fail to comply with an official order to disperse. While demonstrations are rare in practice, several protests against unemployment were held in January 2019, echoing similar incidents a year earlier. Some arrests and brief detentions were reported.

E2. Is there freedom for nongovernmental organizations, particularly those that are engaged in human rights- and governance-related work? 1 / 4

Oman's basic law allows for the formation of nongovernmental organizations, but civic life remains limited in practice. The government has not permitted the establishment of independent human rights organizations and generally uses its registration and licensing process to block the formation of groups it sees as a threat to stability. Individual activists focusing on issues including labor rights and internet freedom continued to risk arrest during 2020. The 2018 penal code includes vague clauses that allow prison terms for individuals who establish, operate, or finance an organization aimed at challenging the "political, economic, social, or security principles of the state" or promoting class conflict.

E3. Is there freedom for trade unions and similar professional or labor organizations? 2 / 4

Omani workers are legally able to organize unions, bargain collectively, and strike. However, there is only one authorized trade union federation, and neither government employees nor household workers are permitted to join unions. Strikes, which are banned in the oil and gas industry, are rare in practice, partly because disputes are often resolved through employer concessions or government mediation.

F. RULE OF LAW: 4 / 16

F1. Is there an independent judiciary? 0 / 4

The judiciary is not independent and remains subordinate to the sultan, who is empowered to appoint and remove senior judges. The sultan also chairs the Supreme Judicial Council, which nominates judges and oversees the judicial system, though a 2012 reform replaced the justice minister with the head of the Supreme Court as the council's deputy chair.

F2. Does due process prevail in civil and criminal matters? 1 / 4

Arbitrary arrest is formally prohibited but suspects arrested in vaguely defined security cases can be held for up to 30 days before being charged, and security forces do not always adhere to other rules on arrest and pretrial detention. Ordinary detainees are generally provided with access to legal representation.

Defendants in politically sensitive cases may face harsher treatment from the justice system. For example, prior to his trial in 2017, Mansour bin Nasser al-Mahrazi, a writer and researcher who was eventually sentenced to three years in prison for offenses including "insulting the sultan," spent at least two months in incommunicado detention, and the judge refused to hear defense witnesses.

F3. Is there protection from the illegitimate use of physical force and freedom from war and insurgencies? 2 / 4

Prisons are not accessible in practice to independent monitors, but former detainees have reported beatings and other abuse. Online activist Hassan al-Basham, who had been sentenced to three years in prison in 2016 for allegedly using the internet in ways that could be "prejudicial to religious values," died in custody in 2018 after reportedly being denied medical care.

The country is generally free from armed conflict, and violent street crime is relatively rare.

F4. Do laws, policies, and practices guarantee equal treatment of various segments of the population? 1 / 4

The 1996 basic law banned discrimination on the basis of sex, religion, ethnicity, and social class, but noncitizens are not protected from discrimination in practice. Women face disparate treatment under personal status laws and de facto bias in employment and other matters. Under the Personal Status Law, a woman must have a male guardian—usually a father—to contract her into marriage. Men are recognized as the head of the household. Same sex relations are punishable with up to three years in prison, and LGBT+ people face societal discrimination.

G. PERSONAL AUTONOMY AND INDIVIDUAL RIGHTS: 5 / 16

G1. Do individuals enjoy freedom of movement, including the ability to change their place of residence, employment, or education? 1 / 4

Most Omani citizens enjoy freedom of movement, but travel bans are often imposed on political dissidents. Foreign workers cannot leave the country without permission from their employer and risk deportation if they change employers without documentation releasing them from their previous contract. During 2020, the government periodically prevented travel internally in the country, initiated a lockdown, and imposed curfews to prevent the spread of COVID-19. These measures were implemented in line with a rise of reported coronavirus cases.

G2. Are individuals able to exercise the right to own property and establish private businesses without undue interference from state or nonstate actors? 2 / 4

While the legal framework protects property rights, state-owned companies and the ruling family are dominant forces in the economy, limiting the role and autonomy of small and other private businesses. Women generally receive less property than men under inheritance laws.

G3. Do individuals enjoy personal social freedoms, including choice of marriage partner and size of family, protection from domestic violence, and control over appearance? 1 / 4

Omani citizens require permission from the Ministry of Interior to marry noncitizens from countries outside the Gulf Cooperation Council. Spouses or children of Omani women cannot gain citizenship. Omani law does not specifically address domestic violence and sexual harassment or criminalize spousal rape, while extramarital sex is criminalized. Women who report rape have at times been prosecuted for engaging in extramarital sex, if authorities do not believe they were assaulted. Women are at disadvantage under laws governing matters such as divorce and child custody. The 2018 penal code included a new provision that criminalized the wearing of women's clothing by men.

G4. Do individuals enjoy equality of opportunity and freedom from economic exploitation? 1 / 4

Oman's labor policies put migrant workers at a severe disadvantage and effectively encourage exploitation. Household workers, who are not covered by the labor law, are especially at risk of abuse by employers. The government has pursued an "Omanization" process to replace foreign workers with native Omanis. Among other tactics, temporary visa bans for foreign workers in various professions have been issued or extended since 2013. Despite a 2008 antitrafficking law and some recent efforts to step up enforcement, authorities do not proactively identify or protect human trafficking victims. The US State Department's *2020 Trafficking in Persons Report* notes that though the government does investigate trafficking cases, there are few cases and convictions are subsequently also uncommon; seven sex trafficking cases achieved convictions in 2019, though three of them were from cases held up in the court system from previous years. Government policies limit shelter stays to victims with cases actively being investigated.

Pakistan

Population: 220,900,000
Capital: Islamabad
Freedom Status: Partly Free
Electoral Democracy: No

Note: The numerical scores and status listed above do not reflect conditions in Pakistani Kashmir, which is examined in a separate report. *Freedom in the World* reports assess the level of political rights and civil liberties in a given geographical area, regardless of whether they are affected by the state, nonstate actors, or foreign powers. Disputed territories are sometimes assessed separately if they meet certain criteria, including boundaries that are sufficiently stable to allow year-on-year comparisons. For more information, see the report methodology and FAQ.

Overview: Pakistan holds regular elections under a competitive multiparty political system. However, the military exerts enormous influence over security and other policy issues, intimidates the media, and enjoys impunity for indiscriminate or extralegal use of force. The authorities impose selective restrictions on civil liberties, and Islamist militants carry out attacks on religious minorities and other perceived opponents.

KEY DEVELOPMENTS IN 2020
- Though the government lockdown to prevent the spread of COVID-19 was still in place, several prominent imams ignored pandemic restrictions and called on worshippers to defy the government's orders. Some who ignored the restrictions attacked police officers attempting to stop them. By the end of the year, over 479,000 people had tested positive for the virus and more than 10,000 people had died, according to government statistics provided to the World Health Organization (WHO).
- In October, the major opposition parties joined together to form the Pakistan Democratic Movement (PDM) and held rallies protesting Prime Minister Imran Khan, who they accused of having been "selected" for office by the military. The PDM emerged after a series of politicized corruption cases were filed against key opposition leaders, and legislation the military supported was railroaded through parliament without opposition support during the year.

POLITICAL RIGHTS: 15 / 40 (−1)

A. ELECTORAL PROCESS: 5 / 12

A1. Was the current head of government or other chief national authority elected through free and fair elections? 1 / 4

A prime minister responsible to the bicameral parliament holds most executive power under the constitution. The president, who plays a more symbolic role, is elected for up to two five-year terms by an electoral college comprising the two chambers of the parliament and the provincial assemblies. PTI-nominated candidate Arif Alvi was elected president in September 2018.

Imran Khan became prime minister in August 2018 when the Tehreek-e-Insaf (PTI) party formed a coalition government, having emerged from the general elections as the largest party in the National Assembly. In the run-up to the polls, observers documented concerted efforts by elements of the country's military and judicial establishment to hamper the Pakistan Muslim League (PML-N) in order to increase the chances that Khan would attain a parliamentary majority. These included corruption, contempt-of-court, and terrorism charges against PML-N leaders and candidates, and their politicized adjudication. Observers also noted pressure on and interference with the media, apparently at the behest of the security services, that resulted in muted coverage of the PML-N's campaign. In 2020, the opposition parties challenged Imran Khan's legitimacy as prime minister in numerous forums, claiming that he had been "selected" by the army and not elected through a fair process.

A2. Were the current national legislative representatives elected through free and fair elections? 2 / 4

The parliament consists of a 342-member National Assembly and a 104-member Senate. Members of the National Assembly are elected for five years. Of the 342 seats, 272 are filled through direct elections in single-member districts, 60 are reserved for women, and 10 are reserved for non-Muslim minorities. The reserved seats are filled through a proportional representation system with closed party lists.

In the Senate, each provincial assembly chooses 23 members, National Assembly members representing the Federally Administered Tribal Areas (FATA) elect 8, and the National Assembly chooses 4 to represent the Islamabad capital territory. Deliberations occurred in 2020 on a formula to replace the old FATA quota as the terms of the incumbents expire. Senators serve six-year terms, with half of the seats up for election every three years.

International and domestic election observers delivered a mixed verdict on the July 2018 National Assembly elections. Polling was orderly and generally took place according to the electoral law, though serious technical difficulties with the Result Transmission System created significant delays in reporting the results. At the same time, the rush of judicial actions against PML-N leaders and restrictions on and interference with media coverage significantly disadvantaged the party, contributing to a spectacular rise in PTI representation in the National Assembly. The PTI received 32 percent of the vote and 149 seats, compared with just 35 seats previously. The PML-N received 24 percent of the vote and 82 seats, down from 157 seats previously. The Pakistan People's Party (PPP) received 13 percent of the vote and 54 seats, an increase of 12 from its previous representation. Notably, parties and candidates linked to active Islamist militant groups, including Tehreek-e-Labaik Pakistan (TLP) and Allah-o-akbar Tehreek (AAT), participated in the elections.

The PTI formed a coalition government at the national level, with the support of the Muttahida Qaumi Movement (MQM), other minor parties, and independents. Voter turnout was 52 percent. The PTI coalition lacks a majority in the current Senate.

A3. Are the electoral laws and framework fair, and are they implemented impartially by the relevant election management bodies? 2 / 4

Elections are administered by the Election Commission of Pakistan (ECP), whose members are current or retired senior judges nominated through a consultative process that includes the government and the parliamentary opposition. In January 2020, the government appointed Sikander Sultan Raja as Chief Election Commissioner, along with two new commissioners, after reaching a consensus with the parliamentary opposition.

The electoral laws are largely fair, and candidates have extensive access to the courts in electoral disputes.

Election observer missions in 2018 acknowledged that the formal electoral framework and its implementation complied with international standards. However, the ECP proved unable to counteract efforts by elements of the judicial and military establishment and their allies to manipulate the campaign environment. According to the Human Rights Commission of Pakistan, politically orchestrated judicial activism resulted in the disqualification of candidates, while the "censorship, intimidation, harassment, and abduction" of journalists who were critical of the security establishment or favored the PML-N or PPP ensured uneven access to the media.

Other, ongoing problems include lower rates of voter registration among women, a requirement that members of the Ahmadi religious minority register as non-Muslims despite considering themselves Muslims, and vague moral requirements for candidate nomination.

B. POLITICAL PLURALISM AND PARTICIPATION: 6 / 16

B1. Do the people have the right to organize in different political parties or other competitive political groupings of their choice, and is the system free of undue obstacles to the rise and fall of these competing parties or groupings? 2 / 4

Several major parties and numerous smaller parties and independents compete in elections and are represented in the parliament and provincial legislatures. However, established parties maintain patronage networks and other advantages of incumbency that hamper competition in their respective provincial strongholds. In recent years, it has become increasingly apparent that major parties' freedom to operate is related to the strength of their relationships with unelected arms of the state, which have sought to sideline figures not to their liking through a variety of legal and extralegal means.

In October, the PML-N and PPP joined together to form the Pakistan Democratic Movement (PDM) and held rallies protesting Prime Minister Imran Khan, who they accused of having been "selected" for office by the military. The PDM emerged to contest several seats in the Senate that are up for election in 2021, after a series of politicized corruption cases were filed against key opposition leaders, and legislation the military supported was railroaded through parliament without the opposition's support during the year.

B2. Is there a realistic opportunity for the opposition to increase its support or gain power through elections? 2 / 4

Opposition parties campaign and contest elections, and each of the last three national elections has resulted in an erstwhile opposition party taking power at the federal level. National opposition parties also continue to hold power or significant shares of assembly seats at the provincial level. However, the military is currently considered more powerful than elected politicians and the judiciary has shown a willingness to engage in politically targeted accountability. Therefore, opposition parties have increasingly concluded that their most plausible route to power is by winning the backing of the unelected establishment rather than through a straight electoral contest. For example, in January 2020, members of the PML-N claimed they could replace the PTI administration by winning army support to form an interim government.

Throughout 2020, the PML-N and PPP, both former governing parties, were profoundly disrupted by a barrage of court cases brought against their first- and second-rank leaders and their family members. The government charged high-profile former officials with corruption, alleged breach of media regulations, and participation in unauthorized demonstrations. Those targeted included former prime minister Nawaz Sharif, his daughter Maryam Nawaz, his younger brother and former Punjab chief minister Shahbaz Sharif, Shahbaz Sharif's son Hamza, and former prime ministers Shahid Khaqan Abbasi and Raja Parvaiz Ashraf, all political figures within PML-N. Former president Asif Ali Zardari and his sister Faryal Talpur, both PPP politicians, were also targeted. Nawaz Sharif travelled to the United Kingdom in 2019 for authorized medical treatment and stayed there throughout 2020 in de facto exile. Hamza and Shahbaz Sharif were jailed. The National Accountability Bureau (NAB)—the government's anticorruption body—and the courts kept the accused occupied with multiple notices and required court appearances. Nevertheless, the parties' senior figures continued to play leadership roles from jail or abroad, and Maryam Nawaz and Bilawal Bhutto Zardari represented the PML-N and PPP in rallies and meetings. The 2020 arrests were a continuation of the 2017–18 dubious court rulings that effectively removed Nawaz Sharif from political life, and subsequently weakened the PML-N.

Throughout 2020, the authorities continued to disrupt the activities of the Pashtun Tahafuz Movement (PTM), which campaigns against violence by both the state and Islamist militants in ethnic Pashtun areas. Security forces dispersed rallies, arrested participants and activists, suppressed media coverage, and charged rally participants with sedition. In January 2020, PTM leader Manzoor Pashteen was arrested on sedition and antistate charges (and released after a month in detention) and PTM's two National Assembly members, Mohsin Dawar and Ali Wazeer, were briefly detained in Islamabad. Wazeer was later arrested again in Karachi. The army reportedly suspects PTM leaders of opposing the Pakistani state and having links to Afghan and Indian intelligence agencies, which PTM supporters deny.

B3. Are the people's political choices free from domination by forces that are external to the political sphere, or by political forces that employ extrapolitical means? 1 / 4

The manipulation of politics by religious extremists has long hampered voters' ability to freely express their political preferences. In recent years, the military has reasserted its role as the political arbiter—more powerful than either the judiciary or the elected government—setting the constraints within which civilian politics play out.

In 2018, the heavy presence of security agents at many polling stations was interpreted by observers, including the Human Rights Commission of Pakistan, as tantamount to voter intimidation. A number of candidates in the 2018 election campaign had links with extremist groups that had advocated or carried out acts of violence, further contributing to a sense of unease among many voters.

B4. Do various segments of the population (including ethnic, racial, religious, gender, LGBT+, and other relevant groups) have full political rights and electoral opportunities? 1 / 4

A joint electorate system allows members of non-Muslim minorities to participate in the general vote while also being represented by reserved seats in the national and provincial assemblies through the party-list system. However, the participation of non-Muslims in the political system continues to be marginal. Political parties nominate members to the legislative seats reserved for non-Muslim minorities, leaving non-Muslim voters with little say in the selection of their supposed representatives. Ahmadis, members of a heterodox Muslim sect, face political discrimination and are registered on a separate voter roll.

Political parties maintain women's wings that are active during elections, but women face practical restrictions on voting, especially in Khyber Pakhtunkhwa and Baluchistan, where militant groups and societal constraints are more prevalent. Women rarely achieve leadership positions in parties or the government. The interests of LGBT+ people are generally not represented by elected officials.

The single member constituency system for national elections ensures that the major ethno-linguistic groups from each province are represented in the National Assembly and participate in party politics, government, and opposition. Although Sindhi, Pashtun, and Baloch figures all play visible roles in national political life—alongside the largest ethno-linguistic group, Punjabis—the military works to marginalize figures from minority groups it suspects of harboring antistate sentiments, as exemplified by its treatment of the PTM.

C. FUNCTIONING OF GOVERNMENT: 4 / 12 (-1)

C1. Do the freely elected head of government and national legislative representatives determine the policies of the government? 1 / 4

Formally, the elected prime minister and cabinet make policy in consultation with the parliament, which holds legislative power. However, there has been a long-running struggle between these civilian structures and the military establishment for control of national security policy. The military has asserted primacy on relations with India, Afghanistan, China, and the United States, as well as on counterterrorism policy within Pakistan. In the last two years of the previous PML-N government, it appeared that the civilian administration aspired to act independently of some military priorities, most notably through exploring détente with India. Since the August 2018 installation of the PTI government, the civilian administration has aligned itself more closely than its predecessor with the military's foreign policy, domestic security, and economic priorities. In early 2020, the government and opposition alike were widely criticized for capitulating to military pressure in extending the Army Chief's term in office.

C2. Are safeguards against official corruption strong and effective? 1 / 4

While there are numerous formal safeguards against official corruption, it is endemic in practice. The use of accountability mechanisms is often selective and politically driven, as demonstrated by the charges brought against PML-N and PPP leaders and former politicians, such as former prime minister Sharif and former president Zardari in 2020. The NAB focuses on cases against politicians and senior officials. By September 2020, it claimed to have launched 3,371 cases, from which it achieved 1,124 convictions (a 58 percent conviction rate), with 1,257 cases pending. The military and judiciary have their own disciplinary systems.

C3. Does the government operate with openness and transparency? 2 / 4 (-1)

The government has relatively progressive laws around public finances, procurement processes, and general government operations. Some effort is put into being seen as complying with international norms.

Access-to-information laws have long been applied in Pakistan; the parliament passed the Right to Access of Information Act in 2017 to update a 2002 law. Information commissions have been established in the provinces supposedly to enable implementation, which is inconsistent. Determined citizens can demand information from departments and complain to the information commissions when departments fail to deliver. Many departments tend to ignore requests.

Vocal civil society groups and journalists often weigh in on policy debates. However, debates about policies with national security implications are closed down quickly. Members of both provincial and national assemblies are expected to make themselves accessible to constituents. Parliament regularly debates and scrutinizes the budget, accompanied by commentary from the media.

There is a procurement regulatory agency that uses many standard transparency tools, including procurement manuals and publication of tenders. However, international bodies such as the World Bank and the Organisation for Economic Co-operation and Development (OECD) have scrutinized Pakistan's public procurements. Members of parliament and select public officials are compelled to submit asset declaration forms that civil society organizations often upload to the internet.

The military—which controls large parts of government functioning under the guise of national security concerns—is deeply opaque in its affairs. Military officials' ability to influence policies, politics, and legislation is formidable, and military intelligence agencies act without oversight and often without the public's knowing of their involvement. Intelligence agencies abduct, detain, interrogate, and torture individuals for extended periods without publicizing information of their whereabouts or the purpose for their detention. The military is also able to censor media and information published about its activity by means of vaguely worded regulations that empower officials to monitor and manage content deemed harmful to "national security interests." Since 2018, multiple high-ranking military officers have been appointed to government positions historically under civilian control.

Score Change: The score declined from 3 to 2 due to the opaque nature and unknown extent of the military's influence in the government.

CIVIL LIBERTIES: 22 / 60
D. FREEDOM OF EXPRESSION AND BELIEF: 6 / 16
D1. Are there free and independent media? 1 / 4

Over the past two decades, Pakistan has boasted a relatively vibrant media sector that presents a range of news and opinions. However, both the civilian authorities and military in recent years have curtailed media freedom. In 2020, the government targeted individual journalists, television programs and stations, and media houses for raising issues authorities considered unpalatable. Authorities employed range of instruments to do so, including the long-used tactic of withdrawing government advertising from critical publications, fines, and temporary bans imposed by the Pakistan Electronic Media Regulatory Authority (PEMRA). In 2020, journalists considered suspect by the state were subject to enforced disappearance, and four local journalists were murdered in unexplained circumstances. Authorities are also believed to rely on "troll farms," which are directed to harass critical commentators. The state continued efforts to enforce a media blackout on the PTM and its members during the year.

The authorities continued to target the Jang media group in 2020 by arresting group owner Mir Shakil ur Rahman, withholding government advertising and temporarily banning operation and distribution of its TV channel Geo. The government continued to withhold public advertising moneys from the Dawn group.

In October 2020, after Nawaz Sharif had received publicity for speeches he made from London, the PEMRA issued an order banning all broadcasters from covering absconders. This order was subsequently challenged in court.

Access to certain regions of the country is prohibited by the military, impeding coverage of issues there. In Baluchistan, local journalists are often caught between authorities who order them not to cover separatist rebel activity, and rebel groups that threaten them for siding with the government.

D2. Are individuals free to practice and express their religious faith or nonbelief in public and private? 1 / 4

Constitutional guarantees of religious freedom have not provided effective safeguards against discriminatory legislation, social prejudice, and sectarian violence. Hindus have complained of vulnerability to kidnapping and forced conversions, and some continue to migrate to India. Members of the Shia sect, Christians, and other religious minorities remain at risk of blasphemy accusations that can arise from trivial disputes and escalate to criminal prosecution and mob violence. The blasphemy laws and their exploitation by religious vigilantes have also curtailed freedom of expression by Muslims.

In October 2020, the Council of Islamic Ideology withdrew its objections to a restored Hindu temple in Islamabad. In December, a violent mob destroyed another Hindu temple in the Karak district of Khyber Pakhtunkhwa province.

Members of the Ahmadi community are legally prohibited from calling themselves Muslims and face discrimination. Four Ahmadis were killed during 2020 in suspected hate crimes.

D3. Is there academic freedom, and is the educational system free from extensive political indoctrination? 2 / 4

Pakistani authorities have a long history of using the education system to portray Hindus and other non-Muslims negatively and to rationalize enmity between Pakistan and India, among other ideological aims. Past attempts to modernize education and introduce tolerance into school textbooks have made little progress, and minority groups consider negative portrayals of non-Muslims in textbooks as a continuing source of hostility towards them. In July 2020, the Punjab government gave itself additional powers to censor publications deemed offensive to Islam. In the course of a review of textbooks taught by private schools in the province, it banned 100 books.

In recent years, scholars have been somewhat more able to discuss sensitive issues involving the military. However, there is no academic freedom on matters pertaining to religion, where academics remain vulnerable to blasphemy accusations.

D4. Are individuals free to express their personal views on political or other sensitive topics without fear of surveillance or retribution? 2 / 4

Pakistanis are free in practice to discuss many topics both online and off, but the 2016 Prevention of Electronic Crimes Act (PECB) gives the executive-controlled Pakistan Telecommunication Authority (PTA) unchecked powers to censor material on the internet. The PTA encourages reporting of websites complainants consider offensive. The level of investment in tracking and blocking sites is typically justified by a professed intention to prevent dissemination of blasphemous and pornographic content. However, the broad and poorly defined censorship mandate of the PTA also includes preventing the maligning of the "state, judiciary, or armed forces." In practice, the agency censors content arbitrarily.

In February 2020, the government adopted a new set of rules, under the PECB, imposing restrictions and obligations on social media companies. The latest rules obliged social media companies to take responsibility for enforcing the government's restrictions on objectionable content and called on them to maintain a physical presence in the country, with threats of fines and service interruption for noncompliance. However, the rules provoked widespread criticism both from Pakistani civil society concerned about the potential for censorship, and from an alliance of major social media companies.

Extralegal violence and allegations of blasphemy also deter unfettered speech.

E. ASSOCIATIONAL AND ORGANIZATIONAL RIGHTS: 6 / 12

E1. Is there freedom of assembly? 3 / 4

The constitution guarantees the right to assemble peacefully, though the government can harness legal provisions to arbitrarily ban gatherings or any activity designated a threat to public order. During 2020, the authorities repeatedly withheld authorization for opposition demonstrations and harassed event organizers—for example, by closing roads leading to rally venues. Despite these obstacles, most demonstrations went ahead. Authorities dispersed the peaceful rallies held by the PTM in major cities including Islamabad, Lahore, Karachi, Loralai, and Bannu.

In response to the COVID-19 pandemic the government installed a lockdown to prevent the spread of the virus. However, several prominent imams ignored pandemic restrictions and called on worshippers to defy the government's orders. Some who ignored the restrictions attacked police officers who attempted to stop them.

E2. Is there freedom for nongovernmental organizations, particularly those that are engaged in human rights- and governance-related work? 1 / 4

The current government has continued a crackdown on nongovernmental organizations (NGOs), both domestic and foreign, initiated by its predecessor in 2015. Organizations are subject to intrusive registration requirements and vetting by military intelligence. Officials can demand that NGOs obtain a "no-objection certificate" (NOC) before undertaking even the most innocuous activity. During 2020, the Khyber Pakhtunkhwa government blocked the bank accounts and froze the registration of 65 percent of the NGOs operating in the province.

E3. Is there freedom for trade unions and similar professional or labor organizations? 2 / 4

The rights of workers to organize and form trade unions are recognized in law, and the constitution grants unions the rights to collective bargaining and to strike. However, these protections are not strongly enforced. Roughly 70 percent of the workforce is employed in the informal sector, where unionization and legal protections are minimal. The procedures that need to be followed for a strike to be legal are onerous. Strikes and labor protests are organized regularly, though they often lead to clashes with police and dismissals by employers.

F. RULE OF LAW: 4 / 16

F1. Is there an independent judiciary? 1 / 4

The judiciary is politicized and has a history of involvement in the power struggles between the military, the civilian government, and opposition politicians, and has often issued rulings aligned with the priorities of the military. During 2020, corruption cases against Nawaz Sharif and other senior PML-N and PPP opposition politicians continued and were widely reported on. The paucity of equivalent cases against PTI figures suggest that the judiciary has allowed itself to be instrumentalized in national politics.

In 2020, Supreme Court Justice Qazi Faez Isa faced complex legal action over allegations of undeclared family property in the United Kingdom. The Law Minister temporarily stepped down in order to represent the government in the case. Fellow Supreme Court

Justice Umar Ata Bandial claimed that the case against Isa was unwarranted and could hurt the independence of the entire judiciary.

The broader court system is marred by endemic problems including corruption, intimidation, insecurity, a large backlog of cases, and low conviction rates for serious crimes.

F2. Does due process prevail in civil and criminal matters? 1 / 4

Police have long been accused of biased or arbitrary handling of initial criminal complaints, and both the police and the prosecution service have been criticized for a chronic failure to prosecute terrorism cases.

In 2019, the mandates of a system of military courts empowered to try civilians lapsed. However, under the Army Act, the military continued to operate its own courts, primarily for its own personnel. However, the army asserted the right to selectively try civilians, on camera, under the Army Act courts, in cases of national security.

Access to due process has increased in the former FATA, which in 2018 was absorbed into Khyber Pakhtunkhwa. Consequently, the Pakistan Penal Code was extended to the former tribal areas, along with the writ of the superior courts. For the first time, the regular police force was established in the old tribal areas.

F3. Is there protection from the illegitimate use of physical force and freedom from war and insurgencies? 1 / 4

In 2020, 509 people were killed in terrorist incidents, up from 370 in 2020. This increase reversed the multiyear decline in terrorist violence over the past decade, since its 2009 peak when over 11,700 people were killed.

Unlike the earlier period of terrorism in Pakistan, large suicide bombings and mass casualty attacks occurred far less frequently in 2020. Only two attacks by suspected Islamic State militants were conducted against madrassahs controlled by the Afghan Taliban Movement: one in Quetta in January killed 15 people, the other in Peshawar in October killed 8.

A low-intensity insurgency continued in Baluchistan, in which the Baloch Liberation Army and several other outfits routinely conducted attacks against security forces, sabotaged infrastructure, and occasionally killed or abducted civilians deemed to be aligned to the state. In response, the Pakistan Army targeted suspected insurgents while conducting numerous operations in insurgency-affected districts. In Khyber Pakhtunkhwa, the Pakistan Taliban Movement conducted multiple terrorist attacks against security forces throughout the year. Although attacks were smaller in scale and less deadly than in 2009, they took place in many of the same areas where militants were previously active.

Civilians face the threat of extralegal violence by state actors, including enforced disappearances. The Voice for Baloch Missing Persons accused the state of operating "death squads" to abduct and kill Baloch people suspected of being sympathetic to the insurgency. The number of pending cases of people registered as missing since 2011 by the official Commission of Inquiry on Enforced Disappearances rose to 6,921 during 2020, of which 4,798 cases had reportedly been resolved by the end of the year. However, the Commission was inactive for much 2020, due to COVID-19 restrictions. The International Commission of Jurists critiqued the Commission, concluding that its approach had enabled impunity by diverting attention away from the judicial process and into an ad hoc process vulnerable to political interference. There was no sign in 2020 that the Commission's deliberations would lead to effective sanctions against agencies involved in the disappearances. For example, in June, the army acknowledge that they were holding human rights defender Idris Khattak, missing since November 2019, and that he was being tried under the Official Secrets Act. However, the Commission treated the case as "disposed of," and did not consider Khattak to be a victim of enforced disappearance. Most victims were from Khyber Pakhtunkhwa, the former FATA, or Baluchistan, and typically were held incommunicado by security and intelligence agencies on suspicion of antistate agitation, terrorism, rebellion, or espionage.

F4. Do laws, policies, and practices guarantee equal treatment of various segments of the population? 1 / 4

Women face discrimination in employment despite legal protections and are placed at a disadvantage under personal status laws. Women are also subject to a number of harmful societal practices and abuses, the perpetrators of which often enjoy impunity. Registration of the "first information report" of a crime is the first hurdle involved in accessing justice; police are often reluctant to proceed in the face of complaints of crimes against women, including so-called crimes of honor.

Other segments of the population that suffer legal or de facto discrimination and violence include ethnic and religious minorities, Afghan refugees, and LGBT+ people. The penal code prescribes prison terms for consensual sex "against the order of nature," deterring LGBT+ people from acknowledging their identity or reporting abuses. Transgender and intersex people are authorized to register for official documents under a "third gender" classification recognized by the Supreme Court since 2009, and some transgender people were recognized in the 2017 census. However, they continue to face targeted violence as well as discrimination in housing and employment.

G. PERSONAL AUTONOMY AND INDIVIDUAL RIGHTS: 6 / 16

G1. Do individuals enjoy freedom of movement, including the ability to change their place of residence, employment, or education? 2 / 4

There are some legal limitations on travel and the ability to change one's residence, employment, or institution of higher learning. The authorities routinely hinder internal movement in some parts of the country for security reasons. The main tool for restricting foreign travel is the Exit Control List (ECL), which blocks named individuals from using official exit points from the country. It is meant to include those who pose a security threat and those facing court proceedings. However, periodically it has been used as a means of controlling dissent.

G2. Are individuals able to exercise the right to own property and establish private businesses without undue interference from state or non-state actors? 2 / 4

In principle, Pakistan's constitution, legal system, and social and religious values all guarantee private property and free enterprise. In reality, however, organized crime, corruption, a weak regulatory environment, and the subversion of the legal system often render property rights precarious. Powerful and organized groups continue to engage in land grabbing, particularly in Karachi and Punjab.

Inheritance laws discriminate against women, and women are often denied their legal share of inherited property through social or familial pressure.

G3. Do individuals enjoy personal social freedoms, including choice of marriage partner and size of family, protection from domestic violence, and control over appearance? 1 / 4

In some parts of urban Pakistan, men and women enjoy personal social freedoms and have recourse to the law in case of infringements. However, traditional practices in much of the country subject individuals to social control over personal behavior, and especially choice of marriage partner. Despite successive attempts to abolish the practice, "honor killing," the murder of men or women accused of breaking social and especially sexual taboos, remains common, and most incidents go unreported.

G4. Do individuals enjoy equality of opportunity and freedom from economic exploitation? 1 / 4

Bonded labor was formally abolished in 1992, and there have been long-standing efforts to enforce the ban and related laws against child labor. Gradual social change has also eroded the power of wealthy landowning families involved in such exploitation. Nevertheless, extreme forms of labor exploitation remain common. Employers continue to use chronic indebtedness to restrict laborers' rights and hold actual earnings well below prescribed levels, particularly among sharecroppers and in the brick-kiln industry.

Palau

Population: 20,000
Capital: Ngerulmud
Freedom Status: Free
Electoral Democracy: Yes

Overview: Palau's presidential republic is maintained through regular democratic elections. The judiciary and the media are independent, and civil liberties are generally upheld. The government has sought to combat official corruption in recent years. Many in the country's large population of foreign workers remain vulnerable to exploitation.

KEY DEVELOPMENTS IN 2020
- Surangel Whipps Jr. was elected president in November, defeating outgoing vice president Raynold Oilouch in a two-round contest. Whipps was not sworn in by year's end.
- Legislative elections were concurrently held with the presidential contest in November. Most members of the House of Delegates were reelected, though only 7 members of the 13-seat Senate won new terms.
- Palau restricted inbound travel in response to the COVID-19 pandemic in March and instituted quarantine policies for travelers in April, effectively prohibiting tourists from visiting the country. Authorities reported no COVID-19 cases or deaths to the World Health Organization (WHO) during the year.

POLITICAL RIGHTS: 37 / 40
A. ELECTORAL PROCESS: 12 / 12
A1. Was the current head of government or other chief national authority elected through free and fair elections? 4 / 4

The president, who serves as both head of state and head of government, is directly elected for up to two consecutive four-year terms using a two-round system, with a runoff if no candidate wins an absolute first-round majority. Surangel Whipps Jr., brother-in-law of term-limited incumbent Tommy Remengesau Jr., was elected in two rounds in November 2020, defeating outgoing vice president Raynold Oilouch. Incoming president Whipps was not sworn in by year's end.

A2. Were the current national legislative representatives elected through free and fair elections? 4 / 4

The bicameral National Congress consists of a 13-member Senate and a 16-member House of Delegates. All members of the National Congress are elected for four-year terms. Congressional elections were held in November 2020, concurrently with the presidential contest. Most House of Delegates incumbents won new terms, while seven senators were reelected.

A3. Are the electoral laws and framework fair, and are they implemented impartially by the relevant election management bodies? 4 / 4

Electoral administration is widely considered to be fair and impartial. A review of the Senate's size and electoral system is undertaken every eight years by a Reapportionment Commission. During the 2016 review, the commission recommended the Senate maintain its current seat count. While the Supreme Court ruled that the body should only contain 11 seats in response to a petition, the court restored the original 13-seat count later that year.

B. POLITICAL PLURALISM AND PARTICIPATION: 15 / 16

B1. Do the people have the right to organize in different political parties or other competitive political groupings of their choice, and is the system free of undue obstacles to the rise and fall of these competing parties or groupings? 4 / 4

There are no laws restricting the formation of political parties, but in practice all candidates run and compete freely as independents. Politicians tend to organize in loose political alliances, often based on clan or family relationships.

B2. Is there a realistic opportunity for the opposition to increase its support or gain power through elections? 4 / 4

Although there are no political parties, lawmakers do organize into informal progovernment and opposition camps, and no single political force has control of the legislature. Power is transferred democratically between rival politicians.

B3. Are the people's political choices free from domination by forces that are external to the political sphere, or by political forces that employ extrapolitical means? 4 / 4

Palau receives financial assistance from the United States under a Compact of Free Association (CoFA), but the US government does not exert improper influence over the country's internal politics. While the political views of traditional chiefs are respected, they do not have authoritative control over the choices of voters.

B4. Do various segments of the population (including ethnic, racial, religious, gender, LGBT+, and other relevant groups) have full political rights and electoral opportunities? 3 / 4

Women generally have equal political rights in law and in practice. Some state-level legislative seats are reserved for male chiefs, who in turn are customarily chosen by councils of women elders. After the November 2020 polls, only one woman held a seat in each house of the National Congress.

About a third of the population consists of foreign nationals who do not have political rights in Palau. Citizenship must be inherited from at least one parent, as there are no provisions for naturalization.

In 2019, former president John Toribiong (2009–13) launched a petition seeking to end the acceptance of absentee ballots, asserting that the petition would combat the political influence wielded by the increasing number of citizens living outside the country.

C. FUNCTIONING OF GOVERNMENT: 10 / 12

C1. Do the freely elected head of government and national legislative representatives determine the policies of the government? 4 / 4

Palau's democratically elected government determines and implements policy without undue interference. Traditional chiefs formally play an advisory role regarding customary matters through the national Council of Chiefs. While they also exercise informal influence over government policy, this is widely seen as a positive check on potential mismanagement or abuse of power by elected officials.

The CoFA, in effect since Palau became independent in 1994, ensures self-government but also provides for close military and economic relations with the United States, including responsibility for Palau's defense. A scheduled 15-year review of the compact resulted in a 2010 bilateral agreement on development aid and other benefits to last until the next review in 2024. In late 2017, US president Donald Trump signed a defense bill that included implementing provisions for the compact review agreement. Meetings over the CoFA's extension began in 2019 and continued in 2020. In August, then US defense secretary Mark Esper became the first to visit Palau. Then president Remengesau invited the United States to establish a military facility in the country during that visit.

Palau maintains diplomatic recognition of Taiwan, amidst several other Pacific nations shifting their recognition to China. In November 2020, the Taiwanese government vowed to develop its relationship with Palau regardless of who won that month's elections.

C2. Are safeguards against official corruption strong and effective? 3 / 4

High-ranking public officials have faced corruption charges in recent years, and several have been convicted. The government and lawmakers have deliberated on strategies to deal with corruption more effectively, and in 2017 the finance minister issued a statement to reiterate the government's ethics rules and a whistleblower protection policy. The Office of the Ombudsman currently operates as part of the president's office under an executive order.

In 2018, the European Union (EU) said that Palau authorities pledged to implement certain reforms and removed the country from its list of tax havens. Palau was returned to the EU's tax-haven list in February 2020, with the bloc saying Palau had not fulfilled its pledge.

C3. Does the government operate with openness and transparency? 3 / 4

A 2014 Open Government Act provides for public access to official documents and hearings, and government officials are obliged to submit annual financial disclosures that are available to the public. However, authorities have sometimes resisted disclosing requested information, particularly at the subnational level.

CIVIL LIBERTIES: 55 / 60

D. FREEDOM OF EXPRESSION AND BELIEF: 16 / 16

D1. Are there free and independent media? 4 / 4

Freedom of the press is respected. There are several independent news outlets, including newspapers and broadcasters, but they often struggle financially. Regional and international news services are also available. Internet access has been hampered by high costs and lack of connectivity outside the main islands.

D2. Are individuals free to practice and express their religious faith or nonbelief in public and private? 4 / 4

Constitutional guarantees of religious freedom are upheld in practice. Although religious organizations are required to register as nonprofit organizations, the process is not onerous or restrictive. Foreign missionaries are also required to obtain a permit.

D3. Is there academic freedom, and is the educational system free from extensive political indoctrination? 4 / 4

There have been no reports of restrictions on academic freedom.

D4. Are individuals free to express their personal views on political or other sensitive topics without fear of surveillance or retribution? 4 / 4

There are no constraints on political discussion, and the government does not monitor personal communications.

E. ASSOCIATIONAL AND ORGANIZATIONAL RIGHTS: 11 / 12
E1. Is there freedom of assembly? 4 / 4

Freedom of assembly is protected by the constitution and respected in practice.

E2. Is there freedom for nongovernmental organizations, particularly those that are engaged in human rights- and governance-related work? 4 / 4

Nongovernmental organizations operate freely, with various groups focusing on issues such as environmental conservation, youth development, public health, and women's rights.

E3. Is there freedom for trade unions and similar professional or labor organizations? 3 / 4

Workers can freely organize unions and bargain collectively, but there are no laws specifically regulating trade unions or strikes or prohibiting antiunion discrimination. Union membership and activity are low in practice, as the private sector consists mostly of small, family-run businesses.

F. RULE OF LAW: 15 / 16
F1. Is there an independent judiciary? 4 / 4

The judiciary has a reputation for independence and integrity. The president appoints judges to lifelong terms based on recommendations from an independent Judicial Nominating Commission, which is made up of three presidential appointees, three jurists named by their peers, and the chief justice.

F2. Does due process prevail in civil and criminal matters? 4 / 4

The authorities generally uphold legal safeguards against arbitrary arrest and detention, and trial proceedings ensure due process.

F3. Is there protection from the illegitimate use of physical force and freedom from war and insurgencies? 4 / 4

Law enforcement agencies maintain internal order, and instances of abuse or impunity are rare, though overcrowding in the country's limited detention facilities remains a problem. In 2019, the vehicle of Narcotics Enforcement Agency chief Ismael Aguon was set ablaze. Aguon believed the action could be interpreted as retaliation for a series of upcoming drug trials.

F4. Do laws, policies, and practices guarantee equal treatment of various segments of the population? 3 / 4

The legal system prohibits discrimination based on gender, race, place of origin, and other categories. Sexual orientation and gender identity are not protected categories, but Palau repealed legal provisions that criminalized consensual same-sex sexual activity in 2014. Then president Remengesau publicly called the country's same-sex marriage ban discriminatory in 2019, though the ban remained in place in 2020. Women generally enjoy equal treatment in practice.

Foreign nationals sometimes face discrimination regarding employment, education, and other matters. Growing tourism from China in particular has created jobs but also raised the cost of living, and some locals regard the presence of Chinese businesses and residents with hostility. However, the number of Chinese tourists has fallen in recent years due to Chinese state policy.

G. PERSONAL AUTONOMY AND INDIVIDUAL RIGHTS: 13 / 16

G1. Do individuals enjoy freedom of movement, including the ability to change their place of residence, employment, or education? 4 / 4

There are usually no significant restrictions on freedom of movement, including internal and international travel. However, Palau restricted inbound travel in response to the COVID-19 pandemic in March 2020 and imposed mandatory quarantine periods for travelers in April. Tourists were effectively unable to visit Palau due to pandemic-related measures.

G2. Are individuals able to exercise the right to own property and establish private businesses without undue interference from state or nonstate actors? 3 / 4

The legal framework generally supports property rights and private business activity, and the government has undertaken reforms to improve conditions in recent years, though some bureaucratic obstacles and corruption-related impediments persist.

Noncitizens cannot purchase land, which is inherited matrilineally among Palauans.

G3. Do individuals enjoy personal social freedoms, including choice of marriage partner and size of family, protection from domestic violence, and control over appearance? 3 / 4

Personal social freedoms are largely respected, and women have equal rights regarding marriage, child custody, and other personal status matters. Rape, including spousal rape, and domestic violence are criminal offenses, though instances of domestic abuse are often not reported to police.

G4. Do individuals enjoy equality of opportunity and freedom from economic exploitation? 3 / 4

Residents generally have access to economic opportunity, and the law provides some protections against exploitative labor practices. However, enforcement of such safeguards is inadequate, and foreign workers remain vulnerable to sexual exploitation, forced labor, or otherwise abusive working conditions in sectors including domestic service and agriculture. The minimum wage law does not apply to foreign workers. Some officials have been accused of complicity in human trafficking.

The 2020 US State Department's *Trafficking in Persons Report* noted that the government made greater efforts to combat human trafficking during its reporting period, including by acceding to a UN antitrafficking protocol. However, the report noted the government's lack of standard operating procedure for identifying trafficking victims, lack of convictions during the reporting period, and did not investigate potential contract violations faced by foreign workers.

Panama

Population: 4,300,000
Capital: Panama City
Freedom Status: Free
Electoral Democracy: Yes

Overview: Panama's political institutions are democratic, with competitive elections and orderly rotations of power. Freedoms of expression and association are generally respected. However, corruption and impunity are serious challenges, affecting the justice system and the highest levels of government. Discrimination against racial minorities is common, and Indigenous groups have struggled to uphold their legal rights with respect to land and development projects.

KEY DEVELOPMENTS IN 2020

- Panama was more severely affected by the COVID-19 pandemic than any other Central American country. According to researchers at the University of Oxford, the country had registered over 246,000 cases and 4,000 deaths at year's end.
- In March, President Laurentino Cortizo declared a state of emergency in response to the pandemic, resulting in large-scale discretionary spending of emergency funds with little transparency.
- Corruption cases against former president Ricardo Martinelli (2009–14) and associates continued. Despite being acquitted in 2019 on corruption charges, Martinelli faced additional trials for graft and for surveilling political rivals and critics. His sons faced extradition to the United States from Guatemala on charges stemming from the notorious Odebrecht corruption scandal.

POLITICAL RIGHTS: 35 / 40 (−1)
A. ELECTORAL PROCESS: 12 / 12
A1. Was the current head of government or other chief national authority elected through free and fair elections? 4 / 4

The president is elected by popular vote for a single five-year term, and cannot serve a second consecutive term. In May 2019, Laurentino Cortizo of the Democratic Revolutionary Party (PRD) was elected president with 33.3 percent of the vote, narrowly defeating Democratic Change (CD) party candidate Rómulo Roux, who won 31 percent of the vote. José Blandón of the then ruling Panameñista Party (PP) won 10.8 percent. Roux initially refused to concede, claiming that the election was marred by voting irregularities. However, Organization of American States (OAS) election monitors described the contest as orderly, and a peaceful transition took place in July.

A2. Were the current national legislative representatives elected through free and fair elections? 4 / 4

Members of the 71-seat unicameral legislature, the National Assembly, are elected for five-year terms. The 2019 elections were held simultaneously with the presidential race and local contests. The PRD won 35 seats, while the CD won 18, the PP won 8, and the United for Change alliance (MOLIRENA) won 5. Another 5 seats went to independents.

A3. Are the electoral laws and framework fair, and are they implemented impartially by the relevant election management bodies? 4 / 4

The country's electoral framework is generally fair and impartially implemented. The Electoral Tribunal of Panama (TE) is responsible for presiding over a multistakeholder commission that reviews the electoral code after each election and submits reform proposals to the National Assembly. In 2017, the legislature adopted reforms proposed by the TE in 2016 that included a 20-day preelection polling blackout—later revised to 48 hours following a Supreme Court ruling that that the longer period was unconstitutional—along with tighter regulation of campaign donations, spending, and advertising.

B. POLITICAL PLURALISM AND PARTICIPATION: 15 / 16

B1. Do the people have the right to organize in different political parties or other competitive political groupings of their choice, and is the system free of undue obstacles to the rise and fall of these competing parties or groupings? 4 / 4

Political parties are free to form and compete in Panama's multiparty system, and since the 2014 elections, candidates have also been able to register as independents. Electoral regulations adopted in 2017 reduced the number of signatures an independent candidate needs to run for office, and specified that only the top three recipients of signatures would be included in the presidential ballot.

B2. Is there a realistic opportunity for the opposition to increase its support or gain power through elections? 4 / 4

Elections are competitive in practice, and orderly transfers of power between rival parties have been the norm since the end of de facto military rule in 1989.

B3. Are the people's political choices free from domination by forces that are external to the political sphere, or by political forces that employ extrapolitical means? 4 / 4

Voters and candidates are generally free from undue interference by groups outside the political system, though the threat that improper donations by drug traffickers and other powerful interests could influence the political process remains a concern, especially given regulatory gaps in campaign financing. Several public officials were charged in cases involving alleged drug and firearms trafficking by in 2020, suggesting a nexus between organized crime and the political system.

B4. Do various segments of the population (including ethnic, racial, religious, gender, LGBT+, and other relevant groups) have full political rights and electoral opportunities? 3 / 4

The law does not limit the political rights of any segment of the citizen population. Women's advocacy organizations have campaigned to improve their representation in elected office, and the electoral code requires gender parity in internal party primaries, but in practice this has not led to more women winning general elections. Only 22.5 percent of National Assembly seats went to women in the 2019 election. That election also saw the first woman from the Guna Indigenous group take her seat.

The country's racial minorities and LGBT+ community continue to face obstacles to the full exercise of their political rights. In 2017, activists created a new progressive party, Creemos, with a platform that included legalization of same-sex marriage, but it failed to gain traction and was deregistered after earning no seats in 2019.

The constitution establishes five Indigenous territories—three at the provincial level and two at the municipal level—and these are duly represented in the system of constituencies for the National Assembly, but the interests of Indigenous people, who make up about 11 percent of the population, remain inadequately addressed by the political system as a whole.

C. FUNCTIONING OF GOVERNMENT: 8 / 12 (−1)

C1. Do the freely elected head of government and national legislative representatives determine the policies of the government? 4 / 4

The elected government and legislature generally determine and implement laws and policies without interference, though evidence of official corruption has raised concerns about the possibility that unelected entities could unduly influence governance.

C2. Are safeguards against official corruption strong and effective? 2 / 4

Safeguards against official corruption are relatively weak and ineffective, due in part to irregular application of the laws and a lack of resources for the judicial system. The Special Anticorruption Prosecutor's Office was formed in 2017 to prosecute those accused of corruption, but has failed to secure convictions in many of these cases.

Investigations have revealed extensive corruption in several presidential administrations. Former president Ricardo Martinelli and multiple top officials were implicated in connection with the Odebrecht case, a corruption scandal centered on a Brazilian construction firm that had repercussions across much of Latin America. Martinelli was arrested in the United States in 2017 and extradited to Panama in 2018, but in August 2019 he was acquitted on charges including wiretapping and the improper use of state funds. In July 2020 prosecutors announced new embezzlement charges, and in December judicial officials stated that a retrial on the surveillance charges would begin in 2021.

Martinelli's two sons were also implicated in the Odebrecht scandal; they were arrested in the United States in 2018 after Panamanian prosecutors accused them of large-scale corruption during their father's term in office. In July 2020, the brothers were arrested in Guatemala, and at year's end they remained in Guatemalan detention pending an extradition petition from the United States, where they were charged with facilitating $28 million in bribes during the Martinelli administration.

The administration of Juan Carlos Varela (2014–19) was also beset by corruption allegations, with several officials and legislators resigning during his term in office. In 2017, Varela admitted that the PP received help from an individual tied to Odebrecht; the former president remained under investigation in subsequent years, and was indicted on new Odebrecht-related bribery charges in July 2020.

In 2019 President Cortizo introduced a constitutional reform package that would have allowed the attorney general to investigate Supreme Court judges and legislators suspected of wrongdoing, but the National Assembly struck the proposals down and sought to increase its own investigative powers, prompting Cortizo to withdraw the reform package altogether. The administration's anticorruption and transparency efforts stagnated in 2020, even as repeated reports of pandemic-related graft and abuses of power led prosecutors to open over a dozen investigations. Critics in civil society described a pattern of unresolved corruption investigations resulting in impunity, a dynamic reinforced by scandals and turnover in the Prosecutor General's Office in recent years.

C3. Does the government operate with openness and transparency? 2 / 4 (−1)

The law provides mechanisms for public access to government information. A transparency law was introduced in 2002, and the Varela administration adopted an open data policy, instructing public institutions to make data accessible to the public in clear, open, and machine-readable formats. However, in 2020 the pandemic and associated state of emergency led to a marked decline in transparency and effective controls on public contracting and procurement processes, as well as unresponsiveness by public officials to public information requests and passivity by the agencies charged with ensuring transparency.

Score Change: The score declined from 3 to 2 due to increased government opacity, reflected in noncompliance with public procurement reporting rules, and refusals to answer freedom of information requests.

CIVIL LIBERTIES: 48 / 60

D. FREEDOM OF EXPRESSION AND BELIEF: 15 / 16

D1. Are there free and independent media? 3 / 4

News consumers have access to a wide variety of private media outlets that present a range of views, but the constitutional guarantee of freedom of the press is not consistently upheld. Independent, critical journalists and outlets reportedly face editorial pressure from the government, and some journalists have experienced harassment when covering stories and opinions unfavorable to the government.

Libel is both a civil and a criminal offense, while defamation and insult have also been defined in the criminal code. Such cases are often filed against journalists and media outlets. Former president Martinelli and his wife have used the courts to stop media discussion of his legal problems; as of October 2020, the Inter American Press Association (IAPA) registered 16 Martinelli lawsuits against 38 journalists and directors of *La Prensa* and *Mi Diario*. In July 2020, former president Ernesto Pérez Balladares also sued *La Prensa* for libel and acquired a court order to seize the paper's assets. According to the Committee to Protect Journalists (CPJ), as of July *La Prensa* faced nearly three dozen criminal and civil suits adding up to $84 million in potential fines and damages. During the COVID-19 lockdown, IAPA also registered cases of police harassment of reporters.

D2. Are individuals free to practice and express their religious faith or nonbelief in public and private? 4 / 4

The constitution recognizes Roman Catholicism as the majority religion and requires general "respect for Christian morality and public order," but freedom of religion is otherwise guaranteed and broadly upheld in practice. Catholic religious instruction is offered but not mandatory in public schools.

D3. Is there academic freedom, and is the educational system free from extensive political indoctrination? 4 / 4

The government generally honors academic freedom, and the schools are free from political indoctrination.

D4. Are individuals free to express their personal views on political or other sensitive topics without fear of surveillance or retribution? 4 / 4

Private discussion is free and vibrant, and use of social media platforms for the expression of personal views, including views on political or social issues, is not restricted.

E. ASSOCIATIONAL AND ORGANIZATIONAL RIGHTS: 11 / 12

E1. Is there freedom of assembly? 4 / 4

Freedom of assembly is generally respected, and peaceful demonstrations are common, though protests that block roads and highways often result in arrests and altercations with police. In October and November 2019, authorities applied disproportionate force against protesters demonstrating in front of the National Assembly to oppose proposed constitutional reforms. During the COVID-19 pandemic in 2020, freedom of assembly was temporarily curtailed, and occasional abuses occurred. In December 2020, police used excessive force to repress a peaceful student demonstration.

E2. Is there freedom for nongovernmental organizations, particularly those that are engaged in human rights- and governance-related work? 4 / 4

Nongovernmental organizations (NGOs) operate freely, but some activists—particularly those focused on environmental issues and Indigenous rights—have complained of harassment and intimidation, including through lawsuits by private companies.

E3. Is there freedom for trade unions and similar professional or labor organizations? 3 / 4

The law generally protects workers' rights to unionize, bargain collectively, and engage in legal, peaceful strikes. However, enforcement of labor protections is inadequate, and labor-related protests frequently feature clashes with police. Public employees are allowed to form associations to engage in collective bargaining and strike activities, but their rights have historically been weaker when compared to those of unions.

F. RULE OF LAW: 10 / 16

F1. Is there an independent judiciary? 2 / 4

The country's judicial system is plagued by corruption and inefficiency. Public disagreements between the Prosecutor General's Office and judges over rulings that impeded major corruption cases in recent years have raised doubts about whether such cases would be heard impartially. The previous Varela administration was criticized over allegations that the National Security Council had interfered with corruption investigations that should have been handled by law enforcement bodies and the judiciary.

F2. Does due process prevail in civil and criminal matters? 2 / 4

Due process is constitutionally guaranteed but inconsistently upheld in practice. The justice system features extensive use of lengthy pretrial detention. According to official statistics, as of December 2020, pretrial detainees represented 39 percent of the country's prison population.

F3. Is there protection from the illegitimate use of physical force and freedom from war and insurgencies? 3 / 4

The country is free from major threats to physical security such as war and insurgencies. However, police have been accused of beatings and other forms of excessive force, including while dispersing protests. The prison system is marked by overcrowding, poor health conditions, and a lack of security. In December 2019, 15 inmates were killed in La Joyita, a prison on the eastern outskirts of Panama City. Spanish news service EFE reported that heavy caliber weapons, including three rifles, were found in the prison after the fighting. The prison system remained afflicted by violence and widespread contraband smuggling in 2020.

The illegal drug trade and related criminal violence remain problems, though the homicide rate is below that of most countries in the region. The Ministry of Public Security reported that the number of homicides rose modestly to 497 in 2020, from 480 in 2019.

F4. Do laws, policies, and practices guarantee equal treatment of various segments of the population? 3 / 4

Discrimination based on gender, race, and other such categories is prohibited by law, but sexual orientation and gender identity are not covered, and racial minorities—including Indigenous people, Panamanians of African descent, and certain immigrant groups—face some discrimination in practice. Indigenous communities enjoy a significant degree of autonomy and self-government, but many Indigenous people live in poverty and lack equal access to basic services. An influx of migrants and asylum seekers from Venezuela, Cuba, and other troubled countries in the region has stoked anti-immigrant sentiment in recent years.

G. PERSONAL AUTONOMY AND INDIVIDUAL RIGHTS: 12 / 16

G1. Do individuals enjoy freedom of movement, including the ability to change their place of residence, employment, or education? 4 / 4

The government generally respects freedom of foreign travel and internal movement, including the freedom to change one's place of residence, employment, or education. These freedoms were temporarily and intermittently curtailed in 2020 as part of efforts to limit the extent of the COVID-19 pandemic.

G2. Are individuals able to exercise the right to own property and establish private businesses without undue interference from state or nonstate actors? 3 / 4

Individuals can own private property and establish businesses freely under the law, but there are some practical impediments to defending property rights and operating businesses, including corruption and interference from organized crime.

Although Indigenous groups have substantial land rights under the law, implementation has been problematic. Such groups have long protested the encroachment of illegal settlers on their lands, government delays in the formal demarcation of collective land, and large-scale development projects that proceed despite dissent within indigenous communities. In 2019, the environment ministry recognized Indigenous claims in 25 areas throughout the country, allowing residents to demarcate collectively held land there.

G3. Do individuals enjoy personal social freedoms, including choice of marriage partner and size of family, protection from domestic violence, and control over appearance? 3 / 4

Personal social freedoms are largely unrestricted. However, domestic violence is a concern; according to the Prosecutor General's Office, over 15,000 domestic violence cases were registered in 2020. Abortion is permitted in cases of rape or incest or to preserve the life or health of the woman, though there are significant procedural obstacles as well as potential penalties for abortions that do not meet the legal standard.

Panama does not recognize same-sex marriage, though it has faced pressure to legalize such unions in recent years. In a 2018 advisory opinion, the Inter-American Court of Human Rights (IACHR) ruled that member states should recognize same-sex unions. Instead, legislators sought to strengthen a ban on same-sex marriage when they altered a package of constitutional reforms in October 2019, but the proposed amendment was scrapped that December. The Supreme Court has yet to rule on several pending cases involving the issue; in October 2020, the IACHR held a hearing on same-sex marriage in Panama.

During the COVID-19 lockdown, the government instituted a quarantine protocol in which women and men were allowed to leave home on alternate days. Human rights groups decried the measure's impact on transgender Panamanians, who were repeatedly subjected to discriminatory or humiliating treatment by police officers.

G4. Do individuals enjoy equality of opportunity and freedom from economic exploitation? 2 / 4

Human trafficking for sexual exploitation and forced labor remains a serious problem despite some government efforts to combat it. Both Panamanian and migrant workers in certain sectors—including the agricultural sector, where many workers are Indigenous people—are subject to exploitative working conditions. Enforcement of basic labor protections is weak in rural areas and among informal workers.

Papua New Guinea

Population: 9,000,000
Capital: Port Moresby
Freedom Status: Partly Free
Electoral Democracy: Yes

Overview: Papua New Guinea is a democracy in which elections are held regularly, but the polls have often been marred by irregularities and violence. Party allegiances are unstable, and only two governments have survived for a full term since independence in 1975. Since the turn of the century, a boom in mineral resources extraction has helped successive incumbent governments to consolidate control. The judiciary retains significant independence, and the media are mostly free to criticize the government. Corruption remains a serious problem.

KEY DEVELOPMENTS IN 2020

- Papua New Guinea managed the COVID-19 pandemic relatively effectively in 2020, registering 780 cases and just 9 deaths, according to researchers at the University of Oxford.
- In December, Prime Minister James Marape survived a rebellion in his cabinet triggered by an opposition attempt to call a no-confidence vote in November.
- Former prime minister Peter O'Neill was arrested in May for corruption and abuse of office in connection with the purchase of two generators from Israel in 2013 without parliamentary approval.

POLITICAL RIGHTS: 23 / 40

A. ELECTORAL PROCESS: 7 / 12

A1. Was the current head of government or other chief national authority elected through free and fair elections? 3 / 4

The governor general represents the British monarch as head of state and formally appoints the prime minister, who is the head of government, following an election process in Parliament. A law provides that the largest political party emerging from a general election has the first right to nominate a prime minister. While the prime minister's legitimacy is partly rooted in the conduct of legislative elections, the election of the prime minister by members of Parliament is a highly competitive process. Peter O'Neill of the People's National Congress party (PNC) resigned in May 2019 after internal party upheaval. Parliament selected former finance minister James Marape, who resigned from the O'Neill-led cabinet that April, to succeed him as prime minister. Opposition leader Belden Namah contested Marape's election before the Supreme Court, but the court threw out the challenge in November 2020.

A2. Were the current national legislative representatives elected through free and fair elections? 2 / 4

Voters elect members of the unicameral, 111-member National Parliament for five-year terms. A limited preferential voting system allows voters to choose up to three preferred candidates on their ballots.

Serious flaws, including bribery and voter fraud, were reported in the 2017 election. Some areas, notably the Highlands Region, experienced election-related violence that resulted in dozens of deaths, as well as severe property damage. Due to irregularities, election results in the Southern Highlands were released several months late and sparked renewed violence in the town of Mendi once made public. The electoral process was smoother in coastal areas, but those regions were not completely free from irregularities and violence. Allegations of voter roll manipulation that favored the incumbent government were widespread, but most clear abuses were localized in the Highlands. Election observers expressed disappointment that recommendations to clean up voter rolls were disregarded.

Parliamentary seats were ultimately divided among numerous small parties, with the PNC taking nearly a quarter of the total and the National Alliance Party (NAP) placing a distant second. Independents made up the third-largest group. After becoming prime minister in 2019, Marape consolidated his position, increased the number of members of parliament affiliated with his Papua and Niugini Union Party (Pangu), and brought Patrick Pruaitch's NAP into government. In June 2020, Marape claimed to have the support of 91 lawmakers in the 111-member parliament, but the end of his 18-month "grace period"—a period in which new prime ministers are immune from no-confidence challenges—in November triggered the movement of key ministers into the opposition. To avoid a planned no-confidence vote, and with the opposition absent, Parliament was adjourned in early December.

Local elections were held in Papua New Guinea in July and August 2019, and were similarly marred by fraud, violence, and voter intimidation. In August 2020, the autonomous region of Bougainville held a delayed but relatively peaceful legislative election. Incumbent president John Momis, who had served the maximum two terms, was replaced by the former commander of the Bougainville Revolutionary Army, Ishmael Toroama.

A3. Are the electoral laws and framework fair, and are they implemented impartially by the relevant election management bodies? 2 / 4

The electoral law, which requires voters to rank three candidates on a preferential ballot, is fair but complex to administer. The voter rolls are poorly maintained. At the local level, election management bodies are chronically lacking in independence, particularly in the Highlands. Irregularities do not necessarily benefit incumbents, more than half of whom usually lose their seats at elections.

Electoral officials have also been accused of corruption in recent years. Electoral Commissioner Patilias Gamato was detained for corruption, money laundering, and conspiracy in 2019. He was released on bail but was rearrested in August 2020 for breaching bail conditions and interfering with state witnesses; he was removed from his position in September.

B. POLITICAL PLURALISM AND PARTICIPATION: 13 / 16

B1. Do the people have the right to organize in different political parties or other competitive political groupings of their choice, and is the system free of undue obstacles to the rise and fall of these competing parties or groupings? 4 / 4

Political parties are able to form and operate freely, but many candidates run as independents and join factions only after reaching Parliament. Electoral loyalties are driven by local and personal factors at the constituency level. Lawmakers frequently switch affiliations and alliances. A law constraining freedom of movement between parties was ruled unconstitutional in 2010.

Prime Minister Marape has transformed the Pangu Party, the country's oldest, into his vehicle for reelection in 2022. A large number of lawmakers defected from their former parties to join Pangu in 2019 and 2020, making it the largest force in Parliament. The NAP, the second-largest parliamentary group after the 2017 election, joined the governing coalition in 2019, but leader Patrick Pruaitch defected in November 2020 and became leader of the opposition.

The law granting the largest party the first opportunity to form a government creates an incentive for parties to register with the Registrar of Political Parties, as does government funding for parties. The 2020 no-confidence challenge was centered on jockeying for positions to enable PNG politicians to enter the 2022 election as incumbents, which confers an electoral advantage; the incumbent government has won all three elections since 2007.

B2. Is there a realistic opportunity for the opposition to increase its support or gain power through elections? 4 / 4

The opposition has a reasonable chance of dislodging the government in elections, mass defections, or through a no-confidence vote on the floor of Parliament. Since independence in 1975, only two governments have served out a full five-year term, the Michael Somare-led 2002–07 government and the O'Neill-led 2012–17 government.

The frequency of no-confidence votes has been diminished somewhat by a provision that grants an incoming prime minister an 18-month "grace period." While Marape's grace period expired in November 2020, he is vulnerable only for eight months before another 12-month grace period kicks in ahead of the 2022 elections. During periods of vulnerability prime ministers often suspend parliament for long periods, which grants significant power to the speaker in Parliament, a position currently held by MP Job Pomat, who was an ally of Marape's predecessor and bitter opponent of Peter O'Neill until resigning from the PNC in June 2020.

B3. Are the people's political choices free from domination by forces that are external to the political sphere, or by political forces that employ extrapolitical means? 2 / 4

Most citizens and candidates are generally free to make political choices without undue interference. However, some local leaders, politicians, and candidate agents control the balloting process, particularly in the Highlands, and complete the ballot papers in bulk—a form of "assisted voting." As a result, the affected citizens are effectively denied the right to vote.

B4. Do various segments of the population (including ethnic, racial, religious, gender, LGBT+, and other relevant groups) have full political rights and electoral opportunities? 3 / 4

Although all citizens have equal political rights under the law, women are underrepresented in elected offices. The 2017 election featured the highest number of women candidates ever, but none won legislative seats, and there are currently no women in the 111-seat Parliament. LGBT+ people face societal discrimination that impedes their ability to advocate for their interests in the political sphere.

A 2005 agreement ended a civil war in Bougainville and provided for an independence referendum to be held between 2015 and 2020. While the Autonomous Bougainville Government has been building its own civil service in preparation for the possibility of independence, central authorities have expressed opposition to the island's possible secession. Over 180,000 people participated in the nonbinding referendum in 2019, and 97.7 percent voted for independence. Following Bougainville's change of government, Papua New Guinean and Bougainville leaders were expected to negotiate a postreferendum agenda in 2021.

C. FUNCTIONING OF GOVERNMENT: 3 / 12

C1. Do the freely elected head of government and national legislative representatives determine the policies of the government? 2 / 4

The prime minister heads the government, but cabinet ministers often exert considerable control over their portfolios without necessarily being answerable to the cabinet. There are no powerful external forces that determine the policies of government, though logging and mining companies have been known to court influence. The government has only a limited ability to implement its policies across the country, as the state's presence in more remote areas is minimal.

C2. Are safeguards against official corruption strong and effective? 0 / 4

Corruption is pervasive and remains the most important hindrance to development. Anticorruption institutions have been subject to political interference. Task Force Sweep was established in 2011 to root out corruption, and it carried out a variety of investigations against politicians, civil servants, and businessmen. However, when the unit turned its attention to millions of dollars' worth of fraudulent payments to Port Moresby law firm Paraka Lawyers that were allegedly authorized by Prime Minister O'Neill, he responded by disbanding the task force; when courts ordered its resurrection, the government cut its funding. The Committal Court dismissed the remaining 22 charges against Paul Paraka in June 2020.

O'Neill was arrested in May 2020 in connection with an investigation into procedural irregularities and possible corruption in the $14 million purchase of generators from Israel in 2013.

Papua New Guinea made strides on legal reforms to combat corruption in 2020. In February, Parliament approved a bill protecting whistleblowers, and in November lawmakers unanimously passed a bill to create a long-promised Independent Commission against Corruption (ICAC). Anticorruption advocates welcomed the move, but cautioned that the ICAC's independence and capacity remained to be determined.

C3. Does the government operate with openness and transparency? 1 / 4

Government operations are generally opaque, and the government does not frequently release accurate information about public expenditures, procurement processes, or officials' assets. Papua New Guinea does not have any access to information law. Government figures, especially regarding public revenue and expenditure, are often inaccurate and are sometimes manipulated. Civil society organizations and opposition politicians criticized the National Pandemic Act passed in June 2020 as the product of a rushed process, and claimed it contained inadequate provisions to ensure transparent management of state funds.

CIVIL LIBERTIES: 39 / 60

D. FREEDOM OF EXPRESSION AND BELIEF: 14 / 16

D1. Are there free and independent media? 3 / 4

Freedom of the press is generally respected. Local media provide independent coverage of the political opposition, as well as controversial issues such as alleged police abuse and official corruption. However, politicians have been known to harass media professionals over negative stories, and journalists can face physical attacks in the course of their work.

Incidents of censorship of journalists during the Marape administration have diminished compared to the frequent violations during the O'Neill government. However, in April 2020 press freedom advocates criticized Police Minister Bryan Kramer after he called for the firing of two journalists who reported on alleged misspending of funds assigned to combat the COVID-19 pandemic.

D2. Are individuals free to practice and express their religious faith or nonbelief in public and private? 4 / 4

Religious freedom is generally upheld. There have been reports of larger churches criticizing newer and smaller groups, and of anti-Muslim rhetoric that has accompanied the arrival of Muslim refugees, but no major infringements on religious liberty have been alleged in recent years.

D3. Is there academic freedom, and is the educational system free from extensive political indoctrination? 3 / 4

Academic freedom is generally respected, though the police have at times violently suppressed student demonstrations on campus.

D4. Are individuals free to express their personal views on political or other sensitive topics without fear of surveillance or retribution? 4 / 4

There are no major constraints on the expression of personal views. However, a 2016 cybercrime law allows the prosecution of people who publish defamatory material or incite violence on social media, raising concerns that it could be misused to punish legitimate speech.

E. ASSOCIATIONAL AND ORGANIZATIONAL RIGHTS: 10 / 12

E1. Is there freedom of assembly? 3 / 4

The constitution provides for freedom of assembly. However, marches and demonstrations require 14 days' notice and police approval, and authorities sometimes deny permits. Prior to the 2019 transfer of nearly all asylum seekers and refugees held on Manus Island under an agreement with the Australian government, police on several occasions used force to suppress demonstrations by detainees.

E2. Is there freedom for nongovernmental organizations, particularly those that are engaged in human rights- and governance-related work? 4 / 4

A number of nongovernmental organizations (NGOs) operate in the country, including groups focused on human rights and environmental causes, as well as some that provide social services. Most are small and lack resources, but they are otherwise free of serious constraints on their activities.

E3. Is there freedom for trade unions and similar professional or labor organizations? 3 / 4

Workers' rights to strike, organize, and engage in collective bargaining are largely respected. However, the government has frequently imposed arbitration in labor disputes to avert strikes, and protections against antiunion discrimination are unevenly enforced. Most workers are employed in the informal sector and lack access to union protections.

F. RULE OF LAW: 7 / 16

F1. Is there an independent judiciary? 3 / 4

While successive governments have exerted political pressure on the court system, the judiciary is generally independent. Judges are appointed by the largely apolitical Judicial and Legal Services Commission and cannot be removed arbitrarily. Laypeople sit on village courts to adjudicate minor offenses under customary and statutory law. In recent years, the higher courts have repeatedly demonstrated their impartiality by ruling against the government and its political interests.

F2. Does due process prevail in civil and criminal matters? 1 / 4

Constitutional guarantees of due process are poorly upheld. Arbitrary detention is relatively common, and opportunities to challenge such abuses are limited in practice. A shortage of trained judicial personnel is a key cause of lengthy detentions and trial delays. The police force is chronically underfunded, and in September 2020 Police Minister Bryan Kramer alleged that the force maintains a "rampant culture of ill-discipline and brutality" and alleged that officers are involved in an array of criminal activities, included drug and firearms trafficking and land theft.

F3. Is there protection from the illegitimate use of physical force and freedom from war and insurgencies? 1 / 4

Law enforcement officials are frequently implicated in brutality and corruption. Prison conditions are poor, and the correctional service is understaffed. Prison breaks are common. Lack of economic opportunities exacerbates social unrest, frequently resulting in violent clashes, injuries, and deaths. An Australian police assistance program exists, but its officers lack powers of arrest and are restricted by a 2005 court ruling that removed immunities from prosecution under local law.

Tribal violence and so-called "payback" attacks are common in the Highlands Region. In March 2020, 11 people were killed in tribal fighting in the region. Killings connected to accusations of sorcery are also common, including five murders in November 2020 in East Sepik Province; according to Human Rights Watch (HRW), most victims are women.

F4. Do laws, policies, and practices guarantee equal treatment of various segments of the population? 2 / 4

The constitution guarantees equality regardless of race, tribe, religion, sex, and other categories, but various forms of discrimination are common in practice. Same-sex sexual relations are a criminal offense that can draw up to 14 years in prison, though the relevant laws are rarely enforced. There is some discrimination against people of Chinese origin, which is mainly linked to resentment toward a growing Chinese business presence that is viewed as disadvantaging other groups. Women face legal discrimination in employment in addition to societal biases. Allegations of sorcery have been used to target women for violence.

Australia paid the Papua New Guinean government to accept asylum seekers who arrived in Australian waters by boat. As the program wound down in recent years, those who were not granted refugee status or did not agree to settle in Papua New Guinea were left in limbo. The Australian government has been reluctant to allow refugees to enter Australia, but some have been sent to the United States as part of a deal between the US and Australian governments.

In 2016, Papua New Guinea's Supreme Court ruled that Australia's Manus Island detention center was unconstitutional, and the facility officially closed in 2017. Many remained in the facility for several years, amid reports of poor living conditions, violence, and mental health problems. In 2019, those remaining on Manus were moved to Port Moresby and held under brutal conditions at the Bomana Immigration Detention Centre. Some eventually agreed to return to their country of origin; as of the end of 2020, 137 people remained in Papua New Guinea, amid criticism of both Papua New Guinean and Australian officials by human rights groups for their treatment of people subjected to the detention regime.

G. PERSONAL AUTONOMY AND INDIVIDUAL RIGHTS: 8 / 16

G1. Do individuals enjoy freedom of movement, including the ability to change their place of residence, employment, or education? 2 / 4

Freedom of movement is somewhat restricted in the Highlands; survivors of tribal violence are known to restrict their domestic travel or go into hiding in the immediate aftermath of skirmishes and attacks, and as many as 2,000 people were internally displaced during acts of violence in mid-2019. Travelers in Port Moresby are subject to roadblocks, where authorities check the registration of their vehicles. Movement is also restricted for refugees and asylum seekers who resided on Manus Island and in Port Moresby.

G2. Are individuals able to exercise the right to own property and establish private businesses without undue interference from state or nonstate actors? 2 / 4

In Papua New Guinea, 97 percent of the land area is theoretically under customary tenure, but Special Agriculture and Business Leases (SABLs) have been used to facilitate land grabs by unscrupulous investors. In 2013, a government commission found that most active SABLs were illegal and recommended their cancellation. In 2017, former premier O'Neill claimed that all SABLs were canceled, but the lands and physical planning minister acknowledged in 2018 that most SABLs were still being contested in court. Many SABLs remained in place in 2020, with local activists warning that large-scale logging was ongoing on land covered by the scheme.

Women face disadvantages regarding property rights and inheritance, particularly under customary law.

G3. Do individuals enjoy personal social freedoms, including choice of marriage partner and size of family, protection from domestic violence, and control over appearance? 2 / 4

The law provides some protections for individual rights on personal status matters like marriage and divorce, but early or forced marriage remains a problem, and legislation meant to combat widespread family violence and aid victims is poorly enforced. About two-thirds of partnered women have experienced physical abuse, according to multiple studies. In June 2020, two high-profile episodes of brutal intimate partner violence prompted heated discussions about gender-based violence. Abortion is illegal except when it is necessary to save the life of the child bearer.

G4. Do individuals enjoy equality of opportunity and freedom from economic exploitation? 2 / 4

Legal safeguards against exploitative working conditions are weakly enforced, and frequent abuses in sectors including logging and mining have been reported. The US Labor Department has previously assembled evidence of child labor in the coffee, cocoa, palm oil, and rubber sectors, as well as in commercial sexual exploitation.

In the 2020 edition of its *Trafficking in Persons Report*, the US State Department reported widespread trafficking of both foreign and domestic victims, including exploitation of children as forced laborers and women in the sex trade, especially in proximity to mining, logging, and fishing operations. The report noted that the country has failed to convict a single trafficker under the 2013 law that criminalized most forms of sex and labor trafficking, and characterized the government's efforts to address the issue as highly apathetic.

Paraguay

Population: 7,300,000
Capital: Asunción
Freedom Status: Partly Free
Electoral Democracy: Yes

Overview: Paraguay's democracy is dominated by the conservative Colorado Party. Corruption remains widespread, while organized crime, environmental destruction, and systemic discrimination damage the rights of rural and Indigenous populations. Poverty and gender-based discrimination also limit the rights of women and children.

KEY DEVELOPMENTS IN 2020

- In response to the COVID-19 pandemic, Paraguay implemented one of most stringent and prolonged lockdowns in the region. Despite early success, the infection rate and death rate eventually started to catch up with regional peers. According to researchers at the University of Oxford, the country registered over 108,000 cases and 2,200 deaths by the end of 2020.

- A September military raid on a camp occupied by Paraguayan People's Army (EPP) guerrillas left two 11-year-old girls dead, and prompted sharp criticism of the government by human rights groups following alleged crime-scene tampering and government misrepresentations of the incident.

POLITICAL RIGHTS: 28 / 40

A. ELECTORAL PROCESS: 10 / 12

A1. Was the current head of government or other chief national authority elected through free and fair elections? 3 / 4

The president is directly elected to no more than one five-year term, although efforts to instate presidential reelection periodically surface. The Colorado Party has held the presidency for most of the past 70 years. The most recent exception, left-wing former president Fernando Lugo (2008–12) was removed from office in a legal, if highly controversial, "express impeachment."

Mario Abdo Benítez of the Colorado Party won the presidency in the 2018 election, taking a little over 46 percent of the vote. Efraín Alegre, the candidate of the opposition Alianza Ganar coalition, took 43 percent. Observers including the European Union (EU) described the election as largely fair, although allegations were made of fraud, vote-buying, and a media blackout affecting other candidates.

A2. Were the current national legislative representatives elected through free and fair elections? 4 / 4

The bicameral Congress consists of an 80-member Chamber of Deputies and a 45-member Senate, with all members elected for five-year terms. The 2018 legislative elections resulted in a majority for the Colorado Party in the Chamber of Deputies, but no party won a majority in the Senate. Monitoring missions considered the polls to be generally competitive and credible.

A3. Are the electoral laws and framework fair, and are they implemented impartially by the relevant election management bodies? 3 / 4

The Superior Electoral Court of Justice (TSJE) regulates electoral processes. The government has yet to implement most recommendations the EU election observation mission issued in 2013 and 2018, including securing the independence of the TSJE, making vote recounts possible, and making it easier for Indigenous peoples to vote. However, EU representatives praised the passage of a campaign finance law in February 2020. Due to the coronavirus pandemic, local elections were delayed from November 2020 to October 2021. Party primaries were also postponed from July 2020 to June 2021.

B. POLITICAL PLURALISM AND PARTICIPATION: 12 / 16

B1. Do the people have the right to organize in different political parties or other competitive political groupings of their choice, and is the system free of undue obstacles to the rise and fall of these competing parties or groupings? 3 / 4

The Colorado Party has been in power for most of the past 70 years. The party dominates the national political scene with the opposition Authentic Radical Liberal Party (PLRA), though both contain rival internal factions.

Several smaller parties emerged or increased their standing in the 2018 elections, including Patria Querida (PPQ), Hagamos (PPH), and Movimiento Cruzada Nacional (MCN), suggesting the grip of the two traditional parties is weakening somewhat.

B2. Is there a realistic opportunity for the opposition to increase its support or gain power through elections? 4 / 4

Despite the dominance of the Colorado Party, opposition parties have a realistic chance of gaining power through elections. Former president Lugo was able to come to power in 2008 due to a split in the Colorado Party, while a liberal-left coalition, Alianza Ganar, came close to taking the presidency in 2018. In addition, rival factions within the Colorado Party serve as a kind of internal opposition and have recently alternated in power.

B3. Are the people's political choices free from domination by forces that are external to the political sphere, or by political forces that employ extrapolitical means? 3 / 4

Citizens are generally free from undue interference in their political choices. However, there is some concern over the growing political influence of Brazilian landowners in eastern regions. The constitution bars military personnel from politics.

B4. Do various segments of the population (including ethnic, racial religious, gender, LGBT+, and other relevant groups) have full political rights and electoral opportunities? 2 / 4

Political office is overwhelmingly dominated by male and White or mestizo individuals. No Afro-Paraguayans or Indigenous people held legislative office in 2020, although an Indigenous political movement, the Movimiento Indígena Plurinacional, has established a grassroots presence in both the Chaco and eastern region. Women held only 21 out of 125 seats in congress in 2020, and no regional governorships.

C. FUNCTIONING OF GOVERNMENT: 6 / 12

C1. Do the freely elected head of government and national legislative representatives determine the policies of the government? 2 / 4

While elected officials determine government policy, the making and implementation of decisions is often influenced or hampered by organized crime and corruption.

A major scandal in July 2019 stoked fears that a renegotiation of the dividends of the Itaipú dam—a publicly owned hydroelectric facility shared with Brazil—due by 2023 will be determined by private interests.

Former president Cartes retains considerable influence over government policy and personnel. At the height of the 2019 Itaipú scandal, only the private intervention of Cartes saved Abdo Benítez from impeachment. Cartes seemingly benefited from special treatment during the COVID-19 pandemic; in July, for instance, he held a private meeting with former Argentine president Mauricio Macri, whose visit was exempted from a flight ban and mandatory quarantine.

In October 2020, the lower house voted to suspend opposition deputy Celeste Amarilla of the PLRA for two months after she alleged that at least 60 of her 80 colleagues held their seats due to "dirty money." Critics said her suspension, driven by the ruling Colorado Party, contravened the constitution and parliamentary privilege.

C2. Are safeguards against official corruption strong and effective? 2 / 4

Corruption and impunity are serious problems, and anticorruption laws have been poorly implemented. Cases often languish for years in the courts without resolution. Anticorruption protests and citizen transparency initiatives have forced the resignation and prosecution of officials from several parties under Abdo Benítez, who has taken a somewhat firmer line against corruption than his predecessors.

In 2020, serious and credible allegations of corruption were made regarding the purchase of coronavirus-related supplies by the Ministry of Health, civil aviation agency DINAC, and state-owned fuels firm Petropar; the latter resulted in the April resignation of Petropar's president.

C3. Does the government operate with openness and transparency? 2 / 4

Government transparency is gradually improving, and the effective implementation of access to information laws has bolstered investigative journalism. Citizens show increasing intolerance for corruption and opaque government, and anticorruption demonstrations are becoming more common.

CIVIL LIBERTIES: 37 / 60

D. FREEDOM OF EXPRESSION AND BELIEF: 12 / 16

D1. Are there free and independent media? 2 / 4

Constitutional freedoms of expression and the press are unevenly upheld. Direct pressure against journalists, including threats by criminal groups and corrupt authorities, encourages self-censorship, and violent attacks against journalists take place occasionally.

In February 2020, Brazilian journalist Lourenço "Léo" Veras was shot and killed in the border city of Pedro Juan Caballero. Veras had reported death threats from narcotraffickers.

In July, soldiers detained and assaulted freelance journalist Roberto Esquivel while he was reporting on lockdown measures in the northern town of Bella Vista Norte. Esquivel was later released without charge.

D2. Are individuals free to practice and express their religious faith or nonbelief in public and private? 4 / 4

Diverse religious groups generally worship freely. However, the cultural dominance of the Catholic Church has spread further into public and private life, sometimes to the detriment of individual rights. Religious groups unaffiliated with the Catholic Church claim the government disproportionately subsidizes Catholic schools. There have also been concerns from human rights groups that Indigenous holidays are not respected by employers of other religious backgrounds.

D3. Is there academic freedom, and is the educational system free from extensive political indoctrination? 3 / 4

Although academia is generally independent, student elections and professional advancement often depend on affiliation with the Colorado Party or the PLRA.

D4. Are individuals free to express their personal views on political or other sensitive topics without fear of surveillance or retribution? 3 / 4

Citizens can, for the most part, engage in free and open private discussion, though the presence of armed groups in some areas can serve as a deterrent.

E. ASSOCIATIONAL AND ORGANIZATIONAL RIGHTS: 8 / 12

E1. Is there freedom of assembly? 3 / 4

Demonstrations and protests are common but sometimes repressed. In October, several thousand smallholder farmers demanding changes to rural land and agriculture policy marched on Asunción without interference.

However, restrictions on public gatherings imposed in response to the COVID-19 pandemic were applied in a politicized manner, with more permissive rules for events involving the ruling Colorado Party. After a high-profile September protest over the military's killing of two 11-year-old girls at a guerrilla camp, prosecutors threatened to bring charges against several demonstrators—initially citing incitement to violence and then the breaking of lockdown restrictions—in an episode widely interpreted as reflecting concerns about a growing authoritarian bent.

E2. Is there freedom for nongovernmental organizations, particularly those that are engaged in human rights- and governance-related work? 3 / 4

Paraguay has a strong culture of largely free nongovernmental organizations (NGOs) working in the field of human rights and governance. However, political access tends to be given to organizations made up of senior business figures or religious groups, while human rights groups are increasingly dismissed as reflecting an international liberal agenda.

E3. Is there freedom for trade unions and similar professional or labor organizations? 2 / 4

Registration procedures for trade unions are cumbersome. Labor activism was nevertheless robust in 2020, with public sector unions protesting in June over proposed pension reforms, and doctors mobilizing to demand unpaid salaries and benefits in September.

F. RULE OF LAW: 7 / 16

F1. Is there an independent judiciary? 2 / 4

The judiciary is nominally independent, but money launderers, drug traffickers, and corrupt politicians have co-opted local judicial authorities. Public prosecutors show increasing signs of co-option by the ruling Colorado Party.

F2. Does due process prevail in civil and criminal matters? 1 / 4

Constitutional guarantees of due process are poorly upheld, largely due to corruption that permeates the judicial system. Individuals with influence or access to money are frequently able to obtain favorable treatment in the justice system. Cases like the 2012 killings of 6 policeman and 11 peasant farmers in Curuguaty are yet to be investigated fully and fairly.

F3. Is there protection from the illegitimate use of physical force and freedom from war and insurgencies? 2 / 4

Paraguay is one of the region's safer countries. However, the Paraguayan People's Army (EPP) guerilla group is still active in the northeast. A September raid on an EPP camp that resulted in the killings of two 11-year-old Argentine girls generated sharp criticism.

According to media reports and a Human Rights Watch (HRW) investigation, officials quickly buried the bodies and burned the girls' clothing, spuriously citing the need to follow COVID-19 sanitation protocols. Officials also made highly disputed claims about the circumstances of the killings and refused to allow independent investigation by respected Argentine forensics officials, despite demands by human rights groups. No video was reportedly filmed of the operation, in violation of standard protocols.

Later in September, an EPP cell kidnapped former vice president Óscar Denis; he had not been released at year's end.

Violence between organized crime groups predominantly takes place along the Brazilian border, but is spreading. Illegal detention and torture by police still occur. Overcrowding and unsanitary conditions are serious problems in prisons.

The police faced multiple accusations in 2020 of inflicting humiliating physical punishment on individuals found violating lockdown, with Interior Minister Euclides Acevedo minimizing the actions and even praising officers' "creativity." In May, a six-year-old boy was wounded when police shot at his parents' car after they turned back from a checkpoint.

In July, soldiers were accused by NGOs of torturing 35 civilians in reprisal after a marine was killed in a shootout with smugglers in Ciudad del Este.

F4. Do laws, policies, and practices guarantee equal treatment of various segments of the population? 2 / 4

Paraguay lacks legislation protecting against all forms of discrimination. While same-sex sexual activity is legal, members of the LGBT+ community face endemic discrimination.

Indigenous people similarly face discrimination and lack access to adequate health care. Rampant deforestation, man-made forest fires, and forced evictions threaten the last Indigenous Ayoreo groups in voluntary isolation and Indigenous Guaraní settlements.

In September 2020, after years of protest by the indigenous Yakye Axa community, the government complied with a 2005 Inter-American Court of Human Rights (IACHR) ruling by initiating construction of road access to lands purchased by the state for the community in 2012.

Mennonite communities in the Chaco are afforded a wide degree of legal forbearance, as are Brazilian and European-descended ranchers in the eastern region.

G. PERSONAL AUTONOMY AND INDIVIDUAL RIGHTS: 10 / 16

G1. Do individuals enjoy freedom of movement, including the ability to change their place of residence, employment, or education? 3 / 4

Freedom of movement is generally respected, though the presence of armed or criminal groups can discourage travel in some areas. Most people can change their employment without legal impediment. For students, moving between educational establishments can prove difficult as faculty often have the power to retain grades.

G2. Are individuals able to exercise the right to own property and establish private businesses without undue interference from state or nonstate actors? 3 / 4

Although there are few formal restrictions on private business activity and property rights, land disputes, often linked to historic misappropriation of public land and disrespect of Indigenous land rights, remain a problem.

The EPP has threatened, kidnapped, and extorted ranchers in northeastern areas.

A September 2020 report by Earthsight linked illegal deforestation for cattle ranching in lands belonging to the Ayoreo Totobiegosode people to leather purchased by European automakers.

G3. Do individuals enjoy personal social freedoms, including choice of marriage partner and size of family, protection from domestic violence, and control over appearance? 2 / 4

Women and children continue to suffer from high levels of gender-based violence and sexual abuse, with authorities receiving a daily average of 80 reports of domestic violence as of April 2020. Abortion, same-sex marriage, and civil unions remain illegal. The LGBT+ community reports feeling increasingly at risk amid the country's conservative shift. Transgender women report that bullying and abuse forces them into homelessness and poverty, and local trans rights group Panambi reported a sharp rise in anti-trans violence in 2020.

G4. Do individuals enjoy equality of opportunity and freedom from economic exploitation? 2 / 4

Approximately 23.5 percent of the population lived in poverty in 2019, with 4 percent living in extreme poverty. Both figures have fallen slightly in recent years, but poverty was expected to rise in 2020 as a result of the COVID-19 pandemic. Indigenous populations are particularly affected. Inequality in land ownership and income is extremely high and social mobility very limited. Employees are often unprotected from employer retaliation. Reports of forced labor and slavery periodically surface.

The ongoing illegal practice of *criadazgo*—temporary adoption whereby children, generally from poor families, work without pay for wealthier ones—severely limits the freedom of roughly 47,000 children across the country.

Peru

Population: 32,800,000
Capital: Lima
Freedom Status: Partly Free
Electoral Democracy: Yes

Status Change: Peru's status declined from Free to Partly Free due to extended political clashes between the presidency and Congress since 2017 that have heavily disrupted governance and anticorruption efforts, strained the country's constitutional order, and resulted in an irregular succession of four presidents within three years.

Overview: Peru has established democratic political institutions and undergone multiple peaceful transfers of power. However, high-profile corruption scandals have eroded public trust in government, while bitter divides within a highly fragmented political class have repeatedly produced political turmoil. Indigenous groups suffer from discrimination and inadequate political representation.

KEY DEVELOPMENTS IN 2020

- Despite a rapidly enacted, stringent lockdown, Peru was the Latin American country most severely affected by the COVID-19 pandemic. By the end of 2020, over 37,000 deaths and 1 million cases had been registered, according to researchers at Johns Hopkins University.
- In November, Peru's Congress voted to remove President Martín Vizcarra following allegations of corruption. The move led to massive protests led by young Peruvians, which was met with a violent police response. The new president, Manuel

Merino, was forced to resign, and Congressman Francisco Sagasti was chosen to fill out the presidential term heading into 2021 elections.
- An off-cycle congressional election held in January resulted in a deeply fragmented Congress, with no party holding even 20 percent of the chamber's 130 seats.

POLITICAL RIGHTS: 29 / 40 (−1)

A. ELECTORAL PROCESS: 10 / 12 (−1)

A1. Was the current head of government or other chief national authority elected through free and fair elections? 3 / 4 (−1)

The president is chief of state and head of government. Presidents are directly elected to a five-year term and may serve nonconsecutive terms. The last president to be seated through a national election was Pedro Pablo Kuczynski. In 2016, Kuczynski won by a historically small margin of 0.2 percent over Keiko Fujimori. The elections took place peacefully, and stakeholders accepted the close result.

Kuczynski resigned in March 2018 as lawmakers prepared to hold an impeachment vote against him over corruption allegations. Vice President Martín Vizcarra was quickly sworn in to replace him, in accordance with legal procedures. Vizcarra repeatedly clashed with legislators, and used his authority to dissolve Congress in September 2019 following a vote of no confidence in his government. Conflict continued following the election of a new Congress in January 2020; Vizcarra survived a first attempt at removal in September, but was ousted in November after congressional opponents mustered the two-thirds vote necessary to invoke the constitution's controversial "moral incapacity" clause. Members of Congress justified the action by highlighting corruption and obstruction-of-justice accusations against Vizcarra, but many outside observers characterized the removal as an abuse of a vague constitutional clause.

Vizcarra was replaced by Manuel Merino, from the center-right Acción Popular party, who selected a conservative cabinet and signaled an aggressive policy agenda. An initial wave of protests in Lima were met with violent police repression, which provoked even larger protests across the country. After less than a week and the resignation of several cabinet members, Merino was forced to resign.

After Merino's resignation, Francisco Sagasti, who had been elected as president of Congress just days earlier, acceded to the presidency with a mandate of seeking unity and shepherding the country to general elections in April 2021.

Score Change: The score declined from 4 to 3 due to Congress's use of a flawed procedure to remove President Martín Vizcarra and replace him with its own handpicked leader, Manuel Merino, leading to mass protests and Merino's resignation after less than one week in office.

A2. Were the current national legislative representatives elected through free and fair elections? 4 / 4

Members of the 130-member unicameral Congress are elected for five-year terms; since a reform in 2018, reelection is not permitted. Congressional balloting employs an open-list, region-based system of proportional representation, with a 5 percent vote hurdle for a party to enter the legislature.

In September 2019, President Vizcarra dissolved Congress, and in mid-January 2020 the Constitutional Court upheld the legality of Vizcarra's decision, leading to extraordinary legislative elections held at the end of the month under conditions observers characterized as largely free and fair. The newly elected Congress—notable mainly in the degree of its party fragmentation, as well as for the collapse of the previously dominant, right-wing Fuerza Popular party—will be replaced by legislators serving full terms following the April 2021 elections.

A3. Are the electoral laws and framework fair, and are they implemented impartially by the relevant election management bodies? 3 / 4

The National Board of Elections (JNE) has taken steps to improve transparency surrounding the electoral process, but insufficiently regulated campaign financing remains a serious issue. A record 22 presidential candidates were registered for the 2021 elections, with 23 parties competing for congressional seats.

B. POLITICAL PLURALISM AND PARTICIPATION: 13 / 16

B1. Do the people have the right to organize in different political parties or other competitive political groupings of their choice, and is the system free of undue obstacles to the rise and fall of these competing parties or groupings? 4 / 4

Peruvian parties, while competitive, are both highly fragmented and extremely personalized. Though there are limits on individual donations, there are no constraints on spending by political parties, offering an outsized advantage to parties able to secure abundant funds.

Since the party system collapsed during Alberto Fujimori's authoritarian regime in the 1990s, the political system in Peru has been described by academic observers as a "democracy without parties." Traditional political parties have been replaced by fragile and opportunistic political organizations that have a very short life and little dedication to democratic practices.

B2. Is there a realistic opportunity for the opposition to increase its support or gain power through elections? 4 / 4

Opposition political parties have a realistic chance of winning power through elections, and the outcomes of elections at both the national and regional levels are subject to effective competition. Fragmentation, rather than lack of political opportunities, is the biggest obstacle faced by political actors attempting to gain and exercise power.

B3. Are the people's political choices free from domination by forces that are external to the political sphere, or by political forces that employ extrapolitical means? 3 / 4

While voters and candidates are generally able to exercise their political choices without undue influence, businesses regularly seek to bribe or otherwise influence political candidates' positions.

B4. Do various segments of the population (including ethnic, racial, religious, gender, LGBT+, and other relevant groups) have full political rights and electoral opportunities? 2 / 4

The concerns of members of ethnic and cultural minority groups, especially in remote mountain and Amazonian areas, remain inadequately addressed in politics. The 2011 Law of Prior Consultation attempted to improve the participation of Indigenous groups by guaranteeing consultation before mining and other development projects are undertaken. However, Indigenous groups have criticized the law, as the process gives Indigenous representatives no veto power, and there are ambiguities as to what qualifies a community as Indigenous.

While the political participation of women has increased over recent years, women held just 26 percent of seats in the Congress elected in 2020, and few leadership roles in local and regional governments. In June 2020, Congress passed a law requiring progressive moves toward full gender parity on party lists.

C. FUNCTIONING OF GOVERNMENT: 6 / 12

C1. Do the freely elected head of government and national legislative representatives determine the policies of the government? 2 / 4

Elected leaders and representatives are the key agents in creating and implementing policy. However, businesses and special interest groups influence officials through bribes and other illicit payments. The last five presidents and longtime opposition leader Keiko Fujimori have all been accused of accepting illegal funds.

Interparty battles, frequently conducted on behalf of party leaders with private stakes in public policy, have disrupted normal government functions in recent years. During his time in office, President Vizcarra constantly battled with Congress over his political and legislative agenda, especially regarding anticorruption reforms. Congress's November 2020 removal of Vizcarra was roundly rejected by the Peruvian public: according to one poll, over 90 percent of Peruvians disapproved of the action, and nearly 80 percent attributed responsibility for the crisis to the legislative branch.

C2. Are safeguards against official corruption strong and effective? 2 / 4

Government corruption remains a critical problem in Peru, though law enforcement authorities frequently investigate and prosecute corruption allegations. Recent years have seen scandals involving allegations of illicit deals between the Brazilian firm Odebrecht and a number of the country's most senior political figures.

After assuming office, President Vizcarra proposed four anticorruption reforms, which were put to a referendum in 2018. Three of the measures—including a ban on consecutive reelection for lawmakers, limits on campaign contributions, and an overhaul of the judicial appointment process—were approved by more than 85 percent of voters. However, Vizcarra's ouster followed allegations that he had received bribes for public works contracts in 2014, while he was serving as governor of the southern region of Moquegua. Vizcarra's proposal to end parliamentary immunity for criminal prosecution was a key point of tension between the president and Congress; 68 of the 130 lawmakers elected in 2020 were subject to open criminal investigations as of November.

C3. Does the government operate with openness and transparency? 2 / 4

Some government agencies have made progress on transparency, but much information related to defense and security policies remains classified under a 2012 law. Vizcarra's administration made a concerted effort to strengthen digital portals that contain public information in order to increase transparency and improve public services.

CIVIL LIBERTIES: 42 / 60

D. FREEDOM OF EXPRESSION AND BELIEF: 15 / 16

D1. Are there free and independent media? 3 / 4

Peru's dynamic press is mostly privately owned, and ownership is highly concentrated. Defamation is criminalized, and journalists are regularly convicted under such charges, though their sentences are usually suspended. In September 2020, criminal proceedings began for investigative journalist Paola Ugaz, who had written a book about alleged physical and psychological abuse within the Sodalitium Christianae Vitae, a Catholic organization. Ugaz and press freedom advocates also denounced a smear campaign targeting her for her reporting.

During the November 2020 political crisis, multiple press freedom watchdogs denounced an attempt by Manuel Merino's short-lived government to curtail the ability of state-run media outlets to cover protests against his administration. Journalists also protested dozens of acts of violence, mainly perpetrated by police, against reporters covering the protests. While murders of journalists have declined in recent years, numerous incidents of intimidation and assault are registered each year.

D2. Are individuals free to practice and express their religious faith or nonbelief in public and private? 4 / 4

The Peruvian constitution guarantees freedom of religion and belief, and these rights are generally respected.

D3. Is there academic freedom, and is the educational system free from extensive political indoctrination? 4 / 4

Academic freedom is unrestricted.

D4. Are individuals free to express their personal views on political or other sensitive topics without fear of surveillance or retribution? 4 / 4

People are generally free to engage in private discussion without fear of retribution or surveillance.

E. ASSOCIATIONAL AND ORGANIZATIONAL RIGHTS: 8 / 12

E1. Is there freedom of assembly? 3 / 4

The authorities generally recognize the constitutionally guaranteed right to peaceful assembly. Local disputes and protests—notably those related to extractive industries, land rights, and resource allocation among marginalized populations—at times result in instances of excessive use of force by security personnel. Efforts in recent years by the state ombudsman and the National Office of Dialogue and Sustainability (ONDS) have contributed to a reduction in protest-related violence during social conflicts.

In November 2020, Congress's removal of President Vizcarra sent Peruvians flooding into the streets, with thousands of people protesting the takeover of power by the conservative Merino government. The youth-led protests were violently repressed by the police, leading to two deaths and hundreds of injuries amid sharp criticism from domestic and international human rights organizations. Protests around the country spiked sharply following the Lima protests, at times including violence by protesters and police use of lethal force.

E2. Is there freedom for nongovernmental organizations, particularly those that are engaged in human rights- and governance-related work? 3 / 4

Freedom of association is generally respected. However, efforts by environmental activists to discourage land development have been met with intimidation.

E3. Is there freedom for trade unions and similar professional or labor organizations? 2 / 4

Peruvian law recognizes the right of workers to organize and bargain collectively. Strikes are legal with advance notification to the Ministry of Labor, but few strikers abide by this regulation. Lengthy processes involved in registering a new union create a window in which labor leaders and activists can be easily dismissed from their jobs. Short-term contracts in many industries make unionization difficult. Less than 10 percent of the formal workforce is unionized.

F. RULE OF LAW: 8 / 16

F1. Is there an independent judiciary? 2 / 4

The judiciary has been perceived as one of the most corrupt institutions in the country. In 2018, secretly recorded tapes revealed five judges trading reduced sentences or judicial appointments in exchange for bribes. All of the judges resigned or were suspended, and the revelations prompted a wave of citizen demonstrations. Later that year, Congress approved a reform leading to the creation of a new National Board of Justice (JNJ) in charge of selecting, evaluating, and disciplining judges. The establishment of the JNJ was widely praised by civil society organizations as well as academia.

Peru's seven-member Constitutional Court has maintained sufficient autonomy to serve as a check on the other branches, and the constant tension between Congress and the executive heightens the importance of both the Court's composition and its decisions. Indeed, observers pointed to the process of appointing six new justices as a key driver of interbranch tensions leading up to the November 2020 political crisis. Some analysts criticized the Court for sidestepping a direct ruling on the constitutionality of Congress's invocation of the moral incapacity clause to remove Vizcarra.

F2. Does due process prevail in civil and criminal matters? 2 / 4

Constitutional guarantees of due process are unevenly upheld. Lawyers provided to indigent defendants are often poorly trained, and translation services are rarely provided for defendants who do not speak Spanish. Impunity for violence against environmental activists who challenge land development remains a problem.

In 2009, former authoritarian president Alberto Fujimori was sentenced to 25 years' imprisonment for human rights abuses committed while in office. Former president Kuczynski issued a controversial medical pardon in 2017, but in 2018 Peru's Supreme Court ordered him back to prison. Police officially returned him to prison in January 2019, and he remained in custody throughout 2020.

F3. Is there protection from the illegitimate use of physical force and freedom from war and insurgencies? 2 / 4

While Peru's murder rate is lower than many regional peers, violent criminal organizations operate in the narcotics and illegal mining industries, and street crime is rampant. A report published in 2019 by the National Statistics Institute (INEI) indicated that between March and August 2019, 26 percent of Peruvians were victimized by crime and 85 percent believed they would be victims of a crime.

Abuses committed by the security forces are rarely punished. In March 2020, Congress passed a law that rights groups including Human Rights Watch criticized as generating additional barriers to police accountability.

F4. Do laws, policies, and practices guarantee equal treatment of various segments of the population? 2 / 4

Discrimination against Indigenous populations and Afro-Peruvians is pervasive. LGBT+ people face discrimination, hostility, and violence. Indigenous Peruvians, who often live vast distances from under-resourced health services, were severely afflicted by COVID-19, while transgender Peruvians were subjected to police abuse during the lockdown.

After Colombia, Peru is the country that has received the highest number of migrants from Venezuela. While the country was initially welcoming, public opinion shifted against tolerance, and a 2019 report by the Ministry of the Interior found that more than half of the Venezuelans residing in Peru have felt or experienced discrimination. Disruptions associated with the COVID-19 pandemic posed additional problems for Venezuelan migrants, who were not eligible for key forms of state assistance.

G. PERSONAL AUTONOMY AND INDIVIDUAL RIGHTS: 11 / 16

G1. Do individuals enjoy freedom of movement, including the ability to change their place of residence, employment, or education? 4 / 4

Peru does not place formal restrictions on movement. Although the use of road blockages as a protest tactic continued in 2020, such actions have generally decreased in recent years, easing movement around the country. People are able to freely change their place of employment or education. While Peru's COVID-19 lockdown was one of the most stringent in Latin America and included significant restrictions on movement, there were fewer accusations of arbitrary or abusive enforcement than in many neighboring countries.

G2. Are individuals able to exercise the right to own property and establish private businesses without undue interference from state or nonstate actors? 3 / 4

The rights to own property and establish business are mostly respected, though tensions persist between extractive industries and Indigenous communities who demand inclusion in land use policy decisions. The Prior Consultation Law is designed in part to better protect Indigenous rights. Its implementation has resulted in some positive outcomes for communities that have taken part in consultation processes—though prior consultation still does not always take place, nor are the requests of Indigenous groups binding.

G3. Do individuals enjoy personal social freedoms, including choice of marriage partner and size of family, protection from domestic violence, and control over appearance? 2 / 4

Gender-based violence is widespread in Peru, with more than half of Peruvian women reporting instances of physical, sexual, or emotional abuse. Proposals to recognize civil unions for same-sex partners have been repeatedly introduced and rejected in Congress, and in November 2020 the Constitutional Court ruled against recognition of a same-sex marriage contracted in Mexico by a Peruvian citizen. Abortion is permitted only in instances where a woman's health is in danger.

G4. Do individuals enjoy equality of opportunity and freedom from economic exploitation? 2 / 4

The large share of Peruvians working in the informal sector leads to widespread economic precarity. Dependence on daily earnings—and the state's inefficiency in distributing aid—contributed to the depth of the COVID-19 pandemic in the country. Peruvian women and girls—especially from the Indigenous community—fall victim to sex trafficking. According to the US State Department's 2020 *Trafficking in Persons Report*, the government of Peru falls short of acceptable standards with respect to combating trafficking, but has attempted to ameliorate the problem, including by prosecuting traffickers and assisting victims.

Philippines

Population: 109,600,000
Capital: Manila
Freedom Status: Partly Free
Electoral Democracy: Yes

Overview: Although the Philippines transitioned from authoritarian rule in 1986, the rule of law and application of justice are haphazard and heavily favor political and economic elites. Long-term violent insurgencies have continued for decades, though their threat to the state has diminished in recent years. Impunity remains the norm for violent crimes against activists and journalists, and President Rodrigo Duterte's war on drugs since 2016 has led to thousands of extrajudicial killings.

KEY DEVELOPMENTS IN 2020

- The Philippine government declared a state of calamity in March in response to the COVID-19 pandemic, and Congress passed an emergency law that contained public health measures but also significantly increased presidential emergency powers, leading to abusive law enforcement actions and freedom of expression restrictions. According to University of Oxford researchers, at the end of 2020 the Philippines had registered approximately 475,000 coronavirus cases and over 9,200 deaths.
- In July, an Anti-Terrorism Act took effect. It established very broad definitions of terrorism, prompting intense criticism and numerous petitions requesting that the Supreme Court rule on the law's constitutionality.
- President Duterte's notorious drug war continued throughout the year, and killings increased by 50 percent during the initial months of pandemic-induced lockdown.
- The press was again the subject of repressive state actions. ABS-CBN, the country's largest and oldest media network, was shut down by the government in May after Congress refused to renew its broadcast license. In June, journalist Maria Ressa was found guilty of cyberlibel and sentenced to up to six years' imprisonment.

POLITICAL RIGHTS: 25 / 40
A. ELECTORAL PROCESS: 9 / 12
A1. Was the current head of government or other chief national authority elected through free and fair elections? 3 / 4

The president is both head of state and head of government, and is directly elected to a single six-year term. Rodrigo Duterte won the 2016 presidential election with 39 percent of the vote. While polling was marked by dozens of violent episodes, including a number of killings, there were fewer such incidents compared to previous election years. Vote buying was also reported.

The vice president is directly elected on a separate ticket and may serve up to two successive six-year terms. Maria Leonor Robredo won the closely contested vice presidency in 2016 with 35 percent of the vote.

A2. Were the current national legislative representatives elected through free and fair elections? 3 / 4

The 24 members of the Senate are elected on a nationwide ballot and serve six-year terms, with half of the seats up for election every three years. The 299 members of the House of Representatives serve three-year terms, with 241 elected in single-member constituencies and the remainder elected through party-list voting.

Midterm elections for both houses of Congress and local government offices were held in May 2019. Despite a ballot redesign that led to a substantial party-list undervote, along with reports of vote buying and some election-related violence, the polls were generally perceived as successful and credible. No single party won an outright majority in either house, but pro-Duterte parties secured majority alliances in both. The opposition Liberal Party alliance did not win a single seat in the Senate.

A3. Are the electoral laws and framework fair, and are they implemented impartially by the relevant election management bodies? 3 / 4

The president appoints the Commission on Elections (Comelec), whose performance was generally praised in 2016 but was criticized for technical glitches and procurement issues that occurred in the 2019 midterm elections. The Comelec performs both election management and adjudication functions; frequent litigation complicates the interpretation of electoral laws and makes the already complex framework even less accessible to the public. The expiration of commissioners' terms presents President Duterte the opportunity to gradually appoint a full Comelec slate in advance of the 2022 elections, and by the end of 2020 four of the seven commissioners were Duterte appointees, all from his home region of Davao.

B. POLITICAL PLURALISM AND PARTICIPATION: 10 / 16

B1. Do the people have the right to organize in different political parties or other competitive political groupings of their choice, and is the system free of undue obstacles to the rise and fall of these competing parties or groupings? 3 / 4

The Philippines has a strong record of open competition among multiple parties, though candidates and political parties typically have weak ideological profiles. Legislative coalitions are exceptionally fluid, and politicians often change party affiliation, typically to join the dominant bloc or the incumbent president's party, a phenomenon that helped boost Duterte's power following the 2016 elections.

In the past three decades, political dynasties have become more prevalent and more powerful, and hold many provincial governorships and a significant number of seats in Congress.

B2. Is there a realistic opportunity for the opposition to increase its support or gain power through elections? 2 / 4

The Philippines has seen regular rotations of power at the national level. However, in recent years opposition politicians have faced increasing harassment, and some have been arrested on charges denounced by the opposition and rights groups as politically motivated.

In 2019, prominent opposition leaders including Vice President Robredo and several sitting senators were charged with sedition as part of an alleged plot to oust Duterte. The charges against them were dropped in February 2020, but former senator Antonio Trillanes and others were indicted. Senator Leila de Lima, one of the most outspoken critics of Duterte's war on drugs, remained in pretrial detention throughout the year. De Lima was arrested in 2017 on charges of accepting money from drug dealers, and is recognized as a prisoner of conscience by international rights groups.

Duterte cracked down on the Communist Party of the Philippines (CPP) and its armed wing, the New People's Army (NPA), after peace talks failed in 2017. The government sought a court petition to declare 649 individuals CPP-NPA members in 2018, effectively designating them as terrorists. The list included actual members of the CPP, critics of the president, a former party-list member of Congress, and the UN special rapporteur on the rights of Indigenous peoples, Victoria Tauli-Corpuz. The list was trimmed to eight alleged CPP members in 2019, and the court dismissed the petition in January 2020 before reversing itself and approving the designation in February.

In November 2020, Duterte labeled the left-wing Makabayan bloc in Congress "legal fronts" of the CPP. The party-list groups that comprise the bloc represent marginalized sectors of society and have often been "red-tagged"—the practice of alleging that targets harbor communist sympathies or connections, resulting in stigmatization and increased risk of physical attack—by the security forces and other government agencies.

B3. Are the people's political choices free from domination by forces that are external to the political sphere, or by political forces that employ extrapolitical means? 2 / 4

Distribution of power is heavily affected by patronage and kinship networks. In the past 30 years, political dynasties have expanded. Groups competing for party-list seats are frequently dominated by traditional political families, and recent elections have resulted in an increasing concentration of power in the hands of a few families. Election-related funding also contributes to the concentration of power: there are no limits on campaign contributions, and a significant portion of political donations come from a relatively small number of donors.

The activities of armed rebel and extremist groups and martial law continue to affect politics in the south of the country. Martial law in Mindanao ended at the beginning of 2020, but the military maintained various restrictions in Marawi Province, the site of a 2017 siege by a group identified with the Islamic State.

Social media platforms, especially Facebook, have been weaponized and exploited by Duterte and his supporters. In October 2020, Facebook removed hundreds of accounts for violating its policy against "coordinated inauthentic behavior on behalf of a foreign or government entity." One network originated in China, while another, which was linked to the Philippine police and military, criticized activists and the political opposition. Without challenging the findings, Duterte issued vague threats regarding Facebook's operations in the country.

B4. Do various segments of the population (including ethnic, racial, religious, gender, LGBT+, and other relevant groups) have full political rights and electoral opportunities? 3 / 4

No laws limit the participation of specific groups in the political process, and the constitution guarantees equal access to opportunities for public service. However, the dominance of political dynasties is an obstacle to the exercise of political rights for some groups. While women make up about 28 percent of the legislature following the 2019 elections, political life is dominated by men and few women are elected without following in the footsteps of a male relative. Muslims and Indigenous groups are not well represented; perceptions of relative socioeconomic deprivation and political disenfranchisement, along with resentment toward Christian settlements in traditionally Muslim areas, have played a central role in the Philippines' Muslim separatist movements.

In 2013, the Supreme Court ruled that the party-list portion of the ballot for the House of Representatives, meant to ensure representation for marginalized or underrepresented groups, could also be open to national political parties, provided that they did not stand in the single-member constituency contests. In 2019, a number of party-list groups gained seats not by representing the sectors or interests as intended, but through substantial support from kinship networks in single geographic regions, and links with the Duterte administration.

C. FUNCTIONING OF GOVERNMENT: 6 / 12

C1. Do the freely elected head of government and national legislative representatives determine the policies of the government? 3 / 4

While elected government officials and legislative representatives determine state policies, the president is able to dominate policymaking due to a political system that grants significant powers to the executive branch. A few dozen families continue to hold a disproportionate share of political authority. Several of Duterte's children hold elected office and exert increasing influence, as evidenced by competitors for the House speakership jockeying for the endorsement of Duterte and his children in 2018 and again in 2020.

C2. Are safeguards against official corruption strong and effective? 1 / 4

Government corruption and impunity for corruption is a serious problem. The courts and other anticorruption institutions have failed to hold powerful politicians and their associates to account for serious allegations.

The official anticorruption agencies, the Office of the Ombudsman and the Presidential Anti-Graft Commission (PAGC), have mixed records. The PAGC lacks enforcement capabilities. The Ombudsman, which is tasked with acting on complaints filed against government workers and officials, is poorly resourced and relies on the solicitor general—the chief counsel of the government—to launch prosecutions. It has focused on major cases against senior government officials and those involving large sums of money, some of which languish for years in the Sandiganbayan (anticorruption court). In 2019, the deputy ombudsman claimed that the Philippines was losing around 700 billion pesos ($13 billion) annually, or around 20 percent of the country's total budget appropriation, due to corruption.

Duterte has fired numerous officials due to corruption, including the interior minister in 2017, but his anticorruption drive has ultimately led to few convictions. In 2018, the Sandiganbayan acquitted Senator Ramon Revilla, Jr. of charges of embezzling over $4 million in government funds during his last term, and Revilla was again elected to the Senate in 2019.

In 2018, the Sandiganbayan found former first lady Imelda Marcos guilty of corruption as governor of Manila in the 1970s and sentenced her to between 6 and 11 years in prison. She remained free on bail throughout 2020 pending appeal to the Supreme Court. Of the 43 cases filed by the Presidential Commission on Good Government (PCGG) against the Marcos family in 1987, 22 have been dismissed, 1 was indefinitely archived, and 20 remain in process.

The government's response to the COVID-19 pandemic has been dogged by allegations of incompetence, negligence, and corruption at the national and local levels. In April, a majority of senators called for the secretary of health's resignation for perceived deficiencies in addressing the pandemic; despite an Ombudsman investigation into the secretary regarding alleged procurement anomalies, Duterte refused to replace him. A spotlight also fell on the national health insurance company after a task force exposed numerous instances of fraud, overpriced supplies, and other misdeeds, leading to charges against high-level officers, including the head of the company. In August, hundreds of elected and appointed local officials faced corruption charges related to the distribution of emergency assistance to vulnerable groups during the national lockdown.

C3. Does the government operate with openness and transparency? 2 / 4

Government transparency remains limited despite some positive initiatives. Local governments have been required to post procurement and budget data on their websites, and the national government has instituted participatory budgeting at various levels. The country's first freedom of information directive was issued by Duterte in 2016, but it mandates public disclosure only in the executive branch and allows major exemptions.

Duterte has refused to release a filing known as a statement of assets and liabilities and net worth (SALN); all previous presidents made the disclosure, pursuant to a 1989 law. In September 2020, the Ombudsman restricted public access to government officials' SALNs, asserting they were being "weaponized," and announced that the office was no longer conducting "lifestyle checks" that investigate officials' apparent unexplained wealth.

Transparency remains deficient in the security sector. A June 2020 report by the UN Office of the High Commissioner on Human Rights (OHCHR) called attention to conflicting data and opacity that impeded the ability to comprehensively tally drug war killings and evaluate the destination of budgeted security funds.

CIVIL LIBERTIES: 31 / 60 (−3)

D. FREEDOM OF EXPRESSION AND BELIEF: 12 / 16 (−2)

D1. Are there free and independent media? 1 / 4 (−1)

The constitution provides for freedoms of expression and the press. Private media are vibrant and outspoken, although content often lacks fact-based claims or substantive investigative reporting. The country's state-owned television and radio stations cover controversial topics and sometimes criticize the government, but they too lack strict journalistic ethics. While the censorship board has broad powers to edit or ban content, government censorship is generally not a serious problem in practice.

The Philippines remains one of the most dangerous places in the world for journalists, and the president's hostile rhetoric toward members of the media exacerbates an already perilous situation. The Philippine Center for Investigative Journalism found attacks and threats on the media have continued relentlessly throughout the Duterte administration, and that there had been no major efforts by state agencies to investigate serious incidents or otherwise address the problem. A coalition of media groups documented 128 attacks and threats against the press between July 2016 and April 2019, including physical attacks; threats, including death threats and bomb threats; smearing journalists as conspiring against the government; red-tagging; and distributed denial-of-service (DDoS) attacks on alternative media sites.

According to the Committee to Protect Journalists (CPJ), 9 journalists have been killed in the Philippines in connection with their work since 2016, including three in 2020. The vast majority of violent attacks remain unpunished. In December 2019, however, a trial court found dozens of defendants guilty for the brutal massacre of 58 people, including 32 journalists, in Maguindanao in 2009. Datu Andal Ampatuan, Jr., the most prominent defendant, was sentenced to life in prison.

Other obstacles to press freedom include Executive Order 608, which established a National Security Clearance System to protect classified information, and the Human Security Act, which allows journalists to be wiretapped based on suspicion of involvement in terrorism. Libel is a criminal offense, and libel cases have been used frequently to quiet criticism of public officials.

Maria Ressa, the founder of the online news site Rappler, was arrested twice in 2019 on charges including tax evasion, libel, cyberlibel, and violations of securities regulations. In June 2020, Ressa and her codefendant, Reynaldo Santos Jr., were found guilty of cyberlibel and sentenced to a minimum of six years in prison. Ressa remained free on bail pending appeal during the rest of the year. In July, Ressa pleaded not guilty to tax evasion, and in November an arrest warrant was issued for a second cyberlibel charge. Rappler, which has run stories critical of Duterte's war on drugs, had its corporate registration revoked by government regulators in 2018 for violating the prohibition on foreign ownership and control of Philippine media outlets. Rappler reporters were accused by Duterte of being part of a "fake news outlet," and blacklisted from government events and interviews with state officials.

In May 2020, ABS-CBN, the oldest and largest media network in the country, shut down its broadcast operations following the expiration of its operating license. Duterte had accused the network of bias against him and openly threatened to close it down since the 2016 campaign. In July, Congress voted against renewal of the license, and ABS-CBN stations remained off the air the rest of the year. The shutdown was condemned by numerous press freedom and human rights advocacy groups.

Score Change: The score declined from 2 to 1 because the government's shutdown of the country's largest media network drastically reduced public access to independent reporting.

D2. Are individuals free to practice and express their religious faith or nonbelief in public and private? 4 / 4

Freedom of religion is guaranteed under the constitution and generally respected in practice. During the COVID-19 lockdown, public religious services were prohibited and all religious centers closed, before gradually reopening at highly reduced capacity.

D3. Is there academic freedom, and is the educational system free from extensive political indoctrination? 4 / 4

Academic freedom at the country's many public and private schools is generally respected. However, authorities closed 55 indigenous primary schools in the Davao region in 2019 following allegations that the schools were teaching leftist ideology.

The security forces have increasingly been monitoring Islamic schools and schools attended by indigenous peoples in areas of the southern Philippines where the military conducts counterinsurgency and antiterror missions. In October 2020, the military's top general stated that the armed forces would monitor the estimated 500 Islamic schools in the country as possible recruitment sites for militants, sparking criticism by Muslim religious leaders. A January 2020 proposal by the police chief of Manila to compile lists of all Muslim students in high schools and universities in the city was rescinded following condemnation by citizens and rights groups.

D4. Are individuals free to express their personal views on political or other sensitive topics without fear of surveillance or retribution? 3 / 4 (−1)

Social media use is very widespread in the Philippines, but rights groups have expressed concern about threats against and censorship of online criticism and the criminalization of allegedly libelous social media posts. In October 2020 a high-ranking military official was criticized by the government's Commission on Human Rights (CHR) for red-tagging after he issued veiled threats to celebrities who participated in an online forum on issues affecting girls and young women.

The Department of Justice began investigating the spread of coronavirus-related misinformation and fake news in early February 2020. Arrests increased following the March enactment of an emergency law, the Bayanihan to Heal as One Act, which criminalized posting fake news in overly broad language and was immediately criticized by rights advocates. Within weeks, investigators had summoned over a dozen persons for their social media posts. A human rights lawyer who described the arrests as having a chilling effect was publicly attacked and insulted by Duterte, and multiple people were charged with crimes, including cyberlibel, for satirical posts or criticism of Duterte and the government.

Score Change: The score declined from 4 to 3 due to the government's aggressive use of emergency powers linked to the pandemic to step up harassment and arrests of ordinary citizens who express dissent on social media.

E. ASSOCIATIONAL AND ORGANIZATIONAL RIGHTS: 6 / 12 (−1)

E1. Is there freedom of assembly? 2 / 4 (−1)

Citizen activism and public discussion are robust, and demonstrations are common. However, permits are required for rallies, and police sometimes use violence to disperse antigovernment protests.

During most of 2020, mass gatherings were prohibited as a preventive measure to stem the spread of the coronavirus. Complaints of insufficient government aid amid the strict lockdown spurred protests that led to dozens of detentions and arrests, even as Duterte defended and subsequently promoted a top police official photographed having a large birthday party. Additional arrests occurred amid protests led by progressive organizations against the Anti-Terrorism Act signed into law in July; protesters were charged with violating both pandemic-related restrictions and public assembly laws.

Score Change: The score declined from 3 to 2 due to selective and sometimes excessive enforcement of COVID-19 assembly restrictions.

E2. Is there freedom for nongovernmental organizations, particularly those that are engaged in human rights- and governance-related work? 2 / 4

Civil society has been historically robust in the Philippines, which hosts a range of active human rights, social welfare, environmental, and other groups. However, assassinations of civil society activists and human rights defenders continue, and President Duterte's public threats against those who oppose his policies have exacerbated an already dangerous atmosphere of impunity.

In July 2020 the CHR published a report describing "a systematic attack on HRDs [human rights defenders] across all sectors of civil society." The agency registered 134 HRDs killed under the Duterte administration, and asserted that the climate of impunity for such killings was connected to frequent presidential pronouncements dismissing human rights and stigmatizing HRDs as tools of drug suspects and communists.

The 2020 OHCHR report also highlighted "red-tagging" as a serious threat to civil society and freedom of expression, noting that red-tagging victims are subjected to death threats or sexually charged comments, and sometimes violence. Prominent killings in 2020 included Randy Echanis, an agrarian leader and peace negotiator, who was killed by police in Manila in August; Zara Alvarez, a farmers' rights advocate monitoring the murders of sugar plantation workers on Negros island, who was slain in August; and Mary Rose Sancelan, a public health official in Negros Oriental province who had been red-tagged by an anticommunist vigilante group before being killed in December.

The OHCHR also noted that police and military intimidation tactics targeting activists continued during the pandemic lockdown. In addition, the COVID-19 emergency law was weaponized against civil society activists during the year. In April, labor advocates attempting to distribute food aid were arrested for violating quarantine rules and then charged with inciting sedition for possessing media content critical of the government.

E3. Is there freedom for trade unions and similar professional or labor organizations? 2 / 4

Trade unions are independent, though less than 10 percent of the labor force is unionized. Collective bargaining is common among unionized workers, however, and strikes may be called as long as unions provide notice and obtain majority approval from their members.

In its 2020 assessment, the OHCHR included trade unionists as a sector targeted for stigmatization and violence. Labor and professional groups have experienced increased harassment, including red-tagging, in recent years, particularly those representing farmers and lawyers. Leaders of such groups have been targeted amid the broader increase in extrajudicial killings that has taken place in the Philippines over the past decade.

F. RULE OF LAW: 3 / 16

F1. Is there an independent judiciary? 1 / 4

Judicial independence has deteriorated during the Duterte administration. Chief Justice of the Supreme Court Maria Lourdes Sereno, a harsh critic of the president, was ousted in 2018 when the court narrowly voted to grant a petition by the solicitor general to cancel Sereno's 2010 appointment due to allegations that she had failed to disclose some of her assets. The decision was sharply criticized by the opposition as a brazen, politically motivated attack on the independence of the judiciary. In December 2020, associates of Imelda Marcos used the same asset disclosure issue to file an impeachment complaint against another Supreme Court justice, Marvic Leonen, who is generally perceived as a human rights advocate.

Judicial independence is also hampered by inefficiency, low pay, intimidation, corruption, and high vacancy rates.

Three judges were assassinated in 2019. In 2020, a Manila prosecutor became the 50th lawyer, judge, or prosecutor killed since 2016, and in October a judge in metro Manila was ambushed but survived.

F2. Does due process prevail in civil and criminal matters? 0 / 4

The justice system fails to guarantee due process rights. Arbitrary detention, disappearances, kidnappings, and abuse of suspects are common. The OHCHR catalogued numerous due process violations linked to Duterte's war on drugs, including the use of watch lists compiled by local officials that identify targets for home "visitations" that do not require warrants and often lead to extrajudicial execution.

The police and military have been implicated in corruption, extortion, and involvement in the illegal drug trade, and in 2019, then national police chief Oscar Albayalde and 13 police officers were charged for involvement in the theft and reselling of confiscated methamphetamine.

Martial law and the suspension of habeas corpus in the southern region of Mindanao ended at the beginning of 2020, but the military presence remained, along with checkpoints and a curfew.

The Anti-Terrorism Act that took effect in July 2020 provides the state significant powers, including the warrantless arrest and detention of people designated as terrorists by an Anti-Terrorism Council appointed by the president. Rights advocates sharply criticized the law's broad definition of terrorism as endangering dissent and free speech, and stated that limits incorporated into the law were too vague to offer effective protection. At least 37 petitions challenging the law's constitutionality were filed in the Supreme Court, with arguments expected in early 2021.

F3. Is there protection from the illegitimate use of physical force and freedom from war and insurgencies? 1 / 4

The Philippines has been afflicted by long-running insurgencies, and more recently, violent extremism in Mindanao. Since his election in 2016, Duterte has waged a violent war on drugs that has led to widespread extrajudicial killing.

Authorities stated in July 2019 that 5,526 people had been killed in Duterte's antidrug campaign as of June 30, 2019. However, human rights groups, drawing in part from a 2017 police report of "deaths under investigation," in 2019 put the number of related deaths at as many as 27,000. The victims include civilians and children who were deliberately targeted.

Convictions for extrajudicial killings and other such crimes are rare, and Duterte has appeared to encourage the actions. In September 2020, Human Rights Watch (HRW) reported that official numbers indicated an increase in killings of more than 50 percent since the start of the COVID-19 lockdown.

The OHCHR summarized the overall findings of its 2020 report by stating that "an overarching focus on national security, countering terrorism, and illegal drugs has resulted in numerous systematic human rights violations, including killings and arbitrary detention, persistent impunity and the vilification of dissent."

In December 2020, the Prosecutor of the International Criminal Court (ICC) reported that its preliminary examination found reasonable basis to believe that state actions connected to the drug war constituted crimes against humanity. Duterte withdrew the country's participation in the ICC in 2018 after the announcement of the investigation into the war on drugs.

The police and military routinely torture detainees, and a lack of effective witness protection has been a key obstacle to investigations against members of the security forces.

Conflict in Mindanao has caused severe hardship, more than 120,000 deaths, and the displacement of tens of thousands of people since it erupted in 1972. Both government and rebel forces have committed summary killings and other human rights abuses. In 2017, a group of Islamic State–linked foreign fighters and local militants attacked the city of Marawi; more than 1,200 people were killed in a five-month siege of the city.

In 2018, pursuant to a 2014 peace treaty with the Moro Islamic Liberation (MILF), President Duterte signed the landmark Bangsamoro Organic Law, which created the self-governing Bangsamoro Autonomous Region in Muslim Mindanao (BARMM). In 2019, the Bangsamoro Transition Authority (BTA) was constituted as the governing body until elections scheduled for 2022. However, militant groups that broke away from the MILF continue to carry out attacks. In December 2020, Duterte endorsed a legislative proposal to extend the BTA and postpone the first BARMM regional elections until 2025.

In 2018, President Duterte ended peace talks with the Communist Party of the Philippines–New People's Army–National Democratic Front of the Philippines (CPP-NPA-NDFP), dashing hopes that the 50-year violent insurgency could reach a peaceful end during his administration. Deadly clashes between the NPA and the Philippine military continue to occur throughout the country. Pursuant to the Anti-Terrorism Act of 2020, the Anti-Terror Council designated the CPP-NPA as terrorist groups in December, allowing the Anti-Money Laundering Council to search for and freeze their assets.

F4. Do laws, policies, and practices guarantee equal treatment of various segments of the population? 1 / 4

Provisions mandating equal treatment are upheld inconsistently, and some groups lack legal protection. LGBT+ people face bias in employment, education, and other services, as well as societal discrimination. An antidiscrimination bill that passed the lower house in 2017 has not advanced further, though several cities, including Manila in October 2020, have passed ordinances recognizing LGBT+ rights and prohibiting acts of discrimination. In the absence of national legislation, birth identification documents cannot be altered, although in 2008 the Supreme Court allowed a change in the registration papers of an intersex individual to reflect his preferred name and gender.

In September 2020, Duterte pardoned a US soldier convicted of killing a Filipino transgender woman in 2014, an act the CHR described as "an affront" to LGBT+ Filipinos. During Manila's pride march in June, 20 LGBT+ people were arrested for violations of public health and public assembly laws, while several LGBT+ people were subjected to humiliating treatment after being arrested in April for violating the COVID-19 curfew.

According to the World Economic Forum, the Philippines features one of the smallest measured gender gaps in the world; women's educational attainment outpaces men's, and women are well represented in professional roles. Women still face some credit constraints and employment discrimination, and the political realm remains male-dominated, with women occupying only 23 percent of national and local elective positions.

Indigenous rights are generally upheld, but land disputes and local development projects regularly cause friction and sometimes lead to violence. Indigenous people often live in conflict areas and are targeted by combatants for their perceived loyalties.

The law mandates that at least one percent of public jobs be reserved for people with disabilities, but this is poorly upheld.

G. PERSONAL AUTONOMY AND INDIVIDUAL RIGHTS: 10 / 16

G1. Do individuals enjoy freedom of movement, including the ability to change their place of residence, employment, or education? 3 / 4

Citizens enjoy freedom of travel and choice of residence, with the exception of areas affected by violent conflict. Although martial law in Mindanao ended at the start of 2020, continuing military counterterrorism measures included checkpoints and a curfew.

The COVID-19 lockdown led to the establishment of several hundred checkpoints manned by the security forces in order to limit intercity travel, with additional localized entry and exit restrictions in villages.

G2. Are individuals able to exercise the right to own property and establish private businesses without undue interference from state or nonstate actors? 2 / 4

Private business activity is often dependent on the support of local power brokers in the complex patronage system that extends throughout the country. Outside of conflict zones, individuals are generally able to exercise the right to own property and establish private businesses without undue interference from state or nonstate actors, notwithstanding the domination and corruption of the economic dynasties.

The coronavirus-related emergency law empowered the president to direct the operations of privately-owned businesses, including medical facilities and businesses in the transportation and hospitality sectors required for quarantine and temporary housing.

G3. Do individuals enjoy personal social freedoms, including choice of marriage partner and size of family, protection from domestic violence, and control over appearance? 3 / 4

Most individuals enjoy personal social freedoms. However, divorce is illegal in the Philippines, though annulments are allowed under specified circumstances, and Muslims may divorce via Sharia (Islamic law) courts. In 2019 the Supreme Court denied a petition to recognize same-sex marriages, with a petition to reconsider denied in January 2020. Domestic violence is a significant problem, and while spousal rape is a crime, very few cases are prosecuted. Police data showed an increase in reported domestic violence against women and children during the COVID-19 lockdown. Abortion is illegal in nearly all circumstances, though unregulated abortions are frequent.

G4. Do individuals enjoy equality of opportunity and freedom from economic exploitation? 2 / 4

The Philippines is a source country for human trafficking, with some Filipinos taken abroad and forced to work in the fishing, shipping, construction, or other industries, or forced to engage in sex work. The country's various insurgent groups have been accused of using child soldiers.

The legal minimum wage in the agricultural sector in some regions falls far short of what is necessary for a family to avoid poverty. Violation of minimum-wage standards is fairly common. Children have been reported working as domestic laborers. There is a shortage of labor inspectors; authorities have acknowledged the problem but say they have limited funds to address it. The Philippines is a global center of online child sexual abuse, and reports indicated an increase during the COVID-19 lockdown.

Poland

Population: 38,400,000
Capital: Warsaw
Freedom Status: Free
Electoral Democracy: Yes

Overview: Poland's democratic institutions took root at the start of its transition from communist rule in 1989. Rapid economic growth and other societal changes have benefited some segments of the population more than others, contributing to a deep divide between liberal, pro-European parties and those purporting to defend national interests and "traditional" Polish Catholic values. Since taking power in late 2015, the populist, socially conservative Law and Justice (PiS) party has enacted numerous measures that increase political influence over state institutions and threaten to reverse Poland's democratic progress. Recent years have seen an increase in nationalist and homophobic rhetoric.

KEY DEVELOPMENTS IN 2020

- President Andrzej Duda was reelected in a July run-off that saw near-record voter turnout, defeating opposition candidate Rafał Trzaskowski by a slim margin. The election was initially scheduled to take place in May, but was delayed due to the government's illegal, last-minute attempt to bypass the electoral commission and administer the poll entirely by mail. The initiative failed, the May election was "abandoned" in the absence of any formal procedure, and a new election was called for June, with a runoff in July.
- After the election, in September, an administrative court ruled that the prime minister had violated the constitution and the electoral code in attempting to transfer the election administration to the post office.
- In April, the European Court of Justice (ECJ) ordered the suspension of the controversial Disciplinary Chamber of the Supreme Court, citing its potential to restrict judicial independence. The European Commission then launched an infringement procedure against Poland over a new law that expanded disciplinary measures against judges. Judges critical of the government's judicial reforms faced sanctions during the year.
- In October, the Constitutional Tribunal (TK) ruled that abortion in cases when the fetus has a congenital disorder is unconstitutional, effectively restricting legal abortion to cases involving rape, incest, or danger to the life or health of the mother. In response, women's rights groups organized mass protests that were attended by hundreds of thousands of people, the largest demonstrations in Poland since the fall of communism in 1989. The government delayed its implementation, and the ruling had not come into effect by the end of the year.

POLITICAL RIGHTS: 34 / 40 (-1)

A. ELECTORAL PROCESS: 10 / 12 (-1)

A1. Was the current head of government or other chief national authority elected through free and fair elections? 3 / 4 (-1)

The president of Poland is directly elected for up to two five-year terms. The president's appointment of a prime minister must be confirmed by the Sejm, the lower house of the parliament. While the prime minister holds most executive power, the president also has some influence, particularly over defense and foreign policy matters.

Andrzej Duda, the candidate of the national-conservative Law and Justice (PiS) party, was reelected in July 2020 in the second round of Poland's presidential election with 51 percent of the vote, narrowly defeating Rafał Trzaskowski of the centrist Civic Platform (PO) party. Voter turnout was 68.1 percent, the second highest since 1989.

The election was originally scheduled for May 2020. Amid political conflict over whether to hold voting during the COVID-19 pandemic, the government in April drafted plans to hold the vote as scheduled in May, but with mail-in ballots, transferring the election's administration to the post office instead of the constitutionally legitimate National Electoral Commission (PKW). However, the government backtracked on these plans, and long-time PiS party chair Jarosław Kaczyński, widely considered Poland's most powerful politician, canceled the election, even though he did not have the constitutional authority to do so. Formally, the May election was "abandoned," not postponed, and a new election was called in June, with a runoff in July. Observers noted that the government had failed to meet its constitutional obligations by abandoning the May vote without any formal procedure, and in September, an administrative court ruled that the prime minister had broken the law in attempting to transfer the election administration to the post office.

Election observers from the Organization for Security and Co-operation in Europe (OSCE) concluded that the election was competitive and well-organized, but tarnished by "hostility" and "biased coverage by the public broadcaster," which PiS had effectively transformed into a government mouthpiece. The OSCE mission noted the insufficiency of regulations governing public officials' campaign activities, with the incumbent receiving an "undue advantage" from campaigning by high-ranking officials, including the prime minister. Further, the OSCE observers raised concerns over the persistent use of homophobic rhetoric by President Duda and his team and media allies.

The current prime minister, Mateusz Morawiecki, was appointed in 2017 with the approval of the PiS majority in the parliament. His mandate was bolstered by PiS's victory in the 2019 legislative elections.

Score Change: The score declined from 4 to 3 because the government attempted to bypass the country's electoral authority to arrange postal voting for the presidential election, delayed the contest extralegally, and misused state resources to benefit the incumbent.

A2. Were the current national legislative representatives elected through free and fair elections? 4 / 4

Members of the bicameral parliament are elected for four-year terms. The 460-seat Sejm, the lower house, is elected by proportional representation and holds most legislative authority. The 100 members of the Senate, the upper house, are elected in single-member constituencies. The Senate can delay and amend legislation, but has few other powers.

In the October 2019 parliamentary elections, PiS won a second term with 43.6 percent of the vote. This represented an increase of 6 percentage points on its results four years earlier, although this translated to the same number of seats in the Sejm, 235. This majority allows

PiS to continue governing without formal coalition partners (although within its electoral lists and parliamentary caucus are two smaller parties, United Poland and Agreement). PO finished second, with 134 seats. Four other parties or coalitions passed the threshold to enter parliament, including left-wing and far-right parties that had been absent during the previous term.

PiS, however, narrowly lost control of the Senate, where an opposition coalition took 51 of 100 seats; PiS took 48.

An OSCE mission concluded that the 2019 elections were generally conducted in a "professional and transparent" manner. However, they expressed concern that recent judicial reforms had left a "lack of trust in prosecutors and courts to handle election-related complaints independently." They also noted that "nationalist and homophobic rhetoric gave rise to a sense of threat," which they echoed in their report on the 2020 presidential election.

A3. Are the electoral laws and framework fair, and are they implemented impartially by the relevant election management bodies? 3 / 4

Poland's electoral framework and its implementation have generally ensured free and fair elections, though legal changes introduced in 2017–18 have increased the potential for political influence over the PKW, which manages elections and oversees party finances, including the power to withhold state subsidies. Previously, all nine members of the PKW were nominated by courts. From the beginning of the new parliamentary term in December 2019, seven members are now chosen by the parliament. As the largest parliamentary grouping, PiS was allowed to nominate a maximum of three members but could also exert influence over the member picked by the Constitutional Tribunal (TK), which is currently led by PiS-installed judges. The new commission was formally approved by President Duda in January 2020.

One of the judicial reforms that came into force in 2018 gave the newly created chamber of the Supreme Court—the Chamber of Extraordinary Control and Public Affairs, whose members are appointed by the now-politicized National Council of the Judiciary (KRS)—the authority to validate or reject election and referendum results. The chamber's substantial power, along with its vulnerability to politicization, further threaten the integrity of electoral oversight.

During the COVID-19 pandemic, the PiS undermined the authority of the PKW by ordering that the May presidential election be held by mail—which would have transferred administration of the election to the postal service—without passing proper legislation to accommodate the changes. The head of the PKW and international democracy watchdogs said voting by mail without proper preparation and legislation would be neither fully free nor fair. Though the election plans were withdrawn, in September 2020, a court in Warsaw ruled that the prime minister's orders had violated the constitution and the electoral code, among other legal breaches.

After the 2020 presidential elections, in August the Supreme Court declared 93 of around 5,800 electoral complaints valid, but that the offenses did not affect the outcome. However, as the OSCE mission noted after the July runoff, complaints to the Supreme Court could only be made after the second round of voting, so that there was no effective legal redress for issues occurring in the first round that could have affected the runoff.

B. POLITICAL PLURALISM AND PARTICIPATION: 16 / 16

B1. Do the people have the right to organize in different political parties or other competitive political groupings of their choice, and is the system free of undue obstacles to the rise and fall of these competing parties or groupings? 4 / 4

Poland's political parties organize and operate freely.

B2. Is there a realistic opportunity for the opposition to increase its support or gain power through elections? 4 / 4

There have been multiple rotations of power among rival parties since the transition from communist rule. However, opposition parties face potential long-term obstacles, including propaganda by PiS-controlled public media and legal changes related to electoral administration.

The PiS victory in the 2015 elections ended two terms of governance by PO, now in opposition. In 2019, PiS won a slim majority in the Sejm but lost control of the Senate. The Democratic Left Alliance (SLD) returned to the parliament, while four new parties entered for the first time.

The 2020 presidential campaign of pro–European Union (EU) Warsaw mayor Rafał Trzaskowski was one of the most significant challenges to PiS's comprehensive grip on power since 2015. The presidential vote ended with the narrowest margin of victory for the incumbent since 1989.

B3. Are the people's political choices free from domination by forces that are external to the political sphere, or by political forces that employ extrapolitical means? 4 / 4

Voters and politicians are generally free from undue interference by outside groups, though there are some concerns that personnel changes associated with the PiS government's assertion of control over various state institutions could be exploited to mobilize political support among public employees ahead of future local and national elections.

Powerful priest Tadeusz Rydzyk, an ally of PiS, uses his media outlets to support the government's message, and has received generous state grants for organizations under his control. Ordo Iuris, a conservative legal nongovernmental organization (NGO), has also gained prominence through its efforts to ban abortion and sex education from schools, as well as its campaign against "gender ideology," which has been endorsed by high-ranking officials in the Catholic Church and PiS.

B4. Do various segments of the population (including ethnic, racial, religious, gender, LGBT+, and other relevant groups) have full political rights and electoral opportunities? 4 / 4

Women have equal political rights and hold 28 percent of the seats in the Sejm. The number of government ministries was reduced from 20 to 14 in September 2020, leaving just one woman in the new cabinet.

Ethnic, religious, and other minority groups enjoy full political rights and electoral opportunities. Though an alliance of three leftist parties nominated Robert Biedroń, an openly gay member of the European Parliament, as their candidate in the 2020 presidential election, LGBT+ people face significant challenges to entering politics and seeing their interests represented in Polish politics in practice. The year's election period was marred by homophobic rhetoric by government figures, including President Duda, whose team and media allies used homophobic rhetoric that warned of the alleged dangers of LGBT+ rights. The minister for science and higher education, appointed in September 2020, had previously stated that LGBT+ people are "not equal to normal people."

Electoral lists representing recognized national minorities are not subject to the minimum vote threshold for parliamentary representation.

C. FUNCTIONING OF GOVERNMENT: 8 / 12

C1. Do the freely elected head of government and national legislative representatives determine the policies of the government? 3 / 4

Freely elected officials generally determine and implement laws and policies without interference, though PiS chair Kaczyński—who was appointed deputy prime minister in

September 2020, and had previously played a dominant role in the government despite not holding any official executive position—retains significant influence on government affairs. Throughout the party's time in power, PiS has sought to limit parliamentary scrutiny of legislation through various means, such as making use of private-members bills that require no consultation or impact assessments; introducing legislation unexpectedly at the last minute, sometimes in the middle of the night; and limiting opportunities for the opposition to question or amend legislation.

C2. Are safeguards against official corruption strong and effective? 3 / 4

PiS came to power promising to clean up corruption, cronyism, and nepotism. While Poles have perceived a steady decline in corruption since 2016, cronyism, a problem under all previous Polish governments, appears widespread under PiS. Since coming to power, the PiS government has altered, lowered, or removed many criteria for staffing of public institutions, allowing for appointments based on party loyalty and personal connections. Following a number of earlier controversies, PiS came under fire in September 2020 for appointments to state-owned firms, including the president's uncle and a minister's wife, though the latter appointment was reversed.

In past years, the Supreme Audit Office (NIK), a state watchdog, has raised concerns about the misuse of public funds by PiS, occasionally prompting the party to take action such as donating scrutinized funds to charity. In 2019, the PiS parliamentary majority appointed the finance minister as the new chair of the NIK. He immediately came under scrutiny for alleged irregularities in his property declarations and links to a criminal group, and subsequently took unpaid leave, rejecting the prime minister's call for his resignation.

In May 2020, Poland's health minister Łukasz Szumowski was accused of cronyism in his acquisition of medical equipment to combat COVID-19: the ministry purchased overpriced respirators that never arrived, as well as face masks for government workers from a family friend of Szumowski that were defective. The ministry notified prosecutors of the defective masks, and the potential fraud the supplier had committed, weeks after the masks were received, and only after media outlets uncovered the story. Szumowski resigned in August from his cabinet position, though he denied any wrongdoing.

C3. Does the government operate with openness and transparency? 2 / 4

The right to public information is guaranteed by the constitution and by the 2001 Act on Access to Public Information, but obtaining records and data from public institutions can be slow and difficult. The Chancellery of the Sejm has refused to release lists of judges who supported controversial new appointees to the KRS, citing personal data protection concerns, despite a ruling from the Supreme Administrative Court (NSA) ordering it to do so.

The current government avoids consulting outside experts or civil society organizations on policy ideas and tends to introduce and pass legislation rapidly, with little opportunity for debate or amendment. In April 2020, the government attempted to pass legislation that would ban abortion and criminalize sexuality education while coronavirus lockdown measures were being enforced. Activists expressed concern that the government was using the lockdown to rush through legislation without public consultation.

CIVIL LIBERTIES: 48 / 60 (−1)

D. FREEDOM OF EXPRESSION AND BELIEF: 13 / 16 (−1)

D1. Are there free and independent media? 3 / 4

The constitution guarantees freedom of expression and forbids censorship. Libel remains a criminal offense, though a 2009 amendment to the criminal code eased penalties.

Reporters Without Borders (RSF), a media watchdog, noted in 2020 "a growing tendency to criminalize defamation" through government lawsuits curbing press freedom.

Poland's media are pluralistic and mostly privately owned. However, the public media and their governing bodies have been purged of independent or dissenting voices since PiS came to power in 2015. TVP, the public television broadcaster, has promoted the government's messages and campaigned on behalf of PiS and President Duda ahead of elections in 2019 and 2020. The station's news broadcasts have sought to discredit the opposition, in flagrant breach of statutory obligations to present news in a "reliable and pluralistic manner." In June 2020, Duda's presidential rival Trzaskowski sued TVP for what he called false and defamatory claims.

TVP also depicts voices critical of the government, including NGOs and judges, as agents of the opposition or foreign forces. The broadcaster's electoral coverage in 2020 was marked by "xenophobic, homophobic and antisemitic" rhetoric, according to the OSCE's observers.

Since 2015, state-controlled companies have shifted their advertising to private media outlets that support the PiS government. More critical outlets have suffered a corresponding drop in advertising revenue, as well as a sharp decline in subscriptions from government ministries.

The PiS leadership has regularly promised to pass a law "deconcentrating" and "repolonizing" private media by reducing foreign ownership, a move that would disproportionately affect the outlets that most vigorously hold the current government to account.

Senior party figures have also suggested that German-owned media critical of the PiS government promote the interest of their German owners in undermining the Polish state. In July 2020, President Duda accused Germany of meddling in the presidential election and singled out *Die Welt*'s Warsaw correspondent by name, who subsequently received thousands of threatening messages.

D2. Are individuals free to practice and express their religious faith or nonbelief in public and private? 4 / 4

The state respects freedom of religion. The PiS government is aligned with the Roman Catholic Church, which wields significant influence in the country. Religious groups are not required to register with the authorities but receive tax benefits if they do. Minority faiths are generally able to obtain registration in practice. There is a formal ban on state funding for church construction, but a church can obtain Culture Ministry funding in practice if, like the Temple of Divine Providence in Warsaw, it includes a museum.

D3. Is there academic freedom, and is the educational system free from extensive political indoctrination? 3 / 4

The ruling party has sought to discredit academics who challenge its preferred historical narrative, particularly with regard to the events of World War II.

The director of the Polin Museum of the History of Polish Jews, Dariusz Stola, who won an open contest for another term in the job in 2019, announced his resignation in February 2020 after the culture minister, Piotr Glinksi, refused to sign off on his reappointment for eight months. Glinski had accused Stola of politicizing the museum after Stola criticized a law that he believed would have a chilling effect on historical research.

D4. Are individuals free to express their personal views on political or other sensitive topics without fear of surveillance or retribution? 3 / 4 (−1)

People are generally free to engage in private discussions on political and other matters without fear of harassment or detention by the authorities.

However, Poland has harsh insult laws, including against offending religious feelings and insulting the president, that have been increasingly used to pursue criminal cases in recent years. In February 2020, a 65-year-old man was arrested and charged with insulting the president for holding up a banner calling the president an "idiot," with a proposed sentence of up to three years in prison. The man was exonerated by a court in July. In December, another man was convicted of insulting the president for drawing obscene graffiti on an election poster of President Duda. He was sentenced to six months' community service. In July, three LGBT+ rights activists were charged with "offending religious feelings" for owning images depicting the Virgin Mary with a rainbow halo. They could face up to two years in prison if convicted.

Score Change: The score declined from 4 to 3 because the government in recent years has pursued a growing number of criminal cases in which activists and government critics were accused of violating insult laws.

E. ASSOCIATIONAL AND ORGANIZATIONAL RIGHTS: 10 / 12

E1. Is there freedom of assembly? 3 / 4

Freedom of assembly is generally respected in law and in practice. Public demonstrations are held with some regularity, though local authorities can limit demonstrations in their districts on grounds of maintaining public order.

In 2020, demonstrations were initially curbed by restrictions imposed during the COVID-19 pandemic. Protesters had to find work-arounds to avoid violating the new rules, gathering to protest in cars, honking their horns, and holding signs to their windows. In May, when business owners in Warsaw held protests calling for government aid in the face of the pandemic, police intervened with force when safety rules were breached, detaining 37 people.

In August 2020, the pretrial detention of an LGBT+ rights activist, accused of assaulting an anti-abortion campaigner and damaging his vehicle, led to protests and the brief detention of a further 48 people. An investigation by Poland's Commissioner for Human Rights found evidence of humiliating treatment of detainees by police, and that some of those detained were merely bystanders.

In October, hundreds of thousands of people protested for over a week against the Constitutional Tribunal's decision to enforce a near-total ban on abortion. Those who gathered formed the largest demonstrations since the fall of communism in 1989.

Greater numbers of LGBT+ pride parades have taken place in Poland in recent years, with many staged in smaller and eastern cities for the first time. Authorities attempted to obstruct these events, including on grounds of safety, but in each case courts prevented authorities from stopping the organizers, arguing that freedom of assembly cannot be denied on the basis of potential violence by opponents. On a few occasions, opposition to the parades turned violent, notably in Białystok in 2019, where police detained over 120 people.

E2. Is there freedom for nongovernmental organizations, particularly those that are engaged in human rights- and governance-related work? 3 / 4

Although NGOs have generally operated without government interference in Poland, public media and top government officials began systematically undermining the credibility of rights and governance-related groups in 2016, accusing many of lacking financial transparency and pursuing an opposition-led political agenda. A 2017 law, which was widely condemned by domestic and international rights activists and by Poland's rights ombudsman, centralized distribution of public NGO funding through a new body called the National

Freedom Institute, indirectly attached to the prime minister's office. As anticipated, when the National Freedom Institute distributed funds in 2019, the money went disproportionately to organizations that fit the government's ideological profile.

The European Commission's September 2020 Rule of Law Report expressed concern at government actions aimed at LGBT+ groups, including arrests, detentions, and smear campaigns.

E3. Is there freedom for trade unions and similar professional or labor organizations? 4 / 4

Poland has a robust labor movement, though certain groups—including the self-employed, private contractors, and those in essential services—cannot join unions. Complicated legal procedures hinder workers' ability to strike. Ahead of the 2020 presidential elections, Poland's largest trade union—Solidarity—in June endorsed the incumbent president for his support of "worker-friendly" government policies, including raising the minimum wage, lowering the retirement age, and a Sunday trading ban phased in since 2018.

F. RULE OF LAW: 11 / 16
F1. Is there an independent judiciary? 1 / 4

Since taking power in 2015, the PiS government has moved aggressively to assert control over the judiciary, passing legislation designed to curb the powers of the TK and to install progovernment judges on its benches. In 2017, three significant judicial reforms were adopted. The first gave the justice minister the power to appoint and dismiss presidents and deputy presidents of courts. The second, which came into force in 2018, mandated that 15 of the 25 members of the KRS, which is responsible for nominating judges, be appointed by the parliament instead of elected by the judiciary. In July 2018, new, lower retirement ages for the Supreme Court came into force, effectively meaning that 27 out of 73 judges had to step down unless they were given the president's approval to remain. These judges were reinstated later that year after an infringement procedure from the European Commission and an interim ruling of the European Court of Justice (ECJ), which later confirmed that the measures had breached European law. The Supreme Court law also created powerful new chambers—the Chamber of Extraordinary Control and Public Affairs (responsible for declaring the validity of elections), and the Disciplinary Chamber.

In 2019, the European Commission launched an infringement procedure alleging that the Disciplinary Chamber undermined the independence of judges. Later that year, the ECJ decided that Poland's own Supreme Court must rule on the independence of the new chamber. The Supreme Court's Labor Chamber promptly decided that the Disciplinary Chamber "is not a court within the meaning of EU and national law." In response, PiS rushed legislation through the Sejm in December to strengthen and expand disciplinary measures to punish individual judges who questioned the validity of the new Disciplinary Chamber or other aspects of the judicial reforms.

In April 2020, the ECJ ordered the suspension of the Disciplinary Chamber, citing its potential to restrict judicial independence. That same month, the European Commission launched a new infringement procedure, this time against the December 2019 law expanding disciplinary measures for judges. In September 2020, the European Parliament passed a resolution noting that there had been a continuing deterioration of judicial independence and the rule of law in Poland and advocating a resumption of the Article 7 (of the Treaty of the European Union) procedure (first triggered by the Commission in 2017). Critics allege that the government has continued to pursue disciplinary action against judges critical of its reforms, in violation of the ECJ ruling. In November, the Disciplinary Chamber suspended judge Igor Tuleya and stripped him of immunity from prosecution. He may now face criminal proceedings for allegedly unlawfully disclosing information when he allowed journalists to attend a politically sensitive hearing.

In September 2020, a Dutch court ruled that the Netherlands would suspend extraditions of criminal suspects to Poland until the ECJ completes its examination of whether there are sufficient guarantees of Polish judges' independence to ensure fair trials.

F2. Does due process prevail in civil and criminal matters? 3 / 4

Defendants generally enjoy due process protections in Poland, though the law allows for extended pretrial detention, and there is a large backlog of cases. The decision by the PiS government to merge the roles of justice minister and prosecutor general "creates potential for misuses and political manipulation" of the justice system, according to the Venice Commission.

Legislation introduced in 2016 gave law enforcement agencies broad authority to monitor citizens' communications activity, including the ability to access metadata without a court order, monitor the movements of foreign citizens without prior court approval, and hold terrorism suspects without charge for up to two weeks. It also contained ambiguous provisions on collecting individuals' data, arresting civilians, prohibiting demonstrations, and blocking internet access.

F3. Is there protection from the illegitimate use of physical force and freedom from war and insurgencies? 4 / 4

Civilians are largely free from extralegal violence, though some incidents of abuse by police have been alleged in the context of antigovernment demonstrations. Human rights groups have reported inadequate medical care in prison facilities.

F4. Do laws, policies, and practices guarantee equal treatment of various segments of the population? 3 / 4

Women and ethnic minority groups generally enjoy equality before the law. LGBT+ people continue to face discrimination. Public support for LGBT+ rights, including same-sex civil partnerships, has risen in recent years. However, 2019 and 2020 saw major setbacks, as an intense anti-LGBT+ campaign led by PiS and parts of the church stoked fears of an "imported LGBT ideology." By the end of 2020, more than 100 local governments had declared themselves "LGBT-ideology-free" zones or established "family charters," in resolutions without specific legal implications that were described by domestic and international rights groups as "manifestations of hate" toward LGBT+ people.

Because Poland's law against inciting hatred does not cover crimes motivated by sexuality or gender identity, public figures have been free to make slurs that would be prosecuted if targeted at other marginalized groups.

G. PERSONAL AUTONOMY AND INDIVIDUAL RIGHTS: 14 / 16

G1. Do individuals enjoy freedom of movement, including the ability to change their place of residence, employment, or education? 4 / 4

People in Poland typically enjoy freedom of travel and choice of residence, employment, and institution of higher education.

G2. Are individuals able to exercise the right to own property and establish private businesses without undue interference from state or nonstate actors? 4 / 4

Citizens have the right to own property and establish private businesses. However, a 2016 law imposed onerous restrictions on sale and ownership of agricultural land, ostensibly to protect small-scale farmers. State and religious institutions are not bound by the new restrictions.

G3. Do individuals enjoy personal social freedoms, including choice of marriage partner and size of family, protection from domestic violence, and control over appearance? 3 / 4

Under Polish law, abortion is permissible through the 12th week of pregnancy if a woman's health or life is in danger or if the pregnancy is a result of a criminal act such as rape. Bills that sought to further restrict abortions, including the imposition of prison terms for illegal abortions, triggered mass protests in 2016 and 2018, prompting the parliament to back down.

Senior PiS figures and the president subsequently made it clear that they still intended to ban what they call "eugenic abortion," in practice meaning cases of a congenital disorder of the fetus. Such cases represent approximately 98 percent of legal abortions in Poland. A group of over 100 lawmakers, mostly from the ruling party, asked the TK to rule on whether such abortions violate the constitution's protection of human life and dignity. In October 2020, the TK ruled that abortion in cases where the fetus has a congenital disorder is unconstitutional, effectively restricting legal abortion to cases involving rape, incest, or danger to the life or health of the mother. In response to the ruling, mass protests with hundreds of thousands of participants took place in Warsaw and other Polish cities. In November, the government delayed implementation of the ruling, despite a court-mandated deadline.

Since 2017, contraceptive pills have been available by prescription only, making Poland one of only two EU countries in which such a restriction is in place. A report by the NIK found that in many, especially rural, parts of Poland, gynecologists are rare. Many women must travel to obtain care, and reliable and timely access to contraception and other sexual-health services is limited. After Poland closed its borders in March 2020 to contain the COVID-19 pandemic, women faced much greater obstacles to travel to less restrictive European states for abortions.

Same-sex civil partnerships and marriages are not permitted, and same-sex couples are not legally allowed to adopt. The constitution places "marriage, as a union of a man and a woman," under the "care and protection" of the state.

In July 2020, Poland's justice minister announced that Poland would withdraw from the Istanbul Convention, a treaty to combat domestic violence and violence against women, on grounds of its alleged promotion of "LGBT and gender ideology." The prime minister in late July referred the matter to the TK, thus delaying any further action. The government passed a law in March mandating the immediate separation of perpetrators of domestic violence from their victims.

G4. Do individuals enjoy equality of opportunity and freedom from economic exploitation? 3 / 4

The law provides meaningful protections against abusive working conditions and child labor, especially in the formal sector. The authorities work to combat human trafficking, but women and children are still subjected to trafficking for sexual exploitation and foreign migrant workers are vulnerable to conditions amounting to forced labor.

State-owned entities have been expanding their already considerable presence in various sectors, such as banking, often by buying out foreign owners, as the government effectively renationalizes parts of the economy. Hiring for senior positions at such firms is often based on political loyalty or connections rather than merit, a longstanding issue under various governments that has grown more widespread under the current administration.

Portugal

Population: 10,300,000
Capital: Lisbon
Freedom Status: Free
Electoral Democracy: Yes

Overview: Portugal is a stable parliamentary democracy with a multiparty political system and regular transfers of power between political parties. Civil liberties are generally protected. Ongoing concerns include corruption, certain legal constraints on journalism, poor or abusive conditions for prisoners, and the effects of racial discrimination and xenophobia. Prosecutors have pursued corruption cases against top officials in recent years.

KEY DEVELOPMENTS IN 2020

- The first wave of the COVID-19 pandemic affected Portugal less severely than other European countries but starting in September infections soared. Collaboration between the government and the opposition, aided by several stringent lockdowns, abetted effective management; nonetheless, according to University of Oxford researchers, the country registered over 413,000 cases and over 6,900 deaths by year's end.
- A report on the rule of law in Portugal issued by the European Commission highlighted the need for improved anticorruption efforts, including within the judiciary, where institutional deficiencies were underscored by the filing of corruption charges against several former judges in September.
- Continuing challenges in addressing racism were illustrated by an allegedly racially motivated murder in July, and a killing and attempted cover-up perpetrated by border police in Lisbon in March.

POLITICAL RIGHTS: 39 / 40
A. ELECTORAL PROCESS: 12 / 12
A1. Was the current head of government or other chief national authority elected through free and fair elections? 4 / 4

In Portugal's parliamentary system, the prime minister holds the most executive power, though the directly elected president can delay legislation through a veto and dissolve the parliament to trigger early elections. The president serves up to two five-year terms. In the 2016 presidential election, center-right candidate Marcelo Rebelo de Sousa, who was supported by the opposition Social Democratic Party (PSD) and its allies, won with 52 percent of the vote, easily defeating a leftist candidate backed by the ruling Socialist Party (PS).

In February 2019, Prime Minister António Costa faced and overcame a motion of no confidence that the opposition put forward in response to a series of public sector strikes. That October, the PS won the general election and Costa resumed his post as head of the new government.

A2. Were the current national legislative representatives elected through free and fair elections? 4 / 4

The 230 members of the unicameral Assembly of the Republic are directly elected every four years using a system of proportional representation in 22 multimember constituencies.

In the October 2019 legislative elections, the governing PS came in first with 106 seats, up from 86 in the previous parliament. The opposition PSD came in second with 77 seats. The Left Bloc (BE) took 19 seats, the Unitary Democratic Coalition (PCP–PEV) secured 12, the conservative-right People's Party (CDS–PP) won 5, and the People-Animals-Nature party (PAN) took 4. Three new parties entered parliament, Iniciativa Liberal (IL), the far-right nationalist Chega (CH), and Livre (L), with one seat each.

A3. Are the electoral laws and framework fair, and are they implemented impartially by the relevant election management bodies? 4 / 4

Elections in Portugal are generally free and fair. The National Elections Commission oversees the process; according to a 2019 preelection visit by representatives of the Organization for Security and Co-operation in Europe (OSCE), the electoral framework merited confidence, though enforcement of campaign finance rules remained uneven.

B. POLITICAL PLURALISM AND PARTICIPATION: 16 / 16

B1. Do the people have the right to organize in different political parties or other competitive political groupings of their choice, and is the system free of undue obstacles to the rise and fall of these competing parties or groupings? 4 / 4

Political parties operate and compete with equal opportunity. There is no legal vote threshold for representation in the parliament, meaning smaller parties can win a seat with little more than 1 percent of the overall vote. Parties espousing racist, fascist, or regionalist values are constitutionally prohibited.

B2. Is there a realistic opportunity for the opposition to increase its support or gain power through elections? 4 / 4

Portugal has established a strong pattern of peaceful power transfers through elections since it returned to democracy in the late 1970s. Three new parties emerged in the 2019 elections: Iniciativa Liberal, Chega, and Livre.

B3. Are the people's political choices free from domination by forces that are external to the political sphere, or by political forces that employ extrapolitical means? 4 / 4

Both voters and politicians are free from undue interference by forces outside the political system.

B4. Do various segments of the population (including ethnic, racial, religious, gender, LGBT+, and other relevant groups) have full political rights and electoral opportunities? 4 / 4

Women and members of ethnic, religious, and other minority groups enjoy full political rights and participate in the political process. Women hold 38 percent of the seats in parliament, and three of them are of African descent—although these women faced racist, xenophobic abuse in 2020, including by their parliamentary colleague from the far-right Chega party. The autonomous regions of Azores and Madeira—two island groups in the Atlantic—have their own political structures with legislative and executive powers.

C. FUNCTIONING OF GOVERNMENT: 11 / 12

C1. Do the freely elected head of government and national legislative representatives determine the policies of the government? 4 / 4

Elected officials are free to determine and implement laws and policies without improper interference by unelected groups. The government used its authority to issue states of emergency during both waves of the COVID-19 pandemic, with little pushback from the opposition.

C2. Are safeguards against official corruption strong and effective? 3 / 4

The country has struggled in recent years with major corruption scandals involving high-ranking politicians, officials, and businesspeople, though many individuals have been duly prosecuted. In September 2020, 17 people, among them three judges, were charged with corruption following a four-year investigation. In February, Portuguese authorities complied with an Angolan government request to freeze bank accounts linked to Angolan businesswoman Isabel Dos Santos, whose assets were divided between Angola and Portugal.

In September, the European Commission published a report assessing the rule of law in Portugal that highlighted deficiencies in Portugal's efforts to combat corruption. While several laws to enhance accountability and transparency for elected officials were approved in 2019, enforcement and effectiveness remain unproven, and resources for auditors, police, and prosecutors remain inadequate. Whistleblower protections are in place, but controversy surrounded the case of Rui Pinto, a hacker-turned-whistleblower who leaked troves of documents related to the business activities of European soccer clubs, as well as many of the documents behind the investigations of Isabel dos Santos. His trial on dozens of charges began in September.

Upon receiving large-scale economic relief funds from the European Union (EU), the government passed a bill simplifying the public procurement process, but in December the president vetoed the bill over concerns regarding lack of transparency and risks of corruption.

C3. Does the government operate with openness and transparency? 4 / 4

Portuguese law provides for public access to government information and judicial proceedings, and state agencies generally respect this right, although several nongovernmental organizations (NGOs), including Transparency International, have unsuccessfully asked the government to release information about the Golden Visas Program.

CIVIL LIBERTIES: 57 / 60

D. FREEDOM OF EXPRESSION AND BELIEF: 16 / 16

D1. Are there free and independent media? 4 / 4

Freedom of the press is constitutionally guaranteed. Public broadcasting channels are poorly funded and face strong competition from commercial television outlets, which provide a wide range of viewpoints, although the risk to pluralism has increased due to media ownership concentration. Internet access is not restricted, but most online media have become paid services and only one national news outlet remains totally open. According to a 2020 report by the European University Institute's Centre for Media Pluralism and Media Freedom, the economic crisis facing news outlets has lowered editorial autonomy and journalistic standards in Portugal.

Portugal remains one of the few countries in Europe where defamation is still a criminal offense, and although prosecutions are uncommon, the European Court of Human Rights (ECHR) has repeatedly ruled against Portuguese authorities for their handling of both civil and criminal defamation cases against journalists.

D2. Are individuals free to practice and express their religious faith or nonbelief in public and private? 4 / 4

Portugal is overwhelmingly Roman Catholic, but the constitution guarantees freedom of religion and forbids religious discrimination. The Religious Freedom Act provides benefits for religions that have been established in the country for at least 30 years or recognized internationally for at least 60 years. However, other groups are free to register as religious corporations and receive benefits such as tax-exempt status, or to practice their faith without registering.

D3. Is there academic freedom, and is the educational system free from extensive political indoctrination? 4 / 4

Academic freedom is respected. Schools and universities operate without undue political or other interference.

D4. Are individuals free to express their personal views on political or other sensitive topics without fear of surveillance or retribution? 4 / 4

There are no significant restrictions on private discussion or the expression of personal views, although defamation laws affect ordinary citizens and politicians.

E. ASSOCIATIONAL AND ORGANIZATIONAL RIGHTS: 12 / 12
E1. Is there freedom of assembly? 4 / 4

Freedom of assembly is upheld by the authorities. In June 2020, protesters in several cities held peaceful marches in support of the Black Lives Matter movement, prompting far-right supporters to hold a march later that month denying that racism exists in Portugal. Authorities refrained from overzealous enforcement of social distancing rules and public assembly restrictions in each case.

E2. Is there freedom for nongovernmental organizations, particularly those that are engaged in human rights– and governance-related work? 4 / 4

Freedom of association is respected. National and international NGOs, including human rights groups, operate in the country without interference. On several occasions in 2020, prominent antiracism NGO SOS Racismo faced threats and vandalism from members of Portugal's small but growing far-right movement.

E3. Is there freedom for trade unions and similar professional or labor organizations? 4 / 4

Workers enjoy the right to organize, bargain collectively, and strike, though there are some limits on the right to strike in a wide range of sectors and industries that are deemed essential.

The state of emergency imposed to limit the spread of COVID-19 included suspension of the right to strike, resulting in the interruption of a dockworkers strike in March.

F. RULE OF LAW: 14 / 16
F1. Is there an independent judiciary? 4 / 4

The judiciary is independent, but staff shortages and inefficiency have contributed to a considerable backlog of pending trials. The situation is more acute in administrative and tax courts, so new specialized courts are being created.

The Council of Europe (CoE) stated in a 2019 report that Portugal's efforts to fight corruption among judges and prosecutors are unsatisfactory. In September, three former judges were charged with corruption in connection with a multiyear investigation that revealed a system of irregular allocation of court cases in order to facilitate graft and influence peddling.

F2. Does due process prevail in civil and criminal matters? 4 / 4

The authorities generally observe legal safeguards against arbitrary arrest and detention, though court backlogs result in lengthy pretrial detention for some defendants. Due process rights are guaranteed during trial.

F3. Is there protection from the illegitimate use of physical force and freedom from war and insurgencies? 3 / 4

Human rights groups and the CoE have expressed concern over abuse of detainees and excessive use of force by police, particularly against members of racial and ethnic minorities. Overcrowding in prisons remains a problem, as do poor health and safety conditions.

In January 2020, police were accused of applying excessive force and expressing racist insults while detaining a Black woman over a minor transit infraction.

In March, border police at the Lisbon airport's detention center allegedly killed a Ukrainian citizen awaiting deportation after arriving without a visa, leading to homicide charges against three border police agents.

F4. Do laws, policies, and practices guarantee equal treatment of various segments of the population? 3 / 4

Equal treatment under the law is guaranteed by the constitution. Various laws prohibit discrimination based on factors including sex, race, disability, gender identity, and sexual orientation. Nevertheless, problems persist with respect to gender bias and discrimination against minorities, particularly Roma and people of African descent.

Racism has become a more prominent issue in the public discourse, due in part to growing far-right support. Antiracism protests occurred in June 2020 in support of the Black Lives Matter movement, and again in July following the murder of a Black man in Lisbon by an assailant who had allegedly used racist insults while threatening the victim.

Although by some measures Portugal is considered a less discriminatory environment for people of African descent than other EU countries, black residents are also susceptible to disparities in housing, education, and employment. A September 2019 study from the European Network Against Racism (ENAR) found "deeply rooted institutional" discrimination at every stage of the judicial process, from reporting through sentencing. Antiracism advocates have accused the state-run Commission for Equality and against Racial Discrimination of negligence in its role as the government's main antidiscrimination agency.

Although Portugal passed an antidiscrimination law in 2017, prejudice and anti-Roma sentiment are still common and rarely punished. Living conditions in Romany communities are generally poor, Romany children face segregation and poor school outcomes, and half of Romany men are employed. Stores in Porto have decorated the entrances to their premises with frogs to deter Roma from entering, as frogs are a symbol of bad luck to many Roma.

Migrants have complained of abusive conduct by state agents, starkly illustrated by the March 2020 killing of a Ukrainian migrant by border police. During the state of emergency proclaimed in response to COVID-19, the government regularized the status of all migrants and asylum seekers while their residency applications remained pending.

G. PERSONAL AUTONOMY AND INDIVIDUAL RIGHTS: 15 / 16

G1. Do individuals enjoy freedom of movement, including the ability to change their place of residence, employment, or education? 4 / 4

Freedom of movement and associated rights are protected in law and by the constitution, and the government respects these rights in practice. The COVID-19 lockdowns resulted in severe restrictions on movement, but the government was not accused of politicizing or abusing lockdown measures.

G2. Are individuals able to exercise the right to own property and establish private businesses without undue interference from state or nonstate actors? 4 / 4

The government does not interfere with the rights to own property, establish private businesses, and engage in commercial activity. Due to a sharp rise in housing prices, a new Basic Housing Law entered into force in October 2019.

G3. Do individuals enjoy personal social freedoms, including choice of marriage partner and size of family, protection from domestic violence, and control over appearance? 4 / 4

There are no major restrictions on personal social freedoms. Portugal legalized same-sex marriage in 2010 and extended adoption rights to same-sex couples in 2015. A 2018 law eliminated the need for transgender people to obtain a medical certificate to formally change their gender or first name. Domestic violence remains a problem despite government efforts aimed at prevention, education, and victim protection. The CoE is concerned that the definition of rape is not based solely on the absence of free consent but requires that there be "duress."

The European Commission has urged Portugal to implement EU rules aimed at reducing child sexual abuse and sexual exploitation.

G4. Do individuals enjoy equality of opportunity and freedom from economic exploitation? 3 / 4

The authorities generally enforce legal safeguards against exploitative working conditions. However, Portugal remains a destination and transit point for victims of human trafficking, particularly from Eastern Europe, Asia, and West Africa. Although forced labor is prohibited by law, there have been some reports of the practice, especially in the agriculture, hospitality, domestic service, and construction sectors. Immigrant workers are especially vulnerable to economic exploitation.

Since February 2019, new legislation obligates all companies to have a transparent compensation policy, an effort to combat the gender pay gap.

The government took steps to support workers affected by economic disruption related to the COVID-19 pandemic. However, the closure of schools amid the pandemic's arrival disadvantaged the approximately 50,000 children in households lacking internet access.

Qatar

Population: 2,800,000
Capital: Doha
Freedom Status: Not Free
Electoral Democracy: No

Overview: Qatar's hereditary emir holds all executive and legislative authority, and ultimately controls the judiciary as well. Political parties are not permitted, and the only elections are for an advisory municipal council. While Qatari citizens are among the wealthiest in the world, the vast majority of the population consists of noncitizens with no political rights, few civil liberties, and limited access to economic opportunity.

KEY DEVELOPMENTS IN 2020

- Access to Doha News, an independent website whose blocking by the Qatari authorities in 2016 had sparked criticism and allegations of censorship, was restored in May, with the outlet resuming operations under new management.
- Also in May, the government rolled out a mandatory contact-tracing application for mobile devices that was designed to help contain the COVID-19 pandemic. The app required access to users' files and location data, raising privacy and security concerns. Cases of the coronavirus peaked in late spring and early summer, but remained relatively low for the rest of the year, with a total of 245 deaths reported at year's end.
- In August, the emir signed two labor laws that allowed migrant workers to change employers without permission and established a monthly minimum wage of 1,000 riyals ($275) for all sectors and nationalities.

POLITICAL RIGHTS: 7 / 40

A. ELECTORAL PROCESS: 2 / 12

A1. Was the current head of government or other chief national authority elected through free and fair elections? 0 / 4

The emir appoints the prime minister and cabinet, and selects an heir-apparent after consulting with the ruling family and other notables. In 2013, Sheikh Hamad bin Khalifa al-Thani abdicated as emir, handing power to his fourth-born son, Sheikh Tamim bin Hamad al-Thani. In January 2020, Sheikh Khalid bin Khalifa al-Thani succeeded Sheikh Abdullah bin Nasser al-Thani, a fellow member of the ruling family, as both prime minister and interior minister.

A2. Were the current national legislative representatives elected through free and fair elections? 1 / 4

The 2003 constitution stipulates that 30 of the 45 seats on the Advisory Council (Majlis al-Shura) should be filled through elections every four years, with the emir appointing the other 15 members. However, elections have been repeatedly postponed, so all members are still appointed. In 2017, the emir renewed the membership of some members and appointed 28 new members. He said the first elections to the Advisory Council would be held in 2019, but at the end of June 2019 he extended the existing council's expiring mandate by another two years. At the opening of the Advisory Council's session in November 2020, the emir announced that elections for two-thirds of the body's seats would take place in October 2021.

Nonpartisan elections have been held since 1999 for the 29-member Central Municipal Council, a body designed to advise the minister for municipal affairs. Members serve four-year terms. Turnout for the April 2019 elections fell to 50.1 percent of registered voters, from the 2015 figure of 70 percent, and two women were elected, the same as in 2015.

A3. Are the electoral laws and framework fair, and are they implemented impartially by the relevant election management bodies? 1 / 4

Electoral laws currently in force cover only the Central Municipal Council elections, and the absence of a legal framework for Advisory Council elections has been a factor in their repeated postponement. Qatari citizens over the age of 18 are eligible to vote, except those in the military or working for the Interior Ministry.

B. POLITICAL PLURALISM AND PARTICIPATION: 2 / 16

B1. Do the people have the right to organize in different political parties or other competitive political groupings of their choice, and is the system free of undue obstacles to the rise and fall of these competing parties or groupings? 0 / 4

The government does not permit the existence of political parties or other political groupings. All candidates for the municipal council elections run as independents.

B2. Is there a realistic opportunity for the opposition to increase its support or gain power through elections? 0 / 4

The ruling family maintains a monopoly on political power, and the system excludes the possibility of a change in government through elections.

As part of the diplomatic clash between Qatar and Saudi Arabia, the United Arab Emirates (UAE), Bahrain, and Egypt that began in 2017, dissident members of the Qatari ruling family living abroad emerged to advocate political change in Qatar, though they did not have any organized public support within the country.

B3. Are the people's political choices free from domination by forces that are external to the political sphere, or by political forces that employ extrapolitical means? 1 / 4

Public participation in the political arena is extremely limited. Voters and candidates who do take part in the municipal elections are often influenced by tribal and family ties.

B4. Do various segments of the population (including ethnic, racial, religious, gender, LGBT+, and other relevant groups) have full political rights and electoral opportunities? 1 / 4

Up to 90 percent of Qatar's population is composed of noncitizens, including expatriates and migrant workers as well as some stateless residents, who have no political rights or electoral opportunities. Citizenship is inherited exclusively from a Qatari father; residents can apply for citizenship after 25 years in the country, but this is rarely granted.

Qatari women enjoy some political rights, though they have little opportunity to organize independently and advocate for their interests. In the 2019 municipal council elections, five of the 85 candidates were women, and two of them—both incumbents—won seats. Four women were among the new Advisory Council members appointed in 2017, becoming the first women to serve on the council.

C. FUNCTIONING OF GOVERNMENT: 3 / 12

C1. Do the freely elected head of government and national legislative representatives determine the policies of the government? 0 / 4

Decision-making authority is concentrated in the hands of the emir and his family, and there is no elected legislature to offset executive power.

C2. Are safeguards against official corruption strong and effective? 2 / 4

The authorities regularly punish lower-level public officials for bribery and embezzlement, but corruption remains a concern, and the country lacks genuinely independent anticorruption mechanisms that can hold senior officials and members of the ruling family publicly accountable for the allocation of state resources. Qatar has been accused of employing corrupt tactics in its successful bid to host soccer's 2022 World Cup.

C3. Does the government operate with openness and transparency? 1 / 4

Official information is tightly controlled, and critics complain of a lack of transparency in state procurement. Although the State Audit Bureau prepares budgets and accounts for government institutions, it does not share their full details with the public or the appointed Advisory Council. A 2016 law empowered the bureau to make some aspects of its audit findings public, but the security ministries remained exempt from its oversight.

CIVIL LIBERTIES: 18 / 60
D. FREEDOM OF EXPRESSION AND BELIEF: 7 / 16
D1. Are there free and independent media? 1 / 4

Both print and broadcast media are influenced by leading families and subject to state censorship. The international television network Al-Jazeera is privately held, but the government has reportedly paid to support its operating costs since its inception in 1996. All journalists in Qatar practice a degree of self-censorship and face possible jail sentences for defamation and other press offenses. Access to the independent English-language website Doha News was restored in May 2020, having been blocked in late 2016 on the grounds that it did not have the required operating permit. The outlet changed ownership in 2017 and again in 2020, shortly before it resumed full operations.

In January 2020, an amendment to the penal code made the sharing or publication of "false news" punishable with up to five years in prison or a maximum fine of 100,000 riyals ($27,500).

D2. Are individuals free to practice and express their religious faith or nonbelief in public and private? 2 / 4

Islam is the official religion, though the constitution explicitly provides for freedom of worship. The Ministry of Islamic Affairs oversees the construction of mosques, the hiring of imams, and guidance for sermons. Churches have been built for Qatar's growing Christian community, but non-Muslims are not allowed to proselytize or worship in public.

D3. Is there academic freedom, and is the educational system free from extensive political indoctrination? 2 / 4

The constitution guarantees academic freedom, but scholars often self-censor on politically sensitive topics. Foreign universities have established branches in Qatar under a program meant to strengthen the country's educational institutions.

D4. Are individuals free to express their personal views on political or other sensitive topics without fear of surveillance or retribution? 2 / 4

While residents enjoy some freedom of private discussion, security forces reportedly monitor personal communications, and noncitizens often self-censor to avoid jeopardizing their work and residency status. Social media users can face criminal penalties for posting politically sensitive content. After Saudi Arabia and its allies imposed their diplomatic boycott and trade sanctions on Qatar in 2017, citizens and residents became more active in debating current affairs and regional developments, without apparent retribution.

In May 2020, the government made it mandatory to use the Ehteraz mobile app to support contact-tracing during the COVID-19 pandemic. The app recorded and uploaded location data and Bluetooth contact between devices, raising concerns about privacy and security. A security flaw that exposed user information was addressed only after Amnesty International reported it to authorities.

E. ASSOCIATIONAL AND ORGANIZATIONAL RIGHTS: 2 / 12
E1. Is there freedom of assembly? 1 / 4

The constitutional right to freedom of assembly is limited by restrictive laws and does not apply to noncitizens. Organizers of public events must obtain a permit from the Interior Ministry, and protests are rare in practice.

E2. Is there freedom for nongovernmental organizations, particularly those that are engaged in human rights- and governance-related work? 0 / 4

All nongovernmental organizations need state permission to operate, and the government closely monitors their activities. There are no independent human rights organizations, though a government-appointed National Human Rights Committee investigates alleged abuses. Independent activists are subject to state harassment. In 2020, human rights lawyer Najeeb al-Nuaimi remained under a travel ban imposed by the attorney general in 2017.

E3. Is there freedom for trade unions and similar professional or labor organizations? 1 / 4

A 2005 labor law expanded worker protections, but the rights to form unions and to strike remain restricted. The only trade union allowed to operate is the General Union of Workers of Qatar, and the law prohibits union membership for noncitizens, government employees, and household workers. Foreign workers who engage in labor protests risk deportation. Nevertheless, thousands of migrant workers employed by multiple companies went on strike in August 2019 to protest poor working conditions and unpaid or reduced wages; the government intervened to resolve the disputes.

F. RULE OF LAW: 5 / 16
F1. Is there an independent judiciary? 1 / 4

Despite constitutional guarantees, the judiciary is not independent in practice. Many judges are foreign nationals serving under temporary contracts that are renewed annually. The Supreme Council of the Judiciary, composed of senior judges, administers the courts and plays a role in nominating judges for appointment by the emir.

F2. Does due process prevail in civil and criminal matters? 1 / 4

Certain laws allow lengthy detentions without charge or access to a lawyer for suspects in cases involving national security or terrorism. Even under normal criminal procedure, judges can extend pretrial detention for up to half of the maximum prison term allowed for the alleged crime. Many laws contain ill-defined offenses and other language that gives prosecutors and judges broad discretion to determine guilt. A 2014 law on cybercrimes has been criticized for the vague wording of several offenses, including online dissemination of content that undermines "general order."

F3. Is there protection from the illegitimate use of physical force and freedom from war and insurgencies? 3 / 4

Violent crime is rare in Qatar, and prison conditions reportedly meet international standards. Legal bans on torture and other mistreatment of detainees have generally been respected in recent years, though international experts have called for further legislative and other improvements. Corporal punishment in the form of flogging, which can be imposed on Muslim defendants for certain offenses under Sharia (Islamic law), is not commonly implemented in practice. The death penalty is permitted, including for crimes other than murder, but no executions have been carried out since 2003.

F4. Do laws, policies, and practices guarantee equal treatment of various segments of the population? 0 / 4

Noncitizens reportedly face discrimination in the courts and from police. While the constitution bars gender-based discrimination, women do not receive equal treatment under a number of laws, and their testimony is worth less than that of men in certain types of cases. LGBT+ people are subject to legal and societal discrimination; vague wording in the penal code can be interpreted to criminalize same-sex sexual activity, and Sharia prohibits any sexual acts outside of heterosexual marriage. Same-sex relationships must be hidden in practice.

In 2018, the government issued a law to permit grants of asylum, making recipients eligible for various forms of state support. The law also provides some protection against refoulement. However, asylum seekers and recognized refugees would be barred from engaging in political activity in Qatar, and they would need government approval to change their place of residence. An asylum committee began receiving applications in 2019, though some asylum seekers reportedly continued to be threatened with deportation, casting doubt on the implementation of the law.

G. PERSONAL AUTONOMY AND INDIVIDUAL RIGHTS: 4 / 16

G1. Do individuals enjoy freedom of movement, including the ability to change their place of residence, employment, or education? 1 / 4

Qataris face no major restrictions on freedom of movement within the country or on type or place of employment. Such freedoms, however, are not extended to noncitizens and foreign workers, who continue to face a variety of constraints despite the enactment of reform laws in recent years. In January 2020, the government expanded migrant workers' ability to leave the country without the permission of their employers, extending the right to sectors that had previously been excluded. In August, the emir signed legislation that would allow migrant workers to change employers before the end of their contract without the existing employer's permission, so long as they provide written notice. However, Amnesty International noted that employers would still manage workers' residence permits, and could still file criminal "absconding" charges against workers who leave their jobs without following the proper procedures.

As part of the diplomatic clash that began in 2017, Saudi Arabia and its allies closed Qatar's only land border, closed their airspace to Qatari flights, expelled Qatari nationals, and banned their nationals from visiting Qatar.

In 2018 the emir signed a law allowing permanent residency—though not citizenship—for the children and foreign spouses of Qatari women as well as for individuals who provide exceptional skills or services to the country. Up to 100 people per year could receive the designation, giving them access to state education and health benefits and greater rights to own property and run businesses in Qatar.

G2. Are individuals able to exercise the right to own property and establish private businesses without undue interference from state or nonstate actors? 1 / 4

Qataris are permitted to own property and start private businesses, although the process of obtaining necessary commercial permits can be cumbersome. With some exceptions, noncitizens are generally barred from owning property and require Qatari partners to own and operate businesses. Women do not have rights equal to those of men under inheritance laws.

G3. Do individuals enjoy personal social freedoms, including choice of marriage partner and size of family, protection from domestic violence, and control over appearance? 1 / 4

There are a number of legal constraints on marriage, and women are typically at a disadvantage to men under laws on personal status matters. Marriage contracts require the consent of the woman's male guardian, and citizens must obtain government permission to marry foreigners. The foreign wives of Qatari men can obtain citizenship, but foreign husbands of Qatari women are eligible only for residency. Domestic violence and spousal rape are not specifically criminalized. Extramarital sex is illegal.

G4. Do individuals enjoy equality of opportunity and freedom from economic exploitation? 1 / 4

Many foreign nationals face economic abuses including the withholding of wages, contract manipulation, poor living conditions, and excessive working hours. However, fear of job loss and deportation often prevents them from asserting their limited rights. Female household workers are particularly vulnerable to abuse and exploitation. International organizations have drawn attention to the harsh working conditions of migrants building the infrastructure for the 2022 World Cup. In 2020, human rights groups reported that withholding of wages and related abuses became more common during the COVID-19 pandemic, with employers using the crisis as a pretext and labor courts limiting their operations.

The government has undertaken reforms to mitigate some of these problems. In 2017, the emir ratified a new law that provided labor rights to household workers, guaranteeing a maximum 10-hour working day, one rest day a week, three weeks of annual leave, and an end-of-service payment, among other provisions, though it failed to set out enforcement mechanisms to ensure compliance. Its standards are also weaker than those in the main labor law. A reform signed into law in August 2020 established a monthly minimum wage of 1,000 riyals ($275) for all workers, regardless of sector or nationality.

Romania

Population: 19,200,000
Capital: Bucharest
Freedom Status: Free
Electoral Democracy: Yes

Overview: Romania's multiparty system has ensured regular rotations of power through competitive elections. Civil liberties are generally respected but have come under growing pressure as entrenched political interests push back against civic and institutional efforts to combat systemic corruption. Discrimination against minorities and other vulnerable groups is a long-standing problem, as is control of key media outlets by businessmen with political interests.

KEY DEVELOPMENTS IN 2020

- The ruling National Liberal Party (PNL) formed a new governing coalition under Florin Cîțu in December, after coming second in that month's lower-house elections. The Social Democratic Party (PSD), which won a plurality of lower-house seats, also won the most Senate seats in concurrent elections.
- The chief prosecutor responsible for organized crime cases, Giorgiana Hosu, resigned in September after her husband, a former police officer, was convicted of illegally accessing a computer system. Hosu's February appointment had been criticized by the Superior Council of Magistrates in an advisory opinion issued that month.

- Romanians encountered a strict COVID-19 lockdown between March and May. Public gatherings were suspended, though some of those restrictions were loosened in September. Sanctions for lockdown violations were invalidated by the Constitutional Court in May, and quarantine-and-isolation measures for some Romanians returning from abroad were ruled unconstitutional in June. Over 627,000 cases and nearly 15,600 deaths were reported to the World Health Organization at year's end.

POLITICAL RIGHTS: 35 / 40

A. ELECTORAL PROCESS 12 / 12

A1. Was the current head of government or other chief national authority elected through free and fair elections? 4 / 4

The president, who holds some significant powers in Romania's semipresidential system, is directly elected for up to two five-year terms. The president appoints the prime minister in consultation with the parliamentary majority, and the prime minister's government requires the confidence of Parliament. Presidential and parliamentary elections held since 1991 have been generally free and fair.

Klaus Iohannis, a centrist who had belonged to the PNL, won a second presidential term in November 2019, winning 66.1 percent of the vote in a runoff. Viorica Dăncilă of the PSD won 33.9 percent.

Ludovic Orban, the prime minister of a PNL-led government, resigned after parliamentary elections were held in December 2020. Florin Cîțu of the PNL, who had served as finance minister, succeeded Orban later that month.

A2. Were the current national legislative representatives elected through free and fair elections? 4 / 4

Members of the bicameral Parliament, consisting of a 136-seat Senate and a 330-seat Chamber of Deputies, are elected to four-year terms in a closed party-list proportional system.

Elections for both houses were held in December 2020, though electoral campaigns were affected by COVID-19-related restrictions. Turnout for the Chamber of Deputies contests stood at 33.3 percent, a record low. The PSD won 28.9 percent of the vote and 110 seats, while the ruling PNL won 25.2 percent and 93 seats. The 2020 USR–PLUS Alliance—consisting of the Save Romania Union and the Party of Liberty, Unity, and Solidarity—won 15.4 percent and 55 seats. The Democratic Union of Hungarians in Romania (UDMR) won 5.7 percent and 21 seats. The nationalist Alliance for the Union of Romanians (AUR) entered Parliament for the first time, winning 9.1 percent and 33 seats. While the PSD won a plurality of seats, the PNL formed a coalition government with the 2020 USR–PLUS Alliance and the UDMR later that month.

In the concurrent Senate elections, the PSD won 29.3 percent of the vote and 47 seats, while the PNL won 25.6 percent and 41 seats. The 2020 USR–PLUS Alliance won 15.9 percent and 25 seats, the AUR won 9.2 percent and 14 seats, and the UDMR won 5.9 percent and 9 seats. Turnout for the upper-house elections stood at 31.9 percent.

Local elections were originally scheduled for June 2020 but were delayed to September due to the COVID-19 pandemic. Pandemic-related measures were enacted at polling places, though social distancing was not consistently observed. The PNL and 2020 USR–PLUS Alliance performed well, with the two groups' candidate for the Bucharest mayoralty defeating PSD incumbent Gabriela Firea. The PSD also lost control of Constanța to the PNL candidate, while the 2020 USR–PLUS Alliance candidate defeated the PNL incumbent in Timișoara.

A3. Are the electoral laws and framework fair, and are they implemented impartially by the relevant election management bodies? 4 / 4

The legal framework generally provides for fair and competitive elections. The Romanian electoral framework relies on a Central Election Bureau, which includes judges and political representatives, and a Permanent Electoral Authority, which manages voter registration, campaign finance, and logistics.

Organization for Security and Co-operation in Europe (OSCE) observers who monitored the December 2020 parliamentary elections noted the complexity of the legal electoral framework. Observers criticized parliamentarians' fast-tracking of electoral-law amendments that September, limiting public debate. OSCE observers also voiced concerns over the electoral authorities' training efforts, which were affected by the COVID-19 pandemic.

B. POLITICAL PLURALISM AND PARTICIPATION: 14 / 16

B1. Do the people have the right to organize in different political parties or other competitive political groupings of their choice, and is the system free of undue obstacles to the rise and fall of these competing parties or groupings? 4 / 4

Romania's multiparty system features active competition between rival blocs. Under the 2015 electoral law, the number of signatures needed to create a new party decreased dramatically, leading to the registration of many new parties. Some 217 parties and alliances competed in the September 2020 local elections; 24 parties and individual candidates competed for Senate seats that December, while 82 groups and candidates, including ethnic minority groups, competed for lower-house seats. The AUR, which was formed in late 2019, entered Parliament for the first time after the December poll.

Critics have argued that signature thresholds to register candidates for local and parliamentary elections still place new and smaller parties at a disadvantage. COVID-19-related legislation reduced the signature requirements for local candidates by half.

B2. Is there a realistic opportunity for the opposition to increase its support or gain power through elections? 4 / 4

The country has established a record of peaceful transfers of power between rival parties, though no-confidence votes have been frequently held in recent years. A minority PNL government led by Ludovic Orban took office in November 2019 after a no-confidence vote removed a PSD-led government the month before.

The Orban government lost a no-confidence vote in early February 2020, though Orban remained in office on an interim basis until a new government under his leadership was formed in March. The PSD attempted to remove the Orban government in August, but that effort failed for lack of a quorum.

B3. Are the people's political choices free from domination by forces that are external to the political sphere, or by political forces that employ extrapolitical means? 3 / 4

People are generally free to make political choices without undue pressure from unaccountable actors. However, clientelism in local politics remains a problem. In small towns and villages, mayors retain significant leverage over voters. Local mayors are known to switch parties to secure funding or other resources.

B4. Do various segments of the population (including ethnic, racial, religious, gender, LGBT+, and other relevant groups) have full political rights and electoral opportunities? 3 / 4

Ethnic, religious, and other minority groups enjoy full political rights under the law. The constitution grants one lower-house seat to each national minority whose representative party or organization wins no seats otherwise, with a maximum of 18 seats allotted in this fashion. President Iohannis, an ethnic German and a Lutheran, is the country's first president from either minority group. The UDMR, which represents the Hungarian minority, is part of the coalition government that took office in December 2020.

Roma, who make up over 3 percent of the population, are underrepresented in politics. Social discrimination against LGBT+ people discourages political advocacy for their rights. Data collection on gender representation is lacking, as is a policy to encourage female political participation. Women represented 23 percent of candidates in the September 2020 local elections, a slight improvement over local elections held in 2016. Women held 18.5 percent of lower-house seats and 18.4 percent of the Senate after the December 2020 elections. Only one female minister was appointed in the Cîțu government.

C. FUNCTIONING OF GOVERNMENT: 9 / 12

C1. Do the freely elected head of government and national legislative representatives determine the policies of the government? 4 / 4

Elected officials are generally able to craft and implement government policy without outside interference.

C2. Are safeguards against official corruption strong and effective? 2 / 4

High levels of corruption, bribery, and abuse of power persist. Romania maintains a comprehensive anticorruption action plan, though the European Anti-Fraud Office (OLAF) noted that anticorruption bodies face pressure when pursuing high-level cases in a report released in September 2020.

A new prosecutor general, chief anticorruption prosecutor, and chief organized-crime prosecutor were appointed in February 2020. In an advisory opinion released that month, the Superior Council of Magistrates criticized the appointments of Gabriela Scutea as prosecutor general and Giorgiana Hosu as chief of prosecution at the Directorate for Investigating Organized Crime and Terrorism. Hosu resigned in September after her husband, a former police officer, was convicted of illegally accessing a computer system.

The National Anticorruption Directorate (DNA) previously won international praise for fairly investigating corruption cases and securing convictions of powerful figures. However, the 2018 dismissal of DNA chief Laura Codruța Kövesi was seen as a blow to its independence. Kövesi was confirmed as head of the European Public Prosecutor's Office by the European Parliament in 2019, though the Romanian government opposed her candidacy. In May 2020, Kövesi won a European Court of Human Rights judgment over her dismissal from the DNA.

Anticorruption bodies pursued cases related to COVID-19-related procurements during 2020, with the DNA disclosing in May that 33 such cases had been opened. In June, the head of a state-owned company was charged with corruption after he was accused of seeking bribes.

C3. Does the government operate with openness and transparency? 3 / 4

Citizens have the legal right to obtain public information and can petition government agencies for it. However, processes for soliciting participation and input from various stakeholders and civil society experts are not well defined, and the government still widely utilizes emergency ordinances for legislating. During the COVID-19-related state of emergency between March and May 2020, authorities had 60 days to respond to information requests, double the preemergency limit. President Iohannis's mid-March pandemic-related decree exempted public procurements from preexisting tender practices.

Pandemic-related information was sometimes withheld by authorities. In March 2020, the Ministry of Internal Affairs ordered local prefects not to publish the number of COVID-19 tests performed or the number of positive results. In a September report, the Center for Independent Journalism (CJI) noted that health-care staff were often prohibited from discussing the pandemic to media outlets.

CIVIL LIBERTIES: 48 / 60
D. FREEDOM OF EXPRESSION AND BELIEF: 13 / 16
D1. Are there free and independent media? 3 / 4

Although the media environment is relatively free and pluralistic, key outlets remain controlled by businessmen with political interests, and their coverage is highly distorted by their owners' priorities. Media outlets increasingly rely on publicly funded advertising and subsidies.

President Iohannis's March 2020 decree allowed authorities to restrict access to web-pages or websites that disseminated purportedly false COVID-19 information. The OSCE criticized the decree that month, warning that users had no avenue to appeal the removal of content. The country's telecommunications regulator restricted access to 15 websites during the pandemic-related state of emergency, though access was restored by May.

OSCE monitors who observed the December 2020 parliamentary elections noted that television channels either did not devote significant airtime to the polls or offered extensive coverage to public officials and President Iohannis.

Media outlets saw private advertising collapse as a result of the COVID-19 pandemic, with the CJI reporting that some outlets saw income fall by at least 70 percent between March and April 2020. In its September report, the CJI warned that authorities were effectively gaining editorial access through publicly funded advertising.

D2. Are individuals free to practice and express their religious faith or nonbelief in public and private? 3 / 4

Religious freedom is generally respected. While the Romanian Orthodox Church remains dominant and politically powerful, the government formally recognizes 18 religions, each of which is eligible for proportional state support. Others can register as religious associations. The have been reports of discrimination and harassment against religious minorities, including vandalism in Jewish cemeteries and media articles referring to Islam and Muslim migrants as threats to Romania. The promotion of antisemitism was banned by legislation adopted in 2018.

Some religious ceremonies were impacted by COVID-19-related measures. In October 2020, the Orthodox Church criticized the government's decision to restrict or cancel major pilgrimages.

D3. Is there academic freedom, and is the educational system free from extensive political indoctrination? 3 / 4

The government generally does not restrict academic freedom, but the education system is weakened by widespread corruption and politically influenced appointments and financing.

Romanian higher-education institutions were affected by an amendment to the National Education Act that banned gender studies programming, which was passed in June 2020. Protesters called on President Iohannis to withhold his assent at a Bucharest demonstration that month. Iohannis sought a ruling from the Constitutional Court in July and the court annulled the amendment in December.

D4. Are individuals free to express their personal views on political or other sensitive topics without fear of surveillance or retribution? 4 / 4

People are generally free to express their opinions without fear of retribution. However, the September 2020 CJI report noted that some social media users received fines after they were accused of insulting police.

E. ASSOCIATIONAL AND ORGANIZATIONAL RIGHTS: 11 / 12

E1. Is there freedom of assembly? 4 / 4

Romania's constitution guarantees freedom of assembly. Public gatherings were restricted in March 2020, when a state of emergency was declared. Public-assembly restrictions were maintained when it expired in May, as the government then declared a state of alert. Some assembly restrictions were loosened in September. Small election-related rallies were held, but attendance was low due to fear of COVID-19 transmission.

Despite these restrictions, demonstrations were held during the year. Several dozen protesters called on President Iohannis to reject a gender-studies ban in Bucharest in June. Protests against COVID-19 measures were also held; protesters who participated in May and July events in Bucharest violated pandemic-related measures, leading to the issuance of several fines.

E2. Is there freedom for nongovernmental organizations, particularly those that are engaged in human rights– and governance-related work? 4 / 4

Nongovernmental organizations (NGOs) operate without major formal restrictions. Nevertheless, many human rights and governance groups suffer from funding shortages and often face hostility and smears from politicians and other actors.

In December 2020, interim premier Nicolae Ciucă removed Adriana Radu, the head of a women's rights NGO, from an advisory council. Radu, who was selected by civil society representatives, was reportedly the only nominated individual to be kept off the council.

E3. Is there freedom for trade unions and similar professional or labor organizations? 3 / 4

Workers have the right to form unions, have a limited right to strike, and can bargain collectively, though laws against the violation of these rights are not well enforced. There are legal constraints on the ability of unions to participate in political activity.

F. RULE OF LAW: 12 / 16

F1. Is there an independent judiciary? 3 / 4

The judiciary is generally independent, but faces pressure from the executive and legislative branches. A special prosecution unit focusing on magistrates has been criticized by magistrates' associations and supranational bodies, who feared it would allow for the intimidation of magistrates and other abuses. The unit remained active in 2020, however.

In September 2020, the Justice Ministry introduced proposed legislative amendments that would affect the judiciary; the public debate period on the amendments was scheduled to conclude in March 2021.

F2. Does due process prevail in civil and criminal matters? 3 / 4

The law provides safeguards against arbitrary arrest and detention which are generally respected. However, the right to a fair and timely trial is often undermined by institutional problems including corruption, political influence, staffing shortages, and inefficient resource allocation. Many government officials and lawmakers have retained their positions despite criminal indictments or convictions by exploiting such weaknesses in the system.

The hearing of noncriminal matters was limited for part of 2020 due to the COVID-19 state of emergency.

F3. Is there protection from the illegitimate use of physical force and freedom from war and insurgencies? 3 / 4

The population faces no major threats to physical security, but prisons and detention centers feature harsh conditions, and the abuse of detainees by police and fellow prisoners remains a problem.

F4. Do laws, policies, and practices guarantee equal treatment of various segments of the population? 3 / 4

The law provides broad protections against discrimination based on gender, race, ethnicity, sexual orientation, and other categories. However, people with disabilities, LGBT+ people, Roma, and HIV-positive children and adults face discrimination in education, employment, medical service provision, and other areas. The constitution guarantees women equal rights, but gender discrimination remains a problem in many aspects of life.

G. PERSONAL AUTONOMY AND INDIVIDUAL RIGHTS: 12 / 16

G1. Do individuals enjoy freedom of movement, including the ability to change their place of residence, employment, or education? 4 / 4

Citizens generally face no significant restrictions on freedom of movement, whether for internal or external travel, and can freely change their place of employment or education.

During the March-to-May 2020 state of emergency, the government instituted a strict COVID-19-related lockdown. In May, the Constitutional Court invalidated legal sanctions over lockdown violations. In June, it ruled that compulsory quarantine and isolation measures for Romanians returning from areas deemed high-risk were unconstitutional. New quarantine and isolation measures came into force in July in response to the ruling.

G2. Are individuals able to exercise the right to own property and establish private businesses without undue interference from state or nonstate actors? 2 / 4

Property rights are protected by law, but despite significant progress, the country has struggled to adjudicate restitution claims for property confiscated during the communist era. Bureaucratic barriers, corruption, and broader weaknesses in the rule of law hamper private business activity.

G3. Do individuals enjoy personal social freedoms, including choice of marriage partner and size of family, protection from domestic violence, and control over appearance? 3 / 4

While personal social freedoms are generally protected, domestic violence remains a serious problem, and laws meant to combat it are poorly enforced. Same-sex marriages are not permitted under Romanian law. However, in 2018, the Constitutional Court recognized the residency rights of same-sex couples married elsewhere, provided that one spouse is a European Union citizen. Antigay rhetoric is still sometimes instrumentalized by political actors in order to galvanize conservative parts of society against political adversaries.

G4. Do individuals enjoy equality of opportunity and freedom from economic exploitation? 3 / 4

The law provides basic protections against exploitative working conditions, though they are unevenly enforced, particularly in the large informal economy. Economic opportunity varies widely between urban and rural areas, and such disparities limit social mobility for some. Human trafficking for the purpose of forced labor and prostitution remains a serious problem. Women and Roma children are especially vulnerable to forced begging.

Russia

Population: 146,700,000
Capital: Moscow
Freedom Status: Not Free
Electoral Democracy: No

Overview: Power in Russia's authoritarian political system is concentrated in the hands of President Vladimir Putin. With loyalist security forces, a subservient judiciary, a controlled media environment, and a legislature consisting of a ruling party and pliable opposition factions, the Kremlin is able to manipulate elections and suppress genuine dissent. Rampant corruption facilitates shifting links among bureaucrats and organized crime groups.

KEY DEVELOPMENTS IN 2020

- Russia experienced a severe outbreak of COVID-19, with at least 3.1 million people testing positive for the virus and 56,000 deaths, according to the government. However, analysts suggested that authorities had downplayed the true number of coronavirus deaths, pointing to, among other things, official statistics that showed a significant increase in the overall number of deaths in the country during the year.
- In July, authorities staged a highly choreographed referendum on extending presidential term limits, with the affirmative result effectively allowing President Putin to remain in office until 2036. Among other changes, the amendments enable the president, with support from Parliament's upper chamber, to remove judges from the Constitutional and Supreme Courts, further reducing the judiciary's already tenuous independence.
- Unsanctioned protests in Khabarovsk began in July and lasted through the end of the year. Authorities largely ignored the protesters until October, when they started making arrests.
- In December, President Putin expanded the law requiring nongovernmental organizations (NGOs) that receive international funding to register as "foreign agents," placing restrictions on their activities and threatening their employees with fines, raids, and arrests.

POLITICAL RIGHTS: 5 / 40

A. ELECTORAL PROCESS: 0 / 12

A1. Was the current head of government or other chief national authority elected through free and fair elections? 0 / 4

The constitution establishes a strong presidency with the power to dismiss and appoint, pending parliamentary confirmation, the prime minister. The president is elected to a six-year term, and can be reelected to one additional term. Constitutional amendments adopted in 2020 allow Putin, but not future presidents, to run for an additional two terms as president, potentially extending his rule to 2036. Like past elections, President Putin's 2018 reelection campaign benefited from advantages including preferential media treatment, numerous abuses of incumbency, and procedural irregularities during the vote count. His most influential rival, Aleksey Navalny, was disqualified before the campaign began due to a politically motivated criminal conviction, creating what the Organization for Security and Co-operation in Europe (OSCE) called "a lack of genuine competition." The funding sources for Putin's campaign were also notably opaque.

A2. Were the current national legislative representatives elected through free and fair elections? 0 / 4

The Federal Assembly consists of the 450-seat State Duma and an upper chamber Federation Council. The 2020 constitutional amendments altered the makeup of the Federation Council to include: two representatives from each of Russia's self-declared 85 regions—including the two regions of occupied Crimea (half appointed by governors and half by regional legislatures, usually with strong federal input)—the president who is a lifetime member, and no more than 30 "representatives of the Russian Federation" appointed by the president, of whom no more than seven can be appointed for life. The rest are appointed for six-year terms.

Half of Duma members are elected by nationwide proportional representation and the other half in single-member districts, with all serving five-year terms. This system was adopted following the 2011 elections, when United Russia garnered just less than 50 percent of the vote under a system that used only nationwide proportional representation. These and other rule changes were designed to benefit United Russia, and were considered to have contributed to the party's 2016 supermajority.

In the 2016 Duma elections, United Russia won 343 seats, securing a supermajority that allows it to change the constitution without the support of other parties. The three main Kremlin-approved "opposition" parties—the Communists, Liberal Democratic Party of Russia (LDPR), and A Just Russia—won the bulk of the remainder, taking 42, 39, and 23 seats, respectively. The Central Electoral Commission reported a turnout of 48 percent, the lowest in Russia's post-Soviet history. The OSCE and the election monitoring group Golos cited numerous violations, including ballot stuffing, pressure on voters, and illegal campaigning. Some opposition candidates were simply not permitted to register, so the outcome of many races was clear even before election day.

In the September 2020 local and regional elections, the Kremlin, as usual, eliminated any serious opposition candidates before the election took place, and their candidates won all 18 governors' races and 11 regional legislative elections. In the 22 regional capital city council elections, Navalny's allies were able to win a few seats in Tomsk and Novosibirsk, preventing the Kremlin from maintaining its majorities and demonstrating Navalny's influence even outside of Moscow and St. Petersburg.

A3. Are the electoral laws and framework fair, and are they implemented impartially by the relevant election management bodies? 0 / 4

Russia's electoral system is designed to maintain the dominance of United Russia. The authorities make frequent changes to electoral laws and the timing of elections in order to secure advantages for their preferred candidates. Opposition candidates have little chance of success in appealing these decisions, or securing a level playing field. In May 2020, Putin signed a law permitting the use of electronic voting across Russia, raising concerns about the security, anonymization, and secrecy of ballots in future elections. In July, Putin also signed a law for all future elections to have a three-day voting period. Critics claimed that the expanded timeframe increases officials' ability to manipulate election outcomes.

Russia adopted extensive changes to its constitution in 2020 through a "nationwide vote" that was set up to avoid full referendum procedures. Voting was originally set for

April 22, but was delayed due to the COVID-19 pandemic. The Central Electoral Commission subsequently adopted a number of provisions that extended the voting period to one week—from June 25 to July 1. Critics charged there was no way to observe or monitor the fairness or integrity of polling. Statisticians claimed it was potentially the most falsified vote in Russian history.

B. POLITICAL PLURALISM AND PARTICIPATION: 3 / 16

B1. Do the people have the right to organize in different political parties or other competitive political groupings of their choice, and is the system free of undue obstacles to the rise and fall of these competing parties or groupings? 1 / 4

The multiparty system is carefully managed by the Kremlin, which tolerates only superficial competition against the dominant United Russia party. Legislation enacted in 2012 liberalized party registration rules, allowing the creation of hundreds of new parties. However, none posed a significant threat to the authorities, and many seemed designed to encourage division and confusion among the opposition. The Justice Ministry has repeatedly refused to register Navalny's political party.

In the 2020 local elections, three new parties met the voting threshold needed to qualify to compete in Russia's 2021 Duma elections: New People, For Truth, and Green Alternative. In practice, each has links to the ruling party, allowing Kremlin-friendly political figures to distance themselves from the increasingly unpopular United Russia while still dominating the vote.

B2. Is there a realistic opportunity for the opposition to increase its support or gain power through elections? 0 / 4

Russia has never experienced a democratic transfer of power between rival groups. Putin, then the prime minister, initially received the presidency on an acting basis from the retiring Boris Yeltsin at the end of 1999. He served two four-year presidential terms from 2000 to 2008, then remained the de facto paramount leader while working as prime minister until he returned to the presidency in 2012, violating the spirit if not the letter of the constitution's two-term limit. A 2008 constitutional amendment extended presidential terms to six years, and a 2020 amendment allowed him to run for an additional two terms, meaning Putin's current term will leave him in office until 2036.

Opposition politicians and activists are frequently targeted with fabricated criminal cases and other forms of administrative harassment that are designed to prevent their participation in the political process. Aleksey Navalny was poisoned with a toxic nerve agent in August 2020 while he was investigating corruption and campaigning in Siberia, with evidence later emerging later that the attack was carried out by the Federal Security Service (FSB). He had to be evacuated to Germany to prevent the authorities from intervening with his treatment.

In December 2020, the Federal Prison Service warned Navalny that he had to return to Russia within 24 hours, or his suspended sentence in the Yves Rocher case would be converted into a real term. The next day, state investigators announced the opening of a new case against Navalny, claiming that he had embezzled money donated to his organization, the Anti-Corruption Foundation (FBK).

B3. Are the people's political choices free from domination by forces that are external to the political sphere, or by political forces that employ extrapolitical means? 1 / 4

Russia's numerous security agencies work to maintain tight control over society and prevent any political challenges to the incumbent regime. The country's leadership is also closely intertwined with powerful economic oligarchs who benefit from government patronage in exchange for political loyalty and various forms of service. Recent reports from the Riga-based online outlet Meduza revealed that authorities are forcing people in the public sector—teachers, doctors, state employees, and others—to vote, so as to reach the government's desired voter turnout; a high enough turnout apparently enables the Kremlin to more easily manipulate election results. The Russian Orthodox Church similarly works to support the status quo, receiving financial support and a privileged status in return.

B4. Do various segments of the population (including ethnic, racial, religious, gender, LGBT+, and other relevant groups) have full political rights and electoral opportunities? 1 / 4

The formation of parties based on ethnicity or religion is not permitted by law. In practice, many regions home to distinct ethnic groups are carefully monitored and controlled by federal authorities. Defenders of minority languages have sought to protect the right to teach them in public schools. Most republics in the restive North Caucasus area and some autonomous districts in energy-rich western Siberia have opted out of direct gubernatorial elections; instead, their legislatures choose a governor from candidates proposed by the president.

Women are underrepresented in politics and government. They hold less than a fifth of seats in the State Duma and the Federation Council. Only 3 of the 31 cabinet members are women, and many issues of importance to women are not prominent in Russian politics.

The July 2020 constitutional amendments contained language defining marriage as between a man and a woman, both reflecting and deepening the systemic challenges LGBT+ people face in gaining political rights and representation.

C. FUNCTIONING OF GOVERNMENT: 2 / 12

C1. Do the freely elected head of government and national legislative representatives determine the policies of the government? 0 / 4

Russia's authoritarian president dominates the political system, along with powerful allies in the security services and in business. These groups effectively control the output of the parliament, which is not freely elected. The 2020 constitutional amendments formalized the power of the president over the legislature and allow Putin to serve as president until 2036, demonstrating his ability to manipulate the system. The federal authorities have limited ability to impose policy decisions in Chechnya, where Chechen leader Ramzan Kadyrov has gained unchecked power in exchange for keeping the republic within the Russian Federation.

C2. Are safeguards against official corruption strong and effective? 1 / 4

Corruption in the government and the business world is pervasive, and a growing lack of accountability enables bureaucrats to engage in malfeasance with impunity. Many analysts have argued that the political system is essentially a kleptocracy, a regime whose defining characteristic is the plunder of public wealth by ruling elites. Some of these elites openly work to fulfill President Putin's policy aims and receive government contracts and protection from prosecution in return for their loyalty.

C3. Does the government operate with openness and transparency? 1 / 4

There is little transparency and accountability in the day-to-day workings of the government. Decisions are adopted behind closed doors by a small group of individuals whose identities are often unclear to the public, and are announced to the population after the fact.

CIVIL LIBERTIES: 15 / 60

D. FREEDOM OF EXPRESSION AND BELIEF: 3 / 16

D1. Are there free and independent media? 0 / 4

Although the constitution provides for freedom of speech, vague laws on extremism grant the authorities great discretion to crack down on any speech, organization, or activity that lacks official support. The government controls, directly or through state-owned companies and friendly business magnates, all of the national television networks and many radio and print outlets, as well as most of the media advertising market. A handful of independent outlets still operate, most of them online and some headquartered abroad. The few that remain in the country struggle to maintain their independence from state interests. Television remains the most popular source of news, but its influence is declining, particularly among young people who rely more on social media.

Attacks, arrests, office raids, and threats against journalists are common and authorities actively targeted journalists outside of Moscow throughout 2020. Ivan Safronov, who had worked as a *Kommersant* and *Vedomosti* correspondent, was arrested in July, and charged with "spying for the West." In September, Ingushetia authorities sentenced journalist Rashid Maisigov to three years in a regime colony for drug possession. He had reported on local protests and the persecution of activists.

Roskomnadzor, the federal media and telecommunications censorship agency, ceased its efforts to eradicate the encrypted messaging service Telegram, lifting its two-year-old ban on the platform in June 2020. The reprieve is contingent upon the company's cooperation in terrorism cases.

D2. Are individuals free to practice and express their religious faith or nonbelief in public and private? 1 / 4

Freedom of religion is upheld unevenly. A 1997 law on religion gives the state extensive control and makes it difficult for new or independent groups to operate. The Russian Orthodox Church has a privileged position, working closely with the government on foreign and domestic policy priorities. Antiterror legislation approved in 2016 grants the authorities power to repress religious groups that are deemed extremist. In 2017, the Supreme Court upheld the Justice Ministry's decision to ban the Jehovah's Witnesses, who at that time numbered about 170,000 in Russia, as an extremist organization. The decision heralded a protracted campaign against the worshippers, marked by surveillance, property seizures, arrests, and torture. At least 339 members of the religion faced persecution for their faith, according to data released in 2020 by the Memorial Human Rights Center. At the end of the year, 45 Jehovah's Witnesses were in prison and 35 were in pretrial detention. The authorities raided the homes of at least 440 Jehovah's Witnesses throughout the year.

Many Muslims have been detained in recent years for alleged membership in banned Islamist groups, including Hizb ut-Tahrir.

D3. Is there academic freedom, and is the educational system free from extensive political indoctrination? 1 / 4

The higher education system and the government-controlled Academy of Sciences are hampered by bureaucratic interference, state-imposed international isolation, and increasing pressure to toe the Kremlin line on politically sensitive topics, though some academics still express dissenting views. New rules limit the political activity of students after some, like Yegor Zhukov, had been involved in the 2019 Moscow protests. Zhukov was admitted to graduate school in fall 2020, but then quickly had his admission revoked. Memorial Human Rights Center currently lists him as "persecuted without imprisonment."

In February 2020, the Education and Science Ministry revoked "recommendations" issued in 2019 requiring government-affiliated scientists to seek permission to meet foreign colleagues and report on such meetings to their superiors.

D4. Are individuals free to express their personal views on political or other sensitive topics without fear of surveillance or retribution? 1 / 4

Pervasive, hyperpatriotic propaganda and political repression—particularly since Russian forces' invasion of Ukraine in 2014—have had a cumulative impact on open and free private discussion, and the chilling effect is exacerbated by growing state efforts to control expression on the internet.

In March 2019, authorities adopted a law imposing fines for insulting officials or state symbols through the use of electronic media. The Presidential Council for Civil Society and Human Rights called the law vague, warning it was subject to abuse.

E. ASSOCIATIONAL AND ORGANIZATIONAL RIGHTS: 3 / 12

E1. Is there freedom of assembly? 1 / 4

The government restricts freedom of assembly. Overwhelming police responses, the excessive use of force, routine arrests, and harsh fines and prison sentences have discouraged unsanctioned protests, while pro-Kremlin groups are able to demonstrate freely. Despite the risks, thousands of people have turned out for a series of antigovernment demonstrations in recent years.

Obtaining permission to hold a protest or rally by groups opposing the Kremlin is extremely difficult. At the regional level, extensive territorial restrictions prohibit assemblies in as much as 70 percent of public space. While some of these restrictions have been invalidated over the years—in prominent Constitutional Court cases in 2019 and 2020—authorities can ban rallies based on "public interest" grounds. In December 2020, two new laws were adopted by the Duma prohibiting single-person pickets and requiring protest organizers to fill out extensive paperwork.

In May 2020, the parliament increased the penalties under Article 212.1 that regulate public gatherings. The Investigative Committee used the updated code in July to file charges against Yulia Galiamina, a member of the Moscow city council and frequent critic of the Russian president, for participating in several protests. In December, Galiamina was convicted and given a two-year suspended sentence.

Unsanctioned protests in Khabarovsk lasted over 150 days, spurred on after the arrest of Governor Sergei Furgal in July 2020. Although the authorities ignored many of the demonstrations, they began arresting activists in October. Furgal, a member of Vladimir Zhirinovsky's opposition party, had defeated a United Russia candidate in the 2018 elections.

E2. Is there freedom for nongovernmental organizations, particularly those that are engaged in human rights- and governance-related work? 0 / 4

The government continued its relentless campaign against NGOs in 2020. Authorities impede activities in part by requiring groups that receive foreign funding and are deemed to engage in political activity to register as "foreign agents." This designation, which is interpreted by much of the Russian public as denoting a foreign spying operation, mandates onerous registration requirements, obliges groups to tag their materials with a "foreign agent" label, and generally makes it extremely difficult for them to pursue their objectives. In December 2020, Putin extended the provisions of the foreign agent law to recognize individuals and informal organizations as potential foreign agents.

Political activities addressed in the law include organizing gatherings, observing elections, issuing public statements aimed at changing legislation, distributing opinions about government decisions, and conducting and publishing public opinion polls. The law also expands the definition of "foreign support" beyond financing and makes it the responsibility of individuals to self-declare their status as foreign agents, or risk fines or prison time. New punishments for violations of the law include up to five years of forced labor in a colony.

By the end of 2020, the Justice Ministry had classified 75 groups as "foreign agents." Among the new designees are No to Violence, which works to recriminalize domestic violence and help its victims. Separately, a total of 29 foreign NGOs have been deemed "undesirable organizations" on the grounds that they threaten national security, including the Jamestown Foundation, Project Harmony, Doctors Against Forced Organ Harvesting, and groups related to Falun Gong. This designation gives authorities the power to issue a range of sanctions against the groups and individuals who work with them. In December, the Justice Ministry added five individuals to its list of mass media foreign agents, two of whom are not members of the media: human rights defender Lev Ponomarev and artist Daria Apakhonchich.

Other forms of harassment and intimidation hinder NGO activities. Aleksey Navalny had to close his Anti-Corruption Foundation in July 2020, due to a lawsuit filed by Putin associate Yevgeny Prigozhin. Navalny released videos that revealed Prigozhin's company sold spoiled food to Moscow's schoolchildren.

E3. Is there freedom for trade unions and similar professional or labor organizations? 2 / 4

While trade union rights are legally protected, they are limited in practice. Strikes and worker protests have occurred in prominent industries, including automobile manufacturing, but antiunion discrimination and reprisals are common. Employers often ignore collective bargaining rights. The largest labor federation works in close cooperation with the Kremlin, though independent unions are active in some industrial sectors and regions.

F. RULE OF LAW: 2 / 16

F1. Is there an independent judiciary? 1 / 4

The judiciary lacks independence from the executive branch, and career advancement is effectively tied to compliance with Kremlin preferences. The Presidential Personnel Commission and court chairmen control the appointment and reappointment of the country's judges, who tend to be promoted from inside the judicial system rather than gaining independent experience as lawyers. Amendments to the constitution adopted in 2020 give the president power to remove judges on the Constitutional Court and the Supreme Court, with the support of the Federation Council, further damaging the already negligible independence of the judiciary.

F2. Does due process prevail in civil and criminal matters? 1 / 4

Safeguards against arbitrary arrest and other due process guarantees are regularly violated, particularly for individuals who oppose or are perceived as threatening to the interests of the political leadership and its allies. Many Russians have consequently sought justice from international courts, but a 2015 law authorizes the Russian judiciary to overrule the decisions of such bodies, and it has since done so on a number of occasions.

Memorial Human Rights Center counted 349 people, including 61 political and 288 religious prisoners in detention at the end of 2020, a marked rise from its 2018 count of 195 prisoners. Those counted included participants of the 2019 Moscow election protests, human rights activists, and advocates for ethnic minority groups.

F3. Is there protection from the illegitimate use of physical force and freedom from war and insurgencies? 0 / 4

Use of excessive force by police is widespread, and rights groups have reported that law enforcement agents who carry out such abuses have deliberately employed electric shocks, suffocation, and the stretching of a detainee's body so as to avoid leaving visible injuries. Prisons are overcrowded and unsanitary; inmates lack access to health care and are subject to abuse by guards. In August 2018, *Novaya Gazeta* posted videos of guards engaging in organized beatings of prisoners in Yaroslavl. The authorities arrested at least 12 guards at the prison after a public outcry, but the NGO Public Verdict reported systematic abuse at another prison in the region in December of that year. In July 2019, Public Verdict released another video showing continued abuse at Yaroslavl. In November 2020, courts convicted 11 prison guards of torture and gave them three- to four- year sentences; the prison directors were acquitted.

Parts of the country, especially the North Caucasus, suffer from high levels of violence; targets include officials, Islamist insurgents, and civilians. Chechen leader Ramzan Kadyrov is accused of using abductions, torture, extrajudicial killings, and other forms of violence to maintain control. This activity sometimes occurs beyond Russian borders: Kadyrov is suspected of arranging the assassination of asylum seekers and political opponents who have fled the country.

F4. Do laws, policies, and practices guarantee equal treatment of various segments of the population? 0 / 4

Immigrants and ethnic minorities—particularly those who appear to be from the Caucasus or Central Asia—face governmental and societal discrimination and harassment. Constitutional amendments establish the primacy of the Russian language within the state, favoring by implication ethnic Russians.

LGBT+ people are also subject to considerable discrimination, which has worsened in the last decade. Since 2013, a federal law banning the dissemination of information on "nontraditional sexual relationships" has been in force, making public discussion of homosexuality illegal. The European Court of Human Rights (ECHR) ruled the law discriminatory in 2017, saying it violated freedom of expression. The ECHR also ruled that Russia was violating human rights by prohibiting LGBT+ demonstrations in 2018. Nevertheless, the law remains in force.

Chechnya remains particularly dangerous for LGBT+ people, with authorities launching a crackdown in January 2019 that ensnared nearly 40 people. According to the Russian LGBT Network, an LGBT+ advocacy group, they were identified when police seized the phone of an LGBT+ social media group's administrator and accessed its contacts. Two detainees reportedly died after they were tortured by police. In May 2019, Maksim Lapunov became the first survivor of a previous 2017 crackdown to file charges at the ECHR, after efforts to have his case heard in Russia failed.

In March 2020, LGBT+ and feminist activist Yulia Tsvetkova was released from house arrest in Khabarovsk on charges of distributing pornography. She faces a six-year prison sentence if convicted in the ongoing case. In 2019, Tsvetkova was fined 50,000 rubles ($720) for administrating two social media pages, one featuring the work of female artists and the other addressing LGBT+ issues.

G. PERSONAL AUTONOMY AND INDIVIDUAL RIGHTS: 7 / 16

G1. Do individuals enjoy freedom of movement, including the ability to change their place of residence, employment, or education? 2 / 4

The government places some restrictions on freedoms of movement and residence. Adults must carry internal passports while traveling and to obtain many government services. Some regional authorities impose registration rules that limit the right of citizens to choose their place of residence, typically targeting ethnic minorities and migrants from the Caucasus and Central Asia. Most Russians are free to travel abroad, but more than four million employees tied to the military and security services were banned from foreign travel under rules issued in 2014.

G2. Are individuals able to exercise the right to own property and establish private businesses without undue interference from state or nonstate actors? 1 / 4

Power and property are intimately connected, with senior officials often using their government positions to amass vast property holdings. State takeovers of key industries and large tax penalties imposed on select companies after dubious legal proceedings have illustrated the precarious nature of property rights under Putin's rule, especially when political interests are involved. Private businesses more broadly are routinely targeted for extortion or expropriation by law enforcement officials and organized criminal groups.

G3. Do individuals enjoy personal social freedoms, including choice of marriage partner and size of family, protection from domestic violence, and control over appearance? 2 / 4

Constitutional amendments adopted in 2020 define marriage as between a man and a woman, a change that makes it impossible to pass legislation legalizing same-sex marriage. The Kremlin used homophobic campaign advertisements to support the amendment's adoption.

Domestic violence receives little attention from the authorities. Instead, domestic violence survivors who kill abusers in self-defense are commonly imprisoned; as many as 80 percent of women imprisoned in Russia may fall under this category. In 2017, Putin signed a law that decriminalized acts of domestic violence that do not result in permanent physical harm. The new law also relieved police from the obligation of automatically opening domestic violence cases, transferring that burden to survivors. During Russia's COVID-19 lockdown, Russian NGOs reported a doubling of domestic violence cases, while official police statistics reported a decrease. In December 2020, the Justice Ministry listed the NGO Nasiliu.net, which fights gender-based violence, as a "foreign agent."

In July 2019, the European Court of Human Rights found that Russia had violated the rights of citizens to be free from torture and inhuman treatment. The Court ruled in favor of Valeriya Volodina, who had experienced extreme physical and psychological abuse from her former husband over the course of several years. Three separate judges found that the severity of the treatment amounted to torture, and declared that the state's negligence in combatting domestic violence amounted to discrimination against women.

Official tolerance of domestic violence was put to the test again in 2020, when Muscovite sisters Angelina, Krestina, and Maria Khachaturyan were charged with their father's 2018 murder, despite a subsequent investigation revealing his history of physical and sexual abuse. The case sparked controversy in Russia, fostering protests and calls for legal reform. By December, murder charges were recommended against the two older sisters, Krestina and Angelina, while Maria faced a separate trial; their cases remained open at year's end.

Residents of certain regions, particularly in the North Caucasus, face tighter societal restrictions on personal appearance and relationships, and some so-called honor killings have been reported. Chechen leader Ramzan Kadyrov has spoken in favor of polygamy and sought to compel divorced couples to remarry.

G4. Do individuals enjoy equality of opportunity and freedom from economic exploitation? 2 / 4

Legal protections against labor exploitation are poorly enforced. Migrant workers are often exposed to unsafe or exploitative working conditions. Both Russians facing economic hardship and migrants to Russia from other countries are vulnerable to sex and labor trafficking. The US State Department's 2020 *Trafficking in Persons Report* criticizes Russia's lack of significant efforts to address trafficking, despite some convictions of traffickers, identification of victims, and return of Russian children from Iraq and Syria. The government enforces a policy of forced labor and records a far lower number of victims than the estimated scope of the problem would suggest. Victims are routinely detained, deported, and prosecuted for activity they were forced to participate in.

Rwanda

Population: 13,000,000
Capital: Kigali
Freedom Status: Not Free
Electoral Democracy: No

Overview: The Rwandan Patriotic Front (RPF), led by President Paul Kagame, has ruled the country since 1994, when it ousted forces responsible for that year's genocide and ended a civil war. While the regime has maintained stability and economic growth, it has also suppressed political dissent though pervasive surveillance, intimidation, rendition, torture, and suspected assassinations.

KEY DEVELOPMENTS IN 2020

- In February, singer Kizito Mihigo, who released a song challenging the official narrative of the genocide in 2014, was arrested near the border with Burundi and died while in detention several days later. While the authorities claimed Mihigo, who planned to flee Rwanda, died by suicide, human rights groups believe he was extrajudicially killed.
- In August, Paul Rusesabagina—who sheltered hundreds of people during the genocide and later resided in Belgium and the United States—was rendered to Rwanda while traveling in the United Arab Emirates (UAE). Rusesabagina, who led an opposition coalition after the genocide, was accused of offenses including terrorism in September, and remained in custody at year's end.
- Scores of Rwandans were arrested and detained by the authorities for violating COVID-19-related face-mask mandates and curfews. Detainees were held in local stadiums, were not offered protection from the elements, and were often forced to attend overnight lectures before they were released. The government instituted travel restrictions in March, though it loosened some of these in June; overnight curfews were introduced in May and remained in force throughout the year. The World Health Organization counted 8,250 COVID-19 cases and 86 deaths at year's end.

POLITICAL RIGHTS: 8 / 40

A. ELECTORAL PROCESS: 2 / 12

A1. Was the current head of government or other chief national authority elected through free and fair elections? 0 / 4

Rwanda's 2003 constitution grants broad powers to the president, who has the authority to appoint the prime minister and dissolve the bicameral Parliament. Amendments passed in 2015 retained a two-term limit for the presidency and shortened terms from seven to five years. The changes also explicitly stated, however, that incumbent Paul Kagame was eligible for an additional seven-year term, after which he could run for two of the new five-year terms. This would extend Kagame's rule until 2034.

Kagame easily won the 2017 presidential election, taking 98.8 percent of the vote according to official results. Frank Habineza of the Democratic Green Party of Rwanda (DGPR) and independent Philippe Mpayimana split the remainder. The electoral process was marred by numerous irregularities, including political intimidation, unfair registration practices, and alleged fraud during the balloting itself.

The National Electoral Commission (NEC) blocked the candidacies of other would-be challengers, including independent and Kagame critic Diane Rwigara, who was barred from running on the grounds that some of the required signatures she had collected were invalid. She claimed that her followers were harassed and jailed as they attempted to gather signatures. The government also orchestrated a campaign of media smears and intimidation against Rwigara, who was subsequently arrested along with her mother and sister.

Local authorities impeded the electoral campaigns of opposition presidential candidates, and some citizens were coerced into attending RPF rallies and voting for Kagame. Rwandans were also made to attend "solidarity" camps and listen to RPF propaganda, while local authorities tasked traditional leaders with persuading their communities to vote for Kagame. Access to the media and the content of electoral coverage were both skewed in favor of the RPF.

On election day, observers reported ballot stuffing, poll workers showing favoritism toward the RPF, and denial of access to the vote-counting process, among other violations. Ballot secrecy was not always respected.

A2. Were the current national legislative representatives elected through free and fair elections? 1 / 4

The 26-seat Senate, the upper house of Parliament, consists of 12 members elected by regional councils, 8 appointed by the president, 4 chosen by the National Consultative Forum for Political Organizations (NCFPO), a public body meant to promote political consensus, and 2 elected by faculty at universities. Senators' terms were shortened from eight to five years as part of the 2015 constitutional reform. The 80-seat Chamber of Deputies, the lower house, includes 53 directly elected members, 24 women chosen by local councils, 2 members from the National Youth Council, and 1 member from the Federation of Associations of the Disabled, all serving five-year terms.

Six incumbent senators, who had served eight-year terms, were replaced in October 2020. Four were appointed by Kagame. Two were selected by the NCFPO.

The RPF dominated the Chamber of Deputies elections held in 2018, capturing 40 of the 53 elected seats. The DGPR gained 2 seats, marking the first time a genuine opposition party has won representation in Parliament. Three other parties allied with the RPF—the Social Democratic Party, the Liberal Party, and the Social Party—won 5, 4, and 2 seats respectively. As with other elections in recent years, the government's repression of legitimate opposition parties and strict control of the media helped to ensure an overwhelming victory for the RPF.

A3. Are the electoral laws and framework fair, and are they implemented impartially by the relevant election management bodies? 1 / 4

The electoral laws are not impartially implemented by the NEC, whose members are proposed by the government and appointed by the RPF-dominated Senate. Rwandan elections routinely feature unfair barriers to registration, campaigning, poll monitoring, and media access for opposition parties and candidates, among other problems.

The 2015 constitutional amendments were adopted through a flawed petition and referendum process. Rights groups and news organizations cited reports that some signatures on the petition were not given voluntarily. The details of the amendments were not widely distributed or discussed ahead of the referendum, in which 98 percent of voters signaled their approval, according to the NEC. The government limited the political activities of groups opposed to the amendments, and the referendum was not monitored by any independent international observer groups.

B. POLITICAL PLURALISM AND PARTICIPATION: 2 / 16

B1. Do the people have the right to organize in different political parties or other competitive political groupings of their choice, and is the system free of undue obstacles to the rise and fall of these competing parties or groupings? 1 / 4

The government-controlled Rwanda Governance Board (RGB) is responsible for registering political parties. In practice it can deny registration at its discretion without proper justification. The government has a long history of repressing its political opponents. Diane Rwigara, who sought to contest the 2017 presidential election, was arrested and imprisoned that year, along with her mother and sister, on multiple charges. The charges against her sister were dropped; Rwigara and her mother were bailed in 2018 and acquitted later that year.

Members of the Dalfa-Umurinzi party, led by 2010 presidential candidate Victoire Ingabire, were targeted in 2020. In January, seven members were convicted of involvement with an "irregular armed force," receiving prison terms varying from 7 to 10 years. Three defendants were acquitted, but one of them, Théophile Ntirutwa, was arrested on charges including murder, theft, and disseminating false information in May. Ntirutwa and three others who were arrested with him awaited trial at year's end. Another acquitted defendant, Venant Abayisenga, was reported missing in June and is believed to have been forcibly disappeared.

B2. Is there a realistic opportunity for the opposition to increase its support or gain power through elections? 0 / 4

The RPF has ruled Rwanda without interruption since 1994, banning and repressing any opposition group that could mount a serious challenge to its leadership. All registered parties currently belong to the NCFPO. While the DGPR won two parliamentary seats in 2018, the RPF maintains a firm hold on power. The DGPR remains vastly outnumbered, holds no other positions of authority, and is unlikely to increase its support to the point where it can viably compete with the RPF in the near future.

B3. Are the people's political choices free from domination by forces that are external to the political sphere, or by political forces that employ extrapolitical means? 0 / 4

Both voters and candidates face significant intimidation aimed at controlling their political choices. Rwandans living outside the country have been threatened, attacked, forcibly disappeared, or killed, apparently in response to their public or suspected opposition to the regime.

B4. Do various segments of the population (including ethnic, racial, religious, gender, LGBT+, and other relevant groups) have full political rights and electoral opportunities? 1 / 4

The constitution calls on the president to ensure "representation of historically marginalized communities" in the Senate through his appointees. However, asserting one's ethnic identity in politics is banned, meaning the level of representation is unclear. The prohibition on discussion of ethnicity makes it nearly impossible for disadvantaged groups, including the indigenous Twa to organize independently and advocate for their interests.

The constitution requires women to occupy at least 30 percent of the seats in each chamber of Parliament. While women currently hold 38.5 percent of Senate seats and 61.2 percent of lower-house seats, they have little practical ability to engage in politics outside the RPF structure. The promotion of gender equity disproportionately privileges English-speaking Tutsis over French-speaking Hutus and rural Tutsis in practice.

C. FUNCTIONING OF GOVERNMENT: 4 / 12

C1. Do the freely elected head of government and national legislative representatives determine the policies of the government? 1 / 4

Government policy is largely set and implemented by the executive, with the security and intelligence services playing a powerful role. Parliament generally lacks independence, merely endorsing presidential initiatives.

C2. Are safeguards against official corruption strong and effective? 2 / 4

The government takes measures to limit corruption, including regular firings and prosecutions of low-level officials suspected of malfeasance. In 2018, President Kagame sacked dozens of civil servants in an ostensible anticorruption effort, and Parliament passed penal-code revisions that expanded the list of corruption-related crimes and increased penalties for those convicted. In 2019, several mayors and other local officials resigned or were dismissed for corruption and other misconduct, though the lack of transparency surrounding the cases made it difficult to assess whether any of the firings were politically motivated.

Despite these actions, graft remains a problem, and few independent organizations or media outlets are able to investigate or report on corruption issues due to the risk of government reprisals.

C3. Does the government operate with openness and transparency? 1 / 4

While a 2013 law provides for public access to government information, implementation has been weak. Data published on Sobanukirwa, a website created by the government to ease the process of requesting access to documents, suggest that only a small fraction of requests result in positive and timely responses. Given the government's active repression of any dissent in recent years, citizens do not have the ability in practice to obtain information about state operations, nor do they have a meaningful opportunity to comment on policy without the threat of punishment.

CIVIL LIBERTIES: 13 / 60 (−1)

D. FREEDOM OF EXPRESSION AND BELIEF: 3 / 16

D1. Are there free and independent media? 0 / 4

The government imposes legal restrictions and informal controls on freedom of the press, and most media outlets practice self-censorship. The few journalists in the country who engage in independent reporting are subject to criminal charges and intimidation. The penal code revisions passed in 2018 criminalized cartoons and writing that "humiliate" Rwandan leaders, but also decriminalized defamation, which the Rwanda Journalists Association considered an improvement to the highly restrictive legal framework.

Many Rwandan journalists have fled the country and work in exile. Due in part to this phenomenon, the government has increasingly blocked access to news services and websites based abroad. The British Broadcasting Corporation's Kinyarwanda-language service has been suspended in the country since 2014.

Authorities continued to target journalists in 2020. In March, four bloggers who reported on alleged abuses perpetrated by security forces and on the effects of COVID-19-related restrictions were arrested, along with a driver. Two of the individuals received charges including the impersonation of a journalist, and their cases were pending at year's end. Later in April, Umubavu TV owner Théoneste Nsengimana was arrested over fraud allegations. Nsengimana was released in May for lack of evidence.

In February 2020, Kizito Mihigo, who released a song challenging the Kagame regime's narrative of the genocide in 2014 and planned to flee Rwanda for fear of detention, was arrested near the border with Burundi. Several days later, Mihigo was found dead in his prison cell. While the authorities claim Mihigo died by suicide, human rights groups believe he was extrajudicially killed.

D2. Are individuals free to practice and express their religious faith or nonbelief in public and private? 2 / 4

Religious freedom has historically been respected, but the government has recently taken steps to assert greater control over religious institutions. In recent years, authorities have shut down Pentecostal churches and some mosques, banned mosques in Kigali from broadcasting the call to prayer, passed a law requiring religious leaders to obtain a theology degree before establishing churches, mandated that religious organizations report grants to the RGB, and required that donations to faith-based groups be deposited in Rwandan banks.

Jehovah's Witnesses face arrest for refusing to participate in security duties or oath-taking involving the national flag.

D3. Is there academic freedom, and is the educational system free from extensive political indoctrination? 1 / 4

The government restricts academic freedom by enforcing official views on the genocide and other sensitive topics. Scholars and students are subject to suspension for "divisionism" and engage in self-censorship to avoid such penalties.

In December 2019, the government announced that primary schools would conduct lessons in English, even though the majority of the population speaks Kinyarwanda. French-speaking students and educators could also be disadvantaged by the decision. Its implementation was delayed due to the COVID-19 pandemic, which prompted the closure of schools between March and November 2020.

D4. Are individuals free to express their personal views on political or other sensitive topics without fear of surveillance or retribution? 0 / 4

The space for free private discussion is limited in part by indications that the government monitors personal communications. Social media are widely believed to be monitored, and the law allows for government hacking of telecommunications networks. In October 2019, WhatsApp disclosed that its messaging service was exploited with Pegasus, a suite of surveillance software, and that Rwandan dissidents were targeted with its use. In addition, the authorities reportedly use informants to infiltrate civil society, further discouraging citizens from expressing dissent.

Rwandan authorities have also employed digital tools as part of its COVID-19 response. The government uses mobile data as part of its contact-tracing efforts, while employing geolocation to track individuals who have been placed in isolation centers.

E. ASSOCIATIONAL AND ORGANIZATIONAL RIGHTS: 2 / 12

E1. Is there freedom of assembly? 0 / 4

Although the constitution guarantees freedom of assembly, this right is limited in practice. Fear of arrest serves as a deterrent to protests, and gatherings are sometimes disrupted even when organizers obtain official authorization. In 2018, police fired live ammunition into two crowds of Congolese refugees in the town of Karongi and Kiziba refugee camp who were protesting cuts in assistance, killing at least 11 people.

Public gatherings were restricted in March 2020 as part of the government's efforts to contain COVID-19, though restrictions on some events, including weddings and funerals, were loosened in October. In April, refugees living in the Gashora camp held a protest after COVID-19 restrictions delayed their resettlement to other countries, though it was quickly dispersed.

E2. Is there freedom for nongovernmental organizations, particularly those that are engaged in human rights- and governance-related work? 1 / 4

Registration and reporting requirements for both domestic and foreign nongovernmental organizations (NGOs) are onerous, and activities that the government defines as divisive are prohibited. Many organizations receive funds from the RGB, which challenges their independence. Several NGOs have been banned in recent years, leading others to self-censor. The government has been accused of employing infiltration tactics against human rights organizations.

E3. Is there freedom for trade unions and similar professional or labor organizations? 1 / 4

The constitution provides for the rights to form trade unions, engage in collective bargaining, and strike, but free collective bargaining and strikes are limited by binding arbitration rules and rare in practice. Public-sector workers and employees in broadly defined "essential services" are generally not allowed to strike. Enforcement of rules against antiunion discrimination is weak. The country's largest union confederation has close ties to the RPF, and the government allegedly interferes in union elections.

F. RULE OF LAW: 2 / 16

F1. Is there an independent judiciary? 0 / 4

The Rwandan judiciary lacks independence from the executive. Top judicial officials are appointed by the president and confirmed by the RPF-dominated Senate. Judges rarely rule against the government in politically sensitive cases.

F2. Does due process prevail in civil and criminal matters? 1 / 4

The police and military regularly engage in arbitrary arrests and detentions, targeting opposition figures and dissidents as well as homeless people, street vendors, and suspected petty criminals. A 2017 Human Rights Watch (HRW) report detailed a system of secret unlawful detention at military facilities for suspected members of armed rebel groups or exiled opposition factions. Such detainees are allegedly denied basic due-process rights, and many who are later brought to trial are convicted based on coerced confessions.

Children facing homelessness also face arbitrary detention. In February 2020, the UN Committee on the Rights of the Child called on the government to refrain from this practice, noting that many detainees were kept in poor conditions and faced physical mistreatment from police and detention staff.

The Rwandan government frequently uses arbitrary arrest and detention against critics and is known to pursue critics abroad. In August 2020, it rendered Paul Rusesabagina—who sheltered hundreds of people during the genocide and later resided in Belgium and the United States—while he was visiting the UAE. Rusesabagina, who later led the opposition Rwanda Movement for Democratic Change (MRCD), was accused of supporting terrorism via the MRCD's armed wing along with other offenses in September. Rusesabagina requested bail in order to seek medical care, but his request was denied that month. He remained in custody at year's end.

F3. Is there protection from the illegitimate use of physical force and freedom from war and insurgencies? 0 / 4

Both ordinary criminal suspects and political detainees are routinely subjected to torture and other ill-treatment in custody. Extrajudicial executions of suspected criminals by security personnel still occur with some frequency. Disappearances, physical assaults, arbitrary detention, and assassinations targeting journalists, opposition members, and other regime critics are commonly reported.

F4. Do laws, policies, and practices guarantee equal treatment of various segments of the population? 1 / 4

Equal treatment for all citizens under the law is guaranteed, and there are legal protections against discrimination. However, the Tutsi minority group is often accused of receiving preferential treatment for high-ranking jobs and university scholarships under the pretext of an affirmative action program for "genocide survivors." English-speaking Tutsis are overrepresented in government. Members of the Hutu majority, who represents 85 percent of the population, face unofficial discrimination when seeking public employment or scholarships. The indigenous Twa minority, meanwhile, continues to suffer from de facto disadvantages in education, employment, and health care.

While women enjoy broad legal equality and have a significant presence in the economy as workers and business owners, gender-based discrimination persists, and gender-equality efforts have largely favored English-speaking Tutsis.

Same-sex activity is not criminalized in Rwanda, though LGBT+ people face strong social stigma. No laws specifically provide protection against discrimination based on sexual orientation or gender identity, and police can arrest individuals using public morality laws.

G. PERSONAL AUTONOMY AND INDIVIDUAL RIGHTS: 6 / 16 (−1)

G1. Do individuals enjoy freedom of movement, including the ability to change their place of residence, employment, or education? 1 / 4 (−1)

An easily obtainable national identity card is required to move within the country. However, all government officials must receive approval from the president or prime minister's office before traveling for personal or professional reasons; some current and former security officials have been arrested for unauthorized travel. Members of opposition groups have also reported restrictions on foreign travel or reentry to Rwanda.

Rwandan authorities introduced COVID-19-related lockdowns and travel restrictions in March 2020. Interregional travel partially resumed in June, though the government reintroduced lockdown measures and travel restrictions in some areas through August. Overnight curfews were introduced in May and were maintained through year's end.

COVID-19-related restrictions were excessively enforced. Individuals accused of violating face-mask mandates and curfews, along with those performing essential errands, were routinely detained in stadiums and were sometimes forced to attend overnight lectures before being released. Some detainees were not offered protection from the elements, nor were they offered food or water. HRW reported that over 70,000 Rwandans were arrested for violating COVID-19 measures during the year.

Score Change: The score declined from 2 to 1 because Rwandan authorities were excessive and disproportionate in their enforcement of COVID-19-related restrictions on movement, leading to tens of thousands of arrests and allegations of ill-treatment in custody.

G2. Are individuals able to exercise the right to own property and establish private businesses without undue interference from state or nonstate actors? 2 / 4

While the government is generally supportive of economic growth through private business activity, it has been criticized for seizing land for infrastructure and development projects without proper compensation, and for imposing agricultural and land-consolidation policies without adequate input from farmers.

The law grants the same property and inheritance rights to men and women, though women are not always able to assert their rights in practice.

G3. Do individuals enjoy personal social freedoms, including choice of marriage partner and size of family, protection from domestic violence, and control over appearance? 2 / 4

The law generally grants equal rights to men and women regarding marriage and divorce, but informal marriages under customary law, including polygamous unions, lack such protections. The penalties for spousal rape are much lighter than for other forms of rape. Domestic violence remains widespread and seldom reported despite government programs to combat it.

Abortion is a criminal offense unless the pregnancy is the result of rape, incest, or forced marriage, or the life of the mother or child is endangered. Abortion convictions can lead to significant prison terms. The 2018 penal code revisions removed language requiring all abortions to be approved by a judge, leaving the final decision in the hands of the patient and her doctor. In May 2020, 50 women who were jailed for having abortions—six of whom were serving life sentences—were released after receiving a presidential pardon. Human rights advocates welcomed the pardons but maintained calls for a liberalization of abortion laws.

G4. Do individuals enjoy equality of opportunity and freedom from economic exploitation? 1 / 4

Regulations governing wage levels and conditions of work in the formal sector are poorly enforced. While Rwanda has increased prosecutions for transnational trafficking in recent years, Rwandan children are trafficked internally for domestic service under abusive conditions, or for commercial sex work, and little effort is made to hold internal traffickers to account. Many children work informally in the agricultural sector. Young Congolese and Burundian refugees are vulnerable to sexual exploitation and coerced recruitment into armed groups linked to Rwandan security forces.

Samoa

Population: 200,000
Capital: Apia
Freedom Status: Free
Electoral Democracy: Yes

Overview: Samoa has a democratic political system with regular elections, though the same political party had been in government for decades as of 2020, and only traditional heads of families are eligible to run as candidates. The judiciary is independent, and civil liberties are generally respected.

KEY DEVELOPMENTS IN 2020

- Samoa was one of the first countries in the world to close its borders in response to the COVID-19 pandemic, and it successfully kept the virus out during the year. Only one case, involving a citizen returning from abroad, was reported.
- In December, the parliament passed a package of three controversial bills that, among other changes, would remove the Land and Titles Court—which adjudicates customary matters—from the jurisdiction of the Supreme Court, potentially endangering the rule of law and exacerbating conflicts between customary authority and individual rights. The measures were awaiting the head of state's formal assent at year's end, and legal challenges were expected.
- Sharp disagreement over the bills, which also drew objections from the Samoa Law Society and other experts, had led to resignations and defections from the ruling Human Rights Protection Party (HRPP) earlier in the year. A new opposition party, Fa'atuatua i le Atua Samoa ua Tasi (FAST), was formed in July, and in September it announced an alliance with two other parties ahead of the April 2021 elections. Deputy Prime Minister Fiame Naomi Mata'afa resigned later in September and joined FAST.

POLITICAL RIGHTS: 30 / 40
A. ELECTORAL PROCESS: 9 / 12
A1. Was the current head of government or other chief national authority elected through free and fair elections? 3 / 4

The parliament elects a ceremonial head of state every five years; a limit of two terms was adopted through a 2019 constitutional amendment. By custom rather than constitutional requirement, the position is given to one of the country's four paramount chiefs. In 2017, the parliament elected Tuimaleali'ifano Va'aletoa Sualauvi II as head of state.

The head of government is the prime minister, who requires the parliament's support. The prime minister as of 2020, Tuila'epa Lupesoliai Neioti Aiono Sa'ilele Malielegaoi of the ruling HRPP, had held his post since 1998, having been reelected most recently in 2016.

A2. Were the current national legislative representatives elected through free and fair elections? 3 / 4

The Legislative Assembly as of 2020 consisted of 47 members elected in traditional village-based constituencies and two members elected by voters in "urban" constituencies—including citizens of mixed or non-Samoan heritage who lacked village ties. Additional members could be added from among the unsuccessful candidates with the most votes in order to meet a minimum 10 percent quota of women members. Elections are held every five years.

In the 2016 parliamentary elections, the HRPP won 35 of the 50 seats; one seat was added to meet the gender quota. Independents took 13 seats, and the opposition Tautua Samoa Party (TSP) held two. After the elections, 12 of the independents joined the HRPP, and the 13th joined the opposition. The next general elections, which would be held under a new constituency system, were scheduled for April 2021.

A3. Are the electoral laws and framework fair, and are they implemented impartially by the relevant election management bodies? 3 / 4

The constitutional and legal framework for elections is largely democratic and fairly implemented. However, only citizens with *matai* status (chiefs or family heads) are allowed to stand as candidates. There are some 17,000 matai, but only about 11 percent are women.

A 2015 amendment to the Electoral Act replaced two at-large seats representing voters of non-Samoan heritage with two "urban" constituencies with defined boundaries. They overlapped with territorial constituencies and pertained to voters who either lacked or chose not to register according to traditional village ties. However, in 2019 the Tuila'epa government won passage of a constitutional amendment that eliminated the special urban constituencies and ensured that all districts—now numbering 51—would be village-based and represented by a single member. The amendment was set to take effect after the current parliament's term ended in 2021.

In September 2020, two potential candidates filed a legal challenge against the 2019 electoral law, arguing that rules requiring candidates to have rendered three years of traditional service to their villages were unclear and discriminatory. The government agreed to amend the law and address the plaintiffs' specific complaints, but disputes over the details of the service requirement continued.

B. POLITICAL PLURALISM AND PARTICIPATION: 12 / 16

B1. Do the people have the right to organize in different political parties or other competitive political groupings of their choice, and is the system free of undue obstacles to the rise and fall of these competing parties or groupings? 3 / 4

There are no major constraints on the formation and operation of political parties, but parties must win a minimum of eight seats to qualify for formal recognition within the legislature. The TSP, which fell from 13 seats to just three after the 2016 elections, lost this status, leading opposition members to criticize the rule for producing a "one-party state."

A number of parties have since emerged to challenge the HRPP. In 2018, Samoa First registered as a political party and aimed to compete in the 2021 elections. In 2019, the Samoa National Democratic Party (SNDP) was reregistered; it had been Samoa's main opposition party between 1988 and 2003. Tumua ma Puleono registered in May 2020, and FAST was formed that July.

B2. Is there a realistic opportunity for the opposition to increase its support or gain power through elections? 3 / 4

There are no obvious obstacles that prevent the opposition from increasing its support and gaining power through elections. However, the ruling HRPP, having been in power since the 1980s, developed an effective campaign machinery during its incumbency, raising concerns about whether its long tenure was due to its popularity or features of the electoral system that may put the opposition at a disadvantage.

In September 2020, FAST, Tumua ma Puleono, and the SNDP announced that they would contest the 2021 elections as an alliance under the FAST banner. They benefited from a number of defections from the HRPP during the year, including that of Deputy Prime Minister Fiame Naomi Mata'afa, who resigned later in September over the government's three controversial reform bills.

B3. Are the people's political choices free from domination by forces that are external to the political sphere, or by political forces that employ extrapolitical means? 3 / 4

While voters and candidates are largely free from undue interference with their political choices, traditional village councils consisting of local leaders with matai titles exercise considerable influence through candidate endorsements. Those who use the electoral laws to challenge the councils' preferred candidates in court have sometimes faced customary penalties such as banishment.

B4. Do various segments of the population (including ethnic, racial, religious, gender, LGBT+, and other relevant groups) have full political rights and electoral opportunities? 3 / 4

While women and members of ethnic minority groups have full voting rights, individuals must hold a customary matai title in order to qualify as electoral candidates, meaning fewer women are eligible in practice. A sizeable minority of villages still do not allow women to hold matai titles.

The 2016 elections marked the first application of the gender quota ensuring that at least five parliamentary seats are held by women. If fewer than that number are elected in normal constituency contests, the unsuccessful female candidates with the most votes are awarded additional seats. One extra seat was consequently added to the 2016 parliament. Few women participate in village council meetings.

Members of the *fa'afafine* community, which includes Samoans who are assigned male gender at birth but maintain a feminine gender identity, can also serve as matai. However, there were no elected fa'afafine parliamentarians as of 2020.

C. FUNCTIONING OF GOVERNMENT: 9 / 12

C1. Do the freely elected head of government and national legislative representatives determine the policies of the government? 3 / 4

The prime minister and cabinet determine and implement government policies without improper interference by outside groups. However, the typically weak opposition presence in the parliament has undermined its role as a check on the executive, and the democratic credentials of the government have been tarnished somewhat by restrictive features of the electoral system.

C2. Are safeguards against official corruption strong and effective? 3 / 4

Independent entities including the Office of the Ombudsman, the Public Service Commission, and law enforcement agencies pursue allegations of corruption by public officials. However, corruption remains a problem and a cause of public discontent, and the government has at times resisted calls for a stronger response.

In April 2020, the *Samoa Observer* reported apparent conflicts of interest within the government, finding that the minister for works, transport, and infrastructure owned several businesses in New Zealand and Samoa and could personally benefit from contracting decisions he helped oversee in his official capacity.

C3. Does the government operate with openness and transparency? 3 / 4

While the government generally operates with transparency, the effectiveness of the state auditing system remains the subject of public debate, and the country lacks a freedom of information law.

In 2019, the government proposed a legislative amendment that would mandate heavy prison terms and fines for public servants who disclose official information to a third party. While the measure had not passed as of 2020, the government responded to leaks to the media by warning of possible prison terms under existing laws for employees who breached confidentiality rules attached to their positions.

The new parliament building, which opened in 2019, lacks a dedicated press gallery, and journalists have often been excluded from the public gallery in practice, limiting the transparency of legislative proceedings.

CIVIL LIBERTIES: 51 / 60
D. FREEDOM OF EXPRESSION AND BELIEF: 14 / 16
D1. Are there free and independent media? 3 / 4

Several public and privately owned print and broadcast news outlets operate in Samoa, and internet access has expanded rapidly in recent years. While press freedom is generally respected, politicians and other powerful actors have used libel or defamation suits to respond to remarks or stories about them. In 2017, the parliament passed legislation that reintroduced criminal libel, which had been abolished in 2013. Artistic works are also subject to government restrictions; in 2019, the feature film *Rocketman* was banned for depicting same-sex sexual activity, which is illegal in Samoa.

The prime minister has repeatedly criticized or refused questions from certain journalists and outlets. He has also threatened to ban social media platforms in response to critical commentary about the government.

D2. Are individuals free to practice and express their religious faith or nonbelief in public and private? 3 / 4

Freedom of religion is constitutionally guaranteed, and is mostly respected in practice. However, a 2017 constitutional amendment shifted references to Samoa being a Christian nation from the constitution's preamble to its body text, meaning it can potentially be used in legal action. There is strong societal pressure at the village level—including from village councils—to participate in the activities of the main local church.

In April and May 2020, the Samoan Law Society and the country's ombudsman expressed concerns that provisions in the government's three proposed reform bills—the Constitution Amendment Bill 2020, the Lands and Titles Court Bill 2020, and the Judicature Amendment Bill 2020—could limit religious freedom by removing the Land and Titles Court from the jurisdiction of the Supreme Court, meaning the latter could no longer review decisions on village customary matters that violated individual rights.

D3. Is there academic freedom, and is the educational system free from extensive political indoctrination? 4 / 4

There are no significant restrictions on academic freedom.

D4. Are individuals free to express their personal views on political or other sensitive topics without fear of surveillance or retribution? 4 / 4

Most Samoans face no serious practical constraints on private discussion or the expression of personal views, though the threat of criminal defamation charges remains a problem for some prominent critics of the government.

E. ASSOCIATIONAL AND ORGANIZATIONAL RIGHTS: 11 / 12

E1. Is there freedom of assembly? 4 / 4

Freedom of assembly is protected by law and respected in practice. Beginning in March 2020, the government-imposed restrictions on public gatherings in response to the COVID-19 pandemic. Demonstrators nevertheless turned out later in the year to protest the government's three controversial bills, avoiding the health restrictions in part by organizing processions of vehicles. Other demonstrations called on the government to help repatriate Samoans stranded abroad by pandemic-related travel bans.

E2. Is there freedom for nongovernmental organizations, particularly those that are engaged in human rights- and governance-related work? 3 / 4

Nongovernmental organizations, including human rights groups, operate freely.

E3. Is there freedom for trade unions and similar professional or labor organizations? 4 / 4

Workers have the right to form and join trade unions, bargain collectively, and strike. Multiple unions exist, representing both public- and private-sector employees; these are often called "associations." The Samoa Workers Congress (SWC) is an umbrella body for all workers' unions.

Union members' rights are governed by the constitution and the 2013 Labour and Employment Relations Act; the latter recognizes unions and employees' roles and rights, the right to collective bargaining, and rights to maternity and paternity leave, and mandates the establishment of a National Tripartite Forum, which provides for workers' benefits and consults on employment policies and conditions. However, some cultural factors hinder the ability of workers and unions to pursue their rights.

Samoa has ratified the International Labour Organization's eight fundamental conventions.

F. RULE OF LAW: 14 / 16

F1. Is there an independent judiciary? 4 / 4

The judiciary is independent. The head of state, on the recommendation of the prime minister, appoints the chief justice. Other Supreme Court judges are appointed by the head of state on the advice of the Judicial Service Commission, which is chaired by the chief justice and includes the attorney general and a Justice Ministry appointee. Judges typically serve until they reach retirement age and cannot be removed arbitrarily.

However, the reform bills adopted in December 2020 featured a number of provisions that could undermine judicial independence and the rule of law. One component would allow the head of state, on the advice of the Judicial Service Commission, to dismiss Supreme Court judges; this had previously required a two-thirds vote in the parliament, which is still required to remove the chief justice. The legislation also separates the judicial system into two distinct and potentially conflicting structures, with one, headed by the Supreme Court, handling civil and criminal matters and the other, the Land and Titles Court, overseeing customary matters including communal land. The Land and Titles Court would have its own appellate body, and individuals would no longer be able to appeal its decisions to the Supreme Court.

F2. Does due process prevail in civil and criminal matters? 3 / 4

The authorities generally observe due process safeguards against arbitrary arrest and detention, and the courts provide defendants with the conditions necessary for a fair trial. However, village councils settle many disputes, and their adherence to due process standards varies; they have the authority to impose penalties including fines and banishment. The December 2020 legal reforms appeared to eliminate individuals' ability to appeal village council decisions to the Supreme Court, raising doubts about how conflicts between customary communal authority and the constitutional rights of individuals would be resolved.

F3. Is there protection from the illegitimate use of physical force and freedom from war and insurgencies? 4 / 4

Violent crime rates are relatively low. Police officers are occasionally accused of physical abuse. Prisons lack adequate resources, resulting in poor conditions including overcrowding, as well as breakdowns in security. In March 2020, as many as 36 people escaped from Tanumalala prison, though all were eventually recaptured. As a result of the incident, which followed an earlier escape in 2019, the prisons commissioner resigned.

F4. Do laws, policies, and practices guarantee equal treatment of various segments of the population? 3 / 4

The constitution prohibits discrimination based on descent, sex, religion, and other categories. The Labour and Employment Relations Act also prohibits discrimination against employees on such grounds as ethnicity, race, color, sex, gender, religion, political opinion, sexual orientation, social origin, marital status, pregnancy, HIV status, and disability. However, these protections are enforced unevenly. In practice women face some discrimination in employment and other aspects of life, and same-sex sexual activity remains a criminal offense for men. Ethnic Chinese residents at times encounter societal bias and restrictions on the location of their businesses.

Members of the fa'afafine community were previously subject to a rarely enforced criminal code provision that prohibited the "impersonation" of a woman; a 2013 amendment removed this stipulation.

G. PERSONAL AUTONOMY AND INDIVIDUAL RIGHTS: 12 / 16

G1. Do individuals enjoy freedom of movement, including the ability to change their place of residence, employment, or education? 3 / 4

While there are few constraints on freedom of movement, village councils still occasionally banish individuals from their communities as a penalty for serious violations of their bylaws.

G2. Are individuals able to exercise the right to own property and establish private businesses without undue interference from state or nonstate actors? 3 / 4

Private business activity is encouraged, and property rights are generally protected, though roughly 80 percent of the country's land is communally owned, meaning it is overseen by matai title holders and other village leaders. The rest consists of freehold and state-owned land.

G3. Do individuals enjoy personal social freedoms, including choice of marriage partner and size of family, protection from domestic violence, and control over appearance? 3 / 4

While personal social freedoms are generally not restricted by law, domestic violence against women and children is a serious problem. The Crimes Act of 2013 made spousal rape a crime, and the Family Safety Act of 2013 empowers the police, public health officials, and educators to assist victims of domestic violence. Nevertheless, many victims do not report abuse due to strong social biases and fear of reprisal.

G4. Do individuals enjoy equality of opportunity and freedom from economic exploitation? 3 / 4

Individuals generally enjoy equality of opportunity and fair working conditions. However, most adults engage in subsistence agriculture, and local custom obliges residents to perform some labor on behalf of the community; those who fail to do so can be compelled.

San Marino

Population: 30,000
Capital: San Marino
Freedom Status: Free
Electoral Democracy: Yes

Overview: San Marino is a parliamentary democracy in which political rights and civil liberties are generally upheld. Corruption is a problem, and while investigative journalists are active, the risk of heavy fines for defamation can encourage self-censorship. The country's judicial system is not sufficiently independent and professional. Women are underrepresented in politics.

KEY DEVELOPMENTS IN 2020

- The San Marino government responded to the COVID-19 pandemic with school closings, bans on public and private gatherings, and movement restrictions in March. However, as the year went on, the government eased restrictions despite outbreaks in the country and in the surrounding regions in Italy. By year's end, over 2,300 people had tested positive for the virus, 59 people died, according to government statistics provided to the World Health Organization (WHO).
- In February, the new government adopted legislation that changed voting rights in the Judicial Council, making the votes of judges and non-judges equal and thereby increasing the influence of political parties. Subsequently, in July, the Judicial Council reinstated the country's former head magistrate and removed the three judges (Buriani, Volpinari, and Di Bona) who had been investigating the so-called Conto Mazzini case, in which 17 high-ranking Sammarinese officials—including 8 former government ministers—were sentenced in 2017 for their involvement in money laundering and other corrupt activities.

POLITICAL RIGHTS: 38 / 40

A. ELECTORAL PROCESS: 12 / 12

A1. Was the current head of government or other chief national authority elected through free and fair elections? 4 / 4

Executive power rests with the 10-member State Congress (cabinet), which is accountable to the parliament and is headed by two captains regent. As the joint heads of state with largely ceremonial roles, the captains are elected every six months by the legislature from among its own members. Although there is no official prime minister, the secretary of state for foreign and political affairs is regarded as the head of government. Following the December 2019 elections, Luca Beccari of the Sammarinese Christian Democratic Party was elected to the post in January 2020.

A2. Were the current national legislative representatives elected through free and fair elections? 4 / 4

The 60 members of the unicameral Great and General Council are elected for five-year terms. The 2019 elections, called about a year early, were considered credible and free, and their results were accepted by stakeholders and the public. The elections were won by the opposition Sammarinese Christian Democratic Party, which obtained 21 seats. The left-wing Tomorrow in Motion coalition came in second with 15 seats, followed by Libera with 10 seats, We for the Republic with 8 seats, and Future Republic with 6 seats. After the elections, the Christian Democrats formed a governing coalition with Tomorrow in Motion and We for the Republic.

A3. Are the electoral laws and framework fair, and are they implemented impartially by the relevant election management bodies? 4 / 4

The electoral laws provide a sound basis for the organization of free and fair elections. In its 2018 compliance report, published in 2019, the Council of Europe's Group of States against Corruption (GRECO) indicated that San Marino had enacted adequate legislation to regulate the financing of political parties.

B. POLITICAL PLURALISM AND PARTICIPATION: 15 / 16

B1. Do the people have the right to organize in different political parties or other competitive political groupings of their choice, and is the system free of undue obstacles to the rise and fall of these competing parties or groupings? 4 / 4

Parties are free to form and operate in San Marino, and a great number of them contest elections. Many parties participate in larger electoral coalitions, as the electoral law gives the largest political grouping the right to take the initiative in government formation.

B2. Is there a realistic opportunity for the opposition to increase its support or gain power through elections? 4 / 4

There are no restrictions preventing the opposition from increasing support through elections, and the country has undergone transfers of power between rival party groupings in recent years. In the 2019 elections, opposition parties defeated the incumbent government and formed a new government. Multiple opposition groups are currently represented in the Great and General Council.

B3. Are the people's political choices free from domination by forces that are external to the political sphere, or by political forces that employ extrapolitical means? 4 / 4

The political choices of voters and candidates are free from undue pressure by unaccountable groups.

B4. Do various segments of the population (including ethnic, racial, religious, gender, LGBT+, and other relevant groups) have full political rights and electoral opportunities? 3 / 4

While citizens generally enjoy full political rights, women are underrepresented in the Great and General Council, where they held 19 seats following the 2019 elections, and in politics generally. An assessment mission from the Organization for Security and

Co-operation in Europe (OSCE) that was deployed ahead of the 2019 polls noted that gender quotas on candidate lists were undercut by the preferential voting system. Women are better represented in the country's Electoral Council and in polling administration.

About 16 percent of the population consists of noncitizens who do not have political rights in the country; most are Italian nationals. Under San Marino's strict naturalization criteria, individuals without a citizen spouse, parent, or grandparent generally must live in the country for over 30 years to be eligible for citizenship.

C. FUNCTIONING OF GOVERNMENT: 11 / 12

C1. Do the freely elected head of government and national legislative representatives determine the policies of the government? 4 / 4

The government and legislature exercise their powers without improper interference from unelected entities.

C2. Are safeguards against official corruption strong and effective? 3 / 4

In response to scandals involving high-ranking officials, San Marino has launched a series of programs to combat corruption and money laundering. In its 2018 report, GRECO found that progress had been made in closing key gaps in the legal framework, but that further improvements were required. GRECO's 2020 report called for structural changes to San Marino's judicial sector in order to prevent unwarranted political influence and to strengthen the country's anticorruption framework. The report also highlighted the need to adopt a code of conduct for members of Parliament, which would require them to declare conflicts of interest and declare assets.

In 2017, several former officials were convicted for their involvement in bribery, corruption, money laundering, and vote buying in the so-called Conto Mazzini case. Multiple former captains regent and ministers received prison sentences ranging from two to eight years. In October 2020, a court held the third hearing on appeal in the case, which was suspended after one of the suspects filed a petition for the recusal of a judge.

C3. Does the government operate with openness and transparency? 4 / 4

Laws providing for the accessibility of government information are in place, and the government generally respects those laws. Public officials are not required to disclose their assets, though political candidates must report their income from the previous year as well as assets or investments.

CIVIL LIBERTIES: 55 / 60 (−2)

D. FREEDOM OF EXPRESSION AND BELIEF: 15 / 16

D1. Are there free and independent media? 3 / 4

Freedom of the press is generally upheld. Local media are pluralistic, and journalists investigate important topics, including financial crimes. However, the risk of heavy fines or civil damages under San Marino's strict defamation laws can prompt self-censorship among journalists. News consumers also have access to Italian media, and internet access is not restricted.

D2. Are individuals free to practice and express their religious faith or nonbelief in public and private? 4 / 4

Religious freedom is broadly upheld in San Marino. Religious discrimination is prohibited by law. There is no state religion, although Roman Catholicism is dominant. Catholic religious instruction is offered in schools but is not mandatory.

D3. Is there academic freedom, and is the educational system free from extensive political indoctrination? 4 / 4

Academic freedom is generally respected.

D4. Are individuals free to express their personal views on political or other sensitive topics without fear of surveillance or retribution? 4 / 4

Freedom of expression is legally safeguarded, and people are generally free to discuss their views on politics and other sensitive topics, though the law prohibits hate speech based on various characteristics.

E. ASSOCIATIONAL AND ORGANIZATIONAL RIGHTS: 12 / 12

E1. Is there freedom of assembly? 4 / 4

Freedom of assembly is upheld in practice. Demonstrations routinely proceed without incident.

E2. Is there freedom for nongovernmental organizations, particularly those that are engaged in human rights- and governance-related work? 4 / 4

Nongovernmental organizations may operate without undue restrictions, and a number of human rights groups are active in the country.

E3. Is there freedom for trade unions and similar professional or labor organizations? 4 / 4

Workers are free to strike, organize in trade unions, and bargain collectively, unless they work in military occupations. Approximately half of the workforce is unionized. The law prohibits antiunion discrimination and provides avenues for recourse for workers penalized for union activity.

F. RULE OF LAW: 13 / 16 (−2)

F1. Is there an independent judiciary? 3 / 4 (−1)

Judicial affairs are managed by a Judicial Council made up of first instance and appellate judges as well as members of Parliament. In 2020 various controversies relating to political interference in the judiciary unfolded. In February 2020, San Marino's new government adopted legislation that changed voting rights in the Judicial Council, making the votes of judges and non-judges equal, and thereby increasing the influence of political parties. Subsequently, in July, the Judicial Council reinstated the country's former head magistrate and removed the three judges (Buriani, Volpinari, and Di Bona) who had been investigating the so-called Conto Mazzini case, in which 17 high-ranking Sammarinese officials—including 8 former government ministers—were sentenced in 2017 for their involvement in money laundering and other corrupt activities.

In response, a September 2020 report from the Council of Europe's Group of States Against Corruption (GRECO) called for structural changes to San Marino's judiciary in order to limit political influence. The report also called for greater transparency and accountability in the country's judicial sector, and for changes in the configuration of the Judicial Council and the appointment of judges. The report was accompanied by a letter from the Council of Europe's Commissioner for Human Rights imploring the Sammarinese government to safeguard the independence of the judiciary. The Sammarinese government responded that the recent changes to San Marino's judicial system were necessary to remedy nonimpartial and unconstitutional decisions made by some of the country's judges.

Score Change: The score declined from 4 to 3 due to a restructuring of the judicial council that increased the representation of political figures as opposed to judges.

F2. Does due process prevail in civil and criminal matters? 3 / 4 (–1)

Due process rights surrounding charges and trials are generally upheld in practice. The authorities respect legal safeguards against arbitrary arrest and detention. However, the 2020 GRECO report on San Marino's judiciary expressed concerns about the lack of professionalism and transparency in San Marino's judicial system, and called for a more consistent, objective, and transparent allocation of cases. In addition, the report expressed a need to increase the accessibility to the public on judicial activity. The government's removal and reassignment of the three judges presiding over the Conto Mazzini case raised questions as to the maintenance of due process in cases of corruption.

Score Change: The score declined from 4 to 3 because the reorganization of the judicial council enabled the politicized reassignment of magistrates overseeing the high-profile Conto Mazzini corruption case.

F3. Is there protection from the illegitimate use of physical force and freedom from war and insurgencies? 4 / 4

The population does not face any major threats to physical security. There is one prison in San Marino, and the inmate population is small, with no reports of serious mistreatment. Law enforcement officers generally operate with professionalism.

F4. Do laws, policies, and practices guarantee equal treatment of various segments of the population? 3 / 4

The law criminalizes the dissemination of ideas related to racial or ethnic superiority; acts of violence or discrimination on various grounds, including sexual orientation and gender identity; and incitement to such acts. However, discrimination based on skin color and language are not covered by these provisions. While San Marino lacks legislation guaranteeing equality and freedom from employment or other discrimination for LGBT+ people, referendum voters in June 2019 approved a constitutional amendment banning all forms of discrimination based on sexual orientation.

A 2018 report from the European Commission against Racism and Intolerance (ECRI) reiterated concerns about the absence of a strong and comprehensive antidiscrimination framework in the country. The Office of the United Nations High Commissioner for Human Rights has also urged San Marino to strengthen its laws against discrimination, in particular gender discrimination. Women face societal prejudices that affect their access to employment and economic opportunity.

G. PERSONAL AUTONOMY AND INDIVIDUAL RIGHTS: 15 / 16

G1. Do individuals enjoy freedom of movement, including the ability to change their place of residence, employment, or education? 4 / 4

There are no restrictions on freedom of movement, and individuals in San Marino may freely change their place of residence, employment, and education.

G2. Are individuals able to exercise the right to own property and establish private businesses without undue interference from state or nonstate actors? 4 / 4

The rights to own property and operate private businesses are upheld.

G3. Do individuals enjoy personal social freedoms, including choice of marriage partner and size of family, protection from domestic violence, and control over appearance? 3 / 4

Personal social freedoms are generally safeguarded in San Marino. A law allowing civil unions for same-sex couples was adopted by the Great and General Council in November 2018 and came into force in February 2019. However, same-sex marriage is not recognized, and same-sex couples do not have the right to adopt children together. Abortion is a criminal offense unless the woman's life is in danger, and reform advocates have met with fierce resistance from conservative Catholic groups in recent years. Reports of domestic violence, which is prohibited by law, are rare.

G4. Do individuals enjoy equality of opportunity and freedom from economic exploitation? 4 / 4

The government generally upholds labor protections for workers and provides assistance to low-income individuals. The Council of Europe's commissioner for human rights in 2015 called on San Marino to continue with efforts to better protect foreign women employed as caregivers or household workers, and ECRI renewed this advice in 2018.

São Tomé and Príncipe

Population: 200,000
Capital: São Tomé
Freedom Status: Free
Electoral Democracy: Yes

Overview: São Tomé and Príncipe holds regular, competitive national elections and has undergone multiple transfers of power between rival parties. Civil liberties are generally respected, but poverty and corruption have weakened some institutions and contributed to dysfunction in the justice system. Threats to judicial independence have been a growing concern in recent years.

KEY DEVELOPMENTS IN 2020

- In November, the National Assembly passed legislation preventing citizens born and living abroad to run for president. The Independent Democratic Action (ADI) party criticized the legislation, saying it was designed to keep Gabon-born party leader Patrice Trovoada from seeking the post.
- COVID-19 cases were detected beginning in April, with transmission progressing through the year. The authorities reported 1,014 cases and 17 deaths to the World Health Organization (WHO) by year's end.

POLITICAL RIGHTS: 35 / 40

A. ELECTORAL PROCESS: 11 / 12

A1. Was the current head of government or other chief national authority elected through free and fair elections? 4 / 4

The president is directly elected for up to two consecutive five-year terms. The prime minister, who holds most day-to-day executive authority, is appointed by the president based on the results of legislative elections. Executive elections are typically considered free and fair.

In the 2016 presidential election, former prime minister and ADI member Evaristo Carvalho led the first round with just under 50 percent of the vote; he was initially credited with over 50 percent, but the National Electoral Commission (CEN) revised the total downward, citing late results. Carvalho's leading opponent, incumbent president and independent Manuel Pinto da Costa, was credited with nearly 25 percent but boycotted the runoff vote, alleging first-round irregularities. Carvalho was consequently elected unopposed. Despite this dispute, African Union observers generally praised the conduct of the election.

In the October 2018 legislative elections, the ADI won the most seats, but failed to form a government. That November, President Carvalho invited the Movement for the Liberation of São Tomé and Príncipe–Social Democratic Party (MLSTP-PSD), under the leadership of Jorge Bom Jesus, and a bloc consisting of the Democratic Convergence Party, the Union of Democrats for Citizenship and Development, and the Force for Democratic Change Movement (PCD-UDD-MDFM), to form a new coalition government. Jesus was appointed prime minister later that month.

A2. Were the current national legislative representatives elected through free and fair elections? 4 / 4

Members of the unicameral, 55-seat National Assembly are elected by popular vote to four-year terms. In the October 2018 legislative elections, the ADI secured 25 seats, followed by the MLSTP-PSD with 23, the PCD-UDD-MDFM with 5, and the Movement of Independent Citizens with 2.

Following the elections, in a bid to secure an absolute majority, then prime minister Trovoada requested that the Constitutional Court order a recount of ballots that had been ruled invalid, which the court agreed to. The opposition condemned the court's decision as biased in favor of the ADI. Demonstrations held outside the site of the recount were violently dispersed by security forces, who fired tear gas into the crowd. Later that month, the Constitutional Court certified the initial election results, and the ADI did not gain any seats. Despite the controversy, international observers deemed the elections largely credible.

A3. Are the electoral laws and framework fair, and are they implemented impartially by the relevant election management bodies? 3 / 4

The electoral laws and framework are generally fair, but implementation suffers from lack of resources and staff.

In November 2020, the National Assembly approved a law preventing citizens born and living abroad to run for president. The ADI criticized it, claiming it was designed to keep Trovoada—who was named party leader the month before and was born in Gabon—from running for president. Also in November, parliamentarians selected new CEN commissioners who will supervise the 2021 presidential election along with a new Constitutional Court judge; the judge succeeded Edite dos Ramos Tem Juá, who was made foreign minister in September.

B. POLITICAL PLURALISM AND PARTICIPATION: 15 / 16
B1. Do the people have the right to organize in different political parties or other competitive political groupings of their choice, and is the system free of undue obstacles to the rise and fall of these competing parties or groupings? 4 / 4

The multiparty system features free and vigorous competition among the ADI, MLSTP-PSD, PCD-UDD-MDFM, and a variety of other parties. Parties are known to fracture, however; in 2019, Trovoada was named leader of the ADI while a splinter faction backed Agostinho Fernandes. Trovoada was named ADI leader by acclamation in October 2020.

B2. Is there a realistic opportunity for the opposition to increase its support or gain power through elections? 4 / 4

Manuel Pinto da Costa and the MLSTP-PSD ruled São Tomé and Príncipe as a one-party state from independence in 1975 until 1991. Since then, there have been multiple democratic transfers of power between rival parties. Individual governments have tended to be short-lived, partly due to the country's system of proportional representation, which encourages coalition or minority governments.

B3. Are the people's political choices free from domination by forces that are external to the political sphere, or by political forces that employ extrapolitical means? 3 / 4

Voters and politicians are generally free from undue interference with their decisions. The practice of vote buying by political parties and candidates remains a problem, though it was reportedly less prevalent during the 2018 elections. While the country experienced military coups in 1995 and 2003, normal civilian rule was swiftly restored in both cases.

B4. Do various segments of the population (including ethnic, racial, religious, gender, LGBT+, and other relevant groups) have full political rights and electoral opportunities? 4 / 4

Women and minority groups enjoy full political rights. While women have made advances in the political sphere, societal discrimination and disparities in access to education inhibit women's participation. Women hold 24 percent of the parliament's seats.

C. FUNCTIONING OF GOVERNMENT: 9 / 12

C1. Do the freely elected head of government and national legislative representatives determine the policies of the government? 4 / 4

The prime minister and cabinet determine the government policy under the supervision of the National Assembly and the president. They implement laws and policies without improper interference from unelected entities.

C2. Are safeguards against official corruption strong and effective? 2 / 4

Corruption is a major problem. Oversight mechanisms, the opposition, and the media have repeatedly uncovered evidence of official malfeasance, sometimes resulting in dismissals and other repercussions, but anticorruption laws are poorly enforced.

In June 2020, the Transparency Observatory claimed that the acquisition of face masks was marred by conflicts of interest among government officials. In September, the cabinet sought to "withdraw its confidence" in Attorney General Kelve Nobre de Carvalho over issues including the disappearance of drugs from Judicial Police premises.

C3. Does the government operate with openness and transparency? 3 / 4

The government generally does not restrict access to information about its operations. However, there is no specific law guaranteeing public access to government information. Officials rarely disclose their assets and income. In August 2020, the Court of Auditors warned of irregularities in the government's 2017 accounts, noting their inability to verify figures related to government debt among other concerns.

CIVIL LIBERTIES: 49 / 60

D. FREEDOM OF EXPRESSION AND BELIEF: 15 / 16

D1. Are there free and independent media? 3 / 4

Freedom of the press is constitutionally guaranteed and largely respected in practice. Public media convey opposition views and grant some access to opposition leaders, but only a handful of private media outlets are available, and a degree of self-censorship is reported at both public and private outlets. There are no restrictions on online media, though the sector is poorly developed. Some 30 percent of the population has internet access.

D2. Are individuals free to practice and express their religious faith or nonbelief in public and private? 4 / 4

The constitution provides for freedom of religion. Religious groups are required to register with the Justice Ministry and can face penalties for failing to do so, but the process is not reported to be biased or restrictive.

D3. Is there academic freedom, and is the educational system free from extensive political indoctrination? 4 / 4

The constitution prohibits political indoctrination in education, and academic freedom is generally respected in practice. However, the quality of education is considered poor. In-person education was suspended during the 2019–20 academic year due to COVID-19, with students relying on remote learning and educational broadcasts. In-person education resumed in September 2020.

D4. Are individuals free to express their personal views on political or other sensitive topics without fear of surveillance or retribution? 4 / 4

There are no restrictions on freedom of expression, which is constitutionally guaranteed. The government is not known to engage in improper surveillance of personal communications or monitoring of online content. Social media is used to express private and political opinions.

E. ASSOCIATIONAL AND ORGANIZATIONAL RIGHTS: 11 / 12
E1. Is there freedom of assembly? 4 / 4

The constitution protects freedom of assembly, which the government generally observes in practice. However, organizers are obliged to give authorities two days' notice before public gatherings.

While COVID-19-related restrictions on public assembly were imposed, several demonstrations were nevertheless held during the year. In September, health workers at Central Hospital held a demonstration after a colleague was killed.

E2. Is there freedom for nongovernmental organizations, particularly those that are engaged in human rights and governance-related work? 4 / 4

Nongovernmental organizations (NGOs), including organizations that focus on human rights and governance issues, are free to operate. The government has not placed any significant restrictions on NGOs in recent years, but a lack of funding limits their activities.

E3. Is there freedom for trade unions and similar professional or labor organizations? 3 / 4

Workers have the legal rights to organize, strike, and bargain collectively. These are mostly respected, though there are no provisions to regulate bargaining or punish antiunion practices by employers. Most union negotiations are conducted with the government, which remains the country's dominant formal-sector employer. In December 2020, employees of the finance and planning ministry held a brief strike over pay and working conditions.

F. RULE OF LAW: 12 / 16
F1. Is there an independent judiciary? 3 / 4

The constitution provides for an independent judiciary, and the courts are relatively autonomous in practice, but they are susceptible to political influence and corruption. The current and previous governments embarked on a series of politically charged judicial appointments and dismissals.

In December 2020, the government launched a three-year modernization program for the justice system. The program is designed, in part, to bolster judicial and prosecutorial independence.

F2. Does due process prevail in civil and criminal matters? 3 / 4

Law enforcement authorities generally observe legal safeguards against arbitrary arrest and detention as well as guarantees for a fair trial, but police corruption is a problem, and indigent defendants are sometimes denied access to a lawyer. Nearly a third of prisoners are in pretrial detention, which can be lengthy in some cases.

F3. Is there protection from the illegitimate use of physical force and freedom from war and insurgencies? 3 / 4

Police are sometimes accused of physically attacking suspects during arrest.

Prisons suffer from overcrowding and other harsh conditions. In June 2020, the UN Development Programme launched a project to improve conditions in São Tomé Prison.

Health workers reportedly faced increased physical attacks and other acts of aggression during the year.

F4. Do laws, policies, and practices guarantee equal treatment of various segments of the population? 3 / 4

Equal treatment is legally guaranteed, but a degree of societal discrimination against women persists, hampering their access to economic and educational opportunities. Although same-sex sexual activity is not criminalized, discrimination against LGBT+ people is sometimes reported, and the law does not specifically address such bias.

G. PERSONAL AUTONOMY AND INDIVIDUAL RIGHTS: 11 / 16

G1. Do individuals enjoy freedom of movement, including the ability to change their place of residence, employment, or education? 4 / 4

The constitution establishes the freedom of internal movement, foreign travel, emigration, and repatriation. The government generally respects these rights, though movement was restricted by COVID-19-related measures during the year.

G2. Are individuals able to exercise the right to own property and establish private businesses without undue interference from state or nonstate actors? 3 / 4

The legal framework and government policies are generally supportive of property rights and private business activity, though bureaucratic obstacles and corruption pose challenges in practice.

G3. Do individuals enjoy personal social freedoms, including choice of marriage partner and size of family, protection from domestic violence, and control over appearance? 2 / 4

There are few formal restrictions on personal social freedoms. However, domestic violence is reportedly common and rarely prosecuted. The minimum age for marriage with parental consent is 14 for girls and 16 for boys, as opposed to 18 without parental consent for both. Roughly a third of girls marry before age 18. In October 2020, several NGOs called on the government to declare a national day of prevention in order to combat sexual violence.

**G4. Do individuals enjoy equality of opportunity and freedom from economic exploitation?
2 / 4**

Forced labor is prohibited and child labor is restricted by law. There are also basic legal protections against exploitative or dangerous working conditions. However, the government lacks the capacity to enforce these rules effectively, particularly in the informal agricultural sector. The economy is heavily reliant on foreign aid.

Saudi Arabia

Population: 35,000,000
Capital: Riyadh
Freedom Status: Not Free
Electoral Democracy: No

Overview: Saudi Arabia's absolute monarchy restricts almost all political rights and civil liberties. No officials at the national level are elected. The regime relies on pervasive surveillance, the criminalization of dissent, appeals to sectarianism and ethnicity, and public spending supported by oil revenues to maintain power. Women and religious minorities face extensive discrimination in law and in practice. Working conditions for the large expatriate labor force are often exploitative.

KEY DEVELOPMENTS IN 2020

- Saudi authorities closed borders, initiated a curfew, and restricted foreign travelers from partaking in the *hajj* pilgrimage as part of its efforts to manage the COVID-19 pandemic. The country reported one of the Middle East's highest infection rates, as infections peaked in June; the World Health Organization reported 362,000 cases and just over 6,200 deaths at year's end.
- In November, the government announced reforms that would dismantle parts of the *kafala* visa-sponsorship system and allow foreign workers to more easily leave Saudi Arabia. The measures are scheduled to take effect in 2021.
- In December, a terrorism court handed women's rights activists Loujain al-Hathloul and Maya'a al-Zahrani, who were arrested in 2018, prison sentences of nearly six years. The sentence of al-Hathloul, who was tortured while in detention, was modified to include time served.

POLITICAL RIGHTS: 1 / 40

A. ELECTORAL PROCESS: 0 / 12

A1. Was the current head of government or other chief national authority elected through free and fair elections? 0 / 4

Saudi Arabia's king is chosen by his predecessor from among male descendants of the country's founder, though the choice must be approved by a council of senior princes, the Allegiance Council. The king rules for life. King Salman bin Abdulaziz al-Saud appointed son Mohammed bin Salman as crown prince in 2017, displacing the prince's older cousin, Mohammed bin Nayef, who was stripped of all official positions. Bin Nayef was detained along with a sibling of King Salman in March 2020 on charges of treason over an alleged plot to overthrow both the king and the crown prince.

The cabinet, which is appointed by the king, passes legislation that becomes law once ratified by royal decree. King Salman also serves as prime minister, and Mohammed bin Salman serves as deputy prime minister and minister of defense.

A2. Were the current national legislative representatives elected through free and fair elections? 0 / 4

The king appoints the 150 members of the Majlis al-Shura (Consultative Council), who serve in an advisory capacity and wield no legislative authority, for four-year terms. King Salman appointed new members in October 2020.

Limited nonpartisan elections for advisory councils at the municipal level were introduced in 2005. In the 2015 elections, two-thirds of the seats on the 284 councils were open to voting, while the rest were filled through appointment by the minister of municipal and rural affairs. Women were allowed to vote and run as candidates for the first time, and a small number won seats. New elections were due in 2019, but were postponed indefinitely without any clear official explanation.

A3. Are the electoral laws and framework fair, and are they implemented impartially by the relevant election management bodies? 0 / 4

The electoral framework lacks constitutional protections, and the 2015 municipal elections were subject to a number of onerous restrictions. The kingdom's rules on gender segregation were applied to campaigns, meaning no candidates could produce posters showing their faces or meet in person with voters of the opposite sex. Candidates were also barred from giving media interviews, leading many to campaign via social media. A number of candidates were disqualified for unclear reasons, though some were reinstated after appeals. Ultimately only a small fraction of the citizen population participated in the elections, reflecting doubts about the effectiveness of the advisory councils.

B. POLITICAL PLURALISM AND PARTICIPATION: 0 / 16

B1. Do the people have the right to organize in different political parties or other competitive political groupings of their choice, and is the system free of undue obstacles to the rise and fall of these competing parties or groupings? 0 / 4

Political parties are forbidden, and political dissent is effectively criminalized. Some of the country's most prominent political rights organizations and activists, including founding members of the banned Saudi Civil and Political Rights Association (ACPRA), have been arrested and sentenced to prison in recent years; one founder, Abdullah al-Hamid, died in custody in April 2020. Many other political activists continue to serve lengthy prison sentences. A new political party, the National Assembly party, was established by Saudi exiles living abroad in October.

B2. Is there a realistic opportunity for the opposition to increase its support or gain power through elections? 0 / 4

The current leadership has given no indication that it plans to allow competitive elections for positions of executive or legislative authority in the future. Opposition movements are banned, and the government is increasingly intolerant even of moderate critics. The Muslim Brotherhood, a Sunni Islamist political organization, is believed to have the sympathy of a substantial minority of Saudis, but has been designated a terrorist group since 2014.

Other groups and individuals that criticize the regime or call for political reform—whether Sunni or Shiite, Islamist or secularist—are subject to arbitrary detention. Prominent reformist clerics Salman al-Awdah, Awad al-Qarni, and Ali al-Omari were arrested in 2017 as part of a crackdown against those who criticized the government campaign to isolate Qatar over its ties to the Muslim Brotherhood and Iran; all three faced the threat of death penalties on terrorism charges, but their cases have been stalled by arbitrary delays—al-Omari's trial was paused several times by June 2020—and they remained in detention at year's end.

B3. Are the people's political choices free from domination by forces that are external to the political sphere, or by political forces that employ extrapolitical means? 0 / 4

The monarchy generally excludes the public from any meaningful political participation. In the absence of political parties, voters in Saudi Arabia's limited municipal elections are heavily influenced by tribal and religious leaders, many of whom benefit from close ties to the ruling establishment.

B4. Do various segments of the population (including ethnic, racial, religious, gender, LGBT+, and other relevant groups) have full political rights and electoral opportunities? 0 / 4

Although political rights are curtailed for all Saudi citizens, women, religious minorities, and LGBT+ people face additional obstacles to participation given the kingdom's strict laws and customs on matters including gender segregation and sexual activity, and its intolerance of religious groups that deviate from Wahhabism, a highly conservative and literalist interpretation of Sunni Islam. Some 30 women served in the last parliament, and a female deputy speaker was appointed in October 2020. Women secured about 1 percent of the seats in the 2015 municipal council elections. Shiites reportedly hold a small number of Majlis al-Shura seats and many municipal council seats in Shiite-majority areas.

Members of religious minorities and women are largely excluded from leadership positions, though some women have held notable roles. A woman was appointed deputy education minister in 2009, and another became deputy labor minister in 2018.

Noncitizens, who make up roughly a third of the population in Saudi Arabia, have no political rights, and citizenship can only be directly transmitted by a citizen father whose marriage is recognized by the state.

C. FUNCTIONING OF GOVERNMENT: 1 / 12

C1. Do the freely elected head of government and national legislative representatives determine the policies of the government? 0 / 4

The kingdom's only elected officials serve on local advisory councils and have little or no influence over national laws and policies.

C2. Are safeguards against official corruption strong and effective? 1 / 4

Corruption remains a significant problem. Although the government generates massive revenue from the sale of oil, which it redistributes through social welfare programs and as patronage, little is known about state accounting or the various direct ways in which public wealth becomes a source of private privilege for the royal family and its clients.

The government has taken some steps to combat corruption and recover misappropriated assets, but its opaque methods have raised serious concerns about politicization and lack of due process. The crown prince heads an anticorruption committee, which in 2017 ordered the detention of more than 300 people, many of whom were coerced into turning over billions of dollars in assets to the state. Bin Salman's campaign has targeted potential rivals within the royal family, leading observers to suggest these crackdowns are meant to consolidate his political and economic control. Major crackdowns and arrests continued in 2020, with 298 government employees being arrested for corruption in March. Another 59 were arrested in October, and over $160 million worth of assets were seized. In November, 226 public- and private-sector officials were arrested.

Independent whistleblowers and anticorruption advocates have faced punishment. *Al-Watan* columnist Saleh al-Shehi received a five-year prison sentence in 2018 after suggesting there was corruption in the royal court in a television appearance.

C3. Does the government operate with openness and transparency? 0 / 4

The functioning of government is largely opaque. The availability of some economic data is improving, but overall, there is little transparency on whether or how state funds are disbursed, or on the internal decision-making process that allocates them; there is no public mechanism for holding senior officials accountable for their decisions. The defense budget is especially shielded from public scrutiny.

The state's oil revenues make up the vast majority of its financial resources, but these are tightly controlled by the royal family, which uses the same income to support itself. In 2018 and 2019, the state oil company, Saudi Aramco, provided more income and expenditure information in preparation for an initial public offering. However, amid ongoing questions about its relationship with the government, the company opted that December to list shares only on a domestic stock exchange, which entailed less transparency than would be required on a major international exchange.

CIVIL LIBERTIES: 6 / 60

D. FREEDOM OF EXPRESSION AND BELIEF: 2 / 16

D1. Are there free and independent media? 0 / 4

The government controls domestic media content and heavily influences regional print and satellite-television coverage. Journalists can be imprisoned for a variety of vaguely defined crimes. In December 2020, the Committee to Protect Journalists reported that 24 journalists were imprisoned in Saudi Arabia.

A 2011 royal decree amended the press law to criminalize, among other things, any criticism of the country's grand mufti, the Council of Senior Religious Scholars, or government officials; violations can result in fines and forced closure of media outlets. All blogs and websites must have a Ministry of Information license or face fines and possible closure.

In October 2018, one of the country's most prominent journalists, Jamal Khashoggi, was murdered by Saudi agents inside the Saudi consulate in Istanbul. Khashoggi, who criticized the government of bin Salman, had been working as a *Washington Post* columnist in the United States. Saudi officials blamed rogue intelligence agents, but according to a UN special rapporteur, the evidence suggested the crown prince's involvement. In December 2019, a Saudi court sentenced five men to death for Khashoggi's murder, and three others received prison sentences; the death sentences were commuted in September 2020. The most senior officials under investigation were acquitted due to a supposed lack of evidence, and bin Salman himself was never officially investigated.

The government maintains an extensive system of social media surveillance and regulation, and invests considerable resources in automated "bot" and other accounts that influence and distort the social media environment and target prominent users. In May 2020, activist Amani al-Zain was reportedly arrested after a video of her criticizing the crown prince—and making a reference to Khashoggi's murder—surfaced. Progovernment social media users targeted al-Zain online before her arrest.

D2. Are individuals free to practice and express their religious faith or nonbelief in public and private? 0 / 4

The 1992 Basic Law declares that the Quran and the Sunna are the country's constitution. Islam is the official religion, and all Saudis are required by law to be Muslims. A 2014 royal decree punishes atheism with up to 20 years in prison. The government prohibits the public practice of any religion other than Islam and restricts the religious practices of Shiites and of those who practice Sufism. The construction of Shiite mosques is constrained through licensing rules and prohibited outside of Eastern Province, where most Shiites live. Although the government recognizes the right of non-Muslims to worship in private, it does not always respect this right in practice.

The government exercises significant influence over Muslim clerics—both officially appointed figures who depend on government patronage and independent religious scholars who need a measure of official goodwill in order to function openly, appear on television, and avoid penalties.

Online commentary that touches on religion can be harshly punished. Among other prominent cases, liberal blogger Raif Badawi, arrested in 2012, received a 10-year prison sentence for blasphemy in 2014 and remained imprisoned in 2020.

D3. Is there academic freedom, and is the educational system free from extensive political indoctrination? 1 / 4

Academic freedom is restricted, and informers monitor classrooms for compliance with curriculum rules, including a ban on teaching secular philosophy and religions other than Islam. Despite changes to textbooks in recent years, intolerance in the classroom remains a significant problem, as some educators continue to espouse discriminatory and hateful views of non-Muslims and Muslim minority sects.

Academics have faced punishment for criticizing government policies or for other reasons. History professor and women's rights activist Hatoon al-Fassi was arrested in 2018, days after her comments on the crown prince's reforms were publicized. She was provisionally released in May 2019, along with three other activists, but still awaits a trial for illegal contact with foreign media, diplomats, and human rights groups. In August 2020, academic Abdullah Ibn Ali Basfar was arrested under unclear circumstances.

D4. Are individuals free to express their personal views on political or other sensitive topics without fear of surveillance or retribution? 1 / 4

Saudis are able to engage in some degree of private discussion on political and other topics, including criticism of certain aspects of government performance, both online and offline. However, severe criminal penalties deter more direct criticism of the regime and free discussion on topics like religion or the royal family. Laws are often vaguely worded, giving the state considerable discretion to determine what constitutes illegal expression.

Surveillance is extensive within Saudi Arabia, and Saudis living and traveling abroad are also subject to spying and intimidation. In November 2019, US prosecutors accused two former Twitter employees of providing information on users, including perceived government critics, to Saudi authorities. The government is also known to use messaging services to track citizens traveling abroad.

The climate for free expression has deteriorated sharply since 2018, with the assassination of Jamal Khashoggi and the arrests of government critics serving as warnings to ordinary Saudis to avoid public dissent.

E. ASSOCIATIONAL AND ORGANIZATIONAL RIGHTS: 0 / 12
E1. Is there freedom of assembly? 0 / 4

Freedom of assembly is not respected, and the government has imposed harsh punishments—including the death penalty—on those who lead or participate in public protests. Hussein al-Rabi was tried in a terrorism court for his involvement in a protest in Eastern Province, and was threatened with torture if he did not confess; al-Rabi was executed in April 2019.

E2. Is there freedom for nongovernmental organizations, particularly those that are engaged in human rights- and governance-related work? 0 / 4

Nongovernmental organizations (NGOs) must obtain a government license to operate. Until the adoption of an NGO law in 2015, officials had approved licenses only for charitable groups; the authorities have expressed a desire to encourage the growth of civil society, but they discourage independent work on human rights and governance issues. Reformist organizations have been denied licenses in practice, in some cases through arbitrary delays.

Human rights activists and other civil society representatives face regular harassment and detention. In 2018, the same year that women were allowed to drive for the first time, authorities arrested 13 women's rights activists; eight were provisionally released by May 2020, though their trials were still pending at year's end. In December, a terrorism court handed two of the remaining detainees, Loujain al-Hathloul and Maya'a al-Zahrani, prison sentences of nearly six years, though al-Hathloul's sentence was modified to include time served.

No domestic NGO openly advocates for LGBT+ rights or issues.

E3. Is there freedom for trade unions and similar professional or labor organizations? 0 / 4

No laws protect the rights to form independent labor unions, bargain collectively, or engage in strikes. Workers who engage in union activity are subject to dismissal or detention. A May 2020 COVID-19-related directive banned "gatherings of workers" to five people, while limits on other gatherings were set at 50.

F. RULE OF LAW: 2 / 16

F1. Is there an independent judiciary? 1 / 4

The judiciary has very little independence in practice. Judges are appointed by the king and overseen by the Supreme Judicial Council, whose chairman is also the justice minister. A special commission of judicial experts issues opinions that serve as guidelines for judges on the interpretation of Sharia (Islamic law), which forms the basis of Saudi law. Judges have significant discretion in how they interpret Sharia and do not have to publish an explanation of their judgments.

F2. Does due process prevail in civil and criminal matters? 1 / 4

Defendants' rights are poorly protected by law. Detainees are often denied access to legal counsel during interrogation, and lengthy pretrial detention and detention without charge are common. Due process is notably lacking in death penalty cases. Statistics on prisoners are lacking, and the number of political prisoners is therefore difficult to assess, but Human Rights Watch counted at least 12 activists serving long prison sentences at year's end.

An antiterrorism law that took effect in 2014 includes lengthy prison sentences for criticizing the monarchy or the government. Among other provisions, it expanded the power of police to conduct raids targeting suspected antigovernment activity without judicial approval.

The hundreds of people arrested in the anticorruption crackdown in 2017 did not pass through the judicial system, but were instead compelled to hand over assets to the government in return for their release. Government supporters claimed that the judicial process would have taken several years due to a lack of capacity.

F3. Is there protection from the illegitimate use of physical force and freedom from war and insurgencies? 0 / 4

Allegations of torture by police and prison officials are common, and access to prisoners by independent human rights and legal organizations is extremely limited. In March 2019, international media published leaked prison medical records indicating that a number of political prisoners suffered from cuts, bruises, burns, and malnutrition. Detained women's rights activists were reportedly given electric shocks, whipped, beaten, sexually abused, and threatened with rape. The family of Loujain al-Hathloul stated she had been offered freedom on the condition that she recant her torture allegations, but she refused.

Corporal punishment, most often lashing, is common in criminal sentencing, though the government ended the use of flogging for some crimes in an April 2020 decision.

Capital punishment is applied to a wide range of crimes other than murder, including drug and protest-related offenses. Defendants facing the death penalty are known to confess under torture, but courts do not consistently investigate subsequent retractions. The use of the death penalty declined in 2020; only 15 people were executed in the first 11 months of the year, compared to 184 in all of 2019. In April 2020, the government restated a previous decision to refrain from using capital punishment against those accused of committing certain crimes as children.

Saudi Arabia has faced cross-border military attacks from Yemen since 2015, when it entered a war against that country's Shiite-led and Iranian-backed Houthi (Ansarallah) movement. In late March 2020, Houthi forces launched missiles at the cities of Riyadh and Jāzān; Saudi authorities reported their interception, along with two civilian injuries. Missiles and armed drones were used against several Saudi cities in June and against Riyadh in September, though Saudi authorities claimed to intercept both. The Houthi movement also launched an attack on an oil facility in February, which was reportedly intercepted.

Saudi authorities were accused of firing on, and later detaining, Ethiopian migrants living in Yemen when Houthi forces expelled several thousand of them to the Saudi border in April 2020. After that incident, in which Saudi forces reportedly killed dozens of people, authorities allowed several hundred migrants into the country, but arbitrarily detained them in unsanitary conditions, engaged in acts of torture, and gave detainees no opportunity to challenge deportation orders. Saudi authorities promised to investigate the matter in September.

F4. Do laws, policies, and practices guarantee equal treatment of various segments of the population? 0 / 4

The courts engage in routine discrimination against various groups, citing their interpretations of Sharia. A woman's testimony is generally given half the weight of a man's, and the testimony of anyone other than observant Sunni Muslims can be disregarded by judges.

Shiites, who make up 10 to 15 percent of the population, face socioeconomic disadvantages, discrimination in employment, and underrepresentation in government positions and the security forces.

Education and economic rights for Saudi women have improved significantly in recent years, but women are still subject to extensive legal and societal discrimination, most notably through the guardianship system, in which women must rely on a close male relative to approve many basic activities. Although legal reforms have recently reduced the scope of the guardianship system, it remains deeply entrenched in societal practices and customs, and an individual woman's degree of freedom depends to a large extent on the attitudes of her family. Reforms announced in August 2019 included a ban on gender discrimination in employment, potentially preventing employers from requiring women to obtain a guardian's permission to work.

Same-sex sexual activity is generally understood to be prohibited under Sharia, and LGBT+ people are at risk of harassment, discrimination, criminal punishment, and violence.

G. PERSONAL AUTONOMY AND INDIVIDUAL RIGHTS: 2 / 16

G1. Do individuals enjoy freedom of movement, including the ability to change their place of residence, employment, or education? 0 / 4

The government punishes activists and critics by limiting their ability to travel outside the country, and reform advocates are routinely stripped of their passports. Family members of activists can also be banned from travel.

Gender segregation restricts freedom of movement for both men and women, but male guardianship and other factors have historically imposed especially onerous constraints on women. The long-standing ban on women driving was lifted in 2018. In August 2019, women over the age of 21 were allowed to apply for a passport without a male guardian's permission.

Foreign workers currently cannot change jobs without a no-objection letter from their existing employer, and some employers confiscate workers' passports to prevent them from leaving. In November 2020, the government announced reforms that will allow foreign workers to more easily leave Saudi Arabia when they take effect in March 2021.

G2. Are individuals able to exercise the right to own property and establish private businesses without undue interference from state or nonstate actors? 1 / 4

While a great deal of business activity in the kingdom is dominated by or connected to members of the government, the ruling family, or other elite families, officials have given assurances that special industrial and commercial zones are free from interference by the royal family.

Women face legal discrimination regarding property rights, with daughters typically receiving half the inheritance awarded to sons. Women are no longer legally required to obtain permission from a male guardian to obtain business licenses.

G3. Do individuals enjoy personal social freedoms, including choice of marriage partner and size of family, protection from domestic violence, and control over appearance? 0 / 4

There are a number of official restrictions on marriage. Muslim women may not marry non-Muslims, citizens require the interior ministry's permission to marry noncitizens, and men are barred from marrying women from certain countries. All sexual activity outside of marriage is criminalized, and the death penalty can be applied in certain circumstances. Women face legal disadvantages in divorce and custody proceedings, and cannot marry without a male guardian's permission. Under reforms announced in August 2019, women can register children's births and oversee children's travel.

A 2013 law broadly defined and criminalized domestic abuse, prescribing fines and up to a year in prison for perpetrators. However, enforcement remains problematic, with some officials prioritizing privacy and family integrity over safety and justice for victims. Prosecutions are extremely rare. Women's practical ability to leave abusive relationships is severely limited. While women are no longer legally required to live with their husbands under the August 2019 reforms, social taboos and other obstacles often deter women from leaving their family home; there are a limited number of shelters for women escaping abuse, but women are not allowed to leave them without their guardians' permission.

The religious police's authority to enforce gender-segregation and personal-attire rules has been sharply curtailed in both law and practice since 2016. Nevertheless, some Saudis have faced penalties for breaching similar rules on social media. In October 2019, an openly gay Saudi man was arrested for electronic crimes and public nudity after using social media to post pictures of himself wearing shorts on the beach.

G4. Do individuals enjoy equality of opportunity and freedom from economic exploitation? 1 / 4

A number of amendments to the labor law that went into effect in 2015 granted broader rights and protections to workers in the private sector. However, the law does not apply to household workers, who are governed by separate regulations that provide fewer safeguards against exploitative working conditions.

Foreign workers—who make up more than half of the active labor force—enjoy limited legal protections and remain vulnerable to trafficking and forced labor, primarily through employers' exploitation of the kafala visa-sponsorship system. In 2014, the Ministry of Labor ruled that expatriate workers who are not paid their salaries for more than three consecutive months are free to switch their work sponsors without approval. In practice, foreign workers are subject to periodic mass deportations for visa violations or criminal activity, though due process is often lacking in such cases. Some components of the kafala system are to be dismantled as part of a labor reform package announced in November 2020.

Government programs give preferential treatment to companies that hire certain percentages of Saudi citizens and penalize those that fail to meet such targets.

Senegal

Population: 16,700,000
Capital: Dakar
Freedom Status: Partly Free
Electoral Democracy: Yes

Overview: Senegal is one of Africa's most stable electoral democracies and has undergone peaceful transfers of power between rival parties since 2000. However, politically motivated prosecutions of opposition leaders and changes to the electoral laws have reduced the competitiveness of the opposition in recent years. The country is known for its relatively independent media and free expression, though defamation laws continue to constrain press freedom. Other ongoing challenges include corruption in government, weak rule of law, and inadequate protections for the rights of women and LGBT+ people.

KEY DEVELOPMENTS IN 2020

- Senegalese authorities declared a COVID-19-related state of emergency in March, and legislators allowed President Macky Sall to issue decrees on several matters for a three-month period. People in several cities held sometimes-violent demonstrations over COVID-19 curfews and travel restrictions in early June, prompting the government to loosen its policies. While the state of emergency expired in July, some measures were reintroduced in August. The World Health Organization recorded nearly 19,000 cases and 402 deaths at year's end.

- In September, then community development minister Mansour Faye, who was accused of mismanaging the government's COVID-19 food aid program, vowed to ignore any summons from the country's anticorruption watchdog. Despite concerns over the program's management, Faye was made infrastructure minister in November.
- In November, President Sall appointed Idrissa Seck, the second-place contestant in the 2019 presidential contest, to chair a government economic council. Two ministries were also assigned to Rewmi members; the move was perceived as part of an effort to clear the field of political opponents.

POLITICAL RIGHTS: 29 / 40

A. ELECTORAL PROCESS: 9 / 12

A1. Was the current head of government or other chief national authority elected through free and fair elections? 3 / 4

The president is chief of state and head of government and is directly elected to a maximum of two consecutive terms. In 2016, the presidential term was reduced via referendum from seven years to five, effective after the end of President Macky Sall's term in 2019.

In the February 2019 presidential election, Sall, of the Alliance for the Republic (APR), defeated four challengers including former prime minister Idrissa Seck of the Rewmi Party and Ousmane Sonko of the Patriots of Senegal for Ethics, Work, and Fraternity (PASTEF) party. Sonko, a former tax inspector, was backed by many young Senegalese frustrated by the Sall administration's policies.

While international observers declared the election credible, it was marred by the exclusion of two prominent opposition politicians, Khalifa Sall and Karim Wade, who might have seriously challenged President Sall. In January 2019, just weeks before the polls, the Constitutional Council ruled they were both ineligible to run for president because they had been convicted in separate, politically fraught corruption cases.

That May, lawmakers approved a controversial constitutional reform that abolished the post of prime minister, and Sall promptly signed it. The move, which had not been a component of Sall's reelection platform, prompted an outcry from critics who accused him of seeking to consolidate power. Separately, that December, President Sall suggested that he could attempt to run for a third term in 2024. In March 2020, two high-profile supporters again raised the possibility of a third term for Sall.

A2. Were the current national legislative representatives elected through free and fair elections? 3 / 4

Members of Senegal's 165-seat National Assembly are elected to five-year terms—105 are elected in single-member districts, and 60 by proportional representation. In the July 2017 parliamentary elections, the ruling United in Hope (BBY) coalition won 125 seats, followed by Abdoulaye Wade's Winning Coalition–Wattu Senegaal with 19. Khalifa Sall's Mankoo Taxawu Senegaal coalition took 7, and 11 groups divided the remainder. International observers deemed the elections credible despite significant procedural errors and logistical challenges.

New biometric voting cards were distributed to only 70 percent of eligible voters before the 2017 elections. To address the problem, the Constitutional Council approved the Sall administration's plan to allow voters to use alternative forms of identification. Some voters were allegedly disenfranchised because of difficulties related to the identification measures, which were approved just four days before the elections.

Local elections, originally due in 2019, were delayed when President Sall entered a dialogue with opposition parties that May. However, that process subsequently stalled, and local elections were consequently not held in 2020.

A3. Are the electoral laws and framework fair, and are they implemented impartially by the relevant election management bodies? 3 / 4

The National Autonomous Electoral Commission (CENA) administers elections. Although the CENA is nominally independent, its members are appointed by the president. The opposition criticized the government for making important changes ahead of the 2017 legislative balloting, including the introduction of the new biometric voting system, without engaging in dialogue or building political consensus. The changes were approved in January 2017, only six months before the elections, which observers argued did not provide sufficient time for logistical information about the new electoral framework to be disseminated in a coordinated fashion.

A new electoral law passed in 2018 requires all aspiring presidential candidates to collect signatures from at least 0.8 percent of the overall electorate before their names could appear on the ballot, and all groups presenting National Assembly lists to obtain signatures from 0.5 percent of voters in at least seven regions. The government asserted that the legislation was necessary to reduce the proliferation of parties that field candidates. Of the 27 candidates who submitted the required signatures prior to the 2019 presidential election, only 5 were approved by the Constitutional Council that January. That June, a European Union election observation mission said the controversial requirement could pose "serious political and organizational problems" in upcoming local elections.

In May 2019, opposition parties and the Sall administration entered talks aimed at resolving voter-roll concerns and reviewing the overarching voting process. However, neither of these goals were reached by the end of 2020, due in part to boycotts from opposition participants.

B. POLITICAL PLURALISM AND PARTICIPATION: 12 / 16

B1. Do the people have the right to organize in different political parties or other competitive political groupings of their choice, and is the system free of undue obstacles to the rise and fall of these competing parties or groupings? 3 / 4

Registration requirements for new political parties are not onerous, and registered parties can organize and operate without government interference. However, opposition candidates still face major financial inequities when competing with incumbents. There is no public financing for political parties, but the ruling party deploys a vast set of state resources to garner support, whereas opposition leaders are often forced to rely on personal wealth to finance party operations or on political alliances to access power.

B2. Is there a realistic opportunity for the opposition to increase its support or gain power through elections? 3 / 4

The opposition can increase its support or gain power through elections. However, the 2018 electoral law was criticized by opposition leaders for making it more difficult for candidates to appear on the ballot and was widely seen as a move to clear the field and ensure President Sall's reelection in 2019.

The prosecutions of some of President Sall's most prominent political opponents in recent years has also reduced the competitiveness of the opposition. In January 2019, the Constitutional Council ruled that Khalifa Sall, a former mayor of Dakar, and Karim Wade, the son of former president Abdoulaye Wade, were both ineligible to run in the 2019 presidential election because both had been sentenced to prison terms for corruption. Karim Wade, sentenced in 2015, received a pardon in 2016, and subsequently went into exile in Qatar. Although Khalifa Sall was supposed to serve a five-year prison sentence for embezzlement, he was eventually pardoned by President Sall in September 2019.

The opposition's ability to compete with President Sall was also lessened by the president's decision to appoint opposition figures to government posts. In November 2020, for example, Sall appointed Rewmi Party presidential candidate Idrissa Seck as head of the Economic, Social and Environmental Council. Two cabinet portfolios were also offered to Rewmi members during the reshuffle.

B3. Are the people's political choices free from domination by forces that are external to the political sphere, or by political forces that employ extrapolitical means? 3 / 4

People's political choices are largely free from domination by groups that are not democratically accountable. Despite the constitutional separation of religion and state, Sufi Muslim marabouts exercise some influence on voters and politicians, particularly on subjects like homosexuality, marriage, and abortion rights.

B4. Do various segments of the population (including ethnic, racial, religious, gender, LGBT+, and other relevant groups) have full political rights and electoral opportunities? 3 / 4

Female representation in the cabinet is relatively poor, with only eight women holding cabinet positions after a November 2020 reshuffle. Women are better represented in the National Assembly, holding 71 seats and representing 43 percent of the body as of December 2020. This is partially due to a 2010 law requiring gender parity on candidate lists. Women's overall rate of participation in politics, such as voting and engaging in local political activities, is nevertheless lower than men's.

Due to high levels of discrimination and social stigma, LGBT+ people have no meaningful political representation.

C. FUNCTIONING OF GOVERNMENT: 8 / 12

C1. Do the freely elected head of government and national legislative representatives determine the policies of the government? 3 / 4

President Sall, his cabinet, and national legislators determine government policies. However, power is concentrated in the executive branch, and the National Assembly is limited in its ability to check the president. The executive has blocked certain parliamentary inquiries into its activities. In May 2019, lawmakers approved a controversial measure to abolish the post of prime minister, which Sall promptly signed. In April 2020, the National Assembly passed COVID-19-related legislation allowing Sall to issue decrees on economic, budgetary, financial, legal, health, and safety matters for three months.

C2. Are safeguards against official corruption strong and effective? 2 / 4

Corruption remains a serious problem, and high-level officials often act with impunity. The Sall administration reactivated the Court of Repression of Illicit Enrichment in 2012, while the National Office for the Fight against Fraud and Corruption (OFNAC), an anticorruption watchdog, was created later that year. However, relevant laws are unevenly enforced, and enforcement actions are sometimes viewed as politically motivated. The corruption case against Khalifa Sall, for example, was widely perceived as an effort to neutralize one of the president's most powerful opponents.

C3. Does the government operate with openness and transparency? 3 / 4

The government generally operates with openness. However, authorities frequently award contracts without any formal tender process, and do not always publicly release contracts or bilateral agreements before they are signed.

Some COVID-19-related decisions were also made opaquely. OFNAC received complaints over the nontransparent process for distributing pandemic-related food aid but then community development minister Mansour Faye, who was accused of mismanagement, vowed to refuse any OFNAC summons in September 2020. Despite these concerns, Faye was appointed infrastructure minister in November.

A 2014 law requires confidential asset disclosures by cabinet members, top National Assembly officials, and the managers of large public funds; the president's asset disclosures are made public.

CIVIL LIBERTIES: 42 / 60

D. FREEDOM OF EXPRESSION AND BELIEF: 13 / 16

D1. Are there free and independent media? 2 / 4

The constitution guarantees freedom of speech, and Senegal is home to many independent television and radio stations and print outlets. Although the overall media situation has improved considerably since President Sall was elected in 2012, several subsequent developments have clouded this positive picture. A controversial press code, proposed in 2017, seeks to increase punishments for defamation offenses, though it remained unsigned by the president in 2020. The 2018 Code on Electronic Communications was ostensibly passed by the National Assembly to guard against disinformation on the internet.

On New Year's Eve 2019, the Audiovisual Regulatory Council (CNRA) suspended television channel Sen TV for seven days. While observers believed the suspension was related to the channel's decision to host PASTEF leader Ousmane Sonko, the CNRA claimed that Sen TV's decision to air cosmetic-depigmentation advertisements prompted the suspension.

D2. Are individuals free to practice and express their religious faith or nonbelief in public and private? 4 / 4

There is no state religion, and freedom of worship is constitutionally protected and respected in practice. Muslims constitute 96 percent of the population.

D3. Is there academic freedom, and is the educational system free from extensive political indoctrination? 4 / 4

Academic freedom is guaranteed by the constitution and generally respected in practice.

D4. Are individuals free to express their personal views on political or other sensitive topics without fear of surveillance or retribution? 3 / 4

Private discussion is generally open and free. However, individuals have occasionally been arrested for social media posts deemed offensive by the government.

In 2018, the National Assembly passed an electronic-communications bill, which included a vaguely worded provision expanding the regulatory power of the government over social media companies. Rights activists expressed concern that the law could be used to shut down, tax, or surveil communications on popular social media platforms.

In January 2020, President Sall proposed an internal security bill that would ostensibly be used to combat online terrorist propaganda and communications. The bill, which was reportedly adopted later that month, was criticized by the Association of ICT Users, which warned that the act would limit the freedom of expression.

E. ASSOCIATIONAL AND ORGANIZATIONAL RIGHTS: 9 / 12
E1. Is there freedom of assembly? 2 / 4

The constitution guarantees freedom of assembly and peaceful demonstrations, but the Ministry of the Interior must approve protests in advance. The government has often cracked down on assembly rights by banning protests around tense political moments and violently dispersing some demonstrations. The government also reserved the right to limit assemblies under a COVID-19-related state of emergency issued in March 2020. While the state of emergency expired in July, some assembly restrictions were reintroduced in August after an increase in COVID-19 transmission and remained in force through year's end.

Senegalese in several cities, including Dakar and Touba, held demonstrations opposing COVID-19 restrictions in early June 2020. Some demonstrations turned violent, with clashes reported between participants and security forces. After a two-day period of rioting, Interior Minister Aly Ngouille Ndiaye announced that over 200 people had been arrested and also announced a loosening of pandemic-related curfew restrictions.

Assembly rights of LGBT+ groups and nongovernmental organizations (NGOs) that support people living with HIV and AIDS are limited.

E2. Is there freedom for nongovernmental organizations, particularly those that are engaged in human rights- and governance-related work? 4 / 4

NGOs generally operate without interference from state or nonstate actors, though the ability of LGBT+ groups to function is impeded by assembly restrictions.

E3. Is there freedom for trade unions and similar professional or labor organizations? 3 / 4

Workers, apart from security employees, have rights to organize, bargain collectively, and strike, though the right to strike is impinged by legal provisions that ban pickets and sit-down strikes, among other activities. Trade unions must be authorized by the Ministry of the Interior, and unions lack legal recourse if registration is denied.

In June 2020, the Union of Justice Workers launched a strike, claiming the government was not fulfilling its obligations under a 2018 agreement, but the union suspended its action in September.

F. RULE OF LAW: 9 / 16
F1. Is there an independent judiciary? 2 / 4

The judiciary is formally independent and enjoys a relatively good reputation, but the president controls appointments to the Constitutional Council, the Court of Appeal, and the Council of State. Judges are prone to pressure from the government on matters involving high-level officials. The Higher Council of the Judiciary, which recommends judicial appointments to the executive branch, is headed by the president and minister of justice, which critics argue compromises its independence.

F2. Does due process prevail in civil and criminal matters? 2 / 4

The law guarantees fair public trials and defendants' rights, but arbitrary arrest and extended detention remains a concern. Though the government is obligated to supply attorneys to felony defendants who cannot afford them, this representation is inconsistent in practice. Lengthy pretrial detention remains a problem. The judicial system's reach does not consistently extend to rural areas, which more often rely on traditional methods of conflict resolution.

F3. Is there protection from the illegitimate use of physical force and freedom from war and insurgencies? 3 / 4

Individuals are generally protected from the illegitimate use of physical force. However, Senegalese prisons are overcrowded, and human rights groups have documented incidents of excessive force and cruel treatment by prison authorities. In an effort to limit the spread of COVID-19 through the prison system, President Sall pardoned over 2,000 prisoners—a fifth of the prison population—in April 2020.

A low-level separatist conflict in the Casamance region is ongoing, though attacks by the Movement of Democratic Forces of Casamance have lessened since a de facto cease-fire was reached in 2012.

F4. Do laws, policies, and practices guarantee equal treatment of various segments of the population? 2 / 4

The caste system is still prevalent among many of Senegal's ethnic groups. Individuals of lower castes are subject to discrimination in employment. Women face persistent inequities in employment, health care, and education.

Same-sex sexual activity remains criminalized. While these laws are rarely enforced, LGBT+ people risk violence, threats, and mob attacks, as well as discrimination in housing, employment, and health care.

G. PERSONAL AUTONOMY AND INDIVIDUAL RIGHTS: 11 / 16

G1. Do individuals enjoy freedom of movement, including the ability to change their place of residence, employment, or education? 3 / 4

Citizens generally enjoy freedom of movement and can change their residence, employment, and educational institution without serious restrictions, though the threat of land mines and rebel activity has hindered travel through parts of the Casamance region.

Movement was restricted under COVID-19-related measures, which were introduced in March 2020. A curfew was introduced that month but was loosened in May. Movement between regions besides Dakar was also restricted that month, though the government loosened restrictions in June after protests were held in several cities. The state of emergency expired in July, though some measures were reintroduced in August and remained in effect through year's end.

G2. Are individuals able to exercise the right to own property and establish private businesses without undue interference from state or nonstate actors? 3 / 4

The civil code facilitates ownership of private property, and property rights are generally respected. Commercial dispute-resolution processes can be drawn out. Property title and land-registration protocols are inconsistently applied, though the government has worked to ease property acquisition and registration. Husbands are legally regarded as heads of households. Traditional customs limit women's ability to purchase property, and local rules on inheritance make it difficult for women to become beneficiaries.

G3. Do individuals enjoy personal social freedoms, including choice of marriage partner and size of family, protection from domestic violence, and control over appearance? 3 / 4

Rates of female genital mutilation (FGM) have declined due in part to campaigns to discourage the practice, but it remains a problem. The government launched a plan to reduce early marriage in 2016, given that almost one in three Senegalese girls married before age 18.

Rape was considered a misdemeanor before President Sall signed into law a measure criminalizing rape in January 2020; this followed 2019 demonstrations which were prompted by the murder of a 23-year-old woman during an attempted rape.

The law allows abortion only to save a woman's life, and abortions for medical reasons are difficult to obtain in practice.

G4. Do individuals enjoy equality of opportunity and freedom from economic exploitation? 2 / 4

Child labor remains a problem, particularly in the informal economy, and laws restricting the practice are inadequately enforced. Forced begging by students at religious schools is common, and teachers suspected of abuse are rarely prosecuted.

According to the 2020 edition of the US State Department's *Trafficking in Persons Report*, the Senegalese government has engaged in ongoing efforts to build a trafficking database and provide support for vulnerable children facing homelessness. However, the report also noted that the authorities rarely investigate or prosecute traffickers who orchestrate forced begging, and convicted traffickers rarely receive sufficiently long prison sentences.

Serbia

Population: 7,000,000
Capital: Belgrade
Freedom Status: Partly Free
Electoral Democracy: Yes

Overview: Serbia is a parliamentary democracy with competitive multiparty elections, but in recent years the ruling Serbian Progressive Party (SNS) has steadily eroded political rights and civil liberties, putting pressure on independent media, the political opposition, and civil society organizations.

KEY DEVELOPMENTS IN 2020

- An electoral list headed by the SNS won the June parliamentary elections, securing a parliamentary supermajority. Opposition parties that held seats during the previous legislative term largely boycotted the contest, saying they were unfairly conducted; in February, weeks before the contest was originally scheduled, legislators lowered the voting threshold to win seats in an apparent effort to lessen the effectiveness of a boycott.
- Riot police responded forcefully to protests in Belgrade in July, with demonstrators rallying against the announcement of a COVID-19 lockdown, other government policies, and of President Aleksandar Vučić's conduct in office. Police were observed attacking protesters, bystanders, and journalists while seeking to disperse the demonstrations, which lasted several days.
- Officials responded to the COVID-19 pandemic opaquely, withholding information on pandemic-related deaths in social care institutions despite calls to release the information in July. Medical professionals who criticized the government's handling of the pandemic faced retaliation and dismissal, with signatories of an open letter published in July subsequently facing disciplinary proceedings.

POLITICAL RIGHTS: 22 / 40 (−1)
A. ELECTORAL PROCESS: 7 / 12 (−1)

A1. Was the current head of government or other chief national authority elected through free and fair elections? 3 / 4

The president is directly elected for up to two five-year terms. In 2017, then prime minister Aleksandar Vučić won the election with 55 percent of the vote in a field of 11 candidates. The campaign was characterized by media bias and allegations of misuse of public resources and vote buying. Vučić remained prime minister throughout that election period, blurring the line between official and electoral activities.

The prime minister is elected by the parliament. Vučić named Ana Brnabić, then the local government minister, to succeed him as prime minister following the 2017 presidential election. In October 2020, Brnabić was again confirmed to the post, after the SNS retained power in the June parliamentary elections.

A2. Were the current national legislative representatives elected through free and fair elections? 2 / 4

The National Assembly is a unicameral, 250-seat legislature whose deputies are elected to four-year terms under a system of proportional representation with a single nationwide constituency. Parliamentary elections were held in Serbia, together with elections in the Autonomous Province of Vojvodina and several municipalities, in June 2020. Initially scheduled for April, they were postponed by a state of emergency put in place due to the COVID-19 pandemic.

The Aleksandar Vučić–For Our Children electoral list, led by the SNS, won 60.7 percent of the vote and 188 seats. The allied Socialist Party and its electoral-list partner, United Serbia, won a combined 32, while the Serbian Patriotic Alliance won 11. Ethnic minority lists, which did not have to surpass the parliamentary threshold to attain representation, won the remaining seats.

Opposition groups that held seats in the previous parliament largely boycotted the June poll, saying the electoral environment was neither free nor fair. Several weeks before the poll was originally scheduled, the parliament reduced the voting threshold to win seats from five percent to three, in what was considered an effort to reduce the effectiveness of the opposition boycott. Turnout was 48.9 percent, the lowest since the introduction of multiparty elections in 1990.

Observers reported numerous irregularities during the campaign and on election day. The Organization for Security and Co-operation in Europe's (OSCE) Office for Democratic Institutions and Human Rights (ODIHR) noted that President Vučić's "continued engagement" as head of state and SNS leader "afforded him unparalleled public exposure, without clear differentiation of his roles." Progovernment parties benefited from a preponderance of television coverage, while voters—especially public-sector workers—were pressured to support the government, according to citizen observers. Parallel voter lists were used to track voters during the poll, while vote buying and the casting of multiple ballots voters were also reported.

A3. Are the electoral laws and framework fair, and are they implemented impartially by the relevant election management bodies? 2 / 4 (−1)

Electoral laws largely correspond to international standards, but aspects of the electoral process are poorly regulated, and implementation of existing rules is flawed in some respects. In its report on the June 2020 elections, ODIHR noted long-running concerns over electoral administration, dispute resolution, and the handling of electoral violations.

Electoral management is often nontransparent; laws, mechanisms, and regulations regarding voter-roll management, campaign finance, compliance with related financial restrictions, candidates' use of their own funds, and the public hearing of electoral challenges are either opaque or lacking.

In February 2020, the parliament enacted electoral amendments that reduced the threshold to win seats from five percent to three and introduced a 40 percent gender quota for party lists. The parliament's decision to lower the threshold weeks before the parliamentary elections were originally scheduled was regarded as an attempt to weaken an opposition boycott.

Score Change: The score declined from 3 to 2 because the electoral framework was amended prior to a regularly scheduled parliamentary election in an attempt to thwart an opposition boycott.

B. POLITICAL PLURALISM AND PARTICIPATION: 10 / 16

B1. Do the people have the right to organize in different political parties or other competitive political groupings of their choice, and is the system free of undue obstacles to the rise and fall of these competing parties or groupings? 3 / 4

Political parties may be established freely and can typically operate without encountering formal restrictions. However, campaign finance regulations are weakly enforced and place no overall cap on the private funds raised and spent by parties and candidates. Following the 2017 presidential election, the OSCE reported that the Anti-Corruption Agency (ACA) had decreased the resources dedicated to proactively monitoring campaign funds and did not thoroughly investigate dubious donations. The Balkan Investigative Reporting Network found that the SNS had orchestrated the use of thousands of proxy donors to bypass legal limits on individual donations and disguise the true source of funding.

B2. Is there a realistic opportunity for the opposition to increase its support or gain power through elections? 2 / 4

There have been peaceful transfers of power between rival parties over the past two decades, and the political system remains competitive. However, the SNS has used various tactics to unfairly reduce the opposition's electoral prospects. These include manipulating the timing of snap elections, exerting pressure on independent state institutions, and mobilizing public resources to support its campaigns.

The SNS has expanded its influence over the media through both state-owned enterprises and an array of private outlets that are dependent on government funding, and has harnessed this influence to strengthen its political position and discredit its rivals, further reducing opposition parties' competitiveness. Opposition figures have also faced escalating harassment and violence in recent years.

B3. Are the people's political choices free from domination by forces that are external to the political sphere, or by political forces that employ extrapolitical means? 2 / 4

Voters enjoy a significant degree of freedom to make political decisions without undue interference, though the ruling party and allied private businesses allegedly use patronage networks to influence political outcomes.

Various incentives have also been employed in recent years to convince hundreds of local elected officials to form alliances with the SNS or change their party affiliation after elections. SNS electoral campaigns have allegedly benefited from the misuse of public resources, such as use of public buses to transport loyalists to rallies. Local observers reported that workers at state-owned enterprises were pressured to support the ruling SNS during the June 2020 elections. SNS operatives have also been known to intimidate voters directly, by appearing at their homes and pressuring them to support the party.

Separately, Russia has been accused of attempting to influence Serbian politics through its state-owned media and an array of small pro-Russian parties, media outlets, and civil society groups in Serbia.

B4. Do various segments of the population (including ethnic, racial, religious, gender, LGBT+, and other relevant groups) have full political rights and electoral opportunities? 3 / 4

The country's electoral threshold for parliamentary representation does not apply to parties representing ethnic minorities. Groups centered on the ethnic Albanian, Bosniak, and Hungarian communities won 19 parliamentary seats in the June 2020 elections. Nevertheless, ethnic minorities have a relatively muted voice in Serbian politics in practice.

Women enjoy equal political rights and benefit from a party-list gender quota. Women won 38.8 percent of parliamentary seats in the June 2020 elections. Ana Brnabić became Serbia's first woman and first gay prime minister in 2017, but critics argued that her appointment was a superficial bid to showcase claims of openness toward the LGBT+ community without systematic engagement on issues important to LGBT+ people.

C. FUNCTIONING OF GOVERNMENT: 5 / 12

C1. Do the freely elected head of government and national legislative representatives determine the policies of the government? 2 / 4

Vučić's move to the presidency in 2017 raised new concerns about the personalization of governance and politicization of state institutions. Vučić has remained the dominant figure in government despite the presidency's limited executive powers under the constitution, creating a de facto presidential system. In October 2020, before a new government was finalized, Vučić announced that early parliamentary elections would be held in April 2022.

Moreover, the executive largely controls the legislative process, and opposition lawmakers are sidelined through the disproportionate use of disciplinary measures, frequent use of accelerated legislative procedures, and late changes to the legislative agenda, among other tactics.

C2. Are safeguards against official corruption strong and effective? 1 / 4

Although the number of arrests and prosecutions for corruption has risen in recent years, high-profile convictions are very rare. Critics have credibly accused Vučić and the SNS government of having ties to organized crime, and cronyism—in the form of jobs provided to allies of the president and the ruling party—is reportedly common. The responsibility for prosecuting corruption cases has been passed among different public prosecutors, who typically fault the police for supplying insufficient evidence in cases against government ministers. The work of the ACA is also undermined in part by the ambiguous division of responsibilities among other entities tasked with combating corruption.

Notable cases that came to light in recent years without being resolved include those of Nenad Popović, a minister without portfolio who was implicated in a questionable privatization that caused an electrical transformer manufacturer to declare bankruptcy; Finance Minister Siniša Mali, whom anticorruption agencies have investigated for suspected money laundering; and Health Minister Zlatibor Lončar, who allegedly has links to an organized crime group.

Senior officials' close relatives and associates have also faced corruption allegations. For example, a series of reports and leaked documents since 2018 tied the father of then interior minister—now Defense Minister—Nebojša Stefanović to an arms-trading scheme and other malfeasance. Aleksandar Obradović, a whistleblower who implicated Stefanović's father in the purchase of arms from the state at reduced rates, was arrested in September

2019, potentially deterring others with knowledge of corruption from coming forward. Obradović remained under investigation, and suspended from his place of work, as recently as September 2020.

C3. Does the government operate with openness and transparency? 2 / 4

The government has received sustained criticism for a lack of transparency in large-scale infrastructure projects and for secrecy surrounding public tenders. For example, details about the state-funded Belgrade Waterfront project, which includes the construction of hotels and luxury apartments and has been beset by controversy since its announcement in 2012, have not been made available to the public. Serbian defense spending is also opaque. In August 2020, the International Monetary Fund (IMF) warned that government aid to the publicly owned Air Serbia was not sufficiently transparent in a regular report on IMF activity in the country.

Legislators do not have adequate opportunities to ask questions about government activities and legislation, and the vast majority of parliamentary questions go unanswered by the government.

Public officials are subject to asset disclosure rules overseen by the ACA, but penalties for violations are uncommon. While a 2004 freedom of information law empowers citizens and journalists to obtain information of public importance, authorities frequently obstruct requests in practice.

The government did release data on the spread of COVID-19, but did initially disclose deaths in social care institutions; it pledged to release those figures in late July 2020 after disability rights groups called for more transparency, but reportedly did not do so by year's end.

CIVIL LIBERTIES: 42 / 60 (−1)

D. FREEDOM OF EXPRESSION AND BELIEF: 12 / 16

D1. Are there free and independent media? 2 / 4

Despite a constitution that guarantees freedom of the press and a penal code that does not treat libel as a criminal offense, media freedom is undermined by the threat of lawsuits or criminal charges against journalists for other offenses, lack of transparency in media ownership, editorial pressure from politicians and politically connected media owners, direct pressure and threats against journalists, and high rates of self-censorship. The Regulatory Body for Electronic Media has been criticized for a lack of independence. Journalists have faced physical attacks, smear campaigns, punitive tax inspections, and other forms of pressure.

The state and ruling party exercise influence over private media in part through advertising contracts and other indirect subsidies. Many private outlets are owned by SNS supporters. Some privately owned national broadcasters and popular tabloids regularly participate in smear campaigns against the political opposition and other perceived government opponents. The incumbent political parties generally receive the majority of media coverage from public broadcasters.

Several acts of violence were committed against journalists in 2020. The Independent Journalists' Association of Serbia counted 28 physical assaults and 33 incidents of intimidation directed at journalists during the first eight months of the year. In July, at least ten journalists who observed COVID-19-related protests in Belgrade were attacked by demonstrators and police officers.

D2. Are individuals free to practice and express their religious faith or nonbelief in public and private? 4 / 4

The constitution guarantees freedom of religion, which is generally respected in practice.

D3. Is there academic freedom, and is the educational system free from extensive political indoctrination? 3 / 4

Academic freedom has largely been upheld, though recent practice and legal changes have raised concerns about political influence. The Law on Higher Education, adopted by the National Assembly in 2017, increased the presence of state-appointed members on the National Council for Higher Education and a national accreditation body; another education law, also adopted in 2017, gave the education minister centralized control over the appointment of school principals.

Over the last several years, senior state officials have been accused of plagiarizing their doctoral theses, stirring debate within academia and casting doubt on the autonomy of university administrative bodies. The officials implicated include Defense Minister Stefanović, Finance Minister Mali, and National Bank Governor Jorgovanka Tabaković. The plagiarism controversies triggered a smear campaign against academics who expressed criticism of the government and the accused officials.

D4. Are individuals free to express their personal views on political or other sensitive topics without fear of surveillance or retribution? 3 / 4

Private discussion is generally free and vibrant, but a pattern of retribution against high-profile critics of the government has contributed to an increasingly hostile environment for free expression and open debate. Perceived government opponents, including journalists, university professors, civil society leaders, celebrities, and ordinary citizens, have faced smear campaigns in progovernment media outlets, criminal investigations, and other retaliatory measures in recent years. In some cases, the government's highest-ranking officials took part in discrediting nonpolitical figures based on their public criticism of government policies.

E. ASSOCIATIONAL AND ORGANIZATIONAL RIGHTS: 9 / 12 (−1)

E1. Is there freedom of assembly? 3 / 4 (−1)

Citizens are generally able to exercise freedom of assembly, though over 30 ongoing prosecutions were launched against activists associated with the protest movement Ne davimo Beograd (Don't Drown Belgrade), which had organized demonstrations against the contentious development project on Belgrade's waterfront, in the recent past.

After the Vučić administration instituted a COVID-19-related lockdown in Belgrade in July 2020, thousands of demonstrators rallied against the announcement, the government's overall pandemic response, and Vučić's conduct as president. Riot police in Belgrade responded forcefully, targeting participants, bystanders, and journalists with physical attacks, chases, and tear gas. Protests, which were also held in several other cities, continued for several days after the government reversed its decision to initiate the lockdown.

Score Change: The score declined from 4 to 3 because protests held in July were met with excessive force by riot police, who attacked protesters, bystanders, and journalists.

E2. Is there freedom for nongovernmental organizations, particularly those that are engaged in human rights- and governance-related work? 3 / 4

Foreign and domestic nongovernmental organizations generally operate freely, but those that take openly critical stances toward the government or address sensitive or controversial topics have faced threats and harassment in recent years.

E3. Is there freedom for trade unions and similar professional or labor organizations? 3 / 4

Workers may legally join unions, engage in collective bargaining, and strike, but the International Trade Union Confederation has reported that organizing efforts and strikes are often restricted in practice, with employers allegedly retaliating against workers and union activists.

F. RULE OF LAW: 9 / 16

F1. Is there an independent judiciary? 2 / 4

The independence of the judiciary is compromised by political influence over judicial appointments, and many judges have reported facing external pressure regarding their rulings. Politicians regularly comment on judicial matters, including by discussing ongoing cases or investigations with the media.

F2. Does due process prevail in civil and criminal matters? 2 / 4

Due process guarantees are upheld in some cases, but corruption, lack of capacity, and political influence often undermine these protections. Among other problems, rules on the random assignment of cases to judges and prosecutors are not consistently observed, and mechanisms for obtaining restitution in civil matters are ineffective. High-profile, politically sensitive cases are especially vulnerable to interference.

In July 2020, an appeals court overturned the convictions of four security officials for the 1999 killing of journalist Slavko Ćuruvija, after the court found that the 2019 verdicts violated criminal procedure. A new trial was pending at year's end.

F3. Is there protection from the illegitimate use of physical force and freedom from war and insurgencies? 3 / 4

The population is generally free from major threats to physical security, though some prison facilities suffer from overcrowding, abuse, and inadequate health care. Radical right-wing organizations and violent sports fans who target ethnic minorities and other perceived enemies also remain a concern.

F4. Do laws, policies, and practices guarantee equal treatment of various segments of the population? 2 / 4

Legal safeguards for socially vulnerable groups are poorly enforced. For example, women are legally entitled to equal pay for equal work, but this rule is not widely respected. The Romany minority is especially disadvantaged by discrimination in employment, housing, and education. LGBT+ people continue to face hate speech, threats, and even physical violence, and perpetrators are rarely punished despite laws addressing hate crimes and discrimination. The government has made some gestures of support for the rights of LGBT+ people, for example by sending representatives to pride events and ensuring adequate police protection for parades.

Individuals living with disabilities are among those who live in social care institutions, and have faced protracted periods of isolation as the COVID-19 pandemic progressed. In July 2020, disability rights groups signed a letter calling on the government to report on COVID-19 deaths in social-care settings and warned that the treatment of residents with disabilities violated the Convention on the Rights of Persons with Disabilities, to which Serbia is a signatory.

G. PERSONAL AUTONOMY AND INDIVIDUAL RIGHTS: 12 / 16

G1. Do individuals enjoy freedom of movement, including the ability to change their place of residence, employment, or education? 4 / 4

There are no formal restrictions on freedom of movement. Serbians are free to change their place of employment and education and have the right to travel.

G2. Are individuals able to exercise the right to own property and establish private businesses without undue interference from state or nonstate actors? 3 / 4

In general, property rights are respected, but adjudication of disputes is slow, and problems such as illegal construction and fraud persist. An estimated two million buildings in Serbia are not registered. Romany residents are often subject to forced evictions, and those evicted are generally not offered alternative housing or access to legal remedies to challenge eviction notices.

G3. Do individuals enjoy personal social freedoms, including choice of marriage partner and size of family, protection from domestic violence, and control over appearance? 3 / 4

Personal social freedoms are generally respected, and men and women have equal legal rights on personal status matters like marriage and divorce. A new law aimed at preventing domestic violence took effect in 2017, but such violence remains a problem; Serbia has one of the highest rates of domestic violence in Europe.

G4. Do individuals enjoy equality of opportunity and freedom from economic exploitation? 2 / 4

Residents generally have access to economic opportunity, but factors such as weak macroeconomic growth and a relatively high rate of unemployment contribute to labor exploitation in some industries. Several reports in recent years have described worsening conditions in factories, particularly those that produce shoes and garments, including low wages, unpaid overtime, and hazardous work environments. Legal protections designed to prevent such abuses are not well enforced. According to the Ministry of Labor, Employment, Veterans Affairs, and Social Affairs, 53 workers died in workplace accidents in 2018, and a similar number of occupational fatalities was reported for 2019.

Seychelles

Population: 100,000
Capital: Victoria
Freedom Status: Free
Electoral Democracy: Yes

Status Change: Seychelles's status improved from Partly Free to Free because a strengthened electoral framework contributed to a more open and competitive presidential election, resulting in the country's first transfer of power to an opposition party.

Overview: Seychelles has seen an increase in political pluralism in recent years, with an opposition coalition winning a parliamentary majority in 2016 and an opposition presidential candidate winning the post in 2020. However, government corruption remains a problem, as does lengthy pretrial detention. Migrant workers remain vulnerable to abuse.

KEY DEVELOPMENTS IN 2020

- Wavel Ramkalawan of the Seychelles Democratic Alliance (LDS) defeated incumbent president Danny Faure in October, becoming the first opposition candidate to win that contest in Seychellois history. The LDS also retained a majority in concurrent National Assembly elections. The contests were considered free and fair, though observers received some reports alleging misuse of state resources.

- Seychelles detected its first COVID-19 case in March, but cases remained low until late December, when transmission increased. Authorities reported 226 cases and no deaths to the World Health Organization (WHO) by year's end.

POLITICAL RIGHTS: 34 / 40 (+5)

A. ELECTORAL PROCESS: 12 / 12 (+2)

A1. Was the current head of government or other chief national authority elected through free and fair elections? 4 / 4 (+1)

The president is chief of state and head of government; the winning candidate is directly elected for up to two five-year terms. The president nominates cabinet ministers and a vice president, all of whom require approval from the National Assembly.

Then vice president Danny Faure became president when James Michel of the People's Party (PL) resigned as president in 2016. Michel had been narrowly reelected in 2015 in a contest marred by vote-buying allegations. In late 2019, Faure was endorsed by the PL, renamed United Seychelles (US), to contest the October 2020 presidential election. Faure lost to Seychelles Democratic Alliance (LDS) candidate Ramkalawan, who received 54.9 percent of the vote. The election marked the first opposition victory in a presidential contest in Seychellois history.

Score Change: The score improved from 3 to 4 because the October presidential election was considered free and fair and there was no repetition of the problems associated with the 2015 election.

A2. Were the current national legislative representatives elected through free and fair elections? 4 / 4

Members of the unicameral National Assembly are directly elected in 26 constituencies, while up to 9 additional seats are assigned by parties according to a proportional calculation of the vote.

The LDS won 25 seats in the October 2020 elections, which were held concurrently with the presidential contest. US won the remaining 10. Observers called the elections free and fair, though they did receive reports alleging misuse of state resources.

A3. Are the electoral laws and framework fair, and are they implemented impartially by the relevant election management bodies? 4 / 4 (+1)

The Electoral Commission has faced criticism from opposition parties and others for enforcing its mandates inconsistently. The 2016 African Union election monitoring mission called for more transparency, better voter-roll scrutiny, and an improved process to inform the public about voter registration. In December 2018, then president Faure approved an amendment to the Elections Act establishing a permanent chief electoral officer. The amendment was also intended to alleviate concerns about the efficiency of the previous system, in which a chief electoral officer was appointed a few months before an election.

Amendments to the electoral law that were proposed by the Electoral Commission were approved in August 2020. The amended legislation includes a clearer definition of what is considered a spoiled ballot, among other provisions.

Score Change: The score improved from 3 to 4 due to electoral reforms enacted over several years, including the parliament's adoption of electoral-law amendments in August.

B. POLITICAL PLURALISM AND PARTICIPATION: 13 / 16 (+2)

B1. Do the people have the right to organize in different political parties or other competitive political groupings of their choice, and is the system free of undue obstacles to the rise and fall of these competing parties or groupings? 4 / 4 (+1)

There are no restrictions on the right to organize political parties or other competitive political groupings. However, during the 2015 presidential election, several opposition parties claimed the government was engaged in systematic harassment and intimidation of candidates.

Political party One Seychelles, which was founded in 2019, fielded presidential and legislative candidates in the October 2020 elections.

Score Change: The score improved from 3 to 4 because political parties operated in a freer environment in 2020 than during past election periods, and a new party was able to field presidential and legislative candidates without incident.

B2. Is there a realistic opportunity for the opposition to increase its support or gain power through elections? 4 / 4 (+1)

The LDS, an alliance of opposition parties, became the first political group to defeat the PL and gain a legislative majority in 2016, reflecting increasing political pluralism in Seychelles. Ramkalawan became the first non-US candidate to win a presidential election in October 2020.

Score Change: The score improved from 3 to 4 after an opposition candidate won the 2020 presidential election, marking Seychelles's first transfer of executive power to an opposition party.

B3. Are the people's political choices free from domination by forces that are external to the political sphere, or by political forces that employ extrapolitical means? 3 / 4

Political choices are generally free from domination by powerful groups that are not democratically accountable. However, there have been reports of vote buying and voter intimidation by political parties.

B4. Do various segments of the population (including ethnic, racial, religious, gender, LGBT+, and other relevant groups) have full political rights and electoral opportunities? 2 / 4

The constitution mandates equal suffrage for adult citizens. Early voting procedures are designed to encourage the participation of some groups, including pregnant women, the elderly, and those with disabilities.

There are still no mechanisms to allow citizens living abroad to vote. Few women hold senior political office because of factors including longstanding traditional beliefs about the role of women and a lack of commitment on the part of political parties to nominate women for office. US is the only party that typically includes high numbers of women among its candidates. Political life is dominated by people of European and South Asian origin.

C. FUNCTIONING OF GOVERNMENT: 9 / 12 (+1)

C1. Do the freely elected head of government and national legislative representatives determine the policies of the government? 4 / 4 (+1)

The head of government and national legislative representatives are generally able to determine the policies of the government, though widespread corruption can influence policymaking. Executive and legislative officials were elected under freer and fairer circumstances in 2020, bolstering the democratic legitimacy of their decisions.

Score Change: The score improved from 3 to 4 because the national representatives in place at year's end were elected through a freer and fairer process, enhancing the democratic legitimacy of their policy decisions.

C2. Are safeguards against official corruption strong and effective? 3 / 4

Concerns about government corruption persist, but there has been significant improvement. In 2016, the National Assembly passed an anticorruption law that established the country's first independent Anti-Corruption Commission (ACC) and strengthened Seychelles's legal anticorruption framework. An ACC official himself received an eight-year sentence for extortion, bribery, and tampering with an investigation in 2018.

In 2019, the National Assembly amended the anticorruption law to increase the number of ACC commissioners, clarify its strength, explicitly give it investigative powers, and enhance its law enforcement provisions.

C3. Does the government operate with openness and transparency? 2 / 4

There are laws allowing public access to government information, but compliance is inconsistent. Some government officials are required to declare assets, but they do not always comply. Declarations are not made public unless a legal challenge forces their release. The Access to Information Act of 2018 seeks to increase openness and transparency of government. Article 54 of the legislation created an Information Commission, established in late 2019, with the responsibility to provide government information and resources to citizens for particular disclosures. It has the power to impose fines when citizens are not provided information in a given time frame.

Concerns about corruption often focus on a lack of transparency in the privatization and allocation of government-owned land, as well as in Seychelles's facilitation of international finance.

CIVIL LIBERTIES: 43 / 60
D. FREEDOM OF EXPRESSION AND BELIEF: 12 / 16
D1. Are there free and independent media? 2 / 4

The Seychelles Media Commission Act of 2010 establishes relatively strict guidelines for journalists. Several newspapers exist besides the state-owned daily, the *Seychelles Nation.* A publicly owned broadcaster provides television and radio programming alongside a private television station and two private radio stations. The law prohibits political parties and religious organizations from operating public radio broadcasts.

Media workers practice a degree of self-censorship to protect their advertising earnings. Newspaper reporting is generally politicized. Although Seychelles has strict defamation laws, they have not been used for years. As the government seeks to maintain the country's image as ideal for tourism, many outlets will temper their commentary on sensitive national issues.

D2. Are individuals free to practice and express their religious faith or nonbelief in public and private? 4 / 4

Religious freedom is generally respected. The government grants larger religious groups programming time on state radio, subject in most cases to advance review and approval. Smaller religious groups do not have access to dedicated broadcast time. Non-Catholic students in public schools providing Catholic instruction have no access to alternative activities during those classes.

D3. Is there academic freedom, and is the educational system free from extensive political indoctrination? 3 / 4

The charter of the University of Seychelles enshrines academic freedom, while the constitution indirectly references academic freedom. A 2016 study from the International Labour Organization (ILO) and the United Nations Education, Scientific, and Cultural Organization (UNESCO) recognized Seychelles as having high compliance in institutional autonomy, tenure, individual rights, and democratic structure in the country's two universities.

In the past, some activists have claimed that educators have had to demonstrate at least nominal loyalty to the PL, which previously controlled the executive and legislative branches, to reach senior bureaucratic positions.

D4. Are individuals free to express their personal views on political or other sensitive topics without fear of surveillance or retribution? 3 / 4

As the government seeks to protect the tourism sector, many sensitive subjects are considered off limits. Individuals who criticize the government publicly or privately sometimes suffer reprisals, such as harassment by police or the loss of jobs or contracts.

E. ASSOCIATIONAL AND ORGANIZATIONAL RIGHTS: 9 / 12
E1. Is there freedom of assembly? 3 / 4

The government passed a revised law in 2015 on public assembly, which several observers credited with permitting a more open and free political environment. However, the law still contains some restrictive provisions, including the need to give five days' notice to the police for assemblies. It also empowers the head of police to disperse public meetings on grounds of preserving public health, morality, and safety, and sets conditions on the timing and location of large gatherings. In 2019, the government established a "Speaker's Corner" in Victoria, where individuals are allowed to make public comments at will.

E2. Is there freedom for nongovernmental organizations, particularly those that are engaged in human rights- and governance-related work? 3 / 4

Human rights groups and other nongovernmental organizations operate without restriction. However, some groups lack the resources necessary to operate and advocate effectively.

E3. Is there freedom for trade unions and similar professional or labor organizations? 3 / 4

Unions are permitted, but only about 15 percent of the workforce is unionized, and collective bargaining is relatively rare. Workers have the right to strike, but only if all other arbitration procedures have been exhausted.

F. RULE OF LAW: 11 / 16
F1. Is there an independent judiciary? 2 / 4

Judges sometimes face interference in cases involving major commercial or political interests. Due to the low number of legal professionals in Seychelles, the country relies on expatriate judges to serve fixed-term contracts on the Supreme Court. The government controls the negotiations and renewal of expatriate contracts, potentially allowing officials to compromise the impartiality of the non-Seychellois magistrates. The judiciary also lacks budgetary independence from the executive and can be subject to external influence. The Supreme Court remains a target of political threats and intimidation.

F2. Does due process prevail in civil and criminal matters? 3 / 4

While constitutional rights to due process are generally respected, prolonged pretrial detention is common. The courts introduced new systems in 2016 intended to expedite the processing of cases, but their effect has been limited.

F3. Is there protection from the illegitimate use of physical force and freedom from war and insurgencies? 3 / 4

Security forces have occasionally been accused of using excessive force, and impunity for such offenses remains a problem. Police corruption continues, particularly the solicitation of bribes. Prisons remain overcrowded.

F4. Do laws, policies, and practices guarantee equal treatment of various segments of the population? 3 / 4

Same-sex sexual activity was decriminalized in 2016, though societal discrimination against LGBT+ activists remains a problem. Prejudice against foreign workers has been reported.

G. PERSONAL AUTONOMY AND INDIVIDUAL RIGHTS: 11 / 16

G1. Do individuals enjoy freedom of movement, including the ability to change their place of residence, employment, or education? 3 / 4

The government does not restrict domestic travel but may deny passports for arbitrary reasons based on "national interest."

G2. Are individuals able to exercise the right to own property and establish private businesses without undue interference from state or nonstate actors? 3 / 4

Individuals may generally exercise the right to own property and establish private business without undue interference from state or nonstate actors. An underdeveloped legal framework can hamper business activities, as can corruption.

G3. Do individuals enjoy personal social freedoms, including choice of marriage partner and size of family, protection from domestic violence, and control over appearance? 2 / 4

Inheritance laws do not discriminate against women, and the government does not impose explicit restrictions on personal social freedoms. However, domestic violence against women remains a problem.

G4. Do individuals enjoy equality of opportunity and freedom from economic exploitation? 3 / 4

Economic life is dominated by people of European and South Asian origin. The government has made minimal progress in preventing or prosecuting instances of human trafficking and labor exploitation. Worker rights in the Seychelles International Trade Zone are different from the rest of the islands, and migrant laborers are vulnerable to abuse there. There were some reports of employers seizing migrant workers' passports upon arrival, a practice that is not currently illegal under Seychellois law.

Bangladeshi workers have been victims of human-trafficking abuses such as seizure of travel documents, unpaid work, and extreme labor exploitation. In 2019, the Seychellois and Bangladeshi governments signed a labor agreement to regulate the recruitment of Bangladeshi workers. Under its terms, designated organizations will assess employment contracts and the language skills of prospective workers.

In the 2020 edition of its *Trafficking in Persons Report*, the US State Department noted that government efforts to address sex-related trafficking were insufficient, and procedures for identifying trafficking survivors went unimplemented.

Sierra Leone

Population: 8,000,000
Capital: Freetown
Freedom Status: Partly Free
Electoral Democracy: Yes

Overview: Sierra Leone has held regular multiparty elections since the end of its civil war in 2002. However, opposition parties have faced police violence and restrictions on assembly. Civic groups are constrained by onerous regulations and government corruption remains pervasive. Other long-standing concerns include gender-based violence (GBV) and female genital mutilation (FGM).

KEY DEVELOPMENTS IN 2020

- Former president Ernest Bai Koroma was questioned by investigators in November after an inquiry documented widespread corruption during his tenure. Koroma and as many as 130 other individuals were barred from leaving the country after a report containing the Commissions of Inquiry's (COI) findings was published in September.
- While Sierra Leoneans faced a COVID-19-related ban on large public assemblies for much of the year, notable protests, including June demonstrations prompted by the rape and murder of a child, took place. The authorities reported 2,560 cases and 76 deaths to the World Health Organization (WHO) at year's end.

POLITICAL RIGHTS: 28 / 40

A. ELECTORAL PROCESS: 10 / 12

A1. Was the current head of government or other chief national authority elected through free and fair elections? 3 / 4

The president is elected by popular vote for up to two five-year terms. In the March 2018 presidential election, Julius Maada Bio of the Sierra Leone People's Party (SLPP) defeated Samura Kamara of the incumbent All People's Congress (APC) and succeeded term-limited predecessor Ernest Bai Koroma. Bio won nearly 52 percent of the vote in the second round. Allegations of violence and voter intimidation marred the campaign period. Nevertheless, international observers determined that the election was credible, praising the National Election Commission (NEC) for effectively fulfilling its duties despite budget constraints, logistical challenges, and pressure from the government, which disbursed election funds late and occasionally threatened to withhold resources.

A2. Were the current national legislative representatives elected through free and fair elections? 3 / 4

In the unicameral Parliament, 132 members are chosen by popular vote, and 14 seats are reserved for indirectly elected paramount chiefs. Parliamentary elections are held every five years, concurrently with presidential elections. During the 2018 parliamentary elections, the APC retained its majority, winning 68 seats, while the SLPP increased its share to 49 seats. The Coalition for Change won 8 seats, the National Grand Coalition (NGC) took 4, and independents captured the remaining 3. Despite some procedural errors, international observers considered the parliamentary elections credible.

In March 2019, APC members of Parliament (MPs) staged a walkout over the SLPP's efforts to remove several APC lawmakers. That May, the High Court ruled in favor of an SLPP petition alleging APC electoral fraud in 2018, resulting in the removal of 10 MPs and a securing a parliamentary majority for the SLPP. The APC filed a petition for the Supreme Court to hear the case in October 2020.

A3. Are the electoral laws and framework fair, and are they implemented impartially by the relevant election management bodies? 4 / 4

The electoral laws and framework are generally deemed to be fair. The NEC, which administers elections, works impartially and independently. However, restrictions that limit who can run for office, such as a requirement that candidates be citizens by birth, have drawn criticism from international observers.

During the 2018 campaign period, the major political parties interpreted the citizenship provision to exclude people with dual citizenship from standing for office. Analysts believe this interpretation was meant to push NGC presidential candidate Kandeh Kolleh Yumkella out of the race. Many other candidates reportedly failed to secure party nominations due to their dual citizenship.

B. POLITICAL PLURALISM AND PARTICIPATION: 11 / 16

B1. Do the people have the right to organize in different political parties or other competitive political groupings of their choice, and is the system free of undue obstacles to the rise and fall of these competing parties or groupings? 2 / 4

Although people have the right to organize in different political parties, opposition parties and leaders have faced intimidation and harassment from the current SLPP government and the APC when it held the presidency.

The APC and SLPP are the country's main political parties, but 17 parties officially registered for the 2018 elections. In 2017, several high-profile figures left the SLPP to form the NGC. While candidate nomination fees are subsidized, the costs of running for office and a rule requiring public-sector personnel to resign 12 months ahead of an election serve as barriers to entry for many candidates, giving an advantage to larger parties and those with greater resources.

B2. Is there a realistic opportunity for the opposition to increase its support or gain power through elections? 3 / 4

The SLPP's presidential victory in 2018, despite the APC's continued use of public resources during the campaign, marked the second peaceful transfer of power between rival parties since the end of the civil war in 2002. The APC had won the previous two presidential elections in 2007 and 2012.

B3. Are the people's political choices free from domination by forces that are external to the political sphere, or by political forces that employ extrapolitical means? 3 / 4

Sierra Leoneans generally enjoy freedom in their political choices, although traditional chiefs and religious leaders exercise influence on voters. Local elites from both major parties often control the selection of candidates for Parliament.

B4. Do various segments of the population (including ethnic, racial, religious, gender, LGBT+, and other relevant groups) have full political rights and electoral opportunities? 3 / 4

Ethnic and religious minorities typically enjoy full political rights and electoral opportunities. Societal impediments to women's political participation remain a challenge, with only 18 of 146 Parliament seats held by women in 2020.

Sierra Leoneans who are not of African descent do not have birthright citizenship and must be naturalized to be able to vote; naturalized citizens cannot run for elected office.

The SLPP has accused the APC of engaging in ethnic discrimination when appointing employees to government agencies.

C. FUNCTIONING OF GOVERNMENT: 7 / 12

C1. Do the freely elected head of government and national legislative representatives determine the policies of the government? 3 / 4

The elected president and Parliament generally determine the government policy, but most power lies within the executive.

China has become the largest investor in Sierra Leone, providing billions of dollars in aid and infrastructure financing since 2013. Beijing cultivated a close relationship with the Koroma administration, which led civil society leaders to claim that China had an undue influence on policymaking. In 2018, the SLPP government cancelled a controversial deal with China to build a new airport near Freetown, though other bilateral projects were ongoing as of 2020.

C2. Are safeguards against official corruption strong and effective? 1 / 4

Corruption remains a pervasive problem at every level of government. Although there has been a decrease in perceived corruption among political institutions, rates of bribery remain high among ordinary citizens seeking basic services.

The Bio administration has promised to tackle systemic corruption and hold perpetrators from the previous government accountable. Commissions of Inquiry (CoI) into Koroma-era corruption presented significant evidence of malfeasance to President Bio in March 2020. A report containing their findings was published in September, with Koroma and as many as 130 other individuals subsequently facing travel bans. Investigators questioned Koroma twice in November, and investigations based on the report's findings were ongoing at year's end.

In March 2020, Labor Minister Alpha Osman Timbo and four other individuals were accused of misappropriating a donation of rice from the Chinese government in 2019, while Timbo was education minister. The High Court discharged the case against Timbo and the other defendants in July, after the ACC declined to offer evidence.

C3. Does the government operate with openness and transparency? 3 / 4

Sierra Leone has an uneven record on transparency. The Right to Access Information Commission was created in 2013 to facilitate transparency and openness in government, but its effectiveness has been hampered by lack of funding and limited public outreach.

The government continues to review and make public all mining and lease agreements, retaining its Extractive Industries Transparency Initiative (EITI) compliance designation. Its 2019 compliance report assessed it as having made meaningful but not satisfactory progress on all requirements. EITI will next validate the government's compliance in October 2021.

CIVIL LIBERTIES: 37 / 60

D. FREEDOM OF EXPRESSION AND BELIEF: 12 / 16

D1. Are there free and independent media? 2 / 4

Numerous independent newspapers circulate freely, and there are dozens of public and private radio and television outlets. However, public officials have previously employed libel and sedition laws to target journalists, particularly those reporting on elections and high-level corruption. In July 2020, Parliament voted to repeal Part V of the 1965 Public Order Act, which criminalized libel and sedition, and introduced the Independent Media Commission Act, which was criticized by some observers who warned that it would no longer allow the registration of newspapers as sole proprietorships.

In April 2020, soldiers in the city of Kenema physically attacked *Standard Times* reporter Fayia Amara Fayia after he photographed a COVID-19 quarantine facility. Fayia was later arrested for attacking a soldier and was denied medication for a preexisting condition while in custody; his case was ongoing as of November.

D2. Are individuals free to practice and express their religious faith or nonbelief in public and private? 4 / 4

Freedom of religion is constitutionally protected and respected in practice.

D3. Is there academic freedom, and is the educational system free from extensive political indoctrination? 3 / 4

Academic freedom is generally upheld, but strained resources within the university system have led to strikes by professors. Student protests have been violently dispersed by security forces in recent years.

D4. Are individuals free to express their personal views on political or other sensitive topics without fear of surveillance or retribution? 3 / 4

Private discussion remains largely open, though freedom of personal expression may be affected by the threat of violence from powerful interests. While authorities reportedly monitor discussions on social media platforms, including WhatsApp, few arrests have been made for online discussions or comments.

E. ASSOCIATIONAL AND ORGANIZATIONAL RIGHTS: 6 / 12

E1. Is there freedom of assembly? 2 / 4

While freedom of assembly is constitutionally guaranteed, the police have repeatedly refused to grant permission to organizers planning protests, and peaceful demonstrations have been violently dispersed in recent years.

Public gatherings of more than 100 people were banned via COVID-19 measures from March through at least early December. Protests and clashes were nevertheless recorded during the year. In June, the rape and murder of a child prompted several days of demonstrations; authorities in Freetown detained at least 20 demonstrators during one of the protests, though they were released soon after. In July, protesters objecting to the relocation of a power station attacked SLPP offices in Makeni. Authorities responded forcefully, killing at least four people.

E2. Is there freedom for nongovernmental organizations, particularly those that are engaged in human rights- and governance-related work? 2 / 4

A variety of nongovernmental organizations (NGOs) and civic groups operate in the country. However, stricter regulations were adopted in 2017 and took effect in 2018, requiring annual renewal of registrations and ministerial approval for projects. The SLPP government upheld the policy after a 2018 review. Many NGOs expressed dissatisfaction with the review's lack of transparency and inclusivity, and concern over the narrowing of space for civil society.

E3. Is there freedom for trade unions and similar professional or labor organizations? 2 / 4

While workers have the right to join independent trade unions, there are no laws preventing discrimination against union members or prohibiting employers from interfering with the formation of unions. Reports of the SLPP replacing union leaders or pressuring them to resign since it returned to government have provoked condemnation from regional union affiliates.

F. RULE OF LAW: 9 / 16

F1. Is there an independent judiciary? 2 / 4

While the constitution provides for an independent judiciary, the courts are prone to executive interference, particularly in corruption cases. A lack of clear procedures for appointing and dismissing judges leaves those processes vulnerable to abuse. Judicial corruption, poor salaries, and inadequate resources also undermine judicial autonomy.

F2. Does due process prevail in civil and criminal matters? 2 / 4

Resource constraints and a shortage of lawyers hinder access to legal counsel. Although the constitution guarantees a fair trial, this right is sometimes limited in practice, largely due to corruption. Pretrial and remand prisoners spend between three and five years behind bars on average before their cases are adjudicated. Police can hold criminal suspects for several days without charge and sometimes engage in arbitrary arrests.

F3. Is there protection from the illegitimate use of physical force and freedom from war and insurgencies? 3 / 4

Detention facilities are under strain, with occupancy levels at 220 percent of official capacity as of 2019. Prisons and detention facilities fail to meet basic health-and-hygiene standards, and infectious disease is prevalent. In April 2020, a riot broke out at the Pademba Road Prison in Freetown after a COVID-19 case was confirmed there. Restrictions on movement within the prison prompted the riot, according to a report issued by prison authorities in July. According to that report, 30 inmates and 1 corrections officer died in the incident.

Police are rarely held accountable for physical abuse and extrajudicial killings, which remain frequent. Police are poorly paid and minimally trained. Civilians can report ill-treatment to the Police Complaints, Discipline, and Internal Investigations Department or the Independent Police Complaints Board, though these agencies have limited capacity and efficacy. At the local level, Police Partnership Boards, whose chairpersons are elected by community members, are intended to provide accountability for arbitrary arrests.

F4. Do laws, policies, and practices guarantee equal treatment of various segments of the population? 2 / 4

LGBT+ people face discrimination in employment and health-care access and are vulnerable to violence. Sex between men is criminalized under a colonial-era law, and anti-LGBT+ discrimination is not explicitly prohibited by the constitution. Women experience discrimination in employment, education, and access to credit. Employers frequently fire women who become pregnant during their first year on the job.

G. PERSONAL AUTONOMY AND INDIVIDUAL RIGHTS: 10 / 16

G1. Do individuals enjoy freedom of movement, including the ability to change their place of residence, employment, or education? 3 / 4

Sierra Leoneans generally enjoy freedom of movement, but the government periodically imposed lockdowns and curfews throughout the year to curb the spread of COVID-19. A national curfew was also employed, though the government shortened it in June and lifted it in October.

Petty corruption is common, and parents often must pay bribes to register their children in primary and secondary school.

G2. Are individuals able to exercise the right to own property and establish private businesses without undue interference from state or nonstate actors? 3 / 4

The government has sought to reduce regulatory barriers to private business in recent years. Property rights are constitutionally guaranteed, though the laws do not effectively protect those rights. There is no land titling system. Outside of Freetown, land falls under customary law, and its use is determined by chiefs. The government often fails to regulate the activities of international investors, exacerbating threats to property rights.

Laws passed in 2007 grant women the right to inherit property, but many women have little power to contest land issues within the customary legal system.

G3. Do individuals enjoy personal social freedoms, including choice of marriage partner and size of family, protection from domestic violence, and control over appearance? 2 / 4

Reports of rape and domestic violence rarely result in conviction, and the police unit responsible for investigating and prosecuting these crimes remains underfunded and understaffed. In 2019, Parliament passed the Sexual Offences Amendment Act, which allows life sentences for those convicted of raping a child.

FGM is not prohibited by law, and the practice remains widespread.

Girls who were pregnant or previously had children were prohibited from attending schools under a 2010 ban which was lifted in March 2020. The Community Court of Justice of the Economic Community of West African States (ECOWAS) ruled the practice was discriminatory in late 2019.

Child marriage has consistently been a problem, with a reported 39 percent of women aged 20–24 having been married by age 18 according to a report published by the Office of the UN High Commissioner for Human Rights (OHCHR) in 2017. In October 2020, the International Rescue Committee (IRC) published the results of a survey of women in 15 African countries, including Sierra Leone; that survey recorded a rise in sexual violence as well as in early or forced marriages when COVID-19 restrictions were imposed.

Women experience discrimination on personal status matters such as marriage and divorce. Customary law governs many of these issues, making it difficult for women to seek legal recourse.

G4. Do individuals enjoy equality of opportunity and freedom from economic exploitation? 2 / 4

Reports of economic exploitation among workers in the natural-resource sector are common. Human trafficking remains a problem, though the 2020 edition of the US State

Department's *Trafficking in Persons Report* noted that the authorities were doing more to investigate trafficking and prosecute suspects. The first trafficking convictions in 15 years were secured in February 2020. Reports of judicial corruption and police abuse of victims remained common, however.

Singapore

Population: 5,800,000
Capital: Singapore
Freedom Status: Partly Free
Electoral Democracy: No

Overview: Singapore's parliamentary political system has been dominated by the ruling People's Action Party (PAP) and the family of current prime minister Lee Hsien Loong since 1959. The electoral and legal framework that the PAP has constructed allows for some political pluralism, but it constrains the growth of opposition parties and limits freedoms of expression, assembly, and association.

KEY DEVELOPMENTS IN 2020

- The COVID-19 pandemic was most acute from March to August, with a lockdown imposed from early April to the beginning of June. Migrant workers were disproportionately affected by both the virus and the related movement restrictions. As of late December, there had been a total of nearly 59,000 cases and 29 deaths.
- In the July parliamentary elections, the ruling PAP won 83 of 93 seats, the same number as in 2015 despite the addition of four new seats to the legislature. The party garnered 61 percent of the popular vote, down from nearly 70 percent in 2015.

POLITICAL RIGHTS: 19 / 40
A. ELECTORAL PROCESS: 4 / 12
A1. Was the current head of government or other chief national authority elected through free and fair elections? 1 / 4

The government is led by a prime minister and cabinet formed by the party that controls the legislature. The current prime minster, Lee Hsien Loong, has been in power since 2004 and secured a new mandate after the July 2020 parliamentary elections. While polling-day procedures are generally free of irregularities, numerous structural factors impede the development of viable electoral competition.

The president, whose role is largely ceremonial, is elected by popular vote for six-year terms, and a special committee is empowered to vet candidates. Under 2016 constitutional amendments on eligibility, none of Singapore's three main ethnic groupings (Chinese, Malays, and Indians or others) may be excluded from the presidency for more than five consecutive terms, and presidential candidates from the private sector, as opposed to senior officials with at least three years of service, must have experience leading a company with at least S$500 million (US$360 million) in shareholder equity. Only one candidate—Halimah Yacob, backed by the PAP—was declared eligible for the 2017 presidential election, making her the winner by default.

A2. Were the current national legislative representatives elected through free and fair elections? 2 / 4

Following a March 2020 recommendation by the Electoral Boundaries Review Committee, the number of directly elected seats in the unicameral Parliament was increased from 89 to 93. The Parliament elected in July 2020 consequently included 14 members from single-member constituencies and 79 members from Group Representation Constituencies (GRCs). The top-polling party in each GRC wins all of its four to five seats, which has historically bolstered the majority of the dominant PAP. As many as nine additional, nonpartisan members can be appointed to Parliament by the president, and a maximum of another 12 can come from a national compensatory list meant to ensure a minimum of opposition representation. Members serve five-year terms, with the exception of appointed members, who serve for two and a half years.

In the 2020 elections, the PAP secured about 61 percent of the popular vote and 83 of the 93 elected seats. The largest opposition group, the Workers' Party (WP), retained the six elected seats it had won in 2015 and gained an additional four, for a total of 10. Two compensatory seats were awarded to the opposition to achieve the minimum of 12.

Elections are largely free of fraud and other such irregularities, but they are unfair due to the advantages enjoyed by the incumbent party, including a progovernment media sector, the GRC system, high financial barriers to electoral candidacy, and legal restrictions on free speech.

A3. Are the electoral laws and framework fair, and are they implemented impartially by the relevant election management bodies? 1 / 4

Singapore lacks an independent election commission; the country's Elections Department is a government body attached to the Prime Minister's Office. The secretary to the prime minister is the head of the Electoral Boundaries Review Committee, which is responsible for reviewing and redrawing the boundaries for electoral constituencies. The prime minister appointed the committee's members in August 2019 in preparation for the 2020 elections. In the past, the PAP-controlled boundaries process has ensured an advantage for the party. The new electoral districts for 2020 were announced in mid-March, four months before the elections, the date of which was announced in June. The electoral framework suffers from a number of other features—including the GRC system and the onerous eligibility rules for presidential candidates—that favor the PAP-dominated political establishment.

B. POLITICAL PLURALISM AND PARTICIPATION: 8 / 16

B1. Do the people have the right to organize in different political parties or other competitive political groupings of their choice, and is the system free of undue obstacles to the rise and fall of these competing parties or groupings? 2 / 4

Singapore has a multiparty political system, and a total of 11 parties contested the parliamentary elections in July 2020. However, a variety of factors have helped to ensure the PAP's dominant position, including an electoral framework that favors the incumbents, restrictions on political films and television programs, the threat of defamation suits, the PAP's vastly superior financial resources, and its influence over the mass media and the courts.

In the midst of the campaign period for the 2020 elections, the police in July investigated a WP candidate for supposedly racially antagonistic posts she made on social media in 2018 and 2020. She received a "stern warning" from the police in September. The Protection from Online Falsehoods and Manipulation Act (POFMA)—which allows any government minister to order correction notices or restrict access to content they deem false or contrary to the public interest—was repeatedly invoked to require corrections regarding comments by opposition candidates in 2020, including during the campaign period. Separately, the Elections Department banned large public rallies during the campaign period, citing the COVID-19 pandemic.

B2. Is there a realistic opportunity for the opposition to increase its support or gain power through elections? 2 / 4

The PAP has governed without interruption since 1959, though the opposition has made some progress in mounting stronger election campaigns over the last decade. Opposition factions collectively put forward candidates for all directly elected Parliament seats in 2020, having done so for the first time in 2015, and ultimately gained four seats.

B3. Are the people's political choices free from domination by forces that are external to the political sphere, or by political forces that employ extrapolitical means? 2 / 4

The corporatist structure of the economy creates dense ties between business and political elites that have been criticized as oligarchic in nature. These networks contribute to the PAP's political dominance.

Many senior government officials formerly served as military officers, and the military has a close relationship with the PAP, but it does not directly engage in politics.

B4. Do various segments of the population (including ethnic, racial, religious, gender, LGBT+, and other relevant groups) have full political rights and electoral opportunities? 2 / 4

Ethnic Chinese Singaporeans make up a majority of the population. Members of minority groups, including Malays and people of Indian descent, have full voting rights, but critics—including academics and civil society organizations—have questioned whether the GRC system really achieves its stated aim of ensuring representation for minority populations. Separately, the rules for presidential candidacy have been criticized for excluding non-Malays from the 2017 election. Malays are generally underrepresented in leadership positions.

Women remain underrepresented in senior government and political positions, though women candidates won 27 of the 93 directly elected Parliament seats in 2020, up from 21 out of 89 in 2015, and the president who took office in 2017 is a woman. The cabinet as of 2020 included three women as full ministers. LGBT+ interest groups operate and are generally tolerated, but they do not have vocal representation in Parliament; open LGBT+ identity can be a barrier to election in practice, in part because sex between men remains a criminal offense.

C. FUNCTIONING OF GOVERNMENT: 7 / 12

C1. Do the freely elected head of government and national legislative representatives determine the policies of the government? 2 / 4

Elected officials determine the policies of the government, but the PAP's political and institutional dominance ensures its victory at the polls, and the party leadership maintains discipline among its members. The constitution stipulates that lawmakers lose their seats if they resign or are expelled from the party for which they stood in elections. This inhibits Parliament's ability to serve as an effective check on the executive.

C2. Are safeguards against official corruption strong and effective? 3 / 4

Singapore has been lauded for its lack of bribery and corruption. However, its corporatist economic structure entails close collaboration between the public and private sectors that may produce conflicts of interest. Lawmakers often serve on the boards of private companies, for example. The current prime minister's wife is the chief executive of Temasek Holdings, a government-linked corporation and sovereign wealth fund; the relationship has drawn accusations of nepotism and cronyism.

C3. Does the government operate with openness and transparency? 2 / 4

The government provides limited transparency on its operations. The Singapore Public Sector Outcomes Review is published every two years and includes metrics on the functioning of the bureaucracy; regular audits of public-sector financial processes are also made accessible to the public. However, other data, including key information on the status of the national reserves, are not made publicly available, and there is no freedom of information law giving citizens the right to obtain government records.

There is a lack of transparency surrounding the activities and salary of the prime minister's wife as the chief executive of Temasek Holdings.

In a move to increase transparency on monetary policy, the Monetary Authority of Singapore released statistics on its foreign exchange intervention operations on a six-month aggregated basis beginning in April 2020.

CIVIL LIBERTIES: 29 / 60 (−2)
D. FREEDOM OF EXPRESSION AND BELIEF: 8 / 16
D1. Are there free and independent media? 2 / 4

All domestic newspapers, radio stations, and television channels are owned by companies linked to the government. Editorials and news coverage generally support state policies, and self-censorship is common, though newspapers occasionally publish critical content. The government uses racial or religious tensions and the threat of terrorism to justify restrictions on freedom of speech. Media outlets, bloggers, and public figures have been subjected to harsh civil and criminal penalties for speech deemed to be seditious, defamatory, or injurious to religious sensitivities. Major online news sites must obtain licenses and respond to regulators' requests to remove prohibited content. However, foreign media and a growing array of online domestic outlets—including news sites and blogs—are widely consumed and offer alternative views, frequently publishing articles that are critical of the government or supportive of independent activism.

In September 2020, the Elections Department filed a police report for "illegal conduct of election activity" against New Naratif, an independent online media outlet that was accused of publishing five paid advertisements on Facebook in July without written authorization from a candidate or the candidate's agent during the election campaign. Also during the year, including the preelection period, government officials repeatedly invoked POFMA to order the publication of correction notices, in some cases targeting online media outlets.

Among other ongoing legal cases against the media, in October 2020 the prime minister went to court in a defamation suit against a prominent blogger who had shared an article online in 2018 that alleged the prime minister's involvement in a Malaysian corruption scandal. The trial was ongoing at year's end.

D2. Are individuals free to practice and express their religious faith or nonbelief in public and private? 3 / 4

The constitution guarantees freedom of religion as long as its practice does not violate any other regulations, and most groups worship freely. However, religious actions perceived as threats to racial or religious harmony are not tolerated, and the Jehovah's Witnesses and the Unification Church are banned. Religious groups are required to register with the government under the 1966 Societies Act.

Muslim religious teachers must be certified by the Asatizah Recognition Board, a body of religious scholars under the purview of the state's Islamic Religious Council of Singapore. The system is seen as an effort to ensure that only state-approved forms of Islam are taught.

D3. Is there academic freedom, and is the educational system free from extensive political indoctrination? 1 / 4

Public schools include a national education component that has been criticized for presenting a history of Singapore that focuses excessively on the role of the PAP. All public universities and political research institutions have direct government links that enable political influence and interference in hiring and firing; recent faculty turnover at two major universities has increased concerns about political pressure. Self-censorship on Singapore-related topics is common among academics, who can face legal and career consequences for critical speech.

D4. Are individuals free to express their personal views on political or other sensitive topics without fear of surveillance or retribution? 2 / 4

While there is some space for personal expression and private discussion, legal restrictions on topics that involve race and religion constrain dialogue. The threat of defamation suits and related charges are also deterrents to free speech, including on social media. In 2019, a judge overseeing a criminal defamation case against the editor of and a contributor to *The Online Citizen* rejected the defendants' argument that the charges were unlawful because the article in question had alleged corruption in the cabinet without identifying any specific person. The ruling effectively allowed defamation charges for criticism of the government in general.

POFMA, which went into effect in October 2019, provides for criminal penalties including fines and up to a year in prison for failure to comply with removal or correction orders. A year after its effective date, POFMA had been invoked some 70 times, including against opposition figures, activists, and social media users.

E. ASSOCIATIONAL AND ORGANIZATIONAL RIGHTS: 3 / 12 (−1)
E1. Is there freedom of assembly? 1 / 4 (−1)

Public assemblies are subject to extensive restrictions. Police permits are required for assemblies that occur outdoors; limited restrictions apply to indoor gatherings. Speakers' Corner at Hong Lim Park is the designated site for open assembly, though events there can likewise be restricted if they are deemed disruptive. Non-Singaporeans are generally prohibited from participating in or attending public assemblies that are considered political or sensitive. A 2017 amendment to the Public Order Act increased the authorities' discretion to ban public meetings and barred foreign nationals from organizing, funding, or even observing gatherings that could be used for a political purpose.

The Public Order and Safety (Special Powers) Act of 2018 granted the home affairs minister and police enhanced authority in the context of a "serious incident," which was vaguely defined to include scenarios ranging from terrorist attacks to peaceful protests. Officials would be permitted to potentially use lethal force and to halt newsgathering and online communications in the affected area. The special powers could even be invoked in advance of a likely or threatened incident.

Authorities in recent years have increasingly punished activists for holding unauthorized events, including even the smallest possible "assemblies." Activist Jolovan Wham was fined in 2019 for "organizing an assembly without a permit," having organized a conference in 2016 that featured a speech via video link by a prodemocracy leader from Hong Kong. Wham's appeal in the matter was dismissed in August 2020, and he elected to spend 10 days in jail rather than pay a fine of S$2,000 (US$1,400), though he paid a separate S$1,200 (US$860) fine for refusing to sign a police statement. In November, Wham was charged with staging an illegal protest for holding a sign with a smiley face near a police station in March, in support of two young activists being investigated by the authorities. The two activists had separately posed for photographs in public that month while holding protest signs about climate change.

Score Change: The score declined from 2 to 1 because authorities in recent years have stepped up arrests and prosecutions of activists for holding events without permits, including those who engage in solitary protests.

E2. Is there freedom for nongovernmental organizations, particularly those that are engaged in human rights- and governance-related work? 1 / 4

The Societies Act requires most organizations of more than 10 people to register with the government; the government enjoys full discretion to register or dissolve such groups. Only registered parties and associations may participate in organized political activity. Despite these restrictions, a number of nongovernmental organizations (NGOs) engage in human rights and governance-related work, advocating policy improvements and addressing the interests of constituencies including migrant workers and women. Prominent activists are subject to police questioning, criminal charges, civil lawsuits, and other forms of harassment in reprisal for their work.

E3. Is there freedom for trade unions and similar professional or labor organizations? 1 / 4

Unions are granted some rights under the Trade Unions Act, though restrictions include a ban on government employees joining unions. Union members are prohibited from voting on collective agreements negotiated by union representatives and employers. Strikes must be approved by a majority of members, as opposed to the internationally accepted standard of at least 50 percent of the members who vote. Workers in essential services are required to give 14 days' notice to an employer before striking. In practice, many restrictions are not applied. Nearly all unions are affiliated with the National Trade Union Congress, which is openly allied with the PAP.

F. RULE OF LAW: 7 / 16

F1. Is there an independent judiciary? 1 / 4

The country's top judges are appointed by the president on the advice of the prime minister. The government's consistent success in court cases that have direct implications for its agenda has cast serious doubt on judicial independence. The problem is particularly evident in defamation cases and lawsuits against government opponents. While judgments against the government are rare, the judiciary is perceived to act more professionally and impartially in business-related cases, which has helped to make the country an attractive venue for investment and commerce.

In September 2020, in a sign of judicial impartiality, the High Court overturned the 2019 conviction of an Indonesian maid, finding her not guilty of stealing from her employer, a powerful executive at a state-owned company. Nevertheless, the courts continued to side with the government and its allies in politically fraught cases during the year.

F2. Does due process prevail in civil and criminal matters? 2 / 4

Defendants in criminal cases enjoy most due process rights; political interference does not occur in a large majority of cases. However, the colonial-era Internal Security Act (ISA) allows warrantless searches and arrests to preserve national security. ISA detainees can be held without charge or trial for two-year periods that can be renewed indefinitely. In recent years it has primarily been used against suspected Islamist militants. The Criminal Law Act, which is mainly used against suspected members of organized crime groups, similarly allows warrantless arrest and preventive detention for renewable one-year periods. The Misuse of Drugs Act empowers authorities to commit suspected drug users, without trial, to rehabilitation centers for up to three years.

F3. Is there protection from the illegitimate use of physical force and freedom from war and insurgencies? 2 / 4

Singaporeans are largely protected against the illegitimate use of force and are not directly exposed to war or insurgencies. Prisons generally meet international standards. However, the penal code mandates corporal punishment in the form of caning, in addition to imprisonment, for about 30 offenses, and it can also be used as a disciplinary measure in prisons. Singapore continues to impose the death penalty for crimes including drug trafficking. Thirteen people were executed during 2018, and four were executed during 2019, according to the Singapore Prison Service. Executions were halted in 2020 as a result of the COVID-19 pandemic, but authorities in September began scheduling them again.

F4. Do laws, policies, and practices guarantee equal treatment of various segments of the population? 2 / 4

The law forbids ethnic discrimination, though members of minority groups may face discrimination in private- or public-sector employment in some instances. Women enjoy the same legal rights as men on most issues, and many are well-educated professionals, but there is no legal ban on gender-based discrimination in employment.

The LGBT+ community faces significant legal obstacles. The penal code criminalizes consensual sex between adult men, setting a penalty of up to two years in prison. The law is not actively enforced, but the courts have upheld its constitutionality in recent years. The Pink Dot parade, held annually in support of equal rights for LGBT+ people since 2009, drew another large turnout in 2019, despite the legal ban on foreign funding and participation. The 2020 parade, scheduled for June, was canceled as a result of the COVID-19 pandemic.

G. PERSONAL AUTONOMY AND INDIVIDUAL RIGHTS: 11 / 16 (−1)

G1. Do individuals enjoy freedom of movement, including the ability to change their place of residence, employment, or education? 2 / 4 (−1)

Citizens enjoy freedom of movement and the ability to change their place of employment. Policies aimed at fostering ethnic balance in subsidized public housing, in which a majority of Singaporeans live, entail some restrictions on place of residence, but these do not apply to open-market housing.

There are practical limits on freedom of movement for foreign migrant workers. In April 2020, due to a surge in cases of COVID-19 among migrant workers, the government imposed a lockdown on worker dormitories, restricting the movement of hundreds of thousands of people and forcing them to stay in overcrowded, dangerous conditions.

Limits on the dormitory residents' movements remained in place for months after broader national lockdown measures had been eased. Nearly half of the foreign workers in the country ultimately tested positive for the virus during the year, accounting for well over 90 percent of Singapore's cases.

Score Change: The score declined from 3 to 2 due to special restrictions on the movement and housing of migrant workers that disproportionately exposed them to the risk of contracting COVID-19.

G2. Are individuals able to exercise the right to own property and establish private businesses without undue interference from state or nonstate actors? 3 / 4

Individuals face no extensive restrictions on property ownership, though public housing units are technically issued on 99-year leases rather than owned outright. While the state is heavily involved in the economy through its investment funds and other assets, private business activity is generally facilitated by a supportive legal framework.

G3. Do individuals enjoy personal social freedoms, including choice of marriage partner and size of family, protection from domestic violence, and control over appearance? 3 / 4

Men and women generally have equal rights on personal status matters such as marriage and divorce, though same-sex marriage and civil unions are not recognized. Social pressures deter some interreligious marriages and exert influence on personal appearance. The government has generally barred Muslim women from wearing headscarves in public-sector jobs that require a uniform, but the issue remains a subject of public debate, and President Yacob herself wears a headscarf. Spousal immunity from rape charges was eliminated through a penal code amendment adopted by Parliament in 2019.

G4. Do individuals enjoy equality of opportunity and freedom from economic exploitation? 3 / 4

Singapore's inhabitants generally benefit from considerable economic opportunity, but some types of workers face disadvantages. The country's roughly 200,000 household workers are excluded from the Employment Act and are regularly exploited. Several high-profile trials of employers in recent years have drawn public attention to the physical abuse of such workers. Laws and regulations governing their working conditions have modestly improved formal protections over the past decade, but the guarantees remain inadequate. In 2018, the Ministry of Manpower issued a new work-permit condition that banned employers from holding the paid wages and other money of foreign household workers for safekeeping. Existing laws such as the Foreign Worker Dormitories Act of 2015 are intended to ensure the food and shelter needs of foreign workers. However, illegal practices such as passport confiscation by employers remain common methods of coercion, and foreign workers are vulnerable to exploitation and debt bondage in the sex trade or industries including construction and manufacturing.

Slovakia

Population: 5,460,000
Capital: Bratislava
Freedom Status: Free
Electoral Democracy: Yes

Overview: Slovakia's parliamentary system features regular multiparty elections and peaceful transfers of power between rival parties. While civil liberties are generally protected, democratic institutions are hampered by entrenched discrimination against Roma and growing political hostility toward migrants and refugees. Political corruption remains a problem.

KEY DEVELOPMENTS IN 2020

- In February, the Ordinary People and Independent Personalities (OL'aNO) party won the general elections and formed a new four-party coalition government, with its leader Igor Matovič as prime minister. OL'aNO, which had campaigned with a strong anticorruption agenda, and its two coalition partners control a three-fifths majority in Parliament, enabling them to pass constitutional amendments. Voter turnout was 65 percent.
- In March, 13 judges and a former Slovak Social Democracy Party (Smer–SD)–nominated deputy secretary of the Justice Ministry were detained on corruption charges, alongside several judges and prosecutors. Evidence retrieved from the phone of Marian Kočner—an oligarch charged with several crimes and who was linked to the murder of investigative journalist Ján Kuciak—and testimony from the arrested judges, prosecutors, and others enabled the police to detain and charge a number of top officials from various law enforcement agencies later in the year.
- Amnesty International raised serious concerns over the government's quarantine of five Roma settlements due to the COVID-19 pandemic in April. Authorities deployed army officers and heavily restricted freedom of movement, despite the low number of confirmed coronavirus cases. Human rights advocates claim that the state targeted Romany communities, further stigmatizing them and inaccurately associating them with high COVID-19 infection rates.

POLITICAL RIGHTS: 37 / 40 (+1)

A. ELECTORAL PROCESS: 12 / 12

A1. Was the current head of government or other chief national authority elected through free and fair elections? 4 / 4

Slovakia is a parliamentary republic whose prime minister leads the government. There is also a directly elected president with important but limited executive powers. In March 2019, an environmental activist and leader of the newly formed Progressive Slovakia party, Zuzana Čaputová, became the first woman elected as president. Čaputová won 58.3 percent of the second round of voting to defeat diplomat Maroš Šefčovič, nominated by Smer–SD, who took 41.7 percent.

Following the general elections held in February 2020, a new four-party coalition government was formed, headed by Prime Minister Igor Matovič of the Ordinary People and Independent Personalities (OL'aNO) party.

A2. Were the current national legislative representatives elected through free and fair elections? 4 / 4

The 150 members of the unicameral parliament, the National Council, are directly elected to four-year terms in a single national constituency by proportional representation. In the February 2020 parliamentary elections, the liberal-conservative OL'aNO party received a plurality of votes (25 percent), defeating the previously dominant incumbent, Smer–SD. Two other previously governing parties, the Slovak National Party (SNS) and Most-Híd, did not clear the 5 percent electoral threshold. OL'aNO entered a coalition government with three other parties that control a three-fifths majority in Parliament (enough to pass constitutional amendments): the conservative We Are Family party, the liberal Freedom and Solidarity, and the newly formed For the People Formation. The vote took place peacefully, and its results were accepted by stakeholders and certified by the state's election management body, the State Commission for Elections and the Control of Funding for Political Parties (known as the State Commission). Voter turnout was 65 percent.

A3. Are the electoral laws and framework fair, and are they implemented impartially by the relevant election management bodies? 4 / 4

The legal framework for elections is generally fair, and 2014 legislation that addressed some gaps and inconsistencies in electoral laws was praised by a 2020 Organization for Security and Co-operation in Europe (OSCE) election monitoring mission. However, electoral legislation does not clarify whether meetings of the State Commission—which is tasked with oversight of party funding, vote tabulation, and electoral preparations—should be open to the public. The parliament in 2019 passed a law that would ban publicizing the result of opinion polls within 50 days of elections. The Constitutional Court ruled that the law would not apply to the 2020 parliamentary polls and did not decide whether the measure was unconstitutional by the end of 2020.

B. POLITICAL PLURALISM AND PARTICIPATION: 15 / 16

B1. Do the people have the right to organize in different political parties or other competitive political groupings of their choice, and is the system free of undue obstacles to the rise and fall of these competing parties or groupings? 4 / 4

Citizens can freely organize in political parties and movements. In 2020, 24 parties competed in the year's elections and 6 of them entered the parliament.

B2. Is there a realistic opportunity for the opposition to increase its support or gain power through elections? 4 / 4

There have been regular transfers of power between parties in the last two decades. President Čaputová, elected in 2019, was the chairwoman of the Progressive Slovakia party, which was formed in 2017. In February 2020, the three governing parties were defeated in the parliamentary elections and the four previous opposition parties formed a coalition government.

B3. Are the people's political choices free from domination by forces that are external to the political sphere, or by political forces that employ extrapolitical means? 4 / 4

The citizens of Slovakia are generally able to make political choices free from external pressures.

B4. Do various segments of the population (including ethnic, racial, religious, gender, LGBT+, and other relevant groups) have full political rights and electoral opportunities? 3 / 4

Nearly all political parties in Parliament have expressed bias against LGBT+ people, who are poorly represented in politics. Roma are also poorly represented, and there have been reports of vote-buying in Romany settlements for local and regional elections.

Women hold thirty-two out of 150 elected seats and are underrepresented in politics generally. The government has worked to implement action plans aimed at increasing parliamentary gender parity, but no significant change has been achieved.

In October 2020, the leader of the far-right Peoples' Party Our Slovakia Marian Kotleba was sentenced to four years and four months in prison for promoting an ideology that aims to suppress democratic rights and freedoms. Kotleba appealed the verdict to the Supreme

Court. If his conviction is upheld, he would serve his prison sentence, lose his parliamentary seat, and be banned from running for future office.

C. FUNCTIONING OF GOVERNMENT: 10 / 12 (+1)

C1. Do the freely elected head of government and national legislative representatives determine the policies of the government? 4 / 4

Democratically elected politicians determine public policy.

C2. Are safeguards against official corruption strong and effective? 3 / 4

Though corruption has long riddled Slovakian institutions, a series of anticorruption police raids in 2020 show significant government effort to address the issue.

In March 2020, 13 judges, several prosecutors, and a former Smer–SD-nominated deputy secretary of the Justice Ministry were detained on corruption charges. Evidence retrieved from the phone of Marian Kočner—an oligarch charged with a number of crimes and who was linked to the murder of investigative journalist Ján Kuciak—and testimony from the arrested judges, prosecutors, and others enabled the police to detain and charge a number of top officials from various law-enforcement agencies, including the former head of the National Criminal Agency, the former head of the Material Reserves Agency, and former high-ranking police officials in November and December. In addition, three highly influential oligarchs with ties to top-level politicians were also detained and charged with corruption and related offences.

In November and December 2020, two former police chiefs were arrested on charges of corruption and obstruction of justice. In October, special prosecutor Dušan Kováčik, who had filed no criminal lawsuits as prosecutor despite his main responsibility to oversee top-level criminal cases, was charged and indicted for colluding with organized crime groups.

C3. Does the government operate with openness and transparency? 3 / 4 (+1)

In 2020, the government introduced two significant measures to increase its transparency: a new prosecutor general was appointed through a new, transparent public interview process. Further, new legislation increases the Judicial Council's oversight powers of judges' property and income declarations. These measures mark a significant effort by the OL'aNO government to ameliorate structural deficiencies in government openness.

Slovak law obliges mandatory publication of all contracts in which a state or public institution is a party, but enforcement is inconsistent. Many business leaders believe that corruption was the main reason behind their failure to secure public tenders.

Score Change: The score improved from 2 to 3 because the government increased oversight of high-ranking judges and introduced a more transparent selection process for prosecutors general.

CIVIL LIBERTIES: 53 / 60 (+1)

D. FREEDOM OF EXPRESSION AND BELIEF: 15 / 16 (+1)

D1. Are there free and independent media? 3 / 4 (+1)

The February 2018 murder of Ján Kuciak, an investigative reporter who was working on corruption and tax fraud cases, represented the worst attack on media freedom in recent Slovak history. In September 2020, the court convicted and sentenced two men for carrying out the murder but acquitted well-known oligarch Marian Kočner and his associate, who were suspected of ordering Kuciak's killing. The prosecutor and the victims' families appealed Kočner's acquittal to the Supreme Court.

In March 2020, Prime Minister Matovič suggested the government create a fund to support the journalists' investigation into corruption. However, local media figures including the head of the Ján Kuciak Centre for Investigative Journalism and the head investigative reporting at the news outlet Aktuality.sk rejected the idea due to concerns that it could threaten media independence.

Verbal harassment of journalists by politicians when Smer–SD was in government were frequent. Though Matovič has spoken poorly of media members who criticize his proposals and performance in office, the OL'aNO government has largely refrained from harassing or intimidating journalists.

Media ownership is concentrated in the hands of a few business groups and individuals. The government postponed legislation that would protect the independence of journalists at the public broadcaster Radio and Television of Slovakia (RTVS) due to the COVID-19 pandemic.

Score Change: The score improved from 2 to 3 because there were fewer reports of the new government harassing or intimidating journalists, though concerns remain.

D2. Are individuals free to practice and express their religious faith or nonbelief in public and private? 4 / 4

Religious freedom is guaranteed by the constitution and generally upheld by state institutions. Registered churches and religious societies are eligible for tax exemptions and government subsidies.

D3. Is there academic freedom, and is the educational system free from extensive political indoctrination? 4 / 4

Academic freedom is guaranteed by the constitution and upheld by authorities.

D4. Are individuals free to express their personal views on political or other sensitive topics without fear of surveillance or retribution? 4 / 4

People may discuss sensitive or political topics without fear of retribution or surveillance. Hate speech laws prohibit the incitement of racial hatred or violence and have been used in recent years to remove a parliamentarian after he made racist remarks toward Roma.

E. ASSOCIATIONAL AND ORGANIZATIONAL RIGHTS: 12 / 12
E1. Is there freedom of assembly? 4 / 4

Freedom of assembly is constitutionally guaranteed and upheld by state authorities, and peaceful demonstrations are common. The government's second lockdown in October 2020 to prevent the spread of the coronavirus included restrictions on the right to public assembly. Several antilockdown demonstrations nevertheless took place in October and November, though police largely refrained from enforcing the restrictions. In October, police dispersed a far-right demonstration in Bratislava with tear gas and water cannon after protesters threw stones and flares.

E2. Is there freedom for nongovernmental organizations, particularly those that are engaged in human rights- and governance-related work? 4 / 4

Nongovernmental organizations (NGOs) are free to operate and criticize state authorities. During former prime minister Robert Fico's tenure, NGOs were accused of seeking to overthrow the legitimate government after some organizations supported and worked for the "For a Decent Slovakia" protests. The far-right Peoples' Party Our Slovakia repeatedly attempted to pass a law that would apply a "foreign agent" label onto any NGO accepting donations from abroad.

E3. Is there freedom for trade unions and similar professional or labor organizations? 4 / 4

Trade unions in Slovakia are pluralistic and operate freely.

F. RULE OF LAW: 12 / 16

F1. Is there an independent judiciary? 3 / 4

The constitution provides for an independent judiciary. However, there is a widespread perception of a lack of transparency and an abundance of corruption in the functioning of the judicial system. According to a September 2020 report by the European Commission, the judiciary is perceived by the public as lacking independence and integrity.

The new coalition government began their ambitious reform of the judiciary with a December 2020 constitutional amendment that changes the composition and powers of the Judiciary Council and incorporates an element of public oversight. A respected former head of the Constitutional Court was appointed its chairman earlier in the year. The Council gained the power to review property declarations of the judges.

The constitutional amendment prevented vacancies on the Constitutional Court, as happened in 2019, by extending the mandate for sitting judges until their replacements are elected by the parliament and appointed by the president. It further introduced a phased partial replacement of future constitutional judges: After the tenure of the present top court expires, new judges will not be appointed with the same term-lengths to prevent any parliamentary majority from packing the courts and endangering the judiciary's independence. The amendment also sets up a new Supreme Administrative Court (to be created in 2021) and overhauls the structure of the judiciary in order to increase the specialization of the district courts.

F2. Does due process prevail in civil and criminal matters? 3 / 4

Due process usually prevails in civil and criminal matters. However, there have been reports of warrantless detentions or detentions otherwise carried out without other appropriate authorization.

F3. Is there protection from the illegitimate use of physical force and freedom from war and insurgencies? 3 / 4

While Slovakia is free from war, insurgencies, and high rates of violent crime, police abuse of suspects is a persistent problem. Reports of police violence against Roma people emerge frequently.

F4. Do laws, policies, and practices guarantee equal treatment of various segments of the population? 3 / 4

Roma face persistent discrimination in many forms, including from public officials and in employment. Romany children in primary schools are regularly segregated into Roma-only classes, and many are educated in schools meant to serve children with mental disabilities. In September 2020, the European Court for Human Rights ruled that two Roma citizens who were beaten in a police raid in a town in eastern Slovakia in 2013 experienced inhumane treatment, and their right to judicial recourse was violated. The court also declared that the authorities had failed to conduct a proper investigation of the police officers involved.

Amnesty International raised serious concerns over the government's quarantine of five Roma settlements in April 2020 due to the COVID-19 pandemic. Authorities deployed army officers and heavily restricted freedom of movement, despite the low number of confirmed coronavirus cases. Human rights advocates claim that the state targeted Romany communities, further stigmatizing them and inaccurately associating them with high COVID-19 infection rates. There were three cases of excessive and unnecessary police violence against Roma between March and May.

Women are underrepresented in senior-level business and government positions. The 2019 Gender Equality Index issued by the European Institute for Gender Equality indicates that in Slovakia the gender pay gap and the percentage of women in top posts in the private sector are among the worst in the European Union.

According to the European Commission against Racism and Intolerance's 2020 report, there has been escalation of hate speech against LGBT+ people, migrants, Muslims, and Jews, especially online. While there are antidiscrimination laws in place, most cases of discrimination are unreported, and police do not always investigate or take action in cases of discrimination on the basis of gender identity or sexual orientation. A 2020 survey found that LGBT+ people have little trust in authorities' antidiscrimination mechanisms.

The number of asylum applications is very low (only 220 in 2020) which reflects the status of Slovakia primarily as a transit country. However, Slovak authorities apply asylum protections very restrictively; by November 2020 just 10 out of 220 applicants had been granted asylum.

G. PERSONAL AUTONOMY AND INDIVIDUAL RIGHTS: 14 / 16

G1. Do individuals enjoy freedom of movement, including the ability to change their place of residence, employment, or education? 4 / 4

The government respects the freedom of movement and the right of citizens to freely change their place of residence, employment, and education.

G2. Are individuals able to exercise the right to own property and establish private businesses without undue interference from state or nonstate actors? 4 / 4

In general, the government does not arbitrarily interfere with citizens' rights to own property and to establish private businesses.

G3. Do individuals enjoy personal social freedoms, including choice of marriage partner and size of family, protection from domestic violence, and control over appearance? 3 / 4

Personal social freedoms, including choice of marriage partner and size of family, are guaranteed and upheld by the state authorities, but a 2014 constitutional amendment defines marriage as a "unique bond" between one man and one woman. Laws neither allow nor recognize same-sex marriages or civil unions. Public opinion has remained against granting couples in same-sex partnerships the same rights granted to unions between a man and a woman.

Slovakia permits abortions, although conservative and far-right groups in Parliament repeatedly propose restrictions, most recently in October 2020.

G4. Do individuals enjoy equality of opportunity and freedom from economic exploitation? 3 / 4

Severe marginalization of Roma harms their opportunities for social mobility. According to the US State Department's *2020 Trafficking in Persons Report*, human trafficking is a problem, and mainly involves the transport of victims to countries in Western and Central Europe, where they are engaged in forced labor, sex work, and begging. The government has significantly increased antitrafficking efforts—including prosecutions and convictions—though victim identification and support services remain inadequate.

Slovenia

Population: 2,100,000
Capital: Ljubljana
Freedom Status: Free
Electoral Democracy: Yes

Overview: Slovenia is a parliamentary republic with a freely elected government. While political rights and civil liberties are generally respected, the right-wing government has verbally attacked democratic institutions including the media and judiciary; this prompted pushback from civil society, and the attacks have failed to yield a systemic weakening of the liberal democratic order. Corruption remains an issue, though media are proactive in exposing it. The judiciary, while somewhat distrusted, has established a record of independent rulings, and the rule of law is generally respected.

KEY DEVELOPMENTS IN 2020

- A new, right-wing government led by Slovenian Democratic Party (SDS) president Janez Janša took office in mid-March.
- Prime Minister Janša and other high-ranking officials verbally attacked the media, the judiciary, and an antigovernment protest movement that organized periodic demonstrations during the year. After the president of the Supreme Court denounced Janša's criticism of the judiciary and public prosecutors as undermining the principle of the separation of powers, the president attempted to quell the dispute in a senior-level meeting in October. It produced no results, and Janša continued his criticism. (The prime minister had been indicted in the fall over a 2005 real estate deal.)
- A procurement scandal involving personal protective equipment (PPE) and ventilators needed amid the COVID-19 pandemic resulted in a number of investigations against high-ranking officials. The whistleblower in this affair was fired from his job in October, and is appealing the termination.
- The government drafted a sweeping overhaul of media legislation that would, if adopted, increase political influence over public media and reduce their funding. The draft law prompted vocal criticism from local and international media organizations and other stakeholders.

POLITICAL RIGHTS: 39 / 40

A. ELECTORAL PROCESS: 12 / 12

A1. Was the current head of government or other chief national authority elected through free and fair elections? 4 / 4

The prime minister heads the executive branch and is appointed by the National Assembly (Državni Zbor) for a four-year term. The president holds the mostly ceremonial position of head of state and is directly elected for up to two five-year terms.

Marjan Šarec, leader of List of Marjan Šarec (LMŠ), resigned as prime minister of a minority government in late January 2020. This allowed Janez Janša, the leader of the right-wing SDS, to form a majority government in mid-March. By mid-December, his government lost majority support as well, making Janša's the second minority government in 2020.

A2. Were the current national legislative representatives elected through free and fair elections? 4 / 4

The legislature is composed of the 40-seat National Council (Državni Svet) and the 90-seat National Assembly. Councilors are indirectly elected to five-year terms by an electoral college. Of the 90 National Assembly members elected to four-year terms, 88 are elected by proportional representation vote. Two additional seats are reserved for lawmakers representing Hungarian and Italian minorities.

Monitors from the Organization for Security and Co-operation in Europe (OSCE) deemed the June 2018 National Assembly elections free and fair. In December 2020, the Democratic Party of Pensioners of Slovenia (DeSUS) quit the ruling coalition, leaving Janša to rule via a confidence-and-supply agreement with the nationalist party, plus two representatives of national minority groups.

A3. Are the electoral laws and framework fair, and are they implemented impartially by the relevant election management bodies? 4 / 4

The National Election Commission is an independent and impartial body that supervises free and fair elections, and ensures electoral laws are properly implemented.

B. POLITICAL PLURALISM AND PARTICIPATION: 16 / 16

B1. Do the people have the right to organize in different political parties or other competitive political groupings of their choice, and is the system free of undue obstacles to the rise and fall of these competing parties or groupings? 4 / 4

The constitutional right to organize in different political parties is upheld in practice. Parties need to pass a 4 percent threshold of votes to win a seat in the parliament. Parties winning less than 4 percent but more than 1 percent of the vote are eligible for a proportional share of national-budget funds.

B2. Is there a realistic opportunity for the opposition to increase its support or gain power through elections? 4 / 4

Political power frequently rotates between parties.

B3. Are the people's political choices free from domination by forces that are external to the political sphere, or by political forces that employ extrapolitical means? 4 / 4

People's political choices are free from domination by powerful groups that are not democratically accountable.

B4. Do various segments of the population (including ethnic, racial, religious, gender, LGBT+, and other relevant groups) have full political rights and electoral opportunities? 4 / 4

Citizens enjoy full political rights and electoral opportunities. Hungarian and Italian minorities each elect their own lawmaker to the National Assembly. Roma councilors sit on 20 municipal councils but are not represented in the national legislature.

The Council of Europe in September 2020 recommended that Slovenia recognize Croatian, Serbian, and German as minority languages and increase funding for television programming in Italian and Hungarian.

A 35 percent gender quota is mandated by law, and parties that fail to adhere to it have had their lists rejected. However, gender quotas are enforced on the precinct level, and NGOs have long complained that women candidates are allotted precincts with lower chances of being elected. Only 24 percent of lawmakers elected in 2018 were women, a decline from the last term.

C. FUNCTIONING OF GOVERNMENT: 11 / 12

C1. Do the freely elected head of government and national legislative representatives determine the policies of the government? 4 / 4

Elected officials are free to set and implement government policy without undue interference.

C2. Are safeguards against official corruption strong and effective? 3 / 4

Corruption in Slovenia primarily takes the form of conflicts of interest between government officials and private businesses. The Commission for the Prevention of Corruption (KPK), mired in controversy in recent years, has seen a change in leadership and, as of February 2020, is headed by Robert Šumi, a lecturer at the police academy. The body has since taken up several notable cases of alleged corruption; these include cases related to procurement of personal protective equipment (PPE) and medical ventilators during the first wave of the COVID-19 pandemic in April, as well as misappropriation of funds by Agriculture Minister Aleksandra Pivec, who resigned in October as a result of the allegations.

In June 2020, the National Assembly, after years of failed attempts, passed its ethics code. In October, Parliament approved a wide-ranging overhaul of the Integrity and Prevention of Corruption Act that expanded the KPK's supervisory role, aimed to improve procedure transparency, and mandated that more officials report assets.

While whistleblower protection is regulated in anticorruption and other laws, NGOs have repeatedly called for comprehensive stand-alone legislation to better protect them.

Corruption and irregularities in the health sector remained in the public focus in 2020—especially in the light of the procurement scandal involving PPE and ventilators, which led to a number of investigations against several high-ranking officials. The whistleblower in this affair was fired from his job in October 2020 in what was widely seen as government retaliation, but is appealing his termination. A wide-ranging investigation by the Court of Audit is proceeding, with suspected criminal acts in at least 13 contracts detected in 2020.

Media continue to be proactive in exposing corruption allegations. This includes allegations in September 2020 of insider trading by a government minister and the indictment in October of Prime Minister Janša over a 2005 real estate deal.

Janša dismissed concerns in the European Commission's September 2020 Rule of Law report about underfunding of anticorruption bodies, saying he was more concerned by the lack of funds for health care than he was about statements by NGOs and other organizations.

C3. Does the government operate with openness and transparency? 4 / 4

The government generally operates with openness and transparency. However, a September 2020 report by the European Commission revealed concerns over lack of resources for key regulators. Additionally, the government proposed a merger of all eight independent regulators into just two superagencies, citing benefits of reduced management costs and increased efficiency. The regulators themselves opposed the merger, claiming it would violate European Union (EU) and international law and curbs their independence.

CIVIL LIBERTIES: 56 / 60 (+1)

D. FREEDOM OF EXPRESSION AND BELIEF: 15 / 16 (+1)

D1. Are there free and independent media? 3 / 4

Freedom of speech and of the press are constitutionally guaranteed, but defamation remains a criminal offense. In a positive development, in 2018 the Supreme Court ruled that journalists cannot legally be compelled to reveal their sources unless there is a clearly demonstratable public good in doing so.

In mid-2020, the government drafted a sweeping overhaul of media legislation that would, if adopted, increase political influence over public media (mostly public broadcaster RTVSLO and the STA press agency) and partially defund them even while their scope of responsibilities remained the same. This drew vocal criticism from local and international media organizations and a plethora of other stakeholders. Some critics assert that the change is aimed at securing public financing for outlets friendly to the SDS. In addition, the affected outlets voiced concerns about having to lay off journalists and other staff should these draft laws be adopted, which in turn would limit their ability to serve the public interest.

Media ownership is sometimes opaque, and journalists are subject to pressure and occasional harassment due to their coverage. Throughout August and September 2020, one outlet became a target of 39 lawsuits from a single individual who is considered to be an associate of the prime minister. The move is considered a collection of SLAPPs (strategic lawsuit against public participation) and was widely condemned by international and local media organizations.

Slovenia was the subject of eight media alerts in 2020 on the Council of Europe Platform to Promote the Protection and Safety of Journalists. Five of these were classified as the state being the source of the threat and include instances of the prime minister denigrating journalists and outlets.

In a July 2020 report, the European Commission raised concerns over media pluralism in Slovenia.

State-owned enterprises continue to hold a stake in several media outlets, leaving them vulnerable to government intervention. Media published by municipalities have been abused as propaganda tools favoring incumbent mayors. Some private outlets have been accused of running stories promoting their owners' business interests. Journalists can also face direct pressure from powerful business interests.

Journalists also face economic threats to their livelihoods, be it by cost-cutting across newsrooms, or outright terminations. These fears have been exacerbated by ownership shifts at various outlets.

D2. Are individuals free to practice and express their religious faith or nonbelief in public and private? 4 / 4 (+1)

The Slovenian constitution guarantees religious freedom and contains provisions prohibiting incitement of religious intolerance or discrimination. However, there are occasional instances of vandalism of religious buildings, and of hate speech by high-profile figures.

Construction of a long-delayed mosque in Ljubljana was completed in 2019. Services began in early 2020 but were soon suspended, along with all other religious services in the country, due to the COVID-19 pandemic.

Score Change: The score improved from 3 to 4 because the country's first mosque officially opened in February, after years of institutional resistance to its construction.

D3. Is there academic freedom, and is the educational system free from extensive political indoctrination? 4 / 4

Academic freedom is generally respected.

D4. Are individuals free to express their personal views on political or other sensitive topics without fear of surveillance or retribution? 4 / 4

Individuals are generally free to express their personal beliefs without fear of reprisal. Defamation remains a criminal offense, though officials may no longer press charges through the state prosecutor. Officials have repeatedly called for authorities to investigate the social media profiles of government critics.

E. ASSOCIATIONAL AND ORGANIZATIONAL RIGHTS: 12 / 12
E1. Is there freedom of assembly? 4 / 4

The rights to peaceful assembly and association are guaranteed by the constitution and respected in practice. Assemblies must be registered with the authorities in advance, and in some instances permits are required.

In 2020, senior government officials called for legal action against protesters attending weekly demonstrations against various government measures and policies. Janša demanded that charges be filed for what he characterized as death threats, though the state prosecutor found no grounds to do so. Interior Minister Aleš Hojs repeatedly demanded that police take a tougher approach with protesters and investigate their social media posts. While the police refused to do so, and the information commissioner warned against such invasions of privacy, protest participants were frequently subject to fines and police procedures based on alleged health violations. At the height of the protest movement, there were instances in which police stopped and searched individuals on grounds related to protest-related activity at locations nowhere near the protests.

E2. Is there freedom for nongovernmental organizations, particularly those that are engaged in human rights– and governance-related work? 4 / 4

Numerous nongovernmental organizations (NGOs) operate freely and play a role in policymaking. However, as a part of one of the coronavirus relief packages, the ruling coalition changed environmental protection acts to (among other things) limit NGO involvement in spatial planning and impact assessments. The Constitutional Court in July 2020 temporarily stayed the NGO-related changes, pending final ruling.

E3. Is there freedom for trade unions and similar professional or labor organizations? 4 / 4

Workers may establish and join trade unions, strike, and bargain collectively.

F. RULE OF LAW: 15 / 16
F1. Is there an independent judiciary? 4 / 4

The constitution provides for an independent judiciary, and efficiency has increased in recent years. However, a significant portion of the general public still has a negative perception of the courts, although this too has improved somewhat in recent years.

Prime Minister Janša continued his regular criticism of the judiciary throughout 2020, prompting the president of the Supreme Court in August to denounce his remarks as undermining the principle of division of power. The president sought to quell the dispute in a senior-level meeting in October, but it solved little, and Janša has since doubled down on his criticism of the courts and public prosecutors.

F2. Does due process prevail in civil and criminal matters? 4 / 4

The rule of law is respected in civil and criminal matters. Programs aimed at reducing court backlogs have seen some success in recent years.

F3. Is there protection from the illegitimate use of physical force and freedom from war and insurgencies? 4 / 4

People in Slovenia are generally free from threats of physical force. Prison conditions meet international standards, though overcrowding has been reported.

Paramilitary groups (called "Wards") became more active in 2020, claiming that their patrols were aimed at protecting the Slovenian border from illegal migrants. After striking down a bill to outlaw these formations in March 2020, Parliament approved a similar measure in September.

F4. Do laws, policies, and practices guarantee equal treatment of various segments of the population? 3 / 4

Some deficiencies exist in the protection of equal rights in Slovenia, including in the treatment of asylum seekers and Roma. In July 2020, the media reported on police restricting the movements of asylum seekers, denying them legal aid, and intentionally conflating the statuses of illegal immigrants and asylum seekers. Proposed amendments to the Aliens Act released in September would allow for stricter asylum measures in case of sudden increases in the number of migrants attempting to enter the country. Advocacy groups said that the amended law would effectively prevent refugees from applying for international protection and would formalize mass deportations.

While their legal status and ability to claim compensation have been resolved to a large extent, some individual cases of "The Erased"—a group of more than 25,000 non-Slovene citizens purged from official records in 1992—relating to restitution and reestablishing legal rights remain pending. Roma face widespread poverty and societal marginalization. Although there are legal protections against discrimination based on sexual orientation, discrimination against LGBT+ people is still present. However, recent research suggests that the social gap experienced by LGBT+ persons is closing. Despite legal protections, people with disabilities still often face workplace discrimination.

G. PERSONAL AUTONOMY AND INDIVIDUAL RIGHTS: 14 / 16

G1. Do individuals enjoy freedom of movement, including the ability to change their place of residence, employment, or education? 4 / 4

Citizens enjoy the right to change their residence, employment, and place of education.

G2. Are individuals able to exercise the right to own property and establish private businesses without undue interference from state or nonstate actors? 4 / 4

Individuals may exercise the right to own property and establish private business in practice.

G3. Do individuals enjoy personal social freedoms, including choice of marriage partner and size of family, protection from domestic violence, and control over appearance? 3 / 4

Individuals generally enjoy personal social freedoms. People entering same-sex partnerships enjoy most of the rights conferred by marriage but cannot adopt children or undergo in-vitro fertilization procedures. Marriage is still legally defined as a union between a man and a woman. Domestic violence is illegal but remains a concern in practice, though nearly all reported cases are investigated. According to the National Institute of Public Health (NIJZ), the number of reported cases increased in 2020, amid the COVID-19 pandemic.

G4. Do individuals enjoy equality of opportunity and freedom from economic exploitation? 3 / 4

Authorities actively prosecute suspected human traffickers and work to identify victims.

Many people at the beginning of their careers or nearing retirement are employed under precarious conditions. According to labor unions and advocacy groups the situation is getting worse every year and was exacerbated by the COVID-19 pandemic. Labor unions cite extended work hours and workplace quality as pressing issues, while experts say that the main problem is lack of oversight.

Solomon Islands

Population: 700,000
Capital: Honiara
Freedom Status: Free
Electoral Democracy: Yes

Overview: Political rights and civil liberties are generally respected in the Solomon Islands. There are weaknesses in the rule of law, and corruption remains a serious concern, but recent governments have taken steps to address it. Violence against women is also a significant problem.

KEY DEVELOPMENTS IN 2020

- Daniel Suidani, the premier of Malaita Province, announced his intentions to hold an independence referendum in September, objecting to a COVID-19 repatriation flight that largely carried Chinese passengers and the national government's developing relationship with China. The national government objected to Suidani's plan that month, calling it illegal.
- The national government proposed a ban on Facebook in November, citing "abusive language" among other concerns. The proposal, which was met with widespread criticism, remained under consideration at year's end.
- Authorities relied on inbound travel restrictions to limit the spread of COVID-19, along with intermittent lockdowns. The first case was detected in October. Solomon Islands authorities reported 17 cases and no deaths by year's end.

POLITICAL RIGHTS: 30 / 40
A. ELECTORAL PROCESS: 9 / 12
A1. Was the current head of government or other chief national authority elected through free and fair elections? 3 / 4

The prime minister, who serves as the head of government, is elected by the National Parliament. Irregularities are frequent in the run-up to prime ministerial elections, known as "second elections." Leading contenders usually separate into camps in Honiara's major hotels and seek the support of other members of Parliament (MPs) with promises of cash or ministerial portfolios.

Following April 2019 elections, Manasseh Sogavare won a fourth nonconsecutive term as prime minister. Solomon Islands Democratic Party (SIDP) leader Matthew Wale attempted to stop Sogavare's selection, saying that Sogavare relaunched the Ownership, Unity, and Responsibility Party (Our Party) too late to abide by a law requiring prime ministerial candidates to maintain party membership; Sogavare was previously aligned with the SIDP before moving to Our Party after the election was held. Sogavare was ruled eligible in late April, while the High Court rejected Wale's legal petition against Sogavare that May.

The National Parliament selects a governor general to represent the British monarch as head of state for five-year terms. The governor general appoints cabinet members on the advice of the prime minister. David Vunagi, a retired Anglican bishop, began serving in that post in July 2019.

A2. Were the current national legislative representatives elected through free and fair elections? 3 / 4

The 50 members of the National Parliament are directly elected in single-seat constituencies by a simple majority vote to serve four-year terms. In the April 2019 elections, the SIDP and the Kadere Party each won 8 seats, while independents won another 21. Another six parties won the remainder. Days after the polls, support among MPs shifted to Our Party, which formed a governing coalition with Kadere, the Democratic Alliance, and the Solomon Islands People First Party.

Commonwealth observers commended the poll's conduct but called for improvements in the voter registration process along with expanded early voting options for individuals living overseas and for essential service personnel.

A3. Are the electoral laws and framework fair, and are they implemented impartially by the relevant election management bodies? 3 / 4

The legal framework generally provides for democratic elections. The electoral rolls have been improved since the 2013 introduction of a biometric voter registration system. Nevertheless, the Solomon Islands Electoral Commission (SIEC) found 4,000 instances of multiple voter registration during the 2018–19 registration period. The SIEC reported its findings to the police but noted that many of these incidents would likely go uninvestigated for a lack of resources.

B. POLITICAL PLURALISM AND PARTICIPATION: 14 / 16

B1. Do the people have the right to organize in different political parties or other competitive political groupings of their choice, and is the system free of undue obstacles to the rise and fall of these competing parties or groupings? 4 / 4

There are no restrictions on the right to organize political parties, but political alliances are driven more by personal ties and local allegiances than formal policy positions or ideology. Party affiliations shift frequently, often as part of efforts to dislodge incumbent governments. MPs shifted to Our Party days after the April 2019 polls were held and defections continued in 2019 and 2020. In September 2019, several Kadere MPs defected to Our Party. In June 2020, a SIDP MP defected to Our Party.

The 2014 Political Parties Integrity Act was meant to encourage a stronger party system through more formalized registration mechanisms. Many formerly party-aligned legislators stood as independents in the 2014 and 2019 elections, calculating that doing so left them with greater flexibility under the legislation. Of the 333 candidates who took part in the April 2019 elections, 170 ran as party candidates, while another 163 ran as independents.

B2. Is there a realistic opportunity for the opposition to increase its support or gain power through elections? 4 / 4

Opposition parties and candidates may campaign freely, and power shifts frequently between rival groups. Since 1978, three governments have been ousted in opposition-led no-confidence votes, and prime ministers have resigned to fend off no-confidence challenges on two occasions. No incumbent premier has been able to win reelection, although both Sogavare and former prime minister Solomon Mamaloni were repeatedly able to return to that post after a period in opposition.

B3. Are the people's political choices free from domination by forces that are external to the political sphere, or by political forces that employ extrapolitical means? 3 / 4

People's political choices are generally unconstrained, though church and tribal leaders exert strong influence in some areas. On the island of New Georgia, the Christian Fellowship Church has secured reelection of its candidate, Job Dudley Tausinga, since 1984. Tausinga lost his seat in 2014 as the church faced a reported internal schism.

China has sought to deepen ties with the Solomon Islands, and won the government's diplomatic recognition in 2019. Concerns over Chinese activity persisted in 2020. In February, a $100 billion loan proposal from Chinese creditors leaked to the public. Observers objected to the proposal, calling it unrealistic. In September, Malaita Province premier Suidani cited a COVID-19 repatriation flight that mostly carried Chinese passengers and the national government's relationship with China when announcing his intentions to hold an independence referendum for the province. The national government objected to the plan, calling it illegal.

B4. Do various segments of the population (including ethnic, racial, religious, gender, LGBT+, and other relevant groups) have full political rights and electoral opportunities? 3 / 4

Women and ethnic minorities enjoy full political rights under the law, but discrimination limits political opportunities for women in practice. While lawmakers have voiced support for increasing women's participation in the National Parliament, including by reserving seats, only four women held seats at the end of 2020.

C. FUNCTIONING OF GOVERNMENT: 7 / 12

C1. Do the freely elected head of government and national legislative representatives determine the policies of the government? 3 / 4

Solomon Islands governments have generally been able to determine national policy without outside interference, but the country's fractious politics hamper efficient policy-making. Prime ministers have struggled to sustain legislative majorities, and cabinet splits are frequent. Ministries are often run as ministers' personal fiefdoms, lacking accountability to the prime minister.

Prime ministers can consequently face significant difficulty when enacting policy choices, with decisions prompting fights for political survival. Sogavare's decision to switch diplomatic recognition from Taiwan to China in 2019 temporarily destabilized his government, with a group of pro-Taiwan MPs—including planning minister and former prime minister Rick "Hou" Houenipwela—being dismissed from cabinet after they abstained from a vote on the matter.

The COVID-19 pandemic impacted representatives' ability to determine policy; budget reviews were disrupted when the parliament was suspended in April, lessening legislative oversight on spending decisions.

C2. Are safeguards against official corruption strong and effective? 3 / 4

Corruption and abuse of office are serious problems. The previous Sogavare government struggled to win support for anticorruption legislation in 2016 and 2017, largely due to resistance from within the cabinet. In 2018, the Hou government secured passage of the Anti-Corruption Act, which establishes an independent anticorruption commission, and the Whistleblowers Protection Act. Some opposition MPs considered the laws, which allowed the use of local custom as a defense in corruption cases and restricted retroactive application, watered down.

Under both the Sogavare and Hou governments, a number of senior officials were investigated or arrested on corruption charges due to the efforts of Task Force Janus, a joint anticorruption initiative between the police force and the Finance Ministry. However, prosecutors have had difficulty winning convictions against politicians accused of corruption. Task Force Janus operations continued in 2020, with an Agriculture Ministry accountant facing corruption charges in September after the task force investigated his activities.

C3. Does the government operate with openness and transparency? 1 / 4

Successive governments have not operated transparently. State dealings with foreign logging companies and mining companies are not open to scrutiny. There is no law stipulating a formal process by which the public may request official information.

Commonwealth observers who monitored the April 2019 elections voiced concern over the possible misuse of the public Rural Constituency Development Fund (RCDF) ahead of the campaign; in late 2018, each MP received funds from the RCDF, which were allegedly used for campaigning purposes. Despite these concerns, efforts to improve accountability for funds spent by MPs in their constituencies have been unsuccessful.

In August 2020, the existence a discretionary fund controlled by Sogavare and funded by China was made public. Previous governments have been accused of benefiting from Taiwan-funded discretionary vehicles.

CIVIL LIBERTIES: 49 / 60

D. FREEDOM OF EXPRESSION AND BELIEF: 16 / 16

D1. Are there free and independent media? 4 / 4

Freedom of the press is usually respected. While politicians and elites sometimes use legal and extralegal means to intimidate journalists, such incidents have been relatively rare in recent years. There are several print newspapers. The government operates a national radio station, and subnational and private radio stations are also available. Subscription television services offer some local content in addition to foreign broadcasts.

In 2018, the Solomon Islands adopted the Whistleblowers Protection Act, which was expected to facilitate journalistic efforts to report on political corruption. In 2019, Reporters Without Borders (RSF) criticized the use of defamation laws, warning that they intimidated journalists and encouraged self-censorship. In May 2020, Solomon Islands police disclosed they were investigating commentator Wendy Amangongo, who wrote several critical articles over the Solomon Islands–China diplomatic relationship, for allegedly breaching emergency measures.

D2. Are individuals free to practice and express their religious faith or nonbelief in public and private? 4 / 4

Freedom of religion is generally respected. Registration requirements for religious groups are not onerous, and religious education is not mandatory.

D3. Is there academic freedom, and is the educational system free from extensive political indoctrination? 4 / 4

Academic freedom is generally respected.

D4. Are individuals free to express their personal views on political or other sensitive topics without fear of surveillance or retribution? 4 / 4

While social taboos persist regarding the open discussion of topics including domestic violence, rape, and child abuse, individuals have historically been free to express their views on politics and other sensitive matters.

However, in November 2020, the government began considering a ban on Facebook, citing concerns including "abusive language." Amnesty International denounced the proposal, which was also criticized by the Chamber of Commerce, government MPs, and members of the opposition. The potential ban remained under consideration at year's end.

E. ASSOCIATIONAL AND ORGANIZATIONAL RIGHTS: 10 / 12
E1. Is there freedom of assembly? 3 / 4

Freedom of assembly is constitutionally guaranteed and generally upheld. However, peaceful demonstrations can give way to civil unrest, particularly during contentious parliamentary debates, elections, or large-scale labor actions.

E2. Is there freedom for nongovernmental organizations, particularly those that are engaged in human rights- and governance-related work? 4 / 4

Nongovernmental organizations (NGOs) often operate informally and the government is not always receptive to the viewpoints of governance-focused groups. Locally based NGOs often lack resources and reportedly grow dependent on the funds and priorities of international donors. Nevertheless, there are no major constraints on NGO activities in the Solomon Islands.

E3. Is there freedom for trade unions and similar professional or labor organizations? 3 / 4

Workers are free to organize, and strikes are permitted with certain restrictions. Laws against antiunion discrimination by employers are reportedly ineffective. The country's main labor union, the Solomon Islands National Union of Workers, was disbanded by court order in 2013 after lengthy litigation over an illegal strike by plantation workers. However, labor activists registered a new entity, the Workers Union of Solomon Islands, in 2014.

In November 2020, the government suspended the country's nurses' association for launching an unapproved strike in October. Participants alleged they did not receive COVID-19-related allowances.

F. RULE OF LAW: 11 / 16
F1. Is there an independent judiciary? 4 / 4

The judiciary has a reputation for independence, though a severe lack of resources has contributed to case backlogs. Judges are appointed by the governor general on the advice of an impartial Judicial and Legal Service Commission. The Court of Appeal is mainly reliant on foreign judges.

F2. Does due process prevail in civil and criminal matters? 2 / 4

Limited resources and capacity restraints are responsible for somewhat common due-process deficiencies. Half of the country's prison inmates are on remand awaiting trial due to case backlogs. Due-process deficiencies also marred the country's COVID-19 response; in April 2020, the chief magistrate released 58 people accused of violating pandemic-related curfew measures that month for want of official charges against them.

F3. Is there protection from the illegitimate use of physical force and freedom from war and insurgencies? 3 / 4

There are few major threats to physical security, though crime remains a problem in some areas. While the country has a history of internal conflict, the threat has subsided over the past two decades, thanks in large part to security aid from international partners.

Rebuilding the police force, which was disarmed in 2003, was the major focus of the Australian-led Regional Assistance Mission to the Solomon Islands (RAMSI), which launched that year. Nearly all Royal Solomon Islands Police Force (RSIPF) officers resigned, retired, or been dismissed since 2003. An extensive training program has since created a force with younger members and with better geographic and gender balance. In 2016, RAMSI undertook a limited rearmament of the police force. RAMSI concluded in 2017, but a residual Australian advisory program continues, while Australia and New Zealand have bilaterally extended RAMSI programs. Mostyn Mangau became the first locally appointed police commissioner in 19 years when he was sworn in in July 2020.

F4. Do laws, policies, and practices guarantee equal treatment of various segments of the population? 2 / 4

The constitution prohibits discrimination based on race, place of origin, sex, and some other categories, but the legal framework does not provide robust protections. De facto discrimination limits economic opportunities for women. Same-sex sexual activity can be punished with up to 14 years' imprisonment. While cases are reportedly rare, the government has resisted international pressure to decriminalize such activity.

Discrimination based on regional differences also remains a factor. The Guadalcanal Plains Palm Oil Ltd. (GPPOL) operation on northern Guadalcanal, one of the country's biggest employers, avoids employing laborers from Malaita, even on a casual basis, for fear of antagonizing local communities.

Ethnic Chinese residents have also faced discrimination; businesses and buildings owned or operated by ethnic Chinese were targeted during the unrest following Sogavare's appointment in 2019. The Malaita provincial government has also terminated licenses for businesses owned and operated by ethnic Chinese. Malaita premier Suidani, meanwhile, has publicly referred to the novel coronavirus as the "Wuhan virus."

G. PERSONAL AUTONOMY AND INDIVIDUAL RIGHTS: 12 / 16

G1. Do individuals enjoy freedom of movement, including the ability to change their place of residence, employment, or education? 3 / 4

Residents generally enjoy freedom of movement, but some impediments exist, particularly in parts of rural Guadalcanal where people from the island of Malaita were expelled during the unrest in 1999–2000. Hostility to Malaitan settlement persists in parts of Western Province.

G2. Are individuals able to exercise the right to own property and establish private businesses without undue interference from state or nonstate actors? 3 / 4

The legal and regulatory framework largely supports property ownership and private business activity. However, property rights are frequently contested. GPPOL administrative buildings have been attacked in the past. Logging concessions have been disputed by local groups, as have tourism operations.

In December 2020, Prime Minister Sogavare voiced his intention to restrict the sale of land to foreign buyers and bolster indigenous land rights via constitutional amendments.

G3. Do individuals enjoy personal social freedoms, including choice of marriage partner and size of family, protection from domestic violence, and control over appearance? 3 / 4

Individual freedoms on personal status issues such as marriage and divorce are generally protected. However, the legal age of marriage is 15, and about a fifth of women are married by age 18. Despite the 2014 Family Protection Act, which formally criminalized domestic violence and enabled victims to apply for protection orders, domestic violence and rape are serious and underreported problems. Victims are reluctant to take their cases to court.

G4. Do individuals enjoy equality of opportunity and freedom from economic exploitation? 3 / 4

Legal protections against exploitative working conditions are not consistently enforced, though authorities have made efforts to update and implement laws against human trafficking in recent years. Local and foreign women and children are vulnerable to sex trafficking and domestic servitude, including through forced marriages or "adoptions" to pay off debts. Migrant workers sometimes face forced labor in the mining, logging, and fishing industries.

Somalia

Population: 15,900,000
Capital: Mogadishu
Freedom Status: Not Free
Electoral Democracy: No

Note: The numerical scores and status listed above do not reflect conditions in Somaliland, which is examined in a separate report. *Freedom in the World* reports assess the level of political rights and civil liberties in a given geographical area, regardless of whether they are affected by the state, nonstate actors, or foreign powers. Disputed territories are sometimes assessed separately if they meet certain criteria, including boundaries that are sufficiently stable to allow year-on-year comparisons. For more information, see the report methodology and FAQ.

Overview: Somalia has struggled to reestablish a functioning state since the collapse of an authoritarian regime in 1991. Limited, indirect elections brought a federal government to power in 2012. By 2016, it had established five federal member states, though these semiautonomous regions are often at odds with the central government. The government's territorial control is also contested by a separatist government in Somaliland and by the Shabaab, an Islamist militant group. No direct national elections have been held to date, and political affairs remain dominated by clan divisions. Amid ongoing insecurity, impunity for human rights abuses by both state and nonstate actors is the norm.

KEY DEVELOPMENTS IN 2020

- The country experienced an initial wave of COVID-19 cases from April to June, followed by an apparent second wave later in the year, though testing and reporting of cases were limited and inconsistent. About 4,700 cases and 130 deaths had been reported by year's end. The authorities harassed journalists who published critical information about the government's response.
- In August, the president signed legislation that granted the government increased oversight of the media sector and included vague provisions criminalizing the publication of content that is deemed false, contrary to the national interest, or incitement of clan divisions.

- Federal and state leaders agreed in September to hold the next parliamentary elections using a clan-based voting system, setting aside plans for direct popular voting. While the elections were initially set for December, ongoing political disagreements about the process led to a postponement, and a new date had yet to be selected at year's end.

POLITICAL RIGHTS: 1 / 40
A. ELECTORAL PROCESS: 0 / 12
A1. Was the current head of government or other chief national authority elected through free and fair elections? 0 / 4

Under the 2012 provisional constitution, the president is elected by a two-thirds vote in the Federal Parliament to serve a four-year term. In February 2017, legislators who were not freely elected themselves chose Mohamed Abdullahi Mohamed, also known as "Farmaajo," as president.

The president shares executive power with a prime minister, who must have the support of Parliament. In September 2020, Parliament confirmed the appointment of Mohamed Hussein Roble to replace Hassan Ali Khaire, who was ousted as prime minister in a July no-confidence vote amid disagreements with the president on a timeline for elections.

A series of indirect elections for state-level executives have been held in recent years, though none were rooted in free or direct legislative elections. Lawmakers in South West State selected a president in 2018, and the parliaments in Puntland and Jubaland chose their state presidents in 2019. The federal government called the Jubaland outcome "unconstitutional" due to problems including registration barriers for some candidates; in June 2020 it recognized the reelected incumbent as an "interim" president with a two-year mandate, while Jubaland authorities insisted that he had a full four-year mandate. Separately, lawmakers in the state of Galmudug elected Ahmed Abdi Kariye as president in February, and the Hirshabelle legislature elected Ali Gudlawe Hussein as that state's leader in November.

A2. Were the current national legislative representatives elected through free and fair elections? 0 / 4

Somalia has not held direct legislative elections since 1969. Limited voting for the bicameral Federal Parliament was held between October 2016 and February 2017. Members of the 54-seat upper house were elected by state assemblies, while the lower house was elected under a system in which 135 clan elders chose 275 electoral colleges, each of which had 51 people and elected one lawmaker. Corruption reportedly played a major role in the elections and the operations of the legislature once constituted. The federal member states have similarly employed clan-based power-sharing systems rather than direct popular elections to form their legislatures.

A3. Are the electoral laws and framework fair, and are they implemented impartially by the relevant election management bodies? 0 / 4

The electoral framework in use for the most recent parliamentary elections did not provide for universal suffrage. The balloting was the result of an ad-hoc process based on lengthy negotiations among the country's main clans.

In September 2020, President Farmaajo and the leaders of the federal member states agreed to hold parliamentary elections in December, again using a system in which clan elders would choose members of electoral colleges, who would in turn elect lawmakers, though the clan delegates would be more numerous than in the last elections. The new Parliament was then scheduled to elect the country's president in February 2021, according to this plan. However, in November the federal government appointed members to the federal election commission and a dispute-resolution commission, drawing strong objections from opposition groups, which argued that the panels were stacked in favor of the incumbent president. As a result of the ongoing dispute, the elections set for December were postponed, and no new date had been established at year's end.

B. POLITICAL PLURALISM AND PARTICIPATION: 1 / 16

B1. o the people have the right to organize in different political parties or other competitive political groupings of their choice, and is the system free of undue obstacles to the rise and fall of these competing parties or groupings? 1 / 4

Legislation enacted in 2016 allowed the first formal registration of political parties since 1969. The National Independent Electoral Commission (NIEC) has since registered more than 100 parties. However, because the September 2020 political agreement on the upcoming parliamentary elections called for a clan-based process and rejected plans for direct popular voting, it was unclear whether political parties would be allowed to play a significant or formal role in the contest. The agreement also called for candidate registration fees that were twice as high as the previous amounts, potentially favoring more established political figures.

State-level authorities exercise varying degrees of control over organized political activity. In May 2020, the police in South West State reportedly renewed the previous year's ban on political gatherings that were not authorized in advance by the state government.

B2. Is there a realistic opportunity for the opposition to increase its support or gain power through elections? 0 / 4

The lack of direct elections prevents any group from gaining power through democratic means. However, there was an orderly transfer of executive power in February 2017, and the federal states and legislature provide platforms for some competing forces to exercise influence and authority.

B3. Are the people's political choices free from domination by forces that are external to the political sphere, or by political forces that employ extrapolitical means? 0 / 4

Ordinary citizens are largely unable to participate in the political process as voters, and the indirect electoral process in 2016–17 was reportedly distorted by vote buying, intimidation, and violence.

B4. Do various segments of the population (including ethnic, racial, religious, gender, LGBT+, and other relevant groups) have full political rights and electoral opportunities? 0 / 4

Presidential candidates are required to be Muslim, according to the provisional constitution.

The current political system is designed to ensure some representation for the country's many clans, but the prevailing "4.5" formula gives the four largest groups—the Hawiye, Darod, Dir, and Rahanweyn—eight out of every nine positions, marginalizing all other clans. The system is also affected by intraclan rivalries and dominated by clan leaders, who do not necessarily represent the interests of their respective groups.

Women's political participation is limited by discriminatory attitudes and hostility from incumbent elites, and the interests of women are poorly represented in practice. Women hold about 24 percent of the seats in both chambers of the Federal Parliament. Lawmakers in 2020 were considering legislation that would mandate a 30 percent quota for women's representation in Parliament, but it had yet to be enacted at year's end.

C. FUNCTIONING OF GOVERNMENT: 0 / 12

C1. Do the freely elected head of government and national legislative representatives determine the policies of the government? 0 / 4

The government, which is not democratically elected, has little practical ability to implement its laws and policies even in parts of the country it controls. Its basic operations are heavily dependent on international bodies and donor governments. Relations between the federal government and the administrations of the federal member states remain poor. Critics and rivals have accused President Farmaajo of seeking to centralize power, and tensions between the president and the leaders of Jubaland and Puntland played a key role in disputes over the electoral process in 2020.

C2. Are safeguards against official corruption strong and effective? 0 / 4

Corruption is rampant in Somalia, and state agencies tasked with combating it do not function effectively. Impunity is the norm for public officials accused of malfeasance.

A 2019 law called for the creation of state and national anticorruption commissions, and a nine-member national commission was nominated in 2020, but the appointments had yet to be approved by the upper house of Parliament at year's end. As part of a national anticorruption strategy adopted by the cabinet in June 2020, the government ratified the African Union Convention on Preventing and Combating Corruption and announced that it would join and sign the UN Convention against Corruption. The lower house of Parliament endorsed the latter convention in December.

In August, a court in the capital sentenced four Health Ministry officials to prison terms ranging from three to 18 years for theft of donor funds meant to address the COVID-19 pandemic. The court acquitted five other defendants for lack of evidence.

C3. Does the government operate with openness and transparency? 0 / 4

Government transparency is limited. Officials are not required to make public declarations of their income and assets, and oversight procedures for public contracts are not well enforced. There is no law guaranteeing public access to government information.

CIVIL LIBERTIES: 6 / 60

D. FREEDOM OF EXPRESSION AND BELIEF: 3 / 16

D1. Are there free and independent media? 1 / 4

While the provisional constitution calls for freedom of the press, journalists regularly face harassment, arbitrary detention and fines, and violence from both state and nonstate actors. Media outlets have also been temporarily suspended by the Ministry of Information in response to their coverage. The Committee to Protect Journalists reported that 69 journalists had been killed since 1992, including at least one in 2020. Freelance broadcast journalist Abdiwali Ali Hassan was fatally shot by two gunmen near his home in Afgooye in February, having received multiple threats related to his work.

Among other cases of harassment and detention during the year, the national intelligence agency detained Radio Hiigsi journalist Mohamed Abdiwahab Nuur in March and charged him with murder and being a member of the Shabaab; a military court acquitted him in August. Also in March, Puntland police arrested a journalist who was asking the public about their views on the government's COVID-19 response, and in April police in Mogadishu arrested Goobjoog Media Group executive Abdiaziz Ahmed Gurbiye after he used social media to criticize the government's performance on the pandemic. Abdiaziz was sentenced in July to six months in prison and a fine for spreading false news, though the prison term was commuted.

In August, the president signed amendments to the media law that included ostensible protections for journalists' rights but also featured vaguely worded provisions criminalizing the dissemination of "false information," reports that conflict with the "national interest," and incitement to violence and clan divisions. The law grants the Ministry of Information broad powers to regulate the media.

D2. Are individuals free to practice and express their religious faith or nonbelief in public and private? 0 / 4

Nearly all Somalis are Sunni Muslims, though there is a very small Christian community whose members generally do not practice their religion in public. Conversion from Islam is illegal in some areas, and suspicions of conversion can draw societal harassment throughout the country. The provisional constitution recognizes Islam as the official religion and forbids the promotion of any other faith. However, it also includes clauses promoting religious freedom and forbidding discrimination based on religion.

In areas under their control, the Shabaab use violence to enforce their interpretation of Islam, including execution as a penalty for alleged apostasy.

D3. Is there academic freedom, and is the educational system free from extensive political indoctrination? 1 / 4

Despite limited funding and infrastructure and other challenges, universities operate in major cities. Academics reportedly practice self-censorship on sensitive topics. Islamic instruction is required in all schools except those operated by non-Muslim minority groups. Schools under Shabaab control integrate radical interpretations of Islam into the curriculum.

D4. Are individuals free to express their personal views on political or other sensitive topics without fear of surveillance or retribution? 1 / 4

Individuals enjoy some freedom of expression in more secure areas of the country, but criticism of powerful figures in the state and society can draw reprisals, and social media posts that touch on sensitive political or religious topics are subject to criminal punishment. Open debate is severely restricted in areas controlled or threatened by the Shabaab.

E. ASSOCIATIONAL AND ORGANIZATIONAL RIGHTS: 3 / 12
E1. Is there freedom of assembly? 1 / 4

Although the provisional constitution guarantees freedom of assembly, security officials require approval for demonstrations and have used violence to suppress unauthorized protests. Some demonstrations proceeded peacefully during 2020, but others were dispersed with lethal force. In July, police in the capital used live ammunition to break up a demonstration against the postponement of elections. Election-related opposition protests in December similarly prompted police violence.

E2. Is there freedom for nongovernmental organizations, particularly those that are engaged in human rights- and governance-related work? 1 / 4

Local civil society groups, international nongovernmental organizations (NGOs), and UN agencies have been able to conduct a wide range of activities in some parts of the country, but they face difficult and often dangerous working conditions. Regional authorities and security forces have reportedly harassed, extorted, obstructed, and attempted to control NGOs and aid groups, and the Shabaab generally do not allow such organizations to operate in their territory.

E3. Is there freedom for trade unions and similar professional or labor organizations? 1 / 4

Independent labor unions are active in Somalia and have worked to expand their operations and capacity. However, constitutional and legal protections for union activity are not always respected. The Federation of Somali Trade Unions has reported threats, dismissals, attempts at co-optation, and other forms of repression and interference from both government officials and private employers.

F. RULE OF LAW: 0 / 16

F1. Is there an independent judiciary? 0 / 4

The judicial system in Somalia is fractured, understaffed, and rife with corruption. Its authority is not widely respected, with state officials ignoring court rulings and citizens often turning to Islamic or customary law as alternatives.

In July 2020, the cabinet approved the appointment of five members to the Judicial Service Commission, a constitutionally required body tasked with overseeing the federal courts. Political opposition groups, the Somali Bar Association, and civil society organizations criticized the appointments, arguing that the individuals were chosen based on clan affiliation rather than the required credentials, and that the cabinet had only caretaker authority given the recent no-confidence vote against the prime minister.

F2. Does due process prevail in civil and criminal matters? 0 / 4

Safeguards against arbitrary arrest and detention are not observed by the country's police, intelligence, and military services, and their work is undermined by corruption. Clan politics and other external factors often play a role in the outcome of court cases. Military courts routinely try civilians, including for terrorism-related offenses, and do not respect basic international standards for due process.

F3. Is there protection from the illegitimate use of physical force and freedom from war and insurgencies? 0 / 4

The ongoing armed conflict has featured numerous terrorist attacks on government, international, and civilian targets, as well as indiscriminate lethal violence and excessive force against civilians by government security services, international troops, and various local militias. The United Nations documented the killing of 557 civilians during 2020, a slight decrease from the previous year. Reported incidents included suicide bombings with civilian targets, clashes between Shabaab militants and villagers, and assassinations.

Authorities carry out executions ordered by military courts after flawed proceedings. Detainees are at risk of torture in custody, and perpetrators generally enjoy impunity. The Shabaab also engage in public executions of those they suspect of working with the government or international forces.

F4. Do laws, policies, and practices guarantee equal treatment of various segments of the population? 0 / 4

While the provisional constitution and legal system offer some formal protections against discrimination based on sex, clan, and other categories, they have little force in practice. Women face widespread disadvantages in areas including housing, education, and employment, while members of marginalized clans and some non-Somali ethnic groups suffer disproportionately from economic exclusion and violence.

LGBT+ people generally do not make their identity public. Same-sex sexual activity can be punished with up to three years in prison under the penal code, and individuals accused of engaging in such activity are subject to execution in Shabaab-controlled areas.

G. PERSONAL AUTONOMY AND INDIVIDUAL RIGHTS: 0 / 16

G1. Do individuals enjoy freedom of movement, including the ability to change their place of residence, employment, or education? 0 / 4

Travel throughout Somalia is dangerous due to periodic combat, attacks on civilians, and the presence of checkpoints controlled by security forces, militias, the Shabaab, and other armed groups that commonly extract arbitrary fees and bribes from travelers.

There were an estimated 2.6 million internally displaced people in Somalia as of 2020, the majority of whom were forced to move due to conflict and insecurity, though flooding and other natural disasters were also factors.

Police reportedly used excessive force when implementing movement restrictions related to COVID-19. In April 2020, an officer killed two civilians while enforcing a curfew in the capital; the alleged perpetrator was sentenced to death by a military court in July.

G2. Are individuals able to exercise the right to own property and establish private businesses without undue interference from state or nonstate actors? 0 / 4

The provisional constitution guarantees property rights, but securing ownership is complicated by a mixture of formal and informal or traditional systems governing land rights. Procedures for registering property and businesses are impeded by corruption and other barriers, and disputes can lead to intimidation and violence. The Shabaab and other extremist groups manage elaborate extortion and "taxation" schemes, placing tremendous pressure on business owners.

Women do not enjoy equal rights to inherit property and are often denied the assets to which they are legally entitled due to discriminatory social norms.

G3. Do individuals enjoy personal social freedoms, including choice of marriage partner and size of family, protection from domestic violence, and control over appearance? 0 / 4

Sexual violence remains a major problem, especially for displaced persons. Perpetrators include government troops and militia members. Forced and early marriage are also widespread in the country. The Shabaab impose forced marriages with their fighters, and individuals can face strong societal pressure to marry or not marry within certain clans. In August 2020 lawmakers began consideration of draft legislation that would effectively permit minors to marry based on physical maturity and make it more difficult to penalize forced marriage. Female genital mutilation is extremely common despite a formal ban.

G4. Do individuals enjoy equality of opportunity and freedom from economic exploitation? 0 / 4

Child labor and trafficking in persons for the purposes of sexual exploitation or forced labor are common. Refugees and displaced persons are particularly vulnerable to exploitation, and these populations also suffered disproportionately from the economic effects of the COVID-19 pandemic and related restrictions in 2020. Children are abducted or recruited to serve as fighters by the Shabaab and to a lesser extent by government and militia forces.

South Africa

Population: 59.6 million
Capital: Pretoria
Freedom Status: Free
Electoral Democracy: Yes

Overview: South Africa is a constitutional democracy. Since the end of apartheid in 1994, it has been regarded globally as a proponent of human rights and a leader on the African continent. However, in recent years, the ruling African National Congress (ANC) has been accused of undermining state institutions in order to protect corrupt officials and preserve its power as its support base began to wane. In 2018, a widely respected anticorruption commission led by a judge began hearing testimony about high-level corruption allegations. The commission will conclude its hearings in 2021.

KEY DEVELOPMENTS IN 2020

- In August, allegations of corruption were brought against high-ranking officials, including in President Cyril Ramaphosa's government, for purchases that were a part of the $26 billion COVID-19 relief package. Private companies charged the government in some cases more than five times the price the national treasury had advised for personal protective equipment.
- At least 10 Black South Africans were killed by police officers and military personnel who enforced COVID-19 lockdowns with violence. In April, Collins Khosa died after he was assaulted in his yard by soldiers and police officers who had accused him of breaking COVID-19 restrictions. A leaked report from the South African National Defense Force (SANDF) claimed the soldiers involved in the incident were not liable for Khosa's death, which caused public outrage. Khosa's family sued the government, and a judge issued a landmark ruling forcing the SANDF to implement codes of conduct around the use of force.
- In November, the secretary general of the ANC, Ace Magashule, was arrested on 21 counts of corruption. In 2014, as premier of the Free State Province, Magashule awarded a 255 million rand ($14 million) asbestos removal contract to close business associates from whom he allegedly received undue benefits.
- Rates of femicide and gender-based violence continued to rise. In April, police minister Bheki Cele reported that the police had received more than 2,300 complaints of gender-based violence in the first week that COVID-19 restrictions were implemented. In September, President Ramaphosa introduced three bills to the National Assembly to combat gender-based violence.

POLITICAL RIGHTS: 33 / 40

A. ELECTORAL PROCESS: 12 / 12

A1. Was the current head of government or other chief national authority elected through free and fair elections? 4 / 4

The National Assembly, the main legislative house of South Africa's bicameral Parliament, elects the president to serve concurrently with its five-year term, and can vote to replace him or her at any time. Presidents can serve a maximum of two terms of five years each.

Former president and ANC leader Jacob Zuma survived four parliamentary no-confidence votes before ANC delegates elected Deputy President Cyril Ramaphosa to become party leader at a 2017 conference. Ramaphosa defeated former African Union (AU) Commission Chairperson Nkosazana Dlamini-Zuma, President Zuma's ex-wife and preferred candidate for the leadership. This defeat made it difficult for Zuma to remain as South Africa's president, and the ANC executive committee forced his resignation in early 2018. The National Assembly then selected Ramaphosa to serve as acting president.

The most recent national election, held in May 2019, was declared free and fair by domestic and international observers. The ANC won 57.5 percent of the vote, and the National Assembly selected Ramaphosa to serve a full term as president later that month.

A2. Were the current national legislative representatives elected through free and fair elections? 4 / 4

The 400-seat National Assembly is elected by party-list proportional representation. The 90 members of the upper chamber, the National Council of Provinces, are selected by provincial legislatures. Parliamentary and provincial elections were concurrently held in May 2019. The ANC won 230 National Assembly seats with 57.5 percent of the vote. The opposition Democratic Alliance (DA) won 84 seats with 20.77 percent of the vote and maintained control over Western Cape Province. The Economic Freedom Fighters (EFF) won 44 seats, the Inkatha Freedom Party (IFP) won 14, Freedom Front Plus (FF+) won 10, and smaller parties won the remaining 18 seats.

A3. Are the electoral laws and framework fair, and are they implemented impartially by the relevant election management bodies? 4 / 4

The Independent Electoral Commission (IEC) is largely considered independent, and the electoral framework is considered fair. However, in recent years concerns have been raised around the integrity of the commission's leadership.

The IEC has been working to comply with a 2016 Constitutional Court directive to accurately record the addresses of all registered voters. In 2018, the IEC received an extension to comply with the court order after citing logistical difficulties, and was given a new deadline of November 2019. By September 2019, as the process neared its conclusion, the IEC reported that only five percent of all registered voters had no address on file.

The IEC is also responsible for enforcing the Political Party Funding Act, which was passed by the National Assembly in 2018 and signed into law by President Ramaphosa in January 2019. The legislation requires political parties to disclose donations worth at least 100,000 rand ($7,100), and prohibits funders from donating more than 15 million rand ($1 million) annually; foreign donations were also prohibited. However, the IEC warned that full implementation would not take place in time for the May 2019 elections. Funding for internal party contests remains relatively opaque; in August 2019, President Ramaphosa declined to name the backers of his successful 2017 ANC leadership campaign, saying no rules were in place to mandate this reporting.

B. POLITICAL PLURALISM AND PARTICIPATION: 13 / 16

B1. Do the people have the right to organize in different political parties or other competitive political groupings of their choice, and is the system free of undue obstacles to the rise and fall of these competing parties or groupings? 3 / 4

The ANC, which is part of a tripartite governing alliance with the Congress of South African Trade Unions (COSATU) and the South African Communist Party (SACP), has won every national election since 1994. Nevertheless, the political environment is generally free from formal constraints, and opposition parties have gained ground in recent elections.

Several new political groups have recently emerged, as well. The National Union of Metalworkers of South Africa, which largely represents private sector workers, sponsored the formation of the Socialist Revolutionary Workers' Party, which launched in April 2019. Patricia de Lille, the former DA mayor of Cape Town, launched the GOOD party after her split from the opposition in 2018. GOOD won two National Assembly seats in May 2019, and de Lille was subsequently named public works minister.

Nontransparent mechanisms for the funding of political parties have benefited the ANC, though reforms to party financing laws were passed by the National Assembly in 2018.

Over 90 political murders have taken place in KwaZulu-Natal Province since 2015. In 2017, the ANC deputy chairperson of the Harry Gwala region, Khaya Thobela, and a former

ANC Youth Leader, Sindiso Magaqa, were killed in separate incidents. In May 2019, ANC councilor Martin Sithole was shot and killed; Sithole was expected to serve as a witness in the murder trial of another ANC member before his own death. In August of that year, IFP councilor Mthembeni Majola was murdered; a second IFP councilor, Khayelihle Sithole, was killed two months later.

In June 2020, the Constitutional Court ruled that individuals are entitled to contest national and provincial elections. Parliament was given 24 months to enact electoral reforms to enable individuals to contest seats in the National Assembly. Since 1994, only political parties were entitled to contest National Assembly seats in a system of proportional representation.

B2. Is there a realistic opportunity for the opposition to increase its support or gain power through elections? 3 / 4

Despite the ANC's political dominance, the party recorded its poorest performance since the end of apartheid in the May 2019 contest. Meanwhile, opposition parties have made local and regional gains; in the 2016 municipal elections, the ANC lost its majorities in the Johannesburg and Tshwane municipalities, the metropolitan area that includes the national capital city of Pretoria. Opposition gains in local elections are especially significant because of the taxation powers and autonomy afforded to municipalities, presenting opposition parties with an opportunity to demonstrate governance capacity.

B3. Are the people's political choices free from domination by forces that are external to the political sphere, or by political forces that employ extrapolitical means? 3 / 4

People's political choices in South Africa are largely free from domination from external actors, and the military is professional and generally stays out of politics. However, there is widespread corruption within the ANC; party officials have been accused of buying delegates' votes to the party conference and paying bribes to influence political appointments. There have also been reports of individuals buying party membership cards in bulk in order to hold full control of specific branches of the party.

The Gupta family's close relationship with and influence over former president Zuma remains a pressing political topic, as well as the subject of an ongoing state capture inquiry. President Ramaphosa has come under scrutiny since revelations emerged in 2018 that 500,000 rands ($38,000) were directed by the South African logistics firm African Global Operations, formerly known as Bosasa, to Ramaphosa's 2017 leadership campaign.

The arrest of ANC secretary general Ace Magashule for corruption could suggest that internal party decisions are influenced by corrupt actors.

B4. Do various segments of the population (including ethnic, racial, religious, gender, LGBT+, and other relevant groups) have full political rights and electoral opportunities? 4 / 4

The constitution prohibits discrimination and provides full political rights for all adult citizens. Women are well represented in government, holding 47 percent of seats in the National Assembly and 2 of 9 provincial premierships. South Africa has one of the world's most liberal legal environments for LGBT+ people. However, discrimination and the threat of violence can discourage LGBT+ people from political participation in practice.

C. FUNCTIONING OF GOVERNMENT: 8 / 12

C1. Do the freely elected head of government and national legislative representatives determine the policies of the government? 3 / 4

Pervasive corruption and apparent interference by nonelected actors have hampered the proper functioning of government, particularly during the Zuma administration, which the Gupta family heavily influenced. In 2018, Zuma was forced by the High Court to appoint a Judicial Commission of Inquiry into state capture, or external influence held over an administration—namely that of the Gupta family and others. When he came into power, Ramaphosa amended the terms of the state capture inquiry to pave the way for evidence gathered to be used in prosecutions. Zuma has since been waging a legal fight to fend off the commission's demands after he had been implicated by over 30 witnesses in several instances of wrongdoing.

Testimony offered at the commission, as well as media reports, suggest that the Gupta family influenced selections to the cabinet and to the board of state-owned companies. At the end of 2018, the Gupta brothers were living in the United Arab Emirates (UAE), having left South Africa to avoid prosecution. In October 2019, the South African government began discussions with the UAE to finalize an extradition treaty in an effort to secure the Guptas' return.

In January and March 2019, the state capture commission, which primarily focuses on the Zuma administration's dealings with the Gupta family, heard the testimony of former Bosasa executive Angelo Agrizzi, who claimed the company had received preferential government contracts since 2004, and that the firm had bribed as many as 38 officials and politicians during the course of business.

In November 2020, Zuma walked out of a commission meeting to which he had been summoned after a failed attempt to secure the recusal of the presiding judge, the country's deputy chief justice. The following month, the Constitutional Court heard an application to compel Zuma to appear and answer questions regarding his involvement in state capture. Zuma has appeared in front of the commission multiple times and denied the allegations against him.

C2. Are safeguards against official corruption strong and effective? 2 / 4

Comprehensive anticorruption laws and several agencies tasked with combating corruption exist, but enforcement has historically been inadequate. The National Prosecuting Authority (NPA) was hobbled by political interference during the Zuma administration; before Zuma became president, a money-laundering investigation stemming from a $2.5 billion arms deal in the 1990s was effectively set aside by the NPA. In 2018, the NPA announced that it would prosecute Zuma over these allegations, but the former president launched an appeal in October 2019, and in December 2020 the case was postponed until at least February 2021.

Since the late-2018 appointment of Shamila Batohi as the head of the NPA and the May 2019 installation of Hermione Cronje as the head of the investigative directorate within the NPA, a series of high-profile businesspeople linked to the ANC have been arrested on corruption charges. In November 2020, ANC secretary general Ace Magashule was charged with 21 counts of corruption linked to a 255-million-rand ($14 million) asbestos removal contract he awarded to close business associates as premier of the Free State Province in 2014, and from which he allegedly received undue personal benefits.

In July 2019, Public Protector Busisiwe Mkhwebane claimed that Ramaphosa deliberately misled the parliament about the Bosasa donation and called for remedial action against him. The president denied the allegations. In March 2020, the High Court in Pretoria found that Ramaphosa did not intentionally mislead Parliament and Mkwhebane's claims had fundamental problems, including a misapplication of the law. In October, Parliament attempted to remove Mkhwebane from office after the Constitutional Court found her to have been dishonest in her investigations.

In August 2020, allegations of corruption were brought against high-ranking officials, including some affiliated with the ANC and in the Ramaphosa government, for purchases that were a part of the $26 billion coronavirus pandemic relief package. Private companies charged the government in some cases more than five times the price the national treasury had advised for personal protective equipment. Provincial governments were implicated as well: The Eastern Cape provincial health department purchased 100 "emergency scooters," allegedly to combat COVID-19, for $5,993 per unit, though their retail price per unit is $2,337. A report from the auditor general flagged over 30,000 relief grants that required investigation. By August, the government's Special Investigating Unit was investigating more than 20 cases of corruption related to COVID-19 relief money.

C3. Does the government operate with openness and transparency? 3 / 4

Section 32(1) of the South African constitution states that everyone has the right to access "any information held by the state" and requires that private bodies release information necessary for the exercise and protection of rights. The 2000 Promotion of Access to Information Act created a framework for access to information procedures in both public and private entities. However, in practice the procedure of accessing information is laborious and bureaucratic.

State contracts worth hundreds of millions of rand have been awarded to companies linked to the Gupta family and other politically connected businesspeople without following proper procedures. A similar lack of transparency and competitive bidding has affected the awarding of other government contracts.

In August 2020, the Ramaphosa administration promised to overhaul the government's procurement system after evidence of wide-scale corruption in the allotment of the $26 billion COVID-19 relief package.

CIVIL LIBERTIES: 46 / 60
D. FREEDOM OF EXPRESSION AND BELIEF: 15 / 16
D1. Are there free and independent media? 3 / 4

Freedom of expression and the press are constitutionally protected and generally respected in practice. South Africa features a vibrant and adversarial media landscape, including independent civic groups that help counter government efforts to encroach on freedom of expression. In 2017, the media played a crucial role in exposing the corruption linked to the Gupta family and the involvement of British public relations firm Bell Pottinger in stirring up racial tensions in the country.

However, journalists face harassment for critical reporting and occasional attacks, with government and opposition parties exerting pressure on both state-run and independent outlets. In March 2020, the government passed new regulations under the 2002 Disaster Management Act, including some that criminalized disinformation about the COVID-19 pandemic. The Committee to Protect Journalists (CPJ), an independent watchdog for freedom of the press issues, warned that the regulations could be used to further censor legitimate press outlets. In May, police harassed, assaulted, and detained journalist Paul Nthoba, editor of the weekly *Mohokare News*, who photographed four officers while on patrol enforcing coronavirus lockdown measures. Nthoba was charged under a COVID-19 regulation of the Disaster Management Act.

Journalists and rights groups have expressed concern that the misuse of surveillance laws, notably the 2002 Regulation of Interception of Communications and Provision of

Communication-Related Information Act (RICA), can enable spying on reporters. In 2017, the amaBhungane Centre launched a constitutional challenge to RICA, and the Gauteng High Court in September 2019 ruled that several sections of the act were unconstitutional. The amaBhungane Centre then applied to the Constitutional Court to uphold the ruling, but police minister Bheki Cele opposed their application; no court ruling had been made by the end of 2020.

D2. Are individuals free to practice and express their religious faith or nonbelief in public and private? 4 / 4

Freedom of religion is constitutionally guaranteed and actively protected by the government. Religious leaders are largely free to engage in discussions of a political nature without fear of adverse consequences.

D3. Is there academic freedom, and is the educational system free from extensive political indoctrination? 4 / 4

Academic freedom in South Africa is constitutionally guaranteed and actively protected by the government.

D4. Are individuals free to express their personal views on political or other sensitive topics without fear of surveillance or retribution? 4 / 4

South Africans are generally free to engage in private conversations of a political nature without harassment. However, a 2016 report from the United Nations Human Rights Committee expressed concern about the government's use of surveillance and about RICA, the law governing surveillance. In September 2019, the High Court found that parts of the RICA law were unconstitutional because it did not, among other things, have sufficient safeguards against state organs abusing intercepted private communication between citizens. The National Assembly was given two years to rectify the defects. The state's legal challenge against the court ruling was ongoing at the close of 2020.

E. ASSOCIATIONAL AND ORGANIZATIONAL RIGHTS: 12 / 12
E1. Is there freedom of assembly? 4 / 4

Freedom of assembly is constitutionally guaranteed and generally respected, and South Africa has a vibrant protest culture. Demonstrators must notify police of events ahead of time, but are rarely prohibited from gathering; in 2018, the Constitutional Court ruled that a failure to notify authorities of intent to protest could not be classified as a crime. Protests over the government's shortcomings in the provision of public services are common in South Africa, and sometimes turn violent. Police have faced accusations of provoking some protest violence.

E2. Is there freedom for nongovernmental organizations, particularly those that are engaged in human rights- and governance-related work? 4 / 4

South Africa hosts a vibrant civil society. Nongovernmental organizations (NGOs) can register and operate freely, and lawmakers regularly accept input from NGOs on pending legislation.

E3. Is there freedom for trade unions and similar professional or labor organizations? 4 / 4

South African workers are generally free to form, join, and participate in independent trade unions, and the country's labor laws offer unionized workers a litany of protections. Contract workers and those in the informal sector enjoy fewer safeguards. Strike activity is very common, and unionized workers often secure above-inflation wage increases. Union rivalries, especially in mining, sometimes result in the use of violent tactics to recruit and retain members and to attack opponents.

F. RULE OF LAW: 9 / 16

F1. Is there an independent judiciary? 3 / 4

The constitution guarantees judicial independence, and courts operate with substantial autonomy in practice. The government lost several cases during 2019, notably the amaBhungane Center's successful challenge of the RICA legislation. The Judicial Services Commission recommends to the president the appointment of Constitutional Court judges based on both merit and efforts to racially diversify the judiciary.

F2. Does due process prevail in civil and criminal matters? 2 / 4

Prosecutorial independence in South Africa has been undermined in recent years, with the National Prosecuting Authority (NPA) experiencing a string of politically motivated appointments and ousters. However, President Ramaphosa appointed a new NPA head in 2018, who has worked to reform the institution. In October 2019, the NPA further bolstered its capacity when it hired several private lawyers to prosecute state capture cases.

Shortages of judicial staff and a lack of financial resources undermine defendants' due process rights, including the right to a timely trial and state-funded legal counsel. Many detainees wait months for their trials to begin, and some are held beyond the legal maximum of two years.

F3. Is there protection from the illegitimate use of physical force and freedom from war and insurgencies? 2 / 4

During the COVID-19 lockdown in 2020, security forces were responsible for the death of at least 10 Black South Africans. In one high-profile case in April, Collins Khosa died following an altercation in his yard with security forces who had accused him of drinking alcohol in public, which was illegal under the COVID-19 lockdown restrictions. Soldiers and police beat Khosa, and a medical examination found blunt force head injury to have caused his death. However, a leaked report on the matter by the military board of inquiry of the South African National Defense Force (SANDF) claimed the soldiers involved in the incident were not liable for Khosa's death. The report caused public outrage and Khosa's family sued the government. In May, a North Gauteng High Court judge ruled the soldiers should be suspended. The judge was critical of the SANDF and its failure to ensure the rights of citizens. In a landmark move, the judge ordered the creation of a code of conduct on the use of force.

According to the Judicial Inspectorate for Correctional Services (JICS) 2018–19 annual report, the most recent report available as of this writing, there was severe overcrowding in some prisons—in part due to delays in holding trials and minimum sentencing guidelines. During this period, 103 unnatural deaths were reported in prisons, and there were 155 complaints of officials assaulting inmates.

Despite constitutional prohibitions, police torture and excessive force during arrest, interrogation, and detention are commonly reported. The Independent Police Investigative Directorate (IPID) is legally required to investigate allegations of police offenses or misconduct. In its annual report for 2019–20, the IPID reported 629 deaths either in police custody or as a result of police action, 120 rapes by police officers, 216 incidents of torture, and 3,820 assaults.

Official statistics released in 2020 continue to show a high rate of violent crimes in some parts of the country.

F4. Do laws, policies, and practices guarantee equal treatment of various segments of the population? 2 / 4

The constitution prohibits discrimination based on a range of categories, including race, sexual orientation, and culture. State bodies such as the South African Human Rights Commission (SAHRC) and the Office of the Public Protector are empowered to investigate and prosecute discrimination cases. Affirmative-action legislation has benefited previously disadvantaged racial groups in public and private employment and in education, but racial imbalances in the workforce persist. White people, constituting a small minority, still own a majority of the country's business assets. The indigenous, nomadic Khoikhoi and Khomani San peoples suffer from social and legal discrimination.

The constitution guarantees equal rights for women, which are actively promoted by the Commission on Gender Equality. Nevertheless, women are subject to wage discrimination in the workplace and are poorly represented in top management positions.

Xenophobic violence against immigrants from other African countries has broken out in recent years. In late March and early April 2019, foreign-owned shops were targeted in the city of Durban; at least three people died in the ensuing violence, and dozens more sought shelter in a police station and local mosque. Xenophobic violence flared in Gauteng Province that September, resulting in the deaths of at least ten South Africans and two foreign nationals. The government's 2019 National Action Plan to Combat Racism, Racial Discrimination, Xenophobia, and Related Intolerance (NAP), though a positive step, has largely failed to improve accountability for perpetrators of xenophobic abuse and provide justice for their victims. Beyond the creation of the NAP, political leadership on countering xenophobic violence has been lacking, and in some cases political leaders have blamed foreign nationals for their own failure to deliver on political promises.

South Africa's asylum system is hampered by delays and administrative errors, leading to a backlog of hundreds of thousands of applications, according to an Amnesty International report issued in September 2019. Asylum seekers living in the country often lack official documentation that guarantees access to local services, and asylum applications are almost always rejected when they are processed.

Services and accommodations for disabled people remain generally inadequate, especially in the education sector. Human Rights Watch (HRW) reported that disabled schoolchildren are often excluded from the mainstream education system and are instead enrolled in special schools that do not consistently support their developmental needs.

G. PERSONAL AUTONOMY AND INDIVIDUAL RIGHTS: 10 / 16

G1. Do individuals enjoy freedom of movement, including the ability to change their place of residence, employment, or education? 3 / 4

While there are no official restrictions on housing, employment, or freedom of movement for most South Africans, travel and some other personal freedoms are inhibited by the country's high crime rate. For many foreigners, the threat of xenophobic violence impedes freedom of movement as well. The legacy of apartheid continues to segregate the population and restrict nonwhite opportunity for employment and education.

G2. Are individuals able to exercise the right to own property and establish private businesses without undue interference from state or nonstate actors? 3 / 4

The state generally protects citizens from arbitrary deprivation of property. However, the vast majority of farmland remains in the hands of white South Africans, who make up some 9 percent of the population. Illegal squatting on white-owned farms is common, as are attacks on white farm-owners.

In a 2017 party conference, the ANC resolved there was a need to expropriate land without compensation for redistribution purposes, on the condition that such expropriation should not negatively affect the economy or compromise food security. Since then, there has been intense public debate about the best way to effect meaningful land reform to address apartheid-era inequalities in property ownership. In July 2019, a presidential panel endorsed the limited use of land expropriation, and an ad-hoc parliamentary committee published a draft constitutional amendment on the matter in December. The committee, interrupted by the COVID-19 pandemic, was reestablished in July 2020 and finished its hearings in November.

G3. Do individuals enjoy personal social freedoms, including choice of marriage partner and size of family, protection from domestic violence, and control over appearance? 2 / 4

Despite a robust legal framework criminalizing domestic violence and rape, gender-based violence remains a grave challenge in South Africa. The South Africa Police Service (SAPS) reported 42,289 rapes during the agency's 2019–20 reporting period. There are frequent reports of physical attacks against LGBT+ people, including instances of so-called corrective rape, in which men rape lesbians, claiming that the action can change the victim's sexual orientation. Sexual harassment is common, and reports of forced marriages persist.

Femicide is also a severe problem, with nearly 2,700 women being murdered during the government's 2019–20 reporting period; many were raped or sexually assaulted before their deaths. In April 2020, police minister Bheki Cele reported that the police had received more than 2,300 complaints of gender-based violence in the first week that COVID-19 restrictions were implemented. Several high-profile acts of violence against women occurred in 2020, including the brutal murder of Tshegofatso Pule in June in a Johannesburg suburb. Pule was eight months pregnant at the time, and her murder sparked nationwide protests. President Ramaphosa has pledged to review legislation on sexual offenses, publish a national sexual offenders list, and launch a public education program on gender-based violence; in September 2020, Ramaphosa introduced three bills to the National Assembly to fight gender-based violence.

Same-sex couples have the same adoption rights as heterosexual married couples, and same-sex marriage is legal.

G4. Do individuals enjoy equality of opportunity and freedom from economic exploitation? 2 / 4

South Africa's deteriorating economic position has triggered some politicians to consider limiting the involvement of foreigners in some business sectors. In September 2020, the country's wealthiest province of Gauteng published a draft provincial ordinance, the Gauteng Township Economic Development Bill, to curtail foreigners from establishing certain types of businesses that locals are capable of establishing. The bill has triggered intense public debate, and its constitutionality will likely be challenged in court.

Inequality levels in South Africa are among the highest in the world. Only a small percentage of the population benefits from large state industries, and the economy is controlled by a relatively small number of people belonging to the political and business elite. The government, businesses, and the biggest labor federation agreed to institute a minimum wage, which was implemented in January 2019. In October of that year, finance minister Tito Mboweni proposed exempting small businesses from the law, but he encountered opposition from the COSATU and SACP, the ANC's coalition partners, later that month. High levels of unemployment persist.

South Africans predominantly from rural regions, as well as foreign migrants, are vulnerable to sex trafficking and forced labor. According to the 2020 *Trafficking in Persons Report*, the government has increased its efforts to combat this issue, prosecuting and convicting traffickers and identifying and referring victims for care. Organized criminal syndicates are responsible for the bulk of trafficking.

South Korea

Population: 51,800,000
Capital: Seoul
Freedom Status: Free
Electoral Democracy: Yes

Overview: South Korea's democratic system features regular rotations of power and robust political pluralism, with the largest parties representing conservative and liberal views. Civil liberties are generally respected, though the country struggles with minority rights and social integration. Legal bans on pro–North Korean activity affect legitimate political expression, and members of the press can face pressure from the government over their coverage of or commentary on inter-Korean relations. Corruption is also a persistent problem, with scandals implicating successive governments and executives from the country's largest companies in recent years.

KEY DEVELOPMENTS IN 2020

- The COVID-19 outbreak in South Korea featured a series of spikes in March, August, and November, with case counts continuing to rise toward the end of the year. However, strict preventative measures and contact tracing were comparatively successful in curbing infections overall. As of late December there had been roughly 64,000 confirmed cases and nearly 1,000 deaths.
- Legislative elections were held on schedule in April, resulting in a victory for the governing liberal Democratic Party (DP). Special safety measures helped to ensure a high voter turnout and prevent a major resurgence of infections.
- In November, Justice Minister Choo Mi-ae attempted to suspend Prosecutor General Yoon Seok-youl after a series of clashes over Choo's attempts to intervene in cases. Her actions were heavily criticized for undermining the independence of the prosecutor's office. Yoon's suspension was eventually blocked by the courts, and Choo resigned at the end of the year.

POLITICAL RIGHTS: 33 / 40

A. ELECTORAL PROCESS: 11 / 12

A1. Was the current head of government or other chief national authority elected through free and fair elections? 4 / 4

The 1988 constitution vests executive power in a directly elected president, who is limited to a single five-year term. Executive elections in South Korea are largely free and fair. Moon Jae-in of the DP, also known as the Minjoo Party, won a 2017 snap presidential election following the impeachment of former president Park Geun-hye. Moon took 41 percent of the vote, followed by Hong Jun-pyo of the conservative Liberty Korea Party (LKP) with 24 percent and Ahn Cheol-soo of the centrist People's Party with 21 percent. About 77 percent of registered voters turned out for the election.

While voters were not unduly pressured by electoral authorities, Kim Kyoung-soo, the governor of South Kyŏngsang Province, collaborated with blogger Kim Dong-won to manipulate the dissemination of 80,000 news articles, so that social media platforms would effectively portray then-candidate Moon more positively. Governor Kim was convicted and sentenced to two years in prison for the scheme in January 2019, and the sentence was upheld on appeal in November 2020; Kim would be forced to leave office if he lost a final appeal to the Supreme Court, which was pending at year's end. His co-conspirator was given a three-year prison sentence in 2019, which was upheld on appeal in February 2020.

A2. Were the current national legislative representatives elected through free and fair elections? 4 / 4

The unicameral National Assembly is composed of 300 members serving four-year terms, with 253 elected in single-member constituencies and 47 through national party lists. In the April 2020 legislative elections, the DP won a total of 180 seats, while the United Future Party—formed in early 2020 through a merger of the LKP and other conservative parties and later renamed the People Power Party—won 103. Smaller parties and independents captured the remainder. Election turnout was expected to drop due to the pandemic, but special measures including staggered voting schedules and social-distancing protocols were implemented to increase the safety of voters, leading to a turnout of 66.2 percent, the highest in 28 years.

Allegations of voter disenfranchisement, election fraud, and Chinese interference surfaced after the elections but were dismissed for lack of evidence. Pandemic-related shut-downs of embassies and consulates around the world prevented more than 87,000 citizens living overseas from voting.

A3. Are the electoral laws and framework fair, and are they implemented impartially by the relevant election management bodies? 3 / 4

Elections are managed by the National Election Commission, an independent nine-member body appointed for six-year terms. Three members are chosen by the president, three by the National Assembly, and three by the Supreme Court. While elections are generally considered free and fair, National Assembly constituencies have historically been affected by malapportionment, giving outsized voting power to thinly populated rural areas. A revised map adopted for the 2016 elections mitigated the problem, in keeping with a 2014 Constitutional Court ruling.

In December 2019, the National Assembly passed an election reform bill that changed the formula for allocation of the 47 proportional seats, allowing the legislature to better reflect the national vote and giving smaller parties a better chance of winning seats. The legislation took effect in time for the April 2020 legislative elections.

B. POLITICAL PLURALISM AND PARTICIPATION: 13 / 16

B1. Do the people have the right to organize in different political parties or other competitive political groupings of their choice, and is the system free of undue obstacles to the rise and fall of these competing parties or groupings? 3 / 4

Political pluralism is robust, with multiple parties competing for power, though party structures and coalitions are very fluid. In addition to the two main parties, the liberal DP and the conservative People Power Party, several smaller groups are represented in the National Assembly, as are a handful of unaffiliated members.

The National Security Law bans pro–North Korean activities, and in one case—that of the United Progressive Party in 2014—the Constitutional Court legally dissolved a political party for violations of the ban.

B2. Is there a realistic opportunity for the opposition to increase its support or gain power through elections? 4 / 4

There have been multiple transfers of power between rival conservative and liberal parties since the early 1990s, and the orderly election and inauguration of President Moon in 2017 reinforced this democratic pattern.

B3. Are the people's political choices free from domination by forces that are external to the political sphere, or by political forces that employ extrapolitical means? 3 / 4

Family-controlled business empires known as *chaebol* dominate the country's economy and have amassed significant political influence, which has historically enabled them to protect their interests despite calls for reform. Corruption scandals involving chaebol bribery have affected almost all of South Korea's former presidents. President Moon came to power promising to reform these large firms, but instead he came to rely on the chaebol to bolster the country's domestic supply chains as it grappled with the continued economic consequences of a trade war with Japan and COVID-19.

The National Intelligence Service (NIS) has been implicated in a series of scandals in recent years, including allegations that it sought to influence the 2012 presidential election and later conducted illegal surveillance targeting President Park's opponents. In December 2020, the legislature passed a reform bill aimed at restricting the agency's involvement in domestic politics and its ability to investigate espionage cases. However, Human Rights Watch argued that the revisions were too vague and would "perpetuate the risk of abuse" by the agency.

B4. Do various segments of the population (including ethnic, racial, religious, gender, LGBT+, and other relevant groups) have full political rights and electoral opportunities? 3 / 4

Although the country's few citizens of non-Korean ethnicity enjoy full political rights under the law, they rarely win political representation. Residents who are not ethnic Koreans face extreme difficulties obtaining citizenship, which is based on parentage. North Korean defectors are eligible for citizenship, and in the 2020 elections, Thae Yong-ho became the first to win a constituency seat in the National Assembly; another defector, Ji Seong-ho, won a seat through proportional representation.

Women enjoy legal equality but remain underrepresented in politics, holding 19 percent of the seats in the National Assembly and six seats in President Moon's cabinet. A group of women lawmakers introduced a reform bill in 2019 that would reserve half of the legislature's seats for women and require gender parity in parties' candidate lists in future races. However, the bill made no progress in 2020. Following the April elections, Kim Sang-hee became the first woman to serve as vice speaker of the National Assembly.

C. FUNCTIONING OF GOVERNMENT: 9 / 12

C1. Do the freely elected head of government and national legislative representatives determine the policies of the government? 4 / 4

Elected officials generally determine and implement state policy without undue interference from unelected entities and interests.

C2. Are safeguards against official corruption strong and effective? 3 / 4

Despite government anticorruption efforts, bribery, influence peddling, and extortion persist in politics, business, and everyday life. The Kim Young-ran Act, or Improper Solicitation and Graft Act, which took effect in 2016, establishes stiff punishments for those convicted of accepting bribes and applies to government officials as well as their spouses, journalists, and educators. The act was revised in September 2020 to temporarily raise the ceiling on gifts allowed for those in public service as one way to help support struggling industries during the pandemic.

Also during 2020, the courts continued to adjudicate cases related to the convictions of former president Park and coconspirator Choi Seo-won for bribery, revealing state secrets, abuse of power, violation of election laws, and illegal receipt of funds from a state agency. In July, Park was given a reduced 20-year sentence, and the Supreme Court in June ordered Choi to serve 18 years in prison with a fine of 20 billion won ($16.9 million). In October, Park's former chief of staff, Kim Ki-choon, was given a one-year prison term for abusing his power and illegally pressuring firms to provide money to support conservative groups. Samsung vice-chairman Lee Jae-yong was handed a five-year prison sentence in 2017 after he directed donations to Choi's group; although he was released in 2018 after the Seoul High Court cut his sentence in half and suspended the remainder, the Supreme Court in 2019 ordered a retrial, which was ongoing at the end of 2020.

Former president Lee Myung-bak (2008–13) was convicted of bribery and embezzlement in 2018 and received a 15-year prison sentence, but an appellate court in February 2020 raised the term to 17 years, which the Supreme Court confirmed in October. Former deputy spy chief Lee Jong-myeong, who served at the NIS under President Lee, was found guilty in September 2020 of illegally spending taxpayers' money and sentenced to eight months in jail.

In 2019 the National Assembly passed legislation to create the Corruption Investigation Office for High-Ranking Officials, which would focus on corruption allegations against public officials, legislators, prosecutors, judges, and the president. It would also have the power to unilaterally indict police officers, prosecutors, and judges. The agency became official in July 2020 but faced delays in the appointment of its leadership due to political disagreements in the National Assembly.

In April 2020, a aide to President Moon was arrested for allegedly accepting bribes and leaking information about a state inspection of a troubled hedge fund during his time in the Blue House. In October, Justice Minister Choo Mi-ae ordered Prosecutor General Yoon Seok-youl to recuse himself from the matter, claiming he had failed to conduct fair, thorough investigations into opposition politicians and prosecutors implicated in the case. The unusual intervention prompted the opposition to claim that Choo was abusing her power, and formed part of the broader clash between Choo and Yoon that eventually led to Choo's resignation in December.

C3. Does the government operate with openness and transparency? 2 / 4

President Moon pledged to fight corruption and improve transparency in the wake of his predecessor's impeachment, but his administration has suffered from a series of scandals involving the transparency of funding decisions, official statistics, and other matters in recent years.

Justice Minister Choo Mi-ae's alleged political meddling in criminal cases during 2020 included a February order to the ministry to stop disclosing information to the National Assembly about indictments against President Moon's allies in connection with a scandal over meddling in a mayoral election.

Overall, however, the government responded to the COVID-19 pandemic with openness and transparency, promoting nationwide testing and contact tracing to contain the virus. The Korea Disease Control and Prevention Agency (KCDA) published health guidelines and daily updates on the number of cases, tests performed, and deaths from COVID-19. Spending decisions were also made in a transparent manner, as the National Assembly approved supplementary budgets to curb outbreaks.

CIVIL LIBERTIES: 50 / 60

D. FREEDOM OF EXPRESSION AND BELIEF: 14 / 16

D1. Are there free and independent media? 3 / 4

The news media are generally free and competitive, reporting aggressively on government policies and allegations of official and corporate wrongdoing. However, a defamation law authorizes sentences of up to seven years in prison or fines of up to 50 million won ($42,000), encouraging a certain degree of self-censorship, and journalists have faced political interference from managers and government officials.

In July 2020, journalist Woo Jong-chang was sentenced to eight months in prison on defamation charges for a 2018 YouTube video about an alleged conspiracy related to former president Park's impeachment. In January 2020, the Supreme Court upheld a lower court ruling that lawmaker Lee Jung-hyun had violated the Broadcast Act by trying to influence media coverage of the *Sewol* ferry tragedy in 2014, when he was a presidential aide. He was the first person to be convicted under that law. Lee was ordered to pay a fine of 10 million won ($8,300) but was able to keep his seat in the National Assembly.

News coverage or commentary that is deemed to favor North Korea can be censored and lead to prosecution under the National Security Law, and access to North Korean media is banned. In addition, the Korea Communications Standards Commission evaluates online content found by its staff or referred to it by other government agencies, and blocks or deletes such content according to vaguely defined standards, though most such material is reportedly related to prostitution or pornography, gambling, promotion of illegitimate food and medicine, and other criminal activity.

D2. Are individuals free to practice and express their religious faith or nonbelief in public and private? 4 / 4

Freedom of religion is guaranteed by the constitution and generally respected in practice. Until recently, the military conscription system made no allowances for conscientious objection, and hundreds of men—nearly all of them Jehovah's Witnesses—were imprisoned each year for refusing military service. However, a 2018 Constitutional Court ruling found that the government had to provide alternative forms of service for conscientious objectors, and in June 2020 the military began accepting applications. The first group of 63 conscientious objectors began their service in October.

Coronavirus cluster cases that were traced back to churches during 2020 led to restrictions on gatherings of large groups of worshippers, with all in-person church activities barred in the greater Seoul area in August and again in December. The Shincheonji Church of Jesus was linked to more than 5,000 cases associated with the country's initial outbreak and was sued by the city of Daegu in June for ignoring quarantine efforts. Its leader, Lee Man-hee, was arrested and indicted in August. The church was also sued by the mayor of Seoul, and members have reportedly faced discrimination and online harassment.

D3. Is there academic freedom, and is the educational system free from extensive political indoctrination? 3 / 4

Academic freedom is mostly unrestricted, though the National Security Law limits statements supporting the North Korean regime and restricts access to material related to North Korea. Separately, the 2016 anticorruption law subjects teachers and administrators to the same tight restrictions as public officials. Certain portrayals of sensitive historical issues—such as imperial Japan's wartime sexual enslavement of Korean women—can be subject to government censorship or prosecution under the country's defamation laws and other statutes.

In January 2020, four teachers in Incheon were arrested for possessing a "variety of banned North Korean texts" and distributing materials in an internal study group. In June, North Korean defector and author Lee Ju-seong was sentenced to six months in jail, suspended for three years, for a book alleging North Korean involvement in the 1980 Gwangju Uprising against military rule in South Korea. In May, President Moon had promised support for an independent fact-finding committee to look into the uprising, also known as the May 18 Democratization Movement, and pushed for recognition of the event in the constitution. A law passed in December prescribed fines and up to five years in prison for dissemination of distorted information about the uprising.

D4. Are individuals free to express their personal views on political or other sensitive topics without fear of surveillance or retribution? 4 / 4

Private discussion is typically free and open, and the government generally respects citizens' right to privacy. However, the government also maintains a robust surveillance apparatus.

An antiterrorism law grants the NIS expansive authority to monitor private communications. The NIS, police, prosecutors, and investigative agencies can also access metadata without a warrant; this includes internet users' national identification numbers, postal addresses, and telephone numbers. During the COVID-19 pandemic in 2020, mobile phone and credit card data were used for contact tracing, raising privacy concerns amid reports that companies had shared data about people who attended antigovernment rallies with health authorities. Information that was publicly released about confirmed coronavirus cases sometimes enabled identification and harassment of infected people. In response to these problems, national health officials and the Personal Information Protection Commission took additional measures to prevent private information from being disclosed.

The National Security Law restricts speech that is considered pro–North Korean. However, the law has not been strictly enforced since a new inter-Korean diplomatic process began in 2018; concerns about potential constraints on free expression shifted to those who opposed or could complicate rapprochement with the North, including North Korean defectors and human rights activists. As of 2020 the Constitutional Court was reviewing the constitutionality of the law's Article 7, which punishes those who praise North Korea's regime or produce, carry, or distribute pro–North Korean materials, but it has repeatedly been upheld in past cases.

E. ASSOCIATIONAL AND ORGANIZATIONAL RIGHTS: 11 / 12
E1. Is there freedom of assembly? 4 / 4

The government generally respects freedom of assembly, which is protected under the constitution. However, several legal provisions conflict with this guarantee, sometimes creating tension between the police and protesters over the application of the law. Large public gatherings were banned starting in February 2020 due to coronavirus concerns.

Despite the health-related restrictions, antigovernment rallies were held in the capital, including large demonstrations in mid-August. Around National Foundation Day in October, the government banned more than 100 planned demonstrations, many of which were also meant to protest President Moon's policies. Numerous police barricades were set up along streets and squares in central Seoul, along with some 90 checkpoints to prevent vehicles from bringing in protesters. Critics said these measures were excessive and politically motivated.

LGBT+ pride events have sometimes been disrupted by counterprotesters. Due to the COVID-19 containment measures in 2020, the annual Seoul Queer Culture Festival was held online.

E2. Is there freedom for nongovernmental organizations, particularly those that are engaged in human rights- and governance-related work? 3 / 4

Human rights groups and other nongovernmental organizations (NGOs) are active and generally operate freely, though they face political pressure when criticizing the government or other powerful interests. Many South Korean NGOs rely on government grants, despite their independent agendas.

NGOs focusing on human rights in North Korea and on support for defectors have come under intense scrutiny and pressure during the tenure of President Moon, who made improving inter-Korean relations a hallmark of his administration. The North Korea Human Rights Foundation (NKHRF), which was established by a 2016 law and provided financial support to human rights activists and organizations, has been largely inactive since funding was cut by 93 percent in 2018. The Moon administration ordered a crackdown in July 2020 on human rights activists who send balloons carrying leaflets across the demilitarized zone, after the North Korean authorities denounced the practice; the government revoked the licenses of two organizations engaged in such activities. In December, lawmakers adopted legislation that banned the transfer of information, goods, and money to North Korea without government approval. Nearly 30 human rights groups filed a constitutional complaint to challenge the law.

E3. Is there freedom for trade unions and similar professional or labor organizations? 4 / 4

Workers have the right to form independent unions and engage in strikes and collective bargaining. The country's independent labor unions advocate for workers' interests in practice, organizing high-profile strikes and demonstrations that sometimes lead to arrests. However, labor unions have diminished in strength, as more South Koreans work on a temporary or part-time basis than in the past.

While South Korea joined the International Labor Organization (ILO) in 1991, as of 2020 it had yet to ratify four of the ILO's eight fundamental conventions on workers' rights. Workplaces with fewer than 30 employees are not obligated to establish or operate collective agreements, and major employers are known to engage in antiunion activity.

F. RULE OF LAW: 12 / 16

F1. Is there an independent judiciary? 3 / 4

The chief justice and justices of the Supreme Court are appointed by the president with the consent of the National Assembly. The appointments are made based on recommendations from the chief justice, who is assisted by an expert advisory committee. The chief justice is also responsible for appointments to the lower courts, with the consent of the other Supreme Court justices. The president, the National Assembly, and the chief justice each nominate three members of the Constitutional Court. The judiciary is generally considered to be independent, but senior judges have also been ensnared in corruption scandals in recent years.

Yang Sung-tae, who served as chief justice from 2011 to 2017, was on trial during 2020 after being accused in 2019 of manipulating high-profile cases in 47 instances to serve the interests of the administration and major businesses. Trials for several other judges who had been indicted for misconduct in 2019 proceeded during 2020, and at least three were found not guilty.

F2. Does due process prevail in civil and criminal matters? 3 / 4

Judges render verdicts in all cases. While there is no trial by jury, an advisory jury system has been in place since 2008, and judges largely respect juries' decisions. Ordinary legal proceedings are generally considered fair, but the courts have sometimes been accused of denying due process and impartiality to defendants in National Security Law cases.

Choo Mi-ae, former chair of the DP, was appointed as justice minister in January 2020 after her predecessor was forced out over ethics violations. Over the subsequent months, Choo repeatedly clashed with Prosecutor General Yoon Seok-youl over the management of cases, especially those involving former or current officials close to President Moon. In November, Choo called for Yoon to be suspended and face disciplinary measures for actions that she said violated ethical codes of conduct. Prosecutors in Seoul and Busan issued statements of protest, calling the suspension a violation of prosecutorial independence. A deputy justice minister resigned in apparent protest, while President Moon endorsed Yoon's suspension. Yoon successfully challenged his suspension in court, and he was reinstated in December, after which Choo resigned. A revised law was passed in September 2020 to prevent justice ministers from abusing their power over prosecutors with respect to disciplinary measures, but it was not set to take effect until January 2021.

F3. Is there protection from the illegitimate use of physical force and freedom from war and insurgencies? 3 / 4

Reports of abuse by guards in South Korea's prisons are infrequent, and prison conditions generally meet international standards. Violent crime is relatively rare, but the country is still technically at war with North Korea, resulting in a heavy military presence in some areas and the constant threat of renewed combat. Minor incidents of violence near the de facto border are not uncommon. In September 2020, a South Korean official allegedly tried to defect to the North but was shot and killed by North Korean soldiers. The South Korean defense ministry reportedly had knowledge of the situation as it was happening but did not take action to intervene or inform other parts of the government. South Korean and international authorities called for further investigations into the event.

F4. Do laws, policies, and practices guarantee equal treatment of various segments of the population? 3 / 4

South Korea lacks a comprehensive antidiscrimination law, though a bill was under consideration in late 2020. Members of the country's small population of non-Korean ethnicity encounter legal and societal discrimination, especially in the workforce. Children of foreign-born residents suffer from systemic exclusion from the education and medical systems. Some foreigners who were not covered by the national health insurance plan were denied access to COVID-19-related benefits and programs during 2020.

There are approximately 33,700 North Korean defectors living in South Korea. While the government aims to integrate this group into South Korean society, defectors can face months of detention and questioning upon arrival. Some defectors have also reported abuse in custody and societal discrimination.

North Korean defectors do not need to apply for asylum using the same process as other applicants. Asylum seekers from other countries are far more likely to have their claims rejected. Of 5,896 such asylum seekers who applied between January and August 2020, only 164 had been accepted as of November. In April, the Justice Ministry said it would allow thousands of applicants to reapply if they were improperly disqualified due to falsified reports of interviews conducted in Arabic by the Korea Immigration Service between 2015 and 2018.

Women generally enjoy legal equality but face significant social and employment discrimination. Women earned 32.5 percent less income than men in 2019, compared with an average of 13 percent among Organization for Economic Co-operation and Development (OECD) countries, and the gap was expected to worsen during the COVID-19 pandemic.

Sexual harassment of women in the workplace is common, and a number of political figures were accused in 2020 as part of the #MeToo movement against such abuses. For example, Seoul mayor Park Won-soon died by suicide in July after a former assistant accused him of sexual assault and harassment; Busan mayor Oh Keo-don stepped down for similar reasons in April. Former Justice Ministry official Ahn Tae-geun was convicted of abuse of power in 2019 and sentenced to two years in prison for sexually harassing public prosecutor Seo Ji-hyeon, but his sentence was overturned in September 2020.

Same-sex relations are not restricted among civilians, and existing human rights legislation bars discrimination based on sexual orientation. However, this legislation does not offer specific penalties, and transgender people are not explicitly protected. In January 2020, a transgender soldier, Byun Hee-soo, was forcibly discharged following her gender confirmation surgery. Byun filed a lawsuit in August, arguing that the constitution does not allow discrimination due to "personal identity"; the case was ongoing at year's end. Soldiers who engage in same-sex sexual activity are subject to a "disgraceful conduct" provision of the Military Criminal Act and face two-year prison terms.

G. PERSONAL AUTONOMY AND INDIVIDUAL RIGHTS: 13 / 16

G1. Do individuals enjoy freedom of movement, including the ability to change their place of residence, employment, or education? 4 / 4

Movement within South Korea and travel abroad are unrestricted, except for travel to North Korea, which requires government approval.

During the COVID-19 pandemic in 2020, residents were urged to self-quarantine and limit travel. Travelers arriving from abroad were required to undergo a 14-day quarantine, and visitors from "high-risk" countries had to submit a negative COVID-19 test result to enter; foreigners who did not abide by the rules faced deportation, and citizens who defied the rules faced fines and arrest. These measures were generally seen as legitimate and proportional to the public health threat.

G2. Are individuals able to exercise the right to own property and establish private businesses without undue interference from state or nonstate actors? 3 / 4

South Korea fully recognizes property rights and has a well-developed body of laws governing the establishment of commercial enterprises. However, the economy remains dominated by chaebol that have colluded with political figures to pursue their own interests, and property ownership for individuals has become especially difficult due to soaring housing prices.

G3. Do individuals enjoy personal social freedoms, including choice of marriage partner and size of family, protection from domestic violence, and control over appearance? 3 / 4

Personal social freedoms are largely respected, and women and men generally have equal rights in divorce and custody matters, though same-sex marriage is not legal in South Korea. Abortion was considered a crime punishable with imprisonment except in cases of rape, incest, threats to the pregnant person's health, or designated disorders or diseases. However, the abortion ban was overturned by the Constitutional Court in 2019, and in October 2020 the government announced that it would alter sections of the law to allow abortions up to 14 weeks into a pregnancy, and in some circumstances up to 24 weeks, though it would not fully decriminalize the procedure. The proposal had not yet been implemented at year's end.

Domestic violence is common, despite laws designed to prevent such crimes. Legislation that would ban men with records of domestic violence or sexual crimes against children from inviting foreign women to immigrate for the purposes of marriage took effect in October 2020. In April, lawmakers adopted a set of bills that strengthened punishments for online sex crimes and raised the legal age of sexual consent from 13 to 16.

G4. Do individuals enjoy equality of opportunity and freedom from economic exploitation?
3 / 4

Protections against exploitative working conditions are enforced by the authorities. Nevertheless, foreign migrant workers remain vulnerable to illegal debt bondage and forced labor, including forced prostitution. In October 2020, a coalition of migrant workers' groups denounced the employment permit system and legislation that makes it difficult for individuals to change their place of employment, which can expose workers to abuses such as reduced pay and long hours without adequate rest periods.

In October 2020, civic, religious, and health groups called for action to address the deaths of couriers from overwork, exacerbated by an increase in online shopping during the pandemic; couriers typically lack the labor protections of full-time employees.

Women in South Korea are vulnerable to recruitment by international marriage brokers and sex traffickers. Although the government actively prosecutes human trafficking cases, those convicted often receive light punishments.

South Sudan

Population: 11,200,000
Capital: Juba
Freedom Status: Not Free
Electoral Democracy: No

Overview: South Sudan, which gained independence from Sudan in 2011, entered a civil war in 2013, when a rift between President Salva Kiir Mayardit and the vice president he dismissed, Riek Machar, triggered fighting among their supporters and divided the country along ethnic lines. A 2018 peace agreement further delayed overdue national elections, instituting an uneasy power-sharing arrangement among political elites who have presided over rampant corruption, economic collapse, and atrocities against civilians, journalists, and aid workers.

KEY DEVELOPMENTS IN 2020

- The government and the Sudan People's Liberation Movement/Army in Opposition (SPLM/A-IO) participated in a cease-fire agreement in January, though it collapsed in April. Cease-fire discussions resumed in October.
- Parties to the Revitalized Agreement on the Resolution of the Conflict in South Sudan (R-ARCSS) implemented a power-sharing agreement in February. Ministerial posts were allocated in March, while Kiir and Machar reached an agreement on allocating gubernatorial posts in 10 states in June.
- Public gatherings were restricted under COVID-19 measures, while South Sudanese faced ill-treatment and arbitrary arrest from authorities enforcing pandemic-related restrictions. South Sudanese authorities reported 3,540 cases and 63 deaths to the World Health Organization (WHO) by year's end.

POLITICAL RIGHTS: -2 / 40

A. ELECTORAL PROCESS: 1 / 12

A1. Was the current head of government or other chief national authority elected through free and fair elections? 0 / 4

Kiir was elected president of the semiautonomous region of Southern Sudan in 2010 and remained president when South Sudan gained independence in 2011. A revised version of Southern Sudan's 2005 interim constitution, adopted at independence, gives sweeping powers to the chief executive. The president cannot be impeached and has the authority to fire state governors and dissolve the parliament and state assemblies. A permanent constitution has not been published.

Elections due in 2015 were postponed due to the civil war. A peace agreement reached that year extended Kiir's mandate until April 2018. That July, the parliament voted to further extend Kiir's term to 2021, along with the mandates of his vice presidents, state legislators, and governors.

In February 2020, parties to the R-ARCSS implemented the peace agreement's power-sharing arrangements, with Kiir serving as president of the Revitalized Transitional Government of National Unity (RTGoNU) and Machar as first vice president. In March, ministerial posts were allocated among the previous government, the SPLM/A-IO, the Sudan People's Liberation Movement–Former Detainees, the South Sudan Opposition Alliance (SSOA), and the Other Political Parties coalition.

A2. Were the current national legislative representatives elected through free and fair elections? 0 / 4

South Sudan has not held elections for its bicameral National Legislature since 2010, and its original mandate expired in 2015; that year's peace agreement extended it to 2018. The R-ARCSS then extended the mandate until May 2022. The lower house, the Transitional National Legislative Assembly (TNLA), currently contains 400 seats and will contain 550 when it is seated; 332 will be allocated to the Kiir government, 128 will be allocated to the Machar-led SPLM faction, and the remainder will go to other groups. In December 2020, South Sudanese leaders reached an agreement on reconstituting the TNLA, though it was not formed by year's end. The upper house, the Council of States, has yet to be reformulated.

In June, Kiir and Machar reached an agreement on allotting gubernatorial positions in 10 states among the government, the SPLM/A-IO, and the SSOA.

A3. Are the electoral laws and framework fair, and are they implemented impartially by the relevant election management bodies? 1 / 4

The R-ARCSS called for a new, impartial National Elections Commission to be established by the end of the first year of the transition. It also mandated changes to the 2012 Electoral Act to bring it in line with international standards. In 2019, the UN Mission in South Sudan (UNMISS) reported that efforts to update the Electoral Act were complete.

The South Sudanese subnational makeup was in flux during 2020. In February, Kiir offered to revert to the country's previous 10-state map to replace the current 32-state arrangement while creating 3 administrative areas. However, a national dialogue that ended in November recommended a 32-state allotment.

B. POLITICAL PLURALISM AND PARTICIPATION: 1 / 16

B1. Do the people have the right to organize in different political parties or other competitive political groupings of their choice, and is the system free of undue obstacles to the rise and fall of these competing parties or groupings? 1 / 4

The SPLM dominates the political landscape, and most competition takes place within the movement, which splintered at the outbreak of the civil war. Kiir's hostility toward dissent within the SPLM contributed to the conflict.

Fragmentation within factions is known to occur. Several SPLM/A-IO members left the faction after ministerial posts were allotted in March 2020.

The R-ARCSS granted non-SPLM parties representation in the TNLA, but they lack the resources to operate effectively and the experience to formulate policy and set party platforms. The agreement tasked a National Constitutional Amendment Committee with reviewing the Political Parties Act of 2012 to ensure that it meets international best practices. In 2019, UNMISS reported that the committee's review was completed.

B2. Is there a realistic opportunity for the opposition to increase its support or gain power through elections? 0 / 4

If fully implemented, the R-ARCSS would eventually provide an opportunity for opposition groups to contest long-overdue elections. However, the 2010 elections featured violence and intimidation against opposition parties and SPLM members whose loyalty to Kiir was in doubt.

B3. Are the people's political choices free from domination by forces that are external to the political sphere, or by political forces that employ extrapolitical means? 0 / 4

The civil war has stifled ordinary politics and created a climate of fear. The country's military, the South Sudan People's Defence Forces (SSPDF), exercises an overbearing influence on political affairs and public life. The autonomous National Security Service (NSS) also maintains a strong hold over South Sudanese politics. The activities of other armed groups tied to partisan and ethnic factions have created an inhospitable climate for political participation by civilians.

B4. Do various segments of the population (including ethnic, racial, religious, gender, LGBT+, and other relevant groups) have full political rights and electoral opportunities? 0 / 4

Under Kiir's leadership, the SPLM has sidelined citizens who are not members of the Dinka ethnic group, of which he is a member. The exclusion of ethnic groups such as Machar's Nuer has gone beyond the denial of political opportunities to include violent attacks, sexual exploitation, and the destruction of property.

While the R-ARCSS established a 35 percent quota for women in the RTGoNU, ministerial appointments made in March 2020 did not meet it. Only 25 percent of ministers are female.

C. FUNCTIONING OF GOVERNMENT: 0 / 12

C1. Do the freely elected head of government and national legislative representatives determine the policies of the government? 0 / 4

The government and legislature, which lack electoral legitimacy, are unable to exercise control over the country's territory.

A clique of Dinka leaders surrounds Kiir and exerts undue influence on decision-making. The UN Security Council has accused the group of deliberately sabotaging peacemaking efforts and stirring up ethnic hatred. In April 2020, a UN expert panel noted that the NSS did not participate in the reunification process of the South Sudanese military.

Sudan and Uganda helped broker the 2018 peace deal but supported opposing sides during the civil war and have maintained subsequent involvement in South Sudanese affairs. Between September 2019 and February 2020, Sudanese general and transitional-government member Mohamed Hamdan Dagalo accompanied Machar to one-on-one meetings with Kiir. An April 2020 report from a UN expert panel noted that the Ugandan military maintained a presence in the state of Central Equatoria, while the Sudanese intelligence apparatus sent weapons to the NSS.

C2. Are safeguards against official corruption strong and effective? 0 / 4

Corruption is pervasive among political and military leaders. State resources, including oil revenues, are concentrated among an elite associated with the president. Military commanders have gained enormous wealth through corrupt procurement deals. President Kiir has facilitated corruption by appointing officials who were previously accused of embezzlement.

An April 2020 report from a UN expert panel noted that the NSS benefited from oil revenue, while the NSS and the SSPDF materially benefited from defending oil fields. In September, the UN Commission on Human Rights in South Sudan reported that South Sudanese officials misappropriated at least $36 million in public funds since 2016.

C3. Does the government operate with openness and transparency? 0 / 4

Under the interim constitution, citizens have the right to access public information and records held by state entities. These rights are not respected in practice by the government, which is hostile to scrutiny and lacks functional capacity. This is notably true for revenue derived from the oil sector, which accounts for a majority of the government's receipts. An April 2020 UN expert-panel report stated that South Sudanese natural resources were illicitly extracted due to nontransparent management. The experts also reported that a 2019 open-tender process did not improve the transparency of oil-related transactions.

ADDITIONAL DISCRETIONARY POLITICAL RIGHTS QUESTION

Is the government or occupying power deliberately changing the ethnic composition of a country or territory so as to destroy a culture or tip the political balance in favor of another group? −4 / 0

Both sides in the civil war have committed atrocities against civilians from rival ethnic groups, but government-aligned forces have been responsible for the worst attacks. The UN and the African Union (AU) have documented numerous incidents of murder, torture, rape, looting, displacement along ethnic lines, and forced starvation. Both organizations have accused Kiir's leadership of planning and coordinating such attacks. UN observers have noted the use of hate speech by senior officials including Kiir.

CIVIL LIBERTIES: 4 / 60

D. FREEDOM OF EXPRESSION AND BELIEF: 2 / 16

D1. Are there free and independent media? 0 / 4

The transitional constitution guarantees freedom of the press, but this right is not respected in practice. The government censors, harasses, and arrests journalists, especially those critical of the government. According to the Committee to Protect Journalists (CPJ), at least six have been killed in the course of their work since 2015, though none were killed in 2020. Defamation is criminally prosecuted, stifling free speech.

In January 2020, the NSS detained radio journalist Ijoo Bosco for reporting on US sanctions against then first vice president Taban Deng Gai. Bosco was released several days later after reportedly apologizing. In February, security agents in Maridi State detained journalist Isaac Van for reporting on corruption allegations against a local football association, but Van was released without charge. In March, the NSS closed the English-language newspaper *Agamlong* after it published an article criticizing a government official. In December, the

United Nations reported that at least five journalists were arbitrarily arrested and detained during a September-to-November reporting period.

D2. Are individuals free to practice and express their religious faith or nonbelief in public and private? 1 / 4

The interim constitution guarantees religious freedom, but houses of worship—used as places of refuge for civilians—have been attacked by gunmen seeking members of rival ethnic groups.

D3. Is there academic freedom, and is the educational system free from extensive political indoctrination? 1 / 4

The education system was seriously disrupted by the civil war, with many schools closed or commandeered for military use. Some schools have reopened in recent years, but some teachers have not returned due to poor pay or delays in receiving pay. Planned activities on campuses require NSS permission, and the agency is known to send undercover agents to universities. As a result, self-censorship occurs in educational institutions.

In February 2020, the University of Juba suspended academic Taban Lo Liyong after he wrote an opinion article on state boundaries.

D4. Are individuals free to express their personal views on political or other sensitive topics without fear of surveillance or retribution? 0 / 4

The NSS has extensive, unchecked powers to conduct surveillance, monitor communications, and infiltrate nongovernmental organizations (NGOs). According to the United Nations, agents have used these powers to intimidate, detain, and murder journalists, opposition activists, civil-society representatives, non-Dinka citizens, and members of faith-based organizations, forcing many to flee the country.

E. ASSOCIATIONAL AND ORGANIZATIONAL RIGHTS: 2 / 12

E1. Is there freedom of assembly? 1 / 4

The government restricts freedom of assembly, despite commitments made in the interim constitution. The authorities also banned public gatherings as part of their COVID-19 response.

E2. Is there freedom for nongovernmental organizations, particularly those that are engaged in human rights- and governance-related work? 0 / 4

The government has adopted a hostile stance toward NGOs. A 2016 law requires NGOs to get written permission from the authorities to conduct activities and hold a bank account in South Sudan, and at least 80 percent of staff must be South Sudanese.

Kiir has accused UN agencies—without foundation—of siding with his rivals. Humanitarian operations have been consistently blocked, workers deliberately targeted, and food supplies looted and extorted at checkpoints. Human Rights Watch (HRW) reported that at least 14 aid workers were killed in South Sudan in 2020, while a UN December 2020 report noted the deaths of at least 124 aid workers since 2013.

In June 2020, the NSS arrested and detained Monday Moses, executive director of the Organization for Non-Violence and Development, after he participated in a campaign calling for government transparency. Moses was released two weeks later.

E3. Is there freedom for trade unions and similar professional or labor organizations? 1 / 4

A 2018 labor law provides for the right to participate in trade unions, bargain collectively, and strike under certain conditions. However, the law has not been effectively implemented, and legal protections for workers are poorly enforced in practice. The country's limited union activity has historically been concentrated in the public sector.

F. RULE OF LAW: 0 / 16

F1. Is there an independent judiciary? 0 / 4

Judicial independence exists in theory but not in practice. There is a severe shortage of judges, partly due to poor pay and working conditions.

In July 2020, the East African Court of Justice ruled that Kiir's 2017 dismissal of judges by decree was unlawful. In September, Kiir issued a directive inviting the 14 affected judges to apply for reinstatement.

F2. Does due process prevail in civil and criminal matters? 0 / 4

Unlawful arrests and detentions are routine according to UN observers. Under the National Security Service Law, the NSS has almost unlimited powers to detain and interrogate suspects. The NSS, which extrajudicially operates detention facilities, is known to hold detainees arbitrarily and incommunicado. Authorities arbitrarily arrest individuals suspected of affiliating with armed organizations that oppose the peace deal, including the National Salvation Front.

Under the peace agreement, all political prisoners are to be released; some were in 2018, while others remain in custody. In 2019, activist Peter Biar Ajak and five other individuals received long sentences for orchestrating protests inside a detention center notorious for squalid conditions and prisoner mistreatment. HRW reported that the detainees were denied a fair trial, in part because they were not informed of the charges against them and were not allowed to speak to lawyers. Ajak was pardoned and released in January 2020.

A UN June 2020 report noted that authorities enforcing COVID-19-related measures engaged in arbitrary arrests, ill-treatment of detainees, and extortion.

F3. Is there protection from the illegitimate use of physical force and freedom from war and insurgencies? 0 / 4

An estimated 400,000 people have died during the South Sudanese civil war. While several groups, including the government and the SPLM/A-IO, committed to a cease-fire in January 2020, that deal failed in April, with fighting resuming in several areas. Cease-fire discussions resumed in October.

South Sudanese face intercommunal violence. In September 2020, UN Deputy High Commissioner for Human Rights Nada al-Nashif warned that such incidents were far more prevalent in the first seven months of the year than over the same period in 2019, and that intercommunal violence was increasingly militarized in nature. Al-Nashif also noted that civil-defense groups were armed and co-opted by other groups. Cattle raids and attacks by armed youth groups were reported during the year.

Physical mistreatment and abuse are widespread within the criminal justice system. Detainees often face torture or sexual assault in custody. Authorities conduct regular executions, including of people who were children when convicted. Three people were executed in 2020 through November.

South Sudanese are also subjected to forced disappearance. In August 2020, the International Committee of the Red Cross (ICRC) reported that it was searching for over 5,000 disappeared people in the country.

There is near-total impunity for perpetrators of wartime violence and sexual abuse. The 2015 and 2018 peace agreements mandated the establishment of an AU-led hybrid court to prosecute these offenses. Little progress was made on establishing the court during the year, however.

F4. Do laws, policies, and practices guarantee equal treatment of various segments of the population? 0 / 4

International monitors have documented repeated, deliberate attacks by government forces against members of non-Dinka ethnic groups, most of them civilians. The perpetrators have not been brought to justice. The UN Commission on Human Rights in South Sudan has concluded that these activities amount to a campaign of ethnic cleansing by the government.

While the interim constitution includes gender-equality guarantees, women are routinely exposed to discriminatory customary practices and gender-based violence (GBV). A June 2020 UN report noted that women, as well as people living with disabilities, were disproportionately affected by COVID-19 mitigation efforts.

While same-sex sexual conduct is not explicitly illegal in South Sudan, "carnal intercourse against the order of nature" is punishable by up to 10 years' imprisonment. LGBT+ people face widespread discrimination and social stigma, including harassment and abuse by security forces.

G. PERSONAL AUTONOMY AND INDIVIDUAL RIGHTS: 0 / 16

G1. Do individuals enjoy freedom of movement, including the ability to change their place of residence, employment, or education? 0 / 4

The interim constitution enshrines free movement and residence, as well as the right to an education. In reality, civil war, multiple local conflicts, and poor-to-nonexistent service delivery have made it impossible for many people to exercise these rights. Illegal roadblocks prevent the free movement of people and goods.

In September 2020, the UN Office for the Coordination of Humanitarian Affairs reported that 1.6 million people were internally displaced in South Sudan, while 2.3 million refugees live abroad.

G2. Are individuals able to exercise the right to own property and establish private businesses without undue interference from state or nonstate actors? 0 / 4

Disputes over land use and ownership are frequent causes of armed conflict in South Sudan, and the return of refugees has exacerbated the problem. Property rights are weak and not respected in practice. Customary practices often deny women their legal rights to property and inheritance.

Legitimate enterprise is stymied by chronic levels of criminality fueled by a war economy that allows armed groups and influential politicians to prosper through corrupt business deals and activities, including the illicit extraction of natural resources like gold and timber.

G3. Do individuals enjoy personal social freedoms, including choice of marriage partner and size of family, protection from domestic violence, and control over appearance? 0 / 4

Rape and other forms of sexual violence have been used extensively as weapons of war against both men and women, without legal consequence for perpetrators. A September 2020 UN report noted that the SSPDF, NSS, militias, and other armed groups all engaged in sexual violence.

Domestic violence is not legally addressed. A 2017 International Rescue Committee (IRC) study found that 65 percent of the women and girls surveyed experienced physical or sexual violence, with 33 percent suffering sexual violence by a nonpartner.

Customary law puts women at a disadvantage in matters of divorce and child custody. Forced and early marriages are common, with about half of girls marrying by age 18. Spousal rape is not a crime.

G4. Do individuals enjoy equality of opportunity and freedom from economic exploitation? 0 / 4

Economic collapse has led to rampant inflation that puts the prices of essential goods out of reach for ordinary people.

Trafficking in persons for forced labor and sexual exploitation is widespread, with rural women and girls, the internally displaced, and migrants from neighboring countries among the most vulnerable to mistreatment. The use of child soldiers is also a serious problem. In 2019, the UN warned that child recruitment was increasing, and that more girls were forced to provide labor, including sex work.

Spain

Population: 47,600,000
Capital: Madrid
Freedom Status: Free
Electoral Democracy: Yes

Overview: Spain's parliamentary system features competitive multiparty elections and peaceful transfers of power between rival parties. The rule of law prevails, and civil liberties are generally respected. Although political corruption remains a concern, high-ranking politicians and other powerful figures have been successfully prosecuted. Restrictive legislation adopted or enforced in recent years poses a threat to otherwise robust freedoms of expression and assembly. A persistent separatist movement in Catalonia represents the leading challenge to the country's constitutional system and territorial integrity.

KEY DEVELOPMENTS IN 2020

- In response to the COVID-19 pandemic, the government declared a national state of alarm between March and June and again from October through the end of the year, with the parliament's approval. The government used its emergency powers to combat the pandemic and its effects, but its decisions and awards of procurement contracts often lacked transparency.
- Health professionals suffered from especially dangerous working conditions, and in October the Supreme Court found that their labor rights had been violated by the failure of governments at all levels to provide adequate protective equipment. The country as a whole recorded nearly two million confirmed cases of the virus and more than 54,000 deaths during the year.
- Regional elections in Galicia and the Basque Country, originally scheduled for April, were postponed due to the pandemic, but they were eventually held in July amid strict health precautions.
- The politically fragmented parliament remained unsuccessful in mustering the three-fifths majority necessary to appoint new members to the General Council of the Judiciary, two years after the terms of the incumbent members had expired.

POLITICAL RIGHTS: 37 / 40 (−1)

A. ELECTORAL PROCESS: 12 / 12

A1. Was the current head of government or other chief national authority elected through free and fair elections? 4 / 4

Following legislative elections, the monarch selects a candidate for prime minister, generally the leader of the party or coalition with a majority in the lower house. The parliament then votes on the selected candidate.

Prime Minister Pedro Sánchez's center-left minority government, which had taken power through a no-confidence vote in the parliament in 2018, failed to win passage for a budget bill in February 2019, and snap elections were scheduled for April. The ruling Spanish Socialist Workers' Party (PSOE) won a plurality of seats but could not secure the majority needed for a new government, triggering repeat elections in November of that year. The PSOE again fell short of a majority, but after reaching a coalition deal with the left-wing party Unidas Podemos and securing the abstentions of Basque and Catalan nationalist lawmakers, Sánchez narrowly won confirmation for a new government in January 2020.

A2. Were the current national legislative representatives elected through free and fair elections? 4 / 4

The lower house of Spain's bicameral parliament, the Congress of Deputies, is composed of 350 members elected in multimember constituencies for each of Spain's provinces, with the exception of the North African enclaves of Ceuta and Melilla, each of which has one single-member constituency. The Senate has 266 members, 208 of whom are elected directly, and 58 of whom are chosen by regional legislatures. Members of both chambers serve four-year terms.

Spain's legislative elections are generally considered free and fair. In the November 2019 balloting, the PSOE secured 120 seats, followed by the conservative Popular Party (PP) with 88, the far-right nationalist party Vox with 52, Unidas Podemos with 35, and the center-right Ciudadanos with 10. Among several other parties, the Basque Nationalist Party (PNV) and the Republican Left of Catalonia–Sovereigntists (ERC-Sobiranistes) won 7 and 13 seats, respectively. In the Senate, the PSOE took 92 seats and the PP won 84.

The regions of Galicia and the Basque Country held elections for their autonomous legislatures in July 2020, after the voting was postponed by three months due to the coronavirus outbreak. Although strict health precautions were enforced at polling places, several hundred people with active infections were barred from leaving their homes to vote. In Galicia, the PP easily secured another absolute majority. In the Basque region, the PNV won nearly 40 percent of the vote and formed a coalition government with the PSOE.

A3. Are the electoral laws and framework fair, and are they implemented impartially by the relevant election management bodies? 4 / 4

Spain's constitution and electoral laws provide the legal framework for democratic elections, and they are generally implemented fairly.

The initiation and conduct of the October 2017 independence referendum in Catalonia featured a number of fundamental flaws. The exercise was prohibited by the courts on constitutional grounds, and the actions of both regional authorities and the PP-led central government at the time contributed to a chaotic environment that did not allow for fair and transparent balloting. However, after the regional government was dissolved that month, elections were held in December, and a new separatist-led government was formed in 2018, largely restoring normal electoral and constitutional conditions in Catalonia even if the underlying dispute remained unresolved.

B. POLITICAL PLURALISM AND PARTICIPATION: 16 / 16

B1. Do the people have the right to organize in different political parties or other competitive political groupings of their choice, and is the system free of undue obstacles to the rise and fall of these competing parties or groupings? 4 / 4

Citizens are free to organize political parties, which are able to function without interference in practice. While the PP and the PSOE once dominated the political system, corruption scandals, persistent economic woes, and the dispute over Catalonia have aided the rise of new alternatives in recent years, including Unidas Podemos on the left and Ciudadanos and Vox on the right.

B2. Is there a realistic opportunity for the opposition to increase its support or gain power through elections? 4 / 4

There have been multiple democratic transfers of power between rival parties since Spain returned to democracy in the late 1970s. By forming a ruling coalition with the PSOE in January 2020, Unidas Podemos became the first party other than the PSOE and the PP to enter national government during the democratic era.

B3. Are the people's political choices free from domination by forces that are external to the political sphere, or by political forces that employ extrapolitical means? 4 / 4

Voting and political affairs in general are largely free from undue interference by unelected or external forces. However, disinformation and other such manipulation in elections is a growing concern.

B4. Do various segments of the population (including ethnic, racial, religious, gender, LGBT+, and other relevant groups) have full political rights and electoral opportunities? 4 / 4

Women and minority groups enjoy full political rights. Women are free to advocate for their political interests, and they are relatively well represented in practice, holding 43 and 38 percent of the seats in the Chamber of Deputies and the Senate, respectively.

Spain's system of regional autonomy grants significant powers of self-governance to the country's traditional national minorities, including Catalans and Basques.

Nine Catalan officials were sentenced to prison on sedition charges in October 2019 for their roles in the illegal 2017 independence referendum. One of them, Oriol Junqueras, was elected to the European Parliament in May 2019 while in pretrial detention, but Spanish authorities denied him the right to go to Strasbourg and take his seat. In December of that year, the Court of Justice of the European Union ruled that his parliamentary immunity had been violated as a result of the continued pretrial detention. However, in January 2020 the Spanish Supreme Court found that Junqueras's October conviction disqualified him from taking his seat. The European Parliament then terminated his mandate and declared the seat vacant.

Separately, in September 2020, the Supreme Court rejected an appeal by incumbent Catalan president Quim Torra and removed him from office; he had been convicted in late 2019 of violating electoral law and disobeying orders from the National Electoral Board by failing to remove separatist symbols from public buildings. The region's vice president became interim president, and regional elections were scheduled for February 2021.

C. FUNCTIONING OF GOVERNMENT: 9 / 12 (−1)

C1. Do the freely elected head of government and national legislative representatives determine the policies of the government? 3 / 4

Elected officials are generally free to make and implement laws and policies without undue interference. However, the political system has failed to produce a stable governing majority in the parliament since 2015, resulting in frequent and inconclusive elections, a sharp decline in the passage of legislation, and an increased use of mechanisms like executive decrees to advance the government's agenda without the approval of lawmakers. The instability has hampered the national government's capacity to address major challenges such as the separatist movement in Catalonia and the COVID-19 pandemic.

In 2020, the government declared a national state of alarm between March and June and again from October through the end of the year, with approval from the parliament. The state of alarm allowed officials to restrict movement and establish curfews, among other health measures. However, the government drew criticism for centralizing the management of the crisis during the first state of alarm, and in June it began empowering the regional authorities to make autonomous decisions about lockdowns and related matters, within a common set of guidelines.

C2. Are safeguards against official corruption strong and effective? 3 / 4

Concerns about official corruption often center on party financing. Though most party expenses are funded by the state, a 2007 law allowed political parties to use commercial bank loans. In 2012, Spain strengthened rules on political financing by restricting access to loans, increasing transparency, and establishing an audit framework. In 2015, new legislation prohibited banks from forgiving debt owed by political parties. Also in the past several years, lawmakers have strengthened rules on asset disclosure and conflicts of interest for high-ranking officials and enacted more severe penalties for corruption-related crimes.

Although the courts have a solid record of investigating and prosecuting corruption cases, the system is often overburdened, and cases move slowly. Among other high-profile proceedings during 2020, the Supreme Court in October confirmed the convictions of 29 defendants in a case involving bribery in exchange for public contracts. The judgment also found that the PP had profited from the scheme and had to return illicit proceeds; the scandal had helped bring down the PP government in 2018. Separately in August, former king Juan Carlos I left the country for the United Arab Emirates amid an ongoing investigation into possible tax evasion and money laundering.

C3. Does the government operate with openness and transparency? 3 / 4 (−1)

Legal safeguards to ensure government transparency include asset-disclosure rules for public officials and laws governing conflicts of interest. The Transparency Act, which took effect in 2014, is meant to facilitate public access to government records, though freedom of information activists have reported onerous procedures and called for improvements to the law, as well as mechanisms to access more judicial and parliamentary documents. The Council of Europe's Group of States against Corruption (GRECO) has noted that the Council of Transparency and Good Governance, the body tasked with monitoring compliance with transparency obligations, lacks adequate financial and human resources. Moreover, civil society organizations reported in 2020 that the Sánchez government frequently resisted complying with requests or orders to disclose information in practice.

During the first state of alarm triggered by the COVID-19 pandemic, the national government and some regional governments suspended their responses to information requests. Even after the suspensions were lifted, the national government often limited public access to information related to the pandemic, including the data and expert advice it used to make decisions. The government also used emergency procedures to award procurement contracts, reducing transparency on government spending and raising concerns about possible abuses.

Score Change: The score declined from 4 to 3 because the government suspended access-to-information mechanisms, restricted information underlying its decisions on public health matters, and awarded contracts using less transparent procedures during the COVID-19 pandemic.

CIVIL LIBERTIES: 53 / 60 (−1)

D. FREEDOM OF EXPRESSION AND BELIEF: 14 / 16

D1. Are there free and independent media? 3 / 4

Spain has a free press that covers a wide range of perspectives and actively investigates high-level corruption. However, consolidation of private ownership poses a threat to media independence, and ownership in the print and online media sectors is less transparent than in broadcast media. While there have been few reports of political interference at the public broadcaster in recent years, the renewal of its board of directors through a competitive process remained incomplete in 2020, having been stalled since 2019 due to a lack of political consensus.

Journalists have sometimes faced physical aggression from protesters and the police while covering demonstrations in recent years, and far-right groups like Vox have been accused of harassing reporters both physically and on social media. Media freedom organizations have also noted a growing tendency by the authorities to override the protection of journalists' sources and to obstruct investigative journalism.

A controversial public safety law that took effect in 2015, nicknamed the "gag law" by its critics, established large fines for offenses including spreading images that could endanger police officers or protected facilities. Journalists have faced penalties in practice for alleged violations of the law while reporting on police actions. In separate 2020 rulings that threatened media freedom, the Supreme Court in June upheld a civil judgment against a news aggregator for insults that a user had posted on the website, and in December confirmed a defamation ruling against a satirical magazine that had published a mocking image of a former bullfighter.

D2. Are individuals free to practice and express their religious faith or nonbelief in public and private? 4 / 4

Religious freedom is guaranteed in the constitution and respected in practice. As the country's dominant religion, Roman Catholicism enjoys benefits not afforded to others, such as financing through the tax system. However, the religious organizations of Jews, Muslims, and Protestants also have certain privileges through agreements with the state, including tax exemptions and permission to station chaplains in hospitals and other institutions. Other groups that choose to register can obtain a legal identity and the right to own or rent property. The penal code contains a provision to punish blasphemy, but prosecutions are rare in practice. In November 2020, a women's rights activist was ordered to pay a fine for offending religious feelings by coordinating a satirical religious procession on International Women's Day in 2013.

D3. Is there academic freedom, and is the educational system free from extensive political indoctrination? 4 / 4

The government does not restrict academic freedom in law or in practice. In October 2020, a court ruled that the public University of Barcelona had violated its obligation to maintain political neutrality by endorsing a 2019 manifesto that condemned the convictions of Catalan officials for their role in the 2017 independence referendum. The university was ordered to pay court costs.

D4. Are individuals free to express their personal views on political or other sensitive topics without fear of surveillance or retribution? 3 / 4

Private discussion remains open and vibrant, but more aggressive enforcement of laws banning the glorification of terrorism has begun to threaten free speech, with dozens of people—including social media users and several performers—found guilty in recent years for what often amounts to satire, artistic expression, or political commentary. In 2017, the Supreme Court ruled that a person could violate the law even if there was no intention to "glorify" a terrorist group or "humiliate" its victims. Individuals have also been prosecuted for insulting the monarchy and other state institutions.

In February 2020, the Constitutional Court overruled the Supreme Court's 2017 conviction of musician César Strawberry for glorification of terrorism in connection with social media posts in 2013 and 2014. In separate cases in June 2020, the Supreme Court sentenced rapper Pablo Hasél and members of a music group to nine and six months in jail, respectively, for insults to the crown and glorification of terrorism. In December, the Constitutional Court ruled that encouraging the burning of the national flag is not protected by freedom of expression.

E. ASSOCIATIONAL AND ORGANIZATIONAL RIGHTS: 11 / 12
E1. Is there freedom of assembly? 3 / 4

The constitution provides for freedom of assembly, and the authorities typically respect this right. However, the public safety act that took effect in 2015 imposed a number of restrictions, including fines of up to €600,000 ($670,000) for participating in unauthorized protests near key buildings or infrastructure. Participants in protests on a variety of local concerns have faced smaller but still substantial fines under the law in practice.

Two of the Catalan independence leaders convicted of sedition in 2019, Jordi Cuixart and Jordi Sànchez, were prosecuted for leading protests aimed at preventing police from halting the banned 2017 referendum. Human rights groups have argued that the 2019 prison sentences were excessive and set a harmful example regarding freedom of assembly.

During 2020, many citizens protested against COVID-19 movement restrictions by demonstrating from their balconies or in the streets, and police generally did not intervene. However, Madrid authorities in September prohibited a planned gathering by pandemic deniers, citing the risk of contagion, and broader protests that accompanied the declaration of a second state of alarm in October featured clashes with police, leading to a number of arrests and injuries.

E2. Is there freedom for nongovernmental organizations, particularly those that are engaged in human rights- and governance-related work? 4 / 4

Domestic and international nongovernmental organizations operate without significant government restrictions.

E3. Is there freedom for trade unions and similar professional or labor organizations? 4 / 4

With the exception of members of the military and national police, workers are free to organize in unions of their choice, engage in collective bargaining, and mount legal strikes. Health workers organized strikes in 2020 to protest dangerous working conditions during the COVID-19 pandemic as well as problems with pay and staffing linked to budget cuts in previous years.

F. RULE OF LAW: 13 / 16 (−1)
F1. Is there an independent judiciary? 3 / 4 (−1)

The constitution provides for an independent judiciary, and the courts operate autonomously in practice. However, the Council of Europe has criticized the fact that under current law, the 12 judges who sit on the 20-member General Council of the Judiciary—which oversees the courts and is responsible for appointing, transferring, and promoting judges—are not directly elected by their peers, but appointed through a three-fifths vote in the parliament, as with the other eight members who are not judges. This arrangement has exposed the body to political disruptions. The council's membership was due to be renewed in late 2018, but the opposition PP denied the governing parties the necessary supermajority; the incumbent council continued to operate on an interim basis at the end of 2020, raising concerns about the legitimacy of its judicial appointments and other decisions.

Score Change: The score declined from 4 to 3 because the parliament failed to elect new members to the judiciary's oversight body for a second consecutive year.

F2. Does due process prevail in civil and criminal matters? 3 / 4

The authorities generally observe legal safeguards against arbitrary arrest and detention, though judges can authorize special restrictions on communication and delayed arraignment for detainees held in connection with acts of terrorism. Defendants typically enjoy full due process rights during trial. However, high-profile cases related to Basque and Catalan nationalism in recent years have featured flaws—including disproportionate charges and penalties as well as unjustified pretrial detention—that drew criticism from international organizations.

In December 2020, the Supreme Court unanimously ruled that Arnaldo Otegi—leader of the Basque separatist party Euskal Herria Bildu, which holds several seats in the parliament—would have to stand trial again on charges for which he had already served a prison sentence. Otegi was originally sentenced in 2011 for attempting to reestablish an outlawed Basque party, Batasuna. He was released in 2016, the trial was deemed unfair by the European Court of Human Rights in 2018, and in July 2020 the Spanish Supreme Court itself agreed to overturn the conviction.

F3. Is there protection from the illegitimate use of physical force and freedom from war and insurgencies? 4 / 4

The population faces no major threats to physical security. The potential for terrorist attacks by radical Islamist groups remains a concern, though Basque Fatherland and Freedom (ETA), a separatist group that carried out terrorist attacks for decades, announced in 2018 that it had formally dissolved, having ended its armed activity several years earlier.

Prison conditions generally meet international standards, but reception centers for irregular migrants suffer from overcrowding and other problems, which were compounded by health risks during the COVID-19 pandemic.

F4. Do laws, policies, and practices guarantee equal treatment of various segments of the population? 3 / 4

Women, racial minorities, and LGBT+ people enjoy legal protections against discrimination and other mistreatment, though a degree of societal bias persists. Some minority groups—including Roma—remain economically marginalized and are allegedly subject to police profiling.

Spain is a major point of entry to Europe for irregular migrants and refugees, with most making the crossing by sea. Some 37,000 people arrived during 2020, a sharp increase from the previous year. Some of the more than 21,000 who came ashore in the Canary Islands were placed in hotels, while others were housed in improvised camps that allegedly violated human rights standards. Separately, thousands of migrants and refugees regularly congregate at the land border between Morocco and the Spanish enclaves of Ceuta and Melilla. In February 2020, the grand chamber of the European Court of Human Rights upheld the legality of a practice in which Spanish authorities summarily return people who cross the enclaves' borders unlawfully, for example by scaling fences. An earlier ruling by the court in 2017 had rejected the practice, but Spain appealed to the grand chamber. Civil society organizations criticized the new ruling.

G. PERSONAL AUTONOMY AND INDIVIDUAL RIGHTS: 15 / 16

G1. Do individuals enjoy freedom of movement, including the ability to change their place of residence, employment, or education? 4 / 4

There are few significant restrictions on individuals' freedom to travel within the country or abroad, or to change their place of residence, employment, or education. However, the authorities have been criticized for failing to grant documented asylum seekers free movement within Spanish territory, despite multiple court rulings on the matter.

During the COVID-19 pandemic, civil society groups registered some cases of discriminatory enforcement of lockdown rules that disproportionately affected racial minority groups or migrant workers. The country's ombudsman launched an investigation into excessive or arbitrary use of fines to punish alleged violations of movement restrictions.

G2. Are individuals able to exercise the right to own property and establish private businesses without undue interference from state or nonstate actors? 4 / 4

The legal framework supports property rights, and there are no major restrictions on private business activity.

G3. Do individuals enjoy personal social freedoms, including choice of marriage partner and size of family, protection from domestic violence, and control over appearance? 4 / 4

Personal social freedoms are generally respected. Same-sex marriage has been legal in Spain since 2005, and same-sex couples may adopt children.

There are legal protections against domestic abuse and rape, including spousal rape; while both remain problems in practice, the government and civil society groups work actively to combat them.

G4. Do individuals enjoy equality of opportunity and freedom from economic exploitation? 3 / 4

Residents generally have access to economic opportunity and protection from exploitative working conditions. Despite strong antitrafficking efforts by law enforcement agencies, however, migrant workers remain vulnerable to debt bondage, forced labor, and sexual exploitation.

The level of income inequality in Spain is among the worst in the European Union. The COVID-19 pandemic exacerbated an already high unemployment rate for the region and drew attention to the poor working and living conditions of seasonal farm laborers, among other disadvantaged groups. In March, the government approved emergency unemployment benefits for domestic workers, who had previously been ineligible for such aid. In October, the Supreme Court found that the national and subnational governments had violated the rights of health workers by failing to ensure that they had adequate access to safety equipment during the pandemic.

Sri Lanka

Population: 21,900,000
Capital: Colombo
Freedom Status: Partly Free
Electoral Democracy: Yes

Overview: Sri Lanka experienced improvements in political rights and civil liberties after the 2015 election of President Maithripala Sirisena, which ended the more repressive rule of Mahinda Rajapaksa. However, the Sirisena administration was slow to implement transitional justice mechanisms needed to address the aftermath of a 26-year civil war between government forces and ethnic Tamil rebels, who were defeated in 2009. Gotabaya Rajapaksa's election as president in November 2019 and the Sri Lanka Podujana Peramuna's (SLPP) victory in the August 2020 parliamentary polls have emboldened the Rajapaksa family, which has taken steps to empower the executive and roll back accountability mechanisms for civil war–era rights violations.

KEY DEVELOPMENTS IN 2020:

- In February, the government withdrew from cosponsorship of UN Human Rights Council Resolution 30/1 on promoting reconciliation, accountability, and human rights in Sri Lanka, which the previous government had signed in 2015. The Rajapaksa government claimed that the goals of the resolution, aimed largely at achieving reconciliation with the ethnic Tamil minority, were unachievable and violated the island's constitution.
- In March, President Gotabaya Rajapaksa pardoned an army staff sergeant sentenced to death for murdering eight Tamils, including three children, in 2000. The island's Supreme Court had upheld the sentence in 2019.
- In March, the government imposed a countrywide curfew to combat COVID-19, and the Elections Commissioner later postponed parliamentary elections twice, from April to June and then to August, on grounds of protecting public health. Polls were finally held in August, with the Rajapaksas' SLPP winning a landslide victory. In October, the SLPP government passed the 20th Amendment, which reintroduced expansive presidential powers.
- In December, the government postponed Provincial Council elections, citing the spread of COVID-19. Council members at year's end were operating under expired mandates.

POLITICAL RIGHTS: 23 / 40

A. ELECTORAL PROCESS: 9 / 12

A1. Was the current head of government or other chief national authority elected through free and fair elections? 3 / 4

Under the constitution as amended in 2015, the president is directly elected for up to two five-year terms and must consult the prime minister on ministerial appointments. The prime minister and cabinet must maintain the confidence of Parliament.

In the November 2019 presidential election, Gotabaya Rajapaksa of the SLPP defeated his main opponent, Housing Minister Sajith Premadasa of the United National Party (UNP), 52 percent to 42 percent. Sirisena, the unpopular incumbent, had decided not to seek a second term. Although international observers deemed the election competitive and largely peaceful, there were reports of violence and intimidation, mostly directed at Muslim voters.

Following the election, Prime Minister Ranil Wickremesinghe of the UNP resigned, and President Gotabaya Rajapaksa appointed his brother, former president Mahinda Rajapaksa, as the new head of government.

A2. Were the current national legislative representatives elected through free and fair elections? 3 / 4

The 225-member unicameral Parliament is elected for five-year terms, with 196 members elected through an open list system at the district level, and 29 members appointed via a national list. In the 2020 parliamentary elections, the SLPP won 145 seats, which when combined with the support of allies, ensured a supermajority. Samagi Jana Balawegaya (SJB) won 54 seats. The UNP, from which the SJB had split in early 2020, managed to acquire only one national-list seat. Sri Lanka's other major party, the Sri Lanka Freedom Party (SLFP), also secured just one seat, although the vast majority of its candidates contested as part of the SLPP, which allied with several parties for the poll.

The 2020 parliamentary elections were notable for how the island's two most consequential parties—the UNP and SLFP—were marginalized. The SLPP is associated with the Rajapaksas (just as the SLFP was long associated with the Bandaranaikes).

While the parliamentary polls were mainly free and fair and saw lower levels of violence compared to previous elections, intimidation and harassment of women, Muslim, and Tamil voters prior to the polls were among the incidents reported.

Provincial council elections were repeatedly postponed due to disputes over the delimitation of voting districts. The last rounds were held in 2012–14, meaning the councils' five-year terms expired in 2017–19. Prominent nationalists, including leading members of the Buddhist clergy, want the councils abolished. They point to how India superimposed the power-sharing system on Sri Lanka via the 13th Amendment, which was adopted as part of the 1987 Indo-Sri Lanka peace accord that attempted to resolve the Sri Lankan civil war. They also point to the wasteful spending associated with the councils, in which 75 percent of council budget goes toward salaries and perks and only 25 percent for development purposes. In 2020, Prime Minister Mahinda Rajapaksa signaled that he wished to hole council elections promptly, but in December the government announced that it was postponing the elections due to COVID-19.

A3. Are the electoral laws and framework fair, and are they implemented impartially by the relevant election management bodies? 3 / 4

The Election Commission (EC) of Sri Lanka, which administers and oversees all elections in the country, has built a reputation for independence. However, the new 20th Amendment, approved in October 2020, compromises the EC's independence by allowing the president sole power to appoint commissioners.

The government has been unable to complete the process for provincial council constituency delimitation required under a 2017 electoral law.

B. POLITICAL PLURALISM AND PARTICIPATION: 10 / 16

B1. Do the people have the right to organize in different political parties or other competitive political groupings of their choice, and is the system free of undue obstacles to the rise and fall of these competing parties or groupings? 3 / 4

A range of political parties are able to operate freely and participate in elections. The success of the SLPP, founded in 2016 and led by Mahinda Rajapaksa, in the 2018 local elections, the 2019 presidential election, and 2020 parliamentary elections, demonstrates that new parties can form and compete without significant interference. However, political debates between parties sometimes involve an element of violence and intimidation.

A total of 35 candidates competed in the 2019 presidential election while over three dozen parties competed during the 2020 parliamentary elections.

B2. Is there a realistic opportunity for the opposition to increase its support or gain power through elections? 3 / 4

Opposition groupings are generally free to carry out peaceful political activities and are able to win power through elections. The opposition SLPP won control of 231 out of 340 local councils in the 2018 elections and captured the presidency in 2019, leading to a peaceful transfer of executive power from the SLFP president and the UNP prime minister. The SLPP, which included many SLFP members that were in opposition, also won the 2020 parliamentary elections in a landslide. However, opposition figures and supporters sometimes face harassment or violence.

B3. Are the people's political choices free from domination by forces that are external to the political sphere, or by political forces that employ extrapolitical means? 2 / 4

Vote buying and political bribery persist as issues that distort the free choices of voters. Monitors said the government offered gifts and handouts to voters ahead of the 2015 presidential election, and Mahinda Rajapaksa's efforts to win lawmakers' support during the 2018 constitutional crisis reportedly included bribery, with dueling allegations that bribes were either offered or demanded.

Many members of the military openly backed then president Mahinda Rajapaksa ahead of the 2015 election, and many among the armed forces recognized his abortive appointment as prime minister in 2018 despite protests that the move was unconstitutional. Former and current military officials supported the candidacy of Gotabaya Rajapaksa in the 2019 presidential election.

B4. Do various segments of the population (including ethnic, racial, religious, gender, LGBT+, and other relevant groups) have full political rights and electoral opportunities? 2 / 4

A number of parties explicitly represent the interests of ethnic and religious minority groups, including several Tamil parties and the Sri Lankan Muslim Congress, the country's largest Muslim party. Systemic discrimination, including via language laws and naturalization procedures, negatively affects Tamils' political participation. When the country celebrated Independence Day in February 2020, the government prevented the national anthem from being sung in Tamil at the official celebration, a practice the previous government had reintroduced.

Women's interests are not well represented in Sri Lankan politics. While a 25 percent quota at the local government level has resulted in an increase in female political candidates, women currently hold only 5.3 percent of seats in Parliament. When President Gotabaya Rajapaksa announced his 27 member cabinet following 2020 parliamentary elections, only one member was a woman. Of the other 26, one was a Muslim and one a Tamil (in a country where Muslims and Tamils amount to 25 percent of the population).

Top Buddhist clergy often pressure governments to pursue certain policies. The Gotabaya Rajapaksa government appears willing to do so, especially when it comes to expanding Buddhist influence in the northeast, which is populated largely by members of various ethnic and religious minority groups.

C. FUNCTIONING OF GOVERNMENT: 5 / 12

C1. Do the freely elected head of government and national legislative representatives determine the policies of the government? 2 / 4

Sri Lanka's constitution prohibits parliament being dissolved for more than three months. Since the legislature was dissolved nearly six months before its term ended, there was pressure on the president in 2020 to reconvene parliament when it became clear that COVID-19 would prevent elections being held before June 2. President Rajapaksa's refusal to do so led to governance without parliamentary input—including the enaction of a curfew, and decisions regarding the budget and public finances—as the military was also becoming more involved in civilian issues. The president's refusal to reconvene parliament, however, was designed to put pressure on the Elections Commission to hold elections early, since he and the SLPP apparently suspected the longer elections were postponed, the more unpopular the president's party would be due to COVID-19-related hardships. In September, the president said his verbal pronouncements were as good as government circulars and instructed officials to obey them.

Earlier, in June, the president created the Presidential Task Force to Build a Secure Country, and a Disciplined, Virtuous, and Lawful Society, comprised of intelligence, military, and police officials. Its expansive remit makes almost anything it decrees legal.

C2. Are safeguards against official corruption strong and effective? 1 / 4

The Sirisena administration's efforts to fight corruption, including arrests and indictments, led to few convictions, partly because there was little will to prosecute those close to the Rajapaksas, and partly because the Sirisena-Wickremesinghe government itself became mired in corruption. While Gotabaya Rajapaksa was indicted in an anticorruption court in 2018 for allegedly misusing public funds to build a memorial to his parents, the charges against him were dropped after he became president in November 2019. There is no expectation that those close to the president or his family will be prosecuted for corruption, although some within the opposition could be held accountable. There appears to be an understanding among major politicians that they ought not prosecute those in opposing parties on corruption allegations, lest they too be held accountable when out of power.

C3. Does the government operate with openness and transparency? 2 / 4

Individuals have used the 2017 Right to Information Act to access government records, but transparency is lacking in procurement and contracting decisions, including for large contracts with Chinese companies. The auditor general in recent years has also noted major discrepancies in the government's assessments of public debt. The draft 20th Amendment sought to abolish the Audit Service Commission, but the version voted on kept it in place.

ADDITIONAL DISCRETIONARY POLITICAL RIGHTS QUESTION

Is the government or occupying power deliberately changing the ethnic composition of a country or territory so as to destroy a culture or tip the political balance in favor of another group? −1 / 0

Following the end of the civil war in 2009, the military presence in the Tamil-populated areas of the north and east increased. While such policies ended after Sirisena took office in 2015, and some land was released from military control, displacement of Tamil civilians remains a concern. The election of Gotabaya Rajapaksa as president in 2019 and the creation of the Presidential Task Force for Archeological Heritage Management in the Eastern Province in June 2020 have led to concerns that the regime may employ the military to back claims pertaining to Buddhist heritage, to further change the region's demographics.

CIVIL LIBERTIES: 33 / 60
D. FREEDOM OF EXPRESSION AND BELIEF: 8 / 16
D1. Are there free and independent media? 2 / 4

Freedom of the press is guaranteed in the constitution, and respect for this right improved following Mahinda Rajapaksa's defeat in 2015. Since the return of the Rajapaksas, however, media and civil society organizations have been more cautious when expressing views that challenge the government—displaying a willingness to criticize policy issues, but muting coverage of corruption. Media criticism of the military is also rare. Journalists covering human rights violations against members of religious and ethnic minority groups often face harassment, including from the authorities. Harassment of Dharisha Bastians, who has covered a number of human rights cases and who has had her equipment seized and her private records leaked, prompted a statement concern from several UN special rapporteurs in July 2020.

D2. Are individuals free to practice and express their religious faith or nonbelief in public and private? 2 / 4

While the constitution gives special status to Buddhism, members of religious minority groups and congregations periodically face discrimination and sometimes deadly violence. While there were no major instances of interreligious violence in 2020, past anti-Muslim rioting has left many Muslims afraid that they may be targeted, and that any attackers may enjoy impunity. Leading up to the 2020 parliamentary elections, some Buddhist figures pledged to prohibit Buddhists from shopping at Muslims stores, ban the burqa, eliminate madrasas, and forcibly reform laws governing Muslim education and marriage. When the spread of COVID-19 became apparent, some government officials blamed the Muslim community for its spread. The government also forced Muslims to cremate relatives thought to have died from the coronavirus, even though the practice is contrary to Islamic beliefs, and the World Health Organization (WHO) had stated that those who died from the virus could be either cremated or buried.

Since Gotabaya Rajapaksa was elected, some Christian places of worship in Northern Province have had military personnel stationed nearby, and pastors have claimed that intelligence agents appear to be monitoring certain religious services.

D3. Is there academic freedom, and is the educational system free from extensive political indoctrination? 2 / 4

Academic freedom is generally respected, but there are occasional reports of politicization at universities and intolerance of dissenting views among both professors and students. Most students and faculty feel pressure to avoid discussing alleged war crimes, human rights for marginalized groups, Islamophobia, or extremist activities by Buddhist clergy.

D4. Are individuals free to express their personal views on political or other sensitive topics without fear of surveillance or retribution? 2 / 4

The civil war remains a sensitive topic. Awareness of state officials' harassment of civil society activists working on human rights issues in the north and east has deterred open discussion of such subjects among ordinary citizens.

E. ASSOCIATIONAL AND ORGANIZATIONAL RIGHTS: 9 / 12
E1. Is there freedom of assembly? 3 / 4

Although authorities sometimes restrict freedom of assembly, assemblies occur regularly, though some demonstrations on sensitive topics like security laws and impunity for forced disappearances are suspected to be subject to surveillance. Demonstrations against the 20th Amendment went forward peacefully in 2020, as did protests prompted by poor access to essential items during COVID-19 lockdowns.

E2. Is there freedom for nongovernmental organizations, particularly those that are engaged in human rights- and governance-related work? 3 / 4

Nongovernmental organizations (NGOs) are generally free to operate without interference, but some NGOs and activists—particularly those in the north and east that focus on sensitive topics such as military impunity—have been subjected to denial of registration, surveillance, harassment, and assaults. Intelligence personnel began attending civil society meetings and questioning some organizations about their personnel and funding sources soon after Gotabaya Rajapaksa became president.

Many NGOs cooperated with the government to distribute aid during COVID-19 lockdowns. Some analysts have expressed concern that the collaboration also provided intelligence officials information about NGO operations and personnel, which may assist authorities should they decide to crack down on those groups.

E3. Is there freedom for trade unions and similar professional or labor organizations? 3 / 4

Trade unions are legally allowed to organize and engage in collective bargaining. Except for civil servants, most workers can strike, though the 1989 Essential Services Act allows the president to declare any strike illegal. Harassment of labor activists and official intolerance of union activities, particularly in export processing zones, is regularly reported. Larger unions are often affiliated with political parties.

F. RULE OF LAW: 8 / 16

F1. Is there an independent judiciary? 3 / 4

Political interference in and intimidation of the judiciary abated somewhat under the Sirisena administration, and the courts have asserted their independence amid political turbulence in recent years, including during the 2018 constitutional crisis. In 2019, the Supreme Court ruled that the president could not unilaterally approve provincial council district boundaries in order to hold overdue elections. In October 2020, the court ruled that four clauses in the proposed 20th Amendment needed approval through a referendum, disagreeing with the attorney general, who claimed the entire amendment could be passed with a two-thirds majority in parliament.

Corruption and politicization remain rife in the lower courts.

F2. Does due process prevail in civil and criminal matters? 2 / 4

Due process rights are undermined by the Prevention of Terrorism Act (PTA), under which suspects can be detained for up to 18 months without charge. The law has been used to hold perceived enemies of the government, particularly Tamils, and many detained under the PTA's provisions have been kept in custody for longer than the law allows. Following the 2019 Easter Sunday bombings, hundreds of Muslim suspects were arrested under the antiterrorism legislation, while Sinhalese anti-Muslim rioters were charged under standard civilian statutes that allowed bail. The police routinely treat government officials and those closely associated with them favorably.

Military personnel accused of committing war crimes during the civil war have received prominent positions in the new government, while others remain in senior military posts. In February 2020, the United States government issued sanctions against Army Commander

Shavendra Silva and his family, barring them from visiting the country, citing allegations of "gross human rights violations."

F3. Is there protection from the illegitimate use of physical force and freedom from war and insurgencies? 2 / 4

Police and security forces have engaged in extrajudicial executions, forced disappearances, custodial rape, and torture, all of which disproportionately affect Tamils. Due to backlogs and a lack of resources, independent commissions have been slow to investigate allegations of police and military misconduct.

In February 2020 the government withdrew cosponsorship of UNHRC Resolution 30/1, on promoting reconciliation, accountability, and human rights in Sri Lanka, a move interpreted by rights groups as a signal that authorities did not intend to hold members of the military accountable for rights violations. In March, President Gotabaya Rajapaksa pardoned an army staff sergeant sentenced to death for murdering eight Tamils, including three children, in 2000. The island's Supreme Court had upheld the sentence in 2019.

The April 2019 bombings and subsequent rioting underscored the threats posed to physical security by terrorism and communal violence.

F4. Do laws, policies, and practices guarantee equal treatment of various segments of the population? 1 / 4

Tamils report systematic discrimination in areas including government employment, university education, and access to justice. Ethnic and religious minorities are vulnerable to violence and mistreatment by security forces and Sinhalese Buddhist extremists.

LGBT+ people face societal discrimination, occasional instances of violence, and some official harassment. A rarely enforced article of the penal code prescribes up to 10 years in prison for same-sex sexual activity. Sexual harassment and employment discrimination against women is common, as are discriminatory legal provisions.

The government does not grant asylum or refugee status under its own laws, nor does it provide services or work permits to asylum seekers and refugees. These individuals rely instead on aid from NGOs, informal employment, and third-country resettlement by the Office of the UN High Commissioner for Refugees (UNHCR).

G. PERSONAL AUTONOMY AND INDIVIDUAL RIGHTS: 8 / 16

G1. Do individuals enjoy freedom of movement, including the ability to change their place of residence, employment, or education? 2 / 4

Free movement is still restricted by security checkpoints, restricted military areas, and military occupation of public and private land. Additional security checkpoints were erected in Northern Province soon after Gotabaya Rajapaksa was elected.

Women with children younger than five years old are not allowed to travel abroad for work. Access to educational institutions is impeded by corruption, with bribes often required to obtain primary school admission.

G2. Are individuals able to exercise the right to own property and establish private businesses without undue interference from state or nonstate actors? 2 / 4

The Sirisena administration claimed that most of the lands occupied by the military during and after the civil war had been returned as of 2019, but ongoing occupations and other forms of land grabbing remain serious problems, especially for Tamils in the northeast. Corruption sometimes hinders the effective enforcement of property rights in general.

Some women face gender-based disadvantages regarding inheritance under the customary laws of their ethnic or religious group, and Muslims reportedly encounter discrimination in property transactions.

In September 2020, a Buddhist monk associated with the Presidential Task Force for Archeological Heritage Management in the Eastern Province prevented farmers from accessing their fields.

G3. Do individuals enjoy personal social freedoms, including choice of marriage partner and size of family, protection from domestic violence, and control over appearance? 2 / 4

Although women have equal rights under civil and criminal law, matters related to the family—including marriage, divorce, and child custody—are adjudicated under the customary laws of each ethnic or religious group, and the application of these laws sometimes entails discrimination against women. Rape of women and children and domestic violence remain serious problems, and perpetrators often act with impunity.

Some very young girls are forced into marriages under Islamic personal law.

G4. Do individuals enjoy equality of opportunity and freedom from economic exploitation? 2 / 4

Although the government has increased penalties for employing minors, many children continue to work as household servants and face abuse from employers. Women and children in certain communities are vulnerable to forced sex work. The government has made some attempts to address human trafficking, but prosecutions and measures to identify and protect victims remain inadequate, and complicity among public officials is a serious problem, according to the US State Department. While most of the mainly Tamil workers on tea plantations are unionized, employers routinely violate their rights. Migrant workers recruited in Sri Lanka are often exposed to exploitative labor conditions abroad.

St. Kitts and Nevis

Population: 50,000
Capital: Basseterre
Freedom Status: Free
Electoral Democracy: Yes

Overview: St. Kitts and Nevis has a history of competitive and credible elections, and civil liberties are generally upheld. There are some concerns about government corruption and transparency. Authorities in recent years have seen some success in addressing a high rate of violent crime. LGBT+ people face discrimination and are politically marginalized.

KEY DEVELOPMENTS IN 2020

- General elections held in June resulted in a landslide victory for the governing Team Unity—a coalition of three-parties—despite low turnout at 58 percent, largely due to the COVID-19 pandemic. The government and the opposition agreed that campaign regulations should be adjusted to prevent the spread of COVID-19. The state-owned ZIZ Broadcasting Corporation provided equal broadcasting time to the registered political parties and any nominated independent candidate.
- In July, the Eastern Caribbean Supreme Court upheld the St. Kitts High Court convictions of Lindsay Grant and Jonel Powell, members of Team Unity in the

National Assembly. The two were at the center of a 2017 corruption case alleging that both men misappropriated $460,000 from a client. Opposition leader Denzil Douglas has called for their resignations.

POLITICAL RIGHTS: 35 / 40 (−1)

A. ELECTORAL PROCESS: 10 / 12

A1. Was the current head of government or other chief national authority elected through free and fair elections? 4 / 4

The prime minister, usually the leader of the largest party in the parliament, is head of government. Prime ministers are normally appointed after legislative elections by the governor general, who represents the British monarch as the largely ceremonial head of state.

After the 2020 elections, Timothy Harris of Team Unity—an umbrella organization of the People's Action Movement (PAM) and the People's Labour Party (PLP) in St. Kitts, and the Concerned Citizens Movement (CCM) in Nevis—was reappointed as prime minister.

A2. Were the current national legislative representatives elected through free and fair elections? 3 / 4

There are 14 seats in the unicameral National Assembly—8 for representatives from St. Kitts, 3 for those from Nevis, and 3 for senators appointed by the governor general (2 on the advice of the prime minister and 1 on the advice of the opposition leader); all serve five-year terms.

Team Unity won the 2020 parliamentary elections with 9 of the 11 directly elected seats. The vote took place peacefully and was considered credible, though turnout was low at 58 percent, largely because of the COVID-19 pandemic. The Caribbean Community (CARICOM) sent a small election monitoring mission, and a coalition of local nongovernmental organizations (NGOs) also observed the polls. The invitation for the Organization of American States (OAS) was revoked due to concerns over COVID-19 quarantine protocols. Several shortcomings, which had been highlighted in previous election observer missions, were not addressed, including an absence of campaign finance legislation. The NGO coalition's final report noted several "administrative and organizational deficiencies."

Despite these shortcomings, the government and the opposition agreed that the state of emergency declared to prevent the spread of COVID-19 should be used consistently regarding campaign regulation. However, there was at least one occasion when Team Unity, with the support of the police, prevented a St. Kitts and Nevis Labour Party (SKNLP) campaign motorcade entering the capital, Basseterre. The state-owned ZIZ Broadcasting Corporation provided equal broadcasting time to the registered political parties and any nominated independent candidate.

Nevis has its own local legislature, with five elected and three appointed members. Elections in 2017 resulted in a win for the incumbent CCM, which took four elected seats, leaving the Nevis Reformation Party with 1.

A3. Are the electoral laws and framework fair, and are they implemented impartially by the relevant election management bodies? 3 / 4

Electoral laws are generally fair and usually implemented impartially by the Electoral Commission. However, the lead-up to the 2015 elections featured an eleventh-hour dispute over district delineations and concerns about the Electoral Commission's independence. In the build up to the 2020 elections, electoral boundaries were again an issue of contention, but the St. Kitts and Nevis High Court threw out an attempt to revise them. One concern was a discrepancy in constituency size of several thousand voters between districts on Nevis.

B. POLITICAL PLURALISM AND PARTICIPATION: 15 / 16 (-1)

B1. Do the people have the right to organize in different political parties or other competitive political groupings of their choice, and is the system free of undue obstacles to the rise and fall of these competing parties or groupings? 4 / 4

There are no major constraints on the right to organize in different political parties and to form new parties.

B2. Is there a realistic opportunity for the opposition to increase its support or gain power through elections? 4 / 4

Opposition candidates are generally able to campaign without restrictions or interference.

There are realistic opportunities for opposition parties to increase their support or gain power through elections. In 2015, the Team Unity coalition unseated the SKNLP, which had been in government since 1995.

In February 2019, opposition leader Denzil Douglas won a legal case in which the government had attempted to remove him from parliament. The High Court ruled that the attempt, based on allegations of improper use of a Dominica diplomatic passport, had no standing.

B3. Are the people's political choices free from domination by forces that are external to the political sphere, or by political forces that employ extrapolitical means? 4 / 4

Candidates and voters can make political choices without undue interference. However, concerns have been raised about the lack of transparency of party and campaign financing, which could enable improper forms of political influence.

B4. Do various segments of the population (including ethnic, racial, religious, gender, LGBT+, and other relevant groups) have full political rights and electoral opportunities? 3 / 4 (-1)

All citizens are formally entitled to equal political rights and electoral opportunities. While women play an active role in political parties and as grassroots organizers, representation in the National Assembly is poor. The population of St. Kitts is primarily Afro-Caribbean and Anglican, but other ethnic and religious groups do engage in the political process.

In 2015 there was one woman elected as a representative; in 2020 there were none, and only one woman in the Nevis Island Assembly was appointed. Discrimination, sexist rhetoric, and intimidation toward them and their families discourage many women from engaging in the political environment. LGBT+ people are marginalized and discriminated against, affecting their ability to engage in frontline politics.

Score Change: The score declined from 4 to 3 because no women were elected as representatives, reflecting the increasing marginalization of women and LGBT+ people from political life.

C. FUNCTIONING OF GOVERNMENT: 10 / 12

C1. Do the freely elected head of government and national legislative representatives determine the policies of the government? 4 / 4

The elected prime minister, cabinet, and national legislative representatives freely determine the policies of the government.

C2. Are safeguards against official corruption strong and effective? 3 / 4

St. Kitts and Nevis's anticorruption laws are mostly implemented effectively. However, while the Integrity in Public Life Act was adopted in 2013, establishing a code of conduct for public officials and financial disclosure guidelines, its implementation rules were not issued until July 2018 and have not yet taken root. For example, Lindsay Grant and Jonel Powell, both Team Unity members of the National Assembly, have been the center of a 2017 case alleging that both men misappropriated $460,000 from a client. In July 2020, the Eastern Caribbean Supreme Court upheld the St. Kitts High Court convictions of Powell and Grant. Opposition leader Denzil Douglas has called for their resignations.

In recent years, concerns, including from the US State Department, have been raised about the country's Citizenship by Investment (CBI) and Residence by Investment Programs. In 2019, two members of the European Parliament sought to have the country's visa-free program with the European Union rescinded because of allegedly "questionable" individuals gaining passports under the CBI program. To address some of these concerns, the St. Kitts government introduced reforms, including expanded background checks and enacting stricter escrow-account rules. However, according to the 2020 CBI Index produced by Professional Wealth Management magazine, a publication from the *Financial Times*, St. Kitts has one of the least corrupt programs.

C3. Does the government operate with openness and transparency? 3 / 4

The government generally operates with transparency, though it long lacked a freedom of information law, which was finally passed in May 2018. The Freedom of Information Act has yet to be implemented due to inadequate resources. Further, the law offers exemptions protecting information related to national security, court proceedings, trade secrets, intellectual property rights, and international relations.

CIVIL LIBERTIES: 54 / 60 (+1)

D. FREEDOM OF EXPRESSION AND BELIEF: 16 / 16 (+1)

D1. Are there free and independent media? 4 / 4 (+1)

Freedom of expression is constitutionally guaranteed, and the government generally respects press freedom in practice. However, the state owns the sole local television station, and the opposition faces some restrictions on access to it. Defamation is a criminal offense that can potentially carry a prison sentence. Some journalists reportedly self-censor in order to avoid pressure from government officials.

Score Change: The score improved from 3 to 4 because the media environment has stabilized in recent years.

D2. Are individuals free to practice and express their religious faith or nonbelief in public and private? 4 / 4

Freedom of religion is constitutionally protected and generally respected in practice.

D3. Is there academic freedom, and is the educational system free from extensive political indoctrination? 4 / 4

The government generally respects academic freedom.

D4. Are individuals free to express their personal views on political or other sensitive topics without fear of surveillance or retribution? 4 / 4

There are no significant constraints on individuals' ability to express their personal views regarding political or other sensitive topics.

E. ASSOCIATIONAL AND ORGANIZATIONAL RIGHTS: 12 / 12

E1. Is there freedom of assembly? 4 / 4

Freedom of assembly is constitutionally guaranteed and generally respected in practice. Demonstrations on various topics routinely proceed without incident.

E2. Is there freedom for nongovernmental organizations, particularly those that are engaged in human rights- and governance-related work? 4 / 4

NGOs generally operate without restrictions.

E3. Is there freedom for trade unions and similar professional or labor organizations? 4 / 4

While workers may legally form unions, employers are not bound to recognize them. A union can engage in collective bargaining only if more than 50 percent of the company's employees are members. Antiunion discrimination is prohibited, and the right to strike, while not protected by law, is generally respected in practice. However, employers, if found guilty of union-based discrimination, are not compelled to rehire employees that had been fired.

F. RULE OF LAW: 13 / 16

F1. Is there an independent judiciary? 4 / 4

The judiciary is largely independent. The highest court is the Eastern Caribbean Supreme Court, but under certain circumstances there is a right of appeal to the Trinidad-based Caribbean Court of Justice and the Privy Council in London.

F2. Does due process prevail in civil and criminal matters? 3 / 4

Defendants are guaranteed a range of due process rights, which are mostly respected in practice; legal provisions for a fair trial are generally observed. Arbitrary arrests are prohibited, and security forces generally operate professionally. However, extended pretrial detention is a problem, with some detainees remaining in custody for more than two years before facing trial or having their cases dismissed.

F3. Is there protection from the illegitimate use of physical force and freedom from war and insurgencies? 3 / 4

While the country is free of war and other such threats to physical security, the government in recent years has struggled to contain a high rate of violent crime, which is linked primarily to criminal groups fighting for territory and control of the domestic drug trade. In 2018, a total of 23 homicides were recorded—which, in a country of 50,000 people, means that St. Kitts and Nevis had one of the world's highest homicide rates per-capita. The government has attempted to address the problem through various means, including a "Peace Initiative," whereby members of criminal groups were encouraged to move out of crime and into legal activities. Police have employed stop-and-search methods extensively. In 2019, Tactical Units of The Royal St. Christopher and Nevis Police Force carried out just over 17,000 stop-and-search exercises. In mid-December 2019, the government said that homicides had fallen by 48 percent over the past 12 months, with crime more generally down by 27 percent. This downward trend continued during 2020.

Prison conditions remain overcrowded.

F4. Do laws, policies, and practices guarantee equal treatment of various segments of the population? 3 / 4

The law protects individuals against discrimination on various grounds, including race, sex, and religion, and these provisions are generally upheld. However, sexual orientation and gender identity are not similarly protected, and societal discrimination against LGBT+ people is pervasive. Under colonial-era laws, same-sex relations between men are illegal and punishable with imprisonment of up to 10 years. No law specifically prohibits workplace sexual harassment.

Rastafarians at times experience barriers to employment and other disadvantages due to discrimination.

G. PERSONAL AUTONOMY AND INDIVIDUAL RIGHTS: 13 / 16

G1. Do individuals enjoy freedom of movement, including the ability to change their place of residence, employment, or education? 4 / 4

There are no significant restrictions on freedom of movement in St. Kitts and Nevis, and individuals freely change their place of residence, employment, and education.

G2. Are individuals able to exercise the right to own property and establish private businesses without undue interference from state or non-state actors? 3 / 4

The legal framework generally supports private business activity, though there have been complaints about timely compensation for land confiscated through eminent domain laws. In the World Bank's 2020 Ease of Doing Business rankings, St Kitts placed 139th, the second lowest in the Caribbean. Enforcing contracts was the highest scoring category, registering property the lowest.

G3. Do individuals enjoy personal social freedoms, including choice of marriage partner and size of family, protection from domestic violence, and control over appearance? 3 / 4

There are few restrictions on individual freedoms pertaining to personal status issues, though same-sex marriage is not recognized. While domestic violence is criminalized, it remains a widespread problem in practice, and spousal rape is not specifically prohibited by law.

G4. Do individuals enjoy equality of opportunity and freedom from economic exploitation? 3 / 4

The law provides safeguards against exploitative working conditions, though lack of resources reportedly affects enforcement. The most recent US State Department *Trafficking in Persons* report from 2019 notes that, while there were no confirmed reports of trafficking during the year, local human rights activists alleged that human smugglers transit through the country regularly, and had in the past brought in sex workers and laborers.

St. Lucia

Population: 200,000
Capital: Castries
Freedom Status: Free
Electoral Democracy: Yes

Overview: St. Lucia is a parliamentary democracy that holds competitive elections and has long experienced peaceful transfers of power between rival parties. Persistent challenges include government corruption and inadequate transparency, police brutality and a perception of impunity for such abuses, and discrimination against LGBT+ people.

KEY DEVELOPMENTS IN 2020

- Authorities declared a COVID-19-related state of emergency in March, which was extended through September. The government then replaced the state of emergency with the COVID-19 (Prevention and Control) Bill, which it attempted to pass in one sitting; when opposition and independent senators denied the body a quorum, temporary members were appointed, allowing the bill to pass in early October. Authorities reported 340 COVID-19 cases and 5 deaths to the World Health Organization (WHO) at year's end.
- Some 55 homicides were recorded in the country by New Year's Eve, the second-highest rate in its history.

POLITICAL RIGHTS: 37 / 40 (−1)

A. ELECTORAL PROCESS: 11 / 12

A1. Was the current head of government or other chief national authority elected through free and fair elections? 4 / 4

The prime minister, usually the leader of the majority party in Parliament, is appointed as head of government by the governor general, who represents the British monarch as the largely ceremonial head of state. Allen Chastanet of the United Workers Party (UWP) was chosen as prime minister following the 2016 legislative elections, which were considered free and fair.

A2. Were the current national legislative representatives elected through free and fair elections? 4 / 4

The bicameral Parliament consists of the 18-seat House of Assembly, with 17 members directly elected to five-year terms, and the 11-seat Senate, whose members are appointed. The prime minister chooses 6 senators, the opposition leader selects 3, and 2 are chosen in consultation with civic and religious organizations.

The most recent House of Assembly elections took place in 2016. The polls were considered competitive and credible, and stakeholders accepted the results. The UWP secured 11 seats, defeating the then governing Saint Lucia Labour Party (SLP), which took 6.

A3. Are the electoral laws and framework fair, and are they implemented impartially by the relevant election management bodies? 3 / 4

Electoral laws are generally fair and implemented impartially by the Electoral Commission. However, differences in the sizes of constituencies have resulted in unequal voting power among citizens. While the largest constituency (Gros Islet) has had more than 20,000 registered voters, the smallest (Dennery South) has had only 5,000.

B. POLITICAL PLURALISM AND PARTICIPATION: 16 / 16

B1. Do the people have the right to organize in different political parties or other competitive political groupings of their choice, and is the system free of undue obstacles to the rise and fall of these competing parties or groupings? 4 / 4

Political parties may organize and operate freely. A number of small parties function, though the UWP and SLP have dominated politics since the 1960s, aided in part by the country's first-past-the-post electoral system. Campaigns are financed entirely through private funds, which can also disadvantage new and small parties.

B2. Is there a realistic opportunity for the opposition to increase its support or gain power through elections? 4 / 4

The country has a long record of democratic transfers of power, with the UWP and SLP regularly alternating in government.

B3. Are the people's political choices free from domination by forces that are external to the political sphere, or by political forces that employ extrapolitical means? 4 / 4

Voters and candidates are generally free to make political choices without undue influence. However, there are few legal controls on the source of funds or on spending by candidates and parties, raising concerns about the potential for improper influence by unaccountable foreign and domestic interests.

B4. Do various segments of the population (including ethnic, racial, religious, gender, LGBT+, and other relevant groups) have full political rights and electoral opportunities? 4 / 4

All citizens are formally entitled to equal political rights and electoral opportunities. Some 85 percent of the population is of African descent, while African-European, East Indian, and other minorities are present.

Women are underrepresented in politics; only three women House of Assembly seats as of 2020. As many as six women were in the Senate as it considered a controversial COVID-19 bill in October. Women have a more significant presence as electoral officials and within party structures. The LGBT+ community is marginalized, affecting its ability to engage fully in political processes.

C. FUNCTIONING OF GOVERNMENT: 10 / 12 (−1)

C1. Do the freely elected head of government and national legislative representatives determine the policies of the government? 3 / 4 (−1)

The elected prime minister, cabinet, and Parliament determine the policies of the government without improper interference from unelected entities.

Parliamentary oversight of COVID-19-related legislation was affected by the government's efforts to attain approval via a shortened process, however. In September 2020, the government introduced the COVID-19 (Prevention and Control) Bill, aiming to pass it in one sitting. The St. Lucia Bar Association objected, calling on the government to consult stakeholders. A group of opposition and independent senators did not attend a scheduled debate, denying the body a quorum and prompting the governor general to appoint two temporary members. The bill was passed in early October.

Score Change: The score declined from 4 to 3 because a controversial COVID-19 prevention bill was approved through an irregular procedure involving the swearing-in of temporary senators.

C2. Are safeguards against official corruption strong and effective? 3 / 4

Several state institutions are responsible for combating corruption, including the parliamentary commissioner, the auditor general, and the Public Service Commission, but their effectiveness is limited somewhat by a lack of resources.

A number of senior officials have faced corruption allegations in recent years. Prime Minister Chastanet and Economic Development Minister Guy Joseph faced long-standing allegations of corrupt behavior regarding an airport redevelopment project during the 2007–11 UWP-led government.

In 2018, an Organization for Economic Co-operation and Development (OECD) report warned that the country's Citizenship by Investment program and other such programs, which offer citizenship and residency rights to foreigners in exchange for large sums of money, carry the potential for misuse.

In September 2020, the St. Lucia Civil Service Association accused the government of retaliating against civil-service members by transferring them to different positions.

C3. Does the government operate with openness and transparency? 4 / 4

The government generally operates transparently. Access to information is legally guaranteed, and government officials are legally required to declare their financial assets annually to the Integrity Commission. However, the commission lacks the enforcement powers necessary to ensure full compliance.

CIVIL LIBERTIES: 54 / 60
D. FREEDOM OF EXPRESSION AND BELIEF: 15 / 16
D1. Are there free and independent media? 3 / 4

The constitution guarantees freedom of expression and communication, and press freedom is largely upheld in practice. A number of private and independent news outlets carry content on a range of issues.

Criminal libel laws remain on the books, with convictions potentially drawing heavy fines and a jail sentence of up to five years, though civil suits are more common. In 2017, Philip Pierre, of the SLP, received libel damages in connection with a 2011 letter to the editor published in the *Mirror* that described Pierre as corrupt.

D2. Are individuals free to practice and express their religious faith or nonbelief in public and private? 4 / 4

Freedom of religion is protected under the constitution and other laws, and these safeguards are largely upheld in practice. However, Rastafarians face some disadvantages as a result of their beliefs, and Muslims have reported occasional harassment.

D3. Is there academic freedom, and is the educational system free from extensive political indoctrination? 4 / 4

Academic freedom is generally respected.

D4. Are individuals free to express their personal views on political or other sensitive topics without fear of surveillance or retribution? 4 / 4

There are no significant restrictions on individuals' ability to express their personal views on political or other sensitive topics.

E. ASSOCIATIONAL AND ORGANIZATIONAL RIGHTS: 12 / 12
E1. Is there freedom of assembly? 4 / 4

The government generally respects the constitutionally protected right to free assembly. In June 2020, protesters organizing under the Black Lives Matter banner held a rally in Castries; while the rally reportedly violated COVID-19 measures, Prime Minister Chastanet spoke in support of the event, which progressed peacefully. In October, the SLP held a reportedly well-attended march.

E2. Is there freedom for nongovernmental organizations, particularly those that are engaged in human rights-and governance-related work? 4 / 4

Independent nongovernmental organizations (NGOs) are free to form and operate.

E3. Is there freedom for trade unions and similar professional or labor organizations? 4 / 4

Most workers have the right under the law to form and join independent unions, go on strike, and bargain collectively. Antiunion discrimination is prohibited.

F. RULE OF LAW: 13 / 16

F1. Is there an independent judiciary? 4 / 4

The judicial system is independent and includes a high court under the Eastern Caribbean Supreme Court (ECSC). Judges are appointed through an impartial Judicial and Legal Services Commission and cannot be dismissed arbitrarily. St. Lucia announced in 2014 that it would adopt the Caribbean Court of Justice (CCJ) as its final court of appeal, replacing the London-based Privy Council. However, its accession to the CCJ had not yet been finalized at the end of 2020.

F2. Does due process prevail in civil and criminal matters? 3 / 4

Detainees and defendants are guaranteed a range of legal rights, which are mostly respected in practice. However, police corruption is a concern, and court backlogs contribute to lengthy pretrial detention. Defendants charged with serious crimes may spend several years awaiting trial behind bars.

F3. Is there protection from the illegitimate use of physical force and freedom from war and insurgencies? 3 / 4

While the population is mostly free from pervasive threats to physical security, violent crime rates remain relatively high on a per capita basis. Some 55 homicides were reported in 2020 through late December, the second-highest figure on record. Other crimes reportedly fell compared to 2019, however.

Police brutality has been seen as a significant problem in St. Lucia in recent years, and there is a widespread perception that members of the Royal Saint Lucia Police Force (RSLPF) enjoy impunity for abusive behavior. In 2013, the United States cut aid to the RSLPF over allegations related to extrajudicial killings that took place in 2010 and 2011. While an international investigation into the matter was completed in 2014, and while RSLPF members were considered culpable, prosecutors took no legal action. St. Lucia receives no US aid due to the so-called Leahy law, though External Affairs Minister Sarah Flood-Beaubrun voiced hope that the incoming administration of US president-elect Joseph Biden would provide aid in November 2020.

In 2019, the government announced that corporal punishment in schools would be suspended starting that May and would be abolished 12 months later. However, this reportedly did not occur in 2020.

F4. Do laws, policies, and practices guarantee equal treatment of various segments of the population? 3 / 4

While discrimination on the basis of race, sex, religion, and other such grounds is generally prohibited, the law does not provide full protection to LGBT+ people. The labor code prohibits dismissal of employees based on sexual orientation. Under an ECSC directive, murders committed when sexual orientation is a motive can be punishable with a life sentence. However, same-sex relations can draw up to 10 years in prison, and LGBT+ people face significant societal prejudice.

Rastafarians face disadvantages because of their beliefs, and Muslims have reported harassment.

G. PERSONAL AUTONOMY AND INDIVIDUAL RIGHTS: 14 / 16

G1. Do individuals enjoy freedom of movement, including the ability to change their place of residence, employment, or education? 4 / 4

There are no serious impediments to freedom of movement in St. Lucia, and individuals are generally free to change their place of residence, employment, or education. While external borders were closed in response to COVID-19 in March 2020, travel restrictions were loosened beginning in June. External travel was still subject to pandemic-related measures as of December.

G2. Are individuals able to exercise the right to own property and establish private businesses without undue interference from state or non-state actors? 4 / 4

The legal and regulatory framework is supportive of property rights and private business activity. The government has actively encouraged both domestic and foreign investors to do business in the country. St. Lucia performs well in World Bank assessments of business conditions in comparison with its neighbors.

G3. Do individuals enjoy personal social freedoms, including choice of marriage partner and size of family, protection from domestic violence, and control over appearance? 3 / 4

The law largely guarantees individual rights with respect to personal status issues like marriage and divorce, but the civil code distinguishes between "legitimate" and "illegitimate" children, which can lead to discrimination against unmarried women and their children in civil and family law cases. Domestic and gender-based violence (GBV) are serious concerns and often go unreported. The law only criminalizes spousal rape when a couple is separated or when a court has issued a protection order.

G4. Do individuals enjoy equality of opportunity and freedom from economic exploitation? 3 / 4

Safety rules and other protections against worker exploitation are typically upheld.

While the government has made some efforts to combat human trafficking, investigations and prosecutions are rare. In its 2020 *Trafficking in Persons Report*, the US State Department reported that the first trafficking survivor since 2015 was identified during the reporting period. However, no prosecutions were reported, and law enforcement officers did not consistently follow procedures on identifying trafficking survivors.

St. Vincent and the Grenadines

Population: 100,000
Capital: Kingstown
Freedom Status: Free
Electoral Democracy: Yes

Overview: St. Vincent and the Grenadines is a parliamentary democracy that holds regular elections and has seen numerous transfers of power between parties. While civil liberties are generally upheld, journalists face the possibility of criminal defamation charges, and same-sex relations remain illegal. Violent crime is a concern.

KEY DEVELOPMENTS IN 2020

- The governing Unity Labour Party (ULP) won the general elections held in November. Although they won fewer votes than the New Democratic Party (NDP), the ULP won 9 of the 15 seats in the parliament, up one seat from the previous elections. It was the ULP's fifth consecutive victory, and the first time since 1998 that the party winning the most votes did not win the most seats. Voter turnout was 67 percent.

- The government took multiple steps to prevent the spread of COVID-19 during the general elections' campaigning period and on election day in November. The Ministry of National Security's Health Services Subcommittee directed campaign rallies and events to be held outdoors and socially distanced and advised all attendees to wear masks; similar guidelines were implemented on voting day. According to government statistics provided to the World Health Organization (WHO), 119 people had tested positive for coronavirus by year's end.

POLITICAL RIGHTS: 36 / 40

A. ELECTORAL PROCESS: 11 / 12

A1. Was the current head of government or other chief national authority elected through free and fair elections? 4 / 4

The prime minister, usually the leader of the majority party in the parliament, is appointed by the governor general, who represents the British monarch as the largely ceremonial head of state. Ralph Gonsalves retained his position as prime minister following the victory of his incumbent Unity Labour Party (ULP) in the 2020 legislative elections, which were considered free and fair.

A2. Were the current national legislative representatives elected through free and fair elections? 4 / 4

The constitution provides for the direct election of 15 representatives to the unicameral House of Assembly. In addition, the governor general appoints six senators to the chamber: four selected on the advice of the prime minister and two on the advice of the opposition leader. All serve five-year terms.

In October 2020, both the ULP and the opposition NDP signed the National Monitoring and Consultative Mechanism "Code of Ethical Political Conduct" to govern the campaign. The elections held in November were won by the ULP, which took 9 seats; its fifth consecutive victory. Although the party increased its majority by one seat, it won around 500 votes less than the NDP. It was the first time since 1998 that the party winning the most votes did not win the most seats. The additional seat gained by the ULP was won by just seven votes. Voter turnout was 67 percent.

The government took multiple steps to prevent the spread of COVID-19 during the campaigning period and on election day in November. The Ministry of National Security's Health Services Subcommittee directed campaign rallies and events to be held outdoors and socially distanced and advised all attendees to wear masks. Similar guidelines were issued for the day of voting, and procedures were established for eligible voters who were under state-mandated quarantine after arriving in the country.

A3. Are the electoral laws and framework fair, and are they implemented impartially by the relevant election management bodies? 3 / 4

Electoral laws are generally fair and impartially implemented. Efforts to update voter lists were initiated in 2013. Ahead of the 2015 elections the legislature passed, with bipartisan support, an amendment to the election law that removed almost 24,000 names from the lists. The 2015 Organization of American States (OAS) election monitoring mission welcomed the change but noted that authorities should implement continuous updating and verification processes; this has not yet been enacted. The mission also called for better standardization of voting procedures across polling sites. Prior to the 2020 elections, the opposition claimed that hundreds of dead people remained on the electoral list.

The 2020 elections were deemed free and fair by a Caribbean Community (CARICOM) observer mission and domestic election observers. Despite the closeness of the vote tallies, the NDP did not challenge the results in court.

B. POLITICAL PLURALISM AND PARTICIPATION: 15 / 16

B1. Do the people have the right to organize in different political parties or other competitive political groupings of their choice, and is the system free of undue obstacles to the rise and fall of these competing parties or groupings? 4 / 4

Political parties can organize freely. While there are a number of smaller political parties in the country, since 1998 only the ULP and NDP have won seats in the parliament. The first-past-the-post electoral system has contributed to this pattern, but there are also concerns that unregulated private campaign financing puts smaller parties at a disadvantage. The limited state funding that is available goes only to parties represented in the previous parliament.

B2. Is there a realistic opportunity for the opposition to increase its support or gain power through elections? 4 / 4

The country has experienced multiple peaceful transfers of power between rival parties after elections, including two since it gained full independence in 1979. The ULP has been in government since 2001, but it has had only a narrow majority over the opposition NDP since 2010.

B3. Are the people's political choices free from domination by forces that are external to the political sphere, or by political forces that employ extrapolitical means? 4 / 4

The political choices of candidates and voters are generally free from interference by extrapolitical forces. However, the OAS raised concerns in 2015 about the lack of transparency regarding party and campaign financing, which could enable undue influence by private actors. Little has been done since to address these concerns.

B4. Do various segments of the population (including ethnic, racial, religious, gender, LGBT+, and other relevant groups) have full political rights and electoral opportunities? 3 / 4

All citizens are formally entitled to full political rights and electoral opportunities, but women remain significantly underrepresented in the legislature and in politics generally. In its report on the 2015 elections, the OAS noted that there was a "pervasive reluctance" on the part of potential women candidates to take part in harsh political campaigns. No women were elected to the House of Assembly in both the 2015 and 2020 elections. Two women were appointed deputy Speaker and Speaker of the House by ULP after the 2020 elections.

LGBT+ people are marginalized, and this affects their ability to engage fully in political processes. There are no openly LGBT+ politicians in the House of Assembly. The St. Vincent population is largely Afro-Caribbean and of mixed African-European decent, with the major religions being Protestantism and Catholicism. These segments of the population and others can engage in the political process. The small Rastafarian community do not engage fully with politics, although politicians canvas for their votes.

C. FUNCTIONING OF GOVERNMENT: 10 / 12

C1. Do the freely elected head of government and national legislative representatives determine the policies of the government? 4 / 4

The elected prime minister, cabinet, and House of Assembly members determine the policies of the government without improper interference from unelected entities.

C2. Are safeguards against official corruption strong and effective? 3 / 4

The independent judiciary and media provide checks on government corruption. However, there is no specialized national anticorruption agency, and claims of petty corruption continue to be reported.

C3. Does the government operate with openness and transparency? 3 / 4

The government generally operates with openness and transparency. Nevertheless, freedom of information legislation that was passed in 2003 has yet to be implemented, and there is no active legislation requiring government officials to disclose assets, income, or gifts. Further, government accounts have not been audited for five years, and it has not released the 2018 poverty assessment report, which allegedly shows that poverty increased from 30 percent to 36 percent in the preceding decade.

CIVIL LIBERTIES: 55 / 60

D. FREEDOM OF EXPRESSION AND BELIEF: 15 / 16

D1. Are there free and independent media? 3 / 4

The constitution guarantees the freedoms of expression and communication, and these rights are usually upheld in practice. The state owns the main local broadcaster, and concerns have been raised, most recently by the NDP in August 2020, about the level of access to the broadcaster given to the political opposition. However, several private newspapers operate consistently, and news consumers also have access to foreign media and online outlets.

Journalists remain subject to criminal and civil defamation laws, and the 2016 Cybercrime Act broadened the definition and scope of defamation to include online publications; violation of its often vaguely worded provisions can carry a fine of as much as EC$500,000 ($185,000) and up to seven years' imprisonment.

D2. Are individuals free to practice and express their religious faith or nonbelief in public and private? 4 / 4

Freedom of religion is constitutionally protected and respected in practice.

D3. Is there academic freedom, and is the educational system free from extensive political indoctrination? 4 / 4

Academic freedom is generally upheld.

D4. Are individuals free to express their personal views on political or other sensitive topics without fear of surveillance or retribution? 4 / 4

There are no significant restrictions on individuals' ability to express their personal views on political or other sensitive topics. However, the threat of defamation is used by politicians. In March 2020, Prime Minister Gonsalves claimed that he could sue speakers at NDP meetings for defamation, though he did not clarify which comments made at those meetings were defamatory.

E. ASSOCIATIONAL AND ORGANIZATIONAL RIGHTS: 12 / 12

E1. Is there freedom of assembly? 4 / 4

Freedom of assembly is constitutionally protected and generally upheld in practice. There were reports of police using excessive force to disperse peaceful protests during the 2015 election period, but no similar such events have taken place in recent years.

E2. Is there freedom for nongovernmental organizations, particularly those that are engaged in human rights–and governance-related work? 4 / 4

Nongovernmental organizations (NGOs) operate freely. However, reported security threats, including a physical attack on a volunteer, apparently prompted the US Peace Corps to withdraw 23 people from the country in August 2018.

E3. Is there freedom for trade unions and similar professional or labor organizations? 4 / 4

The constitution protects the right to form or join trade unions and other such associations. Unions are permitted to strike and engage in collective bargaining. The law prohibits antiunion discrimination and dismissal for engaging in union activities. The right to collective bargaining is generally upheld, though public sector unions have in the past criticized the government for failing to respect the bargaining process.

F. RULE OF LAW: 14 / 16

F1. Is there an independent judiciary? 4 / 4

The judiciary generally operates independently. Judges are appointed through an impartial Judicial and Legal Services Commission and cannot be dismissed arbitrarily. The country is subject to the Eastern Caribbean Supreme Court and recognizes the original jurisdiction of the Caribbean Court of Justice, though the Privy Council in London remains the final court of appeal.

F2. Does due process prevail in civil and criminal matters? 3 / 4

There is due process in civil and criminal matters. Detainees and defendants are guaranteed a range of legal rights, which are mostly respected in practice. However, there is a significant case backlog, which leads to prolonged pretrial detention.

F3. Is there protection from the illegitimate use of physical force and freedom from war and insurgencies? 4 / 4

The population is free from war and other acute threats to physical security. From January to November 2020, there were 27 reported homicides, a slight increase over 2019, but a significant decline from higher rates seen over the past decade.

Prison conditions have improved since a new correctional facility was opened in 2012, but the old prison in Kingstown is still in use and features substandard conditions. Key problems with prison facilities include understaffing, overcrowding, and limited space to segregate noncompliant and juvenile prisoners.

F4. Do laws, policies, and practices guarantee equal treatment of various segments of the population? 3 / 4

The constitution prohibits discrimination based on race, sex, religion, and other such categories, but sexual orientation and gender identity are not similarly protected. Same-sex relations are illegal and carries penalties of up to 10 years in prison. While the law is rarely enforced, societal discrimination against LGBT+ people persists. In July 2019, two gay Vincentian men filed a legal challenge to the law; the government said it would oppose the challenge and received the backing of several Christian groups.

Women reportedly face sexual harassment in the workplace, which is not specifically addressed by law.

G. PERSONAL AUTONOMY AND INDIVIDUAL RIGHTS: 14 / 16

G1. Do individuals enjoy freedom of movement, including the ability to change their place of residence, employment, or education? 4 / 4

There are no significant restrictions on freedom of movement, and individuals can freely change their place of residence, employment, and education.

G2. Are individuals able to exercise the right to own property and establish private businesses without undue interference from state or non-state actors? 4 / 4

Individuals are free to own property and to establish and operate businesses. The government has actively encouraged both domestic and foreign investors to do business in the country, though the World Bank has reported some regulatory difficulties with respect to registering property, obtaining credit, and resolving insolvency.

G3. Do individuals enjoy personal social freedoms, including choice of marriage partner and size of family, protection from domestic violence, and control over appearance? 3 / 4

Individual rights with respect to personal status matters like marriage and divorce are generally protected by law, though same-sex marriage is not recognized. The Domestic Violence Act of 2015, which went into effect in 2016 and provides for protective orders, offers some tools and resources to victims of domestic violence. However, such violence remains a serious and widespread problem, as does sexual assault.

G4. Do individuals enjoy equality of opportunity and freedom from economic exploitation? 3 / 4

The law provides safety and other basic protections against labor exploitation, and these are typically upheld, though there are some reports of inadequate enforcement. The Prevention of Trafficking in Persons Act of 2011 criminalizes forced labor and sex trafficking, and the government has increased its efforts to investigate violations and improve prevention and victim protection, but it has yet to secure any trafficking convictions, the US State Department reported in 2020.

Sudan

Population: 43,800,000
Capital: Khartoum
Freedom Status: Not Free
Electoral Democracy: No

Overview: Since military commanders and a prodemocracy protest movement ousted the repressive regime of Omar al-Bashir and his National Congress Party (NCP) in 2019, Sudan has been ruled by a transitional government in which military and civilian leaders are to share power until national elections can be held. The government has begun to enact reforms, and space for the exercise of civil liberties is slowly opening, but security personnel associated with the abuses of the old regime remain influential. Violence involving security forces, other armed groups, and rival ethnic communities persists in many parts of the country.

KEY DEVELOPMENTS IN 2020

- To prevent the spread of COVID-19 during the year, the government-imposed curfews, banned large gatherings, and limited international travel. More than 1,500 deaths from the disease had been reported by year's end, and the pandemic worsened an already weak economy.
- In October, the transitional government, headed by the Transitional Sovereign Council (TSC), signed the Juba Peace Agreement with an alliance of rebel groups. The accord included provisions for the integration of rebel fighters into the security forces, power-sharing allocations, and commitments to address economic marginalization. It also pushed back national elections until early 2024. Despite the peace agreement, local conflicts among rival ethnic communities increased across the country.
- The TSC stated in February that former president Omar al-Bashir should face charges of genocide and war crimes before the International Criminal Court (ICC), and a delegation from the court visited the country for talks in October. Al-Bashir and other former officials remained in custody in Sudan at year's end.
- In July, Prime Minister Abdalla Hamdok replaced military governors with civilian appointees, and the TSC repealed several repressive laws that had particularly affected the rights of women and members of religious minority groups.
- Citizens continued to organize protests on a variety of issues, including the slow pace of reforms, and security forces often responded with tear gas or live ammunition, though their use of violence was less severe overall than in 2019.

POLITICAL RIGHTS: 2 / 40
A. ELECTORAL PROCESS: 0 / 12
A1. Was the current head of government or other chief national authority elected through free and fair elections? 0 / 4

Former president Omar al-Bashir, who had ruled Sudan since taking power in a 1989 coup, was himself ousted by the military in April 2019, under pressure from a prodemocracy protest movement that began in late 2018. After initially attempting to crack down on the protests, the military leadership held negotiations with an opposition alliance, the Forces of Freedom and Change (FFC), and reached a power-sharing deal in August of that year. The pact created the 11-member TSC, which was to govern Sudan until elections could be held after a 39-month interim period, with the military and the FFC each naming five members and agreeing on the final member, a civilian. General Abdel Fattah al-Burhan was named as the TSC's chair for a 21-month term, after which a civilian would lead the council for 18 months.

Abdulla Hamdok, a former UN official, was named as prime minister. He presided over a cabinet of technocratic ministers who wielded day-to-day executive power under the transitional agreement. The military, however, retained control of the defense and interior ministries.

The October 2020 signing of the Juba Peace Agreement between the TSC and rebel groups led by the Sudan Revolutionary Front (SRF) had the effect of restarting the 39-month transition period prior to national elections. The peace agreement also reorganized the government's power-sharing allocations so that the armed groups would have three seats on the TSC and hold 25 percent of ministerial posts in the cabinet. The new appointments had yet to be made at the end of the year.

The interim constitutional document that emerged from the 2019 power-sharing deal was amended to incorporate the provisions of the Juba Peace Agreement. Among other changes, a new Article 80 created the Council of Partners for the Transitional Period—comprising the prime minister, the FFC, the military, and the rebel groups that signed the peace agreement—with a mandate to discuss major political issues that arise during the transition. Critics of the new body warned that it could come to supersede the authority of the existing governing structures.

A2. Were the current national legislative representatives elected through free and fair elections? 0 / 4

The former parliament was dissolved as part of the 2019 revolution, and the transitional constitution called for the FFC to appoint two-thirds of a 300-seat Transitional Legislative Council (TLC), which was to hold office until elections could be held. Other political factions would select the remaining members. The October 2020 peace agreement revised this structure by allocating 75 seats to the signatory armed groups, 60 to the military, and 165 to the FFC. With consultations pending, the TLC's members had yet to be selected at the end of 2020.

A3. Are the electoral laws and framework fair, and are they implemented impartially by the relevant election management bodies? 0 / 4

The former National Election Commission, which was loyal to al-Bashir and led by an NCP official, was to be replaced by a new commission appointed by the TSC, according to the interim constitution. However, the entity's members had not been named as of late 2020, and the TSC had not developed a legal and administrative framework for elections.

B. POLITICAL PLURALISM AND PARTICIPATION: 4 / 16

B1. Do the people have the right to organize in different political parties or other competitive political groupings of their choice, and is the system free of undue obstacles to the rise and fall of these competing parties or groupings? 1 / 4

The transitional constitution guarantees the right to form political parties, subject to legal regulation. In practice, the FFC and a number of separate parties have continued to operate. However, transitional authorities have arrested high-ranking NCP members associated with the former regime, and in November 2019 the TSC disbanded the NCP altogether and established a committee to seize its assets. In June 2020, the government arrested former NCP leader and foreign minister Ibrahim Ghandour.

Divisions among political parties and activists emerged during 2020. In April, the Umma Party froze its participation in the FFC. A faction of the Sudanese Professionals Association (SPA), which played a crucial role in the 2019 protest movement, withdrew from the FFC in June, and the Sudanese Communist Party did so in November.

B2. Is there a realistic opportunity for the opposition to increase its support or gain power through elections? 1 / 4

Political groupings that were excluded from government under al-Bashir secured participation in the TSC in 2019 and have maintained varying degrees of influence during subsequent negotiations. The transition process more broadly has raised the possibility of future transfers of power through elections. Following the Juba Peace Agreement in October 2020, however, elections were not expected until 2024.

B3. Are the people's political choices free from domination by forces that are external to the political sphere, or by political forces that employ extrapolitical means? 1 / 4

Military and security organizations that used force to oppose the 2019 prodemocracy protests have retained significant power within the TSC. The Rapid Support Forces (RSF), a wing of the military known for human rights abuses during al-Bashir's era and in the crackdown prior to the power-sharing agreement, was incorporated into the transitional government structure, with its commander, General Mohamed Hamdan Dagalo (commonly known as Hemeti), serving as deputy chairman of the TSC.

In 2020, there were several incidents in which violent actors attempted to derail the transition. In January, a shootout broke out in Khartoum between former officers of al-Bashir's National Intelligence and Security Service (NISS) and members of the current General Intelligence Service (GIS). Authorities accused former NISS director Salah Gosh of orchestrating the clashes. In March, Prime Minister Hamdok survived an assassination attempt in the capital. In September, the attorney general announced that between mid-August and early September, RSF officers had seized large amounts of explosives and arrested 41 people while dismantling an alleged terrorist cell.

B4. Do various segments of the population (including ethnic, racial, religious, gender, LGBT+, and other relevant groups) have full political rights and electoral opportunities? 1 / 4

The interim constitution commits Sudan to a plural, decentralized political system in which citizens are free to exercise their rights without discrimination based on race, religion, gender, regional affiliation, or other such grounds. This vision had yet to be implemented as of 2020.

Women played an influential role in the 2019 protest movement and have since demanded greater representation at all levels of government. Two women were named to the TSC in August 2019, though the vast majority of council members and other senior officeholders are men. One woman on the council, Raja Nicola Abdulmessih, is a member of the Coptic Christian minority. Prime Minister Hamdok's cabinet includes four women. In July 2020, the prime minister named two women to serve as state governors. Women are guaranteed 40 percent of the seats on the TLC, which had yet to be formed in 2020.

LGBT+ people remain politically marginalized given the continued criminalization of same-sex sexual activity.

C. FUNCTIONING OF GOVERNMENT: 0 / 12

C1. Do the freely elected head of government and national legislative representatives determine the policies of the government? 0 / 4

While the transitional government includes civilian leaders, it remains unelected. The TSC is chaired by a military officer, and the cabinet's defense and interior ministers are selected by the TSC's military members. In July 2020, Prime Minister Hamdok replaced the military governors of Sudan's 18 states with civilian appointees.

C2. Are safeguards against official corruption strong and effective? 0 / 4

The transitional government had yet to establish an anticorruption commission as of 2020, but it has begun efforts to track down and recover national assets that were stolen by members of al-Bashir's regime. The former president himself was convicted on corruption charges, including receiving illegal funds from Saudi Arabia's crown prince, and sentenced to two years in a reform institution in December 2019.

However, other members of al-Bashir's regime who engaged in corrupt activities have escaped scrutiny. These include senior security officials who sold the services of their troops to foreign powers for use in the ongoing civil war in Yemen. RSF commander Hemeti's rise to high office has been aided by a personal fortune gained through the forcible acquisition of gold mines and other assets.

C3. Does the government operate with openness and transparency? 0 / 4

President al-Bashir's regime lacked transparency before its overthrow, running large off-budget accounts and reserving most of the formal budget for opaque security institutions. In his early engagements with foreign creditors in 2019, Prime Minister Hamdok pledged greater transparency, robust budget management, and an overhaul of the civil service, though these efforts had yet to gain traction in 2020.

The interim constitution requires members of the TSC and TLC, the cabinet, and governors to file disclosures about their personal assets, but there are no clear mechanisms for enforcement, and compliance is reportedly poor in practice.

ADDITIONAL DISCRETIONARY POLITICAL RIGHTS QUESTION:
Is the government or occupying power deliberately changing the ethnic composition of a country or territory so as to destroy a culture or tip the political balance in favor of another group? −2 / 0

Former president al-Bashir faces outstanding arrest warrants from the ICC on charges of war crimes, crimes against humanity, and genocide in Darfur, where an insurgency by members of local ethnic minority groups began in 2003. During peace talks in February 2020, the government reached an agreement with Darfuri rebel groups to turn over to the ICC the five Sudanese suspects accused of war crimes, including al-Bashir. Prime Minister Hamdok reaffirmed this position in August. In June, Ali Kushayb, one of the five suspects, voluntarily surrendered in the Central African Republic. The Sudanese government welcomed and met with ICC representatives in Khartoum in October, but al-Bashir and other suspects remained in Sudanese custody at year's end.

In October 2020, the government signed the Juba Peace Agreement with the SRF alliance and another rebel group, the Sudan Liberation Army (SLA) Minni Minnawi faction. The peace deal, which was meant to end ethnic insurgencies and alleged government war crimes in South Kordofan and Blue Nile States as well as in Darfur, included provisions for a special court for war crimes, the integration of rebels into the security forces and political institutions, economic and land rights, and the creation of a fund to address social and economic marginalization in the conflict areas and support the return of displaced persons. In November, General al-Burhan signed a decree granting general amnesty to the leaders and fighters of the SRF and the SLA Minni Minawi. Other rebel groups in the country were negotiating separately or rejected the peace talks, and some Darfur residents protested the Juba pact, arguing that they were not consulted and that it did not address their needs.

Despite the negotiations, localized ethnic or communal conflict increased across Sudan in 2020. Dozens of people were killed in outbreaks of fighting in West Darfur in January and July, prompting the prime minister to promise to send security forces to the region. Also in July, militias connected with security forces attacked an internally displaced persons (IDPs) camp in North Darfur, killing nine and injuring 20. Amnesty International reported in December that from July to September in Central, North, and West Darfur States, more than 70 people were killed, almost 80 were injured, and houses and businesses were looted and destroyed. According to the International Organization for Migration, more than 8,000 people were displaced during the same time period in Central Darfur. In October, fighting in South Darfur State resulted in dozens of deaths and the displacement of some 4,500 people.

In Red Sea State, in the country's east, fighting between members of the Nuba and Beni Amer ethnic groups in August resulted in at least 34 deaths. In October, members of the Beja community protested against the interim governor, a member of the Beni Amer community, who was subsequently dismissed. Following the dismissal, communal clashes in the cities of Port Sudan and Suakin resulted in the deaths of six Beja members. Subsequent Beni Amer protests turned violent, and security officers opened fire, killing seven people and injuring 19. Ethnic clashes increased in South Kordofan as well. In May, fighting in Kadugli resulted in 26 deaths and injuries to 19 people. The Human Rights and Development Organization (HUDO) reported increased killings and robberies in the state during the year.

In response to local conflicts, the government deployed additional security forces, imposed curfews, and engaged in peacebuilding initiatives. The United Nations reported that there were more than 2.5 million IDPs in Sudan at the end of the year.

CIVIL LIBERTIES: 15 / 60 (+5)

D. FREEDOM OF EXPRESSION AND BELIEF: 7 / 16 (+2)

D1. Are there free and independent media? 1 / 4

The interim constitution guarantees freedom of the press, and the transitional government has pledged to draft legislation that increases protections for journalists. However, a number of repressive statutes—including a 2007 information offenses law, the 2009 press law, and the 2010 national security law—are still in effect, and the government in July 2020 amended the 2018 Law on Combating Cybercrimes to increase the prison sentences for crimes such as disseminating false information.

Journalists have expressed concern that individuals connected with al-Bashir's regime retained positions at media outlets in the country, and key newspapers continued to be closely affiliated with former officials and other political parties. In January 2020, the government committee tasked with recovering assets from the former ruling party suspended the newspapers *Al-Rai al-Am* and Al-Sudani and the television channels Ashorooq and Teiba. In December 2020, more than 80 state media workers were fired for their alleged loyalty to al-Bashir's regime.

Intelligence officers no longer raid and censor newspapers or interfere with printing presses, and institutional censorship in general has declined. However, in July 2020 the military announced that it had appointed a commissioner to bring legal cases against online journalists who insult the armed forces. Journalists reportedly received threats that they would be prosecuted if they did not stop criticizing the military and delete critical reports. In May, two reporters were harassed by intelligence officers in North Darfur State for investigating and reporting on the COVID-19 pandemic.

D2. Are individuals free to practice and express their religious faith or nonbelief in public and private? 2 / 4 (+1)

Sudan's population is mostly Muslim, with a small Christian minority. Under al-Bashir, Christians were persecuted and churches were shuttered, often under the pretext that they lacked appropriate permits. The 2019 interim constitution guarantees freedom of worship and does not give Islam an official status. The new TSC pledged to issue clear guidelines for those seeking permission to build new churches, and Christians welcomed the appointment of a Coptic Christian judge to one of the TSC's civilian seats. Also in 2019, the transitional government repealed the Public Order Act, which had been used to punish both Muslims and non-Muslims for public behaviors that were deemed indecent or immoral according to the official interpretation of Sunni Islam.

Legal reforms continued in 2020, and in July the government adopted the Miscellaneous Amendments Act, which repealed the criminalization of apostasy, abolished corporal punishment for blasphemy, and permitted non-Muslims to trade and consume alcohol, among other provisions.

Score Change: The score improved from 1 to 2 because the government continued to repeal long-standing legislation that had restricted religious freedom, including laws criminalizing apostasy.

D3. Is there academic freedom, and is the educational system free from extensive political indoctrination? 2 / 4 (+1)

Al-Bashir's government regularly interfered with education and worked to suppress dissent on university campuses, using increasingly violent tactics as students became involved with the protest movement that began in late 2018. After the TSC's creation in mid-2019, university students demanded the dismantling of student groups loyal to al-Bashir, the withdrawal of security forces from campuses, and the departure of administrators tied to the former government. In response, the transitional authorities moved to disband NCP groups in higher education and dismissed 28 university chancellors and 35 vice chancellors, many of whom were affiliated with the NCP. The administrators were then replaced with more independent figures. Since campuses reopened in October 2019, after being shuttered early that year, student unions have held elections for their new leaders, and a variety of student groups have been able to organize and hold meetings.

Score Change: The score improved from 1 to 2 due to a reduction in violence and intimidation on university campuses since 2019, the ongoing replacement of university officials and student union leaders who were loyal to the former regime with more independent figures, and a related increase in open debate and activism among students.

D4. Are individuals free to express their personal views on political or other sensitive topics without fear of surveillance or retribution? 2 / 4

The interim constitution affirms the right to privacy, including citizens' right to engage in private correspondence without interference. The transitional government has begun to dismantle the surveillance apparatus associated with the former regime, notably by replacing the NISS with the GIS—which has narrower powers and responsibilities—in 2019. However, the government's decision to increase penalties for disseminating false information and other such offenses in July 2020, and the military's threats to take legal action in response to online insults, raised new doubts about the authorities' commitment to freedom of personal expression. Ongoing violence by security forces and nonstate actors during the year also served to deter unfettered discussion and criticism among ordinary citizens.

E. ASSOCIATIONAL AND ORGANIZATIONAL RIGHTS: 4 / 12 (+1)
E1. Is there freedom of assembly? 1 / 4 (+1)

The security forces repeatedly used lethal violence to suppress protests during the movement to oust al-Bashir. The TSC reaffirmed the right to assemble in the interim constitution, and citizens regularly participated in demonstrations during 2020, calling for more rapid democratic reforms, the advancement of women's rights, accountability for a June

2019 massacre of protesters in Khartoum, and the appointment of civilian state governors, among other demands. In addition, local committees of citizens across the country organized protests to highlight governance problems in their respective areas, and supporters of the former regime protested against reforms that they said were anti-Islamic.

The authorities imposed some restrictions on large gatherings in response to the COVID-19 pandemic, and security forces repeatedly use tear gas and live ammunition to break up demonstrations, though the violence was less extreme and caused fewer deaths than in previous years. In June, for example, police used force to disperse a march calling for a faster pace of reforms, and one person was killed. In July, security forces disrupted a sit-in in North Darfur State, killing one person and injuring a dozen others. In August, neighborhood resistance committees launched demonstrations throughout Khartoum that led to clashes with police and the arrest of 77 people. In October, security officers in Kassala State opened fire on protesters demonstrating against the removal of the interim governor, killing seven and injuring 19.

Score Change: The score improved from 0 to 1 because the authorities' use of force and administrative restrictions against protesters was less severe than in previous years.

E2. Is there freedom for nongovernmental organizations, particularly those that are engaged in human rights- and governance-related work? 2 / 4

Under al-Bashir, international and domestic nongovernmental organizations (NGOs), faced serious legal and administrative obstacles or were banned from operating altogether. Upon taking office, the transitional government signaled a loosening of restrictions on civil society, though it had yet to introduce a new NGO law as of 2020. Local NGOs report being able to register, and organizations that had operated in exile continue to return to and register in Sudan. International humanitarian entities that had been denied access to conflict zones under al-Bashir have similarly been allowed to resume some activities since the second half of 2019.

E3. Is there freedom for trade unions and similar professional or labor organizations? 1 / 4

Independent trade unions were largely absent under al-Bashir; his government banned them after taking power in 1989, and instead co-opted the Sudan Workers' Trade Unions Federation (SWTUF). The independent SPA, founded in late 2016, was instrumental in the protest movement that led to al-Bashir's ouster, and it has since played a role in the transitional government, with one of its members named to the TSC.

The interim constitution affirmed workers' right to form and join trade unions. However, as part of the transitional government's efforts to dismantle the former ruling party and affiliated institutions, it dissolved the SWTUF and the Sudan Journalists Union in late 2019. The International Trade Union Confederation's Africa branch criticized the decision as a violation of freedom of association.

F. RULE OF LAW: 1 / 16

F1. Is there an independent judiciary? 1 / 4

The interim constitution envisages the establishment of an independent judiciary to replace the politically influenced judiciary of the al-Bashir era. The first senior appointments were announced in October 2019, following large protests calling for an acceleration of judicial reform. The new chief justice appointed that month, Nemat Abdullah Khair, became the first woman to hold the position in Sudan's history. The replacement of incumbent judicial officials continued during 2020. In August, the government committee tasked with dismantling the former regime dismissed 151 judges and 21 prosecutors.

F2. Does due process prevail in civil and criminal matters? 0 / 4

The interim constitution called for the establishment of a new public prosecutor's office, and Taj al-Ser Ali al-Hebr was appointed to lead it in October 2019. In addition to the prosecution of former president al-Bashir, the office prosecuted 27 members of the security forces for the detention and killing of a schoolteacher in February 2019, obtaining death sentences against them in late December of that year.

Although the interim constitution enshrines the right to due process, it also contains a provision allowing the government to invoke emergency powers and suspend parts of the document. In practice, security forces continued to engage in arbitrary arrests and detentions during 2020, including in response to protests.

In one high-profile case in August, the authorities arrested and charged 11 artists, including filmmaker Hajooj Kuka, with creating a public disturbance while rehearsing a play—and by chanting prodemocracy slogans at the police station once in custody. The artists reported beatings and other mistreatment in detention, and five of them were sentenced to two months in jail and fines in September, but an appeals court ordered all 11 released in October.

F3. Is there protection from the illegitimate use of physical force and freedom from war and insurgencies? 0 / 4

Torture and abuse of prisoners was rampant under al-Bashir and intensified as antigovernment protests gathered momentum in 2019. Civilians were frequently victims of deadly violence during the final months of al-Bashir's rule and the period of military rule after his ouster. In July 2019, the Central Committee of Sudanese Doctors reported that 246 people had been killed and more than 1,300 had been wounded since the start of the protest movement in December 2018, with most deaths attributed to the security forces.

To date, almost none of the perpetrators of these attacks have been held to account, though eight RSF members were arrested in August 2019 for their involvement in the June massacre of protesters in Khartoum. In September of that year, Prime Minister Hamdok announced the creation of an independent committee to investigate the incident; the findings had not been published as of 2020.

A series of legal amendments adopted by the transitional government in July 2020 banned forced confessions and the "infliction of torture" on suspects, prohibited the death penalty for defendants under age 18, and abolished the penalty of flogging for some criminal offenses, although flogging and other forms of corporal punishment were still prescribed for other crimes.

Despite the October 2020 Juba Peace Agreement, civilians in Sudan continued to suffer from the effects of armed conflict and related lawlessness, and some rebel factions refused to participate in the peace talks. Scores of people were killed and many more were displaced by the rise in communal violence in several parts of the country during the year.

F4. Do laws, policies, and practices guarantee equal treatment of various segments of the population? 0 / 4

Successive governments in Sudan have neglected or abused populations living in the periphery of the country, particularly non-Arab ethnic minority communities, sparking uprisings that were met with indiscriminate force. The 2019 interim constitution commits the transitional government to upholding the human rights of all citizens without discrimination and ensuring their equal treatment under the law. The charter also calls for accountability for war crimes, crimes against humanity, and other serious violations of human rights. The peace deal signed in October 2020 includes provisions to establish a transitional justice commission, a special court to deal with crimes committed in Darfur, and a 10-year, $750 million fund to address social and economic marginalization in the conflict areas and support the return of displaced persons. Implementation of these measures remained uncertain at year's end.

Despite guarantees of equal treatment in the interim constitution and some legal improvements adopted as part of the July 2020 reforms, women continued to face disadvantages in many areas of the law, and perpetrators of widespread crimes against women—including during armed conflicts—have generally enjoyed impunity. Same-sex sexual relations are illegal in Sudan, though the July reforms eliminated flogging and execution as potential punishments. Official and societal discrimination against LGBT+ people remains common.

In 2020, the Sudanese government kept its borders open to allow the entry of Ethiopian refugees fleeing the conflict in that country's Tigray region; as of November, according to UN officials, there were more than 43,000 such refugees in Sudan.

G. PERSONAL AUTONOMY AND INDIVIDUAL RIGHTS: 3 / 16 (+2)

G1. Do individuals enjoy freedom of movement, including the ability to change their place of residence, employment, or education? 1 / 4 (+1)

The 2019 interim constitution affirms freedom of movement and the right to travel—including overseas—for all citizens, but these rights are still impeded in practice by state security forces and other armed groups across the country, including those engaged in clashes between ethnic communities in 2020. Most of the estimated 2.5 million IDPs in Sudan at year's end were concentrated in the long-standing conflict areas of Darfur, South Kordofan, and Blue Nile State.

While some temporary travel restrictions were imposed during 2020 in response to the COVID-19 pandemic, the government removed long-standing legal constraints on travel as part of the July 2020 reform package. The legislation abolished the need for exit permits as well as a rule that had required women to obtain permission from a male guardian in order to travel abroad with children.

Score Change: The score improved from 0 to 1 due to the abolition of exit permits and a rule that had required women to obtain a male guardian's consent to travel abroad with their children.

G2. Are individuals able to exercise the right to own property and establish private businesses without undue interference from state or nonstate actors? 1 / 4

Weak land rights have been a chronic driver of conflict in Sudan. In a succession of opaque deals, al-Bashir's regime leased large parcels of arable land to foreign countries for export crop production. In some cases, local populations were forced from their land or had their water supplies depleted.

The 2019 interim constitution guarantees the right to own property and protects citizens from expropriation by the state without compensation. The government has stated its intention to address land-related grievances, but property seizures by security forces and communal conflicts over land rights continue to be reported.

Women are denied equal rights to property and inheritance under laws based on Sharia (Islamic law) and through discriminatory customary practices.

G3. Do individuals enjoy personal social freedoms, including choice of marriage partner and size of family, protection from domestic violence, and control over appearance? 1 / 4 (+1)

Sharia-based laws deny women equal rights in marriage and divorce. Among other restrictions, a Muslim woman cannot marry a non-Muslim man. Extramarital sex is prohibited, and those convicted of adultery can face flogging or the death penalty. Child marriage is not outlawed, and roughly a third of adult women married before reaching the age of 18.

In 2019, the transitional government repealed the Public Order Act, which had been used in part to punish women for dress or behavior that was deemed indecent. The legal reforms adopted in July 2020 included a provision that criminalized female genital mutilation, which is prevalent among the vast majority of women in Sudan. The first charges under the new law were reported in November.

Sexual violence against women remains a major problem. In March 2020, the government signed a framework of cooperation with the United Nations on preventing and addressing conflict-related sexual violence.

Score Change: The score improved from 0 to 1 due to legislative changes since 2019 that supported women's social freedoms, including the repeal of a public order law that facilitated enforcement of dress codes and the enactment of a ban on female genital mutilation.

G4. Do individuals enjoy equality of opportunity and freedom from economic exploitation?
0 / 4

Bleak economic conditions, mass unemployment, and high prices for basic goods were among the root causes of the revolution that helped topple al-Bashir's regime in 2019. Prime Minister Hamdok's government voiced a commitment to reversing these trends, though the economy worsened in 2020. In September, the International Monetary Fund (IMF) approved a 12-month program to support the government in its efforts to eliminate large fuel subsidies, increase spending for health and social programs, increase its tax base, reduce corruption, and improve the business environment.

The transitional government took early steps to clamp down on hazardous practices and working conditions in the gold-mining sector. In 2019, it announced a ban on the use of cyanide and mercury in gold extraction, following protests in mining areas in South Kordofan that resulted in a heavy-handed response from the RSF. Despite the transitional government's statements and actions regarding labor exploitation, senior military figures who hold positions in the TSC power structure have profited from illicit economic activities, including mining and smuggling operations.

Migrants, refugees, asylum seekers, and IDPs remain especially vulnerable to exploitation, including by criminal networks engaged in human trafficking. Some armed groups in the country have allegedly recruited children as fighters.

Suriname

Population: 600,000
Capital: Paramaribo
Freedom Status: Free
Electoral Democracy: Yes

Overview: Suriname is a constitutional democracy that holds generally free and fair elections. However, corruption and clientelism are pervasive problems in society and in the government, undermining the rule of law. In 2020, a new government was elected, and the country's new leaders have promised to tackle graft and abuses of state power.

KEY DEVELOPMENTS IN 2020

- Suriname was seriously affected by the COVID-19 pandemic. According to researchers at the University of Oxford, the country had registered over 6,200 cases and over 120 deaths by the end of 2020.
- In elections held in May 2020, the administration of President Dési Bouterse was defeated by the Progressive Reform Party (VHP) led by Chandrikapersad Santokhi, who was elected president by the National Assembly in July. Ronnie Brunswijk, the powerful leader of the General Liberation and Development Party (ABOP), was selected as vice president.
- Anticorruption efforts increased during the year. The public prosecutor's office established a dedicated anticorruption unit, and graft investigations resulted in detention orders for several high-ranking officials from the Bouterse government.

POLITICAL RIGHTS: 34 / 40 (+2)

A. ELECTORAL PROCESS: 11 / 12

A1. Was the current head of government or other chief national authority elected through free and fair elections? 4 / 4

The president is chief of state and head of government, and is elected to five-year terms by a two-thirds majority of the 51-seat National Assembly. If no such majority can be reached, a United People's Assembly—consisting of lawmakers from the national, regional, and local levels—convenes to choose the president by a simple majority. In July 2020, the freely elected National Assembly elected President Santokhi and Vice President Brunswijk in accordance with the law.

A2. Were the current national legislative representatives elected through free and fair elections? 4 / 4

The 1987 constitution provides for a unicameral, 51-seat National Assembly. Representatives are elected for five-year terms via proportional representation. Observer missions from the Caribbean Community (CARICOM) and the Organization of American States (OAS) described the May 2020 elections as free and fair, while noting delays in the vote count, which had fueled speculation about fraud. The OAS also noted some problems with election administration, including ballot misprints and deliveries of ballot papers to the wrong polling stations. Nonetheless, no serious concerns were raised about the announced results, and the Independent Electoral Council (OKB) certified the elections in June. The VHP led all parties with 20 seats, Bouterse's National Democratic Party (NDP) followed with 16, the ABOP won 8, and three smaller parties split the remaining seven seats.

A3. Are the electoral laws and framework fair, and are they implemented impartially by the relevant election management bodies? 3 / 4

Electoral laws generally meet international standards of fairness. However, the president appoints the members of the OKB and has the power to fire them, raising concerns about impartiality. In March 2019, the National Assembly approved electoral reforms that had been proposed by the Bouterse government in late 2018, including a prohibition on electoral alliances among political parties. The head of the OKB, Jennifer Van Dijk-Silos, acknowledged significant disorganization in the administration of the 2020 balloting.

B. POLITICAL PLURALISM AND PARTICIPATION: 14 / 16

B1. Do the people have the right to organize in different political parties or other competitive political groupings of their choice, and is the system free of undue obstacles to the rise and fall of these competing parties or groupings? 4 / 4

Suriname's many political parties, which often reflect the country's ethnic cleavages, generally form and operate freely. However, fierce political competition occasionally includes acts of violence or intimidation.

B2. Is there a realistic opportunity for the opposition to increase its support or gain power through elections? 4 / 4

The country has experienced multiple transfers of power between rival parties, and the opposition has a realistic opportunity to increase its support or enter government through elections, as demonstrated by the orderly transition in July 2020.

B3. Are the people's political choices free from domination by forces that are external to the political sphere, or by political forces that employ extrapolitical means? 3 / 4

People's political choices are generally not subject to undue coercion. However, opposition parties have raised concerns about campaign financing—which is unregulated and lacks transparency—and the resulting influence that special interest groups can have on parties and candidates. During the 2020 election campaign, the incumbent NDP was accused of engaging in clientelism by distributing food to citizens. Similar tactics, including distribution of money and funding of community projects using politicians' personal wealth, are used by multiple political parties. The Santokhi government also continued the entrenched practice of dispensing appointments to family members of high-ranking officials.

The period preceding the 2020 elections was characterized by intimidation of supporters of the opposition. In April 2020, assailants attempted to kidnap an opposition parliamentary candidate, Rodney Cairo, who had criticized the military's role in providing security at gold mining operations. National Security Directorate head Danielle Vieira was accused of ordering the act, and an investigation remained ongoing at year's end. Following the inauguration of the Santokhi government, there were no reported cases of intimidation against opponents.

B4. Do various segments of the population (including ethnic, racial, religious, gender, LGBT+, and other relevant groups) have full political rights and electoral opportunities? 3 / 4

Parties are often formed along ethnic lines, meaning most ethnic groups have political representation. Women have historically played a limited role in politics, but have experienced gains in recent years; in 2020, 15 out of the 51 representatives elected to the National Assembly were women, compared with 13 women in 2015. The Santokhi-Brunswijk cabinet included 6 women among its 17 ministers. The interests of Maroons, the descendants of escaped slaves, are directly represented in the government, as Vice President Brunswijk's ABOP party is the largest party among Maroons. Indigenous people are poorly represented in politics, and discrimination against LGBT+ people has resulted in no openly gay politicians in the country.

C. FUNCTIONING OF GOVERNMENT: 9 / 12 (+2)

C1. Do the freely elected head of government and national legislative representatives determine the policies of the government? 4 / 4 (+1)

The country's freely elected representatives are able to determine laws and government policies without undue interference. The Bouterse government used its narrow parliamentary majority to avoid accountability for politically advantageous actions that appeared to exceed its legitimate authority, especially related to state finances and spending. In its initial months, the Santokhi administration refrained from executive overreach.

Score Change: The score improved from 3 to 4 because the Santokhi administration refrained from abusing state power and exhibiting excessive control over other branches of government.

C2. Are safeguards against official corruption strong and effective? 2 / 4

Government corruption is pervasive. In 2017, the National Assembly adopted a new anticorruption law, updating past laws that were severely outdated. The legislation had yet to be implemented as of 2020, but the Santokhi government appointed a commission to plan implementation and funded a special anticorruption unit within the public prosecutor's office that has begun investigating Bouterse-era graft cases. The most prominent case in 2020 involved former finance minister Gillmore Hoefdraad, accused of perpetrating multiple fraud and embezzlement schemes. Hoefdraad fled and was the subject of both a domestic arrest warrant and an Interpol detention request. The former head of Suriname's Central Bank, Robert Van Trikt, was imprisoned for fraud in the same case in February 2020, and remained in custody throughout the year. In a separate case, former vice president Ashwin Adhin was arrested in November 2020 for alleged destruction and misappropriation of property.

C3. Does the government operate with openness and transparency? 3 / 4 (+1)

The government often does not operate with transparency. The Bouterse government channeled almost all information through the National Information Institute (NII), which functions as a centralized state publicity agency. Officials are not required to disclose information about their finances in practice, despite disclosure provisions in the 2017 anticorruption law.

Suriname does not have laws to facilitate access to public information, and access is limited in practice. However, the Santokhi government has communicated with greater transparency, including via regular press conferences at which journalists can ask questions of the president and vice president.

Score Change: The score improved from 2 to 3 because the new government has committed to openly publishing information, and is more responsive to inquiries from the press.

CIVIL LIBERTIES: 45 / 60 (+2)
D. FREEDOM OF EXPRESSION AND BELIEF: 15 / 16 (+1)
D1. Are there free and independent media? 3 / 4

The constitution guarantees press freedom, and the media sector is fairly diverse. The press frequently publishes stories that are critical of the government, though some journalists engage in self-censorship in response to pressure and intimidation from authorities. Bouterse administration officials regularly used state media to verbally attack journalists whose work they found objectionable.

D2. Are individuals free to practice and express their religious faith or nonbelief in public and private? 4 / 4

The constitution guarantees freedom of religion, which is typically upheld in practice.

D3. Is there academic freedom, and is the educational system free from extensive political indoctrination? 4 / 4

Academic freedom is generally respected.

D4. Are individuals free to express their personal views on political or other sensitive topics without fear of surveillance or retribution? 4 / 4

Freedom of expression is enshrined in the constitution, and there are no formal constraints on the expression of personal views among the general public. Government officials' verbal intimidation of perceived critics, which deterred open discussion of sensitive topics in recent years, declined following the 2020 election, as did the overall level of political discord.

Score Change: The score improved from 3 to 4 because the current government has refrained from targeting ordinary citizens and members of political parties who engage in critical speech.

E. ASSOCIATIONAL AND ORGANIZATIONAL RIGHTS: 11 / 12
E1. Is there freedom of assembly? 4 / 4

The constitution guarantees freedom of assembly, which is generally respected in practice.

E2. Is there freedom for nongovernmental organizations, particularly those that are engaged in human rights- and governance-related work? 4 / 4

Nongovernmental organizations (NGOs) function freely in Suriname.

E3. Is there freedom for trade unions and similar professional or labor organizations? 3 / 4

Workers are free to join independent trade unions, which are actively involved in politics. There have been isolated reports of private-sector employers denying collective bargaining rights to unions.

F. RULE OF LAW: 9 / 16 (+1)
F1. Is there an independent judiciary? 2 / 4

The judiciary has enjoyed improved autonomy since the change of government, but is still undermined by corruption and characterized by financial dependence on executive agencies.

F2. Does due process prevail in civil and criminal matters? 2 / 4 (+1)

Obstacles to due process include a lack of capacity and resources that contributes to corruption and trial delays. The public prosecutor's office often pursues cases selectively, and low wages for police encourage bribery and extortion. Payments are sometimes made to obtain favorable outcomes in criminal and civil proceedings. There is a backlog of cases involving non-Dutch speakers, as interpreters who have gone unpaid have refused to work additional cases. Pretrial detention, even for minor crimes, is common and can sometimes last for years. However, the judiciary is operating more independently since the change of administration in 2020, with more investigations for criminal conduct and less evident protection for politically favored allies.

In November 2019, President Bouterse was convicted and sentenced to 20 years' imprisonment for the abduction and murder of 15 political opponents during his time as a military ruler in 1982. Bouterse has accepted "political responsibility" for his involvement, but he long sought to disrupt legal proceedings against him. While his immunity as head of state lapsed with his departure from office in July 2020, the appeal of his conviction remained ongoing, and he remained free throughout the year.

Score Change: The score improved from 1 to 2 because prosecutors have shown more independence in pursuing cases, including those involving alleged corruption by powerful state officials.

F3. Is there protection from the illegitimate use of physical force and freedom from war and insurgencies? 3 / 4

The population is generally free from major threats to physical security. The use of excessive force by law enforcement officials is prohibited, but some cases of police abuse have been reported, including during enforcement of the lockdown imposed in response to the COVID-19 pandemic in 2020.

Temporary detention facilities are characterized by unhygienic conditions, understaffing, and overcrowding. Suriname lies on a major drug-trafficking route, giving rise to some trafficking-related violence. Both former president Bouterse and current vice president Brunswijk have been convicted in absentia of drug trafficking in the Netherlands. Violent crimes such as burglary and armed robbery are common, and police resources are insufficient to address the problem. The gold mining industry, a key export sector, is plagued by organized criminal activity.

F4. Do laws, policies, and practices guarantee equal treatment of various segments of the population? 2 / 2

The constitution prohibits discrimination based on race or ethnicity. Nevertheless, the Maroon and Indigenous people in the hinterland face inequality in areas such as education and employment.

Same-sex sexual relations are legal, though the age of consent differs from that applied to opposite-sex couples. Despite legal protections adopted in 2015, members of the LGBT+ community face societal discrimination, harassment, and abuse by police.

The constitution bars gender discrimination, but in practice, women experience disadvantages in access to employment and education.

G. PERSONAL AUTONOMY AND INDIVIDUAL RIGHTS: 10 / 12

G1. Do individuals enjoy freedom of movement, including the ability to change their place of residence, employment, or education? 3 / 4

The government generally upholds constitutional freedoms of internal movement and residence, though the lack of protections for Indigenous and Maroon lands leaves those communities vulnerable to displacement.

G2. Are individuals able to exercise the right to own property and establish private businesses without undue interference from state or nonstate actors? 2 / 4

Although Suriname's constitution guarantees property rights, they are sometimes inadequately protected. Corruption can hinder private business activity, especially regarding land policy, government contracts, and licensing. Indigenous and other minority groups remain exposed to illegal land expropriation, including by logging and mining operations. Traditional land rights of Indigenous peoples and Maroons are not guaranteed by law, though a draft bill to regulate collective rights was introduced in parliament in 2020. Women face inequality related to inheritance and property due to discriminatory local customs.

G3. Do individuals enjoy personal social freedoms, including choice of marriage partner and size of family, protection from domestic violence, and control over appearance? 3 / 4

Individuals are generally free of undue constraints on personal status decisions such as marriage and divorce. However, domestic violence remains a serious problem, and laws that criminalize it are not well enforced.

G4. Do individuals enjoy equality of opportunity and freedom from economic exploitation? 2 / 4

Despite government efforts to combat it, trafficking in persons remains a serious problem. Women and migrant workers are especially at risk of sexual exploitation and forced labor in various industries. Construction and mining work often do not receive adequate attention from labor inspectors. The deteriorating economy in Venezuela has increased the vulnerability of Venezuelan women to sex trafficking in Suriname. Corruption has facilitated the criminal activities of traffickers.

Sweden

Population: 10,400,000
Capital: Stockholm
Freedom Status: Free
Electoral Democracy: Yes

Overview: Sweden is a parliamentary monarchy with free and fair elections and a strong multiparty system. Civil liberties and political rights are legally guaranteed and respected in practice, and the rule of law prevails. Recent challenges include increases in violent crime and reported hate crimes.

KEY DEVELOPMENTS IN 2020

- The initial Swedish response to the COVID-19 pandemic relied on adherence to voluntary social-distancing guidelines, but stricter regulations came into force after the number of cases spiked in November. There were 457,000 confirmed COVID-19 cases and more than 9,900 deaths in Sweden during the year, according to the World Health Organization (WHO).
- A government-appointed commission in December criticized the government and Swedish society for failing to provide adequate care, amid the pandemic, for elderly people in assisted-living homes. Immigrant communities were also disproportionately affected by the coronavirus.
- Violent crime emerged as a concern, with 163 shootings and 20 shooting deaths in the first six months of the year. New measures to combat the violence include increased search and surveillance powers for police, as well as initiatives aimed at expanding care for people who struggle with substance abuse or psychological conditions. Relatively few shootings have been prosecuted, and little information is available about who is involved in the attacks and why.

POLITICAL RIGHTS: 40 / 40

A. ELECTORAL PROCESS: 12 / 12

A1. Was the current head of government or other chief national authority elected through free and fair elections? 4 / 4

The prime minister is the head of government and is appointed by the speaker of the freely elected parliament, or Riksdag, and confirmed by the body as a whole. Prime Minister Stefan Löfven of the Swedish Social Democrats (SAP) was appointed in January 2019 following parliamentary elections in 2018. King Carl XVI Gustaf, crowned in 1973, is the ceremonial head of state.

A2. Were the current national legislative representatives elected through free and fair elections? 4 / 4

The unicameral Riksdag is comprised of 349 members who are elected every four years by proportional representation. A party must receive at least 4 percent of the vote nationwide or 12 percent in an electoral district to win a seat. Swedish elections are broadly free and fair.

In the September 2018 parliamentary elections, neither main bloc won a majority, with the center-left bloc winning 144 seats and the center-right bloc winning 143 seats. The populist, anti-immigrant party, Sweden Democrats (SD), won 62 seats, up from 49 previously. However, the party's gains fell short of the expectations of many analysts. Parties in both the center-right and center-left blocs refused to form a coalition government with the SD. In January 2019, after over four months without a government, SAP leader Stefan Löfven formed a coalition with the Green Party, the Centre Party, and the Liberals.

A report published in November 2018 by election monitors from the Organization for Security and Co-operation in Europe (OSCE) stated that although the integrity of the elections was not in doubt, the secrecy of the vote was sometimes compromised.

A3. Are the electoral laws and framework fair, and are they implemented impartially by the relevant election management bodies? 4 / 4

Elections are regulated by the Swedish Election Authority, which effectively upholds its mandates. The Election Authority is headed by a government-appointed committee.

B. POLITICAL PLURALISM AND PARTICIPATION: 16 / 16

B1. Do the people have the right to organize in different political parties or other competitive political groupings of their choice, and is the system free of undue obstacles to the rise and fall of these competing parties or groupings? 4 / 4

Political parties may form and operate without restriction.

B2. Is there a realistic opportunity for the opposition to increase its support or gain power through elections? 4 / 4

Sweden has a strong multiparty system with a robust opposition. Eight political parties secured representation in the Riksdag in 2018.

B3. Are the people's political choices free from domination by forces that are external to the political sphere, or by political forces that employ extrapolitical means? 4 / 4

People's political choices are generally free from domination by actors that are not democratically accountable.

B4. Do various segments of the population (including ethnic, racial, religious, gender, LGBT+, and other relevant groups) have full political rights and electoral opportunities? 4 / 4

The country's principal religious, ethnic, and immigrant groups are represented in the parliament, as are many women. There are 161 women (out of 349 members) in Parliament; however, some parties maintain more gender parity than others. Since 1993, the Indigenous Sami community has elected its own legislature, which has significant powers over community education and culture, and serves as an advisory body to the government. There are calls for greater political autonomy of the Sami Parliament, which have been echoed by the United Nations (UN) Special Rapporteur on the rights of Indigenous peoples.

C. FUNCTIONING OF GOVERNMENT: 12 / 12

C1. Do the freely elected head of government and national legislative representatives determine the policies of the government? 4 / 4

Sweden's freely elected representatives develop and implement policy. The strong performance by the far-right Sweden Democrats in the 2018 parliamentary elections, and the refusal of both the center-right bloc and center-left bloc to work with the party, contributed to the failure to form a functioning government for over four months after the general election in 2018. The SAP managed to form a functioning government with the Green Party, Centre Party, and Liberals in January 2019 after a vote in parliament. Three parties abstained from the vote, however.

C2. Are safeguards against official corruption strong and effective? 4 / 4

Corruption is relatively low in Sweden, and anticorruption mechanisms are generally effective. The country's lively free press also works to expose corrupt officials.

C3. Does the government operate with openness and transparency? 4 / 4

The country has one of the most robust freedom of information statutes in the world, and state authorities generally respect the right of both citizens and noncitizens to access public information.

CIVIL LIBERTIES: 60 / 60

D. FREEDOM OF EXPRESSION AND BELIEF: 16 / 16

D1. Are there free and independent media? 4 / 4

Sweden's media are independent. Most newspapers and periodicals are privately owned, and the government subsidizes daily newspapers regardless of their political affiliation. Public broadcasters air weekly radio and television programs in several minority languages. Threats and intimidation of journalists have been reported, particularly against those who report on organized crime, religion, extremist groups, or other sensitive topics.

D2. Are individuals free to practice and express their religious faith or nonbelief in public and private? 4 / 4

Religious freedom is constitutionally guaranteed and generally respected. State authorities document religious hate crimes, investigate and prosecute cases, and provide adequate resources for victims. The police force includes a permanent unit trained to handle hate crimes. However, religiously motivated hate crimes often go unreported. The UN Universal Periodic Review of Sweden in 2020 highlighted numerous such instances, mainly aimed at Muslims and Jews, which included physical assaults and attacks on places of worship.

D3. Is there academic freedom, and is the educational system free from extensive political indoctrination? 4 / 4

Academic freedom is generally respected.

D4. Are individuals free to express their personal views on political or other sensitive topics without fear of surveillance or retribution? 4 / 4

Private discussion is open and vibrant.

E. ASSOCIATIONAL AND ORGANIZATIONAL RIGHTS: 12 / 12

E1. Is there freedom of assembly? 4 / 4

Freedom of assembly is generally respected in law and in practice. However, violence has occasionally erupted between far-right demonstrators and counterprotesters. Sweden introduced a ban on gatherings of more than 50 people, in light of the COVID-19 pandemic.

E2. Is there freedom for nongovernmental organizations, particularly those that are engaged in human rights- and governance-related work? 4 / 4

Nongovernmental organizations of all kinds function freely.

E3. Is there freedom for trade unions and similar professional or labor organizations? 4 / 4

The rights to strike and organize in labor unions are guaranteed. Trade union federations, which represent approximately 70 percent of the workforce, are strong and well organized.

F. RULE OF LAW: 16 / 16

F1. Is there an independent judiciary? 4 / 4

The judiciary is independent.

F2. Does due process prevail in civil and criminal matters? 4 / 4

The rule of law prevails in civil and criminal matters. Defendants are presumed innocent until proven guilty, and the state must provide legal counsel to people accused of criminal offenses.

F3. Is there protection from the illegitimate use of physical force and freedom from war and insurgencies? 4 / 4

While Sweden is free from large-scale insurgencies, rising street violence has emerged as a growing concern. Deadly shootings, arson attacks, and use of hand grenades have taken place in many Swedish cities in recent years, mainly in poor neighborhoods with large immigrant populations. In the first six months of 2020 there were 163 shootings, in which 20 people were killed. Relatively few cases have been prosecuted, and little information is available about who is involved in the attacks or why. In September, the government announced measures to combat the violence, including granting police increased search and surveillance powers that allow them to read encrypted communications on suspects' devices. Other measures included initiatives to increase available care for people who struggle with substance abuse or psychological conditions.

The government introduced new antiterrorism measures following a 2017 attack in which a man drove a truck through central Stockholm and into a department store, killing 5 people and wounding 10 others. The law focused on tighter security in public places, greater information sharing between government agencies, and tighter controls on individuals deemed to pose a security threat.

Conditions in prisons and temporary detention facilities are adequate, but concerns have been raised about excessive use of long detention periods.

F4. Do laws, policies, and practices guarantee equal treatment of various segments of the population? 4 / 4

The Swedish state works to ensure equal protection and rights for all members of the population. An equality ombudsman oversees efforts to prevent discrimination on the basis of gender, ethnicity, disability, and sexual orientation. However, the United Nations has called for the ombudsman's powers to be strengthened and has noted problems with discrimination by police and correctional personnel.

In 2017, in the wake of growing right-wing sentiment and increasing immigration from abroad, the Swedish government voted to place limits on parental leave benefits for immigrants. In 2016, the parliament passed a law that tightened restrictions on asylum seekers, which included limiting family reunification.

In recent years, multiple reports of members of the Sweden Democrats and other parties making antisemitic and anti-Muslim remarks have emerged: these included denials of the Holocaust, antisemitic conspiracy theories, and extreme anti-Muslim rhetoric, sometimes calling for violence. Jewish and Muslim community leaders in Sweden have claimed that the far-right is an indirect but real threat to their communities. Government statistics on hate crimes from 2018, the most recent available, showed that hate crimes were increasing. Authorities recorded 7,090 offences with an identified hate crime motive that year, of which 4,865 had a xenophobic or racist motive.

The United Nations in Sweden's 2020 Universal Periodic Review expressed concern over reports of the profiling of members of minority groups by police, as well as the lack of explicit legal provisions prohibiting organizations that promote and incite racial hatred.

A "Corona Commission" appointed in summer 2020 to evaluate the government's handling of the COVID-19 pandemic reported in December that the Swedish government and society had failed to protect the country's elderly. The report pointed to structural problems that left the country ill-prepared to deal with the pandemic, contributing to the high rate of deaths of elderly people in care homes. Immigrant communities, including those from Somalia and Syria, were also disproportionately harmed by the pandemic.

G. PERSONAL AUTONOMY AND INDIVIDUAL RIGHTS: 16 / 16

G1. Do individuals enjoy freedom of movement, including the ability to change their place of residence, employment, or education? 4 / 4

Freedom of movement is legally guaranteed and generally respected in practice. However, asylum seekers may be assigned to a place of residence, and at times may be forced to change locations. Sweden continues to maintain checkpoints on its external borders that were instituted during the 2015 refugee crisis. Due to the COVID-19 pandemic, the government suspended nonessential travel to Sweden from countries outside of the European Union (EU). The ban did not include those who held a Swedish residency permit or those who had family who are residents in Sweden.

G2. Are individuals able to exercise the right to own property and establish private businesses without undue interference from state or nonstate actors? 4 / 4

The government respects the rights of individuals to own property and establish private businesses. A 2011 Supreme Court ruling granted Sami reindeer herders common-law rights to disputed lands.

G3. Do individuals enjoy personal social freedoms, including choice of marriage partner and size of family, protection from domestic violence, and control over appearance? 4 / 4

Same-sex couples are legally allowed to marry and adopt; lesbian couples have the same rights to artificial insemination and in vitro fertilization as heterosexual couples. The Lutheran Church allows same-sex marriage ceremonies. In 2020, authorities were working to draft a law that would permit people to change their legal gender according to their gender identity.

Despite the country's reputation in the eyes of many as a model for gender equality, Sweden suffers from persistently high levels of rape and sexual assault. To address the issue, the parliament passed a law in May 2018 that legally recognizes that sex without consent amounts to rape. The law distinguishes Sweden from most other European countries, which continue to legally define rape in terms of force, threats, and coercion. In 2020, rape conviction rates in Sweden had increased by 75 percent since the change in the legal definition.

G4. Do individuals enjoy equality of opportunity and freedom from economic exploitation?
4 / 4

People in Sweden generally enjoy equality of opportunity. However, unemployment is higher among immigrants, and particularly immigrant women, than it is among people who were born in Sweden. The United Nations has also noted that the performance gap between foreign-born and native-born children in school remains high.

Sweden is a destination and, to a lesser extent, a transit point for women and children trafficked for the purpose of sexual exploitation, but the Swedish government is proactive in combatting the problem. The government has established antitrafficking working groups and action plans at municipal levels. Nevertheless, the United Nations has pointed out that Sweden lacks robust methods to prevent individuals, especially unaccompanied immigrant children, from falling victim to human trafficking.

Switzerland

Population: 8,600,000
Capital: Bern
Freedom Status: Free
Electoral Democracy: Yes

Overview: The political system of Switzerland is characterized by decentralization and direct democracy. The multilingual state is typically governed by a broad coalition that includes members from four of the largest political parties in the parliament. The 26 cantons of the Swiss Confederation have considerable decision-making power, and the public often weighs in on policy matters through referendums. Civil liberties are generally respected in the country, though laws and policies adopted in recent years have reflected a growing wariness of immigration and minority groups of foreign origin, which sometimes face societal discrimination.

KEY DEVELOPMENTS IN 2020

- In September, voters rejected a proposal to end free movement with the European Union (EU), which the right-wing Swiss People's Party (SVP) called for in 2017. Voters also approved the introduction of paternity leave, agreed to the acquisition of military aircraft, rejected a hunting-law revision, and rejected a tax-break proposal, while voters in the canton of Geneva approved a minimum wage.
- In December, the parliament voted to legalize same-sex marriage and allow transgender and intersex people to update identity documents more easily. Opponents had 100 days to secure a referendum on the decision.

- The cabinet declared a COVID-19-related state of emergency in March, allowing it to issue decrees. The state of emergency expired in June and mass-gathering restrictions introduced in March were also eased that month, though mass-gathering restrictions were reintroduced in October as cases rose. Over 451,000 cases and 7,400 deaths were reported to the World Health Organization at year's end.

POLITICAL RIGHTS: 39 / 40
A. ELECTORAL PROCESS: 12 / 12
A1. Was the current head of government or other chief national authority elected through free and fair elections? 4 / 4

Executive power is exercised by the seven-member Federal Council (cabinet), with each member elected by the bicameral Federal Assembly to four-year terms. The Federal Council represents a consensus-based coalition among most large parties in the Federal Assembly. The presidency is largely ceremonial and rotates annually among the Federal Council's members. In December 2020, Guy Parmelin of the SVP was elected president for 2021 by the Federal Assembly.

A2. Were the current national legislative representatives elected through free and fair elections? 4 / 4

The constitution provides for a Federal Assembly with two directly elected chambers: the 46-member Council of States, in which each canton has two members and each half-canton has one, and the 200-member National Council, whose seats are apportioned among the cantons based on population. All lawmakers serve four-year terms. Switzerland's electoral process is vibrant and pluralistic, garnering high levels of confidence from the public.

The October 2019 elections presented a minor shake-up in Swiss politics. In the National Council, the SVP remained the largest party but lost ground, taking 53 seats, down from 65 in the last parliament. The Social Democratic Party (SP) won 39 seats (losing 4), the Free Democratic Party of Switzerland (FDP) took 28 seats (losing 4), and the Christian Democratic People's Party (CVP) took 25 seats (losing 2). The biggest winners of the election were the Green Party (GPS), which won 28 seats (gaining 17), and the Green Liberal Party (GLP), which won 16 seats (gaining 9).

In the Council of States, the CVP won 13 seats, the FDP secured 12, the SP took 9, the SVP took 6, and the GPS won 5. The GPS made gains, while the SP sustained losses.

A3. Are the electoral laws and framework fair, and are they implemented impartially by the relevant election management bodies? 4 / 4

Switzerland's electoral process is robust and well implemented. Electoral laws are fair, and the Election Commission of Switzerland, which administers elections, is considered impartial.

Referendums scheduled for May 2020 were delayed due to the COVID-19 pandemic but took place in late September. Voters rejected a proposal to end a free-movement agreement with the EU. Voters also supported the introduction of paternity leave, supported the acquisition of new military aircraft, rejected a hunting-law revision, and rejected a tax-break proposal.

B. POLITICAL PLURALISM AND PARTICIPATION: 15 / 16
B1. Do the people have the right to organize in different political parties or other competitive political groupings of their choice, and is the system free of undue obstacles to the rise and fall of these competing parties or groupings? 4 / 4

Political parties are free to form and operate, and a wide range of parties are active at the federal and regional levels. The political system, while stable, remains open to new groups. Party financing and lobbying are relatively opaque, however; the National Council did not support a party-finance transparency bill in September 2020 and rejected a lobbying bill in October.

B2. Is there a realistic opportunity for the opposition to increase its support or gain power through elections? 4 / 4

While most parties govern together by common agreement in the country's consensus-based political system, they compete vigorously in elections and can gain or lose influence depending on their performance at the polls. Contentious policy issues are decided in referendums.

The Federal Council currently comprises two members each from the SVP, the SP, and the FDP, along with one CVP member. After the 2019 elections, the GPS, holds more seats than CVP and as many as the FDP, petitioned the parliament to change the Federal Council's composition to accommodate their electoral success. The GPS lost a parliamentary vote over the issue but will likely renew their bid should they repeat their strong performance in the next election.

B3. Are the people's political choices free from domination by forces that are external to the political sphere, or by political forces that employ extrapolitical means? 4 / 4

People's political choices are generally free from domination by democratically unaccountable entities. However, Switzerland has been criticized for failing to address opacity in party financing. Civil society leaders contend that the campaign finance system allows wealthy interests to influence the platforms of the major political parties.

B4. Do various segments of the population (including ethnic, racial, religious, gender, LGBT+, and other relevant groups) have full political rights and electoral opportunities? 3 / 4

Restrictive citizenship laws and procedures tend to exclude many immigrants, as well as their children, from political participation. Noncitizens represent a quarter of the Swiss population, though more than a third of these are citizens of neighboring countries. Noncitizens cannot vote in federal elections but can vote in some cantonal polls.

Women participate robustly in Swiss politics, both as voters and candidates for office. The 2019 elections saw a record number of women elected to the National Council, where they now represent 42 percent of the body.

C. FUNCTIONING OF GOVERNMENT: 12 / 12

C1. Do the freely elected head of government and national legislative representatives determine the policies of the government? 4 / 4

Switzerland's freely elected officials determine and implement national and local policy through a decentralized system of government.

The 26 cantons have significant control over economic and social policy, with the federal government's powers largely limited to foreign affairs and some economic matters. Extensively used referendums are mandatory for any federal constitutional amendments, the joining of international organizations, and major changes to federal laws.

In March 2020, the Federal Council declared a COVID-19-related state of emergency, allowing it to govern by decree. The state of emergency expired in June and the parliament codified pandemic-related decrees through the adoption of the Federal COVID-19 Act in September.

C2. Are safeguards against official corruption strong and effective? 4 / 4

Safeguards against corruption are generally effective. The trial against Pierre Maudet, a former Geneva cantonal government head who had accepted benefits from the crown prince of Abu Dhabi in 2015, continued in 2020. Maudet held his seat as a Geneva state counsellor but resigned as cantonal business-promotion minister in October, after auditors noted high rates of absenteeism in his department.

A law to improve whistleblower protection was rejected in 2019 and again in March 2020 by the National Council. The reform effort came as a response to criticism by the Organisation for Economic Co-operation and Development (OECD), which criticized Switzerland for failing to fully implement the recommendations of the OECD Anti-Bribery Convention.

C3. Does the government operate with openness and transparency? 4 / 4

The government is generally transparent in its operations. In recent years, an increasing number of cantonal governments have passed transparency laws that make government data more accessible to citizens.

CIVIL LIBERTIES: 57 / 60

D. FREEDOM OF EXPRESSION AND BELIEF: 15 / 16

D1. Are there free and independent media? 4 / 4

Freedom of the press is generally respected in practice. Switzerland has an open media environment, though the state-owned, editorially independent Swiss Broadcasting Corporation dominates the broadcast market. Consolidation of newspaper ownership in the hands of large media conglomerates has forced the closure of some smaller newspapers in recent years.

In November 2020, the Council of States's telecommunications committee voted to support a revision to Article 93 of the constitution that would impose preexisting regulations on radio and television outlets to other media. Reporters Without Borders (RSF) criticized the proposal, warning it would impact the freedom of those outlets.

D2. Are individuals free to practice and express their religious faith or nonbelief in public and private? 3 / 4

Freedom of religion is guaranteed by the constitution, and the penal code prohibits discrimination against any religion. However, Muslims face legal and de facto discrimination. The construction of new minarets and mosques is prohibited as the result of a 2009 referendum.

In 2018, St. Gallen became the second canton to pass its own burqa ban, after Ticino in 2016. In June 2020, the National Council disapproved a proposal to ban burqas, though Swiss voters will consider a proposal to restrict their use in some circumstances in 2021.

D3. Is there academic freedom, and is the educational system free from extensive political indoctrination? 4 / 4

Academic freedom is largely respected.

D4. Are individuals free to express their personal views on political or other sensitive topics without fear of surveillance or retribution? 4 / 4

Individuals are generally able to express their personal views on political issues without fear of retribution, though the law punishes public incitement to racial hatred or discrimination as well as denial of crimes against humanity.

The Federal Intelligence Service (FIS) was granted wider surveillance powers in 2017, allowing it to monitor internet usage, bug private property, and tap phone lines of suspected terrorists. A 2018 law required mobile phone and internet service providers to retain user data, including information on which websites users visited, for six months. Both laws faced subsequent legal challenges. While nongovernmental organization (NGO) Digital Society's legal challenge to FIS surveillance practices failed in an administrative court, the Swiss Federal Court upheld its appeal in December 2020, sending the case back for further review.

According to a 2019 University of Zurich survey, more than half of Swiss internet users practice self-censorship over fears of surveillance. The FIS was also found to have engaged in surveillance of left-wing groups and animal-rights activists during 2020.

E. ASSOCIATIONAL AND ORGANIZATIONAL RIGHTS: 12 / 12
E1. Is there freedom of assembly? 4 / 4

Freedom of assembly is constitutionally guaranteed and is generally respected. Pandemic-related restrictions were imposed in March 2020 but were eased beginning in June. The government introduced new assembly restrictions in October as a second wave of COVID-19 cases was detected; restrictions were further tightened that month and in December.

E2. Is there freedom for nongovernmental organizations, particularly those that are engaged in human rights– and governance-related work? 4 / 4

NGOs operate without undue restrictions.

E3. Is there freedom for trade unions and similar professional or labor organizations? 4 / 4

Workers are generally free to form trade unions and other professional organizations. The right to engage in collective bargaining and strikes is respected. However, the International Labour Organization (ILO) added Switzerland to its blacklist of countries with weak job protection for unionized employees in 2019. While it is improper to dismiss an employee because of union membership or activity, the penalty for such behavior is seen as too low.

F. RULE OF LAW: 15 / 16
F1. Is there an independent judiciary? 4 / 4

While the judiciary is largely independent in practice, judges are affiliated with political parties and are selected based on a system of proportional party, linguistic, and regional representation in the Federal Assembly. The civil society group Justice Initiative has called for an independent, apolitical selection process for federal judges. In September 2020, the SVP sought the removal of federal judge Yves Donzallaz over his perceived disloyalty to the party line. Parliamentarians reelected Donzallaz that month, over the party's objections.

Switzerland, which is not an EU member state, continues to negotiate its relationship with the bloc, though the topic remains contentious within the country. The EU and Switzerland agreed on an institutional framework in late 2018, though its finalization and implementation remained pending at the end of 2020.

F2. Does due process prevail in civil and criminal matters? 4 / 4

Authorities generally observe legal safeguards against arbitrary arrest and detention. The constitution's due-process clause guarantees fair trial proceedings. In September 2020, however, parliamentarians approved legislation allowing police to preventively detain and surveil individuals, including children, suspected of terrorist activities.

F3. Is there protection from the illegitimate use of physical force and freedom from war and insurgencies? 4 / 4

Switzerland is free from war and other major threats to physical security, though violent incidents do occur. In November 2020, a woman attacked two people in a Lugano department store; authorities reported that the assailant had previously communicated with a fighter in Syria, while witnesses claimed she declared her support for the Islamic State (IS) militant group during the attack.

Occasional instances of excessive force by police have been documented, but such abuses are relatively rare. Conditions in prisons and detention centers generally meet international standards, and the Swiss government permits visits by independent observers.

F4. Do laws, policies, and practices guarantee equal treatment of various segments of the population? 3 / 4

Although the law prohibits discrimination on the basis of race, gender, or religion, anti-immigrant attitudes have grown in recent years. A 2016 immigration law included measures meant to curb mass migration from the EU and required employers give preference to Swiss citizens in hiring practices. In 2017, the SVP proposed a referendum on free movement with the EU; voters rejected the proposal to end that arrangement in September 2020.

Switzerland generally respects the rights of refugees. The capacity of centers for asylum seekers was reduced during 2020 due to COVID-19-related measures.

The rights of cultural, religious, and linguistic minorities are legally protected, but minority groups—especially Romany communities and people of African descent—face societal discrimination. The Roma continue to seek official recognition as a minority in Switzerland. A 2018 report by the Federal Commission against Racism noted a strong increase in racial discrimination over the past decade.

While women generally enjoy equal rights, the gender pay gap and discrimination in the workplace persist. The rights of LGBT+ people are generally respected. In February 2020, voters upheld a 2018 amendment to existing antidiscrimination legislation that extended its provisions to include sexual orientation.

G. PERSONAL AUTONOMY AND INDIVIDUAL RIGHTS: 15 / 16

G1. Do individuals enjoy freedom of movement, including the ability to change their place of residence, employment, or education? 4 / 4

Freedom of movement is respected, and there are no undue limitations on the ability to change one's place of residence, employment, or education. Movement within Switzerland and with other countries was limited by COVID-19 measures in March 2020, though border crossings gradually opened beginning in May. Remote-working recommendations were reintroduced in October due to a rise in cases.

G2. Are individuals able to exercise the right to own property and establish private businesses without undue interference from state or nonstate actors? 4 / 4

The rights to own property and operate private businesses remain unrestricted.

G3. Do individuals enjoy personal social freedoms, including choice of marriage partner and size of family, protection from domestic violence, and control over appearance? 4 / 4

Personal social freedoms are protected for most people. In a 2005 referendum, voters approved same-sex civil unions. Recognized since 2007, these unions granted many of the legal benefits of marriage. Limited adoption rights for same-sex civil partners were granted in 2018. Parliamentarians voted to approve same-sex marriage and allow transgender and intersex people to update identity documents more easily in December 2020. Opponents had 100 days to secure a referendum on the decision.

G4. Do individuals enjoy equality of opportunity and freedom from economic exploitation? 3 / 4

The government complies with international standards for combating human trafficking and maintains support programs for survivors according to the 2020 edition of the US State Department's *Trafficking in Persons Report*. Labor regulations are generally enforced, but migrant workers are more vulnerable to exploitative labor practices and dangerous working conditions. While no national minimum wage exists, such rules do exist in two cantons. In Geneva, voters voiced their support for a minimum wage in September 2020. Ticino will introduce its own rules in 2021.

Syria

Population: 19,400,000
Capital: Damascus
Freedom Status: Not Free
Electoral Democracy: No

Overview: Political rights and civil liberties in Syria are severely compromised by one of the world's most repressive regimes and by other belligerent forces in an ongoing civil war. The regime prohibits genuine political opposition and harshly suppresses freedoms of speech and assembly. Corruption, enforced disappearances, military trials, and torture are rampant in government-controlled areas. Residents of contested regions or territory held by nonstate actors are subject to additional abuses, including intense and indiscriminate combat, sieges and interruptions of humanitarian aid, and mass displacement.

KEY DEVELOPMENTS IN 2020

- The regime and its allies continued a military offensive that had begun in late 2019 against antigovernment forces occupying much of Idlib Governorate. The fighting killed hundreds of people and displaced more than 900,000 others before a ceasefire was brokered by Russian and Turkish representatives in March.
- In June, President Bashar al-Assad dismissed the prime minister, who had held his post since 2016. The move came amid deteriorating economic conditions and just ahead of parliamentary elections in July, which were conducted only in regime-held areas and featured no meaningful competition.
- The regime allegedly suppressed information on the true scope of the COVID-19 pandemic in the country, in part by intimidating journalists and medical workers. About 11,300 confirmed cases and 700 deaths were reported for the year, but evident strains on the health system and reports of burials suggested that the actual figures were significantly higher.

POLITICAL RIGHTS: –3 / 40
A. ELECTORAL PROCESS: 0 / 12
A1. Was the current head of government or other chief national authority elected through free and fair elections? 0 / 4

The president, who dominates the executive branch, is empowered to appoint and dismiss the prime minister and cabinet. President Bashar al-Assad was elected for a third seven-year term in 2014 with what the government claimed was 88.7 percent of the vote, defeating two nominal opponents. The balloting was conducted only in government-controlled areas amid war and severe repression. Major democratic states denounced the election as illegitimate.

In June 2020, Assad dismissed Imad Khamis, who had served as prime minister since 2016, and appointed Hussein Arnous, then the water resources minister, to replace him.

A2. Were the current national legislative representatives elected through free and fair elections? 0 / 4

Elections for the 250-seat People's Council were held in July 2020, though only in areas with a regime presence. About half of Syria's population were refugees or internally displaced at the time. The balloting featured no meaningful competition, as Syria's exiled opposition groups did not participate, and the authorities do not tolerate independent political activity in the territory they control. The ruling Baath Party and its National Progressive Front coalition won 183 seats, and the remaining 67 seats went to candidates running as independents, though all were considered government loyalists.

A3. Are the electoral laws and framework fair, and are they implemented impartially by the relevant election management bodies? 0 / 4

There is no transparency or accountability surrounding the official electoral process. The executive authorities, acting through the military-security apparatus, effectively grant or withhold permission to participate in elections in government-held areas. Although some provisional local councils outside government-controlled areas have organized rudimentary elections since 2011, ongoing attacks by progovernment forces and militant groups have largely made such processes untenable. Kurdish-held areas have a provisional constitution that allows local elections, but the Democratic Union Party (PYD) exercises ultimate control.

B. POLITICAL PLURALISM AND PARTICIPATION: 0 / 16

B1. Do the people have the right to organize in different political parties or other competitive political groupings of their choice, and is the system free of undue obstacles to the rise and fall of these competing parties or groupings? 0 / 4

A 2011 decree allowed new political parties to register but also imposed significant obstacles to party formation and prohibited parties based on religion, regional affiliation, and other criteria. In practice, all legal political groups and independents are either part of, allied with, or heavily vetted by the regime.

The local councils active in areas outside of government control are often sponsored or appointed by prominent families, armed groups, or foreign powers. In Kurdish-held areas, decentralized governance theoretically allows for political competition. In practice, however, politics are dominated by the most powerful group, the PYD, whose affiliated security forces frequently detain political opponents.

B2. Is there a realistic opportunity for the opposition to increase its support or gain power through elections? 0 / 4

The Baath Party has governed Syria without interruption since the 1960s, led by Assad or his late father for nearly all of that time. The 2011 decree and 2012 constitutional reforms formally relaxed rules regarding the participation of non-Baathist parties. In practice, the government maintains a powerful intelligence and security apparatus to monitor and punish opposition movements that could emerge as serious challengers to Assad's rule.

B3. Are the people's political choices free from domination by forces that are external to the political sphere, or by political forces that employ extrapolitical means? 0 / 4

In its territory, the regime's security and intelligence forces, militias, and business allies actively suppress the autonomy of voters and politicians. Foreign actors including the Russian government, the Iranian regime, and the Lebanese Shiite militia Hezbollah also exert heavy influence over politics in regime-held areas due to their involvement in the war and material support for the government. In other areas, civilian politics are often subordinated to Turkish-backed armed groups.

The PYD has politically dominated both Arabs and Kurds in the country's Kurdish regions, though the area under its control was reduced after the Turkish-led invasion and occupation of the northwest in 2018 and the northeast in 2019.

B4. Do various segments of the population (including ethnic, racial, religious, gender, LGBT+, and other relevant groups) have full political rights and electoral opportunities? 0 / 4

Although the regime is led primarily by Alawites and presents itself as a protector of that and other religious minorities, the authoritarian government is not an authentic vehicle for minority communities' political interests. Political access is a function not primarily of sect, but of proximity and loyalty to Assad and his associates. Alawites, Christians, Druze, and members of other smaller sects who are outside Assad's inner circle are politically disenfranchised along with the rest of the population. The political elite also includes members of the Sunni sect, but the country's Sunni majority makes up most of the rebel movement and has borne the brunt of state repression as a result.

The opposition's dwindling territory is divided among Turkish-backed rebels, Islamist militias, and radical jihadist militants, with varying implications for ethnic and religious minorities. The Kurdish PYD nominally ensures political representation for Arabs, but it has been accused of mistreating non-Kurdish residents, particularly those suspected of sympathizing with the Islamic State (IS) militant group.

Women have equal formal political rights, holding 11.2 percent of the legislature's seats after the 2020 elections as well as some senior positions in the government. However, they are typically excluded from political decision-making and have little ability to organize independently amid state and militia repression. All leadership positions in Kurdish-held areas are reportedly shared between a man and a woman, though they have limited autonomy outside PYD-led structures.

C. FUNCTIONING OF GOVERNMENT: 0 / 12

C1. Do the freely elected head of government and national legislative representatives determine the policies of the government? 0 / 4

De facto authority in government-controlled Syria lies with the president—who is not freely elected—and his political, security, and business allies rather than with formal institutions such as the cabinet and parliament. Foreign states like Iran and Russia also wield considerable influence over regime policy, and both opposition forces and Kurdish-led fighters have held large swaths of territory with the help of countries including Turkey and the United States, respectively. Ankara's military offensives into Kurdish territory and its subsequent efforts to form a "buffer zone" in the border area have given it an opportunity to expand its influence over Syrian politics.

C2. Are safeguards against official corruption strong and effective? 0 / 4

Members and allies of the regime are said to own or control much of the Syrian economy. The civil war has created new opportunities for corruption among the government, loyalist armed forces, and the private sector. The regime has regularly distributed patronage in the form of public resources and implemented policies to benefit favored industries and companies. Government contracts and trade deals have also been awarded to representatives of foreign allies like Russia and Iran. Even basic state services and humanitarian aid are reportedly extended or withheld based on recipients' demonstrated political loyalty to the Assad regime. Movement restrictions associated with the COVID-19 pandemic created still more opportunities for corruption in 2020, as those who could afford it paid bribes to officials and security forces in order to circumvent the rules.

Individuals in government-held territory who seek to expose or criticize official corruption, for example on social media, face reprisals including dismissal from employment and detention.

Corruption is also widespread in opposition-held areas. Turkish-backed militias have been accused of looting, extortion, and theft. Local administrators and activists complain that little of the international aid reportedly given to opposition representatives abroad seems to reach them, raising suspicions of graft.

C3. Does the government operate with openness and transparency? 0 / 4

The government has long operated with minimal transparency and public accountability, and conditions have worsened during the civil war amid the rise of militias that are nominally loyal to the regime but often free to exploit the population. Officials have broad discretion to withhold government information, and they are not obliged to disclose their assets. Independent civil society groups and media outlets are harshly suppressed and cannot influence or shed light on state policies.

The regime allegedly worked to suppress independent information about the scale of the COVID-19 pandemic in Syria during 2020, in part by warning medical workers not to share their experiences or speak with foreign media outlets. Evidence of strains on the health care system and an increase in burials suggested much larger numbers of cases and deaths than were reflected in official data.

ADDITIONAL DISCRETIONARY POLITICAL RIGHTS QUESTION

Is the government or occupying power deliberately changing the ethnic composition of a country or territory so as to destroy a culture or tip the political balance in favor of another group? -3 / 0

The Syrian government, Kurdish forces, Turkish-backed opposition forces, and Islamist extremist groups have all sought to alter the ethnic composition of their territories, forcing civilians of all backgrounds to seek safety among their respective religious or ethnic communities and contributing to the demographic shifts wrought by the civil war.

Sunni Arab civilians bear the brunt of attacks by the Alawite-led government and loyalist militias. In 2018, the regime forcibly transferred thousands of civilians—most of them Sunni Arabs—from captured opposition areas to Idlib Governorate after bombing and besieging them. The government targeted Idlib again when it launched offensives against rebel forces there in April and December 2019. As many as 900,000 people were internally displaced, some for a second time, and pushed toward the border with Turkey before a March 2020 cease-fire was announced.

In October 2019 the Turkish military launched an offensive into northeastern Syria, aiming to create a buffer zone by pushing out its Kurdish adversaries in the area. A previous Turkish-led offensive in the northwestern district of Afrin in 2018 was reportedly followed by the seizure and destruction of Kurdish civilian property. Turkish-backed militias continued to be accused of expropriating land and homes during 2020.

Sunni Islamist and jihadist groups often persecute religious minorities and Muslims they deem impious. Kurdish militias have been accused of displacing Arab and Turkmen communities in the context of their fight against IS.

CIVIL LIBERTIES: 4 / 60 (+1)

D. FREEDOM OF EXPRESSION AND BELIEF: 3 / 16

D1. Are there free and independent media? 0 / 4

The constitution nominally guarantees freedom of the press, but in practice the media are heavily restricted in government-held areas, and journalists who report critically about the state are subject to censorship, detention, torture, and death in custody. All media must obtain permission to operate from the Interior Ministry. Private media in government-controlled territory are generally owned by figures associated with the regime. Media freedom varies in territory held by other groups, but local outlets are typically under heavy pressure to support the dominant militant faction in the area.

Journalists face physical danger throughout Syria, especially from regime forces and extremist groups. Four were killed in 2020, according to the Committee to Protect Journalists (CPJ), bringing the reported death toll to 139 since the war began in 2011. Three of the four apparently died in Russian air strikes near Idlib; the fourth, Hussain Khattab, was assassinated by gunmen while working for the Turkish state broadcaster in an opposition-held portion of Aleppo Governorate. Also during the year, journalists were increasingly vulnerable to censorship or intimidation by local authorities over reporting on COVID-19.

D2. Are individuals free to practice and express their religious faith or nonbelief in public and private? 2 / 4

While the constitution mandates that the president be a Muslim, there is no state religion, and the regime has generally allowed different confessional groups to practice their faiths as long as their religious activities are not deemed politically subversive. The government monitors mosques and controls the appointment of Muslim religious leaders. Jehovah's Witnesses are banned, proselytizing is restricted, and conversion of Muslims to other faiths is prohibited. The dominance of extremist groups in opposition-held areas of western Syria has threatened freedom of worship for local residents and displaced people.

IS, which persecuted religious activity that did not conform to its version of Sunni Islam, was militarily defeated in Syria when its last population center was captured by US-backed coalition fighters in March 2019. However, the militant group reportedly remains active as a terrorist and guerrilla force, and it continues to recruit from and intimidate the roughly 65,000 IS suspects and family members being held in camps by Kurdish-led forces in eastern Syria.

D3. Is there academic freedom, and is the educational system free from extensive political indoctrination? 0 / 4

Academic freedom is severely restricted. University professors in government-held areas have been dismissed or imprisoned for expressing dissent, and some have been killed for supporting regime opponents. Combatants on all sides of the war have regularly attacked or commandeered schools. Groups including the PYD—and prior to its military defeats, IS—have set up education systems in their territories that feature pervasive political indoctrination.

D4. Are individuals free to express their personal views on political or other sensitive topics without fear of surveillance or retribution? 1 / 4

The government engages in heavy surveillance of private and online discussion and harshly punishes dissent in areas it controls. However, the government has employed its surveillance tools inconsistently in recent years amid deepening criticism from traditionally loyal segments of the population. The environment is somewhat more open in areas where neither the government nor an extremist group has a dominant presence, though the PYD and some opposition factions have allegedly suppressed freedom of speech. During the COVID-19 pandemic in 2020, the regime closely monitored medical staff and warned them against speaking about the scope of the contagion or the government's response.

E. ASSOCIATIONAL AND ORGANIZATIONAL RIGHTS: 0 / 12

E1. Is there freedom of assembly? 0 / 4

Freedom of assembly is severely restricted across Syria. Opposition protests in government-held areas have been met with gunfire, mass arrests, and torture of those detained. Jihadist groups, the PYD, and some rebel factions have also used force to quash civilian dissent and demonstrations.

In June 2020, residents of the largely Druze city of Al-Suwayda engaged in a series of protests against economic deprivation that also criticized the regime. A leading organizer and a number of participants were arrested, while others faced assaults by security forces and government supporters.

E2. Is there freedom for nongovernmental organizations, particularly those that are engaged in human rights- and governance-related work? 0 / 4

The regime generally denies registration to nongovernmental organizations (NGOs) with reformist or human rights missions and regularly conducts raids and searches to detain civic and political activists. A variety of new grassroots civil society networks emerged in many parts of Syria following the 2011 uprising, monitoring human rights abuses by all sides and attempting to provide humanitarian and other services in opposition areas. However, such activists face violence, intimidation, and detention by armed groups and must operate secretly in many cases. Independent groups that attempted to provide aid during the COVID-19 pandemic in 2020 attracted the suspicion of regime intelligence agencies, deterring more widespread or open activism.

E3. Is there freedom for trade unions and similar professional or labor organizations? 0 / 4

Professional syndicates in state-held areas are controlled by the Baath Party, and all labor unions must belong to the General Federation of Trade Unions (GFTU), a nominally independent grouping that the government uses to control union activity. The war's economic and political pressures have made functioning labor relations virtually impossible across the country.

F. RULE OF LAW: 0 / 16

F1. Is there an independent judiciary? 0 / 4

The constitution forbids government interference in the civil judiciary, but judges and prosecutors are essentially required to belong to the Baath Party and are in practice beholden to the political leadership.

F2. Does due process prevail in civil and criminal matters? 0 / 4

Military officers can try civilians in both conventional military courts and field courts, which lack due process guarantees. While civilians may appeal military court decisions to the military chamber of the Court of Cassation, military judges are neither independent nor impartial, as they are subordinate to the military command. Extremist groups have set up religious courts in their territories, imposing harsh punishments for perceived offenses by civilians under their interpretation of religious law. The general breakdown of state authority and the proliferation of militias in much of the country has led to arbitrary detentions, summary justice, and extrajudicial penalties by all sides in the civil war.

F3. Is there protection from the illegitimate use of physical force and freedom from war and insurgencies? 0 / 4

More than 500,000 people have been killed in the civil war since 2011, according to prevailing estimates. While the scale of the fighting has continued to subside with the defeat of IS in 2019 and the Idlib cease-fire in March 2020, the regime and insurgent groups frequently engage in extreme violence against civilians, including indiscriminate bombardment, extrajudicial killings, and torture of detainees, with the government responsible for the greatest number of abuses. Regime forces have detained and tortured tens of thousands of people since the uprising began, and many have died in custody, though detention conditions that amount to enforced disappearance mean the fate of most detainees is unknown. Dire conditions in detention facilities placed detainees at increased risk from COVID-19 in 2020, and repeated regime targeting of health facilities in opposition territories have left populations there especially vulnerable.

Among other violations, the regime has been accused of repeatedly using chemical weapons on civilian targets, including during its 2019–20 offensives into Idlib Governorate. The offensives in Idlib had killed hundreds of people and displaced hundreds of thousands of others by the time of the March 2020 cease-fire.

Although IS lost control of its last population center in March 2019, the group has since resorted to guerrilla and terrorist tactics to attack security forces and local civilian leaders. Separately, Turkish military operations in northern Syria have displaced tens of thousands of people and posed a serious threat to civilians living in the affected area.

Despite a nominal regime victory in the southern governorate of Daraa in 2018, as well as a Russian-brokered reconciliation agreement, violence involving regime forces and local insurgents continued into 2020 and has killed hundreds of people. A general deterioration of the rule of law has also reportedly contributed to violent criminality in the area.

F4. Do laws, policies, and practices guarantee equal treatment of various segments of the population? 0 / 4

Families and networks with ties to the ruling elite receive preferential treatment in legal matters, and are disproportionately Alawite, though Alawites without such connections are far less likely to benefit from any special advantages. Similarly, the armed opposition is overwhelmingly Sunni Arab, and members of this group are consequently likely to face discrimination by the state unless they enjoy close ties with the regime.

The Kurdish minority has faced decades of state discrimination, including restrictions on the Kurdish language and persecution of Kurdish activists, though conditions for Kurds have improved dramatically in areas controlled by Kurdish militias since 2011.

Women are subject to legal and societal inequities, including gender-based disadvantages in social benefits and a severe gender gap in labor force participation. Official mechanisms meant to safeguard women's rights are reportedly not functional, and the general deterioration of law and order has left women exposed to a range of abuses, particularly at the hands of extremist groups that impose their own interpretations of religious law.

Syrian law discriminates against LGBT+ people. According to the 1949 penal code, "unnatural sexual intercourse" is punishable with up to three years in prison. Individuals suspected of same-sex relations are at risk of execution in areas held by extremist groups.

G. PERSONAL AUTONOMY AND INDIVIDUAL RIGHTS: 1 / 16 (+1)

G1. Do individuals enjoy freedom of movement, including the ability to change their place of residence, employment, or education? 0 / 4

Ongoing combat and the proliferation of regime and militia checkpoints have severely restricted freedom of movement. The regime-imposed curfews and other constraints on travel in response to the COVID-19 pandemic in 2020, though enforcement was uneven due to bribery and other factors.

More than six million people remained internally displaced at the end of 2020. Another 5.5 million have sought refuge abroad. Although some Syrians have begun returning to their homes in areas where fighting has subsided, the government offensive in Idlib that began in 2019 had displaced an estimated 900,000 people by early 2020.

G2. Are individuals able to exercise the right to own property and establish private businesses without undue interference from state or non-state actors? 0 / 4

Property rights have been routinely disregarded throughout the civil war. Businesses are frequently required to bribe officials to operate and complete bureaucratic procedures. Access to markets dominated by regime members or allies is restricted. Militias also extort businesses and confiscate private property to varying degrees.

Law No. 10 of 2018 allows the state to designate areas for reconstruction and redevelopment by decree; individuals who cannot meet a number of criteria to prove ownership of affected property risk losing it without compensation.

Personal status laws based on Sharia (Islamic law) discriminate against women on inheritance matters, and societal practices further discourage land ownership by women.

G3. Do individuals enjoy personal social freedoms, including choice of marriage partner and size of family, protection from domestic violence, and control over appearance? 1 / 4 (+1)

Perpetrators of "honor crimes" can receive reduced sentences under the penal code, and rapists can avoid punishment by marrying their victims. Women cannot pass citizenship on to their children. Personal status laws for Muslims put women at a disadvantage regarding marriage, divorce, and child custody. Church law governs personal status issues for Christians, in some cases barring divorce. Early and forced marriages are a problem, with displaced families in particular marrying off young daughters as a perceived safeguard against endemic sexual violence or due to economic pressure. Personal social freedoms for women are uneven in areas outside government control, ranging from onerous codes of dress and behavior in extremist-held areas to formal equality under the PYD in Kurdish areas. However, the defeat of IS, setbacks for other extremist groups, and a decline in the scale of fighting over time has reduced the population's exposure to the most egregious violations of personal social freedoms.

Score Change: The score improved from 0 to 1 because the gradual reduction of territory controlled by radical jihadist groups and affected by heavy fighting has lowered the number of people exposed to extreme forms of organized sexual violence and control over personal dress and social behavior.

G4. Do individuals enjoy equality of opportunity and freedom from economic exploitation?
0 / 4

Many armed groups engage in forced conscription or the use of child soldiers. Displaced people are especially vulnerable to labor exploitation and human trafficking, and there is little equality of opportunity even in relatively stable government-controlled areas, as access to employment and investment is often dependent on personal, political, or communal affiliations. The regime's mismanagement of the COVID-19 outbreak in 2020 led to more dangerous working conditions. Among other measures, the government required state employees to appear for work unless they could confirm that they had COVID-19 by presenting a medical report, the cost of which was prohibitive for many Syrians.

Taiwan

Population: 23,600,000
Capital: Taipei
Freedom Status: Free
Electoral Democracy: Yes

Overview: Taiwan's vibrant and competitive democratic system has allowed three peaceful transfers of power between rival parties since 2000, and protections for civil liberties are generally robust. Ongoing concerns include foreign migrant workers' vulnerability to exploitation and the Chinese government's efforts to influence policymaking, the media, and democratic infrastructure in Taiwan.

KEY DEVELOPMENTS IN 2020

- In January, incumbent president Tsai Ing-wen and her Democratic Progressive Party (DPP) were returned to power in general elections that drew the highest voter turnout since 2008, despite online disinformation and influence operations targeting the vote that were attributed to the Chinese government.
- The government's approach to the COVID-19 pandemic was among the world's most successful. Avoiding any abusive restrictions, officials focused on contact tracing and quarantines for overseas travelers, and provided accurate and timely information to the public. Just seven coronavirus-related deaths were reported for the entire year.

POLITICAL RIGHTS: 38 / 40 (+1)

A. ELECTORAL PROCESS: 12 / 12

A1. Was the current head of government or other chief national authority elected through free and fair elections? 4 / 4

The president, who is directly elected for up to two four-year terms, appoints the premier with the consent of the legislature. The Executive Yuan, or cabinet, is made up of ministers appointed by the president on the recommendation of the premier. In practice, the president holds most executive authority.

Presidential elections have generally been considered credible. In January 2020, President Tsai won a second term in office with 57.1 percent of the vote, defeating Han Kuo-yu of the conservative Kuomintang (KMT), with 38.6 percent, and James Soong of the center-right People First Party, with 4.3 percent. The campaign period featured online disinformation and influence operations that were attributed to the Chinese government, with negative or misleading content targeting Tsai, the DPP, and the democratic process. However, the Taiwanese government, civil society projects, and social media platforms worked to detect and counter the disinformation, which largely failed to shape the election's outcome.

A2. Were the current national legislative representatives elected through free and fair elections? 4 / 4

The unicameral Legislative Yuan has 113 members elected to four-year terms; 73 are directly elected in single-member constituencies, 34 are elected by proportional representation, and 6 are elected by Indigenous voters in two multiseat constituencies. In the January 2020 elections, the DPP secured 61 seats, the KMT won 38, the Taiwan People's Party won 5, the New Power Party won 3, and the Taiwan Statebuilding Party took 1 seat, with the remainder going to independent candidates. The elections were considered free and fair by international observers.

A3. Are the electoral laws and framework fair, and are they implemented impartially by the relevant election management bodies? 4 / 4

Elections in Taiwan are administered by the Central Election Commission (CEC). The law mandates that no political party may hold more than one-third of the seats on the CEC, and it operates impartially in practice.

The 2018 Referendum Act lowered thresholds to permit citizen-initiated ballot measures and decreased the voting age for referendums from 20 to 18 years.

B. POLITICAL PLURALISM AND PARTICIPATION: 15 / 16

B1. Do the people have the right to organize in different political parties or other competitive political groupings of their choice, and is the system free of undue obstacles to the rise and fall of these competing parties or groupings? 4 / 4

The multiparty political system features vigorous competition between the two major parties, the DPP and KMT. Smaller parties are also able to function without interference and have played a significant role in both presidential and legislative contests. Taipei mayor Ko Wen-je formed the new Taiwan People's Party in 2019, and it entered the legislature in 2020.

B2. Is there a realistic opportunity for the opposition to increase its support or gain power through elections? 4 / 4

There have been regular democratic transfers of power between rival parties in recent years, and parties in opposition at the national level often control key municipal governments.

B3. Are the people's political choices free from domination by forces that are external to the political sphere, or by political forces that employ extrapolitical means? 3 / 4

Major business owners with interests in China remain an influential force in Taiwanese politics, largely through their close relationship with the KMT and support for its China-friendly policies. The KMT, which governed Taiwan as an authoritarian, one-party state for decades until democratic reforms took hold in the 1980s and 90s, long enjoyed a considerable financial advantage over rivals like the DPP, which has traditionally favored greater independence from China. However, the KMT's advantage has been whittled away in recent years by DPP government investigations into allegations that the KMT improperly acquired public assets during its rule, leading to the freezing of many of its accounts.

Chinese interference in Taiwan's elections, largely through disinformation campaigns and influence over certain media outlets, remains a serious concern. In December 2019, the legislature passed a new Anti-Infiltration Act that will prohibit foreign powers from funding or directing lobbying efforts, election campaigns, or election-related disinformation in Taiwan. Violations can draw penalties of up to five years in prison. The KMT opposed the measure, warning that it could be used in a politicized manner and violate fundamental rights, though there were no reports of abusive enforcement in 2020.

B4. Do various segments of the population (including ethnic, racial, religious, gender, LGBT+, and other relevant groups) have full political rights and electoral opportunities? 4 / 4

Taiwan's constitution grants all citizens the right to vote. This guarantee applies regardless of gender, ethnicity, religion, sexual orientation, or gender identity. The constitution and electoral laws also provide quotas for women's representation in local councils and at-large seats in the Legislative Yuan. In addition to the presidency, women won 42 percent of the legislature's seats in the 2020 elections. Audrey Tang, who became Taiwan's first transgender cabinet member in 2016, remained a minister in Tsai's government in 2020.

Six seats in the Legislative Yuan are reserved for Indigenous candidates elected by Indigenous voters. An additional two Indigenous candidates won seats in 2016 through normal party-list voting, but none did so in 2020. Members of Taiwan's 16 Indigenous groups make up roughly 2 percent of the population.

C. FUNCTIONING OF GOVERNMENT: 11 / 12 (+1)

C1. Do the freely elected head of government and national legislative representatives determine the policies of the government? 4 / 4

Elected officials in Taiwan are able to set and implement policy without undue interference from foreign or other unelected actors, though consideration of China plays a significant role in Taiwanese policymaking.

Escalating pressure from Beijing continues to threaten Taiwan's sovereignty. Between 2016 and 2020, largely as a result of financial incentives offered by the Chinese government, eight countries severed diplomatic relations with Taiwan. At the end of 2020, Taiwan had diplomatic recognition from just 15 countries, including the Holy See.

C2. Are safeguards against official corruption strong and effective? 3 / 4

Corruption is significantly less pervasive than in the past, but it remains a problem. Political and business interests are closely intertwined, leading to malfeasance in government procurement. The current DPP-led government has moved to reduce these practices, including through amendments to the Government Procurement Act that were adopted by lawmakers in 2019.

Corruption charges have been brought against current and former officials from multiple parties in recent years. Among other cases during 2020, four incumbent lawmakers—two from the KMT, one from the DPP, and one independent—and a former legislator from the New Power Party were charged in September with taking bribes from business magnate Lee Heng-lung, former chairman of Pacific Distribution Investment Co.

C3. Does the government operate with openness and transparency? 4 / 4 (+1)

The 2005 Freedom of Government Information Law enables public access to information held by government agencies, including financial audit reports and documents about administrative guidance. Civil society groups are typically able to comment on and influence pending policies and legislation. In recent years, the open digital platform vTaiwan has gained acceptance among policymakers as a means for the general public to debate and contribute to legislative proposals.

The government's management of the COVID-19 pandemic was widely recognized for its transparency and reliance on scientific data and expertise, as opposed to opaque political or economic interests.

Score Change: The score improved from 3 to 4 due to long-term progress toward greater transparency and public participation in governance and policymaking, as demonstrated by the government's successful management of the COVID-19 pandemic.

CIVIL LIBERTIES: 56 / 60

D. FREEDOM OF EXPRESSION AND BELIEF: 16 / 16

D1. Are there free and independent media? 4 / 4

The news media reflect a diversity of views and report aggressively on government policies, though many outlets display strong party affiliation in their coverage. Beijing continues to exert influence on Taiwanese media. Key media owners have significant business interests in China or rely on advertising by Chinese companies, leaving them vulnerable to pressure and prone to self-censorship on topics considered sensitive by Beijing. The National Communications Commission (NCC) has at times blocked the expansion of such media enterprises to ensure competition and pluralism, and it has fined television news channels for airing false reports. In November 2020, after repeated warnings and fines issued over several years, the NCC decided not to renew the broadcast license of the pro-Beijing television channel CTi News. The outlet—owned by business magnate Tsai Eng-meng's Want Want Holdings conglomerate, which has strong ties to China—went off the air in December after courts upheld the decision. Reporters Without Borders issued a statement to defend the NCC's move, saying it was not contrary to press freedom.

D2. Are individuals free to practice and express their religious faith or nonbelief in public and private? 4 / 4

Taiwanese of all faiths can worship freely. Religious organizations that choose to register with the government receive tax-exempt status.

D3. Is there academic freedom, and is the educational system free from extensive political indoctrination? 4 / 4

Educators in Taiwan can generally write and lecture without interference, and past practices—including prosecutions—aimed at restricting academics' political activism have been rare in recent years.

D4. Are individuals free to express their personal views on political or other sensitive topics without fear of surveillance or retribution? 4 / 4

Personal expression and private discussion are largely free of improper restrictions, and the government is not known to illegally monitor online communication. Human rights experts have recommended improvements to laws meant to combat misinformation, some of which contain vague terms that have the potential to limit legitimate speech, though such laws are generally not enforced in an abusive manner.

E. ASSOCIATIONAL AND ORGANIZATIONAL RIGHTS: 11 / 12

E1. Is there freedom of assembly? 4 / 4

The 1988 Assembly and Parade Act enables authorities to prosecute protesters who fail to obtain a permit or follow orders to disperse, and includes some restrictions on the location of protests, but freedom of assembly is largely respected in practice. During 2020, demonstrations were held on topics including the rights of migrant workers and discrimination against Indigenous people. Taiwan was one of the few countries in the world to hold an LGBT+ pride march, with many others canceled due to the pandemic.

E2. Is there freedom for nongovernmental organizations, particularly those that are engaged in human rights- and governance-related work? 4 / 4

All civic organizations must register with the government, though registration is freely granted. Nongovernmental organizations typically operate without harassment or undue interference.

E3. Is there freedom for trade unions and similar professional or labor organizations? 3 / 4

Trade unions are independent, and most workers enjoy freedom of association, though the government strictly regulates the right to strike. Among other barriers, teachers, workers in the defense industry, and government employees are prohibited from striking.

F. RULE OF LAW: 15 / 16

F1. Is there an independent judiciary? 4 / 4

Taiwan's judiciary is independent. Court rulings are generally free from political or other improper interference.

In July 2020, the legislature adopted the Citizen Judges Act, which would move the country toward a Japan-style system in which professional judges are joined by lay judges from the general public in overseeing trials for serious criminal offenses. Critics of the system continued to call for the introduction of jury trials instead, arguing that juries provide stronger protections against judicial corruption or politicization.

F2. Does due process prevail in civil and criminal matters? 4 / 4

Constitutional guarantees concerning due process and defendants' rights are generally upheld, and police largely respect safeguards against arbitrary detention. Although prosecutors and other law enforcement officials have engaged in abusive practices in the past, particularly in prominent and politically fraught cases, such violations have been less common in recent years.

F3. Is there protection from the illegitimate use of physical force and freedom from war and insurgencies? 4 / 4

Both criminal violence and excessive use of force by police are rare, and attorneys are allowed to monitor interrogations to prevent torture.

After a four-year death penalty moratorium, the government resumed executions in 2010. Between zero and six people have been executed each year since, all for murder or other offenses resulting in death, such as arson. Condemned inmates, after being sedated, are shot from behind at close range.

F4. Do laws, policies, and practices guarantee equal treatment of various segments of the population? 3 / 4

The constitution provides for the equality of all citizens before the law, although Indigenous people continue to face social and economic discrimination, leading to high unemployment, lower wages, and barriers to education and social services. The 2017 Indigenous Languages Development Act designated the languages spoken by 16 officially recognized Indigenous groups as national languages of Taiwan, and authorized their formal use in legislative and legal affairs.

The constitution guarantees women equal rights, though women continue to face discrimination in employment and compensation. Taiwanese law prohibits discrimination in employment and education based on sexual orientation, and violence against LGBT+ people is adequately addressed by police.

Taiwan's National Human Rights Commission was officially launched in August 2020, with a mandate to receive complaints on issues including discrimination, investigate violations, review laws and policies, and work with other entities to promote human rights protections.

Taiwanese law does not allow for asylum or refugee status, but the government has worked to provide visas and humanitarian services to people fleeing persecution in Hong Kong.

G. PERSONAL AUTONOMY AND INDIVIDUAL RIGHTS: 14 / 16

G1. Do individuals enjoy freedom of movement, including the ability to change their place of residence, employment, or education? 4 / 4

Taiwan's residents enjoy freedom of movement, and Taiwanese authorities have gradually eased restrictions on travel between Taiwan and China in recent years. Some travel constraints were enacted in response to the COVID-19 pandemic in 2020, but these were generally regarded as legitimate public health measures.

G2. Are individuals able to exercise the right to own property and establish private businesses without undue interference from state or nonstate actors? 3 / 4

Although property rights are generally respected, urban renewal and industrial projects have been criticized for unfairly displacing residents. Housing advocates have called for legal amendments to clarify residency rights, including protections against forced eviction, and the establishment of an appeals system to review alleged violations. Indigenous groups argue that recent government efforts to return some of their ancestral lands are inadequate.

G3. Do individuals enjoy personal social freedoms, including choice of marriage partner and size of family, protection from domestic violence, and control over appearance? 4 / 4

There are no major restrictions on personal status matters such as marriage and divorce, although people from China who are married to Taiwanese nationals must wait six years before becoming eligible for citizenship, whereas spouses of other nationalities are only required to wait four years. Same-sex marriages have been legal in Taiwan since 2019.

Rape and domestic violence remain serious problems. While the law permits authorities to investigate complaints without victims pressing charges, cultural norms inhibit many women from reporting these crimes to the police. Recent reforms have improved protections for accusers and encouraged reporting of rape and sexual assault, which appears to have increased prosecution and conviction rates.

G4. Do individuals enjoy equality of opportunity and freedom from economic exploitation? 3 / 4

Over 700,000 foreign migrants work in Taiwan; many employed as domestic workers or fishermen are not covered by the Labor Standards Act, excluding them from minimum-wage, overtime, and paid-leave protections. Foreign migrant workers are consequently at substantial risk of exploitation, as indicated by widespread accounts of unpaid wages, poor working conditions, physical and sexual abuse, and extortion and fraud by recruitment and brokerage agencies. Amendments to the Employment Services Act that were adopted in 2018 require employment agencies to swiftly report abuses against migrant workers or face severe fines.

Tajikistan

Population: 9,400,000
Capital: Dushanbe
Freedom Status: Not Free
Electoral Democracy: No

Overview: The authoritarian regime of President Emomali Rahmon, who has ruled since 1992, severely restricts political rights and civil liberties. The political opposition and independent media have been devastated by a sustained campaign of repression, and the government exerts tight control over religious expression and activity. Wealth and authority are concentrated in the hands of Rahmon and his family.

KEY DEVELOPMENTS IN 2020

- The ruling People's Democratic Party of Tajikistan (PDPT) won legislative elections in March, taking 47 lower-house seats in a contest that did not meet democratic standards.
- President Rahmon won a fifth term in office in October, receiving 90.9 percent of the vote according to the electoral authorities. The opposition Social Democratic Party of Tajikistan (SDPT) boycotted the contest, which was marred by reports of fraud.
- At least 20 professors were among those arrested for alleged Muslim Brotherhood membership in January.
- Tajikistani authorities did not report the presence of COVID-19 until the end of April. The intentional spread of the virus and the dissemination of purportedly false pandemic-related news was criminalized in June. Authorities reported 13,665 cases and 90 deaths to the World Health Organization (WHO) by year's end.

POLITICAL RIGHTS: 0 / 40

A. ELECTORAL PROCESS: 0 / 12

A1. Was the current head of government or other chief national authority elected through free and fair elections? 0 / 4

The president is chief of state and is elected for up to two seven-year terms under current rules, but constitutional amendments ratified in 2016 removed term limits for Rahmon, who holds the official status of "leader of the nation."

A presidential election was due in November 2020, but legislators moved the poll to a date in October. President Rahmon won that election and a fifth term with 90.9 percent of the vote according to the Central Commission for Elections and Referendums (CCER). Four candidates from progovernment parties won a combined 7.8 percent, while the SDPT boycotted the contest.

The European Council called the election orderly but noted that previous Organization for Security and Co-operation in Europe (OSCE) recommendations on the media and political environment remained unfulfilled. While independent media outlets were largely unable to observe polling stations, Radio Free Europe/Radio Liberty (RFE/RL) reported incidents of apparent ballot stuffing and of voters submitting ballots on behalf of family members.

A2. Were the current national legislative representatives elected through free and fair elections? 0 / 4

The bicameral Supreme Assembly is composed of an upper house, the National Assembly, and a lower house, the Assembly of Representatives. The National Assembly comprises 25 members chosen by local assemblies and 8 appointed by the president; former presidents are also entitled to a seat. The 63-member Assembly of Representatives is popularly elected through a mixed system of 41 single-member constituencies and 22 proportional-representation seats. Supreme Assembly members serve five-year terms.

In the March 2020 elections, the PDPT won 47 lower-house seats, while progovernment parties divided the remainder. The SDPT did not exceed the 5 percent threshold for representation according to the CCER. OSCE monitors reported that the elections did not meet democratic standards. Reporters for media outlet Asia-Plus documented incidents of officials agreeing to supply ballots to reporters claiming to represent family members.

A3. Are the electoral laws and framework fair, and are they implemented impartially by the relevant election management bodies? 0 / 4

The CCER is subservient to the government and enforces electoral laws in an inconsistent and nontransparent manner. Despite reforms ahead of the 2015 elections, constituencies vary considerably in population, undermining equal suffrage.

B. POLITICAL PLURALISM AND PARTICIPATION: 0 / 16

B1. Do the people have the right to organize in different political parties or other competitive political groupings of their choice, and is the system free of undue obstacles to the rise and fall of these competing parties or groupings? 0 / 4

The government consistently marginalizes independent or opposition parties, which have become excluded from the political process. The Islamic Renaissance Party of Tajikistan (IRPT)—which had been the country's most significant opposition group—lost its legal registration and was declared a terrorist organization in 2015. The 2016 constitutional amendments banned faith-based parties, effectively preventing the IRPT from reforming. The National Alliance of Tajikistan, a Europe-based refugee opposition coalition, was declared a terrorist organization in 2019.

The authorities continued to harass and arrest members of the IRPT, political movement Group 24, and members' extended families during 2020. In March, Hizbullo Shovalizoda was extradited from Austria to Tajikistan and was accused of IRPT membership. Shovalizoda received a 20-year prison sentence in June. In September, Group 24 activist Shobuddin Badalov was detained in the Russian city of Nizhniy Novgorod; Badalov previously organized a rally to protest Rahmon's June visit to Moscow. Two days after his detention, Group 24 reported that Badalov had been extradited to Tajikistan.

Relatives of deceased or imprisoned opposition figures were also targeted. Authorities detained Asroriddin Rozikov in June and accused him of activity in an extremist organization in July. Asroriddin's father, senior IRPT member Zubaidullohi Rozik, was imprisoned in 2016. In August, police detained five sons of IRPT cofounder Said Kiemitdin Gozi, who died in prison in unclear circumstances in 2019.

B2. Is there a realistic opportunity for the opposition to increase its support or gain power through elections? 0 / 4

Tajikistan has no record of peaceful transfers of power between rival parties. Rahmon first became chief executive in 1992, during the country's 1992–97 civil war, and has held the presidency since the office's creation in 1994. Under the 2016 constitutional revisions, he is entitled to run for reelection indefinitely and to overrule cabinet decisions even after leaving office. The amendments also lowered the minimum age for presidents from 35 to 30 years, which would have allowed Rahmon's son, Rustam Emomali, to seek the presidency in 2020. In April, Emomali was named National Assembly chairman, placing him second in the presidential line of succession.

Years of unrelenting repression of independent political activity have left opposition parties unable to compete in elections. The administration exerts complete control over the electoral process and prevents any substantial competition for the presidency or the parliament. Many IRPT members and their relatives were beaten, harassed, and imprisoned before the 2015 elections, with some reportedly tortured in custody or killed in prison.

B3. Are the people's political choices free from domination by forces that are external to the political sphere, or by political forces that employ extrapolitical means? 0 / 4

Political affairs in Tajikistan are controlled almost exclusively by Rahmon and his extended family, leaving citizens with few avenues to participate in the political process. Presidential family members hold numerous public positions and control key sectors of the private economy.

B4. Do various segments of the population (including ethnic, racial, religious, gender, LGBT+, and other relevant groups) have full political rights and electoral opportunities? 0 / 4

No segment of the population enjoys full political rights or electoral opportunities in practice. The regime, which seeks to suppress any genuine dissent, does not permit women, minorities, or religious groups to organize independently to advance their political interests. Women remain underrepresented in the political system, both as voters and in elected positions.

C. FUNCTIONING OF GOVERNMENT: 0 / 12

C1. Do the freely elected head of government and national legislative representatives determine the policies of the government? 0 / 4

The president, who is not freely elected, and his inner circle are virtually unopposed in determining and implementing policy. The PDPT-controlled legislature does not offer a meaningful check on the executive's expansive constitutional authority. Officials from the president's native Kulob District are dominant within government. Rahmon has strengthened his family's grip on power by installing Rustam Emomali as Dushanbe's mayor in 2017 and as National Assembly chairman in April 2020.

C2. Are safeguards against official corruption strong and effective? 0 / 4

Patronage networks and regional affiliations are central to political life, corruption is pervasive, and laws designed to prevent it are routinely ignored. Major irregularities have been reported at the National Bank of Tajikistan and the country's largest industrial firm, the state-owned Tajik Aluminum Company.

C3. Does the government operate with openness and transparency? 0 / 4

Government decision-making and budgetary processes lack transparency, and public officials are not required to disclose financial information. Crackdowns on the media, the opposition, and civil society have further reduced independent scrutiny of state operations. In recent years, the government has concluded extensive infrastructure and resource-extraction agreements with the Chinese government and Chinese companies, with little consultation or transparency.

The government initially denied the presence of COVID-19, with the Health Ministry instead blaming reported pneumonia cases on the weather. The government did not disclose the presence of COVID-19 until April 2020.

CIVIL LIBERTIES: 8 / 60 (−1)

D. FREEDOM OF EXPRESSION AND BELIEF: 1 / 16 (−1)

D1. Are there free and independent media? 0 / 4

The government controls most printing presses, newsprint supplies, and broadcasting facilities, and denies independent media access to these resources. The state shuts out independent outlets and encourages self-censorship. Independent journalists face harassment and intimidation. Civil libel charges have been used to cripple outlets that criticize the government. Authorities routinely block critical websites, news portals, and social media platforms, while using periodic wholesale blackouts of internet and messaging services to suppress criticism.

The government continued to target journalists in 2020. In January, authorities detained journalist Daler Sharifov, accusing him of producing extremist content. Sharifov received a one-year prison sentence in a closed trial in April, and his health has reportedly deteriorated while imprisoned in a penal colony. In late May, Asia-Plus journalist Abdullo Gurbati was assaulted while covering a mudslide in the southern district of Khuroson. The Ministry of Internal Affairs blamed Gurbati for the incident, claiming that he attempted to film residents without their consent. Three people were arrested for assaulting Gurbati in early June and received fines for petty hooliganism.

In April, state news agency Khovar reported the blocking of Prague-based news site Akhbor, which authorities claimed served as a platform for terrorism and extremism; the order had taken effect in March. Before it was blocked, and as the government downplayed the spread of COVID-19, the outlet reported on a rise in illnesses and deaths in Tajikistan. In June, a state-television documentary exposed the personal details of several journalists reportedly affiliated with Akhbor.

D2. Are individuals free to practice and express their religious faith or nonbelief in public and private? 0 / 4

The government imposes severe restrictions on religious freedom, in part by limiting religious activities to state-approved venues and registered organizations. Authorities continue to prosecute individuals for alleged membership in banned religious organizations, including Christian and Muslim groups. Minors are generally barred from attending religious services in mosques, as are women in most cases.

Laws to discourage religious clothing (like the hijab) as well as an unofficial ban on beards for men are arbitrarily enforced. A government-published "guidebook" details recommended dress for women that excludes the hijab and similar garments in favor of "traditional" or "national" alternatives. The government has pressured students to adhere to these dress codes, establishing roadblocks in some areas to search for those who violate them.

D3. Is there academic freedom, and is the educational system free from extensive political indoctrination? 0 / 4 (−1)

The government exerts significant political pressure on universities and academic personnel. In recent years, international scholars have noted the self-exile of Tajikistani academics who faced harassment from security services, surveillance and self-censorship within higher-education institutions, scrutiny of scholars who cooperate with foreign colleagues, and the appointment of officials backed by security services to senior academic posts. Opportunities to study abroad, especially for religious education, are tightly restricted.

In January 2020, authorities arrested at least 113 people for their alleged affiliation to the Muslim Brotherhood, which is banned in Tajikistan; Prosecutor General Yusuf Rahmon reported that over 20 professors were among those arrested that month. At least 30 people were released in February, though 20 defendants received prison sentences in August; their names were not publicly released.

Score Change: The score declined from 1 to 0 because authorities arrested academics over alleged Muslim Brotherhood affiliation.

D4. Are individuals free to express their personal views on political or other sensitive topics without fear of surveillance or retribution? 1 / 4

Restrictive laws and government surveillance serve as deterrents to open discussion of sensitive topics, including criticism of the country's leadership. A 2017 law allows authorities to monitor citizens' online behavior and prescribes fines and prison sentences for those who visit "undesirable websites," among other provisions.

In January 2020, an amended antiextremism law came into effect, allowing the government to block websites without a court order. The dissemination of purportedly false COVID-19-related news was criminalized in June.

E. ASSOCIATIONAL AND ORGANIZATIONAL RIGHTS: 2 / 12

E1. Is there freedom of assembly? 0 / 4

The government strictly limits freedom of assembly. Local government approval is required to hold demonstrations, which officials often refuse to grant.

E2. Is there freedom for nongovernmental organizations, particularly those that are engaged in human rights- and governance-related work? 1 / 4

Nongovernmental organizations (NGOs) must register with the Justice Ministry and are vulnerable to closure for minor technical violations. NGOs must disclose funding from foreign sources. Foreign funds must be logged in a state registry before organizations can access them, and the government oversees operations supported by those funds. Under legislation implemented in 2019, NGOs are obliged to maintain their own websites and publish reports that comply with more expansive and vaguely worded financial reporting to prove they have no "terrorist financing" or "money laundering" links.

E3. Is there freedom for trade unions and similar professional or labor organizations? 1 / 4

Citizens have the legal right to form and join trade unions and to bargain collectively, but these rights and the right to strike are undermined by general legal restrictions on freedoms of assembly and association. There are no laws against antiunion discrimination by employers, and the country's trade union federation is government-controlled.

F. RULE OF LAW: 1 / 16

F1. Is there an independent judiciary? 0 / 4

The judiciary lacks independence. Many judges are poorly trained and inexperienced, and bribery is widespread. The 2016 constitutional amendments abolished the Council of Justice, transferring the authority for most judicial nomination and oversight functions to the Supreme Court. However, these powers remain under executive control in practice. The courts' opaque and biased adjudication of numerous cases against opposition figures and other dissidents, particularly since 2015, has demonstrated their subordination to the political leadership.

F2. Does due process prevail in civil and criminal matters? 0 / 4

Arbitrary arrests and detentions are common, as is corruption among law-enforcement agencies. Defendants are often denied timely access to an attorney, and politically fraught trials are frequently closed to the public. Nearly all defendants are found guilty.

F3. Is there protection from the illegitimate use of physical force and freedom from war and insurgencies? 0 / 4

Civilians are subject to physical abuse by security forces and have no meaningful opportunity to seek justice for such violations. Detainees are reportedly beaten in custody to extract confessions. Overcrowding and disease contribute to often life-threatening conditions in prisons.

Authorities reportedly did little to limit the spread of COVID-19 within the prison system. In July 2020, Justice Minister Muzaffar Ashurion disclosed the pneumonia-related deaths of 98 prisoners, 11 of whom died after the pandemic began. Ashurion also denied the coronavirus's presence in the prison system.

F4. Do laws, policies, and practices guarantee equal treatment of various segments of the population? 1 / 4

Discrimination against ethnic minorities is not a major problem. However, women face bias and disparate treatment in the workplace, and discrimination or violence against LGBT+ people is common. There is no legislation against discrimination based on sexual orientation or gender identity. LGBT+ people frequently face abuse by security forces.

G. PERSONAL AUTONOMY AND INDIVIDUAL RIGHTS: 4 / 16

G1. Do individuals enjoy freedom of movement, including the ability to change their place of residence, employment, or education? 1 / 4

Most citizens can travel within the country but must register their permanent residence with local authorities. Students interested in studying Islamic theology are forbidden from seeking education abroad. Some areas, particularly Gorno-Badakhshan, feature a heavier security presence that includes police checkpoints, which hamper travel and provide opportunities for extortion and other abuses.

G2. Are individuals able to exercise the right to own property and establish private businesses without undue interference from state or nonstate actors? 1 / 4

By law, all land belongs to the state. Corruption and regulatory dysfunction affect enterprises ranging from peasant farms to large companies. The president's extended family and others from his native Kulob District maintain extensive business interests in the country and dominate key economic sectors, impeding business activity by those without such political connections.

G3. Do individuals enjoy personal social freedoms, including choice of marriage partner and size of family, protection from domestic violence, and control over appearance? 1 / 4

Although forced marriage and polygamy are legally prohibited, marriages arranged by parents and religious marriages that allow polygamy are both common in practice. Because of local interpretations of Sharia (Islamic law), women are often unable to exercise their rights to divorce. Domestic violence is widespread, but cases are underreported and seldom investigated adequately.

Reports indicate that women sometimes face societal pressure to wear headscarves. Meanwhile, in addition to restricting hijabs for women and beards for men, the government interferes more broadly in matters of personal appearance. A 2018 guidebook outlined acceptable and unacceptable styles of dress for women, barring clothing that could be deemed immodest or "foreign" in origin.

G4. Do individuals enjoy equality of opportunity and freedom from economic exploitation? 1 / 4

Safeguards against forms of labor exploitation and hazardous working conditions are not well enforced. The scarcity of economic opportunity has compelled citizens to seek work abroad in large numbers, and these migrant workers are at risk of exploitation by human traffickers.

However, the 2020 edition of the US State Department's *Trafficking in Persons* report reported that the Tajikistani government is working to combat human trafficking by prosecuting traffickers and supporting survivors via a state-run shelter, among other activities. However, the report noted that government officials suspected of involvement in trafficking are not investigated.

Tanzania

Population: 59,700,000
Capital: Dodoma
Freedom Status: Partly Free
Electoral Democracy: No

Overview: Tanzania has held regular multiparty elections since its transition from a one-party state in the early 1990s, but the opposition remains relatively weak, and the ruling party, Chama Cha Mapinduzi (CCM), has retained power for over half a century. Since the election of President John Magufuli in 2015, the government has cracked down with growing severity on its critics in the political opposition, the press, and civil society.

KEY DEVELOPMENTS IN 2020

- The October presidential election period was marred by reports of widespread fraud and vote-rigging, widespread arrests, threats and violence against the opposition, the forced dispersal of public gatherings by the authorities, the effective prohibition of independent election monitors, and numerous other serious problems. Official results showed a victory by Magufuli with 84.5 percent of the vote, and the opposition candidate fled the country in November.
- The regime mobilized the army to Zanzibar amid growing unrest ahead of the Zanzibari presidential polls, and both the army and police were implicated in a spate of violence against opposition activists and civilians. As many as nine people were killed in one instance on the island of Pemba, when security forces fired on demonstrators attempting to stop the transport of allegedly fraudulent ballots.
- Tanzania's initial response to the COVID-19 pandemic was in line with that of other countries: distancing, increased hygiene measures, and business and school closures. However, Magufuli declared the pandemic "defeated" in the spring, and authorities worked to suppress discussion of it by firing officials who challenged

the president's narrative, and through the arrests of journalists and ordinary people on charges of spreading fake news.

- The country recorded a total of 509 COVID-19 cases and 21 deaths before officials stopped counting cases in late April. However, reports on social media and from other countries suggest the outbreak was far larger than the regime stated. Mass graves were widely reported on social media early in the pandemic, foreign embassies cited "exponential growth" in cases and organized repatriation flights for their citizens, and truck drivers entering neighboring countries routinely tested positive for COVID-19 at the border.

POLITICAL RIGHTS: 12 / 40 (−5)

A. ELECTORAL PROCESS: 3 / 12 (−3)

A1. Was the current head of government or other chief national authority elected through free and fair elections? 1 / 4 (−2)

The president is elected by direct popular vote for up to two five-year terms. Magufuli won the October 2020 presidential election with 84.5 percent of the vote in a contest that was markedly less free and fair than the 2015 election, which he had won with 58 percent. The 2020 election was marred by widespread fraud and vote-rigging; threats of violence against opposition figures, including the opposition candidate for president, Tundu Lissu; the use of force by police against participants at opposition rallies; the suspension of media outlets and social media; the obstruction and dispersal of Lissu's rallies, and other irregularities. International and local observer missions were denied accreditation, as were many international media outlets. Turnout was just 50 percent, down from 67 percent in the previous poll.

Opposition parties rejected the election's result and called for protests. Soon after, many opposition figures involved in organizing planned demonstrations were arrested, and a widespread protest movement never emerged. Lissu fled to Belgium in November with assistance from several European governments and the United States.

The semiautonomous region of Zanzibar elects its own president, who serves no more than two five-year terms. The 2020 Zanzibar presidential poll, held concurrently with the October general elections, was also marred in controversy. The Zanzibar Electoral Commission (ZEC) announced that CCM candidate Hussein Mwinyi had beat Alliance for Change and Transparency (ACT-Wazalendo) candidate Seif Sharif Hamad, taking 76.3 percent to Hamad's 19.9 percent. The ACT rejected the results of the poll. Ahead of the start of voting in late October, the regime had mobilized the army to Zanzibar, and Hamad was detained by the police. The army and police were accused of firing into a crowd days before the election, killing several people; according to reports, members of the crowd were attempting to stop the delivery of ballots suspected to be fraudulent. Hamad was detained on his way to an early-voting location, and held during the election period. Hamad's close associates, including Nassor Mazrui and Ismail Jussa, were arrested after the election.

Reports of further detentions emerged in the election's aftermath, with killings and torture of detainees reported. Some opposition politicians and activists were detained indefinitely and others were released severely injured from torture. A month after the election, the ACT-Wazalendo agreed to form a unity government in Zanzibar, with Seif Sharif Hamad becoming vice president. The development prompted accusations of co-optation.

Score Change: The score declined from 3 to 1 because the 2020 presidential election period was marred by reports of widespread fraud and vote-rigging, arrests, threats and violence against the opposition, the forced dispersal of public gatherings by authorities, the effective prohibition of independent election monitors, and numerous other problems.

A2. Were the current national legislative representatives elected through free and fair elections? 1 / 4 (-1)

Legislative authority lies with a unicameral, 393-seat National Assembly (the Bunge) whose members serve five-year terms. There are 264 seats filled through direct elections in single-member constituencies, 113 are reserved for women elected by political parties, 10 are filled by presidential appointment, and 5 members are elected by the Zanzibar legislature. The attorney general holds an ex officio seat.

Unlike the 2015 poll, the 2020 legislative election was marred by extensive allegations of fraud and intimidation. Widespread interference in nomination processes, both bureaucratic and physical, led to around 30 opposition candidates being denied a spot on the ballot. Numerous legislative and local government candidates were detained during the campaign period, including high-profile Chadema lawmakers Godbless Lema and Halima Mdee. On election day, opposition politicians complained of election interference and fraud. The results showed that 97 percent of the directly elected seats went to the CCM, substantially increasing the party's majority. Following the elections, key opposition legislative candidates sought asylum, including Godbless Lema, who was granted refugee protection in Canada.

The opposition was granted a small number of women's special seats in line with their share of the vote. Initially, the main opposition party, Chadema, refused to take up these seats. However, a group of 19 women legislators from the party defected and were seated in the legislature; they were then formally expelled by Chadema. Several of these women took their legislative seats upon being released from police custody, prompting speculation of coercion.

Members of Zanzibar's 85-seat House of Representatives serve five-year terms and are installed through a mix of direct elections and appointments. The 2015 legislative elections were annulled along with the concurrent Zanzibari presidential vote, and an opposition boycott of the rerun polling in 2016 left the CCM with full control of the regional legislature. The 2020 legislative elections in Zanzibar were also marred by allegations of fraud.

In 2020, Tanzania also held local government elections. Results of these elections were not released in full. It is thought that CCM won control of each of Tanzania's around 200 local government authorities. From 2015 to 2020, the opposition parties controlled a significant minority of local governments, including all but a handful of Tanzania's urban councils.

Score Change: The score declined from 2 to 1 because the 2020 elections were marred by widespread allegations of fraud, the removal of opposition candidates from the ballot, and the detention of opposition candidates.

A3. Are the electoral laws and framework fair, and are they implemented impartially by the relevant election management bodies? 1 / 4

The National Electoral Commission (NEC) is responsible for overseeing countrywide elections, while the ZEC conducts elections for Zanzibar's governing institutions.

The structures of the NEC and ZEC contribute to doubts about their independence. The NEC is appointed by the Tanzanian president. Magufuli's appointment of Wilson Mahera Charles as the new NEC director in October 2019 was criticized by Chadema and ACT leaders; they argued that Charles, who had previously run for office as a CCM candidate, was a partisan figure. The NEC was criticized for poor administration of voter registration processes ahead of the 2020 elections, and in 2020, the body oversaw the rejection of dozens of legislative and local candidates on technicalities and in early October ordered the suspension of Lissu's presidential campaign for a week, saying he had used incendiary language. Opposition parties accused NEC of being complicit in widespread ballot stuffing and use of "ghost voters" to increase CCM vote shares. The NEC did not release the full results of local government or legislative elections in 2020.

The ZEC is appointed by the Zanzibari president, though the opposition nominates two of the seven members. In 2018, then president Ali Mohamed Shein appointed seven new members to the commission. While some observers approved of Shein's choices, others accused the new members of being CCM partisans whose impartiality could be compromised during the 2020 elections. ACT-Wazalendo presidential candidate Hamad accused the ZEC of failing to register over 100,000 young voters who reached voting age between 2015 and 2020.

B. POLITICAL PLURALISM AND PARTICIPATION: 5 / 16 (−1)

B1. Do the people have the right to organize in different political parties or other competitive political groupings of their choice, and is the system free of undue obstacles to the rise and fall of these competing parties or groupings? 1 / 4

Tanzanians have the right to organize into political parties, but the ruling CCM enjoys considerable incumbency advantages that stifle competition. The system of state funding for parties under the Political Parties Act of 2015 disproportionately benefits the CCM. Political parties are regulated by a presidentially appointed registrar whom the opposition criticizes for partisan bias.

Authorities have stepped up efforts to constrain opposition parties in recent years. In 2016, the government banned all political rallies and demonstrations outside election periods, sharply curtailing parties' ability to mobilize public support. In 2019, the CCM used its parliamentary supermajority to pass amendments to the Political Parties Act that further eroded the rights of opposition groups. The amendments included a provision empowering a government minister to regulate party coalition formation, a ban on political fundraising from international sources, a rule prohibiting political parties from engaging in "activism," and the introduction of a number of tools that the registrar can use to investigate and interfere with the internal operations of targeted parties. The amendments also gave the registrar legal immunity, further reducing accountability for the office. Later in the year, both Chadema and ACT-Wazalendo were threatened with penalties for alleged violations of the Political Parties Act.

The government continued a campaign of repression in 2020, arresting numerous opposition politicians. Zitto Kabwe was once again arrested in June during an internal party meeting for holding an unlawful assembly, with authorities invoking the punitive changes to the Political Parties Act made in 2019. Earlier, in March, several Chadema leaders were convicted of unlawful assembly, rioting, and sedition, among other charges, in connection with a 2018 rally, and ordered to pay fines or face jail. The Office of the UN High Commissioner for Human Rights (OHCHR) called the arrests "troubling evidence of the crackdown on dissent and the stifling of public freedoms in the country." Before and after the election, opposition politicians from all parties were arrested regularly and repeatedly both on the mainland and in Zanzibar.

Opposition figures continued to face threats and physical attacks in 2020. In June, Chadema chairman Freeman Mbowe was attacked in his apartment in Dodoma by unknown assailants. There were also attacks on local Chadema operations including an arson attack of the Arusha regional headquarters. Just ahead of the election, a CCM youth leader threatened to poison Tundu if he attempted to challenge results showing a victory by Magufuli.

The CCM has achieved growing success in its efforts to co-opt opposition politicians, which critics have attributed to bribery, coercion, and other inducements. High-profile defections from opposition to CCM in 2020 included former Chadema secretary general

Vincent Mashinji. A group of women from Chadema defected from the party to take up special seats in Parliament after the 2020 election. Several of these women were released from jail, where they faced politicized charges, in order to be sworn in.

B2. Is there a realistic opportunity for the opposition to increase its support or gain power through elections? 1 / 4

The CCM has governed without interruption for more than 50 years. The electoral prospects of the opposition are limited due to interference; harassment; co-optation; instances of deadly violence against activists, and the risk of such violence; and criminal prosecutions by the government and its allies. Opposition candidates performed better in the 2015 elections than ever before, but still won only 29 percent of the National Assembly seats. The political space for opposition parties narrowed further in 2020, with severe repression leaving little opportunity to win support and even less to gain power.

Chadema lawmaker Tundu Lissu, who traveled abroad to recover after a 2017 attempted assassination in which he was shot 16 times, returned to Tanzania to stand as Chadema's presidential candidate. Despite the intimidation of opposition parties between 2015 and 2020, opposition rallies, particularly those attended by Lissu, drew large crowds; at one point, the NEC suspended his campaign for a week, saying his messaging at a rally was incendiary. After the 2020 election, Lissu and some opposition legislative candidates fled the country. In Zanzibar, the ZEC in October suspended the campaign of Hamad, the ACT-Wazalendo presidential candidate, for five days, similarly on charges of violating electoral ethics.

CCM efforts to convince or coerce opposition politicians to defect to government benches escalated significantly in 2020. Firebrand opposition politicians including Ester Bulaya and Halima Mdee agreed to cooperate with the government as independent politicians in parliament, breaking with Chadema. High-profile government critic and ACT-Wazalendo leader Zitto Kabwe agreed that his party would form a unity government in Zanzibar.

B3. Are the people's political choices free from domination by forces that are external to the political sphere, or by political forces that employ extrapolitical means? 1 / 4 (−1)

Tanzanian voters and politicians are subject to significant undue influence from unaccountable entities using antidemocratic tactics. Magufuli has increasingly exerted pressure through local administrative authorities, particularly the country's presidentially appointed regional and district commissioners. These officials are technically nonpartisan, but most are CCM loyalists or former security personnel. They have significant power within their jurisdictions, and have been especially repressive when overseeing opposition-oriented areas. Civil servants in opposition-controlled councils have been under significant pressure to follow directives from CCM officials, rather than elected opposition politicians. At times they have sought to remove elected municipal leaders, arbitrarily barred the movements and activities of critical nongovernmental organizations (NGOs) and human rights advocates, and reportedly threatened associated individuals. The 2019 local elections, which the opposition boycotted due to widespread candidate disqualifications, were notably managed by the government ministry that also supervises regional and district commissioners.

In 2020, the regime mobilized the army to Zanzibar amid growing unrest ahead of the Zanzibari presidential polls, and both the army and police were implicated in a spate of violence against opposition activists and civilians.

Score Change: The score declined from 2 to 1 because the ruling party has increasingly pressured civil servants to carry out CCM directives, and because the deployment of police and military forces in Zanzibar ahead of elections contributed to an atmosphere of intimidation.

B4. Do various segments of the population (including ethnic, racial, religious, gender, LGBT+, and other relevant groups) have full political rights and electoral opportunities? 2 / 4

Members of ethnic, religious, and other minority groups ostensibly have full political rights, but the participation of some groups is limited in practice.

While the constitution requires that women make up 30 percent of representatives in the parliament, many policies under Magufuli have actively undermined women's rights and obstructed attempts at political advocacy. Since Magufuli came to power, there has been a stark increase in misogynistic language in mainstream politics. In 2017, the President threatened to beat up the paternal aunts (*shangazi*) of rebelling backbenchers. During the 2020 campaign, Chadema candidate Catherine Ruge was arrested, stripped naked, and beaten by police as she stood for election in the heavily male-dominated Serengeti constituency.

LGBT+ people, who face the risk of arrest and harsh discrimination, are unable to openly advance their political interests.

C. FUNCTIONING OF GOVERNMENT: 4 / 12 (−1)

C1. Do the freely elected head of government and national legislative representatives determine the policies of the government? 1 / 4 (−1)

Magufuli has consolidated political power in the presidency since taking office, sidelining the legislature—in part by suppressing dissent within the ruling party—and exerting greater control over cabinet ministers through dismissals and reshuffles. The CCM government has also reasserted its role in managing the activities of legislators, and has threatened those who are frequently absent.

The 2020 election was marred by intimidation, electoral manipulation, fraud, and other problems. The resulting CCM victories have allowed Magufuli to further consolidate control over the legislature and local governments, and locked the opposition out of policymaking.

Score Change: The score declined from 2 to 1 because the CCM government engaged in widespread fraud and coercion to win the year's presidential and legislative elections, undermining the democratic legitimacy of its policy decisions.

C2. Are safeguards against official corruption strong and effective? 2 / 4

Corruption remains a problem in the country, and reform efforts have yielded mixed results. The Prevention and Combating of Corruption Bureau (PCCB) has been accused of focusing on low-level corruption and doing little to address graft committed by senior officials.

In 2020 several scandals emerged in which the apparent perpetrators faced consequences, but which nevertheless reflected negatively on government agencies' ability to enforce their mandates. In July, nine senior PCCB staff were suspended for corruption relating to construction of the agency's buildings. In December, 22 senior officials at the Tanzanian Revenue Authority (TRA) were suspended pending a major corruption investigation.

An audit in 2018 revealed $640 million in missing revenue from the 2016–17 fiscal year. Additional scrutiny in 2019 uncovered more than $1 billion in missing or misappropriated funds. Opposition calls to publish the full report from the auditor general and enforce accountability were rejected. The chair of the parliament's Public Accounts Committee denied any loss or theft.

C3. Does the government operate with openness and transparency? 1 / 4

An access to information act was adopted in 2016, but it gives precedence to any other law governing the handling of government information, and appeals of decisions on information requests are handled by a government minister rather than an independent body. The law imposes prison terms on officials who improperly release information, but assigns no clear penalties for those who improperly withhold information. Local and regional government offices are uneven in their level of responsiveness to requests for information. The Statistics Act was amended in June 2019 to remove criminal liability for publishing information that conflicts with the National Bureau of Statistics, but the government generally continued to resist transparency efforts and punish journalists and civil society groups that attempted to expose official wrongdoing. Live broadcasts of parliament sessions have been suspended since 2016.

The government is suspected of manipulating public statistics on economic performance. In April 2019, Tanzania was accused of blocking the publication of an International Monetary Fund (IMF) report that criticized the country's "unpredictable" economic policies, a claim that was denied by a government spokesman. The World Health Organization (WHO) rebuked Tanzania in September 2019 for not sharing information regarding a death from Ebola-like symptoms in Dar es Salaam. The government insisted that there was no Ebola in the country, described reports about the suspected case as false, and summoned the country's local WHO representative in protest over the announcement. The Tanzanian government's response to the COVID-19 pandemic reflected further declines in government transparency. Magufuli declared the pandemic "defeated" in Tanzania by late spring. The president fired several top officials over their objections to this strategy, including the head of the only COVID-19 testing facility and the deputy health minister. Authorities stopped publishing data from COVID-19 testing in April, and those who tried to report on the extent of the outbreak were subject to legal penalties.

CIVIL LIBERTIES: 22 / 60 (-1)

D. FREEDOM OF EXPRESSION AND BELIEF: 7 / 16

D1. Are there free and independent media? 1 / 4

Independent journalists and media outlets are subject to harsh repression in Tanzania. The 2016 Media Services Act grants the government broad authority over media content and the licensing of outlets and journalists. It also prescribes severe penalties, including prison terms, for publication of defamatory, seditious, or other illegal content.

Sustained legal and regulatory pressure on journalists and the expression of other public figures during 2020 contributed to further self-censorship and other suppression of news coverage. The Tanzania Communications Regulatory Authority (TCRA) penalized numerous media outlets over coverage of the COVID-19 pandemic and the 2020 elections, with research by the Committee to Protect Journalists (CPJ) showing that at least one online television station, a news site, and at least four other broadcasters were ordered to temporarily suspend programming, and that at least 10 additional outlets were fined. Prominent regime critic Khalifa Said was forced out of a commentator position at one newspaper, while comedian Idris Sultan was arrested once again for social media content which was said to be mocking the president. Maxence Melo, founder of online discussion platform Jamii Forums, was convicted of obstructing investigations after refusing to hand over his user data, and given fine and a year in prison, which he is contesting. Prominent investigative journalist Erick Kabendera, who was detained from July 2019 first over citizenship questions, then alleged cybercrimes, and later for money laundering and other financial charges, which do not allow for release on bail, was released in February 2020 but only after accepting a plea deal. Beginning in August 2020, local media must receive explicit permission from the media regulatory body to broadcast content produced outside of Tanzania, limiting citizens' access to information from international broadcasters like BBC World Service and Deutsche Welle.

The 2018 Electronic and Postal Communications (Online Content) Regulations require bloggers and owners of online discussion platforms and streaming services to pay more than $900 in annual registration fees. Many bloggers shut down their outlets as a result.

D2. Are individuals free to practice and express their religious faith or nonbelief in public and private? 3 / 4

Freedom of religion is generally respected, and interfaith relations are largely peaceful, though periodic sectarian violence has occurred. Muslims are believed to be a minority in Tanzania as a whole, but 99 percent of Zanzibar's population practices Islam. Political tensions between mainland Tanzania and Zanzibar often play out along religious lines. The government occasionally raises the specter of interreligious conflict as an excuse to detain political rivals, contributing to a general sense that Muslims are sometimes treated unfairly by authorities. Religious services were not restricted in Tanzania during the COVID-19 pandemic.

D3. Is there academic freedom, and is the educational system free from extensive political indoctrination? 2 / 4

Academic freedom in Tanzania was harmed by the passage of the 2015 Statistics Act, which requires data released publicly to be first approved by the National Bureau of Statistics. In 2018, the parliament passed amendments to the Statistics Act that prescribed fines, a minimum of three years in prison, or both for anyone who disputes official government figures. The law was amended in June 2019 to remove criminal liability for publishing independent data, but given the government's ongoing and general hostility to dissenting views, it was unclear whether the legal change would strengthen academic freedom in practice.

In April 2020, a student from the University of Dar Es Salaam was arrested for spreading false information in connection with publishing remarks about the number of COVID-19 cases in the country.

D4. Are individuals free to express their personal views on political or other sensitive topics without fear of surveillance or retribution? 1 / 4

The government historically monitored the population through a neighborhood-level CCM cell structure, and has increasingly policed personal expression on social media in recent years. Under laws including the 2015 Cybercrimes Act and the 2018 Electronic and Postal Communications (Online Content) Regulations, social media users have been prosecuted for offenses such as insulting the president. Government officials have threatened to prosecute users for supposedly spreading homosexuality through online platforms. Vague prohibitions on communication that "causes annoyance" or "leads to public disorder" have confused users as to what constitutes a violation, and empowered authorities to suppress unfavorable speech at their discretion. The 2018 regulations also require internet cafés to install surveillance cameras. The Electronic and Postal Communications (Online Content) Regulations 2020 took effect in July and prohibits "spreading rumors" or insulting the nation online. In 2020, ordinary citizens were arrested for spreading false information in connection with comments about COVID-19.

Since Magufuli took office, the Tanzanian government has consulted with Hacking Team—a firm that provides electronic surveillance capacity—and signed cybersecurity collaboration agreements with the South Korean and Israeli governments. In 2019, recordings of CCM leaders criticizing Magufuli were publicly leaked in an apparent attempt to demonstrate pervasive surveillance and encourage self-censorship. Magufuli admitted in January 2019 to monitoring the digital communications of some ministers. In the same year, opposition leader Zitto Kabwe's verified Twitter account was hacked and used to promote Magufuli, raising suspicions that the government and its allies, armed with new capabilities, were responsible. In 2020, the Tanzanian authorities reportedly used Twitter copyright rules to force regime critics off the website, which serves as one of the last remaining uncensored spaces for domestic discussion of Tanzanian politics.

E. ASSOCIATIONAL AND ORGANIZATIONAL RIGHTS: 4 / 12
E1. Is there freedom of assembly? 1 / 4

The constitution guarantees freedom of assembly, but the government limits this right through legal mechanisms, restrictions on social media platforms used to organize, and outright violence. Organizers must notify the police 48 hours in advance of any demonstration, and police have broad discretion to prohibit gatherings that could threaten public safety or public order, among other criteria. A ban on political rallies has been in place since mid-2016. The January 2019 amendments to the Political Parties Act further restricted public assembly, in part by broadening the scope of activities that are deemed "political."

Freedom of assembly came under attack in 2020 through a combination of increased violence against demonstrators and limits on communications. During the final week of election campaigns, the main telecommunications providers banned bulk short-message service (SMS) messages, a key tool opposition parties use to organize events and promote turnout. They also blocked any text messages that contained key words associated with the opposition, including the name of presidential candidate, Tundu Lissu. The day before polling opened on the mainland, Twitter and WhatsApp were blocked, further undermining opposition supporters' ability to organize gatherings and coordinate preelection campaigning. At year's end, Twitter was still blocked in Tanzania, and the government has been working to block common virtual private networks (VPNs) used to access it.

Gatherings of opposition supporters at rallies or other election meetings were frequently broken up by force including use of tear gas and live ammunition, with deaths reported in both Zanzibar and on the mainland. In November 2020, the opposition called for national protests after the 2020 election, which they rejected as fraudulent. The organizers of these protests, Freeman Mbowe and Godbless Lema, were arrested and the protests were called off.

E2. Is there freedom for nongovernmental organizations, particularly those that are engaged in human rights- and governance-related work? 1 / 4

Tanzania has a diverse and active civil society sector, but laws that already gave the government broad authority to deregister NGOs were strengthened in 2020. Since then, human rights organizations and activists in particular have been subject to increased restrictions, deregistration, legal harassment, and unlawful arrests. Amendments enacted in June expanded the NGO registrar's discretionary powers to investigate and deregister organizations. Among other changes, the amendments also allow private businesses to be punished if they support the activities of disfavored NGOs, and impose onerous new financial reporting requirements on even small grassroots organizations. Also in June, legal changes made it illegal for NGOs to file public-interest litigation, a process critical to human rights protection in Tanzania.

As a result of these legal changes several organizations, including one of the country's largest human and civil rights organizations, the Tanzania Human Rights Defenders Coalition (THRDC) had their bank accounts suspended, and both THRDC and the Legal and Human Rights Centre (LHRC) were threatened with deregistration in 2020. Both organizations were banned from election observation, voter education, and training lawyers to handle election petitions, all activities they had overseen in previous elections. Human rights lawyer and LHRC employee Tito Magoti and information technology specialist Theodory Giyani were arrested in late December 2019 and arraigned on spurious money laundering and cybercrimes charges. At year's end, they were still being held without charge.

E3. Is there freedom for trade unions and similar professional or labor organizations? 2 / 4

Trade unions are nominally independent of the government and are coordinated by the Trade Union Congress of Tanzania and the Zanzibar Trade Union Congress. The Tanzania Federation of Cooperatives represents most of Tanzania's agricultural sector. The government has significant discretion to deny union registration, and many private employers engage in antiunion activities. Essential public-sector workers are barred from striking, and other workers are restricted by complex notification and mediation requirements. Strikes are infrequent on both the mainland and Zanzibar.

F. RULE OF LAW: 4 / 16 (−1)

F1. Is there an independent judiciary? 1 / 4 (−1)

Tanzania's judiciary suffers from underfunding and corruption. Judges are political appointees, and the judiciary does not have an independent budget, which makes it vulnerable to political pressure. The results of such pressure are particularly evident in cases involving opposition figures and other critics of the government, as well as the recent flurry of legal changes to suppress free and fair competition and protect the regime from prosecution. Politicized courts have enforced new laws that attack human rights and are selectively invoked to keep the government in power. In August 2020, Tanzania's highest court, the Court of Appeal, ruled that it was legal for the government to hold suspects without bail for several offences including money laundering—a charge commonly levied against the government's political opponents, including Erick Kabendera and Tito Magoti. These suspects are then held in jail indefinitely as the courts delay their cases, or until they agree to plead guilty. The Court of Appeals' verdict overruled the High Court's ruling against the government's position.

Lower-level courts were routinely involved in levying politicized charges against opposition activists and remanding them without trial before and after the 2020 election. Eight opposition activists in Singida Region, including Chadema youth leader Nusrat Hanje, were detained without bail in July and charged by the courts with insulting the national anthem. The High Court ruled that they should be released on bail in August but they remained in jail in Dodoma. Hanje was released in December 2020 by the director of public prosecutions and shortly after agreed to take up a parliamentary special seat alongside other women defectors from Chadema.

Score Change: The score declined from 2 to 1 due to the continued subservience of the judicial branch to the CCM government, including through involvement in politicized cases against its political opponents ahead of the 2020 elections.

F2. Does due process prevail in civil and criminal matters? 1 / 4

Due process guarantees are not well upheld in civil and criminal matters. Policies and rules governing arrest and pretrial detention are often ignored, and pretrial detention commonly lasts for years due to case backlogs and inadequate funding for prosecutors. Arbitrary arrests of opposition politicians, journalists, and civil society leaders occurred throughout 2020 as in previous years.

Legal activists have suffered repercussions for their attempts to seek justice through the courts in recent years. The High Court suspended Zanzibari attorney and former head of the Tanganyika Law Society Fatma Karume in September 2019 for filing an "inappropriate" legal challenge on behalf of the opposition that sought to block the appointment of Adelardus Kilangi as attorney general. In 2020, Karume was fired from the firm where she was a senior partner and disbarred for "political activism" after significant government pressure.

In December 2019, Tito Magoti—a rights activist and attorney for Tanzania's Legal and Human Rights Centre—was arrested in a manner that appeared to be an abduction by unidentified men. The regional police commissioner at first denied he was being detained, but Magoti was eventually charged with unbailable economic crimes. At the end of 2020, he was still in jail awaiting trial.

F3. Is there protection from the illegitimate use of physical force and freedom from war and insurgencies? 1 / 4

Reports of abuse and torture of suspects in police custody are common, and police have been accused of extrajudicial killings and other violence over the past four years. There was an increase in violence, abductions, and detentions around the 2020 election, some at the hands of state forces and some by plain clothed assailants.

F4. Do laws, policies, and practices guarantee equal treatment of various segments of the population? 1 / 4

Women's rights are constitutionally guaranteed but not uniformly protected. Women face de facto discrimination in employment, including sexual harassment, which is rarely addressed through formal legal channels. Women's socioeconomic disadvantages are more pronounced in rural areas and in the informal economy.

Same-sex sexual relations are punishable by lengthy prison terms, and LGBT+ people face discrimination and police abuse in practice, leading most to hide aspects of their identities. Men who are suspected of same-sex sexual activity have been arrested and forced to undergo anal examinations.

The repatriation of some 200,000 Burundian refugees slowed in 2020, and at the end of November, 150,000 Burundian refugees remained in Tanzania. In 2020, there was growing fear among refugees in Tanzania that they would be forced to return to Burundi—where many say they would not feel safe in the aftermath of deadly political turmoil in 2015—after the presidents of both countries repeatedly called for them to "go home." In November, Human Rights Watch (HRW) reported that the Burundian and Tanzanian authorities were collaborating to identify Burundian authorities' political opponents and those discouraging repatriation. The group found that refugees were being tortured and then forcibly returned to Burundi in violation of international law.

Pastoralist ethnic groups do not enjoy equal treatment before the law, particularly when it comes to land disputes. These groups often live near Tanzania's lucrative national parks and the government has engaged in heavy-handed treatment of those who refuse to comply with government directives to move. In 2018, opposition leader Zitto Kabwe reported that around a hundred people had died in clashes between local officials and pastoralists in Kigoma Region. In 2020, the government took initial steps toward find a lasting resolution to these disputes.

G. PERSONAL AUTONOMY AND INDIVIDUAL RIGHTS: 7 / 16
G1. Do individuals enjoy freedom of movement, including the ability to change their place of residence, employment, or education? 2 / 4

Residents enjoy some basic freedoms pertaining to travel and changes of residence, employment, and education. The government has wide discretion in enforcing laws that can limit movement, particularly in Zanzibar, where the approval of local government appointees is often required for changes in employment, personal banking, and residency.

Separately, the authorities in recent years have arbitrarily arrested and deported a number of Kenyans, many of whom had been granted Tanzanian citizenship. The government at times imposes travel restrictions on civic activists, human rights researchers, opposition figures facing criminal charges, and other prominent individuals. Opposition politicians who were under threat of violence struggled to leave the country in the aftermath of the election.

G2. Are individuals able to exercise the right to own property and establish private businesses without undue interference from state or nonstate actors? 2 / 4

Tanzanians have the right to establish private businesses but are often required to pay bribes to license and operate them. The state owns all land and leases it to individuals and private entities, leading to clashes over land rights between citizens and companies engaged in extractive industries. These laws have been used to expropriate the resources and lands of wealthy opposition politicians, including Freeman Mbowe's holdings in Hai and Dar es Salaam.

G3. Do individuals enjoy personal social freedoms, including choice of marriage partner and size of family, protection from domestic violence, and control over appearance? 1 / 4

Rape, domestic violence, and female genital mutilation (FGM) are common but rarely prosecuted. An escalating pattern of rapes in which the attackers break into women's homes has been reported in recent years in western Tanzania. Laws and practices regarding marriage, divorce, and other personal status issues favor men over women, particularly in Zanzibar. Tanzania's adolescent fertility rate is more than twice the global average.

The government restricts access to family planning services. In July 2019, Magufuli encouraged women to help increase the country's birth rate and spur the economy. At the same time, girls can be expelled from school for becoming pregnant, and in 2017 the government prohibited those who had given birth from returning to school. In November 2020, a women's rights organization filed a case against the Tanzanian government in the African Court of Human and People's Rights seeking to overturn the ban on pregnant girls from school.

In October 2019, in response to a widely publicized video of a government official caning students who had been accused of setting fire to dormitories, Magufuli applauded the corporal punishment and called for children to be caned both at school and at home so as to create a "disciplined nation."

G4. Do individuals enjoy equality of opportunity and freedom from economic exploitation? 2 / 4

Sexual and labor exploitation remain problems, especially for children living in poor rural areas who are drawn into domestic service, agricultural labor, mining, and other activities. Child labor in gold mines, where working conditions are often dangerous, is common.

Most Tanzanians do not benefit from the country's extensive natural-resource wealth. Tanzania has one of the highest levels of income inequality in the world, and the poverty rate remains high.

Thailand

Population: 66,500,000
Capital: Bangkok
Freedom Status: Not Free
Electoral Democracy: No

Status Change: Thailand's status declined from Partly Free to Not Free due to the dissolution of a popular opposition party that had performed well in the 2019 elections, and the military-dominated government's crackdown on youth-led protests calling for democratic reforms.

Overview: Following five years of military dictatorship, Thailand transitioned to a military-dominated, semi-elected government in 2019. In 2020, the combination of democratic deterioration and frustrations over the role of the monarchy provoked the country's largest antigovernment demonstrations in a decade. In response to these youth-led protests, the regime resorted to familiar authoritarian tactics, including arbitrary arrests, intimidation, lèse-majesté charges, and harassment of activists. Freedom of the press is constrained, due process is not guaranteed, and there is impunity for crimes committed against activists.

KEY DEVELOPMENTS IN 2020

- According to University of Oxford researchers, Thailand registered under 7,500 confirmed cases and 63 COVID-19 deaths, making it one of the countries least severely affected by the pandemic. In March, the government issued an emergency decree, which it subsequently extended and tightened, that included measures widely criticized as empowering the regime against dissent rather than addressing the pandemic's economic and social impact.
- In February, the opposition Future Forward Party was dissolved following a Constitutional Court ruling that its founder had used an illegal donation to fund the party. The Court's ruling also removed several legislators from parliament and banned 10 members of the party's leadership from politics for 10 years.
- Large youth-led protests, which began in February but were curtailed by COVID-19 restrictions, recommenced in July following an easing of lockdown measures. Hundreds of thousands of mostly student protesters participated in multiple antigovernment protests throughout the country, calling for an end to harassment of activists, abolition of Thailand's parliament, constitutional reform, and reform of the powerful monarchy.
- In October, the government declared a "severe" state of emergency, banning gatherings of more than five people and initiating a crackdown against protesters and movement leaders. Beginning in November, lèse-majesté charges were leveled against dozens of activists, prompting human rights groups to express concern over the crackdown.

POLITICAL RIGHTS: 5 / 40 (–1)
A. ELECTORAL PROCESS: 1 / 12
A1. Was the current head of government or other chief national authority elected through free and fair elections? 0 / 4

Thailand is a constitutional monarchy ruled by King Maha Vajiralongkorn, who serves as head of state. Although the monarchy has limited formal power, the king is highly influential in Thai politics, and has significant clout over the military.

The constitution, which was developed by a committee appointed by the military's National Council for Peace and Order (NCPO), was approved in a tightly controlled 2016 referendum and took effect in 2017. According to the charter, Thailand's prime minister is selected by a majority vote of the combined 500-seat elected lower house and the 250-seat upper house, the Senate, whose members are entirely appointed by the military.

The promilitary Palang Pracharat Party, which won only 115 out of 500 lower house seats in the 2019 elections, nominated incumbent prime minister Prayuth Chan-ocha to again serve in that position. In 2014, as army chief, Prayuth had staged a military coup against the democratically elected government and designated himself prime minister. Prayuth maintained the position in 2019 through the support of a promilitary voting bloc in the lower house and votes from 249 appointed senators.

A2. Were the current national legislative representatives elected through free and fair elections? 1 / 4

Under the military-drafted constitution, the bicameral National Assembly consists of the 250-seat Senate, whose members are appointed to five-year terms by the army, and the 500-seat House of Representatives, to which 350 members are directly elected to four-year terms in single-seat constituencies by simple majority vote, and 150 members are elected in a single nationwide constituency by party-list proportional representation vote.

In 2019, after almost five years of postponements, an election for the House of Representatives was contested by 77 political parties, most of which fell into one of two camps: promilitary or antimilitary. The campaign period was marred by political repression, media censorship, unequal access to the media, and a lack of independent and impartial oversight from the Election Commission of Thailand (ECT), whose members were appointed by the junta.

The results, announced six weeks after the polls, were tainted by irregularities, with ballots "lost," and initial vote tallies changed. Additionally, the formula for distributing party seats was altered after the election in order to reduce seats won by opposition parties and redistribute them to military-aligned parties. This resulted in the redistribution of sufficient seats to grant promilitary parties a supermajority.

Only one international election monitoring body, the Asian Network for Free Elections, was permitted to observe the election. Two domestic observer organizations, P-Net and We Watch, were also granted permission to monitor the elections, but all three missions experienced severely restricted access to the polls and voting procedures. We Watch determined that while the election gave the public the opportunity to exercise their voting rights, the process was not free and fair.

In December 2020, Thailand held its first provincial elections since the 2014 coup; candidates associated with locally dominant groups fared well, while those linked to the reform movement made few gains. Elections for other subnational positions remain unscheduled.

A3. Are the electoral laws and framework fair, and are they implemented impartially by the relevant election management bodies? 0 / 4

The 2017 constitution, which governed the 2019 elections, was designed to weaken political parties and elected officials while strengthening unelected institutions. Citizens cast only one ballot in the 2019 elections (rather than distinct votes for constituency and party-list seats, as in previous elections); by design, the system makes it difficult for large parties to gain a majority and form a stable government.

All 250 seats in the Senate were appointed for five-year terms by the military in 2019. Thailand's prime minister is selected through a combined vote of the combined lower and upper house, granting the unelected Senate a powerful role in the selection of the prime minister.

The 2019 elections were overseen by the ECT, whose members were entirely appointed by the junta. Throughout the electoral process, the ECT came under criticism from the public and civil society for its lack of independence and willingness to intervene on behalf of the military and promilitary political parties. For instance, the ECT's post-election change of the seat distribution formula reassigned seats won by the opposition Future Forward Party (FFP) and Pheu Thai Party (PTP) to small military-aligned parties, all of which subsequently voted with the promilitary Palang Pracharat Party and the Senate to retain Prayuth as prime minister.

B. POLITICAL PLURALISM AND PARTICIPATION: 2 / 16 (−1)

B1. Do the people have the right to organize in different political parties or other competitive political groupings of their choice, and is the system free of undue obstacles to the rise and fall of these competing parties or groupings? 1 / 4

From 2014 to 2018, Thailand's military government effectively banned political parties from meeting and conducting activities. In late 2018, the NCPO lifted many restrictions on political parties, allowing them to hold meetings, recruit members, select candidates, and meet with the public. A slew of parties from across the political spectrum began organizing and campaigning in preparation for the 2019 elections, though those opposed to military rule experienced official harassment.

In April 2019, after the FFP's success in the elections, party leader Thanathorn Juangroongruangkit was charged with sedition and other crimes for having allegedly "provided assistance" to democracy activists after a 2015 protest. He was subsequently suspended by the Constitutional Court from taking his parliamentary seat over a complaint that he had held shares in a media company when he applied to serve in the legislature. In February 2020, the FFP was abolished following a Constitutional Court ruling that a loan to the party from Thanathorn constituted an illegal donation. The decision instigated youth-led protests against the ruling government that continued throughout the year.

Opposition parties aligned with exiled former prime minister Thaksin Shinawatra have also suffered attacks by the government. The military-drafted constitution imposes rules designed to weaken existing large parties like PTP, which led the government overthrown in the 2014 coup. To circumvent these limitations, PTP leaders established like-minded parties, including Thai Raksa Chart, to better compete in the 2019 elections. However, after Thai Raksa Chart nominated Princess Ubolratana—the monarch's older sister—as its prime ministerial candidate, the party was dissolved by the Constitutional Court and its candidates were disqualified from running in the election. The development effectively stymied the alliance of Shinawatra-associated opposition parties from electoral success.

B2. Is there a realistic opportunity for the opposition to increase its support or gain power through elections? 0 / 4 (−1)

The junta's ban on activities of political parties, including those opposed to military rule, was lifted in 2018, and numerous parties competed in the 2019 general elections. However, restraints imposed by the military-drafted constitution greatly limited the ability of opposition parties to effectively campaign or gain significant political power through elections.

While parties opposed to military rule, most prominently the PTP and the FFP, won a combined 245 lower house seats, they were unable to advance legislation due to the military's continued control over the chamber.

The February 2020 dissolution of the opposition FFP, whose 80 seats made it the third-largest force in the House of Representatives, was accompanied by a 10-year ban on political participation for 16 party leaders, including Thanathorn and 10 other elected representatives. Following the ruling, the FFP's 55 remaining representatives joined a small political party and rebranded as the Move Forward Party.

Score Change: The score declined from 1 to 0 due to the Constitutional Court's abolition of the opposition Future Forward Party, which held 80 seats in Parliament.

B3. Are the people's political choices free from domination by forces that are external to the political sphere, or by political forces that employ extrapolitical means? 0 / 4

While Thai citizens were able to vote in the 2019 election, the resulting government did not reflect the results of the vote due to a rigged outcome enabled by the military-drafted constitution. The cabinet is stacked with former members of the military, leaders of the 2014 coup, and ministerial holdovers from the junta, including Prime Minister Prayuth.

The 2019 polls were also subject to repeated interventions by the Thai monarchy, which exerts tremendous influence over Thailand's governance and political system. For instance, the Constitutional Court's dissolution order targeting the Thai Raksa Chart party came soon after King Maha Vajiralongkorn made a televised announcement condemning his sister Princess Ubolratana's prime ministerial bid as "extremely inappropriate." On the eve of the 2019 election, King Vajiralongkorn released an unprecedented statement from the monarchy urging citizens to vote for "good people" to prevent "chaos," a message widely understood as a royal endorsement of promilitary parties.

B4. Do various segments of the population (including ethnic, racial, religious, gender, LGBT+, and other relevant groups) have full political rights and electoral opportunities? 1 / 4

In 2019, some political rights denied to the population during military rule were restored with the election of a semicivilian government. Nevertheless, members of minority groups, particularly ethnic minorities and stateless residents of Thailand, are generally unable to choose their representatives or organize independently to assert their interests in the political sphere. Malay Muslims in southern Thailand remain politically marginalized.

Migrant workers, mostly from neighboring Myanmar, Cambodia, and Laos, were believed to number approximately 4.9 million as of 2019, though many left Thailand amid the economic slowdown produced by the COVID-19 lockdown. Migrant workers lack political rights and a path to citizenship.

Women are underrepresented in government at all levels, composing only 16.2 percent of the House of Representatives and 10.4 percent of the Senate. Few women hold leadership roles in political parties, and the interests of women are generally not prioritized in political life, although the 2020 protests included vocal activists advocating for greater attention to women's issues.

The interests of LGBT+ people are increasingly represented in national politics. In July 2020, Thailand's cabinet approved a draft bill that would give same-sex unions many of the same benefits as heterosexual marriages, but Parliament had not given the bill final approval at year's end.

C. FUNCTIONING OF GOVERNMENT: 2 / 12

C1. Do the freely elected head of government and national legislative representatives determine the policies of the government? 0 / 4

Since July 2019, the policies of the Thai government have been determined by the prime minister and the bicameral National Assembly. Despite opposition political parties garnering a significant share of lower house seats in the 2019 elections, Thailand's government remains largely authoritarian due to the unelected Senate, which votes with the lower house to determine the government's long-term strategy and the selection of the prime minister. Consequently, government policies and new legislation continue to be decided and implemented by a clique of former military leaders and their allies.

In recent years, the Thai king has consolidated and expanded the political and military powers of the monarchy. In 2019, King Vajiralongkorn ordered that two elite army units be transferred to the direct command of the palace, citing Article 172 of the constitution, which allows a royal decree to be issued when there is an emergency threatening national security and the monarchy.

C2. Are safeguards against official corruption strong and effective? 1 / 4

Thailand's anticorruption legislation is inadequately enforced, and bribes and gifts are common practice in business, law enforcement, and the legal system. The National Anti-Corruption Commission (NACC) receives numerous complaints each year, and the NCPO passed vague anticorruption laws while in power. However, the military junta engaged in wide-scale corruption, cronyism, and nepotism, and these issues have gone unaddressed since the transition to semicivilian rule in 2019.

C3. Does the government operate with openness and transparency? 1 / 4

Parliamentary oversight of the government that took power in 2019 has resulted in an increase in overall government openness and transparency. However, due to the military's continued sway over government operations and its majority within the National Assembly, high-level decisions continue to be made, and legislation passed, opaquely and with little regard to the protestations of opposition lawmakers.

CIVIL LIBERTIES: 25 / 60 (−1)
D. FREEDOM OF EXPRESSION AND BELIEF: 6 / 16
D1. Are there free and independent media? 1 / 4

Under military rule, the government systematically used censorship, intimidation, and legal action to suppress independent media, and international and domestic news outlets were frequently censored during the election campaign period in 2019. That July, in one of the junta's last acts, several NCPO orders limiting free speech and independent media were lifted, including those banning news reports considered to threaten national security and the NCPO's credibility. However, the new government has retained several laws introduced by the junta that restrict free and independent media, including criminal defamation laws that resulted in Thai journalist Suchanee Cloitre receiving a two-year prison sentence in 2019, though her conviction was overturned in October 2020.

In March 2020, Thailand's government issued an emergency decree that made it illegal to publish information about COVID-19 deemed "false or capable of causing fear in the public," with violators subject to prison terms of up to five years. The decree also empowered authorities to demand that journalists and media groups "correct" reports deemed false or face charges under the Computer Crime Act. Several media organizations faced legal action and content removal requests in 2020 for allegedly breaching the emergency laws.

In October, Twitter disclosed the discovery and suspension of 926 accounts that the company could "reliably link to the Royal Thai Army," which had been "amplifying pro-RTA and progovernment content, as well as engaging in behavior targeting prominent political opposition figures."

Several Thai journalists were arrested while covering the 2020 antigovernment protests, and the government issued shutdown orders to at least four news outlets.

D2. Are individuals free to practice and express their religious faith or nonbelief in public and private? 3 / 4

There is no state religion, and religious freedom is respected in the majority of the country. However, some restrictions exist. Speech considered insulting to Buddhism is prohibited by law. A long-running civil conflict in the south, which pits ethnic Malay Muslims against ethnic Thai Buddhists, continues to undermine citizens' ability to practice their religions. The vast majority of Thais are Buddhist and the king is considered the protector of Buddhism in Thailand, which carries spoken and unspoken authority.

D3. Is there academic freedom, and is the educational system free from extensive political indoctrination? 1 / 4

Academic freedom remains constrained in Thailand. University discussions and seminars on topics regarded as politically sensitive are subject to monitoring or outright cancellation by government authorities. Activist activities on university campuses also continue to be constrained by the government, including through prosecutions for sedition and violations of the country's draconian lèse majesté laws.

Academics working on sensitive topics are subjected to oppressive tactics including summonses for questioning, home visits by security officials, surveillance of their activities, and arbitrary detention for the purpose of questioning. Several Thai academics fled into exile after the 2014 coup.

Thailand's public education system is rife with propaganda aimed at instilling obedience to the country's monarchy and military. In 2020, the education system became a target of student protesters. New youth-led organizations such as Bad Students demanded the government halt harassment of student activists, while collaborating with students on reforms including the abrogation of abusive school regulations.

D4. Are individuals free to express their personal views on political or other sensitive topics without fear of surveillance or retribution? 1 / 4

Despite Thailand's transition from military rule to semicivilian control in 2019, anyone perceived as a critic of the military or the monarchy remains at high risk of surveillance, arrest, imprisonment, harassment, and physical attack. Thailand's post-junta government retained 140 NCPO laws, including laws that restrict freedom of expression. The government also retained the junta's 2016 Computer Crime Act, which gives authorities broad powers to restrict online expression, impose censorship, and enforce surveillance, and extends enforcement of lèse-majesté provisions online. Employment of lèse-majesté laws under the criminal code's Section 112 decreased in the final years of direct military rule, but it returned as a tool of repression in late 2020, with 37 activists facing new prosecutions for having insulted or threatened the monarchy.

E. ASSOCIATIONAL AND ORGANIZATIONAL RIGHTS: 4 / 12 (−1)

E1. Is there freedom of assembly? 1 / 4 (−1)

In March 2020, under the guise of measures to combat COVID-19, Prime Minister Prayuth announced that the state would use broad powers granted by a 2005 emergency decree to protect the "safety of the people," including by prohibiting public assembly and exercising expanded powers of censorship and arrest. The decree, originally scheduled to last a month, was repeatedly renewed; in October, the government declared a more stringent "severe state of emergency" in response to youth-led demonstrations, which prohibited gatherings of more than five people. While the "severe" decree was revoked after a week, the government reintroduced the restrictions in December, citing a rise COVID-19 cases. Human rights groups condemned the government's aggressive use of force and toleration of violence by civilian regime sympathizers during protests in November. More than 170 peaceful protesters were charged with sedition, lèse-majesté, or violations of the prohibition on public gatherings in 2020.

Score Change: The score declined from 2 to 1 because emergency decrees the government said were meant to curb the spread of COVID-19 unduly curtailed youth-led antigovernment demonstrations.

E2. Is there freedom for nongovernmental organizations, particularly those that are engaged in human rights- and governance-related work? 1 / 4

Thailand has a vibrant civil society, but groups focused on defending human rights and freedom of expression, and promoting democracy, continue to face restrictions, criminalization, and prosecution by the state, including under sedition and lèse majesté laws. In 2019, several representatives from Thai democracy groups were attacked by gangs thought to be connected to the military. Civil society groups holding republican views, such as the Organization for Thai Federation, remain forbidden.

Land and environmental activists risk serious and even deadly violence; the environmental rights group Global Witness has described Thailand as among the most dangerous countries in Asia for such activists to operate. Perpetrators of attacks generally enjoy impunity. In January 2020, Thai prosecutors dropped charges lodged in 2019 against four forestry officials in the 2014 disappearance of prominent Thai-Karen environmental activist Porlajee "Billy" Rakchongcharoen.

The 2020 antigovernment protests also led to pressure on Thai human rights and civil society organizations, which were accused by government and right-wing forces of organizing the protests with foreign funding.

E3. Is there freedom for trade unions and similar professional or labor organizations? 2 / 4

Thai trade unions are independent and have the right to collectively bargain. However, civil servants and temporary workers do not have the right to form unions, and less than 2 percent of the total workforce is unionized. Antiunion discrimination in the private sector is common, and legal protections for union members are weak and poorly enforced.

F. RULE OF LAW: 5 / 16
F1. Is there an independent judiciary? 1 / 4

Although Thailand's constitution grants independence to the judiciary, in practice Thailand's courts are politicized, and corruption in the judicial branch is common. The Constitutional Court, which has been accused of favoring the military, has sweeping powers, including the ability to dissolve political parties, overthrow elected officials, and veto legislation. In 2018, the government enacted a law that made criticism of the Constitutional Court with "rude, sarcastic, or threatening words" a criminal offense, further shielding the body from accountability. In February 2020, the Constitutional Court abolished the popular opposition party FFP after what observers characterized as a highly politicized trial.

In 2019, Kanakorn Pianchana, a judge in Yala province, shot himself in court immediately after acquitting five Muslim defendants from Thailand's deep south on murder charges. Before shooting himself, Kanakorn read a statement stating that he had been under intense pressure by superiors to find the five guilty despite a lack of evidence.

F2. Does due process prevail in civil and criminal matters? 1 / 4

Restrictions implemented by the NCPO and retained by the current semicivilian government severely undermine due process rights. Orders issued in 2015 permitted the detention of individuals without charge for up to seven days, and expanded the military's authority in law enforcement, permitting them to arrest, detain, and investigate crimes related to the monarchy and national security, including drug-related crimes. In 2019, much of this authority was transferred from the junta to a newly empowered Internal Security Operations Command (ISOC), which can also summon and detain individuals without a warrant. With the transfer of power from military rule to a semicivilian government, all court cases involving offenses against junta orders were transferred from military to civilian courts.

F3. Is there protection from the illegitimate use of physical force and freedom from war and insurgencies? 1 / 4

The police and military often operate with impunity, which is exacerbated by the absence of any law that explicitly prohibits torture. While most of the country is free from terrorism or insurgency, a combination of martial law and emergency rule has been in effect for over a decade in the four southernmost provinces, where Malay Muslims form a majority and a separatist insurgency has been ongoing since the 1940s. Civilians are regularly targeted in shootings, bombings, and arson attacks, and insurgents have focused on schools and teachers as symbols of the Thai state. Counterinsurgency operations have involved the indiscriminate detention of thousands of suspected militants and sympathizers, and there are long-standing and credible reports of torture and other human rights violations, including extrajudicial killings, by both government forces and insurgents.

Following the 2019 elections, physical attacks on democracy activists by masked assailants widely assumed to be tied to the government increased, with no credible investigations by Thai authorities into any of these assaults.

Extraterritorial executions and disappearances of Thai dissidents-in-exile have also increased in recent years. In December 2018, the bodies of two prominent Thai dissidents in exile in Laos were found stuffed with concrete on the banks of the Mekong River along the Lao-Thai border. In June 2020, Wanchalerm Satsaksit, an exiled Thai activist living in Cambodia, was disappeared off a street in Phnom Penh, presumably by agents connected to the Thai state, and remained missing at year's end.

F4. Do laws, policies, and practices guarantee equal treatment of various segments of the population? 2 / 4

In Thailand's north, so-called hill tribes are not fully integrated into society. Many individuals lack formal citizenship, which renders them ineligible to vote, own land, attend state schools, or receive protection under labor laws. Thailand is known for its tolerance of LGBT+ people, though societal acceptance is higher for tourists and expatriates than for nationals, and unequal treatment and stigmatization remain challenges. Women face discrimination in employment, a problem that was highlighted by the decision of the Royal Police Cadet Academy in 2018 to ban female cadets.

Thailand has not ratified the UN convention on refugees, who risk detention as unauthorized migrants and often lack access to asylum procedures. In 2019, a Lao democracy activist was disappeared from his home in Bangkok, and a Vietnamese journalist who had applied for refugee status was allegedly abducted in Bangkok and returned to Vietnam, likely with the assistance of the Thai state. Antimigrant sentiment in Thailand flared following a coronavirus outbreak in December 2020 thought to have originated in a market near Bangkok where many migrants work.

G. PERSONAL AUTONOMY AND INDIVIDUAL RIGHTS: 10 / 16
G1. Do individuals enjoy freedom of movement, including the ability to change their place of residence, employment, or education? 3 / 4

Thai citizens generally have freedom of travel and choice of residence. However, travel may be restricted in areas affected by civil conflict, and in 2020 freedom of movement was greatly curtailed by the emergency decree rules issued in response to the COVID-19 pandemic.

G2. Are individuals able to exercise the right to own property and establish private businesses without undue interference from state or nonstate actors? 2 / 4

The rights to property and to establish businesses are protected by law, though in practice business activity is affected by bureaucratic delays, and at times by the influence of security forces and organized crime. Court cases related to land and natural resources, particularly those deemed by the junta to be vital to the country's economic development, are susceptible to political interference.

G3. Do individuals enjoy personal social freedoms, including choice of marriage partner and size of family, protection from domestic violence, and control over appearance? 3 / 4

While women have the same legal rights as men, they are vulnerable to domestic abuse and rape, and victims rarely report attacks to authorities, who frequently discourage women from pursuing criminal charges against perpetrators.

G4. Do individuals enjoy equality of opportunity and freedom from economic exploitation? 2 / 4

Exploitation and trafficking of Thailand's large migrant worker underclass and refugees from Myanmar, Cambodia, and Laos are serious and ongoing problems, as are child and sweatshop labor. Sex trafficking remains a problem in which some state officials are complicit. However, the government has made some efforts to prosecute and seize the assets of those suspected of involvement in human trafficking, including police officers and local officials.

Thai companies facing criticism for human rights violations, labor rights abuses, and migrant rights violations continue to file libel lawsuits against activists and human rights defenders. In recent years, poultry producer Thammakaset has filed more than 20 criminal and civil complaints against a wide variety of civil society critics.

Timor-Leste

Population: 1,300,000
Capital: Dili
Freedom Status: Free
Electoral Democracy: Yes

Overview: Timor-Leste has held competitive elections and undergone peaceful transfers of power, but its democratic institutions remain fragile, and disputes among the major personalities from the independence struggle dominate political affairs. Judicial independence and due process are undermined by serious capacity deficits and political influence.

KEY DEVELOPMENTS IN 2020

- The country's governing coalition collapsed after the National Congress for the Reconstruction of Timor-Leste (CNRT) abstained on a budget vote in January. While the CNRT secured a coalition agreement in February, the agreement collapsed in April when the Party for the Enhancement of Timorese National Unity (KHUNTO) broke ranks. A new coalition was formed in May, with Prime Minister Taur Matan Ruak keeping his post.
- The government imposed a COVID-19-related state of emergency in late March, a week after the first case was detected in the country. The state of emergency remained in effect through year's end, and external borders were largely closed to nonresidents. Authorities reported 44 cases and no deaths to the World Health Organization (WHO) by year's end.

POLITICAL RIGHTS: 33 / 40 (+1)

A. ELECTORAL PROCESS: 11 / 12

A1. Was the current head of government or other chief national authority elected through free and fair elections? 4 / 4

The directly elected president is a largely symbolic figure, with formal powers limited to the right to veto legislation and make certain appointments. The president may serve up to two five-year terms. Francisco Guterres, known as Lú-Olo, of the Revolutionary Front for an Independent East Timor (Fretilin) was elected president in 2017, following a campaign period a European Union (EU) observer mission praised for its generally peaceful conduct. The observers also called the election well administered.

The leader of the majority party or coalition in Parliament becomes prime minister and serves as head of government. In June 2018, former independence fighter and former president José Maria Vasconcelos, popularly known as Taur Matan Ruak, was sworn in as prime minister.

A2. Were the current national legislative representatives elected through free and fair elections? 4 / 4

Members of the 65-seat, unicameral Parliament are directly elected and serve five-year terms. Because the minority government seated after the 2017 election could not pass a budget, the president dissolved Parliament in January 2018 and called new elections, which were held that May. The sitting opposition parties—the CNRT, KHUNTO, and the People's Liberation Party (PLP)—formed the Change for Progress Alliance (AMP) coalition and won an outright majority of 34 seats. Fretilin won 23, the Democratic Party won 5, and the Democratic Development Front won 3. An EU observer mission called the elections "transparent, well-managed and credible," and they were generally peaceful and orderly, despite a few violent incidents during the campaign period.

Parliament failed to approve a budget in January 2020 after the CNRT abstained. The CNRT, led by former prime minister Xanana Gusmão, then left the governing coalition, securing an agreement of its own in February. That effort failed in April, when KHUNTO—which originally supported the CNRT—broke from the alliance to support an extension of the COVID-19 state of emergency. A new coalition including the PLP, KHUNTO, and Fretilin was finalized in May, with Taur Matan Ruak remaining as prime minister.

A3. Are the electoral laws and framework fair, and are they implemented impartially by the relevant election management bodies? 3 / 4

The 2017 and 2018 EU election observation missions generally praised the National Election Commission for its oversight of the years' polls but expressed concern that changes to the election laws in 2017 somewhat reduced its supervisory responsibilities. Provisions governing elections are found across several pieces of legislation, and observers have called for legal mandates governing elections to be harmonized into a more coherent framework.

B. POLITICAL PLURALISM AND PARTICIPATION: 14 / 16

B1. Do the people have the right to organize in different political parties or other competitive political groupings of their choice, and is the system free of undue obstacles to the rise and fall of these competing parties or groupings? 4 / 4

Political parties are generally free to operate. Some campaign-finance regulations favor larger parties. These include a lack of spending caps and a system in which government campaign subsidies are awarded after elections, according to the number of votes a party has won.

Two new parties, the youth-aligned KHUNTO and the PLP, concentrated enough support ahead of the 2017 elections to win 13 legislative seats between them that year. They joined AMP in the 2018 elections and formed a governing coalition with Fretilin in May 2020.

B2. Is there a realistic opportunity for the opposition to increase its support or gain power through elections? 4 / 4

The 2018 national elections marked the third time since independence that governing power transferred between parties.

While some smaller parties hold seats in Parliament, parties associated with the independence movement continue to dominate politics. Fretilin participated in governments formed in 2017 and 2020, while the CNRT participated in AMP when that coalition entered government in 2018. The PLP, which is led by Taur Matan Ruak, participated in the 2018 and 2020 governments.

B3. Are the people's political choices free from domination by forces that are external to the political sphere, or by political forces that employ extrapolitical means? 3 / 4

Politics continue to be dominated by independence-movement figures who have formed political parties. Veterans often serve as power brokers and organizers, while local village leaders are known to mobilize voters despite their ostensible nonpartisan status.

B4. Do various segments of the population (including ethnic, racial, religious, gender, LGBT+, and other relevant groups) have full political rights and electoral opportunities? 3 / 4

Ethnic minorities are generally well represented in politics.

Some 38.5 percent of parliamentarians are women. One-third of electoral-list candidates must be female. Women have overwhelmingly expressed the opinion that there would be few if any women candidates on party lists in the absence of parity laws. Women have also been underrepresented at the local level and within the leadership of political parties.

C. FUNCTIONING OF GOVERNMENT: 8 / 12 (+1)

C1. Do the freely elected head of government and national legislative representatives determine the policies of the government? 4 / 4 (+1)

In 2017 and 2018, the government held competitive and peaceful elections without the supervision of a UN mission that had been deployed to help restore security following a 2006 political crisis.

Governments have fallen over their inability to pass budgets in recent years; Parliament was dissolved in early 2018 for this reason. AMP was disrupted after it was unable to pass a budget in January 2020. A 2020 budget was passed in October and a 2021 budget was successfully passed in December.

Six cabinet posts had gone unfilled since 2018, when Lú-Olo rejected several nominees. Taur Matan Ruak announced nominees for those posts, including the health, commerce, and finance ministries, in late April 2020. Nominees were officially appointed in May.

The government was criticized by former president José Ramos-Horta and Fretilin leader Mari Alkatiri for continually extending pandemic-related states of emergency, despite the country's apparent success in containing the virus's spread.

Score Change: The score improved from 3 to 4 because the incumbent prime minister was able to form a new coalition and stabilize the government, filling key positions that had remained vacant since 2018.

C2. Are safeguards against official corruption strong and effective? 2 / 4

The World Bank estimates that Timor-Leste loses from 1.5 to 2 percent of gross domestic product annually to corruption. Anticorruption bodies lack enough funding to operate effectively. The independent Anti-Corruption Commission was established in 2009 and has no powers of arrest or prosecution, relying on the prosecutor general, with input from police and the courts, to follow up on corruption investigations. However, a new anticorruption law, which includes protections for whistleblowers, was gazetted in August 2020.

C3. Does the government operate with openness and transparency? 2 / 4

While the state has attempted to make budgets more accessible, procurement processes remain largely opaque. Requests for public information are not always granted, and at times require applicants to undertake inconvenient travel. Information is often issued exclusively in Portuguese, which most Timorese do not speak.

CIVIL LIBERTIES: 39 / 60
D. FREEDOM OF EXPRESSION AND BELIEF: 14 / 16
D1. Are there free and independent media? 3 / 4

While media freedom is constitutionally protected, domestic media outlets are vulnerable to political pressure due to their reliance on government financial support, in a small media market with limited nongovernmental sources of support. Journalists are often treated with suspicion, particularly by government officials, and self-censor. However, in recent years, journalists have been more willing to produce articles critical of the government.

In June 2020, the government proposed the criminalization of defamation. Reporters Without Borders (RSF) called for the proposal's withdrawal later that month. The Timor-Leste Press Union also voiced its opposition that month. In August, Lú-Olo stated the proposal was not a priority for the government, though it had not been officially withdrawn.

D2. Are individuals free to practice and express their religious faith or nonbelief in public and private? 3 / 4

Freedom of religion is protected in the constitution, and Timor-Leste is a secular state. Approximately 98 percent of the population is Roman Catholic. Protestants and Muslims have reported some cases of discrimination and harassment.

D3. Is there academic freedom, and is the educational system free from extensive political indoctrination? 4 / 4

Academic freedom is generally respected.

D4. Are individuals free to express their personal views on political or other sensitive topics without fear of surveillance or retribution? 4 / 4

There are few constraints on open and free private discussion, and citizens are free to discuss political and social issues. Topics related to the 2006 unrest, in which armed clashes between the police and mobilized civilian groups resulted in numerous deaths and the displacement of some 150,000 people, remain sensitive.

E. ASSOCIATIONAL AND ORGANIZATIONAL RIGHTS: 8 / 12

E1. Is there freedom of assembly? 3 / 4

Freedom of assembly is constitutionally guaranteed. While it is generally respected in practice, some laws can be invoked to restrict peaceful gatherings. Demonstrations deemed to be "questioning constitutional order," or disparaging the reputations of the head of state and other government officials, are prohibited. Demonstrations must be authorized in advance, and laws restrict how close they can be to government buildings and critical infrastructure.

Public gatherings were banned in March 2020 when the government imposed a COVID-19-related state of emergency. A state of emergency remained in force at year's end.

E2. Is there freedom for nongovernmental organizations, particularly those that are engaged in human rights- and governance-related work? 3 / 4

Nongovernmental organizations (NGOs) can generally operate without interference, although all registered NGOs receiving government or donor funds are under the oversight of the Ministry of Planning and Finance. Few NGOs operate outside of the capital.

E3. Is there freedom for trade unions and similar professional or labor organizations? 2 / 4

Workers, other than police and military personnel, are permitted to form and join labor unions and bargain collectively, though a 2011 law requires written notification of demands and allows for five days for a response from employers in advance of striking. If employers do not respond or if an agreement is not reached within 20 days, then five days' notice is required for a strike. In practice, few workers are unionized due to high levels of unemployment and informal economic activity.

F. RULE OF LAW: 8 / 16

F1. Is there an independent judiciary? 2 / 4

Concerns over judicial independence remain for politically sensitive cases, and there is still reported political interference in the judicial system.

After independence, the judicial system depended on contracted foreign judges and lawyers. In 2014, however, the government terminated contracts and visas of foreigners working in judicial, prosecutorial, and anticorruption institutions. As a result, legal proceedings in some courts were delayed or forced to restart with new personnel, and the Legal and Judicial Training Centre was closed. Later, a 2017 law explicitly permitting foreign judges allowed training courses for Timorese judges to recommence after a three-year interruption.

F2. Does due process prevail in civil and criminal matters? 1 / 4

Due process rights are often restricted or denied, owing in part to a dearth of resources and personnel. The training of new magistrates following the 2014 dismissals of foreign judges has been slow, resulting in significant case backlogs, although this is improving with the resumption of training programs. The use of Portuguese for court administration poses an obstacle, and a shortage of Portuguese interpreters often forces the adjournment of trials.

Cases involving past human rights abuses are required by law to be heard by a panel including two international judges, though the 2014 dismissals interrupted these cases.

Alternative methods of dispute resolution and customary law are widely used, though they lack enforcement mechanisms and have other significant shortcomings, including unequal treatment of women.

Geographical access to courts remains a challenge. Many municipalities have no fixed courts and rely on mobile services. The government has established mobile courts as an interim measure and has announced plans for the development of a hybrid justice system, with more harmonization between formal and customary dispute resolution mechanisms.

F3. Is there protection from the illegitimate use of physical force and freedom from war and insurgencies? 3 / 4

Police officers and soldiers are regularly accused of excessive force and abuse of power, though the courts have had some success in prosecuting offenders. Public perception of the police has improved in recent years, as have general feelings of security.

F4. Do laws, policies, and practices guarantee equal treatment of various segments of the population? 2 / 4

While hate crimes based on sexual orientation are considered an aggravating circumstance in the penal code, other protections against discrimination for LGBT+ people are lacking. Gay men and transgender women have particular trouble accessing employment opportunities due to low rates of access to education and discrimination. Lesbian, bisexual, and transgender women report cases of extreme physical violence from strangers and family members, including cases of "corrective" rape and forced marriage or relationships with members of the opposite sex. Equal rights for women are constitutionally guaranteed, but discrimination and gender inequality persist in practice and in customary law.

Religious minorities have reported difficulties in having marriage and birth certificates issued by religious entities readily accepted by the authorities. There have been recent complaints of discrimination against Muslims in civil-service hiring.

G. PERSONAL AUTONOMY AND INDIVIDUAL RIGHTS: 9 / 16
G1. Do individuals enjoy freedom of movement, including the ability to change their place of residence, employment, or education? 3 / 4

Citizens generally enjoy unrestricted travel, though travel by land to the enclave of Oecusse is hampered by visa requirements and Indonesian and Timorese checkpoints. Individuals enjoy free choice of residence and employment, but unemployment rates are high, especially among youth, and most of the population still relies on subsistence farming. External borders were largely closed for much of 2020 as part of the government's COVID-19 response.

G2. Are individuals able to exercise the right to own property and establish private businesses without undue interference from state or nonstate actors? 2 / 4

Timorese have the right to establish businesses. However, practical aspects of establishing and operating a business are complicated by inefficiencies that make it difficult to gain appropriate permits and enforce contracts, as well as difficulties in obtaining credit.

Property rights are complicated by past conflicts and the unclear status of communal or customary land rights. According to a 2019 survey conducted by the Asia Foundation, land problems remain the biggest reported security issue in Timor-Leste, with signs that land-related disputes have increased since 2015. There is no formal mechanism to address competing claims. A national land law designed to establish formal tenure and to help resolve disputes through arbitration was enacted in 2017, but still requires several implementing regulations.

G3. Do individuals enjoy personal social freedoms, including choice of marriage partner and size of family, protection from domestic violence, and control over appearance? 2 / 4

Gender-based violence (GBV) and domestic violence remain widespread. A survey conducted by the Asia Foundation in 2016 found that 59 percent of girls and women aged 15–49 had experienced violence by an intimate partner and 14 percent had experienced rape by someone other than their partner. Civil society groups have criticized the courts' use of prison sentences for only the most severe and injurious such cases, and few reported cases are investigated. A lack of GBV training hampers investigatory procedures into such cases, including investigators' failure to recognize or collect evidence.

According to a 2017 UN Population Fund report, 24 percent of women in Timor-Leste have a child by the time they reach the age of 20, while 19 percent of women aged 20–24 are married by the time they turn 18.

G4. Do individuals enjoy equality of opportunity and freedom from economic exploitation? 2 / 4

Timor-Leste is both a source and destination country for human trafficking. Timorese from rural areas are vulnerable to human trafficking for sexual exploitation and domestic servitude, and children are sometimes placed in bonded labor. The government has increased its efforts to prosecute offenders, including by promulgating the 2017 Law on Preventing and Combating Human Trafficking. However, authorities investigated only 13 trafficking cases in 2019; that figure stood at 65 in 2018, 267 in 2017, and 176 in 2016. No trafficking convictions have been recorded in several years.

Togo

Population: 8,300,000
Capital: Lomé
Freedom Status: Partly Free
Electoral Democracy: No

Overview: While regular multiparty elections have taken place since 1992, Togo's politics have been controlled since 1963 by the late Gnassingbé Eyadéma and his son, current president Faure Gnassingbé. Advantages including security services dominated by the president's ethnic group and malapportioned election districts have helped Gnassingbé and his party retain power. Opposition calls for constitutional and electoral reforms have been harshly repressed for years.

KEY DEVELOPMENTS IN 2020

- President Gnassingbé secured a fourth term in a February election, but the political opposition rejected the official results, alleging fraud. Agbéyomé Kodjo, the main opposition candidate, was arrested in April along with multiple members of his party after he claimed to be the legitimate president. He subsequently went into hiding.
- Beginning in March, the government adopted temporary measures to address the COVID-19 pandemic, including international travel restrictions, curfews, and a

ban on large gatherings. Some of the rules remained in place through the end of the year, by which time about 3,600 confirmed cases and nearly 70 deaths had been reported.

POLITICAL RIGHTS: 15 / 40 (−1)

A. ELECTORAL PROCESS: 4 / 12 (−1)

A1. Was the current head of government or other chief national authority elected through free and fair elections? 1 / 4 (−1)

The president, who serves as head of state and holds most executive power, is elected for five-year terms. The president appoints the prime minister, who serves as head of government. Presidential term limits were eliminated in 2002, then restored through a constitutional amendment in 2019; they did not apply retroactively, meaning the incumbent could seek two additional terms. The two-round presidential election system, requiring a runoff if no candidate wins a majority in the first round, was also restored.

Faure Gnassingbé—who was initially installed as president by the military after the death of his father, Gnassingbé Eyadéma, in 2005—secured a fourth term in the February 2020 election, credited with 71 percent of the vote in the first round against six challengers. Permits for domestic civil society groups to deploy observers were denied or revoked, representatives of the US-based National Democratic Institute were expelled before the election, and mobile messaging applications were blocked on election day. A relatively small number of observers from the African Union and the Economic Community of West African States (ECOWAS) were granted entry and produced largely uncritical reports.

The runner-up, former prime minister Agbeyome Kodjo of the opposition Patriotic Movement for Democracy and Development (MPDD), was credited with 19 percent of the vote. He and other opposition members alleged that the election was stolen, accusing the government of using fake polling stations and engaging in ballot-box stuffing. In the aftermath of the voting, security forces surrounded Kodjo's house and that of a retired archbishop to prevent them from leading demonstrations.

Jean-Pierre Fabre of the National Alliance for Change (ANC), who won 35 percent of the vote in the 2015 presidential election and whose party placed second in 2019 local elections, received less than 5 percent, according to official results. The Independent National Electoral Commission (CENI) reported that turnout had increased from 61 percent in 2015 to over 76 percent in 2020; critics questioned those figures given the scale of recent antigovernment protests.

After Kodjo's lawsuit challenging the election results was rejected by the Constitutional Court in March, his parliamentary immunity was lifted, and he was arrested and temporarily detained in April—along with other members of his party—for asserting that he was the legitimate president. Upon his release, Kodjo went into hiding, and the government issued an international warrant for his arrest in July. He reportedly remained in hiding at year's end.

Score Change: The score declined from 2 to 1 because the presidential election was marred by the exclusion of civil society observers, the blocking of communication tools, and allegations of fraud and vote rigging.

A2. Were the current national legislative representatives elected through free and fair elections? 2 / 4

The constitution calls for a bicameral legislature, but the Senate has never been established. Members of the current 91-seat National Assembly, which exercises all legislative powers, were elected for five-year terms through proportional representation in multimember districts. In the 2018 elections, the main opposition parties led a 14-party boycott, citing a number of unmet demands regarding constitutional and electoral reform. Gnassingbé's Union for the Republic (UNIR) won 59 of the 91 seats, down from 62 in 2013. A party that led the opposition before aligning itself with the government in 2010, the Union of Forces for Change (UFC), won 7 seats. Independents took 18 seats, and smaller parties captured the remainder. Observers from the African Union and ECOWAS said the elections had been held "properly" in a "calm environment," though opposition protests had been violently suppressed in the weeks before the balloting, and voter turnout was low in opposition-leaning areas.

Municipal councillors were elected in 2019 in the first local elections since 1987. The UNIR won more than 60 percent of the council seats; the ANC placed second.

A3. Are the electoral laws and framework fair, and are they implemented impartially by the relevant election management bodies? 1 / 4

Elections are organized and supervised by CENI, whose membership by law should be balanced between the ruling party and the opposition. For the 2020 presidential election, however, only two of the 19 members were from the opposition. Among other irregularities on election day, opposition members were reportedly denied access to some polling places to monitor the vote, and CENI refused to publish detailed results for each precinct. The Constitutional Court, responsible for verifying election results, is also considered to be stacked with close allies of the president. Prominent civil society groups have joined major opposition parties in their calls for a reliable electoral register, fairly apportioned legislative districts, a reorganized CENI, a more independent Constitutional Court, and the announcement of precinct-based election results.

In 2019, the new UNIR-dominated National Assembly adopted a constitutional amendment that established a two-term limit for the presidency with no retroactive effect, allowing Gnassingbé to seek reelection in 2020 and 2025. Other amendments included two-round presidential elections, six-year terms and a two-term limit for lawmakers, and immunity for former presidents regarding acts committed during their terms.

B. POLITICAL PLURALISM AND PARTICIPATION: 6 / 16

B1. Do the people have the right to organize in different political parties or other competitive political groupings of their choice, and is the system free of undue obstacles to the rise and fall of these competing parties or groupings? 2 / 4

There is a multiparty political system, and opposition parties are generally free to form and operate. Candidates can also run as independents. However, the dominance of the UNIR undermines the visibility and competitiveness of other parties. Opposition members are sometimes arrested in connection with peaceful political activities.

In 2017 and 2018, antigovernment protests organized by opposition parties were suppressed with deadly force, and opposition supporters were arrested and tortured. During the run-up to the 2020 presidential election, opposition candidates faced obstacles such as denial of permits to hold rallies. In the weeks after the balloting, several opposition leaders were arrested.

B2. Is there a realistic opportunity for the opposition to increase its support or gain power through elections? 1 / 4

Gnassingbé's family has controlled Togo's powerful presidency since the 1960s. He and the UNIR have retained power thanks in large part to the structure of the electoral system, including district malapportionment in legislative elections and their de facto control over institutions such as the CENI and the Constitutional Court. The return to the two-round presidential election system was not helpful in unifying the opposition during the 2020 contest, as Gnassingbé claimed an outright victory in the first round.

Genuine opposition parties have no presence in the National Assembly following their boycott of the 2018 elections, though they did gain mayoralties and municipal council seats in the 2019 local elections.

B3. Are the people's political choices free from domination by forces that are external to the political sphere, or by political forces that employ extrapolitical means? 1 / 4

The government is dominated by members of Gnassingbé's Kabyé ethnic group, who also make up the vast majority of security personnel. In 2005, the military installed Gnassingbé as president, in violation of the constitution. Since 2017, increased activity by the opposition has been met with increased use of force by the security apparatus. Hundreds of activists have been arrested, and many tortured. In the weeks before the 2018 elections, security forces repeatedly used live ammunition against opposition protesters, killing several people. After the 2020 presidential election, troops surrounded the houses of Kodjo and retired archbishop Philippe Kpodzro after they called for protests.

While security forces defend the regime through intimidation, the UNIR has been accused of relying on patronage and financial incentives, including the distribution of benefits to buy votes at election time.

B4. Do various segments of the population (including ethnic, racial, religious, gender, LGBT+, and other relevant groups) have full political rights and electoral opportunities? 2 / 4

The Éwé, Togo's largest ethnic group, have historically been excluded from positions of influence; they are prominent within the opposition. Since 2010, the community has been politically split, as the Éwé-dominated UFC reached a power-sharing agreement with the government while the majority remained loyal to opposition forces.

Women face some societal pressure that discourages their active and independent political participation. Only 16 percent of the National Assembly members elected in 2018 were women. Candidate registration fees were halved for women ahead of the 2019 local elections. In September 2020, Victoire Tomegah Dogbé became the first woman to serve as Togo's prime minister, and she named women to a record 30 percent of the ministerial posts in her cabinet.

C. FUNCTIONING OF GOVERNMENT: 5 / 12

C1. Do the freely elected head of government and national legislative representatives determine the policies of the government? 2 / 4

The president holds most policymaking power, and the National Assembly, which is controlled by the ruling party, does not serve as an effective check on executive authority. A pattern of flawed elections has undermined the legitimacy of both the executive and the legislature.

C2. Are safeguards against official corruption strong and effective? 1 / 4

Corruption is a serious and long-standing problem. The government has adopted legislation that is ostensibly designed to reduce corruption, such as a 2018 law on money laundering and the funding of terrorism, but these legal changes have not been followed by effective enforcement or convictions of high-ranking officials. The majority of members of the High Authority for the Prevention and Fight against Corruption and Related Offenses (HAPLUCIA) are presidential appointees, raising concerns about the body's independence.

HAPLUCIA cannot prosecute cases itself and must make referrals to the public prosecutor. In recognition of its disappointing performance, the president included a reorganization of the body among his campaign promises ahead of the 2020 election.

C3. Does the government operate with openness and transparency? 2 / 4

A 2016 freedom of information law guarantees the right to access government information, though some information is exempted, and the government does not always respond to requests. Most public officials are not required to disclose their assets.

There is a lack of transparency regarding state tenders. French billionaire Vincent Bolloré was indicted in France in 2018 for allegedly helping Gnassingbé win the 2010 presidential election in exchange for contracts to operate container ports in Lomé. Separately, an investigative media report in June 2020 alleged that officials had embezzled hundreds of millions of dollars in a scheme involving petroleum import contracts. While the government moved to audit the import system in response, the newspaper responsible for the exposé was prosecuted and found guilty of defamation in November.

CIVIL LIBERTIES: 28 / 60
D. FREEDOM OF EXPRESSION AND BELIEF: 9 / 16
D1. Are there free and independent media? 2 / 4

Freedom of the press is guaranteed in the constitution but inconsistently upheld in practice. Although numerous independent media outlets offer a variety of viewpoints, restrictive press laws and a history of impunity for those who commit crimes against journalists encourage self-censorship. There is no mechanism to appeal decisions made by the High Authority for Broadcasting and Communication (HAAC), which can suspend outlets for violations of broadly worded regulations. In March 2020, two newspapers were temporarily suspended for critical reporting on the French government, and a third was suspended for criticizing the first two suspensions. In November, the newspaper *L'Alternative* and its editor were each convicted of defamation and ordered to pay fines for their June report on embezzlement in the petroleum sector. The director of another newspaper, *L'Indépendant Express*, was arrested in late December 2020 after it published a story alleging theft by government ministers.

Police have engaged in violence and other acts of intimidation to discourage press coverage of opposition protests. Authorities have also hampered reporting by cutting mobile phone and internet service during protests; instant messaging apps were blocked on election day in February 2020.

D2. Are individuals free to practice and express their religious faith or nonbelief in public and private? 3 / 4

Religious freedom is constitutionally protected and generally respected in practice. Islam, Roman Catholicism, and Protestant Christianity are recognized by the state as religions; other groups must register as religious associations to receive similar benefits. The registration process has been subject to long delays and a large backlog; approximately 900 applications were pending as of 2020. Senior Catholic clergy are among the government critics who have reportedly been targeted with surveillance software.

D3. Is there academic freedom, and is the educational system free from extensive political indoctrination? 2 / 4

Academics are generally able to engage in political discussions. However, security forces have repeatedly used violence and arrests to quell student protests.

D4. Are individuals free to express their personal views on political or other sensitive topics without fear of surveillance or retribution? 2 / 4

Citizens are able to speak openly in private discussion, but they may be arrested on incitement or other charges for speaking critically about the government to journalists or human rights organizations.

A 2018 cybersecurity law criminalized publication of false information and breaches of public morality, among other problematic provisions that could affect freedom of expression online. The law also granted police greater authority to conduct electronic surveillance. It was reported in 2020 that some government critics have been targeted with surveillance software on their mobile devices.

E. ASSOCIATIONAL AND ORGANIZATIONAL RIGHTS: 6 / 12

E1. Is there freedom of assembly? 1 / 4

While the constitution provides for freedom of assembly, a number of laws allow for its restriction, and police have periodically used deadly violence to disperse assemblies in practice. A 2011 legal reform retained problematic rules on prior notification for demonstrations and limits on their timing. A 2015 revision of the criminal code penalized participation in and organization of protests that had not gone through the necessary administrative procedures. In 2019, the parliament imposed new limits on the timing and location of public demonstrations, and allowed authorities to restrict protests based on the availability of security personnel.

Protests organized in 2017 and 2018 to demand the restoration of presidential term limits attracted hundreds of thousands of participants. Authorities responded with temporary bans and other administrative restrictions, and in some cases police used disproportionate force, resulting in multiple deaths, arrests, and cases of torture.

During the 2020 presidential election campaign, authorities denied permits for several opposition rallies as well as civil society events to protest flawed electoral procedures. In the postelection period, after Kodjo and Kpodzro called for protests, security forces surrounded their homes and restricted access to parts of the capital. Demonstrators who attempted to assemble were dispersed by police, reportedly using excessive force.

E2. Is there freedom for nongovernmental organizations, particularly those that are engaged in human rights- and governance-related work? 2 / 4

Nongovernmental organizations are subject to registration rules that have sometimes been enforced arbitrarily to suppress activism on sensitive topics, such as torture and the rights of LGBT+ people. Several civil society leaders have been arrested and detained for their roles in the protest movement that began in 2017. In April 2020, two members of an antitorture organization were arrested while observing security forces near Kodjo's home, then released without charge. The mobile phones of prodemocracy activists have been targeted with surveillance software.

E3. Is there freedom for trade unions and similar professional or labor organizations? 3 / 4

The government generally protects workers' rights to form and join labor unions, though unions have fewer legal protections in the country's special export-processing zone.

F. RULE OF LAW: 6 / 16

F1. Is there an independent judiciary? 2 / 4

The constitution provides for an independent judiciary, but in practice courts are heavily influenced by the presidency. The Constitutional Court in particular, a majority of which is appointed by the president and the UNIR-controlled National Assembly, is believed to be partial to the ruling party. Judges on other courts are appointed by the executive based on the recommendations of a judicial council, which in turn is dominated by senior judges.

F2. Does due process prevail in civil and criminal matters? 1 / 4

Executive influence and judicial corruption limit constitutional rights to a fair trial. Dozens of people arrested for participating in antigovernment protests in recent years have been charged, tried, and convicted in hasty proceedings. Detainees in general often have no access to counsel.

Corruption and inefficiency are widespread among the police, and there are also reports of arbitrary arrest. The 2018 cybersecurity law contains vague terrorism and treason provisions with heavy prison sentences and grants additional powers to the police without adequate judicial oversight.

F3. Is there protection from the illegitimate use of physical force and freedom from war and insurgencies? 2 / 4

Prisons suffer from overcrowding and inadequate food and medical care, sometimes resulting in deaths among inmates from preventable or curable diseases. The government periodically releases prisoners to address overcrowding, but the process by which individuals are chosen for release is not transparent.

The 2015 penal code criminalizes torture, and a 2016 revision defined torture in line with the UN Convention against Torture. However, instances of torture by security forces continue to be reported, including against participants in recent antigovernment demonstrations.

Islamist militants may present a growing threat to security in Togo, with some fighters from Burkina Faso reportedly taking refuge in the country.

F4. Do laws, policies, and practices guarantee equal treatment of various segments of the population? 1 / 4

Although women and men are ostensibly equal under the law, women continue to experience discrimination, and their opportunities for employment and education are limited. Official and societal discrimination has persisted against people with disabilities, certain regional and ethnic groups, and LGBT+ people, to whom antidiscrimination laws do not apply. Same-sex sexual activity is a criminal offense, and while the law is rarely enforced, LGBT+ people face police harassment.

G. PERSONAL AUTONOMY AND INDIVIDUAL RIGHTS: 7 / 16

G1. Do individuals enjoy freedom of movement, including the ability to change their place of residence, employment, or education? 2 / 4

The law provides for freedom of internal movement and foreign travel, but these rights are sometimes restricted by the authorities in practice. Domestic travel can involve arbitrary traffic stops at which police collect bribes.

The government's response to COVID-19 during 2020 included some international travel restrictions and curfews. Security personnel allegedly used excessive force while enforcing these rules, resulting in several reports of civilian deaths.

G2. Are individuals able to exercise the right to own property and establish private businesses without undue interference from state or nonstate actors? 2 / 4

The country has made regulatory improvements to ease processes such as the registration of companies and property, but in general the business environment is poorly administered, creating opportunities for corruption and driving much economic activity into the informal sector. Women and men do not have equal inheritance rights under traditional or customary law, which is observed mainly in rural areas.

G3. Do individuals enjoy personal social freedoms, including choice of marriage partner and size of family, protection from domestic violence, and control over appearance? 1 / 4

Customary law puts women at a disadvantage regarding matters such as widowhood, divorce, and child custody. Polygamy is widely practiced and legally recognized. Child marriage remains a problem in some regions. Rape is illegal but rarely reported and, if reported, often ignored by authorities. Domestic violence, which is widespread, is not specifically addressed by the law. UN data from 2017 indicated that about 3 percent of women and girls aged 15 to 49 have undergone genital mutilation or cutting, which is illegal and less prevalent among younger girls.

G4. Do individuals enjoy equality of opportunity and freedom from economic exploitation? 2 / 4

Protections against exploitative labor conditions, including rules on working hours, are poorly enforced, and much of the workforce is informally employed. Child labor is common in the agricultural sector and in certain urban trades; some children are subjected to forced labor. According to the US State Department, the government has made efforts to address human trafficking for forced labor and sexual exploitation, but it has struggled to secure convictions against perpetrators.

Tonga

Population: 100,000
Capital: Nuku'alofa
Freedom Status: Free
Electoral Democracy: Yes

Overview: Tonga's constitutional monarchy has featured a prime minister backed by a mostly elected parliament since 2010. However, the king retains important powers, including the authority to veto legislation, dissolve the parliament, and appoint judicial officials. While civil liberties are generally protected, ongoing problems include political pressure on the state broadcaster and land laws that discriminate against women.

KEY DEVELOPMENTS IN 2020

- In December, Tonga's Deputy Prime Minister Sione Vuna Fa'otusia resigned after signaling his support for an impending vote of no-confidence against Prime Minister Pōhiva Tu'i'onetoa. The no-confidence motion was based on seven allegations of wrongdoing against Tu'i'onetoa, mostly involving government spending.
- Police enforced public health restrictions as a part of the state of emergency declared in March in order to prevent the spread of COVID-19. By April, 568 people had been arrested for breaching lockdown rules. The enforced restrictions were implemented even though there were no confirmed cases of the coronavirus throughout the year, according to government statistics provided to the World Health Organization (WHO).

POLITICAL RIGHTS: 30 / 40

A. ELECTORAL PROCESS: 9 / 12

A1. Was the current head of government or other chief national authority elected through free and fair elections? 3 / 4

Though the monarch is no longer the chief executive authority, he retains significant powers, including the ability to veto legislation and dissolve the parliament. King 'Aho'eitu Tupou VI came to the throne in 2012 and is known to hold more conservative views than his late brother and predecessor, George Tupou V.

The prime minister, who chooses the cabinet, is formally appointed by the monarch on the recommendation of the parliament. Veteran democracy campaigner 'Akilisi Pōhiva who initially took office in 2014, died in office in September 2019 after a long illness; he was succeeded by finance minister Pōhiva Tu'i'onetoa, who formed a cabinet that included commoners and members of the nobility. In December 2020, members of Parliament initiated a vote of no-confidence procedure against Prime Minister Tu'i'onetoa, the vote for which would be held in January 2021.

A2. Were the current national legislative representatives elected through free and fair elections? 3 / 4

The unicameral Legislative Assembly (Fale Alea) consists of 17 members who are directly elected by commoners, nine noble members elected by their peers, and up to four additional members whom the prime minister may appoint to the cabinet from outside the parliament and who hold their seats ex officio. The speaker is appointed from among the noble members on the recommendation of the assembly.

In the 2017 snap election, Pōhiva and his supporters in the loosely affiliated Democratic Party of the Friendly Islands won 14 of the 17 popularly elected seats, a sizeable gain from their previous share.

A3. Are the electoral laws and framework fair, and are they implemented impartially by the relevant election management bodies? 3 / 4

The Electoral Commission administers elections competently and fairly, though the framework for parliamentary elections falls short of universal suffrage due to the reservation of nine seats for the nobility.

B. POLITICAL PLURALISM AND PARTICIPATION: 14 / 16

B1. Do the people have the right to organize in different political parties or other competitive political groupings of their choice, and is the system free of undue obstacles to the rise and fall of these competing parties or groupings? 4 / 4

A formal party system has yet to develop, and all candidates technically run as independents in their single-member constituencies. Nevertheless, there are no major restrictions on political competition, and in practice politicians have begun to form loose partisan affiliations. Parliamentarians are also known to shift their allegiances; after former prime minister Pōhiva's death in September 2019, four lawmakers that were associated with the Democratic Party of the Friendly Islands defected to the Peoples' Party, including founder Tu'i'onetoa, effectively leaving the former in opposition by year's end. In April 2020, there were reports of further schisms in the Democratic Party because of the failure to arrange an orderly transition of the leadership after Pōhiva's death. The Democrats supported the motion to initiate a no-confidence vote against Prime Minister Tu'i'onetoa, scheduled for January 2021. The outcome of that vote, if it takes place, could be influenced by the absence of some members of Parliament who are unable to return to Tonga due to COVID-19-related border restrictions.

B2. Is there a realistic opportunity for the opposition to increase its support or gain power through elections? 4 / 4

Rival coalitions led by Pōhiva's popularly elected allies and more conservative politicians of the nobility have alternated in government in recent years. Before Pōhiva took office in 2014, a member of the nobility, Lord Tu'ivakanō, served as prime minister. Prime Minister Tu'i'onetoa governs with the support of popularly elected parliamentarians along with members of the nobility in Parliament.

B3. Are the people's political choices free from domination by forces that are external to the political sphere, or by political forces that employ extrapolitical means? 3 / 4

The monarchy, the nobility, and the country's churches exert considerable political influence, but this has not prevented majority support for prodemocracy candidates in recent elections.

B4. Do various segments of the population (including ethnic, racial, religious, gender, LGBT+, and other relevant groups) have full political rights and electoral opportunities? 3 / 4

Women have the same formal political rights as men, and 15 women ran for seats in the 2017 parliamentary election, but only two won office—an increase from zero in the previous legislature. Cultural biases tend to discourage women's political participation, and women cannot inherit noble titles, meaning the seats reserved for nobility in the parliament are effectively reserved for men. Ethnic minorities face similar obstacles, though the population is mostly homogeneous, and many members of the small Chinese minority have been able to obtain citizenship and its associated political rights.

C. FUNCTIONING OF GOVERNMENT: 7 / 12

C1. Do the freely elected head of government and national legislative representatives determine the policies of the government? 3 / 4

The elected prime minister and his cabinet largely control the formulation and implementation of government policy, but the king continues to rely on a privy council—whose members he appoints himself—for advice regarding the use of his constitutional powers. The Privy Council operates like a shadow government, facilitating a continuing political role for the monarch.

C2. Are safeguards against official corruption strong and effective? 2 / 4

Corruption and abuse of office are serious problems. While public officials and leaders of state-owned companies are sometimes held to account for bribery and other malfeasance, anticorruption mechanisms are generally weak and lacking in resources.

In 2018, Lord Tu'ivakanō was charged with money laundering, perjury, and bribery in a scandal over the sale of passports. Tu'ivakanō appealed for the charges to be dismissed, but the Supreme Court rejected those efforts in October 2019. In April 2020, Tu'ivakanō received a two-year suspended sentence for perjury—he allegedly made false statements about issuing illegal passports to Chinese nationals—and was fined for owning firearms and ammunition without a license. However, upon filing an appeal, Tu'ivakanō was acquitted of the perjury charges in November 2020, after an Appeal Court found that he had not intended to deceive the public. Tu'ivakanō's lost the appeal of the charges for possession of a firearm without a license.

C3. Does the government operate with openness and transparency? 2 / 4

Tonga does not have a law to guarantee public access to government information, which can be difficult to obtain in practice, and officials are not legally obliged to disclose their assets and income. The government has at times resisted public scrutiny of pending policies or auditor general's reports. Nevertheless, the parliament generally operates openly, and the media and civil society are typically able to monitor its proceedings and comment on legislation.

In June 2020, the government announced plans to set up a new National Security and Information Office, in coordination with the police and with ministries in New Zealand and Australia, reportedly to "protect the security of the Tongan people." Critics have claimed that the real objective is to prevent leaks of government information.

In August 2020, media professionals reported that the Ministry of Communication had instituted eight new regulations in May—including a $2,000 Tonga Pa'anga ($867) fine for publishing or broadcasting vaguely defined "sensitive information"—without informing the media industry. The regulations were passed with neither consultation with key stakeholders nor debate in parliament.

CIVIL LIBERTIES: 49 / 60

D. FREEDOM OF EXPRESSION AND BELIEF: 14 / 16

D1. Are there free and independent media? 2 / 4

The constitution guarantees freedom of the press, and a variety of news outlets operate independently, including online. However, politicians have a history of exerting pressure on the media in response to critical coverage.

In May 2020, the Ministry of Communication imposed new regulations that include fines for publishing or broadcasting "sensitive information," a term that is vaguely defined. Journalists argued that the law enables the government to pressure and prevent media outlets and social media users from raising sensitive political issues and critiquing the government. King Tupou VI has a history of supporting media censorship, dating back to his time as prime minister from 2000 to 2006.

D2. Are individuals free to practice and express their religious faith or nonbelief in public and private? 4 / 4

Constitutional protections for religious freedom are generally upheld in practice. Religious groups are not required to register, but those that do receive various benefits. There are some restrictions on commercial activity on Sundays in keeping with a constitutional recognition of the Christian sabbath. Policy guidelines from the Tonga Broadcasting Commission (TBC) bar broadcasts of preaching outside the "mainstream Christian tradition," though this has reportedly not been strictly enforced.

D3. Is there academic freedom, and is the educational system free from extensive political indoctrination? 4 / 4

Academic freedom is generally unrestricted. While there have been reports of self-censorship to avoid friction with the government in the past, no incidents of political interference have been reported in recent years. Tonga hosts one of the regional campuses of the University of the South Pacific as well as the late Tongan scholar Futa Helu's 'Atenisi Institute, which offers tertiary courses. In 2018, Christ's University, which is owned by the Tokaikolo Church and opened in 2015, became Tonga's first locally owned university to be registered and accredited.

D4. Are individuals free to express their personal views on political or other sensitive topics without fear of surveillance or retribution? 4 / 4

The government is not known to monitor personal communications. Though Tongans are generally able to discuss political issues without reprisal, critics saw the May 2020 media regulations as enabling the government to pressure social media users so that they would not raise sensitive political issues. The government began discussing controls over social media after threats were allegedly made against King Tupou IV and his family.

E. ASSOCIATIONAL AND ORGANIZATIONAL RIGHTS: 10 / 12

E1. Is there freedom of assembly? 4 / 4

The constitution protects freedom of assembly, and demonstrations generally remain peaceful. Political protests in 2006 degenerated into violent riots, prompting the government to declare a state of emergency that lasted until early 2011.

E2. Is there freedom for nongovernmental organizations, particularly those that are engaged in human rights- and governance-related work? 3 / 4

Nongovernmental organizations (NGOs) have not reported harassment or other restrictions by the authorities. A number of different laws govern the registration processes for civil society groups, but they are not considered onerous.

E3. Is there freedom for trade unions and similar professional or labor organizations? 3 / 4

Workers have the legal right to organize in trade unions, but implementing regulations have never been issued, meaning the country's various de facto unions generally operate as associations. Tonga joined the International Labour Organization (ILO) in 2016.

F. RULE OF LAW: 12 / 16

F1. Is there an independent judiciary? 3 / 4

The king retains authority over judicial appointments and dismissals. The Judicial Appointments and Discipline Panel, a committee of the privy council, provides advice on appointments, including for the lord chancellor, who has responsibility for administering the courts. The king in privy council has final jurisdiction over cases in the land court relating to hereditary estates and titles.

The judiciary is regarded as largely independent, but the royally appointed attorney general has previously been accused of interfering with judicial rulings. Broader judicial reforms that would have increased the cabinet's influence over judicial appointments were adopted by the parliament in 2014, but the king never gave his assent.

F2. Does due process prevail in civil and criminal matters? 3 / 4

Due process provisions and safeguards against arbitrary arrest and detention are typically respected by the authorities. However, there is no mechanism to guarantee access to counsel for indigent defendants.

The police commissioner, Stephen Caldwell, is a New Zealander. The Police Act of 2010 gives control over the appointment of the police commissioner to the king's privy council, which has raised tensions with elected officials.

F3. Is there protection from the illegitimate use of physical force and freedom from war and insurgencies? 3 / 4

Prison conditions are generally adequate, police brutality is rare, and crime rates remain relatively low. A number of police officers accused of misconduct have been investigated, dismissed, or convicted of crimes in recent years. However, rising public concern has focused on problems including the country's role as a transit point for drug trafficking, drug-related petty crime, and organized crime affecting the Chinese community. Since 2015, Police Commissioner Stephen Caldwell has suspended 64 officers from their duties either for criminal offences or other disciplinary matters. In November 2020, Caldwell released a statement that 21 officers had been dismissed, due to unauthorized absences, failure to complete recruitment requirements, and sexual harassment.

F4. Do laws, policies, and practices guarantee equal treatment of various segments of the population? 3 / 4

The constitution includes a general provision for equality before the law, and this is upheld in many respects. However, women still face some forms of discrimination, including in land and inheritance laws and with regard to employment in practice. Same-sex sexual activity is criminalized, but the ban is not actively enforced.

Continued bias and instances of crime against members of the Chinese minority have been reported, though nothing approaching the scale of the 2006 riots—which targeted Chinese-owned businesses—has occurred since the state of emergency was lifted in 2011.

G. PERSONAL AUTONOMY AND INDIVIDUAL RIGHTS: 13 / 16

G1. Do individuals enjoy freedom of movement, including the ability to change their place of residence, employment, or education? 4 / 4

There are no significant constraints on freedom of movement or the ability to change one's place of residence or employment. Police enforced public health restrictions that were part of the state of emergency declared in March 2020 to prevent the spread of COVID-19, even though there were no confirmed cases of the virus in the country throughout the year. By April, 568 people had been arrested for breaching the lockdown rules.

G2. Are individuals able to exercise the right to own property and establish private businesses without undue interference from state or nonstate actors? 3 / 4

The legal framework generally supports private business activity. However, individuals cannot own or sell land outright, as all land is technically the property of the king. Land rights, once granted by nobles or directly by the crown through an allotment system, can only be leased or inherited, and while women can obtain leases, they are not eligible to receive or inherit land allotments.

G3. Do individuals enjoy personal social freedoms, including choice of marriage partner and size of family, protection from domestic violence, and control over appearance? 3 / 4

Personal social freedoms are typically respected. However, domestic violence remains a problem despite state and civil society efforts to prevent it, and girls as young as 15—the legal minimum age for marriage with parental permission—are sometimes compelled by their parents to marry.

G4. Do individuals enjoy equality of opportunity and freedom from economic exploitation? 3 / 4

The population generally has access to economic opportunities and protection from abusive working conditions, though enforcement of labor laws is affected by resource limitations, and some employers have violated workers' rights. While there is no law specifically regulating child labor, any such work typically entails informal participation in family agriculture and fishing. In August 2020, Tonga signed the ILO's Convention 182, on the Worst Forms of Child Labour.

Trinidad and Tobago

Population: 1,400,000
Capital: Port of Spain
Freedom Status: Free
Electoral Democracy: Yes

Overview: The Republic of Trinidad and Tobago is a parliamentary democracy with vibrant media and civil society sectors. However, organized crime contributes to high levels of violence, and corruption among public officials remains a challenge. Other security concerns center on local adherents of Islamist militant groups. Discrimination against LGBT+ people and violence against women persist, and human trafficking is a significant concern.

KEY DEVELOPMENTS IN 2020

- The incumbent People's National Movement (PNM) led by Prime Minister Keith Rowley won the August general elections with 49 percent of the vote, taking 22 seats. The opposition United National Congress (UNC) earned 47 percent of the vote and 19 seats. Due to the COVID-19 pandemic, no monitoring missions were able to observe the polls. Six constituencies were subject to recounts, causing final results to be delayed by a week.
- In a July press conference, the Minister of National Security claimed that "illegal immigrants" and "boat people"—derogatory terms referring to Venezuelan refugees—presented a potential health risk due to the COVID-19 pandemic. The government targeted asylum seekers with heavier enforcement and created a hotline for residents to report them to report them. Government statistics provided to the World Health Organization (WHO) reported that 7,132 people tested positive for the virus, and 126 people died by year's end.

POLITICAL RIGHTS: 33 / 40

A. ELECTORAL PROCESS: 11 / 12

A1. Was the current head of government or other chief national authority elected through free and fair elections? 4 / 4

The president, the largely ceremonial head of state, is elected to a five-year term by a majority in the combined houses of Parliament. Paula-Mae Weekes, an independent former judge, was elected unopposed in January 2018 and took office that March.

The prime minister, who serves as head of government and is typically the leader of the majority party in Parliament, is appointed by the president. Keith Rowley became prime minister in 2015, after that year's parliamentary elections resulted in a victory for his party, the center-right People's National Movement (PNM). Rowley retained his position after the PNM won the general elections in 2020.

A2. Were the current national legislative representatives elected through free and fair elections? 4 / 4

Parliament consists of the directly elected, 41-member House of Representatives and the 31-member Senate, with members of both houses serving five-year terms. Of the 31 senators, 16 are appointed on the advice of the prime minister, 6 are appointed on the advice of the opposition leader, and 9 are appointed at the president's discretion based on merit.

In the 2020 parliamentary elections, the incumbent PNM won 49 percent of the vote, securing 22 seats. The opposition United National Congress (UNC) took 47 percent of the vote and 19 seats. COVID-19 restrictions prevented observers from monitoring the election. Six constituencies were subject to recounts, causing final results to be delayed by a week.

The semiautonomous island of Tobago has its own House of Assembly, with 12 members elected directly, 3 appointed on the advice of the chief secretary (the island's head of government), and 1 appointed on the advice of the minority leader. The PNM won 10 of the 12 elected seats and the Progressive Democratic Patriots (PDP), a local pro-independence party, won the remainder in the most recent 2017 election.

A3. Are the electoral laws and framework fair, and are they implemented impartially by the relevant election management bodies? 3 / 4

Electoral laws are largely fair. The Elections and Boundaries Commission (EBC) organizes elections and is generally trusted by the public to fulfill its mandate impartially. The EBC recounted the votes in six constituencies after the 2020 election, which were accepted by all parties.

There was no evidence that electoral reforms suggested by 2015 observer missions had been implemented prior to the 2020 elections.

B. POLITICAL PLURALISM AND PARTICIPATION: 13 / 16

B1. Do the people have the right to organize in different political parties or other competitive political groupings of their choice, and is the system free of undue obstacles to the rise and fall of these competing parties or groupings? 3 / 4

Several political parties operate in Trinidad and Tobago. While the PNM dominated the political landscape in the decades following independence, it has weakened in recent years; the national political arena is now largely divided between the PNM and the UNC. Various factors, including the country's first-past-the-post voting system, have made it difficult for less established parties to gain seats in Parliament.

B2. Is there a realistic opportunity for the opposition to increase its support or gain power through elections? 4 / 4

Rival parties consistently transfer power peacefully, with multiple changes in government through elections since the 1980s.

B3. Are the people's political choices free from domination by forces that are external to the political sphere, or by political forces that employ extrapolitical means? 3 / 4

People's political choices are generally free from external pressure. However, observers have raised concerns about lack of transparency in campaign financing, which may enable improper influence and disadvantage opposition parties.

B4. Do various segments of the population (including ethnic, racial, religious, gender, LGBT+, and other relevant groups) have full political rights and electoral opportunities? 3 / 4

All ethnic groups enjoy full political rights, and political parties are technically multiethnic, though the PNM is favored by Afro-Trinidadians and the UNC is affiliated with Indo-Trinidadians.

Women's political participation has increased somewhat in recent years, though they remain generally underrepresented. The speaker of the House of Representatives and 10 out of 41 members of the House are women. In 2018, Paula-Mae Weekes became the first woman to be elected president. Discrimination against LGBT+ people is widespread, affecting their ability to fully engage in political and electoral processes.

C. FUNCTIONING OF GOVERNMENT: 9 / 12

C1. Do the freely elected head of government and national legislative representatives determine the policies of the government? 4 / 4

The country's freely elected executive and legislative officeholders generally determine and implement government policies without undue interference.

C2. Are safeguards against official corruption strong and effective? 2 / 4

Corruption remains a pervasive problem, especially within the police force and among high-ranking government officials and immigration officers. Several pieces of anticorruption legislation exist but are poorly enforced.

In May 2019, former attorney general Anand Ramlogan and former senator Gerald Ramdeen, both of the UNC, were arrested on suspicion of money laundering; Ramlogan was accused of routing kickbacks and legal fees to outside lawyers during his tenure, while Ramdeen was accused of receiving some of the funds. The case against Ramlogan and Ramdeen, who resigned from the Senate in May, was pending at the end of 2020.

C3. Does the government operate with openness and transparency? 3 / 4

Public officials are required to disclose their assets, income, and liabilities, but penalties against those who fail to comply are limited. The Integrity Commission, which is tasked with overseeing these financial disclosures, has been criticized for being ineffective.

The public has the right to access government documents by law, although numerous public institutions are exempt. Furthermore, there is no enforcement of a provision that requires the government to respond to information requests within 30 days. A 2015 law regulating public procurements has not been fully implemented, despite promises by the PNM government to do so. In late 2020, legislation was drafted to fully enact the public procurement regulations, though it excluded government-to-government contracts. Subsequently, the Office of Procurement Regulation would have no oversight of legal, medical, financial, accounting, and auditing services, as well as any other intragovernmental contracts as defined by the Minister of Finance.

CIVIL LIBERTIES: 49 / 60

D. FREEDOM OF EXPRESSION AND BELIEF: 16 / 16

D1. Are there free and independent media? 4 / 4

Freedom of the press is constitutionally guaranteed and generally upheld in practice. Media outlets are privately owned and vigorously pluralistic. However, those regarded as most favorable to the government receive the bulk of state advertising. Under the 2013 Defamation and Libel Act, "malicious defamatory libel known to be false" is punishable by up to two years in prison as well as a fine, but prosecutions are uncommon.

D2. Are individuals free to practice and express their religious faith or nonbelief in public and private? 4 / 4

The constitution guarantees freedom of religion, and the government generally honors this provision. The requirements for registration of a religious organization, which confers tax benefits and other privileges, are not considered onerous. Some restrictions are placed on foreign missionaries; up to 35 per registered religious group are allowed in the country at one time, and they cannot stay longer than three consecutive years.

D3. Is there academic freedom, and is the educational system free from extensive political indoctrination? 4 / 4

Academic freedom is generally upheld.

D4. Are individuals free to express their personal views on political or other sensitive topics without fear of surveillance or retribution? 4 / 4

Individuals are free to express their opinions in private conversations. The government has historically refrained from monitoring online communications; however, the national police launched a Social Media Monitoring Unit charged with monitoring social media platforms to detect evidence of child pornography, prostitution, and human trafficking, in October 2019. According to Police Commissioner Gary Griffith, the unit is not meant to surveil citizens.

E. ASSOCIATIONAL AND ORGANIZATIONAL RIGHTS: 11 / 12
E1. Is there freedom of assembly? 4 / 4

The constitution provides for freedom of assembly, and the government generally respects this right.

E2. Is there freedom for nongovernmental organizations, particularly those that are engaged in human rights–and governance-related work? 4 / 4

Civil society is robust, with a range of domestic and international interest groups operating freely.

E3. Is there freedom for trade unions and similar professional or labor organizations? 3 / 4

Labor unions are well organized and politically active, though union membership has declined in recent years. Strikes are legal and occur frequently. The law contains a provision allowing the Minister of Labor to petition the courts to end any strike deemed detrimental to national interests. Walkouts by workers considered essential, including hospital staff, firefighters, and telecommunication workers, are punishable by up to three years in prison and fines. The government threatened to impose criminal penalties in 2018 prior to a series of strikes protesting the planned closure of the Petrotrin refinery.

F. RULE OF LAW: 9 / 16
F1. Is there an independent judiciary? 3 / 4

The judicial branch is generally independent, but it is subject to some political pressure and corruption. Chief Justice Archie has been suspected of corruption since 2017, when he allegedly sought to influence the Housing Development Corporation.

F2. Does due process prevail in civil and criminal matters? 2 / 4

Due process rights are provided for in the constitution, but they are not always upheld. Rising crime rates and institutional weakness have produced a severe backlog in the court system. Pretrial detainees and remanded individuals account for more than half the prison population. Most detainees' trials begin seven to 10 years after their arrest, often exceeding the maximum sentence for the alleged crime. Corruption in the police force, which is often linked to the illegal drugs trade, is endemic, and inefficiencies have resulted in the dismissal of some criminal cases. Intimidation of witnesses and jurors has been reported by judicial officials.

F3. Is there protection from the illegitimate use of physical force and freedom from war and insurgencies? 2 / 4

The government has struggled in recent years to address criminal violence, which is mostly linked to organized crime and drug trafficking. The national police reported 536 murders in 2019, and 517 in 2018. However, by December 30, 2020, there had been 394 murders, the lowest figure in eight years. In 2017, the Organized Crime Intelligence Unit was established "to pursue, target, dismantle, disrupt and prosecute" organized criminal groups and networks. Police have been criticized for excessive use of force, and many abuses by the authorities go unpunished.

Over a hundred Trinidadians have reportedly sought to join the Islamic State (IS) militant group in recent years. Trinidadian security forces, supported by US military personnel, raided multiple locations in 2018 and arrested individuals suspected of planning a terrorist attack on that year's Carnival celebration.

F4. Do laws, policies, and practices guarantee equal treatment of various segments of the population? 2 / 4

Despite legal protections against discrimination on various grounds, racial disparities persist, with Indo-Trinidadians accounting for a disproportionate share of the country's economic elite. Women continue to face discrimination in employment and compensation.

Human rights groups have criticized the government's unwillingness to address discrimination and violence against LGBT+ people. However, in 2018, the High Court ruled that the provisions of the Sexual Offences Act that criminalized same-sex relations were unconstitutional. The government vowed to appeal that ruling to the London-based Privy Council in late 2018; their case remains pending.

Immigration law does not adequately protect refugees, and Trinidad specifically lacks a system to process asylum claims. As many as 40,000 Venezuelan asylum seekers and refugees have entered the country in recent years, but authorities regularly seek to detain and deport these individuals as illegal immigrants, including those who registered their status with the Office of the UN High Commissioner for Refugees. Local courts have intervened to block deportations.

In June 2019, the government allowed refugees to register for a work permit during a two-week grace period. Over 16,500 Venezuelans applied for permits, which were originally valid for one year; they were subsequently extended until the end of 2020.

In a July 2020 press conference, the Minister of National Security claimed that "illegal immigrants" and "boat people"—derogatory terms for Venezuelan refugees—presented a potential health risk due to the COVID-19 pandemic. The government targeted asylum seekers with more extensive coastal patrols and created a hotline for residents to report them. In December, 31 Venezuelans died after their boat sank en route to Trinidad.

As many as 70 Trinidadians were among those held by Kurdish forces in the Al-Hol camp in Syria, after the IS lost its territorial holdings there in March 2019. In November 2019, Trinidad's national security minister met with US officials to discuss the possibility of repatriating them, though little progress had been made by the end of 2020.

G. PERSONAL AUTONOMY AND INDIVIDUAL RIGHTS: 13 / 16

G1. Do individuals enjoy freedom of movement, including the ability to change their place of residence, employment, or education? 4 / 4

Trinidadians and Tobagonians do not face significant constraints on freedom of movement or on their ability to change their place of residence, employment, or education.

G2. Are individuals able to exercise the right to own property and establish private businesses without undue interference from state or non-state actors? 3 / 4

While the government actively supports both domestic and foreign investment in the country, corruption and weak state institutions can make it more difficult to start and operate businesses. Business owners may face challenges registering property and enforcing contracts.

G3. Do individuals enjoy personal social freedoms, including choice of marriage partner and size of family, protection from domestic violence, and control over appearance? 3 / 4

Most individual rights with respect to personal status issues like marriage and divorce are protected by law. The 2017 Marriage Act raised the legal marriage age to 18, officially making child marriage illegal.

Rape, including spousal rape, is illegal, and domestic violence is addressed by specific legislation. However, enforcement of these provisions remains inadequate. According to 2018 data from the UN Global Database on Violence against Women, 30 percent of women in the country experience physical or sexual violence from an intimate partner in their lifetime, and 19 percent experience sexual violence from a nonpartner. Several high-profile femicides in 2020 and newly published data on violence against women increased public awareness of the issue.

Abortion is illegal in most cases, and there is reportedly little public awareness of legal exemptions for abortions to save a woman's life or preserve her physical or mental health. A woman can be imprisoned for up to four years for obtaining an illegal abortion.

G4. Do individuals enjoy equality of opportunity and freedom from economic exploitation? 3 / 4

The law provides basic protections against exploitative working conditions, though these do not apply or are poorly enforced for informal and household workers in particular. While the government has stepped up efforts to combat trafficking in persons, convictions have been lacking, and funding for services to trafficking survivors has been cut. Venezuelan women are especially vulnerable to sex trafficking.

According to reports, more than two dozen police are under investigation into alleged involvement in sex trafficking between Trinidad and Venezuela as of 2019. The US State Department's *Trafficking in Persons 2020* report notes that government officials and police have at times been facilitated trafficking rings, accepting bribes from brothel owners to transport victims to various locations.

Tunisia

Population: 11,900,000
Capital: Tunis
Freedom Status: Free
Electoral Democracy: Yes

Overview: After ousting a longtime autocrat from power in 2011, Tunisia began a democratic transition, and citizens now enjoy unprecedented political rights and civil liberties. However, the influence of endemic corruption, economic challenges, security threats, and continued unresolved issues related to gender equality and transitional justice remain obstacles to full democratic consolidation.

KEY DEVELOPMENTS IN 2020

- Tunisian authorities instituted a COVID-19-related lockdown in March, which was partially enforced by the army. Mass gatherings were banned before the lockdown was eased by June, though small-scale events took place during the lockdown and larger protests were held later in the year; while authorities responded forcefully to some demonstrations, others proceeded without intervention.
- Travel restrictions and curfews were reintroduced in October, as COVID-19 transmission accelerated, and continued through year's end; nearly 138,000 cases and 4,620 deaths were recorded by the World Health Organization at year's end.
- The proposed cabinet of prime minister-designate Habib Jemli was rejected in January. Ettakatol party leader Elyes Fakhfakh became premier in February but resigned in July after a report highlighted his stakes in firms that earned public contracts; Interior Minister Hichem Mechichi succeeded him after his cabinet was approved in September, and remained in post at year's end.
- In October, parliamentarians considered a draft bill that would provide immunity for security personnel who respond with lethal force while dispersing gatherings. The parliament withdrew the bill later that month, after domestic and international rights groups vehemently opposed it.

POLITICAL RIGHTS: 32 / 40

A. ELECTORAL PROCESS: 12 / 12

A1. Was the current head of government or other chief national authority elected through free and fair elections? 4 / 4

The 2014 constitution lays out a semipresidential system in which a popularly elected president serves as head of state and exercises circumscribed powers, while the majority party in the parliament selects a prime minister, who serves as head of government, following parliamentary elections. The president is directly elected for up to two five-year terms.

The last presidential election took place in October 2019, following the death of President Beji Caid Essebsi that July. Kaïs Saïed, an independent candidate and former constitutional law professor who received an endorsement from the Islamist Ennahda party, won an October runoff against opponent Nabil Karoui with 73 percent of the vote. (Karoui spent most of the campaign in prison on money laundering and tax evasion charges.)

Local observers concluded that the 2019 presidential election was generally competitive and credible, but raised some concerns about Karoui's inability to campaign while in prison.

A2. Were the current national legislative representatives elected through free and fair elections? 4 / 4

Tunisia's 2014 constitution established a unicameral legislative body, the 217-seat Assembly of the Representatives of the People (ARP); 199 members are directly elected in domestic multimember constituencies, while 18 represent multimember constituencies abroad via a party-list system. All members serve five-year terms.

The most recent legislative election took place in October 2019. International and national observers declared the elections generally competitive and credible. Ennahda placed first with 52 seats, Karoui's Qalb Tounes (Heart of Tunisia) party took 38 seats, the progressive Democratic Current took 22, and the al-Karama (Dignity) Coalition took 21. The remaining seats were won by 11 other parties and 17 independent candidates.

The proposed cabinet of the Ennahda-supported prime minister-designate, former junior agriculture minister Habib Jemli, was rejected by parliamentarians in January 2020.

President Saïed then tasked former tourism and finance minister Elyes Fakhfakh, leader of the center-left Ettakatol party, with forming a new cabinet. That cabinet took office in February, but Fakhfakh resigned in July after a report highlighted his holdings in firms that won public contracts. Saïed named Interior Minister Hichem Mechichi to succeed Fakhfakh in late July, and Mechichi's ministerial slate was approved in September.

A3. Are the electoral laws and framework fair, and are they implemented impartially by the relevant election management bodies? 4 / 4

The Independent High Authority for Elections (ISIE), a nine-member commission, is tasked with supervising parliamentary and presidential elections. Since its inception in 2011, the ISIE's political independence and conduct of elections has been well regarded by Tunisian and international observers. In 2019, the ISIE successfully oversaw early presidential elections, including a televised debate between the two candidates in the second round, as well as successful parliamentary elections.

B. POLITICAL PLURALISM AND PARTICIPATION: 14 / 16

B1. Do the people have the right to organize in different political parties or other competitive political groupings of their choice, and is the system free of undue obstacles to the rise and fall of these competing parties or groupings? 4 / 4

Tunisia's numerous political parties represent a wide range of ideologies and political philosophies, and are generally free to form and operate. The 2019 parliamentary elections saw robust competition between political parties and independent candidates within electoral processes that were deemed generally free and credible by observers.

Campaign-finance laws intended to prevent money from determining political outcomes are complex and often unclear. Parties occasionally bend, if not break, the rules in order to campaign effectively.

B2. Is there a realistic opportunity for the opposition to increase its support or gain power through elections? 4 / 4

Opposition parties participate competitively in political processes, and the 2019 elections demonstrated that independents and new parties can win political power through elections. President Saïed is not affiliated with a political party, nor is Prime Minister Mechichi.

B3. Are the people's political choices free from domination by forces that are external to the political sphere, or by political forces that employ extrapolitical means? 3 / 4

Electoral outcomes are the result of transparent balloting. However, domestic economic oligarchies have a high degree of influence over politics. Foreign groups reportedly route funds to preferred campaigns, though these channels of support are opaque.

B4. Do various segments of the population (including ethnic, racial, religious, gender, LGBT+, and other relevant groups) have full political rights and electoral opportunities? 3 / 4

Nongovernmental organizations (NGOs) and international organizations continue working to increase the political participation of marginalized groups. In 2017, the parliament passed a law requiring an equal number of men and women at the top of candidate lists, as well as at least one candidate with a disability and three people under the age of 35 on each list. Representation of women in subsequent elections has been high, and legislation aimed at protecting the rights of women has been passed. Fifty-four women held parliamentary seats after the 2019 elections. Eleven women and one openly gay man requested nomination to stand as candidates in the 2019 presidential election.

The Amazigh ethnic community is underrepresented in electoral politics, but the first party to address their interests, the Akal Movement, was formed in May 2019.

Despite these positive developments, some segments of the population lack full political rights. Only Muslims may run for president. Societal discrimination and laws criminalizing homosexuality preclude many LGBT+ people from active political participation, and political parties largely fail to address LGBT+ issues.

C. FUNCTIONING OF GOVERNMENT: 6 / 12

C1. Do the freely elected head of government and national legislative representatives determine the policies of the government? 3 / 4

The 2011 removal from power of autocrat Zine el-Abidine Ben Ali and his close relatives and associates made way for the establishment of a representative government that is generally accountable to voters. However, late president Essebsi manipulated the national budget in such a way that the legislative branch was deeply underfunded, leaving it with limited ability or resources to craft legislation on its own. As a result, lawmaking has been largely an executive function. The fractured nature of the parliament also interfered in legislative decision-making during 2020, though parliamentarians did pass a national budget in December despite tensions within the body.

C2. Are safeguards against official corruption strong and effective? 1 / 4

Anticorruption legislation has historically been considered weak. The Economic Reconciliation Law of 2017 effectively offered amnesty for those implicated in Ben Ali–era corruption, but was amended due to public disapproval. In July 2018, the parliament approved a new law designed to strengthen the anticorruption legal framework, which requires the president, ministers, and high-level public officials, among others, to publicly declare their assets. Penalties for violating the law include hefty fines and prison terms of up to five years.

The National Commission for the Fight against Corruption (INLUCC) was established in 2011, and a permanent body, the Commission on Good Governance and the Fight against Corruption (IBGLCC) was meant to replace it under the 2014 constitution. While legislation founding the IBGLCC was passed in 2017, the new body remains inactive. INLUCC has continued its operations, notably renewing a partnership with the General Tunisian Labor Union (UGTT) in November 2020, but is underfunded, and cannot compel the judiciary to hear cases.

Corruption remained a significant issue in 2020. In July, then Prime Minister Fakhfakh resigned after Ennahda tabled a no-confidence motion over a report tying firms Fakhfakh held stakes in to public contracts. After he was nominated as premier, Mechichi instructed ministerial nominees to declare assets to INLUCC. In late December, 2019 presidential candidate Nabil Karoui, who was detained on suspicion of money laundering and tax evasion during that campaign, was again arrested over those charges and remained detained at year's end.

The ongoing COVID-19 pandemic has worsened corruption in Tunisia; in December 2020, INLUCC head Imed Boukhris warned that corruption was on the rise, and specifically identified a future vaccination effort as a potential target for illicit behavior.

C3. Does the government operate with openness and transparency? 2 / 4

In 2016, the ARP adopted freedom-of-information legislation, though it was criticized by watchdog groups for its security-related exemptions. Cabinet ministries often refuse public requests for information. Members of the governing coalition voted out in 2019 had frequently crafted policy behind closed doors, without input from other parties.

However, legislation passed in 2018 that required public officials to declare their assets represented a positive step in government transparency. Government officials also operated with relative transparency in response to the COVID-19 pandemic.

CIVIL LIBERTIES: 39 / 60 (+1)

D. FREEDOM OF EXPRESSION AND BELIEF: 12 / 16

D1. Are there free and independent media? 2 / 4

The constitution guarantees freedom of opinion, thought, expression, information, and publication, subject to some restrictions. Press freedom has improved in recent years, and many independent outlets operate. Several online news outlets have launched since the 2011 revolution. Tunisia signed on to the International Declaration on Information and Democracy, which outlines basic principles for the global information and communication space, when the initiative was launched in late 2018.

Some journalists face pressure and intimidation from government officials in connection with their work. Reporters covering the security forces remain particularly vulnerable to harassment and arrest. Moreover, it is difficult to obtain data about the ownership of media companies, their audiences, or the funding of public advertising, and press freedom advocates have expressed concern about significant political influence on a number of major private outlets. Ahead of the 2019 elections, Tunisian journalists expressed concerns about government influence over the public broadcaster.

Journalists and bloggers are also targeted with insult and defamation laws. In April 2020, a blogger was convicted of insulting a public official after posting a video criticizing the effectiveness of a COVID-19-related food distribution effort to Facebook, and received a suspended sentence. Another blogger was charged with causing a disturbance for posting a video of a demonstration that same month, but was acquitted. In July, commentator Taoufik Ben Brik received a modified one-year sentence for defaming and insulting public officials; Ben Brik was charged after criticizing the authorities' treatment of presidential candidate Karoui the previous October. In November 2020, a blogger received a two-year prison sentence for criticizing a prosecutor in a Facebook video posted earlier that month.

D2. Are individuals free to practice and express their religious faith or nonbelief in public and private? 3 / 4

The constitution calls for freedom of belief and conscience for all religions, as well as for the nonreligious, and bans campaigns against apostasy and incitement to hatred and violence on religious grounds. However, blasphemy remains illegal and police may invoke it as a pretext for arrests. Islam is enshrined as the only religion of the state, and Islamic education remains a required component of the curriculum in public schools. In May 2019, during Ramadan, a café owner was arrested and fined for keeping his restaurant open during fast hours in what human rights activists called an arbitrary use of criminal law. Converts to Christianity often experience harassment and discrimination.

D3. Is there academic freedom, and is the educational system free from extensive political indoctrination? 3 / 4

Article 33 of the constitution explicitly protects academic freedom, which continues to improve in practice. However, ingrained practices of self-censorship on the part of academics remain in some instances. Students have reported being unable to pursue dissertation research on topics including sexuality and gender identity, as well as critiques of Islam's role in violent extremism.

D4. Are individuals free to express their personal views on political or other sensitive topics without fear of surveillance or retribution? 4 / 4

Private discussion is generally open and free, though there is some reluctance to broach some topics, including criticism of the military. Homosexuality remains illegal, and the prohibition discourages open discussion of issues affecting LGBT+ people.

E. ASSOCIATIONAL AND ORGANIZATIONAL RIGHTS: 8 / 12 (+1)

E1. Is there freedom of assembly? 3 / 4 (+1)

The constitution guarantees the rights to assembly and peaceful demonstration. Public demonstrations on political, social, and economic issues regularly take place. However, a controversial counterterrorism law adopted in 2015, and successive states of emergency declared in response to political and security situations, have imposed significant constraints on public demonstrations. The latest state of emergency, which was renewed in May and December 2020, allows security forces to ban strikes, meetings, and large gatherings considered likely to incite disorder. The government has called these measures necessary due to security concerns, but analysts have argued the measures are meant to suppress dissent.

Freedom of assembly was also curtailed under COVID-19-related emergency measures enacted in late March 2020, which initially banned all gatherings. That lockdown expired by June, but the government banned protests and limited public gatherings in an October order, citing an increase in COVID-19 cases. Protest bans were included in a November order, but mass-gathering restrictions were loosened in a December order.

Nevertheless, small protests reportedly proceeded in May 2020, with workers in sectors affected by COVID-19 measures demonstrating over a lack of pay. In late June, demonstrators in the city of Tataouine protested over high unemployment, and clashed with authorities after an activist was arrested. The Interior Ministry reported 10 arrests after those clashes. In October, protesters denounced proposed legislation that would provide immunity to security personnel in front of the parliament building in Tunis; participants were physically attacked by security forces, and several were detained. However, other demonstrations proceeded without forceful intervention during the year.

Score Change: The score improved from 2 to 3 because protests and demonstrations were generally able to proceed with less police intervention and fewer arrests than in the previous two years, though police violence remained a problem.

E2. Is there freedom for nongovernmental organizations, particularly those that are engaged in human rights- and governance-related work? 2 / 4

A progressive 2011 decree guarantees the freedom for NGOs to operate and outlines procedures governing the establishment of new groups. Tens of thousands of new NGOs began operating after the revolution, holding conferences, trainings, educational programs, and other gatherings throughout Tunisia in subsequent years.

However, a 2018 law effectively equated NGOs with businesses, and requires them to submit to onerous reporting requirements beyond those codified in the 2011 decree. Under the law, all NGOs (and businesses) are required to register with a new National Registry of Institutions, and to provide data on staff, assets, decisions to merge or dissolve, and operations. Failure to register may result in a year of imprisonment and a fine of $4,000. Critics argue that the requirement increases the monitoring and oversight of civil society by the government. Registration applications can be denied at the discretion of the Council of the National Registry.

E3. Is there freedom for trade unions and similar professional or labor organizations? 3 / 4

The constitution guarantees the right to form labor unions and to strike. The UGTT is the predominant union, though independent unions also exist. The Tunisian economy has seen large-scale strike actions across all sectors since the revolution, with participants demanding labor reform, better wages, and improved workplace conditions. Unions have reported that some employers have taken actions to discourage union activities, including dismissing union activists.

F. RULE OF LAW: 9 / 16

F1. Is there an independent judiciary? 2 / 4

While the constitution calls for a robust and independent judiciary, judicial reform has proceeded slowly since the 2011 revolution, with numerous Ben Ali–era judges remaining on the bench and successive governments regularly attempting to manipulate the courts. Legislation adopted in 2016 established the Supreme Judicial Council, a body charged with ensuring the independence of the judiciary and appointing Constitutional Court judges. Council members were elected in 2016 by thousands of legal professionals. However, the Constitutional Court, which is intended to evaluate the constitutionality of decrees and laws, has not been established via legislation, nor have its members been formally appointed, at year's end.

F2. Does due process prevail in civil and criminal matters? 2 / 4

The state of emergency in place since 2015 and renewed through the end of 2020 gives police broad license to arrest and detain people on security– or terrorism-related charges, and arbitrary arrests continued to take place during the year. Civilians are still tried in military courts, particularly on charges of defaming the army.

In 2014, Tunisia established a Truth and Dignity Commission (IVD) to examine political, economic, and social crimes committed since 1956, and it soon began collecting testimony. In early 2018, the parliament voted against extending the commission's mandate, a decision that drew criticism from rights activists for weakening transitional justice efforts. The commission presented its final report in March 2019 and officially published it in June 2020, drawing on over 62,000 complaints filed by Tunisian citizens against the state for human rights abuses. Tunisian courts were reviewing 69 indictments and 131 referrals from the IVD at year's end.

F3. Is there protection from the illegitimate use of physical force and freedom from war and insurgencies? 3 / 4

Tunisia has recently dealt with periodic terrorist attacks. In June 2019, two suicide bombers detonated their explosives in Tunis, killing a police officer and wounding eight other people; the Islamic State (IS) militant group claimed responsibility.

The police force faces long-standing complaints of officers abusing civilians and detainees with impunity, and the police unions have resisted reform efforts aimed at addressing the problem. Reports of the use of excessive force and torture by security agents continued in 2020.

In October 2020, the parliament considered a bill that would provide immunity for security forces who use lethal force to disperse some gatherings if the action is considered a last resort. National and international rights groups voiced fierce opposition to the bill, which was first proposed in 2013, and the parliament withdrew it.

While the death penalty technically exists, Tunisian authorities have not carried out an execution since 1991. President Saïed drew ire in September 2020 after voicing his support for capital punishment for certain crimes.

F4. Do laws, policies, and practices guarantee equal treatment of various segments of the population? 2 / 4

The constitution prohibits all forms of discrimination and calls for the state to create a culture of diversity. However, LGBT+ people continue to face legal discrimination. Homosexuality remains illegal, and the penal code calls for prison sentences of up to three years for "sodomy." Although the 2014 constitution guarantees gender equality, women experience discrimination in employment, and sexual harassment in public spaces remains prevalent.

Tunisia has no asylum law, leaving the United Nations as the sole entity processing claims of refugee status in the country. Irregular migrants and asylum seekers are often housed in informal detention centers, where they suffer from substandard living conditions. Delays in the issuance of residency permits make it impossible for many to work legally, forcing them to take informal jobs with no labor protections.

G. PERSONAL AUTONOMY AND INDIVIDUAL RIGHTS: 10 / 16

G1. Do individuals enjoy freedom of movement, including the ability to change their place of residence, employment, or education? 3 / 4

Freedom of movement has improved substantially since 2011. The constitution guarantees freedom of movement within the country, as well as the freedom to travel abroad. In 2017, lawmakers approved measures that require authorities to go through more rigorous processes in order to issue travel bans or restrict passports. However, authorities have broad license under the state of emergency to restrict individuals' movement without initiating formal charges, and thousands of people have been affected by such orders.

Freedom of movement was also impacted by COVID-19-related measures. A late March 2020 lockdown order, which was partially enforced by the army, restricted movement and instituted a nationwide curfew, though these initial measures expired by June. Nationwide curfews were reintroduced via October and November orders, which also restricted travel between governorates; some governorates were exempt from travel restrictions in a subsequent December order.

G2. Are individuals able to exercise the right to own property and establish private businesses without undue interference from state or nonstate actors? 2 / 4

The protection of property rights and establishment of new businesses continues to be an area of concern, closely linked to high levels of corruption as well as a large backlog of property disputes.

In November 2018, the cabinet approved a bill that would establish equal inheritance rights for men and women. Currently, women are granted half the share of inheritance that men receive. However, Ennahda expressed opposition to the bill, which did not receive a parliamentary vote by the end of 2020.

G3. Do individuals enjoy personal social freedoms, including choice of marriage partner and size of family, protection from domestic violence, and control over appearance? 3 / 4

Tunisia has long been praised for relatively progressive social policies, especially in the areas of family law and women's rights. However, women face high rates of domestic abuse. In 2017, parliamentarians approved a Law on Eliminating Violence against Women, which addressed domestic violence and also included language intended to protect women from harassment in public, and from economic discrimination. At a conference in November 2018 that brought together government officials, NGO representatives, and domestic abuse survivors, participants noted that the law's implementation was limited by a shortage of trained agents to handle complaints, pressure on women from some agents to avoid taking abusive husbands to court, and logistical barriers to reporting abuse.

Violence against women rose as the COVID-19 pandemic took hold. During the March-to-June national lockdown, the Tunisian Association of Democratic Women's Tunis shelter received four times as many women as it did before.

Homosexuality remains criminalized. A Tunisian appeals court upheld the conviction of two men on sodomy charges in July 2020, resulting in one-year prison sentences for the defendants.

Public displays of affection can lead to charges of violating public morality laws, and jail time.

In 2017, the Justice Ministry repealed a decree that had banned Tunisian women from marrying non-Muslim men.

**G4. Do individuals enjoy equality of opportunity and freedom from economic exploitation?
2 / 4**

Tunisian women and children are subject to sex trafficking and forced domestic work in both Tunisia and abroad. Refugees and other migrants are also susceptible to exploitation by traffickers. Cases of exploitation in the agriculture and textile sectors are prevalent; women often work long hours with no contracts, benefits, or legal recourse. Recent protests have called attention to the lack of economic opportunity for average Tunisians due to high infla-tion, high unemployment, and a lack of meaningful reform to address such issues. Protests throughout 2020 highlighted the continued problem of regional economic inequality, with marginalization, underdevelopment, unemployment, and deteriorating conditions plaguing the country's interior.

Turkey

Population: 83,700,000
Capital: Ankara
Freedom Status: Not Free
Electoral Democracy: No

Overview: President Recep Tayyip Erdoğan's Justice and Development Party (AKP) has ruled Turkey since 2002. After initially passing some liberalizing reforms, the AKP govern-ment showed growing contempt for political rights and civil liberties, and it has pursued a dramatic and wide-ranging crackdown on perceived opponents since an attempted coup in 2016. Constitutional changes adopted in 2017 concentrated power in the hands of the pres-ident. While Erdoğan continues to exert tremendous power in Turkish politics, opposition victories in 2019 municipal elections and the impact of the COVID-19 pandemic on the already shaky economy have given the government new incentives to suppress dissent and limit public discourse.

KEY DEVELOPMENTS IN 2020

- As the COVID-19 crisis threatened the economy and the government's political standing during the year, authorities apparently sought to manipulate official health statistics and launched criminal investigations against medical professionals who released independent information about the outbreak or criticized the official response. Hundreds of ordinary people were also arrested for their social media posts related to the coronavirus.

- Prosecutions and campaigns of harassment against opposition politicians, prominent members of civil society, independent journalists, and critics of Turkey's increasingly aggressive foreign policy continued throughout the year. In December, the European Court of Human Rights (ECHR) called for the immediate release of Selahattin Demirtaş, leader of the Kurdish-oriented People's Democratic Party (HDP), who had been imprisoned since 2016 on politically motivated charges; the court's ruling was ignored. New arrests of HDP members and leaders were carried out during the year, adding to the thousands who have been detained since 2015. The government also continued to replace HDP municipal officials with centrally appointed "trustees."
- Despite a 2019 ECHR ruling that called for the release of philanthropist Osman Kavala, he remained behind bars at year's end facing trumped-up charges. Detained in 2017, he was acquitted in the original case in February 2020, but a new indictment issued in October accused Kavala and a US academic, without evidence, of involvement in the 2016 coup attempt.

POLITICAL RIGHTS: 16 / 40
A. ELECTORAL PROCESS: 5 / 12
A1. Was the current head of government or other chief national authority elected through free and fair elections? 2 / 4

The president is directly elected for up to two five-year terms, but is eligible to run for a third term if the parliament calls for early elections during the president's initial terms. If no candidate wins an absolute majority of votes, a second round of voting between the top two candidates takes place. President Erdoğan has retained a dominant role in government since moving from the post of prime minister to the presidency in 2014. A 2017 constitutional referendum instituted a new presidential system of government, expanding presidential powers and eliminating the role of prime minister.

The snap June 2018 presidential election, which was originally scheduled for November 2019, was moved up at Erdoğan's behest, as he claimed an early election was necessary to implement the new presidential system. The election was held while Turkey was still under a state of emergency put in place after the 2016 coup attempt.

Erdoğan, who leads the AKP, won a second term, earning 52.6 percent of the vote in the first round. Muharrem İnce of the opposition Republican People's Party (CHP) won 30.6 percent. Selahattin Demirtaş of the HDP won 8.4 percent, while Meral Aksenser of the nationalist İyi (Good) Party won 7.3 percent; other candidates won the remaining 1.1 percent. Since Erdoğan's first term ended ahead of schedule, he is eligible for a third term, and could hold office through 2028 if he is reelected again.

Election observers with the Organization for Security and Co-operation in Europe (OSCE) criticized the 2018 poll, reporting that electoral regulators often deferred to the ruling AKP and that state-run media favored the party in its coverage. The OSCE also noted that Erdoğan repeatedly accused his opponents of supporting terrorism during the campaign. İnce, the CHP candidate, also criticized the vote, calling it fundamentally unfair. Demirtaş campaigned from prison, having been charged with terrorism offenses in 2016.

A2. Were the current national legislative representatives elected through free and fair elections? 2 / 4

The 2017 constitutional referendum enlarged the unicameral parliament, the Grand National Assembly, from 550 seats to 600, and increased term lengths for its members from four to five years; these changes took effect with the June 2018 elections. Members are elected by proportional representation, and political parties must earn at least 10 percent of the national vote to hold seats in the parliament.

According to the OSCE, the 2018 legislative elections were marred by a number of flaws, including misuse of state resources by the ruling party to gain an electoral advantage and an intimidation campaign against the HDP and other opposition parties. Reports of irregularities such as proxy voting were more prevalent in the south and southeast.

The People's Alliance, which had formed in February 2018 and included the AKP and the far-right Nationalist Movement Party (MHP), won a total of 344 seats with 53 percent of the vote, while the CHP won 146 seats with 22 percent. The HDP won 11 percent and 67 seats, and the İyi Party entered parliament for the first time with 10 percent of the vote and 43 seats.

In June 2020, two HDP members and one lawmaker from the CHP were expelled from the parliament and detained on espionage and terrorism charges.

A3. Are the electoral laws and framework fair, and are they implemented impartially by the relevant election management bodies? 1 / 4

The judges of the Supreme Electoral Council (YSK) oversee voting procedures. A 2016 law allowed AKP-dominated judicial bodies to replace most YSK judges. Since then, the YSK has increasingly deferred to the AKP in its rulings, most notably in May 2019, when it ordered a rerun of the Istanbul mayoral election; CHP candidate Ekrem İmamoğlu had narrowly won the race in March, but the YSK scrapped the result based on selective technicalities, claiming that some polling documentation went unsigned and that a number of ballot officials were not civil servants as required by law. Despite the annulment of the first election's results, İmamoğlu won the second vote that June, increasing his margin of victory over the AKP candidate.

B. POLITICAL PLURALISM AND PARTICIPATION: 8 / 16

B1. Do the people have the right to organize in different political parties or other competitive political groupings of their choice, and is the system free of undue obstacles to the rise and fall of these competing parties or groupings? 2 / 4

Turkey maintains a multiparty system, with five major parties holding seats in the parliament. However, the rise of new parties is inhibited by the 10 percent vote threshold for parliamentary representation—an unusually high bar by global standards. The 2018 electoral law permits the formation of alliances to contest elections, allowing parties that would not meet the threshold alone to secure seats through an alliance. Parties can be disbanded for endorsing policies that are not in agreement with constitutional parameters, and this rule has been applied in the past to Islamist and Kurdish-oriented parties.

After a cease-fire with the militant Kurdistan Workers' Party (PKK) collapsed in 2015, the government accused the HDP of serving as a proxy for the group, which is designated as a terrorist organization. A 2016 constitutional amendment facilitated the removal of parliamentary immunity, and many of the HDP's leaders have since been jailed on terrorism charges. In September 2018, Demirtaş, the HDP's presidential candidate, was sentenced to four years and eight months in prison for a 2013 speech praising the PKK in the context of peace negotiations. In November 2018, the ECHR ordered his immediate release, finding that his arrest was politically motivated, and his nearly two-year-long pretrial detention was unreasonable. The European court's grand chamber again ordered the HDP leader's release in December 2020, but he remained in prison facing a succession of new charges, along with thousands of other HDP members.

B2. Is there a realistic opportunity for the opposition to increase its support or gain power through elections? 2 / 4

Since coming to power in 2002, the ruling AKP has asserted partisan control over the YSK, the judiciary, the police, and the media. The party has aggressively used these institutional tools to weaken or co-opt political rivals in recent years, severely limiting the capacity of the opposition to build support among voters and gain power through elections.

The government has also resorted to arresting and charging opposition leaders, accusing of them of offenses ranging from terrorism to insulting the president. The HDP has regularly been subjected to this tactic, but Canan Kaftancıoğlu, the chair of the CHP in Istanbul, was also given a prison sentence of almost 10 years in September 2019, after she was charged with insulting the president and spreading terrorist propaganda. In June 2020, Kaftancıoğlu's conviction was upheld by an appeals court; she remained free pending further appeal.

The 2019 municipal elections, in which opposition forces won control of most major urban centers, including Ankara and Istanbul, suggested that there was still space for the opposition to make progress despite the AKP's institutional advantages. However, the central government's continued replacement of dozens of HDP mayors with appointed "trustees" underscored the obstacles opposition leaders can face even after winning election. In most cases these officials have been removed pending trial on dubious terrorism charges.

B3. Are the people's political choices free from domination by forces that are external to the political sphere, or by political forces that employ extrapolitical means? 3 / 4

The civilian leadership has asserted its control over the military, which has a history of intervening in political affairs. This greater control was a factor behind the failure of the 2016 coup attempt, and the government has since purged thousands of military personnel suspected of disloyalty. However, the AKP's institutional dominance threatens to make the state itself an extension of the party that can be used to change political outcomes.

B4. Do various segments of the population (including ethnic, racial, religious, gender, LGBT+, and other relevant groups) have full political rights and electoral opportunities? 1 / 4

Critics charge that the AKP favors Sunni Muslims, pointing to an overhaul of the education system that favored Islamic education in secular schools and promoted the rise of religious schools in the 2010s. The AKP also expanded the Directorate of Religious Affairs, using this institution as a channel for political patronage. Among other functions, the party uses the directorate to deliver government-friendly sermons in mosques in Turkey, as well as in countries where the Turkish diaspora is present.

The non-Sunni Alevi community, as well as non-Muslim religious groups, have long faced political discrimination. While members of religious and ethnic minorities hold some seats in the parliament, particularly within the CHP and HDP, the government's crackdown on opposition parties has seriously harmed political rights and electoral opportunities for Kurds and other minority groups.

Women remain underrepresented in politics and in leadership positions in government, though they won a slightly larger share of seats—104, or about 17 percent—in the 2018 parliamentary elections. While the AKP's policies and rhetoric often do not serve women's interests, opposition parties, notably the HDP, espouse the expansion of rights for women and minority groups.

A small number of openly LGBT+ candidates have run for office. Sedef Cakmak of the CHP was the first such candidate to take part in a city council race; she won her seat in Beşiktaş, a district of Istanbul, in 2014. The first openly gay parliamentary candidate was backed by the HDP in the 2015 general elections but did not win a seat. Despite these efforts,

LGBT+ people remain politically marginalized, and the government has used public morality laws to restrict the formation of organizations that would advocate for their interests.

Refugees residing in Turkey, including an estimated four million Syrians, generally do not have political rights in the country, and much of the Turkish public has resisted the idea of granting them access to citizenship en masse. However, tens of thousands of refugees with special skills or professional qualifications have been naturalized in recent years.

C. FUNCTIONING OF GOVERNMENT: 3 / 12

C1. Do the freely elected head of government and national legislative representatives determine the policies of the government? 2 / 4

The new presidential system instituted in 2018 vastly expanded the executive's already substantial authority. With the elimination of the prime minister's post, President Erdoğan now controls all executive functions; he can rule by decree, appoint judges and other officials who are supposed to provide oversight, and order investigations into any civil servant, among other powers. Erdoğan and his inner circle make all meaningful policy decisions, and the capacity of the parliament to provide a check on his rule is, in practice, seriously limited.

The 2016 state of emergency, which gave the president the authority to suspend civil liberties and issue decrees without oversight from the Constitutional Court, was formally lifted in July 2018 after two years in effect. However, the change has done little to curb the continued consolidation and abuse of executive power.

C2. Are safeguards against official corruption strong and effective? 1 / 4

Corruption—including money laundering, bribery, and collusion in the allocation of government contracts—remains a major problem, even at the highest levels of government. Enforcement of anticorruption laws is inconsistent, and Turkey's anticorruption agencies are generally ineffective, contributing to a culture of impunity. The crackdown carried out since the 2016 coup attempt has greatly increased opportunities for corruption, given the mass expropriation of targeted businesses and nongovernmental organizations (NGOs). Billions of dollars in seized assets are managed by government-appointed trustees, further augmenting the intimate ties between the government and friendly businesses.

In January 2018, Mehmet Hakan Atilla, a key official at Turkey's state-owned financial institution Halkbank, was found guilty in a US court of helping the Iranian authorities evade sanctions, and he was given a 32-month prison sentence that May. During the trial, Turkish-Iranian businessman Reza Zarrab testified that senior Turkish officials had accepted bribes as part of the scheme, and that Erdoğan personally approved some of the bribes during his tenure as prime minister. Erdoğan has lobbied the US government not to continue with its investigations, but Halkbank itself was indicted by US prosecutors in October 2019, and the case was ongoing in 2020.

C3. Does the government operate with openness and transparency? 0 / 4

The political and legal environment created by the government's crackdown since the 2016 coup attempt has made ordinary democratic oversight efforts all but impossible. Although Turkey has access to information law on the books, in practice the government lacks transparency and arbitrarily withholds information on the activities of state officials and institutions. External monitors like civil society groups and independent journalists are subject to arrest and prosecution if they attempt to expose government wrongdoing.

During the COVID-19 pandemic in 2020, authorities allegedly sought to manipulate official health statistics, and medical professionals who released independent information or criticized the state's response faced police questioning and criminal investigations.

CIVIL LIBERTIES: 16 / 60

D. FREEDOM OF EXPRESSION AND BELIEF: 5 / 16

D1. Are there free and independent media? 1 / 4

The mainstream media, especially television broadcasters, reflect government positions and have often carried identical headlines. Although some independent newspapers and websites continue to operate, they face tremendous political pressure and are routinely targeted for prosecution. More than 150 media outlets were closed in the months after the attempted coup in 2016.

In 2019, the parliament further limited media freedom by placing online video services under the purview of the High Council for Broadcasting (RTÜK), the country's broadcast regulator. As a result, online video producers must obtain licenses to broadcast in Turkey, even if they operate abroad. The RTÜK's members are appointed by the parliament and are almost exclusively members of the AKP or its political ally, the MHP.

New outlet closures and arrests of journalists occur regularly. Journalists were arrested or prosecuted during 2020 for their reporting on Turkey's military and intelligence operations in Libya and on the government's response to COVID-19, among other topics. The Committee to Protect Journalists reported that 37 journalists were imprisoned in the country as of December. Kurdish journalists have been disproportionately targeted by the authorities.

The government has continued to expand its attempts to control online sources of news and information. In July 2020, the parliament approved a new law that requires international content providers with more than a million daily users, such as Facebook and Twitter, to have local representation in Turkey and to remove content within 48 hours if so ordered. Companies that fail to comply are subject to heavy fines and eventual restrictions on their bandwidth.

D2. Are individuals free to practice and express their religious faith or nonbelief in public and private? 2 / 4

While the constitution guarantees freedom of religion, the public sphere is increasingly dominated by Sunni Islam. Alevi places of worship are not recognized as such by the government, meaning they cannot access the subsidies available to Sunni mosques. The number of religious schools that promote Sunni Islam has increased under the AKP, and the Turkish public education curriculum includes compulsory religious education courses; while adherents of non-Muslim faiths are generally exempted from these courses, Alevis and nonbelievers have difficulty opting out of them.

Three non-Muslim religious groups—Jews, Orthodox Christians, and Armenian Christians—are officially recognized. However, disputes over property and prohibitions on training of clergy remain problems for these communities, and the rights of unrecognized religious minorities are more limited. Non-Muslims were increasingly targeted with hate speech during 2020, with Armenians in particular subjected to public vilification as the Turkish government supported the Azerbaijani military in its offensive against ethnic Armenian forces in Nagorno-Karabakh.

D3. Is there academic freedom, and is the educational system free from extensive political indoctrination? 1 / 4

Academic freedom, never well respected in Turkey, was weakened further by the AKP's purge of government and civil society after the 2016 coup attempt. Schools tied to Fethullah Gülen—the Islamic scholar whose movement was blamed for the coup attempt and deemed a terrorist organization in Turkey—have been closed. Thousands of academics have been summarily dismissed for perceived leftist, Gülenist, or PKK sympathies.

In 2018, President Erdoğan issued a decree giving him the power to appoint rectors at both public and private universities. The government and university administrations now routinely intervene to prevent academics from researching sensitive topics, and political pressure has encouraged self-censorship among many scholars.

In January 2020, a group of 20 students from Boğaziçi University were sentenced to 10 months in prison for a campus protest against Turkey's military actions in Syria. Another seven students were fined. In June, the president issued a decree to close İstanbul Şehir University; the institution had been cofounded by former prime minister Ahmet Davutoğlu, a former ally and current political rival of President Erdoğan. In July, it was reported that Uludağ University had opened an investigation into professor Kayıhan Parla over his reports on the COVID-19 pandemic, which had cast doubt on official statistics regarding case counts and fatalities.

D4. Are individuals free to express their personal views on political or other sensitive topics without fear of surveillance or retribution? 1 / 4

While many Turkish citizens continue to voice their opinions openly with friends and relations, more exercise caution about what they post online or say in public. The arbitrariness of prosecutions for alleged dissent, which often result in pretrial detention and carry the risk of lengthy prison terms, is increasingly creating an atmosphere of self-censorship. During 2020, hundreds of social media users were arrested for "provocative" posts about the COVID-19 pandemic, and others continued to be detained and prosecuted for speech on topics such as the economy, "terrorism," or military operations.

E. ASSOCIATIONAL AND ORGANIZATIONAL RIGHTS: 3 / 12

E1. Is there freedom of assembly? 1 / 4

Although freedom of assembly is theoretically guaranteed in Turkish law, authorities have routinely disallowed gatherings by government critics on security grounds in recent years, while progovernment rallies are allowed to proceed. Restrictions have been imposed on May Day celebrations by leftist and labor groups, protests by purge victims, and opposition party meetings. Police use force to break up unsanctioned protests. Pandemic-related rules on social distancing were often cited selectively to justify the dispersal of unauthorized demonstrations during 2020.

Commemorations by Saturday Mothers, a group that protests forced disappearances associated with a 1980 coup d'état, have been routinely broken up by police; many participants, including elderly people, have been arrested. In July 2020, riot police prevented the group from gathering publicly to mark the 25th anniversary of their first protests.

The government has also targeted LGBT+ events in recent years. Istanbul's pride parade, which once drew tens of thousands of participants, was banned for the fifth consecutive year in 2019. Participants who tried to march faced tear gas and rubber bullets when police dispersed their gathering. Rallies were also banned in Ankara and the coastal city of Izmir. In 2020, pride events were organized entirely online.

E2. Is there freedom for nongovernmental organizations, particularly those that are engaged in human rights- and governance-related work? 1 / 4

The government has cracked down on NGOs since the 2016 coup attempt, summarily shutting down at least 1,500 foundations and associations and seizing their assets. The targeted groups worked on issues including torture, domestic violence, and aid to refugees and internally displaced persons. NGO leaders also face routine harassment, arrests, and prosecutions for carrying out their activities.

In July 2020, a court convicted four human rights defenders, including former Amnesty International Turkey chair Taner Kılıç, on groundless charges of aiding a terrorist organization; they were among several activists arrested in July 2017, most of whom were acquitted.

Osman Kavala, a prominent civil society leader and philanthropist, was arrested in November 2017 and charged in early 2019 with attempting to overthrow the government by supporting a protest in Istanbul's Gezi Park in 2013. The indictment was heavily criticized by human rights organizations for lacking credible evidence. Kavala and 15 other defendants from Turkish civil society were finally put on trial in June 2019. In December of that year, the ECHR ruled that Kavala's detention was unjustified and called for his release. He was acquitted in February 2020, but prosecutors immediately brought new charges against him and US academic Henri Barkey, accusing them, without evidence, of involvement in the 2016 coup attempt. The two were formally indicted in October; Kavala remained in custody at year's end, while Barkey was facing trial in absentia.

E3. Is there freedom for trade unions and similar professional or labor organizations? 1 / 4

Union activity, including the right to strike, is limited by law and in practice; antiunion activities by employers are common, and legal protections are poorly enforced. A system of representation threshold requirements make it difficult for unions to secure collective-bargaining rights. Trade unions and professional organizations have suffered from mass arrests and dismissals associated with the 2016–18 state of emergency and the general breakdown in freedoms of expression, assembly, and association. Union leaders were among those arrested while attempting to hold May Day demonstrations in 2020.

F. RULE OF LAW: 3 / 16

F1. Is there an independent judiciary? 1 / 4

The appointment of thousands of loyalist judges, the potential professional costs of ruling against the executive in a major case, and the effects of the postcoup purge have all severely weakened judicial independence in Turkey. More than 4,200 judges and prosecutors were removed in the 2016 coup attempt's aftermath. The establishment of the new presidential system in 2018 also increased executive control over the judiciary; members of the Board of Judges and Prosecutors (HSK), a powerful body that oversees judicial appointments and disciplinary measures, are now appointed by the parliament and the president, rather than by members of the judiciary itself.

Though the judiciary's autonomy is restricted, judges sometimes ruled against the government in significant cases in 2020, for example in the acquittals of Kavala and several other civil society figures.

F2. Does due process prevail in civil and criminal matters? 0 / 4

Due process guarantees were largely eroded during the state of emergency between 2016 and 2018, and these rights have not been restored in practice since the emergency was lifted. Due process and evidentiary standards are particularly weak in cases involving terrorism charges, with defendants held in lengthy pretrial detention for periods lasting up to seven years. According to the Justice Ministry, more than 130,000 people were under investigation for terrorism offenses related to the Gülen movement as of mid-2020, and nearly 60,000 were on trial. In many cases, lawyers defending those accused of terrorism have faced arrest themselves. A new law adopted in July 2020 allowed the formation of multiple bar associations in each province; human rights groups criticized the measure, arguing that the creation of progovernment rivals would effectively undercut the existing bar associations, which have remained largely apolitical.

F3. Is there protection from the illegitimate use of physical force and freedom from war and insurgencies? 1 / 4

Torture at the hands of authorities remains common in the wake of the 2016 coup attempt and subsequent state of emergency. Human Rights Watch has reported that security officers specifically target Kurds, Gülenists, and leftists with torture and degrading treatment, and operate in an environment of impunity. In September 2020, two Kurdish farmers were allegedly thrown from a military helicopter after soldiers detained them in their village, and one later died of his injuries. Prosecutors do not consistently investigate allegations of torture or abuse in custody, and the government has resisted the publication of a European Committee for the Prevention of Torture report on its detention practices.

The threat of terrorism decreased in 2018 with the weakening of the Islamic State (IS) militant group in neighboring Syria and Iraq; no large-scale terrorist attacks were reported during 2019 or 2020. However, civilians in the Kurdish southeast endured another year of conflict between security forces and the PKK, and residents have been subject to curfews as part of a new strategy to limit PKK activity. The conflict has killed more than 5,000 people within Turkey and in northern Iraq since July 2015, most of them soldiers or Kurdish militants.

F4. Do laws, policies, and practices guarantee equal treatment of various segments of the population? 1 / 4

Although Turkish law guarantees equal treatment, women as well as ethnic and religious minority groups suffer varying degrees of discrimination. For example, Alevis and non-Muslims reportedly face discrimination in schools and in employment, particularly when seeking senior public-sector positions. Gender inequality in the workplace is common, though women have become a larger part of the workforce since the beginning of the century.

The conflict with the PKK has been used to justify discriminatory measures against Kurds, including the prohibition of Kurdish festivals for security reasons and the reversal of Kurdish municipal officials' efforts to promote their language and culture. Many Kurdish-language schools and cultural organizations have been shut down by the government since 2015.

Turkey hosts 3.6 million refugees from Syria, in addition to 400,000 refugees and asylum seekers from other parts of the world. While the government has worked to provide them with basic services, a large minority of refugee children lack access to education, and few adults are able to obtain formal employment. Popular resentment against this population has been rising for years and is felt across the political spectrum. In response to public pressure, the Turkish government in October 2019 announced a plan to resettle as many as one million Syrian refugees in a new buffer zone in northern Syria. That month, the Turkish military launched an offensive to capture the territory in question from the Syrian Democratic Forces, a US-backed and Kurdish-led militia group that had waged a successful multiyear campaign against IS in Syria, but that Ankara opposed due to its alleged ties to the PKK. Also in October 2019, Turkish authorities forced Syrian refugees to secure new residency permits or risk deportation. In February 2020, the government announced that it would not block asylum seekers who sought to cross into the European Union, encouraging large-scale attempts that were met with violence and pushbacks by Greek security forces. Turkish authorities restored border controls in March, though crossing attempts and pushbacks continued during the year.

Same-sex relations are not legally prohibited, but LGBT+ people are subject to widespread discrimination, police harassment, and occasional violence. There is no legislation to protect people from discrimination based on their sexual orientation or gender identity. LGBT+ people are banned from openly serving in the military.

G. PERSONAL AUTONOMY AND INDIVIDUAL RIGHTS: 5 / 16

G1. Do individuals enjoy freedom of movement, including the ability to change their place of residence, employment, or education? 1 / 4

An upsurge in fighting between the government and the PKK in 2015 and 2016 resulted in the displacement of hundreds of thousands of people in southeastern Turkey, and freedom of movement remains limited in the region as low-level clashes continue.

More than 125,000 public-sector workers have been fired in the purges that followed the 2016 coup attempt, and those who were suspended or dismissed have no effective avenue for appeal. Many purge victims were unable to find new employment in the private sector, due to an atmosphere of guilt by association.

The authorities also targeted purged workers and their spouses with the revocation of their passports. The government stated in 2019 that it was working to reinstate passports after the Constitutional Court overturned the regulation that allowed their original revocation. However, the matter remained unresolved in 2020.

Refugees in Turkey continue to face legal and practical obstacles to free movement within the country.

G2. Are individuals able to exercise the right to own property and establish private businesses without undue interference from state or nonstate actors? 1 / 4

Private property rights are legally enshrined, but since 2013 many critics of the government have been subjected to intrusive tax and regulatory inspections. In the aftermath of the 2016 coup attempt, the assets of companies, NGOs, foundations, individuals, media outlets, and other entities deemed to be associated with terrorist groups have been confiscated. According to a survey published in 2018, at least $11 billion in private business assets, ranging from corner stores to large conglomerates, had been seized.

G3. Do individuals enjoy personal social freedoms, including choice of marriage partner and size of family, protection from domestic violence, and control over appearance? 2 / 4

The government has shown increasing disinterest in protecting vulnerable individuals from forced marriage and domestic violence. Child marriages, often performed at unofficial religious ceremonies, are widespread, and Syrian refugees appear to be particularly vulnerable. The Directorate of Religious Affairs briefly endorsed the practice, suggesting that girls as young as nine years old could marry when it published a glossary of Islamic terms in early 2018. The same document, which was retracted after public outcry, also defined marriage as an institution that saved its participants from adultery.

Despite legal safeguards, rates of domestic violence remain high; police are often reluctant to intervene in domestic disputes, and shelter space is both extremely limited and often geographically inaccessible. The AKP considered weakening domestic violence protections as part of a larger effort to dissuade women from seeking divorce; a parliamentary report published in 2016 recommended that women should be required to prove their partner's violence in order to receive extended police protection. The recommendation was retracted after sparking public criticism.

G4. Do individuals enjoy equality of opportunity and freedom from economic exploitation? 1 / 4

The weakness of labor unions and the government's increasing willingness to take action against organized labor have undermined equality of opportunity, protection from economic exploitation, and workplace safety. Workplace accidents have become more frequent in recent years, and laborers have little recourse if injured. According to the Workers' Health and Work Safety Assembly (İSİGM), more than 2,400 workers died in workplace incidents in 2020, including at least 741 who died of COVID-19. The large refugee population is especially vulnerable to exploitative employment conditions.

Turkmenistan

Population: 6,000,000
Capital: Ashgabat
Freedom Status: Not Free
Electoral Democracy: No

Overview: Turkmenistan is a repressive authoritarian state where political rights and civil liberties are almost completely denied in practice. Elections are tightly controlled, ensuring nearly unanimous victories for the president and his supporters. The economy is dominated by the state, corruption is systemic, religious groups are persecuted, and political dissent is not tolerated.

KEY DEVELOPMENTS IN 2020

- The government denied the presence of COVID-19 in Turkmenistan throughout the year, despite evidence of widespread respiratory infections and a surge in deaths.
- Constitutional changes that were approved in September called for the abolition of the Khalk Maslahaty (People's Council) and the creation of an upper house of parliament with the same name. The new chamber was set to be convened in 2021.
- Citizens engaged in a series of rare demonstrations during the year to protest the worsening economic situation. The events were typically triggered by local breakdowns in public services.

POLITICAL RIGHTS: 0 / 40
A. ELECTORAL PROCESS: 0 / 12
A1. Was the current head of government or other chief national authority elected through free and fair elections? 0 / 4

The president is directly elected for an unlimited number of seven-year terms, extended from five years under a 2016 constitutional revision. Gurbanguly Berdimuhamedov, the incumbent, was reelected for a third term in 2017 with 97.69 percent of the vote amid turnout of over 97 percent, according to official results. His eight token opponents were either nominees of state-backed parties or members of the ruling Democratic Party of Turkmenistan (DPT) who ran as independents. The Organization for Security and Co-operation in Europe (OSCE) criticized the election process for failing to present voters with a genuine choice and noted that it took place in a strictly controlled political and media environment.

A2. Were the current national legislative representatives elected through free and fair elections? 0 / 4

The unicameral Mejlis is composed of 125 members elected from individual districts to serve five-year terms. Parliamentary elections are tightly controlled by the state and feature no genuine competition from opposition candidates.

In the March 2018 elections, the DPT won 55 seats, the Party of Industrialists and Entrepreneurs and the Agrarian Party each took 11, and candidates nominated by groups of citizens secured 48. Voter turnout was reported to be approximately 92 percent. The OSCE found that the elections "lacked important prerequisites of a genuinely democratic electoral process." Observers said that while there was a semblance of pluralism, all parties and candidates supported the president, and the absence of media diversity interfered with citizens' ability to make a free and educated choice.

In September 2020, the parliament and president approved amendments to the constitution that abolished the 2,500-seat Khalk Maslahaty, a body that included Mejlis members as well as a variety of unelected officials and community leaders. It was set to be replaced in early 2021 with an upper chamber of parliament that would have the same name, leaving the Mejlis as the lower house. The new 56-seat chamber would include eight members each from the country's five provinces and Ashgabat, selected by the respective governors, plus eight members appointed by the president. The speaker of the new chamber would also be the president's constitutionally designated successor should he fall ill or die in office.

A3. Are the electoral laws and framework fair, and are they implemented impartially by the relevant election management bodies? 0 / 4

The legal framework for elections is neither fair nor impartially implemented. The Central Election Commission (CEC) is appointed by the president and operates with little transparency. The law allows virtually no opportunity for independent fundraising or campaigning. In the 2017 presidential and 2018 parliamentary elections, the CEC organized and funded all campaign activities, according to international monitors.

The constitution and electoral code were amended in 2016 to remove the upper age limit of 70 for presidential candidates, extend the presidential term from five to seven years, and eliminate the right of public associations to nominate presidential candidates.

B. POLITICAL PLURALISM AND PARTICIPATION: 0 / 16

B1. Do the people have the right to organize in different political parties or other competitive political groupings of their choice, and is the system free of undue obstacles to the rise and fall of these competing parties or groupings? 0 / 4

The party system is dominated by the ruling DPT and controlled by the executive branch. The 2012 law on political parties specified the legal basis for citizens to form independent parties, but barred parties formed on professional, regional, or religious lines, and those created by government officials. Nevertheless, Berdimuhamedov subsequently announced plans to form two new groups—the Party of Industrialists and Entrepreneurs and the Agrarian Party. Both were then openly organized by sitting members of the DPT and formally registered in 2012 and 2014, respectively. The Agrarian Party won its first parliamentary seats in 2018.

B2. Is there a realistic opportunity for the opposition to increase its support or gain power through elections? 0 / 4

Turkmenistan has never experienced a peaceful transfer of power between rival parties through elections. Berdimuhamedov had served in the government of his late predecessor, Saparmurat Niyazov, who in turn had ruled the country since before its independence from the Soviet Union. The Soviet-era Communist Party became the DPT in 1991 and remains in power to date. All genuine opposition groups operate either illegally or in exile.

B3. Are the people's political choices free from domination by forces that are external to the political sphere, or by political forces that employ extrapolitical means? 0 / 4

The authoritarian political system offers voters no meaningful alternatives to the ruling party. At an informal level, politics within the regime are thought to be influenced by regional patronage networks, or "clans," that control different parts of the state and economy.

B4. Do various segments of the population (including ethnic, racial, religious, gender, LGBT+, and other relevant groups) have full political rights and electoral opportunities? 0 / 4

Members of the ethnic Turkmen majority and the president's tribal subdivision in particular are favored for leadership positions. While women and members of ethnic or religious minority groups formally have full political rights, no segment of the country's population enjoys the practical ability to engage in independent political activity. About a quarter of candidates elected to the Mejlis in 2018 were women.

C. FUNCTIONING OF GOVERNMENT: 0 / 12

C1. Do the freely elected head of government and national legislative representatives determine the policies of the government? 0 / 4

The president, who is not freely elected, has ultimate decision-making authority. The executive branch determines laws and policies with no meaningful input or oversight from the rubber-stamp legislature. The Khalk Maslahaty that was abolished in 2020 had been revived in 2018 after being previously abolished in 2008. It was formally considered the country's top representative body, surpassing the role of the much smaller Mejlis. However, it met infrequently and mainly endorsed the president's decrees and policies.

C2. Are safeguards against official corruption strong and effective? 0 / 4

There are no independent institutions tasked with combating corruption, which is widespread in Turkmenistan. Anticorruption bodies have allegedly been used to extort revenue from wealthy officials and businesspeople. Crackdowns on corruption are typically selective and related to conflicts within the ruling elite.

In July 2020, Bakhtiyar Bashekov, a former district leader in Ashgabat, was sentenced to 22 years in prison for embezzlement, only two days after being removed from his post. It was reported in October that Merdan Govshudov, the deputy minister of education until his dismissal in September, had been tried, convicted, and sentenced to imprisonment for corruption in the education sector.

Genuine checks on nepotism and conflicts of interest are lacking. Serdar Berdimuhamedov, the president's son and presumed political heir, was appointed governor of Ahal Province in mid-2019. In February 2020, he was appointed minister of industry and construction operations. The president's brother-in-law, Nazar Rejepov, has benefited from preferential government contracts; his firm is a subcontractor for the construction of a highway between Ashgabat and Türkmenabat.

C3. Does the government operate with openness and transparency? 0 / 4

Decisions on monetary policy, large-scale contracts with foreign companies, and the allocation of state profits from hydrocarbon exports are largely opaque and ultimately controlled by the president, without effective legal limits or independent oversight. Government officials and state-owned companies are not required to disclose their basic financial information to the public.

Throughout the COVID-19 pandemic in 2020, the government refused to admit to the disease's presence in the country and failed to publish any data regarding the number of cases and deaths. This denial directly contradicted independent evidence of increased respiratory ailments and deaths, as well as the government's own belated introduction of measures such as mandatory mask wearing and movement restrictions. Health workers faced tight controls on their communications, among other hardships. The lack of publicly available information led to a surge in rumors, and many ailing citizens opted to avoid seeking care because they feared how they might be treated in state hospitals.

CIVIL LIBERTIES: 2 / 60
D. FREEDOM OF EXPRESSION AND BELIEF: 0 / 16
D1. Are there free and independent media? 0 / 4

Press freedom is severely restricted. The state controls nearly all broadcast and print media, and the state-run internet service provider blocks websites that carry independent news coverage or opposition-oriented content. Some citizens are able to access foreign satellite broadcasts, but the government continues efforts to remove receivers from houses in the countryside.

Independent journalists, particularly those affiliated with Radio Free Europe/Radio Liberty (RFE/RL), are subject to harassment, detention, physical abuse, and prosecution on trumped-up charges.

In September 2020, Ashgabat resident Nurgeldy Halikov was found guilty of fraud and sentenced to a prison term of four years after reportedly sharing a photo of a World Health Organization (WHO) delegation's July visit to Turkmenistan with the independent news website Turkmen.news; the photo was also shared on Instagram.

D2. Are individuals free to practice and express their religious faith or nonbelief in public and private? 0 / 4

Legal restrictions, state monitoring and harassment, and the risk of penalties including fines and imprisonment have virtually extinguished the ability of individuals to freely practice religion. A 2016 law on religion maintained existing bans on religious activity outside state control, imposed a higher membership threshold for the registration of religious groups, and required all registered groups to reapply for registration. Senior Muslim clerics are appointed by the government, and Muslims who do not follow the officially approved interpretation of Islam are subject to persecution, including lengthy prison terms.

Members of unregistered religious minority groups continue to face raids, beatings, and other forms of harassment. Turkmenistanis who conscientiously object to compulsory military service for religious reasons risk imprisonment. In September 2020, Myrat Orazgeldiyev, a conscientious objector and Jehovah's Witness, was sentenced to a one-year prison term for refusing military service, despite his pleas to undertake a civilian alternative. Four other conscientious objectors had been imprisoned earlier in the year, according to the nongovernmental organization (NGO) Forum 18.

D3. Is there academic freedom, and is the educational system free from extensive political indoctrination? 0 / 4

The government places significant restrictions on academic freedom, limiting research on politically sensitive topics and imposing onerous obstacles to the recognition of degrees from foreign institutions. Curriculums in schools and universities are controlled by the government.

In August 2019, schools were instructed to celebrate the government's achievements since Turkmenistan gained independence from the Soviet Union. That October, educators were instructed to review and teach Berdimuhamedov's writings.

In 2020, public health social-distancing measures were used as a pretext to sharply reduce classes in the country's schools that used Russian as the language of instruction.

D4. Are individuals free to express their personal views on political or other sensitive topics without fear of surveillance or retribution? 0 / 4

Private discussion and the expression of personal views are highly restricted due to intrusive supervision by state security services, including physical surveillance, monitoring of telephone and electronic communications, and the use of informers.

In recent years, the government has employed increasingly sophisticated methods to monitor the population. Authorities have reportedly used special software to eavesdrop on voice over internet protocol (VoIP) calls, operate computer cameras remotely, and record keystrokes. Social media users who post critical comments about the government are subject to intimidation and imprisonment, and restrictions on social media sites, cloud storage services, and virtual private networks (VPNs) have intensified. The government also reportedly monitors the online contacts and posts of its citizens abroad.

A 2019 law further expanded the government's ability to monitor communications systems, regardless of their ownership. Also that year, the National Security Ministry reportedly enlarged its system of informers in universities to identify students who were critical of the government.

E. ASSOCIATIONAL AND ORGANIZATIONAL RIGHTS: 0 / 12

E1. Is there freedom of assembly? 0 / 4

The constitution guarantees freedom of assembly, and the 2015 Law on Assemblies defines the right of individuals and groups to hold peaceful gatherings with prior authorization. However, the law grants officials broad discretion to block assemblies, and the authorities do not allow organized antigovernment demonstrations.

A number of small, spontaneous demonstrations took place during 2020, with citizens protesting economic deterioration and local breakdowns in public services. For example, a protest in Türkmenabat in May came in the wake of powerful wind storms in April that had damaged property and led to electricity shortages. More than a thousand people were reported to have participated, demanding that local authorities assist with cleanup efforts and restore electricity. In September and October 2020, protesters successfully opposed the attempted closure by police of flea markets in Türkmenabat and Bayramali, where people had begun selling their belongings in response the dire economic situation. Authorities generally responded to the year's protests with a combination of concessions and police intimidation.

E2. Is there freedom for nongovernmental organizations, particularly those that are engaged in human rights– and governance-related work? 0 / 4

Onerous registration and regulatory requirements effectively prevent most independent NGOs from operating legally or receiving foreign funding, and activities by unregistered groups can draw fines, detention, and other penalties. Individual activists face intimidation and harassment, as do the family members of human rights activists working in exile. Among other cases during 2020, lawyer Pygambergeldy Allaberdyev was arrested in Balkanabat on hooliganism charges in September, reportedly for his alleged links to activists abroad; he was tried later in the month and sentenced to six years in prison.

E3. Is there freedom for trade unions and similar professional or labor organizations? 0 / 4

Workers have a legal right to join trade unions, but there are no protections against antiunion discrimination, and strikes are prohibited. The government-controlled Association of Trade Unions of Turkmenistan is the only union organization permitted to operate.

F. RULE OF LAW: 0 / 16

F1. Is there an independent judiciary? 0 / 4

The judicial system is subservient to the president, who appoints and dismisses judges unilaterally. In practice, the courts are commonly used to punish dissent and remove potential threats to the president's political dominance.

F2. Does due process prevail in civil and criminal matters? 0 / 4

Arbitrary arrests and detentions are common, particularly for dissidents, members of unapproved religious groups, activists, and journalists who work with foreign organizations. The authorities frequently deny defendants' basic rights of due process, including public trials and access to defense attorneys.

F3. Is there protection from the illegitimate use of physical force and freedom from war and insurgencies? 0 / 4

Prison conditions are extremely harsh, and security forces routinely use torture to extract confessions or punish inmates, which can result in deaths in custody. Turkmenistanis are also subject to enforced disappearance; in a 2019 report, the Prove They Are Alive! human rights campaign identified 121 people who remained forcibly disappeared in the country. Physical abuse and hazing in the military have reportedly led to several deaths among conscripts in recent years.

F4. Do laws, policies, and practices guarantee equal treatment of various segments of the population? 0 / 4

Employment and educational opportunities for members of non-Turkmen ethnic minorities are limited by the government's promotion of Turkmen national identity, and activists who advocate for minority rights have faced persecution. Traditional social and religious norms help to restrict women's access to education and economic opportunity; there are no legal protections against sexual harassment in the workplace.

The law does not protect LGBT+ people from discrimination, and sexual activity between men can be punished with up to two years in prison. In May 2020, a well-known entertainer and several other young men were sentenced to two years in prison on "sodomy" charges.

G. PERSONAL AUTONOMY AND INDIVIDUAL RIGHTS: 2 / 16

G1. Do individuals enjoy freedom of movement, including the ability to change their place of residence, employment, or education? 0 / 4

Freedom of movement is restricted, with frequent reports of individuals being barred from traveling abroad; officials are reportedly instructed to prevent Turkmenistanis under the age of 40 from leaving the country. The government is known to prohibit the families of dissidents and prisoners from leaving. Internal passports and a residency permit system also obstruct travel within the country. Despite these restrictions, unpublished government statistics suggest that nearly two million people emigrated during a 2008–18 reporting period, with many of them seeking to escape the dire economic situation.

Although the government refused to admit to the presence of COVID-19 in the country in 2020, additional restrictions on freedom of movement were imposed as illnesses and deaths increased. Under rules in place for part of the year, citizens seeking to travel across the country were required to undergo an examination at a clinic, obtain permission from the police, buy a plane ticket, and take a COVID-19 test. In November, a stricter two-month ban on such travel was imposed, with any exceptions requiring approval from special local commissions. Bribery reportedly played a role in the permit process throughout the year.

G2. Are individuals able to exercise the right to own property and establish private businesses without undue interference from state or nonstate actors? 1 / 4

The constitution establishes the right to property ownership, but the deeply flawed judiciary provides little protection to businesses and individuals, and the president's relatives monopolize key sectors of the economy that are not directly state controlled. Arbitrary evictions and confiscation of property are common.

G3. Do individuals enjoy personal social freedoms, including choice of marriage partner and size of family, protection from domestic violence, and control over appearance? 1 / 4

Domestic violence is reportedly common, but few victims file complaints with the authorities, and the government has not made significant efforts to monitor, prevent, or combat the problem. Reporting and prosecution of rape are similarly limited. While polygamy has long been illegal, it apparently persists in practice; a 2018 law was meant to reinforce the ban. Schoolgirls in Mary Province were ordered to undergo mandatory gynecological tests in 2019 after local officials claimed that some girls were secretly giving birth to children or undergoing abortions.

G4. Do individuals enjoy equality of opportunity and freedom from economic exploitation? 0 / 4

The government forces thousands of students, public employees, and other citizens to participate in the annual cotton harvest with little or no pay. Impoverished residents of rural areas are especially vulnerable to trafficking abroad for forced labor or sexual exploitation, and the government does little to address the problem.

The state's mismanagement of a weak economy, including soaring inflation, has inhibited opportunity and imposed hardship on the population. Persistently low oil and gas prices have driven down vital export revenues in recent years, leading to reports of unpaid wages and shortages of basic goods. To raise funds, the government has at times increased various fees, cut subsidies, and pressured officials, businesspeople, and ordinary workers to make "voluntary" contributions. The COVID-19 pandemic exacerbated the existing crisis, especially in relation to food shortages and rationing. Also during the pandemic, medical personnel were reportedly forced to work in dangerous conditions and locations, and to pay for their own protective equipment.

Tuvalu

Population: 10,000
Capital: Funafuti
Freedom Status: Free
Electoral Democracy: Yes

Overview: Tuvalu is a parliamentary democracy that holds regular, competitive elections. Civil liberties are generally upheld. Ongoing problems include a lack of antidiscrimination laws to protect women and LGBT+ people, and there are concerns about child labor in some industries.

KEY DEVELOPMENTS IN 2020

- There were no reported cases of COVID-19 in Tuvalu. Other than the closure of borders in mid-March virus-related lockdown measures were minimal, as no wave of infections arrived to disrupt everyday life and business. The government implemented a strict, 14-day quarantine protocol for repatriation of citizens abroad and similarly careful measures for repatriation of foreign citizens in Tuvalu. Commercial flights to the islands remained suspended at year's end.
- The pandemic drew attention to the islands' vulnerabilities, with government officials and others remarking that an outbreak could have had alarming effects due to the country's geographic isolation and reliance on imports. In June, Prime Minister Kausea Natano, in his role as Pacific Island Forum chair, called for sustainable international assistance for Tuvalu and other fragile regional economies to recover from economic struggles related to the pandemic, as well as to protect against natural disasters and the impact of climate change.
- Cyclone Tino struck the country in January, causing extensive property damage and prompting concerns about food insecurity. A state of emergency was declared, and the World Bank granted the country $6 million to aid recovery efforts.

POLITICAL RIGHTS: 37 / 40

A. ELECTORAL PROCESS: 12 / 12

A1. Was the current head of government or other chief national authority elected through free and fair elections? 4 / 4

A governor general represents the British monarch as ceremonial head of state. The prime minister, chosen by Parliament, leads the government, thus the legitimacy of the presidential election depends in part on the conduct of parliamentary elections. Independent candidate Kausea Natano became prime minister after the September 2019 elections, which were considered free and fair. He defeated another independent, Enele Sopoaga, in a secret ballot, receiving 10 of the 16 ministers' votes.

A2. Were the current national legislative representatives elected through free and fair elections? 4 / 4

The unicameral House of Assembly has 16 members who are directly elected through contests in eight geographical constituencies, each of which are represented by two members. The attorney general has an advisory role and does not vote. In the September 2019 elections, all candidates ran as independents. Two women ran for seats in Parliament, though only the incumbent Puakena Boreham was elected. Each of the main inhabited islands in Tuvalu is also governed by an elected local council.

A3. Are the electoral laws and framework fair, and are they implemented impartially by the relevant election management bodies? 4 / 4

Tuvalu's legal framework provides for democratic elections, and the laws are fairly and impartially implemented. An appointed secretary to the government is responsible for the supervision of elections and maintenance of voter rolls. Local polling officers are authorized to adjudicate election-related disputes in their districts, and there is a mechanism through which appeals may be filed. The September 2019 elections were accepted by all relevant stakeholders and constituencies.

B. POLITICAL PLURALISM AND PARTICIPATION: 15 / 16

B1. Do the people have the right to organize in different political parties or other competitive political groupings of their choice, and is the system free of undue obstacles to the rise and fall of these competing parties or groupings? 4 / 4

There are no formal political parties, though no law bars their formation. Candidates typically run as independents and form loose, frequently shifting alliances once in office.

B2. Is there a realistic opportunity for the opposition to increase its support or gain power through elections? 4 / 4

Tuvalu has an established pattern of democratic transfers of power. Individual prime ministers and governments have seldom lasted a full term in office in recent decades, with intense political rivalries sometimes prompting no-confidence votes in Parliament.

B3. Are the people's political choices free from domination by forces that are external to the political sphere, or by political forces that employ extrapolitical means? 4 / 4

Traditional elders and the main Protestant church play an influential role in society, but they do not exercise undue control over the political choices of voters and candidates.

B4. Do various segments of the population (including ethnic, racial, religious, gender, LGBT+, and other relevant groups) have full political rights and electoral opportunities? 3 / 4

All Tuvaluans aged 18 and over who are present in the country on polling day but not imprisoned are eligible to vote. Politics are generally dominated by older, well-educated men. While women formally have full political rights, in practice their participation is somewhat inhibited by discriminatory and widespread biases. Two women ran in the 2019 parliamentary elections, and one of them (an incumbent) won a seat. A move to add two reserved seats for women was considered as part of a constitutional review process in 2018. No action appears to have been taken as of the end of 2019.

C. FUNCTIONING OF GOVERNMENT: 10 / 12

C1. Do the freely elected head of government and national legislative representatives determine the policies of the government? 4 / 4

Tuvalu's elected officials are able to develop and implement government policies and legislation without improper interference from any unelected entity. The country often receives funding from other countries and international entities to implement policies and programs. The Asian Development Bank (ADB), the World Bank, and partner countries provide the country with grants, but there have been no reported concerns of undue influence on government.

In August 2019, the Tuvalu government reaffirmed its commitment to its relationship with Taiwan, which precludes any diplomatic ties with China, and thus any influence China might have on Tuvalu's government. China's influence has grown in the Pacific, which has raised concerns of undue influence on the independence of policymaking in several other countries in the region.

C2. Are safeguards against official corruption strong and effective? 3 / 4

Corruption is not a severe problem in Tuvalu, and the country's independent auditing and law enforcement bodies are generally effective in combating graft, though there have been some corruption scandals in recent years.

Tuvalu is among the countries included in a new initiative, led by New Zealand in cooperation with the United Nations, to strengthen anticorruption laws in the Pacific Island region.

C3. Does the government operate with openness and transparency? 3 / 4

Government operations and legislative processes are generally transparent, though there is no freedom of information law to guarantee and regulate public access to official records. While officials are legally obliged to disclose their assets and income, the rules are not consistently enforced, according to the US State Department.

In November 2019, the Tuvalu Parliament livestreamed government proceedings on social media for the first time. Information about changes in policy or circumstance in Tuvalu can take days to reach the body of the population, as well as the rest of the world; livestreaming parliamentary sessions sought to ameliorate these challenges.

In December 2020, the government announced plans to become a "paperless society," by using blockchain technology to create a national digital ledger in which all public data would be stored.

CIVIL LIBERTIES: 56 / 60
D. FREEDOM OF EXPRESSION AND BELIEF: 16 / 16
D1. Are there free and independent media? 4 / 4

The constitution provides for freedom of the press, and there are no reported restrictions on this right, though the small media market does not support independent domestic news outlets. The government operates a radio station and a national newspaper. Many residents use satellite dishes to access foreign programming. Internet coverage has grown somewhat in recent years, though access is largely limited to the main island, and is expensive, inconsistent, and limited everywhere else.

D2. Are individuals free to practice and express their religious faith or nonbelief in public and private? 4 / 4

The constitution and laws provide for freedom of religion, and this right is generally respected in practice. A Protestant church, the Congregational Christian Church of Tuvalu, has official status under the law, and about 97 percent of the population belongs to it. Cultural leaders are empowered to regulate local religious activities, and on smaller islands they sometimes discourage minority groups from proselytizing or holding public events.

D3. Is there academic freedom, and is the educational system free from extensive political indoctrination? 4 / 4

Academic freedom is generally respected.

D4. Are individuals free to express their personal views on political or other sensitive topics without fear of surveillance or retribution? 4 / 4

There are no significant restrictions on freedom of expression. The government does not improperly monitor personal communications or social media activity.

E. ASSOCIATIONAL AND ORGANIZATIONAL RIGHTS: 12 / 12
E1. Is there freedom of assembly? 4 / 4

The constitution provides for freedom of assembly, and the government typically upholds this right in practice.

E2. Is there freedom for nongovernmental organizations, particularly those that are engaged in human rights- and governance-related work? 4 / 4

Freedom of association is respected. Nongovernmental organizations operate without interference, providing a variety of health, education, and other services.

E3. Is there freedom for trade unions and similar professional or labor organizations? 4 / 4

Workers in the private sector have the right to organize unions, bargain collectively, and strike. Public-sector employees can join professional associations and engage in collective bargaining, but they are not permitted to strike. Most labor disputes are resolved through negotiations in practice. The only registered union represents seafarers.

F. RULE OF LAW: 15 / 16

F1. Is there an independent judiciary? 4 / 4

The judiciary is independent. The chief justice is appointed by the head of state on the advice of the cabinet, and other judges are appointed in the same manner after consultation with the chief justice. Judges cannot be removed arbitrarily.

F2. Does due process prevail in civil and criminal matters? 4 / 4

The authorities generally uphold due process during arrests, detentions, and trials. A public defense lawyer is available to detainees and defendants. However, the limited capacity of the legal system can lead to delays in court proceedings and access to counsel.

F3. Is there protection from the illegitimate use of physical force and freedom from war and insurgencies? 4 / 4

There were no reports of physical abuse by police or in the prison system during the year. Criminal activity does not pose a major threat to physical security.

F4. Do laws, policies, and practices guarantee equal treatment of various segments of the population? 3 / 4

While women generally enjoy equality before the law, discriminatory biases and social norms limit women's role in society, and there are no specific legal protections against gender discrimination in employment.

Same-sex sexual activity is illegal and can be punished with imprisonment, though the law is not actively enforced. Discrimination based on sexual orientation or gender identity is not specifically banned.

There is no national legal framework for providing refuge to asylum seekers, nor were there any such applications reported in 2020.

G. PERSONAL AUTONOMY AND INDIVIDUAL RIGHTS: 13 / 16

G1. Do individuals enjoy freedom of movement, including the ability to change their place of residence, employment, or education? 4 / 4

Tuvaluans are free to travel within the country and abroad, and to relocate for purposes including employment and education. The country's borders were closed to international travel in 2020 due to the COVID-19 pandemic. The government implemented a strict, 14-day quarantine protocol for repatriation of citizens abroad, and similarly careful measures for repatriation of foreign citizens in Tuvalu. Commercial flights to the islands remained suspended at year's end.

G2. Are individuals able to exercise the right to own property and establish private businesses without undue interference from state or nonstate actors? 3 / 4

Tuvalu's legal framework and government policies are generally supportive of property rights and private-business activity. However, laws and practices surrounding land ownership and inheritance favor men over women.

In June and July 2019, a dispute over a leasing agreement for the island's airport escalated between landowners on the island Funafuti and the government. The landowners believed that the lease had expired after 25 years—in 2017—while the government claimed the original lease for the airport was set for 99 years. After landowners blockaded the runway, and the two parties went into negotiations, a case for the incident and dispute was filed in the High Court, which determined that the landowners had violated their lease agreement. Police were ordered to arrest anyone who interfered with flights, as the blockade was deemed to pose a "significant sovereign risk."

G3. Do individuals enjoy personal social freedoms, including choice of marriage partner and size of family, protection from domestic violence, and control over appearance? 3 / 4

Although personal social freedoms are generally respected, domestic violence often goes unreported because it is viewed as a private matter. There are no specific laws against spousal rape.

G4. Do individuals enjoy equality of opportunity and freedom from economic exploitation? 3 / 4

Forced labor is prohibited, and the government mandates basic protections against exploitative or dangerous working conditions, though enforcement is not proactive or consistent. Most of the labor force works in the informal sector or in small-scale fishing and agriculture. No law addresses forms of harmful or hazardous child labor, and the US State Department's 2019 Findings on the Worst Forms of Child Labor, the most recent available, stated that there was evidence of child labor in the fishing industry and among domestic workers.

In 2018, Tuvalu created its first national human rights institution (NHRI) and will give the country's ombudsman additional powers to promote and protect human rights on the island. The new NHRI was created to be aligned with the Paris Principles for independent and effective human rights institutions.

Uganda

Population: 45,700,000
Capital: Kampala
Freedom Status: Not Free
Electoral Democracy: No

Overview: While Uganda holds regular elections, their credibility has deteriorated over time, and the country has been ruled by the same party and president since 1986. The ruling party, the National Resistance Movement (NRM), retains power through the manipulation of state resources, intimidation by security forces, and politicized prosecutions of opposition leaders. Uganda's civil society and independent media sectors suffer from legal and extralegal harassment and state violence.

KEY DEVELOPMENTS IN 2020

- Between March and May, police arrested and assaulted at least 10 journalists while enforcing COVID-19-related restrictions, taking advantage of the pandemic to further curtail freedom of the press. In April, police arrested Rogers Asiimwe of Freedom Radio, raided his office, and questioned him about his discussion of the coronavirus, its origins, and the Ugandan government's lockdown measures.

- In October, a combined military and police force raided the campaign headquarters of the singer and parliamentarian Robert Kyagulanyi—better known as Bobi Wine—ostensibly to recover red berets the campaign had stashed, a part of military uniform. Wine's campaign uses the berets as a symbol of resistance, which the government claims is illegal. While opposition parties' rallies were violently dispersed by security forces and participants were arrested throughout the year, the NRM was able to hold campaign events without interference.
- Following the November 2020 arrest of Bobi Wine at a political rally, security forces violently dispersed protests organized by Wine's party, killing 54 people. Multiple videos shared on social media during protests show the military and plain-clothes gunmen firing high-caliber rifles in populated urban centers. The government failed to hold any of the attackers responsible for killing unarmed civilians.

POLITICAL RIGHTS: 11 / 40
A. ELECTORAL PROCESS: 3 / 12
A1. Was the current head of government or other chief national authority elected through free and fair elections? 1 / 4

The president is directly elected to serve five-year terms. In the 2016 election, incumbent Yoweri Museveni won with 60.6 percent of the vote, according to official results. Kizza Besigye of the opposition Forum for Democratic Change (FDC) placed second, with 35.6 percent. The integrity of the election was undermined by problems including the misuse of state resources and flawed administration by the Electoral Commission (EC).

A 2017 constitutional amendment removed the presidential age limit of 75, allowing the president to seek reelection in 2021. Opposition parties and other critics challenged the validity of the change, citing procedural problems and intimidation, but the Supreme Court upheld the amendment in April 2019.

A2. Were the current national legislative representatives elected through free and fair elections? 1 / 4

The 2016 elections for the unicameral Parliament were held concurrently with the presidential vote. A total of 426 members were chosen, including 289 elected in single-member districts, 112 elected to reserved seats for women, and 25 chosen to represent special interest groups (the military, youth, people with disabilities, and trade unions). Members serve terms of five years. The ruling NRM won an absolute majority with 293 seats. Independents won 66 seats, the opposition FDC took 36, and smaller parties divided the remainder. As with the presidential election, the integrity of the balloting was undermined by problems including the misuse of state resources and flawed administration by the EC. Ahead of the 2021 elections, in November 2020 the government introduced a ban on campaign rallies, citing the COVID-19 pandemic. Subsequently, stringent restrictions prohibiting public campaigning events were introduced, though they were not uniformly applied. Ruling-party politicians were allowed to hold rallies and campaign freely while opposition rallies were violently dispersed by police and military.

A3. Are the electoral laws and framework fair, and are they implemented impartially by the relevant election management bodies? 1 / 4

Independent observers, civil society, and opposition leaders have long critiqued and called for substantive reforms to Ugandan electoral laws. On election day in 2016, the EC experienced significant technical and logistical problems. It extended the voting time for polling stations that opened late, with voting in some areas continuing for an extra day even as counting was well under way. This exacerbated existing mistrust of the EC and raised suspicions of malfeasance.

Following the flawed 2016 elections, the Supreme Court called on the attorney general to implement electoral reforms to address these issues within two years and update the court on the progress of the changes. The deadline passed in March 2018 with no meaningful reforms advanced. Between February and March 2020, the parliament passed five electoral reform bills that they had been ordered to draft in 2019. President Museveni assented to four of the laws in July 2020.

Between July 2018 and February 2019, the EC suspended the Citizens' Coalition for Electoral Democracy in Uganda (CCEDU), a prominent nongovernmental organization (NGO), from election observation and voter education, claiming the group is partisan and undermines the integrity of elections. However, after representatives from the CCEDU met with the EC in October of that year, both sides indicated that they had reached an agreement to allow the group to resume its work.

B. POLITICAL PLURALISM AND PARTICIPATION: 5 / 16

B1. Do the people have the right to organize in different political parties or other competitive political groupings of their choice, and is the system free of undue obstacles to the rise and fall of these competing parties or groupings? 1 / 4

The formation of political parties is protected by law, and multiple parties exist and compete in practice. However, the activities of opposition groups are hindered by restrictive party registration requirements and candidate eligibility rules, a lack of access to state media coverage, and violence or harassment by state authorities and paramilitary groups.

Police used tear gas and live ammunition to break up FDC rallies in the towns of Lira and Kasese in April 2019, and used similar tactics throughout 2019. When FDC leaders tried to organize the party's national conference in November, heavily armed police and military officers cordoned off the venue and forcibly dispersed party supporters. Besigye and a number of other FDC members were arrested and temporarily detained.

In June 2020, the Ugandan government prohibited all political gatherings, ostensibly to curtail the spread of COVID-19. Candidates were forced to campaign using radio, TV, leaflets, and social media; media the ruling party has substantial influence over. The government's enforcement of the ban disproportionately targeted opposition party activities, particularly of Bobi Wine's People Power group. In October, a combined military and police force raided Wine's campaign headquarters, claiming the raid was intended to recover red berets, a part of military uniform, that Wine's campaign use as a symbol of resistance; the government claims they are illegal. While opposition parties' rallies were violently dispersed by security forces and participants were arrested throughout the year, the NRM was able to hold campaign events without interference.

Following the November 2020 arrest of Bobi Wine at a political rally, security forces violently dispersed protests organized by Wine's party, killing 54 people. Multiple videos shared on social media during protests show the military and plainclothes gunmen firing high-caliber rifles in populated urban centers. The government failed to hold any of the attackers responsible for killing unarmed civilians.

B2. Is there a realistic opportunity for the opposition to increase its support or gain power through elections? 1 / 4

The ruling party dominates all levels of government. There are several dozen opposition lawmakers in Parliament, as well as numerous independents, though some of the latter support the NRM. Presidential and parliamentary election campaigns are characterized by violence, intimidation, and harassment toward opposition parties.

Leaders of opposition parties and political movements are sometimes arrested on trumped-up criminal charges. There were multiple arrests of FDC leaders during 2019, and Bobi Wine was arrested in November 2020 and harassed throughout the year. At the end of 2020, Wine and more than 30 others were still awaiting trial on treason charges arising from a 2018 incident in the Arua district; police alleged that Wine and his supporters obstructed President Museveni's motorcade and threw stones at the vehicles. Charges of annoying, alarming, or ridiculing the president were added to the case in August 2019.

B3. Are the people's political choices free from domination by forces that are external to the political sphere, or by political forces that employ extrapolitical means? 1 / 4

The military is closely aligned with Museveni and the NRM, and holds 10 seats in Parliament. The government and ruling party also reportedly use public resources and patronage networks to build political support among religious leaders and other influential figures.

B4. Do various segments of the population (including ethnic, racial, religious, gender, LGBT+, and other relevant groups) have full political rights and electoral opportunities? 2 / 4

Although Uganda has a large number of diverse ethnic groups, they lack equal representation and opportunities. Small ethnic groups like Alur, Ik, Bagungu, Bakonzo, Kakwa, Batwa, and Karamojong are disproportionately affected by violent conflicts, and have less access to education and inadequate healthcare.

The dominant position and coercive tactics of the NRM impede free political participation and advocacy of interests by Uganda's various ethnic groups, including those affiliated with subnational kingdoms and smaller Indigenous groups. An assessment of women's participation in the 2016 elections by the Women's Democracy Group, a coalition of Ugandan civil society organizations, noted a widespread perception that because a certain number of legislative seats are reserved for women, "they should not contest for direct positions so as to reduce on the competition for male contestants." Due to severe legal and societal discrimination, the interests of LGBT+ people are not represented in politics.

C. FUNCTIONING OF GOVERNMENT: 3 / 12

C1. Do the freely elected head of government and national legislative representatives determine the policies of the government? 1 / 4

Power is concentrated in the hands of the NRM leadership, the security forces, and especially the president, who retains office through deeply flawed electoral processes. Lawmakers have little practical ability to influence legislation in which the government has a particular interest, though there is more consultation on ordinary policy matters. The executive has secured passage of key legislation through inducement, harassment, and intimidation of the legislative branch. For example, several opposition lawmakers were assaulted and forcibly removed from Parliament by plainclothes military officers during the reading of the 2017 constitutional amendment bill that removed the presidential age limit.

C2. Are safeguards against official corruption strong and effective? 1 / 4

Corruption is a serious problem. There are laws and institutions designed to combat official malfeasance, including the Anti-Corruption Act of 2009 and the Inspectorate of Government, and instances of alleged graft have led to investigations and intense media attention. However, the system has not been effective at addressing corruption in a sustained manner, and top government officials are rarely prosecuted in practice.

C3. Does the government operate with openness and transparency? 1 / 4

Many government departments deny requests for information under the country's Access to Information Act. Other laws related to national security and confidentiality also impede open access to information in practice. The Access to Information Act is not uniformly applied. Government agencies seem to release information that only favors the regime. For example, in September 2020, the Electoral Commission made public the academic documents of Bobi Wine while refusing to release those of President Museveni, despite numerous petitions. Wine described the Commission's decision as intended to raise questions about his eligibility to run for president.

Public procurement decisions are generally opaque.

CIVIL LIBERTIES: 23 / 60
D. FREEDOM OF EXPRESSION AND BELIEF: 8 / 16
D1. Are there free and independent media? 1 / 4

The media sector features many independent outlets, but their journalists face arrest, harassment, intimidation, and assault in reprisal for their work. Authorities routinely raid and shut down radio stations and other outlets, and will take away accreditation from journalists in retribution for their reporting.

Throughout 2020, journalists covering the campaign events of Bobi Wine were harassed, assaulted, and detained, on various charges. The Committee to Protect Journalists, a press freedom watchdog, reported that at least seven journalists were harassed and attacked by police and members of the public between November and December while covering campaigns for the 2021 presidential elections. Further, authorities issued new guidelines for foreign journalists, requiring them to reapply for accreditation within a week of the guidelines being announced. At least one foreign news crew was deported.

Between March and May, police arrested and assaulted at least 10 journalists while enforcing COVID-19-related restrictions. In April, police arrested Rogers Asiimwe of Freedom Radio, raided his office, and questioned him about his discussion of the coronavirus, its origins, and the lockdown measures instituted by the Ugandan government.

D2. Are individuals free to practice and express their religious faith or nonbelief in public and private? 3 / 4

There is no state religion, and freedom of worship is both constitutionally protected and generally respected in practice. However, the government has restricted religious groups whose members allegedly pose security risks. It has also sought to control political statements by religious leaders, tolerating those who express support for President Museveni and the ruling party while subjecting those with more critical views to intimidation, harassment, and arrest

A series of Muslim clerics have been murdered in recent years, and the investigations into the crimes have not yet led to any convictions.

D3. Is there academic freedom, and is the educational system free from extensive political indoctrination? 2 / 4

Academic freedom has been undermined by alleged surveillance of university lectures by security officials, and by the need for professors to obtain permission to hold public meetings at universities. In December 2018, 45 staff members at Makerere University in Kampala were dismissed for indiscipline, but critics argued that the dismissals were meant to silence critics of the government within the university. The 2019 imprisonment of prominent Makerere University academic, Stella Nyanzi, under the Computer Misuse Act for cyber harassing President Museveni was annulled in February 2020, after a judge ruled that she had not been given a fair trial.

Authorities have responded harshly to campus protests by student groups.

D4. Are individuals free to express their personal views on political or other sensitive topics without fear of surveillance or retribution? 2 / 4

Private speech is relatively unrestrained, and Ugandans openly criticize the government on social media. However, individuals are at risk of criminal penalties for such speech, and the government reportedly monitors social media platforms. Media reports in August 2019 indicated that Ugandan intelligence officials, with assistance from a Chinese telecommunications firm, had hacked into the accounts and devices of opposition figures to track their communications and movements; the same techniques could presumably be used against ordinary citizens.

In 2018, the government implemented a controversial social media tax, requiring users on platforms like Facebook, Twitter, and WhatsApp to pay a daily fee of $0.05, which is prohibitively expensive for many. Critics assailed the tax as an attack on freedom of expression and an attempt to limit the exchange of criticism of the government and mobilization of the opposition online. According to the UCC, the tax led to a decline in the number of social media users in the months following its introduction.

In August 2019, the UCC issued an order requiring all social media bloggers, YouTubers, and online influencers to be registered. In September 2020, the UCC announced that all online content creators must register by October 5. The registration process includes a $27 fee, and applicants have to provide their passport, national identification information, and contact information. Critics claim the regulations curtail freedom of speech for Ugandans who use social media to criticize the government.

E. ASSOCIATIONAL AND ORGANIZATIONAL RIGHTS: 4 / 12

E1. Is there freedom of assembly? 1 / 4

In March 2020, the Constitutional Court annulled the Public Order Management Act (POMA), the 2013 public order law that required groups to register with local police in writing three days before any gathering, public or private, to discuss political issues. The government relied on the law to prevent opposition rallies, as it gave police the authority to deny approval for such meetings if they are not deemed to be in the "public interest," and to use force to disperse assemblies judged unlawful.

In 2020, the number of unlawful, unjustified, and disproportionate use of force against protesters dramatically increased. The military and police killed 54 people during protests in Kampala and other towns on November 18 and 19, which was condemned local and international human rights activists, donors, and civil society organizations as blatant human rights violations.

The annulment of POMA did not stop police from repeatedly using tear gas, live ammunition, and arrests to disrupt opposition events in 2020. During the COVID-19 pandemic, security forces used public health measures to violently disperse rallies and meetings associated with Wine's campaign.

E2. Is there freedom for nongovernmental organizations, particularly those that are engaged in human rights- and governance-related work? 1 / 4

Civil society in Uganda is active, and several NGOs address politically sensitive issues. However, their operations are vulnerable to various legal restrictions, burdensome registration requirements, and occasional threats. NGOs that work on human rights issues have reported break-ins at their offices and burglaries in recent years, and the police have failed to adequately investigate the incidents.

In August and September 2019, the government required NGOs to submit information to the National Bureau for NGOs on their staffing, finances, and activities. In November 2019, the interior minister ordered some 12,000 NGOs to shut down for failing to renew their registration, though the bureau said the groups would still have an opportunity to re-register. Only about 2,000 groups had successfully navigated the process.

E3. Is there freedom for trade unions and similar professional or labor organizations? 2 / 4

Workers' rights to organize, bargain collectively, and strike are recognized by law, except for workers providing essential government services. As of 2018, there were 42 trade unions in Uganda, representing close to one million people. Most are grouped under two umbrella entities—the National Organization of Trade Unions (NOTU) and the Central Organization of Free Trade Unions (COFTU). Despite their legal and institutional protections, trade unions have been undermined in practice by co-optation, intimidation, and manipulation designed to frustrate their organizing and bargaining efforts.

F. RULE OF LAW: 4 / 16

F1. Is there an independent judiciary? 1 / 4

Executive influence weakens judicial independence, as does systemic corruption. In August 2019, the chief justice established an internal task force to investigate widespread allegations of judicial corruption, but the FDC called for an independent probe by outside lawyers and experts.

F2. Does due process prevail in civil and criminal matters? 1 / 4

Police routinely engage in arbitrary arrests and detentions, despite legal safeguards against such practices. Other impediments to due process include prolonged pretrial detention, inadequate access to counsel for defendants, and corruption. A number of reform initiatives in recent years, including the introduction of plea bargaining in 2015, have reportedly had some success in reducing large case backlogs.

F3. Is there protection from the illegitimate use of physical force and freedom from war and insurgencies? 1 / 4

Rape, extrajudicial violence, and torture and abuse of suspects and detainees by security forces are persistent problems, and prosecutions of the perpetrators are rare. The alleged torture of Bobi Wine and other opposition politicians in August 2018 led to protests against police brutality. The government said it would investigate Wine's allegations of torture, but no charges had been filed as of 2020.

On December 27, 2020, Bobi Wine's bodyguard, Francis Senteza Kalibala, was run over and killed by a military vehicle. Wine said the killing was "deliberate," which the military denied. On December 30, boxer Isaac "Zebra" Ssenyange was shot dead by security officers at his home. After reports emerged that Ssenyange supported the ruling party, President Museveni described his death as a mistake and apologized to his family.

Prison conditions are poor, as the prison system is operating at about three times its intended capacity, with pretrial detainees constituting nearly half of the inmate population.

F4. Do laws, policies, and practices guarantee equal treatment of various segments of the population? 1 / 4

Ugandan laws prohibit discrimination based on ethnic origin, religion, age, race, disability, color, and sex. However, the LGBT+ community continues to face overt hostility from the government and much of society. Same-sex relations are criminalized under a colonial-era law. Men and transgender women accused of consensual sex are sometimes forced to undergo an anal exam that Human Rights Watch (HRW) says could amount to torture. In October 2019, LGBT+ activist Brian Wasswa was fatally attacked at his home in Jinja. In October and November 2019, police carried out two groups of mass arrests of LGBT+ people in Kampala.

The law prohibits employment discrimination based on gender and other criteria, but it does not cover the informal sector, in which most women work, and women are subject to de facto discrimination in employment and other matters.

There were about 1.4 million refugees living in Uganda at the end of 2020, and the United Nations has praised the government for its progressive asylum policies. However, it struggles to fund basic services for some refugee populations.

G. PERSONAL AUTONOMY AND INDIVIDUAL RIGHTS: 7 / 16

G1. Do individuals enjoy freedom of movement, including the ability to change their place of residence, employment, or education? 3 / 4

Freedom of movement in Uganda is largely unrestricted, including for refugees, most of whom live outside of camps and have been able to move more freely in recent years. However, bribery is common in many facets of life, such as interacting with traffic police, gaining admittance to some institutions of higher education, and obtaining government jobs.

During the COVID-19 pandemic, the Ugandan government implemented strict measures and movement restrictions to prevent the spread of the virus, which were at times violently enforced by security forces.

G2. Are individuals able to exercise the right to own property and establish private businesses without undue interference from state or nonstate actors? 2 / 4

Customary land tenure is widespread in the north, and land disputes—some of them violent—are common, particularly when private development projects are at stake. Forced evictions sometimes occur in northern and central Uganda. In 2018, police detained 26 land rights activists and two local NGO staff for mobilizing residents of Mubende district to resist illegal evictions; a related clash with employees of a businessman carrying out evictions had led to one death. The 28 individuals were charged in late 2018 with nine counts, including murder and aggravated robbery. In October 2019, their counsel was briefly detained when he demanded access to his clients. The trial was adjourned in November 2019 and resumed in 2020.

The law allows women to inherit land, but local customary rules and societal practices put women at a disadvantage regarding land tenure and inheritance.

G3. Do individuals enjoy personal social freedoms, including choice of marriage partner and size of family, protection from domestic violence, and control over appearance? 1 / 4

Domestic violence is widespread and underreported, and underage marriages are common in some communities. Some 34 percent of women aged 20 to 24 are married by age 18 and more than 60 percent of young adults experienced physical abuse as children, according to a 2019 UN Children's Fund report. In November 2018, courts across the country began holding special sessions to address a backlog of thousands of rape and domestic violence cases.

G4. Do individuals enjoy equality of opportunity and freedom from economic exploitation? 1 / 4

Poor enforcement of labor laws contributes to unsafe or exploitative conditions for some workers, including extremely low pay. Child labor in agriculture, domestic service, and a variety of other industries is a significant problem, and the issue is most prevalent in rural areas. Sexual exploitation of minors is also an ongoing problem.

While Uganda has in place a number of domestic laws to promote workers' rights, the government has failed to regulate the recruitment and transfer of Ugandan domestic workers to Middle Eastern countries. Accounts that surfaced in the media in 2019 described Ugandan workers in the Middle East experiencing sexual abuse, beatings, exploitation, and torture. Draft legislation to regulate the employment of Ugandans abroad was under consideration in late 2019.

Ukraine

Population: 41,800,000
Capital: Kyiv
Freedom Status: Partly Free
Electoral Democracy: Yes

Note: The numerical scores and status listed here do not reflect conditions in in the occupied Ukrainian territories of Crimea and Eastern Donbas, which are examined in separate reports. *Freedom in the World* reports assess the level of political rights and civil liberties in a given geographical area, regardless of whether they are affected by the state, nonstate actors, or foreign powers. Disputed territories are sometimes assessed separately if they meet certain criteria, including boundaries that are sufficiently stable to allow year-on-year comparisons. For more information, see the report methodology and FAQ.

Overview: Ukraine has enacted a number of positive reforms since the protest-driven ouster of President Viktor Yanukovych in 2014. However, corruption remains endemic, and the government's initiatives to combat it have met resistance and experienced setbacks. Attacks against journalists, civil society activists, and members of minority groups are frequent, and police responses are often inadequate. Russia occupies the autonomous Ukrainian region of Crimea, which it invaded in the aftermath of Yanukovych's ouster, and its military supports armed separatists in the eastern Donbas area.

KEY DEVELOPMENTS IN 2020

- More than one million people tested positive for COVID-19, and 18,533 people died during the year. Though the government-imposed restrictions on movement and public space, most measures were deemed to be proportionate.

- In October 2020, multiple reports alleged that the head of the Constitutional Court, Oleksandr Tupytsky, had obtained land in occupied Crimea, failed to declare luxurious real estate in Kyiv, and was linked to a prominent case of judicial fraud.
- Also in October, the Constitutional Court annulled multiple anticorruption laws that required the public declaration of government officials' and representatives' assets and mandated criminal punishments for not doing so. Multiple judges who published their financial holdings had been under investigation because of these laws.
- During November and December, President Volodymyr Zelenskyy attempted to dissolve the Constitutional Court after it annulled significant anticorruption legislation. Though the Court was not dissolved, the parliament passed new, albeit weakened legislation replacing the annulled anticorruption measures.

POLITICAL RIGHTS: 26 / 40 (−1)

A. ELECTORAL PROCESS: 9 / 12

A1. Was the current head of government or other chief national authority elected through free and fair elections? 4 / 4

The president is directly elected for a maximum of two five-year terms. In the 2019 election, held in two rounds in March and April, Zelenskyy defeated incumbent president Petro Poroshenko with 73.2 percent of the second-round vote, winning a majority of votes in all but one Ukrainian region. International observers deemed the vote competitive and credible, although polling could not take place in Crimea and separatist-held parts of Donbas.

A2. Were the current national legislative representatives elected through free and fair elections? 3 / 4

The 450 members of the unicameral Supreme Council, or Verkhovna Rada, have been elected to five-year terms through a mixed system in which half of the members are chosen by closed-list proportional representation and the other half in single-member districts. Future elections will be held under a new system approved in December 2019.

In early elections held in July 2019, President Zelenskyy's Servant of the People party won 254 seats, giving them an outright majority—the first time since independence any party had crossed that threshold. The incumbent Poroshenko bloc, which had rebranded in May as European Solidarity, took just 25 seats. The Opposition Platform–For Life grouping took 43 seats, Fatherland 26, and the Voice Party 20.

The elections were deemed generally competitive and credible, despite some problems. Voting was again impossible in Crimea and separatist-held parts of Donbas. Consequently, the elections filled only 424 of the 450 seats. Additionally, approximately one million Ukrainian citizens are unable to vote because they do not have a registered address. An Organization for Security and Co-operation in Europe (OSCE) election monitoring mission cited some irregularities, including "widespread vote-buying, misuse of incumbency, and the practice of exploiting all possible legislative loopholes" that contributed to inequalities among competitors.

In October 2020, Ukraine held its first local elections under the reforms and revisions to the electoral framework passed in December 2019. Despite the Central Election Commission's generally timely and professional administration of the election during the pandemic, the OSCE observer mission expressed concern about the often-politicized work of territorial commissions, widespread allegations of vote-buying, and abuse of state resources, among other issues.

A3. Are the electoral laws and framework fair, and are they implemented impartially by the relevant election management bodies? 2 / 4

The mixed electoral system for the parliament that has governed past polls, including those in 2019, has been criticized as prone to manipulation and vote-buying. President Zelenskyy attempted to introduce an entirely party list–based system prior to the 2019 parliamentary election, but could not garner enough parliamentary support. However, in December 2019, the new parliament adopted an electoral code that partially implemented a proportional representation voting system, with open party lists for both parliamentary and local elections, and Zelenskyy enacted it at the end of the year.

In October 2020, the Central Election Commission decided not to conduct local elections in 18 communities of the Donetsk and Luhansk regions in eastern Ukraine, located close to the contact line with noncontrolled territories. The decision affected 475,000 voters, who continued to be governed by military-civil administrations, which are appointed directly by the president.

B. POLITICAL PLURALISM AND PARTICIPATION: 12 / 16

B1. Do the people have the right to organize in different political parties or other competitive political groupings of their choice, and is the system free of undue obstacles to the rise and fall of these competing parties or groupings? 3 / 4

With the exception of a ban on the Communist Party, there are no formal barriers to the creation and operation of political parties. New political parties organize frequently. A law that came into force in 2016 provides parliamentary parties with state funding, but the provision effectively favors established parties over newcomers. Party financing in Ukraine remains opaque, despite robust laws to regulate it.

B2. Is there a realistic opportunity for the opposition to increase its support or gain power through elections? 4 / 4

Ukrainian politics feature dynamic competition among parties. Opposition groups are represented in the parliament, and their political activities are generally not impeded by administrative restrictions or legal harassment. Generally, grassroots parties have difficulty competing with more established parties that enjoy the support and financial backing of politically connected business magnates, known as oligarchs.

In the second election round held in April 2019, Zelenskyy won the presidency by a large margin, defeating incumbent president Poroshenko. In July's elections, President Zelenskyy's new Servant of the People's party took an absolute majority of seats in the Rada, defeating the incumbent European Solidarity grouping.

B3. Are the people's political choices free from domination by forces that are external to the political sphere, or by political forces that employ extrapolitical means? 2 / 4

Russian influence in Ukrainian politics has continued to decline since Yanukovych's ouster, though Moscow retains influence in some eastern and southern regions.

Ukraine's oligarchs exert significant influence over politics through their financial support for various political parties, and lobby for the appointment of loyalists to key institutional positions.

Although electoral laws forbid the use of public resources in election campaigns, incumbent officials used administrative resources during the local election campaign, while law enforcers turned a blind eye to the practice.

B4. Do various segments of the population (including ethnic, racial, religious, gender, LGBT+, and other relevant groups) have full political rights and electoral opportunities? 3 / 4

There are no formal restrictions on the participation of women and members of ethnic, racial, or other minority groups in political life. However, their voting and representation are hindered by factors including discrimination that discourages their political participation, the conflict in the east, lack of identity documents for many Roma, and rules against running as an independent for many local, district, and regional offices. Internally displaced persons (IDPs), of which there are over 1.5 million, face legal and practical barriers to voting. Societal discrimination against LGBT+ people affects their ability to engage in political and electoral processes.

The Law on Local Elections mandates a 30 percent quota for women on party lists, but it is not effectively enforced. A record 87 women were elected to parliament in 2019, though this amounts to only 20 percent of all seats.

C. FUNCTIONING OF GOVERNMENT: 5 / 12 (−1)

C1. Do the freely elected head of government and national legislative representatives determine the policies of the government? 3 / 4

Elected officials craft and implement reforms, though many initiatives stall due to opposition from powerful business groups and other special interests. The main obstacle to effective governance in government-controlled parts of Ukraine is corruption.

C2. Are safeguards against official corruption strong and effective? 1 / 4

Corruption remains a serious problem, and even the little remaining political will to fight it is eroding, despite strong pressure from civil society. Anticorruption agencies have repeatedly been ensnared in politically fraught conflicts with other state entities and elected officials. In September 2020, the Constitutional Court ruled that a prominent anticorruption agency created by the ruling party was unconstitutional and shut down multiple investigations that had been opened by the agency. The agency had been investigating multiple sitting judges. The High Anti-Corruption court, created in September 2019, convicted 16 high-ranking officials in 2020.

In October 2020, multiple reports claimed that Constitutional Court Chief Justice Oleksandr Tupytsky allegedly had illegally obtained and owned land in Russia-occupied Crimea, omitted recording his luxurious real estate in Kyiv among his assets, and had ties to a prominent case of judicial fraud. Tupytsky denied any wrongdoing. The State Bureau of Investigation opened a criminal investigation alleging that Tupytsky had committed treason by owning land in Russian-occupied Crimea.

C3. Does the government operate with openness and transparency? 1 / 4 (−1)

In previous years, Ukraine made some progress in advancing transparency, for example by requiring that banks publish the identity of their owners, and by passing a 2016 law obliging politicians and bureaucrats to file electronic declarations of their assets. However, in October 2020, the Constitutional Court annulled the asset-declaration law, as well as a law that dictates criminal punishments for falsified asset reporting. Law enforcement agencies were forced to close some high-level corruption cases and remove the full database of official declarations from public access. Parliament reinstated a weakened version of the law in December.

In July 2020, the director and several high-ranking officials of the National Bank, a historically independent regulator, resigned due to systemic political pressure and the installation of a presidential loyalist as the bank's new leader.

After making progress to enhance the accessibility of information about public procurements in recent years, Ukraine failed to set up a centralized system about the purchasing medical equipment—including vaccines—to fight the coronavirus pandemic in a timely and transparent manner. Moreover, the Finance Ministry reported in December that about 26 percent of the money allocated to the COVID-19 emergency fund was spent on building roads.

Score Change: The score declined from 2 to 1 because a Constitutional Court ruling significantly weakened asset-declaration requirements and rolled back criminal penalties for the falsification of asset declarations.

CIVIL LIBERTIES: 35 / 60 (−1)

D. FREEDOM OF EXPRESSION AND BELIEF: 11 / 16

D1. Are there free and independent media? 2 / 4

The constitution guarantees freedoms of speech and expression, and libel is not a criminal offense. The media landscape features considerable pluralism, and open criticism of the government and investigation of powerful figures. However, business magnates own and influence many outlets, using them as tools to advance their agendas. President Zelenskyy has received significant support from media outlets controlled by banking magnate Igor Kolomoisky. Other parties also receive favorable coverage from "friendly" media. Zelenskyy at times has also refused to take reporters' questions, and his staff has occasionally refused access to spaces journalists are legally permitted to enter.

A number of Russian news outlets and their journalists are prohibited from entering the country. Various language laws impose upon news outlets requirements that certain content be in the Ukrainian language. In April 2020, the National Security Council and President Zelenskyy extended a ban on Russian social media in Ukraine.

Journalists continued to face threats of violence and intimidation in 2020, and Ukraine's courts and law enforcement agents often fail to protect their rights. In August, several international media watchdogs urged Ukrainian authorities to investigate the torching of a car affiliated with an investigative television program and the alleged surveillance of its journalists. By the end of the year, the police reportedly had identified three suspects.

The independent Institute of Mass Information recorded 205 media-freedom violations in 2020, including 19 cases of physical violence, 11 cyberattacks, 111 incidents of interference, 18 incidents of threats, 17 cases of restricting access to public information, and 2 cases of direct censorship. The National Police initiated 200 investigations of various crimes against journalists in 2020.

D2. Are individuals free to practice and express their religious faith or nonbelief in public and private? 3 / 4

The constitution and a 1991 law define religious rights in Ukraine, and these are generally respected. However, smaller religious groups continue to report some discrimination. Vandalism of Jewish structures and cemeteries continues. Acknowledging one's atheism may result in discrimination.

In October 2018, Ukrainian Orthodox clerics received permission from religious authorities in Istanbul, the historical seat of the Eastern Orthodox Church, to create their own autocephalous church and remove it from the canonical jurisdiction of the Russian Orthodox Church. A new Orthodox Church of Ukraine was then formed in December to unite existing factions. The Kremlin and church leaders in Moscow strongly objected to the move, and Ukrainian officials said they anticipated provocations, including disputes over church property. However, tensions between the new Orthodox Church of Ukraine and the Ukrainian branch of the Russian Orthodox Church have decreased in recent years.

D3. Is there academic freedom, and is the educational system free from extensive political indoctrination? 3 / 4

A 2014 law dramatically reduced the government's control over education and allowed universities much greater freedom in designing their own programs and managing their own finances.

A law adopted in 2017 was designed to align the country's education system with those in the European Union (EU), but it drew criticism for provisions that mandate the use of Ukrainian as the primary language of instruction in most publicly funded secondary schools by 2020, affecting numerous schools taught in minority languages.

D4. Are individuals free to express their personal views on political or other sensitive topics without fear of surveillance or retribution? 3 / 4

Ukrainians generally enjoy open and free private discussion, although the polarizing effects of the conflict have weighed on political expression, especially when it relates to questions of individual and national identity. Heated exchanges in the media and instances of violence against those expressing views considered controversial are not uncommon, likely contributing to self-censorship among ordinary people.

E. ASSOCIATIONAL AND ORGANIZATIONAL RIGHTS: 7 / 12

E1. Is there freedom of assembly? 2 / 4

The constitution guarantees the right to peaceful assembly but requires organizers to give the authorities advance notice of demonstrations. Ukraine lacks a law governing the conduct of demonstrations and specifically providing for freedom of assembly.

Threats and violence by nonstate actors regularly prevent certain groups from holding events, particularly those advocating equal rights for women and LGBT+ people. In August 2020, police arrested 16 people after fights broke out during a march for LGBT+ rights in Odessa.

E2. Is there freedom for nongovernmental organizations, particularly those that are engaged in human rights- and governance-related work? 2 / 4

Numerous civic groups emerged or were reinvigorated following the departure of Yanukovych in 2014, and many are able to influence decision-making at various levels of government. In 2019, the Constitutional Court struck down a law that had required leaders, staff, and contractors of nongovernmental organizations (NGOs) focused on corruption to submit asset and income declarations. Populist lawmakers had used the information made public through the law to smear the groups as working to harm Ukraine on behalf of malicious "foreign agents."

However, in recent years, NGOs have faced growing threats of violence, and those responsible are rarely brought to justice. In July 2020, the house of Vitaliy Shabunin, head of the board of the Anti-corruption Action Centre, was set on fire. The police started a criminal investigation but had no suspects by the end of the year.

E3. Is there freedom for trade unions and similar professional or labor organizations? 3 / 4

Trade unions function in the country, but strikes and worker protests are infrequent, as the largest trade union, stemming from the Soviet-era labor federation, lacks independence from the government and employers in practice. Factory owners are still able to pressure their workers to vote according to the owners' preferences.

F. RULE OF LAW: 6 / 16 (−1)

F1. Is there an independent judiciary? 1 / 4

Ukraine has long suffered from corrupt and politicized courts, and recent reform initiatives aimed at addressing the issue have stalled or fallen short of expectations.

In October 2020, President Zelenskyy attempted to dissolve the Constitutional Court after it annulled laws aimed at fighting corruption; multiple Constitutional Court judges had been under investigation because of those laws. Shortly thereafter, the State Bureau of Investigation opened a criminal case against several Constitutional Court judges for allegedly attempting to seize state power. Though he was unable to dissolve the body, Zelenskyy ordered by presidential decree in December the suspension of Constitutional Court Chief Justice Oleksandr Tupytsky, who was also being investigated for bribery and witness tampering. The court claimed that Tupytsky's suspension was unconstitutional, though it then opened an inquiry into removing him from his position. The crisis was unresolved at year's end.

F2. Does due process prevail in civil and criminal matters? 1 / 4 (−1)

Although due process guarantees exist, in practice individuals with financial resources and political influence can escape prosecution for wrongdoing. According to statistics from the World Prison Brief published in April 2020, about 37 percent of prisoners are in pretrial detention.

The government has made little progress in meeting domestic and international demands to investigate and prosecute crimes committed during the last months of the Yanukovych administration in late 2013 and early 2014, which included the shooting of protesters.

Judges consistently move to stymie corruption investigations into high-profile officials, including within the judiciary. In September and October 2020, the Constitutional Court annulled a series of anticorruption laws that required asset declarations of public officials, created anticorruption institutions, and empowered key anticorruption actors. The National Anticorruption Bureau and the National Agency for Prevention of Corruption reportedly were forced to close multiple ongoing investigations because of the ruling.

In December 2020, the National Anticorruption Bureau complained about the presidentially appointed prosecutor general's "unprecedented meddling" in the investigation of a bribery case related to deputy head of the president's office.

Score Change: The score declined from 2 to 1 because judges have prevented corruption investigations from proceeding, and the prosecutor general meddled in the investigation of high-level officials.

F3. Is there protection from the illegitimate use of physical force and freedom from war and insurgencies? 2 / 4

The security situation is generally stable outside of the occupied areas. However, there have been a number of high-profile assassinations and assassination attempts in recent years, some of which targeted political figures. Conditions in many prisons are squalid and dangerous.

F4. Do laws, policies, and practices guarantee equal treatment of various segments of the population? 2 / 4

A 2012 law introduced a nonexclusive list of grounds on which discrimination is prohibited. Gender discrimination is explicitly banned under the constitution. However, these protections are inconsistently enforced, and the Romany minority and LGBT+ people experience significant discrimination in practice. Roma and LGBT+ people and groups generally only receive police protection or justice for attacks against them when there is intense pressure from civil society or international observers. Rights groups have reported that employers openly discriminate on the basis of gender and age.

In September 2020, President Zelensky signed a decree aimed at creating a network for fighting domestic abuse, citing a spike in domestic violence in the first half of the year as a result of a nationwide lockdown.

G. PERSONAL AUTONOMY AND INDIVIDUAL RIGHTS: 10 / 16

G1. Do individuals enjoy freedom of movement, including the ability to change their place of residence, employment, or education? 3 / 4

Freedom of movement is generally not restricted in areas under government control. Ukraine's cumbersome system requiring individuals to be legally registered at an address to be able to vote and receive some services, however, creates a barrier to full freedom of movement, in particular for the displaced and those without an address where they could be registered for official purposes.

Movement restrictions in Ukraine due to the COVID-19 pandemic disproportionately impacted the elderly, the poor, and families with children.

G2. Are individuals able to exercise the right to own property and establish private businesses without undue interference from state or nonstate actors? 2 / 4

The government has taken steps to scale back regulation of private businesses in recent years. However, the business environment is negatively affected by widespread corruption, and a moratorium on the sale of agricultural land remains in effect until July 2021.

The COVID-19 lockdown was not enforced equally for all businesses in Ukraine. Some businesses that belong to politically connected individuals were allowed to operate with few restrictions, while other nonessential businesses were forced to close down.

G3. Do individuals enjoy personal social freedoms, including choice of marriage partner and size of family, protection from domestic violence, and control over appearance? 3 / 4

The government generally does not restrict social freedoms, though same-sex marriages are not recognized in Ukraine. Domestic violence is widespread, and police responses to the few victims who report such abuse are inadequate.

G4. Do individuals enjoy equality of opportunity and freedom from economic exploitation? 2 / 4

The trafficking of women domestically and abroad for the purpose of prostitution continues. IDPs are especially vulnerable to exploitation for sex trafficking and forced labor.

Labor laws establish a minimum wage that meets the poverty level, as well as a 40-hour work week and workplace safety standards. However, workers at times go unpaid, and penalties for workplace safety violations are lenient.

United Arab Emirates

Population: 9,800,000
Capital: Abu Dhabi
Freedom Status: Not Free
Electoral Democracy: No

Overview: The United Arab Emirates (UAE) is a federation of seven emirates led in practice by Abu Dhabi, the largest by area and richest in natural resources. Limited elections are held for a federal advisory body, but political parties are banned, and all executive, legislative, and judicial authority ultimately rests with the seven hereditary rulers. The civil liberties of both citizens and noncitizens, who make up an overwhelming majority of the population, are subject to significant restrictions.

KEY DEVELOPMENTS IN 2020

- After signing a US-brokered agreement to normalize relations with Israel in September, the Emirati government took steps to suppress public criticism of the move, including the imposition of a travel ban on a writer and the promotion of a mobile application that encourages residents to report illegal speech.
- The effects of the COVID-19 pandemic seriously harmed the Emirati economy and resulted in a significant outflow of migrant workers. The government warned residents that spreading false information about the disease was a criminal offense. By year's end, after two waves of infections that peaked in May and October, the country had reported more than 206,000 confirmed cases and 665 deaths.

POLITICAL RIGHTS: 5 / 40

A. ELECTORAL PROCESS: 1 / 12

A1. Was the current head of government or other chief national authority elected through free and fair elections? 0 / 4

The Federal Supreme Council, comprising the dynastic rulers of the seven emirates, is the country's highest executive body. It selects a president and vice president from among its members, and the president appoints a prime minister and cabinet. The emirate of Abu Dhabi has controlled the federation's presidency since its inception in 1971; the current president, Sheikh Khalifa bin Zayed al-Nahyan, succeeded his father in 2004. In 2006, Sheikh Mohammed bin Rashid al-Maktoum succeeded his late brother as ruler of the emirate of Dubai and as vice president and prime minister of the UAE.

A2. Were the current national legislative representatives elected through free and fair elections? 1 / 4

The unelected Federal Supreme Council is also the country's highest legislative authority, but it is advised by the 40-seat Federal National Council (FNC), which can review proposed laws and question government ministers.

Since 2006, half of the FNC's members have been elected for four-year terms on a nonpartisan basis by an electoral college chosen by the rulers of each emirate, while the government directly appoints the other half. The size of the electoral college has expanded over time. For the October 2019 elections it grew to 337,000 members, up from 224,000 in 2015, though this still fell far short of the entire voting-age citizen population. Close to 500 candidates vied for the 20 elected seats. Voter turnout remained low at about 35 percent, matching the 2015 level.

There are no elected legislative bodies in the individual emirates.

A3. Are the electoral laws and framework fair, and are they implemented impartially by the relevant election management bodies? 0 / 4

The UAE's electoral framework applies only to the advisory FNC, and it lacks universal suffrage. While the electoral college has expanded, and overseas voting was permitted for the first time in 2015, there is no accountability for the procedures by which the rulers of each emirate draw up the lists of eligible voters. The geographical allocation of FNC seats results in significant overrepresentation for the smaller emirates.

B. POLITICAL PLURALISM AND PARTICIPATION: 2 / 16

B1. Do the people have the right to organize in different political parties or other competitive political groupings of their choice, and is the system free of undue obstacles to the rise and fall of these competing parties or groupings? 0 / 4

Political parties are banned, and all electoral candidates run as independents.

Since 2011, the UAE has aggressively cracked down on opposition activists, particularly if they are suspected of belonging to the Association for Reform and Guidance (Al-Islah), a group formed in 1974 to advocate for democratic reform. The government has accused members of Al-Islah of being foreign agents of the Muslim Brotherhood intent on overthrowing the regime and designated the Muslim Brotherhood as a terrorist organization in 2014. Qatar's support for the Muslim Brotherhood has been a factor in efforts by the UAE, Saudi Arabia, and their regional allies to isolate that country since 2017. Dozens of activists, civil society leaders, academics, and students remained imprisoned during 2020 as part of the broader crackdown, including the prominent economist Nasser bin Ghaith, lawyer Mohammed al-Roken, and human rights advocate Ahmed Mansoor.

B2. Is there a realistic opportunity for the opposition to increase its support or gain power through elections? 0 / 4

The political system grants the emirates' hereditary rulers a monopoly on power and excludes the possibility of a change in government through elections.

B3. Are the people's political choices free from domination by forces that are external to the political sphere, or by political forces that employ extrapolitical means? 1 / 4

The political choices available to eligible voters are severely limited in practice, and the alignments of both voters and candidates are heavily influenced by tribal networks.

B4. Do various segments of the population (including ethnic, racial, religious, gender, LGBT+, and other relevant groups) have full political rights and electoral opportunities? 1 / 4

Approximately 90 percent of the population of the UAE consists of noncitizens who lack political rights and electoral opportunities, including thousands of stateless residents. There is no clear process for obtaining citizenship without Emirati parentage or marriage to an Emirati man; children of Emirati mothers and foreign fathers must apply for naturalization.

Women make up about 50 percent of the FNC electoral college, and approximately 180 women ran as candidates in the 2019 elections, more than double the 78 who ran in 2015. Women won seven of the elected seats on the council, and the authorities appointed 13 women in keeping with a pledge to ensure equal representation in the 40-member body.

In practice, however, ordinary women have little opportunity to organize independently and advance their interests through the political system.

C. FUNCTIONING OF GOVERNMENT: 2 / 12

C1. Do the freely elected head of government and national legislative representatives determine the policies of the government? 0 / 4

Government policies are determined by the dynastic rulers of the seven emirates. The FNC performs only advisory functions and has struggled to arrange hearings with government ministers. In practice, policymaking authority has coalesced around the crown prince of Abu Dhabi, Mohammed bin Zayed al-Nahyan, since the titular UAE president suffered a stroke in 2014. The president, Khalifa bin Zayed al-Nahyan, has made occasional appearances in state media since 2018, but there has been no obvious change to the crown prince's de facto leadership.

C2. Are safeguards against official corruption strong and effective? 2 / 4

The UAE is considered one of the least corrupt countries in the Middle East, and the government has taken steps to increase efficiency and streamline the bureaucracy. Nevertheless, there are no genuinely independent anticorruption mechanisms, and senior members of the ruling families are able to shield themselves and their associates from public scrutiny.

The collapse of the Abraaj Group private equity firm beginning in 2018, several months after institutional investors questioned its alleged mismanagement of funds, highlighted regulatory and oversight weaknesses in the financial sector in Dubai that could also have implications for the strength of the country's safeguards against public-sector malfeasance.

C3. Does the government operate with openness and transparency? 0 / 4

The government generally lacks transparency, and despite legal provisions for access to public information, it remains difficult in practice. The State Audit Institution does not release public information about its reports, and its remit is limited to federal entities and state-owned companies, whereas most spending takes place in the individual emirates; the institution can conduct audits of an emirate's entities if asked by its ruler.

CIVIL LIBERTIES: 12 / 60

D. FREEDOM OF EXPRESSION AND BELIEF: 3 / 16

D1. Are there free and independent media? 0 / 4

The 1980 Publications and Publishing Law, considered one of the most restrictive press laws in the Arab world, regulates all aspects of the media and prohibits criticism of the government. Journalists commonly practice self-censorship, and outlets frequently publish government statements without criticism or comment. Media operate with more freedom in certain "free zones"—areas in which foreign media outlets can produce news content intended for foreign audiences—but the zones remain subject to UAE media laws and have additional regulatory codes and authorities.

Emirati-owned and UAE-based media outlets have participated actively in a government-backed media campaign against Qatar that began in 2017. The attorney general warned that year that anyone who showed sympathy or favoritism toward Qatar in any medium could be punished with three to 15 years in prison and a fine of at least 500,000 dirhams ($136,000) under the penal code and a highly restrictive 2012 cybercrime law.

A number of well-known commentators have been jailed in recent years for criticizing the authorities, expressing support for dissidents or human rights, or calling for political reform. Leading human rights activist Ahmed Mansoor, who was sentenced to 10 years in prison in 2018 for using social media to "publish false information that damages the country's reputation," was among those who remained behind bars in 2020. Following the September 2020 agreement to normalize relations with Israel, Emirati authorities barred writer Dhabia Khamis al-Maslamani from leaving the country, and prosecutors began an investigation into her for social media posts that allegedly threatened national security by criticizing normalization.

In November 2020, a court sentenced two men to two years in prison for airing a fabricated story about COVID-19 deaths in a television interview.

D2. Are individuals free to practice and express their religious faith or nonbelief in public and private? 1 / 4

Islam is the official religion, and the majority of citizens are Sunni Muslims. Blasphemy is a criminal offense, as is proselytizing to Muslims by non-Muslim groups. The General Authority of Islamic Affairs and Endowments provides regular guidance to Muslim preachers; it and a Dubai counterpart appoint the country's Sunni imams. Shiite clergy have their own council to manage religious affairs.

There have been some allegations of noncitizen Shiite Muslims facing discrimination or deportation in recent years. Christian, Hindu, and Sikh places of worship have been built on plots of land donated by ruling family members. Pope Francis became the first Roman Catholic pontiff to visit the Arabian Peninsula when he traveled to the UAE in 2019 as part of a bid by Emirati officials to emphasize the country's religious tolerance. Later that year, the authorities announced plans to open an Abrahamic Family House, to include a mosque, a church, and a synagogue, in 2022.

D3. Is there academic freedom, and is the educational system free from extensive political indoctrination? 1 / 4

The Ministry of Education censors textbooks and curriculums in both public and private schools. Islamic education is required in public schools and for Muslims in private schools. Several foreign universities have opened satellite campuses in the UAE, although faculty members are generally careful to avoid criticizing the government. At least 10 faculty members from New York University (NYU) have been denied entry to teach or conduct research at NYU's Abu Dhabi campus. Students, staff, and support personnel have also been denied entry. The UAE authorities have placed scholars and students who have criticized aspects of government policy on a unified Gulf Cooperation Council (GCC) security list, barring them from the wider region.

In 2018, British doctoral student Matthew Hedges was arrested after completing a research trip to the country. He was held in solitary confinement in Abu Dhabi for five months, convicted on espionage charges after a trial that lasted five minutes, and sentenced to life imprisonment. Under international pressure, he was then pardoned by the UAE president and promptly deported.

D4. Are individuals free to express their personal views on political or other sensitive topics without fear of surveillance or retribution? 1 / 4

A number of laws give authorities broad discretion to punish individuals' speech on sensitive topics. The 2012 cybercrime law, which amended and replaced one passed in 2006, introduced lengthy prison terms for vaguely worded offenses such as damaging "the reputation or the stature of the state or any of its institutions." A 2014 counterterrorism law prescribes punishments including the death penalty for offenses like "undermining national security" and possession of material that opposes or denigrates Islam. A 2015 law against hate speech and discrimination contained loosely worded definitions and criminalized a wide range of free speech activities. These and other criminal laws have been actively enforced, including against ordinary social media users.

Human Rights Watch reported in 2019 that the authorities had systematically persecuted the relatives and associates of jailed or exiled dissidents, for example by revoking their citizenship, withholding identity documents, banning travel, denying them access to education and employment, and subjecting them to surveillance and intimidation. Such practices serve as a further deterrent to unfettered speech.

During 2020, the government sought to control speech pertaining to the COVID-19 pandemic as well as its decision to normalize relations with Israel. The country's chief prosecutor warned in March that spreading false information about the pandemic was a criminal offense. In September, following the normalization agreement, government-linked accounts on social media reportedly promoted the My Safe Society mobile application; first launched in 2018 by the prosecution service, the app encourages users to report content or activities that threaten the UAE's security.

E. ASSOCIATIONAL AND ORGANIZATIONAL RIGHTS: 2 / 12

E1. Is there freedom of assembly? 1 / 4

The government places restrictions on freedom of assembly. Public meetings require government permits, and unauthorized political or labor protests are subject to dispersal by police. Demonstrations are rare in practice.

E2. Is there freedom for nongovernmental organizations, particularly those that are engaged in human rights- and governance-related work? 0 / 4

Nongovernmental organizations (NGOs) must register with the Ministry of Social Affairs and can receive subsidies from the government, though they are subject to many restrictions. International human rights groups have been denied entry to the UAE. Local human rights activists are at serious risk of detention, prosecution, and mistreatment in custody, and their relatives may be subject to various forms of harassment.

E3. Is there freedom for trade unions and similar professional or labor organizations? 1 / 4

Workers—most of whom are foreign—do not have the right to form unions, bargain collectively, or strike. They can seek collective redress for grievances through state mediation or the courts, and the government sometimes arranges concessions and settlements. Workers occasionally protest against unpaid wages and poor working and living conditions, but such demonstrations are typically dispersed by security personnel, and noncitizens who participate risk deportation. Professional associations require government licenses and are closely monitored by the authorities.

F. RULE OF LAW: 3 / 16

F1. Is there an independent judiciary? 0 / 4

The judiciary is not independent, with court rulings subject to review by the political leadership. Judges are appointed by executive decree, and the judiciary as an institution is managed largely by executive officials. Many judges are foreigners working on short-term contracts.

F2. Does due process prevail in civil and criminal matters? 1 / 4

Detainees are often denied adequate access to legal counsel during interrogations, and lengthy detention without charge is not uncommon. Judges are empowered to extend such detention indefinitely. Systematic violations of international due process standards have been observed in numerous high-profile trials involving political dissidents, human rights defenders, and foreigners, among others. Some of those convicted have their detentions arbitrarily extended after their sentences are complete.

F3. Is there protection from the illegitimate use of physical force and freedom from war and insurgencies? 1 / 4

Authorities have been criticized by international human rights organizations for failure to investigate allegations of torture and mistreatment in custody, including denial of medical care. Detainees regularly report abuse by the authorities. Ahmed Mansoor went on hunger strikes during 2019 to protest the conditions of his detention, having been harshly beaten by prison authorities for his complaints; in October 2019 more than 100 organizations joined a global call for his immediate release, but he remained imprisoned throughout 2020.

Sharia (Islamic law) courts sometimes impose flogging sentences for offenses including drug use, prostitution, and extramarital sex.

F4. Do laws, policies, and practices guarantee equal treatment of various segments of the population? 1 / 4

Discrimination against noncitizens and foreign workers is common, and they are at risk of deportation for relatively minor offenses. Women face legal and societal discrimination on a variety of issues, including employment. Same-sex sexual relations can draw harsh criminal penalties under vaguely worded laws, and LGBT+ people are subject to widespread social stigma.

G. PERSONAL AUTONOMY AND INDIVIDUAL RIGHTS: 4 / 16

G1. Do individuals enjoy freedom of movement, including the ability to change their place of residence, employment, or education? 1 / 4

Emirati citizens face few apparent restrictions on freedom of movement within the UAE or on their ability to change their place of employment, though societal norms sometimes constrain a woman's ability to work or travel without the consent of her husband, father, or other male guardian.

Under the country's *kafala* system, migrant workers' legal status is tied to their employers' sponsorship, meaning they can be punished or deported for leaving employment without meeting certain criteria. Stateless residents' freedom of movement is limited by their lack of travel documents; under a government program, many stateless people have received passports from the Comoros that ease travel and other activities but do not confer full citizenship. Qatari nationals have been barred from the UAE since 2017.

During the COVID-19 pandemic in 2020, restrictions on movement varied among the emirates. Relatively strict lockdowns were imposed in March and April, but tourism-dependent Dubai opened to international visitors a few months later, even as Abu Dhabi maintained tighter travel rules. Basic social-distancing measures remained in place for most of the year.

G2. Are individuals able to exercise the right to own property and establish private businesses without undue interference from state or nonstate actors? 1 / 4

The UAE has enacted reforms in recent years to ease procedures for establishing and operating businesses. However, the government and ruling families exercise considerable influence over the economy and are involved in many of the country's major economic and commercial initiatives, limiting the space for genuinely private business activity.

Citizens of the UAE and other GCC states are able to own property, though in practice Qatari citizens have been restricted from exercising this right since the 2017 diplomatic rift with Qatar began. In 2019, the emirate-level authorities in Abu Dhabi allowed foreigners to own freehold property in designated investment zones for the first time. Dubai has permitted non-GCC nationals to own property in designated zones since 2001.

Women generally receive smaller inheritances than men under Sharia, and women are excluded from state benefits aimed at supporting home ownership.

G3. Do individuals enjoy personal social freedoms, including choice of marriage partner and size of family, protection from domestic violence, and control over appearance? 1 / 4

Women are generally placed at a distinct disadvantage under laws governing marriage and divorce. Among other disparities, a Muslim woman's male guardian must approve her marriage. Muslim women are forbidden to marry non-Muslims, while Muslim men may marry Christian or Jewish women. Some categories of extramarital sex are criminal offenses, which deters victims from reporting rape. No laws prohibit spousal rape. A measure adopted in late 2019 introduced orders of protection and new criminal penalties to address domestic violence, but its wording appeared to allow some forms of control or punishment by male guardians.

In November 2020, the government announced changes to Sharia-based laws that decriminalized cohabitation by unmarried couples; eliminated penalties for the possession, purchase, or consumption of alcohol by people age 21 or older; and repealed legal provisions that assigned lighter penalties for "honor crimes" against women. The amendments would also allow couples who married in another country to adhere to that country's laws regarding divorce and inheritance.

G4. Do individuals enjoy equality of opportunity and freedom from economic exploitation? 1 / 4

Foreign workers are often exploited and subjected to harsh working conditions, physical abuse, and withholding of passports with little to no access to legal recourse. A series of ministerial decrees issued in 2015 aimed to give migrant workers more flexibility to terminate employment under certain conditions. Foreign household workers were not covered by those decrees or by labor laws in general, leaving them especially vulnerable. A law adopted in 2017 guaranteed such household workers basic protections and benefits including sick leave and daily rest periods, though they were inferior to those in the national labor law, and household workers would still be unable to leave their employers without a breach of contract.

Large numbers of foreign workers reportedly left or sought to leave the country during 2020 after losing their jobs due to economic dislocation caused by the COVID-19 pandemic and related lockdowns. In May, Indian authorities announced that nearly 200,000 Indians resident in the UAE had registered for repatriation flights.

A competitive rivalry between Abu Dhabi and Dubai for eye-catching development projects masks deeper sensitivities in relations between these two emirates and the five less affluent emirates in the northeast. Economic disparities also persist among UAE citizens across the seven emirates and between citizens and the noncitizen majority.

United Kingdom

Population: 67,200,000
Capital: London
Freedom Status: Free
Electoral Democracy: Yes

Overview: The United Kingdom (UK)—which includes the constituent countries of England, Scotland, and Wales along with the territory of Northern Ireland—is a stable democracy that regularly holds free elections and is home to a vibrant media sector. While the government enforces robust protections for political rights and civil liberties, recent years have seen concerns about increased government surveillance of residents, as well as rising Islamophobia and anti-immigrant sentiment. In a 2016 referendum, UK voters narrowly voted to leave the European Union (EU), through a process known colloquially as "Brexit," which will have political and economic reverberations both domestically and across Europe in the coming years.

KEY DEVELOPMENTS IN 2020

- In January, the regional government of Northern Ireland resumed after a hiatus of nearly three years, in a wide-ranging deal backed by the UK and Irish governments.
- In December, the UK and the EU finalized an agreement to govern their future relationship and finalize the UK's departure from the bloc. Under its terms, UK travelers to EU member states will need visas in more circumstances, while EU citizens in the UK are required to seek settled status with the authorities.
- The government instituted a nationwide COVID-19-related lockdown in March before loosening some restrictions in May, though another lockdown was reimposed in England in late October and stricter restrictions were instituted throughout Great Britain in December. Police forces were criticized for using new and existing powers to disproportionately target racial and ethnic minorities throughout the crisis. The World Health Organization recorded 2.4 million cases and nearly 72,600 deaths at year's end.

POLITICAL RIGHTS: 39 / 40

A. ELECTORAL PROCESS: 12 / 12

A1. Was the current head of government or other chief national authority elected through free and fair elections? 4 / 4

Executive power rests with the prime minister and cabinet, which must have the support of the House of Commons. The leader of the majority party or coalition usually becomes prime minister, and appoints the cabinet. A snap general election was held in December 2019, where a majority Conservative government, led by Prime Minister Boris Johnson, was elected.

A2. Were the current national legislative representatives elected through free and fair elections? 4 / 4

The UK has a bicameral Parliament. The more powerful lower chamber, the House of Commons, has 650 members directly elected to serve five-year terms. Members of the unelected House of Lords are appointed by the monarch. There were 793 members in December 2020. The body largely plays an oversight role in reviewing legislation passed by the House of Commons.

A general election was not due until 2022, but Prime Minister Johnson, who led a minority government after winning the premiership in July 2019, secured a new election from Parliament. The Conservatives, who focused their campaign on their intention to stop further delays to the Brexit process, won 365 seats in the December election, up from 318 in the last Parliament, and secured an 81-seat majority. The opposition Labour Party won 203 seats, down from 262 in the last Parliament.

The Scottish National Party, which campaigned to remain in the EU and advocates for Scottish independence from the UK, remained the third-largest party in the House of

Commons, gaining 13 seats over its 2017 result and winning 48 of Scotland's 59 parliamentary seats. The Liberal Democrats, the fourth-largest party, won 11 seats nationwide.

Elections for some local councils, police commissioners, and mayoralties in parts of England and Wales were scheduled for May 2020, but were delayed to May 2021 due to the COVID-19 pandemic.

A3. Are the electoral laws and framework fair, and are they implemented impartially by the relevant election management bodies? 4 / 4

The UK's electoral framework is robust and well implemented, though a limited Organization for Security and Co-operation in Europe mission that observed the 2017 election urged lawmakers to boost transparency surrounding campaign financing. Despite this recommendation, no individual donation caps currently exist. In September 2020, the Electoral Reform Society (ERS), a nongovernmental organization (NGO), called for the regulation of internet-based campaign and financing activities.

Parliament maintains a direct role in electoral management, notably through its involvement in the seat boundary drawing process. The Parliamentary Constituencies Act 2020, which was enacted in December, will limit its future involvement. The Fixed-term Parliaments Act 2011, meanwhile, limits a prime minister's ability to force a snap election, but the government introduced a bill to repeal it in December 2020.

Conservative governments have moved towards requiring voters to produce identification in order to vote. In August 2019, the ERS noted that 2,000 prospective voters living in English authorities participating in a pilot voter identification scheme were turned away from polling stations in that May's local elections, and that a permanent requirement would disproportionately impact Black, Asian, and minority ethnic (BAME) voters.

The UK's electoral infrastructure has contended with Russian interference dating back to the 2016 referendum on EU membership. In July 2020, a parliamentary intelligence committee criticized the government's inability to investigate potential Russian interference in the referendum.

B. POLITICAL PLURALISM AND PARTICIPATION: 16 / 16

B1. Do the people have the right to organize in different political parties or other competitive political groupings of their choice, and is the system free of undue obstacles to the rise and fall of these competing parties or groupings? 4 / 4

Parties do not face undue restrictions on registration or operation. The Conservative and Labour parties have dominated politics for decades, though other parties regularly win seats.

B2. Is there a realistic opportunity for the opposition to increase its support or gain power through elections? 4 / 4

Opposition parties operate freely, and have a realistic opportunity to increase their support and gain power through elections.

B3. Are the people's political choices free from domination by forces that are external to the political sphere, or by political forces that employ extrapolitical means? 4 / 4

People's political choices are generally free from domination by groups using extrapolitical means.

B4. Do various segments of the population (including ethnic, racial, religious, gender, LGBT+, and other relevant groups) have full political rights and electoral opportunities? 4 / 4

Under the UK's system of devolution, Parliament has granted different degrees of legislative power to the Northern Ireland Assembly, the Welsh Assembly, and the Scottish Parliament, augmenting the political representation of regional populations.

Women, LGBT+ people, and members of racial and ethnic minority groups are active in UK politics. After the December 2019 general election, a record 220 members of Parliament (MPs), representing 34 percent of the lower house, are female. LGBT+ and BAME representation also improved.

C. FUNCTIONING OF GOVERNMENT: 11 / 12

C1. Do the freely elected head of government and national legislative representatives determine the policies of the government? 4 / 4 (+1)

Freely elected officials can generally make and implement national policy without significant influence from actors who are not democratically accountable. Parliament approved the Coronavirus Act 2020, which includes a two-year sunset clause and is subject to parliamentary review, to initiate a COVID-19 lockdown in March 2020.

Elections to the Northern Ireland Assembly took place in March 2017, but legislators did not form a functioning government for a record-breaking 1,045 days after that poll. An agreement, which was facilitated by the UK and Ireland, was finalized in January 2020.

Score Change: The score improved from 3 to 4 because Northern Irish legislators agreed on the formation of a regional government in January after a deadlock lasting nearly three years.

C2. Are safeguards against official corruption strong and effective? 3 / 4 (−1)

Large-scale official corruption is not historically pervasive, and anticorruption bodies are generally effective. However, the UK government issued numerous COVID-19-related tenders to politically connected recipients or to firms without relevant experience according to a December 2020 *New York Times* report examining $22 billion worth of contracts. A National Audit Office report issued in November highlighted conflict-of-interest and bias concerns in the tender process.

Politically connected firms also received tenders for other purposes; in March 2020, a firm connected to Conservative minister Michael Gove and then staffer Dominic Cummings received £840,000 ($1.04 million) to conduct Brexit-related focus group research without a public bidding process.

The UK faces scrutiny for the ways in which its banking and financial sectors, property market, and offshore services in overseas territories enable money laundering and facilitate corruption globally.

Score Change: The score declined from 4 to 3 due to reports of firms and individuals connected to the governing Conservative Party receiving COVID-19-related and other public tenders despite conflict-of-interest and bias concerns.

C3. Does the government operate with openness and transparency? 4 / 4

MPs are required to disclose assets and sources of income, and this information is made available to the public. Freedom-of-information legislation is reasonably well implemented, and journalists can generally access information to report to the public. However, in November 2020, NGO openDemocracy reported that requests deemed sensitive are vetted by a government office.

CIVIL LIBERTIES: 54 / 60 (−1)

D. FREEDOM OF EXPRESSION AND BELIEF: 14 / 16

D1. Are there free and independent media? 4 / 4

Press freedom is legally protected. The media environment is lively and competitive, espousing viewpoints spanning the political spectrum. The publicly owned British Broadcasting Corporation, which relies on dedicated license fees for most of its funding, is editorially independent and competitive with its commercial counterparts. The Conservative government has considered decriminalizing nonpayment of license fees, though the *Daily Telegraph* reported in December 2020 that the government was delaying its plans to 2022.

In 2018, the culture secretary announced that Section 40 of the Crime and Courts Act would not be implemented, and ultimately would be repealed. Section 40 stipulates that, in media-related court cases, publishers who are not members of a recognized self-regulator can be ordered to pay opponents' legal costs, even if they win. Section 40 was not repealed by the end of 2020.

Journalists have faced blacklisting from government officials during 2020. In May, the prime minister's office banned a journalist working for openDemocracy from participating in daily press conferences, after the outlet reported on COVID-19 testing failures. In September, the Council of Europe (CoE) criticized the government after the Ministry of Defence blacklisted journalists from online news outlet Declassified UK the month before. The ministry apologized to the CoE later that month, and promised to conduct a review.

D2. Are individuals free to practice and express their religious faith or nonbelief in public and private? 4 / 4

Freedom of religion is protected in law and practice. A 2006 law bans incitement to religious hatred, with a maximum penalty of seven years in prison. Nevertheless, minority groups, particularly Muslims, continue to report discrimination, harassment, and occasional assaults. In October 2020, the Home Office reported 105,000 hate crimes in England (barring Greater Manchester) and Wales during its 2019–20 reporting period, an eight percent increase over 2018–19.

Muslims have been reluctant to discuss religious subjects or their identity in some settings, especially in the classroom, due to Prevent, a strategy designed to divert individuals vulnerable to terrorist or extremist recruitment. Educators and human rights groups have criticized the policy for forcing Muslims to self-censor, for fear of being referred to the program.

D3. Is there academic freedom, and is the educational system free from extensive political indoctrination? 3 / 4

Academic freedom is generally respected, though the government has recently made political forays into the academic curriculum. In October 2020, Women and Equalities Minister Kemi Badenoch commented that teaching critical race theory was partisan and illegal. That same month, the Department for Education issued guidance calling anticapitalism an "extreme political stance."

The Counter-Terrorism and Security Act 2015 requires schools and universities to help divert students from recruitment into terrorist groups, as part of the government's long-standing Prevent strategy. Educators are expected to report students suspected of terrorist or extremist sympathies to a local government body, and vet the remarks of visiting speakers, among other obligations. Human rights NGO Liberty criticized the strategy in 2019, saying it stifled open debate and academic inquiry. That January, the government agreed to launch an independent review into Prevent, but its chair was dismissed that December, and the post remained empty at the end of 2020.

D4. Are individuals free to express their personal views on political or other sensitive topics without fear of surveillance or retribution? 3 / 4

Concerns about the effects of mass surveillance on unfettered private discussion have persisted for several years. The Investigatory Powers Act 2016 required communications companies to store customer metadata for 12 months and, in some cases, allowed this information to be accessed by the authorities without a warrant. The government later limited access to metadata for serious criminal investigations with the approval of an independent commission after the High Court ruled the legislation incompatible with EU jurisprudence in 2018.

The Coronavirus Act 2020 extended the deadline for the review of urgent surveillance warrants obtained without initial judicial authorization from 3 days to 12, and allows authorities to store biometric data for longer periods.

The UK government has advocated for the use of automated facial recognition (AFR), which builds "faceprints" of individuals based on recordings taken in public gatherings. In August 2020, the Court of Appeal ruled the South Wales Police's use of AFR unlawful, but did not preemptively ban its use throughout the UK.

The government launched a contact tracing system meant to control the spread of COVID-19 in May 2020, but in July, it admitted that it did not conduct a required privacy assessment before launching the system. The system was also affected by at least three data breaches by that month.

E. ASSOCIATIONAL AND ORGANIZATIONAL RIGHTS: 12 / 12

E1. Is there freedom of assembly? 4 / 4

Freedom of assembly is generally respected, though peaceful protesters have found themselves under police surveillance for attending public events in recent years.

Major protests were held under the Black Lives Matter banner in May and June 2020 in response to the police killing of George Floyd in the US. Many of these protests were peaceful, though acts of violence and vandalism, notably against statues commemorating slaveholders and historical figures accused of racism, were reported. Right-wing counterprotesters and members of football networks notably clashed with police during a mid-June protest in London, which ended with over 100 arrests.

Demonstrations against COVID-19-related measures also took place through much of 2020, with large monthly events taking place in London beginning in August. An early September demonstration was dispersed by police, who arrested 32 people amid clashes. Antilockdown protests also ended with arrests in late September, October, November, and December.

E2. Is there freedom for nongovernmental organizations, particularly those that are engaged in human rights- and governance-related work? 4 / 4

NGOs generally operate freely. However, in recent years, disclosures of surveillance of NGOs and political organizations have drawn criticism. In October 2020, the Metropolitan Police apologized to an individual whose father, an undercover officer, engaged in a long-term relationship with his mother while surveilling animal rights and environmental organizations. In November, an inquiry into the conduct of undercover officers, which was originally announced in 2014, heard evidence, and remained in session at year's end.

E3. Is there freedom for trade unions and similar professional or labor organizations? 4 / 4

Workers have the right to organize trade unions, which have traditionally played a central role in the Labour Party. The rights to bargain collectively and strike are also respected.

F. RULE OF LAW: 13 / 16 (−1)

F1. Is there an independent judiciary? 4 / 4

The judiciary is generally independent, and governmental authorities comply with judicial decisions. A new Supreme Court began functioning in 2009, improving the separation of powers by moving the highest court out of the House of Lords.

F2. Does due process prevail in civil and criminal matters? 3 / 4 (−1)

While due process generally prevails in civil and criminal matters, rights groups and some figures within the judiciary have criticized severe cuts in legal aid under reforms that took effect in 2013, which left many vulnerable people without access to legal counsel. The cuts notably affected immigration-related and family court cases.

The Coronavirus Act 2020 provided police with new enforcement powers, which have been criticized as disproportionately broad in scope. In July 2020, the *Guardian* reported that the Metropolitan Police was disproportionately fining BAME London residents for violating COVID-19 measures. UK police have also been accused of using existing stop-and-search powers disproportionately. In December, an individual claiming to have been stopped dozens of times by the Metropolitan Police and the City of London Police vowed to sue both forces for racial profiling.

The Counter-Terrorism and Security Act 2015 allows authorities to seize travel documents of individuals attempting to leave the country if they are suspected of planning to engage in terrorist-related activities abroad, and to forcibly relocate terrorism suspects within the country. The Counter-Terrorism and Border Security Act 2019 makes viewing terrorist content online punishable by up to 15 years in prison, and allows law enforcement agencies to keep fingerprints and DNA of terrorism suspects for up to five years, even if no charges are ultimately filed.

The UK justice system still grapples with cases stemming from the Troubles, the 1968–98 conflict over the partition of the island of Ireland. In September 2020, territorial prosecutors upheld a previous decision not to prosecute 15 individuals allegedly involved in the 1972 Bloody Sunday massacre. Separate charges against "Soldier F," who is accused of murder and attempted murder for participating in the massacre, remained pending. In November 2020, the UK government declined to open an inquiry into the 1989 murder of Belfast lawyer Pat Finucane, who was allegedly killed by a loyalist organization with the assistance of a soldier and a police informant.

Parliament began considering the Covert Human Intelligence Sources (Criminal Conduct) Bill, which would allow undercover officers to engage in criminal offenses to perform their roles, in September 2020. In November, a parliamentary human rights committee criticized it, warning it would allow agents to engage in especially violent activity.

Score Change: The score declined from 4 to 3 because residents belonging to racial and ethnic minority groups were disproportionately stopped and searched by police forces using existing and COVID-19-related powers.

F3. Is there protection from the illegitimate use of physical force and freedom from war and insurgencies? 3 / 4

Individuals living in the UK are largely free from violence, but acts of terrorism did occur in 2020. In February, two people were injured in a stabbing attack in London. In a June incident, three people were stabbed to death in the English town of Reading.

Northern Ireland has seen continued paramilitary activity. The Police Service of Northern Ireland reported two security-related deaths, 17 bombing incidents, and 79 terrorism-related arrests throughout 2020.

While prisons generally adhere to international guidelines, problems of overcrowding, violence, self-harm, and drugs in prisons worsened in the 2010s. In an August 2020 report, Her Majesty's Inspectorate of Prisons called prisons' response to the COVID-19 pandemic swift, but noted that COVID-19-related measures caused "increasing levels of stress and frustration among many prisoners," who consequently had little human contact.

F4. Do laws, policies, and practices guarantee equal treatment of various segments of the population? 3 / 4

Foreign residents in the UK have been subject to increasing scrutiny since the 2010s. Under the ongoing "hostile environment" policy, which aims to persuade undocumented immigrants to voluntarily leave the UK or refrain from immigrating, individuals seeking public and private services face stringent immigration checks. In a September 2020 report, the Institute for Public Policy Research concluded that immigrants faced heightened racist treatment and poverty due to the policy. That same month, a parliamentary public accounts committee accused the Home Office of formulating biased immigration policies in a separate report.

The Windrush scandal of 2018 has spurred debate over the treatment of immigrants and minorities. Thousands of people arrived from Caribbean countries including Jamaica, Trinidad and Tobago, and Barbados at the UK government's invitation between 1948 and 1971, and received indefinite leave to remain in 1971. However, many Windrush-era immigrants and their children, who often traveled on their parents' passports, were denied health coverage and housing in recent years, and at least 164 may have been wrongfully deported by February 2020. An independent report commissioned by the House of Commons, published in March, did not make a definitive finding of institutional racism within the Home Office, but did accuse it of "institutional ignorance and thoughtlessness."

Asylum seekers and migrants can be detained indefinitely, and there have been persistent reports of poor conditions and abuse in immigration detention centers. Asylum seekers also have reported difficulty finding suitable housing from landlords while their applications are processed. The government also vowed to end reunion rights for minor refugees and asylum seekers living outside the UK with family members living in the country. The House of Lords approved a legislative amendment to protect such rights in October 2020, though the lower house was expected to overrule it. In September, the Home Office began evicting refused asylum seekers from emergency accommodation provided at the beginning of the COVID-19 pandemic, sparking fierce criticism from local government officials and NGOs.

Citizens of EU member states may encounter difficulties remaining in the UK. While many in this group of 3.4 million people should be eligible to remain after the UK's departure from the EU, securing this status has proven difficult for some applicants. In September 2020, a University of Oxford report warned that a large portion of this group may not realize they are required to apply for "settled status," or may face barriers to applying.

The UK has recorded a sustained rise in hate crimes against LGBT+ residents for much of the 2010s. The Home Office recorded nearly 16,000 such crimes during its 2019–20 reporting period in England (barring Greater Manchester) and Wales, a 19 percent increase over the 2018–19 reporting period.

The authorities actively enforce a 2010 law barring discrimination on the basis of factors including sexual orientation and gender reassignment. While women receive equal treatment under the law, gender discrimination persists in the workplace and elsewhere in society.

BAME residents face continued discrimination, including by the authorities. Stop-and-search powers are disproportionally used against BAME people; the Metropolitan Police initiated 105,000 such stops between April and June 2020, but only a fifth of such stops ended with an arrest, fine, or warning. According to Home Office internal data, this tactic is 40 times more likely to be directed at Black people in the UK. BAME people have also disproportionately contracted and died of COVID-19, according to a government report published in June.

G. PERSONAL AUTONOMY AND INDIVIDUAL RIGHTS: 15 / 16

G1. Do individuals enjoy freedom of movement, including the ability to change their place of residence, employment, or education? 4 / 4

While UK residents generally enjoy freedom of internal movement, travel has been affected by COVID-19-related lockdowns. A strict lockdown was introduced in March 2020, though many measures were eased by the end of May. A four-week lockdown was initiated in England at the end of October, as the rate of COVID-19 infections increased, and stricter measures were implemented in Great Britain in late December. Varying restrictions in localities and constituent countries remained in force throughout the year.

UK passport holders saw their freedom to travel to EU member states lessened when an agreement on the UK's departure from the bloc was reached in December 2020. Under its terms, visitors from the UK will require a visa for extended travel to EU member states in the Schengen border area beginning in January 2021.

G2. Are individuals able to exercise the right to own property and establish private businesses without undue interference from state or nonstate actors? 4 / 4

Individuals may freely exercise the right to own property and establish private businesses.

G3. Do individuals enjoy personal social freedoms, including choice of marriage partner and size of family, protection from domestic violence, and control over appearance? 4 / 4

The government generally does not place explicit restrictions on personal social freedoms. Abortion and same-sex marriage were heavily proscribed or prohibited in Northern Ireland until Parliament passed the Northern Ireland (Executive Formation) Act 2019.

Domestic violence is common in the UK. The Office for National Statistics (ONS) reports that nearly a third of English and Welsh women between the ages of 16 and 59 experience domestic abuse. Domestic violence increased during COVID-19-related lockdowns, with police data showing that two-thirds of women in abusive relationships experienced more violence during the first national lockdown.

G4. Do individuals enjoy equality of opportunity and freedom from economic exploitation? 3 / 4

A 2016 report by a government commission expressed concern about the social and economic isolation of many members of ethnic and religious minorities, and of the poor. According to the ONS, income inequality rose to 34.6 percent in 2020.

The Modern Slavery Act 2015 increased punishments for human traffickers and provides greater protections for victims, but implementation has been weak. Children and migrant workers are among those most vulnerable to forced labor and sex trafficking. In June 2020, the International Organization for Migration reported that trafficking referrals and investigations fell in the UK during the first national lockdown.

UK workers have encountered unsafe and exploitative conditions during the COVID-19 pandemic. For example, in July 2020, an undercover reporter revealed that workers in a Leicester garment factory were paid less than the minimum wage, and that COVID-19 mitigation measures were not enforced in the facility.

United States

Population: 329,900,000
Capital: Washington, DC
Freedom Status: Free
Electoral Democracy: Yes

Overview: The United States is a federal republic whose people benefit from a vibrant political system, a strong rule-of-law tradition, robust freedoms of expression and religious belief, and a wide array of other civil liberties. However, in recent years its democratic institutions have suffered erosion, as reflected in partisan pressure on the electoral process, bias and dysfunction in the criminal justice system, harmful policies on immigration and asylum seekers, and growing disparities in wealth, economic opportunity, and political influence.

KEY DEVELOPMENTS IN 2020

- The COVID-19 pandemic swept through the country in successive waves during the year, leaving some 340,000 people dead and more than 19 million confirmed cases by year's end. The government response was seriously compromised by politicized misinformation from President Donald Trump and related attempts within the administration to manipulate or control health information. These problems were compounded by similar missteps among some state governments.
- In February, the Senate, led by a Republican Party majority, acquitted President Trump on charges that he abused his office by attempting to extort a personal political favor from the Ukrainian government and obstructed Congress by ordering the executive branch not to cooperate with the impeachment inquiry in the House of Representatives, where the Democratic Party held a majority.
- The May killing of George Floyd, a Black civilian, by police in Minnesota sparked one of the largest protest movements in modern US history, as millions of people took to the streets in hundreds of cities to decry systemic racism and police violence against Black Americans. While the vast majority of demonstrations were peaceful, some were accompanied by significant property damage, and others featured police brutality or violence involving armed vigilantes. Large numbers of journalists faced assaults or arrests while covering such protests.
- Democratic Party presidential candidate and former vice president Joe Biden— along with the Democrats' vice presidential nominee, Senator Kamala Harris—defeated Trump and Vice President Mike Pence in the November general elections. Democrats also retained a majority in the House of Representatives, but Senate control was contingent on the outcome of two runoff elections in the state of Georgia, scheduled for January 2021. President Trump refused to concede his loss,

instead attacking the legality of state electoral rules, floating false conspiracy theories about large-scale fraud, and pressuring Republican officials in key states to overturn the results. His claims were consistently rejected by electoral authorities, overwhelmingly dismissed by the state and federal courts, and unsuccessful in halting the formal vote of the Electoral College in December, but they were echoed by numerous Republican politicians. Final certification of the vote and Biden's inauguration were expected in January 2021.

POLITICAL RIGHTS: 32 / 40 (−1)
A. ELECTORAL PROCESS: 10 / 12
A1. Was the current head of government or other chief national authority elected through free and fair elections? 3 / 4

The president, who serves as both head of state and head of government, is elected for up to two four-year terms. Presidential elections are decided by an Electoral College, with electors apportioned to each state based on the size of its congressional representation. In most cases, all of the electors in a particular state cast their ballots for the candidate who won the statewide popular vote, regardless of the margin. Two states, Maine and Nebraska, have chosen to divide their electoral votes between the candidates based on their popular-vote performance in each congressional district. The Electoral College makes it possible for a candidate to win the presidency while losing the national popular vote, an outcome that took place in the presidential elections of 2000 and 2016.

In the 2020 election, Biden won 306 Electoral College votes, leaving Trump with 232, and Biden defeated Trump by more than seven million votes, or approximately 4.4 percentage points, in the national popular balloting. Turnout was the highest recorded in more than a century, with roughly two-thirds of the eligible population casting a ballot.

The COVID-19 pandemic impeded in-person public events as a focal point of campaigning, but Trump eventually returned to his preferred format of large rallies, even as he and dozens of staff and associates contracted the coronavirus, leading in the president's case to a brief hospitalization. The pandemic also compelled many states to adjust their voting systems to accommodate more early and mail-in balloting, which would help prevent dangerous crowding at polling sites. This led to a series of legal battles, with the Trump campaign and other Republican litigants generally arguing against the changes and claiming that they would open the door to fraud. The balloting itself unfolded with few significant disruptions, though existing obstacles to voting—such as strict voter-identification requirements and inadequate numbers of polling sites—remained a factor, with long lines exacerbated by both the high turnout and pandemic-related shortages of poll workers.

The Homeland Security Department assisted states in their efforts to safeguard the election against foreign and other illegal interference, in part by upgrading voting equipment to include paper records and monitoring their systems for potential hacking. Social media companies, which had been criticized for failing to prevent foreign actors from using their platforms to fraudulently influence the political process in the past, made greater efforts to delete fake accounts, imposed varying restrictions on political advertising, and attempted to thwart disinformation campaigns. These measures were deemed successful in many respects: despite some reported attempts by Russian, Chinese, and Iranian state actors to hack voting infrastructure and spread disinformation on social media, there was little evidence that such efforts had a meaningful impact. Disinformation and other interference from President Trump and his domestic allies were far more damaging.

Despite a vote-tabulation process that was lauded by observers as transparent and professional, Trump refused to concede defeat, and demanded a halt to the count in states where the late tally favored Biden. In the weeks after the election, Trump launched continual volleys of fraud allegations focused on pivotal states, and openly pressured election officials in those states, particularly Republicans, to make decisions that would support his claims regardless of the facts and the law. During the counting and certification process and in the period surrounding the formal Electoral College voting on December 14, state election workers reported intimidation and death threats. A raft of lawsuits by the Trump campaign and its allies—alleging wide-ranging misconduct, challenging the legality of various electoral rules, and seeking to block states from certifying Biden's victory—were almost universally dismissed by state and federal courts. Evidence of large-scale fraud was nonexistent, as the Justice Department eventually acknowledged despite pressure from the president, but the Trump camp's disinformation, complemented by the reluctance of leading Republicans to explicitly acknowledge Biden as the president-elect, helped to convince many Trump supporters that voter fraud was widespread and Biden was not the rightful winner.

Among Republicans, a divide emerged between state officials involved in administering the elections, who generally defended the fairness of the process and the accuracy of the results, and many members of Congress, who gave credence to Trump's claims and cast doubt on Biden's victory. Following the Electoral College vote, Senate majority leader Mitch McConnell recognized Biden as the president-elect, but other Republican leaders, including several senators and House minority leader Kevin McCarthy, continued to support efforts to contest the results. At the end of the year, there was no plausible legal or constitutional means for Trump to change the outcome. Many Republicans nevertheless refused to acknowledge the legitimacy of Biden's planned accession to the presidency in January 2021.

Earlier in 2020, the Senate acquitted Trump in an impeachment process that began in September 2019. Democratic leaders in the House of Representatives had launched the inquiry following allegations that the president had misused his authority to benefit his reelection prospects by pressuring the president of Ukraine to announce investigations into supposed misdeeds by Biden; Biden's son, who sat on the board of a Ukrainian energy company that had been scrutinized for possible malfeasance; and an unfounded theory that Ukrainians had framed Moscow for the theft of Democratic Party emails in 2016. The House adopted two articles of impeachment in a nearly party-line vote in December 2019, determining that Trump had abused his office in the Ukrainian affair and obstructed Congress by ordering the executive branch to withhold documents and testimony from the House investigators even when subpoenaed. The Senate trial, in which conviction would have resulted in Trump's removal from office, began in January 2020. The Senate voted to exclude new testimony from the trial, and in February only one Republican joined all 47 Democrats in voting for conviction on the abuse of office count, while the obstruction count failed on a party-line vote.

A2. Were the current national legislative representatives elected through free and fair elections? 4 / 4

Elections for the bicameral Congress are generally free and competitive. The House consists of 435 members serving two-year terms. The Senate consists of 100 members—two from each of the 50 states—serving six-year terms, with one-third coming up for election every two years. All national legislators are elected directly by voters in the districts or states that they represent.

The capital district, Puerto Rico, and four overseas US territories are each represented by an elected delegate in the House who can perform most legislative functions but cannot participate in floor votes.

Following the 2020 elections, the Republican Party retained control of 50 Senate seats, a confirmed loss of one. Democrats held 46 Senate seats, and there were two independent senators who generally vote with the Democrats. The remaining two seats were to be determined in a January 2021 runoff election in Georgia; Republicans needed to win one of the seats to maintain a majority in the chamber, while Democrats needed to win both to achieve control via the tie-breaking vote of the incoming vice president, Kamala Harris, whose own vacated Senate seat would be temporarily filled through an appointment by California's Democratic governor in January 2021. In the House, the Democratic majority was reduced to 222, while the number of Republicans rose to 211; results in one district remained pending at year's end, and one elected Republican died of COVID-19 in late December.

Unlike in 2018, when the election in a North Carolina House district was nullified on grounds of fraud committed by the Republican side, there were no serious accusations of result-altering fraud in any race in 2020. Republican lawmakers who supported Trump's objections to the presidential results notably did not question the validity of their own elections.

A3. Are the electoral laws and framework fair, and are they implemented impartially by the relevant election management bodies? 3 / 4

The electoral framework is generally fair, though it is subject to some manipulation. The borders of House districts, which must remain roughly equal in population, are redrawn regularly—typically after each decennial census. In the practice known as partisan gerrymandering, House districts, and those for state legislatures, are crafted to maximize the advantage of the party in power in a given state. The redistricting system varies by state, but in most cases it is overseen by elected officials, and observers have expressed alarm at the growing strategic and technical sophistication of partisan efforts to control redistricting processes and redraw maps. Historically, gerrymandering has also been used as a tool of racial disenfranchisement, specifically targeting Black voters, as well as Hispanic and Native American populations. The Voting Rights Act of 1965 generally prohibits racially discriminatory voting rules, and racial gerrymandering is subject to reversal by federal courts, but it remains a problem in practice, in large part because partisan gerrymandering efforts tend to identify Black voters and other members of racial and ethnic minority groups as likely supporters of the Democratic Party.

In 2019 the Supreme Court ruled that the federal judiciary has no authority to prevent politicians from drawing districts to preserve or expand their party's power. However, some state courts have struck down partisan-gerrymandered maps based on their own constitutions, and state-level reforms have begun to address the issue, with a handful of states establishing independent bodies to manage redistricting in recent years. In 2020, Missouri referendum voters backtracked on one such reform, but voters in Virginia approved a plan to create a bipartisan redistricting commission.

Some states have adopted strict voter-identification laws whose documentation requirements can disproportionately limit participation by poor, elderly, or racial minority voters; people with disabilities; and university students. Proponents of such laws argue that they prevent voter fraud, despite research showing that fraud is extremely rare. Separately, reductions in the number of polling places in several states in recent years are thought to have suppressed turnout by groups such as low-income hourly workers, who are less able to travel to distant polling locations or wait in long lines. Restrictions on voter identification and access to polling places tend to affect demographic groups that are seen as likely to support Democratic candidates, and they are typically adopted by Republican state lawmakers.

Some of these obstacles may have had less effect in 2020, in part because the requirements for voting by mail were eased in most states and localities. In some jurisdictions, the number of votes cast prior to Election Day exceeded the total votes cast in 2016. At the same time, COVID-19 contributed to shortages of poll workers and changes to polling locations, and long lines remained a problem. Democrats strongly endorsed voting by mail, while President Trump called the practice a "scam" and discouraged Republican participation, as did some Republican state officials. Cuts to US Postal Service operations and consequent mail delivery delays aroused fears of late or undelivered ballots, but such problems did not appear to affect the outcome.

Critics have argued that the Electoral College system for presidential elections is undemocratic, as it violates the principle that each citizen's vote should carry equal weight. Similar critiques have been directed at the constitution's allocation of two Senate seats to each state regardless of population. Defenders of these systems argue that they are fundamental to the United States' federal structure, in which the states enjoy a substantial degree of autonomy, and claim that they ensure due political attention to parts of the country's territory that might otherwise be neglected.

The six-member Federal Election Commission is tasked with enforcing federal campaign finance laws, but vacancies on the panel meant that it lacked a quorum during nearly the entirety of the 2020 campaign.

B. POLITICAL PLURALISM AND PARTICIPATION: 14 / 16

B1. Do the people have the right to organize in different political parties or other competitive political groupings of their choice, and is the system free of undue obstacles to the rise and fall of these competing parties or groupings? 4 / 4

The intensely competitive US political environment is dominated by two major parties: the Republicans on the right and the left-leaning Democrats. The country's prevailing "first past the post" or majoritarian electoral system discourages the emergence of additional parties, as do a number of specific legal and practical hurdles. However, the two parties' primary elections allow for a broad array of views and candidates to enter the political system, even if those in several states fully exclude unaffiliated voters. The 2020 general elections featured participation by ideologically diverse candidates across the country, as did the primary contests that produced the nominees for the November balloting. For the many seats at all levels that are regarded as "safely" Democratic or Republican, due in part to partisan gerrymandering, primaries often represent the main battleground for opposing views. Republicans, especially in the House, have faced sharp competition from more right-wing challengers in recent voting cycles, and left-wing Democrats—many of them aligned with or endorsed by the Democratic Socialists of America—challenged a number of moderate, party-backed candidates in 2020.

Independent or third-party candidates have sometimes influenced presidential races or won statewide office, and small parties and ideological factions—such as the Libertarian Party, the Green Party, and the Democratic Socialists of America—have also modestly affected state and local politics in recent years. In 2019, the state of Maine became the first to adopt a system of ranked-choice voting for both primary and general elections, which could prove more hospitable to third parties than the majoritarian system, though it generated no notable change in the 2020 elections. Also in 2020, voters in Alaska approved the adoption of another ranked-choice voting system, while Massachusetts voters rejected one.

B2. Is there a realistic opportunity for the opposition to increase its support or gain power through elections? 4 / 4

Power changes hands regularly at the federal level, and while certain states and localities are seen as strongholds of one party or the other, even they are subject to intraparty competition and interparty power transfers over time. After the 2020 elections, the Democrats held 23 state governorships, while Republicans held 27; Republicans maintained control over a majority of state legislatures.

In an unusual development following the 2018 midterms, outgoing Republican-led legislatures in Michigan and Wisconsin attempted to strip powers from executive offices that had just been captured by Democrats. The moves largely failed in Michigan, due in part to vetoes by the outgoing Republican governor, but the relevant measures were adopted in Wisconsin, where Democrats became governor and attorney general. The Republican-controlled legislature in North Carolina had pioneered such moves after a Democrat won the governorship in 2016.

President Trump's efforts to overturn his loss to Biden in 2020 put extreme pressure on the political and electoral systems, eroding the long-standing tradition of respect for official results and highlighting potential structural weaknesses that could be exploited by future candidates. Nevertheless, these efforts were ultimately unsuccessful, with Republican officials in the targeted states generally adhering to their legal duties, and transfers of power below the presidential level proceeded without similar contestation.

B3. Are the people's political choices free from domination by forces that are external to the political sphere, or by political forces that employ extrapolitical means? 3 / 4

Various interest groups have come to play a potent role in the nominating process for president and members of Congress, as the influence of traditional party leadership bodies has declined in recent decades. This is partly because the expense and length of political campaigns place a premium on candidates' ability to raise large amounts of funds from major donors, especially at the early stages of a race. While there have been a number of attempts to restrict the role of money in political campaigning, most have been thwarted or watered down as a result of political opposition, lobbying by interest groups, and court decisions that protect political donations as a form of free speech.

The 2020 election campaigns were by far the most expensive ever. As with other recent campaigns, much of the spending was routed through various types of "super PACs" (political action committees) and other legal vehicles designed to minimize restrictions on donor anonymity and on the size and sources of contributions. Small donations made up an important share of candidates' fundraising, but extremely wealthy contributors played an outsized role in overall spending. Expenditures did not always correlate with electoral success: former New York City mayor Michael Bloomberg gained little traction during his short-lived Democratic presidential primary campaign despite spending roughly $1 billion, while Democratic Senate candidates challenging Republican incumbents in states such as Kentucky, Iowa, Maine, and South Carolina were defeated despite far outspending their opponents.

Concerns about undue influence have also focused on lobbyists and other figures working for foreign governments who associate themselves with political campaigns. A Justice Department probe into foreign interference with the 2016 presidential election uncovered a number of cases of undisclosed consultant work for foreign powers and led to increased enforcement of the Foreign Agents Registration Act (FARA). In October 2020, a top Trump fundraiser, Elliott Broidy, pleaded guilty to illegal lobbying on behalf of Chinese and Malaysian clients.

Threats against elected officials from far-right extremists rose substantially in 2020. Restrictions imposed by states to combat the COVID-19 pandemic served as an early focal point of radical antigovernment sentiment, with armed demonstrations in several states, notably Michigan, where armed protesters entered the state capitol and attempted to intimidate lawmakers in April. In October, 13 far-right militia members were arrested in connection with a plot to kidnap the state's Democratic governor. Violent far-right groups participated in postelection protests against Trump's defeat, some of which led to clashes with counterprotesters.

The Trump campaign in 2020 drew criticism for a pattern in which administrative resources were misused to support the president's candidacy. Administration officials routinely promoted Trump's reelection or attacked his Democratic opponents, which apparently violated federal laws barring government employees from engaging in electioneering and other political activities. The president also repeatedly used the White House, his official plane, and other government facilities for campaign events. Separately, Trump on multiple occasions threatened or sought to withhold federal resources from states and cities whose Democratic leaders opposed him politically. Examples included his objections to economic relief for Democratic-led states during the COVID-19 pandemic, and his reluctance to release federal emergency aid to California as it faced catastrophic wildfires in August.

B4. Do various segments of the population (including ethnic, racial, religious, gender, LGBT+, and other relevant groups) have full political rights and electoral opportunities? 3 / 4

A number of important laws are designed to ensure the political rights of members of racial and ethnic minority groups, and the 2020 elections featured increased participation as candidates by women and representatives of such groups. The Congress elected in 2020 included the first openly gay Black House members and record or near-record numbers of Black, Hispanic, Native American, Asian American and Pacific Islander, LGBT+, and women lawmakers. Kamala Harris, whose mother and father were Indian and Jamaican immigrants, respectively, became the first Black American, the first Asian American, and the first woman to win election as vice president. Nevertheless, White Americans and men have remained highly overrepresented in Congress and senior policymaking positions.

De facto disenfranchisement has persisted among racial and ethnic minority communities, which are disproportionately affected by laws and policies that create obstacles to voting and winning elected office. In 2013 the Supreme Court invalidated portions of the Voting Rights Act of 1965, allowing certain states that previously had to submit legal changes for preclearance by federal authorities to adopt election laws without prior review. In the years since, in addition to adopting voter-identification requirements and limiting polling locations, a number of states—including some that were never subject to the preclearance rule—have rolled back innovations like early voting that contributed to higher rates of participation among minority groups.

Various other state election-management policies have been criticized for having a disparate impact on these communities. In Georgia in 2018, for example, the registrations of some 53,000 voters—most of them Black—were stalled due to applicant information that did not exactly match government records, and hundreds of thousands of other voters had been purged from the rolls for failing to vote in recent elections. The efforts by President Trump and his allies to overturn the 2020 election results centered on cities with large Black populations—such as Detroit, Philadelphia, Milwaukee, and Atlanta—where the margins heavily favored Biden, triggering legal complaints in response that accused the Trump camp of a racially discriminatory attempt to disenfranchise Black voters.

State laws that deny voting rights to citizens with felony convictions continue to disproportionately disenfranchise Black Americans, who are incarcerated at significantly higher rates than other populations. All but two states suspend voting rights during incarceration for felonies; the majority provide for automatic restoration, either upon release or after parole or probation, though in some cases financial penalties must also be paid, and 11 states impose additional steps and obstacles to restored suffrage. A growing number of states have eased these restrictions in recent years, but the issue remains controversial. In September 2020, an appeals court upheld a Florida requirement that former felons pay all outstanding case-related fines and debts to regain their voting rights, leaving hundreds of thousands of people unable to vote in the November elections. Overall, researchers estimated that more than five million people remained disenfranchised in 2020 due to felony convictions.

C. FUNCTIONING OF GOVERNMENT: 8 / 12 (–1)

C1. Do the freely elected head of government and national legislative representatives determine the policies of the government? 3 / 4

After Democrats gained a majority in the House of Representatives in the 2018 elections, the Trump administration frequently clashed with Congress in ways that challenged the legislature's constitutional authority. For example, in 2019 the president declared a national emergency so as to redirect congressionally appropriated funds to pay for the construction of a wall along the border with Mexico, a project that he had prioritized during his presidential campaign but which had failed to win sufficient financing from lawmakers. Later that year, Trump's irregular obstruction of appropriated military aid to Ukraine and his orders to defy subpoenas culminated in the House impeachment inquiry. During 2020 the administration continued its refusal to comply with a host of congressional reporting requirements, information requests, and subpoenas on various oversight matters.

The Trump administration consistently left large numbers of vacant positions across the higher levels of government departments and agencies, undercutting Congress's authority to confirm such appointees and making it difficult or impossible for the agencies to operate as intended by law. The problem was exacerbated by a high rate of departures by senior officials under Trump. In August 2020, the Government Accountability Office found that Chad Wolf, the acting secretary of homeland security, was serving in violation of laws governing such temporary appointments; the finding cast doubt on the legal validity of several controversial department decisions. Executive branch functions and continuity were further threatened following the November elections, when the outgoing administration broke precedent by hampering cooperation with incoming Biden administration officials, even after the General Services Administration formally set the transition in motion by "ascertaining" Biden's evident victory.

C2. Are safeguards against official corruption strong and effective? 3 / 4

The United States benefits from strong safeguards against official corruption, including a traditionally independent law enforcement system, a free and vigorous press, and an active civil society sector. A variety of regulations and oversight institutions within government are designed to curb conflicts of interest and prevent other situations that could lead to malfeasance.

Beginning in 2017, however, the Trump administration presented a number of challenges to existing norms of government ethics and probity. Anticorruption watchdogs criticized President Trump for shifting management of his real-estate development empire to his children rather than divesting ownership or establishing a stronger structural barrier between himself and his businesses. They argued that without such separation, the president could use his office for personal enrichment or allow his official decisions to be influenced by his private business interests. Lawsuits that were ongoing during 2020 focused on a constitutional rule that forbids officeholders from receiving compensation, or "emoluments," from other governments, which Trump was accused of doing through his businesses; one such case ended in October, when the Supreme Court declined to hear an appeal of a lower court judgment that the plaintiffs lacked standing to file suit. The president, his staff, and special interest groups of foreign and domestic origin all frequently visited and held events at Trump-branded properties in the United States throughout his term in office, generating publicity and income; the *Washington Post* reported in October that Trump had visited such properties 280 times during his presidency, spending $2.5 million in taxpayer dollars. Trump's decision to appoint his daughter and son-in-law as presidential advisers created potential conflicts involving their own business interests and personal relationships.

The Trump administration also notably undercut conflict-of-interest restrictions for other White House and executive branch appointees. Although the president issued an executive order in 2017 that limited appointees' ability to shift to lobbying work after leaving government, the same order eased restrictions on lobbyists moving into government, and the administration initially resisted efforts to disclose waivers allowing appointees to skirt the rules that remained. In practice, many Trump nominees received such waivers. Journalistic and congressional investigations routinely found conflicts of interest and other ethical violations among nominees and appointees.

An anonymous whistleblower from the Central Intelligence Agency who filed the complaint that touched off the impeachment inquiry in 2019 faced extreme pressure from the president and his allies, including attempts to publicize their identity. Although the whistleblower's identity was never publicly confirmed, the individual was forced into protective surveillance amid threats of violence. Following his February 2020 acquittal in the Senate, President Trump fired or forced the resignation of several officials who offered testimony that harmed his case during the House impeachment process. Observers warned that the situation could deter officials from reporting possible corruption in the future. In October, the president signed an executive order calling for many senior civil servants to be reclassified in a manner that could allow them to be fired for political or other arbitrary reasons, further weakening their ability to report malfeasance; implementation of the order remained unclear at year's end.

Also in 2020, several senators came under scrutiny for profitable stock trades during a period of market volatility that accompanied the COVID-19 outbreak. Most of the legislators were cleared of allegations that they illegally made trades based on their exclusive briefings about the pandemic, though an investigation into one senator was still open at year's end.

C3. Does the government operate with openness and transparency? 2 / 4 (−1)

The United States was the first country to adopt a Freedom of Information Act (FOIA) over 50 years ago, and the law is actively used by journalists, civil society groups, researchers, and members of the public. A 2016 reform law was designed to improve government agencies' responsiveness to FOIA requests, and reporters and activists were able to use FOIA filings to obtain important documents on the Trump administration that congressional investigators could not access through normal oversight requests or subpoenas. Nevertheless, government performance on FOIA requests declined during Trump's presidency, and in 2020 the coronavirus-induced transition to remote work by government employees produced a sharp drop in responsiveness to information requests at the federal, state, and local levels.

The pandemic intensified the Trump administration's existing lack of transparency in a number of other ways. Since assuming office, the president and members of his administration had frequently made statements that were either misleading or untrue, and typically failed to correct the record when such statements were challenged by the press and others. The administration also operated with greater opacity than its immediate predecessors, for example by making policy and other decisions without meaningful input from relevant agencies and their career civil servants and removing information on certain issues—such as climate change—from government websites. Throughout 2020, Trump and a number of his aides consistently promoted false and misleading information about COVID-19 for political reasons, playing down the severity of the outbreak and claiming that state and local social-distancing restrictions were unnecessary constraints on the economy. Political appointees in the administration also interfered with the analysis and recommendations of federal public health professionals, seeking to control data collection and official guidance. Such practices were echoed by some likeminded governments at the state and local levels.

In a break with presidential tradition, Trump refused to voluntarily release his personal tax records as a candidate, and he resisted formal requests for them from congressional and state investigators after taking office. The Supreme Court in June 2020 rejected Trump's novel claim of presidential immunity from criminal investigation in a New York case, and attempts to obtain his tax and business records were ongoing in the lower courts at year's end.

The executive branch includes a substantial number of auditing and investigative agencies that are independent of political influence; such bodies are often spurred to action by the investigative work of journalists. Trump left vacancies in several inspector general offices across the federal government during his presidency, and in April and May 2020 he arbitrarily fired or replaced a series of inspectors general who had documented or investigated malfeasance by administration officials, prompting bipartisan criticism from members of Congress.

Also in 2020, the administration persisted in its unusual attempts to tally noncitizens in connection with the decennial census in order to exclude some from the population count used for reallocating congressional seats. The effort, which appeared to break from a constitutional requirement that the "whole number of persons" in each state be counted for reapportionment, led to disruptions that threatened the accuracy of the overall count. The Census Bureau in April asked for an extension of its year-end deadline due to the effects of the pandemic, but the president in July ordered it to meet the deadline, and required both the traditional census results and a parallel version that excluded undocumented immigrants; it remained unclear how such immigrants would be enumerated. A series of court challenges added uncertainty to the bureau's task. The Supreme Court in December declined to block its attempts to fulfill Trump's instructions, but the count was still incomplete at year's end.

Score Change: The score declined from 3 to 2 due to a pattern of politically motivated disinformation and attempts to control or manipulate official findings related to the COVID-19 pandemic by the federal and some state governments, the president's abrupt dismissal of several inspectors general who had documented or investigated malfeasance by administration officials, and further administration interference with the collection and reporting of decennial census data, among other problems.

CIVIL LIBERTIES: 51 / 60 (–2)

D. FREEDOM OF EXPRESSION AND BELIEF: 15 / 16 (–1)

D1. Are there free and independent media? 3 / 4 (–1)

The United States has a free and diverse press, operating under some of the strongest constitutional protections in the world. The media environment retains a high degree of pluralism, with newspapers, newsmagazines, traditional broadcasters, cable television networks, and news websites competing for readers and audiences. Internet access is widespread and unrestricted. While many larger outlets have prospered, however, independent local sources of news have struggled to keep up with technology-driven changes in news consumption and advertising, contributing to significant ownership consolidation in some sectors, and a number of communities with just one or no local news outlet. News coverage has also grown more polarized, with certain outlets and their star commentators providing a consistently right- or left-leaning perspective. The cable network Fox News in particular grew unusually close to the Trump administration; several prominent on-air personalities and executives migrated to government jobs beginning in 2017, and key hosts openly endorsed Republican candidates or participated in campaign rallies. Following the 2020 elections, however, Fox joined other networks in calling the presidential race for Biden, and Trump subsequently denigrated the outlet, directing his followers to smaller, more extreme channels that fully endorsed his attempts to overturn the election results.

Trump was harshly critical of the mainstream media throughout his presidency, routinely using inflammatory language to accuse them of bias and mendacity. He maintained a drumbeat of verbal attacks on individual journalists and established outlets, describing them as—among other things—"fake news" and the "enemy of the American people." Trump allies have allegedly sought to collect and release embarrassing personal information about critical journalists, and certain reporters or outlets have been excluded from specific government or Trump campaign events. As of 2020 the president had not followed through on threats to strengthen libel laws or review certain outlets' broadcast licenses, as he largely lacked the authority to do so, though he has been accused of interfering with the other business interests of critical outlets' owners. Trump's reelection campaign filed defamation suits against a number of news outlets in early 2020, the administration filed an unsuccessful lawsuit to block the publication of a critical book by a former national security adviser, and the president's brother similarly filed an unsuccessful lawsuit to block a critical book by his niece. In July, a judge found that federal probation officers had revoked the prison furlough of Trump's former personal lawyer, Michael Cohen, in retaliation for his plans to publish his own book about the president.

In June 2020, Trump appointee Michael Pack was confirmed as the head of the US Agency for Global Media, which oversees government-funded news outlets serving audiences abroad. Pack quickly undertook major personnel and policy changes, undermining the news operations' editorial independence and declining to renew the visas of foreign journalists at the agency, including those vulnerable to repression in their home countries. The steps drew fierce criticism from agency employees, media watchdogs, and members of Congress; in November, a federal judge granted an injunction preventing Pack from directing news coverage.

Despite increased hostility from political figures and their supporters on social media, the mainstream media—including national television networks and major newspapers—have devoted considerable resources to independent coverage of national politics. Outlets like the *New York Times*, the *Washington Post*, and CNN have conducted investigations into the business affairs of Trump and his associates, closely examined the facts at the heart of the impeachment inquiry and other scandals, and regularly assessed the accuracy of the administration's claims.

A growing number of Americans look to social media and other online sources for political news, increasing their exposure to disinformation and propagandistic content of both foreign and domestic origin. The larger platforms have struggled to control false or hateful material without harming freedom of expression or their own business interests, though they have announced multiple mass removals of accounts linked to Russia, Iran, and China that were being used to spread disinformation. False content from certain far-right sources has also been removed from major platforms. In 2020, both social media platforms and mainstream outlets, particularly some Fox News programs, served as conduits for questionable or false information about the nature and spread of the coronavirus.

While violence against journalists in the United States has been rare in recent decades, media watchdog groups registered widespread press freedom violations, including police violence and arbitrary arrests targeting journalists, in the context of the nationwide protests sparked by the police killing of George Floyd. The US Press Freedom Tracker, a joint project of multiple nongovernmental organizations (NGOs), documented a total of 123 arrests of journalists and 334 assaults on journalists for 2020, compared with just 9 arrests and 34 assaults in 2019.

Score Change: The score declined from 4 to 3 due to a dramatic increase in arrests of and physical assaults on journalists across the country during the year, with most cases linked to coverage of protests.

D2. Are individuals free to practice and express their religious faith or nonbelief in public and private? 4 / 4

The United States has a long tradition of religious freedom. The constitution protects the free exercise of religion while barring any official endorsement of a religious faith, and there are no direct government subsidies to houses of worship. The debate over the role of religion in public life is ongoing, however, and religious groups often mobilize to influence political discussions on the diverse issues in which they take an interest. The Supreme Court regularly adjudicates difficult cases involving the relationship between religion and the state.

In 2020, multiple state and local governments-imposed restrictions on the size of religious gatherings to slow the spread of the coronavirus, prompting legal challenges. The Supreme Court issued somewhat conflicting rulings on the subject, though the restrictions in question differed in their details: in May and July the justices upheld attendance limits in California and Nevada, respectively, but in November the court—with a newly appointed justice reinforcing the conservative majority—struck down a New York order that strictly capped the number of congregants allowed to attend religious services in high-risk areas.

Hate crimes based on religion are generally prosecuted vigorously by law enforcement authorities. Federal Bureau of Investigation (FBI) statistics for 2019, released in November 2020, showed an increase of more than 6 percent in such crimes from 2018; incidents involving Jewish targets rose 14 percent and constituted over 60 percent of the year's religion-based hate crimes. Anti-Muslim crimes were the next most common, and Christian churches with predominantly Black congregations have also experienced attacks in recent years.

D3. Is there academic freedom, and is the educational system free from extensive political indoctrination? 4 / 4

The academic sphere has long featured a high level of intellectual freedom. While it remains quite robust by global standards, this liberty has come under pressure in recent years. University faculty have reported instances of harassment—including on social media—related to curriculum content, textbooks, or statements that some students strongly disagreed with. As a consequence, some professors have allegedly engaged in self-censorship. Students on a number of campuses have obstructed guest speakers whose views they find objectionable. In the most highly publicized cases, students and nonstudent activists have physically prevented presentations by controversial speakers, especially those known for their views on race, gender, immigration, Middle East politics, and other sensitive issues. Separately, the American Association of University Professors has complained that the politicization of climate change and other scientific topics is contributing to a more hostile environment for those working in related fields, including instances of harassment by private individuals.

The Trump administration in September 2020 ordered recipients of federal funds, including universities, to avoid diversity training that includes "divisive concepts" related to racism and sexism, prompting expressions of concern regarding impingements on academic freedom from numerous university administrators. A federal judge blocked implementation of the order in December.

D4. Are individuals free to express their personal views on political or other sensitive topics without fear of surveillance or retribution? 4 / 4

Americans are generally free to engage in private discussion and air their personal views in public settings, including on the internet, though a number of threats to this freedom exist.

Civil libertarians, many lawmakers, and other observers have pointed to the real and potential effects of the collection of communications data and other forms of intelligence-related monitoring on the rights of US residents, despite the adoption of significant reforms since such activities surged following the terrorist attacks of September 11, 2001. Separately, surveillance programs run by federal and local law enforcement agencies have long raised concerns among civil liberties groups, due in part to allegations of a disproportionate focus on religious, racial, and ethnic minority communities. A growing number of law enforcement and other government agencies are monitoring public social media content, with targets including applicants for US visas and participants in peaceful protests. The frequent use of drone aircraft and camera networks, sometimes in conjunction with facial-recognition technology, to monitor protest activity in 2020 prompted complaints about privacy violations and led some protesters to adapt their tactics to make identification more difficult.

A public debate about law enforcement access to encrypted communication services continues, with some officials warning that their technical inability to break encryption even with a judicial warrant posed a threat to the rule of law, and opponents arguing that any weakening of encrypted services' security would expose all users to criminal hacking and other ill effects.

Aside from concerns about government surveillance, internet users in the United States have faced problems such as aggressive disinformation efforts, intimidation, and frequently sexualized harassment on social media that may deter them from engaging in online discussion and expressing their views freely.

E. ASSOCIATIONAL AND ORGANIZATIONAL RIGHTS: 10 / 12 (−1)

E1. Is there freedom of assembly? 3 / 4 (−1)

In general, officials respect the constitutional right to public assembly. Demonstrations on political and other topics are common and typically proceed without incident. In response to acts of violence committed in the course of some past demonstrations, local authorities often place restrictions on the location or duration of large protests. Since 2017, legislative initiatives aiming to criminalize or stiffen penalties for certain forms of protest, or to shield perpetrators of violence against protesters from legal liability, have been proposed in most states. Numerous such bills were introduced in 2020, and at least seven were passed into law.

In recent years, large protests and aggressive law enforcement responses have been sparked by highly publicized police killings of Black civilians, many of which were recorded on video. In May 2020, outrage over the killing of George Floyd by police in

Minneapolis inspired one of the largest waves of protests in US history. Under the banner of the Black Lives Matter (BLM) movement, marches occurred in hundreds of cities and smaller communities. Estimated participation in May and June ranged from 15 to 26 million people, and daily protests occurred well into the summer in some cities. An overwhelming majority of the protests were peaceful, but in some settings they were accompanied by violence against police and significant damage to public and private property; local officials in certain cities complained of intimidating demonstrations outside their private homes. Human rights groups and academic experts found that aggressive police tactics were often the cause or prime escalating factor in violent episodes, and hundreds of instances of unprovoked or disproportionate police brutality were documented on video. At least 10,000 people had been arrested in connection with the protests by early June, though minor charges were frequently dropped.

Observers noted that police violence against protesters rarely resulted in accountability, and that police often exercised greater restraint toward anti-BLM counterprotesters and participants in separate demonstrations against COVID-19-related restrictions, many of whom were armed and displayed far-right or White supremacist symbols. Several people were killed in confrontations involving armed protesters, counterprotesters, or vigilantes during the year, including one prominent shooting by a left-wing gunman in Oregon who was later killed by police.

The Trump administration and its political allies frequently denounced the BLM movement and offered unqualified support to police, downplaying the extent of police violence. The president threatened to deploy active-duty military units in cities experiencing unrest, and in June a combination of federal law enforcement agents and National Guard members used chemical irritants and physical force to clear peaceful protesters from a plaza adjacent to the White House. In Portland, Oregon, where nightly protests repeatedly ended in clashes with law enforcement agents, city and state officials accused the administration of purposefully inflaming tensions by deploying federal agents to protect a federal courthouse; the agents' uniforms at times lacked any identifying insignia, and some detainees were taken away in unmarked vehicles.

Score Change: The score declined from 4 to 3 due to excessive police and federal agency responses to racial justice protests during the year, including thousands of arrests and numerous documented instances of police brutality, as well as multiple cases of intimidation and lethal violence involving armed protesters, counterprotesters, or vigilantes.

E2. Is there freedom for nongovernmental organizations, particularly those that are engaged in human rights– and governance-related work? 4 / 4

US laws and practices give wide freedom to NGOs and activists to pursue their civic or policy agendas, including those that directly oppose government policies. Organizations committed to the protection of civil liberties, immigrants' rights, equality for women and minority groups, and freedom of speech have become more active since 2016, mounting campaigns and filing lawsuits to block actions by the Trump administration that they considered harmful. A number of privately supported projects have also been established in recent years to address deficiencies in the electoral and criminal justice systems.

E3. Is there freedom for trade unions and similar professional or labor organizations? 3 / 4

Federal law generally guarantees trade unions the right to organize and engage in collective bargaining. The right to strike is also protected, though many public employees are prohibited from striking. Over the years, the strength of organized labor has declined, and just 6.3 percent of the private-sector workforce belonged to unions in 2020. While public-sector unions have a higher rate of membership, with 34.8 percent, they have come under pressure from officials concerned about the cost of compensation and pensions to states and municipalities. The overall unionization rate in the United States rose slightly to 10.8 percent in 2020, but this reflected the year's pandemic-related job losses rather than an actual increase in the number of unionized workers. The country's labor code and decisions by the National Labor Relations Board (NLRB) during Republican presidencies have been regarded as impediments to organizing efforts, but even Democratic administrations have largely failed to reverse the deterioration. Union organizing is also hampered by resistance from private employers. Among other tactics, many employers categorize workers as contractors or use rules pertaining to franchisees to prevent organizing.

A 2018 Supreme Court decision that government employees cannot be required to contribute to unions that represent them in collective bargaining has led to further losses in union membership. Organized labor scored a modest victory the same year when referendum voters in Missouri overturned a 2017 law that would have similarly allowed private-sector workers who benefit from union bargaining to opt out of paying union dues or fees. That left 27 states with such "right-to-work" legislation in place.

Strike activity proceeded largely without incident in 2020. Many well-publicized strikes and labor protests involved accusations that employers were providing insufficient protective equipment and hazard pay to employees who were unable to work remotely during the COVID-19 pandemic.

F. RULE OF LAW: 11 / 16

F1. Is there an independent judiciary? 3 / 4

The American judiciary is largely independent. The courts regularly demonstrated their autonomy during the Trump presidency by blocking or limiting executive actions.

However, judicial appointments in recent years have added to existing concerns about partisan distortion of the appointment and confirmation process. Republican leaders in the Senate had stalled many federal judicial nominations in the final years of Barack Obama's presidency, resulting in an unusually large number of vacancies at the beginning of 2017. The most prominent was a seat on the Supreme Court that the Senate had held open during 2016 by refusing to allow hearings on Obama's nominee. In 2017, the Senate confirmed Trump's nominee for the position, appellate court judge Neil Gorsuch, but only after the Republican leadership changed Senate rules that had required a supermajority to end debate on Supreme Court nominations, meaning the confirmation could proceed with a simple-majority vote. Democrats had enacted a similar rule change for lower court nominations in 2013.

The president filled a new vacancy on the Supreme Court in 2018, when federal appellate court judge Brett Kavanaugh narrowly won confirmation after contentious Senate hearings involving accusations of sexual assault; Kavanaugh denied the allegations and angrily denounced the campaign against him as a "political hit" orchestrated by "left-wing opposition groups." In 2020, Trump filled a third Supreme Court vacancy by nominating appellate court judge Amy Coney Barrett, who was confirmed in October, with one Republican senator joining all Democrats in opposition. Democrats stridently objected to the confirmation process, noting that Republicans had justified blocking Obama's 2016 nominee by claiming that when vacancies arise in election years, appointments should not be made prior to the balloting. Coney Barrett's appointment cemented a conservative Supreme Court majority; many Democrats suggested that the Republicans' actions justified the introduction of legislation to expand the size of the court and add new justices under a Democratic president.

By the end of 2020, Trump had successfully appointed a record 234 federal judges in all, including 54 appellate court judges. In a break with precedent, a number of his nominees were confirmed by the Senate even after he lost the November election.

Trump repeatedly responded to adverse court rulings by verbally attacking the judges and courts responsible and accusing them of political bias, earning a rare rebuke from Chief Justice John Roberts in 2018. The president also used his pardon power in an arbitrary or politicized fashion, bypassing Justice Department processes, overturning the convictions of several individuals whose cases were championed by his political allies, and publicly discussing possible pardons for himself or other individuals in a position to provide evidence against him in various investigations. In the weeks following his defeat in the November 2020 election, he pardoned longtime associate Roger Stone, who had been convicted in 2019 of lying to Congress and witness tampering; his first national security adviser, Michael Flynn, who had pleaded guilty to lying to the FBI in 2017; former campaign chairman Paul Manafort, who was convicted of tax fraud and other offenses and was considered a key link to Russian interference in the 2016 election; and 2016 campaign aide George Papadopoulos, who in 2017 pleaded guilty to lying to the FBI. These were among a larger raft of pardons issued to individuals with personal or political connections to Trump, including three former Republican congressmen convicted of fraud or misusing funds and four former military contractors convicted for their roles in a notorious 2007 massacre of civilians in Iraq.

In many states, judges are chosen through either partisan or nonpartisan elections, and a rise in campaign fundraising for such elections over the last two decades has increased the threat of bias and favoritism in state courts. In addition, executive and legislative officials in a few states have attempted to increase their control over state supreme courts, including through impeachments and constitutional changes.

F2. Does due process prevail in civil and criminal matters? 3 / 4

The United States has a deeply rooted rule-of-law tradition, and legal and constitutional protections for due process are widely observed. However, the criminal justice system suffers from a number of chronic weaknesses, many of which are tied to racial discrimination and contribute to disparities in outcomes that disadvantage people of color, particularly Black Americans. Media reports and analyses in recent years have drawn new attention to the extensive use of plea bargaining in criminal cases, with prosecutors employing the threat of harsh sentences to avoid trial and effectively reducing the role of the judiciary; deficiencies in the parole system; long-standing funding shortages for public defenders, who represent low-income defendants in criminal cases; racial bias in risk-assessment tools for decisions on pretrial detention; and the practice of imposing court fees or fines for minor offenses as a means of raising local budget revenues, which can lead to jail terms for those who are unable to pay.

These problems and evolving enforcement and sentencing policies have contributed to major increases in incarceration over time. The population of sentenced state and federal prisoners soared from about 200,000 in 1970 to some 1.4 million as of 2019. The incarceration rate based on such counts rose from around 100 per 100,000 US residents in 1970 to a peak of more than 500 in the late 2000s, then slipped to 419 as of 2019. There are also hundreds of thousands of pretrial detainees and short-term jail inmates behind bars. Despite gradual declines in the number of Black prisoners, Black and Hispanic inmates continue to account for a majority of the prison population, whereas Black and Hispanic people account for roughly a third of the general US population. Lawmakers, elected state attorneys, researchers, activists, and criminal justice professionals have reached a broad consensus that the current level of incarceration is not needed to preserve public safety. Civil liberties organizations and other groups have also argued that prison sentences are often excessive and that too many people are incarcerated for minor drug offenses.

In 2018, under pressure from a bipartisan coalition advocating for reforms to curb mass incarceration, Congress passed and the president signed a law that eased federal mandatory-minimum sentencing rules, among other modest changes. A majority of states have also passed laws in recent years to reduce sentences for certain crimes, decriminalize minor drug offenses, and combat recidivism; such gradual steps continued in 2020. Some states have restricted the use of cash bail, which can unfairly penalize defendants with fewer resources and enlarge pretrial jail populations. In November 2020, voters in Oregon approved a ballot measure to decriminalize possession of all drugs, the first state to take such a step; several others have decriminalized the recreational use of marijuana.

While accusations of prosecutorial misconduct and partiality are frequent at the state and local levels, the federal Justice Department has generally been regarded as more professional and independent. In 2020, however, Attorney General William Barr stirred controversy through statements and decisions on a variety of topics—including personnel changes, ongoing investigations, prosecutions of Trump associates, and civil suits against Trump—that appeared to serve the president's personal or political interests. The perceived improprieties prompted multiple federal prosecutors to withdraw from specific cases or resign in protest during the year. They also drew public rebukes from former Justice Department officials and in some instances from federal judges.

F3. Is there protection from the illegitimate use of physical force and freedom from war and insurgencies? 3 / 4

The US homicide rate, at 5.0 per 100,000 inhabitants as of 2019, remains low by regional and historical standards, and overall crime rates have declined since the 1990s. However, murder rates reportedly rose by more than 20 percent in the first nine months of 2020, with even higher spikes in a number of large cities.

The increased policy focus on reforming the criminal justice system in recent years has coincided with a series of widely publicized incidents in which police actions led to civilian deaths. Most of these prominent cases involved Black civilians, while Native Americans are reportedly killed by police at a higher rate per capita than any other group. Only a small fraction of police killings lead to criminal charges; when officers have been brought to trial, the cases have typically ended in acquittals or sentences on reduced charges. In many instances, long-standing and rigid labor protections prevent municipal governments and police departments from imposing significant administrative sanctions on allegedly abusive officers. Under the Trump administration, the Justice Department pulled back from previous federal policies aimed at imposing reforms on troubled local police departments through court-approved agreements.

Several high-profile police killings in 2020 stirred particular outrage. The March death of Breonna Taylor in Louisville, Kentucky, which occurred during a raid targeting a suspect who was not present in Taylor's apartment, sparked months of protests in the city. An investigation yielded "wanton endangerment" charges against one officer but no charges related to Taylor's death, prompting allegations that the Kentucky attorney general failed to adequately present the case to the grand jury. In May, a Minneapolis police officer killed George Floyd, who had allegedly used a fake bill at a corner store, by kneeling on his neck for nearly eight minutes as three other officers stood by. The officers were fired and charged with offenses including murder, with a trial expected to occur in 2021.

Opinion polling suggested that the year's protests against police violence and racial injustice were successful in shifting White Americans' attitudes and raising their awareness of the problems; attempts by some protest leaders to mobilize support for structural reforms that would strip police departments of funding fared less well. The protests also succeeded in drawing media and advocacy attention to many police departments' deep resistance to any reform or accountability mechanisms and putting a spotlight on the presence within law enforcement of some officers with direct links to racist and White supremacist groups.

Conditions in prisons, jails, and pretrial detention centers are often poor at the state and local levels, and in 2020 COVID-19 outbreaks occurred at facilities across the country, producing infections and deaths at much higher rates than in the general population. Many jurisdictions and the federal government took steps to ease crowding by releasing suspects and convicted inmates who were deemed less dangerous.

Use of the death penalty has declined significantly in recent years. There were seven executions across five states in 2020—down from 22 in 2019 and a peak of 98 in 1999. The death penalty has been formally abolished by 22 states, with Colorado joining the list in 2020; in another 17 states where it remains on the books, executions have not been carried out for the past five years or more. However, in July 2020 the federal government resumed executions for the first time since 2003, and 10 federal executions were carried out by the end of the year, provoking widespread criticism from religious leaders and criminal justice advocates. Factors encouraging the decline of the death penalty include clear racial disparities in its application, with death sentences far more likely in cases involving White murder victims than Black murder victims; a pattern of exonerations of death-row inmates, often based on new DNA testing; states' inability to obtain chemicals used in lethal injections due to objections from producers, as well as legal challenges to the constitutionality of the prevailing methods of lethal injection; and the high costs to state and federal authorities associated with death penalty cases. The US Supreme Court has effectively ruled out the death penalty for crimes other than murder and in cases where the perpetrator is a juvenile or mentally disabled, among other restrictions.

F4. Do laws, policies, and practices guarantee equal treatment of various segments of the population? 2 / 4

An array of policies and programs are designed to protect the rights of individuals against discrimination based on race, ethnicity, gender, and other categories, including in the workplace. However, women and some minority groups continue to suffer from disparities on various indicators, and a number of recent government policies have infringed on the fundamental rights of refugees, asylum seekers, and immigrants.

Although women constitute almost half of the US workforce and have increased their representation in many professions, the average compensation for female workers is roughly 80 percent of that for male workers, a gap that has remained relatively constant over the past several decades. Meanwhile, the wage gap between White and Black workers has grown in recent decades, meaning Black women, who are affected by both the gender and racial components of wage inequality, made about 61 cents for every dollar earned by White male workers as of 2017. Women are also most often affected by sexual harassment and assault in the workplace. A popular social media campaign that began in late 2017, the #MeToo movement, encouraged victims to speak out about their experiences. The phenomenon has led to the sudden downfall of powerful men in the worlds of politics, business, news, and entertainment, while underscoring the scale of the problem in American society.

In addition to structural inequalities and discrimination in wages and employment, racial and ethnic minority groups face long-running and interrelated disparities in education and housing. De facto school segregation is a persistent problem, and the housing patterns that contribute to it are influenced by factors such as mortgage discrimination, which particularly affects Black and Hispanic homeowners. Black homeownership has fallen steadily from a peak in 2004, despite gains for other groups in recent years. This in turn influences overall gaps in wealth and social mobility. For example, the median wealth of White families is 12 times the median wealth of Black families. Black people also face discrimination in health care and experience worse outcomes than their White counterparts, and during the COVID-19 pandemic, people of color experienced strikingly higher mortality from the virus. Asian Americans were the victims of a surge in discrimination and harassment in 2020, attributed in part to President Trump's attempts to focus blame for the pandemic on China, where the initial outbreak occurred.

The Supreme Court issued landmark decisions involving gender and the rights of minority groups in 2020. In June, the court reaffirmed the validity of an 1866 treaty and recognized that much of eastern Oklahoma remained under the sovereignty of the Muscogee (Creek) Nation, a Native American tribe. Also that month, the Supreme Court ruled that federal civil rights legislation includes LGBT+ people as a class protected from workplace discrimination. The decision was a rebuke to the Trump administration, whose effort to roll back previous administrations' moves to uphold the rights of LGBT+ people through executive actions and rulemaking for federal agencies and contractors continued in 2020. A ban on transgender people serving in the military, announced in 2017, took effect in 2019, even as court challenges continued; existing service members who had already received a diagnosis of gender dysphoria and had begun gender-affirming medical processes would be allowed to openly identify as their gender, but others, including new recruits, had to adhere to their "biological sex."

The Trump administration in 2020 intensified its efforts to reduce the number of legal immigrants, refugees, asylum seekers, and undocumented immigrants entering and residing in the country. Such moves since 2017 had in many cases been hasty, uncoordinated, and underfunded, leading to implementation problems as well as conflicts with existing laws, constitutional protections, and international human rights standards. While the administration typically cited exaggerated security concerns as justification for its policies, the COVID-19 pandemic provided a new rationale and helped the administration achieve larger declines in the number of newly arriving immigrants and asylum claimants than had previously been possible.

Beginning soon after his inauguration in 2017, the president issued a series of three executive orders barring travel from a group of Muslim-majority countries on security grounds, twice revising the original order in response to lawsuits claiming that the bans were blatantly discriminatory. In 2018 the Supreme Court upheld the third version, which banned most entries by citizens of Iran, Syria, Yemen, Libya, Somalia, and one non-Muslim country, North Korea. Less severe bans were imposed on six additional countries in early 2020. These orders, combined with other administration changes, helped to reduce the number of refugees admitted to the United States for resettlement to its lowest point since the program began in 1980. The refugee resettlement cap for the 2021 fiscal year was slashed to 15,000 people, down from 18,000 in fiscal 2020, and actual admissions remained far below the cap in 2020; prior to the Trump administration, the annual caps had generally surpassed 70,000.

A succession of other Trump administration policies have focused on curbing the arrival of asylum seekers at the southern border, most of whom have come from Central America in recent years. The policies consistently drew legal challenges on the grounds that they denied asylum seekers basic due process, violated statutory rules on asylum applications, and breached international prohibitions on returning asylum seekers to unsafe countries, among other objections. In 2019, the administration unveiled a new program allowing border authorities to force non-Mexican asylum seekers to wait in Mexico while their claims are adjudicated in the United States; tens of thousands of people were returned to Mexico under the program, joining a large preexisting set of would-be applicants often living in difficult and dangerous conditions there. The administration also announced in 2019 that individuals generally could not seek asylum in the United States if they passed through a third country without seeking and being denied asylum in that country, effectively blocking claims from Central Americans who travel through Mexico. Over the course of 2019, the United States signed agreements with Guatemala, El Salvador, and Honduras—all poor countries with high crime rates that have generated large numbers of migrants—allowing US authorities to deport asylum seekers there if they passed through without applying for asylum. The administration has also gradually adjusted rules to extend permissible detention periods and broaden the list of deportable offenses. In 2020, the administration cited the COVID-19 pandemic to justify a broad slate of restrictions. A March order closed the border to asylum claimants, and federal agents began immediately returning all irregular border-crossers to Mexico or their countries of origin, including unaccompanied children. Separately in February, the Supreme Court allowed implementation of a new rule permitting the denial of permanent residency to applicants deemed likely to make use of state social benefits; immigrants' rights advocates claimed the rule deterred immigrants from accessing necessary public health services, among other objections.

The Trump administration attempted to ramp up arrests and deportations of both undocumented immigrants, regardless of whether they had committed crimes, and legal immigrants or refugees who committed crimes in the United States, even if they had long since completed their sentences. The previous practice had been to focus deportation efforts on the most dangerous criminal immigrants with the weakest ties to American communities. The COVID-19 pandemic forced Immigration and Customs Enforcement (ICE) to scale back its arrests and return to the focus on dangerous criminals, but the administration continued efforts to punish cities that refused to assist ICE agents in identifying and detaining undocumented immigrants. The administration's enforcement drive has added to an existing backlog of cases in immigration courts; as of December 2020 there were more than a million pending cases, roughly double the number pending when Trump took office. The pandemic exacerbated poor conditions in immigration detention facilities; as of mid-November, over 7,300 detainees had tested positive for the virus. Under pressure from immigrants' rights advocates, the administration took steps to reduce the population of ICE detainees, which declined by more than 50 percent between February and November. A surge of criticism followed revelations in September that a doctor at an immigration detention center in Georgia had performed invasive and unnecessary medical procedures, including hysterectomies, on detained women. Separately in June, the Supreme Court ruled, on procedural grounds, against the administration's effort to end the Deferred Action for Childhood Arrivals (DACA) program, which prevents the deportation of undocumented immigrants who were brought to the United States as children; legal wrangling over reimplementation of the program continued at year's end.

G. PERSONAL AUTONOMY AND INDIVIDUAL RIGHTS: 15 / 16

G1. Do individuals enjoy freedom of movement, including the ability to change their place of residence, employment, or education? 4 / 4

There are no significant undue restrictions on freedom of movement within the United States, and residents are generally free to travel abroad without improper obstacles. A patchwork of temporary movement restrictions were imposed across the country in response to the COVID-19 pandemic, with states acting independently based on local conditions and strategies, though the rules were loosely enforced and relied mainly on voluntary compliance.

G2. Are individuals able to exercise the right to own property and establish private businesses without undue interference from state or nonstate actors? 4 / 4

Property rights are widely respected in the United States. The legal and political environments are supportive of entrepreneurial activity and business ownership. President Trump's shifting and exemption-filled tariff policies prompted concern throughout his administration that political favoritism was distorting markets involving tariff-sensitive businesses. Similarly, perceived support for the administration allegedly influenced the awarding of government aid and contracts, including during the COVID-19 pandemic. Coronavirus-related business restrictions at the state and local levels caused significant disruption and confusion, prompting civil disobedience and public protests by some private business owners.

G3. Do individuals enjoy personal social freedoms, including choice of marriage partner and size of family, protection from domestic violence, and control over appearance? 4 / 4

Men and women generally enjoy equal rights in divorce and custody proceedings, and there are no undue restrictions on choice of marriage partner, particularly after a 2015 Supreme Court ruling that all states must allow same-sex marriage. In recent years, a growing number of states have passed laws to eliminate exemptions that allowed marriages of people under age 18 in certain circumstances. Rape and domestic or intimate-partner violence remain serious problems. The applicable laws vary somewhat by state, though spousal rape is a crime nationwide. Numerous government and nongovernmental programs are designed to combat such violence and assist victims. In the past several years, a series of new state laws have reduced women's access to abortion without overtly breaching prior Supreme Court decisions on the issue, and some have survived judicial scrutiny, adding to state-by-state variation in access. In June 2020, however, the Supreme Court struck down a Louisiana law that would have significantly reduced abortion access in that state.

G4. Do individuals enjoy equality of opportunity and freedom from economic exploitation? 3 / 4

The "American dream"—the notion of a fair society in which hard work will bring economic and social advancement, regardless of the circumstances of one's birth—is a core part of the country's identity, and voters tend to favor government policies that they believe will enhance equality of opportunity. In recent decades, however, studies have shown a widening inequality in wealth and a narrowing of access to upward mobility. Inequality concerns mounted in 2020 as the recession linked to the COVID-19 pandemic caused a massive spike in unemployment—especially for Black and Hispanic workers—leading to record demand for food banks and other community services. Economic stimulus legislation passed by Congress in April and December mitigated the damage, in part by expanding unemployment benefits, but widespread hardship persisted at year's end.

One key aspect of inequality is the growing income and wealth gap between Americans with university degrees and those with a high school degree or less; the number of well-compensated jobs for the less-educated has fallen over time as manufacturing and other positions are lost to automation and foreign competition. These jobs have generally been replaced by less remunerative or less stable employment in the service and retail sectors, where there is a weaker tradition of unionization. The coronavirus-related economic shock amplified this dynamic, disrupting employment and income for lower-earning, less-educated workers far more than for college-educated professionals. Although the country has legal safeguards against unsafe working conditions, workers in essential industries such as meat processing faced a high risk of contracting COVID-19 in practice, with inadequate protective equipment and hazard pay. Poorer children who lacked the resources to adapt to remote learning were also most harmed by pandemic-linked school closures, which threatened to exacerbate educational inequality.

The inflation-adjusted national minimum wage has fallen substantially since the 1960s, with the last nominal increase in 2009, though many states and localities have enacted increases since then. Other obstacles to gainful employment include inadequate public transportation and the high cost of living in economically dynamic cities and regions. The latter problem, which is exacerbated by exclusionary housing policies in many jurisdictions, has also contributed to an overall rise in homelessness in recent years.

Uruguay

Population: 3,500,000
Capital: Montevideo
Freedom Status: Free
Electoral Democracy: Yes

Overview: Uruguay has a historically strong democratic governance structure and a positive record of upholding political rights and civil liberties while also working toward social inclusion. Although all citizens enjoy legal equality, there are still disparities in treatment and political representation of women, transgender people, Uruguayans of African descent, and the indigenous population.

KEY DEVELOPMENTS IN 2020

- Uruguay's COVID-19 response was lauded for much of the year, as the country avoided the devastation experienced by neighboring countries. However, cases began rising rapidly late in the year. According to researchers at the University of Oxford, the country had registered over 19,000 cases and 180 deaths at year's end.
- President Luis Lacalle Pou, a member of the center-right Partido Nacional, took office in March 2020 following his election victory in November 2019.
- Human rights activists criticized the Law of Urgent Consideration, a broad-based public sector reform passed in July, for weakening freedom of association and empowering police to expand the use of force.

POLITICAL RIGHTS: 40 / 40

A. ELECTORAL PROCESS: 12 / 12

A1. Was the current head of government or other chief national authority elected through free and fair elections? 4 / 4

The president is directly elected to a five-year term, and may hold nonconsecutive terms. The most recent general elections were held in two rounds in October and November 2019. The ticket of Luis Lacalle Pou and Beatriz Argimón of the center-right Partido Nacional captured the presidency and vice presidency after a close runoff decided by approximately 37,000 votes. Lacalle Pou—a senator and son of a former president—defeated former Montevideo mayor Daniel Martínez of the center-left Frente Amplio in the runoff. The election took place peacefully and stakeholders accepted the results, and Lacalle Pou was inaugurated in March 2020.

A2. Were the current national legislative representatives elected through free and fair elections? 4 / 4

The bicameral General Assembly consists of the 99-member Chamber of Representatives and the 30-member Senate, with all members directly elected for five-year terms. No single party achieved a majority in the October 2019 elections. The Frente Amplio retained the most representatives, but went from 50 seats in the Chamber of Representatives to 42, and from 15 to 13 seats in the Senate. Lacalle Pou's Partido Nacional built a predominantly center-right coalition with four other parties—the Partido Colorado, the newly formed Cabildo Abierto, the Partido de la Gente, and the Partido Independiente—that together won 57 seats in the Chamber of Representatives and 17 seats in the Senate. The elections took place peacefully, and stakeholders accepted the results.

A3. Are the electoral laws and framework fair, and are they implemented impartially by the relevant election management bodies? 4 / 4

Uruguay's Electoral Court serves as the highest authority on elections and supervises the National Electoral Office, which oversees voter registration and has one office in each of the country's regional departments. Electoral laws are generally fair, and the Electoral Court, whose nine members are elected by both houses of Parliament with a two-thirds majority, is generally viewed as impartial. Voting is compulsory. In September 2020, Uruguay held municipal elections after delaying voting from May due to the COVID-19 pandemic.

B. POLITICAL PLURALISM AND PARTICIPATION: 16 / 16

B1. Do the people have the right to organize in different political parties or other competitive political groupings of their choice, and is the system free of undue obstacles to the rise and fall of these competing parties or groupings? 4 / 4

Uruguay's multiparty system is open and competitive. The major political groupings are the Colorado Party, the Frente Amplio coalition, the Independent Party, and the Partido Nacional (also known as Blanco). The Partido Nacional, accompanied by its coalition partners, took power in early 2020.

B2. Is there a realistic opportunity for the opposition to increase its support or gain power through elections? 4 / 4

Opposition parties are competitive.

B3. Are the people's political choices free from domination by forces that are external to the political sphere, or by political forces that employ extrapolitical means? 4 / 4

People's political choices are generally free from undue influence from undemocratic actors.

B4. Do various segments of the population (including ethnic, racial, religious, gender, LGBT+, and other relevant groups) have full political rights and electoral opportunities? 4 / 4

The Afro-Uruguayan minority, which accounts for approximately 8 percent of the population, is significantly underrepresented in government and professional jobs. In 2019, voters elected the first Afro-Uruguayan women senator. Indigenous peoples are also severely underrepresented, although there is a currently a grassroots campaign that aims to gain formal government recognition of the Indigenous Charrúa people.

Representation of women in national, regional, and local government is low. Eight out of 30 senators and 19 of 99 representatives (21 percent of total legislators) elected in 2019 were women, a slight decrease from the number elected in 2014.

C. FUNCTIONING OF GOVERNMENT: 12 / 12

C1. Do the freely elected head of government and national legislative representatives determine the policies of the government? 4 / 4

The head of government and national legislature determine the policies of the government without undue interference.

C2. Are safeguards against official corruption strong and effective? 4 / 4

The level of corruption in Uruguay is low by regional standards. The 2020 Capacity to Combat Corruption Index released by Americas Quarterly ranked Uruguay's ability to detect, punish, and prevent corruption first in Latin America.

C3. Does the government operate with openness and transparency? 4 / 4

Government institutions have established a robust record of accountability to the electorate. Enforcement of the Transparency Law, which prohibits a range of offenses related to abuse of office, is relatively strong at the national level. However, civil society groups criticized the government for insufficient transparency in the administration of the COVID-19 Solidarity Fund in 2020.

CIVIL LIBERTIES: 58 / 60

D. FREEDOM OF EXPRESSION AND BELIEF: 16 / 16

D1. Are there free and independent media? 4 / 4

Constitutional guarantees regarding free expression are generally respected. The press is privately owned; the broadcast sector includes both commercial and public outlets. There are numerous daily and weekly newspapers, some of which are connected to political parties. The Center for Archives and Access to Public Information registered 26 press freedom violations between April 2019 and March 2020, the majority of which involved denials of access to information or threats and assaults. Freedom of expression advocates also criticized a provision of the Law of Urgent Consideration (LUC) passed in July that criminalizes insulting the police.

D2. Are individuals free to practice and express their religious faith or nonbelief in public and private? 4 / 4

Freedom of religion is legally protected and broadly respected.

D3. Is there academic freedom, and is the educational system free from extensive political indoctrination? 4 / 4

Academic freedom is upheld.

D4. Are individuals free to express their personal views on political or other sensitive topics without fear of surveillance or retribution? 4 / 4

Discussion of personal and political topics is generally open and robust, and there is little fear of government surveillance or retribution.

E. ASSOCIATIONAL AND ORGANIZATIONAL RIGHTS: 12 / 12

E1. Is there freedom of assembly? 4 / 4

Freedom of assembly is protected by law, and the government generally respects this right in practice. The LUC contains provisions that, according to human rights advocates, could result in greater police use of force to disperse protests.

E2. Is there freedom for nongovernmental organizations, particularly those that are engaged in human rights- and governance-related work? 4 / 4

A wide array of community organizations and national and international human rights groups are active in civic life, and do not face government interference. The conduct of state agents during Uruguay's military dictatorship (1973–85) remains a sensitive topic; in September 2020, a human rights group, the Mothers and Relatives of Detained Uruguayans, denounced a social media smear campaign—in which a sitting senator was an allegedly central participant—targeting the group for its efforts at pursuing justice for dictatorship-era crimes.

E3. Is there freedom for trade unions and similar professional or labor organizations? 4 / 4

Workers are free to exercise the right to join unions, bargain collectively, and hold strikes. Unions are well organized and politically powerful. Labor advocates were among the most vocal opponents of the LUC, and following its approval the country's main labor union began mobilizing for a referendum to overturn dozens of articles in the law, including provisions that place limits on strike activity.

F. RULE OF LAW: 15 / 16

F1. Is there an independent judiciary? 4 / 4

Uruguay's judiciary is generally independent.

F2. Does due process prevail in civil and criminal matters? 3 / 4

The courts in Uruguay remain backlogged, and prisons are violent and operate at or near capacity. However, recent changes to criminal procedure have reduced pretrial detention, and proposals to divert people convicted of low-level drug crimes from prisons to addiction treatment centers were under discussion in 2020. Some prisoners convicted of minor offenses were released to house arrest during the COVID-19 pandemic in order to limit the virus's spread inside prisons.

Efforts to seek justice for human rights violations committed under the military regime have been slow and inconsistent. In September 2020, human rights groups denounced the right-wing Cabildo Abierto party's introduction of a proposed amnesty law for members of the military, and in December 2020 the Inter-American Court of Human Rights (IACHR) expressed concern at Uruguay's lack of compliance with rulings requiring judicial processes for dictatorship-era rights violations.

F3. Is there protection from the illegitimate use of physical force and freedom from war and insurgencies? 4 / 4

Uruguay is free from large-scale violence and civil strife. The LUC included language that was criticized by domestic observers as well as multiple United Nations special rapporteurs for potentially granting members of the security forces overly broad discretion to use coercive force.

Criminal violence and insecurity have increased in Uruguay in recent years, although murders in 2020 were down roughly 20 percent from the record set in 2018.

F4. Do laws, policies, and practices guarantee equal treatment of various segments of the population? 4 / 4

Transgender people have historically been discriminated against in Uruguay. However, in 2018 the executive promulgated a law allowing transgender people to change relevant information on their identification documents. The law also allows minors to have gender confirmation hormone therapy without parental or guardian permission, and set aside funds to help ensure that transgender people have access to education and health care, and to provide a pension for transgender people who were persecuted by the military dictatorship. However, violence against transgender people remains widespread.

The Afro-Uruguayan minority continues to face economic and social inequalities. While a 2013 affirmative action law was enacted to combat persistent inequality, Afro-Uruguayans experience high unemployment rates, and they were disproportionately affected by the economic dislocation resulting from the COVID-19 pandemic. In November, antiracism groups criticized the violent dispersal of a gathering of largely Afro-Uruguayan people by the police, which resulted in 11 arrests.

Women enjoy equal rights under the law but face discriminatory attitudes and practices, including a persistent wage gap.

G. PERSONAL AUTONOMY AND INDIVIDUAL RIGHTS: 15 / 16

G1. Do individuals enjoy freedom of movement, including the ability to change their place of residence, employment, or education? 4 / 4

Freedom of movement is protected, and individuals are free to change their residence, employment, and institution of higher education without interference.

G2. Are individuals able to exercise the right to own property and establish private businesses without undue interference from state or nonstate actors? 4 / 4

The right to own property and establish private business is respected.

G3. Do individuals enjoy personal social freedoms, including choice of marriage partner and size of family, protection from domestic violence, and control over appearance? 4 / 4

Violence against women remains a serious concern, but authorities are making efforts to combat gender-based violence. The legislature in 2017 voted to designate femicide a special circumstance that can increase sentences, and has begun confiscating guns from policemen who have been convicted of domestic violence. However, levels of gender-based violence have risen in the country, sparking calls for stronger protections. In December 2019, President Vázquez issued a resolution declaring a national emergency on gender-based violence, which would expand monitoring and rehabilitation programs for convicted offenders. The issue remained prominent in 2020, as calls to domestic abuse hotlines and formal gender-based violence complaints rose substantially amid the isolation induced by COVID-19 lockdowns.

The legislature voted overwhelmingly to legalize same-sex marriage in 2013. Abortion for any reason during the first trimester has been legal since 2012. However, many women, especially in rural areas, lack access to legal abortions. Stigma connected to the procedure continues to impede full access for women.

G4. Do individuals enjoy equality of opportunity and freedom from economic exploitation? 3 / 4

Individuals generally enjoy equality of opportunity, although certain barriers persist for Afro-descendants, women, transgender, and Indigenous Uruguayans. The LUC was criticized by labor rights advocates for allegedly weakening labor protections and the public education system.

According to reports, the government is not doing enough to combat transnational trafficking, and laws do not prohibit internal trafficking.

Uzbekistan

Population: 34,200,000
Capital: Tashkent
Freedom Status: Not Free
Electoral Democracy: No

Overview: While reforms adopted since President Shavkat Mirziyoyev took office in 2016 have led to improvements on some issues, Uzbekistan remains an authoritarian state with few signs of democratization. No opposition parties operate legally. The legislature and judiciary effectively serve as instruments of the executive branch, which initiates reforms by decree, and the media are still tightly controlled by the authorities. Reports of torture and other ill-treatment persist, although highly publicized cases of abuse have resulted in dismissals and prosecutions for some officials, and small-scale corruption has been meaningfully reduced.

KEY DEVELOPMENTS IN 2020

- Reacting to the first wave of COVID-19 infections in March, the government imposed a lockdown that lasted some two months and offered the public detailed health information. A more serious second wave that began in July temporarily overwhelmed the health care system, however, and official reporting diverged from observable reality. By year's end, public health measures had helped to suppress the surge. A total of about 77,000 cases and 614 deaths were reported for the year.
- In June, the death of a businessman who was severely beaten while in police detention sparked public outrage after three years of official pledges regarding reform of the security sector. In response, the prosecutor general's office swiftly brought charges against the officers implicated in the case and publicized data on torture investigations for the first time.
- Despite new openness from within government agencies about corruption and abuse of power, critical journalists and social media activists continued to face dismissal or police interrogation during the year. In August, independent journalist Bobomurod Abdullaev, who had been accused of operating a popular anonymous social media account that made corruption allegations, was extradited from Kyrgyzstan to face charges in Uzbekistan, though the case was eventually dropped.

POLITICAL RIGHTS: 2 / 40

A. ELECTORAL PROCESS: 1 / 12

A1. Was the current head of government or other chief national authority elected through free and fair elections? 0 / 4

The president, who holds most executive power, is directly elected for up to two five-year terms. Longtime prime minister Shavkat Mirziyoyev was named acting president through an irregular parliamentary process in 2016, after Islam Karimov, who had held the presidency since Uzbekistan's independence from the Soviet Union in 1991, suffered a stroke and died. The constitution called for the Senate chairman to serve as acting president, but the chairman declined the post. Mirziyoyev won a special presidential election at the end of 2016, taking a reported 88.6 percent of the vote and defeating nominal challengers whose parties in some cases openly campaigned for the incumbent. Election monitors from the Organization for Security and Co-operation in Europe (OSCE) concluded that "the dominant position of state actors and limits on fundamental freedoms undermine political pluralism and led to a campaign devoid of genuine competition."

A2. Were the current national legislative representatives elected through free and fair elections? 0 / 4

Uzbekistan has a bicameral legislature. The lower house is composed of 150 seats, with members directly elected in individual constituencies. The 100-member upper house, or Senate, includes 84 members who are elected by regional councils and 16 who are appointed by the president. All members of the parliament serve five-year terms.

The December 2019 lower house elections again offered voters no meaningful choice, as all participating parties supported the government. The final results that followed January 2020 runoffs in 25 districts closely mirrored those from the previous lower house elections. The president's party, the Liberal Democratic Party of Uzbekistan (O'zLiDeP), maintained the largest share with 53 of 150 seats. Milliy Tiklanish (National Revival) won 36, the Adolat (Justice) Social Democratic Party won 24, and the People's Democratic Party (XDP) won 22. The Ecological Party of Uzbekistan, which directly competed for the first time after previously having its seats automatically allocated, won the same total of 15 delegates that it had been granted in the previous parliament. OSCE election monitors noted numerous irregularities, including procedural violations, the use of multiple ballots by voters, and ballot-box stuffing.

A3. Are the electoral laws and framework fair, and are they implemented impartially by the relevant election management bodies? 1 / 4

The electoral laws and framework are implemented in ways that offer no opportunities for independent political actors or parties to participate in elections at any level. Election management bodies are closely controlled by the government.

Mirziyoyev has presided over some electoral reforms during his tenure. A 2017 law allowed the election of 11 district councils within Tashkent, in addition to the existing council for the city as a whole; Tashkent has the status of a region, and districts in the country's other regions already had elected councils. Another set of reforms enacted in 2019 ended indirect representation for the Ecological Party, removed voting restrictions on those with past criminal convictions, and allowed voters to add their names to more than one party roll; these lists are required for political parties to participate in elections.

B. POLITICAL PLURALISM AND PARTICIPATION: 0 / 16

B1. Do the people have the right to organize in different political parties or other competitive political groupings of their choice, and is the system free of undue obstacles to the rise and fall of these competing parties or groupings? 0 / 4

Only five political parties are registered—O'zLiDep, the XDP, Adolat, Milliy Tiklanish, and the Ecological Party. They engage in mild criticism of one another and occasionally of government ministers, but all are effectively progovernment.

B2. Is there a realistic opportunity for the opposition to increase its support or gain power through elections? 0 / 4

No genuine opposition parties operate legally. Unregistered opposition groups function primarily in exile. Domestic supporters or family members of exiled opposition figures have been persecuted, and they are barred from participating in elections.

B3. Are the people's political choices free from domination by forces that are external to the political sphere, or by political forces that employ extrapolitical means? 0 / 4

Regional alliances of political elites hold the levers of government at all levels, creating economic oligarchies and patronage networks that stifle political competition. There is some intra-elite competition, but without the patronage of the established networks, political and economic advancement is all but impossible.

B4. Do various segments of the population (including ethnic, racial, religious, gender, LGBT+, and other relevant groups) have full political rights and electoral opportunities? 0 / 4

No registered party represents the specific interests of ethnic or religious minority groups, and no other parties or actors have the opportunity to achieve political representation. Women formally enjoy equal political rights, but they are unable to organize independently to advance their political interests in practice, and they remain underrepresented in leadership positions.

A component of the electoral reform package enacted in 2019 required 30 percent of legislative candidates to be women. Women now hold 33 percent of the seats in the lower house and 23 percent of the seats in the Senate. No women ran for president in 2016.

C. FUNCTIONING OF GOVERNMENT: 1 / 12

C1. Do the freely elected head of government and national legislative representatives determine the policies of the government? 0 / 4

The country's leadership is not freely elected, and the legislature serves as a rubber stamp for the executive branch.

C2. Are safeguards against official corruption strong and effective? 0 / 4

Corruption is pervasive. Graft and bribery among low- and mid-level officials remain common and are at times conducted overtly and without subterfuge. However, petty corruption among traffic police and officials granting identification documents and registrations has been notably reduced in recent years by pilot programs that introduced video surveillance and traffic cameras.

President Mirziyoyev has overseen an ongoing purge of the notoriously corrupt security and law enforcement services. In February 2020, former prosecutor general Otabek Murodov was convicted on graft charges, becoming the third prosecutor general to be prosecuted in two years. Analysts contend that the purge is largely meant to neutralize security officials from the Karimov era and shift power to the president's personal security service and the reformed National Guard, both of which are overseen by Mirziyoyev's family members.

Media discussion of corrupt practices has cautiously expanded since Karimov's death, but in some cases the journalists and commentators involved have come under pressure. In August 2020, the Senate admitted that public health officials in five different regions may have embezzled COVID-19 emergency funds. A few weeks earlier, in July, a Tashkent-based blogger had been summoned for questioning by the security services after he made similar allegations on social media and called on Uzbekistan's international creditors to investigate.

C3. Does the government operate with openness and transparency? 1 / 4

Government operations remain mostly opaque, but one of Mirziyoyev's first acts as president in late 2016 was the creation of new online mechanisms that offered citizens the opportunity to file complaints, report problems, and request services. The initial program was overwhelmingly popular and was quickly expanded to all ministries and local government offices, requiring local officials to interact with citizens and demonstrate responsiveness. The innovations contributed to a cultural change in governance, though they frequently encountered resistance at the local level.

While the government was considered to have communicated well with the public during the early months of the COVID-19 pandemic, dubious official statements and statistics during a second wave in the summer conflicted with direct evidence of a more severe crisis that temporarily overwhelmed the health care system.

CIVIL LIBERTIES: 9 / 60 (+1)

D. FREEDOM OF EXPRESSION AND BELIEF: 3 / 16 (+1)

D1. Are there free and independent media? 1 / 4 (+1)

Despite constitutional guarantees, press freedom remains severely restricted. The state controls major media outlets and related facilities, and independent outlets were mostly shuttered or blocked under Karimov. However, domestic media, including news websites and live television programs, now cautiously discuss social problems and criticize local officials, reflecting a slight reduction in media repression since Mirziyoyev took power. Some independent news sources have emerged and are not subject to overt censorship, though most outlets still avoid openly criticizing Mirziyoyev and the government.

The presence of independent international outlets is limited; several foreign reporters have been granted press passes since 2017, although other journalists working for outlets like Radio Free Europe/Radio Liberty (RFE/RL) have been denied entry. Access to news and information via popular social media sites like YouTube and Facebook became more reliable after the government stopped blocking those sites at the end of 2018, and social media platforms have become lively forums for political discussion.

Journalists continue to face criminal penalties for a variety of possible offenses related to their work. In December 2020, the president signed legal amendments that eliminated prison terms for libel and insult, but compulsory labor and other penalties remained in place, and dissemination of false information was added to the criminal and administrative codes. An earlier law adopted in March had criminalized dissemination of false information related to COVID-19.

Under Mirziyoyev, a number of journalists have been released from prison, and 2018 marked the first year in two decades that no journalists were imprisoned, but the government handed down a jail sentence to a blogger in 2019. The state also used the Soviet-era practice of forced psychiatric hospitalization against journalist Nafosat Olloshukurova during 2019, and she fled the country in January 2020 after being threatened with further confinement. In August, authorities in Kyrgyzstan detained and extradited journalist Bobomurod Abdullaev at the request of Uzbek authorities, who reportedly accused him of operating an anonymous social media account that made allegations of corruption. The US State Department and human rights organizations objected to the move, citing his past persecution in Uzbekistan. After a brief detention in Tashkent, Abdullaev was released, and the case against him was eventually dropped.

Score Change: The score improved from 0 to 1 because some independent media sources have emerged in recent years and avoided overt censorship, though journalists still face intimidation by authorities, and self-censorship remains common.

D2. Are individuals free to practice and express their religious faith or nonbelief in public and private? 0 / 4

The government permits the existence of approved Muslim, Jewish, and Christian denominations, but treats unregistered religious activity as a criminal offense. Suspected members of banned Muslim organizations and their relatives have faced arrest, interrogation, and torture. Arrested believers are frequently accused of founding previously unknown religious organizations, a charge that carries high penalties. In most cases, little evidence of the existence of such organizations is presented at the closed trials. In 2017, Mirziyoyev announced that some 16,000 individuals had been removed from an official list of roughly 17,000 people who had been suspected or previously convicted of religious extremism. Individuals on the list were kept under close surveillance or on probation. In May 2020, the Interior Ministry announced that some previously released prisoners who had been members of the Islamist group Hizb ut-Tahrir were being rearrested on allegations of continuing to proselytize for the group or possessing its literature.

Since 2019, Islamic activists and bloggers not affiliated or accused of affiliation with Hizb ut-Tahrir have faced fewer arrests; many of the country's most prominent activists were already arrested or jailed on administrative charges in 2018 after criticizing a state decision to effectively ban the hijab in schools and universities.

In August 2020, the Interior Ministry announced that minors would again be allowed to attend prayers in public mosques, reversing a Karimov-era ban. In September, the parliament introduced new proposed amendments that would potentially loosen or reverse the controversial prohibition on wearing religious clothing in state and educational institutions, as well as somewhat simplify the requirements for religious organizations to register. The legislation had not been passed as of year's end. Human rights activists and international monitors noted that the proposals would not fundamentally change the state's authority to license religious organizations, censor religious literature, and prosecute anyone participating in religious activities or teaching outside state-approved forums.

D3. Is there academic freedom, and is the educational system free from extensive political indoctrination? 1 / 4

The government has long limited academic freedom, in part by controlling contacts between universities or scholars and foreign entities. Universities in Uzbekistan have slowly expanded their cooperation with foreign counterparts since 2016.

Texts that glorify former president Karimov are no longer required reading at universities.

D4. Are individuals free to express their personal views on political or other sensitive topics without fear of surveillance or retribution? 1 / 4

The freedoms of personal expression and private discussion have long been limited by *mahalla* committees—traditional neighborhood organizations that the government transformed into an official system for public surveillance and control. The government also engages in extensive surveillance of electronic communications.

Through its various reforms since 2016, the Mirziyoyev administration has signaled a greater tolerance for public criticism, modestly improving the climate for expression of personal views on sensitive topics. However, the 2020 legal amendments that criminalized dissemination of false information, including about COVID-19, indicated ongoing pressure to set limits on public debate.

E. ASSOCIATIONAL AND ORGANIZATIONAL RIGHTS: 1 / 12

E1. Is there freedom of assembly? 0 / 4

Despite constitutional provisions for freedom of assembly, authorities severely restrict this right in practice, breaking up virtually all unsanctioned gatherings and detaining participants. In August 2020, officials published draft legislation proposed by the Interior Ministry that would permit and set rules for public assemblies, but would allow them only on weekdays at specific times, limit their duration to two hours, and require preapproval of applications submitted at least 15 days in advance, among other restrictions.

E2. Is there freedom for nongovernmental organizations, particularly those that are engaged in human rights- and governance-related work? 1 / 4

Unregistered nongovernmental organizations (NGOs) have faced severe repression and harassment. A new organization designed to oversee the activities of registered NGOs, the Center for the Development of Civil Society (CDCS), was formed in 2019, but new legislation governing NGO registration had yet to be adopted as of 2020.

The government remained unwilling to register local or international NGOs that address human rights issues during the year. A special commission set up to deal with the COVID-19 pandemic created new formal restrictions on distribution of pandemic and natural disaster aid by charity organizations, effectively banning many local and independently organized efforts to fill gaps during times of crisis, though these rules largely went unenforced in practice.

E3. Is there freedom for trade unions and similar professional or labor organizations? 0 / 4

The Federation of Trade Unions is controlled by the state, and no genuinely independent union structures exist. Organized strikes are extremely rare.

F. RULE OF LAW: 1 / 16

F1. Is there an independent judiciary? 0 / 4

The judiciary remains subservient to the president. In 2017, however, a number of judicial reforms were enacted through constitutional and legislative amendments, establishing specific terms in office for judges and creating a Supreme Judicial Council (OSK) to oversee appointments and disciplinary action, among other changes. The council, whose chairperson is approved by the Senate on the president's recommendation, replaced a commission that was directly subordinate to the president.

F2. Does due process prevail in civil and criminal matters? 0 / 4

Due process guarantees are extremely weak. Law enforcement authorities have routinely justified the arrest of suspected religious extremists or political opponents by planting contraband, filing dubious charges of financial wrongdoing, or inventing witness testimony. The Lawyers' Chamber, a regulatory body with compulsory membership, serves as a vehicle for state control over the legal profession. The judicial reforms adopted in 2017 gave judges rather than prosecutors the authority to approve certain investigative steps, such as exhumations and some forms of surveillance. In August 2020, a presidential decree introduced an option for defendants to enter plea bargains for a range of offenses and included provisions to improve detainees' access to lawyers.

F3. Is there protection from the illegitimate use of physical force and freedom from war and insurgencies? 1 / 4

A 2016 law on police prohibits torture, and a 2017 presidential decree that bars courts from using evidence obtained through torture took effect in 2018. Despite the reforms, reports of physical abuse against detainees continued to appear on social media in 2020.

In June, the family of Andijon businessman Alijon Abdukarimov, who had been detained the previous month by police investigating a theft, published videos on social media showing him in an intensive care unit as a result of severe torture during interrogation. Abdukarimov died from his injuries days later, sparking widespread public outrage. The prosecutor general's office brought charges against the officers implicated in the case, and six officers received sentences ranging from one to 10 years in prison in November. Also in June, the prosecutor general's office publicized data on torture investigations for the first time, admitting that of 757 cases investigated in three years, only 33 had led to prosecution. It promised additional reforms and a state commission to prevent police torture. The human rights ombudsman acknowledged the same month that torture remained a serious problem, and the Interior Ministry announced that video cameras would be installed in police interrogation facilities across the country.

Prisons suffer from severe overcrowding and shortages of food and medicine. As with detained suspects, prison inmates—particularly those sentenced for their religious beliefs—are often subjected to torture and other ill-treatment. Jaslyk prison, a correctional facility where torture was especially widespread, was ordered closed by President Mirziyoyev in 2019.

F4. Do laws, policies, and practices guarantee equal treatment of various segments of the population? 0 / 4

Although racial and ethnic discrimination are prohibited by law, the belief that senior positions in government and business are reserved for ethnic Uzbeks is widespread. Women's educational and professional prospects are limited by discriminatory cultural and religious norms. Women are also barred from certain jobs under the labor code.

Sex between men is punishable with up to three years in prison. The law does not protect LGBT+ people from discrimination, and social taboos deter the discussion of LGBT+ issues.

G. PERSONAL AUTONOMY AND INDIVIDUAL RIGHTS: 4 / 16

G1. Do individuals enjoy freedom of movement, including the ability to change their place of residence, employment, or education? 1 / 4

Permission is required to move to a new city, and bribes are commonly paid to obtain the necessary documents. Bribes are also frequently required to gain entrance to and advance in exclusive universities. The government took steps to ease travel within the country and to neighboring states beginning in 2017, when it removed police checkpoints at internal borders, resumed direct flights to Tajikistan, and opened border crossings as part of an agreement with Kyrgyzstan. The Mirziyoyev administration abolished exit visas in 2019, ending a system that was used to proscribe travel beyond other member states of the Commonwealth of Independent States.

The government imposed tight restrictions on movement in March 2020 to prevent COVID-19 infections, easing the rules in May as cases declined. A second lockdown was imposed in July and lifted beginning in September. The moves were generally seen as legitimate public health measures.

G2. Are individuals able to exercise the right to own property and establish private businesses without undue interference from state or nonstate actors? 1 / 4

Widespread corruption and extensive state control over the economy limit private business opportunities and make property rights tenuous in practice.

G3. Do individuals enjoy personal social freedoms, including choice of marriage partner and size of family, protection from domestic violence, and control over appearance? 1 / 4

While the law generally grants men and women equal rights in matters such as marriage and divorce, women often face de facto disadvantages. Extralegal child marriage is reportedly practiced in some areas. Victims of domestic violence are discouraged from pressing charges against perpetrators, who rarely face prosecution. Rape is also seldom reported or prosecuted, and spousal rape is not explicitly criminalized.

G4. Do individuals enjoy equality of opportunity and freedom from economic exploitation?
1 / 4

Economic exploitation remains a serious domestic problem, as does the trafficking of men and women abroad for forced labor and sex work. A 2009 law imposed stronger penalties for child labor, and in 2012 Mirziyoyev, then the prime minister, pledged to end the practice completely. In 2017, the president issued a decree to formally ban forced agricultural labor by students, health workers, and teachers. During the subsequent cotton harvests, the government increased incentives for voluntary labor and granted access to international observers. In 2018, the International Labor Organization (ILO) noted that 93 percent of cotton workers were voluntarily employed for that year's harvest, while child labor was not an issue.

In March 2020, President Mirziyoyev signed a decree to fully end the state quota system for cotton that had motivated local officials to require forced labor. While some wheat quotas remained, these were also scheduled to be reduced beginning in 2021. In September, the Agriculture Ministry mandated higher pay rates for cotton harvesters. Despite these improvements, some evidence of forced labor has continued to be reported in recent years, and prosecutions of suspected traffickers remain rare.

Vanuatu

Population: 300,000
Capital: Port Vila
Freedom Status: Free
Electoral Democracy: Yes

Overview: Vanuatu conducts democratic elections but suffers from a pattern of unstable coalition governments that do not complete their terms. Although political corruption is a problem, the largely independent judiciary has been able to hold elected officials accountable in high-profile cases. Other persistent problems include domestic violence and societal discrimination against women.

KEY DEVELOPMENTS IN 2020

- In December, former prime minister Charlot Salwai and three other former ministers were acquitted on bribery and corruption charges, but Salwai was convicted of perjury, for making a false sworn statement to mislead the court. The corruption charges were in relation to a vote of no confidence that was withdrawn when Salwai was in office in 2016. Deputy Prime Minister Ishmael Kalsakau, who was leader of the opposition at the time, claimed that Salwai bribed two parliamentarians to withdraw their signatures from the no-confidence motion.
- After the March 2020 general elections, the Vanua'aku Pati party formed a coalition government with the Union of Moderate Parties, The National United Party, the Nagriamel political movement, and the Green Confederation Party. Bob Loughman of Vanua'aku Pati was named prime minister in April. The COVID-19 pandemic, as well as an extreme weather event, significantly impacted voter turnout, which was around 51 percent.

POLITICAL RIGHTS: 33 / 40
A. ELECTORAL PROCESS: 10 / 12
A1. Was the current head of government or other chief national authority elected through free and fair elections? 3 / 4

The prime minister, who holds most executive authority and appoints their own cabinet, is chosen by Parliament from among its members. Prime ministerial elections and votes of no confidence often feature improprieties, as rival coalitions seek to entice members to shift allegiances with offers of cash or ministerial portfolios. Bob Loughman became prime minister in April 2020, after the March general elections, winning 31 of the 52 votes in the parliament.

The largely ceremonial president is elected to serve a five-year term by an electoral college consisting of Parliament and the heads of the country's provincial councils. A two-thirds majority is required, and multiple rounds of voting can be held to reach this threshold. In 2017, Presbyterian pastor Tallis Obed Moses was elected to replace President Baldwin Lonsdale, who died in office.

A2. Were the current national legislative representatives elected through free and fair elections? 4 / 4

The 52-seat unicameral Parliament is directly elected for four-year terms in 18 constituencies ranging from one to seven members in size. In the March 2020 elections, Graon Mo Jastis Pati won nine seats, the Union of Moderate Parties and Leaders Party of Vanuatu both won five seats, and the National United Party won four. In total, 18 different parties and individuals were seated in Parliament, including Vanua'aku Pati, which formed a coalition government with the Union of Moderate Parties, The National United Party, the Nagriamel political movement, and the Green Confederation Party. Bob Loughman of Vanua'aku Pati was named prime minister in April. The COVID-19 pandemic, as well as an extreme weather event, significantly impacted voter turnout, which was around 51 percent.

A3. Are the electoral laws and framework fair, and are they implemented impartially by the relevant election management bodies? 3 / 4

The electoral framework is generally fair, and elections are administered without bias, but international observers have noted problems including an inaccurate voter roll and understaffing of election management bodies. Moreover, the use of the single-nontransferable-vote system, particularly in larger multimember constituencies, is believed to weaken political parties and encourage fragmentation. It is also especially unfair at by-elections when voters may be filling only one vacant seat in a multiseat district.

B. POLITICAL PLURALISM AND PARTICIPATION: 15 / 16
B1. Do the people have the right to organize in different political parties or other competitive political groupings of their choice, and is the system free of undue obstacles to the rise and fall of these competing parties or groupings? 4 / 4

Numerous political parties operate without restrictions in Vanuatu. A total of 18 parties and independents won seats in the 2020 elections. Politicians frequently switch allegiances. In mid-2018, the government withdrew proposed constitutional reforms that were meant in part to address party switching and political instability, having failed to reach consensus with the parliamentary opposition. Plans to put these reform proposals to a referendum were abandoned in May 2019.

B2. Is there a realistic opportunity for the opposition to increase its support or gain power through elections? 4 / 4

The country has a record of frequent democratic transfers of power between rival parties.

B3. Are the people's political choices free from domination by forces that are external to the political sphere, or by political forces that employ extrapolitical means? 4 / 4

There are no major undue constraints on the choices of voters or candidates from outside the political system. Traditional chiefs—represented by the National Council of Chiefs, a consultative body for customary and language matters—exert some influence, but they do not control electoral decisions.

B4. Do various segments of the population (including ethnic, racial, religious, gender, LGBT+, and other relevant groups) have full political rights and electoral opportunities? 3 / 4

Ethnic minorities enjoy equal political rights. Political groupings have historically been divided in part along linguistic lines, with an Anglophone majority and a Francophone minority.

Women's political participation is impaired by customary biases, and they are severely underrepresented in elected offices. No women were elected to Parliament in 2020. Only 18 women contested seats in the elections. Some seats are reserved for women at the municipal level, and women's rights groups have lobbied for a quota at the national level as well.

C. FUNCTIONING OF GOVERNMENT: 8 / 12

C1. Do the freely elected head of government and national legislative representatives determine the policies of the government? 3 / 4

The elected prime minister and cabinet determine and implement government policies without improper interference, and the legislature serves as a check on executive power. However, party fragmentation and frequent no-confidence votes have long disrupted governance. Charlot Salwai's government was the first since 1995 to complete a full four-year term (2016–20).

In June 2020, the ruling coalition voted to suspend 22 opposition parliamentarians, after the opposition boycotted the parliament's first sitting. The opposition subsequently challenged its suspension in the Supreme Court. Opposition leader Ralph Regenvanu claimed that such boycotts were a regular feature of postindependence parliaments.

C2. Are safeguards against official corruption strong and effective? 2 / 4

Abuse of office and corruption are serious problems, but prosecutors, the ombudsman, and other independent institutions are sometimes effective in combating them.

In December 2020, former prime minister Salwai and three other former ministers were acquitted on bribery and corruption charges, but Salwai was convicted of perjury for making false sworn statement to mislead the court. The corruption charges were in relation to a vote of no confidence that was withdrawn when Salwai was in office in 2016. Deputy Prime Minister Ishmael Kalsakau, who was leader of the opposition at the time, claimed that Salwai bribed two parliamentarians to withdraw their signatures from the no-confidence motion.

In July 2020, Vanuatu's President Tallis pardoned nine former parliamentarians imprisoned on 2015 conspiracy charges.

C3. Does the government operate with openness and transparency? 3 / 4

The government largely operates with transparency. Parliament sessions are streamed live on the internet, and elected officials are required to submit financial disclosure reports that can be investigated by the ombudsman's office, but the documents are not made public. However, leader of the opposition Ralph Regenvanu claimed that the ruling coalition had suspended 22 opposition parliamentarians in June 2020 in order to avoid scrutiny of the government's financial plans for the coronavirus pandemic.

A new freedom of information law that was adopted in 2016 took effect in 2017, and the government issued an order on implementation later that year. The law was widely welcomed as a positive step, though observers remained concerned about the establishment of fees and other potential obstacles to timely fulfillment of information requests.

CIVIL LIBERTIES: 49 / 60

D. FREEDOM OF EXPRESSION AND BELIEF: 14 / 16

D1. Are there free and independent media? 2 / 4

The government generally respects freedom of the press, though elected officials have sometimes been accused of threatening journalists for critical reporting. Publicly and privately owned newspapers publish in English and French. There are a small number of private broadcasters, but the state-owned broadcaster has a dominant position in the sector. Foreign news services are also available, and about a quarter of the population has access to the internet.

In November 2019, the government rejected a work-permit renewal request from journalist Dan McGarry, publisher of the *Daily Post* newspaper, and barred him from returning to the country later that month. McGarry claimed that the government retaliated against the newspaper's coverage of Chinese influence in Vanuatu, which the government denied; the Supreme Court revoked the travel ban in December, allowing McGarry to return to Vanuatu.

D2. Are individuals free to practice and express their religious faith or nonbelief in public and private? 4 / 4

The constitution's preamble states that the republic is founded on "Christian principles," but there is no official religion, and adherents of other faiths can worship freely. Authorities do not enforce a legal registration requirement for religious groups.

D3. Is there academic freedom, and is the educational system free from extensive political indoctrination? 4 / 4

There are no constraints on academic freedom.

D4. Are individuals free to express their personal views on political or other sensitive topics without fear of surveillance or retribution? 4 / 4

The government does not monitor personal communications, and individuals are able to discuss politics and other matters without interference.

E. ASSOCIATIONAL AND ORGANIZATIONAL RIGHTS: 11 / 12

E1. Is there freedom of assembly? 4 / 4

The law provides for freedom of assembly, and the government typically upholds this right in practice. Public demonstrations generally proceed without incident.

E2. Is there freedom for nongovernmental organizations, particularly those that are engaged in human rights- and governance-related work? 4 / 4

There are no significant constraints on the formation and operations of nongovernmental organizations (NGOs), which are not required to register with authorities.

E3. Is there freedom for trade unions and similar professional or labor organizations? 3 / 4

Workers can join unions, bargain collectively, and strike. The right to strike is somewhat impaired by notification rules and the government's ability to bar such actions in essential services; violations can draw criminal penalties. The umbrella Vanuatu Council of Trade Unions (VCTU) is an affiliate of the International Trade Union Confederation (ITUC). Union leaders have raised concerns about antiunion pressure on seasonal workers who travel to New Zealand, including from recruiting agents within Vanuatu.

F. RULE OF LAW: 13 / 16

F1. Is there an independent judiciary? 4 / 4

The judiciary is largely independent, but a lack of resources hinders the hiring and retention of qualified judges and prosecutors. The president appoints the chief justice after consulting with the prime minister and the opposition leader. Other judges are appointed by the president on the advice of the Judicial Service Commission (JSC); judges cannot be removed arbitrarily. Tribal chiefs and island courts empowered to hear customary law cases adjudicate local disputes.

Vanuatu's courts have demonstrated impartiality in recent years through their adjudication of cases involving senior political figures. In 2018, the Court of Appeal ruled against former deputy prime minister Joe Natuman, who appealed his ejection from Parliament after receiving a two-year suspended prison sentence for interfering with a police inquiry when he was prime minister in 2014.

Viran Molisa Trief became the first woman to be a Supreme Court judge in the country in July 2019.

F2. Does due process prevail in civil and criminal matters? 3 / 4

Due process rights are guaranteed by law. However, police do not always uphold legal safeguards against arbitrary arrest and detention. Long periods of pretrial detention are not uncommon, largely due to case backlogs in the courts. However, Vanuatu's pretrial population is relatively low for the region.

Fourteen police officers were suspended in July 2020 after they assaulted villagers on the island of Santo, using firearms and burning private property. The officers had been sent to the island to respond to a land dispute.

F3. Is there protection from the illegitimate use of physical force and freedom from war and insurgencies? 3 / 4

The police paramilitary unit, the Vanuatu Mobile Force (VMF), has a reputation for heavy-handed treatment of citizens. Civilian authorities have not been effective in punishing and preventing cases of police brutality. Natuman's 2018 conviction stemmed from interference with an investigation regarding high-ranking officers charged with mutiny. In his defense, Natuman claimed he was seeking to bring unity to the troubled police force.

Prisons have suffered from overcrowding, violence, poor living conditions, and lax management that contributes to frequent escapes.

F4. Do laws, policies, and practices guarantee equal treatment of various segments of the population? 3 / 4

Women are guaranteed legal equality, but in practice they continue to face societal discrimination that affects their access to employment and economic opportunity. LGBT+ people are not protected by antidiscrimination laws.

The rapid expansion of Chinese-owned businesses has sometimes fueled resentment toward Chinese residents. Certain occupations are reserved for ni-Vanuatu as part of a policy to boost employment for the native population.

G. PERSONAL AUTONOMY AND INDIVIDUAL RIGHTS: 11 / 16

G1. Do individuals enjoy freedom of movement, including the ability to change their place of residence, employment, or education? 4 / 4

The constitution protects freedom of movement, which is also respected in practice. In March 2020, President Obed Moses declared a state of emergency to respond to the COVID-19 pandemic, which included travel restrictions and other public health measures to prevent the spread of the virus.

G2. Are individuals able to exercise the right to own property and establish private businesses without undue interference from state or nonstate actors? 3 / 4

The legal framework is generally supportive of property rights and private business activity. However, irregularities surrounding land deals, and corruption in the Lands Ministry, are persistent problems. Legislation adopted in 2017 was designed to strengthen oversight for the leasing of customary land.

G3. Do individuals enjoy personal social freedoms, including choice of marriage partner and size of family, protection from domestic violence, and control over appearance? 2 / 4

Domestic violence is widespread. Social stigma and fear of reprisal inhibits reporting, particularly in more remote rural areas, and police and courts rarely intervene or impose strong penalties. Government and civil society efforts to combat the problem are inadequately funded. Spousal rape is not specifically criminalized. Women pursuing civil cases related to personal status matters face difficulties paying the required court fees. Only fathers can automatically pass citizenship to their children at birth.

G4. Do individuals enjoy equality of opportunity and freedom from economic exploitation? 2 / 4

Poverty is extensive, and more than three-quarters of the population rely on subsistence agriculture. The government does not properly enforce health and safety standards, leaving employees in construction, logging, and other industries exposed to hazardous working conditions. Children often perform agricultural work at the family level, and laws on child labor do not meet international standards.

Venezuela

Population: 28,500,000
Capital: Caracas
Freedom Status: Not Free
Electoral Democracy: No

Overview: Venezuela's democratic institutions have deteriorated since 1999, but conditions have grown sharply worse in recent years due to harsher crackdowns on the opposition and the ruling party relying on widely condemned elections to control all government branches. The authorities have closed off virtually all channels for political dissent, restricting civil liberties and prosecuting perceived opponents without regard for due process. The country's severe humanitarian crisis has left millions struggling to meet basic needs, and driven mass emigration.

KEY DEVELOPMENTS IN 2020

- In January, the ruling United Socialist Party of Venezuela (PSUV) attempted to undercut the legitimacy of Juan Guaidó, the interim president backed by the democratic opposition, by engineering the election of Luis Parra as National Assembly president. Military forces barred opposition members from entering the chamber to participate in the vote, and the Constitutional Chamber of the Nicolás Maduro-aligned Supreme Tribunal of Justice (TSJ) ratified Parra's election in May.
- Tightly controlled National Assembly elections went forward in December despite an opposition boycott, leading to a new body with a ruling-party majority. The old opposition-led legislature in response extended its own term, in an attempt to keep control of the legislative branch. At the end of the year, Venezuela had rival presidents and legislatures, with Maduro firmly in control and the democratic opposition severely weakened.
- Opposition figures, journalists, activists, protesters, and others perceived as dissidents faced relentless repression, including arbitrary arrests and extrajudicial executions.
- A state of emergency was enacted in March in response to the COVID-19 pandemic, upending everyday life. Authorities and armed groups enforced movement restrictions with violence, while alongside the pandemic, Venezuelans suffered from an acute shortage of gasoline that exacerbated widespread misery. Venezuelans continued to flee the country in massive numbers due to the country's worsening crises; in August, the International Monetary Fund (IMF) released a report estimating that 10 million people could emigrate by the end of 2023.

POLITICAL RIGHTS: 1 / 40 (−1)

A. ELECTORAL PROCESS: 0 / 12

A1. Was the current head of government or other chief national authority elected through free and fair elections? 0 / 4

Venezuela's president serves six-year terms, and is not subject to term limits. In January 2019, incumbent president Nicolás Maduro was sworn in for a new term after winning the 2018 snap presidential election. The poll saw record-low turnout, with only 46 percent of voters participating, and by most international accounts lacked even a veneer of competitiveness. That month, Venezuela's democratically elected National Assembly declared its head, Juan Guaidó, to be Venezuela's interim president as a constitutional response to Maduro's reelection in a fraudulent poll.

The ruling United Socialist Party of Venezuela (PSUV) attempted to undercut Guaidó's legitimacy by engineering the election of Luis Parra as National Assembly president in January 2020, with military forces barring opposition members from entering the chamber to participate in the vote. The Constitutional Chamber of the Maduro-aligned Supreme Tribunal of Justice (TSJ) ratified Parra's election in May. Meanwhile, more than 50 countries that had recognized Guaidó as Venezuela's acting president in 2019 continued to do so, but some critics have begun to express concerns about Guaidó's capacity to challenge *chavismo*. Maduro is recognized by fewer than 20 countries, generally Venezuela's historical allies and governments with an economic or other interest in the country—most prominently Russia, China, and Cuba.

During the year, the Lima Group, composed of mostly Latin American governments; the International Contact Group, which brings together a number of European and Latin American governments; the United States; and the European Union (EU) called for a transitional government to organize free and fair presidential elections, to little effect.

A2. Were the current national legislative representatives elected through free and fair elections? 0 / 4

The unicameral National Assembly is popularly elected for five-year terms, using a mix of majoritarian and proportional-representation voting. Three seats are reserved for Indigenous representatives. Ahead of the December 2020 elections, electoral authorities announced that the new National Assembly would have 277 seats, up from 167.

The major opposition parties refused to participate in December's vote for the 2021–26 National Assembly term, saying they had no reason to believe the Maduro administration would oversee a fair election, and pointed in particular to the installation of new election commissioners without input from opposition lawmakers in the National Assembly. The ruling party and its allies won 91 percent of seats, though most of the world's democracies, including the United States, rejected the results as illegitimate. In late December, the outgoing, opposition-controlled National Assembly voted to extend its term into 2021 in an effort to keep control of the legislative branch. Also in December, Maduro announced that the National Constituent Assembly—a body established in 2017 to supplant the National Assembly, and filled with regime loyalists elected in a nondemocratic process—would be shuttered.

A3. Are the electoral laws and framework fair, and are they implemented impartially by the relevant election management bodies? 0 / 4

Venezuela's electoral system is heavily influenced by political manipulation and institutional interference in favor of the PSUV. The new members of the National Electoral Council (CNE), appointed by the TSJ in 2020 without input from opposition lawmakers, are all aligned with the PSUV or minor parties that are not aligned with the main opposition parties. In September, the United States sanctioned Indira Alfonso Izaguirre, the new president of the CNE, and other state officials, citing their efforts to prevent free and fair elections.

Recent polls, including the 2018 presidential election and the 2020 legislative elections, have been characterized by disqualifications of prominent opposition candidates, government abuse of public resources, uneven access to the state-dominated media, the diminished presence of international observers, and intimidation of state employees.

B. POLITICAL PLURALISM AND PARTICIPATION: 1 / 16 (−1)

B1. Do the people have the right to organize in different political parties or other competitive political groupings of their choice, and is the system free of undue obstacles to the rise and fall of these competing parties or groupings? 0 / 4

Opposition leaders have long been harassed, attacked, imprisoned, and otherwise impeded from participating in political processes or leading political parties in peaceful activities. In September 2020, an independent UN fact-finding mission concluded, after investigating over 200 cases since 2014 and reviewing thousands more, that the Venezuelan government had ordered the arrest and torture of numerous dissidents, and that "even conservative estimates suggest that Venezuela has one of Latin America's highest rates of killings by state agents."

A slew of further violations, apparently intended to impede party activities and competition, were recorded in 2020. In late February, chavismo supporters shot at an opposition demonstration in Barquisimeto. Six people were injured, and Guaidó's vehicle was shot at.

In June and July, the TSJ suspended the leaders of the most prominent opposition parties—Acción Democrática (Democratic Action) and Voluntad Popular (Popular Will)—and placed in charge figures who had previously been suspended from the parties for supporting Parra's election as president of the National Assembly, and negotiating with the Maduro regime.

Former chavistas also continued to be targeted in 2020. According to Provea (Provide), a Venezuelan rights organization, 44 former government loyalists have faced persecution including violations of their rights to association, but also to their personal freedom and integrity, since 2017. Among them was Alí Domínguez, an activist and journalist, who was murdered in 2019.

There were 351 political prisoners in Venezuela at the end of 2020, according to rights group Foro Penal (Criminal Forum). Leopoldo López, founder of two opposition parties who in 2019 had taken refuge in the house of the Spanish ambassador to Venezuela after escaping from house arrest, fled to Spain in October.

In May 2020, 82 people were arrested for being part of an alleged plan to kidnap Maduro to take him to the United States, where officials in March had offered a $15 million reward for information leading to his capture or conviction. Seventeen of the detainees confessed and gave information about opposition leaders that were related to the plot, according to the national prosecutor's office, which is controlled by the ruling party.

B2. Is there a realistic opportunity for the opposition to increase its support or gain power through elections? 0 / 4

While discontent with the Maduro administration remains widespread, the government has cut off virtually all avenues for political change. The opposition has boycotted recent national elections after claiming that the international criteria of competitiveness could not be met. Both López and Henrique Capriles Radonski, a prominent opposition figure and former governor of Miranda State, remain banned from holding public office.

B3. Are the people's political choices free from domination by forces that are external to the political sphere, or by political forces that employ extrapolitical means? 0 / 4

The Maduro regime increasingly relies on the military, paramilitary forces, and opaque support from foreign states in order to retain political power. Military leaders have taken control of numerous offices, and Maduro has continued to strengthen the Bolivarian Militia, a civilian militia group established by the late president Hugo Chávez Frías in 2008 to support the military; the government claimed the group had over 4 million members in 2020. In January, the National Constituent Assembly approved legislation to consider the militia a part of Venezuela's official military and Maduro claimed that every member of the militia should be provided with a gun.

Separately, irregular, state-affiliated armed groups known as *colectivos* routinely commit acts of violence against civilians, particularly at antigovernment protests, and carry out government-backed voter intimidation efforts. The Office of the UN High Commissioner for Human Rights (OHCHR) attributed a number of deaths that occurred during protests between January and May 2019 to colectivos.

The Maduro regime has become increasingly dependent on economic, medical, military, and other assistance from foreign allies to maintain power, particularly from Russia, Cuba, Turkey, and Iran.

B4. Do various segments of the population (including ethnic, racial, religious, gender, LGBT+, and other relevant groups) have full political rights and electoral opportunities? 1 / 4 (−1)

The PSUV's increasing political dominance leaves little opportunity for ethnic, minority, and other groups to advocate for their interests.

Indigenous people in Venezuela are poorly represented in politics, and members of these groups struggle to bring government attention to issues of importance, including economic inequality and destructive incursions on ancestral lands. Indigenous people were further marginalized in 2020 through changes to the structure of the National Assembly: while the total number of legislators was significantly increased from 167 to 277, the number of seats reserved for Indigenous representatives remained the same. Separately, in July, the CNE revoked Indigenous groups' right to vote directly and secretly to choose their representatives to the National Assembly, passing the changes without consulting Indigenous communities. Under the new rules, the three seats reserved for Indigenous representatives would be chosen by previously selected delegates of the Indigenous groups in an open assembly, which in effect was likely to hand the seats to PSUV allies. After an outcry, the reform was rolled back in August.

Though several women hold senior positions in government, there remains a lack of policy discussion regarding issues that primarily affect women. Almost no LGBT+ people living openly hold senior political or government positions in Venezuela.

Score Change: The score declined from 2 to 1 due to the marginalization of Indigenous representatives in the legislature.

C. FUNCTIONING OF GOVERNMENT: 0 / 12

C1. Do the freely elected head of government and national legislative representatives determine the policies of the government? 0 / 4

Venezuela does not function as a representative democracy. The opposition-controlled legislature had no practical ability to carry out its constitutional mandate between 2015 and 2020 and since August 2017 was supplanted by the National Constituent Assembly, a body packed with regime loyalists who were elected under undemocratic conditions. After the opposition announced that it would boycott the 2020 National Assembly elections, effectively securing PSUV control of the chamber, Maduro announced the closure of the National Constituent Assembly.

C2. Are safeguards against official corruption strong and effective? 0 / 4

Corruption is rampant in Venezuela. The government's economic policies—particularly its currency and price controls—offer significant opportunities for black-market activity and collusion between public officials and organized crime networks. The United States, Canada, Panama, the EU, and others continue to sanction Venezuelan officials for corruption and other offenses that go uninvestigated in Venezuela. For example, in March 2020, then US Attorney General William Barr, accused Maduro and other high-ranking officials of drug trafficking.

C3. Does the government operate with openness and transparency? 0 / 4

There is virtually no transparency regarding government spending. The Maduro regime has moreover consistently failed to publish reliable crime and economic data, including monthly inflation statistics and annual gross domestic product.

In 2020, watchdogs and others raised serious doubts about the veracity of government data on the COVID-19 health crisis. According to opposition lawmakers, there had been 1,412 COVID-19-related deaths as of October 5th, more than two times the number reported by the government at the time. In a report released in August, Amnesty International denounced authorities for failing to disclose the number of health workers who had died of COVID-19; the Medical Union of Venezuela put the number of deaths at 295 at the end of the year. Amnesty International also expressed doubts about the veracity of the official number of COVID-19 cases, while Human Rights Watch and Johns Hopkins University called the official death count "absurd" and "not credible" in May.

CIVIL LIBERTIES: 13 / 60 (−1)

D. FREEDOM OF EXPRESSION AND BELIEF: 6 / 16

D1. Are there free and independent media? 1 / 4

Venezuela's independent journalists operate within a highly restrictive regulatory and legal environment, and risk arrest and physical violence in connection with their work. Most of the country's independent newspapers have shut down or moved to an exclusively digital format, where they are subject to frequent blocking.

In the first half of 2020, there were at least 12 arbitrary arrests of journalists in connection with their coverage of the COVID-19 pandemic, according to the Institute of Press and Society in Venezuela (IPYS). Journalists were also detained for other reasons during that period, mostly related to media coverage of a gasoline shortage. The nongovernmental organization (NGO) Public Space documented 112 freedom-of-speech violations in Venezuela through May, including intimidation and censorship, mostly against journalists and mostly committed by security forces or other state agents. In August, two journalists from the television channel Guacamaya TV were killed by members of the Special Action Forces (FAES) of the Bolivarian National Police. The public prosecutor's office is investigating the crime. In July, political scientist Nicmer Evans was arrested and accused of "hate speech" over comments on social media that were critical of Maduro's policies.

The Maduro regime maintains a state communications infrastructure used to propagate its political and ideological program. Maduro had made 151 televised appearances in the first ten months of 2020. In contrast, live-streamed speeches by Guaidó are frequently blocked.

D2. Are individuals free to practice and express their religious faith or nonbelief in public and private? 3 / 4

Constitutional guarantees of religious freedom are generally respected, though tensions between the government and the Roman Catholic Church remain high. Government relations with the small Jewish community have also been strained at times.

D3. Is there academic freedom, and is the educational system free from extensive political indoctrination? 1 / 4

Academic freedom has come under mounting pressure since chavismo arrived to power. Budget cuts and other funding problems have undermined universities' autonomy and prompted an exodus of academics from the country. In 2020, public universities in many cases received as little as 10 percent of their requested funding for various programs for the whole year.

In August 2019, the TSJ suspended the head of the Central University of Venezuela, the biggest and highest-ranked university in the country, changed voting rules for the election of school authorities, and ordered elections at nine public universities that are considered opposition strongholds. Under the directive, if elections were not held within six months of the decision, the court will choose the new authorities. However, after a series of student protests, the TSJ in February 2020 allowed more time to hold the elections. A March 2020 TSJ ruling contained related directives that university leaders characterized as confusing, and which rights advocates said could further damage universities' autonomy.

Classes have been conducted virtually since March 2020 due to the COVID-19 pandemic, and largely abandoned universities have been subsequently targeted with vandalism. NGO Aula Abierta (Open Classroom) counted 112 security incidents at universities during the year.

D4. Are individuals free to express their personal views on political or other sensitive topics without fear of surveillance or retribution? 1 / 4

Free private expression is severely constrained in Venezuela. In August 2020, IPYS detailed concerted government efforts to control information on social networks and suppress protected speech. According to the report, authorities employ cybertroops to disseminate purportedly false news and hack adversaries to gather information and use it against them, especially on Twitter and Facebook.

The government increased surveillance of the population in 2020 through social service and health-care systems. Health-related measures were linked to the Fatherland ID card, which is required to access social services. Between July and August, the government activated so-called Popular Prevention Brigades to identify people potentially infected with COVID-19 and to monitor their adherence to health advice. According to the government, the brigades have over 70,000 members, all of them community leaders with close ties to the PSUV. In July, Maduro alleged that the number of COVID-19 cases was increasing because of Venezuelans who returned to the country using illegal pathways. Maduro urged Venezuelans to denounce returnees, whom he labeled "bioterrorists."

Health workers were arrested for publishing information on social media about possible COVID-19 cases, and for protesting against the lack of proper equipment and working conditions. Meanwhile, Diosdado Cabello Rondón, president of the National Constituent Assembly, threatened health experts on public television for questioning the official number of COVID-19 cases.

E. ASSOCIATIONAL AND ORGANIZATIONAL RIGHTS: 2 / 12
E1. Is there freedom of assembly? 0 / 4

While guaranteed by the constitution, freedom of assembly is severely restricted in practice. While protests were nevertheless common despite government restrictions and the threat of deadly crackdowns by security forces, their numbers fell dramatically due to the state of emergency and lockdowns declared to prevent the spread of COVID-19. More than half of the roughly 4,400 protests recorded by the Venezuelan Observatory of Social Conflicts in the first half of the year were motivated by the lack of public services, especially electricity, water, and gasoline; others were explicitly related to politics, and some were related to a lack of protective or medical equipment. The group reported that 221 of those were repressed by security forces or paramilitary groups, that 129 people were arrested, and 2 were killed.

In recent years, there have been violent clashes between protesters and security forces. In 2017, there were more than 1,900 protest-related injuries and 136 deaths, with at least 102 people apparently killed by security forces or state-affiliated colectivos.

E2. Is there freedom for nongovernmental organizations, particularly those that are engaged in human rights- and governance-related work? 1 / 4

Activists and NGOs are routinely harassed, threatened, and subject to legal and administrative sanctions for their work. Dozens of civil society activists have been physically attacked in recent years and the government has attempted to delegitimize rights organizations by accusing them of conspiring with foreign governments.

E3. Is there freedom for trade unions and similar professional or labor organizations? 1 / 4

Workers are legally entitled to form unions, bargain collectively, and strike, with some restrictions on public-sector workers' ability to strike. Control of unions has shifted from traditional opposition-allied labor leaders to new workers' organizations that are often aligned with the government. The competition has contributed to a substantial increase in labor violence as well as confusion and delays during industry-wide collective bargaining.

In December 2018, Ruben González, head of the union for workers at the public company Ferrominera Orinoco, was arrested and sentenced to almost six years in prison by a military tribunal. In 2020, he was one of 110 political leaders pardoned by the government.

F. RULE OF LAW: 1 / 16
F1. Is there an independent judiciary? 0 / 4

Politicization of the judicial branch increased dramatically under Chávez and has progressed further under Maduro. Political control of the judiciary was reinforced through the appointment of new, regime-loyal judges in 2010 and again in 2015.

In recent years, the TSJ has issued numerous decisions that have bolstered Maduro's power. In 2020, the reelection of Juan Guaidó as president of the National Assembly was overruled, the leadership of major opposition political parties was changed, and the court choose the new members of the CNE without legally required input from the opposition-led National Assembly.

A 2020 UN report on rights in Venezuela noted that the lack of judicial independence contributes to authorities' inability to protect human rights.

F2. Does due process prevail in civil and criminal matters? 0 / 4

Opponents of the government and the PSUV are routinely detained and prosecuted without regard for due process, and victims of violence at the hands of the state have no realistic avenue for redress.

In September 2020, a UN report claimed that Maduro and his government committed at least 223 human rights violations since 2014, including torture and extrajudicial executions. The report identified three police and intelligence forces as primarily responsible: the Body of Penal, Criminalistic, and Scientific Investigations; the Bolivarian National Intelligence Service (SEBIN); and FAES. In 2019, the UN had asked Venezuela's government to dissolve FAES, but the body is still operating. In recent years, SEBIN has increasingly carried out policing functions and arrested opposition politicians and journalists without informing the Public Ministry or presenting official charges.

The military has also assumed roles previously reserved for civilian law enforcement institutions. According to Venezuelan human rights groups, hundreds of civilians have been tried in military court proceedings since 2017.

Many courts were closed in 2020 due to the COVID-19 pandemic, resulting in significant delays of trials and other proceedings.

F3. Is there protection from the illegitimate use of physical force and freedom from war and insurgencies? 0 / 4

Statistics for 2019, released in January 2020 by the Venezuelan Violence Observatory, placed the country's homicide rate at 60.3 per 100,000 people, a decline from 2018 but still among the highest in the world.

Prison conditions in Venezuela remain among the worst in the Americas. *Pranes*, or gang leaders who operate from prisons, freely coordinate criminal networks throughout Venezuela. In May 2020, 46 people were killed and more than 70 were wounded, most of them inmates, during unrest at a prison in the state of Portuguesa that broke out over new, pandemic-related restrictions on the food visitors were allowed to bring in.

F4. Do laws, policies, and practices guarantee equal treatment of various segments of the population? 1 / 4

The rights of Indigenous people, who make up 2.5 percent of the population, are upheld by the constitution but poorly protected by authorities. In practice, Indigenous groups face discrimination and unequal treatment, especially in Bolívar, where Indigenous people experience labor exploitation, extortion by paramilitary groups, sex trafficking of some women, and land grabs related to illegal mining, which also results in the destruction of forests and other natural features on Indigenous lands. The OHCHR documented seven instances of deadly violence against Indigenous people in the first five months of 2019.

Although discrimination based on sexual orientation is barred, LGBT+ Venezuelans face widespread intolerance and are occasionally subjected to violence.

G. PERSONAL AUTONOMY AND INDIVIDUAL RIGHTS: 4 / 16 (−1)

G1. Do individuals enjoy freedom of movement, including the ability to change their place of residence, employment, or education? 1 / 4 (−1)

The government declared a COVID-19-related state of emergency in March 2020, placing harsh restrictions on Venezuelans. Authorities and paramilitary groups arbitrarily detained, beaten, and tortured civilians who did not follow quarantine and other security instructions. Venezuelans returning home from neighboring countries by foot were subject to harsh restrictions on their mobility upon arrival. According to human rights organizations, they were forced to quarantine for 25 days in squalid public centers that lack health and other basic supplies, and were guarded by the military and colectivos.

Venezuelans continued to flee the country in massive numbers due to the country's ongoing social and economic crises. In August 2020, the IMF reported that Venezuelan emigration could reach 10 million people by the end of 2023.

Score Change: The score declined from 2 to 1 because security forces and government-allied militias used abusive methods to enforce COVID-19 movement restrictions, using disproportionate punishments including arbitrary detention, assault, and torture.

G2. Are individuals able to exercise the right to own property and establish private businesses without undue interference from state or nonstate actors? 1 / 4

Property rights have been damaged by years of price controls, nationalizations, overregulation, and corruption. Accusations of mismanagement, underinvestment, graft, and politicized hiring practices within state-owned enterprises are common.

G3. Do individuals enjoy personal social freedoms, including choice of marriage partner and size of family, protection from domestic violence, and control over appearance? 2 / 4

The politically driven economic collapse in Venezuela has reduced the availability of reproductive health care. Maternal and infant mortality has increased. Due to restrictive legislation on abortion, many women and girls resort to clandestine abortions that are frequently unsanitary and unsafe.

Women relatives of political prisoners are subjected to sexual and gender-based violence and humiliation during visits in detention centers, security operations, and house raids. Women who have been political prisoners have reported attacks by security forces including sexual violence, threats of rape, and forced nudity.

A 2007 law was designed to combat violence against women, but domestic violence and rape remain common and are rarely punished in practice. COVID-19 lockdowns increased the risk of gender-based violence. During the first quarter of 2020, 137 women were killed, 67 percent more than during the same period in 2019, according to NGO Femicide Monitor.

The LGBT+ community in Venezuela still lacks fundamental rights like legal marriage, child adoption, and the right to one's gender identity.

G4. Do individuals enjoy equality of opportunity and freedom from economic exploitation? 0 / 4

Venezuelan women and children are increasingly vulnerable to sex trafficking within Venezuela and in neighboring countries, as well as in Europe, with the problem exacerbated by worsening economic conditions and the COVID-19 crisis.

With job opportunities growing even scarcer during the COVID-19 pandemic, and hyperinflation outpacing wages, more Venezuelans have sought employment in the informal sector, where they are exposed to dangerous or exploitative working conditions. Among businesses that are legally registered, sanctions for labor law violations, when levied, generally target private-sector operations instead of those that are state-run.

Vietnam

Population: 96,200,000
Capital: Hanoi
Freedom Status: Not Free
Electoral Democracy: No

Overview: Vietnam is a one-party state, dominated for decades by the ruling Communist Party of Vietnam (CPV). Although some independent candidates are technically allowed to run in legislative elections, most are banned in practice. Freedom of expression, religious freedom, and civil society activism are tightly restricted. The authorities have increasingly cracked down on citizens' use of social media and the internet to voice dissent and share uncensored information.

KEY DEVELOPMENTS IN 2020

- Journalists, bloggers, and human rights activists continued to face arrests, criminal convictions, and physical assaults during the year.
- Enforcement of a cybersecurity law that took effect in 2019 began to seriously restrict online speech. Facebook, for instance, reportedly removed an increasing amount of content within Vietnam, and the government allegedly threatened to completely exclude the platform from the Vietnamese market if it did not more thoroughly censor local content.
- Vietnamese authorities adopted one of the world's most effective strategies against the COVID-19 pandemic, using mass testing, contact tracing, travel restrictions, and social-distancing measures to keep the total number of cases for the year below 1,500, with just 35 deaths reported by the end of December. However, the government also used the pandemic to help justify further restrictions on speech, implementing a new decree in April that imposed fines on internet users for sharing false and other harmful information online.

POLITICAL RIGHTS: 3 / 40

A. ELECTORAL PROCESS: 0 / 12

A1. Was the current head of government or other chief national authority elected through free and fair elections? 0 / 4

The president is elected by the National Assembly for a five-year term, and is responsible for appointing the prime minister, who is confirmed by the legislature. However, all selections for top executive posts are predetermined in practice by the CPV's Politburo and Central Committee.

In 2016, nominees for president and prime minister were chosen at the CPV's 12th Party Congress, which also featured the reelection of Nguyễn Phú Trọng as the party's general secretary. In April of that year, the National Assembly formally confirmed Trần Đại Quang as president and Nguyễn Xuân Phúc as prime minister.

President Trần Đại Quang died in September 2018, and the National Assembly confirmed Nguyễn Phú Trọng as his replacement in October; Trọng retained the post of party general secretary. The next party congress was scheduled for January 2021.

A2. Were the current national legislative representatives elected through free and fair elections? 0 / 4

Elections to the National Assembly are tightly controlled by the CPV, which took 473 of the body's 500-seat maximum in the 2016 balloting. Candidates who were technically independent but vetted by the CPV took the other 21 seats filled that year. More than 100 independent candidates, including many young civil society activists, were barred from running in the elections.

A3. Are the electoral laws and framework fair, and are they implemented impartially by the relevant election management bodies? 0 / 4

The electoral laws and framework ensure that the CPV, the only legally recognized party, dominates every election. The party controls all electoral bodies and vets all candidates, resulting in the disqualification of those who are genuinely independent.

B. POLITICAL PLURALISM AND PARTICIPATION: 1 / 16

B1. Do the people have the right to organize in different political parties or other competitive political groupings of their choice, and is the system free of undue obstacles to the rise and fall of these competing parties or groupings? 0 / 4

The CPV enjoys a monopoly on political power, and no other parties are allowed to operate legally. Members of illegal opposition parties are subject to arrest and imprisonment.

B2. Is there a realistic opportunity for the opposition to increase its support or gain power through elections? 0 / 4

The structure of the one-party system precludes any democratic transfer of power. The Vietnam Fatherland Front (VFF), responsible for vetting all candidates for the National Assembly, is ostensibly an alliance of organizations representing the people, but in practice it acts as an arm of the CPV.

B3. Are the people's political choices free from domination by forces that are external to the political sphere, or by political forces that employ extrapolitical means? 0 / 4

The overarching dominance of the CPV effectively excludes the public from any genuine and autonomous political participation.

B4. Do various segments of the population (including ethnic, racial, religious, gender, LGBT+, and other relevant groups) have full political rights and electoral opportunities? 1 / 4

Although members of ethnic minority groups are nominally represented within the CPV, they are rarely allowed to rise to senior positions, and the CPV leadership's dominance prevents effective advocacy on issues affecting minority populations. Vietnam has enacted policies and strategies aimed at boosting women's political participation, but in practice the interests of women are poorly represented in government.

C. FUNCTIONING OF GOVERNMENT: 2 / 12

C1. Do the freely elected head of government and national legislative representatives determine the policies of the government? 0 / 4

The CPV leadership, which is not freely elected or accountable to the public, determines government policy and the legislative agenda.

C2. Are safeguards against official corruption strong and effective? 1 / 4

CPV and government leaders have acknowledged growing public discontent with corruption, and there has been an increase in corruption-related arrests in recent years. The government reported in 2019 that it had disciplined over 53,000 officials and other party members for graft. Multiple senior officials, including two members of the Central Committee, have faced discipline including jail time.

Despite the crackdown, enforcement of anticorruption laws is generally selective and often linked to political rivalries. Many top officials who have been detained or jailed belonged to a different political faction than Trọng. The CPV does not tolerate journalistic investigations, independent courts, or other autonomous bodies that might serve as a check on corruption.

C3. Does the government operate with openness and transparency? 1 / 4

The CPV leadership operates with considerable opacity. The National Assembly passed an access to information law in 2016, but its provisions are relatively weak. Information can also be withheld if it is deemed to threaten state interests or the well-being of the nation. Independent journalists and civil society groups are not permitted to scrutinize or critique government activities.

CIVIL LIBERTIES: 16 / 60 (−1)

D. FREEDOM OF EXPRESSION AND BELIEF: 3 / 16 (−1)

D1. Are there free and independent media? 0 / 4 (−1)

Although the constitution recognizes freedom of the press, journalists and bloggers are constrained by numerous repressive laws and decrees. Those who dare to report or comment independently on controversial issues also risk intimidation and physical attack.

The criminal code prohibits speech that is critical of the government, while a 2006 decree prescribes fines for any publication that denies revolutionary achievements, spreads "harmful" information, or exhibits "reactionary ideology." Decree 72, issued in 2013, gave the state sweeping new powers to restrict speech on blogs and social media. The state controls all print and broadcast media.

A cybersecurity law that was adopted in 2018 and took effect in 2019 includes several provisions that could restrict access to uncensored news and information. It requires companies like Facebook and Google to store information about Vietnamese users in Vietnam and allows the government to block access to a broad range of content that could be defined as dangerous to national security. Under pressure from the government, Facebook agreed to increase its removals of allegedly illegal content in Vietnam during 2020, and officials reportedly threatened to block the platform if it did not restrict even more content. Radio Free Asia found that some of its Vietnamese Facebook posts were removed. Google's YouTube video-sharing platform also reportedly complied with government censorship demands during the year.

New arrests, beatings, criminal convictions, and cases of mistreatment in custody involving journalists and bloggers continued to be reported in 2020. Among other cases during the year, a Radio Free Asia blogger was sentenced to 10 years in prison in March, a prominent dissident writer was arrested in May and charged with subversion, and a blogger was reportedly beaten while confined to a psychiatric hospital in July. Also in July, the well-known writer and journalist Phạm Đoan Trang ended her association with her publisher due to what she claimed was intense police harassment. Trang was arrested in October on charges of "propaganda against the state," which carries a prison term of up to 20 years. In November, prosecutors indicted three leaders of an independent journalists' association on similar charges.

Score Change: The score declined from 1 to 0 due to the intensifying persecution of independent writers and journalists.

D2. Are individuals free to practice and express their religious faith or nonbelief in public and private? 1 / 4

Religious freedom remains restricted. All religious groups and most individual clergy members are required to join a party-controlled supervisory body and obtain permission for most activities. The 2016 Law on Belief and Religion reinforced registration requirements, allowed extensive state interference in religious groups' internal affairs, and gave authorities broad discretion to penalize unsanctioned religious activity. Unregistered and unrecognized religious groups face routine harassment, including violence, criminal charges, and property damage.

D3. Is there academic freedom, and is the educational system free from extensive political indoctrination? 1 / 4

Academic freedom is limited. University professors must refrain from criticizing government policies and adhere to party views when teaching or writing on political topics.

D4. Are individuals free to express their personal views on political or other sensitive topics without fear of surveillance or retribution? 1 / 4

Although citizens enjoy more freedom in private discussions than in the past, authorities continue to attack and imprison those who openly criticize the state, including on social media. The government engages in surveillance of private online activity.

In 2020, the authorities imposed fines on hundreds of people for allegedly sharing false information about COVID-19 online. The crackdown was carried out under existing laws as well as a new decree implemented in April that prescribed fines for the use of social media to disseminate content that reveals state secrets or is deemed false or misleading, slanderous, or harmful to moral or social values.

E. ASSOCIATIONAL AND ORGANIZATIONAL RIGHTS: 1 / 12
E1. Is there freedom of assembly? 1 / 4

Freedom of assembly is tightly restricted. Organizations must apply for official permission to assemble, and police routinely use excessive force to disperse unauthorized demonstrations. After nationwide anti-China protests in 2018, during which dozens of participants were assaulted and arrested, the courts convicted well over a hundred people of disrupting public order, and many were sentenced to prison terms.

E2. Is there freedom for nongovernmental organizations, particularly those that are engaged in human rights– and governance-related work? 0 / 4

A small but active community of nongovernmental organizations (NGOs) promotes environmental conservation, land rights, women's development, and public health. However, human rights organizations are generally banned, and those who engage in any advocacy that the authorities perceive as hostile risk imprisonment.

Criminal prosecutions and violence against activists persisted in 2020. In June it was reported that an Australian citizen who had been jailed in Vietnam for membership in the banned opposition Viet Tan movement had been held incommunicado for months. In July, a court imposed lengthy prison terms on eight activists who had planned protests calling for the protection of constitutional rights on National Day in 2018. Also in July, a court sentenced a prominent prodemocracy activist to eight years in prison for his antigovernment posts on Facebook.

E3. Is there freedom for trade unions and similar professional or labor organizations? 0 / 4

The Vietnam General Conference of Labor (VGCL), the only legal labor federation, is controlled by the CPV. The right to strike is limited by tight legal restrictions.

A 2019 revision of the labor code, adopted to comply with international trade agreements, would theoretically allow workers to form their own representative bodies after taking effect in 2021, but the government was expected to limit such groups' independence in practice.

F. RULE OF LAW: 4 / 16

F1. Is there an independent judiciary? 1 / 4

The judiciary is subservient to the CPV, which controls the courts at all levels. This control is especially evident in politically sensitive criminal prosecutions, with judges sometimes displaying greater impartiality in civil cases.

F2. Does due process prevail in civil and criminal matters? 1 / 4

Constitutional guarantees of due process are generally not upheld. Defendants have a legal right to counsel, but lawyers are scarce, and many are reluctant to take on cases involving human rights or other sensitive topics. Defense lawyers do not have the right to call witnesses, and often report insufficient time to meet with their clients. In national security cases, police can detain suspects for up to 20 months without access to counsel.

Amendments to the penal code that took effect in 2018 included a provision under which defense lawyers can be held criminally liable for failing to report certain kinds of crimes committed by their own clients.

F3. Is there protection from the illegitimate use of physical force and freedom from war and insurgencies? 1 / 4

There is little protection from the illegitimate use of force by state authorities, and security personnel are known to abuse suspects and prisoners, sometimes resulting in death or serious injury. In June 2020, family members of jailed activist Nguyễn Văn Đức Độ claimed in a petition that he had been beaten and fed human feces while incarcerated in Đồng Nai Province. Prison conditions are generally poor. The death penalty can be applied for crimes other than murder, including drug trafficking.

F4. Do laws, policies, and practices guarantee equal treatment of various segments of the population? 1 / 4

Members of ethnic minority groups face discrimination in Vietnamese society, and some local officials restrict their access to schooling and jobs. They generally have little input on development projects that affect their livelihoods and communities. Members of ethnic and religious minorities also sometimes face monitoring and harassment by authorities seeking to suppress dissent and suspected links to exile groups.

Men and women receive similar treatment in the legal system. Women generally have equal access to education, and economic opportunities for women have grown, though they continue to face discrimination in wages and promotions.

The law does not prohibit discrimination based on sexual orientation or gender identity, and societal discrimination remains a problem. Nevertheless, LGBT+ pride events are held annually across the country.

G. PERSONAL AUTONOMY AND INDIVIDUAL RIGHTS: 8 / 16

G1. Do individuals enjoy freedom of movement, including the ability to change their place of residence, employment, or education? 2 / 4

Although freedom of movement is protected by law, residency rules limit access to services for those who migrate within the country without permission, and authorities have restricted the movement of political dissidents and members of ethnic minorities on other grounds. Vietnamese citizens who are repatriated after attempting to seek asylum abroad can face harassment or imprisonment.

G2. Are individuals able to exercise the right to own property and establish private businesses without undue interference from state or nonstate actors? 1 / 4

All land is owned by the state, which grants land-use rights and leases to farmers, developers, and others. Land tenure is one of the most contentious issues in the country, and is the subject of regular protests. The seizure of land for economic development projects is often accompanied by violence, accusations of corruption, and prosecutions of those who voice objections. A dispute over the leasing of land to a state-owned company in a village outside Hanoi turned deadly in January 2020, when a police raid on protesting residents led to the killing of a village leader and three police officers; officials later indicted 25 people on murder and other charges in connection with the incident.

G3. Do individuals enjoy personal social freedoms, including choice of marriage partner and size of family, protection from domestic violence, and control over appearance? 3 / 4

The government generally does not place explicit restrictions on personal social freedoms. Men and women have equal rights pertaining to matters such as marriage and divorce under the law. In 2015, Vietnam repealed a legal ban on same-sex marriage, but the government still does not grant such unions legal recognition.

Domestic violence against women remains common, and the law calls for the state to initiate criminal as opposed to civil procedures only when the victim is seriously injured.

G4. Do individuals enjoy equality of opportunity and freedom from economic exploitation? 2 / 4

Human trafficking is a problem in Vietnam, although the US State Department reported in 2020 that the government has taken some steps to boost antitrafficking efforts. Internationally brokered marriages sometimes lead to domestic servitude and forced prostitution. Male and female Vietnamese migrant workers are vulnerable to recruitment for forced labor abroad in a variety of industries. Enforcement of legal safeguards against exploitative working conditions, child labor, and workplace hazards remains poor.

Yemen

Population: 29,800,000
Capital: Sanaa
Freedom Status: Not Free
Electoral Democracy: No

Overview: Yemen, home to a long-running series of smaller internal conflicts, has been devastated by a civil war involving regional powers since 2015. Saudi Arabia, the United Arab Emirates (UAE), and their allies intervened that year to support the government of President Abd Rabbu Mansur Hadi against Ansar Allah (Supporters of God), also known as the Houthis—an armed rebel movement that is rooted in the Zaidi Shiite community, which forms a large minority in northwestern Yemen. The civilian population has suffered from direct violence by both sides, as well as from hunger and disease caused by the interruption of trade and aid. Elections are long overdue, normal political activity has halted, and many state institutions have ceased to function.

KEY DEVELOPMENTS IN 2020

- In January, the Southern Transitional Council (STC)—a separatist group backed by the UAE—pulled out of a 2019 Saudi-brokered agreement that had ended an outbreak of fighting between the Hadi government and the STC in a number of southern cities. The STC declared self-rule in the city of Aden in April but reached a new cease-fire with the government in June and returned to the original agreement in July. In December, Hadi formed a new power-sharing government that included STC representatives and other anti-Houthi factions.
- Yemen's humanitarian crisis worsened during the year, with civilians facing hardships including cholera, growing malnutrition, and an ongoing fuel shortage in addition to the new COVID-19 pandemic. The first case of COVID-19 was confirmed in April, and reported infections surged over the summer. By year's end at least 611 deaths had been confirmed, though the country's capacity to track the spread of the coronavirus was extremely limited, and both the Hadi government and the Houthi rebels allegedly withheld data related to the pandemic.

POLITICAL RIGHTS: 1 / 40

A. ELECTORAL PROCESS: 0 / 12

A1. Was the current head of government or other chief national authority elected through free and fair elections? 0 / 4

Under the existing constitution, the president is elected for seven-year terms. In 2011, after sustained pressure from the United States, the United Nations, and the Gulf Cooperation Council, longtime president Ali Abdullah Saleh signed a Saudi-brokered agreement that transferred his powers to then vice president Hadi in exchange for immunity from prosecution for his role in a violent crackdown on antigovernment protests. In 2012, Yemeni voters confirmed Hadi, who ran unopposed, as interim president with a two-year term. In 2014, the multiparty National Dialogue Conference (NDC), a months-long initiative in which more than 500 delegates aimed to reach agreement on Yemen's political future, concluded with a plan to transform the country into a federated state of six regions. The NDC also extended Hadi's term by one year so that the proposed reforms could be finalized in a new constitution.

However, the constitutional drafting process and election schedule were thrown into disarray by the Houthis, who took over large swaths of the country, eventually occupying Sanaa in September 2014. The Houthis subsequently refused to evacuate the capital as part of a tentative power-sharing agreement, leading Hadi and his cabinet to flee into exile in early 2015. Meanwhile, the Houthis assumed control of state institutions in the areas they held. Hadi retained international recognition as president but had no clear mandate and little control over the country.

In keeping with the Saudi-brokered Riyadh Agreement of 2019, a power-sharing government was formed by anti-Houthi factions in December 2020. Hadi loyalists retained control of the most powerful ministries, but the government included representatives from the STC, the Islamist party Al-Islah, and other political blocs. Maeen Abdelmalek Saeed, Hadi's prime minister since 2018, kept his post.

A2. Were the current national legislative representatives elected through free and fair elections? 0 / 4

According to the constitution, the president selects the 111 members of the largely advisory upper house of Parliament, the Majlis al-Shura (Consultative Council). The 301 members of the lower house, the House of Representatives, are elected to serve six-year terms. The original six-year mandate of the last Parliament expired in 2009, and elections were put off again in 2011 amid the popular uprising against Saleh. In January 2014, the NDC declared that parliamentary elections would occur within nine months of a referendum on the new constitution then being drawn up. The constitutional drafting committee completed its work in January 2015, but due to the outbreak of the civil war and the Saudi-led intervention in March of that year, no vote has yet taken place. The incumbent Parliament was disbanded after the Houthis seized control of the capital.

A3. Are the electoral laws and framework fair, and are they implemented impartially by the relevant election management bodies? 0 / 4

Presidential and legislative elections are now many years overdue, and no side in the civil war has been able to assert enough territorial control to implement any electoral framework.

B. POLITICAL PLURALISM AND PARTICIPATION: 1 / 16

B1. Do the people have the right to organize in different political parties or other competitive political groupings of their choice, and is the system free of undue obstacles to the rise and fall of these competing parties or groupings? 1 / 4

Political parties continue to exist in Yemen, but they face severe repression by different authorities and armed groups across the country.

The Houthis have harshly suppressed political dissent in areas under their control since 2015. Yemeni forces associated with the UAE have used arbitrary arrests, detentions, and enforced disappearances to persecute certain political groups, including members of Al-Islah, an offshoot of the Muslim Brotherhood in Yemen.

In 2019, after clashes broke out in the southern city of Aden between the Saudi-backed Hadi government and the STC, an ally of convenience against the Houthis that enjoys UAE support, the STC detained dozens of progovernment politicians, clerics, and activists. The

Saudi-brokered Riyadh Agreement, reached in late 2019, temporarily ended the infighting, but in January 2020 the STC pulled out of the deal, and in April it declared self-rule in Aden, leading to a new round of clashes in the southern governorates. A cease-fire was reached in June, and the STC returned to the Riyadh Agreement process in July.

The power-sharing government formed by anti-Houthi factions in December included Hadi's General People's Congress (GPC), the STC, Al-Islah, the Socialist Party, and a number of smaller parties and independents. It remained unclear whether the arrangement would lead to a meaningful decrease in political persecution for the participating groups in areas outside Houthi control.

B2. Is there a realistic opportunity for the opposition to increase its support or gain power through elections? 0 / 4

Parliamentary elections have not been held in Yemen since 2003 and were last due in 2009. The most recent presidential election, in 2012, featured only one candidate. No date had been set for future elections as of 2020, and peaceful political opposition has been suppressed in the context of the civil war.

B3. Are the people's political choices free from domination by forces that are external to the political sphere, or by political forces that employ extrapolitical means? 0 / 4

Ordinary political activity is impeded by the presence of multiple armed groups throughout Yemen, including Houthi-led rebel forces, extremist groups, southern separatists, foreign troops from the Saudi-led coalition, Hadi government troops, and local or partisan militias.

B4. Do various segments of the population (including ethnic, racial, religious, gender, LGBT+, and other relevant groups) have full political rights and electoral opportunities? 0 / 4

All segments of the population lack political rights under current conditions in Yemen. Thirty percent of the NDC's delegates were women, and its final agreement called for similar representation in all branches of government under a new constitution, but the draft constitution has been on hold since the outbreak of war. Only one woman won a seat in the last parliamentary elections, and no women were appointed to the December 2020 power-sharing government. A caste-like minority group with East African origins, known as the Akhdam or Muhamasheen, accounts for as much as 10 percent of the population but has long been marginalized in politics and in society. The group had one representative at the NDC.

C. FUNCTIONING OF GOVERNMENT: 0 / 12

C1. Do the freely elected head of government and national legislative representatives determine the policies of the government? 0 / 4

Yemen has no functioning central government with full control over its territory, and any state institutions that continue to operate are controlled by unelected officials and armed groups. The Hadi government is largely dependent on its foreign patrons, particularly Saudi Arabia and the UAE, which also have parallel relationships with other anti-Houthi groups. The Houthis receive at least some support from Iran.

C2. Are safeguards against official corruption strong and effective? 0 / 4

Government probity was minimal even before the outbreak of war in 2015, as a network of corruption and patronage established under Saleh remained entrenched in public institutions, and formal anticorruption mechanisms were largely ineffective. The disruption to legal commerce caused by the civil war has increased the role of smuggling and created further opportunities for graft. In June 2020, STC forces seized a convoy that was reportedly carrying 64 billion riyals ($255 million) in banknotes to the central bank in Aden. Food aid is often stolen and sold illegally by officials on all sides of the conflict, including Houthis and armed forces linked to the Saudi military coalition, exacerbating a food-security crisis that has left millions at risk of malnutrition. The obstruction of aid also increased the difficulty of international efforts to contain and treat COVID-19 in the country.

C3. Does the government operate with openness and transparency? 0 / 4

Government transparency, already limited prior to 2015, has deteriorated along with state institutions during the war. The only truly national institution that had initially continued to function during the conflict, the central bank, has been split between a government-backed version in Aden and a rebel-backed version in Sanaa since 2016. This has caused politicized disruptions to public-sector salaries, aid, and commerce, and further reduced the transparency of state finances and monetary policy. Both the Houthis and the Hadi government allegedly undercounted COVID-19 cases and withheld related data during 2020.

CIVIL LIBERTIES: 10 / 60
D. FREEDOM OF EXPRESSION AND BELIEF: 3 / 16
D1. Are there free and independent media? 0 / 4

The state has historically controlled most terrestrial television and radio, though there have been several privately owned radio stations. Since the outbreak of the war, the belligerents have either taken over or enforced self-censorship at any surviving media outlets in the country. Houthi-backed authorities reportedly block certain news websites, online messaging and social media platforms, and satellite broadcasts. The Houthis, the Saudi-led coalition, and Hadi government forces have also harassed and detained reporters.

In April 2020, the Houthi-controlled Specialized Criminal Court in Sanaa issued death sentences against four journalists accused of espionage; they remained in custody at year's end. Six journalists who had been arrested with the others in 2015 were convicted on lesser charges.

Journalists endure violent attacks and enforced disappearances committed by all sides in the conflict. In June 2020, Nabeel Hasan al-Quaety, a photojournalist, was assassinated in front of his house in Aden by unidentified gunmen. In December, television reporter Adeeb al-Janani was killed in an attack on Aden's airport while attempting to cover the arrival of the newly appointed power-sharing government.

D2. Are individuals free to practice and express their religious faith or nonbelief in public and private? 1 / 4

Islam is the official religion, and the constitution declares Sharia (Islamic law) to be the source of all legislation. Yemen has few non-Muslim religious minorities; their rights have traditionally been respected in practice, though conversion from Islam and proselytizing to Muslims is prohibited. Members of the Baha'i community in the north have reported increased persecution under Houthi rule. In March 2020, Houthi officials ordered the release of six Baha'i men, one of whom had been arrested in 2013 and later sentenced to death; the five others had been among a group of 24 Baha'is arrested in 2017. All six were released and expelled from the country in July, but legal proceedings against the larger group arrested in 2017 apparently continued at year's end.

Since the outbreak of the war in 2015, assassinations and other violent attacks on religious clerics have increased, and combatants on all sides have destroyed many religious buildings across the country.

D3. Is there academic freedom, and is the educational system free from extensive political indoctrination? 1 / 4

Strong politicization of campus life, including tensions between supporters of the ruling GPC and Al-Islah, which had long been in opposition, historically infringed on academic freedom at universities. Since 2015, Houthi forces have repeatedly detained scholars as part of their crackdown on dissent, and Houthi officials have been accused of skewing the curriculum in public schools and promoting their political ideology.

The war has caused damage to educational facilities across the country, suspension of classes and other activities at schools and universities, and deaths of children caught in either errant or deliberate military attacks on schools. Millions of students no longer attend school due to the war, and thousands have been recruited by armed groups.

D4. Are individuals free to express their personal views on political or other sensitive topics without fear of surveillance or retribution? 1 / 4

Freedom of personal expression and private discussion is severely limited as a result of intimidation by armed groups and unchecked surveillance by the Houthi authorities, who have detained critics of their rule and used courts under their control to issue harsh penalties, including death sentences, for some perceived opponents.

E. ASSOCIATIONAL AND ORGANIZATIONAL RIGHTS: 3 / 12

E1. Is there freedom of assembly? 1 / 4

Yemenis have historically enjoyed a degree of freedom of assembly, with periodic restrictions and at times deadly interventions by the government. Demonstrations against both the Hadi government and Houthi authorities occurred during 2020, resulting in arrests and alleged torture of detainees in some cases. In September, UAE-backed security forces fired live ammunition to disperse demonstrators in the governorate of Hadhramaut who were protesting a breakdown in public services. Also that month, STC forces that had taken over the Yemeni island of Socotra in June used live fire to suppress protests against their presence and alleged plans for an Emirati military base.

E2. Is there freedom for nongovernmental organizations, particularly those that are engaged in human rights- and governance-related work? 1 / 4

A number of nongovernmental organizations (NGOs) work in the country, but their ability to function is restricted by interference from armed groups, and the spread and politicization of COVID-19 has made their work even more dangerous. Houthi forces have closed or raided NGO offices and detained workers, and both sides in the civil war have blocked or seized humanitarian aid. Human rights defenders risk arrest and detention by both Houthi and anti-Houthi forces.

E3. Is there freedom for trade unions and similar professional or labor organizations? 1 / 4

The law acknowledges the right of workers to form and join trade unions, but in practice these organizations have had little freedom to operate. Virtually all unions belong to a single labor federation, and the government is empowered to veto collective bargaining agreements. Normal union activity has been disrupted by the civil war and the related breakdown of the economy.

F. RULE OF LAW: 2 / 16

F1. Is there an independent judiciary? 1 / 4

The judiciary, though nominally independent, is susceptible to interference from various political factions and armed groups. Authorities have a poor record of enforcing judicial rulings, particularly those issued against prominent tribal or political leaders. Lacking an effective court system, citizens often resort to tribal forms of justice and customary law—practices that have increased as state institutions continue to deteriorate. Criminal courts in Houthi-controlled areas remain active, but they are used as a political instrument by the Houthi leadership, according to UN experts. The judicial system is mostly inoperative in other parts of the country.

F2. Does due process prevail in civil and criminal matters? 0 / 4

Arbitrary detention is common, with hundreds of cases documented in recent years. Many amount to enforced disappearances, with no available information about the victims' status or location. Detainees are often held at unofficial detention sites. As with other state institutions, security and intelligence agencies like the Political Security Organization have been split into parallel structures aligned with the different sides in the civil war. In areas that lie within the UAE's sphere of influence in southern Yemen, Emirati special forces have operated a network of secret prisons and detention centers where torture is said to be rife.

F3. Is there protection from the illegitimate use of physical force and freedom from war and insurgencies? 0 / 4

The civil war has included periods of acute violence across the country. Saudi-led coalition air strikes have failed to distinguish between military and civilian targets, and artillery fire from Houthi forces has been similarly indiscriminate. A number of other armed factions, including foreign military units and extremist groups like Al-Qaeda in the Arabian Peninsula (AQAP), operate in the country with impunity for any abuses. According to the Armed Conflict Location & Event Data Project, some 130,000 people have been killed in the conflict since the beginning of 2015, including more than 19,000 in 2020. Among other flashpoints of fighting during the year, a number of attacks took place in Aden, including an assault at the airport in December that killed at least 25 people and wounded 110 as ministers from the newly formed power-sharing government arrived. The government blamed the Houthis, who denied responsibility.

In addition to reports of torture and other abuse in prisons and detention centers, detainees faced a heightened risk of disease due to the COVID-19 pandemic in 2020. Both the government and the Houthis released hundreds of prisoners to ease crowding, though a number of journalists and political opponents remained behind bars. In October the warring parties agreed to exchange 1,081 prisoners, including 15 Saudis, in what amounted to the largest such exchange since late 2018.

F4. Do laws, policies, and practices guarantee equal treatment of various segments of the population? 1 / 4

Despite the growing sectarian rift between the Sunni Muslim majority and the large Zaidi Shiite minority, Yemen is relatively homogeneous in terms of language and ethnicity. However, the Muhamasheen face severe social discrimination and poverty. Women also continue to face discrimination in many aspects of life, and their testimony in court is equivalent to half that of a man. Same-sex sexual activity is illegal, with possible penalties including lashes, imprisonment, and death. Due to the severe threats they face, few LGBT+ Yemenis reveal their identity.

Migrants and refugees fleeing war and poverty in the Horn of Africa continue to arrive in Yemen. Roughly 283,000 refugees and asylum seekers remained in Yemen as of September 2020, according to UN data. Many of those entering were seeking work in the Gulf states but faced harsh conditions, violence, and barriers to further travel once in Yemen. The combination of war and the pandemic in 2020 worsened conditions for migrants. In April, Houthi forces expelled thousands of Ethiopian migrants from northern Yemen, blaming them for spreading COVID-19; dozens were killed, and the others were forced to the Saudi border.

G. PERSONAL AUTONOMY AND INDIVIDUAL RIGHTS: 2 / 16

G1. Do individuals enjoy freedom of movement, including the ability to change their place of residence, employment, or education? 0 / 4

There were 3.7 million internally displaced people (IDPs) in Yemen as of June 2020, according to figures released by the Office of the UN High Commissioner for Refugees (UNHCR) in December. Movement within the country is impaired by combat, landmines, damage to infrastructure, and checkpoints at which a variety of armed groups engage in harassment and extortion. IDPs in 2020 were disproportionately affected by loss of livelihood due to the COVID-19 pandemic, since most performed unskilled jobs in the informal economy, and many were blamed for spreading the virus.

Even in peacetime, a woman must obtain permission from her husband or father to receive a passport and travel abroad.

G2. Are individuals able to exercise the right to own property and establish private businesses without undue interference from state or nonstate actors? 1 / 4

Property rights and business activity have been severely disrupted by the civil war and unchecked corruption, as well as the retreat of state authorities from large areas of Yemen and the division of the country into spheres of influence controlled by different armed groups. Women do not have equal rights in inheritance matters.

G3. Do individuals enjoy personal social freedoms, including choice of marriage partner and size of family, protection from domestic violence, and control over appearance? 1 / 4

Women face disadvantages in divorce and custody proceedings and require a male guardian's permission to marry. Child marriage is a widespread problem. There are some restrictions on marriage to foreigners; a woman can confer citizenship on a child from a foreign-born spouse if the child is born in Yemen. The penal code allows lenient sentences for those convicted of "honor crimes"—assaults or killings of women by family members for alleged immoral behavior. Although female genital mutilation is banned in state medical facilities, it is still prevalent in some areas. Extremist groups have attempted to impose crude versions of Sharia in territory under their control, harshly punishing alleged violations related to sexual activity, personal appearance, and other matters.

G4. Do individuals enjoy equality of opportunity and freedom from economic exploitation? 0 / 4

The war has increased the risk of human trafficking, and after 2015 the government was no longer able to pursue antitrafficking efforts it had previously begun. Migrants, refugees, and the internally displaced are especially vulnerable to exploitation. Children have reportedly been recruited as fighters by all sides in the war. Border controls and naval blockades imposed by the Saudi-led coalition have contributed to shortages of food, medicine, fuel, and other essential imports, leaving the public more exposed to famine and disease as well as coercion and deprivation by armed groups and illegal traders. The World Food Programme reported in December 2020 that 16.2 million people were food insecure in Yemen and 24.3 million were in need of humanitarian assistance. A cholera outbreak continued in 2020. As of the end of the year, the World Health Organization had reported 2,101 confirmed cases of COVID-19 and 611 deaths, though limited testing and other factors meant that both cases and deaths were likely undercounted.

Zambia

Population: 18,400,000
Capital: Lusaka
Freedom Status: Partly Free
Electoral Democracy: No

Overview: Zambia's political system features regular multiparty elections, and some civil liberties are respected. However, opposition parties face onerous legal and practical obstacles to fair competition, and the government regularly invokes restrictive laws to curb freedom of expression and ban peaceful demonstrations and meetings. Political violence remains a problem.

KEY DEVELOPMENTS IN 2020

- In April, the country's media regulator forced the closure of a popular private television station that had a history of tensions with the government. The move came after the station's owner said it would not air government advertisements related to the COVID-19 pandemic for free, citing unpaid debts for previous state advertisements.
- An audit report released in November found that some 1.3 billion kwacha ($70 million) in public funds pertaining to COVID-19 had been mismanaged between February and July, including through dubious procurement contracts. Health Minister Chitalu Chilufya had been acquitted in August of unrelated corruption charges.
- Chishimba Kambwili, leader of the opposition National Democratic Congress (NDC) party, was sentenced in October to a year in prison on forgery charges and released on bail pending an appeal. Opposition members criticized the case as a politically motivated attempt to eliminate Kambwili from the 2021 presidential race.
- Also in October, the parliament rejected constitutional amendments introduced by the ruling Patriotic Front (PF) that would have increased the power of the presidency and allowed major changes to the electoral system.

POLITICAL RIGHTS: 20 / 40 (−2)

A. ELECTORAL PROCESS: 6 / 12

A1. Was the current head of government or other chief national authority elected through free and fair elections? 2 / 4

The president is directly elected to serve up to two five-year terms. In 2016, Edgar Lungu of the PF was narrowly reelected with 50.35 percent of the vote, defeating Hakainde Hichilema of the United Party for National Development (UPND), who took 47.67 percent. The 2016 polls were marred by election-related violence between PF and UPND supporters, restrictions on opposition-aligned media, misuse of public resources by the ruling PF, and invocation of the Public Order Act to restrict opposition rallies. While expressing serious concern over these problems, international election monitors deemed the results credible.

A2. Were the current national legislative representatives elected through free and fair elections? 2 / 4

The unicameral National Assembly comprises 156 elected members, up to 8 members appointed by the president, and 3 seats allocated for the vice president, the speaker, and a deputy speaker. The 2016 legislative polls were held concurrently with the presidential election and featured the same problems, though international monitors found the outcome generally credible. The PF won 80 seats, followed by the UPND with 58; independents and smaller parties took the remainder.

During the 2016 campaign period, 64 of Lungu's ministers failed to vacate their government posts while running for parliament seats, giving them improper access to government resources. In December 2020, the Constitutional Court reaffirmed a four-year-old order calling on them to return the public funds they received during the illegal overstay.

The PF won two September 2020 by-elections to fill seats that were left vacant by the deaths of the incumbents, retaining one seat and gaining another that was held by an independent.

A3. Are the electoral laws and framework fair, and are they implemented impartially by the relevant election management bodies? 2 / 4

The Electoral Commission of Zambia (ECZ) is responsible for managing the election process but lacks capacity. The US-based Carter Center, which was among groups that monitored the 2016 polls, criticized the ECZ for "ineffective" management of vote tabulation and verification.

In August 2020, multiple lawsuits challenged the ECZ's decision to discard the existing voter rolls and embark on a new, 30-day registration drive ahead of the 2021 elections. Litigants from the opposition and civil society argued that the move amounted to a breach of the constitution and electoral laws. The matter had not been resolved at year's end, but in December the ECZ announced that it had registered over seven million of the targeted 8.4 million eligible voters.

In October, a PF-sponsored package of constitutional amendments failed to reach the necessary two-thirds majority in the parliament, effectively ending the initiative. The controversial amendments would have given the president greater control over the judiciary, the electoral system, and monetary policy.

B. POLITICAL PLURALISM AND PARTICIPATION: 10 / 16

B1. Do the people have the right to organize in different political parties or other competitive political groupings of their choice, and is the system free of undue obstacles to the rise and fall of these competing parties or groupings? 2 / 4

Political parties are registered under the Societies Act and do not regularly face onerous registration requirements; independent candidates may also run for office. However, the Registrar of Societies deregistered the opposition NDC in 2019 on the grounds that its party constitution was flawed. A court restored the party's registration in August 2020.

Opposition parties continued to face harassment, intimidation, arrests, and other significant obstacles to their activities during 2020. In October, NDC leader Chishimba Kambwili was sentenced to a year in prison on forgery charges that his supporters said were politically motivated. He was granted bail pending an appeal of the conviction, which threatened to affect his 2021 presidential bid. In late December, police summoned UPND leader Hakainde Hichilema for questioning in a fraud investigation. After hundreds of UPND supporters gathered nearby to protest police harassment of Hichilema, officers attacked the crowd, and two people—a UPND supporter and a state prosecutor—were shot dead in the confusion that followed. Facing a public outcry, Lungu dismissed two senior police officials. Meanwhile, prosecutors organized a work stoppage to demand justice for the killing of their colleague.

B2. Is there a realistic opportunity for the opposition to increase its support or gain power through elections? 2 / 4

Zambia has experienced two democratic transfers of power between rival groups. The current ruling party, the PF, took power in 2011. Opposition parties have regularly won seats in the legislature, and the UPND nearly doubled its representation in the 2016 elections, but its ability to compete was impeded by intense pressure on the private media, use of the Public Order Act to restrict opposition events, and political violence.

Laws against election-related violence are poorly enforced, and violent incidents involving the PF and opposition groups remain common, especially in the run-up to parliamentary and local elections.

B3. Are the people's political choices free from domination by forces that are external to the political sphere, or by political forces that employ extrapolitical means? 3 / 4

The people's political choices are for the most part free from domination by groups that are not democratically accountable, though the ruling party has at times been accused of undemocratic tactics including vote buying and political pressure on public employees to ensure election victories.

B4. Do various segments of the population (including ethnic, racial, religious, gender, LGBT+, and other relevant groups) have full political rights and electoral opportunities? 3 / 4

Suffrage in Zambia is universal for adult citizens. Women have equal political rights according to the constitution, but only 30 women secured parliament seats in 2016, and few hold key positions in government. A requirement that elected officials be educated at least through high school effectively prevents many rural women from declaring political candidacies, given their low educational completion rates.

Presidents since independence have failed to honor the 1964 Barotseland Agreement, which promised the Western Province, which is home to the Lozi ethnic group, limited local self-governance. Several people accused of leading a separatist movement there remained in prison for treason at the end of 2020. In August, one leading Barotse separatist died in prison of unknown causes.

Criminalization of sexual activity between members of the same sex poses a major barrier to the ability of LGBT+ people to advocate for their interests through the political system.

C. FUNCTIONING OF GOVERNMENT: 4 / 12 (−2)

C1. Do the freely elected head of government and national legislative representatives determine the policies of the government? 2 / 4

Flawed elections undermine the democratic legitimacy of both the president and the National Assembly, and the executive exhibits excessive dominance over the legislature. A third of the PF's lawmakers hold positions in the cabinet, and the ruling party is able to push legislation through the National Assembly with little effective resistance from the opposition.

C2. Are safeguards against official corruption strong and effective? 1 / 4 (−1)

Corruption in government is widespread, and impunity is common. Prosecutions and court decisions on corruption charges, when they do occur, are often thought to reflect political motivations. Limited funding and enforcement restrict the efficacy of institutional safeguards against corruption, and PF leaders and the government sometimes undermine the work of anticorruption bodies. In 2018, the United Kingdom, Ireland, Finland, and Sweden withdrew aid to Zambia amid allegations that donor funds had been embezzled by government ministries.

The Financial Intelligence Centre (FIC), a government anticorruption watchdog, released its 2019 report in September 2020, observing that government officials used their positions to award noncompetitive contracts in exchange for kickbacks, or to sell favors to businesspeople, particularly foreign actors. While a number of the president's aides and associates faced corruption charges during 2020, their cases ended without convictions. In August, for example, Health Minister Chitalu Chilufya was acquitted of charges that he had amassed illicit wealth from public office between 2016 and 2018.

In November 2020, the Auditor General's Office reported that some 1.3 billion kwacha ($70 million) in public funds pertaining to COVID-19 had been mismanaged between February and July, including through dubious procurement contracts. More than two dozen officials were reportedly cited for possible disciplinary action.

Score Change: The score declined from 2 to 1 due to the authorities' failure to successfully prosecute senior officials despite evidence of corruption in recent years.

C3. Does the government operate with openness and transparency? 1 / 4 (−1)

Zambia continues to struggle with government transparency and accountability. There is no law guaranteeing public access to information, and while the Anti-Corruption Act requires some public officeholders to make financial declarations, it is only loosely enforced.

In addition to the irregular transfers and contracts involving COVID-19 funds that were identified by the Auditor General's Office during 2020, some donated equipment also reportedly went missing. For example, of the one million masks and 200,000 test kits provided to Zambia by China's Jack Ma Foundation in March, only about 20,000 masks and 200 test kits were recorded as received by the government's medical supplies entity, according to the audit report.

President Lungu dismissed the central bank governor, a former World Bank official, in the middle of his contract without explanation in August 2020, adding to concerns about the transparency of Zambia's fiscal and economic management. Lungu named a close ally, Christopher Mvunga, to fill the post, and the appointment was confirmed by the parliament in October even as some lawmakers questioned Mvunga's qualifications.

Score Change: The score declined from 2 to 1 due to the president's abrupt replacement of the central bank governor with a close political ally and reports of irregularities surrounding public funds, contracts, and supplies related to the COVID-19 pandemic.

CIVIL LIBERTIES: 32 / 60

D. FREEDOM OF EXPRESSION AND BELIEF: 9 / 16

D1. Are there free and independent media? 1 / 4

Freedom of the press is constitutionally guaranteed but restricted in practice. Self-censorship remains common. Public media provide government points of view and neglect coverage of the opposition, though some private outlets carry sharp criticism of the government. Outlets that are perceived as aligned with the opposition are subject to arbitrary closure by authorities, while critical journalists risk damage to equipment, frivolous lawsuits, arrest, and harassment by the government and political party supporters.

In April 2020, the Independent Broadcasting Authority (IBA) permanently shut down the privately owned outlet Prime TV following a protracted dispute with the government. The station had refused to air the government's COVID-19 awareness advertising free of charge, citing outstanding payments for previous government ads. Prior to its license revocation, Prime TV was officially banned from receiving government advertising, its journalists were excluded from official events, and its signal was removed from a partly state-owned carrier. In 2019, the IBA had temporarily suspended the station's license after the PF accused it of favoring the opposition.

Also during 2020, police and PF supporters repeatedly interfered with local radio stations to prevent opposition leaders from appearing on call-in or prerecorded programs. In July, PF supporters threatened to burn down Mafken Radio in Mufulira, and similar incidents were reported at other radio stations in Muchinga Province earlier in the year. In August, PASME community radio station in Petauke, Eastern Province, accused the district commissioner of illegally disrupting the broadcast of a prerecorded interview with the leader of the UPND.

D2. Are individuals free to practice and express their religious faith or nonbelief in public and private? 3 / 4

Constitutional protections for religious freedom are generally respected. However, the constitution declares Zambia to be a Christian nation, and the government has been criticized for increasingly engaging in activities that blur the separation of church and state, including backing an annual National Day of Prayer, building an interdenominational church, and attempting to include "Christian morality" in the constitution through the proposed amendments that failed in the parliament in October 2020. Religious groups must belong to approved umbrella bodies and are subject to regulations imposed by the Ministry of National Guidance and Religious Affairs.

D3. Is there academic freedom, and is the educational system free from extensive political indoctrination? 3 / 4

The government generally does not restrict academic freedom. However, authorities do place pressure on student unions in response to protests, and student demonstrators risk arrest and violent dispersal by the police.

D4. Are individuals free to express their personal views on political or other sensitive topics without fear of surveillance or retribution? 2 / 4

There is some freedom of private discussion and personal expression in Zambia, though the government appears to monitor citizens' speech on live radio call-in shows and social media, at times resulting in legal penalties.

In March 2020, police announced several cases in which social media users faced questioning or arrest for online speech. A 15-year-old boy from Kapiri Mposhi was arrested for insulting the president and making other defamatory remarks on Facebook. Four other Facebook users were arrested for similar offenses, and police summoned four WhatsApp group administrators for conversations they moderated on that platform.

E. ASSOCIATIONAL AND ORGANIZATIONAL RIGHTS: 7 / 12
E1. Is there freedom of assembly? 2 / 4

Freedom of assembly is guaranteed under the constitution but is not consistently respected by the government. Peaceful protests against the government and political meetings organized by the opposition are frequently restricted under the Public Order Act. Police must receive advance notice before all public meetings and often assert that such events do not have permission to proceed. Police repeatedly arrested activists and opposition party supporters on charges of unlawful assembly in 2020. In July, for example, a group of UPND members were arrested while conducting intraparty elections on a farm.

E2. Is there freedom for nongovernmental organizations, particularly those that are engaged in human rights- and governance-related work? 2 / 4

Nongovernmental organizations (NGOs) operate in a restrictive environment and are required to register every five years under the 2009 NGO Act. In October 2020, the government approved draft legislation that would amend the 2009 law to increase monitoring of NGO funds for possible illegal activities such as money laundering and the financing of terrorism. The measure was under consideration in the parliament at year's end.

E3. Is there freedom for trade unions and similar professional or labor organizations? 3 / 4

The law generally provides for the right to join unions, strike, and bargain collectively, though workers in essential services do not have the right to strike, and the category is defined to include the mining industry. Historically, Zambia's trade unions were among Africa's strongest, but their leading bodies, including the Zambia Congress of Trade Unions (ZCTU), have faced interference and marginalization under PF rule.

F. RULE OF LAW: 8 / 16

F1. Is there an independent judiciary? 2 / 4

Judicial independence is guaranteed by law, but in practice the judiciary is subject to political pressure. In November 2018, for example, Lungu warned that chaos would erupt if the Constitutional Court attempted to block his bid to run for a third term in 2021. In December of that year, the court, composed entirely of Lungu appointees, issued a unanimous ruling that appeared to support Lungu's eligibility for another term, though legal experts and political figures continued to debate the issue as of 2020. Lungu had first taken office in 2014, after the death of then president Michael Sata, and won election to a full five-year term in 2016.

F2. Does due process prevail in civil and criminal matters? 2 / 4

Pretrial detainees are sometimes held for years under harsh conditions, and many of the accused lack access to legal aid, owing to case backlogs and limited resources. Bail is frequently denied to detainees. In rural areas, customary courts of variable quality and consistency—whose decisions often conflict with the constitution and national law—decide many civil matters.

F3. Is there protection from the illegitimate use of physical force and freedom from war and insurgencies? 2 / 4

Allegations of police brutality, including the use of torture to extract confessions, are widespread, and security forces generally operate with impunity. Conditions in pretrial detention facilities and prisons are poor, with reports of forced labor, abuse of inmates by authorities, and deplorable health conditions.

F4. Do laws, policies, and practices guarantee equal treatment of various segments of the population? 2 / 4

Women are constitutionally guaranteed the same rights as men, but gender-based discrimination and sexual harassment are prevalent in practice. Same-sex sexual activity is illegal and can be punished with between 15 years and life in prison. The law is actively enforced.

Refugees are protected under local and international law, and there were about 70,000 refugees in Zambia as of 2020. However, they often suffer from limited access to basic services and particular vulnerability to gender-based violence.

G. PERSONAL AUTONOMY AND INDIVIDUAL RIGHTS: 8 / 16

G1. Do individuals enjoy freedom of movement, including the ability to change their place of residence, employment, or education? 3 / 4

The government generally respects the constitutionally protected right to free internal movement and foreign travel. However, internal movement is often impeded by petty corruption, such as police demands for bribes at checkpoints. In the spring of 2020, some government officials and police officers reportedly advocated or engaged in beatings to enforce social-distancing regulations meant to prevent the spread of COVID-19.

G2. Are individuals able to exercise the right to own property and establish private businesses without undue interference from state or nonstate actors? 2 / 4

Most agricultural land is administered according to customary law. However, the president retains ultimate authority over all land and can intercede to block or compel its sale or transfer. Women frequently experience discrimination in matters involving property and inheritance rights. The process of meeting regulatory requirements for starting and operating businesses can be lengthy and opaque.

G3. Do individuals enjoy personal social freedoms, including choice of marriage partner and size of family, protection from domestic violence, and control over appearance? 2 / 4

Personal status issues such as marriage and divorce are governed by either statutory or customary law, with customary practices varying among different ethnic groups. Due in large part to a government-backed strategy in place since 2016, the rate of child marriage has decreased significantly in recent years, though more than 30 percent of women aged 20 to 24 were married before age 18, according to 2018 data from the UN Children's Fund.

In 2020, plans by the Education Ministry to fully integrate comprehensive sexuality education (CSE) into the school curriculum met with opposition from a church group, the Evangelical Fellowship of Zambia, as well as the religious affairs minister. Supporters of the plan said it would help address high rates of child marriage, sexually transmitted diseases, and school dropouts due to pregnancy, while opponents alleged that it would promote immorality and extramarital sex. The matter remained under discussion at year's end.

Domestic abuse is common, and traditional norms inhibit many women from reporting assaults. Rape can draw a maximum penalty of life in prison with hard labor, but the problem is widespread, and the law is not frequently enforced.

G4. Do individuals enjoy equality of opportunity and freedom from economic exploitation? 1 / 4

Labor exploitation, child labor, and human trafficking remain prevalent despite laws meant to prevent them. The authorities have struggled to sustain antitrafficking efforts, notably decreasing investigations of related crimes and funding for victim assistance, according to the US State Department's 2020 report on trafficking in persons. Most human trafficking in the country reportedly entails the exploitation of women and children from rural areas in economic pursuits ranging from domestic work to mining and agriculture, but victims from other African countries and China have also been drawn into exploitative working conditions.

Zimbabwe

Population: 14,900,000
Capital: Harare
Freedom Status: Not Free
Electoral Democracy: No

Status Change: Zimbabwe's status declined from Partly Free to Not Free due to the authorities' intensifying persecution of opposition figures and civic activists.

Overview: The Zimbabwe African National Union–Patriotic Front (ZANU-PF) has dominated Zimbabwean politics since independence in 1980, in part by carrying out severe and often violent crackdowns on the political opposition, critical media, and other sources of dissent. President Emmerson Mnangagwa took power in 2017 after the military intervened to remove longtime president Robert Mugabe amid factional divisions within the ruling party. However, the new administration has largely retained the legal, administrative, and security architecture it inherited from the Mugabe regime, and it has stepped up repression to consolidate its authority. Endemic corruption, weak rule of law, and poor protections for workers and land rights remain among Zimbabwe's critical challenges.

KEY DEVELOPMENTS IN 2020

- Authorities used COVID-19 lockdown measures to restrict Zimbabweans' freedom of movement, forcing travelers to undergo stringent document checks at roadblocks. Journalists were also targeted by the authorities, despite being classified as essential, with two arrested for violating lockdown measures in May.
- Authorities forcibly dispersed an antigovernment protest in Harare in July, physically attacking and arresting participants. Earlier that month, journalist Hopewell Chin'ono and civil society leader Jacob Ngarivhume were arrested in connection with the rally; Ngarivhume was bailed in September, while Chin'ono was arrested on other charges in November.
- In March, the Supreme Court ruled that Movement for Democratic Change Alliance (MDC Alliance) leader Nelson Chamisa was not the legitimate opposition leader, replacing him with Movement for Democratic Change–Tsvangirai (MDC-T) leader Thokozani Khupe in a move that was regarded as a ZANU-PF attempt to fracture the opposition. Khupe recalled at least 31 MDC Alliance legislators as the year progressed, forcing them to surrender their seats.

POLITICAL RIGHTS: 11 / 40 (−1)
A. ELECTORAL PROCESS: 3 / 12
A1. Was the current head of government or other chief national authority elected through free and fair elections? 1 / 4

The president is directly elected and limited to two five-year terms under the 2013 constitution. President Mugabe was forced to resign after 37 years in power as a result of the 2017 coup. ZANU-PF then selected Mnangagwa, whom Mugabe had dismissed as vice president, to succeed him.

A presidential election, alongside parliamentary and local polls, was held as planned in July 2018. Mnangagwa was credited with 50.8 percent of the vote, followed by MDC Alliance candidate Nelson Chamisa with 44.3 percent and MDC-T candidate Thokozani Khupe with 9 percent.

International and local observers reported a peaceful campaign but raised concerns about its overall conduct and integrity. Southern African Development Community observers noted challenges including parties having difficulty accessing voter rolls, progovernment bias by state media, contested postal voting, and the denial of the diaspora's right to vote. A European Union mission noted similar bureaucratic challenges and problems with state media, as well as reports of assisted voting, and of inducements and intimidation meant to aid the ruling party.

Vote-tallying irregularities and delays led to postelection tensions. The MDC Alliance leadership declared victory in the presidential election before the official results and accused ZANU-PF of attempting to rig the vote during the delay. Postelection opposition protests erupted in Harare, and the military was deployed to disperse them, leading to several deaths. The Zimbabwe Electoral Commission (ZEC) ultimately declared Mnangagwa the winner but the MDC, whose factions had reunited after the elections, refused to recognize the legitimacy of Mnangagwa's victory.

A2. Were the current national legislative representatives elected through free and fair elections? 1 / 4

Zimbabwe has a bicameral legislature. In the lower chamber, the 270-seat National Assembly, 210 members are elected through a first-past-the-post system with one member per constituency, and 60 women are elected by proportional representation. The 80-seat Senate includes six members from each of Zimbabwe's 10 provinces who are elected through proportional representation. Sixteen are indirectly elected by regional councils, two seats are reserved for people with disabilities, and two are reserved for tribal chiefs. Members in both houses serve five-year terms.

ZANU-PF won 180 of the 270 National Assembly seats in the 2018 parliamentary elections. The MDC Alliance won 87, and the MDC-T won 1 via proportional representation. An independent former ZANU-PF member and the National Patriotic Front, a ZANU-PF splinter faction, each took one seat. In the Senate, ZANU-PF secured 34 elected seats, the MDC Alliance took 25, and the MDC-T took 1. Bureaucratic irregularities and media bias that affected the presidential election also marred the parliamentary elections. Traditional leaders ignored the constitutional ban on their participation in partisan politics.

In March 2020, the Supreme Court ruled that Chamisa was not the legitimate opposition leader, replacing him with MDC-T leader Khupe. Khupe subsequently recalled 31 MDC Alliance legislators of both houses as the year progressed, forcing them to surrender their seats in what observers considered a ZANU-PF attempt to fracture the opposition. Another 15 MDC Alliance members reportedly defected to the MDC-T by October to retain their seats.

ZANU-PF won most local and national by-elections held during 2019, though observers raised concerns about the interference of traditional leaders, reports of violence, intimidation, alleged ballot-box stuffing, and the distribution of food and medicine to secure votes.

A3. Are the electoral laws and framework fair, and are they implemented impartially by the relevant election management bodies? 1 / 4

The ZEC is responsible for election management and oversight, but its independence from ZANU-PF has long been questioned. International election monitors criticized aspects of its management of the 2018 polls, noting vote-count stewardship, opaque procurement processes, and the irregular arrangement of the ballots themselves, which appeared to favor certain candidates. Political parties and civil society had difficulty accessing voter rolls, affecting audit and verification processes envisioned by the Electoral Act.

The introduction of biometric voter registration since 2017 has been problematic, and on election day in 2018 there was no biometric voter authentication. Separately, there was a noticeable decline in voter registration in Harare and Bulawayo, possibly due in part to fewer registration kits having been allocated there.

Weeks ahead of the 2018 elections, the Constitutional Court ruled that Zimbabweans abroad must return to the country to register to vote, effectively contravening constitutional provisions guaranteeing every citizen the right to vote.

In July 2019, the ZEC appointed a former military figure as its chief elections officer. The opposition criticized the move, noting his long history of overseeing flawed elections and previous tenure as acting chief elections officer during the 2018 balloting.

B. POLITICAL PLURALISM AND PARTICIPATION: 5 / 16 (−1)

B1. Do the people have the right to organize in different political parties or other competitive political groupings of their choice, and is the system free of undue obstacles to the rise and fall of these competing parties or groupings? 2 / 4

Political parties may generally form without interference. However, state media tend not to cover opposition parties, impacting their competitiveness. Authorities have often suppressed opposition gatherings. While opposition groups were able to hold most meetings with limited disruption in the run-up to the 2018 elections, the MDC and its supporters faced postelection raids, arrests, and prosecutions.

MDC members were also targeted in 2020; one parliamentarian and two members were arrested in June after claiming that security agents sexually assaulted and tortured them while detaining them the month before. Also in June, several high-ranking MDC Alliance members were arrested after trying to enter a building occupied by the MDC-T. In August, MDC Alliance parliamentarian and vice chairman Job Sikhala was arrested, but was bailed in September.

Groups such as Mthwakazi Liberation Front (MLF) have been blocked from conducting memorial meetings for victims of Gukurahundi massacres in the 1980s. The MLF is regarded by the government as a secessionist political party, and its leaders have faced persecution.

B2. Is there a realistic opportunity for the opposition to increase its support or gain power through elections? 1 / 4 (−1)

ZANU-PF has dominated the government without interruption since independence, though the MDC held the post of prime minister as part of a power-sharing deal with Mugabe between 2009 and 2013.

The MDC managed to increase its share of parliamentary seats in the 2018 elections despite the uneven playing field, and Chamisa secured almost a million more votes in the 2018 presidential contest than the MDC candidate had in 2013. However, postelection violence and a subsequent crackdown limited the opposition's ability to operate and gain support, as reflected in the 2019 by-election results.

The opposition has more recently been weakened by factional infighting, which ZANU-PF reportedly fostered. The conflict notably affected the MDC's legislative presence, with MDC-T leader Khupe forcing MDC Alliance legislators to surrender their seats. That conflict was ongoing at year's end; Khupe lost a leadership contest in December, but vowed to appeal the results in court.

Score Change: The score declined from 2 to 1 due to mass arrests, intimidation, and harassment targeting opposition party officials, as well as the ruling party's alleged efforts to exploit divisions within the opposition by coopting one of the rival factions.

B3. Are the people's political choices free from domination by forces that are external to the political sphere, or by political forces that employ extrapolitical means? 1 / 4

The military has continued to play a critical role in political affairs since Mugabe's ouster in 2017. Many senior military officials assumed leadership positions in ZANU-PF and the government.

Traditional leaders, who wield influence over public resources such as food aid, have intimidated villagers, restricted opposition access to their areas, and issued political statements in support of the ruling party, despite constitutional provisions and court orders requiring them to abstain from partisan politics. The president of the National Council of Chiefs, Fortune Charumbira, publicly supported Mnangagwa and ZANU-PF ahead of the 2018 elections, and he defied a court order to retract his statements.

B4. Do various segments of the population (including ethnic, racial, religious, gender, LGBT+, and other relevant groups) have full political rights and electoral opportunities? 1 / 4

Zimbabwe's ethnic Shona majority dominates ZANU-PF, and members of the Ndebele minority have at times complained of political marginalization by both ZANU-PF and the MDC.

Women and their interests are underrepresented in the political system. The 2018 elections featured a slight decline in the number of women elected outside proportional representation. After the vote, women made up 34 percent of the parliament, down from the post-2013 35 percent figure. The proportional representation quota expires in 2023, raising concerns about whether progress in women's representation will be sustained. Four of 23 presidential candidates in 2018, or 17 percent, were women.

LGBT+ advocacy groups exist, but severe discrimination limits their ability to advance their interests in the political sphere.

C. FUNCTIONING OF GOVERNMENT: 3 / 12

C1. Do the freely elected head of government and national legislative representatives determine the policies of the government? 1 / 4

The president and parliament generally determine policies and legislation, but they lack strong electoral legitimacy, and the parliament does not serve as an effective check on executive power. In October 2019, after MDC lawmakers staged a walkout during Mnangagwa's state of the nation address, the speaker imposed heavy financial penalties.

The military continues to play an outsized role in civilian governance. Some officers received cabinet appointments following the 2017 coup, and senior commanders were rewarded with prominent ambassadorships during 2019. The government was compelled to deny rumors of another coup in June 2020, which were prompted by the military's involvement in seizing MDC property and in enforcing COVID-19-related lockdown measures.

C2. Are safeguards against official corruption strong and effective? 1 / 4

Corruption is endemic, and past revelations of large-scale graft did not consistently lead to successful prosecutions. The Zimbabwe Anti-Corruption Commission (ZACC) was disbanded in early 2019, with President Mnangagwa naming the wife of a former general, a retired major, former opposition politicians, and civil society leaders to the body that July. Despite this disruption, ZACC referred over 90 cases to prosecutors in 2020.

Corruption featured heavily in the government's COVID-19 response. In June 2020, Health Minister Obadiah Moyo was arrested after ZACC accused him of steering a $42 million contract to a firm outside the pharmaceutical sector. While Moyo was bailed in the case, which remained ongoing at year's end, he was dismissed from his post in July.

In September 2020, ZACC reported that the National Pharmaceutical Company allegedly violated procurement rules when acquiring equipment and chemicals for COVID-19-related work earlier in the year, and noted that Deputy Health Minister John Mangwiro unsuccessfully steered a related tender to a firm that offered inflated prices. Despite speculation that Mangwiro would be arrested, he remained in post at year's end. That same month, several high-ranking members of the national police were arrested after ZACC accused them of corrupt acts.

C3. Does the government operate with openness and transparency? 1 / 4

Government processes are generally opaque. Access to information is constitutionally protected, but restrictive laws limit the ability of media outlets and ordinary citizens to obtain government information. In July 2020, new freedom-of-information legislation, which aimed to make some information more freely available and replace the restrictive Access to Information and Protection of Privacy Act, was enacted.

CIVIL LIBERTIES: 17 / 60

D. FREEDOM OF EXPRESSION AND BELIEF: 7 / 16

D1. Are there free and independent media? 1 / 4

The constitution protects media freedom, but restrictive laws undermine this guarantee. The possibility of harsh penalties, including prison sentences, for violations of laws like the Criminal Law (Codification and Reform) Act (CLCRA) contributes to self-censorship among journalists.

The state-controlled Zimbabwe Broadcasting Corporation (ZBC) has historically dominated broadcast media. Many Zimbabweans rely on radio for information, but media diversity is limited by authorities' sustained refusal to grant licenses to community radio stations. Commercial radio licenses usually go to state-controlled companies or individuals with close links to ZANU-PF. The government controls Zimbabwe's two main daily newspapers, though there are several independent print outlets. In November 2020, the Broadcasting Authority of Zimbabwe issued new television broadcasting licenses, breaking the ZBC's monopoly. All six awardees were connected to the government or ruling party, and one was owned by the Defense Ministry.

Journalists continued to face detention and arrest throughout the year. In May 2020, two journalists were arrested for violating COVID-19 lockdown measures when they tried to interview MDC members who alleged abuse at the hands of the authorities, even though journalists were considered essential workers. The two were bailed later that month. In late June, a freelance journalist working with Voice of America was reportedly charged with undermining the president's authority and was released pending a trial, though police denied he was a suspect. In July, Hopewell Chin'ono, who reported on corruption within the Health Ministry, was arrested in Harare, as authorities sought to crack down on an upcoming protest. Chin'ono, whose reporting helped prompt Health Minister Moyo's resignation, was bailed in September, but was rearrested on contempt charges in November and remained in detention at year's end.

D2. Are individuals free to practice and express their religious faith or nonbelief in public and private? 3 / 4

Freedom of religion is generally respected in Zimbabwe. However, congregations perceived to be critical of the government have faced harassment. In August 2020, Catholic bishops criticized the government in pastoral letter, and authorities called on congregants to "ignore" the letter later that month.

D3. Is there academic freedom, and is the educational system free from extensive political indoctrination? 2 / 4

The Ministry of Higher Education supervises education policy at universities, and the president serves as chancellor of all eight state-run universities. The government has the authority to discipline students and faculty at state-run universities. Students have at times faced violent police responses to campus protests.

D4. Are individuals free to express their personal views on political or other sensitive topics without fear of surveillance or retribution? 1 / 4

Zimbabweans have enjoyed some freedom and openness in private discussion, but official surveillance of political activity is a deterrent to unfettered speech. Individuals have been arrested for critical posts on social media, prompting self-censorship online. However, some social media users did criticize the government in 2020, with the brief use of #ZimbabweanLivesMatter in August.

E. ASSOCIATIONAL AND ORGANIZATIONAL RIGHTS: 3 / 12

E1. Is there freedom of assembly? 1 / 4

Freedom of assembly is constitutionally guaranteed but poorly upheld in practice. In November 2019, the Maintenance of Peace and Order Act (MOPA) replaced the more repressive Public Order and Security Act, though MOPA retains heavy assembly restrictions. Zimbabwean authorities instituted a strict COVID-19 lockdown in March 2020, limiting the size of public gatherings. Gathering restrictions persisted through year's end.

Opposition groups attempted to organize a major antigovernment rally in July, but authorities responded by deploying the army to patrol Harare. Scores of participants were reportedly arrested and assaulted by security forces. Journalist Chin'ono and nongovernmental organization (NGO) leader Jacob Ngarivhume were arrested earlier in the month in connection to the planned rally; Ngarivhume was granted bail in September, but was ordered to report to a police station on a regular basis through year's end.

E2. Is there freedom for nongovernmental organizations, particularly those that are engaged in human rights- and governance-related work? 1 / 4

NGOs face restrictions under laws including the CLCRA and the Private Voluntary Organisations Act, despite rights laid out for them in the constitution. NGO leaders and members faced detentions, abductions, and continued scrutiny in 2020.

E3. Is there freedom for trade unions and similar professional or labor organizations? 1 / 4

The Labour Act gives the government broad authority to veto collective bargaining agreements it deems economically harmful, and to regulate unions' internal operations. Strikes are banned in "essential" industries and subject to procedural restrictions, though they occur in practice. Due to the unemployment and heightened informal employment that have accompanied Zimbabwe's economic crisis, unions are grossly underfunded. Strikes are sometimes tolerated, though authorities have been known to charge union leaders with subversion for such activity.

In March 2020, doctors and nurses working in public hospitals launched a strike over a lack of protective equipment. In June, the Zimbabwe Nurses Association launched a strike aimed at securing pay in US dollars, which disrupted hospital services. The union called for an end to the strike in September, after the departure of former health minister Moyo. In October, teachers held a strike over pay and working conditions.

F. RULE OF LAW: 2 / 16

F1. Is there an independent judiciary? 1 / 4

Pressure on the courts to endorse executive actions and protect ZANU-PF's interests has eroded the judiciary's independence. Judges occasionally rule against the government in sensitive cases, but this is rare, and such rulings are not always respected.

Individual judges faced a further loss in independence when Chief Justice Luke Malaba issued a directive instructing them to clear rulings with superiors in July 2020. Malaba rescinded his directive after facing fierce criticism later that month.

F2. Does due process prevail in civil and criminal matters? 0 / 4

Constitutionally stipulated due process protections are not enforced. Police and other security personnel frequently ignore basic rights regarding detention, searches, and seizures, and accused persons are often held and interrogated for hours without legal counsel or explanation of the reason for their arrest. Lawyers also face detention and arrest on spurious charges. Perceived opponents of the regime faced arrests and detentions throughout 2020.

F3. Is there protection from the illegitimate use of physical force and freedom from war and insurgencies? 0 / 4

Security forces backed by ZANU-PF have long engaged in acts of extralegal violence, including against opposition supporters, with impunity. Detainees and protesters often face police brutality, sometimes resulting in death. Overcrowded prisons are unsanitary, food shortages have been reported, and prisoners risk contracting illnesses including COVID-19.

F4. Do laws, policies, and practices guarantee equal treatment of various segments of the population? 1 / 4

While discrimination on the basis of a broad range of characteristics is prohibited under the 2013 constitution, discrimination on the basis of sexual orientation or gender identity is not expressly prohibited. Sex between men is a criminal offense and can be punished with a fine and up to a year in prison. Land and indigenization policies have previously been criticized for discriminating against white Zimbabweans. Despite legal protections against gender discrimination, women face significant disadvantages in practice, including in employment and compensation.

G. PERSONAL AUTONOMY AND INDIVIDUAL RIGHTS: 5 / 16

G1. Do individuals enjoy freedom of movement, including the ability to change their place of residence, employment, or education? 2 / 4

Movement has been restricted by the extensive use of police roadblocks, which have been deployed in recent years to impede protests. Authorities also used roadblocks and documentation checks to enforce COVID-19 lockdown measures, which grew more stringent in July 2020 after some Zimbabweans reportedly offered forged documentation.

G2. Are individuals able to exercise the right to own property and establish private businesses without undue interference from state or nonstate actors? 1 / 4

Land rights are poorly protected, and in rural areas, the nationalization of land has left both commercial farmers and smallholders with limited security of tenure. Controversies persist over efforts to enact new land reforms. Women face discrimination in terms of access to and ownership of land, particularly communal or family land controlled by traditional leaders or male relatives.

In August 2020, the government launched a compensation scheme to support white and foreign-born farmers affected by a 2000s land reform program. Under the program, some landowners may regain lost property.

G3. Do individuals enjoy personal social freedoms, including choice of marriage partner and size of family, protection from domestic violence, and control over appearance? 1 / 4

Laws on personal status matters such as marriage and divorce are generally equitable, but customary practices put women at a disadvantage. Domestic violence is a problem, and sexual abuse is widespread, especially against girls.

Child marriages were banned in 2016, but factors including poverty, certain religious views, and lack of enforcement have sustained the practice; a third of girls are married by age 18. In June 2020, NGO CAMFED reported that more children were considering marriage in response to the COVID-19 pandemic's economic effects.

The Termination of Pregnancy Act makes abortion illegal except in very limited circumstances. Same-sex marriages are constitutionally prohibited.

G4. Do individuals enjoy equality of opportunity and freedom from economic exploitation? 1 / 4

Due to an ongoing economic crisis, many workers are not adequately compensated, and can go unpaid for months. Inflation has accelerated, with the government reporting a figure of 837 percent in August 2020. The International Trade Union Confederation Global Rights Index categorized Zimbabwe as one of the worst countries to work in its 2020 assessment.

The government has continued efforts to combat human trafficking, though it remains a serious problem. Men, women, and children can be found engaged in forced labor in the agricultural sector, forced begging, and forced domestic work. Women and girls remain particularly vulnerable to sex trafficking.

Territory Reports

Abkhazia

Population: 243,000
Freedom Status: Partly Free

Note: *Freedom in the World* reports assess the level of political rights and civil liberties in a given geographical area, regardless of whether they are affected by the state, nonstate actors, or foreign powers. Disputed territories are sometimes assessed separately if they meet certain criteria, including boundaries that are sufficiently stable to allow year-on-year comparisons. For more information, see the report methodology and FAQ.

Overview: Abkhazia, a breakaway region of Georgia, has maintained de facto independence since the end of a civil conflict in 1993. The government is financially dependent on Russia, which has a military presence in Abkhazia and is one of a handful of states that recognizes the territory's independence. The tumultuous political environment features significant opposition and civil society activity. Ongoing problems include a flawed criminal justice system, discrimination against ethnic Georgians, and a lack of economic opportunity.

KEY DEVELOPMENTS IN 2020

- In early January, opposition protesters took over the main governmental headquarters, and the Supreme Court annulled the results of the 2019 presidential election, leading to the resignation of President Raul Khajimba. Khajimba's main political opponent, Aslan Bzhania, won a snap presidential election in March.
- In June, a recently established human rights office released its first annual report on conditions in Abkhazia. In response to some of its findings, President Bzhania abolished certain regulations that discriminated against ethnic Georgians and called for a major reform of the law enforcement system.
- Abkhazian authorities closed border crossings between Abkhazia and Georgian-controlled territory beginning in March, citing the COVID-19 pandemic. The crossings were periodically reopened for essential travel or returning residents. Meanwhile, the border with Russia was closed in early April and reopened in early August despite increases in COVID-19 cases. By year's end, more than 8,200 confirmed cases and 100 deaths had been reported.

POLITICAL RIGHTS: 17 / 40

A. ELECTORAL PROCESS: 5 / 12

A1. Was the current head of government or other chief national authority elected through free and fair elections? 2 / 4

Abkhazia's 1999 constitution established a presidential system, in which the president and vice president are directly elected for five-year terms.

President Khajimba, who was first elected in 2014, appeared to win reelection in a two-round contest that ended in September 2019. The balloting was originally scheduled for June, but was postponed after candidate Bzhania was hospitalized with mercury poisoning. Bzhania ended his candidacy in favor of former Sukhumi mayor Alkhas Kvitsinia. According to the initial results, Khajimba won the second round with 47 percent of the vote, while Kvitsinia took 46 percent. Kvitsinia sued to overturn those results, alleging that the Central Electoral Commission (CEC) misinterpreted electoral law when verifying them; his lawsuit was rejected by the Supreme Court in late September.

In a rapid series of events in early January 2020, opposition protesters broke into the government headquarters to demand Khajimba's resignation, a majority of lawmakers similarly called on the president to step down, and the Supreme Court—ruling on an appeal of its September 2019 decision—annulled the results of the presidential election. Khajimba tendered his resignation a few days later, and a snap election was scheduled for March.

Bzhania won the new election, taking more than 56 percent of the vote in the first round. Two lesser-known candidates divided the remainder; Khajimba did not participate. Most established election monitors do not assess Abkhazia's elections. However, notwithstanding the circumstances that led to the new presidential vote, informal observations indicated that the balloting and campaign period were relatively free. The campaign proceeded even as Bzhania was temporarily hospitalized with a respiratory ailment, which for a time raised suspicions of a second poisoning. COVID-19 was also a concern, but political rallies continued during the election period.

Under the constitution, the prime minister and cabinet are appointed by and accountable to the president. In April 2020, President Bzhania appointed Aleksandr Ankvab as prime minister; Ankvab had served as president in 2011–14 before being forced to resign amid street protests by Khajimba and his supporters.

A2. Were the current national legislative representatives elected through free and fair elections? 2 / 4

The parliament, or People's Assembly, comprises 35 members elected for five-year terms from single-seat constituencies. The 2017 parliamentary elections were marred by instances of intimidation, with violent attacks on two candidates. The voting was voided and rescheduled in one district due to ballot irregularities. Independent deputies dominated the new legislature, and many were oriented toward the opposition. However, about 20 legislators were considered supporters of Khajimba, as was the new speaker, Valeriy Kvarchia.

Following the March 2020 presidential election, four members of parliament left their seats to join the executive branch, including the new president himself and his prime minister. Their seats were filled through snap elections July and September 2020.

A3. Are the electoral laws and framework fair, and are they implemented impartially by the relevant election management bodies? 1 / 4

The legal framework does not support fully democratic elections. Eight members of the CEC are chosen by the parliament, and seven are appointed by the president. While elections in recent years have been competitive, all elections are predicated on the exclusion of ethnic Georgians.

B. POLITICAL PLURALISM AND PARTICIPATION: 8 / 16

B1. Do the people have the right to organize in different political parties or other competitive political groupings of their choice, and is the system free of undue obstacles to the rise and fall of these competing parties or groupings? 2 / 4

A large number of parties and social organizations participate in Abkhazia's fractious political system, and these movements generally enjoy freedom of association. Organizations representing veterans of the 1992–93 war with the Georgian government are particularly influential.

However, corruption within parties hampers their democratic functions, and a 2009 law forbids the formation of parties catering to the interests of any particular ethnic, religious, racial, or professional group. Parties are relatively weak as electoral vehicles and as forces within the parliament, with most candidates campaigning and serving as independents. In the 2017 parliamentary contest, 112 of 137 candidates ran as independents.

B2. Is there a realistic opportunity for the opposition to increase its support or gain power through elections? 3 / 4

Although independent candidates are not able to draw on the sort of support or infrastructure typically associated with membership in an established political party, those running against incumbents have enjoyed some success. For example, while no candidates for the opposition groups Amtsakhara or United Abkhazia were elected in 2017, most incumbent legislators—including government ministers—lost their seats.

After winning the 2020 presidential election, Bzhania invited representatives of alternative political groups to join his government, including Ankvab, who became prime minister, and Sergey Shamba of United Abkhazia, who became secretary of the Security Council. Meanwhile, Khajimba supporters quickly formed at least one new political group aimed at competing in the next parliamentary elections.

B3. Are the people's political choices free from domination by forces that are external to the political sphere, or by political forces that employ extrapolitical means? 2 / 4

While voters' choices influence domestic politics, the functioning of Abkhazia's political institutions remains dependent on economic and political support from Moscow.

B4. Do various segments of the population (including ethnic, racial, religious, gender, LGBT+, and other relevant groups) have full political rights and electoral opportunities? 1 / 4

Under the constitution, only a person of Abkhaz nationality who is a citizen of Abkhazia can be elected to the presidency. The Armenian and Russian communities traditionally have an informal agreement whereby parties nominate members of ethnic minorities to represent districts where they predominate. Ethnic Abkhaz dominate the political sphere; of the 35 members of the parliament, 32 have Abkhaz surnames and 3 are Armenian. The ethnic Georgian population is routinely excluded from elections and political representation. As with other recent elections, authorities argued ahead of the 2020 presidential vote that the majority of residents in the ethnic Georgian district of Gali were Georgian citizens and therefore not permitted to cast ballots.

Societal norms discourage women from running for office, and women and their interests remain underrepresented in the political sphere. In 2020, only one cabinet-level position and one parliamentary seat were held by women.

C. FUNCTIONING OF GOVERNMENT: 4 / 12

C1. Do the freely elected head of government and national legislative representatives determine the policies of the government? 1 / 4

While Abkhazia's president sets the tone for most domestic policy, the overall ability of elected authorities to determine and implement policies is limited by the economic and political influence of Moscow. The Russian government supplies most of the state budget, though its contributions have started to decline.

Several thousand Russian troops are permanently stationed in the territory. However, there has been significant pushback against a 2014 Russian-Abkhazian treaty, with critics arguing that some of its provisions threaten Abkhazia's autonomy. In November 2020, faced with a pandemic and an economic downturn, Abkhazian leaders withdrew many of their previous concerns and signed an agreement with Russia that called for changes to a number of laws, including amendments that would give broader rights to Russian investors and impose restrictions on local nongovernmental organizations (NGOs) that receive foreign funding. The Russian state remains influential in Abkhazia's security apparatus; the territory's State Security Service (SGB) includes a representative of the Russian government in its leadership.

In addition to foreign influence, Abkhazia's government has been affected by a pattern of political instability in recent years. Prime ministers have been frequently replaced, and Khajimba was the second consecutive president to be forced out of office amid antigovernment protests. In 2020, President Bzhania pledged to pursue constitutional reforms that would shift more power from the executive branch to the parliament.

C2. Are safeguards against official corruption strong and effective? 1 / 4

Corruption is believed to be extensive and is tolerated by the government, despite promises to combat it. In recent years, Russian officials have voiced concern about the large-scale embezzlement of funds provided by Moscow, but efforts to investigate and punish such malfeasance have been largely ineffective. After the change in government in 2020, prosecutors launched investigations into allegations of embezzlement and fraud at state-owned companies.

C3. Does the government operate with openness and transparency? 2 / 4

Legal amendments from 2015 allow citizens to request information about any government decisions that are not classified as state secrets, and to receive a response within a month. Nevertheless, the territory's political culture is nontransparent, and social stigmas prevent citizens from requesting information.

In February 2020, after roughly a year of discussion, the parliament adopted legislation requiring declarations of income, property, and expenses for all public officials and their close relatives. The law, which was also intended to improve the transparency of recruitment for public officials, was amended in March to expand its asset declarations to more relatives after activists organized a hunger strike in front of the parliament. However, the new rules would not come into force until lawmakers adopted parallel changes to the law on the civil service.

In June, the Office of the Commissioner for Human Rights released its first annual report on conditions in Abkhazia, having been established in late 2018. The office noted that it remained underfunded, with no basic security provided for its staff. It also reported that law enforcement agencies largely ignored the concerns it raised, refused to provide complete and relevant information, and did not respond to requests in a timely manner. The SGB was deemed the most opaque state structure. President Bzhania praised the report and promised to make it a basis for his planned reform of the law enforcement system.

CIVIL LIBERTIES: 23 / 60
D. FREEDOM OF EXPRESSION AND BELIEF: 8 / 16
D1. Are there free and independent media? 2 / 4

The local media sector is dominated by the government, which operates the Abkhaz State Television and Radio Company (AGTRK), a newspaper, and a news agency, though there are also some private outlets. Journalists have criticized AGTRK for failing to air material that could be perceived as unflattering to the government. News websites and social media have become increasingly popular sources of information. Major Russian television stations broadcast into Abkhazia, and residents of the Gali district have access to Georgian broadcasts. Some legal restrictions apply to both traditional and online media, including criminal libel statutes.

D2. Are individuals free to practice and express their religious faith or nonbelief in public and

Orthodox Christianity is the dominant religion in Abkhazia, but the Georgian Orthodox Church faces discrimination and restrictions. Most practicing Christians adhere to one of two branches of the Abkhazian Orthodox Church.

Muslims are allowed to practice freely, though some community leaders have been attacked in the past. In 2020, local Muslim leaders reported ongoing difficulties in their efforts to obtain permission for the construction of an official mosque; Islamic religious services have generally been held in private homes, some of which were renovated and expanded during the year to accommodate increased participation.

There are no widely reported restrictions on the minority who identify with Abkhazia's traditional pre-Christian religion. Jehovah's Witnesses are formally banned under a 1995 decree.

D3. Is there academic freedom, and is the educational system free from extensive political indoctrination? 1 / 4

The education system is affected by the separatist government's political priorities. Schools providing instruction in Russian and Armenian generally operate without interference. However, Georgian-language schools in Gali have been undergoing reorganization since 2015 with the aim of replacing Georgian with Russian. In August 2020, days before the start of a new school year, the education minister ordered all new pupils of Abkhaz origin to register at schools teaching only in the Abkhaz language; however, the prime minister reversed the decree after it faced criticism from civil society.

Universities in the capital have recently become more lenient about the enrollment of Gali Georgians, who are educated in Russian and lack Abkhaz passports. Nevertheless, bureaucratic complications still arise with respect to obtaining a diploma, and some argue that requiring aspiring university students to take Abkhaz-language proficiency exams as part of their graduation from secondary school disadvantages members of ethnic minorities.

D4. Are individuals free to express their personal views on political or other sensitive topics without fear of surveillance or retribution? 3 / 4

The freedoms of personal expression and private discussion are not severely restricted in practice. Social media platforms host vibrant discussions on political and other topics in Abkhazia. However, there is some self-censorship on sensitive subjects, especially those relating to ethnic Georgians and relations with Tbilisi, or to the families of senior officials or local businessmen. In October 2020, a young ethnic Georgian was detained in Gali after setting fire to the Abkhazian flag during public celebrations marking the anniversary of the end of the 1992–93 war.

Criminal code amendments adopted in late 2019 prescribe up to 15 years' imprisonment for "actions against the sovereignty of Abkhazia." The code also mandates prison sentences for the discussion of "anticonstitutional agreements" on the political status of Abkhazia. Some local observers expressed concerns that the legislation could have negative repercussions for freedom of speech.

E. ASSOCIATIONAL AND ORGANIZATIONAL RIGHTS: 6 / 12

E1. Is there freedom of assembly? 3 / 4

Freedom of assembly is largely respected, and opposition and civil society groups regularly mount protests. While violent confrontations have occurred in the past, protests during 2020 largely proceeded without excessive uses of force by police. In early January, a small group of activists took over the main governmental headquarters to call for the resignation of then president Khajimba, resulting in damage to government property. In March, a hunger strike by local anticorruption activists contributed to the expansion of long-sought legislation requiring asset declarations for all state officials and their family members.

E2. Is there freedom for nongovernmental organizations, particularly those that are engaged in human rights– and governance-related work? 2 / 4

Civil society organizations, particularly groups representing Abkhazia's war veterans, exert influence on government policies. Some 300 NGOs are registered, though only a fraction of these are active. Many groups struggle to secure sustainable funding, in part because partnerships with foreign or international NGOs are complicated by Abkhazia's disputed status. NGOs that receive funding from foreign governments or entities that do not recognize Abkhazia's independence face criticism from local journalists and authorities. While its November 2020 policy agreement with Russia called for special restrictions on groups that receive foreign funding, the government had not adopted such legislation at year's end.

E3. Is there freedom for trade unions and similar professional or labor organizations? 1 / 4

Trade unions exist, but unions and labor activists have struggled to effectively defend the rights of workers. In recent years the territory's federation of independent trade unions has clashed with the government over the distribution of social insurance funds.

F. RULE OF LAW: 4 / 16
F1. Is there an independent judiciary? 1 / 4

Despite attempts to introduce more parliamentary oversight of the judiciary, nepotism and corruption reportedly have a significant impact on judicial independence. Implementation of judicial decisions remains inconsistent.

The 2017 pardon of Giorgi Lukava, a Georgian guerrilla leader who fought separatist authorities and was serving a 20-year prison sentence imposed in 2013, raised questions about respect for judicial rulings and judicial independence. Critics said the pardon was illegal, as then president Khajimba made the decision without the approval of the pardons commission. The Constitutional Court ruled the pardon constitutional in 2019.

The Supreme Court's handling of the 2019 presidential election case raised a number of questions about judicial impartiality. Hearings on Kvitsinia's appeal of the initial September 2019 decision were delayed for weeks, contributing to the political crisis in early January 2020. Just a day before the final ruling, which was issued in the midst of an opposition occupation of government offices, Kvitsinia's lawyers successfully petitioned for the replacement of a judge on the case whose term had expired and who was therefore dependent on the president for extensions. Khajimba initially rejected the objectivity of the court's decision to annul the 2019 results, citing pressure from the protesters, but he eventually agreed to end the crisis by resigning.

F2. Does due process prevail in civil and criminal matters? 1 / 4

The criminal justice system is undermined by limited defendant access to qualified legal counsel, violations of due process, and lengthy pretrial detentions.

In September 2020, in response to the first annual report by the human rights commissioner's office as well as recent cases of serious misconduct by law enforcement officials, President Bzhania launched consultations with law enforcement and judicial agencies on the potential for systemic reforms.

F3. Is there protection from the illegitimate use of physical force and freedom from war and insurgencies? 1 / 4

Isolated acts of criminal and political violence occur in Abkhazia, though government data have shown declines in the overall crime rate in recent years. Conditions in prisons and detention centers are reportedly poor, and the 2020 report by the human rights commissioner's office highlighted cases of alleged torture and mistreatment in custody.

Organized crime remains a crucial problem. In November 2019, two suspected members of a criminal organization, along with one bystander, were killed by assailants in Sukhumi. After the change in leadership in 2020, at least one of the former president's private bodyguards was arrested for alleged involvement in the incident. Newly elected president Bzhania, who pledged to crack down on organized crime, ordered officials to compile a list of people who were granted firearms by his predecessor and recover the weapons from anyone with a criminal history.

F4. Do laws, policies, and practices guarantee equal treatment of various segments of the population? 1 / 4

Ethnic Georgian residents of the Gali district continue to face discrimination, including police harassment and unequal access to documentation, education, and public services. In 2017, Sukhumi began issuing residence permits to Gali Georgians for five-year renewable terms. Permit holders may retain Georgian citizenship, reside in Gali, and cross the de facto border into Georgia proper. The separatist authorities stated that they would grant Abkhazian citizenship to any Georgian willing to "rediscover their Abkhaz ethnic heritage." Local officials warned Gali Georgians against attempting to hold both passports amid complaints of bureaucratic hurdles in obtaining residency permits.

The 2020 report by the human rights commissioner's office noted the government's discriminatory policies toward ethnic Georgians and called for reforms to address them. In July, in response to some of the report's recommendations, President Bzhania reduced especially high land taxes in Gali that dated to 2003 and reversed a 2019 order requiring extra payments from NGOs that sought to carry out projects in the district.

Many women in Abkhazia reportedly experience gender-based violence, with higher rates in rural areas. The territory lacks robust legal protections against discrimination affecting LGBT+ people.

G. PERSONAL AUTONOMY AND INDIVIDUAL RIGHTS: 5 / 16

G1. Do individuals enjoy freedom of movement, including the ability to change their place of residence, employment, or education? 1 / 4

Freedom of movement is limited by the ongoing dispute over Abkhazia's status. Travel permits remain expensive and burdensome to obtain. More than 70 percent of Abkhazia's residents hold Russian passports, as Abkhaz travel documents are not internationally recognized.

Crossings between Georgian-controlled territory and Abkhazia generally remained closed after March 2020, with authorities claiming the closures were necessary to prevent the spread of the coronavirus; the crossings were opened for short periods during the year to allow essential travel and the return of local residents. Meanwhile, crossings on the border with Russia closed in early April, reopened in early August, and remained open despite subsequent increases in COVID-19 cases.

G2. Are individuals able to exercise the right to own property and establish private businesses without undue interference from state or nonstate actors? 1 / 4

Criminal activity hampers the operations of local businesses. The constitution forbids foreigners, including Russians, from buying real estate in Abkhazia, a rule that has broad support in Abkhazian society. However, the 2020 bilateral agreement with Russia envisioned changes that could clear the way for Russian acquisition of Abkhazian land, for example by allowing Russians to obtain dual citizenship. Uncertainty persists regarding property rights for ethnic Georgians in Gali, whose residency permits do not allow them to officially own or inherit property. The legal status of properties whose owners were expelled from Abkhazia during the 1990s is also unclear, as displaced people cannot return to claim them.

G3. Do individuals enjoy personal social freedoms, including choice of marriage partner and size of family, protection from domestic violence, and control over appearance? 2 / 4

Personal freedoms are somewhat inhibited by conservative social mores and societal disapproval of certain identities and behavior, including "nontraditional" sexual orientations and gender nonconformity. A 2016 law banned abortions in all circumstances apart from prior fetal death. In its 2020 report, the human rights commissioner's office called on authorities to overturn the abortion ban.

NGOs have expressed concern about so-called honor killings of young women accused of moral transgressions. Domestic violence and rape are serious problems, and victims lack access to effective remedies for such abuse. There is no specific law to address domestic violence.

G4. Do individuals enjoy equality of opportunity and freedom from economic exploitation? 1 / 4

Equality of opportunity is limited by Abkhazia's international isolation, as well as by corruption and criminality. In 2018, Russian and other foreign businessmen complained that criminal activity and arbitrary expropriations severely impaired their ability to work and invest in the territory. NGOs have expressed concern about human trafficking in Abkhazia.

Crimea

Population: 2,350,000
Freedom Status: Not Free

Note: *Freedom in the World* reports assess the level of political rights and civil liberties in a given geographical area, regardless of whether they are affected by the state, nonstate actors, or foreign powers. Disputed territories are sometimes assessed separately if they meet certain criteria, including boundaries that are sufficiently stable to allow year-on-year comparisons. For more information, see the report methodology and FAQ.

Overview: In early 2014, Russian forces invaded the autonomous Ukrainian region of Crimea and quickly annexed it to the Russian Federation through a referendum that was widely condemned for violating international law. The occupation government severely limits political and civil rights, has silenced independent media, and employs antiterrorism and other laws against political dissidents. Many Ukrainians have been deported from or otherwise compelled to leave Crimea. Members of the indigenous Crimean Tatar minority, many of whom continue to vocally oppose the Russian occupation, have faced acute repression by the authorities.

KEY DEVELOPMENTS IN 2020

- Crimean authorities initiated strict assembly restrictions in March in response to the COVID-19 pandemic, but those restrictions were selectively applied, with a June military parade celebrating the Soviet Union's involvement in World War II proceeding with reportedly little modification. Territorial authorities were accused of underreporting COVID-19 deaths by health-care workers in September.
- In September, the Office of the United Nations High Commissioner for Human Rights (OHCHR) published a report on human rights in Crimea, noting ongoing arbitrary arrests and searches, torture of detainees, interference with the work of journalists, due process violations, and other serious abuses.
- Territorial courts issued the first prison sentences against Jehovah's Witnesses for their religious activity in March, when a church member received a six-year sentence for attempting to form a congregation. In September, a prison sentence lodged against another adherent was upheld in a separate case.

POLITICAL RIGHTS: −2 / 40

A. ELECTORAL PROCESS: 0 / 12

A1. Was the current head of government or other chief national authority elected through free and fair elections? 0 / 4

Under the administrative system established by Russia, the Crimean Peninsula is divided into the Republic of Crimea and the federal city of Sevastopol, a port of roughly 436,600 residents. Sevastopol's political institutions largely mirror those of Crimea proper.

The head of the Republic of Crimea is elected by its legislature, the State Council of Crimea, for up to two consecutive five-year terms. Lawmakers choose the leader based on a list of nominees prepared by the Russian president. In October 2014, the legislature unanimously elected Sergey Aksyonov as the head of the republic in a process that did not conform to democratic standards. (Aksyonov had led Crimea since February 2014, when a group of armed men forced legislators to elect him prime minister at gunpoint.) He was unanimously reelected in 2019.

An Organization for Security and Co-operation in Europe (OSCE) election monitoring mission noted that polling for Ukraine's presidential election, held in two rounds in March and April 2019, could not be organized in Crimea.

A2. Were the current national legislative representatives elected through free and fair elections? 0 / 4

The State Council consists of 75 members elected to five-year terms. Two-thirds of the members are elected by party list and one-third in single-member districts. Legislative elections in 2014 under the Russian-organized Crimean constitution were contested exclusively by candidates who backed the Russian occupation, and Ukrainian parties were banned. Conditions for the September 2019 elections were similar, though the ruling party in Russia, United Russia, lost some support, and won 60 seats, down from 70 previously. The ultranationalist Liberal Democratic Party of Russia (LDPR) secured 10 seats, and the Communist Party won 5.

OSCE election monitors noted that polling for Ukraine's parliamentary elections in July 2019 could not be organized in Crimea. Crimeans were similarly unable to participate in Ukraine's October 2020 local elections.

A3. Are the electoral laws and framework fair, and are they implemented impartially by the relevant election management bodies? 0 / 4

The Russian occupation authorities have tailored the electoral system to ensure maximum control by Moscow. Legislators electing the chief executive are limited to candidates chosen by the Russian president. In the legislative elections, legitimate opposition forces are denied registration before the voting begins, leaving voters with the choice of either abstaining or endorsing pro-Russian candidates.

B. POLITICAL PLURALISM AND PARTICIPATION: 0 / 16

B1. Do the people have the right to organize in different political parties or other competitive political groupings of their choice, and is the system free of undue obstacles to the rise and fall of these competing parties or groupings? 0 / 4

Ukrainian political parties are banned, allowing Russia's ruling party and other Kremlin-approved factions to dominate the political system. The Russian Federal Security Service (FSB), local police, and pro-Russian "self-defense" units use intimidation and harassment to suppress any political mobilization against the current government or the annexation of Crimea.

As in Russia, the authorities in the territory consistently crack down on opposition political activity. Crimean Tatars have continued to voice dissent and openly oppose the Russian occupation, but they risk harassment, arrest, and imprisonment for their actions. Other opposition figures also experience intimidation and police surveillance. In early 2018, Yevgeniy Karakashev, an opposition political activist, was arrested in Crimea on terrorism charges, and in April 2019 was convicted by a Russian court and sentenced to six years in a penal colony. In October 2019, pro-Ukraine activist Oleh Prykhodko was arrested in Crimea and accused of terrorism; his trial was still ongoing at the end of 2020.

B2. Is there a realistic opportunity for the opposition to increase its support or gain power through elections? 0 / 4

Because Ukrainian political parties are not allowed to compete in elections and Russia tightly controls the political and electoral systems, there is no opportunity for a genuine political opposition to form, compete, or take power in Crimea.

B3. Are the people's political choices free from domination by forces that are external to the political sphere, or by political forces that employ extrapolitical means? 0 / 4

Sergey Aksyonov, the chief executive, was originally installed by Russian security forces, and subsequent elections have been carefully controlled by the Russian government, which pressures citizens to vote. Among other abuses, during the 2016 Russian parliamentary elections, public- and private-sector workers were threatened with dismissal from their jobs if they failed to vote. During the March 2018 Russian presidential election and September 2019 local elections, public employees were again threatened with termination if they did not vote.

B4. Do various segments of the population (including ethnic, racial, religious, gender, LGBT+, and other relevant groups) have full political rights and electoral opportunities? 0 / 4

Occupation authorities deny full political rights to all Crimea residents, but Crimean Tatars and ethnic Ukrainians are regarded with particular suspicion and face greater persecution than do ethnic Russians.

The headquarters of the Mejlis, the Crimean Tatars' representative body, was closed by the authorities in 2014. The Mejlis's incumbent chairman, Refat Chubarov, and Crimean Tatar leader Mustafa Dzhemilev have since been banned from the territory. The Mejlis was officially banned by Crimea's Supreme Court in 2016. In March 2020, Chubarov was charged with organizing riots for participating in a 2014 demonstration, while Dzhemilev was charged with "illegally crossing the state border of the Russian Federation" in April. Both cases were still ongoing at year's end.

The prohibition on Ukrainian political parties leaves ethnic Ukrainians with limited options for meaningful representation.

Women formally have equal political rights, but they remain underrepresented in leadership positions in practice, and government officials demonstrate little interest in or understanding of gender-equality issues. After the September 2019 election, women held 21 percent of the seats in the State Council.

C. FUNCTIONING OF GOVERNMENT: 0 / 12

C1. Do the freely elected head of government and national legislative representatives determine the policies of the government? 0 / 4

All major policy decisions are made in Moscow and executed by Russian president Vladimir Putin's representatives in Crimea or the local authorities, who were not freely elected and are beholden to the Kremlin.

C2. Are safeguards against official corruption strong and effective? 0 / 4

Corruption is widespread in Crimea and occurs at the highest levels of government. Generally, efforts to investigate and prosecute corruption are inadequate. Some elements of the Russian-backed leadership, including Aksyonov, reputedly have ties to organized crime. In recent years, the Russian FSB has arrested a number of Crimean officials as part of an ostensible campaign against graft; many of the arrests were related to allegations that local authorities embezzled Russian funds meant to support the occupation. However, some have also been linked to infighting between Crimean and Russian officials over control of the peninsula's assets.

C3. Does the government operate with openness and transparency? 0 / 4

With strict controls on the media and few other means of holding officials accountable, residents struggle to obtain information about the functioning of their government. Budget processes are opaque, and input from civil society, which is itself subject to tight restrictions, is limited.

Authorities are similarly opaque about the course of the ongoing COVID-19 pandemic. In September 2020, Crimean health-care workers warned that the occupation authorities were underreporting pandemic-related deaths. In October, former Mejlis chairman Chubarov claimed that Russian authorities were withholding pandemic-related information, and claimed that services in Sevastopol were overwhelmed to the point that some patients could not access care.

ADDITIONAL DISCRETIONARY POLITICAL RIGHTS QUESTION

Is the government or occupying power deliberately changing the ethnic composition of a country or territory so as to destroy a culture or tip the political balance in favor of another group? −2 / 0

Since the occupation began, the Russian government has taken decisive steps to solidify ethnic Russian domination of the peninsula and marginalize the Ukrainian and Crimean Tatar communities. The elimination of the Ukrainian language from school curriculums and the closure of most Ukrainian Orthodox churches since 2014 are indicative of this attempt to Russify the population.

Russian and local pro-Russian officials' policies and actions in Crimea have led to an influx of hundreds of thousands of people from Russia, including Russian troops, civilian personnel, and their families. People displaced by fighting and deprivation in eastern Ukraine—home to many ethnic Russians—have also come to Crimea. Ukrainian citizens from Crimea have been drafted into compulsory military service in the Russian armed forces, in contravention of international law. By 2020, more than 25,000 Crimeans had been drafted into the Russian military, with many of them forced to serve far from Crimea.

Meanwhile, political persecution has led to an outflow of ethnic Ukrainians and Crimean Tatars. Russia instituted a policy of mass Russian naturalization for all residents of Crimea in 2014, in violation of international law. Once the policy was enacted, Crimeans had only 18 days to opt out of Russian citizenship. Ukrainian citizens, many of them long-term residents with immediate family on the peninsula, continue to be deported from Crimea, often for opting out of Russian citizenship.

CIVIL LIBERTIES: 9 / 60 (−1)

D. FREEDOM OF EXPRESSION AND BELIEF: 2 / 16 (−1)

D1. Are there free and independent media? 0 / 4

Media freedom is severely curtailed in Crimea. In addition to other restrictive Russian laws, a penal code provision prescribes imprisonment for public calls for action against Russia's territorial integrity, which has been interpreted to ban statements against the annexation, including in the media.

Journalists in Crimea risk harassment, arrest, and imprisonment for carrying out their work. In 2019, Crimean Tatar citizen journalist Nariman Memedeminov was handed a two-and-a-half-year prison sentence over YouTube videos he posted in 2013 about the activities of Hizb ut-Tahrir, a pan-Islamist movement that seeks to establish a caliphate but does not advocate violence to achieve it; the group operates legally in Ukraine but is designated as a terrorist group in Russia. Memedeminov's YouTube channel has more recently covered abuses against Crimean Tatars. Memedeminov was released from a Russian prison in September 2020. In December, a territorial court handed Lenur Islyamov, owner of Crimean Tatar television station ATR, a 19-year prison sentence in absentia on charges including "sabotage."

Independent and pro-Ukraine media outlets do not openly function on the peninsula. A 2015 reregistration process overseen by the Russian media and telecommunications regulator Roskomnadzor effectively reduced the number of media outlets in Crimea by more than 90 percent. The occupation authorities have cut Crimea off from access to Ukrainian television, and Crimean internet service providers must operate under draconian Russian media laws. Russian authorities continued to block a number of Ukrainian news sites, and interfered with Ukrainian radio signals by transmitting Russian programming on the same frequencies in 2020. The September 2020 OHCHR report noted continued interference with journalistic work by Russian law enforcement agents.

D2. Are individuals free to practice and express their religious faith or nonbelief in public and private? 0 / 4 (−1)

The occupation authorities forced religious organizations to reregister under new rules, sharply reducing the number of registered groups. All 22 Jehovah's Witnesses congregations were deregistered after the Russian Supreme Court ruled in 2017 that the group had violated laws against extremism. In March 2020, authorities began issuing prison sentences to adherents for their activity. That month, a Jehovah's Witness received a six-year sentence for attempting to organize a congregation. In September, the territory's supreme court upheld a conviction against another member for his religious activity and handed him a six-year sentence.

Mosques associated with Crimean Tatars have been denied permission to register, and Muslims have faced legal discrimination. At least 10 Crimean Tatars received prison sentences for their alleged Hizb ut-Tahrir membership in 2020. A December 2020 report from the Crimean Human Rights Group, a local nongovernmental organization (NGO), separately counted the detention of 69 individuals accused of membership in "extremist" Muslim organizations in the previous month.

Occupation authorities have confiscated numerous properties in Crimea from the Orthodox Church of Ukraine (OCU); in June 2019, a de facto court nullified a prominent Simferopol cathedral's lease with Ukrainian authorities; it was the last cathedral in Crimea to have maintained an affiliation with the Ukrainian church authorities. (Earlier that year, police detained Ukrainian archbishop Clement in Simferopol, but he was released a few hours later in the face of international pressure.) In July 2020, authorities ordered the demolition of a smaller OCU structure in Yevpatoria.

Score Change: The score declined from 1 to 0 due to escalating persecution of the Muslim, Ukrainian Orthodox, and Jehovah's Witness communities.

D3. Is there academic freedom, and is the educational system free from extensive political indoctrination? 1 / 4

Schools must use the Russian state curriculum. Schoolchildren in Crimea are exposed to Russian military propaganda. Some schoolchildren have also received basic military training in recent years. Instruction in the Ukrainian language has been almost completely eliminated. In a 2017 ruling, the International Court of Justice ordered Russia to ensure the availability of education in Ukrainian, but the authorities did not comply with this order. Access to education in the Crimean Tatar language has been more stable, declining only slightly since 2014.

D4. Are individuals free to express their personal views on political or other sensitive topics without fear of surveillance or retribution? 1 / 4

The FSB reportedly encourages residents to inform on individuals who express opposition to the annexation, and a climate of fear and intimidation seriously inhibits private discussion of political matters. Social media comments are reportedly monitored by authorities. The FSB frequently opens criminal cases against those who criticize the occupation and the oppression of Crimean Tatars.

E. ASSOCIATIONAL AND ORGANIZATIONAL RIGHTS: 1 / 12
E1. Is there freedom of assembly? 0 / 4

Freedom of assembly is severely restricted. Public events cannot proceed without permission from the authorities, and the Crimean government lists only 366 locations where they can be held. Permission to hold demonstrations is frequently denied, and when protests do proceed, participants are often arrested. Authorities have at times handed activists advance warning notes threatening them with administrative or criminal prosecution for holding events. A number of such warning notes were handed to Crimean Tatar activists before the anniversary of the Stalin-era mass deportations and Crimean Tatar Flag Day.

Authorities further restricted public gatherings in March 2020 in response to the COVID-19 pandemic, but were selective in enforcing those restrictions. A June military parade celebrating the anniversary of the Soviet Union's World War II victory proceeded without significant modification. In comparison, Venera Mustafayeva, the mother of imprisoned human rights activist Server Mustafayev, was cited for violating COVID-19-related restrictions when she held a one-person protest in the town of Bakhchysarai in September, and received a fine in December.

E2. Is there freedom for nongovernmental organizations, particularly those that are engaged in human rights- and governance-related work? 0 / 4

The de facto authorities, including the FSB, repress all independent political and civic organizations. NGOs are subject to harsh Russian laws that enable state interference and obstruct foreign funding. NGO leaders are regularly harassed and arrested for their activities.

In September 2020, Server Mustafayev, a coordinator for NGO Crimean Solidarity, was sentenced to 14 years' imprisonment in a Russian penal colony for his alleged ties to Hizb ut-Tahrir.

E3. Is there freedom for trade unions and similar professional or labor organizations? 1 / 4

Trade union rights are formally protected under Russian law but limited in practice. As in both Ukraine and Russia, employers are often able to engage in antiunion discrimination and violate collective-bargaining rights. Pro-Russian authorities have threatened to nationalize property owned by labor unions in Crimea.

F. RULE OF LAW: 0 / 16

F1. Is there an independent judiciary? 0 / 4

Under Moscow's rule, Crimea is subject to the Russian judicial system, which lacks independence and is effectively dominated by the executive branch. Russian laws bar dual citizenship for public officials, and Crimean judges were required to obtain Russian citizenship in order to retain their positions after the annexation.

In recent years, Russian judges have been transferred to from Russia to work in Crimea. These judges regularly hand down politically motivated judgements against residents who oppose the annexation.

F2. Does due process prevail in civil and criminal matters? 0 / 4

Russian authorities replaced Ukrainian laws with those of the Russian Federation. In December 2020, Russian president Putin enacted criminal code amendments allowing for harsher punishments against those accused of "violating" or "alienating" Russian territorial integrity.

Many detainees and prisoners are transferred from occupied Crimea to Russia, in violation of international law; the September 2020 OHCHR report noted that individuals accused of membership in banned religious groups, espionage, or subversion are often tried in Russian military courts.

Arbitrary arrests and detentions, harsh interrogation tactics, falsification of evidence, pressure to waive legal counsel, and unfair trials are common. The OHCHR report noted that prosecutors are heavily favored in military court proceedings, and separately noted that state-appointed defense lawyers participating in cases in Crimea were often ineffective.

F3. Is there protection from the illegitimate use of physical force and freedom from war and insurgencies? 0 / 4

The Russian occupation authorities commonly engage in torture of detainees and other abuses. The September 2020 OHCHR report noted accounts of "mock executions, beatings, electric shocks, and sexual violence." Victims of torture have no legal recourse, allowing security forces to act with impunity.

Detention centers are often overcrowded and unhygienic, and detainees do not consistently receive medical attention; Server Mustafayev and two codefendants did not receive timely medical treatment after contracting a respiratory infection in March 2020.

Ongoing Russian-Ukrainian tensions threaten Crimea's security. In November 2018, Russian forces attacked and seized three Ukrainian naval vessels in the Black Sea near Crimea as they attempted to enter the Sea of Azov through the Kerch Strait. Russia then took the 24 Ukrainian military personnel on board into custody; they were released in September 2019 as part of a prisoner swap. (The International Tribunal for the Law of the Sea had ordered their release that May.) Russia continues to conduct large-scale war exercises in Crimea.

F4. Do laws, policies, and practices guarantee equal treatment of various segments of the population? 0 / 4

In addition to official discrimination and harassment against ethnic Ukrainians and Crimean Tatars, women face de facto discrimination in the workplace, and the legal situation for LGBT+ people has worsened under the Russian occupation. After 2014, Crimea became subject to Russia's 2013 law banning dissemination of information that promotes "nontraditional sexual relationships," which tightly restricts the activities of LGBT+ people and organizations.

G. PERSONAL AUTONOMY AND INDIVIDUAL RIGHTS: 6 / 16

G1. Do individuals enjoy freedom of movement, including the ability to change their place of residence, employment, or education? 1 / 4

The occupation authorities have sought to compel Crimea's residents to accept Russian citizenship and surrender their Ukrainian passports. Those who fail to do so face the threat of dismissal from employment, loss of property rights, inability to travel to mainland Ukraine and elsewhere, and eventual deportation as foreigners.

G2. Are individuals able to exercise the right to own property and establish private businesses without undue interference from state or nonstate actors? 1 / 4

Property rights are poorly protected, and the Russian annexation has resulted in a redistribution of assets in favor of Russian and pro-Russian entities. After the occupation, the properties of many Ukrainian companies were seized by Russian authorities. In May 2018, a court in The Hague ordered Russia to pay $159 million to Ukrainian companies that had their property confiscated. The properties of Crimean Tatars who returned in the 1990s—after a Soviet-era mass deportation—and built houses without permits are also vulnerable to seizure by Russian authorities.

In March 2020, Putin signed an edict banning foreign individuals from owning coastal land in the territory; the edict also included new restrictions on property rights which do not apply for Crimean residents holding Russian passports.

G3. Do individuals enjoy personal social freedoms, including choice of marriage partner and size of family, protection from domestic violence, and control over appearance? 2 / 4

Domestic violence remains a serious problem in Crimea, and Russian laws do not offer strong protections. In 2017, Putin signed legislation that partly decriminalized domestic abuse in Russia, prescribing only small fines and short administrative detention for acts that do not cause serious injuries. Russian law does not recognize same-sex marriage or civil unions.

G4. Do individuals enjoy equality of opportunity and freedom from economic exploitation? 2 / 4

Economic opportunity has been limited since the occupation due to international sanctions, restrictions on trade via mainland Ukraine, and reliance on trade with Russia. Pollution problems in Crimea are associated with sulfur dioxide emitted from a chemical factory led to the evacuation of over 4,000 children in the town of Armyansk in 2018. Emissions were recorded again in 2019. Residents' access to goods and services remains constrained, and vital industries like tourism and agriculture have stagnated.

As in both Ukraine and Russia, migrant workers, women, and children are vulnerable to trafficking for the purposes of forced labor or sexual exploitation.

Eastern Donbas

Population: 1,800,000 (est.)
Freedom Status: Not Free

Note: *Freedom in the World* reports assess the level of political rights and civil liberties in a given geographical area, regardless of whether they are affected by the state, nonstate actors, or foreign powers. Disputed territories are sometimes assessed separately if they meet certain criteria, including boundaries that are sufficiently stable to allow year-on-year comparisons. For more information, see the report methodology and FAQ.

Overview: Eastern Donbas comprises the portions of Ukraine's Donetsk and Luhansk regions that have been occupied by Russian and Russian-backed separatist forces since 2014. It covers about a third of the two regions' territory; the current population cannot be determined with precision, but is likely not more than two million people. Local authority lies in the hands of the so-called People's Republics of Donetsk and Luhansk (DNR and LNR, respectively), which claim to be independent states but are not recognized by any country, including Russia. Both are entirely dependent on Moscow for financial and military support, and their leaders have openly proposed joining the Russian Federation. Politics within the territories are tightly controlled by the security services, leaving no room for meaningful opposition. Local media are also under severe restrictions, and social media users have been arrested for critical posts. The rule of law and civil liberties in general are not respected.

KEY DEVELOPMENTS IN 2020

- The coronavirus pandemic had significant detrimental effects on both public health and the area's struggling industrial economy, with reports of crowded hospital wards and shortages of medical staff and medical equipment, as well as recurring labor unrest over wage arrears. Separatist suppressed two miners' strikes in the spring with a mix of repression and financial concessions.
- Crossing points with government-controlled Ukraine were closed in mid-March and only partially reopened in the summer, making it impossible for many pensioners to pick up state payments in government-controlled areas. Bureaucratic and arbitrary movement restrictions also interfered with delivery of aid shipments from Russia, the United Nations, and the International Committee of the Red Cross (ICRC).
- The issuing of Russian passports to Ukrainian nationals residing in the occupied areas under simplified procedures resumed after a quarantine-related hiatus between March and July. As of mid-December, more than 350,000 locals are thought to

have received Russian citizenship, although the rate at which Russian documents are issued seems to be slowing.

- The number of local residents remained unclear, as separatist authorities did not release any results of a census carried out in October 2019.

POLITICAL RIGHTS: −1 / 40

A. ELECTORAL PROCESS: 0 / 12

A1. Was the current head of government or other chief national authority elected through free and fair elections? 0 / 4

Under the two separatist entities' constitutions, executive authority is exercised by a directly elected "head of the republic," who appoints a prime minister and cabinet with the consent of the legislature.

The winners of the deeply uncompetitive and fraudulent leadership elections in November 2018 remained in place. Both Donetsk leader Denis Pushilin and Luhansk leader Leonid Pasechnik are believed to be widely unpopular but sufficiently loyal to Moscow.

A2. Were the current national legislative representatives elected through free and fair elections? 0 / 4

The DNR and LNR constitutions call for "People's Councils" of 100 and 50 seats, respectively. Legislative elections in November 2018 were held under the same flawed conditions as the concurrent leadership elections, with no meaningful competition permitted. Both entities feature only two authorized political "movements." In the DNR, the ruling Donetsk Republic movement was credited with 72.5 percent of the vote, while Peace for Luhansk took 74.1 percent in the LNR. The remaining seats went to the two secondary movements, Free Donbas and the Luhansk Economic Union.

A3. Are the electoral laws and framework fair, and are they implemented impartially by the relevant election management bodies? 0 / 4

The separatist electoral authorities implemented their entities' laws and regulations arbitrarily in 2018, allegedly manipulating the declared election results and using technicalities to exclude challengers perceived as being able to consolidate enough support to defeat preferred candidates. For example, the DNR election commission approved each of the officially sanctioned candidates' lists of signatures, but it rejected the list submitted by separatist businessman Pavel Gubarev on the grounds that it contained fake signatures.

B. POLITICAL PLURALISM AND PARTICIPATION: 0 / 16

B1. Do the people have the right to organize in different political parties or other competitive political groupings of their choice, and is the system free of undue obstacles to the rise and fall of these competing parties or groupings? 0 / 4

The separatist entities feature political duopolies, with both officially sanctioned parties supporting roughly the same policy agenda. Any other political organizations, even if they are also pro-Russian in orientation, are effectively banned. The Communist Party, for instance, has been denied registration in occupied Donetsk.

B2. Is there a realistic opportunity for the opposition to increase its support or gain power through elections? 0 / 4

The run-up to the 2018 elections showed that meaningful competition, even within the pro-Russian separatist movement, is not tolerated. Authorities have made efforts to co-opt dissident separatists, and this continued in 2020. In May, Donetsk field commander turned opposition figure Alexander Khodakovsky was rehabilitated when separatist leader Pushilin honored fighters of his "Vostok" militia group. However, former separatist leader Pavel Gubarev remained sidelined.

B3. Are the people's political choices free from domination by forces that are external to the political sphere, or by political forces that employ extrapolitical means? 0 / 4

Russia has established a complex web of control over the "People's Republics" that affects all aspects of daily life, including political affairs. Local media, schools and universities, public services, and business structures are dominated by people loyal to the separatist leadership. While many of them are locals, some key positions are held by Russian citizens. Political control is ultimately enforced by the secretive "state security" ministries of the two entities, which are thought to be directed by Russia's Federal Security Service (FSB). The military formations known as "people's militias," which have tens of thousands of men under arms, are believed to be commanded by regular Russian military officers.

B4. Do various segments of the population (including ethnic, racial, religious, gender, LGBT+, and other relevant groups) have full political rights and electoral opportunities? 0 / 4

While the separatist constitutions guarantee equal rights regardless of ethnicity, race, or religious beliefs, in practice ethnic and religious groups not affiliated with the Russian government are excluded from politics, and no segment of society is able to organize independently to advocate for its interests in the political sphere. Professing pro-Ukrainian sentiment is outright dangerous.

C. FUNCTIONING OF GOVERNMENT: 0 / 12

C1. Do the freely elected head of government and national legislative representatives determine the policies of the government? 0 / 4

None of the separatist officials in Donbas are freely elected, and their de facto governments operate with extreme opacity, making it difficult to discern how much autonomy they have in practice vis-à-vis the Russian government. For example, DNR prime minister Alexander Ananchenko, appointed in 2018, was rarely seen in public until in November 2019. He and the key ministers for the Interior and State Security remain without photographs on the official government website.

Russian officials exert considerable influence on politics in the region. Vladislav Surkov, an adviser to the Russian government whose portfolio included oversight of the two entities, resigned in February 2020 and was replaced by Dmitry Kozak—a rival whose appointment as a deputy head of the Kremlin administration in January apparently triggered Surkov's resignation. Kozak is widely seen as a more pragmatic policymaker than Surkov, who tended to install loyalists into the regions' political positions. However, Russia's policies towards the Donbas did not change significantly after the transition.

C2. Are safeguards against official corruption strong and effective? 0 / 4

Corruption is thought to be widespread in occupied Donetsk and Luhansk, and there are no effective mechanisms in place to combat it. The assassination of Donetsk separatist leader Alexander Zakharchenko in 2018 and the ouster of Luhansk counterpart Igor Plotnitsky one year earlier have been explained by analysts as a reaction from Moscow to excessively corrupt practices among local elites. While separatist authorities regularly report arrests among customs and police officials, there is no evidence that corruption is effectively curtailed.

C3. Does the government operate with openness and transparency? 0 / 4

Lack of transparency is an overarching feature of both separatist regimes, and levels of secrecy increased over the past year. In early 2020, the DNR information ministry ended the tradition of interviews with separatist officials, which had previously allowed some limited insight into the separatist administration's functioning. Both republics continued the practice of communicating the removal of cabinet members by presenting successors without explanation or public discussion.

ADDITIONAL DISCRETIONARY POLITICAL RIGHTS QUESTION

Is the government or occupying power deliberately changing the ethnic composition of a country or territory so as to destroy a culture or tip the political balance in favor of another group? −1 / 0

Professing Ukrainian identity in the separatist-controlled areas of Donbas is considered dangerous, and most residents who identified as Ukrainian have left since 2014. Both entities abolished the official-language status to Ukrainian in the first half of 2020, making Russian the sole official language. School is conducted in Russian, and Ukrainian-language materials were eliminated from school curriculums at the start of the 2020–21 academic year.

CIVIL LIBERTIES: 4 / 60 (−1)

D. FREEDOM OF EXPRESSION AND BELIEF: 2 / 16

D1. Are there free and independent media? 0 / 4

No free and independent media have operated in the occupied Donbas since 2014. The local media landscape remains in the hands of "official" DNR and LNR broadcasters and websites. The relatively insignificant local print media have also been brought under control. Separatist outlets largely republish information and quotes from separatist and Russian officials. Reports about the armed conflict are exclusively based on statements from separatist militias, which blame the Ukrainian government side for every cease-fire violation. Coverage of government-controlled Ukraine is almost always negative, whereas reporting on the local economy is restricted to positive events like the opening of new coalfaces.

Pro-Ukrainian bloggers and journalists have been silenced by long prison sentences and eventual deportation to government-controlled Ukraine via prisoner exchanges. The most prominent example is that of Stanislav Aseyev, a freelancer for Radio Free Europe/Radio Liberty (RFE/RL); he was convicted of "organizing an extremist organization" and espionage, and handed a 15-year sentence before being returned to Ukrainian government-controlled territory in 2019, after two years in detention. Pro-Russian bloggers critical of the separatist leadership remain, but usually operate anonymously.

Ukrainian journalists generally do not enter the DNR and LNR for safety reasons, and most foreign media remain subject to extremely restrictive accreditation policies, with the result amounting to a virtual prohibition on reporting.

D2. Are individuals free to practice and express their religious faith or nonbelief in public and private? 1 / 4

Although both "People's Republics" guarantee freedom of religion in their constitutions, adherents of faiths that are not affiliated with the Russian Orthodox Church remain subject to persecution. The most severely affected are Jehovah's Witnesses, who in 2018 were banned completely as an extremist organization and had their properties seized. Also that year, a mandatory reregistration process left many groups without recognition, and raids or other pressure were directed at Baptists, members of the Orthodox Church of the Kyiv

Patriarchate, the Greek Catholic Church, and some Muslim communities. Most members of religious minority groups, including Roman Catholics and Jews, are thought to have left the separatist-held areas since 2014.

D3. Is there academic freedom, and is the educational system free from extensive political indoctrination? 0 / 4

Local universities were brought under separatist control in 2014. Some, like Donetsk National University, split into two rival institutions, with one established in government-controlled territory and the other run by separatist authorities at the old location. Political indoctrination remains rampant in the occupied areas; high schools were forced to switch to Russian standards in September 2020, having previously introduced new curricula with revised history lessons and reduced Ukrainian-language instruction.

Political indoctrination is rampant, especially for the younger generation. Both republics have set up militarized youth organizations for this purpose. Membership in the "Young Guards–Yunarmia" is open to children as young as eight years old, prompting allegations of a children's army.

D4. Are individuals free to express their personal views on political or other sensitive topics without fear of surveillance or retribution? 1 / 4

Any public expression of criticism is highly risky, and private citizens' online activities are monitored. In December 2020, for example, Donetsk-based pro-Russian commentator Roman Manekin was detained and accused of cooperating with Ukrainian intelligence on the basis of both public and private Facebook exchanges. He has been detained at least twice before, in 2017 and 2018, for criticizing the DNR leadership on social media.

Testimony from former prisoners about abuse in custody also serves to deter free expression.

E. ASSOCIATIONAL AND ORGANIZATIONAL RIGHTS: 0 / 12

E1. Is there freedom of assembly? 0 / 4

No significant protests have been held in the separatist-held areas since 2014, when most pro-Ukrainian activists fled. Even gatherings of nationalists who favor integration with Russia are not tolerated if they are critical of separatist authorities. In the spring of 2020, relatives and colleagues of striking coal miners held unauthorized rallies in support of them in the Luhansk region. The protests ebbed after the miners were paid some of their wages and members of the separatist security ministry detained some protesters; there were reports that some miners were tortured while in detention, or that their family members were arbitrarily detained.

E2. Is there freedom for nongovernmental organizations, particularly those that are engaged in human rights- and governance-related work? 0 / 4

Independent nongovernmental organizations (NGOs) are not permitted to operate. The last independent NGO in the separatist-held areas, the Responsible Citizens volunteer group, stopped functioning in 2016 when several of its leaders were forcibly deported to government-controlled Ukraine. Foreign aid organizations like the Czech group People in Need were also expelled. The only remaining international organizations operating in the area are the ICRC, some UN agencies, and the Organization for Security and Co-operation in Europe (OSCE).

E3. Is there freedom for trade unions and similar professional or labor organizations? 0 / 4

The DNR and LNR have official trade union federations, and both are headed by separatist lawmakers who defer to the local leadership. The officially sanctioned unions' purpose is to rally workers' support for separatist authorities, rather than to defend their labor rights. In 2020, for example, LNR miners' union leaders supported the "restructuring" of 56 mines, a process that came with significant wage and job losses.

F. RULE OF LAW: 0 / 16

F1. Is there an independent judiciary? 0 / 4

There are no signs of judicial independence in the two separatist entities. Courts continued to hand down lengthy prison sentences against alleged Ukrainian agents and other perceived enemies of the local authorities, validating spurious charges regardless of the evidence. The work of the judiciary is entirely opaque, and outside observers are not known to have attended court hearings.

F2. Does due process prevail in civil and criminal matters? 0 / 4

Basic due process guarantees are not observed by separatist authorities or affiliated armed groups. Arbitrary arrests and detentions remain common, and interrogators have reportedly used force and torture to extract confessions. The United Nations' Human Rights Monitoring Mission in Ukraine said in a report released in September 2020 that interviews with released prisoners "confirmed patterns of torture and ill-treatment."

F3. Is there protection from the illegitimate use of physical force and freedom from war and insurgencies? 0 / 4

Combat between Russian-backed separatist forces and the Ukrainian military continued in the first half of 2020, frequently endangering civilians. The second half of the year was much calmer, as a renewed ceasefire, brokered in July, continued to hold. More than 13,000 people have been killed since the conflict began in April 2014, including more than 3,300 civilians, according to the Office of the UN High Commissioner for Human Rights (OHCHR). The OHCHR has condemned the lack of institutional mechanisms to prevent and punish enforced disappearances, which have been reported during the conflict, particularly in its early years.

There have been numerous reports of abuse, sexual violence, and torture in separatist prisons and detention centers. The self-proclaimed state security ministries of both entities regularly publish videos in which detainees confess to spying and other forms of subversive activity while showing signs of physical abuse or severe psychological pressure.

F4. Do laws, policies, and practices guarantee equal treatment of various segments of the population? 0 / 4

The deeply flawed legal system operating in the occupied regions offers little recourse for women facing gender-based discrimination, and the basic rights of LGBT+ people are not recognized. In 2018, two Russian transgender activists traveled to Donetsk with the aim of carrying out an art performance in support of transgender rights. They were quickly arrested and expelled.

In addition to the prevailing hostility toward the Ukrainian ethnic identity, there are no provisions to protect the separatist-held areas' other ethnic minority groups—such as Greeks, Azerbaijanis, and Armenians—from discrimination.

G. PERSONAL AUTONOMY AND INDIVIDUAL RIGHTS: 3 / 16 (−1)

G1. Do individuals enjoy freedom of movement, including the ability to change their place of residence, employment, or education? 0 / 4 (−1)

Travel between the separatist-held areas and government-controlled Ukraine was already severely restricted, and in response to the COVID-19 pandemic, harsh, excessively bureaucratic, and frequently arbitrary additional restrictions were implemented. All five crossing points between separatist and government-held areas were closed between late March and mid-June, and thereafter only two reopened. Restrictions in the DNR were more severe than in the LHR, allowing entry only for previously approved individuals, who were then forced to undergo two weeks of "observation" in a hospital. Crossings between the two territories themselves did not reopen at all. Most of those affected by the restrictions were the more than one million old-age pensioners, who could no longer travel to government-controlled Ukraine to pick up state payments, receive health care, or conduct other important personal business. Travel to and from Russia was less impeded, but senior separatist officials must still inform their leaders before leaving the territories.

The Russian government's distributing of Russian passports to residents of the occupied territories continued in 2020, and the separatists claimed in December that more than 350,000 had been issued. At least 1.5 million of the areas' 3.6 million prewar residents are believed to have left their homes since 2014, suggesting that no more than 14 percent have accepted Russian passports. However, the intensifying campaign against the Ukrainian language and Ukrainian identity has raised fears that Ukrainian passport holders will face increasing difficulties in the future.

Score Change: The score declined from 1 to 0 because COVID-19-related restrictions on movement were selectively implemented to limit travel to and from government-controlled parts of Ukraine.

G2. Are individuals able to exercise the right to own property and establish private businesses without undue interference from state or nonstate actors? 0 / 4

The separatists continued to ignore property rights. In the LNR, the de facto authorities regrouped coal mines into a state-run holding called Vostok-Ugol, including enterprises previously nationalized by separatist authorities under the pretext of "external administration." The main external administrator in both "republics" is a secretive holding firm with Russian management, reportedly registered in the Russian-occupied Georgian region of South Ossetia. There have been numerous reports of other property seizures, including the expropriation of apartments whose lawful owners have fled.

G3. Do individuals enjoy personal social freedoms, including choice of marriage partner and size of family, protection from domestic violence, and control over appearance? 2 / 4

Domestic violence is a serious problem, and both separatist entities have taken nominal steps to improve the protection of women and children. However, the loss of Ukrainian government and NGO services has negatively affected conditions for victims. Neither separatist entity recognizes same-sex marriage.

G4. Do individuals enjoy equality of opportunity and freedom from economic exploitation? 1 / 4

Economic opportunity is impaired by the ongoing conflict, trade barriers with government-controlled Ukraine, international sanctions, and the concentration of wealth and resources in the hands of Russian- and separatist-affiliated elites. Many residents are dependent on humanitarian assistance. Exploitative working conditions, including low or unpaid wages, have been reported even by separatist-controlled media. Separatist forces have allegedly trained and enlisted minors for participation in armed conflict.

Gaza Strip

Population: 1,900,000
Freedom Status: Not Free

Note: Prior to its 2011 edition, *Freedom in the World* featured one report for Israeli-occupied portions of the West Bank and Gaza Strip and another for Palestinian-administered portions. *Freedom in the World* reports assess the level of political rights and civil liberties in a given geographical area, regardless of whether they are affected by the state, nonstate actors, or foreign powers. Disputed territories are sometimes assessed separately if they meet certain criteria, including boundaries that are sufficiently stable to allow year-on-year comparisons. For more information, see the report methodology and FAQ.

Overview: The political rights and civil liberties of Gaza Strip residents are severely constrained. Israel's de facto blockade of the territory, periodic military incursions, and rule-of-law violations have imposed serious hardship on the civilian population, as has Egypt's tight control over the southern border. The Islamist political and militant group Hamas gained control of Gaza in 2007, following its victory in the preceding year's legislative elections and a subsequent conflict with Fatah, the ruling party in the West Bank. The subsequent schism between Hamas and the Fatah-led Palestinian Authority (PA) has contributed to legal confusion and repeated postponement of elections, which have not been held in Gaza since 2006.

KEY DEVELOPMENTS IN 2020

- Hamas and Fatah launched a new round of talks aimed at reconciling the two factions in February. In September, the two participants announced a deal to hold new legislative and presidential elections, though details on electoral management remained pending and the polls were ultimately not held by year's end.
- Israel launched a monthlong air campaign against sites in Gaza in early August, in response to a rocket attack launched from the territory. Israeli authorities tightened restrictions on the flow of materials, including fuel and construction materials, into Gaza that month, though the additional restrictions were loosened by early September. Further exchanges of fire were reported in mid-September and late October.
- Gazans faced COVID-19-related restrictions in March, when access to the Erez and Rafah crossings were severely reduced and when Gazan authorities introduced restrictions on gatherings and nonessential businesses that lasted through May. Gazan authorities initiated a lockdown and movement restrictions in the territory in August after community spread was detected; lockdown and curfew measures were reintroduced in November as the pandemic continued. At year's end, the UN Office for the Coordination of Humanitarian Affairs (UNOCHA) counted nearly 40,000 COVID-19 cases and 356 deaths.

POLITICAL RIGHTS: 3 / 40

A. ELECTORAL PROCESS: 0 / 12

A1. Was the current head of government or other chief national authority elected through free and fair elections? 0 / 4

The PA has not held a presidential election since 2005, when the Fatah faction's Mahmoud Abbas won with 62 percent of the vote. Following its win in 2006 legislative elections and a violent rift with Fatah and the West Bank–based PA in 2007, Hamas seized control of the Gaza Strip. Abbas's four-year electoral mandate expired in 2009, though he has continued to govern in the West Bank.

Under PA laws, the prime minister is nominated by the president and requires the support of the Palestinian Legislative Council (PLC). Hamas leader Ismail Haniya was nominated and sworn in as prime minister following the 2006 elections, and again in 2007 as part of a short-lived unity government, but he was dismissed by President Abbas after the Fatah-Hamas conflict that year. Hamas did not recognize the dismissal. Because repeated attempts to form new PA unity governments have failed, Hamas has exercised de facto executive authority in the Gaza Strip since 2007. The de facto head of government, Yahya Sinwar, was chosen in a closed election by Hamas members in 2017.

In October 2017, Hamas and Fatah signed a reconciliation agreement brokered by Egypt to work toward a consensus government and new elections, though its implementation subsequently stalled. In late September 2020, Fatah and Hamas agreed to hold presidential and parliamentary elections within six months, though those polls were ultimately not held by year's end.

A2. Were the current national legislative representatives elected through free and fair elections? 0 / 4

The PA has not held elections for the 132-seat PLC since 2006, when Hamas won 74 seats and Fatah took 45. The subsequent Fatah-Hamas schism and Israel's detention of many lawmakers left the full PLC unable to function, and the body's electoral mandate expired in 2010. Nonetheless, a Hamas-led rump legislature continued to operate in the Gaza Strip. In 2018, President Abbas ordered the formal dissolution of the PLC, backed by a Supreme Constitutional Court ruling that also called for legislative elections within six months. Hamas rejected the decision. In September 2020, Hamas and Fatah agreed to schedule parliamentary elections, though polls were not held by year's end.

A3. Are the electoral laws and framework fair, and are they implemented impartially by the relevant election management bodies? 0 / 4

No open elections for any office have been held in Gaza since 2006. Decisions about the conduct of elections are highly politicized. For example, Hamas refused to participate in the 2017 PA municipal elections, which had been postponed from the previous year amid disputes between Hamas and Fatah over candidate lists. Following a 2016 PA court ruling to exclude the Gaza Strip from the elections, ostensibly due to concerns about judicial oversight, no agreement could be reached on how to arrange balloting in Gaza. While Fatah and Hamas reached an initial September 2020 agreement to hold elections, a specific electoral-management plan was not finalized by year's end.

B. POLITICAL PLURALISM AND PARTICIPATION: 2 / 16

B1. Do the people have the right to organize in different political parties or other competitive political groupings of their choice, and is the system free of undue obstacles to the rise and fall of these competing parties or groupings? 1 / 4

Since 2007, Gaza has functioned as a de facto one-party state under Hamas rule, although smaller parties—including Islamic Jihad, the Popular Front for the Liberation of Palestine (PFLP), the Democratic Front for the Liberation of Palestine (DFLP), and a faction of Fatah that opposes President Abbas—are tolerated to varying degrees. Some of these groups have their own media outlets and hold rallies and gatherings. However, those affiliated with President Abbas and his supporters in Fatah are subject to persecution.

B2. Is there a realistic opportunity for the opposition to increase its support or gain power through elections? 0 / 4

The postponement of elections has prevented any opportunities for a change in the political status quo. The formation of an interim consensus government between Hamas and Fatah, or at least a reconciliation on issues of administration, is widely seen as a necessary precursor to the holding of new elections. Reconciliation efforts have previously foundered due to disputes about control of Gaza's internal security, border crossings, and payment of salaries. Hamas and Fatah launched a new round of talks in February 2020, which were ongoing at year's end.

B3. Are the people's political choices free from domination by forces that are external to the political sphere, or by political forces that employ extrapolitical means? 0 / 4

Israel's ongoing blockade of Gaza, which comprises strict limits on the movement of goods and people in and out of the territory, and the ongoing Hamas-Fatah rift hamper the development of normal civilian political competition. Armed groups, including the Israeli military and militias such as those affiliated with Hamas and Islamic Jihad, exercise disproportionate control over the day-to-day lives of Palestinians in Gaza and leave them with virtually no ability to shape policies that affect them.

B4. Do various segments of the population (including ethnic, racial, religious, gender, LGBT+, and other relevant groups) have full political rights and electoral opportunities? 1 / 4

Hamas makes little effort to address the rights of marginalized groups within Gazan society. Women enjoy formal political equality under PA laws, and some women won seats in the PLC in 2006. However, women are mostly excluded from leadership positions in Hamas and absent from public political events in practice. Gazan women do actively participate in civil society gatherings that touch on political issues. The political interests of LGBT+ people, who face widespread discrimination in Gaza, are not represented by those in power.

C. FUNCTIONING OF GOVERNMENT: 1 / 12

C1. Do the freely elected head of government and national legislative representatives determine the policies of the government? 0 / 4

The expiration of the presidential and parliamentary terms has left Gaza's authorities with no electoral mandate. In 2020, Hamas continued to govern Gaza unilaterally, assigning responsibilities to its own officials as the reconciliation deal with Fatah remained unfulfilled.

The ability of Palestinian officials to make and implement policy in Gaza is severely circumscribed by Israeli and Egyptian border controls, Israeli military actions, and the ongoing schism with the PA in the West Bank. Israel maintains a heavy security presence around Gaza's land and sea perimeters, using live fire to keep anyone from entering buffer zones near these boundaries, which further reduces local control over the territory.

C2. Are safeguards against official corruption strong and effective? 1 / 4

Hamas has been accused of corruption in public service delivery and aid distribution, which is crucial to daily life in Gaza given that over 80 percent of the population depends on international assistance due to the blockade. In its October 2020 report, the Coalition for Accountability and Integrity (AMAN) noted that the continuing Fatah-Hamas schism, issues regarding judicial integrity, and specific issues regarding the procurement process have impeded the prosecution of corruption cases.

C3. Does the government operate with openness and transparency? 0 / 4

The Hamas-controlled government has no effective or independent mechanisms for ensuring transparency in its funding, procurements, or operations. AMAN's October 2020 report noted that political decision-making remained out of public view.

CIVIL LIBERTIES: 8 / 60
D. FREEDOM OF EXPRESSION AND BELIEF: 4 / 16
D1. Are there free and independent media? 0 / 4

The media are not free in Gaza. West Bank–based newspapers have been permitted in the territory since 2014, and a number of political factions have their own media outlets. However, Gazan journalists and bloggers continue to face repression from the Hamas government's internal security apparatus and from Israeli forces. In a 2018 report, Human Rights Watch (HRW) detailed a pattern of arrests, interrogations, and in some cases beatings and torture of journalists in Gaza.

While press-freedom violations declined in 2020, partially due to the suspension of Great March of Return events, Gazan authorities continued to target journalists during the year. In late March, police physically attacked journalist Yasser Abu Athara as he filmed a COVID-19-related protest, seizing his mobile phone. Cartoonist Ismael el-Bozom was arrested twice in late March for producing material that criticized Hamas, but was ultimately released without charge due to a COVID-19-related mitigation policy. El-Bozom reported he was beaten by interrogators after his first arrest. In July, media outlets al-Arabiya and al-Hadath were banned from operating in Gaza after they reported on a Hamas officer's apparent defection to Israel; Hamas branded the report as "fake news."

D2. Are individuals free to practice and express their religious faith or nonbelief in public and private? 1 / 4

Freedom of religion is restricted. The PA Basic Law declares Islam to be the official religion of Palestine and states that "respect and sanctity of all other heavenly religions (Judaism and Christianity) shall be maintained." Blasphemy is a criminal offense. Hamas authorities have enforced conservative Sunni Islamic practices and attempted to exert political control over mosques. However, they have not enforced prayers in schools or compelled women to wear hijab in Gaza's main urban areas to the extent that they did in the early years of Hamas control.

D3. Is there academic freedom, and is the educational system free from extensive political indoctrination? 1 / 4

Primary and secondary schools in the Gaza Strip are run by Hamas, the UN Relief and Works Agency (UNRWA), or private entities. In the Hamas-run Islamic University, people are separated by gender, and women are obliged to cover their hair. Hamas intervenes in the schools under its control to uphold its views on Islamic identity and morality. It does not intervene extensively in private universities, but Hamas-led police have violently suppressed student demonstrations. Some Gazan academics are believed to practice self-censorship. Israeli and Egyptian restrictions on trade and travel limit access to educational materials and academic exchanges.

D4. Are individuals free to express their personal views on political or other sensitive topics without fear of surveillance or retribution? 2 / 4

Intimidation by Hamas militants and other armed groups has some effect on personal expression and private discussion in Gaza, and the authorities monitor social media for critical content. A 2018 HRW report documented a number of incidents in which Hamas intimidated, detained, or abused individuals in response to their social media activity or attendance at political events, most notably those perceived to be supportive of Fatah or opposed to the Hamas government. For example, individuals have been detained and questioned about social media posts that were critical of the Hamas leadership and its handling of electricity shortages.

E. ASSOCIATIONAL AND ORGANIZATIONAL RIGHTS: 2 / 12

E1. Is there freedom of assembly? 0 / 4

Israeli forces use violent and sometimes lethal methods to disperse demonstrations near the de facto border. The Great March of Return began in 2018 as a weekly demonstration to demand the return of Palestinian refugees to what is now Israel. Israeli forces positioned along the border regularly fired on demonstrators with live ammunition, resulting in scores of fatalities. According to the UN Office for the Coordination of Humanitarian Affairs (UN-OCHA), more than 210 people were killed and some 36,000 injured by the end of 2019, with many wounded by shrapnel, rubber-coated bullets, or direct hits from tear-gas canisters in addition to live gunfire. Organizers effectively halted these protests in March 2020 due to the COVID-19 pandemic.

Hamas also significantly restricts freedom of assembly, with security forces violently dispersing unapproved public gatherings. In response to 2019 protests against the economic situation under the slogan We Want to Live, Hamas security forces arrested more than 1,000 demonstrators and allegedly beat some participants in a particularly harsh crackdown. We Want to Live demonstrations were not held in 2020.

E2. Is there freedom for nongovernmental organizations, particularly those that are engaged in human rights- and governance-related work? 1 / 4

There is a broad range of Palestinian nongovernmental organizations (NGOs) and civic groups, and Hamas operates a large social-services network. However, Hamas has restricted the activities of organizations that do not submit to its regulations, and many civic associations have been shut down for political reasons since the 2007 PA split. Aid and reconstruction efforts by NGOs after the 2014 conflict with Israel have been held up in part by disagreements over international and PA access to the territory and control over border crossings. The Israeli government also imposes restrictions on access to Gaza for human rights researchers and NGO staff.

E3. Is there freedom for trade unions and similar professional or labor organizations? 1 / 4

The Fatah-aligned Palestinian General Federation of Trade Unions, the largest union body in the territories, has seen its operations curtailed in Gaza. Workers have little leverage in labor disputes due to the dire economic situation, extremely high unemployment, and the dysfunctional court system, which impedes enforcement of labor protections.

Hamas sometimes intervenes in labor union elections or in the activities of professional associations that are linked to Fatah. Hamas has established its own, parallel professional associations to compete with existing organizations that are more strongly affiliated with Fatah and rival groups. The civil servants' union for the Hamas-controlled public sector occasionally holds rallies and strikes.

F. RULE OF LAW: 0 / 16

F1. Is there an independent judiciary? 0 / 4

Hamas maintains an ad hoc judicial system that is separate from the PA structures headquartered in the West Bank, which do not operate in Gaza. The system is subject to political control, and Palestinian judges lack proper training and experience. There are also reportedly long delays in hearing cases related to a range of issues, including land disputes and personal status matters.

F2. Does due process prevail in civil and criminal matters? 0 / 4

Hamas security forces and militants regularly carry out arbitrary arrests and detentions. The court system overseen by Hamas generally fails to ensure due process, and in some cases civilians are subject to trial by special military courts.

Some 254 Palestinian security detainees and prisoners from Gaza were held in Israeli prisons as of the end of September 2020, according to Israeli NGO B'Tselem, which has noted that transporting prisoners outside of occupied territory is a breach of international law. Israeli military courts, which handle the cases of such detainees, lack the full due process guarantees of civilian courts.

F3. Is there protection from the illegitimate use of physical force and freedom from war and insurgencies? 0 / 4

The number of Palestinians in Gaza killed by Israeli forces fell in 2020. UNOCHA counted 3 conflict-related fatalities and 56 injuries in the territory that year, while B'Tselem separately counted a total of 105 deaths caused by Israeli forces in 2019. However, fighting between Hamas and Israel did occur during the year. In late January 2020, the Israeli military reported that mortar shells were fired from Gaza but reported no deaths. Israel attacked Hamas targets in the territory in response. Israeli forces launched a monthlong air campaign in early August, bombing targets in response to a rocket attack launched in Gaza. Exchanges of fire were again reported in mid-September and late October.

Those fishing in the waters off of Gaza or were otherwise close to the de facto border with Israel were also at risk during 2020. UNOCHA counted a monthly average of 74 shooting incidents involving Israeli forces and Palestinians in Gazan waters or near the border during the first nine months of the year.

Hamas-led authorities have applied the death penalty without due process or adequate opportunity for appeals and without the legally required approval from the PA president. Sixteen death sentences were issued through mid-December 2020, though no executions were carried out.

F4. Do laws, policies, and practices guarantee equal treatment of various segments of the population? 0 / 4

The legal system operating in Gaza offers few protections against harassment and discrimination for women and other vulnerable groups, including LGBT+ people. Laws dating to the British Mandate era authorize up to 10 years' imprisonment for sexual acts between men.

Gazan residents living with disabilities face significant barriers, with a December 2020 HRW report noting pervasive stigma against this population. The report noted that people with disabilities were especially affected by Israeli restrictions on imports, impeding their ability to access medical equipment. In addition, little regulation is dedicated to the needs of this group.

G. PERSONAL AUTONOMY AND INDIVIDUAL RIGHTS: 2 / 16

G1. Do individuals enjoy freedom of movement, including the ability to change their place of residence, employment, or education? 0 / 4

Freedom of movement for Gaza residents is severely limited. Israel and Egypt exercise tight control over border areas, and Hamas imposes its own restrictions on travel. Israel often denies Gaza residents permits to travel outside of the territory on security grounds, permitting only certain medical patients and other individuals to leave. University students have difficulty acquiring the necessary permits to leave the territory to study abroad. Hamas allowed PA officials to deploy to Gaza's border crossings in 2017, but this did not lead to any practical changes in freedom of movement for Gazans. Corruption and the use of bribes at crossing points is common.

Beginning in mid-2018, Egypt partially reduced its restrictions on the Rafah crossing. However, it is still difficult for many Palestinians to receive appropriate permits from Hamas and the Egyptian government, with wealthier individuals paying brokers to arrange "expedited" processing. The Rafah crossing between Gaza and Egypt was mostly closed to passengers in 2020 due to COVID-19-related restrictions, however; Palestinians were only been able to exit through Rafah four times in 2020.

While Israeli policies governing the Erez crossing were loosened in 2019, travel through the crossing was restricted in 2020 when the Israeli government instituted COVID-19 measures. In a December update, UNOCHA reported that the Erez crossing was primarily accessible for medical patients and exceptional cases, and that 250 people entered the territory through the crossing per week.

COVID-19 also impacted Gazans living in the territory, with territorial authorities introducing restrictions between March and May. A lockdown was declared in August after community spread was detected in Gaza, though it expired at the end of the month. Movement restrictions were introduced in several towns in September as viral spread continued. New lockdown and curfew measures were introduced in November, and remained in force within the territory at year's end.

The Israeli army prevents Palestinians from approaching the Israel-Gaza border fence and a surrounding "buffer zone" extending up to 300 meters into the territory, despite the border not being accepted or recognized by the international community or any key actors. While several hundred Palestinians were shot while approaching the buffer zone during Great March of Return protests in 2018 and 2019, B'Tselem counted one death in 2020, due to the protests' COVID-19-related suspension.

Israel periodically restricts or closes Gaza's offshore fishing zone. In February 2020, Israel temporarily reduced the permitted fishing zone from 15 to 10 nautical miles offshore. In August, it temporarily shut the zone altogether as part of its response to attacks originating in Gaza.

Gazan Christians were unable to travel to the West Bank town of Bethlehem for the Christmas holiday due in part to Israeli COVID-19 restrictions.

G2. Are individuals able to exercise the right to own property and establish private businesses without undue interference from state or nonstate actors? 1 / 4

While Gaza residents are able to own property and engage in business activity, their rights have been seriously undermined by the effects of periodic conflicts between Hamas and Israel, among other factors. Only a fraction of the homes damaged or destroyed during the 2014 conflict had been reconstructed by the end of 2019, and approximately 16,500 people remained in temporary housing by the middle of that year. Impediments to private enterprise in Gaza include persistent Israeli bans on imports of many raw materials. While there were indications that export restrictions on certain food products and import restrictions on other items loosened at the end of 2019, the importation of many goods was restricted by Israel in August 2020. These additional restrictions were again loosened by September.

G3. Do individuals enjoy personal social freedoms, including choice of marriage partner and size of family, protection from domestic violence, and control over appearance? 1 / 4

Palestinian laws and societal norms, derived in part from Sharia (Islamic law), put women at a disadvantage in matters such as marriage and divorce. Hamas has enforced restrictions on personal attire and behavior it deems immoral, though enforcement has relaxed in recent years.

So-called honor killings reportedly continue to occur, though information on the situation in Gaza is limited. In 2019, the #MeTooGaza hashtag was launched on social media, encouraging Palestinian women to share their own experiences with abuse and harassment.

Domestic violence is common in Gaza, with nearly four in ten Gazan women facing such violence according a 2019 PA survey. Rape and domestic violence go underreported and are historically unpunished, as authorities are allegedly reluctant to pursue such cases. In 2019, the PA began drafting legislation that would establish a minimum age for marriage, institute harsher punishments towards those who engage in domestic violence, and improve protections for domestic-violence survivors. In September 2020, Hamas called on the PA to revoke the law until a new PLC was seated.

G4. Do individuals enjoy equality of opportunity and freedom from economic exploitation? 0 / 4

The blockade of the Gaza Strip's land borders and coastline has greatly reduced economic opportunity in the territory. Nearly half of Gaza's labor force was unemployed in the second quarter of 2020. Israel's intermittent restrictions on the entry of construction materials have hampered the economy. Israeli forces also prevent farming near the border fence and limit Gazan fishermen's access to coastal waters. Hamas has imposed price controls that may further dampen economic activity.

Inconsistent access to fuel imports and electricity due to Israeli, PA, and Egyptian policies hinders all forms of development in the territory, including domestic desalination that could improve access to clean water. In 2018, Israel lifted some fuel-transfer restrictions, and Qatar began financing fuel and other aid to improve electricity generation and overall economic conditions. However, Israel temporarily suspended fuel deliveries in 2019 and again in August 2020, in response to attacks originating from the territory. The August restriction on imports, which also included construction materials and other essential goods, was loosened by September.

PA officials have little ability to enforce legal protections against exploitative labor conditions in Gaza, and most private-sector wage earners receive less than the legal minimum, which is itself lower than the poverty threshold.

Hong Kong

Population: 7,500,000
Freedom Status: Partly Free

Note: *Freedom in the World* reports assess the level of political rights and civil liberties in a given geographical area, regardless of whether they are affected by the state, nonstate actors, or foreign powers. Territories are sometimes assessed separately if they meet certain criteria, including boundaries that are sufficiently stable to allow year-on-year comparisons. For more information, see the report methodology and FAQ.

Overview: The people of Hong Kong, a special administrative region of China, have traditionally enjoyed substantial civil liberties and the rule of law under their local constitution, the Basic Law. However, the chief executive and about half of the Legislative Council (Legco) are chosen through indirect electoral systems that favor pro-Beijing interests, and the territory's freedoms and autonomy have been sharply reduced in recent years amid growing political intervention from the mainland.

KEY DEVELOPMENTS IN 2020

- A prodemocracy protest movement that arose in 2019 continued into the new year, with participants calling for the resignation of Chief Executive Carrie Lam, direct elections for her post and all seats in the Legco, the release and exoneration of detained protesters and activists, and an independent inquiry into police conduct, among other priorities. The mass protests eased for a time as the COVID-19 pandemic prompted social-distancing rules and restrictions on movement, though demonstrations and activism continued on a smaller scale.
- In April, police arrested 15 leading figures in the democracy movement, including current and former legislators, and charged them with participation in unlawful assemblies in connection with the 2019 protests.
- At the end of June, the Standing Committee of China's National People's Congress (NPC) abruptly passed a new National Security Law (NSL) for Hong Kong, with immediate effect and no public consultation. The measure created broadly worded new offenses—separatism, subversion of state power, terrorism, and collusion with foreign states—and asserted universal jurisdiction. It also allowed for the transfer of cases to mainland China for trial, established a secretive new security apparatus to enforce its provisions, and provided for closed trials by hand-picked judges. The law was used for the rest of the year to arrest and charge prominent media figures, politicians, and activists associated with the protest movement.
- In July, prodemocracy parties held primary elections ahead of Legco elections scheduled for September, but Lam invoked emergency powers two weeks later to postpone the Legco elections by a year, citing a rise in COVID-19 infections. The government also launched an investigation into whether the primary voting violated the NSL.
- In November, Legco members from the prodemocracy opposition resigned en masse after four of their colleagues were disqualified and unseated by the Hong Kong government under a new directive from the NPC in Beijing.

POLITICAL RIGHTS: 15 / 40 (−1)

A. ELECTORAL PROCESS: 2 / 12

A1. Was the current head of government or other chief national authority elected through free and fair elections? 0 / 4

The chief executive, who serves a five-year term, is chosen by a 1,200-member election committee. Some 200,000 "functional constituency" voters—representatives of elite business and social sectors, many with close Beijing ties—elect 900 of the committee's members, and the remaining 300 consist of Legco members, Hong Kong delegates to China's NPC, religious representatives, and Hong Kong members of the Chinese People's Political Consultative Conference (CPPCC), a Chinese government advisory body.

In 2017, Carrie Lam, a former deputy to outgoing chief executive Leung Chun-ying and Beijing's favored candidate, was chosen as Hong Kong's fourth—and first woman—chief executive, with 777 election committee votes. Her main opponent, former financial secretary John Tsang, received just 365 votes despite drawing far more support than Lam in public opinion polls. As in the past, the selection process featured reports of heavy lobbying by central government representatives.

A2. Were the current national legislative representatives elected through free and fair elections? 1 / 4

Of the Legco's 70 seats, 30 are elected by functional constituency voters, 35 are chosen through direct elections in five geographical constituencies, and the remaining five are directly elected after nominations by Hong Kong's 18 district councils from among their own members. Members serve four-year terms.

In the September 2016 elections, a growing movement emphasizing localism and self-determination emerged to compete with existing pro-Beijing and prodemocracy camps. Candidates from this movement, which grew out of the 2014 Umbrella Movement, captured six seats. Other prodemocracy parties took 23 seats, while pro-Beijing parties won 40; an independent took the remaining seat.

Authorities responded to the new opposition dynamic by tightening qualification rules, forcing out lawmakers, and making it increasingly difficult for localist and prodemocracy candidates to win office. In October 2016, after some localist and prodemocracy Legco members altered their oaths of office as a form of protest, the oaths of two of them were rejected. The NPC in Beijing issued an unusual Basic Law interpretation soon afterward, requiring oaths to be taken "sincerely and solemnly," and the courts then upheld the two disqualifications. In July 2017, the government received court approval to remove four other Legco members who made political statements during their 2016 swearing-in ceremonies.

Following months of dramatic prodemocracy protests in 2019, prodemocracy candidates won a record-breaking 389 of 452 elected seats in district council elections that November, with pro-Beijing candidates obtaining just 58 seats, down from 300 in the previous elections. The polls featured the highest voter turnout since Hong Kong began holding district council elections, and were seen as a ringing endorsement of the protest movement. Prodemocracy parties were left in control of 17 of the 18 district councils. The elections were, however, marred by an Electoral Affairs Commission (EAC) decision to disqualify activist Joshua Wong on the grounds that "advocating or promoting 'self-determination'" made his candidacy invalid. The election period also featured violent physical attacks on a number of candidates on both sides.

In July 2020, Chief Executive Lam invoked emergency powers to postponed by a year the Legco elections due in September, citing the threat of COVID-19. The NPC Standing Committee in Beijing then approved the extension of the existing legislature's term. In

November, the NPC Standing Committee issued a directive allowing the Hong Kong government to summarily remove—without judicial review—lawmakers whom it deemed to have promoted or supported Hong Kong independence, solicited foreign forces to interfere in Hong Kong's domestic affairs, refused to recognize China's sovereignty over Hong Kong, or engaged in behavior that endangered national security. Lam's government quickly ousted four Legco members under the new authority, prompting all 15 of the remaining prodemocracy opposition lawmakers to resign in protest.

A3. Are the electoral laws and framework fair, and are they implemented impartially by the relevant election management bodies? 1 / 4

Universal suffrage, meaning direct elections, is the "ultimate aim" under the Basic Law, but Beijing and the Hong Kong leadership have permitted only incremental changes to the electoral system since its inception. The system continues to favor pro-Beijing interests and prevents direct elections for many offices, and the most recent changes have had the effect of excluding opposition candidates and views. Ahead of the 2016 Legco elections, the EAC required all candidates to attest in writing to their belief that Hong Kong is unquestionably a part of China, based on certain Basic Law provisions. The EAC invalidated the nominations of six localist candidates for failure to comply, preventing them from running. The 2016 Basic Law interpretation concerning "sincerity" and "solemnity" in oath-taking bolstered the EAC's power to block candidates on similar grounds, and the NPC's two major decisions in 2020—the adoption of the NSL and the November directive on removing lawmakers who pose a threat to national security—gave the government far-reaching authority to shape future electoral outcomes.

B. POLITICAL PLURALISM AND PARTICIPATION: 7 / 16 (−1)

B1. Do the people have the right to organize in different political parties or other competitive political groupings of their choice, and is the system free of undue obstacles to the rise and fall of these competing parties or groupings? 2 / 4

The political choices of Hong Kong residents are limited by the semidemocratic electoral system, which ensures the dominance of pro-Beijing parties and candidates. The largest pro-Beijing party is the Democratic Alliance for the Betterment and Progress of Hong Kong. The main parties in the prodemocracy camp are the Civic Party and the Democratic Party, and key localist groupings include Youngspiration and Civic Passion. The Chinese Communist Party (CCP) is not formally registered in Hong Kong but exercises considerable influence.

In 2018, Hong Kong's secretary for security officially banned the proindependence Hong Kong National Party (HKNP), alleging that that its activities were likely to threaten national security, public safety, and public order. The move marked the first blanket prohibition of a political party in Hong Kong since the territory's 1997 handover from Britain to China.

The government took more aggressive steps in 2020 to outlaw localist and prodemocracy political activity. In addition to the politicians and activists who were arrested during the year for alleged violations of the NSL and for organizing unlawful assemblies, arrest warrants were issued for prodemocracy figures who had recently sought safety abroad. Individuals accused of helping such people to flee the territory were similarly subject to arrest. The government declared that the slogans used in the 2019 protest movement, such as "liberate Hong Kong, revolution of our times," connoted support for Hong Kong independence in violation of the NSL, and authorities arrested people for carrying materials displaying versions of these slogans.

B2. Is there a realistic opportunity for the opposition to increase its support or gain power through elections? 1 / 4 (-1)

Prodemocracy legislators have historically enjoyed substantial minority representation alongside their pro-Beijing counterparts. However, after a series of disqualifications and expulsions that began in 2016 culminated in the mass resignation of prodemocratic lawmakers in November 2020, there were no democratic opposition candidates in the Legco at year's end, and the postponement of Legco elections meant that this would remain the case for at least another year.

The subjective nature of the NPC's standards for oath-taking, the expansive criminalization of speech and political activity under the NSL, and the chief executive's discretionary authority to remove Lecgo members under the NPC's November 2020 directive all invite arbitrary enforcement and pose serious obstacles for the opposition in future elections. In July, for example, the Hong Kong government used the NSL to disqualify a dozen prodemocracy candidates from running in Legco elections. Also that month, Beijing declared that the opposition's Legco primary elections were "illegal," and the Hong Kong government launched an investigation into whether the primary organizers had violated the NSL; Lam argued that by planning to win a majority in the Legco and use parliamentary procedures to force her resignation, the participating opposition figures could have violated the security law's prohibition on subversion of state power.

Score Change: The score declined from 2 to 1 because authorities used the Beijing-imposed National Security Law to disqualify and arrest opposition politicians, and because a decision by the Chinese government empowered the Hong Kong government to summarily remove opposition legislators, prompting the prodemocracy bloc in the Legislative Council to resign en masse.

B3. Are the people's political choices free from domination by forces that are external to the political sphere, or by political forces that employ extrapolitical means? 1 / 4

The unelected CCP leadership in Beijing exerts a powerful influence on politics in Hong Kong through a variety of channels, including the NPC's ability to issue interpretations of the Basic Law, the cooptation of Hong Kong business leaders through their mainland assets and membership in the NPC or CPPCC, and lobbying or harassment of election committee members and other political figures to ensure favorable electoral outcomes. In what was interpreted as a threat to prodemocracy protesters, Chinese troop carriers were seen massing near the Hong Kong border in Shenzhen in August 2019. In October 2019, Chinese president Xi Jinping issued a warning that attempts to divide China—a reference to Hong Kong protesters—would end in "bodies smashed and bones ground to powder." The 2020 NSL, imposed without consultation by the central government, gives Beijing vastly expanded powers in Hong Kong, in part by establishing a centrally controlled security apparatus in the territory, and by allowing defendants in some NSL cases to be transferred to the mainland for prosecution and punishment.

B4. Do various segments of the population (including ethnic, racial, religious, gender, LGBT+, and other relevant groups) have full political rights and electoral opportunities? 3 / 4

While there are no formal restrictions preventing women or members of ethnic minority groups from voting or running for office, their participation is limited in practice, with just 12 women and no ethnic minority candidates elected to the Legco in 2016. Approximately 8 percent of Hong Kong's population consists of non-Chinese ethnic minorities, and more than half of such residents are foreign nationals working as domestic helpers. Most have origins in South or Southeast Asia.

Hong Kong's first and only openly gay Legco member, Raymond Chan, was initially elected in 2012 and reelected in 2016, but he resigned in September 2020 to protest the postponement of elections; he was later arrested for having disrupted legislative sessions in May.

C. FUNCTIONING OF GOVERNMENT: 6 / 12

C1. Do the freely elected head of government and national legislative representatives determine the policies of the government? 1 / 4

Directly elected officials have little ability to set and implement government policies under the territory's political system, and unelected mainland authorities are highly influential. The Basic Law restricts the Legco's lawmaking powers, prohibiting legislators from introducing bills that would affect Hong Kong's public spending, governmental operations, or political structure.

As a result of the 2017 removal of some prodemocracy lawmakers and the outcome of 2018 by-elections, the prodemocracy camp lost an important legislative veto power that requires control over a majority of geographical constituency seats. In May 2020, pro-Beijing lawmakers took control of a key Legco committee amid scuffles between opposition members and security guards, further reducing the prodemocracy camp's ability to block controversial legislation. By year's end, with the NSL in force, elections postponed, and all prodemocracy opposition members ousted or resigned from their seats, what remained of the Legco offered few meaningful checks on executive authority.

C2. Are safeguards against official corruption strong and effective? 3 / 4

Hong Kong is regarded as having generally low corruption rates, and some high-ranking officials have been successfully prosecuted for graft-related offenses in the past. However, residents perceive the government to be lagging in the fight against corruption. In January 2019, Secretary for Justice Teresa Cheng survived a motion of no confidence in the Legco after consistently rejecting calls to explain why she dropped a corruption case against former Hong Kong chief executive Leung Chun-ying.

An increasing source of concern has been the apparently politicized application of anti–money laundering and anticorruption laws against organizations connected with the 2019 protest movement. In December 2020, for example, a church that had promoted de-escalation of clashes between police and protesters had its accounts frozen, its staff arrested, and its premises raided over claims that it had hidden or misused donations.

C3. Does the government operate with openness and transparency? 2 / 4

Hong Kong has no freedom of information law, nor does it have any specific legislation relating to the management of government records and archives. Although an administrative code—the Code of Access to Information—is intended to ensure open access to government records, it includes broad exemptions, and official adherence is inconsistent.

Consultations between Hong Kong officials and the Beijing government, represented by a Liaison Office in the territory, are largely opaque, leaving the extent of Beijing's influence on the local government's decisions unclear to the public. There is no transparency regarding central government processes that directly affect Hong Kong. The 2020 NSL was drafted in secret and announced without public consultation, taking effect almost immediately after the text was first published.

CIVIL LIBERTIES: 37 / 60 (–2)

D. FREEDOM OF EXPRESSION AND BELIEF: 9 / 16 (–1)

D1. Are there free and independent media? 2 / 4

The Basic Law has historically acted as a bulwark for press freedom, and the mainland's internet censorship regime does not yet apply in Hong Kong. Residents have long had access to a variety of print, broadcast, and digital news sources.

However, in recent years the Hong Kong and Chinese governments, alongside businesses with close Beijing ties, have increased political and economic pressure on the media. Some local news outlets have been acquired by mainland businesses. These trends have resulted in self-censorship among journalists, changes in editorial content, and a rise in mainland-style practices. Certain outlets have carried propagandistic content, such as dubious "confessions" by mainland political detainees. In 2018, the Hong Kong government refused to renew an employment visa for Victor Mallet, a veteran journalist for the *Financial Times* and vice president of Hong Kong's Foreign Correspondents' Club (FCC), after he chaired an FCC event featuring a leader of the HKNP. In July 2020, Hong Kong denied a work permit to *New York Times* correspondent Chris Buckley, who had been expelled from the mainland in May.

During the protests of 2019, journalists were assaulted, detained, sprayed with blue dye (used by police to identify protesters) and tear gas, struck by projectiles, and threatened with live ammunition.

In August 2020, prodemocracy media owner Jimmy Lai was arrested along with several others on suspicion of "colluding with foreign forces," and police executed search warrants at the headquarters of his *Apple Daily* newspaper. In December, about 100 workers at the i-Cable news network, including the entire staff of a respected investigative news program, were laid off, prompting mass resignations by other employees to protest what they considered to be politically motivated firings. Also that month, longtime Hong Kong journalist Kent Ewing reported that the planned publication of his book, a history of Hong Kong from 1997 to the present, had been canceled because, due to "political circumstances," printers and bookstores refused to handle it.

D2. Are individuals free to practice and express their religious faith or nonbelief in public and private? 4 / 4

Religious freedom is generally respected in Hong Kong. Adherents of the Falun Gong spiritual movement, which is persecuted in mainland China, are free to practice in public. However, they have complained of counterdemonstrations and harassment by members of the Hong Kong Youth Care Association (HKYCA), which has ties to the CCP.

D3. Is there academic freedom, and is the educational system free from extensive political indoctrination? 1 / 4

University professors have historically been able to write and lecture freely, and political debate on campuses has been lively. However, since its enactment in June 2020, the NSL has been used aggressively to suppress discussion of Hong Kong independence and control discussion of the 2019 protest movement. Both public and private schools, colleges, and universities have been affected. In the years preceding the new law, government-led revisions of history curriculums and textbooks, and attempts to instill Chinese patriotism, had stirred accusations of a pro-Beijing agenda in primary and secondary education.

During the 2019 protest movement, Hong Kong's education bureau reportedly instructed teachers to avoid questions about the demonstrations and declared that class boycotts by students were illegal. In November 2019, police laid siege to protesters on two campuses—the

Chinese University of Hong Kong and Hong Kong Polytechnic University—and standoffs took place at the City University of Hong Kong and Hong Kong University. The siege at Polytechnic University lasted almost two weeks; thousands of tear gas canisters were used at the school, and over a thousand people were arrested. Multiple universities in Hong Kong canceled classes for the remainder of the term. Professors found guilty of involvement in protests have since faced dismissal by their universities.

In July 2020, the Hong Kong government instructed schools to pull books that might breach the NSL. As part of its enforcement of the ban on discussions of independence on school campuses, the government deregistered a primary school teacher for life in September.

D4. Are individuals free to express their personal views on political or other sensitive topics without fear of surveillance or retribution? 2 / 4 (−1)

Hong Kong has a tradition of free personal expression and private discussion, but local and mainland security agencies have been suspected of monitoring the communications of prodemocracy activists for some years, and they now have a specific mandate to do so under the NSL, which permits warrantless surveillance and wiretapping. The law also allowed mainland authorities to establish security agencies in the territory under their own jurisdiction, and people charged with NSL offenses can be detained and tried on the mainland. The NSL's enactment reportedly prompted many social media users to self-censor, shutter their accounts, or delete existing content that could run afoul of the law.

Surveillance of demonstrators was already a serious concern during the 2019 protests, with police and the government using facial recognition technology and blue dye to identify participants. The government enacted a ban on face masks at all demonstrations under the Emergency Regulations Ordinance, in a bid to prevent participants from avoiding identification. There were also reports of Hong Kong authorities seizing protesters' phones and searching them.

In another blow to free expression, the Legco in June 2020 adopted a controversial law that criminalized disrespect for China's national anthem, with penalties of up to three years in prison.

Score Change: The score declined from 3 to 2 because the National Security Law introduced mainland security agencies into Hong Kong and allowed authorities to surveil and arrest ordinary citizens and activists based on their personal communications, leading to a marked increase in self-censorship.

E. ASSOCIATIONAL AND ORGANIZATIONAL RIGHTS: 6 / 12

E1. Is there freedom of assembly? 1 / 4

The Basic Law guarantees freedom of assembly, but the Public Order Ordinance requires organizers to give police seven days' notice before protests and to obtain official assent. Signs of authorities' growing intolerance of prodemocracy demonstrations had emerged during the 2014 Umbrella Movement, which featured increased use of baton charges, pepper spray, and arrests by police. Protesters' encampments also faced assaults by counterdemonstrators, many of whom were later found to have links with criminal gangs. In 2019, numerous defendants received prison sentences in connection with their participation in the Umbrella Movement protests.

Since 2019, police have frequently used excessive violence against prodemocracy demonstrators. In November 2019, police fired on protesters with live rounds, resulting in the hospitalization of one person. At the same rally, a police officer drove a motorcycle into a crowd of protesters. Separately, attacks on protesters by mobs linked to organized crime groups caused hundreds of injuries and dozens of hospitalizations, and police often failed to intervene.

In 2020, the government repeatedly used COVID-19 as a pretext to ban public assemblies, including the annual June vigil to commemorate the 1989 Tiananmen Square massacre, and the NSL was invoked to arrest individuals for actions as trivial as carrying stickers inscribed with the slogan "liberate Hong Kong" or even holding blank placards.

E2. Is there freedom for nongovernmental organizations, particularly those that are engaged in human rights and governance-related work? 3 / 4

Historically, Hong Kong has hosted a vibrant nongovernmental organization (NGO) sector, including a number of groups that focus on human rights in mainland China. However, early in 2019, there was a sophisticated cyberattack on the Hong Kong branch of Amnesty International, reportedly originating on the mainland. Later in the year, police and nonstate actors attacked protest leaders and peaceful activists at the Lennon Walls (walls covered with notes bearing messages of support for the protest movement). In October, Jimmy Sham, head of the Civil Human Rights Front, was attacked by a group of men armed with hammers, resulting in his hospitalization. Chinese officials verbally attacked activists speaking about Hong Kong at the United Nations as they delivered their addresses.

The introduction of the NSL in 2020 dramatically changed the environment for civil society in Hong Kong. The entire staff of some organizations quit on the eve of the law's introduction. While arrests under the NSL during the year focused primarily on persons and organizations connected with the 2019 demonstrations and the democratic opposition rather than NGOs as such, the crackdown had a chilling effect on the entire sector.

E3. Is there freedom for trade unions and similar professional or labor organizations? 2 / 4

Trade unions are independent, but collective-bargaining rights are not recognized, and protections against antiunion discrimination are weak. Some trade unions took an active role in the 2019 protest movement, and attempted to organize an unofficial referendum on whether to call a general strike in June 2020, but the effort fell short of its turnout goal and drew warnings from government ministers. Lee Cheuk-yan, general secretary of the Hong Kong Confederation of Trade Unions, was among those arrested and charged for their involvement in organizing protests during the year.

F. RULE OF LAW: 9 / 16 (−1)

F1. Is there an independent judiciary? 2 / 4

The Hong Kong judiciary is largely independent and remained so during the 2019 crisis. However, Judge James Spigelman resigned from the Court of Final Appeal in September 2020, citing the content of the NSL. Several provisions of the law undermined judicial autonomy, for instance by allowing the government to select judges for NSL trials.

The NPC has historically reserved the right to make final interpretations of the Basic Law, limiting the independence of the Court of Final Appeal. Such interventions were rare prior to the NPC's 2016 interpretation regarding oaths of office, which was also unusual for being issued without a request from the Hong Kong government and before the local courts had ruled on the matter in question. It was seen as a blow to the autonomy of the territory's legal system. The 2020 NSL was imposed on Hong Kong through a Basic Law provision that allows the NPC to list national laws that must be applied locally, bypassing both the Legco and Hong Kong's courts.

Since the beginning of the 2019 protests, the Hong Kong judiciary has faced political pressure and criticism over various decisions, with complaints coming from the Hong Kong government, mainland Chinese media, and protesters. In November 2019, a Hong Kong court struck down the emergency decree banning the use of face masks as unconstitutional, a decision which was promptly met with criticism from the NPC. The Court of Appeal partly overturned that ruling in April 2020, finding that the ban was only unconstitutional when applied to legal gatherings, as opposed to unlawful assemblies; the Court of Final Appeal then fully upheld the ban in December.

F2. Does due process prevail in civil and criminal matters? 2 / 4 (−1)

The courts have typically upheld due process rights and adjudicated civil and criminal matters fairly and efficiently in the past. Following the thousands of arrests made during the protests that began in 2019, courts came under pressure to process cases faster, and pro-Beijing politicians and media called on them to side with the prosecution and hand down heavier sentences. In August 2020, a private prosecution brought by a prodemocracy lawmaker against a police officer who had fired a live round at a protester was quashed after the justice secretary intervened.

Under the NSL, individuals charged with national security offenses are tried by judges selected by the chief executive, and the central government wields influence over the appointment of prosecutors. In cases involving offenses against public order or state secrets, the trials may be closed to the public. The central government's new Office for Safeguarding National Security in Hong Kong can assert jurisdiction over some cases and have them tried on the mainland. The NSL includes a presumption against granting bail to suspects and defendants. Some high-profile defendants, such as Jimmy Lai and politician Agnes Chow, were denied bail in non-NSL cases during the year.

Score Change: The score declined from 3 to 2 due to multiple provisions of the National Security Law that undermined defendants' rights, including the power of the chief executive to assign specific judges and magistrates to national security cases, the ability of central government authorities to assume control of certain cases and try them in mainland courts, and a presumption against granting bail to pretrial detainees.

F3. Is there protection from the illegitimate use of physical force and freedom from war and insurgencies? 2 / 4

Police are forbidden by law from employing torture, disappearance, or other forms of abuse. However, the 2019 protest movement featured frequent episodes of police violence, which have generally gone unaddressed. There were also credible allegations of arbitrary detention and even torture of protesters in 2019. Late that year, a group of foreign experts appointed by the Independent Police Complaints Council (IPCC) to study police practices during the protests stepped down, citing concerns about whether the council was capable of engaging in a sufficiently robust, independent inquiry. The IPCC issued a report in May 2020 that generally defended police conduct.

In addition to police violence, the protest movement brought about a more general climate of unrest, due to both clashes that accompanied demonstrations and violent attacks committed by nonstate actors against protesters, activists, and bystanders at locations far from where protest actions were taking place.

The 2015 disappearances of five Hong Kong booksellers into police custody on the mainland continue to cast doubt on the local government's capacity to protect residents from abuses by Chinese authorities, particularly in light of the new jurisdictional powers provided by the NSL. Four of the booksellers were eventually released, but they reportedly faced surveillance and harassment in Hong Kong; the fifth, Swedish citizen Gui Minhai, remained in detention on the mainland and was sentenced to 10 years in prison in February 2020 for supposedly providing intelligence to foreign entities.

F4. Do laws, policies, and practices guarantee equal treatment of various segments of the population? 3 / 4

Citizens are generally treated equally under the law, though people of South Asian origin or descent face language barriers and de facto discrimination in education and employment. Women are also subject to some employment discrimination in practice. Antidiscrimination laws do not specifically protect LGBT+ people.

G. PERSONAL AUTONOMY AND INDIVIDUAL RIGHTS: 13 / 16

G1. Do individuals enjoy freedom of movement, including the ability to change their place of residence, employment, or education? 3 / 4

Hong Kong residents generally enjoy freedom of movement, though authorities periodically deny entry to visiting political activists and Falun Gong practitioners, raising suspicions of Beijing-imposed restrictions. Some Hong Kong activists and politicians have also faced difficulty traveling to the mainland. In 2019, there were reports that people traveling into China from Hong Kong were subjected to checks by mainland authorities, who searched their phones for protest photos and related communications. In 2020, a number of countries, including Britain and Australia, offered special visas and other pathways for Hong Kong residents to escape political repression, though in retaliation Beijing threatened to refuse recognition of the relevant documents.

G2. Are individuals able to exercise the right to own property and establish private businesses without undue interference from state or nonstate actors? 3 / 4

While property rights are largely respected, collusion among powerful business entities with political connections is perceived as an impediment to fair competition.

G3. Do individuals enjoy personal social freedoms, including choice of marriage partner and size of family, protection from domestic violence, and control over appearance? 4 / 4

Hong Kong residents are legally protected from rape and domestic abuse, and police generally respond appropriately to reports of such crimes. Men and women enjoy equal rights in personal status matters such as marriage and divorce. A constitutional challenge to Hong Kong's restrictions on same-sex marriage was rejected by a court in 2019. In two separate cases in September 2020, a court ruled in favor of inheritance rights for a gay couple but rejected a bid to compel the territory to fully recognize same-sex marriages undertaken abroad.

G4. Do individuals enjoy equality of opportunity and freedom from economic exploitation? 3 / 4

While most Hong Kong residents enjoy equality of opportunity and freedom from economic exploitation, certain marginalized groups face substantial risks of exploitation and abuse. For instance, foreign household workers, who make up roughly 4.4 percent of Hong Kong's population, remain vulnerable to a wide range of exploitative practices. Since they may face deportation if dismissed, many are reluctant to bring complaints against employers. Hong Kong is also a significant site for human trafficking, but the city still lacks comprehensive antitrafficking legislation.

Indian Kashmir

Population: 13,900,000
Freedom Status: Not Free

Note: *Freedom in the World* reports assess the level of political rights and civil liberties in a given geographical area, regardless of whether they are affected by the state, nonstate actors, or foreign powers. Disputed territories are sometimes assessed separately if they meet certain criteria, including boundaries that are sufficiently stable to allow year-on-year comparisons. For more information, see the report methodology and FAQ.

Overview: Control of Kashmir has been divided between India and Pakistan since 1948, and Indian-administered Kashmir long enjoyed substantial autonomy under India's constitution. However, the region's autonomous status was revoked in 2019, and what had been the state of Jammu and Kashmir was reconstituted as two union territories under the direct control of the Indian central government. The move stripped residents of many of their previous political rights. Civil liberties have also been curtailed to quell ongoing public opposition to the reorganization. Indian security forces are frequently accused of human rights violations, but few are punished. Separatist and jihadist militants continue to wage a protracted insurgency.

KEY DEVELOPMENTS IN 2020

- In the wake of the region's 2019 political reorganization, internet access and freedom of assembly remained severely restricted in 2020, and many of the thousands of Kashmiris who were detained during the previous year's crackdown were still in confinement.
- The Indian government issued legal amendments in March and October that made it possible for more Indians to claim permanent residency and buy land in Jammu and Kashmir, raising concerns that the government was attempting to change the ethno-religious composition of the Muslim-majority territory.
- The killing of a militant leader by Indian forces in May set off a wave of protests and a violent response from police that left at least one person dead and dozens injured.
- Economic conditions worsened during the year due to the ongoing security clampdown as well as new movement restrictions that were imposed in response to the COVID-19 pandemic.

POLITICAL RIGHTS: 7 / 40 (−1)

A. ELECTORAL PROCESS: 2 / 12

A1. Was the current head of government or other chief national authority elected through free and fair elections? 0 / 4

Prior to 2019, the state of Jammu and Kashmir enjoyed special autonomy under Article 370 of the Indian constitution. A chief minister—typically the head of the largest party in the state legislature's lower house—was entrusted with executive power. Under the Jammu and Kashmir Reorganisation Act 2019, adopted by the Indian Parliament that August, the region's autonomous status was revoked, it was downgraded from a state to a union territory, and the Ladakh area was separated to form a second union territory. Executive authority in each now rests with a lieutenant governor appointed by the president of India on the advice of the Indian prime minister. In Jammu and Kashmir, the lieutenant governor is to be assisted by a chief minister and cabinet responsible to an elected legislature with limited powers, though no such legislature had been elected by the end of 2020. Manoj Sinha, a former Indian minister belonging to India's ruling Bharatiya Janata Party (BJP), was appointed as lieutenant governor of Jammu and Kashmir in August 2020. Radha Krishna Mathur, a former bureaucrat who was appointed as lieutenant governor of Ladakh in 2019, remained in office during 2020.

The process by which Jammu and Kashmir's autonomous status and statehood were revoked drew criticism and doubts about its legality. Opponents and other observers argued that the central government had improperly delayed state elections beginning in 2018 and then hastily adopted the reorganization law with little debate.

A2. Were the current national legislative representatives elected through free and fair elections? 0 / 4

Until the passage of the Jammu and Kashmir Reorganisation Act in 2019, the region had a bicameral legislature. The lower chamber, the Legislative Assembly, was composed of 87 members directly elected for six-year terms to single-member districts. The upper chamber, called the Legislative Council, comprised 28 indirectly elected members and eight members nominated by the governor. The 2014 elections were broadly free and fair, with reduced levels of voter intimidation, harassment, and violence compared to past elections. The state legislature was dissolved by the governor in late 2018, ending attempts by local parties to form a new governing majority after the BJP's withdrawal brought down the last coalition government, but central authorities then extended direct rule and postponed new state elections through the summer of 2019, when the Reorganisation Act rendered them moot.

Under the arrangements adopted in 2019, the new union territory of Jammu and Kashmir would have a unicameral legislature with limited powers and at least 83 elected members. (As in the old assembly, another 24 seats associated with constituencies in Pakistani-controlled Kashmir would be left vacant.) However, elections were not expected until 2021, following the demarcation of constituencies. The new union territory of Ladakh will continue to be administered solely by the lieutenant governor, with no legislature of its own.

Local elections to Block Development Councils in October 2019 were extensively boycotted by local mainstream political parties. However, in elections for District Development Councils that were held in November and December 2020, an alliance of Kashmiri parties that supported regional autonomy won control of 13 of the 20 councils, despite complaints that its candidates faced restrictions on media coverage and freedom of movement during the campaign. The BJP, whose workers were subjected to militant violence ahead of the vote, placed second and emerged as the largest single party. Separately, the BJP suffered losses but retained control in October elections for the Autonomous Hill Development Council in Leh, a district in Ladakh.

A3. Are the electoral laws and framework fair, and are they implemented impartially by the relevant election management bodies? 2 / 4

The legal framework governing statewide elections prior to 2019 was broadly perceived as fair. While intimidation of election workers and electoral authorities by militant groups sometimes interfered with the orderly implementation of electoral laws and regulations, the process was overseen by the Election Commission of India, a respected and largely independent body.

The Indian Parliament adopted the Jammu and Kashmir Reorganisation Act swiftly and without significant input from Kashmiris, fundamentally altering the electoral system and effectively stripping residents of substantial voting power.

B. POLITICAL PLURALISM AND PARTICIPATION: 3 / 16 (−1)

B1. Do the people have the right to organize in different political parties or other competitive political groupings of their choice, and is the system free of undue obstacles to the rise and fall of these competing parties or groupings? 1 / 4

Until 2019, a competitive multiparty system had operated in the region. While new political parties had to register with the Election Commission, parties were generally able to form freely, and there were mechanisms by which independent candidates could stand for office. Notable impediments to normal party politics included militant violence, intimidation, and separatist boycotts.

Political activities were almost completely suspended after August 2019, as security forces detained thousands of party members and activists without charge, including the leaders of mainstream Kashmiri parties and the local branch of India's opposition Congress party. Former chief ministers and incumbent lawmakers were among those detained, and despite a series of releases, many remained in detention for much of 2020.

After the last elected chief minister, Mehbooba Mufti, was released in October, her People's Democratic Party (PDP) formed the People's Alliance for Gupkar Declaration (PAGD) with several other Kashmiri parties, including its former rival, the Jammu and Kashmir National Conference (JKNC). The new group sought to restore the region's autonomy under the Indian constitution.

B2. Is there a realistic opportunity for the opposition to increase its support or gain power through elections? 1 / 4

For more than a decade, state-level power had rotated between the two largest Kashmiri parties: the PDP and the JKNC. The Hindu nationalist BJP, which currently governs in New Delhi, has made significant electoral inroads in recent years; it participated in a coalition government with the PDP from 2015 to 2018.

The postponement of state elections, the 2019 reorganization of the region, and the related mass detentions effectively reduced the ability of opposition groups to compete and enter government in Jammu and Kashmir for the foreseeable future. The PAGD accused the government of curtailing its ability to campaign freely ahead of the District Development Council elections in November and December. While the alliance won those elections overall, the councils manage local development matters and have little governmental authority.

The union territory of Ladakh has a centrally appointed executive and no legislature, meaning no rotations of power through elections are possible at the territory level. Elections are still held for district-level development councils, but as in Jammu and Kashmir, their powers are greatly overshadowed by those of appointed officials.

B3. Are the people's political choices free from domination by forces that are external to the political sphere, or by political forces that employ extrapolitical means? 0 / 4

The activities of separatist militants and a heavy Indian security presence have long impaired the ability of people in certain areas to participate freely in political processes. Since August 2019, tens of thousands of additional Indian troops have been deployed to the region to quash any public expressions of opposition to the Reorganisation Act. The deployment was accompanied by reports of intimidation and violence against civilians, and more than 5,000 people, including peaceful protesters, were arrested in the second half of 2019.

B4. Do various segments of the population (including ethnic, racial, religious, gender, LGBT+, and other relevant groups) have full political rights and electoral opportunities? 1 / 4 (−1)

The former state constitution granted all permanent residents over 18 the right to vote in state assembly elections. While the region had a female chief minister until early 2018, women have generally been underrepresented in politics.

Prior to the 2019 reorganization, historical refugees from Pakistan, who are disproportionately Hindu, were not entitled to permanent residency rights and could not vote in state elections, though they were able to vote in Indian parliamentary elections. Such individuals were allowed to vote in the development council polls in Jammu and Kashmir for the first time in November 2020.

During the campaign period for the council elections, Muslim Kashmiri candidates and their parties were allegedly disadvantaged by continued detentions, police interference, and movement restrictions, many of which were imposed for security reasons.

The 2019 reorganization left the largely Buddhist and Shiite Muslim population of Ladakh without elected government institutions at the territory level. There are still two Autonomous Hill Development Councils representing Ladakh's two districts, Leh and Kargil, but many in Kargil vocally opposed the 2019 changes, and a broad coalition of political groups in Leh—including the local BJP branch—threatened to boycott the October 2020 council elections until the central government promised to address local concerns about land rights and other implications of Ladakh's new status.

Score Change: The score declined from 2 to 1 because the region's 2019 reorganization left the largely Buddhist and Shiite Muslim population of Ladakh with no elected government institutions at the territory level, and ongoing detentions and other restrictions in Jammu and Kashmir were reported to have disproportionately affected Muslim politicians and parties ahead of District Development Council elections in late 2020.

C. FUNCTIONING OF GOVERNMENT: 2 / 12

C1. Do the freely elected head of government and national legislative representatives determine the policies of the government? 0 / 4

India has never held a referendum on allowing Kashmiri self-determination, as called for in a 1948 UN resolution. Jammu and Kashmir long enjoyed substantial autonomy under India's constitution, but since 2019 it has been ruled directly by the central government through an appointed lieutenant governor, as has the newly separated territory of Ladakh. There are legal provisions for an elected legislature in Jammu and Kashmir, although its powers will ultimately be limited, and no legislature was in place during 2020. Many laws that had been passed by the state government have been subject to repeal or amendment under the new system, and more laws passed by the Indian Parliament now apply to Jammu and Kashmir. The union territory will no longer be permitted to formulate its own laws regarding policing and public order.

C2. Are safeguards against official corruption strong and effective? 1 / 4

Corruption is widespread. A 2011 law established an anticorruption commission with far-reaching investigatory powers. The panel, known as the State Vigilance Commission, processed more than a thousand complaints after the first commissioners were appointed in 2013, and it filed a handful of bribery charges against public officials. However, few corruption cases result in convictions. In 2020, the commission was dissolved after the Jammu and Kashmir territorial government repealed the underlying law.

C3. Does the government operate with openness and transparency? 1 / 4

The administration generally operates with opacity, and the changes in the administrative status of the region in 2019, coupled with severe restrictions on press freedom, have further impeded transparency. Several official agencies intended to promote transparency and good governance, including the State Information Commission, were shut down in 2019 and 2020.

CIVIL LIBERTIES: 20 / 60

D. FREEDOM OF EXPRESSION AND BELIEF: 6 / 16

D1. Are there free and independent media? 1 / 4

Until mid-2019, print media were thriving in Jammu and Kashmir. Online media had proliferated, providing new platforms for news and information. The announcement of the region's changed administrative status was accompanied by a severe clampdown on the activities of local and foreign journalists. The authorities continued to disrupt internet service during 2020; limited mobile and fixed-line service was gradually restored, but high-speed mobile connectivity remained blocked at year's end. Protracted curfews and restrictions on movement, caused in part by COVID-19 lockdowns, also made it difficult for media outlets to operate for much of the year.

A new media policy introduced in June 2020 gave government officials the authority to examine and censor content for "fake news, plagiarism, and unethical or antinational activities." Several journalists were questioned or charged over their work during the year. In April, for example, journalists Masrat Zahra and Gowhar Geelani were placed under investigation for allegedly "glorifying antinational activities" and "glorifying terrorism," respectively, through their social media posts. In October, authorities raided the offices of *Greater Kashmir*, a prominent English-language newspaper, as part of a larger series of raids targeting alleged funding for "separatist activities." Also during 2020, there were reports of journalists being beaten in connection with their work by police and other security forces.

D2. Are individuals free to practice and express their religious faith or nonbelief in public and private? 2 / 4

Freedom of worship is generally respected by the authorities. However, communal violence between Muslims and Hindus periodically flares up, and many have been injured or killed as a result. A ban on Shiite Muslims' Muharram processions, which take place during a period of mourning at the Islamic new year, has been upheld for decades. Authorities closed some mosques for months in the wake of the 2019 revocation of autonomy, and many were shuttered again for about five months during a COVID-19 lockdown before restrictions were eased in August 2020. Also that month, security forces violently dispersed Muharram processions in Srinagar, causing multiple injuries.

D3. Is there academic freedom, and is the educational system free from extensive political indoctrination? 1 / 4

Academic freedom is often circumscribed. Authorities monitor the research produced at Kashmiri universities, and a combination of censorship and self-censorship discourages students and professors from pursuing sensitive topics of inquiry. Colleges, universities, and schools were shuttered for most of 2020, first on security grounds and then because of the coronavirus pandemic. Remote learning was severely impeded by the ongoing restrictions on internet access.

D4. Are individuals free to express their personal views on political or other sensitive topics without fear of surveillance or retribution? 2 / 4

While private discussion has sometimes been robust, fear of reprisals by government or militant forces can serve as a deterrent to uninhibited speech. The mass arrests of politicians, activists, protesters, and others after the revocation of autonomy in 2019, which continued into 2020, were apparently aimed at curbing free expression and likely had a chilling effect on the rest of the population.

E. ASSOCIATIONAL AND ORGANIZATIONAL RIGHTS: 3 / 12

E1. Is there freedom of assembly? 0 / 4

Freedom of assembly is frequently restricted during times of unrest. The authorities often reject requests for permits for public gatherings submitted by the separatist All Parties Hurriyat Conference (APHC). Separatist leaders are frequently arrested prior to planned demonstrations, and violent clashes between protesters and security forces are not uncommon.

Curfews were in force in parts of the region during 2020—including in the period surrounding the anniversary of the revocation of the region's autonomy—and lockdowns to stem the spread of the coronavirus further curtailed people's ability to congregate and express dissent. The ongoing disruptions to phone and internet services served to prevent the planning of protests. Nevertheless, security forces clashed with protesters on multiple occasions, using tear gas and shotguns that fire metal pellets to disperse crowds. The killing of a top militant commander, Riyaz Naikoo, by Indian forces in May set off a wave of protests that left one person dead and dozens injured.

E2. Is there freedom for nongovernmental organizations, particularly those that are engaged in human rights- and governance-related work? 1 / 4

Although local and national civil rights groups are generally permitted to operate, they are routinely harassed by security forces. The separatist APHC is technically allowed to function, but its leaders are frequently subjected to detention. In 2019, the central government imposed a five-year ban on the group Jamaat-e-Islami (Jammu and Kashmir) and arrested its top leadership, claiming that it was engaged in separatist activities. Many of the arrests that followed the revocation of autonomy in 2019 targeted independence advocates, human rights lawyers, and other civic activists. Efforts by civil society to monitor human rights violations during the subsequent crackdown were hampered by the suspension of internet and telephone services. In October 2020, the National Investigation Agency conducted raids at the offices and homes of human rights activists and nongovernmental organization (NGO) workers as part of a probe into alleged funding for "separatist activities."

E3. Is there freedom for trade unions and similar professional or labor organizations? 2 / 4

Although workers have the right to form unions and engage in collective bargaining under Indian law, union rights are inconsistently upheld in practice.

F. RULE OF LAW: 4 / 16

F1. Is there an independent judiciary? 1 / 4

Courts in the region are politicized and typically act as an extension of Indian executive and military authority. The government and security forces frequently disregard court orders that impose constraints on their actions. In January 2020, the Indian Supreme Court ruled that the indefinite internet shutdown in Kashmir was unjustified and violated constitutional rights to free speech and expression, but authorities were slow to ease the shutdown, and mobile internet access remained restricted at year's end.

F2. Does due process prevail in civil and criminal matters? 1 / 4

Due process rights, including access to a timely trial, are hampered in part by large backlogs of cases and intermittent lawyers' strikes. In addition, broadly written legislation, such as the unpopular Armed Forces Special Powers Act (AFSPA) and the Disturbed Areas Act, allow security forces to search homes and arrest suspects without a warrant, shoot suspects on sight, and destroy buildings believed to house militants or arms. Under the AFSPA, prosecutions of security personnel cannot proceed without the approval of the central government, which is rarely granted. Following the 2019 reorganization of the region, the central government now has the sole authority to declare an area "disturbed" under the AFSPA, which activates enhanced powers for security forces. The Public Safety Act allows detention without charge or trial for up to two years, though 2012 amendments barred the detention of minors. The law was used to jail mainstream political leaders and others in 2019 and 2020. Many such detainees were held in parts of India outside Kashmir.

F3. Is there protection from the illegitimate use of physical force and freedom from war and insurgencies? 1 / 4

After several years of relative stability, security deteriorated sharply following the 2016 killing of Burhan Muzaffar Wani, a popular separatist militant leader. The situation remained volatile in 2020. At least 321 civilians, security personnel, and militants were reportedly killed in conflict-related violence over the course of the year.

Indian security personnel have continued to engage in torture, forced disappearances, and custodial killings of suspected militants and their alleged civilian sympathizers, and they generally enjoy impunity for such abuses. In 2019, the Office of the UN High Commissioner for Human Rights (OHCHR) released a report highlighting human rights violations in the Kashmir region over the previous year, updating a similar 2018 document; the report condemned excessive and extrajudicial violence committed by Indian security forces, and criticized the Indian government's refusal to investigate reported violations.

Militant groups have killed pro-India politicians, public employees, suspected informers, members of rival factions, soldiers, and civilians. The militants also engage in kidnapping, extortion, and other forms of intimidation. The OHCHR report detailed severe rights violations committed by active militant groups. Among other types of incidents during 2020, militants were suspected of having targeted and killed several BJP workers ahead of development council elections.

F4. Do laws, policies, and practices guarantee equal treatment of various segments of the population? 1 / 4

A pattern of violence targeting Pandits, or Kashmiri Hindus, has forced several hundred thousand Hindus to flee their homes in the region over the years, and many continue to reside in refugee camps. Other religious and ethnic minorities, including Sikhs and Gurjars, have been targeted in the past, but such reports have become less frequent. Women face societal discrimination. They are also subject to harassment, intimidation, and violent attacks, including rape and murder, at the hands of both the security forces and militants. Gay, transgender, and other LGBT+ people are generally marginalized in Kashmiri society.

G. PERSONAL AUTONOMY AND INDIVIDUAL RIGHTS: 7 / 16

G1. Do individuals enjoy freedom of movement, including the ability to change their place of residence, employment, or education? 1 / 4

Freedom of movement has been heavily curtailed by the authorities. Strict curfews were imposed in connection with the region's 2019 reorganization, and coronavirus-related lockdowns were added during 2020, with the severity varying somewhat by location and over time. Even when curfews are not in place, internal movement is disrupted by roadblocks, checkpoints, and periodic protest-related impediments. Kashmir residents face delays of up to two years to obtain and renew passports due to heightened levels of scrutiny.

In March 2020, the Indian government altered domicile legislation to make it easier for refugees and Indian nationals from outside Kashmir to establish permanent residency and obtain government jobs in the region, extending eligibility to those who had lived there for 15 years or studied there for seven years. The change would benefit many long-term residents who had lacked domicile status, but critics alleged that the government's aim was to alter the Muslim-majority territory's demographic composition. Tens of thousands of new domicile certificates were issued during the year.

G2. Are individuals able to exercise the right to own property and establish private businesses without undue interference from state or nonstate actors? 2 / 4

Property rights are undermined by displacement and military activity related to the conflict, and the regulatory environment constrains the establishment and operation of new businesses. In October 2020, the Indian government substantially altered dozens of laws governing land ownership in Jammu and Kashmir, ending long-standing restrictions on property acquisition by people who were not permanent residents of the region. Ladakh was not immediately affected by those changes. The new legal framework also gave the government and the military enhanced powers to reserve and manage land for development and strategic purposes.

G3. Do individuals enjoy personal social freedoms, including choice of marriage partner and size of family, protection from domestic violence, and control over appearance? 2 / 4

Many women face domestic violence and other forms of abuse. There have been reports of women being killed in dowry disputes, and conservative social customs limit the choice of marriage partners for individuals.

G4. Do individuals enjoy equality of opportunity and freedom from economic exploitation? 2 / 4

Certain social groups are subject to economic marginalization, though some are also eligible to benefit from affirmative-action policies in areas such as employment and education. Child labor is reportedly prevalent in the region, and the government has taken few steps to combat it. Militant groups have been accused of recruiting children as fighters.

Nagorno-Karabakh

Population: 150,000 (2015 census)
Freedom Status: Partly Free

Note: *Freedom in the World* reports assess the level of political rights and civil liberties in a given geographical area, regardless of whether they are affected by the state, nonstate actors, or foreign powers. Disputed territories are sometimes assessed separately if they meet certain criteria, including boundaries that are sufficiently stable to allow year-on-year comparisons. For more information, see the report methodology and FAQ.

Overview: The Republic of Nagorno-Karabakh, which also calls itself the Republic of Artsakh, has enjoyed de facto independence from Azerbaijan since a 1994 cease-fire agreement ended roughly two years of open warfare, though its independence is not recognized by any UN member states, and cease-fire violations were common in the decades after the agreement. The territory's population is mostly ethnic Armenians, and given its geographic and diplomatic isolation, it is dependent on close political, economic, and military ties with Armenia. Competitive elections in 2020 featured robust debate, an orderly vote in spite of the COVID-19 pandemic, and the acceptance of the election's results by stakeholders. A large-scale attack by Azerbaijani forces later in the year gave way to six weeks of war; local officials, rights groups, and journalists documented dozens of war crimes during this period, including by Azerbaijani forces against civilians.

KEY DEVELOPMENTS IN 2020

- Six weeks of warfare followed a large-scale attack on the territory on September 27 by Azerbaijani forces. The fighting was ended by a November 9 cease-fire agreement that placed large portions of the conflict zone under Azerbaijan's direct control. This included about a third of Nagorno-Karabakh itself along with seven territories adjacent to the region, which had remained under the Armenian administration since the end of the war in the early 1990s.
- At least 52 ethnic Armenian civilians were reported killed during the period of open hostilities, more than 160 were wounded, and tens of thousands of people by some counts were displaced. Local officials, rights groups, and journalists documented dozens of war crimes, including Azerbaijani soldiers beheading Armenian civilians and military and mutilating their corpses, and torturing war prisoners.
- A record number of new political parties and politicians took part in parliamentary and presidential elections held in March and April, making them the most competitive polls in the region's recent history.

POLITICAL RIGHTS: 16 / 40 (+3)

A. ELECTORAL PROCESS: 7 / 12 (+3)

A1. Was the current head of government or other chief national authority elected through free and fair elections? 2 / 4 (+1)

The president is directly elected for up to two five-year terms, and is both head of state and head of government, with authority to appoint and dismiss cabinet members.

The presidential election of spring 2020 was widely acknowledged as the most competitive in the recent history of Nagorno-Karabakh. An unprecedented 14 candidates engaged in an intense electoral campaign that featured extensive campaign activities in person and on social media. Weeks of televised presentations of candidates' programs culminated in the region's first-ever televised debates.

Despite calls of local health workers and some political activists from Armenia to postpone the election due to the COVID-19 pandemic, the vote took place on schedule, in two rounds in accordance with the local electoral code. Seventy-two percent of eligible voters participated in the first round, though turnout declined to 45 percent in the second. The electoral commission asked voters to wear face masks, which were provided; use their own pens; and follow social-distancing rules at polling stations. After the second round concluded, the local leadership declared a state of emergency, put in place restrictions on travel between regions, and introduced a ban on mass gatherings.

Arayik Harutyunyan, a former prime minister and local businessman, won a majority of votes in the second round of the election. His main rival, acting foreign minister Masis Mayilyan, was one of only two candidates who refused to participate in the televised debates. Mayilyan received 12 percent of votes in the second round even after calling on supporters not to cast a vote, to prevent the further spread of the COVID-19 in the region. Both candidates criticized Nagorno-Karabakh's previous leadership figures allied with Armenia's former president, Serzh Sargsyan, who himself had resigned amid the 2018 mass street protests in that country.

Many foreign observers were not able to attend due to the COVID-19-related closure of international borders. Local observers, including those trained and supported by Armenia's leading nongovernmental organizations (NGOs), said the vote was free and fair despite reports of a few administrative irregularities and verbal clashes at some polling stations. Past elections were marred by problems including a lack of genuine competition and alleged abuses of administrative resources.

Score Change: The score improved from 1 to 2 because the presidential election was competitive and free of major irregularities.

A2. Were the current national legislative representatives elected through free and fair elections? 3 / 4 (+1)

Of the unicameral National Assembly's 33 members, all are elected by party list. Elections took place in spring 2020 in parallel with the presidential race. Ten political parties—almost twice more than in the 2015 elections—participated and organized into two blocs. Parties campaigned freely in towns and villages and participated in televised presentations and debates.

The Free Motherland (Azat Hayrenik) party, founded by Harutyunyan, maintained its dominant position in the legislature, winning 16 seats. The newly formed Miasnakan Hayrenik (United Motherland) party, led by opposition politician Samvel Babayan, came in second with nine seats. The remaining seats went to three other parties— the Armenian Revolutionary Federation (ARF)–Dashnaktsutyun, which won three seats; Ardarutyun (Justice), which also won three; and Artsakhi Zhoghovrdarakan Kusaktsutyun (Democratic Party of Artsakh), which won two; these were generally associated with politicians from past ruling coalitions.

Score Change: The score improved from 2 to 3 because the 2020 parliamentary election was more competitive than previous polls.

A3. Are the electoral laws and framework fair, and are they implemented impartially by the relevant election management bodies? 2 / 4 (+1)

Amendments passed in 2014 led to some improvements to the electoral code. Among other changes, the number of parliamentary seats under the proportional system increased, and the vote threshold for representation decreased to 5 percent for political parties and 7 percent for electoral coalitions, allowing for broader political participation. Electoral code changes adopted in July 2019 for the 2020 elections shifted the parliament to a fully proportional system, eliminating the individual constituencies.

In contrast to past elections and the 2017 referendum, the spring 2020 presidential and parliamentary votes were not marred by significant criticism of electoral administration.

Score Change: The score improved from 1 to 2 due to improvements in election management.

B. POLITICAL PLURALISM AND PARTICIPATION: 7 / 16 (+1)

B1. Do the people have the right to organize in different political parties or other competitive political groupings of their choice, and is the system free of undue obstacles to the rise and fall of these competing parties or groupings? 3 / 4 (+1)

There are few formal restrictions on the freedom to form and join political parties, but the political landscape in past years has been constrained in practice. Given the territory's contested status, open dissent and vigorous competition have been regarded as signs of disloyalty or even as a security risk.

Nagorno-Karabakh, however, has seen greater political activity since the 2018 revolution in Armenia. The spring 2020 campaign featured open and vigorous competition between existing and newly formed political parties. Politicians freely discussed domestic issues, and some presented detailed plans to improve transparency, implement anticorruption reforms, and improve diversity in government. There were no reports of serious, undue pressure or attacks against candidates during the 2020 campaign. Local politicians remained vocal and united in their criticism of any attempt to propose unilateral concessions in peace talks with Azerbaijan and called for international recognition of the region's independence.

Score Change: The score improved from 2 to 3 because political parties were generally able to organize events and compete freely during the spring election campaign.

B2. Is there a realistic opportunity for the opposition to increase its support or gain power through elections? 2 / 4

During the past decade, the leading political parties have tended to form broad coalitions and co-opt potential rivals, precluding genuine opposition. However, the so-called Velvet Revolution in Armenia in 2018 has brought considerable change to the political environment in Nagorno-Karabakh, with a number of prominent politicians refraining from forming coalitions with the ruling elites ahead of the spring 2020 elections and instead campaigning independently.

The elections saw a record number of presidential candidates and political parties competing for power. Two leading presidential candidates stood in an open opposition to the region's previous leadership. Five out of 14 candidates for the presidency did not represent any political party and ran independently. Two newly formed political parties gained seats, including Miasnakan Hayrenik (United Motherland), which came second in the race and took nine out of 33 seats in the local parliament.

The September 2019 local elections also featured strong performances by independent and opposition candidates. Many seats went to candidates with no party affiliation, who made up more than half of the registered contenders for local leadership posts.

B3. Are the people's political choices free from domination by forces that are external to the political sphere, or by political forces that employ extrapolitical means? 1 / 4

Politics in Nagorno-Karabakh are heavily influenced by the threat of military aggression and the 2020 war with Azerbaijan, which increased the territory's political, military, and financial dependence on Armenia. This dependence provides leverage for interference by the Armenian leadership in Nagorno-Karabakh's domestic political affairs, although local elites also have political influence, including over the selection of senior leadership positions.

In December 2019, Armenian prime minister Nikol Pashinyan met with some of the top candidates in the 2020 presidential race; the move was widely interpreted as Pashinyan's personal endorsement of those he believed were prepared to cooperate with his government, rather than criticizing it or siding with Armenia's former leadership. Since then, Pashinyan and key representatives of his government refrained from meetings with Nagorno-Karabakh's presidential candidates and their affiliated political parties.

Since February 2020, Armenia provided financial support to two NGOs that trained region's specialists in support to the independent observance of the spring 2020 elections. Despite strong calls from Armenian civil society, Armenia's leadership refused to interfere in Nagorno-Karabakh's dispute over whether to postpone the 2020 elections in light of the COVID-19 pandemic and expressed a need for local electoral processes to be implemented independently.

After the close of the 2020 war, a number of Armenia's and Nagorno-Karabakh's officials complained about poor relations between Yerevan and Stepanakert, which, they said, had emerged as among the key reasons for the defeat in fighting with Azerbaijan. Soon after the war, President Arayik Harutyunyan returned to senior positions some controversial politicians, who had previously left due to conflicts with Pashinyan.

B4. Do various segments of the population (including ethnic, racial, religious, gender, LGBT, and other relevant groups) have full political rights and electoral opportunities? 1 / 4

Before the 2020 war, the population was almost entirely ethnic Armenian as a result of displacement during the war in the 1990s. In accordance with the November 9, 2020, cease-fire agreement, thousands of Armenians fled from territories assigned to Azerbaijan, not including residents from about one-third of Nagorno-Karabakh itself.

Formally, women have equal political rights, but social constraints and a prevailing sense of militarization in local life limit their participation in practice, and they are poorly represented in leadership positions. While the 2014 electoral code required parties to ensure that women hold one in five of the places on their parliamentary lists, only five women won seats in the parliament in 2015. Before the spring 2020 elections, the gender quota was further increased to one in every four candidates on party lists, resulting in seven women taking seats at the newly formed parliament. For the first time ever, the 2020 race included two female candidates for presidency. Both received hundreds of votes. One of them, Bella Lalayan, campaigned for women's and social rights. In the 2019 local elections, women won about 11 percent of council seats and 2 percent of local leadership posts.

C. FUNCTIONING OF GOVERNMENT: 3 / 12

C1. Do the freely elected head of government and national legislative representatives determine the policies of the government? 1 / 4

The ability of locally elected officials to set and implement government policies is limited in practice by security threats along the line of contact between Nagorno-Karabakh and Azerbaijani forces, warnings from Baku, and the dominant role played by the Armenian government. The constitution calls for close cooperation with Armenia on political, economic, and military policy.

C2. Are safeguards against official corruption strong and effective? 1 / 4

Nagorno-Karabakh continues to suffer from significant corruption, particularly in the construction and infrastructure-development sectors. Officials practice favoritism in filling civil service positions.

C3. Does the government operate with openness and transparency? 1 / 4

A freedom of information law was adopted in 2004, but the government operates with little transparency in practice. Key decisions are negotiated by political actors, with few meaningful opportunities for public input. After the spring 2020 elections, new president Arayik Harutyunyan invited his main opponents to join leading positions in the government, suggesting this could result in more transparency for decision-making processes.

ADDITIONAL DISCRETIONARY POLITICAL RIGHTS QUESTION

Is the government or occupying power deliberately changing the ethnic composition of a country or territory so as to destroy a culture or tip the political balance in favor of another group? -1 / 0

The Azerbaijani military's operation in 2020 aimed at gaining control of Nagorno-Karabakh ruptured a cease-fire that, while frequently violated, had mostly prevented large-scale violence since 1994. That Russian-brokered agreement had been reached after Armenian forces captured the territory and seven adjacent Azerbaijani districts, and ethnic Azerbaijani residents fled or were expelled from the affected region. During the six weeks of fighting between September 27 and November 9, 2020, human rights groups as well local and international journalists documented attacks or evidence of attacks against the ethnic Armenian civilian population, as well as atrocities against ethnic Armenian soldiers. Tens of thousands of ethnic Armenian civilians consequently fled the territory, with many saying they felt that their lives would be at risk if they stayed. Only a fraction of those who left chose to return after the fighting ended.

Score Change: The score declined from 0 to -1 because attacks on civilian targets and atrocities by Azerbaijani troops against ethnic Armenian soldiers compelled tens of thousands of people to flee the territory.

CIVIL LIBERTIES: 19 / 60 (-1)

D. FREEDOM OF EXPRESSION AND BELIEF: 7 / 16

D1. Are there free and independent media? 2 / 4

The most popular local television station is the government-run Artsakh TV. The station's editorial policy has changed significantly since the political opening in Armenia in 2018, and it has in recent years hosted a greater plurality of opinion, notably during the intense campaign period before the spring 2020 elections. Critics of the territory's leadership who were previously prevented from making even short appearances became regular guests on current-affairs programs. In addition, regular debates were organized to address prominent topics in local public life, including the first-ever debate of presidential candidates in March.

Social media platforms are increasingly used by the public and government officials for the dissemination and discussion of news. Young opposition leaders are also well connected with independent media outlets in Armenia, which are able to convey their views to news consumers in Nagorno-Karabakh. Additionally, one popular Armenian media outlet, CivilNet, opened a permanent office in Stepanakert and hired local reporters for regular coverage of developments in Nagorno-Karabakh.

Nevertheless, many domestic journalists continue to practice self-censorship, primarily on subjects related to security and the peace process. The internet penetration rate is low and has been slow to expand. Mobile internet service remains unaffordable for most residents. One of the most prominent presidential candidates, Masis Mayilyan, campaigned on a promise to make affordable mobile internet services accessible to all residents of the region.

D2. Are individuals free to practice and express their religious faith or nonbelief in public and private? 1 / 4

The constitution guarantees religious freedom but allows for restrictions in the name of security, public order, and other state interests. The charter also recognizes the Armenian Apostolic Church as the "national church" of the Armenian people. The religious freedom of other groups is limited in practice. A 2009 law banned religious activity by unregistered groups and proselytism by minority faiths and made it more difficult for minority groups to register.

In 2019, restoration of the main mosque in the town known as Shushi to Armenians and Shusha to Azerbaijanis was completed, and the mosque was formally reopened that October. Services resumed when Azerbaijani military took over the town during the 2020 war. During the war, the Azerbaijani army fully or partially destroyed a number of Armenian religious objects, notably Sourp Ghazanchetsots Cathedral and Kanach Zham, in the same town. Russian peacekeepers took control of at least two important Armenian cathedrals, which are in the vicinity of or located inside the Azerbaijani-controlled territory as a result of the November cease-fire agreement. It remains unclear whether residents of Armenia and Nagorno-Karabakh will be allowed to attend services at these cathedrals.

D3. Is there academic freedom, and is the educational system free from extensive political indoctrination? 1 / 4

Schools and universities are subject to political influence and pressure to avoid dissenting views on sensitive topics, particularly those related to the territory's status and security. Educators engage in a degree of self-censorship on such issues.

D4. Are individuals free to express their personal views on political or other sensitive topics without fear of surveillance or retribution? 3 / 4

Private discussion is generally open and free, though expression of dissent may be inhibited somewhat by the prevailing nationalist sentiment in politics and society.

E. ASSOCIATIONAL AND ORGANIZATIONAL RIGHTS: 5 / 12
E1. Is there freedom of assembly? 2 / 4

Freedom of assembly has been respected unevenly. In March and April 2020, Stepanakert saw its largest street rallies related to the parliamentary and presidential elections, including those calling for the vote to be postponed due to the COVID-19 pandemic, and events decrying alleged electoral irregularities. In contrast to past decade, there were no attempts to disrupt the rallies.

E2. Is there freedom for nongovernmental organizations, particularly those that are engaged in human rights– and governance-related work? 2 / 4

More than 250 NGOs are registered in the territory, but most are inactive. Many groups struggle to secure sustainable funding, in part because partnerships with foreign or international NGOs are complicated by Nagorno-Karabakh's disputed status. Civil society groups also face competition from government-organized entities.

Armenia funded the monitoring of Nagorno-Karabakh's parliamentary and presidential elections in March and April 2020 by Transparency International's affiliate in Armenia, and the Stepanakert office of the Yerevan-based Union of Informed Citizens. Shortly before the vote, the Transparency International affiliate refused to send observers, citing the spread of COVID-19 in the region. Nevertheless, some of their local activists still participated in observation missions and in some cases continued cooperating with the NGOs after the elections.

E3. Is there freedom for trade unions and similar professional or labor organizations? 1 / 4

Trade unions are allowed to organize, but in practice they are weak and relatively inactive, with little practical ability to assert workers' interests. Many labor disputes are resolved through personal connections and family links before they reach local courts.

F. RULE OF LAW: 3 / 16 (−1)

F1. Is there an independent judiciary? 1 / 4

The judiciary is not independent in practice. The courts are influenced by the executive branch as well as by powerful political, economic, and criminal groups.

F2. Does due process prevail in civil and criminal matters? 1 / 4

The constitution guarantees basic due process rights, but police and the courts do not always uphold them in practice. Outspoken political dissidents have been subject to harassment by the authorities.

F3. Is there protection from the illegitimate use of physical force and freedom from war and insurgencies? 0 / 4 (−1)

The civilian population of Nagorno-Karabakh was subjected to indiscriminate violence and targeted atrocities by Azerbaijani forces during the six-week conflict. Abuses included the use of cluster munitions, white phosphorous bombs, and other heavy weapons in attacks that failed to distinguish between military and civilian targets, including against residential areas in the main towns and villages. Rights groups and journalists reported instances of civilians being beaten, detained, subject to degrading treatment, and tortured by Azerbaijani forces; Britain's *Guardian* newspaper conducted an investigation confirming the identities of two elderly noncombatant men beheaded by Azerbaijani forces, videos of which had been shared on social media. Attacks on dual-use infrastructure, such as facilities providing telecommunications and electricity services, damaged civilian sites such as churches, schools, and private businesses. Nagorno-Karabakh's human rights ombudsman reported that 52 ethnic Armenian civilians were killed by Azerbaijani attacks on the territory. In accordance with the November 9, 2020, cease-fire statement, Azerbaijan gained control over seven adjacent territories and parts of Nagorno-Karabakh itself, with the new line of contact running close to or inside civilian-populated areas.

Local officials and international human rights groups documented beheadings of Armenian soldiers, mutilation of their corpses, and torture of war prisoners by Azerbaijani soldiers, with footage of many such instances shared widely on social media. Footage also circulated of Azerbaijani soldiers desecrating graveyards.

Amnesty International reported instances where ethnic Armenian forces committed abuses against their counterparts during the conflict, including several instances of corpse mutilation and one of violence against a prisoner of war resulting in death.

Score Change: The score declined from 1 to 0 due to reports of wartime atrocities and indiscriminate, lethal military attacks on civilian areas.

F4. Do laws, policies, and practices guarantee equal treatment of various segments of the population? 1 / 4

The constitution bans discrimination based on gender, ethnicity, religion, and other categories. However, women are underrepresented in the public and private sectors and remain exposed to discrimination in practice. To preserve the Armenian character of the territory, state policies promote Armenian language and culture and have encouraged ethnic Armenians to migrate to Nagorno-Karabakh, partly through housing and other subsidies.

G. PERSONAL AUTONOMY AND INDIVIDUAL RIGHTS: 4 / 16 (−1)

G1. Do individuals enjoy freedom of movement, including the ability to change their place of residence, employment, or education? 0 / 4 (−1)

Freedom of movement within Nagorno-Karabakh is hindered by its ambiguous legal and diplomatic status, the instability of the cease-fire, and the presence of land mines, which continue to cause deaths and injuries, and in 2020, open warfare.

During the 2020 war, half to over 70 percent of the population of Nagorno-Karabakh fled the conflict zone. Around 50,000 returned as part of a process organized by the Russian peacekeepers. Only some were able to return to homes located in the areas transferred to Azerbaijani control as a result of the November 9, 2020, cease-fire agreement.

Score Change: The score declined from 1 to 0 because the military conflict caused mass displacement and severely impaired civilians' ability to safely leave or travel within the territory.

G2. Are individuals able to exercise the right to own property and establish private businesses without undue interference from state or nonstate actors? 1 / 4

Most major economic activity is tightly controlled by the government or a small group of powerful elites with political connections. The property rights of displaced Azerbaijanis have yet to be adequately addressed.

G3. Do individuals enjoy personal social freedoms, including choice of marriage partner and size of family, protection from domestic violence, and control over appearance? 2 / 4

Men and women have equal legal rights with respect to marriage and divorce, though the constitution defines marriage as a union between a man and a woman, precluding same-sex marriage. The government offers material incentives to encourage couples to have children. Domestic violence is common and not effectively prosecuted.

G4. Do individuals enjoy equality of opportunity and freedom from economic exploitation? 1 / 4

Employment opportunities remain scarce and are mostly confined to the state sector or state-subsidized businesses.

Northern Cyprus

Population: 382,000
Freedom Status: Free

Note: *Freedom in the World* reports assess the level of political rights and civil liberties in a given geographical area, regardless of whether they are affected by the state, nonstate actors, or foreign powers. Disputed territories are sometimes assessed separately if they meet certain criteria, including boundaries that are sufficiently stable to allow year-on-year comparisons. For more information, see the report methodology and FAQ.

Overview: The Turkish Republic of Northern Cyprus (TRNC) is a self-declared state recognized only by Turkey. Civil liberties are generally upheld, and the multiparty political system is largely democratic, though it has experienced growing interference from the Turkish government. Other ongoing concerns include corruption, discrimination against minority communities, and human trafficking.

KEY DEVELOPMENTS IN 2020

- In early March, in response to the COVID-19 pandemic, the government closed all borders and imposed movement restrictions on the population that lasted in whole or in part until June. As of mid-May there were no coronavirus patients in local hospitals. However, a number of entry restrictions remained in place, and social-distancing measures were tightened again in December as case numbers rose. Despite the upward trend, only six deaths were reported for the year.
- A new information technology law enacted in July empowered the government to shut down websites that carry illegal content, including defamatory material.
- In the October presidential election, which featured heavy-handed interference by the Turkish government, center-left incumbent Mustafa Akıncı was defeated by Prime Minister Ersin Tatar, a right-wing nationalist with close ties to Ankara.
- Days before the election, the People's Party (HP), led by Foreign Minister Kudret Özersay, withdrew from the ruling coalition. Tatar's National Unity Party (UBP) formed a new coalition in December with two smaller parties, and the resulting government was narrowly approved by the legislature later that month.

POLITICAL RIGHTS: 28 / 40 (−3)

A. ELECTORAL PROCESS: 9 / 12 (−2)

A1. Was the current head of government or other chief national authority elected through free and fair elections? 2 / 4 (−2)

The president, who serves as head of state and represents the TRNC internationally, is popularly elected to five-year terms. The 2020 presidential election was originally scheduled for April, but it was postponed until October due to the COVID-19 pandemic. Akıncı, the incumbent, ran for reelection as an independent with the backing of the social democratic Communal Democracy Party (TDP). He was defeated by Prime Minister Tatar of the UBP, the Turkish government's preferred candidate, who took nearly 52 percent of the vote in the second round.

The election period featured highly unusual and overt interference by Turkish authorities on Tatar's behalf; during his term as president, Akıncı had repeatedly criticized the Turkish government, including for meddling in TRNC politics. In early October, before the first round of voting, the communications adviser for Turkish vice president Fuat Oktay arrived to aid Tatar's campaign, while a member of the Turkish parliament from the far-right Nationalist Movement Party (MHP) canvassed 69 villages to support Tatar. The Turkish embassy allegedly contacted mayors and village leaders to ask them what they needed in exchange for their support. Reports later emerged that Turkish government and intelligence officials had threatened Tatar's opponents, including Akıncı, as well as Turkish Cypriot businesses with interests in Turkey. The public interventions polarized the electorate between those who condemned Ankara's interference and those who wanted to maintain Turkish support. Possibly due to the extreme polarization, only 58 percent of eligible voters went to the polls in the first round, the lowest figure in the history of the TRNC. In the week before the second-round vote, the UBP distributed favors in villages, while Tatar's government disbursed financial aid, ostensibly to compensate for losses during the COVID-19 lockdown. Turnout for the runoff balloting was 67 percent.

The president appoints the prime minister and cabinet members, who must have the support of a legislative majority. After winning election as president, Tatar resigned as prime minister and head of the UBP. Ersan Saner, a seasoned lawmaker and former minister, became the new UBP leader and eventually formed a ruling coalition with the center-right Democratic Party (DP) and the Rebirth Party (YDP), a right-wing group backed primarily by settlers from Turkey. The previous coalition, between the UBP and HP, had collapsed ahead of the election when the HP withdrew. In late December, Saner's cabinet narrowly won approval from the legislature in a 24–20 vote, with some members abstaining.

Score Change: The score declined from 4 to 2 because the government of Turkey openly intervened to support its preferred candidate—the incumbent prime minister—in Northern Cyprus's presidential election, deploying personnel and financial resources to aid his campaign.

A2. Were the current national legislative representatives elected through free and fair elections? 4 / 4

For elections to the 50-seat Assembly of the Republic, the TRNC employs a mixed voting system, with the proportional representation component setting a 5 percent vote threshold for parties to win seats. Members serve five-year terms. In the 2018 elections, the UBP led with 21 seats, followed by the center-left Republican Turkish Party (CTP) with 12 seats, the HP (9), the TDP (3), the DP (3), and the YDP (2). The HP had initially formed a government with the CTP, the TDP, and the DP, but withdrew and formed a new coalition with the UBP in 2019, before withdrawing from that alliance as well ahead of the 2020 presidential vote.

A3. Are the electoral laws and framework fair, and are they implemented impartially by the relevant election management bodies? 3 / 4

The Supreme Election Committee is an independent body composed of judges, and elections in the TRNC have generally been considered free and fair, though the degree of Turkish government interference in the 2020 presidential vote called this into question.

A complex new election law that came into effect in 2018 allowed voters to choose a single party, individual candidates from multiple parties, or a combination of the two; voters were also able to choose candidates across more than one multimember constituency. The law made it more complicated to vote for individual candidates and therefore encouraged party voting.

During the 2020 presidential election, several hundred citizens were prohibited from voting because they were under quarantine in connection with the COVID-19 pandemic.

B. POLITICAL PLURALISM AND PARTICIPATION: 12 / 16 (−1)

B1. Do the people have the right to organize in different political parties or other competitive political groupings of their choice, and is the system free of undue obstacles to the rise and fall of these competing parties or groupings? 4 / 4

Turkish Cypriots are free to organize in political parties, and several parties compete in practice. Six parties were represented in the legislature in 2020, including two—HP and YDP—that entered the chamber for the first time after the 2018 elections. Under a 2015 law, parties that receive at least 3 percent of the vote may obtain state funding.

B2. Is there a realistic opportunity for the opposition to increase its support or gain power through elections? 4 / 4

There have been multiple transfers of power between rival parties over the past two decades, with shifts in both the presidency and the premiership. Akıncı ousted the incumbent president in the 2015 election, only to lose office himself in the 2020 balloting. Three different governing coalitions have controlled the cabinet since the 2018 legislative elections, and opposition parties retained a strong position in the assembly as of 2020.

B3. Are the people's political choices free from domination by forces that are external to the political sphere, or by political forces that employ extrapolitical means? 2 / 4 (-1)

Although the Turkish government has always exercised considerable influence over the TRNC, in the past it had little direct control over voters, many of whom have supported candidates and parties that displayed independence from Ankara. In the 2020 presidential election, however, the Turkish government for the first time engaged in an explicit campaign of inducements and threats against Akıncı and in support of his main rival, Tatar. Support for Tatar's UBP party had already been strong in rural areas, particularly among those who viewed the party's patronage network as a way to access jobs and favors. That network, in turn, depended in part on a steady flow of economic support from Turkey, and Ankara's open opposition to Akıncı raised the prospect that such support could be cut off if he won reelection.

The Turkish government's interference in the process reportedly continued when, following Tatar's election as president in October, the UBP began an intraparty contest to decide on a new party leader and prime minister. Pressure from Turkish government representatives allegedly resulted in the withdrawal of the two leading candidates in favor of a third candidate, Ersan Saner, who was supported by Ankara and ultimately succeeded.

Score Change: The score declined from 3 to 2 due to increased interference by the government of Turkey in Northern Cyprus's political processes, including the presidential election and the contest within the ruling party to replace the prime minister.

B4. Do various segments of the population (including ethnic, racial, religious, gender, LGBT+, and other relevant groups) have full political rights and electoral opportunities? 2 / 4

All adult citizens may vote, but the rights of minority populations remain a concern. The few hundred Maronite and Greek Cypriots living in the TRNC are issued special identity cards and are unable to vote in TRNC elections. While small numbers of Maronites from the south have been allowed to resettle in their ancestral villages in the north since 2017, there has been no significant progress on expanding Maronite political rights.

Women have full political rights, and a 2015 law requires 30 percent of a party's parliamentary candidate list to consist of women. However, women's political participation is limited in practice, particularly in leadership positions. In the 2018 elections, women won nine seats out of 50, an improvement from four in the previous legislature. No female candidates ran in the 2020 presidential race, and the new coalition government formed in December 2020 had no female ministers.

There have been recurring questions about the number of naturalized TNRC citizens originally from Turkey, their voting habits, and the manner in which they acquired citizenship. Immediately after Cyprus's division in 1974, an agreement between the Northern Cyprus administration and the Turkish government brought around 25,000 Turkish farmers and workers to the island and gave them citizenship rights. This group primarily comprised people who had been displaced by development projects in Turkey and came from many ethnic backgrounds and political persuasions. After 1979, this facilitated migration ended, and Turkish civilians arriving in Northern Cyprus since then have come on their own initiative. Naturalized citizens account for about a third of the citizen population, according to some estimates. Their voting patterns remain pluralistic, with most endorsing conservative parties but many also supporting the CTP.

C. FUNCTIONING OF GOVERNMENT: 7 / 12

C1. Do the freely elected head of government and national legislative representatives determine the policies of the government? 3 / 4

While elected officials have generally developed and implemented policies and legislation without direct interference from Ankara, the TRNC remains diplomatically, militarily, and financially dependent on Turkey, and this dependence sometimes allows the Turkish government to influence policymaking.

President Akıncı showed considerable independence from the Turkish government, creating a rift with Turkish president Recep Tayyip Erdoğan that resulted in overt Turkish intervention in the 2020 presidential election. The TRNC coalition government formed in 2019 was more aligned with Ankara's position on reunification talks with the Republic of Cyprus. Whereas Akıncı had long supported a federal model, for example, the new UBP-led government called for consideration of alternatives, including a two-state solution. After Tatar's election as president in 2020, the TRNC was expected adhere more closely to Ankara's policy aims.

C2. Are safeguards against official corruption strong and effective? 2 / 4

Corruption, cronyism in the distribution of civil service jobs, and nepotism are serious impediments to good governance, and the media have exposed a number of scandals in recent years. Surveys of businesspeople in Northern Cyprus have shown that large majorities consider corruption and bribery to be significant problems, including in the public sector and government services.

C3. Does the government operate with openness and transparency? 2 / 4

Although there is a law providing for access to information, there has been very little progress in making government records available to the public in practice. Information is not always kept in an accessible form, and officials reportedly withhold data on sensitive topics such as the naturalization of Turkish settlers as TRNC citizens.

CIVIL LIBERTIES: 50 / 60

D. FREEDOM OF EXPRESSION AND BELIEF: 15 / 16

D1. Are there free and independent media? 4 / 4

Freedom of the press is guaranteed by law, and TRNC authorities generally respect it in practice. The media often carry sharp criticism of both the TRNC and Turkish governments. However, a new information technology law enacted in July 2020 enables the authorities to shut down websites that carry illegal content, including material that is deemed to violate existing laws on libel and insult. Consolidation of private media ownership is also a concern.

D2. Are individuals free to practice and express their religious faith or nonbelief in public and private? 3 / 4

The TRNC is a secular state and legally guarantees freedom of worship, which is mostly respected in practice. However, authorities continue to impose restrictions on access to churches and otherwise interfere with church services. Christians and non-Sunni Muslims have complained that the government favors Sunni Islam in its policies on religious education and places of worship. The government's Religious Affairs Department staffs Sunni mosques with imams.

D3. Is there academic freedom, and is the educational system free from extensive political indoctrination? 4 / 4

Academic freedom is generally respected. While large numbers of teachers and professors have been fired or jailed for political reasons in Turkey since 2016, no similar purges had occurred in the TRNC as of 2020.

D4. Are individuals free to express their personal views on political or other sensitive topics without fear of surveillance or retribution? 4 / 4

There are no significant restrictions on freedom of private discussion, and individuals generally do not face repercussions for expressing their political views on social media. While the information technology law enacted in July 2020 included provisions that could restrict online speech, no significant enforcement actions were reported during the year.

E. ASSOCIATIONAL AND ORGANIZATIONAL RIGHTS: 11 / 12

E1. Is there freedom of assembly? 4 / 4

Freedom of assembly is guaranteed by the constitution and generally upheld in practice. The health threat posed by COVID-19 resulted in some limitations on public gatherings during 2020, though the restrictions were not considered to be abusive or disproportionate.

E2. Is there freedom for nongovernmental organizations, particularly those that are engaged in human rights- and governance-related work? 4 / 4

Numerous nongovernmental organizations are registered in the TRNC, and they typically operate without restrictions. Many such groups have worked with Greek Cypriot partners to advance reunification efforts.

E3. Is there freedom for trade unions and similar professional or labor organizations? 3 / 4

Workers may form independent unions, bargain collectively, and strike. Collective bargaining is reportedly common in the public sector. However, the government can limit strikes in ill-defined essential services, and employers are reportedly able to obstruct unionization in the private sector without legal repercussions.

F. RULE OF LAW: 13 / 16

F1. Is there an independent judiciary? 4 / 4

The judiciary is independent, and courts have often ruled against the government in recent years. The system is overseen by the Supreme Council of Judicature, which is headed by the president of the Supreme Court and includes that court's seven judges as well as one member each appointed by the president, the legislature, the attorney general, and the bar association. The council is responsible for judicial appointments, promotions, assignments, and disciplinary measures.

F2. Does due process prevail in civil and criminal matters? 3 / 4

Although due process rights are typically respected, police have been accused of violating protections against arbitrary detention and coerced confessions in some cases, for example by improperly denying suspects access to a lawyer.

There had been no large-scale purges of TRNC security forces or other public employees in connection with the 2016 coup attempt in Turkey as of 2020, but due process has been a concern in the clusters of cases that have emerged. Investigations and dismissals of police officers have been reported, for example, with those fired accused of ties to the movement of US-based Islamic preacher Fethullah Gülen, which is blamed for the coup attempt and considered a terrorist organization in Turkey. Some Turkish military personnel stationed in Northern Cyprus have been arrested on similar allegations.

F3. Is there protection from the illegitimate use of physical force and freedom from war and insurgencies? 3 / 4

The population is generally free from threats to physical security, but police have been accused of abusing detainees, and prisons feature overcrowding and other harsh conditions.

F4. Do laws, policies, and practices guarantee equal treatment of various segments of the population? 3 / 4

Women enjoy legal equality, but in practice they encounter some discrimination in employment, education, and other areas.

The tiny Greek and Maronite minority communities live in enclaves and suffer from social and economic disadvantages. The small Kurdish population is reportedly subject to discrimination in employment. Both groups have complained of surveillance by TRNC authorities.

LGBT+ people reportedly face social stigmatization, though same-sex sexual activity was decriminalized in 2014, and discrimination based on sexual orientation or gender identity is prohibited by law.

The TRNC lacks legal protections for asylum seekers, raising concerns about possible refoulement. Some Turkish nationals suspected of belonging to the Gülen movement have been deported to Turkey, where they face persecution.

G. PERSONAL AUTONOMY AND INDIVIDUAL RIGHTS: 11 / 16

G1. Do individuals enjoy freedom of movement, including the ability to change their place of residence, employment, or education? 3 / 4

Movement within the TRNC territory is generally unrestricted. However, travel abroad is complicated by the TRNC's lack of international recognition. The only direct flights from the TRNC are to Turkey. Most governments do not accept TRNC travel documents, so many Turkish Cypriots carry Republic of Cyprus passports, for which they are eligible. Movement across the UN buffer zone dividing the island has improved since 2004 due to the opening of new border crossings.

A number of former civilian municipalities have been under Turkish military control since 1974, with bans on settlement or resettlement. In October 2020, with Ankara's support, the government partially opened the closed town of Varosha (Maraş), which had once been a popular tourist destination. The move drew objections from Varosha's former Greek Cypriot residents and the UN Security Council, which had long warned against any unilateral change in the town's status or settlement by people other than its previous inhabitants. The action was seen as part of the Turkish government's bid to assist Tatar's presidential election campaign.

During 2020, the government installed hundreds of surveillance cameras in a integrated system across the territory. Similar systems have been deployed in Turkey to monitor the population, particularly in cities. In Northern Cyprus, the cameras were installed even in small villages, and it was not clear how the information collected would be used. They were expected to be operated by police, but the chain of command for the Turkish Cypriot police is tied to the Turkish military.

G2. Are individuals able to exercise the right to own property and establish private businesses without undue interference from state or nonstate actors? 3 / 4

The authorities recognize the rights to own property and establish businesses. In practice these rights are somewhat limited, as authorities have in various ways attempted to prevent the sale of historically Turkish Cypriot properties to foreigners. The TRNC formed the

Immovable Property Commission (IPC) in 2006 to resolve claims by Greek Cypriots who owned property in the north before the island's 1974 division. In 2010, the European Court of Human Rights recognized the commission as an "accessible and effective" mechanism. However, its work has been seriously impaired in recent years by a lack of funding from the government and Ankara.

G3. Do individuals enjoy personal social freedoms, including choice of marriage partner and size of family, protection from domestic violence, and control over appearance? 3 / 4

Personal social freedoms are generally respected, though women's organizations have criticized the government for failing to adequately address the problems of rape and domestic violence. According to multiple surveys in recent years, about one in three women have experienced such violence. However, figures released in December 2019 suggested that reporting of such abuse was increasing significantly, with police in 2018 receiving 1,047 reports—four times the average from previous years.

G4. Do individuals enjoy equality of opportunity and freedom from economic exploitation? 2 / 4

While TRNC citizens generally have access to economic opportunity and protections from abusive working conditions, noncitizens often experience exploitation and lack mechanisms for appeal. During the COVID-19 pandemic in 2020, many temporary workers from Turkey were returned to that country without pay. The pandemic led to hardships for many local workers as well, though civil servants received their pay without interruption even during the lockdown period.

Human trafficking and forced prostitution are serious problems, despite a nominal legal ban on prostitution. The TRNC does not have adequate antitrafficking legislation and does not fund antitrafficking efforts. Observers also report that some authorities are complicit in trafficking.

Pakistani Kashmir

Population: 5,500,000
Freedom Status: Not Free

Note: *Freedom in the World* reports assess the level of political rights and civil liberties in a given geographical area, regardless of whether they are affected by the state, nonstate actors, or foreign powers. Disputed territories are sometimes assessed separately if they meet certain criteria, including boundaries that are sufficiently stable to allow year-on-year comparisons. For more information, see the report methodology and FAQ.

Overview: Pakistani Kashmir is administered as two territories: Azad Jammu and Kashmir (AJK) and Gilgit-Baltistan (GB). Each has an elected assembly and government with limited autonomy, but they lack the parliamentary representation and other rights of Pakistani provinces, and Pakistani federal institutions have predominant influence over security, the courts, and most important policy matters. Politics within the two territories are carefully managed to promote the idea of Kashmir's eventual accession to Pakistan. Freedoms of expression and association, and any political activity deemed contrary to Pakistan's policy on Kashmir, are restricted.

KEY DEVELOPMENTS IN 2020

- Rigorous lockdown measures to combat the COVID-19 pandemic were implemented in both AJK and GB in March and April, and restrictions were reimposed more briefly during a second wave of infections in the autumn. Journalists were exempted from the restrictions, and normal life—including the limited freedom of assembly—resumed outside the lockdown periods.

- Elections for the GB legislature were held in November. The ruling party in Pakistan, Pakistan Tehreek-e-Insaf (PTI), initially won fewer than half of the directly elected seats, but several independents quickly joined the party, giving it a majority. Khalid Khurshid Khan of the PTI was duly elected as chief minister in December. Opposition parties complained of election rigging but took up their seats in the new assembly.

- Pakistani and Indian forces exchanged fire across the Line of Control (LoC) separating their de facto Kashmiri territories throughout the year. Pakistan reported over 3,000 Indian violations of the 2003 cease-fire arrangement, which allegedly killed 28 civilians and injured more than 249 others in 2020.

- The prospect that GB could be granted provisional provincial status in Pakistan remained under discussion during the year, but no substantive changes were made.

POLITICAL RIGHTS: 9 / 40

A. ELECTORAL PROCESS: 4 / 12

A1. Was the current head of government or other chief national authority elected through free and fair elections? 1 / 4

Both AJK and GB have locally elected executive leaders. However, the Pakistani government also controls—directly and indirectly—key executive functions, and it is not accountable to voters in the two territories.

Under AJK's 1974 interim constitution, a president elected by the Legislative Assembly serves as head of state, while the elected prime minister is the chief executive. After the 2016 elections, the new assembly elected the local leader of Pakistan's then ruling Pakistan Muslim League–Nawaz (PML-N), Raja Farooq Haider, as prime minister, and Masood Khan, formerly a senior Pakistani diplomat, as president. They remained in office during 2020, despite the presence of a PTI government in Pakistan since 2018. An AJK Council based in Pakistan's capital, Islamabad, comprises both Kashmiri and Pakistani officials and is chaired by the Pakistani prime minister. The council holds a number of executive, legislative, and judicial powers, such as control over the appointment of superior judges and the chief election commissioner.

Under the Government of Gilgit-Baltistan Order 2018—adopted by the Pakistani government to replace GB's previous basic law, the 2009 Gilgit-Baltistan Empowerment and Self-Governance Order (GBESGO)—executive functions are shared between a Pakistani-appointed governor and a chief minister chosen by the GB Assembly (GBA). The governor signs legislation and has significant power over judicial appointments; the governor's decisions cannot be overruled by the GBA. The order also grants extensive authority to the Pakistani prime minister, including exclusive executive and legislative powers on a long list of topics.

GB residents who sought de facto provincial status challenged the 2018 order, and in 2019 the Pakistani Supreme Court instructed the Pakistani government to fully address GB's constitutional status. In May 2020, the Pakistani president amended the 2018 order to provide for a caretaker administration in GB that would preside over elections in November. In September, Pakistan's chief of army staff chaired a meeting at which Pakistani politicians apparently agreed on a shift toward provincial status for GB, and the PTI campaigned on the pledge ahead of the elections. The PTI duly won the balloting, in keeping with a long-standing pattern in which elections in AJK and GB are won by the local branch of the party in power in Pakistan. Khalid Khurshid Khan of the PTI was elected as GB chief minister in December, and Pakistani prime minister Imran Khan formed a committee tasked with making recommendations on GB's constitutional status. Despite these moves, there was still significant opposition to a change in GB's status in both AJK and the Pakistani establishment.

A2. Were the current national legislative representatives elected through free and fair elections? 2 / 4

Neither AJK nor GB is represented in the Pakistani Parliament.

The AJK Legislative Assembly as of 2020 had 49 seats; the region's election commission in 2019 finalized the creation of four new seats, which were due to be filled in the 2021 elections. Of the existing seats, 41 were filled through direct elections: 29 with constituencies based in the territory and 12 meant to represent Kashmiri refugees throughout Pakistan. Another eight were reserved seats: five for women and one each for representatives of overseas Kashmiris, technocrats, and religious leaders. The PML-N won the 2016 elections with 31 seats. The local branch of the Pakistan People's Party (PPP) won three seats, as did the Muslim Conference, while the PTI secured two. The remaining two seats were won by the Jammu Kashmir Peoples Party and an independent. The election process was largely peaceful, though both the PPP and the local PTI leader complained of preelection manipulation, including the use of federal development funds to boost support for the PML-N.

The 33-member GBA is composed of 24 directly elected members, six seats reserved for women, and three seats reserved for technocrats. The GBA's legislative authority is limited to certain subjects, and even discussion of some topics—foreign affairs, defense, internal security, and judicial conduct—is prohibited by the Government of Gilgit-Baltistan Order 2018. However, the order does allow the GBA to exercise legislative powers that were previously allocated to the Gilgit-Baltistan Council (GBC). The council, which now has an advisory role, is headed by the Pakistani prime minister and vice-chaired by the GB governor and includes six members chosen by the GBA and six Pakistani ministers or Parliament members chosen by the Pakistani prime minister. The GB chief minister also has a seat.

Elections to the GB Assembly were held in November 2020. The PTI emerged as the largest party, with 10 of the 24 directly elected seats. Several independents then opted to join the PTI, and after the reserved seats were filled through proportional representation, the party controlled 22 out of 33 seats. All the main Pakistani parties campaigned extensively in GB. The PPP and PML-N—which took five and three seats, respectively—both initially complained of election rigging and refused to accept the results, but they eventually took up their seats in the new assembly. Smaller parties secured the remaining three seats.

A3. Are the electoral laws and framework fair, and are they implemented impartially by the relevant election management bodies? 1 / 4

The electoral framework in both territories facilitates indirect control by the Pakistani authorities. For example, the AJK Council appoints the chief election commissioner, and the electoral system for the AJK Legislative Assembly disproportionately favors nonresident refugees over AJK residents. The nonresident elections are more vulnerable to manipulation by federal Pakistani authorities, and the party in office at the federal level tends to win these seats. Candidates in the AJK elections must formally endorse "the ideology of Pakistan" and Kashmir's accession to Pakistan.

The Pakistani president's May 2020 order to set the stage for the November GBA elections applied Pakistan's 2017 election law to GB and called for a neutral caretaker administration to replace the incumbent GB government until the elections. The election code of conduct for GB requires parties and candidates to refrain from any action or speech that could be deemed prejudicial to the "ideology of Pakistan" or the country's security. Like the similar rule in AJK, this vague provision can be used to exclude candidates associated with nationalist parties or those disapproved of by the Pakistani authorities.

B. POLITICAL PLURALISM AND PARTICIPATION: 4 / 16

B1. Do the people have the right to organize in different political parties or other competitive political groupings of their choice, and is the system free of undue obstacles to the rise and fall of these competing parties or groupings? 1 / 4

Politics in both AJK and GB are dominated by local branches of the main Pakistani parties and some local parties, such as AJK's Muslim Conference, that are closely allied with the Pakistani establishment. Small nationalist parties that are opposed to union with Pakistan are actively marginalized or barred outright from the political process, and they played no significant role in the 2020 GB elections. Activists accused of opposition to Pakistani rule have been subject to surveillance, harassment, and sometimes imprisonment. The interim constitution of AJK bans political parties that do not endorse the territory's eventual accession to Pakistan, and similar rules prevail in GB.

The issue of jailed GB political activists emerged again during the 2020 election campaign. Supporters and family members of 14 activists from Hunza, including Baba Jan of the Awami Workers Party, who were jailed in 2011 for protests over government mishandling of a natural disaster staged a seven-day sit-in in October 2020 and blocked the Karakorum Highway. The caretaker administration promised to have the men released, and the last members of the group were freed by late November 2020.

B2. Is there a realistic opportunity for the opposition to increase its support or gain power through elections? 1 / 4

There is ample precedent for transfers of power between the major parties, though these are typically dictated by parallel changes at the federal level in Pakistan. The installation by the PTI government in Islamabad of a caretaker administration in GB prior to the 2020 elections may be interpreted as a move to eliminate the advantage of local incumbency, but it also underscored the institutional benefits that accrue to the incumbent party in Pakistan with regard to AJK and GB elections. While the PML-N was in power in Islamabad, federal authorities were similarly accused of working to manipulate the 2016 AJK Legislative Assembly elections in favor of that party.

B3. Are the people's political choices free from domination by forces that are external to the political sphere, or by political forces that employ extrapolitical means? 1 / 4

Because voters in GB and AJK cannot participate in Pakistani elections, Pakistani federal officials and entities are not democratically accountable to them. Security agencies operating in both territories are federal institutions. They work to block and suppress any parties or politicians that adopt positions deemed to conflict with Pakistani interests.

B4. Do various segments of the population (including ethnic, racial, religious, gender, LGBT+, and other relevant groups) have full political rights and electoral opportunities? 1 / 4

Men and women have the right to vote in both territories. Although there is no bar on women contesting general seats, women rarely exercise this right in practice. Instead, general seats tend to be filled by men. The seats reserved for women are filled proportionally from party lists based on the general vote, meaning the parties themselves determine who will represent women's interests. In the 2020 GB elections, only four women stood for general seats. The election observation group Free and Fair Election Network (FAFEN) analyzed new voter registrations and highlighted a persistent gender gap, with nearly 9 percent fewer women than men among all registered GB voters.

Shiite Muslims, Sunni Muslims, and members of the Ismaili offshoot of Shia Islam are represented in the GBA, having won directly elected seats. A small Shiite party allied itself with the PTI in the 2020 balloting. The heterodox Ahmadi sect, which suffers systematic discrimination in Pakistan, is poorly represented in GB's political system, as is the Christian minority.

C. FUNCTIONING OF GOVERNMENT: 3 / 12

C1. Do the freely elected head of government and national legislative representatives determine the policies of the government? 1 / 4

The powers of the elected chief executives in AJK and GB are limited by the fact that the Pakistani prime minister, the Pakistani minister for Kashmir Affairs and Gilgit-Baltistan, and through them the federal civil service, exercise effective control over government operations in both territories. As in Pakistan, federal military and intelligence agencies also play a powerful role in governance and policymaking.

The territories lack any meaningful fiscal autonomy, as federal taxes are imposed on both, and they receive a share of the resulting funds from the federal government. The territories' local representatives are excluded from the Pakistani bodies that negotiate interprovincial resource allocation.

There has been a sustained debate on the idea of enhancing GB's status in the Pakistani constitution by designating it as a provisional province, granting its legislators powers on par with those delegated to Pakistan's four existing provinces, and giving GB representation in the federal Parliament. Proponents have claimed that this would reduce any legal concerns hampering Chinese investment as part of the China-Pakistan Economic Corridor (CPEC) infrastructure project and grant GB residents the constitutional rights enjoyed by Pakistani citizens. However, figures associated with the struggle against Indian control of Kashmir have criticized the GB proposal as a weakening of the commitment to full Kashmiri accession to Pakistan. While the debate continued in 2020, decision-making authority regarding a new status remained concentrated in Islamabad rather than GB itself.

C2. Are safeguards against official corruption strong and effective? 1 / 4

Both territories have formal safeguards against official corruption, and GB is within the jurisdiction of Pakistan's National Accountability Bureau, which has a field office in Gilgit. However, as in Pakistan, corruption is believed to remain endemic, with enforcement actions subject to political influence.

C3. Does the government operate with openness and transparency? 1 / 4

Transparency and access to government information are limited in practice. The AJK and GB governments have made gestures toward transparency by posting basic information about their operations online, but such disclosures remain infrequent and inadequate.

ADDITIONAL DISCRETIONARY POLITICAL RIGHTS QUESTION
Is the government or occupying power deliberately changing the ethnic composition of a country or territory so as to destroy a culture or tip the political balance in favor of another group? -2 / 0

The Sunni Muslim share of the population in GB—historically a Shiite-majority region—has increased significantly in the decades since a pre-1947 rule was abolished to allow immigration from different parts of Pakistan. State agencies are suspected of deliberately encouraging this migration to engineer a demographic change. Under the 2009 GBESGO, settlers were given formal citizenship rights in GB; critics of a clause in the Government of Gilgit-Baltistan Order 2018 have argued that it appears to extend GB citizenship rights to all Pakistani citizens, further encouraging settlement. The pre-1947 restrictions on acquiring residency and citizenship are still in place in AJK and have assumed greater significance since the Indian authorities eased similar restrictions in Indian-administered Jammu and Kashmir in early 2020.

CIVIL LIBERTIES: 19 / 60
D. FREEDOM OF EXPRESSION AND BELIEF: 6 / 16
D1. Are there free and independent media? 1 / 4

AJK and GB are subject to laws that curb freedom of expression, particularly regarding reporting or commentary on the political status of the territories. Media houses need permission from the AJK Council and the federal Ministry of Kashmir Affairs and Gilgit-Baltistan to operate. A wide range of outlets are present and active. However, coverage of news and politics does not diverge from official Pakistani narratives, including the notions that India's hold over the Kashmir Valley is illegitimate and all Kashmiris seek accession to Pakistan. This compliance is achieved through a mixture of censorship, self-censorship, and harassment. A number of outlets have faced closure by authorities in recent years.

D2. Are individuals free to practice and express their religious faith or nonbelief in public and private? 1 / 4

Both territories have a predominantly Muslim population, and there is no official or social tolerance of nonbelief. Tools used to compel expressions of belief and conformity with official interpretations of religious doctrine include laws criminalizing blasphemy, rules requiring observance of Ramadan, and an obligation to denounce the heterodox Ahmadi sect to obtain a Pakistani passport. Although there is a history of Sunni-Shiite sectarian violence in GB, no major incidents have been reported in recent years.

D3. Is there academic freedom, and is the educational system free from extensive political indoctrination? 2 / 4

Each territory is home to a growing education system, and education is much valued as a path to migration and employment. However, in academia there are acute sensitivities around the issue of constitutional status, and debate or materials questioning Pakistan's claims over Kashmir are not tolerated. Student union activity has long been subject to state monitoring for signs of nationalist political views. Local languages and scripts are not taught in government schools. There is a history of attacks on schools in the Darel Valley by Islamist militants who oppose secular and girls' education.

D4. Are individuals free to express their personal views on political or other sensitive topics without fear of surveillance or retribution? 2 / 4

Federal intelligence agencies maintain a prominent and intrusive presence in both territories. Discussion of heterodox political or religious views consequently carries significant risks. The authorities have increased their monitoring of social media and sporadically punish expression of anti-Pakistan or separatist opinions.

E. ASSOCIATIONAL AND ORGANIZATIONAL RIGHTS: 4 / 12

E1. Is there freedom of assembly? 1 / 4

The authorities' observance of freedom of assembly is highly discretionary. The Pakistani state traditionally uses AJK as a platform to protest against Indian control of Jammu and Kashmir and the treatment of the population on the Indian side of the LoC. Protests that do not directly challenge Pakistani control or the territories' constitutional status are more likely to be tolerated. The authorities rely on harassment, intimidation, and the use of security checkpoints to deter protests in opposition to government policies.

In August 2020, despite the pandemic, ruling and opposition parties participated in highly choreographed anti-India speeches, demonstrations, and a special sitting of the AJK Assembly to mark the first anniversary of the Indian government's revocation of Jammu and Kashmir's autonomy.

Among other examples of tolerated protests during the year, medical professionals demonstrated in GB in June over their working conditions amid the pandemic. In October, the prisoner support group Aseeran-i-Hunza Rihaee Committee held its sit-in and blockade of the Karakoram Highway, which helped prompt the release of the political activists detained in 2011. The main political parties were all able to campaign and hold meetings ahead of the tightly controlled GBA elections, although not on the scale of those prior to the pandemic. The PPP and PML-N also organized protest demonstrations after the elections.

In February 2020, the proindependence Jammu and Kashmir Liberation Front (JKLF) asserted its freedom of assembly by organizing rallies in AJK to commemorate leaders killed on the Indian-held side, but three participants in one of the rallies were injured by Indian forces firing across the LoC.

E2. Is there freedom for nongovernmental organizations, particularly those that are engaged in human rights- and governance-related work? 1 / 4

Humanitarian nongovernmental organizations (NGOs) are subject to strict registration requirements and thus operate at the pleasure of the authorities. NGOs working on political or human rights issues face more intrusive government scrutiny and, in some cases, harassment.

E3. Is there freedom for trade unions and similar professional or labor organizations? 2 / 4

AJK is subject to labor laws similar to those in Pakistan. However, unions and professional organizations are frequently barred. Labor laws and union activities are poorly developed in GB.

F. RULE OF LAW: 3 / 16

F1. Is there an independent judiciary? 1 / 4

Both territories have nominally independent judiciaries, but the Pakistani federal government plays a powerful role in judicial appointments. On politically sensitive issues, the AJK and GB courts are not considered to operate with independence from the executive in Pakistan.

The president of AJK, in consultation with the AJK Council, appoints the chief justice of the territory's Supreme Court. Other judges of the superior courts are appointed by the

AJK president on the advice of the council, after consultation with the chief justice. The chief judge and other judges of GB's Supreme Appellate Court are appointed for three-year terms by the prime minister of Pakistan on the recommendation of the governor. In its 2019 ruling on GB's 2018 governance order, the Pakistan Supreme Court essentially extended its jurisdiction to GB residents and courts, adding to the legal ambiguity surrounding the territory's constitutional status, which remained unresolved in 2020.

F2. Does due process prevail in civil and criminal matters? 1 / 4

The civilian court systems in both territories feature basic due process guarantees, including defense lawyers and a right to appeal, but arbitrary arrests and other violations are not uncommon, particularly in security-related cases. Pakistan's Anti-Terrorism Act (ATA), which is often used to suppress dissent, includes vaguely defined offenses, allows extended detention without trial, and applies to juveniles, among other problematic features. Since 2015, the Pakistani government has allowed civilians facing charges of terrorism or sectarian violence to be tried in military courts, which have fewer due process protections and can impose the death penalty.

F3. Is there protection from the illegitimate use of physical force and freedom from war and insurgencies? 1 / 4

Torture and deaths in custody at the hands of security forces have been reported, especially for independence supporters and other activists. Separately, armed extremist groups devoted largely to attacks on Indian-administered Jammu and Kashmir operate from AJK and GB and have links with similar factions based in Pakistan and Afghanistan.

A 2003 cease-fire agreement between the Indian and Pakistani armies is supposed to protect AJK from attacks across the LoC. However, the two armies engaged in near-constant exchanges of fire during 2020, after a 2019 suicide attack on the Indian side killed more than 40 paramilitary police officers and set off a period of intensified hostilities. Pakistan reported over 3,000 Indian violations of the cease-fire in 2020, which allegedly killed 28 civilians and injured more than 249 others. Although some of the firing struck military targets, it was often directed at civilians, damaged their residences, and left them at risk of injuries from unexploded ordnance. The Pakistani army reported that the Indian military used cluster munitions, which are particularly dangerous to civilians.

F4. Do laws, policies, and practices guarantee equal treatment of various segments of the population? 0 / 4

As in Pakistan, women in the territories face economic discrimination, disadvantages under personal status laws, and abusive customary practices, the perpetrators of which often enjoy impunity. LGBT+ people, members of ethnic minorities, and non-Sunni religious groups also suffer from discrimination, and Afghan refugees have encountered increased harassment and pressure to return to Afghanistan since 2015. Pakistani authorities have been reluctant to offer citizenship to migrants displaced from Indian-administered Jammu and Kashmir. These refugees have periodically been subjected to abuse and arbitrary arrest for demanding greater rights.

G. PERSONAL AUTONOMY AND INDIVIDUAL RIGHTS: 6 / 16

G1. Do individuals enjoy freedom of movement, including the ability to change their place of residence, employment, or education? 2 / 4

The people of AJK and GB have Pakistani national identity cards and passports. They are internationally recognized as Pakistani nationals. However, there are reports of passports or passport renewals being denied for those suspected of questioning Pakistani control over the region. The territories' heavy military presence and the threat of shelling and other violence along the LoC restricts internal movement for civilians. Residents and travelers also risk accidentally straying across the LoC and being stranded or detained.

Rigorous lockdown measures were implemented in both AJK and GB in March and April 2020 in response to the COVID-19 pandemic, and restrictions were reimposed more briefly during a second wave of infections in the autumn. They were not seen as unusually onerous or disproportionate.

G2. Are individuals able to exercise the right to own property and establish private businesses without undue interference from state or nonstate actors? 2 / 4

AJK's pre-1947 state subject law, which bars outsiders from seeking permanent residency, allows only legal residents to own property. In GB, residents have raised concerns about possible displacement by CPEC development projects, and at least some forcible evictions have been reported to date. Procedures for establishing private enterprises in the territories are onerous in practice.

G3. Do individuals enjoy personal social freedoms, including choice of marriage partner and size of family, protection from domestic violence, and control over appearance? 1 / 4

In both territories, the legal framework criminalizes domestic violence and so-called honor killings, but harmful traditional practices related to sex, marriage, and personal behavior often prevail amid weak enforcement of formal protections, especially in more conservative areas. Informal justice mechanisms operating at the village level are the first point of recourse for many incidents involving sexual or domestic violence against women, and their judgments can inflict further harm on victims.

G4. Do individuals enjoy equality of opportunity and freedom from economic exploitation? 1 / 4

Both territories, but particularly GB, have historically been less economically developed than Pakistan, and their population has depended on labor migration to supplement incomes. The lack of local control over extractive industries prompts periodic complaints that residents are being deprived of the benefits of natural resources. There are divergent views in GB regarding the extent to which local people stand to gain from economic activity generated by the centrally managed CPEC.

Child labor is known to occur, though the AJK government banned the practice by passing the Restriction of Employment of Children Act 2016 and amending it in 2017. Under this legislation, businesses in AJK cannot hire residents under the age of 17. Laws against sex and labor trafficking in general are poorly enforced.

Somaliland

Population: 4,500,000
Freedom Status: Partly Free

Note: *Freedom in the World* reports assess the level of political rights and civil liberties in a given geographical area, regardless of whether they are affected by the state, nonstate actors, or foreign powers. Disputed territories are sometimes assessed separately if they meet certain criteria, including boundaries that are sufficiently stable to allow year-on-year comparisons. For more information, see the report methodology and FAQ.

Overview: Somaliland—whose self-declared independence from Somalia is not internationally recognized—has seen a consistent erosion of political rights and civic space. Journalists and public figures face pressure from authorities. Years-long election delays leave elected officials in posts well beyond their original mandates. Minority clans are subject to political and economic marginalization, and violence against women remains a serious problem.

KEY DEVELOPMENTS IN 2020

- In August, the three major political parties and the National Election Commission (NEC) agreed to schedule local and parliamentary elections for May 2021. The parties had previously agreed to hold elections by year's end but delayed them after the NEC warned it could not meet the envisioned timeframe.
- In August, the House of Representatives approved a bill that would allow for child marriages, criminalize "false" rape reports, and narrow the definition of rape. The upper house was still considering the bill at year's end.
- The first COVID-19 cases in Somaliland were detected in late March. The Somaliland Ministry of Health reported over 1,200 COVID-19 cases and 42 deaths as of mid-December.

POLITICAL RIGHTS: 18 / 40 (+1)
A. ELECTORAL PROCESS: 5 / 12
A1. Was the current head of government or other chief national authority elected through free and fair elections? 3 / 4

The president is directly elected for a maximum of two five-year terms and appoints the cabinet. In 2017, after two years of delay, Somaliland held its third presidential election. Muse Bihi Abdi of the Peace, Unity, and Development Party (Kulmiye) won the contest with 55 percent of the vote, followed by Abdurahman Mohamed Abdullahi of the Waddani party with 40 percent, and Faisal Ali Warabe of the For Justice and Development (UCID) party with 4 percent. International observers concluded the process was credible; some instances of bribery and intimidation at polling places did not significantly affect the final result.

A2. Were the current national legislative representatives elected through free and fair elections? 0 / 4

Members of the 82-seat lower legislative chamber, the House of Representatives, are directly elected for five-year terms, while members of the 82-seat upper chamber, the Guurti, are clan elders indirectly elected for six-year terms. The last lower-house elections were held in 2005, and new elections due in 2010 have been repeatedly postponed. Local council elections, last held in 2012, have similarly been delayed. Guurti members were chosen for an initial term in 1993, but due to a lack of legal clarity on electing their replacements, their mandates have been repeatedly extended.

In July 2020, Kulmiye, Waddani, and the UCID agreed to hold parliamentary and local elections before year's end. In August, the NEC warned that their timeframe could not be met. Later that month, the NEC and the parties agreed to schedule the polls for May 2021.

A3. Are the electoral laws and framework fair, and are they implemented impartially by the relevant election management bodies? 2 / 4

The legal and administrative framework for elections is largely fair, but ambiguities in some laws as well as technical and logistical challenges have led to chronic election delays. The House of Representatives approved a new composition for the NEC in June 2020 and began considering a revised electoral law in July. The electoral law was gazetted in October.

In July, a Technical Election Unit, which is envisioned to compose of three members from the international community, was established to advise the NEC. A voter-registration drive for the 2021 polls began in late November 2020.

B. POLITICAL PLURALISM AND PARTICIPATION: 9 / 16 (+1)

B1. Do the people have the right to organize in different political parties or other competitive political groupings of their choice, and is the system free of undue obstacles to the rise and fall of these competing parties or groupings? 3 / 4 (+1)

The constitution allows for a maximum of three officially recognized political parties. The three groups that receive the most votes in local council elections are declared eligible to contest national elections and compete freely in practice. The system is meant to encourage alliances across clan divisions, but clan and party affiliation remain closely aligned.

Score Change: The score increased from 2 to 3 because there was no repetition of the previous year's arrests of opposition figures.

B2. Is there a realistic opportunity for the opposition to increase its support or gain power through elections? 2 / 4

The political system allows democratic transfers of power between rival parties, with the most recent handover at the presidential level in 2017. Opposition parties hold positions in the legislature and in subnational governments, though election delays—most recently occurring in August 2020—have impaired their ability to challenge incumbents.

B3. Are the people's political choices free from domination by forces that are external to the political sphere, or by political forces that employ extrapolitical means? 2 / 4

Clan elders play an influential role in politics, both directly with their kinsmen and through the currently unelected Guurti, which has the authority to extend officials' terms in office and approve election dates.

B4. Do various segments of the population (including ethnic, racial, religious, gender, LGBT+, and other relevant groups) have full political rights and electoral opportunities? 2 / 4

Women and various clans formally enjoy equal political rights. However, larger clans tend to dominate political offices and leadership positions. Cultural barriers also limit women's political participation. In a 2019 report, the Hargeisa-based Centre for Policy Analysis noted that only 12 of 173 appointments that had been made by President Bihi were given to women. A proposed parliamentary gender quota was not included in the October 2020 electoral law.

C. FUNCTIONING OF GOVERNMENT: 4 / 12

C1. Do the freely elected head of government and national legislative representatives determine the policies of the government? 1 / 4

The 2017 election improved the democratic legitimacy of the president in determining government policy, and decisions made by national authorities are implemented in most of Somaliland's claimed territory. However, the consistent delays of legislative elections threaten this legitimacy.

C2. Are safeguards against official corruption strong and effective? 1 / 4

Somaliland has few institutional safeguards against corruption and nepotism. Prosecutions of officials for malfeasance are rare. Former president Ahmed Mohamed Mohamoud "Silanyo" took some measures to combat corruption, but the anticorruption commission he created in 2010 has been ineffective. A new commission chairman was appointed in February 2020.

In September 2020, Auditor General Ahmed Yusuf Dirir disclosed the arrests of several officials over corruption-related charges. The auditor general also disclosed that several other individuals were accused of forging documents.

C3. Does the government operate with openness and transparency? 2 / 4

The government operates with relative transparency in many respects but is more opaque regarding contracts for major projects. Journalists and civil society activists who attempt to scrutinize government activities often face harassment.

CIVIL LIBERTIES: 24 / 60
D. FREEDOM OF EXPRESSION AND BELIEF: 6 / 16
D1. Are there free and independent media? 1 / 4

A variety of print, television, and online news outlets operate, but many have political affiliations, and the state-run broadcaster has a monopoly in the radio sector. The penal code criminalizes defamation and other vaguely defined press offenses, such as circulation of "false, exaggerated, or tendentious news." The government has restricted the registration of new newspapers.

The government continued to target journalists and outlets in 2020. In January, Eryal TV reporter Abdirahman Mohamed Hiddig was arrested after the deputy manager of a state-owned printing press filed a complaint over Abdirahman's social media comments. Abdirahman received a 21-month prison sentence later in January. In mid-June, Somali Cable TV journalist Khadar Mohamed Tarabi and Universal TV journalist Khadar Farah Rigah were briefly detained after filming a Las Anod protest over Somalia-Somaliland talks held that month in Djibouti. Horyaal24 TV journalist Jabir Said Duale was arrested for similar reasons in Erigavo but was released without charge.

In late June, police officers ordered the staff of Star TV to vacate their Hargeisa office. Two days later, Hargeisa police raided the offices of Universal TV and ordered their staff to vacate. Star TV was reportedly raided for hosting a debate that focused on the Somalia-Somaliland talks, while Universal TV was accused of broadcasting events celebrating Somalian independence. The authorities revoked the licenses of both stations that month.

Astaan TV director Abdimanan Yusuf was detained by authorities in July and was initially accused of entering Somaliland illegally and collaborating with Somalian intelligence services. Yusuf received a five-year prison sentence and a fine from a Hargeisa court in November, while Astaan TV was shuttered indefinitely.

D2. Are individuals free to practice and express their religious faith or nonbelief in public and private? 2 / 4

Islam is the state religion. The constitution allows for freedom of belief but prohibits conversion from Islam and proselytizing by members of other faiths. Places of worship must obtain government permission to operate, though there is no mechanism to register religious organizations.

D3. Is there academic freedom, and is the educational system free from extensive political indoctrination? 2 / 4

Teachers and professors are often able to pursue academic activities of a political and quasi-political nature without fear of intimidation. While funds allocated for public schools are uneven across the regions, they are generally free from overt political manipulation.

D4. Are individuals free to express their personal views on political or other sensitive topics without fear of surveillance or retribution? 1 / 4

While individuals can express themselves with relative freedom on political matters, remarks on sensitive social and cultural issues are increasingly subject to censure and retribution. Recent arrests and convictions for controversial social media posts has contributed to greater self-censorship online among residents.

E. ASSOCIATIONAL AND ORGANIZATIONAL RIGHTS: 5 / 12
E1. Is there freedom of assembly? 1 / 4

The constitution allows for freedom of assembly, but organized public demonstrations are infrequent, and the authorities have sometimes employed violence to disperse protests.

E2. Is there freedom for nongovernmental organizations, particularly those that are engaged in human rights- and governance-related work? 2 / 4

Local and international nongovernmental organizations (NGOs) often operate without serious interference, but such groups can face harassment for their work. NGOs documenting human rights note that their work and events are not covered by government media outlets.

In October 2020, the Somaliland government suspended cooperating with UN agencies, after the United Nations finalized a sustainable development cooperation framework with the Somalian government. In early November, Somaliland officials began holding talks with the United Nations on a new relational framework, which were not concluded by year's end.

E3. Is there freedom for trade unions and similar professional or labor organizations? 2 / 4

The constitution does not explicitly protect the right to strike, though it does permit collective bargaining. The right to belong to a union is generally respected.

F. RULE OF LAW: 7 / 16
F1. Is there an independent judiciary? 2 / 4

Although some progress has been made in reforming the judicial system in recent years, the judiciary lacks independence, sufficient funding, and proper training. Judges are often selected on the basis of clan or political affiliation and are subject to interference from the government.

F2. Does due process prevail in civil and criminal matters? 2 / 4

Due process is observed unevenly. Poverty and political factors play a role in how cases are charged and investigated, and whether there is adequate and timely representation for the defendant. Both customary law and Sharia (Islamic law) are used alongside civil law, which complicates adherence to statutory procedure. In practice, police arrest individuals arbitrarily and hold detainees without charge for extended periods. Lawyers are frequently denied access to detained clients. Long delays in court cases are common.

F3. Is there protection from the illegitimate use of physical force and freedom from war and insurgencies? 1 / 4

Somaliland's police and security forces have been accused of using excessive force, and conditions in detention centers are harsh and overcrowded. In an effort to limit the spread of COVID-19 in Somaliland detention centers, President Bihi pardoned 574 prisoners in April 2020 and 365 in May.

F4. Do laws, policies, and practices guarantee equal treatment of various segments of the population? 2 / 4

Members of smaller clans face discrimination, limited access to public services, and prejudice in the justice system. Clan connections play a critical role in securing employment. Women also suffer from inequality, including in the Sharia and customary legal systems. Homosexuality is a criminal offense, and LGBT+ people generally do not acknowledge their sexual orientation or gender identity publicly.

G. PERSONAL AUTONOMY AND INDIVIDUAL RIGHTS: 6 / 16

G1. Do individuals enjoy freedom of movement, including the ability to change their place of residence, employment, or education? 2 / 4

Freedom of movement is respected to some extent, but traffic between Somaliland and Puntland is restricted, and the Somaliland government limits travel to and from Somalia's federal capital, Mogadishu. Clan divisions hinder individuals' relocation within the territory.

G2. Are individuals able to exercise the right to own property and establish private businesses without undue interference from state or nonstate actors? 2 / 4

Individuals are able to own property and operate private businesses without undue interference from the government. However, land disputes are common, as tenure is often complicated by lack of documentation and inconsistencies among different legal systems and state authorities. In 2019, police and military officials forcefully evicted several families to build a new presidential palace. No compensation was paid to the affected families.

G3. Do individuals enjoy personal social freedoms, including choice of marriage partner and size of family, protection from domestic violence, and control over appearance? 1 / 4

Personal social freedoms are constrained by several factors. Marriages between members of major and minor clans are stigmatized. Female genital mutilation (FGM) is common. In 2018, the Ministry of Religious Affairs released a religious edict banning one common type of FGM, but human rights groups criticized the edict for not fully prohibiting the practice.

Domestic violence remains a serious problem, and rape is rarely reported to authorities due to social pressures against such complaints. The Sexual Offenses Bill, which criminalized many forms of gender-based violence (GBV), was signed in 2018 by President Bihi, but was subsequently suspended by the Ministry of Religious Affairs after an outcry from religious leaders. In August 2020, the House of Representatives approved the Rape, Fornication and Other Related Offences Bill, which would allow for child marriages, criminalize reports of rape deemed "false," and would narrow the definition of rape. The bill was still being considered by the Guurti at year's end.

G4. Do individuals enjoy equality of opportunity and freedom from economic exploitation? 1 / 4

The informal sector, including traditional pastoral activities, accounts for much of the economy, and many households rely on remittances from relatives working in other countries. Trafficking in persons for forced labor or sexual exploitation abroad is a serious problem. Refugees from neighboring countries, including Yemen and Ethiopia, and internally displaced people are also vulnerable to exploitation.

South Ossetia

Population: 53,400
Freedom Status: Not Free

Note: The numerical scores and status listed here do not reflect conditions in Georgia, which is examined in a separate report. *Freedom in the World* reports assess the level of political rights and civil liberties in a given geographical area, regardless of whether they are affected by the state, nonstate actors, or foreign powers. Disputed territories are sometimes assessed separately if they meet certain criteria, including boundaries that are sufficiently stable to allow year-on-year comparisons. For more information, see the report methodology and FAQ.

Overview: Large parts of South Ossetia, a breakaway territory of Georgia, enjoyed de facto independence after a civil conflict ended in 1992. A 2008 war that drew in Russian forces resulted in the expulsion of the remaining Georgian government presence and many ethnic Georgian civilians. Only Russia and a handful of other states have since recognized South Ossetia's independence. The territory remains almost entirely dependent on Russia, and Moscow exerts a decisive influence over its politics and governance. Local media and civil society are largely controlled or monitored by the authorities, and the judiciary is subject to political influence and manipulation.

KEY DEVELOPMENTS IN 2020

- The suspicions death of a local resident, Inal Dzhabiev, at the Tshkhinvali detention center in August provoked street protests and led to a number of resignations in the government. The demonstrations went forward without interference from authorities, marking a tentative break from the restrictive environment of past years.
- Citing a need to sustain contact exclusively with Russia, and no states or institutions that did not recognize the sovereignty of South Ossetia, authorities refused to accept support from the World Health Organization (WHO) and UN agencies during the COVID-19 pandemic—despite shortages of protective equipment and other supplies.
- For almost the entire year, the local leadership kept border crossings with Georgia proper closed, leading to shortages and restricted access to emergency medical care for many ethnic Georgians living in the region.
- The South Ossetian journalist and activist Tamara Mearakishvili continued to face harassment from authorities.

POLITICAL RIGHTS: 2 / 40

A. ELECTORAL PROCESS: 2 / 12

A1. Was the current head of government or other chief national authority elected through free and fair elections? 0 / 4

Although South Ossetia's elections occur regularly, they are severely restricted at all stages of the process, and are not monitored by independent observers or recognized by the international community. In the most recent presidential election, in April 2017, former military leader Anatoly Bibilov was elected to a five-year term with 58 percent of the vote; he defeated the incumbent, Leonid Tibilov, who took 30 percent, and State Security Committee (KGB) official Alan Gagloyev, who took 11 percent.

Political analysts said that the conduct of the 2017 election was an improvement on the 2011 poll, the results of which had been disputed. Nevertheless, political debate and competition only occurred within a narrow field of candidates allowed by Russia and pro-Russian authorities.

A2. Were the current national legislative representatives elected through free and fair elections? 1 / 4

In June 2019, residents of South Ossetia elected parliamentarians through a new voting system: half of the 34 seats went to political parties in a proportional representation system, and the remaining spots were designated to single-member constituencies. Legislative elections are not internationally recognized, and the extent of Russian influence in the territory's politics precludes truly competitive contests.

The parliamentary elections yielded some positive developments. In contrast to previous years, political parties reported few problems with registration, campaigned in the region, and took part in televised debates. However, more than half of the candidates for the single-member constituencies, mainly private individuals, were unable to register their candidacies. The United Ossetia party of President Bibilov won 14 seats, followed by the Unity of the People party with 5 seats, and the Nykhas movement with 4 seats. Smaller parties captured the remainder.

A3. Are the electoral laws and framework fair, and are they implemented impartially by the relevant election management bodies? 1 / 4

According to electoral laws, candidates must have permanently resided in South Ossetia for 10 years. Authorities continue to restrict voting rights of ethnic Georgian residents remaining in South Ossetia. Russian political influence undermines the independence of the election commission.

B. POLITICAL PLURALISM AND PARTICIPATION: 2 / 16

B1. Do the people have the right to organize in different political parties or other competitive political groupings of their choice, and is the system free of undue obstacles to the rise and fall of these competing parties or groupings? 1 / 4

Moscow exerts a decisive influence over politics and governance, effectively placing significant restrictions on the ability of political parties outside of a narrow political spectrum to operate freely. However, a number of new parties have registered over the past decade, including the ruling United Ossetia, which has governed the territory since winning the most seats in the 2014 elections. United Ossetia controls the local Ministry of Justice and thus oversees the party registration processes. The body has inspected party-member lists, but upon identifying mistakes has allowed parties to resolve them without negative consequences for elections.

However, individual candidates have faced difficulties registering with the Central Election Commission (CEC) to participate in elections. Ahead of the June 2019 parliamentary polls, a number of opposition politicians and individuals responded to new legislation that allowed both proportional representation and single-member constituencies (decided by a "first-past-the-post" or majoritarian election). Ninety-nine candidates applied to stand in the elections for single-member constituencies, but only 39 received approval from the CEC to register, and appeals of CEC decisions were unsuccessful.

B2. Is there a realistic opportunity for the opposition to increase its support or gain power through elections? 1 / 4

While Bibilov, the opposition candidate, challenged and defeated the incumbent in the 2017 presidential election, the success or failure of opposition politicians is largely determined by Moscow. South Ossetian government sources implied that banned presidential candidate Kokoity was not in Moscow's favor. Opposition lawmakers have some influence in the legislature and criticize the ruling party on occasion.

In September 2020, mass street rallies provoked by the suspicious death in August of a local resident, Inal Dzhabiev, while in police custody at the Tskhinvali detention center led to widespread calls for Bibilov's resignation. Around that time, local law enforcement conducted surprise searches at the office of the main opposition party, Nykhas, and at the private home of its leader. Most opposition parliamentarians have boycotted parliamentary sessions since early September, demanding the resignation of the general prosecutor in order to ensure a transparent investigation into Dzhabiev's death.

B3. Are the people's political choices free from domination by forces that are external to the political sphere, or by political forces that employ extrapolitical means? 0 / 4

South Ossetia's institutions are almost entirely dependent on economic and political support from Moscow. There are few avenues for people to meaningfully participate in political processes if they wish to advocate for interests that fall outside of the narrow political spectrum defined by Russia and the territory's Russian-aligned authorities and their private business interests.

B4. Do various segments of the population (including ethnic, racial, religious, gender, LGBT+, and other relevant groups) have full political rights and electoral opportunities? 0 / 4

While the South Ossetian government includes several women ministers, the interests of women and minority groups are not represented politically. Most ethnic Georgian residents have either declined or have been denied the ability to participate in elections.

C. FUNCTIONING OF GOVERNMENT: 0 / 12

C1. Do the freely elected head of government and national legislative representatives determine the policies of the government? 0 / 4

The ability of elected officials to determine and implement policy is heavily influenced by the Russian government. A sweeping 2015 treaty between Russia and South Ossetia closely integrates the territory's defense, security, and customs mechanisms with those of Russia, charging Moscow with protection of South Ossetia's borders. Russian aid comprises almost the entirety of South Ossetia's budget. Private emails leaked in 2016 that were apparently tied to a senior Kremlin adviser described Moscow-based working groups that reviewed legislation drafted by the authorities in Tskhinvali. Media reports detailing the increasingly important role of South Ossetia as a conduit for funds from Russia to the breakaway territories of eastern Ukraine continue to surface; details of the reports reflect the ability of Russian authorities to shape South Ossetia's financial and business regulations and infrastructure to serve their own purposes. Like his predecessors, many of Bibilov's ministerial appointments are of Russian citizens, and Bibilov has spoken repeatedly of formally uniting the territory with Russia's North Ossetia–Alania or joining the Russian Federation as a separate region.

During the 2020 COVID-19 pandemic, Bibilov declined humanitarian support from the World Health Organization (WHO) and United Nations agencies, citing a need to sustain contact exclusively with Russia, and no states or institutions that did not recognize the sovereignty of South Ossetia. This effectively left South Ossetian medical institutions with a shortage of protective equipment, medication, and disinfectants.

C2. Are safeguards against official corruption strong and effective? 0 / 4

Official corruption is widespread in South Ossetia, and there is little to no systematic attempt to fight it. However, a rare parliamentary review of the presidential fund in June 2020 identified purchases of luxury cars for parliamentarians and officials loyal to the president and United Ossetia. Soon after, in July, parliament adopted and the president signed a new law that introduced annual declarations for all civil servants and restrictions on conflicts of interest. Adoption of the law was delayed for five years.

C3. Does the government operate with openness and transparency? 0 / 4

Due in large part to the significant level of Russian influence on domestic politics and decision-making, South Ossetia's government does not operate with transparency. Officials have not identified a lack of transparency as a policy priority.

ADDITIONAL DISCRETIONARY POLITICAL RIGHTS QUESTION:

Is the government or occupying power deliberately changing the ethnic composition of a country or territory so as to destroy a culture or tip the political balance in favor of another group? -2 / 0

During the 2008 war, Ossetian forces seized or razed property in previously Georgian-controlled villages, and large numbers of ethnic Georgians fled the fighting. Authorities in South Ossetia have since barred ethnic Georgians from returning to the territory unless they renounce their Georgian citizenship and accept Russian passports. Of approximately 20,000 ethnic Georgians displaced from their homes in South Ossetia, most have not been able to return.

Conditions for remaining local residents have largely stabilized since the war, particularly due to the absence of open conflict across the administrative line separating the territory from Georgia. Nevertheless, the weeks-long restrictions of movement between the territory and Georgia proper in January and September 2019 provoked a temporary rush of dozens of fleeing ethnic Georgians fearful of permanent closure of crossing points. A similar outflow of local Georgians took place in January 2020, when region's leadership agreed to open crossings with Georgia proper for 10 days: people left for Georgia, many due to hardships and shortages caused by border closures.

CIVIL LIBERTIES: 8 / 60

D. FREEDOM OF EXPRESSION AND BELIEF: 3 / 16

D1. Are there free and independent media? 0 / 4

Local media, including the television channel Ir, the newspapers *Yuzhnaya Osetiya* and *Respublika,* and the online portal Res, are almost entirely controlled by the authorities. Self-censorship is pervasive, and defamation charges are often employed against critical media. An increasing number of residents rely on online outlets for news and other information, and foreign media, including broadcasts from Russia and Georgia, remain accessible. The local version of Russian news portal Sputnik, accessible in both Russian and Ossetian, is increasingly popular.

Social media platforms are also popular among the region's residents, who maintain both public and private groups to discuss politics and everyday problems. Some discussions attract parliamentarians, officials, and even President Bibilov. People mainly use mobile internet, which is of a low speed and relatively expensive, but still accessible to many users.

In 2020, authorities continued to press charges against Tamara Mearakishvili, a journalist and activist who works with Georgian and international media outlets including Radio Free Europe/Radio Liberty (RFE/RL). After the South Ossetian Supreme Court dismissed three previous criminal accusations against Mearakishvili in July 2019 (concerning illegal acquisition of documents and defamation), Mearakishvili has stated that authorities continued to harass her and to demand her imprisonment. In January 2020, the Supreme Court overturned its 2019 verdict and returned Mearakishvili's case to the first instance court for retrial. In September, the prosecutor's office cut off the electricity at Mearakishvili's apartment for almost a month, claiming she owed a payment from 2017. The issue was resolved at the request of the region's parliamentarians.

Prominent journalist Irina Kelekhsaeva also faced possible criminal charges related to her work. In January 2020, the Justice Minister sued Kelekhsaeva for defamation for a 2019 RFE/RL story on poor conditions and abuses in prisons. The case was sent to the prosecutor general office's for review in February.

D2. Are individuals free to practice and express their religious faith or nonbelief in public and private? 1 / 4

While the majority of the population is Orthodox Christian, there is a sizeable Muslim community. Followers of Russian Orthodoxy and Ossetian neopaganism also inhabit the territory. Some property of the Georgian Orthodox Church is controlled by the South Ossetian Orthodox Church (called the Eparchy).

In 2017, South Ossetia's de facto Supreme Court outlawed Jehovah's Witnesses as an "extremist" organization; the group had been banned in Russia earlier that year.

D3. Is there academic freedom, and is the educational system free from extensive political indoctrination? 1 / 4

The government exerts strong influence over the education system. In 2017, the ministry of education began to phase out Georgian-language education, and this process continued throughout 2020. In February 2020, Nino Amiranashvili, the director of a Georgian school, lost her job after she refused to expel five ethnic Georgian students who had enrolled in 2019. She appealed this decision in court, which ruled in July against her dismissal, asked the government to reinstate her, and ordered that she be compensated for lost wages and moral damages.

D4. Are individuals free to express their personal views on political or other sensitive topics without fear of surveillance or retribution? 1 / 4

Private discussion is constrained by the sensitivity of certain topics, particularly the territory's geopolitical standing. Speaking of the property rights and expulsion of the Georgian population is assumed to attract unwanted attention.

E. ASSOCIATIONAL AND ORGANIZATIONAL RIGHTS: 2 / 12 (+1)

E1. Is there freedom of assembly? 2 / 4 (+1)

Residents occasionally demonstrate against environmental degradation, the sluggish pace of postwar reconstruction, animal rights, and, more rarely, overtly political grievances.

However, in past years, freedom of assembly has been strictly limited. Participants in unsanctioned gatherings risk being charged with crimes, and authorities have responded to demonstrations by closing roads and deploying security forces to patrol.

However, an antigovernment protest movement that emerged in 2020 proceeded without interference from authorities, marking a tentative break from the restrictive environment of past years. In late August, the death in police custody of local resident Inal Dzhabiev, 28, who had been detained for alleged involvement in a gunfire attack on the interior minister's vehicle, provoked mass protests in the Tskhinvali central square. Photos of his corpse depicting extensive bruises were widely shared on social media, providing apparent evidence for accusations that he had been tortured. Thousands turned out to demand the resignation of the president and punishment of those responsible for the death; Dzhabiev's funeral, at the end of August, turned into the largest mass protest seen in the region in years. Protests continued into September, when supporters of both the opposition and the president held rallies, and beginning in December, relatives and friends of Dzhabiev held a nonstop protest and vigil in Tskhinvali's central square demanding punishment of those responsible for the death. Police made no attempts to prevent or disperse any of these rallies throughout the year. A number of senior officials, including the prime minister and interior minister, resigned amid the movement, though not the president, who promised a transparent investigation.

Score Change: The score improved from 1 to 2 because large antigovernment protests over the suspicious death of a young man in police custody proceeded without interference from the authorities.

E2. Is there freedom for nongovernmental organizations, particularly those that are engaged in human rights- and governance-related work? 0 / 4

Nongovernmental organizations (NGOs) that operate in the territory are subject to government influence and, by extension, influence from Russia. Legislative amendments in 2014 increased the oversight capacity of authorities over NGO activity, subjecting organizations that receive foreign funding to broader and more frequent reporting requirements and branding them "foreign partners." In recent years, a handful of organizations have officially received funding from Russia, while at least one took part in a United Nations–run project. NGOs engaged in conflict resolution and reconciliation are smeared by the authorities and progovernment media as agents of Tbilisi or western intelligence services.

E3. Is there freedom for trade unions and similar professional or labor organizations? 0 / 4

Trade unions in South Ossetia largely defer to the policies of the separatist government. Conflict with Georgia has left trade unions weak and geographically divided.

F. RULE OF LAW: 1 / 16

F1. Is there an independent judiciary? 0 / 4

South Ossetia's judiciary is not independent. The justice system is manipulated to punish perceived opponents of the separatist leadership. In July 2019, after more than a year in pretrial detention, a local court sentenced former official Georgy Kabisov, accused of embezzlement of state funds, to seven years in prison. The case is seen as highly political due to personal problems between Kabisov and President Bibilov. Later in July 2019, the court launched a closed-door investigation into the case of an official in the presidential administration, Sergey Lipin, as well as Lipin's wife and two administrators of a local computer center: all were accused of state espionage for the Georgian government. In July 2020, Lipin and his wife were sentenced to 16 and 13 years in prison, respectively, for treason.

In 2020, President Bibilov further consolidated his control over the courts, proposing to replace a number of district judges. Despite criticism of the opposition, the parliament approved the president's proposal.

F2. Does due process prevail in civil and criminal matters? 0 / 4

South Ossetia uses a modified version of the Russian criminal code. Government allies reportedly continue to violate the law with relative impunity. Russian prosecutors have attempted to curb malfeasance by local officials, but the Russian court system itself remains deeply flawed.

Criminal prosecutions are used to punish activists and individuals that question or inconvenience the authorities, as reflected by multiple criminal accusations made against journalist Kelekhsaeva and activist and journalist Mearakishvili. In April 2019, a Russian businessman, Kurban Buganov, who had received no repayment for massive public works projects completed over the previous decade, became the focus of a criminal investigation by the office of the prosecutor general, despite no apparent evidence of wrongdoing. The investigation appears to be a means for the South Ossetian government to avoid payment for the public infrastructure projects completed by Buganov's company.

F3. Is there protection from the illegitimate use of physical force and freedom from war and insurgencies? 0 / 4

Victims of human rights violations committed during the 2008 conflict have few avenues for legal recourse. Physical abuse and poor conditions are reportedly common in prisons and detention centers. At court sessions, prisoners often speak about floods and freezing conditions at an old building that was built decades ago merely as a temporary detention center, and not as a long-term prison. In October 2019, 56 inmates of the only local prison located in Tskhinvali went on hunger strike with the demand for better food and more opportunities to exercise. Negotiations with the local justice minister ended with the prisoners being physically assaulted, which was filmed by CCTV cameras, leaked, and shared widely on social media.

In late August 2020, after Inal Dzhabiev died while in police custody, photos of his corpse that circulated on social media depicted extensive bruises. Two detainees implicated alongside Dzhabiev in a gunfire attack on the interior minister's vehicle were released after promising not to leave the region; one of them could not walk after leaving the detention center and spent weeks undergoing medical care. At least eight police officers were detained on charges related to Dzhabiev's death. The opposition and Dzhabiev's family rejected investigations by local officials.

F4. Do laws, policies, and practices guarantee equal treatment of various segments of the population? 1 / 4

Discrimination against ethnic Georgians continues. Reports of arbitrary discrimination and detention of ethnic Georgians continue to arise. There are no initiatives to support the rights of LGBT+ people.

G. PERSONAL AUTONOMY AND INDIVIDUAL RIGHTS: 2 / 16 (−1)

G1. Do individuals enjoy freedom of movement, including the ability to change their place of residence, employment, or education? 0 / 4 (−1)

Restrictions on freedom of movement between South Ossetia and Georgia proper remain in place. In 2019, border crossings were closed for long periods with no prior notification with one action ostensible to prevent the spread of influenza prompting denunciations by the European Union (EU), Organization for Security and Co-operation in Europe (OSCE), and UN mediators.

The crossings were closed for most of 2020, in part due to the COVID-19 pandemic. Security services granted almost no requests to cross into Georgia proper, even for people with emergency health problems. The Georgian government reported that at least 16 people had died by mid-November due to a lack of timely medical assistance. Crossings into Russia were also restricted at times due to the pandemic.

Score Change: The score declined from 1 to 0 due to arbitrary restrictions on travel across both the Russian border and the de facto border with government-controlled Georgia, resulting in denial of access to life-saving medical care during the COVID-19 pandemic.

G2. Are individuals able to exercise the right to own property and establish private businesses without undue interference from state or nonstate actors? 0 / 4

The territory's political and military situation has negatively affected protections of property rights, particularly for residents close to the administrative border. The separatist authorities have consistently refused to countenance the return of ethnic Georgians expelled from their homes before or during the 2008 war. Small businesses risk being seized or subjected to predatory behavior by larger, more powerful corporations.

In July 2020, several businesses from Tskhinvali established a new association with their counterparts in Russia's North Ossetia, aimed at gaining additional authority and protections in light of new Russian customs regulations.

G3. Do individuals enjoy personal social freedoms, including choice of marriage partner and size of family, protection from domestic violence, and control over appearance? 2 / 4

While no laws officially regulate individuals' public appearance, statements by public officials reflect intolerance for behavior that deviates from the territory's conservative norms. No laws or government programs specifically protect victims of domestic violence.

G4. Individuals enjoy equality of opportunity and freedom from economic exploitation? 0 / 4

Economic opportunity is been limited by the territory's unrecognized status, among other reasons. Populations living along the administrative border with Georgia proper face economic uncertainty due to divisions created by shifting and uncertain borders.

Tibet

Population: 3,510,000 [Note: This figure covers only the Tibet Autonomous Region.]
Freedom Status: Not Free

Note: *Freedom in the World* reports assess the level of political rights and civil liberties in a given geographical area, regardless of whether they are affected by the state, nonstate actors, or foreign powers. Disputed territories are sometimes assessed separately if they meet certain criteria, including boundaries that are sufficiently stable to allow year-on-year comparisons. For more information, see the report methodology and FAQ.

Overview: Tibet is ruled by the Chinese Communist Party (CCP) government based in Beijing, with local decision-making power concentrated in the hands of Chinese party officials.

Residents of both Han Chinese and Tibetan ethnicity are denied fundamental rights, but the authorities are especially rigorous in suppressing any signs of dissent among Tibetans, including manifestations of Tibetan religious beliefs and cultural identity. State policies, including incentives for non-Tibetan people to migrate from other parts of China and the relocation of ethnic Tibetans, have reduced the ethnic Tibetan share of the population.

KEY DEVELOPMENTS IN 2020

- Beginning in January, Chinese government officials effectively leveraged the COVID-19 pandemic to close Buddhist temples and monasteries for many months. Authorities required temples and monasteries to participate in political indoctrination sessions and display political loyalty to the CCP in order to reopen after lockdown restrictions were lifted. The CCP also expanded the "intelligent temple management" system, often as another requirement for their reopening, and included enhanced video surveillance in all temples and monasteries.
- In June, the Chinese government enhanced the requirements for disabled Tibetans seeking jobs in government departments, as well as those who receive state benefits, stipulating that they must denounce the Dalai Lama, abandon their political beliefs, and swear loyalty to the CCP. The new requirements fell in line with the government's abusive "vocational training," "labor transfer," and "poverty eradication" campaigns that undermine Tibetans' cultural and social identity and consolidate the CCP's control over the region. By July, 543,000 Tibetans had received "vocational training."

POLITICAL RIGHTS: –2 / 40

A. ELECTORAL PROCESS: 0 / 12

A1. Was the current head of government or other chief national authority elected through free and fair elections? 0 / 4

The Chinese government rules Tibet through administration of the Tibetan Autonomous Region (TAR) and 12 Tibetan autonomous prefectures or counties in the nearby provinces of Sichuan, Qinghai, Gansu, and Yunnan. Under the Chinese constitution, autonomous areas have the right to formulate their own regulations and implement national legislation in accordance with local conditions. In practice, however, decision-making authority is concentrated in the hands of unelected ethnic (Han) Chinese officials of the CCP, which has a monopoly on political power. In 2016, Wu Yingjie replaced Chen Quanguo as TAR party secretary.

The few ethnic Tibetans who occupy senior executive positions serve mostly as figureheads or echo official doctrine. Che Dalha, one of two ethnic Tibetan members of the CCP's 205-member Central Committee, has served as chairman (governor) of the TAR since January 2017. The chairman is formally elected by the regional people's congress, but in practice such decisions are predetermined by CCP leadership.

A2. Were the current national legislative representatives elected through free and fair elections? 0 / 4

The regional people's congress of the TAR, which is formally elected by lower-level people's congresses, chooses delegates to China's 3,000-member National People's Congress (NPC) every five years. In practice, all candidates are vetted by the CCP. The current TAR people's congress held its first session in January 2018, and the current NPC was seated that March.

A3. Are the electoral laws and framework fair, and are they implemented impartially by the relevant election management bodies? 0 / 4

As in the rest of China, direct elections are only permitted at the lowest administrative levels. Tight political controls and aggressive state interference ensure that competitive races with independent candidates are even rarer in Tibet than in other parts of the country. Regulations published in 2014 placed significant restrictions on candidates for village elections, excluding those who have attended religious teachings abroad, have communicated with overseas Tibetans, or have relatives studying at monasteries outside China.

B. POLITICAL PLURALISM AND PARTICIPATION: 0 / 16

B1. Do the people have the right to organize in different political parties or other competitive political groupings of their choice, and is the system free of undue obstacles to the rise and fall of these competing parties or groupings? 0 / 4

All organized political activity outside the CCP is illegal and harshly punished, as is any evidence of loyalty to or communication with the Tibetan government in exile, based in Dharamsala, India.

The exile government includes an elected parliament serving five-year terms, a Supreme Justice Commission that adjudicates civil disputes, and a directly elected prime minister, also serving five-year terms. Votes are collected from the Tibetan diaspora around the world. The unelected Dalai Lama, the Tibetan spiritual leader who also traditionally served as head of state, renounced his political role in 2011. Lobsang Sangay was elected prime minister in the same year, replacing a two-term incumbent and becoming the exile government's top political official; he was reelected in 2016.

B2. Is there a realistic opportunity for the opposition to increase its support or gain power through elections? 0 / 4

As in China as a whole, the one-party system structurally precludes and rigorously suppresses the development of any organized political opposition. Tibet has never experienced a peaceful and democratic transfer of power between rival groups.

B3. Are the people's political choices free from domination by forces that are external to the political sphere, or by political forces that employ extrapolitical means? 0 / 4

The authoritarian CCP is not accountable to voters and denies the public any meaningful influence or participation in political affairs.

B4. Do various segments of the population (including ethnic, racial, religious, gender, LGBT+, and other relevant groups) have full political rights and electoral opportunities? 0 / 4

Political opportunities for ethnic Tibetans within Tibet remain limited by the dominance of ethnic Chinese officials in top-level and strategic party and government positions, while ethnic Tibetans are restricted to lower-level and rubber-stamp positions. Engagement by ethnic Tibetans on local community issues is vigorously suppressed and harshly punished.

Women are well represented in many public-sector jobs and CCP posts within the TAR, though most high-level officials are men, and women are unable to organize independently to advance their political interests.

C. FUNCTIONING OF GOVERNMENT: 1 / 12

C1. Do the freely elected head of government and national legislative representatives determine the policies of the government? 0 / 4

As elsewhere in China, unelected CCP officials determine and implement government policies in Tibet. Constitutionally, the TAR, like other ethnic minority regions, should enjoy greater autonomy than other provinces, but in practice it is controlled even more tightly by the central government.

In March 2018, the CCP Central Committee announced significant structural reforms that reduced the already limited separation between the party and state governance, placing CCP entities—like the United Front Work Department—more explicitly in charge of policy areas including religious affairs and ethnic minorities, which are especially relevant for Tibet.

C2. Are safeguards against official corruption strong and effective? 1 / 4

Corruption is believed to be extensive, as it is in China more generally, though little information is available on the scale of the problem.

There have been moves in recent years to curb graft among the region's officials as part of Chinese president Xi Jinping's nationwide anticorruption campaign. However, many prosecutions are believed to be politically selective or amount to reprisals for perceived political and religious disloyalty. Tibetan residents who seek to expose official misdeeds have been jailed. For example, anticorruption activist Anya Sengdra of Qinghai Province was arrested in September 2018 and sentenced in December 2019 to seven years in prison on vague charges of disturbing social order.

C3. Does the government operate with openness and transparency? 0 / 4

Governance is opaque in all of China but even more so in Tibet. A study by the Chinese Academy of Social Sciences, published in 2017, ranked cities and counties nationwide by their level of government transparency; Lhasa, the capital of the TAR, scored lowest among the cities, and the TAR's Nang county was the lowest among the counties under examination.

ADDITIONAL DISCRETIONARY POLITICAL RIGHTS QUESTION
Is the government or occupying power deliberately changing the ethnic composition of a country or territory so as to destroy a culture or tip the political balance in favor of another group? −3 / 0

The Chinese government accelerated policies that reduce Tibetans as a proportion of the population and undermine their cultural and religious identity in 2020. The implementation of the "2019-2020 Farmer and Pastoralist Training and Labor Transfer Action Plan" continued, forcing tens of thousands of additional Tibetan farmers and nomads to give up their land rights, become wage laborers, and move to urban areas where they are crowded into large apartment blocks. While the Plan's stated goal is to alleviate rural poverty, in practice it has alienated tens of thousands of Tibetans from their cultural way of life, means of livelihood, and connection to the land. Government policies also continue to incentivize ethnic Chinese in-migration, further eroding Tibetans' distinct cultural and religious identity. Tibetans are being forced to give up their land-use rights and turn them over to state-run collectives. Military-led "vocational training" is used for political indoctrination and to pressure participants to abandon their religious beliefs and "backward thinking." According to 2020 official figures, 543,000 Tibetans had received "vocational training" by July.

In 2020, local officials were, for the first time, given specific quotas for the number of Tibetans they needed to enroll in vocational training programs. According to official statistics, at least 26,000 Tibetans in one county alone—Chamdo county—have been relocated from their land and moved to urban areas since 2016, while the government brought in thousands of Han Chinese workers, claiming they were needed for large infrastructure projects. As Han Chinese who move to the region do not typically change their household registration, their numbers are not reflected in official statistics. Hundreds of thousands of Tibetans forced into wage labor are dependent on the state for their income, and thus are subject to new rules issued in June requiring all those who receive state benefits, as well as state employees, to denounce the Dalai Lama, abandon their religious beliefs, and profess political loyalty to the CCP.

Authorities also use the creation of national parks in Tibet to further justify the forcible relocation of Tibetans from their ancestral land, with 4,000 people reportedly ordered to leave an area bordering Qinghai and Gansu Provinces before the end of 2020. May 2020 "ethnic unity" regulations, which promote intermarriage between Han Chinese and Tibetans through financial incentives, advance Sinicization policies and the dilution of Tibetan identity.

CIVIL LIBERTIES: 3 / 60

D. FREEDOM OF EXPRESSION AND BELIEF: 0 / 16

D1. Are there free and independent media? 0 / 4

Chinese authorities tightly restrict all news media in Tibet. Individuals who use the internet, social media, or other means to share politically sensitive news content or commentary face arrest and heavy criminal penalties. Tibetan cultural expression, which the authorities associate with separatism, is subject to especially harsh restrictions; those incarcerated in recent years have included scores of Tibetan writers, intellectuals, and musicians.

Deliberate internet blackouts occur periodically in Tibet, including in areas where public demonstrations have occurred. International broadcasts are jammed, and personal communication devices are confiscated and searched. The online censorship and monitoring systems in place across China are applied even more stringently in the TAR, while censorship of Tibet-related keywords on the popular messaging application WeChat has become more sophisticated.

The TAR is the only region of China that requires foreigners to get a special permit to enter, with foreign journalists regularly prevented from visiting. Journalists also face barriers to access Tibetan areas of Sichuan and other provinces, though no permission is technically required to travel to those places. Tibetans who communicate with foreign media without permission risk arrest and prosecution.

D2. Are individuals free to practice and express their religious faith or nonbelief in public and private? 0 / 4

Freedom of religion is harshly restricted in Tibet, in large part because the authorities interpret reverence for the Dalai Lama and adherence to the region's unique form of Buddhism as a threat to CCP rule. New regulations on religious affairs came into effect in 2018, reiterating many existing restrictions and strengthening controls on places of worship, travel for religious purposes, and children's religious education, including in Tibetan areas.

The CCP's Central Committee, which absorbed the former religious affairs body in 2018, controls who can study in monasteries and nunneries and enforces a minimum age requirement of 18 for those who wish to become monks or nuns, although some institutions continue to accept younger children without registration. Monks and nuns are required to sign a declaration rejecting Tibetan independence, expressing loyalty to the government, and denouncing the Dalai Lama. Since 2012, the CCP has set up committees of government officials within monasteries to manage their daily operations and enforce party indoctrination campaigns. Police posts are increasingly common even in smaller monasteries. Possession of Dalai Lama–related materials—especially in the TAR—can lead to harassment, arrest, and punishment, including restrictions on commercial activity, loss of welfare benefits, and imprisonment.

Authorities took advantage of the coronavirus pandemic in 2020 to further restrict and surveil Buddhist Tibetans. In order to reopen after COVID-19 restrictions were lifted, temples and monasteries were required to participate in political indoctrination sessions and expand the "intelligent temple management" system, which includes enhanced video surveillance in all temples and monasteries. Participants were required to study Xi Jinping Thought, a collection of Xi's statements; recognize the CCP's claim that China "liberated" Tibet; and denounce the Dalai Lama. A new June campaign of "behavioral reform" and an "environmental clean-up drive" removed Tibetan prayer flags, a cultural object that wards off evil spirits. Authorities also restricted Tibetans' access to important religious sites and places of worship. Months after construction work was completed in October around Jokhang Temple in Lhasa, Tibetan worshippers' access to the site was strictly controlled and many were denied entry. Chinese tourists—whose numbers reportedly quadrupled after COVID-19 restrictions were lifted, averaging around 4,000 per day at Potala Palace—enjoyed unfettered access.

The Chinese government has asserted its intention to select the successor of the current Dalai Lama, who turned 85 in July 2020, and has promoted its own appointee to serve as the Panchen Lama, a religious figure who plays an important role in identifying the reincarnation of a Dalai Lama, according to Tibetan Buddhist rituals. The location of the Panchen Lama, who was originally recognized by the current Dalai Lama, remains unknown after he was abducted by Chinese officials in 1995, when he was six years old.

D3. Is there academic freedom, and is the educational system free from extensive political indoctrination? 0 / 4

University professors cannot lecture on certain topics, and many must attend political indoctrination sessions. The government restricts course materials to prevent circulation of unofficial versions of Tibetan history and has reduced the use of Tibetan as the language of instruction in schools in recent years.

D4. Are individuals free to express their personal views on political or other sensitive topics without fear of surveillance or retribution? 0 / 4

Freedom of private discussion is severely limited by factors including authorities' monitoring of electronic communications, a heavy security presence, recruitment of informants, and regular ideological campaigns in Tibetan areas. In 2020, authorities in Tibet expanded the invasive security and censorship system that features pervasive video surveillance, use of facial recognition technology, "smart" identity cards, and integrated surveillance to track residents and tourists in real time. Hundreds of "security centers" were set up across the region, with more than 130 in Lhasa alone.

Ordinary Tibetans continued to be detained or sentenced to prison for actions like verbally expressing support for the Dalai Lama and freedom for Tibet, sharing images of the Dalai Lama or the Tibetan flag on social media, or sending information abroad about recent self-immolation protests. In July 2020, Khando (or Khadro) Tseten was sentenced to seven years in prison on charges of "inciting state subversion" and "sharing state secrets" in connection with a song he composed that praised the Dalai Lama.

After the implementation of the 2017 Cybersecurity Law, authorities held meetings with managers of WeChat groups in Tibetan areas, warning them to ensure that online discussions remained "appropriate," while informing residents at monasteries of the risks of sharing illicit information.

Estimates for the number of Tibetan political prisoners in detention in 2020 range from 500 to more than 2,000, according to US Congressional reports and the Tibetan Centre for Human Rights and Democracy, respectively.

E. ASSOCIATIONAL AND ORGANIZATIONAL RIGHTS: 0 / 12
E1. Is there freedom of assembly? 0 / 4

Chinese authorities severely restrict freedom of assembly as part of the government's intensified "stability maintenance" policies in Tibet. Control and surveillance of public gatherings extend beyond major towns to villages and rural areas. Even nonviolent protesters are often violently dispersed and harshly punished. Nevertheless, Tibetans continue to seek ways to express dissatisfaction with government policies; sporadic solo or small-scale protests in public places persist, with participants briefly calling for the return of the Dalai Lama, the release of the Panchen Lama, or independence for Tibet, before being seized by police.

Abusive government policies and responses to those who self-immolate decreased the number of incidents in 2020. Officials have implemented information blackouts, heightened the security presence, increased surveillance, and arrested those associated with self-immolators en masse. Engaging in self-immolation and organizing, assisting, or gathering crowds related to such acts are considered criminal offenses, drawing charges of intentional homicide in some cases. In addition to mass arrests, the government employs collective-punishment tactics—for both self-immolations and other forms of protest—that include financial penalties for protesters' families, cancellation of public benefits for their households, and termination of state-funded projects in their communities.

E2. Is there freedom for nongovernmental organizations, particularly those that are engaged in human rights- and governance-related work? 0 / 4

Nongovernmental organizations (NGOs) are even more highly restricted in Tibetan areas than elsewhere. Even nonpolitical social and community engagement, including initiatives to promote the Tibetan language and to protect the environment, is harshly punished. Ten Tibetans, including two monks, from Sangchu county in Gansu Province were sentenced in June 2020 to prison terms ranging from 8 to 13 years for their efforts to block the construction of a slaughterhouse in their area and for demanding compensation for land confiscated for the project.

E3. Is there freedom for trade unions and similar professional or labor organizations? 0 / 4

Independent trade unions are illegal in Tibet, as they are in China as a whole. The only legal union organization is the government-controlled All-China Federation of Trade Unions, which has long been criticized for failing to properly defend workers' rights. Labor activism in Tibet is riskier and therefore much rarer than in other parts of China. According to the China Labour Bulletin, no strikes were documented in the TAR during 2020, compared with some 800 labor actions, including strikes and sit-ins, elsewhere in the country.

F. RULE OF LAW: 0 / 16
F1. Is there an independent judiciary? 0 / 4

The CCP controls the judicial system, and courts consequently lack independence. Courts at all levels are supervised by party political-legal committees that influence the appointment of judges, court operations, and verdicts and sentences. Given the political sensitivity of Tibetan areas, the scope for autonomous judicial decision-making is even more limited than elsewhere in China.

F2. Does due process prevail in civil and criminal matters? 0 / 4

Tibetans are routinely denied due process in criminal matters, including arbitrary detention, denial of family visits, long periods of enforced disappearance, solitary confinement, and illegal pretrial detention. Authorities often fail to inform families of the police detention, whereabouts, and well-being of loved ones. Businessman Tenzin Choephel, who had sought to raise awareness of environmental issues impacting Tibetan areas, has been detained since March 2018 and no information about his whereabouts had been released by the end of 2020. In a raid, police had found photos of the Dalai Lama in his home. Tibetans have even less access to legal representation of their choice than Han Chinese; lawyers seeking to defend them are routinely harassed, denied access to their clients, blocked from attending relevant hearings, and in some cases disbarred in retaliation. Trials are closed if state security interests are invoked, which sometimes occurs even when no political crime is listed.

F3. Is there protection from the illegitimate use of physical force and freedom from war and insurgencies? 0 / 4

Detained suspects and prisoners are subject to torture and other forms of abuse. Tibetan prisoners of conscience have died in custody under circumstances indicating torture, and others have been released in poor health, allegedly to avoid deaths in custody. According to a partial database maintained by the US Congressional-Executive Commission on China, there were still hundreds of Tibetan political prisoners at the end of 2020.

Four Tibetans died in detention or immediately following their release in the first half of 2020. Many more Tibetans were released from custody in extremely poor health. A woman who had served a 15-month prison term, for sharing information about her nephew's four-and-a-half-year sentence for calling for release of the Panchen Lama, was released from jail in August disabled from the torture and ill-treatment she had suffered in detention.

F4. Do laws, policies, and practices guarantee equal treatment of various segments of the population? 0 / 4

Ethnic Tibetans face a range of socioeconomic disadvantages and discriminatory treatment by employers, law enforcement agencies, and other official bodies. The dominant role of the Chinese language in education and employment limits opportunities for many Tibetans; Tibetans receive preferential treatment in university admission examinations, but this is often not enough to secure entrance. Tibetans who apply for all public sector jobs—including cleaners and other low-level staff—are now required to denounce the Dalai Lama, renounce their religious beliefs, and demonstrate their political loyalty in other ways that fundamentally negate their ethnic and cultural identity.

As in the rest of China, gender bias against women remains widespread, despite laws barring workplace discrimination. LGBT+ people suffer from discrimination, though same-sex sexual activity is not criminalized. Social pressures discourage discussion of LGBT+ issues.

G. PERSONAL AUTONOMY AND INDIVIDUAL RIGHTS: 3 / 16

G1. Do individuals enjoy freedom of movement, including the ability to change their place of residence, employment, or education? 0 / 4

The TAR has extreme restrictions on freedom of movement, particularly affecting ethnic Tibetans. Obstacles including troop deployments, checkpoints, roadblocks, required bureaucratic approvals, and passport restrictions impede freedom of movement within and beyond Tibetan areas, particularly for travel to and from the TAR. Chamdo city has been completely closed off to foreigners since 2008.

While Han Chinese tourists were encouraged to visit the TAR—particularly after the lifting of COVID-19 restrictions—and enjoy relative freedom of movement there, foreign tourists, journalists, diplomats, and others are tightly controlled and often denied entry. Foreign tourists must travel in groups with state-approved tour guides and obtain official permission to visit the TAR. Even then, last-minute travel bans are periodically imposed. Foreign nationals of Tibetan origin face enormous challenges in getting a visa, in some cases waiting for years only to be denied one.

Increased security efforts and Nepalese government cooperation have made it difficult for Tibetans to cross the border into Nepal. Obtaining a passport for foreign travel is extremely difficult for Tibetans, and in recent years some Tibetan pilgrims who have traveled abroad have faced detention upon return to China.

G2. Are individuals able to exercise the right to own property and establish private businesses without undue interference from state or nonstate actors? 1 / 4

The economy is dominated by state-owned enterprises and private businesses with informal ties to officials. Tibetans reportedly find it more difficult than ethnic Chinese residents to obtain permits and loans to open businesses.

The multi-year policy of forcing Tibetans off the land and into the wage economy has given the state additional leverage over a growing proportion of Tibetans, as they lose their self-reliance and depend on the government for their income. The government has used this leverage to force Tibetans to give up their religious beliefs, to denounce the Dalai Lama, and in other ways to show political fealty to the CCP.

G3. Do individuals enjoy personal social freedoms, including choice of marriage partner and size of family, protection from domestic violence, and control over appearance? 1 / 4

China's restrictive family-planning policies are formally more lenient for Tibetans and other ethnic minorities. Officials limit urban Tibetans to two children and encourage rural Tibetans to stop at three. As a result, the TAR is one of the few areas of China without a skewed sex ratio. Nevertheless, the authorities continue to regulate reproduction, and related abuses are occasionally reported. State policies actively encourage interethnic marriages with financial and other incentives, and couples must designate a single ethnicity for their children. Separately, Tibetan women are vulnerable to human trafficking schemes that result in forced marriage.

G4. Do individuals enjoy equality of opportunity and freedom from economic exploitation? 1 / 4

Exploitative employment practices are pervasive in many industries, as is the case across China, though ethnic Tibetans reportedly face additional disadvantages in hiring and compensation. Human trafficking that targets Tibetan women can lead to prostitution or exploitative employment in domestic service and other sectors elsewhere in China.

Transnistria

Population: 465,000
Freedom Status: Not Free

Note: *Freedom in the World* reports assess the level of political rights and civil liberties in a given geographical area, regardless of whether they are affected by the state, nonstate actors, or foreign powers. Disputed territories are sometimes assessed separately if they meet certain criteria, including boundaries that are sufficiently stable to allow year-on-year comparisons. For more information, see the report methodology and FAQ.

Overview: Transnistria is a breakaway region of Moldova in which ethnic Russians and Ukrainians together outnumber ethnic Moldovans. The territory has operated with de facto independence since a brief military conflict in 1992, though it is internationally recognized as a part of Moldova. Its government and economy are heavily dependent on subsidies from Russia, which maintains a military presence and peacekeeping mission in the territory. Political competition is increasingly restricted, and the ruling political group is aligned with powerful local business interests. Impartiality and pluralism of opinion in the media is very limited, and authorities closely control civil society activity.

KEY DEVELOPMENTS IN 2020

- Beginning in March, the separatist authorities tightened travel restrictions in response to the COVID-19 pandemic, disrupting civilian life and livelihoods along the de facto border with government-controlled Moldova. Approximately 26,000 confirmed cases of the coronavirus were reported during the year, as were more than 500 deaths.
- The Transnistrian government escalated its crackdown on dissent during the year, initiating criminal cases against several political and civic activists.
- The legislative elections in November featured low voter turnout and a lack of basic competition, with candidates in more than two-thirds of the districts running unopposed. The ruling party captured nearly all of the seats, and no genuine opposition parties won representation.

POLITICAL RIGHTS: 8 / 40 (−1)

A. ELECTORAL PROCESS: 2 / 12 (−1)

A1. Was the current head of government or other chief national authority elected through free and fair elections? 1 / 4

The president is elected for up to two consecutive five-year terms. Parliament speaker Vadim Krasnoselsky, an independent candidate closely associated with the Renewal (Obnovleniye) Party, won the 2016 presidential election with 62 percent of the vote in the first round, defeating incumbent Yevgeniy Shevchuk, who took 27 percent. Four other candidates divided the remainder. The campaign featured mutual accusations of corruption between the two main candidates, and Shevchuk lost even though his campaign was aided by administrative resources. State media heavily favored him and sought to portray Krasnoselsky as a crony of Sheriff Enterprises, the powerful business conglomerate that dominates the Transnistrian economy and backs Renewal; Krasnoselsky previously served as the company's security chief. Given Transnistria's political status, established international election monitors did not send missions to oversee the contest.

Constitutional amendments approved in 2011 created a relatively weak post of prime minister. The president appoints the prime minister, who must be approved by the parliament. Krasnoselsky named Aleksandr Martynov to serve as prime minister in late 2016.

A2. Were the current national legislative representatives elected through free and fair elections? 0 / 4 (−1)

Legislation adopted in July 2019 reduced the size of the unicameral Supreme Council from 43 to 33 members, all serving five-year terms. Elections for the body were held in

November 2020. A total of 51 candidates applied to run for seats, and only 45 were registered, with four denied registration and two withdrawing their applications. In 23 of the 33 electoral districts, the candidates ran unopposed; by comparison, only two candidates had run unopposed in each of the previous two legislative elections. Voter turnout was just 28 percent of the eligible electorate. The Renewal Party won 29 seats, and the remainder went to candidates who also had links to Sheriff Enterprises. As Transnistria is not internationally recognized, no established election monitoring organization sent a mission to observe the balloting.

Score Change: The score declined from 1 to 0 because the legislative elections offered voters almost no meaningful choice, with ruling party candidates running unopposed in most districts.

A3. Are the electoral laws and framework fair, and are they implemented impartially by the relevant election management bodies? 1 / 4

The Electoral Commission has long been criticized by various political figures for an alleged lack of impartiality and independence. In 2020, at least one would-be candidate claimed that he was denied registration for political reasons.

Changes to the electoral code in 2018 abolished the 25 percent minimum turnout threshold for an election to be considered valid, though the officially reported voter turnout for the 2020 Supreme Council elections would still have cleared the former minimum.

B. POLITICAL PLURALISM AND PARTICIPATION: 4 / 16

B1. Do the people have the right to organize in different political parties or other competitive political groupings of their choice, and is the system free of undue obstacles to the rise and fall of these competing parties or groupings? 1 / 4

Transnistria's entire political establishment, including opposition parties, supports the separatist agenda and Russia's role as the territory's foreign patron.

While the opposition Communist Party was formerly able to hold some events and criticize the government, it has faced growing political repression in recent years. In 2018, party leader Oleg Horzhan was arrested, stripped of his parliamentary immunity, and jailed for organizing illegal demonstrations, criticizing officials, and interfering with law enforcement agents. He received a four-and-a-half-year prison sentence.

In September 2020, the authorities initiated a criminal case against Nadezhda Bondarenko, the acting chair of the Communist Party and the editor of its newspaper, for allegedly insulting the president. Aleksandr Samoniy, a Tiraspol city councilman for the Communist Party, was charged in June for posting critical and insulting posts against the authorities on Facebook. He subsequently fled the territory.

B2. Is there a realistic opportunity for the opposition to increase its support or gain power through elections? 1 / 4

The Renewal Party has long controlled the legislature, and its defeat of the incumbent president in 2016 cemented its control over the executive branch as well. The territory's persecuted opposition parties did not play a significant role in the 2020 legislative elections, which left the Supreme Council with no genuine opposition members.

B3. Are the people's political choices free from domination by forces that are external to the political sphere, or by political forces that employ extrapolitical means? 1 / 4

The ruling Renewal Party and the political establishment more broadly are dominated by the monopolistic business conglomerate Sheriff Enterprises. In addition, the political influence of the Russian government is undergirded by the presence of Russian troops, who are ostensibly stationed in the territory to guard a Soviet-era ammunition depot and, as peace-keepers, to uphold a 1992 cease-fire between Transnistrian and Moldovan forces. Moscow has also financially supported the territory's pension system and provided subsidized energy.

B4. Do various segments of the population (including ethnic, racial, religious, gender, LGBT+, and other relevant groups) have full political rights and electoral opportunities? 1 / 4

Both men and women have the legal right to vote, participate in campaigns, and run for office. However, the system in practice allows little opportunity for independent political activity by any segment of the population, and few women are included in the political leadership; only two women hold seats on the Supreme Council.

While Transnistria has three official languages—Russian, Ukrainian, and Moldovan—Russian is used in governmental affairs. Authorities do not allow voting in Moldovan elections to take place in Transnistrian-controlled territory, though residents who sought to vote in Moldova's February 2019 elections were observed traveling into Moldova proper to participate. Residents with Russian citizenship had access to polling stations during Russia's tightly controlled 2018 presidential election.

C. FUNCTIONING OF GOVERNMENT: 2 / 12

C1. Do the freely elected head of government and national legislative representatives determine the policies of the government? 1 / 4

Transnistria's flawed elections undercut the democratic legitimacy of both execu-tive leaders and legislative representatives. Sheriff Enterprises exerts a strong influence on elected officials' policy decisions, which are also closely monitored by the Russian government.

C2. Are safeguards against official corruption strong and effective? 0 / 4

Transnistrian politics have long been built on personal business interests, nepotism, and favoritism. There are few visible safeguards against official corruption.

C3. Does the government operate with openness and transparency? 1 / 4

Although officials publish some government information on websites and are occa-sionally interviewed by media outlets about their policies, the public is generally excluded from decision-making processes, and governmental openness and transparency are limited in practice.

CIVIL LIBERTIES: 12 / 60 (−1)

D. FREEDOM OF EXPRESSION AND BELIEF: 4 / 16 (−1)

D1. Are there free and independent media? 0 / 4

Authorities closely monitor and control the public media, and Sheriff Enterprises dominates private broadcasting, leading to widespread self-censorship. The territory's few independent print outlets have limited circulation. Critical reporting can result in reprisals including criminal charges, and the government also uses bureaucratic obstruction and with-holding of information to inhibit independent journalism.

Legislation adopted in 2016 gave authorities even greater control over state media outlets, including the power to appoint editorial staff, and enabled officials to limit media access to their activities and bar the use of recording devices.

Travel restrictions related to COVID-19 further limited access to the territory for Mol-dovan and foreign journalists during 2020. Separately, telecommunications regulators in

January suspended the license of LinkService, a smaller competitor of Transnistria's leading internet service provider, which is owned by Sheriff Enterprises. An appellate court blocked the decision in April and allowed LinkService to continue operating at least through the end of the public health emergency.

D2. Are individuals free to practice and express their religious faith or nonbelief in public and private? 2 / 4

Most of the population is Orthodox Christian, and authorities have denied registration to several smaller religious groups, which at times face harassment by police and Orthodox opponents. The law imposes restrictions and penalties related to unauthorized distribution of religious literature, preaching in public spaces, and organized religious activities in residential buildings. Foreign religious groups are not permitted to register, and foreign individuals may not found or join registered groups.

Jehovah's Witnesses have been unable to obtain registration in Transnistria. Members of the Muslim community report a reluctance to practice their faith openly due to past intimidation by authorities, and they have struggled to advance plans to establish a mosque in Tiraspol.

D3. Is there academic freedom, and is the educational system free from extensive political indoctrination? 1 / 4

Academics and students may take part in international forums, but potential reprisals by Transnistrian authorities are a deterrent to participation in programs sponsored by Moldova. Academic analysis of topics such as the 1992 conflict, the role of the Russian Federation and peacekeeping forces, and Transnistrian statehood are subject to censorship.

The few Latin-script schools in Transnistria that are overseen by the Moldovan state face pressure from Transnistrian authorities. During 2020, travel restrictions imposed in response to COVID-19 disrupted the routine movement of the schools' students and staff.

D4. Are individuals free to express their personal views on political or other sensitive topics without fear of surveillance or retribution? 1 / 4 (−1)

Legal restrictions on certain kinds of speech discourage free discussion. Among other provisions related to defamation or insult of the authorities, the criminal code penalizes public expression of disrespect for the Russian peacekeeping mission.

Speech-related prosecutions of dissidents, activists, and ordinary social media users have become more common in recent years, inhibiting expression by other residents. In addition to the cases against Communist Party politicians during 2020, a criminal investigation regarding incitement to extremism was opened in March against Larisa Kalik, who had recently published a book documenting abusive conditions in the Transnistrian military. She fled the territory as a result. Also in March, it was reported that pensioner Tatiana Belova and her husband, Serghei Mirovici, had been sentenced to three years in prison for "extremism" and "insulting the president" via posts on Telegram in 2019. Belova was released in July, but Mirovici reportedly remained in prison.

Score Change: The score declined from 2 to 1 because prosecutions on charges such as inciting extremism or insulting the authorities have discouraged free expression in recent years.

E. ASSOCIATIONAL AND ORGANIZATIONAL RIGHTS: 1 / 12
E1. Is there freedom of assembly? 0 / 4

Freedom of assembly is tightly restricted. Authorities consistently reject applications for permits to hold meetings and protests, and participants in unauthorized actions face administrative penalties or criminal prosecution.

In July 2020, the authorities dispersed a public protest in Rîbnița in which participants voiced objections to pandemic-related travel restrictions that prevented them from reaching their places of employment. Activist Gennadiy Chorba was arrested on extremism charges for organizing the protest and was placed in pretrial detention; the case was pending at year's end. Separately in September, security forces raided an unauthorized dance party at a farm and arrested 47 people, some of whom were reportedly mistreated in custody.

E2. Is there freedom for nongovernmental organizations, particularly those that are engaged in human rights and governance-related work? 1 / 4

Nongovernmental organizations (NGOs) and civic activists operate in a repressive environment. Groups that work on human rights issues or other topics deemed politically sensitive are subject to surveillance and harassment. The local Coordination Council for Humanitarian and Technical Assistance, which is controlled by the prime minister, must approve governance-related work.

A 2018 law requires more burdensome reporting by NGOs, including on foreign funding, and prohibits foreign-backed NGOs from engaging in broadly defined "political activities." In 2020 the authorities continued to smear and harass the Apriori Center, an NGO that provides legal advice and capacity-building support to individual activists and other NGOs.

E3. Is there freedom for trade unions and similar professional or labor organizations? 0 / 4

The trade union system in Transnistria has not been reformed since the Soviet era, and unions are manipulated by the political leadership in practice. Independent labor activism is not tolerated.

F. RULE OF LAW: 2 / 16

F1. Is there an independent judiciary? 0 / 4

The judiciary serves the interests of the political authorities and Sheriff Enterprises. The European Court of Human Rights has asserted that Moscow is responsible for the decisions of Transnistrian courts, and that these courts do not meet minimum standards of fairness.

F2. Does due process prevail in civil and criminal matters? 0 / 4

Security and law enforcement agencies in Transnistria regularly engage in arbitrary arrests and detentions and deny detainees access to attorneys. Trials and other criminal proceedings lack safeguards for due process and are frequently held without public scrutiny, with the outcomes announced after the fact.

F3. Is there protection from the illegitimate use of physical force and freedom from war and insurgencies? 1 / 4

Police mistreatment of suspects is common, and physical abuse is employed to obtain confessions. Prison conditions remain poor; denial of proper medical care has been reported, including in the case of jailed Communist Party leader Oleg Horzhan during 2020. The authorities have been accused of engaging in forced disappearances and abductions in recent years.

F4. Do laws, policies, and practices guarantee equal treatment of various segments of the population? 1 / 4

While the Transnistrian constitution guarantees people's rights and freedoms "without distinction as to sex, race, nationality, language, religion," and other such categories, these protections are frequently violated with impunity. Members of the Moldovan-speaking minority face discrimination and harassment. Women are also subject to discrimination in practice; among other problems, they are formally excluded from numerous occupations that are considered hazardous or physically difficult. Same-sex sexual activity is illegal in Transnistria, and members of the LGBT+ community generally do not identify themselves publicly due to widespread government and societal discrimination.

G. PERSONAL AUTONOMY AND INDIVIDUAL RIGHTS: 5 / 16

G1. Do individuals enjoy freedom of movement, including the ability to change their place of residence, employment, or education? 2 / 4

Approximately 300,000 people in Transnistria hold Moldovan citizenship and can travel freely to European Union (EU) countries. Since 2018, Transnistria residents have been able to obtain neutral license plates for use on international roads. Moldovan authorities also began recognizing Transnistrian educational documents that year.

New checkpoints and travel restrictions were imposed beginning in March 2020 in response to the COVID-19 pandemic, substantially reducing freedom of movement in and out of Transnistria as well as within the territory. Among other effects on civilian life, the measures disrupted the movement of health workers to their places of employment.

G2. Are individuals able to exercise the right to own property and establish private businesses without undue interference from state or nonstate actors? 1 / 4

Full private property rights are only recognized for housing; other property rights, including land ownership, remain restricted. Procedures for establishing a private business are hampered by bureaucratic impediments.

G3. Do individuals enjoy personal social freedoms, including choice of marriage partner and size of family, protection from domestic violence, and control over appearance? 1 / 4

Same-sex marriage is not permitted. Domestic violence is a persistent concern, and it is not considered a criminal offense in the absence of serious physical injury. However, the problem has become more public in recent years, including through television reports. Dedicated services, including psychological aid, a hotline for victims, and shelters, are operated by civil society organizations supported by international donors.

G4. Do individuals enjoy equality of opportunity and freedom from economic exploitation? 1 / 4

Economic opportunity remains very limited. Sheriff Enterprises dominates the economy. Despite increased international aid meant to ensure better opportunities for women, many still fall victim to traffickers who subject them to forced labor or sex work.

West Bank

Population: 2,949,000
Freedom Status: Not Free

Note: Prior to its 2011 edition, *Freedom in the World* featured one report for Israeli-occupied portions of the West Bank and Gaza Strip and another for Palestinian-administered portions.

Freedom in the World reports assess the level of political rights and civil liberties in a given geographical area, regardless of whether they are affected by the state, nonstate actors, or foreign powers. Disputed territories are sometimes assessed separately if they meet certain criteria, including boundaries that are sufficiently stable to allow year-on-year comparisons. For more information, see the methodology and FAQ.

Overview: The West Bank is under Israeli military occupation, which entails onerous physical barriers and constraints on movement, demolition of homes and other physical infrastructure, restrictions on political and civil liberties, and expanding Jewish settlements. Jewish settlers in the West Bank are Israeli citizens and enjoy the same rights and liberties as other Israelis. The West Bank's Palestinian residents, excluding those living in East Jerusalem, fall under the partial jurisdiction of the Palestinian Authority (PA), which is operating with an expired presidential mandate and has no functioning legislature. The PA governs in an authoritarian manner, engaging in acts of repression against journalists and human rights activists who present critical views on its rule. East Jerusalem Palestinians are governed directly by Israel. While a small minority of them have Israeli citizenship, most have a special residency status that provides them with a restricted set of rights compared with those of Israeli citizens.

KEY DEVELOPMENTS IN 2020

- Over 114,000 confirmed cases of COVID-19 and over 1,100 deaths were recorded in the West Bank and East Jerusalem during the year, according to the United Nations Office for the Coordination of Humanitarian Affairs (UNOCHA). The economic fallout of the pandemic was compounded when the PA refused to receive tax revenue transfers from Israel and cut off security coordination beginning in May—a protest against Israel's declaration of plans to annex portions of the West Bank. However, the PA resumed coordination with Israel in November, and Israel transferred over $1 billion of accrued tax revenues in December.
- In November, Israeli authorities demolished the hamlet of Humsah al-Baqaia in the Jordan Valley, under the pretext that it was unlawfully constructed. They destroyed over 70 structures, the largest single demolition in the past 10 years. During the year, 989 Palestinians were rendered homeless because of building demolitions, including over 300 in East Jerusalem—the most of any year in East Jerusalem since 2004.

POLITICAL RIGHTS: 4 / 40

A. ELECTORAL PROCESS: 1 / 12

A1. Was the current head of government or other chief national authority elected through free and fair elections? 0 / 4

The Palestinian Authority (PA) has not held a presidential election since 2005. The four-year term of Mahmoud Abbas, who won that year with 62 percent of the vote, expired in 2009, but he has continued to rule with the support of the Palestine Liberation Organization (PLO), led by his party, Fatah. The rift between the West Bank–based PA government, under the control of Fatah, and the de facto Hamas government in the Gaza Strip has impeded the resumption of regular elections. Hamas, an Islamist political movement and militant group, seized control of Gaza in 2007. This followed its victory in the 2006 legislative elections and a period of armed struggle between Hamas and Fatah that left each in control of a separate territory. A 2014 agreement between the two groups to form a unity government did not result in actual power sharing. In 2017, the two sides committed to a reconciliation deal brokered by Egypt, but there has been little progress on implementation. In September 2020, Fatah and Hamas announced that they had agreed to hold legislative and presidential elections within six months, though no official date was set at year-end. Both parties have demanded that Israel allow East Jerusalem residents to participate.

Under PA laws, the prime minister is nominated by the president and requires the support of the Palestinian Legislative Council (PLC). However, the PLC elected in 2006 was unable to function due to the Fatah-Hamas division and Israel's detention of many lawmakers. Abbas has since appointed prime ministers and cabinets without legislative approval. Mohammad Shtayyeh was appointed and sworn in as prime minister along with a new Fatah-led cabinet in April 2019. Hamas opposed Shtayyeh's appointment.

A2. Were the current national legislative representatives elected through free and fair elections? 0 / 4

Palestinians in the West Bank do not have a functioning legislative body. Elections for the 132-seat PLC have not been held since 2006, when Hamas won 74 seats and Fatah took 45. Israel's suppression of Hamas and fighting between Fatah and Hamas left the PLC unable to function. Israeli forces have repeatedly detained elected PLC members since 2006, and the legislature's electoral mandate expired in 2010. In December 2018, President Abbas ordered the formal dissolution of the PLC, backed by a Supreme Constitutional Court ruling that also called for legislative elections within six months. Hamas rejected the decision. In September 2020, Fatah and Hamas announced that they had agreed to hold legislative and presidential elections within six months, though no official date was set at year-end.

The majority of Palestinian residents in East Jerusalem do not hold Israeli citizenship and thus did not have the right to vote in Israel's 2019 and 2020 Knesset (parliamentary) elections. Noncitizen Palestinian residents are permitted to vote in Israeli municipal council elections in Jerusalem, but historically most have boycotted.

Israeli citizens living in West Bank settlements are represented by the Israeli Knesset and participated in the 2019 and 2020 Israeli legislative elections.

A3. Are the electoral laws and framework fair, and are they implemented impartially by the relevant election management bodies? 1 / 4

Palestinian residents of the West Bank cannot vote in Israeli general elections. PA laws provide a credible framework for presidential and legislative elections, but neither have been held since 2005 and 2006, respectively. The Palestinian Central Elections Commission oversees elections in the West Bank and Gaza. The body's nine commissioners are appointed by the president, although the law requires them to be experienced and politically impartial judges, academics, or lawyers.

Israel's Central Elections Committee oversees Knesset elections, and its Interior Ministry manages Israeli municipal elections, including in Jerusalem. These elections are generally free and fair, but Palestinians in the occupied West Bank are excluded from participating. Noncitizen Palestinians in East Jerusalem are also excluded from participating in Knesset elections.

B. POLITICAL PLURALISM AND PARTICIPATION: 4 / 16

B1. Do the people have the right to organize in different political parties or other competitive political groupings of their choice, and is the system free of undue obstacles to the rise and fall of these competing parties or groupings? 1 / 4

In addition to Fatah, a number of small Palestinian parties operate relatively freely in the West Bank. However, the PA deals harshly with supporters of Hamas and rivals of

President Abbas within Fatah. Israel detains and arrests political activists if they are perceived as threats to Israeli security.

Since 2007, the PA and Israeli forces in the West Bank have collaborated in surveillance and repression of Hamas, periodically engaging in mass arrests and closures of affiliated institutions.

East Jerusalem Palestinians can form party lists to run in the city's Israeli municipal elections but doing so may lead to increased scrutiny by Israeli authorities and harassment from Palestinians who oppose participation.

B2. Is there a realistic opportunity for the opposition to increase its support or gain power through elections? 0 / 4

The prolonged and indefinite postponement of presidential and legislative elections has prevented any rotation of power in the West Bank. The PA leadership has been accused of avoiding any contest that could lead to a Hamas victory. Moreover, the boycott of the 2017 local elections by opposition groups left them largely unrepresented in West Bank municipal councils.

B3. Are the people's political choices free from domination by forces that are external to the political sphere, or by political forces that employ extrapolitical means? 1 / 4

Israeli authorities regularly surveil, detain, and harass political figures from the Popular Front for the Liberation of Palestine (PFLP), Hamas, Islamic Jihad, and other factions that Israel considers terrorist groups. In addition, Israel's restrictions on freedom of movement—including checkpoints, roadblocks, and permit restrictions, as well as the continuous barrier it has constructed along the West Bank side of the pre-1967 border—can impede Palestinian political organizing and activity.

Foreign government donors sometimes exert influence over the PA to promote or marginalize certain politicians or political factions. For example, following the 2006 legislative elections, the United States and other members of the Middle East "Quartet" (Russia, the United Nations, and the European Union) temporarily suspended aid to the PA. Further, in 2018 and 2019, the US government halted aid to the United Nations Relief and Works Agency (UNRWA), shuttered US Agency for International Development (USAID) programs in the occupied territories, and dramatically reduced aid to the PA in what was widely seen as a pressure campaign to encourage the Palestinian leadership to negotiate with Israel under the Trump administration's terms.

B4. Do various segments of the population (including ethnic, racial, religious, gender, LGBT+, and other relevant groups) have full political rights and electoral opportunities? 2 / 4

Women and religious and ethnic minorities enjoy formal political equality under PA laws, and both women and Christians have held PLC seats and cabinet positions. There are legislated gender quotas for party lists in legislative and local elections, which tend to result in approximately 20 percent of candidates being women. In some districts of the West Bank (Ramallah and Bethlehem), seats are set aside for Christian candidates. Reforms to increase Christian representation in local councils prior to the 2017 elections were interpreted by opponents of Fatah to have political aims.

Palestinian residents of East Jerusalem have the option to apply for Israeli citizenship, though most decline for political reasons, and about half or more of those who apply each year are unsuccessful. In November 2020, an Israeli court ordered the Interior Ministry to implement a 1968 legislative clause that would facilitate the process by which young Palestinians obtain Israeli citizenship. While noncitizen residents can vote in Israeli municipal elections in Jerusalem, historically most people have boycotted; noncitizens cannot vote in Knesset elections. A Palestinian Jerusalem resident who is not a citizen cannot become mayor under current Israeli law. East Jerusalem Palestinians are only entitled to vote in PA elections with Israel's approval.

As of 2020, there were over 475,000 settlers in the West Bank excluding East Jerusalem, and over 200,000 Jewish settlers in East Jerusalem, all of whom are Israeli citizens with full political rights in Israel.

C. FUNCTIONING OF GOVERNMENT: 2 / 12

C1. Do the freely elected head of government and national legislative representatives determine the policies of the government? 0 / 4

The PA lacks an elected executive and legislature. Because the legislature has not functioned since 2007, new laws are introduced via presidential decree. The ability of the PA president and ministries to implement policy decisions is limited in practice by direct Israeli military control over much of the West Bank. The PA has virtually no ability to provide services, access farming communities, or develop water, waste management, or land resources in Area C—a largely rural area that makes up more than 60 percent of West Bank territory and is under exclusive Israeli control. Israel periodically withholds the transfer of tax revenues to the PA, which affects salary payments and policy implementation. In an act of protest against Israel's declared intention to annex portions of the West Bank, the PA refused to accept tax revenue transfers from and halted security coordination with Israel in May 2020, compounding the economic hardship brought on by the COVID-19 pandemic. The PA resumed coordination with Israel in November, and Israel transferred over $1 billion of accrued tax revenues in December.

C2. Are safeguards against official corruption strong and effective? 1 / 4

Official corruption remains a major problem that is widely recognized by the public, according to opinion surveys. The PA's Anti-Corruption Commission is responsible for implementing an anticorruption strategy, but a December 2019 report released by Transparency International showed that 78 percent of Palestinians are unfamiliar with the body. In their October 2020 report covering developments in 2019, the Coalition for Accountability and Integrity (AMAN) noted some improvements in legislation to curb bribery, refine procurement procedures, and enhance protections for whistleblowers. However, ensuring transparency, combating nepotism and favoritism in appointments and promotions, and safeguarding a strong and fair judiciary remain prominent challenges.

Documents published online in June 2019 revealed that PA cabinet members under former prime minister Rami Hamdallah had secretly received large salary increases in 2017, during a time of economic stagnation, with approval from Abbas. Prime Minister Shtayyeh suspended the raises and pledged to investigate them.

C3. Does the government operate with openness and transparency? 1 / 4

Government transparency is generally lacking in the PA, and in the absence of basic accountability mechanisms including regular elections and legislative oversight, the administration has little incentive to make substantive improvements. Journalists, activists, and others who attempt to scrutinize PA policies or internal operations are subject to intimidation and harassment.

The operations of Israeli military authorities in the West Bank are opaque, and the Israeli military and civil administrations are not accountable to Palestinians.

ADDITIONAL DISCRETIONARY POLITICAL RIGHTS QUESTION

Is the government or occupying power deliberately changing the ethnic composition of a country or territory so as to destroy a culture or tip the political balance in favor of another group? –3 / 0

The growth of Jewish settlements, seizures of Palestinian land, and the demolition of Palestinian homes in the West Bank continued in 2020. Under the pretext of unlawful construction, Israel demolished 272 housing units and hundreds of other structures in the West Bank and East Jerusalem, leaving 989 homeless, according to the Israeli human rights group B'Tselem. The November demolition of the hamlet Humsah al-Baqaia in the Jordan Valley destroyed over 70 structures and was the largest single demolition in the past 10 years. Demolitions in East Jerusalem in 2020 left more Palestinians homeless there than any year on record since 2004. The Israeli Civil Administration (ICA) employs 2017–18 occupation policies (including Military Order 1797) that remove options for Palestinians to challenge demolition orders and allow the ICA to confiscate portable buildings without a hearing or right to objection. In 2018, the Knesset passed a law limiting Palestinians' direct access to the Israeli Supreme Court for petitions against the construction of Jewish settlements.

A 2017 Israeli law authorized the retroactive, formal seizure of private Palestinian land, with compensation, where settlements had been built illegally. But, following petitions, the law was frozen, and in June 2020, the High Court of Justice nullified it. In a rare decision in August 2020, the Supreme Court overturned a 2018 district court decision and ruled for the removal of a settlement outpost in the West Bank that had been built on privately owned Palestinian land.

CIVIL LIBERTIES: 21 / 60

D. FREEDOM OF EXPRESSION AND BELIEF: 7 / 16

D1. Are there free and independent media? 1 / 4

The news media are generally not free in the West Bank; journalists are surveilled and repressed by both Palestinian and Israeli authorities, and social media companies have sometimes blocked Palestinian journalists' accounts. Under PA law, journalists can be fined and jailed and newspapers closed for publishing information that might harm national unity, contradict national responsibility, or incite violence.

According to the Palestinian Center for Development and Media Freedoms (MADA), the closures associated with the COVID-19 pandemic in March and April 2020 resulted in a decline in overall violations of media freedom in the occupied territories during that time frame. Violations of media freedom by Palestinian and Israeli authorities in the West Bank included the summons, interrogation, and arrest of journalists, confiscation of equipment, and restrictions on reporting.

In 2017, President Abbas issued the Electronic Crimes Law (ECL), prescribing heavy fines and lengthy prison terms for a range of vaguely defined offenses, including the publication or dissemination of material that is critical of the state, disturbs public order or national unity, or harms family and religious values. In October 2019, a Palestinian court in Ramallah ordered 59 websites, many of which carried news content, and social media pages to be blocked under the ECL, claiming that they disturbed public order and threatened civil peace. The sites featured criticism of Abbas, were affiliated with opposition groups, or focused on combating corruption. The decision was appealed and referred to the Constitutional Court, which had conferred no ruling by the end of 2020.

Reporters are subject to surveillance, assault, and detention by Israeli forces. Israeli authorities were responsible for 210 media freedom violations in the West Bank and East

Jerusalem in 2020, according to MADA. These violations included physical assault, preventing journalists from covering certain events, interrogation, arrest, and detention. Facebook also shut down pages and accounts of Palestinian journalists due to alleged incitement to violence and terrorism.

D2. Are individuals free to practice and express their religious faith or nonbelief in public and private? 2 / 4

The PA Basic Law declares Islam to be the official religion of Palestine and states that "respect and sanctity of all other heavenly religions (Judaism and Christianity) shall be maintained." Blasphemy is a criminal offense. The ECL criminalizes expression aimed at harming moral and religious values without defining those values, allowing for arbitrary enforcement.

Security-related restrictions on movement, and vandalism or physical assaults against worshippers or places of worship, affect Jewish, Muslim, and Christian residents of the West Bank to varying degrees. The Israeli authorities regularly prevent Palestinian Muslims in the West Bank from reaching Jerusalem to pray, and generally restrict access for young adult males to the Temple Mount/Haram al-Sharif compound on Fridays.

D3. Is there academic freedom, and is the educational system free from extensive political indoctrination? 2 / 4

The PA has administrative authority over Palestinian education. Political activism is common on university campuses, and student council elections generally proceed freely—an Islamist bloc sympathetic to Hamas has performed strongly in several of the past Birzeit University student council elections, for example. However, students affiliated with the bloc have been detained by Israeli and Palestinian authorities. In March 2019, Israeli forces entered Birzeit University, arrested three students, and raided the office of the student council.

According to the Association for Civil Rights in Israel, East Jerusalem's schools are underfunded compared with schools in West Jerusalem, and East Jerusalem severely lacks physical classrooms.

Israeli authorities have more actively restricted visas for foreign academics attempting to visit Palestinian universities in the West Bank since 2016, according to the Right to Enter Campaign.

D4. Are individuals free to express their personal views on political or other sensitive topics without fear of surveillance or retribution? 2 / 4

Residents have some freedom to engage in open private discussion, though Israeli and PA security forces are known to monitor online activity and arrest individuals for alleged incitement or criticism of Palestinian authorities, respectively. The adoption and enforcement of the ECL has increased concerns about the freedom of personal expression online.

Human rights organizations have accused the PA of monitoring social media posts and detaining individuals for harsh questioning related to their comments. In 2018, evidence emerged that the PA has engaged in extensive electronic surveillance of lawyers, activists, political figures, and others, which could have a deterrent effect on expression more broadly. Issa Amro, a prominent human rights activist who was allegedly beaten and tortured in detention in 2017, faced a potential prison term for "disturbing public order" under the ECL and has been arrested on multiple other charges since. Throughout 2020, individuals were detained for their posts on social media, including for posts that discussed planning a protest; that denounced the government's response to the COVID-19 pandemic; that "defam[ed] authorities"; and that criticized the PA's resumption of relations with Israel.

E. ASSOCIATIONAL AND ORGANIZATIONAL RIGHTS: 5 / 12

E1. Is there freedom of assembly? 1 / 4

In 2020, the PA restricted freedom of assembly as a part of the state of emergency enacted to combat the COVID-19 pandemic. In September, PA security forces reportedly fired sound grenades and tear gas on peaceful demonstrators in Ramallah, dispersing the group.

The PA requires permits for demonstrations, and those that protest PA policies are generally dispersed by security forces. In 2019, hundreds of women peacefully demonstrated in the West Bank to call for an end to gender-based violence following the August murder of a 21-year-old Palestinian woman, Israa Ghrayeb, allegedly by her male relatives.

Israel's Military Order 101 (1967) requires a permit for all political demonstrations of more than 10 people. Israeli Military Order 1651 (2009) is used to prosecute and sentence those who are accused of harming public order or engaging in alleged incitement. Israeli authorities frequently restrict and disperse demonstrations, some of which become violent, and certain protest areas are designated as closed military zones. Protesters are at risk of injury by tear-gas canisters, rubber-coated bullets, or live ammunition, and clashes between demonstrators and Israeli troops periodically result in fatalities.

E2. Is there freedom for nongovernmental organizations, particularly those that are engaged in human rights- and governance-related work? 2 / 4

A broad range of nongovernmental organizations (NGOs) operate in the West Bank. However, Israeli restrictions on movement can impede civil society activity, Islamist groups have been periodically shut down by Israeli or PA officials, and activists who criticize the PA leadership can face harassment and abuse by security services.

A 2017 Israeli law bars entry for any foreign individual who publicly supports a boycott of Israel or its West Bank settlements. In August 2019, the law was used to prevent US congresswomen Ilhan Omar and Rashida Tlaib from visiting Israel and the West Bank; while Tlaib's prohibition was modified later in the month so that she could visit relatives in the West Bank, she rejected the offer. The law was also used in November 2019 to expel Omar Shakir, the Israel and Palestine representative for Human Rights Watch (HRW), for his advocacy against Israeli settlements in the West Bank.

In July 2020, Israeli authorities reportedly raided the offices of three artistic and cultural organizations in East Jerusalem—the Edward Said National Conservatory of Music, the Yabous Cultural Centre, and the Shafaq Cultural Network—seizing documents and materials, ransacking the offices, and detaining the groups' directors.

E3. Is there freedom for trade unions and similar professional or labor organizations? 2 / 4

Teachers in the West Bank staged a strike in October 2020 after not receiving their full salaries for months. Some teachers were reportedly arrested after taking part in the strikes. The official teachers' union warned that they would not be able to protect teachers taking part in unauthorized actions from being arrested. In December, the union called on teachers to strike after the government stated it would not pay them the full amount of their delayed salaries.

Workers may establish unions without government authorization, but labor protections in general are poorly enforced. Palestinian workers seeking to strike must submit to arbitration by the PA Labor Ministry, and various other rules make it difficult to mount a legal strike. Palestinian workers in Jerusalem are subject to Israeli labor law.

F. RULE OF LAW: 4 / 16

F1. Is there an independent judiciary? 2 / 4

Palestinians in the West Bank are subject to the jurisdiction of both the Palestinian judiciary and the Israeli military court system, neither of which is fully independent. In July 2019, President Abbas issued two decrees, the first dissolving the existing High Judicial Council and replacing it with a transitional body, and the second lowering the retirement age of judges. A number of judges and human rights organizations denounced the moves as an effort to increase executive control over the judicial branch. Although the transitional council included former members of the High Judicial Council, it was given an expanded mandate to restructure the judicial system.

Enforcement of judicial decisions is impeded by PA noncompliance as well as lack of Palestinian jurisdiction in Area C, where the Israeli military exerts exclusive control.

The Israeli civilian courts, which have jurisdiction over Israeli settlers in the West Bank, are independent.

F2. Does due process prevail in civil and criminal matters? 1 / 4

The opaque distinction between criminal and security-related offenses, the regular use of detention without trial by Palestinian and Israeli security forces, and the use of martial law and a military court system that applies exclusively to Palestinians in the West Bank all violate the due process rights of Palestinians. Jewish settlers are tried in Israeli civilian courts, which generally provide due process protections.

Human rights groups regularly document allegations of arbitrary detention by PA security forces. Palestinians are also regularly detained without charges for extended periods by Israeli authorities. The Israeli military frequently conducts home raids without a warrant. According to B'Tselem, there were over 3,900 Palestinian security detainees and prisoners from the West Bank being held in Israeli prisons as of September 2020, and 157 Palestinian minors from the occupied territories (which includes the Gaza Strip). Minors being held are usually interrogated without a lawyer or parental guardian present and are tried by a special military court. Acquittals are very rare, and the courts have been criticized for a lack of due process protections. East Jerusalem Palestinian minors are tried in Israeli civilian juvenile courts.

Maher al-Akhras, a 49-year-old man from the West Bank, was detained without charge by Israeli authorities in July 2020 and went on a hunger strike for more than 100 days protesting his detention. He was released at the end of November.

F3. Is there protection from the illegitimate use of physical force and freedom from war and insurgencies? 0 / 4

Penal codes applicable in the West Bank permit capital punishment, but no executions have been carried out since 2005. In 2018, the State of Palestine became a signatory to the International Covenant on Civil and Political Rights, which severely restricts the use of capital punishment.

Physical abuse of detainees by PA authorities in the West Bank has been documented by human rights organizations. Individual testimonies also attest to the use of excessive violence by the Israeli military.

Israeli soldiers accused of excessive force or abuse of Palestinian civilians are subject to Israeli military law, though convictions, which are rare, typically result in light sentences. Jewish settlers who attack Palestinian individuals, property, and agricultural resources generally enjoy impunity. B'Tselem reported that 23 Palestinians were killed by Israeli security forces in the West Bank, including East Jerusalem, in 2020. There were also hundreds of cases of violence against Palestinians by settlers.

Israeli security personnel and civilians face small-scale terrorist attacks in the West Bank. According to B'Tselem, three Israeli civilians and two security personnel were killed in the West Bank by Palestinians during 2019.

F4. Do laws, policies, and practices guarantee equal treatment of various segments of the population? 1 / 4

The legal arrangements operative in the West Bank are fundamentally discriminatory: Israelis and Palestinians who reside or commit crimes in the same location are subject to different courts and laws.

Palestinian women are underrepresented in most professions and encounter discrimination in employment, though they have equal access to universities. Women are legally excluded from what are deemed dangerous occupations. Gender-based harassment and violence remain major problems in the West Bank.

Although LGBT+ people in the West Bank do not face prosecution for same-sex sexual activity, they have been subject to harassment and abuse by PA authorities and members of society.

G. PERSONAL AUTONOMY AND INDIVIDUAL RIGHTS: 5 / 16

G1. Do individuals enjoy freedom of movement, including the ability to change their place of residence, employment, or education? 1 / 4

The PA employed movement restrictions between towns and districts and curfews to respond to the COVID-19 crisis in 2020. Closures were in place from March through May, then reimposed again in November. While some Palestinian workers from the occupied territories were prevented from traveling into Israel for work due to the declaration of a March lockdown there, others in construction, agriculture, and health were allowed to cross the border.

Israeli checkpoints, travel permits, and other restrictions continue to seriously constrain freedom of movement, stunt trade, and limit Palestinian access to jobs, hospitals, and schools.

The Israeli separation barrier, 85 percent of which lies in West Bank territory and which was declared illegal in 2004 by the International Court of Justice, divides Palestinian communities and causes general hardship and disruption of services.

East Jerusalem Palestinians are vulnerable to revocation of their residency status if they leave the city for extended periods of time, affecting their freedom to travel, or if they are deemed to be a threat to public safety, security, or the state of Israel.

G2. Are individuals able to exercise the right to own property and establish private businesses without undue interference from state or nonstate actors? 1 / 4

While Palestinians are able to own property and engage in business activity, their rights are seriously undermined by Israel's movement and access restrictions and the expansion of Israeli settlements, which is encouraged by the Israeli government and private groups. Israeli authorities employ a variety of methods to prevent Palestinians from developing their privately owned land, particularly in Area C, for example by declaring nature reserves, denying permit requests, and demolishing structures. In East Jerusalem, demolitions in 2020 left more Palestinians homeless in the city than any year on record since 2004. In 2020, Israel carried out its largest single demolition in the West Bank in a decade in the hamlet of Humsah al-Baqaia. Palestinian property is also illegally damaged by Israeli settlers.

Palestinian structures built in and around Jerusalem are consistently under threat of demolition by Israeli security forces, even if they fall in the area of the West Bank technically under the jurisdiction of the PA.

G3. Do individuals enjoy personal social freedoms, including choice of marriage partner and size of family, protection from domestic violence, and control over appearance? 2 / 4

Palestinian laws and societal norms, derived in part from Islamic law, put women at a disadvantage in matters such as marriage and divorce. For Christians, personal status issues are governed by ecclesiastical courts. Rape and domestic abuse remain underreported and frequently go unpunished, as authorities are allegedly reluctant to pursue such cases.

The widely publicized August 2019 murder of Israa Ghrayeb drew attention to the problem of so-called honor killings and other gender-based violence. Ghrayeb was allegedly killed by three of her male relatives who objected to her posting a photo of herself with her fiancé online. The men were charged with her murder the next month, and the case was still pending at the end of 2020. A 2018 law amended a provision in the penal code that had been used to grant leniency to the perpetrators of honor killings, prohibiting its application in cases of serious crimes against women and children. However, activists argue that the practical effects of these changes have been minimal.

G4. Do individuals enjoy equality of opportunity and freedom from economic exploitation? 1 / 4

Unemployment rates in the Palestinian territories are high compared with the rest of the Middle East and global averages. The excess supply of workers creates conditions in which labor exploitation is more likely. Unemployment rates also increased in the occupied territories due to the COVID-19 pandemic and the impact of closures on the Palestinian economy, especially during the stricter lockdowns.

In 2017, the PA signed international protocols dealing with human trafficking, child trafficking, and child prostitution. However, child labor is still prevalent in the occupied territories.

Many West Bank Palestinians, mostly male, work in Israel and the settlements, where the PA has no jurisdiction. While these workers are covered by Israeli labor laws, the International Labour Organization (ILO) reported in 2018 that inconsistent application of these laws remains a concern. The Palestinians' work permits usually tie them to a single employer, creating a relationship of dependency, according to the ILO. Nonetheless, some laborers have achieved collective bargaining agreements with their Israeli employers. Tens of thousands of Palestinians work without permits, making them vulnerable to greater exploitation. Many Palestinians lose considerable income to "brokers" who are needed to connect Palestinian workers to jobs. Israel has revoked work permits for those who share last names with individuals whom Israel considers to be security threats, even if they are not related.

Western Sahara

Population: 597,000
Freedom Status: Not Free

Note: *Freedom in the World* reports assess the level of political rights and civil liberties in a given geographical area, regardless of whether they are affected by the state, nonstate actors, or foreign powers. Disputed territories are sometimes assessed separately if they meet certain criteria, including boundaries that are sufficiently stable to allow year-on-year comparisons. For more information, see the report methodology and FAQ.

Overview: Morocco has claimed authority over Western Sahara since 1975, but the United Nations (UN) does not recognize Moroccan control, calling Western Sahara a "non-self-governing territory." Morocco controls the most populous area along the Atlantic coastline, more than three-quarters of the territory. While the UN brokered a cease-fire in 1991, a long-promised referendum on the territory's status has yet to be held. The Moroccan-controlled area, which Rabat calls its "Southern Provinces," is represented in the Moroccan parliament. However, civil liberties are severely restricted, particularly as they relate to independence activism.

KEY DEVELOPMENTS IN 2020

- The proindependence Polisario Front declared an end to its cease-fire with Morocco in November, after Moroccan forces cleared a road that was reportedly blocked by Polisario supporters. The Polisario subsequently engaged in fighting with Moroccan forces.
- In December, the United States recognized Moroccan sovereignty over Western Sahara.
- According to Reuters, 766 COVID-19 cases were detected in Western Sahara throughout the year, while 2 people died of the illness.

POLITICAL RIGHTS: –3 / 40
A. ELECTORAL PROCESS: 0 / 12
A1. Was the current head of government or other chief national authority elected through free and fair elections? 0 / 4

Morocco controls more than three-quarters of Western Sahara, and Moroccan authorities allow no proindependence candidates to run for office.

The Polisario Front is based in Tindouf, Algeria, and leads a nationalist movement comprised of members of the Sahrawi ethnic group. It controls the less-populated interior of the territory. The constitution of the government-in-exile states that the leader of the Polisario Front is the territory's president, but it does not hold regular elections within the territory.

A2. Were the current national legislative representatives elected through free and fair elections? 0 / 4

In the Moroccan-controlled portion of the territory, voters elect 13 representatives to the Moroccan parliament. Representatives who serve in Rabat cannot contest the region's status. Turnout in municipal and parliamentary elections in Western Sahara is difficult to ascertain, but reports are that it is chronically low.

The Sahrawi Arab Democratic Republic (SADR), the breakaway government, maintains a 51-member Sahrawi National Council, which is indirectly elected by the General Popular Congress of the Polisario Front. Most voting occurs in refugee camps in Algeria. The Polisario Front organizes the elections and does not allow any political parties to compete.

A3. Are the electoral laws and framework fair, and are they implemented impartially by the relevant election management bodies? 0 / 4

The electoral framework is not fair, given the constraints on representation in the Moroccan-controlled territory, the prohibition of any candidate who challenges Moroccan control of the territory to run for Parliament, and Moroccan control of the media.

B. POLITICAL PLURALISM AND PARTICIPATION: 0 / 16

B1. Do the people have the right to organize in different political parties or other competitive political groupings of their choice, and is the system free of undue obstacles to the rise and fall of these competing parties or groupings? 0 / 4

The Polisario Front, which controls the government-in-exile and the eastern portion of the territory, does not allow other political parties to compete. In recent years, the Polisario has cracked down on political dissent, imprisoning a number of opponents of the regime. In 2018, a vocal critic, who was imprisoned for his activity, was found dead at the Dheibya prison, apparently from hanging. The Polisario stated he died by suicide, but the man's family claimed he was assassinated.

In Moroccan-controlled areas, the Polisario Front is banned, and proindependence parties are not allowed to form.

B2. Is there a realistic opportunity for the opposition to increase its support or gain power through elections? 0 / 4

Since political parties that advocate for Sahrawi independence or autonomy cannot function in Moroccan-controlled areas, the most salient opposition elements cannot gain power through elections. No credible opposition exists in territory controlled by the Polisario Front due to the ban on other political parties.

B3. Are the people's political choices free from domination by forces that are external to the political sphere, or by political forces that employ extrapolitical means? 0 / 4

People's political choices in Moroccan-controlled areas are dominated by the Moroccan government. The government-in-exile in Tindouf is ostensibly autonomous but works closely with Algerian authorities. As a "non-self-governing territory," the people in the region are unable to elect an independent government.

B4. Do various segments of the population (including ethnic, racial, religious, gender, LGBT+, and other relevant groups) have full political rights and electoral opportunities? 0 / 4

Due to the territory's lack of sovereignty, no segment of the population has full political rights or electoral opportunities. However, women play a significant role in politics. Many women are leaders in the independence movement and organize the refugee camps in Algeria.

C. FUNCTIONING OF GOVERNMENT: 0 / 12

C1. Do the freely elected head of government and national legislative representatives determine the policies of the government? 0 / 4

Western Sahara has no freely elected leaders. Representatives from the "Southern Provinces" serve in the lower house of the Moroccan parliament, which is dominated by the monarchy. The monarchy determines government policies regarding the territory. The Polisario Front governs portions of the territory in its control.

The Polisario has accused Morocco of exploiting Western Sahara's natural resources, and Morocco–European Union (EU) trade agreements have included Polisario-claimed territory. The European Parliament approved agricultural and fisheries agreements with Morocco in 2019; the European Council also approved the fisheries agreement that year. While a European Court of Justice (ECJ) ruling required the EU to seek local consent on agreements covering the disputed territory, the Polisario Front did not participate in consultations on the agreements and launched a legal action against them at the ECJ that year. The case remained pending at the end of 2020.

In February 2020, the Moroccan parliament adopted legislation meant to formalize Rabat's control over Western Saharan territorial waters. In December, the United States recognized Moroccan sovereignty over Western Sahara.

C2. Are safeguards against official corruption strong and effective? 0 / 4

Corruption among Moroccan state officials and in the economy is widespread and investigations are rare. Corruption occurs primarily to facilitate the exploitation of natural resources—phosphates, hydrocarbons, and fisheries—by Moroccan and international interests. In Tindouf, official corruption among members of the Polisario is similarly widespread and endemic.

C3. Does the government operate with openness and transparency? 0 / 4

Moroccan access-to-information laws apply to Western Sahara. Information about Western Sahara is nearly nonexistent, which severely limits transparency. The Moroccan government publishes budget and financial information online, and public officials—including parliament members, judges, and civil servants—are required to declare their assets. However, nongovernmental organizations (NGOs) assert that many officials do not hand over this information, and the law provides no penalties for noncompliance.

ADDITIONAL DISCRETIONARY POLITICAL RIGHTS QUESTION

Is the government or occupying power deliberately changing the ethnic composition of a country or territory so as to destroy a culture or tip the political balance in favor of another group? −3 / 0

Before and since the establishment of the UN Mission for the Referendum in Western Sahara (MINURSO) in 1991, Morocco has endeavored to tip the population's balance in its favor. By some counts, Moroccans now outnumber Sahrawis in Western Sahara. Morocco continues to work to prevent a referendum over the territory's final status. Morocco constructed a sand berm to divide territory under its control from Sahrawi-controlled territory in the east.

CIVIL LIBERTIES: 7 / 60
D. FREEDOM OF EXPRESSION AND BELIEF: 3 / 16
D1. Are there free and independent media? 0 / 4

Some pro-Sahrawi media outlets do operate, such as the all-volunteer Equipe Media group, but they face regular harassment by Moroccan authorities, who ensure that reporting does not dispute Morocco's sovereignty over Western Sahara. The Moroccan 2016 Press Code criminalizes challenging its "territorial integrity," which potentially criminalizes independent journalism that focuses on the dispute in Western Sahara. Print outlets found to violate this provision risk suspension, while news sites face potential blocking. Journalists accused of challenging Morocco's territorial integrity could face prison sentences of between six months and two years. Reporting by Moroccan journalists working in the territory is sharply constrained.

International media are carefully vetted and scrutinized during their visits to Moroccan-controlled territory. Reporters visiting Tindouf are said to enjoy greater freedom of movement and inquiry, but such claims are difficult to substantiate. In Sahrawi-controlled territory in the east, press freedoms are also limited, with television and radio coverage reflecting the ideology and viewpoints of the Polisario. Some exiled groups provide coverage from outside Western Sahara. Internet access is limited throughout the territory.

Journalists in Moroccan- and Polisario-controlled territory faced detention or trial in 2020. In May, journalist Ibrahim Amrikli was arrested for breaching health measures and insulting public officials; Amrikli reported that he was ill-treated while in custody. Amrikli was conditionally released but was in hiding as of December. In June, Algargarat Media founder Essabi Yahdih was interrogated by Laâyoune police while visiting a police station for administrative purposes. Police accused Yahdih of offending the Moroccan king and threatened to harm him while in custody, but Yahdih was released without facing prosecution. In August, journalist Mahmoud Zeidan was detained in Tindouf after criticizing the distribution of pandemic-related aid but was released after a day.

D2. Are individuals free to practice and express their religious faith or nonbelief in public and private? 2 / 4

Moroccan authorities generally do not interfere with religious practices, though as in Morocco proper, mosques are closely monitored by authorities. Moroccan law prohibits any efforts to convert a Muslim to another faith. It is illegal to publicly criticize Islam.

D3. Is there academic freedom, and is the educational system free from extensive political indoctrination? 0 / 4

Educators practice self-censorship around the status of Western Sahara, as Moroccan law criminalizes debate that calls this into question. Other sensitive topics include the monarchy and Islam. The University of Tifariti was established in 2013 as the first university in Polisario-controlled territory.

D4. Are individuals free to express their personal views on political or other sensitive topics without fear of surveillance or retribution? 1 / 4

As in Morocco proper, there is concern about state surveillance of online activity and personal communications, and people do not feel free to speak privately about the status of Western Sahara and other sensitive topics. Freedom of expression is profoundly curtailed in Polisario-controlled areas as well.

E. ASSOCIATIONAL AND ORGANIZATIONAL RIGHTS: 0 / 12

E1. Is there freedom of assembly? 0 / 4

Demonstrations and protests are broken up regularly, particularly on sensitive issues such as self-determination and Sahrawi prisoners held by Morocco. Protesters are frequently arrested and beaten.

E2. Is there freedom for nongovernmental organizations, particularly those that are engaged in human rights- and governance-related work? 0 / 4

NGOs that advocate for independence or question Islam as the state religion are denied official registration by the Moroccan government. Organizations that meet the government's criteria are frequently denied registration as well. Foreign NGO representatives observing the human rights situation of Moroccan-controlled areas of Western Sahara have been expelled in recent years.

In March 2020, a Laâyoune court handed Sahrawi activist Khatri Dada a 20-year sentence for vandalism and offending public officials. Dada denied the charges, saying that his confession was the result of coercion. In September, a Laâyoune prosecutor opened an investigation into the Sahrawi Organ against Moroccan Occupation, a proindependence group.

E3. Is there freedom for trade unions and similar professional or labor organizations? 0 / 4

Moroccan unions have a presence in Western Sahara, but they are largely inactive. Government restrictions limit the right to strike. Most people in unions work for the Moroccan government.

The Polisario Front has a trade union called the Sahrawi Trade Union (UGTSARIO), which is also inactive; there is little economic activity in the refugee camps in Tindouf, and there is no functioning labor market in Polisario-controlled territory.

F. RULE OF LAW: 0 / 16

F1. Is there an independent judiciary? 0 / 4

Courts in Western Sahara are controlled by Morocco and their rulings reflect its interests. Executive interference and corruption significantly impede judicial independence.

F2. Does due process prevail in civil and criminal matters? 0 / 4

Due process rights are not respected. In 2017, a Moroccan appeals court issued prison sentences to 23 Sahrawis over the 2010 deaths of Moroccan security personnel during an uprising at the Gdeim Izik protest camp; confessions that were allegedly obtained by torture were used as trial evidence.

Proindependence advocates and other civil society leaders are often arbitrarily arrested, particularly in the aftermath of demonstrations. International human rights groups view many Sahrawis in Moroccan prisons, including human rights activists and proindependence advocates, as political prisoners.

F3. Is there protection from the illegitimate use of physical force and freedom from war and insurgencies? 0 / 4

Tensions remain between the Moroccan military and the Polisario Front, with periodic mobilization of forces. Moroccan forces cleared a Western Sahara road in November 2020, after supporters of the Polisario Front reportedly blocked it. The Polisario then declared an end to its cease-fire with Morocco and subsequently engaged in fighting with Moroccan forces.

In 2018, the first UN-brokered talks between the Polisario and the Moroccan government in six years took place. Both sides agreed to continue talks in 2019, but little progress was made. The UN's envoy to Western Sahara, former German president Horst Köhler, resigned in 2019 for health reasons; his position remained unfilled at the end of 2020. Morocco ritually offers autonomy to the Western Sahara, but the Polisario demands an independence referendum.

Torture and degrading treatment by Moroccan authorities continues to be a problem, especially against proindependence advocates.

F4. Do laws, policies, and practices guarantee equal treatment of various segments of the population? 0 / 4

Sahrawis experience discrimination in access to education and employment. According to Sahrawi activists, Moroccan settlers are favored by employers in the phosphate mining industry, which is a predominant source of employment.

Women play leadership roles at the Sahrawi camps in Algeria, and some Sahrawi have described life in these camps as matriarchal. However, cultural norms also dictate that women stay at home and manage the household.

Moroccan law prohibits same-sex sexual acts.

G. PERSONAL AUTONOMY AND INDIVIDUAL RIGHTS: 4 / 16

G1. Do individuals enjoy freedom of movement, including the ability to change their place of residence, employment, or education? 1 / 4

Morocco and the Polisario Front both restrict free movement in Western Sahara. The sand berm, constructed by Morocco in the 1980s, is 1,700 miles long. The wall, which is surrounded on both sides by land mines, constitutes what may be the longest continuous minefield in the world.

G2. Are individuals able to exercise the right to own property and establish private businesses without undue interference from state or nonstate actors? 1 / 4

The territory's occupied status leaves property rights insecure. No credible free market exists within the territory. The SADR government routinely signs contracts with firms for the exploration of oil and gas, although these cannot be implemented given the territory's status.

G3. Do individuals enjoy personal social freedoms, including choice of marriage partner and size of family, protection from domestic violence, and control over appearance? 2 / 4

In Polisario-controlled territory and in Tindouf, women have a relatively higher social status than in Morocco. However, social freedoms are curtailed. Moroccan law criminalizes both adultery and premarital sex. Spousal rape is not considered a crime.

G4. Do individuals enjoy equality of opportunity and freedom from economic exploitation? 0 / 4

Economic opportunity is inhibited by the territory's undetermined status. The economic activity generated by companies that exploit the country's natural resources generally does not benefit the Sahrawi population. Sex trafficking, often affecting young girls, takes place in coastal fishing villages.

Freedom in the World 2021
Methodology Questions

A. ELECTORAL PROCESS

A1. Was the current head of government or other chief national authority elected through free and fair elections? (Note: Heads of government chosen through various electoral frameworks, including direct elections for president, indirect elections for prime minister by parliament, and the electoral college system for electing presidents, are covered under this question. In cases of indirect elections for the head of government, the elections for the legislature or other body that chose the head of government, as well as the selection process for the head of government itself, should be taken into consideration. In systems where executive authority is formally divided between a head of state and a head of government, greater weight should be given to elections for the official with the most executive authority.)

- Did independent, established, and reputable national and/or international election monitoring organizations judge the most recent election for head of government to have met democratic standards?
- Was the most recent election for head of government called in a timely manner, without undue, politically motivated delays or an accelerated schedule that unfairly limited campaign opportunities for some candidates?
- Was the registration of voters and candidates conducted in an accurate, timely, transparent, and nondiscriminatory manner?
- Were women allowed to register and run as candidates?
- Could all candidates make speeches, hold public meetings, and enjoy fair or proportionate media access throughout the campaign, free of intimidation?
- Did voting take place by secret ballot?
- Were voters able to vote for the candidate or party of their choice without undue pressure or intimidation?
- Was the vote count transparent and timely, and were the official results reported honestly to the public?
- Could election monitors from independent groups and representing parties/candidates watch the counting of votes to ensure its honesty?
- Did voters have equal access to polling places and opportunities to cast ballots?
- Has the most recently elected head of government been removed from office through violent, irregular, unconstitutional, or otherwise undemocratic means? (Note: Although a bloodless coup may ultimately lead to a positive outcome—particularly if it removes a head of government who was not freely and fairly elected—the new leader has not been freely and fairly elected and cannot be treated as such.)
- Has the head of government's electorally mandated term expired or been extended without new elections?

- In cases where elections for regional, provincial, or state governors and/or other subnational executive officials differ significantly in conduct from national elections, does the conduct of the subnational elections reflect an opening toward improved political rights in the country, or, alternatively, a worsening of political rights?

A2. Were the current national legislative representatives elected through free and fair elections?

- Did independent, established, and reputable domestic and/or international election monitoring organizations judge the most recent national legislative elections to have met democratic standards?
- Were the most recent legislative elections called in a timely manner, without undue, politically motivated delays or an accelerated schedule that unfairly limited campaign opportunities for some parties or candidates?
- Was the registration of voters and candidates conducted in an accurate, timely, transparent, and nondiscriminatory manner?
- Were women allowed to register and run as candidates?
- Could all candidates make speeches, hold public meetings, and enjoy fair or proportionate media access throughout the campaign, free of intimidation?
- Did voting take place by secret ballot?
- Were voters able to vote for the candidate or party of their choice without undue pressure or intimidation?
- Was the vote count transparent and timely, and were the official results reported honestly to the public?
- Could election monitors from independent groups and representing parties/candidates watch the counting of votes to ensure its honesty?
- Have members of the most recently elected national legislature been removed from office through violent, irregular, unconstitutional, or otherwise undemocratic means? (Note: Although a bloodless coup may ultimately lead to a positive outcome—particularly if it removes a legislature that was not freely and fairly elected—an appointed postcoup legislative body has not been freely and fairly elected and cannot be treated as such.)
- Has the legislature's electorally mandated term expired or been extended without
- new elections?
- In cases where elections for subnational councils/parliaments differ significantly in conduct from national elections, does the conduct of the subnational elections reflect an opening toward improved political rights in the country, or, alternatively, a worsening of political rights?

A3. Are the electoral laws and framework fair, and are they implemented impartially by the relevant election management bodies?

- Is there a clear, detailed, and fair legislative framework for conducting elections? (Note: Changes to electoral laws should not be made immediately preceding an election if these changes infringe on the ability of voters, candidates, or parties to fulfill their roles in the election.)
- Does the composition of election commissions ensure their independence?
- Are election commissions or other election authorities free from government or other pressure and interference?
- Do adult citizens enjoy universal and equal suffrage?

- Is the drawing of election districts conducted in a fair and nonpartisan manner, as opposed to malapportionment or gerrymandering for personal or partisan advantage?
- Has the selection of a system for choosing legislative representatives (such as proportional versus majoritarian) been improperly manipulated to advance certain political interests or to influence the electoral results?
- Are procedures for changing the electoral framework at the constitutional level, including referendums, carried out fairly and transparently, with adequate opportunity for public debate and discussion?

B. POLITICAL PLURALISM AND PARTICIPATION

B1. Do the people have the right to organize in different political parties or other competitive political groupings of their choice, and is the system free of undue obstacles to the rise and fall of these competing parties or groupings?

- Do political parties encounter undue legal or practical obstacles in their efforts to form and operate, including onerous registration requirements, excessively large membership requirements, etc.?
- Do parties face discriminatory or onerous restrictions in holding meetings or rallies, accessing the media, or engaging in other peaceful activities?
- Are laws and regulations governing party financing fair and equitably enforced? Do they impose excessive obstacles to political and campaign activity, or give an effective advantage to certain parties?
- Are party members or leaders intimidated, harassed, arrested, imprisoned, or subjected to violent attacks as a result of their peaceful political activities?
- In systems dominated by political parties, can independent candidates register and operate freely?

B2. Is there a realistic opportunity for the opposition to increase its support or gain power through elections?

- Are various legal/administrative restrictions selectively applied to opposition parties to prevent them from increasing their support base or successfully competing in elections?
- Are there genuine opposition forces in positions of authority, such as in the national legislature or in subnational governments?
- Does intimidation, harassment, arrest, imprisonment, or violent attack as a result of peaceful political activities affect the ability of opposition party members or leaders to increase their support or gain power through elections?
- Is there a significant opposition vote?
- Did major opposition parties choose to boycott the most recent elections rather than participate in a flawed process?

B3. Are the people's political choices free from domination by forces that are external to the political sphere, or by political forces that employ extrapolitical means?

- Do entities that are external to the political system (the military, foreign powers, economic oligarchies, criminal organizations, armed militants, or any other powerful group) intimidate, harass, or attack voters or political figures in order to influence their political choices?
- Do such groups offer bribes or other incentives to voters or political figures in order to influence their political choices?

- Do entities within the political system, such as major parties and incumbent leaders, use extrapolitical means (corrupt patronage networks, control over land or employment, control over security forces, control over party militias, manipulation of state institutions or resources) to exert improper influence over the political choices of voters or political figures?
- Do traditional or religious leaders use extrapolitical means (control over communal land or resources, bribes or economic incentives, violence or intimidation) to exert improper influence over the political choices of voters or political figures?
- Do major private or public-sector employers directly or indirectly control the political choices of their workers?
- Do major private donors to political parties or causes use opaque or illegal methods to exert improper influence over voters or political figures?
- Does the formal structure of the political system give overriding authority to entities that are not accountable to voters (hereditary monarchs, religious hierarchies, unelected military or party officials, the sole legal party in one-party states), thus excluding the public from meaningful political participation?

B4. Do various segments of the population (including ethnic, racial, religious, gender, LGBT+, and other relevant groups) have full political rights and electoral opportunities?

- Do national political parties of various ideological persuasions address issues of specific concern to these groups?
- When other parties fail to address the interests of certain groups, are political parties that are focused on those groups—provided they espouse peaceful, democratic values—legally permitted and de facto allowed to operate?
- Does the government inhibit the participation of certain groups in national or subnational political life through laws and/or practical obstacles—for example, by limiting access to voter registration or failing to publish public documents in certain languages?
- Are the interests of women represented in political parties—for example, through party manifestos that address gender issues, gender equality policies within parties, and mechanisms to ensure women's full and equal participation in internal party elections and decision-making?
- Are there unusually excessive or discriminatory barriers to acquiring citizenship that effectively deny political rights to a majority or large portion of the native-born or legal permanent population, or is citizenship revoked to produce a similar result?

C. FUNCTIONING OF GOVERNMENT

C1. Do the freely elected head of government and national legislative representatives determine the policies of the government? (Note: Because the score for question C1 is partly dependent on the presence of a freely elected head of government and national legislative representatives, under most circumstances it will not exceed the average of the scores for questions A1 and A2.)

- Are the candidates who were elected freely and fairly duly installed in office, and were they able to form a functioning government within a reasonable period of time?
- Do other appointed or non–freely elected state actors interfere with or prevent freely elected representatives from adopting and implementing legislation and making meaningful policy decisions?

- Do nonstate actors, including criminal gangs and insurgent groups, interfere with or prevent elected representatives from adopting and implementing legislation and making meaningful policy decisions?
- Do the armed forces or other security services control or enjoy a preponderant influence over government policy and activities, including in countries that are nominally under civilian control?
- Do foreign governments control or enjoy a preponderant influence over government policy and activities by means including the presence of foreign military troops and the use of significant economic threats or sanctions? (Note: If a treaty was signed and ratified by a freely elected government, adherence to that treaty is typically not considered an improper external influence on policymaking, even if it limits a government's options in practice.)
- Is the freely elected government able to implement its decisions across the entire territory without interference from nonstate actors?
- Does the executive exhibit excessive dominance over the legislature?
- Has partisan polarization or obstructionism seriously impaired basic executive or legislative functions, such as approving a budget or filling important vacancies?

C2. Are safeguards against official corruption strong and effective?

- Has the government implemented effective anticorruption laws or programs to prevent, detect, and punish corruption among public officials, including conflicts of interest?
- Is the government free from excessive bureaucratic regulations, registration requirements, or other controls that increase opportunities for corruption?
- Are there independent and effective auditing and investigative bodies that function without impediment or political pressure or influence?
- Are allegations of corruption involving government officials thoroughly investigated and prosecuted without prejudice or political bias?
- Are allegations of corruption given extensive and substantive airing in the media?
- Do whistleblowers, anticorruption activists, investigators, and journalists enjoy legal protections that allow them to freely and safely report abuses?

C3. Does the government operate with openness and transparency?

- Do citizens have the legal right and practical ability to obtain information about state operations and the means to petition government agencies for it?
- Does the government publish information online, in machine-readable formats, for free, and is this information accessible by default?
- Are civil society groups, interest groups, journalists, and other citizens given a fair and meaningful opportunity to comment on and influence pending policies or legislation?
- Are elected representatives accessible to their constituents?
- Is the budget-making process subject to meaningful legislative review and public scrutiny?
- Does the state ensure transparency and effective competition in the awarding of government contracts?
- Are the asset declarations of government officials open to public and media scrutiny and verification?

ADDITIONAL DISCRETIONARY POLITICAL RIGHTS QUESTION
(SEE EXPLANATION IN ANALYST GUIDELINES):

Q: Is the government or occupying power deliberately changing the ethnic composition of a country or territory so as to destroy a culture or tip the political balance in favor of another group?

- Is the government providing economic or other incentives to certain people in order to change the ethnic composition of a region or regions?
- Is the government forcibly moving people in or out of certain areas in order to change the ethnic composition of those regions?
- Is the government arresting, imprisoning, or killing members of certain ethnic groups in order change the ethnic composition of a region or regions?

CIVIL LIBERTIES

D. FREEDOM OF EXPRESSION AND BELIEF

D1. Are there free and independent media? (Note: "Media" refers to all relevant sources of news and commentary—including formal print, broadcast, and online news outlets, as well as social media and communication applications when they are used to gather or disseminate news and commentary for the general public. The question also applies to artistic works in any medium.)

- Are the media directly or indirectly censored?
- Is self-censorship common among journalists (the term includes professional journalists, bloggers, and citizen journalists), especially when reporting on sensitive issues, including politics, social controversies, corruption, or the activities of powerful individuals?
- Are journalists subject to pressure or surveillance aimed at identifying their sources?
- Are libel, blasphemy, security, or other restrictive laws used to punish journalists who scrutinize government officials and policies or other powerful entities through either onerous fines or imprisonment?
- Is it a crime to insult the honor and dignity of the president and/or other government officials? How broad is the range of such prohibitions, and how vigorously are they enforced?
- If media outlets are dependent on the government for their financial survival, does the government condition funding on the outlets' cooperation in promoting official points of view and/or denying access to opposition parties and civic critics? Do powerful private actors engage in similar practices?
- Do the owners of private media exert improper editorial control over journalists or publishers, skewing news coverage to suit their personal business or political interests?
- Is media coverage excessively partisan, with the majority of outlets consistently favoring either side of the political spectrum?
- Does the government attempt to influence media content and access through means including politically motivated awarding or suspension of broadcast frequencies and newspaper registrations, unfair control and influence over
- printing facilities and distribution networks, blackouts of internet or mobile service, selective distribution of advertising, onerous operating requirements, prohibitive tariffs, and bribery?

- Are journalists threatened, harassed online, arrested, imprisoned, beaten, or killed by government or nonstate actors for their legitimate journalistic activities, and if such cases occur, are they investigated and prosecuted fairly and expeditiously?
- Do women journalists encounter gender-specific obstacles to carrying out their work, including threats of sexual violence or strict gender segregation?
- Are works of literature, art, music, or other forms of cultural expression censored or banned for political purposes?

D2. Are individuals free to practice and express their religious faith or nonbelief in public and private?

- Are registration requirements employed to impede the free functioning of religious institutions?
- Are members of religious groups, including minority faiths and movements, harassed, fined, arrested, or beaten by the authorities for engaging in their religious practices?
- Is state monitoring of peaceful religious activity so indiscriminate, pervasive, or intrusive that it amounts to harassment or intimidation?
- Are religious practice and expression impeded by violence or harassment by nonstate actors?
- Does the government appoint or otherwise influence the appointment of religious leaders?
- Does the government control or restrict the production and distribution of religious writings or materials?
- Is the construction of religious buildings banned or restricted?
- Does the government place undue restrictions on religious education? Does the government require religious education?
- Are individuals free to eschew religious beliefs and practices in general?

D3. Is there academic freedom, and is the educational system free from extensive political indoctrination?

- Are teachers and professors at both public and private institutions free to pursue academic activities of a political and quasi-political nature without fear of physical violence or intimidation by state or nonstate actors?
- Does the government pressure, strongly influence, or control the content of school curriculums for political purposes?
- Is the allocation of funding for public educational institutions free from political manipulation?
- Are student associations that address issues of a political nature allowed to function freely?
- Does the government, including through school administration or other officials, pressure students and/or teachers to support certain political figures or agendas, including by requiring them to attend political rallies or vote for certain candidates? Conversely, does the government, including through school administration or other officials, discourage or forbid students and/or teachers from supporting certain candidates and parties?

D4. Are individuals free to express their personal views on political or other sensitive topics without fear of surveillance or retribution?

- Are people able to engage in private discussions, particularly of a political nature, in public, semipublic, or private places—including restaurants, public transportation, and their homes, in person or on the telephone—without fear of harassment or detention by the authorities or nonstate actors?

- Do users of personal online communications—including direct messages, voice or video applications, or social media accounts with a limited audience—face legal penalties, harassment, or violence from the government or powerful nonstate actors in retaliation for critical remarks?
- Does the government employ people or groups to engage in public surveillance and to report alleged antigovernment conversations to the authorities?

E. ASSOCIATIONAL AND ORGANIZATIONAL RIGHTS

E1. Is there freedom of assembly?

- Are peaceful protests, particularly those of a political nature, banned or severely restricted?
- Are the legal requirements to obtain permission to hold peaceful demonstrations particularly cumbersome or time-consuming?
- Are participants in peaceful demonstrations intimidated, arrested, or assaulted?
- Are peaceful protesters detained by police in order to prevent them from engaging in such actions?
- Are organizers blocked from using online media to plan or carry out a protest, for example through DDoS attacks or wholesale blackouts of internet or mobile services?
- Are similar restrictions and obstacles used to impede other public events, such as conferences, panel discussions, and town hall–style meetings?
- Are public petitions, in which citizens gather signatures to support a particular policy or initiative, banned or severely restricted?

E2. Is there freedom for nongovernmental organizations, particularly those that are engaged in human rights– and governance-related work? (Note: This includes civic organizations, interest groups, foundations, think tanks, gender rights groups, etc.)

- Are registration and other legal requirements for nongovernmental organizations particularly onerous or intended to prevent them from functioning freely?
- Are laws related to the financing of nongovernmental organizations unduly complicated and cumbersome, or are there obstacles to citizens raising money for charitable causes or civic activism?
- Are donors and funders of nongovernmental organizations free from government pressure?
- Are members of nongovernmental organizations intimidated, arrested, imprisoned, or assaulted because of their work?

E3. Is there freedom for trade unions and similar professional or labor organizations?

- Are trade unions allowed to be established and to operate without government interference?
- Are workers pressured by the government or employers to join or not to join certain trade unions, and do they face harassment, violence, or dismissal from their jobs if they fail to comply?
- Are workers permitted to engage in strikes, and do participants in peaceful strikes face reprisals? (Note: This question may not apply to workers in narrowly defined essential government services or public safety jobs.)
- Are unions able to bargain collectively with employers and negotiate agreements that are honored in practice?
- For states with primarily agricultural economies that do not necessarily support the formation of trade unions, does the government allow for the establishment

of agricultural workers' organizations or their equivalents? Is there legislation expressly forbidding the formation of trade unions?

- Are professional organizations, including business associations, allowed to operate freely and without government interference?

F. RULE OF LAW

F1. Is there an independent judiciary?

- Is the judiciary subject to interference from the executive branch of government or from other political, economic, or religious influences?
- Are judges appointed and dismissed in a fair and unbiased manner?
- Do judges rule fairly and impartially, or do they commonly render verdicts that favor the government or particular interests, whether in return for bribes or for other reasons?
- Do executive, legislative, and other governmental authorities comply with judicial decisions, and are these decisions effectively enforced?
- Do powerful private entities comply with judicial decisions, and are decisions that run counter to the interests of powerful actors effectively enforced?

F2. Does due process prevail in civil and criminal matters?

- Are defendants' rights, including the presumption of innocence until proven guilty, protected?
- Do detainees have access to independent, competent legal counsel regardless of their financial means?
- Are defendants given a fair, public, and timely hearing by a competent, independent, and impartial tribunal?
- Is access to the court system in general dependent on an individual's financial
- means?
- Are prosecutors independent of political control and influence?
- Are prosecutors independent of powerful private interests, whether legal or illegal?
- Do law enforcement and other security officials operate professionally, independently, and accountably?
- Do law enforcement officials make arbitrary arrests and detentions without warrants, or fabricate or plant evidence on suspects?
- Do law enforcement and other security officials fail to uphold due process because of influence by nonstate actors, including organized crime, powerful commercial interests, or other groups?

F3. Is there protection from the illegitimate use of physical force and freedom from war and insurgencies?

- Do law enforcement officials beat detainees during arrest or use excessive force or torture to extract confessions?
- Are conditions in pretrial detention facilities and prisons humane and respectful of the human dignity of inmates?
- Do citizens have the means of effective petition and redress when they suffer physical abuse by state authorities?
- Does the law allow corporal punishment, and are such penalties employed in practice?
- In countries that allow the death penalty, is it applied for crimes other than murder or in a manner that violates basic standards of justice?
- Is violent crime common, either in particular areas or among the general population?

- Is the population subjected to physical harm, forced removal, or other acts of violence or terror due to civil conflict or war?

F4. Do laws, policies, and practices guarantee equal treatment of various segments of the population?

- Are members of various distinct groups—including ethnic, racial, religious, gender, LGBT+, and other relevant groups—able to effectively exercise their human rights with full equality before the law?
- Is violence against such groups considered a crime, is it widespread, and are perpetrators brought to justice?
- Do members of such groups face legal and/or de facto discrimination in areas including employment, education, and housing because of their identification with a particular group?
- Do noncitizens—including migrant workers and noncitizen immigrants—enjoy basic internationally recognized human rights, including the right not to be subjected to torture or other forms of ill-treatment, the right to due process of law, and the freedoms of association, expression, and religion?
- Do the country's laws provide for the granting of asylum or refugee status in accordance with the 1951 UN Convention Relating to the Status of Refugees, its 1967 Protocol, and other regional treaties regarding refugees? Has the government established a system for providing protection to refugees, including against *refoulement* (the return of persons to a country where there is reason to believe they would face persecution)?

G. PERSONAL AUTONOMY AND INDIVIDUAL RIGHTS

G1. Do individuals enjoy freedom of movement, including the ability to change their place of residence, employment, or education?

- Are there restrictions on foreign travel, including an exit visa system, which may be enforced selectively?
- Is permission required from the authorities or nonstate actors to move within the country?
- Do state or nonstate actors control or constrain a person's ability to change their type and place of employment?
- Are bribes or other inducements needed to obtain the necessary documents to travel, change one's place of residence or employment, enter institutions of higher education, or advance in school?
- Is freedom of movement impaired by general threats to physical safety, such as armed conflict? Do such threats lead to forced displacement?
- Do women enjoy the same freedom of movement as men?

G2. Are individuals able to exercise the right to own property and establish private businesses without undue interference from state or nonstate actors?

- Are people legally allowed to purchase and sell land and other property, and can they do so in practice without undue interference from the government or nonstate actors?
- Do women face discrimination in property and inheritance rights?
- Is fair business competition heavily skewed by political favoritism, cronyism, or other improper interference?
- Are individuals protected from arbitrary expropriation, and do they receive adequate and timely compensation when property is seized?
- Are people legally allowed to establish and operate private businesses with a reasonable minimum of registration, licensing, and other requirements?

- Are bribes or other inducements needed to obtain the necessary legal documents to operate private businesses?
- Do private/nonstate actors, including criminal groups, seriously impede private business activities through such measures as extortion?

G3. Do individuals enjoy personal social freedoms, including choice of marriage partner and size of family, protection from domestic violence, and control over appearance?

- Are personalized forms of violence—including domestic violence, female genital mutilation/cutting, sexual abuse, and rape—widespread, and are perpetrators brought to justice?
- Does the government directly or indirectly control choice of marriage partner or other personal relationships through means such as bans on interfaith marriages, failure to enforce laws against child marriage or dowry payments, restrictions on same-sex relationships, or criminalization of extramarital sex?
- Do individuals enjoy equal rights in divorce proceedings and child custody matters?
- Do citizenship or residency rules undermine family integrity through excessively high or discriminatory barriers for foreign spouses or transmission of citizenship to children?
- Does the government determine the number of children that a couple may have, including by denying access to or imposing birth control, or by criminalizing or imposing abortion?
- Does the government restrict individuals' choice of dress, appearance, or gender expression?
- Do private institutions or individuals, including religious groups or family members, unduly infringe on the personal social freedoms of individuals, including choice of marriage partner, family size, dress, gender expression, etc.?

G4. Do individuals enjoy equality of opportunity and freedom from economic exploitation?

- Do state or private employers exploit their workers through practices including unfairly withholding wages, permitting or forcing employees to work under unacceptably dangerous conditions, or adult slave labor and child labor?
- Does tight government control over the economy, including through state ownership or the setting of prices and production quotas, inhibit individuals' economic opportunity?
- Do the revenues from large state industries, including the energy sector, benefit the general population or only a privileged few?
- Do private interests exert undue influence on the economy—through monopolistic practices, concentration of ownership, cartels, or illegal blacklists— that impedes economic opportunity for the general population?
- Do laws, policies, or persistent socioeconomic conditions effectively impose rigid barriers to social mobility, generally preventing individuals from rising to higher income levels over the course of their lives?
- Is the trafficking of persons for labor, sexual exploitation, forced begging, etc., widespread, and is the government taking adequate steps to address the problem?

KEY TO SCORES, PR AND CL RATINGS, STATUS

TABLE 1		TABLE 2	
Political Rights (PR)		**Civil Liberties (CL)**	
Total Scores	**PR Rating**	**Total Scores**	**CL Rating**
36–40	1	53–60	1
30–35	2	44–52	2
24–29	3	35–43	3
18–23	4	26–34	4
12–17	5	17–25	5
6–11	6	8–16	6
0–5*	7	0–7	7

TABLE 3

Combined Average of the PR and CL Ratings (Freedom Rating)	Freedom Status
1.0 to 2.5	Free
3.0 to 5.0	Partly Free
5.5 to 7.0	Not Free

* It is possible for a country's total political rights score to be less than 0 (between −1 and −4) if it receives mostly or all 0s for each of the 10 PR questions *and* it receives a sufficiently negative score for the additional discretionary PR question. In such a case, a country would still receive a final PR rating of 7.

Tables and Ratings

Countries

Country	PR	CL	Freedom Status
Afghanistan	5	6	Not Free
Albania	3	3	Partly Free
Algeria	6	5	Not Free
Andorra	1	1	Free
Angola	6	5	Not Free
Antigua and Barbuda	2	2	Free
Argentina	2	2	Free
Armenia	4	4	Partly Free
Australia	1	1	Free
Austria	1	1	Free
Azerbaijan	7	6	Not Free
Bahamas	1	1	Free
Bahrain	7	6	Not Free
Bangladesh	5	5	Partly Free
Barbados	1	1	Free
Belarus	7	6	Not Free
Belgium	1	1	Free
Belize	2	1 ▲	Free
Benin	4	2	Partly Free
Bhutan	2 ▲	4	Partly Free
Bolivia	3	3	Partly Free
Bosnia and Herzegovina	4	4	Partly Free
Botswana	3	2	Free
Brazil	2	3 ▼	Free
Brunei	6	5	Not Free
Bulgaria	2	2	Free
Burkina Faso	4	4	Partly Free
Burundi	7	6	Not Free
Cabo Verde	1	1	Free
Cambodia	7	5	Not Free
Cameroon	6	6	Not Free
Canada	1	1	Free

Country	PR	CL	Freedom Status
Central African Republic	7	7	Not Free
Chad	7	6	Not Free
Chile	1	1 ▲	Free
China	7	6	Not Free
Colombia	3	3	Partly Free
Comoros	5 ▼	4	Partly Free
Congo (Brazzaville)	7	5	Not Free
Congo (Kinshasa)	7	6	Not Free
Costa Rica	1	1	Free
Côte d'Ivoire	5 ▼	4	Partly Free
Croatia	1	2	Free
Cuba	7	6	Not Free
Cyprus	1	1	Free
Czech Republic	1	1	Free
Denmark	1	1	Free
Djibouti	7	5	Not Free
Dominica	1	1	Free
Dominican Republic	3	3	Partly Free
Ecuador	3	3	Partly Free
Egypt	6	6	Not Free
El Salvador	2	4	Partly Free
Equatorial Guinea	7	7	Not Free
Eritrea	7	7	Not Free
Estonia	1	1	Free
Eswatini	7	5	Not Free
Ethiopia	6	6	Not Free
Fiji	3	3	Partly Free
Finland	1	1	Free
France	1	2	Free
Gabon	7	5	Not Free
Georgia	4 ▼	3	Partly Free
Germany	1	1	Free
Ghana	2	2	Free
Greece	1	2	Free
Grenada	1	2	Free
Guatemala	4	4	Partly Free
Guinea	5	5	Partly Free
Guinea-Bissau	5	4	Partly Free
Guyana	2	3	Free

Country	PR	CL	Freedom Status
Haiti	5	5	Partly Free
Honduras	4	5 ▼	Partly Free
Hungary	3	3	Partly Free
Iceland	1	1	Free
India	2	4 ▼	Partly Free ▼
Indonesia	2	4	Partly Free
Iran	6	6	Not Free
Iraq	5	6	Not Free
Ireland	1	1	Free
Israel	2	3	Free
Italy	1	1	Free
Jamaica	2	2	Free
Japan	1	1	Free
Jordan	6 ▼	5	Not Free ▼
Kazakhstan	7	5	Not Free
Kenya	4	4	Partly Free
Kiribati	1	1	Free
Kosovo	4 ▼	4	Partly Free
Kuwait	5	5	Partly Free
Kyrgyzstan	7 ▼	5 ▼	Not Free ▼
Laos	7	6	Not Free
Latvia	1	2	Free
Lebanon	5	4	Partly Free
Lesotho	3	3	Partly Free
Liberia	3	4	Partly Free
Libya	7	6	Not Free
Liechtenstein	2	1	Free
Lithuania	1	2 ▼	Free
Luxembourg	1	1	Free
Madagascar	3	4 ▼	Partly Free
Malawi	3	3	Partly Free
Malaysia	4	4	Partly Free
Maldives	4	5	Partly Free
Mali	6 ▼	5	Not Free ▼
Malta	2	1	Free
Marshall Islands	1	1	Free
Mauritania	5	5	Partly Free
Mauritius	1	2	Free
Mexico	3	4 ▼	Partly Free

Country	PR	CL	Freedom Status
Micronesia	1	1	Free
Moldova	3	3 ▲	Partly Free
Monaco	3	1	Free
Mongolia	1	2	Free
Montenegro	3 ▲	3	Partly Free
Morocco	5	5	Partly Free
Mozambique	5	4	Partly Free
Myanmar	5	6	Not Free
Namibia	2	2	Free
Nauru	2	3	Free
Nepal	3	4	Partly Free
Netherlands	1	1	Free
New Zealand	1	1	Free
Nicaragua	6	5	Not Free
Niger	4	4	Partly Free
Nigeria	4	5	Partly Free
North Korea	7	7	Not Free
North Macedonia	3	3	Partly Free
Norway	1	1	Free
Oman	6	5	Not Free
Pakistan	5	5	Partly Free
Palau	1	1	Free
Panama	2 ▼	2	Free
Papua New Guinea	4	3	Partly Free
Paraguay	3	3	Partly Free
Peru	3 ▼	3	Partly Free ▼
Philippines	3	4	Partly Free
Poland	2	2	Free
Portugal	1	1	Free
Qatar	6	5	Not Free
Romania	2	2	Free
Russia	7	6	Not Free
Rwanda	6	6	Not Free
Samoa	2	2	Free
San Marino	1	1	Free
São Tomé and Príncipe	2	2	Free
Saudi Arabia	7	7	Not Free
Senegal	3	3	Partly Free
Serbia	4	3	Partly Free

Country	PR	CL	Freedom Status
Seychelles	2 ▲	3	Free ▲
Sierra Leone	3	3	Partly Free
Singapore	4	4	Partly Free
Slovakia	1	1 ▲	Free
Slovenia	1	1	Free
Solomon Islands	2	2	Free
Somalia	7	7	Not Free
South Africa	2	2	Free
South Korea	2	2	Free
South Sudan	7	7	Not Free
Spain	1	1	Free
Sri Lanka	4	4	Partly Free
St. Kitts and Nevis	2 ▼	1	Free
St. Lucia	1	1	Free
St. Vincent and the Grenadines	1	1	Free
Sudan	7	6	Not Free
Suriname	2	2 ▲	Free
Sweden	1	1	Free
Switzerland	1	1	Free
Syria	7	7	Not Free
Taiwan	1	1	Free
Tajikistan	7	6	Not Free
Tanzania	5	5	Partly Free
Thailand	7 ▼	5 ▼	Not Free ▼
The Gambia	4	4	Partly Free
Timor-Leste	2	3	Free
Togo	5	4	Partly Free
Tonga	2	2	Free
Trinidad and Tobago	2	2	Free
Tunisia	2	3	Free
Turkey	5	6	Not Free
Turkmenistan	7	7	Not Free
Tuvalu	1	1	Free
Uganda	6	5	Not Free
Ukraine	3	4 ▼	Partly Free
United Arab Emirates	7	6	Not Free
United Kingdom	1	1	Free
United States	2	2 ▼	Free
Uruguay	1	1	Free

Country	PR	CL	Freedom Status
Uzbekistan	7	6	Not Free
Vanuatu	2	2	Free
Venezuela	7	6	Not Free
Vietnam	7	6 ▼	Not Free
Yemen	7	6	Not Free
Zambia	4	4	Partly Free
Zimbabwe	6 ▼	5	Not Free ▼

PR and CL stand for political rights and civil liberties, respectively; 1 represents the most free and 7 the least free rating.

▲ ▼ up or down indicates an improvement or decline in ratings or status since the last survey.

NOTE: The ratings reflect global events from January 1, 2020, through December 31, 2020.

Territories

Territory	PR	CL	Freedom Status
Abkhazia	5	5	Partly Free
Crimea	7	6	Not Free
Eastern Donbas	7	7	Not Free
Gaza Strip	7	6	Not Free
Hong Kong	5	3	Partly Free
Indian Kashmir	6	5	Not Free
Nagorno-Karabakh	5	5	Partly Free
Northern Cyprus	3 ▼	2	Free
Pakistani Kashmir	6	5	Not Free
Somaliland	4 ▲	5	Partly Free
South Ossetia	7	6	Not Free
Tibet	7	7	Not Free
Transnistria	6	6	Not Free
West Bank	7	5	Not Free
Western Sahara	7	7	Not Free

PR and CL stand for political rights and civil liberties, respectively; 1 represents the most free and 7 the least free rating.

▲ ▼ up or down indicates an improvement or decline in ratings or status since the last survey.

NOTE: The ratings reflect global events from January 1, 2020, through December 31, 2020.

Freedom Ratings—Countries

FREE	Panama	Paraguay	Brunei
1.0	Slovakia	Peru	Iraq
Andorra	St. Kitts and Nevis	Senegal	Jordan
Australia		Sierra Leone	Myanmar
Austria	**2.0**		Mali
Bahamas	Antigua and Barbuda	**3.5**	Nicaragua
Barbados	Argentina	Bhutan	Oman
Belgium	Bulgaria	Georgia	Qatar
Cabo Verde	Ghana	Liberia	Turkey
Canada	Jamaica	Madagascar	Uganda
Chile	Monaco	Mexico	Zimbabwe
Costa Rica	Namibia	Nepal	
Cyprus	Panama	Papua New Guinea	**6.0**
Czech Republic	Poland	Philippines	Cambodia
Denmark	Romania	Serbia	Cameroon
Dominica	Samoa	Ukraine	Congo (Brazzaville)
Estonia	São Tomé and Príncipe		Djibouti
Finland	Solomon Islands	**4.0**	Egypt
Germany	South Africa	Armenia	Eswatini
Iceland	South Korea	Bosnia and Herzegovina	Ethiopia
Ireland	Suriname	Burkina Faso	Gabon
Italy	Tonga	Guatemala	Iran
Japan	Trinidad and Tobago	Kenya	Kazakhstan
Kiribati	United States	Kosovo	Kyrgyzstan
Luxembourg	Vanuatu	Malaysia	Rwanda
Marshall Islands		Niger	Thailand
Micronesia	**2.5**	Singapore	
Netherlands	Botswana	Sri Lanka	**6.5**
New Zealand	Brazil	The Gambia	Azerbaijan
Norway	Guyana	Zambia	Bahrain
Palau	Israel		Belarus
Portugal	Nauru	**4.5**	Burundi
San Marino	Northern Cyprus	Comoros	Chad
Slovakia	Peru	Côte d'Ivoire	China
Slovenia	Seychelles	Guinea-Bissau	Congo (Kinshasa)
Spain	Timor-Leste	Honduras	Cuba
St. Lucia	Tunisia	Lebanon	Laos
St. Vincent and the		Maldives	Libya
Grenadines	**PARTLY FREE**	Mozambique	Russia
Sweden	**3.0**	Nigeria	Sudan
Switzerland	Albania	Togo	Tajikistan
Taiwan	Benin		United Arab Emirates
Tuvalu	Bhutan	**5.0**	Uzbekistan
United Kingdom	Bolivia	Bangladesh	Venezuela
Uruguay	Colombia	Guinea	Vietnam
	Dominican Republic	Haiti	Yemen
1.5	Ecuador	Kuwait	
Belize	El Salvador	Mauritania	**7.0**
Croatia	Fiji	Morocco	Central African Republic
France	Hungary	Pakistan	Equatorial Guinea
Greece	India	Tanzania	Eritrea
Grenada	Indonesia		North Korea
Latvia	Lesotho	**NOT FREE**	Saudi Arabia
Liechtenstein	Malawi	**5.5**	Somalia
Lithuania	Moldova	Afghanistan	South Sudan
Malta	Montenegro	Algeria	Syria
Mauritius	North Macedonia	Angola	Turkmenistan
Mongolia			

Freedom Ratings – Territories

FREE
2.5
Northern Cyprus

PARTLY FREE
4.0
Hong Kong

4.5
Somaliland

5.0
Abkhazia
Nagorno-Karabakh

NOT FREE
5.5
Indian Kashmir
Pakistani Kashmir

6.0
Transnistria
West Bank

6.5
Crimea
Gaza Strip
South Ossetia

7.0
Eastern Donbas
Tibet
Western Sahara

Freedom in the World 2021 Contributors

DONORS
This report was made possible by the generous support of the National Endowment for Democracy, the Merrill Family Foundation, and the Lilly Endowment.

RESEARCH AND EDITORIAL TEAM
Elisha Aaron, Editorial Research Assistant
Ever Bussey, Research Associate
Noah Buyon, Research Associate
Cathryn Grothe, Research Associate
David Meijer, Associate Editor
Shannon O'Toole, Managing Editor
Sarah Repucci, Vice President for Research and Analysis
Tyler Roylance, Staff Editor
Amy Slipowitz, Research Manager
Mai Truong, Director of Research Operations
Tessa Weal, Research Assistant

ANALYSTS
Aalaa Abuzaakouk, Youth program manager for the Middle East and North Africa region, Georgetown University

Elen Aghekyan, Yale University

Tiago Aguiar, Independent researcher

Ibrahim Al-bakri Nyei, PhD candidate, School of Oriental and African Studies

Aurora Almada e Santos, NOVA University of Lisbon

Ibrahima Amadou Niang, Independent researcher

Ignacio Arana Araya, Assistant Teaching Professor, Carnegie Mellon University

Bojan Baća, Re:constitution Research Fellow, Max Weber Institute of Sociology, Heidelberg University

Slava (Veaceslav) Balan, PhD candidate, University of Ottawa

Gerald Bareebe, Assistant Professor, York University

Chantal Berman, Georgetown University

Bruno Binetti, Inter-American Dialogue

Mamadou Bodian, West Africa Research Center

Gustavo Bonifaz Moreno, Independent researcher

Brett L. Carter, University of Southern California

Annie Barbara Chikwanha, University of Johannesburg

Peter Clegg, University of the West of England

Jack Corbett, Professor of politics, University of Southampton

Olga de Obaldía, Fundación Libertad Ciudadana – Capítulo Transparencia Internacional Panamá

Karin Deutsch Karlekar, Director, Free Expression at Risk Programs, PEN America.

Neil DeVotta, Wake Forest University

Jake Dizard, Independent researcher

Juan Carlos Donoso, Institute for Social Research, University of Michigan

Boniface Dulani, University of Malawi

Howard Eissenstat, Department of History, St. Lawrence University

Anthony Elghossain, lawyer, writer, and nonresident scholar, Middle East Institute.

Donika Emini, Executive Director, Balkan Research Institute

Golnaz Esfandiari, Senior correspondent, Radio Free Europe

Jon Fraenkel, Professor of Comparative Politics, Victoria University of Wellington

Michael Freedman, University of Haifa

Michael Fusi Ligaliga, Te Tumu, School of Māori, Pacific & Indigenous Studies, University of Otago

Dustin Gilbreath, Caucasus Research Resource Centers Georgia

Katya Gorchinskaya, Independent Consultant

Liutauras Gudžinskas, Vilnius University.

Ted A. Henken, Baruch College, City University of New York

Hannah Hills, The Governance Group.

Jonathan Hulland, American Jewish World Service

Niklas Hultin, George Mason University.

Harry Hummel, Independent researcher

Salomé Ietter, PhD candidate, Queen Mary University of London

Rico Isaacs, University of Lincoln

Faysal Itani, Center for Global Policy

Valery Kavaleuski, Independent researcher

Jane Kinninmont, European Leadership Network

Marko Kmezić, University of Graz

Niklas Kossow, Independent researcher

Ágnes Kovács, Assistant professor, Eötvös Loránd University, Budapest

Josh Kurlantzick, Council on Foreign Relations

Lone Lindholt, Independent researcher

Alyssa Maraj Grahame, Bates College

Richard R. Marcus, Professor and Director, The Global Studies Institute and the International Studies Program, California State University, Long Beach

David McGrane is an associate professor of political studies at St. Thomas More College at the University of Saskatchewan.

Rachael McLellan, London School of Economic

Mushfiq Mohamed, Maldivian Democracy Network

Kacey Mordecai, Robert F. Kennedy Human Rights

Jasmin Mujanović, Political scientist, cohost of "Sarajevo Calling"

Harris Mylonas, Associate professor of political science and international affairs, George Washington University; Editor-in-chief, *Nationalities Papers*

Joachim Nahem, The Governance Group

Kuniaki Nemoto, Musashi University

Lucas Olo Fernandes, Independent researcher

Robert Orttung, George Washington University

Susan L. Ostermann, University of Notre Dame

Ana Pastor, Independent researcher

Aljaž Pengov Bitenc, Radio KAOS

Nicole Phillips, UC Hastings College of the Law.

Enrica Picco, International lawyer and researcher

Elizabeth M. Ramey, Independent researcher

Adrien M. Ratsimbaharison, Benedict College

Corina Rebegea, Center for European Policy Analysis

Elizabeth Rhoads, Centre for East and South-East Asian Studies, Lund University

Tyson Roberts, University of California, Los Angeles

Michael Runey, Enact Sustainable Strategies

Marek Rybar, Masaryk University, Brno

Debbie Sharnak, Rowan University

Elton Skendaj, Manchester University, USA

Olga Skrypnyk, human rights defender, head of the board of the Crimean Human Rights Group

Ruzha Smilova, Sofia University and Centre for Liberal Strategies

Jared Thompson, Master of Arts candidate, Johns Hopkins School of Advanced International Studies

Jenny Town, Fellow, Stimson Center

Elizabeth Tsurkov, Princeton University

Noah Tucker, Central Asia Program, George Washington University

Olesya Vartanyan, Senior analyst, International Crisis Group

Wouter Veenendaal, Leiden University

Diego Velazquez, Journalist

David Vivar, Academic coordinator,FLACSO-Honduras and Professor, National Autonomous University of Honduras

Franz von Bergen Granell, Journalist

Gregory White, Smith College

Tricia Yeoh, Chief Executive Officer, Institute for Democracy and Economic Affairs

Faiz Zaidi, Research officer, Institute for Democracy and Economic Affairs

ADVISERS
Alejandro Anaya-Muñoz, ITESO, Jesuit University of Guadalajara

Florian Bieber, University of Graz

Julio F. Carrión, University of Delaware

Licia Cianetti, Royal Holloway, University of London

Javier Corrales, Amherst College

Mai El-Sadany, Managing Director and Legal and Judicial Director, Tahrir Institute for Middle East Policy

Sumit Ganguly, Indiana University, Bloomington.

Julie A. George, Queens College and the Graduate Center, City University of New York

Lane Greene, the *Economist*

Idayat Hassan, Centre for Democracy and Development

Steven Heydemann, Smith College

Peter Lewis, Johns Hopkins School of Advanced International Studies

Peter Mandaville, Professor of International Affairs, Schar School of Policy and Government at George Mason University

Yaël Mizrahi-Arnaud, The Forum for Regional Thinking

Sana Ali Mustafa, Associate Director, Partnerships, Asylum Access

Houda Mzioudet, University of Toronto

Catherine Putz, Managing editor, *The Diplomat*

Samer Shehata, University of Oklahoma

Dan Slater, University of Michigan

Bridget Welsh, University of Nottingham Malaysia

Susanna D. Wing, Haverford College

Sources for
Freedom in the World 2021

Freedom in the World relies on analysts to assess political rights and civil liberties in each of the countries and territories covered by the report, using a combination of on-the-ground research, consultations with local contacts, and information from news articles, nongovernmental organizations, governments, and a variety of other sources. Expert advisers and regional specialists then vet the analysts' conclusions. Research is bolstered by a vigorous fact-checking process. The end product represents the consensus of the analysts, outside advisers, and Freedom House staff, who are responsible for any final decisions.

Please send inquiries about *Freedom in the World*'s sources to research@freedomhouse.org.

FREEDOM HOUSE BOARD OF TRUSTEES

Michael Chertoff, *Chair*

Carol C. Adelman, Goli Ameri, Peter Bass, David E. Birenbaum, Sewell Chan, Jørgen Ejbøl, Martin Etchevers, Francis Fukuyama, Jonathan Ginns, Dionisio Gutierrez, Robert Keane, Rachel Kleinfeld, Jim Kolbe, Faith Morningstar, Monde Muyangwa, Sushma Palmer, Vivek Paul, Maurice A. Perkins, Andrew Prozes, Ian Simmons, Thomas Staudt, Robert H. Tuttle, Anne Wedner, Norman Willox

Michael J. Abramowitz, *President*

Freedom House

Freedom House supports global freedom through comprehensive analysis, dedicated advocacy, and concrete assistance for democratic activists around the world.

Founded in 1941, Freedom House has long been a vigorous proponent of the right of all individuals to be free. Eleanor Roosevelt and Wendell Willkie served as Freedom House's first honorary co-chairpersons.

Michael Chertoff
Chair
Freedom House Board of Trustees

Michael J. Abramowitz
President

Arch Puddington
Distinguished Fellow for Democracy Studies

www.freedomhouse.org

Support the right of every individual to be free.
Donate now.